CW01669266

Reader's Digest

FAMILY WORD FINDER

Reader's Digest

FAMILY WORD FINDER

A new thesaurus of synonyms and antonyms in dictionary form

Published by The Reader's Digest Association Limited
LONDON · NEW YORK · MONTREAL · SYDNEY · CAPE TOWN

UK edition prepared by the editors of
The Reader's Digest Association Limited
in association with Oxford University Press

US edition prepared by the editors of
The Reader's Digest Association Inc.
in association with Stuart B. Flexner

First UK edition Copyright © 1978
Reprinted 1985
The Reader's Digest Association Limited
25 Berkeley Square, London W1X 6AB

Copyright © 1978
Reader's Digest Association Far East Limited

Philippines Copyright 1978
Reader's Digest Association Far East Ltd

All rights reserved. No part of this book
may be reproduced, stored in a retrieval
system, or transmitted in any form or by
any means, electronic, electrostatic,
magnetic tape, mechanical, photocopying,
recording or otherwise, without permission
in writing from the publishers.

® READER'S DIGEST is a registered trademark of
The Reader's Digest Association, Inc. of
Pleasantville, New York, U.S.A.

Printed in Great Britain by
Thomson Litho Ltd, East Kilbride

Bound by Mackays of Chatham Ltd

Typesetting in Great Britain by
Vantage Photosetting Co. Ltd, Eastleigh and London

How to Use the Family Word Finder

The *Family Word Finder* is a thesaurus, or treasury, of synonyms and antonyms, grouped into over 10,000 main entries which appear in alphabetical order. Each main headword is printed in **bold** type, as in a dictionary.

Synonyms

Making up the bulk of each *Word Finder* entry are lists of synonyms and other words related to the headword. These lists are the most important feature of this book. By scanning them you will be able to find words expressing precisely what you want to say. The chances are that the word you seek is already lurking somewhere in your subconscious mind. Scanning the lists of synonyms is in that case simply a convenient means of nailing your word down immediately. The list will often do more than that for you, however. It may contain yet another word that is even more precise or expressive than the one you had in mind. It may also lead you to a brand-new idea and a turn of phrase that will express your idea in a nutshell.

Immediately following each headword is its part of speech: *n.* for noun, *v.* for verb, *adj.* for adjective, *adv.* for adverb, *prep.* for preposition, *conj.* for conjunction, *pron.* for pronoun, and *interj.* for interjection. If the headword is used as more than one part of speech, the synonyms for each are listed in separate paragraphs. Since many words have more than one meaning, we have numbered each separate meaning with a numeral in **bold** type.

Every headword and every numbered meaning is followed by an illustrative sentence. Often, when the synonym list combines several different shades of meaning or use, we give more than one sentence for it. There are approximately 25,000 such illustrative sentences in this book, to enable you to locate the appropriate list and to illustrate the exact meaning and proper use of all the headwords.

Synonyms within each list are arranged where possible in decreasing order of use, from commonest to least common. Thus, synonyms you might be most likely to need appear near the beginning of each list, whereas less common synonyms and related words, including technical terms, foreign words and slang, come towards the end of the list. We have also labelled some synonyms *Medical, Nautical, Latin, Archaic,* and so on, for your convenience.

Other specialized synonyms are separated from general synonyms by the label *variously*. For those who wish to make extensive use of the lists of synonyms as a writing aid, we have freely expanded the lists to include many words that are not actually synonymous but only loosely equivalent in sense. These we have labelled *loosely*, especially in cases where their unqualified inclusion might otherwise be misleading.

The simplest definition of a synonym is "a word that means the same thing as another word." Unfortunately, this definition takes no account of the very aspect of synonyms that makes a book of synonyms useful. This aspect of synonyms was well described by the famous statesman and author Lord Chesterfield (1694–1773), when he pointed out that there is invariably "some little difference, some distinction between all those words that are vulgarly called synonymous — one hath always more energy, extent, or delicacy than another."

That is exactly why we use a thesaurus, or word finder. It assists us in our search for the exact nuance of feeling or meaning that will give perfect expression to our thought.

Antonyms

Following the lists of synonyms, many entries have lists of antonyms, indicated by the **bold** abbreviation **Ant.** When necessary, such antonyms are grouped together and numbered **1, 2, 3,** etc., to match the corresponding numbered senses in the synonym lists.

Spelling and Pronunciation Tips

Notes on spelling and pronunciation follow hundreds of main entries whose headwords are widely misspelt or mispronounced. Many of these notes include not only the facts and rules, but also simple hints and memory aids to help you to remember them. They contain the most up-to-date, commonsense information from the most reliable authorities. Many variant spellings and pronunciations have also been included.

In cases where there is wide uncertainty, we have provided guidance as to the currently preferred forms. Our rendering of the pronunciations is self-explanatory — no obscure symbols are used.

Usage

The *Word Finder* provides usage guidance on three levels: illustrative sentences, usage labels, and usage notes.

For example, these illustrative sentences answer such questions as: Does one *coerce* another *to do* something or *into doing* it? Implicit in the illustrative sentence is the answer to this question: *Prisoners of war were coerced into writing letters praising their captors.*

Explicit information on the status of a given synonym is furnished by usage labels within the lists. For example, "kids" as in the sentence *The kids had a great time at the party* is colloquially synonymous with "children." Since it belongs to the informal, conversational level of usage, we have labelled it *Informal.* On the other hand, "crate" meaning "aeroplane" or "soft soap" meaning "cajolery" belong to the non-standard style of usage known as *Slang* and are so labelled.

Finally, hundreds of *Usage notes* answer more complex questions such as: What is the difference between *historic* and *historical*? Answer: *Historic* means famous in history, celebrated, whereas *historical* merely means belonging to history and not to legend: *Tolstoy's War and Peace is a great historical novel.* But: *Plymouth Hoe is a historic spot.*

Word Origins

Following very many entries in this book are *Word origins*. These tell you where many of our common words come from and can help you to remember their meaning and use. If you get into the habit of reading the *Word origins* every time you use the book, you will gain some understanding of how our language grew.

English belongs to the Indo-European family of languages, which consists of about 100 related tongues, all descended from the prehistoric language of a pastoral, bronze-working, horse-breeding people, the Aryans, who inhabited the steppes of Central Asia about 4500 B.C. Scholars refer to their language at this stage as Indo-European.

Over the next 3,000 years or so, the community of Indo-European speakers splintered off, to Iran and India (where their idiom developed into the sister languages, Old Persian and Sanskrit) and elsewhere in many other directions, mainly westward. The farther afield they ranged, the farther their manner of speaking the ancestral tongue diverged. The old national name, *Aryan* (meaning "noble"), survived in both Persia and India and is in fact the source of the present-day name of *Iran.*

A few hundred years after the primeval Aryan community started to break up, there were already several Indo-European languages where there once had been only one. Derivative idioms grew even farther apart, so that by the dawn of recorded history a dozen branches of the Indo-European language family overspread most of western Eurasia from the Himalayas to the Atlantic.

The most important of these branches are: the Indo-Iranian, which comprises Persian (in Iran), Sanskrit, together with the derivatives Hindi, Urdu, and Bengali (in India) and several other languages, including Romany, the language of the Gipsies; the Slavic branch, which includes Russian, Polish, and others; the Hellenic branch, Greek; the Italic branch, which includes Latin and the derivative Romance languages such as French, Romanian and Italian; the Celtic branch, from which are descended Gaelic, Welsh and Breton; and finally the Germanic branch, including English, Dutch, German, Yiddish and the Scandinavian languages.

To illustrate the family relationship of these languages, here are the words for *mother* and *brother* in languages belonging to the above-mentioned branches and also in the common ancestor tongue, Indo-European:

English	mother	brother
German	mutter	bruder
Gaelic	máthair	braithair
Latin	mater	frater
Greek	mētēr	phratēr
Old Church Slavonic	mati	bratru
Sanskrit	mātr	bhrātr
Indo-European	*māter-	*bhrāter-

(*Note:* Indo-European forms are preceded by asterisks, indicating that they are *reconstructions* — that is, educated guesses by scholars as to the word's original form; also, because word endings are the least predictable, most changeable aspect of language, scholars place hyphens instead of conjectural endings at the end of each reconstructed Indo-European word.)

Because words like the *mother* words cited on the previous page have common ancestry, it is customary to refer to them as *cognates*. Thus, English *mother* is *cognate* with Latin *mater*, although it does not derive directly from it. The following diagram shows derivations of different *mother* words from their common ancestor.

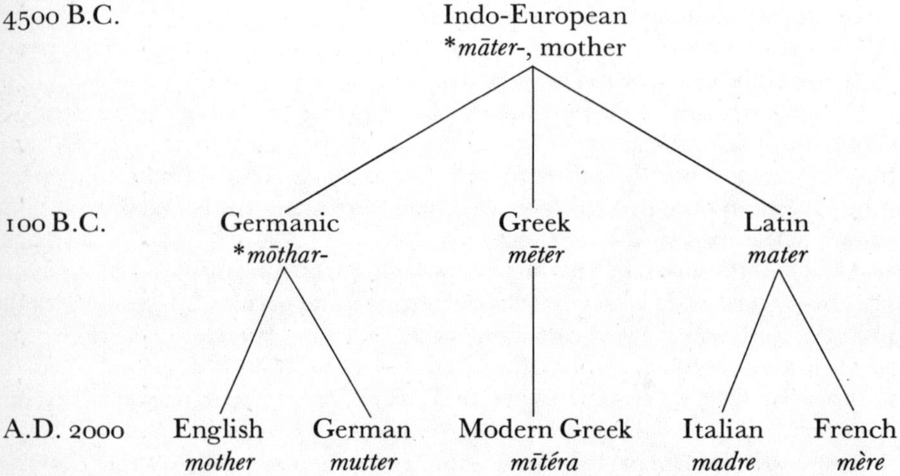

During the Roman occupation of Britain in the first four centuries of the Christian era, many Britons and Romans were bilingual, but as far as we know it never occurred to any of them that their respective languages were long-lost cousins. Still less could it have occurred to them that the speech of the Jutes, Saxons, Angles, and Frisians (who were then encamped on the North Sea from Jutland down to the mouth of the Rhine) might also be kin. It was with the coming of these Germanic tribes, however, after the collapse of Roman authority in A.D. 410, that the history of our language really began. We now refer to their descendants as the *Anglo-Saxons* and to their language as *Old English*. They were eventually to give Britain a new name: *England*, "Land of the Angles."

The Anglo-Saxon era lasted 500 years. During the second half of the period (from A.D. 800 onwards), successive waves of Viking invaders took over much of England, reaching the height of their influence with the reign of Canute (994–1035), King of England, Denmark, and Norway. Though the Viking invaders eventually integrated with their Anglo-Saxon cousins, these Norse-speaking newcomers left an indelible mark on our vocabulary.

The language of 10th-century England is as far removed from us today as are the longships of the Vikings. In order to understand Old English we must study it like a foreign language. Here, for example, are the opening verses of the Lord's Prayer as recited by Englishmen in the year 1000:

Old English (*c.* A.D. 700–1100)	**Modern English (*c.* A.D. 1500–)**
Fæder ūre,	Our Father
thū the eart on heofonum,	which art in heaven,
sī thīn nama gehālgod.	hallowed be thy name.
Tōbecume thīn rīce.	Thy kingdom come.
Gewurthe thīn willa on eorthan	Thy will be done in earth,
swā swā on heofonum . . .	as it is in heaven . . .

The Norman Conquest in 1066 heralded the end of the Old English period. French became the language of the Court and of state business, while ordinary folk continued to speak English. At the same time, William the Conqueror promoted marriages between Normans and English — a far-sighted policy that led in the long run not only to a national reconciliation but also to the formation of a new type of English in which the basic native tongue was richly blended with the imported French word-stock. We call this language *Middle English*, and in it we can readily recognize the immediate ancestor of Modern English.

Emerging during the 12th and early 13th centuries, Middle English became a polished literary language during the 14th century, with the classic *Canterbury Tales* of Geoffrey Chaucer (1340–1400). The following refrain from Chaucer's "Merciless Beauty" well illustrates the blend of French and English vocabularies characteristic of the new composite idiom:

Your yën two wol slee me sodenly,
I may the beauté of hem not sustene . . .
[Your two eyes will slay me suddenly,
I may the beauty of them not sustain . . .]

Sodenly, *beauté*, and *sustene* are French-derived; the other words are all native English. This proportion has remained more or less the same since the 13th century. More than half of the words in typical speech or writing which relate to abstract concepts tend to be borrowed — mainly from French or Latin. At the same time, if you counted *all* words in a typical segment of speech or writing, the native English words substantially outnumber the borrowed ones.

The dialect of the East Midlands around London was closer to *Modern English* than any of the other dialects of England. In 1476 the printer William Caxton used this dialect when he set up a press at Westminster and printed *The Dictes and Sayenges of the Phylosophers*, the first book ever to be published in England. In this, as in many subsequent — enormously influential — translations from the classics, Caxton used the current speech of London and thus helped to establish its predominant status.

By the reign of Henry VIII a generation later, London English was becoming the national standard. A contemporary style manual advises the writer: "Ye shall therefore take the usual speech of the Court and that of London and the shires lying about London within 60 miles, and not much above." The language of this exhortation is somewhat old-fashioned — but it is Modern English none the less.

While London town and London English were growing by leaps and bounds, Humanism — the revival of Classical learning — was becoming a major movement in England as elsewhere in Europe. During the 16th century, Humanists introduced Greek and Latin words into the language by the thousand. A large number of these words survived and now belong to our basic vocabulary.

The departure of colonists for Virginia and New England in the early 17th century took English to the New World. Since the first settlers had grown up under Queen Elizabeth and James I, their language might be called Elizabethan. Thrown together at first in small settlements under conditions of isolation and hardship, and joined sooner or later by immigrants from all over Europe, they were soon speaking a new kind of English. Now, more than 300 years after the beginnings of the split between Old World and New World English, we are experiencing a reversal of influence as more and more American idioms are absorbed into our language.

The connection of our Court with France in the late 17th century was reflected in additions to the vocabulary of art and literature. During the 18th century, French was regarded as the language of culture, and it was used throughout Europe in "polite society." The increasing ease of travel, too, brought many influences from Europe which are reflected in our language.

During the 19th century, as British commerce and colonization spread across the globe, French gave way to English as the most influential language in Europe and elsewhere. At the same time, the Industrial Revolution, closely followed by the march of technology, occasioned a vast increase in scientific and technical terminology, and English became the *lingua franca* of the scientific world.

In the 20th century, the rapid growth in power and population, first of the British Empire, then of the United States of America, gave the English language pride of place. Now, English is the mother tongue of millions of people in Britain, North America, Australia, New Zealand, the West Indies, and South Africa; it is a language of state business and commerce in India, Pakistan, and much of Africa and the rest of the world. As a language of diplomacy it has become universal. It was even the first language uttered by man on the moon! The *Word origins* in this book reflect the history of the language over the centuries.

In order to present this kind of survey, we have often grouped together related words and told you their histories in special boxes entitled *Exploring the Word.* Many of these appear throughout the book. You will also find on a number of pages quotations from famous writers and public figures, each illustrating the effective use of a nearby headword.

Thus the *Family Word Finder* can be used in many ways — as a thesaurus, or word finder; as a simple dictionary; as a guide to spelling, pronunciation, and usage; or simply as a book to browse in, to improve your vocabulary and familiarity with words and their stories. Keep it next to your dictionary, your writing desk, or your favourite reading chair. We believe you and your family will find it easy and enjoyable to use, and we hope you will use it often.

A

abandon *v.* **1** *She abandoned her child on the doorstep. Abandon ship!:* desert, forsake, leave, depart from, leave behind, withdraw from, evacuate; give up, quit, relinquish, let go, cast aside, forswear, abdicate, renounce. **2** *The scientist abandoned his research for lack of funds:* discontinue, give up, drop, forgo, waive, scrap, wash one's hands of, relinquish, forfeit, surrender.
—*n.* **3** *The Gipsies danced with gay abandon:* lack of restraint, freedom; immoderation; recklessness, impulsiveness, impetuosity, spontaneity; enthusiasm, gusto, exuberance, spirit, dash, verve, ardour, animation.
Ant. **1** claim, take; keep, hold, possess. **2** continue, maintain. **3** restraint, control; moderation, tameness.
◇ *Word origin: Abandon* comes from the Old French phrase *laisser à bandon,* to relinquish to another's control.

abandoned *adj.* **1** *The abandoned house was torn down:* deserted, forsaken, vacant, unoccupied; discarded, cast aside, cast away, relinquished, rejected, left behind, neglected. **2** *The pleasure-seeker led an abandoned life:* debauched, debased, dissipated, dissolute, degraded, profligate, reprobate, shameless, immoral, disreputable, sinful, wicked, loose, wanton, unprincipled; impure, unchaste, lewd; irreformable, irreclaimable, unrepentant.
Ant. **1** occupied; well-kept, kept, claimed. **2** virtuous, reputable, upright, high-principled, worthy, elevated, healthy, conscientious; moral, sinless, pure, chaste; reformed, redeemed, penitent, regenerate.

abase *v. The Bible says that the proud man shall be abased:* humble, bring low, cast down; *Informal* bring down a peg, cut down to size; humiliate, disgrace, dishonour, defame, belittle, vilify, denigrate, vitiate; downgrade, degrade, devalue, debase; shame, mock, mortify.
Ant. elevate, raise, uplift, lift; dignify, honour, acclaim, praise, laud, extol; promote, upgrade, inflate.
◇ *Word origin: Abase* comes from Late Latin *bassus,* low.

abashed *adj. He was abashed at forgetting his wife's birthday:* embarrassed, ashamed, chagrined, mortified, humiliated, humbled, self-conscious, dismayed, bewildered, confused, dumbfounded, nonplussed, disconcerted, confounded, fazed; shy, bashful, cowed, subdued, crushed, intimidated.
Ant. proud, pleased, elated, exalted, buoyed; confident, poised, emboldened, reassured.
◇ *Word origin: Bah!* was an exclamation of astonishment in Old French. Our own word *abashed* comes from Old French *esbahir,* to get a *bah* out of someone.

abate *v. The wind abated after the storm:* decrease, diminish, reduce, lessen, subside, decline, fade, fade away, dwindle, moderate, mitigate, weaken, wane, curtail, slack, slacken, go down, lower, fall off, fall away, taper off, lighten, soften, quiet, quell, slow, slake off, temper, cool, blunt; ease, relieve, alleviate, assuage, soothe, allay, mollify, dull; dampen, restrain, restrict.
Ant. increase, intensify, magnify, enhance, heighten, aggravate, amplify; multiply, rise, come up, strengthen, sharpen, heat up; quicken, accelerate, hurry, speed, speed up; prolong, extend.
◇ *Word origin: Abate* comes from Old French *abatre,* to beat down.

abbey *n. The monks live in their abbey in the mountains. Westminster Abbey is in London:* monastery, friary, cloister, priory, hermitage; convent, nunnery; church, cathedral, chapel.

abbreviate *v. As time was short, he abbreviated his visit:* shorten, abridge, curtail, condense, contract, reduce; cut, cut down, cut short, compress, trim, clip, truncate.
Ant. lengthen, extend, elongate, stretch, stretch out, draw out; expand, enlarge, amplify, increase, augment, add to, pad out; prolong, protract; write out, write in full.

abbreviation *n. "Mr." is the abbreviation of "Mister":* shortened form, short form, shortening, condensed form, reduced form, compressed form, contracted form, cut-down form; contraction, abridgement, condensation, digest, synopsis, summary; lessening, trimming, curtailment, cutting, clipping, pruning.
Ant. full form, written-out form; lengthening, extending, extension, elongation, stretching, stretching out, drawing out; expansion, enlargement, amplification, increasing, augmentation, prolongation.
◇ *Usage note: G.B., CBI, Yorks.,* and *Dr.* are abbreviations, shortened forms of a word or phrase to represent the full term. NATO, ERNIE, and UNICEF are a type of *abbreviation* called *acronyms,* abbreviations that may be pronounced as a word rather than as a series of letters. Thus, an *abbreviation* is pronounced as separate letters (G.B., CBI) while an *acronym* may be pronounced as a word (NATO, ERNIE).

abdicate *v. King Edward VIII abdicated to marry a commoner. He abdicated his responsibilities and fled:* resign, vacate the throne; relinquish, give up, abandon, surrender, quit, forgo, cede, yield.

Ant. accede to the throne; claim, possess, keep.
◇ *Word origin: Abdicate* comes from Latin *ab-*, away, + *dicare*, to proclaim. Thus, when a king *abdicates*, he "proclaims away" his throne.

abduct *v. Kidnappers abducted the child:* kidnap, carry off, make off with, run off with, steal, bear off, seize.
Ant. return, bring back; free, set free; restore, relinquish, surrender.

aberration *n.* **1** *The flaw in a lens that doesn't focus properly is called spherical aberration. The new rules were confusing and full of aberrations:* irregularity, deviation, abnormality, anomaly, divergence, aberrancy; wandering, rambling, straying, lapse. **2** *His only aberration was an occasional lapse of memory:* minor mental disorder, mental lapse, abnormality, quirk, peculiarity, idiosyncrasy, eccentricity, unconformity, nonconformity, oddity, strangeness; illusion, delusion, self-deception, hallucination; madness, insanity, lunacy, derangement.
Ant. 1, 2 normality, regularity, uniformity, conformity. **2** sanity, soundness of mind.

abet *v. The criminal was aided and abetted by his brother:* encourage, support, sustain, back, give moral support to, sanction, uphold; urge, urge on, goad, spur, incite; lead on, egg on; assist, help, aid.
Ant. discourage, talk out of, dissuade, expose, denounce; deter, stop, hinder, impede, thwart, obstruct, balk.
◇ *Word origin: Abet* comes from Old French *abeter*, to incite, tease, or bait another.

abeyance *n. The project will be held in abeyance until spring:* postponement, suspension, deferral, adjournment, discontinuance, inaction, dormancy, latency; pause, cessation, recess, hiatus.

abhor *v. Nature abhors a vacuum. She abhors snakes:* detest, hate, loathe, despise, abominate, execrate; feel aversion towards, be revolted by, find repulsive, shudder at, recoil from, shrink from, regard with repugnance, view with horror, eschew, can't stand, can't stomach, be nauseated by.
Ant. love, adore, like, delight in, dote on, cherish, relish, treasure, prize, value, enjoy, admire; desire, crave, covet.
◇ *Usage note:* See HATE.
◇ *Word origin: Abhor* comes from Latin *abhorrere*, meaning to shrink away from something.

abide *v.* **1** *I can't abide loud noise:* bear, stand, tolerate, put up with, endure, stomach, brook; suffer, submit to, stand for. **2** *Abide with me a while longer:* stay, remain, tarry, linger, stop; live, reside, dwell; visit, sojourn, sit; *Slang* stick with.
Ant. 2 go, leave, quit, depart; escape, flee, fly; abandon, avoid; move, migrate, journey.

abiding *adj. Saint Augustine had an abiding faith in God:* lasting, everlasting, enduring, eternal, unending, continuing, permanent, durable, firm, fast; changeless, unchanging, steadfast, constant, unshakable, immutable, indissoluble.
Ant. temporary, passing, momentary, impermanent, ephemeral; weak, shaky, failing; changeable, fickle.

ability *n. A good salesman has the ability to sell anything:* capability, capacity, power, facility, faculty, aptitude, proficiency, knack, competence, qualification; skill, talent, know-how, expertise, adeptness, acumen; flair, genius, gift, bent.
Ant. inability, incapacity, incapability, inaptitude, incompetence, maladroitness; weakness, powerlessness, helplessness.

"It is a great ability to be able to hide one's ability." —*La Rochefoucauld*

---

abject *adj.* **1** *The old couple lived in abject poverty:* hopeless, inescapable, complete, thorough; wretched, miserable, deplorable, terrible, horrible. **2** *The soldier deserted like an abject coward:* lacking courage, spiritless, cringing, grovelling; contemptible, despicable, vile, base, mean, low, ignoble, sordid.
Ant. 1 hopeful; partial; dignified, honourable. **2** courageous, spirited, bold, staunch; manly, domineering, vain, arrogant, haughty, insolent; admirable, respected, esteemed.

abjure *v.* **1** *Pacifism abjures the use of deadly force:* disclaim, disallow, repudiate, reject. **2** *Some of the prisoners abjured their heresies and lived:* renounce, forswear, recant.

able *adj.* **1** *Our case was handled by two able lawyers:* skilful, proficient, capable, competent, expert, good, talented, highly qualified, accomplished, masterful, effective, efficient, adroit, adept, apt; experienced, practised, learned. **2** *The starving man was barely able to walk. We are not able to grant your request:* capable, fit, fitted, competent, having the means; equal to, adequate, qualified.
Ant. 1 unskilful, incapable, incompetent, inexpert, inept, inefficient, ineffective, amateurish; mediocre, indifferent, fair. **2** incapable, unfit, incompetent, inadequate, unqualified.

ablution *n.* **1** *After ablutions in the river, the holy man continued on his way:* ceremonial washing, ritualistic washing; bathing, cleansing. **2** *He had no time for his morning ablutions:* washing, bathing, cleaning, lavation; wash, bath.
◇ *Word origin: Ablution* comes from Latin *ab-*, away, + *luere*, to wash.

abnegation *n. In a mood of abnegation, he gave up sweets and milk shakes:* self-denial, renunciation, relinquishment, giving up, eschewal, forbearing; abstinence, temperance, continence; rejection, refusal.

Ant. self-indulgence, indulgence, abandon; intemperance, incontinence; affirmation, concession.

abnormal *adj. The cat has an abnormal fear of birds. An abnormal amount of snow fell in October:* unnatural, atypical, unusual, irregular, aberrant, anomalous; uncommon, unconventional, exceptional, unexpected, unaccustomed, inordinate; strange, peculiar, rare, queer, odd, freakish, eccentric, bizarre, curious, outlandish, unheard of, grotesque, weird, monstrous, deformed.

Ant. normal, natural, typical, usual, ordinary, common; conventional, routine, regular, expected, customary, familiar, unexceptional.

◇ *Usage note: Abnormal* can mean either below or above normal, either better or worse than normal: *Einstein had an abnormal IQ. An idiot has an abnormal IQ.* On the other hand, *subnormal* always means below or worse than normal.

◇ *Word origin:* This word was once spelt *anormal* and came from the Greek *anōmalos*, meaning irregular. Later the *b* was added by analogy with the Latin word for irregular, *abnormis*, based on Latin *ab-*, from, + *norma*, norm, hence away from the norm.

abnormality *n. A club-foot is an abnormality that can often be corrected by surgery:* deformity, malformation; irregularity, aberration, anomaly, deviation; oddity, peculiarity, idiosyncrasy, eccentricity, unconformity.

abode *n. The hermit's abode was a cave:* residence, place of residence, dwelling-place, dwelling, habitation; house, home, living quarters, domicile, lodging.

abolish *v. Capital punishment was abolished some years ago:* eliminate, eradicate, extinguish, exterminate, terminate, end, put an end to, wipe out, stamp out, blot out, do away with, quash; repeal, revoke, annul, nullify, invalidate, rescind, cancel; abrogate, vitiate, set aside, repudiate.

Ant. establish, institute, introduce, create, found; support, promote, increase, sustain, continue; revive, reinstate, renew, repair, restore, reintroduce; authorize, legalize, enact.

◇ *Word origin: Abolish* and *abolition* are based on the Latin *abolere*, to destroy, do away with.

abolition *n. The M.P. fought for the abolition of income tax:* elimination, ending, termination, eradication, extinction, abolishment; repeal, annulment, nullification, revocation, cancellation, rescinding, repudiation, abrogation.

Ant. establishment, institution, introduction, creation, founding; authorization, legalization, enactment, passing; promotion; continuation; reinstatement, restoration, reintroduction.

◇ *Word origin:* See ABOLISH.

abominable *adj.* **1** *Murder is the most abominable crime:* detestable, despicable, contemptible, reprehensible, loathsome, hateful, abhorrent, disgusting, revolting, repulsive, repugnant, repellent, odious; vile, base, wretched, heinous, ignominious, villainous, infamous, atrocious, horrid, horrible, foul, hellish, damnable, cursed, accursed. **2** *The weather was abominable:* very unpleasant, disagreeable, miserable, terrible, foul, extremely bad, unsuitable, awful, *Informal* lousy.

Ant. 1 laudable, praiseworthy, commendable, admirable, respectable, desirable, applaudable; satisfactory, gratifying, charming, enchanting, likeable. **2** pleasant, agreeable, enjoyable, pleasing, delightful, good, wonderful, charming, suitable, *Informal* beautiful.

◇ *Word origin: Abominable* is ultimately derived from Latin *abominari*, to detest something as an ill omen. But from the 14th until the 17th century the word was spelt *abhominable* because people imagined it to have come from the Latin phrase *ab homine*, meaning away from man, hence inhuman, beastly. This misunderstanding permanently affected the meaning of the word.

abomination *n.* **1** *The dirty streets of this city are an abomination!:* abhorrence, anathema, evil, horror, torment, plague, affliction, annoyance, bugbear, *French* bête noire. **2** *Decent people regard concentration camps with abomination:* loathing, repugnance, disgust, hate, hatred, abhorrence, antipathy, aversion.

Ant. 1 delight, joy, pleasure, treat; benefit, blessing, boon, satisfaction, gratification. **2** love, liking, affection, relish, regard; admiration, appreciation, respect, approval, esteem.

aboriginal *adj. The Indians were the aboriginal people of America:* native, indigenous, original, autochthonous; earliest, first, ancient, primordial, primeval, primitive, primary.

Ant. alien, foreign, immigrant, imported, exotic; late, recent, subsequent, successive, modern.

aborigine *n. The Australian aborigines hunted with boomerangs:* original inhabitant, primitive inhabitant, indigenous person; native, aboriginal.

Ant. alien, foreigner, immigrant; newcomer, new boy, late arrival, Johnny-come-lately.

◇ *Word origin:* The *Aborigines* were a tribe of ancient Italy from whom the Latins were said to be descended, and their name is traditionally supposed to be based on the phrase *ab origine*, from the beginning. The Roman statesman and orator Cicero was the first to use the word in its present sense.

abort *v.* **1** *Cows with Bang's disease often abort their calves:* miscarry, terminate the pregnancy of. **2** *The astronauts aborted the space flight when their engine caught fire:* terminate, end, halt, call off; fail, fail to develop fully.

Ant. 1 give birth, bear, deliver. 2 carry through, see through, conclude, complete, finish; execute, perform, effect, achieve.

◇ *Word origin: Abort* comes from *abortus*, a form of the Latin verb meaning to miscarry.

abortion *n.* 1 *Her pregnancy ended in an abortion:* miscarriage, termination of pregnancy. 2 *The attempt to redesign the aeroplane was an abortion:* failure, unsuccessful attempt, fruitless attempt, fiasco, disaster; halting, calling off, ending, termination.

Ant. 1 childbirth, parturition, giving birth, delivery. 2 success, successful completion, realization, achievement.

abound *v. Our garden abounds with roses. Tulips abound in Holland:* teem, overflow, be filled, have plenty of, be well supplied, be rich in, swarm, superabound; exist in great numbers, be plentiful, proliferate, be numerous, flourish.

Ant. lack, want, have too few, be deficient in, fall short, be scant; be in short supply.

◇ *Word origin:* See ABUNDANT.

"A faithful man shall abound with blessings." —*Proverbs* 28: 20

---

abrasion *n.* 1 *The abrasion on his knee soon healed:* scraped spot, scrape; scratch, lesion. 2 *Years of abrasion had worn the stones smooth:* scraping, grating, rubbing, friction, scouring, chafing; erosion, wearing away, wearing down.

abrasive *n.* 1 *Use sandpaper or some other abrasive to remove the paint:* scraping material, grinding material, scouring material; smoothing substance.

—*adj.* 2 *The speaker's abrasive remarks insulted the audience:* harsh, irritating; rasping, rough, caustic, chafing.

Ant. 2 mild, soothing, healing.

abreast *adv., adj. The soldiers marched three abreast:* side by side, in a line across, in rank.

Ant. one behind another, in single file, Indian file.

abridge *v.* 1 *The book was abridged to a more readable length:* shorten, condense, reduce, compress, digest, abbreviate, cut, cut down, scale down, pare down, trim. 2 *No one can abridge your legal rights:* restrict, limit, curtail, diminish, lessen, reduce, decrease; deprive one of, take away.

Ant. 1 expand, enlarge, lengthen, increase, extend, amplify; prolong; augment, add to, supplement. 2 increase, augment, add to.

◇ *Word origin: Abridge* is from Old French *abregier*, which in turn was taken from Latin *abbreviare*, the same word that gives us *abbreviate*.

abridgement *n.* 1 *Have you seen the new abridgement of Gibbon's Roman History?:* shortened form, condensed form, condensation, abbreviation, digest. 2 *The town council voted for an abridgement of the mayor's power:* restriction, limitation, restraint, curtailment, reduction, lessening, decrease, diminishing, diminution.

Ant. 1 lengthened version. 2 expansion, enlargement, amplification, increase, augmentation, extension.

abroad *adv.* 1 *On our trip abroad we visited relatives in Belgium:* overseas, out of the country. 2 *It's unsafe to be abroad at night if you're not wearing something white:* out of doors, outside, out, out of the house, forth, out in the open air. 3 *A thousand rumours were abroad:* in circulation, at large, doing the rounds, all around, round and about; spread far and wide, rife, astir.

Ant. 1 nearby, near home; in one's native land, within the country. 2 indoors, inside, in, in the house, at home, within four walls; *French* chez soi, *German* zu Hause.

abrogate *v. Parliament must abrogate the new tax law:* abolish, cancel, put an end to, end, do away with, quash; repeal, revoke, rescind, annul, nullify, void, invalidate, set aside, override, reverse, undo, dissolve; retract, countermand, recall, withdraw, repudiate, renounce, abjure; *Informal* scrap, throw out.

Ant. institute, establish, create, found; enact, ratify; confirm, sustain, uphold, support, sanction; continue; revive, renew.

abrupt *adj.* 1 *The car came to an abrupt stop at the barricade:* sudden, unexpected, unforeseen, unanticipated, unlooked-for, unannounced; hasty, quick, rapid, swift, instantaneous, precipitate. 2 *His abrupt reply hurt our feelings:* curt, brusque, blunt, gruff, short; discourteous, impolite, uncivil, ungracious, unceremonious, rude, rough. 3 *The cliff made an abrupt descent to the sea:* steep, sheer, sharp, precipitous.

Ant. 1 gradual, leisurely, unhurried, deliberate, slow, easy. 2 courteous, polite, gracious, thoughtful, civil; gentle, easy. 3 gradual, easy, slow.

abscond *v. The thief absconded with the jewels:* flee, take flight, fly, depart hastily, leave suddenly; make off, steal off, steal away; escape, run away, run off.

absence *n.* 1 *The teacher noted the pupil's absence:* not being present, non-attendance, non-presence, non-appearance, absenteeism; truancy. 2 *He shows an absence of initiative:* lack, unavailability, non-existence; scarcity, deficiency, insufficiency, scantiness, want.

Ant. 1 presence, attendance, appearance. 2 existence, supply; abundance, sufficiency, adequacy, surfeit.

absent *adj.* 1 *Why were you absent from school yesterday?:* not present, non-attendant; away, gone, missing, out, truant. 2 *He gave her an absent look:* inattentive, unthinking, heedless, unaware, unconscious, absent-minded, preoccupied, distracted; vacant, blank, empty, vague, dreamy, musing.

—*v.* **3** *Why did you absent yourself from the meeting yesterday?:* cause to be not present, fail to attend, not appear, stay away, keep away, play truant, *Informal* not show up, cut.

Ant. 1 present, in attendance, attendant. **2** attentive, thoughtful, meaningful, conscious, aware, alert. **3** attend, appear at, show up.

absolute *adj.* **1** *The Dalai Lama was an absolute monarch:* unrestricted, unrestrained, unlimited, unconditional, unqualified, unbounded; complete, supreme, pure, full, *Informal* out and out. **2** *His story was an absolute lie:* complete, pure, total, thorough, unqualified, unrestricted, unadulterated, utter, unlimited; perfect, outright; *Informal* out and out, through and through. **3** *The police have absolute proof of his guilt:* positive, definite, conclusive, certain, sure, decisive; real, genuine, reliable, unqualified, unquestionable, confirmed, infallible, unequivocal.

Ant. 1 restricted, restrained, conditional, limited, qualified; constitutional. **2, 3** qualified, limited, conditional, questionable, dubious, unconfirmed, equivocal; not complete, incomplete.

absolutely *adv.* **1** *I am absolutely sure that these are the facts:* entirely, completely, thoroughly, wholly, utterly, definitely, positively; unconditionally, without limitation. **2** *Good nutrition is absolutely essential for your health:* positively, certainly, utterly, definitely, decidedly, truly, really, indeed; undoubtedly, unquestionably, unequivocally, indubitably.

Ant. 1 somewhat, fairly, reasonably, approximately. **2** probably, conditionally.

absolve *v.* **1** *The jury absolved him of the crime:* acquit, find not guilty, judge innocent; exonerate, vindicate, clear. **2** *I was absolved from having to pay my partner's debts. The priest absolved them from their sins:* release, free, set free, excuse, exempt, discharge, loose, deliver; pardon, forgive, shrive.

Ant. 1 convict, charge, find guilty. **2** obligate, oblige, bind, hold to, be held responsible; accuse, blame, condemn.

◇ *Word origin: Absolve* comes from the Latin *absolvere,* which in Roman law meant to acquit, to pronounce not guilty.

absorb *v.* **1** *The sponge absorbed all the spilt water:* soak up, take up, suck up, swallow up, drink in, sponge up. **2** *Can the students absorb this lesson in an hour?:* take in completely, assimilate, digest; *Informal* drink in, make part of oneself. **3** *I was so absorbed in this book that I didn't hear you:* engross, immerse, occupy, preoccupy, engage, enwrap; arrest, rivet, fix, fascinate.

Ant. 1 exude, eject, cast off, cast out, disperse, dispel; drip. **2** give out, disperse, impart. **3** unoccupy; distract.

◇ *Spelling tip:* Remember that the final *b* of *absorb* changes to *p* in *absorPtion.*

◇ *Word origin: Absorb* comes from Latin *absorbere,* to swallow up or devour (in the sense that quicksand or whirlpools devour) or more mildly, to engross.

absorbing *adj. Boys find stamp-collecting an absorbing pastime:* fascinating, interesting, engrossing, captivating, intriguing, engaging; exciting, thrilling.

abstain *v. Vegetarians abstain from eating meat:* refrain, desist, forbear, eschew, avoid, forgo, decline, refuse; deny oneself.

Ant. partake of, indulge in, yield to, give in to; overdo, abandon oneself to, make a slave of oneself to.

abstention *n. Vegetarians are known for their abstention from eating meat:* abstaining, non-indulgence, refraining, desisting, forbearance, eschewing, eschewal, avoidance, refusal; non-participation, denying oneself.

Ant. indulgence, abandon.

abstinence *n. I much admire Quakers for their abstinence:* non-indulgence, self-denial, self-restraint, self-control, forbearance, abstention; (*variously*) temperance, sobriety; continence, chastity.

Ant. indulgence, self-indulgence, abandon, excess; (*variously*) intemperance, dissipation; wantonness; gorging, gluttony; greediness, covetousness, graspingness, acquisitiveness.

"To many, total abstinence is easier than perfect moderation." —*St. Augustine*

---

abstract *adj.* **1** *Abstract ideas may lead to concrete plans:* theoretical, theoretic, conceptual, general, generalized, imaginary, visionary, hypothetical, indefinite, impractical; subtle, profound, abstruse, intellectual.

—*n.* **2** *Please write an abstract of this scientific article:* summary, synopsis, précis, recapitulation; digest, condensation, abridgement; outline.

—*v.* **3** *The thief abstracted £5 from my wallet:* extract, remove, withdraw, take out, take; separate, dissociate, isolate. **4** *Please abstract this scientific article:* summarize, précis; digest, condense, abridge; outline.

Ant. 1 concrete, specific, material; practical; factual, definite, real, actual. **2** amplification, enlargement, expansion. **3** add, inject; mix, unite, combine.

abstruse *adj. Mathematics can be an abstruse subject:* hard to understand, obscure, incomprehensible, unfathomable, complex, puzzling, perplexing, arcane, enigmatic; profound, deep, subtle, abstract, remote, esoteric.

Ant. simple, easy, obvious, clear; superficial, light, amusing, entertaining.

absurd *adj. It's absurd to believe that the earth is flat. The clown wore an absurd costume:* unreasonable, illogical, irrational, preposterous, senseless; ridiculous, foolish, silly, stupid, ludicrous, nonsensical, asinine, comical, farcical; funny, laughable; *Informal* crazy, wild.

Ant. reasonable, logical, sensible, rational, sound; smart, intelligent, sagacious, judicious, prudent.

◇ *Word origin: Absurd* is from Latin *absurdus*, meaning senseless, formed from *ab-*, completely + *surdus*, deaf; hence *absurd* implies deaf to the truth, deaf to reason.

absurdity *n. His story of being kidnapped by little green men was sheer absurdity. The absurdities of the playful little monkeys amused us:* nonsense, unreasonableness, incredibility, idiocy, inanity, asininity, irrationality, ridiculousness, drivel; falsehood, fallacy, delusion; foolishness, buffoonery, comicalness, silliness.

Ant. truth; reasonableness, credibility; wisdom, sagacity.

abundance *n. There was such an abundance of food that we all overate:* ample amount, great supply, full measure, profusion, excess, more than enough, surplus, glut, plenitude, repletion, plethora, surfeit, copiousness; heap, flood, bounty, wealth.

Ant. scarcity, deficiency, lack, dearth, scantiness, sparseness, paucity.

abundant *adj. There is abundant water despite the dry spell:* ample, sufficient, enough, more than enough, profuse, copious, prolific, bounteous, bountiful, abounding, lavish, brimming, teeming; rife, replete.

Ant. insufficient, scant, sparse, meagre, uncommon, scarce, skimpy, sparing.

◇ *Word origin: Abundant* comes from Latin *abundare*, to overflow. Our word *abound* also comes from this Latin word.

abuse *v.* **1** *A good workman doesn't abuse his tools. Stop abusing that dog!:* misuse, use improperly, ill-use; mistreat, maltreat, ill-treat; harm, hurt, injure; impose upon. **2** *The old shrew abused everyone in a loud voice:* insult, speak ill of, scold, berate, carp at, rail at, revile, vilify, castigate; speak harshly to, reproach, criticize, censure, bawl out, upbraid; belittle, malign, slur, denigrate; curse, slander, denounce, defame, disparage, inveigh against. —*n.* **3** *Borrowing money is an abuse of friendship:* misuse, unfair use, improper use, misapplication, misemployment; imposition. **4** *Child abuse is a punishable offence:* mistreatment, maltreatment, ill-use, cruelty; injury, harming, beating, assault. **5** *I'll listen to no more of your abuse!:* insulting language, insults, harsh language; berating, railing, invective, tirade; reproach, criticism, censure, scolding, upbraiding, castigation, carping; belittling, sneering, disparagement, slander, vilification; cursing, defamation.

Ant. **1** respect, protect, care for. **2** praise, speak well of, compliment, extol, laud, flatter, commend, acclaim. **5** praise, compliment, acclaim; flattery.

abusive *adj.* **1** *Please don't use such abusive language:* insulting, harsh, vituperative, mean, railing, acrimonious; offensive, obscene, foul-mouthed, vile, rude, gross; derogatory, disparaging, defamatory, scurrilous, deprecatory, castigating, critical, censorious, slanderous, reviling, maligning, vilifying, scornful. **2** *He was arrested for his abusive treatment of the dog:* cruel, improper; harmful, hurtful, injurious.

Ant. **1** laudatory, flattering, complimentary, praising, extolling, mild, courteous, respectful, polite. **2** kind; just.

abut *v. There is a fence where the two yards abut:* meet end to end, meet, join, adjoin, touch; be contiguous, be adjacent to, be next to.

abysmal *adj. The serfs were maintained in a state of abysmal ignorance:* thorough, endless, unending, complete; bottomless, boundless, unfathomable, deep, profound, extreme, vast.

"Man is a rope stretched between the animal and the Superman — a rope over an abyss." —*Nietzsche*

---

abyss *n.* **1** *One slip on this mountain and you'll fall into the abyss:* bottomless pit, vast chasm, crevasse, fissure, gorge, gully; void, depth, nadir, gulf. **2** See HELL.

Ant. **1** elevation, height; mountain, hill, mount; summit, zenith.

◇ *Word origin: Abyss* goes back to the Greek word *abyssos*, bottomless. The modern senses of the word first appeared in Biblical Greek, where *abyssos* was used for the great deep of Genesis 1: 2 and for the bottomless pit of Revelation 9: 1.

academic *adj.* **1** *He remembered his academic days fondly:* school, scholastic, educational; polytechnic, university. **2** *A good historian must have an academic mind:* scholarly, studious; learned, educated, erudite; pedantic, bookish. **3** *How to talk to a Martian is rather an academic question:* theoretical, hypothetical, abstract, speculative, conjectural; not practical, remote, ivory-towered.

Ant. **2** non-scholarly, non-studious, uneducated, unschooled, untaught, unlettered, unlearned. **3** practical, immediate, common sense; everyday, ordinary, matter-of-fact.

◇ *Word origin: Academy* comes from *Akadēmeia*, name of the gymnasium on the outskirts of ancient Athens where Plato taught. It was named after *Akadēmos*, a legendary hero of Attica.

accede *v.* **1** *The mayor acceded to the citizens' demands:* consent to, approve, agree to, grant, assent to, accept, concur with; concede, permit, yield to, submit to, defer to, acquiesce in; surrender to, subscribe to, abide by, comply with, conform to; admit, acknowledge. **2** *When the king dies, the Crown prince will accede to the throne:* succeed to, inherit.

Ant. 1 reject, refuse, disallow, spurn, decline, veto; oppose, object to, resist, protest, disapprove, demur; shy away from, balk at.

◇ *Spelling tip: Cede* means to yield, surrender, or transfer. *Accede* means to consent, to yield, surrender, or transfer to; thus, *accede* ends in *-cede, acCEDE.*

◇ *Usage note:* Don't confuse *accede* and *exceed. Accede* means to consent or agree; *exceed* means to surpass, to go beyond the limit of.

accelerate *v.* **1** *The car suddenly accelerated:* go faster, move faster, speed up, pick up speed, quicken pace. **2** *Fertilizer will accelerate the growth of these tomato plants:* speed up, hurry, quicken, hasten, rush, step up, spur; expedite, further, promote, advance, precipitate, facilitate, intensify.

Ant. 1, 2 slow, slow down, decelerate. **2** delay, retard, hinder, impede, hamper, obstruct.

◇ *Word origin: Accelerate* comes from Latin *celer*, quick.

accent *n.* **1** *The word "woman" has its accent on the first syllable:* stress, emphasis; primary accent, primary stress. **2** *She speaks with a German accent:* pronunciation, enunciation, articulation, inflection; intonation, tone, modulation. **3** *The room was all white with a few red accents:* hint, touch, embellishment, detail; ornament, adornment, trimming.

—*v.* **4** *Accent the word "woman" on the first syllable:* stress, emphasize, accentuate.

◇ *Word origin:* Classical Greek was a sing-song language. To describe the *accent* of his native tongue, a Greek author of the 1st century B.C. used a word meaning song. More than a thousand years later, medieval grammarians put the same word into Latin as *accentus*, or song added to speech.

accept *v.* **1** *She accepted his invitation to dance:* take something offered, receive willingly, receive with favour. **2** *I accept your apology. The police accepted his story as true:* agree to, consent to, grant as satisfactory, accede to, assent to, receive with approval, acknowledge. **3** *The boy accepted full responsibility for breaking the window:* assume, undertake, bear, acknowledge, admit, avow.

Ant. 1, 2 refuse, reject, decline, spurn. **3** disown, repudiate; deny, disavow, disacknowledge.

◇ *Usage note:* Do not confuse *accept* and *except. Accept* means to take something offered: *I accept your invitation, apology, gift,* etc. *Except* means to exclude or leave out; with the exception of: *I like everyone except Bill. No one is excepted from paying taxes.*

acceptable *adj.* **1** *The lawyers found the contract acceptable:* capable of being accepted, agreeable, proper, suitable, satisfactory; worthy, good. **2** *His work is acceptable, but he has not won a prize:* adequate, suitable, passable, tolerable, allowable; barely satisfactory, *Informal* so-so.

Ant. 1, 2 unacceptable, unsatisfactory, unsuitable.

acceptance *n.* **1** *His acceptance of bribes led to his arrest:* accepting, taking, receiving; receipt, reception. **2** *The employer gave his acceptance to the worker's suggestions:* approval, consent, agreement, permission, concession, acquiescence; *Informal* O.K., stamp of approval; sanction, endorsement, affirmation. **3** *It took years for Einstein's theory to gain acceptance:* approval, approbation, belief, recognition, acknowledgement; affirmation, confirmation.

Ant. 1, 2 rejection, refusal, repudiation; disapproval. **3** rejection; disavowal.

accepted *adj. Camels are the accepted means of transport in the desert:* agreed upon, approved, acceptable, confirmed, acknowledged, established; common, normal, usual, conventional, standard, regular, customary, universal, time-honoured.

access *n.* **1** *How could the thief have gained access to the vault? Each constituent has access to his M.P.:* admittance; entrance, entrée. **2** *Switzerland has access to the sea via the River Rhine:* a means of reaching, an approach, passage, passageway, gateway, entrance, entry; road, path.

◇ *Usage note:* A few people always confuse *access* and *excess. Access* is a way of getting to something or someone; *excess* is a surplus, a state of overabundance. Thus, *How could the thief have gained access to the vault? Dieting will take off your excess weight.*

accessible *adj.* **1** *A doctor must have a telephone accessible at all times:* available, ready, at hand, on hand, handy, nearby; obtainable, attainable, reachable. **2** *The principal was always accessible to the students:* available, approachable, reachable.

Ant. 1 unavailable, far-off, unobtainable; hidden, hidden away, secreted. **2** unapproachable, unavailable, inaccessible, unreachable.

accessory *n.* **1** *The new swimming-pool was a welcome accessory to the school:* addition, supplement; adjunct, attachment, component, extension. **2** *This belt makes a beautiful accessory to your dress:* accompaniment, adornment, decoration; complement, accent, detail. **3** *The get-away driver was convicted as an accessory to the robbery:* accomplice, confederate, partner; associate, colleague, assistant.

◇ *Pronunciation tip:* Don't be careless in pronouncing *accessory*. Remember that it has a *k* sound at the beginning and ends in *-ory*, not merely *-ry*. Thus: *aK-sessory.*

accident *n.* **1** *Columbus discovered America by accident:* chance, luck, pot luck, good fortune, fortuity. **2** *An ambulance rushed to the scene of the accident. He broke his leg in a skiing accident:* collision, crash, wreck, smash-up; mishap, misadventure, mischance; bit of bad luck, piece of misfortune.

Ant. 1 plan, intention, intent, design, calculation, purpose.

accidental *adj. Our meeting on the street was purely accidental:* unplanned, unintentional, unpremeditated, uncalculated, unforeseen; unexpected, fortuitous; chance, haphazard, random, inadvertent.

Ant. planned, intentional, intended, premeditated, calculated; foreseen, expected; prepared, designed, projected.

acclaim *v.* **1** *Critics acclaimed the new play:* greet with praise, loudly approve, applaud, cheer, hail; laud, extol, commend, sing the praises of, exalt, compliment, eulogize; honour, celebrate. **2** *The people acclaimed him king:* name by acclamation.

—n. **3** *The new opera was greeted with universal acclaim:* great praise, loud approval, applause, plaudits, cheering, acclamation, rejoicing.

Ant. **1** criticize, denounce, condemn, disapprove, *Informal* slam, boo, hiss, shout down, give the raspberry.

◇ *Word origin: Acclaim* comes from Latin *acclamare,* meaning (1) to jeer, (2) to cheer, and (3) to name by acclamation. It is also related to *clamour.*

acclamation *n. The queen was received with acclamation by the crowd. He was elected president of the society by acclamation:* ovation, burst of applause, cheering, shout of approval; acclaim, homage, tribute, approbation, plaudits, adulation; cheers, hurrahs, hosannas.

Ant. booing, hissing, raspberry; disapproval, denunciation, censure, disapprobation, execration, excoriation.

◇ *Word origin:* See ACCLAIM.

acclimatize *v. In a few days you'll be acclimatized to the cold weather:* get used to, accustom, adapt, adjust, habituate, become seasoned to, inure.

◇ *Pronunciation tip: Acclimatize* is usually pronounced so that the second syllable is stressed, said strongest, *ak-LIE-mut-eyes.*

accolade *n. The Nobel prize is the highest accolade a writer can receive:* award, honour, tribute, prize, trophy, decoration, citation; praise, compliment, commendation, acclaim, admiration.

◇ *Word origin:* Originally, *accolade* meant "hug round the neck" and stood for a ceremonial embrace confirming the bestowal of knighthood.

accommodate *v.* **1** *Can you accommodate me with a loan?:* do a kindness for, do a favour for; oblige, help, aid, assist; supply, provide, furnish. **2** *This hotel can accommodate 500 guests:* have capacity for, furnish room for, billet, shelter, bed down; entertain; hold, contain; lodge, put up. **3** *You'll have to accommodate yourself to the situation:* adapt, adjust, fit, bring into line; conform, modify, reconcile.

Ant. **1** inconvenience, disoblige, trouble.

accommodating *adj. The taxi-driver was very accommodating:* obliging, helpful, considerate, kind, hospitable, *Informal* neighbourly; polite, courteous, gracious; conciliatory, yielding.

Ant. disobliging, inconsiderate; rude, churlish.

accommodation *n.* **1** *What kind of accommodation did you have on the ship?:* rooms, quarters, lodgings, housing; arrangements. **2** *If labour and management don't reach an accommodation there will be a strike:* compromise, settlement, adjustment; agreement, concord.

accompany *v.* **1** *My daughter accompanied me on the trip. Secret Service agents accompany the Ambassador everywhere:* go in company with, go along with, attend; conduct; escort, chaperon, convoy, usher, guard. **2** *Suffering accompanies war:* to occur with, go together with, go hand in hand with, go hand in glove with, be connected with, coexist with, follow. **3** *The pianist accompanied her singing:* play accompaniment for, supply music for.

◇ *Usage note: Accompanied by* literally means in the company of or escorted by: *Shirley came to the party accompanied by her brother. The aircraft-carrier was accompanied by three destroyers. Accompanied with* means as a supplement to: *His words were accompanied with angry gestures.*

◇ *Word origin:* See COMPANION.

accomplice *n. The butler was an accomplice in the robbery:* confederate, accessory, partner, collaborator; associate, colleague, ally; assistant, subordinate, aide, helper, supporter, abettor; participant.

accomplish *v.* **1** *Robin Hood always accomplished what he set out to do:* achieve, succeed at, carry out, do; perform, realize, execute, attain, fulfil; bring about, produce. **2** *If you organize your work you'll accomplish more:* do, get done; finish, complete.

Ant. **1** fail, fall short, miss the mark; give up, forsake. **2** leave undone.

accomplished *adj.* **1** *Space flight is an accomplished fact:* existing, realized, effected, completed, consummated; established, proven, accepted, proved. **2** *Cicero was an accomplished orator:* expert, able, proficient, capable, fine, skilled, skilful; masterly, practised, finished, experienced, eminent, polished, cultivated; talented, gifted, brilliant, adroit, deft, apt.

Ant. **1** non-existent, unrealized, unestablished, unproven. **2** unskilled, poor, incompetent, incapable, inexpert; inexperienced; unpolished; untalented, amateurish.

accomplishment *n.* **1** *All nations must work for the accomplishment of peace:* achievement, realization, execution, attainment, fulfilment, carrying out; culmination, consummation. **2** *Developing the supersonic jet was quite an accomplishment:* achievement, feat, attainment, exploit; deed, act. **3** *Playing the piano is but one of her accomplishments:* achievement, feat, skill; talent, gift, proficiency, capability.

Ant. 1 failure. **2** blunder. **3** lack, deficiency, lacuna, incapacity.

accord *v.* **1** *The views of the Liberal and Labour Parties accord on the new tax bill:* agree, concur; conform, correspond, be in unison, match, tally, coincide, harmonize; *Informal* square, be in tune. **2** *High honours were accorded him when he graduated:* grant, present, give, bestow, render, tender, bequeath, vouchsafe; concede, allow, cede.

—*n.* **3** *Our views on politics are not in accord:* agreement, harmony, accordance, concurrence, concert, conformity; rapport, sympathy.

Ant. 1 differ, disagree, conflict, clash, collide, contrast. **2** withhold, deny, refuse, hold back. **3** conflict, discord, disagreement, dissension; variance, contention.

accordingly *adv.* **1** *I'm an adult and I expect to be treated accordingly:* in accordance with the fact, correspondingly, suitably, appropriately. **2** *This furnace cost a lot of money; accordingly, it should perform perfectly:* therefore, thus, so, hence, wherefore, whereupon, consequently, as a result; in which case, then, whence, thence, in due course.

Ant. 1 conversely.

accost *v. A beggar accosted me in front of the hotel:* hail, call to, speak to suddenly, greet, salute, address; confront, approach, buttonhole, waylay, stop, halt; solicit, make an appeal to, proposition.

Ant. evade, avoid, ignore, overlook, slight, shun.

◇ *Usage note:* Although *accost* means to approach and speak to, to stop and greet, it has taken on somewhat unpleasant connotations, especially of being stopped by someone whom one does not particularly wish to meet or talk to. Thus, we usually say *I was greeted by a friend* but *I was accosted by a beggar* or *A stranger stopped him in the street to tell him his shoe was untied* but *The policeman accosted him to warn him against jay-walking.*

◇ *Word origin:* Accost comes from Latin *costa*, rib. (If you *accost* someone, the two of you are standing rib to rib.)

account *n.* **1** *Give us a full account of your holiday:* description, report; story, history, record, chronicle, tale, narrative, narration, commentary; explanation, version, statement, enumeration. **2** *The student disobeyed the rules and on this account is being expelled from school:* reason, cause, grounds, sake, consideration, regard, *Informal* score. **3** *These old letters are of no account:* importance, import, worth, significance, consequence, note; value, use, merit; esteem, honour, repute, distinction, dignity, standing, rank. **4** *My wife handles our household accounts:* financial record, financial statement, bookkeeping, books, accounting.

—*v.* **5** *He accounts himself the equal of any man at ballroom dancing:* consider, regard, believe, look upon as, view as, think, judge, count, deem, hold, take to be; rate, estimate, calculate, reckon, value, appraise, weigh, gauge.

accountant *n. An accountant helped me to fill up my income-tax form:* chartered accountant, bookkeeper, auditor, actuary.

accredit *v.* **1** *The new ambassador is fully accredited by his government:* furnish with credentials, certify, license, endorse, commission, authorize, sanction, officially recognize; empower. **2** *The invention of the electric light is accredited to Thomas Alva Edison:* attribute, ascribe, assign, credit.

accrue *v. Interest on money in a savings account accrues regularly:* accumulate, collect, build up, amass, pile up, add up; grow, increase.

Ant. dwindle, decrease, diminish, lessen, wane, dribble away.

accumulate *v. Snow accumulated on the ground. He accumulated a fortune buying and selling used cars:* gather, gather together, pile up, heap up, amass, collect, assemble, aggregate; grow, congregate, cumulate, garner; save up, store up, hoard.

Ant. scatter, disperse, distribute; dissipate, waste.

◇ *Word origin: Accumulate* is related to Latin *cumulus*, heap, which also gives us the name of the heaped or piled up *cumulus* clouds.

accumulation *n.* **1** *Let's throw out that accumulation of junk in the attic:* collection, assemblage, conglomeration; mass, heap, pile, hoard, store; stock, supply, aggregation, accrual. **2** *The accumulation of rare books is his pastime:* collecting, amassing, gathering; acquiring, agglomerating, hoarding.

Ant. 2 distribution, dispersing, dispersal, scattering.

accuracy *n. The Inland Revenue checks tax returns for accuracy:* accurateness, correctness, freedom from error; exactness, exactitude, precision; truth, truthfulness, verity, fidelity, faithfulness.

Ant. error, inaccuracy, incorrectness, carelessness, slovenliness; lies, lying, fallaciousness.

"In all pointed sentences, some degree of accuracy must be sacrificed to conciseness."

—*Samuel Johnson*

---

accurate *adj. The drawing of the house is accurate in every detail. He is an accurate mathematician:* correct, without error, unerring, true, truthful, faithful, perfect, faultless, exact, right, precise, scrupulous.

Ant. incorrect, wrong, inaccurate, fallacious; inexact, defective, imperfect, faulty; careless, slipshod, slovenly.

◇ *Word origin: Accurate* comes from Latin *accuratus*, done with care. (The Latin word *cura* means "care.")

accusation *n. Your accusation that I lied is untrue.*

The accusation is wilful murder: charge, allegation, complaint, imputation, citation, indictment.

Ant. reply, answer, plea; denial, rebuttal.

accuse *v.* **1** *The prosecutor accused the defendant of murder:* charge, lodge a complaint against, arraign, indict, cite. **2** *You can't accuse him of laziness:* charge, reproach, take to task, call to account, upbraid; blame.

Ant. 1, 2 reply, answer, plea, rebut; deny, defend; acquit, absolve, vindicate, exonerate.

◇ *Word origin: Accuse* comes from Latin *accusare,* to call to account (from *causa,* cause or lawsuit).

accustomed *adj.* **1** *He spoke with his accustomed courtesy:* usual, common, normal, regular, general, customary, habitual, established, conventional, set, routine, commonplace, ordinary, familiar, prevailing, prevalent, fixed, ingrained. **2** *Laplanders are accustomed to cold weather:* used to, acclimatized, seasoned, familiarized, inured, in the habit of, given to, habituated, wonted, prone.

Ant. 1 unusual, uncommon, rare, strange, unfamiliar, foreign, exotic; singular, infrequent, occasional; peculiar, abnormal, unconventional, odd, queer, erratic. **2** unused, unaccustomed.

acerbity *n.* **1** *The butler addressed the uninvited callers with acerbity:* ill-tempered manner, brusqueness, sarcastic irritability, sarcasm, irascibility, acrimony, pointed rudeness. **2** *The acerbity of some wines is such as to make them an acquired taste:* acidity, tartness, astringency.

Ant. 1 good nature, cordiality, good humour, affability, pleasantness, mellowness, complaisance. **2** blandness, tastelessness, lifelessness, indifference.

◇ *Word origin: Acerbity* comes from Latin *acerbitas,* bitterness, harshness. When Romans used the word literally, it referred to the taste of unripe fruit.

ache *n.* **1** *A dentist can cure that ache:* pain, throb, twinge, pang, hurt.

—*v.* **2** *The blow made my head ache:* hurt, feel pain, be sore, smart, throb.

achieve *v.* **1** *The Restoration Fund has achieved its goal of collecting one thousand pounds:* accomplish, attain, realize, reach, fulfil; bring to pass, bring about, carry out, effect, do, dispatch. **2** *Can a mere mortal achieve perfect happiness?:* attain, obtain, gain, get, earn, win, acquire, procure.

Ant. 1 fail in, fall short of. **2** lose, be deprived of.

◇ *Word origin:* The *-chieve* in *achieve* is related to *chief,* in the sense of "head." Thus, literally, to *achieve* is to bring something to a head.

achievement *n.* **1** *Man's first walk on the moon was a stunning technological achievement:* accomplishment, attainment, realization, fulfilment; feat, exploit, effort, act, deed. **2** *Climbing Ben Nevis is just one of her achievements:* accomplishment, attainment, acquirement; skill, mastery, expertise, command.

Ant. 1 failure, defeat, frustration, fiasco.

acid *adj.* **1** *These lemons are more acid than usual:* sour, tart, astringent, pungent, sharp, biting, harsh, vinegarish. **2** *That film critic has an acid wit:* sharp, biting, stinging, cutting, scalding, harsh, bitter, caustic, nasty, crabbed; sarcastic, satirical, ironic.

Ant. 1 sweet, succulent; alkaline; pleasant-tasting, mild, gentle, bland. **2** kindly, gentle, sweet, mild, soft; pleasant; warm-hearted, benign, compassionate.

acknowledge *v.* **1** *The losing candidate acknowledged his defeat. We acknowledge that night must follow day:* recognize, accept, admit, own, own up to, confess, allow, grant, concede, accede, concur, yield, assent. **2** *The chairman acknowledges the delegation from France:* recognize, extend cognizance to, take notice of; call upon, call upon to speak, call upon to vote. **3** *Did he acknowledge your greeting?:* respond to, reply to, answer; express appreciation for, thank for.

Ant. 1 disclaim, repudiate, reject, renounce, contradict; deny, disavow. **2, 3** ignore, disregard, disdain, slight, spurn, reject; deny.

acknowledgement *n.* **1** *He gave his wife full acknowledgement for her help in starting the business:* recognition, recognizance, credit. **2** *His acknowledgement that he stole the necklace cleared his sister of blame:* affirmation, admission, confession, concession. **3** *Accept our grateful acknowledgement with this note:* thanks, gratitude, appreciation; response, answer, reply.

Ant. 1, 2 denial, disavowal, disclaimer, demurrer.

acme *n. Appearing in the West End was the acme of his theatrical career:* height, peak, pinnacle, zenith, high point, highest point, climax, summit; heyday, flowering; crown, crest, apex, culmination, apogee.

Ant. depth, low point, worst point, bottom, nadir.

◇ *Word origin: Acme* comes from Greek *akmē,* point or sharp edge. But the Greeks used the word figuratively, too, just as we do. According to them, for example, the "acme of youth" was the best time to be alive.

acolyte *n.* **1** *Two acolytes attended the priest at Mass:* altar boy, attendant, server; novice, assistant. **2** *The famous film director arrived, surrounded by his acolytes:* follower, admirer, adherent, assistant, helper, attendant.

acquaint *v.* **1** *Have you two just met, or were you acquainted before? Our minister believes in getting acquainted with everybody in town:* introduce, make known socially, meet. **2** *It takes time to acquaint yourself with a new job. Let me acquaint you with the facts of the matter:* familiarize, apprise, disclose, reveal, advise, tell, inform,

notify, enlighten, make aware, divulge to.
Ant. **2** hide, conceal, keep secret, keep private; withhold, reserve, retain, hold back.

acquaintance *n.* **1** *He's not really a friend, just an acquaintance:* person slightly known, distant friend. **2** *We had a brief acquaintance with her a while ago:* friendship, relationship, association, dealings. **3** *The school's curriculum stresses acquaintance with the sciences:* familiarity, awareness, knowledge.
Ant. **1** stranger; good friend, intimate, bosom friend, buddy. **3** unfamiliarity, ignorance.

acquiesce *v. I don't like the idea but I will acquiesce in it:* consent, agree, assent, accede, allow; bow to, yield, submit, give in; admit, concede, grant, comply, concur, conform, fall in with; resign oneself, reconcile oneself.
Ant. resist, fight, contest, refuse, balk at, veto; protest, object, disagree, dissent, demur.
◇ *Word origin: Acquiesce* is based on Latin *acquiescere*, to rest.

acquire *v. Paul Getty acquired a fortune in the oil business. She has acquired a working knowledge of French:* get, obtain, attain, gain, secure, procure; achieve; earn, win, pick up; cultivate.
Ant. lose, be deprived of; relinquish, give up, forgo.

acquisition *n.* **1** *This painting is the museum's most recent acquisition:* acquirement, procurement, possession, property, gain, purchase, prize. **2** *Informal. Leonardo devoted his life to the acquisition of knowledge:* attainment, obtainment, achievement, acquirement, procurement, gain.
◇ *Usage note:* In formal speech and writing, an *acquisition* is a material possession while an *acquirement* is a personal skill or knowledge gained through practice or study: *The Rembrandt painting was the museum's major acquisition. An ability to read the music of Bartok at sight is a difficult acquirement.*

acquisitive *adj. She is an acquisitive person, always wanting things:* covetous, grasping, greedy, avaricious; materialistic.
Ant. self-denying, abstemious, non-possessive; altruistic; generous.

acquit *v.* **1** *The jury acquitted the defendant on all charges:* declare not guilty, declare innocent, clear; exonerate, vindicate, absolve, let off, discharge, release, relieve, deliver, liberate, set free; exempt, excuse. **2** *A gentleman must acquit himself well in any situation:* conduct, behave, comport, act.
Ant. **1** charge, indict, blame; convict, declare guilty; condemn, damn, doom.

acrid *adj.* **1** *The burning rubber gave off acrid smoke:* caustic, harsh, sharp, bitter, burning, stinging, irritating, biting, pungent; smelly, foul-smelling, malodorous. **2** *A political cartoonist must have an acrid sense of humour:* harsh, sharp, biting, bitter, nasty, acrimonious, vitriolic, acid; sarcastic, ironic, satirical.
Ant. **1** sweet, pleasing; fragrant, aromatic. **2** kindly, gentle, sweet, sweet-natured, good-natured; benign. compassionate.
◇ *Word origin:* The story goes that about 300 years ago an English chemist was trying to think of a word meaning bitter and fiery. *Acrimonious* and *acid* were the first words that came to mind; so he combined them in one word, and the result was *acrid.*

acrimonious *adj. You may not like my decision, but don't be acrimonious about it:* sarcastic, spiteful, rancorous, bitter, peevish, ill-natured, nasty; venomous, caustic, corrosive, sour, cutting, splenetic, irascible.
Ant. forgiving, benign, benignant, good-humoured, kind-hearted.

acrimony *n. The election campaign led to bitter acrimony between the candidates:* ill will, hard feelings, rancour, anger, bitterness; animosity, hostility, spitefulness, antagonism, asperity, malignity, spite, malignancy, spleen, animus.
Ant. goodwill, good feelings, love, liking, friendliness.
◇ *Word origin: Acrimony* comes from Latin *acrimonia,* meaning sharpness and pungency of flavour.

act *n.* **1** *He was criticized for one careless act:* deed, action, performance, step, move; feat, exploit, accomplishment, achievement. **2** *The thief was caught in the act:* action, process of doing. **3** *This area was declared a National Park by an act of Parliament:* official decision, law, edict, decree, bill, resolution, statute, ordinance, measure. **4** *Romeo dies in the last act of* Romeo and Juliet. *His song and dance act was a sensation in vaudeville:* segment of a play, main division of a play; short performance, routine. **5** *Her sickness is just an act to get sympathy:* pretence, pose, fake, insincere act.
—*v.* **6** *Act now and save money during our annual sale:* do it, perform, do, function, execute, operate, move; press on, put forth; commit oneself. **7** *Act your age! The car acted as if it was about to run out of petrol. Mr. Smith will act as chairman of the committee:* behave, comport oneself; work, operate, function. **8** *When you see the gift, act surprised:* pretend to be, feign, fake, affect, simulate, counterfeit. **9** *He has acted the part of Hamlet three times:* perform, play, enact; represent; impersonate.
Ant. **1** inactivity, inaction. **6** stay, stop, rest, procrastinate, put off.

acting *adj.* **1** *Mr. Smith will be acting mayor until new elections are held:* temporary, substitute, surrogate, provisional, interim; simulated, ersatz.
—*n.* **2** *Acting can be a difficult profession:* dramatics, thespianism; theatre, dramaturgy, stagecraft.
Ant. **1** permanent; real, true.

action *n.* **1** *The action of this crank turns the wheel:* power, force, work, effort; effect, influence. **2** *The fire brigade was called into action when the* *alarm sounded:* operation, activity, functioning, performing, performance; process; production. **3** *Increasing the tax was an unpopular action:* act, deed, step, move; exploit, feat, achievement. **4** *We expect action on our complaint before next Friday:* activity, work, effort, exertion, movement, enterprise; committed attention, achievement, accomplishment, progress, execution. **5** *The general has seen action in three wars:* combat, battle, fighting, conflict, warfare. **6** *It was a boring film with no action:* movement, excitement. **7** *My lawyer will take action against you in the courts:* legal proceedings, prosecution, suit, redress.

Ant. 2 inaction, inactivity, rest. **4** complacency. **6** dialogue, exposition.

activate *v. These push-buttons activate the lift:* start, turn on, actuate, put into action, set going, stimulate; drive, impel, energize; vitalize, mobilize.

Ant. deactivate; stop, turn off, halt.

> **Exploring the Word:** *Act, action, activity, active, actor, actual, activate, agent, agency, agenda,* and *agile* all come from Latin *agere,* to do. Thus an *act, action,* or *activity* is something done; *active* means doing many things; an *actor* is one who does something; *actual* means done, in existence; and *activate* means to start or cause to do. Similarly, an *agent* or an *agency* is one who does or acts for another, an *agenda* is a list of things to be done, and *agile* means able to act quickly or effortlessly.

active *adj.* **1** *No one is more active than a teenager. He is the most active member of the team:* energetic, vigorous, lively, animated, indefatigable; busy, on the go, occupied, engaged, industrious, enterprising, ambitious, go-getting, forceful, assertive. **2** *Skiing is an active sport:* strenuous, energetic; vigorous; lively, animated. **3** *Invitations went to all active members of the club. Mount Vesuvius is an active volcano:* functioning, operative, working, acting, effectual; in force, at work. **4** *She may be eighty, but she has an active mind:* alert, quick, vigorous, alive, lively; agile, nimble, sprightly, animated, imaginative, industrious, diligent.

Ant. 1-4 inactive. **1** unoccupied; torpid, sluggish, indolent, idle, lazy. **2** sedentary; inert. **3** non-functioning, inoperative; dormant. **4** sluggish, slow, dull; unimaginative.

activity *n.* **1** *The schoolroom was full of bustling activity:* movement; enterprise; hustle, bustle, stir, hurly-burly; sprightliness, vivacity, liveliness, animation. **2** *We need a little activity to keep ourselves warm:* exercise, exertion, movement. **3** *What school activities interest you?:* undertaking, enterprise, venture, endeavour, avocation, occupation.

Ant. 1 inactivity, torpor, dullness. **2** relaxation, rest.

actor *n.* **1** *A good actor can play any role:* performer, thespian, dramatic artist, trouper, player; (*variously*) star, leading actor, supporting actor, character actor, working actor, extra, walk-on; starlet. **2** *We are all actors in the drama of life:* participant, doer, functionary, perpetrator.

actual *adj.* **1** *This book is based on an actual case:* real, existing, factual, true, genuine, authentic, confirmed. **2** *What is the actual location of the ship now?:* real, physical, corporeal, existent, existing, concrete, tangible, certain, sure; current, present, prevailing.

Ant. 1 fictional, fictitious, made-up; hypothetical, theoretical. **2** probable, supposed, projected, conjectured.

actually *adv. The events depicted in the film did not actually take place:* in fact, really, truly, genuinely, literally, indeed.

actuate *v.* **1** See ACTIVATE. **2** *Everything he does is actuated by greed:* motivate, prompt, cause, induce, stimulate, instigate, incite, move, drive, impel, arouse, rouse; influence, inspire, excite, stir, animate.

Ant. 1 See ACTIVATE. **2** check, curb, restrain, hinder, deter, dampen, retard, inhibit, thwart.

acumen *n. His business acumen will help the company:* keenness, acuteness, smartness, astuteness, shrewdness, cleverness; discernment, intelligence, wisdom, perspicacity, sound judgement; clear-headedness, sagacity, insight, perception, ingenuity.

Ant. obtuseness, dullness, ignorance, stupidity, folly, bad judgement.

acute *adj.* **1** *Angles of less than 90° are called acute angles:* sharply pointed, sharp, needle-shaped, peaked. **2** *She had an acute headache. He's suffering from acute appendicitis:* severe, intense, fierce, very great, very bad; excruciating, distressing, piercing, agonizing. **3** *Einstein was a man of uncommonly acute intelligence:* keen, penetrating, piercing; discriminating, discerning, sensitive, ingenious.

Ant. 1 obtuse, dull, blunt, blunted. **2** mild, moderate, *Medical* chronic. **3** obtuse, dull, dense, stolid.

adage *n. "Live and let live" is an old adage:* saying, proverb, maxim, axiom, motto; dictum, truism, wise observation, precept, *Informal* saw, old saw.

adamant *adj. Her mother is adamant in demanding that she be home by eleven:* insistent, unyielding, inflexible, fixed, set, firm, immovable, uncompromising, unbending, determined, stubborn, obdurate, *Slang* uptight.

Ant. yielding, flexible, lax, undemanding, easy-going, indifferent, *Slang* easy; submissive, capitulating, pliant, compliant, compromising.

◇ *Word origin: Adamant* comes from Greek *adamas,* unbreakable. The Greeks and Romans came to use it as a poetic word for diamond. The Greek verb *daman,* from which it is derived, means to tame an animal, subdue an enemy, or marry a girl. It is also cognate with our English word *tame.*

adapt *v.* **1** *The chameleon adapts to its surroundings by changing colour:* adjust, conform, accommodate, fit, suit, assimilate, co-ordinate, harmonize, reconcile, attune to. **2** *The play is adapted from a short story:* reshape, shape, fashion, frame, transform, rework, convert, make suitable, make fit, recompose, remodel, modify, change, alter.

◇ *Usage note:* See ADOPT.

"The reasonable man adapts himself to the world: the unreasonable one persists in trying to adapt the world to himself. Therefore all progress depends on the unreasonable man."
—*George Bernard Shaw*

---

adaptable *adj.* **1** *An adaptable person is at ease anywhere:* flexible, pliant, compliant, unrigid, open-minded, easy-going; conformable, malleable, amenable. **2** *The new auditorium is adaptable for either theatrical or sports events:* usable, serviceable, applicable, accommodative; changeable, adjustable, alterable.

Ant. 1 inflexible, rigid, fixed, closed-minded, *Slang* uptight. **2** inflexible, non-adjustable, unalterable; unusable, unserviceable.

adaptation *n.* **1** *The building is undergoing adaptation from garage to living quarters:* alteration, modification, remodelling, conversion; refitting; adjustment, change, shift. **2** *The TV series is an adaptation of a novel:* altered version, modification, reworking, revision, reshaping.

add *v.* **1** *Let's add up the cost of all our purchases:* total, sum up, count up, figure up, compute, calculate, reckon. **2** *Add one more item to the list. May I add a point or two?:* include, attach, append, join, join on, tack on; offer in addition, supplement, increase by, enlarge by.

Ant. 1 subtract, deduct. **2** remove, exclude, eliminate, withdraw; take away, reduce.

◇ *Word origin:* When you *add* something, you put it with something else—*add* comes from Latin *addere,* to put.

addendum *n. The report has an addendum clarifying certain points:* added section, supplement, addition, codicil, postscript; appendage, attachment.

addict *n.* **1** *Addicts must be identified and treated at once:* drug addict, *Slang* user, tripper, freak, dope-fiend. **2** *She's an opera addict:* devotee, fan, adherent, habitué, acolyte, votary, *Slang* nut, hound.

—*v.* **3** *She was addicted to sweets:* give (oneself) habitually, yield obsessively, surrender, submit; *Slang* hook, turn on.

Ant. 3 withdraw, break the habit; renounce, give up, eschew.

◇ *Word origin:* An *addict* is a slave to his habit. The word comes from Latin *addictus,* which in Roman law meant a debtor awarded as a slave to his creditor.

addition *n.* **1** *Addition is taught before subtraction:* mathematical sum, totalling, counting up, summing up, summation, reckoning, enumeration. **2** *The addition of a baby to the household changed our lives. The addition of a porch will increase the value of the house:* adding, including, encompassing, embracing; joining, adjoining, annexing, appending, attaching; extending, increasing. **3** *The addition in cost of tuition over last year is £200:* increase, increment; extension, enlargement, extra, additive, augmentation. **4** *The addition to the town library will double its size:* annex, wing, extension, appendage; adjunct, appurtenance, addendum, added contribution.

Ant. 1-3 subtraction. **2** subtracting, removing, removal, detaching, detachment. **3** decrease, reduction, deduction, lessening, diminution.

additional *adj. The charge for the delivery of the furniture is additional:* extra, added, added on, supplementary, appended, over-and-above.

addled *adj. The witness became addled by the cross-examination. My brain may be old but it's not addled:* confused, mixed-up, muddled, befuddled, nonplussed; foolish, silly.

◇ *Word origin:* If you are *addled,* you are mixed-up; if an egg is *addled,* it is rotten. The word comes from Old English *adela,* meaning something slimy and nasty.

address *n.* **1** *Please print your name and address:* place of residence, abode, place of business; location, locality. **2** *The Presidential address will be broadcast at 8 o'clock:* speech, talk, statement, oration, discourse.

—*v.* **3** *Address this letter to the Postmaster-General:* write for delivery to, put an address on. **4** *The general addressed his troops before the battle:* give a formal talk, talk to, speak to, orate, lecture, salute in words; write to.

◇ *Word origin: Address* is ultimately derived from Latin *directum,* straight, direct. Thus, when you *address* someone, you are (literally speaking) *directing* your words to him; and when you *address* a letter, you are likewise *directing* it to the addressee.

adept *adj. She's adept at organizational work. He's adept in needlecraft:* skilled, skilful, expert, proficient, accomplished, masterly, masterful, practised; good, apt, able, adroit, dexterous, gifted.

Ant. amateurish, beginning; unskilled, inept, unaccomplished, clumsy, awkward.

◇ *Word origin:* An *adept* person has attained skill. The word is from Latin *adeptus,* having attained.

adequate *adj. Our hotel room wasn't luxurious, but it was adequate:* suitable, satisfactory, sufficient, equal to need, passable, fitting, fit; enough, ample.

Ant. inadequate, unsuitable, unsatisfactory, insufficient; imperfect, defective; too little, not enough.

adhere *v.* **1** *The wallpaper won't adhere to the ceiling:* stick, stick fast, hold, cling, cleave; glue, glue on, paste, cement; fix, fasten. **2** *He adhered to the faith of his fathers:* be faithful, be loyal, be constant, be true, keep, keep to, hold closely, maintain, cling, stick, cleave, stand by, remain fixed.

Ant. 1 come unstuck, come loose, come unglued; detach, unfasten. **2** break with, part from, separate from, leave, be disloyal, be untrue.

"... . they do no more adhere and keep place together than the Hundredth Psalm to the tune of 'Green Sleeves'."
—*William Shakespeare*

adherence *n. The teacher demanded adherence to the rules:* strict observance, attachment, keeping to, obedience; loyalty, fealty, faithfulness, fidelity, constancy, allegiance, devotion.

Ant. breaking, disobedience; disloyalty, unfaithfulness, infidelity.

adherent *n.* **1** *He is a leader with many adherents:* follower, supporter, advocate, disciple, upholder; devotee, partisan, fan; acolyte, pupil. —*adj.* **2** *Scrape off that adherent substance with a razor-blade:* adhesive, sticky, sticking, gummy, viscous, viscid, clinging, adhering, holding fast.

Ant. 1 opponent, detractor. **2** loose; watery.

adhesive *adj.* **1** *Glue and paste are adhesive substances:* adherent, adhering, sticky, sticking, clinging; gummy, glutinous; gummed. —*n.* **2** *You need an adhesive to hold these cut-outs in place:* sticky substance, adhering substance, gummy substance; glue, paste, cement, solder, mortar, plastic wood.

Ant. 2 solvent.

◇ *Usage note:* Don't confuse *adhesive* and *cohesive. Adhesive* refers to one thing sticking to another thing. *Cohesive* refers to particles of the same substance sticking together; thus cake mixture may be *cohesive* and a group that is united and sticks together may be *cohesive*, or a story whose facts all make sense and fit together may be *cohesive*.

adjacent *adj. Our farm is adjacent to yours:* next to, beside, right beside, abutting, touching, bordering, next door to; contiguous with, conterminous, proximate, juxtaposed.

Ant. far from, remote from, separated from.

◇ *Usage note: Adjacent* means next to, but not necessarily connected with, while *adjoining* means next to and connected. Thus *adjacent* hotel rooms are separated by a wall, while *adjoining* rooms are connected by a common door.

◇ *Word origin: Adjacent* is from Latin *ad-*, to, near, + *jacere*, to lie, hence lying near to (something).

adjoining *adj. The two sisters had adjoining rooms at the hotel:* joining, joined, touching, connected, interconnected, next-door.

Ant. separate, detached, discrete, individual.

◇ *Usage note:* See ADJACENT.

adjourn *v.* **1** *He adjourned the meeting until tomorrow at 10 a.m.:* recess, suspend, interrupt, discontinue, put off, postpone; close, end, dismiss, dissolve. **2** *When dinner had finished, they adjourned to the living-room:* repair, remove, move; depart for.

Ant. 1 convene, be in session, call to order, open, reopen; assemble, gather, convoke, continue. **2** remain, stay, stay put.

◇ *Word origin: Adjourn* comes from Old French *adjorner*, to set a day for the reopening of a meeting, from the phrase *à jorn nomé*, to an appointed day.

adjunct *n. The American Civil War was the first to see railways used as an adjunct to military operations:* accessory, supplement, complement, auxiliary part, secondary feature; appurtenance.

adjust *v.* **1** *It's cold in here; can you adjust the thermostat?:* set, fix, move, regulate, change, order. **2** *My eyes haven't adjusted to the dark yet:* accustom, acclimatize, accommodate, adapt, reconcile, conform; fix, alter, modify, regulate.

Ant. 1 leave as it is, let remain as it is, leave alone.

◇ *Word origin:* When you *adjust* something you bring it closer to a standard. The word is based on Latin *juxta*, close to, which is also found in *juxtaposition*.

adjustment *n.* **1** *These spectacles need adjustment:* adjusting, alignment, straightening; fixing, regulation, regulating, modification; bringing into agreement, justification, reconciliation, rectification; focusing. **2** *This knob on the TV set is the vertical adjustment:* control, regulator, adjusting device; setting. **3** *The newlyweds need a period of adjustment:* settling in, settlement, acclimatization, adapting, *Informal* getting used to; orientation.

adjutant *n. The general chose his friend the major as his adjutant:* assisting staff officer, aide, assistant, right-hand man, aide-de-camp.

◇ *Word origin:* An *adjutant* assists or aids a superior officer. The word is ultimately derived from Latin *ad-*, to, + *juvare*, to help, hence one who gives help to.

ad lib *adv.* **1** *She ended up talking ad lib about nothing:* continuously, non-stop, endlessly, ceaselessly. —*v.* **2** *If you forget your speech, just ad-lib:* improvise, extemporize, speak extemporaneously, speak off the cuff, speak impromptu, make up.

Ant. 2 follow the script, speak from notes.

◇ *Word origin: Ad lib* is short for Latin *ad*

libitum, meaning according to one's pleasure. It has long been used on musical scores to mean that the performer is free to slow or accelerate the tempo, or even pause, as he sees fit.

administer *v.* **1** *It takes brains to administer a large corporation:* manage, run, direct, administrate, govern, supervise, superintend. **2** *Administer the lotion to the sunburned area with a cotton swab:* dispense, apply, give, tender.

administration *n.* **1** *The administration of justice is often difficult:* administering, application, execution, management; dispensation, distribution, tendering. **2** *An executive should be experienced in administration:* management, executive duty, superintendence, leadership, overseeing; governing, government. **3** *The teachers are responsible to the Provost and the administration:* officers, executives; governing body, management, managerial organization, government.

administrative *adj. How best to expand the factory is an administrative problem:* executive, managerial, management, supervisory, organizational.

admirable *adj. His honesty is admirable:* worthy of admiration, commendable, praiseworthy, laudable, estimable.

Ant. deplorable, reprehensible, censurable, disappointing; bad, untrustworthy, worthless, faulty.

admiration *n. My admiration for his courage knows no bounds:* high regard, high opinion, esteem; veneration, honour, commendation, praise, approval, respect.

Ant. low regard, low opinion, disdain.

"Admiration is a very short-lived passion, that immediately decays upon growing familiar with its object." —*Joseph Addison*

---

admire *v. I admire your courage. He's so conceited he stops to admire himself in front of every mirror:* view with approval, hold in high regard, hold in esteem, think highly of, respect, esteem, value, prize, take pleasure in.

Ant. hold in low regard, hold a low opinion of, view with disapproval, disdain, abhor.

◇ *Word origin: Admire* comes from Latin *admirari*, to wonder at, and is also related to our words *miracle, mirage*, and *mirror*.

admissible *adj. Only a few errors are admissible. Hearsay is not admissible evidence in court:* capable of being admitted, permitted, allowed, allowable, permissible, acceptable, admittable, tolerated, tolerable, passable.

Ant. inadmissible, unacceptable, disallowed, non-permissible, intolerable.

admission *n.* **1** *Admission is limited to persons whose names appear on the guest list:* admittance, permission to enter, entry, entrance, entrée, access. **2** *Admission to the lecture is £2.50:* price of admission, entrance fee, ticket; fee, charge, tariff. **3** *Your admission of guilt will reduce the court's sentence:* acknowledgement, confession, profession, concession, declaration: assent, affirmation.

Ant. 3 denial, disavowal; rejection, negation.

admit *v.* **1** *Please admit the guests of honour. Only 15 new lawyers were admitted to the bar:* let in, allow to enter, let enter, give access to, grant entrance; appoint, induct, invest; receive. **2** *Did the thief admit his guilt?:* acknowledge, confess, concede, profess, declare. **3** *The rules of chess do not admit touching a piece without moving it:* allow, permit, grant, let.

Ant. 1 exclude, keep out, debar; dismiss, reject. **2** deny, disavow, reject, negate. **3** prohibit, forbid, disallow.

admonish *v.* **1** *The captain admonished the guards to be on the alert:* warn, caution, put on guard; advise, counsel, enjoin. **2** *The preacher admonished his congregation for failure to attend weekly services:* reprove, censure, reprimand, rebuke, reproach, remonstrate, chide, chasten, scold, upbraid, criticize, take to task, call to account, rap on the knuckles.

Ant. 2 praise, compliment, commend.

◇ *Word origin: Admonish* comes from the Latin prefix *ad-*, to, at, + *monere*, to warn.

admonition *n. The Bishop's admonitions were ignored by the rebel priest:* reprimand, mild reproof, scolding, reproach, remonstrance, rebuke, rap on the knuckles; warning, cautionary reminder, advice.

Ant. compliment, commendation, bit of praise, pat on the back.

◇ *Word origin: Admonition* comes from Latin *admonitio*, a friendly warning.

adolescent *n.* **1** *Over 70 per cent of today's adolescents are apolitical:* teenager, juvenile, youngster, young man or woman, minor, youth, schoolboy, schoolgirl, lad, lass, lassie; stripling, fledgling.

—*adj.* **2** *The film's attitude toward life is adolescent:* for a teenager, befitting a teenager, not adult; immature, puerile, pubescent, juvenile; callow, undeveloped; youthful, boyish, girlish; childish, babyish.

Ant. 1 adult; child. **2** adult, mature.

◇ *Word origin: Adolescent* and *adult* come from different forms of the Latin verb *adolescere*, to grow up; and in Latin they mean "growing up" and "grown-up," respectively.

adopt *v.* **1** *Many childless couples adopt children:* become the legal parent of, take as one's own child. **2** *We've adopted a motto for our club. The schools must adopt new methods of teaching foreign languages:* formally approve, accept, choose, appropriate, take up, follow, embrace, espouse; assume, affect; acknowledge, conform to.

Ant. 1 give up for adoption, place; disinherit. **2** give up, cast aside, cast off; spurn, forswear, repudiate, reject, disclaim; annul, abrogate.

◇ *Usage note: Adopt* means to take as one's own, and *adapt* means to adjust. Thus: *Living in Japan, I adopted Oriental customs.* And thus: *She adapted the Japanese recipe to British tastes.*

adorable *adj. The little girl was adorable. There is the most adorable dress on sale at the shop!:* lovable, delightful, precious, likeable, pleasing, divine; appealing, charming, captivating, engaging, fetching, irresistible.

Ant. hateful, unlovable, unlikeable, hard to like, despicable; displeasing, unappealing.

adoration *n. The monks devote their lives to the adoration of God:* worship, worshipping, glorification, exaltation, veneration, reverence, adulation, devotion; honour, idolization, magnification.

Ant. blasphemy, denunciation, reviling, execration, belittling.

adore *v.* **1** *He adores his wife and children. I simply adore your new hat:* love, hold dear, cherish; *Informal* worship, revere, glorify; fancy, like, prize, dote on; admire. **2** *O, come let us adore Him:* worship, glorify, exalt, revere, venerate, idolize.

Ant. 1 hate, dislike, abhor, loathe, despise. **2** blaspheme, revile, denounce, execrate, belittle.

◇ *Word origin: Adore* comes from the Latin *adorare, ad-*, to, + *orare*, to pray, to speak, hence literally to pray to, speak to. The same Latin verb *orare*, to pray, to speak, is also found in *oration* and *oratory*.

◇ *Usage tip:* Commenting on *adore* in the sense of "worship as a god," the *Oxford English Dictionary* notes: "Now almost confined to poetry."

adorn *v. A simple gold pin adorned her dress:* ornament, decorate, embellish, array, bedeck, bejewel, *Informal* deck out; beautify, set off to advantage, furbish.

Ant. strip, bare; simplify.

◇ *Word origin: Adorn* comes from Latin *ad-*, to, at, + *ornare*, to adorn, from which we also get *ornate* and *ornament*.

adornment *n. They said that her greatest adornment was her beauty:* ornament, ornamentation, decoration, jewellery, embellishment; finery, attire.

adroit *adj. A sculptor must have adroit hands. Politicians must be adroit speakers:* dexterous, nimble; deft, apt, proficient, skilled, skilful, expert, masterful; clever, artful, facile, cunning.

Ant. clumsy, awkward, maladroit, unhandy.

adulation *n. The official adulation of Stalin in the Soviet Union ended suddenly after his death:* flattery, fawning, fulsome praise.

Ant. condemnation, denunciation, defamation, aspersion, abuse, vituperation, censure, ridicule; hatred, dislike, loathing.

◇ *Word origin: Adulation* is ultimately derived from Latin *adulari*, to engage in fawning, cringing, or tail-wagging like a dog.

adulterate *v. The ancient Greeks often adulterated their wine with water:* thin, water, water down, qualify.

advance *v.* **1** *The troops advanced twenty miles. We will advance hard workers to the top of the class:* go forward, come forward, bring forward, send forward, progress, bring up, move up, send up, move onward, press on; put up front, promote. **2** *The biologist advanced a new theory of life:* proffer, bring forward, offer, bring to notice, bring to attention, lay down, assign. **3** *The Apollo landings advanced our knowledge of the moon:* bring forward, further, increase, improve, promote, add to, multiply, further the growth of, take a step forward. **4** *My boss advanced me £10 against next week's wages:* pay beforehand, give beforehand; pay on account, pay now.

—*n.* **5** *The enemy advance must be stopped!:* forward movement, progress, onward movement. **6** *Discovering a cure for cancer would be a major medical advance. His advance in the firm led him from office-boy to director:* improvement, advancement, progress, furthering, promotion, step, breakthrough, growth, gain. **7** *The plumber wanted an advance of £50 before he started work:* prepayment, down payment; retainer. **8** *If you don't stop making advances to all the girls, you'll get your face slapped!:* pass, amorous overture, overture; proposition.

—*adj.* **9** *The advance troops have sighted the enemy:* forward, foremost, before all others, in front, up front. **10** *The advance sale of tickets made the play a success despite the bad reviews:* previous, prior, before the fact.

Ant. 1 retreat, go backwards, regress, retrogress, move back, withdraw; demote, degrade. **2** hide, keep secret, withhold, suppress, hold back, keep to oneself; recall. **3** decrease, lessen, diminish, subtract from, set back, retard, weaken. **4** defer payment, withhold payment. **5** retreat, withdrawal, regression, retrogression. **6** worsening, regression, retrogression, set-back. **7** deferred payment. **9** rear, hindmost, at the back.

advantage *n.* **1** *Being able to speak French is a great advantage on a trip to the Continent:* help, benefit, aid, service, profit; blessing, boon, support, comfort, convenience. **2** *The taller team has an advantage in a game of netball:* edge, upper hand, initial supremacy, precedence, dominance; superiority, success.

Ant. 1, 2 disadvantage. **1** hindrance, difficulty, drawback, deterrent, disservice, curse; discomfort, inconvenience. **2** handicap, *Slang* short end of the stick.

advantageous *adj.* **1** *You'll find it advantageous to learn Spanish before visiting South America:* helpful, beneficial, useful, profitable, of assistance, of service. **2** *Taking his opponent's queen put the chess player in an advantageous position:* superior, favourable, dominating, enviable, fortunate.

Ant. 1 unhelpful, useless, detrimental; harmful, injurious. **2** inferior, unfavourable, unfortunate, *Informal* up a gum-tree, up the creek.

adventure *n. Have you read about the adventures of Marco Polo?:* enterprise, undertaking, venture, *Poetic* emprise, quest.

◇ *Word origin:* The early meaning of *adventure* was chance or fortune. The word has retained this kernel of meaning ever since. Adventures usually involve chance and taking chances, and adventurers are always in some sense people seeking their fortune.

adventurous *adj.* **1** *Her father was an adventurous man, unafraid of risks:* seeking excitement, eager for experience, daring, bold, venturesome, audacious; brave, courageous, valiant, intrepid. **2** *The trip promised to be long but adventurous:* challenging, risky, hazardous, dangerous, perilous.

Ant. 1 unadventurous, cautious, hesitant. **2** dull, boring, routine; completely safe.

adversary *n. Yorkshire and Lancashire are adversaries on the cricket field:* opponent, rival, competitor, foe, antagonist, enemy.

Ant. ally, accomplice, colleague, team-mate; friend.

adverse *adj. Adverse winds prevented our plane from arriving on time. Don't be discouraged by adverse criticism:* unfavourable, contrary, opposing, unpropitious, detrimental, negative, difficult; hostile, antagonistic, unfriendly, inimical harmful, injurious.

Ant. favourable, helpful, beneficial, supporting, agreeable; auspicious.

◇ *Usage note:* Don't confuse *adverse* and *averse. Adverse* means in opposition, unfavourable: *Father ignored all adverse comments on his extravagant life-style. Averse* means feeling a dislike for, having an inclination against something: *Father is always averse to spending money.*

adversity *n. She tried to be brave in the face of adversity:* unfavourable circumstances, misfortune, calamity, disaster, ill-fortune, bad luck, catastrophe, mishap; affliction, trial, trouble, distress, woe.

Ant. good fortune, success, breakthrough, lucky stroke, blessings.

"In the day of prosperity be joyful, but in the day of adversity consider." —*Ecclesiastes 7: 14*

---

advertise *v. If you want to sell your product you must advertise it. Don't advertise your shortcomings:* publicize, call attention to, give public notice to, proclaim, vaunt, tout, noise abroad; display, reveal, show.

Ant. hide, conceal, keep hidden, keep under cover, keep secret, keep indoors.

advice *n.* **1** *Get a lawyer's advice on the matter:* recommendation, counsel, suggestion, opinion, view; help, guidance. **2** *Advice from abroad indicates that war is about to begin:* information, intelligence, word, tidings, news, report, notification, message, account.

◇ *Usage note: Advice* (rhyming with *ice*) is a noun meaning counsel, suggestion, information. *Advise* (rhyming with *eyes*) is a verb meaning to give advice or suggestions to. To keep *advice* and *advise* straight in your mind, remember these two sentences: *My advice is not to drive on the ice. I advise you to have your eyes checked.*

advisable *adj. It's advisable for all children to have polio jabs:* recommendable; prudent, judicious, wise, smart; suitable, seemly, expedient, sound, proper, fitting, fit; *Informal* best, a good bet.

Ant. unsuitable, unsound, improper; inexpedient, stupid, silly; unfitting.

advise *v.* **1** *I advise you to reconsider your decision:* counsel, recommend, recommend to, suggest, suggest to, offer an opinion, offer the opinion that; commend, urge, encourage, enjoin; caution, warn, admonish. **2** *We have been advised that the roads are too icy for the trip:* inform, tell, notify, apprise, report, give notice, make known, communicate.

◇ *Usage note:* See ADVICE.

adviser *n. The doctor is chief medical adviser to this car manufacturer:* consultant, counsellor, mentor; aide, surrogate, assistant.

advocacy *n. Mrs. Pankhurst was famed for her advocacy of equal rights for women:* championship, campaigning for, pleading the case of, speaking out for, support, supporting, backing, espousal, pressing for, advancement, furthering, promotion, propagation; recommendation, endorsement, defence.

Ant. opposition; combatting, assault, attacking.

advocate *v.* **1** *The committee advocates revising the licensing laws:* recommend, advise, propose, prescribe; champion, urge, promote, campaign for, plead the cause of, argue for, speak out for, stand up for, push for; endorse, support, back, press for, espouse; advance, further, propagate.

—*n.* **2** *The gamekeeper is an advocate of environmental protection laws:* champion, backer, supporter, proponent, promoter, spokesman for; believer, upholder, apostle, patron; defender, pleader, apologist, propagandist. **3** *He hired the best advocate he could find to represent him in court:* lawyer, legal adviser, counsel, counsellor, barrister, solicitor, *Slang* mouthpiece.

Ant. 1 oppose, combat, attack, assail, impugn. **2** opponent, adversary, enemy, antagonist, detractor; attacker, accuser.

◇ *Word origin: Advocate* comes from Latin *advocatus*, someone who has been called in to help. Originally used in the sense of legal adviser or friendly witness, the word became a term in Roman law designating the professional who defends one's interests in a court case.

aerial *n.* 1 *If you had a roof-top aerial you could get a better picture on your television set:* antenna.
—*adj.* 2 *Sea-gulls glided overhead on aerial currents:* air, in the air, from the air, by air, airborne; by aircraft, of aircraft, flying, capable of flight; atmospheric, airy, wind-created.
Ant. 2 land, on the ground; by land.
◇ *Word origin: Aerial* is ultimately derived from Latin *aer,* air.

aeroplane *n. The aeroplanes flew overhead in V-formation:* plane, aircraft, fixed-wing aircraft; (*variously*) jet, prop-jet, propeller-driven plane, biplane, seaplane; *Slang* bird, crate, bus.

aesthetic *adj. The course in art history is designed to develop the student's aesthetic judgement:* appreciative of beauty, appealing to artistic taste, having artistic tastes, artistic; sensitive, discriminating, cultivated, refined, fastidious.
Ant. unaesthetic, unappreciative; insensitive, undiscriminating.
◇ *Word origin: Aesthetic* comes from Greek *aisthētikos,* perceptive, responsive, appreciative.

affable *adj. The elderly woman proved an affable companion:* amiable, genial, congenial, friendly, cordial, gracious, sociable, compatible; good-natured, good-humoured, pleasant, warm, easy-going, open; courteous, civil, mannerly.
Ant. unfriendly, unsociable, unapproachable, inaccessible, distant, haughty, *Informal* stand-offish; ill-humoured, unpleasant, cold; discourteous, uncivil, ungracious, rude, brusque, curt, surly.

affair *n.* 1 *What I do in my spare time is my own affair:* personal business, private matter, concern, business; personal problem, interest, pursuit. 2 *The Foreign Office handles international affairs. Running a household is a complex affair:* undertaking, activity, matter, business, operation, function, transaction, effort; incident, occurrence, episode, event, happening, proceeding, circumstance, adventure. 3 *Christmas was a merry affair:* celebration, festivity, party, social gathering, social function, occasion. 4 *The affair between the two film stars caused a scandal:* love affair, romance, relationship, liaison, intrigue, amour.

affect *v.* 1 *The rain will affect our plans for a picnic:* influence, be of importance to, impinge upon, act on, produce an effect on, change, modify concern, relate to, pertain to, interest, regard. 2 *The speech deeply affected the audience:* have an emotional effect on, move, touch, stir, impress. 3 *She's from Devon but she affects a Welsh accent:* make a pretence of, feign, put on, pretend to, assume, adopt, imitate, counterfeit, simulate; fancy, show a preference for, tend towards, embrace, be inclined towards.
Ant. 2 leave unmoved, *Informal* leave cold; bore. 3 repudiate, scorn, reject, shed, *Informal* cast aside, cast off.
◇ *Usage note:* Too many people still confuse *affect* and *effect. Affect* means to influence, *effect* means to bring about a result, to produce or accomplish something. Thus: *The girl's tears affected him deeply.* And thus: *Her tears effected the desired result — he forgave her.*

affectation *n. Her finishing-school accent is just an affectation:* false mannerism, pretence, pretension, sham; airs, false air, insincerity, artificiality, *Slang* put-on.
Ant. the genuine article; naturalness, sincerity, genuineness, artlessness, simplicity.

affected *adj.* 1 *The affected workers said that the lay-off was unfair:* acted upon, concerned, pertinent, interested; influenced, changed. 2 *The sad story left him deeply affected:* moved, touched, stirred, impressed; grieved, sorry, sorrowful, troubled, distressed, afflicted. 3 *The disease left his sense of hearing affected:* upset, harmed, injured, impaired. 4 *Wealth and fame have made him so affected that I don't like him any more:* pretentious, pompous, conceited, vain; vainglorious; artificial, unnatural, mannered, unreal, not genuine, phoney, assumed, contrived, studied.
Ant. 1–4 unaffected. 1 unconcerned, uninterested. 2 unmoved, untouched, *Informal* cold. 3 healed, cured; unharmed, uninjured, untouched. 4 natural, unpretentious, genuine, real; modest.

affection *n.* 1 *He feels great affection for his parents:* emotional attachment, fondness, love, tenderness, warmth; liking, proclivity, kind disposition. 2 *Chopin died of a consumptive affection:* sickness, illness, disease, ailment, malady, disorder, physical complaint.
Ant. 1 hate, loathing, antipathy, enmity; dislike, coldness, coolness. 2 healthiness, well-being, healthfulness, salubriousness.
◇ *Word origin: Affection* comes from Latin *affectio,* meaning a condition or state of body or mind, usually an agreeable one. 16th-century medical writers were the first to use *affection* in its now-rare sense of "pathological condition, ailment" (see sense 2 above).

"Affection is the broadest basis of a good life."
—*George Eliot*

---

affectionate *adj. The affectionate child loved to be cuddled. She has an affectionate relationship with her grandparents:* loving, demonstrative; warm-hearted, tender, tender-hearted, fond, doting, caring; ardent.
Ant. cold, cool, undemonstrative, impassive, stolid; apathetic, callous.

affiance *v. The king affianced his daughter to a neighbouring prince:* engage to marry, betroth, pledge, solemnly promise.

affiliate *v.* 1 *Businessmen should always affiliate*

themselves to the local Chamber of Commerce: associate, connect; join, unite, ally, incorporate, band together; fraternize, consort. —*n.* **2** *Our company is an affiliate of a large corporation:* close associate, legally connected associate, colleague; branch, chapter, part, arm, division, subdivision.

Ant. 1 dissociate; leave, quit, resign from.

affiliation *n. The two hospitals have a close affiliation with each other, sometimes sharing equipment:* association, relationship, alliance, connection, union.

affinity *n.* **1** *A natural affinity drew these two musicians together:* natural liking, partiality, fancy, liking, fondness; leaning, bent, proclivity, propensity; sympathy, rapport. **2** *There is a close affinity between lemons and limes:* family resemblance, similarity, likeness, parallelism, homology; relation, connection, compatibility.

Ant. 1 aversion, repulsion, antipathy, disliking. **2** dissimilarity.

◇ *Word origin: Affinity* is from Latin *affinitas*, which means kinship by marriage, as distinct from blood kinship. In the late 18th century, naturalists began to use *affinity* to mean a family resemblance (as between cats and lions).

affirm *v.* **1** *We affirm these statements to be true:* declare, assert, aver, avow, maintain, proclaim; profess, allege, hold, contend, claim. **2** *Posterity will doubtless affirm my judgement:* confirm, sustain, ratify, validate, endorse, approve, warrant.

Ant. 1 deny, refute, repudiate, disavow, renounce. **2** reject, deny, rescind, nullify, veto, disallow, contravene, forswear.

affirmation *n.* **1** *The White Paper was a forceful affirmation of the Government's views:* strong assertion, avowal, declaration. **2** *The Director is awaiting the Board's affirmation of his nominee:* confirmation, ratification, endorsement, approval, consent, corroboration, certification.

Ant. 1 denial, refutation, repudiation, disavowal, renunciation. **2** nullification, veto, rejection.

affirmative *adj.* **1** *Please give an affirmative answer if you agree:* yes, assenting, positive, affirmatory; approving, concurring, confirmatory. **2** *The medical tests are affirmative:* positive, confirming, confirmatory, corroborative, ratifying, affirming, concurring; emphatic, conclusive, categorical. —*n.* **3** *Our debating team gave the arguments for the affirmative:* side in favour of a question; positive side, optimistic side. —*adv.* **4** *When asked if the spaceship was in orbit, the astronaut replied "Affirmative!":* yes.

Ant. 1–4 negative. **1** negating, no. **2** nonconfirming; inconclusive, doubtful. **4** no.

affix *v. Affix the parking permit to your windscreen:* attach, fasten, fix, add on, put on; seal, stick, glue, paste, post, tag.

Ant. detach, unfasten, take off; unglue.

afflict *v. Famine and war still afflict mankind:* distress, oppress, torment, plague.

Ant. relieve, comfort, console, solace, assuage; bless, delight.

◇ *Word origin:* If you are *afflicted*, your health or hopes have been dashed or struck down. *Afflict* comes from Latin *afflictus*, cast down, wretched.

affliction *n. Faith permitted him to endure every affliction:* distress, hardship, trouble, trial, tribulation, torment, adversity, misfortune, ordeal, calamity, pain, misery, wretchedness, curse.

Ant. relief, comfort, consolation, solace; blessing, joy, delight.

affluent *adj. In a truly affluent society there's more than enough for all:* rich, wealthy, prosperous, well-to-do, moneyed, well-off, well-heeled, flourishing.

Ant. poor, impoverished, impecunious; destitute, indigent.

◇ *Word origin: Affluent* is ultimately derived from Latin *affluere*, to flow freely and in abundance.

◇ *Usage note:* Don't confuse *affluent*, well off, wealthy, and *effluent*, outflowing. Thus, we speak of an *affluent* society but of an *effluent* stream.

afford *v.* **1** *We can afford the house if we save our pennies:* have the money for, bear, support. **2** *A mountain climber can't afford to take chances with inferior equipment:* bear the consequences of, bear, sustain; risk, chance. **3** *A four-day working week will afford us more leisure time. The terrace affords a fine view:* give, provide, offer, supply, furnish, command, grant, yield, lend, impart.

affront *v.* **1** *Don't affront the speaker by asking rude questions:* offend, insult, outrage. —*n.* **2** *His rejection of my plan was a personal affront!:* offence, insult, slur, slight, indignity; rudeness, discourtesy, contemptuousness; insolence, impertinence; outrage, dishonour, disgrace, ignominy, humiliation, mortification; wrong, abuse, ill-treatment, injury.

Ant. 1 pamper, flatter, humour, indulge, gratify; honour, please; appease, smooth the feathers of. **2** courtesy, deference, compliment, honour; apology.

◇ *Word origin: Affront* comes from Old French *afronter*, to push someone's face in. By the time the word entered English (around 1300) it merely meant to insult someone to his face. The word is ultimately derived from Latin *frons*, forehead, which is also the basis of *front* and *frontal*.

afraid *adj.* **1** *I'm afraid of lightning:* scared, fearful, terrified, terror-stricken, alarmed, anxious, anxiety-ridden, apprehensive, timorous, panicky, panic-stricken; fainthearted, cowardly, *Informal* lily-livered,

chicken-livered, chicken-hearted, *Slang* chicken. **2** *I'm afraid I can't come to your party:* regretful, sorry, unhappy; disappointed.
Ant. 1 fearless; bold, audacious, venturesome; indifferent. **2** happy, pleased.
◇ *Usage note: Afraid, scared, frightened,* and *terrified* are very close in meaning and are often used interchangeably. *Afraid* is the most general term, sometimes used to express a vague, general fear, ranging from a small fear to a large one: *afraid of the dark, afraid of mice, afraid for his life. Scared, frightened,* and *terrified* all imply fear. *Scared* is somewhat informal and suggests a fairly mild fear, often quickly passing, a being startled, a fear that causes one to look up or turn around: *Oh, you scared me; I didn't know you were there. Frightened* is more formal than *scared* and suggests a greater degree of fear: *She was too frightened to move. Terrified* suggests extreme fear for one's life or safety: *Not knowing how to swim, he was terrified of falling in the water. The young soldier was terrified by the battle.*
◇ *Word origin: Afraid* was originally a form of the word *affray,* brawl or fray. It replaced an older form *afeared* (meaning "afraid"), which may still be heard in some dialects.

aftermath *n. The picnic had an unfortunate aftermath — we all had food poisoning the next day:* consequence, outcome, result; sequel, follow-up, upshot, offshoot, by-product.
◇ *Word origin: Aftermath* comes from *after* + *math,* an obsolete word meaning "a mowing." Hence, *aftermath* originally meant a second crop of grass after mowing. It has been used in its present sense, however, for more than 300 years.

agape *adv.* **1** *She just stood there with her mouth agape, not knowing what to say:* wide open, gaping. **2** *The symphony left the audience agape:* thunderstruck, spellbound, struck dumb, dumbfounded, stupefied, amazed, astonished, awestruck, flabbergasted, agog.

age *n.* **1** *The child was about three years of age. The days of our age are three score years and ten:* period of existence, duration of life, life span; lifetime, generation. **2** *His face was wrinkled with age. You can't get a driving-licence until you're of age:* old age, advanced age, seniority; adulthood. **3** *Geologists say this valley was formed by the last ice age. We reach middle age before we know it:* era, epoch, period; stage of time, time of life. **4** *It seemed an age before he arrived:* a long time, aeon, millennium; for ever.
—*v.* **5** *Children seem to age before our eyes. The tragedy has aged him:* advance in age, grow older; make old. **6** *The cheese was aged for two years before being ready for market:* mature, ripen, develop.
Ant. 2 youth, childhood, adolescence. **4** short time, instant, second.
◇ *Usage note:* See ERA.

aged *adj.* **1** *The tribe was ruled by an aged and venerable man:* old, elderly, of advanced age, advanced in years, ancient. **2** *A pretty little girl, aged 3:* of the age of, as old as, having lived for. **3** *Do you have any aged Cheddar cheese?:* mature, ripe, ripened, mellow.
Ant. 1 young, youthful, juvenile. **3** unripe, immature.

agency *n.* **1** *I got the job through an employment agency:* service organization, bureau, department. **2** *The hero was granted a pension through the agency of the king:* power, action, activity, operation; intervention, mediation, force, influence, charge, means, instrument, instrumentality.

agenda *n. What's on your agenda today?:* list of things to be done, schedule, programme; timetable, diary, items of business.
◇ *Usage note: Agenda* was originally the plural of Latin *agendum,* "thing to be done." In modern English, however, *agenda* is sometimes considered as the singular form with *agendas* the plural. Thus, *What's on the agenda for the meeting? The secretary kept track of the two executives' agendas.*

agent *n.* **1** *She's not a good actress, but she gets a lot of parts because she has a good agent:* representative; emissary, envoy, deputy, advocate; intermediary, negotiator, go-between. **2** *Gravity is the agent that draws objects to earth:* force, power, agency, mover, effective principle; means, instrument, cause, author, vehicle. **3** *England's wingers were the leading agents of their recent success:* doer, perpetrator, performer, practitioner, worker, mover, operator, executor.
Ant. 2 counteragent, hindrance, opponent, neutralizer.

aggravate *v.* **1** *Don't scratch — you'll only aggravate the itch:* make worse, worsen, make more severe; intensify, inflame, irritate, increase, heighten. **2** *His bossy attitude aggravates me:* irritate, annoy, exasperate, anger, vex, nettle, affront.
Ant. 1 improve; soothe, relieve, assuage, alleviate, ease; lessen, mitigate, pacify. **2** please; soothe, calm, placate, ease.
◇ *Usage note: Aggravate* really means to make worse: *The cold weather aggravated his rheumatism.* For a long while, many teachers and critics said that the word should not be used to mean to irritate, annoy, or vex. Today this use is considered acceptable by a vast majority of teachers, critics, and linguists. Thus, you may say or write *Stop aggravating me* without feeling guilty.

aggregate *n. The final plan was an aggregate of all our ideas:* composite, compound, union, combination, gathering, accumulation, blend, collection, amassing, bringing together, summation, mixture, mix, mass, conglomeration, conglomerate.
◇ *Word origin: Aggregate* comes from Latin

aggregatus, brought to the flock, from *grex*, flock. Latin *grex* also gives us *gregarious*, sociable, seeking out others, associating in a group or flock.

aggression *n. Deer show less aggression than tigers. Sinking our ship was an act of open aggression:* hostile behaviour, hostility, fighting spirit, active anger, viciousness, pugnacity, belligerence; act of war, hostile act, assault, invasion, raid, offensive.

Ant. peacefulness, friendliness, submissiveness; peace, pacification.

aggressive *adj.* **1** *Aggressive nations must turn to peace. Dogs can become aggressive if provoked:* hostile, belligerent, pugnacious, vicious, tending to attack, contentious, warring, *Informal* nasty. **2** *An aggressive young man can go far in this firm:* self-assertive, forceful, bold; enterprising, energetic, zealous.

Ant. 1 peaceful, friendly; submissive. **2** retiring, quiet, shy, bashful, mild; lazy.

aghast *adj.* **1** *We were completely aghast at his failure:* astonished, amazed, stunned, astounded, thunderstruck. **2** *She was aghast at the brutal way prisoners were treated:* filled with horror, horrified, terrified, horror-struck, shocked, appalled; fear-struck, frightened.

Ant. 1 expectant, expecting, confident; nonplussed. **2** pleased, calmed; indifferent, unmoved, unaffected, unexcited.

◇ *Word origin: Aghast* is a form of the Middle English word *agasten*, to frighten. The *h* was added because people associated the word with *ghastly*.

agile *adj. With an agile leap, the boy escaped his captor. The job requires an agile mind:* nimble, spry, supple, limber, lithe, dexterous, graceful, quick, swift, fleet, alert, active.

Ant. clumsy, awkward, heavy, ponderous; slow, sluggish, lethargic, inactive, torpid.

◇ *Pronunciation tip: Agile* may be pronounced either as *aj-uhl* or as *aj-ile* in America, but as *aj-ile* in Britain.

agitate *v.* **1** *A cement mixer agitates the cement until it is ready to pour:* stir, stir up, shake, shake up, churn, mix; beat, rock, jar. **2** *The fiery speech agitated the crowd:* upset, excite, work up, bring to fever pitch; disquiet, trouble, disturb, alarm, foment.

Ant. 2 calm, calm down, soothe, pacify, quiet, compose, still.

agog *adj. The teenagers were agog at the sight of the film star:* awestruck, enthralled, thrilled, excited, worked up, astir, eagerly expectant.

Ant. indifferent, uninterested; bored.

◇ *Word origin: Agog* comes from Old French *en gogues*, in a merry mood.

agonize *v. The man agonized over the guilt that he felt:* feel pain, be in agony, suffer, be in anguish, be tormented, be tortured, be distressed; worry, strain, struggle, labour, wrestle, *Slang* sweat.

Ant. enjoy, exhilarate; relax.

agony *n.* **1** *This country must not again go through the agony of war:* suffering, pain, torment, throes, torture; anguish, distress, misery, affliction, woe; sorrow, anxiety. **2** *She went through agonies finishing her exam paper:* effort, striving, struggle, strain; trial, tribulation.

Ant. 1, 2 pleasure, joy, enjoyment; comfort, ease; relief, consolation.

◇ *Word origin: Agony* comes from Greek *agonia*, mental anguish. It was first used as an English word by the religious reformer John Wycliffe (1320?-84) in his translation of the passage in Luke 22:44 that recounts the agony and arrest of Jesus in the garden of Gethsemane.

agrarian *adj. Does Holland have a primarily agrarian economy?:* agricultural, farming, crop-raising, agronomical.

Ant. manufacturing, industrial.

agree *v.* **1** *I can't agree to the terms of this contract:* assent, consent, accede, go along with; think alike, be of one mind, side with, subscribe, come to the same conclusion, admit, grant, concede, allow. **2** *Since the two stories don't agree, someone is lying:* concur, accord, coincide, conform, correspond; fit, match, square, harmonize, chime, tally. **3** *The union and management have agreed on a new contract:* settle, come to an understanding, see eye to eye.

Ant. 1–3 disagree, differ. **1** dissent, dispute, refute, deny, oppose. **2** contradict.

◇ *Usage note:* We *agree to* a plan, idea, scheme, etc., but *with* a person. Thus: *I agree* TO *the terms of the contract* but *I agree* WITH *you.*

agreeable *adj.* 1 *Our new neighbour was an agreeable person. I hope you will find your room agreeable:* pleasing, pleasant, gratifying; to one's liking, to one's taste, acceptable, suitable, appropriate, fitting. **2** *Are you agreeable to my plans for a picnic?:* in accord, consenting, complying, amenable, going along with; approving, concurring.

Ant. 1 disagreeable, unpleasant, displeasing, unlikeable, offensive; unacceptable, unsuitable, inappropriate, unfitting. **2** disapproving.

"My idea of an agreeable person is a person who agrees with me." —*Benjamin Disraeli*

---

agreement *n.* **1** *The meeting ended in friendly agreement:* mutual understanding, accord; concord, concordance, harmony, concert, meeting of minds. **2** *There is so much agreement between the answers to the exam papers, that the teacher suspects plagiarism:* harmony, in keeping, compliance, congruity, conformity, compatibility, accordance, affinity; similarity, analogy, correspondence. **3** *They made an agreement to rent the house:* promise, contract, compact, pact, arrangement, settlement, covenant, *Informal* deal.

Ant. 1 disagreement, discord, dissension. **2** disagreement, discord; inconsistency, dissonance, difference, dissimilarity, discrepancy.

agriculture *n. Better methods of agriculture are needed to feed the world's population:* farming, husbandry, crop-raising, cultivation, tillage, market gardening; agronomy, agronomics, rural economy, land use.

aground *adj., adv. The ship was aground in shallow water:* stranded, grounded, foundered, stuck, beached, ashore.

Ant. afloat.

aid *v.* **1** *At Christmas, many organizations aid the poor:* help, assist, abet, lend assistance, give a helping hand; support, give support to, sustain, minister to, serve; contribute, give alms to. **2** *A good dictionary can aid the student by enlarging his vocabulary:* foster, further, promote, advance; facilitate, make easy, serve.

—*n.* **3** *The stranded climbers needed aid to get back down the mountain:* help, assistance, helping hand; support. **4** *Many charitable organizations in Britain give aid to the disaster victims. The family lived on government aid for two years:* relief, dole; charity, donation, contribution; subsidy, allowance. **5** Usually **aide**. *His political aides worked hard during the election campaign:* assistant, right-hand man, associate, subordinate, adjutant, auxiliary, girl Friday, man Friday; helper, abettor; follower, adherent, retainer; *Religious* acolyte, *Military* aide-de-camp.

Ant. 1 hurt, harm, injure; oppose, hinder. **2** hinder, obstruct, block, *Informal* hold up; oppose, discourage, thwart, impede, detract from. **3** hindrance. **5** superior, boss; leader.

◇ *Spelling tip: Aid* is the standard English spelling for all but an aide-de-camp. Americans, however, use the French spelling *aide* to mean any high-ranking assistant.

ail *v.* **1** *What's ailing you today?:* bother, annoy, trouble, distress, worry; be the matter with, afflict, sicken, make ill; pain. **2** *My grandmother is ailing again:* be sick, be ill, be unwell, be indisposed; fail in health, be infirm; *Slang* be on the sick list.

Ant. 1 make happy; comfort, solace, console. **2** be in good health, make well; be strong, thrive, flourish.

ailment *n. Back pains and an upset stomach are just two of his ailments:* disorder, complaint, malady, infirmity, affliction, disability; illness, sickness, disease, infection; indisposition, weakness.

Ant. good health, healthy sign; fitness.

aim *v.* **1** *Aim the gun at the target:* point, direct, level, train on; take aim, sight. **2** *We aim to please. He aimed for the top:* try, strive, aspire to, work toward, endeavour, seek, attempt, be after; intend, mean, want, wish, desire, essay, have in mind; have in view, have an eye to.

—*n.* **3** *The gunner's aim was on target:* aiming, line of sighting; marksmanship. **4** *His aim is to retire to Cornwall:* desire, wish, intention, intent; aspiration, goal, ambition, target, purpose, object; plan, scheme, design.

◇ *Word origin:* When you *aim* a weapon, you are estimating the path of the missile to the target. *Aim* ultimately comes from Latin *aestimare*, to estimate, which also gives us our word *estimate*.

air *n.* **1** *Air is composed mainly of oxygen, nitrogen, carbon dioxide, and water vapour:* the air we breathe. **2** *The glider soared high in the air:* atmosphere, stratosphere, sky, *Poetic* ether. **3** *Cold air blew in through the open window:* wind, breeze, draught, air current, air flow, blast, puff, zephyr, whiff, waft, breath of air. **4** *An air of mystery pervaded the abandoned house. She has a certain air of sadness all the time:* atmosphere, aura, feeling, ambience; quality, manner, style, look. **5 airs.** *Don't put on airs with me!:* affectations, affectedness, pretensions, pretence, artificial manners; haughtiness, hauteur, arrogance, superciliousness, swank. **6** *The child sang a delightful air:* tune, ditty, melody, song, strain; ballad, lay, carol.

—*v.* **7** *The blankets were aired on the line:* ventilate, expose to air, aerate. **8** *The People's Party candidate aired his views on television:* voice, express, declare, vent, tell, utter proclaim, make public, reveal, disclose, divulge, display, exhibit, publicize, expose.

Ant. 8 keep silent; suppress, repress, hide, conceal.

airport *n. Be at the airport half an hour before the plane leaves:* airfield, landing ground, runway; airstrip, landing strip, terminal, aerodrome; air base.

airship *n. The airship floated high above the trees:* lighter-than-air craft; (*variously*) dirigible, blimp, rigid balloon.

◇ *Usage note:* The difference between a *dirigible* and a *blimp* is that a *dirigible* has a supporting framework to make the gasbag rigid whereas a *blimp* does not, relying on the gas to keep the bag rigid and collapsing when the gas is removed. Technically, a large *balloon* is not truly an airship because it cannot be steered. Technically, also, a *glider* is an aeroplane and not an airship, because it is heavier than air, even though powered by up-currents and winds.

airy *adj.* **1** *The castle's halls were large and airy:* open to the air, well-ventilated, sunny, spacious; windy, breezy, draughty. **2** *The little goats hopped about in an airy way. The band played an airy tune:* jaunty, sprightly, lively, frolicsome; light-hearted, light, light-of-heart, merry, cheerful, cheery. **3** *His head was full of airy thoughts:* imaginary, fanciful, dreamy, ethereal, unsubstantial, immaterial, unrealistic, illusory, idealized.

Ant. 1 airless, stifling; gloomy, dark, dank. **2**

ponderous, heavy, sluggish, clumsy, slow; cheerless, doleful. **3** material, substantial, factual, realistic; solid, hard.

"And as imagination bodies forth
The forms of things unknown, the poet's pen
Turns them to shapes and gives to airy nothing
A local habitation and a name."
— *William Shakespeare*

aisle *n. The aisle was crammed with people:* passageway, passage; pavement, walk, path, way, corridor, lane; ambulatory, cloister.
◇ *Usage note:* See ISLAND.
◇ *Word origin: Aisle* comes from French *aile*, wing (or wing of building), which comes from the Latin word for wing, *ala*. (French *aile* also gives us *aileron*, "little wing.")

ajar *adv. The door was left ajar:* partly open; open, unclosed, agape, gaping.

akin *adj., adv.* **1** *Wolves and dogs are closely akin:* related by blood, related, kin, kindred; of the same stock, having a common ancestor, consanguineous; connected, allied, affiliated. **2** *Her thoughts on the subject are akin to mine:* alike, like, identical, uniform; similar, resembling, parallel, comparable, corresponding, analogous; agreeing, congenial, correlative.
Ant. 1, 2 unrelated, unconnected; foreign, alien. **2** unlike, different, divergent, dissimilar, disparate; disagreeing, non-congenial.

alacrity *n.* **1** *She answered his call for assistance with alacrity:* willingness, enthusiasm, eagerness, zeal, avidity; alertness, promptness, dispatch, readiness. **2** *Despite his 80 years, he moved with alacrity:* liveliness, briskness, sprightliness; agility, nimbleness.
Ant. 1 unwillingness, indifference, unconcern, apathy, impassiveness, reluctance, disinclination; languor, lethargy, dullness. **2** slowness, sluggishness.

alarm *n.* **1** *The building was evacuated at the first alarm:* warning, danger signal, alert. **2** *A sentry gave the alarm to the troops:* call to arms, summons to arms, war cry; hue and cry, beat of drum. **3** *She responded with alarm to the news:* apprehension, trepidation, consternation, agitation, dismay, distress, perturbation, misgiving; fear, fright, affright, panic, terror.
—*v.* **4** *The sight of smoke alarmed them. I am alarmed by your irresponsible attitude:* unnerve, frighten, scare, terrify; panic; dismay, disturb, make uneasy, distress, trouble, make anxious, make nervous, agitate, appal.
Ant. 1 all clear. **3** composure, self-possession, equanimity, sang-froid, calmness, coolness, serenity, tranquillity. **4** give courage; calm, assure, relieve, comfort.
◇ *Word origin: Alarm* comes from the Italian phrase *all' arme*, to arms!

album *n. They pasted the photos in the album:* scrap-book, book, portfolio; register.
◇ *Word origin:* An *album* is a book with blank pages for preserving photographs, stamps, etc. The word comes from Latin *album*, meaning white tablet—the term used by the Romans for tablets on which they inscribed state records and lists of names. The first modern *albums* were autograph books, which came into fashion in the 17th century.

alcoholic *adj.* **1** *It is against the law to serve alcoholic beverages to minors:* intoxicating, spirituous, hard, strong; fermented, distilled; *Slang* with a kick.
—*n.* **2** *He became an alcoholic and lost his job:* drunkard, drunk, dipsomaniac, inebriate; hard drinker, sot, bibber, tippler, imbiber, toper; *Slang* wino, sponge, barfly, soak, boozer, toss-pot, froth-blower.
Ant. 1 non-alcoholic, non-intoxicating, soft. **2** teetotaller, abstainer.
◇ *Word origin: Alcohol* is derived from Arabic *al-kohl*, powdered antimony used to darken the eyelids. This cosmetic was obtained by a process similar to distillation and the similarity in manufacture gave modern *alcohol* its name.

alcove *n. The living-room had a dining alcove at one end:* recess, niche, nook, bay; cubicle, corner, opening.
◇ *Word origin: Alcove* is derived from Arabic *al-gobbah*, vaulted chamber.

alert *adj.* **1** *For a two-month-old, the baby was exceptionally alert:* aware, attentive, wide-awake, observant; active, quick, lively, sprightly, nimble. **2** *The alert guard foiled the robbery:* watchful, vigilant, diligent, keen-eyed, wary, on guard, careful, heedful.
—*n.* **3** *The air-raid alert sounded at noon:* alarm, siren; warning, signal.
—*v.* **4** *The sign alerted us to the thin ice:* warn, forewarn, make aware of, signal, notify, inform.
Ant. 1 unaware, oblivious, half-asleep; slow, listless, sluggish, inactive, lethargic, languid. **2** unwary, careless, heedless, lackadaisical, unconcerned, dilatory. **3** all clear. **4** lull.
◇ *Word origin: Alert* comes from the Italian phrase *all' erta*, on the look-out.

alias *n. To avoid reporters, the film star registered under the alias of Jim Jones:* assumed name, pseudonym, *nom de guerre*.
◇ *Usage note:* Do not italicize *alias* when you use it to mean an assumed name: "The spy used the alias of George Brown on his mission." On the other hand, italicize *alias* when you use it to mean "otherwise known as": John Smith *alias* Machine Gun Johnny (literally "John Smith, otherwise known as Machine Gun Johnny").

alibi *n. The defendant had no alibi for the night of the crime:* defence of being elsewhere; excuse, explanation, justification, pretext, *Slang* story.
◇ *Usage note:* Basically, an *alibi* is a legal term, a claim that an accused person was

elsewhere at the time a crime was committed: *His alibi was that he was in Lincoln when the Chelsea bank was robbed.* Today *alibi* is used informally to mean excuse, but carries the connotation that the excuse is contrived.

Exploring the Word: *Alias, alien,* and *alienate* come from Latin *alius,* another, otherwise. (The word is cognate with *else.*) An *alien* is a native of another country; to *alienate* means to "make other"—to transfer (something) by sale or to make (someone) a stranger or enemy.

alien *n.* **1** *During World War II all aliens had to register with the government:* resident foreigner, foreigner, outsider, stranger; immigrant, newcomer.
—*adj.* **2** *Orange trees are alien to Canada:* foreign, not native, strange; remote, distant, outlandish, exotic. **3** *Cheating is alien to my nature:* contrary, opposed, contradictory, inconsistent, incompatible, conflicting; unlike, different, dissimilar, unconnected, unrelated, incongruous; separated, estranged.
Ant. 1 citizen, subject, countryman; native, naturalized citizen. **2** native, indigenous. **3** in accordance with, agreeable, compatible, consistent, congenial; like, related, relevant, congruous.
◇ *Usage note: Alien* and *foreigner* both refer to people staying in a country of which they are not citizens. *Foreigner* is the more general and friendly term and sometimes carries connotations of an exotic guest: *Most foreigners want to see the Tower of London and visit Saint Paul's. Foreigners have a hard time learning our language. Alien* is a more legal and unfriendly term, emphasizing that a person is not a native or naturalized citizen and may owe his allegiance to a foreign country: *Enemy aliens were imprisoned during the war. Homeless aliens who fled their country have difficulty finding work.*

alienate *v. His increasing belligerence alienated him from his old friends:* estrange, separate, divorce, turn away, set against.
Ant. make friendly, draw close, unite; reunite, reconcile, turn to.

align *v.* **1** *She neatly aligned the flowerpots on the window-sill:* arrange in line, line up: straighten, even, even up; make parallel, put in a row. **2** *He aligned himself with those who voted against the tax bill:* join, ally, side; associate.
◇ *Word origin: Align* comes from French *aligner,* to place in line, which is based on Latin *linea,* line.

alike *adj.* **1** *He and his brother are very much alike:* same, identical, uniform, equal, even, of a piece, one and the same; corresponding, equivalent, synonymous, homogeneous, analogous, parallel.
—*adv.* **2** *A good teacher treats all his pupils alike:* equally, in the same way, similarly, identically, evenly, uniformly.
Ant. 1 different, unlike, dissimilar, distinct, separate, divergent, diverse. **2** differently, unequally, unevenly, distinctly, separately, disparately, diversely.
◇ *Usage note:* Do not precede *alike* with *both.* Thus, *The two houses are alike,* not "The two houses are both alike."

alive *adj.* **1** *My brother is alive and well in Mexico. Despite the hard winter, the rose-bush is still alive:* living, among the living, animate, breathing, subsisting, *Archaic* quick, *Informal* alive and kicking, above ground. **2** *My grandmother is more alive than a lot of young people:* full of life, vital, lively, vivacious, animated, vigorous, energetic, spry; aware, eager, alert, spirited. **3** *Our plans to remodel the house are still alive:* in existence, extant, in force, operative, in operation; not dead, unextinguished, unquenched; possible, viable.
Ant. 1 dead, deceased, expired, defunct, lifeless, departed, no more; inanimate. **2** lifeless, unanimated, dispirited, spiritless, apathetic; inactive, unaware. **3** extinct, inactive, inoperative, inoperable; gone, lost, down the drain.
◇ *Word origin:* The word *alive* grew out of the Old English phrase *on life,* meaning "in life."

all *adj.* **1** *We drank all the coffee:* the whole of, the total of; the entire contents of, every part of. **2** *All children must be asleep before Father Christmas comes:* every one of, each of, each and every one of; any of, any one of; the whole number of, the total of, the sum of; to a man. **3** *In all fairness I have to warn you of his plans:* complete, total, full, entire, perfect, utter, utmost, the greatest possible.
—*adv.* **4** *This shirt is all worn out. She's all excited about going to the party:* completely, entirely, totally, utterly, wholly, altogether; very, exceedingly, in the highest degree, fully.
—*pron.* **5** *Is that all you can carry?:* everything, every item; the whole quantity, the greatest number, the whole amount, the greatest amount, the total, the entirety, the utmost possible. **6** *He gave presents to all of us:* everyone, each, every member.
Ant. 1, 2 none of; some. **3** partial. **4** somewhat, partially, a little. **5** nothing, none; some. **6** no one, none; some.

allay *v.* **1** *His reassuring words allayed my fears:* calm, quiet, put to rest, soothe; subdue, cause to subside, quell, smooth, appease, pacify, mollify. **2** *This medicine will allay the pain:* relieve, ease, alleviate, lessen, assuage, reduce, diminish, check; lighten, soften, mitigate, mollify; blunt, dull, moderate, slake, slacken, subdue, quiet, quench.
Ant. 1 arouse, awake, kindle, stir, stir up, excite, provoke; stimulate, fan. **1, 2** make worse, aggravate, increase, intensify, heighten, enhance, magnify, multiply.
◇ *Word origin: Allay* comes from Old English *alecgan,* to lay aside.

allegation *n. Your allegation that the mayor is corrupt must be proved:* assertion, declaration, claim, avowal, profession, contention, statement; charge, accusation.
Ant. retraction; denial, disavowal, refutation.

allege *v. The newspaper article alleges that the hostage is dead:* claim, declare, state, assert, maintain, say, avow, contend, affirm, aver, profess; charge, accuse.
Ant. retract; disclaim, deny, disavow, refute.
◇ *Usage note: Allege* means to state or claim without proof or strong conviction, to put forward as an idea to be debated or analysed. Thus an *alleged* criminal is a person said to have committed a crime but not proved guilty. *Assert* means to state positively, with strong conviction or supporting arguments: *The teacher alleged that the student might have cheated in the exam. The student asserted that he had not cheated.*

allegiance *n., I'm proud to pledge allegiance to the flag and to my country. My first allegiance is to my family, then to my friends:* loyalty, faithfulness, fidelity, adherence, constancy; deference, devotion, homage.
Ant. disloyalty, betrayal, treachery, perfidy, deceit, faithlessness; treason, traitorousness, sedition, rebellion; alienation.

allegory *n. George Orwell's* Animal Farm *is generally interpreted as an allegory about the Russian Revolution:* fable, parable.
Ant. true story, history.

alleviate *v. This ointment will alleviate the soreness:* relieve, ease, allay, assuage; lessen, reduce, diminish, check, lighten, soften, mitigate, mollify; blunt, dull, moderate, slake, slacken, subdue, quench.
Ant. make worse, aggravate, increase, intensify, heighten, enhance, magnify, multiply.

alley *n. There was a boulevard in front of the house and an alley behind it:* narrow back street, byway; passageway, passage, pathway, lane.
◇ *Spelling tip: Alley* follows the simple rule of adding an *-s* to become a plural: *alley-alleys.* Thus *Dustbins littered the back streets and alleys.* Do not confuse *alleys* with *allies*, the plural of *ally: France and its allies won the First World War.*

"It is our true policy to steer clear of permanent alliance with any portion of the foreign world." —*George Washington*

---

alliance *n.* **1** *England and France formed an alliance against Germany:* agreement, pact, compact, treaty, concordat, entente cordiale. **2** *The American colonies joined in an alliance against the British:* association, partnership, league, company; confederation, confederacy, federation, union, coalition.
Ant. 2 separation, secession.

allied *adj.* **1** *The allied armies of Britain, the United States, Canada, and France invaded Hitler's Europe:* joint, combined, united; associated; affiliated; incorporated, corporate, amalgamated. **2** *Music and drama are allied arts:* related, kindred, akin, cognate; similar, resembling, alike, like.
Ant. 1 unallied, uncombined, disunited; individual. **2** alien, foreign to each other, unrelated; different, dissimilar, unalike, disparate; divergent.

allocate *v. The town allocated funds for the new school:* set aside, designate, earmark, allot, assign, apportion; budget, appropriate.
Ant. withhold, hold back, deny, refuse, veto.

allot *v. The factory allotted a parking-space to each employee:* assign, allocate, earmark, give out, appoint, consign, grant, allow, dispense; apportion, portion out, distribute, parcel out, dole out, divide up, mete out, provide.
Ant. withhold, retain, keep; deny, refuse.

allotment *n.* **1** *When petrol is scarce, rationing will ensure that each driver gets his fair allotment:* share, portion, quota, measure, apportionment, allocation, consignment; allowance, appropriation, grant, dispensation. **2** *I grow peas and beans on my allotment:* portion of land, plot, patch, kitchen garden.

allow *v.* **1** *My salary doesn't allow me to live extravagantly. The teacher allowed us to leave school early:* permit, let, give permission to, give leave to; authorize, concede to, sanction, agree to, approve. **2** *Allow yourself an hour to get to the airport:* allot, allocate, assign, grant, give, provide.
Ant. 1 forbid, refuse, prohibit, disallow, deny.

allowance *n.* **1** *When I was a boy my allowance was 50p a week. Disabled veterans deserve a government allowance:* allotment, subsidy, stipend, grant, bounty; annuity, pension. **2** *Trade in your old car and you'll get an allowance on the new one:* discount, deduction, reduction, concession, rebate.
Ant. 2 increase, increment.

all right *adj., adv.* **1** *She felt all right in spite of her accident:* well, healthy, in good health, hale, hearty; safe, uninjured, unharmed, unimpaired, *Informal* O.K. **2** *The new cake recipe turned out all right:* satisfactorily, acceptably, *Informal* O.K.; correctly, properly. **3** *All right, I'll do as you wish:* yes, very well, *Informal* O.K.; certainly, absolutely.
Ant. 1 bad, poorly, in bad health, incapacitated; injured, harmed. **2** badly, poorly, unsatisfactorily, unacceptably; incorrectly. **3** no, not at all; absolutely not.
◇ *Usage note:* Many people unite the phrase *all right* as one word "alright." No such word exists in formal usage, so don't write *alright* unless you mean to be informal or slangy. If you are writing an exam paper or an application for a job, you had better spell it *all right.*

allude *v. He frequently alluded to his childhood on the farm:* mention, refer, speak of, touch upon; hint, suggest, intimate.

Ant. keep secret, keep quiet about, be close-mouthed about.

◇ *Usage note:* Although *allude* and *refer* are synonyms, their connotations and proper use are quite different. *Allude* means to mention indirectly or briefly in passing, to hint at: *He's often alluded to his army experiences but he's never told me about them. Refer* means to mention directly or in detail: *I refer to Shakespeare's* Hamlet, *Act III, Scene I—"To be, or not to be: that is the question."*

allure *v.* **1** *He was allured by her wealth and sophistication:* lure, attract, entice, tempt, lead on, bait, seduce; fascinate, beguile, charm, enchant, intrigue, captivate.
—*n.* **2** *He found a strange allure in the foreignness of her accent:* attraction, enticement, lure, temptation; fascination, enchantment, charm, intrigue.

Ant. 1 repel, alienate, drive away, deter, damp one's enthusiasm, *Slang* turn off; bore, be indifferent to.

allusion *n. Even the slightest allusion to the larder might make their mother suspect!:* reference, mention; hint, suggestion.

◇ *Usage note:* Don't confuse *allusion* and *illusion.* An *allusion* is a reference or mention; an *illusion* is a false impression, something that seems to be something else, or something that seems to exist but doesn't. Thus: *The teacher made an allusion to Shakespeare. The sky-blue ceiling gives one the illusion that one is out of doors.*

ally *n.* **1** *Britain and her allies won through in two world wars:* partner, associate, confederate, affiliate; collaborator, accomplice, accessory; colleague, confrère.
—*v.* **2** *The townspeople allied themselves in the fight for lower taxes:* unite, join together, join forces, band together, combine, bind together; affiliate, confederate, league.

Ant. 1 enemy, foe, adversary, opponent; rival, competitor, antagonist. **2** go separate ways; separate.

almighty *adj.* **1** *Judaism was the first religion to teach the existence of a supreme deity with almighty power:* unlimited, absolute, supreme, infinite, invincible, omnipotent.
—*n.* **2 The Almighty.** See GOD.

◇ *Usage note: Almighty* is almost never, in formal usage, applied to anything other than the attributes of God *Almighty.* In informal speech, however, the word is commonplace, as in the sentence *There was an almighty bang,* meaning an extremely or excessively loud bang.

"Holy, holy, holy, Lord God Almighty,"
—*Revelation 4: 8*

---

almost *adv. She almost fell off her horse. It's almost ten miles from here to Norwich market:* nearly, very nearly, about, just about, approximately, close to, all but, not quite, not far from, within an inch of.

Ant. exactly, definitely; certainly, surely.

aloft *adv. The glider soared aloft. They held their heads aloft:* in the air, above, overhead, in the sky, in the clouds, skyward, heavenward; up, high up, way up, on high, in a higher place.

Ant. down, low, low down; lower, below, beneath; earthward.

alone *adv., adj.* **1** *She's too young to go to the party alone. The house stood alone on the hill:* by oneself, without others, unaccompanied, separately, singly, solitarily; single, solitary, isolated; unescorted, unattended, unchaperoned. **2** *It's too big a job for one man to do alone. The Queen alone has the power to invest one with a knighthood:* without help, unaided, unassisted, single-handedly, with one's own two hands; all by oneself, only, on one's own, solely, sole. **3** *Mount Everest stands alone in its magnificence:* unique, uniquely, singular, singularly; unsurpassed, unequalled, unmatched, matchless, peerless, without peers, unparalleled, incomparable. **4** *After her husband's death she felt terribly alone:* lonesome, lonely, forsaken, deserted, abandoned, isolated, separated; forlorn, desolate.

Ant. 1 accompanied, with others, together, jointly; escorted, attended, chaperoned. **2** with assistance, assisted, with help, helped, aided; jointly, together, with others. **3** among others, equally, equalled; surpassed, overshadowed.

aloof *adj.* **1** *Her aloof manner gained her few friends:* cool, cold, detached, indifferent, stand-offish, distant, remote, unsociable, reserved, unapproachable, unsympathetic, unresponsive, haughty, high-hat, formal. **2** *The Royal Family stands aloof from politics:* apart, at a distance, above.

Ant. 1 warm, friendly, familiar, open, sociable, gregarious, neighbourly; sympathetic, compassionate.

aloud *adv. If you want to say it aloud, don't be bashful. The ancients were in the habit of reading aloud even when alone:* not in a whisper; in a normal speaking voice, audibly.

Ant. in a whisper; quietly, inaudibly, silently.

alter *v. The blonde wig completely altered her appearance:* change, transform, make different, amend, convert; modify, vary, recast.

Ant. keep, retain, *Informal* stick to.

◇ *Usage note:* Some students tend to confuse *alter* and *altar.* An *altar* is a table, platform or raised area for the performance of religious rites, as in a church; whereas to *alter* is to change. Thus, *The bridesmaids lead the bride to the altar. If it rains we'll have to alter our plans for the barbecue.*

alteration *n. If we remodel the shop we'll have to close for alterations:* change, modification, remodelling; transformation, transmutation, conversion; adjustment.

Ant. permanence, changelessness, stability.

altercation *n. Their frequent altercations destroyed their friendship:* dispute, argument, quarrel, row, *Informal* scene, wrangling; discord, falling-out, disagreement; fight, scrape, fracas, scuffle, affray, rumpus, brawl, mêlée, *Slang* broil.

Ant. agreement, accord, concord, harmony, peace; making-up.

alternate *v.* **1** *My sister and I alternate in washing the supper dishes. The desert temperatures alternate from 120° at noon to 40° at night:* take turns, perform by turns, rotate; interchange, intersperse; vary, change, alter.

—adj. **2** *Each of the two chemists works on alternate Sundays. The awning had alternate red and white stripes:* every other, every second; alternating, reciprocal, consecutive, successive.

◇ *Pronunciation tip: Alternate* has two different pronunciations, one for the adjective, and one for the verb. The adjective is pronounced *al-TER-nate, on al-ter-nate Sundays.* The verb, to *alternate,* is pronounced *AL-ter-nate: We al-ter-nate jobs.*

"In the development of this organization [the United Nations] rests the only true alternative to war." *—J. F. Kennedy*

---

alternative *n. If he wants to get to Leith by tonight he has no alternative but to go by plane:* choice, other choice, option, recourse; selection, substitute.

> **Exploring the Word:** When we *alter* something we change it into something other than it was. *Alter* comes from Latin *alter,* meaning "other." This same Latin word also gives us *alternative,* not one's first choice but the "other" or second choice; *altercation,* a dispute in which one person says or wants one thing and someone else says or wants the other; and *altruist,* a person devoted to the welfare of others.

altogether *adv.* **1** *The actor gave an altogether magnificent performance:* completely, entirely, utterly; absolutely, totally, wholly, thoroughly, perfectly, fully, out and out; in general, on the whole, quite. **2** *The bill came to £67 altogether:* in all, as a whole, in toto, in sum; collectively, all inclusive. **3** *Altogether, I'm glad we're moving:* all told, all in all, on the whole, in sum, *Informal* when all is said and done.

Ant. 1 partially, partly, incompletely. **2** in part; separately, individually. **3** partially, partly; somewhat.

◇ *Usage note: Altogether* is one word, meaning completely, absolutely. *All together,* two words, means all at once, in the same place or at the same time. Thus: *You're altogether wrong. All together, pull!*

altruistic *adj. Her altruistic deeds helped many people:* unselfish; generous, benevolent, large-hearted; humanitarian, charitable, philanthropic, public-spirited.

Ant. selfish, self-seeking, covetous, greedy; egoistic, egocentric, self-centred; malevolent, mean, grudging.

◇ *Word origin: Altruistic* is derived from *altruisme* (altruism), a term coined by the French philosopher Auguste Comte (1795-1857) to stand for the opposite of *egoism.* The word consists of Italian *altrui,* someone else (Latin *alter,* other) + *-ism.*

always *adv.* **1** *Work always begins at nine:* every time, on every occasion, without exception; regularly, invariably, consistently. **2** *Will you love me always?:* for ever, for ever and ever, for all time, eternally, everlastingly, perpetually, evermore; continually, unceasingly, unremittingly, incessantly.

Ant. 1 never; rarely.

amalgamate *v. Silver must be amalgamated with a harder material to make durable jewellery. The two shipping companies amalgamated into one:* combine, blend, merge, fuse, mix, commingle; unite, unify, join together, consolidate, incorporate, integrate.

Ant. separate, part, divide, disunite.

amass *v. The campers amassed a large pile of branches before starting their fire. He amassed a fortune in the oil business:* accumulate, gather, collect, assemble, compile, heap up, pile up.

Ant. scatter, disperse, distribute, dispense.

amateur *n.* **1** *Amateurs are not allowed to play in most professional golf tournaments. An amateur shouldn't play roulette for high stakes:* non-professional, dabbler, dilettante; beginner, novice, neophyte, greenhorn, tiro.

—adj. **2** *Acting with an amateur theatrical group can be fun:* non-professional; unprofessional, unpolished, inexperienced; unskilled, inexpert.

Ant. 1, 2 professional, expert. **2** experienced, practised, polished, finished; skilled.

◇ *Word origin:* An *amateur* does what he does for love of doing it, rather than for money. The word comes from Latin *amator,* lover, friend, or admirer.

amaze *v. Her rapid progress in karate amazed the teacher:* surprise, astonish, astound; flabbergast, awe, daze, shock, dumbfound, stupefy, stun, stagger.

Ant. expect, anticipate.

amazement *n. Imagine my amazement when the 70-year-old man beat me at tennis:* astonishment, surprise, shock, stupefaction; disbelief, bewilderment; wonder, awe.

Ant. anticipation, expectation; calmness, composure, indifference.

ambiguity *n. The ambiguities of his statement led us to suspect that he might be lying:* equivocation, vagueness, uncertainty, indefiniteness.

Ant. clarity, clearness, explicitness, definiteness, certainty.

ambiguous *adj. "Indian" is an ambiguous word because it can mean an American Indian or a native of India:* equivocal, vague, unclear, cryptic, enigmatic, indefinite, uncertain; misleading, having a double meaning.
Ant. explicit, definite, specific, direct, conclusive; clear, plain, frank, unmistakable, obvious, simple, lucid; unquestionable, honest.
◇ *Word origin: Ambiguous* comes from Latin *ambiguus*, ambiguous. Its ultimate derivation is from *ambigere*, to go round and round, shilly-shally.

ambition *n.* **1** *An executive has to have a lot of ambition to reach the top:* drive, zeal, desire, push, striving. **2** *His ambition is to be a lawyer:* aspiration, goal, aim, intent, objective, purpose, design; desire, dream, hope, longing, yearning.
Ant. 1 indifference; indolence, sloth.
◇ *Word origin: Ambition* came into English through French from Latin *ambitio*, which is made up of two elements, *amb-* (about) and *ire* (to go), the same source as in our word *ambit*, the compass or extent of something. *Ambition* entered English in the 14th century, and was soon regarded as a despicable vice: for example, one writer talked heatedly, in about 1450, of "vices [such] as pride, ambition, vainglory."

"Most people would succeed in small things if they were not troubled with great ambitions."
—*Henry Wadsworth Longfellow*

---

ambitious *adj.* **1** *Ambitious students get the best marks:* aspiring; zealous, eager, intent, desirous, ardent, avid. **2** *Building your own garage is a rather ambitious undertaking:* enterprising, industrious, energetic; strenuous, difficult.
Ant. 1 unambitious, unaspiring; apathetic, indolent, slothful, lazy. **2** modest, humble, lowly; easy, simple.

ambivalent *adj. I have ambivalent thoughts on where to spend my holiday:* contradictory, conflicting, opposing, clashing, warring; mixed, wavering, fluctuating, *Informal* wishy-washy.
Ant. definite, positive; unwavering.

amble *v. We ambled across the meadow enjoying the fresh air:* stroll, walk leisurely, wander aimlessly, ramble, meander, saunter.
Ant. rush, run, race.
◇ *Word origin: Amble* and *ambulatory* are derived from Latin *ambulare*, to walk.

ambulatory *adj. Young doctors sometimes perform surgery on ambulatory patients:* up and about, not confined to bed; walking, moving, mobile, peripatetic.
Ant. bedridden; not walking, immobile.

amen *interj. All Christian and Jewish prayers end with an "Amen!":* so be it, it is so, let it be so, so shall it be, would that it were so; truly, verily; *Informal* hear hear, yes indeed.
◇ *Word origin: Amen* goes back to Hebrew *āmēn*, verily, truly, so it is. It was taken into Christian use from Mosaic law: "And the Levites shall speak, and say unto all the men of Israel with a loud voice, Cursed be the man that maketh any graven or molten image . . . And all the people shall answer and say, Amen." (Deuteronomy 27: 14–15.)

amenable *adj. The committee is amenable to any suggestions. Are you amenable to having the meeting next Tuesday?:* agreeable, willing to agree, willing to listen; favourably disposed, cordial, persuadable, open, open-minded, acquiescent, willing, obliging, sympathetic, yielding, submissive.
Ant. closed-minded, obstinate, stubborn, headstrong, truculent, recalcitrant, autocratic, autonomous.

amend *v.* **1** *The members of the club voted to amend the constitution:* change, revise, modify, alter, emend. **2** *I would advise you to amend your manners:* improve, better, perfect, develop, polish, enhance; emend, correct, rectify, reform, remedy, mend, fix.
Ant. 2 corrupt, spoil, damage, harm, injure, hurt, impair, blemish; vitiate.
◇ *Usage note:* Although *amend* and *emend* overlap in meaning, there is a distinct difference that it is well to maintain. To *amend* is to change something in order to improve it: *He amended the speech by making some additions and deletions.* To *emend* is to change something in order to correct it: *He emended the report by substituting the correct figures for the erroneous ones.* Because *emend* seems to be losing favour and *amend* is taking over both meanings, we have given "correct, rectify," etc., as synonyms at def. **2** above, but precise writers would still consider these as proper synonyms only for *emend*, not *amend.*

amendment *n.* **1** *The Prime Minister hopes the bill will be passed without further amendment:* addition, adjunct. **2** *Amendments must be made to the blueprints before the builder will accept them:* revision, modification, change, alteration, emendation; improvement, correction, rectification, reform.

amends *n. Is there any way I can make amends for ruining your party?:* apology, defence, redress, justification, explanation, vindication; restitution, recompense, retribution, compensation, reparation, indemnification, restoration, payment, requital, expiation, *Informal* peace-offering; atonement, acknowledgement, satisfaction.

amenity *n.* **1** Plural **amenities**. *Children should be taught the social amenities:* good manners, politeness, courtesies, niceties, gallantries, etiquette; refinement, gentility. **2** *These forests were planted for amenity, not for timber:* agreeableness, pleasantness, pleasure, advantage, attractiveness, beauty.
Ant. 1 bad manners, rudeness, boorishness,

impoliteness, discourtesy. **2** unpleasantness, surliness, incivility.
◇ *Word origin: Amenity* is based on Latin *amoenus,* pleasant.

amiable *adj. Amiable neighbours help make a house a home. He has an amiable personality:* friendly, agreeable, amicable, pleasant, good-natured, kindly, obliging, cordial, sociable, affable; pleasing, attractive, engaging, winning, charming; polite, genial, gracious.
Ant. unfriendly, hostile, disagreeable, unpleasant, ill-humoured, sullen, surly, sour; displeasing, unattractive, repellent, repugnant, loathsome, offensive.
◇ *Usage note: Amiable* is usually used to describe persons and *amicable* to describe actions, gestures, etc. Thus, *The next-door neighbours are amiable people. The union and the company reached an amicable settlement in their contract dispute.*

amicable *adj. If wars are to end, nations must learn amicable means of settling their disputes:* friendly, peaceable, agreeable, amiable, amenable, harmonious, cordial, civil, polite, courteous, kind, kindly, kind-hearted, benevolent; sociable, neighbourly.
Ant. unfriendly, belligerent, antagonistic, contentious, pugnacious, bellicose, quarrelsome, hostile; disagreeable, nasty, unsociable, unkind, cold.
◇ *Pronunciation tip: Amicable* is stressed on the first syllable: *AMicable.*
◇ *Usage note:* See AMIABLE.

amiss *adj.* **1** *I knew something was amiss from her startled expression:* wrong, awry, inappropriate, unsuitable, improper, out of order, *Informal* up; faulty, mistaken, incorrect, erroneous; false, fallacious, mixed-up; untoward.
—adv. **2** *Did I speak amiss when I mentioned the surprise?:* wrongly, inappropriately, unsuitably, improperly, mistakenly, untowardly, out of order, *Informal* out of line; incorrectly, erroneously, falsely, faultily, inaccurately, awry, astray.
Ant. 1 right, proper, appropriate, suitable, *Informal* perfect, O.K.; in order; correct, true. **2** rightly, properly, appropriately, suitably; correctly, truly.

amity *n. Canada and the United States have lived side by side in amity for generations:* friendship, harmony, goodwill, understanding, sympathy; agreement, accord, concord; cordiality, fellowship, fraternity, brotherhood.
Ant. enmity, antagonism, hostility, animosity, conflict, contention, ill will; disagreement, dissension, discord, strife.

amnesty *n. The king granted an amnesty to the rebels:* pardon, reprieve; forgiveness, absolution, reconciliation; immunity.
◇ *Word origin:* Both the concept of *amnesty* and our word for it come to us from the ancient Greeks: *amnestia* means literally "non-remembrance" but was regularly used in the legal sense of pardon. (The word, because also relating to forgetfulness, gave rise to *amnesia,* memory loss, a term which first appeared in medical writing about 200 years ago.)

amorous *adj. The young man gave his fiancée an amorous glance:* loving, enamoured, lovesick; ardent, passionate, impassioned; fond, affectionate, tender, doting.
Ant. unloving, indifferent, uncaring, cold, frigid; hateful.

amorphous *adj. An amorphous haze hung over the city:* shapeless, formless, unshapen; vague, nondescript, indeterminate, characterless, anomalous.
◇ *Word origin: Amorphous* comes from Greek *amorphos,* meaning (1) shapeless, and (2) unshapely or misshapen. To the ancient Greeks the concepts of "form" and "beauty" were one and the same, and a single word, *morphē,* stood for both.

amount *n.* **1** *What is the amount of my bill?:* total, sum, sum total, aggregate; extent, magnitude. **2** *The recipe calls for a small amount of sugar:* quantity, measure; volume, bulk, mass.
◇ *Usage note: Amount* and *number* confuse some people. Use *amount* when referring to quantities that can't be counted: *a large amount of snow, a small amount of money.* Use *number* when referring to things that can be counted: *a large number of people, a small number of pounds.*

amour *n. He's always bragging about his amours:* love affair, affair, romance, intrigue, liaison.
◇ *Word origin:* Speakers of English have been using the originally French word *amour* for "love" or "love affair" since about 1300. But, says the *Oxford English Dictionary,* the word has for some time been used "only humorously of honourable love-making."

ample *adj.* **1** *This country has an ample supply of fuel oil if we don't waste any. We have ample time for a leisurely lunch:* enough, sufficient, adequate, satisfactory; more than enough, plenty, abundant, plentiful, bountiful, profuse, copious, generous, liberal. **2** *A wrestler must have ample muscles:* large, big, immense, huge, vast; wide, broad, extensive, expansive, outspread, extended, roomy, spacious, voluminous, commodious.
Ant. 1 insufficient, inadequate, unsatisfactory; limited, restricted; scant, scanty, sparse, meagre, skimpy, scrimpy; niggardly, stingy. **2** small, little, minute, wee.

amplification *n.* **1** *The amplification of the project will take more time:* enlargement, expansion, increasing, development, extension; heightening, broadening, widening. **2** *His story needs amplification:* elaboration, rounding out, developing, augmentation, added detail.
Ant. 1 reduction, decreasing, curtailment,

contraction, cutting down, paring down; narrowing. **2** simplification, simplifying; condensing, abridging, cutting, boiling down.

amplify *v.* **1** *We must amplify our effort by working a lot harder:* increase, intensify, strengthen, heighten, raise; expand, extend, enlarge, widen, lengthen, deepen. **2** *Please amplify your remarks by giving us some examples:* elaborate on, expatiate on; expand, develop, add to, augment, supplement, fill out, complete.

Ant. 1 reduce, decrease, curtail, cut down, pare down. **2** simplify, condense, abbreviate, abridge; summarize, boil down.

amplitude *n.* **1** *The amplitude of the universe is awesome:* magnitude, extent, size; vastness, largeness, bigness; spaciousness, capaciousness; dimension, breadth, width; bulk, volume, mass. **2** *Leonardo da Vinci is remembered for the great amplitude of his creative powers:* range, scope, extent, compass, sweep, reach; expanse; completeness, fullness, richness; abundance, profusion, plenitude, copiousness, plethora.

Ant. 1 smallness, littleness, minuteness, exiguity. **2** limitation, narrowness, restriction, circumspection.

amply *adv. The troops were amply supplied with provisions:* adequately, sufficiently, satisfactorily, thoroughly, completely, fully; suitably, abundantly, plentifully, profusely, copiously, bountifully, generously, liberally, lavishly, richly, unstintingly.

Ant. inadequately, insufficiently; scantily, meagrely, skimpily.

amputate *v. The surgeon had to amputate the patient's leg:* cut off, sever, excise, remove; *Informal* lop off.

amulet *n. The witch-doctor wore an amulet on a string round his neck:* charm, talisman.

amuse *v. We amused ourselves by playing games:* entertain, divert, occupy interest, engross, absorb, beguile; please, gladden, cheer, enliven.

Ant. bore; tire, weary; vex, annoy.

"Scarfs, garters, gold, amuse his riper stage,
And beads and prayer-books are the toys of age."
—*Alexander Pope*

---

amusement *n.* **1** *Reading is my favourite amusement. There is a time for work and a time for amusement:* pastime, diversion, distraction; entertainment, recreation, avocation, hobby; play, game, revel. **2** *He smiled with amusement at the child's prank:* merriment, pleasure, delight, enjoyment.

Ant. 1 bore, boredom, tedium, monotony, ennui. **2** sadness; displeasure, disgust.

amusing *adj.* **1** *Charades is an amusing game:* entertaining, diverting, interesting, beguiling, engrossing, absorbing; pleasant, delightful, pleasurable, pleasing, cheering. **2** *His jokes were amusing:* funny, comical, humorous, witty, droll, farcical, waggish.

Ant. 1 boring, dull, tedious, monotonous. **2** sad, depressing.

anaemic *adj.* **1** *He felt weak because he was anaemic:* deficient in haemoglobin, thin-blooded. **2** *That anaemic-looking room needs some bright paint:* pale, pallid, wan, dull, colourless, subdued, quiet; weak, characterless.

Ant. 2 bright, colourful, florid, loud, flashy; strong, powerful.

anaesthesia *n. His state of anaesthesia lasted several hours after the operation:* insensibility to sensations, loss of feeling, insentience, numbness; unconsciousness, stupor.

anaesthetic *n. The doctor used a new anaesthetic on the patient:* pain-killer, analgesic, narcotic.

Ant. stimulant, analeptic.

analgesic *n. The most common analgesic is aspirin:* pain-killer, anodyne; (*variously*) anaesthetic, narcotic, opiate.

Ant. irritant.

analogous *adj. The heart is analogous to a pump:* similar, like, comparable, akin, equivalent, parallel, correlative, corresponding.

Ant. dissimilar, unlike; different, divergent.

analogy *n. The doctor pointed out the analogy between the heart and a pump:* similarity, likeness, resemblance, similitude; comparison, correspondence, parallelism, correlation; simile, metaphor.

Ant. dissimilarity, difference.

◇ *Word origin: Analogy* comes from Greek *analogia*, meaning a proportion like the following: 2/10=10/x. This method of stating proportions was invented by Greek mathematicians, as was the familiar method of calculating unknown quantities in ratios (which in the present example would yield x=50).

analyse *v.* **1** *The doctor analysed the blood sample for anaemia:* separate and examine the parts of. **2** *The mathematician analysed his figures again:* examine, study, investigate, question, search; evaluate, consider, judge, think through, reason out.

Ant. 2 ignore, overlook, pay no heed to, shut one's eyes to; neglect, slight, pass over, brush aside.

analysis *n.* **1** *Chemical analysis of water yields hydrogen and oxygen:* separation, breakdown, break-up, reduction, resolution, partition, dissociation. **2** *Scotland Yard wants a complete analysis of how the crime was committed:* examination, investigation, inquiry, observation, study, test, search. **3** *The newscaster's analysis of the election results was interesting:* judgement, evaluation, reasoning, thinking, interpretation, speculation, estimation; summary, review, outline, synopsis, abstract, précis, digest, brief. **4** *The psychiatrist recommended analysis:* psycho-analysis, psychotherapy, therapy.

Ant. 1 synthesis, uniting, union, combining, combination.

◇ *Word origin:* If you take something apart in order to study it, you are performing an *analysis.* The 4th-century B.C. Greek philosopher Aristotle was the first to use this word (which originally meant "loosening, dissolving, or dissolution") as a technical term, and the word has been associated with problem-solving ever since.

analyst *n.* **1** *The neurotic patient was sent to an analyst:* psycho-analyst, *Slang* head-shrinker, shrink. **2** *A football coach has to be a good analyst of his players' abilities:* judge, evaluator, estimator; examiner, investigator, observer, tester.

analytic, analytical *adj. A chess player must have an analytic mind:* logical, systematic, organized, problem-solving; inquiring, studious, searching, testing.

Ant. illogical, disorganized, unsystematic, chaotic.

anarchist *n. Anarchists burned down the palace:* rebel, revolutionary, insurgent, terrorist, mutineer; syndicalist; nihilist.

Ant. loyalist, Tory, conservative; disciplinarian.

anarchy *n. Any form of government is better than anarchy:* absence of government, disorder, lawlessness, chaos.

Ant. order, discipline, authority; government, organization, control; regimentation, subjection.

◇ *Word origin:* In Classical Greek *anarchia* means the state of a people without government: *an-*, without, + *archon*, leader. Borrowed into modern languages via Medieval Latin, the word has been associated with rebellion since Renaissance times and with the ideal state advocated by anarchists only since about the time of the French Revolution.

anathema *n.* **1** *That traitor's name is anathema in this house!:* an abomination, taboo, unmentionable. **2** *The papal anathema was pronounced chiefly against heretics:* curse, malediction; excommunication, ban, proscription; denunciation.

Ant. 1 beloved; welcomed. **2** blessing, benediction.

anathematize *v. We declare him excommunicated and anathematized and we judge him condemned to eternal fire:* excommunicate, damn; condemn, accurse, imprecate, execrate, abominate, hold in abomination.

ancestor *n.* **1** *His ancestors were pioneers:* forefather, forbear; progenitor, procreator, begetter. **2** *The bone-shaker is an ancestor of the modern bicycle:* forerunner, predecessor, antecedent, precursor.

Ant. 1 descendant, inheritor; progeny, issue, offspring. **2** successor.

ancestry *n.* **1** *Many Mexicans are of Spanish ancestry:* descent, extraction, derivation; origin, stock, heredity, race. **2** *My aunt has always made much of her ancestry:* ancestors, lineage, progenitors; family, line, parentage, house; genealogy, pedigree, blood, family tree.

Ant. 1 posterity. **2** descendants, progeny, issue.

"People will not look forward to posterity, who never look backward to their ancestors."
—*Edmund Burke*

---

anchor *n.* **1** *Drop the anchor when the boat passes the sand-bar: Informal* hook; ground tackle, mooring. **2** *The Bible is the anchor of our faith:* mainstay, support, bulwark, strong point, basis, foundation; safeguard, security, defence.

—*v.* **3** *They anchored their boat in the outer bay:* secure by anchor, moor; drop anchor, cast anchor, ride at anchor. **4** *We anchored the hammock to the trees:* secure, fix, affix, fasten.

Ant. 3 lift anchor, weigh anchor, break free.

ancient *adj.* **1** *The pyramids were built in ancient times:* long past, remote, olden, old; early, primeval, primitive, prehistoric; *Historical use* Graeco-Roman, classical, prior to A.D. 476. **2** *The Lord of a manor was loath to infringe the ancient rights of the peasants. He drives an ancient machine:* old, very old, aged, age-old; antique, timeworn, hoary. **3** *That the woman's place is only in the home is an ancient idea:* out-of-date, old-fashioned, out-of-fashion, outmoded, antiquated, passé, bygone, *Informal* old hat; obsolete, obsolescent, archaic.

Ant. 1 recent, late. **2** new, brand new, spanking new, young. **3** modern, fresh, novel, modernistic; current, up-to-date, newfangled, new-fashioned, in vogue, modish, *Slang* with-it.

ancillary *adj. The main clause of the contract concerns the amount of money to be paid, and all the whens and wherefores are ancillary to it:* supplementary, auxiliary, accessory, contributory; secondary, subordinate, subsidiary; minor, dependent, subservient, inferior.

Ant. main, major, primary, prime; independent; counteractive, contrary, at odds with.

anecdote *n. Public speakers often begin their talks with humorous anecdotes:* story, tale, yarn, short narrative, brief account, sketch, reminiscence.

◇ *Usage note:* Be sure to spell and pronounce *anecdote* (*an-ek-dote*) properly. Don't confuse it with *antidote* (*anti-dote*). An *anecdote* is a short narrative, often humorous. An *antidote* is something that counteracts, acts *anti-* to or against, a poison or disease. Thus: *Annie told an anecdote about her childhood. Is there an antidote for strychnine?*

◇ *Word origin: Anecdote* comes from the title of a 6th-century A.D. book by the historian

Procopius, who held high office under Emperor Justinian at Constantinople and did an exposé on the private lives of Justinian and Theodora which appeared posthumously as *Anekdota*, "Unpublished Titbits," now widely available in English under the title *Secret History*.

anew *adv. After the applause the performers began anew. If the experiment doesn't work this time, you'll have to begin your research anew:* again, once more, over again; from scratch, in a new way, afresh, newly.

Ant. never again, nevermore.

angel *n.* **1** *The angel Gabriel is mentioned in the Bible at Daniel 8: 16 and Luke 1: 26:* messenger of God, heavenly spirit, celestial being; (*variously*) seraph, cherub, throne, domination, virtue, power, principality, archangel. **2** *I married an angel:* angelic person, *Slang* doll, gem, jewel, saint.

Ant. 1 devil.

angelic *adj.* **1** *The music had an angelic quality:* ethereal, celestial, heavenly, divine, spiritual, saintly, beatific; seraphic, cherubic. **2** *What an angelic child!:* angel-like, good, ideal, pure, innocent; beautiful, lovely, enrapturing, rapturous, entrancing, adorable.

Ant. 1, 2 demonic. **1** hellish, infernal, **2** diabolical, fiendish; ugly, ugly as sin, repulsive.

anger *n.* **1** *My anger grew as he continued his insults:* rage, outrage, fury, wrath, ire, temper, gall, bile, choler, spleen, pique; indignation, resentment, exasperation, petulance, vexation, irritation, annoyance, displeasure, umbrage, disapprobation; antagonism, animosity, hostility, hatred, enmity, acrimony; ill temper, hot temper.
—*v.* **2** *I did not mean to anger you:* infuriate, enrage, outrage, madden, incense, inflame, pique, rile, gall, nettle, chafe, ruffle, exacerbate; provoke, exasperate, vex, irritate, annoy, displeasure; antagonize, embitter, cause ill feelings; *Informal* make bad blood, ruffle one's feathers, get one's hackles up.

Ant. 1 love, liking, fondness; goodwill, peacefulness, mildness, amiability; approval, acceptance, condonation; calmness, equanimity; pleasure, gratification; forgiveness. **2** placate, appease, pacify, mollify, propitiate, calm, soothe; please, delight, gladden, gratify, *Informal* tickle.

angle *n.* **1** *A vertical line will meet a horizontal line at an angle of 90°: Geometry* space between two lines or planes that meet; divergence. **2** *The road makes a sharp angle just over that hill:* bend, corner, edge, cusp. **3** *Try to look at the situation from my angle. The view of the valley is beautiful from this angle:* point of view, viewpoint, standpoint, side, aspect, slant; outlook, focus, perspective.

◇ *Word origin: Angle* is from Latin *angulus*, corner, angle.

angry *adj. Her rudeness makes me angry. She's in an angry mood:* mad, furious, infuriated, enraged, outraged, raging, fuming, incensed, inflamed, irate, indignant, exasperated, resentful, vexed, piqued, riled, nettled, galled; provoked, irritated, annoyed, displeased, offended, affronted; hostile, hateful, antagonistic, acrimonious, embittered; ill-tempered, petulant, irascible, splenetic, huffy.

Ant. loving, fond, friendly; calm, soothing, peaceful, mild, complaisant, agreeable, pleasant, amiable; happy, pleased, pleasing, gratified, gratifying; good-natured, even-tempered; apologetic, forgiving, unresentful, placating.

"Be not hasty in thy spirit to be angry: for anger resteth in the bosom of fools."
—*Ecclesiastes 7: 9*

---

anguish *n. The mother waited in anguish for news of the missing child:* distress, pain, agony, suffering, torment, misery; anxiety, heartache, grief, woe; remorse, sorrow.

Ant. comfort, ease; relief, solace, consolation, alleviation.

angular *adj.* **1** *The mountain track is angular and difficult to follow:* sharp-cornered, bent, crooked, jagged. **2** *The old mountaineer had an angular face:* bony, gaunt, spare, lean, rawboned, scrawny, lanky, lank.

Ant. 1 straight; rounded. **2** chubby, fleshy, rotund, plump, stout, portly.

animal *n.* **1** *Human beings are social animals. Corals are secreted by marine animals:* living being, creature, organism, biological system. **2** *No animals are allowed in the restaurant:* dumb animal; (*variously*) wild animal, beast, farm animal, pet. **3** *The zoo has collections of animals, birds, and reptiles:* mammal, quadruped. **4** *Those teen-age hooligans behaved just like animals:* brute, beast.

animate *v.* **1** *All living forms are animated by a mysterious force sometimes known as the "life force":* make alive, vivify, vitalize, quicken. **2** *Her gaiety animated the entire group:* make lively, enliven, invigorate, give energy to, add spirit to, energize; excite, fire, warm. **3** *She was animated by the best of intentions:* stimulate, arouse, stir, inspire, spur on, move, impel, set on, incite, instigate, activate, actuate; goad, urge, prompt, provoke, work up.
—*adj.* **4** *Do you think animate beings exist on Mars?:* alive, having life; moving.

Ant. 1 kill, deaden, make lifeless, devitalize. **2** depress, dishearten, cool, put a damper on, dull; bore. **3** discourage, dampen; deter, restrain, inhibit, curb, check. **4** inanimate, dead, lifeless.

◇ *Word origin: Animate* is ultimately derived from Latin *anima*, breath, life, soul, the vital principle. *Animal, animation,* and even *animosity* are derived from the same Latin stem.

animated *adj. The party was filled with animated conversation:* lively, spirited, active, vivacious, vigorous, zestful, invigorating, energetic, exciting, elated, vibrant, vivid, bright, fervent, ardent, zealous, passionate, hot, glowing, buoyant, airy, sprightly, quick, brisk, breezy, blithe, gay, sportive.

Ant. dull, deadly, lifeless, boring, monotonous; depressed, dejected; inactive, listless, spiritless, lethargic, torpid, slow, apathetic, passive; dispirited.

animation *n. The children sparkled with animation:* liveliness, life, spirit, high spirits, good spirits, animal spirits, blithe spirit, vivacity, vitality, vital power, zest, vigour, vim, verve, exhilaration, eagerness, enthusiasm; excitement, ardour, elation, glow, vibrancy, fire, alertness, brightness, alacrity, sprightliness, buoyancy, briskness, gaiety, good cheer, sportiveness; action, activity.

Ant. lifelessness, dullness, spiritlessness; lethargy, apathy, passivity, inertness, stolidity, sluggishness, dejection, depression, low spirits.

animosity *n. The animosity between Castlereagh and Canning finally resulted in a duel:* ill will, antagonism, bitterness, dislike, unfriendliness, malice, malevolence, malignity, hatred, hate, hostility, enmity, antipathy, anger, resentment, rancour, acrimony.

Ant. goodwill, love, friendship, friendliness, harmony, congeniality, kindness, sympathy.

◇ *Word origin:* Latin *animosus* means bold and spirited, like a good horse. About the year 1450 *animosity* entered English as a literary word meaning "boldness, high spirits."

annals *n. We found the information in the annals of the society. Never in the annals of crime has there been such a daring robbery:* yearly records, chronological records; chronicles, historical rolls, records, registers; history, chronology; minutes.

annex *v.* **1** *The city annexed the area across the river:* attach, add, incorporate, acquire, appropriate, expropriate, seize, merge, connect, join, subjoin, adjoin, affix, append, tack on, *Informal* grab.

—*n.* **2** *A new annex is being added to the school:* addition, attachment, appendage.

Ant. 1 detach, separate, disconnect, remove, disengage. **2** separation, detachment.

annihilate *v. Hitler sought to annihilate resistance movements throughout Europe:* wipe out, exterminate, liquidate, *Slang* mop up; destroy completely, reduce to nothing, lay waste, obliterate, end, abolish, eradicate, erase, extirpate.

Ant. let live; build, construct, create, make.

◇ *Pronunciation tip: Annihilate* is pronounced *an-I-ilate.*

annotate *v. The famous classicist Richard Porson annotated the plays of Aeschylus in 1795:* explicate, elucidate, interpret, expound; construe, explain, comment, commentate, remark; gloss.

annotation *n. The annotations were printed in italics:* note, footnote, gloss; remark, comment, observation; commentary, elucidation, interpretation, explication, explication de texte, exegesis, apparatus criticus.

Ant. main text, text.

announce *v.* **1** *The Prime Minister announced his cabinet appointments:* publish, promulgate, proclaim, declare; broadcast, advertise, disseminate, give out, sound abroad, trumpet; disclose, divulge, reveal. **2** *The dark clouds announced the coming of a storm:* herald, harbinger, foretell, presage, augur, betoken, portend, signify, signal.

Ant. 1, 2 suppress, secrete, hide, cover up, conceal, bury, withhold, hush, keep back, keep secret, repress; hold back, reserve.

annoy *v. You children must stop annoying me by asking for sweets all day long. I'm annoyed every day by the slow bus service in this town:* disturb, bother, pester, badger, harry, harass, nag, tax, hector, tease; trouble, worry, torment, plague, inconvenience, distract; irritate, provoke, exasperate, vex, gall, ruffle, rile, nettle.

Ant. calm, soothe, comfort, relieve, solace, console; please, gratify; appease, mollify.

◇ *Word origin:* Our word *annoy* goes back to the Latin phrase *mihi in odio est,* it is hateful to me. Latin *odium,* hate, also gives us our words *odium* and *odious.* But most closely related to *annoy* is *ennui,* a French import naturalized in our language toward the end of the 18th century.

annul *v. The contract was annulled because it had not been legally signed by both parties:* render null and void, nullify, invalidate, cancel, void; abrogate, revoke, rescind, retract, recall, repeal, reverse; abolish, dissolve, undo.

Ant. validate; enact, perform.

annulment *n. The annulment of the marriage was granted by the judge:* nullification, invalidation, cancellation, voiding; abrogation, revocation, retraction, recall, repeal, reversal; dissolution, undoing, repudiation, abolition.

Ant. validation.

anoint *v.* **1** *She anointed herself with sun-tan lotion:* put oil on, smear with oily liquid, pour oil on, oil. **2** *And the men of Judah came, and there they anointed David king:* consecrate by unction, make holy by anointing, sanctify by anointing.

anomalous *adj.* **1** *An Eskimo in native dress would cut an anomalous figure in Cardiff:* incongruous, out of keeping, bizarre. **2** *Cats with six toes are anomalous but not uncommon:* irregular, abnormal, atypical; monstrous.

Ant. 1 common, usual, standard, typical, familiar, unexceptional, ordinary, natural, normal, regular, conventional, customary. **2** normal, typical.

anomaly *n. His mature behaviour was an anomaly*

in someone so young: irregularity, exception to the rule; oddity, rarity; abnormality, deviation; eccentricity, peculiarity, incongruity.
Ant. the norm, the rule, the common thing.

anonymous *adj. They did not know whom to thank for the anonymous gift:* nameless, un-named, bearing no name, unsigned; unidentified, unacknowledged, of unknown authorship.
Ant. named, signed; identified, acknowledged, known.

answer *n.* **1** *Please send an answer to my letter soon:* reply, response, acknowledgement, rejoinder. **2** *How many students had the correct answer?:* solution, explanation, resolution.
—v. **3** *Answer your sister's letter when you have the time. Please answer the doorbell:* reply, respond, acknowledge, react to; write, say, rejoin, retort. **4** *I answered the problems in the test quickly and got them all right:* give a solution to, solve, resolve. **5** (usually followed by **for**) *He will answer for his mistakes:* be responsible, be accountable, be liable; pay for, suffer for, make amends for, atone for, expiate. **6** *His qualifications answer the requirements of the job:* meet, fill, fulfil, serve, suit; be sufficient, be adequate, be enough, pass muster, be satisfactory, do well enough; conform, correspond, be similar, be like, be equivalent, be the counterpart of, be correlated.
Ant. **1** question, query, inquiry, interrogation; summoning, summons, call, challenge. **2** problem. **3** question, ask, query, inquire, interrogate; summon, call, challenge. **4** ask. **6** fail; differ.
◇ *Word origin:* An *answer* was originally a solemn affirmation rebutting an accusation. The Old English verb *andswerian* combines *and-*, against or opposite, with *swerian*, to swear. The accused thus *answered* by swearing the opposite of what had been charged by his accuser.

answerable *adj. An 18-year-old is answerable for his behaviour:* accountable, responsible, liable.
Ant. unaccountable, not responsible.

antagonism *n. The unfairness of the will caused antagonism between the brothers:* hostility, opposition, conflict, friction, clashing, discord; animosity, enmity, antipathy; animus, rancour, spite, resentment; hatred, dislike, aversion, detestation.
Ant. love, friendship, friendliness, amity, liking; peacefulness, agreement, accord, concord, harmony; sympathy, understanding.

antagonist *n. His antagonist in the debate was quicker than he:* opponent, adversary, rival, competitor, opposer, contestant, disputant; enemy, foe, attacker, assailant.
Ant. ally, partner, colleague, team-mate; supporter, patron, defender; friend.

antagonize *v. His rude remarks antagonized the guests:* alienate, repel, offend.
Ant. conciliate, placate, pacify, appease, mollify, propitiate.

ante *n. He thinks nothing of a game where £100 is the ante and £500 the limit:* stake, bet, beginning bet, wager, pot.
◇ *Word origin:* An *ante* is a poker stake put up to "sweeten the pot," usually before the deal (*ante* means "before" in Latin). The word first appeared in its present gambling sense in the United States about 150 years ago, and is now used in the United Kingdom in this sense, and also meaning an amount of money paid in advance, a subscription.

> **Exploring the Word:** Latin *ante*, before, is found in *ante-bellum*, before the war, especially before the American Civil War; *anterior*, literally "more before," hence earlier; *antecedent*, a person or thing that has gone before in time; *anticipate*, literally to take beforehand, hence to expect; and *ancient* and *antique*, before the present, hence very old. *Ante* is also found in our Italian borrowing *antipasto*, before the meal, the term we occasionally use for cold, mixed hors d'oeuvres, Italian style.

antecedent *adj.* **1** *The harpsichord was antecedent to the pianoforte:* precursory, pre-existent, anterior, precedent, previous, prior.
—n. **2** *The horse and trap was the antecedent of the motor car:* precursor, forerunner, predecessor, precedent, ancestor; harbinger, herald, pioneer. **3** **antecedents**. *My antecedents were all farmers:* ancestors, forefathers, forbears, family, predecessors, ancestry; family tree, lineage, pedigree, stock, house, extraction, progeniture.
Ant. **1** subsequent, following, posterior; later, after. **2** successor, sequel; consequence, result, aftermath, upshot. **3** descendants, progeny, issue, offspring.

antedate *v. The American Revolution antedates the French Revolution by 14 years:* precede, come first, be of older date than, occur earlier than, predate, go before, happen before, anticipate, antecede.
Ant. follow, succeed, come after, postdate.

antediluvian *adj. Uncle Jim's antediluvian business methods prevented him from ever making any money:* antiquated, antique, archaic, obsolete.
◇ *Word origin: Antediluvian* is formed of two Latin words: *ante*, before, + *diluvium*, flood. The word was coined more than 300 years ago, and one of its first users was Sir Thomas Browne (1646) in writing about "antediluvian chronology," that is, the dating of events that occurred prior to the Flood described in the Book of Genesis.

anterior *adj.* **1** *Architects often embellish the anterior wall of a building and leave the rear wall blank:* front, in front, forward, placed before. **2** *Magna Carta is anterior to the United States Constitution by more than 500 years:* previous, prior, antecedent.

Ant. 1 posterior, rear, back. 2 subsequent, posterior.

anthology *n. He bought an anthology of Conan Doyle's stories:* collection, compilation, choice; treasury, chap-book, garland, florilegium; selections, extracts, miscellanea, scrap-book, commonplace-book, miscellany, analects, gleanings, collectanea.

◇ *Word origin: Anthology* comes from Greek *anthologia,* flower gathering (from *anthos,* flower, + *legein,* to pick).

antic *n.* usually **antics**. *The clown's lively antics made the children laugh:* pranks, tricks, monkey-tricks, tomfoolery, clownishness, buffoonery, sport, practical jokes; playful behaviour, fanciful acts, ridiculous acts, skylarking, larks, escapades.

Ant. seriousness, solemnity, gravity.

◇ *Word origin: Antic* and *antique* are just different forms of the same word, going back to Latin *antiquus,* previous or ancient. The special meaning of *antic* arose in Renaissance Italy during excavations of ancient Roman remains. Great numbers of grotesque masks and figurines turned up, and the excavators took to calling them *anticos,* "oldies." Soon the word came to stand for anything having to do with clowns or clowning.

anticipate *v. We anticipate a lot of snow this winter:* expect, look for, await; count on, prepare oneself for, look toward; look forward to, long for, pin hope on; foresee, forecast, predict, foretell.

Ant. despair of, doubt; dread, fear; remember, recollect.

anticipation *n.* 1 *As Christmas drew near, the children were filled with anticipation:* expectation, expectancy, hope. 2 *The soldier polished his boots in anticipation of the inspection:* expectation, preparation.

anticlimax *n. After the excitement of the campaign, election day was an anticlimax:* let-down, comedown, disappointment, dull ending.

Ant. climax, culmination, lofty ending.

antidote *n.* 1 *Doctors rushed an antidote to the boy who had been bitten by the snake:* antipoison, antitoxin. 2 *A hobby is a good antidote for boredom:* remedy, cure, corrective.

◇ *Usage note:* see ANECDOTE.

◇ *Word origin:* An *antidote* is given to counteract a poison. The word is from Greek *anti-,* against, + *didonai,* to give.

antipathy *n. I try to be broad-minded but I do feel antipathy towards people who are dirty and unkempt:* dislike, aversion, distaste; disgust, repulsion, loathing, repugnance, abhorrence; antagonism, animosity, ill will, enmity, rancour, hostility, unfriendliness.

Ant. affinity, fellow-feeling, regard, sympathy, attraction, partiality; love, affection, attachment.

antiquated *adj. Grandmother has antiquated ideas about etiquette:* antique, old-fashioned, outmoded, passé, dated, out-of-date, out-dated, of the old school; obsolete, archaic, obsolescent.

Ant. modern, new, young, current, recent, fresh, novel; up-to-date, new-fashioned, fashionable, newfangled, stylish, modish, smart.

antique *adj.* 1 *She has a fine collection of antique furniture:* old, antiquated.

—*n.* 2 *The museum has a display of valuable antiques:* relic, rarity, curio, objet d'art, bibelot, trinket.

Ant. 1 modern, new, fashionable, recent, current.

◇ *Usage note:* In the specific usage of antique dealers and of various customs laws, an *antique* is a work of art or manufacture that is more than 100 years old.

antiquity *n.* 1 *The vase in the museum is valuable because of its great antiquity:* ancientness, great age, oldness. 2 *"Classical Antiquity" means the period of the ancient Greeks and Romans:* ancient times. 3 **antiquities.** *We went to the British Museum to look at the Elgin Marbles and other antiquities:* relics, monuments.

Ant. 1 modernity, newness. 2 modern times, the present, today.

antiseptic *n.* 1 *You'd better put an antiseptic on that cut:* disinfectant, germicide, germ-killer, bactericide, prophylactic.

—*adj.* 2 *The operating-theatre must be made antiseptic before the heart transplant begins:* sterile, germ-free, aseptic.

antisocial *adj.* 1 *I don't know whether he's antisocial or just shy:* unfriendly, unsociable, retiring; unsocial, asocial, misanthropic. 2 *Someday his antisocial behaviour will land him in gaol:* hostile, menacing, antagonistic, belligerent; alienated, rebellious.

Ant. 1 gregarious, friendly, sociable, social. 2 conformist, well-adjusted, normal.

antithesis *n.* 1 *Good is the antithesis of bad:* direct opposite, reverse, converse, opposite extreme, contrast, antipode. 2 *"To be, or not to be" is an example of literary antithesis:* opposition of one idea to another in the same sentence, stating opposites in one sentence, setting of one clause against another in a sentence.

◇ *Word origin:* In Greek as in English, *antithesis* means the combining of two contradictory concepts in one sentence, as a rhetorical device. The following slogan was cited by Noah Webster in his *Dictionary* (1828) as an example of *antithesis:* "Liberty with laws, and government without oppression."

antonym *n. An antonym is a word that is opposite in meaning to another:* antithesis, opposite; *abbreviation* ant.

◇ *Word origin: Antonym* comes from French *antonyme,* which is in turn made up of Greek word elements *anti-,* opposite, + *onuma,* word. The term first appeared in English in

C. J. Smith's *Synonyms and Antonyms* (1870).

anxiety *n. Our anxiety grew when the climbers hadn't returned by nightfall:* uneasiness, unease, worry, apprehension, misgiving, foreboding, distress, concern, tension, anguish, suspense, fretfulness, disquiet, disquietude; dread, fear, alarm; solicitude.

Ant. relief; assurance, certainty, confidence; calmness, tranquillity, serenity, composure, self-possession, aplomb.

> **Exploring the Word:** Has a tight, choking collar ever caused you *anguish?* Or have you ever been so *anxious* about something that you were "all choked up"? If so, you will be pleased to know that our words *anguish, anxious, anxiety* come from Latin *angere*, to choke. Thus the idea of choking with *anguish* or *anxiety* has been around for a long time.

anxious *adj.* **1** *She was anxious about her friend's illness:* uneasy, distressed, apprehensive, tense, disturbed, worried, troubled, disquieted, concerned, fretful, fraught with anxiety, anguished, fearful, alarmed, overwrought. **2** *The children are anxious to go to the party:* eager, impatient, desirous, wanting, expectant; earnest, intent, keen, ardent, fervent, avid, zealous.

Ant. **1** relieved, assured, sure, confident; calm, composed, cool, collected, unruffled, unperturbed, nonchalant. **2** reluctant, averse, hesitant, loath, disinclined, indisposed.

◇ *Usage note:* Basically, *anxious* means distressed, worried: *Dad's illness gave us some anxious moments.* Although generally acceptable, it is not considered the best usage to use *anxious* to mean eager or expectant. Thus, in formal situations it is better to say or write *The child was eager for Christmas to come* rather than *The child was anxious for Christmas to come.*

anyhow *adv. A well-groomed woman can't wear her hair just anyhow:* carelessly, haphazardly, indifferently, without concern, sloppily.

Ant. with care, carefully, perfectly, neatly. See also ANYWAY.

anyway *adv.* **1** *The weather was uncertain but we went hiking anyway:* anyhow, nevertheless, all the same. **2** *It's too cool to go swimming anyway:* in any case, in any event, at any rate, anyhow.

◇ *Usage note: Anyway* and *anyhow* sometimes mean exactly the same thing and are both informal. If you want to sound more formal, you should use *nevertheless* (sense **1**) or *in any case* or *at any rate* (sense **2**).

apart *adv.* **1** *The toy fell apart the first time the child played with it:* into pieces, into parts, asunder. **2** *The two shops are only a few streets apart. Our birthdays are only a week apart:* distant, one from another, afar; separate. **3** *The shy child sat apart from the other children:* aside, to one side, by oneself, by itself, alone, aloof; isolated, separate, cut off, divorced.

Ant. **1** together. **2** near; together, adjoining. **3** in the midst of, surrounded.

apathetic *adj. Today's students are not apathetic about religion. The castaways lost hope and grew apathetic:* indifferent, unconcerned, uninterested, unresponsive, uncommitted, disengaged, impassive, impossible, unmoved; listless, unemotional, emotionless, unfeeling, cold, passionless, spiritless.

Ant. concerned, interested, responsive, committed, active; stirred, aroused, roused, excited; emotional, passionate, zealous, vehement, hot.

> "The long mechanic pacings to and fro,
> The set grey life, and apathetic end."
> —*Alfred, Lord Tennyson*

apathy *n. Public apathy can lead to bad government:* indifference, unconcern, lack of interest, inattention, unresponsiveness, passiveness, lassitude; lack of feeling, emotionlessness, coolness, impassibility, impassivity.

Ant. concern, interest, attention, responsiveness, action; emotion, feeling, excitement, passion, zeal, vehemence, enthusiasm, fervour.

◇ *Word origin: Apathy* comes from Greek *apatheia*, impassivity. Aristotle used the word as an antonym of *pathos*, feeling. To Stoics it meant freedom from emotion, a desirable state according to them. In his *Ladder of Divine Ascent* Saint John Climacus (A.D. 525–606) uses the word as a term for the state of grace you will reach if you make it to the top of the Ladder.

ape *n.* **1** *Gorillas are the largest of the apes:* tailless monkey, primate, (*loosely*) monkey.
—*v.* **2** *He apes his older brother in everything he does:* mimic, imitate, copy, echo, parrot, mirror, emulate, follow; mock, parody, caricature, burlesque, travesty.

◇ *Word origin:* The origin of the word *ape* is unknown, but the fact that apes were transported along the trade routes of northern Europe during the Dark Ages is demonstrated by cognate forms of the word all the way from Old Russian to West Germanic—including Old English, which had two forms: masculine *apa* and feminine *ape.*

aperture *n. The light came in through an aperture in the roof:* opening, hole, orifice, slit, space, interstice, slot; rift, rent, cleft, gap; chink, fissure, breach.

Ant. closure.

apex *n. The apex of the pyramid looms 80 feet above the desert. Winning the Nobel prize was the apex of William Faulkner's career:* summit, highest point, pinnacle, peak, tip, zenith, vertex, crown, crowning point, cap; climax, acme, apogee, culmination, consummation.

Ant. bottom, base, foot; lowest point, low point, depth, nadir, perigee.

◇ *Word origin: Apex* is the Latin word for the highest point or tip.

aphorism *n. The statement "A man is known by the company he keeps" is an aphorism:* maxim, epigram, proverb, adage, axiom, apothegm, dictum, *Slang* old saw.

◇ *Word origin: Aphorism* comes from the title of a 5th century B.C. book by the famous Greek physician Hippocrates. His book *Aphorismoi,* meaning "Terse Sentences," opens with one of the most famous of all *aphorisms,* "Art is long, life is short."

apiece *adv. The rings cost three pounds apiece. Mother gave us two cup-cakes apiece:* each, individually, severally, respectively.

Ant. together, all together, overall, collectively, en masse, as a group.

aplomb *n. A good hostess can handle an embarrassing situation with great aplomb:* composure, self-composure, self-possession, calmness, coolness, equanimity, level-headedness, stability, poise, balance; self-assurance, self-confidence, confidence, intrepidity, savoir-faire, sang-froid.

Ant. awkwardness, confusion; embarrassment.

◇ *Word origin:* If you do something with *aplomb,* you do it with level-headed assurance. The word comes from French *à plomb,* "according to the plumb or plummet," i.e. straight up and down, perfectly balanced.

apocryphal *adj. Many of the miracles ascribed to Thomas à Becket are apocryphal:* probably untrue, doubtful, questionable, dubious, unauthentic; unauthenticated, unverified, unsubstantiated, disputed; unauthorized, unofficial, uncanonical, spurious.

Ant. undisputed, unquestionable, without a doubt, authentic, credible, true, factual; verified, authenticated, substantiated, attested; authorized, approved, official, sanctioned, canonical.

apologetic *adj.* **1** *If you're truly apologetic, why not say that you're sorry?:* regretful, contrite, remorseful, self-reproachful. **2** *Good students don't need to be apologetic about their marks:* making excuses, defensive, excusatory, extenuatory, vindicatory, justificatory, exonerative, mitigatory, apologetical.

Ant. 2 proud.

apologize *v. He apologized for his rude behaviour:* express regret, make apology, beg pardon, say one is sorry.

apology *n.* **1** *She made an apology for breaking the glass:* expression of regret, saying one is sorry, begging pardon; acknowledgement of error. **2** *The writer's autobiography was really an apology for the way he had lived:* explanation, justification, defence, vindication, excuse.

◇ *Word origin: Apology* comes from Greek *apologia,* a speech in defence, such as the famous discourse by Socrates when on trial for his life before the Athenian assembly in 399 B.C.

apostle *n.* **1** *Paul was an apostle of Christ:* missionary, evangelist, proselytizer, disciple, witness; envoy, emissary, messenger, zealot. **2** *Thomas Paine was an apostle of free speech. Florence Nightingale was an apostle of hospital nursing:* advocate, pioneer, supporter, proponent, exponent, propagator, propagandist, activist, zealot.

Ant. opponent, detractor.

◇ *Word origin: Apostle* comes from Greek *apostolos,* meaning one sent forth on a mission, a delegate or envoy. The word entered our language via the New Testament, in which it occurs 80 times, notably in Luke 6:13: "And [Jesus] called his disciples, and chose from them twelve, whom he named apostles."

◇ *Usage hint:* The term *apostles* is correct both for the twelve disciples who were thus designated by Christ and for the missionary companions of Saint Paul.

appal *v. The sinking of the* Lusitania *by a German U-boat in 1915 appalled all Britons:* horrify, dismay, shock, offend, outrage; disgust, sicken, repel, revolt, nauseate; terrify, alarm, unnerve, dishearten, abash, frighten.

Ant. please, gladden; attract; reassure, calm, comfort, console.

appalling *adj. The plight of the starving natives is appalling:* dreadful, horrible, horrifying, horrific, awful, terrible, dire, grim, dismaying, horrid, frightful, fearful, ghastly, shocking, outrageous, intolerable, insufferable, abominable; disgusting, sickening, revolting, nauseating, repulsive, repellent; alarming, disheartening, terrifying, frightening.

Ant. pleasing, pleasant; reassuring, comforting.

apparatus *n.* **1** *This apparatus can purify a thousand gallons of water a minute:* equipment, machinery, mechanism, machine, contraption, device, contrivance, appliance; tools, implements, instruments, utensils, gear, paraphernalia, outfit, tackle; materials, material. **2** *The apparatus of government must not be obstructed by dissidents:* system, organization, set-up.

◇ *Pronunciation tip: Apparatus* may be pronounced as *apparATus* or as *apparATEus.* Both pronunciations are completely acceptable, though the second is more popular today.

apparel *n. The new apparel for this spring features bright plaids. The nun packed all her apparel in one small suitcase:* clothing, clothes, garments, dress, attire, *Slang* duds, togs; vestments, vesture, raiment, robes, habit, garb, costume; equipment, gear, array, trappings, accoutrements.

apparent *adj.* **1** *Her love for the child was apparent.*

The correct answer is apparent: obvious, evident, manifest, self-evident, plain, open, patent, marked, overt, conspicuous, clear, clear as day, clear-cut; understandable, unmistakable. **2** *It was an apparent stroke, but the doctors aren't certain yet:* probable, seeming, according to appearances, likely, presumable, ostensible. **3** *The boat slowly became apparent through the fog:* visible, discernible, perceivable, perceptible, distinct.

Ant. 1 unclear, uncertain, doubtful, ambiguous; hidden, covered up, veiled, disguised. **2** improbable, doubtful, unlikely, obscure. **3** invisible, hidden, concealed, indiscernible, imperceptible; dim, fuzzy.

◇ *Spelling tip:* A few people are never sure if this word ends in *-ant* or *-ent.* Remember: *It is appaRENT that you will have to pay the RENT.*

apparition *n.* **1** *After hearing the ghost stories, the children thought that they saw an apparition:* ghost, phantom, spectre, spirit, phantasm, wraith, shade, revenant, spook; materialization, manifestation, presence. **2** *Snow is quite an apparition in the Scillies:* unusual sight, strange spectacle, phenomenon.

appeal *n.* **1** *The appeal for funds for the flooded city was highly successful:* plea, request, entreaty, petition, supplication, solicitation, adjuration, suit, *Informal* S.O.S. **2** *The kitten's appeal was hard to resist:* attraction, charm, fascination, interest, allure, charisma, *Informal* pull. —*v.* **3** *The besieged nation appealed to the United Nations for aid:* plead, entreat, implore, call upon, petition, apply, solicit, beseech, invoke, adjure, sue to, beg, supplicate. **4** *The idea of learning to ski appeals to me:* attract, interest, allure, entice, invite, tempt, fascinate, excite, charm, engage, *Slang* turn one on.

Ant. 1 refusal, rejection, repudiation, denial. **2** repulsiveness, alienation. **3** refuse, reject, repudiate, deny, rebuff. **4** repel, repulse, alienate, revolt, disgust, sicken, *Slang* turn one off; bore.

appear *v.* **1** *Dark clouds appeared on the horizon:* come into view, become visible, show, show up, turn up, crop up, loom up, come to light; materialize, emerge. **2** *She appears older than she is:* look, seem, strike one as being. **3** *It appears that supper will be late:* be evident, be apparent, be obvious, be clear, be plain, be manifest, be patent. **4** *The story will appear in tomorrow's paper. Fritz Kreisler appeared in concert halls all over the world:* be published, come out, be placed before the public; be on the stage, come before the public, perform.

Ant. 1 disappear, disappear from sight, vanish. **3** be uncertain, be unclear, be unknown; be doubtful.

appearance *n.* **1** *The sudden appearance of the bull terrified the hikers. After the cold winter everyone looked forward to the appearance of spring:* appearing, coming into view, showing up, turning up; coming, advent, emergence, materialization, manifestation. **2** *An applicant for a job should try to have a neat appearance:* look, aspect. **3** *He gave the appearance that he was doing well until he goofed:* outward show, pretence, guise, pretext.

Ant. 1 disappearance, vanishing; departure, passing.

appease *v.* **1** *Nothing would appease the crying baby:* calm, make peaceful, pacify, quiet, soothe, solace, mollify, lull, compose, placate. **2** *That sandwich appeased my appetite:* satisfy, ease, allay, abate, assuage, alleviate, temper, mitigate, relieve; slake, quench, quell, blunt, still, quiet, dull. **3** *Chamberlain should never have tried to appease Hitler:* conciliate, accommodate, propitiate.

Ant. 1–3 aggravate, provoke, inflame, arouse. **1** disturb, upset, bother, annoy, dissatisfy, perturb. **3** anger, enrage, infuriate; antagonize, *Informal* cross.

◇ *Word origin: Appease* is ultimately derived from Latin *pax,* peace.

appeasement *n.* **1** *Is appeasement of an enemy better than war?:* acceding to demands, conciliation, propitiation, accommodation; submission, giving in. **2** *Music is an appeasement for shattered nerves:* means of quieting, means of calming, pacification, easing; alleviation, allaying, abating, mollification, assuagement, assuasion, mitigation, abatement, dulling, blunting, quenching; satisfaction, gratification.

Ant. aggravation, provocation, arousal; disturbance, annoyance.

appellation *n. Richard I was given the appellation "The Lion-Hearted":* name, title, designation, epithet, cognomen, sobriquet, nom de guerre, *Slang* monicker, label.

append *v. The professor will append a glossary to his new book:* add, affix, attach, join, subjoin, tack on, tag on, supplement; suspend, hang on.

Ant. remove, omit, leave out; subtract, take away, detach, disconnect, disengage, separate.

appendage *n.* **1** *The porch wasn't part of the original house but added later as an appendage:* addition, attachment, adjunct; supplement, auxiliary, accessory. **2** *The insect had lost one of its appendages and moved awkwardly:* extremity, member, projecting part; (*variously*) limb, arm, leg, feeler, tentacle, tail.

Ant. 1 main body. **2** body.

appendix *n. The book's appendix included a list of important dates in history:* supplement, codicil; addendum, addition, postscript.

Ant. preface, introductory material; main body, body of the text.

appertain *v. The responsibilities that appertain to parenthood were discussed at the meeting:* belong to, be part of, pertain to, be characteristic of, inhere in; relate to, apply to, concern, be

proper to, refer to, touch upon, bear upon.
Ant. be unrelated, be irrelevant, have no bearing upon.

appetite *n.* **1** *The diet pills made her lose her appetite:* hunger, thirst. **2** *He has an enormous appetite for classical music:* desire, craving, yearning, passion, inclination, penchant, proclivity; relish, zest, gusto, fondness, liking, stomach.
Ant. 2 surfeit, fill; distaste, aversion, dislike, detestation, disgust, loathing, revulsion, repugnance, repulsion.

appetizing *adj. The smell of the over-cooked food was not very appetizing:* mouth-watering, appealing, tempting, inviting, tantalizing; attractive; savoury, palatable, succulent.
Ant. unappetizing; nauseating, sickening, repulsive; unpalatable, unsavoury, distasteful.

applaud *v.* **1** *Please don't applaud until everyone has performed:* clap. **2** *The mayor, in his speech, applauded the fireman's bravery:* praise, laud, congratulate, commend, compliment; acclaim, hail, extol, sing the praises of, eulogize.
Ant. 1 boo, hiss, *Slang* give a raspberry. **2** criticize, censure; disparage, deride, ridicule, decry, deprecate, belittle.

> **Exploring the Word:** *Applaud, applause, plaudit,* and *plausible* all come from Latin *plaudere,* to clap. Thus *applause* is clapping; a *plaudit* is an expression of praise, a kind of verbal clapping; and *plausible,* praiseworthy, hence acceptable.

applause *n.* **1** *The applause for the pianist was deafening:* clapping, ovation. **2** *Critics seldom give playwrights the applause they want:* praise, acclaim, plaudits, compliments, approval.
Ant. 1 booing, hissing, *Informal* raspberries. **2** criticism, condemnation, derision, ridicule.

appliance *n. The kitchen is equipped with modern appliances:* device, apparatus, machine, mechanism, contraption, contrivance, implement; equipment, gear.

applicable *adj. Yesterday's solutions are not always applicable to today's problems:* relevant, pertinent, adaptable, germane, apt, useful, suitable, fit, befitting, fitting, apropos.
Ant. inapplicable, inappropriate, wrong, useless, unsuitable, unfit, irrelevant.

applicant *n. There were three applicants for the job:* candidate, aspirant, hopeful; job hunter; petitioner, suppliant, claimant.

application *n.* **1** *The burn needs an application of ointment three times a day:* spreading on, putting on. **2** *The liquid application was less effective against sunburn than the cream:* ointment, salve, unguent, lotion, balm, wash, solution, poultice, emollient. **3** *The application of French cooking terms to English cooking is open to debate:* relevance, pertinence, germaneness, appositeness. **4** *Have you made out your application for a passport?:* request, requisition, form; petition, claim, appeal, suit, entreaty, solicitation. **5** *His application to his studies was rewarded by an A:* attention, attentiveness, diligence, industry, perseverance, persistence, dedication, commitment, assiduity.
Ant. 5 inattention, *Slang* skiving off; laxness, indolence.

apply *v.* **1** *Apply two coats of varnish to the wood:* put on, lay on, spread on. **2** *He applied what he had learnt in class to the experiment:* use, utilize, employ, exercise, practise, implement, bring to bear. **3** *The rules of safe driving apply to everyone:* be applicable, refer, pertain, relate, have bearing upon, be appropriate, fit, suit. **4** *Job seekers should apply at the personnel office:* make application, request, petition. **5** *It's difficult to apply oneself to a boring task:* devote, dedicate, direct, address.
Ant. 1 remove, take off. **3** be inapplicable, be irrelevant, be inappropriate, be unsuitable.

appoint *v.* **1** *The Prime Minister appointed a new cabinet member:* name, designate, assign, choose, commission, delegate; select, nominate. **2** *Let's appoint a time for our next meeting:* designate, set, fix upon, determine, establish, prescribe; decide on, choose, settle, arrange. **3** *The new hotel was lavishly appointed with ultra-modern furnishings:* furnish, equip, fit out, provide, supply.
Ant. 1 dismiss, discharge, cashier, fire. **2** cancel; change, rearrange. **3** strip, divest, denude, dismantle.

appointment *n.* **1** *The cabinet appointments will be announced on Tuesday:* designation, assignment, commissioning; naming, selection, choosing, nomination. **2** *The appointment as ambassador will be difficult for one with no experience:* assignment, position, office, situation, post, station, spot, place, berth. **3** *What time is your lunch appointment?:* meeting, engagement, date, rendezvous; meeting time, meeting-place. **4 appointments.** *The room's appointments were in Queen Anne style:* furnishings, furniture; accoutrements, outfit, equipment, equipage, gear.
Ant. 1 dismissal. **3** accidental meeting; cancellation.

apportion *v. Apportion your income so that 25 per cent goes for housing and 10 per cent for food:* allocate, allot, distribute proportionally, prorate, portion out, parcel out, measure out, mete out, deal out, dole out, ration; divide, disperse, consign, partition, share.
Ant. collect, receive, gather, assemble; keep, retain; give all, dispense all at once.

appraisal *n.* **1** *What's your appraisal of the situation?:* evaluation, judgement, estimate. **2** *The building society commissioned an appraisal of the flat before fixing the mortgage:* monetary evaluation, estimated value, valuation; assessment.

appraise *v.* **1** *The house is appraised at £25,000 for tax purposes:* value, estimate to be worth, assay; assess. **2** *The personnel manager personally* *appraises each applicant:* evaluate, judge, examine, inspect, review, *Informal* size up.

appreciable *adj. There is an appreciable difference between the two cars:* noticeable, obvious, evident, definite, clear-cut, substantial; recognizable, perceptible, perceivable, discernible, detectable, ascertainable.

Ant. unnoticeable, imperceptible, immaterial, unsubstantial, indistinguishable, undetectable; minor, small.

appreciate *v.* **1** *I appreciate all that you've done for me:* be grateful for, be thankful for, regard highly, feel indebted. **2** *Van Gogh's paintings weren't appreciated until after his death. You don't have to be a connoisseur to appreciate good wine:* realize the worth of, estimate justly; value, rate highly, hold in high regard, esteem, prize, cherish, relish, treasure, savour; like, admire, respect. **3** *Many men don't appreciate how much work it takes to keep house and cook three meals a day:* realize, understand, comprehend, recognize, perceive, sympathize, be conscious of, be aware of, be cognizant of. **4** *Land will continue to appreciate in the years ahead:* rise in value, inflate, improve, enhance.

Ant. 1 be ungrateful. **2** undervalue, underrate, underestimate; belittle, disparage, scorn, disdain, ignore. **3** be unaware, be insensitive to; misunderstand, misjudge, misconceive. **4** depreciate; devaluate, deflate.

appreciation *n.* **1** *How can we express our appreciation for your help?:* gratitude, gratefulness, thankfulness, thanks, regard. **2** *An educated person should have an appreciation of good music:* awareness, understanding, comprehension, clear perception, cognizance, recognition of worth; admiration, relish, liking, sympathy. **3** *The appreciation of real estate values has been phenomenal:* increase in value; growth, rise.

Ant. 1 ingratitude; disregard. **2** ignorance, incomprehension; dislike, antipathy, aversion. **3** depreciation, devaluation; fall, decline, drop.

"By appreciation we make excellence in others our own property." — *Voltaire*

---

apprehend *v.* **1** *The police expect to apprehend the kidnappers before nightfall:* arrest, take into custody, take prisoner; catch, seize, capture, *Informal* nab, bag. **2** *The public doesn't fully apprehend the complexity of space flight:* comprehend, understand, perceive, discern, see; realize, recognize, know, sense.

Ant. 1 release, free, let go; discharge; liberate. **2** be unaware of, be unconscious of; misunderstand, misconceive, miss, lose.

apprehension *n.* **1** *He was filled with apprehension about the future:* foreboding, uneasiness, misgiving, dread, dismay, anxiety, alarm, suspicion, mistrust, apprehensiveness; worry, concern, distress; presentiment of evil, premonition of trouble. **2** *The apprehension of the murderer was announced by the police:* arrest, capture, seizure. **3** *Quickness of apprehension is the mark of a good student:* grasp, comprehension, perception, understanding.

Ant. 1 confidence, assurance; trust; unconcern, nonchalance, composure. **2** release, freeing; discharge; liberation. **3** incomprehension, lack of understanding.

apprehensive *adj. The prospect of major surgery would make anyone apprehensive:* uneasy, filled with misgiving, anxious, disquieted, distressed, alarmed, worried, concerned, fearful, afraid, *Informal* scared; nervous, jittery; suspicious, distrustful.

Ant. confident, assured, calm, at ease, cool, composed, unruffled, nonchalant; unafraid.

apprentice *n. My grandfather learnt shoemaking as an apprentice to a master craftsman:* indentured assistant, learner, student, pupil; beginner, novice, tiro, neophyte.

Ant. expert, master, professional, *Informal* pro.

◇ *Word origin: Apprentice* comes from Old French *aprendre*, to learn, teach. In the trade guilds of the Middle Ages an *apprentice* was of the lowest rank, being below a journeyman.

apprise *v. Police should apprise an arrested person of his right to remain silent and to be represented by a lawyer:* inform, notify, advise, tell, make acquainted, make aware, make cognizant of, enlighten.

Ant. keep secret, keep quiet about.

approach *v.* **1** *The car slowed down as it approached the corner. Summer is approaching. John is approaching manhood:* come to, near, come near, draw near, come nearer to, come close to, move towards, gain upon. **2** *Few actors approach Laurence Olivier in ability:* come close to, approximate; equal, match, be like, resemble. **3** *The Inspector of Schools has approached several educators about filling the principal's post:* make overtures to, broach a subject to, make advances to, make a proposal to, sound out. **4** *Approach each new job with enthusiasm:* embark on, undertake, set about, enter upon, begin, begin work on, initiate.

—*n.* **5** *The dog's barking announced our approach:* drawing near, coming nearer, advance. **6** *The approach to the castle leads through the woods:* access, way; road, avenue, passage, passageway. **7** *His whole approach to the problem is wrong:* way of handling, method of attack, attitude; method, procedure, technique.

Ant. 1 leave, go, draw away; retreat, withdraw, retire, go back. **2** be different, diverge. **3** ignore, overlook, pass over, pass by. **4** leave, finish, end. **5** departure, leaving, withdrawal. **6** exit.

approbation *n. The architect received approbation for his new office-building design:* praise, congratulation, compliment, good word,

applause, acclaim; approval, acceptance, support, endorsement, ratification, commendation, laudation, official sanction.
Ant. censure, condemnation, criticism: disapproval, dissatisfaction, protest, rejection, veto.

appropriate *adj.* **1** *A long dress is appropriate for a formal wedding:* suitable, proper, well-suited, congruous, fitting, befitting, correct, seemly, apt, apropos, well-chosen; characteristic, belonging, pertinent, relevant, germane, to the purpose, to the point, opportune.
—*v.* **2** *The city will appropriate money for two new schools:* allocate, set apart, allot, apportion, assign, earmark. **3** *The council should appropriate land for a new motorway:* take possession of, take, confiscate, expropriate.
Ant. **1** inappropriate, improper, ill-suited, unsuitable, unsuited, unfitting, incongruous, unbefitting, unseemly; incorrect, wrong, inconsonant, incompatible; uncharacteristic, out of place, inopportune, irrelevant. **2** withhold. **3** give, bestow, donate; relinquish, cede, dispose of.
◇ *Pronunciation tip: Appropriate* has two different pronunciations. The adjective is pronounced *a-PRO-priate,* thus *Let's buy Mary an a-PRO-priate gift.* The verb is pronounced *a-pro-pri-ATE,* thus *to a-pro-pri-ATE funds.*
◇ *Word origin:* What is *appropriate* is proper to one's own self. The word is ultimately derived from Latin *proprius,* one's own, which is also the basis of our words *proper* and *property.*

appropriation *n.* **1** *The mayor approved the appropriation for the new building:* allocation, money set aside, apportionment of funds, allotment. **2** *The treasurer was gaoled for his appropriation of company funds:* taking for one's own use, taking, misappropriation, expropriation, arrogation, confiscation, usurpation.
Ant. **1** withholding of funds. **2** return, reimbursement, repayment, paying back, recompense.

approval *n.* **1** *He studied hard to win his teacher's approval:* good opinion, regard, admiration, respect, esteem, appreciation, approbation, favour, liking. **2** *In this country, parental approval is necessary before a seventeen-year-old may get married:* permission, consent, concurrence, agreement, compliance, acquiescence, leave, sanction, countenance, licence; authorization, mandate.
Ant. **1** disapproval, disfavour, dislike, dissatisfaction, displeasure, censure, criticism, rebuke, reproof, reproach, disparagement. **2** disapproval, objection; refutation, veto.

approve *v.* **1** *The family approves of her new fiancé:* consider favourably, judge as good, regard as worthy, think highly of, have a good opinion of, be pleased with, receive with favour; esteem, respect, appreciate, praise, like, accept; believe in. **2** *No teacher can approve of cheating in exams:* permit, allow, consent to, countenance, assent to, concur in, accede to, advocate, go along with, subscribe to, second. **3** *Parliament approved the new housing bill:* confirm, affirm, sustain, uphold, ratify, pass, authorize, endorse, sanction, rubber-stamp; permit, allow.
Ant. **1** disapprove, dislike; criticize, disparage, condemn. **2** disallow, repudiate, reject, object to, refute. **3** reject, disapprove, veto.

approximate *adj.* **1** *The approximate time of our arrival will be two o'clock:* rough, very near, estimated, relative; nearly accurate, almost exact; inexact.
—*v.* **2** *The colour of these curtains approximates that of the rug:* almost match, approach, come close to, border on, verge on, nearly equal; look like, closely resemble.
Ant. **1** exact, precise, correct, accurate; definite, specific. **2** differ completely, be nowhere near.

approximately *adv. The time is approximately ten o'clock:* just about, almost, around, more or less, very nearly, close to, not far off, in the vicinity of, in the neighbourhood of, generally.
Ant. exactly, precisely, on the dot; definitely, specifically.

apropos *adj. The speaker's jokes were not apropos to such a solemn occasion:* appropriate, fitting, befitting, suitable, well-suited, opportune, just the thing, congruous, correct, seemly, apt; pertinent, relevant, germane, applicable, related, to the point.
Ant. inappropriate, unsuitable, ill-suited, unsuited, inapt, unfitting, unseemly, incorrect, wrong, incongruous, out of place, inopportune, irrelevant, untimely, unrelated.
◇ *Word origin: Apropos* comes from the French phrase *à propos,* to the purpose.

"Apt words have power to suage
The tumours of a troubled mind."
—*John Milton*

---

apt *adj.* **1** *That dog is apt to bite if he's teased:* likely, liable; inclined, prone, given to, disposed to, predisposed. **2** *Alert children are usually apt students:* bright, clever, intelligent, gifted. **3** *The doctor made a few apt remarks about nutrition and health:* appropriate, suitable, well-suited, proper, fitting, befitting, congruous, seemly, apropos; pertinent, relevant, germane, opportune.
Ant. **1** unlikely; averse, disinclined. **2** slow to learn, slow, dull. **3** inappropriate, unsuitable, ill-suited, unsuited, improper, unfitting, incongruous, unseemly; irrelevant, inopportune.
◇ *Usage note:* See LIKELY.
◇ *Word origin:* Both *apt* and *aptitude* come from Latin *aptus,* fitted, suited.

aptitude *n. She has a natural aptitude for music:*

ability, capacity, capability, talent, gift, faculty, genius, knack, flair, facility, proficiency, endowment, quickness, cleverness; inclination, tendency, predisposition, leaning, turn, bent, propensity, penchant, proclivity, proneness, predilection.
Ant. inaptitude, ineptitude; aversion, disinclination.
◇ *Word origin:* See APT.

aquatic *adj.* **1** *Ducks are aquatic creatures:* at home in water, living in or near water, growing in water; marine (*salt water*), oceanic, pelagic (*open sea*), thalassic (*seagoing*), lacustrine (*lake-dwelling*), fluvial, fluviatile (*river and stream*), neritic (*offshore*), abyssal (*deepest parts of the ocean*). **2** *Water-skiing is a popular aquatic sport:* occurring on water, carried on in water.
Ant. 1 land, terrestrial.

aqueduct *n. The Romans built aqueducts to transport water from the mountains:* conduit, channel, watercourse, duct.

arable *adj. The land is too rocky to be arable:* cultivable, farmable, ploughable, tillable; productive, fruitful, fertile, fecund.
Ant. uncultivable, unfarmable, untillable; unproductive, barren, infertile.
◇ *Word origin: Arable* comes from Latin *arare*, to plough.

arbiter *n. Judges are the arbiters of fair punishment:* judge, referee, umpire, arbitrator; authority, pundit.
◇ *Word origin: Arbiter* is Latin for "one who goes to see," hence a judge.

arbitrary *adj.* **1** *A judge can't make arbitrary decisions — he must follow the rules of law:* subjective, personal, wilful, chance, random, summary; capricious, whimsical, fanciful, inconsistent. **2** *Dictators are arbitrary rulers:* absolute, unlimited, unrestrained, uncontrolled, autocratic.
Ant. 1 objective, impersonal. **2** constitutional, lawful.

arbitrate *v.* **1** *The United Nations will try to arbitrate in the international dispute:* decide, settle, mediate, reconcile, bring to terms, sit in judgement; judge, adjudge, adjudicate; umpire, referee. **2** *The union agreed to arbitrate its differences with the company:* submit to arbitration, allow to be decided by an arbitrator.
Ant. negotiate.
◇ *Usage note:* See MEDIATE.

arbitrator *n. If negotiations are deadlocked, an arbitrator must be called in:* mediator, arbiter, adjudicator, judge; referee, umpire; (*loosely*) negotiator, moderator, intermediary, go-between.
◇ *Usage note:* See MEDIATE.

arc *n. The rainbow formed a beautiful arc in the sky:* curve, arch, crescent, half-moon, bow.
◇ *Word origin:* Both *arc* and *arch* come from the Latin word *arcus*, bow. *Archery* and *archer* also come from this word.

arcane *adj. Astrology is an arcane subject:* mysterious, esoteric, occult, recondite, obscure, hermetic, mystic, mystical.
Ant. clear, obvious, evident, understood, known, well-known, open, revealed.

arch[1] *n.* **1** *The arch of the ceiling spans 50 feet:* curved span, vault, dome. **2** *Her eyebrows have a naturally high arch:* curvature, curve, arc, bow-shape, bend.
—v. **3** *The trees arched over the garden path:* span, curve, bend. **4** *The cat arched its back:* curve, bend.
Ant. 2 straightness. **4** straighten, straighten out, unbend.
◇ *Word origin: Arch, arc,* and *archer* all ultimately come from the Latin word *arcus*, bow.

arch[2] *adj.* **1** *The butler was the arch-villain of the piece:* chief, principal, major. **2** *She gave him an arch look:* mischievous, sly, wily, roguish, saucy, designing, cunning.
Ant. 1 minor, petty, lesser. **2** frank, open, forthright.
◇ *Usage note:* When *arch* is used in the sense of "principal" (as in *arch-criminal*) it is customary to connect it with the word it modifies by hyphenation.

archaic *adj. Warming-pans have been archaic for years:* antiquated, obsolete, obsolescent, gone out of use, out-of-date, old-fashioned, bygone, passé, behind the times, ancient, antique.
Ant. modern, current; new, fresh, novel, up-to-date, fashionable, newfangled, modish, *Slang* trendy.
◇ *Word origin: Archaic* comes from Greek *archaios*, ancient, which also gives us *archaeology*, the scientific study of ancient things.

Exploring the Word: The Greeks used the prefix *arch-* to mean "boss," chief, master. It is the basis of our words *architect*, master builder, and *architecture*, the work of a master builder. In religion, it is found in *archangel*, an angel of the highest rank; *archbishop*, the chief bishop of a province; and in *archdeacon* and *archdiocese*. Originally *archipelago* meant an important or "chief" sea with many islands, though today it just refers to a chain of islands. In politics, a *monarch* is one who is the sole chief or master, one who rules alone, while a *matriarch* is a female ruler or leader, and *anarchy* literally means "the state of being without a leader."

archetype *n. Satan is the archetype of evil-doers:* original, prototype, classic, model, exemplar, prime example.
◇ *Pronunciation tip:* The *ch* in *archetype* is pronounced as *k*. Thus the proper pronunciation is *ar-ki-type*. This same *k* sound is also found in *archaic* (*ar-ka-ic*), *archangel* (*ark-ane-gel*), and *archipelago* (*ar-ki-pel-a-go*).

architect *n.* **1** *Christopher Wren is my favourite architect:* building designer, master builder. **2**

Each man is the architect of his own happiness: originator, creator, author, designer, planner, deviser, contriver, founder, artificer; instigator, prime mover, shaper, innovator.

architecture *n.* **1** *The study of architecture includes both engineering and aesthetics:* science of building, art of designing buildings; structural design, construction, architectonics. **2** *I like the wood and stone architecture of our Tudor period houses:* design, construction, structuring, style.

archives *n. pl.* **1** *The* Fidelio *sketch-book is in the Beethoven archives in Bonn:* library, depository, museum. **2** *The museum's Civil War archives are valuable:* documents, papers, records, memorabilia.

arctic *adj.* **1** *Permafrost occurs only in arctic regions:* north of the Arctic Circle, near the North Pole; polar, far-northern; septentrional, hyperborean. **2** *Napoleon's army became bogged down in the arctic Russian winter:* bitter, icy, frigid, glacial, freezing, frost-bound, icebound, frozen, gelid.

—*n.* **3 Arctic.** *Admiral Byrd explored the Arctic:* region north of the Arctic Circle, North Pole, north polar region.

Ant. 2 torrid, hot, warm, summery. **3** Antarctica, the Antarctic, South Pole.

◇ *Spelling tip:* Don't forget the first *c* in *arCtic.* Remember, the *ARCtic Circle* has an *arc* in it!

◇ *Word origin: Arctic* comes from *Arktos,* "Bear," the Greek name of the constellation *Ursa Major,* the Great Bear, which describes a circle around the pole-star.

ardent *adj. Roger Casement was an ardent patriot. Don Juan was an ardent lover:* impassioned, passionate, zealous, eager, fervent, fervid, fiery, tempestuous, vehement, emotional, enthusiastic, intense, fierce, keen, earnest; lusty, spirited, feverish.

Ant. indifferent, half-hearted, nonchalant, dispassionate, unenthusiastic, apathetic, impassive, phlegmatic, detached; unloving, unamorous, cold, cool, frigid.

◇ *Word origin:* An *ardent* lover burns with passion. *Ardent* comes from Latin *ardere,* to burn.

ardour *n.* **1** *Van Gogh began each new painting with great ardour:* feeling, passion, fervour, intensity, zeal, vehemence, fierceness, warmth, excitement, eagerness, enthusiasm, spirit, feverishness, animation, vigour, verve. **2** *Women spoke of Rudolph Valentino with ardour:* passion, rapture, amorousness, devotion, love, warmth.

Ant. 1 indifference, unconcern, disinterestedness, apathy, detachment, dispassion, languor, languidness; coldness, coolness, frigidity.

arduous *adj. Crossing the continent in a covered wagon was an arduous undertaking:* difficult, hard, laborious, toilsome, wearisome, exhausting, fatiguing, tiring, burdensome, heavy, tough, troublesome, onerous, trying, full of hardships, formidable, severe, Herculean; vigorous, strenuous, energetic.

Ant. light, facile, easy, simple, effortless, smooth.

area *n.* **1** *The pineapple plantation occupies a large area of the island:* expanse, extent, stretch, portion, zone, space. **2** *Alligators are found in marshy areas:* region, locality, terrain, territory, section, tract, range, district. **3** *France has always excelled in the area of the arts:* field, sphere, realm, domain, province, arena, scope.

arena *n.* **1** *The city built a new sports arena:* stadium, amphitheatre, bowl, gymnasium, field, hippodrome, circus; ring, stage, platform. **2** *After World War II Japan entered the arena of international trade:* field, realm, area, province, domain, sphere, scene, theatre, stage; battleground, battlefield, lists, playing field, market-place.

◇ *Word origin:* Early *arenas,* like modern bullfighting arenas and some circus arenas, had sand surfaces which could be swept between contests or performances. *Arena* comes from Latin *harena,* sand, sandy place, sand-strewn place of combat.

argot *n. Jean Genet used the argot of pickpockets in some of his stories:* criminal jargon, cant; (*loosely*) lingo, vernacular, idiom, slang, patois.

◇ *Word origin: Argot* is a recent import from French. (It entered English only about 100 years ago.) Emile Littré in his monumental *Dictionnaire de la langue française* (1881) suggests that *argot* may be related to English *argue, argument.*

argue *v.* **1** *The local shopkeepers argued that a new municipal car-park was necessary:* reason, contend, maintain, assert, claim, hold, plead, expostulate, remonstrate. **2** *The children argued about whose turn it was to sit in the front seat:* have an argument, quarrel, dispute, debate, bicker, quibble, wrangle. **3** *Her flower arrangements argue her artistic tastes:* show, indicate, exhibit, display, manifest, demonstrate, evince; express, imply, denote, point to.

Ant. 2 agree, concur. **3** hide, conceal; raise doubt, disprove.

"Arguments out of a pretty mouth are unanswerable." —*Joseph Addison*

---

argument *n.* **1** *Arguments about matters of taste are futile:* quarrel, bickering, squabble, row, clash, altercation, fight, tiff, imbroglio, embroilment; disagreement, dispute, debate, controversy, heated discussion, war of words. **2** *The town has a powerful argument for turning the land into a park:* reason, line of reasoning, case, line of argument, argumentation. **3** *It used to be the custom to print the argument of a play before the main text:* outline, abstract, summary, plot, synopsis, story, central idea, contents, gist.

Ant. 1 agreement, accord, concord, concurrence, harmony. 2 rebuttal, refutation, retort, rejoinder, response, answer.

arid *adj.* 1 *Land reclamation has made a garden out of an arid waste:* dry, dried-up, waterless, parched, drought-scourged, desertlike; barren. 2 *Dr. Johnson's table-talk was never arid:* dull, lifeless, uninteresting, dreary, uninspired, unimaginative, dry as dust; pedantic.

Ant. 1 well-watered; lush, verdant. 2 lively, full of life, interesting, exciting, spirited, imaginative, pithy.

arise *v.* 1 *A plume of smoke arose from the volcano:* rise, move upward, ascend, go up, mount, climb. 2 *Resentment can arise between two men who want the same job. Accidents can arise from carelessness:* come into being, occur, spring up, crop up, set in, emanate, ensue; originate, stem from, start, begin, commence, dawn, result, appear, make its appearance, emerge, show itself, come to light.

Ant. 1 descend, come down, fall. 2 cease, stop, end, die; disappear, go away, fade away, be suppressed, be hidden.

aristocracy *n. The highest-ranking members of the Spanish aristocracy are the grandees:* nobility, peerage, patricians; upper class, élite, beau monde, high society, upper crust, gentry.

Ant. commons, common people, plebs, commoners, populace, masses; lower classes, working class, proletariat, hoi polloi, rabble, canaille.

◇ *Word origin: Aristocracy* comes from Greek *aristokratia,* "rule by the best citizens," from *aristos,* best, + *krateein,* to rule. John Calvin used *aristocracy* this way in his *Institution of the Christian Religion* (1561): "Aristocracy [is] the government of the best choicest men."

aristocrat *n. Jockey Club membership was once limited to aristocrats:* noble, nobleman, lord, peer, grandee; gentleman, squire, patrician.

Ant. commoner, plebeian.

◇ *Word origin:* The word *aristocrat* first appeared in English during the summer of 1789, when the struggles of the French *aristocrates* (royalists) to hold their own against the Jacobins (revolutionaries) were the principal topic of conversation throughout Europe.

aristocratic *adj. She comes from an aristocratic family. The Minister had an aristocratic bearing:* noble, titled, lordly, royal, regal, courtly, blue-blooded; high-born, well-born, well-bred, of gentle blood, of high rank, patrician, gentlemanly, upper-class; refined, dignified.

Ant. common; middle-class, lower-class, working-class, plebeian, ill-bred; unrefined, crude.

arm *n.* 1 *Put the bracelet back on your arm. He broke his arm. Most starfish have five arms:* (*of humans*) upper limb, forearm, upper arm; (*of certain animals*) anterior limb. 2 *The English Channel is an arm of the sea:* appendage, offshoot, branch, projection. 3 *The convalescent home is just another arm of the hospital:* branch, division, department, section, sector, detachment. 4 **arms** *The army can't advance until the new shipment of arms arrives:* firearms, guns, weapons; ordnance, weaponry, armament, matériel. 5 *The procession was led by a soldier carrying the royal arms:* coat of arms, heraldic emblem, insignia, crest, blazonry.

Ant. disarm.

—*v.* 6 *The cowboys armed themselves to fight the rustlers. During World War II the United States armed many of its allies:* take up arms, obtain arms; furnish with weapons, prepare for war. 7 *He armed himself for the long night's drive by drinking black coffee:* prepare, make ready, prime, forearm; equip, outfit, fortify, strengthen, protect.

> **Exploring the Word**: Virgil's *Aeneid* begins with the words, *Arma virumque cano,* "I sing of arms and the man." The Latin words *arma,* arms, and *armare,* to arm or equip, give us *arms, firearms, armour, armament, armada,* an armed fleet, *army,* armed men, and *armoury,* a place where arms are kept.

armada *n. The armada was lined up off the coast ready for battle:* fleet, flotilla, squadron, escadrille, navy.

◇ *Word origin: Armada* is an originally Spanish word meaning armed force. It is still mainly used (with a capital *A*) as a designation for the ill-fated "Invincible Armada," the fleet of 130 ships sent against England in 1588 by Philip II of Spain.

armament *n.* 1 *The battleship's armament included cannon, rocket-launchers, anti-aircraft guns, and six inches of steel plating:* weapons, arms, guns, ordnance, equipment, outfitting, munitions. 2 *The armament of any of the great powers could destroy civilization:* military might, war-making machine, weaponry.

armistice *n. Armistice was declared on November 11, 1918:* suspension of hostilities, ceasefire, truce; peace.

Ant. outbreak of war, attack; war, hostilities.

◇ *Spelling tip: Armistice* ends in *-ice.* An *armistice* is an agreement to stop fighting for a time; it puts the fighting "on ICE."

armour *n.* 1 *Bullet-proof cars are sheathed in armour. The priest felt protected by the armour of his faith:* protective covering, protection, shield. 2 *Knights fought in armour:* suit of armour, coat of mail, mail, chain.

armoury *n. Many old armouries are now used to house reserve units:* arsenal, arms depot, ordnance depot.

◇ *Usage note:* Technically, the difference between an *armoury* and an *arsenal* is that only arms or weapons are stored or made in an *armoury*, whilst an *arsenal* also handles munitions.

army *n.* **1** *The Allied Army invaded Nazi-occupied France on June 6, 1944:* military force, military machine, military; land forces, land force, troops, soldiers, soldiery, fighting men, legions, legion, militia. **2** *An army of ants swarmed over the sand-hill:* host, horde, swarm, pack, multitude, legion, throng, force, crowd, mob, band, gang, crew, bevy; mass, aggregation.

Ant. 1 civilians. **2** small number.

aroma *n. The aroma of cooking made me hungry:* good smell, pleasant odour, scent, fragrance, bouquet, redolence, savour.

Ant. stench, stink.

◇ *Word origin: Aroma* comes from Greek *arōma*, spice, which may be ultimately derived from the verb *arōmenai*, to plough — from the *aroma* of earth upturned by the plough.

aromatic *adj. He smokes an aromatic pipe tobacco:* fragrant, sweet-smelling, sweet-scented, scented, perfumed, odoriferous, odorous; piquant, spicy, pungent.

Ant. non-aromatic, unscented; bad-smelling, stinking, malodorous, noisome, rank, putrid, fetid, acrid.

arouse *v.* **1** *She aroused the children from their nap:* awaken, wake up, waken, rouse. **2** *A walk before dinner will arouse your appetite. Don't arouse my anger!:* summon up, call forth, excite, stimulate, provoke, spur, incite, kindle, stir up, foster, foment, move, quicken; sharpen, whet, goad, fan, heat up, warm.

Ant. 1 put to sleep, lull. **2** end, kill, still, quench; damp, dampen, dull, calm, quell, quiet, allay, mitigate, assuage, alleviate, relieve, pacify, moderate, placate, mollify.

arraign *v.* **1** *The superintendent asked that the suspect be arraigned immediately:* indict, charge. **2** *The medical association met to arraign the doctor for his unethical behaviour:* accuse, charge, indict; call to account, take to task, denounce, censure, criticize, find fault with, impute.

Ant. 2 withdraw charges, drop charges; exonerate, absolve, excuse, pardon, exculpate, overlook; defend, vindicate; condone, approve, support, praise, acclaim.

arrange *v.* **1** *She arranged the flowers beautifully. The books were arranged in alphabetical order:* group, array, set out, range, pose; order, set in order, organize, sort, assort, assign places to, file, classify, marshal, rank, line up, systematize, methodize. **2** *The travel agent arranged the flight with a night in Rome:* plan, schedule, lay out, prepare, devise, contrive, provide, design, fix up; settle, agree to. **3** *The musician arranged the symphony so that it could be performed without violins by a marching band:* orchestrate, score, adapt.

Ant. 1 disorganize, disarrange, jumble, disturb, mess up; scatter, disperse.

arrangement *n.* **1** *Flower arrangement can be an art. The arrangement of the files makes it easy to find what one needs:* grouping, arraying, disposal, assortment, distribution, ordering; order, organization, systematization, classification, categorization, methodization. **2** Often **arrangements**. *The bride's family is responsible for the wedding arrangements. The arrangements for a truce were made at last:* plans, preparations, measures, provisions; settlement, agreement, terms, compact. **3** *The symphony orchestra played a special arrangement of "Silent Night":* orchestration, score, adaptation.

Ant. 1 disorder, disorganization, disarray, topsy-turviness.

arrant *adj. That is nothing but an arrant lie! The highwayman is an arrant knave:* thorough, thoroughgoing, utter, confirmed, outright, downright, unmitigated, out and out, extreme, notorious; undisguised.

Ant. partial, sometimes, incomplete, inconsistent, modified.

◇ *Word origin: Arrant* was originally a variant of *errant*, and meant "wandering," as in the phrases *knights errant* and *errant thieves*, so called because both types were proverbially on the move. Later, *errant* came to be reserved for knightly wanderers, and the spelling *arrant* stuck with knavish drifters, acquiring the denotation of outright, confirmed, manifest, and the connotation of notoriously bad or unacceptable.

array *n.* **1** *The shops have set out their array of Christmas merchandise:* display, exhibition, arrangement, disposition, marshalling, order, show, parade, pageantry; collection, assortment, supply. **2** *The women were decked out in their best array for the charity ball:* finery, fine clothes, attire, clothing, apparel, raiment, garments, dress, garb, *Informal* glad rags, Sunday best.

—*v.* **3** *Array the paintings so that everyone can see them:* arrange, group, order, organize, marshal, align, range, rank: set out, place, display, deploy, pose. **4** *The child was arranged in silk and lace for its christening:* clothe, attire, dress, adorn, bedeck, deck, fit out, outfit, robe, wrap.

Ant. 1 disarray, hodge-podge, odds and ends. **2** rags. **3** disarrange, mix up, mess up.

arrears *n. He hasn't paid the arrears on his mortgage yet:* overdue debt, unpaid debt, outstanding debt; indebtedness, liability, obligation, debit, balance due.

Ant. prepayment, early payment.

arrest *v.* **1** *The police arrested the suspect a mile away from the scene of the crime:* take into custody, apprehend, catch, seize, capture, take prisoner, collar; detain, hold, secure, *Slang* nick. **2** *A speck on the horizon arrested the navigator's attention:* catch, attract; fix, hold, seize, capture, occupy, engage, rivet, absorb, engross. **3** *The new drug arrested the spread of the disease:* check, block, stay, halt, stop, end, bring to a standstill; delay, slow, retard, inhibit, hold back, restrain, hinder, suppress, interrupt.

—*n.* **4** *Fingerprints on the safe led to the robber's arrest:* apprehension, capture, seizure, taking into custody, *Slang* cop. **5** *The arrest of the flood-waters saved many homes:* stopping, stoppage, halt, blocking, checking, staying; slowing, inhibiting, holding back, retention, slow down.

Ant. **1** release, free, set free, let go. **2** be ignored, be passed over. **3** encourage, quicken, speed up. **4** releasing, freeing. **5** quickening.

arrival *n.* **1** *The celebrity's arrival was greeted with loud cheers:* arriving, coming, advent, appearance, approach. **2** *The motel had no rooms for late arrivals:* comer, visitor, visitant, newcomer.

Ant. **1** departure, leaving, going, withdrawal.

arrive *v.* **1** *Firemen arrived at the house within ten minutes of the alarm. The plane is arriving now:* come, reach, get to, appear, show up, turn up, reach a destination; approach, near, draw near, go toward. **2** *Good weather has arrived at last:* come, occur, happen, befall, take place, come to pass, appear. **3** *With the film's huge success, the leading actor has really arrived:* achieve recognition, succeed, make good, reach the top.

Ant. **1, 2** depart, go, go away, leave, withdraw, retire, *Slang* scram, beat it, scarper, make tracks; set out, set forth, be off. **3** fail, fall.

arrogance *n.* *The arrogance of the aristocracy helped to lead to the French Revolution:* overbearing pride, haughtiness, assurance, presumption, pretension, loftiness, imperiousness; vanity, conceit, egoism, bluster, swagger, vainglory, self-importance, braggadocio; insolence, disdain, contempt, scorn, lordliness.

Ant. humility, modesty, simplicity, politeness, self-effacement, diffidence, bashfulness, meekness, shyness.

"When men are most sure and arrogant, they are commonly most mistaken." —*David Hume*

---

arrogant *adj.* *The boss's son was arrogant to all the employees:* overbearing, haughty, presumptuous, pretentious, imperious, overweening, high and mighty; vain, conceited, egotistical, vainglorious, self-important, self-assuming, swaggering; insolent, disdainful, contemptuous, scornful, lordly, pompous, supercilious.

Ant. unassuming, polite, considerate, modest, diffident, deferential; self-effacing, bashful, meek, shy.

arsenal *n.* **1** *The gun collector's home looked like an arsenal. This arsenal produces two tons of gunpowder a day:* armoury, arms depot, ordnance depot, military storehouse; ammunition dump, magazine; arms factory, munitions factory. **2** *The police found an arsenal in the boot of the robbers' car:* cache of weapons, weapon collection, weapons, military stores.

◇ *Usage note:* See ARMOURY.

◇ *Word origin:* Early *arsenals* were workshops for making ships and arms. *Arsenal* comes from Arabic *dār al sinā' ah*, maritime arsenal or, literally, court of manufacture. The word *arsenal* entered English around 1500 from the name of the great Venetian navy yard, the *Arzanà*, where visitors would see up to 200 galleys and great quantities of ships' stores at once.

art *n.* **1** *Music and ballet are my favourite forms of art:* artistic activity, creative work, artistry. **2** *The museum has a fine collection of modern art:* works of art, objects of art. **3** *Caruso's great art is demonstrated in this recording:* artistry, genius, mastery, expertise, skill, facility, virtuosity. **4** *I received my bachelor of arts degree:* liberal arts, humanities. **5** *She is accomplished in the art of flattery:* craft, technique, methods, principles, strategy; fine points, subtleties, finesse.

Ant. **1** science. **2** junk, worthless objects. **3** lack of skill, ineptitude, incompetency, inability.

artful *adj.* **1** *He used an artful excuse to get out of doing the work:* cunning, crafty, sly, wily, foxy, strategic, diplomatic, politic, scheming, designing, contriving, machinating, manœuvring; deceitful, deceptive, underhand, shifty, tricky. **2** *That artful dodger has taken my place in the queue:* skilful, smart, clever, shrewd, sharp, astute, quick, adroit, deft, resourceful, ingenious, inventive, nimble-minded, dextrous, knowing, subtle; able, apt, adept, masterly, proficient, gifted, talented.

Ant. **1** artless; simple, natural, candid, open, frank, straightforward, unsophisticated, ingenuous, naïve. **2** dull, clumsy, plodding; ungifted, untalented, unadept, unskilled.

article *n.* **1** *Today's newspaper has an article about conservation:* piece, write-up, story, item, essay, paper, theme, sketch, commentary, review. **2** *Every article in the shop is on sale:* item, thing, piece, object, product, commodity; substance, matter. **3** *We discussed every article of business on the agenda. The negotiators agreed to all the articles of the settlement:* item, piece, point, count, particular, matter, detail; clause, paragraph, part, division, portion; term, condition, stipulation, proposition, provision, proviso.

◇ *Word origin: Article* comes from Latin *articulus*, joint or jointed part. The word first appeared in English during the reign of Henry III, with reference to the 12 *articles* of the Apostles' Creed.

articulate *adj.* **1** *The lecturer stated that the first human language consisted of "articulate cries":* enunciated, intelligible, meaningful, speechlike, expressive. **2** *Porpoises communicate with*

one another but are not truly articulate: capable of speech. **3** *He's a highly articulate speaker. They engaged in an articulate argument:* eloquent, expressive, fluent, facile; clearly expressed.
—*v.* **4** *Please articulate clearly so that everyone can hear you:* enunciate, utter, pronounce, enounce. **5** *A good debater must articulate his ideas well enough to convince others:* express, convey, state, voice; formulate, organize. **6** *The hand articulates with the forearm at the wrist:* hinge, connect, join, fit together, hook up.
Ant. 1–3 inarticulate. **1** unintelligible, incomprehensible, indistinct. **2** dumb, mute, aphasic. **3** inexpressive, non-fluent. **4** mumble, murmur, swallow words.
◇ *Word origin: Articulate* comes from Latin *articulare,* to utter distinctly, which was formed from *articulus,* joint. The Romans thus pictured speech as an *articulated* whole, like the body with its jointed members.

articulation *n.* **1** *Clear articulation was the first thing we worked on in the speech class:* utterance, enunciation, pronunciation; diction, elocution. **2** *The knee joint forms a ball-and-socket articulation:* joint, juncture, connection, hinge.
◇ *Word origin:* As a term for a joint of the body and for utterance of speech sounds, *articulation* has been a part of the international scientific vocabulary since the 1500's. *Articulatio* exists as a word in Classical Latin as well, where it means (1) the putting forth of new shoots in a grape-vine, and (2) "fan-leaf," a disease characterized by abnormalities in the joints of the vine.

artifice *n.* **1** *Being able to palm a card is an artifice every magician must know:* trick, device, stratagem, manœuvre, contrivance; subterfuge, ruse, dodge, feint, wile; hoax, blind, trap. **2** *A master spy must be full of artifice:* cunning, craftiness, guile, slyness, wiliness, artfulness, intrigue, trickery, machination, scheming, foxiness; deceit, deception, duplicity, imposture, falsehood; ingenuity, inventiveness, invention, cleverness.
Ant. 2 frankness, candour, openness, artlessness, ingenuousness, sincerity; truthfulness, honesty.

artificial *adj.* **1** *The new dam will form a large artificial lake behind it. Fill the vase with artificial flowers:* man-made, manufactured, synthetic, non-natural; imitation, simulated, fake, counterfeit, false, sham, phoney, spurious, specious, ersatz. **2** *The film star flashed an artificial smile at the crowd:* insincere, feigned, pretended, phoney, forced, laboured, unnatural, affected, mannered, factitious.
Ant. 1 natural, real, genuine, authentic, bona fide, true, actual. **2** sincere, natural, honest, frank, candid, open; unaffected.

artillery *n. Wellington had numerical superiority in troops and artillery:* cannon, big guns, mounted guns, ordnance.
◇ *Word origin: Artillery* comes from Old French *artiller,* to arm. The word came into English before the introduction of firearms in warfare and originally meant catapults, crossbows, and the like.

artisan *n. The carpenter was a talented artisan:* craftsman, handicraftsman; skilled worker, technician; master, master craftsman.

artist *n.* **1** *The artist's works were displayed at the museum. Joan Sutherland is an operatic artist:* practitioner of a fine art. **2** *She's an artist in the kitchen:* master, expert, virtuoso.
Ant. 2 amateur, beginner, tiro, novice.

artistic *adj.* **1** *The museum has high artistic standards:* aesthetic. **2** *Picasso's artistic ability was apparent in his early youth:* befitting an artist, of an artist, of art, in art. **3** *The flower arrangement is very artistic:* elegant, exquisite, attractive, handsome, aesthetic, stylish, graceful.
Ant. 1 inartistic, unaesthetic. **3** tasteless, inelegant, unattractive; unpolished, uncultured, unrefined; unaccomplished, untalented, inexpert.

artistry *n. Duke Ellington's artistry will long be admired:* artistic ability, mastery, talent, proficiency, sensibility, taste, touch; accomplishment, virtuosity.
◇ *Word origin:* The word *artistry* was coined a little more than 100 years ago by the poet Robert Browning.

artless *adj.* **1** *Her love was as artless as a child's:* frank, candid, open, honest, true, guileless, innocent, naïve, simple, straightforward; sincere, trusting, undesigning, open-hearted, ingenuous, unsophisticated, unaffected, unself-conscious. **2** *Nothing can compare to the artless beauty of a waterfall:* natural, pure, unadorned, plain, simple. **3** *The painting was completely artless:* inartistic, lacking art; without artistic talent, untalented.
Ant. 1 cunning, crafty, sly, wily, dishonest, deceitful, designing, artful, insincere, pretended, faked, phoney, false, counterfeit; sophisticated, affected, self-conscious; suspicious, distrustful. **2** artificial, unnatural, synthetic. **3** artistic, aesthetic.
◇ *Usage note:* The older meaning of *artless* was "untalented" or "inartistic." This use is rare nowadays. The word's now-predominant sense of "unartificial" was coined in 1672 by the poet John Dryden with the following line: "Such artless beauty lies in Shakespeare's wit . . ."

ascend *v.* **1** *The balloon ascended quickly. The climbers slowly ascended the mountain:* rise; climb, mount, scale. **2** *Queen Elizabeth II ascended the throne when her father died:* succeed to, inherit.
Ant. 1 descend; fall.

ascendancy, ascendency *n. The Labour Party is gaining ascendancy in Parliament:* power, control, domination, dominance, predominance, superiority, supremacy, mastery, pre-eminence, leadership, advantage, edge, sway, upper hand, whip hand; command, authority, influence, rule, reign, sovereignty

Ant. inferiority, weakness, subordination, subjection, servility; disadvantage, defeat.

ascent *n.* **1** *The steeplejack made a careful ascent of the roof of the building:* ascension, climb, climbing, scaling, mounting, rise, rising, upward movement. **2** *The road made a sharp ascent to the top of the hill:* gradient, grade, incline, slope. **3** *His ascent from office-boy to president of the company took fifteen years:* advancement, advance, rise, progress, progression, climb, ascension.

Ant. descent. **3** fall, retrogression.

◇ *Usage note:* See ASSENT.

ascertain *v. The insurance adjuster had to ascertain the exact value of the missing jewels:* find out, establish, determine, learn, discover, detect, unearth, ferret out.

"The ascetic, rejoicing in his heart because he has been liberated from desire, lives as peacefully and happily as if he were ruler of the universe." —*Bhartrihari*

---

ascetic *n.* **1** *Most of the early saints were extreme ascetics:* self-denier, abstainer, self-mortifier; hermit, recluse, solitary, eremite, anchorite, celibate, cenobite; religious, monk, nun, flagellant; yogi, fakir, dervish.

—*adj.* **2** *Trappist monks lead an ascetic existence:* austere, self-denying, abstemious, strict, rigorous, self-mortifying.

Ant. 1 hedonist, sensualist, voluptuary, sybarite, bon vivant. **2** self-indulgent, indulgent, pampered, luxurious, comfortable; abandoned, dissolute, voluptuous, sensuous, sensual, sybaritic.

◇ *Word origin: Ascetic* goes back to Greek *askētēs*, an athlete in training. The Greek word for athletic training is *askēsis*, and from it we get *ascesis*, which means rigorous self-discipline or training. Very much the same thing is denoted by *asceticism*, which was first used in English by Sir Thomas Browne in 1646.

ascribe *v. Scholars ascribe the unsigned painting to Rubens. He ascribes his good health to proper diet and exercise:* attribute, credit, accredit, charge to, assign, trace to.

Ant. discredit, deny, discount; dissociate.

◇ *Word origin: Ascribe* comes from Latin *ad-* (to) + *scribere* (to write), which also gives us *script, scribe* and *conscription.* The word was first used in English during the 14th century in the translation by John Wyclif of the Second Book of Samuel.

ashamed *adj. He was ashamed of his bad manners. Modern women aren't ashamed to wear slacks in public:* feeling shame, put to shame, mortified, embarrassed, humiliated, chagrined, discomfited, disconcerted, distressed, crestfallen, chap-fallen, shamefaced; shy, bashful, prudish, squeamish; guilt-stricken, conscience-stricken.

Ant. proud, honoured; arrogant, vain; gratified, satisfied, pleased, comforted.

ashen *adj. The sick woman had an ashen complexion:* wan, pale, pallid, grey, leaden, livid.

Ant. bright, vivid, colourful, warm-hued; rosy, red-cheeked, blushing, robust, ruddy, rubicund.

◇ *Word origin: Ashen* is a poetic word and was first used in 1808 by Sir Walter Scott in referring to ". . . the ashen hue of age."

ashore *adv. All ashore that's going ashore! The wreckage of the boat washed ashore:* to shore, onto the shore, on shore, on land, on dry land.

Ant. on board, at sea, sailing; to the sea, on the sea, in the sea.

asinine *adj. It's asinine to build a house so close to a river that floods every year:* stupid, foolish, silly, ridiculous, absurd, senseless, brainless, idiotic, moronic, imbecilic, feeble-minded, witless, half-witted, insane, crackers, simple-minded, irrational, muddle-headed, dunderheaded, thick-headed, thick-skulled, thick-witted.

Ant. smart, wise, intelligent, clever, sage; sensible, rational, reasonable, sane.

◇ *Word origin: Asinine* means stupid, like an ass. It comes from Latin *asinus*, ass, donkey.

ask *v.* **1** *May we ask where you've been all this time? The driver asked directions from the petrol-station attendant:* inquire, query, request an answer to; request information about, request information from, question, interrogate, quiz, pump, grill, sound out. **2** *Ask the Johnsons to come to dinner tomorrow:* invite, request, bid, summon. **3** *I asked for a bicycle for Christmas. Don't ask for a rise. Ask for help:* express a desire for, seek, request, call, apply, petition, solicit, sue, appeal, plead, urge, implore, entreat, beseech, beg, supplicate, press. **4** *The antique dealer is asking £25 for that old watch:* state as a price, charge, demand, claim; request, desire, seek, expect.

Ant. 1 answer, inform, supply information. **2** ignore, pass over; blackball; accept; refuse, decline, reject. **3** grant, give; refuse, reject, deny, spurn. **4** declare not for sale; offer, pay, give, shell out.

askance *adv. The shopkeeper looked askance at the crowd of young rowdies who entered his shop:* distrustfully, mistrustfully, suspiciously; disdainfully, disapprovingly.

Ant. trustfully, unsuspiciously.

askew *adv., adj. His tie was hanging askew:* crooked, crookedly, awry, lopsided, aslant.

Ant. straight, centred, even, right, true, in line, in a line, aligned, plumb, *Informal* straight as an arrow.

asleep *adj., adv. The little boy was asleep before the bedtime story was finished:* sleeping, slumbering; (*variously*) sound asleep, fast asleep, dead to the world, dozing, napping, taking a siesta.

Ant. awake, wide awake; up.

aspect *n.* **1** *The valley took on a mysterious aspect at dusk:* look, air, appearance. **2** *Consider the economic aspects of owning your own house:* feature, point, side, facet, consideration.

aspersion *n. It's not fair to cast aspersions on someone that you know nothing about:* slur, abuse, smear, slander, deprecation, disparagement, detraction, defamation, reproach, censure, vilification, railing, reviling, calumny, obloquy.

Ant. praise, laudatory remark, plaudit, compliment, commendation, *Informal* pat on the back.

asphyxiate *v. Carbon monoxide asphyxiates dozens of people every year:* suffocate, smother, stifle, choke, strangulate.

Ant. breathe, inhale, take in oxygen.

aspiration *n. Marcus Garvey's aspiration was to re-establish the Jamaican blacks in Africa:* ambition, object, objective, day-dream, end, mark, endeavour, design, purpose, intent, intention, hope, desire, longing, wish, yearning, craving, hankering.

aspire *v. As a model, Marilyn Monroe always aspired to an acting career:* desire, wish for, hope for, long for, yearn for, crave, covet, hanker after, thirst after, hunger over, pine for, pant after; seek, pursue, aim at.

◇ *Word origin: Aspire* comes from Latin *ad-* (to) + *spirare* (to breathe), meaning to strive or, literally, to pant after something desired.

ass *n.* **1** *The asses were hitched to the cart:* donkey, neddy, moke. **2** *Don't be an ass and leave your job without having another:* fool, idiot, numskull, blockhead, bonehead, twerp, nitwit, nincompoop, ninny, half-wit, moron, imbecile, dunce, dunderhead, goon, booby, jerk.

Ant. 2 sage; brain, genius.

◇ *Usage note:* Do not confuse an *ass* and a *mule.* An *ass* is a distinct species, but a *mule* is a hybrid between an ass and a horse, almost always the offspring of a male ass and a mare.

assail *v. A mugger assailed him in the dark street:* attack, assault, set upon, lunge at, pitch into, fly at, descend upon.

Ant. defend, support; retreat, withdraw.

assailant *n. The assailant was identified by the man he had beaten:* attacker, mugger, assaulter, assailer, aggressor.

assassin *n. The assassin had gone into hiding:* killer, murderer, slayer, executioner, desperado, sniper, gunman.

◇ *Word origin: Assassin* comes from Arabic *hashshāshīn,* "hashish-users," name of an Islamic order founded around the year 1090, whose members were said to take hashish before being sent forth to assassinate leading Crusaders.

assassinate *v. President John F. Kennedy was assassinated in Dallas in 1963:* kill, murder, slay, put to death, do to death, *Slang* bump off, do in.

assault *n.* **1** *The Battle of Britain was an air assault that lasted many months. The stick-up man was charged with robbery and assault with a deadly weapon:* attack, onslaught, assailing, aggression: (*variously*) raid, strike, foray, charge, sally, lunge, thrust, drive, push, offensive, invasion, storming, bombardment, siege.
—*v.* **2** *The king's troops assaulted the castle on all sides:* attack, assail, set upon, strike at, fall upon, lunge at, fly at, lash out at, (*variously*) raid, strike, charge, thrust at, invade, storm, bombard, besiege.

Ant. 1 defence, resistance, protection; retreat, withdrawal. **2** defend, protect, resist, withstand; retreat, withdraw.

◇ *Usage note:* In the term "assault and battery" *assault* refers to a threatened or attempted attack which may precede the actual physical one. Thus, if a person raises his arm to strike another, grabs him by the shoulder, etc., that is *assault.* If the person follows through with an actual blow, that is *battery,* and both together are "assault and battery."

"Words ought to be a little wild for they are the assault of thoughts on the unthinking."
—*J. M. Keynes*

---

assay *v. The ore was assayed, and found to contain 75 per cent gold:* analyse, assess, evaluate, appraise, rate, estimate; test, try, prove.

assemblage *n. The zoo has a remarkable assemblage of animals:* collection, gathering, assembly, aggregation, aggregate, congregation, concentration, accumulation; bunch, group, body, company, store, stock, throng, conclave, flock, herd, pack, cluster, clump, mass, pile, heap, batch.

assemble *v.* **1** *The club members assembled in the meeting room:* gather, convene, come together, congregate, meet, flock, convoke, call together, summon. **2** *Assemble your papers and put them in this file:* gather, collect, accumulate, round up, bring together, group together, amass, muster, marshal, compile, heap up, pile up. **3** *It took two hours to assemble the bicycle:* put together, fit together, fabricate; join, connect.

Ant. 1 disperse, scatter, go separate ways; disband, adjourn, dismiss. **2** disperse, scatter, distribute, divide, dispense. **3** disassemble, take apart, *Informal* knock down, break up.

assembly *n.* **1** *The assembly of doctors discussed the latest medical research:* assemblage, gathering, company, congregation, convocation, group, body, conclave, crowd, throng, flock, herd, pack, troop; collection, aggregate, aggregation, cluster, mass. **2** *The United Nations Assembly passed a new measure:* legislative body,

representative body, parliament; Commons, council, conference, meeting, chamber.
Ant. **1** dispersion, dismissal, disunion, disruption.

assent *v.* **1** *The majority assented to my views on the matter, though some begged to disagree:* agree, concur, accept, subscribe to, fall in with, concede, approve, allow, grant; acquiesce, defer to, consent, comply, yield, accord, permit.
—*n.* **2** *The teacher answered with a brief nod of assent:* agreement, concurrence, acceptance, consent, approval, compliance, accord, acquiescence, concession, confirmation, approbation, admission, affirmation, ratification, endorsement, sanction, acknowledgement, recognition, corroboration, verification.
Ant. **1** dissent, disagree, differ, disapprove, protest, object, reject, refuse, deny, negate, spurn, disallow. **2** disagreement, dissent, dissension, difference, disapproval, protest, objection; refusal, rejection, unacceptance; denial, negation, disavowal, disallowance, veto.
◇ *Usage note:* Don't confuse *assent* and *ascent.* An *assent* is an act or gesture of agreement or permission: *The sovereign gave his assent to the Bill although it restricted his freedom.* An *ascent*, of course, is an upward climb or movement: *the ascent of Mount Everest, the ascent of a submarine from the bottom.*

"However loudly we may assert our own unworthiness, few of us are really offended by hearing the assertion contradicted by a disinterested party." —*Dorothy L. Sayers*

---

assert *v. The old man asserts that eating garlic prevents rheumatism:* maintain, contend, insist, avow, claim, uphold, affirm, swear, declare, aver, profess, propound, advocate, argue, advance, put forward, set forth, avouch; stress, accent, emphasize.
Ant. deny, disavow, disclaim, refute; laugh off, *Informal* put down; retract, take back.
◇ *Usage note:* See ALLEGE.

assertion *n. The assertion that gout is caused by eating luscious food has not been proved:* claim, contention, dictum, upholding, insistence, argument, protestation; avowal, averment, allegation.
Ant. denial, disavowal, disclaimer; retraction.

assertive *adj. A good army officer must be assertive:* positive, forceful, strong-willed, confident, self-assured, self-assertive, insistent, emphatic; aggressive, domineering, pushy, outspoken, cocksure.
Ant. retiring, reserved, shy, bashful, meek, timid, timorous, submissive; uncertain, fearful.

assess *v.* **1** *The house was assessed at £30,000:* value for taxation, estimate, appraise, value. **2** *The club assessed each member at £25 each for the damage:* levy a charge on, tax. **3** *The general assessed the situation and called for reinforcements:* judge, evaluate, appraise, look over.
◇ *Spelling tip: Assess* has four *s*'s. If you leave off the final *s*, you will have written *asses* (ass + es), the plural of the *ass!*

assessment *n.* **1** *The home owner protested at the high assessment on his house:* value for taxation, rate; appraisal. **2** *The council levied an assessment on each property owner when it put in the new sewers:* tax, tariff, impost, fine, toll, charge, fee, dues. **3** *The critic's assessment of the book is that it is beautifully written:* judgement, evaluation, appraisal, estimation.

asset *n.* **1** *A knowledge of German can be a great asset when travelling in Europe:* benefit, advantage, help, aid, service, boon, advantage. **2** **assets.** *This bank has assets of over five million pounds:* financial resources, means, wealth; money, cashable possessions; (*loosely*) cash, property, effects, belongings, capital, money.
Ant. **1** liability, handicap, disadvantage, disservice, drawback, hindrance. **2** liabilities, debts.

assiduous *adj. It takes assiduous work to learn Russian. I admire an assiduous student:* diligent, industrious, hard-working, laborious, unremitting, determined, persistent, persevering, earnest, steadfast, constant, tenacious, dogged, untiring, tireless, indefatigable, sedulous.
Ant. indolent, lazy, idle; haphazard, casual, cavalier, lax, hit-or-miss, undetermined, inconstant, happy-go-lucky.

assign *v.* **1** *A locker was assigned to each student:* allot, allocate, consign, set apart, distribute, apportion, mete out; dispense, grant, give. **2** *The reporter was assigned to cover international news:* designate, name, appoint, commission, delegate, choose; charge, entrust, invest. **3** *Let's assign a day for the next meeting:* name, fix, set, appoint, specify, designate, stipulate, prescribe, determine.
Ant. **2** dismiss, discharge, divest, relieve. **3** keep open, hold in abeyance.

assignation *n. Their assignation had to be kept a secret:* tryst, secret meeting, rendezvous.
◇ *Usage note:* Do not use the word *assignation* unless you mean a meeting of lovers.

assignment *n.* **1** *The student's assignment was to write a composition:* homework, lesson, chore, job, duty. **2** *The ambassador's next assignment will be to India:* post, appointment, designation, commission. **3** *The foreman is responsible for the assignment of jobs:* distribution, apportionment, parcelling out, dealing out, doling out, allotment, allocation.

assimilate *v. What we eat is assimilated into our systems. A good student assimilates knowledge quickly:* absorb, take in, digest, incorporate, imbibe, ingest.

Ant. keep out, reject; keep apart, segregate, isolate.

assist *v. The nurse assisted the doctor in the operating theatre:* help, aid, abet, serve, accommodate, work for, lend a hand, wait on; work with, collaborate, co-operate, support, benefit, sustain, uphold, back up, reinforce.

Ant. hinder, hamper, impede, obstruct; oppose, counteract.

assistance *n.* **1** *The pilot needed the co-pilot's assistance in landing the plane:* help, aid, support, helping hand, service; collaboration, co-operation, reinforcement. **2** *The public's assistance is needed to build the orphanage:* financial support, contribution, charity, alms, relief, subsidy, sustenance, stipend.

Ant. 1 hindrance, obstruction; opposition, resistance, counteraction.

◇ *Spelling tip:* Students often can't remember whether this word ends in *-ance* or *-ence*. Remember this sentence: *I don't need your assistANCE to dANCE!*

assistant *n. The boss's new assistant is a hard worker:* helper, subordinate, aid, second-in-command, subaltern, lieutenant, adjutant, associate, help, auxiliary, mate, aide, helping hand; colleague, co-worker, collaborator, partner, accessory, confederate, accomplice, co-operator, ally, supporter.

"Strike the right of associating for the sake of labour from the privileges of a free man, and you may as well at once bind him to a master."
— *William Cullen Bryant*

---

associate *v.* **1** *In the children's minds summer is associated with picnics:* identify, relate, link, connect, affiliate, ally, league, couple, pair, bind; tie, yoke, combine, unite, join, correlate. **2** *They associate with all the right people socially:* fraternize, be friends, consort, mix, mingle, club together, run around, hob-nob, hang out, rub shoulders.

—*n.* **3** *The doctor's associates agreed that the operation was necessary:* colleague, confrère, collaborator, co-worker, peer, partner, confederate, ally, intimate, confidant, accomplice, fellow. **4** *My associates on the walk included my brother and three neighbours:* comrade, companion, friend, pal, buddy, chum, mate, crony.

—*adj.* **5** *He became an associate member of the club, though one day he hoped to become a full member:* subordinate; closely connected, affiliated, related, allied.

Ant. 1 separate, disconnect, dissociate, divorce; distinguish. **2** avoid, ignore; alienate, estrange. **4** stranger. **5** full, major, main, leading, chief; unaffiliated, unrelated, unallied.

◇ *Pronunciation tip:* The third syllable in *associate* may be pronounced either *-she-* or *-see-*. Both are correct.

association *n.* **1** *The local farmers' association markets all our produce:* organization, federation, confederation, confederacy, alliance, league, union, combine, syndicate, coalition, fraternity, society, body, group, club; company, corporation, partnership. **2** *The salesman's association with the firm lasted 20 years. My association with Tom goes back to our days in the Navy:* affiliation, connection, alliance, participation, membership, relation, relationship, relations, collaboration; friendship, acquaintance, familiarity, intimacy, friendliness, fraternization, companionship, fellowship, camaraderie. **3** *In Great Britain, fireworks have a strong association with November 5th, but in China, fireworks are associated with New Year:* identification, connection, relation, correlation, linkage, bond, tie, affiliation, alliance. **4** *The football team was a rare association of brains and brawn:* combination, mixture, blend, pastiche, mingling, union, community.

Ant. 2 disassociation, dissociation, separation, independence; alienation, estrangement.

assorted *adj. The jar contained assorted boiled sweets:* mixed, various, varied, diverse, diversified, sundry, miscellaneous, different, heterogeneous.

Ant. identical, uniform, like, unvaried, all the same.

assortment *n. Modern chemists have a wide assortment of merchandise:* variety, mixture, selection, conglomeration, diversity, miscellany, choice, medley, hodgepodge, mélange; array, collection, stock, store, quantity.

Ant. uniformity, sameness, monotony.

assuage *v. Liniment will assuage the pain, but soaking in hot water does the injury more good:* allay, ease, mitigate; lighten, lessen, soften; mollify, alleviate, soothe, calm, quiet, still, pacify, appease, temper, take the edge off, tone down.

Ant. intensify, aggravate, heighten, increase, augment; provoke, excite, arouse, kindle, inflame.

assume *v.* **1** *I assume that I'll see you at the meeting on Tuesday. Scientists assume that there is no animal life on Mars:* take for granted, suppose, presume, suspect, believe, think, understand, guess, imagine, gather, fancy; infer, postulate, theorize, deduce, hypothesize, surmise, speculate, conjecture, judge. **2** *The new buyer assumed the mortgage on the house. The new admiral will assume command of the Pacific Fleet:* take on, take up, take over, become responsible for, take care of, shoulder, attend to, accept, enter upon, undertake, set about. **3** *The Bolsheviks assumed power by means of the October Revolution:* seize, take, appropriate, usurp, arrogate, commandeer, expropriate.

Ant. 1 know, prove. **2, 3** relinquish, give up, give over, hand over, put aside, divest oneself of, leave.

◇ *Usage note:* To *assume* means to suppose, to put forward as a hypothesis or possibility: *Let's assume you don't get a rise — could we still afford a new car?* To *presume* means to consider likely, to expect or think to be a fact: *Since the firm is prosperous and my work's been good, I presume I'll get a rise.* In modern use, *assume* is often used for both meanings.

"We must never assume that which is incapable of proof." —*George Henry Lewes*

assumed *adj.* **1** *The reporter agreed to quote his informant under an assumed name:* pseudonymous, pretended, fictitious, make-believe, made-up, phoney, falsified, false. **2** *The assumed time of his arrival was 2p.m.:* supposed, presupposed, presumed.

Ant. 1 real, authentic, actual, true, original, natural. **2** stated, known, proved; positive, absolute.

assumption *n.* **1** *They rented the old house on the assumption that the landlord would paint it. A basic assumption of physics is that all celestial objects have gravitational fields:* belief, supposition, presumption, presupposition, premise, postulate, postulation. **2** *His assumption of his father's debts was admirable. The new governor's assumption of office takes place next Tuesday:* taking on, taking up, becoming responsible for, assuming, shouldering, accepting, acceptance, entering upon, undertaking. **3** *The general's assumption of power was the start of a dictatorship:* seizure, taking, appropriating, usurpation, arrogation.

assurance *n.* **1** *The plumber gave us his assurance that he would fix the pipes tomorrow. The customer said that he would be back with a cheque for the car and left £50 assurance:* pledge, promise, word of honour, vow, oath, profession, averment, affirmation; guarantee, warranty, binder. **2** *Winston Churchill had the natural assurance of a born leader:* self-assurance, assuredness, confidence, self-confidence, self-possession, certitude, certainty, sureness, poise, coolness; boldness, aggressiveness, self-reliance. **3** *Bob's a salesman for a life assurance company:* insurance.

Ant. 1 lie, fib, falsehood, fiction, tall story, cock-and-bull story, fishing story, whopper; doubt, uncertainty, scepticism, suspicion, distrust, disbelief. **2** shyness, timidity, bashfulness; timorousness, self-doubt, uncertainty, hesitancy; nervousness, apprehension.

assure *v.* **1** *The witness assured the judge that he was telling the truth. The office manager assured the secretary that she would receive a rise:* vow to, promise, pledge to, give one's word to, guarantee. **2** *One more try will assure victory:* make sure, make certain, guarantee, ensure; clinch, secure, confirm. **3** *Assure the house for its full value:* insure.

Ant. 1 deny, refute, disavow, disclaim; lie, fib; doubt, express doubt, disbelieve. **2** be uncertain, be unsure, be up in the air; make doubtful.

◇ *Word origin: Assure* is ultimately derived from Latin *ad-* (to) + *securus* (sure, safe). The Latin word *securus* also gives us *secure.*

assured *adj.* **1** *The old family retainer had an assured position for life. After winning the Academy Award the actor's next film was an assured success:* guaranteed, certain, sure, secure, dependable, settled, fixed, positive; undoubted, unquestionable, irrefutable, indisputable, indubitable. **2** *Lord Nelson was an assured man:* self-assured, self-confident, self-possessed, confident.

Ant. 1 uncertain, unsure, insecure, unsettled; questionable, doubtful, disputable, dubious. **2** timid, timorous, shy, bashful; self-doubting, uncertain; nervous, apprehensive, fearful.

astern *adv. The tugboat drew astern of the ship:* to the stern, toward the stern, aft, abaft, to the rear, behind.

Ant. fore, afore, forward; ahead, before, in front.

astir *adj., adv. The campers were astir at dawn:* awake, roused, out of bed, up, up and about, afoot, moving about, on the move, in motion, active, bustling about.

Ant. asleep, napping, in bed, lying down, reclining; quiet, still.

astonish *v. The magician's next trick will astonish you:* surprise, astound, amaze, overwhelm, take aback; startle, stun, shock, electrify, stupefy, daze, dazzle, stagger, strike dumb, dumbfound, flabbergast, make one's eyes pop, take one's breath away; perplex, bewilder, confound, confuse.

Ant. come as no surprise, be expected, anticipate, foresee, count upon; bore.

◇ *Word origin:* See ASTOUND.

astonishing *adj. The small shop had an astonishing selection of watches for sale:* overwhelming, surprising, astounding, amazing, overpowering; startling, breath-taking, striking, staggering, impressive, shocking, electrifying, stupefying, dazzling; perplexing, bewildering, confounding, confusing.

Ant. expected, anticipated, foreseen, looked for.

astonishment *n. Imagine the astonishment of prehistoric man when a comet appeared in the sky:* amazement, surprise, shock, wonder, wonderment, awe; bewilderment, perplexity, confusion, stupefaction.

Ant. calmness, indifference; boredom.

astound *v. Alexander Graham Bell astounded the world with his invention of the telephone:* astonish, amaze, overwhelm, stun, startle, electrify, shock, stupefy, stagger, dazzle, daze, strike dumb, dumbfound, flabbergast, surprise, take back, make one's eyes pop, take one's breath away.

◇ *Word origin: Astound, astonish,* and *stun* are all ultimately derived from Latin *ex-* (out) + *tonare* (to thunder). All three words originally connoted extreme shock, such as that suffered by one who was literally thunderstruck.

astray *adj., adv. We went astray at the crossroads and were lost. The police were led astray by false clues:* off the right track, off course, off the mark, amiss, afield, off, into error.
Ant. on the right track, on course.
◇ *Word origin: Astray* is ultimately derived from Latin *extra-* (out of bounds) + *vagari* (to wander). Our words *vague* and *vagrant* are also related to Latin *vagari.*

astute *adj. Sam is an astute judge of character. You'd better hire an astute business man:* shrewd, smart, sagacious, clever, keen, keen-minded, sharp, bright, intelligent, perceptive, discerning, knowing, penetrating, subtle; cunning, sly, foxy, wily, crafty; adroit, machiavellian, artful, politic, designing, calculating.
Ant. dull, slow, thick, unknowing, unintelligent, stupid, dumb, gullible, naïve.
◇ *Word origin: Astute* comes from Latin *astus,* which has both the good sense of adroitness or dexterity and the bad sense of craft or cunning.

asunder *adj., adv. The election debate tore the country asunder:* apart, into pieces, to shreds; in pieces, rent, torn apart, broken apart.
◇ *Usage note: Asunder* is hardly ever used except in highly formal prose.

asylum *n.* **1** *It is no longer fashionable to call a mental hospital an asylum. The abandoned children were put into an asylum:* institution, home; (*variously*) sanatorium, mental hospital, mental institution, madhouse; poor-house, almshouse, eleemosynary institution, orphanage, children's home, *Informal* madhouse, loony-bin. **2** *Belgium granted asylum to the political refugees:* refuge, haven, harbour; shelter, home; place of immunity, sanctuary.
◇ *Word origin: Asylum* comes to us (via Latin) from Greek *asulon,* right of sanctuary. The word first appeared in English in the sense of "hospital" or "institution" during the reign of George III.

atheism *n. The priest was shocked by the youth's atheism:* disbelief, unbelief, godlessness, irreligion, apostasy.
Ant. religion, belief.
◇ *Word origin:* The word *atheism* first entered English in the 16th-century translations of works by Calvin and his followers. The Calvinists modelled the words *atheism* and *atheist* on Greek *atheos,* formed from *a-* (without, no) + *theos* (god), which means (1) godless, (2) God-denying, and (3) God-forsaken.

atheist *n. I believe in God but my brother is an atheist:* disbeliever, unbeliever, non-believer, denier of God's existence, godless person.
Ant. believer, religionist, God-fearing person.
◇ *Usage note:* An *atheist* believes that there is no God whilst an *agnostic* holds that nothing is known, or likely to be known, of the existence of God or of anything beyond material phenomena.

"Our programme necessarily includes the propaganda of atheism." —*Lenin*

---

athlete *n. British athletes won five gold medals in the Olympics:* person active in physical exercise and sports, sportsman, games player; contestant, contender, champion.
◇ *Word origin: Athlete* comes from Greek *athlētēs,* meaning "a contestant in the games." It is based on Greek *athlon,* winner's prize.

athletic *adj.* **1** *King Alfred was supposedly sickly as a youth but built himself up into an athletic man:* strong, able-bodied, muscular, brawny, powerful, sturdy, strapping, hardy, robust, husky, stalwart, burly; manly, masculine, virile. **2** *In the old days sailors led athletic lives:* physically active, vigorous, hardy.
Ant. 1 frail, weak, fragile, feeble, run down, out of shape, sickly. **2** sedentary, inactive.
◇ *Spelling tip:* See ATHLETE.

athletics *n. pl. A well-balanced student should like both intellectual things and athletics:* exercise, exercises, sports, gymnastics, physical training.

athwart *adv., prep. Our defensive position lay athwart the enemy's line of advance:* across, astride; perpendicular to, sidewise, sideways, transversely, from side to side of, at right-angles to.
Ant. parallel to, to the side of.

atmosphere *n.* **1** *Man must stop polluting the earth's atmosphere:* gaseous envelope, air. **2** *We all love the cheerful atmosphere of Christmas:* mood, spirit, feeling, feel, ambience, aura, quality, tone, colour, flavour; environment, surroundings.
◇ *Word origin: Atmosphere* was coined by a 17th-century scientific writer from Greek *atmos* (vapour) + *sphaira* (sphere) to denote the envelope of gases surrounding our sphere, the earth.

atom *n.* **1** *The splitting of the atom was a milestone in the history of science:* smallest part of a chemical element; (*loosely*) indivisible particle. **2** *There was not an atom of evidence to convict him:* particle, scrap, shred, speck, grain, iota, bit, whit, jot, spot, inch, trace, mite, dot, morsel, crumb, fragment, scintilla, tittle, mote.
Ant. 1 compound; subatomic particle. **2** mass, load, quantity, heap.
◇ *Word origin:* An *atom,* the smallest identifiable part of an element capable of existing alone, was once thought to be the smallest indivisible particle of matter. The word comes from Greek *atomos,* indivisible, and the

concept was first set forth by the 5th-century B.C. Greek philosopher Democritus.

atone *v. The errant father promised to atone for the way he had neglected his children:* do penance for, make amends for, make up for, expiate, make expiation, pay for, compensate, recompense, remunerate, make reparation for, render satisfaction for, redeem, shrive.

◇ *Word origin: Atone* is *at one* written together. It comes from Early Modern English *at onement* (atonement), "harmony, reconciliation."

atonement *n. The criminal reformed and promised atonement for his acts:* penance, penitential act, amends, satisfaction, shrift, expiation, redress, reparation, compensation, recompense, redemption, reconciliation, restoration, propitiation.

atrocious *adj.* **1** *Murder is the most atrocious crime of all:* cruel, brutal, inhuman, heinous, monstrous, horrible, terrible, villainous, outrageous, nefarious, enormous, infamous, grievous, pitiless, merciless, ruthless, flagrant, vile, evil, bad, savage, barbarous, vicious, fiendish, diabolical, hellish, infernal, black, dark. **2** *It was an atrocious play:* bad, dreadful, execrable, terrible, tasteless, uncouth, vulgar, tawdry, vile, rude, low.

Ant. 1 humane, kind, benevolent, generous, merciful, gentle, tender, civilized; virtuous, honourable; admirable, wonderful. **2** good, fine, elegant, tasteful, high-class.

◇ *Word origin: Atrocious* comes from Latin *atrox*, black-looking, dreadful, cruel.

atrocity *n. The mercenaries ravaged the countryside, committing one atrocity after another:* crime against humanity, savage deed, atrocious deed, outrage, horror, villainy, enormity; barbarity, barbarism, brutality, inhumanity, heinousness, savagery.

Ant. humaneness, kindness, benevolence, mercifulness, gentleness, tenderness; good deed, kind act.

atrophy *n. A bedridden person should exercise to prevent atrophy of his muscles:* wasting away, withering, degeneration, shrivelling, drying up, decaying, decline; lack of development, lack of use.

Ant. growth, development, strengthening; exercise, use.

◇ *Word origin:* A living thing will *atrophy* if it is not nourished. The word comes from Greek *a-* (not, without) + *trephein* (to nourish).

attach *v.* **1** *Attach the trailer to the car. Attach a stamp to the envelope and post it:* fasten to, make fast, join, connect, couple: affix, fix, secure, stick; append, annex. **2** *The submarine was attached to the Western Fleet:* assign, allocate, allot, designate, detail, destine, earmark; associate, affiliate, connect. **3** *The boy was so attached to the new puppy that he refused to leave it:* be fond of, be devoted to, be in love with; feel affection for, be bound by love of.

Ant. 1 detach, unattach, unfasten, disconnect, unconnect, remove, release, separate, disengage. **2** withdraw, recall; dissociate, separate, retire.

attachment *n.* **1** *The attachment of the new engine to the train only took a few minutes:* attaching, fastening, coupling, connection; affixing, fixing, securing. **2** *She has a great attachment to her sister:* love, devotion, affection, fondness, tenderness, bond; friendship, liking, regard, respect. **3** *The vacuum cleaner has four different attachments. The attachment to the contract must be signed by two witnesses:* accessory, fixture; supplement, addition, adjunct, appendage, addendum, appendix.

Ant. 1 aversion, antipathy, hatred, animosity, enmity, dislike; estrangement, alienation, indifference, coolness.

attack *v.* **1** *Lord Kitchener arrived too late to attack the enemy. A good chess player must always attack his opponent's king:* assault, assail, take the offensive, begin hostilities against, set upon, fall upon, bear down upon, descend upon, charge, fly at, lunge at, pitch into. **2** *The book attacks the Navy for being unprepared for World War II:* censure, denounce, disparage, damn, denigrate, impugn, blame, criticize, fault. **3** *Attack each new task with enthusiasm:* set about, undertake, go to work on, go at, approach, tackle.

—*n.* **4** *The enemy attack came at dawn:* offensive, rush, assault, onslaught, aggression, charge, onset. **5** *The newspaper's attack on the mayor's plans aroused public indignation:* censure, impugnment, denigration, abuse, disparagement, criticism. **6** *His attack was brought on by over-excitement:* seizure, stroke, fit, spasm, paroxysm, spell.

Ant. 1 withdraw, retreat; defend, guard, protect, resist. **2** defend, support, uphold, sustain, vindicate, excuse, whitewash. **4** retreat, withdrawal; defence, resistance. **5** defence, support, vindication, excuse, whitewash.

attain *v. He attained success through hard work:* achieve, gain, procure, win, earn, obtain, secure; accomplish, effect, acquire, reach, realize, reap, bring off.

Ant. lose, let go, give up, forfeit; fail at, fall short of.

attainment *n.* **1** *The attainment of an engineering degree is no easy task:* attaining, obtaining, gaining, getting, winning, earning, securing, acquirement, acquiring, acquisition, procuring, procurement. **2** *He's a man of great attainments in several fields:* achievement, accomplishment, acquirement; proficiency, competence, mastery, skill, talent.

attempt *v.* **1** *The expedition will attempt to climb the Matterhorn:* try, strive, endeavour, venture, undertake, essay, aim, work at, make an effort, have a go at, have a bash at, have a crack at, tackle, hazard.

—*n.* **2** *Hannibal's attempt at invading Italy by crossing the Alps was successful:* effort, undertaking, try, endeavour, venture, essay, aim. **3** *An unsuccessful attempt was made on the Tsar's life:* assault, attack, onslaught.

attend *v.* **1** *All students must attend classes in French and German:* be present at, go to, appear at, frequent; visit. **2** *Don't worry about the work, I'll attend to it tomorrow. The nurse is attending the patient now:* take care of, tend to, look after, mind, serve, service, be attendant on, minister to, wait upon, care for, provide for. **3** *Each child must be attended by a parent:* accompany, conduct, escort, convoy, squire, usher, watch over, oversee, superintend, have charge of. **4** *Her illness was attended by weakness:* accompany, be associated with, be connected with, go hand in hand with; follow. **5** *Attend to my words of warning:* heed, mind, listen to, hearken to, give thought to, consider, pay attention to, note, observe, mark, take to heart.

Ant. 1 absent oneself from, be absent, play truant, miss, *Informal* cut, skip. **2** ignore, disregard, neglect, slight. **4** dissociate, be unrelated to. **5** disregard, turn a deaf ear to.

attendance *n.* **1** *Your attendance at the club meeting is necessary:* presence, attending, being there, appearance. **2** *The employee's attendance was so poor that he was fired after six months:* record of attendance. **3** *The attendance at Wembley was over 90,000:* number present, audience, crowd, house, gate.

Ant. 1 absence, non-attendance.

◇ *Spelling tip:* Does this word end in *-ance* or *-ence?* Remember: *What was the AttenDANCE at the DANCE?*

attendant *n.* **1** *The queen was always surrounded by her attendants:* servant, underling, menial, lackey, flunkey, aid, helper; companion, escort, chaperon; follower, adherent.

—*adj.* **2** *We always dread winter and its attendant hardships:* accompanying, associated, related; accessory, consequent.

> "I open with a clock striking, to beget an awful attention in the audience: it also marks the time, which is four o'clock. . . ."
>
> —*Richard Brinsley Sheridan*

attention *n.* **1** *Nobody paid any attention to the warning:* heed, regard, note, notice, mind, concern, consideration; observance, alertness, vigilance, wariness. **2** *A scientist must give his full attention to any problem he wants to solve:* concentration, thought, thoughtfulness, deliberation, contemplation. **3** *The attention of the host pleased the guests:* courtesy, civility, thoughtfulness, politeness, deference, respect; service, care, homage. **4** *The young man showered his attentions on his fiancée:* devotion, suit, court, wooing; gallantries, compliments, assiduities.

Ant. 1–4 inattention, disregard, neglect, negligence, indifference, unconcern. **2** distraction, thoughtlessness, carelessness. **3** thoughtlessness, discourtesy, incivility, rudeness, impoliteness.

attentive *adj.* **1** *A good speaker deserves an attentive audience:* heedful, mindful, intent, awake, wide awake, alert, listening, observant. **2** *She's always an attentive hostess:* thoughtful, considerate, obliging, accommodating, courteous, polite; dedicated, devoted, diligent, painstaking, zealous.

Ant. 1 inattentive, indifferent, unconcerned, heedless, neglectful. **2** thoughtless, inconsiderate, unaccommodating; discourteous, impolite, rude; negligent, remiss, careless.

attenuate *v.* **1** *The silversmith attenuated the ingot into one long thread:* draw out, make thin, make fine, make slender, spin out. **2** *Aspirin only attenuated the pain:* weaken, reduce, diminish, lessen, decrease; dilute, water down, adulterate, impair, enervate, enfeeble.

Ant. 1 broaden, make thick, make coarse, make fat, enlarge, expand. **2** increase, amplify, intensify, augment, strengthen, develop.

◇ *Word origin: Attenuate* comes from Latin *attenuare,* to make thin, which is based on *tenuis,* thin, from which we get *tenuous.*

attest *v. The lawyer attested to the validity of the will. The success of the operation attests the surgeon's skill:* testify, swear to, verify, confirm, corroborate, vouch for, certify, warrant, affirm, assert, evince, assure, declare; prove, demonstrate, exhibit, show, display, support, substantiate, give evidence, bear witness, bear out.

Ant. refute, deny, disavow; controvert, contradict, disprove, gainsay, belie, cut the ground from under.

◇ *Word origin: Attest* comes from Latin *attestari,* to bear witness, and is related to *testify* and *testimony.*

attire *v.* **1** *The mourners were attired in black:* dress, clothe, garb, robe, gown, deck out, array, costume, don, invest, fit out, turn out, rig out.

—*n.* **2** *Her wedding attire was all satin and lace:* dress, garments, apparel, clothing, clothes, costume, outfit, garb, wardrobe, habiliments, raiment, vestments, *Slang* togs; finery, array, glad rags.

Ant. 1 undress, disrobe, unclothe, strip, bare, denude.

◇ *Word origin: Attire* comes from Old French *atirer,* to equip. It is likely that a car's *tyre* is so called because it is equipment or *attire* for a wheel.

attitude *n.* **1** *Why do you have such a belligerent attitude?:* disposition, frame of mind, outlook, point of view, perspective, manner, demeanour, air. **2** *The listeners stood in an attentive attitude:* posture, stance, pose, position.

attract *v.* **1** *Sugar attracts flies. The zoo attracted* *many visitors:* draw, lure, allure, entice, pull; interest, appeal to, fascinate; captivate, charm, enchant, bewitch. **2** *Try not to attract attention:* draw, induce, provoke, cause, bring about, precipitate, evoke.

Ant. repel, repulse; disgust, antagonize, affront, offend, outrage.

attraction *n. Detective novels hold a special attraction for me:* appeal, fascination, allure, lure, enticement, inducement, magnetism, drawing power, pull, temptation, enchantment, captivation, tendency, affinity; charm, glamour, attractiveness.

Ant. repulsion, repugnance; aversion, disinclination, indifference, apathy.

attractive *adj. The new dress styles are very attractive:* appealing, pleasing, likeable, agreeable, pleasant; charming, delightful, enchanting, engaging, winning; lovely, beautiful, pretty, handsome, becoming, fetching, fair, sightly, chic, elegant, tasteful; inviting, tempting, enticing, fascinating, alluring, bewitching, captivating, seductive.

Ant. unappealing, displeasing, unlikeable, unpleasant, unpleasing, offensive, repellent, repugnant, repulsive, revolting, obnoxious, distasteful; ugly, unbecoming, unsightly, inelegant; uninviting.

attribute *v.* **1** *The car accident was attributed to faulty brakes:* ascribe, credit, assign, allege to belong; charge to, set down to, lay to, account for by, trace to, blame on, bring home to, saddle with, lay at the door of; cause by, derive from.

—*n.* **2** *Generosity is but one of her many fine attributes:* characteristic, trait, quality, virtue, aspect, facet, feature, character, property; accomplishment, acquirement, attainment, faculty, ability, distinction, grace, gift, talent, endowment.

◇ *Pronunciation tip: Attribute* has two pronunciations. The verb, *to attribute,* is pronounced *a-TRIB-yoot.* The noun, *an attribute,* is pronounced *A-tri-byoot.*

attrition *n.* **1** *Attrition over thousands of years formed a cave in the rocks:* wearing down, wearing away, friction, abrasion, erosion, grinding, scraping. **2** *The Arab forces gradually gained victory over their enemies after tactics of attrition:* tiring, breaking one's morale, weakening by harassment or siege.

attune *v. Astronauts have to attune themselves to weightlessness in space:* adapt, accustom, familiarize, acclimatize.

Ant. resist, fight against; alienate.

atypical *adj. Seasickness is an atypical ailment among experienced sailors:* unusual, uncommon, untypical, non-typical, anomalous, unrepresentative, out of keeping, unlooked for, contrary, abnormal, unnatural, irregular.

Ant. typical, representative; common, familiar, ordinary, usual, customary, in keeping, normal, natural, regular, expected.

auburn *adj.* **1** *She has pure auburn hair, now that the bleach has been washed out:* reddish-brown, golden-brown, tawny, chestnut-coloured, nut-brown, cinnamon, russet, rust-coloured, copper-coloured, henna.

◇ *Word origin: Auburn* comes originally from Latin *alburnus,* whitish, which is itself based upon *albus,* white. It used to designate a yellowish-white colour, but *burnus* seems to have been confused with *brown* during the Middle Ages, and *auburn* is now known as a reddish-brown colour.

audacious *adj.* **1** *Napoleon was an audacious leader:* bold, daring, adventurous, venturesome, enterprising; brave, courageous, fearless, unafraid, valiant, dauntless, stouthearted, lion-hearted, stalwart, valorous, plucky, *Slang* gutsy. **2** *We admired the audacious feats of the trapeze artists:* bold, daring, reckless, rash, risky, daredevil, devil-may-care, death-defying, breakneck; heedless, foolhardy, injudicious, imprudent, desperate, hotheaded, self-willed, wild. **3** *Her audacious behaviour shocked us all:* impudent, impertinent, insolent, brazen, fresh, shameless, outrageous, defiant, unabashed, presumptuous, assuming, forward, saucy, cheeky, bossy, pert; disrespectful, rude, discourteous.

Ant. 1 unadventurous, unenterprising; cowardly, faint-hearted, craven, frightened, timid, pusillanimous, *Slang* yellow, chickenhearted, lily-livered. **2** careful, guarded, discreet; prudent, circumspect, cautious, judicious. **3** tactful, gracious, cordial, amiable, ingratiating, unassuming, deferential, reverential, obsequious, *Informal* smarmy; polite, courteous, mannerly, well-mannered, ladylike, gentlemanly, refined, polished, formal.

audacity *n.* **1** *Sky-diving takes both audacity and skill:* boldness, daring, nerve, spunk, grit, pluck, *Slang* guts; derring-do, venturesomeness; fearlessness, valour, bravery, courage; recklessness, rashness, foolhardiness. **2** *She had the audacity to walk out during the sermon:* impudence, impertinence, insolence, brass, brashness, effrontery, brazenness, shamelessness, cheek, gall, presumption, forwardness, bumptiousness.

Ant. discretion, prudence, caution, wariness, circumspection; cowardice, timorousness, faint-heartedness, timidity.

audible *adj. The music was barely audible. He heaved an audible sigh:* loud enough to be heard, heard, perceptible, discernible, clear, distinct.

Ant. inaudible, muffled, faint.

audience *n.* **1** *The audience applauded the performance:* listeners, spectators, assembly, house. **2** *Shakespeare has always had a large audience:* public, following. **3** *They requested an audience with the Pope:* interview, personal meeting, hearing, audition, reception; conference, discussion, consultation, talk, parley.

◇ *Usage note:* Don't worry about whether you should follow *audience* by a singular or plural verb. Technically *audience* is a collective noun and you can consider it singular or plural as you see fit, depending on whether or not you consider the *audience* as a single unit or as made up of many individuals. Thus, you might say *The audience is happy with the new play* (all of them as one unit) or *The audience are dressed in a variety of ways, some in suits and dresses, some in jeans* (considering the audience as made up of separate units). But don't waste time worrying about it — just use the verb form, singular or plural, that sounds right to you.

Exploring the Word: Latin *audire*, to hear, gives us *audible*, loud enough to hear; *audience*, those who hear, a group or meeting of listeners; and *audio*, broadcast or recorded sound, sound quality, or the sound or "hearing" part of a TV programme or of *audio-visual* material. To *audit* is to hear or examine something and an *auditor* is a financial examiner, one who "hears" accounts; an *audition* is a test hearing of a singer or actor, and an *auditorium* is a room or building where lectures, plays, etc. are heard. The *auditory canal* is a passage in the ear; both it and the *auditory nerve* are concerned with our hearing.

audit *v.* **1** *Accountants audit the company's books every year:* examine, inspect, check, go over, investigate, scrutinize; verify, balance, review, take stock of.
—*n.* **2** *The stockholder demanded an audit of the firm's accounts:* examination, inspection, investigation, scrutinizing; verification, review.

audition *n.* **1** *The actor's audition landed him a role in the new play:* try-out, hearing, test performance.
—*v.* **2** *The dance company is auditioning new dancers for the chorus:* try out, give a test performance.

auditor *n.* **1** *The auditor checked the firm's books:* financial examiner; (*loosely*) accountant, book-keeper, comptroller. **2** *I'm not a regular student, but just an auditor of the course:* one who listens, listener.

auditorium *n. The graduation assembly took place in the college auditorium:* assembly hall, lecture hall, concert hall, auditory; arena, theatre.

aught *pron. For aught I know, she's gone, and for aught I care, she can stay:* all.
◇ *Usage note: Aught* (meaning "all") is never used nowadays except in the phrases illustrated by the above sentence. Until the end of the last century *aught* was also used as a literary word meaning "anything at all," as in the following line by Tennyson: "Unfaith in aught is want of faith in all."

augment *v. The boy augmented his allowance by mowing lawns:* add to, increase, enlarge, expand, extend, raise, boost, swell, inflate, amplify, magnify, intensify; heighten, lengthen, widen, deepen.
Ant. decrease, reduce, diminish, lessen, lower; curtail, cut back, abridge, shorten, narrow, contract, shrink, moderate, subside.

augur *n.* **1** *Roman augurs predicted the future by interpreting flights of birds and other natural occurrences:* oracle, prophet, seer; diviner, prognosticator, soothsayer.
—*v.* **2** *Dark clouds augured the coming of the thunderstorm:* prophesy, predict, prognosticate, presage, bode, intimate, be an omen of; be a sign of, signify, portend, forecast, foretell, forewarn, foreshadow, promise.

augury *n.* **1** *Augury was commonly performed by inspecting the flight of birds or the entrails of sacrificial victims:* prophecy, divination, prognostication; auspice, sortilege. **2** *The rainbow was an augury of clear weather:* omen, portent, sign, token, warning, forewarning, indication; herald, forerunner, precursor, promise, harbinger.

august *adj. Gladstone is one of the most august figures of English history:* awe-inspiring, monumental, majestic, magnificent, impressive, imposing, sublime, grand, grandiose, noble, dignified, distinguished, eminent, illustrious, stately, solemn, venerable, exalted, glorious, supreme, superb, lofty, high-ranking, regal.
Ant. unawesome, unimpressive, unimposing, uninspiring; mean, common, commonplace, undistinguished, undignified, unstately, ignoble, unmajestic, unexalted; paltry, insignificant; ridiculous, comic.

aura *n. There was an aura of warmth about her:* atmosphere, mood, feeling, feel, character, quality, suggestion, air, essence, aroma, emanation.
◇ *Word origin: Aura* means "breeze" in Latin.

auspice *n.* **1** *The break in the clouds was an auspice of better weather to come:* indication, sign, portent, omen, warning, augury, prognostication. **2 auspices.** *The free concerts were given under the auspices of the opera company:* sponsorship, patronage, support, advocacy, aegis, championship; care, charge, authority, control, countenance, guidance, influence, protection.
◇ *Word origin:* Among the Romans, an *auspicium* (auspice) was an omen divined by watching the flight of birds. The word comes from Latin *avis* (bird) + *specere* (to watch).

auspicious *adj.* **1** *The amount of business that the new shop did on its first day was most auspicious:* being a good omen, encouraging, favourable, promising, propitious, heartening, reassuring, hopeful. **2** *On this auspicious occasion I would like to toast the bride and groom:* happy, felicitous, benign, good, fortunate, successful, lucky, opportune, timely, red-letter.

Ant. inauspicious. **1** ill-omened, ominous, discouraging, unfavourable, unpromising, unpropitious, disheartening, adverse, sinister, unsatisfactory. **2** sad, unhappy, sorrowful, baleful, melancholy, cheerless, joyless, pathetic, dismal; unfortunate, unlucky, black.

austere *adj.* **1** *In the old days, schoolmasters were thought of as austere men:* stern, strict, severe, ascetic. **2** *The Puritans led austere lives:* rigorous, spartan, ascetic, self-denying, abstemious, strict, strait-laced.

Ant. **1** permissive, lenient, indulgent, easy, flexible, lax; frivolous, gay, cheerful, joyful, merry, light-hearted, jovial, jolly, jaunty, nonchalant, lively, exuberant, vivacious, effervescent, high-spirited, playful, convivial; kindly, kind, sweet, genial. **2** luxurious, lush, comfortable, easy; sophisticated, cosmopolitan; loose, corrupt, dissolute, dissipated, debauched, degenerate, depraved, wanton, abandoned, self-gratifying, free-and-easy, immoral, wicked, evil, sinful, impure, lewd, licentious, lascivious.

◇ *Word origin: Austere* and *austerity* go back to Greek *austeros,* harsh, bitter.

authentic *adj.* **1** *This is an authentic Persian rug:* genuine, real, true, actual, bona fide, legitimate, original. **2** *This book tells the authentic story of a doctor's life:* true, actual, real; factual, accurate, faithful, veritable, valid; verified, authenticated, attested, accredited, unquestioned, pure, unadulterated; reliable, dependable, trustworthy, authoritative.

Ant. **1** imitation, counterfeit, simulated, synthetic, fake, sham, phoney, bogus, mock, specious. **2** unreal, false, untrue, inaccurate, unfaithful; fictitious, pretended, make-believe, hypothetical, supposed, unverified, unreliable, untrustworthy, undependable; deceptive, misleading, fraudulent, corrupt, adulterated.

authenticate *v. The lawyer authenticated the will:* establish as genuine, verify, confirm, attest, vouch for, avouch, validate, certify, guarantee, warrant, endorse.

Ant. impugn, gainsay, invalidate, negate, contravene; repudiate, deny, reject, spurn.

author *n.* **1** *Mark Twain is the author of* Tom Sawyer: writer; (*variously*) novelist, short-story writer, poet, essayist, playwright. **2** *The Chancellor of the Exchequer is the author of present British financial policy:* creator, originator, maker, prime mover, innovator, initiator, inventor, father, framer; founder, producer, planner, organizer.

authoritarian *adj.* **1** *Their country has an authoritarian government:* favouring authority, repressing individual freedom; strict, harsh, severe, unyielding, inflexible, uncompromising, austere, disciplinary, disciplinarian, dogmatic, doctrinaire; dictatorial, tyrannical, fascist; by the rule, by the book.

—*n.* **2** *The drill sergeant was a strict authoritarian:* disciplinarian, rule follower; martinet, tyrant, dictator.

Ant. **1** revolutionary, insurgent, mutinous, dissenting, nonconformist; lenient, permissive, flexible. **2** anarchist, rebel, revolutionary, insurgent, mutineer; malcontent, dissenter, nonconformist.

authoritative *adj.* **1** *Is this an authoritative order from the general or merely a personal request?:* official, sanctioned, commanding, commanding obedience; administrative, sovereign, ruling. **2** *He was a small man but there was an authoritative tone in his voice:* showing authority, commanding, imperative, decisive, masterful, imposing, impressive, peremptory; arrogant, lordly, autocratic, dogmatic, dictatorial, tyrannical. **3** *Read a good, authoritative book on Queen Victoria:* trustworthy, reliable, dependable, sound, valid, authentic, definitive, factual, scholarly, learned.

Ant. **1** unofficial, unsanctioned, unauthorized, without authority; facetious, frivolous. **2** subservient, servile; weak, indecisive, meek, timid, humble, modest. **3** untrustworthy, unreliable, undependable, invalid; deceptive, misleading.

authority *n.* **1** *The referee's authority ends at the final whistle. Speak to someone in a position of authority:* command, control, power, sway, force, weight, rule, supremacy, domination, dominion, strength, might, influence, importance, respect, prestige, esteem; jurisdiction, administration. **2 authorities.** *You had better notify the authorities that the child is missing:* powers that be, government administration; officialdom, police. **3** *A leading agricultural authority predicts that farm prices will hold firm:* expert, specialist, scholar, mastermind, pundit; accepted source, trustworthy source.

Ant. **1** servility, servitude, weakness. **2** follower; public, masses.

authorize *v.* **1** *The law authorizes policemen to carry truncheons:* give authority to, empower, permit, allow, commission, license, entitle, invest, enable, give leave. **2** *The firm's bookkeeper has to authorize all payments:* give authority for, approve, sanction, confirm; certify, accredit, warrant, vouch for.

Ant. **1** enjoin, prohibit, forbid, proscribe, preclude, interdict; prevent, disallow.

autocrat *n. One of the Tsar's titles was "Autocrat of all the Russias." My father was the autocrat in our house:* absolute ruler, ruler, monarch, overlord; tyrant, despot.

◇ *Word origin:* The word *autocrat* entered English (via the political vocabulary of the French Revolution) from Greek *autokrator,* "ruler by himself," a term designating the Roman emperor.

autocratic *adj. The emperor was an autocratic ruler. The governor had an autocratic attitude to-*

wards his prisoners: having absolute power, dictatorial, monarchical, tsaristic; tyrannical, tyrannous, despotic, imperious, repressive, oppressive, iron-handed.
Ant. limited, constitutional, democratic, egalitarian; lenient, permissive, indulgent, forbearing, tolerant.

automatic *adj.* **1** *Use an automatic dishwasher:* self-operating, self-acting, self-moving, self-propelling, electric, mechanical, push-button, automated. **2** *Breathing and blinking are automatic reactions:* occurring independently, involuntary, reflex, instinctive, unconscious, spontaneous, non-volitional, uncontrolled, unwilled, inherent; mechanical, routine, habitual.
Ant. 1 manual. **2** voluntary, conscious, intentional, controlled, deliberate.
◇ *Spelling tip: Automatic* is easy to spell, but some people have problems with *automatically.* Remember that *automatically* is spelt with two *l's*: *automatic* + *-ALLY.*

> **Exploring the Word**: Greek *autos* means "self" and gives us many words including: *autobiography,* writing about one's own life; *autocrat,* one who rules by himself, an absolute ruler; *autograph,* literally to write one's own name; *automatic,* self-acting; *automotive,* concerned with self-moving vehicles; *autonomy,* self-rule, self-governing; and even *autopsy,* literally a seeing for oneself, a doctor's seeing for himself the cause of a death by a post-mortem examination of a body. (Our word *automation* is a modern blend of *autom*[atic] + [oper]*ation.*)

automation *n. We're living in the age of automation:* automatic machinery, machine-operated machinery.

autonomous *adj. The school of adult education was an autonomous extension of the university:* self-governing; independent, sovereign, free.
Ant. governed, dependent, subject.

autonomy *n. After World War II, Britain granted many of its colonies autonomy:* self-government, home rule; independence; sovereignty, freedom, liberation.
Ant. foreign rule, dependency; colonial status.

autumn *n. Autumn is the season when leaves turn brown and days get shorter:* harvest-time; autumnal equinox, Indian summer.

auxiliary *adj.* **1** *If the main power line fails, the hospital will use its auxiliary generator:* supplementary, ancillary, subordinate, secondary, subsidiary, accessory; reserve, emergency, back-up.
—*n.* **2** *The helicopters will serve as an auxiliary to the fast reconnaissance planes:* supplement, subsidiary, accessory; partner, companion, accomplice, associate; helper, assistant, giver of aid, helping hand; reserve, back-up.
Ant. 1 main, chief, primary, first-line. **2** main body, major item; opponent, antagonist, hindrance, drawback.

avail *n.* **1** *Efforts to save the sinking ship were of no avail:* use, usefulness, advantage, purpose; service, benefit, success, profit; help, aid.
—*v.* **2** *Avail yourself of every opportunity to get a good education. Our efforts to save the burning building availed us little:* use, utilize, profit from, take advantage of; benefit, help, aid, assist, serve, be of use, be of advantage, profit.
Ant. 1 detriment, disadvantage, disservice, harm. **2** overlook, neglect, ignore, slight, pass up, spurn; hinder, harm, hurt, be useless.

available *adj. The hotel had no available rooms. Is there a doctor available?:* ready for use, ready for service, free, open, obtainable, accessible, at one's disposal, convenient, on hand, at hand, handy, at one's elbow, on tap, vacant.
Ant. unavailable, unobtainable, in use, occupied, spoken for, taken, engaged; inconvenient, inaccessible; unusable, unserviceable.

avalanche *n.* **1** *The avalanche trapped the climbers:* snow-slip; earthslide, landslide. **2** *The post office expects an avalanche of letters at Christmas:* overwhelming amount, flood, deluge, inundation, torrent, cascade, blizzard, heap, mass.
Ant. 2 paucity, scantiness; dearth, lack, deficiency, insufficiency, shortage, drought.

avant-garde *n. In the 1920's Picasso was still considered a member of the avant-garde:* artistic innovators, advance guard, vanguard, trailblazers, trend-setters, pioneers, leaders, forerunners, originators.
◇ *Word origin: Avant-garde* is French for "advance guard."

avarice *n. His avarice led him into unethical business deals:* lust for money, greed, greediness, money-grubbing, rapacity, venality, graspingness, covetousness, worship of Mammon; miserliness, stinginess, parsimony, penny-pinching, niggardliness, close-fistedness, penury.
Ant. generosity, benevolence, magnanimity, munificence, charitableness, unselfishness; extravagance, liberality, open-handedness.

avenge *v. The crowd avenged the burning of the monastery by wrecking the Viking boats:* take vengeance for, wreak vengeance, revenge, retaliate, get even for, repay, punish, exact satisfaction for, inflict injury for, injure, exact an eye for an eye.
Ant. excuse, forgive, pardon, overlook; accept, be resigned to, tolerate.
◇ *Usage note:* See REVENGE.

avenue *n.* **1** *The avenue was lined with modern shops:* tree-lined road; boulevard, thoroughfare, broad street. **2** *The only avenue of escape is over that mountain:* way, route, road, course, path, pathway, passage, passageway, direction; opportunity, chance, access, approach, gate, gateway, outlet.
Ant. 1 alley, lane.

◇ *Pronunciation tip:* The correct pronunciation of *avenue* is *avenyew.* It was originally a French word, but its pronunciation has been anglicized.

aver *v. The witness averred that he had seen the suspect at the scene of the crime:* assert, declare, affirm, state, avow, avouch, maintain, swear, insist, emphasize, contend, profess, represent, proclaim, pronounce, protest, asseverate; certify, verify, guarantee.

Ant. deny, disavow, disclaim, repudiate; doubt, be uncertain, gainsay.

average *n.* **1** *The average of 2, 3, and 7 is 4. He maintained a batting average of about 40:* mean amount; (*loosely*) mean, ratio, medium, norm, midpoint, par; standing, accomplishment. **2** *He bowls better than average:* the ordinary, the standard, the typical, the general, the usual, normal, the run of the mill, the rule.

—*adj.* **3** *Including stops for petrol and a traffic jam, our average speed was still 40 miles an hour:* mean, par; (*loosely*) medium, median, medial. **4** *Yesterday was an average working day. He is of average height. It was only an average film:* typical, ordinary, common, normal, usual, standard, moderate; fair, passable, so-so, tolerable, mediocre, indifferent, not bad, run-of-the-mill, betwixt and between, rank and file.

Ant. 1, 3 maximum; minimum. **4** unusual, uncommon, different, special, remarkable, exceptional, extraordinary, extreme, abnormal; memorable, conspicuous, noticeable, prominent; outstanding, superlative, surpassing, excellent, wonderful, terrific, stupendous, tremendous, great, fine, good; awful, bad, dreadful, terrible, horrible, lousy.

◇ *Usage note:* See MEDIOCRE.

averse *adj. I don't approve of whisky but I'm not averse to a glass of wine now and then:* opposed, loath, disinclined, unwilling, reluctant, indisposed, ill-disposed, unfavourable, recalcitrant, antipathetic, unamenable, inimical.

Ant. agreeable, amenable, willing, inclined, disposed, favourable; eager, avid, ardent, desirous, intent, keen.

◇ *Usage note:* See ADVERSE.

"Aversion we have for things, not only which we know have hurt us, but also that we do not know whether they will hurt us or not."
—*Thomas Hobbes*

---

aversion *n. Cats have an aversion to getting wet:* dislike, unwillingness, reluctance, antipathy, disinclination; distaste, repugnance, prejudice against, opposition; abhorrence, loathing, hatred, disgust, detestation, revulsion, repulsion, animosity, horror.

Ant. willingness, inclination; eagerness, desire, love, liking.

avert *v.* **1** *She averted her head so that we couldn't see her face:* turn aside, turn away, turn. **2** *The quick arrival of fire-fighters averted a major forest fire:* prevent, forestall, preclude, ward off, stave off, keep off, fend off, beat off, keep at bay, nip in the bud, frustrate.

Ant. 1 hold steady. **2** allow, permit, let.

aviation *n. The Wright brothers were pioneers in aviation:* flying, flight, aeronautics, aerodynamics.

aviator Also (for a woman flyer) **aviatrix** *n. Baron von Richthofen was a famous German aviator:* pilot, flyer, air-man.

◇ *Usage note: Aviatrix* has been little used since the 1940's. Most present-day women pilots prefer to be called aviators. The first *aviatrix* was Hélène Dutrieu of France, who got her flying licence in 1910.

◇ *Word origin:* An *aviator* soars through the air in his aeroplane like a bird. Both *aviator* and *aviation* come from the Latin word for bird, *avis. Aviation* was originally a French word. The first recorded use of it in English comes from a book called *The Right to Fly*, as long ago as 1866!

avid *adj.* **1** *People who are too avid for success may miss some of the joys of life:* eager, greedy, hungry, desirous, keen, anxious; grasping, covetous, acquisitive, voracious, rapacious. **2** *He was an avid football fan:* devoted, enthusiastic, intense, zealous, rabid, fanatic.

Ant. indifferent, apathetic. **1** unconcerned, disdainful; indisposed, disinclined, loath. **2** reluctant, recalcitrant, unwilling.

avocation *n. The doctor's avocation was painting:* sideline, secondary occupation; hobby, diversion, pastime, distraction, recreation, entertainment.

Ant. vocation, occupation, work, business, *Informal* line.

◇ *Usage note:* If you tend to confuse *avocation* and *vocation*, see the usage note at VOCATION.

avoid *v. How did the robbers avoid the guards? Avoid fried foods for a while:* evade, elude, dodge, escape, avert, side-step, skirt, fight shy of; keep away from, shun, keep clear of, steer clear of, refrain from, eschew, forsake, forbear, boycott.

Ant. meet, face, confront, incur, contact; approach, find, seek out, invite, solicit; pursue, embrace.

avoidance *n. Constant avoidance of exercise is unhealthy:* keeping away from, shunning, evasion, eluding, shirking, skirting.

Ant. search, invitation, soliciting; pursuit, embrace; meeting, facing, confronting.

avow *v. He avowed his love to her:* declare, admit, confess, own, disclose, proclaim, profess, affirm; assert, state, swear, aver.

Ant. disavow, disclaim, deny, repudiate; keep hidden, keep secret.

avowal *n. The criminal's avowal of guilt closed the case:* admission, confession, profession, declaration, proclamation, acknowledgement; affirmation, assertion, statement, protestation, assurance, word, averment.

Ant. disavowal, disclaimer, repudiation; hiding, keeping secret.

avowed *adj. Bernard Shaw was an avowed vegetarian:* self-declared, professed, self-proclaimed, confessed, sworn; acknowledged, declared.

Ant. secret, undisclosed, unrevealed, private, clandestine, surreptitious, furtive.

await *v. The audience eagerly awaited the speaker's arrival. Your Highness, your coach awaits you:* wait for, look for, look forward to, anticipate, expect; be in readiness for, be in waiting, attend.

awake *v.* **1** *We awake every morning at six. The alarm awoke everyone in the house:* wake, wake up, awaken, raise from sleep. **2** *The fuel shortage awoke the country to the need of developing atomic energy:* make awake, arouse, alert, make aware, make heedful.

—*adj.* **3** *The campers lay awake listening to the night sounds:* not sleeping, wide awake, open-eyed. **4** *A pilot must be awake to changes in the weather:* alert, aware, attentive, watchful, vigilant, heedful, mindful, conscious, wide awake, alive to.

Ant. 1 sleep, go to sleep; doze, nap. **2** put to sleep, make unaware; dull. **3** asleep, sleeping, dozing, napping; dormant, hibernating. **4** unaware, inattentive, unmindful, unconscious.

awaken *v.* **1** *The parents were awakened by the child's coughing:* wake, wake up, awake, rouse from sleep. **2** *Seeing the Giant's Causeway awakened my interest in Irish mythology:* arouse, kindle, call forth, make aware, stimulate, stir up, excite; revive, fan, fire, give new life to.

Ant. 1 go to sleep, put to sleep. **2** quiet, dampen, dull, subdue, check.

awakening *n.* **1** *After an early awakening, we had a big breakfast:* awaking, waking, waking up; arising, getting up, rising from sleep. **2** *If you think this is an easy job, you're in for a rude awakening. The child had a gradual awakening to the joys of music:* arousal.

award *v.* **1** *They award a scholarship to the student with the highest marks. The grandparents were awarded custody of the children:* grant, accord, confer on, bestow, give; assign, allot, allow, concede; decree, appoint.

—*n.* **2** *The Academy Awards are given out once a year:* prize, trophy; medal, decoration, laurels, honour, citation, tribute.

Ant. 1 withhold; refuse, disallow; deny. **2** booby prize.

aware *adj. Everyone should be aware of the dangers of cigarette smoking:* conscious, cognizant, familiar with, acquainted with, informed, apprised, enlightened on, knowledgeable, sensible, sentient, conversant, mindful, awake to, alert to, alive to.

Ant. unaware, unfamiliar with, ignorant, unacquainted with, uninformed about, unknowledgeable, non-conversant, unmindful, insensible, oblivious, unenlightened on.

awareness *n. A good parliamentarian must have an awareness of what the people at home want:* realization, recognition, cognizance, familiarity, sensibility, understanding, mindfulness, acquaintance, appraisal, alertness, consciousness, perception, acuteness; knowledge, information.

Ant. unawareness, unfamiliarity, insensibility, obliviousness, ignorance, unenlightenment.

awe *n.* **1** *The sight of Notre Dame Cathedral filled the tourists with awe:* wonder, reverence, veneration, solemnity, exaltation, respect, adoration, amazement, astonishment, abashment. **2** *The approaching exam struck awe in our hearts:* fright, fear, terror, dread, panic, dismay, alarm, apprehension, consternation, disquietude, perturbation, trepidation, shock, horror, trembling, quaking, quivering.

—*v.* **3** *The natives of New Guinea were awed when they saw their first aeroplane:* strike with wonder, amaze, astonish, abash, overawe, cow, intimidate, fill with reverence; frighten, beset by fear, terrify, fill with dread, dismay, alarm, disquiet, perturb, shock; panic.

Ant. 1 contempt, scorn, disdain; irreverence, disrespect, insolence, arrogance, superciliousness, levity. **2** scorn, disdain. **3** take in one's stride.

awesome *adj. The eruption of a volcano is an awesome sight:* solemn, inspiring, majestic, magnificent, wondrous, astonishing, amazing, awe-inspiring, breath-taking, stupefying, fearsome, fearful, frightening, terrifying, dreadful, alarming, disquieting, perturbing, intimidating.

awful *adj.* **1** *What awful weather! She gave me an awful book. He was guilty of the awful crime of murder:* bad, dreadful, terrible, horrible, horrendous, deplorable, distressing, lousy, unpleasant, displeasing, appalling, frightful, ghastly, fearful, horrifying, hideous, ugly, gruesome, monstrous, shocking, revolting, reprehensible, despicable, contemptible, mean, low, base, heinous; dire, redoubtable, formidable, alarming. **2** *The astronauts know the awful expanse of the solar system:* awe-inspiring, awesome; wondrous, solemn, majestic, amazing, stupefying; fearsome, terrifying, dreadful, disquieting.

Ant. 1 good, fine, O.K., wonderful, terrific, tremendous, pleasant, pleasing; attractive, beautiful, pretty; admirable, likeable.

◇ *Usage note:* (1) Some pedants think *awful* still means only awesome, inspiring awe (def. **2** above). In present-day English, however, *awful* almost always means bad, unpleasant. Thus, *I feel awful, It was an awful film*, etc., are completely correct.

(2) One of the main reasons why certain people would like to see sense **1** proscribed, is that *awful* in this sense tends to get overused, and weakened, because of all the differing contexts it can occur in. Thus, not only do we say *That's awful weather!*, but even *What an awful joke!* or *You are awful!* So try some of the synonyms listed in this book. That's one thing a thesaurus is for, to prevent over-using certain words when others can be more precise, fresher, or add variety to your style.

awfully *adv. It's awfully cold today:* very, extremely, quite, exceptionally, terribly, horribly, dreadfully, immensely, excessively.
Ant. somewhat.

awkward *adj.* **1** *She was an awkward skier:* clumsy, unco-ordinated, without grace, ungainly; inexpert, unskilful, inept, bungling, gauche, maladroit. **2** *The heavy axe was awkward to use:* unwieldy, unhandy, cumbersome, inconvenient, troublesome, difficult, unmanageable. **3** *The scandal caused an awkward situation for the entire family:* embarrassing, unpleasant, trying, difficult, uncomfortable, ticklish, touchy, troublesome, inconvenient.
Ant. 1 graceful, well-co-ordinated, effortless, dexterous; skilful, adept. **2** handy, convenient. **3** proud; pleasing, pleasant, easy, comfortable.

"God may forgive sins, but awkwardness has no forgiveness in heaven or earth."
—*Ralph Waldo Emerson*

---

awry *adj., adv.* **1** *The picture is hanging awry:* askew, crooked, crookedly, unevenly, uneven, turned to one side, twisted, out of line, obliquely. **2** *The game was supposed to start at two, but something went awry and it didn't start until three:* wrong, amiss, askew.
Ant. 1 straight, even, evenly, in line, true; horizontally, vertically. **2** right, perfectly, as expected, smoothly.

axiom *n. The statement that all men are created equal is an axiom of democracy:* basic principle, postulate, fundamental law.
Ant. contradiction, paradox; absurdity.
◇ *Word origin: Axiom* is ultimately derived from Greek *axios*, worthy, self-evident. The related Greek word from which it is directly derived is *axioma*, and it was the philosopher Aristotle who gave the word its permanent sense of "self-evident principle."

axis *n.* **1** *The globe spun on its axis:* line around which a rotating body turns, line of rotation, line of symmetry, centre line; shaft, spindle, stem; pivot, pivotal point. **2** *Germany, Italy, and Japan formed an axis against the Allies in World War II:* alliance, coalition, alignment, compact, entente.
◇ *Word origin: Axis* comes from Latin *axis*, axle.

aye *n. All those in favour, say "Aye." The ayes have it:* yes, yea; affirmative vote.
Ant. nay, no; negative vote.

azure *n.* **1** *Azure goes well with her blonde hair:* sky-blue, clear blue, cerulean, cobalt.
—*adj.* **2** *The ship sailed under azure skies:* clear blue, sky-blue, cobalt, cerulean; cloudless.
◇ *Word origin:* The word *azure* goes back to *al-lāzward*, the Arabic term for the blue gem *lapis lazuli.*

B

babble *n.* **1** *The salesman kept up his babble until we shut the door in his face:* gabble, drivel, twaddle, blab, gab, jabber, jabbering, prattle, chit-chat, gibberish. **2** *The speaker shouted over the babble of the crowd:* murmur, clamour, hubbub, hum, din. **3** *We could hear the babble of a brook:* murmur, murmuring, babbling, burble, gurgle.
—*v.* **4** *The baby babbled happily:* gurgle, murmur, gibber, coo. **5** *Don't babble on the phone all day:* talk, talk incoherently, talk foolishly, prattle, jabber, chatter, chit-chat, blather, blab, gab, gabble, prate, rattle on, run on. **6** *The brook babbled merrily:* murmur, gurgle.
Ant. 2 silence, stillness, quietness. **4** articulate, enunciate.

babe *n. The mother cuddled the babe in her arms:* baby, infant, child, tot.

babel Sometimes **Babel**. *n. The conference became a babel of conflicting opinions:* tumult, confusion, turmoil, uproar, pandemonium, bedlam, hullabaloo, clamour, hubbub, din.
Ant. stillness, silence, quiet, quietness; calm, tranquillity.
◇ *Word origin: Babel* comes from the Tower of Babel, the tower which according to Genesis 11:4–9 was begun by descendants of Noah to reach heaven but was abandoned when God confused the language of the builders. The city of Babel in Shinar (of the Biblical account) is now identified with Babylon.

baby *n.* **1** *The baby slept in its cot:* infant, babe, babe in arms, newborn child, neonate. **2** *Dr. Anderson is the baby of our bridge club:* youngster; junior member, youngest member, newest member. **3** *Take your medicine and don't be such a baby about it:* sniveller, cry-baby, coward.

—*v.* **4** *Her older sisters always babied her:* pamper, indulge, over-indulge, spoil, coddle, molly-coddle, humour.
—*adj.* **5** *The baby bird fell out of the nest. Her garden is full of baby marigolds:* young; small, diminutive, miniature, tiny, little, minute, petite, wee, midget, pygmy, dwarf, dwarfish, tiddly, pocket-sized.
Ant. 1 adult; elder, old man, old woman, ancient. **2** oldest, doyen, senior member, oldest member. **3** adult; stoic, good sport. **4** mistreat, abuse. **5** adult, mature; giant, large, great, huge, enormous.

babyish *adj. The actress was known for her babyish temper tantrums:* childish, infantile, immature, juvenile, puerile.

Bacchanal *n. That New Year's Eve party was a real Bacchanal!:* drunken party, spree, orgy, debauch, debauchery, carouse, carousal, revel, wassail, revelry, festival, carnival, frolic, merry-making, feast.
◇ *Word origin:* In ancient Rome, *Bacchanal* was the name of the place where the orgies of Bacchus, god of wine, were held. The orgies (called *Bacchanalia,* held once every three years, always by night) were so wild that they were banned by a decree of the Senate in 186 B.C.

bachelor *n. Distrusting women, he remained a bachelor all his life:* unmarried man, single man.
Ant. husband; bridegroom, groom.
◇ *Spelling tip:* Some hard-working married men think *bachelors* lead a life of ease (*e*'s). Remember there is an *e* in *bachElor.*

"When I said I would die a bachelor, I did not think I should live till I were married."
— *William Shakespeare*

---

back *n.* **1** *Lie flat on your back. You were lucky that you didn't break your back in the accident:* rear part of the body; backbone, spine, spinal column, dorsum; hindquarters. **2** *Did you paint the back of the bookcase? Please move to the back of the bus:* rear, rear end, posterior, hind part, tail, far end; reverse, reverse side, far side, stern.
—*v.* **3** *Back the car out of the garage. The trainer backed away from the enraged tiger:* move backwards; move away, retreat, retire, withdraw, pull back, fall back, draw back, back down, turn tail, beat a retreat; reverse, retract, revert, retrogress, recede, ebb; return, rebound, recoil, spring back. **4** *Which candidate will you back in the election? Can you back your story with facts?:* help, assist, support, aid, abet, sustain, maintain; endorse, sponsor, vouch for, advocate, promote, encourage, sanction, uphold, countenance, second, reinforce, corroborate, substantiate, confirm, bear witness, attest, testify for, validate, certify, affirm, verify, bolster, hold up, take sides with; praise, protect, guard, succour; patronize, finance, subsidize, underwrite, warrant.
—*adj.* **5** *The dog stood up on its back legs and begged. Put this flowerpot in the back porch:* rear, hindmost, hind, hinder, behind, after; posterior, dorsal, caudal, tail, tail-end, tergal; furthermost, farthermost. **6** *The library has 50 years of the newspaper's back issues:* past, previous, former, earlier; out-of-date, obsolete, expired, elapsed, behind, bygone, gone. **7** *He owed three months' back rent:* overdue, tardy, late, belated, delayed, past, elapsed; in arrears, not paid.
Ant. 1 front; face, stomach. **2** front, head, fore. **3** move forward, move ahead, move toward, approach, advance, progress; attack. **4** hinder, oppose, resist, combat, block; repudiate, invalidate, negate, weaken, undermine, subvert, *Slang* knock. **5** front, fore. **6** future, late. **7** advance.

"Our self-feeling in this world depends entirely on what we *back* ourselves to be and do."
— *William James*

---

backbone *n.* **1** *Good posture results from holding the backbone straight:* spine, spinal column, vertebrae, vertebral column, back; chine, dorsum. **2** *Have you the backbone to overcome hard luck?:* strength of character, character, fortitude, resolve, resoluteness, resolution, strength, mettle, tenacity, spunk, pluck, nerve, firmness, spirit, grit, will, guts, intrepidity, steadfastness; bravery, courage, dauntlessness, manliness. **3** *The cotton industry was the backbone of Lancashire:* mainstay; basis, foundation, strength.
Ant. 2 spinelessness; cowardliness, cowardice.

backer *n. To win the election you'll need some powerful political backers. The backers of the play doubled their money:* supporter, champion, advocate, promoter; adherent, ally, follower, well-wisher; sponsor, patron, guarantor, angel, underwriter, investor, financier.
Ant. detractor; hinderer, enemy, competitor, adversary, opponent.

background *n.* **1** *The painting showed trees in the foreground and mountains in the background:* distance, rear, landscape, *Theatre* mise-en-scène, backdrop, setting, set, flats. **2** *Abraham Lincoln came from an impoverished background. His background qualifies him for his office:* environment, circumstances, milieu, context; upbringing, rearing, family connections, antecedents, breeding, heritage, life story; training, experience, education, preparation, grounding, past, history, credentials.
Ant. 1 foreground; fore, forefront. **2** future.

backing *n.* **1** *The bill won't pass the Committee stage without the Minister's backing:* help, support, aid, assistance; endorsement, sanction, sponsorship, patronage, advocacy, aegis, championing, encouragement, prompting, sustenance, succour, co-operation, helping hand. **2** *The plaster wall has a backing of asbestos:* back, interior, core, inner layer.

Ant. 1 hindrance, opposition, resistance; repudiation, subversion. **2** front, covering, cover, exterior, outer layer.

backwards Also **backward**. *adv.* **1** *Take two steps backwards:* towards the rear, rearwards, to the rear, back, in reverse, back away from, in retreat. **2** *Can you somersault backwards? Your pullover's on backwards. You did the job backwards, but at least it was done:* with the back first, back; (*variously*) upside down, inside out, wrong side out, topsy-turvy, wrong, improperly, disorderly, chaotically, messily. **3** *Count backwards from 10 to 1:* in reverse.

—adj. Only **backward 4** *She gave the homestead a sad backward glance:* turned away from the front, turned towards the back, reversed, inverted. **5** *He's a little backward in his studies:* slow, slow-paced, retarded, behind, undeveloped, remiss, tardy, impeded, sluggish, laggard; slow-witted, dull, dense. **6** *Why do you act so backward with strangers?:* shy, bashful, timid, withdrawn, reserved, reticent, uncommunicative. **7** *We watched the backward flow of the tide:* reverse, ebbing, receding, retreating, withdrawing, returning, retrograde, regressive, retrogressive.

Ant. 1 forwards, frontward. **2** right side up, right side out; properly, correctly. **3** forwards. **5** advanced, ahead. **6** forward, bold, brazen, brash, precocious; eager, willing. **7** forward.

◇ *Usage note: Backward* is a perfectly good word, both as an adverb and as an adjective. *Backwards* can get you into trouble because it can be used only as an adverb. Thus one can only use *He never took a backward glance*, not "backwards" as an adjective, but one can use either *He glanced backward* or *He glanced backwards.* Unless you are absolutely sure about your grammar, there is a simple solution: always use *backward* and be safe.

"Life can only be understood backwards; but it must be lived forwards."

—Sören Kierkegaard

---

backwoods *n. My new guests had unfortunately lived all their lives in the backwoods of civilization:* remote area, unpopulated area, hinterland, country, rural area; woodland, countryside, *Slang* sticks, back of beyond.

Ant. city, metropolis, metropolitan area, urban area, populated area.

bacteria *n. Some bacteria are beneficial, as in cheese-making:* germ, microbe, microorganism, virus, *Slang* bug; bacillus, pathogen.

◇ *Usage note: Bacteria* is actually a plural form and should take a plural verb: *Bacteria are in the air we breathe and in the food we eat.* The singular form *bacterium* is hardly ever used except by biologists.

◇ *Word origin: Bacteria,* the plural of *bacterium,* comes from the diminutive of Greek *baktron,* staff, stick, hence literally "little stick." The first bacteria to be microscopically observed (and hence described) were stick-like in appearance.

bad *adj.* **1** *She's a very bad singer. It's a bad workman who blames his tools. We expect bad weather. She gets bad marks:* not good, poor, inferior, wretched, awful, terrible, dreadful, below standard, below par, second-rate, lousy; faulty, defective, imperfect, deficient, lacking, inadequate, valueless, useless, unproductive, unfit, baneful. **2** *Lying is a bad thing to do:* immoral, unethical, sinful, evil, wicked, wrong, offensive, corrupt, unprincipled, opprobrious, villainous, false, disreputable, criminal, detestable, deplorable, perfidious, reprehensible, base, mean, vile, nefarious, beastly, rotten. **3** *You exercised bad judgement. Her bad spelling kept her from becoming a secretary:* erroneous, wrong, incorrect, not correct, imperfect, unsound, fallacious, faulty, questionable; inefficient, ineffective. **4** *Too many sweets are bad for your teeth:* harmful, unhealthy, hurtful, injurious, detrimental; disadvantageous, troublesome, nonproductive; risky, dangerous, hazardous, menacing. **5** *We were prepared for bad news. He's in a bad mood. Don't feel bad about breaking the glass:* unpleasant, unwelcome, disappointing, distressed, distressing, discouraged, sorry, discouraging, disturbing, regrettable, troubled, troubling; gloomy, glum, melancholy, joyless, grim, disheartening, unnerving, dreadful; cross, angry, short-tempered, irascible, irritable, touchy. **6** *I feel bad about not being able to help you:* sorry, sad, regretful, remorseful, contrite, guilty, conscience-stricken. **7** *Bad milk can make you sick:* spoiled, rotten, decayed, foul, decomposed, turned, rank, putrescent, mouldy, mildewed; polluted, tainted. **8** *What's that bad smell?:* disagreeable, unpleasant, sickening, loathsome, odious, nasty, distasteful, foul, disgusting, nauseating, fetid, unpalatable, bitter, acrid, revolting, repulsive, vile, repugnant. **9** *I feel bad enough to go to hospital:* ill, sick, sickly, unwell, ailing, infirm, indisposed, unhealthy, under the weather. **10** *He has a bad toothache. They were in a bad accident:* severe, harsh, terrible, serious, disastrous, painful, acute, frightful, dreadful, calamitous, tragic; agonizing, distressing, searing, excruciating, grievous, wretched, miserable.

—n. **11** *You must learn to take the bad with the good:* harmful things, sad events, disappointment, misfortune. **12** *The bad that men do can be forgiven by God:* evil, wickedness, immorality, sin, offences, wrongs, villainy, crimes.

Ant. 1–9, 11, 12 good. **1** fine, excellent, above average, superior, first rate. **2** virtuous, moral, ethical, right, righteous, exemplary, high-minded. **3** correct, right, perfect, sound, intelligent. **4** beneficial, healthful, salubrious; harmless, safe. **5** pleasant, welcome, heartening, encouraging, promising, hopeful, cheerful, cheering, happy, joyful, joyous, sweet, smiling, good-tempered, sweet-tempered. **7** fresh, sweet. **8** agreeable, pleasant, fragrant, aromatic, sweet. **9** well, healthy, sound, fit. **10** mild, light, frivolous, trivial, unimportant, minor.

◇ *Usage note:* When a person feels sorry about something (def. **5**, above), he feels *bad* about it, not "badly." *Badly* only means "improperly, in an unsatisfactory manner," as *The child behaved badly in school,* and "very much," as in *She badly wants a new hat.*

badge *n. The policeman wore his badge proudly. The war veteran considers his scar a badge of honour:* emblem, insignia, medallion, ensign, shield, seal, brand, device; symbol, sign, hallmark, mark, token, stamp.

badger *v. You can't badger me into going to the party!:* goad, bully, provoke, bait, pester, nag, harass, hector, harry, hound, persecute, tease, annoy, vex, irritate, nettle, chafe, trouble, torment, plague, coerce, beset.

badly *adv.* **1** *He did the work very badly. You judged him badly:* poorly, improperly, incorrectly, not well, in an inferior way, wretchedly, shoddily, imperfectly, defectively, deficiently, inadequately, erroneously, wrongly, wrong, faultily, unsoundly, unsatisfactorily, incompetently, ineptly, carelessly, sloppily. **2** *The army behaved badly toward the prisoners of war:* immorally, unethically, sinfully, wickedly, wrongly, offensively, corruptly, without principle, villainously, disreputably, criminally, basely, vilely, nefariously. **3** *The boy badly wants a new bicycle. The tooth hurts badly:* very much, greatly, exceedingly, extremely, desperately; intensely, severely, acutely, sorely, horribly, terribly, dreadfully, frightfully.

Ant. 1 well, excellently, superbly; properly, correctly, perfectly, competently, ably, splendidly, satisfactorily; right, rightly. **2** well, morally, virtuously, righteously, ethically.

◇ *Usage note:* See BAD.

"Held we fall to rise, are baffled to fight better,
Sleep to wake." —*Robert Browning*

baffle *v. The unexpected news baffled us:* confuse, bewilder, perplex, mystify, confound, befuddle, stump, puzzle, muddle, nonplus; daze, astonish, astound, disconcert, dumbfound, amaze, surprise.

Ant. clarify, explain, elucidate, clear up.

bag *n.* **1** *We brought home three bags of groceries:* sack, paper bag; packet, bundle, pouch, receptacle. **2** See SUITCASE. **3** See PURSE.
—*v.* **4** *Since you've lost weight that suit bags on you:* sag, droop, hang loosely; bulge, swell out, protrude. **5** *The hunters bagged three deer:* kill in hunting, shoot; capture, catch, trap, entrap, snare, ensnare; get, take, collect, obtain, acquire.

baggage *n.* **1** *Customs officers examined all baggage at the airport:* luggage, suitcases, bags, travelling-bags, valises, grips, trunks. **2** *The king's army travelled with much baggage:* equipment, gear, paraphernalia, accoutrements, impedimenta; belongings, effects.

baggy *adj.* **1** *Circus clowns always wear baggy trousers:* sagging, droopy, loose-fitting, slack, limp; unshapely, unpressed. **2** *His eyes are baggy with fatigue:* flabby, flaccid, paunchy, bulbous, swollen, puffed.

Ant. 1 tight, tight-fitting, close-fitting; well-cut, shapely; neat, pressed.

bail[1] *n.* **1** *The accused are being held on £5,000 bail:* bond, security, surety.
—*v.* **2** *The accused's brother bailed him out of prison:* stand bail or security for.

◇ *Word origin: Bail,* security, comes from Old French *baillier,* to hand over, which goes back to Latin *baiulare,* to bear a burden, to carry something heavy.

bail[2]. Also **bale** *v. Bail the water out of the boat:* scoop, ladle, dip, spoon, shovel.

◇ *Word origin: Bail,* to scoop out water, comes from Old French *baille,* bucket, which may also be related to Latin *baiulare,* to carry something heavy (See BAIL[1]).

"Beauty without grace is the hook without the bait." —*Ralph Waldo Emerson*

bait *n.* **1** *Worms are good bait for perch:* lure. **2** *The shop offered a free gift as bait to get customers:* lure, allure, allurement, inducement, enticement, temptation, attraction, bribe.
—*v.* **3** *Bait your hook with a worm:* put bait on. **4** *He baited his sister unmercifully:* tease, torment, tantalize, antagonize, annoy, vex, harry, harass, hound, hector, badger, worry; *Slang* needle.

balance *n.* **1** Also **balances.** *Weigh that side of beef on the balance:* scales, scale. **2** *A counterweight keeps the machine in balance:* equilibrium, stability, equipoise, counterpoise, weight equality; symmetry, parity. **3** *The speech struck a perfect balance between humour and seriousness:* equilibrium, ratio, proportion, harmony; middle ground, mean. **4** *She's young but she has a great deal of emotional balance:* stability, steadiness, poise, composure, equanimity, equilibrium, equipoise, self-possession, level-headedness, coolness, presence, judgement. **5** *On balance, his accomplishments outweigh his faults:* comparison, evaluation, appraisal,

consideration, estimate, opinion. **6** *The balance on your account is £5. Leave the balance of the work until tomorrow:* amount owed, amount credited, sum minus payment; remainder, rest, left-over, residue, remnant, outstanding portion.
—*v.* **7** *Can you balance on one foot? Balance that big rock with these two small ones:* steady, keep steady, hold equilibrium, stabilize, poise, counterpoise; make level, level off, parallel. **8** *The good balances the bad:* offset, set off, counterbalance, equate, counteract, neutralize, compensate for. **9** *We balanced the benefits against the costs of medical insurance:* compare, contrast, evaluate, weigh; consider, estimate, deliberate, reflect, ponder, cogitate, sum up. **10** *The company balances its accounts every month:* compute, calculate, sum up, total, tally, reckon, tot up, square; pay.
Ant. **3** imbalance, disproportion. **4** instability, self-doubt, uncertainty, incertitude, shakiness. **8** upset, overbalance, outweigh, underbalance.
◇ *Usage note: Balance* is technically a financial term to be used in referring to the difference between two amounts. Thus, *She paid the balance of the money in July.*
◇ *Word origin: Balance* comes from the Latin phrase *libra bilanx*, two-scale balance. *Libra* means both pound (unit of weight) and set of scales (weight-measuring instrument); and the *lanx* in *bilanx* (*bi-*, two-) means dish or scale.

balanced *adj. The book gives a balanced account of the history of apartheid:* fair, equitable, just, impartial, unprejudiced, disinterested.
Ant. one-sided, lopsided, prejudiced, biased, slanted, distorted, unfair.

balcony *n.* **1** *Many of the old Spanish houses have wrought-iron balconies:* deck, veranda, portico, loggia, terrace. **2** *We had cheap seats in the balcony of the theatre:* loges, upper circle, boxes; upper floor, *Slang* gods.
◇ *Word origin: Balcony* comes from Italian *balcone*, whose basis is Old High German *balcho*, scaffold, beam.

bald *adj.* **1** *When he grew bald he bought a toupee:* bald-headed, bald-pated, hairless, depilated, smooth, glabrous. **2** *The mountain is bald above the tree line:* bare, without cover, treeless, denuded, naked, barren. **3** *That is a bald falsehood!:* open, bare, undisguised, flagrant, blunt, flat, obvious, unadorned, stark, naked, straightforward, plain, simple, unvarnished, unembellished; outright, out and out, categorical, unequivocable, unqualified, utter.
Ant. **1** hairy, hirsute, coiffed. **2** overgrown, forested. **3** elaborate, complicated, embellished, fancy; hidden, disguised, devious, roundabout, underhand, surreptitious.
◇ *Word origin: Bald* comes from Middle English *balled*, hairless, having a white patch or white blaze. This original use of *bald* survives in *bald eagle* and *piebald*.

balderdash *n. That story is 10 per cent fact and 90 per cent balderdash:* nonsense, tommy rot, tomfoolery, stuff-and-nonsense, drivel, trash, rot, claptrap, bunk, buncombe (or bunkum), bosh, twaddle, *Slang* bull; gibberish, double-talk, obfuscation, flummery.
Ant. sense, good sense; truth, fact.

bale *n. The farmers loaded the bales of hay on to the cart:* bound bundle, bundle, pack, packet, parcel, package, case; load.
◇ *Word origin:* See BALL[1].

baleful *adj. She gave him a baleful stare:* sinister, ominous, threatening; evil, malignant, malign, malevolent, malicious, baneful, venomous, spiteful, dire, furious, cold, cold-hearted, icy; hurtful, deadly, harmful.
Ant. kindly, friendly, benevolent, beneficent, benign, salutary, warm; favourable.
◇ *Word origin: Baleful* comes from Old English *balu*, evil.

"No themes are so human as those that reflect for us, out of the confusion of life, the close connection of bliss and bale, . . ."
—*Henry James*

---

balk Also **baulk**. *v.* **1** *The donkey balked at climbing the path:* shirk, refuse, resist, demur, recoil, shrink from, shun, evade, hesitate, eschew. **2** *The kidnapping attempt was balked by the police:* thwart, stall, forestall, stymie, frustrate, prevent, hinder, defeat, check, baffle, foil, impede, block, obstruct, bar, inhibit, derail.
Ant. **1** accept willingly, do eagerly, submit; relent, yield, acquiesce. **2** aid, help, assist, abet; further, promote, advance, support, encourage, expedite, facilitate, smooth; allow, permit.
◇ *Pronunciation tip: Balk* rhymes with *walk*. Be sure to write the *l* but do not pronounce it.

ball[1] *n.* **1** *The cat played with the ball of twine:* round mass, sphere, spheroid, pellet, globe, globule, orb. **2** *Four boys were playing ball in the field:* game of ball; cricket, football, catch. **3** *The muskets were loaded with powder and ball:* shot, bullets, projectiles.
Ant. **1** cube.
◇ *Word origin: Ball* (sphere) comes from a Common Germanic word meaning "ball, sphere." This same word is the ancestor of our word *bale* (because of its rounded contours).

ball[2] *n. The banquet was followed by a ball:* dance, dancing party, social evening, soirée, *Slang* disco, hop.
◇ *Word origin: Ball* (formal dance) comes from French *bal*, a dance, which is derived from Late Latin *ballare*, to dance.

ballad *n.* **1** *He read the class one of the great Scottish ballads:* narrative poem, narrative verse, rhyming story. **2** *We sat round the camp-fire, while a folk-singer sang ballads:* folk song, song, lay; ditty, shanty, carol.

◇ *Word origin: Ballad* is from Old French *balade,* dancing song.

"... And then the lover,
Sighing like furnace, with a woful ballad
Made to his mistress' eyebrow...."
—*William Shakespeare*

---

ballast *n. The ship carried bags of sand as ballast:* stabilizing material, counterweight, counterpoise, weight, dead weight; makeweight; balance, counterbalance, ballasting, control, equipoise, stabilizer.

balloon *n.* **1** *The child's balloon floated into the air. The weather balloon carried scientific instruments several miles above the clouds:* air-filled bag, gas-filled bag, inflatable bag.

—*v.* **2** *His coat ballooned in the high wind:* billow, swell out, puff out, fill with air, inflate, blow up, distend, expand, bloat, enlarge, dilate.

◇ *Spelling tip:* This word is in many school spelling tests. Remember to double both the *l* and the *o.*

◇ *Word origin: Balloon* comes from Italian *ballone,* large ball, sphere.

ballot *n. Three of the candidates listed are to be chosen by ballot. The matter was decided by a secret ballot:* vote, round of voting, voting, poll, polling.

"The ballot is stronger than the bullet."
—*Abraham Lincoln*

---

ballyhoo *n.* **1** *Weeks of ballyhoo preceded the film's premiere:* promotion, publicity, advertising, public relations, propaganda, hullabaloo.

balm *n.* **1** *You'd better put some balm on that sunburn:* ointment, salve, unguent, emollient, lotion, cream, balsam. **2** *The music was balm for his jangled nerves:* solace, comforter, comfort, restorative, curative, anodyne, palliative.

Ant. irritant. **2** annoyance, vexation, affliction.

◇ *Pronunciation tip:* The *l* in *balm* is silent; the word is pronounced to rhyme with *charm.*

◇ *Word origin: Balm* comes from Greek *balsamon,* the balsam tree, which yields the resinous substance used as an ointment.

balmy *adj.* **1** *By April the weather had turned balmy. The rain brought a balmy breeze:* gentle, mild, soft, fair, clement, bland, temperate, summery, warm, pleasant, refreshing, agreeable; calm, calming, easing, soothing, salubrious. **2** *A balmy aroma came from the evergreen forest:* fragrant, sweet-smelling, aromatic, perfumed, ambrosial, refreshing, redolent.

Ant. 1 harsh, raw, strong, intense, severe, inclement, rough, discomforting, irksome, vexing, annoying; stormy, unseasonable. **2** stinking, smelly, malodorous, foul, offensive, rank, fetid, putrid, putrescent.

baluster *n. The balcony railing is supported by a series of vase-shaped balusters:* post, support, upright, rail, column, pillar, pilaster.

bamboozle *v. The con man bamboozled him out of £500:* dupe, deceive, trick, cheat, swindle, victimize, defraud, cozen, gull, rook, gyp; delude, mislead, hoodwink, fool, hoax; lure, beguile, coax, con.

ban *v.* **1** *Bicycles are banned from the new motorway. They threatened to ban the book:* prohibit, bar, exclude, banish, debar, disallow, enjoin, forbid; proscribe, suppress, interdict.

—*n.* **2** *The police lifted the ban against parking in this street:* prohibition, forbidding, barring, proscription, taboo, interdiction, interdict, exclusion, restriction, restraint, embargo, banishment, stoppage.

Ant. 1 allow, permit, let, approve, authorize, O.K., countenance, endorse, sanction. **2** approval, permission, allowance.

banal *adj. There were no new ideas in his banal lecture:* stale, trite, unoriginal, commonplace, hackneyed, ordinary, pedestrian, unexciting, unimaginative, everyday, stock, humdrum, dull, uninteresting, conventional, stereotyped, insipid, threadbare, shopworn, tired, corny, cliché-ridden, vapid, platitudinous, jejeune.

Ant. original, new, novel, unique, exciting, fresh, unusual, extraordinary, innovative, distinctive, stimulating, stimulative, gripping, provocative, challenging, imaginative, interesting.

◇ *Pronunciation tip:* The first syllable of this word may be pronounced either as *bay-* or *ban-*. Thus, both *BAY-nal* and *ban-AHL* are correct pronunciations.

◇ *Word origin: Banal* comes from an old meaning of *ban,* "force of vassals called to arms," hence common people. The ending *-al* was later added to form an adjective: *banal.* In medieval France and England, a *banal* mill was a mill where feudal tenants were legally obliged to have their wheat ground, and the *banal* oven was where bread was baked. The word almost died out but was revived in 18th-century journalese as a synonym for "vulgar" or "commonplace".

band[1] *n.* **1** *A band of students brought their grievances before the dean:* group, company, party, body, troop, crowd, gang, party, pack, bunch, throng, assembly, multitude; confederacy, confederation, association, society, clique, crew, fellowship, league, club, set, circle. **2** *The band played until midnight:* orchestra, ensemble, group.

—*v.* **3** *If we band together we can give our argument strength:* unite, join, consolidate, gather.

Ant. 3 split up, divide, disperse.

◇ *Word origin: Band,* a group, comes from Gothic *bandwa,* sign. Later the word came to mean "banner" and then a group acting under one flag or standard.

band² *n. Her hair was held in place by a velvet band. A dark band of clouds was on the horizon:* strip, stripe, streak, ring, fillet, circlet, strap, hoop, binding; ribbon, sash, belt, collar, bandeau, thong, girdle, surcingle, cincture.

bandage *n.* **1** *Wrap the bandage round your injured arm:* dressing, binding, compress, plaster. —*v.* **2** *Disinfect the wound before you bandage it:* cover with a bandage, dress, bind.

bandanna *n. She put a bandanna on her head to keep her hair from blowing:* kerchief, neckerchief, silk square, handkerchief, scarf.

◇ *Word origin: Bandanna* comes from Hindustani *bāndhnū*, a method of tie-dyeing cloth with bright colours.

bandit *n. The stage-coach was held up by two bandits:* outlaw, robber, desperado, highwayman, thief, brigand, burglar, crook, gangster, gunman, hijacker, pirate; *Obsolete* knight of the road, footpad.

◇ *Word origin: Bandit* comes from Italian *bandito*, outlaw, and is ultimately derived from Medieval Latin *bannire*, to banish.

bandy *v. We can't take you seriously when you just bandy words:* toss back and forth, trade, swap, exchange, interchange, barter, shuffle, play with, toss about.

bane *n.* **1** *Dirt and noise from the nearby motorway were the bane of her existence:* plague, curse, scourge, torment, nuisance; affliction, blight, burden, woe, canker, poison, ruin, ruination; pain in the neck, thorn in the flesh, fly in the ointment; disaster, calamity, tragedy, detriment, destroyer. **2** *Beware, my lord — there's bane in that cup:* poison, toxin, venom.

Ant. 1 blessing, treasure, treat, prize, bright spot, joy, pleasure; comfort, consolation, solace, balm, apple of one's eye. **2** antitoxin.

◇ *Word origin: Bane* comes from Old English *bana*, murderer. The word first appeared in the sense of "poison" in a 1398 treatise *On the Properties of Things*, which states that "henbane is mannis bane" — in other words, henbane is poisonous to man. It is still found in the names of poisonous plants.

bang *n.* **1** *The balloon burst with a bang. He closed the door with a bang:* loud sound, sudden noise, report, boom, pop, clap, burst, slam, crash, explosion. **2** *The falling branch gave her a terrific bang on the head:* blow, hit, knock, smack, clout, rap, box, wallop, whack, tap, slap, cuff, thwack, thump, buffet.
—*v.* **3** *The baby kept banging his spoon on the plate. Don't bang the door!:* strike noisily, beat, close loudly, slam.
—*adv.* **4** *The car rolled bang into the telegraph pole:* headlong, suddenly, smack, slap, crashingly.

◇ *Word origin: Bang*, a heavy, noisy blow, comes from Old Norse *bang*, hammering (from *banga*, hammer). Our other word *bang*, a fringe of hair, is a shortened form of *bangtail*, a horse with a short tail, so called because it is cut off abruptly or quick as a *bang*.

"This is the way the world ends
Not with a bang but a whimper."— *T. S. Eliot*

---

banish *v.* **1** *The king banished the traitor from the realm:* exile, expel, eject, evict, outlaw, deport, cast out, turn out, drive out, send away, dismiss, send to Coventry; excommunicate. **2** *Banish gloom from your thoughts:* ban, shut out, bar, dismiss, put away, exclude; cast out, drive out, eliminate, remove, get rid of, erase, cast away, send away, drop, dispel, dislodge, discharge, eradicate, evict, oust, discard, eject, reject.

Ant. 1, 2 invite, admit, accept, receive, receive with open arms, welcome, entertain; harbour, shelter; foster, nourish, cherish.

bank¹ *n.* **1** *A high bank of earth surrounded the fortress:* embankment, mound, heap, pile, mass; ridge, rise, knoll, dune, dike, parapet, barrow, terrace. **2** *The boaters picknicked on the bank of the river:* shore, side, edge, margin, strand, brink. **3** *The fishing boats headed for Dogger Bank:* shoal, reef, shallow, bar, shelf, sandbank, flat.
—*v.* **4** *The plough banked up the snow along the side of the road:* pile up, heap, amass. **5** *The road banks sharply on that curve:* have one side higher than the other, slope, slant, tilt, tip.

Ant. 1 ditch, trench; valley, dip. **3** deep water, depths. **4, 5** level, plane, smooth out.

bank² *n. A bank of spotlights lit up the scene:* row, tier, rank, line, file, string, series, array, succession, train, chain.

bank³ *n.* **1** *The bank cashed his cheque:* banking house, financial institution; trust company, savings bank, commercial bank; exchequer. **2** *The hospital maintained its own blood bank:* repository, depository, storehouse; store, stockpile, supply, accumulation, fund, savings, reserve, reservoir.
—*v.* **3** *I bank at the National Westminster. She banks £10 a week:* transact business with a bank; deposit money in a bank, save, keep.

◇ *Word origin: Bank* comes from French *banc*, bench. This originally meant a money-changer's counter. The diminutive form of the same French word gives us *banquet* (literally, "little table").

bankrupt *adj. Severe business losses left the company bankrupt:* ruined, failed, without funds, unable to pay debts, insolvent, broke, wiped out; destitute, indigent, penniless, impoverished, depleted, exhausted.

Ant. solvent, sound; prosperous.

◇ *Word origin:* The *-rupt* in *bankrupt* is ultimately derived from Latin *ruptus*, broken, which also gives us *rupture*. The expressions "break the bank" and "broke" (meaning insolvent) are related.

banner *n. The king's banner showed his coat of arms. Welcoming banners hung from the balconies:* standard, flag, colours, ensign, pennant, pendant, streamer, burgee.

banquet *n.* **1** *A victory banquet was served in the royal dining-room:* feast, repast, dinner, symposium.
—*v.* **2** *The guests banqueted until midnight:* feast, dine, eat one's fill, revel.
Ant. 1 snack, light meal; fasting, starvation; abstinence. **2** fast, starve; abstain.
◇ *Word origin: Banquet* entered English from French in the late 15th century. The French word means literally a small bench, as does the corresponding Italian word *banchetto.*

"Be not made a beggar by banqueting upon borrowing." —*Ecclesiasticus 18: 33*

---

banter *n.* **1** *We laughed at the banter of the two old friends:* kidding, joking, ribbing, persiflage, jesting, repartee, word play, waggery, raillery, ragging, badinage, chaff, chaffing.
—*v.* **2** *He stood on the corner bantering with friends:* kid, rib, taunt, mock, jolly, twit, chaff, joke, ride, needle, tease.

baptism *n.* **1** *The baptism of new members of the church will take place tomorrow:* Christian sacrament of initiation, christening; sprinkling, immersion; spiritual rebirth, purification. **2** *The battle was his baptism as a soldier:* initiation, rite of passage; introduction, beginning.
Ant. 2 last act; farewell.

baptize *v.* **1** *The minister baptized the baby:* administer the Christian sacrament of baptism to. **2** *The child was baptized Robert:* christen, name, dub.
◇ *Word origin: Baptize* comes from Greek *baptizein,* to dip or immerse.

bar *n.* **1** *The monkey rattled the bars of his cage:* pole, rod, stick, stake, rail, pale, paling, grating, rib; (*variously*) cross-piece, crossbar, lever, crowbar, jemmy, spar, sprit. **2** *The bar of soap slipped from his grasp:* block, tablet, cake. **3** *The boat ran aground on the bar:* sandbar, reef, shoal, shallow, spit, bank, shelf, flat. **4** *We had a sandwich and a beer at a neighbouring bar. He opened a snack-bar. Take your glass to the bar:* tavern, saloon, taproom, cocktail lounge, lounge; public house, pub, alehouse, inn; serving counter, long table; canteen, sandwich-bar. **5** *A bar of light fell across the darkened room:* band, strip, stripe, ribbon, streak, stroke, beam, belt, slice, line. **6** *Near-sightedness is a bar to becoming a pilot:* obstacle, barrier, obstruction, impediment, stumbling-block, block, check, curb, snag, catch, hindrance, constraint, restraint, restriction, limitation. **7** *After finishing her legal studies she was called to the bar:* legal profession, body of lawyers. **8** *His misbehaviour brought him before the bar of public opinion:* court, tribunal; judgement. **9** *The song has 24 bars:* measure.
—*v.* **10** *Bar the barn door so that the cows can't get out:* put a bar across, lock, bolt, fasten; block up, close up, barricade. **11** *He has been barred from practising medicine:* ban, prohibit, enjoin, stay, stop, restrain, prevent, forbid, obstruct, block, debar, disallow, restrict, limit, exclude, preclude, impede. **12** *Reporters were barred from the court:* exclude, shut out, lock out; banish, expel, evict, eject, exile, oust, cast out.
Ant. 3 deep water, depths. **6** aid, help, advantage, boon, benefit, edge. **10** open, unlock, clear. **11, 12** allow, permit, let, accept; admit, invite, welcome, receive.
◇ *Spelling tip:* Remember the spelling rule: before adding a suffix beginning with a vowel, double the final consonant of all one-syllable words that end in a single consonant preceded by a single vowel. Thus, *bar* becomes *baRRed* and *baRRing.*

barb *n.* **1** *The fish-hook has a barb at the tip:* spur, backward point, point, spike, prong, tine, snag, bristle, nib, cusp, prickle, barbule, spicule. **2** *We're tired of your nasty barbs:* disagreeable remark, sarcasm, insult, complaint, criticism, dig, jibe, cut.
◇ *Word origin: Barb* comes from Latin *barba,* beard, beardlike projection. This same Latin word also gives us *barber.*

barbarian *n.* **1** *The city barricaded itself against the invading barbarians:* savage, alien, outlaw. **2** *Young barbarians have defaced public buildings:* hoodlum, ruffian, rowdy, tough, punk, hood, hooligan, delinquent, vandal, bully, lout. **3** *Barbarians in the audience jeered at the composer's new work:* anti-intellectual, lowbrow, philistine, vulgarian, illiterate, ignoramus, troglodyte, yahoo.
—*adj.* **4** *The emperor commanded a great wall to be built against barbarian invaders:* savage, alien. **5** *The artist accused the public of having barbarian tastes:* uncultivated, uncultured, lowbrow, crude, philistine, unsophisticated, uncouth.
Ant. 1 native, citizen. **3** highbrow, intellectual, connoisseur, sophisticate; *plural* literati, cognoscenti. **5** cultivated, cultured, highbrow, intellectual; refined, literate, humane, liberal.
◇ *Word origin: Barbarian* comes from Greek *barbaros,* non-Hellenic, hence foreign, rude.

barbaric *adj.* **1** *The Huns were notorious for their barbaric cruelty. The tribal dance was a spectacle of barbaric splendour:* barbarian, uncivilized, barbarous, savage, wild. **2** *His behaviour to the guests was barbaric and embarrassing:* coarse, uncouth, crude, ill-mannered, vulgar, rude, unpolished, uncivilized, boorish.
Ant. civilized, cultivated, gentlemanly, gracious, polite.
◇ *Usage note: Barbaric* means of or like a barbarian, but its connotations are not always unfavourable (def. **1,** above): *barbaric customs, barbaric splendour. Barbarous,* however,

only means of or like the cruelty or coarseness associated with barbarians and is always unfavourable: *a barbarous murder, a barbarous tyrant, barbarous taste.*

barbarity *n. The pirates treated their captives with barbarity:* savageness, cruelty, brutality, ruthlessness.
Ant. humaneness, gentleness, mildness.

barbarous *adj.* **1** *It's barbarous to keep a large dog cooped up like that:* cruel, brutal, mean, inhuman, vicious, harsh, barbaric, outrageous. **2** *The letter was written in barbarous English:* coarse, crude, rough, vulgar, crass, impolite.
Ant. 1 humane, merciful, compassionate, lenient, humanitarian, benevolent, benign.
◇ *Usage note:* See BARBARIC.

barber *n.* **1** *My barber recommended a new hair tonic:* hairdresser, hair-stylist.
—*v.* **2** *You need to barber that beard of yours:* cut, trim, tonsure, shave; dress, arrange.
◇ *Word origin: Barber* goes back to Latin *barba*, beard.

bard *n.* **1** *The Homeric poems were composed and sung by bards:* poet-singer, epic poet, poet. **2** *A local bard read his poetry at the eisteddfod:* narrative poet, writer, versifier, rhymer, rhymster, poetaster; minstrel, troubadour.
◇ *Word origin: Bards* held an important place in early Celtic society. According to a second-century A.D. Roman writer, "*Bardus* is the Gaulish name for a member of the class of poet-singers who sing the praises of brave men." Ultimately, the word goes back to an Indo-European root meaning praise.

bare *adj.* **1** *The engineers worked bare to the waist in the boiling sun:* stripped, naked, nude, undressed, unclothed, unrobed, disrobed, uncovered, unclad, exposed, peeled. **2** *Let's hang up some paintings on those bare walls. The cupboard was bare:* empty, without contents, void, vacant, blank; unadorned, unembellished, naked, undecorated, unornamented; austere, stark, plain. **3** *The carpet was worn bare from years of use:* threadbare, bald, thin, napless, worn. **4** *We existed on nothing but the bare necessities:* just sufficient, just enough, scant, mere, marginal, meagre, supportable, endurable. **5** *The detective outlined the bare facts of the case. Let's have the bare truth:* plain, undisguised, stark, bald, simple, fundamental, essential, elementary, unelaborated, straightforward, unadorned, unembellished, unvarnished, uncoloured.
—*v.* **6** *Bare your head when the flag is hoisted:* uncover, undress, strip, unveil, undrape; unsheathe, denude. **7** *The poet bared his heart to the world:* open, reveal, uncover, show, expose, divest, unmask, offer.
Ant. 1 clothed, dressed, clad, covered, attired, robed, apparelled. **2** full, overflowing, well-stocked, crammed; adorned, embellished, ornamented, dressed up. **3** thick. **4** abundant, profuse, copious, plentiful, bounteous, ample. **6** cover, clothe, dress, veil, robe. **7** hide, conceal, mask; suppress.
◇ *Spelling tip:* Remember the spelling rule: a one-syllable word ending in a consonant and a silent *e* drops the silent *e* before adding a suffix beginning with a vowel. Thus *bare* becomes *baring.*

barefaced *adj. He persisted in the most barefaced lies about the accident:* brazen, impudent, shameless; transparent, palpable, bald; bold, unabashed, insolent, brash, fresh, cheeky, forward, flippant, glib.
Ant. modest, reticent, shy.

barely *adv. When the rescuers found the castaway he was barely alive. A pound of sugar is barely enough for a week:* almost not, only just, just, scarcely, hardly, no more than, just about, almost, slightly, sparingly, scantily, meagrely, faintly; by the skin of one's teeth.
Ant. fully, completely; abundantly, amply, copiously, profusely.
◇ *Usage note: Barely* means "almost not" and thus has negative force.

bargain *n.* **1** *We made a bargain that I would do the work and you would supply the materials:* agreement, compact, pact, promise, pledge, accord, understanding, settlement, arrangement, contract, transaction, covenant, treaty. **2** *At that low price the house is a bargain:* fair deal, good buy.
—*v.***3** *I refuse to bargain over the price:* negotiate, haggle, dicker, barter, higgle, deal.
Ant. 2 extravagance, white elephant, swindle.

bark[1] *n.* **1** *The bark of a dog sounded in the night:* yelp, yap, howl, howling, bay, cry; woof.
—*v.* **2** *The dog barks at strangers:* yelp, woof, yap, howl, bay. **3** *The captain barked a command at the troops:* shout, bellow, yell, roar, shriek, cry out.

bark[2] *n.* **1** *Beavers had stripped away the tree's bark:* covering, husk, sheathing, skin, casing, rind, peel, *Scientific* periderm.
—*v.* **2** *He barked his shins on the doorpost:* scrape, skin, abrade, rub, flay, strip.

baroque *adj. The mansion was built in a baroque style:* extravagant, florid, ornate, flamboyant.
Ant. classical, simple.
◇ *Usage note:* Although *baroque* is often used in a general way, technically it refers to an ornate style of architecture, furniture, and art popular in Europe in the late 17th and early 18th centuries.
◇ *Word origin: Baroque* comes from Portuguese *barroco*, an irregular pearl, or, figuratively, something grotesque, odd, whimsical — and hence quintessentially *baroque.*

barrage *n.* **1** *The cannons kept up a barrage of fire over the enemy lines:* bombardment, shelling, salvo, volley, cannonade, fusillade, battery, curtain of fire. **2** *The reporters fired a barrage of questions at the mayor:* volley, salvo, fusillade, deluge, outpouring, blast, burst, stream, shower, spray.

barrel *n.* **1** *The grocer offered barrels full of biscuits and pickles. We bought a barrel of apples:* cask, keg, tub, hogshead, butt, drum, tun: the amount a barrel can hold, **2** *The rifle barrel was hot:* tube, tubular part (as of a gun or a pen).

barren *adj.* **1** *The farmer was cheated when he bought a barren cow:* infertile, sterile, infecund, (*of cows*) farrow. **2** *No one could raise crops on this barren land:* infertile, unproductive, unfruitful, depleted, waste, desolate, austere; arid, dry. **3** *It's a barren topic, not worth discussion:* unproductive, unfruitful, fruitless, unrewarding, ineffectual, useless, futile; uninteresting, dull, prosaic, uninformative, lacklustre, uninstructive, uninspiring, stale.

Ant. productive, fertile. **1** fecund, prolific. **2** lush, rich, luxuriant. **3** useful, worthwhile, fruitful, profitable, interesting, instructive.

barricade *n.* **1** *The rebels fired from behind barricades:* barrier, rampart, bulwark, blockade, obstruction, impediment, obstacle, fence.

—v. **2** *The police barricaded the streets and so prevented the robber from escaping:* block, protect or shut in with a barrier.

◇ *Word origin: Barricade* is from Spanish *barrico*, barrel. (The first barricades were barrels filled with earth and stones, set up in Paris on the Day of the Barricades in 1588, when supporters of the Catholic League rebelled against Henry III of France.)

barrier *n.* **1** *The stallion leapt over the wooden barrier. The castle's defensive barrier was 20 feet deep:* obstruction; (*variously*) obstacle, barricade, blockade, fence, wall, hedge; ditch, trench, moat. **2** *Not knowing a foreign language is a barrier to enjoying travel abroad. The country set up trade barriers against imported goods:* obstacle, obstruction, impediment, hindrance, handicap, bar, difficulty, restriction, limitation, stumbling-block, hurdle.

Ant. 1 entrance, opening, passage, way. **2** aid, help, advantage; encouragement, spur.

barter *v. The Indians would barter beaver pelts for weapons:* trade, swap, exchange, interchange.

◇ *Word origin: Barter* comes from Old French *barater*, to exchange.

base[1] *n.* **1** *The lamp stands on a circular base:* support, pedestal, stand, bottom, foundation, underpinning, substructure, ground, groundwork, bed. **2** *The base of his argument is that our price is too high:* foundation, essence, principle, root, core, heart, key, rudiment, ground, source. **3** *The soup has a tomato base:* essential ingredient, principal constituent. **4** *The weary troops marched back to the base:* camp, station, post, billet, installation, garrison.

—v. **5** *This song is based on an old folk tune:* derive from, model on, found on. **6** *The company's headquarters is based in Paris. The British home fleet was based at Scapa Flow until 1957:* station, garrison, locate, situate, install, billet, ground, establish, place.

Ant. 1 top, summit, apex, zenith, peak, pinnacle; superstructure. **2, 3** non-essentials, frills.

◇ *Word origin: Base, basic, basis,* and even *basement* go back to Greek *basis*, pedestal.

base[2] *adj.* **1** *Zinc and brass are base metals:* inferior, poor quality; alloyed, impure, debased, adulterated, spurious. **2** *Cheating at cards is a base practice:* mean, vile, low, contemptible, despicable, ignoble, shameful, immoral, bad, scoundrelly, villainous, sinful, wicked, dishonourable, dastardly, scurvy, iniquitous, depraved, degenerate, vulgar, gross, cowardly, corrupt, sordid, craven, foul, faithless, nefarious, ignominious, infamous, dissolute, debased, degraded, unworthy, disgraceful, black-hearted, evil-minded, unprincipled, insidious, detestable, reprehensible, discreditable, disreputable, sneaky, underhand, *Slang* dirty, fast.

Ant. 1 precious, valuable, rare; pure, unadulterated, unalloyed. **2** virtuous, honourable, honest, just, above-board, righteous, upright, moral, ethical, lofty, good, admirable, heroic.

◇ *Word origin: Base,* mean or vile, goes back to Late Latin *bassus*, low, short. This may be related to Greek *basis*, meaning pedestal, base, which gives us *base*[1] (see above).

baseless *adj. The story is founded on a baseless rumour:* unfounded, groundless, ungrounded, without basis, unsupported, unsubstantiated, uncorroborated, unjustified, unjustifiable, unsound.

Ant. well-founded, well-grounded, supported, substantiated, corroborated, factual.

bashful *adj. She is too bashful to speak to strangers:* shy, timid, easily embarrassed, demure, retiring, unconfident, timorous, modest, diffident, reticent, reserved, shrinking, constrained, uncertain, shame-faced, sheepish, confused, blushing.

Ant. aggressive, brash, bold, brazen, impudent, immodest, forward, shameless, intrepid; conceited, egoistic, egotistic, confident, self-assured, fearless, arrogant.

◇ *Word origin: Bashful* is a variant of *abash* plus the suffix *-ful*, hence "full of shame or confusion."

"Strange to the world, he wore a bashful look,
The Fields his study, Nature was his book."

—*Robert Bloomfield*

---

basic *adj.* **1** *The basic ingredient of the dish is ham:* fundamental, elementary, essential, key, core, base, prime, primary, foundational.

—n. **2** *Reading ability is one of the basics of education:* fundamental, essential, core, base, foundation, underpinning.

Ant. 1 accompanying, supporting, supplementary, complementary, secondary; unimportant, trivial, minor. **2** unessential; frill, frivolity, triviality.

◇ *Word origin:* See BASE[1].

basis Plural **bases** *n. Charity toward others is the basis of her philosophy:* base, underpinning, ground, foundation, touchstone, cornerstone, fundamental, essential, principle.
◇ *Word origin:* See BASE[1].

bask *v.* **1** *The skiers basked by the fire:* warm oneself, toast oneself, soak up warmth; sunbathe. **2** *He basked in his wife's admiration:* revel, wallow, luxuriate, delight.

bastard *n.* **1** *The king sired three bastards:* illegitimate child, natural child, love-child.
—*adj.* **2** *He learned to speak a kind of bastard French:* impure, irregular, imperfect, inferior, hybrid, counterfeit, misbegotten, spurious.
◇ *Word origin: Bastard* comes from an Old French phrase *fils de bast,* meaning "child of the pack-saddle," referring to the use of the saddle as an impromptu bed.

bastion *n.* **1** *Foot soldiers stormed the mighty bastion:* fortress, fort, citadel; rampart, breastwork, barbette. **2** *The university is a bastion of intellectual freedom:* bulwark, stronghold, citadel.

batch *n. The first batch of cakes was burnt. The prisoners were led out in batches and shot:* group, bunch, lot, amount, stock, collection, crowd, number, aggregate, quantity.

bathos *n. The play is full of melodramatic bathos:* sentimentality, sentimentalism, mawkishness, false pathos, soppiness, slush, slushiness, mush, mushiness, corn.

batter *v.* **1** *Enemy fire battered the walls of the fort:* beat, buffet, smash against, pound, pummel, smite, lash. **2** *Police battered down the door of the thieves' hide-out:* pound, smash, break, beat, shatter; crush. **3** *The old hat was battered beyond recognition:* beat up, maul, mangle, knock out of shape.

battle *n.* **1** *The Battle of Waterloo was decisive. The two boxers had a championship battle:* combat, clash, campaign, war, warfare, skirmish, set-to, fight; contest, encounter, affray, fray, conflict, engagement, action; duel, bout. **2** *Martin Luther King led the battle for equal rights for blacks:* struggle, fight, contest; dispute, controversy, agitation, debate, confrontation, crusade.
—*v.* **3** *The two armies battled all night. The two boxers battled until the final bell. He battled his way against the wind:* war, fight, clash, skirmish, duel, meet, engage; struggle, contend, contest, combat, brawl, tussle.
Ant. 1 armistice, peace, truce; concord, agreement. **2** agreement, accord.
◇ *Word origin: Battle, batter,* and *battery* come from Latin *battuere,* to beat.

bawdy *adj. The old drinking-song was bawdy but amusing:* earthy, lusty, risqué, ribald, indecent, coarse, gross, licentious, blue, suggestive, sexual, sexy, indecorous, immodest, improper, indelicate, vulgar, lewd, dirty, rude.
Ant. decent, modest, delicate, clean.

bawl *v.* **1** *The nursery was full of babies bawling:* cry, wail, howl, yowl, squall, blubber, weep. **2** *The captain bawled for the sergeant:* shout, bellow, yell, roar, cry out, howl, call, call out, clamour.
Ant. 1 laugh. **2** whisper, murmur, mutter.

bay[1] *n. The ship dropped anchor in a quiet bay:* cove, inlet, estuary, arm of the sea, sound, basin, natural harbour; firth, fiord, bight, road, lagoon.

bay[2] *n. A small table and chair stood in the dining bay:* alcove, nook, niche, recess, compartment, carrel.

bay[3] *n.* **1** *The hunters followed the bay of the hounds:* barking, howling, cry, clamour, yelping, yapping. **2 at bay.** *A bear at bay is very dangerous:* cornered, trapped, forced to stand and fight.
—*v.* **3** *The hound bayed mournfully:* howl, bark, yelp, yap, cry.

bazaar *n.* **1** *We bought this rug at the bazaar in Marrakesh:* market, market-place, outdoor market, mart, shopping-centre, exchange. **2** *Mother baked this cake for the church bazaar:* charity fair, charity sale; fair, bring-and-buy sale.
◇ *Usage note:* See BIZARRE.
◇ *Word origin: Bazaar* comes from Persian *bāzār,* market.

be *v.* **1** *There are five of us in our family:* exist, live, subsist. **2** *The party will be in a week:* occur, happen, come to pass, take place, befall. **3** *Will you be at the party after I get there?* Gone With the Wind *will always be my favourite film:* be present, endure, last, continue, remain, stay, persist.
◇ *Word origin: Be* is related to words meaning much the same thing throughout the Indo-European languages. The equivalent word in Greek means "to bring forth, grow." The Sanskrit equivalent means "to become."

beach *n. The waves receded from the beach:* shore, sea-shore, strand, coast.

beacon *n. The ship's crew watched for the flashing beacon of their home port:* light, beam, signal; (*variously*) lighthouse, lighted buoy, landmark, sea-mark, watch-tower, pharos; watch-fire.
◇ *Word origin: Beacon* comes from Old English *bēacn,* sign, portent. The related Old English verb *bēcnan,* meaning "make a mute signal to," gives us *beckon.*

bead *n.* **1** *She wore a string of beads round her neck:* small pieces of glass, stones, wood, etc., used for ornament, as on a necklace. **2** *Beads of sweat covered his brow. Beads of gold dust covered the counter top:* drop, droplet, globule, little ball, blob, pellet, spherule, bubble; speck, particle, dot, pill.
◇ *Word origin:* The first *beads* were rosary beads used in counting prayers. The word comes from Old English *gebed,* prayer.

beam *n.* **1** *The carpenter was raising the roof-beam:* (*in technical use*) horizontal support; structural support, prop, girder, rafter, joist, brace, spar, stud, trestle, timber. **2** *A beam of light penetrated the darkness:* ray, streak, stream, gleam, glimmer, glint, glow, radiation. **3** *The ship was very broad in the beam:* widest part, width, expanse, breadth.
—*v.* **4** *Television and radio stations beamed the news to the country. A searchlight beamed in the distance:* transmit, emit, radiate, broadcast; gleam, glimmer, glitter, glow, glare, shine. **5** *Her entire face beamed with happiness:* shine, gleam, glow, radiate.
◇ *Word origin: Beam* comes from Old English *bēam*, tree.

bear *v.* **1** *These columns bear the weight of the roof. Our office bears the brunt of the work. He bears responsibility well:* support, sustain, maintain, carry, uphold, shoulder, take on, endure, hold up under, tolerate; underpin, bolster. **2** *Donkeys bore supplies up the steep mountain track:* transport, carry, tote, convoy, bring, haul, take, convey. **3** *She bore three fine sons:* give birth to, bring into being, bring forth, deliver; reproduce, propagate, germinate, spawn, hatch, whelp, drop. **4** *Apple trees bear blossoms in early spring:* produce, develop, bring forth, give, yield; engender, create, generate, render. **5** *Bear these thoughts with you as you go out into the world:* carry, keep in mind, hold close, harbour, cherish, take. **6** *She can't bear the sound of chalk scraping on a blackboard:* tolerate, abide, endure, stand, put up with, stomach, brook, take, undergo, submit to, suffer, brave. **7** *This information bears strongly on the matter under discussion:* pertain, relate, apply, refer, appertain, concern, be pertinent to, affect, have bearing on, have respect to, touch upon. **8** *This matter bears investigation:* warrant, invite, admit, be susceptible of, permit, allow, encourage. **9** *You bear a strong likeness to my sister. The letter bears the salutation "Dear Sir":* exhibit, manifest, display, show, have, carry, contain, possess, be marked with, be equipped with, be furnished with, wear. **10** *To get this door open you have to bear hard against it:* press, push, bear down, force, drive. **11** *Bear right at the junction:* go in the direction of, aim for, turn, tend, bend, curve, diverge, deviate.
Ant. **1** rest on; reject, cast off, throw off. **2** put down; leave. **4** shed, drop, loose. **5** put aside, forget; relinquish. **9** hide, conceal. **10** pull.
◇ *Usage note:* The basic forms of the verb *to bear* are *bear* (present tense), *bore* (past tense), and *borne* (past participle). Thus: *The tree bears fruit every year. The tree bore fruit last year. It has borne fruit before.*

beard *n.* **1** *The prospector had a long beard. John sported a two-day growth of beard:* whiskers; bristles, stubble, *Slang* five-o'clock shadow.
—*v.* **2** *Daniel bearded the lion in its den:* corner, bring to bay, trap, confront, face, defy, brave, dare.

bearded *adj. The penny shows George V with a bearded face:* bewhiskered, whiskered, unshaven, hairy, hirsute, shaggy, bushy, bristly.
Ant. clean-shaven, smooth-shaven.

bearing *n.* **1** *The old judge has a regal bearing:* carriage, mien, manner, air, presence; demeanour, behaviour, attitude, comportment, deportment, port. **2** *Your remarks have no bearing on our discussion:* relevance, pertinence, significance, reference, application, applicability, connection, concern, relation, relationship, association; sense, meaning, import, importance. **3** *These fruit trees are past bearing:* reproducing, reproduction, giving birth, germination, procreation, propagation, producing, breeding, conception. **4** **bearings.** *We lost our bearings in the darkness:* sense of direction, orientation, direction, way, course, position.
Ant. **2** irrelevance, insignificance.

beast *n.* **1** *The lion is the king of beasts:* animal, brute. **2** *You were a beast to insult her needlessly:* brute, cad, swine, pig, cur, rat.
Ant. **1** man. **2** gentleman, lady; *Informal* angel, sweetheart, gem.

beastly *adj. The weather has been beastly. He's a beastly little man:* unpleasant, disgusting, disagreeable, nasty, vile, loathsome, abominable, contemptible; cruel, inhuman, bestial, gross, coarse, depraved, swinish; bad, terrible, awful, dreadful, deplorable.
Ant. pleasant, agreeable, appealing, admirable; humane, sweet, sensitive, gentlemanly, ladylike; good, fine, wonderful.

beat *v.* **1** *Stop beating on the door! Hear how he beats that drum:* hit, strike, pound, wallop, whack, thwack, knock, smack, punch, slap, smite, clout, flail, bat, tap, rap, bang, hammer. **2** *They beat him within an inch of his life:* thrash, pummel, batter, maul, trounce; whip, flog, flail, scourge, switch, strap, club, cane. **3** *Alexander the Great beat every opponent between Greece and India:* defeat, be victorious over, triumph over, win over, overcome, overpower, vanquish, best; conquer, crush, rout, destroy, repel, repulse, quell, put down, master, subdue, whip, lick, clobber, trounce, drub. **4** *He beat all competition in the elections:* win over, excel, surpass, outdo, prevail over, predominate, eclipse, overcome, defeat, thrash, carry all before one. **5** *Her heart beat madly with fright. The sea-gull beat its wings against the air:* pulsate, pulse, throb, pound, palpitate, flutter, quiver, fluctuate, vibrate, quake, shake, twitch, go pit-a-pat; flap. **6** *Beat the egg whites until they are stiff:* whip; stir vigorously, mix.
—*n.* **7** *The room resounded with each beat of the gong:* blow, stroke, strike, hit, whack, rap, slap. **8** *The music had the familiar beat of a waltz:* cadence, time, rhythm, metre, measure,

stress, accent. **9** *They felt safer knowing that the policeman was on his beat:* route, rounds, circuit, path, course, way; area, zone, territory, domain, realm.

Ant. 1, 2 caress, stroke, pat, pet; soothe, comfort; shield, protect, guard. **3, 4** lose, suffer defeat, go down in defeat, surrender; fall, fail, get the worst of, go under.

beatific *adj. The Madonna's smile was beatific:* blissful, serene, heavenly, divine, sublime, glorious, exalted, transcendental, angelic, saintly; enraptured, rapturous, rapt, ecstatic.

Ant. worldly, sophisticated; mundane, common, coarse, crude.

◇ *Word origin: Beatific* is ultimately derived from Latin *beatus*, happy.

beatitude *n. Prolonged meditation had given him an aura of beatitude:* bliss, felicity, blessedness, saintliness; exaltation, exaltedness, transcendence, transfiguration; rapture, ecstasy, euphoria.

Ant. despair, hopelessness, dolour.

beau Plural **beaux** *n.* **1** *Do you think Helen will marry her new beau?:* boy-friend, sweetheart, young man, fellow, suitor, admirer, flame, gentleman caller, squire, swain; fiancé, betrothed; love, beloved, lover. **2** *The young beau flirted with all the ladies:* ladies' man, cavalier, dandy, fop, swell, playboy, gay blade, blade; young blood, popinjay, coxcomb; nob, spark, lad, buck, toff.

beautiful *adj.* **1** *His sister is a beautiful woman. The music is beautiful:* pretty, handsome, good-looking, fine-looking, lovely, gorgeous, attractive, exquisite, ravishing, comely, fair, bonny, seemly, beauteous, pulchritudinous, resplendent; pleasing, enjoyable, captivating. **2** *You did a beautiful job of cleaning up the kitchen:* very good, excellent, first-rate, wonderful, fine, splendid, admirable, great, stupendous, commendable, estimable, worthy.

Ant. 1 ugly, unattractive, ill-looking, hideous, grotesque; unpleasant, bad, awful, disgusting, repulsive, repugnant, revolting. **2** bad, awful, terrible, lousy, second-rate.

> **Exploring the Word:** The Latin word *bellus* means pretty and gives us our words *beauty* and *bauble*, literally a pretty toy. The French masculine form based on this Latin word gives us *beau*, literally "pretty man" (*"Beau"* was the nickname of the dandy, George Brummell), and the French feminine form gives us *belle*, literally "pretty girl."

beautify *v. Planting flowers along the promenade will help to beautify the town:* enhance, embellish, adorn, ornament, improve, grace, dress up, smarten up.

Ant. spoil, mar, disfigure, deface, besmirch.

beauty *n.* **1** *Paris is a city of great beauty:* loveliness, handsomeness, good looks, pulchritude, attractiveness, splendour, resplendence, magnificence. **2** *The actress is one of the great beauties of our time:* beautiful woman, beautiful girl, belle, goddess, Venus; *Slang* knock-out, beaut, doll, stunner, pin-up, good-looker. **3** *One of the beauties of the plan is its simplicity:* advantage, attraction, feature, good thing, excellence, benefit, grace.

Ant. 1 ugliness, repulsiveness, unpleasantness. **2** *Slang* witch, bag, hag. **3** disadvantage, detraction, shortcoming, flaw.

◇ *Spelling tip:* As is common in English, the *y* of *beauty* changes to an *i* when a suffix is added: *beautY, beautIes, beautIfy, beautIful.* But *beautEous* is unusual, the *y* of *beauty* becomes an *e!*

beckon *v.* **1** *The leader beckoned the others to follow him:* signal, motion, wave at, wave on, gesture, gesticulate, crook a finger at. **2** *The romance of the sea beckoned the old sailor:* entice, lure, allure, invite, attract, draw, pull, call, summon, coax.

Ant. 2 repel, repulse, *Informal* put off.

◇ *Word origin: Beckon* comes from Old English *bēcnan*, to signal or beckon. A related Old English word meaning "a signal" gives us *beacon.*

becoming *adj.* **1** *His behaviour was not very becoming for a gentleman:* suitable, appropriate, proper, seemly, fit, fitting, befitting, worthy, meet, congruous, consistent, in keeping. **2** *Blue is a very becoming colour:* flattering, enhancing, attractive, pretty, good-looking; apt, harmonious, congenial, compatible.

Ant. unbecoming. **1** unsuitable, inappropriate, improper, unseemly, unfit, unfitting, unbefitting, unworthy, incongruous, inconsistent with, out of keeping, indecorous. **2** ugly, unattractive.

bed *n.* **1** *The bed needs a new mattress. The cowboy made a bed on the ground out of his saddle and blankets:* bedstead, place to sleep, bunk, pallet, berth; (*for infants*) cradle, cot. **2** *Serve the shrimp cocktail on a bed of lettuce:* base, bottom, floor, foundation. **3** *There's a bed of anthracite in this mountain:* layer, stratum, band, belt, zone; seam, deposit, vein, lode. **4** *Plant a bed of roses by the garage:* plot, patch, bank.

bedazzle *v.* **1** *The bright lights bedazzled her:* daze, confuse, dumbfound, bewilder, stupefy, nonplus, disconcert, befuddle, fluster. **2** *Her charm bedazzled him:* dazzle, confound, astound, stagger, flabbergast, overwhelm, overpower, enchant, captivate, sweep one off one's feet.

bedlam *n. The argument turned the party into bedlam:* scene of wild confusion, uproar, pandemonium, madhouse, tumult, turmoil.

◇ *Word origin: Bedlam* comes from the name of *St. Mary of Bethlehem*, a lunatic asylum in London during the Middle Ages. (The old pronunciation of *Bethlehem* was *bedlam.*)

bedroom *n. The house has three bedrooms:* sleeping room, bedchamber, boudoir, dormitory.

beer *n. He ordered a cheese sandwich and a bottle of beer:* (*variously*) lager, ale, stout, porter, mild, dark, bitter, light, small beer, bock; *Slang* booze, nog.

◇ *Word origin: Beer* is ultimately derived from Latin *bibere,* to drink.

"Oh, Elizabeth, your justice would freeze beer!" —*Arthur Miller*

---

befall *v. Bad luck may befall you at any time:* happen, occur, come to pass, ensue, chance, fall, follow, betide.

befitting *adj. A formal gown is befitting if you wish to attend the diplomatic reception:* suitable, appropriate, fitting, fit, proper, apt, seemly, right, decent, becoming; relevant.

Ant. unsuitable, inappropriate, unfit, unfitting, unbecoming, improper, unseemly, wrong; irrelevant, meaningless.

beforehand *adv. If you wanted soup for lunch you should have told me beforehand:* earlier, sooner, before, before now, ahead of time, in advance, before the fact, in time.

Ant. afterwards, after.

befriend *v. He has always tried to befriend the down-and-outs:* make friends with, get acquainted with, associate with, consort with, fraternize with; assist, help, help out, give aid to, succour, comfort, minister to, protect, defend, hold out a helping hand to, look after, sympathize with, embrace, welcome, support, sustain, stick by, stand by, side with, uphold, take under one's wing.

Ant. alienate, estrange.

befuddle *v.* **1** *The new arrival was befuddled by the rapid-fire conversation:* confuse, perplex, bewilder, puzzle, baffle, confound, disorganize, daze, unsettle, rattle, fluster, muddle, mix up, knock off balance. **2** *The wine had befuddled him:* addle, stupefy, make groggy, intoxicate, make drunk, make tipsy, inebriate.

Ant. **1** make clear to, illuminate, bring into focus. **2** sober, clear one's head.

beg *v.* **1** *During the Depression, many men had to beg for a living:* seek charity, solicit, crave alms, *Informal* cadge, sponge, hustle, go from door to door, be on one's uppers. **2** *The accused begged for the court's understanding:* plead, entreat, implore, beseech, supplicate, sue, appeal to, importune, pray. **3** *Your reply begs the question:* evade, avoid, dodge, shirk, shun, escape, avert, eschew, parry, fend off, sidestep, steer clear of, shrug off, duck.

Ant. **1** give, contribute, present, bestow, donate, confer. **2** demand, exact, insist, grant, give, accord.

◇ *Word origin:* Lambert (le) Bègue ("the Stutterer") was not a beggar, but the word *beg* may possibly come from his name. In the 12th century in The Netherlands, he founded the Beguine Sisterhood, a lay Roman Catholic order; later, several lay fraternities arose in imitation of this order and the members were called Beghards, many of whom depended on alms for a living. Thus, inadvertently, Lambert Bègue gave his name to our word *beg.*

beget *v.* **1** *The old patriarch is said to have begotten more than 20 children in his lifetime:* father, sire, get, propagate, breed, engender, procreate, spawn. **2** *Evil deeds may beget dire consequences:* bring about, result in, cause, effect, occasion, lead to, produce, give rise to, call forth, engender, generate.

Ant. **2** prevent, forestall, foil, ward off, deter, save.

beggar *n.* **1** *A ragged beggar held out his hand asking for a coin:* almsman, mendicant, parasite, cadger, tramp, *Slang* sponger, scrounger. **2** *The poor beggar looked silly trying to portray the role of Hamlet:* fellow, chap, guy, *Slang* devil.

—*v.* **3** *Her hat was so funny it beggars description:* make inadequate, be beyond, surpass; challenge, baffle.

Ant. **1** giver, contributor, bestower, donor, donator, benefactor, philanthropist.

begin *v.* **1** *Please begin work. School term begins on Monday:* start, commence, initiate, set out, embark on, take the first step. **2** *This has been true since the world began:* come into existence, bring into existence, be born, start, commence, initiate, undertake; originate, establish, introduce, found, institute, launch, inaugurate; arise, burst forth, break out, crop up, set in motion.

Ant. **1, 2** end, finish, terminate, conclude, complete; stop, cease, quit.

beginner *n. I'm just a beginner in woodwork. Tommy can now read excellently, but he was a late beginner:* novice, neophyte, student, tiro, learner, fledgling, tenderfoot, greenhorn, starter, apprentice, *Slang* baby, babe in the woods.

Ant. expert, professional, master, authority, virtuoso, old hand.

"Youth, what man's age is like to be doth show;
We may our ends by our beginnings know."
—*Sir John Denham*

---

beginning *n.* **1** *Start at the beginning and play the piece again. This is only the beginning!:* start, commencement, starting-point, onset; zero hour. **2** *The beginning of the scandal was a small item in the newspaper:* origin, source, foundation, fountain-head, well-spring, spring, spring-board; embryo, inauguration, birth, inception, seed, introduction, launching.

Ant. **1, 2** end, ending, conclusion, finish, closing, termination, expiration.

begone *v. Begone with you!:* go away, away, be

off, get out, depart, leave, *Slang* scram, scarper, beat it, scat, shoo, get lost.
Ant. come here, come.

begrudge *v. Why do you begrudge him his success?:* grudge, resent, hold against; envy, be jealous of.
Ant. congratulate, wish well; be happy for.

beguile *v.* **1** *The boy was beguiled into thinking he could become a famous singer:* delude, lead astray, deceive, dupe, ensnare, lure, trick, cheat, hoodwink, hoax. **2** *Beguiled by the warm day, the students fell to day-dreaming:* lull, distract, enchant, charm, bewitch, captivate, please, cheer; entertain, divert, amuse, occupy.
Ant. 1 enlighten, disabuse, make wary, correct, put right. **2** alert, alarm, bring to one's senses, jar.

behave *v.* **1** *Why can't that child behave?:* conduct oneself properly, comport oneself well, act correctly, control oneself. **2** *You behave as if you'd been wronged:* act, conduct oneself, comport oneself, deport oneself, acquit oneself.
Ant. 1 misbehave.

behaviour *n.* **1** *His behaviour under stress is admirable:* conduct, manner, attitude, control, self-control, comportment, deportment, bearing, demeanour. **2** *The compass is showing strange behaviour:* response, reaction, functioning, conduct, operation, action, performance. **3** *The naturalist studied the behaviour of lions in their natural habitat:* acts, deeds, actions, activity, conduct, practice, habits.

"The sum of behaviour is to retain a man's own dignity, without intruding on the liberty of others." —*Francis Bacon*

---

behead *v. Henry VIII gave the order to behead Anne Boleyn:* decapitate, send to the scaffold, bring to the block; guillotine.

behold *v. The strollers could behold the beautiful sunset. Behold, the new king is crowned!:* look, look at, look upon, observe, note, see, gaze at, stare at, view, discern, survey, regard, watch, examine, inspect, notice, scan, scrutinize, witness; attend, pay attention, heed, mark, contemplate.
Ant. overlook, disregard, ignore, miss.

beholden *adj. Your help has made us beholden to you:* under obligation, obligated, obliged, indebted, in one's debt, bound, liable; answerable, accountable, responsible.

behove *v. It would behove you to take better care of your health:* be advantageous, benefit, be advisable, be wise; be fitting, befit, be proper, be necessary, be apt, be appropriate.

being *n.* **1** *A new world came into being:* existence, existing, occurrence, reality, actuality, life, living, subsistence. **2** *His very being felt the need of love:* nature, soul, spirit, psyche, essence, true being, core, inner person, persona. **3** *Can there be beings on other planets?:* living creature, creature, human being, human, person, fellow creature, mortal, individual.
Ant. 1 nothingness, non-existence, nullity.

belated *adj. Our good wishes are belated but sincere:* late, tardy, past time, overdue, behind, behind time, slow, delayed, deferred, unpunctual, after the fact, behindhand.
Ant. early, ahead of time, beforehand, before the fact.

belch *v.* **1** *After the feast the king belched loudly:* eructate, burp; hiccup. **2** *The volcano belched fire:* emit, discharge, spew, spout, spurt, eject, issue, send forth, gush, roar forth, expel, erupt, disgorge, vomit, vent, cough up.
—*n.* **3** *The gluttonous king gave forth a belch:* burp, eructation. **4** *A belch of flame came from the rocket's exhaust:* emission, discharge, spurt, spout, gush, ejection, issuing, eruption.

beleaguer *v.* **1** *Enemy troops beleaguered the city:* besiege, surround, blockade, bombard. **2** *He beleaguered her with pleas for forgiveness:* harass, badger, pester, bother, annoy, hector, vex, bombard, besiege.
◇ *Word origin: Beleaguer* comes from Dutch *belegeren, be-* (about) + *leger* (camp), to camp about, hence, to surround with armed forces.

belfry *n. Mischievous boys climbed up to the belfry and rang the bells at midnight:* bell tower, campanile: (*loosely*) steeple, spire.
◇ *Word origin: Belfry* is from Old French *berfrei*, movable siege-tower. Over the centuries, the *ber-* has been replaced by *bel-*, since people associate the tower with the *bell* it contains.

belie *v.* **1** *The facts belie your story:* disprove, refute, contradict, controvert, repudiate, show to be false, give the lie to, invalidate, gainsay, negate, betray, deny. **2** *The author's smile belied his anger with the critic:* misrepresent, falsify; disguise, camouflage, mask, conceal, cloak.
Ant. 1 prove, verify, attest to, validate, support, confirm, corroborate. **2** represent, reveal, disclose, indicate.

belief *n.* **1** *The prevailing belief is that Mars is uninhabited. It is my belief that it's going to rain:* conviction, firm notion, opinion, view, theory, persuasion; conclusion; assumption, supposition, presumption, feeling, expectation, judgement, impression, hypothesis, deduction, inference, guess. **2** *I have complete belief in my friends:* confidence, trust, faith, assurance, reliance, certitude. **3** Often **beliefs**. *Could you defend your political beliefs?:* conviction, persuasions, principle, way of thinking; morality, morals, teachings, ethics; faith, creed, dogma, doctrine, canon.
Ant. 2 distrust, mistrust, doubt. **3** disbelief, unbelief, scepticism; denial, disavowal.

believable *adj. The story is hardly believable:* plausible, credible, convincing, possible, imaginable, acceptable.

Ant. unbelievable, incredible, doubtful, dubious, unconvincing, implausible, questionable; unacceptable; fabulous.

believe *v.* **1** *Don't believe everything you hear. We all believe in good, free education for our children:* trust, put faith in, place confidence in, be certain of, credit, rely on, depend on; presume true, accept as true, hold, be assured by, be convinced by, be persuaded by, judge accurate, count on, be sure of, swear by; swallow, fall for. **2** *I believe it's going to rain:* presume, think, imagine, guess, surmise, suspect, judge, suppose, assume, consider, speculate, conjecture, presuppose; theorize, hypothesize, deduce, infer; maintain, hold.

Ant. 1 doubt, question, distrust, mistrust, discredit, disbelieve. **2** know, know for sure.

belittle *v. Don't belittle her piano-playing just because you're jealous:* make light of, disparage, deride, scorn, disdain, sneer at, malign, cast aspersions on, minimize, mitigate, underrate, undervalue, underestimate, depreciate; *Slang* knock, run down, put down, pooh-pooh.

Ant. overpraise, praise, vaunt, elevate, exalt, magnify; boast about, crow over, make a big fuss over.

bell *n. The church bells called the worshippers to prayer. The fire bell woke us in the middle of the night:* tocsin, chime, carillon, gong; peal of bells, peal, ringing, tintinnabulation.

belle *n. The film is about belles and their dashing Regency beaux. That gown will make you the belle of the ball:* beautiful girl, beautiful woman, beauty; most beautiful woman, most beautiful girl, star, queen; charmer; *Slang* heart-throb.

bellicose *adj.* See BELLIGERENT.

belligerence, belligerency *n. The two hostile nations regarded each other with belligerence:* warlike attitude, hostility, aggressiveness, combativeness, pugnacity, antagonism, unfriendliness, animosity.

Ant. peacefulness, friendliness.

> **Exploring the Word:** The Latin *bellum*, war, gives us *belligerent*, warlike, warring; *bellicose*, warlike; *ante-bellum*, before the war, especially before the American Civil War; and *rebel, rebellion*, literally to make war back, fighting back against an oppressor. Our word *revels* is also based on this Latin word for war and means merry-making or festivities so uproarious and noisy as to sound like a war!

belligerent *adj.* **1** *Why do nations maintain belligerent attitudes toward each other?:* warlike, warring, hostile, antagonistic, aggressive, combative, martial, bellicose. **2** *Why do you have such belligerent feelings toward your neighbours?:* unfriendly, hostile, antagonistic, bellicose, pugnacious, quarrelsome, contentious, irritable, bad-tempered, cantankerous, irascible, inimical, truculent.

—*n.* **3** *Switzerland was not a belligerent in World War II. The larger nation was the belligerent:* warring country, nation at war, combatant, fighter, adversary; aggressor, attacker, antagonist.

Ant. 1, 2 peaceful, peaceable. **1** pacific; neutral. **2** friendly, amicable, neighbourly. **3** neutral, non-combatant; the attacked, defender.

bellow *v.* **1** *The bull bellowed with rage. The captain bellowed a command at the troops:* roar; shout, yell, bawl, cry, scream, shriek, whoop.

—*n.* **2** *The wrestler gave a loud bellow and attacked his opponent:* roar, shout, yell, shriek, scream.

Ant. 1, 2 whisper. **1** murmur, mutter.

belly *n.* **1** *Eating green apples gave the boy a pain in the belly:* stomach, tummy, abdomen, paunch, vitals, *Slang* gut, guts, midriff; corporation. **2** *He has no belly for adventure:* liking, desire, appetite, stomach, hunger, taste. **3** *The luggage is in the belly of the plane:* bowels, depths, recesses, interior, insides.

◇ *Usage note: Belly* was once the common term for the middle or lower part of the human trunk. Later, people thought the word indelicate and began to use the more scientific word *abdomen* or the word *stomach* (actually the internal digestive organ). Thus, today *belly* is more often than not used informally to mean a large protruding abdomen and *abdomen* and *stomach* are most often used to refer to the middle or lower part of the human trunk.

◇ *Word origin: Belly* comes from Old English *belig*, bag.

belong *v.* **1** *These boots belong in the closet. Do these woods belong to the property that's for sale?:* have as a proper place; be part of, attach to, go with; concern, pertain to, be connected with. **2** *This book belongs to the school:* be the property of, be owned by, be held by. **3** *We belong to the country club:* be a member of, be included in; be associated with, be allied to.

belongings *n. Pack up your belongings and leave!:* possessions, effects, personal property, luggage, goods; gear, paraphernalia, accoutrements, things, stuff.

beloved *adj.* **1** *It was given me by a beloved friend:* loved, cherished, dear, precious, treasured, adored, endeared; respected, admired, highly valued, esteemed, revered.

—*n.* **2** *He received a long letter from his beloved:* sweetheart, loved one, love, dearest, precious; (*variously*) lover, boy-friend, beau, girlfriend, fiancé(e), spouse, husband, wife.

belt *n.* **1** *This dress comes with a red leather belt:* sash, band, cummerbund, waistband, girdle. **2** *A belt of trees encircled the field:* circle, band, strip, stripe, layer. **3** *The drought damaged crops in the green belt:* area, district, region, zone, country, land.

—*v.* **4** *The coat is belted at the waist:* encircle by a belt, fasten with a belt, wrap up, girdle, encircle.

◇ *Word origin: Belt* comes to us via Old Norse from Latin *balteus,* sword belt.

bemoan *v. Stop bemoaning the loss of your job and go out and look for a new one:* grieve over, weep over, lament, bewail, mourn, regret, rue.

Ant. laugh at; celebrate, exult.

bemused *adj.* **1** *He gave the child a bemused look:* mildly amused, lovingly amused; engrossed, thoughtful. **2** *The wine left him somewhat bemused:* confused, muddled, bewildered, fuzzy, dull-witted, stupefied, dazed, stunned.

Ant. 1 angry, stern, unsympathetic. **2** clear-headed, perceptive, *Slang* sharp.

bench *n.* **1** *The old man sat on the park bench and fed the pigeons:* seat, settle, pew, rigid couch, backless couch, backless chair, stool. **2** *The carpenter's bench was covered with tools:* workbench, work-table, counter, trestle, board, table. **3** *The accused will be brought before the bench:* court, tribunal, judiciary, seat of justice, magistrates; judge's chair.

◇ *Word origin: Bench* comes from an Old English word *benc.* It derives ultimately from the same root as our word *bank,* a grassy slope. *Bench* was used in a legal context as early as the 13th century.

bend *v.* **1** *Be careful or you'll bend that spoon. The mountain road bends treacherously:* twist, make crooked, become crooked, warp, buckle, contort; curve, arc, loop, turn, wind. **2** *Bend at the knee when you ski downhill:* flex; crouch, stoop, lean; bow, buckle, genuflect. **3** *We will not bend to the will of a tyrant. No tyrant can bend us to his will:* bow down, submit, yield, give in, accede, relent, succumb, be subjugated, surrender, capitulate, *Informal* knuckle under; force to submit, cause to yield, cause to give in, cause to defer, cause to relent, force to surrender, force, compel, coerce, control, shape, mould, influence, sway. **4** *The welder bent to his work with determination:* apply oneself, attend, give oneself to, buckle down, put one's heart into.

—*n.* **5** *Steer round that bend in the river:* curve, turn, crook, arc, hook, twist.

Ant. 1, 2 straighten; stiffen.

benediction *n. At the end of the service the bishop gave the benediction:* blessing, closing prayer.

Ant. malediction, curse, imprecation, censure.

benefactor *n. The new wing of the hospital is the gift of a generous benefactor:* supporter, patron, sponsor, upholder, backer, helper, friend; contributor.

beneficial *adj. Exercise is extremely beneficial to good health:* helpful, advantageous, propitious, useful, valuable, contributive, favourable, profitable, productive; healthful, healing, good.

Ant. useless, detrimental, detractive, disadvantageous; unfavourable, harmful, pernicious, unwholesome.

beneficiary *n. Fill in the name of your beneficiary on the insurance policy:* inheritor, legatee, heir, successor, receiver, recipient.

benefit *n.* **1** *Your advice was of great benefit to me. The new factory will be a great benefit to the town:* help, aid, avail, profit, value, gain, worth, advantage, good, betterment, blessing; behalf, interest. **2** *The theatre benefit collected £100,000:* charity affair, charity performance.

—*v.* **3** *The new hospital will benefit the entire community. I benefited from my father's advice:* help, aid, assist, serve, be useful to, be an advantage to, do good for, advance, better, profit; be helped, be aided, be served, gain, profit from.

Ant. 1 damage, harm, injury, impairment, privation; loss, disservice, disadvantage, drawback. **3** harm, injure, hurt, damage, impair, deprive; lose, detract from, be useless to, be bad for, worsen, hold back.

◇ *Spelling tip: Benefit* is based on the Latin word *bene* (related to Latin *bonus,* good), which also gives us *bene*volence, *bene*volent, *bene*diction, *bene*ficial, and *bene*ficiary. This Latin *bene* gives *bene*fit its two *e*'s, *bEnEfit.*

> **Exploring the Word:** A charity *benefit* does good for charity, a workman's sickness *benefit* can do him good. *Benefit* is based on Latin *bene,* well, which also gives us *beneficial,* doing good, helpful; *benefactor,* one who does good for another; *benevolent,* doing good; and *benediction,* the saying of good, especially the calling down of divine favour on a person. A *beneficiary* is, of course, one who receives benefit as from someone else's will or insurance policy.

benevolence *n.* **1** *The playground leader smiled with benevolence at the noisy children:* good will, kindliness, kind-heartedness, kindness, compassion, benignity. **2** *The Restoration Fund depends on the public's benevolence:* generosity, charity, charitableness, humanitarianism, bountifulness, liberality.

Ant. 1 ill-will, unkindness, unkindliness, malevolence, malignity. **2** selfishness, greediness; stinginess, illiberality, niggardliness.

benevolent *adj.* **1** *The old woman had a benevolent feeling towards all cats. He gave her a benevolent gaze:* kind-hearted, kind, compassionate, tender, full of goodwill, benign, benignant, humane. **2** *The church women are forming a benevolent society. The club received a benevolent donation:* unselfish, charitable, philanthropic, humanitarian; generous, liberal, bountiful, bounteous, large-hearted.

Ant. 1 unkind, cruel, malevolent, malicious, malignant. **2** selfish, greedy; stingy, miserly, niggardly, illiberal.

benign *adj.* **1** *The benign uncle tended to spoil the boy:* kind, kindly, kind-hearted, tender, tender-hearted, soft-hearted, soft, gentle, benevolent, humane; gracious, affable. **2** *The decrease of the patient's fever was a benign sign:* good, favourable, salutary, auspicious, encouraging, propitious, lucky. **3** *Tasmania has a benign climate:* mild, pleasant, nice; healthful, harmless, innocuous.
Ant. **1** unkind, unkindly, hard-hearted, harsh, stern, malicious, malevolent, hateful, malign, inhumane, ungracious. **2** bad, unfavourable, discouraging, threatening, ominous, unlucky. **3** harsh, severe, extreme, unpleasant.

bent *adj.* **1** *At eighty my grandfather was bent and wizened. Fix it with a bent pin:* angled, twisted, crooked, curved, arched, contorted, stooped, hunched, bowed.
—n. **2** *If the boy has a bent for music, give him piano lessons:* leaning, tendency, inclination, propensity, penchant, proclivity, disposition, predisposition; mind, liking, fondness, bias, partiality, attraction, predilection; talent, gift, flair, knack, faculty, facility, ability, aptness, capacity, endowment, aptitude, genius.
Ant. **1** unbent, straight, straight as an arrow, rigid, uncurved, unbowed. **2** aversion, disinclination, dislike, antipathy, hate, hatred, abhorrence.

bequeath *v. Most men bequeath their property to their wives and children:* will, leave, hand down, endow.

bequest *n. Grandfather left a bequest to each of the grandchildren:* legacy, inheritance, endowment.

berate *v. The principal berated the student for his tardiness:* scold, upbraid, reprimand, rebuke, reprove, reproach, criticize, castigate, take to task, rail at, *Slang* bawl out, slam, tell off.
Ant. praise, compliment, laud, thank, congratulate.

bereave *v. The accident bereaved Jane of her husband. The refugees arrived bereft of their possessions. The looters behaved as if altogether bereft of their senses:* deprive, strip, dispossess.
◇ *Usage note: Bereaved* and *bereft* are used in two entirely different ways, and you must never mix them up. *Bereaved* refers exclusively to *bereavement* (losing someone you love). *Bereft* refers to the other kinds of loss or dispossession: *bereft of one's inheritance, bereft of all hope.*

berth *n.* **1** *Have you ever slept in the upper berth of a sleeping-car?:* bunk, bed, sleeping-place. **2** *The ship rested in its berth:* dock, pier, slip, quay, anchorage, wharf; haven, resting-place. **3** *The salesman found a new berth with a shoe company:* job, position, situation, place, office, post, spot, niche, appointment, employ, billet.

beseech *v. I beseech you to forgive me:* beg, plead with, implore, adjure, supplicate, pray.

beset *v.* **1** *The complaints department was beset by angry customers:* attack on all sides, besiege, surround, hem in, assail, set upon; beleaguer, bedevil, plague, pester, badger, harass, hound, annoy, worry, dog. **2** *The crown was beset with rubies, emeralds, and pearls:* set, stud, array, deck, embellish, bead; set upon, place upon.

besiege *v.* **1** *The Indians besieged the fort:* lay siege to, surround and attack, beleaguer; assail, assault. **2** *He was besieged with requests for money:* beset, plague, pester, badger, harass, hound, bedevil, annoy, dog.
◇ *Spelling tip:* Like *siege, besiege* follows the basic spelling rule "*i* before *e* (except after *c* or when sounded like *a* as in *neighbour* and *weigh*)." Thus, *i* before *e*: *besIEge.*

best *adj.* **1** *This film was voted the best picture of the year. What's the best medicine for a cold?:* most excellent, superior, finest, choice, highest quality, top-notch, unrivalled, unsurpassed, unequalled; most helpful, most desirable. **2** *It rained for the best part of a week:* largest, greatest, most.
—adv. **3** *Which vacuum cleaner picks up dirt best? Which coat do you like best? Which job pays best?:* most excellently, most successfully, beyond all others; in the highest degree; most, most of all, above all others; most profitably, most advantageously, to the greatest advantage. **4** *The company hired the man best able to do the job:* to the highest degree, most fully, most, most of all.
—n. **5** *Even the best of us make mistakes. The dog won a prize for being the best of the breed:* finest, most excellent, choice, élite, greatest, pick, cream, top. **6** *Do the best you can:* utmost, hardest, all that one can, the most that can be done, highest endeavour. **7** *I'm not at my best unless I've had a good night's sleep:* most pleasant, nicest, loveliest, most competent, highest perfection. **8** *Aunt Ellen sends her best to all:* best wishes, kindest regards, greetings, compliments.
Ant. **1, 3, 6, 7** worst. **2, 4, 6** least. **1** poorest. **3** most poorly.

bestial *adj. The prisoners received bestial treatment:* brutal, cruel, beastly, ruthless, merciless, barbaric, barbarous, savage, depraved, inhumane.
Ant. tender, humane; kind, gentle, merciful.

bestow *v.* **1** *The country bestowed its highest medal on the war hero:* grant, confer, present, give, award, accord, render, impart, mete, dispense, honour with; give away, donate, hand out, consign, turn over to, deliver, settle upon, apportion, deal out. **2** *You should bestow more time on work and less on day-dreaming:* apply, expend, devote, occupy; use, utilize, employ, spend, consume.
Ant. **1** get, receive, acquire, procure, obtain, gain, earn, take, collect. **2** waste, fritter away.

◇ *Word origin: Bestow* is based on the word *stow,* to place, hence to place with someone, to give or present.

bet *v.* **1** *Over two million pounds was bet on the Grand National last year:* wager, gamble, make a bet, stake, risk, venture, chance, hazard, plunge.
—*n.* **2** *Put your bet down before the wheel stops spinning:* wager, stake, gamble, ante.

"Verily I say unto you, that one of you shall betray me." —*St. Matthew* xxvi. 21

betray *v.* **1** *Judas Iscariot betrayed his master:* be disloyal, be treacherous, be unfaithful, break faith with, sell out, inform against, play false with, double-cross, two-time, con, deceive, trick, dupe. **2** *Don't ever betray a confidence. Her eyes betrayed her sadness:* violate, let down; reveal, disclose, divulge, expose, uncover, show, tell, tell on, unmask, give away, lay bare, let slip, blurt out.
Ant. **1** be loyal, be faithful, be true, keep the faith. **2** keep, guard, safeguard; preserve, hide, conceal, cover, mask.

betrayal *n.* **1** *The Bible tells of the betrayal of Christ by Judas:* treachery, treason, disloyalty, unfaithfulness. falseness, breach of faith, bad faith, perfidy, double-dealing, double-cross, two-timing; deception, duplicity, trickery. **2** *Nothing is worse than the betrayal of a confidence:* revelation, disclosure, divulgence, telling, giving away, blurting out, violation.
Ant. **1** loyalty, faithfulness. **2** keeping, guarding, safeguarding; preserving.

betroth *v. She is betrothed to her childhood sweetheart:* engage, affiance, promise, pledge, contract, commit.
◇ *Word origin: Betroth* and *betrothal* are ultimately derived from Old English *trēowth,* faith or trust, which also gives us *true, truth, troth, truce,* and *trust.*

betrothal *n. A feud between the two families prevented Romeo and Juliet's betrothal:* engagement, affiancing, troth, betrothing.
◇ *Word origin:* See BETROTH.

better *adj.* **1** *She's a better dancer than I. A down-filled jacket is better than a woollen one for really cold weather:* superior, finer, more excellent, of higher quality, greater; preferable, more useful, of greater value, more suitable, more desirable, more acceptable. **2** *The better part of the day was spent working:* greater, larger, longer, bigger. **3** *The patient is better today:* healthier, more healthy, stronger, fitter; improving, improved, mending, progressing, recovering.
—*adv.* **4** *Learn to play the violin a little better before joining the orchestra. You understand the problem better than I do:* in a superior way, more completely, more thoroughly.
—*v.* **5** *He tried to better himself by going to night-school:* improve, advance, further, forward, raise, upgrade, uplift, elevate, enhance, enrich, cultivate, refine, promote, increase, heighten, strengthen. **6** *The pole-vaulter bettered the world record by six inches:* surpass, exceed, outdo, outstrip, top.
Ant. **1, 3, 4** worse. **1** inferior, lesser. **2** lesser, smaller; shorter. **3** sicker, weaker; failing, sinking. **5** worsen, lessen, weaken; lower, downgrade, devaluate, depress, impoverish.

bevy *n.* **1** *The beaters flushed a bevy of quail:* flock, flight; covey, (*loosely*) herd, pack, drove, swarm, school, shoal. **2** *A bevy of beautiful girls was in the beauty contest:* company, body, crowd, assemblage, gathering, collection, multitude, horde, band, party, host, throng.

bewail *v. The boy bewailed the loss of his dog:* lament, mourn, grieve over, bemoan, moan over, cry over, weep over; regret, rue, deplore.
Ant. rejoice over, laugh over, celebrate, delight in.

beware *v. Beware of the dog. Caesar was warned to beware the Ides of March:* look out, look out for, watch out for, take warning, guard against, take care, take precautions, be on the alert, be careful, be cautious, be wary, take heed, mind.
Ant. ignore, pay no attention to.

bewilder *v. The motorist was bewildered by the conflicting road signs:* confuse, puzzle, perplex, baffle, befuddle, mix up, muddle, addle, disconcert, nonplus, mystify, stupefy, fluster.
Ant. enlighten, inform, instruct, edify, educate, straighten out, advise, set straight, awaken.

bewilderment *n. Imagine my bewilderment when the plane landed at the wrong airport!:* confusion, puzzlement, perplexity, mystification, frustration.
Ant. enlightenment, edification.

bewitch *v.* **1** *Half the village accused Goodwife Osborne of having bewitched the cow:* put under a spell, cast a spell on; bedevil. **2** *Shirley Temple bewitched a generation of film-goers:* charm, enchant, entrance, captivate, fascinate, beguile, delight, enrapture, *Slang* turn on.
Ant. **2** repulse; repel, disgust, displease, *Slang* turn off.

bias *n.* **1** *Some people have a bias against foreigners. The pianist has a bias in favour of Chopin:* prejudice, leaning, inclination, bent, predilection, proneness, propensity, proclivity, tendency, feeling; fixed idea, preconceived idea, preconception, narrow view, slant, one-sidedness, unfairness, narrow-mindedness; bigotry, intolerance; partiality. **2** *The dress was cut on the bias:* angle, slant, diagonal line, cross.
—*v.* **3** *Don't let his insults bias you against her:* prejudice.
Ant. **1** fairness, impartiality, disinterestedness, dispassionateness, objectivity; open-mindedness, tolerance.

Bible *n.* **1** *We studied the Bible in Sunday school:* the Holy Scriptures (*Hebrew and Christian*); the Scriptures, Holy Writ, the Good Book, the Book. **2 bible.** *To spell well, let a dictionary be your bible:* authority, guide; guidebook, reference book, handbook, manual.
◇ *Usage note: Bible* is always capitalized when it refers to the Holy Scriptures. Thus, *The preacher read from the Bible, Bible stories, Bible-thumping.* The word *bible* is not capitalized when used to refer to a non-religious written authority: *When learning to make sauces, let a good cookery book be your bible.*

"The American mind, unlike the English, is not formed by books, but . . . by newspapers and the Bible." —*Van Wyck Brooks*

bicker *v. The children constantly bicker over their toys:* squabble, wrangle, quarrel, argue, spar, dispute, disagree, fight.
Ant. agree, concur, accord, be of one mind; assent, consent, concede, acquiesce.

bicycle *n.* **1** *It's dangerous to ride a bicycle on the main road:* bike, two-wheeler, cycle.
—*v.* **2** *In Europe, many workmen bicycle to work:* bike, cycle, ride.
◇ *Word origin: Bicycle* literally means two-wheeled. It comes from Latin *bi-* (two, twice) + Greek *kuklos* (circle), which is also the basis of our *cycle, motor-cycle,* and *tricycle.*

bid *v.* **1** *The queen bids all her subjects to pay the tax. I bid you join our party:* command, order, direct, require, charge, call upon, enjoin, insist, instruct, demand, ordain; invite, summon, ask, request, call, beckon. **2** *He bade us farewell:* tell, say, wish, greet. **3** *The antique dealer bid £200 for the rug. The aircraft company bid for the Air Force contract:* offer, proffer, tender, propose; submit an offer.
—*n.* **4** *What was the highest bid for the painting!:* offer, offering, proposal, bidding; invitation. **5** *After three gruelling matches, England had to concede that her bid to regain the Ashes had failed:* try, attempt, effort, endeavour.
Ant. 1 forbid, prohibit, disallow, ban, bar.
◇ *Usage note:* Remember that *bid* has a tricky past tense: *He bade his mother goodbye* and *He bid £1,000 at the auction.*

bidding *n.* **1** *The dog came at his master's bidding:* command, order, request, behest, demand, direction, charge, injunction, instruction, mandate, dictate; summons, summoning, invitation, bid, call, beck. **2** *The bidding at the auction reached £500 for one antique chair:* offer, offering, offers, proffering, tendering, proposal.

bide *v. Bide with us awhile:* wait, stay, abide, dwell.
Ant. go, depart, leave.
◇ *Usage note: Bide* and *abide* both have a strongly old-fashioned flavour and are best avoided.

big *adj.* **1** *Brazil is a big country. Farmers expect a big corn crop this year. Wrestlers have to be big men:* large, huge, enormous, vast, gigantic, mammoth, great, colossal, monumental, grandiose; considerable, sizeable, substantial, abundant, prodigious; strapping, husky, bulky, hulking, heavy, massive. **2** *The Prime Minister has a big decision to make. Clark Gable was a big star in his day:* important, vital, major, consequential, significant, momentous, weighty; prominent, leading, eminent, notable, top, chief, main, prime, head, high. **3** *No one likes his big talk:* pretentious, arrogant, boastful, conceited, bragging, haughty. **4** *Your charitable contribution shows that you have a big heart. It takes a big man to admit his mistakes:* generous, magnanimous, benevolent, liberal, gracious, kind; noble, humane, honourable, just, princely, high-minded, chivalrous, heroic. **5** *You're a big boy now:* mature, grown, grown-up, adult.
Ant. 1 little, small, diminutive, microscopic, wee, tiny, petite, minute, miniature, tiddly, pigmy, dwarf, pocket-sized, teeny, teeny-weeny, itsy-bitsy. **2** unimportant, insignificant, inconsequential, minor; low-ranking, subordinate, unknown. **3** ordinary, commonplace, modest, humble, unassuming, meek, unpretentious, mild, unpresuming, reserved, restrained, diffident. **4** stingy, cheap, petty, dishonourable, unjust, unchivalrous; ignoble, inhumane, unkind, cruel. **5** little, young, immature.

bigoted *adj. Bigoted people can never bring themselves to admit that the other fellow may be right:* prejudiced, intolerant, biased, narrow-minded.
Ant. unbigoted, unprejudiced, tolerant, unbiased, broad-minded, open-minded.

bigotry *n. At one time or another, every race and religion has been the object of bigotry:* prejudice, intolerance, narrow-mindedness; racism, discrimination, bias.
Ant. tolerance, open-mindedness, broad-mindedness.

bilious *adj.* **1** *That sausage roll gave me a bilious feeling:* sick, queasy, nauseous, green at the gills, sickly, sickening; greenish. **2** *The boss was in a bilious mood today:* irritable, peevish, ill-tempered, ill-humoured, angry, grumpy, nasty, cranky, crabby, cross, grouchy, petulant, testy, touchy, snappish, short-tempered, cantankerous, huffy, out of sorts.
Ant. 1 good, fine, healthy; attractive. **2** happy, pleasant, good-tempered, amicable, genial, cordial; agreeable, sympathetic, compliant.
◇ *Word origin: Bilious* acquired its sense of "peevish" because irritability was thought to be caused by an excess of bile in the body.

bilk *v. The lad was bilked of his inheritance:* swindle, cheat, defraud, victimize, trick, dupe, deceive, bamboozle, fleece, con, gyp, rook, gull, cozen.

bill *n.* **1** *Did you pay the phone bill?:* statement, invoice, account, charge, charges, reckoning, tally. **2** *How many bills are before Parliament this session?:* piece of legislation, proposal; measure, act; law, statute, regulation, ordinance, decree. **3** *On the wall was a sign reading "Stick no bills":* poster, placard, advertisement, bulletin; handbill, leaflet, circular, brochure. **4** *The Palace Theatre used to have the best variety bill. The waiter brought us a bill of fare:* programme, schedule, list, agenda, card, roster, calendar, catalogue, inventory, ticket, register, docket, menu.

"It's true I've got no shirts to wear;
It's true my butcher's bill is due;
It's true my prospects all look blue—
But don't let that unsettle you!"
— *W. S. Gilbert*

---

billow *n.* **1** *The yacht was tossed by the billows:* wave, swell, breaker; surge, crest. **2** *A billow of steam rose from the basement:* wave, cloud, surge.
—*v.* **3** *The sails billowed in the wind:* swell, puff up, balloon, belly; surge, roll.
Ant. 1 trough. **3** deflate, collapse.

bind *v.* **1** *Bind those boxes together with a rope. Bind the layers of wood together with glue:* fasten, secure, tie, tie up, truss, gird, strap, rope, lash, hitch; join, attach, affix, stick, glue, paste. **2** *The doctor bound the wound with gauze. The book was bound in red leather:* bandage, swathe; cover, encase, wrap. **3** *The contract binds the company to pay royalties to the inventor:* obligate, require, necessitate, oblige, compel, coerce, force, prescribe. **4** *The seamstress bound the hem of the dress with a ruffle:* border, edge, trim, rim, frame, fringe.
Ant. 1 untie, unbind, unfasten, unloose, loosen; free, set free, separate. **2** unbandage; unwrap, uncover. **3** free, release, exempt, absolve.

birth *n.* **1** *The child's birth occurred at 2 a.m. The mother had a difficult birth:* being born; childbirth, bearing, delivery, parturition. **2** *The imposter claimed to be of royal birth:* descent, ancestry, family, parentage, extraction, lineage, derivation, breeding, genealogy, blood, stock, strain, origin, beginnings, background. **3** *The birth of jazz was in New Orleans:* start, beginning, commencement, origin, source, genesis, emergence.
Ant. 1 death; miscarriage, abortion. **3** conclusion, finale, end, finish, death.

bisect *v. The new railway bisects the town:* cut in two, cut in half, divide in two, split, split down the middle; intersect, cross.

bit *n.* **1** *The glass broke into bits:* small piece, piece, fragment, particle, chip. **2** *A bit of carrot fell on the floor:* small amount, trace, scrap, morsel, speck, dab, pinch, whit, iota, mite, finger, trifle, crumb, shred, snip, paring, shaving, grain, granule, drop, droplet, sprinkling, dollop. **3** *Stay a bit longer:* short while, short time, brief period, moment.
Ant. 1 whole, entity, aggregation. **2** lot, mass, hunk, block, heap, the lion's share. **3** long time.
◇ *Word origin:* See BITE.

bite *v.* **1** *Be careful, that dog bites! A mosquito just bit me:* seize with the teeth, eat into, nip, gnash, champ, gnaw, nibble; sting, pierce, prick. **2** *The tyres bit into the snow and we were on our way:* take hold, dig, grip.
—*n.* **3** *I just want a bite of that pie:* small portion, small piece, mouthful, bit, speck, morsel, taste, scrap, crumb, shred, dab, snip. **4** *The dog gave the postman a nasty bite. He was scratching an insect bite:* tooth wound, nip; sting, prick. **5** *The cold bite of the wind drove us indoors:* sting, stinging, nip, smart.
◇ *Word origin: Bite* comes from Old English *bita*, a bite of food or a morsel, which also gives us *bit*.

biting *adj.* **1** *The biting cold froze the sailor's hands:* stinging, piercing, sharp, harsh, smarting, nipping, cutting, bitter. **2** *She loves to make biting remarks:* trenchant, mordant, cutting, stinging, piercing; scathing, withering, caustic.
Ant. 1 mild. **2** pleasant, gentle, soothing, genial, flattering, complimentary.

> **Exploring the Word:** Our word *bill* comes from Latin *bulla*, which meant an official seal and later an official document, edict, or decree which bore such a seal. Thus a *Divorce Bill, bill of lading, bill of sale*, and *bill* meaning receipt are all official documents and still often bear an official seal, stamp, or signature. A Papal *bull* is an official document, edict, or decree issued by the Pope and sealed with his official seal, which is still called a *bulla*. The diminutive of Latin *bulla* gives us *bulletin*, literally a small, official document, and now a brief news account.

bitter *adj.* **1** *Vinegar has a bitter taste:* sour, acid, acerbic, acrid, tart, sharp, caustic, biting, stinging, harsh, astringent. **2** *The children shouldn't be outdoors in this bitter cold:* stinging, smarting, piercing, sharp, biting, severe. **3** *Failing maths was a bitter blow to the boy's pride:* grievous, cruel, harsh, painful. **4** *Being left out of his father's will made him bitter. The brothers had a bitter argument:* resentful, sullen, morose, spiteful, crabbed, sour, rancorous, scornful, mean, angry.
Ant. 1 sweet, sugary, saccharine, cloying; bland, mild, insipid, flat, dull. **2** mild, gentle, balmy. **3** happy, joyful, delightful, pleasant, gay; fortunate, lucky. **4** grateful, thankful, appreciative; friendly, amiable, genial, pleasant.
◇ *Word origin: Bitter* is closely related to *bite*

and originally meant "biting, cutting, cruel."

bizarre *adj. Children like to wear bizarre costumes at Hallowe'en:* strange, fantastic, weird, queer, freakish, outlandish, odd, unusual.
Ant. subdued, ordinary.
◇ *Usage note:* Don't confuse a *bazaar,* a fair for the sale of goods, as for charity, with *bizarre,* meaning unusual, weird. *We bought a cake at the church bazaar* but *She wore a rather bizarre dress.*

black *adj.* **1** *A black cat crossed our path:* coal-black, jet, raven, ebony, sable, swarthy, inky. **2** *It was a cold, black night:* dark, murky, lightless, stygian, sunless, moonless, unilluminated, unlighted. **3** Often **Black.** *She hoped to become the first Black member of Parliament:* Negro, coloured, dark-skinned. **4** *Cynics have a black outlook on the state of the world:* gloomy, grim, dismal, sombre, dim, calamitous. **5** *The bus-driver stopped short and gave the pedestrian a black look:* sullen, hostile, dark, furious, angry, threatening. **6** *The villain had a black heart:* evil, wicked, bad, nefarious.
—*n.* **7** *Black is the most sombre colour:* ebony, jet, raven, sable. **8** Often **Black.** *Martin Luther King was the first American Black to win a Nobel prize:* Negro, Afro-American, black man, coloured man, man of colour.
Ant. **1** white, snow-white, chalky, whitish. **2** bright, light, sunny, moonlit, illuminated, lighted, well-lighted, lit. **3** white, Caucasian. **4** optimistic, bright, happy, gay. **5** friendly, amiable, amicable, congenial, warm, pleased. **6** good, virtuous, wholesome, righteous, moral, honourable, upright, exemplary, pure. **7** white. **8** white, white man, Caucasian.

blacken *v.* **1** *The commandos blackened their faces with charcoal:* make black, become black; darken, black. **2** *Don't blacken my name by spreading rumours:* defame, dishonour, defile, disgrace, discredit, denigrate, stigmatize, tarnish, sully, stain, smear, befoul, besmirch, revile, slander.
Ant. **1** lighten, whiten; clear. **2** exalt, honour, credit, uplift, eulogize, praise.

blackguard *n. In the old play, the blackguard was outwitted by the hero:* villain, scoundrel, knave, rogue, rascal, cad, scamp, miscreant, rat.
Ant. hero; gentleman.
◇ *Pronunciation tip: Blackguard* is pronounced as if it were spelt "blaggard."
◇ *Word origin:* In the 16th and 17th centuries, *blackguard* was a common designation for criminals, drifters, and camp-followers, but the actual origin of the term is unknown.

blacklist *v. Communists were blacklisted from working in the motion-picture industry:* blackball, bar, debar, ban, preclude, exclude, reject, ostracize.
Ant. welcome, accept, invite, meet with open arms, acclaim, go all the way with.

blackmail *n.* **1** *For not turning the evidence over to the police, she demanded £10,000 blackmail from him:* hush-money, extortion, pay-off, tribute; ransom.
—*v.* **2** *Threatening a scandal, he blackmailed the firm into paying him for keeping quiet:* extort, demand a pay-off; threaten, force, coerce, hold to ransom.
◇ *Word origin: Blackmail* has nothing to do with the postman's *mail.* It comes from Scottish *mail,* payment, tax. This "black-tax" was originally extorted by freebooting Scottish chiefs in exchange for "protection."

blade *n.* **1** *The blade needs sharpening:* cutting edge, cutter; (*variously*) sword, knife, scalpel, razor; skate runner, sledge runner. **2** *The boy chewed on a blade of grass:* leaf, frond, needle, switch.

blame *v.* **1** *The police blame the accident on the driver who was attempting to pass. I don't blame you for being angry:* hold responsible, accuse, charge; fault, find fault with, reproach, reprove, censure, condemn, rebuke, castigate, criticize, disapprove.
—*n.* **2** *The accountant accepted the blame for the error. Mother's going to put all the blame on me:* responsibility, accountability, liability, guilt, onus, fault, culpability, burden; accusation, charge, recrimination; reproach, censure, condemnation, reproof, rebuke, criticism, denunciation, castigation, remonstrance.
Ant. **1** exonerate, vindicate, absolve, acquit, clear, exculpate; excuse, justify, forgive; praise, laud, acclaim, commend, compliment, approve of. **2** exoneration, vindication, absolution; excuse, alibi; praise, acclaim, commendation, compliment, congratulation, tribute, credit, honour, glory, distinction.
◇ *Word origin: Blame,* like *blasphemy,* comes from the Greek adjective *blasphēmos,* meaning "evil-speaking."

"I loved thee once, I'll love no more,
Thine be the grief, as is the blame."
—*Sir Robert Aytoun*

---

blameless *adj. The jury found the building contractor blameless. She's always had a blameless reputation:* not responsible, not at fault, guiltless, not guilty, innocent, unblameable, clear, inculpable; irreproachable, spotless, unspotted, unsullied, untainted, unstained, unblemished, uncorrupted, unimpeachable.
Ant. responsible, at fault, guilty, implicated, culpable; sullied, tainted, censurable, reprovable.

blanch *v. Blanch celery by keeping it in a dark place. He blanched with fright:* bleach, fade, lighten; whiten, turn pale.
Ant. darken, blacken, obscure; brighten, redden, colour, stain, dye.

◇ *Word origin: Blanch* comes from French *blanc,* white. *Blank* and *blanket* also come from this French word.

bland *adj.* **1** *They put him on a bland diet. What a bland film!:* uninteresting, unexciting, dull, uninspiring, unstimulating, tedious, tiresome, monotonous, humdrum, flat, vapid, prosaic, weak. **2** *These bland spring days are meant for day-dreaming:* mild, balmy, calm, calming, tranquil, quiet, moderate, temperate, unruffled, even, smooth, soothing, benign, peaceful, peaceable, untroubled, non-irritating.

Ant. **1** interesting, exciting, electrifying, sensational, thrilling, astonishing, stimulating, inspiring, stirring, rousing, overpowering, moving. **2** turbulent, tempestuous, excited, volatile, explosive; harsh, severe, rough, irritating, annoying.

◇ *Word origin: Bland* and *blandishment* come from Latin *blandus,* smooth, caressing, flattering.

blandishment, Often **blandishments** *n. Even her blandishments couldn't win him over:* flattery, cajolery, coaxing, wheedling, inveiglement, ingratiation, blarney.

Ant. intimidation, threats, scolding, insults, bullying, browbeating.

◇ *Word origin:* See BLAND.

blank *adj.* **1** *Take a blank sheet of paper and write your name at the top. Never sign a blank cheque:* not written on, clean, unmarked, unused, not filled out, not filled in; empty, vacant, clear, plain. **2** *The stranger returned my greeting with a blank look:* vacant, empty, inexpressive, expressionless, unrecognizing, inane, uninterested, thoughtless, dull, vacuous, hollow, void. **3** *The invalid spent long blank days alone:* empty, idle, meaningless, futile, wasted, unrewarding, useless, worthless, insignificant, valueless, inconsequential, profitless, unprofitable, fruitless, unproductive.

—*n.* **4** *Fill in the blanks to complete the crossword. My memory is a blank!:* empty space, space, void, gap; emptiness, hollowness, vacuum, vacancy.

Ant. **1** marked, filled out, filled in, full, completed. **2** thoughtful, interested, meaningful, expressive, intelligent, alert, sharp. **3** full, filled, busy; rewarding, valuable, worthwhile, useful, meaningful, significant, consequential, profitable, fruitful, productive.

◇ *Word origin: Blank,* like *blanch* and *blanket,* comes from French *blanc,* white; hence, unmarked or uncoloured.

blanket *n.* **1** *Put another blanket on the bed:* counterpane, coverlet, quilt, bedspread, Afghan. **2** *A blanket of snow covered the ground:* covering, cover, coating, coat, mantle, carpet, overlay, film, veneer.

—*v.* **3** *Confetti blanketed the ballroom floor:* cover, carpet, coat, overlay, cloak.

◇ *Word origin:* A *blanket* was originally a sheet of white woollen cloth. It comes from the French word for white, *blanc,* from which we also get *blanch* and *blank.*

blare *v. The loudspeaker blared the music over the park. The horns blared:* sound loudly, blast, resound, scream, bellow, roar; trumpet, make a fanfare, peal, honk.

Ant. mute, stifle; hum, murmur, whisper.

blarney *n. He was a ladies' man with quite a line in blarney:* flattery, fawning, overpraise, honeyed words, sweet words, line; cajolery, wheedling, inveigling, coaxing; fanciful talk, exaggeration, overstatement, hyperbole, stories, fibs, *Slang* hot air.

Ant. truth, frankness, candidness, guilelessness, directness.

◇ *Word origin:* Our word *blarney* comes from the famous Blarney Stone in Blarney, County Cork, that reputedly gives all who kiss it great skill in flattery.

blasé *adj. Don't be so blasé about your good fortune:* bored, unexcited, unenthusiastic, unconcerned, uninterested, indifferent, insouciant, nonchalant, world-weary, spiritless, unmovable, apathetic; jaded, surfeited, gorged, full, glutted, saturated, satisfied.

Ant. enthusiastic, excited, interested, concerned, spirited.

◇ *Word origin: Blasé* is the French word for being satiated or sick with over-indulgence.

blasphemous *adj. "God is dead" is a blasphemous statement:* irreverent, profane, sacrilegious, irreligious, impious, ungodly, godless.

Ant. reverent, religious, pious, godly.

blasphemy *n. Taking the name of the Lord in vain is pure blasphemy:* profanity, irreverence, sacrilege, impiousness; cursing, swearing.

Ant. prayer, praying; veneration, reverence, adoration; blessing, benediction, thanksgiving.

◇ *Usage note:* See OBSCENITY.

◇ *Word origin:* See BLAME.

blast *n.* **1** *A blast of wind shook the house:* gust, gale, surge, rush, roar. **2** *The blast of the factory whistle could be heard for miles:* loud noise, blare, scream, roar, bellow, bleat, shriek, toot, honk, peal. **3** *The blast completely demolished the building:* explosion, detonation, report, burst, discharge, eruption.

—*v.* **4** *Music blasted from the little radio:* sound loudly, blare, resound, scream, shriek, roar, bellow, honk, peal, toot. **5** *The construction crew blasted a tunnel through the mountain. Heavy bombers blasted the enemy positions:* explode, dynamite, torpedo, bomb, shell; burst, level, bore.

blatant *adj.* **1** *There's a blatant error in this bill:* obvious, unmistakable, clear, conspicuous, prominent, overt. **2** *He's so blatant no one wants anything to do with him:* loud, obtrusive, offensive, crude, uncouth, gross, crass, coarse, vulgar, undignified, indelicate, cheap, tawdry, ill-mannered, unrefined, tasteless, unsubtle, ungenteel, unpolished; noisy, blar-

ing, clamorous, harsh, ear-splitting, deafening, piercing.
Ant. inconspicuous, subtle. **1** unnoticeable, hidden. **2** unobtrusive, agreeable, acquiescent, refined, genteel, dignified, delicate, well-mannered, tasteful, in good taste, cultured, polished, high-class, *Informal* classy; quiet, subdued, soft.
◇ *Word origin: Blatant* was coined by the 16th-century poet Edmund Spenser, who described a bellowing, thousand-tongued monster as "the Blatant Beast." He may have based the word on Latin *blaterare*, to babble or bleat.

blaze *n.* **1** *The ice-skaters huddled round the blaze of the bonfire:* fire, flame, flames, conflagration. **2** *The blaze of sunlight on the water was breathtaking:* glow, gleam, shimmer, glitter, flash, shine, glare, flare, beam, ray; radiance, brilliance, brightness, effulgence, resplendence. **3** *The trouble-maker stalked out in a blaze of anger:* outburst, burst, blast, flash, rush; eruption, outbreak, torrent, explosion.
—v. **4** *The fire blazed all night:* burn brightly, burn, flame. **5** *Her eyes blazed with happiness:* glow, gleam, shine, glisten, glitter, shimmer, be resplendent, be bright, be brilliant; flash, beam, glare, flame, flare.

bleach *v. The sun bleached the life-guard's hair:* whiten, blanch, lighten, fade, make pale, wash out.
Ant. blacken, darken; colour, stain, dye.

bleak *adj.* **1** *The North of Scotland is bleak and damp:* bare, barren, windswept, weather-beaten, desolate. **2** *The world situation seems bleak. Saturday was a bleak winter's day:* gloomy, dreary, dismal, grim, depressing, cheerless; unpromising, distressing, sombre, forbidding. **3** *A bleak wind blew from the north:* bitter, raw, cold, icy, piercing, biting, nipping, frosty, chill, wintry.
Ant. **1** covered with vegetation, wooded, forested; sheltered, protected, warm, cheerful, comfortable. **2** bright, cheerful, cheery, sunny; pleasant, genial; promising, encouraging. **3** mild, balmy, soft, warm, springlike.

blemish *n.* **1** *Because of the blemish in the wood, the table was half-price. A pimple is a skin blemish:* flaw, imperfection, defect, disfigurement; spot, blotch, blot, mark, stain, taint.
—v. **2** *The one loss blemished the team's otherwise perfect record:* flaw, mar, spoil, tarnish, sully, taint, stain, smudge, smirch; spot, mark, blot, blotch, blur, disfigure.
Ant. **1** perfection, improvement; decoration, ornament, complement, refinement. **2** perfect, improve, complete, refine, enhance; purify, purge, reclaim, restore, rectify, correct.

blend *v.* **1** *Blue and yellow blend to make green:* mix, merge, combine, unite, mingle, intermingle; fuse, compound, melt together, incorporate. **2** *The curtains blend with the rug:* harmonize, go well, complement.
—n. **3** *Mocha icing is a blend of coffee and chocolate:* mixture, mix, combination, merger, mergence, mingling, concoction; compound, fusion.
Ant. **1** separate, divide. **2** clash. **3** separation, division.

bless *v.* **1** *The bishop blessed the new chapel:* make holy, consecrate, sanctify, hallow, dedicate, give benediction; anoint, baptize. **2** *Fate blessed him with great talent:* favour, oblige, benefit, endow, bestow, grace, give. **3** *God bless you:* guard, protect, watch over, support.
Ant. **1** curse, anathematize. **2** curse, condemn, disfavour; handicap, harm, injure.
◇ *Word origin: Bless* comes from Old English *bloedsian*, to mark with blood so as to make holy. During the Christianization of the Saxons, missionaries used the word to translate Latin *benedicere* ("bless").

blessed *adj.* **1** *He prayed to the Blessed Virgin:* revered, holy, hallowed, sacred, sanctified, consecrated, adored. **2** *The birth of a baby is truly a blessed event:* joyous, joyful, happy, felicitous, blissful, wonderful. **3** *Having a healthy body and a sound mind, I consider myself twice-blessed:* fortunate, favoured, lucky, well-endowed, graced.
Ant. **1** cursed, accursed, anathematized. **2** unhappy, sad, unfortunate, grievous. **3** condemned, deprived.
◇ *Pronunciation tip:* When used to mean sacred or joyous, *blessed* is pronounced as two syllables, *bless-id: the Bless-id Virgin; a bless-id event.* When used to mean fortunate, *blessed* is often pronounced and spelt as one syllable: *a twice-blest man.*

blessing *n.* **1** *The rabbi officiated at the blessing of the new temple. Do you ask a blessing before meals?:* consecration, dedication, hallowing, invocation, benediction; grace, prayer of thanks, thanksgiving. **2** *He knew the blessings of a happy childhood:* advantage, benefit, good, good fortune, favour, gift, bounty, gain, profit. **3** *The engaged couple had the blessing of their families:* approval, consent, concurrence, permission, leave, support, sanction, backing, good wishes, favour, regard.
Ant. curse. **1** imprecation, malediction, anathema. **2** deprivation, misfortune, disadvantage, detriment, drawback, harm, injury, damage. **3** disapproval, objection, disapprobation, condemnation, denunciation, censure, reproof; ill will, disfavour.

blight *n.* **1** *A mysterious blight destroyed the corn crop:* plant disease, pestilence; (*loosely*) dry rot, rot, rust, fungus, mildew, decay. **2** *Greed is a blight on mankind:* affliction, curse, scourge, pestilence; canker, contamination, corruption.
—v. **3** *Lack of education blighted his chances of success:* spoil, ruin, wreck, kill, destroy,

smash, demolish, blast, crush; wither, shrivel, cripple, thwart, rot, injure, harm, frustrate.
Ant. **2** blessing, good, favour, service, boon, bounty. **3** benefit, help, aid, improve, better, advance, further, foster, promote.

blind *adj.* **1** *Milton died an old and blind man:* sightless, unable to see, unseeing. **2** *The teacher was blind to the fact that some students were cheating. We must not be blind to the suffering of others:* ignorant, unaware, unknowing, unobserving, unobservant, incognizant, uncomprehending, unconscious of, unseeing, obtuse; unmindful, unfeeling, dull, insensitive, unperceptive or imperceptive, undiscerning, indifferent, neglectful, inattentive, heedless, unconcerned, uninterested, insouciant. **3** *The argument put him in a blind rage:* uncontrolled, uncontrollable, unthinking, mindless, unreasonable, irrational, senseless, insane. **4** *A car entered the main road from the blind drive:* hidden, concealed, obscure, unnoticeable, unnoticed.
—*n.* **5** *The blinds keep the sun out:* Venetian blind. **6** *The night-club was just a blind for the gambling casino:* cover, screen, front, subterfuge, disguise, masquerade, camouflage; dodge, ruse, pretext, deception.
Ant. **1** sighted, seeing. **2** aware, conscious, knowledgeable, observant, cognizant, alive to, awake to; mindful, sensitive, discerning, attentive, heedful, concerned. **3** controlled, controllable, rational. **4** in full view, obvious, noticeable, open.

"There's none so blind as they that won't see."
—*Jonathan Swift*

bliss *n.* *Being home again was pure bliss:* happiness, joy, ecstasy, delight, rapture, glee, gladness, luxury, heaven, paradise; exhilaration, exaltation, jubilation.
Ant. misery, agony, anguish, torment, distress; sorrow, sadness, grief, unhappiness; dejection, depression, gloom.
◇ *Word origin: Bliss* comes from Old English *blīths*, joy, and is related to *blithe* (Old English *blīthe*), joyous.

blithe *adj.* **1** *The child had a wonderfully blithe personality:* joyous, merry, happy, cheery, cheerful, sunny, radiant, glad, gleeful, jolly, jovial, mirthful; carefree, light-hearted, frolicking, sprightly, lively, ebullient, exultant, airy, blithesome. **2** *Don't act with such a blithe disregard of others:* heedless, careless, thoughtless, unmindful, insensitive, unconscious, uncaring, unfeeling, indifferent, unconcerned, blind, casual, inconsiderate.
Ant. **1** sad, unhappy, sorrowful, dejected, depressed, gloomy, cheerless, glum, morose, dour, melancholy, heavy-hearted. **2** thoughtful, considerate, concerned, solicitous, obliging, kind-hearted.
◇ *Word origin:* See BLISS.

bloat *v.* *The cow's stomach was bloated from eating the wet fodder:* distend, swell, puff up, expand, inflate, balloon, enlarge.
Ant. shrink, contract, shrivel.
◇ *Word origin: Bloat* probably comes from Old Norse *blautr*, soaked. The smoked herring called a *bloater* has been "soaked" in smoke.

bloc *n.* *He expected some support from the Third World bloc:* faction, group, wing, clique, body, ring, cabal; alliance, coalition, combination, combine, union.
◇ *Usage note: Bloc, wing,* and *faction* all refer to loosely organized groups within a larger group or society. A *bloc* is a group interested in promoting certain interests, regardless of the political affiliation of its members: *the Communist bloc includes both hard-liners and revisionists, who favour better relations with the West.* A *wing* is one of two directly opposed subgroups of the same political party or bloc: *The conservative wing of the farm bloc, the liberal wing of the Christian Democrat party.* A *faction* is usually a disruptive or a minority subgroup: *A small faction of M.P.s attempted to prevent a vote on the bill.*

block *n.* **1** *The garage was made of concrete blocks:* brick, bar, cube, square. **2** *The landfall proved an unsurpassable block:* obstruction, barrier, obstacle, blockade, bar, impediment; hindrance, interference, blockage.
—*v.* **3** *Snow-drifts blocked our progress towards the frontier:* obstruct, blockade, bar, choke, stop up, jam; hinder, impede, check, halt, prevent, thwart.
Ant. **3** clear, unblock, unbar, open, free; advance, further, forward, promote, foster.

blond, blonde *adj.* **1** *He has blond hair and blue eyes:* light-coloured, yellowish, yellow, gold, golden, flaxen. **2** *The Nordic peoples tend to be blond rather than dark:* fair, fair-skinned, light-complexioned, light, pale, fair-haired.
—*n.* **3** *Is it a legend that gentlemen prefer blondes?:* blonde-haired woman; person having fair skin and hair.
Ant. brunette, brunet. **1** dark, black. **2** dark, dark-skinned, olive-complexioned.

blood *n.* **1** *The boxer had blood running down his nose:* vital fluid, gore. **2** *Tolerance of others is the very blood of democracy:* life-blood, source, vital principle. **3** *He's a terror when his blood is up:* temper, passion, temperament, spirit. **4** *The king must marry a woman of noble blood:* extraction, lineage, descent, ancestry, heritage, family, family line, birth.

bloom *n.* **1** *This plant has one white bloom. The dogwood had a heavy bloom this spring:* blossom, flower, bud; blossoming, florescence. **2** *Her face shone with the bloom of youth:* glow, flush, rosiness, radiance, lustre, shine, beauty, vigour, zest, strength, prime, heyday; flowering, blossoming, flourishing.

—*v.* **3** *The century plant blooms only once in its lifetime:* flower, blossom, burgeon, sprout, bear fruit, fructify. **4** *Musical talent usually blooms at an early age:* flourish, thrive, fare well, prosper, succeed, bear fruit, burgeon; develop, grow.

Ant. 2 pallor, greyness, wanness, ashenness; decay, decadence, blight. **3** wither, die; be sterile. **4** wither, fade, fail, wane.

◇ *Word origin: Bloom* comes from Old Norse *blōm,* flower.

blossom *n.* **1** *Orange blossoms have a lovely scent:* flower, bloom.

—*v.* **2** *Did the wisteria blossom this year?:* flower, bloom, burgeon. **3** *Their romance was blossoming:* bloom, grow, develop; flourish, thrive, burgeon, progress.

Ant. 2 wither, die, be sterile. **3** wither, fade, fail, diminish.

blot *n.* **1** *Will that ink blot come out?:* blotch, spot, splotch, smudge, smear, stain, mark, discoloration. **2** *The one poor mark was a blot on the student's record:* blemish, flaw, blotch, taint, stain, stigma, bad mark, smirch.

—*v.* **3** *The ink blotted on the paper:* smear, smudge, splotch, blotch; spot, stain, besmirch. **4** *Blot the wet ink with a clean blotter:* soak up, absorb, take up; remove, dry.

Ant. 2 credit, distinction, honour, feather in one's cap.

blotch *n. Measles gave him red blotches all over his face:* spot, splotch, mark, blot.

◇ *Word origin: Blotch* is a blend of *blot* + *botch.*

blow *n.* **1** *The fighter was punch-drunk from too many blows to the head:* hit, knock, punch, smack, whack, clout, thump, sock, wallop, box, jab, bash, crack, bang, belt. **2** *The failure of his business was a terrible blow to him:* shock, jolt, upset, disappointment, rebuff, reversal, detriment; tragedy, disaster, calamity, misfortune, catastrophe, affliction.

—*v.* **3** *The leaves are blowing away. The wind is blowing:* move by wind; gust, puff. **4** *Blow on your hands to keep them warm:* exhale, puff. **5** *Little Boy Blue, come blow your horn:* sound, toot, honk, whistle, blast, play. **6** *The explosion blew the bridge to smithereens. My curling-iron always blows a fuse:* burst, explode, blow out, pop, burn out.

Ant. 1 caress, pat. **2** comfort, relief, blessing, consolation; achievement, victory. **3** still. **4** inhale.

blue *adj.* **1** *The sky is very blue today:* bluish, azure, cerulean, sky-blue, cobalt-blue, cobalt, Prussian-blue, navy-blue, navy, sea-blue, powder-blue, sapphire, indigo, aqua, aquamarine, turquoise. **2** *She feels homesick and blue:* depressed, dejected, sad, gloomy, despondent, downcast, low, down-hearted, disconsolate, morose, melancholy, down, down in the dumps, down in the mouth.

Ant. 2 elated, exultant, excited, exhilarated, jubilant, happy, overjoyed, joyful, pleased, delighted, blithe, glad, gay, merry, jolly, up in the clouds, in high spirits.

"Why make so much of fragmentary blue
In here and there a bird, or butterfly,
Or flower, or wearing-stone, or open eye,
When heaven presents in sheets the solid hue?"
—*Robert Frost*

---

bluff[1] *adj.* **1** *Henry VIII had a bluff and hearty nature:* outspoken, plain-spoken, blunt, frank, open, unceremonious, candid, direct, straightforward, forthright, bold, headlong; abrupt, brusque, curt, rough, crusty.

—*n.* **2** *The farm was perched on a bluff high above the river:* promontory, cliff, scar, headland, bank, ridge, precipice, escarpment, crag, peak.

Ant. 1 retiring, reticent, repressed, hesitant, unsure, mealy-mouthed, shy; indirect, roundabout, deceptive; formal, ceremonious, mannered, tactful.

bluff[2] *v.* **1** *The poker player bluffed his opponents into thinking he had a good hand. He's just bluffing about his rise:* deceive, delude, humbug, mislead, fool; fake, sham, lie, counterfeit, pretend, hoax.

—*n.* **2** *The bully's claim to be a professional boxer was just a bluff to scare you:* pretence, fake, sham, fraud, lie, humbug, deception, subterfuge; idle boast, boast, bragging.

Ant. 2 truth, fact.

blunder *n.* **1** *Sending the bill to the wrong customer was a terrible blunder. His remark was a social blunder:* mistake, error, slip; impropriety, indiscretion, gaucherie, gaffe, faux pas; *Slang* boner, goof, boob, clanger.

—*v.* **2** *The clerk blundered when he added up the bill:* make a mistake, be in error, be at fault, slip up, *Slang* goof, make a boob. **3** *How did you manage to blunder onto the wrong aeroplane?:* flounder, bumble, bungle, stumble, stagger.

Ant. 1 achievement, success. **2** be correct, be accurate, be exact. **3** go alertly, move purposefully.

◇ *Word origin: Blunder* is related both to Norwegian *blundra,* shut the eyes, and to our word *blind.*

blunt *adj.* **1** *It's hard to carve a roast with a blunt knife:* dull, dulled, unsharpened; thick, edgeless, unpointed. **2** *You can hurt people's feelings by being too blunt:* frank, open, outspoken, candid, straightforward, explicit, to the point; abrupt, rough, tactless, insensitive, curt, trenchant, assertive.

—*v.* **3** *Lack of sleep blunted his thinking:* dull, numb, benumb, deaden, make insensitive, stupefy; moderate, mitigate, soften, lighten.

Ant. 1 sharp, keen, acute; edged, serrated, pointed. **2** tactful, subtle, diplomatic, politic, sensitive, polite, courteous, polished. **3** sharpen, hone, put an edge on, make keen; stimulate, excite, animate, vitalize.

blur *v.* **1** *Mist often blurs the landscape:* cloud, becloud, fog, befog, make hazy, dim, bedim, darken, obscure, make indistinct. **2** *The damp paper caused the ink to blur:* smear, smudge, blotch, spread, run, blot.
—*n.* **3** *The water made a blur on the paper:* smudge, smear, blotch, splotch, blot. **4** *I was so exhausted that the evening was just a blur:* confusion, fog, haze, cloud, obscurity.
Ant. 1 clear, brighten, outline, spotlight.

blush *v.* **1** *She blushes every time a boy talks to her:* flush, redden, turn red, colour, grow red.
—*n.* **2** *At the first blush of dawn, the cock will crow:* reddening, rosy tint, pinkish tinge.
Ant. 1 blanch, turn pale, pale, turn ashen.

bluster *v.* **1** *He blusters so much that it's hard to believe him:* boast, swagger, rant, brag; protest, threaten, storm, bully.
—*n.* **2** *His bragging and bluster made him unpopular:* bluff, swagger, swaggering, bravado, bombast, boasting, ranting, boisterousness, noisy talk, noise.
Ant. 1 be retiring, be reticent, be shy. **2** shyness, meekness, mildness, reticence.

board *n.* **1** *Saw this board in half:* plank, piece of timber; slat, weatherboard, panel, deal, batten. **2** *How much is bed and board?:* meals, daily meals, food. **3** *The founder of the company is chairman of the board:* board of directors, directors, council, tribunal.
—*v.* **4** *My aunt boards holiday-makers during the summer:* lodge, house, quarter, put up; billet, bed; feed. **5** *The passengers boarded the aeroplane at noon:* enter, get on, go onto, embark.
Ant. 5 leave, disembark, deplane.

boast *v.* **1** *He boasted that he was the best swimmer in school:* brag, crow; vaunt, blow one's own trumpet. **2** *The city boasted two new schools:* be proud of, speak proudly of, show off, exhibit, flaunt; have, contain, possess.
—*n.* **3** *Mother's favourite boast was that no one had more beautiful children:* brag, vaunt.
Ant. 1 disclaim, disavow, deprecate, depreciate. **2** be ashamed, cover up. **3** disclaimer, disavowal.

boastful *adj. The team's full-back is extremely boastful. Discount his boastful claim:* conceited, cocky, vainglorious, puffed up, full of swagger, pretentious, pompous, cocksure, bragging, braggadocio; vaunting, exaggerated, crowing, inflated, swollen.
Ant. modest, self-disparaging, deprecating, self-belittling.

boat *n. The fishing-boat left the dock at dawn:* vessel, craft, ship.
◇ *Usage note:* In general usage, a *boat* is a small, open craft that can be hauled out of the water: *a rowing-boat, a lifeboat. My father traded in his sailing-boat for a motor-boat.* A *ship* is a larger craft, one that can't be hauled out of the water but requires a dry dock: *a warship, a transatlantic steamship. Sailing-ships were once used to hunt whales.*

bob[1] *v. The skiff bobbed in the water. A boxer learns to bob and weave:* move up and down; bounce, hop, leap, jump about, dance; duck, nod.

bob[2] *v. Women began to bob their hair in the 1920's:* crop, shorten, cut, clip, shear, trim; dock.

body *n.* **1** *And what sort of a body is she? The house faces a body of water. Stars are the heavenly bodies:* person, being, thing, quantity, mass. **2** *He developed a muscular body. The wings are soldered to the body of the aeroplane:* physique, figure, build, form, shape; frame, main part, torso, trunk. **3** *The police took the body to the morgue:* corpse, remains, cadaver, carcass. **4** *The body of the populace supported the mayor. A large body of people attended the outdoor concert:* majority, mass, group, throng, mob, multitude. **5** *The school's governing body meets once a term:* assembly, confederation, committee, congress, council, faction, bloc, coalition, combine, league, society, force, brotherhood. **6** *Flour will give the gravy more body:* thickness, stiffness, cohesion.
Ant. 2 soul, spirit; mind, intellect, intelligence, psyche; limb, wing, protuberance. **4** minority; handful, scattering, few.

> "The utmost glory of the human body is a mean subject of contemplation compared to the emotion, exertion and character of that which animates it." —*John Ruskin*

bog *n.* **1** *Walking is difficult in the bog:* marsh, marshland, swamp, moorland, wetlands, mire, fen, spongy ground, quagmire, morass.
—*v.* **2** *The car was bogged down in the mud:* be stuck, mire, sink, be partially buried, be partially immersed.
Ant. 1 dry ground, firm ground.

bogus *adj. The cashier was reprimanded for not spotting the bogus cheque. She wore the bogus diamonds and left the real ones in the bank:* counterfeit, fraudulent, spurious, forged; artificial, synthetic, fake, imitation, simulated, phoney, sham, false, feigned, make-believe, pretend.
Ant. genuine, real, authentic, true, bona fide, actual, natural.
◇ *Word origin: Bogus* was originally an American slang term for a counterfeiter's press. Later, it came to mean counterfeit money, and much later Mark Twain popularized it in its present sense of "fake, sham." More recently, it has found its way into standard English.

Bohemian, Also **bohemian** *n.* **1** *Greenwich Village is the home of many artists and bohemians:* nonconformist, hippie, beatnik.
—*adj.* **2** *The poet lived a bohemian life in Paris:* nonconformist, unconventional.
Ant. 1 conformist, *Slang* square, straight. **2** conventional, conformist, *Slang* square, straight.
◇ *Word origin:* The Celtic people who in

Roman times inhabited what is now western Czechoslovakia were called *Boii*, "fighters," and their name survives in *Bohemian*. During the Middle Ages a belief arose that *Bohemia* was the homeland of the Gipsies, so *Bohemian* came to mean not only "native of Bohemia" but "Gipsy." The term was introduced into English by the novelist William Makepeace Thackeray (1811–63).

boil *v.* **1** *Boil the water for the tea:* simmer, seethe, brew; parboil, stew. **2** *The waves boiled around the ship:* bubble, froth, foam, churn, well up, toss, simmer. **3** *His rudeness made me boil with anger:* range, rave, storm, seethe, fume, fulminate, rant, burn, sizzle, smoulder, foam, quiver, chafe, bristle.
—*n.* **4** *The doctor had to lance the boil:* sore, fester, carbuncle.
Ant. **1** freeze; cool. **2** subside, calm. **3** calm, appease, assuage, simmer down.

boisterous *adj. The children became boisterous when their mother left the room:* clamorous, uproarious, noisy, loud; disorderly, wild, rowdy, unruly, obstreperous, out of hand, unrestrained.
Ant. quiet, silent, still, calm, peaceful, tranquil, serene, sedate; well-behaved, restrained.

bold *adj.* **1** *Don Quixote thought he was a bold adventurer. The engineer had a bold plan to build a bridge over the English Channel:* brave, courageous, valiant, unafraid, fearless, heroic, valorous, stalwart, dauntless, indomitable, stout-hearted, lion-hearted, intrepid, unshrinking; daring, audacious, adventuresome, daredevil, imaginative, creative. **2** *I was offended by his bold remarks:* rude, impudent, fresh, insolent, brazen, impertinent, defiant, saucy, brash, forward; fiery, spirited. **3** *The room was decorated in bold colours:* colourful, loud, hot, warm, flashy.
Ant. **1** cowardly, faint-hearted, fearful, shrinking, flinching; *Slang* chicken, chicken-hearted, yellow; mundane, ordinary, modest, unimaginative, uncreative or non-creative. **2** meek, timid, timorous, retiring, bashful, shy; courteous, polite, gracious, tactful. **3** pale, dull, soft, colourless, pastel, conservative, cold, cool.

bolster *v.* **1** *More timbers are needed to bolster the roof of the mine:* support, brace, prop up, hold up, buttress, reinforce, shore up, shoulder, cradle. **2** *More facts are needed to bolster your argument:* support, uphold, strengthen, add to, help, aid, assist.
—*n.* **3** *Put the bolster on the couch:* cushion, pillow.
Ant. **1** weigh down. **2** diminish, lessen, weaken, tear down.

bolt *n.* **1** *Is the bolt on the door closed?:* sliding bar, bar, catch, fastener, rod, latch, lock. **2** *The engine is held in place by two strong bolts:* fastening rod, pin, peg, dowel, rivet. **3** *The suspect made a bolt for the door:* dash, rush, run, sprint; spring, jump, leap. **4** *It took two bolts of cloth to make the curtains:* roll, length. **5** *A bolt of lightning lit up the sky:* thunderbolt, shaft, dart, stroke, flash, brand.
—*v.* **6** *Bolt the windows before you leave:* bar, latch, lock, fasten, secure. **7** *He bolted out of the room in a rage:* dash, rush, run, fly, speed, hasten, hurry, scoot, flee, tear, hurtle, sprint; spring, jump, leap, bound. **8** *Eat slowly and don't bolt your food:* eat rapidly, gobble, gulp, swallow whole, wolf.
Ant. **6** unbolt, unlatch, unbar, unlock, unfasten, open. **7** saunter, stroll, amble, creep, sneak.
◇ *Word origin:* Originally, a *bolt* was an arrow for a crossbow. Later, the word became generalized to include a variety of long or cylindrical objects or to leaving as quickly as an arrow from a crossbow.

bomb *n.* **1** *The war-plane carries 5,000 pounds of bombs:* explosive device, explosive missile, grenade, mine, *Slang* egg.
—*v.* **2** *The rebels bombed the munitions factory:* set off a bomb in, drop a bomb on, throw a bomb at, bombard.
◇ *Word origin:* Both *bomb* and *bombard* go back to the Greek word *bombos*, meaning the booming of thunder.

bombard *v.* **1** *Planes, ships and artillery bombarded the enemy port:* rain explosives upon, fire upon, batter, pepper, open fire on, shell, bomb, cannonade, strafe. **2** *During the storm the telephone exchange was bombarded with reports of dead lines:* barrage, besiege, beset, pepper, assail, assault, attack; harass, pester, hound, worry.
◇ *Word origin:* See BOMB.

bombastic *adj. No one believed his bombastic claims:* grandiloquent, pompous, windy, padded, inflated, magniloquent, tumid, turgid, verbose, wordy.
Ant. temperate, unpretentious, modest, natural, simple, unaffected, deflated, quiet.
◇ *Word origin: Bombastic* comes from French *bombace*, cotton padding, which may be ultimately derived from Persian *pamba*, cotton.

bona fide *adj. This is a bona fide £20 note. He made a bona fide offer and I accepted:* genuine, real, actual, true, authentic, legitimate; honest, sincere, in good faith, honourable, lawful, legal.
Ant. counterfeit, fraudulent, spurious, forged; artificial, synthetic, imitation, simulated, fake, phoney, sham, bogus, false, feigned, make-believe, pretended.
◇ *Word origin: Bona fide* is a Latin phrase meaning "in good faith," hence genuine.

bonanza *n. His modest investment grew into a bonanza:* windfall, sudden profit, gold mine.
Ant. disaster, loss.
◇ *Word origin: Bonanza* comes from American Spanish *bonanza*, good luck, hence a rich vein of gold or silver. The word is ultimately

derived from Latin *bonus,* good, which also gives us *bonus, bonny,* and *boon,* as in the phrase "a boon companion."

bond *n.* **1** Usually **bonds**. *The captive could not break his bonds:* bindings, fastenings; (*variously*) rope, cord, chains, shackles, manacles, irons, fetters. **2** *There is a strong bond between the two brothers:* tie, affinity, union, connection, knot, link. **3** *An honest man's word is his bond:* guarantee, pledge, compact, agreement, obligation, stipulation, promise. **4** *Stocks and bonds can be good investments:* promissory note, security, certificate; scrip.

◇ *Word origin: Bond* is a variant form of *band.*

bondage *n. Wilberforce sought to end the bondage of slavery:* slavery, servitude, enslavement, vassalage, serfdom, captivity, yoke; bonds, shackles, chains, fetters.

Ant. freedom, liberty, emancipation, independence, liberation.

◇ *Word origin: Bondage* comes from Old English *bonda,* meaning serf, peasant. That a person in *bondage* may also be said to be in *bonds* is just a coincidence, as the words *bonds* and *bondage* are not related.

bonus *n. The workers are expecting a large Christmas bonus. If you order three books you will receive a fourth one as a bonus:* gratuity, gift, premium, dividend, prize, reward, benefit, bounty.

Ant. fine, penalty, tax.

◇ *Word origin: Bonus* is the Latin word for good. The word was probably first used in English in a jocular, or ignorant, fashion to signify a "good thing", Latin *bonum.*

book *n.* **1** *The best way to get a child to read is to have many books in the house:* volume, written work, bound work, tome, publication. **2** *You should keep an address book. Write in my autograph book:* notebook; album, tablet.

—*v.* **3** *The travel agent booked our sunshine cruise. The night-club has booked an excellent floor show:* reserve, make reservations, arrange for, engage, procure, schedule, programme, organize, line up, bill. **4** *The police booked him for dangerous driving:* register, list, record, enter, put down, write down, mark down, note, insert, post, enrol; file, catalogue, index; charge, accuse, indict.

Ant. 3 cancel, disengage.

boom¹ *n.* **1** *The boom of the explosion could be heard for miles:* bang, roar, rumble, blast, thunder. **2** *After the depression, there was a business boom:* prosperous period, successful period, good times; upsurge, upturn, boost, spurt, thrust, push, expansion, growth, development, increase, gain, improvement, advance.

—*v.* **3** *The drums boomed:* bang, rumble, roar, blast, thunder. **4** *The business boomed whilst the old man lived:* thrive, flourish, prosper, increase, grow, develop, spurt.

Ant. 2 depression, recession, bad times, hard times, slump, downturn, decrease; bust, burst. **4** fail, slump.

boom² *n. Lower the boom and take in the sail:* horizontal pole, spar; beam, shaft, bar.

boor *n. He's a clumsy boor:* lout, oaf, yokel, bumpkin, clodhopper, peasant, rustic; vulgarian, philistine.

Ant. sophisticate, cosmopolitan; gallant.

◇ *Usage note:* See BORE¹.

◇ *Word origin: Boor* comes from Dutch *boer,* meaning farmer, a word familiar to us from the *Boer War* (1899–1902) in South Africa between Great Britain and the Transvaal, which had been settled by Dutch farmers, the *Boers.*

boorish *adj. She considers the peasants boorish:* crude, rude, coarse, vulgar, unrefined, unpolished, uncouth, gauche, loutish, oafish, rustic, peasantlike.

Ant. genteel, polite, polished, gentlemanly, cultured, refined, cultivated, courtly, gallant, ladylike; sophisticated, urbane, cosmopolitan.

boost *v.* **1** *Boost me up so that I can look in the window:* lift, raise, heave, hoist, elevate, push, shove, pitch, give a leg up. **2** *The new assembly line boosted production by twenty per cent:* increase, raise, advance, raise upward, add to, enlarge, expand, advance, develop, improve. **3** *The Chamber of Commerce boosts local business:* promote, advance, foster, further, forward, support, sustain, nurture; speak well of, propound, praise, extol, acclaim, laud, urge on, put in a good word for, stick up for.

—*n.* **4** *Give me a boost onto the horse:* lift, heave, hoist, raise, shove, push. **5** *I received a pay boost. Last month saw a boost in sales:* increase, rise, jump, addition, increment; growth, development, enlargement, expansion, advance, improvement, rise, pick-up, upsurge, upswing, upward trend. **6** *The charity bazaar got a boost in the local newspaper:* favourable mention, good word, good review, free ad, *Informal* plug, promotion, praise, compliment, applause.

Ant. 1, 2 lower, let down, push down, drop. **2** decrease, reduce, diminish, lessen, subtract from, deduct, cut, curtail, crop, pare, whittle down, scale down, moderate, ease. **3** hinder, hold back, condemn, criticize, *Informal* knock. **5** decrease, reduction, cut-back, curtailment, lessening, decline, fall, falling off, diminution, dwindling, wane, ebb, deterioration. **6** condemnation, criticism, *Informal* knock.

booth *n.* **1** *She called from a phone booth. Each voter went into a polling booth:* compartment, cubbyhole, nook; hutch, coop, pen. **2** *I won a kewpie doll at the hoop-la booth at the fair:* stall, stand, counter, table; tent.

◇ *Word origin: Booth* is related to old Icelandic *būth,* dwelling.

booty *n. The pirates buried their booty on a desert island:* loot, plunder, spoils, pillage, takings, pickings; prize, gain, winnings.

Ant. fine, forfeiture.

border *n.* **1** *Summer cottages were built all along the border of the lake. The bedspread had a fringed border:* edge, rim, periphery, perimeter, circumference, extremity, verge, margin, brim, brink, curb, skirt, frame, outskirts, fringe, pale, limit. **2** *Do you need a passport to cross the Scottish border?:* frontier, boundary, line.
—*v.* **3** *Ireland borders the Atlantic Ocean:* be next to, adjoin, join, flank, touch, neighbour on, abut, skirt, verge upon. **4** *The seamstress bordered the dress with flowers:* edge, trim, fringe, befringe, frame, bind, rim, hem, skirt.
Ant. **1** interior, inside, middle, centre.

bore[1] *v.* **1** *Long stories about "the good old days" bore me:* be tedious to, tire, weary, fatigue, exhaust, tax one's patience, wear out, *Slang* be a drag.
—*n.* **2** *The guest speaker turned out to be a deadly bore:* dull person, tiresome thing, *Slang* drag.
Ant. **1** excite, interest, amuse, stimulate, delight. **2** life and soul of the party, *Slang* gas.
◇ *Usage note:* Don't confuse *boor* and *bore.* A *boor* is an oafish, unmannerly person; a *bore* is a dull, tiresome, person or thing.

"A bore is a man who deprives you of solitude without providing you with company."
—*Gian Vincenzo Gravina*

bore[2] *v.* **1** *To reach the iron ore deposit engineers had to bore through solid rock:* drill, tunnel, hollow out, gouge out, sink, pierce, burrow, drive.
—*n.* **2** *In general, rifles have smaller bores than shot-guns:* inside diameter, calibre.
Ant. **1** fill, plug.
◇ *Word origin: Bore* comes from Old Norse *bora,* hole.

boredom *n. The patient spent long days of boredom in the hospital:* dullness, tedium, ennui, monotony, tediousness, doldrums, weariness.
Ant. excitement, interest, stimulation, amusement, entertainment, diversion.

boring *adj. Playing canasta all evening is boring:* dull, unexciting, uninteresting, tiresome, monotonous, repetitious, tedious, wearisome, flat, insipid, tiring.
Ant. exciting, interesting, stimulating, exhilarating; amusing, entertaining.

born *adj.* **1** *George Gershwin was a born musician:* natural, innate, intuitive; endowed from birth.
—*v.* **2** *Charles Dickens was born in 1812:* given birth to, brought forth, delivered.

borrow *v.* **1** *May I borrow your car?:* use, take on loan, take and return. **2** *The playwright borrowed the essence of the plot from Shakespeare:* appropriate, take, get, obtain, acquire, copy, use, usurp; filch, pirate, plagiarize, pilfer, steal, commandeer.
Ant. lend. **1** return. **2** contribute, give, present.
◇ *Word origin:* When we *borrow* something, we pledge to return it. The word comes from Old English *borgain,* to take on pledge or credit.

bosom *n.* **1** *She clutched the child to her bosom:* breast, bust, chest. **2** *Conflicting emotions wrestled in his bosom:* heart, innermost being, inmost nature, soul, spirit, core, breast, centre. **3** *Every young man must leave the bosom of his family to seek his own fortune:* midst, inner circle, heart, centre, nucleus, core.
—*adj.* **4** *John is my bosom friend:* close, intimate, cherished, dear, beloved.
Ant. **4** distant, remote.

boss *n.* **1** *A good boss tries to keep his workers happy:* employer, supervisor, foreman, manager, superintendent, administrator, executive, chief, leader, head, master.
—*v.* **2** *Don't try to boss me around!:* order, command, *Informal* push.
Ant. **1** employee, worker, man in the ranks, subordinate, underling; follower.
◇ *Word origin: Boss* comes from Dutch *baas,* master. The word was first used by a British writer at the beginning of the 19th century, but it was used in American English from the time of the earliest contact between Dutch and English colonists in and around New York during the 17th century.

botch *v.* **1** *The typist botched the job and had to start again:* spoil, muff, bungle, make a mess of, do unskilfully, butcher, mar, mismanage; blunder, fail, err, fumble.
—*n.* **2** *The cook made a botch of the dinner:* mess, bungle, blunder, failure, hash, fumble, flop.
Ant. **1** master, perfect, do well at, do skilfully, make a success of, triumph at. **2** success, triumph, achievement, *Informal* hit.

bother *v.* **1** *My cold still bothers me:* annoy, trouble, distress, inconvenience, dismay, disquiet, worry, disturb, upset, pester, nag, harass, harry, aggravate, fret, vex, irk, try, irritate, tax, strain. **2** *She didn't even bother to say she was sorry:* trouble, attempt, make an effort.
—*n.* **3** *Having an extra guest at dinner will be no bother at all. Don't make such a bother over deciding which dress to wear:* inconvenience, problem, trouble, difficulty, hardship, strain, stress, load, tax, onus, encumbrance, nuisance, trial, affliction, *Slang* drag; hindrance, impediment, worry, responsibility, care, aggravation, vexation, irritation, *Informal* headache, pain in the neck; fuss, disturbance, commotion, tumult, stir, ado, flurry, rumpus, racket.
Ant. **1** help, aid, comfort, solace, console, calm, quiet, appease, placate, pacify, mollify. **2** neglect. **3** convenience, help, aid, solution, answer, pleasure, delight, comfort.

bothersome *adj. Being without a car for the day was bothersome:* troublesome, annoying, inconvenient, aggravating, vexing, taxing, distressing, disturbing, worrisome.

Ant. convenient, helpful, comforting, consoling; pleasant, delightful, comfortable.

bottle *n. The milkman leaves us a pint bottle of milk every day:* glass container, vessel; (*variously*) phial, vial, jar, canteen, carafe, flask.

◇ *Word origin: Bottle* comes from the diminutive of Late Latin *buttis*, cask. *Buttis* also gives us *butt*, which is a specialized term for a big wine cask.

bottom *n.* **1** *Attach the cord to the bottom of the lamp. The main entrance is at the bottom of the mountain:* base, foot, pedestal, foundation. **2** *The shoes are in the bottom of the trunk:* lowest part, deepest part. **3** *Is that chewing-gum stuck to the bottom of your shoe?:* underside, underpart, lower side, belly, sole. **4** *The ship sank to the bottom:* ocean floor, riverbed, depths. **5** *She spanked the child on its bottom:* rump, backside, buttocks, seat, fundament; *Slang* bum. **6** *Let's get to the bottom of this mystery:* basis, base, root, heart, core, centre, substance, essence, principle; gist, quintessence, foundation, source, origin, beginning, cause, ground, rudiments, mainspring, spring, well-spring.

—*adj.* **7** *The cat slept on the bottom step of the stairs:* lowest, lower; deepest, deeper.

Ant. 1-4, 7 top. **1** crown, peak, summit, height, acme, apex. **2** cover, lid. **4** surface. **7** highest, uppermost, higher, upper.

bough *n. During the storm a bough broke off the tree:* branch, limb.

◇ *Word origin: Bough* comes from the Old English *bōg*, shoulder, hence a "shoulder" of a tree.

boulevard *n. The boulevard was lined with two rows of lime trees arrayed in ranks:* avenue, wide street, tree-lined street.

Ant. alley, back street.

bounce *v.* **1** *The ball bounced against the wall:* rebound, ricochet, bound, recoil, bob, jounce, bump, thump.

—*n.* **2** *In tennis you must return the ball before the second bounce:* rebound, bound, hop. **3** *A good night-club entertainer has to have a lot of bounce:* vitality, liveliness, pep, animation, vivacity, vigour, verve, energy, life, dynamism, spirit.

Ant. 3 staidness, calmness, calm, tranquillity, composure; weariness, tiredness.

◇ *Word origin: Bounce* comes from Middle English *bunsen*, to thump, beat.

bound¹ *adj.* **1** *Bound newspapers will be collected for the scrap-paper drive:* tied, tied up, fastened, secured, trussed, lashed together; in bonds. **2** *The author gave his manuscripts and bound books to the local library:* encased, wrapped, covered. **3** *The roses are bound to die in this frost:* sure, certain, fated, destined, doomed. **4** *The borrower is bound by contract to pay off the debt in two years:* required, obliged, constrained, limited, forced; determined, resolved, resolute.

Ant. 1 unbound, untied, loose. **3** unsure, uncertain; avoidable, escapable. **4** free, unlimited, unrestrained; irresolute.

bound² *n.* **1** *There are a hunting-lodge and an orchard within the bounds of the estate. Her flashy evening gown oversteps the bounds of good taste:* limit, boundary, border, confine, line; periphery, extremity, rim, pale. **2** *Rescuers are hunting for the lost climbers somewhere within the bounds of Snowdonia:* area, territory, region, compass, range, domain, province, district; realm, orb, orbit.

—*v.* **3** *A stone wall bounds the property:* surround, enclose, encircle, circumscribe, border, edge, hedge, fringe; mark, define, limit, confine.

bound³ *v.* **1** *The dog bounded out of the house:* leap, jump, vault, spring; bounce, bob, prance, dance, gambol, romp, flounce.

—*n.* **2** *In one bound, the boy jumped the fence:* leap, jump, vault, spring, bounce, rebound, flounce, bob.

Ant. 1 crawl, creep, amble, hobble, limp.

◇ *Word origin: Bound³* comes from French *bondir*, to rebound, jump. The word entered English during the reign of Elizabeth I, and Shakespeare was one of the first to use it in writing.

bound⁴ *adj. We're Morocco bound:* going to, heading for, destined.

◇ *Word origin: Bound⁴* comes from Middle English *boun*, prepared, ready to go.

boundary *n. The Tamar River forms the boundary between Devon and Cornwall:* border, dividing line, line, frontier, barrier; landmark, rim, edge, margin, pale, periphery, extremity.

◇ *Pronunciation tip: Boundary* may be pronounced with either two or three syllables. Both *bound-ry* and *boun-duh-ry* are correct. But beware! In spelling, you must include the *-a-*, *boundary*.

boundless *adj. Teenagers seem to have boundless appetites:* vast, immense; limitless, unlimited, unbounded, endless, inexhaustible, measureless, immeasurable, infinite, incalculable, without end, unending, unrestricted.

Ant. limited, restricted, bounded, circumscribed; small, little.

bounteous *adj.* **1** *The crops were bounteous this year:* abundant, plentiful, plenteous, bountiful, profuse, copious, ample, prolific, lavish, large, rich, full, teeming, overflowing, abounding. **2** *Many bounteous donors contributed to the charity:* generous, bountiful, munificent, unstinting, unsparing, magnanimous, charitable, beneficent, liberal, free, large, philanthropic, benevolent.

Ant. 1 sparse, spare, meagre, scant, scanty, scrimpy, lean, slender, modest, small, limited, restricted, inadequate. **2** stingy, miserly, niggardly, sparing, stinting, close, penurious, uncharitable, frugal, parsimonious; greedy, covetous, avaricious.

◇ *Word origin:* See BOUNTY.

bountiful *adj.* See BOUNTEOUS.

bounty *n.* **1** *In olden days the poor had to depend on*

the parish's bounty: generosity, benevolence, munificence, charitableness, charity, philanthropy, assistance, aid, help, giving, liberality, open-handedness, alms-giving. **2** *Every soldier was promised ten acres of land as a bounty:* grant, reward, recompense, bonus, tribute, bestowal, benefaction, endowment; present, favour, gratuity, donation, contribution.
Ant. 1 stinginess, closeness, niggardliness, miserliness; greed, covetousness, avarice.
◇ *Word origin:* Both *bounty* and *bounteous* can be traced back to Latin *bonitas*, goodness.

bouquet *n.* **1** *The bride carried a bouquet of white roses:* bunch of flowers, nosegay; boutonnière. **2** *The wine has a marvellous bouquet:* aroma, scent, odour, fragrance.
◇ *Pronunciation tip:* The preferred pronunciation is *boo-KAY.*
◇ *Word origin: Bouquet* is the diminutive of Old French *bos*, woods, hence a little wood or little thicket of flowers.

bourgeois *n.* **1** *The princess was ostracized for marrying a rich bourgeois:* member of the middle class, burgher, (*disparagingly*) Babbitt.
—*adj.* **2** *The furnishings were in bourgeois taste:* middle-class.

> **Exploring the Word**: Late Latin *burgus* means fort or castle. It gives us *borough*, a town or part of a town having its own local government; *burgess*, an inhabitant of a town or borough; *burgher* and *bourgeois*, both literally meaning "townsman," hence tradesman or member of the middle class as opposed to the landed gentry. Latin *burgus* also gives us the endings *-burg, -burgh*, or *-berg* found in the names of many towns in both Europe and North America, as *Edinburgh, Hamburg* and *Pittsburgh.*

bout *n.* **1** *I've never attended a championship bout:* fight, boxing match, match, battle, contest, conflict, struggle, fray, brush, tilt, skirmish, embroilment, scuffle, clash, encounter, engagement, contention, affair. **2** *I've just had a bout of flu:* spell, session, turn, course, interval, period, term, siege, spree, series, cycle.
◇ *Word origin: Bout* goes back to Low German *bucht*, bend or turn. Originally, it meant a going and coming back as in a round of ploughing, later a spell or spree, as a drinking *bout*, and then a contest, as a boxing *bout.*

bow¹ *v.* **1** *The duke bowed and kissed her hand. Bow your head when the flag passes:* bend, salaam, stoop; (*of a woman*) curtsy. **2** *The City Council refused to bow to the wishes of the mayor:* yield, give in, submit, surrender, defer, comply, relent, agree, acquiesce, concede.
—*n.* **3** *The conductor made a deep bow to the audience:* bend, salaam.
Ant. 2 fight, battle, contest, resist, stand fast.

bow² *n. The captain walked towards the bow of the ship:* forward end, front, prow.
Ant. stern.

bowl *n.* **1** *What lovely salad bowls! Would you like another bowl of soup?:* deep dish, vessel, container, receptacle; (*variously*) tureen, porringer, boat; bowlful, dishful, portion, helping. **2** *Unless there is rain, the entire area will be a dust bowl. The bathroom has no wash-bowl:* basin; hollow, depression, cavity, valley. **3** *Outdoor concerts are given in the Crystal Palace concert bowl:* stadium, amphitheatre, arena.

box¹ *n.* **1** *He bought me a box of sweets:* carton, cardboard container, container, receptacle; crate, chest, caddy; coffer. **2** *We have a box at the opera:* stall, compartment, booth.
◇ *Word origin:* The first wooden *box* may have been made from boxwood. In any event, our word *box* can be traced back to Greek *pyxos*, the *Buxus sempervirens* or boxwood tree.

box² *v.* **1** *Father used to box our ears when we were bad:* cuff, slap, bat, hit, strike, whack, thwack, buffet. **2** *The champion was asked to box in an exhibition bout:* fight, spar, exchange blows, engage in fisticuffs.
—*n.* **3** *One more smart-alec remark and you'll get a box on the ears!:* cuff, slap, whack, thwack, hit; buffet, thumping.

boy *n. We have two boys and a girl:* male child; man-child, lad, youth, stripling, youngster.

boycott *n.* **1** *Housewives organized a meat boycott to protest against high prices:* refusal to buy, rejection, spurning, exclusion, ostracism, blacklisting.
—*v.* **2** *The townspeople boycotted the overpriced shop:* refuse to have dealings with, reject, spurn, ostracize, exclude, blacklist.
Ant. 1 mass patronage, group support, usage, acceptance. **2** patronize, support, welcome, use, accept.
◇ *Word origin: Boycott* comes from the name of Captain C. C. Boycott, a 19th-century landlord's agent in County Mayo, Ireland, who was obstructed and ostracized by tenants in the first "boycott" (1880).

boyish *adj. The actor had boyish good looks. He was punished for a boyish prank:* youthful, boylike, juvenile, innocent, fresh, tender; childish, childlike, immature, puerile; awkward, unfledged, callow.
Ant. manly, rugged; adult, mature, grown-up, experienced, sophisticated, worldly.

brace *n.* **1** *The table is shaky because the braces are loose:* reinforcement, support, bracket, prop, stanchion, stay, strut, bracer. **2** *We caught a brace of partridge:* pair, couple, duo, twosome.
—*v.* **3** *Brace those sagging shelves with more cross-pieces. Brace yourself for some bad news:* reinforce, strengthen, steady, prop, prop up, shore, shore up, bolster, buttress, support, sustain, hold up.
Ant. 3 weaken, loosen; let fall.

bracelet *n. She's wearing a beautiful charm bracelet:* armlet, bangle.
◇ *Word origin: Bracelet* is ultimately derived

from Latin *bracchium*, arm, which also gives us *brace*, literally "a supporting arm," and *embrace*.

bracing *adj. A steam-bath followed by a cold shower is very bracing:* invigorating, stimulating, energizing, restorative, refreshing, arousing; strengthening, fortifying, reviving.
Ant. soporific, restful, dulling, depressing; weakening, debilitating, enervating.

bracket *n.* **1** *The shelf was supported by a bracket at each end:* support, brace, stay, strut, prop, stanchion. **2** *What tax bracket are you in?:* group, grouping, class, classification, category, range, division, designation, status.
—*v.* **3** *You'd better bracket those shelves with two-by-fours:* support, brace; prop, prop up, shore, shore up. **4** *All able-bodied men will be bracketed as A.1 in the doctor's report:* class, classify, group, categorize, designate.
◇ *Word origin: Bracket* comes from Old French *braguette*, codpiece, diminutive form of *bragues*, breeches. The term may have arisen from a fancied resemblance between a bracket and a pair of breeches. The word is derived from Latin *bracae*, term for the breeches worn by Gaulish tribesmen.

brackish *adj. The water is too brackish to drink:* salty, briny, saline, salt.
Ant. fresh, clear, sweet.
—*Word origin: Brackish* comes from Dutch *brak*, salty.

brag *v. He constantly brags about how well he plays golf:* boast, extol oneself, vaunt, crow, puff oneself up, blow one's own trumpet, pat oneself on the back.
Ant. be humble, be self-deprecating, deprecate, depreciate, disclaim, disavow; be ashamed, cover up.

braggart *n. He's so proud of his success that he's become a braggart:* bragger, boaster, bluffer, *Slang* blow-hard.
Ant. humble person, self-effacing person, modest person.

braid *v. The mother braided the girl's hair into two pigtails:* plait, weave, intertwine, entwine, twine, interlace, twist, ravel, lace.

brake *n.* **1** *This car has four-wheel brakes. Higher taxes will put a brake on inflation:* stopping device; curb, constraint, restraint, rein, check, drag.
—*v.* **2** *Don't brake the car abruptly on an icy road. The increase in the crime rate must be braked:* stop, halt, arrest, stay, check; reduce speed, slow; curb, control.
Ant. **1** starter, accelerator; acceleration, stimulus; freedom. **2** start; move, accelerate, speed up, hasten, quicken, expedite.
◇ *Usage note:* See BREAK.

branch *n.* **1** *There's a bird's nest on the branch of that tree:* limb, bough, spray. **2** *There's good fishing in the west branch of the river:* leg, prong, channel, tributary, feeder; extension, section, part. **3** *The local branch of the union is very small. Theatre is a branch of the arts:* section, part, segment, component, arm, wing, member, extension, division, subdivision, chapter, offshoot; bureau, office, branch office, department, agency.
—*v.* **3** *The main road branches into three B-roads after the roundabout:* divide, diverge, radiate, separate, fork, shoot off, ramify, bifurcate.
Ant. **1** trunk. **2** main channel. **3** complex, composite, mass, conglomerate, union, affiliation, alliance; main office, home office.
◇ *Word origin: Branch* comes from Late Latin *branca*, paw. (Boughs branch off from trees, and small rivers branch off from bigger ones in the same way as an animal's toes branch off from its feet.)

"Now golden fruits on loaded branches shine,
And grateful clusters swell with floods of wine."
—*Alexander Pope*

---

brand *n.* **1** *The farm's brand is an X. The timbers were marked with red letters or brands:* branding iron; mark made by branding; label, mark, emblem, stamp, sign, trade mark. **2** *Which brand of peanut butter is cheapest?:* brand name, make, manufacture; type, kind, sort, variety, grade, class, quality. **3** *After the scandal he carried the brand of an informer wherever he went:* stigma, stain, mark, disgrace, smirch, smear, slur, taint, spot, blot, imputation, blemish.
—*v.* **4** *The farmer branded a hundred calves in one afternoon:* mark with a branding iron, mark, sear, burn in. **5** *His criminal record branded him for life:* stigmatize, mark, stain, taint, besmirch, spot, blemish, disgrace, discredit.
Ant. **3** trophy, laurel, honour. **5** bring honour to, commemorate.
◇ *Word origin: Brand* is an Old English word for a piece of burning wood, or torch, and also for a sword. Our word *brandish*, to wave, comes from it.

brandish *v. The cavalry officer brandished his sword and the charge began:* flourish, wave, shake, swing, wield, waggle; flaunt, display, exhibit, show off.
Ant. sheathe, put away; put up, lower.
◇ *Word origin:* See BRAND.

brash *adj. He's such a brash young man, that I shouldn't be surprised if he finds himself in deep trouble soon:* impudent, impertinent, brazen, forward, rude; bold, heedless, overconfident, know-it-all.
Ant. cautious, prudent, careful, well-considered, thoughtful, circumspect, respectful, deferential, polite, reserved; hesitant, uncertain, timid, timorous.

brat *n. That little brat needs spanking:* spoilt child, rude child, hoyden, whelp, chit, rascal, imp.
Ant. little angel, little darling.
◇ *Word origin: Brat* originally meant any child and may come from the Scottish word *brat*, bib.

bravado *n. His bravado hides his real fear:* show of courage, swaggering, swagger, braggadocio, boasting, boastfulness, bragging, vaunting, crowing, bombast, bluster, blowing.

Ant. nervousness, trembling, quaking; shame.

◇ *Word origin: Bravado* entered English during the reign of Queen Elizabeth I, coming either from Spanish *bravata* or French *bravade,* both of which mean *bravado.* See also BRAVE.

brave *adj.* **1** *A brave fireman rescued the woman:* courageous, valiant, valorous, heroic, fearless, dauntless, undaunted, stout-hearted, lion-hearted, intrepid, unafraid, unflinching, unshrinking; plucky, game, doughty, stalwart, *Slang* gutsy.

—*v.* **2** *The rescue party braved the storm to reach the sinking ship:* dare, confront, challenge, face, defy, overcome, breast, stand up to, look in the eye; endure, bear, withstand, tolerate, take, put up with, suffer, sustain, stand, weather, brook, abide, stomach, undergo.

Ant. 1 cowardly, cringing, frightened, fearful, afraid, craven, faint-hearted, *Slang* chicken, chicken-hearted, yellow, lily-livered; timid, timorous, shrinking. **2** retreat from, back away from, give in to, surrender to, give up in the face of, *Informal* turn tail.

◇ *Word origin: Brave* comes to us via Italian *bravo,* brave, which is ultimately derived from Greek *barbaros,* meaning non-Hellenic, and (after the Persian War) brutal, barbarous.

"To a brave man, good and bad luck are like his right and left hand. He uses both."

—*St. Catherine of Siena*

---

bravery *n. The policemen showed great bravery in the face of danger:* courage, valour, heroism, fearlessness, intrepidity, dauntlessness; boldness, daring, pluck, spunk, audacity, spirit, mettle, *Slang* grit.

Ant. cowardice, fright, fearfulness, faintheartedness, timidity, *Slang* chickenheartedness, yellowness.

brawl *n. Most Westerns include a scene with a bar-room brawl:* fight, scuffle, fracas, fray, mêlée, row, ruckus, scrap, broil, clash, battle, uproar, rumpus, embroilment, altercation, imbroglio; quarrel, squabble, tiff, dispute, wrangle.

brawn *n. It takes brawn to be a weight-lifter:* brawniness, muscle, muscular development, robustness, huskiness, beefiness, sturdiness, ruggedness; strength, might, power.

Ant. slightness, scrawniness, leanness, thinness, skinniness, slenderness; weakness, feebleness, fragility.

◇ *Word origin: Brawn* comes from Old French *braon,* fleshy part (of the hind leg). The word refers to boar or swine's flesh and entered English during the 1300's. *Brawn* is also related to the German word *Braten,* roast meat.

brawny *adj. Most wrestlers are very brawny:* muscular, burly, robust, husky, rugged, sturdy, strapping, strong, powerful, mighty.

Ant. scrawny, gaunt, slender, slight, skinny, thin, slim, lean, lanky, lank; weak, feeble, fragile, delicate.

brazen *adj. How can you believe such a brazen lie?:* brassy, impudent, shameless, bold, boldfaced, barefaced, brash, unabashed, insolent, saucy, forward, immodest, audacious; open, arrogant, cheeky.

Ant. reserved, reticent, diffident, respectful, decorous, well-mannered, mannerly, polite; cautious, modest, timid, timorous, shy, bashful; underhand, secret, stealthy, surreptitious.

◇ *Word origin: Brazen* comes from Old English *bræs,* brass. Thus, to be *brazen* is to be brassy. (*Brazen* still is used to mean "made of brass," but this use is now rare.)

breach *n.* **1** *The explosion made a breach in the dam. Armoured units poured through the breach in the enemy's lines:* opening, break, hole, rift, gap, gash, rent, crack, split, chink, cleft, crevice, slit, rupture, fissure. **2** *If the actor isn't paid he'll sue the director for breach of contract. Police arrested the demonstrators for committing a breach of the peace:* violation, infringement, infraction, transgression, disobedience, trespass, defiance; non-observance, non-compliance; disregard, neglect, dereliction, failure.

Ant. 1 closure; stoppage, blockage. **2** adherence to, observance, compliance with, obedience, fidelity to; attention, heed, regard.

breadth *n.* **1** *The length multiplied by the breadth will give you the area of the field:* width, wideness, broadness, latitude. **2** *Thomas Jefferson, writer, politician, architect, and farmer, had a mind of great breadth. We were stunned by the breadth of the mountain range:* broadness, scope, range, reach, spread, compass, stretch, span, expanse, extent, extensiveness; size, area, dimensions, measure.

Ant. 1 length, longness, longitude. **2** narrowness, confinement, circumscription, restrictedness, slightness, scantiness.

◇ *Word origin: Breadth* comes from Middle English *brēde,* breadth. The *-th* ending first appears in a document from the reign of Henry VIII. Within a couple of generations *breadth* became the standard form of the word, doubtless because people preferred it as an analogue of *width* and *length.*

break *v.***1** *If you break that vase you'll have to pay for it. I broke my leg skiing:* shatter, fragment, burst, crack, fracture, snap, split, chip, splinter; crush, pulverize, granulate, powder, disintegrate, demolish. **2** Often **break off, break away**. *Break off a piece of liquorice* *for me. The mainmast broke away in the storm:* detach, separate, pull off, tear off, wrench away, sever, divide, cleave, sunder, rive, rend, disjoint, disconnect, dismember. **3** *The telly is broken again:* be inoperative, work improperly, become useless; ruin, destroy. **4** Usually **break off**. *The union broke off negotiations and called a strike:* end, stop, cease, halt, suspend, shut down, interrupt, discontinue. **5** *Who's going to break the bad news to her?:* disclose, reveal, divulge, announce, proclaim, tell, inform, make public, give out. **6** *When the storm breaks run for the house. The audience broke into applause:* erupt, burst out, come forth suddenly; happen, occur, appear. **7** Often **break in (out)**. *Horses must be broken in before they can be ridden. You must break yourself of the cigarette habit:* tame, train, master, discipline, subdue, overcome, bend to one's will. **8** *Paying for the house will just about break me:* bankrupt, ruin, cripple financially, clean out, strap for funds, impoverish, make insolvent, make impoverished, take all one's money, put on the rocks. **9** *The net broke the acrobat's fall:* take the force of, soften, diminish, weaken, lessen, lighten. **10** *This winter broke the record for rainfall:* surpass, exceed, better, top, outdo, beat, cap, excel, go beyond. **11** *The convict broke out of gaol. The full back broke through the defensive line and scored a try:* escape, get away from, make a get-away, slip away, take to one's heels, flee, run, run away, fly, dash, make a dash, take flight. **12** *Did you ever break the law? I hate to break my promise:* violate, be guilty of infraction of, infringe, transgress against, disobey, defy; disregard, ignore, pay no heed to, neglect, shirk, fall back on, renege on.

—*n.* **13** *The break in the pipe caused thousands of gallons of oil to be lost. Water seeped through the break in the basement wall:* breach, opening, rupture, fissure, hole, rent, crack, fracture, gap, gash, rift, tear, split, cleft, division, separation. **14** *Let's take a short break for lunch:* interruption, interlude, recess, interval, intermission, hiatus, lapse, rest, respite, pause. **15** *The actress's big break came when she stood in for the ailing star:* stroke of luck, opportunity, chance, fortune.

Ant. 1 repair, fix, mend, heal. **2** connect, join, unite, fasten, secure, attach, bind, weld. **3** repair, fix. **4** start, begin, commence, open; continue, preserve, prolong. **5** keep quiet about, conceal, hide, secrete, cover up. **6** end, stop, cease, halt; die down, die away, diminish. **7** submit to, yield to, acquiesce; free. **8** make wealthy, make prosperous, enrich, fill one's pockets, feather one's nest, give one money to burn. **9** increase. **10** fall short of, be under, be lower than. **11** capture, catch. **12** obey, adhere to, comply with; heed, observe, regard. **13** closing, stopping, blockage. **14** continuation, resumption.

breakable *adj. Those plates are too breakable for everyday use:* fragile, delicate, brittle, crumbly, frail, flimsy.

Ant. unbreakable, sturdy, strong.

breakdown *n.* **1** *The train had a breakdown outside Adelaide. I hear she had a nervous breakdown:* failure, collapse; disorder, mishap, deterioration. **2** *Give me a complete breakdown of all the supplies you need:* division, categorization, detailed list, item-by-item count, step-by-step instructions.

"One of the symptoms of approaching nervous breakdown is the belief that one's work is terribly important." —*Bertrand Russell*

breakup *n. The ship can't get through until the breakup of the ice in the spring. The argument between the friends led to their breakup:* separation, breaking, dispersal, split, splitting, disintegration, crack-up, parting.

breast *n.* **1** *He beat his breast in agony:* chest, bosom. **2** *The father's breast was filled with pride over his son's accomplishments:* heart, innermost self, very marrow.

breath *n.* **1** *It's so cold you can see your breath:* air breathed in and out. **2** *The patient's breath grew stronger:* breathing, respiration, wind, inhalation, exhalation. **3** *The puppets were so real they seemed to have the very breath of life:* spirit, vital spirit, vital spark, divine spark, life force, life-blood, animation, vitalization.

◇ *Usage note: Breath* (without a final *e*) is a noun meaning air from or in the lungs. *Breathe* (with a final *e*) is a verb meaning to inhale or exhale.

◇ *Word origin: Breath* and *breathe* come from Old English *brǣth*, vapour, exhalation, odour.

breathe *v.* **1** *Breathe that clear mountain air!:* draw breath, draw in air, inhale and exhale, respire; gasp, pant, puff, huff. **2** *Don't breathe a word of this to anyone:* whisper, murmur, impart.

◇ *Usage note and word origin:* See BREATH.

breath-taking *adj. The trapeze artists performed breath-taking feats:* exciting, awesome, amazing, astonishing, startling, surprising.

breech *n.* **1** *"Breech" is an old-fashioned word for "backside":* buttocks, rump, seat, behind, posterior, fundament; hindquarters, hind part, haunches. **2 breeches** *Jodhpurs are a type of riding breeches:* knee-breeches; (*also loosely*) trousers, pants.

◇ *Word origin: Breeches* comes from Latin *bracae*, term for the trousers worn by Gaulish tribesmen. In Caesar's day the barbarian and Romanized regions of Gaul were distinguished from each other by the names *Gallia Bracata* ("breeches-wearing Gaul") and *Gallia Togata* ("toga-wearing Gaul").

breed *v.* **1** *Mosquitos breed in stagnant water. Brecon farmers breed the best pigs in the world:*

reproduce, propagate, beget, multiply, procreate, produce offspring, bear, bring forth, give forth, raise, grow. **2** *Familiarity breeds contempt:* foster, nurture, develop, cultivate, promote, mother, father; generate, produce, give rise to, cause, lead to, occasion, sire.
—*n.* **3** *The collie is a beautiful breed of dog:* species, strain, race, stock, order, family, variety, type, sort, kind.
Ant. **2** destroy, extinguish, kill, wipe out, eradicate, erase, demolish, extirpate; stifle, hinder, harm, injure, block, obstruct, stop, stay.

breeding *n.* **1** *Cattle breeding is big business. Tsetse-fly breeding is reduced by draining swamps:* raising, producing, production, growing; reproduction, propagation, begetting, multiplying, mating, procreation, generation, germination, bearing, spawning, hatching, bringing forth. **2** *The value of a racehorse depends on its breeding:* lineage, blood line, line, heredity, ancestry, parentage, extraction, pedigree, family tree, descent, genealogy. **3** *People of good breeding seldom lose their tempers:* manners, refinement, polish, gentility, background, politeness, courtesy, grace, cultivation; upbringing, training, rearing.

breeze *n.* **1** *A warm breeze blew from the south:* gentle wind, light wind, current of air, puff of wind, light gust, zephyr, waft.
—*v.* **2** *She breezed out of the room without a backward glance:* move in a carefree manner, sweep, sail, glide, flit, float, coast, waft, pass.
◇ *Word origin: Breeze* comes from Spanish *brisa,* north-east wind. The word passed into English during the 16th century, when maritime rivalry between England and Spain was at its height.

breezy *adj.* **1** *It's breezy out on deck today:* windy, windswept, gusty, blowy, blustery, squally. **2** *The speaker's short breezy talk cheered up the audience:* light, carefree, free and easy, blithesome, buoyant, lively, animated, vivacious, gay, cheerful, sunny, merry, jaunty, pert, debonair, fresh, airy, brisk, peppy, spry, frisky, sprightly, spirited, energetic, bouncy, resilient.
Ant. **1** calm, still, windless. **2** heavy, careworn, depressed, dull, sad, mournful, morose, lifeless, inanimate, unspirited; serious, pompous, heavy-handed.

"Therefore, since brevity is the soul of wit,
And tediousness the limbs and outward flourishes,
I will be brief: . . ." —*William Shakespeare*

---

brevity *n. Brevity is the opposite of prolixity. The brevity of life should make one live each day to the full:* briefness, shortness, quickness, conciseness, pithiness, succinctness, terseness; impermanence, transience, ephemerality.
Ant. long-windedness, prolixity; lengthiness.

brew *v.* **1** *Let the tea brew a little longer. To make beer, grain, hops, and malt must be brewed:* boil, steep, seethe; ferment, soak. **2** *The children are brewing up a surprise for your birthday. A storm is brewing on the horizon:* concoct, contrive, scheme, plot, devise, plan, think up, arrange, prepare, make produce, foment; originate, initiate, germinate, hatch, start, begin, form, formulate, gather, ripen.
—*n.* **3** *Milk with honey and an egg yolk is a delicious brew. The beer here is a mild brew:* beverage, drink, concoction, mixture; (*variously*) beer, ale, stout, porter.
Ant. **1** chill; drain, distill. **2** cancel, disperse, break up, die away.

bribe *n.* **1** *The inspector was accused of accepting a bribe:* pay-off, hush money, illegal gift, graft, *Slang* payola.
—*v.* **2** *The criminal tried to bribe the policeman:* buy off, pay off, suborn, *Informal* grease the palm of.

bric-à-brac *n. Her home is filled with bric-à-brac:* baubles, ornaments, knick-knacks, gimcracks, gewgaws, kickshaws.
◇ *Usage note:* Although *bric-à-brac* means knick-knacks or decorative objects, it is a collective noun and takes a singular verb: *Bric-à-brac is out of place in modern décor.*

bridal *adj. Her bridal gown was of pure silk. The bridal party arrived at the church:* bride's; wedding, marriage, matrimonial, nuptial.
◇ *Word origin: Bridal* originates from Old English *brȳdealu,* meaning bridal feast or wedding-feast, from *brȳd* (bride) + *ealu* (ale, ale-drinking).

bridge *n.* **1** *London Bridge crosses the Thames. They built a bridge over the railway:* span, overpass; catwalk. **2** *We must build a strong bridge of friendship with America:* bond, link, tie, band, connection, union, association, alliance, liaison.
—*v.* **3** *A wooden plank bridged the stream. Both parents and teenagers must try to bridge the generation gap between them:* span, cross, cross over, traverse, go over, extend across, reach across; link, connect, bind, band, unify.
Ant. **2** separation, division, schism, split, break, dissociation. **3** widen, separate, divide, split, break.

bridle *n.* **1** *Grab the horse by the bridle:* head harness; (*loosely*) bit and brace; restraint, check, curb.
—*v.* **2** *Bridle the horses:* put on the head harness; harness. **3** *You must learn to bridle your temper:* curb, check, restrain, control, restrict, suppress, repress, constrain, inhibit, hinder, arrest; master, manage, harness, direct, rule. **4** *Anyone would bridle at such insults:* thrust up one's head, rear up, draw up; recoil, draw back, flinch.
Ant. **2** unbridle, unharness. **3** express, voice, utter, air, vent, let out, let go, free. **4** cringe, cower, grovel.

brief *adj.* **1** *There will be a brief stop for lunch:* short, short-lived, momentary, temporary, quick, hasty, swift, fleeting, transient, transitory. **2** *Each student is to write a brief outline of the book:* short, concise, succinct, terse, pithy, compact, thumb-nail; abbreviated, condensed, abridged, compressed, limited, shortened, curtailed, summarized, summary.
—*v.* **3** *The Minister of Defence briefed the Prime Minister on the enemy's strength:* inform, inform quickly, give a run-down, fill in on, give the details of, describe to, advise, instruct, prepare.
—*n.* **4** *The law journal printed the brief of the case:* legal summary; (*loosely*) argument, contention, case, defence.
Ant. 1, 2 long, lengthy, extended, prolonged, protracted, extended, extensive. **3** keep uninformed, conceal, keep secret, hide, cover up.

Exploring the Word: *Brief* and *brevity* come from the Latin word *brevis,* meaning short. This same Latin word gives us *abbreviate,* to shorten, especially to make a short form of a word; *breve,* a mark ˇ used to indicate a short vowel sound or unstressed syllable in poetry; and *breviary,* a book of short daily prayers and offices for the canonical hours in the Catholic church.

brigade *n.* **1** *A brigade is usually commanded by a brigadier-general:* (*technically, two or more*) regiments, battalions, army groups, squadrons; (*loosely*) military unit, unit, legion, contingent, body of troops, detachment. **2** *The little town has a volunteer fire brigade:* company, corps, unit, force, squad, contingent, outfit, crew, group, organization.
◇ *Word origin: Brigade* and *brigand* come from Italian *brigata* and *brigante,* meaning "troop" and, originally, "soldier" respectively. Both words are based on *brigare,* to contend, fight.

brigand *n. In the old days, wild brigands plundered farmhouses and held up stage-coaches:* outlaw, bandit, desperado, ruffian, cutthroat, gunman, hoodlum; plunderer, looter, vandal, pillager, spoiler, despoiler, pilferer; (*variously*) highwayman, robber, thief, rustler, pirate, buccaneer, privateer, corsair.
◇ *Usage note:* Specifically, a *brigand* is a member of a roving and plundering gang, such as a highwayman, cattle thief, or pirate. Thus, an outlaw who works alone, plans specific robberies, or breaks and enters, is not technically a *brigand.* Captain Hook was a *brigand,* but Jesse James was a robber.

bright *adj.* **1** *The bright lights hurt my eyes. Children love bright colours:* brilliant, blazing, dazzling, shimmering, vivid, intense, shining, glowing, gleaming, beaming, radiant, sparkling, glittering, resplendent; luminous, lustrous, lambent, effulgent; illuminated, light-filled, sunny, warm. **2** *Only bright students are given scholarships. He came up with a bright idea:* intelligent, smart, brainy, brilliant; wise, profound, sage, sagacious, shrewd, keen, clever, inventive, resourceful, ingenious, perceptive, discerning, alert, wide-awake, clear-headed, aware, quick, quick-witted, sharp, acute, astute; talented, gifted, capable, competent, proficient, masterful, excellent, great, illustrious, grand, magnificent, outstanding, remarkable, splendid. **3** *The children's bright laughter could be heard throughout the house:* merry, gay, happy, joyous, joyful, cheerful, glad; jolly, lively, exhilarating, sparkling. **4** *The young lawyer has a bright future ahead of him:* promising, favourable, auspicious, propitious, hopeful, optimistic, exciting, rosy successful, prosperous, happy, healthy, sunny, excellent, grand, good.
Ant. dull. **1** dim, pale, subdued, dark, drab, gloomy, murky, obscure, dusky, cloudy, misty, cool. **2** dumb, stupid, muddle-headed, slow-witted, witless, brainless, simple-minded, simple, foolish, unwise, rattle-brained, feather-brained, doltish, oafish, dunder-headed, moronic, idiotic, imbecilic, half-witted, asinine, thick, slow, retarded, lethargic, sluggish, ignorant; untalented, ungifted, incapable, incompetent. **3** sad, glum, dreary, joyless, gloomy, forlorn, unhappy, dismal, cheerless, grim, depressed, dejected, doleful, melancholy, downcast, downhearted, heavy-hearted. **4** unpromising, inauspicious, hopeless, pessimistic, dim, grim; failing, unsuccessful, unhappy, cloudy, bad, awful, terrible, poor.
◇ *Usage note:* Both *bright* and *brightly* may be used as adverbs. Thus *The sun shines bright* is as correct as *The sun shines brightly.*

brighten *v.* **1** *Brighten the kitchen by painting it yellow:* make brighter, lighten, enliven, perk up, illuminate, light. **2** *Your visit brightened my day:* gladden, cheer, make happy, perk up, buoy up, lift, lift up, enliven, animate, stimulate.
Ant. 1 darken, dull, blacken. **2** sadden, depress, make downcast.

brilliance, brilliancy *n.* **1** *The diamond glowed with a pure white brilliance:* brightness, radiance, sparkle, glitter, lustre, gleam, glow, shine, sheen, shimmer, dazzle, blaze, resplendence, splendour, luminosity, effulgence, intensity, vividness. **2** *The brilliance of Louis Pasteur led to important advances in medicine and chemistry:* intelligence, smartness, braininess, wisdom, profundity, sagacity, shrewdness, keenness, cleverness, inventiveness, resourcefulness, ingenuity, perception, discernment, alertness, clear-headedness, awareness, quickness, sharpness, acuity; genius, talent, gift, capability, competence, proficiency, masterfulness, excellence, greatness, illustriousness, magnificence, grandeur, distinction.

Ant. 1 dullness, dimness, paleness, darkness, drabness, obscurity. 2 stupidity, dumbness, dullness, idiocy, asininity, imbecility, thickness, simple-mindedness, doltishness, oafishness, folly, silliness; inanity, ineptitude, incompetence, mediocrity.

brilliant *adj.* 1 *The crown was brilliant with jewels:* See BRIGHT, def. **1.** 2 *Einstein had a brilliant mind. Rachmaninov was a brilliant pianist:* See BRIGHT, def. **2.**

Ant. See BRIGHT, Antonym list **1** and **2.**

◇ *Word origin: Brilliant* comes from Greek *berillos*, beryl, a stone of which some brilliant varieties are used as gems.

brim *n.* 1 *Fill the cup to the brim:* upper edge, brink, rim, border, margin, verge; projecting rim.

—*v.* 2 *Her eyes brimmed with tears:* fill, fill up, overflow.

brine *n. To make dill pickles, soak cucumbers in brine:* salt water, salt solution, pickling solution; the sea, sea-water.

Ant. fresh water, clear water.

bring *v.* 1 *Bring the dessert to the table:* carry, convey, bear, tote, fetch, deliver, transport, take. 2 *April showers bring May flowers. My son brought ruin on my house:* bring about, cause, induce, effect, institute, begin, start, initiate; create, engender, generate, originate, produce. 3 *I just can't bring myself to apologize:* compel, force, make, persuade, convince. 4 *How much did the house bring on the market?:* sell for; fetch.

Ant. 1 take away, send, remove. 2 quash, kill, prevent, suppress, quell, crush, repress, extinguish, put down, squelch, squash, dispel, nullify, abolish, void, revoke.

brink *n. The tree grew on the brink of the cliff. The world is on the brink of war:* edge, margin, rim, brim, verge, border, skirt, shore, bank; threshold, point.

brisk *adj.* 1 *The hikers kept up a brisk pace:* quick, swift, lively, active, sprightly, spry, energetic, vigorous, snappy, peppy, alert, animated, spirited, vivacious, nippy, breezy, bustling, busy, dynamic. 2 *It's great to work outdoors during brisk autumn days:* bracing, invigorating, refreshing, fresh, stimulating, stirring, rousing, exhilarating, vivifying.

Ant. 1 sluggish, torpid, lethargic, lazy, indolent, slothful, inactive, unenergetic, heavy, dull. 2 tiring, exhausting, fatiguing, wearisome; boring, monotonous, dull.

brittle *adj. This chalk is too brittle to write with:* breakable, fragile, frangible, crumbly, friable.

Ant. strong, sturdy, supple, elastic, resilient, flexible; unbreakable.

broach *v. He's been seeing her for years but has never broached the subject of marriage:* mention, suggest, introduce, bring up, touch on, pose, propose, advance, submit, institute, open up, launch.

Ant. repress, suppress, keep hidden, conceal, secrete; close, end.

broad *adj.* 1 *He was tall and had broad shoulders:* wide; outspread. 2 *Can you imagine crossing the broad expanse of Australia on a motor bike?:* expansive, extensive, extended, spacious, immense, capacious, roomy, rangy, large, ample, sizeable, thick. 3 *A zoo-keeper has to have a broad knowledge of the animal kingdom:* extensive, comprehensive, sweeping, general, inclusive, far-reaching, universal, wide, wide-ranging, all-embracing, immense, unlimited; non-specific, undetailed. 4 *Give me a broad hint. They robbed the bank in broad daylight:* full, plain, open, clear, obvious.

Ant. narrow. 1 long, lengthy. 2, 3 limited, confined, circumscribed, restricted, small, slight, scant. 3 specific, detailed. 4 partial, veiled, obscure, hidden, enigmatical.

broadcast *v.* 1 *The World Cup match is broadcast in Europe, Asia, and the Americas:* transmit, send out, beam, put on the air, radio; televise, relay; cable.

—*n.* 2 *The special election broadcast will be on the box at eight tonight:* programme, show; announcement, talk, statement.

◇ *Word origin: Broadcast* originally referred to the technique of scattering seed over the whole surface to be sown, rather than planting it in rows.

broaden *v. The road was broadened into a four-lane motorway. The company broadened its line by adding three new items to sell to supermarkets:* widen, spread out, stretch, enlarge, expand, extend, distend, dilate, swell; increase, raise, boost, build up, amplify, augment, supplement, develop, advance, improve, strengthen, reinforce, intensify.

Ant. narrow, squeeze, contract, decrease; reduce, simplify, subtract from, diminish.

broad-minded *adj. The new priest is a flexible and broad-minded man:* open-minded, tolerant, catholic, unprejudiced, unbiased, flexible, unbigoted, undogmatic, liberal, unprovincial, charitable, amenable, magnanimous.

Ant. narrow-minded, closed-minded, intolerant, prejudiced, biased, bigoted, inflexible, dogmatic, provincial, uncharitable.

brochure *n. The company sent out an advertising brochure:* pamphlet, leaflet, circular, booklet, folder.

◇ *Word origin:* Originally a *brochure* was a pamphlet whose pages were stitched together. It is based on French *brocher*, to stitch.

broil *v.* 1 *Don't fry the steaks, broil them:* cook by direct heat. 2 *This sun will broil you:* make very hot, burn, scorch, sear, cook, blister, bake, roast, fry, parch.

◇ *Word origin: Broil* comes from Old French *brouiller*, to burn.

broke *adj. I'm afraid I'm flat broke:* without

funds, bankrupt, penniless, insolvent, impoverished, *Slang* cleaned out.
Ant. wealthy, rich, prosperous, affluent, solvent.

bronze *adj. The coast-guard's skin was bronze from the sun:* reddish-brown, copper-coloured, chestnut, reddish-tan, tan, brownish.
◇ *Word origin: Bronze* comes from Italian *bronzo*, bronze, which itself derives from the Latin. It first appeared in medieval documents listing bronze objects of antiquity. The word has passed into virtually all European languages.

brooch *n. The dress was ornamented with a brooch on the lapel:* pin, clasp.

brood *n.* **1** *The hen drove the intruders away from her brood:* hatchlings, chicks, young, offspring, litter, spawn, family, children.
—*v.* **2** *The hen is brooding her eggs:* sit upon, incubate, hatch, cover. **3** *Don't brood over lost opportunities:* worry, fret, mope, sulk, dwell, mull, chew.

brook[1] *n. There are trout in this brook:* stream, streamlet, rivulet, rill, beck, burn, gill.

"The music of the brook silenced all conversation."
—*Thomas Hood*

---

brook[2] *v. I will not brook any more of your insolence!:* take, stand, abide, allow, tolerate, bear, suffer, endure, stomach.
Ant. reject, refuse, dismiss, forbear, forbid, prohibit, disallow, bar, banish, resist, repudiate, rebuff, renounce.

broth *n. Instead of coffee try a cup of beef broth for breakfast:* stock, thin soup, bouillon, consommé.

brothel *n. New Orleans was once notorious for its brothels:* whore-house, house of prostitution, red-light district, bawdy-house, house of ill-repute, house of ill-fame, bordello, bordel, stew, disorderly house, seraglio; *French* maison de passe, maison close.
◇ *Word origin: Brothel* is the Middle English word for "worthless, lewd person, prostitute."

brother *n.* **1** *Jakob and Wilhelm Grimm were the scientist brothers who collected fairy-tales:* male sibling, blood-brother. **2** *We are all brothers under the skin. Brother, your nomination has been accepted. The soldiers were brothers in arms:* fellow member, kinsman, peer, (*female*) sister; fellow-man, fellow citizen, countryman, landsman; comrade, companion; colleague, confrère, associate, partner, pal, mate, chum. **3** *Trappist brothers take vows of silence:* monk, friar, religious, cleric.
Ant. 1 sister, female sibling. **2** non-member, foreigner, stranger.
◇ *Usage note:* In religious use, a *brother* is a member of a religious order who is not a priest. Thus, to refer to a priest as a *brother* is incorrect.

brow *n.* **1** *The blacksmith wiped the sweat from his brow:* forehead. **2** *The lighthouse is on the brow of the cliff:* edge, brink, brim, rim, periphery, verge, margin, side, border, boundary.

browbeat *v. The lawyer browbeat the witness into confessing that he had seen the crime committed:* bully, intimidate, cow, domineer, tyrannize, abash, *Slang* bulldoze; badger, harass, hector; threaten, terrorize, frighten.
Ant. coax, persuade, flatter, invite, charm, beguile, seduce.

brown *adj. Pot-roast with brown gravy is delicious:* brownish, brunette, chocolate, coffee, mahogany, walnut, nut-brown, drab, khaki, greenish-brown, dirt-coloured, beige, liver-coloured, chestnut, tawny, sorrel, hazel, bay, purplish-brown, puce, umber, reddish-brown, terra-cotta, rust, russet, roan, bronze, yellow-brown, buff, golden-brown, copper, auburn, light-brown, dun, sand-coloured, cinnamon, ginger, tan, camel, fawn.

browse *v.* **1** *Two cows were browsing in the field:* graze, pasture, nibble, feed, eat. **2** *I just browsed through the paper. We browsed through the bookshop:* peruse, look through, look over, glance through, examine cursorily, check over, skim, scan, survey, dip into; wander through.

bruise *v.* **1** *I was cut and bruised by the fall. Don't bruise the tomatoes:* discolour, mark, blacken, mar, blemish; injure, hurt, damage. **2** *The insult bruised her feelings:* offend, wound, hurt, injure, abuse.
—*n.* **3** *The blow caused a large bruise on his arm:* contusion, black mark, discoloration, mark, blemish; injury.

brunette *adj.* **1** *He prefers brunette women to blonde:* dark-haired, brown-haired; brown-haired and brown-eyed, dark, olive skinned.
—*n.* **2** *She was a brunette until she dyed her hair red:* a dark-haired woman or girl.
Ant. blond, blonde. **1** fair, light, light-haired, light-skinned.
◇ *Word origin: Brunette* is an old diminutive form of French *brun*, brown.

brunt *n. The Norfolk coast bore the brunt of the storm:* full force, force, impact, main shock, violence, stress.

brush[1] *n.* **1** *Paint goes on more slowly with a brush than with a roller:* bristled tool; (*variously*) paintbrush, whisk, duster, clothes-brush, hairbrush, nail-brush, scrubbing-brush, broom, besom, tooth-brush, shoe-brush. **2** *She removed the speck of dust with a brush of her hand:* brushing, sweep, whisk, flick, grazing, dusting; touch, stroke. **3** *The arrest for speeding was his first brush with the law:* encounter, meeting, confrontation, skirmish, engagement, fracas, scuffle, battle, set-to.
—*v.* **4** *Brush your teeth three times a day:* use a brush on; (*variously*) wash, clean, cleanse, scrub, dust, groom, paint, polish, varnish,

shine. **5** *He brushed the papers aside. The spider's web brushed my forehead:* sweep, whisk, flick; graze, touch, stroke, caress.

brush[2] *n. The rabbit disappeared into the brush:* underwood, brushwood, undergrowth, bush, bushes, shrubbery, shrubs; thicket, bracken, fern, copse, sedge, scrub, forest, woodland, woodlands, bush country.

brusque *adj. Being busy is no excuse for being brusque:* abrupt, curt, short, gruff, bearish, crusty, blunt, bluff, harsh, rough, tart; rude, impolite, ungracious, unceremonious, discourteous, ungentle.

Ant. civil, considerate, patient, gentle, courteous, polite, gracious, cordial, genial.

◇ *Word origin: Brusque* comes from Italian *brusco,* sour, sharp, disagreeable. The same word has long been a plant name in the western Mediterranean area for a prickly shrub known in English as "butcher's-broom." *Brusque* originally meant sharp and disagreeable, like butcher's-broom.

brutal *adj. In* Peter Pan, *Captain Hook is a brutal pirate. Murder is a brutal crime:* cruel, vicious, savage, inhuman, barbaric, barbarous, ruthless, hard-hearted, heartless, pitiless, merciless, remorseless, unfeeling, bloody, brutish, fierce, demoniacal, bloodthirsty, atrocious, hellish; harsh, crude, coarse.

Ant. humane, gentle, sweet, kind, soft-hearted, merciful, sympathetic, sensitive; noble, civilized, refined.

◇ *Word origin:* See BRUTE.

brutality *n. The kidnappers subjected their prisoners to extreme brutality:* cruelty, viciousness, savagery, savageness, inhumanity, ruthlessness, barbarity, brutishness, ferocity, harshness.

Ant. humaneness, gentleness, kindness, tenderness.

brute *n.* **1** *Hunger can turn men into brutes:* savage, barbarian, cruel person, monster, demon, fiend, devil, swine. **2** *Alexander Pope said that man is "the middle link between angels and brutes":* beast, wild animal, animal, dumb creature, beast of the field.

Ant. 1 gentleman, angel. **2** human, man.

◇ *Word origin:* Both *brute* and *brutal* come from Latin *brutus,* heavy, stupid, or dull.

bubble *n.* **1** *A bubble of paint ruined the smooth wall. Children love to blow bubbles:* air ball, globule, blister, bleb. **2 bubbles** foam, froth, fizz, effervescence.

"Like a hell-broth boil and bubble.
Double, double, toil and trouble;
Fire burn and cauldron bubble."
—*William Shakespeare*

—*v.* **3** *The water began to bubble in the kettle:* boil, percolate, seethe; foam, froth, fizz, effervesce, sparkle, gurgle, burble.

Ant. 3 be flat.

buccaneer *n. Buccaneers attacked Spanish treasure galleons in the Caribbean:* pirate, privateer, freebooter, corsair.

◇ *Word origin: Buccaneer* was originally a French word, *boucanier,* meaning a French settler in Haiti who had gone so far native as to cook and dry meat over a Haitian *boucan,* a large cooking-grill. Some such settlers turned to piracy, and the word *buccaneer* (those who cook over a *boucan*) came to mean "pirate."

bucket *n. The water-bucket leaks:* pail, tub, vessel; scoop, scuttle, hod; bucketful, pailful.

◇ *Word origin: Bucket* is a Norman French diminutive of Old English *būc,* belly, pitcher.

buckle *n.* **1** *The cowboy wore a wide belt with a silver buckle:* clasp, hasp, fastener, catch, clip. —*v.* **2** *Buckle the strap tighter:* clasp, fasten, catch, secure, hook, couple. **3** *The walls of the building buckled during the fire:* bend, belly out, bulge, sag, warp, curl, crinkle, wrinkle, contort, distort; collapse, cave in, crumple.

Ant. 2 unbuckle, unfasten, unhook, uncouple, release, loosen. **3** straighten.

◇ *Word origin: Buckle* comes from French *boucle,* the boss or knob by which a shield was held. (A small shield was called a *buckler.*) Later the word was applied to the strap of a shield and then the cheek-strap of a helmet, which had adjustable buckles. *Buckle* still refers to a knob or projection used for lacing on some types of boots and shoes.

bud *n.* **1** *The plant's first buds will open soon:* unopened flower; shoot, sprout.

—*v.* **2** *The rose-bushes are budding:* put forth shoots, sprout, open; begin to grow, begin to bloom, develop, burgeon.

budge *v.* **1** *We couldn't budge the heavy rock:* stir, move, shift, dislodge, push, slide, roll. **2** *Once Dad had made a decision, no one could budge him:* move, change, shift, influence, persuade, sway, convince.

Ant. 1 stick, remain, stay.

◇ *Word origin: Budge* comes from French *bouger,* to stir, move.

budget *n.* **1** *The Chancellor's budget must be approved by Parliament. Our household budget is £30 a week:* financial plan, spending plan, financial statement; allowance, allotment, allocation, funds, monies, resources, means, cost.

—*v.* **2** *Sensible people budget their incomes:* allocate, schedule, plan, apportion, portion out, arrange, ration.

◇ *Word origin: Budgets* sometimes *bulge* and both words ultimately come from Latin *bulga,* leather bag. *Budget* comes to us from this Latin word via French *bougette,* little purse.

buff *n.* **1** *I bought a jacket made of buff:* leather, buffalo hide. **2** *The boys went swimming in the buff:* nakedness, bare skin, *Informal* the raw, altogether, birthday suit.

—*adj.* **3** *The child has buff-coloured hair:* yellowish-brown, tan, tawny; straw, sandy, yellowish.
—*v.* **4** *She buffed the wood until it shone:* polish, rub, burnish, smooth.
◇ *Word origin: Buff* comes from the French word for buffalo, *buffle*, hence a buffalo skin, later any skin (including our own in the phrase "in the buff"), then the colour of leather, and finally came to mean to clean or polish with a piece of leather, velvet, or the like.

buffer *n. After World War I several small countries were created to serve as buffers between major powers:* shield, cushion, protector, bumper.

buffet *v. The boxer buffeted his opponent about the head. The wind buffeted the sails:* hit, strike, beat, box, jab, wallop, cuff, slap, knock, baste, pound, thump, bang, rap, thwack, pummel, thrash; push, bump, shove.

buffoon *n. The class buffoon made funny faces while the teacher was speaking:* clown, jester, joker, prankster, trickster, funny-man, mimic, zany, silly-billy, comedian, comic, merry andrew, madcap, wag; fool, harlequin, pantaloon, Punchinello, Punch, scaramouch, pierrot.
◇ *Word origin: Buffoon* comes from Italian *buffone*, clown, jester. In opera, a *buffo*, another Italian word, is a male singer of comic roles, usually a bass.

bug *n.* **1** *This bed is riddled with bugs:* small aphid-like insect, *in technical use* Hemiptera. **2** *A lot of people have caught the flu bug now:* virus, germ.

build *v.* **1** *The school is building a new gym. This factory builds cars:* construct, erect, make, put up, set up, put together, fabricate, fashion, manufacture, produce. **2** *My father built this business with years of hard work. You must build up your strength again:* increase, enlarge, greaten, extend, develop, raise, enhance, build up, improve, intensify, multiply, augment, supplement, amplify, strengthen, renew, reinforce, harden, steel, brace; establish, found, originate, launch, institute, begin, start, initiate, inaugurate, set up, open, embark on, undertake. **3** *The army tries to build men:* form, shape, mould, produce, create.
—*n.* **4** *His build is too small for playing football:* physique, form, figure, body, construction, structure, shape.
Ant. 1–3 demolish, tear down, dismantle, destroy. **2** decrease, diminish, reduce, lessen, lower, contract, attenuate, curtail, shrink, scale down; weaken, dilute, deplete, decline, impair, sap, undermine, debilitate, cripple, harm, injure; end, stop, terminate, finish, conclude, wind up, close, discontinue, suspend, relinquish.
◇ *Word origin: Build* originates from Old English *bold*, house.

building *n. That building was designed by Frank Lloyd Wright:* structure, edifice, construction.

bulge *n.* **1** *What's that bulge in your pocket?:* lump, bump, protuberance, protrusion, projection, swelling, prominence, curve; sagging, bagginess, excess.
—*v.* **2** *The Christmas stocking bulged with presents:* swell, swell out, puff out, protrude, project, stand out, stick out, bag, sag.
Ant. 1 hollow, cavity, hole, pocket. **2** shrink, cave in, collapse.
◇ *Word origin: Bulge* comes from Latin *bulga*, leather bag, which also gives us our word *budget*.

> **Exploring the Word:** The names for the parts of a building have some interesting stories. Originally *attic* was an architectural term meaning a small top storey with square columns of the *Attic* order (from *Attica*, the region of Athens in Greece). An attic may also be called a *garret*, which was originally the highest part of a castle or fort built for look-outs, and comes from Old French *garite*, watch-tower. *Basement* comes from Greek *basis* (pedestal), hence that which is the pedestal for a building. A basement may also be called a *cellar* from Latin *cella*, meaning a cell or small room. Our words *floor* and *roof* come from Old English, as does *door*, which originally meant a gate. *Wall* is from Latin *vallus*, meaning palisade or rampart, the breastwork of stakes round a fort. *Window* comes from Old Norse *vindauga*, "wind-eye."

bulk *n.* **1** *The sheer bulk of an elephant is startling:* mass, massiveness, largeness, bigness, amplitude, magnitude, size, volume, weight, dimensions, proportions, extent, quantity, measure, substance, greatness, hugeness, enormity. **2** *He left the bulk of his estate to his wife:* main part, major part, greater part, principal part, best part, lion's share, body, most, majority, preponderance, plurality.
Ant. 2 lesser part, minor part, smallest part.
◇ *Word origin: Bulk* comes from Old Norse *bulki*, cargo.

bulky *adj. The package is light but it's too bulky to carry:* cumbersome, unwieldy, clumsy, awkward, unhandy, ungainly, unmanageable, lumpish; large, big, huge, massive, immense, voluminous, enormous, hulking, extensive, capacious, sizeable.
Ant. handy, manageable, wieldy, small, little, petite, diminutive, slim.

bull *n. The elephant herd contained three bulls and seven cows:* male; (*variously*) male bovine animal, ox, male elephant, male whale, male seal, male elk, male moose.

bulletin *n. The TV programme was interrupted by a news bulletin:* brief announcement, news report, report, dispatch, release, communiqué, communication, statement, message, notification, note.

◇ *Word origin: Bulletin* comes from Latin *bulla*, edict, seal, or official document. Latin *bulla* also gives us *bill* (receipt), *bill* of sale, *bill* of lading, and papal *bull*.

bully *n.* **1** *The bully terrorized the small boys:* tormentor, intimidator, autocrat, petty tyrant, despot, oppressor, coercer; tough, ruffian.
—*v.* **2** *He loved to bully his younger brother:* intimidate, cow, browbeat, bulldoze, tyrannize, domineer, terrorize, frighten, coerce, harass, annoy, ride roughshod over, tread on.
—*interj.* **3** *Bully for you, mate!:* hurray, hurrah, good, well done.
Ant. 2 lure, entice, flatter, coax, cajole, urge, persuade.
◇ *Word origin: Bully* came from Dutch *boele*, meaning "sweetheart or fine fellow," in the 1500's. Later, it came to mean "swashbuckler or hired tough." Throughout the 18th century, it meant "pimp."

bulwark *n.* **1** *A bulwark surrounded the old fort. Aswan Dam stands as a bulwark against flooding of the Nile:* defensive wall, earthwork, embankment, rampart, parapet; barrier, guard. **2** *Universal suffrage is the bulwark of democracy:* support, mainstay.
Ant. 2 weakness, weak link.

"Britannia needs no bulwarks,
No towers along the steep;
Her march is o'er the mountain waves,
Her home is on the deep."
— *Thomas Campbell*

---

bump *v.* **1** *The child bumped his head on the table. The two cars bumped together:* hit, strike, knock, slam, bang, smack, whack, crack, thump, rap; collide, crash into, crash, smash into, run into, butt, buffet, clash. **2** *The old van bumped along the rocky road:* bounce, jolt, jar, jounce, jostle; shake, rattle.
—*n.* **3** *His amnesia was caused by a bump on the head:* blow, rap, knock, impact, hit, whack, wallop, slam, smack, sock, smash, bang, crack, slap, punch, crash, jolt, collision. **4** *His legs were covered with bumps and bruises. Watch that bump in the road:* lump, swelling; hump, knob, protuberance, bulge, excrescence, node, knot, nodule.
Ant. 2 roll, glide, sail, flow, slide, slip, glissade, coast.

bun *n.* **1** *Currant buns are good for tea:* roll, soft roll, sweet roll. **2** *Aunt Mary always wore her hair in a bun:* coil, knot.

bunch *n.* **1** *A bunch of grapes makes a pretty centre-piece. Let's throw out that old bunch of newspapers:* cluster, clump; bundle, batch, collection, assortment, accumulation, array, stack, heap, pile, quantity, lot, mass, number, amount; shock, knot. **2** *A bunch of children surrounded the ice-cream man:* group, band, flock, bevy, troop, pack, multitude, crowd, host, company, gang, tribe, team, mob, string, gathering; assembly.
—*v.* **3** *We bunched around the fire for warmth:* huddle, crowd, gather, cluster, group, mass, collect, draw together, congregate, assemble, pack, flock, herd, cram together.
Ant. 3 separate, disperse, scatter, leave.

bundle *n.* **1** *The Christmas shopper was loaded down with bundles. A bundle of books was donated to the library:* package, parcel, packet; bale, sheaf, pack, stack, heap, pile, array, bunch, batch, collection, assortment, accumulation, multitude; mass, group, amount, quantity.
—*v.* **2** *Newspapers were bundled on the van:* tie together, wrap, package, bind, truss, bale, stack.
Ant. 2 disperse, scatter.
◇ *Word origin: Bundle* comes from Middle Dutch *bundel*, sheaf of papers, bundle. It is related to our words *bond, band*, and *bind*, and to the German word *Bund*, confederation or society.

bungle *v. The plumber bungled the job and now the pipe leaks. I bungled in thinking that £100 would be enough for the holiday:* blunder, botch, mismanage, do badly, spoil, ruin, mar, butcher, mess up, make a mess of, miscalculate, misreckon, misestimate, miscompute, misjudge, *Slang* foul up, louse up, goof.
Ant. succeed, accomplish, effect, carry off, carry out, triumph.

bunk[1] *n. First-class passengers sleep in staterooms, third-class sleep in bunks:* berth, built-in bed, tiered bed, bed, pallet.

bunk[2] *n. Informal. His claiming to be a good swimmer is a lot of bunk:* poppycock, baloney, hokum, tommy-rot, rot, hog-wash, claptrap, humbug, hooey, drivel, piffle, hot air, stuff and nonsense, stuff, bull, bunkum, blather; nonsense, foolishness, inanity, ridiculousness.
◇ *Spelling tip: Bunk* is a short form of *buncombe. Bunkum* is nowadays the usual spelling of this word.
◇ *Word origin: Bunk,* empty talk, is a short form of *buncombe*, from *Buncombe* County, in North Carolina, U.S.A., whose congressman was known for making unimportant speeches in Congress, saying he was "making a speech for Buncombe."

"History is bunk." —*Henry Ford*

---

buoy *n.* **1** *The coast-guard replaced the buoy in the channel:* floating marker, bell-buoy, float, beacon, bell.
—*v.* **2** *Flotation collars are used to buoy up space capsules that land in the sea:* keep afloat, keep from sinking. **3** *There's nothing like a good joke to buoy one's spirits:* lift, uplift, raise, boost, elevate, lighten, cheer, cheer up, gladden, brighten.

Ant. 2 sink, drown. **3** lower, crush, dash, cast down, depress, deject, deaden, sadden, dull, darken, chill, damp, dampen.

◇ *Word origin: Buoy* comes from Old High German *bouhhan*, buoy, and is related to *beacon*. The word can be found in most European languages: French *bouée*, Italian *boia*, Spanish *boya*, Russian *buī*.

buoyancy *n.* **1** *Modern life-jackets have a great deal of buoyancy:* floatability; lightness, weightlessness. **2** *The host's buoyancy ensured that the guests had a good time:* good spirits, animation, vivacity, enthusiasm, exhilaration, good humour, cheerfulness, cheeriness, gladness, joyousness, sunniness, brightness, glee, gaiety, light-heartedness, joviality, jollity.

Ant. 2 depression, dejection, low spirits, bad humour, cheerlessness, sadness, gloom, melancholy, tears; dullness, lethargy.

buoyant *adj.* **1** *Taking a deep breath and holding it can keep a person buoyant in the water:* afloat, floating, floatable; light, weightless. **2** *Her buoyant personality made her many friends:* animated, vivacious, enthusiastic, exhilarated, elated, cheerful, happy, glad, joyful, joyous, sunny, bright, gay, light, light-hearted, blithe, merry, jolly; optimistic, hopeful, carefree, free and easy, breezy, sportive; energetic, peppy, lively, sprightly.

Ant. 2 gloomy, glum, dour, sullen, moody, sad, joyless, cheerless, unhappy, tearful, depressed, dejected, morose, doleful, melancholy, despondent; pessimistic, careworn forlorn, hopeless, despairing; dull, lethargic.

◇ *Word origin: Buoyant* comes from Spanish *boyante*, light-sailing (from *boyar*, to float, which in turn comes from *boya*, buoy).

burden *n.* **1** *A horse can easily carry a burden of several hundred pounds:* load, weight; cargo, freight. **2** *She bore the burden of raising two children alone:* weight, load, strain, stress, care, responsibility, onus, trouble, anxiety; encumbrance, hardship.

—*v.* **3** *The hiker was burdened with a heavy pack. I don't like being burdened with someone else's problems:* weigh down, load with, load, overload; make responsible for, obligate, saddle with, trouble, encumber, try, tax, vex, press down, afflict, handicap, oppress, hamper, hinder.

Ant. 2 freedom, ease. **3** lighten, free, ease.

bureau *n.* **1** *Put the envelopes in the top drawer of the bureau:* desk, writing-desk, cabinet. **2** *The Marriage Bureau has moved just down the road:* agency, department, office, division, station, administration, branch, service.

◇ *Word origin: Bureau* was borrowed from the French during the 17th century. In French it means (1) desk, (2) office, and (3) agency.

burglar *n.* *The burglar has robbed eight houses in two weeks:* housebreaker, prowler, robber, thief, pilferer, purloiner; picklock, cracksman.

◇ *Spelling tip:* The *-ar* ending trips up some people. Just remember the term *burglAr Alarm* — and let the *a* in *Alarm* remind you of the *a* in *burglAr*.

◇ *Word origin: Burglar* comes from Germanic *burg* (fort, town, dwelling) + Latin *latro* (robber), hence the robber of a dwelling.

burglary *n.* *The burglary took place when no one was at home:* breaking and entering, break-in, theft, robbery, housebreaking, thieving, stealing, larceny, felony; filching, pilfering, purloining.

burial *n.* *The burial was held at a non-sectarian cemetery;* inhumation, interment, entombment; funeral, obsequies, rites.

Ant. exhumation, disinterment.

burlesque *n.* *The magazine contained a burlesque on absent-minded professors:* satire, parody, farce, take-off, spoof, caricature, mockery, ridicule, travesty; comedy, slapstick comedy, buffoonery.

Ant. factual representation, history, portrait; tragedy.

◇ *Word origin: Burlesque* is from Italian *burlesco*, comical (from *burla*, joke).

burly *adj.* *The wrestler was a burly man:* sturdy, strapping, hefty, bulky, brawny, beefy, thickset, big, large, sizeable, strong, ponderous, hulking.

Ant. puny, weak, thin, slim, skinny, scrawny, lean, spare, lanky, gaunt, angular, rawboned; small, diminutive.

burn *v.* **1** *The building burned as crowds watched helplessly. The lights in the kitchen burned all night:* be on fire, blaze, be ablaze, flame, be in flames, smoke, smoulder; incandesce, glow, flare, flash, flicker. **2** *Wet wood won't burn. Rake up the leaves and burn them. The toast burned:* ignite, kindle, fire; set on fire, set fire to, incinerate, consume with flames, reduce to ashes, cremate; char, scorch, sear, scald, singe, wither, shrivel, parch. **3** *This car burns too much oil:* use as fuel, consume. **4** *The child burned with fever:* be feverish, be hot, swelter, be flushed. **5** *The cut burns from the iodine. Holding the rope burned his hands:* pain, hurt, smart, sting, tingle, prickle, prick, bite, nip; chafe, abrade, scrape, skin, blister, irritate, nettle. **6** *I burn too easily to stay on the beach for long:* sunburn, tan, sun-tan, brown, bronze.

—*n.* **7** *The fireman suffered severe burns. The burn of the antiseptic made him wince. The lariat gave me a rope-burn:* (*variously*) first-degree burn, reddening, second-degree burn, blistering, blister, third-degree burn, charring; smart, sting, tingle, pain, prickle, bite; abrasion, chafe, scrape, irritation.

Ant. 1, 2 extinguish, put out, go out, burn out, smother. **4** be cold, shiver, have a chill, chill. **5** tickle, cool, assuage, soothe. **6** whiten, pale, fade.

◇ *Usage note: Burned* and *burnt* are both correct as the past tense and past participle of *burn.* Thus, *I burned my hand, I burnt my hand* and *I have burned my hand, I have burnt my hand* are all correct. *Burned* seems to be the more frequently used except in an adjectival position before a noun: *I burned my hand* but *a burnt offering.*

burning *adj.* **1** *The burning building gave off an eerie light:* flaming, aflame, afire, blazing, fiery, ignited, kindled, smouldering, smoking, raging, sizzling, glowing, flaring, flickering, flashing. **2** *She had a burning desire to be an actress:* all-consuming, raging, fervent, fervid, passionate, impassioned, ardent, eager, fanatic, zealous, intense, frantic, frenzied, fiery, red-hot, glowing, boiling, hot, heated, aglow; resolute, compelling, sincere, earnest. **3** *The hot mustard left a burning sensation on his tongue:* stinging, smarting, piercing, irritating, prickling, tingling; painful, caustic, biting, sharp, astringent, acrid, corroding, pungent.

Ant. 2 half-hearted, indifferent, lukewarm, mild, perfunctory, faint, passive, apathetic, lethargic, laconic, phlegmatic, lackadaisical. **3** soothing, cooling, numbing.

burnish *v. The silver bracelet was burnished to a bright finish:* polish, buff, shine, smooth, rub up.

Ant. abrade, scratch, mar.

◇ *Word origin: Burnish* comes from Old French *burnir,* to polish, which is related to *brun,* brown. *Burnir* also means "to make brown."

burrow *n.* **1** *The rabbit's burrow is under the flower-bed:* hole, furrow, den, lair, tunnel.

—*v.* **2** *The steam-shovel burrowed into the soft ground:* dig, tunnel, excavate, scoop out, hollow out.

Ant. 2 fill in, cover over.

bursar *n. Cheques for tuition are made out to the college bursar:* treasurer, purser, cashier, purse-bearer, paymaster.

◇ *Word origin: Bursar* has its root in Late Latin *bursa,* bag or purse, which also gives us *purse, purser,* and *disburse.*

burst *v.* **1** *The balloon burst. He watched the bombs bursting in the air. This dress is so tight that the seams are bursting:* break, break open, shatter, fly apart, fragment, disintegrate; explode, blow up, blast, detonate, discharge, pop; rupture, fracture, split, crack, splinter, pull apart, tear apart, separate, detach, divide, sunder, rend, disjoin, disconnect. **2** *She burst into tears. He burst into the room ranting and raving:* erupt, break, break out, gush forth, spout; rush, run, spring forth, barge, fly.

—*n.* **3** *The soldiers heard the burst of guns in the distance:* explosion, detonation, discharge, blast, bang, pop; breaking, shattering, crashing, cracking, splitting. **4** *With a great burst of speed the aeroplane took off:* outburst, outpouring, outbreak, eruption, rush, torrent.

Ant. 1 put together, hold together, connect, join, unite, fasten, secure, attach. **4** cessation, stopping; slowing down, deceleration.

◇ *Usage note: Burst* has only one form, *burst* — that is its present form, the past, and the past participle: *The balloon burst; it burst yesterday; it had burst before.* Remember: *Last winter the water-pipes burst in the cold weather. She bursts into tears whenever you mention his name.*

bury *v.* **1** *Sir Winston Churchill is buried in Bladon churchyard:* inter, entomb, inhume, lay in the grave, consign to the grave, deposit in the earth. **2** *The letter was buried under a pile of papers on the desk:* hide, conceal, secrete, cover, cover up, submerge, submerse, immerse, engulf, enclose, encase.

Ant. 1 exhume, disinter; resurrect. **2** unearth, uncover, discover, find, bring to light, reveal, expose, show, exhibit, display.

bush *n.* **1** *The lawn was bordered by rose-bushes:* plant, shrub, shubbery, hedge. **2** *The safari headed off into the bush:* woods, woodlands, forest, jungle.

business *n.* **1** *What business are you in?:* job, profession, vocation, occupation, career, calling, pursuit; work, employment, line, industry, trade, field, activity, speciality, specialization, function, duty, position, place, province, assignment, mission, livelihood, living, means of support, walk of life, bread and butter. **2** *A financier must have a keen understanding of business:* commerce, industry, manufacturing, trade, buying and selling, merchandising; dealing, transaction, negotiation, bargaining, affairs. **3** *My father owns a small business in Wales:* firm, establishment, concern, store, shop, factory, office, enterprise, venture, undertaking, corporation, company, partnership. **4** *My personal life is none of your business! Let's get down to the business in hand:* concern, affair, problem, question, responsibility; matter, job, task, duty, chore, situation, case, subject, topic, point.

Ant. 1 unemployment, inactivity; avocation, hobby, entertainment, relaxation.

◇ *Word origin: Business* originates from Old English *bisignis,* "busyness."

"Half the time when men think they are talking business, they are wasting time."

—*E. W. Howe*

---

businesslike *adj. Let's conduct this meeting in a businesslike manner:* orderly, organized, systematic, methodical, regular, efficient, practical, professional, correct, serious, careful, thorough, diligent, industrious, sedulous, assiduous, painstaking.

Ant. disorderly, disorganized, unorganized, unsystematic, irregular, miscellaneous, catch-as-catch-can, frivolous; inefficient, unprofessional, impractical, careless, sloppy, messy, untidy, slipshod.

bust *n.* **1** *The sweater had red sleeves and a blue stripe across the bust:* bosom, breast, chest. **2** *The sculptor made a bust of Beethoven:* sculpture of a person's head and shoulders.
◇ *Word origin: Bust* comes from Italian *busto,* torso, which means (1) portrait bust, (2) bosom, and (3) corset. The word entered English about 300 years ago, and for quite a while people said and wrote "busto" before shortening it to *bust.*

bustle *v.* **1** *The clerk bustled about trying to wait on three customers at once:* scurry, hurry, rush, hustle, scamper, dash, scramble, tear, fly, flit, scuttle, flutter, fluster; stir, bestir, be active, press on, make haste, be quick, make the most of one's time, work against time, not let the grass grow under one's feet.
—*n.* **2** *The bustle of Tokyo is very confusing:* commotion, flurry, tumult, hustle, stir, agitation, activity, fuss, hurry, excitement; pother, to-do, ado.
Ant. 1 move slowly, crawl, creep, drag one's feet, procrastinate, waste time; loaf, relax, rest. **2** inactivity, quiet, peacefulness, tranquillity.

busy *adj.* **1** *The secretary was busy all day typing the reports:* occupied, active, engaged, employed, working, hard at work, labouring, toiling, industrious, slaving, on duty, in harness, engrossed, absorbed, intent. **2** *This is one of my busy days:* active, strenuous, full, bustling.
—*v.* **3** *Grandmother busied herself with sewing:* occupy, keep occupied, engage, employ, work at, labour at, be engrossed in, be absorbed in.
Ant. 1, 2 idle, inactive, unoccupied, unemployed, at leisure, off duty. **2** lazy, slothful, indolent, relaxed, slack.

busybody *n. That old busybody wants to know everyone's business:* meddler, snooper, pry, Paul Pry; gossip, scandalmonger, tell-tale, tattle-tale, blabber-mouth, blabber, chatterbox, newsmonger, talebearer.

butt[1] *n. A cigar butt lay in the gutter. The rifle barrel is firmly attached to the butt:* end, blunt end, bottom, shank, stub, stump.
Ant. front, top.
◇ *Word origin: Butt*[1] comes from Middle English *butte,* thicker end of a thing. The word may be related to Old Norse *būtr,* block of wood.

butt[2] *n. It's no fun being the butt of a joke:* target, victim, mark, object, laughing-stock, dupe, Aunt Sally.
◇ *Word origin: Butt*[2] comes from Old French *but,* target.

butt[3] *v. The rams butted each other playfully: (with the head or horns)* push, shove, bump, knock, hit, strike, smack, thump, thwack, rap, ram, thrust, buffet, jostle, jab, slap.
◇ *Word origin:* See BUTTRESS.

buttocks *n. The trousers are too tight across the buttocks:* posterior, rump, seat, rear, rear end, fundament, nates, hindquarters, haunches.

buttress *n.* **1** *The north wall of the cathedral had a beautiful stone buttress:* support, brace, prop, stanchion, abutment, stay, shoulder.
—*v.* **2** *Buttress that fence with some two-by-fours. You'd better buttress your argument with more facts:* prop, prop up, brace, shore, shore up, reinforce, strengthen, bolster, support.
◇ *Word origin: Buttress* comes from Old French *bouter,* to push or thrust. The same Old French word gives us to *butt* with the head or horns, as a goat does.

buxom *adj. Nowadays, women want to be thin rather than buxom:* (*of women*) plump, robust, strapping, large-breasted, bosomy.
Ant. frail, delicate, thin, slender, slim, skinny, lean; pale, wan.

buy *v.* **1** *Many families buy a new car every two years:* purchase, put money into, pay for, invest in, acquire, procure, obtain, gain, get. **2** *Honest politicians cannot be bought:* bribe, buy off, corrupt, influence, suborn, offer an inducement, seduce.
—*n.* **3** *The coat was a good buy at £39:* bargain, worthy purchase.
Ant. 1 sell, vend, retail, auction, hawk; rent, lease.

buzz *n.* **1** *The audience made such a buzz that I couldn't hear the play. The buzz in the room stopped when he got up and spoke:* murmur, whisper; buzzing, hum, humming sound.
—*v.* **2** *Insects buzzed around the flowers:* hum, drone, whirr.
◇ *Word origin:* The word *buzz* was coined about 600 years ago. It is an onomatopoeic word — that is, it mimics the sound it represents.

bygone *adj. The old man told stories of bygone days:* gone by, past, former, departed, of yore, olden, ancient.
Ant. future, to come, coming, prospective, subsequent, succeeding, later, unborn.

bypass *v. The coach bypasses Coventry to avoid city traffic:* go round, go by, circumvent, avoid, dodge, avert.
Ant. go through, bisect, cross, meet, confront.

bystander *n. The boy wasn't involved in the fight — he was just an innocent bystander:* onlooker, looker-on, spectator, witness, observer, beholder, viewer, watcher, attender; passer-by.
Ant. participant, principal.

byword *n. From now on, "More haste, less speed" is going to be my byword:* rule, dictum, principle, precept, law, truth; pet phrase, slogan, motto, saying, maxim, proverb, axiom, adage, aphorism, apothegm, catchword, shibboleth, saw.

C

cab *n. Don't wait for a bus, hail a cab:* taxi, taxi-cab, hackney carriage.
◇ *Word origin: Cab* is a shortened form of *cabriolet,* a light one-horse carriage with two seats.

cabal *n.* **1** *The government was toppled by a cabal of dissident generals:* junta, faction, combination, band, ring, league. **2** *The Russian émigrés were constantly engaged in anti-Soviet cabals:* intrigue, conspiracy, plot, design, scheme, plan, machination, connivance.

cabaret *n. Berlin between the wars was famous for its political cabarets:* night-club, bistro, café, *Informal* club.
◇ *Pronunciation tip:* Put the stress on the first syllable: *CAB-a-ray.*

cabin *n.* **1** *See Father Christmas in his log cabin! Many fishermen own cabins along the lake:* hut, shack, shanty, chalet, hutch; lodge, cottage, bungalow. **2** *The captain's cabin is near the bridge of the ship:* stateroom, quarters, room; compartment.
Ant. 1 mansion, palace, castle.
◇ *Word origin:* Late Latin *capanna,* cabin, gives us our word *cabin.* The word has been in English since as long ago as 1400.

cabinet *n.* **1** *The Secretary of State is an important member of the cabinet:* council, group of counsellors, official advisers, advisory board, ministry. **2** *Put the dishes in the cabinet:* cupboard, kitchen cabinet, china-closet, china cabinet, desk, bureau; case, chest, chest of drawers, file, box, receptacle.

cable *n.* **1** *The telephone company laid their cables beneath the streets. The tarpaulin was held in place by two cables:* bundle of wires, electric wire, wires, line, wire rope; rope, cord, thread, twisted strand; chain, mooring, hawser; fastening. **2** *Send a cable to our overseas office:* cablegram, overseas telegram, wire.

cache *n.* **1** *The reels had a cache of firearms in the mountains:* store, stockpile, stock, secret repository. **2** *Pirates buried their gold in a cache near here:* hiding-place, secret place.
Ant. 1 display, exhibition, show, array.
◇ *Pronunciation tip:* The *ch* in *cache* is pronounced *sh,* so the word is pronounced *kash.* Thus, the words *cache* and *cash* are pronounced exactly alike. You can remember the proper way to pronounce *cache* by this sentence: *Hide that cash in the cache.*
◇ *Word origin: Cache* comes from French *cacher,* to hide.

cad *n. Only a cad would strike a woman:* dishonourable man, bounder, rotter, churl, dastard, *Slang* cur, louse, heel, rat; villain, scoundrel, rascal, knave, rogue, caitiff.
Ant. gentleman, cavalier; hero, champion, worthy, *Informal* prince.

cadaver *n. The cadaver was taken to the morgue:* corpse, dead body, body, remains, *Slang* stiff.
◇ *Word origin: Cadaver* is the Latin word for corpse.

cadaverous *adj. His long illness gave him a cadaverous appearance:* corpselike, deathlike, deathly; pale, ashen, chalky, pallid, bloodless, blanched.

cadence *n. The soldiers marched to the cadence of the band:* rhythmic pattern, beat, tempo, swing, throb, pulse, accent, measure, metre, rhythm.

cage *n.* **1** *The lion paced back and forth in his cage:* barred enclosure, enclosure, pen.
—*v.* **2** *In modern zoos animals are not caged but are confined by walls and moats:* lock up, shut in, pen, pen in, coop up, encage, impound; confine, restrict, restrain.
Ant. 2 let out, free, liberate.
◇ *Word origin:* A *cage* is, figuratively, a man-made cave. It goes back to Latin *cavea,* a hollow, enclosure, stall, or *cage* (from *cavus,* empty or hollow, which also gives us *cave, cavern,* and *cavity*).

cagey *adj. The cagey deer avoided the hunter's traps:* wary, cautious, chary, careful, prudent, alert, watchful, heedful, discreet; wily, cunning, crafty, sly, foxy, artful, shrewd, sharp, keen.
Ant. unwary, careless, heedless, reckless, rash, unthinking, imprudent, indiscreet; dense, dull, slow-witted, stolid.

cajolery *n. The mother used threats and cajolery to get the child to eat his spinach:* wheedling, coaxing, inveigling, enticement, beguilement, promises, *Slang* soft soap; persuasion; flattery, fawning, adulation, blandishment, blarney.
Ant. threats, extortion, coercion, force.

cake *n.* **1** *The birthday cake had chocolate icing:* (*variously*) layer cake, loaf cake, cup-cake, gâteau; (*loosely*) pastry, sweet rolls, éclairs. **2** *Cakes of ice floated downstream. Buy a cake of soap;* block, bar; mass, lump.
—*v.* **3** *The mud caked on the side of the car;* harden, solidify, dry, coagulate, congeal, thicken, crust; mass, compress, consolidate.
◇ *Word origin: Cake* comes from Old Norse *kaka,* cake. By "cake" the Vikings may actually have meant a kind of oatmeal baked in thin loaves. "Cake" of this sort is referred to in the old byword for Scotland — *Land of Cakes.* The German form *Kuchen* means coffee cake. The Dutch word is *koek,* and its diminutive form *koekje* gives the American *cookie.*

calamitous *adj. A drought would be calamitous for the region's crops:* disastrous, catastrophic, ruinous, cataclysmic, adverse, destructive,

fatal, detrimental, harmful, deleterious, pernicious, blighting; tragic, distressful, dreadful, woeful, baleful, unfortunate, unlucky.
Ant. beneficial, advantageous, favourable, helpful, valuable, fortunate, good, convenient.

calamity *n. The recent flooding in the south was a calamity:* disaster, catastrophe, tragedy, cataclysm, adversity, affliction, hardship, misfortune, tribulation, trial, undoing, downfall, reverse, blow, failure, scourge, ruin; mishap, mischance, ill fortune, bad luck, stroke of ill luck; distress, misery, woe, trouble, sea of troubles, ill, ill wind.
Ant. benefit, blessing, advantage, help, aid, boon, good fortune, good luck, piece of luck.

"Public calamity is a mighty leveller."
—*Edmund Burke*

---

calculate *v.* **1** *Income tax is calculated on a percentage of net income minus exemptions and deductions:* compute, figure, reckon, determine, ascertain, work out; count, sum up, add up, measure. **2** *I calculate that we'll be in Salisbury in six more hours:* judge, estimate, figure, reckon. **3** *The President's speech was calculated to ease world tensions:* design, intend, plan, devise, project, mean, aim at.
◇ *Word origin: Calculate* can be traced back to Latin *calculus*, pebble, referring to the early use of pebbles in counting.

calculating *adj. He's a cold, calculating man who will do anything to get to the top:* scheming, designing, plotting, contriving, intriguing, Machiavellian, crafty, devious, cunning, wily, tricky, artful; shrewd, foxy, sly.
Ant. open, candid, frank, direct, plain-spoken, sincere, above-board, honest; naïve, artless, guileless, ingenious, undesigning.

calculation *n.* **1** *The scientist's calculations proved exactly right:* computation, figuring, reckoning; answer, result. **2** *By my calculation, Arsenal will win the game by one goal:* judgement, estimation, reckoning.

calendar *n.* **1** *The calendar showed that Christmas fell on a Tuesday:* chart of days, weeks, and months. **2** *The executive noted the appointment on his calendar:* agenda, day-book, diary, schedule, list, register, programme, table.
◇ *Usage note:* Do not confuse the two words *calendAr* and *calendEr*. *Calendar* is the word you probably want; it is a record of days and dates. (A *calendEr* is a machine for making paper, cloth, or rubber smooth or glossy by pressing between rollers.)
◇ *Word origin: Calendar* comes from Latin *Kalendarium*, a money-lender's account book. The Roman term arose from Latin *Kalendae* (Calends, first day of the month) because monthly payments were due on the first of the month.

calibre *n.* **1** *The calibre of a gun determines the weight of its projectile:* bore, inside diameter. **2** *His character was of the highest calibre:* worth, merit, excellence, quality, ability, competence, capability, capacity, talent, gifts, skill, power, scope; stature, reputation, repute, importance, prominence, prestige, eminence, distinction, estimation, achievement, position, rank, place.

call *v.* **1** *Did you hear someone call for help? Please stand when the teacher calls your name:* call out, cry out, cry, shout, yell, bellow, scream, roar, clamour, bawl, speak loudly, shriek, hail, halloo. **2** *Call the children in for supper. Call a meeting of the club members:* summon, ask, bid, invite, order, command, demand, require, direct, instruct, charge; call together, convene, assemble, convoke, muster, collect, gather, rally. **3** *The hospital calls on everyone to support the fund-raising drive:* appeal to, ask, ask for, call upon, entreat, bid, request, petition, invoke, summon, invite, supplicate, pray to. **4** *Some old friends came to call. Our salesman will call to pick up the order:* visit, pay a visit, look in on, drop in, come round. **5** *The union called a strike:* proclaim, announce, declare, decree, order, command, convoke. **6** *Just call me Bob. The publisher decided to call the book* The Golden Flower. *The play was called a masterpiece:* name, dub, christen, title, entitle, identify, designate, style, label, characterize, describe as, known as, specify. **7** *I'll call you long distance tonight:* telephone, phone, contact, ring up.
—*n.* **8** *Did you hear a call?:* outcry, crying out, cry, shout, yell, scream, bellow, clamour; hail, halloo. **9** *He got a call for jury duty. The Prime Minister put out a call for greater effort. The explorer answered the call of the wild:* summons, order, notice, command, demand, direction, instruction, charge; invitation, request, bid, appeal, entreaty, petition, supplication, plea; announcement, proclamation, declaration, decree. **10** *Let's make a call on the Johnsons. The doctor doesn't make house calls:* visit. **11** *The secretary took all calls:* telephone call, phone call, telephone message. **12** *You had no call to do that. There's no call to take skis on our holiday this year:* right, need, cause, reason, grounds, claim, occasion, justification, excuse, warrant.
Ant. 1 be silent, be still, be quiet; whisper, murmur. **2** excuse, dismiss, release, disperse, scatter. **3** grant, give. **5** call off, cancel, renounce. **8** whisper, murmur. **9** excuse, dismissal, release.

calling *n.* **1** *We could hear his calling to us from over the field:* calling out, crying out, outcry, crying, shouting, yelling, screaming, bellowing, hailing, hallooing. **2** *Art is his calling:* main interest, mission, first love, attachment, dedication, devotion, passion, enthusiasm, preferred pursuit, province, forte, speciality, specialization, métier; life's work, career, profession, vocation, occupation, trade, employment, business, job, work, line, field, craft, activity, function, assignment, livelihood, living, means of support, walk of life, bread and butter.

Ant. 1 whispering, murmuring. **2** hobby, avocation; bane, nuisance, affliction, scourge, curse, plague, aversion, dislike, anathema, abomination, bane of one's existence, thorn in the flesh.

callous *adj.* **1** *The farmer's hands were callous from years of toil:* callused, hard, hardened, horny, tough, thick-skinned, pachydermatous. **2** *Years of pain made him callous to the suffering of others:* unsympathetic, unfeeling, insensitive, uncaring, cold, hard, hardened, hard-hearted, heartless, cruel, apathetic, dispassionate, unresponsive, indifferent.

Ant. 1 tender, soft, thin-skinned. **2** compassionate, sympathetic, sensitive, soft, soft-hearted, warm-hearted, caring, responsive, gentle.

◇ *Usage note:* Don't confuse *callOUS*, an adjective, with *callUS*, a noun, meaning a hardened or thickened area of skin. Don't confuse either of these words with *callow*, meaning inexperienced, immature: *a callow youth.* A *callous* soldier and a *callow* youth are just the opposite.

◇ *Word origin: Callous* comes from Latin *callus,* hard skin, callus.

callow *adj. The callow youth didn't know enough to be polite to the old man:* immature, inexperienced, unseasoned, untried, green, raw, unschooled, uninitiated, uninformed, ignorant, shallow, awkward, unsophisticated, naïve, artless; childish, juvenile, infantile.

Ant. mature, grown-up, adult, experienced, tried and true, finished; informed, sophisticated, polished.

◇ *Usage note:* See CALLOUS.

◇ *Word origin: Callow* comes from Old English *calu,* bare, bald, or unfledged, as a young bird.

calm *adj.* **1** *The water was so calm that it looked like glass:* motionless, smooth, quiet, still, unruffled, undisturbed, placid, mild, balmy, bland, pacific, gentle, tranquil, serene. **2** *The defendant remained calm throughout the trial:* unperturbed, unexcited, composed, self-possessed, unagitated, collected, cool, cool-headed, impassive; passionless, imperturbable, untroubled, serene, placid, peaceful, tranquil; *Slang* unflappable.

—*n.* **3** *Peace and calm are the only cure for jangled nerves. Her calm in the face of disaster is amazing:* calmness, quiet, quietness, peacefulness, tranquillity, restfulness, stillness, smoothness; windlessness, stormlessness; composure, placidity, repose, self-possession, impassivity, imperturbability, coolness, *Slang* cool.

—*v.* **4** *She had to calm herself after all the excitement:* calm down, compose, collect, quieten, pacify, cool off, becalm, *Slang* simmer down. **5** *This ointment will calm the pain:* allay, assuage, soothe, quell, mollify, mitigate, relieve, alleviate, moderate, subdue, cause to subside, placate, tranquillize, ease, lessen, diminish, reduce.

Ant. 1, 2 agitated, disturbed, ruffled, violent, raging, fierce, wild. **1** turbulent, stormy, rough. **2** excited, aroused, hot-headed, heated, passionate; troubled, perturbed, worried, upset, uncollected, discomposed, shaken, jolted, rocked, frantic, frenzied. **3** disturbance, agitation, violence, fierceness, wildness, tempestuousness. **4** excite, agitate, disturb, arouse, work up. **5** irritate, aggravate, intensify, inflame.

◇ *Word origin: Calm* goes back to Greek *kauma,* meaning heat of the day, the period when people take a siesta in Mediterranean countries.

"Calm soul of all things! make it mine
To feel, amid the city's jar,
That there abides a peace of thine,
Man did not make and cannot mar!"

—*Matthew Arnold*

---

camouflage *n.* **1** *The tanks' camouflage prevented enemy planes from seeing them. His friendliness is just camouflage to put us off our guard:* deceptive markings, protective colouring, disguise; mask, masqerade, subterfuge, false appearance, blind, cover, screen, cloak, concealment.

—*v.* **2** *A chameleon camouflages itself by changing colour:* cover with a disguise, disguise, give a false appearance to; mask, screen, cloak, conceal, hide, cover up, veil, shroud.

Ant. 2 show, expose, display, exhibit.

camp *n.* **1** *The hikers set up camp for the night. The army camp wasn't far from town:* encampment, camping ground, temporary shelter, tents, tent, bivouac, lodging, quarters; army base, barracks.

—*v.* **2** *The family camped in the Lake District this summer:* lodge in temporary quarters, encamp, pitch a tent; bivouac; rough it.

◇ *Word origin: Camp* comes from Latin *campus,* field, level plain where Roman military exercises and games were held, field of battle. This Latin word also gives us *campus* and *campaign.*

campaign *n.* **1** *The desert campaign was won with tanks and armoured vehicles:* military operation, operation, offensive, regional battle, battle series, action. **2** *The company started its new sales campaign with massive advertising on television:* drive, effort, push, movement, endeavour, offensive, action.

—*v.* **3** *The Member is campaigning for re-election:* electioneer, solicit votes, canvass, compete for office, stand, run.

◇ *Word origin:* See CAMP.

canal *n.* **1** *The Panama Canal connects the Atlantic and Pacific oceans:* artificial waterway, man-made waterway; channel, conduit, aqueduct; arm of the sea. **2** *Food is digested in the alimentary canal:* duct, tube, passage, channel.

◇ *Word origin: Canal* and *channel* both come from Latin *canalis,* groove, pipe, channel, canal.

cancel *v.* **1** *We cancelled our hotel reservations and stayed with friends. The general cancelled all military leave:* call off, set aside, quash, do away with, dispense with, abolish, revoke, recall, call back, rescind, repeal, countermand, retract, recant, vitiate; annul, nullify, invalidate, abrogate, repudiate, void, declare null and void. **2** *This show of kindness cancels the cruelty shown yesterday:* offset, make up for, compensate for, atone for, redeem, counterbalance, balance out, neutralize.

Ant. 1, 2 confirm, affirm, reaffirm, ratify; implement, enact, enforce, uphold, sustain, maintain.

◇ *Word origin: Cancel* comes from Latin *cancellare,* to make a lattice of scratches over. (*Cancelli* means a lattice-work gate or grille.)

cancer *n.* **1** *Cigarette smoking can cause lung cancer:* malignant growth, malignancy, malignant tumour, carcinoma, sarcoma, neoplasm. **2** *By the late 1920's, the cancer of Hitlerism was widespread in Germany:* malignancy, plague, sickness, rot.

◇ *Word origin:* As anyone interested in astrology knows, *Cancer,* the constellation and fourth sign of the zodiac, is also called "the Crab." Why did this Latin word for crab come to signify a malignant tumour, or any spreading evil? Perhaps because of a crab's slow stretching or spreading way of walking. Our words *canker* and *chancre* are also based on the Latin word *cancer,* crab.

candid *adj.* **1** *To be candid, I don't think you have the talent to be a great violinist:* frank, open, honest, truthful, sincere, blunt, straightforward, forthright, plain-spoken, outspoken, direct, plain, outright, downright, free, unvarnished, fair, just. **2** *Candid photographs can be very revealing:* unposed, informal, relaxed, natural.

Ant. 1 diplomatic, flattering, fawning, honeyed, subtle, mealy-mouthed, complimentary, kind. **2** formal, posed.

"But of all plagues, good Heaven, thy wrath can send,
Save me, oh, save me, from the candid friend!" —*George Canning*

---

candidate *n. There are three candidates for the foreman's job. Who will be the Republic's presidential candidate?:* applicant, nominee, aspirant, possibility, hopeful, competitor, contestant; office seeker, job seeker.

◇ *Word origin: Candidate* comes from Latin *candidatus,* "wearing white" (because office seekers in Rome wore white togas).

candle *n. The candles gave a warm glow to the room:* taper; (*archaic and literary*) tallow, light, rush light, wax, dip, bougie, *French* cierge.

◇ *Word origin: Candle* comes from Latin *candere,* to gleam, glow white. The same Latin verb gives us *candour,* clearness or sincerity, and *incandescent.*

"It is better to light one candle than curse the darkness." —*Motto of the Christopher Society*

---

candlestick *n. Before the dinner party, the hostess put fresh candles in the candlesticks:* candleholder, candelabrum, sconce, chandelier, girandole; *Eastern Orthodox Church* dikerion, trikerion; *Judaism* menorah.

◇ *Usage note:* Although *candelabrum* is about the only common synonym for *candlestick* today, the other synonyms indicate the importance candles had before electric lights. *Candelabrum* and *girandole* both refer to a branched candlestick holding more than one candle, and the plural of *candelabrum* is *candelabra* (two or more such candlesticks). In Eastern Orthodoxy, a *dikerion* is a *candelabrum* with two branches (symbolizing the twofold nature of Christ, human and divine), and a *trikerion* has three (symbolizing the Trinity). Today a *chandelier* refers to an ornamental light hanging from a ceiling, but originally it was a branched support of a number of candles hanging from a ceiling. A *sconce* is an ornamental wall bracket for holding a candle. A *menorah* is both the seven-branched candelabrum of the Jewish temple and the nine-branched candelabrum for lighting the eight candles of the eight days of Hanukkah successively, using the ninth candle to light them.

candour *n. A good critic must be a man of great candour:* frankness, openness, honesty, truthfulness, sincerity, bluntness, straightforwardness, forthrightness, plain-spokenness, directness, artlessness, fairness, justness, impartiality, freedom from prejudice.

Ant. diplomacy, flattery, subtlety, evasiveness, deceit, artfulness, dishonesty, insincerity, hypocrisy, unfairness, partiality, bias, prejudice.

◇ *Word origin:* See CANDLE.

cane *n.* **1** *Since he broke his hip, he's had to walk with a cane:* walking-stick, stick, staff, rod.
—*v.* **2** *Schoolmasters used to cane disobedient children:* (*with a cane*) flog, thrash, beat, whip, flail, trounce, baste, drub, tan, lash, switch; strike, hit, whack, wallop, rap, smite.

◇ *Word origin: Cane* comes from Greek *kanna,* reed or cane.

canker *n.* **1** *The canker caused her lip to swell:* mouth sore; ulcer, sore. **2** *Organized crime, the*

speaker said, is a canker in our way of life: source of corruption, cancer, blight.
◇ *Word origin:* See CANCER.

canny *adj. The old squire was a canny politician:* artful, skilful; knowing, wise, astute, shrewd, sharp, clever, subtle, convincing, cunning, crafty, foxy, wily, cagey; wary, careful, judicious, sagacious, intelligent, perspicacious, circumspect.
Ant. unskilled, inept, dumb, obtuse, blatant; bumbling, fumbling.

canon *n. The canons of the Roman Catholic Church permit divorce only by dispensation. The canons of good behaviour apply to everyone:* rule, principle, precept, code, standard, yardstick, criterion; regulation; order, ordinance, law, decree, statute.
◇ *Word origin: Canon* comes from Latin *canon,* rule or law, which comes from Greek *kanōn,* measuring-rod, rule, standard. Our other word *canon,* a clergyman assigned to a large church or who is a member of a special religious order, means one who lives according to a religious rule or *canon.*

canopy *n. A canopy shaded the entrance to the building:* awning, covering, tester, hood.
◇ *Word origin: Canopy* goes back to the Greek word for mosquito, *kōnōps,* and the first *canopies* were mosquito-nets arranged over a bed.

cant *n.* **1** *The thief's claim that he was going to give the money to the poor was just a lot of cant:* hypocrisy, insincerity, humbug, pretentiousness, pretence, sham, sanctimoniousness. **2** *Thieves' cant is unintelligible to outsiders:* jargon, lingo, talk, parlance, slang, argot, vernacular.
◇ *Word origin: Cant* goes back to Latin *cantus,* song, singing, and may have first been applied in this contemptuous sense to the singsong whining of beggars at church doors.

cantankerous *adj. When the team loses, the team manager is in a cantankerous mood:* quarrelsome, argumentative, contentious, contrary, testy, touchy, peevish, fretful, huffy, ill-tempered, ill-natured, ill-humoured, disagreeable, grouchy, grumpy, irascible, irritable, cranky, cross, bearish, surly, churlish, snappish, waspish, crabbed, morose, sullen, sulky, short, crusty, mean, choleric, splenetic.
Ant. agreeable, good-humoured, good-natured, pleasant; amiable, affable, genial, kindly; placid, calm, complaisant, mellow; merry, gay, happy, jolly, jaunty, breezy, vivacious, cheerful, light-hearted.

canteen *n.* **1** *We bought tea and biscuits in the office canteen:* mess, refreshment room, restaurant, snack-bar. **2** *She received a canteen of cutlery as a wedding-present:* box, case (divided into compartments), presentation case.
◇ *Word origin: Canteen* comes from Italian *cantina,* a cellar.

canvas *n.* **1** *Gym-shoes are made of canvas. The Scouts spent the night under canvas:* sailcloth, tent cloth, duck; tarpaulin. **2** *The artist set his canvas on the easel:* painting, picture (*on canvas*).
◇ *Word origin: Canvas* comes from the Latin (and Greek) word for hemp, *cannabis.*

cap *n.* **1** *The nurse wore a pleated cap on her head:* brimless *hat,* visored *hat,* head-dress. **2** *Put the cap back on the bottle of soda:* top, lid, seal.
—*v.* **3** *The Wright brothers capped their first flight with many longer ones:* better, surpass, exceed, outdo.

capability *n. Only pilots of the highest capability are chosen to become test pilots. The country has the capability to defeat any aggressor:* ability, competency, competence, attainment, proficiency, facility, faculty, capacity, skill, art, know-how, qualification; power, efficacy, potential, potentiality, talent, gift, flair, knack.
Ant. incompetence, ineptitude, inadequacy, inability, inefficiency, impotency, powerlessness.

capable *adj. Napoleon was one of the most capable generals in history:* able, competent, expert, skilful, skilled, masterly, accomplished, gifted, talented, proficient, adept, apt, deft, adroit, effective, efficacious; clever, intelligent, artful, ingenious.
Ant. incapable, incompetent, unaccomplished, unqualified, inexpert, unskilled, inept, ineffective, amateurish.

capacity *n.* **1** *The hot-water tank has a fifty-gallon capacity:* maximum contents, limit, extent, volume, size, amplitude, room, space. **2** *The United States has the capacity to produce more than any other nation:* ability, power, capability, faculty, facility, strength, might. **3** *Einstein was a man of outstanding capacity:* ability, endowment, talent, gifts, faculty, aptitude, potential; intelligence, intellect, sagacity, brainpower, mind; perspicacity, discernment, judgement. **4** *In her capacity as Commander in Chief, the Queen is head of the armed forces:* role, function, position.
Ant. 2, 3 inability, incapacity.

cape *n.* **1** *The nurses' uniform includes a cape:* cloak, mantle, shawl, pelisse, tabard, poncho, serape. **2** *Steer the boat round the cape and into the harbour:* peninsula, point, promontory, headland.
◇ *Word origin:* A *cape* is a headland and comes via French from Latin *caput,* head.

caper *v.* **1** *The fawns capered about in the forest:* prance, gambol, frisk, cavort, romp, frolic; leap, jump, hop, skip, bounce, bound.
—*n.* **2** *The students' latest caper was putting frogs in all the drinking fountains:* lark, escapade, caprice, adventure, spree, fling, frolic; trick, prank, practical joke, antic, stunt, tomfoolery, high jinks, jape, monkey business.
◇ *Word origin: Caper* is a shortened form of *caprile,* an upward leap with all four feet off the ground, made by a trained horse.

capital *n.* **1** *Rome is the capital of Italy. Paris under Louis XIV was the cultural capital of Europe:* seat of government; chief city, first city, centre, headquarters. **2** *The child wrote his name in capitals:* capital letter, upper-case letter, large letter, majuscule. **3** *The corporation has enough capital to build another factory:* investment funds, working capital, income-producing property, resources, available means, cash, cash in hand, wealth, financing, principal, working assets, wherewithal. —*adj.* **4** *It was a capital idea!:* excellent, great, fine, super, superb, first-rate, first-class.
Ant. **2** small letter, lower-case letter, minuscule. **3** debts, debits. **4** bad, poor, inferior, awful, lousy, second-rate.
◇ *Word origin: Capital* comes from Latin *capitalis,* which means (1) affecting the head (as in *capital* crime) and (2) pre-eminent. *Capital* in the sense of "chief place, seat of government" was coined by the poet John Milton and first used in *Paradise Lost.* In the sense of accumulated wealth, capital did not become current until the 18th century.

capitalism *n. Under capitalism, we can own our own business:* free enterprise, private ownership.
Ant. socialism, communism, collectivism.

capitalist *n.* **1** *Small capitalists own most of the businesses:* investor, businessman. **2** *The Rockefellers and the DuPonts are leading capitalists:* financier, tycoon, plutocrat, mogul.
Ant. worker, labourer, proletarian; socialist, communist, collectivist.

capitol *n. The Capitol is one of the most beautiful buildings in Washington:* government house, legislative building.

Exploring the Word: The word *capitol* goes back to the temple of Jupiter Capitolinus, a temple to the god Jupiter which stood on the Capitoline Hill in ancient Rome. This was the crowning or "head" hill on which Rome was built (the word comes from Latin *caput,* head, which also gives us *cap* and *cape,* which originally was a cloak with a hood for covering the head). Our words *chief, captain,* and *chef* also come from *caput,* a *chief* being a head man or leader, a *captain* the head of a ship or army company, and a *chef* the head of a kitchen. The same Latin word also gives us *capsize,* via Spanish *capazar,* and literally means to sink head first.

capitulate *v. Lack of supplies caused the enemy to capitulate:* surrender, acknowledge defeat, give up, yield, succumb, lay down one's arms, come to terms, sue for peace, hoist the white flag, throw up the sponge, throw in the towel.
Ant. defeat, win over, be victorious.

caprice *n. Is your decision to become a vegetarian serious, or just a caprice?:* whim, fancy, quirk, notion, impulse; eccentricity, idiosyncrasy, oddity, peculiarity, crotchet, vagary; lark, escapade, caper, stunt, prank, antic, spree, fling; craze, fad.

capricious *adj. The capricious woman bought and exchanged three dresses in a week:* changeable, fickle, variable, impulsive, erratic, flighty, skittish, mercurial, fanciful, faddish; indecisive, undecided, irresolute, uncertain, wavering, vacillating, shilly-shallying; irresponsible, inconsistent, unsteady, unstable, fitful, uneven, eccentric, quirky.
Ant. consistent, unchangeable, inflexible, unmovable, firm, fixed, unwavering, invariable, unswerving; resolute, determined, steadfast, certain, decided, decisive; serious, responsible, steady, stable, even.

capsize *v. The boat capsized when all the cargo shifted to one side:* overturn, turn over, keel over, tip over, upset, turn turtle.
Ant. right, upright.

captain *n.* **1** *Bligh was the captain of the* Bounty *when the crew mutinied:* commanding officer, commander, master, skipper, *Slang* old man; pilot. **2** *Six first lieutenants were promoted to captain:* company commander, commanding officer, commandant, chief officer. **3** *Robin Hood was the captain of a famous robber band:* leader, head man, chief, chieftain, head, boss.
Ant. **1** able-bodied seaman, deck-hand. **3** follower, member.

"I am the captain of the *Pinafore*;
And a right good captain too!"
—*W. S. Gilbert*

---

captivate *v. The actor's talent and good looks captivated the audience:* fascinate, charm, enchant, bewitch, dazzle, hypnotize, mesmerize, enthrall, delight, enrapture, transport, carry away, win over, lure, seduce, attract, infatuate, enamour, take the fancy of, turn the head of.
Ant. repulse, repel, alienate, turn away, disenchant, antagonize; disgust, nauseate, make sick.

captive *n.* **1** *Captives were kept in POW camps until the war was over:* prisoner; hostage. —*adj.* **2** *The captive airmen were released after the war. The captive peoples of Europe formed underground groups to fight the Nazis:* imprisoned, incarcerated, confined, penned, caged, locked up; subjugated, enslaved, oppressed.
Ant. **1** captor, guard; free man. **2** free, unconfined, at liberty freed, liberated, independent, emancipated.

capture *v.* **1** *The army captured the town. The boys captured a hawk. The police captured the criminal:* seize, take; take prisoner, take captive, catch, trap, ensnare, snare, bag, snag, lay hold of; arrest, apprehend, take into custody, *Slang* pinch, collar, nab.

—*n.* **2** *The capture of the white whale was Captain Ahab's obsession:* seizure, taking, capturing, taking prisoner, taking captive, catching, trapping, snaring, ensnaring, bagging, collaring, laying hold of; arrest, apprehension.
Ant. 1 release, free, let go, liberate. **2** release, freeing, liberation; escape.

car *n.* **1** *The new car had disc brakes:* motor car, motor, machine, vehicle, motor vehicle, *Slang* jalopy, old crock, hot rod, tin lizzie. **2** *The railway bought 200 new cars:* railway carriage; (*variously*) coach, carriage, sleeping-car, Pullman car, sleeper, dining-car, diner, cable-car; wagon, guard's van.
◇ *Word origin: Car* comes from Latin *carrus*, a kind of two-wheeled wagon for transporting heavy loads.

Exploring the Word: *Car, chariot,* and *carriage* all come from Latin *carrus*, wagon. Related Latin words also give us *cargo*, literally the load transported in a wagon; *carry*, originally meaning to take in a wagon; *charge*, to put a load in a wagon; and even *career*, the road or course one takes in life.

card *n.* **1** *In bridge, each player is dealt thirteen cards:* playing-card. **2** *Amy sent a card from France:* postcard, (*variously*) picture postcard, greetings card, birthday card, Christmas card, anniversary card, New Year card, Easter card, good-luck card, Valentine, get-well card. **3** *The salesman left his card:* (*variously*) business card, visiting card. **4** *The race was fourth on the card:* programme, time-table.
◇ *Word origin: Card,* like *chart*, comes from Greek *chartēs*, leaf of papyrus. (The Greek word is probably from Egyptian.)

cardinal *n.* **1** *The Pope appointed the archbishop cardinal*: member of the College of Cardinals in the Roman Catholic Church.
—*adj.* **2** *Decorum was the cardinal rule in the office:* first, foremost, basic, prime, primary, fundamental, elementary, chief, main, key, principal, central, leading, most important, paramount, highest, greatest, outstanding, dominant, predominant, pre-eminent, uppermost, top, head, underlying; vital, necessary, essential, indispensable, intrinsic. **3** *The king wore a cardinal robe trimmed with ermine:* deep red, cherry, blood-red, carmine, wine-coloured, claret, scarlet.
Ant. 2 second, secondary, subordinate, least important, unessential, unnecessary, dispensable; lowest, smallest.
◇ *Word origin: Cardinal* came from Latin *cardo*, hinge, that on which something turns or depends, of prime importance, and thus came to be applied to members of the College of Cardinals in Rome. Since cardinals wore cassocks of deep scarlet, *cardinal* came to mean that colour. Later when a bird of approximately the same colour was found in the New World, *cardinal* became a bird, and much later even an American baseball team using this bird as a symbol. Thus from a hinge to a principal of the Roman Catholic Church, to a colour, to a bird, to a baseball team, *cardinal* illustrates how a word can change and grow in meaning.

care *n.* **1** *Handle these fragile glasses with care. Answer all the questions with care:* carefulness, caution, precaution, circumspection, diligence, attention, attentiveness, heed, watchfulness, vigilance, thought; regard, concern, effort, pains, consideration, discrimination, solicitude, conscientiousness, application, fastidiousness, meticulousness, exactness, scrupulousness. **2** *He hasn't a care in the world. The mother's major care was the safety of her children:* concern, worry, responsibility, load, anxiety, strain, stress, pressure; bother, annoyance, nuisance, vexation, tribulation, heartache, distress, trouble, hardship, affliction, sorrow, grief, misery, anguish, sadness, unhappiness. **3** *The sick man is still under the doctor's care:* ministration, attention, supervision, charge, keeping, protection.
—*v.* **4** *Do you care what happens to the house?:* be concerned, be interested in, be worried, mind, regard, bother about, trouble about. **5** *The guests didn't care to have coffee after dinner:* want, wish, desire.
Ant. 1 carelessness, neglect, negligence, abandon, recklessness, unconcern, disregard, inattention, thoughtlessness, heedlessness, indifference. **2** relaxation; pleasure, delight, happiness. **4** disregard, forget about. **5** dislike, hate, detest, abhor, loath; reject.

career *n. Florence Nightingale made nursing her career:* profession, vocation, calling, occupation, employment, work, job, business, livelihood, activity, line, pursuit, walk of life.
Ant. hobby, avocation, sideline, diversion, entertainment, relaxation.

carefree *adj. Oh, to be young and carefree again!:* free of care, careless, without worry, without a worry in the world, untroubled, happy-go-lucky, light-hearted, relaxed, easy-going, free-and-easy; in high spirits, joyous, elated, jaunty, optimistic, buoyant, jubilant, breezy; happy, cheerful, sunny, glad, laughing, smiling, radiant, full of life, gleeful, jolly, gay.
Ant. careworn, heavy-hearted, worried; unhappy, sad, sorrowful, joyless, cheerless, melancholy, crestfallen, blue, gloomy, dismal, dreary, depressed, dejected, disconsolate, desolate, despondent.

careful *adj.* **1** *Be careful crossing the street. My mother was careful to show no favouritism:* cautious, watchful, wary, guarded, chary, alert, observant, attentive, on guard, vigilant, diligent, concerned, thoughtful, mindful, regardful, heedful, prudent, painstaking, scrupulous, circumspect, discreet, tactful, judicious, solicitous. **2** *The teacher expects careful handwriting:* precise, punctilious, exact, fastidious, particular, meticulous, conscientious, fussy, painstaking, fine, nice, scrupulous, accurate, correct.

Ant. 1 careless, reckless, rash, abandoned, slack, lax, neglectful, negligent, remiss, heedless, thoughtless, unthinking, inattentive, unconcerned, improvident. **2** careless, sloppy, slipshod, slovenly, slapdash, casual; inexact, imprecise, inaccurate; unrigorous, slack.

careless *adj.* **1** *A careless mistake cost the company millions of pounds. Careless remarks hurt the girl's feelings:* thoughtless, unthinking, heedless, unmindful, absent-minded, sloppy, slipshod, lax, slack, negligent, rash; inconsiderate. **2** *The student was careless about his personal appearance:* nonchalant, offhand, indifferent, heedless, thoughtless, unconcerned, forgetful, negligent, neglectful, lackadaisical, carefree, untroubled, casual, lax, slack, slipshod, slapdash; untidy, slovenly, sloppy, messy, disorderly; inexact, imprecise, incorrect, inaccurate. **3** See CAREFREE.

Ant. 1 careful, cautious, wary, alert, attentive, diligent, watchful, mindful, concerned. **2** careful, fastidious, neat, tidy, meticulous, fussy, painstaking, orderly; scrupulous, correct, precise, exact, accurate.

caress *n.* **1** *The grandmother gave each of the children a kiss and a caress:* gentle touch, stroking, pat, petting, fondling; embrace, hug.

—*v.* **2** *The old man caressed his youngest grandchild:* stroke, fondle, toy with, pet, pat, touch; embrace, hug, clasp; cuddle.

Ant. 1 hit, blow, slap, cuff, box. **2** hit, beat, thrash, slap, cuff, box.

◇ *Word origin: Caress* goes back to the Latin word for dear, *carus.*

caretaker *n. John was the caretaker of the old mansion:* custodian, keeper, overseer, curator, steward, warden; janitor, porter; watchman, gatekeeper.

cargo *n. The cargo was put in the hold of the ship;* freight, shipment, load, lading, burden; goods, merchandise.

caricature *n.* **1** *The comedian's caricature of a fat man running for a bus was very amusing:* lampoon, take-off, burlesque, parody, satire, travesty, mockery; distortion, absurdity, exaggeration.

—*v.* **2** *The cartoonist caricatured workmen sleeping on the job:* lampoon, burlesque, parody, satirize, mock.

◇ *Word origin: Caricature* comes from Italian *caricare,* to overload, exaggerate. Its Latin origin *carricum,* a load, gives us *cargo.*

carnage *n. Those who have seen the carnage of war will never forget:* slaughter, butchery, great bloodshed, mass killing, massacre.

carnal *adj. A chaste mind has no room for carnal thoughts:* sexual, sensual, erotic, voluptuous, sensuous, prurient, lustful, libidinous, fleshly, unchaste, lewd, lascivious, lecherous, salacious, immoral, sinful, impure, venereal, wanton.

Ant. chaste, modest, virginal, pure.

carnival *n. The village held an annual carnival:* fair, festival, jamboree, celebration, jubilee, fête, gala, pageant; Shrove Tuesday; holiday.

carnivorous *adj. Lions are carnivorous animals:* meat-eating, flesh-eating, predatory, predaceous.

Ant. herbivorous; vegetarian.

> **Exploring the Word:** Latin *carnalis,* fleshly (from *carno,* flesh) gives us *carnal,* fleshly, worldly; *carnivorous,* flesh-eating; *carrion,* a feeder on dead flesh, as a vulture; *carnage,* destruction of flesh, killing; and even *carnival,* literally "the lifting of meat," i.e. the festival of meat-eating prior to the fasting of Lent — in other words, our present-day Shrove Tuesday. The same Latin word is also in our Mexican dish *chile con carne,* chilli with meat.

carol *n. "Silent Night" is a favourite carol:* Christmas carol, hymn, song of praise, song of joy.

Ant. dirge, lament.

◇ *Word origin: Carol* goes back to Greek *khoros* (dance) + *auleein* (to play the flute), hence Greek *khoraulēs,* meaning "a dance accompanied by flute music" and, later, "a song of joy or praise."

carouse *v. The sailors caroused in the pub:* revel, make merry; drink, tipple, imbibe, guzzle, quaff, wassail.

◇ *Word origin: Carouse* comes from the first word of the German phrase *garaus trinken,* to drink "all out."

carp *v. The old man carped continually about the hotel's service:* complain, find fault, fault-find, nag, cavil, criticize, disapprove, deride, belittle, knock, condemn, deprecate, disparage, chide, decry, reproach, censure, impugn, pick on, jibe at, pull to pieces.

Ant. compliment, praise, applaud, laud, approve.

carpet *n.* **1** *Our living-room is covered with a wall-to-wall carpet:* rug; matting, mat. **2** *A carpet of leaves covered the ground:* blanket, layer, covering, sheet.

carriage *n.* **1** *The queen rode in an ornate carriage pulled by four white horses:* coach, horse-drawn coach; landau; vehicle, conveyance. **2** *The prima ballerina was a woman of erect and handsome carriage:* bearing, posture, comportment; demeanour, mien, attitude, appearance, air, poise, aspect; presence, manner, behaviour, deportment.

carry *v.* **1** *The porter carried the luggage upstairs:* take, bring, tote, bear, fetch, haul, lug, cart, lift; move, transport, transmit, convey,

transfer, conduct, shift, displace, ship, deliver. **2** *The money will carry me through the week. The walls carry the weight of the roof:* support, sustain, maintain, bear, uphold, hold up, prop, brace, shoulder, lift. **3** *All the newspapers carried the story:* communicate, transmit, disseminate, publish, run, print, broadcast, release, offer. **4** *The shop carries only good brands:* supply, stock, keep, display, offer.
Ant. 1 throw down, drop, let go. **3** withhold, reject, delete, censor; cover up, keep secret.

cart *n.* **1** *The farmer sold fresh corn from his roadside cart:* wagon, tumbrel, wain, curricle, trap; two-wheeler, dog-cart, gig, dray, tip-cart; go-cart, push-cart, handcart, barrow, wheelbarrow, hand-barrow.
—v. **2** *Lorries carted the rubbish to the city refuse dump:* transport, haul, lug, tote, carry; bear, move; take, bring, fetch, convey, transmit, transfer, transplant.

carte blanche *n. The interior decorator was given carte blanche in decorating the house:* a free hand, free reign, full authority, unconditional power, open sanction.
◇ *Word origin: Carte blanche* is French for a blank piece of paper. Thus, when the French say they give someone *carte blanche,* it is the same as our saying we give someone a "blank cheque."

carton *n. The books were packed in cartons:* box, cardboard box, container, cardboard container; packing-case, case, packing-crate, crate.

carve *v.* **1** *The statue was carved out of marble. The boys carved their initials in the tree:* sculpture, sculpt, chisel, hew; shape, mould, model, fashion, pattern, form, work, turn; engrave, etch, incise. **2** *Dad carved the Christmas turkey:* slice, cut up, dissever, saw, hack, slash; cleave, rend, split, divide, quarter, apportion, allot.

cascade *n.* **1** *The water formed a cascade down the mountain:* waterfall, falls, cataract, Niagara; rapids, chute.
—v. **2** *The water cascaded over the cliff:* surge, pour, gush, rush, fall.
Ant. 2 trickle, drip, drop, seep.

case[1] *n.* **1** *In this case, it is clear that no further action is necessary. It was a case of love at first sight:* instance, incidence, incident, occurrence, situation, event, episode, happening, condition, example, illustration, circumstance; matter, business, affair, concern. **2** *The case was brought before a jury:* lawsuit, suit, litigation, action; dispute, controversy, debate, argument, inquiry, hearing, proceeding; plea, appeal, cause. **3** *A doctor attended the case:* patient, sick person, invalid, victim, sufferer; injury.

case[2] *n.* **1** *Put the books in a packing-case. The thieves took a jewel case:* box, crate, carton, chest, container, receptacle; tray, cabinet, display case, bin. **2** *The driving-licence was kept in a plastic case:* wrapper, cover, covering, sheath, sheathing, jacket, envelope, overlay, housing, protection.
◇ *Word origin:* See CASH.

cash *n.* **1** *The purchases were paid for with cash:* money, currency, legal tender, paper money, bank notes, coins, change; *Slang* bread, dough; coin of the realm, ready money.
—v. **2** *The bank will cash your cheque:* turn into money, give cash for, obtain cash for; redeem, exchange, change.
Ant. 1 cheque; charge, chit, promissory note, note, IOU.
◇ *Word origin: Cash* and *Case*[2] come to us via French *caisse,* cash box, from Latin *capsa,* box; hence *cash* literally means "that which is kept in a box."

cashier *n. Please pay the cashier:* bank clerk; teller; bursar, purser, treasurer, banker.

cask *n. The wine was fermented in large casks:* vat, barrel, keg, hogshead, tub, butt, tun.

casket *n. Caskets of jewels were found in the pirate's cave:* jewel box, chest, coffer, case.

cast *v.* **1** *Let him who is without sin, cast the first stone:* pitch, toss, fling, hurl, throw, let fly, sling, heave; propel, launch, fire, shoot, discharge, project, catapult. **2** *The candles cast a warm glow on the table:* shed, spread, diffuse, direct, deposit, scatter, disseminate, disperse, distribute, circulate, broadcast, sow. **3** *The producer cast leading actors in the parts:* assign, appoint, pick, choose, give parts to. **4** *The statue was cast in bronze:* mould, form, shape, model, set, sculpt; mint.
—n. **5** *The fisherman caught a trout with his first cast:* pitch, toss, throw; fling, hurl, heave, sling; propulsion, launch, launching. **6** *The play's cast was given a standing ovation:* performers, actors, company, troupe, players; list of characters, dramatis personae. **7** *The plaster was poured into a bronze cast:* mould, form, shape, pattern, casting, casing, impression, stamp, set, model. **8** *Her face has a distinctly Oriental cast:* look, appearance, mien, stamp.
◇ *Word origin: Cast* comes from Old Norse *kasta,* to throw.

caste *n. Hindu society is based on a system of castes:* hereditary social class, rank, condition, station.
◇ *Word origin: Caste* is ultimately derived from Latin *castus,* pure. Hence *half-caste* means "half pure-blooded." The Latin *castus,* pure, also gives us *chastity* and *castigate,* to chastise for not being pure.

castigate *v. The principal castigated the students for their unruly behaviour:* chastise, upbraid, rebuke, censure, reprimand, reproach, chasten, reprove, berate, scold, admonish, criticize, chide, dress down, haul over the coals, take to task; *Slang* tear off a strip; punish, discipline, correct, penalize.
Ant. praise, laud, compliment, honour; reward, encourage.
◇ *Word origin:* See CASTE.

castle *n. The king's castle stood on a hill:* palace, mansion, hall, manor; fortified residence, stronghold, citadel, fortress, tower, keep.
◇ *Word origin: Castle* comes from a diminutive form of Latin *castrum*, camp, fort. Many English towns and villages have *caster/chester/cester* in their names, showing that they were originally Roman camps, as *Lancaster, Winchester, Worcester.*

casual *adj.* **1** *The two old friends had a casual meeting:* chance, unexpected, accidental, unplanned, unarranged, unforeseen, unpremeditated, unintentional, undesigned, unlooked for. **2** *I have a casual interest in golf:* incidental, informal, haphazard, random, undirected, offhand, vague, so-so, half-hearted, indiscriminate, passing, relaxed, easy-going, lackadaisical, indifferent. **3** *The guests wore casual attire:* informal, non-dressy, sporty; haphazard, random.
Ant. formal. **1** intentional, calculated, planned, fixed, arranged, designed, deliberate, intentional, premeditated, foreseen, expected; studied, considered, well-advised. **2** serious, committed, concerned, specific, direct, systematic, professional; all-consuming, whole-hearted, fanatic, passionate, enthusiastic. **3** dressy, ceremonial, formal.

> **Exploring the Word**: *Casual, accidental,* and *incidental* all refer to somewhat unplanned-for things that just happen or fall on us. They all come (in one way or another) from Latin *cadere*, to fall, befall, which also gives us *casualty*, a person hurt or killed by the fall of chance; and *accident, incident, occasion,* and *case*, an event or state of things that befalls on us, as if by chance. It also gives us *cadence*, the fall or beat of music or poetry; *coincide*, to fall or happen together; *decadence*, a falling into decay, a moral decline; and *cascade*, a falling, as of water.

casualty *n. The earthquake caused many casualties:* injured, wounded, or dead person; injury, fatality.

cat *n.* **1** *The neighbours have a dog and a cat:* feline, house cat, pussy-cat, pussy, puss, tabby, tabby cat, mouser; (*young*) kitten, kitty; (*male*) tom-cat, tom. **2** *At the zoo, the bears are next to the cats:* (*loosely*) lions and tigers; (*variously*) lion, tiger, leopard, panther, puma, lynx, ocelot, wild-cat.

cataclysm *n. The weakened government could not withstand another cataclysm:* catastrophe, calamity, disaster, débâcle, upheaval.
Ant. triumph, victory, success; benefit, good fortune, boon.
◇ *Word origin: Cataclysm* comes from Greek *kataklusmos*, the Deluge, the Flood. Among the ancients, the word had a figurative political sense of "public calamity," as it does today. *Cataclysm* is also used by geologists to denote a sudden violent change in the earth's surface.

catalogue *n.* **1** *The farmer ordered new seed from the seed-catalogue:* list, listing, inventory, file, record, index, roll, roster, register, directory. —*v.* **2** *The librarian catalogues the books alphabetically:* list, inventory, classify, file, record, index, register.

catapult *n.* **1** *The catapult hurled the missile two hundred yards:* hurling engine, sling. —*v.* **2** *The shove catapulted the boy into the room:* hurl, be hurled, fling, throw, propel, heave, pitch, cast, toss, shoot.

cataract *n.* **1** *Only experienced canoers should attempt to ride over the cataracts of the Colorado River:* rapids, falls, waterfall, cascade. **2** *A cataract of rain washed out the road:* deluge, torrent, downpour; flood, inundation.
◇ *Spelling tip:* Don't be tempted to put an *e* in *cataract* — all the vowels are *a's*. Remember, *cAtArAct* is a giant waterfall of *A's*.
◇ *Word origin: Cataract* comes from Greek *katarrhaktēs*, "down-crashing." The word is formed from *kata-* (down) + *rhassein* (to smash).

catastrophe *n. The flood in Venice was a major catastrophe:* disaster, calamity, misfortune, mishap, tragedy; affliction, scourge, cataclysm, devastation, havoc, ravage, blow.
Ant. benefit, good fortune, boon.

catcall *n. The auditorium was filled with catcalls from the hostile audience:* boo, hiss, hoot, whistle, jeer, gibe, heckling; *Slang* raspberry.
Ant. applause, cheering; hurrah, hurray.

catch *v.* **1** *The children learned to catch glow-worms and put them in a jar. The police caught the thief:* seize, seize and hold, capture, take captive, take, lay hold of, trap, snare, bag, grab, snag, hook, corner; arrest, apprehend, take into custody, collar, snatch, nab. **2** *The winning runner caught up with his opponent at the finishing-line. Leave now if you want to catch the train:* overtake, reach, get to, intercept, make. **3** *The thief was caught in the act:* discover, detect, come upon, discern, find out, spot, descry; surprise, take off guard. **4** *I was caught by his false promises:* deceive, fool, trick, dupe, take in, delude, mislead, betray, play false, hoodwink, bamboozle; lure, trap, ensnare, bait. **5** *A snowball caught the passer-by in the shoulder:* strike, hit, belt, bang, bump, bat, buffet, whack, smack, smite. **6** *Children catch cold easily:* contract, get, come down with, become infected with, break out in. **7** *The charming child caught the group's fancy:* captivate, attract, allure, charm, enchant, bewitch, enthral, transport, carry away; delight, dazzle, enrapture; *Slang* turn on. **8** *I caught something of his sadness from the tremor in his voice:* sense, feel, discern, grasp, understand, perceive, recognize, comprehend, fathom. **9** *This belt buckle doesn't catch:* fasten, hook, latch, clasp, lock.

—*n.* **10** *The fielder made a good catch on the boundary:* catching, seizure, snatch, snap, grab, snare, capture. **11** *The fisherman's catch was two trout:* take, haul, bag, capture, seizure, find, pickings, yield, prize, booty. **12** *The catch on the cupboard door is loose:* fastening, latch, hook, clasp, hasp, closure, coupling, lock. **13** *It looks so easy that there must be a catch:* hitch, snag, drawback, stumbling-block, disadvantage; trick, hoax, deceit. **14** *There was a catch in the speaker's voice when he spoke of the tragedy:* break, crack, rasping.

Ant. 1 free, release, loose, let go, give up, liberate; drop, fumble. **2** miss. **3** to be undetected, to be undiscovered. **4** undeceive, untrick, undupe, undelude. **5** miss. **6** avoid, evade; be resistant to. **7** repel, alienate, turn away; *Slang* turn off. **9** unfasten, unhook, unlatch, unlock. **10** drop; fumble. **11** loss, miss. **13** advantage, benefit, boon, reward.

catching *adj. Chicken-pox is catching. Her laughter was so catching that we all joined in:* contagious, communicable, infectious, transmittable.

Ant. non-catching, non-contagious, uncommunicable, non-infectious, non-transmittable.

catchword *n.* **1** *Children know all the catchwords used in television commercials:* slogan, motto, byword, watchword, password; war-cry, battle-cry. **2** *The catchwords at the top of the page make it easier to find entries in a dictionary:* headword.

categorical *adj. The politician made a categorical denial of the charges that he had taken bribes:* absolute, unconditional, unqualified, unequivocal, unmistakable, unreserved, express, flat, sure, certain, emphatic, explicit, pronounced, definite.

Ant. conditional, qualified, equivocal, ambiguous, vague, dubious, doubtful, questionable, indefinite, unsure, uncertain, hesitant, enigmatic.

category *n. The social services department has specialists for each welfare category:* classification, class, grouping, division.

◇ *Spelling tip:* The *e* is the tricky letter here. Remember: *catEgory.*

cater *v. The doting husband catered to his wife's every wish:* humour, pamper, indulge, pander; satisfy, gratify, please.

caterwaul *v. The caterwauling of the cats kept the neighbourhood awake all night:* howl, wail, cry, scream, shriek, screech, whine, yelp, squawk, squeal, bawl, clamour, rend the air.

◇ *Word origin: Caterwaul* comes from Low German *katerwaulen: kater* (tom-cat) + *waulen* (to screech, howl).

catharsis *n. Aristotle said that tragic drama provides catharsis of the emotions by arousing people's pity and fear:* purification, cleansing, purging, release, venting.

◇ *Word origin: Catharsis* comes from Greek *katharsis,* a purgation, a cleansing from guilt or defilement.

catholic *adj.* **1 Catholic.** *My son attends a Catholic school:* Roman Catholic. **2 Catholic.** *Pope John XXIII aimed for a truly catholic ecumenical Christianity:* universal, world-wide, all-inclusive, all-embracing. **3** *Our young people distinguish themselves with more catholic sympathies and tastes than ever before:* broad, comprehensive, universal.

Ant. 1 non-Catholic. **2, 3** sectarian, parochial, provincial, narrow, exclusive, limited.

◇ *Word origin: Catholic* comes from Greek *katholikos,* meaning universal.

"I bless my stars for a taste so catholic, so unexcluding." —*Charles Lamb*

---

cattle *n. Rearing cattle is an important branch of agriculture:* cows, *Archaic* kine; (*male*) bulls, bullocks, steers, oxen; (*female*) cows, milk cows, dairy cattle; (*young*) calves, heifers.

◇ *Word origin:* In some countries a man's wealth is still reckoned by the number of *cattle* he owns. *Cattle* comes from Medieval Latin *capitale,* wealth, capital. The same word gives us *capital* and *chattel.*

catty *adj.* **1** *That gossip always has something catty to say about others:* spiteful, malicious, mean, malignant, malevolent. **2** *The room had a catty smell:* catlike, of cats.

◇ *Word origin: Catty* is of fairly recent origin and the first use recorded by the Oxford English Dictionary was in 1886.

caucus *n. The delegates held a caucus before the convention to elect a chairman:* assembly, meeting, conclave, council, conference, session.

◇ *Word origin: Caucus* probably comes from the Virginian Algonquian word *caucawasu,* meaning tribal elder or adviser, as first recorded in about 1610 by Captain John Smith.

cause *v.* **1** *Icy roads cause many accidents:* bring about, lead to, give rise to, bring to pass, produce, generate, create, effect, make, provoke, incline, precipitate; motivate, incite, stimulate, stir up, impel, inspire.

—*n.* **2** *Differences over money were the cause of the argument:* reason, source, root, prime mover; provocation, inducement, motivation, motive, grounds, incentive, instigation, origin, inspiration, initiation, occasion, stimulus, foundation, mainspring, spring, genesis. **3** *We must not be traitors to the cause of liberty:* goal, aspiration, object, purpose, principle, ideal, belief, conviction, tenet, persuasion, side.

Ant. 1 prevent, forestall, deter, inhibit, ward off, stop, foil. **2** effect, result, consequence, fruit, outcome, final outgrowth, end.

◇ *Word origin: Cause* comes from Latin *causa,* cause, reason, lawsuit.

caustic *adj.* **1** *Acid is caustic:* burning, corrosive, corroding, erosive; astringent, stinging,

biting, sharp. **2** *His caustic tone hurt our feelings:* sarcastic, biting, stinging, cutting, scathing, sharp, harsh, acrid, acrimonious, tart, bitter.
Ant. 1 soothing, healing; bland, mild. **2** flattering, complimentary; sweet, kind, loving, pleasant, pleasing, gentle, gracious, agreeable, mild, bland.

caution *n.* **1** *Cross the street with caution:* care, carefulness, wariness, alertness, watchfulness, vigilance, prudence, precaution, heed, heedfulness, concern, thought, regard, discretion, restraint, circumspection, deliberation, guardedness, mindfulness. **2** *The policeman let the driver off with a caution:* warning, forewarning, alarm, tip-off, admonition, caveat.
—*v.* **3** *The weather-forecaster cautioned us about the icy roads:* warn, forewarn, alert, put on one's guard, tip off, advise; alarm, notify.
Ant. 1 carelessness, recklessness, foolhardiness, rashness, heedlessness, imprudence, daring, daredevilry. **2** put off one's guard; dare.

cautious *adj. Be cautious when swimming in deep water:* careful, wary, alert, watchful, vigilant, attentive, prudent, circumspect, judicious.
Ant. careless, reckless, rash, foolhardy, heedless, inattentive; daring, impetuous, adventurous, venturous, venturesome.

cavalcade *n. The circus cavalcade marched round the ring before the show:* parade, procession, column; caravan.
◇ *Word origin:* See CAVALRY.

cavalier *n.* **1** *The Queen's Horse Guards had 20 cavaliers:* cavalry-man, mounted soldier, horse-soldier, horse trooper, horseman; knight, lancer, dragoon, hussar. **2** *Beau Brummell was the epitome of a cavalier:* gallant, beau, courtier, fine gentleman; dandy, fop; man-about-town, playboy, blade.
—*adj.* **3** *Don Juan was known for his cavalier treatment of women's deeper feelings:* disdainful, uncaring, off-hand, thoughtless, cursory, indifferent, nonchalant; arrogant, haughty.
Ant. 1 infantryman, foot-soldier. **2** conscientious, considerate, diligent, caring, thoughtful, sincere.
◇ *Word origin:* See CAVALRY.

cavalry *n. My grandfather joined the cavalry because he loved horses:* mounted troops, horse-soldiers, horse troops, mounted men; lancers, dragoons, hussars.
Ant. infantry, foot-soldiers.
◇ *Usage note: Lancers* are cavalrymen who carry lances; *dragoons* are heavily armed cavalry troops; and *hussars* are lightly armed cavalry troops.
◇ *Word origin: Cavalry, cavalier,* and *cavalcade* come from Latin *caballus,* horse. Thus *cavalry* means troops on horseback, a *cavalier* was originally a gallant knight on horseback, and a *cavalcade* was a company or procession of horsemen.

cave *n. Bears often hibernate in caves:* underground chamber, cavern, grotto; dug-out, hollow, den, cavity.
◇ *Word origin: Cave, cavern,* and *cavity* all come from Latin *cavus,* hollow, empty.

cavern *n. Limestone caverns attract many potholers:* large cave, large underground chamber, pot-hole.
◇ *Word origin:* See CAVE.

cavil *v. My boss cavils at the least detail:* complain, find fault, faultfind, criticize, disparage, deprecate, belittle, discredit, deride, quibble, pick to pieces.
Ant. praise, applaud, compliment, flatter, approve.

cavort *v. The ponies cavorted in the paddock:* caper, prance, frisk, frolic, gambol, bound, romp, play.

cease *v. The general ordered his troops to cease fire. The music ceased:* stop, halt, leave off, desist, conclude, end, bring to an end, finish, terminate, forbear, break off, adjourn, discontinue, suspend, pause, refrain from, abstain from; die away, pass, abate, come to a standstill.
Ant. begin, commence, start, initiate, continue, persist.
◇ *Word origin: Cease* and *cessation* come from Latin *cessare,* to stop. The same Latin word gives us *incessant,* without stopping.

"Can a woman's tender care
Cease, towards the child she bare?
Yes, she may forgetful be
Yet will I remember thee." *William Cowper*

---

cede *v. Mexico ceded New Mexico to the United States in 1848:* yield, grant, deliver, deliver up, hand over, surrender, give, tender, relinquish, release, abandon, leave, transfer.
Ant. keep, retain, withhold, maintain one's hold on, hold back, cling to, hang on to, hold tight, adhere.

celebrate *v.* **1** *The party celebrated the couple's fiftieth anniversary:* commemorate, observe; engage in festivities. **2** *Conservatives celebrate free enterprise:* proclaim, broadcast; acclaim, praise, extol, venerate, honour, exalt, applaud, laud, cheer, commend, revere. **3** *Jews celebrate Yom Kippur by fasting and going to the synagogue:* observe, solemnize, hallow, consecrate, honour, ritualize, bless, glorify.
Ant. 1 ignore, disregard, overlook. **2** condemn, despise, dishonour, profane. **3** desecrate, dishonour, profane.
◇ *Word origin: Celebrate* and *celebrity* come from Latin *celeber,* famous. Thus *celebrate* means to make famous or to observe a famous occasion whilst, of course, a *celebrity* is a famous person.

celebrated *adj. Rabindranath Tagore was a celebrated Hindu poet:* famous, famed, renowned, well-known, prominent, distinguished, acclaimed, noted, notable, eminent, illustrious, respected, revered, venerable, honoured, treasured, prized.

Ant. unknown, little-known, forgotten, undistinguished, unacclaimed, insignificant, trivial, paltry; dishonoured, degraded, unpopular, unnotable.

celebration *n. The birthday celebration went on all day:* celebrating, party, festivity, festival, feast, gala, fête, jubilee, carnival, revelry; commemoration, ritual, observance, ceremony, ceremonial, solemnization, hallowing, memorialization, sanctification.

celebrity *n.* **1** *Gracie Fields was a leading celebrity of her day:* famous person, star, notable, luminary, personality, name; dignitary, personage, person of note; *Slang* big shot, bigwig, V.I.P. **2** *W. G. Grace gained celebrity both for his character and ability:* fame, stardom, renown, note, notoriety, notability, distinction, glory, prominence, eminence, popularity, a name for oneself.

Ant. **1** unknown, nobody, nonentity; has-been. **2** obscurity, oblivion.

◇ *Word origin:* See CELEBRATE.

celestial *adj.* **1** *As a child, the saint had the celestial beauty of an angel:* heavenly, divine, angelic, seraphic, blissful, hallowed, sublime, beatific, ethereal, Elysian, other-worldly, unearthly, empyrean, paradisal. **2** *A celestial map shows the positions of the planets:* astral, astronomical, solar, planetary, stellar; sky.

Ant. **1** earthy, earthly, mundane, worldly, mortal; hellish, infernal, satanic. **2** earthly, terrestrial.

◇ *Word origin: Celestial* comes from Latin *caelum,* heaven or sky, which also gives us *ceiling.*

celibacy *n. Catholic priests must take vows of celibacy:* chastity, virginity, continence, abstinence; bachelorhood, spinsterhood.

◇ *Word origin:* See CELIBATE.

celibate *adj. Unlike priests, ministers need not lead celibate lives:* unmarried, unwed, single, bachelor, spinster; chaste, virginal, continent, abstinent, pure.

Ant. married, wed, wedded; unchaste, incontinent, impure; promiscuous, loose, wanton.

◇ *Word origin: Celibate* and *celibacy* come from the Latin *caelebs,* unmarried.

cellar *n. The furnace is down in the cellar. Do you keep a wine cellar? We're building a coal-cellar:* basement, downstairs; underground room, subterranean room; cave, den, dug-out.

Ant. attic, garret; upstairs.

◇ *Spelling tip:* This word ends in *-ar,* not *-er.* Remember, a *cellAr* is for storing *Apples.*

◇ *Word origin:* Our words *cellar* and *cell* come from Latin *cella,* small room.

cement *n.* **1** *The boys wrote their initials in the cement before it dried. Paste the picture in the album with rubber cement:* (*loosely*) concrete, mortar; glue, paste.

—*v.* **2** *Let's cement the parts together:* glue, paste, stick, fix, seal, weld, set; unite, join, secure.

◇ *Usage note: Cement* is a powder made of limestone and clay and is used to make concrete and mortar. Thus, technically, a pavement may be made of concrete if it contains cement to bind the other ingredients together. In non-technical, general use, however, cement and concrete are synonyms.

◇ *Word origin: Cement* comes from Latin *caementum,* meaning "stone chips," and was originally made by binding together small stones and chips in mortar.

cemetery *n. We went to the cemetery to visit Grandfather's grave:* graveyard, burial-ground, memorial park, churchyard, burying-ground, necropolis, catacomb, ossuary, (of paupers) potter's field; *Slang* bone-yard.

◇ *Word origin: Cemetery* comes from Greek *koimētērion,* dormitory. Greek Christian writers first used the word to mean burial-ground.

censure *n.* **1** *The sleeping sentry received strong censure from his commanding officer:* reprimand, reproof, upbraiding, rebuke, reprobation, reproach, admonition, castigation, scolding, chiding, remonstrance, criticism, complaint, condemnation, disapproval, disapprobation, dressing-down, tongue-lashing.

—*v.* **2** *The dean censured the students for breaking rules:* rebuke, reprimand, admonish, upbraid, reproach, castigate, denounce, condemn, chide, berate, disapprove, criticize, reprove, scold, reprehend; *Slang* tear off a strip, haul over the coals, rap on the knuckles, pan, rap.

Ant. praise. **1** approval, eulogy, commendation, compliment, encouragement. **2** commend, applaud, compliment, eulogize, laud.

◇ *Usage note:* Don't confuse *censure,* to reprimand or rebuke someone, with *censor,* to prohibit or remove objectionable material, or the person who does it. Thus, *The judge censured the driver but didn't fine him. The censor censored a scene from the film.*

central *adj.* **1** *The bull's-eye is the central part of the board:* in the centre, middle, middlemost, midmost, interior, inner, inmost. **2** *The firm's central office is in Johannesburg. The Prime Minister is the central figure in the government:* major, main, principal, most important, chief, key, leading, primary, paramount, prime, dominant, predominant, foremost, focal, pivotal, basic, fundamental, essential.

Ant. **1** outermost, outside, outer, exterior. **2** minor, subordinate, subsidiary, secondary.

centre *n.* **1** *He hit the centre of the target:* middle point, dead centre, hub; middle, mid, central part; core, heart, interior, pivot, axis, nucleus. **2** *Broadway is the theatrical centre of the United States:* focal point, main point, main place, hub, heart, crux, essence.

—*v.* **3** *Please centre your attention on the front of the room:* concentrate, direct, address, fix, focus, converge, gather.
Ant. 1 exterior, outside; perimeter, edge, rim, circumference. **3** diffuse, scatter, disperse.

> **Exploring the Word:** Greek *kentron,* centre, gives us our words *centre; central; centrifugal,* force directed away from the centre, as by a whirling motion; *concentric,* having the same centre; *eccentric,* off-centre, hence deviant; and *concentrate,* to gather together at the centre.

ceremonial *adj.* **1** *The King loved to behave in a ceremonial manner:* formal, ceremonious, ritualistic. **2** *Bach wrote the ceremonial music for the Easter service:* used in ceremonies, liturgical, solemn.
—*n.* **3** *Mother enjoys the ceremonial of the mass:* ritual, rite, service, ceremony, liturgy, sacrament; formality, celebration, observance.
Ant. 1 informal, relaxed, casual, down-to-earth, plain, simple.

ceremonious *adj. The host's greetings were too ceremonious to be friendly:* formal, stiff, correct, over-polite, proper, starchy, rigid, meticulous, careful, precise, methodical, exact, fussy, prim, solemn, dignified, pompous.
Ant. unceremonious, informal, relaxed, careless, casual, down-to-earth, plain, simple.

ceremony *n.* **1** *The inauguration ceremony was brief:* rite, ritual, service, observance, ceremonial, celebration, function, formalities, commemoration. **2** *Lack of ceremony caused the conference to break up in chaos:* formality, formal behaviour, etiquette, politeness, decorum, protocol, propriety, custom, conventionality; nicety, amenity.
Ant. 2 informality.
◇ *Word origin:* A *ceremony* is a ritual which expresses our veneration for something. The word comes from Latin *caerimonia,* religious worship.

certain *adj.* **1** *I'm certain that I put the book on the table:* sure, positive, confident, convinced, undoubting, undoubtful, satisfied, secure, assured, cocksure. **2** *After the Boston Tea Party, war between England and America seemed certain. That the diamonds are real is certain:* definite, inevitable, positive, inescapable, bound to happen, settled; conclusive, indubitable, unequivocal, unmistakable, unquestionable; unqualified, indisputable, undisputed, undeniable, incontrovertible, incontestable, irrefutable, reliable, absolute, unalterable, unchangeable, unshakeable, well-grounded, valid. **3** *A certain person has been asking questions about you:* specific, particular, individual, special, express.
Ant. 1 uncertain, doubtful, dubious, unconvinced. **2** doubtful, unlikely, questionable, unclear, unsure, unsettled, indefinite, inconclusive, undecided, disputable, unreliable, unfounded, equivocal, qualified, fallible.

certainty *n.* **1** *The forecast of rain was given with such certainty that everyone carried an umbrella:* positiveness, confidence, certitude, assurance, surety, sureness, conclusiveness; conviction, belief, trust, faith, presumption, authoritativeness. **2** *It is a certainty that the new bypass will be built:* fact, reality, actuality, inevitability, inescapability, sure thing, sure bet.
Ant. uncertainty. **1** indecision, inconclusiveness, unsureness; scepticism, disbelief, faithlessness, doubt.

certificate *n. Have you a certificate of ownership for this car?:* document, certification, credential, licence, affidavit, voucher, authorization, authentication.

certify *v. Two witnesses must certify that this is your signature. Ask the bank manager to certify this cheque:* confirm, corroborate, attest, substantiate, validate, verify, witness, testify to, vouch, swear, guarantee, warrant, endorse, authorize, ratify, underwrite, second, support, sanction, authenticate, assure, declare, aver, give one's word.
Ant. repudiate, disavow, deny, disprove.

cessation *n. The warring nations agreed on a cessation of hostilities:* stopping, stop, ceasing, halting, halt, desisting, ending, end, concluding, termination, surcease, leaving off, breaking off; discontinuing, discontinuance, suspension, adjournment, stay, respite, pause, interruption, recess.
Ant. starting, start, beginning, commencement, initiation; continuance, continuation, persistance; resumption.
◇ *Word origin:* See CEASE.

chafe *v.* **1** *The tight collar chafed his neck:* rub, scratch, scrape, rasp, abrade. **2** *The bus-driver chafed at the slowness of the traffic:* be irritated, be exasperated, be annoyed, rage, rankle, seethe, boil, burn, fume, foam.
Ant. 1 soothe, cool, heal, protect. **2** pacify.
◇ *Word origin: Chafe* comes to us via Old French *chaufer,* to warm, from Latin *calor,* heat, from which we also get *calorie.* A *chafing-dish* is a vessel for heating or warming food at the table.

chagrin *n. The man resigned his job with chagrin, admitting he could not do the work:* shame, humiliation, embarrassment, mortification.
Ant. pride, glory, triumph, exultation.

chain *n.* **1** *Where can I buy a bicycle-chain? Grandfather always wore a watch on a chain:* linked cable, metal links; fob. **2** Usually **chains.** *The prisoners were put in chains:* shackles, fetters, bonds, irons; manacles, handcuffs, leg-irons. **3 chains.** *The slaves were freed from their chains:* bondage, subjugation, enslavement, slavery, servitude, serfdom, thraldom. **4** *A bizarre chain of events caused the accident on the Orient Express:* series, sequence, succession, string, train.

—*v.* **5** *Chain the dog securely to the fence:* shackle, fetter, fasten, tie, tie up, secure, bind, lash, tether, moor; put in irons, manacle.

Ant. 5 unchain, unfasten, untie, unshackle, unstrap; free, let go, let loose, liberate.

chalice *n. The priest poured wine into the chalice:* goblet, cup, vessel.

◇ *Word origin: Chalice* comes from Latin *calix*, cup, which is still sometimes used to refer to the ecclesiastical chalice. Note, however, that the cup-shaped part of certain flowers and organs, *calyx*, is spelt with a *y*. (Both words come from Greek *kalux*, cup of a flower.)

challenge *n.* **1** *He received a challenge to a duel. The champion issued a challenge to all other boxers to fight him:* summons, dare, defiant bid, hostile invitation, demand. **2** *Mt. Everest is the supreme challenge to a climber:* test, trial, gage.

—*v.* **3** *The fathers challenged the sons to a race:* dare, summon, bid, invite to compete, defy, fling down the gauntlet. **4** *I challenge the truth of your story:* question, impute, dispute, take exception to, doubt. **5** *The new job challenged his skill:* test, try, tax.

Ant. 4 accept, believe, agree with; concede, yield, acquiesce.

chamber *n.* **1** *The lawyers met in the judge's chambers. The crowd waited outside the council chamber:* room, inner room, office; apartment; hall. **2** *The king retired to his chamber:* bedroom, boudoir; sitting-room, parlour, drawing-room, salon. **3** *The Upper Chamber approved the amendment:* legislative body; council, House of Commons, House of Lords, assembly, congress, board, diet.

◇ *Word origin: Chamber* comes from Greek *kamara*, vault. *Kamara* also gives us *bicameral* (two chambers or houses, as of a legislature) and *camera* (a lightproof chamber in which an image is projected on a film).

champion *n.* **1** *Joe Louis was the world heavyweight boxing champion for many years:* title holder, contest winner; victor, winner, conqueror, vanquisher. **2** *Mahatma Gandhi was a champion of peaceful relations among all countries:* upholder, advocate, defender, supporter, protector, backer, promoter.

—*v.* **3** *Octavia Hill championed the establishment of the National Trust:* fight for, battle for, uphold, support, back, stand up for, defend, promote, advocate, aid, abet, speak for, espouse.

Ant. 1 loser; contender. **2** opponent, enemy, detractor. **3** oppose, combat; hinder.

◇ *Word origin: Champion* comes from Late Latin *campio*, fighter, from *campus*, field (which also gives us *campus, camp*, and *campaign*).

chance *n.* **1** *The two friends met by chance in the street:* accident; fortune, luck, destiny, fate. **2** *There's a chance of rain today:* possibility, likelihood, likeliness, probability. **3** *Candidates who fail the driving test will have another chance next year:* opportunity, try, attempt, occasion, possibility. **4** *Don't take chances by driving too fast:* risk, danger, hazard; gamble, speculation, jeopardy.

—*v.* **5** *It chanced that someone found the lost ring:* happen, occur, come to pass, come about, turn out, fall, befall, fall to one's lot. **6** *Should we chance getting home before it snows?:* take a chance, risk, hazard, venture, gamble, try, attempt, rely on fortune.

—*adj.* **7** *A chance meeting brought the two old friends together again:* accidental, unintentional, unexpected, unlooked for, unplanned, unforeseen, random, undesigned, unpremeditated, fortuitous, fortunate, lucky.

Ant. 1 plan, design, intent, intention, premeditation. **2** unlikelihood, impossibility, improbability, certainty. **4** surety, certainty, sure thing. **7** intentional, planned, premeditated; designed, arranged, expected, foreseen, looked for.

"A wise man turns chance into good fortune."
—*Thomas Fuller*

---

change *v.* **1** *Rain made us change our plans for the picnic. The caterpillar changed into a butterfly:* alter, modify, make different, shift, vary, recast, restyle, remodel, reorganize, reform, revolutionize; transfer, transmute, mutate, transform, turn, convert, metamorphose. **2** *You'd better change that shirt for a larger one:* exchange, replace, substitute, swap, trade, switch, shift, interchange, shuffle; remove and replace.

—*n.* **3** *After the warm days, this cold weather is quite a change. The new owner made a lot of changes in the business:* difference, modification, switch, shift, variation, deviation, variety, fluctuation, veering; alteration, conversion, substitution, swapping, reform, reformation, revolution, reorganization, remodelling, restyling; metamorphosis, transformation, conversion, transmutation, transfiguration. **4** *Let's eat out for a change:* novelty, something different, exception; diversion. **5** *Have you any change for the tip?:* coins, small coins, silver.

Ant. 1 hold, keep, bide, stay, remain. **2** keep. **3** uniformity, permanence, immutability, fixedness, constancy, stability, invariability, unchangeableness, monotony. **5** notes, paper money.

◇ *Word origin: Change* comes from Late Latin *cambiare*, to exchange. The word entered Latin during the Roman occupation of Gaul and Britain and is probably of Celtic origin, related to Irish *gaimbim*, tax.

changeable *adj. Her moods are as changeable as the weather:* variable, varying, erratic, irregular, alternating, deviating, fickle, flighty, volatile, fluctuating, mercurial, capricious, fitful, vacillating, unsteady, uncertain, unstable, capricious; mutable, reversible, transformable, modifiable, convertible.

Ant. unchangeable, invariable, regular, undeviating, constant, steady, certain, reliable, stable, immutable, irreversible, inconvertible.

◇ *Spelling tip:* Remember that *change* keeps its *e* in *changeable*. In fact, all words ending in *-ge* keep the *e* before adding *-able*.

channel *n.* **1** *We sailed across the English Channel:* strait, passage, watercourse, narrows. **2** *Heavy rains wore a channel in the yard:* groove, furrow, trough, gash, cut, gutter. **3** *It takes a week for a memo to reach the boss by the normal channels:* route, course, avenue of communication.

—*v.* **4** *The requests for transfers are channelled through the personnel office:* route, direct, send, convey, guide, steer, lead.

◇ *Word origin: Channel* and *canal* come to us from Latin *canalis*, groove.

chaos *n. Without rules, people would live in a state of chaos:* turmoil, upheaval, confusion, tumult, uproar, furore, bedlam, pandemonium, turbulence, commotion; disorder, disarray, disarrangement, mess, muddle, jumble, discomposure.

Ant. order, organization, routine, efficiency; calmness, calm; quiet, composure, peacefulness.

◇ *Word origin: Chaos* comes from Greek *khaos*, vast chasm, void.

chaperon *n.* **1** *Débutantes used to be accompanied by chaperons:* adult overseer, adult attendant; guardian, protector, custodian, attendant, duenna.

—*v.* **2** *A group of parents chaperoned the school dance:* oversee, keep an eye on, shepherd; guard, safeguard, watch, accompany, escort.

◇ *Word origin: Chaperon* is the French word for a cape or riding hood. The present-day sense of the word arose because a human *chaperon* was supposed to protect as closely as a hood or cape.

chapter *n.* **1** *Read chapters 1 to 5 of the textbook. The Renaissance was an important chapter in European history:* part, section, division, subdivision, portion; clause, period, span. **2** *The Dean and Chapter met to discuss Cathedral business:* body of canons; assembly of members of religious order.

char *v. The sparks from the fireplace charred the carpet:* singe, scorch, sear, burn; incinerate, reduce to charcoal, carbonize.

◇ *Word origin: Char* is presumably a shortening of the word *charcoal*.

character *n.* **1** *Each individual should be judged by his own character:* qualities, traits, attributes, nature, self, being, make-up, individuality, distinctiveness. **2** *A person who cheats has little character:* honour, integrity, moral strength, morality, honesty, goodness, rectitude, uprightness. **3** *The police were tracking a suspicious character:* person, individual, specimen, being, personality. **4** *My old aunt is a priceless character:* oddity, eccentric, original, queer fish, card. **5** *Ophelia is the main female character in* Hamlet: fictional person, person, persona; role, part; (*plural*) dramatis personae.

Ant. **2** dishonour, dishonesty, moral weakness.

characteristic *adj.* **1** *Windy days are characteristic of March:* typical, representative, indicative, symbolic, emblematic, distinctive, distinguishing.

—*n.* **2** *Tactfulness is one of his nicest characteristics:* attribute, trait, quality, aspect, feature, property, mark, earmark; mannerism, peculiarity, speciality, trade mark.

Ant. **1** uncharacteristic, unusual, atypical, unrepresentative, rare.

characterization *n. The characterization of librarians as old maids is unfair and untrue. The actress's characterization of Juliet was superb:* representing, representation, portrayal, portrait, picturing, depiction; delineation, description.

charge *v.* **1** *The hotel charges seven pounds a day for this room:* fix as a price, put a value on, ask, demand, require, exact, price; request payment, assess, levy. **2** *Did the customer pay cash for the shoes or charge them?:* put on one's account, incur a debit, take credit, delay payment; debit. **3** *The air was charged with electricity:* load, fill, lade, pack, stuff; pile, stack, heap. **4** *The major charged his soldiers to stand firm:* command, order, direct, instruct, bid, call upon, summon, enjoin. **5** *The traffic policeman charged the young man in the sports car with driving recklessly:* attribute, ascribe, fix responsibility for, lay the blame for, impute, assign; accuse, incriminate, blame, indict, lodge a complaint against, prefer charges against. **6** *The cavalry charged the enemy fort:* rush, attack, storm, come at, make a dash at, beset, assail, assault, make an onslaught.

—*n.* **7** *The charge for admission is fifty pence:* fee, cost, price, expense, assessment, rate, payment; payment due, toll, duty. **8** *The Earl of Cardigan led the Charge of the Light Brigade:* attack, onslaught, assault, storming, rush, onset, sortie. **9** *The children are in the charge of a nursemaid:* care, custody, keeping, safe keeping, guardianship, protection; jurisdiction, superintendence, supervision, administration, control, command, management. **10** *The suspect was booked on a charge of theft:* allegation, accusation, complaint; arraignment, indictment. **11** *The judge made a brief charge to the jury:* direction, advice, instruction, injunction; order, command, bidding, dictate, enjoining; rule of conduct.

Ant. **1** give away, give. **2** pay, pay cash. **3** empty, unload. **5** absolve, exculpate; vindicate, exonerate, pardon, acquit. **6** retreat, withdraw. **8** retreat, withdrawal. **10** pardon, reprieve, vindication, exoneration; acquittal, absolution, clearance.

◇ *Spelling tip:* Remember that *charge* keeps its final *e* in *chargeable* and *rechargeable.* In fact, all words ending in *-ge* keep the *e* before adding *-able.*

charitable *adj.* **1** *Christian Aid asks us to be charitable in our gifts this year. The children's home is a charitable organization:* generous, giving, bountiful, bounteous, munificent, open-handed, lavish; philanthropic, almsgiving, eleemosynary, benevolent. **2** *A more charitable person would forgive the boy's errors:* forgiving, understanding, sympathetic, sympathizing, kindly, kind, kind-hearted, warm-hearted, gracious, considerate, magnanimous; lenient, liberal, tolerant, indulgent.

Ant. **1** uncharitable, stingy, parsimonious, ungiving, ungenerous. **2** unforgiving, strict, rigid, unkind, unsympathetic, hard-hearted, cold-hearted, inconsiderate.

charity *n.* **1** *The orphanage is supported by the charity of the townspeople. The Red Cross is my favourite charity:* philanthropy, contributions, donations, donating, alms, alms-giving, giving, financial help, help, aid, gift, assistance, offering, endowment, benefaction, fund-raising, hand-out; generosity, munificence, open-handedness, bounty, benefaction; charitable institution, fund. **2** *Faith, hope, and charity can make the world a better place:* goodwill, love of mankind, humanity, compassion, love, sympathy, kindness, goodness, benevolence, affection, benignity, tolerance, graciousness.

Ant. **1** uncharitableness, stinginess, parsimony. **2** malice, ill will, hate, hatred, selfishness, cruelty, intolerance.

◇ *Word origin: Charity* comes from Latin *caritas,* love, akin to *carus,* dear. The same word gives us *caress* and *cherish.*

charlatan *n. It's been proved that fortune-tellers are charlatans:* fake, fraud, deceiver, quack, imposter, cheat, swindler, trickster, cozener, confidence man, mountebank.

◇ *Pronunciation tip:* The initial *ch* in *charlatan* is pronounced *sh,* the same as the initial sound in *shoe.*

◇ *Word origin: Charlatan* comes from Italian *ciarlatano,* babbler, idle talker.

charm *n.* **1** *The chairman of a TV talk programme must have lots of charm. The girl's warm personality is her greatest charm:* power to please, fascination, allure, allurement, attraction, magnetism, lure, draw. **2** *The fairy godmother's magic charm turned Cinderella's rags into a beautiful gown:* spell, incantation, conjuration; sorcery, black magic. **3** *Some men used to carry a rabbit's foot as a charm:* lucky charm; amulet, talisman trinket, bauble, ornament.

—*v.* **4** *Everyone was charmed by the child's graciousness:* please, give pleasure, delight, gratify, make happy, enrapture, enthral; fascinate, attract, allure, engage, entrance, enchant, grip, captivate, take, bewitch, *Slang* turn on. **5** *His daughter charmed him into buying her a car:* lure, seduce, cajole, win over, beguile, bewitch. **6** *The witch charmed the prince, turning him into a frog:* change by magic, work magic on, cast a spell, conjure.

Ant. **1** unattractiveness, repulsiveness. **4** repel, alienate, disgust, displease; *Slang* turn off.

◇ *Word origin: Charm* comes from the Latin *carmen,* song, verse, incantation, oracular response. It is closely related to *chant, enchant,* and *incantation.*

"Charming people live up to the very edge of their charm, and behave as outrageously as the world will let them." —*Logan Pearsall Smith*

---

charming *adj. She gave us a charming smile. Jim has developed a charming personality:* attractive, pleasing, delightful, agreeable, lovely, graceful, winning, winsome, likeable; entrancing, fascinating, captivating, engaging, enthralling, bewitching, enchanting, fetching, enticing, magnetic, irresistible, alluring.

Ant. unattractive, unpleasing, unpleasant, unlikeable, repulsive, repellent, disgusting.

chart *n.* **1** *The navigator plotted the ship's course on the chart. The chart showed the decline in the company's sales during the year:* map, navigator's map, mariner's map; diagram, graph, table, tabulation; blueprint, scheme.

—*v.* **2** *The pilot charted the plane's course:* map out, draw up, diagram; draft, plan, delineate, design, outline, lay out.

◇ *Word origin: Chart, charter,* and *card* come from Greek *chartēs,* sheet of papyrus, originally an Egyptian name for the reed from which the first paper was made.

charter *n.* **1** *The organization operates under charter:* permit, licence, authority, franchise, agreement, contract, concession, sanction, deed.

—*v.* **2** *The College was chartered by the King two hundred years ago:* establish by charter, license, commission, grant, authorize. **3** *The holiday-makers chartered a boat to go fishing:* rent, hire, lease, let, engage.

chase *v.* **1** *The policeman chased the thief down the street. Huntsmen chased the deer silently:* pursue, go in pursuit of, go after, run after, try to overtake, try to catch up with; hunt, stalk, trail, track, follow, tail, dog, hound, shadow. **2** *Mother chased the cat from the bedroom:* drive, put to flight; evict, oust, send away, drive away, rout, shoo, send packing, cast out; scatter, dispel.

—*n.* **3** *Many huntsmen find the chase more exciting than the kill:* hunt, hunting, quest, pursuit, pursuing, following, stalking, tracking.

Ant. **1** let go, let escape, lose, lose track of, escape, flee, elude.

chasm *n. The earthquake left a deep chasm in the earth's surface:* abyss, fissure, rift, split, gorge, ravine, gap, crevasse, divide, gulf, break, cleft, crack, breach; pit, crater, hold, cavity.
◇ *Pronunciation tip:* Remember to pronounce *chasm* with a *k* sound: *Kas'm.*

chaste *adj.* **1** *Boy Scouts are enjoined to remain chaste in mind and body:* virginal, pure, continent, clean-living, wholesome, decent, virtuous, sinless, clean, untainted, uncorrupted, unsullied, immaculate. **2** *The author's chaste style is elegant but boring:* pure, classic, restrained, austere, severe, strict, precise; unadorned, unornamented, unembellished.
Ant. 1 unchaste, incontinent, impure, lewd, obscene, wanton, promiscuous, licentious, ribald; married, wed, corrupt, unwholesome, dishonourable, immoral, sinful, immodest; impure, unclean, tainted, sullied, soiled, dirty, blemished, tarnished. **2** ornate, flashy, gaudy, unrestrained, self-indulgent, vulgar.

chasten See CHASTISE.

chastise *v. The teacher chastised the child for arriving late:* punish, discipline, penalize, beat, whip, spank, thrash, flog, strap; reprimand, scold, castigate, upbraid, rebuke, reproach, admonish, chasten, reprove, correct, censure, criticize, chide, call down, berate, scourge, take to task, fulminate against; *Informal* call on the carpet, give a tongue-lashing to, haul over the coals.
Ant. reward, honour, praise, compliment, applaud, commend, congratulate, give kudos to.

chastity *n. Nuns must take two vows of chastity:* celibacy, purity, virginity, innocence, continence, abstemiousness.
Ant. incontinence; promiscuity, lewdness, wantonness, licentiousness.

Exploring the Word: The Latin word *castus* means pure. It gives us *chaste* and *chastity.* Closely related is the word *incest,* from Latin *incestus,* impure, unchaste. *Castus* also gives us *chastise, castigate,* and *chasten,* all of which mean to punish in order to keep pure or to make pure again.

chat *v.* **1** *Stop and chat a while:* talk, converse, chatter, chit-chat, prate, prattle; *Slang* palaver, chew the rag, chew the fat.
—*n.* **2** *Call me tomorrow and we'll have a chat:* talk, conversation; chit-chat, gab, palaver, natter, confabulation, talk session, heart-to-heart talk.
◇ *Word origin: Chat* is a short form of *chatter.*

chattel *n. The will says that "all goods and chattels" are left to his brother:* personal possessions, personal effects, belongings, effects, movable property, movables; paraphernalia, gear, things, trappings, accoutrements.
◇ *Word origin: Chattel* comes from Medieval Latin *capitale,* property, which also gives us *capital* and *cattle.*

chatter *v.* **1** *The guests chattered as they waited for dinner:* talk, talk idly, babble, jabber, prattle, prate, gabble, chit-chat, palaver, confabulate, gossip, twaddle, blather, blab, patter, *Slang* gas. **2** *My teeth are chattering from the cold:* clatter, click, clank.
—*n.* **3** *The children's constant chatter was irritating:* jabber, gibber, babble, talk, talking, gossip, chit-chat, gabble, palaver, twaddle, blather, blabbing, patter, idle talk.
◇ *Word origin:* The word *chatter* is onomatopoeic; that is to say, it imitates the sound it represents.

chauvinism *n. The minister's chauvinism made him intolerant of other countries:* super-patriotism, jingoism, my country right or wrong, militarism, nationalism.
◇ *Word origin: Chauvinism* comes from the name of Nicolas Chauvin, legendary veteran of the French armies of the First Republic and Empire. According to the Littré *Dictionnaire de la langue française* (1881), Chauvin "became a popular cartoon character who, by his blind and narrowly patriotic sentiments concerning the fortunes and reverses of Napoleon I, now lends his name to anyone with exaggerated and ridiculous notions of patriotism and war."

"What we obtain too cheap we esteem too lightly; it is dearness only that gives everything its value." —*Thomas Paine*

cheap *adj.* **1** *Chicken is not as cheap as it was:* inexpensive, low-priced, economical, reasonable. **2** *Talk is cheap:* effortless, costless, easy. **3** *The coat may be expensive but it looks cheap:* shoddy, shabby, inferior, worthless, poor, second-rate, trashy, meagre, paltry, gimcrack; flashy, gaudy, in bad taste, tawdry, seedy, common, inelegant. **4** *Spreading gossip is a cheap thing to do:* contemptible, petty, despicable, sordid, ignoble, wretched, mean, base; vulgar, immoral, indecent. **5** *He's too cheap to pick up the bill:* tight, stingy, miserly, penurious, tight-fisted, close.
Ant. 1 expensive, costly, high-priced, high, overpriced. **2** worthwhile, valuable; difficult, troublesome. **3** superior, good, fine, first-rate, worthy; tasteful, high-class, classy, in good taste, elegant, chic, smart. **4** admirable, commendable; moral, decent. **5** generous, charitable, open-handed.
◇ *Usage note: Cheap* and *inexpensive* may be used interchangeably. However, *cheap* can have connotations of inferiority or low rank which *inexpensive* does not have. Thus *an inexpensive dress* and *a cheap dress* both cost little, but a *cheap* dress may also be low in quality, depending on the context of the statement. Likewise, a *cheap* cut of meat is not

an *inexpensive* steak but is a cheap*er*, less valuable cut, as chuck opposed to sirloin.
◇ *Word origin: Cheap* comes from the old phrase *good cheap*, a bargain, a good trade, from the Old English word *ceāp*, barter, bargain, market.

cheat *v.* **1** *Her uncle cheated her out of her inheritance:* swindle, defraud, trick, bilk, gyp, fleece; *Slang* rook; deceive, dupe, victimize, betray, delude, hoodwink, bamboozle, humbug, cozen, hoax, gull; *Slang* con. **2** *Only a cad would cheat at cards:* practise fraud, practise trickery, break the rules, act unfairly. **3** *You can't cheat fate for long:* escape, thwart, foil, circumvent, outwit, frustrate, baffle, fool, defeat.
—n. **4** *That cheat would defraud his own mother!:* swindler, trickster, con man, shark, double-crosser, deceiver; fraud, charlatan, mountebank, crook; quack, fake, imposter, chiseller, dodger.

check *v.* **1** *Inflation must be checked if the pound is to have any value. The sandbags will check the flood-waters temporarily:* stop, bring to a standstill, stay, halt, restrain, slow, hold back, curb, limit, brake, inhibit, arrest, constrain, rein in, rein, harness, bridle, stall; impede, obstruct, choke, prevent, suppress, block, muzzle, retard, smother, frustrate, thwart, circumvent, hold, gag. **2** *Please check the broken light switch. Did you check your purse for the keys?:* inspect, look at, test, examine; search, look into, peruse, explore. **3** *Check on the problem and report the results at the next meeting:* investigate, study, take stock of, review, probe, inspect, survey, look over, examine, explore.
—n. **4** *A system of checks and balances keeps the various branches of local government equal. The anchor served as a check to the boat's forward progress:* restraint, limit, limitation, restriction, control, curb, prevention, prohibition, constraint, hindrance, impediment, barrier, bar, block, obstacle, obstruction, repression, bridle; stop, stoppage, halt, end, stay, cessation. **5** *The plumber made a careful check of the pipes:* test, inspection, scrutiny, examination, survey, search, perusal, probe, investigation, exploration, study.
Ant. **1** begin, initiate, start; accelerate, speed up, spur, let loose, give free rein, unleash, release; foster, encourage, further, urge on; help, abet, aid, support. **2, 3** ignore, overlook, disregard. **4** accelerator, spur, encouragement, fostering, furthering, help, aid; start, beginning.
◇ *Word origin:* All meanings of the word *check* stem from its use in chess, indicating that the king is in danger, hence meaning "defeat or stop." The word comes from Arabic and Persian *shāh*, king.

cheek *n.* **1** *Don't put too much rouge on your cheeks:* jowl, side of the face. **2** *I wouldn't have the cheek to go to a party uninvited:* impudence, impertinence, nerve, insolence, arrogance, effrontery, audacity, brazenness, brass, boldness, forwardness, brashness, temerity.
Ant. **2** reserve, reticence, shyness, bashfulness, timidity, timorousness, humility, self-effacement.

cheep *v.* **1** *Listen to the little chicks cheep!:* peep, chirp, chirrup, tweet, twitter.
—n. **2** *The cheeps of the birds delighted the children:* chirp, peep, chirrup, tweet, twitter.

cheer *n.* **1** *The goal brought loud cheers from the crowd:* approving shout, encouraging cry, hooray, huzzah, yell, shriek. **2** *The nurse always had words of cheer for the patients:* assurance, reassurance, encouragement, comfort, hopefulness, hope; optimism, buoyancy. **3** *The party sparkled with cheer:* gaiety, fun, merriment, animation, joy, joviality, liveliness, revelry, gladness, high spirits, vivacity, buoyancy, joyfulness, delight, pleasure, glee, geniality, rejoicing, jubilation, merry-making, festivity.
—v. **4** *The visiting fans cheered their team to victory:* support, hail, encourage, hurrah, shout, yell, cry. **5** *A vase of roses cheered up the room. The minister's words cheered the family:* brighten, enliven, gladden, animate; assure, reassure, encourage, comfort, hearten, warm, inspire, fortify, buoy up, uplift.
Ant. **1** boo, catcall, hiss, whistle, raspberry. **2** gloom, discouragement, hopelessness, pessimism. **3** gloom, sadness, despair, depression, despondency. **4** deride, discourage, taunt, ridicule, boo, hiss. **5** darken, sadden; discourage, dispirit, depress, dishearten.
◇ *Word origin: Cheer* comes from Old French *chere*, face, countenance. Hence, to be of good cheer literally means to put on a happy face.

cheerful *adj.* **1** *It's wonderful to see you so cheerful:* cheery, gay, joyful, joyous, light-hearted, happy, glad, gladsome, merry, sunny, high-spirited, in a good humour, jovial, buoyant, elated, gleeful, jolly, agreeable, pleasant; breezy, jaunty, blithe, optimistic, airy, lively, sprightly. **2** *Yellow is a cheerful colour:* bright, lively, cheery, gay, sparkling, sunny.
Ant. **1** cheerless, glum, gloomy, sullen, dour, morose, dejected, depressed, depressing, downcast, down-hearted, melancholy, sad, doleful, despondent, disconsolate, dismal, rueful, unhappy, joyless, miserable; dispiriting, unpleasant; lifeless, dull. **2** cheerless, dull, sombre, lifeless, depressing.

cheerless *adj. The host's cheerless mood cast a pall on the party. It was a cheerless autumn day:* gloomy, downcast, dreary, glum, dispirited, despondent, dolorous, forlorn, down-hearted, funereal, doleful, spiritless, grim, dejected, joyless, desolate, heavy-hearted, solemn, austere, saturnine, morose, sullen, sad, melancholy, miserable, mournful, lugubrious, woebegone, unhappy, disconsolate, rueful, woeful; bleak, grey, dull, sunless, sombre, dismal, uninviting, depressing, comfortless.

Ant. cheerful, gay, joyful, light-hearted, happy, merry, jolly, gleeful, elated.

chequered *adj.* **1** *The table had a red and white chequered table-cloth. The fields were chequered with patches of light and shade:* checked, particoloured, variegated, motley, mottled, dappled, piebald, pied. **2** *He had a chequered career of failure and success:* varied, uneven, motley, inconstant, irregular, fitful, fluctuating, vacillating, up-and-down, seesaw.

Ant. 1 solid. **2** consistent, constant, unvarying, unvaried, unvariable, unchanging, steady, stable, even, smooth.

cherish *v.* **1** *Some people cherish possessions more than friends:* love, hold dear, revere, treasure, value, prize, dote on, appreciate, venerate, honour, esteem, idolize, nurse, nourish, nurture, sustain, shelter. **2** *The bride and groom promised to cherish each other through sickness and health:* care for, take care of, sustain, succour, nurture.

Ant. 1 hate, dislike, scorn, despise, disdain. **2** desert, forsake, abandon, renounce, neglect, ignore.

◇ *Word origin: Cherish* goes back via Old French to Latin *carus*, dear, which also gives us *caress* and *charity*.

chew *v. Chew your food slowly:* masticate; champ, gnaw, crunch, munch, grind, crush; ruminate.

chic *adj. The film star wore a very chic dress:* fashionable, stylish, smart, elegant; modish, voguish.

Ant. unfashionable, unstylish, passé; dowdy, inelegant, shabby, shoddy.

◇ *Pronunciation tip: Chic* is pronounced *sheek*, not *chick*. Remember the *sh* sound and the long *e* sound: *sheek*.

◇ *Word origin:* English has borrowed *chic* directly from French. The French word comes from German *Schick*, meaning taste, elegance, fitness.

chide *v. Mother chided me for being late:* admonish, reprimand, scold, chasten, rebuke, reproach, reprove, upbraid, berate, take to task; find fault, criticize, censure, denounce.

Ant. praise, commend, laud, extol, applaud, compliment.

chief *n.* **1** *The chief of the Italian delegation addressed the U.N.:* head, leader, director, chairman; boss, overseer, administrator, superintendent, supervisor; commander, captain; ringleader, master; ruler, chieftain, monarch, overlord, sovereign, potentate, lord.

—*adj.* **2** *His patient's well-being was the doctor's chief concern:* major, main, prime, primary, first, foremost, highest-ranking, greatest, dominant, predominant, paramount, uppermost, prevailing, highest, supreme, principal, preponderant, key, leading, outstanding; governing, ruling, crowning, leading.

Ant. 1 subordinate, underling, follower, hanger-on; subject. **2** minor, least, last, subordinate, secondary, subsidiary.

◇ *Word origin: Chief* comes from Old French *chef*, head. In French *chef* also means "chief" and, as in present-day English, "chief cook." The word is ultimately derived from Latin *caput*, head, which also gives us *cap, capital*, and *captain*.

chiefly *adv. Shakespeare thought of himself chiefly as a poet but is admired above all as a playwright:* primarily, principally, mainly, in the main, mostly, most of all, predominantly, particularly, above all, expressly, especially.

Ant. least, last, least of all, in a small way.

child *n. The child is only six years old. The average family has two children:* youth, youngster, juvenile, kid, boy, lad, girl, lass; baby, infant, tot, little one, son, daughter, offspring.

Ant. adult, grown-up, man, woman; parent.

"He who pleases children will be remembered with pleasure by men." —*James Boswell*

---

childbirth *n. Many obstetricians encourage some form of natural childbirth:* child-bearing, giving birth, delivery, parturition.

childhood *n. A happy childhood helps to give children security:* youth, boyhood, girlhood; nursery days, school-days, adolescence.

Ant. adulthood, maturity.

childish *adj. Her behaviour is extremely childish:* immature, childlike, infantile, puerile, juvenile, callow, adolescent, babyish; silly, foolish, naïve, simple, asinine.

Ant. mature, grown-up, adult, sophisticated; manly, manful, womanly.

◇ *Usage note: Childish* usually refers to the unattractive characteristics of children, such as lack of seriousness, temper, tantrums, etc.: *Don't be childish! Her childish remark embarrassed everyone. Childlike* usually refers to the attractive characteristics of children, enthusiasm, innocence, etc.: *a wonderful childlike faith in people.*

chill *n.* **1** *There's a chill in the air this morning:* chilliness, coolness, iciness, frostiness, frigidity; crispness, sharpness, nip, bite, rawness. **2** *He caught a chill from being out in the rain:* cold; fever.

—*adj.* also **chilly. 3** *A chill wind blew from the North:* chilling, cold, wintry, arctic, icy, frigid, frosty, penetrating, cool; brisk, biting, bitter, raw, keen, shivery, crisp, sharp, cutting, nippy. **4** *We received a chilly greeting from our opponents:* icy, frigid, cold, aloof, hostile, unfriendly, stony, callous, indifferent, uncaring, unresponsive, stiff, unfeeling, passionless, forbidding, harsh.

Ant. 1 warmth, warmness. **3** warm, warming, hot, tropical, balmy, mild. **4** warm, friendly, cordial, congenial, emotional.

chime *n.* **1** *Our church chimes were installed 10 years ago:* set of bells, carillon. **2** *I love to listen to the chime of the grandfather clock:* peal, pealing, ring, ringing, toll, tollings, knell, tinkling, jingle, ding-dong, gong, tintinnabulation; striking, strike.
—*v.* **3** *The bells chimed as the bride and groom left the church:* peal, ring, sound, toll, knell, tintinnabulate, jingle, tinkle, strike.
◇ *Word origin: Chimes* and *cymbals* sound completely different from each other, but both words come from Latin *cymbalum*, cymbal.

china *n. Set the table with the best china:* dishes, cups and saucers, plates, tableware, chinaware, bone china; pottery, crockery, earthenware, stoneware, porcelain, ceramic ware, slip-ware.
◇ *Word origin:* Today few of us have crockery imported from China, yet there was a time when all true *china* came from China.

chink[1] *n. The rain came in through a chink in the roof:* crack, slit, rift, rent, crevice, cleft, breach, fissure, cut, split, gap, gash, cut, break; hole, opening, aperture.

chink[2] *v. The coins chinked in my pocket:* clink, jingle, jangle, clank, tinkle, ring, rattle.

chip *n.* **1** *Gather some wood chips for the fire. Buy a packet of potato chips:* small piece, fragment, scrap, sliver, chunk, shaving, splinter, shred, slice, paring, cutting; flake, crumb, morsel, bit, wafer. **2** *This glass has a chip in the rim:* nick, gash.
—*v.* **3** *I chipped the dish when I dropped it:* nick, gash, split, splinter. **4** *The sculptor chipped away at the block of marble:* hew, chop, cut, whittle, hack, chisel.

chirp *v.* **1** *Listen to the birds chirping:* chirrup, tweet, twitter, sing, cheep, peep.
—*n.* **2** *The chirps of the crickets keep us awake:* chirrup, tweet, twitter, cheep, peeping, cheeping, chirr.

chivalrous *adj. Chivalrous men treat women with great respect:* gallant, courtly; mannerly, polite.
Ant. ungallant, loutish, boorish, discourteous, rude, unmannerly, disloyal, untrustworthy, inconstant, dishonourable; cruel.

chivalry *n. His considerate treatment of his fiancée shows that chivalry isn't dead:* knighthood; gallantry, courtliness, politeness, courtesy.
Ant. loutishness, boorishness, rudeness, impoliteness, unmannerliness, discourtesy, disloyalty, inconstancy; cruelty, inhumanity.
◇ *Word origin: Chivalry* comes from Latin *caballus*, horse, a possibly Celtic word which also gives us *cavalry* and *cavalier*.

choice *n.* **1** *The worker left the job of his own choice. The child had no choice but to go to bed:* choosing, decision, deciding, discretion, opting, determination; alternative, option, voice, vote, say. **2** *My choice for dessert is ice cream:* selection, preference, pick, appointment. **3** *The boutique has a poor choice of dresses:* selection, variety, pick, stock, supply, store, collection, assemblage, assortment, array, display.
—*adj.* **4** *The market only carries choice fruit and vegetables:* select, well-chosen, superior, first-rate, first-class, best, better, prime, prize, preferred, preferable, exclusive, special, excellent, fine; exceptional, superlative, élite, tip-top, extraordinary, consummate.
Ant. **1** coercion, force; command, order. **4** poor, inferior, worse, second-rate, second-class, mediocre, fair, average, common, ordinary, indifferent.
◇ *Usage note:* See ALTERNATIVE.

choke *v.* **1** *The Boston Strangler choked his victims. The rescuers were choking from the heavy smoke:* strangle, throttle; smother, asphyxiate, suffocate, gag, stifle. **2** *Mud choked the river:* stop up, clog, obstruct, constrict, blockade, block, congest, plug, plug up, dam, dam up, stuff; impede, retard, hold back, arrest, check, hinder, constrain, restrain, hamper, inhibit, bridle, suppress.
Ant. **2** clear, unclog, unstop, unblock, unplug; spur, speed, accelerate, aid, help, encourage.

choose *v.* **1** *Which dress did the girl choose?:* select, pick out, pick, take, decide on, settle on, fix upon, single out, opt for, extract; make up one's mind, resolve, espouse, embrace, adopt. **2** *The defeated candidate chose not to stand for Parliament again:* decide, determine, prefer, commit oneself, elect, see fit, desire, wish, be inclined, like.
Ant. **1** reject, eschew, refuse, decline, spurn, repudiate, cast away, cast out, leave, throw aside, disclaim, dismiss; forgo, forbear.

choosy *adj. Weight-watchers must be very choosy about the food they eat:* fussy, finicky, particular, fastidious, discriminating.

chop *v.* **1** *George Washington chopped down the cherry tree. Chop some wood for the fire:* cut, fell; sunder, hew, hack, split, cleave, slash, gash, lop, crop. **2** *Chop the carrots for the stew:* cut up, dice, mince, chip, cube; pulverize, fragment.
—*n.* **3** *The forester gave the tree one last chop and it fell:* stroke, whack, blow, hit, cut, hack, swipe. **4** *Pork chops and apple are a good combination:* cutlet, rib, slice, cut, *French* côtelette.
◇ *Word origin: Chop* comes from Middle English *choppen*, to cut, hew. It is closely related to *chap*, to crack or make rough. Oddly, neither word is in any way related to *chip*.

chore *n.* **1** *Children should help with the household chores:* household task, domestic work, farm task, small job, task, job, duty, work, assignment, stint, errand. **2** *Filling in complicated tax forms is a real chore:* unpleasant task, difficult job, strain, burden, tedious job, exacting task.
◇ *Word origin:* In our grandparents' day, the usual form of the word was *char* (as in *charwoman*). *Chore*, commoner in North America,

has superseded it and is now the standard form.

chortle *v.* **1** *Father used to chortle over the funny cartoons every Sunday:* chuckle, snort merrily, laugh.

—*n.* **2** *The child gave a merry chortle:* chuckle, merry snort, laugh, gleeful whoop.

◇ *Word origin: Chortle* was coined by Lewis Carroll in *Through the Looking-Glass* (1871): "'O frabjous day! Calooh! Callay!' He chortled in his joy." The word is a blend of *chuckle* + *snort.*

chorus *n.* **1** *Sing the last chorus again:* refrain, antiphony, response. **2** *The chorus sang Christmas carols:* choir, singing group, glee club, choral society; line of dancers; group of speakers. **3** *The union members shouted their assent in chorus:* concert, unison, unity, one voice; accord, concord, concordance, consensus, unanimity.

◇ *Word origin: Chorus* comes from Greek *choros*, dance. The same Greek word gives us *choir.* Both words come from the ancient Greek drama in which the *chorus* (chorus) were the performers who danced and sang in accompaniment to the dramatic action.

christen *v. The baby was christened in St. Paul's Cathedral:* baptize, sprinkle, dip, immerse; name, designate, dub, dedicate.

◇ *Word origin: Christen* comes from Greek *khriein*, to anoint. This same Greek word gives us *Christ* (literally "The Anointed One").

> **Exploring the Word:** The Greek *khronos* means time. It gives us *chronic*, lasting for a long time, as a chronic illness; *chronological*, in order of time; *chronometer*, a device for measuring time; *chronicle*, an account of events in order of time, as an historical record; *anachronism*, out of the proper time, as something left over from the past or a modern object wrongly assumed to have existed in the past; and *synchronize*, to come together in time, to coincide. Our word *crony* also has this Greek base and originally meant one who had attended a university at the same time as someone else, a fellow student, and later came to mean any close friend.

chronic *adj. She's developed a chronic cough. He's become a chronic complainer:* habitual, long-standing, continual, continuous, constant, persistent, persisting, enduring, lasting, abiding, confirmed, inveterate, perennial, ingrained, deep-seated, deep-rooted; recurring, recurrent, periodic, intermittent.

Ant. temporary, infrequent, once-in-a-lifetime, occasional, fleeting.

◇ *Usage note:* A *chronic* illness continues. An *acute* illness comes to a crisis quickly. Thus we speak of *chronic rheumatism* but *acute appendicitis.*

chronicle *n.* **1** *The Anglo-Saxon Chronicle is one of the earliest written records of England:* record, history, chronology, journal, account, log, annals; narrative, story, epic, saga.

—*v.* **2** *The historian chronicled the main events of the decade:* record, set down, list, log, note, enter; recount, relate, report, narrate.

chuck *v.* **1** *He chucked the child under the chin:* poke lovingly, pat, tap, pet, tickle. **2** *Chuck the suitcase onto the back seat:* toss, fling, sling, cast, throw, heave, pitch.

chum *n. Bobby and I were childhood chums:* friend, close friend, pal, mate, bosom friend, companion, comrade, intimate, confidant, crony; playmate, playfellow.

Ant. stranger, casual acquaintance; enemy, antagonist.

◇ *Word origin: Chum* may be short for *chamber fellow*, a room-mate.

chummy *adj. The two girls seemed very chummy:* friendly, close, intimate, familiar, congenial, affectionate, devoted; *Slang* pally, thick.

Ant. estranged, alienated, unfriendly, antagonistic, distant, aloof, cool.

chunk *n. Chunks of ice were floating in the cold water:* lump, hunk, piece, mass, clod, block, square, wad, nugget.

church *n.* **1** *St. Peter's in Rome is the largest church in Christendom:* place of worship, house of God, Lord's house, tabernacle, chapel, temple; cathedral, basilica, mosque, synagogue. **2** *Did you attend church last Sunday?:* religious service; service, divine worship, devotions. **3** *I belong to the Methodist Church:* religion, denomination, faith, affiliation, persuasion, belief, sect, cult.

> **Exploring the Word:** *Church* comes from Greek *kūriakon* (*dōma*), the Lord's (house); whilst *cathedral* comes from Greek *kathedra*, seat, hence a bishop's seat. *Altar* comes from Latin, *altus*, high, and originally was a raised place for Roman sacrifices to the gods. *Pew* is from Greek *podion*, base, pedestal. A *sacristy* is the room in a church where sacred vessels and vestments are kept and comes from Latin *sacer*, sacred. A *vestry* is a room where the clerical garments are kept or put on, and comes from Latin, *vestis*, garment. Sailors should feel at home in the *nave* of a church, the main part between the two side aisles, because the word comes from Latin, *navis*, ship, which its shape sometimes resembles.

churlish *adj. Many people tend to be churlish before they've had breakfast:* surly, grouchy, sullen, crabbed, bearish, brusque, crusty, quarrelsome, ill-tempered, irascible, petulant, testy, irritable, rancorous, bilious, choleric, splenetic, captious, waspish, sour, tart; uncivil, ill-mannered, unmannerly, boorish, rude, impolite, insulting, discourteous; ill-bred, crude, uncouth, dastardly, contemptible, arrogant, impudent, insolent.

Ant. pleasant, agreeable, amiable, easy-going, sweet, kind, good-humoured, even-tempered; civil, polite, courteous, gallant, mannerly; well-bred, noble, admirable, cultivated, gentlemanly, humble.

◇ *Word origin: Churl* comes from Old English *ceorl*, man, free man. After the Norman conquest in 1066, most of the common people who had been free were bound to the land as serfs, and *churl* became a term of contempt, like "peasant."

churn *v. Butter is made by churning cream. The sea was churning furiously:* beat, whisk, whip, shake, shake up, stir up, agitate, vibrate; toss, heave, swirl, roll, roil, foam, rage, convulse, disturb, pulsate, palpitate.

cinder *n. A cinder blew into my eye. The kitchen-maid cleaned the cinders from the grate:* ember, ash; piece of burned coal or wood or iron slag; (*also in plural*) embers, ashes, clinkers, scoria, slag, dross.

◇ *Word origin: Cinder* comes from Old English *sinder*, slag. Its meaning has been influenced since Elizabethan times by French *cendre*, ash, on the model of which it was respelt with a *c*.

cinema *n. Mary Pickford was one of the first stars of the cinema:* motion pictures, pictures, films, *Slang* flicks.

◇ *Word origin: Cinema* is a short form of *cinematograph*, which is formed from Greek *kinēma* (movement) + *-graph* (writing, picture), hence moving pictures or motion picture. The technique and name of *cinematography* were invented by the Lumière brothers in France during the 1890's.

cipher *n.* **1** *One followed by two ciphers is 100:* zero, nought, aught; nothing, nil. **2** *He was determined not to remain a cipher all his life:* nobody, nonentity, nullity, nothing, naught, obscurity. **3** *The spy's report was written in cipher:* code, secret writing; cryptogram; anagram, acrostic.

Ant. 1 infinity, something. **2** somebody, something, notable, personage, star.

◇ *Word origin: Cipher* comes from Arabic *sifr*, which also gives us our word *zero.*

circle *n.* **1** *The children gathered round in a circle. There's a circle of haze round the moon tonight:* ring, circuit; halo, corona, hoop, belt, girdle, cordon, circlet, ringlet, girth, girt. **2** *He is not in my circle of friends. Sports are not within my circle of interests:* group, set, coterie, clique, society, cabal, knot, crowd, company; sphere, field, realm, compass, circuit, bounds, region, domain, range, reach, arena, theatre, sweep, swing, province, dominion, territory. **3** *After colliding with the lorry, the car turned full circle:* cycle, round, revolution, circuit, sequence, progression, turn.

—*v.* **4** *The fence circles the yard:* encircle, surround, ring, ring round, border, enclose, hedge in, hem in, border, circuit, belt, gird, girdle, wind about, loop, bound, envelop, encompass, circumscribe. **5** *Our plane circled the airport for an hour before landing. The children circled round and round:* revolve round, curve round, move round, circumnavigate, circumrotate; revolve, pivot, reel, curve, curl, turn.

Ant. 1 square.

circuit *n.* **1** *The circuit of the earth round the sun takes about a year:* circling, orbiting, revolving; revolution, pivoting. **2** *It rained within a fifty mile circuit of the centre of the storm:* circumference, perimeter, compass, area, distance round; border, bounds, limit, confine, extremity, edge, margin, frontier. **3** *The athletes ran three times round the circuit:* beat, route, round, course, run, territory, tour, lap; journey, jaunt, excursion, trek, walk.

circuitous *adj. We took a circuitous path. I couldn't follow his circuitous reasoning:* circular, winding, roundabout, indirect, devious, meandering, rambling; tortuous, twisting, turning, serpentine.

Ant. direct, straight, undeviating, as the crow flies.

◇ *Spelling tip: Circuitous* is spelt *circuit* + *-ous.*

circular *adj.* **1** *The kitchen has a circular table. A circular drive leads to the house:* round, rounded, ring-shaped, curved, winding, circuitous. **2** *The circular motion of the merry-go-round made the girl dizzy:* turning, rotary, revolving, spinning, twirling, winding, pivoting, spiralling, coiling, curling, swivelling, gyrating; rolling, rocking.

—*n.* **3** *The firm printed a circular advertising the sale:* handbill, bill, broadsheet, leaflet, advertisement, bulletin, notice, announcement.

Ant. 1 square, rectangular, straight. **2** linear.

◇ *Spelling tip:* This word ends in *-ar*, not *-er.* Remember a *circulAR ARmband.*

circulate *v.* **1** *Blood circulates in the veins and arteries. Waiters circulated among the guests serving champagne:* flow, circle, move around, pass through, radiate; go around, make the rounds, move about; get abroad, go forth, visit around. **2** *Pictures of the wanted men were circulated to police around the country:* distribute, disperse, disseminate, pass round, issue, put forward, put about, give out; make public, spread, scatter, strew, publicize, announce, make known, publish.

Ant. 1 stop, stagnate. **2** keep, hold back; keep secret, hide, conceal, suppress.

circulation *n.* **1** *The 17th-century English physician William Harvey discovered the circulation of the blood:* flow, flowing, circling, rotation, motion. **2** *The groat, or fourpenny piece is no longer in circulation. The local newspaper has a circulation of 10,000 copies a day:* distribution, dissemination, dispersion, diffusion, radiation, propagation, transmission, promulgation.

Ant. 1 stagnation.

circumference *n. The circumference of a circle is equal to pi times the diameter. We sailed round the entire circumference of the island:* distance around, periphery, perimeter, circuit; boundary, bounds, extremity, border, edge, margin, rim, girdle, girth, outline, compass, limits, fringe.
Ant. centre, interior.

> **Exploring the Word:** The Greek word *kirkos* means ring, circle. In its Latin form *circus,* it gives us *circus, circle, circuit,* and *circulate,* as well as *circumference,* the distance round a circle; *circumscribe,* to draw a circle round, hence to limit or restrict; *circumstance,* something that stands or exists all around an act, hence a limited or particular event or fact; *circumvent,* to go round, hence to evade or escape; *circumspect,* to look around in a circle or in all directions, hence cautious; and *circumlocution,* speaking in a circle, a roundabout way of saying something.

circumlocution *n. The speaker's point could have been made with less circumlocution:* roundabout expression, wordiness, meandering, verbiage, garrulity, verbosity, discursiveness, long-windedness, rambling, digression.
Ant. directness, conciseness, terseness, succinctness, brevity, briefness.
◇ *Word origin: Circumlocution* comes from Latin *circumlocutio: circum-*(round) + *locutio* (speaking). The term was introduced by the Roman grammarian Quintilian as a literal rendering of Greek *periphrasis,* periphrasis, circumlocution.

circumscribe *v.* **1** *On this map, major cities are circumscribed in red:* circle, encircle, outline, delineate; surround, enclose, encompass. **2** *His illness circumscribed his activities:* limit, restrict, restrain, confine, constrain, hem in, check, curb, bridle, fix.
Ant. 2 expand, extend, enlarge, open, throw open, unfetter.

circumspect *adj. Be circumspect in making important decisions:* careful, cautious, guarded, vigilant, alert, wide-awake; watchful, discreet, deliberate, wary, thoughtful, judicious, prudent, sagacious, sage, discriminating, contemplative, discerning, particular, perspicacious.
Ant. rash, reckless, foolhardy, heedless, careless; audacious, adventurous, venturous, daring, venturesome, bold.

circumstance *n.* **1** *Bad weather is a circumstance that we cannot control:* fact, factor, occurrence, event, incident, happening, phenomenon, condition, state of affairs, vicissitude, detail, particular, item, thing, point, element, matter. **2** *The king's coronation was an occasion of much pomp and circumstance:* ceremony, pageantry, ritual, formality; splendour, resplendence, magnificence, brilliance.

circumvent *v. The pilot circumvented the storm by flying farther south. The swindler tried to circumvent the law:* circle, circumnavigate, go round, bypass, skirt; escape, avoid, elude, evade, keep away from, shun, miss, dodge, thwart, outwit, frustrate.
Ant. face, confront, meet, meet head on, go through; follow, conform to.

citadel *n. Soldiers took up defensive positions behind the walls of the citadel:* fortress, fort, stronghold, bastion, fortification.
◇ *Word origin: Citadel* is from the diminutive of the Italian *città,* city, hence little city, a fortress commanding a city.

citation *n.* **1** *The Oxford English Dictionary contains citations of the written language to illustrate how words have been used:* quotation, quote, excerpt, passage, extract, gobbet; illustration, example, instance. **2** *The soldier won two citations for bravery:* commendation, official praise; medal, award, honour.

cite *v.* **1** *The lawyer cited a previous case to support his argument:* allude to, refer to, specify, quote, mention, note, bring forward, indicate, give as example, advance, present, exemplify, document, enumerate. **2** *The corporal was cited for bravery in battle:* commend, praise, honour, mention, name.
Ant. 1 ignore, disregard; conceal, keep secret. **2** condemn, rebuke, chastise, chasten, criticize; dishonour.
◇ *Usage note:* See SITE.

citizen *n. Only citizens of France may vote in the election. The citizens of Paris live in a beautiful city:* national, subject; inhabitant, resident, denizen, native.
Ant. alien, foreigner; non-resident, visitor, transient, tourist, outsider.

> **Exploring the Word:** The Latin words *civis,* citizen, and *civitas,* body politic, city, give us *citizen* and *city.* Latin *civis* also gives us *civil* and *civic,* belonging to a citizen or a city, as *civil rights* (the rights of a citizen) and *civic centre* (the physical, business, or cultural centre of a city). A *civilian* is literally a citizen, as opposed to the state itself or a person representing the state, as a soldier; while *civilization* literally means city culture and people. *Civvies,* of course, are citizen's clothes or, as we would say, "civilian clothes."

city *n.* **1** *The city is an exciting place to live:* town, big town, metropolitan area, megalopolis, metropolis; incorporated town, municipality, township. **2** *The entire city turned out for the celebration:* population of a city, townspeople, inhabitants, residents, denizens.

civic *adj.* **1** *Voting is your civic duty:* citizen's, public. **2** *Keeping your lawn clean should be part of civic pride:* communal, community, local, public.

civil *adj.* **1** *Martin Luther King devoted his life to* *civil rights:* citizen, citizen's, individual. **2** *The governors met to discuss civil problems:* community, communal, state, city, municipal, civic, public. **3** *Public education is under civil rather than religious control:* communal, secular, lay, civic, public; non-military. **4** *It was all I could do to be civil to the rude man:* polite, courteous, well-mannered, mannerly, respectful, gentlemanly; affable, gracious, cordial, neighbourly, amiable, obliging, conciliatory, genial, decorous, civilized.

Ant. **1** state. **3** religious; military. **4** uncivil, impolite, rude, discourteous, ill-mannered, unmannerly; uncordial, ungracious.

◇ *Word origin: Civil* has also meant "polite" ever since Augustus Caesar was called *civilis* (citizenly) because he acted like an ordinary citizen.

civilian *n. What does it feel like to be a civilian after 20 years in the army?:* private citizen, non-military person, non-uniformed person; lay person.

Ant. soldier, military man; uniformed fireman, uniformed policeman.

civility *n. Even though angry, he treated us with civility:* politeness, courtesy, courteousness, good manners, manners, respect, respectfulness, tact; graciousness, agreeableness, affability, amiability, cordiality, good temper, pleasantness.

Ant. impoliteness, discourtesy, discourteousness, bad manners, disrespect; unfriendliness, hostility, unpleasantness, disagreeableness, ungraciousness.

civilization *n.* **1** *The missionary returned to civilization after two years in the jungle:* civilized life or society. **2** *Ancient Greek civilization was one of the highest man has achieved:* culture, cultivation, enlightenment, refinement.

Ant. **1, 2** barbarism, barbarity, barbarousness, savagery.

clad *adj. The beggar was clad in rags:* clothed, dressed, attired, garbed, arrayed.

Ant. undressed, unclothed, naked.

◇ *Usage note: Clad* is an alternative past tense of *clothe* — we may use either. The following two lines show classic uses of each: "Hast thou *clothed* his neck with thunder?" (Authorized Version of the Bible); "He *clad* their nakedness with skins of beasts" (John Milton).

claim *v.* **1** *She claimed that the ring was stolen, not lost:* assert, profess, declare, maintain, avow, allege, affirm, charge. **2** *Has anyone claimed the gloves you found?:* lay claim to, seek as due, demand, exact, command, insist on; call for, collect, pick up, ask, request, take.

—*n.* **3** *The jury believed the defendant's claim of innocence:* assertion, avowal, affirmation, declaration, profession, protestation, postulation, statement, plea, allegation. **4** *The doctor's work makes too many claims on his time. His claim to the property was declared valid:* demand, call, requirement, exaction, request; right, title, ownership, access, pretension.

Ant. **1** disavow, deny. **2** disclaim, renounce, disown, reject, repudiate, refuse, relinquish, forgo, abnegate, abjure, waive, cede. **3** disclaimer, disavowal, denial, repudiation.

clammy *adj. She has a chill and her hands are clammy:* cold and damp, damp, sticky, slimy, pasty; wet, sweaty, perspiring.

Ant. dry, cool.

◇ *Word origin: Clammy* comes from the same root as *clam* (the shellfish), *clay*, and *glue*. All four words refer to qualities of wetness and stickiness.

clamour *n.* **1** *The clamour of the traffic gave me a headache:* noise, uproar, din, blast, hubbub, jangle, racket, clangour, rumpus, commotion, shouting. **2** *A clamour of protest went up from the crowd:* cry, outcry, hue and cry, shout, call, bellow, yell, howl, wild chorus, storm, thunder.

—*v.* **3** *The audience clamoured for the show to begin:* shout, cry out, cry, call out, call, bellow, howl, yell, vociferate, make a racket.

Ant. **1 – 3** whisper, murmur. **1** silence, quiet.

clamp *n.* **1** *Hold the parts together with a clamp until the glue hardens:* clip, clasp, grip, vice, fastener.

—*v.* **2** *Clamp the two-by-fours together securely. He clamped his jaws in anger:* clinch, clench, clip, clasp, fasten, secure.

clan *n.* **1** *What clan do your Scottish ancestors belong to?:* tribal family, family group, house; line, lineage, lineal group, strain, stock. **2** *The same clan of actors always spend their holidays at this resort:* circle, group, gang, party, alliance, ring, knot, crowd, company; society, brotherhood, cabal, guild, fraternity, league, affiliation, association.

◇ *Word origin:* Although we use *clan* to refer to any group of relatives or clique, we associate the word with the famous clans of Scotland — rightly so, because *clan* is an originally Scottish Gaelic word.

clandestine *adj. The spy had a clandestine meeting to receive confidential information:* secret, undercover, hidden, covert, cloaked, secretive, masked, underground, veiled, concealed; private, confidential, secluded, undisclosed, unrevealed; stealthy, sneaking, surreptitious, furtive, underhand, underhanded.

Ant. open, out in the open, public, above-board, disclosed, revealed, unconcealed; straightforward, forthright, frank, candid.

◇ *Pronunciation tip: Clandestine* should be pronounced so that the *DES-* is stressed. Thus, *clan-DES-tin*, not *CLAN-des-tin*.

clang *v.* **1** *The bells clanged:* ring loudly, resound, peal, gong, chime, toll, knell, jangle.

—*n.* **2** *The clang of pots and pans woke us:* clash, clashing, din, clangour, clank; ringing, resounding, peal, tolling, knell, gong, jangle, chime.

◇ *Word origin: Clang* comes from Latin *clangere*, to resound. The word passed from Latin into Germanic in Roman times. *Clank* and *clink* arose from *clang*, and each has had its own distinct imitative connotation ever since.

clank *n.* **1** *The woman heard the pots and pans clanking in the kitchen:* rattle, clang, clash, clashing, clink, clangour, chink, jangle.
—*v.* **2** *The towing-chains clanked every time that the car moved:* rattle, clang, clink, chink, clash, jangle, clatter.

clannish *adj. The older families in town are very clannish and have little to do with newcomers:* cliquish, exclusive, snobbish, unreceptive, cold, aloof, distant, unfriendly; sectarian, narrow, restricted, parochial, insular.
Ant. open, friendly, hospitable, receptive, warm.

clap *v.* **1** *The audience stood and clapped at the end of the performance:* applaud. **2** *The victorious players clapped each other on the back:* slap, smack, rap, strike, whack, thump, swat, hit, smite, thwack; bump, buffet, bang, crack. **3** *A detective clapped the handcuffs on the suspect. He clapped the door shut:* set suddenly, cast, thrust, slam, hurl, rush, propel, pitch, fling, force, dash, toss, push, shove, drive, plunge.
—*n.* **4** *I received a sudden clap on the shoulder:* slap, slam, rap, bat, tap, smack, swat, hit, whack, strike, cuff, thump, crack, wallop, thwack. **5** *The clap of thunder woke everyone:* peal, burst, roar, crack, bang, clack, clatter, slam, explosion.
Ant. 1 boo, hiss, blow a raspberry.

clarify *v.* **1** *How do you clarify syrup?:* clear, purify, refine, purge. **2** *His explanation clarified the mystery:* explain, clear up, make clear, resolve, solve, disentangle, illuminate, elucidate, explicate, lay open, make plain, make understandable, bring to light, shed light on.
Ant. 1 cloud, muddy. **2** obscure, confuse, mix up, entangle, cloud, muddle.
◇ *Word origin: Clarify* comes from Latin *clarus* (clear) + *facere* (to make).

clarion *adj. The clarion call of a bugle rent the air:* clear, shrill, high-pitched, ringing, sharp, acute, piercing, blaring; distinct, stirring, compelling, commanding, imperative.
Ant. dull, muted, muffled, soft; low.
◇ *Word origin:* A *clarion* call can be heard loud and clear. The word comes from Latin *clarus*, clear, the same Latin word that gives us *clear* and *clarify*.

clarity *n.* **1** *The news commentator analysed the situation with clarity:* clearness, lucidity, intelligibility, comprehensibility, plainness, simplicity, directness; precision, exactness, explicitness. **2** *The clarity of the spring water was amazing:* clearness, transparency, purity, translucence, lucidity; brightness, brilliance, glassiness, luminosity, radiance, effulgence.
Ant. 1 obscurity, confusion; imprecision, complexity. **2** cloudiness, muddiness, murkiness; dullness, opaqueness.
◇ *Word origin:* Like *clear* and *clarify, clarity* comes from Latin *clarus*, clear.

clash *v.* **1** *The dustbins clashed as the men emptied them:* crash, clang, clank, rattle, clatter, crash. **2** *The two armies clashed on the plains below the city:* battle, fight, contest, contend, combat, grapple, skirmish, tussle, cross swords, exchange blows. **3** *The two lawyers clashed in court:* argue, dispute, quarrel, wrangle, squabble, boil, altercate, tiff, feud, lock horns.
—*n.* **4** *The clash of swords signalled the start of the battle:* crash, crashing, clang, clank, rattle, clatter, clangour, jangle. **5** *The clash between the armies occurred at dawn:* battle, fight, combat, conflict, contest, fray, skirmish, encounter, struggle; fracas, set-to. **6** *The clash of opinions caused tension in the room:* conflict, disagreement, difference, opposition, discord, dissidence, disharmony, jarring, friction, antagonism.
Ant. 2 make peace. **3** agree, concur; make up. **5** peace, truce. **6** concord, accord, harmony, agreement.

clasp *n.* **1** *The bracelet has a gold clasp:* fastening, fastener, catch, latch, grip, hook, coupler, hasp, link, clinch, bolt, clamp, buckle, lock, snap. **2** *He held her in a tight clasp:* hold, grip, embrace, hug, grasp, clutch, squeeze.
—*v.* **3** *Clasp the two halves of the broken necklace together:* latch, catch, hook, clamp, lock, hasp, buckle, clinch, link, couple, secure, fasten, clip, snap. **4** *The child clasped the doll tightly:* hold, grip, grasp, hug, embrace, clutch, grapple, press, squeeze.
Ant. 3 unclasp, unfasten, open, unlock, unlatch, unhook, unbuckle, uncouple, unsnap. **4** let go, drop; release, give up.

class *n.* **1** *Pine trees belong to the evergreen class:* classification, category, group, type, kind, sort, order, variety, division, genre, breed, species, genus. **2** *No-one in my class likes history:* set of pupils, form, group, section. **3** *Professor Johnson takes the nine o'clock history class:* course, session, section; lesson. **4** *She was born into the middle class. Class distinctions have diminished in recent years:* social stratum, social rank, station, status, position, caste, condition, sphere, state; circle, clique, set, group.
—*v.* **5** *Francis Bacon is classed as a Cubist painter:* classify, group, categorize, type, rank, rate, brand, label, pigeon-hole, catalogue, size, arrange, index, order; grade, number.
◇ *Usage note: Class* can be followed either by a singular or a plural verb, depending on whether you consider the *class* as one unit or as composed of individual members. Thus you may correctly say *The class has elected its leader* (which implies that you consider the class as a unit, acting together) or *The class are, in general, very bright* (implying that you

consider the class as composed of a number of very bright individuals). And if you had used *is* or *are* in either of these examples that would be all right, too, because it is how you feel about the class, if you feel *it* is a unit or that *they* are individuals. Thus, whichever one you use is correct.
◇ *Word origin: Class* and *classify* come from Latin *classis,* group or class.

"The world is divided into two classes, those who believe the incredible, and those who do the improbable."
—*Oscar Wilde*

---

classic, classical *adj.* **1** *Theyer wrote a classic biography of Beethoven. Sneezing and a sore throat are classic symptoms of a cold:* definitive, authoritative, absolute, accepted, traditional, model, archetypal, prototypal, exemplary; excellent, outstanding, distinguished, distinguishing, first-class, first-rate, consummate, masterly, ageless, heroic, enduring, epic. **2** *Latin is a classical language. Caesar was a hero of classical antiquity:* ancient Greek or Roman; Graeco-Roman.
—*n.* **3** *Dickens'* A Tale of Two Cities *is a literary classic:* masterpiece, standard work; prototype, archetype, model, first-class example, paragon.
Ant. 1 bad, poor, inferior, awful, terrible, lousy, second-rate; unrepresentative, atypical. **2** modern. **3** piece of junk, trash.
◇ *Usage note:* Both *classic* and *classical* can be used to mean standard, typical, or the highest or memorable class: *a classic* (or *classical*) *case of measles, The model-T Ford is a classic* (or *classical*) *car.* However, *classical* is preferred when referring to the ancient Greeks and Romans or their literary *classics*: *The classical culture of Rome* (of ancient Rome as opposed to modern Rome), *a classical beauty* (like that of ancient Greek or Roman statues).
◇ *Word origin: Classic* comes from Latin *classicus,* meaning "first-class." The word first came to be applied to the standard Greek and Roman authors in the phrase *scriptores classici,* "first-class writers."

classification *n.* **1** *The classification of books in the library follows the Dewey Decimal System:* grouping, categorization, categorizing, classing, arrangement, arranging, gradation, organization, organizing, ordering, codification, systematization, assortment, disposition. **2** *Aspirin belongs to the classification of non-prescription drugs:* group, grouping, class, category, division, section, designation, order, rank, series, family, species, genus, kind, sort, type.

classify *v. Eggs are classified according to size:* organize, class, grade, type, rank, rate, distinguish, categorize, group, assort, range, arrange, pigeon-hole, segregate; label, catalogue, index, brand, list, codify, tag, ticket; size, number, order.
◇ *Word origin:* See CLASS.

clatter *v.* **1** *The shutters clattered in the wind:* clash, clack, rattle, bang, clump, crash, clang, clank, clink, jangle.
—*n.* **2** *The shop was filled with the clatter of machinery:* clattering, clack, clank, rattling, racket, jangle, crashing, clamour, chatter.

clause *n.* **1** *In general, a grammatical clause contains a subject and a predicate:* simple sentence or part of a sentence. **2** *The third clause of the contract specifies when payments are due:* provision, proviso, stipulation, specification, condition, article, covenant, proposition, term.

claw *n.* **1** *The cat tore the chair with its claws:* talon, animal nail. **2** *The animal's claw was caught in the trap. The boy was gnawing on a lobster claw:* paw, foot; clawed hand, pincer.
—*v.* **3** *He clawed at the door trying to open it:* tear, maul, lacerate, slash, scratch; clutch, seize, grip.

clean *adj.* **1** *Put on a clean shirt. I like a clean room:* unsoiled, spotless, immaculate, sanitary, unblemished, unspotted; cleaned, cleansed, washed, scrubbed, bathed, scoured, laundered, fresh; neat, tidy, orderly. **2** *The cabinetmaker did a clean job:* perfect, flawless, faultless, neat, fine, trim, well-made. **3** *In the country we breathed clean air:* unpolluted, pure, clear, uncontaminated, unadulterated, untainted, uninfected, undefiled. **4** *He leads a clean life:* wholesome, honourable, upright, virtuous, moral, decent, decorous, innocent, healthy, chaste, unsoiled, exemplary, untainted, stainless, unsullied, unblemished, unspotted.
—*v.* **5** *The curtains were cleaned beautifully. Clean your room before going to school:* cleanse, wash, scour, scrub, launder, bathe, shampoo; sweep, vacuum, mop, dust; tidy, tidy up, order, neaten.
Ant. 1 dirty, filthy, soiled, stained, spotted; unwashed, unbathed; messy, untidy, disorderly. **2** flawed, imperfect, faulty, crude, ragged, awkward, sloppy, messy. **3** contaminated, polluted, impure, infected, tainted. **4** unwholesome, dishonourable, indecorous, immoral, indecent, stained, unhealthy, tainted, sullied, blemished; evil, wicked, depraved. **5** soil, dirty, stain; mess up, disorder.

cleanse *v.* **1** *Cleanse your face thoroughly before going to bed:* clean, wash, bathe, launder, scrub, scour, shampoo. **2** *The minister's soothing words cleansed my heart of guilt:* rid, free, expunge, expurgate, clear, flush, sweep out, erase, absolve; release, unburden, deliver.
Ant. 1 soil, dirty, befoul, stain. **2** burden, weigh down, charge, fill, load.

clear *adj.* **1** *The day dawned with a clear sky. The water in the bay was as clear as glass:* unclouded, cloudless, unobscured, fair, halcyon, serene, sunny; bright, brilliant, radiant, gleaming, dazzling, luminous, shining light, glistening, glowing, sparkling; lucid, transparent, translucent, crystalline, pellucid; gauzy, diaphanous. **2** *The singing was loud and clear:* distinct, audible, intelligible, distinguishable, plain, recognizable, articulate. **3** *His meaning was as clear as the nose on your face:* plain, obvious, unmistakable, evident, self-evident, comprehensible, clear-cut, undisguised, unambiguous, straightforward, explicit, inescapable, apparent, unhidden, unconcealed, positive, certain, definite, unequivocal, unqualified, undeniable, pronounced, patent, express. **4** *This problem requires clear thinking:* unconfused, unmuddled, unencumbered, alert, keen, wide-awake, sharp, discerning. **5** *The path was clear:* open, free, unobstructed, unimpeded, unblocked.

—*adv.* **6** *The message came over the wireless loud and clear:* clearly, distinctly, plainly, audibly, articulately. **7** *The prisoner escaped clear away:* entirely, wholly, completely.

—*v.* **8** *The skies finally cleared:* become unclouded, brighten, lighten; become fair. **9** *The snow-ploughs cleared the streets. Machines have cleared the way for progress:* unblock, unstop, empty, rid, clean, open; remove, free, remove obstacles from. **10** *The small plane cleared the trees easily:* pass over, fly over; vault over, leap over, skip over, hop over, bound over. **11** *A surprise witness cleared him of the crime:* vindicate, exculpate, exonerate, free, absolve, acquit.

Ant. **1** cloudy, clouded, obscured, hazy, stormy, murky, muddy, unclear, opaque. **2** inaudible, unclear, indistinguishable, indistinct, unrecognizable, inarticulate. **3** unclear, ambiguous, uncertain, hidden. **4** confused, muddled. **5** obstructed, blocked, barricaded, clogged, closed. **6** unclearly, indistinctly, inarticulately. **8** cloud, darken. **9** obstruct, block, clog, close. **11** convict; accuse, blame.

clearly *adv. The country is clearly in the midst of a drought:* undoubtedly, beyond doubt, beyond question, unquestionably, decidedly, palpably, undeniably, certainly, plainly, evidently, unmistakably, assuredly, recognizably, patently, distinctly, noticeably, unequivocally, indubitably, perceptibly, surely, obviously, observably, markedly.

cleave[1] *v. His wet shirt cleaved to his back. Honest men always cleave to their principles:* cling, stick, hold, hold fast, adhere, fuse, be joined, unite; be faithful, be constant, be true, stand by.

Ant. separate, come loose, slip off; let go, release, free; forsake, abandon, relinquish.

cleave[2] *v.* **1** *With one blow of his axe, the forester clove the tree stump down the centre. The ice-breaker cleft a passage through the frozen river:* split, divide, bisect, halve, rend, slit, slice, part, crack, rive; cut, slash, chop, hack, hew, lay open, open, plough, furrow, tear. **2** *The butcher cleft the bones from the side of beef:* sever, cut off, disjoin, detach, separate, chop off, disengage, dismember, break off.

Ant. **1, 2** unite, join. **2** attach, affix.

cleft *n.* **1** *The mountain climbers found shelter in a cleft in the ice:* split, crack, crevice, crevasse, rift, fissure, rent, cranny, opening, aperture, break, breach, gap, cleavage, notch, indentation, slit, furrow, trough, trench.

—*adj.* **2** *Swine have cleft feet. The boys built a tree house on a cleft branch of the tree:* divided, cloven, bisected, split, slotted, notched; forked, branched.

clemency *n.* **1** *The defendant was grateful for the judge's clemency:* mercy, mercifulness, charity, forbearance, forgivingness, magnanimity, tolerance, sympathy, compassion, humanity, benevolence, kindness, indulgence, leniency. **2** *Cornwall is known for the clemency of its weather:* mildness, moderation, softness, pleasantness, temperance.

Ant. **1** sternness, strictness; cruelty, mercilessness, hard-heartedness. **2** harshness, inclemency, severity.

◇ *Word origin: Clemency* comes from Latin *clemens*, mild.

clench *v.* **1** *The boy clenched his fists in anger:* close tightly, set, set firmly, stiffen, strain tight. **2** *The patient clenched the arms of the dentist's chair:* grasp firmly, clinch, clasp, clutch, fasten on, grip, hold fast.

Ant. **1** unclench, loose, loosen, relax. **2** unclench, unclasp, release, let go.

◇ *Usage note:* See CLINCH.

clergy *n. Many members of the clergy went to Rome for the ecumenical council:* ministry, priesthood, pastorate, the cloth; clergymen, preachers, churchmen, ministers, pastors, prelates, clerics, archdeacons, deans, bishops, vicars, rectors, curates, deacons, priests, rabbis.

clergyman *n. Only a clergyman can help you with your religious problems:* member of the clergy, minister, priest, rabbi; preacher, pastor, chaplain, parson, cleric, churchman; *Slang* padre, sky pilot.

Ant. layman.

"A man who is good enough to go to heaven, is good enough to be a clergyman."
—*Samuel Johnson*

clerical *adj.* **1** *The new employee must be good at filing and other clerical work:* of clerks, of general office work, clerkly, office; (*variously*) bookkeeping, accounting, record-keeping, filing, typing. **2** *The priest donned his clerical robes:* ecclesiastical, religious, cleric, pastoral, ministerial, priestly, rabbinical.

clerk *n. The new clerk is an excellent typist:* clerical worker, office worker; (*variously*) filing clerk, bookkeeper, typist.

◇ *Pronunciation tip: Clerk* is pronounced *clark* in Britain and *clerk* in America.

clever *adj.* **1** *A clever student should have no trouble with maths:* smart, bright, intelligent, sharp, keen, astute, quick, quick-witted, able, adroit. **2** *He has a clever plan. We laughed at her clever remark:* inventive, ingenious, imaginative, deft, adroit, artful, crafty, expert; cute, humorous, witty, keen, acute, sharp, smart.
Ant. **1** dull, stupid, witless, dim-witted, dense, slow-witted, unaccomplished, slow. **2** clumsy, awkward; unimaginative, uninventive, boring, tedious, dull.

cleverly *adj. The escape was cleverly executed:* ingeniously, inventively, imaginatively, craftily, artfully, adroitly, sharply, expertly, deftly, intelligently, smartly; wittily, humorously.
Ant. unimaginatively, inexpertly, stupidly, clumsily, awkwardly.

cliché *n. "Her lips are as red as roses" is a cliché:* hackneyed expression, banality, platitude, stereotyped or trite phrase, bromide.
◇ *Pronunciation tip:* The only proper pronunciation of *cliché* is *clee-shay.* All other pronunciations are so wrong as to "stick out like a sore thumb," to quote an old cliché.
◇ *Word origin: Cliché* comes from French *clicher,* to stereotype, make a printing plate to reproduce many copies of the same material. Thus, an expression that has been repeated many times has come to be termed a *cliché.*

click *n.* **1** *I heard the click of a key in the door:* sharp sound, clack, clink, snap.
—*v.* **2** *The lock clicked shut. The dancer clicked her castanets:* clack, clink, clap, crack, crackle, snap, tap, rattle.

client *n. The lawyer believed in his client's innocence. The furrier has many wealthy clients:* person represented, patron, customer, buyer, purchaser, shopper.
◇ *Word origin: Client* comes from Latin *cliens,* listener. In ancient Rome the word actually meant a person under the protection of a patron, a "listener" in the sense that he was at his patron's beck and call. The word came to mean a lawyer's client during the Middle Ages, and acquired its present-day sense of "customer" about the time of the Gunpowder Plot.

cliff *n. The castle was perched on the top of a cliff:* bluff, precipice, promontory; ledge, crag.
Ant. flat ground, plain, level country; hollow, abyss, hole.

climate *n.* **1** *The Virgin Islands have a mild climate. Millionaires often move to a warm climate:* usual weather, weather pattern, weather; weather region, weather zone. **2** *After the revolution, the climate of the country remained tense:* general feeling, mood, atmosphere, disposition, frame of mind, attitude, spirit, tone, character, temper, quality, air, ambience.
◇ *Word origin: Climate* comes from Greek *klima,* region, hence the weather typical of a region.

climax *n.* **1** *Seeing the Vatican was the climax of our trip:* highest point, high point, culmination, supreme moment, crowning point, best part, height, acme, summit, peak, pinnacle, apex, crown. **2** *The climax of the play came in the last act:* turning-point, decisive point, critical point, crisis, moment of revelation, point of highest development.
Ant. **1** nadir, bottom. **2** anticlimax.
◇ *Word origin: Climax* comes from Greek *klimax,* ladder.

climb *v.* **1** *The cat climbed the tree. The plane climbed to 40,000 feet:* ascend, mount, clamber up, scramble up, scale, rise steadily; rise, go up, come up.
—*n.* **2** *The climb to the mountain top took ten hours:* ascent, climbing.
Ant. **1** descend, go down, come down, climb down. **2** descent.

clinch *v.* **1** *A final-minute goal clinched the match. The business man clinched the deal with a handshake:* make sure of winning, win, insure victory; make sure of obtaining, obtain, make sure, assure, settle, secure, decide; close, conclude, establish, fix, bind, verify, confirm, cap, crown, complete, culminate, wind up, finish off. **2** *Clinch the boards together:* tie, rope; clamp, bolt, couple, fasten, make fast. **3** *The boxer clinched his opponent:* clasp, clutch, grab hold of, grasp, grip, grapple, hold firmly, seize and hold.
◇ *Usage note:* Don't confuse *clench* and *clinch. Clench* means to close or hold tightly: *to clench one's teeth, to clench one's fist, Clench this rope. Clinch* means to secure, fasten, or grapple: *A handshake clinched the deal ten minutes before the deadline, The boxer went into a clinch in the middle of the ring.*

cling *v. Wet clothes cling to the body. The shy child clung to her mother. Always cling to your beliefs:* stick, hold, hold fast, adhere, cleave, fuse; stay close; grasp, grip, hang on to, hold on to, clasp, hug, clutch, grab hold of; be faithful, be constant, be true, stand by, maintain.
Ant. separate, come loose, slip off; let go, release, free; forsake, abandon, relinquish, give up.

clinic *n. The public health clinic is giving free X-rays this week:* medical centre, out-patients' ward, polyclinic; infirmary.

clink *n.* **1** *The keys clinked in his pocket:* jangle, clank, jingle, tinkle, ring sharply; click, clack; rattle.
—*n.* **2** *The diners toasted each other with a clink of glasses:* tinkle, ting, jingle, jangle, sharp ring, clank, click, clack.
◇ *Word origin:* See CLANG.

clip *v.* **1** *The gardener clipped the shrubbery:* cut off, cut short, cut out, shorten, trim, crop, bob, shear. **2** *Please clip these cards together:* clamp, staple, fasten, couple, attach, fix, secure, pin.
—*n.* **3** *The veterinary surgeon gave the dog a close clip:* clipping, trim, crop, cropping, cut, bob,

shearing, cutting, snipping, paring. **4** *My hair clip came unfastened:* fastener, hook, grip, clasp; hook, buckle.

Ant. 1 unclip, unstaple, unfasten, uncouple, separate.

clique *n. The summer visitors have their own clique and seldom mingle with townspeople:* group, coterie, circle, set, faction, clan, crowd, gang.

cloak *n.* **1** *The queen wore an ermine cloak:* cape, mantle, robe, tunic, burnous, pelisse. **2** *The invaders attacked under a cloak of fog. The negotiations were conducted under a cloak of secrecy:* cover, screen, curtain, shield, concealment, mantle, veil, curtain.

—*v.* **3** *The magician was cloaked in black silk:* robe, shroud, wrap. **4** *The soldiers cloaked their fear with joking and bravado:* hide, mask, screen, veil, conceal, secrete, disguise, camouflage.

Ant. 4 reveal, show, display, expose, bare, uncover.

◇ *Word origin: Cloak* comes from Medieval Latin *cloca,* bell, from its bell-like shape.

clock *n. The clock on the mantelpiece showed the right time:* timepiece, watch, horologe, chronometer.

◇ *Word origin: Clock* come from Medieval Latin *cloca,* bell. The word was introduced into England by Flemish clock-makers brought to England by Edward I towards the end of the 13th century.

clod *n.* **1** *Some clods of dirt stuck to the uprooted plants:* lump, clump, chunk, wad. **2** *That clod wouldn't know a gentleman if he saw one:* boor, yokel; dolt, chump, dope, cretin, blockhead, clown, dunce, moron, imbecile, ignoramus, numskull, oaf.

Ant. 2 sophisticate, gentleman; genius, savant.

clog *v.* **1** *Leaves and twigs clogged the gutter:* stop up, stop, block, obstruct, choke, congest, close, dam up.

—*n.* **2** *There's a clog somewhere in the drain-pipe:* stoppage, obstruction, block, blockage; obstacle, impediment, barrier, restraint, check.

Ant. 1 unclog, unblock, clear, free, open.

◇ *Word origin: Clog* comes from Middle English *clogge,* block of wood — hence our word *clogs* for wooden-soled shoes.

cloistered *adj. The child led a cloistered life, seeing only her guardian and tutor:* secluded, sheltered, insulated, isolated, withdrawn, dissociated, aloof, recluse, sequestered, closeted, confined, solitary, alone, separate, apart, detached; hidden, concealed, secreted.

Ant. public, social, gregarious.

close *v.* **1** *Close the door tightly. The handyman closed the hole in the wall with plaster. The stableboy closed the horse in the stall:* shut, secure; close up, stop up, stop, fill up, fill, fill in, stuff, clog, clog up, plug, plug up, shut off, blockade, block, obstruct, seal off; shut in, shut up, confine, pen in, enclose, pen, coop up. **2** *The soldiers closed ranks. The surgeon closed the two edges of the incision with surgical thread:* join, link, connect, couple, unite, fuse, bring together. **3** *The pianist closed the concert with a Gershwin medley. Schools closed for the Christmas holiday:* end, finish, conclude, terminate, stop, halt, cease, bring to an end, wind up; adjourn, go into recess, suspend, discontinue, dismiss, leave off, break off, shut down.

Exploring the Word: *Close* comes from Latin *claudere,* to shut. From this same word comes *disclose,* to "un-close," i.e. to uncover or expose; *enclose,* to shut in; *include,* to put in together with; *exclude,* to shut out; *preclude,* to shut out in advance, hence to prevent; *recluse,* a person shut away from others; *seclude,* to shut away from others; and *conclude,* to shut so thoroughly as to end the matter. It also gives us *clause,* a self-contained or "shut-off" part of a sentence or a contract; *cloister,* an enclosure or place of seclusion for monks or nuns inside a monastic establishment; and *claustrophobia,* morbid fear of being shut in.

—*adj.* **4** *The house is close to the park. The migration of the ducks southward showed that winter was close:* near, nearby, next to, neighbouring, approximate, hard by; imminent, at hand, impending, forthcoming, nigh. **5** *Keep a close grip on your purse. Keep a close watch on the children:* tight, firm, secure, fast, fixed, solid; alert, intense, intent, watchful, careful, attentive, vigilant, keen, sharp, thorough. **6** *Living at such close quarters makes privacy difficult. The fabric was of a close weave:* congested, crowded, teeming, swarming, populous; tight, cramped, confined, narrow, restricted, compact, compressed, pinched, stuffed, squeezed, jammed; dense, solid, impenetrable, impermeable. **7** *The air in this room is very close:* stuffy, suffocating, stagnant, unventilated; muggy, humid, stifling, sweltering, hot, warm. **8** *The two brothers are very close:* attached, friendly, intimate, familiar, loving, warm, devoted; inseparable, allied, *Informal* thick as thieves. **9** *The colour is close to what I want, but the style is wrong. It was a close race:* near, similar, akin, almost like, almost alike, much the same as, resembling, approaching; nearly even, nearly equal, well-matched, neck and neck. **10** *He's as close with his money as Scrooge:* stingy, miserly, tight, tight-fisted, penurious, parsimonious, niggardly, stinting, scrimping, penny-pinching, ungenerous, grudging. **11** *A straight razor gives a close shave:* near to the skin, smooth, trim, neat, short.

—*n.* **12** *The crowd began to leave before the close of the game:* end, finish, conclusion, termination, wind-up, completion; closing, ending, finale.

—*adv.* **13** *Come close so that I can see you:* near, nearby, in proximity.

Ant. 1–3, 5, 6, 10 open. **1** unstop, unplug, unclog; free, release, let out. **2** widen, spread, expand; separate, part, divide, disunite. **3** begin, start, commence, inaugurate, initiate. **4** far, far off, distant, a long way off. **5** loose, weak, relaxed; careless, inattentive. **6** spacious, roomy, uncrowded, uncongested, vacant, empty; open wide, spread out, unrestricted, unconfined; loose, porous, lacy. **7** fresh, refreshing; cool, airy. **8** unfriendly, estranged, alienated, distant, detached, aloof, cold, cool, indifferent, hateful. **9** far, dissimilar; unequal, uneven, unmatched. **10** extravagant, generous, open-handed, free, liberal, unstinting, magnanimous, charitable, bountiful, lavish. **12** beginning, start, commencement, initiation, inauguration. **13** far, far away.

closely *adv. Listen closely to the instructions:* carefully, diligently, attentively, heedfully, alertly, intently, sharply, watchfully, vigilantly, keenly; intensely, vigorously.

Ant. carelessly, inattentively.

clot *n.* **1** *The medication dissolved the blood clot:* coagulation, gob, mass, thrombus.

—*v.* **2** *In haemophilia the blood doesn't clot properly:* coagulate, congeal, thicken, solidify.

cloth *n. Two yards of cloth will be enough for the dress:* fabric, piece-goods, linen, material.

> **Exploring the Word:** *Cloth* comes from an Old English word, but *fabric* comes from Latin *fabrica*, artisan's workshop. *Wool* also comes from Old English, but *cotton* comes from Arabic *qutun*. Both *silk* and *serge* come from *Seres*, Greek name for an Oriental people on the silk route with whom European traders dealt to obtain their materials. *Twill* comes from Old English *twili*, "two-threaded." *Tweed* is just a Scottish variant of the word *twill*, influenced by the name of the river Tweed which flows through the district where it is woven. *Duck* comes from the Dutch word *doek*, cloth, while *denim* is a shortening of the French phrase *serge de Nîmes*, serge of Nîmes, after the French city where it was made. *Calico*, the cotton cloth printed in bright figured patterns, comes from the term *calicut cloth*, because it was originally imported from Calicut in India.

clothe *v.* **1** *After showering, I clothed myself for the party. The charity feeds and clothes the needy:* dress, attire, robe, garb, array, drape, cloak, don; deck, deck out, bedeck, bedizen, rig out, costume. **2** *A dense fog clothed the road:* cover, envelop, wrap, enwrap, sheathe, shroud, encase, case, swaddle, cloak, coat, screen, cloud, veil.

Ant. 1 undress, disrobe, strip, unclothe; divest, dismantle. **2** uncover, lay bare, expose, exhibit.

clothes *n. pl. The seamstress made all her own clothes:* clothing, wearing apparel, apparel, garments, wardrobe, wear, attire, habiliments, dress, raiment, garb, costume, ensemble, finery, regalia, *Slang* get-up, togs, rags.

◇ *Word origin: Clothes* comes from the plural of *cloth.*

clothing *n.* See CLOTHES.

cloud *v.* **1** *The sunny sky suddenly clouded. Fog clouded the road ahead:* grow cloudy, overcast, darken, dim; overshadow, shadow, shade, eclipse; obscure, blur, shroud, cover, veil, cloak, screen, conceal, hide, curtain. **2** *A foolish misunderstanding clouded his good name:* place under suspicion, call in question, cast doubt on, tarnish. **3** *Personal involvement clouded his sense of fair play:* impair, distort, upset, disturb; confuse, bias, muddle, muddy, blind, make vague.

Ant. 1 clear, uncloud; uncover, unveil, show, reveal, uncloak. **2** recommend, honour, confirm, second; clear, exonerate. **3** clear, clarify, purify; restore, cure.

◇ *Word origin: Cloud* comes from Old English *clūd*, hill or rocky mass. During the 1200's people started using the word for masses of vapour in the sky, and the old meaning was soon forgotten. Old English *clūdig* ("rocky") underwent the same change and became our word *cloudy.*

cloudy *adj.* **1** *Cloudy skies drove the bathers off the beach:* clouded, overclouded, overcast, dark, grey, leaden, dreary, gloomy, hazy, murky, sunless. **2** *The reason for her anger is rather cloudy:* unclear, vague, confused, confusing, nebulous, hazy, indefinite, undefined, mysterious, obscure, veiled.

Ant. 1 uncloudy, clear, bright, fair, sunny, sun-filled. **2** clear, transparent, plain, obvious, straightforward, distinct, definite, well-defined.

◇ *Word origin:* See CLOUD.

clown *n.* **1** *Coco was the most famous circus clown of his time. The boy plays the clown to get attention:* buffoon, jester, harlequin, comic, comedian, fool, mime, zany, funny man, joker, madcap; merry andrew; wit, wag, card, humorist.

—*v.* **2** *Don't clown around any more — it's time to get down to business:* joke, jest, mess about, kid around, fool around.

◇ *Word origin:* The word *clown* for a circus or stage buffoon appeared in English (from an unknown source) about 400 years ago. Several European languages have borrowed the word. The French spell it *clown* and pronounce it *kloon.*

club *n.* **1** *The vicious-looking club was undoubtedly the murder weapon:* truncheon, bludgeon, stick, bat, mace, shillelagh, cudgel. **2** *The bridge club meets every Wednesday:* group, society, league, association, affiliation, union, alliance, guild; fraternity, chapel, brotherhood, lodge.

3 *Dances were held at the club twice a year:* clubhouse; country club.
—*v.* 4 *The farmer clubbed the snake with a stick:* beat, strike, pummel, bat, batter, bash, buffet, cudgel, bludgeon, flail, flog, lay about.

clue *n. The pirates left no clues as to where the treasure was hidden:* sign, hint, trace, cue, indication, evidence, mark, key, scent, glimmer, inkling; guide, indicator, pointer; intimation, inference, suggestion, insinuation.

clump *n.* 1 *Clumps of daisies grew wild in the field:* cluster, group, mass, batch, shock, bunch, assemblage, collection, aggregate; thicket, grove, copse. 2 *The plough threw up clumps of soil:* lump, mass; bump, knot, knob. 3 *The book fell from the table with a clump:* thump, thud, clunk, clomp, plunk, bump.
—*v.* 4 *The skiers clumped into the lodge in their heavy boots:* tramp, stomp, stamp, plunk, clunk; plod, bang.

clumsy *adj.* 1 *The clumsy waiter spilt the soup:* blundering, bungling, maladroit, careless, butter-fingered, heavy-handed, unhandy, like a bull in a china shop, inept, graceless, ungraceful, awkward, gawky. 2 *The toy windmill was a clumsy package to carry. The carpenter did a clumsy piece of work repairing the banister:* unhandy, cumbersome, bulky, unwieldy, unmanageable, ungainly; awkward, crude, rough, unskilled, inept, ill-contrived, makeshift, careless.
Ant. 1 dexterous, deft, handy, adroit, careful; graceful, smooth. 2 handy; professional, expert, skilful.

cluster *n.* 1 *Clusters of four-leaved clovers grew in the yard. People were standing in a cluster at the bus-stop:* clump, bunch, sheaf, batch, shock, mass; group, crowd, block, knot, band, collection, assemblage, throng, aggregate, congregation, company, swarm, herd, pack, bevy, accumulation, agglomeration, conglomeration.
—*v.* 2 *The Boy Scouts clustered round the bonfire for warmth:* gather, group, crowd, bunch, collect, congregate, assemble, throng, swarm, muster, flock, herd, converge; mass, amass, heap, pile, accumulate, aggregate.
Ant. 2 disperse, scatter, fan out.

clutch *v.* 1 *The little girl clutched her doll tightly:* grasp, clasp, hold, grip, clench, hug, embrace, squeeze, hang on to, cling to.
—*n.* 2 *The man held the money in a tight clutch:* grasp, hold, grip, clasp, hug, embrace.
Ant. 1 let go, let loose, loose, free.

clutter *v.* 1 *The child cluttered his room with toys and pictures:* strew, scatter, litter, fill, pile, heap.
—*n.* 2 *A clutter of dirty dishes filled the sink. The clutter in this room is disgraceful:* pile, heap, mess, litter, hodgepodge, jumble, tangle, disorder, disarray, confusion, chaos.
Ant. 1 straighten, straighten up, tidy, arrange, order, organize, clean. 2 neatness, tidiness, order, orderliness, organization.

coach *n.* 1 *Cinderella rode to the ball in a coach pulled by white horses:* carriage, four-wheeler, four-in-hand; stage-coach. 2 *The train was made up of an engine and four coaches. The bus company is putting new coaches on all its routes:* railway passenger car; motor coach, charabanc, bus, omnibus; motor car, car, limousine. 3 *A football team needs a good coach if it's going to win any matches. The professor agreed to be the boy's maths coach:* trainer, athletic director; tutor, private teacher, preceptor, mentor.
—*v.* 4 *I coach a youth club soccer team during the spring:* train, instruct, tutor, teach, drill; advise, guide, direct.
Ant. 3 player; student. 4 learn.
◇ *Word origin: Coach,* a carriage, comes from the name of *Kocs,* Hungary, where the first "kocs carts" were built around 1475. The word did not enter the English language until the mid-16th century.

coagulate *v. Certain drugs cause blood to coagulate:* clot, congeal; solidify, set, gel, jell, jellify, harden, curdle; thicken.
Ant. liquefy, melt, dissolve, soften.
◇ *Word origin: Coagulate* comes from the Latin prefix *co-* (together) + *agulare* (to force or impel), hence to force together, bind. The Romans used the word to mean "curdle."

coalesce *v. The flour and milk coalesced into a pasty batter. The various Left-wing parties coalesced to back one candidate:* unite, combine, fuse, form, join, amalgamate, mix, blend; join forces, band together, come together, form an alliance, ally, consolidate, become one, merge.
Ant. separate, divide, disunite, part; split, disintegrate, dissolve.
◇ *Word origin: Coalesce* comes from the Latin prefix *co-* (together) + *alescere* (to grow), hence to grow together or fuse.

coalition *n. The United Fund is a coalition of several charities:* union, alliance, partnership, league, affiliation, federation, association, confederacy, combination, syndicate, society; fusion, consolidation, conglomeration, amalgamation, agglomeration.

coarse *adj.* 1 *The recipe calls for coarse salt. Father has a heavy, coarse beard:* coarse-grained, unrefined; rough, rough-textured, harsh, scratchy, prickly, nubbly, shaggy, bristly, bristling. 2 *He was a coarse, loud-mouthed man:* crude, crass, unrefined, lacking taste, rough, unpolished; ungentlemanly, ill-bred, uncouth, boorish, loutish, inelegant, common, brutish, rude, impolite, ill-mannered; vulgar, indelicate, indecent, improper, indecorous, offensive, gross, foul-mouthed, obscene, dirty, lewd, licentious, lascivious, ribald; sordid, odious, repulsive, revolting, scurrilous, vile, disgusting.
Ant. 1 fine-grained, fine, refined, smooth,

soft, silky, satiny. **2** refined, gentlemanly, genteel, well-bred, cultivated, cultured, civilized, polished, elegant, urbane; polite, well-mannered, mannerly; decent, delicate, proper, decorous, inoffensive, clean; pleasant, pleasing, appetizing.
◇ *Usage note:* See COURSE.

coast *n.* **1** *Fishing boats were anchored all along the coast:* sea-coast, shore, shore-line, sea-shore, seaside; seaboard.
—*v.* **2** *The glider coasted down onto the landing-strip. The sledge coasted down the slope:* glide, glissade, float, drift, waft, sweep, skim; slide, slip.
Ant. 1 interior, midlands, hinterland.
◇ *Word origin: Coast* comes from Latin *costa*, rib or flank.

coat *n.* **1** *It's very cold, so wear a heavy coat:* top-coat, overcoat; raincoat, waterproof, duffle-coat, anorak, mackintosh; jacket, sports coat, blazer. **2** *The horse's coat was kept shiny by brushing:* hair, fur, hide, pelt. **3** *Two coats of paint were needed to cover the old colour:* coating, covering; layer, overlay.
—*v.* **4** *Coat the table-top with a thin layer of varnish. The furniture was coated with dust:* cover, spread, overlay, smear; envelop, encase, encrust; (*variously*) paint, enamel, lacquer, glaze, whitewash, plaster, laminate.
Ant. 4 remove, uncover, clear; clean, wash, dust, scrape, dissolve.

coating *n. The walk was covered with a thin coating of snow:* coat, covering, layer, overlay, film, sheet, veneer, skin, envelope.

coax *v. John coaxed his father into letting him use the family car:* wheedle, cajole; inveigle, talk into; *Informal* soft-soap, butter up.
Ant. intimidate, cow, threaten, menace, pressure, bully, bulldoze, browbeat; coerce, force, compel.

cobbler *n. The cobbler repaired the shoes:* shoemaker, shoe-repairer, boot maker.

cock *n.* **1** *The cock crowed in the farmyard:* rooster; male bird. **2** *Turn the cock to increase the flow of oil:* valve, tap, faucet, stopcock, handle, knob.
—*v.* **3** *The soldiers cocked their rifles:* draw back the hammer, raise the hammer of. **4** *The puppy cocked its ear at the sound of footsteps:* turn to one side, raise, tip, stand up, perk up; set erect, bristle up.
Ant. 1 hen; chick. **3** uncock.

coddle *v.* **1** *His parents coddled him because he was an only child:* pamper, spoil, indulge, baby, molly-coddle, humour, dote on. **2** *I like a coddled egg for breakfast:* lightly boiled.
Ant. 1 neglect, ignore, deny.

code *n.* **1** *The spy sent his message in code:* secret writing, cipher; cryptogram. **2** *The club's code of dress requires men to wear ties at dinner:* laws, rules, regulations, standards, principles, proprieties, precepts; statute, ordinance.
◇ *Word origin: Code* comes from Latin *codex*, book.

codicil *n. A codicil was attached to the will:* added clause, addendum, rider; postscript, subscript; addition, supplement, extension, appendix.
◇ *Word origin: Codicil* comes from *codicillus*, diminutive of Latin *codex*, book, hence little book or supplement.

coerce *v. Prisoners of war were coerced into writing letters praising their captors:* force, pressure, compel, drive, oblige, make, intimidate, cow, dragoon, bully, browbeat, bulldoze, threaten.
Ant. free, allow, permit; coax, cajole, flatter.
◇ *Word origin: Coerce* comes from the Latin prefix *co-* (together) + *arcere* (to restrain).

"What has been the effect of coercion? To make one-half of the world fools and the other half hypocrites." —*Thomas Jefferson*

---

coercion *n. The boy attended school only under coercion:* force, pressure, compulsion, intimidation, threats, duress, bullying, browbeating.
Ant. choice, one's own free will, volition, desire, preference, self-motivation.

coffer *n.* **1** *A coffer of gold coins was found in the pirate's cave:* chest, treasure chest, box, case. **2** **coffers.** *The nation's coffers are empty:* treasury, money supply, vaults, safes, cash boxes.
◇ *Word origin:* See COFFIN.

coffin *n. The coffin was transported to the cemetery in a hearse:* pall, box, catafalque, sarcophagus, cist.
◇ *Word origin: Coffin*, like *coffer*, comes from Greek *kophinos*, basket.

cogitate *v. The professor cogitated in front of the fire for hours. I need a few days to cogitate on the problem:* think, ponder, contemplate, deliberate, ruminate, meditate, reflect; think about, think over, reflect upon, deliberate on, mull over, consider thoroughly, study, concentrate upon, weigh.
◇ *Word origin: Cogitate* comes from Latin *cogitare*, to ponder or turn over in the mind. It is related to the word *agitate*.

cognate *adj.* **1** *We were cognate on our mothers' sides. French and Italian are cognate languages:* related, akin, kindred, relative, consanguine. **2** *Jogging and bicycling are cognate forms of exercise:* similar, like, alike.
—*n.* **3** Kaiser *and* Tsar *are German and Russian cognates of Latin* Caesar: word that is related to another word or words by derivation, borrowing, or descent.
Ant. 1, 2 unrelated. **2** unlike, not alike, dissimilar, different, opposite, contrary, contradicting, conflicting; unassociated, unallied, unaffiliated, diverse.

cognizance *n.* **1** *Most tourists take little cognizance of Alpine flowers:* notice, note, heed, attention, recognition, cognition, awareness; regard, observation, scrutiny. **2** *Cognizance of* *all available facts was necessary to solve the mystery:* knowledge, awareness, cognition, familiarity; apprehension, comprehension, grasp, perception, understanding; sensibility, consciousness.

Ant. **1** inattention, disregard, nonobservance, neglect, oversight. **2** ignorance, unfamiliarity, unawareness, incomprehension; insensibility, unconsciousness.

cognizant *adj. Is the prisoner cognizant of his rights?:* aware, informed, knowledgeable, knowing, familiar, acquainted, conversant, no stranger to, understanding, enlightened, versed in, instructed, posted, mindful, conscious.

Ant. unaware, uninformed, ignorant, unfamiliar, unknowledgeable, unknowing, unacquainted, unenlightened, unapprised, oblivious, unconscious, insensible.

cohere *v.* **1** *The powdery snow wouldn't cohere into snowballs:* stick together, hold together, unite, join, fuse, cling, bind, cement, glue, stick, hold, combine, consolidate; set, solidify, congeal, coagulate. **2** *The witnesses' accounts didn't cohere:* agree, coincide, correspond, match, fit, tally, harmonize, conform, concur, be consistent, square, dovetail; be related, be connected.

Ant. **1** separate, fall apart, come apart, unstick, detach, disjoin; scatter, disperse. **2** disagree, differ, diverge, be inconsistent, be at odds, be unlike; be disconnected, be unrelated.

coherent *adj. A good reporter can write a coherent account of confusing events:* logical, meaningful, intelligible, rational, clear, lucid, connected, comprehensible, understandable; consistent, harmonious, corresponding, congruous, in agreement, in keeping.

Ant. disjointed, disconnected, rambling, inconsistent, incongruous; irrational, illogical, meaningless, confusing, chaotic, vague, hazy, unintelligible, incomprehensible.

cohesive *adj. Tar is a cohesive substance:* coherent, cohering, viscous, sticky, sticking; inseparable, connected, consolidated, solid, cemented, indivisible, set.

◇ *Usage note:* See ADHESIVE.

cohort *n. Jim and his cohorts had blasted the safe open, but the police caught them before they could make off with the money:* fellow, companion, mate, henchman, associate, accomplice, follower, myrmidon.

◇ *Word origin: Cohort* is from Latin *cohors,* a troop of soldiers that was a tenth of an ancient Roman legion, or 300 to 600 men. Latin *cohors* also means "enclosed yard," and based on the same stem is *hortus,* garden. Both words travelled all over Europe with the Roman legions and made their way into indigenous languages from Britain to Russia. Here are some cognates of *cohors* and *hortus:* the words *yard, garden,* and *court* in English; German *Garten,* garden; and Russian *gorod,* town, as in *Novgorod* ("New-Town").

◇ *Usage note:* Conservative authorities condemn all uses of *cohort* save in the original sense of a troop of Roman soldiers. But most people nowadays accept the colloquial meaning, and (say many grammarians) if most accept it, it must be right. Be guided by your own judgement.

coil *v.* **1** *Vines coiled round the oak tree:* wind, spiral, loop, twist, twine; entwine, circle, encircle, curl, writhe.

—*n.* **2** *The seaman tripped over a coil of rope:* loop, spiral, ring, circle, curl, roll, braid.

coin *n.* **1** *The gold sovereign has become a rare coin in our day. The bank clerk counted out five pounds in coin:* metal piece of money, piece; change, silver, coin of the realm.

—*v.* **2** *These pennies were coined at the mint in London:* mint, strike. **3** *Who coined the phrase "Life is not a bowl of cherries"?:* create, make up, conceive, originate, fabricate, invent, devise, concoct, think up, dream up, hatch.

◇ *Word origin: Coin* is from Latin *cuneus,* wedge or die. Our word *cuneiform,* referring to wedge-shaped characters of some ancient inscriptions (and to wedge-shaped bones in the wrist and foot), has the same Latin basis.

coincide *v.* **1** *The two paths coincide a few yards above the beach. My birthday coincides with my wedding anniversary:* meet, come together, converge, cross; be concurrent, occur simultaneously. **2** *Does the witness's story coincide with that of the defendant?:* agree, concur, accord, correspond, match, tally, fit, conform, square, dovetail.

Ant. **1** diverge, separate, divide, part, split. **2** disagree, differ, contradict, counter, be unlike, be at odds, be inconsistent.

coincidence *n.* **1** *Running into my uncle at the races was pure coincidence:* chance, accident, luck, fate, fortuity. **2** *The coincidence of smoking and cancer suggests that the disease may be caused by the habit:* simultaneous occurrence, concurrence.

Ant. **1** design, plan, premeditation, purpose.

coincidental *adj.* **1** *These meetings happen too often to be coincidental:* accidental, unplanned, chance, fortuitous. **2** *The drop in the stockmarket was coincidental with the bad news from abroad:* simultaneous, synchronous, contiguous, concomitant.

cold *adj.* **1** *Would you like a glass of cold milk? The coffee is cold:* cool, cooled, chilled, chilly, icy, ice-cold, gelid, frosty, frosted, frigid; unheated, unwarmed. **2** *The rain brought a cold wind. Last week we had some cold weather:* wintry, freezing, chilling, chilly, chill, cool, icy, ice-cold, frigid, glacial, arctic, polar, brisk, crisp, snappy, nippy, nipping, bitter, sharp, harsh, severe, cutting, biting, penetrating, piercing, stinging, marrow-chilling, bone-

chilling, teeth-chattering. **3** *You must be cold without a coat:* chilled, chilly, cool, ice-cold, chilled to the bone, chilled to the marrow, freezing, frozen, frozen stiff, numbed. **4** *Her sister was a cold person. His wife gave us a cold reception:* unemotional, passionless, frigid, unresponsive, unfeeling, undemonstrative, unmoved, unimpressionable, impervious, passive, impassive, unexcitable, stiff, unstirred; apathetic, antipathetic; unsympathetic, unconcerned, uninterested, indifferent, phlegmatic, uncaring, unloving; unfriendly, reserved, detached, distant, remote, aloof, haughty, supercilious, disdainful, reticent, uncommunicative, inaccessible, unapproachable, forbidding, steely, stony, heartless, cold-hearted, cold-blooded, cruel, hard, hardened, inured, harsh, callous. **5** *The news item was cold by morning. The scent of the fox was cold:* old, stale, flat, uninteresting; faint, faded, dead. **6** *Informal The fighter was knocked out cold:* unconscious, insensible, insensate.
—*n.* **7** *Some people feel the cold more than others:* coldness, coolness, chill.

Ant. 1–5 hot, warm. **1** red-hot, steaming; heated, warmed. **2** sweltering, scorching, warming, balmy, mild, summery, sunny. **3** sweltering, roasting, perspiring, sweating. **4** emotional, passionate, ardent, fervent, responsive, demonstrative, alive, vital, animated, excitable, spirited, gay; sympathetic, compassionate, concerned, caring, interested; loving, friendly, open, unreserved, warm-hearted. **5** new, fresh; sharp, strong. **6** conscious; semi-conscious. **7** heat, warmth.

"God sends cold according to clothes."
—*George Herbert*

---

cold-blooded *adj.* **1** *Few men could have made the difficult decision in such a cold-blooded way:* cold, unfeeling, unemotional, heartless, cold-hearted, hard-hearted, passionless, unimpassioned, unsympathetic, unfriendly, stiff, reserved, formal, unresponsive, insensitive; unconcerned, uninterested, detached, disinterested, indifferent, uncaring, unmoved, unimpressible, unimpressionable, impervious, passive, impassive, unexcitable, unstirred; contemptuous, disdainful; calculating, deliberate; steely, flinty, stony, hard, cruel, callous, hardened, inured, harsh. **2** *The cold-blooded murder shocked the town:* brutal, inhuman, inhumane, bloodthirsty, savage, barbarous, fiendish, evil, ruthless, merciless, unmerciful, unpitying, pitiless, diabolical, demonic, satanic, villainous.

Ant. 1 warm, feeling, emotional, heartfelt, kind-hearted, soft-hearted, passionate, excitable, impassioned, sympathetic, compassionate, friendly, open, responsive, sensitive, concerned, interested, involved, caring, loving, kind, gentle, humane. **2** humane, civilized, merciful, benevolent, charitable.

collaborate *v.* **1** *Rodgers and Hammerstein collaborated on many famous musicals:* work together, work side by side, team up, join forces, create together, co-operate, unite. **2** *Few townspeople collaborated with the occupying army:* co-operate, collude.

◇ *Word origin: Collaborate* comes from the Latin prefix *com-* (with) + *laborare* (to work), hence "to work with." Strangely, the verb *to collaborate* is not recorded in English until 1871, some seventy years after *collaborator.* The reason for this anomaly seems to be that *collaborator* is an anglicization of the French *collaborateur,* which first appears in English in 1801. It did not become really accepted *as* English, with a verbal form, and inflected forms, until some time later.

collaborator *n.* **1** *Gilbert and Sullivan were collaborators on "The Mikado":* associate, colleague, confederate, co-worker, team-mate, co-partner, ally. **2** *Following the Liberation of Paris, many collaborators were executed:* collaborationist, puppet, quisling, traitor.

◇ *Word origin:* (Sense **1**) see COLLABORATE; *Collaborator* (sense **2**) goes back to Italian *collaborazione,* collaboration, which at the time of Mussolini's take-over in Italy (1922) was a special term for coalition among rival factions. Less than 20 years later in France (1940–41) the term acquired its present sense of "co-operation with German occupation forces." With the Allied invasion of Europe (1944) *collaborator* became synonymous with "traitor."

collapse *v.* **1** *The earthquake caused many buildings to collapse:* cave in, fall, buckle, fall to pieces, give way, break apart, crumple. **2** *The negotiations collapsed when no agreement could be reached:* break down, fail, fall through, come to nothing, be in vain, flounder, run aground, *Slang* flop, fizzle out, fold. **3** *The fireman collapsed from inhaling too much smoke. We collapsed with laughter:* fall prostrate, become unconscious, swoon, *Slang* keel over; take sick, be stricken, become ill, suffer a breakdown; fall helpless, give way, break up.
—*n.* **4** *The collapse of the old bridge forced the ferry back into operation. The collapse of the government left the country in chaos:* fall, falling apart, disintegration, downfall, breakdown, failure, cave-in, buckling, giving way. **5** *The actress's collapse was brought on by overwork:* breakdown, sudden illness, crack-up, seizure, attack; fall, faint, swoon; coma.

Ant. 1 stand. **2** succeed, triumph, flourish. **3** stand up; get well, recover. **5** good health.

◇ *Spelling tip:* Many people hesitate when writing *collapsible* because they can't remember if it ends in *-able* or *-ible.* Remember: *I will collapse during the spelling test if I don't remember the I in* collapsible.

collateral *n.* **1** *The house served as collateral for the*

loan: security, pledge, warranty, warrant, guarantee, insurance, endorsement.
—*adj.* **2** *The information was collateral to the main issue, but still important. The student needs collateral tutoring in maths:* secondary, subordinate, incidental; auxiliary, supplementary, ancillary, accessory, additional, extra, supporting, supportive, contributory, parallel.
Ant. **2** superior, overshadowing; primary, essential, fundamental, basic, chief, key.

colleague *n. The judge was highly respected among his colleagues:* confrère, associate, fellow; partner, co-partner, co-worker, fellow worker, confederate, team-mate, collaborator, mate.
Ant. rival, competitor, opponent, adversary, antagonist.

collect *v.* **1** *A crowd collected to watch the fight:* gather, congregate, flock together, cluster around, herd together, rally, meet, come together, get together, draw together, convene, bring together. **2** *Dust collects on the furniture overnight:* accumulate, amass, pile up, heap up, aggregate, compile. **3** *The Earl Haig Fund collected £1,000 in town this year:* raise, obtain, receive, solicit, amass, get, scrape up, scrape together, muster. **4** *The refuse men collect the rubbish every Wednesday:* pick up, call for, gather up. **5** *Give the speaker a few minutes to collect herself and then begin the programme:* compose, calm, control, get hold of, get together, pull together; prepare, muster, rally.
Ant. **1–4** disperse, scatter. **3, 4** distribute, disperse.

collected *adj. The witness was remarkably collected under cross-examination:* self-controlled, self-assured, self-possessed, composed, confident, poised, calm, cool, cool-headed, restrained, level-headed, steady, even-tempered; quiet, serene, tranquil, peaceful, placid, unruffled, unperturbed, undisturbed, unemotional, unflappable.
Ant. nervous, perturbed, disturbed, ruffled, unsteady, shaky, troubled, distressed; unpoised, uncontrolled, excitable, irritable, emotional.

collection *n.* **1** *A strange collection of people attended the party. A collection of old books filled the attic:* group, gathering, assembly, assemblage, aggregation, crowd, bunch, pack, body, throng, mob, drove, swarm, flock, bevy; accumulation, assortment, jumble, clutter, miscellany, hodgepodge, variety, heap, array, pile, cluster, clump, mass. **2** *As a child I had a stamp collection. She has written a collection of short stories:* assemblage, aggregation, compilation, treasury, anthology, corpus. **3** *The collection was made before the last hymn:* collecting, gathering, amassing, accumulating, muster, receiving, soliciting; gift, offertory, oblation.

collective *adj. If the team makes a strong collective effort, we'll win the game:* unified, joint, combined, co-operative, mutual, integrated; collected, gathered, aggregate, cumulative, accumulated, composite.
Ant. individual, separate, divided, uncombined, unco-operative, fragmented, piecemeal.

collide *v.* **1** *The cars collided at the junction:* run into one another, crash, hit, smash, meet, meet head on, bash together; strike against, hurtle against, beat against, knock into, bump into. **2** *The brothers' political views usually collide:* disagree, conflict, clash, diverge.
Ant. **1** miss; avoid, evade. **2** agree, coincide, accord, harmonize, mesh, fit, square.
◇ *Word origin: Collide* comes from the Latin prefix *com-* (together) + *laedere* (to strike).

collision *n.* **1** *There was a three-car collision on the motorway. The collision could be heard from my house:* crash, smash-up, accident; impact, smash, clash, bump, striking together. **2** *The collision of the opposing armies ravaged the countryside:* conflict, clash of arms, battle, combat, fight, encounter, engagement, skirmish, struggle.

colloquial *adj. The politician's colloquial language endeared him to small-town voters:* folksy, homespun, homely, chatty, ordinary, vernacular, idiomatic, common, everyday, workaday, plain, informal, casual, unsophisticated, conversational, familiar, demotic.
Ant. formal; sophisticated, literary, cultured, refined.

collusion *n. The diplomat was arrested for acting in collusion with the enemy:* secret agreement, conspiracy, intrigue, guilty association, connivance, complicity; treason; fraud.

colony *n.* **1** *Australia was originally a British colony:* settlement, province, territory, dependency, dominion, protectorate, possession, satellite state. **2** *A colony of gulls and terns inhabits the island:* community, group.
◇ *Word origin: Colony* comes from Latin *colonus,* farmer, because it was farmers who settled new colonies and expanded national borders into unknown or hostile territory.

colour *n.* **1** *Children love bright colours. Many artists mix their own colours:* colouring, coloration, tint, hue, shade, tone, tinge; pigment, pigmentation, paint, dye, dyestuff. **2** *A few weeks in the country brought back her healthy colour:* natural complexion, skin hue; bloom, rosiness, glow, blush, redness, flush. **3** *It wasn't the words so much as the colour of his criticism that hurt her:* tone, feeling, spirit, mood, intent, intention, force, stress, effect, implication, insinuation, intimation, connotation, import, significance, sense, meaning, drift.
—*v.* **4** *Let's colour the walls green and the ceiling white:* paint, stain, dye, tint, pigment, tinge, crayon, chalk, wash. **5** *A judge can't let personal feelings colour his decisions:* prejudice, influence, affect, bias, distort, slant, warp, twist, pervert, taint. **6** *Her face coloured when she was*

embarrassed: redden, blush, flame, burn, flush, glow, go crimson, become florid; change colour.

Ant. 2 paleness, pallor, wanness, sallowness, whiteness. **3** denotation. **6** blanch, go white.

"Among the several kinds of beauty the eye takes most delight in colours."

—Joseph Addison

---

colourful *adj.* **1** *Colourful wallpaper would brighten up the room:* brightly coloured, bright, brilliant, vibrant, full-toned, gay, florid, loud, showy; multicoloured, many-coloured, particoloured, variegated. **2** *He wrote of the colourful characters that he met on his trip:* picturesque, interesting; unusual, distinctive, unique; graphic, vivid, vivacious, animated, spirited, vigorous, zestful, dynamic, forceful, compelling.

Ant. 1 dull, drab, dingy, dreary, monotonous, dark, grey, faded, washed out, pale. **2** dull, uninteresting, colourless, unexciting, lifeless, flat, boring.

colourless *adj.* **1** *Continuous washings gave the shirt a colourless appearance:* without colour, undyed, natural, neutral; white, whitened, greyed, pale, bleached, faded, washed out, dull, drab, dingy, dreary. **2** *Her colourless skin could take a bit of rouge:* pale, pallid, ashen, ashy, wan, blanched, white, sallow, pasty, anaemic, bloodless, sickly, cadaverous, ghastly, ghostly. **3** *Her boy-friend has a colourless personality:* dull, unexciting, uninteresting, lifeless, monotonous, boring, dreary, drab, lack-lustre, flat, unanimated, spiritless, uninspired, ordinary, commonplace, prosaic, neutral, vapid, insipid, pale, anaemic, bloodless.

Ant. 1 bright, brilliant, lustrous, colourful. **2** ruddy, glowing, healthy, robust. **3** colourful, bright, exciting, interesting, lively, full of life, animated, spirited, vigorous, dynamic, forceful, compelling, strong; distinctive, unusual, unique.

colossal *adj. Samson was feared for his colossal strength. I have just made a colossal blunder:* extremely large, huge, vast, immense, massive, enormous, gigantic, giant, great, titanic, mammoth, grand, almighty, extreme, exceeding, excessive, extravagant, tremendous, spectacular, prodigious, inordinate, incredible, overwhelming, imposing, awe-inspiring, monumental.

Ant. small, little, tiny, minute, diminutive, miniature; slight, weak, feeble; ordinary, common, average, so-so.

◇ *Word origin: Colossal* comes from Greek *kolossos*, statue. The word got its added connotation of bigness by association with the famous *Colossus of Rhodes*, a giant statue of the god Apollo at the harbour entrance of ancient Rhodes. Then counted as one of the Seven Wonders of the World, it stood, according to Pliny, seventy cubits high.

column *n.* **1** *The dome was supported by white marble columns:* pillar, support, upright, post, pilaster, pylon. **2** *The accounts ledger had many columns for entries:* vertical row, vertical list; row, line. **3** *A column of soldiers marched down the road:* row, line, queue, file; procession, formation, parade, caravan, cavalcade, train, phalanx.

comb *n.* **1** *Bring me the comb and brush:* toilet comb, dressing comb, fine-tooth comb. **2** *The cock had a red comb:* cockscomb, topknot, head tuft; tuft, plume, panache.

—v. **3** *The mother combed the child's hair:* dress, groom, untangle; style, arrange; curry. **4** *Police combed the house for clues:* search, hunt throughout, seek through, look through, scour, cast about, explore.

combat *n.* **1** *The enemy battleship was sunk in combat:* military action, action, fighting, battle, engagement, clash, skirmish. **2** *Conservatives and Socialists are engaged in a combat over the new housing bill:* conflict, battle, clash, struggle, fight, fighting, encounter, confrontation, contest, contention.

—v. **3** *The nation will combat all invaders. The Salk vaccine did much to combat polio:* fight, battle, do battle with, war against, wage war, go to war, make warfare, attack, contest, march against, grapple with, come to blows, struggle; oppose, work against, contest against, make a stand against.

Ant. 1 peace time, peace; armistice, truce; surrender, capitulation. **2** agreement, accord, concord, compliance, concurrence, acquiescence. **3** make peace, declare a truce; surrender, capitulate, give up; support, uphold, accept, comply, assent, concur, acquiesce, welcome.

combatant *n. How many combatants were killed during D-Day?:* fighting man, soldier, serviceman, man-at-arms, warrior, fighter.

Ant. non-combatant, non-fighting man; civilian.

combination *n.* **1** *The actress had the right combination of looks and talent to become a star. The combination of yellow and blue forms green:* combining, mixture, mix, mixing, blend, blending, pooling, union, joining, composition, compound, composite, synthesis, amalgamation, amalgam, alloy, fusion; medley, variety, assortment. **2** *The combination of the 50 states forms the United States of America:* union, federation, confederation, confederacy, merger, alliance, association, coalition, league, joining, combining, coalescing.

Ant. 1, 2 division, separation; dissolution, dissolving.

combine *v. Combine ketchup and horse-radish to make the shrimp sauce. The two boys combined their resources to buy a bicycle:* unite, unify, join, bring together, put together, consolidate, merge, couple, pool, lump together, league; mix, blend, mingle, compound, amalgamate, incorporate, fuse, synthesize.

Ant. separate, divide, part, sever, sunder, detach; dissolve, dissociate, disunite.

combustible *adj. Petrol is highly combustible:* flammable, inflammable, incendiary, burnable, combustive, ignitable.

combustion *n. The spontaneous combustion of the oil-soaked rags caused the barn to catch fire:* burning, ignition, kindling, incineration, conflagration, flaming, firing.

come *v.* **1** *Come here!:* move toward, go toward, approach, draw near, advance; present oneself. **2** *What time are the guests coming?:* arrive, reach a destination; appear, show up, turn up, drop in. **3** *Christmas comes but once a year. Spring is coming:* take place, fall, occur, happen, come about, come to pass, rise, arise, emerge, appear, materialize, arrive, spring forth, rear its head; advance, approach, be imminent, impend, loom, be in the wind, be on the horizon, bear down upon. **4** *The belt came unbuckled. Dreams can come true:* become; be, grow to be. **5** *My uncle comes from Queensland. This radio comes from Japan:* be a resident, be a native; issue, spring, arise, descend, follow; bud, germinate be a product of, originate in, emanate. **6** *The curtains come just to the window-sill:* reach, extend, go, stretch, range, spread. **7** *The blouse comes in all colours:* be made, be produced, be available, be offered.

Ant. 1–3 go, go away, depart, leave, withdraw, retreat.

◇ *Spelling tip:* Many people are confused by the fact that *beginning* has two *n*'s and *coming* has only one *m*. The rule is, if the final *e* of a word is squeezed out when you combine it with *-ing*, you *never* in that case go on to double the consonant. Thus: *come + -ing = coMing.*

comedian *n. The star of the show was a very funny comedian:* comic, (*fem.*) comedienne, joker, funny man, humorist, wag; clown, jester, buffoon, fool, madcap, zany, prankster, practical joker; comic actor.

comedy *n.* **1** *Shakespeare wrote comedies, histories, and tragedies:* play with a happy ending, farce, satire, light entertainment; travesty, burlesque. **2** *The seriousness of the situation left no room for comedy:* joking, jesting, humour, wit, drollery, banter, raillery; fun, silliness, pranks, foolery, tomfoolery, fooling around, monkey business, buffoonery, horseplay.

Ant. 1 tragedy, tragic drama, high drama, serious play, melodrama; opera. **2** seriousness, solemnity, sobriety; tears, sadness, melancholy.

◇ *Word origin: Comedy* comes from Greek *kōmos*, revel or revelry.

comely *adj.* **1** *The prince fell in love with a comely young maiden:* pretty, fair, sightly, well-favoured, attractive, bonny, winsome, fetching, pleasing, engaging, winning; wholesome, blooming. **2** *The girl's comely behaviour was a delight to her parents:* seemly, becoming, suitable, tasteful, proper, decorous, nice, correct, fitting; appealing, pleasing, pleasant, agreeable, engaging, winning, charming; natural, simple, unaffected.

Ant. 1 ugly, homely, plain, unsightly, unlovely, unattractive, ill-favoured, repulsive, disagreeable; jaded, faded. **2** unseemly, unbecoming, unsuitable, tasteless, distasteful, tactless, indecorous, inappropriate, unfitting, improper, scandalous; disagreeable, unappealing, unpleasant, repellent, repulsive; unnatural, affected, pretentious.

comfort *v.* **1** *The mother comforted the crying child:* console, solace, soothe, quiet, calm, compose, ease, reassure, lighten one's burden, quiet one's fears cheer, cheer up, hearten, encourage, bolster up, bolster one's spirits. —*n.* **2** *After the disaster, he found comfort in his old friends:* solace, reassurance, consolation, serenity, composure, peace, calm, cheering up, encouragement, help. **3** *The child is a great comfort to his grandparents:* consolation, solace, satisfaction, pleasure, source of serenity, source of encouragement, comforter. **4** *The hotel provides all the comforts of home:* creature comforts, ease, satisfaction, pleasure, gratification, well-being, contentment, warmth, coziness, relaxation, freedom from distress; luxury, opulence.

Ant. 1–4 discomfort, distress, torment, bother, burden, trouble. **1** aggravate, annoy, irk, rile, ruffle, stir up, excite; sadden, depress, dishearten, discourage. **2–4** aggravation, irritation, annoyance, sadness, discouragement, dissatisfaction, displeasure. **3** bane. **4** poverty, hardship, inconvenience.

comfortable *adj.* **1** *Air-conditioning makes for a comfortable house:* providing comfort, giving ease; pleasurable, pleasant, congenial, agreeable, gratifying; suitable, satisfactory, adequate. **2** *Are you comfortable? Shy people don't feel comfortable with strangers:* at ease, easy, at home, relaxed, contented, serene, untroubled, undisturbed; free from distress.

Ant. uncomfortable. **1** unsatisfactory, unsuitable, displeasing, unpleasant, disagreeable, uncongenial. **2** uneasy, nervous, tense, fretful, worried, troubled, disturbed, distressed, miserable, wretched, discontented.

comic Also **comical** *adj. It was such a comic state of affairs that we had to laugh:* funny, humorous, laughable, amusing, ridiculous, ludicrous, silly, farcical, absurd, nonsensical, mirthful, merry, risible, whimsical, jocose, jocular, jovial, droll, witty, rich, facetious.

Ant. tragic; serious, grave, solemn, sober; pathetic, touching, poignant, melancholy; sad, depressing, doleful, dolorous.

◇ *Word origin:* See COMEDY.

coming *n.* **1** *The dark clouds foretold the coming of rain:* arrival, arriving, approach, approaching, nearing; appearance, advent, occurrence, emergence, materializing.
—adj. **2** *The new hospital will be built in the coming year:* next, forthcoming, subsequent, arriving, advancing, approaching; future, imminent, impending, to come, on the way, in view, on the horizon, in the wind.
Ant. **1** departure, withdrawal, disappearance. **2** departing; past, previous, prior.
◇ *Spelling tip:* See COME.

command *v.* **1** *The king commanded the guards to raise the drawbridge:* order, direct, bid, charge, require, adjure, call upon, instruct; call for, summon, enjoin. **2** *Wellington commanded the English soldiers at Waterloo:* direct, lead, head, have authority over, have charge of, be master of, rule, boss, govern; guide, conduct, manage, supervise, superintend, administer. **3** *Toscanini commanded the admiration of music lovers all over the world:* call forth, elicit, receive, get, deserve, compel, draw, extract, evoke, induce, prompt, provoke, inspire, motivate, kindle, incite.
—n. **4** *Who issued the command to fire?:* order, direction, directive, demand, charge, ultimatum, summons, behest, bid, call, instruction, edict, decree. **5** *The dictator assumed command of the country:* control, domination, rule, grip, grasp, hold, power, authority; direction, charge, conduct, governing, leadership, management, administration, supervision. **6** *The teacher had a good command of French:* mastery, comprehension, understanding, grasp, knowledge, familiarity.
Ant. **1** plead, beg, supplicate; obey. **2** follow. **3** repel; deter, discourage.

"The reward of the general is not a bigger tent, but command." —*Oliver Wendell Holmes*

---

commandeer *v. The policemen commandeered a taxi to chase the robbers:* appropriate, expropriate, seize, take, usurp.

commander *n. General Eisenhower was commander of the Allied forces during World War II:* commanding officer, commander-in-chief; chief, leader, head; ruler, director, conductor, manager, boss.
Ant. subordinate, follower; inferior.

commanding *adj.* **1** *The speaker's commanding manner quieted the crowd:* authoritative, imposing, forceful, compelling, powerful, strong, dynamic, gripping, arresting; impressive, important, striking; distinguished, stately, grand, lofty. **2** *The soldier reported directly to his commanding officer:* in command, directing, controlling, leading, governing; chief, head, ruling, superior, senior. **3** *The penthouse offered a commanding view of the city:* dominating, towering, imposing, prominent, overshadowing.
Ant. **1** shrinking, retiring, timid, shy, modest, weak; unimposing, unimpressive. **2** subordinate, subservient, junior.

commemorate *v.* **1** *The monument commemorates local war heroes:* memorialize, honour, pay homage to, pay tribute to, acclaim, hallow. **2** *York Minster's 500th anniversary is commemorated this year:* celebrate, observe, salute, hail, mark, acknowledge, show respect for, glorify, extol, solemnize, revere, venerate.
Ant. **1, 2** dishonour, shame, degrade. **2** overlook, ignore, pass over, forget.

commence *v. The dancing will commence immediately after the dinner:* begin, start, get started, get going; inaugurate, initiate, originate.
Ant. end, conclude, finish, stop, halt, terminate.
◇ *Word origin: Commence* is from the Latin prefix *com-* (thoroughly) + *initiare* (to begin), which also gives us *initial* and *initiate.*

commencement *n.* **1** *For the first few weeks after the commencement of her job, Sally found that she frequently mislaid the office keys:* beginning, start, initiation, inauguration, outset, dawn, morning; onset, inception, genesis, birth, origination; first step. **2** *The dean gave a short speech at commencement:* graduation, graduation day, graduation ceremonies.
Ant. **1** end, ending, close, conclusion, finish.

commend *v.* **1** *The student's teachers commended him to his prospective employers. The critics commended the director's new film:* recommend, endorse, put in a good word for, support, back, stand by; speak highly of, laud, praise, extol, approve, acclaim, *Informal* O.K. **2** *The old man commended his business responsibilities to his grandson:* entrust, give over, hand over, leave in the hands of, give, commit, consign, confer, convey, pass over, relegate, delegate, transfer.
Ant. **1** denounce, renounce, condemn, blackball; criticize, censure, deride, attack. **2** withhold, keep; withdraw.

commendable *adj. Perseverance is a commendable trait:* to be commended, worthy, praiseworthy, admirable, laudable, meritorious, honourable, creditable, exemplary, deserving, estimable.
Ant. unworthy, dishonourable, discreditable, disreputable, undeserving.
◇ *Spelling tip:* Some people hesitate when writing this word, not being sure if it ends in *-able* or *-ible.* Remember, if you are *able* to *commend* someone, he is *commendABLE.*

commensurate Also **commensurable** *adj. Her salary is commensurate with her ability and experience:* in accord, consistent, fitting, in agreement, suitable, appropriate, compatible, corresponding, proportionate, comparable, on a proper scale, relative, equal, equivalent, even, balanced, meet, parallel, relative, square.

Ant. inconsistent, unsuitable, inappropriate, unfitting, incompatible, disproportionate, dissimilar, incomparable, unequal, discordant.

comment *n.* **1** *The teacher wrote his comments in the margin of the composition:* commentary, criticism, remark, explanation, observation, reflection, elucidation, clarification, explication, exemplification; note, annotation. **2** *The speaker's proposal drew angry comments from the crowd:* remark, statement, commentary, observation, reflection; word, utterance, expression, assertion.
—*v.* **3** *Would the councillor care to comment on why he voted against the new housing project?:* explain, clarify, elucidate, expound, expand on, shed light; discuss, talk about, remark, make a statement.
◇ *Word origin: Comment* is from Latin *commentum,* something thought up in the mind (*mens* = mind). *Commentum* was first used in the sense of interpretation or comment by the 6th century A.D. encyclopaedist, Isidore of Seville.

commentary *n.* **1** *Students were asked to write a commentary on one of Shakespeare's plays:* series of comments, explanatory essay, critique, explanation, explication, exposition, interpretation; treatise, dissertation. **2** See COMMENT (senses **1, 2**).

commentator *n. The TV sports commentator said that our team won fairly:* newscaster, news analyst, columnist, critic, reviewer; explainer, interpreter, speaker, writer.

commerce *n. Overseas commerce increased by 20 per cent in the last month:* business, trade, trading, buying and selling, exchange, mercantilism; industry.
◇ *Word origin: Commerce* is from the Latin prefix *con-* (together, with) + *merx* (merchandise), which also gives us *merchant, merchandise,* and *mercantile.*

commercial *adj.* **1** *He wanted to make his living in the arts rather than in the commercial world. Christmas has become too commercial:* business, trade, mercantile, buying-and-selling, sales, profit-making.
—*n.* **2** *The TV show was interrupted by too many commercials:* advertisement, ad.
Ant. **1** artistic, professional; non-profit-making, philanthropic, eleemosynary, charitable.

commiserate *v. Friends commiserated with the bereaved family:* feel for, express sorrow, sympathize with, show pity, have compassion for, express fellow-feeling, condole with, grieve with, lament with, share one's sorrow.
◇ *Word origin: Commiserate* is based on the Latin prefix *con-* (together, with) + *miser* (wretched), which also gives us *miser, misery,* and *miserable.*

commission *n.* **1** *He was indicted for the commission of a felony:* committing, committal, carrying out, act, acting out, performing, performance, doing, perpetration, transacting, exercise, conduct. **2** *The ambassador was given the commission to negotiate the treaty:* authority, authorization, power, capacity, mandate, charge, duty, task, appointment, mission, assignment, office, function, role, deputation, warrant, licence, proxy, commitment, entrusting, trust. **3** *I will take a week's leave when I've been granted my commission:* officer's rank, rank, position, appointment, office; appointment papers, document, certificate, written orders. **4** *All tenants' complaints should be sent to the Housing Commission:* commissioners, board, agency, council, committee; delegation, representatives, deputation. **5** *The insurance agent earned a commission on every policy that he sold:* percentage, cut, portion, piece, fee; *Slang* rake-off.
—*v.* **6** *An architect was commissioned to design the new building:* authorize, empower, appoint, assign, name, delegate, charge, bid, order, direct, give the go-ahead, engage, employ, hire, contract, charter. **7** *Sandhurst graduates are commissioned as army officers:* grant officer's rank, appoint; give a document, certify.
Ant. **1** non-commission, omission, non-committal, non-performance. **5** salary, straight salary. **6** release, fire, let go.

commit *v.* **1** *He was accused of committing robbery:* perform, carry out, do, act, enact, transact, practise, perpetrate, execute, effect, pursue, participate in; *Slang* pull, pull off. **2** *The company committed its profits to building new factories. The court committed the man to a lunatic asylum:* consign, put in the custody of, give over, put in the hands of, deliver, entrust, transfer, place, put, assign, deposit; confine, intern, institutionalize. **3** *The government committed itself to spending ten million pounds on new roads:* obligate, bind, make liable, engage, decide, determine, resolve.
Ant. **1** omit. **2** withhold, hold back, take from; receive, accept; release, free. **3** disavow, disregard; waver, vacillate, shilly-shally.

commitment *n.* **1** *The factory requested a larger commitment of coal for its needs. The prisoner's period of commitment to the prison lasted five years:* consignment, assignment, delivery, dispatching, transfer, giving over; confinement, internment, institutionalizing, imprisonment, detention, incarceration, restraint. **2** *Most citizens have a commitment to a political party. By signing the lease you made a commitment to pay £30 a month rent:* obligation, liability, responsibility; bond, guarantee, warranty, pledge, assurance, vow, word, promise; resolution, decision, determination, stand.
Ant. **1** withholding; release, freeing, liberation. **2** negation, disavowal; indecisiveness, wavering, vacillation, shilly-shallying.

commodious *adj. Is the house commodious enough for a large family?:* roomy, spacious, large, capacious, unconfining, uncramped, ample, expansive, extensive.

Ant. cramped, confining, small, narrow.

commodity *n.* **1** *Wheat is a valuable commodity:* article of trade, article of commerce, merchandise, product, ware, goods, staple. **2** *A good reputation is a valuable commodity:* asset, possession, property, belonging, holding, convenience, advantage.

Ant. 2 liability, handicap, disadvantage, hindrance, burden.

common *adj.* **1** *We must all work for the common good. That the couple argue a lot is common knowledge:* public, general, joint, shared, collective, communal; widespread, universal. **2** *Train accidents are far too common. "More haste, less speed" is a common saying:* commonplace, ordinary, frequent, often met with, routine, regular; customary, conventional, standard, settled, established, familiar, everyday, well-known, widely known, popular, traditional, oft-repeated; stock, common or garden, household, homespun, prosaic, threadbare, moth-eaten, old-hat, worn-out, worn thin; informal, colloquial. **3** *He wasn't a hero but just a common man:* ordinary, plain, simple, average, normal; *Slang* workaday, unknown, undistinguished, obscure, nameless, unnoticed, inglorious, ignoble, unexalted, middle-class, plebeian, bourgeois; without rank, unimportant, insignificant, lowly, low, minor, lesser, subordinate, mediocre. **4** *His common manners repelled her:* coarse, crude, crass, uncouth, insensitive, callous, brutal, boorish, loutish, brash, brazen, shameless, shameful, unblushing, disagreeable, unrefined, uncultured, unpolished, tasteless, gross, base, mean, cheap, tawdry, bad, deficient; rude, impolite, ill-mannered, ill-bred, low-bred, ignoble; vulgar, obnoxious, offensive, contemptible, vile, disgraceful, low-minded, lewd, smutty, obscene, ribald.

Ant. 1 private, personal, individual, separate, secret. **2** uncommon, unusual, rare, infrequent, strange, unique, odd, exceptional, unfamiliar, extraordinary, unpopular, unorthodox, unconventional, unheard of, abnormal, scarce, unknown, little-known; formal, sophisticated; literary. **3** outstanding, superior, exceptional, extraordinary, important; distinguished, famous, renowned, noble, noteworthy, glorious, exalted. **4** polished, refined, cultured, gentle, delicate, sensitive, gentlemanly, gallant, noble; polite, well-mannered, well-bred, becoming, pleasing, modest, unassuming.

commonly *adv. Barbara was commonly known as Babs:* usually, ordinarily, generally, normally, customarily, regularly, routinely, traditionally, conventionally, habitually, frequently, often, most often, in most instances, by and large, in general, as a rule, for the most part, generally speaking, as a matter of course, by force of habit, popularly, widely; familiarly, informally.

Ant. rarely, seldom, infrequently, scarcely; privately, secretly; formally, politely.

commonplace *adj.* **1** *Horses and traps were commonplace sights in 1900:* common, ordinary, usual, routine, everyday, familiar, regular, standard, traditional, customary, general, widespread. **2** *The film's commonplace plot bored the audience:* common, dull, banal, pedestrian, humdrum, uninteresting, unimaginative, unoriginal, trite, hackneyed, stereotyped, stale, old, old-hat, oft-repeated, worn-out, worn thin, threadbare, moth-eaten.

—*n.* **3** *"East, West, home's best" is a well-known commonplace:* hackneyed expression, banality, platitude, cliché, bromide, received idea.

Ant. 1, 2 uncommon, unusual, unfamiliar, rare, strange, unique, odd, extraordinary, exceptional, infrequent. **2** exciting, interesting, imaginative; original, distinguished, new.

◇ *Word origin: Commonplace* is a translation of Latin *locus communis,* common or oft-cited place (in a book), hence stock theme or subject.

common sense *n. Though he wasn't well educated, his common sense guided him through life:* native reason, good sense, good judgement, natural sagacity, basic intelligence; *Slang* horse sense.

◇ *Usage note: Common sense,* when used as an adjective meaning "practical, clear," is spelt as one word: *The country doctor was known for his commonsense approach to life.*

"Common sense in an uncommon degree is what the world calls wisdom."
—*Samuel Taylor Coleridge*

---

commotion *n. What's all the commotion about?:* hullabaloo, fuss, bustle, stir, ado, to-do; excitement, tumult, furore, uproar, turmoil, agitation, perturbation, fussing and fuming, racket, clatter.

Ant. peace, tranquillity, calm, calmness, serenity; quiet, quietness.

communal *adj. The park was communal property:* community, common, collective, mutual, joint, public.

Ant. private, personal, individual.

communicable *adj. Measles is a communicable disease:* contagious, catching, infectious, transmittable, transmissible, transferable.

Ant. uncommunicable, uncontagious.

communicate *v.* **1** *The radio stations communicated the storm warnings to the islanders:* make known, inform of, announce, apprise of, tell, notify, advise, pass on, convey, disclose, divulge, reveal, relate, bring word, proclaim, broadcast, publish, publicize; state, declare, say, mention; show, exhibit, signify. **2** *School children often communicate colds to each other:* give, transmit, impart, pass on; convey. **3** *The two friends hadn't communicated with each other for years:* exchange information, express feelings; converse, speak together, talk, correspond, write.

Ant. 1 keep secret, hush up, suppress, repress, withhold, hold back, cover up.

communication *n.* **1** *There can be no mutual understanding without communication between people:* exchanging information, expressing feelings; conversation, speaking, correspondence, writing. **2** *The latest communication from the ship indicates that the danger has passed:* notices, report, message, news, information; intelligence, communiqué; (*variously*) bulletin, directive, statement, declaration, proclamation; correspondence, letter, missive, missal, dispatch, document, note; telephone call, telegram, wire, cablegram, cable, radio message, broadcast.

communicative *adj. If he were more communicative we would know his true feelings. This letter is not very communicative:* talkative, free-spoken, unreserved, loquacious, voluble, chatty, outgoing, sociable, friendly, open, candid; informative, expressive, revelatory, revealing.

Ant. uncommunicative, untalkative, quiet, reserved, introverted, unsociable, secretive, guarded; uninformative.

communion *n.* **1** *The family took Communion at midday Mass:* Holy Communion, the Eucharist. **2** *The old couple had a perfect communion of thoughts:* sharing, harmony, concord, accord, agreement, affinity, sympathy. **3** *The gamekeeper spent the day in communion with nature:* spiritual concentration, contemplation, rapport.

Ant. 2 alienation, disunion, division, separation; disharmony, discord, disagreement.

community *n.* **1** *This is a good community in which to bring up children:* neighbourhood, district, locale, area, vicinity, quarter, residential suburb, environs; environment, surroundings. **2** *The entire community is behind the charity appeal. The scholarly community welcomed the new library:* group, social group, interest group; populace, population, citizenry, public, people, folk, society. **3** *Archaeologists and anthropologists share somewhat the same community of interest:* area, sphere, field, range, realm, scope, province, arena; sameness, similarity, likeness, affinity, agreement.

Ant. 3 difference, dissimilarity, disparity, disagreement, conflict.

compact[1] *adj.* **1** *The primitive hut was made of compact mud and branches:* compressed, pressed, tightly packed, dense, concentrated, clustered, crammed, stuffed. **2** *The flat has a compact but well-equipped kitchen:* small, little, snug, tidy.

—*v.* **3** *Try to compact the sand into the mould:* pack closely, compress, press, pack, stuff, cram.

Ant. 1 loosely packed, loose, spread-out, dispersed, scattered, sprawling. **2** spacious, rambling, roomy, large, big, huge. **3** disperse, loosen; separate.

◇ *Word origin: Compact*[1], pressed together, comes from the Latin prefix *com-* (together, with) + *pangere* (to fasten).

compact[2] *n. The two nations made a compact to preserve the peace:* agreement, pact, treaty, covenant, contract, concordat, bond; understanding, arrangement, alliance, bargain.

◇ *Word origin: Compact*[2], an agreement or contract, comes from the Latin prefix *com-* (together, with) + *pax* (peace), which also gives us *pact, peace,* and *pacific.*

companion *n.* **1** *Bad companions can lead a youth astray:* associate, friend, comrade, crony, chum, pal, buddy, mate. **2** *The doctor recommended hiring a companion for the elderly woman:* attendant, helper, assistant, escort.

Ant. 1 stranger; enemy, foe.

◇ *Word origin: Companion* and *company* come from Vulgar Latin *companio* (*com-*, with + *panis,* bread), hence someone you break bread with.

companionship *n. The lonely man longed for companionship:* friendship, friendly relations, close acquaintance, fellowship, comradeship, camaraderie, sociability, familiarity; friends, companions, company, associates, comrades, chums, pals, mates.

Ant. isolation, solitude, loneliness, insularity.

company *n.* **1** *We are having company for dinner:* guest, guests, visitor, visitors, callers. **2** *I enjoy her company. Dad didn't want any company around when he was working:* presence, companionship, friendship, fellowship, comradeship, camaraderie, society, sociability; people, friends, comrades, companions. **3** *There are advantages in working for a large company:* business concern, concern, firm, business corporation, establishment; *Slang* outfit. **4** *A large company of men gathered outside the court:* assembly, assemblage, congregation, gathering, group, band, mob, multitude, throng, bunch, party, gang.

Ant. 1 host, hostess. **2** isolation, solitude, loneliness, insularity.

◇ *Word origin:* See COMPANION.

comparable *adj. Being granted a yearly bonus can be considered comparable to getting a rise in pay. This dinner is comparable to the best French cooking:* similar, like, equal, equivalent, as good as, on a par with, roughly the same as, analogous, tantamount, commensurable, commensurate; parallel, approximate, approaching, close, a match for, in a class with, up to.

Ant. incomparable, different, unlike, dissimilar, incommensurable, incommensurate, unequal.

◇ *Spelling tip:* Does this word end in *-able* or *-ible?* Remember if you are *able* to compare something it is *comparABLE.*

◇ *Pronunciation tip: Comparable* and *incomparable* should be pronounced so that the *COM-* is stressed. Thus *COM-par-a-ble* and *in-COM-par-a-ble.*

comparative *adj. I'm a comparative newcomer:* relative, by comparison; near, approximate.

compare *v.* **1** *Compare food costs today with those of a year ago:* note the similarities of, note the differences of, contrast, balance against. **2** *Many people compared Marilyn Monroe to Jean Harlow:* liken, equate, describe as similar, draw a parallel between, correlate, relate, identify with. **3** *Tinned soup can't compare with the homemade variety:* be comparable, match, equal, compete with, approach, be as good as, bear comparison, hold a candle to, be in a class with, be on a par with, be up to.

Ant. 3 bear no comparison, be unlike, be dissimilar, be incomparable, be unequal.

◇ *Usage note:* Many people use *contrast* as a synonym of *compare.* In good usage, however, one *compares* like things, things of the same class or kind. Thus: *Compare the size of these two oranges. How does your new house compare with your old one?* One *contrasts* unlike things, things of different classes or kinds. Thus: *Contrast the size of the cherry and the water-melon. How does living in a tent contrast with living in a modern flat?*

◇ *Word origin: Compare* comes from the Latin prefix *com-* (together, with) + *par* (equal).

comparison *n.* **1** *The traveller made a comparison between the Alps and the Rocky Mountains:* comparative estimate, selective judgement, notation of similarities and differences, contrast. **2** *There was no comparison between the two voices:* similarity, likeness, resemblance, equality, analogy, relation, correlation, parallel, kinship, connection.

Ant. 2 difference, dissimilarity, inequality.

compassion *n. The nurse had great compassion for her patients:* sympathy, empathy, commiseration, feeling, fellow-feeling, pity, tenderness, tender-heartedness, heart, humanity.

Ant. apathy, unconcern, indifference, detachment, disdain; cold-heartedness, hard-heartedness.

"The wretched have no compassion."

—*Samuel Johnson*

---

compassionate *adj. The compassionate judge gave the young offender a light sentence:* sympathetic, pitying, humane, kind-hearted, kind, tender-hearted.

Ant. uncompassionate, inhumane, unfeeling, unsympathetic, unpitying, pitiless.

compatibility *n. The couple attributed their happy marriage to complete compatibility:* affinity, harmony, rapport, aggreement, accord, like-mindedness, congeniality, concord.

Ant. incompatibility, disharmony, disagreement, disaccord, discord.

compatible *adj. The two sisters couldn't live together because they weren't compatible. Giggling is not compatible with serious discussion:* in harmony, like-minded, congenial, mutually sympathetic; fitting, fit, suitable, in accord, in keeping, seemly, apt, appropriate.

Ant. incompatible, unharmonious, uncongenial; contradictory, unfitting, unsuitable, out of keeping, unseemly, inapt, inappropriate, inconsistent, counter.

compel *v. Bad health compelled him to resign from his job:* force, drive, require, necessitate, oblige, make, give no choice but.

Ant. stop, deter, thwart, hinder, prevent.

compensate *v.* **1** *The firm compensated the injured worker for the time lost:* recompense, reimburse, make restitution, pay back, repay, make up, cover, redress, redeem, make compensation, indemnify; pay, remunerate. **2** *The marvellous acting compensated for the play's weak script:* make up, offset, balance, counter-balance, make amends, excuse.

Ant. 2 emphasize, exaggerate, worsen, add insult to injury.

compensation *n. The injured man was granted £10,000 compensation:* recompense, redress, reimbursement, restitution, repayment, indemnity; benefits, settlement, satisfaction, consideration.

Ant. loss, expenditure, time and trouble.

compete *v. Professional football teams compete for the best young players:* contend, contest, vie, match strength, oppose, be rivals; match wits, fight, combat, battle, lock horns, strive against.

Ant. surrender, give up, yield.

competence *n. The young surgeon showed exceptional competence:* ability, ableness, capability, competency, proficiency, skill, expertness, mastery, expertise; *Slang* the goods, what it takes.

Ant. incompetence, inability, incapacity, inadequacy.

competent *adj. Be sure to get a competent electrician for the job:* skilled, skilful, expert, proficient, efficient; qualified, fit, experienced, trained, practised, versed, dependable, responsible, trustworthy.

Ant. incompetent, incapable, unskilled, unskilful, inexpert; unqualified, unfit, inexperienced, inadequate, undependable, irresponsible, untrustworthy.

◇ *Spelling tip:* An easy way to remember that this word ends in *-ent* is to remember that a *competENT* man can always pay his *rENT.*

competition *n.* **1** *Competition between business firms keeps prices down:* competing, rivalry, contention, opposition, struggle, conflict. **2** *Who will be the team's competition in next week's game?:* opposition, rival, opponent, contender. **3** *The figure-skating competition was judged by an international panel:* contest, event, match, tournament, tourney.

Ant. 1 co-operation, collaboration, concert, joint effort, team-work. **2** partner, helper, aider, abettor.

"Government and co-operation are in all things the laws of life; anarchy and competition the laws of death." —*John Ruskin*

competitive *adj. The city asked for competitive bids for the housing project. An athlete must have a competitive spirit:* competing, opposing, contending; fighting, combative, striving, aggressive.
Ant. co-operative, mutual, joint; non-combative, unaggressive.

competitor *n. The firm's largest competitor is going out of business. The heavyweight champion is fighting an unknown competitor:* rival, opposition, opponent, contestant, contender, fighter.
Ant. ally, partner, collaborator.

compilation *n.* **1** *The compilation of data for the report took six months:* compiling, collecting, gathering, accumulating, mustering, marshalling, garnering, assembling, aggregating, drawing together. **2** *The newspaper published a compilation of local recipes:* assemblage, group, aggregation, body; assortment, accumulation.
Ant. 1 distribution, dispersal, scattering, disbanding, dispelling, dissipation.

compile *v. Doctors compiled thousands of case histories to prove the relationship between smoking and cancer:* collect, accumulate, assemble, amass, heap up, gather, muster, marshal, bring together, draw together, garner.
Ant. distribute, disperse, scatter.
◇ *Word origin: Compile* comes from the Latin prefix *com-* (thoroughly) + the verb *pilare* (to plunder, strip). Thus *compilare* means to gather for oneself by plundering or stripping from others. The word first appeared in something akin to its modern sense as a nickname applied to the poet Virgil by an irreverent contemporary who called him *compilator*, "the plunderer," on account of his imitation of Homer and other ancient authors.

complacent *adj. Ever since he got a rise he's been too complacent to work hard:* self-assured, content, contented, self-satisfied, smug; untroubled, unbothered, at ease.
Ant. unsatisfied, insecure, discontent, discontented, troubled, uneasy, soul-searching, self-questioning.
◇ *Usage note:* Don't confuse *complacent*, pleased with or willing to accept things as they are, with *complaisant*, anxious to please. Thus, *If you weren't so complacent you could change things for the better*, but *A good servant should be complaisant but not servile.*

complain *v. The tenants complained that there was not enough hot water:* state a grievance, express dissatisfaction, find fault, criticize, carp, cavil, nag, whine; *Informal* beef, gripe, kick, grouse, grouch, grumble, bellyache.
Ant. compliment, praise, laud, commend; approve, appreciate.
◇ *Word origin: Complain* and *complaint* come from the Latin prefix *com-* (thoroughly) + *plangere* (to lament).

complaint *n.* **1** *The department store has a special section to handle customers' complaints:* grievance, dissatisfaction, criticism, faultfinding, protest, objection, tirade; *Informal* beef, gripe. **2** *Arthritis is a common complaint among the elderly:* disorder, malady, infirmity, debility, ailment, impairment, sickness, illness, disability.
Ant. 1 compliment, praise, commendation; approval, appreciation. **2** remedy, salve, balm, ointment.
◇ *Word origin:* See COMPLAIN.

complaisant *adj. The host's complaisant manner made everyone feel welcome:* obliging, solicitous, pleasing, agreeable, compliant, cordial, congenial, affable, warm, gracious, friendly, pleasant, pleasing, amiable, good-natured, good-humoured, easy-going.
Ant. unobliging, contrary, unsolicitous, unco-operative, indifferent; disagreeable, unpleasant, cold, unfriendly, ungracious.
◇ *Usage note:* See COMPLACENT.

complement *n.* **1** *Travel can be an excellent complement to one's education:* completion, consummation, rounding-off; supplement, companion. **2** *The farm was sold along with its complement of livestock:* full amount, full number, total, ensemble, aggregate; completion, whole, entirety; required number, necessary amount.
—*v.* **3** *A delicious dessert complemented the dinner:* make complete, round off, perfect, crown, cap, consummate; match, serve as a companion, supplement.
◇ *Usage note:* See COMPLIMENT.

complementary *adj. The period costume calls for a complementary hair-style:* integral, corresponding, correspondent, interrelated, compatible, companion, matched.
Ant. uncomplementary, incompatible, incongruous, inconsistent; different, diverse; contradictory.

complete *adj.* **1** *The library has a complete set of Robert Louis Stevenson's books:* entire, whole, full, unbroken, intact, undivided. **2** *Our triumph was complete:* thorough, absolute, total, utter, conclusive, perfect, consummated, fully realized, accomplished, achieved, performed, executed, carried out, settled.
—*v.* **3** *The workmen haven't completed the house yet:* make complete, make whole; finish, end, conclude, terminate, make an end of, accomplish, achieve, perform, execute, carry out, fulfil, discharge, close, settle, consummate;

Informal polish off, wrap up. **4** *A good brandy completes a fine meal:* complement, round off, perfect, crown, cap.

Ant. 1, 2 incomplete, partial. **2** inconclusive, imperfect, deficient, spoilt, marred, blemished, tainted, unfinished, unsettled, unachieved, unaccomplished, undone. **3** start, begin, commence, initiate; undo. **4** spoil, ruin, mar, taint.

completion *n.* **1** *The completion of the new road is scheduled for June:* completing, finishing; concluding, ending, closing, terminating, wind-up. **2** *The teacher retired at the completion of the school year:* conclusion, end, close, termination, finish, expiration, wind-up; fulfilment, consummation.

Ant. 1 beginning, starting, initiating, commencing. **2** start, beginning, commencement, initiation.

complex *adj.* **1** *The new manager must deal with many complex problems:* complicated, intricate, involved, difficult, perplexing, bewildering, puzzling, enigmatic; composite, compound, manifold, multiple, multifarious, variegated, mixed, tangled, knotty, perverse, labyrinthine.

—*n.* **2** *We live in a large housing complex. A new computer complex will be installed in the new year:* system, network, aggregate. **3** *Don't let him give you an inferiority complex:* subconscious idea, fixed idea, psychological feeling; obsession, preoccupation.

Ant. 1 simple, uncomplicated, easy, uninvolved, clear, obvious, unconfused.

◇ *Word origin: Complex* comes from the Latin prefix *com-* (together, with) + *plexus* (plaited). It is closely related to *complicated* and *complexion.*

"Each human being is a more complex structure than any social system to which he belongs." —*Alfred North Whitehead*

---

complexion *n.* **1** *Blondes often have fair complexions:* skin colouring, colouring, pigmentation, coloration, colour, hue, tone; skin texture. **2** *Knowing that one of the witnesses lied puts a different complexion on the case:* appearance, impression, aspect, look, outlook, guise, slant, image, countenance, character.

compliance *n. Compliance with the traffic laws is necessary for safe driving. Yes-men are known for their compliance:* conformity, conforming, obedience, yielding, giving in, submission, deference; assent, acquiescence, complaisance, pliancy, non-resistance, passivity, docility, meekness.

Ant. non-compliance, non-conformity, disobedience, resistance, rebelliousness, revolt, assertiveness, individuality, stubbornness, opposition, defiance, obstinacy.

complicate *v. Don't complicate the problem by raising new issues:* make complex, make intricate, make difficult, involve, confound, confuse, muddle, entangle, knot, snarl, ravel, tangle.

Ant. uncomplicate, simplify, clarify, unsnarl, untangle, disentangle, unknot, clear up.

complication *n. Bad flying conditions were an unexpected complication:* problem, difficulty, aggravation, disadvantage, handicap, drawback, hitch, snag, obstacle, stumbling-block, hindrance, impediment, quandary, dilemma, predicament, perplexity.

Ant. answer, solution; boon, bonus, help, aid, asset, advantage, benefit, boost.

compliment *n.* **1** *The hostess received glowing compliments on the dinner:* expression of praise, approving remark, commendation, praise, laudation, adulation, flattery, acclamation, tribute, honour, homage, congratulation. **2** **compliments.** *Please give my compliments to your parents:* regards, respects, good wishes, best wishes, best greetings, felicitations, salutations; congratulations, praise, homage; salute, toast.

—*v.* **3** *The mayor complimented the city on the good voting turn-out:* pay a compliment to, praise, pay tribute to, laud, applaud, salute, commend; speak highly of, sing the praises of, extol, exalt.

Ant. 1 insult, denunciation, condemnation, criticism, depreciation, disparagement, reproach, complaint; *Informal* beef, gripe. **3** insult, criticize, denounce, decry, disparage, condemn, censure, reprehend, reproach.

◇ *Usage note: Compliment* and *complement* look and sound so much alike that they cause problems. A *complIment* is an expression of praise or admiration: *I compliment you for good work.* On the other hand *complEment* means something that completes or perfects: *A good cup of coffee is a necessary complement to a well-cooked meal.*

complimentary *adj.* **1** *The reviews were full of complimentary remarks on the actress's performance:* commendatory, praising, praiseful, admiring, laudatory, extolling, panegyric; appreciative, congratulatory, flattering, adulatory. **2** *Each player was given four complimentary tickets to the game:* free, gratis, gratuitous, without charge.

Ant. 1 uncomplimentary, disparaging, abusive, insulting, critical, disapproving, fault-finding, carping, unflattering.

comply *v. Visitors to the factory must comply with the rules:* conform, accede, adhere, abide by, follow, obey, mind, observe, fulfil, meet, satisfy, be faithful to; surrender, submit, yield, give in, defer, acquiesce, bow, bend.

Ant. disobey, break, reject, repudiate, spurn, disregard, ignore; resist, fight, oppose.

component *adj.* **1** *Iron and carbon are two component elements of steel:* constituent, ingredient, member, composing, material, elementary, elemental.

—*n.* **2** *A component had to be replaced in the stereo system:* part, component part, constituent, member, element, ingredient, piece, item; detail, particular.

Ant. 1, 2 whole, complex, compound.

comport *v. The prisoner of war comported himself with dignity:* conduct, carry, deport, bear; behave, acquit.

compose *v.* **1** *The poet composed a new sonnet:* create, make, form, frame, shape, fashion, devise, write. **2** *The United Kingdom is composed of Great Britain and Northern Ireland:* be part of, be a portion of, make up, form, constitute, belong to. **3** *Compose yourself before answering that nasty letter:* calm, settle, collect, quiet, relax, lull, soothe, pacify, placate, quell, modulate, smooth down one's feathers.

Ant. 1 destroy, demolish, obliterate, tear up. **2** contain, include, embrace, enfold, encompass, comprise, embody. **3** excite, upset, agitate, rouse, stir up, antagonize, inflame, become nervous, fly off the handle, lose one's cool.

◇ *Usage note:* See COMPRISE.

composed *adj. The captain remained composed throughout the raging storm:* calm, serene, at ease, placid, peaceful, tranquil, sedate, quiet, quiescent, cool, cool-headed, steady, collected, poised, controlled, level-headed, even-tempered, unflappable, imperturbable, unperturbed, unagitated, undisturbed, unexcited, unruffled, untroubled, unemotional, restrained, dispassionate, undemonstrative.

Ant. hot-headed, unpoised, uncontrolled, perturbed, agitated, disturbed, anxious, upset, distraught, nervous, uneasy, ruffled, excited, stirred up, steamed up, inflamed.

composite *adj. The artist made a composite drawing of the two faces:* combined, compound, compounded, blended, mosaic.

Ant. uncombined, single, uncompounded, unmixed, unblended.

composition *n.* **1** *The orchestra played a modern composition:* work, piece, creation; concoction, production, product, exercise. **2** *The composition of the report took two months:* composing, forming, formulation, creating, creation, making, framing, shaping, fashioning, preparation, devising, compilation, organizing, organization. **3** *The composition of the painting is very graceful. The composition of brass includes copper and zinc:* structure, design, configuration, arrangement, form, organization, framework, layout; make-up, constitution, combination.

composure *n. The speaker retained his composure throughout the heckling:* poise, aplomb, calm, calmness, serenity, ease, cool, coolness, coolheadedness, self-possession, control, self-control, self-restraint, calmness, even-temperedness, self-assurance, equanimity, level-headedness, patience, dignity, unexcitability, imperturbability, unflappability.

Ant. discomposure, nervousness, uneasiness, disquiet, impatience, excitability, agitation, hot-headedness, perturbation, unrestraint, instability.

compound *adj.* **1** *Bronze is a compound metal made of copper and tin:* combined, complex, composite, conglomerate, mixed, blended.

—*n.* **2** *Water is a compound of hydrogen and oxygen:* combination, composition, composite, blend, mixture, union, fusion, amalgam, alloy, conglomeration.

—*v.* **3** *The chemist compounded several elements to form the antidote:* put together; combine, blend, mix, mingle, unite, fuse, alloy, incorporate, formulate, prepare, devise, make, concoct, fabricate, synthesize, **4** *The player compounded his mistake by arguing with the referee:* add to, augment, increase, heighten, enlarge, magnify, amplify, reinforce, boost.

Ant. 1 single, simple, pure, unmixed, unblended, uncompounded. **2** element. **3** separate, part, divide, disunite, divorce, split; isolate, segregate, sift. **4** lessen, decrease, ameliorate, palliate, mitigate, modify, minimize, moderate.

comprehend *v. The child couldn't comprehend the advanced textbook:* understand, grasp, fathom, make out, perceive, conceive, penetrate, absorb, assimilate, digest; *Informal* savvy, get.

Ant. misunderstand, mistake, misapprehend, misinterpret, misconceive, miss the point of.

> **Exploring the Word:** The Latin word *prehendere* means to grasp or seize. It gives us *comprehend,* to grasp with the mind; *apprehend,* to seize; *reprehensible,* seized in order to blame, hence deserving blame; *prison,* a place where seized persons are kept; and *prehensile,* adapted for use in grasping, as the prehensile tails of certain Latin American monkeys.

comprehension *n. The teacher had no comprehension of the boy's problems at home:* understanding, conception, grasp, perception, insight, apprehension, realization, awareness, consciousness, acquaintance.

Ant. misunderstanding, misconception, incomprehension, misapprehension, unawareness.

comprehensive *adj. The book is a comprehensive study of the 1930's:* all-inclusive, all-embracing, overall, extensive, expansive, broad, sweeping, widespread, universal, general; exhaustive, complete, thorough, full, copious, compendious.

Ant. limited, restricted, narrow, specialized, specific; exclusive, incomplete.

compress *v. Compress this clay into a small ball. Can you compress your speech into five minutes?:* press, squeeze, compact, cram, pack; condense, reduce, shrink, shorten, curtail, abbreviate, abridge.

Ant. stretch, spread, expand, enlarge, increase, lengthen.

comprise *v.* **1** *The lunch comprises sandwiches and beer. A full deck comprises 52 cards:* include, contain, be composed of, consist of, be made of. **2** *Some 20,000 persons comprised the upper-class reading public in Jane Austen's day:* constitute, make up, form, compose.

◇ *Usage note:* Ever since about 1850, people have been using *compose* and *comprise* interchangeably in the sense of "constitute, compose" (sense **2** above).

compromise *n.* **1** *A compromise was finally reached after days of arbitration:* mutual concession, accommodation, agreement, settlement, adjustment, arrangement, rapprochement; balance, happy medium; truce, compact.

—*v.* **2** *Let's compromise and each pay half the damages:* make mutual concessions, adjust differences, come to an understanding, strike a bargain, come to terms, make a deal, settle, agree, meet half-way; *Slang* split the difference. **3** *The malicious rumours compromised her reputation:* endanger, jeopardize, imperil, risk; discredit, undercut, make suspect, make vulnerable, implicate, embarrass.

Ant. 1 difference, dispute, disagreement, contention, controversy, quarrel, strife. **2** differ, disagree, dispute, contest, argue, quarrel. **3** enhance, support, boost; establish, assure, save.

◇ *Word origin: Compromise* is from Latin *compromittere*, to promise mutually.

compulsion *n. The suspect said that he signed the confession under compulsion. It took a lot of compulsion to get Dad to wear a dinner-jacket:* coercion, duress, force, pressure, domineering; obligation, necessity, requirement, demand; strong inducement, urging.

Ant. choice, free will, option.

compulsive *adj.* **1** *The pregnant woman had a compulsive desire for pickles. An organization has been formed to help compulsive gamblers:* unable to resist, uncontrollable, obsessive, fanatic, compelled, compelling, driving, driven, addicted, habitual; *Slang* hooked. **2** See COMPULSORY.

Ant. 1 non-compulsive, resistible, controllable, uncompelling; weak, wishy-washy.

compulsory *adj. The nation has compulsory education for everyone between the ages of five and sixteen:* mandatory, obligatory, required, imperative, requisite, demanded, prescriptive, binding, unavoidable; enforced, compulsive, coercive, forcible.

Ant. voluntary, optional, discretionary, non-obligatory, non-required, non-requisite, unimperative, unnecessary, non-binding.

compunction *n. The student seemed to have no compunction about cheating:* pang of conscience, qualm, demur, misgiving, anxiety, concern, unease, distress of mind, scruple.

Ant. pride, self-respect, righteousness; shamelessness.

◇ *Word origin: Compunction* is formed from the Latin prefix *com-* (thoroughly) + *pungere* (to prick or sting). *Pungere* is also the base of the words *punctual, punctuate, puncture,* and *pungent.*

compute *v. Can you compute the distance of the moon from the earth?:* add, add up, total, sum up, count up, tally; calculate, determine mathematically, reckon, ascertain, figure out, work out.

Ant. guess, suppose, conjecture, surmise, estimate, approximate, make a stab at.

◇ *Word origin: Compute* is from the Latin prefix *com-* (together, with) + *putare* (to reckon, to think), which also gives us *dispute* and *reputation.*

comrade *n. The boys have been comrades since kindergarten days:* companion, boon companion, friend, crony, confrère, intimate, pal, chum, mate, bosom friend, confidant; colleague, fellow member, associate, helpmate, co-worker, ally, partner, confederate, collaborator.

Ant. stranger; enemy, foe, antagonist.

◇ *Word origin: Comrade* comes from Spanish *comarada*, room-mate. It is ultimately derived from Latin *camera*, room, which also gives us *chamber, camera* and *bicameral* (having two chambers, as a legislative body with both a lower and an upper house).

concave *adj. His concave cheeks emphasized his thinness:* curving inward, sunken, hollow, depressed, indented.

Ant. convex, protuberant, rounded.

◇ *Word origin: Concave* comes from Latin *con-* (thoroughly) + *cavus* (hollow), which also gives us *cave* and *cavity.*

conceal *v. The robber concealed the weapon under his coat. You can't conceal the truth for ever:* hide, cover, cover up, keep out of sight, secrete, keep secret, disguise, mask, screen, cloak, camouflage.

Ant. reveal, disclose, divulge, expose, exhibit, display, show, lay bare, uncover, unmask, uncloak, unveil, flash.

◇ *Word origin: Conceal* comes from Latin *con-* (thoroughly) + *celare* (to hide).

concealment *n.* **1** *Concealment of evidence is against the law:* concealing, hiding, covering, covering up, secreting, secretion, masking, screening. **2** *The boy remained in concealment until the bully went away:* hiding, hiding-place, hide-out, cover, secret place.

Ant. 1 disclosure, developing, revealing, revelation, exposure, exhibition, displaying, display, showing, show, uncovering; leak, give away, indiscretion.

concede *v.* **1** *I concede that your request is reasonable:* grant, agree, acknowledge, be persuaded, vouchsafe, acquiesce, accept, recognize, own, allow, confess. **2** *After his queen was* *captured the chess player conceded the game to his opponent:* surrender, give up, yield, abandon, relinquish, resign, cede, hand over, deliver, tender.

Ant. 1 deny, refute, reject, repudiate, disclaim, dissent, contest, protest, contradict, controvert, debate, dispute, argue. **2** make a stand, fight to the bitter end; win, defeat, beat.

> **Exploring the Word:** Latin *cedere* means both to yield and to go. Meaning "to yield" it give us *concede, concession,* and *accede* (to yield to); *necessary,* that which can't be yielded or given up, hence, something required or essential. Meaning "to go" this same root gives us *exceed* and *excess,* to go beyond, a going beyond limits: *precede, predecessor,* and *precedent,* to go before, one who has gone before, something that has gone before and serves as a standard or guide; *proceed* and *proceeding,* to go forward, a course of going or of action; *process, procedure,* and *procession,* a method of going forward or of doing something, a parade of onward moving things; *recede, recess,* and *recession,* to go back, a going back or withdrawal for a time, a going back to a lower economic level; *succeed,* to go next, follow closely; *succession,* a series of people or things *succeeding* one another; and *success,* the happy result of getting somewhere.

conceit *n. She is good-looking but her conceit is unbearable:* vanity, pride, vainglory, self-love, self-esteem, self-importance; bragging, boastfulness.

Ant. humility, modesty; self-depreciation.

conceited *adj. The conceited actor thinks that he's better than John Barrymore:* vain, overweening, arrogant, egotistical, self-important, bigheaded, vainglorious, puffed up; boasting, bragging, strutting, smug.

Ant. humble, modest, unassuming, unaffected; self-effacing.

conceivable *adj. There is no conceivable way to raise a thousand pounds:* imaginable, thinkable, perceivable, knowable, believable, credible, supposable.

Ant. inconceivable, unthinkable, unimaginable, unbelievable, incredible.

conceive *v.* **1** *The Chamber of Commerce conceived a plan to encourage business:* think up, produce, form, create, hatch, contrive, frame, concoct, invent, dream up; initiate, originate, start. **2** *Some people couldn't conceive of living without a telephone:* imagine, envision, envisage, understand, comprehend; think of, consider.

◇ *Spelling tip: Conceive* follows the old spelling rule "*i* before *e* except after *c*."

concentrate *v.* **1** *The enemy concentrated its attack on the right flank. Please concentrate on the lesson:* focus, centre, converge, bring to bear, direct toward; give full attention to, fasten on, pay heed, consider closely, be engrossed in, put one's mind to. **2** *Many holiday resorts are concentrated in the south:* mass, amass, congregate, accumulate, assemble, gather, bunch, heap up. **3** *Concentrate the soup by boiling it:* reduce, condense, thicken.

Ant. 1 spread out, deploy, dissipate; let one's mind wander, pay no attention. **2** scatter, spread, spread out, disperse, diffuse. **3** dilute, water down, thin.

concentration *n.* **1** *Chess requires great concentration:* concentrating, close attention, fixed regard, mental application, deep thought, intentness, absorption, engrossment, diligence. **2** *There's a concentration of play-grounds in our area:* mass, cluster, assemblage, collection, accumulation, aggregation, gathering; centralization, convergence, consolidation, focus; boiling down, reduction, thickening.

Ant. 1 inattention, inattentiveness, disregard, distraction, absent-mindedness. **2** scattering, spreading out, dispersion, diffusion, divergence; dilution, thinning.

concept *n. The astronomer presented a new concept of the beginning of the universe:* idea, conception, theory, hypothesis, postulate, notion, surmise, supposition, impression, image, view; opinion, belief, conviction.

> "The trouble with Lloyd George is that he thinks in images, not in concepts."
>
> —*Viscount Haldane*

conception *n.* **1** *The conception of the plan occurred at a meeting of scientists:* conceiving, envisaging, imagining, forming, formation, concocting, devising, creating, originating; genesis, birth, invention, initiation, start, beginning, hatching, launching. **2** *The architect's conception of the building was a glass skyscraper. Have you any conception of how I feel?:* idea, image, picture, concept; perception, understanding, apprehension, notion. **3** *Conception occurred in Europe but the baby was born in America:* becoming pregnant, getting with child, fertilization, inception of pregnancy.

Ant. 1 completion, finish, ending, termination; outcome, result, issue.

concern *v.* **1** *Good government concerns every citizen:* affect, touch, bear upon, involve, be relevant to, relate to, pertain to, appertain to, apply to, interest, occupy, be one's business. **2** *Mrs Smith was most concerned about her son's health:* worry, trouble, disturb, make anxious, distress.

—*n.* **3** *Earning a living was his first concern:* business, interest, matter, affair, involvement, thing of moment; job, duty, chore, charge, mission. **4** *The teacher began to feel concern about the child's frequent absences. He showed concern for the feelings of others:* worry, anxiety, trouble, care, distress, disturbance; thoughtfulness, regard, solicitude, consideration, heed, attention. **5** *The two big banking* *concerns merged:* firm, establishment, company, corporation, business, enterprise, undertaking; shop, house.

Ant. 1 be irrelevant to, be unrelated to, be of no interest to. **4** unconcern, indifference, disregard, inattention, heedlessness, carelessness.

◇ *Word origin: Concern* comes from Latin *con-* (together) + *cernere* (to distinguish, see), hence to see completely in one's mind, to worry.

concerned *adj.* **1** *Good citizens must be concerned in civic affairs:* involved, committed, engaged, participating, active; caring, interested, solicitous, attentive. **2** *The sailor was concerned about the approaching storm:* worried, anxious, disturbed, troubled, distressed.

Ant. 1 unconcerned, indifferent, aloof, detached, uninterested; neglectful, remiss. **2** undisturbed, untroubled, carefree, without a care.

concerted *adj. The team made a concerted effort to win the game:* united, joint, co-operative, by assent; planned, predetermined, prearranged, premeditated, agreed upon.

Ant. disunited, separate, individual, unco-operative; unplanned, unpremeditated, uncontrived.

concession *n.* **1** *The lawyer's concession on that point will help your case:* admission, acknowledgement, assent, acquiescence. **2** *The union made concessions at the bargaining table:* compromise, adjustment, modification; yielding, giving in.

Ant. 1 denial, disavowal, dissent.

conciliatory *adj. One conciliatory remark would make them friends again:* peacemaking, reconciling, friendly, placatory, pacifying, mollifying, accommodative, appeasing.

Ant. antagonistic, hostile, unfriendly, unforgiving.

◇ *Word origin: Conciliatory* comes from Latin *conciliare,* to call together, which is also the basis of our word *council.*

concise *adj. Write a concise summary of the book:* terse, to the point, pithy, condensed, brief, short, abbreviated.

Ant. rambling, discursive, wordy, verbose.

conclave *n. The committee members held a conclave before the public meeting:* private meeting, secret council, private gathering; meeting, convocation, assembly, council, conference, session, convention, parley.

◇ *Word origin: Conclave* comes from Latin *con-* (together) + *clavis* (key), hence literally "locked together with a key." Latin *clavis,* key, also gives us *clavichord,* a keyboard instrument, and *clavicle,* the collar-bone, which has something of a key-like appearance and rotary motion.

conclude *v.* **1** *The pianist concluded the recital with a Chopin étude:* close, draw to a close, finish, end, complete discontinue, stop, terminate, halt, break-off, bring down the curtain on. **2** *The peace negotiations were successfully concluded:* settle, decide, resolve, arrange; effect, accomplish, bring to pass, carry out. **3** *After waiting an hour they concluded that she wasn't coming:* decide, determine, judge; deduce, reason, surmise, infer.

Ant. 1 begin, commence, start, initiate, inaugurate, open; prolong, protract, extend.

conclusion *n.* **1** *The lovers are united at the conclusion of the play:* end, finish, close, completion, wind-up, termination, finale, final part, dénouement, resolution. **2** *The company announced the conclusion of a new union contract:* arrangement, settlement, resolution, agreement, working out, completion. **3** *It was the astronomer's conclusion that the moon was never part of the earth. One conclusion of the meeting was that the club must raise its fees:* finding, determination, decision, judgement, deduction, inference, presumption; result, outcome, resolution, upshot.

Ant. 1 beginning, commencement, start, initiation, inauguration, opening.

"Conclusions are not often reached by talk any more than by private thinking."

—*Robert Louis Stevenson*

---

conclusive *adj. Fingerprints on the gun were conclusive evidence that the suspect was guilty:* decisive, determining, compelling, convincing, definite, absolute, clinching, certain, categorical; undeniable, irrefutable, incontrovertible, unquestionable, incontestable, inescapable, unanswerable, unimpeachable; clear, demonstrable, manifest, obvious, patent, palpable.

Ant. inconclusive, indecisive, unconvincing, indefinite, uncertain; deniable, refutable, doubtful, dubious, questionable, disputable, contestable, impeachable; vague, obscured, confused.

concoct *v. The cook concocted a delicious stew. He'll concoct some excuse to get out of cutting the grass:* cook up, mix, brew, compound, formulate; make up, think up, create, invent, fabricate, frame, devise, contrive, hatch.

◇ *Word origin: Concoct* comes from Latin *con-* (together) + *coquere* (to cook). Other forms of Latin *coquere,* to cook, give us *biscuit* (twice cooked), *cook,* and even *kitchen.*

concoction *n. The dessert was a concoction of bananas, custard, and breadcrumbs. The story was a fantastic concoction of lies:* mixture, brew, conglomeration, blend, compound, creation, invention, fabrication, contrivance.

concomitant *adj. His wit was a concomitant reason for his success:* attendant, accompanying, contributing, additional, related, connected, corollary, secondary, accessory, complementary, supplementary.

Ant. non-contributory, unconnected.

concord *n. Wales and England have lived in concord for many years:* peace, harmony, agreement, co-operation, mutual understanding, goodwill, cordial relations, accord; amity, friendship, amicability.
Ant. discord, conflict, strife, disagreement, dissension, contention; animosity, ill will.

concrete *n.* **1** *The path was paved with concrete:* fused stones, alloyed rocks, (*loosely*) cement; mixture of cement, sand, lime and water. —*adj.* **2** *The lawyer had concrete evidence of his client's innocence. The remark was a concrete example of his rudeness:* real, material, tangible, solid, substantial; definite, specific, explicit, express, particular.
Ant. 2 theoretical, abstract, immaterial, intangible, insubstantial; vague, indefinite, inexplicit, unspecified.
◇ *Usage note:* See CEMENT.
◇ *Word origin: Concrete* comes from Latin *con-* (together) + *crescere* (to grow), hence grown or blended together. The same root gives us *increase* and *accretion.*

concur *v. My political views concur with his. The two accounts concur in all major points:* agree, be in accord, correspond, coincide, conform, be uniform, tally, square, match, go hand in hand, go along with, hold with.
Ant. disagree, differ, diverge, be at odds.

concurrence *n.* **1** *When the two parties reach concurrence they will sign a contract:* agreement, accord, concord, harmony, unanimity, mutual consent, consensus, meeting of the minds; co-operation, collaboration, working together. **2** *The concurrence of the two events made for an exciting day:* simultaneous occurrence, happening at the same time, coincidence, correspondence, conformity, conjuncture, coexistence, synchronism.
Ant. 1 disagreement, discord, difference, divergence, disharmony.

concurrent *adj.* **1** *Our views of popular music are concurrent:* agreeing, in agreement, in accordance, of the same mind, harmonious; commensurate, consonant, correspondent, aligned; allied, congenial, sympathetic, compatible; matching, congruous, coincident. **2** *St George's Day and Shakespeare's birthday are concurrent. The concurrent political rallies caused a traffic jam:* occurring at the same time, coinciding, simultaneous, synchronous, coexisting; contemporary, contemporaneous.
Ant. 1 in disagreement, different, unsympathetic, incompatible.

condemn *v.* **1** *In 1915 women were condemned for wearing short skirts:* censure, disapprove, criticize, decry, denounce, reprehend. **2** *The thief was condemned to a year of hard labour. The refugee was condemned to a life of wandering:* sentence, doom, damn, proscribe.
Ant. 1 praise, compliment, commend, applaud, acclaim, laud, extol, condone, approve. **2** free, liberate.
◇ *Spelling tip:* Since the final *n* is not heard when this word is spoken, some people forget to add it when they spell the word. Remember the final *n: condemN.*
◇ *Word origin: Condemn* comes from Latin *con-* (thoroughly) + *damnare* (to condemn, punish), which also gives us *damn, damage,* and *indemnity,* freedom from punishment.

condemnation *n.* **1** *Cheating deserves our harshest condemnation:* censure, disapproval, criticism, reprehension, reproach, reproof, rebuke, denunciation, disapprobation. **2** *The jury's condemnation was a shock to the suspect:* pronouncement of guilt, conviction, judgement; punishment, sentence.
Ant. 1 praise, compliment, commendation, approval, acclaim, lauding, extolling. **2** acquittal, exoneration, exculpation, reprieve, vindication, clearance.

condensation *n. The magazine published a condensation of the new novel:* abridgement, condensed version, digest, shortened form.

condense *v.* **1** *Moisture in the atmosphere condensed into dew during the night:* liquefy, precipitate. **2** *The editors condensed the manuscript to half its original length:* abridge, digest, shorten, abbreviate, reduce, cut, trim, pare down, boil down, blue-pencil. **3** *Condense the mixture by boiling down some of the liquid:* thicken, concentrate, reduce, boil down; compress, compact, consolidate, contract.
Ant. 1 evaporate, vaporize. **2** expand, lengthen, enlarge, increase, pad, round out. **3** dilute, water down; amplify.
◇ *Word origin: Condense* comes from Latin *con-* (together) + *densus* (crowded, close), which also gives us *dense.*

condescend *v.* **1** *The director condescended to take advice from the stage-hand:* humble oneself, lower oneself, deign, stoop, submit, descend, *Informal* unbend, come down a peg, come down off one's high horse. **2** *Don't condescend to me!:* patronize, talk down to, look down on, treat with disdain, *Informal* get on one's high horse with.
Ant. 1 scorn, spurn, disdain. **2** accept, treat as an equal, respect.
◇ *Usage note: Condescend* and its related word, *condescension,* are used in two almost opposite senses. The first sense implies an actual lowering or descending to another person's level; the second implies looking or talking down in a patronizing way from a lofty perch.

condescending *adj. I dislike his condescending manner towards his employees:* patronizing, superior, disdainful, overbearing, *Informal* high-hat.

condescension *n.* **1** *I admire the king's condescension towards his subjects:* assumption of equality, self-effacement, humbleness, humility, modesty, self-abasement, graciousness, deference. **2** *The duke's condescension infuriates me:*

haughtiness, loftiness, disdain, hauteur, patronizing attitude, *Informal* high-and-mighty attitude, airs.

Ant. 1 arrogance, haughtiness, superiority, pride.

condition *n.* **1** *The business is in good financial condition:* state, situation, circumstances, state of affairs, shape, standing, position, status. **2** *The doctor says his condition is better. She has a heart condition:* state of health, state, physical fitness, shape, fettle; ailment, malfunction, malady, complaint, problem. **3** *What are the conditions of the contract? We agreed to rent the house on condition that the roof be repaired:* term, provision, proviso, stipulation, demand, arrangement, agreement; prerequisite, requisite, contingency; qualification, restriction, limitation, reservation.

—*v.* **4** *Practice had conditioned her for skiing:* prepare, ready, equip, fit, put in shape, tone up, accustom, make used to.

Ant. 4 disqualify, incapacitate; unaccustom.

"To be a poet is a condition rather than a profession." —*Robert Graves*

---

conditional *adj. The warring nations agreed to a conditional truce:* provisional, tentative, with reservations, qualified, limited, restricted, contingent.

Ant. unconditional, absolute, unlimited, unrestricted, categorical.

condolence *n. The widow received many letters of condolence:* sympathy, commiseration, solace, compassion, consolation, pity.

Ant. congratulation, felicitation.

◇ *Word origin: Condolence* comes from Latin *con-* (together, with) + *dolere* (to feel pain, grieve), which also gives us *doleful* and *indolent.*

condone *v. Parents must not condone their children's bad behaviour:* overlook, let pass, ignore, disregard, put up with, wink at; forgive, forget.

Ant. condemn, denounce, censure, disapprove; punish, castigate.

◇ *Word origin: Condone* comes from the Latin prefix *con-* (altogether) + *donare* (to give), hence to be generous in overlooking an offence. (The Latin word *condonare,* to overlook and forgive, is a specialized term in canon law — the law of the Roman Catholic Church — where it means to forgive one's spouse for a breach of marital duties, such as adultery, on condition that the offence will not be repeated.) The stem of the same Latin word, *don-,* give, also gives us *donate* and *donor.*

conducive *adj. Exercise is conducive to good health:* contributive, contributory, favourable, instrumental, calculated to produce, helpful in bringing about, helpful, promotive, beneficial; salutary.

Ant. harmful, hurtful, deleterious, damaging.

conduct *n.* **1** *The student's conduct in class was disruptive:* behaviour, comportment, deportment, ways, manner, action, deeds. **2** *His conduct of the business was very successful:* management, administration, direction, guidance, supervision, leadership, government, generalship.

—*v.* **3** *The mayor conducted the visitors through town. He should learn how to conduct a meeting:* guide, lead, escort, usher, convey, convoy, pilot, steer, attend, accompany; preside over, chair. **4** *The children conducted themselves well at the party:* behave, comport, act, carry, bear. **5** *The eldest son conducts the family's business affairs:* manage, administer, direct, guide, regulate, rule, govern, superintend, supervise; perform, transact, carry on, carry out, discharge, dispatch, execute, operate, enact, look after.

Ant. 3 follow, trail.

conduit *n. The water flows through this underground conduit:* main, pipe, duct, tube, canal, channel, passage; (*variously*) watercourse, aqueduct, sewer, gutter, trough, drain.

◇ *Pronunciation tip: Conduit* is pronounced either as *CONduit* or *CUNdit.*

confederacy *n. The Spanish seaports formed a confederacy against pirates:* alliance, league, coalition, association, federation, union, combine, fusion; guild, society, band, syndicate.

◇ *Word origin: Confederacy* and *confederate* come from Latin *con-* (together) + *foedus* (league), hence joined in a league. Latin *foedus,* league, also gives us *federal* and *federation.* It is cognate with *fides,* faith.

confederate *n. Darbyshire was Jennings' confederate in various pranks:* ally, colleague, partner, associate, collaborator, co-worker, fellow-conspirator, accessory, helper, abettor, cooperator, comrade, companion, right-hand man, helping hand.

Ant. opponent, rival, enemy, foe.

◇ *Word origin:* See CONFEDERACY.

confederation *n. The United Nations is a confederation of many countries:* league, association, alliance, coalition, federation, union, combine, fusion; society, band, guild, syndicate.

confer *v.* **1** *Diplomas were conferred on members of the graduating class:* present to, bestow upon, award, accord, give. **2** *The two lawyers conferred on the best way to handle the case:* consult, discuss, hold a conference, deliberate together, parley, talk together, converse, compare notes, palaver.

Ant. 1 withdraw, take away; withhold, deny.

conference *n. The teacher had a conference with each student during the term. The annual conference of botanists will be held in Oslo this year:* discussion, talk, consultation, deliberation, parley; meeting, convention, symposium, conclave, council.

confess *v. The murderer confessed his crime to the*

police. He confessed his love to the girl: admit, acknowledge, reveal, disclose, divulge, make known, bring to light, expose, lay bare, declare, avow, blurt out, make a clean breast of, unbosom one's self, own up, *Slang* come clean, sing.

Ant. disavow, repudiate, disown; deny, hide, conceal, cover; remain silent, keep mum, button one's lips.

confession *n.* **1** *The thief's confession of guilt closed the case:* admission, acknowledgement, revelation, disclosure, divulgence, declaration, avowal. **2** *He made his confession at St. Patrick's:* priestly confession, confessional, acknowledgement of one's sins, *Archaic* shrift.

Ant. 1 denial, disavowal, refutation, concealment, hiding.

confidant, confidante (*fem.*) *n. She is my confidante in all matters:* intimate, friend, trusty companion, crony, bosom friend.

◇ *Usage note:* A *confidant* is a person to whom one confides personal thoughts and feelings; *confident* means assured.

◇ *Word origin: Confidant* was originally a French word which first occurred in English in 1714. It was first used exclusively of someone entrusted with the secrets of another's love affairs, but is now used more widely.

confide *v. Did she confide her plans to you?:* tell secretly, tell privately, reveal, disclose, make known, impart, divulge, let know, let in on; confess, lay bare, unbosom one's self.

Ant. keep one's own counsel, keep secret, remain silent, keep mum, button one's lips; deny, repudiate.

confidence *n.* **1** *The bank manager has complete confidence in the cashiers:* trust, faith, conviction, belief, reliance, credence. **2** *He would be a good pianist if he had more confidence:* self-confidence, self-assurance, faith in oneself, certainty, certitude; self-reliance, courage, intrepidity, mettle, spirit, nerve, boldness, daring, audacity; *Informal* spunk, pluck, grit, *Slang* guts. **3** *The old friends exchanged confidences:* secret, intimacy, private matter, confidential matter, inside information.

Ant. 1 distrust, mistrust, doubt, misgiving, apprehension, disbelief. **2** self-doubt, uncertainty, timidity, bashfulness, shyness.

◇ *Usage note:* See TRUST.

"..., confidence is a plant of slow growth in an aged bosom..." — *William Pitt*

---

confident *adj.* **1** *The team is confident that it will win the game:* convinced, certain, sure, positive, secure, assured, optimistic, expectant. **2** *A champion bridge player must be very confident:* self-confident, self-assured, sure of oneself, self-reliant, intrepid, dauntless, daring, bold.

Ant. 1 unconfident, uncertain, unsure, distrustful, dubious, doubtful, apprehensive, fearful, pessimistic. **2** self-doubting, unsure, insecure, hesitant, nervous, jittery.

◇ *Spelling tip:* a good way to remember the -ENT at the end of this word is to remember that a landlord must be *confidENT* that you are going to pay the *rENT*.

◇ *Usage note:* See CONFIDANT.

confidential *adj. Please lock up these confidential reports:* secret, private, not to be disclosed, privy, undisclosed, off-the-record, top-secret, *Informal* hush-hush.

Ant. public, open; published, publicized.

confidentially *adv. She told me the news confidentially:* in strict confidence, in secret, secretly, privately, behind closed doors, between ourselves, sub rosa, between you and me.

Ant. openly, publicly.

confine *v.* **1** *Please confine your remarks to the topic under discussion:* limit, restrict, restrain, keep, regulate, govern. **2** *The prisoner was confined in a fenced enclosure because he was thought to be dangerous:* keep in, shut in, shut up, coop up, hold, fence in, cage, pen, tie; imprison, gaol, incarcerate, hold in custody, lock up, impound.

Ant. 1 extend, expand, amplify. **2** release, free, liberate, loose, let out.

confinement *n.* **1** *Expectant mothers used to spend a long time in confinement:* lying in, accouchement, childbirth. **2** *The unruly prisoner was put in solitary confinement:* detention, constraint, custody, shutting in, cooping up, imprisonment, incarceration, restriction, limitation, restraint, circumscription.

Ant. 2 release, freeing, liberation.

confines *n. pl. The lost sheep must be somewhere within the confines of this farm:* limits, border, bounds, boundaries, edge, circumference.

confirm *v.* **1** *The witnesses' testimony confirmed the suspect's story:* corroborate, bear out, uphold, sustain, verify, validate, substantiate, authenticate, establish, prove, clinch. **2** *The hotel confirmed our reservations by telegram:* acknowledge, agree to, approve, accept; make firm, make certain, make binding; validate, authorize, certify, ratify.

Ant. 1 contradict, refute, repudiate, deny, disavow, disprove, impugn, contravene, controvert. **2** cancel, reject, refuse; annul, abrogate, repeal.

confirmation *n.* **1** *The newspaper received confirmation of the story:* substantiation, verification, corroboration, authentication, validation, proof. **2** *The executive committee's choice of location requires confirmation by a majority of club members:* acceptance, approval, endorsement, ratification, sanction; assent, accord, accordance, agreement.

Ant. 1 denial, repudiation, refutation, contradiction, disavowal, recantation. **2** rejection, refusal, disapproval, cancellation, annulment.

confirmed *adj.* **1** *Confirmed reports from the front tell of a great victory by our infantry, supported by tanks:* corroborated, substantiated, authenticated, verified, proven true, validated, established. **2** *My brother is a confirmed bachelor:* established, inveterate, ingrained, chronic, set, fixed, dyed-in-the-wool, deep-seated, deep-rooted, hardened.
Ant. 1 unconfirmed, unsubstantiated, unverified, unproven; contradicted, refuted, repudiated, denied. **2** temporary, sometimes, occasional, off-and-on, now-and-then.

confiscate *v. The customs officer confiscated the smuggled goods:* seize, commandeer, appropriate, pre-empt, take, take over, impound, expropriate.
Ant. release, return, restore.
◇ *Word origin: Confiscate* comes from the Latin prefix *con-* (together) + *fiscus* (purse, chest, treasury), hence literally "to force someone to put his property in a common treasury." Latin *fiscus* also gives us *fiscal.*

conflict *v.* **1** *Our political views conflict:* disagree, oppose, be contrary, clash, collide, be inharmonious, be contradictory.
—*n.* **2** *Nations must not settle their differences by armed conflict:* fight, combat, battle, struggle, clash, warfare, hostility, encounter, action, skirmish, engagement, fray, scuffle, mêlée, set-to, fracas, tussle. **3** *The conflict between the brothers' political views caused a row:* disagreement, difference, discord, division, dissent, dissension; antagonism, friction, strife.
Ant. 1 agree, harmonize, coincide, reconcile. **2** peace truce, treaty. **3** agreement, harmony, accord, concord.
◇ *Word origin: Conflict* comes from Latin *con-* (together) + *fligere* (to strike).

conform *v.* **1** *All students must conform to the rules:* follow, comply with, obey, submit to, be guided by, adhere to, fall in with, act in agreement with. **2** *The dressmaker made the dress conform to the pattern. He conformed the plans to the new specifications:* correspond, agree with, tally with, square with, fit, dovetail; reconcile, adjust, adapt.
Ant. 1 disobey, oppose, diverge, differ. **2** differ, be dissimilar.

"I would to God they would either conform, or be more wise, and not be catched."

—*Samuel Pepys*

---

conformation *n. The horse had the conformation of a thoroughbred:* form, shape, formation, configuration, structure, framework, arrangement, anatomy.

conformity *n. Every man must live in conformity with his own beliefs:* agreement, harmony, accord, compliance, observance, acquiescence, assent, obedience, submission, likeness, uniformity, resemblance, correspondence, similarity.
Ant. disagreement, disharmony, discord, disobedience, opposition, rebellion; difference, dissimilitude, divergence.

confound *v. The patient's unusual symptoms confounded the doctor:* perplex, confuse, baffle, bewilder, puzzle, mystify, mix up, disconcert, unsettle, nonplus, rattle, fluster, throw off the scent; amaze, astound, astonish, surprise, startle, dumbfound, strike with wonder.
Ant. enlighten, explain, solve, clear up, clarify.

confront *v. We must confront the future with optimism. The boy confronted his accuser and denied the charges:* face, face up to, meet, encounter, cope with; withstand, challenge, dare, brave, defy, throw down the gauntlet.
Ant. avoid, evade, flee, turn tail; surrender to, yield to.
◇ *Word origin: Confront* comes from the Latin prefix *con-* (together) + *frons* (face, forehead). This Latin word *frons* also gives us *front, frontier, affront,* and *effrontery.*

confuse *v.* **1** *The road signs confused the driver:* perplex, bewilder, baffle, puzzle, mystify, fluster, rattle, muddle, addle, befuddle, mix up, confound, disconcert, unsettle, nonplus, discompose. **2** *You confused me with my twin brother. This new clue confuses the case against him:* mix up, mistake; confound, make perplexing, make baffling, make unclear, muddle, befog, throw into disorder.
Ant. 1 enlighten. **2** differentiate, untangle; explain, solve, clarify, clear up.

confusion *n.* **1** *Imagine our confusion when we found that the invitation was for the following week:* bewilderment, stupefaction, bafflement, perplexity, puzzlement, mystification; disconcertion, discomposure, abashment. **2** *The room was in a state of confusion. The painting was a confusion of colours:* chaos, disorder, disarrangement, disarray, disorganization, untidiness, shambles, upheaval, mess; muddle, clutter, jumble, hodgepodge, tangle, snarl-up; riot, tumult, madhouse, turmoil, pandemonium, hullabaloo, hubbub, commotion, ferment, disturbance, bedlam, uproar.
Ant. 1 enlightenment, explanation, solution, clarification; composure, calm. **2** organization, order, orderliness, arrangement, tidiness, neatness.

congeal *v. The gelatin will congeal quickly in the refrigerator:* harden, set, stiffen, solidify, thicken, curdle, clot, coagulate, jell, gelatinize; freeze.
Ant. dissolve, soften, melt, thaw.
◇ *Word origin: Congeal* comes from Latin *con-* (together) + *gelare* (to freeze), which also gives us *gelatin* and *jelly.*

congenial *adj.* **1** *The two friends had congenial tastes:* similar, compatible, kindred, harmonious, well-suited, consistent, like, agreeing, related, sympathetic, corresponding. **2**

The girl has a warm, congenial disposition: agreeable, pleasing, pleasant, gracious, affable, genial, cordial, companionable, social, sociable, convivial.

Ant. 1 dissimilar, different, incompatible, opposite, unrelated, unlike. **2** disagreeable, displeasing, unpleasant, ungracious.

congenital *adj. Left-handedness is a congenital trait:* innate, inherent, inborn, inbred, hereditary, inherited, ingrained; natural, native.

Ant. acquired, assumed, learned.

◇ *Usage note: Congenital* means at, with, or during birth, having occurred before or during birth: *Birthmarks are congenital. If a pregnant woman doesn't take care of herself she can give her baby congenital defects. Hereditary* refers only to those characteristics inherited from one's parents at the time of conception: *Haemophilia is hereditary, Red hair is a hereditary characteristic of George's family.*

congested *adj. The roads are becoming more and more congested:* crowded, overcrowded, filled, packed, jammed, gorged, saturated.

Ant. uncongested, empty, uncrowded, free.

congestion *n. The congestion at the beach at week-ends is unbelievable:* crowding, overcrowding, jam, mass, mob, pile-up, obstruction, bottle-neck, snarl-up.

Ant. uncrowding, emptiness, desertedness.

conglomeration *n. The stew was a conglomeration of fish, potatoes, and left-over vegetables:* mixture, collection, combination, aggregate, aggregation, agglomeration; jumble, mishmash.

◇ *Word origin: Conglomeration* comes from Latin *con-* (together) + *glomus* (ball). (*Glomus* is related to *globus*, globe.)

congratulate *v. I congratulate you on your 20th anniversary:* give one's best wishes, wish one joy, salute, felicitate, hail, compliment, rejoice with, wish many happy returns of the day, applaud.

Ant. rebuke, reprove, censure, condemn, criticize, reprehend.

congratulations *n. pl. Let's telegraph our congratulations to the new parents:* best wishes, good wishes, greetings, well-wishing, salute, felicitations, many happy returns of the day.

Ant. rebuke, reproof, censure, condemnation, criticism, reprehension.

congregate *v. A crowd congregated round the soap-box orator:* assemble, gather, collect, cluster, come together, crowd together, mass, amass, throng, flock.

Ant. disperse, scatter, separate, part.

◇ *Word origin: Congregate* and *congregation* come from Latin *con-* (together) + *grex* (flock). Latin *grex*, flock, is also the basis of *aggregate* and *gregarious.*

congregation *n.* **1** *The guru spoke before a large congregation:* audience, assembly, gathering, crowd, group, throng, multitude, horde, flock. **2** *The congregation welcomed its new minister:* church membership, religious assembly, parishioners, parish, brethren, laity.

◇ *Word origin:* See CONGREGATE.

◇ *Usage note:* Whilst the verb *congregate* is typically used with secular connotations, the noun *congregation* almost always denotes a group who have assembled for purposes of religious instruction.

congress *n.* **1** *A congress of heart specialists is meeting in Paris:* conference, convention, assembly, council, gathering, discussion group; delegates, representatives. **2** *American;* usually **Congress**. *The United States Congress handles over 200 bills a session:* Parliament, legislature, legislative body, national council, federal council; (*variously*) Chamber of Deputies, diet.

conjecture *n.* **1** *Do you know for sure or is it only conjecture?:* guesswork, supposition, inference, deduction, surmise, guess, view, judgement, speculation, suspicion, opinion, notion, idea, theory, hypothesis, assumption, augury, *Informal* shot in the dark.

—*v.* **2** *The old man conjectured that it would be an unusually cold winter:* guess, suppose, think, calculate, reckon, surmise, theorize, imagine, infer, forecast, speculate, hypothesize, presume, presuppose, judge, fancy.

Ant. 1 fact, surety, certainty. **2** know.

conjugal *adj. There is a vast difference between infatuation and conjugal love:* marital, wedded, married, matrimonial, nuptial, connubial.

Ant. single, unmarried, unwedded.

conjunction *n. The conjunction of heavy rains and high winds caused flooding:* combination, union, joining, meeting, association, concurrence.

conjure *v. Witches are supposed to be able to conjure up the Devil:* call forth, make appear, raise, command, invoke; call away, make disappear, allay; practise sorcery, bewitch, charm, enchant, cast a spell.

connect *v.* **1** *Please connect the two wires:* join, attach, unite, fasten together; couple, tie, combine, merge. **2** *A good student must connect what he reads with what he sees around him:* associate, relate, compare, correlate, combine,

Ant. 1 disconnect, detach, unfasten, disjoin, sunder, separate, divide, part. **2** dissociate, separate.

◇ *Word origin: Connect* and *connection* come from Latin *con-* (together) + *nectere* (to bind).

connection *n.* **1** *The connection between the throttle and the carburettor is broken:* coupling, coupler, fastening, link, linkage, connector, attachment, tie, junction. **2** *There is no connection between the two incidents:* relation, relationship, interrelation, association, correlation, affinity, attachment, alliance. **3** *They have connections somewhere in Devon. He's just a business connection:* relative, relation, family, kin, kinfolk, kinsfolk, kinsman, kith and kin, flesh

and blood; friend, associate, acquaintance, contact.
Ant. 1 disconnection, detachment. **2** detachment, dissociation. **3** stranger.
◇ *Word origin:* See CONNECT.
connive *v. The two gangs connived in the smuggling of goods:* conspire, plan, plot, co-operate secretly, participate surreptitiously, collude, be a party to, be accessory to, be in collusion with, lend oneself to, aid, abet; allow, shut one's eyes to, wink at.
Ant. have no part, be innocent of, deter, resist; censure, deplore, condemn, expose.
◇ *Word origin: Connive* literally means to shut one's eyes to wrongdoing. It comes from Latin *conivere*, to wink, shut the eye.
connoisseur *n. The old gentleman was a connoisseur of fine wines:* expert, judge, authority, man of good taste, cognoscente; epicure, gourmet.
◇ *Spelling tip:* If you're a *connoisseur* you may know *twice* as much as anyone else. Thus, two *n*'s and two *s*'s: *coNNoiSSeur.*
◇ *Word origin: Connoisseur* comes ultimately from Latin *cognoscere*, to know, understand. The same Latin verb gives us *recognize*, to know again, and *incognito*, unknown.
connotation *n. The word "winter" has the connotation of ice skating and skiing. His speech wasn't openly contemptuous, but its connotations were insulting:* suggested meaning, suggestion, implication, undertone, insinuation, colouring, intimation, spirit, drift, evocation.
Ant. denotation, basic meaning, literal meaning.
◇ *Usage note:* When referring to words many people confuse *denotation* and *connotation. Denotation* is the actual, specific meaning of a word, the physical aspect or basic concept: *The denotation of "car" is a four-wheeled, self-propelled vehicle. Connotation* is what a word or object suggests or implies: *The connotations of "car" include speed, convenience, and travel.*
connubial *adj. The couple celebrated their tenth anniversary of connubial bliss:* conjugal, wedded, married, marital, matrimonial, nuptial.
Ant. single, unmarried, unwedded.

"The conquered almost always conquer."
—*G. K. Chesterton*

---

conquer *v.* **1** *The Allies conquered Germany in World War II:* defeat, vanquish, win over, overcome, overpower, triumph over, prevail over, beat, whip, thrash, drub, trim, rout, lick, best, floor, subjugate, humble; occupy, possess, rule. **2** *You must conquer your fear of heights:* overcome, surmount, master, prevail over, get the better of, get the upper hand over, quell.
Ant. 1 be defeated, be beaten, lose, surrender, capitulate, give up, bow to. **2** give in to, yield to, surrender to.
conqueror *n. The conqueror marched into the defeated country:* victor, vanquisher, subjugator, subduer, winner; champion.
Ant. conquered, conquest, defeated, vanquished, subjugated, loser.
◇ *Spelling tip:* One who conquers is a *conquerOR.* Remember, the word ends in *-or* not *-er.*
conquest *n.* **1** *Faith will help in your conquest of fear:* conquering, defeat, vanquishment, mastery, overcoming, victory, triumph, winning, ascendancy, subjugation, dominion, upper hand, sway, whip hand. **2** *In World War II one of Japan's aims was the conquest of China. Her beauty won her many conquests:* captured territory, captive, acquisition; adherents, follower, fan, lover, adorer.
Ant. 1 failure, surrender, submission, loss.
conscience *n. George Washington's conscience would not let him lie:* moral sense, sense of right and wrong, ethical feelings.
◇ *Spelling tip: Conscience* is a spelling demon to some people. Remember, it is spelt with *science* at the end, *con-SCIENCE.*
◇ *Word origin:* Both *conscience* and *consciousness* come from Latin *conscire*, to know inwardly. *Conscience* is an inward knowing of right and wrong, *consciousness* an inward alertness or awareness. Latin *conscire*, to know inwardly, is itself based on Latin *scire*, to know, which also gives us our word *science.*
conscientious *adj. A conscientious worker arrives on time and leaves no mess behind him:* high-principled, dutiful, scrupulous, responsible, honest, ethical, trustworthy; painstaking, careful, exact, particular, meticulous.
Ant. unconscientious, unscrupulous, unreliable, untrustworthy; careless, neglectful, remiss, negligent, heedless, thoughtless, slack, lax, feckless, irresponsible.
conscious *adj.* **1** *Is the patient conscious yet?:* able to feel and think, sentient, sensible, aware. **2** *Were you conscious of his hostility?:* aware, cognizant, discerning, knowledgeable, perceiving, noticing, observing, apperceptive, awake to, alert to, alive to, in the know. **3** *His rudeness was conscious, not accidental:* deliberate, calculated, studied, premeditated.
Ant. 1–3 unconscious. **2** unaware, ignorant, insensible, oblivious.
◇ *Word origin:* See CONSCIENCE.
consciousness *n.* **1** *The accident victim never lost consciousness:* awareness, sensibility, mental activity. **2** *That people on the other side of the world are starving never entered his consciousness:* awareness, cognizance, perception, mind, thoughts, senses, feelings, discernment.
Ant. 1 unconsciousness; unawareness, insensibility.
consecrate *v. The shrine was consecrated by the Church:* declare sacred, make sacred, sanctify, hallow, bless, glorify, immortalize.
Ant. desecrate, profane, defile.

◇ *Word origin: Consecrate* comes from Latin *con-* (thoroughly) + *sacrare* (to treat as sacred, make holy), which also gives us *desecrate* and *sacred.*

consecutive *adj. The amazing gymnast performed innumerable consecutive somersaults:* successive, following one another, progressive, sequential, serial, continuous, uninterrupted, unbroken, in turn.

Ant. non-consecutive, random, haphazard, hit-or-miss, disordered.

consensus *n. The consensus of the voters was to defeat the referendum. A large group will seldom reach a consensus:* general agreement, majority opinion, general opinion; common consent, unanimity, concord, accord, concurrence.

Ant. minority opinion; disagreement, discord, difference.

◇ *Usage note:* The expression *consensus of opinion* is widely used. However, since *consensus* by itself means a general opinion, the longer expression is redundant. Try to use *consensus* by itself, leaving off the "of opinion."

consent *v.* **1** *The firm will consent to your taking leave of absence:* agree, concur, assent, approve, accept, accede, acquiesce, concede; yield, submit, fall in with, permit, allow, sanction, confirm, ratify, endorse.

—*n.* **2** *Roland had to obtain the consent of Mary's father before they could get married:* agreement, concurrence, assent, approval, acceptance, willingness, permission, sanction, confirmation, ratification, endorsement, accord, concord, acquiescence.

Ant. 1 dissent, refuse, disallow, decline, resist, balk, demur, disagree, disapprove. **2** refusal, non-acceptance, unwillingness, disapproval, dissent, disagreement.

consequence *n.* **1** *As a consequence of his laziness, he was fired:* result, outcome, development, upshot, outgrowth, issue, aftermath, end, sequel, fruit. **2** *An event of great consequence took place in 1914:* importance, import, significance, note, moment, magnitude, distinction, prominence, notability, seriousness, gravity, influence, avail, worth, value, account, usefulness.

Ant. 1 prelude, source, root, cause, determinant, reason. **2** insignificance, unimportance, paltriness, triviality.

conservation *n. The world will run out of oil unless it practises conservation:* preservation, husbandry, care, careful use, protection, maintenance, upkeep.

Ant. waste, destruction, decay, loss, neglect.

conservative *adj.* **1** *Lord Tweedsmuir reflected the conservative views of his day. The professor is a radical in politics but a conservative dresser:* non-liberal, unprogressive, right-wing, reactionary; established, cautious, moderate, undaring, quiet, middle-of-the-road.

—*n.* **2** *Usually* **Conservatives.** *The Conservatives voted against building the new road:* opponent of change, champion of the status quo, middle-of-the-roader, moderate, right-winger, reactionary.

Ant. 1 radical, liberal, progressive; innovative, imaginative, speculative, faddish. **2** radical, innovator, changer, progressive.

conservatoire *n. The pianist is a graduate of the Swiss Conservatoire:* music school, art school, academy.

conservatory *n. Orchids grow all the year round in the conservatory:* greenhouse, hot-house, nursery, glasshouse.

conserve *v. The public must conserve electricity to prevent black-outs:* preserve, save, use less, use sparingly, not waste, cut back on; maintain, care for, safeguard, guard.

Ant. waste, squander.

◇ *Word origin: Conserve* comes from Latin *con-* (thoroughly) + *servare* (to keep, save). It is closely related to *save* and *serve.*

consider *v.* **1** *Consider the consequences before deciding:* think about, reflect on, envisage, contemplate, regard, weigh, appraise, gauge, examine, review, mull over, ponder, turn over in one's mind, study, cogitate on, deliberate on, bear in mind, be aware of, pay heed; respect, honour, make allowances for. **2** *The critics considered the play excellent:* regard, hold to be, judge, deem, think, believe, hold, opine.

Ant. 1 ignore, neglect, overlook, disregard.

◇ *Usage note:* Good writers do not use *consider as* when *consider* alone will do. Thus, *I consider him as a good doctor* should be simply *I consider him a good doctor.*

◇ *Word origin: Consider* was originally an astrological term meaning to deliberate on the positions of the stars and planets. It comes from Latin *con-* (thoroughly) + *sidus* (star).

"Consider the lilies of the field, how they grow; they toil not, neither do they spin."

—*Matthew 6: 28*

---

considerable *adj. Just reading 'War and Peace' to the end is a considerable achievement:* sizeable, substantial, large, great, goodly, tidy, of some size, ample, not small, a good deal of; of some importance, significant, notable, noticeable; estimable, noteworthy, remarkable, impressive.

Ant. insubstantial, meagre, small, insignificant; ordinary, average, unimportant, workaday, unremarkable.

◇ *Spelling tip: Considerable* ends in *-able,* not "-ible." Remember this: *ConsiderAble* means *lArge.*

considerably *adv. Losing 30 pounds changed her appearance considerably:* substantially, significantly, noticeably, notably, sizeably, largely, greatly, amply, abundantly, remarkably, estimably.

Ant. minimally, unnoticeably, insignificantly, little.

considerate *adj. It was very considerate of you to send me a get-well card:* thoughtful, kind, kindly, solicitous, attentive, concerned, obliging, mindful.

Ant. inconsiderate, thoughtless, oblivious, heedless, selfish.

consideration *n.* **1** *Please give this suggestion serious consideration:* thought, regard, attention, concern, heed, notice, deliberation, contemplation, meditation, cogitation, reflection, study, review, examination. **2** *Consideration for others is the basis of good manners:* thoughtfulness, regard, considerateness, respect, solicitude, tact, honour, kindliness. **3** *Cost is a major consideration in buying a new car:* factor, point, concern, interest; inducement, motive, reason, cause, ground. **4** *I'll do the job for you, if you like — but for a consideration:* reward, recompense, remuneration, fee, tip, compensation, requital, reparation.

Ant. 1 disregard, inattention. **2** thoughtlessness, heedlessness, selfishness.

consign *v. The father consigned his property to his eldest son:* hand over, transfer, deliver, entrust, commit, deposit with, convey, remit, remand, assign, relegate, delegate, commend to.

Ant. receive; keep, retain, withhold.

consignment *n.* **1** *The consignment of the property to the new owners will take place tomorrow:* transfer, delivery, committing, depositing, assignment, handing over, consigning, entrusting, relegation, delegation, committing. **2** *The consignment of merchandise arrived on time:* shipment, goods shipped, goods for sale, goods sent on approval.

Ant. 1 reception, receiving; keeping, retention, storage.

consist *v.* **1** *This fudge consists largely of chocolate and sugar:* be composed of, be made up of, comprise, contain, include. **2** *Happiness consists in appreciating what you have:* lie, be found in, reside.

◇ *Word origin: Consist* comes from Latin *con-* (together) + the verb *sistere* (to stand).

consistency, consistence *n.* **1** *This sauce has a thin consistency:* texture, viscosity, density, thickness, firmness, stiffness, compactness; body, composition, construction, structure, make-up. **2** *A good batsman must prove his consistency throughout the season:* constant performance, undeviating behaviour, steady effort, uniform standards, persistence; steadfastness, faithfulness. **3** *There is no consistency in the furniture styles in this room:* harmony, congruity, agreement, accordance, coherence, correspondence, correction, compatibility.

Ant. 2 inconsistency, erratic behaviour, volatility. **3** inconsistency, disharmony, incongruity, disagreement, discordance, incompatibility.

◇ *Usage note: Consistence* means exactly the same thing as *consistency*, but in general use *consistency* occurs much more frequently than *consistence.*

consistent *adj.* **1** *A golf champion must be a consistent winner:* constant, steady, regular, persistent, unchanging, undeviating, conforming to type. **2** *Choose furniture that's consistent with the modern style of the house:* harmonious, consonant, in agreement, agreeing, of a piece, unified, compatible, congenial, meet, correspondent, congruous, suitable.

Ant. 1 inconsistent, irregular, erratic, nonuniform, changing, deviating. **2** inconsistent, in disagreement, incompatible, uncongenial, incongruous, discordant, contradictory, contrary, unsuitable.

consolation *n. Words are little consolation when tragedy strikes:* solace, comfort, relief, succour, assuagement, help, alleviation, soothing, easement, support, encouragement, cheer; condolence, sympathy.

Ant. depression, disappointment, discouragement, dissatisfaction.

console *v. The mother consoled the boy, then bandaged his scuffed knee:* soothe, comfort, calm, succour, cheer, ease, support, sustain; condole with, commiserate with, lament with, express sorrow, express sympathy for, sympathize.

Ant. distress, trouble, discompose, upset, annoy, disturb, perturb, agitate, aggravate, grieve, sadden, hurt, wound, disquiet.

◇ *Word origin: Console* comes from Latin *con-* (together) + *solari* (to solace). The older English word for *console* was *consolate,* but the poet John Dryden coined the new form in 1693 and launched it in one of his many popular plays with the following awe-inspiring verse: "Till I, thy consul sole, consol'd thy doom." The fearsomeness of the line did not prevent people from repeating the word and using it.

consolidate *v.* **1** *The two railway tracks were consolidated into one line:* combine, unify, incorporate, unite, emerge, bring together, band together, join, fuse, amalgamate, league, integrate, federate, compress, condense, concentrate. **2** *The team's victory consolidated its chance for the championship:* strengthen, solidify, make solid, make sure, make firm.

Ant. 1 separate, divide, part, sever, sunder; dissolve. **2** weaken, make uncertain.

◇ *Word origin: Consolidate* comes from the Latin prefix *con-* (together) + *solidus* (solid).

consort *n.* **1** *Prince Albert was the consort of Queen Victoria:* spouse, mate, husband, wife; partner, companion, associate.

—v. **2** *The police suspect him because he consorts with known criminals:* keep company, accompany, associate, go around with, fraternize, mingle, mix, pair off, club together, hang out, rub elbows.

Ant. 2 dissociate, separate, part, estrange.
◇ *Word origin: Consort* comes from Latin *con-* (together) + *sors* (lot, condition), hence one who shares another's condition or lot in life.

conspicuous *adj.* **1** *That red hat makes her conspicuous. The Borgia family were conspicuous violators of the laws of God and men:* standing out, easily seen, easily noticed, highly visible, obvious, striking; plain, clear, evident, manifest, patent, distinct, glaring, prominent, arresting, flagrant. **2** *Man's first moon landing was a conspicuous achievement:* outstanding, striking, notorious, remarkable, notable, illustrious, distinguished, glorious, memorable, celebrated, prominent, well-known, eminent, renowned, famous, splendid, brilliant, great.
Ant. 1 inconspicuous, unnoticeable, concealed, hidden, unseen, invisible, imperceptible, unapparent, indiscernible. **2** inconspicuous, undistinguished, trifling, unmemorable, common, ordinary, modest, humble; mediocre, average, commonplace.

conspiracy *n. Those who planned the rebellion were indicted for conspiracy against the king:* criminal plan, treasonous plan, secret plan, plot, intrigue, collusion, connivance, machination; sedition, treason, treachery.

conspirator *n. Three nights later, all the conspirators had been hanged:* plotter, schemer, traitor, intriguer.

conspire *v.* **1** *Guy Fawkes and his associates were tried for conspiring to blow up Parliament:* scheme, intrigue, collude, connive, machinate, plot treason. **2** *Bad weather and car trouble conspired to ruin our excursion:* contribute jointly, combine, unite, co-operate, concur, work together.
◇ *Word origin: Conspire* comes from Latin *con-* (together) + *spirare* (to breathe), hence to breathe — or whisper — together.

constant *adj.* **1** *Keep the chemicals at a constant temperature of 40 degrees:* fixed, uniform, steady, regular, even, unchanging, invariable, unalterable, unvaried, undeviating, permanent, stable, immutable, unswerving, unfailing. **2** *Her constant nagging drives me crazy:* incessant, unceasing, ceaseless, unrelenting, continual, endless, everlasting, eternal, interminable, perpetual, persistent, unbroken, uninterrupted, sustained. **3** *The guide-dog was the blind man's constant companion:* loyal, devoted, faithful, true, tried-and-true, trustworthy, trusty, steadfast, dependable, resolute, abiding, unwavering, enduring.
Ant. 1 variable, fluctuating, changing, changeable, erratic, irregular, uneven, unfixed, deviating, alterable, unstable. **2** occasional, intermittent, irregular, spasmodic, sporadic, fitful, random, unsustained. **3** inconstant, disloyal, unfaithful, faithless, false, perfidious; untrustworthy, undependable, irresolute, wavering, flagging, fickle.

consternation *n. To their complete consternation the swimmers saw a shark approaching:* paralysing fear, panic, shock, terror, horror, fright, alarm; dismay, apprehension, trepidation.
Ant. composure, calmness, equanimity, aplomb, self-possession, sang-froid, presence of mind; fearlessness, boldness.
◇ *Word origin: Consternation* literally means throwing oneself down on the ground in panic or dismay. It comes from the Latin prefix *con-* (thoroughly) + *sternere* (to lay low).

constitute *v.* **1** *Meat, milk, vegetables, fruit and starches constitute a balanced diet:* form, compose, make up, make, compound. **2** *A committee was constituted to investigate rising prices:* establish, create, set up, institute, found; appoint, delegate, commission, authorize, name, invest.

constitution *n.* **1** *The fabric's open-weave constitution makes it unsuitable for curtains:* composition, make-up, construction, structure, configuration, figuration, formation, texture. **2** *The old man still has a strong constitution:* physical condition, physique, figure, health, strength, mettle, stamina, vitality. **3** *The general meeting voted to amend the Constitution:* governing charter, charter, fundamental principles, basic laws.

"I am of a constitution so general, that it consorts and sympathiseth with all things."
—*Sir Thomas Browne*

---

constitutional *adj.* **1** *His limp is constitutional, not the result of an accident:* organic, physical, internal, congenital, natural, inborn, intrinsic. **2** *Freedom of speech is a constitutional guarantee:* of the constitution, chartered, basic, fundamental, vested.
—*n.* **3** *My father takes his daily constitutional:* walk, stroll, ramble, turn.
Ant. 1 inorganic, non-physical, external, fortuitous; foreign, alien, extraneous, extrinsic, acquired, environmental, accidental. **2** unconstitutional, unlawful, illegal.

constraint *n.* **1** *The manufacturer was forced to return the money under constraint of law:* force, obligation, coercion, pressure, compulsion, necessity, duress, enforcement. **2** *He stopped shouting and began to speak with constraint:* restraint, reserve, suppressed feelings, diffidence.
Ant. 1 free will; desire, wish. **2** naturalness, openness, frankness, boldness.

constrict *v. Doesn't that tight bracelet constrict your arm?:* squeeze, cramp, pinch, strangle, choke, bind; contract, compress, shrink.
Ant. free, release, loosen, unbind, untie; distend, swell.

constriction *n. Constriction in the patient's chest made breathing difficult:* tightness, compression, contraction, narrowing, stricture, con-

straint; squeezing, cramping, choking, pinching, binding, shrinking, strangling.
Ant. loosening, freeing, releasing, unbending; expansion, widening, dilation, distension, swelling.

construct *v. To construct a building. To construct a plan:* build, erect, make, fabricate, set up; create, formulate, frame, design, devise, fashion, shape, organize, arrange.
Ant. demolish, destroy, raze, tear down, take apart.
◇ *Word origin: Construct, construction,* and *construe* come from Latin *con-* (together) + *struere* (to build), which also gives us *structure* and *destruction.*

construction *n.* **1** *The construction of the bridge took two years:* constructing, building, putting together, erecting, rearing, raising, fabrication, fashioning, creation, production, manufacture. **2** *The construction will be used to store farm equipment:* building, structure, edifice. **3** *The construction of the new school is simple and modern:* style, form, configuration, build, conformation, composition, make. **4** *What construction do you put on the witness's account of the crime?:* interpretation, explication, elucidation, reading, rendition, version, explanation.
Ant. 1 demolition, razing, destruction, tearing down.
◇ *Word origin:* See CONSTRUCT.

constructive *adj. The painter gave the art students constructive criticism of their work:* helpful, productive, practical, handy, useful, beneficial, advantageous, valuable.
Ant. destructive, unhelpful, useless.

construe *v. Do you construe that remark as favourable or critical?:* interpret, understand, comprehend, take, read, decipher, translate, make out, figure out; explain, elucidate.
◇ *Word origin:* See CONSTRUCT.

consul *n. The French consul in Toronto will stamp your visa:* diplomatic agent, representative, foreign officer, minister, envoy, emissary.
◇ *Usage note:* See COUNCIL.

consult *v.* **1** *Did anyone consult the boss about this job?:* refer to, inquire of, ask advice of, seek counsel from, seek the opinion of; take into account, consider, regard, have an eye to. **2** *The two lawyers consulted on the case:* confer, exchange views, deliberate together, talk over, discuss together, compare notes.
Ant. 1 ignore, disregard, bypass.

consultation *n. The doctor is in consultation with a patient:* meeting, conference, council, deliberation, hearing, discussion, interview.

consume *v.* **1** *The small car consumed very little petrol:* use up, expend, spend, deplete, exhaust, drain; waste, squander, dissipate, fritter away. **2** *The children consumed all the lemonade and cream buns:* eat, devour, eat up, swallow up, gulp down, guzzle, drink up. **3** *The entire building was consumed by fire:* destroy, lay waste, ravage, devastate, demolish, annihilate. **4** *He was consumed with envy:* absorb, engross, eat up, devour.
Ant. 1 conserve, preserve, save; provide, supply.
◇ *Word origin: Consume* and *consumption* come from Latin *con-* (thoroughly) + *sumere* (to use, take).

consumer *n.* **1** *Consumers want better, safer products:* user, customer, buyer, purchaser, patron, client. **2** *Worry is a great consumer of energy:* user, spender; waster, dissipater, squanderer.
Ant. 1 manufacturer, maker, seller. **2** saver, preserver, conserver; supplier, provider.

consummate *v.* **1** *The marriage was declared void because it had not been consummated:* complete, perfect, fulfil, execute, accomplish, achieve, realize, effect, bring about, carry out, perform, do.
—*adj.* **2** *After years of study and practice he is a consummate pianist:* finished, complete, accomplished, faultless, perfect; thorough, absolute, utter, unquestioned, unconditional, undisputed, supreme, unmitigated, sheer, total, through-and-through.
Ant. 1 begin, start, initiate, conceive, inaugurate. **2** unfinished, incomplete, imperfect, deficient; crude, rough, raw; partial, conditional, deficient.

consummation *n. The signing of the treaty was the consummation of long negotiations:* achievement, realization, fulfilment, attainment, execution, accomplishment; completion, finish, conclusion, close, culmination, end.
Ant. beginning, inception, start, initiation; failure, breakdown.

consumption *n.* **1** *Increased consumption of paper is depleting our forests:* use, using up, consuming; expenditure, depletion, exhaustion. **2** *In the 19th century consumption was a frightening disease:* tuberculosis, T.B.
Ant. 1 conservation, preservation, saving.
◇ *Word origin:* See CONSUME.

"I can get no remedy against this consumption of the purse: borrowing only lingers and lingers it out, but the disease is incurable."
— *William Shakespeare*

---

contact *n.* **1** *The car turned over when the rear wheels lost contact with the road:* touch, connection; meeting, touching, junction, union, adjacency, abutment. **2** *The pilot lost contact with the control tower:* communication, connection, association.
—*v.* **3** *I finally contacted him by phone:* communicate with, reach, get in touch with.
◇ *Usage note:* Although *contact,* meaning to get in touch with (def. **3** above), has been in general use for over 50 years, many people still object to it. Whatever your position on this disputed usage happens to be, bear in

mind that conservatism in usage is mainly a good thing. If language changes too rapidly, communication breaks down; and if we can't *contact* our neighbours efficiently, we are all in serious trouble.

contagious *adj. Chicken-pox is a contagious disease:* catching, infectious, communicable, transmittable, spreading, communicable by contact.

Ant. non-contagious, non-catching, non-infectious.

◇ *Word origin: Contagious* comes from Latin *con-* (together) + *tangere* (to touch), so a contagious disease is spread by actually touching a sick person or his possessions.

contain *v.* **1** *The suitcase contained nothing but dirty clothes. The story contained some humorous passages:* hold, include, enclose; accommodate, incorporate, embody, embrace, involve. **2** *Try to contain your anger:* control, hold back, hold in, repress, restrain, keep within bounds, curb, check.

Ant. 2 express, vent, release, let out.

container *n. Is that container large enough to hold all the books?:* receptacle, holder; (*variously*) vessel, carton, box, bag, can, bucket, pail, bottle, jar, vat, barrel.

contaminate *v. The chemicals contaminated the river:* taint, pollute, dirty, soil, infect, foul, befoul, make impure, spoil, blight, poison, corrupt, defile.

Ant. purify, clean, cleanse.

contamination *n. The contamination of the water made it unfit to drink:* polluting, dirtying, soiling, fouling, poisoning, defilement, spoiling, adulteration; impurity, pollution, dirtiness, foulness, uncleanness, filth, putridity.

Ant. purity, cleanness.

contemplate *v.* **1** *The Roman augurs contemplated the stars for signs of things to come:* regard, survey, examine, inspect, scan, note, look at fixedly, view attentively, stare at, gaze at, observe. **2** *Contemplate the problem before making a final decision:* ponder, mull over, reflect upon, think about, consider fully, deliberate on, cogitate on, weigh, meditate on, speculate about, muse about, ruminate. **3** *The travel agent contemplates trouble in obtaining hotel reservations. Our neighbour contemplates moving to Cardiff:* expect, anticipate, envisage, imagine, project; plan, intend, look forward to, think of, aspire to, have in view.

Ant. 1 disregard, overlook, ignore.

◇ *Word origin: Contemplate* and *contemplation* come from Latin *con-* (together) + *templum* (open space for observation of the stars). The corresponding Latin words belonged in Roman times to the specialized vocabulary of augury (see AUGUR). We don't know very much about the actual techniques of *contemplation* in this sense, because the information was kept secret. Latin *templum* also gives us our word *temple*.

contemplation *n.* **1** *The tourists' contemplation of the Alps was obstructed by fog:* viewing, observation, inspection, examination, seeing, survey, scanning, looking, gazing. **2** *The governor reached his decision after a great deal of contemplation:* thought, thinking, reflection, cogitation, pondering, meditation, study, deliberation, consideration, musing, rumination, reverie.

◇ *Usage note:* In technical Christian use, *contemplation* is the state to which mystics aspire: union with God. In this sense it is often called "mystical union," "ecstasy," or "meditation." However, meditation is only a prelude to mystical contemplation — typically, a mental prayer based on a concentrated devotional reflection. "Meditation" is also now a general term for various psychosomatic techniques associated with Yoga and other traditions of spirituality imported from the Far East.

contemplative *adj. De Gaulle personified the "man of action," so some of us were surprised by the contemplative tone of his writings:* thoughtful, reflective, meditative, musing, ruminating, cogitative, pensive, speculative, introspective, studious, engrossed, lost in thought.

Ant. active, practical, pragmatic.

◇ *Usage note:* The commonplace distinction between the *contemplative* and the *active* goes all the way back to Aristotle's distinction between *praktikos* (practical) and *theōrētikos* (contemplative, speculative, "theoretical").

contemporary *adj.* **1** *Do you prefer contemporary furniture?:* modern, up-to-date, up-to-the-minute, current, present-day, recent, late, new, newfangled, brand-new, ultra-modern, advanced. **2** *Hitler was contemporary with Mussolini:* of the same time, coexistent, concurrent, contemporaneous, coincident, simultaneous.

Ant. 1 antique, old-fashioned, old, early, out-of-date, archaic, obsolete.

◇ *Usage note: Contemporary* refers to people who lived at the same period or live at the present time: *Theda Bara and Rudolph Valentino were contemporary with each other. Contemporary cars are more streamlined than older ones. Contemporaneous* refers chiefly to events or works that occurred at the same period in the past: *The poems of Keats and of Shelley are contemporaneous. The invention of the car was contemporaneous with that of the telephone.*

contempt *n. Traitors have always been treated with contempt:* scorn, disdain, derision, shame, humiliation, disgrace, dishonour; disrepute, disfavour, disregard, disgust, distaste, repugnance, revulsion, aversion, detestation, loathing, hatred, hate, abhorrence, antipathy.

Ant. honour, respect, esteem, admiration, regard; liking, love.

◇ *Usage note: Contempt, disdain,* and *scorn* all imply looking down on others. *Contempt* is the strongest term and means a looking down with total lack of respect. *Disdain* suggests a looking down with an unwillingness to touch or get involved, because one feels oneself to be too good to do so. *Scorn* doesn't necessarily mean one feels superior but only that one has a low opinion of others. Thus, *The king felt contempt for his would-be assassin, disdain for beggars, and scorn for fools.*

contemptible *adj. Spreading wicked gossip is contemptible:* mean, vile, low, base, shameful, ignominious, miserable, unworthy, abject, cheap, shabby, paltry; disgusting, repugnant, revolting, despicable, detestable.

Ant. honourable, admirable, laudable, praiseworthy, worthy; pleasant, attractive, appealing.

◇ *Usage note:* Many people confuse the words *contemptible* and *contemptuous. Contemptible* means despicable, deserving of contempt. *Contemptuous* means feeling contempt for someone or something: *The Kaiser was contemptuous of Kitchener's forces and allegedly described them as a contemptible little army.*

◇ *Spelling tip:* Does this word end in *-able* or *-ible?* Remember: *I will be contemptIble if I don't remember the I in contemptIble.*

contemptuous *adj. Snobs are usually contemptuous of people they feel to be beneath them:* scornful, disrespectful, insolent, disdainful, arrogant, snobbish, haughty, pompous, supercilious, lordly.

Ant. humble, awestruck; respectful, deferential, obliging, gracious, friendly, amicable, admiring, civil.

◇ *Usage note:* See CONTEMPTIBLE.

contend *v.* **1** *It is hard to contend with poverty. Three students contended for the prize:* fight, struggle, strive, contest, combat, battle, war, wrestle, grapple, tussle, jostle, spar, clash, skirmish; complete, vie, be a rival. **2** *The suspect contended that the witness was lying:* assert, declare, avow, aver, claim, insist, hold, maintain, put forward, allege, propound; argue, quarrel, debate, dispute.

Ant. 1 concede, yield, surrender, give up. **2** deny, disavow, refute.

content[1] *n.* **1** (*Often plural*) *Empty out the contents of your purse. The content of this tin is seven ounces of tuna fish:* thing contained, what is inside, load; capacity, volume, area, size. **2** *The content of his argument was weak:* substance, essence, thoughts, ideas, matter, meaning, gist, thesis, text.

content[2] *adj.* **1** *Many men are content with a routine life:* satisfied, gratified, wanting no more, pleased, happy, comfortable, complacent; untroubled, unconcerned, unmoved, at ease, serene, at rest.

—*v.* **2** *The cosy fire and good company contented him:* satisfy, suffice, comfort, gratify, please, make easy, cheer, set at ease, appease.

—*n.* **3** *The children ate to their heart's content:* satisfaction, contentment, gratification, comfort, peace of mind, peace, serenity, pleasure, delight, happiness.

Ant. 1–3 discontent. **1** dissatisfied, unsatisfied, unhappy, displeased, uncomfortable; troubled, concerned, worried, restless. **2** dissatisfy, displease, provoke, pique, upset, annoy. **3** dissatisfaction, discomfort, unhappiness, displeasure.

"My motto is 'Contented with little, yet wishing for more.'"

—*Charles Lamb*

---

contented *adj. Are you contented with things as they are?:* satisfied, content, gratified, pleased, happy; comfortable, at ease, serene, at peace.

Ant. discontented, dissatisfied, displeased, uncomfortable, uneasy, worried, troubled, concerned, annoyed, piqued.

contentment *n. The baby finished his milk with a smile of contentment:* satisfaction, content, contentedness, gratification, happiness, pleasure, peace, ease, serenity, comfort.

Ant. discontent, dissatisfaction, unhappiness, displeasure, discomfort.

contest *n.* **1** *It was a bitter contest of wills. She will enter the beauty contest:* conflict, struggle, fight, battle, combat, war, encounter, bout, engagement, dispute; competition, match, tournament, tourney, rivalry, game.

—*v.* **2** *The soldiers contested their fort to the end:* fight for, battle for, combat for, struggle for, compete for, contend for, vie for. **3** *The referee's decision was contested by the loser:* dispute, call in question, argue against, challenge, debate, oppose, controvert, object to.

Ant. 1 agreement, accord, peace. **2** relinquish, surrender, yield, give up. **3** accept, agree to, approve, support, maintain.

◇ *Pronunciation tip: Contest* is correctly pronounced one way as a noun and another as a verb. The noun is stressed on the first syllable, a *CON-test: Did you enter the CON-test?* The verb is stressed on the second syllable, to *con-TEST: He con-TEST-ed the judge's decision.*

continence *n. The doctor advised continence:* self-restraint, forbearance, abstinence, moderation; (*variously*) purity, chastity, sobriety, temperance.

Ant. incontinence, abandon, self-indulgence, licentiousness, wantonness, drunkenness, intemperance, excess, lack of moderation.

contingency *n. We must be prepared for any contingency:* emergency, unforeseen event, accident; extremity, urgency, predicament.

contingent *adj. Whether the picnic is held or not is contingent upon the weather:* dependent, subject to, controlled by, conditioned by.

Ant. independent, uncontrolled, unrelated.

continual *adj.* **1** *The noise from the children's*

playground was continual: ceaseless, unceasing, continuous, constant, incessant, unremitting, perpetual, perennial, never-ending, unending, endless, interminable, everlasting, unbroken, uninterrupted. **2** *She was tired by the continual trips to the grocer's, school, and office:* frequent, habitual, constant, recurring, persistent, oft-repeated.

Ant. 1 ceasing, terminable, broken, fitful, spasmodic, intermittent, irregular. **2** infrequent, rare, occasional, sporadic, spasmodic, exceptional.

continuance *n. Businessmen hope for a continuance of prosperity:* continuation, continuing, persistence, perseverance, permanence, extension, protraction, prolongation, stay, lasting.

Ant. end, cessation, stopping, termination.

continuation *n. This new stretch of track is just a continuation of the old railway:* addition, continuance, continuing, extension, prolongation, protraction, sequence, sequel, supplement.

Ant. end, cessation, termination.

continue *v.* **1** *The rain continued all day. After the diversion, the road continues all the way to York:* keep on, keep up, go on, proceed, persist, persevere, last, endure, carry on, drag on; resume. **2** *Mr. Heppel will continue as headmaster of the school:* remain, stay, stay on, keep on, carry on, abide.

Ant. 1 discontinue, stop, cease, desist, pause, stay. **2** leave, resign, retire, quit, step down.

continuity *n. When the typist fell sick another typist was employed to keep up the continuity of the work:* flow, progression, succession, continuation, continuance, continuum, chain.

continuous *adj.* **1** *A continuous line of cars stretched as far as the eye could see:* unbroken, successive, progressive, consecutive; linked, connected. **2** *This continuous hot weather is oppressive:* unremitting, constant, uninterrupted, unceasing, incessant, interminable, continual, continuing, lasting, ceaseless, steady, endless, perpetual, everlasting, eternal, persistent, persevering, enduring, extensive, protracted, prolonged.

Ant. 1 intermittent, broken, disconnected. **2** passing, spasmodic, sporadic, occasional; inconstant, interrupted, ending, ceasing.

contort *v. His face was contorted with rage:* twist, bend, distort, deform, warp, be misshapen.

Ant. straighten, unbend.

contour *n. The chair follows the contours of the body:* outline, shape, form, figure, lines, physiognomy.

contraband *n. Customs agents checked the ship for contraband:* prohibited articles, illegal imports, illegal exports, smuggled goods, unlicensed goods.

contract *n.* **1** *The solicitor drew up a binding contract:* written agreement, legal document, compact, pact, arrangement.

—*v.* **2** *When you bend your elbow, the muscles of the arm contract:* draw together, become smaller, compress, tighten, constrict; shorten, narrow, shrink, dwindle, condense, reduce. **3** *He contracted huge debts by rash spending:* acquire, incur, get, take, develop, assume, absorb, enter into, engender. **4** *The firm contracted to deliver the merchandise in six months:* sign an agreement, agree, pledge, promise, make a bargain, undertake, negotiate, come to terms.

Ant. 2 expand, stretch, distend, enlarge, dilate, swell, lengthen, widen, grow, increase. **3** avoid, evade, elude, escape, shun, eschew; avert, ward off. **4** disagree, refuse.

contraction *n. Cold weather causes a contraction of two inches in the bridge:* drawing in, constriction, compression, tightening, shrinkage, shrivelling, decrease, reduction, lessening, shortening, narrowing, condensation, abbreviation.

Ant. expansion, extension, increase, stretching, swelling, enlargement, lengthening, widening, broadening.

contradict *v. The witness contradicted the defendant's testimony:* refute, deny, confute, controvert, impugn, oppose, counter, be contrary to, gainsay, rebut; disprove, belie.

Ant. corroborate, confirm, verify, substantiate, authenticate, affirm, sustain, support, endorse.

contradiction *n. One story is a direct contradiction of the other. The chairman wouldn't listen to any contradiction of his opinions:* refutation, denial, confutation, rebuttal, counter, negation.

Ant. corroboration, confirmation, verification, substantiation, affirmation, support, endorsement; agreement, accord.

"Contradiction should awaken attention, not passion." —*Thomas Fuller*

---

contradictory *adj. The two experts had contradictory views on the matter:* conflicting, opposing, contrary, disagreeing, countervailing, antithetical, discrepant, irreconcilable, adversative, inconsistent.

Ant. similar, like, parallel, agreeing.

contrary *adj.* **1** *Lying is contrary to my code of ethics. The boy was swimming in a direction contrary to the current:* opposed, opposite, contradictory, counter, at variance, at cross purposes, conflicting, incompatible, antithetical, inimical, converse, discordant, disparate. **2** *Don't be so contrary!:* disagreeing, contradictory, unaccommodating, stubborn, obstinate, intractable, refractory, balky, recalcitrant, wilful, headstrong, perverse, obstreperous, froward, wayward; hostile, antagonistic. **3** *A contrary wind held the ship in port:* unfavourable, adverse, unpropitious, untoward, inauspicious, unsuitable, unfitting, inexpedient.

Ant. 1 consistent, parallel, accordant. **2** complaisant, compliant, obliging, acquiescent, accommodating, tractable, agreeing, unassuming, submissive; good-natured, agreeable, pleasant, peaceful. **3** favourable, propitious, auspicious, suitable, fitting.
◇ *Usage note:* In sense **2**, *contrary* is usually stressed on the second syllable, not the first.

contrast *v.* **1** *Contrast Keats's poetry with Dylan Thomas's. This cold weather contrasts with last week's heat:* differentiate, set in opposition; differ, diverge, deviate, depart, disagree with.
—*n.* **2** *In contrast to our old house, the new one is a mansion! There's a remarkable contrast between England and Scotland:* comparing differences, comparison, differentiation; difference, dissimilarity, unlikeness, variance, disparity, divergence, distinction.
Ant. 1 liken, compare, resemble, parallel. **2** similarity, likeness, comparison, parallelism, sameness, similitude, agreement.
◇ *Usage note:* See COMPARE.

contribute *v.* **1** *Every household contributed to the rescue fund:* give, donate, bestow, grant, confer, hand out, present, endow. **2** *Air pollution contributes to respiratory diseases:* advance, influence, lead to, help bring about, forward, be conducive to, have a hand in, bear a part.
Ant. 1 take, receive; withhold, deny. **2** curb, check, slow, impede, detract.

contribution *n. Each two-pound contribution will buy the orphans milk for a week:* donation, gift, bestowal, endowment, grant, benefaction, dispensation, offering; charity, alms.

contrite *adj. His contrite manner made us forgive him:* conscience-stricken, sorrowful, regretful, repentant, penitent, remorseful, chastened, humbled.
Ant. proud, pleased, uncontrite, unrepentant, unapologetic.

contrition *n. Did Judas feel contrition for his betrayal of Christ?:* self-reproach, regret, remorse, qualms of conscience, compunction; repentance, penitence, penance, atonement.

contrivance *n.* **1** *This contrivance peels and cores apples:* device, contraption, gadget, instrument, apparatus, implement, tool, machine, mechanism, invention; *Slang* whatsit, doodah, thingumajig. **2** *The boy tried every contrivance he knew to get the puppy to follow him home:* plan, trick, stratagem, plot, artifice, intrigue, measure, design, machination.

contrive *v.* **1** *She contrived a bookcase out of bricks and boards:* devise, create, concoct, invent, design. **2** *The youths contrived to stow away on the ship:* scheme, plot, plan, devise a plan; manœuvre, manage, effect by stratagem.

control *v.* **1** *The pilot controls the plane from the cockpit. The treasurer controls the expenditure of funds:* command, govern, rule, master, regulate, manipulate, manage, have charge of, superintend, supervise; dominate, reign over. **2** *Control your temper:* restrain, restrict, repress, subdue, contain, master, bridle.
—*n.* **3** *The small island was under the control of Great Britain. The driver lost control of the car:* command, management, mastery, regulation, direction, sway, rule, dominion, domination, jurisdiction, authority, supervision, charge. **4** *Aspirin serves as an effective control for most headaches:* curb, restraint, suppressant, brake.
Ant. 2 free, release, let loose, give vent.
◇ *Usage note: Comptroller* is only a variant spelling for *controller*, a high-ranking accountant who verifies or "controls" financial records.
◇ *Spelling tip:* Remember that the final *l* in *controL* doubles in *controLLed* as it does in *controLLing.*
◇ *Word origin:* The best way to *control* or check accounts is to compare them with a duplicate list or "counter list." *Control* comes from Medieval Latin *contrarotulus*, a "counter roll" or check-list (from *contra-*, against, + *rotulus*, list).

controversial *adj. James Joyce's* Ulysses *was a controversial book. Abortion is a highly controversial subject:* widely discussed, causing debate; debatable, disputable, arguable, open to discussion, questionable, at issue.
Ant. non-controversial, undebatable, indisputable, incontrovertible, unquestionable, proven, sure, certain.

controversy *n. There was a heated controversy over the plans for the new school:* debate, discussion, dispute, contention, argument, quarrel, wrangle, squabble, altercation; disagreement, dissension.
Ant. agreement, unanimity, accord.

convalescence *n. Fresh air and sunshine helped the patient's convalescence:* recovery, recuperation, restoration, *Archaic* recruitment.
◇ *Spelling tip: Convalescence* can be a spelling demon. You'll get it right if you pronounce it slowly to yourself and then spell all the syllables carefully: *con-va-les-cence.*

convene *v. The club convenes every month. The chairman convened the committee to put the issue to a vote:* gather, come together, assemble, hold a session, bring together, summon, call together, convoke, muster, collect, round up.
Ant. adjourn, disperse, dissolve, dismiss, disband.

convenience *n.* **1** *The campers missed the convenience of a refrigerator:* usefulness, utility, service; handiness, accessibility, availability. **2** *The new house has every modern convenience:* comfort, accommodation, facility; appliance, work saver. **3** *Shopping bags are provided for the customers' convenience:* accommodation, use, ease, enjoyment, pleasure, satisfaction. **4** *Please call at your earliest convenience:* opportunity, chance, convenient time, suitable time.
Ant. 1 inconvenience, uselessness, hardship.

3 inconvenience, dissatisfaction, discomfort, annoyance.

convenient *adj.* 1 *The height of this lamp isn't convenient for reading:* suitable, suited, useful, helpful, adapted, easy to use, serviceable, advantageous, beneficial. 2 *The car-park is convenient for the office:* easily accessible, nearby, at hand.

Ant. 1 inconvenient, unsuitable, awkward, useless, unhandy. 2 inconvenient, inaccessible, distant.

convent *n. The religious girl wanted to enter a convent:* society of nuns, nunnery, cloister.

convention *n.* 1 *A psychologists' convention is at least a chance to meet old friends:* assembly, conference, congress, convocation, conclave, meeting, gathering. 2 *Youth often questions the conventions of society:* custom, social rule, standard, precept, practice, propriety, protocol, formality.

conventional *adj. White is the conventional colour for a wedding dress:* traditional, customary, accepted, proper, orthodox; normal, standard, regular, common, routine.

Ant. unconventional, unorthodox, extraordinary, uncommon, abnormal.

"Conventional people are roused to fury by departure from convention, largely because they regard such departure as a criticism of themselves." —*Bertrand Russell*

---

converge *v. This play touches the region where comedy converges with tragedy:* come together, meet, approach; focus, concentrate, run together.

Ant. diverge, separate, part, scatter, disperse.

conversation *n. We had a long telephone conversation:* talk, discourse, dialogue, chat, chit-chat, tête-à-tête, palaver, confabulation; *Slang,* rap, gab, session.

converse[1] *v. We conversed for hours on the phone:* talk, speak together, engage in conversation, chat, chit-chat, confabulate, palaver; *Slang* chin-wag, jaw, chew the rag, rap.

◇ *Pronunciation tip:* See CONVERSE[2].

converse[2] *n. His political views are the converse of mine:* opposite, reverse, contrary, antithesis.

Ant. same.

◇ *Pronunciation tip: Converse*[1] and *converse*[2] are pronounced differently. The noun is stressed on the first syllable, *CON-verse: I maintain that just the CON-verse is true.* The verb is stressed on the second syllable, *to conVERSE: I would like to con-VERSE with you.*

conversion *n.* 1 *The conversion of a caterpillar into a butterfly is miraculous:* change, transformation, transfiguration, metamorphosis, transmutation. 2 *Saint Patrick is traditionally regarded as responsible for Ireland's conversion to Christianity:* change, change of religion, change-over, change of heart, change in beliefs.

convert *v.* 1 *The plant converts crude oil into petrol:* change, transform, turn. 2 *He was converted to Judaism. The explanation converted him to our point of view:* cause to change one's religion, change one's belief; cause a change of opinion, proselytize.

—*n.* 3 *He is a convert to Buddhism:* converted person; proselyte, neophyte, novice.

convex *adj. The outside of a spectacle lens is convex:* curved outward, rounded, protuberant, bulging.

Ant. concave, sunken, hollowed out.

◇ *Word origin: Convex* comes from Latin *convexus,* arched, rounded.

convey *v.* 1 *The pipeline conveys natural gas to the Midlands:* carry, transport, bear, conduct, bring, move, transmit. *Please convey my best wishes to your parents:* communicate, make known, impart, relate, give, tell, disclose, reveal, divulge, confide to. 3 *The old man conveyed the family farm to his son:* transfer, deliver over, cede, deed, grant; will, bequeath, leave.

Ant. 2 conceal, hide, receive, listen. 3 retain, keep, hold on to, cling to.

◇ *Word origin: Convey* and *convoy* both come from Latin *con-* (together) + *via* (road, way), hence to travel the same road, to transport or escort.

conveyance *n.* 1 *The removal firm handles the conveyance of furniture to new homes:* conveying, transport, transportation, carrying, transfer, carriage, movement, transmission. 2 *What kind of conveyance does the dairy use to deliver the milk?:* transportation, vehicle; (*variously*) bus, car, lorry, carriage, van, wagon, cart.

convict *v.* 1 *He was convicted of manslaughter:* declare guilty, find guilty; condemn, doom.

—*n.* 2 *All the convicts complained bitterly about prison conditions:* prisoner, felon, inmate, offender; *Slang* gaolbird, con.

Ant. 1 acquit, find innocent.

◇ *Pronunciation tip: Convict* has two pronunciations, one for the noun and the other for the verb. The noun, a *convict,* should be clearly stressed on the first syllable: *The CON-vict was recaptured by the police.* The verb, to *convict,* should be stressed on the second syllable: *The jury will con-VICT him for armed robbery.*

◇ *Word origin:* See CONVINCE.

conviction *n.* 1 *His political convictions are radical:* belief, view, opinion, judgement, principle, tenet, faith, persuasion, creed, doctrine, dogma. 2 *The audience was swayed by the speaker's conviction:* certainty, certitude, assurance, firm persuasion, steadfastness, intensity, ardour, earnestness, fervour, fever, zeal.

Ant. 2 uncertainty, misgiving, hesitation, doubt.

convince *v. The politician's speech convinced the voters that he was the man for the job:* persuade, prevail upon, sway, win over, bring round, influence, assure, satisfy.

◇ *Word origin: Convince* and *convict* both come from Latin *con-* (thoroughly) + *vincere* (to conquer). Latin *convincere* has two meanings: (1) to *convict* of a crime, and (2) to show conclusively or prove. The word *convince* arose from this second sense.

convivial *adj. It's fun to make a tour with convivial people:* sociable, friendly, companionable, genial, affable, agreeable, fun-loving, merry, jovial, gregarious, festive.

Ant. unsociable, unfriendly, reserved, reticent, serious, sober, grave, sedate, solemn.

convocation *n. A convocation of experts was called to debate the issue:* convention, congress, conference, caucus, council, conclave, assembly, gathering, meeting, round-up, roster, muster.

Ant. adjournment, dismissal, disbanding.

convolution *n. The children were fascinated by the convolutions of the snake:* coiling, coil, twisting, twist, winding, undulation, contortion; sinuosity, sinuousness, tortuousness; maze, labyrinth.

Ant. uncoiling, unwinding.

convoy *v.* **1** *A Royal Navy frigate convoyed the ship into the port:* escort, conduct, accompany, go along with.

—*n.* **2** *Seven destroyers formed the troop-ship's convoy:* escort, armed guard; (*variously*) column, fleet, formation.

◇ *Word origin:* See CONVEY.

convulsion *n.* **1** *The patient had an epileptic convulsion:* spasm, fit, contortion, seizure, paroxysm. **2** *Plural, The audience broke into convulsions of laughter:* outburst, fit, spasm; commotion, disturbance, tumult, agitation.

cool *adj.* **1** *Today was a cool day for July:* slightly cold, somewhat cold, chill, chilly, not warm. **2** *The announcer had a cool, unruffled manner:* calm, unexcited, composed, unflappable, self-possessed, collected, deliberate, cool-headed, undisturbed, untroubled, unemotional, dispassionate, impassive, serene. **3** *He seemed so cool that I feared I had offended him:* unfriendly, uncordial, unsociable, distant, reserved, aloof, offish, unresponsive, indifferent, nonchalant, cold, icy, frosty.

—*v.* **4** *Cool the soup before freezing it:* make cool, become cool, chill, lose heat.

Ant. **1** warm, *Informal* warmish. **2** excited, frenzied, frantic, wild, delirious, impassioned, highly strung, nervous, tense, wrought-up, overwrought, hysterical, agitated, perturbed, disturbed, troubled, upset. **3** friendly, cordial, warm, responsive. **4** warm, heat.

◇ *Spelling tip:* Remember that *coolly* has two *l*'s. It is made up of *cooL + Ly, cooLLy.*

co-operate *v. Please co-operate with us in evacuating the island quickly:* work together, participate, collaborate, unite, act jointly, join, join forces, take part, share in, pitch in, work side by side, go along, take part in, stand shoulder to shoulder, join hands, pull together.

Ant. oppose, fight, conflict, rival; counteract, negate, neutralize, nullify.

◇ *Word origin: Co-operate* comes from Latin *co-* (together) + *operari* (to work), which also gives us *operate* and *operation.*

co-operation *n. With the co-operation of all the employees the work was done on time:* co-operating, working together, participation, collaboration, joint action, team-work, give and take, pulling together; concurrence, agreement, accordance, concert.

Ant. opposition, hindrance, conflicting, rivalry, dissension, infighting; disagreement, discord.

co-ordinate *v.* **1** *Try to co-ordinate the work so that the plasterers finish before the painters arrive:* organize, order, arrange, systematize, relate, match, mesh, harmonize.

—*adj.* **2** *The army, navy, and air force are co-ordinate branches of the armed services:* equal, coequal, equally important.

Ant. **1** disorganize, muddle. **2** unequal, disparate.

◇ *Word origin: Co-ordinate* comes from Latin *co-* (together) + *ordo* (series, row, order). Latin *ordo* also gives us our word *order.*

cope *v. An executive has to cope with many business problems every day:* contend, spar, wrestle, face, strive, struggle, tussle, hold one's own; manage, hurdle.

copious *adj. The secretary took copious notes on everything that was said at the meeting:* profuse, plentiful, abundant, bountiful, extensive, full, ample, liberal, generous, lavish, plenteous.

Ant. skimpy, sparse, meagre, scanty, scant, spare.

◇ *Word origin:* See COPY.

copy *n.* **1** *The copy of the painting is very close to the original:* reproduction, facsimile, duplicate, replica, representation; imitation, counterfeit, forgery. **2** *The reporter's copy was due at four:* text, story, written material, reportage, manuscript.

—*v.* **3** *Please copy this letter in triplicate:* make a copy of, reproduce, duplicate; photostat, Xerox. **4** *Don't copy everything your elder brother does!:* emulate, follow, imitate, mimic, ape, mirror, repeat.

Ant. **1** original, archetype, prototype, model, pattern. **3** originate, create.

◇ *Spelling tip:* A *copyright* is the exclusive *right to copy*, i.e., to publish or reproduce a literary or artistic work — hence, the word is spelt *copyright.* In advertising a *copywriter* is so called because he is a *writer of copy* — hence, the word is spelt *copywriter.*

◇ *Word origin:* To make *copies* of something is to make a supply or an abundance of it. *Copy* comes from Latin *copia*, supply, abundance. The same Latin word gives us *copious* and *cornucopia* (horn of plenty).

coquette *n. Be careful that the little coquette doesn't steal your boy-friend:* flirt, vamp, heart-breaker, *Slang* tease.

◇ *Word origin: Coquette* comes from Latin *coquet*, a little cock, referring to a cock's strutting — hence, it literally means a little "strutter" or show-off.

cord *n. Wind the cord tightly round the box:* twine, thin rope, braid, heavy string.

◇ *Usage note:* Some people confuse *cord* and *chord*. A *cord*, of course, is a rope, electric wire, or a ropelike part of something. *Chord* refers to a combination of musical tones, a string for a musical instrument, a straight line that intersects a curve in geometry, or a strong emotional response. Thus, *Tie the package with a strong piece of cord,* but *Play a few chords on the guitar and I'll sing.* In parts of the body usage varies; thus you may say either *vocal cord* or *vocal chord.*

◇ *Word origin: Cord* comes from Greek *khordē*, gut, string of a musical instrument made from gut, *chord*. The "gut, string" sense of *chord* and *cord* is also present in the cognate word *yarn*.

cordial *adj. The hostess gave each guest a cordial greeting:* friendly, gracious, genial, amiable, affable, warm, affectionate, sincere, heart-felt, whole-hearted, hearty, good-natured.

Ant. unfriendly, ungracious, cool, cold, frigid, indifferent, distant, detached, reserved, aloof, formal, ceremonious.

core *n.* **1** *Cut out the core of the apple:* kernel, centre, central part, innermost part, nucleus. **2** *Let's get to the core of the matter:* essence, essential part, gist, heart, centre, pith, substance, crux, meat; *Slang* guts, brass tacks, nitty-gritty.

coronet *n. The duke wore his coronet and ceremonial robes:* small crown, diadem; chaplet, tiara.

◇ *Word origin: Coronet* is originally a diminutive form of French *couronne*, crown, hence literally "little crown." A *coronet* is worn by royalty below the rank of king and queen and by the nobility.

corporal *adj. I don't believe in corporal punishment, but I'd love to give that boy a spanking:* bodily, physical, *Archaic* corporeal.

> **Exploring the Word:** Latin *corpus*, body, gives us *corpse; corps; corporation*, a group permitted by law to act as one body or legal entity; *corpulent*, having a fleshy body, fat; *corpuscle*, literally a "little body"; *corsage*, a body or group of flowers; *corset*, via French, meaning "little body," that which fits over the body; and *corporal* (bodily) punishment.

corporation *n. The corporation has branch offices in several cities:* incorporated group, corporate body, association, legal entity; (*loosely*) company, holding company, association, syndicate, combine.

corporeal *adj. Spiritualists believe that an aura surrounds our corporeal being:* physical, bodily; mortal, worldly, non-spiritual, material, perceptible.

Ant. spiritual, heavenly, ethereal, astral, religious; intellectual, mental.

corps *n.* **1** *His father served in the signals corps during the First World War:* military branch; organized body of troops, combat unit. **2** *A corps of doctors arrived to inoculate the recruits:* team, crew, force, troop, party, band.

◇ *Spelling tip: "Dear Joe, I have just joined the diplomatic corps. P.S. Remember to spell the PS in 'corps' but not to pronounce it."* If you remember that *P.S.* you will remember to spell *corps* correctly and also to pronounce it correctly, as *kor* (*core*).

◇ *Usage note:* A *corps* is an organized unit of people, *the diplomatic corps, the press corps.* A *corpsE* is a *dEad* body. A core is the centre, as of fruit: *an apple core. There is lots of iron* ore *in the* core *of the earth.*

corpse *n. The coroner was called to examine the corpse:* dead body, body, cadaver, remains; *Slang* stiff.

◇ *Usage note:* (1) See CORPS. (2) It's a widespread misconception that *corpus delicti* refers only to the corpse of a murder victim. Actually, in legal use the *corpus delicti* is any essential item or fact proving that a crime has been committed. In a murder case this could include not only the body but also blood-stained clothing, or in a burglary a damaged safe or a broken lock.

corpulent *adj. Overeating had made him corpulent:* fat, obese, overweight, rotund, fleshy, portly, stout, plump, well-padded, chubby, roly-poly, chunky; well-fed, hefty; dumpy, lumpish.

Ant. emaciated, thin, slender, slim, lean, gaunt, skinny, scrawny; raw-boned, lanky.

correct *v.* **1** *Please correct any misspellings in this letter. Wearing glasses should correct your eyesight:* make right, remove the errors of, amend, rectify, repair, remedy, improve; alter, change, adjust, modify; regulate, fix; rework, revamp, revise. **2** *His father corrected him when he misbehaved:* chasten, reprimand, admonish, berate, scold, rebuke, censure, reprove, lecture, chide, dress down, take to task, haul over the coals, read the riot act to; punish, castigate, discipline, chastise.

—*adj.* **3** *Each correct answer earned ten marks in the exam:* free from error, accurate, right, faultless, flawless, perfect; exact, precise, true, factual, unerring. **4** *Correct behaviour should be taught in the home:* proper, fitting, fit, appropriate, suitable, seemly, becoming; conventional, acceptable.

Ant. 1 spoil, mar, ruin, damage, harm, hurt, injure, impair. **2** excuse, condone, praise, compliment, laud. **3** incorrect, wrong, inaccurate, false, untrue. **4** improper, unfitting, inappropriate, unsuitable, unseemly, unbecoming, unconventional.

correction *n.* **1** *Make any final corrections before handing in your examination papers. The navigator made a correction to bring the ship back on course:* rectification, improvement, emendation; alteration, change, revision, modification, adjustment. **2** *Unruly children need correction:* discipline, punishment, reformation, chastisement, castigation.

corrective *adj. The upsurge in crime calls for strong corrective measures. A hearing-aid is a corrective device:* counter, counteractive, counterbalancing; reformatory, rectifying; improving, ameliorative, therapeutic, remedial, compensatory: restorative, palliative.

correlate *v. The barrister tried to correlate the testimony of the two witnesses:* relate, show relationship between, connect, correspond, parallel.

Ant. disconnect, contradict, oppose.

correspond *v.* **1** *The two sisters correspond every week:* exchange letters, write letters, communicate, drop a line to. **2** *The news report doesn't correspond with the facts. His sporty clothes don't correspond with his shy behaviour:* agree, conform, concur, coincide, accord, parallel, harmonize, equate, match, fit, suit, tally, dove-tail, square; be similar, be like, be equivalent, be complementary.

Ant. 2 differ, disagree, belie, diverge.

◇ *Word origin: Correspond* and *correspondence* both come from the Late Latin prefix *cor-* (together, thoroughly) + *respondere* (to answer, undertake in return).

correspondence *n.* **1** *Our correspondence is limited to a few friendly letters. The latest correspondence from the front tells of a great victory:* post, letters, missives, epistles; dispatches, bulletins, communiqués. **2** *There is no correspondence between the two stories:* similarity, resemblance, relation, association.

◇ *Spelling tip:* A good speller writes all of his *correspondence* with *E*'s (ease): *corrEspondEncE.*

◇ *Usage note:* A *coRRespondent* corresponds with other people by writing letters or news items: *Who will serve as the correspondent to write the club's letters? The newspaper has a foreign correspondent. A co-Respondent* is a joint defendant who *co*-responds with another in a court of law, especially a person charged with having committed adultery with a husband or wife in a divorce case: *The young actress was a co-respondent in the director's divorce case.*

corridor *n. Each office opens onto the corridor:* hallway, hall, passageway; passage; aisle, lobby, gangway; approach, way, road, artery.

corroborate *v. Recent experiments seem to corroborate Einstein's theory:* prove, verify, confirm, uphold, support, sustain, substantiate, affirm, validate, bear out, vindicate, authenticate, certify, back, back-up.

Ant. disprove, contradict, refute, nullify, negate, invalidate.

◇ *Spelling tip:* Beware! you must remember the 3R's to spell *coRRoboRate.*

corrode *v. Battery acid had corroded the inside of the torch:* eat away, wear away, erode; rust, oxidize.

◇ *Word origin: Corrode* comes from the Latin prefix *con-* (thoroughly) + *rodere* (to gnaw), hence to eat away, consume. The Latin verb *rodere,* to gnaw, also gives us *erode* and *rodent* (one of the Rodentia or "gnawing" order of mammals).

corrugated *adj. The box is made of corrugated cardboard:* bent into folds, ridged, furrowed, puckered, pleated, fluted, grooved, creased, wrinkled, crinkled.

corrupt *adj.* **1** *Corrupt politicians must be thrown out of office:* dishonest, dishonourable, crooked, shady, unscrupulous, fraudulent, unethical, unprincipled. **2** *Corrupt friends led him astray:* wicked, immoral, depraved, debased, iniquitous, base, mean, low, sinful, evil.

—*v.* **3** *Criminal parents could corrupt any child:* make immoral, deprave, debase, subvert, lead astray, debauch; contaminate, poison; pervert, seduce.

Ant. 1 honest, honourable, upright, ethical, principled, scrupulous, righteous, moral; *Slang* straight. **2** virtuous, moral, ethical, righteous, noble, high-minded. **3** reform, uplift.

corruption *n.* **1** *Our police force seems free of corruption:* dishonest practices, dishonesty, graft, bribery, fraud, shady dealings. **2** *The Bible warns against sin and corruption:* wickedness, depravity, evil ways, immorality, iniquity, sinfulness, debauchery, turpitude, vice, wrongdoing, degeneracy, decadence, looseness.

Ant. 1 honesty, righteousness, scrupulousness, trustworthiness, integrity. **2** goodness, good, righteousness, morality, nobility, purity.

"He that accuses all mankind of corruption ought to remember that he is sure to convict only one."
—*Edmund Burke*

---

corset *n. She needs a corset to control her ample figure:* girdle, foundation garment, corselet, laces.

cosmic *adj.* **1** *Our science library has a history of cosmic theory since Galileo. Without maths and physics, cosmic space and time can't be understood:* of the universe, (*especially*) extra-terrestrial, of outer space, interplanetary, interstellar. **2** *This is a matter of cosmic importance:* vast, immense, widespread, stupendous, grandiose; global, infinite, universal.

Ant. 2 minor, small, minute, infinitesimal.

◇ *Word origin:* See COSMOS.

cosmopolitan *adj.* **1** *London is a very cosmopolitan city:* international, not provincial, sophisticated, broadminded, worldly, worldly-wise.
—*n.* **2** *A true cosmopolitan is as much at home in Tokyo as in London:* man of the world, sophisticate, cosmopolite, citizen of the world.
Ant. 1 provincial, insular, parochial, narrow-minded, bigoted, hidebound, rigid, isolated; rustic, countrified. **2** provincial, rustic, boor.
◇ *Word origin:* See COSMOS.

cosmos *n. There may be other intelligent life elsewhere in the cosmos:* universe, interstellar system, macrocosm, earth and the heavens, the whole wide world; heavenly bodies, starry host, vault of heaven, stars.
◇ *Word origin: Cosmos* and *cosmic* come from Greek *kosmos*, ordered system, universe. The same Greek word gives us *microcosm* ("little world"), *macrocosm* ("big world," i.e. universe), *cosmopolitan* (at home in all parts of the world), and *cosmopolite* ("world-citizen"), a term dating back to ancient Alexandria.

cost *n.* **1** *What's the cost of a cruise to Majorca?:* price, charge, amount, outlay, expense, expenditure, market price, bill, toll, fee; worth, value, face value, valuation. **2** *The soldiers captured the hill at great cost:* loss, sacrifice; expense, price, penalty; pain, distress, suffering, hurt, harm, injury, damage.
—*v.* **3** *This mink coat costs £3,000:* sell for, be priced at, go for, fetch, bring in, take, amount to, come to. **4** *That mistake will certainly cost you!:* harm, injure, hurt, damage, burden, weigh down; cause suffering to, cause to lose, make sacrifice.

costly *adj.* **1** *The house is too costly for us to buy:* expensive, high-priced, dear, precious, stiff, steep, exorbitant. **2** *The general's decision to invade was a costly mistake:* causing much loss, disastrous, catastrophic; harmful, damaging, deleterious.
Ant. 1 cheap, inexpensive; reasonable, fair.

costume *n. The peasants danced in their native costumes:* national dress, indigenous garb, historical dress; outfit, attire, dress, raiment, garb, apparel, garments, clothing, clothes; uniform, livery.
◇ *Word origin: Costume* and *custom* both come from Latin *consuetudo*, custom. A *costume* is really just the clothes it is the *custom* to wear on certain occasions or for specific activities.

cosy *adj. We spent a cosy evening chatting by the fire:* snug, snugly warm, comfortable, comfy, relaxing, easy, restful, snug as a bug in a rug; homelike, homy, *Spanish* simpático, *German* gemütlich.

coterie *n. The literary coterie lunches at the hotel every Thursday:* set, clique, faction, camp, circle, crowd, group, band, clan, crew, brotherhood, club, gang.
◇ *Word origin: Coterie* is originally a French word meaning a group of tenants or *cottagers* who held land together or from the same landlord, and thus had common interests.

cottage *n. The wood-carver lived in a cottage on the side of the hill:* simple house, rustic house, cot, bungalow; lodge, chalet; hut, shack.
Ant. palace, castle, château, mansion, manor house, town house.

couch *n.* **1** *Sit beside me on the couch:* sofa, divan, settee; (*variously*) lounge, chesterfield, love-seat, day-bed, chaise longue.
—*v.* **2** *He couched his demands in careful, polite language:* express, voice, word, utter, put, state, set forth, phrase, frame; draw up, draft.

council *n.* **1** *A council of leading educationalists is meeting in Stoke:* convention, conference, congress, conclave, assembly, convocation, synod; gathering, congregation. **2** *The city council met to discuss the new proposal:* legislative body, assembly, governing body, representatives; cabinet, privy council, chamber, ministry, board, panel, committee.
◇ *Usage note:* It's easy to keep *council, counsel,* and *consul* straight. A *council* refers to a group of people who rule or deliberate, or to one of their meetings: *The CIty counCIL voted against the parking proposal. Counsel* is advice, to give advice, or an adviser or lawyer: *My counSEL counSELLed me to SELL the land.* A *consul* is a foreign-based government official below the rank of ambassador. *The SULtan's conSUL examined my visa.* Remember the three spellings: *the CIty counCIl, my counSEL counSELLed me to SELL the land,* and *the SULtan's conSUL.*

counsel *n.* **1** *Seek an architect's counsel before building the house:* advice, opinion, guidance, recommendation, suggestion; consultation, thoughts. **2** *On advice of counsel they settled out of court:* lawyer, legal adviser, counsellor, counsellor-at-law, barrister, solicitor; *American* attorney.
—*v.* **3** *The teacher counselled the boy to study harder:* advise, recommend, suggest, advocate, prompt, urge, charge, call for, instruct; warn, admonish, caution.
◇ *Usage note:* See COUNCIL.

counsellor *n. The queen met with her counsellor before she gave her opinion to the Prime Minister:* adviser, instructor, tutor, mentor; cabinet member, minister.

count *v.* **1** *Count from one to ten:* add one by one, number, enumerate, numerate, tick off; add up, total. **2** *Six people are on the trip if you count the children. The old friend was counted a member of the family:* include, take into account, consider; regard, look on, ascribe, attribute, impute. **3** *Count yourself lucky to have escaped serious injury:* consider, regard, deem, hold, look upon, rate, reckon, estimate, judge. **4** *Every penny counts:* matter, be worthwhile, tell, be effective, carry weight, be important, enter into consideration, add to the number.

5 *According to my count 27 people were present:* total, tally, calculation, enumeration, computation, reckoning, numbering, numeration.

Ant. 2 exclude, except, leave out, ignore.

◇ *Word origin: Count* comes from Latin *computare,* to compute: *com-,* together, + *putare,* to calculate or reckon, the same word as is the base of our electrical *computer.* This is hardly surprising, as a *computer* is fundamentally a machine for *counting* up a series of digits extremely rapidly. *Count* first appeared in English during the 14th century: the modern sense of *computer* in 1897. Incidentally, the noble rank of *count* has nothing to do with counting. It is an entirely different word, coming from Latin *comes,* an official (of the Roman administration).

countenance *n.* **1** *At the news of the fatal accident, his countenance fell:* expression, look, mien, appearance, air, aspect, presence, visage, traits; face, features, build, physiognomy. **2** *The mayor will not give his countenance to the new proposal:* approval, sanction, approbation, moral support, advocacy, auspices, encouragement, championship; assistance, help, aid, promotion.

—*v.* **3** *The navy will countenance longer shore leave for all personnel:* permit, approve, sanction, endorse, condone; advocate, support, promote, further, advance, uphold, forward, favour, champion, back, work for.

Ant. 2 disapproval, discouragement, disapprobation, disfavour, opposition. **3** prohibit, disapprove, oppose, condemn; discourage, hinder, thwart, frustrate, block.

counter[1] *n.* **1** *Take your groceries to the check-out counter. Watches are at the jewellery counter:* table, stand, display case. **2** *In Monopoly each player receives £200 when his counter passes "Go":* playing piece, piece, disc, man.

◇ *Word origin:* A *counter,* a board or table on which to transact business, or something to count or keep score with, comes from Latin *computare,* to reckon, compute, or calculate.

counter[2] *adv. & adj.* **1** *The election results are running counter to all predictions:* contrary, contrary to, contradictory, in the opposite way, at variance, in defiance of, opposite, opposed, against, conflicting, in conflict.

—*v.* **2** *After being hit by a left, the boxer countered with a left of his own:* retaliate, strike back, fight back, hit back, get even, pay back; oppose, offset, reverse, resist, defy.

Ant. 1 in agreement, similar to, parallel to, in unison with, as planned, as expected, accordant with, coincident with, consonant with. **2** accept, take; yield, give in, give up, surrender.

◇ *Word origin: Counter,* an opposite, to oppose or parry, comes from Latin *contra,* against.

counteract *v. This medicine should counteract the effects of the fever:* act against, nullify, negate, neutralize, undo, offset, counterbalance; fight, oppose, check, thwart, hinder, restrain, repress, curb, resist; alleviate, assuage; clash with, conflict with; overpower, overcome, defeat, annihilate.

Ant. aid, assist, abet, reinforce, support, help, co-operate with, promote, advance, forward, further, encourage.

counterfeit *adj.* **1** *The counterfeit money fooled many bank clerks:* forged, fake, phoney, not genuine, bogus, sham, imitation, simulated, artificial, ersatz, spurious, feigned.

—*n.* **2** *The painting is not really a Rembrandt but a counterfeit:* forgery, fake, phoney, fraud, sham, imitation.

Ant. 1 genuine, authentic, real, the real McCoy, good, original.

◇ *Spelling tip: Counterfeit* is not genuine in that it does *not* follow the spelling rule "*i* before *e* except after *c*. . ." Remember, *counterfeit* is like counterfeits of all kinds: it doesn't follow the rule.

counterpart *n. Canada's Prime Minister is to meet his counterpart in France. The two cars are exact counterparts in make, model, and colour:* equal, one comparable to another, correspondent, correlative, parallel; match, twin, double, fellow, duplicate, copy, mate, the spitting image.

Ant. antithesis, opposite, contradiction, contrast.

countless *adj. There are countless stars in the sky:* innumerable, numberless, infinite, endless, myriad, multitudinous, unlimited, limitless, untold, immeasurable, measureless, unnumbered, incalculable.

Ant. finite, limited, enumerable.

country *n.* **1** *The plane flew over mountainous country:* terrain, land, area, region, district, territory; countryside, landscape, scenery. **2** *Over 130 countries are members of the United Nations:* nation, state, kingdom, commonwealth, realm. **3** *The country will hold an election this year:* nation, population, populace, inhabitants, citizens, people, natives, public, community, countrymen. **4** *His father's country was Czechoslovakia:* native country, native land, mother country, homeland, fatherland, native soil; nationality. **5** *City people often dream of buying a house in the country:* rural areas, countryside, hinterlands, farming area, wide open spaces; *Slang* sticks, outback, backwoods.

—*adj.* **6** *She was born in a little country village in the Fens:* rural, farming, farm, provincial, rustic, back country; unsophisticated, simple.

Ant. 5 city, town, urban area, metropolis. **6** urban, cosmopolitan, city, urbane, sophisticated, citified.

◇ *Word origin: Country* comes from Latin *contra,* against, hence a region or land set against another, a separate or distinct region or nation. Latin *contra* also gives us such words as *contrary, contradict, counter, counteract, counterbalance, counterpoint,* etc.

countryman *n.* **1** *"Friends, Romans, countrymen, lend me your ears":* compatriot, fellow citizen, fellow countryman. **2** *The city slicker tried to outwit the innocent countryman:* rustic, farmer, peasant, yeoman, provincial; *Slang* yokel, gaffer, country bumpkin, clodhopper.

Ant. 1 alien, foreigner, stranger. **2** city dweller, townsman, urbanite, metropolitan, cosmopolitan, city slicker.

coup de grâce *n. After the firing-squad finished, an officer administered the coup de grâce with a pistol:* death-blow, finishing stroke, mercy stroke.

◇ *Word origin: Coup de grâce* is a French phrase meaning "stroke of mercy."

coup d'état *n. French army leaders ousted the president in the latest coup d'état:* overthrow, rebellion, revolution, palace revolution; subversion, uprising, mutiny.

◇ *Word origin:* Spelt *coup d'état* in modern French usage, this phrase means literally "stroke of state," hence an unexpected stroke of policy, especially a sudden seizure of power.

couple *n.* **1** *Bring a couple of chairs for John and Joan:* pair, two of a kind, combination of two, doublet. **2** *Mr. and Mrs. Cutler are a nice-looking couple:* twosome, pair, duo; man and wife, husband and wife, married pair, engaged pair, man and woman.

—*v.* **3** *The guard's van is coupled to the last goods wagon:* connect, join, link, fasten, hitch, tie, bind, yoke.

Ant. 3 detach, separate, disconnect, part, unfasten, unhitch, untie.

◇ *Word origin: Couple* comes from Latin *copula,* bond, band, which also gives us *couplet* (two successive lines of verse, usually rhymed, forming a single unit).

courage *n. He was mentioned in dispatches for his courage in battle:* bravery, valour, fearlessness, dauntlessness, stout-heartedness, daring, boldness, hardiness, nerve; *Slang* guts, pluck, spunk, mettle, grit.

Ant. cowardice, faint-heartedness, pusillanimity, timidity; terror, fear, dread.

course *n.* **1** *The ship was 200 miles off course:* route, direction, path, channel, passage, road, track, way; orbit, trajectory. **2** *In the course of the discussion many views were heard:* progression, development, onward movement, unfolding, flow, march. **3** *Your best course would be to accept his offer:* procedure, action, conduct, method, mode, behaviour. **4** *The college offers courses in science and in the humanities:* classes, lessons, lectures; course of study, curriculum, subject. **5** *The country club has a golf course. The riders must follow the course round to the left:* circuit, circle, round, run; racecourse, track.

—*v.* **6** *The trout stream courses over the rocks:* run, flow, race, pour, surge, gush, stream.

◇ *Usage note:* Some people find it difficult to separate the meanings of *coarse* and *course. Coarse* is an adjective meaning: rough, unrefined, hence vulgar. *Course,* on the other hand, is a noun meaning: direction, passage of time, progress, a series of events, line of conduct, a class or curriculum of studies, a portion of a meal, or land passed over. Thus, *The best wholemeal bread is made from* coarse *flour, His wife blushed at his* coarse *joke.* But *The plane's* course *was due south, In the* course *of one year her hair turned completely grey, The disease must run its* course, *Wars have influenced the* course *of history, What* course *of action should I follow? When you finish the Red Cross* course, *you can be a midwife, The final* course *was apple pie with ice cream, Have you played on this golf-*course *before?*

> **Exploring the Word**: Latin *cor,* heart, gives us *courage,* having heart; *concord* and *accord,* being of one heart, agreement; *discord,* with the hearts apart, hence, lack of agreement; *cordial,* from the heart, friendly, and also a drink that invigorates or stimulates the heart; and even *record,* which literally means to bring something back to the heart or mind, as does a written record, a photographic record, or a gramophone record. (Our word *cardiac* doesn't come from Latin *cor* but from its Greek cognate *kardia,* heart.)

court *n.* **1** *Some of Shakespeare's plays were performed before the court of Queen Elizabeth I:* royal household, staff, entourage, retinue, train, advisers, council, following, cortège, attendants. **2** *The king held court every day:* audience, hearing, assembly, meeting. **3** *Hampton Court was the country home of Henry VIII:* palace, castle, château, hall, manor. **4** *The new block is built round a court:* courtyard, yard, enclosed area, quadrangle, quad. **5** *The knight paid court to his fair lady:* courtship, homage, respects, address, solicitations, flattering attention; suit, wooing. **6** *The young lawyer made his first appearance before the court:* court of law, court of justice, bench, bar, judicial tribunal.

—*v.* **7** *Some businessmen court only wealthy clients:* curry favour with, fawn upon, pander to; woo, pay suit to, pay one's addresses to; pursue, run after. **8** *Don't court disaster by driving too fast:* invite, attract, induce, provoke, seek.

Ant. 7 avoid, shun, ignore, refuse, repudiate, reject, turn down, turn away.

◇ *Word origin: Court* comes to English via Old French *cort,* from Latin *cohors,* troop of soldiers — hence, later, a king's troop of advisers and friends, a king's council and retinue. Latin *cohors* also gives us our word *cohort,* while Old French *cort* also gives us our words *courtesy* and *courteous*, literally "befitting a royal court."

courteous *adj. They wrote us a courteous thank-you note. Bill is always a courteous youth:* polite, well-mannered, mannerly, well-behaved, refined, well-bred, civil, respectful, tactful, diplomatic, kind, gracious, considerate; soft-spoken, mild.

Ant. discourteous, impolite, rude, uncivil, curt, ill-mannered, unmannerly, insolent, disrespectful, unkind, ungracious.

◇ *Word origin:* See COURT.

courtesy *n.* **1** *Friend or foe, king or fool, treat everyone with courtesy:* politeness, courteousness, good manners, manners, good behaviour, civility, respect, deference, kindly consideration, graciousness, gentility, gentle breeding, cultivation, refinement, courtliness, gallantry. **2** *Each woman shopper was given a rose by courtesy of the management:* courteous act, favour, considerate gesture, kindness, consideration, indulgence; regards, respects.

Ant. 1, 2 discourtesy. **1** impoliteness, discourteousness, bad manners, unmannerliness, rudeness, incivility, disrespect, insolence; churlishness, boorishness.

◇ *Word origin:* See COURT.

courtly *adj. The old man was esteemed for his courtly manners:* refined, genteel, polished, elegant, decorous, civilized, gallant, chivalrous, dignified, stately; aristocratic, blue-blooded, well-bred; polite, courteous, mannerly, gentlemanly.

Ant. unrefined, inelegant, ungentlemanly, undignified, unpolished, impolite; coarse, vulgar, base, low, boorish, loutish, plebeian; ill-mannered, discourteous, rude, uncivil.

courtship *n. They were married after a courtship of nine years:* wooing, courting, suit, engagement period, keeping company.

cove *n. The boat was anchored in the cove:* bay, inlet, lagoon, estuary.

◇ *Word origin: Cove* comes from Old English *cofa*, a cave, cavelike room.

covenant *n. The Old Testament tells of the covenant God made with the Jews:* solemn agreement, pledge, vow, promise, oath, bond; pact, treaty, contract.

cover *v.* **1** *Grandmother always covered the table with a lace cloth:* put on, put over, lay on, overlay, blanket, clothe, sheathe, shroud, envelop, wrap, enwrap. **2** *The raincoat covered him from top to toe:* protect, shield, guard, shelter, defend. **3** *She covered her face with her hands:* hide, conceal, obscure, secrete; cloak, veil, screen; mask, disguise, camouflage. **4** *The history book covers the years of Queen Anne's reign. The reporter covered the convention for the local newspaper:* deal with, include, involve, contain; embrace, encompass, take in, comprehend; report, tell of, write up. **5** *We covered three countries in two days:* travel through, pass over, pass through, traverse, cross.

—*n.* **6** *The jewel box had a carved wooden cover. Don't judge a book by its cover:* lid, top, cap, covering; wrapper, case, encasement, envelope, jacket, sheath, binding. **7** *Do you want another cover on the bed?:* blanket, bedspread, quilt, coverlet, eiderdown. **8** *When the rain started, we took cover under a large tree:* shelter, protection, shield, guard, defence; asylum, refuge, sanctuary, concealment, hiding-place. **9** *This insurance policy provides cover for all types of accident:* protection, indemnity; payment, reimbursement.

Ant. 1 uncover, remove, take off; unclothe, unwrap, expose. **2** expose. **3** uncover, reveal, exhibit, show, unmask, expose. **4** exclude, omit, leave out. **6** base, bottom, stand. **8** exposure.

coverage *n. The newscaster received an award for his coverage of the election:* reporting, description, analysis; publishing, broadcasting.

covering *n.* **1** *The lampshade was wrapped in a cellophane covering:* cover, wrapper, wrapping, casing, envelope, sheath.

—*adj.* **2** *Send a covering letter with your résumé:* descriptive, explanatory.

covert *adj. The police had a covert meeting with the kidnappers to arrange for release of the captive:* secret, clandestine, hidden, concealed, unknown, veiled, disguised.

Ant. overt, known, open, public; candid, frank, plain, clear, evident, obvious.

covet *v. The assistant coveted his boss's job:* desire, desire greedily, crave, lust after, yearn for, want, long for, aspire to, have an eye on, fancy, hanker after.

Ant. reject, forswear, decline, refuse, renounce, relinquish.

covetous *adj. Poverty made him covetous of others' wealth:* craving, desirous, lustful, yearning; greedy, avaricious, rapacious, grasping, mercenary, selfish; envious, jealous.

Ant. self-denying, self-abnegating, forswearing, renouncing, abjuring; liberal, generous, bountiful, unselfish.

cow *v. The smaller boys were cowed by the form bully:* intimidate, frighten, make cringe, terrorize, terrify, scare, browbeat, bully, bulldoze; dishearten, dismay, abash, discourage, deter.

Ant. calm, soothe, quiet, encourage, support.

"Cowards die many times before their deaths;
The valiant never taste of death but once."
— *William Shakespeare*

---

coward *n. Only a coward would run from danger:* uncourageous person, dastard, caitiff, craven, poltroon; *Slang* cry-baby, yellow-belly; milksop, molly-coddle, sissy.

Ant. brave person, hero, champion, daredevil.

◇ *Word origin: Coward* comes from Latin *cauda*, tail, perhaps because a coward is one who, like a dog, sneaks away with his tail between his legs.

cowardly *adj. Sending anonymous letters is a cowardly act:* uncourageous, faint-hearted, timorous, timid, dastardly, craven, pusillanimous; showing the white feather; *Slang* chicken-hearted, yellow, yellow-bellied, lily-livered, gutless; frightened, afraid, fearful, apprehensive, anxious, nervous, shaky, tremulous.

Ant. brave, courageous, valiant, valorous, dauntless, stout-hearted, lion-hearted, plucky, spunky; bold, daring, audacious, intrepid, doughty.

cower *v. The serfs cowered before the lord of the manor:* crouch in fear, cringe, draw back, shrink, bow, flinch, quail, tremble; grovel, crawl, truckle, toady.

Ant. swagger, strut, stand up to; intimidate, bully, terrorize, cow, browbeat.

coy *adj. She always gets coy when asked to recite:* shy, modest, bashful, sheepish, shrinking, timid, timorous, skittish; overmodest, prudish, blushing, demure; pretending to be shy, coquettish, kittenish.

Ant. brash, brazen, bold, forward, impudent, impertinent, flippant, flip, pert, saucy, immodest.

◇ *Word origin: Coy* comes to us via Old French *quei*, from Latin *quietus*, quiet.

crack *v.* **1** *The whip cracked as the wagon driver started the horses:* sound sharply, snap, pop, crack, crackle, clap, thunder; strike sharply. **2** *The plate cracked when I dropped it:* split, fracture, cleave, chip, splinter, break partially. **3** *Anyone can crack under extreme pressure:* break, break down, give way, lose control, become irrational, go to pieces.

—*n.* **4** *There was the crack of rifle fire in the distance:* sharp sound, report, snap, pop, clap, crackle. **5** *The earthquake caused huge cracks in the earth:* split, fissure, rift, rent, cleft, slit, gash, crevice, rupture. **6** *Don't make any cracks about her funny-looking hat:* wisecrack, joke, quip, gag, jest, gibe, funny remark, teasing remark, witticism; insult, critical remark, taunt.

cradle *n.* **1** *The child slept soundly in her cradle:* bed on rockers, baby's bed; (*loosely*) crib, bassinet. **2** *Athens was the cradle of democracy:* beginning place, birthplace, nursery, source, fountain, fountain-head, fount, well-spring, spring.

—*v.* **3** *The nurse cradled the infant in her arms:* rock, cuddle, snuggle, enfold, hug, clasp tenderly.

craft *n.* **1** *Thatching is a craft that is fast dying out:* skill, ability, adeptness, deftness, fineness, proficiency, adroitness, knack, competency, expertise, expertness, know-how, technique, mastery. **2** *Weaving was the town's chief craft:* trade, business, occupation, vocation, employment; industry, commerce, pursuit, calling; handicraft, art. **3** *Magicians use craft to hoodwink an audience:* craftiness, cunning, artifice, ruse, wile, trickery, chicanery; deception, guile, duplicity, deceit; intrigue, sharp practice. **4** *The small craft skimmed over the water:* ship, boat, vessel; aircraft, aeroplane, plane.

Ant. **1** inaptitude, unskilfulness, maladroitness, inaptness, ineptitude, ineptness, inability, incompetency, clumsiness. **2** manual labour; intellectual pursuit. **3** openness, candour, frankness, straightforwardness, sincerity, ingenuousness.

crafty *adj. The crafty business partner wound up with all the money:* cunning, shrewd, sharp, wily, foxy, tricky, sly, guileful, artful, shifty, underhand, devious, deceptive, deceitful, unethical, dishonest; intriguing, scheming, designing, calculating, plotting astute, canny, suspicious.

Ant. honest, open, candid, frank, above-board, ethical; naïve, innocent, simple, ingenuous.

cram *v.* **1** *He couldn't cram any more into the bulging suitcase:* jam, pack, stuff, fill, fill to overflowing, crowd, overcrowd, congest; force, press, compress, squeeze, ram. **2** *Informal The student had to cram for her history test:* study hastily, study hard, grind.

Ant. **1** empty, deplete, drain, exhaust, clear.

cramp *n.* **1** *She got cramp in her leg whilst swimming:* muscular contraction, spasm, stitch, crick, stiffness; sharp pain, pang.

—*v.* **2** *Lack of education cramped his chances of getting a good job:* hamper, hold back, restrict, limit, check, hinder, thwart, frustrate, handicap, obstruct, block, stymie.

Ant. **2** help, aid, advance, forward, expand, increase; free, release, loose.

◇ *Word origin: Cramp* comes from Middle Dutch *krampe*, hook.

cranky *adj. My husband is always cranky in the morning until he's had his coffee:* grouchy, cross, bearish, crotchety, ill-tempered, ill-humoured, out of sorts, irascible, captious, splenetic, cantankerous, peevish, waspish, testy, petulant.

Ant. good-natured, good-humoured, cheerful, gay, happy, amiable, agreeable, complaisant; placid, calm, serene.

crash *v.* **1** *The flowerpot crashed to the pavement:* fall heavily, dash, strike noisily, smash, shatter, clatter; topple, hurtle, tumble, plunge. **2** *The two cars crashed at the junction:* collide, strike together, dash together, hit together, smash, bump, bang. **3** *Five boys tried to crash her birthday party:* enter without invitation, come uninvited to, enter without a ticket, slip in, sneak in, invade, intrude.

—*n.* **4** *We could hear the crash of pots and pans in the kitchen:* clatter, bang, din, racket, clangour, crack, boom; noisy breaking, shattering, smashing; noisy striking, hitting, bumping; falling, toppling, plunging, tumbling.

5 *Several persons were injured in the crash:* collision, smash-up, crack-up, accident, wreck. **6** *The stock-market crash of 1929 ruined many people:* financial collapse, financial disaster, failure, bankruptcy, ruin; (*loosely*) depression, recession, slump, decline, set-back.

Ant. 4 silence; murmur, whisper. **6** prosperity, upsurge, flourishing, success.

crass *adj. His crass manners made others dislike him:* coarse, crude, vulgar, gross, unrefined, unpolished, inelegant; uncaring, insensitive, boorish, oafish, unsympathetic, unfeeling, hard-hearted, cruel.

Ant. refined, polished, elegant; deferential, obliging, sympathetic, kind, warm-hearted, soft-hearted.

◇ *Word origin: Crass* comes from Latin *crassus,* thick, fat.

crave *v. Since going on the diet she craves sweets:* pine for, sigh for, wish for, hope for, desire, want, long for, yearn for, hunger for, thirst for, hanker after, have a fancy for, lust after, covet; require, need.

Ant. reject, spurn, repudiate, renounce, scorn, refuse, decline; detest, abominate, loathe, hate, despise, abhor.

craven *adj. Refusing to stand and fight was a craven thing to do:* cowardly, dastardly, pusillanimous; timid, timorous, fearful, frightened, scared; *Slang* yellow, lily-livered, chicken-hearted; mean-spirited, base, low, low-down.

Ant. brave, courageous, heroic, fearless, valorous, valiant, dauntless; bold, daring, audacious.

crawl *v.* **1** *The caterpillar crawled across the rock:* move by dragging the body, creep, slither, squirm, wiggle, writhe, worm; move on hands and knees, go on all fours. **2** *The holiday traffic crawled along the motorway:* go at snail's pace, inch, drag, worm, potter, mosey.

Ant. 1 walk; run. **2** race, rush, dash, dart, spurt, hurry, hasten, tear, go like a bat out of hell, go like the wind.

craze *v.* **1** *The shipwrecked men were crazed with thirst:* drive mad, make crazy, make insane, drive wild, send berserk, derange, unhinge, cause to run amok.

—*n.* **2** *Hula hoops were a craze some years ago:* fad, rage, popular whim, mania, passion, infatuation.

Ant. 1 calm, soothe, ease.

crazy *adj.* **1** *Not all crazy people are in asylums:* insane, mad, demented, deranged, maniac, daft, unbalanced, unhinged; *Slang* cracked, touched, nuts, nutty, off one's head, mad as a hatter, mad as a March hare. **2** *She always wears a crazy hat:* bizarre, weird, odd, unusual, peculiar, strange, uncommon, silly, absurd, outrageous, laughable; *Slang* far-out. **3** *You children are crazy to get married so young:* foolish, imprudent, unwise, foolhardy; senseless, stupid, silly, ridiculous, idiotic, absurd. **4** *All the girls are crazy about the good-looking football star:* mad, smitten with, taken with, fanatical, wild, keen, rabid, avid, zealous, frantic, hysterical, excited; very fond, infatuated, passionate, enthusiastic.

Ant. 1 sane, mentally sound, rational, reasonable, sensible, well-balanced. **2** sensible, practical; acceptable, conservative, common, average, usual, run-of-the-mill. **3** smart, wise, prudent, sensible. **4** unenthusiastic, uncaring, unexcited, cool, indifferent.

creak *v. The rusty hinges creaked when the gate opened:* rasp, squeak, screech, grate, grind.

crease *n.* **1** *Iron the creases out of this blouse:* fold, wrinkle, ridge, crinkle, rumple, pucker, corrugation.

—*v.* **2** *Years of worry had creased his brow:* wrinkle, pucker, crinkle, rumple, corrugate; fold, pleat, rumple.

Ant. 2 smooth, flatten, straighten out.

create *v.* **1** *The chemist worked for years to create a waterproof glue:* originate, invent, develop, devise, formulate, make, concoct, contrive, fashion, fabricate, design, form, mould, erect, construct, bring into being, give birth to; cause, bring to pass. **2** *The government has created a new department of sport:* found, establish, set up, institute, form, organize, appoint.

Ant. 1 destroy, demolish, annihilate. **2** close, shut down.

◇ *Word origin: Create* comes from Latin *creare,* to produce, create. The same Latin verb gives us *procreate, recreation,* and *creature.*

"Vitality in a woman is a blind fury of creation." —*George Bernard Shaw*

---

creation *n.* **1** *The whale is the largest mammal in creation:* the world, the universe, nature; all things, all living things. **2** *The creation of new playgrounds will benefit the local children:* creating, making, institution, origination, development, devising, establishment, founding, production, bringing into existence, formation; building, construction, fabrication, fashioning, erection. **3** *The designer's latest creation is a backless evening dress:* original work, imaginative work, invention, brainchild, concoction, production, handiwork.

Ant. 2 destruction, demolition, annihilation.

◇ *Word origin: Creation* and *creator,* like *create,* come from Latin *creare,* to produce, but are rare in classical use. Latin-speaking Christians coined both words in translating the Old and New Testaments from Hebrew and Greek. Our use of "creation" to mean "the world" (sense **1** above) comes from the King James version of Romans 8.22: "For we know that the whole creation groaneth and travaileth in pain together until now."

creative *adj. James Joyce was one of Ireland's most creative writers:* original, imaginative, fertile, ingenious, inventive, fanciful, visionary.

creator *n.* **1** *Captain W. E. Johns was the creator of "Biggles":* originator, author, framer, designer, producer, architect, maker, initiator, inventor, founder, father, generator, begetter. **2 The Creator.** See GOD.

creature *n. All creatures great and small inhabit the earth:* living being, living thing; animal, lower animal, dumb animal, beast; (*variously*) quadruped, vertebrate, invertebrate, mammal, bird, fish, reptile, insect; human being, human, mortal, man, person, individual.

◇ *Word origin:* See CREATE.

credentials *n. The new ambassador will present his credentials to the Queen this morning. A scholar's publications are his credentials:* (*diplomatic*) letter of credence; official testimonials; (*general*) written proof of status or qualifications, certificate, diploma, reference, letter of recommendation, testimonial, authorization.

credible *adj. Is the witness's story credible?:* believable, plausible, reasonable, likely, possible, probable, tenable; conceivable, thinkable, imaginable; reliable, trustworthy, dependable.

Ant. incredible, unbelievable, implausible, unreasonable, unlikely, improbable, inconceivable; unreliable, untrustworthy, dubious, doubtful, questionable, unthinkable.

◇ *Usage note: Credible, creditable,* and *credulous* confuse some people. *Credible* means believable: *Do you think his story is credible — or incredible? Creditable* means to one's credit, praiseworthy: *My son gets very creditable marks at school. Credulous* means gullible, believing too easily: *Con men love to cheat credulous women.*

credit *n.* **1** *The photographer was given credit in the programme:* recognition, acknowledgement; honour, high regard, esteem, glory, acclaim. **2** *We bought the sofa on credit:* the instalment plan, account, H.P. **3** *You have a credit of £10 towards your next purchase:* allowance, prepayment.

—*v.* **4** *Edison is credited with the invention of the phonograph:* attribute, ascribe, assign, acknowledge, recognize; honour, acclaim. **5** *How could you credit such a wild story?:* believe, trust, have faith in, put confidence in, rely on, accept; *Informal* swallow, fall for, buy.

Ant. 1 disgrace, shame, censure, ignominy. **2** cash, cash on the nail. **3** debit, charge. **5** doubt, disbelieve, distrust, question.

creditable *adj. The coach did a creditable job in bringing the team through to the final:* admirable, commendable, praiseworthy, meritorious, laudable; reputable, estimable, respectable, worthy.

Ant. blameable, censurable, discreditable; disreputable, dishonourable.

◇ *Usage note:* See CREDIBLE.

credo *n. His credo is to work hard and save every penny:* creed, set of beliefs, doctrine, tenet, code, rule, maxim, motto, philosophy.

credulous *adj. Anne is so credulous she'll believe anything you tell her:* ready to believe, easily convinced, gullible, believing; too trustful, over-trustful, unsuspecting, unsuspicious, unquestioning.

Ant. incredulous, unbelieving; suspicious, suspecting, wary, cynical.

◇ *Usage note:* See CREDIBLE.

creed *n. The minister explained the church's creed to the visitors:* religious belief, belief, profession of faith, doctrine, dogma, set of principles, credo, group of tenets, canons, gospel.

creek *n. The children love to wade in the creek:* inlet, fiord, estuary, bay, cove, firth, mouth, arm of the sea.

creep *v.* **1** *The snake crept along the garden wall:* crawl, slither, writhe, worm, wriggle, squirm. **2** *The hunter crept up as close to the deer as possible:* advance secretly, walk stealthily, come unnoticed, sneak, steal. **3** *The old car crept down the road:* move slowly, inch, crawl, dawdle, potter along, go at snail's pace.

Ant. 1 run. **2** blunder, bluster, trample. **3** race, rush, fly, tear, hasten, hurry, sprint, dart, dash, go like the wind, *Slang* go like a bat out of hell, go like the clappers.

crest *n.* **1** *The bird has a crest of white feathers:* tuft, topknot, comb, plume, crown. **2** *The look-out tower is on the crest of the hill:* top, summit, pinnacle, highest point, peak, tip, apex, height. **3** *They proudly displayed their family crest above the mantelpiece:* coat of arms, arms, armorial bearings, escutcheon.

Ant. 2 bottom, base.

crestfallen *adj. The team was crestfallen after losing the game:* down-hearted, downcast, dejected, depressed, disappointed; discouraged, disheartened, dispirited, low-spirited, despondent, woebegone.

Ant. elated, exuberant, happy, joyful, up in the clouds, in seventh heaven; encouraged, heartened, uplifted.

crevice *n. A huge crevice split the iceberg almost in two:* fissure, crack, cleft, split, fracture, rift, rent, slit; chasm, crevasse.

◇ *Usage note: Crevice* is a general word, meaning any crack or fissure. *Crevasse* is a mountaineering word, meaning a deep chasm or fissure in a glacier.

crew *n.* **1** *The television crew began to film the interview:* work gang, squad, corps, force, team, company, party. **2** *The ship's crew mutinied:* work-force, company of sailors, company, complement, hands, sailors, mariners, seafarers, seamen; air crew, plane crew. **3** *The rebels were a motley crew:* band, body, pack, group, mob, throng, troop, horde; assemblage, multitude, mass, herd.

Ant. 2 officers.

crime *n.* **1** *He was convicted of the crime of embezzling:* unlawful act, violation of the law, lawbreaking, foul play, offence; capital crime, felony, misdemeanour, malfeasance. **2** *It's a*

crime to waste so much food: wrong, wrongdoing, misdeed, blameworthy action, misconduct; senseless act, wasteful act, outrage, villainy, abomination; sin, transgression, iniquity, wickedness.
Ant. **1** lawful act; retribution, pardon. **2** good deed, right, virtue, virtuous act; benefit, boon.

> **Exploring the Word**: The Latin word *crimen* means both accusation and judgement. It gives us *crime: criminal* (originally an accused person but now one judged guilty); *incriminate,* to charge with a crime; and *discriminate,* to judge by making a distinction between persons, concepts, or things.

criminal *adj.* **1** *Robbery is a criminal act:* illegal, unlawful, law-breaking, lawless, felonious, illicit, crooked, guilty, delinquent. **2** *It's criminal to let such a fine garden go to rack and ruin:* wrong, blameworthy; senseless, wasteful; outrageous, wicked, villainous, abominable. —*n.* **3** *The criminal was sent to prison for ten years:* guilty person, person convicted of a crime; culprit, law-breaker, outlaw, felon; *Informal* crook; wrongdoer, transgressor, malefactor, offender.
Ant. **1** lawful, legal, licit; honest, law-abiding; innocent. **2** right, just, commendable, admirable, meritorious, honourable, praiseworthy. **3** innocent person.
cringe *v. The child cringed every time his father raised his voice:* cower, flinch, shrink, quail, blench, recoil, dodge, duck; grovel, be servile, toady, truckle.
Ant. strut, swagger.
cripple *n.* **1** *Before the Salk vaccine infantile paralysis made cripples of many people:* lame person, the halt, the disabled, the handicapped; *Slang* old crock.
—*v.* **2** *The accident crippled her permanently:* make lame, disable, incapacitate; damage, harm, maim. **3** *The snowstorm crippled rail transport:* impair, disable, incapacitate, render impotent, debilitate, hamstring, inactivate; stop, halt, bring to a standstill.
Ant. **3** help, aid, assist, ease, facilitate.
◇ *Word origin: Cripple* comes from Old English *crēopan,* to creep.
crisis *n. Negotiations between the two countries are approaching a crisis:* turning-point, climax; emergency, critical stage, crux.
◇ *Word origin: Crisis* comes from Greek *krisis,* turning-point, point of decision.
crisp *adj.* **1** *These potato crisps are not very crisp:* crispy, brittle, snappy, crunchy. **2** *It was a delightful evening of crisp conversation:* brisk, sharp, pointed, snappy, incisive, candid, terse; vivacious, energetic, lively, sparkling, witty. **3** *Yesterday was a crisp autumn day:* brisk, pleasantly cool, chilly, nippy, bracing, refreshing, fresh, invigorating.
Ant. **1** limp, soft, wilted. **2** dull, slow, cautious, insipid. **3** warm, balmy.
◇ *Word origin: Crisp* comes from Latin *crispus,* curled.
criterion *n. What is the major criterion for judging a symphony?:* standard, measure, gauge, yardstick, rule, principle, law, norm; model, precedent, example, touchstone.
◇ *Usage note: Criterion* is the singular form of the word: *What is your one criterion for judging the value of diamonds?* The plural is *criteria,* which must take the plural verb: *The criteria for judging show dogs are complex.*
◇ *Word origin: Criterion* comes from Greek *kritērion.* Its source is Greek *krinein,* to decide, judge, which also gives us *critic.*
critic *n.* **1** *I like painting, but I'm no critic of modern art:* judge, connoisseur, expert, authority, virtuoso; evaluator, analyst, arbiter; professional reviewer, commentator. **2** *The Minister called a press conference to answer his critics:* detractor, antagonist, attacker, fault-finder, censor, criticizer; carper, scold, back-biter, reviler, vilifier; *Informal* knocker.
◇ *Word origin: Critic, critical, criticism,* and *criticize* come from Greek *kritēs,* judge, one who decides.
critical *adj.* **1** *Don't be so critical of everyone else:* censorious, faultfinding, disparaging, derogatory, fussy, nagging, cavilling, carping, nit-picking, disapproving, finicky, hair-splitting. **2** *It takes years to develop one's critical faculties:* judging, discriminating, analytical, diagnostic; perspicacious, judicious. **3** *This is a critical time in the nation's economy:* decisive, crucial, grave, serious, urgent, momentous, pressing, vital; dangerous, perilous, precarious, hazardous, risky.
Ant. **1–3** uncritical. **1** complimentary, approving, laudatory; inexact, haphazard, permissive. **2** undiscriminating, unanalytical, shallow. **3** secure, settled, calm, tranquil; safe.
criticize *v. She's always criticizing her husband for being sloppy:* find fault with, disapprove of, disparage, cast aspersions on, reprove, reproach, denounce, censure; nag at, fuss, carp, cavil, pick to pieces.
Ant. compliment, praise, commend, laud, extol, applaud.
critique *n. The students were required to write a critique of a Hemingway novel:* critical essay, criticism, critical commentary, critical examination; review.
crook *n.* **1** *Shepherds in the West Country still carry their traditional crooks:* staff, stock, support, crutch, hook, arc, bow. **2** *The crook in the road hides the cottage from view:* bend, curve, turn, twist, angle, curvature. **3** *Only a crook would charge for work and not do it:* cheat, dishonest person, knave, criminal, robber, thief, bandit, swindler, embezzler; outlaw, thug, burglar, robber.

crooked *adj.* **1** *Please straighten that crooked picture. The old mill is on a crooked road:* askew, awry, not straight; curved, twisted, twisting, winding, meandering, tortuous, sinuous, serpentine, zigzag, spiral; bent, bowed, hooked; distorted, deformed, warped, out of shape. **2** *The agent was suspected of crooked dealings:* dishonest, corrupt, unscrupulous, dishonourable, criminal, unlawful; deceptive, fraudulent, unethical, underhand, deceitful, nefarious; sneaky, shifty, shady, wily, crafty.

Ant. 1 straight, straight as an arrow; flat. **2** honest, legal, lawful, ethical, scrupulous, honourable, fair, above-board, upright.

crop *n.* **1** *This year's corn crop will set a new record:* harvest, yield, gleaning, gathering, reaping.
—*v.* **2** *His hair was cropped when he entered the army:* cut short, clip, shear, trim, lop, snip, cut, bob, prune.

cross *n.* **1** *The church has a cross on top of its steeple:* rood, crucifix. **2** *Her illness is a cross she will have to bear:* burden, misfortune; affliction, suffering, ordeal, trial, tribulation, trouble. **3** *The mule is a cross between a female horse and a male donkey:* cross-breed, hybrid, half-breed; blend, combination, amalgam.
—*v.* **4.** *Cross the eggs off the shopping list:* delete, strike out, cancel, cross out, obliterate. **5** *We crossed the river in a rowing-boat:* go across, traverse, cut across, go over, pass over, travel over, travel through; intersect, meet, criss-cross. **6** *They tried to cross a beagle with a Saint Bernard:* cross-breed, interbreed, mix, intermix; hybridize, cross-pollinate, cross-fertilize.
—*adj.* **7** *The roof is supported by cross beams:* intersecting, lying crosswise; athwart, transverse, oblique. **8** *Why is Mother so cross today?:* angry, mad, ill-tempered, annoyed, in a bad mood, cranky, petulant, surly, disagreeable, ill-humoured, grouchy, peevish, touchy, snappish, shirty, churlish, gruff, out of sorts, irritable, waspish, irascible, testy, choleric, cantankerous, crotchety, captious, splenetic; contrary, querulous, intractable.

Ant. 2 relief, respite; boon, benefit. **3** thoroughbred. **4** write down, add, include. **8** good-humoured, good-natured, good-tempered; agreeable, amenable, sweet.

◇ *Word origin:* The word *cross* comes from Latin *crux*, cross, which also gives us *crucifix, crusade*, and *crucial.*

> "Don't cross the bridge till you come to it,
> Is a proverb old, and of excellent wit."
> —*Henry Wadsworth Longfellow*

crotchety *adj. Grandfather has grown crotchety with age:* cranky, contrary, fussy, grouchy eccentric, odd, peculiar, erratic.

◇ *Word origin:* A *crotchety* person is full of stubborn or eccentric ideas, full of little twists. The word comes from *crochet*, the diminutive of French *croc*, hook.

crow *v.* **1** *The cock crows at daybreak:* utter the cry of a cock, cackle, call. **2** *I wish he would stop crowing about his promotion:* gloat, boast, brag, strut, swagger, vaunt; *Slang* blow; exult, rejoice, triumph, trumpet.

crowd *n.* **1** *Shop early and avoid the crowd:* throng, multitude, horde, mob, swarm, herd, flock, host, legion; gathering, assemblage, congregation. **2** *She's started to go around with a rather fast crowd:* set, circle, circle of friends, clique, claque, group, coterie.
—*v.* **3** *We crowded round the platform to hear the speaker:* congregate, flock, swarm, gather, assemble; cluster, mass, herd, throng, huddle, concentrate. **4** *The eager spectators crowded into the stadium:* shove, push, press, cram, jam, squeeze, swarm, surge, elbow in.

Ant. 3 disperse, scatter; draw back, draw away, retreat.

crowded *adj. Trafalgar Square is always crowded on New Year's Eve:* crammed, jammed, jam-packed, packed, full, filled, mobbed, congested, teeming, swarming, thronged, overflowing.

Ant. empty; half-full.

crown *n.* **1** *The queen wore a crown encrusted with diamonds:* coronet, tiara, diadem, circlet. **2** *The winning athlete was given a crown of laurel leaves:* wreath, garland, circlet, chaplet. **3** *The ambassador is a respresentative of the Crown:* royalty, sovereignty, monarchy, royal dominion. **4** *The crown of the hat is covered with lace:* highest part, top, summit, pinnacle, peak, crest, apex, zenith, acme. **5** *Jack fell down and broke his crown:* top of the head, pate, head; *Slang* noddle, bonce.
—*v.* **6** *Our Kings and Queens are crowned in Westminster Abbey:* invest with a crown, give royal power to, put a crown upon. **7** *Winning an Academy Award crowned the actor's career:* top, top off, bring to the highest point, climax, complete, fulfil, perfect, round off, reach a peak.

Ant. 4 bottom, base, foot. **6** dethrone, depose.

◇ *Word origin: Crown* comes from Latin *corona*, crown, which also gives us *coronation* (the crowning of a new king or queen), the *coronary arteries* (two arteries which encircle the heart like a crown), and *coronary* (*thrombosis*), a thrombosis (blood clot) in one of these two arteries.

> "The poorest man may in his cottage bid defiance to all the forces of the Crown."
> — *William Pitt*

crucial *adj. Father made all the crucial decisions in our family:* decisive, critical, determining, significant, momentous, important, pressing, urgent; grave, serious.

crude *adj.* **1** *The crude sugar was shipped to the*

refinery: raw, unrefined, unprocessed, unprepared; coarse. **2** *The client was shown the crude sketches of the architect's plans:* uncompleted, incomplete, unfinished, rough, undeveloped, sketchy, imperfect. **3** *I've never appreciated his crude sense of humour:* vulgar, obscene, unrefined, coarse, tasteless, crass, gross, uncouth, unpolished.

Ant. 1 refined, processed, prepared; fine, fine-grained. **2** final, finished, completed. **3** refined, polished, tasteful, subtle, urbane.

cruel *adj. Attila the Hun was a cruel tyrant:* inhuman, inhumane, sadistic, brutal, vicious, savage, merciless, unmerciful; heartless, pitiless, uncompassionate, unfeeling, hard-hearted, ruthless, remorseless, cold-blooded.

Ant. humane, benevolent, merciful, compassionate, kind, warm-hearted, sympathetic, tender, gentle, mild.

crumb *n. Slicing the bread left crumbs all over the table:* scrap, shred, bit, morsel, sliver, minute portion, particle, fragment, speck, grain.

crumble *v.* **1** *Crumble the biscuits to make the base:* break into crumbs, fragment, splinter; crush, grind, pulverize, powder, grate. **2** *After years of neglect the house began to crumble:* decay, disintegrate, fall apart, break up, waste away, wear away, go to rack and ruin.

crumple *v.* **1** *The new synthetic fabrics won't crumple when folded:* wrinkle, rumple, crease, crinkle, crush; pucker, corrugate. **2** *The staircase crumpled under his weight:* collapse, give way, cave in, fall, fall to pieces, break up.

crunch *v. The squirrels crunched the nuts:* chew noisily, chomp, gnaw, gnash, grind, munch; chew, masticate.

crusade *n.* **1** *The First Crusade departed for the Holy Land in 1096:* military expedition against non-Christians. **2** *The city is launching a crusade to clean up the slums:* reform movement, idealistic campaign, movement, drive; rally, mass meeting.

◇ *Word origin:* The word *crusade* (related to Latin *crux*, cross) refers to the fact that the Christian knights' arms were marked with the sign of the Cross when they warred against the Saracens in Palestine.

crush *v.* **1** *To make wine you first crush the grapes:* mash, squash, squeeze, press, compress; crumble, crumple, pulverize, break, shatter, granulate, pulverize. **2** *The hero crushed the heroine in his arms:* hug tightly, embrace, squeeze, press. **3** *The army quickly crushed the uprising:* subdue, suppress, quash, smash, squash, put down, quell; overcome, overpower, overwhelm; quench, extinguish.

crux *n. The crux of the matter is that he's going to resign:* main point, decisive point, essence, essential, basis, heart, core, central issue; *Slang* brass tacks, nitty-gritty.

cry *v.* **1** *Many mourners were crying at the funeral:* weep, shed tears, sob, bawl, blubber, snivel; keen, mourn, lament, whimper, moan, wail, howl, groan. **2** *He cried out just as the boat struck the rocks:* call, call out, shout, yell, scream, roar, bellow, shriek, howl, screech, exclaim, utter; whoop, cheer; hail. **3** *The prisoner cried for mercy:* beg, plead, implore, importune; appeal, sue, petition. **4** *The hawker cried his wares throughout the town:* proclaim, make public, call out, blare, trumpet, hawk, blazon; advertise, promulgate.

—*n.* **5** *He gave a cry of alarm:* call, shout, yell, scream, yelp, screech, roar, bellow, shriek, howl, exclamation; outcry, clamour, whoop, cheer, hurrah, huzzah. **6** *Hear our cry, O Lord!:* plea, entreaty, appeal, supplication, petition, prayer; request, solicitation.

Ant. 1 laugh, snicker, giggle. **2, 5** whisper, murmur, mutter.

"She would have made a splendid wife, for crying only made her eyes more bright."

—*O. Henry*

---

crypt *n. The bishop was buried in a crypt beneath the altar:* underground chamber, vault, tomb, sepulchre, catacomb.

◇ *Word origin:* See CRYPTIC.

cryptic *adj. The fortune-teller kept muttering cryptic warnings:* puzzling, perplexing, enigmatic, mysterious, obscure; ambiguous, vague; secret, hidden, mystical, strange, dark, cabalistic, arcane, occult, esoteric.

◇ *Word origin: Cryptic* and *crypt* come from Greek *kruptos*, hidden, which also gives us the name of the colourless gaseous element *krypton.*

cuddle *v.* **1** *The little girl cuddled the rabbit:* hug tenderly, embrace, hold warmly, snuggle, nuzzle, cling to, clasp; caress, fondle, pet. **2** *The children cuddled up in the warm bed:* snuggle, nestle, huddle, lie snug, draw close, curl up.

cudgel *n. The pedlar always carried a cudgel for protection:* club, bludgeon, shillelagh, truncheon, staff, stick, cosh, quarterstaff, baton.

cue *n. Her wink was my cue to leave the party:* actor's signal; signal, sign, hint, clue, key, intimation, insinuation, tip, inkling.

◇ *Word origin:* An actor's *cue* is a word or action that tells him *when* to begin his speech, make an entrance on stage, etc. Some etymologists believe this word *cue* is a spelling of the letter *Q*, said to have been an abbreviation of the Latin word *Quando*, "When," formerly written on actors' scripts to mark their entrances. (Incidentally, the other word *cue* for a billiards stick or *curlicue*, a curl of hair, comes from French *queue*, tail.)

culminate *v. Their disagreement culminated in a fight:* conclude, end, end up, result, wind up, terminate, finish.

◇ *Word origin: Culminate* comes from Latin *culmen*, top, highest point.

culpable *adj. The insurance company is trying to*

find out which driver is culpable: guilty, at fault, liable, blameworthy, blameable, censurable, to blame.

Ant. innocent, blameless.

culprit *n. Police apprehended the culprit two miles from the scene of the crime:* guilty party, offender; law-breaker, criminal, felon; malefactor, miscreant, evil-doer, sinner, transgressor, wrongdoer.

◇ *Word origin: Culprit* and *culpable* come from latin *culpa*, guilt, fault. The phrase *mea culpa* comes from the Roman Catholic liturgy (*mea culpa, mea culpa, mea maxima culpa:* "through my fault, through my fault, through my most grievous fault") in which each member of the congregation acknowledges his sinfulness. The phrase is often loosely used in English to mean any formal acknowledgement of guilt or error.

cult *n.* **1** *The evangelist broke away from the church and formed his own cult:* religious rites, religious observances; sect, religious group, faction. **2** *The cult of youth places emphasis on good intentions rather than on hard work:* devotion, admiration; disciples, admirers, zealots, followers, devotees.

◇ *Word origin:* See CULTIVATE.

cultivate *v.* **1** *They invented better implements to cultivate the soil:* till, farm, raise crops from, garden; plough, hoe, spade, dig, weed; sow, plant, grow. **2** *She cultivated her mind by reading many books:* develop, improve, enrich, enhance, elevate, advance. **3** *Get out more and cultivate new friends:* acquire, develop, seek, court; ingratiate oneself with, run after.

Ant. 1 be fallow. **2** impoverish, bankrupt.

◇ *Word origin: Cultivate, cult,* and *culture* come from Latin *colere*, to cultivate, care for.

cultivation *n.* **1** *Most of the land has been improved by cultivation:* agriculture, farming, agronomy, husbandry, gardening; tilling, planting, sowing. **2** *Cultivation of the mind is one of the primary aims of education:* culture, refinement, polish, elevation, gentility, manners, grace, good breeding, good taste.

culture *n.* **1** *A child should be exposed to culture from an early age:* art, music, and literature; the arts; good taste, enrichment, enlightenment, learning, accomplishments, erudition, knowledge. **2** *Ancient Egypt had an advanced culture:* civilization, state of refinement, level of progress.

◇ *Word origin:* See CULTIVATE.

cultured *adj.* **1** *One doesn't have to be cultured to enjoy good music:* well-educated, artistically knowledgeable, learned, well-read. **2** *She learned her cultured manners in a Swiss finishing school:* cultivated, refined, polished, genteel, elegant, well-bred.

Ant. 1 uncultured, uncultivated, unenlightened, uneducated. **2** uncultivated, unrefined, unpolished, inelegant, coarse, crass, lowbred, common, vulgar.

cumbersome *adj. The packages are too cumbersome to carry:* unwieldy, clumsy, cumbrous, unmanageable, awkward, ungainly, bulky; ponderous.

Ant. compact, manageable, wieldy.

cumulative *adj. Obesity is the cumulative result of years of overeating:* accumulative, collective, aggregate, conglomerate, amassed, heaped up.

◇ *Word origin: Cumulative* comes from Latin *cumulus*, heap, which also gives us *accumulate* and *cumulus*, clouds (which look like a heap or pile).

cunning *n.* **1** *The prime minister retained power by employing great cunning:* craftiness, slyness, shrewdness, guile, artifice, wiliness, foxiness; deviousness, duplicity, deception, deceit, trickery, chicanery. **2** *The inlaid desk had been made with great cunning:* cleverness, art, craft, skill, dexterity, adroitness, deftness, finesse, subtlety; ability, aptitude, expertness, talent, genius.

—*adj.* **3** *By a cunning trick he became the queen's confidant:* shrewd, crafty, sly, artful, canny, ingenious, guileful, wily, foxy, machiavellian, deceptive, deceitful, devious, shifty, underhand, tricky.

Ant. 1 sincerity, candour, ingenuousness. **2** clumsiness. **3** ingenuous, artless.

cupboard *n. There's another box of salt in the cupboard:* kitchen cabinet, cabinet, closet; buffet, sideboard, china-closet; bureau, chiffonier, armoire.

cur *n.* **1** *You'd better put a muzzle on that cur before he bites someone:* mean dog, unfriendly dog; mongrel. **2** *Only a cur would treat a woman like that!:* blackguard, scoundrel, villain, varlet, rascal, wretch.

curb *n.* **1** *The nation must put a curb on its spending to balance the economy:* restraint, restriction, control, check, bridle, halter, rein, hindrance, limitation, retardant.

—*v.* **2** *Try to curb your wild enthusiasm:* restrain, restrict, check, control, bridle; repress, suppress, inhibit, limit, moderate, retard, slow down, slow up, hold back; slacken, decelerate.

◇ *Word origin: Curb* comes from the same word as *curve*, the Latin *curvus*, bent, curved. Originally a *curb* was any curved or flexible strap or chain used to restrain an animal,but it is now used of many other kinds of restraint.

cure *v.* **1** *Moving to the South of France cured her of asthma:* restore to health, make well, heal, eradicate sickness from, rid of an illness. **2** *The hams were cured over an open fire:* preserve, smoke, dry, salt.

—*n.* **3** *Scientists are working on a cure for the commom cold:* remedy, corrective, curative treatment, means of healing, antidote.

◇ *Word origin: Cure* comes from Latin *cura*, care.

curiosity *n.* **1** *She's full of curiosity about our new house:* inquisitiveness, interest, questioning; prying; *Slang* nosiness. **2** *This red and yellow striped sea shell is quite a curiosity:* rare object, rarity, curio, novelty; phenomenon, marvel, wonder, sight, oddity, freak.
Ant. 1 indifference, apathy, disregard.

"Curiosity is one of the permanent and certain characteristics of a vigorous intellect."
—*Samuel Johnson*

---

curious *adj.* **1** *Man is naturally curious about the universe:* inquisitive, interested in, eager to learn, anxious to know, inquiring, questioning, searching; nosey, snooping, prying. **2** *She has a curious way of talking:* unusual, odd, peculiar, bizarre, strange, queer; novel, quaint, singular, uncommon, unique, rare.
Ant. 1 incurious, uninterested, unconcerned, indifferent, apathetic. **2** customary, commonplace, common, usual, familiar, average, everyday.
◇ *Word origin:* Like *cure, curious* comes from Latin *cura*, care. (An early meaning of *curious* was "carefully made.")

curl *v.* **1** *Her mother curled her hair:* form into ringlets, coil, wave; twist, frizz, frizzle, crimp. **2** *Smoke curled from the chimney:* coil, curve, swirl, wind, twist, twirl, spiral.
—*n.* **3** *The little girl had blonde curls:* ringlet, coil of hair, lock. **4** *Curls of smoke wafted out of the chimney:* coil, spiral, twist; curlicue, wave, corkscrew.
◇ *Word origin: Curl* comes from Middle Dutch *krull*, curl.

curmudgeon *n. The old curmudgeon never smiled at anyone:* grouch, grumbler, crank, gruff person, irritable person, irascible person; *Slang* grump, crab, sourpuss.

currency *n.* **1** *The pound sterling is the currency of Great Britain:* medium of exchange, legal tender, money; cash, coin, coinage, notes, bank notes, paper money, ready money. **2** *That style enjoyed great currency in the 1920's:* popularity, vogue, acceptance, prevalence, predominance, universality.

current *adj.* **1** *Current fashions are more casual than those of the 1950's:* present, present-day, up-to-date, contemporary, modern, existing; popular, prevailing, prevalent, in vogue, in style; *Slang* now, with-it.
—*n.* **2** *The glider soared upward on a current of air:* flow, stream, tide; draught, flux. **3** *There was a current of unrest among the students:* undercurrent, tendency, inclination, drift, trend; feeling, mood, atmosphere.
Ant. 1 past, out-of-date; old-fashioned, out of style, outmoded, obsolete, passé, archaic.
◇ *Usage note:* Some people have difficulty distinguishing between *currant* and *current.* A *currant* is a small berry used in buns and for making jam: *Ants love to eat currAnts. Current,* of course, means a continuous onward flowing as of water or electricity, or belonging to the present, up-to-date: *Swim with the currEnt, currEnt events.*

> **Exploring the Word**: *Current* may mean the running of water in a river or stream or of electricity in a wire, while something that is *current* refers to that which is happening or "running by" now. The word comes from Latin *currere*, to run, which also gives us *concur,* to run together, hence to agree; *occur,* to run towards, hence to take place, come about; and *recur,* to run again, happen again. The same root also gives us *currency,* the "current" medium of exchange; *discourse,* an outpouring or running of words; *course,* the direction of running; *cursory,* hasty, superficial, or "done on the run"; *precursor,* one who has run ahead to announce something that follows, a herald; and *excursion,* literally a "run out" or a short trip.

curse *n.* **1** *The witch put a curse on the princess:* evil spell, evil eye; *Slang* jinx; malediction, denunciation, anathema, imprecation. **2** *His curse made her blush:* swearing, oath; expletive, profanity, blasphemy, obscenity. **3** *Housework was the curse of her life:* burden, ordeal, affliction, misfortune, trouble, trial, tribulation, bane, annoyance, torment, vexation, plague, scourge, cross.
—*v.* **4** *When angry, he cursed everyone in sight:* swear at, swear, utter a profanity, utter a blasphemy, utter an obscenity; damn, blast, denounce, condemn, execrate; invoke evil on, anathematize. **5** *The family has been cursed with poor health:* afflict, trouble, burden, torment, vex, plague, scourge.
Ant. 1, 2 blessing, benediction. **3** joy, boon, benefit; relief, respite. **4** compliment, praise, laud, extol; bless. **5** benefit, relieve, help, aid.

cursory *adj. He gave the report a cursory glance and tossed it aside:* quick, hasty, hurried, swift, brief, passing, perfunctory, random, haphazard, casual, offhand, superficial, desultory, careless, inattentive.
Ant. slow, careful, painstaking, meticulous, scrupulous, searching, profound, elaborate.

curt *adj. I was surprised at his curt reply:* abrupt, blunt, bluff, brusque, short, terse, summary, peremptory; petulant, snappy, gruff, crusty, rude.
Ant. warm, friendly, courteous, polite.
◇ *Word origin: Curt* and *curtail* come from Latin *curtus*, cut short.

curtail *v. The trip was curtailed because of bad weather:* cut short, cut, shorten, pare down, clip, trim; reduce, decrease, diminish, abridge, abbreviate, condense, contract.
Ant. lengthen, extend, prolong, elongate, protract, expand.
◇ *Word origin:* See CURT.

curve *n.* **1** *This road is full of sharp curves:* bend, turn, crook, arc, arch, bow, curvature, loop. —*v.* **2** *The ball curved to the right:* turn, bend, hook, curl, wind, arch, twist, swerve, coil, spiral.
◇ *Word origin: Curve* comes from Latin *curvus,* bent, curved, crooked.

cushion *n.* **1** *The children sat on cushions on the floor:* pillow, pad, bolster. —*v.* **2** *The batsman's pads cushion the impact of the ball:* soften, suppress, damp, dampen, stifle; muffle, quiet, deaden.

custodian *n.* **1** *The museum's custodian locked the doors promptly at five:* caretaker, janitor, superintendent, concierge, watchman. **2** *Who is the child's custodian?:* guardian, keeper; chaperon, duenna.

custody *n.* **1** *The mother was given custody of the children:* guardianship, charge, care, trusteeship, safe-keeping, protection, watch; preservation, conservation. **2** *The police have taken the suspect into custody:* detention, confinement; possession.
◇ *Word origin: Custody* and *custodian* come from Latin *custos,* guard. The Romans used the job title *custos* for a remarkably broad range of occupations. Here's a sample: guard, overseer, bodyguard, teacher of youth, eunuch attendant of women, counting agent, supply officer, spy, gaoler.

custom *n.* **1** *It is the custom for gentlemen to remove their hats indoors:* habitual practice, convention, usage, fashion, mode, form, habit. **2** **customs** *We had to pay customs on the camera equipment that we bought abroad:* duty, import tax, tariff; toll, assessment; Customs and Excise department, custom-house.
Ant. **1** rarity, phenomenon, curiosity.
◇ *Usage note:* See HABIT.
◇ *Word origin: Custom* and *customary* come from Latin *consuetudo,* custom, what one is used to, which also gives us *accustom* and *costume.*

customary *adj. He arrived with his customary promptness:* usual, habitual, normal, regular, routine, wonted, typical, accustomed, conventional, traditional, general, common, ordinary, everyday.
Ant. unusual, uncommon, rare, exceptional; occasional, infrequent, irregular, sporadic.

customer *n. The shop has more customers than it can take care of:* patron, shopper, buyer, purchaser; client, habitué.
◇ *Word origin: Customer* originally meant an habitué, one who deals with a particular establishment by *custom.*

cut *v. He cut his chin whilst shaving. Cut the cake:* lacerate, incise, gash, slash, hack, nick, lance, slit; slice, carve, saw, chop, dice, cube, mince; divide, section, split, dissect; sever, sunder, rive. **2** *It's time to cut the lawn again:* trim, clip, shear; mow, prune, pare, crop, snip, shave. **3** *Cut the report down to four pages:* condense, abridge, contract, précis, abbreviate, pare down, reduce, diminish, curtail, decrease; leave out, delete. **4** *We spoke to her, but she cut us:* snub, ignore, refuse to recognize, refuse to greet, turn one's back on, give one the cold shoulder. **5** *The road cuts through the forest:* cross, intersect, bisect, divide, go through, go across, move, change direction. —*n.* **6** *Put a bandage on that cut. The bulldozer made a cut for the railway lines:* incision, wound, gash, nick; slit, rent, opening; hollow, furrow, indentation, trench, excavation, cutting, channel, passage, course. **7** *This is a good lean cut of beef. The actor's agent gets a 10 per cent cut:* piece, portion, share, slice, section. **8** *Some retailers have announced a price cut:* reduction, decrease, abatement, decline, fall, diminution, contraction, shortening, shrinkage, curtailment, lessening.
Ant. **3** expand, enlarge, increase, lengthen. **4** welcome, greet. **8** increase, rise, surge; expansion, enlargement.

cute *adj. That was remarkably cute of you!:* acute, sharp, clever, perceptive, incisive, quick, quick-witted, adroit, keen, astute, ingenious; attractive, pretty.
◇ *Word origin: Cute* is a short form of *acute.*

cutting *adj.* **1** *That north wind is cutting:* piercing, sharp, harsh, stinging, nipping, biting, penetrating, smarting; cold, raw, bitter. **2** *She replied with a cutting remark:* harsh, sharp, caustic, biting, bitter, sarcastic, disparaging, acrimonious.
Ant. **1** balmy, soothing, pleasant. **2** gratifying, flattering; soothing, consoling, kind, mild.

cycle *n. We studied the cycle of the seasons in our biology class:* series, connected group, progression, sequence.
◇ *Word origin: Cycle* comes from Greek *kuklos,* circle, wheel, from which we also get *bicycle, tricycle, and cyclone.*

cynic *n. A cynic attributes selfish motives to all acts:* sceptic, scoffer, misanthrope, misogynist; pessimist.
Ant. humanitarian; optimist.
◇ *Word origin: Cynic* goes back to the Greek word *kuon,* dog, and its adjective *kunikos,* doglike, snarling. A group of Greek philosophers of the 4th century B.C., who held that virtue was the only goal of life, eventually became so self-righteous that they were called *hoi kunikoi,* "the snarlers." This expression gives us our word *cynic,* a fault-finding person.

cynical *adj. With that cynical outlook he doesn't trust anyone:* misanthropic, misogynic, sceptical, sneering, sardonic, scornful, scoffing, derisive, sarcastic.
Ant. philanthropic, humanitarian; hopeful, optimistic; credulous, ingenuous.

D

dab *v.* **1** *She dabbed some cold cream on her face:* pat, tap, apply gently.
—*n.* **2** *Put a dab of butter on your toast:* pat, bit, small quantity; small lump, little chunk. **3** *She applied her make-up with quick dabs:* pat, stroke, tap, light slap.

dabble *v.* **1** *The child dabbled in her bath. We dabbled our feet in the brook:* splash, slosh, spatter, sprinkle; play in water; dip in and out of water. **2** *She dabbles in politics:* potter, do something superficially, work on something casually.

dainty *adj.* **1** *The tiny statue has dainty hands:* delicate, fine, refined, lovely, pretty, beautiful, exquisite; attractive, pleasing, elegant. **2** *Old people are often dainty eaters:* fussy, choosy, fastidious, particular. **3** *Dainty sandwiches were served with tea:* small, neat, delicious, choice, tasty.
Ant. 1 gross, coarse, vulgar. **2** easily satisfied. **3** thick, clumsy, unappetizing.
◇ *Word origin: Dainty* goes back to Latin *dignitas*, worth, beauty. We get *dignity* from the same word.

dally *v.* **1** *Come straight home from school and don't dally:* dawdle, dilly-dally, trifle, loiter, linger, waste time, fritter away time. **2** *In the novel, the prince dallied with the servant girl:* flirt, toy, play, trifle, fool around.
Ant. 1 hurry, hasten, speed.

dam¹ *n.* **1** *The beavers built a dam across the stream:* barrier, wall, obstruction, hindrance.
—*v.* **2** *Engineers dammed the river to control flooding:* block, barricade, obstruct, hinder, confine.
◇ *Usage note:* Do not confuse *dam*, a barrier to hold back water, with *damn*, a curse, to swear at. Thus: *The Kariba Dam is a great feat of engineering* but *He doesn't give a damn.*

dam² *n. The word* cow *is used to indicate the dam of some animals, such as elephants or moose:* female parent of an animal.
Ant. sire, bull.
◇ *Word origin: Dam* (an animal's mother) is a variant of *dame.*

damage *n.* **1** *The flood caused great damage to the town:* injury, harm, hurt, impairment, loss. **2** *The court ordered the defendant to pay £1,000 damages for the accident:* cost, compensation for a loss.
—*v.* **3** *The fire damaged our house:* injure, hurt, harm, mar, impair, spoil.
Ant. 1 improvement, betterment; reparation. **3** improve, repair, mend, better.
◇ *Word origin: Damage* is from Latin *damnum*, loss, hurt.

damn *v.* **1** *The reviewer damned the new novel:* condemn, blast, criticize, censure, disparage, denounce, bring condemnation on, inveigh against, rail at. **2** *Should all sinners be damned?:* doom, condemn, sentence to hell.
Ant. 1 commend, praise, laud, applaud, speak well of, declare successful. **2** redeem, bless.
◇ *Usage note:* See DAM¹.
◇ *Word origin: Damn* comes from Latin *damnare*, to inflict loss upon (see DAMAGE, to which it is related). *Damnare* also means "to condemn," and it is from this use that *damn* is ultimately derived.

damp *adj.* **1** *My clothes are damp from the rain:* moist, wet, wettish, soggy, clammy, sodden, soaked, sopping, dripping. **2** *It was a cold, damp day:* humid, muggy, dank, wet, rainy, drizzly, foggy, misty, dewy.
—*n.* **3** *The damp is bad for my rheumatism:* moisture, humidity, mist; clamminess, mugginess, dankness.
—*v.* **4** *His loss didn't damp his zest for living:* check, curb, restrain, hinder, hamper, inhibit; discourage, depress; reduce, diminish, dull, deaden.
Ant. 1, 2 dry. **1** watertight. **2** arid, without rain. **3** dryness, aridity, aridness.
◇ *Word origin: Damp* comes from Middle Low German *damp*, steam.

dampen *v.* **1** *She dampened a sponge and cleaned the counter:* moisten, wet; make damp. **2** See DAMP, sense **4.**

damsel *n. The novel tells a tale of a man who enjoys rescuing damsels in distress:* girl, lass, maiden.
◇ *Usage note:* Apart from the phrase *damsel in distress*, the word *damsel* is now rare outside story-books.

dance *v.* **1** *The couple danced a polka:* move the feet and body to music, perform. **2** *We danced with glee at the good news:* leap, skip, jump, cavort, bounce, prance, frolic, gambol.
—*n.* **3** *Do you know any new dances?:* rhythmical steps or motions, usually to music, a specific set of steps or motions (fox-trot, Charleston, jitterbug, Lancers, cakewalk, twist, polka, etc.); choreography. **4** *Do you know Beethoven's* German Dances*?:* dance music, music to dance to. **5** *He studied dancing:* the art of dancing. **6** *They're having a dance on Saturday night at the club:* ball, party; disco, hop.

dandy *n.* **1** *Beau Brummel was a famous English dandy:* fop, clothes-horse, beau, coxcomb, fashion-plate, man of fashion; masher; natty dresser. **2** *My new car is a dandy:* beauty; fine thing, something first-rate.
—*adj.* **3** *She thinks giving a party is a dandy idea:* fine, great, excellent, superb; splendid, super; first-rate, very good.
Ant. 1 slob, sloppy person. **3** bad, terrible, awful.
◇ *Word origin:* No one seems to know why

but the personal name Andrew or Andy must once have been associated with fine clothes and good humour. *Dandy* is based on the name *Andy*.

danger *n. A fireman's life is full of danger:* peril, risk, hazard, jeopardy; exposure to injury, state of being exposed to harm.

Ant. security, safety, immunity, exemption; safeguarding, safeguard, protection.

◇ *Word origin: Danger* is from Old French *dangier*, meaning "power to harm," i.e. the power of a lord. The word is ultimately derived from Latin *dominus*, lord.

"Dangers bring fears, and fears more dangers bring." —*Richard Baxter*

---

dangerous *adj. It's dangerous to skate on thin ice:* risky, perilous, hazardous, chancy, unsafe, precarious, treacherous, menacing, full of risk, threatening; apt to harm.

Ant. safe, steady, secure; shielded.

dank *adj. The bear entered the dark, dank cave:* damp, moist, wet; humid, muggy, clammy, sticky, soggy, sodden; chilly, cold.

dapper *adj. He looks very dapper in his tailored jacket:* smart, neat, trim, spruce, modish, stylish, natty, well-groomed.

dappled *adj. The children rode a dappled mare:* spotted, mottled, variegated.

dare *v.* **1** *She dared to walk the tightrope without a net:* venture, have the courage or nerve. **2** *I dare you to jump across the brook:* challenge, defy.

—*n.* **3** *For a dare I jumped off the high diving-board:* challenge; provocation; taunt.

◇ *Usage note:* You may have noticed that *dare* is often used where you might normally expect *dares*. Thus: *He dare not* as well as *He dares not*. Both are correct. To complicate things even further, *dare* is often used without *to*, mainly in negative or interrogative constructions: *He dare not speak but doesn't dare hold his peace. I wonder if she dared come home. How dare he behave like that? Dare we proceed?* There is no hard-and-fast rule — trust your ear.

daring *n.* **1** *Douglas Bader's daring made him a famous pilot:* boldness, courage, bravery; audaciousness, audacity, adventurousness.

—*adj.* **2** *The soldier was decorated for daring acts behind enemy lines:* bold, gallant, valiant, courageous, brave, adventurous, venturesome, dauntless, undaunted, intrepid; plucky, game; audacious.

Ant. **1** cowardice, timidity, timorousness. **2** cowardly, uncourageous.

dark *adj.* **1** *The streets were very dark during the black-out:* black, obscure, opaque, dim, dusky, shadowy, shady; overcast, murky, dingy; sunless; without light. **2** *She had beautiful big dark eyes:* deeply coloured, not light, not pale. **3** *The war was a dark period for us:* gloomy, dismal, bleak, dreary, joyless, sorrowful, sombre; disheartening, discouraging, hopeless. **4** *The witch in the story practised the dark arts of sorcery:* evil, wicked, sinister. **5** *His dark expression showed his angry mood:* angry, sullen, sombre, gloomy, frowning; forbidding, ominous, bleak, sinister, threatening. **6** *There seemed to be some dark meaning in his remark:* hidden, concealed, secret; obscure, deep.

—*n.* **7** *It was hard to find a seat in the dark of the theatre:* darkness; absence of light, partial absence of light. **8** *The children got home before dark:* nightfall, night, night-time; evening, twilight, eventide.

Ant. **1, 2, 3, 5, 7, 8** light. **1, 2, 3, 5** bright. **1** luminous, lit, illumined, illuminated; dazzling, radiant. **2** pale, fair, white. **3** happy, joyful, hopeful. **5** happy, joyful, cheerful. **6** open, known; clear, lucid, plain, transparent; comprehensible. **7** lightness, brightness. **8** dawn, morning, daytime, daybreak, afternoon.

darken *v.* **1** *We drew the curtains and darkened the room:* dim, blacken, obscure, make dark, make darker, make dim, exclude light from. **2** *She used a tint to darken her hair:* colour, dye, tint; make less pale or fair; colour deeper, shade a deeper hue. **3** *The argument darkened her mood:* cloud, dispirit, sadden; make despondent, make gloomy, fill with gloom.

Ant. **1, 2, 3** lighten, brighten. **3** make happy.

darkness *n.* **1** *Darkness comes early in winter:* night-time, night, dark; evening, twilight, dusk, nightfall, eventide. **2** *The interior of the cave was in complete darkness:* dark, blackness, dimness, shade.

darling *n.* **1** *Darling, we'll be married in June!:* beloved, dear, dearest, sweetheart, love.

—*adj.* **2** *My darling wife and I are going to Paris:* beloved, dear, dearest; precious, loved, lovable, adored; sweet, charming, enchanting, lovely. **3** *I bought a darling hat:* cute, attractive; charming, enchanting, captivating; adorable.

dart *n.* **1** *We each threw two darts at the board:* missile, spear, javelin, projectile; small arrow. **2** *The small boy's dart across the High Street caused a fatal accident:* dash, rush, sprint, run; spurt, leap, jump, bound, fling; sudden movement.

—*v.* **3** *The bird darted from branch to branch:* dash, rush, bolt, tear, run, race, sprint; hurry, hasten; spring, leap, jump, bound; flit; fly quickly, move quickly.

dash *v.* **1** *She dashed the plate against the door in anger:* hurl, throw, fling, thrust, slam, smash, shatter, crash, splinter. **2** *Upon hearing the scream, he dashed out of the room and up the stairs:* dart, bolt, tear, race, rush, run, speed, hurry, hasten. **3** *Don't dash the paint on the wall like that:* splash, splatter, spatter. **4** *Rain dashed our plans for hiking:* ruin, spoil; thwart, frustrate, foil; discourage, disappoint, put a damper on.

—*n.* **5** *He made a dash for the train just as it began to leave the station:* dart, bolt, race, rush, run, sprint. **6** *A dash of vinegar might improve the salad:* pinch, bit, little, drop, touch, small addition, slight amount, *French* soupçon. **7** *She conducted the orchestra with great fire and dash:* verve, vigour, spirit, flair, zeal, animation, élan, vivacity, energy.

dashing *adj.* **1** *He always played dashing buccaneer types in films:* impetuous, daring, audacious, bold, swashbuckling, gallant, spirited; brave, courageous, fearless, plucky, unafraid.

dastardly *adj. A hit-and-run driver must be a dastardly person:* cowardly, mean, sneaky, base, vile, despicable, atrocious, shameful, low.

Ant. gallant, valiant, valorous, brave, courageous.

data *n. pl. The files contain data on the company's progress:* information, facts, figures; documents, evidence, dossier.

◇ *Pronunciation tip: Data* is pronounced *DAY-tuh.*

◇ *Usage note:* In present-day English *data* is occasionally used with a singular verb: *The data is correct.* However, in Latin, *data* is the plural of *datum,* and most people prefer to treat it as a plural in English: *Numerical data are obtained by counting and measuring.* (The traditional plural construction is still very much favoured by schoolteachers and textbook writers.)

"My mind lets go a thousand things,
Like dates of wars and deaths of kings."
—*T. B. Aldrich*

---

date *n.* **1** *The date of the attack on Pearl Harbor was December 7, 1941:* particular point or period of time, day, month, or year. **2** *The date of the Renaissance is usually considered to be from the 14th to the 16th century:* period, age, era, stage, epoch, historical period. **3** *Didn't we have a date for lunch today?:* appointment, engagement, rendezvous, agreement to meet.

—*v.* **4** *The cathedral of Notre Dame dates from the 12th century:* originate, exist from, bear a date. **5** *Please date all your business letters. This statue has been dated as 5th century B.C.:* put a date on, affix a date to, mark with a date, ascertain the date of, fix the time of.

◇ *Word origin: Date* comes from the phrase written in ancient Roman letters and documents *data Romae* (written or given in Rome), accompanying the date on which it was written. Soon the first word *data* came to mean "the first line of a letter or document telling when and where it was written," and later grew to mean the words or numbers telling when anything was written or done.

dated *adj.* **1** *Dress styles become dated very quickly:* old-fashioned, unfashionable, out-of-date, outmoded, passé, antiquated, obsolete. **2** *We bought a dated engraving by Rembrandt:* showing a date, having a date.

daub *v.* **1** *First daub the surface with plaster, then paint:* coat, cover, smear, paint. **2** *The walls were daubed with finger-marks:* smear, smudge, spot, soil, dirty, stain, smirch.

—*n.* **3** *The child's clothes were covered with daubs of mud:* blot, blotch, spot, splotch, stain.

◇ *Word origin: Daub,* to smear or coat as with plaster or paint, comes from Latin *dealbare,* to whitewash.

dauntless *adj. The dauntless troops charged the enemy stronghold:* fearless, unafraid, bold, courageous, brave, valiant, valorous, heroic, gallant, daring, resolute, stout-hearted, undaunted.

Ant. cowardly, fearful, afraid, apprehensive, faint-hearted, irresolute.

dawdle *v. If you dawdle on the way home, you won't have time for your homework:* dally, dilly-dally, idle, loiter, loaf, delay; procrastinate; potter around, loll around, fool around; kill time, waste time, fritter away time.

Ant. hurry, hasten, speed.

dawn *n.* **1** *Did you hear the cock crow at dawn?:* daybreak, sunrise, daylight, dawning. **2** *The book is about the dawn of civilization:* beginning, birth, rise, inception, origin, advent, start, unfolding; first appearance.

—*v.* **3** *Day will dawn at 5:03 tomorrow:* begin to grow light in the morning. **4** *A new age for mankind is dawning:* begin, appear, rise, commence; develop, unfold, emerge. **5** *It dawned on me that I'd left the oven on:* occur, strike, come to one's mind, begin to see or understand, begin to make an impression.

◇ *Word origin: Dawn* comes from Old English *dagung* "daying," i.e., becoming day.

day *n.* **1** *She never goes out during the day:* time between sunrise and sunset; period of 12 daylight hours; period of 24 hours. **2** *What day is her birthday?:* date; particular day. **3** *The day of the horse and cart is long past:* heyday, period, time, epoch, age; period of ascendancy. **4** *Do you still work an 8-hour day?:* working day, period of activity. **5** *Australia is three days from here by air:* day's journey, distance that can be travelled in a day.

Ant. 1 night, night-time.

◇ *Word origin: Day* is from Old English *daeg,* time of sunlight.

"All comes out even at the end of the day."
—*Winston Churchill*

---

daybreak *n. He was up at daybreak:* dawn, break of day; sunrise.

day-dream *v.* **1** *She day-dreamed about a carefree holiday:* muse, imagine, fantasize, fancy; wool-gather, dream.

—*n.* **2** *His day-dream is to retire to a tropical island:* fantasy, dream, pipe-dream.

daylight *n.* **1** *Wear these dark glasses in the daylight:* sunlight, sunshine; light of day. **2** *A farmer must finish his work during daylight:* daytime, day; the period between sunrise and sunset, the period between dawn and dusk, the daylight hours, the period of 12 daylight hours. **3** *In winter he feeds the livestock before daylight:* dawn, daybreak, sunrise, morning; beginning of day. **4** *Certain facts in the case have not been brought out into the daylight:* public attention, full view; openness.

daze *v.* **1** *The blow dazed me, but I wasn't hurt:* stun, shock, stupefy; stagger, confuse, bewilder; numb, benumb. **2** *The natural beauty of the Cheddar Gorge dazed all of us:* amaze, astound, astonish, surprise, dazzle, startle, stun, flabbergast; excite, electrify.
—*n.* **3** *After the accident, she walked around in a daze:* stupor, shock, bewilderment; astonishment, surprise.

dazzle *v.* **1** *The bright array of candles dazzled the guests:* daze, blind, confuse, blur; blind temporarily, as with strong light; dim the vision. **2** *The film star dazzled us with her glamour:* awe, overawe, overwhelm, overpower; excite, electrify; impress greatly.

dead *adj.* **1** *The doctor pronounced him dead on arrival at the hospital:* deceased, expired, perished, lifeless; no longer living, having no life. **2** *Scientists believe that Mercury is a dead planet:* lifeless, inorganic, inanimate; incapable of life; devoid of life, having no life. **3** *A language that is no longer spoken is called a dead language:* defunct, extinct; obsolete; no longer in use. **4** *The battery was dead and the car wouldn't start:* inoperative, inactive; not working, not responsive; out of operation. **5** *That colour looks dead next to your skin. This town is dead after 10 p.m.:* dull, lack-lustre, unexciting, vapid, flat, insipid. **6** *The arrow hit the dead centre:* exact, unerring, precise. **7** *The company's lack of profits is the result of too much dead capital:* unproductive, ineffectual, unused, useless; unemployed, unprofitable, stagnant. **8** *There was dead silence after the announcement:* total, complete, utter, absolute, thorough, entire. **9** *After a day of shopping, I'm usually dead:* exhausted, tired, spent; worn-out.
—*n.* **10** *The furnace broke down in the dead of winter:* midst, depth, middle; period of greatest darkness, cold, quiet, or gloom. **11 the dead.** *We must pray for the dead:* dead people; those who have died.
—*adv.* **12** *The deer stopped dead in her tracks:* abruptly, suddenly. **13** *I am dead certain that I saw him:* absolutely; completely, entirely.
Ant. 1 alive, living, live, animate; breathing. **2** living, animate. **3** existing, living, in use. **4** working, responsive, operative, operating, active, in motion; alive. **5** lively, vivacious, exciting. **6** inaccurate, inexact. **7** productive, effective, useful. **8** partial, incomplete. **9** active, energetic.

deaden *v.* *Two of these pills will deaden the ache. A new silencer will deaden the noise that your car's exhaust makes:* blunt, dull, diminish, subdue, moderate, mitigate; abate, lessen, weaken; soothe, assuage, alleviate; numb, drug, anaesthetize, dope; muffle, smother, mute.

deadlock *n.* *The negotiations soon reached a deadlock:* standstill; checkmate, impasse.

deadly *adj.* **1** *Cancer is a deadly disease:* fatal, lethal, mortal, death-dealing, deathly; malignant; destructive, baneful. **2** *He has become my deadly enemy:* dangerous enough to kill, destroy, or harm; relentless, unrelenting. **3** *The lecture is deadly — let's leave:* boring, dull, tedious; terrible, awful, dreadful.
—*adv.* **4** *It was a deadly boring play:* completely, entirely, fully, thoroughly, totally; terribly, awfully, horribly.
Ant. 1 vital, wholesome, life-giving. **2** relenting, appeasable, placable. **3** exciting.
◇ *Usage note: Deadly* and *lethal* both mean causing death or likely to cause death. *Deadly* is usually applied to diseases, accidents, snakes, and other animate factors: *a deadly disease, a deadly enemy* (an enemy seeking or desiring one's death). *Lethal* is usually applied to poisons and other chemicals: *Cyanide is lethal.*

deal *v.* **1** *Next time the problem comes up, I'll deal with it:* treat, handle, oversee; attend to, see to, take care of, cope with, dispose of. **2** *His book dealt with the life of Augustus John:* concern, consider; have to do with, be occupied with. **3** *It is important to know how to deal effectively with one's co-workers:* act, behave. **4** *This gallery deals in 19th century paintings:* trade, market, buy and sell; do business. **5** *The challenger dealt the champion a swift blow:* give, deliver, administer. **6** *The person on the left deals the cards now:* distribute, dispense, apportion, give out, mete out, parcel out, dole out.
—*n.* **7** *The deal rotates clockwise. I lost on that last deal:* distribution, apportionment, round, hand, single game. **8** *The terms are agreeable — it's a deal:* bargain, agreement, arrangement.
Ant. 1 ignore, overlook, disregard; neglect, leave undone. **6** receive, gather, collect, take back.

dealing *n.* **1** Usually **dealings.** *We have dealings with their firm from time to time:* relations, transactions, traffic, trade; business. **2** *She has a reputation for honest dealing:* treatment, practice; method or manner of conduct.

dear *adj.* **1** *She's very dear to us. Letters often begin "Dear Sir or Madam":* precious, beloved, loved, cherished, much loved, fondly regarded, favourite; esteemed, respected, highly regarded (used in a salutation: "Dear Dr. Jones"). **2** *Diamonds are very dear:* expensive, costly, high-priced; at a premium.
—*n.* **3** *You're a dear to look after the children for me:* darling, sweetheart, love, angel, good person, kind person, generous person.

Ant. 1 hated, abhorred, disliked. **2** inexpensive, cheap, low-priced; common; worthless.

dearth *n. There is a dearth of skilled workers in this area:* scarcity, lack, shortage, paucity; deficiency; insufficient supply.

Ant. abundance, superabundance, plenty; adequate supply.

"Because I could not stop for Death,
He kindly stopped for me."
—*Emily Dickinson*

---

death *n.* **1** *He mourned the death of his best friend:* dying, demise, passing, decease, expiration; loss of life. **2 Death.** *Death is often pictured as a skeleton carrying a scythe:* grim reaper, angel of death.

Ant. 1 life; birth, beginning, rise, growth.

deathless *adj. Only the body dies — the soul is deathless:* immortal, eternal, perpetual, everlasting, not subject to death.

Ant. mortal; perishable; transitory; passing.

deathly *adj.* **1** *She looked deathly after the accident:* deathlike, resembling death, cadaverous, ashen, pale, wan. **2** *There was a deathly silence in the theatre as the curtain went up:* extreme, terrible, intense.

—*adv.* **3** *The man is deathly ill:* extremely, very.

Ant. 1 lifelike, lively.

debase *v. Inflation has debased the country's currency. Don't debase yourself by accepting a bribe:* lower, degrade, defile, disgrace; befoul, desecrate, corrupt, deteriorate; adulterate; impair the worth of, reduce the quality of.

Ant. enhance, elevate, uplift, improve, heighten.

debatable *adj. It's debatable whether I shall go abroad this summer:* questionable, doubtful, dubious, undecided, uncertain, unsure; problematical, arguable, disputable, controvertible.

Ant. certain, sure, settled, decided, beyond question.

debate *n.* **1** *The two colleges will hold a debate on Saturday:* argument, discussion, dispute; formal discussion of opposing points of view, disputation. **2** *After much debate, I refused their offer:* deliberation, consideration, reflection, meditation.

—*v.* **3** *The council debated whether the new bypass should be built or not:* argue, dispute, discuss. **4** *I debated whether to accept the job:* deliberate, consider, reflect, ponder, think about, meditate upon.

◇ *Word origin:* The *-bate* in *debate* comes from Latin *battuere*, to beat, which gives us our words *beat* and *battle.*

debauchery *n. The carnival nights were full of rioting and debauchery:* excess, intemperance, immoderation, self-indulgence, dissipation.

debilitate *v. She was debilitated by a bad cold:* weaken, devitalize, enervate; make feeble, deprive of strength, wear out.

Ant. strengthen, invigorate, energize, vitalize, rejuvenate, renew, restore.

debonair *adj.* **1** *The young gentleman was smiling, blithe and debonair:* charming, urbane, gracious, suave; refined, elegant, well-bred, sophisticated, genteel, carefree, lighthearted, jaunty, dapper, buoyant, sprightly, free and easy.

Ant. 1 awkward, rude, gauche, uncivil, serious, gloomy.

◇ *Word origin: Debonair* comes from the Old French phrase *de bon aire*, of good mien.

debt *n. I'll pay off all my debts with this cheque:* liability, obligation, debit, bill, arrears, deferred payment; that which is owed.

◇ *Spelling tip: Debt* is easy to spell but *debtor* can cause problems because it ends in *-or* rather than the more common *-er.* Remember: *A debtOR must pay OR else.*

début *n.* **1** *The young actress made her début in the new comedy:* first public appearance. **2** *She made her début at the ball last year:* coming out, presentation, formal introduction into society.

decadence *n. A long period of decadence preceded the fall of the Roman empire:* decline, deterioration, decay, corruption, immorality, degeneration, degeneracy, debasement.

decadent *adj. The country got rid of its powerful, rich, and decadent aristocracy:* corrupt, immoral, decaying, degenerate, debased, depraved, debauched, perverse, perverted, dissolute.

decamp *v.* **1** *The army decamped during the night:* depart from camp, break camp; move off, march off. **2** *The treasurer decamped with part of the company's pay-roll:* depart suddenly, abscond, leave quickly or secretly, make off quickly, run away, sneak off, take off.

decay *v.* **1** *The tree began to decay as soon as it was cut down:* rot, decompose, disintegrate, spoil, putrefy; corrode.

—*n.* **2** *The decay of the tooth could have been prevented by proper dental care:* decomposition, rot, rotting, putrefaction; spoiling.

Ant. 1 flourish, flower, expand, grow, increase.

deceased *adj.* See DEAD **1**.

◇ *Usage note:* Don't confuse *diseased*, afflicted with an illness, with *deceased*, dead.

deceit *n. There is too much deceit practised against consumers:* deception, cheating, fraud, dishonesty, deceitfulness; duplicity, trickiness, trickery, underhandedness; misrepresentation.

Ant. honesty, frankness, sincerity, openness, candour, forthrightness; truthfulness; fair dealing.

deceitful *adj. Her saying one thing and doing the other shows that she's deceitful:* untrustworthy, insincere, hypocritical; underhand, false, dishonest, deceptive, treacherous; sneaky, double-dealing; tricky, cunning, crafty.

deceive *v. He deceived me by pretending to be a*

famous film star: mislead, delude, trick, fool, cheat; swindle, defraud.
Ant. enlighten; guide; tell the truth to, be true to, be honest to.
◇ *Spelling tip: Deceive* is not deceiving, it follows the rule of "*i* before *e* except after *c*," hence de*CEI*ve.
◇ *Usage note: Deceive* and *mislead* both mean to cause someone to believe something that isn't true. *Deceive* means to give a false impression or to be false, usually intentionally or knowingly: *She deceived her fiancé by secretly seeing other men. The general used a mock attack to deceive the enemy. Her haughty manner was meant to deceive us into thinking she was an aristocrat. Mislead* often means to give a false impression or information unintentionally or unknowingly: *The sunny morning misled us and we were caught in the afternoon rain. The boy's directions misled us, and we never did find the lake.*

"Who is right—the man who believes that he is being deceived, or the man who believes that he is not?"

—*G. C. Lichtenberg*

---

decency *n. Please have the decency to apologize:* propriety, decorum, respectability, modesty, appropriateness; quality of being decent.
Ant. indecency.
decent *adj.* **1** *I'm not sure that the film is decent enough for the children to see:* proper, suitable, fitting, appropriate; seemly, correct. **2** *He is rather fat, but he has a decent face:* fair; fairly attractive, honest. **3** *The workers went on strike for decent working conditions:* adequate, satisfactory; passable, fair; ample, sufficient, reasonably satisfying. **4** *He was decent enough to say thank you:* courteous, accommodating, obliging, gracious.
Ant. 1 improper, unsuitable, inappropriate, unseemly, incorrect, unbecoming; immodest, indecent, obscene, lewd. **3** inadequate, unsatisfactory, unfair, intolerable. **4** awkward, gauche, inept, maladroit, clumsy, crude; discourteous.
◇ *Usage note:* See DESCENT.
deception *n.* **1** *There was some deception in the advertisement claims:* deceit, deceitfulness, deceptiveness, fraud, fraudulence; trickery, trickiness; duplicity, insincerity, double-dealing, treachery; cunning. **2** *The magician's disappearing act was done by deception:* trick, artifice, illusion.
Ant. 1 candour, honesty, sincerity, truthfulness.
deceptive *adj. The magazine won't accept deceptive ads:* misleading, dishonest, deceitful, fraudulent.
Ant. truthful, honest, trustworthy.
decide *v.* **1** *I have decided to learn shorthand. We've decided to buy the house in the country:* determine, resolve, settle; choose, elect, select; make up one's mind. **2** *The court decided against the defendant:* settle, decree, rule; judge; come to a decision; make a decision.
Ant. 1 vacillate, waver, hesitate, falter, fluctuate.
decided *adj.* **1** *It was a decided win for our team:* clear-cut, certain, unquestionable, unmistakable, definite, indisputable; beyond all question. **2** *She coped with the problems in a decided manner:* determined, decisive, definite, unhesitating, unwavering, resolute, deliberate, assertive, firm, strong-willed.
Ant. 1 dubious, doubtful, questionable, ambiguous. **2** undetermined, indecisive, hesitating, wavering, irresolute, weak, weak-willed.
decision *n.* **1** *After much debate, I came to a decision to accept the job:* conclusion, judgement, verdict; resolution; determination; result arrived at after consideration. **2** *The court's decision will be made known tomorrow:* ruling, verdict, finding, decree; pronouncement by a court. **3** *The job demands a man of decision:* determination, decisiveness, decidedness, resolution, resoluteness, resolve, purpose, purposefulness.
Ant. 3 indecision, uncertainty, vacillation, vagueness.
decisive *adj.* **1** *The last battle ended in a decisive victory:* conclusive, undeniable, indisputable, final, convincing, definitive. **2** *A decisive person is needed to deal with the situation:* resolute, determined, decided, positive, definite, absolute; firm.
Ant. 1 inconclusive, disputable, dubious. **2** indecisive, irresolute, wavering, fluctuating; hesitant, reluctant.
declaim *v.* **1** *Mark Antony declaimed over the body of Caesar:* orate, recite, utter aloud in rhetorical manner, make a formal speech. **2** *The farmers declaimed against the imposition of higher taxes:* rail, inveigh.
declaration *n.* **1** *His signed declaration presented the facts as he knew them:* statement, affirmation; attestation, testimony, deposition; avowal, acknowledgement, assertion. **2** *We read the declaration posted on the notice-board:* announcement, proclamation; notification, notice, publication, document.
Ant. 1 denial; disavowal, retraction.
declare *v.* **1** *The combatants declared a truce. Having nothing to declare, they passed quickly through Customs:* proclaim, pronounce, announce. **2** *Their appearance at the meeting declared their willingness to compromise:* affirm; reveal, show, give evidence of.
Ant. 1 suppress, withhold. **2** hide, conceal.
decline *v.* **1** *I declined to go along with such a wild scheme:* refuse, reject, spurn; fail to accept, turn down, balk at. **2** *The road declines sharply at this point:* slope downward, incline downward, slope down. **3** *Her health has been declining these past months. The pound declined on the open market. His popularity declined after the*

1950's and he retired: weaken, fail, flag, sink, deteriorate, worsen; ebb, diminish, dwindle, decrease, lessen.

—*n.* **4** *The path follows a sharp decline to the lake:* down grade, declivity, drop; downward incline, downward slope. **5** *We are studying the decline of ancient Rome:* deterioration, decay. **6** *Our business has gone into a decline this year:* slump, recession, downward tendency. **7** *With his life in decline, he waited for death:* last part, period close to the end, sinking.

Ant. **1** accept, consent. **2** rise. **3** improve, increase, strengthen. **5, 6** rise, improvement.

◇ *Word origin: Decline* is from Latin *de-* (away, down) + *clinere* (to lean). The Latin verb *clinere* also gives us *incline* and *recline.*

decompose *v.* **1** *The dead tree began to decompose and had to be uprooted:* rot, decay, putrefy, spoil; disintegrate; go to pieces. **2** *Salt decomposes into sodium and chlorine:* separate; break up, disintegrate, break down.

decontaminate *v. The laboratory was sprayed with chemicals to decontaminate it:* purify, sterilize, disinfect.

Ant. contaminate, infect.

décor *n. The décor in the drawing room was late Victorian:* decoration, ornamentation; style of decorating.

◇ *Word origin:* See DECORATE.

decorate *v.* **1** *We decorated the house for Christmas:* ornament, adorn, bedeck, deck, array, trim, garnish, embellish. **2** *The soldier was decorated for bravery:* honour; award a decoration to, confer distinction upon.

◇ *Word origin: Decorate, décor, decorum,* and *decorous* come from Latin *decor,* grace, elegance through French *décorer.*

decoration *n.* **1** *He specializes in the decoration of private houses:* adornment, ornamentation, beautification, embellishment. **2** *The decorations for the party were bright and cheery:* ornament, ornamentation, trimming, trim, embellishment, adornment, garnish. **3** *The admiral's uniform was covered with decorations:* medal, award, emblem, ribbon, badge.

decorous *adj. The investiture is an occasion calling for decorous behaviour:* proper, correct, suitable, dignified, becoming, seemly, fit, appropriate; decent, polite, mannerly, respectful.

Ant. improper, unfit, unbecoming, unsuitable, undignified.

◇ *Word origin:* See DECORATE.

decorum *n. Jennifer can be relied on to act with decorum:* propriety, politeness; tact, gentility, respectability, dignity, taste.

Ant. impropriety, inappropriate behaviour, bad manners.

◇ *Word origin:* See DECORATE.

decoy *n.* **1** *The poachers used wooden ducks as decoys to attract the flock. The Trojan Horse was used as a decoy:* enticement, bait, lure, inducement; smoke-screen; deceptive stratagem.

—*v.* **2** *He used a whistle to decoy the birds into range:* bait, entice, lure, allure; attract by some deceptive device.

◇ *Word origin:* Originally a *decoy* was a cage or trap into which game was lured. It comes from Dutch *de kooi,* "the decoy." *Kooi* is ultimately derived from Latin *cavea,* cage.

decrease *v.* **1** *Water consumption decreased during the summer:* diminish, lessen, reduce, dwindle, drop, subside; slacken, ease, abate, taper, decline.

—*n.* **2** *A big decrease in sales caused the shop to close:* reduction, lessening, loss, decline, abatement, diminution, dwindling, cutback; falling-off.

Ant. **1** increase, augment, enlarge, extend, lengthen, expand. **2** growth, extension, expansion, swelling.

decree *n.* **1** *The king issued a decree that all prisoners should be granted amnesty:* order, command, proclamation, dictum, law, edict, ruling.

—*v.* **2** *The king decreed an amnesty:* order, command, proclaim.

decrepit *adj. This decrepit building shows many years of negligence:* broken-down, dilapidated, battered, rickety.

decry *v. The king decried the lack of support he received from the people:* criticize, denounce, condemn; disparage, deprecate, censure.

Ant. extol, acclaim, laud, commend, praise.

dedicate *v.* **1** *She dedicated herself to conserving the country's natural resources:* devote, commit, pledge; give completely. **2** *The bishop dedicated the new building on Sunday:* launch, present; devote to a special use. **3** *She dedicated the novel to her husband:* inscribe, address.

dedication *n.* **1** *The archbishop attended the dedication of the new church:* ceremony or act of dedicating for a specific use. **2** *His dedication to teaching won the respect of his pupils:* devotion, devotedness, commitment. **3** *The book's dedication reads "To Mother":* prefatory inscription or address.

deduce *v. From her conversation, I deduced that she had a large family:* conclude, reason, gather, infer, comprehend, understand.

deduct *v. They deducted the cost of the broken window from his allowance:* subtract, remove, take, withdraw; decrease by, take from.

Ant. add, enlarge, amplify; add to.

◇ *Spelling tip: Deduct* is easy to spell but some people hesitate over *deductible,* not being sure if it ends in *-able* or *-ible.* Remember: If you can claim a tax *deductIon,* it must be deductIble.

deed *n.* **1** *He is remembered for his many good deeds:* act, action, feat, achievement, accomplishment; effort. **2** *Did you have the deeds of the house?:* legal document showing ownership of property.

deem *v. I deem it advisable to buy property now:* think, believe, judge, regard, consider, hold.

deep *adj.* **1** *Don't go into deep water unless you can swim. They drilled a deep hole in the earth's crust:* of great depth, far below the surface, extending far downwards. **2** *A deep wardrobe can hold two rods:* far in or back, extending inwards from front to back. **3** *Rip Van Winkle lay in a deep sleep for many years:* intense, profound, extreme. **4** *The child sat there deep in thought:* absorbed, involved, immersed, engrossed; lost. **5** *He's certainly a deep thinker:* intelligent, astute, sagacious, discerning, wise, learned; profound, philosophical. **6** *The matching skirt is deep blue:* dark, strong, intense; rich, vivid. **7** *Don't you love his deep, rich voice?:* resonant, sonorous; low in pitch, not high, not sharp.
—*n.* **8** *The ill-fated* Titanic *rests in the deep:* ocean, sea.
—*adv.* **9** *They dug deep for the treasure:* deeply; far down.
Ant. 1, 2 shallow. **3** light. **4** uninvolved. **5** superficial; slow. **6** light, pale, faded; dull. **7** high, sharp; light.
◇ *Usage note:* In many contexts, *deep* may be used as an adverb, just as *deeply* is. Thus, *Drink deep* is as correct as *Drink deeply.*

> **Exploring the Word:** Latin *ducere,* to lead, gives us *duct* and *viaduct,* passages leading from one place to another: *abduct,* to lead away; *conduct,* to lead or escort or the way that one "leads" or behaves oneself; *deduce* and *deduction,* literally to lead down, hence to track down to an origin, a conclusion; *induct,* to lead in, as into military service; *introduce,* to lead another into something, as a friendship or a group of people; *produce* and *production,* to lead forward, hence to bring forth or yield something, that which is brought forth; *reduce,* to lead back, as to a lower or lesser condition, size, amount, or the like; and *seduce* and *seduction,* to lead astray, a leading astray.

deeply *adv.* **1** *How deeply did the needle penetrate?:* deep; far below the surface, far down. **2** *I was deeply moved by her testimony:* greatly, profoundly, intensely; passionately; acutely; completely, thoroughly, entirely. **3** *Who can gaze deeply into the future?:* far on in time or place. **4** *He spoke deeply in an emotional voice:* resonantly, sonorously; with a deep tone, at a low pitch. **5** *The fabric is deeply dyed red:* vividly, intensely, richly. **6** *I'm amazed to learn that he's deeply in debt:* seriously, gravely; up to one's neck.
Ant. 1 shallowly. **2** hardly, very little. **4** with a high tone, at a high pitch. **5** lightly, dully. **6** not seriously.

deface *v. He defaced the book by writing on it:* mar, damage, disfigure, impair; spoil, injure, bruise, mark, scar.
Ant. beautify; improve the looks of.

de facto *adv.* **1** *Though the King had absolute authority, the noblemen ruled their own lands de facto:* actually, really; in fact.
—*adj.* **2** *Elections meant nothing — he was the de facto head of state:* actual, real, in existence.
◇ *Word origin: De facto* is Latin for "from the fact," hence existing in fact with or without legal sanction. In law, *de facto* is the opposite of *de jure,* "by right, according to law." Thus if both an owner of a piece of land and a squatter who lives on that land claim it, the owner may claim it *de jure,* according to law, but the squatter may claim it *de facto,* from the fact that he actually lives on it.

defamation *n. He sued the newspaper for defamation of character:* slander, libel, disparagement, calumny, vilification.

defamatory *adj. I won't stand for any more of his defamatory remarks:* libellous, slanderous, disparaging, derogatory, calumnious, vilifying.

defame *v. We expect politicians to defame one another in an election speech:* slander, libel, malign, disparage, discredit, denigrate, degrade, vilify; speak ill of, attack the good reputation of.
Ant. praise, laud, applaud, extol.

default *n.* **1** *If the team doesn't show up, it will lose by default:* failure to appear or otherwise act. **2** *His car was repossessed because of default of the monthly instalment:* non-payment; failure to pay.

defeat *v.* **1** *The British fleet defeated the French at Trafalgar:* overcome, conquer, overthrow, rout, vanquish, overpower, overwhelm, quell, crush; gain a victory over an opponent, prevail over. **2** *This kind of problem always defeats me:* confound, baffle, thwart, foil, frustrate; elude, get the better of.
—*n.* **3** *The new housing bill suffered defeat in the House:* loss of a contest, failure to win. **4** *Losing the scholarship meant the defeat of all her hopes:* frustration, disappointment, thwarting.
Ant. 1 lose, succumb, surrender, capitulate, bow, yield, submit. **3** success, triumph, victory.

defect *n.* **1** *The television set was returned because of a defect:* fault, flaw, imperfection; blemish, spot, blotch, stain; scar, crack, break. **2** *Her insensitivity is a defect in her character:* deficiency, omission, incompleteness, shortcoming, fault, default; weakness, frailty, failing; weak point.
—*v.* **3** *The scientist defected to another country:* desert (one's country), leave (one's land for another) without permission.
Ant. 1 perfection, completeness. **2** strength.

defective *adj.* **1** *May I return this toaster if it's defective?:* faulty, imperfect, lacking, deficient, flawed, impaired, inadequate, insufficient, wanting, broken; out of order. **2** *Owing to brain damage, his speech was defective:* abnormal: subnormal; lacking in normal development.
Ant. 1 perfect, adequate; intact, entire, whole. **2** normal.

defence *n.* **1** *Many men enlisted for the defence of their country:* protection, preservation, security, safeguard, guard; maintenance; care, safe-keeping, custody. **2** *We must strengthen our defences on the western border:* fortification, stronghold, barricade; means of defending. **3** *I want to speak in defence of anti-pollution laws:* upholding, justification, support, advocacy. **4** *The defence rests its case on the evidence of Smith:* the defendant(s) and their counsel in a court of law. **5** *Three people from our school played for the defence:* the part of a team which tries to prevent the other team from scoring.
Ant. 4 prosecution. **5** attack.

defend *v.* **1** *A family must defend its home against attack:* protect, preserve; secure, shield, shelter, guard, safeguard; keep safe, watch over. **2** *Freedom from tyranny is a principle we should always defend:* uphold, support, maintain; endorse, advocate, champion; stand by.

defer[1] *v. You may defer payment until next month:* delay, postpone, table, shelve, suspend, put off.
Ant. expedite.

defer[2] *v. The child always deferred to his elder brother:* yield, submit, obey, capitulate, accede; respect; give in; pay respect to.
Ant. disobey, disrespect.

deference *n. Out of deference to her age and position, the committee followed her suggestions:* respect, reverence, honour, regard; obedience, capitulation.
Ant. disrespect, contempt; defiance, disobedience.

deferential *adj. Her treatment of the elderly people was affectionate and deferential:* respectful, courteous, civil, polite, reverential, reverent, regardful, dutiful, obedient, submissive, acquiescent.

deferment Also **deferral** *n. She arranged with the finance company for the deferment of payment:* postponement, delay, extension, stay.

defiance *n. The child showed defiance by refusing to eat:* disobedience, rebelliousness, rebellion.

defiant *adj. His defiant attitude was a challenge to fight:* rebellious, disobedient, provocative; aggressive, bold; truculent.
Ant. meek, timid; obedient, yielding, submissive.

deficiency *n.* **1** *I suffer from a calcium deficiency:* shortage, insufficiency, inadequacy. **2** *In spite of her mental deficiencies, she manages to do a good job:* flaw, defect, imperfection, failing, frailty, shortcoming, weakness.
Ant. 1 sufficiency, adequacy, abundance.

deficient *adj.* **1** *A diet deficient in vitamins is unhealthy:* lacking, inadequate, insufficient, short of. **2** *Tests indicate that he is mentally deficient:* flawed, defective, inferior, weak, unsatisfactory.
Ant. 1 sufficient, adequate. **2** up to par.

deficit *n. After all those expenses we ended the year with a deficit:* shortage, deficiency.
◇ *Word origin: Deficit* is Latin for "it is lacking."

defile *v.* **1** *Insults alone cannot defile a person's honour:* dirty, soil, befoul, besmirch, spoil, stain, taint, tarnish, dishonour, debase, disgrace, degrade. **2** *The infidels defiled the shrine:* desecrate, profane; treat sacrilegiously.
Ant. 1 honour. **2** hallow, consecrate, sanctify.
◇ *Word origin: Defile* seems to be a combination of Old French *defouler,* to trample down, and Old English *befȳlan,* to befoul.

define *v.* **1** *Can you define the word* defile*?:* state the meaning of. **2** *This booklet defines the committee's functions:* specify, describe, state, designate, delineate; spell out. **3** *The black tree was clearly defined against a yellow sky:* delineate, silhouette.
Ant. 3 obscure, hide, conceal, camouflage.

definite *adj.* **1** *The club has a definite meeting time each week:* precise, exact, fixed. **2** *She was definite about the caller's message:* sure, positive, certain; clear-cut.
Ant. 1, 2 indefinite, undetermined, indeterminate, unclear, uncertain.

"The difference between the first- and second-best things in art absolutely seems to escape verbal definition." — *William James*

---

definition *n.* **1** *Write a clear definition of the word* deep*:* statement of meaning. **2** *The club must give a clear definition of its goals:* description, precise nature, purpose, limits. **3** *The photo has good definition:* clarity, distinctiveness.

definitive *adj. This is the definitive account of the affair:* complete, reliable, conclusive, decisive, perfect; exact, decided.
Ant. incomplete, unreliable, inconclusive; imperfect, inexact.

deflect *v. The policeman's badge deflected the bullet:* divert, swerve; cause to run aside, alter the course.

deform *v. Open-cast mining deforms the landscape:* mar, disfigure, distort, contort, twist; mangle, maim; make ugly.

deformity *n. She has a deformity that makes walking difficult:* deformation, malformation.

defraud *v. Land speculators tried to defraud her of her savings:* cheat, bilk, fleece, swindle, rook.

deft *adj. The tennis player returned the service with a deft backhand:* skilful, expert; dextrous, adroit, able, apt; quick, sure.
Ant. unskilful, inexpert, maladroit, gauche, inept; slow, unsure.

defunct *adj. The company has been defunct since the war:* extinct, dead.
Ant. alive, live, living; in force, in vigour.

defy *v.* **1** *They believe that it is essential to defy convention:* challenge, confront, resist, stand up to, oppose; disregard, disdain, spurn. **2** *The plane defied the laws of gravity:* resist, withstand; be beyond the power of.
Ant. 1, 2 encourage. **1** support, help.

degradation *n. In his degradation he drank heavily and considered suicide:* humiliation, disgrace.
Ant. exaltation; honour, dignity, uprightness.

degrade *v. Marion wouldn't degrade herself by cheating:* lower, shame, debase, dishonour, disgrace; corrupt; bring contempt upon.
Ant. dignify.

degree *n.* **1** *The office-boy worked his way up, a degree at a time:* step, grade, mark, point; phase, stage. **2** *She shows a high degree of intelligence:* level, order, grade. **3** *The summer months had an average temperature of more than 80 degrees. A right angle has 90 degrees:* division, interval, unit.

deign *v. I would not deign to comment on such behaviour:* stoop, condescend, think fit, consent, deem; see fit.
◇ *Spelling tip: Deign* follows the spelling rule "*i* before *e* except after *c* or when sounded like *a*, as in *neighbour* and *weigh.*"

dejected *adj. He was dejected when she turned down his proposal of marriage:* depressed, downhearted, low, disheartened, despondent, sad, desolate, disconsolate; sorrowful, unhappy, discouraged, doleful, dispirited, spiritless.
Ant. happy, elated, joyous, light-hearted; encouraged, cheerful, blithe.

de jure See DE FACTO.

delay *v.* **1** *The committee delayed action on the matter until next month:* postpone, suspend; retard; shelve, table, put off. **2** *A snowstorm delayed the plane for two hours:* detain; hinder, impede; slow, check, suspend; inhibit, hamper, obstruct; hold up, keep back. **3** *If you delay now, you'll have to do more later:* procrastinate, dawdle.
—*n.* **4** *Please finish your work without delay:* loitering, tarrying, lingering, dawdling, postponement, deferment, suspension, stay. **5** *The delay was caused by a road accident:* stoppage, slowing; hindrance to progress.
Ant. 1, 2, 3 expedite, hasten, speed, hurry. **4** progress without hindrance.

delectable *adj. Both the dinner and the conversation were delectable:* delightful, enjoyable, pleasurable, pleasant, agreeable, gratifying; delicious.
Ant. offensive, repulsive, disagreeable, revolting; distasteful.

delegate *n.* **1** *Every county will send a delegate to the convention:* representative, agent, deputy, envoy.
—*v.* **2** *We have delegated her to represent our school at the conference:* designate, name; appoint as a representative. **3** *She delegated her power of attorney to her nephew:* entrust, assign, give, hand over, charge, transfer; commit to the care of.
◇ *Word origin:* A *delegate* is a person sent with authority to represent another or others; to *delegate* work or authority is to transfer or send it to someone else. *Delegate* comes from Latin *de-* (down) + *legare* (to send).

delegation *n.* **1** *We did not approve of his delegation of so much responsibility to one man:* commissioning, entrustment, authorization; designation; act of delegating. **2** *A delegation was sent to the capital to meet the minister:* body of delegates.

delete *v. It will be clearer if you delete the last paragraph:* remove; cut, cancel, erase; take out, strike out.

deleterious *adj. Smoking cigarettes may be deleterious to your health:* harmful, hurtful, detrimental; dangerous, destructive, ruinous, injurious.
Ant. beneficial; healthy, healthful, helpful, advantageous.

deliberate *adj.* **1** *It was a deliberate attempt to bring discredit on the minister:* intentional, premeditated, planned, pre-arranged, purposeful, express, wilful; calculated, careful, considered, circumspect, cautious, wary, prudent, thoughtful. **3** *The cortège proceeded at a deliberate pace:* leisurely, slow, easy, unhurried, slow-paced; measured.
—*v.* **4** *He deliberated his decision for several days:* examine, consider, weigh; meditate, contemplate; mull over, reason out. **5** *The board deliberated for two days before they reached a decision:* confer, debate, discuss; talk over.
Ant. 1, 2 impulsive, rash, impetuous, sudden, hasty. **3** fast, hurried.

deliberation *n.* **1** *The judge could not be hurried in his deliberation:* careful consideration before decision. **2** *The board of directors held their deliberation in the conference room:* discussion, conference, debate. **3** *He spoke with deliberation, choosing his words very carefully:* care, carefulness, circumspection, steadiness. **4** *The crime was planned with great deliberation:* forethought, premeditation, calculation, distinct intention, conscious purpose.

delicacy *n.* **1** *We admired the delicacy of the imported cloth:* fineness, exquisiteness, elegance, softness, smoothness, lightness. **2** *The carving was executed with great delicacy:* precision, perfection, accuracy; fine workmanship. **3** *Pheasant is a delicacy we can seldom enjoy:* choice food, something pleasing to the palate. **4** *Religion is a subject to be approached with great delicacy:* tact, taste, discrimination; consideration; sensitiveness, sensitivity, sensibility. **5** *The delicacy of his health has alarmed us all:* weakness, frailness, frailty, fragility, unsoundness.
Ant. 1, 2 coarseness, roughness, inelegance, grossness. **4** insensitiveness, insensibility, inconsiderateness, rudeness. **5** strength, vigour, vitality; energy.

delicate *adj.* **1** *She wore a long gown of delicate silk:* fine, dainty, exquisite, elegant. **2** *The plate was so delicate that I was afraid to wash it:* breakable, fragile, frail, flimsy, perishable; dainty. **3** *We were concerned over his delicate condition:* frail, feeble, debilitated, weakened;

infirm, unwell, sickly, ailing. **4** *Paint the walls a delicate blue:* soft, muted, subdued. **5** *Did you see the delicate workmanship on the bronze doors?:* exquisite, minute, detailed. **6** *He handled the situation in a delicate manner:* tactful, tasteful, diplomatic, careful, sensitive, fastidious, scrupulous, refined. **7** *Sex education is a delicate subject:* touchy, ticklish, sensitive; difficult, precarious.

Ant. 1 coarse, crude, rough, inelegant, gross. **2** unbreakable, strong. **3** strong, healthy, well; good. **4** harsh, bright, glaring. **5** careless; crude, rough. **6** indifferent, inconsiderate, careless, insensitive, unrefined, vulgar.

delicious *adj. Try some of this delicious chocolate cake:* delectable, palatable, savoury, tasty, luscious, appetizing; pleasant, pleasurable, delightful, joyful, charming.

Ant. distasteful, unpleasant, disagreeable.

delight *n.* **1** *They got a great deal of delight from their children:* pleasure, happiness, enjoyment, joy, gratification. **2** *The zoo is a delight for people of all ages:* something that gives joy or pleasure.

—v. **3** *Your visit last week delighted us:* please, gratify, cheer; charm, fascinate, enchant, amuse. **4** *I delight in browsing through antique shops:* revel; take great pleasure in, take delight in.

Ant. 1 disappointment, discontent, pain; displeasure. **3** displease; irk, bother. **4** dislike; take no pleasure in.

delighted *adj. A delighted audience demanded four encores:* pleased, captivated, enthralled, enraptured, enchanted; elated, ecstatic.

Ant. displeased, disgusted.

delightful *adj. With dinner and the theatre, it was a delightful evening:* enjoyable, pleasing, pleasurable, pleasure-giving; agreeable, charming, engaging, entertaining, amusing, enchanting; amiable, congenial.

Ant. displeasing, unpleasant, distressing; disagreeable, distasteful.

delinquency *n. There was no excuse for the well-educated boy's delinquency:* misbehaviour, misconduct.

delinquent *n. The robbery was committed by a group of delinquents:* misdoer, miscreant, wrong-doer; juvenile delinquent, young offender.

delirious *adj.* **1** *She was delirious from the high fever:* incoherent; raving. **2** *The crowd became delirious when the astronaut appeared on the terrace:* frantic, frenzied, carried away, excited, ecstatic.

Ant. 1 coherent, rational. **2** calm.

deliver *v.* **1** *I delivered the cheques to the bank. This supermarket delivers only on Saturdays:* carry, bear, bring, convey; surrender; give over, hand over, turn over. **2** *The Chancellor delivers his speech tomorrow:* give, utter, say, proclaim. **3** *The champion delivered a series of punches to the challenger:* launch, aim, throw, direct, deal, strike. **4** *They were delivered from slavery:* save, rescue, liberate, emancipate, free, release; set free.

Ant. 1 keep, hold. **4** enslave, oppress.

◇ *Word origin:* To *deliver* a package means to give it freely into the recipient's hands, *"Deliver* us from evil" means free us from evil, and when an obstetrician *delivers* a baby he sets it free from the womb. Thus *deliver* basically means to set free. The word is ultimately derived from Latin *liber,* free, which also gives us *liberty.*

deliverance *n. The village owes its deliverance to the army:* liberation, release, emancipation; rescue, salvation.

delivery *n. We awaited the delivery of the documents:* transfer, transmittal, transmission, handing over, giving over.

delude *v. I may be deluding myself, but I think I'm losing weight:* mislead, deceive, fool, trick, dupe.

deluge *n.* **1** *Noah built the ark in readiness for the Deluge:* flood, inundation. **2** *A deluge of requests for autographed pictures was received daily by the star:* inundation, flood, barrage; overwhelming amount.

—v. **3** *The spring thaw caused the river to deluge the town:* overwhelm with a flood of water, flood, inundate, drown, submerge, engulf, flow over, overflow; bury, swamp, swallow up. **4** *The written requests for pictures deluged the star's office:* overwhelm, overrun, swamp, flood, inundate, glut.

Ant. 1 drought, dearth, aridity, aridness; ebb, abatement. **3** dry out.

delusion *n. He suffered from the delusion that he was a young boy:* illusion, misbelief, misconception.

de luxe *adj. It is one of Oxford's de luxe restaurants:* elegant, grand, fine, luxurious, splendid, choice.

◇ *Word origin: De luxe* is French for "of luxury," referring to luxury articles.

delve *v. We delved into the newspaper files to find out the facts:* search, probe, dig into, examine, explore, look into.

demand *v.* **1** *She demanded a room all to herself:* exact, order, require; insist upon, lay claim to. **2** *The situation demands immediate attention:* need, require, call for.

—n. **3** *Her every demand was carried out:* command, order; act of demanding, something that is demanded. **4** *There was a huge demand for experienced workers:* need, requirement, want.

demean *v. Could you demean yourself by stealing from that poor woman?:* debase, lower, humble, humiliate, shame.

Ant. dignify, honour; glorify, elevate.

demeanour *n. He's a young man of pleasing demeanour:* conduct, behaviour, deportment, comportment, bearing, presence, appearance.

demented *adj. Because of all her ranting, I thought that she must be demented:* insane, mad, lunatic, crazy, crazed, deranged.
Ant. sane, rational.

demise *n.* **1** *His untimely demise was the result of a sudden heart attack:* death, decease, passing, expiration. **2** *The demise of the empire was caused by internal strife:* end, fall, collapse, ruin.
Ant. 1 birth.

democracy *n.* **1** *What are the principles of democracy? A true democracy allows free speech:* government by the people, representative government; state having government by the people. **2** *The democracy of the courts affords justice for all:* fairness, equality, political equality.
◇ *Word origin: Democracy* is from Greek *dēmos* (people) + *krateein* (to rule), hence a form of government in which the people have and exercise political power. A *democrat* is thus one who advocates or upholds such a form of government.

"Democracy is still upon its trial. The civic genius of our people is its only bulwark."
—*William James*

democratic *adj.* **1** *He staunchly defended democratic principles:* advocating democracy, characterized by principles of political equality. **2** *These democratic gatherings are attended by all kinds of people:* characterized by social equality, tending to level distinctions in rank.
Ant. 1 autocratic, despotic, tyrannical. **2** socially unequal.

demolish *v.* **1** *They are going to demolish the old armoury:* wreck, destroy, level, raze; tear down. **2** *The evidence demolished the plaintiff's case:* ruin, devastate; put an end to.
Ant. 1 build, create; restore, repair. **2** strengthen.

demolition *n. We watched the demolition of the old tower:* destruction, wrecking, razing, levelling.

demon *n.* **1** *They held an elaborate ceremony to exorcise the demons:* devil; evil spirit, malignant spirit. **2** *The demon held her prisoner in the tower:* fiend, monster. **3** *She's a demon to have on any committee:* go-getter; energetic person.
Ant. 1, 2 angel. **1** cherub; good spirit. **2** kind person, good person. **3** lazy person.
◇ *Word origin: Demon* goes back to Greek *daimōn,* divinity or tutelary genius (the ancient Greek equivalent of a guardian angel). The authors of the New Testament and the Church Fathers, writing in Greek and Latin, gave the word its present meaning of "evil spirit."

demonic Also **demoniac, demoniacal** *adj. She attacked the problem with demonic energy:* fiendish, devilish; frantic, hellish, hectic, frenzied, furious, like one possessed.
Ant. calm, cool.

demonstrate *v.* **1** *The instructor demonstrated the proper way to sew in a zip-fastener:* teach, show; describe, illustrate, explain. **2** *The fireman demonstrated great courage in saving the child:* show, reveal, display, exhibit, manifest. **3** *The lawyer demonstrated that the witness was lying:* prove, show, establish; make clear by reasoning, make evident. **4** *The miners demonstrated for better working conditions:* picket, parade, march, hold a protest meeting.
◇ *Word origin: Demonstrate* comes from the Latin prefix *de-* (completely) + *monstrare* (to show, point out).

demonstration *n.* **1** *We attended a demonstration of the new manufacturing process:* exhibition, display; illustration. **2** *His new book seems an ample demonstration of his patriotism:* expression, manifestation, display. **3** *We watched the demonstration from our window:* parade, march, picketing; protest meeting, rally.

demonstrative *adj.* **1** *The puppy was very demonstrative:* affectionate; effusive, gushing, openly expressive. **2** *The exhibition is demonstrative of many problems in the city:* serving to demonstrate, offering proof.

demoralize *v. Talk of defeat had demoralized the team:* discourage, dishearten, undermine, disorganize, disconcert; break down the morale of.
Ant. stimulate, encourage.

demote *v. As a punishment, the corporal was demoted to private:* lower in rank, downgrade.

demur *v.* **1** *The majority were in favour of the plan, but a few demurred:* object; take exception.
—*n.* **2** *The lieutenant was a man who would follow any order without demur:* hesitation, scruple, qualm, compunction, misgiving, objection, protest.

demure *adj. She seemed demure when her parents were around:* shy, modest, prim, reserved, unassuming.
Ant. brazen, brash, impudent, barefaced; shameless, immodest.
◇ *Usage note:* Don't confuse *demure* and *demur. Demure* means prim or sedate: *a demure young girl. Demur* means to make objections, to take exception: *The others signed the contract, but I demurred.*

den *n.* **1** *The cave made a good den for the foxes:* lair, earth, shelter, retreat. **2** *The place is a den of thieves:* haunt, hide-out; hotbed. **3** *Mother won't let any of us into her den:* study, library, private room.

denial *n.* **1** *The colonel issued a denial of any wrongdoing:* disowning, disavowal, disclaimer. **2** *His denial of the petition caused the students to rebel:* rejection, refusal.
Ant. 1 affirmation, avowal, acknowledgement, admission. **2** granting.

denizen *n. The denizens of the forest came alive at night:* inhabitant, resident, dweller.

denomination *n.* **1** *The various required subjects fall under several denominations:* designation, name, category, class, grouping. **2** *He's a church-goer, but I don't know of what denomination:* sect, religious group. **3** *The bank sent the money in three denominations:* value, size.

denote *v. The flashing lights denote dangerous roads ahead:* indicate, mark, signal, signify, mean, name.

dénouement *n. The dénouement was so ridiculous that it ruined the whole play:* outcome, solution; finale, conclusion, termination, end.

◇ *Word origin:* A *dénouement* is the final unravelling of the plot of a play, novel, etc. It comes from French *dénouer,* to unknot, and was introduced as a loan-word into English around the year 1750.

denounce *v.* **1** *The council denounced the new law:* condemn, criticize, censure, vilify. **2** *She was denounced as a thief:* accuse; inform against.

Ant. 1 commend, praise, extol, laud. **2** vindicate, exonerate.

dense *adj.* **1** *The crowd was so dense that we could hardly move. It was difficult to see through the dense fog:* crowded, compressed, compact, close, concentrated, thick, impenetrable, heavy, intense. **2** *He's so dense that he'll never understand your message:* dumb, stupid, dull, ignorant, thick, thick-headed, slow.

Ant. 1 sparse, scattered, dispersed; thin, transparent, light. **2** alert, bright, intelligent, quick, quick-witted, clever.

dent *n. The body of the car is full of dents:* depression, pit, hollow, indentation.

◇ *Word origin: Dent* was originally a variant pronunciation of *dint,* which comes from an old word meaning a blow or hit.

denunciation *n. The candidate's speech was a denunciation of dishonest government:* condemnation, censure, denouncement; attack against.

Ant. defence, apology; acclamation, recommendation.

deny *v.* **1** *The defendant denied ever making such a statement:* contradict, disavow, disclaim, refute. **2** *He denied the students a chance to speak:* refuse, disallow; withhold from. **3** *Atheists deny the existence of God:* refuse to acknowledge, not recognize; contradict, declare untrue.

Ant. 1 confirm, concede, admit, affirm, assert. **2** grant. **3** acknowledge, recognize; believe in.

◇ *Word origin: Deny* comes from the Latin prefix *de-* (completely) + *negare* (to refuse, say no), which also gives us *negate* and *negative.*

depart *v.* **1** *Before you depart, let me give you a word of advice:* go, leave; exit, go away, set out, start out, set forth, go forth. **2** *He departed from the text to tell an anecdote:* digress, turn aside, deviate.

Ant. 1 arrive; remain, stay.

department *n.* **1** *I work in the wages department:* division, bureau, branch, section. **2** *Bordeaux is in the department of Gironde:* district, division, province, sector.

departure *n.* **1** *Our departure is scheduled for 6 a.m. tomorrow:* leaving, going, exit; going away. **2** *His new work is a departure from what he wrote before:* digression, divergence, deviation.

Ant. 1 arrival, return.

depend *v.* **1** *The farmers here depend heavily on the weather forecast:* rely, count. **2** *You can always depend on her:* place trust, have faith. **3** *The party depends on whether or not we collect enough money:* hinge, rest, be determined by, be contingent upon, hang on, be dependent on.

dependable *adj. My secretary is skilful and dependable:* reliable, trustworthy, unfailing, trusty, trusted; loyal, faithful, steady, steadfast; sure, true.

Ant. untrustworthy, unreliable, doubtful, questionable, unsteady, fickle, unstable.

dependence *n.* **1** *The old lady's dependence on her children was absolute:* dependency. **2** *Her dependence on religion is very great:* reliance, trust, confidence.

dependency *n. There is a difference between a dependency and a colony:* province; territory subject to another.

dependent *adj.* **1** *Too many young people are dependent on their parents:* reliant; needing help. **2** *Good health is largely dependent on proper nourishment:* determined by; contingent on; subject to.

Ant. 1 self-reliant, independent.

◇ *Spelling tip:* Remember: *Your young children are dependEnt on you* but while they are living in your house *they are your dependAnts.*

deplete *v. The drought has depleted our supply of water:* exhaust, use up, drain; lessen, reduce, decrease, consume.

Ant. increase, augment.

deplorable *adj.* **1** *The family lived in a deplorable slum:* wretched, awful, miserable. **2** *The soldier's actions were deplorable:* deserving reproach, reprehensible, blameworthy.

Ant. 1 acceptable, good.

deplore *v.* **1** *The citizens deplored the death of their king:* lament, mourn, bemoan, bewail, grieve for. **2** *We all deplored his lack of good manners:* censure, condemn; disapprove of.

◇ *Word origin: Deplore* comes from Latin *de-* (completely) + *plorare* (to cry out, bewail).

> "Talkative people say many things in company which they deplore when alone."
> —*Antonio de Guevara*

---

deport *v.* **1** *The authorities deported him for illegal entry:* oust, expel; banish, exile, expatriate. **2** *She deported herself in a manner becoming to a duchess:* behave, act, carry; conduct oneself.

deportment *n. If her deportment doesn't improve, the school may expel her:* conduct, behaviour; comportment, demeanour.

depose *v. The nobles deposed the king:* dethrone; oust; remove from office.

deposit *v.* **1** *Deposit your lunch tray at the cafeteria door:* put, place; set down. **2** *The soil was deposited on the banks:* accumulate, place; put down. **3** *I deposited ten pounds in my savings account:* place for safekeeping; put in the bank, give in trust, commit to custody.
—*n.* **4** *The flood left a large deposit of mud in the street:* accumulation, sediment, pile. **5** *I left a £5 deposit on a new winter coat:* down payment, partial payment, instalment.
◇ *Word origin: Deposit* means to put away, and a *depot* is where something is put away or stored. Both words come from Latin *de-* (down, away) + *ponere* (to put, place).

deposition *n.* **1** *The deposition of Charles I took place in 1649:* the act of deposing. **2** *The witnesses gave their pre-trial depositions:* testimony, declaration. **3** *There was a deposition of soil on the banks:* deposit, accumulation.

depot *n.* **1** *I went to the depot to collect the umbrella that I'd left on the bus:* bus station. **2** *Enemy bombs demolished our supply depot:* military storage place, dump.
◇ *Word origin:* See DEPOSIT.

depraved *adj. A person of such depraved appetites has no place in our community:* corrupt, perverted, wicked, debased, debauched, degenerate, vile, degraded.
Ant. moral, virtuous, wholesome.
◇ *Word origin: Depraved* comes from Latin *de-* (completely) + *pravus* (perverse, bad).

deprecate *v. The townspeople deprecated the new monument:* protest against, condemn; express strong disapproval of.
Ant. approve, favour, endorse, sanction.
◇ *Word origin:* To *deprecate* originally meant to pray for deliverance from something unfavourable or disapproved. It comes from Latin *de-* (away) + *precari* (to pray, request), which also gives us *pray* and *prayer.*
◇ *Usage note: Deprecate* has been mixed up with *depreciate* for so long that the two words are now synonymous in the sense of "belittle." Purists deplore this usage, however, so you had better familiarize yourself with both words before using either in formal writing.

depreciate *v.* **1** *Runaway inflation has depreciated the country's currency. The car has depreciated £200 since last year:* reduce or lower the value of; lose value. **2** *He depreciates all my efforts to help him:* belittle, disparage, downgrade, scorn, denigrate; run down.
Ant. 1 appreciate. **2** appreciate, cherish, esteem, prize.
◇ *Word origin: Depreciate* comes from Latin *depretiare,* to reduce the price of, hence to make light of.

depress *v.* **1** *Her sad news depressed me all day:* dispirit, sadden, dishearten, deject, lower in spirits. **2** *The new bypass depressed business along the old road:* lessen, weaken, diminish. **3** *Depress the lever to start the machine:* lower; press down.
Ant. 1 elate, cheer, gladden, hearten. **2** heighten, increase, strengthen.
◇ *Word origin: Depress* comes from Late Latin *depressare,* to press down.

depression *n.* **1** *She suffered from serious depression after losing her job:* sadness, gloom, dejection, discouragement, down-heartedness; melancholia, melancholy, despondency, desolation. **2** *There was a depression in the carpet where the lamp had stood:* indentation, hollow. **3** *During the 1930's we experienced a severe depression:* economic decline, recession.
Ant. 1 cheerfulness, gladness; lightheartedness, joyousness. **3** boom.

deprive *v. She was deprived of her membership for not paying her dues:* dispossess, divest, strip, confiscate; take from.
◇ *Word origin: Deprive* comes from Latin *de-* (completely) + *privare* (to deprive).

"To weep is to make less the depth of grief."
—*William Shakespeare*

---

depth *n.* **1** *The lake reaches a depth in the middle of 300 feet:* downward measurement, perpendicular measurement. **2** *Her latest poem shows remarkable depth of feeling:* profundity, deepness. **3** *The depth of his voice gives him a good tone for recording:* timbre, deepness.
Ant. 1 height. **2** superficiality.

deranged *adj. She became so deranged that she had to be put in an institution:* insane, irrational, unbalanced; crazy.
Ant. sane, normal, rational.

derelict *adj.* **1** *There are many old and derelict ships in the bay:* abandoned, deserted.
—*n.* **2** *They run a home for derelicts:* vagrant, outcast, tramp, down-and-out.
◇ *Word origin: Derelict* comes from Latin *de-* (completely) + *relinquere* (to abandon). The same Latin verb gives us *relinquish.*

deride *v. They derided the new music:* ridicule, mock, scoff, scorn.

derision *n. The losing players were the target of derision of their erstwhile supporters:* ridicule, mockery, disdain, scorn.
◇ *Word origin: Derision* comes from Latin *de-* (completely) + *ridere* (to laugh, mock).

derivation *n.* **1** *He is working on the derivation of a new plastic from chemicals:* deriving, acquiring, obtaining, getting. **2** *The waltz is probably of German derivation:* origin, source, ancestry. **3** *The dictionary gives the derivation of many words:* etymology; historical development.

derive *v.* **1** *She derives great satisfaction from her coin collection:* gain, obtain, glean. **2** *Many English words are derived from Latin and Greek:* descend; originate, arise; stem from.
◇ *Word origin: Derive* comes from Latin *de-* (from) + *rivus* (stream), also giving us *river.*

derogatory *adj. They made derogatory remarks about their opponents:* belittling, disparaging, uncomplimentary, unfavourable.

Ant. flattering, complimentary, favourable.
◇ *Word origin: Derogatory* comes from Latin *de-* (away) + *rogare* (to ask, propose), hence taking away by talking, detracting.

descend *v.* **1** *The lift descended slowly to the ground floor:* drop, come down, go down, move downward. **2** *The path descends sharply:* incline, dip, slope, slant. **3** *The estate descended through the male heirs for two centuries:* to be inherited, pass, be handed down. **4** *The troops descended upon the village and destroyed it:* swoop, invade; come in force.
Ant. 1 ascend, climb, go up.
◇ *Word origin: Descend* and *descent* come from Latin *de-* (down) + *scandere* (to climb).

> **Exploring the Word:** Latin *scandere,* to climb, gives us *ascend,* to climb to, rise up, and the *Ascension,* the rising of Christ into Heaven after the Resurrection; *condescend,* to climb down to the level of an inferior; *descend,* to climb from, come down; *scan,* to pass the eyes up and down quickly, read hurriedly; and *transcend,* literally to climb across, hence to overcome or rise above something.

descendant *n. The royal family are descendants of Queen Victoria:* offspring, issue, progeny, scion.
Ant. ancestor, progenitor, forefather.
◇ *Spelling tip:* A *descendant* is an offspring, and many parents think their young *descendANTS* have *ANTS* in their pants! Remember, *descendANT.*

descent *n.* **1** *The spectators watched the descent of the balloon:* fall, drop, coming down. **2** *There is a gradual descent from the house to the lake:* slope, slant, decline, declivity. **3** *She is very proud of her descent from a Russian aristocrat:* ancestry, origin, lineage. **4** *The town was destroyed by the descent of barbarians:* sudden visit, surprise attack, raid, assault, incursion.
Ant. 1 ascent, rise; upward climb.
◇ *Usage note: Descent, decent* and *dissent* look and sound a little too much alike for the comfort of some students. *Descent* is the act of coming down: *After SCaling the mountain, we made our deSCent. Decent,* of course, means respectable, suitable: *He dresses deCENTly even though he doesn't have a CENT to his name. Dissent* means to differ, disagree, a disagreement: *To DISsent is to DISagree.*
◇ *Word origin:* See DESCEND.

describe *v.* **1** *They described their journey in vivid detail:* detail, narrate, relate, recount, recite, explain; illustrate, characterize, portray; depict. **2** *Describe a circle on the floor with a piece of chalk:* draw, trace, outline; delineate, mark out.
◇ *Word origin:* To *describe* something originally meant to write it down, and the written-down piece was a *description.* The words come from Latin *de-* (down) + *scribere* (to write).

description *n.* **1** *She gave an accurate description of the man's appearance:* account, depiction, portrayal, characterization; narration. **2** *The show featured dogs of every description:* kind, sort, type, ilk, variety; species, class, genus, nature, manner, brand.
◇ *Word origin:* See DESCRIBE.

desecrate *v. Vandals desecrated many tombstones in the cemetery:* defile, violate, profane, dishonour.
Ant. honour, esteem.
◇ *Word origin: Desecrate* comes from Latin *de-* (undoing, reversing) + *sacer* (holy, sacred), hence to divert from a sacred use, to profane. Latin *sacer* also gives us *sacred.*

desert[1] *n.* **1** *Some animals can survive in the desert on very little water:* waste; arid region, barren wilderness.
—*adj.* **2** *The speculators bought a large desert tract and sold lots:* barren, desolate; infertile, arid, waste, uncultivated, untilled, wild, uninhabited.

desert[2] *v. The police are looking for a woman who deserted her children:* abandon, forsake, leave; run away from.
◇ *Spelling tip:* It is too easy to confuse the spelling of *dessert* and *desert.* A *dessert* is a sweet course at the end of a meal; you want two helpings of the *s: Give me two helpings of deSSert.* On the other hand, a *desert* is an arid, sandy region, one that you would want to get out of quickly, so use only one *s: Let's get out of this deSert.*

deserts *n. pl. The new film was praised beyond its deserts. The bad boy got his deserts in the end:* due.

deserve *v. He deserves the award for his acts of bravery:* merit, rate; be worthy of, be entitled to, earn as due, be deserving of.

design *v.* **1** *She designed a new generator that saved the company millions:* plan, conceive, fashion, devise; draw, draft, sketch; draw up plans for. **2** *This fund is designed to help worthy students:* intend, destine, set up.
—*n.* **3** *She wasn't happy about the designs for the book:* sketch, drawing, outline, blueprint, diagram. **4** *The quilt has a sunburst design:* pattern, motif; form, arrangement. **5** *He has a design for becoming a millionaire in five years:* plan, project, blueprint, intention, purpose, goal, target, objective, end, aim. **6** *The group had designs against the government:* plan, scheme, plot; intrigue.

designate *v.* **1** *He designated the place where we were to meet:* specify, indicate, name, pinpoint; select, call, term, label, identify. **2** *I asked that Martha be designated co-chairman:* appoint, choose, elect, select, name, nominate, assign.

designing *adj. They are so designing that you can't help questioning their motives:* scheming, conniving, crafty, cunning, wily, artful, plotting.
Ant. candid, frank, honest, open, guileless, artless.

desirable *adj.* **1** *We're moving to a more desirable* *neighbourhood:* pleasing, fine; worth desiring, worth having, in demand. **2** *Such changes are desirable:* advisable, advantageous, beneficial.

Ant. 1 undesirable, disagreeable. **2** harmful, inadvisable, improper.

desire *v.* **1** *All men desire happiness:* crave, want, wish; long for; yearn for. **2** *We desire your early reply to this inquiry:* request, urge; ask for. —*n.* **3** *The desire for fame drove him relentlessly:* longing, craving, need, wish, yearning.

Ant. 1 spurn, reject, refuse, decline, repudiate. **3** distaste, aversion, dislike.

◇ *Word origin:* One's *desires* were once thought to be influenced by the stars. The word comes from Latin *desiderare,* to desire or to investigate closely. Latin *sidus* (constellation, star) also gives us *consider* (which among the Romans was an astrological term used in augury meaning "to consider the stars carefully").

desist *v. The company agreed to desist from false advertising:* cease, stop; discontinue, suspend; refrain from, leave off.

Ant. begin, persist, continue, persevere.

◇ *Word origin: Desist* comes from Latin *de-* (off) + *sistere* (to stand), hence to "stand off" from or stop doing something.

desolate *adj.* **1** *After the war the town was a desolate place:* deserted, uninhabited, empty, bare, barren, bleak, forsaken, abandoned. **2** *She has been desolate since losing her husband:* despondent, dejected, forlorn, downcast, depressed, sad, melancholy; sorrowful, wretched, miserable; bereft, lonely, solitary. —*v.* **3** *Many coastal towns were desolated by the hurricane:* ruin, ravage, devastate; destroy, demolish; lay waste. **4** *We were desolated by the death of our good friend:* sadden, grieve, depress, distress, dishearten; discourage.

Ant. 1 inhabited, populous. **2** cheerful, light-hearted, joyous, happy, glad. **3** develop, nourish, cultivate. **4** cheer, hearten, encourage.

◇ *Word origin: Desolate* originally meant "friendless, forsaken." It comes from Latin *de-* (completely) + *solus* (alone), which also gives us *solo, solitary,* and *solitude.*

desolation *n.* **1** *The desolation of the town was accomplished with one bomb:* ruin, devastation, destruction. **2** *We couldn't stay out there in that desolation another day:* barrenness, emptiness, bleakness, dreariness, bareness, wilderness. **3** *Her desolation is greater now that the children are away:* loneliness, seclusion, solitariness, solitude. **4** *That's too much desolation for anyone to bear:* sadness, melancholy, unhappiness, sorrow, depression, dejection, distress, misery.

despair *n.* **1** *He sank into despair after his business failed:* hopelessness, discouragement, despondency, gloom, depression. **2** *That child has been the despair of all her teachers:* burden, ordeal, trial. —*v.* **3** *I despair of ever finding her again:* have no hope, lose heart, lose faith in.

Ant. 1 hopefulness, cheerfulness. **2** delight, joy, pride. **3** have faith in, have confidence in.

◇ *Word origin: Despair, desperate,* and *desperation* come from Latin *de-* (away, without) + *sperare* (to hope), hence to be without hope.

◇ *Spelling tip: Despair* begins with a *des-*, not a "dis-." Remember this silly sentence: *If you were lost in a DESert you would DESpair.*

desperate *adj.* **1** *He was a desperate criminal on the loose:* reckless, dangerous, wild, frantic. **2** *Even his desperate schemes could not save the project:* daring, rash. **3** *She's in hospital with a desperate illness:* grave, critical, dangerous, serious; hopeless, incurable. **4** *She became so desperate that we feared for her sanity:* despairing, despondent, wretched; beyond hope. **5** *The family is in desperate need of help:* extreme, great, dire.

Ant. 1 cautious, careful. **2** sensible, safe. **3** hopeful, promising; curable. **4** elated, joyful, happy; hopeful, optimistic.

◇ *Word origin:* See DESPAIR.

desperation *n. In desperation, he finally broke down the door:* despair, hopelessness, recklessness.

despicable *adj. How can you forgive such despicable behaviour?:* contemptible, detestable, vile, mean, base, disgraceful, outrageous.

Ant. praiseworthy, laudable, worthy.

◇ *Pronunciation tip: Despicable* may properly be pronounced in either of two ways, as *des-PIK-a-ble,* with the second syllable stressed, or as *DES-pi-ka-ble,* with the first syllable stressed. The former is more common.

despise *v. I despise anyone who is cruel to animals:* dislike, scorn, loathe, detest, abhor; condemn, disdain; look down on.

Ant. like, admire, appreciate, respect, esteem.

despoil *v. Barbarians despoiled the northern towns:* rob, plunder, pillage, loot.

despondent *adj. It's easy to grow despondent when plans go awry:* discouraged, depressed, dejected, down-hearted, downcast, hopeless, disheartened, low.

Ant. encouraged, light-hearted, joyful, joyous, happy, glad.

◇ *Word origin: Despondent* comes from the Latin prefix *de-* (away, without) + *spondere* (to promise), hence without promise, without hope.

despot *n. The citizens revolted against the despot's rule:* tyrant, dictator, autocrat, oppressor.

◇ *Word origin: Despot* comes from the Greek *despotēs,* master, lord, despot. Although *Despotēs* was a title given to some Byzantine emperors and high-ranking bishops and patriarchs of the Eastern Orthodox Church, the word has had mostly bad connotations in English from its earliest recorded use.

dessert *n. Does the price of the meal include dessert?:* final course; (*variously*) pudding,

pie, tart, cake, sweet, ice cream, fruit, nuts.
◇ *Word origin: Dessert* is eaten after the table is cleared of the main course. It comes from French *desservir*, to clear a table.
◇ *Spelling tip:* See DESERT[2].

destination *n. My destination is Lahore but I'm stopping off at Calcutta:* journey's end, goal, plan, purpose, ambition, objective, aim, end, object.
◇ *Word origin: Destination* and *destiny* come from Latin *de-* (completely) + *stare* (to stand), hence to make fast, the place at which one stands still or makes fast, as a home port.

destiny *n.* **1** *Do you believe that our destiny is predetermined?:* future, fate, fortune, lot. **2** *Are you willing to let your life be controlled by destiny?:* fate, necessity, fortune, kismet, *Greek* moira.
◇ *Word origin:* See DESTINATION.

"I have learned that it is not the mountains that makes destiny, but the grains of sand and the little pebbles." —*B. Traven*

---

destitute *adj. The collection will be used to aid destitute families:* poor, poverty-stricken, needy, indigent, penniless, broke.
Ant. rich, affluent, opulent, wealthy.

destroy *v. Fire destroyed several shops in the town centre:* ruin, demolish, wreck, waste, ravage, devastate.
Ant. save, preserve, conserve; establish, found, institute; make, form.
◇ *Word origin: Destroy* and *destruction* come from Latin *de-* (down) + *struere* (to build), hence to undo construction, to "destruct." Latin *struere* also gives us *construct* and *structure.*

destruction *n. The fire caused the destruction of two landmarks:* destroying; ruin, demolition, wrecking, wreckage, devastation.
Ant. preservation, conservation; institution, organization.

destructive *adj.* **1** *It was the most destructive storm in 30 years:* damaging, ruinous, detrimental, injurious, devastating; harmful, hurtful. **2** *Criticism should not be destructive:* not constructive, negative.
Ant. **1** beneficial, constructive, creative, restorative, preservative. **2** constructive.

detach *v.* **1** *They detached their trailer and pitched camp:* separate, disconnect, disengage, sever, unhitch, disentangle, loosen. **2** *A plane was detached to survey the area:* send on a special mission, assign to special service.
Ant. attach, fasten, connect, engage, tie, bind.
◇ *Word origin: Detach* literally means to untack. It comes from French *dé-* (un-) + *tache* (tack, nail).

detached *adj.* **1** *The coupon is not valid if detached:* separated, disconnected; unfastened, unhitched, unconnected, uncoupled, severed. **2** *A judge must be detached when summing up:* impartial, neutral, unbiased, unprejudiced, disinterested, objective, dispassionate, fair. **3** *She's so detached that it's hard to get to know her:* aloof, distant, reserved, indifferent.
Ant. **1** attached, joined, connected, fastened. **2** partial, biased, prejudiced. **3** concerned, involved; warm, close, inviting.

detachment *n.* **1** *The crash was caused by the detachment of two coaches from the train:* separation, disconnection, disengagement, severing, severance, cutting off. **2** *You need a sense of detachment to arrive at a just decision:* impartiality, objectivity, fairness, neutrality. **3** *His air of detachment lost him many friends:* aloofness, indifference, coolness; isolation, preoccupation. **4** *A detachment of guards was sent to investigate the trouble:* unit, force, special task force.

detail *n.* **1** *The likeness was perfect in every detail:* particular, item, fact, component, feature, aspect, respect. **2** *The detail in the statue is very fine:* particulars or items seen as a group. **3** *An extra detail of police was sent to the area:* special duty, particular assignment, detachment. —*v.* **4** *The men were asked to detail their grievances:* itemize, enumerate, particularize, specify, delineate; relate, recount. **5** *She was detailed to act as special courier:* select for special duty; assign to a task, appoint.
Ant. **1** whole, aggregate, total, sum. **4** generalize.

detain *v.* **1** *The bad weather detained us for several hours:* delay, stop; hinder, retard, slow, slow down, slow up. **2** *The police detained the suspect at the border:* confine, hold, keep in custody; arrest.

detect *v. We detected the robbers as they entered the bank. I detected a note of pity in her voice:* discover, uncover, notice, note, observe, perceive, see, spot; catch.
◇ *Word origin: Detect* comes from the Latin prefix *de-* (away, off) + *tegere* (to cover), hence to uncover, reveal. A *detective* is thus literally one who "uncovers" crimes.

detective *n. The police assigned several detectives to apprehend the murderer:* investigator; special investigator; *Slang* sleuth, C.I.D. man, cop, private eye.
◇ *Word origin:* See *Exploring the Word* at POLICE.

detention *n.* **1** *The detention of the whole class after school was unfair:* detainment, holding, keeping in, holding back. **2** *He was kept in detention until he could raise bail:* custody, confinement; imprisonment, incarceration.
Ant. release, liberation.

deter *v. Bad weather didn't deter us from starting our holiday:* discourage, hinder, prevent, dissuade; stop, impede.
◇ *Word origin: Deter* literally means "to frighten away." It comes from Latin, *de-* (away) + the verb *terrere* (to frighten), which also gives us *terror* and *terrify.*

deteriorate *v. The weather has deteriorated these past few days. The patient's condition has deteriorated since the operation:* worsen, degenerate, decline, wane, lapse, fade; disintegrate, decay, crumble, fall off.
Ant. improve, ameliorate, advance.

determination *n.* **1** *That was one determination the judge never regretted:* decision, resolution, resolve; judgement, solution, verdict, conclusion. **2** *The determination of our slogan was arrived at by a contest:* determining, settling, resolving, reasoning, fixing, act of deciding. **3** *If she had more determination, she could be a success at anything:* resolution, resoluteness, perseverance, tenacity, persistence, steadfastness; boldness, spunk, power, pluck.
Ant. 1, 2 irresolution, indecision, doubt. **3** instability, hesitancy, hesitation, weakness.

determine *v.* **1** *I tried to determine the reason for her actions:* ascertain, discover, learn, establish, detect; find out, work out. **2** *Present decisions will determine the future of the company:* control, regulate, affect; decide, influence; give direction to. **3** *She determined that they would stay in Cape Province:* settle, decide, resolve, conclude; come to a decision.

deterrent *n. Punishment is not necessarily a deterrent:* restraint, curb, hindrance, check, discouragement.
◇ *Spelling tip:* Don't let the three *e*'s be a *deterrent* for spelling this word correctly: *dEtErrEnt.*

detest *v. I detest looking at snakes:* abhor, despise, loathe, hate; dislike intensely, recoil from.
Ant. like, love, adore, relish, cherish.
◇ *Word origin: Detest* comes from Latin *detestari,* to bear witness against, denounce, and hence to hate. The word is based on Latin *testis,* witness, which also gives us *attest, testify,* and even *testis* and *testicle* (the organ having been considered by medieval physicians as a "witness" of virility).
◇ *Usage note:* See HATE.

detestable *adj. Selfishness is a detestable trait in anyone:* hateful, obnoxious, abhorrent, loathsome; unpleasant, disagreeable; repulsive, revolting, disgusting, offensive.
Ant. likeable, lovable, agreeable, attractive.

detract *v. The peeling walls detract from the beauty of the room:* diminish, reduce, lower, lessen; take away from, subtract from.
Ant. increase, heighten, enhance; add to.

detriment *n. Staying up late will work to the detriment of your school-work:* injury, damage, harm, loss; impairment, disadvantage.
Ant. improvement, enhancement; aid, advantage.

devastate *v. The hurricane devastated a large section of the coast:* waste, destroy, ravage, desolate, despoil, spoil, ruin, wreck, demolish, level, lay waste.
Ant. create, erect, develop; build up.
◇ *Word origin: Devastate* comes from Latin *de-* (completely) + *vastare* (to lay waste).

devastation *n. The explosion caused complete devastation of the factory:* ruination, destruction.

develop *v.* **1** *The children developed their reading skills further during this year:* expand, broaden, improve, advance; mature, grow, flower, ripen. **2** *If you develop the idea further, I shall be interested in discussing it:* expand, enlarge; elaborate on. **3** *I developed a cold this week:* acquire, contract, pick up, come to have. **4** *It developed that they had an alibi for the night:* evolve, turn out, unfold, come to light. **5** *The builders are developing that part of town:* build up, convert. **6** *Let's have these negatives developed:* process, finish, print.
◇ *Word origin:* To *develop* something literally means to unfold or unwrap it. The word comes from the Old French prefix *des-* (un-) + *voloper* (to fold, wrap up). Old French *voloper* also gives us *envelop.*
◇ *Spelling tip:* If you wait and see what *develops,* you will still *never* see a final *e* on this word. Remember, *develop* ends in *-lop;* a final *e* never develops.

development *n.* **1** *Scientists have studied the development of man:* progress, growth, evolution, history. **2** *What are the latest developments in medicine?:* event, advance. **3** *There are several new developments in the case:* event, result.

deviate *v. The witness deviated from the truth:* part, stray, wander, depart, vary; turn aside, go astray.
Ant. continue, remain; stick to.
Word origin: To *deviate* is to stray from the straight and narrow path. Both *deviate* and *devious* come from the Latin prefix *de-* (from) + *via* (road), hence "from the road, away from the right or expected route."

device *n.* **1** *She invented a device that automatically closes windows when it rains:* invention, contrivance, apparatus, contraption, gadget, mechanism. **2** *He is full of devices for getting sympathy:* plan, plot, scheme, trick, design, artifice; strategy, stratagem, wile, ruse.
◇ *Usage note:* A *device* (rhymes with *ice*) is a tool, contrivance, or aid: *This device crushes ice-cubes. Devise* (rhymes with *eyes*) means to invent or construct: *He devised a sunshade for his eyes.*

devil *n.* **1 the Devil** *The preacher said that the Devil would take over their souls:* Satan, prince of darkness, chief enemy of God, Lucifer, Beelzebub, spirit of evil. **2** *The window was broken by those young devils:* mischief-maker, scamp, scoundrel, rogue, villain, ruffian. **3** *The poor devil never knew what hit him:* wretch, creature, unfortunate, thing; *Informal* fellow, chap, bloke.

devious *adj. His devious business methods landed him in trouble:* dishonest, deceitful, tricky, sly, treacherous, dishonourable, crooked, double-dealing.

Ant. forthright, above-board, straightforward; open, frank, honest.
◇ *Word origin:* See DEVIATE.

devise *v. He tried to devise a foolproof plan for getting rid of termites:* design, invent, conceive, concoct, contrive, think up, frame, prepare, formulate, map out, plot, forge, construct.
◇ *Usage note:* See DEVICE.

Exploring the Word: The *Devil* slanders God and righteousness — his name comes from Greek *diabolos*, slanderer, backbiter. *Satan* comes from Hebrew *sātān*, enemy. *Lucifer* comes from Latin *lux* (light) + *ferre* (to bear), light-bearer. *Mephistopheles* was the malevolent spirit to whom Faust sold his soul in medieval legend, and not originally the same as Satan. But when this story was retold in Marlowe's play *The Tragical History of Doctor Faustus* (1593), Goethe's two-part drama *Faust* (written between 1808 and 1832), and Gounod's opera *Faust* (first performed in 1859), *Mephistopheles* did become synonymous with Satan. *Beelzebub*, a devil mentioned in both Old and New Testaments, comes from Hebrew *ba'al-z'būb*, "fly-lord," "lord of the flies." Another Biblical name for the Devil is *Belial*. The word comes from Hebrew *b'liya'al*, worthlessness, destruction.

devoid *adj. The jury was devoid of sympathy when I presented my case:* lacking, barren, wanting, bereft of, destitute, empty, without, unblest with.
Ant. full, abounding, replete, flush, rich, abundant, overflowing.
◇ *Word origin:* In Middle English, *devoid* meant to empty out.

devote *v. She devoted her life to helping struggling actors:* dedicate, give over to, direct, apply, address, utilize, centre one's attentions on, give oneself up to; consecrate.
◇ *Word origin: Devote* literally means to vow completely. It comes from Latin *de-* (completely) + *vovere* (to vow).

devoted *adj. Be wary of politicians who claim to be devoted public servants:* dedicated, earnest, strongly committed, staunch, zealous, steadfast, unwavering; ardent, fond, loving, passionate; faithful, true, loyal, adhering.
Ant. uncommitted, undedicated, indifferent, dispassionate, unimpassioned, inconstant, unloving; unfaithful, disloyal.

devotion *n.* **1** *His wife resents his devotion to his mother:* attentiveness, dedication, commitment, devotedness, earnest attachment; regard, reverence, love, fondness, concern for; loyalty, adherence, faithfulness, fealty, allegiance, zeal, ardour. **2** *The spirit of devotion in the monastery communicated itself to the guests:* devoutness, religious fervour, holiness, piety, reverence, godliness, spirituality; religiosity. **3** (*Usually plural*) *Devotions are held every Sunday morning:* act of religious worship, service, religious observance, meditation, prayer meeting.
Ant. 1 indifference, unconcern, disinterest, disregard; irreverence, negligence, aversion; unfaithfulness, disloyalty, faithlessness, inconstancy, infidelity. **2** impiety, irreverence.

devour *v.* **1** *He was so hungry that he devoured several helpings:* eat voraciously, consume greedily, take in ravenously, gobble up, wolf down, stuff in, bolt down, gulp down. **2** *She devours several historical novels a week:* read eagerly and swiftly, read widely or compulsively, knock off, go through; absorb oneself in, become engrossed in.
Ant. refuse, pass up, ignore, be indifferent to. **1** disgorge, vomit, regurgitate.
◇ *Word origin: Devour* comes from Latin *de-* (completely) + *vorare* (to swallow), which also gives us *voracious*.

devout *adj.* **1** *The more devout members of the sect were wary of changing the ritual:* religious, orthodox, pious, godly, reverent. **2** *She is a devout admirer of French painting:* ardent, fervent, earnest, intense, serious, passionate, zealous.
Ant. 1 irreligious, impious, irreverent, sacrilegious. **2** passionless, passive, indifferent.

dew *n. Beads of dew still clung to the leaves and flowers:* moisture, condensation, film of precipitation, night or morning wetness; droplets of moisture.

dexterity *n. A surgeon must have great dexterity to handle precision instruments:* manual skill, deftness, adroitness, handiness, nimbleness with the fingers, proficiency, facility.

dextrous Also **dexterous** *adj. Her dextrous fingers moved effortlessly over the piano keys:* skilful, nimble, agile, adroit, deft; ingenious, resourceful, active, quick, gifted, efficient, able.
Ant. clumsy, awkward, maladroit, inept.
◇ *Pronunciation tip: Dextrous* may be pronounced either with two syllables, *DEX-trous*, or with three, *DEX-ter-ous*.
◇ *Word origin: Dextrous* comes from the Latin word *dexter*, right hand. Since most people are right-handed, something done with the right hand was considered skilfully done.

diabolic Also **diabolical** *adj. They were unaware of his diabolic intent to sabotage the factory:* devilish, satanic, fiendish, wicked, evil, impious, villainous, nefarious, monstrous, heinous, vicious, foul.
Ant. angelic, good, saintly, pious.

diagnosis *n. The doctor's diagnosis indicated heart disease. The committee undertook a comprehensive diagnosis of the city's problems:* identification of a disease, specification of illness, determination from examination, summary or conclusion from symptoms, medical or scientific report; investigation, study, examination, analysis, scrutiny.

◇ *Word origin: Diagnosis* comes from the Greek prefix *dia-* (across, between, through) + the verb *gignōskein* (to know), hence to know the difference or distinguish between diseases. *Prognosis* is based on the same Greek verb.

diagram *n. The company sent us a diagram of the new aircraft:* outline, representation, plan, drawing, map, line drawing, sketch, illustration, chart, rough projection, breakdown.

dialect *n. Cockney is the colourful dialect spoken in the East End of London:* variety of a language, vernacular, idiom, lingo, jargon, argot, patois.
◇ *Word origin:* See DIALOGUE.

dialogue *n.* **1** *The stubborn manager finally consented to a dialogue with the strike leaders:* formal discussion, conference, talk, exchange of viewpoints, parley, personal meeting. **2** *The dialogue of the play was hilariously stilted, but the plot was quite conventional:* direct or spoken discourse in literature, verbal exchange, conversation in a book or play, lines, speech; literary piece in the form of a conversation.
Ant. monologue, soliloquy.
◇ *Word origin: Dialogue* and the related word *dialect* come from Greek *dia-* (across, between, through) + *legein* (to speak).

diaphanous *adj. The fabric was as diaphanous as a spider's web:* translucent, transparent, sheer, filmy, gossamer, gauzy, flimsy, pellucid, lucid, limpid.
Ant. opaque, solid, thick, heavy.
◇ *Word origin: Diaphanous* comes from Greek *dia-* (across, between, through) + *phainein* (to show, to appear), to show through, hence transparent or translucent. The Greek word *phainein*, to show or appear, is also the source of our words *phantom, phenomenon*, and *fantasy*.

diary *n. She writes faithfully in her diary every night:* daily journal, day-to-day record, journal, day-book; log, chronicle.
◇ *Usage note:* A *diary* is a daily or personal record or journal: *I keep a dIAry of my daily activities.* A *dAIry* is a farm or barn where cows are kept or a place where milk and milk products are prepared and sold. *An AIry dAIry keeps the cows healthy.*
◇ *Word origin: Diary*, a record of daily events, comes from Latin *dies*, meaning *day*.

diatribe *n. In her diatribe she gave vent to all her resentments against him:* verbal or written castigation, bitter harangue, tirade, violent denunciation, stream of abuse, accusatory language, invective, vituperation, contumely.

dictate *v.* **1** *I'm dictating an answer to your letter now:* say to a person for writing down, utter for another to record, speak into a machine for recording, transmit a message through. **2** *The conqueror dictated the terms of surrender:* lay down, set forth, ordain, determine, order, direct, prescribe, pronounce, decree, declare with directive authority.
—*n.* **3** *We must all follow the dictates of the law:* requirement, mandate, stricture, rule, ruling, order, edict, dictum; bidding, urging, inclination, counsel, prompting, exhortation.
Ant. 1 record, write down. **2** follow, submit to, obey.

"It is a paradox that every dictator has climbed to power on the ladder of free speech." —*Herbert Hoover*

---

dictator *n. Stalin was one of the most feared dictators of modern history:* absolute ruler, despot, autocrat, tyrant; (*variously*) emperor, tsar, Kaiser, duce, Fuehrer, Caesar.

dictatorial *adj.* **1** *A constitutional president has no dictatorial powers:* absolute, authoritative, unlimited, unrestricted, categorical, arbitrary. **2** *I resent his dictatorial manner:* domineering, imperious, inclined to command, tyrannical, despotic, autocratic, magisterial, peremptory, lordly, wilful, overbearing, haughty.
Ant. 1 democratic, constitutional, limited, restricted. **2** suppliant, agreeable, humble, considerate, tentative.

> **Exploring the Word:** *Dictate, dictation*, and *dictator* come from Latin *dicere*, to say, to speak. To *dictate* is to speak so that the words can be recorded or obeyed, *dictation* is what is said or the act of saying it, and a *dictator* is one whose *dictates*, or sayings, must be obeyed, one who speaks the orders. Latin *dicere* is the source of many other English words, including: *diction*, way of speaking; *dictum*, a saying or pronouncement; *addict*, literally one who is assigned by decree to another (as a slave); *contradict*, to speak against or the opposite of another's words; *benediction*, a saying of good words, a blessing; *malediction*, a saying of bad words, a curse; *edict*, a speaking out, hence a proclamation or decree; *predict*, to say beforehand, to tell the future; and *jurisdiction*, exercise of judicial authority.

diction *n.* **1** *Bad diction marred the effectiveness of her speech:* choice of words, command of language, verbal style, rhetoric, wording, manner of expression, turn of expression, use of idiom, vocabulary, phraseology, verbiage. **2** *The actor was told to improve his diction:* enunciation, distinctness of speech sounds, articulation, pronunciation, elocution.

dictum *n.* **1** *We must not question the boss's dictum:* dictate, edict, decree, pronouncement, authoritative statement, order, dogmatic bidding. **2** *There's an old dictum that blood is thicker than water:* saying, saw, adage, maxim, axiom, proverb, truism, precept.

didactic *adj.* **1** *The sociologist's talk was didactic but entertaining:* instructive, prescriptive, educational, tutorial, doctrinal, intended for instruction, edifying. **2** *He couldn't shake off his didactic manner after teaching for so long:* lecturelike, preachy, inclined to lecture, pedantic, pedagogic, academic, donnish; moralizing, homiletic; dogmatically overbearing.

◇ *Word origin: Didactic* comes from Greek *didaktikos*, apt to teach, tending to teach.

die *v.* **1** *Her husband died in the war:* perish, suffer death, expire, pass away, pass on, pass over, leave this world, depart, meet death, come to one's end, be heard of no more, draw the last breath, go the way of all flesh, go to one's glory, go from dust to dust. **2** *The chiming of the bells died out but the sound seemed to linger in the air:* wane, ebb, decline, recede, fade away, subside, melt away, fade, gradually diminish, become fainter and fainter, slowly disappear, wither, pass, come to an end, die away. **3** *The electric train stopped when the batteries died:* fail, expire, become inoperative or inactive, run out, lose power, stop, break down, degenerate, rot, wear away, go flat; go stale, lose force, run down. **4** *I'm dying to see Jamaica:* yearn, be eager, be anxious, long, desire greatly, pine with desire, want keenly, wish ardently, be consumed with desire, ache, be beside oneself with desire.

Ant. 1 live, be born, survive, exist, flourish, begin, be immortal. **2** increase, build, become strong.

◇ *Usage note:* Some people forget that *die* means to perish, stop, or diminish, whilst *dye* means to colour by a chemical process, or the colouring matter used. Thus, *The rose-bushes will die without water. The sound died away,* but *Dye these Easter eggs. She dyed her hair blonde. Add more dye to the water.*

diet[1] *n.* **1** *She's on a diet because of her high blood pressure:* nutritional regimen, particular selection of food for health or other reasons, prescribed food and drink, limitation of fare. **2** *A balanced diet is necessary for good health:* nutrition, nourishment, eating habits, eating regimen, nutriment, nurture, board, sustenance, subsistence, victuals, provisions, edibles, comestibles.

—*v.* **3** *You will have to diet before you can wear that dress:* eat abstemiously, take food according to a regimen, follow prescribed eating habits, regulate one's food, restrict one's intake; eat sparingly, eat restrictedly; abstain from over-indulgence.

◇ *Word origin:* As doctors tell us, the way to lose weight is to change our long-term eating habits and way of living. Indeed, *diet* comes from Greek *diaita*, course of life.

diet[2] *n. The measure was unanimously approved by a vote of the diet:* lawmaking body, legislature, bicameral assembly, representative body for acting upon public affairs; congress, convention, convocation, general assembly, parliament, synod; assemblage.

differ *v.* **1** *This photograph differs markedly from the other one:* contrast, stand apart from, deviate from, depart from, diverge from; be unlike, be dissimilar, be distinct, be disparate. **2** *I differ with my partner sometimes, but usually we agree:* disagree, take issue, be of a different opinion, be at variance, stand opposed to, fail to go along, demur, think differently; dissent, dispute.

Ant. 1 ape, mimic, copy. **2** concur, coincide, agree.

◇ *Usage note:* To *differ from* means to be *different from,* to be unlike. To *differ with* means to *disagree with,* to differ in opinion, but *to differ from* can also sometimes be used with this meaning. Thus, *This house differs from our old one in having an extra bedroom,* but *I differ with* (or *from*) *him over politics.*

difference *n.* **1** *She doesn't know the difference between asking and demanding:* distinction, contradistinction, lack of resemblance, dissimilarity, unlikeness, dissimilitude, contrast, variation, disagreement, contrariety, deviation, divergence, contradiction; distinguishing characteristic, point of dissimilarity. **2** *There is a difference in their ages of six years:* discrepancy, disparity. **3** *They haven't spoken since their difference last year:* dispute, argument, disagreement, clash, falling out, contretemps, quarrel, squabble, fight, set-to.

Ant. 1 resemblance, similarity, likeness, similitude, analogy, affinity, agreement, uniformity, unity, consonance, identity, harmony, sameness. **3** agreement, concurrence, harmony, compatibility.

different *adj.* **1** *Her hat is different from yours:* unlike, dissimilar, not identical, not alike, distinct, disparate, other than, divergent, contrasting. **2** *We put the cakes in three different boxes:* separate, distinct, individual. **3** *I heard the news from different sources:* several, various, sundry, divers, variegated, manifold, miscellaneous, diversified, unrelated. **4** *He has a different outlook on things:* unconventional, unusual, not ordinary, uncommon, rare, unique, singular, distinctive; foreign, strange, peculiar, anomalous, bizarre.

Ant. 1 identical, alike, same, similar, like. **4** ordinary, common, usual, typical, conventional.

differentiate *v.* **1** *I learnt to differentiate between the French white wines:* discriminate, distinguish, see the difference in. **2** *The sun-roof differentiates the de luxe model from the standard:* distinguish, set off, set apart, constitute a difference between, make different; contrast, separate, draw the line.

◇ *Usage note:* See DISTINGUISH.

difficult *adj.* **1** *Moving the boulders was a difficult task:* hard, onerous, laborious, strenuous, demanding, requiring much effort, arduous, not easy, burdensome, exhausting, wearisome, toilsome, formidable, troublesome, exacting, trying, uphill, Herculean, Sisyphean, tough; complex, complicated, intricate, problematical, hard to solve, thorny, ticklish, knotty; perplexing, bewildering, hard to understand. **2** *She was always a difficult child:* hard to please, hard to satisfy, hard to deal with; unpredictable, unaccommodating; hard to manage, unruly, froward, obstinate, stubborn, wilful, perverse, unmanageable, obstreperous, unyielding, intractable, fractious, inflexible; critical, fastidious. **3** *Times were difficult during the Depression:* hard, grim, rough, full of hardship, not easy, tough, trying, troublesome.

Ant. 1 simple, easy, facile, light; clear, uncomplicated, lucid; plain, manifest. **2** easy, pleasant, amenable, co-operative, accommodating, manageable, flexible, tractable. **3** easy, pleasant, halcyon.

difficulty *n.* **1** *I finally overcame my difficulty in meeting people:* trial, troublesomeness, arduousness, laboriousness, uphill work, rough going, tough job, severe test; obstacle, impediment, obstruction, barrier, snag, stumbling-block, hindrance; problem, dilemma, puzzle, quandary, intricacy, perplexity. **2** *Because of some difficulty with her husband she had to return the coat:* trouble, predicament, pickle, critical situation, crisis, straits, hot water, mess, jam, deep water, muddle.

Ant. 1 ease.

diffidence *n. His diffidence keeps him from making friends:* timidity, timidness, timorousness, shyness, meekness, insecurity, retiring disposition, reserve, constraint, introversion; bashfulness, extreme modesty, humbleness, want of self-confidence, unassertiveness, sheepishness, lack of self-assurance; hesitancy, reluctance.

Ant. boldness, audaciousness, forwardness, assertiveness, aggressiveness; self-confidence, confidence.

diffuse *adj.* **1** *The room was bathed in soft diffuse light:* scattered, spread out, unconcentrated, dispersed, extended widely; vaguely defined. **2** *His talk was so diffuse that I missed his point:* wordy, verbose, discursive, rambling, long-winded, lacking conciseness, disjointed, digressive, not concentrated, desultory, roundabout, wandering, maundering, meandering, circumlocutory.

Ant. 1 concentrated. **2** succinct, concise, terse, pithy, compact; methodical, organized.

diffusion *n.* **1** *The diffusion of knowledge was accelerated by the invention of printing:* spread, dispersal, scattering. **2** *The diffusion of his prose style is confusing:* verbosity, diffuseness, wordiness, prolixity, verbiage, profuseness; circumlocution, indirection, roundaboutness, rambling, maundering, disjointedness, discursiveness.

Ant. 1 concentration, centralization, congestion. **2** conciseness, succinctness, terseness, condensation, compactness.

dig *v.* **1** *The kids dug a tunnel in the sand. We dug for worms to use as bait:* excavate, scoop out, gouge, penetrate and loosen ground, hollow out; bring to the surface, disinter, unearth, exhume, retrieve from the soil. **2** *Can you dig the material out of the archives?:* search and find, retrieve, extricate, find among, come up with, pin-point, salvage, bring to view. **3** *He dug his elbow into my ribs:* poke, drive, jab, thrust, prod.

—*n.* **4** *He gave me a dig in the ribs:* poke, thrust, punch, jab, prod. **5** *She couldn't resist a dig about my freckles:* cutting remark, gibe, jeer, verbal thrust, wry comment, taunt, aside.

digest *v.* **1** *Some foods are hard to digest:* assimilate, convert into an absorbable form, transform for bodily use, dissolve. **2** *It took her a while to digest the bad news:* grasp, comprehend, absorb, assimilate mentally, understand, realize, take in mentally, appreciate, take in wholly, fathom.

—*n.* **3** *The digest of the two-volume novel included the most exciting scenes:* condensation, abridgement, summary, synopsis, précis, résumé, abstract.

◇ *Spelling tip: Digest* is easy to spell, but *digestible* causes some people to hesitate because they are not sure if it ends in *-able* or *-ible.* Remember: *If it agrees with your digestIon, it is digestIble.*

◇ *Word origin: Digest* comes from Latin *digerere*, meaning to break things down and rearrange them, or to digest (food). Underlying both meanings is the idea of assimilation, which is at the source of the derivative Latin word *digesta*, "digested writings." This originally designated a condensed selection arranged according to subject headings. From this in turn comes the title of the emperor Justinian's code of laws, the *Digest* (6th century A.D.), which by extension gives us the common term *digest*, a comprehensive summary of a body of information.

dignified *adj. My father is too dignified to do anything so silly:* full of dignity, decorous, self-respecting, circumspect, reserved, distinguished, upright, honourable, upstanding, proud.

Ant. undignified, crass, vulgar.

"It is only people of small moral stature who have to stand on their dignity."

—*Arnold Bennett*

---

dignity *n.* **1** *She maintained her dignity throughout the trial:* comportment, dignified behaviour, respectful deportment, self-possession, decorum; stateliness, lofty bearing, proud demeanour, impressiveness of character; majesty, augustness. **2** *We must respect the dignity of the high court:* loftiness, high position, honour, station, official prerogatives, importance.

◇ *Word origin: Dignity* and the related words *dignified, dignify,* and *dignitary* are based on Latin *dignus,* worthy.

digress *v. Let me digress for a moment to tell you a little story:* depart from the subject, stray, wander, deviate, turn aside.

Ant. proceed, advance, continue.

digression *n. His long digression made him forget his main point:* divergence, departure, straying, wandering; diversion, obiter dictum, side remark, divagation.

dilapidated *adj. We bought a dilapidated house and tried to repair it:* run-down, decrepit, broken-down, tumbledown, falling to pieces, falling into decay, ruined, ramshackle, deteriorated, crumbling in disrepair, shabby, rickety, falling apart, battered, worn-out; *Slang* shot, beaten-up.

◇ *Spelling tip:* We are aware that a building is *dilapidated* when we see it with our two eyes. This word has two *i*'s: *dIlapIdated.*

◇ *Word origin: Dilapidated* literally means thrown apart or scattered, as stones from a building. The word comes from Latin *di-* (away) + *lapis* (stone). The Latin word for a stone, *lapis,* also gives us *lapidary* (one who collects or works with precious stones) and the blue gem *lapis lazuli.*

dilate *v. This medicine will dilate the blood vessels and prevent clotting:* expand, swell, enlarge, distend, inflate, puff out; make wider, widen, broaden.

Ant. constrict, contract, shrink, compress, condense, narrow.

◇ *Word origin: Dilate* comes from the Latin prefix *di-* (apart) + *latus* (wide).

dilatory *adj. The younger girl was dilatory about doing her homework:* inclined to delay, slow, procrastinating, remiss, tardy, sluggish, reluctant; dawdling, lackadaisical, negligent; indolent, slothful, lazy.

Ant. diligent, assiduous, sedulous, industrious, conscientious; punctual, prompt.

dilemma *n. The doctor's dilemma was whether he should tell the patient the truth or risk his refusing the treatment:* plight, difficult choice, choice between two evils, problem, quandary, predicament; impasse, deadlock, stalemate; Hobson's choice.

◇ *Word origin:* To be caught on the horns of a *dilemma* is to be forced to choose between two equally undesirable alternatives or propositions. *Dilemma* comes from the Greek prefix *di-* (two) + *lēmma* (a premiss, proposition).

dilettante *n. His inheritance allows him to pursue the arts as a dilettante:* one who pursues various arts; dabbler, amateur, trifler, experimenter.

Ant. artist, expert, professional.

diligent *adj. He was a diligent worker and deserved promotion:* industrious, hard-working, zealous, persevering, active, sedulous, assiduous, persistent, earnest, pertinacious, untiring, plodding, studious, painstaking; careful, thorough, well-intentioned, patient, concerted.

Ant. dilatory, lazy, careless, laggard, indifferent, inconstant, erratic.

dilute *v.* **1** *Dilute the ammonia with water:* thin, make thinner, thin out, make less concentrated, make weak, weaken, adulterate; thin with water, water down, add water to; make more fluid, make more liquid. **2** *His love for the boy tended to dilute his anger:* diminish, mitigate, temper, lessen the force of, decrease, weaken, attenuate, reduce, diffuse.

—*adj.* **3** *I've heard that the public bar serves diluted whisky:* watered down, watery, weak, weakened, adulterated, thinned out, reduced in strength by admixture.

Ant. **1** thicken, concentrate, strengthen. **2** strengthen, intensify.

◇ *Word origin: Dilute* comes from Latin *dis-* (away) + *luere* (to wash). This same Latin verb also gives us *ablution.*

dim *adj.* **1** *The room was too dim for me to be able to read:* lacking light, not bright, lacking luminosity, unilluminated, obscure from lack of light, darkened, dusky, tenebrous, shadowy, murky, adumbrated, indistinct, obscured, clouded, ill-defined, faint, nebulous, hazy; blurry, blurred; muffled, low, soft, weak, muted, feeble. **2** *I had a dim suspicion that trouble was near:* vague, intangible, faint, indefinite, indistinct, remote, foggy.

Ant. **1** bright, brilliant, radiant, luminous, effulgent. **2** distinct, plain, clear, palpable, definite, pronounced, well-defined.

dimension *n.* Often **dimensions.** **1** *The dimensions of the supposed flying saucer were quite improbable:* measurements, size, length, width, height, thickness; physical extent, mass, massiveness, bulk, volume. **2** *No one realized the dimensions of his problem:* scope, magnitude, extent, importance, volume, amplitude, weight, greatness, massiveness.

◇ *Word origin: Dimension* comes from the Latin prefix *dis-* (apart) + *metiri* (to measure), which also gives us *measure, metre* and *meter.*

diminish *v.* **1** *The cold spell quickly diminished our supply of firewood:* reduce, lessen, shrink, decrease, make smaller, shorten, lower. **2** *Time will never make our friendship diminish:* become smaller, lessen, shrink, dwindle, narrow, be reduced, shrivel, wane, decline, subside, fall off, ebb, peter out.

Ant. enlarge, augment, increase, amplify, enhance, heighten, magnify; expand, grow, burgeon, increase.

◇ *Word origin: Diminish* and *diminutive* come from the Latin prefix *de-* (down) + the verb *minuere* (to lessen), from which we also get *miniature.*

diminutive *adj.* **1** *Gulliver then encountered a*

diminutive people: tiny, little, small, short, slight, stunted, undersized, petite, minute, lilliputian; teeny, wee, elfin, dwarfish; on a small scale, insignificant, unimportant, inconsiderable.
—*n.* **2** *Maggie is a diminutive for Margaret:* short form, affectionate expression, nickname, pet name, hypocoristic term.
Ant. 1 enormous, immense, gigantic, oversized, huge, vast, colossal, mammoth, monumental.
◇ *Word origin:* See DIMINISH.

din *n. There was such a din that I didn't hear the phone:* clamour, uproar, loud confused noise, hubbub, racket, hullabaloo, tumult, clangour, stir, babble, clattering, rumpus.
Ant. quiet, silence, calm, stillness.

dingy *adj. The meeting was held in a dingy storeroom in the old building:* dirty and drab, dusty, lacking brightness, shabby, miserable, grimy, dreary, gloomy, dismal.
Ant. bright, burnished, radiant, glittering, luminous, shining, lustrous; gay, cheerful.
◇ *Usage note: Dingy,* meaning darkened or discoloured, should not be confused with *dingHy,* the small boat used as a tender for large vessels. The first is pronounced *DIN-ji,* the second *DING-i.*

dip *v.* **1** *She dipped the blouse into the hot suds:* dunk, place momentarily in a liquid, submerge, immerse briefly. **2** *She dipped up the soup into individual bowls:* take out with a ladle, scoop, lift by scooping, dish, dish up, dish out, ladle, spoon, bail; shovel. **3** *The moon dipped behind the trees:* droop, descend, slope, incline downward, turn down, decline, sink, drop down. **4** *I've only dipped into politics:* dabble, try tentatively, involve oneself slightly; study slightly, read here and there in a book, peruse, skim, take a cursory view of, glance at, run over.
Ant. 3 rise, climb, ascend. **4** involve deeply, immerse.
◇ *Word origin: Dip* comes from the Old English verb *dyppan,* to dip. It is closely related to our word *deep.*

diplomacy *n.* **1** *He is highly experienced in international diplomacy:* conduct of international relations, statesmanship, national spokesmanship, discourse between nations, foreign affairs, foreign negotiation, international politics. **2** *She used great diplomacy in handling the awkward situation:* tact, finesse, discretion, savoir-faire; artful management, skill, subtlety, delicacy, manœuvring, craft, artfulness.
Ant. 2 tactlessness, crassness, awkwardness, clumsiness, ineptness.
◇ *Word origin:* See DIPLOMAT.

diplomat *n.* **1** *He's a French diplomat assigned to the embassy in London:* government negotiator with foreign countries, statesman, national representative, international affairs expert, negotiator, interlocutor; ambassador, consul, minister, envoy, attaché, emissary. **2** *We need a diplomat to deal with these prima donnas:* tactful person, one who is artful in coping with situations, artful handler of people, public relations expert.
◇ *Word origin: Diplomat* and the related words *diplomacy* and *diplomatic* are based on Greek *diplōma,* a paper folded double, a letter. Our word *diploma* comes from this same Greek word.

diplomatic *adj.* **1** *He has a diplomatic post in Ethiopia:* involving diplomatic service, ambassadorial, foreign-office. **2** *He's so diplomatic that he can get on with anyone:* tactful, discreet, politic; sensitive, prudent, attuned, smoothly skilful in handling others, skilful in attaining one's ends, strategic, artful, adept.
Ant. 2 tactless, rude, unthinking, clumsy.
◇ *Word origin:* See DIPLOMAT.

dire *adj.* **1** *Any refusal to meet their demands will bring dire consequences:* dreadful, awful, appalling, horrible, terrible, woeful, harrowing, grave; calamitous, catastrophic, ruinous, cataclysmic, disastrous; urgent, desperate, extreme, fearful, crucial, critical. **2** *We were frightened by her dire prediction:* ill-boding, grim, ominous, portentous, dreadful, ill-omened, apocalyptic, dismal, inauspicious.
Ant. 1 happy, pleasing, good, favourable. **2** favourable, auspicious, promising.
◇ *Word origin: Dire* comes from Latin *dirus,* awful.

"I have neither eye to see, nor tongue to speak here, but as the House is pleased to direct me."
—*William Lenthall*

---

direct *v.* **1** *Mr. Kelly directs the activities of the community centre. I was directed to cut the budget:* supervise, manage, oversee, head, serve as director for, handle, conduct, control, superintend, lead, preside over; advise, urge, instruct, order, command, enjoin, charge. **2** *The policeman directed us to the shopping centre:* point the way, usher, indicate, put on the right track, conduct to, lead, guide, pilot, navigate. **3** *She directed her remarks to the speaker:* level at, aim, train at, point toward, address, intend for, earmark, designate.
—*adj.* **4** *They insisted upon direct negotiations between the leaders of the two countries:* face-to-face, head-on, personal, firsthand, without intervening agent, without intercessor, unmediated. **5** *He surprised me with several direct questions:* straightforward, without circumlocution, frank, candid, clear, explicit, plainspoken, point-blank, going straight to the point; sincere, honest, pointed, forward, forthright, blunt.
Ant. 4 indirect, meandering, roundabout, circuitous; mediated, by proxy. **5** indirect, devious, subtle, ambiguous, sly, oblique.

direction *n.* **1** *The research centre will be under his direction:* management, superintendence, headship, supervision, guidance, leadership, control, charge; administration, command, care. **2** *In which direction is the beach?:* way, line along which anything moves or lies, path, track, route, line of march, alignment; point of compass, course, bearing. **3** *You're thinking in the right direction:* line of thought or action, inclination, aim, tendency, bent, course, trend, track, bearing, drift, current. **4** (*Usually plural*) *Follow the directions carefully:* instruction, order, regulation, prescription, guide-lines, recipe.

directly *adv.* **1** *She drove directly to school. He lives directly across the street from me:* straight, in a straight line, on a straight course, not obliquely, unswervingly, as the crow flies, in a bee-line, without deviation from course; exactly, precisely. **2** *The guests will arrive directly:* soon, presently, momentarily; forthwith, at once, immediately, right away, promptly, as soon as possible. **3** *I spoke directly to the manager:* face-to-face, in person, personally. **4** *I hope you will answer me directly:* openly, honestly, frankly, straightforwardly, candidly, without circumlocution, in plain terms, unambiguously, unequivocally.

Ant. 1 indirectly, circuitously, crookedly; imprecisely, obliquely, inexactly. **2** later, eventually. **3** indirectly. **4** ambiguously, equivocally, cryptically, deceitfully, dishonestly.

director *n. What the camp needs is a vigorous entertainments director:* supervisor, manager, controller, superintendent, conductor, head, leader, organizer, overseer, administrator, boss, governor, chief, curator, foreman, commander, chairman, master.

dirge *n. He composed a dirge to honour the war dead:* funeral song, requiem, death song, death march, lament, burial hymn, threnody, mournful composition; mournful sound.

◇ *Word origin: Dirge* comes from the first word of the Latin verse *Dirige, Domine, Deus meus, in conspectu tuo viam meam,* "Direct, O Lord, my God, my way in thy sight," pronounced in the Roman Catholic burial service and adopted from Psalms 5: 8. (*Dirige* is the imperative of *dirigere,* to *direct.*)

dirt *n.* **1** *We need more sweepers to keep the gutters free of dirt:* mud, mire, dust, filth, filthy substance, impurity, foul matter, trash, sweepings, refuse, garbage, rubbish, muck, grime, soot, slime, scum, slops, leavings, dross, excrement, offal. **2** *The archaeologists removed quantities of dirt from the site:* soil, earth. **3** *Those shops still peddle their dirt to the tourists:* smut, filth, pornography, muck, obscenity, moral filth, vileness, squalidness, scurrility, scabrousness, salaciousness, indecency, profanity, unclean language. **4** *Her column is filled with dirt about famous people:* gossip, rumour, defamation, scandal, sensational exposé.

◇ *Word origin:* Dirt was originally an Old Norse word *drit,* meaning mud or excrement.

dirty *adj.* **1** *Scrape your dirty shoes on the doormat:* unclean, grimy, soiled, begrimed, muddied, grubby, filthy, foul, besmeared, messy, unwashed, untidy, smudgy, befouled, sullied, tarnished, polluted. **2** *He got involved in some dirty dealings on the stock-market:* unscrupulous, illegal, illicit, base, mean, contemptible, despicable, low-down, devious, deceitful, vile, shabby, nasty, sordid, squalid, dishonest, fraudulent, crooked, dishonourable, corrupt, perfidious, deceitful, villainous, treacherous. **3** *His company publishes dirty books:* obscene, vulgar, off-colour, scabrous, pornographic, morally unclean, indecent, blue, prurient, immoral, smutty, coarse, lewd, filthy, licentious; risqué. **4** *I seem to get all the dirty jobs:* distasteful, unpleasant, disagreeable, foul; hard, difficult.

—*v.* **5** *We have certainly dirtied this floor:* soil, make dirty, mess up, sully, smear, besmear, smudge, muddy, stain, tarnish, begrime, blacken; pollute, ruin, muck up.

Ant. 1 clean, washed, pure, spotless. **2** honest, respectable, above-board, honourable. **3** moral, respectable, decent, reputable. **4** easy, agreeable, pleasant. **5** clean, tidy up.

disability *n.* **1** *His disability prevents him from holding down a job:* handicap, particular incapacity, disablement, unfitness, infirmity, impairment, defect, affliction, debilitation, impediment, weakness, inadequacy. **2** *He suffers the disability of being still under age:* disadvantage, disqualification, handicap.

Ant. 1 fitness, capability, ability, capacity, strength. **2** advantage, merit, qualification.

disable *v. The plane was critically disabled when one of the engines caught fire:* incapacitate, render inoperative, damage, cripple, impair; deprive of strength, weaken, hinder, handicap.

disabuse *v. Someone ought to disabuse her of those star-struck notions:* enlighten about, free from error, clear the mind of, rid of deception, relieve of, set straight, set right, open the eyes of, free of a mistaken belief.

disadvantage *n.* **1** *His years of experience in the job put me at a disadvantage:* weak position, unfavourable condition, handicap; in arrears. **2** *What are the disadvantages of owning your own home?:* drawback, handicap, detriment, weakness, weak point, inconvenience, impediment, hindrance, fly in the ointment, trouble, hardship, nuisance, burden, flaw.

Ant. 1 advantage. **2** advantage, convenience, merit, desirability, benefit, perquisite; gain, profit.

disadvantaged *adj. Several disadvantaged countries need immediate help:* underprivileged, underdeveloped, impoverished, struggling, deprived, handicapped, troubled.

Ant. advantaged, privileged, affluent.

disagree *v.* **1** *My total disagrees with yours. We disagree completely on politics:* differ, be unlike, fail to agree, not coincide, vary, be at variance, conflict, be discordant, deviate, be dissimilar, diverge, depart; be of different opinion, think differently, stand apart, oppose one another, be unreconciled, differ in opinion, entertain contradictory views; be at loggerheads, clash. **2** *Too much sun disagrees with her:* be injurious, cause problems, disconcert, distress, discomfort, make ill, be unfavourable in effect, upset.

Ant. 1 agree, coincide, correlate.

disagreeable *adj.* **1** *The weather has been thoroughly disagreeable all week:* unpleasant, nasty, displeasing, distasteful, unpalatable, grating, repugnant, harsh, repellent, repulsive; uninviting, uncomfortable, unwelcome. **2** *She is always so disagreeable when we ask her to help:* unpleasant, ill-natured, irritable, difficult, uncongenial, unamiable, ill-tempered, churlish, nasty, bad-tempered, grouchy, cross, peevish, surly, petulant, testy, acrimonious, irascible.

Ant. 1 agreeable, pleasant, propitious, delightful, inviting, welcome. **2** agreeable, pleasant, congenial, amiable, personable.

disagreement *n.* **1** *There was apparent disagreement between their stories:* difference, lack of agreement, variance, discrepancy, unlikeness, disparity, failure to correspond, lack of harmony, deviation, divergence, diversity, dissimilarity, incongruity, dissimilitude, discord, incompatibility. **2** *They haven't spoken since their disagreement:* quarrel, squabble, fight, argument, difference, falling-out, misunderstanding, discord, dispute, clash.

Ant. 1 agreement, unity, likeness, similarity, correspondence, convergence, congruity, accord, harmony.

Exploring the Word: The Latin verb *parere,* to appear, come forth, gives us *appear, disappear,* literally "to appear away"; *reappear,* to appear again; *appearance,* the way things appear or look; *apparent,* literally "appearing," hence obvious or evident; and *apparition,* a ghost or other materialization that just seems to appear out of thin air.

disappear *v.* **1** *The sun disappeared behind the clouds:* vanish from sight, become obscured, cease to be seen, pass out of sight, be lost to view, cease to appear; withdraw, retire, go, be gone, depart, exit, flee, leave, fade, fade away. **2** *The spot disappeared when the shirt was washed:* melt away, vanish, evaporate, end, cease to exist, leave no trace, be no more, die out, cease to be known.

Ant. 1 appear, arrive. **2** appear, materialize.

◇ *Spelling tip:* This word has one *s* and two *p*'s. It is formed from *dis-* + *appear.*

disappearance *n.* *The disappearance of the secret documents created a scandal:* act of disappearing, vanishing, evanescence, sudden or unexplained loss, passing from sight.

Ant. appearance, materialization, manifestation.

disappoint *v.* *You disappointed us by not coming to our party:* fail to live up to the expectations of, let down, sadden, disillusion, chagrin, dishearten; thwart, frustrate.

Ant. satisfy, gratify, fulfil.

◇ *Spelling tip:* It might surprise you to know that many university students misspell this word. It has one *s* and two *p*'s and is formed from *dis-* + *appoint.*

disappointment *n.* **1** *Rover has been a disappointment to us as a watch-dog:* let-down, failure, dissatisfaction, something that disappoints, disillusionment, wash-out, fiasco, disaster. **2** *She says that she's finally learnt to accept disappointment:* thwarted expectation, miscarriage of plan, unrealization, unfulfilment, loss, bad news, frustration, set-back, dissatisfaction, defeat, failure.

Ant. 1, 2 satisfaction, fulfilment.

disapprove *v.* *Her parents disapprove of her going to dances alone:* view with disfavour, frown upon, discountenance, object to, find unacceptable, condemn, regard as wrong, think ill of, dislike, take exception to, look askance at; censure, criticize, deprecate, denounce, disparage, deplore, decry.

Ant. approve, commend, recommend, applaud, compliment, endorse, sanction, like.

disarming *adj.* *He has a most disarming smile:* winning, winsome, magnetic, charming, ingratiating, beguiling, melting, irresistible, captivating, entrancing, appealing, bewitching.

Ant. irritating, annoying, exasperating, infuriating.

disarrange *v.* *Please don't disarrange all of my papers:* scramble, disorder, mix up, displace, put out of order, disarray, upset, jumble, scatter, disorganize, confuse, put askew, muddle, turn topsy-turvy; rumple, dishevel, ruffle.

Ant. arrange, order, systematize, methodize.

disarray *n.* *The room was in complete disarray after the party:* disorder, messiness, sloppiness, upset, disarrangement, dishevelment, untidiness, confusion, disharmony, disorganization, chaos, jumble, clutter, shambles, mix-up.

Ant. order, arrangement, organization.

"So weary with disasters, tugg'd with fortune,
That I would set my life on any chance,
To mend it or be rid on't."

— *William Shakespeare*

disaster *n.* *The fire was the worst disaster that ever hit the town:* catastrophe, calamity, adverse happening, misfortune, crushing reverse, great mishap, cataclysm, tragedy, trouble, scourge, accident, adversity, ruination, blight, harm, misadventure, wreck, fiasco.

Ant. blessing, benefit, good fortune, profit, gain, boon, windfall.

◇ *Word origin: Disaster* comes from the negative prefix *dis-* + Latin *astrum* (star), hence the unfavourable aspect of one's star.

disastrous *adj. Investing his savings in that dubious stock was disastrous:* ruinous, catastrophic, calamitous, critically injurious, devastating, ill-fated, ill-starred, inauspicious, dire, harmful, destructive, fatal, dreadful, terrible, tragic, adverse, unfortunate, grievous, desolating, horrendous, harrowing.

disavow *v. He disavowed the rumours that he would stand for mayor:* repudiate, deny, contradict, denounce, reject, abjure, gainsay; disclaim knowledge of, deny responsibility for, deny connection with, disown, divorce oneself from, refuse to acknowledge.

Ant. acknowledge, admit; claim, accept.

disbelief *n. I stared at him in complete disbelief:* scepticism, lack of credence, doubt, doubtfulness, unbelief, dubiety, incredulity, distrust, mistrust.

Ant. belief, credulity, trust, faith, credence.

disburse *v. The company tried to disburse the cost over several years:* pay out, lay out, allocate, give out in payment, distribute; *Slang* shell out, fork out.

◇ *Word origin: Disburse* comes from the Old French prefix *des-* (away) + *bourse* (purse), hence to pay out. The French word *bourse*, purse, gives its name to the *Bourse*, the Paris Stock Exchange. It also gives us our word *purse* and goes all the way back to Greek *bursa*, leather bag.

discard *v. Let's discard some of these old newspapers:* get rid of, throw away, throw out, weed out, thrust aside, cast aside, remove; abandon, shelve, have done with, relinquish, drop, shed, ditch, dispose of, dispense with, dump, scrap, throw overboard, jettison.

Ant. retain, keep, preserve.

discern *v. She could discern a faint light at the end of the forest:* detect, make out, perceive, espy, catch sight of, descry, see, observe, behold, notice, pick out.

◇ *Word origin:* See DISCREET.

discerning *adj. The discerning speaker presented a splendid analysis of the problem:* perceptive, acute, perspicacious, sharp, astute, penetrating, keen-sighted, sensitive, piercing, discriminating, shrewd, intelligent, wise, judicious, sage, sagacious, clear-sighted, sharp-sighted; showing discernment, quick to discern, having keen insight.

Ant. undiscerning, unperceptive, indiscriminate.

discharge *v.* **1** *We feared that he would discharge his gun:* set off, shoot, activate, touch off, fire off, detonate, trigger, explode; send forth a missile from, eject, launch, propel, let fly. **2** *The boiler discharged steam:* emit, throw off, pour forth, send forth, project, give forth, exude, gush. **3** *His boss discharged him because of habitual absenteeism:* fire, dismiss, release, oust, let go, terminate, sack, get rid of, give the boot to, axe, give one his marching orders, lay off, send packing, cashier, remove from office. **4** *The prisoners were discharged from the detention centre:* release, allow to go, let go, free, set free, liberate.

—*n.* **5** *The discharge of the revolver was accidental:* firing, discharging, detonating, triggering, firing off, activating, exploding; detonation, explosion, blast, fusillade, shot, report, burst. **6** *He framed his honourable discharge from the army:* release, release document; demobilization. **7** *The discharge from the wound contained pus:* flow, suppuration, drainage, emission, ooze, issue, secretion, seepage.

disciple *n. She is an ardent disciple of yoga:* pupil, student, follower, devotee, aficionado, pursuer; adherent, believer, admirer, supporter, partisan; proselyte, neophyte, convert; *Informal* nut, freak.

Ant. master, teacher, leader, guru.

◇ *Word origin: Disciple* and *discipline* go back to Latin *discipulus*, learner, from *discere*, to learn.

disciplinarian *n. The teacher was no disciplinarian and his class always ran wild:* one who maintains discipline, enforcer of rules and order, stickler for rules, hard taskmaster, martinet, authoritarian, one who goes by the book.

discipline *n.* **1** *The discipline at the military academy is extraordinary:* training, drill, drilling, schooling, indoctrination, enforcement of rules, rigour, diligent exercise, practice, preparation. **2** *Daily practice is a discipline observed by most musicians:* method, regulated activity, prescribed habit, regimen, self-enforced practice, course of exercise.

—*v.* **3** *You must discipline yourself not to eat ice cream:* train, instruct, teach by exercise, drill, prime, break in. **4** *He severely disciplined his students by keeping them in after school:* punish, chastise, chasten.

◇ *Word origin:* See DISCIPLE.

disclaim *v. He disclaimed all responsibility for the accident:* disavow, disaffirm, deny, repudiate, renounce, decline, disown, forswear, abnegate, wash one's hands of.

Ant. claim, avow, affirm, acknowledge, accept, admit.

disclose *v.* **1** *The lawyer disclosed the details of the merger:* tell, reveal, divulge, make known, lay bare, bare, uncover, unveil, communicate, broadcast, publish, make public, impart. **2** *Daylight disclosed a chain of mountains in the distance:* uncover, allow to be seen, reveal, expose, bring into view, cause to appear, bring to light.

Ant. 1 conceal, hide. **2** cloak, mask, cover, veil.
◇ *Word origin: Disclose* comes from the Latin prefix *dis-* (not) + the root *clos-/clud-* (to shut), not shut, hence not hidden away but revealed. The same Latin root is found in *enclose* and *include.*

discolour *v. Water discoloured the carpet:* stain, spoil the colour of, change the colour of, tarnish, streak, bleach, tinge.

discomfort *n.* **1** *The discomfort from the stitches was not too great:* ache, hurt, pain, soreness, irritation, affliction; hardship, absence of comfort, uncomfortableness, trouble, trial, disquietude; vexation, annoyance, distress, malaise, misery.
—*v.* **2** *We were slightly discomforted by her cool manner:* make uneasy, embarrass, make uncomfortable, discomfit, distress, try, discompose, disquiet.
Ant. 1 comfort, ease, pleasure.
◇ *Usage note:* A person may be *discomforted,* made uncomfortable or uneasy, in body or mind: *The extreme cold discomforted the mountain climbers. News of the accident discomforted him* (made him mentally uneasy). Another word, *discomfit,* now little used, means to be mentally confused, frustrated, or embarrassed: *The actress was discomfited when anyone asked her age. The speaker was discomfited by the heckler.*

discomposure *n. She was outwardly calm and betrayed no sign of discomposure:* perturbation, agitation, uneasiness, distraction, disturbed condition, confusion, disquietude, discomfiture, embarrassment, discomfort, flurry, anxiety, nervousness.
Ant. composure, poise, equanimity, impassiveness, easiness, quietude.

disconcerted *adj. The performers were disconcerted by the late-comers:* distracted, ruffled, nonplussed, agitated, unsettled, confused; upset, annoyed, disturbed, troubled, perturbed, thrown, rattled.
Ant. unruffled, impassive, undistracted.

disconnected *adj. The plot was too disconnected to make sense:* confused, rambling, jumbled, disorganized, illogical, incoherent, mixed-up, disjointed, irrational.
Ant. connected, organized, logical, coherent.

disconsolate *adj. She is disconsolate over the loss of her job:* depressed, downcast, unhappy, inconsolable, desolate, sad, dejected, crushed, despondent, miserable, forlorn, broken-hearted, pessimistic, heavy-hearted, sorrowful, dispirited, woeful, woebegone, discouraged, doleful, low-spirited, melancholy, wretched, blue.
Ant. happy, joyous, cheerful, hopeful, optimistic, comforted.

discontented *adj. She was discontented with her dull life:* unhappy, dissatisfied, regretful, displeased, bored, disgruntled, miserable.
Ant. contented, satisfied, happy.

discontinue *v. I had to discontinue my keep-fit class after spraining my ankle:* stop, break off, terminate, suspend, drop, cease, give up, bypass, quit, abstain, abandon, leave off, end, put an end to.
Ant. continue, further, extend.

discord *n.* **1** *There was considerable discord between the three scientists' ideas:* dispute, disagreement, conflict, quarrelling, contention, discordance, dissension, disunity, division, lack of concord, being at odds, clashing, wrangling, friction, strife, incompatibility. **2** *The discord of his music is hard on the ear:* discordance, dissonance, disharmony, harshness, grating noise, cacophony, unpleasant sounds.
Ant. 1 harmony, consonance, accord, agreement, amity, unity, solidarity, compatibility. **2** harmony, consonance.

discount *n. Students get a discount on air fares:* reduction, deduction, subtraction, concession, cut, break, allowance, abatement; rebate.

discourage *v.* **1** *The second failure utterly discouraged him:* daunt, lessen the self-confidence of, dishearten, deject, unnerve, do in, dispirit, depress, prostrate; dash one's hopes, dampen one's spirits, decimate, destroy confidence in, unman. **2** *They discouraged him from investing in the stock:* dissuade, deter, divert from, restrain, keep back, disincline, advise against, express disapproval of, attempt to prevent.
Ant. 1 encourage, hearten, fortify, inspire, embolden. **2** encourage, urge, bid; welcome, support.

discouragement *n.* **1** *At the moment my discouragement has reached its lowest ebb:* depression, dejection, melancholy, hopelessness, despair, despondency, low spirits, downheartedness, gloom, dismay, pessimism, moroseness, lack of spirit, heaviness of spirit. **2** *That's about all the discouragement I can take:* consternation, worry, damper, constraint, restraint, curb, hindrance, obstacle, impediment.
Ant. 1 encouragement, hopefulness, high spirits, optimism, cheerfulness. **2** encouragement, boost, uplift.

discourse *n.* **1** *The lawyers enjoyed hours of leisurely discourse at their club:* conversation, talk, intercourse, converse, discussion, colloquy, dialogue, chat. **2** *We listened to a discourse on the evils of drugs:* lecture, address, speech, sermon, oration; dialogue, formal discussion of a subject; harangue, diatribe; essay, dissertation, treatise.
—*v.* **3** *The professors discoursed on Mycenaean civilization for an hour:* talk, talk together, converse, confer, discuss.

discourteous *adj. I was offended by his discourteous reply:* rude, impolite, ungracious, uncivil, uncourteous, unmannerly, boorish, ill-mannered, ungallant, disrespectful, impertinent, fresh, insolent, impudent; ill-bred, ill-behaved, ungentlemanly, uncourtly, unladylike, uncouth.

Ant. courteous, civil, polite, gracious, mannerly, respectful; well-bred, well-behaved, gentlemanly, ladylike.

discover *v.* **1** *Columbus discovered America in 1492:* come upon, come across, find, learn of, detect, gain sight or knowledge of, stumble upon, chance upon, light upon, uncover, unearth, locate, bring to light, ferret out, dig up; find out, ascertain. **2** *I discovered my error too late:* realize, notice, see, become cognizant of, recognize, perceive, spot, discern, learn of, determine, find, detect, uncover, unearth, locate.

◇ *Usage note:* Don't use *discover* when you mean *invent.* To *discover* is to find something that was already there before someone found it: *Balboa discovered the Pacific Ocean.* To *invent* is to create something new that was not in existence before: *Alexander Graham Bell invented* (not "discovered") *the telephone.*

discredit *v.* **1** *She discredited his good name with ugly gossip:* defame, abuse, dishonour, impair the reputation of, disgrace, vilify, disparage, smirch, smear, debase, degrade, vitiate, tarnish, taint, undermine, sully, stigmatize, drag through the mud. **2** *The insurance investigator discredited his false claim:* prove false, deny, disallow, disprove, reject; destroy confidence in, shake one's faith in, undermine belief in; dispute, challenge, question.

Ant. 1 credit, praise, laud. **2** credit, prove, support, accept, verify.

discreet *adj. I made discreet inquiries about his private life:* prudent, careful, tactful, judicious, cautious, circumspect, diplomatic, polite, politic.

Ant. indiscreet, rash, heedless, imprudent, careless, incautious, impetuous.

◇ *Word origin: Discreet, discretion,* and *discern* come from the Latin prefix *dis-* (apart) + the root *cret-/cern-* (to distinguish, separate), hence to perceive as unique, to know enough to keep separate.

◇ *Usage note:* Don't confuse *discrEET*, meaning "tactful, careful not to say or do the wrong thing," and the less common *discrETE*, meaning "distinct, separate." Thus, *A politician must be discrEET*, but *Charity and compassion are two discrETE qualities.*

discrepancy *n. There is a great discrepancy between his version of the accident and yours:* difference, inconsistency, variance, disagreement, lack of correspondence, disparity, dissimilarity, divergence, incongruity.

Ant. correspondence, accord.

◇ *Word origin: Discrepancy* comes from Latin *dis-* (apart) + *crepare* (to creak). The same Latin verb *crepare,* to creak, gives us *decrepit* ("creaky," as with age).

discretion *n.* **1** *Use your own discretion in choosing a restaurant:* good judgement, power of choosing, preference, individual choice, predilection, inclination, volition, option. **2** *He showed little discretion in handling the awkward situation:* good sense, judgement, sound judgement, judiciousness, sagacity, acumen, discernment, prudence, discrimination, tact.

Ant. 2 indiscretion, rashness, thoughtlessness, recklessness, irresponsibility, insensitivity, heedlessness, tactlessness, carelessness.

◇ *Word origin:* See DISCREET.

"The better part of valour is discretion."

— *William Shakespeare*

---

discriminate *v.* **1** *Many businesses are accused of discriminating against women:* demonstrate bias, set apart as different, show disfavour towards, make a distinction against, disfranchise, disdain, treat as inferior. **2** *Can you discriminate between good and bad art?:* differentiate, draw a distinction, separate.

◇ *Word origin: Discriminate* comes from Latin *dis-* (apart) + *crimen* (charge, accusation), hence to make a judgement separating things. Latin *crimen* also gives us our words *crime, criminal,* and *incriminate.*

◇ *Spelling tip:* Some people find the three *i*'s in this word a problem: *dIscrImInate.* And — the next time people ask you to name a word having four *i*'s in it, don't use the expected word Mississippi — surprise them with *dIscrImInatIng* or *dIscrImInatIon.*

◇ *Usage note:* See DISTINGUISH.

discrimination *n.* **1** *Laws have been passed against religious discrimination:* bias, prejudice, differential treatment, bigotry, distinction, inequity, favouritism. **2** *He shows a fine discrimination in choosing wines:* discretion, discernment, judgement, distinction; taste, refinement; astuteness, acumen, shrewdness, keenness, perspicacity.

discursive *adj. His discursive style makes his writing hard to follow:* digressive, rambling, roundabout, wandering, circuitous, diffuse, long-winded.

Ant. direct, methodical, coherent, succinct.

discuss *v. We were all eager to discuss yesterday's match:* talk about, go over, speak of, discourse about, review, exchange views on, converse about, debate, consider, examine, dissect.

◇ *Word origin:* To *discuss* literally means to shake apart. It comes from Latin *dis-* (apart) + *quatere* (to shake).

discussion *n. All members are invited to take part in a discussion of the proposed by-laws:* talk, dialogue, discourse, debate, parley, argument, disputation, review, consideration, deliberation; study, scrutiny, investigation, analysis; *Slang* thrashing-out, powwow.

disdain *v.* **1** *The proud man disdained all offers of*

help: look down upon, frown upon, think unworthy of notice, spurn, despise, abhor, treat with contempt, loathe, detest, discountenance, snub, deride; recoil from with pride, deem unbecoming, consider beneath oneself, deem unacceptable.
—*n.* **2** *I have nothing but disdain for bigots:* scorn, contempt, abhorrence, dislike, disrespect, distaste; feeling of superiority, haughty indifference, icy aloofness, intolerance.
Ant. **1** favour, admit, admire, like, love. **2** regard, admiration, respect, esteem, reverence, awe, fear.
◇ *Usage note:* See CONTEMPT.

disease *n. Doctors hope that someday they can eradicate all disease:* illness, sickness, ill health, physical disorder, ailment, malady, infirmity, morbid condition.
Ant. health, salubriousness, healthiness.
◇ *Word origin:* A *disease* is literally that which makes one uncomfortable or not at ease: "dis-ease." When it was first borrowed from French *desaise* during the reign of Richard II, it meant what both languages now express by the word *malaise.*

disembark *v. The assault troops disembarked on the beach just before dawn:* land, leave a ship, go ashore from a ship, get off a ship, debark.
Ant. embark, go aboard.

disfavour *n.* **1** *She incurred the doctor's disfavour by ignoring her diet:* disapproval, disapprobation, displeasure, dislike, disregard, dissatisfaction, odium, disrespect; disgrace, unacceptableness, ignominy. **2** *We did ourselves a disfavour by inviting the rude girl:* disservice, harmful act, ill turn, discourtesy.
Ant. **1** favour, approval, approbation, esteem, respect. **2** favour, service, kindness, courtesy.

disfigure *v. Was she disfigured by the accident?:* mar the features of, deform, deface, cut up, injure the appearance of, render unsightly, maim, make ugly, scar, scarify, blemish; mutilate, damage, impair.

disgorge *v. Her dog luckily disgorged the bone from his throat:* dislodge, throw up, discharge, regurgitate, throw out from the throat or stomach, spout, vomit forth, spew, eject, expel, cough up, spew up, cast up.

disgrace *n.* **1** *That scrap-yard is a disgrace to the neighbourhood:* shame, reproach, dishonour, blot, smirch, blemish, discredit, stain, embarrassment, tarnish, scandal, eyesore. **2** *He is in disgrace for revealing defence secrets:* disfavour, ill favour, contempt, disrepute, discredit; *Slang* in the doghouse.
—*v.* **3** *She disgraced herself by passing out at the garden party:* embarrass, humiliate, dishonour, debase, bring reproach upon, shame, degrade, abase, bring shame upon, cause to lose favour; blot, smirch, taint, derogate.
Ant. **1** grace, honour, credit, glory. **2** grace, favour, esteem. **3** grace, honour, credit, distinguish.

disgraceful *adj. He was chastised for his disgraceful manners:* shameful, dishonourable, scandalous, shocking, appalling, disreputable, discreditable, outrageous, ignominious; unworthy, unseemly, unbecoming; degrading, low, mean, inglorious, base, detestable, opprobrious, infamous, odious, despicable, vile.
Ant. honourable, reputable, creditable, worthy, seemly, becoming.

disgruntled *adj. Father becomes disgruntled when dinner is late:* sulky, grumpy, vexed, peevish, displeased, irritated, discontented, malcontent, dissatisfied, sullen, petulant, testy, shirty.
Ant. happy, contented, pleased, satisfied.

disguise *v.* **1** *She came to the ball disguised as Marie Antoinette:* assume a false identity, camouflage one's outward appearance, dress up, garb, mask, cloak, camouflage, veil; simulate, counterfeit, feign. **2** *She tried to disguise her real feelings:* conceal, hide, falsify, dissemble, cover up, mask, veil, misrepresent, gloss over.
—*n.* **3** *His disguise did not conceal his identity:* cover, counterfeit appearance, masquerade, get-up, deceptive covering, camouflage, concealment, guise, costume, false appearance; veil, cover-up, mask, screen, blind, false front, sham, pretence, pose.

disguised *adj. The disguised commandos slipped through the enemy's defences:* camouflaged, in disguise, unrecognizable, undercover, incognito, masked; cloaked, dressed up, veiled.

disgust *v.* **1** *His crudeness disgusted us:* repel, revolt, be repulsive to, appal, put off, offend, fill with loathing, cause aversion; sicken, nauseate, turn one's stomach.
—*n.* **2** *He couldn't hide his disgust at the news:* revulsion, repugnance, loathing, distaste, abhorrence, repulsion, aversion, contempt, hatred, detestation, antipathy, disaffection, displeasure, dislike, disrelish.
Ant. **1** please, delight, impress. **2** liking, taste, relish, fondness, love, satisfaction, affection, pleasure.

dish *n.* **1** *Put the potatoes in the blue dish:* plate, serving dish, platter, shallow bowl, flat receptacle. **2** *Wasn't that a dainty dish to set before a king?:* food, recipe, particular food, fare, article of food, victuals, edibles, comestibles. **3** *Would you like a dish of peaches?:* dishful, portion, plateful, bowlful, serving.
—*v.* **4** *Dish the berries into the bowl:* place, transfer, scoop, spoon, ladle; dole, portion, serve, dispense.
◇ *Word origin: Dish,* like *disc,* comes from Latin *discus,* Greek *diskos,* meaning disc, dish, platter.

dishearten *v. It disheartens any writer to have a novel rejected:* dispirit, dismay, discourage, daunt, deject, depress, dash, abash, weaken the resolution of, crush, take the heart out of.

Ant. encourage, uplift, hearten, make determined.

dishevelled *adj. She awoke from her nap with her hair dishevelled:* unkempt, ruffled, rumpled, disorderly, disordered, disarrayed, disarranged, messy, sloppy, untidy, in disorder, tousled, frowzy, blowzy, uncombed, bedraggled.

Ant. ordered, orderly, unruffled, neat, tidy; kempt, groomed.

◇ *Word origin: Dishevelled* comes from Middle French *des-* (away) + *chevel* (hair), to put the hair away from its arrangement, hence to have tousled the hair.

◇ *Spelling tip:* If you aren't neat, you can get *dishevelled* with *e*'s (ease) and this word has three *e*'s in it: *dishEvEllEd.*

dishonest *adj.* **1** *I wouldn't do business with such a dishonest man:* corrupt, not honest, untrustworthy, disposed to cheat, false, lacking integrity, perfidious, destitute of good faith, faithless, crooked, unscrupulous, deceitful, dishonourable, disingenuous, unprincipled, false-hearted, two-faced, fraudulent, underhand. **2** *The commercial was taken off the air because of its dishonest claims:* not honest, misleading, specious, deceptive, false, fraudulent, mendacious, untruthful, spurious.

Ant. 1 honest, upright, honourable, forthright, above-board, law-abiding, principled, lawful. **2** honest, true, supportable, demonstrable.

dishonour *n.* **1** *His collaboration with the enemy brought dishonour to the family:* shame, dishonourableness, disgrace, ill repute, discredit, ignominy, odium, disrepute, public disgrace, infamy, derogation, disfavour, humiliation, scandal; stigma, blot, blemish, stain. **2** *Sir, you have done me a grave dishonour!:* slight, affront, insult, offence, discourtesy.
—*v.* **3** *Rumours of corruption dishonoured the minister:* disgrace, shame, bring shame on, bring reproach upon, defame, deprive of honour, discredit, abase, blacken, tarnish, stain the character of, sully, debase, stigmatize, disparage, degrade.

Ant. 1 honour, glory, renown, repute, fame; reverence, veneration; esteem, respect, regard, admiration. **2** honour, compliment, courtesy. **3** honour, credit.

disillusion *v. I hate to disillusion you, but your chances of winning are nil:* undeceive, shatter one's illusions, free from illusion, open the eyes of, burst the bubble, disenchant, disenthral, disabuse, bring one down to earth, break the spell.

Ant. deceive, lead on, beguile.

disintegrate *v. The plane would probably disintegrate at that high speed:* fall apart, break up, break apart, go to pieces, shatter, crumble, crumble to fragments, reduce to particles, reduce to fragments, splinter, cause to fall to pieces.

Ant. blend, fuse, merge, coalesce; unite, combine, link up, join, connect.

disinterested *adj. We need a disinterested party to settle the argument:* impartial, unbiased, neutral, free from bias, unprejudiced, impersonal, outside, uninvolved, dispassionate, free from self-interest.

Ant. partial, biased, prejudiced, selfish, having an axe to grind.

◇ *Usage note:* Remember that *disinterested* means impartial, unbiased: *A judge must be disinterested in the cases he tries.* Don't confuse it with *uninterested,* which means not interested, not caring: *I like music but am uninterested in art.*

disjointed *adj.* **1** *The structure of the house seemed somehow disjointed:* disconnected, detached, having the joints separated, unconnected, unattached, split, divided, apart, disarticulated, helter-skelter. **2** *The film was too disjointed to make any sense:* rambling, mixed-up, confused, disconnected, disorganized, jumbled, tangled, chaotic, disharmonious, heterogeneous, incoherent, illogical.

Ant. 1 jointed, connected, attached. **2** sensible, coherent, logical.

dislike *v.* **1** *I dislike selfish people:* regard with disfavour, not like, feel repugnance toward, hold as disagreeable, regard with displeasure, have no taste for, object to, look on with aversion, consider obnoxious; loathe, abhor, despise, hate, detest, abominate, scorn.
—*n.* **2** *Her dislike for the catty woman was obvious:* distaste, aversion, antipathy, disaffection; loathing, repugnance, hatred, repulsion, revulsion, abhorrence, abomination, detestation, disgust; antagonism, hostility, malice, animosity, disdain, animus, enmity, rancour.

Ant. 1 like, esteem, favour. **2** liking, relish, delight, inclination, attraction, esteem, admiration.

"If people are made to do what they dislike, you must allow for a little ill-humour."
—*Lord Melbourne*

---

dislocate *v. He gave up bowling when he dislocated his elbow:* put out of joint, disjoint, disconnect, disarticulate, unhinge, uproot, disengage, separate, disunite.

dislodge *v. It took a bulldozer to dislodge the rock:* dig out, remove, displace, force out, eject, disturb, oust, uproot, extricate, disentangle, expel, dispel.

Ant. lodge, situate, bury, embed, root, plant, establish, seat.

disloyal *adj. She felt disloyal for giving up her citizenship:* unfaithful, inconstant, untrue, false to one's obligations, recreant, dishonourable, undutiful; perfidious, seditious, treasonable, treacherous, traitorous, faithless, subversive.

Ant. loyal, faithful, constant, true, steadfast.

disloyalty *n. He proved his disloyalty by betraying my secret:* faithlessness, unfaithfulness, apostasy, betrayal of trust, infidelity, lack of fidelity, breaking of faith, recreancy, perfidy, deceitfulness, falseness, falsity, breach of trust, inconstancy, double-dealing; treachery, treason, subversive activity.

Ant. loyalty, fealty, allegiance, fidelity, constancy.

dismal *adj.* **1** *She works in a dismal little room in the attic. His dismal attitude is infectious:* gloomy, cheerless, sombre, bleak, dreary; doleful, mournful, dolorous, despondent, sad, joyless, dejected, pessimistic, hopeless, morbid, downcast, depressed, unhappy, lugubrious, sorrowful, disheartened, heavy-hearted, desolate, woeful, melancholy, down in the dumps, disconsolate, rueful, down-in-the-mouth, woe-begone, forlorn; grim-visaged, long-faced. **2** *The show was dismal and a waste of time:* poor, unmentionable, awful, terrible, abysmal, very bad, abominable, dreadful, horrible.

Ant. 1 cheerful, bright, inviting, gay, happy. **2** good, fine, excellent, admirable.

◇ *Word origin: Dismal* comes from the Latin phrase *dies mali*, evil days, from the days that were marked as unlucky on medieval calendars.

dismay *v.* **1** *The boy's recklessness dismayed his mother:* fill with consternation, alarm, frighten, distress, appal, scare, unnerve, horrify; cow, daunt, dishearten, abash, intimidate, discourage; disillusion, disappoint, put off. —*n.* **2** *Imagine our dismay at the sight of the gun:* alarm, apprehension, anxiety, distress, concern, complete loss of courage, consternation, perturbation, trepidation; panic, terror, dread, fright, affright, horror, scare; utter disheartenment, discouragement, intimidation. **3** *I couldn't hide my dismay over her poor marks:* disappointment, disillusionment, discouragement, exasperation.

Ant. 1 cheer, reassure, relieve, encourage, hearten. **2** confidence, assurance, aplomb, self-possession, encouragement. **3** satisfaction, happiness, joy, reassurance, relief.

dismiss *v.* **1** *The workers were dismissed for lunch. Dismiss the meeting:* allow to leave, permit to go, release, excuse, send forth, let go, disperse; dissolve, adjourn, disband; free, liberate. **2** *She was dismissed for idling on the job:* fire, oust, discharge from office, put out of a job, sack, let go, terminate, remove from service, send packing, give one his marching orders, cashier. **3** *I trust her and dismiss any suggestion of dishonesty:* put out of mind, reject, set aside, disregard, disclaim, discard, lay aside, repudiate, eliminate.

Ant. 1 hold, detain, recall. **2** hire, employ, accept, admit. **3** welcome, accept.

disobedient *adj. The disobedient boy seemed incorrigible:* insubordinate, unsubmissive, rebellious, non-compliant, unmanageable, ungovernable, obstinate, recalcitrant, intractable, contrary, stubborn, refractory, fractious, froward, defiant, wayward, haughty, undutiful, perverse, unruly, disorderly, unyielding, seditious, insurgent, mutinous.

Ant. obedient, submissive, compliant, manageable, governable, dutiful, yielding, well-behaved.

disobey *v. He was finally expelled for disobeying the headmaster:* disregard, ignore, defy, not listen to, go counter to, refuse to obey, violate, overstep, transgress, resist, refuse to submit to, fail to comply with, infringe on.

Ant. obey, follow, abide by.

disorder *n.* **1** *I can't stand the disorder in this garage:* disarray, mess, muddle, disorderliness, disarrangement, disorganization, chaos, disruption, confusion. **2** *He was in hospital with a kidney disorder:* ailment, illness, sickness, affliction, disease, organic disturbance, malady, indisposition, complaint. **3** *The student disorder featured on tonight's news:* commotion, disturbance, public disturbance, fracas, turmoil, riot, rumpus, uproar, dissension, minor uprising, disturbance of peace, breach of order.

Ant. 1 order, orderliness, organization, neatness.

disordered *adj. His papers were too disordered for me to handle alone:* disorganized, confused, disarranged, jumbled, haphazard.

disorderly *adj.* **1** *Help me to straighten out these disorderly files:* disordered, out of order, unsystematized, disarranged, disorganized, unsystematic, pell-mell, unsorted, chaotic, jumbled, confused, topsy-turvy, helter-skelter; untidy, messy, sloppy, dishevelled, slipshod, straggling, unkempt, careless, slovenly. **2** *The demonstrators were gaoled for their disorderly conduct:* unlawful, disruptive, wayward, violating constituted order, lawless, constituting a nuisance; unruly, undisciplined, wild, boisterous, obstreperous, riotous, noisy, rowdy, improper, bad, disreputable.

Ant. 1 orderly, ordered, arranged, organized, methodical, neat, tidy.

disorganized *adj. His plan is too disorganized:* confused, disordered, jumbled, muddled, unsystematic, disordered, chaotic.

Ant. organized, ordered, systematic, systematized, methodized.

◇ *Usage note:* See UNORGANIZED.

disoriented *adj. I feel distinctly disoriented by the whole situation:* not adjusted, confused, distracted, mixed up, out of touch, out of joint; unstable.

disown *v. He disowned his reprobate son:* disinherit, disclaim, disavow, repudiate, renounce, cast off, forsake, denounce, reject, refuse to acknowledge, refuse to recognize.

Ant. claim, accept, acknowledge, recognize.

disparage *v. Don't disparage his attempts at bettering himself:* belittle, ridicule, discredit, run down, put down, mock, denigrate, undervalue, underrate, depreciate, slight, detract from, derogate.

Ant. applaud, praise, laud, extol, acclaim, commend, compliment, appreciate.

◇ *Word origin: Disparage* comes from Old French *des-* (away) + *parage* (equality of rank), hence to take away equality of rank, to discredit or belittle. The root behind Old French *parage* is Latin *par,* which also gives us *peer* and *par,* as in the golfing term *par for the course.*

disparate *adj. Their views are unusually disparate for brothers:* dissimilar, different, unlike, contrasting, at odds, at variance, discrepant, discordant.

Ant. similar, like, homogeneous, parallel, accordant.

dispassionate *adj. He described the problem in a dispassionate and objective way:* unemotional, cool, unexcited, unimpassioned, undisturbed, imperturbable, unmoved, calm, serene, collected, composed, level-headed, unruffled, uninvolved, detached; impartial, unbiased, unprejudiced, fair, impersonal, disinterested, neutral.

Ant. passionate, impassioned, emotional, excited, apprehensive, concerned, disturbed, partial, biased, prejudiced, interested.

dispatch *v.* **1** *They dispatched the report to the field commander:* send off, send on the way, transmit rapidly, post, forward. **2** *The business was dispatched in record time:* finish, complete, conclude, execute quickly, wind up, carry out, dispose of rapidly, expedite, settle, discharge speedily, carry out speedily, make short work of. **3** *The injured horse was summarily dispatched by its owner:* kill, finish off, execute, put to death, slay, put an end to; summarily shoot; murder, assassinate, bump off; slaughter, massacre.

—n. **4** *The correspondent sent his dispatch from Hong Kong:* message, report, missive, bulletin, official communication, flash; letter, story, news account, item, piece, telegraphic message, communiqué. **5** *The deed must be done with dispatch:* promptness, haste, quickness, expedition, swift execution, swiftness, rapidity, speed, celerity, alacrity.

◇ *Pronunciation tip:* Be careful to pronounce *dispatch* so that the *PATCH* sound is stressed. Thus *dis-PATCH,* not "DIS-patch."

dispel *v. The surprise attack dispelled the enemy infantry. Let me dispel your doubts:* scatter, drive away, drive away by scattering, expel, repel, rout, drive off; put an end to, make disappear, resolve, allay, eliminate, remove, dismiss, banish.

dispensable *adj. Trying to economize, they found many dispensable items in their budget:* unnecessary, expendable, non-vital, disposable, unessential, non-essential, unimportant, of secondary importance, accessory, extrinsic, superfluous.

Ant. indispensable, necessary, essential, needed, important.

◇ *Spelling tip:* Unless she's very wealthy, a woman will have to dispense with a *SABLE* coat — remember: *dispenSABLE.*

dispensation *n.* **1** *She directed the dispensation of blankets and hot coffee:* distribution, dispensing, allocation, designation, dealing out, meting out, apportioning, consignment, allotment, bestowal, conferment, division; reparation, remuneration. **2** *Catholics may obtain a divorce only with special dispensation from the Pope:* permission, authorization, decree, credential, exemption, relaxation of a law, approval.

Ant. 2 prohibition.

disperse *v. A thunderstorm struck and dispersed the picnickers:* drive off, scatter, dissipate, send scurrying, send off, rout, dispel, disband; distribute, spread throughout.

Ant. assemble, gather, amass, call in, collect, pool, congregate, convene, summon, muster, concentrate, recall.

◇ *Word origin: Disperse* comes from Latin *dis-* (away) + *spargere* (to scatter), hence to scatter away. Latin *spargere* also gives us *sparse.*

displace *v.* **1** *The car quickly displaced the horse and trap as the most popular method of transport:* supplant, supersede, replace, take the place of; crowd out. **2** *Many of the inhabitants were displaced by the rising flood-waters:* dislocate, dislodge, move, shift; put out of the usual place, put in a wrong place. **3** *An object will displace its own volume of water:* fill the space of, take the place of.

display *v.* **1** *The fireman displayed great courage in saving the child. The boat displayed all her flags as she came into port:* exhibit, show, demonstrate, bring into view, make visible.

—n. **2** *The shop has a large display of gift suggestions:* exhibition, show; presentation, demonstration; manifestation.

Ant. 1 disguise, cloak, hide, conceal.

displease *v. Nothing displeases me more than boasting:* annoy, irritate, offend, disturb.

Ant. please, gratify.

displeasure *n. The TV commercial incurred the displeasure of many viewers:* annoyance, vexation, irritation, wrath, indignation; dissatisfaction, dislike, disapproval.

Ant. pleasure, satisfaction, approval, endorsement.

dispose *v.* **1** *The committee was not disposed to hold another meeting:* incline, motivate; be willing. **2** *The shop disposed the jewellery in an attractive display:* arrange, array, place; organize, order, rank, classify. **3** *His vast property was disposed of in his will:* distribute, deal out; get rid of.

Ant. 2 disarray, disarrange, disorganize.

◇ *Word origin: Dispose* and *disposition* come from Latin *dis-* (apart) + *ponere* (to put, place, position), hence to put away. *Disposition* is the way in which something is positioned, as the *disposition of troops*, or put away, as the *disposition of funds*, whilst a *sunny disposition* refers to a person's temperament.

disposition *n.* **1** *Did you ever meet anyone with such a cheerful disposition?:* spirit, nature, temperament, mental constitution, characteristic mood. **2** *Her natural disposition to criticize has lost her many friends:* tendency, inclination; predisposition. **3** *The disposition of the troops preceded the battle itself:* organization, arrangement, grouping, placement, distribution. **4** *The foundation has funds at its disposition for the aid of schools:* control, disposal, power to dispose of.
Ant. 1 disaffection, unwillingness.
◇ *Word origin:* See DISPOSE.

dispossess *v. If you pay your rent, they can't dispossess you:* deprive of, take away, take back; evict, oust, expel.

disprove *v. Evidence has now disproved that theory:* refute, discredit; prove to be false or wrong, prove to the contrary.
Ant. prove, demonstrate; show to be true.

disputable *adj. It's disputable whether the two groups will agree to work together:* questionable, debatable, doubtful, uncertain, dubious.

dispute *v.* **1** *The expert disputed the authenticity of the document:* doubt, question, contradict; call in question, question the truth of. **2** *The strikers began to dispute hotly with members of the management:* argue, quarrel, wrangle, squabble, clash.
—n. **3** *The dispute concerns capital punishment:* controversy, debate, argument; quarrel, disagreement, squabble, bickering, clash, altercation, feud, wrangle.
Ant. 1 agree to, concede, concur with.
◇ *Word origin: Dispute* comes from Latin *dis-* (apart) + *putare* (to think), to think apart, think differently, hence to disagree or argue.

"Truths turn into dogmas the moment they are disputed." —*G. K. Chesterton*

---

disqualify *v.* **1** *Lack of education will disqualify you for most good jobs:* disable, make unqualified, make unfit. **2** *They disqualified her for being late for the final:* pronounce unqualified, declare ineligible, deny participation.

disquieting *adj. He has a disquieting way of staring at people:* disturbing, upsetting, vexing, troubling; disconcerting, unsettling, distressing, perturbing, annoying, irritating, bothersome.

disregard *v.* **1** *Disregard the mess and keep working:* overlook, ignore; pay no heed to, pay no attention to, take no notice of.
—n. **2** *His complete disregard of others lost him the respect of his friends:* lack of regard or respect, lack of attention, wilful oversight.
Ant. 1 heed; pay attention to, regard. **2** consideration, esteem, appreciation.

disreputable *adj.* **1** *They used to run around with several disreputable people:* shady, dishonourable, unprincipled; having a bad reputation, not reputable, of bad character. **2** *This house is in a disreputable condition:* shameful, disgraceful, shocking; not respectable.
Ant. 1 reputable, honourable; principled. **2** respectable, admirable.

disrespect *n. The disrespect she shows her parents is shocking:* contempt, dishonour, irreverence, disregard, impoliteness, rudeness, discourtesy, lack of respect.
Ant. respect, esteem, regard, reverence.

disrespectful *adj. He was sent to the headmaster's study for his disrespectful behaviour:* rude, impolite, discourteous, contemptuous.
Ant. respectful, courteous, polite.

disrupt *v.* **1** *The special TV report disrupted regular programmes:* interrupt, interfere with. **2** *The war disrupted many lives:* upset; throw into disorder.

dissatisfied *adj. She was dissatisfied with the results:* displeased, unhappy, discontented; not satisfied.
Ant. satisfied, pleased, content.

dissect *v.* **1** *In biology we had to dissect a frog:* cut apart, anatomize, separate into pieces. **2** *Dissect the poem and find out the author's meaning:* analyse, study; examine part by part, break down.

"Like following life through creatures you dissect,
You lose it in the moment you detect."
—*Alexander Pope*

---

dissemble *v. He tried to dissemble his disappointment with a joke:* hide, mask, disguise, feign, conceal, dissimulate.
Ant. show, manifest, evidence, reveal.
◇ *Word origin:* If you are a good *dissembler*, you have mastered the art of *dissimulation.* Both *dissemble* and *dissimulate* come from Latin *dissimulare*, to feign that a thing is not that which it is. This Latin verb comes from *dissimilis*, dissimilar — the *dis-* in this case being equivalent to our prefix *un-*. Latin *similis*, similar, is also the source of our word *resemble.*

disseminate *v. Plato's philosophy has been disseminated throughout the world:* scatter, spread, diffuse, disperse, broadcast.
◇ *Word origin: Disseminate* comes from Latin *dis-* (apart) + *semen* (seed), thus to scatter or spread in the manner of sowing seeds. Ever since its first recorded uses in Latin the word has always been used figuratively, just as we use it today. For example, the 3rd-century Church Father Tertullian refers to Gospel preaching as *disseminatio evangelii*, "sowing of the good news."

dissent *v.* **1** *If enough members dissent, the new bill won't be approved:* disagree, protest; withhold assent, withhold approval.
—*n.* **2** *A conclusion cannot be reached whilst there is dissent among the leaders:* disagreement, difference, dissension, discord.
Ant. **1** agree, concur; think in like manner. **2** agreement, concurrence, accord.

dissertation *n.* **1** *In order to receive the degree she had to present a dissertation:* thesis. **2** *The women's group are drawing up a dissertation on natural childbirth:* treatise, disquisition, tractate, monograph, memoir, discourse.
◇ *Usage note:* In sense **1** *dissertation* is strictly confined to the long, written essay or thesis, which counts as all, or part, of the work submitted for a (usually higher) degree in a university or college. The synonyms given at sense **2** above are no longer exclusively confined to the academic sphere.

disservice *n. He did you a grave disservice by refusing to help:* hurt, wrong, injustice, injury, harm, bad turn.
Ant. service, favour; good turn.

dissident *adj.* **1** *The dissident members kept the measure from coming to a vote:* disagreeing, differing, dissenting.
—*n.* **2** *The dissidents are saying that the plan is unproductive:* dissenter, rebel.
Ant. **1** agreeing, consenting, contented, satisfied. **2** conformist.

dissimilar *adj. Jane and Edna were so dissimilar that you wouldn't believe they were sisters:* unlike, different, distinct; not similar.
Ant. alike, similar, corresponding, akin; identical.

dissimulate *v. They dissimulated their true intentions:* hide, conceal, dissemble, mask, disguise.
◇ *Word origin:* See DISSEMBLE.

dissipate *v.* **1** *He dissipated his inheritance in less than six months:* squander, waste, misspend, fritter away, spend foolishly. **2** *The police managed to dissipate the mob without any arrests. The fog dissipated when the sun came out:* disperse, dispel, scatter; break up and drive off.
◇ *Word origin: Dissipate* comes from Latin *dissipare,* to scatter, disperse, squander.

dissociate *v. His marriage forced him to dissociate himself from his former companions:* separate, disconnect, break off with.

dissolute *adj. He was a dissolute young man who thought only of his own pleasure:* dissipated, corrupt, loose, debauched, immoral; unrestrained, abandoned.
Ant. moral, upright, temperate, sober, prudent, circumspect.

dissuade *v. My teacher dissuaded me from accepting the job:* discourage; persuade not to, advise against, urge not to.
Ant. persuade to, advise in favour of, urge to.
◇ *Word origin: Dissuade* is from Latin *dis-* (away, apart) + *suadere* (to persuade), to persuade away, advise against doing something.

distance *n.* **1** *The distance between the shop and my house is 3 miles:* span, gap, interval, intervening space. **2** *There was some distance between them at the last meeting:* reservation, restraint, reserve, formality; coldness, coolness, aloofness, stiffness.
Ant. **1** closeness, nearness. **2** warmth, friendliness, familiarity, closeness.
◇ *Word origin:* See DISTANT.

distant *adj.* **1** *I'd like to travel to distant lands:* far, far-off, remote, far-removed. **2** *Her distant relatives lived in this village:* remote; not closely related. **3** *She was so distant with me that I thought she was angry:* unfriendly, cool, cold, aloof, restrained, reserved.
Ant. **1, 2** near, close. **2** close. **3** friendly, cordial, warm, affectionate.
◇ *Word origin: Distant* and *distance* come from Latin *dis-* (apart, away) + *stare* (to stand), hence standing away, separation in space.

distasteful *adj. Asking people for money is distasteful to most of us. The medicine is distasteful, but it's good for you:* unpleasant, displeasing, disagreeable, disgusting.
Ant. pleasant, pleasing, delightful; tasty.

distend *v. The children's stomachs were strangely distended by malnutrition:* swell, bloat, swell out, expand, bulge, inflate, billow, puff out.

distil *v.* **1** *The liquid distils when heated:* evaporate, condense, vaporize. **2** *Whiskey is distilled from a fermented mash of grain. Impurities are removed by distilling the water:* separate by evaporation, produce by vaporization and condensation, purify by distillation; extract, draw out, draw forth.

distinct *adj.* **1** *Her business life is kept distinct from her social life:* separate, different, dissimilar, diverse, individual, not identical. **2** *The photograph showed a distinct image:* clear, lucid, plain; definite, well-defined, clear-cut. **3** *It was our distinct pleasure to entertain the ambassador:* well-defined, unmitigated, explicit, unquestionable; extraordinary, supreme.
Ant. **1-3** indistinct. **1** same, similar, identical; connected. **2** unclear, vague, obscure, indefinite, blurred. **3** usual, common.
◇ *Word origin:* See DISTINGUISH.

distinction *n.* **1** *Being colour-blind, he can't make any distinction between red and green:* differentiation, separation, discernment, discrimination. **2** *Is there a subtle distinction between theology and theosophy?:* difference, differential, contrast. **3** *She has become a painter of distinction:* excellence, note, superiority; eminence, notability, prominence, importance, pre-eminence, greatness.

distinctive *adj. She has a very distinctive way of speaking:* unique, different, characteristic, uncommon, individual, original, singular, atypical, special, extraordinary.
Ant. typical, common, ordinary.

distinguish *v.* **1** *His red hair distinguished him from his brothers:* differentiate, set apart, single out, make distinctive, characterize. **2** *You should be able to distinguish between right and wrong:* discriminate, decide; note differences. **3** *She distinguished herself as a great lawyer:* make well known, make famous, make celebrated, make prominent.

◇ *Word origin: Distinguish* and *distinct* come from Latin *distinguere,* to separate, distinguish. The basic idea of the word is "to mark apart, to separate by points." It is related to Greek *stigma,* mark; to our English words to *stick* and to *stitch;* and even to *tiger*—which in its Old Iranian form *tigra* means "sharp" (presumably with reference to the animal's teeth and claws).

◇ *Usage note: Distinguish, discriminate* and *differentiate* all refer to the act of telling apart things that are somewhat similar. *Distinguish* usually suggests the making of fine distinctions requiring skill, as: *Only an expert can distinguish the two types of porcelain. Discriminate* implies making a choice based on values: *You must try not to discriminate between men and women. Differentiate,* on the other hand, implies no qualitative judgement and is most often used to describe the technical telling apart of very similar things, as: *The scientist differentiated over 100 species of sea snail.*

distinguished *adj.* **1** *The award went to a distinguished playwright:* notable, renowned, famous, celebrated, prominent, eminent; great. **2** *The men looked distinguished in their tailor-made suits:* dignified, refined, elegant; grand, splendid, magnificent, superb.

Ant. 1-2 undistinguished. **1** unknown, uncelebrated. **2** inelegant, common, inferior.

Exploring the Word: *Distort, contortion, extortion, retort, torture,* and *torque* all come from Latin *torquere,* to twist. Thus to *distort* is to twist out of shape, to twist the truth out of shape; a *contortion* is a twisting of the body into an unusual posture; *extortion* is the twisting or wringing of money out of someone by threats or violence; to *retort* is to twist a speaker's words back at him, an accusation directed back at the accuser; *torture* means to cause pain, as by twisting someone's arm, while a *tortuous* road is a twisting or devious one; and *torque* is a degree of twist.

distort *v.* **1** *The bias of a reporter can easily distort the news:* misrepresent, twist the meaning of, give a one-sided view of. **2** *Years of pain had distorted his face:* contort, deform; twist out of shape.

distract *v.* **1** *The decoy distracted her attention whilst his mate stole the bag:* draw away (the attention), divert, side-track. **2** *Fear distracted her so that she could hardly think straight:* disturb, trouble, perplex, agitate, worry, disorder, confuse, bewilder, torment, madden, craze.

distraction *n.* **1** *Tennis is one of the many distractions we can offer:* diversion, amusement, entertainment, pastime, recreation. **2** *I was worried almost to distraction:* madness, desperation, frenzy, mental distress or upset.

distraught *adj. The distraught mother waited for news of her missing child:* distressed, agitated, distracted, frantic; beside oneself, extremely troubled; mad, seething, frenzied.

Ant. collected, calm, serene, cool, composed.

distress *n.* **1** *His distress was shared by all his neighbours:* pain, torment, agony, anguish, torture; need, want, acute suffering; trouble, danger.

—*v.* **2** *The news of his death distressed us greatly:* grieve, trouble, upset, disturb, torment.

Ant. 1 comfort, solace, relief; happiness; safety. **2** relieve, console, make happy.

"Wealth in modern societies is distributed according to opportunity."
—*Richard H. Tawney*

distribute *v.* **1** *The agency will distribute the food among several countries:* divide, apportion, allot; dispense, dole out, give out. **2** *The Post Office distributes the post by district:* deliver, circulate, disseminate. **3** *The lessons were distributed over 24 chapters:* classify, class, separate, arrange, systematize, catalogue, tabulate, methodize.

Ant. 1, 2 collect, amass, gather.

◇ *Word origin: Distribute* literally means to give out or allot to others. It comes from Latin *dis-* (away, apart) + *tribuere* (to grant, assign). The same Latin verb also gives us *tribute, attribute,* and *contribute.*

distribution *n.* **1** *The distribution of news is vital for an informed public:* dissemination, scattering, spreading, circulation. **2** *The distribution of schools in our city has been criticized:* arrangement, grouping, sorting, organization. **3** *The distribution of property is clearly stated in her will:* apportionment, allotment, allocation, division.

district *n. A person must vote in his or her own district:* neighbourhood, ward, parish, area, region.

distrust *v.* **1** *I have distrusted him ever since he sold me that defective refrigerator:* suspect, doubt, mistrust, question; feel distrust of, regard with suspicion.

—*n.* **2** *My parents' distrust of Bill has made our friendship difficult:* suspicion, doubt, mistrust; lack of faith.

Ant. 1 trust; depend on; have confidence in, have faith in, believe in. **2** confidence, trust, reliance.

disturb *v.* **1** *She will be angry if you disturb her whilst she's asleep:* interrupt, bother, intrude on, annoy; destroy the quiet of. **2** *Only bad weather can disturb our plans:* disorganize,

unsettle, disarrange, disrupt, dislocate, put out of order. **3** *The students' arrest disturbed their friends:* worry, distress, trouble, upset, perturb.
Ant. 2 establish, organize; put in order.
◇ *Word origin: Disturb* comes from Latin *dis-* (completely) + *turbare* (to stir up), hence to agitate. The Latin *turbare* also gives us *turbulence.*

disturbance *n.* **1** *You can work in here without any disturbance:* interruption, distraction, bother, annoyance, perturbation, upset. **2** *There was some kind of disturbance outside the Town Hall:* outbreak, rioting, disorder, uproar, turmoil, tumult.
Ant. 1 calm, serenity, quiet. **2** order.

ditch *n.* **1** *The car skidded and went into the ditch:* pit, trench; hollow, excavation.
—*v.* **2** *The robbers ditched the getaway car:* get rid of, discard; scrap, abandon, dump.
◇ *Word origin: Ditch* comes from Old English *dic,* moat, ditch, which also gives us *dike.*

dive *v.* **1** *The parachutists dived from the plane:* fall, plunge, leap, jump.
—*n.* **2** *The policeman made a dive for the attacker's legs:* lunge, dash, plunge; jump, leap. **3** *Informal We had a few drinks in some Soho dive:* shabby bar, sleazy night-club, gin-palace, honky-tonk.

diverge *v.* **1** *The path diverges off to the right after the pond:* separate, deviate, split, swerve, deflect. **2** *Our views of politics diverge greatly:* differ, conflict, disagree, be at odds.
Ant. 1 converge, agree, concur.
◇ *Word origin: Diverge* comes from the Latin prefix *di-* (apart) + *vergere* (to incline). *Divergere,* to turn aside, is Late Latin and first entered our language in anglicized form as an antonym of *converge* in a mid-17th-century study of the physical nature of light.

divergent *adj.* **1** *The two roads run parallel for a mile, then become divergent:* separate, splitting off, drawing apart. **2** *He tried to reconcile their divergent views:* different, disagreeing, conflicting.
Ant. 1 convergent. **2** agreeing, concurring, similar, like; identical.

diverse *adj.* **1** *My sister and I have diverse ideas on how to bring up children:* different, differing, dissimilar, disparate, contradictory, conflicting, opposite. **2** *She has diverse interests:* varied, of many kinds, sundry, far-flung.
Ant. identical, same.

diversify *v. A wise investor is careful to diversify his holdings:* vary; increase the variety of, variegate; diffuse, divide up, spread out.

diversion *n.* **1** *The diversion of the stream changed the land:* drawing away, turning aside, deflection. **2** *His only diversion is an occasional game of golf:* distraction, pastime, amusement; hobby, avocation.

diversity *n. Diversity of opinions makes for an interesting discussion:* difference, variance, diversification, divergence; variety, assortment.
Ant. likeness, similarity, sameness.

divert *v.* **1** *During the storm the controller diverted our plane to another airport:* deflect, side-track, turn aside from a path, draw away from a course. **2** *The children were diverted by his funny stories:* distract, amuse, entertain; turn from serious thoughts, draw onto a different subject.

divest *v. He divested himself of his clothing:* strip or remove (clothing), disrobe; take off, get out of, peel off, rid, free.
Ant. clothe, dress, cover.

divide *v.* **1** *The builder will divide the land into thirteen separate sites:* separate, split, subdivide, part, partition. **2** *We divided the pie amongst the three of us:* distribute, share; allocate, apportion, deal out. **3** *The new proposal divided the committee members:* disunite, cause to disagree, split, cause to take sides. **4** *She divided the shirts according to size:* classify, arrange, sort, separate, put in order.
Ant. 1 connect, unite, join, attach. **3** unite, cause to agree.

"A house divided against itself shall not stand." —*Matthew* xii:25

---

divination *n.* **1** *The high priest's powers of divination held sway over the people:* augury, soothsaying, prophecy. **2** *Not many of her divinations have been accurate:* guess, premonition, conjecture, foreboding.

divine *adj.* **1** *Zeus gave his divine blessing to the union:* heavenly, holy, celestial. **2** *She made the most divine chocolate cake that I have ever tasted:* excellent, wonderful, marvellous, admirable.
—*v.* **3** *The oracles were expected to divine the future:* foretell, prophesy, predict, forecast; fathom, surmise, guess, suspect.
◇ *Word origin: Divine* comes from Latin *divus,* god. To *divine* in the sense of "foretell" comes from the related Latin word *divinus,* which in this case means "god-inspired one," because practitioners of divination were believed to be thus inspired.

divinity *n.* **1** *He was punished for challenging the divinity of Zeus:* holiness, divine nature. **2** *He is a student of divinity and hopes to become a priest:* religion, theology, science of divine things, theosophy, science of God. **3** *In ancient Greece the divinities ruled over the life of man:* god, goddess, deity; divine being, celestial being.

division *n.* **1** *I call for a clearer division of labour on this site:* separation, splitting up. **2** *They put up a division between the kitchen and dining-room:* partition, divider, artificial wall, room-divider. **3** *I think that he works for a division of the company:* part, branch, department, section, wing. **4** *A sharp division of opinion was evident among the members:* split, difference, variance,

disagreement, divergence, discord, disunion.
Ant. **4** agreement, accord, union.

divorce *n.* **1** *Why must there be a divorce between feelings and actions?:* separation, rupture, breach.
—*v.* **2** *Is he still unable to divorce fantasy from reality?:* separate, segregate, disunite, dissociate, divide.
Ant. **1** unity. **2** unite, join.

divulge *v. Did the director ever divulge the reasons for his decision?:* disclose, tell, impart, relate, communicate; make known.
Ant. conceal, hide; keep secret.
◇ *Word origin:* To *divulge* means to make a secret commonly known. It comes from the Latin prefix *di-* (apart) + *vulgare* (to propagate), from *vulgus,* the common people. Latin *vulgus* also gives us *Vulgate* (the 4th century Latin version of the Bible), *vulgar,* and *vulgarity.*

dizzy *adj.* **1** *I always feel dizzy after riding on the merry-go-round:* shaky, giddy, reeling, off balance, vertiginous. **2** *The marchers kept up a dizzy pace:* rapid, quick, fleet, swift.
Ant. **1** steady, calm, composed.
◇ *Word origin: Dizzy* comes from Old English *dysig,* a word which has been in the language for considerably over a thousand years. However, when it was first used, it meant foolish or stupid, and the present sense did not arise until the mid 14th century.

do *v.* **1** *Has she agreed to do the work?:* perform, execute, administer, carry out. **2** *Have you done what I told you?:* accomplish, conclude, finish, fulfil, complete, achieve. **3** *They do the kitchen and bathrooms every day:* clean, put in order, prepare, arrange, organize. **4** *You'd better get used to doing as you're told:* behave, comport oneself, conduct oneself. **5** *We used to do business in Oxford Street:* conduct, proceed, carry on. **6** *Will this table-cloth do or should I use another?:* suffice, serve; be satisfactory, be enough. **7** *She's doing as well as can be expected:* fare, get on, make out. **8** *Informal Last summer we did 10 countries in three weeks:* cover, travel through, visit, look at, stop in.

docile *adj. We bought a docile old horse for the children:* manageable, tractable, compliant, tame, obedient, complaisant, agreeable, obliging, willing.
Ant. unruly, wild, ungovernable, disobedient, untrainable.

dock[1] *n.* **1** *We took the children down to the dock to see the ships:* wharf, pier, quay, waterfront.
—*v.* **2** *The tanker will dock in Hull for the installation of new equipment:* berth, come into port, guide a ship into dock, go into dry dock for repairs. **3** *The two modules docked in outer space:* couple, hook up, link up, join, fasten together, unite, rendezvous.
◇ *Word origin:* Many of our naval and seafaring terms come from Holland and the Scandinavian countries. *Dock* comes from Middle Dutch *docke.*

dock[2] *v.* **1** *The tail of the pony was docked:* crop, cut short; cut off. **2** *They docked his salary because of absence:* deduct a part from; deduct from the wages of, subject to loss.

doctor *n.* **1** *If you're ill, you'd better see a doctor:* physician, medical practitioner, person licensed to practise medicine; (*variously*) general practitioner, GP, dentist, paediatrician, oculist, veterinary surgeon.
—*v.* **2** *Doctor that cut before it becomes infected:* treat, apply medication to, give medical treatment to. **3** *He was gaoled for doctoring his tax return:* falsify, change, alter, tamper with.

> **Exploring the Word**: Latin *docere,* to teach, gives us *docile,* easy to teach, train, or manage; *doctor,* a teacher, as one holding the degree of doctor of philosophy (Ph.D.), or a doctor of medicine (M.D.) — the abbreviations stand for the Latin forms of the two titles, *philosophiae doctor* and *medicinae doctor* respectively; *doctrine,* a teaching or body of teachings; and *document,* a piece of writing used as a means of teaching or conveying information.

doctrine *n. The Church propounds the doctrine of free will:* principle, belief, conviction, philosophy, tenet, teaching, dogma.

document *n.* **1** *There are many documents containing the king's signature:* official paper, instrument, legal form.
—*v.* **2** *The lawyer gathered evidence to document the charges:* support, back up, give weight to, verify, substantiate.

doddering *adj. He helped the doddering old man across the street:* shaking, trembling, tottering, weak, feeble, decrepit, senile.
Ant. spry, agile, nimble; healthy, strong.
◇ *Word origin: Doddering* comes from Middle English *didder,* to tremble. Our phrase *all of a dither* literally means "all in a tremble, trembling all over," and is based on the same Middle English word *didder.*

dodge *v.* **1** *He threw a chair at me, but luckily I dodged in time:* duck, swerve, side-step. **2** *The reporters gathered round him, but he dodged their queries:* evade, avoid, elude; equivocate, hedge, fend off.
—*n.* **3** *Informal She found a new dodge to evade paying her taxes:* trick, stratagem, wile, device, machination.

doer *n. Bill is the talker, but Fred is the doer:* active person, activist, go-getter, hustler, dynamo.
Ant. do-nothing, idler, loafer, good-for-nothing.

dog *n.* **1** *What kind of dog makes the best pet for a child?:* canine; pup, puppy, mongrel, cur. **2** *Only a dirty dog like him would evict his own mother:* heel, scoundrel, villain, beast, blackguard, cur.

◇ *Word origin: Dog* comes from Old English *docga,* mastiff or bulldog. (The general term for "dog" in Old English is *hund,* hound.) In its "mastiff" sense the English word has been borrowed throughout western Europe — in Germanic languages *dogge,* in French *dogue,* and in other Romance languages *dogo.* But the ultimate source of the original Old English word remains unknown.

dogma *n. You can't embrace a religion without accepting its dogmas:* doctrine, teachings, set of beliefs, principles, philosophy; convictions, credo, tenet.

◇ *Word origin: Dogma* and *dogmatic* come from Greek *dogma,* tenet, that which is deemed right, from *dokein,* to seem, seem good, think, suppose.

dogmatic *adj.* **1** *She's so dogmatic that you can't tell her anything:* opinionated, arbitrary, biased, prejudiced; imperious, dictatorial, domineering; stubborn, obstinate. **2** *The Nicene Creed is one of the most important dogmatic statements of the Christian faith:* doctrinal, expressing dogma.

Ant. diffident, vacillating, uncertain; docile, complaisant.

◇ *Word origin:* See DOGMA.

doldrums *n. pl. I've been in the doldrums ever since she left:* depression, gloom, blues, dumps.

◇ *Word origin:* The *doldrums* were originally the part of the ocean near the equator where the winds are calm or dull. The *dol-* of *doldrums* comes from Old English *dol,* dull, and the word seems to have been formed by analogy with *tantrum.*

◇ *Usage note: Doldrums* is always preceded by *the.*

dole *n.* **1** *Many families have been living on the dole since the strike:* welfare benefits, allotment, apportionment, allocation, share, hand-out; food or clothing distribution.

—*v.* **2** *The organization doled out many gifts to the needy over Christmas:* give, hand out, distribute as charity, deal, parcel.

◇ *Word origin:* A *dole* is something given or dealt out. *Dole* comes from Old English *daelan,* which also gives us our word *deal.*

doleful *adj. The funeral was a long, doleful ceremony:* sad, gloomy, sorrowful, woeful, unhappy, joyless, dreary, dismal.

Ant. happy, joyful, cheerful, light-hearted.

◇ *Word origin: Doleful* comes from Latin *dolus,* pain. The same Latin word is the source of our archaic and poetic words *dole* and *dolour,* pain, grief. (There is thus no connection with the *dole,* charity, of Old English origin, which appears in the preceding entry.) Also descended from Latin *dolus,* pain, are *condole, condolence,* and *dolorous.*

doll *n.* **1** *She asked me to make some clothes for her doll:* dolly, figurine, dummy; (*variously*) baby doll, rag doll, teddy bear, golliwog, puppet, marionette. **2** *Informal Cathy is a little doll:* a pretty child, beauty, dear; honey, sweetheart, darling.

◇ *Word origin: Doll* was originally a common nickname for *Dorothy.* Thus somewhere in the distant past there was a little girl who named her toy Dorothy and then Doll and the name stuck for all "dolls."

dolt *n. One of the dolts in the office has mislaid my application:* idiot, clod, imbecile, fool, blockhead, bonehead, moron, half-wit.

Ant. whiz-kid, brain, genius, boffin.

◇ *Word origin: Dolt* comes from Old English *dol,* which also gives us *dull.*

domain *n.* **1** *His domain extends for 20 miles in every direction:* estate, land, territory, fief. **2** *The conspirators were banished from the king's domain:* dominion, territory, province, kingdom, empire. **3** *He lived his life in the ethereal domain of thought:* sphere, area, field, region.

◇ *Word origin: Domain* comes from Latin *dominium,* property, ownership rights, from *dominus,* proprietor, owner, lord.

domestic *adj.* **1** *Most family pets are domestic animals:* domesticated, tame; house-trained. **2** *Their new car is for domestic use:* home use, native, not foreign.

—*n.* **3** *It takes a staff of domestics to run that big house:* attendant; household help; (*variously*) maid, chamber-maid, cook, butler, houseboy, etc.

Ant. **1** wild, ferocious, untame. **2** foreign, imported.

◇ *Word origin: Domestic* and *domicile* come from Latin *domus,* house.

domicile *n. For voting purposes his domicile is in Melbourne:* residence, legal residence, dwelling, home, house, place where one lives.

◇ *Word origin:* See DOMESTIC.

dominant *adj.* **1** *The dominant powers took control of the conference:* ruling, controlling, predominating, predominant, superior, commanding, authoritative, principal, chief. **2** *The new tower will be the dominant building in the city:* outstanding, most important, most prominent.

dominate *n.* **1** *She completely dominates her family and makes all the decisions:* rule, govern, direct, control, domineer; preside over, be the head of. **2** *A ring of huge oak trees dominated the house:* occupy a commanding position, command visually; tower over, dwarf.

◇ *Word origin: Dominate* comes from the Latin *dominus,* lord, owner.

domination *n. She has been under the domination of her father since her childhood:* rule, control, authority, command, power, mastery, superiority.

Ant. subjection, inferiority, subordination.

domineering *adj. He was a domineering man, allowing no one to overrule him:* tyrannical, dictatorial, despotic, imperious, commanding, dogmatic; overbearing, arrogant.

Ant. subservient, submissive; timid, shy.

dominion *n.* **1** *"I have sole dominion over this land," declared the king:* rule, sovereignty, jurisdiction, supremacy, command, mastery. **2** *The law was put into effect throughout all of his dominions:* domain, empire, realm; territory, land, region.
◇ *Word origin: Dominion,* like *domain,* comes from Latin *dominium,* property. You will have noticed that all of the foregoing *dom-* entry words from Latin have to do with property and ownership. They go back beyond Latin to a root *dem-* meaning "house, household." Our English word *indomitable,* "untamable," is not related, however, as has often been erroneously supposed, perhaps from the connotations of *dominate* and *domineer. Indomitable* is based on Latin *domare,* to tame. Greek *damân,* Old English *temian,* and German *zähmen* are related and mean the same thing.
don *v. We donned our best clothes for the party:* wear, put on, dress in, invest oneself with, get into, pull on.
◇ *Word origin: Don,* to put on a garment, is a contraction of *do on.* The antonym *doff,* to take off a garment, especially one's hat, is a contraction of *do off.*
donate *n. She donated a large sum to the college endowment fund:* contribute, give, present, bequeath; make a gift of.
◇ *Word origin: Donate* and *donor* come from Latin *donare,* to give.
donation *n. Many donations of money and clothing poured in for the flood victims:* present, gift, contribution.
done *adj. The pie isn't done until the crust has gone brown:* ready; cooked sufficiently, cooked enough, prepared, finished.
donkey *n.* **1** *Donkeys are better than horses on mountain trails:* ass; (*variously*) mule, Neddy, jackass. **2** *Don't be such a donkey about accepting help from your friends:* fool, idiot, ass, jackass.
◇ *Word origin:* No one knows where the word *donkey* comes from. It first appeared in English some time before 1785. It originally rhymed with *monkey.* A possible derivation is from the proper name *Duncan.*
donor *n. The new arts foundation won't survive without more donors:* contributor, benefactor, giver; philanthropist, humanitarian.
◇ *Word origin:* See DONATE.
doom *n.* **1** *The condemned woman could only await her doom:* fate, lot, portion, destiny; destruction, ruin, death. **2** *The preacher warned his congregation about the day of doom:* The Last Judgement, Judgement Day, doomsday, end of the world, Armageddon, resurrection day.
—*v.* **3** *Many landmarks are doomed because of the public's indifference:* mark for demolition, consign to ruin, consign to destruction.
◇ *Word origin: Doom* comes from Old English *dōm,* judgement. Thus, doomsday means "Judgement Day."
doomsday *n. On doomsday, the preacher said, we shall have to account for our sins:* Day of Judgement, end of the world, Judgement Day, The Last Judgement.
◇ *Word origin:* See DOOM.
◇ *Usage note: Doomsday* is often colloquially used as a synonym for "the end of time, eternity" as in the following sentence: *You can lecture that child until doomsday but you'll never knock any sense into his head.*
door *n. Barbara stood at the door and greeted everyone:* doorway, entrance, entry, ingress, hallway; exit, egress.
dope *n.* **1** *Slang He was accused of peddling dope:* narcotics, drugs. **2** *Slang He gave me some dope on the fifth race:* tip, news; inside information. **3** *Slang The dope never knows when I'm kidding her:* dummy, fool, *Yiddish* klutz.
—*v.* **4** *Louise was heavily doped before the operation:* drug, sedate, anaesthetize.
◇ *Word origin: Dope* comes from Dutch *doop,* sauce.
dormant *adj. The geyser has been dormant for five years now:* inactive, quiescent, idle; sleeping, somnolent; hibernating.
Ant. active, operative, moving, awake.
◇ *Word origin: Dormant* comes from Latin *dormire,* to sleep, which also gives us *dormitory,* a room with sleeping accommodation for several people, and even *dormouse,* literally a dozing mouse.
dossier *n. The office keeps a dossier on every employee:* file, record, portfolio, brief, report.
dot *n.* **1** *She bought a blue dress with white dots:* mark, speck, small spot; period, point.
—*v.* **2** *Dot the pie-filling with bits of butter:* dab, dapple, spot.
◇ *Word origin: Dot* is probably an old variant form of *teat* or *tit,* nipple.
dotage *n. He's in his dotage and has difficulty remembering things:* senility, feeble-mindedness, second childhood.
Ant. youth, heyday, salad days.
◇ *Word origin:* See DOTE.
dote *v. Grandparents often dote on their grandchildren:* bestow excessive love on, fuss over, lavish foolish fondness on.
◇ *Word origin: Dote* and *dotage* come from Middle Dutch *doten,* to be silly. Hence to *dote* on someone is literally to be so fond of that person as to seem foolish, and *dotage* is silliness due to old age, senility.
double *adj.* **1** *The workers receive double pay for working on Sundays:* multiplied by two, twice as much, twice as great, as much again. **2** *The house has double doors in the dining-room:* paired, twin, two-part. **3** *His statement had a double meaning:* two-sided, dual, ambiguous; twofold in character. **4** *We sleep in a double bed:* meant for two; accommodating two.
—*n.* **5** *She is the double of her mother as a girl:* twin, counterpart, duplicate; *Slang* spitting image, ringer.
—*v.* **6** *That new stock has doubled my income:*

make twice as great, multiply by two, increase twofold.
◇ *Word origin: Double* comes from Latin *duplex*, double, twofold, which also gives us *duplex*, *duplicate*, and *duplicity*.

doubt *v.* **1** *She doubts that anyone is truly clairvoyant:* question, wonder; be sceptical concerning, have doubts about, be doubtful, feel uncertain, waver in opinion. **2** *He promised to repay the money, but I doubt his word:* distrust, mistrust, suspect; lack confidence in.
—*n.* **3** *Is there any doubt about your willingness to accept the job?* uncertainty, indecision, question, lack of conviction. **4** *She has her doubts about lending him any more money:* misgiving, mistrust, suspicion, apprehension, qualm.
Ant. 1 believe, feel certain. **2** trust, believe, rely on. **3** resolve. **4** trust, belief, confidence, faith.

doubtful *adj.* **1** *She's still doubtful about the wisdom of her choice:* undecided, uncertain, unconvinced, unsettled; hesitating, irresolute. **2** *I think the manuscript is of doubtful authenticity:* dubious, suspicious, suspect, questionable. **3** *The results of the experiment are doubtful:* unclear, vague, uncertain, inconclusive.
Ant. 1 decided, certain, positive. **2** indubitable, incontrovertible; definite.

doughty *adj. He was a doughty little man who could never be bullied:* courageous, brave, bold, intrepid, fearless, unafraid, dauntless, stouthearted; strong, confident, determined.
Ant. cowardly, timid.
◇ *Pronunciation tip:* The pronunciation of this word is difficult to arrive at from its spelling and should not be confused with either *dough* or *tough*. The correct pronunciation is *DOW-tee.*

dour *adj. She has a dour expression that discourages friendship:* gloomy, sullen, morose, sour; unfriendly, solemn, forbidding.
Ant. happy, bright, sweet; soft.
◇ *Word origin: Dour* comes from French *dur*, hard, and is derived from Latin *durus*, hard, which also gives us *durable*.
◇ *Pronunciation tip:* In its traditionally preferred pronunciation, *dour* rhymes with *poor*. It is thus pronounced in Scotland to this day, but in other parts of the English-speaking world *dour* also rhymes with *sour*.

douse *v. He doused his hair in the sink to rinse off all the shampoo:* drench, submerge, immerse, soak, plunge into water, souse, saturate.

dovetail *v.* **1** *The sides of the drawer dovetail at the corners:* unite, join, fit together, connect by interlocking. **2** *If our schedules dovetail, I'll see you in Birmingham:* harmonize, coincide, match.

dowdy *adj. She's much too young to look so dowdy:* drab, shabby, sloppy, slovenly, frumpy, unattractive.
Ant. smart, well-dressed, fashionable, chic; neat, trim, tidy.
◇ *Word origin: Dowdy* comes from Middle English *doude*, slut.

down *adj.* **1** *I've felt down ever since I heard the news:* downcast, disheartened, dejected, depressed; down-and-out. **2** *He's down with a nasty cold:* sick, ill, ailing.
—*v.* **3** *He downed the champion with a left hook:* fell, floor, drop, knock down; knock out, K.O. **4** *She usually downs three martinis before dinner:* swallow, gulp; drink down, put away.
Ant. 1 gladdened, glad, happy, spirited.
◇ *Word origin: Down* comes from Old English *ofdūne*, "off-hill." Old English *dūn*, hill, has other interesting Germanic and Celtic relatives: Middle Dutch *dūne*, sandy hill, which gives us our word *dune*; and a Celtic word which became Old English *tūn*, town. (Remember that many towns were hill forts in the north-western Europe of the Dark Ages.)

downcast *adj. There's no need to be downcast just because you lost:* unhappy, sad, disconsolate, disheartened, cheerless, depressed, dejected, low, blue, discouraged.
Ant. happy, glad, encouraged, spirited.

downfall *n.* **1** *The revolution brought about the dictator's downfall:* fall, ruin, ruination, destruction, collapse. **2** *A downfall is expected, so take an umbrella:* downpour, shower, rainstorm, rain shower.

down-hearted *adj. The student is down-hearted because the professor failed her thesis:* unhappy, sorrowful, depressed, sad, disheartened, dejected, discouraged, downcast.
Ant. happy, glad, encouraged, spirited.

downpour *n. We got caught in a sudden downpour and were soaked:* shower, cloudburst, rainstorm, rain shower.

downright *adj.* **1** *She told a downright lie:* absolute, total, thoroughgoing, complete, out and out. **2** *Her downright answer startled him:* direct, straightforward, candid, open, frank, blunt; sincere, honest, above-board, straight-from-the-shoulder.
—*adv.* **3** *He was downright rude to us:* completely, thoroughly, unmistakably, unequivocally; utterly, plainly; actually, really, in truth.
Ant. 1 indefinite, unclear. **2** indirect, devious; insincere, dishonest.

downtrodden *adj. He vowed to do all he could to help the downtrodden masses:* oppressed, tyrannized, subservient; harshly ruled; exploited.

doze *v.* **1** *She was dozing in the hammock when I phoned:* nap, snooze; sleep lightly.
—*n.* **2** *There's nothing like a little doze after lunch:* nap, snooze, light sleep, forty winks, catnap.

drab *adj. She works in a drab little office:* dreary, gloomy, dull, dingy, dismal, cheerless, sombre, grey.
Ant. 1 bright, cheery, cheerful, colourful.
◇ *Word origin: Drab* was originally a yellowish-brown colour. The word comes from

French *drap*, cloth, which also gives us our words *drape* and *drapery*.

draft *n.* **1** *She has just finished the first draft of her new play:* sketch, outline, rough sketch; preliminary version. **2** *He sent a draft for £100 to his cousin in Ireland:* postal order, money order.

—*v.* **3** *He drafted the model of the atomic engine:* outline, diagram, sketch.

◇ *Usage note: Draft* is a phonetic spelling of *draught.* In English it is usual to spell it thus in the above senses. See also DRAUGHT.

drag *v.* **1** *Drag the chair over here so that I can stand on it:* pull, haul, lug; draw with effort, pull forcibly. **2** *The bride's long train dragged behind her:* trail; be drawn, be pulled along. **3** *Traffic during the rush-hour just drags along:* crawl, creep, inch; move slowly.

—*n.* **4** *Don't be such a drag — come along with us: Slang* spoil-sport, damper, killjoy, wet blanket.

drain *v.* **1** *Drain the oil out of the crankcase:* draw fluid from, pump off; remove by degrees, empty out. **2** *Most of the river drains into the Bristol Channel:* discharge, flow off gradually, flow out, debouch. **3** *He drained his parents of every penny they had:* sap, empty, deplete; dissipate, use up.

—*n.* **4** *What could have stopped up the main drain?:* tube, pipe, outlet; conduit, sewer, channel. **5** *This car has really been a drain on my income:* sap, drag, strain; depletion, continuous strain.

Ant. 3 fill, supply, replenish.

drama *n.* **1** *He has written a historical drama:* play, theatrical piece, dramatic composition. **2** *She wants to study drama and become an actress:* dramatic art, acting, direction, mise-en-scène, the stage, the theatre. **3** *The film had the drama of a real-life adventure:* excitement, suspenseful events; dramatic quality, intense interest, vividness.

◇ *Word origin: Drama* comes from Greek *drāma*, action, deed. The Greeks often used the word in the sense of "stage-action, play."

dramatic *adj.* **1** *Dramatic talent must be trained like any other gift:* theatrical; of the drama, for the theatre. **2** *There was a dramatic confrontation between the two leaders:* emotional, striking, sensational, climactic, melodramatic, suspenseful.

drastic *adj. He's liable to do something drastic in his present state of mind:* extreme, radical; bizarre, outlandish; dire, dreadful; dangerous, deleterious,

draught *n.* **1** *Close the window and stop that draught:* wind, breeze; current of air. **2** *This team of horses has a draught of 16 tons:* drag, pull, haul. **3** *The knights drained their draughts of wine:* drawing from a cask; drinks, gulp, swallow.

draw *v.* **1** *How many horses will draw the royal coach?:* pull, drag, haul, pull along. **2** *They will draw the winner's name out of the barrel:* extract, pull out, take out, draw out. **3** *Cover the food so that it won't draw the flies:* attract, lure; allure, entice, charm; evoke, elicit, bring forth, make appear. **4** *The real test is to draw a horse in motion:* sketch, etch, limn, picture with pencil or crayon, make a picture of. **5** *She agreed to draw up a proper contract:* draft, write, make, make out. **6** *She drew the wrong conclusion from the meeting:* get, take, make, deduce, infer. **7** *The strands of rubber were drawn to test their strength:* stretch, attenuate, elongate; extend, protract.

—*n.* **8** *Free rides used to be a big draw at this playground:* attraction, lure, enticement. **9** *The competition was a draw, so they awarded two first prizes:* tie, stalemate; deadlock.

Ant. 1 push, shove. **2** put in. **7** contract. **8** repellent.

drawback *n. Lack of funds can be a drawback if you want to invest in a dead cert:* obstacle, hindrance, detriment, impediment, stumbling-block.

drawing *n.* **1** *His drawing of the village green was quite good:* sketch, picture, study, illustration, delineation, depiction. **2** *The drawing for prizes will take place at 8 p.m.:* selection of winners, lottery.

dread *v.* **1** *I dread the thought of coming home late at night:* fear, be afraid of, anticipate with horror, shrink from, cringe at, cower at.

—*n.* **2** *Her dread of staying at home alone made her extremely nervous:* fear, fright, terror, fearfulness, apprehension, anguish, anxiety, trepidation.

—*adj.* **3** *He prepared to face the dread consequences:* frightening, alarming, terrifying, fearful, awful, horrifying.

Ant. 1 be unafraid. **2** confidence, courage, fearlessness, bravery.

dreadful *adj. She had a dreadful accident:* awful, terrible, horrible, tragic; fearful, frightful, alarming, shocking, distressing.

dream *n.* **1** *I had another dream about a far-away place:* sleeping vision; nightmare, incubus. **2** *Her dreams of success kept her from concentrating:* day-dream, fantasy, reverie. **3** *The Ambassador's dream is of a lasting peace:* desire, wish, goal, hope; prospect, expectation. **4** *That new sports car is an absolute dream:* joy, pleasure, delight.

—*v.* **5** *I dreamed that I won a chariot race with Ben-Hur:* have a dream. **6** *Stop dreaming and get on with your work!:* day-dream, be lost in thought, pass time in reverie. **7** *I wouldn't dream of asking her to my home:* consider, think, give serious thought to. **8** *The delegates dreamed of peace:* desire, wish, hope for, have as a goal, look forward to.

◇ *Word origin: Dream* comes from old English *drēam*, which meant joy, jubilation. Thus when we say someone is a real "dream" or has a "dream" job, we are using *dream* in something approaching its original sense.

dreary *adj. She rented a dreary little room on the top*

floor: gloomy, depressing, cheerless, sad, dismal, mournful, forlorn, melancholy.
Ant. cheerful, joyful, happy, bright.
◇ *Word origin: Dreary* comes from Old English *drēorig,* gory, bloody, gruesome.

dregs *n. pl.* **1** *Let the coffee dregs settle to the bottom of the pot:* residue, sediment, grounds, deposit. **2** *Some of his clients really are the dregs of humanity:* the coarse part, lowest and worst part, lower depths; riff-raff, rabble, canaille.

drench *v. If you don't take your raincoat, you may get drenched:* douse, saturate, wet, soak.
◇ *Word origin: Drench* comes from a form of the Old English verb *drincan,* to drink. In Elizabethan times, a *drench* was a medicinal potion for a sick animal. Farmers and vets still use *drench* in its original way to mean a liquid medicine forced down an animal's throat.

dress *n.* **1** *She buys several new dresses every season:* gown, frock, robe. **2** *The dress of the natives is unique:* clothing, clothes, costume, attire, apparel.
—*v.* **3** *Try to dress appropriately for each occasion:* clothe oneself, attire, put on clothes. **4** *The shop dressed its display windows for the Christmas season:* trim, adorn, ornament, decorate, deck, embellish. **5** *She often spends hours just dressing her hair:* arrange, curl, groom; comb out, do up. **6** *He was released after his wounds had been dressed:* treat, bandage, apply a dressing to, cleanse, disinfect.
◇ *Word origin: Dress* comes from French *dresser,* meaning to arrange.

dressmaker *n. The dressmaker hemmed several of my dresses:* seamstress; couturier, (*fem*) couturière, *French* midinette.

dribble *v. Cereal dribbled from the baby's mouth:* drip, fall in drops, run bit by bit. **2** *He dribbled the ball down to the goal and scored:* bounce; kick, manœuvre.
◇ *Word origin: Dribble* comes from our word *drip* and, except for its meaning in sports, means the same as *drip.*

drift *v.* **1** *The boat drifted dangerously near the weir. Some people drift through life without caring very much about anything:* be carried by a current, be borne along; wander, ramble, amble. **2** *The wind drifted the leaves across our yard:* pile up, amass, gather, accumulate.
—*n.* **3** *They reported an easterly drift of winds:* direction, course, current, flow, stream; movement. **4** *Wind left the snow in 10-foot drifts:* heap, pile, mass, accumulation. **5** *The drift of his question seemed to embarrass the speaker:* implication, meaning, gist, sense; object, objective, aim, direction, purpose, intention.

drill *n.* **1** *I need a drill to make a hole for the rod:* machine for drilling, boring tool. **2** *The soldiers practised their gun drill daily:* practice, training, repeated exercises.
—*v.* **3** *You'll have to drill holes in that plank:* punch, pierce, puncture, bore. **4** *The teacher drilled the class in the pronunciation of Latin words:* instruct by repetition, train, exercise, work with.
◇ *Word origin: Drill* comes from Dutch *drillen,* to bore.

drink *v.* **1** *Do you want tea or coffee to drink?:* imbibe, absorb, take in, partake of. **2** *We drank each other's health at the end of the meal:* toast, salute, drink in honour of.
—*n.* **3** *We stopped at the well for a cool drink:* beverage, liquid refreshment. **4** *He took to drink after his wife left him:* alcohol, alcoholic liquor; alcoholism, drunkenness, heavy drinking, *Informal* the bottle. **5** *Give me a drink of your lemonade:* sip, gulp, swallow, taste.
◇ *Word origin: Drink* comes from Old English verb *drincan.*

"We are fighting Germany, Austria and drink, and as far as I can see, the greatest of these three deadly foes is drink."
—*David Lloyd George*

---

drip *v.* **1** *He got out of the shower and dripped water all over the floor:* trickle, dribble; splash, sprinkle, drizzle; let fall in drops.
—*n.* **2** *We heard the drip of a leaky tap:* trickle, dribble, dripping. **3** *Slang That drip can't take no for an answer:* ass, jerk, creep, bore, dummy, wet, *Yiddish* klutz.

drive *v.* **1** *They drove the cows along the country lane:* move, advance; push forward, spur, urge along. **2** *The boss drives her workers hard:* press, urge, prod, goad; incite, impel. **3** *Our troops are driving toward the enemy stronghold:* advance, press forward; rush. **4** *We usually drive into the country on Sundays. She drives a car skilfully:* go by car, ride, go driving, motor; guide, steer; operate. **5** *His pride drove him to complete the job:* motivate; force, compel, coerce. **6** *Just what are you driving at?:* suggest, intend, mean, insinuate.
—*n.* **7** *Why not come with us for a drive in the country?:* ride, outing, excursion; trip by car. **8** *The team did not relent in their drive toward the goal:* push, surge, advance, campaign, onward course. **9** *She has tremendous drive in everything she does:* motivation, ambition, push.

drivel *v.* **1** *The baby sat and drivelled in his high-chair:* drool, slobber, slaver. **2** *When I left she was still drivelling on about her popularity at school:* ramble, babble, talk foolishly, talk nonsense.
—*n.* **3** *We listened to a lot of drivel about the sagging economy:* gibberish, rambling, babbling, nonsense, senseless talk.

driver *n.* **1** *He hired a car and driver for the evening:* chauffeur. **2** *She took a heavy driver for her first shot:* wooden golf-club.

droll *adj. We found the play very droll, but some people disliked it:* humorous, whimsical, oddly amusing, funny, laughable; off-beat.
Ant. ordinary, common; dull, boring.

◇ *Word origin: Droll* comes from French *drôle,* facetious, amusing, which in turn comes from Middle Dutch *drolle,* "little man." The latter is probably related to the trolls, or mischievous dwarfs, of Scandinavian folklore.

drone[1] *n. He was a drone who took advantage of everyone's hard work:* parasite, idler, loafer, lazy person.

◇ *Word origin: Drone* comes from Old English *drān,* male honey-bee. Its root meaning is "droner, buzzer." A related Old English word is *dora,* bumble-bee, surviving in the rare word *dor,* a small insect which makes a loud humming noise as it flies. Related are the Greek words *thrōnāx,* drone, male of the honey-bee, *anthrēnē,* wild bee, and *tenthrēnē,* ground-nesting wasp. Both the English and the Greek words go back to an Indo-European root meaning "buzz, hum, drone."

drone[2] *v.* **1** *The air-conditioner droned on throughout the night:* hum, buzz, whirr, vibrate.

—*n.* **2** *The drone of the machines distracted me:* hum, buzz, whirr, vibration, murmuring.

drool *v. The dog drooled in anticipation of his dinner:* slobber, slaver, dribble, water at the mouth, drivel.

droop *v.* **1** *The branches of the tree drooped after the heavy rain:* sag, hang down, hang listlessly, incline downwards. **2** *Our spirits drooped as we watched our team lose:* weaken, wither, lower, dim; lose vigour, sink, diminish.

Ant. 1 rise. **2** revive, rally, flourish, perk up.

drop *n.* **1** *Drops of water sparkled in the sunlight:* droplet, drip, driblet, globule, tear. **2** *Add a drop of Tabasco and mix well:* dash, dab, pinch, trace, smack, sprinkling, *French* soupçon. **3** *It's almost a 20-foot drop to the ground. The road ends abruptly in a drop to the sea:* descent, fall; declivity, slope, plunge; precipice, abyss. **4** *The drop in temperature was a relief:* decline, fall, lowering, decrease.

—*v.* **5** *Water dropped from the ceiling into the pan on the floor:* drip, dribble, trickle, fall in drops. **6** *The sky-diver dropped towards the earth:* fall, plunge, plummet, dive, descend. **7** *If it's going to start an argument, let's drop the subject:* abandon, leave, forsake, give up; bring to an end, terminate, cease to consider. **8** *Sales always drop in the spring:* fall, lower, lessen, dwindle, decline, slacken, slide, sink. **9** *The boss dropped him from the staff after two weeks:* discharge, dismiss, fire, *Informal* sack. **10** *Don't drop the "g" in "dancing" and "walking":* leave out, omit, fail to include, fail to pronounce.

Ant. 2 much, lots, loads, quantities. **3** rise. **4** rise, increase. **6** rise, soar, shoot up. **7** take up, discuss, consider, talk over. **8** rise, increase, go up. **9** hire, sign on, add. **10** include, pronounce.

drought also **drouth** *n.* **1** *The drought caused famine throughout the country:* aridity; period of dry weather, lack of rain. **2** *At the moment there's a drought of new playwriting talent:* scarcity, lack, shortage, deficiency, want, dearth, need, insufficiency.

◇ *Word origin: Drought* comes from Old English *drugath,* dryness. Both *drought* and *dry,* as well as *drain,* come from a common Germanic root meaning "dry."

drown *v.* **1** *How many drowned when the boat capsized?:* asphyxiate, suffocate; go to Davy Jones's locker, go down for the third time, meet a watery end. **2** *The crops were drowned by the heavy rainfall:* inundate, flood, deluge, immerse, submerge, drench, soak. **3** *She was irked because the audience's coughing drowned her words:* overpower, overwhelm, overcome, engulf, swallow up.

Ant. 2 dry, drain.

drowsy *adj.* **1** *That medicine made me drowsy:* sleepy, dozy, lethargic, languid, listless, slow, lazy, tired. **2** *The drowsy music was relaxing:* hypnotic, soporific, somnolent.

Ant. 1 alert, lively.

drub *v. The man was severely drubbed for stealing the horse:* beat, chastise, whip, bastinado, cane, thrash, flog, hit.

◇ *Word origin: Drub* comes from Arabic *daraba,* to beat as with a stick. The word seems to have passed directly into English during the early 1600s via the unpleasant experiences of English-speaking prisoners on the Barbary Coast.

drudge *n.* **1** *He's merely a drudge in his uncle's office:* menial, lackey, toiler, grubber, underling, subordinate, inferior.

—*v.* **2** *She drudges daily with no hope of bettering herself:* toil, grub, plod, labour, struggle.

drudgery *n. Doing these monthly reports is sheer drudgery:* distasteful work, menial labour, toil, travail, grind.

"The test of a vocation is the love of the drudgery it involves."

—*Logan Pearsall Smith*

---

drum *n.* **1** *Oil is shipped in large drums:* barrel, keg, cask, tub.

—*v.* **2** *The rain drums on the window-pane:* rap, tap, beat, beat rhythmically, tattoo. **3** *The sound of the surf drummed in our ears:* roll, roar, beat, rumble, reverberate, din, beat a tattoo; pulsate. **4** *They will drum him out of the corps for insubordination:* expel, discharge, dismiss, drive out. **5** *His father drummed it into him that he had to succeed:* repeat persistently, reiterate, drive home, force, hammer at, din, din in the ear, harp on.

drunk *adj.* **1** *He was drunk and surly when he arrived at the party:* intoxicated, inebriated, sodden, besotted, under the influence of alcohol; *Slang* soused, smashed, zonked, paralytic, pie-eyed.

—*n.* **2** *You had to be careful not to meet a drunk at*

that time of night: drunkard, boozer, sot, soak, bibber, tosspot, toper, barfly; alcoholic, wino, dipsomaniac.

Ant. 1 sober, abstemious, abstinent, temperate.

dry *adj.* **1** *This dry weather is bad for the crops:* arid, rainless, free from moisture. **2** *I'm so dry, let's stop here for a pint:* thirsty; desiring liquid, suffering from lack of water, dehydrated. **3** *He gives the driest speeches that I've ever listened to:* uninteresting, dull, tedious, monotonous, boring, wearisome. **4** *He has a dry wit that I don't always understand:* dead-pan, low-key; droll, quietly humorous.

—*v.* **5** *Dry the dishes and then put them away. Dry your eyes, everything's all right:* blot, wipe; remove the moisture from, mop up, make dry. **6** *The river dried up during the hot spell:* become dry, shrivel up, desiccate, dehydrate.

Ant. 1 wet, damp, moist, humid, dank. **3** interesting, fascinating, lively, entertaining.

dual *adj. The programme has a dual purpose:* two-fold, double.

Ant. single, singular.

◇ *Word origin: Dual* comes from Latin *duo*, two, which also gives us such words as *duet* and *duplex*.

dubious *adj.* **1** *I was dubious about his ability to help:* doubtful, uncertain, sceptical, unconvinced. **2** *She spends too much time with dubious friends:* questionable, suspicious, suspect, shady; unreliable, untrustworthy, undependable.

Ant. 1 sure, positive, certain, definite. **2** reliable, trustworthy, dependable.

◇ *Word origin: Dubious* comes from the Latin word *dubium*, meaning doubt.

duck *v. I ducked when I saw the rock falling:* swerve, veer, dodge, side-step; crouch, stoop.

◇ *Word origin: Duck*, the aquatic bird that can dive beneath the water for food, comes from Old English *dūce*, duck, literally "diver."

due *adj.* **1** *How much is still due on your car?:* unpaid, owing, owed, outstanding; in arrears. **2** *She is entitled to all the respect due to a distinguished scholar:* suitable, fitting, rightful, deserved, merited, appropriate, becoming, proper; sufficient, adequate. **3** *The plane is due in at 4:15 this afternoon:* scheduled, expected to arrive. **4** *The child gave her parents due cause to be upset:* sufficient, adequate, enough, ample, plenty of.

Ant. 2 inappropriate, unbecoming. **4** insufficient, inadequate, scanty, scant.

dulcet *adj. The dulcet tones of her voice floated down the hall:* pleasing, mellifluous, melodious, sonorous; lyrical, musical, tuneful.

◇ *Word origin: Dulcet* comes from Latin *dulcis*, sweet. The same word is the basis of *dulcimer*, the musical instrument; *dolce*, the musical direction: "sweetly"; and our facetious word for a sweetheart: *Dulcinea* — after *Dulcinea* del Toboso, the beloved of Don Quixote.

dull *adj.* **1** *This knife is so dull that the blade won't cut at all:* blunt; not sharp, not keen. **2** *He was a dull man and you had to explain things very carefully and slowly to him:* slow, dense, thick, obtuse, dim-witted, stupid. **3** *The stock-exchange had a very dull day:* slow, inactive, uneventful; not brisk. **4** *How did such a dull book become a best-seller?:* boring, uninteresting, vapid, unimaginative, prosaic, trite. **5** *The walls were painted a dull blue:* lack-lustre, muted, subdued, quiet. **6** *I thought I heard a dull sound in the kitchen:* muffled, indistinct, subdued, deadened.

Ant. 1 sharp. **2** intelligent, clever, bright. **3** active, lively, spirited. **4** interesting, imaginative, exciting. **5** bright. **6** distinct, clear, well-defined.

◇ *Word origin: Dull* comes from Old English *dol*, stupid.

dullard *n. People took advantage of him because he was a dullard:* dunce, dolt, nitwit, half-wit, imbecile, dumb-bell, dummy.

duly *adj.* **1** *The hostess was duly thanked for her hospitality:* rightfully, properly, suitably, deservedly; correctly, appropriately. **2** *The witness duly arrived and was put on the stand:* punctually; on time, at the proper time.

dumb *adj.* **1** *She had always worked with deaf and dumb children:* mute, aphasiac, incapable of speech. **2** *Everyone else spoke up, but Alan remained dumb:* silent, mute, mum, refusing to speak. **3** *Informal She says she's tired of being called dumb:* stupid, unintelligent; foolish, dopey; dull, dense, dim-witted.

Ant. 1 articulate; capable of speech. **3** smart, intelligent, clever, bright.

"Children are dumb to say how hot the day is,
How hot the scent is of the summer rose."
—*Robert Graves*

---

dumbfound also **dumfound** *v. We were dumbfounded at all the damage done by the storm:* stun, astonish, startle, amaze, flabbergast.

dummy *n. The shop's display windows had dummies in beautiful silk gowns:* mannequin, model, form, figure.

dump *v.* **1** *The delivery boy dumped the groceries in the back yard:* toss, drop heavily, unload carelessly. **2** *The lorry dumped three loads of gravel in the drive:* unload, empty; dispose of, get rid of.

—*n.* **3** *The refuse men won't take this; it'll have to go to the dump:* dumping ground, rubbish heap, refuse pile. **4** *Slang How can anybody live in a dump like this?:* hovel, hole; shack, shanty.

◇ *Word origin: Dump* comes indirectly from Norwegian *dumpa*, to fall suddenly, make a thump. Incidentally, to be "down in the dumps" has nothing to do with this *dump* but is from a completely different word, Dutch *domp*, gloom.

dunce *n. Who was the dunce that left the door open?:* dummy, idiot, fool, moron, imbecile, simpleton, dim-wit.

◇ *Word origin: Dunce* comes from the name of the Sottish philosopher and theologian John *Duns* Scotus (died 1308). His influence lasted for more than 200 years in the schools of Europe. In 1530 he was denounced in the following vigorous terms by the Luther-inspired reformer and Bible translator William Tyndale: "Remember ye not how the old barking curs, *Duns' disciples*, and like draff called Scotists, the children of darkness, raged in every pulpit against Greek, Latin and Hebrew?" The new term of contempt was soon shortened to *dunce*, and within fifty years designated any common fool.

dupe *n.* **1** *He was the dupe of the racketeers:* pawn, sucker, fall guy, cat's-paw, scapegoat.

—*v.* **2** *The agency duped her into signing up for £200 worth of lessons:* trick, fool, mislead, deceive; humbug, bamboozle.

◇ *Word origin: Dupe* comes from the last part of the Middle French phrase *teste d'uppe*, head of a hoopoe — a trophy from an easy victim, since the hoopoe is a bird that was considered easy to catch or kill.

duplicate *n.* **1** *The duplicate looks like a Rembrandt, but it won't fool the experts:* facsimile, reproduction, replica, imitation; copy, carbon copy.

—*v.* **2** *It'll be a long time before he can duplicate that performance:* match, parallel, repeat, make again, copy.

Ant. 1 original.

◇ *Word origin: Duplicate* and *duplicity* come from Latin *duplex*, double, twofold, which also gives us *double.*

duplicity *n. The duplicity apparent in his past actions astounded her:* deceit, deceitfulness, fraud, dishonesty, guile, cunning, falseness.

Ant. straightforwardness, forthrightness, candour.

◇ *Word origin:* See DUPLICATE.

durable *adj. This raincoat is made of very durable material:* enduring, lasting, sound, substantial, sturdy, tough, strong, hard-wearing.

Ant. fragile, frail, weak, flimsy.

duration *n. We will remain closed for the duration of the strike:* continuance, extent, term, period, continuation, length.

duress *n. He testified that he had signed the contract under extreme duress:* force, constraint, threat, coercion; compulsion, pressure.

dusk *n. At dusk the lights of the city are turned on:* twilight, sunset, sundown, nightfall.

dusky *adj.* **1** *I hardly recognised him in the dusky light:* dim, veiled, cloudy, gloomy, murky. **2** *The natives had dusky complexions:* dark, swarthy, dark-hued.

Ant. 1 bright, clear. **2** fair, light.

dutiful *adj. For many years she was a dutiful secretary:* diligent, faithful, loyal; obedient, conscientious.

Ant. uncaring; disrespectful; disobedient; careless, remiss.

duty *n.* **1** *He felt that it was his duty to report the matter to the police:* obligation, responsibility; business, province. **2** *One of her duties is to report any absentees:* function, task, assignment, charge. **3** *How much duty did you have to pay on that camera?:* tax, tariff, customs, levy.

dwarf *n.* **1** *"Snow White and the Seven Dwarfs" is a charming story:* fairy, pixie, sprite, elf, gnome, leprechaun, imp, goblin, troll, pygmy, little man.

—*adj.* **2** *This border was planted with dwarf marigolds:* diminutive, small, tiny, pygmy, miniature, petite, baby.

—*v.* **3** *This present trouble dwarfs the other matter:* overshadow, dim, diminish.

Ant. 2 huge, gigantic.

"The dwarf sees farther than the giant, when he has the giant's shoulders to mount on."
—*Samuel Taylor Coleridge*

---

dwell *v.* **1** *He dwells in the country for most of the year:* reside, live, inhabit, abide. **2** *She dwelt at length on the similarities in the two paintings:* linger over, continue for a time, harp on.

Ant. 1 roam.

◇ *Word origin: Dwell* and *dwelling* come from Old English *dwellan*, to linger, influenced by Old Norse *dvelja*, to sojourn, dwell. Remember that the Vikings (speakers of Old Norse) and the Anglo-Saxons(speakers of Old English) were still restless and unsettled when the two meanings blended. Living in a place seldom meant more than "sojourning" there.

dwelling *n. The ancient Britons lived in primitive dwellings, hardly sheltered from the weather:* house, home, residence, abode, habitation.

◇ *Word origin:* See DWELL.

dwindle *v. Our food supply dwindled as we got more and more lost in the woods:* diminish, decrease, decline, lessen, shrink, become smaller; wane, fade.

Ant. increase, grow; burgeon, flourish.

dye *n.* **1** *Try some red dye on that old sweater:* colour, colouring, tint, shade, coloration, stain.

—*v.* **2** *Maybe you could dye that skirt to match your blouse:* colour, tint, stain.

dynamic *adj. We need a dynamic person to head the board:* active, vigorous, vital, energetic, forceful, driving, powerful.

◇ *Word origin: Dynamic* comes from Greek *dynamis*, power, potency. The same Greek word is the basis for *dynamite, dynamo,* and even *dynasty.*

E

eager *adj.* **1** *The children were eager to go on the picnic:* excited, avid, keen, desirous, yearning, longing, impatient, raring, athirst, thirsting, hungering, agog. **2** *He is an eager student:* earnest, enthusiastic, intent, intense, fervent, fervid, ardent, impassioned, passionate, zealous, spirited; industrious, enterprising, hard-working, persevering, diligent, resolute; ambitious, aggressive.

Ant. 1 indifferent, unconcerned, uninterested; opposed, adverse. **2** indifferent, uninterested, apathetic, impassive, heedless, unmindful, inattentive, irresolute, unambitious, unenterprising, unaggressive; lazy, negligent.

early *adv.* **1** *My dental appointment is early next week:* during the first part, near the beginning. **2** *The speaker arrived early for the meeting:* ahead of time, in advance, beforehand; too soon, prematurely, before the usual time; betimes, in good time.

—*adj.* **3** *The Smiths were among the early arrivals:* first, initial. **4** *The salesman was early for the appointment:* ahead of time, before-hand, premature. **5** *The archaeologists uncovered an early Egyptian city:* ancient, very old, primitive, prehistoric, archaic, primeval, primordial.

Ant. 1-5 late. **1** later, near the end. **2** late, tardily. **3** latter, later, last. **4** tardy. **5** modern.

◇ *Word origin: Early* is made up of the following word elements: an old form of our poetic word *ere* (before) + *-ly.*

earn *v.* **1** *The average skilled worker now earns over £4,000 a year:* make, receive, gain, get, collect, draw, realize, clear, net, pick up, bring home. **2** *You won't get promotion unless you earn it:* deserve, merit, rate, warrant, be entitled to; attain, achieve, secure.

Ant. 1 waste, lose, spend, forfeit, squander. **2** lose, forfeit.

◇ *Word origin: Earn* comes from Old English *earnian,* to reap. The ancestor word in Germanic meant harvest or harvest work, but by the time Old English became a written language (early 700's A.D.) *earnian* had also come to mean "earn or gain" as wages.

earnest *adj.* **1** *Only earnest chess players become champions:* serious, intent, eager, determined, resolute, purposeful, diligent, hard-working, persevering, industrious, assiduous, ambitious, devoted. **2** *The earnest young man had no time for jokes:* sober, serious, thoughtful, grave, solemn, staid, sedate; stable, constant, fixed, steady, firm. **3** *She ignored his earnest request for forgiveness:* sincere, honest, heartfelt, deeply felt, whole-hearted; impassioned, passionate, intense, ardent, zealous, fervent, fervid, urgent, insistent, vehement; spirited, eager, enthusiastic.

Ant. 1, 2 frivolous, capricious, trifling, irresolute, apathetic; sportive, jesting; unsteady, unstable; flippant, light. **3** insincere, indifferent, half-hearted, unimpassioned; unspirited, unenthusiastic.

earnings *n. pl. Income tax is based on one's earnings:* money earned, income, wages, salary, pay, payment, compensation, profits, receipts, proceeds.

Ant. costs, expenditure, outlay.

earth *n. The farmer examined a handful of earth:* soil, ground, land, topsoil, sod, turf, clay, dust.

◇ *Word origin: Earth* comes from Old English *eorthe,* which means both "ground" and "world." (Incidentally, the related word for *earth* in Dutch is *aarde,* and from it we get, via Afrikaans, the name of the *aardvark,* literally "earth-pig.")

earthly *adj.* **1** *Is man too occupied with earthly matters?:* worldly, terrestrial, mundane; secular, non-spiritual, ungodly, temporal, material, materialistic; corporeal, physical, bodily. **2** *Informal This gadget is of no earthly use:* possible, practical; conceivable, imaginable, feasible.

Ant. 1 unearthly, celestial, heavenly, spiritual, divine, godly; non-materialistic.

earthquake *n. The earthquake in San Francisco was one of the worst catastrophes of the century:* quake, tremor, earth tremor, shock, seismic disturbance, upheaval.

ease *n.* **1** *The lotion brought ease to the athlete's aching body:* comfort, relief, assuagement, solace, easement, freedom from pain. **2** *The retired couple lived a life of ease:* comfort, leisure, relaxation, restfulness, rest, quiet, repose, serenity, tranquillity, security, peace of mind, freedom from worry; prosperity, luxury, luxuriousness, abundance, plenty, affluence. **3** *Our team won the game with ease:* easiness, effortlessness, facility, readiness. **4** *The hostess greeted her guests with ease:* naturalness, relaxed manner, unaffectedness, unconstraint, aplomb, poise, composure, confidence.

—*v.* **5** *The aspirin eased his headache. The pilot's calm manner eased the passengers' fears:* relieve, assuage, mitigate, abate, allay, alleviate, mollify, palliate, lessen, lighten, diminish; comfort, soothe, console, quiet, still, calm, pacify, disburden. **6** *The removal men eased the piano through the door:* move carefully, manœuvre gently, handle with care, slip, slide.

Ant. 1 pain, discomfort, misery, irritation. **2** hardship, difficulty, travail, misery, poverty, worry, concern, distortion; turmoil, disturbance, agitation, annoyance, toil, hard work, sweat. **3** difficulty, effort, exertion, great pains; clumsiness, awkwardness. **4** stiffness, formality, affectedness, tension, constraint; embarrassment, self-consciousness, discomposure, awkwardness. **5** worsen, irritate, aggravate, discomfort; make uneasy, make nervous, make tense.

◇ *Word origin: Ease* comes from Latin *adjacens*, close at hand, within easy reach. This same Latin word gives us *adjacent*.

easily *adv.* **1** *A good carpenter can mend the chair easily:* with ease, without difficulty, without trouble; handily, without a hitch; effortlessly, lightly, freely, smoothly. **2** *He is easily the school's best student:* beyond question, certainly, surely, far and away, by far, clearly, plainly, undoubtedly, undeniably, beyond doubt, beyond a shadow of doubt.

Ant. 1 with difficulty; awkwardly, clumsily. **2** by a hair, by the skin of one's teeth; questionably, doubtfully.

East, the *n. More Britons visit America than the East:* the Orient, the Far East, Asia; the Near East; the eastern hemisphere.

Ant. the West, western hemisphere, the Occident.

easy *adj.* **1** *It was an easy job:* not difficult, not hard, easily done, effortless, simple, not burdensome, light, painless. **2** *With no worries and plenty of servants, she's always led an easy life:* comfortable, untroubled, unworried, carefree; leisurely, relaxed, restful, serene, tranquil, peaceful, calm, composed, secure; wealthy, luxurious, well-to-do, affluent; *Slang* cushy. **3** *His easy manner made him many friends:* relaxed, unaffected, natural, easy-going, informal, friendly, outgoing, unconstrained, pleasant, gracious, open, candid, frank, unforced. **4** *The professor has an easy manner:* not strict, lenient, permissive, not harsh, not oppressive, indulgent, accommodating, yielding, tractable, compliant, soft, gentle, benign, mild, docile; unsuspicious, gullible, too trusting, naïve.

—*adv.* **5** *Mother won't rest easy until all the children are home:* easily, comfortably, without worry, without tension, serenely, peacefully, calmly, leisurely.

Ant. 1 difficult, hard, arduous, burdensome, exhausting. **2** hard, difficult, uncomfortable, impoverished, poor; troubled, worried, anxious, insecure. **3** stiff, rigid, formal, unnatural, affected, forced, tense, anxious; *Slang* uptight; introverted, constrained, self-conscious, embarrassed, secretive, mysterious. **4** hard, strict, harsh, rigid, difficult, demanding, exacting, authoritarian, dictatorial, oppressive, unyielding; suspicious, guarded.

easy-going *adj. Easy-going people seldom get ulcers:* calm, relaxed, carefree, happy-go-lucky, nonchalant, casual, offhand, unexcitable, insouciant, unruffled; even-tempered, mild-tempered, patient, unconcerned, unworried.

Ant. tense, worrying, compulsive, rigid, excitable, volatile, impatient, explosive: *Slang* uptight.

eat *v.* **1** *Did you eat anything at the party? The boys ate a hearty lunch:* feed, take nourishment, take sustenance, take a meal, break bread; (*variously*) breakfast, lunch, dine, sup; feast, gormandize; consume, take, ingest, dispatch, bolt, gulp, wolf down, gobble, nibble. **2** *The harsh chemical had eaten into the metal:* corrode, waste away, dissolve, rust, wear away.

Ant. 1 fast, abstain; starve, go hungry, be famished.

"Part of the secret of success in life is to eat what you like and let the food fight it out inside." —*Mark Twain*

---

ebb *v.* **1** *A crab was left stranded on the beach when the tide ebbed:* recede, go out, flow away, flow back, fall away, move back, go down, retreat, withdraw. **2** *The old man's strength began to ebb:* decline, fade away, abate, subside, dwindle, shrink, slacken, lessen, decrease, weaken, deteriorate, waste away, degenerate.

Ant. 1 flood, rise, swell, ascend, flow. **2** increase, grow, mount, build, climb, advance, progress, improve, wax, flourish.

eccentric *adj.* **1** *Comets move in eccentric orbits:* off-centre, not circular, parabolic, elliptical. **2** *Wearing evening dresses all day is just part of her eccentric behaviour:* peculiar, odd, strange, queer, weird, bizarre, unusual, extraordinary, unique, singular, uncommon, outlandish, freakish; quaint, whimsical, capricious, quixotic, rash; curious, unconventional, unorthodox, erratic, irregular; *Slang* funny, nutty, freaky, sick; abnormal, aberrant, unnatural; psychotic, insane.

—*n.* **3** *The old eccentric left a fortune to her pet cat:* character, peculiar person, odd person, unconventional person, crackpot; *Slang* curio, odd fish, nut, crank, weirdo, weirdie.

Ant. 1 concentric; circular, round, centred. **2** common, ordinary, usual, conventional, customary, normal, natural, typical, regular. **3** normal person, conformist; *Slang* square.

◇ *Word origin: Eccentric* comes from Greek *ek-* (out) + *kentron*, centre, and means literally "out of centre," or off-centre.

ecclesiastic *n. The dean of the divinity school has to be an ecclesiastic:* clergyman, cleric, churchman, minister, priest, rabbi, preacher, pastor, parson, chaplain, curate, prelate, rector, vicar, deacon.

ecclesiastical *adj. The bishop is responsible for all ecclesiastical matters in this diocese:* clerical, parochial, pastoral, episcopal.

Ant. secular, lay.

◇ *Word origin: Ecclesiastical* comes from *ekklēsiastēs*, Greek rendering of Hebrew *qōheleth*, preacher. (Hence the Old Testament book of *Ecclesiastes.*) The word *ek-*

klēsiastēs originally meant a member of the political assembly, or *ekklēsia*, of a Greek city-state. Both words are based on the verb *ekkalein*, to summon and hold a meeting (from *ek-* + *kalein*, call).

echelon *n. Major decisions are made in the higher echelons of the company:* level, rank, authority, position, office; file, tier, line, rung.
◇ *Word origin: Echelon* comes from French *échelle*, meaning ladder. *Echelle* comes from Latin *scala*, ladder, from which we also get *scale* (both the musical *scale* and *scale* in the sense of scaling a wall) and *escalator.*

echo *n.* **1** *The cavern is famous for producing echoes:* reflection of sound, reverberation.
—*v.* **2** *The cowbells echoed across the valley:* resound, reverberate, ring. **3** *His speech echoed my own feelings:* match, follow, parallel, reflect, mirror, duplicate, reproduce, take after, simulate, imitate, copy, repeat; ape, parrot.
Ant. 3 contradict, be at odds with, differ from, oppose, deny.
◇ *Usage note:* The plural of *echo* is *echoES*, the past tense of the verb is *echoED.*
◇ *Word origin: Echo* comes from Greek *ēkhō*, meaning sound or noise.

eclipse *n.* **1** *A solar eclipse occurs when the moon passes between the sun and the earth:* obscuring, darkening, veiling, cloaking, masking, covering, shadowing. **2** *The scandal caused an eclipse of the minister's reputation:* diminishing, clouding, loss; blotting out, obliteration, overshadowing, annihilation, erasing, eradicating, wiping out.
—*v.* **3** *Tomorrow the moon will partially eclipse the sun:* cast a shadow upon, obscure, darken, cover, mask, cloak, conceal, hide. **4** *The author's latest book eclipses all his previous ones:* overshadow, outshine, dim, surpass, outdo, exceed, excel, transcend, tower above, outrival; wipe out, obliterate, blot out.
Ant. 2 brightening, increase, enhancement. **3** illuminate, unveil, uncover, expose, display, show.
◇ *Word origin: Eclipse* comes from Greek *ekleipsis: ek-* (out) + *leipein* (to leave).

economic *adj.* **1** *Good transport is needed for the economic growth of a country:* material, monetary, productive, distributive. **2** *We bought a small car for economic reasons:* monetary, pecuniary, financial, fiscal, budgetary. **3** See ECONOMICAL.

economical *adj. Economical shoppers wait for special sales:* thrifty, economizing, economic, saving, frugal, prudent, careful, not wasteful; tight-fisted, close-fisted, parsimonious, penurious, niggardly, chary, sparing, scrimping, spartan; low-priced, cheap, reasonable, modest.
Ant. extravagant, spendthrift, uneconomical, wasteful, imprudent; generous, liberal, lavish; expensive, high-priced, exorbitant.
◇ *Usage note:* Although *economic* and *economical* both mean thrifty, money-saving, and may be used interchangeably, many people use only *economical* in this sense and restrict *economic* to senses having to do with the science of economics: *an economical housekeeper* but *the nation's economic policy.*

economize *v. Their reduced income forced them to economize:* cut expenses, cut costs, be economical, practise economy, avoid waste, avoid extravagance, be prudent, be frugal, be parsimonious, tighten one's belt, save, conserve, skimp, scrimp, stint, pinch, use sparingly, husband, retrench.
Ant. be extravagant, squander, waste, dissipate, misuse.

economy *n.* **1** *To run a large household one has to practise economy:* thrifty management, thriftiness, thrift, frugality, prudence, providence. **2** *Inflation dealt a savage blow to the nation's economy:* material well-being, financial status, monetary resources, productive power, financial management, resources management.
Ant. 1 extravagance, lavishness, wastefulness, imprudence, improvidence.
◇ *Word origin: Economy* comes from Greek *oikos* (house) + *nemein* (to manage). Actually *oikonomia* (the Greek word corresponding to our word *economy*) had much the same range of meanings as our word — it meant thrift and household management, as well as spareness, as in architecture or a work of art. It also meant the public revenue of a city-state.

ecstatic *adj. The couple were ecstatic at the birth of their son:* full of ecstasy, joyful, joyous, overjoyed, happy, glad, delighted, rapturous, enraptured, rapt, transported, entranced, blissful, elated, exalted, ebullient, enthusiastic, excited, beside oneself, delirious.
Ant. unhappy, wretched, miserable, sorrowful, grief-stricken, down-hearted, joyless, saddened, displeased; unexcited, unenthusiastic, indifferent, blasé.
◇ *Word origin: Ecstatic* comes from Greek *ekstasis*, displacement, from *ek-* (dis-) + *stasis*, placing. The New Testament authors were the first to use the word to mean "entrancement, trance," and the 3rd-century A.D. neo-Platonist Plotinus was the first to use the word in its present-day sense.

eddy *n. The river is dangerous for swimmers because of its eddies:* current, whirling current, whirlpool, maelstrom, vortex.
Ant. flow, drift, course, stream.

edge *n.* **1** *The river runs along the edge of the property:* boundary line, line, bound, border, periphery, margin, rim, fringe, side, extremity, limit; dividing line, brink, verge, threshold.
—*v.* **2** *The blouses were edged with ribbon:* border, trim, rim, bind, fringe, hem. **3** *Towards the end of the speech some members of the audience*

began to edge towards the door: steal, sneak, move sideways, sidle, inch, advance slowly, creep, move with caution, move slyly, slink.
Ant. 1 centre, interior, middle. **3** rush, run, sprint, bound, leap, speed, hasten.

edible *adj. Are those mushrooms edible?:* eatable, fit to be eaten, suitable for eating, comestible, consumable; non-poisonous, safe for eating; digestible.
Ant. inedible, uneatable; poisonous, dangerous, indigestible.
◇ *Usage note: Edible* has largely replaced *eatable* in the sense of being generally fit to eat, safe or nourishing to eat, or an acceptable part of the diet: *Some mushrooms are edible, toadstools are inedible. Eggs are edible, wood is inedible.*

edict *n. The dictator's edict forbids speaking against the regime:* decree, proclamation, pronouncement, pronunciamento, edict, ukase, dictate, command, order, ordinance, mandate, dictum, injunction, manifesto, public notice; law, statute, regulation, prescript, enactment, ruling; bull.

edification *n. Some religious instruction is necessary for the edification of the young:* elevation, enlightenment, uplifting, moral improvement, advancement, education, educational benefit, indoctrination, instruction, guidance, direction; information.
◇ *Word origin:* See EDIFICE.

edifice *n. A 50-storey edifice will be built on this site:* building, structure, construction.
◇ *Word origin: Edifice* and *edification* come from the Latin elements *aedis* (dwelling) + *facere* (to make). Thus *edifice* literally means a building that has been made, while *edification* figuratively means an intellectual or moral building or benefit.

"It is only the 'educated' man, especially the literary man, who knows how to be a bigot."
—*George Orwell*

---

educate *v. The primary schools educate the greatest number of children:* teach, instruct, train, school, develop, tutor, coach; enlighten, inform, edify, civilize.

education *n.* **1** *The job demands someone with a university education:* schooling, training, instruction, teaching, learning, academic learning, study; information, knowledge, enlightenment, edification, cultivation, culture, mental development, scholarship, erudition. **2** *You need to take six more papers in education to earn your teacher's certificate:* art of teaching, teaching, pedagogics, pedagogy, tutelage, instructing.

eerie *adj. Seeing the old graveyard gave us an eerie feeling:* inspiring fear, fearful, frightening, ominous, ghostly, spooky, creepy, weird, mysterious, odd, queer, uncanny, strange, uneasy, apprehensive.
Ant. soothing, comforting, consoling, relaxing; calm, tranquil, easy.
◇ *Word origin:* Something that is *eerie* makes us afraid or timid. *Eerie* comes from the Old English word for timid, *earg.*

efface *v. Time had effaced the ancient inscription:* wipe out, obliterate, eradicate, erase, delete, blot out, rub out, expunge, cancel, extirpate; destroy, annihilate, raze.
Ant. restore, replace, reinstate, renew, revive; keep, retain.
◇ *Word origin:* When we *efface* something, we literally obliterate its face or appearance. The word comes from the Latin prefix *ex-* (out) + *facies* (face).

effect *n.* **1** *Farmers felt the effect of the drought for years:* result, consequence, upshot, outcome, development, aftermath, after-effect, outgrowth, sequel. **2** *The plea for clemency had no effect on the judge:* influence, power, force, effectiveness, efficacy, impact, impression, weight, validity. **3** *The law came into effect yesterday:* operation, action, execution, force, enforcement; function, accomplishment. **4** *In effect, her insult meant the end of our friendship:* fact, actuality, reality, truth; significance, meaning, gist, general idea, purport, import, intent, intention; implication, essence, drift, tenor. **5** (*Usually plural*) *Before moving, the family sold as many of their effects as possible:* personal property, possessions, things, goods, movables, furniture, trappings; personal estate, commodities, holdings, assets, chattels.
—*v.* **6** *The new hair-do effected a startling change in her appearance:* produce, accomplish, bring about, make, cause, achieve, carry out, execute, perform, create, realize, attain.
Ant. 1 cause, occasion, inducement, incitement, foundation, source; beginning, origin. **6** prevent, hinder, deter, block, obviate, cancel out, frustrate.
◇ *Usage note:* See AFFECT.

effective *adj.* **1** *The business needs a more effective sales programme:* effectual, efficacious, efficient, productive, useful, serviceable, capable, competent, forceful, forcible, dynamic, powerful, strong, influential, potent. **2** *The new interest rate becomes effective next month:* operative, in operation, active, activated, in effect, a reality; actual, real; current. **3** *The book has a very effective closing chapter:* impressive, cogent, telling, convincing, compelling, persuasive; striking, forceful, powerful, strong, incisive, moving, eloquent.
Ant. 1-3 ineffective. **1** ineffectual, inefficient, unproductive, bootless, inadequate, incompetent, useless, insufficient, impractical; forceless, powerless, impotent, weak. **2** inoperative, inactive. **3** weak, wishy-washy, tame, unimpressive, unconvincing; disappointing, unsatisfactory.
◇ *Usage note: Effective* and *effectual* both refer

to the ability to achieve a desired result. *Effective* is the more general term and may be used to apply to both persons and things, while *effectual* often refers to things, to past actions, or to negative judgements: *John has become an effective leader. His reorganization plan proved less than effectual.*

effeminate *adj. To everyone's surprise, the burly man had an effeminate voice:* womanish, unmanly, sissy.

Ant. manly, manlike, masculine, virile.

effervescence *n.* **1** *The bottle of fizz had lost its effervescence:* bubbliness, bubbling, bubbling up, fizz, fizzle, fizziness, froth, foaming. **2** *The old lady's effervescence amused us:* liveliness, ebullience, buoyancy, enthusiasm, life, vitality, vigour, vivacity, animation, spirit, zip, dash, gaiety.

Ant. **1** flatness. **2** despondency, tiredness, lethargy, seriousness, gravity, sedateness.

◇ *Spelling tip:* Like *effervescent,* the word bubbles over with two *f*'s at the beginning: *eFFervescence.*

effervescent *adj.* **1** *Champagne and sparkling Burgundy are effervescent wines:* bubbling, bubbly, fizzy, fizzing, sparkling, foaming. **2** *The effervescent youngsters brought life to the staid resort:* lively, vivacious, ebullient, animated, exuberant, sparkling, bubbling, gay, merry, irrepressible.

Ant. **1** flat. **2** subdued, sedate, sober, grave, staid.

effete *adj. Over the years the nation's aristocracy had grown effete:* decadent, morally corrupt, depraved, degenerate; unproductive, unprolific, barren, sterile, enervated, worn-out, wasted, spent, exhausted.

Ant. healthy, wholesome, vital, productive, vigorous.

◇ *Word origin: Effete* originally meant incapable of further production, worn-out. It comes from Latin *ex-* (out) + *fetus* (bearing), which also gives us *foetus.*

efficient *adj. A lawyer needs an efficient secretary:* effective, productive, proficient, businesslike, workmanlike, capable, competent, apt; work-saving, time-saving, unwasteful, effectual.

Ant. inefficient, ineffectual, ineffective, unproductive, unworkmanlike, unbusinesslike; useless, wasteful.

effigy *n. The mob burned an effigy of the dictator:* representation, image, likeness; (*variously*) statue, dummy, doll, puppet, mannequin, manikin, marionette, straw man, scarecrow.

◇ *Word origin:* An *effigy* is a likeness or image fashioned out of clay, wood, straw, etc., to look like someone. The word comes from Latin *ex-* (out) + *fingere* (to fashion), which also gives us *feign.*

effort *n.* **1** *The chair can be lifted with little effort:* exertion, power, force, energy, labour, work, industry, strain, struggle, toil, stress, pains, travail, trouble, elbow-grease. **2** *The factory made an effort to provide better working conditions:* endeavour, attempt, try.

effortless *adj. A good player can make tennis look effortless:* easy, uncomplicated, simple, not difficult, painless.

Ant. hard, difficult, complicated, tough.

effrontery *n. What effrontery to barge in uninvited like that!:* shamelessness, brazenness, brashness, impertinence, insolence, impudence, presumption, arrogance, audacity, temerity, cheek, nerve, gall, brass, *Yiddish* chutzpah.

Ant. modesty, reserve, shyness, timidity, bashfulness; respect, diffidence.

◇ *Word origin: Effrontery* comes from Latin *ex-* (out) + *frons* (forehead, face), "barefaced."

effusive *adj. The effusive praise embarrassed the chef:* lavish, unrestrained, profuse, gushy, gushing, unreserved, extravagant, expansive, copious, free-flowing; ebullient, exuberant.

Ant. restrained, reserved, sparing, sparse.

egoism *n. Extreme egoism prevented him from thinking of anyone but himself:* self-centredness, self-importance, self-absorption, self-love, narcissism, overweening pride, vanity.

Ant. humility, modesty; self-distrust, self-doubt, altruism.

◇ *Word origin: Egoism* comes from the Latin word *ego,* which means "I".

egoist *n. The egoist believes that everyone is motivated by self-interest:* self-centred person, narcissist; selfish person.

egotism *n. Her letters are filled with overwhelming egotism:* self-admiration, self-praise, bragging, boastfulness, braggadocio, immodesty, conceit, vanity, vainglory, smugness, arrogance.

Ant. modesty, humility, bashfulness, self-criticism, self-abnegation.

"Conscience makes egotists of us all."
—*Oscar Wilde*

---

egotist *n. I couldn't bear listening to that egotist talk about himself a minute longer!:* self-admirer, boaster, braggart, swaggerer, Gascon, braggadocio; *Slang* blow-hard.

egregious *adj. Introducing the speaker by the wrong name was an egregious blunder:* conspicuously bad, gross, flagrant, glaring, outrageous, shocking, notorious, monstrous, heinous, insufferable, intolerable, grievous.

Ant. tolerable, moderate, minor, unnoticeable.

egress *n.* **1** *The thieves made their egress through a rear door:* exit, departure, withdrawal, escape; discharge, issue, outflow, seepage, leakage. **2** *Each flat must have egress to a fire escape:* way out, passage out, outlet, exit; aperture, vent.

Ant. **1, 2** entrance.

eject *v.* **1** *The volcano ejected lava and ashes:*

discharge, emit, spew, spout, disgorge, exude, throw out, cast out. **2** *The police ejected the demonstrators from the hall:* oust, evict, expel, remove, force out, turn out, kick out, drive out; exile, banish, deport, dispossess.
Ant. 1 take in, inject; retain, withhold, keep, house, store. **2** move in, bring in, receive, admit, introduce.

elaborate *adj.* **1** *The elaborate lighting system took months to install:* complex, involved, complicated, intricate; painstaking, laboured. **2** *The actresses were dressed in elaborate costumes:* fancy, elegant, ornate; ostentatious, showy, flashy, gaudy, garish.
—*v.* **3** *The reporter asked the general to elaborate on his statement:* expand, add details, particularize, specify, clarify, embellish.
Ant. 1, 2 simple, plain. **3** digest, condense, abbreviate, summarize, sum up.

elapse *v. Twenty years have elapsed since our first meeting:* pass, pass by, lapse, go by, slip by, slip away, glide by, roll by, slide by.

elastic *adj.* **1** *The slacks have an elastic waistband:* stretchable, flexible, resilient, supple, rubbery, recoiling, springy, rebounding. **2** *People with elastic dispositions recover quickly from disappointment:* flexible, supple, pliant, pliable, tolerant, complaisant, yielding, accommodating, adaptable, responsive; recuperative, readily recovering.
Ant. 1 stiff, inflexible, rigid. **2** inflexible, intolerant, unyielding, unaccommodating.

elated *adj. The ski-jumper was elated at setting a new record:* overjoyed, jubilant, exalted, exhilarated, in high spirits, ecstatic, excited, animated; happy, delightful, joyful, joyous, pleased, glad, gleeful, rejoicing; proud, blissful, flushed with success.
Ant. dejected, depressed, dashed, dispirited, discouraged, blue, sad, unhappy; humbled, abashed, chagrined.

elder *adj.* **1** *The elder son is at school, the younger in kindergarten:* older, firstborn, senior.
—*n.* **2** *Young people should have respect for their elders:* senior, older adult. **3** *All elders of the church are members of the council:* patriarch, presbyter, head; church dignitary, church official.
Ant. 1, 2 younger, junior. **3** neophyte; layman.

elderly *adj. The elderly man lived on a small pension:* old, aged, venerable; past one's prime.
Ant. young, youthful.
◇ *Usage note:* See OLD.

elect *v.* **1** *I declare that the President has been elected by unfair means!:* select by vote, vote into office, choose by ballot; choose, pick, select. **2** *Gauguin elected painting as a career when he was in his thirties:* choose, select, decide on, opt for, adopt, resolve upon, fix upon, settle on, single out, pick out, espouse, embrace, take up, determine in favour of.
Ant. 1 defeat, vote down, vote out. **2** reject, repudiate, decline, abjure, renounce, dismiss, turn one's back on.

election *n.* **1** *The municipal elections are in November:* voting, choosing by vote, vote, balloting, poll. **2** *The election of a new auditor is up to the board of directors:* choice, selection, decision, option, alternative, determination, resolution, resolve.

elective *adj. Many people feel that directorships should never be elective positions:* chosen by election, filled by election, passed by vote.
Ant. appointed, named; inherited.

electric, electrical *adj.* **1** *I got an electric shock from the metal railing:* of electricity, for electricity, operated by electricity, power-driven. **2** *The band gave an electric rendering of the national anthem:* thrilling, stirring, exciting, electrifying, spirited, stimulating, exalting, rousing, inspiring, soul-stirring, full of fire, galvanizing.
Ant. 2 dull, flat, unexciting, spiritless, unmoving, uninspiring, tedious, boring, colourless, insipid, ordinary, prosaic.
◇ *Usage note:* It has become our custom to refer to *electric power* or an *electric stove* but to refer to *electrical energy*. In general, *electric* is used to mean "using electricity" and *electrical* to mean "concerning the use of electricity," as in *electrical engineering*. This is a rather fine distinction, so it's best to learn whichever of the two applies in a specific context.
◇ *Word origin: Electric* comes from Greek *ēlektron*, amber, because rubbing a piece of amber was the first known way of producing a spark, shock, or magnet, later associated with electricity. The same Greek word also gives us *electron* and *electrode*.

electrify *v.* **1** *A neon sign must be electrified:* supply with electricity, equip for the use of electricity; pass an electric current through, charge with electricity. **2** *The trapeze artist's act electrified the audience:* thrill, stir, excite, rouse, stimulate, galvanize, quicken, animate, fire; amaze, astound, astonish, startle, stun, daze, dazzle, surprise, take one's breath away.

eleemosynary *adj. The orphanage is an eleemosynary institution:* charitable, depending on donations; altruistic, benevolent, philanthropic, non-profit-making.
Ant. profit-making, business.
◇ *Word origin:* Both *eleemosynary* and *alms* come from Greek *eleēmosynē*, alms. The latter is an Old English simplification of the Church Latin form.

elegance *n. The mansion was furnished with supreme elegance:* luxuriousness, exquisiteness, sumptuousness, grandeur, richness; class; taste, refinement, delicacy, grace, gracefulness; purity, balance, symmetry.
Ant. plainness; bad taste, crudeness.

elegant *adj.* **1** *The table was covered with an elegant lace cloth:* exquisite, fine, grand, sumptuous, luxurious, ornate, artistic; tasteful, delicate, refined, graceful, classic, symmetrical, well-proportioned; beautiful, handsome, stylish, lovely, attractive. **2** *His mother is an elegant lady in her seventies:* refined, genteel, well-bred, polished, cultivated, dignified, gracious, charming, polite, courtly; *Slang* classy; fashionable, stylish, debonair, urbane, dapper.

Ant. 1 plain, inelegant; tasteless, tawdry, crude, coarse, rough; ugly, hideous, misshapen; clumsy. **2** unrefined, coarse, lowbred, boorish, undignified, rude, ungraceful; unfashionable.

elegy *n. The poet laureate composed an elegy upon the death of the king:* poem of lamentation, lament for the dead, melancholy poem, sad poem; requiem, funeral song, song of lamentation, melancholy piece of music.

Ant. paean, jubilee, hallelujah, anthem.

◇ *Word origin: Elegy* goes back to Greek *elegeiā*, song of lament.

element *n.* **1** *Hydrogen is the lightest of all elements:* basic chemical substance, uncompounded substance, simple body; *Ancient Classical* earth, air, fire, water. **2** *Cells are the elements of the human body:* basic part, basic unit, constituent, component part, component, ingredient, building block, member, subdivision. **3** usually **elements.** *The elements of physics are difficult to grasp:* principles, rudiments, foundations, basic ideas, origins, essence, features, factors; *Informal* basics. **4** *The artist was out of his element amongst the bankers and stockbrokers:* natural habitat, native state, natural medium, environment; milieu.

Ant. 1 compound. **2** whole, entity, total, sum, system. **3** advanced concept; frills, supplement.

◇ *Word origin: Element* comes from Latin *elementum*, principle, rudiment.

elementary *adj. The student took a course in elementary maths:* basic, basal, fundamental, rudimentary, elemental; simple, plain, uncomplicated, primitive, primary, original, first, undeveloped, crude.

Ant. advanced, higher, complex, complicated.

elevate *v.* **1** *A special device elevated the stage for the finale:* raise, upraise, raise aloft, lift up, uplift, move up, hoist, heave, boost, place high, heighten. **2** *The vice-president was elevated to the rank of president of the company:* raise, move up, promote, advance; improve, better, refine, dignify, ennoble, enhance. **3** *The good news elevated everyone's spirits:* elate, boost, lift, raise, uplift, cheer, exhilarate, animate, excite, inspire, perk up.

Ant. 1–3 lower. **1** lower, drop. **2** demote, degrade; *Slang* kick downstairs, bust; humble, demean. **3** depress, sadden, deject; deaden, numb.

elevation *n.* **1** *Mexico City stands at an elevation of 7,500 feet:* height, altitude, height above sea-level; prominence, lift. **2** *We picnicked on an elevation overlooking the entire park:* elevated place, rising ground, acclivity, ascent, rise, hill, mountain. **3** *The sergeant's elevation to lieutenant was richly deserved:* rise, promotion, advancement, boost; improvement, bettering, refinement, cultivation.

Ant. 1 depth. **2** low ground, valley, depression, dip. **3** demotion.

elf *n. Elves inhabited the enchanted forest:* pixie, puck, brownie, fairy, sprite, leprechaun, troll, gnome; gremlin, goblin, hobgoblin.

elicit *v. The magistrate's remark elicited a flood of letters:* bring forth, draw forth, draw out, call forth, evoke, extract, exact, extort, derive, fetch, cause, educe, bring to light.

Ant. repress, discourage.

◇ *Usage note:* See ILLICIT.

◇ *Word origin: Elicit* comes from Latin *e-* (out) + *lacere* (to deceive), hence to draw out by deceit or magic.

eligible *adj. You have to meet the qualifying standard to be eligible to run in the Olympic Games:* qualified, able to be chosen, acceptable, authorized, appropriate, proper, suitable, applicable; desirable, worthwhile.

Ant. ineligible, unacceptable, inappropriate, unsuitable.

◇ *Spelling tip: Eligible* has an *e* at each end and two *i's* in the middle: *ElIgIblE.*

eliminate *v. Can the government eliminate poverty?* get rid of, do away with, banish, abolish, eradicate, erase, exterminate, cut out, annihilate, weed out, stamp out; remove, throw out, exclude, reject, drop, leave out, omit; eject, expel, cast out, exile, dismiss, oust.

Ant. obtain, get, invite, establish; add, include, inject, accept, admit, incorporate.

◇ *Word origin: Eliminate* comes from the Latin prefix *e-* (out) + *limen* (threshold), hence to expel.

élite *n. Rhodes scholarships are given only to the élite among students:* best, choice, best group, choice class, select body, the pick, top, cream, flower; crème-de-la-crème, upper class, wealthy, society, high society, aristocracy, *French* haute monde; notables, celebrities, personages; *Slang* bigwigs, big shots.

Ant. worst, dregs, scum; lower class, working class; rabble, hoi polloi, riff-raff.

◇ *Pronunciation tip:* The first syllable of *élite* should be pronounced as *ay-*, the second syllable as *-leet*; this second syllable is always stressed. Thus *ay-LEET* is the correct pronunciation.

elocution *n.* **1** *The actor is famous for his clear elocution:* manner of speaking, pronunciation, intonation, diction. **2** *If you want to be a politician, you should take a course in elocution:* public speaking, oratory, speech, diction, articulation, enunciation, pronunciation.

elongate *v. The metal bar could be elongated under intense heat:* lengthen, extend, make longer, draw out, stretch out, prolong, protract.

Ant. shorten, curtail, contract, abbreviate, abridge.

eloquent *adj. The counsel for the defence made an eloquent plea for his client's acquittal:* persuasive, forceful, striking, stirring, moving, spirited, emphatic, passionate, impassioned, vivid.

Ant. routine, ordinary, commonplace, pedestrian, unimpressive, weak, dull, prosaic.

elucidate *v. The footnotes elucidated the text:* clarify, explain, explicate, make plain, clear up, throw light upon, illuminate, illustrate, describe, expound, detail, interpret, spell out, delineate, comment upon.

Ant. confuse, obscure, becloud, muddle.

elude *v. The robber eluded his pursuers:* evade, avoid, escape, escape the notice of, dodge, shun, keep clear of, get away from.

Ant. confront, meet, encounter; challenge.

> **Exploring the Word**: The ancient Romans liked to play and to tease people as much as we do. Their word *ludere*, to play, make sport of, gives us *allude*, literally to play at something, hence to refer sportively to something already said; *elude*, literally to play away from another — the word (*eludere*) was a gladiator's technical term meaning to elude or parry an enemy's blow; *illusion* (from *illudere*, to mock) comes from Latin *illusio*, mocking, jeering, or irony (the word acquired its modern sense of "illusion" only in Church Latin); and finally *ludicrous*, from Latin *ludicrus*, sportive, joking, done in jest. The neuter form of the word, *ludicrum*, meant "stage play" or "public games" to the Romans. (Their term for the Olympic Games was *Olympiorum ludicrum.*) Our word *ludicrous*, as used in Shakespeare's day, still evoked these old Roman meanings; the word acquired its present sense of "ridiculous" or "absurd" around the 1870's.

elusive *adj.* **1** *Antelope are among the most elusive animals to hunt:* hard to catch, evasive; tricky, slippery, shifty, wily, crafty, foxy. **2** *Metaphysics is full of elusive concepts:* hard to grasp, difficult to comprehend; baffling, puzzling, hard to express.

emaciated *adj. The survivors were emaciated after weeks without food:* undernourished, starving, underfed, sickly, thin, wasted, gaunt, haggard, skinny, lean, scrawny, lank, skeletal, cadaverous.

Ant. robust, hardy, stout, fat, plump, chubby, beefy.

◇ *Word origin: Emaciated* comes from Latin *e-* (out) + *macer* (lean), hence "thinned out" or reduced to a state of leanness.

emanate *v. The brook emanates from an underground spring. The command emanated from headquarters:* flow, issue, come forth, send forth, spring, well, exude, give off; originate, stem, proceed, rise.

Ant. end, terminate, culminate.

◇ *Word origin: Emanate* comes from Latin *e-* (out) + *manare* (to flow).

emancipate *v. Have you always wanted women to be emancipated?:* free, set free, liberate, set at liberty, manumit; unfetter, unchain, unshackle.

Ant. enslave, subjugate; chain, manacle, shackle.

emasculate *v.* **1** *The RSPCA has recommended emasculating tom-cats to reduce the cat population:* castrate, geld. **2** *The law against speeding is emasculated by fining offenders only trivial amounts:* weaken, make less forceful, undermine, devitalize, soften, render impotent.

Ant. 2 strengthen, reinforce, vitalize.

embark *v.* **1** *The last passengers embarked at noon:* board ship, go aboard; put on board. **2** *He is about to embark on a new business venture:* start, begin, commence, undertake, launch, enter upon, set out.

Ant. 1 disembark, go ashore; land, arrive. **2** conclude, finish, end, terminate.

◇ *Word origin: Embark* goes back to the Latin prefix *in-* (in) + *barca* (boat), hence to get or put in a boat.

embarrass *v. The mother was embarrassed by her child's bad behaviour:* make self-conscious, make ill at ease, mortify, shame, abash, chagrin, discomfit, disconcert, upset, distress, discountenance; fluster, rattle, confuse, faze, nonplus.

Ant. put at ease, be self-confident.

embattled *adj. The embattled troops called for reinforcements:* engaged in battle, hard-pressed, fighting, embroiled; equipped for battle, battle-ready, arrayed in battle order, prepared for battle, fortified.

embellish *v. He embellished his signature with a series of curlicues:* enhance, elaborate, ornament, decorate, adorn, beautify, garnish, gild, colour, embroider, dress up, set off, *Slang* gussy up.

Ant. simplify, strip bare.

◇ *Word origin: Embellish* comes from Latin *in-* (in) + *bellus* (pretty), which gives us *belle, belles-lettres*, and *beauty*.

ember *n. Stir the embers and the fire may revive:* live coal, smouldering remains; cinder, ash, clinker, slag.

embezzle *v. The girl's guardian embezzled the money that had been left to her:* misappropriate, defalcate; defraud, swindle, cheat; *Slang* fleece, filch, rip-off, bilk, rook.

embitter *v. Being fired without cause is enough to embitter anyone:* envenom, make bitter, make resentful, make rancorous, rankle, sour, make cynical, make pessimistic.

Ant. comfort, please; gladden, delight.

emblem *n. The fleur-de-lis is the armorial emblem of the kings of France:* insignia, badge, symbol, hallmark, device, sign, design, representative figure, colophon.

embody *v.* **1** *The sculpture embodies the artist's love*

of animals: express, represent, personify, exemplify, realize, typify, manifest, substantiate. **2** *The testimony is embodied in the court's records:* include, incorporate, collect, contain, organize, bring together, assimilate, blend, merge, fuse.
Ant. 1 disembody. **2** exclude, except; scatter, disperse.

embrace *v.* **1** *The two sisters embraced each other warmly:* hug, clasp in the arms; grasp, clasp. **2** *Iceland embraced Christianity in about the year 1000:* accept, espouse, adopt. **3** *The study embraced all aspects of the housing problem:* include, contain, embody, comprise, incorporate, cover, encompass, comprehend.
Ant. 2 spurn, reject, refuse, decline, repudiate, scorn, disdain, rule out. **3** omit, delete, exclude, except; ignore, disregard.
◇ *Spelling tip:* Remember that *embrace* keeps its final *e* in *embraceable.*
◇ *Word origin: Embrace* ultimately comes from Latin *in-* (in) + *bracchium* (arm), hence to hold in one's arms. Latin *bracchium*, arm, also gives us our word *bracelet.*

embroider *v.* **1** *The seamstress embroidered a flower on the dress:* decorate with stitches, make of decorative stitches. **2** *The old soldier embroidered his adventures more and more as the years passed:* embellish, adorn with fictitious details, exaggerate, colour; romanticize.
◇ *Word origin: Embroider* comes from Old French *en-* (in) + *brouder* (to stitch). Old French *brouder* comes not from Latin but from Frankish (the language of the Franks — Charlemagne was a Frank) in which it meant "embroider," too. The root meaning is "point." Related words are: *bass* (because of its spiny dorsal fin), *bristle, burr* (both the clinging seed and the cutting tool), *brad* (the nail), and even *borsch* — because the original base of the soup was cow parsnip (Russian *borshch*), a coarse, prickly plant.

embryonic *adj. The class studied the frog in its embryonic state. The plan is still in an embryonic stage:* undeveloped, beginning, rudimentary, incipient, immature; unfinished, imperfect, incomplete, rough.

emend *v. The report must be emended by inserting the right figure:* correct, revise, rectify, improve, change.
◇ *Usage note:* See AMEND.
◇ *Word origin: Emend* comes from Latin *e-* (out) + *mendum* (fault). Latin *mendum*, fault, is also the source of *amend* and *mend.*

emerge *v.* **1** *Venus emerged from the sea:* rise, surface, issue, come up, come forth, come into view; discharge, emit, stream, gush, run, escape, flow, pour. **2** *After long negotiations, a possible solution emerged:* develop, arise, dawn, become apparent, surface, appear, become visible, loom, become manifest, come to light, come out of hiding, crop up, turn up.
Ant. 1 submerge, sink, fall, recede. **2** disappear, hide, fade away; retreat, depart, withdraw.

emergency *n. Sound the alarm only in cases of extreme emergency:* unforeseen danger, pressing necessity, contingency, exigency, crisis, urgency, pinch.

emigrant *n. The emigrants scattered far and wide in their search for a new way of life:* émigré, expatriate; (*loosely*) wanderer, wayfarer.
Ant. immigrant.
◇ *Word origin: Emigrant* goes back to the Latin prefix *e-* (out) + *migrare* (to move, to migrate), hence one who moves out of one country or place to settle in another. Latin *migrare* also gives us the words *immigrate* and *migrate.*

emigrate *v. The young doctor emigrated to Canada:* move, migrate, remove; leave, depart, quit.
Ant. immigrate.

eminence *n.* **1** *Toscanini's eminence as a conductor is undisputed:* high position, elevated rank, repute, public esteem, pre-eminence, importance, standing, prominence, distinction, note, notability, fame, celebrity, conspicuousness, reputation, glory, greatness, excellence. **2** *The hotel was built on an eminence overlooking the sea:* elevation, high place, height, high point, prominence, promontory, hill, hillock, summit, rise, upland, ridge, mountain, peak, bluff, cliff, knoll, hummock.
Ant. 1 lowliness, unimportance, lack of distinction; disrepute, dishonour, infamy, notoriety. **2** lowland, declivity, valley.

eminent *adj.* **1** *Winston Churchill was one of the world's most eminent statesmen:* illustrious, pre-eminent, high-ranking, top, important, elevated, esteemed, distinguished, famous, renowned, prominent, exalted, celebrated, well-known, outstanding, noted, notable, signal, great, glorious, grand, imposing, paramount. **2** *The explosive situation was handled with eminent restraint:* extraordinary, remarkable, outstanding, notable, noted, noteworthy, unusual, utmost, memorable.
Ant. 1 lowly, unimportant, undistinguished; little known, unknown; infamous, notorious. **2** unremarkable, ordinary; inconspicuous.
◇ *Usage note:* Too many people still confuse *eminent* and *imminent. Eminent* means esteemed, highly respected, distinguished, well-known: *Joseph Conrad was an eminent writer. Imminent* means about to happen, impending: *A storm is imminent.* Remember *Eminent — Esteemed; Imminent — Impending.*
◇ *Word origin: Eminent* comes from Latin *e-* (out) + *manere* (to stand), hence outstanding.

emissary *n. The prime minister met with the queen's emissary:* delegate, ambassador, envoy, legate, representative, deputy, agent; go-between, messenger, courier.

emission *n.* **1** *All cars must have devices to reduce*

exhaust emissions: discharge, ejection, voidance, expulsion; (*variously*) smoke, fumes, pollutant, impurity, waste. **2** *The emission of radio signals was interrupted by a power failure:* sending out, emitting, transmission, issuance; throwing out, ejection, expulsion.
Ant. 2 injection, reception.

emit *v. The old radiator emits little heat:* send out, give forth, give, discharge, issue, transmit, pour forth, shed, dispatch, expel, throw out, cast out, vent, beam.
Ant. inject; receive, retain, withhold.

"The advantage of the emotions is that they lead us astray." —*Oscar Wilde*

---

emotion *n.* **1** *The candidate addressed the crowd with emotion:* strong feeling, fullness of heart, excitement, agitation, passion, sentiment, zeal, ardour, vehemence, fervour, heat, warmth. **2** *Jealousy can be a destructive emotion:* concern, strong feeling; (*variously*) love, hate, anger, jealousy, sorrow, sadness, fear, despair, happiness, satisfaction, pride.
Ant. 1 indifference, impassiveness, apathy,

emotional *adj.* **1** *Weddings are emotional occasions:* appealing to the emotions, sentimental, warm, moving, touching, stirring, soul-stirring, heart-warming, thrilling. **2** *She has always been an emotional girl:* easily affected by emotion, temperamental, hypersensitive, vulnerable, responsive, demonstrative, sentimental; passionate, impassioned, fervent, fiery, ardent, zealous, enthusiastic, impetuous; excitable, hysterical, wrought-up, highly strung.
Ant. 1, 2 unemotional, cold, dull. **2** insensitive, unfeeling, indifferent, apathetic, dispassionate, undemonstrative, unsentimental, unresponsive, unexcitable.

emotionalism *n. The defendant's emotionalism embarrassed the jurors:* show of emotion, demonstrativeness, sentimentality, mawkishness, gush, hysteria, hysterics; theatrics, melodramatics, melodrama.
Ant. impassivity, impassiveness, detachment, matter-of-factness.

emperor, *fem.* **empress** *n. The emperor of Japan is venerated by his subjects:* ruler, monarch, sovereign; (*variously*) king, Caesar, tsar, mikado, sultan, Kaiser, shah; (*fem.*) queen, tsarina, sultana.
◇ *Word origin:* See EMPIRE.

emphasis *n.* **1** *The emphasis of the new plan must be on cutting costs:* stress, prominent point, feature, weight, underscoring. **2** *In the word "pillow" the emphasis is on the first syllable:* stress, accent, accentuation.

emphasize *v. The biography emphasized the general's French campaign:* stress, accent, feature, dwell on, press home, iterate, underscore, underline, punctuate, accentuate, point up, bring into relief.
Ant. de-emphasize, play down, underplay; equalize, balance.

emphatic *adj.* **1** *The defendant made an emphatic denial of the charges:* strong, vigorous, forceful, decisive, flat, unqualified, absolute, unequivocal, unyielding, insistent, unwavering, categorical. **2** *The writer's second novel was an emphatic success:* definite, unmistakable, striking, certain, distinct, decided, telling, momentous, marked, express, pronounced, conspicuous, significant.
Ant. 1 hesitant, unsure, uncertain, weak, irresolute, qualified, equivocal. **2** uncertain, indistinct, insignificant, unremarkable, commonplace, average.

empire *n. India was once part of the British Empire:* sovereignty, rule, dominion, realm, domain, commonwealth, imperium.
◇ *Word origin: Empire, emperor,* and *empress* all come from Latin and are closely related to our word *imperative.* Latin *imperare* means to rule, govern, control. *Imperium* means power, rule, or government; it was the name Romans gave to their empire. *Imperator* was the title of Roman emperors.

empirical *adj. The old sailor had never studied navigation, but he had a good empirical knowledge of it:* practical; experimental, first-hand.
Ant. theoretical, secondhand.
◇ *Word origin:* There is no connection between *empire* and *empirical. Empirical* goes back to Greek *em-* (in) +*peira* (trial, experiment), hence skill based on trial and error. The word owes its existence in English to the Empiric school of physicians, who believed in practice and observation rather than in training and theory. Their writings, called the *empeirika,* have survived in a few sentences quoted by the 2nd-century A.D. Greek anatomist and medical writer, Galen.

employ *v.* **1** *The mill employs a thousand workers:* hire, use, engage, retain, take on. **2** *You must employ your leisure hours to good effect:* use, utilize, make use of, put to use, apply, engage, keep busy, occupy, devote, exercise.
—*n.* **3** *The geologist is in the employ of a large oil company:* service, employment; retainership.
Ant. 1 discharge, dismiss, fire, let go, *Slang* sack. **2** waste, fritter away; misuse, misapply.
◇ *Word origin: Employ* goes back to Latin *implicare,* to enfold or involve. The word came into English from French *employer,* to utilize, to use the services of. The original English meaning of *employee* was someone working in a government office or house of business, and the original spelling, standard until the 1840's, was *employé.* The modern spelling of this word is first recorded in 1850.

employee *n. The management has authorized wage increases for all employees:* worker, wage earner, hand, job holder, staff member, member; underling, hireling.
Ant. employer, boss.

employer *n. The secretary worked for the same employer for 20 years:* boss; proprietor, business owner; business, firm, company, establishment, organization, outfit.

Ant. employee, worker, wage earner, job holder, staff member; underling, hireling.

employment *n.* **1** *The student was looking for employment during the summer:* work, job, employ, service; occupation, business, profession, vocation, calling, pursuit, trade, field, line; task, chore, preoccupation. **2** *The scheme requires the employment of great ingenuity:* utilization, exertion, using, use, employing, application, exercise, service, engagement.

Ant. 1 unemployment, leisure, inactivity; avocation, hobby, sideline. **2** disuse, disregard, neglect, foregetting, putting aside.

emporium *n. If the emporium doesn't sell the item, no one will:* large shop, department store, general store; market, bazaar, warehouse.

◇ *Word origin: Emporium* comes from the name of the famous Exchange (*Emporion*) in ancient Athens, from *emporos*, commercial traveller, merchant, from *em-* (in) + *poros* (route), hence literally an "en-router." Other English words related to Greek *poros*, route, are *port, ford, ferry*, and *fare* (to travel).

empower *v. French law empowers the police to search any suspicious persons:* authorize, sanction, invest, vest, license, endow; permit, allow, enable; commission, delegate.

Ant. restrain, disbar, divest of power; disallow, forbid, enjoin.

empty *adj.* **1** *Our voices echoed through the empty house:* vacant, unoccupied, uninhabited, bare. **2** *He didn't want to retire and lead an empty life:* aimless, meaningless, without substance, insignificant, worthless, purposeless, futile, unfulfilled, idle, hollow; shallow, banal, trivial, inane, insipid, frivolous.

—*v.* **3** *Empty the glass before putting it in the dishwasher. The Fal empties into the English Channel:* pour out, drain, dump, void, evacuate; discharge, flow, debouch.

Ant. 1 full, stuffed, crammed, packed, jammed; occupied, inhabited. **2** meaningful, significant, substantial, useful, valuable, worthwhile, purposeful, fulfilled, busy, full, rich, vital, interesting, serious. **3** fill, pack, put in, stuff, cram, jam; receive.

emulate *v. Politicians would do well to emulate Disraeli:* take as a model, follow the example of, pattern oneself upon, follow, copy, imitate; try to equal, rival; mimic, ape.

◇ *Word origin: Emulate* comes from Latin *aemulus*, rival, which is related to Latin *imitari*, to imitate. It is also related to our word *aim*.

enable *v. A university education enables a person to get a better job:* make able, empower, qualify, capacitate, make possible for, allow, permit; aid, assist, support, benefit.

Ant. prevent, bar, disqualify, prohibit, incapacitate; hinder, thwart, frustrate, block, keep back, hold back.

enact *v. Parliament enacted the new farm bill:* pass into law, pass, legislate, vote to accept, authorize, ratify; proclaim, decree; sanction, approve.

Ant. reject, turn down, vote down, fail to pass, veto; abolish, annul, repeal, rescind, cancel.

enamour *v. John is enamoured of Mary. Most visitors to London are enamoured of the City:* inflame with love, affect with fondness, enrapture, infatuate, allure, draw to, attach; enthral, charm, enchant, entrance, captivate, bewitch, fascinate, excite, take a fancy to.

Ant. repel, repulse, revolt, disgust, disenchant, put off, *Slang* turn off.

enchant *v.* **1** *The sorcerer enchanted the beautiful princess:* cast a spell over, place under a spell, bewitch, charm; hypnotize, mesmerize. **2** *The family was enchanted with the sweet little girl:* charm, delight, entrance, enthral, captivate, enrapture, fascinate, bewitch, transport.

Ant. 1 release, free, exorcise. **2** repel, repulse, revolt, disgust, sicken, *Slang* turn off.

enchantress *n.* **1** *The enchantress turned the prince into a frog:* sorceress, witch, vampire, siren. **2** *Men flocked around the beautiful enchantress:* seductress, temptress, vamp, charmer, femme fatale.

encircle *v. A heavy wire fence encircles the compound:* circle, ring, surround, wreathe, girdle, gird, circumscribe, encompass; enclose, fence, wall, hem in.

enclose Also **inclose** *v.* **1** *A high stone wall enclosed the estate:* surround, ring, circle, encircle, girdle, encompass, circumscribe, fence in, wall in, shut in. **2** *Please enclose a cheque with your order:* include, send with, put in the same envelope, put in the same package.

encompass *v.* **1** *High mountains completely encompass the little ski resort:* surround, encircle, circle, enclose, ring, girdle, fence in, wall in, hem in. **2** *The encyclopædia encompasses scientific, historical, and cultural information:* include, cover, embrace, contain, comprise, incorporate, embody, hold, involve, take in, touch on.

Ant. 2 exclude, leave out, omit; ignore.

encounter *v.* **1** *She encountered an old friend in the street. The plane encountered a storm over the Alps:* meet, meet with, chance upon; sustain, confront, run into, experience, come upon; endure, undergo, suffer. **2** *Napoleon encountered Wellington at the Battle of Waterloo:* clash with, meet and fight, do battle with, contend against, engage in combat, grapple with, skirmish with, cross swords with, come face to face with.

—*n.* **3** *Many men were lost in the encounter:* battle, combat, fight, confrontation, engagement,

hostile meeting, bout, affray, fracas, skirmish, clash, brush.
Ant. 1 escape, shun, miss, elude, avoid. 3 retreat, withdrawal.
◇ *Word origin: Encounter* comes from the Latin prefix *in-* (to become) + *contra* (against), to come against something.

encourage *v.* 1 *Many letters of support encouraged the mayor to stand again:* inspire, give confidence to, inspirit, embolden, induce, give hope to, hearten, rally, egg on; spur, exhort, impel, sway; reassure, hearten, cheer. 2 *Good health encourages clear thinking:* foster, promote, advance, further, boost, forward, assist, help, prompt, aid.
Ant. 1 discourage, dissuade, deter, depress, deject, dishearten, dispirit. 2 retard, hinder, prevent, inhibit, hamper.

encouragement *n. A little encouragement is all that some people need:* encouraging, approbation, praise, support, reassurance; boost, lift, *Slang* shot in the arm.
Ant. discouragement, criticism; disparagement, ridicule.

encroach *v. The neighbour's hedge is encroaching on our property. Social security "snoopers" encroach on a person's right to privacy:* intrude, infringe, invade, impinge, make inroads on, overrun, overstep, violate, break into, trespass, transgress, interfere.
Ant. respect, honour, recognize, observe; safeguard, protect.
◇ *Word origin: Encroach* comes from Old French *en* (in) + *crochier* (to hook), literally to get a hook into something that belongs to someone else. The related French word *croc*, hook, does not go back to Latin but instead to Germanic origins — it is related to Old Norse *krokr*, hook, and to our word *crook*.

encumber *v. The walker was encumbered with a heavy pack:* burden, weigh down, load, load down, lade, saddle; tax, inconvenience, hinder, impede, slow down, obstruct.
Ant. unload, unburden, disencumber.

encyclopædic *adj. In matters of general science, his knowledge is encyclopædic:* comprehensive, all-encompassing, exhaustive, universal, wide-ranging; scholarly, erudite.

end *n.* 1 *Put the vegetables at the end of the table. The school is at the southern end of the town:* extremity, terminus; edge, limit, boundary, border. 2 *We stayed to the very end of the concert:* conclusion, ending, termination, close, finish, expiration, cessation, completion, finale, wind-up, culmination, consummation. 3 *What will be the end of their constant arguments?:* outcome, upshot, result, consequence, effect, issue, fulfilment, settlement. 4 *He used unscrupulous methods to achieve his end:* aim, goal, purpose, object, objective, result, intention, design. 5 *Another world war could mean the end of civilization as we know it. He met an untimely end:* extinction, extermination, destruction, termination, ruin; death, demise. 6 *This end of cloth is enough for a dress:* remnant, left-over, fragment, scrap.
—*v.* 7 *The book ends on page 364. The meeting ended at ten o'clock:* conclude, halt, draw to a close, terminate, cease, finish, stop, leave off, call an end to, run out, wind up, close, bring down the curtain. 8 *The Spanish Conquistadors ended the Aztec civilization:* destroy, eradicate, kill, annihilate, exterminate, extinguish, finish off.
Ant. 1, 2, 3, 5 beginning, start, commencement, inauguration; inception, birth. 7, 8 begin, start, commence.

endanger *v. The spread of urban areas endangers our wildlife:* threaten, put in danger, imperil, jeopardize, hazard, risk.
Ant. protect, safeguard, preserve, defend, shield, save.

endear *v. Smoking a cigar in a lift won't endear you to the other passengers:* make beloved, make dear; create goodwill among, ingratiate with, make attractive.
Ant. alienate, estrange.

endearment *n. His letters to his fiancée were full of fond endearments:* loving word, fond utterance, sweet nothings; pet name, affectionate term.
Ant. curse, malediction.

endeavour *v.* 1 *We should all endeavour to be more considerate to others:* try, attempt, make an effort, strive, work at, undertake, take pains, labour, struggle, do one's best; aspire, aim, seek.
—*n.* 2 *The boy made an honest endeavour to do the work well:* attempt, effort, try, essay, exertion, striving, struggle. 3 *Portrait painting has been his lifelong endeavour:* undertaking, enterprise, work, preoccupation, interest; occupation, vocation, job, career.
Ant. 1 neglect, ignore, pass up, overlook; abandon, dismiss.

ending *n. The film has a happy ending:* conclusion, end, close, finish, wind-up, finale, termination, cessation, expiration, completion, culmination, consummation.
Ant. beginning, start, opening, inception.

endless *adj. Endless desert stretched out before us. Their endless bickering got on everyone's nerves:* without end, unending, uninterrupted, unbroken, interminable, boundless, infinite, measureless, unlimited; perpetual, everlasting, eternal, constant, continuous, continual, persistent.
Ant. finite, limited, bounded, circumscribed; temporary, short-lived, brief, passing, transitory, transient.

endorse *v.* 1 *I find it impossible to endorse the application of a candidate with a record like his:* support, back, champion, approve, sanction, recommend, vouch for, subscribe to, stand behind, affirm, ratify, OK, second, lend one's name to. 2 *Endorse the cheque on the back:*

sign, countersign; authorize, validate, certify.
Ant. 1 disapprove, denounce, condemn, discredit, disavow, reject, repudiate, spurn.

endow *v.* **1** *Grandfather endowed each child with a trust fund:* bestow a fund upon, provide with an income; bequeath, settle on, leave, will; award, confer, grant, bestow. **2** *Nature endowed her with extraordinary beauty:* supply, equip, provide, accord, invest, bestow, grant, furnish; bless, grace, favour.
Ant. 2 divest, deprive, take.
◇ *Word origin: Endow* comes from the Old French prefix *en-* (in) + *douer* (to give, as a marriage portion), which also gives us *dowry* and *dower.*

endowment *n.* **1** *The businessman left an endowment of a million pounds to each son:* legacy, bequest, bestowed fund, willed income; benefaction, grant, gift, donation, award. **2** *A natural bent for music is just one of her endowments:* natural gift, talent, flair, ability, aptitude, faculty, attribute.

endurance *n. Sailing the Atlantic single-handed requires great endurance:* stamina, hardihood, durability, strength; fortitude, perseverance, tenacity, pertinacity, tenaciousness, persistence, resolution, permanence, durableness; immutability, changelessness, stability.
Ant. frailty, weakness.
◇ *Spelling tip:* Some people hesitate over this word, not knowing if it ends in *-ance* or *ence.* Remember: *It takes a lot of endurANCE to dANCE all night.*

endure *v.* **1** *The company has endured tremendous losses:* sustain, bear, withstand, stand, experience, undergo, go through, weather, suffer, bear up under, brave; tolerate, countenance, brook. **2** *They vowed that their love would endure for ever:* last, persist, prevail, live, live on, continue, remain.
Ant. 1 escape, evade, avoid, bypass, side-step; lose to, be defeated by, surrender to. **2** perish, die, fail, succumb, subside, crumble, decay.
◇ *Word origin: Endure* comes from the Latin prefix *in-* (to become) + *durus* (hard), which also gives us *durable* and *duration.*

"The deadliest enemies of nations are not their foreign foes; they always dwell within their own borders." —*William James*

---

enemy *n.* **1** *His thoughtless behaviour earned him many enemies:* antagonist, detractor, opponent, adversary, foe, rival, competitor. **2** *The enemy was advancing towards the city:* opposing military force, armed foe; hostile nation, belligerent state; assailant, attacker.
Ant. 1 friend, supporter, well-wisher. **2** ally, confederate.
◇ *Word origin: Enemy* and *enmity* come from the Latin prefix *in-* (not) + *amicus* (friend), not a friend.

energetic *adj. I never saw such an energetic child. The old lady has an energetic mind:* full of energy, active, vigorous, lively, spry, animated, restless, spirited; forceful, dynamic, brisk, robust, go-getting, high-powered, hard working, industrious; alert, enthusiastic, quick-witted.
Ant. enervated, languid, inactive, lethargic, sluggish, listless; phlegmatic.

energy *n.* **1** *The new power plant supplies energy for the entire city:* power, force; (*variously*) hydroelectric power, electric power, atomic energy, nuclear energy. **2** *Even after hours of work his energy never seems to give out:* vitality, vim, vigour, verve, pep, go, vivacity, liveliness, animation, zest, zeal, enterprise, drive, hustle.
Ant. 2 inertia, lassitude, listlessness, sluggishness.
◇ *Word origin: Energy* comes from Greek *energeia,* vigour of expression, activity. The word was coined by the philosopher Aristotle from the word elements *en-* (in) + *ergon* (work). A century or so after Aristotle the term *hai energiai,* expressing the concept "cosmic forces," entered Western thought through the popular occult writings of a group of philosophers centred in Alexandria. The psychological meaning of *energy,* "vigour or intensity of action," was introduced into our language early in the 19th century by the poet Samuel Taylor Coleridge; the scientific meanings of the word have sprung up over the past 150 years.

enervate *v. The long march in the sun enervated the soldiers:* exhaust, weary, weaken, debilitate, devitalize, enfeeble, sap one's energy, deplete, wash out, fatigue, tire, *Slang* whack out, fag.
Ant. energize, invigorate, strengthen, vitalize, stimulate, quicken.

enforce *v. The police must enforce the law:* carry out, administer, keep in force, compel obedience to, insist on, impose, implement, execute, apply, exact support, defend.
Ant. ignore, disregard; waive, forgo.
◇ *Spelling tip:* Remember that *enforce* keeps its final *e* in *enforceable.*

engage *v.* **1** *The children are engaged in a great many outdoor activities:* involve, occupy, engross, absorb; take part, participate, partake; undertake, set about, enter into, embark on. **2** *The house was so large that it was necessary to engage an extra maid:* employ, hire, take on, retain, secure, take into service. **3** *The couple got married after being engaged for only a month:* betroth, affiance, pledge, promise. **4** *The battleship engaged the enemy at the mouth of the harbour:* begin conflict with, encounter in battle, fight with, give battle to, war with, combat.
Ant. 2 fire, lay off, let go, *Slang* sack. **4** flee, retreat, withdraw.

engagement *n.* 1 *Have you a luncheon engagement?:* appointment, date, commitment, meeting, arrangement; obligation, duty. 2 *The couple announced their engagement at the party:* betrothal, troth, plighted faith, affiancing. 3 *The singer had a brief engagement at a suburban night-club:* employment, job, position, situation, *Slang* gig; post, berth, billet. 4 *The general had won three engagements with the enemy:* battle, fight, encounter, combat, conflict, action, skirmish, brush, bout, contest, scuffle, fray.

engaging *adj. It's hard to scold a child who has such an engaging manner:* winning, attractive, disarming, winsome, enchanting, charming, captivating, pleasing, likeable, lovable, agreeable, appealing, ingratiating.

Ant. offensive, disagreeable, displeasing, unattractive, unpleasant, unlikeable, unlovable; repulsive, repellent.

engender *v. Respect can engender love:* give rise to, cause, bring about, beget, breed, generate, produce, occasion, precipitate.

Ant. kill, end, crush.

engross *v. I was completely engrossed in the book when the phone rang:* absorb, occupy, preoccupy, involve, immerse, engage, hold, arrest, take up.

Ant. bore, tire, weary; vex, annoy, irritate.

engulf *v. The flood-waters engulfed the entire village:* swallow up, envelop, bury, swamp, overrun, inundate, submerge, immerse, deluge.

enhance *v. The splendid dress enhanced her beauty:* intensify, heighten, magnify, make more attractive, make more appealing; elevate, lift, raise, boost; redouble, embellish, augment, add to, complement.

Ant. diminish, reduce, lessen, decrease, minimize, depreciate, detract from.

◇ *Word origin: Enhance* comes from Old French *enhaucer,* to lift up, ultimately derived from Latin *in-* (in) + *altus* (high).

enigma *n. Just why he suddenly switched political parties remains an enigma:* puzzle, riddle, question, perplexity, mystery, secret, hidden meaning.

◇ *Word origin: Enigma* is from Greek *ainigma,* riddle.

enigmatic, enigmatical *adj. The Mona Lisa has an enigmatic smile:* mysterious, secretive, puzzling, indecipherable, cryptic, baffling, perplexing, inscrutable, elusive, ambiguous, equivocal, paradoxical.

Ant. candid, frank, open, straightforward, self-explanatory, intelligible, lucid; explicit, expressive, express, definite, clear, manifest.

◇ *Pronunciation tip: Enigmatic* rhymes with *automatic.*

enjoin *v.* 1 *The firemen enjoined the public to stand clear:* advise, counsel, warn, admonish, command, bid, charge, direct, instruct, call upon; beg, entreat, ask, urge. 2 *The judge enjoined the strikers from picketing inside company property:* prohibit, forbid, restrain, place an injunction on, restrict, ban, bar, proscribe, interdict.

Ant. 2 permit, allow, let.

enjoy *v.* 1 *The audience enjoyed the new opera:* like, appreciate, admire, think well of, take pleasure in, be pleased with, rejoice in, delight in, fancy, relish; savour; *Slang* lap up, get a kick out of. 2 *The Scots enjoy some of the world's most beautiful scenery:* have the benefit of, be blessed with, have, possess, own.

Ant. 1 dislike, hate, detest, loathe, abhor, abominate, despise.

◇ *Word origin: Enjoy* is from Latin *in-* (in) + *gaudere* (to rejoice), hence to rejoice in something.

enjoyable *adj. Was it an enjoyable film? We all had a most enjoyable evening:* pleasant, pleasing, providing enjoyment, pleasurable, agreeable, fun-filled, delightful, satisfying, rewarding, gratifying.

Ant. unpleasant, disagreeable, unenjoyable, unpleasurable, unsatisfying; hateful, detestable, loathsome, abominable, despicable.

"If a man cannot enjoy the return of spring, why should he be happy in a labour-saving Utopia?" —*George Orwell*

---

enjoyment *n.* 1 *The guests sipped the fine wine with enjoyment:* pleasure, delight, satisfaction, happiness, gratification, joy; fun, entertainment, amusement, diversion, good time. 2 *Be pleased that you have at least the enjoyment of your liberty:* benefit, advantage, blessing, privilege, right, prerogative, exercise, possession.

Ant. 1 displeasure, dissatisfaction, detestation, loathing, abhorrence, aversion, repugnance, hatred, dislike. 2 disadvantage, handicap.

enlarge *v.* 1 *The magnifying glass enlarges the image 50 times. The hotel is being enlarged to accommodate more guests:* make larger, increase, expand, swell, extend, inflate; augment, add to, multiply; magnify, amplify, lengthen, widen, broaden, elongate; become bigger, grow, develop. 2 *In the discussion period the speaker enlarged on his opening statement:* expand, amplify, elaborate, expound, expatiate, discourse.

Ant. 1 decrease, shorten, curtail, shrink, contract, reduce, diminish, lessen. 2 condense, abridge, abbreviate, narrow.

enlighten *v. The tour of our country enlightened the foreign visitors on the workings of democracy:* inform, instruct, educate, edify, make aware, illuminate, cause to understand, apprise, advise; civilize, sophisticate.

Ant. mystify, perplex, puzzle, bewilder, mislead, confound, confuse.

enlist *v.* 1 *Were you press-ganged into the navy or*

did you enlist voluntarily?: join, join up, enrol, sign up, volunteer. **2** *The mayor tried to enlist the support of every citizen in the anti-litter campaign:* recruit, engage, obtain, gain the assistance of.

Ant. 1 withdraw, resign, retire, leave. **2** reject, refuse, dismiss.

enliven *v. His jokes enlivened the party:* make lively, animate, pep up, cheer up, brighten, excite, quicken, vitalize, vivify, wake up, fire; renew, rejuvenate.

Ant. dampen, chill, cast a pall over, deaden, make dull, make boring, subdue, depress, weigh down.

en masse *adv. The audience booed and then walked out en masse:* in a group, in a body, together, all together, as a whole, as a group.

Ant. individually, separately, one by one.

◇ *Word origin: En masse* is French for "in a mass."

enmity *n. Despite the truce, strong enmity remains between the two nations:* hostility, ill will, hatred, rancour, acrimony, animosity, animus, bitterness, antipathy, malice.

Ant. goodwill, amity, friendliness, friendship, amicability, love, affection, cordiality.

◇ *Word origin:* See ENEMY.

ennui *n. An idle life left the heiress in a state of ennui:* weariness, boredom, tedium, languor, listlessness, lassitude; apathy, indifference.

Ant. excitement, eagerness, interest, curiosity, commitment.

◇ *Word origin: Ennui* is the French for "boredom." It derives ultimately from the Latin phrase *in odio,* in detestation, i.e. detestable. (Our word *annoy* comes from Old French *anoi,* which is the ancestor of present-day French *ennui.*)

enormity *n.* **1** *The enormity of the crime shocked the public:* monstrousness, atrociousness, outrageousness, offensiveness, vileness, villainy, depravity, viciousness, wickedness, evilness, malignity, heinousness, baseness. **2** *The enormity of the task overwhelmed them:* immensity, hugeness, vastness, largeness, enormousness.

Ant. 1 inoffensive, innocuousness, harmlessness, innocence. **2** smallness, insignificance, meagreness.

enormous *adj. The banquet was held in an enormous room:* huge, vast, immense, tremendous, colossal, gigantic, mammoth, gargantuan, Brobdingnagian, titanic, elephantine; massive, prodigious.

Ant. small, little, tiny, minute, miniscule, lilliputian, diminutive, trivial, insignificant, meagre, midget, dwarf, tiddly, itsy-bitsy, teeny, (*fem.*) petite.

◇ *Word origin: Enormous* literally means "exceeding the norm." It comes from Latin *e-* (out) + *norma* (norm), hence, outside the norm.

enough *adj.* **1** *Is there enough food for everyone?:* adequate, sufficient, ample, plenty, abundant, copious.

—*pron.* **2** *I know that the paint is the right shade, but did you buy enough of it?:* sufficient amount, sufficiency, ample supply, competence, plenty, plenitude, full measure.

—*adv.* **3** *I'm hungry enough to eat an ox:* adequately, sufficiently, satisfactorily, amply, abundantly; passably, tolerably, reasonably.

Ant. 1 inadequate, insufficient; skimpy, scant, meagre. **2** insufficiency, inadequacy, paucity, scarcity. **3** inadequately, insufficiently.

enrage *v. Sloppy work enrages a meticulous person:* infuriate, incense, make furious, anger, madden, inflame, provoke the wrath of, throw into a rage, make one's blood boil.

Ant. placate, pacify, appease, mollify, conciliate, soothe, calm, allay, quiet, assuage.

enrapture *v. Her beautiful singing voice enraptured audiences everywhere:* enthral, hold rapt, transport, entrance, enchant, captivate, beguile, charm, bewitch, delight, thrill.

Ant. bore, put off, fail to interest.

enrich *v.* **1** *The development of oil fields enriched the Arab nations:* make rich, make wealthy, *Slang* feather the nest of. **2** *British culture may be enriched by Oriental immigrants. The breakfast cereal is enriched with vitamins and minerals:* elevate, improve, enhance, upgrade, fortify, refine; adorn, embellish.

Ant. 1 impoverish. **2** degrade, downgrade, bastardize, weaken, divest, strip.

enrol *v. The evening class will enrol new students during the first week in September:* register, sign on, enter, take on; admit, accept, engage; enlist, join, join up, recruit.

Ant. withdraw, drop out, retire; dismiss, expel.

enrolment *n. Today is the last day for enrolment in the YMCA swimming classes:* enrolling, registration, matriculation, signing on; enlistment, recruiting, admittance.

Ant. withdrawing, dropping out.

en route *adv. Try to visit Stonehenge en route to Cornwall:* in transit, on the way, on the road.

ensemble *n.* **1** *Mixing antique and modern furniture in a room can make a striking ensemble:* totality, entirety, general appearance, overall effect; assembly, aggregate. **2** *She wears a different ensemble every day of the week:* outfit, costume, attire, *Slang* get-up. **3** *At the end of the performance the entire ensemble of dancers and singers took a bow:* group of performers, company, troupe.

◇ *Pronunciation tip: Ensemble* should be pronounced *ahn-SAHM-ble.*

ensign *n. The ship's ensign was flown at half-mast:* flag, banner, standard, pennant, pennon, colours, jack.

enslave *v. The Tsar enslaved the peasants. There is a danger of patients becoming enslaved to pain-killing drugs:* hold in bondage, make a slave

of, enthral, indenture, enchain, shackle, put in shackles; subjugate, capture, control, dominate; addict.
Ant. free, emancipate, release, liberate.

ensue *v. After the heavy rains, flooding ensued:* follow, result, come to pass, derive, succeed.
Ant. herald, precede, introduce.

ensure *v.* **1** *Come early to ensure a good seat:* assure, be sure of, make sure, make certain of, clinch; guarantee, warrant, secure. **2** *Some people used to think that carrying a rabbit's foot would ensure them from harm:* protect, guard, safeguard, make safe, secure.
◇ *Usage note:* Do not confuse *ensure* and *insure*, even though they sound very similar. We have seen what *ensure* means. *Insure* can only be used to mean to guarantee against loss of property, life, etc., with an *insurance policy: The house is insured for £20,000.*

entail *v. The new job entails setting up sales conferences:* require, necessitate, demand, call for; include, involve, incorporate, occasion.
Ant. eliminate, cut out; exclude, leave out.

entangle *v.* **1** *He awoke with a start, entangled in the collapsed mosquito-net:* tangle, enmesh, ensnare, snare, enravel, snarl, encumber, intertwine, twist up. **2** *The witness entangled himself in a web of lies:* tangle, catch, trap, ensnare, involve, embroil; complicate, mix up, confuse, muddle, foul up; implicate, compromise, embarrass.
Ant. 1 disentangle, free, extricate, unravel.

enter *v.* **1** *The thief entered by a rear window:* come in, go in, pass into, proceed into, make an entrance, arrive, penetrate, intrude into. **2** *If you plan to enter the diplomatic service, study history and foreign languages. I refused to enter into the discussion:* join, commit oneself to, embark upon, set out on, bind oneself, become a member of, participate in, take part in. **3** *Are you going to enter the pie-baking contest?:* enrol in, sign up for, register for, enlist in, join; list, record, post, inscribe.
Ant. 1 exit, leave, depart, go out, go. **2, 3** leave, withdraw from, drop out of, take out of, resign from, retire from.
◇ *Word origin: Enter, entrance, entrée,* and *entry* come to us from French *entrer*, to enter, ultimately derived from Latin *intra*, inside.

"It is easier for a camel to go through the eye of a needle, than for a rich man to enter into the kingdom of God." —*St. Matthew* xix. 24

---

enterprise *n.* **1** *The firm's latest enterprise will require an enlarged staff:* undertaking, venture, endeavour, project, operation, effort. **2** *The manager was pleased with the salesman's enterprise:* initiative, drive, aggressiveness, push, ingenuity, ambition, energy, enthusiasm, eagerness, zeal, willingness, spirit, alertness, vigour, daring, boldness, adventurousness.
Ant. laziness, spiritlessness, indolence.

enterprising *adj. The company can always find room for an enterprising young man:* ambitious, aggressive, industrious, hard-working, active, energetic, venturesome, intrepid, self-reliant, bold, eager, enthusiastic, zealous, earnest, alert, keen, wide-awake.
Ant. lazy, indolent, timid, cautious, wary, conservative.

entertain *v.* **1** *The magician entertained the children with a variety of tricks:* amuse, divert, give enjoyment to, beguile, please, regale, delight, enthral, charm, engage pleasantly, interest, absorb. **2** *Diplomats often entertain on a large scale:* have guests, give a party, play host, keep open house, offer hospitality. **3** *We simply cannot entertain such outrageous ideas:* consider, admit, contemplate, harbour, think about, keep in mind, heed, muse over, dwell on, ponder, cogitate on.
Ant. 1 bore, weary, tire; displease, disgust. **3** reject, ignore, disregard.
◇ *Word origin:* To *entertain* a person is to hold his attention agreeably. The word comes from Latin *inter-* (among) + *tenere* (to hold).

entertainment *n. The city offers all kinds of entertainment for both young and old:* amusement, diversion, distraction, recreation, fun, play, good time, pastime, leisure activity, novelty; pleasure, enjoyment, satisfaction.
Ant. work, job, preoccupation.

enthral *v.* **1** *The acrobats enthralled a large audience:* intrigue, spellbind, fascinate, enchant, captivate, charm, enrapture, entrance, transport, thrill, beguile, hypnotize. **2** *The emperor enthralled all of his military prisoners:* enslave, put into slavery, keep in bondage, subjugate.
Ant. 1 bore, fail to interest. **2** free, emancipate, liberate.

"There is a melancholy which accompanies all enthusiasm." —*Sir Anthony Ashley Cooper*

---

enthusiasm *n.* **1** *We are looking forward with enthusiasm to your visit:* eagerness, keenness, anticipation, excitement, fervour, zest, ardour, exuberance, elation. **2** *One of her great enthusiasms is skiing:* interest, passion, devotion, craze, mania, rage, pet activity; hobby, hobby-horse, diversion, distraction.
Ant. 1 apathy, indifference, unconcern, detachment, aloofness, calmness, coldness, coolness.
◇ *Usage note:* Many teachers and others feel that the verb *enthuse*, to express or feel enthusiasm, to be enthusiastic, is not a true word. They feel that such sentences as *Mother enthused about her new dress* and *He was enthused about his holiday* should be phrased as *Mother talked enthusiastically* (or *expressed enthusiasm*) *about her new dress* and *He was enthusiastic about his holiday.* In modern usage, then, *enthuse* is a borderline case; it's best to avoid it in formal writing and speaking.

◇ *Word origin: Enthusiasm* comes from Greek *enthousiasmos* "god-insideness" — prophetic or poetic frenzy, divine inspiration. The main word elements are *en-* (in) and *theos* (god). The word was brought over into English about 400 years ago and first used in the sense of "misguided religious emotion."

enthusiast *n. Dad's a football enthusiast:* fan, devotee, aficionado, fanatic, addict, *Slang* maniac, nut, freak.

enthusiastic *adj. Sam is an enthusiastic golfer. The diplomat received enthusiastic praise:* wholehearted, ardent, fervent, fervid, eager, zealous, passionate, spirited, exuberant; unqualified, unstinting.
Ant. blasé, dispassionate, cool, lukewarm, unenthusiastic, uninterested, half-hearted, faint, feeble.

entice *v. Isn't there any way of enticing you to come to the party?:* induce, tempt, beguile, lure, allure, incite, attract, seduce; persuade, coax, inveigle, wheedle.
Ant. repel, discourage, dissuade.

entire *adj.* **1** *The entire school turned out for the football match:* whole, total, full, gross; complete, all-inclusive, thorough, absolute. **2** *The ancient vase was found entire and unblemished:* intact, unbroken, undamaged, unimpaired, in perfect condition.
Ant. 1 partial, incomplete. **2** broken, fragmented, defective, damaged, impaired.
◇ *Word origin: Entire* comes from Latin *integer*, whole. The same Latin word gives us *integer* (a whole number), *integrate*, and *integrity*.

entirely *adv. He's entirely wrong:* completely, wholly, fully, totally, thoroughly, altogether, utterly, absolutely, unreservedly.
Ant. partially, somewhat, slightly, moderately, partly, tolerably.

entitle *v.* **1** *This coupon entitles you to a free dancing lesson:* give the right to, authorize, qualify, make eligible, allow, permit. **2** *The book is entitled* Russia Before The Revolution*:* title, name, designate, call, style, dub, label.
Ant. 1 disable, disqualify.

entity *n. The moon is an entity whose origins are unknown:* real thing, thing, object, article, structure, body, matter, substance, quantity; creature, being, individual.
Ant. non-entity, fantasy, hallucination, illusion, mirage, delusion, chimera, phantom.

entourage *n. The king travelled with an entourage of 200 servants, courtiers, and guards:* retinue, attendants, train, cortège, escort, following, convoy, staff, court; companions, followers, associates.
◇ *Pronunciation tip:* The preferred pronunciation of *entourage* is *ahn-too-RAHZH*.

entrails *n. pl. The soothsayer tried to foretell the future by examining the entrails of sacrificial animals:* viscera, intestines, insides, innards, guts, bowels.
◇ *Word origin: Entrails* comes from the Medieval Latin word *intralia*, insides, intestines, whose source is *inter*, within. (Latin *inter* also gives us *interior*.)

entrance[1] *n.* **1** *The management placed a guard at the front entrance:* entry, way in, access, approach, ingress; (*loosely*) door, doorway, gate, gateway, portal, passageway, opening. **2** *Men without ties and jackets will be refused entrance:* permission to enter, entry, admittance, access, ingress, entrée. **3** *Her entrance in the red dress caught everyone's attention:* entry, coming in, approach, ingress; appearance, introduction.
Ant. exit, departure, egress.
◇ *Word origin:* See ENTER.

entrance[2] *v.* **1** *It was a gift bound to entrance any child:* delight, gladden, enrapture, fill with wonder, spellbind, fascinate, transport, captivate, enthral, charm, bewitch. **2** *A hypnotist looks for subjects who are easily entranced:* put into a trance, hypnotize, mesmerize.
Ant. 1 bore, fail to interest.
◇ *Pronunciation tip:* Remember that *entrance*[1] is pronounced *EN-trance*, whereas *entrance*[2], to put into a *trance*, is pronounced *en-TRANCE*.

entreat *v.* **1** *I entreat you to contribute generously to the building fund:* ask earnestly, beseech, implore, plead with, appeal to, exhort, request, beg, supplicate, adjure, enjoin, petition, importune.
Ant. command, direct, demand.

entreaty *n. The king was deeply affected by the prisoner's sad entreaty:* earnest request, plea, appeal, supplication, petition, importunity.
Ant. demand, ultimatum.

entrée *n.* **1** *His family's position gives him entrée into the best social circles:* admittance, admission, entry, entrance, ingress, access; acceptance, acknowledgement. **2** *If you would like to choose the entrée, Sally can choose the meat:* dish or course served between fish and meat courses.
◇ *Pronunciation tip:* The *en-* of *entrée* should be pronounced *ahn-*. Thus, the correct pronunciation is *AHN-tray*.
◇ *Word origin:* See ENTER.

entrench Also **intrench** *v. Most habits are firmly entrenched during childhood. He has entrenched himself so thoroughly as president of the club that he can't be dispensed with:* establish solidly, fix, set, install; embed, anchor, dig in, plant, root; put in a strong position.

entre nous *adv. Entre nous, I think they're getting married in May:* between the two of us, between you and me, between ourselves, confidentially, privately, in strict confidence.
◇ *Word origin: Entre nous* is French for "between us."

entrepreneur *n. He makes his living as entrepreneur for various musical groups:* impresario, manager, organizer, director.
◇ *Pronunciation tip:* The first syllable of *entrepreneur* is pronounced *ahn-* whereas the last

syllable is *nur.* Thus the correct pronunciation is *AHN-truh-pruh-NUR.*

entrust Also **intrust** *v. The manager is entrusted with full responsibility for running the office:* trust, put in trust of, charge with, authorize, give the custody of, hand over, turn over, commit, consign, assign, delegate.

entry *n.* **1** *The entry to the estate is behind those trees:* way in, way, approach, ingress, access; (*loosely*) door, doorway, gate, gateway, portal, passageway. **2** *Please wait in the entry:* entrance hall, foyer, doorway, vestibule. **3** *An ovation greeted the conductor's entry into the hall. Only persons with tickets will be allowed entry:* approach, introduction, appearance; entrance, entrée, admission, admittance, ingress. **4** *Make an entry of the amount in your cheque-book:* record, account, registration; note, memo, memorandum, minute, item, jotting. **5** *Only entries posted before midnight will be considered. The stable's entry in this race is the black horse:* thing entered, person entered, contestant, competitor.

Ant. **1** exit, egress. **3** exit, departure, leaving, leave-taking, withdrawal.

◇ *Word origin:* See ENTER.

enumerate *v.* **1** *The teacher enumerated the students' spelling mistakes:* specify, numerate, cite, relate, detail, recount, spell out. **2** *Enumerate the items again to make sure that none is missing:* count, count up, add, add up, sum up, total, tally, tabulate, number, list, tick off.

◇ *Word origin: Enumerate* comes from the Latin prefix *e-* (out) + *numerare* (to count), hence to count out or name one by one. The related Latin *numerus,* number, gives us *number* and *numeral.*

enunciate *v. The boy must learn to enunciate his consonants correctly:* pronounce clearly, utter distinctly; articulate, sound, speak, voice.

Ant. mutter, mumble, stammer, stutter.

envelop *v. Fog enveloped the town. The plan is enveloped in secrecy:* wrap, enwrap, cover, encase, sheathe, enfold, enclose, blanket, cloak, shroud, veil, contain, swathe, swaddle, surround, encompass; hide, conceal, obscure.

Ant. unwrap, uncover, expose, reveal, lay bare.

◇ *Usage note:* See ENVELOPE.

◇ *Word origin: Envelop* and *envelope* both come from Old French *en-* (in) + *voluper* (to wrap), which also gives us *develop.*

envelope *n. Fold the letter carefully and put it in an envelope:* letter covering, paper wrapper, gummed wrapper; wrapping, jacket, cover, covering.

◇ *Pronunciation tip: Envelope* can be pronounced with the English *en-* sound, *EN-va-lope,* or the French *ahn-* sound, *AHN-va-lope.*

◇ *Usage note:* Don't confuse the verb *to envelop,* meaning to wrap or enclose, with the noun *envelope,* the paper wrapper for a letter.

◇ *Word origin:* See ENVELOP.

enviable *adj. He is in the enviable position of being able to choose between two highly paid jobs:* worthy of envy, covetable; desirable, advantageous, agreeable, excellent, beneficial, salutary, fortunate, lucky.

envious *adj. The woman was too envious to enjoy her friend's good fortune:* jealous, filled with envy, green with envy, covetous; grudging, resentful, spiteful.

"The greatest harm that you can do unto the envious is to do well." —*John Lyly*

---

environment *n. Mould grows best in a warm, damp environment. A happy family provides a loving environment for children:* medium, habitat, element; surroundings, setting, locale, scene, milieu, environs, atmosphere, situation, background; living conditions.

◇ *Word origin: Environment* and *environs* come from French *environ,* around. Hence *environment* is the total of the things or circumstances around us and the *environs* are the surrounding neighbourhood of a place.

environs *n. pl. However ugly you consider the town to be, its environs are indisputably charming:* outskirts, suburbs, surrounding area, vicinity, adjacent district, purlieus, green belt.

Ant. city centre, core city, inner city; slums.

◇ *Word origin:* See ENVIRONMENT.

envoy *n. Cyprus sent a special envoy to the peace talks. My envoy will pick up the contract at your office tomorrow:* representative, delegate, ambassador, agent, deputy, minister, intermediary, middle man; courier, messenger.

◇ *Usage note:* Although *envoy* is used in a general sense, in the diplomatic service it refers specifically to a diplomatic representative ranking between an ambassador and a chargé d'affaires

◇ *Word origin: Envoy* comes to us from Old French *en voie,* on the way. (*Voie* comes from Latin *via,* road.) Hence an *envoy* is literally someone who has been sent on the way to carry out a mission, as a diplomat.

envy *n.* **1** *He found it hard to suppress his envy of his brother's success:* jealousy, enviousness, resentfulness, resentment, grudging, covetousness, spite, malevolence, *Informal* the green-eyed monster.

—*v.* **2** *It's hard not to envy a woman who has everything:* feel envious toward, be jealous of, resent, be spiteful toward, begrudge.

epic *n.* **1** *The* Aeneid *is one of the great epics of Western culture:* epic poem, historic poem, heroic poem, saga; heroic adventure, drama.

—*adj.* **2** *Ulysses is one of the epic characters of literature:* heroic, great, majestic, imposing, superhuman, noble, exalted; legendary, fabled, storied, fabulous.

◇ *Word origin: Epic* comes from Greek *epos,* extended poetic narrative of the deeds of gods and heroes.

epicure *n. Only an epicure would spend so much time choosing wine and cheese:* gourmet, gastronome, fastidious connoisseur, bon vivant; gourmand, glutton.
◇ *Word origin: Epicure* comes from the name of the Greek philosopher *Epicurus*, who believed that the highest good in life was pleasure.

epicurean *adj.* **1** *The statesman's epicurean life has been harshly criticized:* devoted to luxury, pleasure-seeking, voluptuous, sensual, libertine, hedonistic, self-indulgent, intemperate. **2** *The banquet was an epicurean feast:* fit for an epicure, gourmet, luxurious, lavish, rich, sybaritic, Lucullan.
—n. **3** *Nero was one of history's most famous epicureans:* voluptuary, sensualist, libertine.
Ant. 1, 2 Spartan, austere, simple, plain, humble, modest. **3** Spartan; puritan, ascetic.

epidemic *n.* **1** *Thousands died in the flu epidemic of the First World War:* outbreak, contagion, infection; plague, pestilence.
—adj. **2** *Thanks to the Salk vaccine, polio is no longer an epidemic disease:* dangerously contagious, pandemic, rampant, widespread, rife, prevailing; catching, infectious.
◇ *Word origin: Epidemic* comes from Greek *epidēmia*, prevalence of a disease among the people. The word elements are *epi-* (over) and *dēmos* (people). This term was coined by Hippocrates.

epigram *n. The plays of Oscar Wilde are celebrated for their epigrams:* witty saying, clever comment, bon mot, witticism, quip; maxim, aphorism, adage.

epilogue *n. The book's epilogue hints at what the author thinks the future will bring:* final section, concluding addition, addendum, rider, afterword; concluding speech.
Ant. preface, prologue, introduction.

episode *n.* **1** *The Battle of Hastings was an important episode in our history. We'll forget this little episode, but don't let me catch you lying again!:* milestone, event, occurrence, period; incident, affair, experience, adventure. **2** *One of the most famous episodes in Dickens's* Oliver Twist *is about the little boy who dared to ask for 'more':* scene, passage, part, section, chapter; instalment.

episodic *adj. The book's episodic style made the plot hard to follow:* rambling, wandering, loosely connected, meandering, digressive, discursive, halting, segmented, discontinuous.

epistle *n.* **1** *The courier brought an epistle from the king. The sermon was based on St. Paul's Epistle to the Ephesians:* letter, formal letter, missive, written communication, message; text in letter form.
◇ *Word origin: Epistle* comes from Greek *epi-* (over) + *stellein* (to send), something sent over to another, hence a letter or message.

epithet *n.* **1** *"The Conqueror" was an epithet which described King William I:* appellation, designation, sobriquet, nickname. **2** *He screamed several well-chosen epithets into the phone and slammed down the receiver:* curse, abusive name, insult, expletive, obscenity, blasphemy.
◇ *Word origin: Epithet* comes from Greek *epi-* (upon) + *tithēnai* (to place), hence to place a descriptive name or phrase on a person.

epitome *n. Money and good taste made her the very epitome of fashion:* embodiment, exemplification, representation, essence, résumé, summary, sum and substance; ideal, peak, height.

epoch *n. The Renaissance was an epoch of unparalleled cultural achievement:* period, age, era, time, interval.
◇ *Usage note:* See ERA.
◇ *Word origin: Epoch* comes from Greek *epi-* (over) + *ekhein* (to hold). This combination gives *epokhē*, stoppage, station. Later scientific meanings included "fixed point in time," "position at such a point," "period of vibration." The word has been used in English in its present sense for the past 300 years.

equable *adj.* **1** *A good travelling companion should have an equable disposition:* even-tempered, easy-going, calm, tranquil, serene, placid, unexcitable, unruffled, *Slang* unflappable; good-natured, agreeable, pleasant, sunny. **2** *Italy has a more equable climate than England:* uniform, constant, unvaried, unchanging, even, steady, regular, consistent, dependable, stable, predictable.
Ant. 1 fitful, nervous, tense, excitable; disagreeable, unpleasant, harsh, gruff. **2** variable, fluctuating, changeable, inconsistent, uneven, varied, irregular, unstable, unpredictable.

equal *adj.* **1** *The two men were of equal height. The calories in this piece of bread are equal to those in four cream crackers:* the same, even, like, uniform; identical, one and the same, matched, evenly matched, of a piece; equivalent, proportional, corresponding, correlative, symmetrical, balanced, evenly balanced, tantamount, comparable, commensurate.
—n. **2** *The young reporter was considered to be the equal of many veteran journalists:* peer, match; equivalent, counterpart, parallel, opposite number.
—v. **3** *The debits must equal the credits on the balance sheet:* be the same as, be even with, equate with, be identical to, accord with, agree with, tally with, match, square with, balance with, correspond to, parallel; equalize.
Ant. 1 unequal, different, uneven, unlike, dissimilar, varied, diverse, disparate, disproportionate, incommensurate, irregular, unbalanced. **3** be unequal, be uneven, be different, disagree, diverge.

equality *n.* **1** *Democracy must offer every citizen*

equality: equal opportunity, justice, fairness, impartiality, fair treatment, fair play. **2** *The organization seeks to ensure equality of pay for men and women:* parity, coequality, evenness, sameness, uniformity, equivalency, correspondence; balance, similarity.
Ant. 1 inequality, injustice, unfairness, bias, prejudice. **2** inequality, dissimilarity, difference.

> **Exploring the Word:** *Equal, equality, equivalent,* and *even* all come from Latin *aequalis* and *aequus,* equal, even, which also gives us *adequate,* equal to the task; *egalitarian,* one who believes in political and social equality; *equable,* steady; *equate,* to express as being equal, and *equation,* a mathematical statement expressing the equality of two quantities; *equanimity* (Latin *anima* means life, mind, spirit), evenness of mind, calmness, composure; *equilibrium* (Latin *libra,* balance), equal balance, hence a state of balance, stability; *equator,* the imaginary line round the centre of the earth, so called because day and night are equal when the sun crosses it; and *equinox* (Latin *nox,* night), the time when the hours of daylight and night are equal, about March 21st for the *vernal* (Latin *ver,* spring) *equinox* and about September 21st for the *autumnal equinox.*

equanimity *n. We must keep our equanimity during times of crisis:* calmness, composure, self-possession, steadiness, poise, aplomb, coolness, imperturbability, presence of mind, self-control, tranquillity, sang-froid.
Ant. panic, hysteria, disquiet, perturbation, agitation, discomposure.

equate *v.* **1** *You can't equate investment and profitability:* equal out, even out, match, be equivalent to, be proportionate to, be commensurate, equalize, average, balance. **2** *Don't equate his failure with laziness:* think of as, consider as, draw a parallel between, compare.

equilibrium *n. When the two weights match, the scale is said to be in equilibrium:* balance, stability, equipoise; sense of balance.

equip *v. Equip yourself with everything you'll need on safari:* furnish, supply, fit out, appoint, prepare, provide, provision, accoutre; rig, caparison.
Ant. divest, denude, strip.
◇ *Spelling tip: Equip* follows the rule that words ending in a single consonant with the accent on the last syllable double that consonant before a suffix beginning with a vowel. Hence, *equiP,* but *equiPPed, equiPPing.*
◇ *Word origin: Equip* and *equipment* come from Old French *esquiper,* which in turn comes from Old Norse *skipa,* to fit out a ship. Thus our words *equip* and *ship* have the same root.

equipment *n. A good sleeping-bag is an essential part of every camper's equipment:* apparatus, gear, material, paraphernalia, outfit, matériel, supplies, furnishings, accoutrements, tackle, stuff.
◇ *Word origin:* See EQUIP.

equitable *adj. The lawsuit ended with an equitable settlement:* fair, just, even-handed, impartial, reasonable, proper, due.
Ant. inequitable, unfair, unjust, unreasonable.

equity *n.* **1** *The High Court must judge each case with complete equity:* impartiality, fairmindedness, fairness, justness, even-handedness, reasonableness; fair dealings, justice. **2** *The family has over £10,000 equity in the house:* assets over liabilities, assets after mortgage, cash value; (*loosely*) cash, value, profit, assets, investment.
Ant. 1 unfairness, partiality, bias, prejudice, unreasonableness; injustice.

equivalent *adj.* **1** *An old florin is equivalent to ten new pence:* equal, the same as, comparable, commensurate with, tantamount, corresponding, correspondent, correlative; even, one and the same, of a piece.
—*n.* **2** *That dress cost the equivalent of a week's wages:* equal amount, comparable sum; correspondent, peer, counterpart, parallel, match.
Ant. 1 unequal, dissimilar, incomparable, incommensurate, different.

equivocate *v. Please stop equivocating and give me a straight answer:* evade, avoid the issue, hedge, stall, dodge, beat about the bush, be ambiguous, mince words, prevaricate.
◇ *Word origin: Equivocate* comes from two Latin words, *aequus* (equal, even) and *vox* (voice), to have two equal voices, hence to have a double meaning, to be purposely misleading or vague.

era *n. The birth of Christ ushered in the Christian era:* period, age, epoch, time, interval.
◇ *Usage note:* Only in the specific field of geology do *era, period,* and *epoch* have distinct and specific meanings: an *era* being a long span of time divided into *periods* that may in turn be subdivided into *epochs.* However, despite a lot of argument, *era, epoch,* and *period* may be used interchangeably in general speech and writing: *The jazz age* (or *era,* or *epoch,* or *period*) *of the 1920's, The Elizabethan age* (or *era,* or *epoch,* or *period*). *Age* and *period* seem to be the more common uses, but only because *era* and *epoch* seem more formal. Incidentally, strictly speaking, an *epoch* is not so much a period of time as a point in time during which some drastic change or event takes place that sets the tone for the following age. Thus, technically, *The epoch of New Orleans' jazz bands led to the jazz age.*
◇ *Word origin: Era* comes from Late Latin *aera,* counters for calculation, hence a fixed date from which time is counted.

eradicate *v. Diligent police work will help to eradicate crime:* eliminate, annihilate, exterminate, erase, expunge, extinguish, extirpate, uproot, destroy, wipe out, do away with, abolish, remove, blot out, obliterate.
Ant. establish, originate, implant, engender, create, breed.
◇ *Word origin: Eradicate* comes from Latin *e-* (out) + *radix* (root), hence to pull out by the roots.

erase *v. Erase the pencilled notes in the margins:* wipe away, rub out, eradicate, expunge, remove, eliminate.
Ant. write, draw, print, stamp, mark, record.
◇ *Word origin: Erase* comes from Latin *e-* (out) + *radere* (to scrape), which also gives us *abrade, raze,* and *razor.*

erect *adj.* **1** *The old man had an erect posture:* upright, vertical, straight, unstooped, unbent; stiff, rigid.
—*v.* **2** *The town will erect a monument to its war heroes:* construct, build, put up, raise. **3** *The flag-pole toppled over, and a crane had to be used to erect it:* place upright, stand up, put in a vertical position, set right side up.
Ant. 1 horizontal, supine, leaning, stooped, bent; limp, relaxed, flaccid. **2** raze, demolish, tear down, destroy.

erode *v. Salt spray eroded the bridge. Wind eroded the loose topsoil:* corrode, eat away; wear away, waste, ravage, spoil, disintegrate, despoil.
Ant. build up, strengthen, reinforce.
◇ *Word origin: Erode* literally means to eat away. It comes from Latin *e-* (out, off) + *rodere* (to gnaw), which also gives us our word *rodent,* animal known for gnawing.

erotic *adj. At one time, women's short-sleeved bathing-suits were considered erotic. John Donne wrote several famous erotic poems to his mistress:* unchaste, immodest, ribald, wanton, impure, suggestive, risqué; obscene, indecent, lascivious, lewd, bawdy, salacious; sexual, sexy, sexually stimulating, carnal; amorous, passionate, ardent, amatory, impassioned.
◇ *Word origin: Erotic* comes from Greek *erōs,* sexual love, which in turn corresponds to the name of *Eros,* god of love.

err *v.* **1** *Banks rarely err in totting up the balance in a current account:* make a mistake, slip up, be incorrect, be in error, be inaccurate, miscalculate, mess up. **2** *"To err is human, to forgive divine":* lapse from virtue, transgress, sin, fall from grace, go astray, misbehave, do wrong, do a bad thing.
◇ *Word origin:* See ERROR.

errand *n. The boy had to go to town on an errand for his mother:* mission, task, assignment, undertaking, duty, office, minor chore.
◇ *Word origin:* An *errand* was originally a trip to carry a message and comes from Old English *aerende,* message.

erratic *adj. March weather is often erratic. The boy's erratic behaviour worried his parents:* inconsistent, unpredictable, unstable, shifting, changeable, variable, fitful, capricious, odd, queer, strange, peculiar, unusual, unnatural, aberrant, wayward, abnormal.
Ant. consistent, invariable, regular, undeviating, unchanging, stable, steady, certain, sure, reliable, predictable, dependable; typical, normal, customary, natural.
◇ *Word origin:* See ERROR.

erroneous *adj. The facts are correct, but your conclusion is erroneous:* inaccurate, incorrect, untrue, wrong, false, fallacious, faulty, mistaken, unfounded, unsound, spurious.
Ant. correct, accurate, true, factual, well-founded.
◇ *Word origin:* See ERROR.

error *n. The bill contains an error in addition:* mistake, inaccuracy, miscalculation, fault, flaw, *Slang* bungle, botch, bloomer, howler, boner; misconception, misunderstanding, misapprehension, misinterpretation, fallacy, oversight.
Ant. accuracy, flawlessness, correctness.
◇ *Word origin: Error, err, erroneous,* and *erratic* come from Latin *errare,* to wander, hence a wandering from what is correct, true, or good.

"Error is always in haste." —*Thomas Fuller*

---

ersatz *adj. During the war we made do with ersatz coffee:* synthetic, artificial, imitation, not genuine, counterfeit, sham, fake, phoney, pretended.
Ant. real, genuine, authentic, natural.
◇ *Pronunciation tip:* The English pronunciation of the German word *ersatz* is with the stress on the first syllable.

erstwhile *adj. My erstwhile friend refused to lend me the money:* former, past, bygone, previous.
Ant. current, present.
◇ *Word origin: Erstwhile* comes from Old English *erst* (before) + *while* (time), hence "of former time."

erudite *adj. The professor was an erudite man. The TV interviewer was known for his erudite comments:* learned, well-informed, well-educated, well-versed, literate, well-read, cultured, cultivated, scholarly, thoughtful, intelligent, well-reasoned, wise, sapient.
Ant. uninformed, uneducated, illiterate, unscholarly; shallow, unthinking; rash, ill-advised.
◇ *Word origin: Erudite* comes from Latin *e-* (out) + *rudis* (untrained), literally out of an untrained state, hence trained, educated, very learned.

erupt *v. Mount Vesuvius erupted in 79 A.D., destroying Pompeii. Laughter erupted from the audience:* burst forth, break out, explode, blow up, pour forth, belch forth, discharge, be ejected, throw off, emit, vent, flow forth, gush.

Ant. retain, contain, hold, hold back; be dormant, subside.

eruption *n.* **1** *The eruption of hot springs is a major feature of Iceland's geological history:* discharge, emission, ejection, venting, bursting forth, outburst, outbreak, pouring forth, outpouring, belching forth, flowing forth, gushing, explosion, blowing up. **2** *The patient has a painful skin eruption:* rash, inflammation, breaking out; dermatitis, eczema, pimples, festering.

Ant. 1 retention, repression; dormancy, quiescence; inactivity, subsidence.

escalate *v.* **1** *With prices escalating, a pound buys a lot less than it used to:* rise, increase, advance, ascend, elevate, mount, boost, swell. **2** *The enemy escalated the war by sending more troops to the front:* intensify, step up, expand, extend, enlarge, amplify, magnify, broaden, aggrandize.

Ant. 1 lower, decrease, fall, subside, descend, retreat. **2** de-escalate, lessen, limit, narrow, contract, minimize.

escapade *n. The student's latest escapade consisted of painting the statue purple:* prank, caper, antic, trick, caprice, mischief; lark, fling, spree, adventure, revel, high old time.

◇ *Word origin:* An *escapade* is an escape from restraint or convention. It comes to us from the Spanish word for escape, *escapada.* See ESCAPE.

escape *v.* **1** *Three prisoners escaped from the gaol:* break free, break out, get away, make a get-away, make off, slip away, run away, flee, skip, bolt, cut and run, abscond, steal off, avoid capture. **2** *The skiers only just escaped the avalanche. There's no way to escape doing the work:* avoid danger, get away safely, avert; avoid, elude, dodge, shun, eschew. **3** *Gas is escaping from the broken pipe:* issue, emerge, emanate, be emitted, be discharged, pour forth, flow, stream, gush. **4** *The exact date of our meeting escapes me:* elude, be forgotten by, slip from the memory of.

—*n.* **5** *How did the prisoners manage their escape?:* break-out, exodus, gain of freedom, flight, decampment, get-away. **6** *That was a very lucky escape! The back door is your only means of escape:* avoidance of danger, safe get-away, extrication, deliverance; means of fleeing danger, exit, egress. **7** *Television programmes are a favourite escape for many people:* diversion, distraction, evasion of worry, avoidance of problems, way of getting away from it all. **8** *The escape of oil caused the motor to break down:* discharge, emission, outflow, leakage, seepage, outpour, issuing forth, pouring forth, outburst, egress, efflux, effluence.

Ant. 1 capture, recapture, apprehend; stay. **2** meet, encounter, face; seek, hunt, chase; trap, catch. **3** retain, hold, contain; inject, pour in. **4** come to mind, be on the tip of one's tongue; remember, recollect. **5** capture, recapture, apprehension. **8** retention, containment; injection, influx.

◇ *Word origin: Escape* comes from Latin *ex-* (out) + *cappa* (cloak, cape), "out of one's cloak," hence to throw off restraint, to get away from confinement.

eschew *v. Eschew fattening foods if you want to lose weight:* abstain from, forgo, give up, forbear, avoid, shun, steer clear of, fight shy of.

Ant. seek, chase after, hunt out; indulge in, welcome, embrace.

escort *n.* **1** *The king's escort totalled 50 men:* accompanying guard, guard, protective screen; attendant body, retinue, cortège, entourage, attendants, company. **2** *Her cousin will be her escort to the dance:* squire; companion, conductor, chaperon.

—*v.* **3** *Let me escort you to the door:* conduct, guide, lead the way, take, usher; squire, chaperon.

esoteric *adj.* **1** *Some fields of science seem hopelessly esoteric to the layman:* incomprehensible, abstruse, recondite, arcane, cryptic, inscrutable, mysterious, obscure. **2** *The tribe has an esoteric ritual that no outsider may witness:* secret, undisclosed, private, confidential, inviolable, hidden, concealed, covert, veiled, cloaked; mystical, occult.

Ant. 1 obvious, clear, plain, simple. **2** public, open, exoteric.

◇ *Word origin:* An *esoteric* thing is understood only by an inner circle of people. The word comes from Greek *esōterikos,* inner, innermost.

especial *adj.* See SPECIAL.

especially *adv.* **1** *The cabinet was made especially for the dining-room:* expressly, specifically, exclusively; principally, particularly, primarily. **2** *The sunsets in the Pacific are especially beautiful:* exceptionally, outstandingly, particularly, uncommonly, extraordinarily, unusually, singularly, notably, really, intensely.

◇ *Usage note:* See SPECIAL.

espouse *v. The council will espouse the cause of conservation:* adopt, take up, embrace; support, champion, back, advocate, promote, further, side with, stand up for, express belief in, boost.

Ant. reject, renounce, abjure; denounce, hinder, obstruct, block, thwart.

esprit de corps *n. An enthusiastic coach can give a team great esprit de corps:* team spirit, group unity, group enthusiasm, group pride, high morale, solidarity.

◇ *Word origin: Esprit de corps* is a French term used in English, and literally means "spirit of the corps."

essay *n.* **1** *The homework consisted of writing an essay on "What Democracy Means to Me":* short composition, theme, paper; dissertation, treatise, tract, editorial, article, commentary, critique. **2** *His first essay at flying an*

aeroplane was a near disaster: attempt, effort, try, venture, endeavour, bid, undertaking, experiment.
—*v.* **3** *Who will essay the crossing first?:* try, attempt, take on, undertake, venture, make an effort at, take a crack at, have a go at, make a stab at.

essence *n.* **1** *The very essence of justice lies in the right of every man to a fair trial. The essence of his long speech was that we must all work harder:* basic quality, essential character, quintessence, nature, principle, substance, life-blood, spirit, heart, core, soul; meaning, significance, gist, point, pith. **2** *Use essence of turpentine to remove the paint spot:* concentrate, tincture, elixir, spirits, extract. **3** *Her favourite essence smells like gardenias:* perfume, scent, cologne, fragrance, toilet water.

essential *adj.* **1** *Water is essential to the growth of crops:* indispensable, requisite, necessary, needed, crucial, vital. **2** *The essential purpose of a holiday is to allow you to relax:* basic, fundamental; main, key, principal, cardinal, leading, important, inherent, intrinsic, ingrained.
—*n.* **3** *Petroleum is an essential of modern industry. The crash course teaches the essentials of French in six weeks:* basic need, requisite, necessity, indispensable element, key element, vital part, primary constituent; basics, fundamentals, rudiments, principles.
Ant. 1, 2 dispensable, superfluous, unimportant, incidental, unnecessary, immaterial, secondary, minor, lesser, minimal, trivial. **3** accessory, extra, option.

establish *v.* **1** *Father established this business forty years ago:* found, set up, bring about, bring into existence, form, organize, create, begin, start, inaugurate, institute, open, initiate. **2** *The young man established himself as an expert on foreign stamps:* gain recognition for, win acceptance for, make secure, install, settle, sustain, fix, implant. **3** *The new evidence establishes the suspect's guilt:* prove, show, confirm, verify, corroborate, authenticate, sustain, uphold, validate, put to rest any doubts about; justify, warrant.
Ant. 1 close, disband, dissolve, liquidate, eradicate, destroy. **2** uproot, unsettle, dethrone. **3** refute, invalidate, deny, cast doubt on, bring into question, throw suspicion upon.

establishment *n.* **1** *The committee will work toward the establishment of a school for the handicapped:* establishing, setting up, instituting, founding, bringing about, formation, development, organization, creation, building. **2** *The mill is the oldest establishment in the town:* business, company, concern, firm, outfit, organization, institution, building, plant, factory, office. **3** **Establishment.** *The student protesters blame the Establishment for all social problems:* traditional leaders, entrenched leaders, ruling class; established order, entrenched social order, system.
Ant. 1 closing, dissolution, disbanding, liquidation, eradication, destruction. **3** revolutionaries, rebels, activists, anarchists, radicals, upstarts.

estate *n.* **1** *The estate consists of the main house, servants' quarters, stables, and 200 acres of woods:* country estate, large residential property, landed property, manor, country mansion. **2** *He left an estate of over a million pounds to be divided among his children:* assets at death, assets, fortune, wealth, money, property, material possessions, belongings; inheritance, legacy, bequest, will. **3** *At the age of 18 a boy reaches a man's estate:* state, station, condition, status, situation, period of life; rank, grade, class, order.

"It is the first part of intelligence to recognize our precarious estate in life."
—*Robert Louis Stevenson*

---

esteem *v.* **1** *History esteems Sigmund Freud as the father of psycho-analysis:* venerate, revere, hold in high regard, value, honour, think highly of, attach importance to, set store by, prize, treasure, admire, respect, cherish, look up to. **2** *I should esteem it gracious of you to join us for dinner:* consider, regard, believe, think, hold, deem, judge, reckon, calculate.
—*n.* **3** *I hold your honesty in the highest esteem:* regard, respect, favourable opinion, estimate, approval, admiration, veneration, appreciation, reverence.
Ant. 1 disdain, scorn, disparage, deprecate; decry, detest, despise, dislike, abominate, abhor, loathe; undervalue, belittle, underrate; devaluate, degrade. **3** disrespect, contempt, disdain, scorn, depreciation; hate, aversion, dislike, detestation, abhorrence, repugnance, loathing.
◇ *Word origin: Esteem* comes from Latin *aestimare,* to value, evaluate, which also gives us *estimate.*

"Everything that man esteems
Endures a moment or a day.
Love's pleasure drives his love away,
The painter's brush consumes his dreams."
—*W. B. Yeats*

---

estimable *adj. Robert Frost was an estimable poet:* highly regarded, worthy of esteem, worthwhile, admired, treasured, prized, good, important, respected, revered, praiseworthy, commendable, laudable, honourable, admirable.
Ant. scorned, disdained, disparaged, deprecated, despised, disliked; unworthy, undeserving, inferior, bad.

estimate *v.* **1** *The dealer estimated the worth of the used car at £350:* evaluate, reckon, calculate, judge, appraise, value, assess, assay, guess. **2** *The archaeologist estimated that the vase was 3,500 years old:* think, consider, believe, surmise, guess, conjecture, opine, conclude. —*n.* **3** *The expert's estimate is that the painting is worth £2,500:* evaluation, estimation, assessment, appraisal, calculation, assay; opinion, judgement, reckoning, thinking, surmise, view, belief.

◇ *Pronunciation tip: Estimate* has two different pronunciations, one for the noun and one for the verb. The noun, an *estimate,* is pronounced *ES-ti-muht.* The verb, to *estimate,* is pronounced *ES-ti-mate.*

◇ *Word origin:* See ESTEEM.

estimation *n. According to the estimation of the critics this is the best film of the year:* opinion, judgement, appraisal, estimate, view, belief, consideration, evaluation, reckoning.

"The angels keep their ancient places;
Turn but a stone, and start a wing!
'Tis ye, 'tis your estrangèd faces,
That miss the many-splendoured thing."
—*Francis Thompson*

---

estrange *v. Strong political differences estranged the two old friends:* alienate, drive apart, disaffect, part, destroy the affection of; antagonize, make hostile.

Ant. unite, join, link, bind; reconcile; conciliate.

estuary *n. The boat anchored in the estuary:* tidal basin, inlet, arm of the sea; river mouth, firth.

◇ *Word origin:* Technically, an *estuary* is that part of a river where its current meets the sea and becomes influenced by the tides. The word comes from Latin *aestuarium,* tidal channel, from *aestus,* tide.

etc., &c. *The cat show featured Persians, Siamese, Abyssinians, etc.:* and others, and the rest, and so forth, and so on.

◇ *Usage note: Etc.* is the legitimate abbreviation for *et cetera* and may be used in all contexts; the full form is never necessary. *Et cetera* (or *caetera*) is Latin for "and others" and also can mean "and so forth." You should never write *and etc.* Also, never use *etc.* when only one item has been stated; use it only after two or more similar items have been listed. Thus, *He likes football, rugby, etc.,* not *He likes football, etc.*

◇ *Pronunciation tip:* The first *t* in *et cetera* is clearly pronounced *eT cetera.*

eternal *adj.* **1** *The vicar spoke of the soul's eternal life:* lasting for ever, everlasting, infinite, timeless, endless, immortal, without end. **2** *I can't stand any more of her eternal nagging:* continual, unending, never-ending, perpetual, ceaseless, constant, endless, interminable, abiding, persistent, relentless, uninterrupted.

Ant. 1 transient, transitory, fleeting, perishable, finite, evanescent, ephemeral, mortal, temporal. **2** occasional, infrequent, rare, spasmodic, irregular, scattered, random, temporary, patchy, on-and-off.

◇ *Word origin: Eternal* and *eternity* come from Latin *aeternalis* and *aeternitas.* Their base is *aevum,* age.

eternity *n.* **1** *The stars will exist throughout eternity. The dull play seemed to last an eternity:* for ever, infinity, time without end, endlessness, ages and ages. **2** *The minister's sermon was about the joys of eternity:* everlasting life, immortality, the here-after, the next world, the after life, the world to come; Heaven, paradise, Zion, New Jerusalem.

Ant. 1 instant, moment, a second, a split second. **2** the here and now, life on earth, mortality.

◇ *Word origin:* See ETERNAL.

ethereal *adj. Her ethereal beauty couldn't be captured by the greatest painter:* sublime, celestial, exquisite, aerial, airy, unearthly, unworldly, delicate; elusive, rare, rarefied.

Ant. earthly, mundane, worldly; statuesque, monumental, solid.

◇ *Word origin: Ethereal* comes from Greek *aithēr,* ether, the heaven.

ethical *adj. Forcing the farmer to sell his land wasn't illegal, but it wasn't ethical either:* moral, decent, virtuous, upright, right, proper, fitting, correct, just, fair, above-board, straight-forward, open and above-board. *Slang* kosher.

Ant. unethical, underhand, shady, improper, unfair, low-down, nefarious, unbecoming, unseemly, indecorous, immoral, indecent.

"An act has no ethical quality whatever unless it be chosen out of several all equally possible."
—*William James*

---

ethics *n. pl. (Sometimes sing.) Her ethics would never allow her to betray a friend. The Protestant ethic is that each man must work for his own sustenance:* moral code, rules of conduct, moral principle, principles, morality, moral philosophy, sense of right and wrong, sense of duty, conscience.

◇ *Word origin: Ethics* comes from Greek *ēthikos,* moral, ethical. (The plural *ēthika* became the title, "Ethics," of several treatises on the subject — Aristotle's *Nicomachean Ethics* is the most famous of them.) The basic word is *ēthos,* character, disposition, characteristic spirit, which of course gives us our word *ethos.*

ethnic *adj. Every country has its ethnic dishes:* native, national, indigenous; racial, cultural; original, unique.

◇ *Word origin: Ethnic* comes from Greek *ethnos,* nation.

etiquette *n. The book on etiquette detailed the*

wedding procedure: rules of behaviour, amenities, protocol, conventions, behaviour, proprieties, civilities, manners, usage, decorum, politeness, courtesy; gentility, good form, good taste.
Ant. impropriety, boorishness, rudeness, impoliteness, vulgarity, indecorum.
◇ *Word origin: Etiquette* comes from French *étiquette*, originally a soldier's billet for lodgings, later an identification label or ticket. Still later, the word came to designate the complex body of ceremonial rules governing the royal court of France. Finally, it entered English in its present sense about 1750 and was much used by such writers as Lord Chesterfield and Horace Walpole.

Eucharist *n. Members of the congregation took the Eucharist:* Communion, Holy Communion. Sacrament of the Lord's Supper, Mass; consecrated wafer, consecrated elements of bread and wine; (*when given to a person in danger of dying*) viaticum.
◇ *Word origin: Eucharist* comes from Greek *eukharistia*, thanksgiving, which in the usage of first the Greek and then the Latin Church Fathers acquired its present sense of "Sacrament of the Lord's Supper." The original word may still be heard in the Modern Greek for "thank you": *evkharistō!*

eulogize *v. The deceased was eulogized by his closest friend:* praise highly, laud, panegyrize, extol, glorify, acclaim, hail, exalt, magnify; compliment, boost, commend, pay tribute to.
Ant. malign, defame, vilify, slander, libel, criticize, condemn.

eulogy *n. His obituary in the* Times *was a great eulogy:* oration of praise, praise of the dead, encomium, panegyric; high praise, tribute, homage, hosanna, acclamation, laudation, citation, paean, plaudit.
Ant. condemnation, criticism; vilification, defamation, aspersion, calumny, slander, libel.
◇ *Word origin: Eulogy* and *eulogize* come from Greek *eu-* (well) + *legein* (to speak), hence to speak well of someone.

euphemism *n. "Maiden lady" is a euphemism for "old maid":* mild expression, restrained expression, inoffensive expression, delicate term, refined term; prudish phrase, over-delicacy, over-refinement, prudishness.

evacuate *v.* **1** *When the fire-drill starts, students will evacuate the building:* leave withdraw from, vacate; abandon, desert, forsake. **2** *The fireman evacuated the guests from the burning hotel:* remove, move out, take out, order out.
Ant. 1 enter, go in, occupy. **2** take in, move in.

evade *v. The thief evaded the police by dodging into an alley. The stranger evaded all questions about his past:* avoid, dodge, elude, steer clear of, duck, parry, shun, escape, eschew, side-step, circumvent, fend off, hedge; equivocate.
Ant. face, face up to, meet face to face, confront; encounter, meet, meet head-on.

evaluate *v. The teacher evaluated the performance of each student:* appraise, rate, assess, weigh, judge, estimate, value, assay.

evaporate *v.* **1** *The spot of water evaporated in the sun:* dry up, vaporize, melt away; dehydrate, dessicate. **2** *The magician made a handkerchief evaporate into thin air. When the fight was over the crowd evaporated:* disappear, vanish, fade away, melt away, dissolve, evanesce; scatter, dispel, dissipate.
Ant. 1 condense, concentrate; reconstitute, reconstruct. **2** appear, materialize, emerge, gather, collect, converge.
◇ *Word origin: Evaporate* comes from Latin *e-* (out, away) + *vapor* (vapour, steam), to remove moisture or liquid.

evasion *n. The witness's evasion of the question was obvious:* avoidance, dodging, eluding, attempt to escape, ducking, shrinking from, shunning, side-stepping, circumventing.
Ant. confronting, facing up to, meeting head-on; frankness, candour.

evasive *adj. The politician's evasive answers infuriated the reporters:* elusive, elusory, ambiguous, equivocal, equivocating, dodging, hedging, devious, dissembling, shifty, deceptive, misleading, deceitful.
Ant. candid, straightforward, frank, direct, open, honest, truthful, guileless.

even *adj.* **1** *An even road makes driving easy. Plant the rose-bushes in an even row:* level, smooth, flat, plane; plumb, straight, parallel, flush, true, uniform. **2** *The plane flew at an even speed:* constant, regular, steady, uniform, unvarying, unwavering. **3** *Pour even amounts of milk into each cup. You buy the tickets next time and we'll be even:* equal, identical, the same, uniform; equitable, level, matching, balanced, square. **4** *A teacher should have an even disposition:* even-tempered, calm, steady, placid, unruffled, unexcitable; balanced, fair, just, dispassionate, impartial, unbiased.
Ant. 1-4 uneven. **1** wavy, undulating, rough, bumpy; crooked, curving, twisting, turning; slanted, awry, irregular. **2** variable, changing, fluctuating, non-uniform, irregular. **3** unequal, different, unidentical, inequitable, unbalanced. **4** emotional, hot-tempered, quick-tempered, excitable, easily ruffled, biased, unfair, unjust, prejudiced.

evening *n. Evening in the country is a very peaceful time:* sundown, sunset, twilight, dusk, gloaming; close of day; eve, eventide, nightfall.
Ant. dawn, dawning, sunrise, daybreak, daylight, morning.

event *n.* **1** *Winning the scholarship was a great event in the boy's life:* occurrence, momentous occurrence, milestone; occasion, episode, happening, experience, incident. **2** *Track and field events are held at the new sports ground:* contest, competition, tournament, game, bout.

eventful *adj. The birthday party and the film have made this an eventful day. The High Court's decision was an eventful one:* noteworthy, notable, memorable, thrilling, exciting, unforgettable; momentous, historic, epoch-making, important, significant, weighty, consequential; critical, crucial, fateful.
Ant. ordinary, dull, unexciting, uninteresting, trivial, trifling, unimportant, insignificant, inconsequential, irrelevant.

eventual *adj. My father bought a country house for his eventual retirement:* future, prospective, coming, later; impending, imminent, ultimate, final; following, consequent, resulting, ensuing.
Ant. past, previous, prior.

eventually *adv. The house will have to be repainted eventually:* in the course of time, sometime, one day, ultimately, sooner or later, finally, in the end.
Ant. never; immediately, at once.

everlasting *adj.* **1** *Heaven will give him everlasting peace:* eternal, immortal, perpetual, lasting, never-ending, infinite. **2** *The poet wrote of the beauty of the everlasting hills:* long-lasting, ever-living, imperishable, durable, indestructible, undying, continual. **3** *Your everlasting complaints annoy everyone:* constant, endless, ceaseless, unceasing, incessant, perpetual, continuous, interminable, wearisome, tiresome, tedious.
Ant. 1, 2 transitory, temporary, passing, fleeting, ephemeral, momentary, short-lived, transient. **3** intermittent, occasional.

everyday *adj.* **1** *Cooking breakfast is an everyday job:* daily, quotidian. **2** *After church, change into your everyday clothes:* routine, ordinary, common, commonplace, workaday, usual, customary, familiar, established, regular; conventional, stock, run-of-the-mill, dull, mundane, unimaginative; trite, hackneyed, stereotyped.
Ant. 1 occasional, infrequent, irregular, now and then, incidental, periodic, sporadic. **2** original, imaginative, extraordinary, uncommon, unusual, special, best, individual, exciting, interesting, fantastic, outlandish.

everywhere *adv. Flags flew everywhere to celebrate the Jubilee:* in every place, in all places, far and wide, far and near; extensively, ubiquitously; universally, all over, the world over; throughout, to the four winds.
Ant. nowhere, here and there.

"Man is born free, and everywhere he is in chains." —*J. J. Rousseau*

---

evict *v. The landlord evicted the tenant for not paying the rent:* turn out, remove, dispossess, dislodge, expel, eject, oust, kick out.

evidence *n. The suspect's fingerprints on the gun were the main evidence against him. Her smile was sufficient evidence of her happiness:* proof, facts, material proof, data; documentation, corroboration, confirmation, affirmation, authentication; substantiation; exhibit, testimony, indication, sign, token; illustration, exemplification.

evident *adj. The applause made it evident that the play was a hit:* clear, plain, obvious, apparent, manifest, conspicuous, perceptible, noticeable; certain, patent, unmistakable, unquestionable, undeniable, plain as the nose on your face; visible, tangible.
Ant. unclear, obscure, inconspicuous, imperceptible, doubtful, vague, questionable, uncertain, dubious; secret, covert, hidden, undisclosed, unknown, concealed, undiscovered.

evidently *adv. He's been sniffling all day and evidently has a cold:* apparently, assumedly, to all appearances; obviously, clearly, plainly, certainly, unquestionably, unmistakably, undeniably, doubtless, without a doubt.

evil *adj.* **1** *Shakespeare characterizes Richard III as an evil king:* bad, wicked, iniquitous, immoral, sinful, base, unprincipled, sinister, malevolent, malicious, malignant, vile, villainous, vicious, nefarious, heinous.
—n. **2** *The curate preached against evil:* sin, wickedness, immorality, wrongdoing, vice, baseness, iniquity, depravity, corruption.
Ant. 1 good, honourable, worthy, moral, exemplary wholesome, upright, virtuous, benevolent, kind, human, humane, merciful, sympathetic, benign. **2** good, goodness, virtue, morality, righteousness.

evoke *v. The book evoked memories of his boyhood:* bring forth, call forth, call up, summon, invoke, conjure up, elicit, induce, produce, suggest, stimulate, provoke, excite, stir, arouse, rouse, waken, awaken.
Ant. repress, suppress, restrain, hold back, inhibit, stifle, curb, check, crush; prevent, subdue, silence, stop, extinguish.

evolution *n. The 20th century has seen a startling evolution in medical research:* growth, development, unfolding, rise, increase, expansion, enlargement; maturation, fruition.
Ant. deterioration, withering, contraction, shrinking, decrease, diminution, falling off.

evolve *v. The simple plan evolved into a complicated scheme:* develop, grow, expand, enlarge, increase, unfold, unroll, mature.
Ant. deteriorate, wither, contract, shrink, decrease.

exact *adj.* **1** *Please give your exact age:* correct, accurate, specific, explicit, precise, right, true; clear-cut, unequivocal, to the letter, literal. **2** *Mathematics is an exact science:* meticulous, painstaking, exacting, strict; careful, punctilious, scrupulous, systematic, methodical.
—v. **3** *The victors exacted ransom for their hostages:* demand, claim, extract, wrest, force, require, compel, squeeze, mulct, extort.

Ant. 1 approximate, imprecise, inaccurate, incorrect. 2 sloppy, careless, slovenly, devil-may-care.

exacting *adj.* 1 *General Montgomery was an exacting commander:* demanding, meticulous, unsparing, critical, strict, rigid, unbending, stern, severe, harsh, hard, hard-headed, hard-nosed, no-nonsense. 2 *Volunteers are needed for an exacting assignment:* demanding, hard, arduous, difficult, tough, trying, strenuous.

Ant. 1 easy, easy-going, carefree, nonchalant, devil-may-care, soft, soft-hearted, lenient, permissive. 2 easy, effortless, undemanding.

exactly *adv.* 1 *Where exactly is the pain?:* precisely, specifically, explicitly; accurately, correctly, truly, literally. 2 *You may do exactly as you like:* just, entirely, absolutely, fully, wholly, precisely, quite, strictly. 3 *Exactly, we agree:* quite so, that's right, indeed, of course, precisely, certainly, assuredly, just so.

Ant. 1 approximately, loosely, more or less; inaccurately, incorrectly, vaguely.

exaggerate *v. The fisherman exaggerated the size of his catch:* overstate, magnify, amplify, hyperbolize, enlarge on, stretch, embroider, overdo.

Ant. understate, minimize, disparage, qualify.

◇ *Spelling tip:* Remember that there is a double *g* in this word. Don't forget to *exaggerate* the number of *g*'s to two: *exaGGerate.*

◇ *Word origin: Exaggerate* comes from Latin *ex-* (out) + *aggerare* (to heap), hence to heap to a greater size, heap on size or importance.

exalt *v.* 1 *The humbly born Roman was exalted by his emperor:* laud, praise, pay tribute to, honour, applaud, acclaim, cheer, commend, make much of; glorify, magnify, worship. 2 *The orchestra gave a performance that truly exalted the audience:* uplift, elevate, inspire, ennoble, elate.

Ant. 1 damn, condemn, disgrace, degrade, dishonour, shame, debase, demean, lower, humble, humiliate, disparage, depreciate, belittle. 2 depress, dispirit, dishearten, weary; dismay, appal.

◇ *Usage note:* See EXULT.

◇ *Word origin: Exalt* comes from Latin *ex-* (up) + *altus* (high), to lift up, glorify. The Latin *altus*, high, also gives us *altitude* (height above sea-level) and *alto* (the highest male singing voice).

exaltation *n.* 1 *The soldier's victories soon led to his exaltation in rank:* elevation, promotion, uplift, raising; eulogizing, panegyric, honour, dignity, glory; grandeur, nobility; worship, deification. 2 *Her exaltation at visiting the Vatican lasted many days:* elation, ecstasy, rapture, transport, happiness, bliss.

Ant. 1 damnation, condemnation, depreciation, debasement, belittling, degradation, dishonouring, humiliation. 2 depression, dejection, melancholia, gloom, despondency, blues; sorrow, sadness, misery.

exalted *adj.* 1 *Kings are the most exalted of men. The poet Milton wrote in an exalted style:* high-ranking, noble, lordly, august, lofty, illustrious; magnificent, glorious, grand, elevated, dignified, honourable, notable. 2 *The play put us in an exalted mood:* ecstatic, rapturous, inspired, excited, happy, elated, blissful, heightened, lofty, uplifted.

Ant. 1 lowly, vulgar, ignoble, base, modest, unassuming; low-born, low-bred, plebeian, servile. 2 depressed, dejected, glum, gloomy, despondent, blue; sorrowful, sad, low, miserable.

examination *n.* 1 *The surveyor made a thorough examination of the house:* inspection, scrutiny, survey, perusal, looking over, analysis, investigation, review, study, assay, audit; physical check-up. 2 *The examination consisted of 50 true-or-false questions:* exam, test, review, quiz; *(variously)* oral, viva voce, entrance, G.C.E., tripos, final.

examine *v.* 1 *Examine the merchandise carefully:* look over, inspect, scrutinize, view, survey, observe, peruse, scan. 2 *Examine the facts carefully:* study, probe, look into, inquire into, consider, investigate, explore, ponder, review; audit, take stock of. 3 *The teacher examined the students in chemistry. The lawyer examined the witness:* test, quiz; question, query, interrogate, pump, grill.

Ant. 1 ignore, overlook. 2 accept at face value.

◇ *Word origin: Examine* comes from Latin *examen*, the tongue of a scale, hence a weighing, consideration, or *examination.*

example *n. Notre Dame cathedral is an outstanding example of Gothic architecture:* sample, illustration, representation, exemplification, specimen, case in point, archetype, prototype, pattern, model, ideal, standard, exemplar, paragon, paradigm.

Ant. anomaly, paradox; abnormality, aberration, contradiction, incongruity.

◇ *Word origin: Example* and *sample* are really the same word. They come from Latin *exemplum*, model, instance, *example.*

"The first great gift we can bestow on others is a good example." —*Thomas Morell*

---

exasperate *v. Constant interruptions exasperated the speaker:* irritate, annoy, rile, irk, anger, madden, incense, infuriate, enrage; rankle, aggravate, provoke, try the patience of; offend, ruffle, chafe, harass, vex, pique, bother; *Slang* turn off.

Ant. mollify, pacify, placate, appease, propitiate, conciliate; calm, assuage, tranquillize.

excavate *v. The engineers excavated a chamber in the mountain. Heinrich Schliemann excavated the ruins of ancient Troy:* make a hole in, hollow

out, tunnel, dig, dig out, scoop out; gouge, mine, quarry, cut out; burrow, furrow, groove; unearth, uncover, dig up.
Ant. fill, fill in, fill up, bury, cover up.
◇ *Word origin: Excavate* comes from Latin *ex-* (out) + *cavus* (hollow), which also gives us *cave, cavern,* and *cavity.*

exceed *v.* **1** *The police will stop you if you exceed the speed limit:* go beyond, go over, pass, overdo, outreach, outrun, outpace, outstrip, overshoot, transcend, surmount. **2** *In his enthusiasm for training he exceeded all the other footballers in the team:* excel, predominate, surpass, come first, be superior, outrival, outrank.
Ant. 1 stay within, keep in, keep under. **2** fail, be inferior.
◇ *Spelling tip:* Only three common words in the English language end in *-ceed: exceed, proceed,* and *succeed* (along with their common forms, such as *exceeds, exceeding, proceeded, succeeding,* etc.). Learn these three *-ceed* words now: *exCEED, proCEED, sucCEED.*
◇ *Usage note:* See ACCEDE.

exceedingly *adv. The children were exceedingly well behaved:* very, extremely, greatly, especially, notably, very highly; vastly, enormously, outstandingly, impressively, eminently, pre-eminently, supremely, surpassingly, immeasurably, excessively, superlatively, extraordinarily, unwontedly, unusually, inordinately, amazingly, astonishingly.

excel *v. In international competition, the Australians excel at tennis:* exceed, surpass, prevail, predominate, rank first, tower above, outstrip, outrival, outdo, walk off with the honours, *Slang* take the cake.
Ant. fail, fall behind, fall short, be inadequate, be inferior to.
◇ *Spelling tip: Excel* doubles its final *l* in *exceLLing* and *exceLLed* and in the related words *exceLLence* and *exceLLent.*

excellence *n. Swiss watches are renowned for their excellence:* high quality, quality, superiority, perfection, greatness, merit, eminence, pre-eminence, transcendence, distinction.
Ant. inferiority, poor quality, imperfection, deficiency; fault, blemish, defect, flaw, shortcoming, inadequacy, failing, frailty.

excellent *adj. Franz Liszt was a first class composer and pianist:* outstanding, superior, superlative, superb, classic, choice, capital, sterling, great, tremendous, fine, top-notch, first-rate, first-class; admirable, notable; matchless, peerless, pre-eminent, exemplary; *Informal* prime, super, the tops, A–1.
Ant. bad, poor, imperfect, inferior, terrible, awful, substandard, second-rate, second-class, below par, incompetent, inexpert, unskilled, faulty, *Slang* lousy.

except *prep.* **1** *Put everything except the vase in the box:* excepting, excluding, exclusive of, but, save, saving, other than, barring, besides.
—*v.* **2** *The students were excepted from taking the exam:* exempt, excuse, exclude, omit, eliminate; bar, ban, shut out, enjoin, remove, pass over, count out, disallow, reject.
Ant. 1 including. **2** include, reckon, count.
◇ *Usage note:* See ACCEPT.

exception *n.* **1** *All the houses in the row are brick, with the exception of the corner house:* exclusion, exemption, omission, elimination, removal, debarment separation, segregation, seclusion, isolation; leaving out, shutting out, disallowment; rejection, renunciation, repudiation. **2** *This case is an exception to the rule:* deviation, special case, anomaly, rarity, inconsistency, irregularity, oddity, peculiarity, difference.
Ant. 1 inclusion, taking in, counting. **2** consistency, regularity, conformity.

exceptional *adj.* **1** *Such hot weather is exceptional in October:* unusual, extraordinary, unique, uncommon, rare, singular, irregular, anomalous, abnormal, peculiar, unwonted, unnatural, queer, odd, aberrant, unprecedented, unheard of, phenomenal, freakish. **2** *The film was good but not exceptional:* better than average, outstanding, superior, excellent, first-class; wonderful, terrific, great, marvellous, special, extraordinary, remarkable, incomparable, inimitable, *Slang* out of this world.
Ant. 1 common, ordinary, usual, normal, typical, regular, natural, expected, customary, familiar. **2** average, mediocre, bad, terrible, awful, second-rate; *Slang* lousy, crummy, so-so.

excerpt *n. The parson read an excerpt from the Book of Genesis:* extract, selection, portion, section, piece, part, abstract, quotation, quoted passage.
◇ *Word origin: Excerpt* comes from Latin *ex-* (out) + *carpere* (to pluck, pick). Hence the Roman word for an extract or passage from a book or writing was *excerptum,* excerpt.

excess *n.* **1** *The child had an excess of energy:* surplus, over-abundance, superabundance, undue amount, too much, over-supply, surfeit, plethora; profusion, fullness, lavishness, avalanche, flood, inundation, overflow; glut, repletion.
—*adj.* **2** *The excess furniture was stored in the cellar:* surplus, extra, excessive, overflow; remainder, residue, spare.
Ant. 1 deficiency, lack, shortage, scarcity, dearth, paucity, inadequacy, insufficiency, scantness. **2** insufficient, inadequate, scanty, scarce.
◇ *Usage note:* See ACCESS.

excessive *adj. Excessive spending can lead to bankruptcy:* excess, over-abundant, undue, too much, profuse; extreme, superfluous, extravagant, immoderate, inordinate, exaggerated, unreasonable, needless, unnecessary, disproportionate, senseless.

Ant. insufficient, deficient, inadequate, lacking, wanting, scarce, meagre, scanty, scant, skimpy, sparse.

exchange *v.* **1** *The trapper will exchange furs for flour, coffee, and gunpowder:* trade, swap, barter, trade off, convert into. **2** *My cousins and I always exchange Christmas gifts:* swap, interchange, give and take, reciprocate.
—*n.* **3** *There was an exchange of greetings among the old friends:* interchange, reciprocity, give and take; trade, swap, switch, bandying, tit for tat, *Latin* quid pro quo.
Ant. 1 keep, hold on to.

excise[1] *n. Alcohol and tobacco are subject to excise:* tax, duty, surcharge.
◇ *Word origin: Excise*[1] comes from the Latin phrase *ad censum*, "taxable."

"*Excise.* A hateful tax levied upon commodities." —*Samuel Johnson*

---

excise[2] *v. The surgeon excised the abscess with great skill:* remove, cut out, cut off, eradicate, extract, pluck out.
◇ *Word origin: Excise*[2] comes from Latin *ex-*, out + *caedere*, to cut.

excite *v.* **1** *News of the discovery of oil in the North Sea excited the nation:* thrill, electrify, galvanize, rouse, arouse, spur on, stir up, agitate, move, stimulate, energize, kindle, fire, inflame, provoke, animate, incite; titillate, *Slang*: get a kick out of. **2** *The professor's lecture on Bernard Shaw excited our interest:* evoke, elicit, waken, awaken, stimulate, whet, pique, arouse.
Ant. 1 dull, lull, bore, soothe, quiet, calm, pacify. **2** allay, appease, mollify, diminish; deaden, kill, quench.

excitement *n. The canoe trip over the rapids was full of excitement:* thrill, adventure, *Slang* kicks; stimulation, interest, animation, enthusiasm, elation, action, activity, furore, ferment, commotion, ado, turmoil, tumult, agitation, flurry, flutter, frenzy, stir.
Ant. serenity, peace; inactivity, lethargy, sluggishness; dullness, boredom.

exciting *adj. That was the most exciting film of the year:* thrilling, electrifying, breath-taking, hair-raising, spine-tingling, rousing, sensational, stirring, impelling, provocative, stimulating, moving, affecting, inspiring, dazzling, zestful; titillating, spicy, risqué.
Ant. unexciting, uninteresting, dull, boring, monotonous, wearisome, humdrum, drab, dreary, soporific.

exclaim *v. "You're a liar!" she exclaimed:* cry out, call out, ejaculate, shout, yell, bellow, howl, proclaim, vociferate.

exclamation *n. With an exclamation of surprise she recognized her long-lost relative:* ejaculation, vociferation, outcry, cry, shout, yell, shriek, bellow, howl, squeal, screech, yelp; interjection, expletive.
Ant. whisper, mutter, murmur, mumble; statement, question.

exclude *v.* **1** *The men's club voted to exclude women:* keep out, bar, ban, shut the door on, shut out, prevent entrance of, blackball, boycott, reject, prohibit, forbid, refuse; evict, remove, banish, expel, oust, eject, throw out. **2** *The doctor excluded food poisoning as the cause of the illness:* rule out, omit, except, set aside, leave out; repudiate.
Ant. 1 invite, welcome; admit, include, accept.

> **Exploring the Word**: *Exclaim*, to cry out, and *exclamation*, an outcry, come from Latin *clamare*, to shout, cry out, which also gives us: *claim*, to declare; *clamour*, shouting, noise; *acclaim*, to praise or endorse by a shout; *declaim*, to speak or utter aloud; *disclaim*, to shout against, deny or disavow; *proclaim* and *proclamation*, to cry out before someone, a public announcement; and *reclaim*, to call back, to call back to a previous state or in order to make useful again.

exclusion *n. The court ruled that the exclusion of women from the college was illegal:* keeping out, barring, non-admission, debarment, rejection, prohibition, refusal; restraint, exile, prevention, preclusion; eviction, removal, banishment, dismissal, ejection, expulsion, throwing out.
Ant. admittance, inclusion, acceptance.

exclusive *adj.* **1** *The Athenaeum is an exclusive men's club:* select, elect; restricted, restrictive; closed, private; clannish, cliquish; aloof, snobbish. **2** *The estate agent has the exclusive right to sell the house:* sole, single, private, unshared, undivided; complete, entire, total, full.
Ant. 1 open, unrestricted; popular, common. **2** non-exclusive, shared, divided; partial, incomplete.

excommunicate *v. The church has the power to excommunicate heretics:* remove, exclude from sacraments, anathematize, divest of membership, unchurch; expel, eject, banish, ban, oust.
Ant. admit, enrol; readmit, reinstate.

excruciating *adj. The ointment eased the excruciating pain:* extremely painful, unbearable, insufferable, unendurable, agonizing, torturous, racking, tormenting; acute, severe, extreme, fierce, intense, violent, cutting, lacerating.
Ant. bearable, tolerable, endurable; mild, slight, gentle, trivial.
◇ *Word origin: Excruciating* comes from Latin *ex-* (completely) + *cruciare* (to torture), whose base is *crux*, rack, gallows, cross. Thus, *excruciating* literally means "racking," because *excruciare* means to torture on the rack.

excursion *n. The family made a weekend excursion to a campsite:* outing, trip, pleasure trip, short journey, tour, jaunt, sally, expedition, sortie; (*variously*) ride, drive, voyage, cruise, flight, walk, stroll, hike, tramp, ramble, trek; *Slang* junket.

excuse *v.* **1** *Please excuse me for interrupting:* forgive, pardon, make allowance for, pass over, bear with, indulge, accept one's apology. **2** *Don't excuse his rudeness by saying he was in a hurry:* apologize for, justify, explain, defend, vindicate, ask forgiveness for, condone, pardon, let off, absolve, acquit, exonerate, exculpate, clear; mitigate, palliate, extenuate, gloss over, overlook, whitewash. **3** *People over 65 may be excused from jury duty if they wish:* release, exempt, free, spare, let off, relieve of.
—*n.* **4** *Ignorance of the law is no excuse:* justification, defence, vindication, acceptable explanation, absolution, exoneration, argument, plea for forgiveness.
Ant. 1, 2 censure, blame, criticize; chastise, castigate, discipline, chasten, correct, punish, charge, accuse, condemn, convict, sentence. **3** hold liable for, hold responsible for, subject to; compel, obligate, oblige, force into. **4** accusation, charge.

execute *v.* **1** *The general's plans were executed by his subordinates:* carry out, effect, put into effect, discharge, administer, accomplish, fulfil, achieve, complete, effectuate, consummate, realize, carry through, perpetrate, enforce. **2** *Murderers are still occasionally executed in France:* put to death, inflict capital punishment on; kill, slay; murder, assassinate, massacre. **3** *The violin concerto was executed with great flair:* perform, render, play, do; act, enact.

execution *n.* **1** *The execution of our plans must be completed quickly:* carrying out, effecting, accomplishment, administration, performance, discharge, transaction, realization, fulfilment, achievement, completion. **2** *France uses the guillotine for executions:* putting to death, infliction of capital punishment; killing, slaying. **3** *The artist's execution of the oil painting was flawless:* performance, doing, rendition, interpretation.

executive *n.* **1** *An executive should have wide business experience:* administrator, administrative head, director, manager; (*variously*) president, chairman, superintendent, supervisor, overseer.
—*adj.* **2** *The company is always looking for young men with executive potential:* administrative, managerial, supervisory, leadership.
Ant. 1 labourer, worker, subordinate, hired hand, menial, underling.

exemplary *adj. The older boy's exemplary behaviour had a good influence on the younger:* worthy of imitation, emulative, model; admirable, praiseworthy, commendable, laudable, noteworthy, estimable, sterling, ideal, meritorious.
Ant. objectionable, blameworthy, punishable.

exemplify *v. The novel* Tom Sawyer *exemplifies 19th-century life in the United States:* typify, epitomize, illustrate, represent, demonstrate, instance, embody, personify.
Ant. misrepresent, falsify.

"True nobility is exempt from fear."
— *William Shakespeare*

---

exempt *v.* **1** *A doctor's note will exempt you from physical education:* except, excuse, relieve, free, release, spare, absolve, clear, privilege, grant, immunity to.
—*adj.* **2** *Church property is usually exempt from taxation:* not subject to, immune, excepted, excused, relieved, freed, absolved, spared, cleared, not liable to, released from; privileged.
Ant. 1 subject, oblige, liable, expose. **2** liable, subject; responsible, chargeable, answerable.

exemption *n.* **1** *Father was given exemption from military service during World War II because of poor eyesight:* release, immunity, freedom, absolution, dispensation, exception, excuse. **2** *Children may be listed as exemptions on your income-tax return:* deduction, allowance; expense.
Ant. 1 responsibility, obligation, liability.

exercise *n.* **1** *Exercise stimulates the flow of blood:* physical activity; callisthenics, daily dozen, *Slang* physical jerks. **2** *Singing scales is the best exercise a singer can give her vocal cords. The army is having military exercises this week:* practice, training, schooling, drill. **3** *The exercise of caution is necessary when driving:* use, practice, employment, utilization, application, discharge.
—*v.* **4** *If you want to stay healthy you must exercise:* be physically active, do callisthenics; train, drill, follow a training regimen, discipline, school, break in, give lessons, tutor, teach, develop, prepare, inculcate. **5** *To lose weight, exercise restraint in eating:* carry out, perform, execute, discharge, employ, utilize, wield; apply, practise, exert, display, show, exhibit.
Ant. 1 inactivity, idleness. **3** avoidance, evasion, ignoring, overlooking. **4** be sedentary, be inactive. **5** avoid, evade, ignore, overlook, eschew.

"Whenever I feel like exercise I lie down until the feeling passes." —*Robert M. Hutchins*

---

exert *v. If you exert all your strength you can move that rock. The manager exerts most of the authority in this office:* put forth, put in action, set in motion, exercise, employ, wield, use, utilize, make use of, apply, discharge, resort to, avail oneself of.

exertion *n. It took a great deal of exertion to push the car up the hill. Chess requires a lot of mental exertion:* effort, energy, strength, labour, toil, work, pains, trouble, struggle, travail, endeavour, industry, application, activity, *Slang* elbow-grease.

Ant. idleness, inertia; rest, repose, ease, leisure.

exhale *v. When we exhaled in the cold we could see our breath:* breathe out; respire, expire, emit breath, breathe; pant, puff, huff.

Ant. inhale, breathe in.

◇ *Word origin: Exhale* comes from Latin *ex-* (out) + *halare* (to breathe), which also gives us *inhale* (to breathe in) and *halitosis* (bad breath).

exhaust *v.* **1** *The soldiers had exhausted their supply of ammunition:* use up, run through, expend, deplete, spend, consume, finish. **2** *The fast game of tennis exhausted me:* wear out, tire, overtire, fatigue, drain, enervate, sap one's energy; tax, strain, weaken, debilitate, disable, *Slang* poop, fag. **3** *The chemist made a vacuum in the bell-jar when he exhausted the air from it:* empty, draw out, draw off, drain.

Ant. 1 amass, obtain, get, re-stock, replenish; save, conserve, preserve, keep, store, hoard. **2** invigorate, refresh, renew, revive, vivify, animate, enliven, strengthen.

◇ *Word origin: Exhaust* comes from Latin *ex-* (out) + *haurire* (to draw).

exhausted *adj.* **1** *The children were exhausted after the day's play:* tired out, dead tired, fatigued, worn out, played out, all in, done in, drained, spent, wearied; *Slang* dead beat, flaked out, pooped. **2** *The campers' supply of food was exhausted:* used up, finished, spent, depleted, consumed, drained, expended, emptied; bankrupt, impoverished.

Ant. 1 full of pep, ready to go, full of vim and vigour; invigorated, refreshed, revived, vivified, animated, enlivened. **2** replenished, restored, saved, conserved, preserved, kept.

exhaustion *n.* **1** *The walkers were ready to drop with exhaustion:* fatigue, weariness, tiredness, enervation. **2** *The exhaustion of the army's rations caused its defeat:* using up, spending, consumption; depletion, draining.

Ant. 1 energy, pep, vim, vigour, new strength. **2** replenishment; conservation, preservation.

exhaustive *adj. The student did exhaustive research before writing the paper:* comprehensive, all-inclusive, thorough, complete, sweeping, all-out, all-embracing.

Ant. hit-or-miss, incomplete, cursory, superficial.

exhibit *v.* **1** *Manufacturers will exhibit their new cars at the Motor Show:* display, show, put on view, present for inspection, reveal, make public, parade, demonstrate, unveil, bring to light, air, flaunt, brandish.

—*n.* **2** *The curator has rearranged the exhibits at the museum:* item on display, object in an exhibition, object on show.

Ant. 1 hide, conceal, suppress, repress, mask, secrete, bury.

◇ *Word origin: Exhibit* and *exhibition* come from Latin *ex-* (out) + *habere* (to hold, have), hence to hold out to be seen.

exhibition *n. There will be an exhibition of antique glassware at the fair:* show, showing, public showing, display, exposition, public presentation, demonstration, unveiling, array.

exhilarate *v. The walk in the beautiful woods exhilarated the hikers:* fill with high spirits, excite, stimulate, invigorate, hearten, lift, enliven, animate, quicken, elate, gladden, delight, cheer.

Ant. depress, dispirit, sadden, deject.

◇ *Word origin: Exhilarate* comes from the Greek *hilaros,* cheerful, which also gives us *hilarious* (causing so much cheerfulness that we burst out laughing).

exhilaration *n. The team was full of exhilaration after winning the game:* high spirits, exaltation, elation, liveliness, animation, excitement, vivacity, delight, gladness, joyousness, lightheartedness, gaiety.

Ant. dejection, depression, sadness, gloom.

exhort *v. The general exhorted his troops to stand fast:* encourage, spur, goad, press, prod, urge, plead with, beseech, enjoin, implore, appeal to, persuade; advise, advocate, recommend, admonish, bid; *Slang* egg on, give a pep talk to.

Ant. dissuade, discourage; forbid, prohibit.

exigency *n.* **1** *A ship's captain must be able to cope with any exigency:* emergency, contingency, crisis, circumstance, predicament, quandary, plight, extremity, difficulty, hardship; *Slang* pickle, pinch, scrape, jam. **2** *Plural We have to cope with the exigencies of daily living:* requirements, necessities, demands, needs, constraints, urgencies.

exile *v.* **1** *Russia exiled Alexander Solzhenitsyn for writing political novels:* banish, deport, expel, eject, oust, expatriate, drive out, deprive of citizenship.

—*n.* **2** *The king drove his enemy into exile:* banishment, expulsion, expatriation. **3** *Political exiles seek refuge in friendly countries:* exiled person, banished person, expellee, displaced person; outcast, pariah, expatriate.

Ant. 1 grant refuge, grant citizenship; welcome, accept, embrace.

exist *v.* **1** *A few old whaling ships still exist:* be in existence, survive, endure, last, remain, stay, abide. **2** *Humans could not exist on Mars:* live, survive, maintain life, breathe. **3** *A life free from worry just doesn't exist:* occur, have existence, prevail, happen, ensue, obtain.

Ant. 1 pass away, disappear, vanish. **2** die, perish.

existence *n.* **1** *Do you believe in the existence of the Loch Ness monster?:* actuality, reality, presence, animation; tangibility, materialization. **2** *The patient's very existence depends on the doctor's skill:* life, being, survival; subsistence, continuance, endurance.

Ant. 1 non-existence, nothingness. **2** death, passing away.
◇ *Spelling tip:* This word ends in *-ence*, not "-ance." A good way to remember this *e* is to remember that your landlord's *existEnce* depends on your paying the *rEnt.*

"It is man's destiny to ponder on the riddle of existence." —*C. F. Kettering*

exit *n.* **1** *There is only one exit from the theatre:* way out, egress, outlet, passage out. **2** *We made a hasty exit when the fight started:* departure, withdrawal, retreat, exodus, escape.
—*v.* **3** *Please exit by the rear door:* leave, depart, go out, withdraw, escape, retire; *Slang* blow.
Ant. 1, 2 entrance. **3** enter, come in.
◇ *Word origin: Exit* comes from Latin *ex-* (out) + *ire* (to go).

exodus *n. At weekends the motorways are filled by the exodus from the city:* departure, going forth, exit, flight, hegira, migration; emigration, exile.
◇ *Word origin: Exodus* comes from Greek *ex-* (out) + *hodos* (way). *Exodus,* the second book of the Old Testament, describes the departure of the Jews from Egypt under Moses.

exonerate *v. New evidence exonerated the prisoner. The jury exonerated the accused:* clear, free, absolve, vindicate, exculpate; find innocent, acquit.
Ant. prove guilty, condemn, blame; find guilty.
◇ *Word origin: Exonerate* comes from Latin *ex-* (out, away) + *onus* (burden), to remove the burden or "onus" of guilt.

exorbitant *adj. That restaurant charges exorbitant prices:* excessive, enormous, unreasonable, preposterous, outrageous, extreme, undue, out-of-line, inordinate, extortionate; overpriced, high-priced, expensive, extravagant, costly, dear.
Ant. fair, equitable; cheap, reasonable, inexpensive, *Slang* dirt cheap.
◇ *Word origin: Exorbitant* comes from Latin *ex-* (out) + *orbita* (track), off the track, deviating. Latin *orbita,* track, also gives us *orbit* (the track a planet, spacecraft, etc., follows in the sky).

exotic *adj.* **1** *Palm trees are exotic imports into northern countries:* foreign, not native, not indigenous, from abroad, alien. **2** *She was famed for her exotic hats:* unusual, different, unique, striking, exceptional, peculiar, strange, unfamiliar.
Ant. 1 native. **2** commonplace, run-of-the-mill, ordinary.
◇ *Word origin: Exotic* comes from Greek *exōtikos,* from outside, foreign.

expand *v.* **1** *The business has expanded by 50 per cent this year:* grow, increase, enlarge, magnify, multiply, amplify, develop, evolve, heighten, aggrandize, augment; widen, dilate, swell, distend, fatten, inflate. **2** *The eagle expanded its wings as it rose in the air:* stretch, spread, spread out, outspread, extend, open, unfold, unfurl, unroll, unravel.
Ant. 1 decrease, fall off, shrink, contract, curtail, condense. **2** close, fold, furl, roll up.

expanse *n. Covered wagons had to cross the vast expanse of the desert:* extent, area, space, range, sweep, field, stretch, reach, breadth, magnitude, compass.
Ant. limit, confine, enclosure.

expansion *n. Future expansion of the business calls for two new factories. The runway is undergoing expansion to accommodate larger planes:* enlargement, enlarging, increase, growth, development, magnifying, multiplying, amplifying; extension, spreading, lengthening, widening, stretching; swelling, distention, dilation.
Ant. decrease, shrinkage, contraction, shortening, curtailment, cut-back.

expansive *adj.* **1** *A good salesman usually has an expansive personality:* open, free, effusive, exuberant, extroverted, outgoing, unrestrained, liberal, uninhibited, unrepressed; generous, bountiful, bounteous. **2** *A judge must have an expansive knowledge of the law:* extensive, broad, comprehensive, wide-ranging, wide, far-reaching, voluminous, capacious.
Ant. 1 reserved, restrained, repressed, stiff, inhibited, introverted, shy, antisocial; taciturn, silent, reticent. **2** narrow, limited, restricted, circumscribed.

expatriate *n. During World War II, many German expatriates settled in the United States:* exile, émigré, refugee, displaced person, political refugee, banished person, deported person, outcast, pariah.

expect *v.* **1** *The skiers expect deep snow in Chamonix:* look forward to, look for, envisage, anticipate, foresee, contemplate, reckon on, bargain for. **2** *The company expects punctuality of every employee:* demand, look for, require, trust, rely upon, reckon upon, count on, hope for. **3** *I expect that she will be here soon:* assume, presume, suppose, believe, surmise, imagine, calculate, contemplate, conjecture, *Informal* reckon, guess.
Ant. 1 despair of, lose faith in; dread, fear.

expectation *n. The team has every expectation of winning the championship:* expectancy, anticipation, likelihood, prospect, presumption, assurance, confidence, hope, trust, reliance, belief, contemplation.
Ant. memory, recollection; unlikelihood, despair, discouragement, hopelessness.

expedient *adj.* **1** *The professor found it expedient to lecture from notes:* useful, helpful, worthwhile, advantageous, beneficial, practical, effective; desirable, advisable, wise, judicious. **2** *In an expedient move, the Members voted to raise their salaries:* self-serving, self-seeking, conniving, calculating, selfish, self-interested; opportune, politic.

—*n.* **3** *The neon sign is ugly, but it's a necessary expedient to our business:* practical aid, help, advantage, benefit, profitable practice, resort; makeshift device, stopgap.

Ant. 1 inexpedient, impractical, ineffective, detrimental, disadvantageous, harmful, undesirable, inadvisable, futile, vain, fruitless. **2** unselfish, altruistic; just, ethical, right.

expedite *v. Using postal codes expedites the delivery of letters:* hasten, speed up, accelerate, quicken, promote, further, facilitate, forward, advance, dispatch, push through.

Ant. slow, slow down, retard, impede, hinder, block, obstruct.

expedition *n.* **1** *The scientists went on an expedition into the Brazilian jungle:* scientific trip, exploration; journey, voyage, trek; mission, enterprise, campaign. **2** *The expedition slept in tents in the desert:* travellers, voyagers, wayfarers, adventurers, explorers.

expeditious *adj. The emergency demands expeditious action:* prompt, speedy, hasty, ready, quick, fast, swift, rapid, immediate, instant, punctual; alert, ready, snappy, bright-eyed, effective, efficacious.

Ant. slow, dilatory, sluggish, leisurely, deliberate, inefficient, ineffective, ineffectual.

expel *v.* **1** *The whale expelled water from his blow-hole:* force out, drive out, cast out, eject, discharge, excrete, evacuate, eliminate, void, dislodge, spew. **2** *The treasurer was expelled from the club for breaking the rules:* eject, oust, remove, throw out; discharge, fire, dismiss, cashier, drum out; sack; banish, exile, evict.

Ant. 1 take in, ingest, inhale. **2** admit, accept, invite, welcome; hire, engage.

expend *v.* **1** *The class expended a great amount of time on the project:* use up, spend, consume, go through; dissipate, drain, exhaust, empty, wear out, squander, waste. **2** *The treasury expended £50,000 on public works:* spend, pay out, pay, disburse, give, donate, contribute; *Informal* fork out, shell out, lay out.

Ant. 1, 2 conserve, save, preserve, hoard. **2** earn, receive, collect.

expendable *adj.* **1** *The city has a million pounds of expendable funds for street repairs:* spendable, available, disbursable, payable. **2** *Lives must be saved, but the equipment is expendable:* able to be sacrificed, relinquishable, consumable, forgoable, replaceable; dispensable, superfluous, non-essential.

expenditure *n.* **1** *Expenditure should always be less than income:* expenses, money spent, spending, disbursement, outlay, outgoings, paying out; payment, cost, price, charge. **2** *The project entailed a great expenditure of energy:* spending, expending, exertion, application, output, use, employment, consumption.

Ant. 1 receipts, income, profit. **2** conservation, saving, preservation, hoarding.

expense *n. The expense of remodelling the house is more than we can afford:* cost, price, charge, outlay; amount, quotation, rate, figure; source of expenditure, item paid for; drain, depletion; financial burden.

Ant. income, proceeds, return, profit, receipts, gain.

expensive *adj. The shop carries very expensive clothes:* costly, high-priced, dear; overpriced, exorbitant, extravagant, excessive, unreasonable, immoderate, uneconomical, beyond one's means.

Ant. cheap, inexpensive, economical, reasonable, low-priced, cut-price, *Slang* two-a-penny.

experience *n.* **1** *Experience is the best teacher:* personal knowledge, first-hand knowledge, observation, doing, practice, training, seasoning, familiarity. **2** *Meeting the Japanese emperor was a memorable experience:* event, episode, incident, adventure, happening, occurrence, affair.

—*v.* **3** *Few Western Europeans experience real hunger:* know, undergo, live through, go through, encounter, meet, endure, suffer, sustain, bear; feel, sense, perceive, see, behold, view, observe; withstand.

Ant. 1 inexperience; theory. **3** escape, miss.

◇ *Word origin:* The Latin word *experiri,* to try out, gives us *experience* (trying out something for oneself), *experiment* (a try out or test), and *expert* (one who has tried out or experienced something thoroughly).

experienced *adj. This work demands an experienced bookkeeper:* accomplished, practical, trained, seasoned, qualified, well-versed, knowing, veteran, skilled, expert, able, capable, competent, efficient, master; sophisticated, wise, worldly-wise.

Ant. inexperienced, impractical, untrained, unqualified, untried, green, apprentice, unskilled; inept, incompetent.

experiment *n.* **1** *As an experiment she substituted honey for sugar in the pudding. The Research Institute conducts experiments on jet engines:* test, trial, tentative procedure, try-out, venture; feeler; research, investigation, examination, analysis, experimentation.

—*v.* **2** *The chemist experimented with a new formula for dyes:* test, try-out, explore, *Slang* mess around with; research, investigate, analyse, seek proof for.

◇ *Word origin:* See EXPERIENCE.

> "I would rather have you know me merely as the result of one of my father's early experiments." —*Charles Edison, son of Thomas Edison*

experimental *adj. The architect produced several experimental designs:* tentative, speculative, conjectural, conceptual, trial, test, trial-and-error, rough, first-draft, new, radical, fresh.

Ant. traditional, proven, tried-and-true; hackneyed, commonplace, routine.

expert *n.* **1** *Jane has become an insurance expert:*

authority, specialist, master, professional, connoisseur, ace, veteran, *Slang* wizard.
—*adj.* **2** *The riders were all expert horsemen:* skilled, skilful, masterly, professional, experienced, master, accomplished, trained, practised, knowledgeable, qualified, proficient, able, apt, adept, deft, adroit, competent, capable, first-class; *Informal* ace, crack, A-1.
Ant. 1 amateur, tiro, novice; dabbler, dilettante. **2** unskilled, amateurish, inexperienced, untrained, unqualified, inept, incompetent.
◇ *Word origin:* See EXPERIENCE.

expertise *n. Landing a plane in fog takes a great deal of expertise:* special skill, skill, know-how, expertness, specialization, professionalism, *Informal* savvy.

expire *v.* **1** *The magazine subscription expires next month:* come to an end, run out, lapse, cease, discontinue, end, terminate, conclude, finish. **2** *In the old play the heroine expired of a broken heart:* die, pass away, perish, decease, *Informal* give up the ghost.
Ant. 1 continue, renew, begin, start, commence. **2** live; be born.

explain *v.* **1** *Can you explain how an aircraft flies?:* describe, demonstrate, make clear, make plain, illustrate. **2** *The students were asked to explain the meaning of the poem. How do you explain such rude behaviour?:* clarify, clear up, resolve, elucidate, interpret, account for, give a reason for, fathom, justify, give an explanation for.
Ant. 2 confuse, obscure, misinterpret.

explanation *n.* **1** *The astronomers gave an explanation of the way in which the orbits of the planets are related:* explication, account, description, elucidation. **2** *There doesn't seem to be any explanation for the boy's erratic behaviour:* reason, warrant, accounting, answer, cause, motive, motivation; justification, excuse.
◇ *Spelling tip:* Note that although *explain* has an *ai, explanation* has only an *a: explAIn,* but *explAnation.* If in doubt when writing *explanation,* just pronounce it slowly to yourself, *ex-plan-a-tion,* and the *-an-* sound should lead you to the correct spelling.

explicit *adj. She gave explicit directions on the way to clean the rug:* specific, definite, precise, exact, express, certain, distinct, absolute, categorical, unequivocal, unqualified, clear, clearly expressed, straightforward; candid, frank, plain, direct, outspoken, blunt, pointed, unreserved.
Ant. vague, general, indefinite, inexact, ambiguous, equivocal, uncertain, enigmatic, cryptic, obscure; implicit, implied, indirect, oblique; suggested, hinted.
◇ *Usage note:* Beware of confusing *explicit* and *implicit*. *Explicit* means specific or clearly expressed: *The lease is explicit in saying the rent must be paid by the 10th of every month. Implicit* means implied or understood but not directly stated: *It's not in the lease, but it's implicit that the rent is to be paid in sterling, not in foreign currency.*

explode *v.* **1** *Fortunately, no one was hurt when the gas main exploded:* blow up, burst loudly, burst violently, go off; erupt, blast, discharge violently; set off, detonate. **2** *The boss exploded with anger when he saw the sales report:* burst out emotionally, erupt, utter noisily, express noisily. **3** *New facts explode the theory that the moon was once part of the earth:* disprove, prove wrong, prove false, belie, refute, expose, discredit, repudiate, invalidate, burst, destroy.
Ant. 1 implode, fizzle out.
◇ *Word origin:* The first *explosions* were used to drive bad actors off the stage! *Explode, explosion,* and *explosive* come from Latin *ex-* (out) + *plaudere* (to clap, applaud), literally a loud outburst of applause, which the Romans used to drive inept performers off the stage, in the same way as we hiss, boo, or give a slow handclap.

exploit *n.* **1** *Flying the Atlantic alone was a brilliant exploit:* achievement, feat, accomplishment, heroic act, brave deed, adventure, daring deed.
—*v.* **2** *You must exploit every opportunity to learn new things:* use to advantage, turn to practical account, utilize, make use of, put to use, capitalize on, profit by. **3** *The company exploited its workers with long hours and low pay:* take advantage of, make selfish use of, abuse, misuse, take unfair advantage of.
Ant. 1 failure, defeat. **2** pass up, ignore. **3** pamper, coddle, spoil.

explore *v.* **1** *Captain Scott explored the Antarctic:* scout, range over, travel over, travel to observe, travel and map, traverse, penetrate. **2** *We must explore all possible ways of increasing food production:* look into, examine, scrutinize, investigate, search into, plumb, analyse, probe, pry into, inquire into, try, try out, experiment with.
◇ *Word origin: Explore* comes from Latin *ex-* (out) + *plorare* (to shout), literally to cry out when one finds something new. Latin *plorare,* also gives us *deplore* (to cry out against something) and *implore* (to cry out urgently, make an entreaty).

explosion *n.* **1** *The explosion at the munitions depot shook the entire town:* blowing up, detonation, blast; violent bursting, eruption, discharge, fulmination; report, crack, clap. **2** *She felt better after her explosion of anger:* outburst, outbreak, eruption, paroxysm, fit.
◇ *Word origin:* See EXPLODE.

explosive *n.* **1** *Dynamite and other explosives must be handled with care:* blasting material; ammunition; pyrotechnics.
—*adj.* **2** *The balloon should never have been filled with an explosive gas:* liable to explode, capable of exploding, unstable, volatile. **3** *The charge*

of spying created an explosive international situation: dangerous, tense, volatile, perilous, critical, precarious, strained, touchy, ticklish, shaky; emotional, keyed up.

◇ *Word origin:* See EXPLODE.

exponent *n. The delegate is a leading exponent of free trade:* advocate, supporter, champion, proponent, backer, promoter, expounder, spokesman, defender, propagandist.

Ant. opponent, foe, enemy, detractor, critic.

export *v.* **1** *We export cars to America and import silk from Japan:* sell abroad, ship overseas, send out, dispatch.

—*n.* **2** *Germany's export of small cars totalled two million this year:* foreign sale, selling abroad, marketing abroad, shipping overseas. **3** *Cheese and watches are two of Switzerland's chief exports:* exported commodity, trade commodity, shipped wares, material sent abroad, article of foreign trade.

expose *v.* **1** *The small craft was exposed to the dangers of the open sea:* subject, force to endure, leave unprotected, submit; endanger, imperil, jeopardize, hazard, risk. **2** *In some Muslim countries women do not expose their faces in public:* bare, uncover, show, display, exhibit, lay open to view; strip, denude, divest, exhibit nakedness. **3** *The child exposed the plans for the surprise party:* disclose, reveal, divulge, let out, let slip, uncover, bring to light, unearth. **4** *Education should expose students to good painting and music:* familiarize with, put in contact with, acquaint with, make conversant with, offer. **5** *The magazine exposed the politician as a crook:* disclose to be, reveal to be, show in one's real light; denounce, brand, betray.

Ant. 1, 2 hide, conceal, cover, shield. **1** protect, guard. **3** conceal, keep secret.

exposé *n. The newspaper printed an exposé of local crime:* exposure, scandalous disclosure, sensational report, divulgence, revelation, baring.

Ant. suppression, whitewash.

exposition *n. He gave a clear exposition of his views:* explanation, elucidation, clarification, account, exegesis, commentary; presentation, demonstration, description.

exposure *n.* **1** *The company feared exposure of its shaky cash position:* disclosure, divulging, divulgence, revelation, laying open, bringing to light, bringing out in the open, public notice, unmasking, uncovering. **2** *Her skin was dry after exposure to the wind:* subjection, submission, laying bare, laying open, making vulnerable.

Ant. 1 hiding, concealment, cover-up. **2** cover, covering, shelter, refuge, protection, shield.

expound *v. The candidate expounded his views on foreign policy:* state in detail, give a full account of, hold forth, explain, describe, elucidate, make clear, explicate; defend, uphold.

express *v.* **1** *It's not easy to express such a complex idea:* put into words, articulate, phrase, word, couch, relate, communicate, state, say, speak, utter, declare, describe, verbalize, voice. **2** *Her face expressed her bitter disappointment:* reveal, divulge, disclose, show, exhibit, evidence, evince, convey, communicate, make known.

—*adj.* **3** *The doctor gave express orders that the patient was to have no visitors:* explicit, definite, specific, unequivocal, categorical, exact, clear, lucid, precise, direct, plain, certain, particular; vivid, forceful. **4** *The express train is an hour faster than the slow one:* non-stop, stopping infrequently; fast, high-speed, quick, swift, rapid.

Ant. 1 remain silent, be quiet, be still. **2** hide, conceal, cover, veil, mask, cloak; suppress, repress. **3** implicit, implied, indirect, oblique, hinted, suggested, vague, general, indefinite, obscure, enigmatic, ambiguous, equivocal.

"True wit is nature to advantage dressed,
What oft was thought, but ne'er so well expressed." —*Alexander Pope*

---

expression *n.* **1** *Shelley's poems are famous for their beauty of expression. In a democracy everyone is entitled to the expression of his views:* wording, phraseology, style, language; stating, saying, speaking, voicing, airing, venting, telling, uttering, declaration, assertion, setting forth, relating, communication. **2** *"Round the bend" is a colloquial expression meaning, "crazy":* term, word, phrase, turn of phrase, phrasing, phraseology, idiom, locution. **3** *She has such a happy expression on her face:* look, appearance, aspect, mien, countenance. **4** *An actor must speak his lines with a great deal of expression:* eloquence, emotion, meaning; modulation, enunciation, articulation, tone.

Ant. 1 suppression, restraint, repression.

"Law is merely the expression of the will of the strongest for the time being." —*Brooks Adams*

---

expressly *adv.* **1** *I expressly told him I wouldn't go:* explicitly, definitely, pointedly, unequivocally, categorically, decidedly, clearly, distinctly, plainly, in no uncertain terms. **2** *The tourist went to the Alps expressly to ski:* specifically, particularly, specially, precisely.

Ant. 1 implicitly, indirectly, obliquely; vaguely, indefinitely, equivocally.

expropriate *v. The new government expropriated all property of foreigners:* confiscate, appropriate, take, take over; seize, commandeer.

◇ *Word origin: Expropriate* comes from Latin *ex-* (out) + *proprius* (one's own), hence to take out of "one's own" (the owner's) possession. The Latin *proprius,* one's own, also gives us *property* and *appropriate.*

expulsion *n. Expulsion from school is the penalty for cheating. The expulsion of exhaust fumes from the engine made a loud noise:* expelling, ejection, ousting, removal; exile, banishment, eviction, exclusion, debarment, prohibition, proscription; discharge, elimination.
Ant. acceptance, entering, entrance, welcoming, inclusion; injection.

expurgate *v. The censors expurgated several passages from the book:* cut, cut out, remove, delete, censor, remove as offensive, bowdlerize, purge, *Informal* blue-pencil.
◇ *Word origin: Expurgate* comes from Latin *ex-* (out) + *purgare* (to cleanse). The same Latin word gives us *purge, purgative,* and *Purgatory* (the place where the soul may be cleansed).

exquisite *adj.* **1** *She bought an exquisite china figurine:* delicate, fine, elegant; particularly beautiful, beautifully dainty, lovely, precious. **2** *The bracelet was made with exquisite workmanship:* superb, superlative, consummate, matchless, peerless, flawless, incomparable, excellent, fine, choice, admirable, splendid. **3** *The hostess had exquisite taste in clothes:* discriminating, admirable, impeccable, faultless, perfect, fastidious, meticulous.
Ant. 1 clumsy, bulky, ugly, hideous. **2** sloppy, clumsy; mediocre, ordinary; inferior, bad. **3** common, unrefined, indiscriminate, careless, slovenly.

extant *adj. The Dead Sea Scrolls are the earliest extant manuscripts of many sections of the Bible:* in existence, existing, existent, surviving, to be found; present, living.
◇ *Word origin: Extant* used to mean "conspicuous, standing out," rather than merely "existing or surviving." It comes from Latin *ex-* (out) + *stare* (to stand).

extemporaneous *adj. When the guest speaker failed to arrive, the club's president gave an extemporaneous talk on conservation:* impromptu, improvised, extemporary, ad-lib, without notice, extempore, unprepared, unpremeditated, unrehearsed, off the top of one's head, spur-of-the-moment, offhand, without notes.
Ant. well-rehearsed, prepared, planned; premeditated.

extend *v.* **1** *Extend the line to the edge of the paper. We extended the meeting another 15 minutes:* stretch out, draw out, lengthen, make longer, elongate; continue, protract, prolong. **2** *He extended his hand in greeting. The professor extended an invitation to all the students to come to tea:* advance, submit, put out, stretch forth, reach out; offer, give, hold out, proffer, bestow, impart, grant. **3** *The course will extend the students' knowledge of nature:* broaden, widen, expand, enlarge, increase, spread, stretch, amplify, augment.
Ant. 1 shorten, curtail, abbreviate, abridge, contract, shrink, condense. **2** withdraw, take back. **3** narrow, decrease, restrict, limit, reduce.

extended *adj.* **1** *The birds began their flight with extended wings:* spread out, stretched out, unfolded, unfurled. **2** *The play was so successful that it had an extended run at the local theatre:* prolonged, long, continued, protracted, lengthened, drawn out. **3** *An extended search turned up the missing ring:* widespread, extensive, comprehensive, thorough; widened, broadened, expanded, enlarged.
Ant. 1 folded, furled, contracted. **2** short, shortened, curtailed, abbreviated, abridged. **3** narrow, limited, restricted.

extension *n.* **1** *The soldier was granted a two-day extension of his leave:* lengthening, continuation, increase, prolongation; delay, postponement. **2** *The garage was built as an extension of the house:* wing, appendage, annex, addition, appendix; enlargement, expansion.
Ant. 1 shortening, curtailment, decrease.

extensive *adj.* **1** *An extensive desert covers much of northern Africa:* wide, broad, large, vast, huge, extended, voluminous, great; lengthy, long, protracted. **2** *The professor had an extensive knowledge of Oriental history:* wide, broad, comprehensive, all-inclusive, far-flung, thorough, universal, capacious.
Ant. 1, 2 narrow. **1** small, little, tiny; short. **2** restricted, specialized.

extent *n. The extent of the forest was unknown to the settlers. The new laws limit the extent of the king's powers:* expanse, stretch, area; scope, range, compass, breadth, magnitude, size, sweep, dimensions, amplitude, amount, degree, reach; duration, time, length.
Ant. limitation, limits.

extenuating *adj. He was not fined for speeding because his need to get to the hospital quickly was an extenuating circumstance:* justifiable, serving as an excuse, explanatory; mitigating, attenuating, qualifying, tempering, moderating, lessening, diminishing.
Ant. unjustifiable, inexcusable; aggravating, intensifying.

exterior *adj.* **1** *The seed has a hard exterior covering:* outside, outer, outermost, external, superficial, outward. **2** *The nation must follow its own policy and not be influenced by exterior events:* external, foreign, alien, exotic, extrinsic, extraneous.
—*n.* **3** *The exterior of the house is red brick:* outside, outer side, surface; façade, face, coating, covering, finish, shell, skin. **4** *Her calm exterior belied her agitation:* outward appearance, manner, demeanour, bearing.
Ant. 1 inside, internal, inner. **2** internal, domestic, native; intrinsic, inherent, ingrained. **3** interior, inside, core.

exterminate *v. The new chemical will exterminate the cockroaches:* destroy, wipe out, kill, annihilate, eliminate; eradicate, abolish, root out, erase, expunge; extinguish, demolish.

Ant. increase, develop, foster, build up; create, generate, originate, beget; replenish, restore.

external *adj.* **1** *The external layer of skin is called the epidermis:* outside, outer, outermost, exterior, surface, superficial, outward. **2** *The flat needs better insulation to keep out external noise:* from the outside, extraneous, extrinsic; foreign, alien.

Ant. 1 internal, inner, innermost, interior, inward, inside. **2** internal; intrinsic, inherent.

extinct *adj.* **1** *The passenger-pigeon is extinct:* defunct, dead, vanished, lost, gone, no longer in existence, died out, no longer surviving. **2** *Popocatepetl is not an extinct volcano but a dormant one:* no longer burning, quenched, extinguished, put out, gone out.

Ant. 1 extant, surviving, living; flourishing, thriving. **2** burning; active.

◇ *Word origin:* See EXTINGUISH.

extinguish *v.* **1** *Firemen extinguished the blaze quickly:* put out, douse, quench, smother; blow out, snuff out. **2** *Failing medical exams extinguished his hopes of becoming a doctor:* wipe out, destroy, end, abolish, eliminate, kill, demolish, dispel, eradicate, cancel, crush, quash, stifle.

Ant. 1 ignite, light, fire. **2** increase, foster, promote, forward, build up; secure, establish, confirm, maintain, support.

◇ *Word origin: Extinguish* and *extinct* come from Latin *ex-* (completely) + *stinguere* (to quench).

extol *v. The general extolled the bravery of his men:* praise, laud, commend, compliment, acclaim, applaud, eulogize, sing the praises of.

Ant. decry, denounce, damn, curse, condemn, censure, criticize; belittle, denigrate.

extortion *n. The gangster was arrested for extortion:* blackmail; threats, force, coercion; forced payments, hush-money, ransom, tribute.

extra *adj.* **1** *The shop hired extra assistants for Christmas. Why did you buy all those extra eggs?:* additional, supplementary, further, more, spare, auxiliary, accessory; superfluous, surplus, redundant, unneccessary.

—n. **2** *The new car has every extra:* accessory, additional feature, special accompaniment, adjunct, appurtenance, attachment, complement, luxury.

—adv. **3** *The coffee is extra strong this morning:* unusually, uncommonly, exceptionally, especially, particularly, additionally, remarkably, extraordinarily.

Ant. 1 fewer. **2** basic necessity. **3** less.

◇ *Word origin: Extra* means "beyond" in Latin.

extract *v.* **1** *The dentist extracted her wisdom teeth:* pull out, take out, draw out, prize out, remove, extricate, pluck out, root out, extirpate. **2** *He manages to extract some humour from every situation:* get, glean, obtain, derive, exact, wrest, evoke, bring out, elicit, deduce, educe. **3** *The new process extracts oil from shale:* process chemically, separate, take out, draw out, squeeze out, press out, distil. **4** *The newspaper extracted several passages from the speech and printed them on the front page:* excerpt, choose, select, cull, abstract, copy out; cite, quote.

—n. **5** *Add a teaspoon of vanilla extract to the milk shake:* concentrate, essence, distillate, juice. **6** *The book contains extracts from famous poems:* excerpt, selection, passage, abstract; quotation, citation.

Ant. 1, 2 insert, embed, implant, inject, infuse.

extraneous *adj.* **1** *The witness's extraneous remarks were struck from the record:* irrelevant, unrelated, inappropriate, immaterial, inadmissible. **2** *Our language has been affected by extraneous influences:* foreign, alien, exotic, extrinsic, strange, adventitious.

Ant. 1 relevant, pertinent, germane, appropriate, material, connected, related, essential. **2** native, intrinsic, inherent.

◇ *Word origin: Extraneous,* like *strange,* comes from Latin *extraneus,* foreign, unfamiliar (from *extra,* outside, beyond).

extraordinary *adj. What an extraordinary dress! The dog is an extraordinary size:* unusual, uncommon, remarkable, phenomenal, unique, rare, out of the ordinary, exceptional, notable; amazing, incredible, unbelievable, inconceivable, unheard of; strange, odd, queer, monstrous.

Ant. usual, common, average, ordinary, unremarkable, run-of-the-mill, everyday, familiar, customary.

"He calls his extravagance, generosity; and his trusting everybody, universal benevolence."
—Oliver Goldsmith

---

extravagance *n.* **1** *His extravagance led him into bankruptcy:* excessive spending, overspending, inordinate outlay; waste, wastefulness, improvidence, prodigality. **2** *She was misled by the extravagances of the travel brochure. Dancing all night was an extravagance that his health could not afford:* excess, excessiveness, unrestraint, immoderation; unreasonableness, absurdity, folly, caprice, capriciousness, recklessness, profligacy.

Ant. 1 economy, frugality, saving, stinginess, tight-fistedness, miserliness. **2** moderation, restraint, reasonableness.

◇ *Spelling tip:* To remember that this word ends in *-ance* and not "-ence," remember this sentence: *Her new dress for the dANCE was an extravagANCE.*

extravagant *adj.* **1** *Extravagant people never save money. Watering the lawn daily is an extravagant use of water:* profligate, spending readily, prodigal, overspending, lavishly spending, open-handed, spendthrift; wasteful, squandering, imprudent, improvident. **2** *The firm made extravagant claims for the new soap. Did the singer deserve such extravagant praise?:* excessive, immoderate, unrestrained, inordinate, unreasonable, outlandish, preposterous, outrageous, absurd, fantastic, fabulous, unreal, high-flown, foolish, wild, exaggerated.

Ant. **1** thrifty, economical; frugal, stingy, tight-fisted, miserly, close; conservative, saving, prudent. **2** moderate, restrained, reasonable, sensible, serious, realistic, sober, down-to-earth; careful, cautious.

extreme *adj.* **1** *Extreme cold will cause the engine to fail:* severe, intense, very great, excessive, immoderate, extraordinary, unusual, uncommon; inordinate, exaggerated. **2** *Sidney Webb's political views were extreme for his time:* radical, advanced, avant-garde; outrageous, extravagant. **3** *Plant the tree in the extreme corner of the garden:* most distant, farthest, outermost, farthest removed.

—*n.* **4** *She will go to any extreme to get her way:* ultimate limit, extremity, boundary, height, end; excess, excessive degree, *Informal* nth degree.

Ant. **1** moderate, mild, reasonable, common, average, ordinary. **2** traditional, conservative. **3** near, nearest.

◇ *Word origin: Extreme* and *extremity* come from Latin *extremus,* outermost, utmost, *extreme.*

extremely *adv. It's extremely warm for this time of year:* very, unusually, exceptionally, especially, extraordinarily, uncommonly, excessively, immoderately, singularly, surprisingly, intensely, remarkably; unnaturally, abnormally, freakishly, peculiarly, curiously.

extremity *n.* **1** *They fenced in the western extremity of the estate. The spacecraft reached the extremity of its orbit:* end, farthest point, terminus, extreme, edge, outer edge, tip, margin; most distant point, reach, limit, boundary, bound, border, confine. **2** *The illustrator was good at drawing faces and bodies but not extremities:* hand, foot; limb, arm, leg; finger, toe.

Ant. **1** beginning, start, commencement; nearest point.

◇ *Word origin:* See EXTREME.

extricate *v. The fox tried desperately to extricate itself from the trap. Let's see how she extricates herself from this embarrassing situation!:* free, release, get out, loose, rescue, liberate, deliver; untangle, disentangle, disengage, wriggle out of.

Ant. catch, trap, snare, ensnare, tangle, entangle, trip up, tie, tie up.

extrovert *n. Jim is an extrovert who loves to meet people:* outgoing person, gregarious person, sociable person, hail-fellow-well-met; exhibitionist, show-off, *Informal* life and soul of the party.

Ant. introvert; loner.

exuberance *n. The children are always full of exuberance:* enthusiasm, energy, liveliness, spirit, zeal, vigour, buoyancy, sprightliness, vivacity, animation, life, eagerness, excitement.

Ant. despair, dejection; lethargy.

exuberant *adj.* **1** *The crew gave an exuberant shout when the boat got under way:* enthusiastic, lively, spirited, sprightly, animated, eager, excited, energetic, zealous, vigorous. **2** *The hillside is covered with an exuberant growth of weeds:* growing thickly, lavish, profuse, copious, abundant, superabundant, luxuriant, lush, plenteous.

Ant. **1** despairing, dejected, unenthusiastic, dispirited, dull, lethargic. **2** thin, sparse, scant, scanty, meagre, sporadic.

exult *v. The children exulted as the end of term drew near:* rejoice, be jubilant, be elated, be delighted, be exhilarated, be in high spirits, glory; *Informal* jump for joy; crow, gloat.

Ant. be downcast, be gloomy, be blue, feel sad.

◇ *Usage note:* Don't confuse *exult,* to rejoice, with *exalt,* to honour. Thus, *The country exulted when the war was over,* but *The king was exalted by his subjects.*

eye *n.* **1** *She shaded her eyes from the sun:* (*variously*) eyeball, iris, pupil; *Informal* orb, peeper. **2** *Are your eyes good enough for you to drive without glasses?:* eyesight, vision, sight; *He has an artist's eye:* perception, discrimination, taste.

—*v.* **3** *She eyed the stranger with amusement:* glance at, look at, gaze at, view, scan, observe, study, inspect, scrutinize, survey, stare at, watch, behold.

◇ *Usage note:* Words for eye doctors and spectacle makers and sellers can be confusing. An *ophthalmologist* or an *oculist* (an older word) is a doctor who specializes in diseases of the eye. An *ophthalmic optician* is a specialist who measures visual accuracy and orders and fits lenses for spectacles.

F

fable *n.* **1** *Tell them the fable about the fox and the grapes:* parable, tale, fairy-tale, legend, romance, allegory, myth. **2** *That story about his pirate ancestor is probably a fable:* tall story, untruth, fiction, fabrication, falsehood, invention, fib, hoax, lie; *Slang* whopper, yarn, leg-pull.

◇ *Word origin: Fable* comes from Latin *fari*, to speak (our words *fame* and *fate* are from the same root). Greek *phāmā*, fame, and *phanai*, to speak, are also related.

fabled *adj. Some people still believe in the fabled Loch Ness monster:* fanciful, imaginary, unreal, fictitious; legendary, mythical, mythological, fabulous, storied.

Ant. real, authentic, historical, factual, honest-to-goodness.

fabric *n.* **1** *Wash this fabric in cold water:* cloth, textile, material. **2** *The fabric of the nation is weakened when its citizens mistrust the government:* framework, structure, frame, make-up, superstructure, organization, substance; foundation, substructure, infrastructure.

◇ *Word origin: Fabric* was originally woven in small workshops and comes from French *fabrique*, workshop.

fabricate *v.* **1** *All of the furniture is fabricated on the premises:* build, form, construct, assemble, frame, manufacture, produce, erect, fashion, shape, compose. **2** *She fabricated a good excuse for staying at home:* invent, concoct, make up, hatch, devise, design, contrive, formulate, embroider, counterfeit, falsify, simulate, forge, feign; *Slang* fake, trump up.

Ant. **1** destroy, raze, demolish, dismember.

fabrication *n.* **1** *Our company is engaged in the fabrication of aeroplane parts:* building, construction, constructing, manufacture, assemblage, production, erection, composition, make-up, fashioning, creation. **2** *His alibi was a complete fabrication:* falsehood, invention, lie, untruth, fiction, fib, concoction, fable, prevarication, myth, forgery, yarn, fairy-tale; *Slang* cock-and-bull story.

Ant. **1** destruction, razing. **2** truth.

fabulous *adj.* **1** *The explorer talked about his fabulous adventures in Africa:* amazing, marvellous, extraordinary, astonishing, astounding, incredible. **2** *We're still talking about the fabulous party you gave:* marvellous, wonderful, fantastic, superb, great, spectacular; *Informal* smashing. **3** *The story is about the fabulous unicorn:* fabled, legendary, mythical, mythological, fanciful, imaginary, apocryphal, fictitious, invented, fantastic.

Ant. **1** credible, ordinary, routine. **2** ordinary, common, fair, commonplace. **3** genuine, authentic, real, natural, historical, actual, true.

façade *n.* **1** *The façade of our building is yellow brick:* building front, frontage, front view, face. **2** *She puts on a façade of confidence to hide her uncertainty:* false appearance, pretence, superficial manner, false front, mask, veneer.

◇ *Usage note: Façade* is a French word, and the correct way to spell it is with the cedilla. This little mark is placed under *c* in French and Portuguese to indicate that it is pronounced *s* instead of *k* before *a, o,* and *u. Cedilla* means "little zed" in Old Spanish; it still does look like a lower-case *z* in a medieval manuscript.

◇ *Word origin:* Latin *facies*, face, gives us *face; façade*, the face of a building; *facet*, one of the small "faces" or surfaces of a gem; and *surface*, literally the "above face," the exterior of something. All these words are related to Latin *facere*, to do or make—the root meaning of *face* is "shape imposed on something."

"And how am I to face the odds
Of man's bedevilment and God's?"

—*A. E. Housman*

---

face *n.* **1** *She powdered her face before going to dinner:* visage, countenance, features, facial features, physiognomy; *Slang* mug, phiz. **2** *Put on a happy face. Don't make a face at me:* expression, aspect, look, countenance, air; grimace, facial contortion, pout, look of annoyance. **3** *Pioneers cleared the forests and changed the face of the countryside:* appearance, look, semblance, external aspect. **4** *The scandal was hushed up in an effort to save face:* reputation, good name, dignity, repute, image, prestige, self-respect. **5** *I scratched the face of my belt buckle:* front surface, obverse side, principal side, finished side, façade, frontage, forepart. **6** *After forgetting my lines, I didn't have the face to go back on stage:* nerve, boldness, daring, pluck, self-assurance, mettle, spunk, confidence, grit, hardihood; cheek, front, brass, gall, effrontery, impudence.

—*v.* **7** *The opponents faced each other across the chess-board:* encounter, confront, meet face to face, turn toward, look toward. **8** *The chalet faces the skiing slopes:* front on, give toward, overlook. **9** *The cabinet is faced with a walnut veneer:* surface, cover, coat, overlay.

Ant. **5** back, underside, reverse side. **6** shyness, timidity.

facet *n.* **1** *The many facets in the diamond make it sparkle:* surface, polished surface, plane, cut. **2** *Generosity is one of the nicer facets of his character:* aspect, side, phase, part, angle.

facetious *adj. He kept us laughing with his facetious remarks:* humorous, funny, amusing, jocular, joking, jovial, jesting, witty, jocose, droll, comic, comical, playful.

Ant. solemn, serious, sober, lugubrious, grave, sedate, staid, sad, dull.

◇ *Word origin: Facetious* comes from Latin *facetia*, a jest, witticism. The plural form of this word has been borrowed directly into English: *facetiae* (pronounced *fuh-SEE-shee-ee*), meaning "merry sayings, ribaldries." This word is not related to the *face* words—its pre-Latin origin is unknown.

facile *adj.* **1** *The weaver was extremely facile with his hands. Our guide spoke facile English:* skilful, adroit, handy, quick, artful, clever, apt, adept, proficient; fluent, effortless, smooth. **2** *I don't trust his facile way of passing over the weakest points in his argument:* glib, slick, careless, casual, superficial, shallow, cursory.

Ant. 1 clumsy, awkward, plodding, halting, maladroit, unskilful, slow. **2** determined, serious, careful, thoughtful, penetrating.

◇ *Word origin: Facile* comes from Latin *facilis*, easy, and is related to *facere*, to do, and thus to our word *fact*.

facilitate *v. An addressograph facilitates the handling of bulk mail:* expedite, speed up, accelerate, ease, simplify, help in, make less difficult, make easier, assist the progress of, lessen the labour of, lighten, smooth; forward, help to advance, promote, further, advance, aid, foster.

Ant. hinder, hamper, complicate, encumber, slow down.

facility *n.* **1** *She speaks German with great facility:* ease, fluency, expertness, skill, proficiency, efficiency, readiness, effortlessness, adroitness, aptness, dexterity, knack, deftness, smoothness, bent, capability, competence. **2** *Modern stoves can be used with greater facility than the old wood-burners:* ease, practicability, effortlessness, easiness, smoothness. **3** *This kitchen has a waste disposal unit and other modern facilities:* appliance, convenience, aid, advantage, resource, means.

Ant. 1 ineptness, clumsiness, awkwardness, maladroitness; rigidity, woodenness, effort, exertion, pains. **2** difficulty, hardship, labour.

facsimile *n. This is a facsimile of Magna Carta:* copy, reproduction, replica, imitation, duplicate, reprint, likeness, transcript; photostat, Xerox.

fact *n. The lawyer tried to establish the facts of the case:* happening, deed, occurrence, event, act, circumstance, incident, thing done, particular, specific; reality, actuality, truth, certainty, verity.

Ant. fiction, supposition, fancy, opinion, unreality, falsehood, lie, delusion, invention.

◇ *Usage note:* (1) *Fact* is a useful word but *the fact that* is usually a sloppy, unnecessary expression. For example, do not say or write *owing to the fact that* when you can use *since* or *because*; and don't say or write *in spite of the fact that* when you can use *though* or *although.* (2) If you want to state a *fact*, do so directly, without introducing it with *the fact is.* Thus *The fact is, it's raining* is a careless and wordy way of simply saying *It's raining.* (3) Don't use the trite and redundant expression *the true fact. Facts* by their very nature are always true!

Exploring the Word: *Fact*, something already done or existing, a *factor*, something that contributes to doing, *factory*, a place where work is done or things are made, and *factotum*, one who does everything, a jack of all trades, come from Latin *facere*, to do or make. This Latin verb gives us many words including: *defeat*, a failure, *defect*, a flaw, and *deficient*, lacking something or unable to do something; *effect*, to do, bring about, and *efficient*, doing with little effort; *facile, facilitate,* and *facility*, respectively meaning able to do something easily, to make easy to do, and ease of doing, hence skill; *facsimile* and *counterfeit*, the first being something made similar, a copy, and the second being something made *counter*, or against, an original for comparison so as to make a fraudulent imitation that is as close to the original as possible; *feasible*, capable of being done; *infect*, literally to work in, dye, taint (before the discovery of microbes, *infections* were thought to be caused by something analogous to a dye, tainting one's physical being); *manufacture* (Latin *manus*, hand), originally to make by hand, now to make a product by hand or machinery; *perfect*, to do thoroughly, done complctcly; *proficient*, literally going forward, advancing, hence advanced, expert; *profit*, progress, advantage; and *unify* (Latin *unus*, one), to make one, combine into a unit.

faction *n.* **1** *The liberal faction of the party is demanding reforms:* group, side, subdivision, clique, combine, ring, set, circle, coterie, gang, cabal, bloc, minority, splinter group. **2** *The convention broke up in bitter faction:* discord, dissension, conflict, disagreement, dissidence, division, contention, strife, rebellion, insurgency, schism, split, incompatibility, breach, quarrelling, sedition, rupture, clash, disruption.

Ant. 2 agreement, harmony, concord.

factor *n. Lack of money was the main factor in my decision not to buy a car:* consideration, reason, circumstance, element, influence, cause.

factotum *n. Our factotum, John, has cared for our estate for years:* handyman, jack of all trades, right-hand man, man Friday, girl Friday.

factual *adj. The reporter gave a factual account of the accident:* full of facts, matter-of-fact, plain, circumstantial, literal; genuine, actual, authentic, real, correct, exact, faithful, scrupulous, accurate; unadorned, unembroidered.

Ant. fanciful, imaginary, embellished, unreal, illusory, figurative.

faculty *n.* **1** *He joined the faculty of English at Manchester University:* department, branch, school, teaching staff, teaching body, professors, teachers. **2** *He has a faculty for putting people at ease:* knack, capacity, capability, special ability, skill, gift, talent, genius, quality, bent, penchant, power, skilfulness, aptitude, adeptness, flair. **3** *The stroke deprived him of the faculty of speech:* power, capability of the mind, inherent physical capability, function, endowment. **4 faculties.** *The old shepherd still enjoys the full possession of his faculties even at the age of 95:* wits, senses, reason, normal intelligence, mental powers.

Ant. **2** inability, incapacity, unskilfulness, weakness, failing.

fad *n. Miniskirts were a widespread fad in the 1960's:* craze, rage, fashion, mania, latest word, latest thing, vogue, mode; whim, whimsy, fancy.

fade *v.* **1** *The blue rug has faded over the years. The light faded as the sun went down:* pale, dim, dull, bleach, lose lustre, lose colour, lose brightness, make pale, become colourless, make colourless, grow dim, become dull, lose clarity, whiten. **2** *His strength seemed to fade after the operation:* decline, dwindle, flag, fail, diminish, wither, fall off, lessen, taper, ebb, shrivel, languish, crumble, droop, wane, slowly disappear; dissolve, evanesce, evaporate, recede, melt away, dissipate; die gradually, pass away.

Ant. **1, 2** brighten. **2** flourish; rise, increase, bloom, grow; endure, abide, last, stand.

fail *v.* **1** *He failed to reach the finals of the tennis tournament. Our plans failed:* not succeed, stop short of, be unsuccessful, miss the mark, fall short of; come to nothing, come to naught, abort, fall through, turn out badly, miscarry, founder, be defeated, run aground, collapse, misfire, meet with disaster, be in vain, prove of no use, turn out badly; *Informal* come to grief, fizzle out, go up in smoke, end in smoke, meet one's Waterloo, be stillborn, slip up; *Slang* bomb, flop. **2** *I failed maths. He failed no students this term:* get less than the pass-mark; give less than the pass-mark. **3** *I thought we could depend on the neighbours for help, but they failed us:* disappoint, let down, forsake, desert. **4** *The battery failed because the lights were left on. His energy failed after his illness:* decline, dwindle, fade away, waste away, die, wane, become weaker, languish, deteriorate, flag, droop, perish gradually, disappear, give out, ebb, lose vigour, collapse; stop working, stop operating. **5** *Bad investments caused the company to fail:* go bankrupt, go under, become insolvent, go out of business, crash, *Informal* fold up.

Ant. **1** succeed. **2** pass. **4** grow, bloom, strengthen, flourish, prosper, gain.

failure *n.* **1** *Her failure to get the job surprised us:* failing, proving unsuccessful; lack of success, vain attempt, ill success, labour in vain; non-fulfilment, wash-out, botch. **2** *The bank warned him about his failure to meet the payments:* neglecting, dereliction, negligence, non-performance, remissness, default, non-observance. **3** *The failure of the bank caused a fall in shares:* bankruptcy, crash, financial disaster, insolvency, ruin, ruination, folding, collapse, downfall. **4** *The party was a failure:* not a success, disappointment, wash-out, botch, muddle, mess, misfire, mishap; *Slang* flop, dud, ne'er-do-well, loser. **5** *The failure of her eyesight makes reading difficult:* decline, loss of strength, failing, deterioration, deteriorating, breakdown.

Ant. **1** success; fulfilment. **2** observance, care. **3** success, prosperity. **4** success, effectiveness, adequacy. **5** strength, strengthening, improvement.

"There is the greatest practical benefit in making a few failures early in life."

—*T. H. Huxley*

---

faint *adj.* **1** *The music was too faint to hear. There was a faint trace of lipstick on the glass:* soft, inaudible, remote, low, dulcet, indistinct, weak, muffled, whispered, muted; dim, pale, almost imperceptible, faded, subtle, delicate, obscure, inconspicuous. **2** *He needed more than faint encouragement:* feeble, weak, slight, small, inconsiderable, meagre, thin, frail, fragile, little. **3** *Climbing those stairs caused her to feel faint:* dizzy, light-headed, vertiginous, about to swoon, giddy; feeble, weak, exhausted, lacking strength, drooping, torpid, lethargic, fatigued, languid, worn out. **4** *Faint heart never won fair lady:* timorous, timid, lacking spirit, fearful, lacking courage, cowardly, lily-livered.

—*v.* **5** *She fainted when she read the telegram:* swoon, black out, lose consciousness, collapse.

Ant. **1** bright, brilliant, clear, conspicuous, fresh, hearty, vigorous, loud, blaring, distinct, glaring. **2** strong, considerable, vigorous. **3** strong, steady, sturdy, hearty. **4** strong, brave, bold, courageous.

◇ *Usage note:* Don't confuse *faint* and *feint. Faint* means to lose consciousness briefly, and also "feeble, timid." To *feint* means to make a mock blow or attack to divert attention from a real one. Thus, *She fainted from the heat. Only a faint sound came over the radio. Faint heart never won fair maid,* but, *The feint on the army's left flank was followed by a frontal attack.*

faint-hearted *adj. He made only a faint-hearted attempt to win the race:* weak, irresolute, half-hearted, indifferent; lily-livered, cowardly, craven, lacking courage, timid.

Ant. strong-hearted, brave, courageous, bold.

fair *adj.* **1** *The lottery was fair, since everyone had an* *equal chance of winning:* unprejudiced, impartial, equitable, even-handed, treating all sides alike, just, unbiased, affording no undue advantage, dispassionate, objective, legitimate, disinterested; honest, reasonable, square, upright, honourable, above-board; according to the rules, proper, justified; *Slang* kosher. **2** *He is a good fielder, but only a fair batsman:* average, moderate, pretty good, middling, mediocre, passable, reasonable, satisfactory, decent, tolerable, respectable, medium, ordinary, indifferent, run-of-the-mill. **3** *The day is warm and the sky is fair:* cloudless, unclouded, rainless, sunny, sunshiny, pleasant, fine, bright. **4** *She has fair hair, unlike her sisters:* light-coloured, not dark, pale, blond, creamy; fair-skinned, light-skinned. **5** *The old song was about a fair maiden and her suitors:* attractive, lovely, good-looking, pretty, comely, well-favoured, beautiful, bonny.

—*adv.* **6** *He was accused by his opponents of not playing fair:* justly, truthfully, honestly, honourably, legally, ethically, squarely, forthrightly, candidly.

Ant. 1 unfair, prejudiced, partial, inequitable, biased; dishonest, dishonourable, improper. **2** exceptional, poor, bad. **3** cloudy, stormy, dark, foul, threatening. **4** dark. **5** ugly, homely. **6** unfairly, dishonestly.

◇ *Usage note:* In some contexts *fair* may be an adverb, just as *fairly* is. So don't let people criticize you for saying *play fair.* It is just as correct as *play fairly.*

fairly *adv.* **1** *We hope the case will be decided fairly:* justly, honourably, honestly, squarely, equitably, in a fair manner, even-handedly, in a just way, rightly, impartially, dispassionately, objectively, legitimately, properly. **2** *He's fairly bright but not up to scholarship standard:* rather, tolerably, passably, moderately, reasonably, somewhat. **3** *The children fairly raced out of school:* actually, really, fully, completely, absolutely, positively; so to speak, in a manner of speaking.

Ant. 1 unfairly, unjustly, inequitably, wrongly, partially, dishonestly, improperly. **2** extremely, very, immoderately, exceptionally.

faith *n.* **1** *I have faith in Dick's integrity. You must have faith in God's wisdom:* belief, confidence, trust, security, certitude, reliance, assurance, certainty, credence, conviction. **2** *He is a member of the Catholic faith:* religion, creed, persuasion, denomination, sect, church. **3** *Keep faith by paying your debts:* obligation, verbal pledge, word of honour, promise; fidelity, constancy, loyalty, fealty.

Ant. 1 doubt, uncertainty, scepticism, dubiety; unbelief, disbelief; mistrust, suspicion; misgiving, apprehension, denial, dissent, distrust, incredulity, discredit, infidelity, rejection, agnosticism.

◇ *Usage note:* See TRUST.

◇ *Word origin: Faith* comes from Latin *fides,* faith. The word is also related to the *-fé* of *auto-da-fé* (the "act of faith" whereby the Inquisition burned heretics).

faithful *adj.* **1** *She was a faithful employee for 40 years. She prided herself on being a faithful wife:* loyal, devoted, steadfast, steady in the performance of duty, tried, conscientious, staunch, true, constant, reliable, unwavering, trustworthy, dependable, worthy of confidence, incorruptible, unswerving, resolute, trusty, scrupulous, honest, upright, truthful. **2** *She gave a faithful account of the accident:* exact, strict, truthful, precise, accurate, verifiable; true-to-life, lifelike; close, similar.

Ant. 1 faithless; disloyal, false, perfidious, traitorous, treacherous; fickle, inconstant, unstable, unfaithful, untrue, untrustworthy, wavering. **2** inexact, imprecise, inaccurate, dissimilar.

fake *v.* **1** *He faked a nervous disorder to stay out of the army:* pretend, feign, simulate, fabricate, dissemble, dissimulate, hoax, sham. **2** *He was arrested for faking some famous paintings:* counterfeit, fabricate, contrive, forge, trump up, falsify.

—*n.* **3** *Only an expert could tell that the pearls were fakes:* counterfeit, imitation, forgery, fraud, sham, dummy, make-believe; contrivance, trick, hoax, fabrication, imposture, delusion, deceit, deception, artifice, ruse, dodge. **4** *The travelling medicine-men were fakes:* imposter, poseur, fraud, pretender, faker, quack, phoney, charlatan, deceiver, humbug.

—*adj.* **5** *He wore a fake moustache to the party:* not real, false, bogus, counterfeit, phoney, pseudo, spurious, sham, fabricated, contrived, forged, simulated, specious, artificial, invented, concocted, make-believe, fictitious.

Ant. 5 real, authentic, actual.

fall *v.* **1** *The apple fell from the tree. He fell down the stairs:* drop, drop down, tumble, plunge, topple, plop, crumble, come down suddenly, collapse, crash down. **2** *The price of meat finally fell:* decline, become less, decrease, become lower, cheapen, depreciate. **3** *Her dress falls in pleats from the waist:* extend down, hang down, slope, droop, cascade; descend, drop. **4** *The town fell on the third day of the attack:* surrender, be captured, be overthrown, be defeated, be taken, pass into enemy hands, capitulate, succumb; be destroyed, come to destruction; be wounded, be slain, perish, die. **5** *How many innocents have fallen and become hardened sinners!:* transgress, give in to temptation, succumb, go astray, lapse, sin, depart from rectitude, err. **6** *My birthday falls on a Sunday this year:* occur, come to pass, happen, take place, come off, crop up, come around.

—*n.* **7** *The net broke the tightrope walker's fall:* plunge, descent, drop, falling, dropping, spill, tumble, slip, plummet. **8** *Yesterday saw a* *sudden fall in stock prices:* drop, decline, lowering, sinking, diminution, decrease, reduction, slump, depreciation; ebb, subsidence, wane. **9 falls.** *We could see the spray from the falls downriver:* waterfall, cascade, cataract. **10** *The play was about the fall of an honest man:* corruption, ruin, loss of innocence, deviation from virtue, slip, going astray, lapse into sin, surrender to temptation, subversion; disgrace, downfall, come-down, loss of eminence, debasement. **11** *The fall of the city followed heavy bombardment:* surrender, capitulation, overthrow, capture, downfall, collapse, defeat.

Ant. 1-2 rise, climb, ascend, mount, soar, increase. **4** triumph, prevail, endure, hold out, survive. **7** rise, ascent. **8** climb, increase, advance, appreciation.

fallacy *n.* **1** *It's a fallacy that everyone needs the same amount of sleep:* misconception, error, false notion, misleading notion, mistake, false belief, misbelief, delusion, illusion, misapprehension. **2** *The fallacy in that argument is that taste is unpredictable:* fault, faultiness, flaw, inconsistency, erroneous reasoning, mistake, pitfall, catch.

Ant. 1 truism, surety, verity, sureness, fact, certainty. **2** logic, proof, soundness, verity, truth, surety, certainty, consistency.

◇ *Word origin: Fallacy, fallible,* and *false* all come from the same Latin word: *fallere,* to deceive.

fallen *adj.* **1** *The fallen king was exiled:* overthrown, deposed; ousted, discharged, turned out. **2** *The fallen player was helped to his feet:* tumbled, sprawled, toppled, dropped, spilled. **3** *The mission catered for derelicts and fallen women:* immoral, sinful, loose, disgraced, ruined, debased. **4** *The fallen soldiers were eulogized as heroes:* dead, slain; massacred, slaughtered, butchered.

fallible *adj. He's usually right, but his judgement is fallible:* imperfect, frail, liable to error; human, mortal; faulty, unsure, unreliable.

Ant. infallible, perfect; divine, superhuman.

◇ *Word origin:* See FALLACY.

"He who would distinguish the true from the false must have an adequate idea of what is true and false." —*Spinoza*

---

false *adj.* **1** *Columbus had a false impression of the size of the earth:* faulty, incorrect, untrue, wrong, fallacious, apocryphal, not correct, erroneous, mistaken, inaccurate, invalid, unsound, inexact, unfounded; delusive, misleading, deceptive, deceiving, spurious, factitious, **2** *She trusted him till he proved to be a false friend:* disloyal, faithless, unfaithful, false-hearted, two-faced, untruthful, double-dealing, devious, hypocritical, dishonest, treacherous, perfidious, traitorous, inconstant, deceitful, tricky. **3** *She removed her false eyelashes:* artificial, bogus, counterfeit, fake, imitation, forged, spurious, feigned, sham, phoney, unreal.

Ant. 1 true, correct, right, accurate, valid, sound, exact. **2** loyal, true, faithful, constant, sincere, steadfast, honest. **3** real, genuine, authentic, bona fide.

◇ *Word origin:* See FALLACY.

falsehood *n.* **1** *He told a falsehood to avoid being punished:* lie, untruth, false statement, fabrication, falsification, canard, invention, fiction, story, figment; *Informal* fib, whopper; white lie. **2** *The boy's father punished him for falsehood:* lying, untruthfulness, falseness, dishonesty, falsity, falsification, deceptiveness, deception, misrepresentation, inaccuracy, deceit, distortion, mendacity, perjury, misstatement, dissimulation, double-dealing, dissembling; perfidy, hypocrisy, duplicity, bad faith, two-facedness, insincerity.

Ant. 1 truth, verity, fact. **2** veracity, genuineness, honesty, honour.

falsify *v.* **1** *He falsified his birth certificate to get a passport:* alter fraudulently, misrepresent, fake, distort, doctor, represent falsely, tamper with, pervert, misuse. **2** *The theory has been falsified by new evidence:* disprove, belie, rebut, show to be false, prove unsound, refute, confute.

Ant. 2 verify, confirm, certify, justify.

falter *v.* **1** *My uncle never faltered in his belief in the value of self-reliance:* hesitate, be undecided, waver, vacillate, fluctuate, demur, be irresolute, show weakness, shrink, lag; *Informal* dilly-dally, blow hot and cold. **2** *The boy faltered when the policeman demanded his name:* stammer, speak haltingly, pause nervously, stutter, mumble, halt. **3** *She faltered toward the door in the dark:* stumble, move unsteadily, teeter, stagger, totter, reel; shamble, shuffle, dodder.

Ant. 1 persevere, persist, proceed.

fame *n. Charles Lindbergh achieved great fame as an aviator:* eminence, prominence, repute, renown, celebrity, public esteem, glory, popularity, illustriousness, prestige, notability, pre-eminence, distinction, note, laurels, glory.

Ant. obscurity, oblivion; disgrace, dishonour, disrepute, discredit, infamy, ignominy.

"Fame is proof that people are gullible." —*Ralph Waldo Emerson*

---

familiar *adj.* **1** *The boy and his pony are a familiar pair around town:* often encountered, well-known, known, seen frequently, generally seen; frequent, habitual, commonplace, ordinary, everyday, common, proverbial, customary, usual, general; conventional, accepted, stock, traditional. **2** *Are you familiar with the rules?:* acquainted, cognizant of, conversant, informed about, versed in, abreast of, no stranger to, apprised of,

experienced at, at home in; skilled in, proficient at, seasoned. **3** *After a good dinner, we all loosened up and became quite familiar:* friendly, informal, amicable, close, intimate, confidential, unreserved, cosy, snug, chummy, hand in glove, brotherly, fraternal, accessible, companionable, *Spanish* simpático, *German* gemütlich; forward, unduly intimate, free, bold, impertinent, taking liberties, disrespectful, intrusive.
—*n.* **4** *Not even his familiars knew of his marriage:* friend, close aquaintance, crony, buddy, intimate, chum, pal, confidant, boon companion.
Ant. 1 unfamiliar, unknown, uncommon, new, unusual, unconventional, infrequent, rare, unaccustomed, extraordinary. **2** unfamiliar, ignorant, unversed, unacquainted, uninformed; unskilled, unseasoned. **3** distant, detached, indifferent, formal, aloof, cold.
◇ *Word origin:* See FAMILY.

familiarity *n.* **1** *I asked him to translate the words on the coin because of his familiarity with Latin:* knowledge, acquaintance, acquaintanceship, intimacy, comprehension, skill, proficiency, conversance, experience. **2** *She boasts about her familiarity with the duchess:* closeness, intimacy, friendship, association, close acquaintance; fellowship, brotherhood, amity, fraternity, brotherliness; *Informal* cosiness, chumminess. **3** *He treated us with familiarity:* informality, ease, absence of ceremony, naturalness, unconstraint, unreserve. **4** *I dislike that shop assistant because of his familiarity:* impertinence, disrespect, impudence, forwardness, presumption, undue intimacy, over-familiarity, undue liberty, intrusiveness, impropriety, unseemliness, indecorum.
Ant. 1 unfamiliarity, ignorance, inexperience. **2** unfamiliarity, distance. **3** formality, constraint, reserve. **4** propriety, properness, respect, decorum.

familiarize *v. Deborah needs to familiarize herself with her new camera:* acquaint, make familiar, accustom, make conversant, instruct, educate, edify, inculcate, teach, school, inform, tutor, enlighten; make used to, acclimatize, habituate, season.

family *n.* **1** *Our family needs a larger house. Do you want a large family?:* parents and children; children of two parents, issue, offspring, progeny, brood. **2** *My family all get together at Christmas:* relatives, kin, kinsmen, kith and kin, kinfolk, kinsfolk, relations. **3** *The Hapsburg family ruled Austria for years:* house, lineage, ancestry, line, dynasty, clan, tribe, breed; genealogy, race, stock, blood, extraction; forbears, parentage, forefathers. **4** *Both English and Russian belong to the Indo-European family of languages:* group, division, class, classification, kind, order, set, category.
◇ *Word origin: Family* comes from Latin *familia*, household. The root word is Latin *famulus*, servant. *Famulus* may be a survival from a language spoken in Italy previous to the coming of the Italic-speaking ancestors of the Romans.

famine *n.* **1** *Crop failures are causing famine in Asia:* general scarcity of food, short rations, starvation, extreme hunger, acute shortage, want, deficiency, paucity, dearth, lack, scarcity, scantiness, insufficiency, exhaustion, meagreness, depletion, destitution, poverty, short supply.
Ant. 1, 2 abundance, surfeit, sufficiency, feast, bounty, glut.
◇ *Word origin:* See FAMISH.

famish *v. I'm famished because I missed lunch:* be eager for food, be ravenous, suffer extreme hunger, distress with hunger, deprive of nutriment.
◇ *Word origin: Famish* and *famine* come from Latin *fames*, hunger.

famous *adj. Elizabeth Taylor is a famous film star:* well-known, noted, celebrated, prominent, renowned, far-famed; eminent, illustrious, notable, distinguished; conspicuous, notorious.
Ant. obscure, unknown, undistinguished, unsung, inglorious, obscure, forgotten, uncelebrated.

fan *n. He is such a devoted football fan that he travels with his team:* enthusiast, follower, supporter, partisan, admirer, zealot, fanatic; *Slang* nut, freak, booster.

fanatic *n. The fanatics on both sides want a civil war:* zealot, enthusiast, extremist, maniac, member of the lunatic fringe; activist, radical, militant.
Ant. unbeliever, cynic; Laodicean.
◇ *Word origin: Fanatic* literally means "pertaining to a temple." It comes from Latin *fanum*, temple, from which we also get our poetic word *fane*, temple. The *fanatici* ("fanatics") of classical antiquity were priests of the temples of Cybele and other goddesses whose worship involved frenzy. Such people were considered to be maniacs.

fanaticism *n. His religious fanaticism led him to execute heretics:* zealotry, enthusiasm, extreme zeal, intemperance, ruling passion, obsession, monomania, extremism, wild and extravagant notions; activism, militantism, radicalism, dogmatism.
Ant. cynicism, scepticism, indifference, apathy, latitudinarianism.

fanciful *adj.* **1** *She has a fanciful way of calling her plants by name:* whimsical, flighty, imaginative, capricious, humorous, inventive, odd, romantic, fantastic, bizarre, quixotic, eccentric, curious, unusual, unpredictable. **2** *His stories for children are filled with fanciful characters:* unreal, imaginary, fictitious, fabulous, based on fancy, fey, fantastic, chimerical, apocryphal, mythical, legendary.

Ant. 1 unimaginative, conventional, conservative, sensible, sober, ordinary; prosaic, predictable. **2** real, realistic, true.

fancy *n.* **1** *It suited the little girl's fancy to give a tea-party for her dolls:* imagination, whimsy, caprice, fantasy. **2** *She had a fancy that Prince Charming would come along:* illusion, fantasy, figment, day-dream, reverie, conceit, vagary, crotchet, vision, notion, dream, caprice. **3** *She has a fancy for rich desserts:* leaning, liking, longing, fondness, predilection, inclination, relish, penchant, partially, capricious preference, taste, desire, *Informal* hankering.
—*adj.* **4** *The stationery was decorated with a fancy border. The shop handles fancy foods:* showy, not plain, unusual, ornamental, decorative, ornate, intricately wrought, elegant, elaborate; florid, rococo, gingerbread, baroque; fine, special, distinctive, superior, superfine, exceptional, specially selected, de luxe, epicurean, gourmet; expensive, high-priced, extravagant.
—*v.* **5** *Do you fancy marrying an Indian prince?:* imagine, dream of, picture, conceive of. **6** *I fancy he'll get the promotion:* suspect, suppose, think, assume, opine, conjecture, imagine, surmise, presume, be inclined to think, suspect, take it. **7** *She fancies the man with the blue eyes:* like, have a mind to, take a liking to, be bent upon, take to, have an eye for, want, long for, favour, be fond of, be pleased with, crave, yearn for, *Informal* hanker after; relish, enjoy.
Ant. 2 conviction, certainty. **3** dislike, distaste, aversion. **4** plain, ordinary, undecorated; common, inferior; low-priced, cheap, modest, inexpensive.
◇ *Word origin:* See FANTASY.

fantastic *adj.* **1** *She had some fantastic idea that I was poisoning her:* weird, odd, queer, freakish, antic, bizarre, amazing, wild, extravagant, absurd, mad, ridiculous, preposterous, outlandish, grotesque, implausible, unbelievable, incredible, strange, irrational, extreme, far-fetched; romantic, visionary, imaginary, chimerical, fanciful, quixotic, illusory. **2** *The writer received a fantastic amount of praise for his new play:* great, extravagant, extreme, huge, enormous, tremendous. **3** *Informal This is a fantastic dessert:* marvellous, extremely good, wonderful, sensational, great, superb.
Ant. 1 reasonable, sensible, credible, ordinary, rational, common. **2** ordinary, moderate, limited. **3** common, ordinary, poor; *Slang* crummy.
◇ *Spelling tip:* Remember that *fantastically* is spelt with two *l's*: *fantastic + -ALLY.*

fantasy Also **phantasy** *n.* **1** *We all have the occasional fantasy of telling the boss what we think of him:* fancy, imagination, realm of dreams, mind, make-believe, unreality. **2** *Some of the old fantasies about the space age are coming true:* illusion, day-dream, imagining, dream, reverie, invention, visionary idea, fiction, figment, supposition, caprice, whimsy; nightmare, vision, chimera, apparition, mirage, phantasm, phantom, hallucination.
Ant. 1, 2 reality, actuality, fact.
◇ *Word origin: Fantasy* comes from Greek *phantasia*, appearance, phantasm, imagination. *Fantasy* has been used in English now for about 600 years and for much of that time it has been merely an alternative spelling for *fancy. Fancy* was originally a contraction of *fantasy.*

far *adv.* **1** *Our land extends far beyond the fence:* a long way, at a great distance, distantly, deeply, to a remote point, to a distant point, yonder, afar, beyond range. **2** *The weather was far worse than we expected:* very much, much, incomparably, to a great degree, immeasurably, greatly, transcendently, a great deal, considerably.
—*adj.* **3** *I long to travel to places that are far away:* far-off, remote, way-off, yonder, out-of-the-way, far-removed.
Ant. 1 close, near, nigh. **2** less, little. **3** near, nearby, close.

farce *n.* **1** *His new farce got very good reviews:* satirical comedy, broad comedy, burlesque, harlequinade, parody, low comedy. **2** *There is a great deal of farce in this novel:* buffoonery, horse-play, tomfoolery, ridiculousness, absurdity, nonsense, drollery. **3** *Freedom of the press is a farce under a dictatorship:* sham, mockery, travesty, pretence, make-believe, absurdity, parody.
Ant. 1 tragedy. **2** seriousness. **3** reality.
◇ *Word origin: Farce* goes back to Medieval Latin *farsa*, stuffing (forcemeat), which in turn comes from *farcire*, to stuff. The word entered English in this sense around the year 1400. The kind of entertainment we today call *farce* acquired its present name at about the same time. This may well have been a figurative extension of the culinary meaning. *Farce* has an important characteristic in common with *stuffing:* it has got to be light yet highly seasoned or it is altogether indigestible.

fare *n.* **1** *The bus fare has gone up another penny:* charge for journey, passage-money, ticket price, fee, cost of transport. **2** *The taxi-driver stopped to pick up a fare:* paying passenger, rider, customer, client. **3** *The fare served on the cruise was excellent:* food, food and drink, provisions, victuals, diet, table, menu, board.
—*v.* **4** *He has fared well in the construction business:* manage, get on, get along, experience good or bad fortune, go through an experience, turn out, do, perform.

farewell *interj.* **1** *Now we must say "farewell":* goodbye; *Informal* so long, Godspeed; *French* adieu, au revoir, *Spanish* adios, *Italian* arrivederci, ciao, *German* auf Wiedersehen, *Japanese* sayonara.

—*n.* 2 *We exchanged hasty farewells and parted:* goodbye, parting wish, parting compliment, valediction. 3 *It was a painful farewell:* leave-taking, departure, departing, parting, adieu.
Ant. 1 hello, greetings. 2 salutation, welcome, greetings. 3 meeting, arrival.
◇ *Word origin:* Farewell is short for the older *fare thee well.*

far-fetched *adj. His theory of a coming invasion from outer space is far-fetched:* improbable, unlikely, implausible, doubtful, dubious, preposterous, unconvincing, strained.
Ant. likely, probable, plausible.

farm *n.* 1 *Her uncle grows corn and soya beans on a 200-acre farm:* tract, spread, land, holding, property, estate, grange, plantation, country place.
—*v.* 2 *He now farms almost all of his land:* cultivate, have under cultivation, use for raising crops, produce crops, till the soil, plant, engage in agronomy, practise husbandry; (*variously*) plough, harvest, reap, sow.
◇ *Word origin: Farm* comes to us via French *ferme* from Latin *firma,* a lease or fixed payment, as those under which farmers obtained their land.

farmer *n. His father is a tobacco farmer:* grower, raiser, planter, cultivator of land, agriculturist, person who runs a farm, agrarian, yeoman, agronomist, tiller of the soil, agricultural labourer, husbandman, harvester, reaper, tenant-farmer, smallholder.

far-sighted *adj.* 1 *Far-sighted people usually need glasses for reading:* long-sighted, hyperopic. 2 *A more far-sighted person would have anticipated war:* foresighted, forehanded, far-seeing, long-sighted, foreseeing, prescient, clairvoyant, provident, wise, judicious, prudent, level-headed, commonsensical, acute, shrewd; wisely planned.
Ant. 1 near-sighted, myopic, short-sighted. 2 short-sighted, improvident, injudicious.

farther *adv.* 1 *Didn't you walk farther than you'd intended? I'm farther into the book than you are:* further, to a greater distance, past the point that, at a greater distance; beyond, at or to a more advanced point; to a greater degree or extent, deeper.
—*adj.* 2 *The bar is at the farther end of the room:* more distant, more remote, remoter, further, more removed. 3 *The trip from London to Sydney is farther than I thought:* longer, lengthier.
Ant. 2 closer, nearer. 3 shorter.
◇ *Usage note: Farther* and *further* may be used interchangeably. If you want to be precise, however, use *farther* to mean "at a greater distance" and *further* to mean "more, in addition." Thus, *The petrol station is three miles fArther down the road, I have nothing fUrther to say.*
◇ *Word origin:* See FURTHER.

fascinate *v. The magician fascinated the children. The snake was fascinated by the charmer's music:* charm, captivate, bewitch, attract and hold, beguile, entrance, enchant, allure, grip the attention of, engross, delight, enthral, enrapture, allure, spellbind, absorb, interest greatly, enravish; transfix, hold motionless, rivet, overpower, spellbind, hold spellbound.
Ant. bore, repel.
◇ *Word origin: Fascinate* comes from Latin *fascinare,* to put under a spell, from *fascinum,* witchcraft.

fascinating *adj. The book is so fascinating that I can't put it down:* gripping, engrossing, enthralling, absorbing, riveting, overpowering, charming, captivating, enchanting, bewitching, beguiling, entrancing, alluring, interesting, delightful, spellbinding.
Ant. boring, uninteresting, dull; repellent.

fascism *n. Fascism is right-wing dictatorship with a government-controlled economy and no opposition:* right-wing dictatorship, corporate state, corporatism, corporativism; (*variously*) national socialism, Nazism; totalitarianism, police state; plutocracy, oligarchy.
Ant. socialism, democracy.
◇ *Word origin: Fascism* comes from Italian *Fascismo,* ideology of the government of Benito Mussolini (formed in 1919). The word comes from Latin *fasces,* bundle of rods around an axe (the emblem of the magistrates' power in ancient Rome). The *fasces* of Mussolini's *fascism* symbolized the anti-communist coalition that had brought it into being. In economic theory, *fascism* is often called *corporatism* and the fascist state the *corporate state.* Although Italian *fascism* has been extinct since World War II, the word is still much used in a way that makes it virtually synonymous with "right-wing dictatorship."

fashion *n.* 1 *She always dresses according to the latest fashion:* style, custom, mode, trend, general practice, usage, habit, prevailing taste, vogue, craze, fad, rage; conventionality, convention, form. 2 *She moves in a graceful fashion:* way, manner, demeanour, air, mode of action, attitude; tenor, behaviour.
—*v.* 3 *She fashioned a necklace from paper-clips:* shape, create, make, form, contrive, design, frame, devise, forge, pattern, fabricate, hew, mould, construct; compose, produce, manufacture, carve.
◇ *Usage note:* See HABIT.

fashionable *adj. We ate at a fashionable new restaurant:* in fashion, stylish, in style, modish, smart, in vogue, voguish, all the rage, chic, current, prevailing, popular; *Slang* in, with-it, hip.
Ant. unfashionable, old-fashioned, out-of-date, dated, unstylish, passé; *Slang* old hat.

fast[1] *adj.* 1 *Gazelles are very fast animals. She did a fast job. The clock is fast:* swift, quick, fleet, moving quickly, able to move rapidly, rapid,

winged; brisk, hasty, flying, hurried; accelerated; taking only a short time, done in little time, speedy, expeditious; ahead, in advance. **2** *Does she still run around with that fast crowd?:* wild, reckless, pleasure-mad, immodest, extravagant, dissipated, profligate, intemperate, wanton, dissolute, self-indulgent, rakish, free in behaviour and morals, immoral, loose, lustful, debauched, licentious. **3** *The wives soon became fast friends:* steadfast, firm, constant, unwavering, abiding, enduring, resolute, durable, steady, unswerving; loyal, devoted, staunch, stable, true, lasting, faithful. **4** *The cargo was made fast in the hold:* secure, fastened, firm, steady, immovable, rigid, firmly fixed in place, firmly tied, resistant, securely attached, stationary, taut, tight. **5** *Is the dye fast or will it run?:* permanent, ineradicable, lasting, durable, unfading.
—adv. **6** *With that extra glue the stamp ought to stick fast:* firmly, fixedly, tightly, securely, tenaciously, immovably, solidly. **7** *The child was fast asleep:* soundly, fully, completely. **8** *Don't drive so fast:* swiftly, rapidly, speedily, quickly, hastily, hurriedly. **9** *My watch is running fast:* ahead, in advance.
Ant. 1 slow. **2** upright, moral, steady, sober, virtuous. **3** unsteady, wavering, inconstant, irresolute, unstable; disloyal, unfaithful. **4** loose, weak, movable, insecure, unsteady. **6** loosely, insecurely. **8** slowly, slow, dawdlingly. **9** slow, behind, late.

fast² *v.* **1** *They always fast during the religious holidays:* refrain from eating, deny oneself food, go without food, abstain from food, go hungry; starve, famish.
—n. **2** *He will continue his fast until his demands are met:* fasting, doing without food, abstinence from food, hunger-strike; fast day, period of fasting.
Ant. 1 eat. **2** eating, feast.

fasten *v.* **1** *Fasten the mirror securely to the wall. Fasten the ends together. Fasten the lock:* attach, tie, fix firmly in position, make fast, hold fixed, hold immovable, secure, make secure, anchor, affix; (*variously*) lash, hitch, moor, truss, pin, bolt, screw, rivet, weld, pinion, bind, stick, yoke, clamp, cement, solder, fuse; unite, join, connect, adhere, put together, hold together, (*variously*) close, hook, lock, button, couple, dovetail, link, dowel. **2** *She fastened her eye on the child:* fix, direct, focus, rivet, hold.
Ant. 1 unfasten; loosen, loose; separate, untie, part, sever, sunder, divorce, divide, undo, relax, remove, detach, unbolt, unhitch, disunite, uncouple, disconnect.

fastidious *adj. She's too fastidious to enjoy roughing it:* fussy, particular, excessively critical, hard to please, pernickety, difficult, finicky, meticulous, proper, hypercritical, choosey, exacting, over-precise; over-delicate, dainty, over-refined, precious; squeamish.
Ant. remiss, neglectful, slack, casual, lax; uncritical, indulgent, easy; indelicate, unrefined, coarse.
◇ *Word origin:* A *fastidious* person often feels disgust at things that are not delicate, refined, or neat. The word comes from Latin *fastidium*, disgust.

fat *n.* **1** *I try not to eat much fat:* grease, greasy substance, animal fat, adipose tissue.
—adj. **2** *He's too fat and needs to diet:* stout, heavy, plump, chubby, overweight, obese, thickset, fleshy, pudgy, rotund, paunchy, portly, beefy, pot-bellied, lumpish, corpulent. **3** *The doctor told him to keep off fat foods:* fatty, greasy, oily, containing fat, unctuous, suety, blubbery. **4** *Informal His new venture is making a fat profit:* lucrative, rewarding, remunerative; fortunate, productive, fruitful, fertile. **5** *The gambler took out a fat wallet:* well-stocked, full, replete, plentiful, plenteous, flush, abundant, copious, well-furnished, chock-full, stuffed.
Ant. 2 lean, spare, lank, lanky, skinny, gaunt, scrawny, raw-boned, angular; thin, slender, slim, slight, cadaverous. **3** lean. **4** lean, unprofitable, unlucrative, poor, scarce, scanty, unrewarding, unremunerative, unfruitful, unproductive. **5** barren, empty, lean.

"I find no sweeter fat than sticks to my own bones." — *Walt Whitman*

---

fatal *adj.* **1** *Only her friends knew that she had a fatal illness:* terminal, deadly, mortal, causing death, lethal; virulent. **2** *Disagreement among the architects was fatal to the project:* ruinous, lethal, destructive, calamitous, disastrous, catastrophic.
Ant. 1 harmless, slight, minor, non-lethal. **2** life-giving, constructive, beneficial, vitalizing, restorative, helpful.

fatalism *n. She accepted her child's illness with a kind of fatalism:* submission to fate, passive acceptance, stoicism, predestination; helplessness, powerlessness.

fate *n.* **1** *By a twist of fate, I found myself travelling on the same train as my uncle:* destiny, predestination, predetermination; providence, will of heaven. **2** *Always losing at cards seemed to be his fate:* fortune, lot, destiny, portion, doom, kismet, *Greek* moira. **3** *The fate of the proposed bill in the Commons is uncertain:* future, outcome, upshot, prospect, ultimate fortune, chances; consequence, effect.
Ant. 1 will, choice, decision, independence, freedom, chance.

fateful *adj. Meeting you was a fateful moment in my life:* momentous, decisively important, critical, decisive, determinative, crucial, significant; ominous, portentous; fatal, disastrous.
Ant. unimportant, ordinary, insignificant.

father *n.* **1** *He resembles his father:* male parent,

sire, (*variously*) dad, daddy, pa, papa, pater, *Slang* old man. **2** *They work the land as their fathers did:* forefather, ancestor, progenitor. **3** *Alexander Graham Bell was the father of the telephone:* inventor, creator, begetter, originator, founder, author, maker. **4** *I studied with the fathers at St. Joseph's Academy:* priest, padre, abbé, pastor, curé, parson, preacher, dignitary of the church, confessor.
—*v.* **5** *A son owes a debt to the man who fathered him:* sire, act as the father of, beget, engender, procreate. **6** *The plan was fathered by a local banker:* found, originate, create, begin, hatch, author.
◇ *Word origin: Father* is *faeder* in Old English, *pater* in Latin, *patēr* in Greek, and *pəter* in Indo-European, the ancestral tongue from which Greek, Latin, English, and roughly 100 other languages have evolved throughout Europe and much of Asia over the past 5,000 years.

fatherland *n. After the war he returned to his fatherland:* homeland, native land, native soil, native country, mother country, motherland; *Latin* patria.

fathom *v. Can anyone fathom the meaning of that story?:* penetrate, work out, comprehend, understand, follow, sort out, divine, discover, get to the bottom of, ferret out, unravel, uncover.
◇ *Word origin: Fathom* comes from Old English *fæthm*, the length of span of two outstretched arms, or six feet.

fatigue *n.* **1** *I felt great fatigue after looking unsuccessfully for a job all day:* tiredness, exhaustion, weariness, debilitation, lassitude, enervation, heaviness, listlessness, languor, drowsiness, tedium, overtiredness.
—*v.* **2** *Climbing the mountain fatigued the whole scout troop:* exhaust, tire, overtire, weary, wear out, enervate, debilitate, drain, weaken; *Informal* bush, fag, whack.
Ant. 1 energy, alertness, vigour, indefatigability. **2** rest, refresh, restore, rejuvenate, renew, relieve.

fatty *adj. Butter and bacon are fatty foods:* greasy, containing fat, shortened, buttery, oily, suety, lardy, blubbery.

fatuous *adj. Everything she says is completely fatuous:* foolish, inane, silly, vacant in mind, simple, stupid, brainless, witless, asinine, imbecile, idiotic, puerile, obtuse, besotted, senseless, moronic, ridiculous.
Ant. sensible, prudent, judicious, wise, sage, sapient, clever, bright, intelligent, smart, witty.

fault *n.* **1** *His only fault is that he lacks ambition:* shortcoming, defect, deficiency, insufficiency, imperfection, flaw, failing, infirmity, frailty, weakness, weak point, drawback; taint, stain, foible, blemish. **2** *It would be wise to confess your fault:* error, blunder, wrong, mistake, misdeed, transgression, sin, oversight, offence, wrong-doing, dereliction, indiscretion, slip, cause for blame, peccadillo, misdemeanour, crime. **3** *Whose fault is it that the plan fell through?:* responsibility, guilt, answerability, accountability, culpability, blame, negligence, error of judgement.
—*v.* **4** *We can't fault his work at all:* find fault with, blame, censure, criticize.
Ant. 1 merit, excellence, virtue, perfection, strength, sufficiency. **3** credit. **4** praise.

faultless *adj. She practised the speech until her delivery and timing were faultless:* perfect, without blemish, free from imperfection, flawless, without fault, ideal, irreproachable, immaculate, unblemished, impeccable, unimpeachable; correct, accurate.
Ant. faulty, incomplete, imperfect, incorrect, defective, inaccurate, erroneous.

faulty *adj. I'd better get that faulty exhaust fixed:* unsound, defective, impaired, imperfect, injured, awry, out of order, amiss, inadequate, deficient, inferior; incorrect, mistaken, erroneous, unsatisfactory, bad, unreliable, wrong, false.
Ant. sound, perfect, complete, adequate, blameless, faultless, correct, accurate.

faux pas *n. Insulting the guest was a terrible faux pas:* breach of etiquette, mistake, blunder, gaffe, indiscretion, false step, error, impropriety, lapse; *Slang* goof, howler.
◇ *Pronunciation tip:* Neither the *x* of *faux* nor the *s* of *pas* is pronounced. The correct pronunciation is *foe-pah.*
◇ *Word origin: Faux pas* means "false step" in French.

favour *n.* **1** *Would you do me a favour and post this letter?:* good turn, kind act, good deed, service, accommodation; benefaction, largesse, courtesy, dispensation, act of grace. **2** *Punctuality is a good way to win the boss's favour:* approval, goodwill, friendly disposition, esteem, kindly regard, good opinion, approbation; support, patronage, commendation, countenance; championship, advocacy, espousal. **3** *I shall wear her favour in the tournament:* gift, present, goodwill token, memento, souvenir.
—*v.* **4** *How many board members favour the merger?:* approve, be in favour of, support, endorse, back, be for, go in for, like, commend, sanction, esteem, countenance, encourage, smile upon, side with, uphold. **5** *The teacher favours serious students. I must favour my weak ankle when I walk:* prefer, have a preference for, fancy, side with, patronize, be partial to; pamper, deal gently with, humour, indulge, use lightly, use gently. **6** *They favoured our programme with a large contribution:* support, aid, help, assist, oblige, succour, foster, accommodate, abet, show favour to, do a kindness for. **7** *She favours her grandmother more than her mother:* look like, resemble, take after, be the image of.

Ant. 1 injury, disservice, harm, hurt. **2** ill will, disfavour, malice, malevolence, antipathy, prohibition, animosity, enmity, hostility, disapproval. **4** oppose, be against, disapprove, dislike. **5** dislike, object to. **6** hurt, harm, inconvenience, thwart, foil.

"A denial of a favour is not an invasion of a right." —*James Fenimore Cooper*

---

favourable *adj.* **1** *With favourable winds, a sailing ship could outrun a steamship:* advantageous, good, giving help, affording aid, helpful, beneficial, serviceable, convenient, timely, fair. **2** *The credit agency gave him a favourable report:* approving, showing favour, commendatory, salutary, good, showing approval, well-disposed; friendly, kind, benign, amicable, sympathetic. **3** *Indications are favourable for an upsurge in business:* promising, propitious, auspicious, good, hopeful, conducive, predisposed.

Ant. 1-3 unfavourable. **1** disadvantageous, unhelpful. **2** disapproving, ill-disposed, unfriendly, unsympathetic. **3** unpromising, inauspicious.

favourite *n.* **1** *The eldest boy was her favourite:* preferred one, choice, pet, fancy, jewel, darling, blue-eyed boy, apple of one's eye. **2** *The incumbent is the favourite in the election:* probable winner, one favoured to win, front-runner. —*adj.* **3** *I can't find my favourite tie:* best-liked, preferred, pet, choice, most popular, special.

favouritism *n. A wise teacher never shows favouritism:* partiality, bias, favouring of one over others, one-sidedness, partisanship.

fawn *v. The waiters fawned over the rich guest in the hope of a tip:* be servile, be obsequious, ingratiate oneself, truckle, toady, pander, seek favour, bow and scrape, flatter, pay court.

Ant. be insulting, ignore.

faze *v. The roof could fall in and it wouldn't faze her:* disconcert, fret, rattle, daunt, worry, disturb, upset, discompose, perturb, discomfit, embarrass, abash, confound, fluster, flurry.

◇ *Word origin: Faze* comes from Old English *fēsian,* to drive away.

fear *n.* **1** *She has a great fear of the dark:* dread, fright, foreboding, terror, panic, threat, horror, affright, apprehension, alarm, dismay, trepidation, consternation, disquietude, quaking, perturbation, qualm, anxiety, worry, concern, fearfulness, cowardice. **2** *High places are her biggest fear:* qualm, phobia, apprehension, source of anxiety, dread; nightmare, bugaboo, bugbear, spectre, bogy; worry, concern, care. **3** *The immense space and quiet inside the cathedral gave one a proper fear of God:* reverence, awe, reverential regard, wonder, veneration, esteem, deep respect. —*v.* **4** *I fear his wrath more than anything:* be afraid of, dread, be frightened of, regard with fear, be apprehensive of, take fright, be scared of, tremble at, shudder at. **5** *The children were taught to fear God:* feel awe for, revere, respect deeply, honour humbly, venerate, reverence, esteem.

Ant. 1 fearlessness, bravery, intrepidity, courage, confidence, security, calm, assurance, aplomb; backbone, endurance, grit, guts, heroism, pluck.

◇ *Word origin: Fear* comes from Old English *faer,* danger, sudden calamity. It is related to Old Saxon *vār,* ambush. Also related is the Latin *periculum,* danger, from which we get our word *peril.*

fearful *adj.* **1** *A fearful bolt of lightning split the sky:* frightening, frightful, dreadful, causing fear, terrible, dread, alarming, formidable, appalling, macabre, ominous, ghastly, terrifying, distressing, shocking, portentous, horrible, sinister, dire, horrid, eerie, lurid, awful. **2** *We were fearful that she might harm herself:* afraid, frightened, apprehensive, alarmed, aghast, panicky, haunted by fear, anxious, worried, scared, full of fear, uneasy, concerned, nervous. **3** *Strangers alarm the fearful child:* frightened, tremulous, nervous, showing fear, intimidated, diffident, timid, timorous, anxious, panic-stricken, panicky, scared, faint-hearted, chicken-hearted, apprehensive.

Ant. 1 reassuring, encouraging, pleasant, benign. **2** fearless, unafraid, confident. **3** fearless, audacious, brave, courageous, bold, dauntless, valiant, intrepid.

fearless *adj. The soldiers followed their fearless leader into battle:* dauntless, bold, undaunted, unafraid, confident, intrepid, brave, courageous, undismayed, without fear, unflinching, unshrinking, gallant, daring, venturesome, adventurous, unabashed, valiant, indomitable, valorous, heroic, audacious, doughty, lion-hearted, plucky, gritty.

Ant. fearful, cowardly, timorous, daunted, afraid, dismayed, apprehensive, flinching, shrinking, terrified.

feasible *adj. It's not feasible to make the trip in one day:* practicable, possible, conceivable, workable, achievable, attainable; desirable, advisable, appropriate, fitting, suitable, politic.

Ant. unfeasible, infeasible, unworkable, unachievable, impractical, impossible, unsuitable, impracticable.

◇ *Usage note:* See POSSIBLE.

feast *n.* **1** *Our host provided a feast fit for a king:* banquet, sumptuous repast, festive board, large dinner, elegant meal, large spread, Bacchanal; rich supply, surplus, bounty. **2** *When is the feast of St. Stephen:* holiday, festival, feast day, celebration, festal day, fête, jubilee, saint's day, *Italian* festa. —*v.* **3** *The lords and ladies feasted on venison:* eat richly, dine, have a feast, fare sumptuously, wine and dine, banquet, gorge, gluttonize, eat one's fill, gormandize. **4** *How many guests were feasted at the château?:* feed luxuriously, entertain expensively, wine and dine, entertain with a feast.

Ant. 1 fast, famine, fasting. **2** fast, fast day, fasting.

◇ *Word origin: Feast* goes back to Latin *festum,* holiday, festal banquet, which also gives us *festive* and *festival.* The related Latin word *feriae,* holidays, gives us our words *fair* and *ferial.* A *ferial day* was once a "church festival day" but is now a day of the week on which no feast is observed. (Words often reverse meanings — in the above case the process took hundreds of years.) Also related is Latin *fanum,* temple, from which we get our words *fane, fanatic,* and *profane.*

feat *n. The circus acrobats performed staggering feats of dexterity and strength:* deed, act, action, task, achievement, accomplishment, exploit, performance, attainment; manœuvre, stroke; adventure, enterprise, triumph, tour de force.

feature *n.* **1 features.** *The veil she was wearing obscured her features:* parts of the face, visage, aspect, lineaments, physiognomy. **2** *The landscaping is the dominant feature of the estate:* attribute, quality, hallmark, trait, characteristic, mark, property, earmark, character, important part. **3** *The high-wire act is the feature of the circus:* highlight, main item, special attraction, specialty, crowd-puller.

—v. **4** *The variety show featured a ventriloquist:* represent prominently, display, spotlight, present.

"She was a lady of incisive features bound in stale parchment." — *George Meredith*

---

federation *n. He is president of the new federation of garment manufacturers:* union, united group, league, confederation, confederacy, alliance, association, coalition, combine, syndicate.

fee *n. The doctor's fee was higher than we expected:* charge, consideration, payment for professional services, compensation, price, commission, honorarium, stipend, emolument, remuneration, salary, wage, hire; tariff.

◇ *Word origin: Fee* comes from Middle English *fe,* inherited estate, from Old French *fe,* fief. This goes back to a Frankish word meaning "cattle-property" from which we also get the word *feudal.* The *fee* word is also to be found in Modern German *Vieh* (pronounced *fee* and meaning "cattle") and in our word *fellow,* which comes from Old Norse *felagi,* originally one's business partner, or "wealth-sharer": *fe* (cattle, wealth, fief) + *lagi* (to share, lay). These are all related to Latin *pecu* (flock), the plural of which, *pecua,* means money, and gives us our word *pecuniary.*

feeble *adj.* **1** *The old woman is too feeble to do her own shopping:* enfeebled, weak, weakened, infirm, sickly, disabled, not strong, ailing, fragile, debilitated, delicate, frail, decrepit, enervated, powerless, impotent, puny, forceless, senile, doddering, declining. **2** *We were embarrassed by his feeble attempts to be funny:* ineffective, poor, flat, spiritless, thin, frail, lacking force, tame, meagre, vapid, faint, weak, flimsy, flabby, slight, insipid, lame, ineffectual, paltry, wishy-washy, colourless, inadequate.

Ant. 1 robust, strong, sturdy, stout, stalwart, vigorous, lusty, energetic, hale, healthy. **2** effective, effectual, successful; forceful, cogent, vehement, ardent; hearty, strong, spirited.

◇ *Word origin:* It is sad to see a person who is *feeble.* The word comes from Latin *flebilis,* sad, lamentable.

feeble-minded *adj. The feeble-minded child needed special tuition:* mentally slow, retarded, subnormal, half-witted, moronic, imbecilic; senile; weak-minded, stupid, childish, senseless.

Ant. bright, intelligent, smart.

feed *v.* **1** *She must struggle to feed and clothe such a large family:* supply with nourishment, provide food for; feast, cater for, wine and dine; give as food. **2** *Pigs will feed on almost anything:* eat, take nourishment, consume, take food, devour, fare; graze, pasture. **3** *Applause feeds his ego:* nourish, nurture, support, augment, encourage, maintain, strengthen, bolster, sustain, foster; gratify, satisfy, minister to.

—n. **4** *I bought a sack of cattle feed:* foodstuff, nourishment, food for animals, provisions, fodder, victuals, provender, viands, comestibles, forage, mash, pasture.

Ant. 1 starve. **3** starve, thwart, deny, stifle.

◇ *Word origin: Feed, food,* and *fodder* all come from the same Old English word *fōda,* food.

feel *v.* **1** *I love to feel silk pyjamas against my skin:* perceive by touch, sense, touch, examine by touching, have the feeling of; palpate, paw, handle, finger, manipulate, press. **2** *He feels the cold more than most. I feel a sense of guilt about what happened:* have a sensation of, experience, sense, perceive, suffer from, be aware of; understand, comprehend, know, see, discern, observe, notice. **3** *He had to feel for the light switch in the dark. Can you feel your way in the dark?:* grope, find by touching, fumble, search with the hands; reach, probe. **4** *I feel that he should resign:* be of the opinion that, believe, think, be convinced, sense, have an impression. **5** *It's hard to feel for someone so selfish:* have sympathy, sympathize with, share the feelings of, have compassion, be moved by, be touched by, be stirred by.

—n. **6** *Don't you like the feel of this material?:* feeling, sensation, touch, texture, composition, character, make-up.

◇ *Usage note: Feel* is a good word, but some people over-use it as a synonym for *think, believe*, or even *know* (def. **4**). It's as if by saying "I feel this is wrong" they aren't committing themselves as fully as saying more definitely *I think this is wrong, I believe this is wrong, I know this is wrong.* Don't be wishy-washy and hide behind the word *feel.* If you *think, believe*, or *know*, say so!

"She had a mannish manner of mind and face, able to feel hot and think cold." —*Joyce Cary*

---

feeling *n.* **1** *He has no feeling in his left hand. The feeling of warmth from the fire was lovely:* sense of touch, sensation, tactile sense, perception by touch, sensibility, awareness, consciousness. **2** *He had a feeling of intense joy when his son was born:* emotion, sense, sensation, thrill, reaction, impression, response, sentiment; aura, atmosphere. **3** *She has no feeling for the suffering of others. He played the piece with great feeling:* sympathy, compassion, concern, sensitivity, susceptibility, passion, emotion, ardour, affection, sentiment, fervour, vehemence, zeal, pity, earnestness, verve, enthusiasm, warmth, gusto, spirit. **4** *My feeling is that we should postpone the meeting:* opinion, view, point of view, attitude, impression, instinct, inclination, sentiment.

Ant. 1 numbness, insensibility, insensateness. **3** insensitivity, unconcern, imperturbability, coldness, apathy. **4** unfeeling, unemotional, dispassionate, cold.

feelings *n. pl. He doesn't care about the feelings of others:* sensibilities, susceptibilities, emotions, sensitivities; pride, ego, self-esteem.

feign *v.* **1** *She feigned surprise and they believed her:* simulate, affect, pretend, fake, make believe, sham, imitate deceptively, put on, make a show of. **2** *He feigned an alibi for the time of the robbery:* make up, invent, forge, concoct, counterfeit, devise deceptively, fabricate, fake, *Slang* cook up.

◇ *Spelling tip: Feign* and *feint* follow the spelling rule "*i* before *e* except after *c* or when sounded like *a* as in *neighbour* and *weigh.*" There is that *a* sound in *feign* and *feint*, thus they are spelt *fEIgn* and *fEInt.*

◇ *Word origin:* When we *feign* something, we give it a false appearance or shape. *Feign* comes from Latin *fingere*, to shape, to mould clay with the fingers. Our word *feint* has the same origin, as do *fiction* and *figure.*

feint *n. The dogs made a few feints at each other, then backed away without fighting:* feigned attack, pass, bluff, deceptive movement, move; artifice, stratagem, pretence, manœuvre, ruse, ploy, trick, gambit, hoax, subterfuge, wile, dodge, pretext; mask, blind.

◇ *Spelling tip:* See FEIGN.

◇ *Usage note:* See FAINT.

◇ *Word origin:* See FEIGN.

felicitous *adj.* **1** *Champagne is for weddings and other felicitous occasions:* happy, joyful, joyous, fortunate, propitious. **2** *The young man searched hard for a felicitous last line to his poem:* apt, appropriate, suitable, fitting, well-chosen, pleasing, happy, inspired; effective.

Ant. 1 infelicitous, solemn, inappropriate. **2** infelicitous, awkward, clumsy, unfortunate.

◇ *Word origin:* See FELICITY.

felicity *n.* **1** *Her felicity knew no bounds when he asked her to marry him:* happiness, blissfulness, bliss, ecstatic joy, delight, delectation, paradise, heavenly contentment, heaven, beatitude, ecstasy. **2** *He usually expresses himself with felicity:* aptness, charm, grace, nicety, fitness, effectiveness, suitability, appropriateness; skill, knack, ingenuity.

Ant. 1 sorrow, misery, sadness, unhappiness. **2** inappropriateness, clumsiness, awkwardness.

◇ *Word origin: Felicity* and *felicitous* come from Latin *felix*, happy.

fell *v. One more blow was needed to fell the tree:* knock down, cut down, cause to fall, hew down, prostrate; demolish, destroy, raze.

fellow *n.* **1** *Harry is certainly a nice fellow:* boy, man, chap; *Slang* bloke. **2** *The boy went to join his fellows on the playing-field:* companion, associate, friend, comrade, consort, chum, coworker, compatriot, colleague, pal, mate; peer, equal.

Ant. 1 girl, woman, lass. **2** foe, opponent, antagonist, stranger.

◇ *Pronunciation tip: Fellow* should, of course, be pronounced *fell-o* and not "fell-er" or "fell-a." These last pronunciations may sound right in films, but they are not generally acceptable.

◇ *Word origin:* See FEE.

fellowship *n. He enjoys the fellowship of his co-workers:* companionship, comradeship, friendliness, cordiality, friendship, sociability, amicability, intimacy, familiarity, amity, affability; society, association, fraternity, brotherhood.

Ant. unfriendliness, unsociability; antagonism, hostility.

female *adj.* **1** *She is the eldest female child:* girl, woman; offspring-bearing, child-bearing. **2** *Sewing is considered a female occupation:* feminine; womanly, ladylike, womanlike. —*n.* **3** *There are more females than males in our society:* woman, girl. **4** *This litter consists of 2 males and 7 females:* female animal, offspring-bearing animal; (*variously*) mare, dam, sow, heifer, cow, bitch, hen.

Ant. 1 male, **2** male, masculine, manly, virile. **3** male, man, boy. **4** male.

◇ *Word origin:* See FEMININE.

feminine *adj.* **1** *Gentleness was long considered a feminine trait:* womanly, female, female-like, like a woman, girlish, ladylike, gentle, soft; dainty, delicate.

Ant. 1 masculine, male, manly, virile; indelicate, rough, mannish, unfeminine.

◇ *Word origin: Feminine* comes from Latin *femina*, woman, whose diminutive form *femella* gives us *female.* The root meaning is "she who suckles" (Latin *felare*, to suckle young). The same Indo-European root gives the same association of meanings in Greek: *thēlē*, nipple, and *thēlus*, female.

femininity *n. She was a tough-minded executive, but she never lost her femininity:* womanliness, female quality, girlishness, femaleness, feminineness; softness, gentleness.

Ant. masculinity, manliness, virility; toughness, mannishness.

fence *n.* **1** *We built a fence round the yard to keep the dog in:* barrier, protective enclosure, palings, palisade, rail, barricade, stockade.

—*v.* **2** *It took miles of barbed wire to fence in the farm:* enclose with a fence, surround, secure, encompass, gird, hedge, pen, encircle, hem in, wall in, coop, confine. **3** *He fenced with his new sword:* duel, cross swords, engage in sword-play.

◇ *Word origin:* A *fence* is a means of defence. In fact, the word *fence* grew out of shortening the word *defence.*

"Good fences make good neighbours."

—*Robert Frost*

---

fend *v.* **1** *The minister fended off a mass of reporters and got into his car:* ward off, avert, push away, keep off, avoid, repel, repulse, parry. **2** *As a grown-up, you must fend for yourself from now on:* manage, provide, shift, survive, take care of, support.

◇ *Word origin:* When you *fend* something off you are defending yourself. *Fend* is just a short form of *defend*, formed over the centuries by dropping the first syllable.

ferment *v.* **1** *We decided to let a jug of raw apple-juice ferment into cider:* turn partly into alcohol, undergo fermentation, turn; sour, seethe, bubble up, foam, froth, effervesce. **2** *Student politics fermented during the late 1960's:* seethe, be turbulent, smoulder, fester, agitate, inflame.

—*n.* **3** *What kind of ferment do the wine-makers use?:* fermentation, fermentation agent; yeast, mould, enzyme, leaven, leavening. **4** *The ferment among the students caused the college to close:* unrest, disruption, agitation, inflammation, turmoil, turbulence, tumult, commotion, uproar.

Ant. 4 calmness, quiet.

◇ *Usage note:* See FOMENT.

ferocious *adj. Tigers are among the most ferocious of animals:* savage, bestial, rapacious, brutish, ravening, predatory, fierce, violent; relentless, merciless, barbarous, ruthless, atrocious, murderous, maddened, enraged, bloodthirsty, fiendish, brutal, deadly.

Ant. tame, domesticated, subdued, submissive, mild, calm.

fertile *adj.* **1** *Anything grows in this fertile ground. We were surprised that the old mare was still fertile:* productive, fruitful, fructuous, fecund, vegetative, plenteous, luxuriant, loamy, rich; generative, reproductive, capable of bearing offspring, prolific; capable of developing, fertilized, fecundated, fructified. **2** *His fertile mind keeps turning out new schemes:* imaginative, productive, inventive, creative; original, ingenious.

Ant. 1 infertile, barren, unproductive, unfertilized, poor, dry, unfruitful; impotent, sterile. **2** unproductive, uninventive, unimaginative, uncreative.

fertilize *v. The male fish fertilizes the female's eggs. The garden soil needs fertilizing:* make fertile, render productive, impregnate, make fruitful, fructify, furnish with pollen, fecundate, pollinate, inseminate; enrich, feed with nutrients, manure.

fervent *adj. The lawyer made a fervent plea for clemency:* earnest, impassioned, fervid, warm-hearted, passionate, ardent, devout, zealous, intense, keen, eager, vehement, spirited, fierce, heartfelt, whole-hearted, hearty, fiery, enthusiastic.

Ant. cool, cold, chilly, frigid; apathetic, impassive, phlegmatic, unfeeling, unimpassioned.

fester *v.* **1** *Her boil festered and had to be lanced:* form pus, suppurate, become infected, inflame, ulcerate, blister; rot, putrefy. **2** *Her resentment had festered for many years:* rankle, smoulder, intensify, grow, grow virulent; gall, chafe, fret, nettle, pique, rile.

◇ *Word origin: Fester* comes from Latin *fistula*, ulcer.

festival *n. The church was decked out for the harvest festival:* feast, celebration, holiday, carnival, fête, festivities, jubilee, gala day, gala, jamboree, fiesta.

◇ *Word origin:* See FEAST.

festive *adj. We all wore festive costumes to the ball:* festal, joyous, gala, merry, jolly, gay, convivial, light-hearted, celebratory; larkish, playful, sportive, frolicsome.

Ant. funereal, gloomy; sad, lugubrious, glum, drab, dreary.

◇ *Word origin:* See FEAST.

fetch *v.* **1** *Throw a stick and watch the dog fetch it:* get and bring back, retrieve, get, obtain, bring. **2** *The load of furniture should fetch a good price:* sell for, bring, procure, yield, realize, get; cost, afford, amount to.

◇ *Word origin: Fetch* comes from Old English *fetian*, to fetch, and is related to Old English *fōt*, foot. (To *fetch* a thing involves leg-work.)

fête *n.* **1** *They held a lavish fête at their country house:* party, feast, celebration, gala, garden party, banquet, carnival; *French* bal masqué, fête champêtre; festival, holiday.

—*v.* 2 *The ambassador will fête the visiting dignitaries:* wine and dine, give a party for, feast, banquet; treat, regale.

◇ *Word origin: Fête* was originally a French word, a festival, celebration, feast.

fetid *adj. The room reeks of that fetid cigar smoke:* stinking, malodorous, rank, foul, ill-smelling, noisome, stenchful, stenchy, mephitic; rotten, putrid; gamy, nasty, tainted, rank, rancid; musty, fusty, mouldy; suffocating, stifling.

Ant. fragrant, odorous, odoriferous, balmy, aromatic, redolent; perfumed, scented; clean, fresh, pure.

◇ *Word origin: Fetid* literally means "stinking." It comes from Latin *fetere,* to stink.

fetish *n.* **1** *A rabbit's foot carried for good luck is a fetish:* charm, talisman, magic object; superstition; idol, image, amulet, scarab, phylactery. **2** *Cleanliness is admirable, but don't make a fetish of it:* preoccupation, obsession, craze, mania, passion, idée fixe.

fetter *n.* **1** *The guards put fetters on all the prisoners:* foot shackle, ankle irons, bond, chain; manacle, handcuff. **2** *Education aims at removing fetters from the mind:* hindrance, obstruction, curb, restraint; confinement, imprisonment, durance, duress.

—*v.* **3** *We had to fetter the horse to keep it from straying:* shackle, hobble, put into bilboes, confine, trammel, pin down, tie down, tie up, truss up, bind hand and foot; manacle, handcuff, chain. **4** *Many people are fettered by lack of self-confidence:* hamper, hold back, impede, restrain, bind, encumber; confine, cage, shut in.

Ant. 3, 4 free, unfetter, liberate, release; extricate, disencumber. **4** encourage, promote.

◇ *Word origin: Fetter* goes back to Old English *feter,* fetter, shackle. It is cognate with Latin *pedicula* and Greek *pedē,* having the same meaning. They all come from the same ancestor-word in Indo-European which gave us Old English *fōt,* from which we get our word *foot.*

feud *n.* **1** *The feud caused many deaths in the two families:* bad blood, vendetta, dispute, strife, quarrel; conflict, altercation, disagreement, bickering, falling out, argument; hostility, animosity, ill will, enmity, hard feelings, bad blood, discord, controversy; schism, faction; breach, rupture; fracas, affray, clashing, brawl, wrangle; *Informal* fuss, tiff, set-to, squabble.

—*v.* **2** *Martha and her sister have been feuding for years:* quarrel, dispute, be at odds, disagree, argue, bicker; clash, brawl, wrangle; *Informal* squabble, row.

◇ *Word origin:* See FOE.

feverish *adj.* **1** *I've been feeling feverish all morning:* fevered, hot, febrile, flushed, pyretic; fiery, red-hot, inflamed, burning, parched. **2** *He had a feverish desire to begin the race:* ardent, fanatic, impatient, over-eager, passionate, fervent, zealous, impassioned; excited, restless, wrought-up, highly-strung.

Ant. 2 composed, collected, cool; calm, unruffled, serene, tranquil; offhand, nonchalant.

few *adj.* **1** *Few countries can survive without trade:* not many, scarcely any, hardly any; scant, scanty, thin, sparse, skimpy, rare, exiguous, scarce; occasional, sporadic, infrequent, few and far between; limited, piddling, paltry, meagre, inconsiderable, infinitesimal, insignificant, unusual, uncommon, unique.

—*n.* **2** *Don't give me any more peas—I still have a few:* small number, some, several, handful.

Ant. 1 many, abundant, numerous, abounding, plentiful, bounteous; unstinted, inexhaustible.

◇ *Usage note:* (1) *Few* and *several* both refer to a small quantity or number. *Few* is pessimistic, stressing the smallness of the quantity, which may be only two; *several* can be optimistic and stresses a somewhat larger quantity, and means more than two. Note the difference in emphasis between *The team won a few games* (only a few) and *The team won several games* (more than a few, enough to be proud of). (2) If you sometimes don't know when to use *fewer* and when to use *less,* see the Usage note at LESS.

fiasco *n. My attempt to get Bill and Jane acquainted was a fiasco:* complete failure, disaster; non-success, débâcle, labour in vain, miscarriage; *Slang* flop, botch, wash-out.

Ant. success, triumph, coup.

◇ *Word origin: Fiasco* means "flask" (bottle) in Italian; and *far fiasco* is Italian slang for having a failure, a flop.

fib *n.* **1** *That compliment was a fib, but it made her feel better:* harmless lie, half-truth, white lie; untruth, prevarication, misrepresentation, falsification, fiction, fabrication, invention.

—*v.* **2** *I fibbed and told him he'd be up and about in no time:* lie, tell a white lie, tell a half-truth, stretch the truth, prevaricate, equivocate, hedge.

◇ *Word origin: Fib* comes from *fable.*

"O fortune, fortune! all men call thee fickle."
—*William Shakespeare*

fickle *adj. She's so fickle that she has a new boy-friend every week:* changeable, unpredictable, vacillating, inconstant, irresolute, inconsistent, mercurial; whimsical, capricious, volatile; giddy, feather-brained, frivolous, light-headed, flighty, erratic, fitful, spasmodic, feather-headed, wavering, fluctuating, unstable, unsteady, variable, shifting; unreliable, untrustworthy.

Ant. constant, true, faithful, loyal, staunch, steadfast, firm, resolute, changeless, invariable; settled, stable, steady, sure, reliable, trustworthy.

fiction *n.* **1** *Hemingway and Lawrence were masters of fiction:* imaginative literary work, prose narration, romance; (*variously*) narrative, novel, novella, short story, short novel, tale, play; invention, imagination, fantasy, story-telling. **2** *That story about her rich grandfather was certainly a fiction:* falsehood, fabrication, prevarication, made-up story, fable, fib, tall story, concoction, lie, forgery; *Slang* whopper, yarn, cock-and-bull story.
Ant. **1** non-fiction, journalism. **2** certainty, fact, history; reality, truth, verity.

fictitious *adj. The spy registered at an hotel under a fictitious name:* unreal, false, untrue, assumed, feigned, invented, fanciful, imaginary, unfounded, counterfeit, forged, fabricated, bogus, fraudulent, spurious, supposititious, not genuine; artificial, sham, fake, phoney, trumped-up, simulated; legendary, mythical, apocryphal.
Ant. real, true, actual; genuine, authentic, veritable; veracious, truthful.

fidelity *n.* **1** *My grandfather always votes Labour out of fidelity to the party:* devotion, loyalty, faithfulness, adherence, constancy, fealty, true-heartedness; trustworthiness, integrity, honesty, truthfulness, probity; honour, allegiance, staunchness; sincerity, good faith, earnestness. **2** *The artist portrayed the lady with great fidelity:* accuracy, exactness, exactitude, faithfulness, correspondency, adherence to fact; closeness, precision; reliability.
Ant. faithlessness, unfaithfulness, perfidy, perfidiousness, falseness, falsity, disloyalty, treacherousness, treachery, traitorousness, untruthfulness; disaffection, infidelity; inexactness, inaccuracy.

> **Exploring the Word:** Latin *fides*, trust, faith, and the related *fidelis*, faithful, give us *faith*, *fidelity*, and *hi-fi*, literally "high faithfulness" of sound reproduction. The same Latin base gives us *affiance*, *fiancé*, and *fealty* (a vassal's obligation of *fidelity* to his lord under the feudal system); *affidavit*, an oath of trust, as a sworn statement; *confide*, to entrust a secret to someone, *confidence*, faith in someone or a secret entrusted to another, and *confidential*, "in trust"; *infidel*, one who is "unfaithful" (not a believer); and *infidelity*, unfaithfulness.

fidgety *adj. The children get fidgety when we take them to church:* restless, restive, impatient; unquiet, jumpy, jittery, jerky, twitchy, nervous, uneasy, apprehensive; irritable; tremulous.

field *n.* **1** *The horses were turned loose in the field:* meadow, grassland, pasture, grazing land, lea, mead, greensward; lawn, green, common; heath, clearing. **2** *Soccer is played on a rectangular field:* playing-field; turf, court, course, pitch; lists. **3** *The general serves better in the field than at a desk:* battlefield, battleground, theatre of war, front, front line. **4** *She is a leader in the field of cosmetics:* realm, domain, province, territory, region, sphere, department, area; occupation, profession, calling, line. **5** *The eye-specialist will examine your field of vision:* scope, range, area, extent, reach, expanse, sweep, stretch, orbit, circle, spectrum.
—*v.* **6** *The square leg fielded the ball and threw down the wicket:* pick up, catch; collect, grab, retrieve, secure.

fiend *n.* **1** *People used to blame illness and misfortune on fiends:* evil spirit, demon, incubus, succubus; devil, Satan, hell-hound, prince of darkness. **2** *The police will spare no effort to capture the fiend who murdered the children:* wicked person, demon, monster, brute, beast, devil incarnate; barbarian.
◇ *Word origin:* A mean person can be a *fiend*, and the Devil is sometimes called the *Arch Fiend*. *Fiend* comes from Old English *fēond*, which meant both "the devil" and "an enemy."

fierce *adj.* **1** *The boar, when cornered, is a fierce and dangerous animal:* wild, savage, ferocious, menacing, fearful, threatening, bloodthirsty, violent, brutal, cruel, fell, feral, barbarous, merciless; enraged, raging, furious, tigerish, leonine; truculent, bellicose; voracious, ravenous, ravening; horrible, terrible. **2** *The wind was so fierce that we could hardly stand up:* powerful, strong, violent, vehement, intense, overpowering, extreme, inordinate, immoderate, overwhelming; unrestrained, unbridled, uncurbed, untamed; passionate, fiery, fervent, fervid, intensely eager, impetuous.
Ant. **1** tame, docile, gentle, harmless, domesticated; cool, civilized; kind, patient; submissive, affectionate, sweet. **2** mild, peaceful, temperate, calm.

fiery *adj.* **1** *Shadrach, Meshach, and Abednego were thrown into the fiery furnace:* full of fire, flaming, burning; intensely hot, sweltering, torrid, blazing, alight, ablaze, afire; glowing, glaring, red-hot, flashing. **2** *The doctor felt the patient's fiery cheek:* feverish, fevered, burning, febrile, inflamed, flaming, pyretic. **3** *The lovers were reunited in a fiery embrace:* ardent, passionate, fervent, fervid, violent, impassioned; highly-strung, impulsive, fierce, impetuous, demonstrative, temperamental; spirited, mettlesome, enthusiastic; zealous, vehement. **4** *He'd better learn to control that fiery temper:* hot-headed, hot-tempered, easily angered, excitable, headlong, readily provoked, impetuous, precipitate, choleric, peppery, irascible; angry, irate, violent, wrathful, irritable.
Ant. **1** extinguished, quenched. **2** cool, chilly, cold, icy, frigid. **3** indifferent, passionless, phlegmatic, unimpassioned; dispassionate; mild, tame.

fight *n.* **1** *The two gangs had a fight in the*

playground: skirmish, struggle, fray, mêlée, strife, contest, duel, tussle, scuffle, scrimmage, quarrel, fracas, brush, bout, dogfight; battle, combat, armed action, clash of arms, war, armed conflict, pitched battle, battle royal. **2** *The shop-steward always had plenty of fight in him:* spirit, pluck, grit, toughness, combativeness, militancy, mettle, gameness; belligerency, pugnacity, bellicosity. **3** *She had an awful fight with the refuse collector:* dispute, altercation, discord, contention, quarrel, feud, difference, controversy, wrangling, set-to, tussle, bickering, dissension; *Informal* squabble, brawl, scrap, row, brush, tiff. **4** *A fight was arranged between the champion and the challenger:* bout, match, prize-fight, event, tournament, tourney, round; joust, tilt.
—*v.* **5** *The story tells how David fought Goliath:* battle, do battle with, join battle with, take up arms against, cross swords with, come to blows with, combat, struggle with, encounter, engage, battle; rise up in arms, go to war, wage war, exchange blows, take up the cudgels, scuffle, brawl, skirmish, tussle, scrap, box, spar, duel; joust, tilt. **6** *She fought back the tears as she spoke:* resist, contend against, strive with, struggle against, oppose, repulse. **7** *They fought the war all across Europe:* wage, conduct, carry on. **8** *I separate the children when they start fighting:* argue, dispute, clash, feud, wrangle, bicker, squabble.
Ant. 1 pacification, reconciliation, reconcilement; appeasement, compromise.

"To fight against the shoddy design of those goods by which our fellow-men are surrounded becomes a moral duty."
—*Nikolaus Pevsner*

fighter *n.* **1** *Will both fighters last 15 rounds?:* boxer, pugilist, prize-fighter; sparring partner. **2** *If you come from the slums, you have to be a fighter in order to survive:* person with spirit, scrapper. **3** *The king decorated him as a brave fighter:* warrior, soldier, military man, combatant, fighting man; belligerent, militarist.

figment *n. The prowler on the roof turned out to be a figment of my imagination:* fabrication, fancy, fantasy, fiction, invention, concoction; story, fable, canard; falsehood.
Ant. fact, reality, actuality, certainty.

figurative *adj. She used the word "dead" in its figurative sense to mean "tired":* metaphorical, not literal, symbolic, involving a figure of speech; ironic, satirical, humorous; hyperbolical; allegorical; flowery, florid, ornate.
Ant. literal, precise, verbatim, faithful, exact; prosaic, unpoetical, plain.
◇ *Usage note:* To clarify the difference between *figuratively* and *literally*, see the usage note at LITERAL.

figure *n.* **1** *The figure for "one" is "1":* numerical symbol, digit, number, cipher, numeral. **2** *He named a figure that was much more than we could pay:* price, amount, rate, cost, quotation, sum, value. **3 figures.** *I was never much good at figures:* arithmetic, sums, calculations. **4** *The gown showed off her lovely figure:* form, shape, outline, silhouette, body, physique, build; contour, cut, cast; configuration, frame, anatomy. **5** *Michelangelo was one of the great figures of the Renaissance:* personage, character, person, notable, eminence, force, leader, factor, presence, man, woman. **6** *She bought a scarf printed with a spiral figure:* pattern, design, device, motif, emblem; sign, symbol, plan, schema; diagram, illustration, drawing.
—*v.* **7** *Figure out the total and I'll pay it with a cheque:* calculate, compute, count up, add up, sum, reckon, cast, find the amount of, total, tot up, foot; assess, appraise, estimate. **8** *The wallpaper was figured with rose-buds:* embellish, adorn, ornament, mark, pattern, variegate, diversify. **9** *Historical events figure in Tolstoy's novel,* War and Peace*:* have a part, play a part, be mentioned, appear; be conspicuous, be prominent, be placed, count, shine forth, appear.
◇ *Pronunciation tip: Figure* is normally pronounced as if it were spelt "figger."
◇ *Word origin: Figure* comes from Latin *figura*, figure, from *fingere*, to make, form, mould with the hands or fingers.

figure-head *n. His title was "President," but he was only a figure-head:* authority in name only, puppet, front man; cipher, nonentity, tool.
◇ *Word origin: Figure-head* in its main sense of ornamental figure on the prow of a ship (for which there is no synonym) is a relatively recent word. It apparently first appeared in print around 1770.

file *n.* **1** *This room has been set aside for the department files:* collection of papers or documents, information for reference; archives, stacks; filing cabinet, folder, drawer, dossier. **2** *A file of customers was waiting when the shop opened:* line, queue, rank, row; string, chain, tier.
—*v.* **3** *Please file these letters under "Smith":* store, put away, arrange for later reference, classify, catalogue, index, place on file; record, list, chronicle, make an entry of. **4** *The duchess filed a petition for divorce:* apply, submit a claim, petition, put in, request. **5** *The students filed into the assembly hall:* walk in line, march in a file, follow the leader, walk in Indian fashion, move forward in a line or crocodile, advance in a queue.
◇ *Word origin: File* comes from French *fil*, string or thread, from Latin *filum*, which means the same. In Shakespeare's day, a *file* was a wire on which papers were strung and also a collection of papers *filed* in this manner. The originally military expression *file* (as in *single file*) means a row of people lined

up one after another, like papers strung on the old-fashioned *file* wire.

filial *adj. There was much filial affection in the hug she gave her father:* befitting one's child, sonlike or daughterly; respectful, dutiful.

fill *v.* **1** *Ask him to fill the bottle with turpentine:* make full, fill up; pervade, permeate, overspread, charge; saturate, impregnate, infuse, suffuse; load, lade, pack; cram, glut; feed fully, gorge, sate, satisfy, satiate. **2** *Has that secretarial position been filled?:* occupy, take up, assign, fulfil, supply; function, serve, act; preside, do duty; execute, discharge, carry out. **3** *Does John need help in filling those orders?:* make up, furnish, replenish, supply, provide; provision, outfit, stock; lay in, lay by, store. **4** *This new medicine fills an urgent need:* satisfy, meet, supply, answer, take care of. **5** *Breathe in until your lungs fill with air:* expand, inflate, dilate, distend; blow up, puff.
—*n.* **6** *Have you had your fill of cashew nuts?:* full amount, sufficiency, surfeit.
Ant. drain; empty, evaporate, shrink, diminish, ebb, subside; exhaust, vacate.

film *n.* **1** *There seems to be a film of oil on the water:* thin layer, coat, coating, membrane, skin, sheet; veil, cloud, haze, mist. **2** *Who stars in his latest film?:* motion picture, movie, *Slang* flick. **3 films.** *She always wanted to work in films:* the film industry, cinema, silver screen.
—*v.* **4** *The old woman's eyes filmed over as she thought of the past:* haze, veil, mist. **5** *They're filming a detective drama here now:* make a film of, shoot.

filter *n.* **1** *The lake water passes through a filter before it is piped in to our homes:* strainer, sieve, screen, purifying device.
—*v.* **2** *The dehumidifier filters the moisture out of the air:* strain, pass through a filter, cleanse, refine, purify, clarify, filtrate. **3** *Sunlight was filtering through the venetian blinds:* seep, dribble, leak, trickle; ooze, drain, well out, exude, effuse.
Ant. 2 muddle, disturb, befoul; thicken; mix, merge, combine.
◇ *Word origin: Filter* comes from Medieval Latin *filtrum,* felt. (Felt was once a common filter.)

filth *n.* **1** *The pavements and gutters were full of filth:* foul matter, dirt, rubbish, ordure, sewage, muck, slime; contamination, squalidness, squalor, nastiness, filthiness, pollution, defilement, impurity; dung, excrement, faeces, excreta, manure; slop, refuse, garbage, offal, carrion, putridness; mud, mire, sludge, slush. **2** *They're trying to shut down those shops that sell filth:* pornography, obscenity, smut; grossness, indecency, immorality, lewdness; foul language, dirty-mindedness, vileness, corruption; suggestiveness, indelicacy; ribaldry.

final *adj.* **1** *Our final meeting of the season is next Wednesday:* last, closing, concluding; rear, rearmost, hindmost; ending, terminating, terminal; latest, last-minute; extreme, ultimate. **2** *She said "No, and that's final":* decisive, conclusive, definitive, determinative; complete, thorough, finished, exhaustive; irrevocable, unchangeable, unappealable.
Ant. 1 opening, first, initial. **2** preliminary; inconclusive, incomplete, changeable.
◇ *Usage note: Final* is a good word and today *finalize* (to put into final form) is accepted, too. *Finalize* has been in the vocabulary for about 50 years now, though it was criticized when U.S. President Eisenhower used it frequently, and is still considered by many to be a part of the "in" vocabulary of business and politics. However, in referring to putting something like a contract or political bill into final form, there is really no good synonym for it — so *finalize* it is.

finale *n. The finale of the pageant was a spectacular fireworks display:* last part, conclusion, close, end, epilogue, curtain, finish, finis, wind-up, termination, swan-song, crowning glory.
◇ *Pronunciation tip: Finale* may be pronounced as *fi-NAHL* or the Italian way *fi-NAH-lay.*

finally *adj.* **1** *Finally, the report mentions a decline in profits:* in the end, lastly, at the last, in conclusion, ultimately; eventually, at length. **2** *The gunman's fate was finally sealed when he resisted arrest:* conclusively, definitively, once and for all; inescapably, inexorably, incontrovertibly.

> **Exploring the Word:** *Finish, final,* and *finale* come from Latin *finis,* end, limit. This same Latin word gives us *confine,* to limit; *define,* to tell what the ends or limits of the meaning of a word or of a task are; *finite,* having an end, having limits; *fine,* literally ended, hence thoroughly done, excellent, delicate; and *refine,* to make finer, improve.

finance *n.* **1** *The company needs a man who knows finance:* money management, banking, investment banking, investment counselling, fiscal matters, economics, accounts.
—*v.* **2** *The bank will help me finance my new car:* pay for, raise money for, supply money for, underwrite.
◇ *Word origin: Finance* formerly meant payment, final settlement of a bill. Its source is Latin *finis,* end, which also gives us *final* and *finish.*

financier *n. The library got a large contribution from a wealthy financier:* expert in money matters, broker, banker, large-scale investor; rich man, man of means, man of substance, moneyed man, millionaire, capitalist.

find *v.* **1** *She found a diamond ring on the bus:* come upon, light upon, stumble upon, come across, chance upon; meet with, encounter, bump into. **2** *Doctors hope to find a way of beating* *cancer:* uncover, discover, hit upon, come by; unearth, dig up, disinter; track down, ferret out; detect, expose, learn, ascertain, determine. **3** *We were surprised to find you at the party:* discern, catch sight of, espy, spot, meet. **4** *They all helped me to find the ring I had lost:* regain, recover, get back, retrieve, repossess. **5** *She found peace of mind through the study of yoga:* acquire, gain, attain, achieve, get, procure, win, earn. **6** *The jury found for the plaintiff. The accused woman was found guilty of shop-lifting:* declare a verdict, determine, pronounce; decide, rule, decree, judge, adjudge, adjudicate, award.

—n. **7** *That mahogany table was a real find:* bargain, good buy, discovery; bonanza, windfall; catch, acquisition; godsend, lucky hit.

Ant. 1 lose, miss, overlook; mislay, misplace.

fine[1] *adj.* **1** *This shop has some very fine furs:* high-quality, choice, top-grade, exceptional, first-class, superior, superb, splendid, admirable, excellent, flawless, exquisite, magnificent; tasteful, smart; rare; *Slang* dandy, nifty, neat, great, spiffy. **2** *Fine hair just won't keep its curl:* thin, slender; silky, silken, delicate; light-weight, flimsy, gossamer, cobwebby, diaphanous, sheer, transparent; airy, ethereal. **3** *The hourglass contains fine sand:* powdery, pulverized, powdered, ground, refined. **4** *See if you can put a fine edge on this knife:* keen, sharp; precise, perfect; polished, brilliant, accomplished, consummate. **5** *Her new tea-set is of fine china:* delicate, fragile, exquisite, dainty, ethereal, gauzy. **6** *We complimented the child on her fine manners:* elegant, refined, fastidious, well-bred, exquisite; smart, chic, stylish, modish. **7** *If those clouds drift away, we'll have a fine afternoon:* clear, bright; pleasant, sunny, rainless, cloudless, fair. **8** *He says there's a fine distinction between "wealthy" and "rich":* subtle, hard to discern, minute, small, nice, hair-splitting; slight, tenuous, thin, unsubstantial. **9** *Bob and Edna have two fine children:* handsome, attractive, comely, good-looking, well-favoured, fair; beautiful, pretty, bonny, lovely.

—adv. **10** *Sam is doing fine in his new business:* very well, excellently, swimmingly.

Ant. 1 coarse, rough, unfinished, plain, crude. **2, 3** thick, coarse, rough, heavy, stout. **4** dull, blunt. **5** poor, inferior. **6** rough, crude, clumsy. **7** cloudy, dark, foul. **8** broad, clear, obvious. **9** ill-favoured, disagreeable. **10** poorly, badly.

fine[2] *n.* **1** *The fine for excess parking is outrageously high:* penalty, sum demanded as punishment, assessment, charge, damages, forfeit, mulct.

—v. **2** *The judge fined her £25 for loitering:* punish by a fine, penalize, assess, charge, mulct.

◇ *Word origin: Fine,* a penalty, is related to our word *finance,* which originally meant a payment, final settlement of a debt.

finery *n. She bought lots of new finery for her Caribbean cruise:* showy dress, elegant clothing, fine things, frippery, frills; trimmings, paraphernalia, trappings; gewgaws, tinsel, spangles, trinkets, baubles.

> "A modest woman, dressed out in all her finery, is the most tremendous object of the whole creation." —*Oliver Goldsmith*

finesse *n. What could have been a nasty situation was handled with great finesse:* delicacy, tact, discretion, artful management, *savoir-faire,* artfulness, craft; wile, ruse, subterfuge, artifice, stratagem; trickery, cunning, dodge, guile; intrigue, deception.

finger *n.* **1** *How do you get a child to stop sucking his finger?:* organ of touch, digit; (*variously*) thumb, forefinger, middle finger, ring-finger, little finger; pointer.

—v. **2** *The grocer asked us not to finger the tomatoes:* handle, touch, feel, caress, toy with, manipulate, play with, meddle with; poke, punch, squeeze; *Informal* paw, fiddle with, maul, twiddle.

finish *v.* **1** *We finished dinner about 9 o'clock:* end, conclude, bring to a close, complete, wind up, bring to an end; terminate, discontinue; stop, cease; seal, clinch; draw to a close; get done, accomplish, carry out, carry through, achieve, fulfil, consummate, make good; close, put an end to; get out of the way, dispose of, *Informal* knock off; realize, discharge, do thoroughly, settle. **2** *Finish these chips and I'll get some more:* use up, dispatch; consume, devour. **3** *What can we use to finish off these weeds?:* eradicate, exterminate, destroy, kill, get rid of, put out of the way; defeat, overcome completely. **4** *Why not finish the table with a walnut stain?:* surface, veneer, face, glaze, gild; lacquer, varnish, coat.

—n. **5** *At the finish no one applauded:* conclusion, end, close, termination, completion; finale, finis, fall of the curtain, ending, curtain; epilogue, dénouement; final event, wind-up, closing period, last, last stage; goal, objective. **6** *Does all the furniture have that glossy finish?:* surface, exterior, coating, veneer, lacquer; polishing, finishing touches, last touch.

Ant. 1 begin, start, undertake, commence; originate, create. **5** beginning, commencement, genesis; inauguration, inception; birth, conception.

finished *adj.* **1** *The finished job was a great satisfaction to him:* completed, concluded, ended; complete, final; consummated, perfect; entire, full, whole. **2** *The portrait was executed with finished artistry:* faultless, flawless, consummate, accomplished, skilled, impeccable; elegant, refined; beautiful, shapely, well-set; classic, ideal; cultivated, urbane, exquisite, well-bred, trained, polished, well-mannered.

Ant. **1** unfinished, incomplete, imperfect; begun. **2** green, callow, raw; inexperienced, unskilled; unrefined, inelegant, inartistic; rough, rude, coarse, crude.

finite *adj. Distances between stars are immense, but finite:* measurable, limited, bounded, countable, circumscribed, terminable, subject to limitations, confined, restricted; not everlasting, temporal, short-lived.

Ant. infinite, unlimited, unbounded, boundless, measureless; endless, perpetual.

fire *n.* **1** *Keep an extinguisher in case a fire breaks out in the house:* conflagration, blaze, flame, bonfire; flash, spark, flare; inferno, holocaust. **2** *Napoleon roused his troops with a speech full of fire:* ardour, vigour; power, intensity, force, genius, inspiration, imaginativeness, vehemence, spirit, burning passion, fervour, fervency; enthusiasm, eagerness, vivacity, gusto, earnestness; dash, élan, punch, verve, vim; splendour, brilliance, effulgence, lustre, radiance. **3** *The soldiers were ordered to hold their fire:* discharge of firearms, firing; salvo, fusillade, bombardment, volley, cannonade, broadside, enfilade; sniping, sharp-shooting.

—*v.* **4** *The guns began firing at daybreak:* shoot, discharge, project a missile, open fire, bombard, shell, fusillade, enfilade; fire off, make go off, hurl, project, eject. **5** *It took several bundles of twigs to fire the logs:* ignite, kindle, light, set on fire, set fire to, set burning, inflame; burn, catch fire. **6** *It was a speech to fire the heart of every true patriot:* arouse, stimulate, rouse, vivify, spark, inspire, animate, excite, inspirit; fill with ardour, inflame, incite, stir, stir up, quicken, instigate, foment, galvanize, trigger. **7** *The pottery was glazed and then fired at an intense heat:* bake, cook. **8** *Informal She was fired for spending too much time on the phone:* dismiss, let go, oust, remove from service, cashier; *Slang* sack, boot out, show the door, give marching orders; depose.

◇ *Word origin: Fire* comes from Old English *fȳr*, fire. This is related to Greek *pūr*, fire, from which we get our word *pyrotechnics*. Another Greek word, *purā*, taken over by the Romans into Latin as *pyra*, gives us (thanks to Sir Thomas Browne) our word *pyre*.

firearm *n. The villagers are buying firearms to protect their homes:* gun, small arm, side-arm; *Informal* shooting-iron; (*variously*) pistol, rifle, shotgun, revolver, machine-gun, submachine-gun.

firm[1] *adj.* **1** *The plastic was poured into the mould and left to set until it was firm:* stiff, hard, rigid; unbending, unyielding; solid, compressed, dense, compact; rocky, stony, adamantine; steely, flinty. **2** *The price was firm and not subject to bargaining:* settled, fixed, established, confirmed; unalterable, indissoluble. **3** *Put another nail in the frame to make it firm:* steady, not shaking, stable, fast, secure; rooted, moored, anchored; immovable; close, taut, tight, rigid, inflexible. **4** *Mother was firm in her resolve not to move away:* resolute, steadfast, determined, unwavering, resolved, staunch, persistent, unflinching, unshaken, unfaltering; earnest, serious, decided, intent, constant, steady; strong-willed, strong-minded, dogged, dead-set; obstinate, bent, inflexible, inexorable; grim, tenacious, obdurate, adamant; fearless, invincible.

Ant. loose, flabby; soft, flaccid, limp; flimsy, sleazy; unsteady, unstable; wavering, irresolute, inconstant, unreliable.

Exploring the Word: Latin root *firmus*, firm, strong, unyielding, gives us *firm; affirm*, to make firm, to ratify; *confirm*, to make thoroughly strong, to verify; *confirmation*, the act of making firm or verifying, as the *confirmation* of a hotel reservation or a religious *confirmation* in which a person is verified as to his faith and admitted to membership in a church; *firmament*, the expanse of the heavens the ancients thought was firmly supported on the back of Atlas or other deities; *infirm*, not strong, weak or sick, *infirmary*, the place for "not strong" or sick people, and *infirmity*, the weakness or sickness itself, the cause of one's lack of strength.

firm[2] *n. Rosemary has worked for our firm ever since she left school:* company, concern, organization, business, establishment, house; commercial house, partnership, corporation.

first *adj.* **1** *This painting received first prize in the contest:* foremost, leading, chief among others, principal, main, prime, head, highest; superior, pre-eminent, supreme, paramount; vital, essential. **2** *Norsemen may have been the first European settlers in the New World:* earliest, original, premier, eldest; primitive, primal, aboriginal; beginning, maiden. **3** *He teaches the first principles of life-saving:* basic, elementary, rudimentary, primary, introductory, beginning.

—*n.* **4** *We were friends from the first:* beginning, introduction, commencement, start, outset, inception, starting-point.

—*adv.* **5** *She asked first if we were free on Tuesday evening:* before anything else, to begin with, at the outset, initially; first and foremost. **6** *They want me to apologize, but I'd shoot myself first:* by preference, by choice, before; rather, sooner, preferably.

Ant. **1** secondary, subordinate, lesser. **2** later, subsequent.

◇ *Word origin: First* was the superlative of Old English *fore*, before, hence literally means "foremost."

fiscal *adj. The job as treasurer naturally entails fiscal responsibility:* financial, monetary, pecuniary, budgetary, economic.

◇ *Word origin: Fiscal* comes from Latin *fiscus*, treasury, purse, rush basket. The same Latin word gives us *confiscate.*

fish *v.* **1** *Every morning we fished off the end of the pier:* attempt to catch fish, angle, cast; hook, net, troll, trawl, seine. **2** *She opened her purse and began fishing for her lipstick:* search, hunt, grope, rummage, ferret, look for.

fishy *adj. Informal* **1** *There's something fishy about his diplomatic background:* doubtful, dubious, improbable; suspicious, suspect, unreliable, questionable; peculiar, strange, odd; extravagant, exaggerated, far-fetched; slippery, shady, dishonest, unscrupulous. **2** *She fixed me with a fishy stare:* glassy-eyed, dull, vacant, expressionless, blank.

fit[1] *adj.* **1** *Is this water fit to drink? The lorry with four-wheel drive is fit for rough use on bumpy roads:* suitable, good, adapted, appropriate; right, proper, meet, correct; seemly, fitting, becoming, befitting, decorous; pertinent, relevant, applicable, consonant; timely, seasonable; opportune, convenient; apposite, apropos. **2** *Only fit applicants need apply:* qualified, competent, trained, able; capable, capacitated, efficient; prepared, initiated; mature, ripe; ready, eligible. **3** *These days he looks fitter than I've ever seen him:* healthy, hale, well, in good physical condition, strong, robust, toned up, in good trim. **4** *She's not fit to associate with decent people:* worthy, deserving, suitable, acceptable; good enough, sufficiently virtuous.

—v. **5** *The house fits nicely in that wooded environment. Does a 12 o'clock lunch fit in with your plans?:* be suitable for, be adapted to; agree, harmonize, accord; conform, be adapted to; be the right size or shape for, correspond; become, befit; match, equal; coincide, concur. **6** *After she has fitted the dress it should be ready in a week:* try on for size, adjust, make suitable, suit, adapt; shape, alter, fashion; graduate, calibrate; correct, rectify. **7** *Money was needed to fit out the expedition:* equip, outfit; prepare, ready, make qualified, qualify, make competent; enable, empower, capacitate, train.

Ant. 1 unfit, ill-suited, unsuitable, inappropriate; unprepared, ill-fitted, inadequate, improper, unseemly; inexpedient, ill-timed, untimely, amiss.

fit[2] *n.* **1** *From early childhood she was subject to fits and loss of memory:* epileptic seizure, convulsion, spell; (*variously*) grand mal, petit mal. **2** *She had a sudden fit of coughing that she couldn't control:* spell, sudden acute attack, spasm, paroxysm, seizure, outbreak. **3** *In a fit of pique she told him to go home:* outburst, explosion, burst, access; passing mood, whim, caprice, crotchet, whimsical notion.

◇ *Word origin: Fit*[2], a seizure or convulsion, comes from Middle English *fit*, painful spell, from Old English *fitt*, conflict. Nothing further is known about the origin of the word, and in fact Old English *fitt* is what students of language call a *hapax legomenon* (from Greek *hapax*, "once only" and *legō*, "to say"). A *hapax legomenon* is a word that occurs only once in all the recorded writings of a language. Thus, our commonplace synonym for "convulsion" was a rare and obscure word in King Alfred's day.

fitful *adj. The rain has been fitful all afternoon:* irregular, intermittent, periodic, sporadic, spasmodic, now-and-then, now-and-again; unsteady, changeable, erratic, fluctuating, uneven, random, variable, convulsive; weak, listless.

Ant. constant, steady, incessant; even, equable, regular, uniform; orderly, systematic, methodical; predictable, calculable; changeless, unchanging, immutable.

fitting *adj. The visiting head of state was given a fitting welcome:* suitable, proper, decorous, seemly, appropriate, apt, befitting, meet, fit, congruous.

Ant. unfitting, unsuitable, improper, unseemly, ill-suited.

"The Turtle lives 'twixt plated decks
Which practically conceal its sex,
I think it clever of the turtle
In such a fix to be so fertile."

—Ogden Nash

---

fix *v.* **1** *The workmen fixed the aerial to the roof of the house:* fasten, attach, affix, moor, make fast, implant, rivet, anchor, place permanently, connect. **2** *The dealer fixed the price at £50:* set, settle, determine definitely, decide, establish, stabilize, prescribe. **3** *Is something added to fix the cement?:* harden, solidify, make rigid, make firm, become stable, become set; congeal, consolidate. **4** *Investigators fixed the blame for the fire on the night-watchman:* place, put, impose, affix. **5** *You'd better call someone to fix that tap:* repair, mend, patch up, correct, set right, put to rights, adjust, renovate, put in good condition, rebuild; adjust, regulate. **6** *Informal What time are you going to fix dinner for?:* prepare, make, put together, assemble. **7** *Informal If he tries that again I'll really fix him:* get even with, get revenge on, get back at; *Slang* sort him out, give him what for, settle his hash, cook his goose; retaliate, take action against.

—n. **8** *After accepting two invitations for the same evening he was really in a fix:* predicament, embarrassing situation, plight, difficulty, dilemma, awkward spot, quandary, ticklish situation; *Slang* spot, jam, pickle, scrape, hot water; muddle, mess, entanglement, involvement.

◇. *Word origin: Fix* comes from Latin *fixus*, fastened.

fixation *n. She has a fixation about birds hating*

her: obsession, preoccupation, fixed idea; delusion, complex, monomania; quirk, fetish.

fixed *adj.* **1** *France's Maginot Line was a series of fixed fortifications:* stationary, immovable, fast, firmly implanted; firm, stable, fastened, set, rooted, motionless, still, rigid. **2** *Shop owners are protesting about fixed prices. I was embarrassed by her fixed stare:* not varying, not fluctuating, constant, steady; intent, steadily directed, persistent, determined; unbending, unpliant, inflexible, firm, unwavering.

Ant. moving, mobile, wavering, unstable, unsteady, inconstant; bending, pliant; varying.

fixture *n.* **1** *The light fixture was installed on the living-room ceiling:* apparatus, appliance, equipment; attachment, appendage, appointment, equipage, paraphernalia. **2** *We lunch there so often that we're considered fixtures:* devotee, habitué; *Informal* familiar sight, old faithful, *Slang* addict.

fizzle *v.* **1** *The wet match fizzled but didn't light:* sputter, hiss; bubble, gurgle, fizz. **2** *Informal The plan fizzled out for lack of interest:* come to nothing, fail, abort, misfire, fall through, miscarry, come to grief, fall short, miss the mark; *Slang* flop; break down, collapse, founder.

—*n.* **3** *The hot coals made a fizzle as they hit the water:* hiss, sputter.

flabby *adj.* **1** *His muscles had become flabby from lack of exercise:* limp, flaccid, soft, yielding, inelastic; feeble, weak, hanging loosely, slack, floppy, drooping limply; baggy. **2** *The author's ideas were flabby and entirely conventional:* feeble, enervated; adulterated, ill-defined, emasculated, spiritless, effete, impotent, listless, lame, flimsy.

Ant. **1** firm, hard, solid; tight, taut, tense; tough, sturdy, strong. **2** plucky, gritty, tenacious.

◇ *Word origin: Flabby* is a variant of *flappy*—so weak or soft as to *flap.*

flag *n.* **1** *The country's flag was displayed in every window:* banner, emblem, standard, ensign, streamer, pennant, colours; *(in Great Britain)* Union Jack; *(in the U.S.)* stars and stripes, Old Glory, stars and bars.

—*v.* **2** *The police patrol flagged us away from the accident:* signal, warn, wave. **3** *My energy flagged after climbing all those steps:* decline, grow weak, wilt, give way, languish; grow spiritless, fall off in vigour, abate, slump, succumb, subside, sag, pall; fade, grow weary, tire, totter, dodder; faint, sink, ebb, wane, fail.

Ant. **3** freshen, recover, brace up.

flagrant *adj. That was a flagrant abuse of his authority:* shockingly bad, shameless, brazen, flaunting, audacious, immodest; glaring, gross, sheer, obvious, crying, arrant, barefaced; notorious, scandalous, conspicuous, outrageous, heinous, monstrous.

◇ *Word origin: Flagrant* comes from Latin *flagrare,* to blaze, from which we also get our word *conflagration.* Our word *blaze* is in fact related to it, as are many other Indo-European words relating to fire, burning, shining, and dazzling. Latin *flagrare* also appears in our legal phrase *in flagrante delicto* (often shortened to *in flagrante*) which means "red-handed" or literally "while the crime is blazing" (Latin *delictum* means criminal offence).

flair *n. Jane has a great flair for designing hats:* bent, knack, talent, aptitude, gift; keen perception, discernment, ingenuity, faculty, capacity; style, taste; verve, dash, panache.

◇ *Usage note:* Some people write *flare* when they mean *flair.* A *flair* is a talent or aptitude: a *flair for painting.* A *flare* is, of course, a light or a torch, or an outburst as of fire or of anger: *Flares lit up the sky. After a quick flare of temper the child calmed down.*

◇ *Word origin: Flair* comes from French *flair,* sense of smell, especially a dog's sense of smell. The French also use the word figuratively in the sense of "discernment, perceptiveness." It comes from Latin *fragrare,* to smell, from which we get our words *fragrance* and *fragrant.*

flake *n.* **1** *Snow was falling in large flakes:* flat thin piece, scale, sheet, bit, patch.

—*v.* **2** *This new coat of paint has already started to flake:* peel off, peel, come off in flakes, scale off, chip off, chip, crumble.

flamboyant *adj.* **1** *The room was decorated in flamboyant reds and purples:* ornate, gaudy, florid; baroque, rococo; showy, flashy, ostentatious. **2** *She was one of the most flamboyant actresses in the theatre:* dashing, colourful, exciting, sensational.

flame *n.* **1** *The flame of the match was visible for miles:* flare, blaze, fire, burning vapour, light, conflagration; spark, glare, gleam, glow, flash. **2** *The flame of his ambition seemed to grow with time:* ardour, passion, fervour, intensity, fervency, glow, excitement, burning zeal; enthusiasm, warmth, affection. **3** *Informal His old flame turned up at the school reunion:* sweetheart, girl-friend, beau, lover, swain, boy-friend.

—*v.* **4** *The petrol flamed up instantly when touched by the match:* burst into flames, fire, flare, kindle, light, ignite, blaze, burn with a flame; glare, shine brilliantly, flash; flush, redden, blush.

◇ *Word origin:* Latin *flamma,* a blaze, gives us *flame* and *flammable;* and also, via French, *flamboyant,* literally "flaming," and *flambé,* served flaming, as food topped with ignited brandy.

flaming *adj.* **1** *The flaming wreckage burned for hours:* blazing, burning, fiery, afire, ablaze, alight; igneous, inflammable, smouldering, glowing; bright, brilliant, shining. **2** *The bad news put the boss in a flaming rage:* violent, stormy, ardent, intense, vehement, fervid, fervent, passionate; conspicuous, flagrant, glaring, egregious.

flammable *adj. Flammable material should not be stored next to the chimney:* inflammable, combustible, igneous, combustive, incendiary.

Ant. non-flammable.

◇ *Usage note: Flammable* has now replaced its older synonym *inflammable* (from Latin *inflammare,* to kindle) in technical and commercial usage, where the word FLAMMABLE on a dangerously combustible product is thought to serve as a more unmistakable warning. It is to be hoped that everyone will eventually adopt the terms *flammable* and *non-flammable* in preference to *inflammable* and *non-inflammable.*

flank *n.* **1** *He slapped the horse on the flank to make it move:* side, haunch, loin, hip. **2** *The attack was aimed at the enemy's left flank:* side, wing, edge, border.

—*v.* **3** *Long rows of poplars flanked the avenue:* line, border, skirt; edge, fringe; lie along, wing; screen, shield, cover.

flap *v.* **1** *That shutter flaps every time there's a wind:* wave about, swing loosely, flop, flutter; shake, beat, vibrate, oscillate, agitate, move to and fro, bang.

—*n.* **2** *We heard the flap of the cat-door on the back step:* flop, flapping, bang, banging, flutter. **3** *A flap covered the entrance to the tent:* hanging piece, lap, lappet, fly, tab; skirt, apron.

flash *n.* **1** *A flash of lightning preceded the crash of thunder:* streak, blaze, glare, gleam, flare, flame; radiance, coruscation, incandescence, fulmination. **2** *The speech was lightened by some flashes of humour:* outburst, instance, occurrence, spark, glimmer, touch. **3** *Informal The waitress was back in a flash with the menus:* instant, moment, jiffy, minute, second, split second, trice, twinkling of an eye, shake, wink.

—*v.* **4** *The light on top of the police car was flashing:* blink, go on and off, flicker, sparkle, glitter; shine, blaze, glare, flame, glow, gleam; scintillate, coruscate glisten, glimmer.

flashy *adj. Her wardrobe is full of flashy clothes:* dazzling, flamboyant, showy; smart, sporty; pretentious, gaudy, garish, loud, tawdry, ostentatious; bedizened, tinsel, raffish, vulgar, in bad taste.

Ant. plain, modest, simple, natural, unaffected.

flat[1] *adj.* **1** *The lower meadow is absolutely flat:* level, horizontal, smooth; plane, planar, regular, equal, unbroken. **2** *They took their naps, lying flat in the floor:* recumbent, prostrate, prone, lying at full length, flush, low, reclining, supine, levelled, laid low. **3** *The manager issued a flat denial of all charges:* unqualified, unequivocal, thorough, out and out, positive, downright, absolute, complete, total, peremptory; clear, direct, plain, unmistakable. **4** *The ginger-ale went flat after being left open:* lacking effervescence; stale, tasteless, insipid, flavourless; dull, vapid, dead, unpalatable.

—*n.* **5** Often **flats.** *The poachers waded into the flats, looking vainly for duck:* level land, flat ground, lowlands; open country, prairie, plain; shallow, shoal, marsh. **6** *The motorway is the worst possible place to have a flat:* flat tyre, blow-out, deflated tyre, blown-out tyre, puncture.

—*adv.* **7** *Lie down flat and breathe deeply:* horizontally, levelly, prostrate. **8** *Dinner will be ready in two minutes flat:* exactly, precisely.

Ant. **1** uneven, rough, rugged, broken, irregular, scabrous, hilly, rolling; slanting, sloping; vertical, upright, perpendicular. **4** bubbly, effervescent, sparkling, fizzy; flavoursome, tasty, savoury; palatable.

flat[2] *n. The couple moved into a new three-room flat:* set of rooms, suite of rooms on one floor, rented (often furnished) rooms, apartment.

flatten *v.* **1** *Flatten the dough with the palms of your hands:* make flat, smooth, level; plane, even; press down, compress; deflate. **2** *The champion flattened his opponent in the first round:* knock down, floor, fell, ground, prostrate; *Slang* drop; crush, defeat, overwhelm, overcome.

flatter *v.* **1** *At the retirement dinner everyone flattered him shamelessly:* overpraise, compliment, praise lavishly, gratify by praise; eulogize, adulate, laud, extol, panegyrize, honour; court, cajole, blandish, beguile, wheedle; curry favour with, truckle to, toady; *Slang* butter up, soft-soap, suck up to. **2** *The films flatter him — he's not really as handsome as all that:* represent too favourably, become, show off well. **3** *I flattered myself that they really wanted to know what I thought:* delude, deceive, mislead, fool.

◇ *Word origin: Flatter* and *flattery* come from Old French *flater,* to caress with the hand (from Frankish *flat,* flat of the hand).

flatterer *n. The boss is the type who needs a staff of flatterers:* fawner, adulator, sycophant, wheedler, truckler, toady, eulogist; *Slang* yes-man, bootlicker, crawler, lickspittle.

"Just praise is only a debt, but flattery is a present." —*Samuel Johnson*

---

flattery *n. Thirty years of flattery got him nowhere when she made her will:* excessive compliment, false praise; sycophancy, toadyism, toadying, obsequiousness, fawning, wheedling, servility; cajolery, blandishment, soft soap, truckling, jollying, blarney; adulation, eulogy, panegyric, encomium.

◇ *Word origin:* See FLATTER.

flaunt *v.* **1** *We know that she has money, so she doesn't have to flaunt it:* show off, parade, exhibit, brandish, vaunt, air, make a show of, advertise, broadcast, strut; boast, brag. **2** *Everyone along the parade route seemed to be flaunting a flag:* flourish, brandish, wave, sport, blazon, dangle.

Ant. conceal, hide, screen; cloak, mask, disguise, dissemble.

◇ *Usage note: Flaunt* and *flout* are fairly uncommon words, and there is a tendency to confuse their separate meanings. *Flaunt* means to make an ostentatious display, to show off something; *flout* means to show contempt for, to defy. Thus, *She flaunted her big diamond ring, Don't flout the rules or you'll be kicked out of the team.*

flavour *n.* **1** *The shop sells ice cream in eight different flavours:* characteristic taste, savour; tang, piquancy; relish, seasoning, flavouring; lacing. **2** *The novelist has captured the flavour of life in the cities today:* subtle quality, distinctive character, essence, soul, spirit; style, tenor, aura, ambience, tone, gusto.

—*v.* **3** *Mother flavours her custards with lemon extract:* give flavour to, season, spice, lace.

Ant. 1 tastelessness, flatness; odourlessness, scentlessness; insipidity, vapidity, mawkishness.

flaw *n.* **1** *Her beauty is without flaw. Lack of civilian clothes was the one flaw in our plan of escape:* defect, blemish, fault, imperfection, marring feature, weakness, weak spot, fallacy, shortcoming, frailty; error, mistake; deformity, injury, defacement, disfigurement; spot, speck; blot, smudge, stain, blotch; failing, foible, vice.

—*v.* **2** *The artist's garish use of colour flawed the painting:* mar, impair, harm; weaken, compromise, detract from, make defective, blemish, deface, injure, disfigure.

flawless *adj. We heard a flawless performance of Beethoven's Ninth Symphony:* faultless, errorless, impeccable, perfect; sound, without blemish, immaculate.

Ant. defective, flawed, marred, impaired.

flay *v.* **1** *Eskimos flay the reindeer they kill and use the hides for garments:* skin, scalp, peel, decorticate, pare, bark; strip, fleece, plunder. **2** *The headmaster flayed the boys for their irresponsible behaviour:* chastise severely, castigate, excoriate, censure harshly; scold, rebuke, upbraid, punish.

fleck *n.* **1** *His hair already had flecks of grey:* spot, patch of colour, mark, speck, freckle, dot, speckle; mole, blemish; small bit, drop, jot, tittle, particle.

—*v.* **2** *The damask wallpaper was flecked with gold:* speckle, mark with flecks, spot, spatter, dapple, bespeckle, bespot, dot, besprinkle; streak, stipple, mottle.

fledgling *n. As a pilot, he's still a fledgling:* inexperienced person, novice, beginner, tiro, freshman, apprentice; *Informal* greenhorn, tenderfoot.

◇ *Word origin: Fledgling* comes from Middle English *flegge,* "feathered," said of a young bird that has just grown enough feathers to begin flying.

flee *v.* **1** *He fled the kidnappers and phoned the police:* escape from, run away from, get away from, hasten away from, make one's escape from; make a getaway, take to one's heels, take flight, abscond, skip, cut and run; decamp, desert, make off, hasten off, speed off, fly away; vanish, disappear, *Slang* scarper. **2** *Why does she always flee any kind of responsibility?:* evade, avoid, shun, wriggle out of; elude, dodge.

fleet *n.* **1** *Thousands waited at the dock for the fleet to come in:* naval force, navy, naval division, group of warships, armada; flotilla, squadron. **2** *He made his money with a fleet of removal vans:* large group, number, array, band, squadron.

—*adj.* **3** *Antelopes are among the fleetest animals:* swift, rapid, speedy, fast, swift-footed, fast of foot, light-footed, nimble-footed, nimble; hurried, quick, expeditious, hasty, cursory; transient, brief, evanescent; sudden, instantaneous, momentary; short, transitory.

Ant. 3 deliberate, slow, laggard, tardy.

◇ *Word origin: Fleet* comes from Old English *flēotan,* to float, drift. The related Old English *flēot* means a group of ships.

fleeting *adj. We caught only a fleeting glimpse of the Queen's car:* swiftly passing, brief, flitting, passing, momentary, evanescent, short-lived, quick; fugitive, transitory, transient, fugacious, ephemeral, temporary, temporal; perishable, impermanent; precarious, unenduring.

Ant. lasting, permanent, enduring, imperishable, durable, long-lived.

flesh *n.* **1** *The wound was merely a superficial penetration of the flesh:* muscular tissue, soft tissue of a body, muscle and fat, brawn; meat, animal food; fat, fatness. **2** *The spirit is willing, but the flesh is weak:* body, physical nature, physique, flesh and blood, materiality; strength, vigour, power, muscular energy, animal force; carnality, sensuality, bodily desire. **3** *The minister said that such was the way of all flesh:* mankind, humanity, human race, man, people, living creatures. **4** *The flesh of the peach was sweet and juicy:* pulp, substance, meat, edible part.

—*v.* **5** *Three good meals a day should flesh him out in no time:* fatten, fill out, make plump, become plump. **6** *The playwright often fails to flesh out his characters:* fill out, characterize fully, realize, individualize, particularize, give depth to.

flexible *adj.* **1** *The springs were made of flexible steel:* easily bent, elastic, resilient, springy, extensible, bendable, ductile, plastic, malleable, tractable, pliable, pliant; supple, limber, lithe, soft. **2** *We need a foreign policy that is more flexible:* adaptable, changeable, yielding, responsive, manageable, malleable, compliant, complaisant; docile, submissive, easily managed; amiable, genial; mild, gentle.

Ant. 1 inflexible, stiff, rigid, inelastic. 2 intractable, unyielding, inexorable; absolute, dogmatic.

> **Exploring the Word:** *Flex* and *flexible* come from Latin *flectere*, to bend, which also gives us: *deflect*, to bend something away; *inflection*, the "bending" of a pitch or tone of voice; *inflexible*, unbending; *reflect*, to bend or send back light, sound, or heat waves, or to bend one's thoughts; and *reflection*, an image or light rays bent back as from a mirror or thoughts bent back into one's mind.

flicker *v.* **1** *The candle flickered in the draught:* flutter; glow, glisten, glitter, glimmer, shimmer; flare, blaze, flash; sparkle, coruscate, wave to and fro, quiver, flit, vibrate; waver, quaver, wriggle, tremble; undulate, oscillate; shake, waggle; throb, pulsate; sway; fluctuate, vacillate.

—n. **2** *There was a brief flicker and the flashlight went dead:* unsteady light, glitter, flare, gleam, spark, flash. **3** *Whilst there is a flicker of hope we will continue the search:* small amount, vestige, modicum, spark, glimmer, trace.

flight *n.* **1** *Some birds are incapable of flight. Our cross-channel flight took an hour:* air travel, flying, winging, soaring; aeronautics, plane trip; space travel. **2** *A flight of geese passed overhead:* flock, flying group, squadron, wing. **3** *There is no way to stop the flight of time:* rush, swift movement, quick passage. **4** *The defeated army took flight:* hasty departure, running away, rout, fleeing, retreat, escape, withdrawal; exodus, hegira.

flighty *adj. Her parents decided that she was too flighty to get much out of university:* unstable, frivolous, irresponsible, fickle, impractical, whimsical, capricious, changeable, mercurial, inconstant, volatile, quixotic; scatter-brained, hare-brained, dizzy, reckless, thoughtless, light-headed, giddy; irresolute, indecisive.

flimsy *adj.* **1** *These shirts are so flimsy that I'm afraid to put them in the washing machine:* unsubstantial, thin, slight, frail, fragile, delicate; diaphanous, sheer, filmy, gossamer, gauzy, cobwebby; shoddy, ill-made, jerry-built; ramshackle, shabby, sleazy, dilapidated, cheap, trashy. **2** *Does she really expect us to believe a flimsy excuse like that?:* feeble, weak, inadequate; poor, worthless, foolish; trivial, trifling, petty, frivolous; shallow, superficial.

Ant. 1 stout, sturdy, strong; heavy, weighty. 2 sound, cogent; substantial, solid.

flinch *v. She flinched as she touched the hot stove:* wince, draw back, jerk back, shrink, recoil, start, cringe, blench, shy, shudder, falter, shiver, quiver, quake, quaver, cower, quail; grimace, contort; retreat, fly, give ground.

fling *v.* **1** *Please don't fling books around like that:* throw with force, hurl, heave, pitch, toss, cast, dash, let fly, precipitate, propel, sling; eject, emit, expel.

—n. **2** *Next weekend let's have a fling at the fair:* spree, bit of fun; *Slang* ball, bash, lark.

"Come, fill the Cup, and in the Fire of Spring
The Winter Garment of Repentance fling."
—Edward Fitzgerald

---

flip *v.* **1** *Let's flip a coin to see who goes first:* toss, flick, throw, spin. **2** *He flipped through the pages of the phone book looking for the number:* turn, thumb, turn over.

—n. **3** *He removed the crumb with a flip of the thumb and forefinger:* tap, flick, fillip; toss, throw, spin.

flippant *adj. The young man shocked everyone by making flippant remarks while the will was being read:* impudent, brash, impertinent, disrespectful, saucy, insolent, pert, rude; *Informal* cheeky, flip; trifling, frivolous; presumptuous, bumptious.

Ant. respectful, considerate.

flirt *v.* **1** *She flirts with every man in the office:* toy, play at love, dally, trifle in love, tease, *Slang* make eyes at. **2** *Uncle Ted flirted with the idea of opening a bookshop:* toy, play, trifle; entertain an idea.

—n. **3** *He stopped going out with her when she turned out to be a flirt:* flirter, tease, heart-breaker, philanderer; (*fem.*) coquette, vamp.

flit *v. The honey-bees were flitting from flower to flower:* dart, skim, move lightly and swiftly, flicker, flutter; fly rapidly, wing, hasten, speed, scud.

float *v.* **1** *When you're tired of swimming just float for a while:* rest on water; be poised in air; drift, hover, waft, slide, move gently, bob, be buoyant, be buoyed up; levitate. **2** *Is there enough water in the tub to float your boat?:* make buoyant, buoy up, bear up, hold up, keep afloat, give support to; launch.

Ant. 1, 2 sink, settle, go to the bottom, submerge.

◇ *Word origin: Float* comes from Old English *flēotan,* to float or swim, which also gives us our word *fleet* (ships). *Flotsam* (as in the phrase *flotsam and jetsam*) is also related, although more remotely than its spelling suggests.

flock *n.* **1** *A flock of sheep blocked the road:* herd, pack, bunch, group, troop, drove, multitude; band, company, bevy, collection, aggregation; brood (of young birds), school (of fish), swarm (of insects), pride (of lions), pod (of seals or whales), covey (of game birds). **2** *A flock of customers waited for the shop to open:* crowd, mob, gang, throng, large number; gathering, assemblage; congregation.

—*v.* **3** *Birds of a feather flock together:* go, run, gather, assemble, muster, converge, swarm, cluster, congregate, herd; crowd, surge, mass, throng, huddle, stream, rush.

flog *v. The quartermaster flogged a sailor caught napping on watch:* whip, lash, thrash, beat, horsewhip, scourge, flail, flagellate, drub; strike, smite, lambaste, cuff; club, maul, cudgel; cane, birch, slipper, switch; strap, hide.

◇ *Word origin: Flog* comes from Latin *flagellare,* to whip, which also gives us *flail* and *flagellation.*

flood *n.* **1** *During the flood many people were stranded in their homes:* inundation, great overflowing of water, overflow; deluge, cloudburst, downpour. **2** *A flood of tears didn't make her story any more convincing:* torrent, stream, flow, outpouring, tide, cascade, downpour, deluge, current, gush.

—*v.* **3** *The rains flooded the fields and destroyed all the crops:* inundate, deluge, submerge, cover with a flood, wash over, fill to overflowing, flow over. **4** *The market has been flooded with electronic gadgets:* oversupply, glut, inundate, deluge; shower, drench.

Ant. 1 drought, scarcity, lack, shortage, subsidence, stoppage.

floor *n.* **1** *The glass fell off the table and shattered on the floor:* bottom surface, bottom, flooring, base, ground; pavement, parquet. **2** *Her rooms are on the third floor:* storey, stage, level; deck. **3** *The government has put a floor under certain farm prices:* base rate, base, minimum, bottom.

—*v.* **4** *The challenger was floored with a solid right hook:* knock down, ground, fell, level, prostrate, *Slang* down, drop.

flop *v.* **1** *The puppy just flopped around on the slippery floor:* move clumsily or heavily; fall heavily, tumble, topple, drop, plop, flap awkwardly. **2** *Informal After only three performances, the play flopped:* fail, close, close down, go under, give up, fold, wash out.

—*n.* **3** *Informal The dinner party was a flop because the guest of honour didn't show up:* failure, fiasco, disaster, disappointment, labour in vain, wash-out; *Slang* non-starter, bust.

Ant. 2 succeed, triumph, make a hit; flourish, prosper. **3** success, triumph, hit.

◇ *Word origin: Flop* is a variant of the word *flap.*

floral *adj. Her bedroom wallpaper had a floral pattern:* of flowers, flowery, blossomy, bloomy; botanical, herbaceous; verdant.

florid *adj.* **1** *It may be his high blood pressure that gives him such a florid complexion:* ruddy, rosy, reddish, high-coloured, rubicund; ruddy-faced, red-faced, flushed, sanguine, red-complexioned; inflamed, blowzy, hectic. **2** *We listened to a long florid speech about the greatness of our founder:* flowery, showy, ornamented, elaborate, ornate, ostentatious, highly embellished, flamboyant, high-flown, grandiloquent; rococo, baroque.

Ant. 1 pallid, anaemic, bloodless. **2** unadorned, bare, prosaic, matter-of-fact.

◇ *Word origin:* See FLOWER.

Exploring the Word: The names of flowers are interesting, and from them we often get the names of colours and even girls (Rose, Violet, Iris, Lily, Daisy, etc.). The star-shaped *aster* comes from the Greek word for star, *aster* (which also gives us *astronomy, astrology,* and *asterisk*). The *chrysanthemum* now comes in a variety of colours but originally was a yellow gold and comes from Greek *chrysos,* gold, + *anthemon,* flower. The *dahlia* is named in honour of the 18th-century Swedish botanist Anders *Dahl.* The *poinsettia* is named after the U.S. Secretary of War Joel R. *Poinsett,* who brought the plant back from Mexico where he had served as the first U.S. minister from 1825 to 1829. A *daisy* looks like an eye and comes from the Old English name for the flower, *daegas ēage,* "day's eye." A *nasturtium* is a strong-smelling, almost pungent, flower whose name comes from Latin *nasus,* nose, + *torquere,* to torture or twist — a "nose-twister." *Pansy* comes from the French *pensée,* thought, though no one seems to know why. *Lilac* comes from Persian *līak,* blue, indigo; the name of the intertwined, turban-like *tulip* comes from Turkish *tülbend,* turban. *Iris* is Latin for rainbow (the *iris* of the eye is the coloured, circular part).

Many of the rest of our common flowers take their name from their Latin names, as the *rose* (Latin *rosa*), *lily* (Latin *lilium*), *daffodil* (Latin *asphodelus*), *poppy* (Latin *papaver*), and *violet* (Latin *viola*).

flotsam *n. We spotted a great deal of flotsam that could have been from the missing ship:* floating wreckage, floating goods, debris; cast-offs, odds and ends, refuse, junk.

◇ *Usage note:* The phrase *flotsam and jetsam* refers to anything discarded, whether on land or sea. Technically, however, *flotsam* is a ship's cargo or equipment found *floating* in the water, as from a ship that has sunk; whereas *jetsam* is cargo or equipment thrown overboard, or *jettisoned,* in order to lighten a ship in distress.

flounce[1] *v.* **1** *She was so furious that she turned and flounced off the stage:* strut, hurl oneself, fling oneself, storm, stamp; stride, spring, bound; trip, skip, prance, caper, gambol.

—*n.* **2** *With an angry flounce he was gone from the house:* flouncing movement, bound, spring, leap.

flounce[2] *n.* **1** *Her dress had so many flounces that she kept getting them caught on things:* ruffle, frill, ornament, furbelow; valance, fringe, trimming; hem, edging, skirting.

—*v.* **2** *The gown was flounced with tiers of pink lace:* trim, ruffle, frill, ornament, fringe, hem, edge.

flounder *v.* **1** *The car floundered in the icy slush:* struggle, move unsteadily, proceed clumsily, stumble, stagger; pitch, toss about, plunge clumsily; wallow, welter; lurch, totter, flop, shamble, tumble; limp, hobble. **2** *When she forgot her speech she floundered hopelessly:* falter, waver, hesitate, be uncertain, halt; lose oneself, miss one's way, blunder, muddle, wander aimlessly.

◇ *Usage note:* Don't confuse *flounder* and *founder.* To *flounder* is to struggle clumsily, to thrash about (like a fish): *The child floundered about in the water until the coastguard got to him. A good speaker doesn't flounder.* To *founder* means to sink after filling with water or to fail completely: *The ship foundered before it could be towed to port. The tax bill was endorsed by our committee but foundered in Parliament.*

◇ *Word origin: Flounder* is a blend of *flounce* + *founder.*

flourish *v.* **1** *His dry-cleaning business really flourished this year:* prosper, thrive, grow, succeed, turn out well, fare well, be successful; get ahead, get on, rise in the world, go up in the world, *Informal* make one's pile; have a run of luck, feather one's nest; bloom, blossom, flower, burgeon. **2** *Flourishing their swords and muskets, the troops attacked:* brandish, wave about in the air, swing, flaunt, wield, shake; twirl, sweep, swish.

—*n.* **3** *The armies met with a flourish of swords and bayonets:* waving, shaking, brandishing, agitation, wielding, twist, swinging, thrashing; ostentatious display, show, parade, ostentation; swagger, strut, swashbuckling; pomp, glitter, splash, dash. **4** *The actor signed his contract with a flourish:* embellishment, decorative figure, curl, curlicue, decoration; musical ornament, turn, grace-note, appoggiatura, cadenza. **5** *The teacher always speaks with a lot of flourish:* bravado, bluff, braggadocio, boasting, vaunting; rant, fustian, hot air, grandiloquence, magniloquence. **6** *The coronation got under way with a great flourish of horns and trumpets:* trumpet-call, fanfare, fanfaronade.

Ant. **1** decline, fail, fade.

◇ *Word origin: Flourish* is from Latin *florere,* to bloom, whose root is Latin *flos,* flower. See FLOWER.

flout *v. She flouted convention by wearing black at her wedding:* scorn, show contempt for, scoff at, spurn, laugh at, jeer at, gibe at, sneer at, defy, treat with disdain, mock, poke fun at; twit, taunt, chaff, rag, insult.

Ant. revere; regard, respect, esteem.

◇ *Usage note:* See FLAUNT.

◇ *Word origin: Flout* seems to come from *flute,* and may literally mean to play the flute to mock someone. Today flutes are not very common in comedy acts, but comedians still may have a member of a band sound the drums or blow several raucous notes on a trumpet to emphasize a mocking remark.

flow *v.* **1** *The Thames flows eastwards into the sea:* course, roll along, move in a stream, run, pour, stream; rush, gush, well out, issue, effuse; discharge, debouch, drain; surge, deluge, swirl; filter, seep; move gracefully, glide, sweep, pass, drift, float. **2** *It was a party flowing with champagne:* abound, be full of, overflow, run, be copious.

—*n.* **3** *The flow of melted snow cascaded down the mountainside and into the river:* stream, course, torrent, flood; current, tide; rapids, millrace. **4** *A steady flow of good ideas has come from the publicity department:* outpouring, effusion, outflow, flux, tide, discharge; efflux, effluence, emanation, debouchment; spurt, spout, gush, jet; train, succession, sequence, progression; abundance, plenty, plethora.

flower *n.* **1** *He sent her flowers to mark their anniversary:* blossom, bloom, posy floret, bud; nosegay, bouquet, floral tribute. **2** *The army boasted that it had the flower of the nation's youth:* best, pick, choicest part, finest part, cream; élite, aristocracy.

—*v.* **3** *Your peonies will flower in late spring. Mozart's genius flowered at a very early age:* bloom, produce blossoms, produce flowers, blossom, open, be in flower, blow; burgeon; bud; develop fully, mature, flourish, prosper.

Ant. **2** dregs, residue.

◇ *Word origin: Flower* comes from Latin *flos,* flower. From this the Romans named their goddess of flowers *Flora;* from the same stem we get *floral, florid* (flowery, ornate, ruddy-coloured), *florist,* and *florescence.*

flowery *adj.* **1** *The rose bush was never so flowery before:* covered with blossoms, flowering, burgeoning, blooming, blossoming; florescent, efflorescent; decorated with flowers, floral. **2** *His language was embarrassingly flowery:* ornate, ornamental, embellished, fancy, euphuistic, florid; rhetorical, figurative, grandiloquent, magniloquent.

fluctuate *v.* **1** *With prices fluctuating so much, it's hard to plan a budget:* rise and fall, change often, vary irregularly, shift, bob up and down, wobble, veer; come and go, ebb and flow. **2** *All the year she has fluctuated between optimism and despair:* waver, vacillate, sway, oscillate, swing, be irresolute, be unsettled, hesitate, be undetermined, falter, shift, alternate, be inconstant; dawdle, dilly-dally.

Ant. hold fast, persist, stand fast, stand firm.

fluent *adj. Joan is fluent in both Spanish and German:* able to speak readily, ready in speech; glib, smooth-spoken, vocal, voluble, eloquent, articulate, smooth-tongued, silver-tongued; effortless, facile; effusive, talkative, garrulous; self-assured, well-versed.

Ant. hesitant, stammering, halting.

fluffy *adj. Her divan is covered with fluffy pink pillows:* soft and light as fluff, feathery, downy; fuzzy, fleecy, woolly; light and airy.

fluid *n.* **1** *A few drops of cleaning fluid should take out that spot:* liquid, solution.
—*adj.* **2** *The doctor prescribed a fluid diet for two weeks:* liquid, liquefied, of fluids, watery. **3** *Keep your plans fluid until we decide what we're going to do:* flexible, adaptable, adjustable; changeable, indefinite; unstable, shifting, floating, liquid.
Ant. **1** solid. **2** solid, hard, firm. **3** definite, fixed, settled.

> **Exploring the Word**: *Flux, fluid,* and *fluctuate* come from Latin *fluere,* to flow. This same Latin word also gives us *fluent,* flowing easily, able to let words flow easily; *affluent,* having wealth or possessions flow towards one, wealthy; *influx,* a flowing in, pouring in; *influence,* the power of importance flowing into one person or thing from another; and *influenza,* the Italian form of *influence,* so called because the illness was once thought to be due to the influence of the stars.

fluke *n. By some fluke the judges passed over the obvious winners and chose her:* accident, unlikely event, quirk of fate, chance, mischance, hap,vicissitude, freak; stroke of luck, piece of luck, windfall, miracle.

flurry *n.* **1** *A sudden flurry sent the paper flying all over the yard:* sudden wind, gust, windy blast, breeze, puff, squall; shower, light snowfall. **2** *There was quite a flurry when the queen visited the college:* bustle, sudden excitement, commotion, fuss, to-do, ado, fluster, flutter, stir, pother, nervous hurry, agitation, turbulence, tumult, disturbance, perturbation, discomposure, restlessness, fidgets, confusion, trepidation; fever, heat, flush; haste.
—*v.* **3** *Don't be flurried by her checking on your work:* make nervous, put into a flurry, fluster, agitate, disquiet, disturb, perturb; rattle, confuse, discompose, disconcert, flutter, confound; panic, alarm.

flush[1] *n.* **1** *Her complexion has a flush that I have never seen before:* blush, rosiness, rosy glow; bloom, tinge of colour, high colour, tint; redness, ruddiness. **2** *Give the drain a flush, and hope it clears itself:* cleansing flow, watery gush, wash, douche, deluge. **3** *In a flush of anger he hurled the chair across the room:* rush of emotion, impulse, access; tremor, flutter, quiver; thrill, shock; jubilation, exultation. **4** *She was a beautiful girl in the first flush of youth:* bloom, glow, glowing, strength, freshness.
—*v.* **5** *She flushed with pleasure when we complimented her:* blush, redden, colour, grow crimson, glow. **6** *Once a year they have to flush the city's sewers:* cleanse by flooding, wash out, flood, douche; rinse, scour, scrub, sponge, swab; drench, dampen, moisten. **7** *The returning army was flushed with victory:* animate, elate, make proud, puff up; thrill, excite.

flush[2] *adj.* **1** *I want the table-top flush with the back of the sofa:* even, level, on the same plane.
—*adv.* **2** *Put the bookcase flush against the wall:* squarely, in contact with, so as to touch.

fluster *v.* **1** *I was flustered when company arrived unexpectedly:* disconcert, ruffle, make nervous, disturb, perturb, agitate, shake, startle, upset, discompose, discomfit, befuddle, muddle, confuse; perplex, daze, bewilder, throw off balance.
—*n.* **2** *I was in such a fluster over the affair that I didn't know whether I was coming or going:* nervous excitement, confusion, flutter, agitation, turmoil, flurry, dither, discomposure, discomfiture, bewilderment.
◇ *Word origin:* If you try to *hurry* too much you may get *flustered. Fluster* comes from Icelandic *flaustra,* to bustle.

flutter *v.* **1** *The flag fluttered from the top of the pole:* wave, toss about, flap, flitter; throb, tremble, shake, pulsate; bob, wobble, quiver; palpitate. **2** *The butterfly fluttered from leaf to leaf:* flit, flitter; wing, soar.
—*n.* **3** *There was a great flutter of wings as the gulls rose in the air:* agitation, vibration, flapping, beating; quiver, tremble, tremor. **4** *Meeting celebrities always puts her in a flutter:* twitter, fluster; confusion, flurry, perturbation; hurry, commotion; thrill, sensation, tingling; ripple, stir.

flux *n.* **1** *The boat battled against the mighty flux of the river:* flow, current, course, flood, stream, tide. **2** *Scientific knowledge is always in a state of flux:* continuous change, fluctuation, alteration, modification; shifting, transition, mutation, transformation.

fly *v.* **1** *The new aeroplane flies at twice the speed of sound:* travel through the air; pilot a plane; wing, take wing, take the air, take off, soar, glide, sail, coast, swoop. **2** *The king's banner was flying above his tent:* wave, flutter, float, undulate, flap, vibrate, hover, display in the air, hoist in the air. **3** *The days really flew by during our holiday:* move quickly, pass rapidly, go suddenly. **4** *He was warned to fly from the emperor's wrath:* flee, run away, hasten away, make one's escape, make one's getaway, take flight, take to one's heels, hasten, hustle, hurry.

foam *n. The glass of beer was mostly foam:* mass of tiny bubbles, froth, head, fizz, sparkle, effervescence, bubbling; scum, spume; suds, lather.

foamy *adj. I'd like a cold, foamy glass of lemonade:* frothy, bubbling, effervescent, sparkling, fizzy; lathery.

focus *n.* **1** *He took out the binoculars and adjusted the focus:* focal length, focal point, point of concentration, converging point. **2** *The café is the focus of social life in many French towns:* centre, hub, middle, heart; meeting-place,

gathering place, headquarters, rallying point; rendezvous, trysting place; haunt, retreat, resort; heart, core, nucleus.
—*v.* **3** *Focus the telescope on that distant lighthouse:* bring into focus, adjust, centre; converge, bring to a point, concentrate; fix, centre, direct, aim, bring to bear.
◇ *Word origin:* The *focus* of life in ancient times was the hearth. *Focus* is the Latin word for "hearth, fireplace," from which come Italian *fuoco*, Spanish *fuego*, and French *feu*, all meaning "fire." The modern sense of *focus* was coined by the German astronomer Johannes Kepler (1571–1630) and was first used by him to designate the point at which a parabolic mirror concentrates light rays to cause burning.

fodder *n. Most cattle fodder contains chemicals these days:* feed, foodstuffs, silage, forage, provender.

foe *n. Our foes made peace with us, and we became friends:* enemy, adversary, opponent, foeman, antagonist; attacker, assailant; rival, competitor.
Ant. friend, comrade, companion; ally, confederate.
◇ *Word origin: Foe* comes from Old English *gefāh*, related to Old English *fēhida*, from which we get our word *feud.* In Anglo-Saxon times, *foes* in a *feud* were enemies locked in a mortal vendetta. The *feud* generally ended in money and property settlements being made by surviving "foes" to the bereaved kinsmen of their adversaries. Many cheated on the settlement agreement or kept on feuding. Some of these were proclaimed outlaws — a status then as now even more uneasy than that of a *foe.*

fog *n.* **1** *When the fog closed in we couldn't see the top of the hill:* thick mist, haze, smog, murk, murkiness; *Slang* pea souper. **2** *Early in the morning my brain was in a fog:* daze, haze, stupor, bewilderment.
—*v.* **3** *When foul weather fogged the port, the ships anchored outside:* cover with fog, enclose in mist or fog. **4** *Lack of sleep has fogged his mind:* befog, bewilder, muddle, daze, confuse, perplex, obscure, dim, cloud, darken.
Ant. **2** clarity, comprehension, perspicuity. **3** clear, brighten, clarify, purge, purify.
◇ *Word origin:* Although *fogs* can occur almost anywhere, they occur most frequently over wet, marshy ground. *Fog* comes from the Scandinavian *fogg*, long grass on wet ground, a marsh.

"Fear death? — to feel the fog in my throat,
The mist in my face." —*Robert Browning*

---

foggy *adj.* **1** *At sunrise we walked through the foggy fields:* misty, hazy, brumous; clouded, cloudy, beclouded, filmy, overcast, murky, smoggy; vaporous, nebulous. **2** *He has only a foggy notion of what he wants to do:* unclear, confused, vague, fuzzy, misty, cloudy, dim, obscure, indistinct; resembling fog, shadowy, dusky, dark.
Ant. **2** lucid, distinct, decisive, accurate, clear, bright; shrewd, sharp; alert, alive, awake.
◇ *Usage note:* Don't confuse *foggy* and *fogey.* The *g* in *fog* doubles in *foGGy: a foggy night.* An *old fogey* (one *g*) is a person who is behind the times.

foible *n. Is vanity a cardinal sin or merely a foible?:* minor fault, weakness, shortcoming, frailty, failing, imperfection, weak point, weak side, infirmity, defect, deficiency; quirk, kink, whimsy.
Ant. strength, forte, virtue, perfection; crime, atrocity; sin, enormity, abomination.
◇ *Word origin:* The *foibles* or personal weaknesses of people are sad to contemplate. *Foible* comes from Latin *flebilis*, sad, lamentable, which also gives us *feeble.*

foil[1] *v. The revolt was foiled by troops loyal to the king:* frustrate, balk, thwart, scotch; hinder, prevent, check, nip in the bud.
Ant. advance, further, forward; endorse, promote, abet, sustain, foment, incite, instigate.

foil[2] *n.* **1** *The dome of the temple was covered with gold foil:* leaf, flake, lamina, sheet, film, wafer. **2** *Her wry humour is a perfect foil for his gushiness:* contrast, antithesis, complement, supplement, match, counterpart, correlative.
◇ *Word origin:* Gold *foil* is also called gold "leaf." *Foil* comes from Latin *folium*, leaf, which also gives us our word *foliage* (leaves).

foist *v. Don't let them foist shop-soiled goods onto you:* pass off, palm off, impose, unload, get rid of.

fold[1] *v.* **1** *Fold the napkins and put one by each plate:* double, crease, pleat, lap; gather, tuck, dog-ear, pucker; wrinkle, rumple, crumple; crinkle, curl. **2** *Fold the scarf in some tissue-paper:* wrap, wrap up, envelop, enfold. **3** *She folded the child in her arms:* embrace, embosom, clasp, enfold, entwine, hug.
—*n.* **4** *The poison capsule was concealed in a fold of her dress:* gather, tuck, pleat, layer, crinkle, pucker, ruffle, flounce. **5** *The map has begun to split along the fold:* crease, folding, doubling, bend.
Ant. **1, 2** unfold, unwrap, uncover; expose, exhibit, disclose, reveal.

fold[2] *n.* **1** *How many sheep are kept in each fold?:* pen, enclosure, close, yard; barnyard, stockade, stable. **2** *The preacher said that one of the brothers had strayed from the fold:* religious life, straight and narrow; the church, congregation, flock, parish.

foliage *n. The red and gold foliage of the trees was lovely:* leaves, foliation, leafage, verdure.

folks *n. pl.* **1** *Folks are talking about her scene in the nativity play:* people, the public, everyone. **2** *Informal My folks will be here for Christmas and*

New Year: parents, family, family members, relatives, kinsfolk, kinfolk, kith and kin, kinsmen, blood relations.

◇ *Usage note:* Apart from phrases such as *ordinary folk, young folk,* or *the common folk* (all of which take plural verbs), we nowadays occasionally say *folks* when we're talking about people or kinsmen. We still of course use the singular form *folk* as a descriptive word: *folk customs, folk-music.*

◇ *Word origin: Folk* goes back to Old English *folc,* the people, tribe, nation. German *Volk* means the same and stems from the same ancestor-word.

folklore *n. Witches frequently occur in tales based on folklore:* legends, lore, traditions, folk-tales, fables, myths, fairy tales.

follow *v.* **1** *"Q" follows "P" in our alphabet:* come after, go behind, tread on the heels of, walk in the steps of, tread in the rear of, proceed in the wake of; bring up the rear. **2** *Who will follow the prime minister when he retires?:* succeed, come next, come after, step into the shoes of; replace, supplant, take the place of. **3** *The citizens agreed to follow their civic leaders:* accept as an authority, give allegiance to; follow the example of, emulate, imitate, copy, take after. **4** *There is no excuse for not following instructions:* obey, heed, act in accordance with, comply with, observe, mind, conform to, be guided by; notice, watch, regard, note. **5** *The detectives followed the gang to their hide-out:* pursue, chase, go after, run after; track, stalk, trail, trace, hunt; *Informal* shadow, tail, dog, hound; attend, accompany. **6** *Everyone ought to have some ideals to follow:* emulate, cherish, strive after, aim at; cultivate. **7** *He followed law after he left the Navy:* take up, engage in, practise, carry on; be concerned with, attend to, prosecute. **8** *Could you follow what he was saying?:* understand, grasp, comprehend, catch on; keep up with.

Ant. 1 precede, lead, guide; pilot, steer. **3** forsake, desert, abandon. **4** disobey, ignore, flout. **5** elude, evade, escape. **7** avoid, shun; quit, abandon, renounce, give up.

follower *n.* **1** *He eluded his followers by crossing the river:* pursuer, stalker, chaser; *Slang* tail, shadow; hunter. **2** *Mahatma Gandhi had many followers throughout the world:* disciple, adherent, apostle; devotee, admirer, partisan, supporter, advocate; pupil, protégé, *Slang* fan. **3** *The queen's retinue included 300 followers:* attendant, servant, servitor, retainer, dependent; henchman, accessory, satellite, stooge; hanger-on, parasite, toady, sycophant.

Ant. 2 leader, teacher, guru; enemy, foe, antagonist; rival, opponent, contender.

following *n.* **1** *I hated the show, but it has a large following:* audience, public, patronage, body of followers, attendance, clientele; partisans, adherents; suite, retinue, train, entourage.

—*adj.* **2** *She stayed with us until the following afternoon:* next, succeeding, subsequent, ensuing; successive, consecutive; consequent, sequential. **3** *The Prime Minister has issued the following statement:* ensuing, subsequent, below, now to be mentioned, coming next.

folly *n.* **1** *It would be folly for you to try to lift that piano:* foolishness, senselessness, idiocy, brainlessness, imbecility, inanity, asininity; fatuousness, silliness, doltishness, irrationality. **2** *Please talk to her about the folly of leaving school:* imprudence, indiscretion; foolishness, frivolity, absurdity, tomfoolery, nonsense, giddiness, levity, trifling.

Ant. 1 wisdom, prudence, sound judgement, good sense; sobriety, sober-mindedness, level-headedness; rationality, moderation, sanity, lucidity.

◇ *Word origin:* See FOOL.

foment *v. He did his best to foment a quarrel between the brothers:* stir up, incite, foster, promote, instigate, provoke, urge, excite, stimulate, galvanize, foster; rouse, arouse, kindle, inflame, spur, goad, agitate; irritate, aggravate, exacerbate, quicken, fan the fire, fan into flame, blow the coals.

Ant. quell, suppress, repress, quench; check, curb, restrain; allay, discourage, destroy, extinguish, extirpate.

◇ *Usage note: Foment* means to stir up discontent or discord, to cause external agitation: *The king's enemies fomented a rebellion.* It should not be confused with *ferment,* which means to undergo or cause fermentation, the gradual decomposition of an organic compound induced by enzymes, bacteria, yeast, etc., or to be in a state of internal excitement or agitation: *We ferment hops and barley in the making of beer. His mind was in a ferment.*

"If woman could be fair and yet not fond."
—*Edward de Vere, Earl of Oxford*

---

fond *adj.* **1** *Did you ever see anyone so fond of desserts?:* having a liking for, enamoured, addicted to, crazy about. **2** *What can I do to discourage her fond looks?:* loving, tender, affectionate, amorous, devoted, passionate, impassioned, ardent, enamoured, infatuated, sentimental, desirous; doting, indulgent, over-affectionate, foolishly loving, overfond. **3** *She has fond hopes of becoming a film star:* cherished, held dear, preserved, harboured, sustained; naïve, somewhat foolish.

Ant. 1 averse, indifferent. **2** unconcerned, aloof; unloving, unaffectionate, undemonstrative; strong-minded, rational, austere.

◇ *Word origin:* Today, *fond* means feeling affection for someone or something, but its older meaning is "naïve, foolish." It comes from Middle English *fonned,* foolish.

fondle *v. She has fondled that kitten all morning:*

caress, stroke, touch fondly; cuddle, hug, embrace, nestle, fold in one's arms, clasp to one's bosom; nuzzle, spoon, bill and coo.
Ant. worry, annoy, chafe, irritate; ruffle, tease, heckle, badger, bait; torment, aggravate.

fondness *n. Her fondness for him seems to be genuine:* tenderness, affection, attachment, devotion; love, amorousness, desire, passion, ardour. **2** *If I could only curb my fondness for rich food!:* partiality, predilection, penchant, preference, inclination, propensity, bent, fancy, liking; weakness, susceptibility.
Ant. 1 antagonism, hostility, antipathy; hatred, contempt, loathing; harshness, brutality. **2** dislike, aversion, repulsion, revulsion.

food *n.* **1** *It takes most of his wages to buy food for the family:* foodstuffs, provisions, comestibles, victuals, viands, provender, eatables, edibles, nourishment, nurture, nutrition, subsistence, sustenance; *Slang* grub, chow. **2** *We use the clover as food for the livestock:* fodder, forage, feed, silage, provender; pasture, pasturage.
◇ *Word origin: Food, fodder,* and *feed* are all from Old English *fōda*, food.

"Countries are populous according to the quantity of human food which they produce or can acquire." — *Thomas Robert Malthus*

---

fool *n.* **1** *Only a fool would let his inheritance slip through his fingers:* stupid person, idiot, dolt, blockhead, bonehead, simpleton, charlie, nitwit, dummy, imbecile, moron, nincompoop, dunderhead, numskull, ignoramus, ass, dunce, ninny, oaf, clod, chump, goose; *German* dummkopf, *Yiddish* klutz. **2** *The king relied on his fool for wise counsel:* jester, clown, buffoon, dunce, merry andrew; harlequin, Punchinello, pierrot.
—*v.* **3** *I thought that I had bought a good car, but I was fooled:* trick, deceive, make a fool of, dupe, flimflam, hoodwink, cheat, defraud, hoax, bilk, gull, con, beguile, bamboozle, cozen, humbug, diddle. **4** *When he seems to be fooling he may be quite serious:* joke, jest, play the fool, cut capers, monkey about, frolic; pretend, feign, make believe, tease.
Ant. 1 genius, wise man, savant, sage, pundit, guru; adept, expert, scholar, master.
◇ *Word origin:* We sometimes call a *fool* a windbag. So did the Romans. Our word *fool* comes from Latin *follis*, a pair of bellows, or an air-inflated playing ball. By late imperial times the word took on the figurative sense that has come down to us, so that when Saint Augustine applies the phrase *follis inflatus* to a person he mentions unfavourably in one of his works, he means "a puffed-up windbag," i.e. a fool. The same Latin word also gives us our word *folly*.

foolhardy *adj. Walking a tightrope across the Niagara Falls was a foolhardy venture:* rash, reckless, incautious, impulsive, impetuous, imprudent, daredevil, madcap, hot-headed, hare-brained, headstrong, brash, hasty; heedless, careless, thoughtless.
Ant. wary, cautious, circumspect; prudent, careful, heedful, mindful, watchful, alert; calculating, shrewd, far-sighted, judicious.

foolish *adj. That was a very foolish thing to say:* unwise, imprudent, ill-considered, indiscreet, ill-advised, incautious, short-sighted, irresponsible; unintelligent, absurd, inane, fatuous, witless, senseless; stupid, half-witted, brainless, boneheaded, silly, simple-minded; moronic, asinine, idiotic, imbecilic; preposterous, ridiculous, ludicrous.
Ant. intelligent, bright, smart; quick-witted, brilliant, sane, rational, sensible; wise, sage, sagacious, sapient; judicious, prudent, circumspect, cautious; clear-sighted, perspicacious, strong-minded, sound; clever, calculating, sharp.

foolishness *n. Because of her foolishness they're now deeply in debt:* imprudence, folly, extravagance, irresponsibility, indiscretion; absurdity, preposterousness, ridiculousness, asininity; injudiciousness, senselessness, witlessness, brainlessness, unwisdom; childishness, silliness, puerility; stupidity, fatuousness, idiocy, lunacy, imbecility.

foot *n.* **1** *She's been limping since she dropped the frying-pan on her foot:* terminal part of the leg, lower extremity; *Slang* tootsy; (of animals) hoof, paw, trotter, pad. **2** *Reinforcements of 1,000 foot were sent up to the front:* foot-soldiers, infantry. **3** *We placed a wreath at the foot of the statue:* base, lower part, bottom, foundation.
◇ *Pronunciation tip: Foot* is easy to pronounce, but the word for a foot doctor, *chiropodist*, isn't. The initial *ch* may be pronounced as a *k*, or as *sh*, *ki-ROP-uh-dist, shi-ROP-uh-dist.*
◇ *Word origin: Foot* comes from Old English *fōt*, which is related to Latin *pes*, foot, Greek *pous* and *peza*, foot, Sanskri *pada*, foot, and many more foot-words, all of which come to us from the Indo-European root *ped-*, foot.

foothold *n. The hill was so slippery that it was hard to get a sure foothold:* footing, purchase, toe-hold; firm place, stable position, firm footing.

footloose *adj. Now that her children have grown up, she's footloose:* free, unattached, uncommitted, unencumbered, fancy-free.

fop *n. In olden days such a vain, conceited ass would have been called a fop:* dandy, coxcomb, toff, popinjay, beau, Beau Brummel, masher, peacock, fashion-plate.
◇ *Word origin: Fop* comes from Dutch *foppen*, to fool, gull, hoax. During the first 200 years of its existence in English (1450–1650) *fop* meant "fool." Later the word acquired its

present-day sense of "dandy", probably because during the period of the Restoration (1660–88) *foppery* was very prevalent at the court of Charles II.

foppish *adj. He wears such foppish clothes that the other youths laugh at him:* dandyish, foplike, showy, ostentatious, dandiacal; gaudy, ornate, over-elaborate; vain, affected, finical.

Ant. unassuming, modest, unostentatious, unpretentious, unaffected; dowdy, seedy, slovenly; clownish, gauche, yokelish, rustic, provincial, awkward.

forage *n.* **1** *Do the cattle have enough forage?:* fodder, feed, provender, silage; food, provisions; pasture, pasturage. **2** *The platoon went out on a forage and returned with several chickens:* search for provisions, foray.

—*v.* **3** *The survivors of the plane crash had to forage about for something to eat:* search, rummage, seek, hunt, explore, look about, cast about; scrounge, come up with; raid, strip of supplies, plunder, despoil, ravage.

◇ *Word origin: Forage* comes from French *fourrage*, forage, fodder. The French word goes back to Germanic and is related to our words *food* and *fodder*.

foray *n.* **1** *The Vikings made regular forays on the weakly-defended coastal towns:* raid, sudden attack, invasion, depredation, incursion, inroad; sally, thrust; expedition, venture.

—*v.* **2** *The soldiers forayed into the surrounding countryside when their provisions were low:* plunder, pillage, ravage, raid; invade, attack, make an incursion.

◇ *Word origin:* A *foray* was originally a raid (or *forage*) for *fodder* or other provisions.

forbear *v.* **1** *She should try to forbear from saying such cruel things:* refrain, desist, abstain, do without, hold back, give up; eschew, renounce, forgo, abnegate, discontinue, leave off, stop, cease, break off. **2** *I wanted to curse him, but I had to forbear:* restrain oneself, be patient, be tolerant, tolerate, show indulgence; suffer, endure, bear.

forbearance *n. It takes considerable forbearance to overlook his faults:* patience, leniency, resignation, tolerance, indulgence, self-restraint, command of temper, endurance, longanimity; mildness, meekness, submission; mercy, mercifulness, clemency, pity, pardon; moderation, abstinence, temperance.

Ant. anger, impatience, intolerance.

forbid *v. I forbid you to stay out after midnight:* prohibit, not allow, command not to, order not to, interdict, proscribe; ban, veto, taboo, bar, exclude, disallow; hinder, prevent, render impossible, preclude, obviate, obstruct, inhibit, impede; oppose, gainsay; refuse, restrain, reject.

Ant. permit, allow, let, suffer; authorize, bid, license; approve, sanction, endorse; order, command.

forbidding *adj. When I saw that forbidding watch-dog, I went no further:* disagreeable, unpleasant, dour, inhospitable, unapproachable, unfriendly; dangerous-looking, sinister, ominous, grim, threatening, prohibitive, prohibitory; ugly, repellent, odious, offensive, horrible, repulsive, abhorrent, hideous.

Ant. attractive, alluring, inviting.

"Other nations use 'Force'; we Britons alone use 'Might'." —*Evelyn Waugh*

---

force *n.* **1** *The force of her personality can be seen in the way her friends imitate her:* energy, power, vigour, strength; vim, vitality, animation; effectiveness, efficacy; attraction, magnetism, charisma. **2** *A poet must carefully weigh the force of each word he uses:* significance, meaning, value, import, weight, weightiness, signification; effect, impact; cogency, validity, emphasis. **3** *Push with as much force as you can:* power, might, strength, potency, pressure, energy, momentum, stress, impact, puissance, stamina. **4** *The police had to use force to hold back the crowd:* coercion, constraint, duress, compulsion, enforcement; violence. **5** *How many employees are in your work-force?:* group, body, team, unit, squad, crew; army, corps, detachment.

—*v.* **6** *Bad weather forced us to call off the picnic:* oblige, compel, push, make necessary, necessitate, require, constrain, enjoin, make, impel, drive, overpower; persuade, induce. **7** *We forced water into the pipe to clean it:* thrust, propel, push, press, drive, coerce, urge, impel; impose, intrude, obtrude. **8** *The police tried to force the truth from the suspect:* obtain by force, pull, wrest, squeeze, pry, wrench, drag; coerce, extort; coax, elicit. **9** *He had forgotten his key and had to force the door:* break, break open, use violence on.

Ant. 1 weakness, frailty; ineffectiveness, inefficiency, inefficacy.

◇ *Word origin: Force* comes from Latin *fortis*, strong, which also gives us *fort*, fortified place, *forte*, strength or strong point, *fortify*, to make strong, *fortitude*, strong-mindedness, and *fortress*, stronghold.

forced *adj.* **1** *The bridge had been built with forced labour:* enforced, compelled, coerced, involuntary, unwilling, obliged, obligatory, required, constrained, compulsory, bound, mandatory; slave, enslaved, impressed. **2** *Her forced smile indicated that something was wrong:* strained, laboured, not natural; artificial, mannered, affected.

Ant. 2 easy, natural, simple, unforced, unpretending.

forceful *adj. The politician gave a brief but forceful speech:* powerful, strong, full of force, puissant, dynamic, vigorous, potent, energetic, emphatic; effective, vivid, pithy, valid, cogent; robust, virile.

Ant. feeble, weak, spent, exhausted.

◇ *Usage note: Forceful* means strong, vigorous, effective: *a forceful personality, a forceful speech.* The less common word *forcible* means brought about by or having force: *Press-ganging, or the forcible enlistment of sailors by paid recruiters was one of the least popular aspects of the navy.*

fore *adj. He stood watch in the fore part of the ship:* front, forward, frontal, headmost, anterior.

Ant. rear, aft, posterior, back, hindmost.

forebear Also **forbear** *n. Our forebears came from eastern Europe:* ancestor, forefather, progenitor, antecedent, forerunner; procreator, begetter.

◇ *Word origin: Forebear* means literally "forebe-er," i.e. one who has been before, namely one's ancestor.

foreboding *n. She had a foreboding that the trip would end in disaster:* premonition, presentiment, apprehension; omen, prognostic, forewarning, augury, portent; dread, boding; misgiving.

forecast *v.* **1** *Experts have forecast an upturn in the stock-market:* predict, prognosticate, project; prophesy, augur, foresee; expect, anticipate, calculate, extrapolate; envisage, envision, divine; foretell, presage, portend, foreknow. —*n.* **2** *The forecast for tonight is rain changing to snow by morning:* prediction, prognostication, prophecy, prognosis, outlook; projection, foreknowledge, precognition, prevision, prescience, presentiment; presage, augury; anticipation, conjecture.

forefather *n. He wants to visit Scotland where his forefathers lived:* ancestor, forebear, progenitor, antecedent; patriarch, forerunner; originator, begetter, procreator, author, father.

Ant. descendant, progeny, child.

forefront *n. A new group of young popular singers is coming to the forefront:* lead, head, vanguard, position of prominence, fore; public attention, widespread acceptance, fame, celebrity.

foreign *adj.* **1** *He's thinking of buying a new foreign car:* from another land, alien, not domestic, not native; imported, introduced; strange, exotic, outlandish; distant, remote; unfamiliar, unknown; heathenish, barbarous. **2** *The doctor cleansed the wound of foreign matter. Spite is foreign to her nature:* extraneous, extrinsic, unconnected, unrelated; uncharacteristic, inappropriate, antipathetic, inconsistent, incongruous, incompatible, inconsonant; not pertinent, irrelevant, inapplicable, beside the point, inadmissible.

Ant. 1 domestic, native. **2** relevant, pertinent, applicable; intrinsic, characteristic; congenial, agreeable, suited.

◇ *Word origin:* What do our words *foreign* and *forest* have in common? They both ultimately come from the Latin word *foris,* meaning "out of doors."

◇ *Spelling tip: Foreign* is a *foreign* word in that it does *not* follow the rule "*i* before *e* except after *c* or when sounded like *a* as in *neighbour* and *weigh.*" Remember: *The forEIgn soverEIgn did not dEIgn to rEIgn.*

foreigner *n. This year many foreigners are visiting our country:* alien, outlander, non-native; immigrant, newcomer, émigré, outsider, stranger; barbarian, pagan.

Ant. native, citizen, aborigine.

◇ *Usage note:* See ALIEN.

foreknowledge *n. Did anyone have foreknowledge of the stock-market crash?:* prior knowledge, advance notice; foresight, foresightedness; clairvoyance, second sight, precognition, prescience, prevision; presentiment, anticipation, apprehension, premonition.

foreman *n. For years he worked as a foreman in a steel yard:* manager, overseer, supervisor, shop-steward, chief workman, boss, coordinator, superintendent; spokesman, chairman, president, presiding juryman.

foremost *adj. Shakespeare's birthplace is one of our foremost tourist attractions:* principal, leading, main, pre-eminent, chief, head; paramount, supreme, capital, cardinal; vital, essential.

forerunner *n.* **1** *The penny farthing was a 19th-century forerunner of the modern bicycle:* precursor, predecessor, prototype; ancestor, forebear, forefather, progenitor; trial balloon, *ballon d'essai,* stalking-horse. **2** *A promise of leaves on the trees and buds waiting to flower are forerunners of spring:* herald, harbinger, foretoken, omen, portent, sign, presage, precursor, prognostic, token, augury, premonition, forewarning.

foresee *v. The prophet foresaw a severe famine in the land:* anticipate, expect, look forward to, envisage, look ahead to; prophesy, foretell, predict, prognosticate, forecast; be clairvoyant, be prescient, foreknow, have second sight; augur, presage; divine, forebode.

foresight *n.* **1** *The oracle was believed to have foresight in predicting future events:* clairvoyance, foreknowledge, prescience, power of foreseeing, second sight, prevision, precognition. **2** *Through lack of foresight he found himself out of petrol on a country road:* preparedness, prudence, far-sightedness, forethought, anticipation, provision for the future, planning, provident care, providence, long-sightedness; shrewdness, perspicacity, sagacity; discretion, precaution, wisdom; premeditation.

Ant. 1 hindsight, retrospection. **2** unpreparedness, carelessness, neglect, improvidence.

"What need a man forestall his date of grief,
And run to meet what he would most avoid?"
—*John Milton*

---

forestall *v. Labour and management have agreed on a temporary settlement, thereby forestalling a strike:*

prevent, thwart, ward off, avert, avoid, head off, circumvent; block, preclude, obviate; anticipate, guard against; *Informal* steal a march on.

forest *n. The forest was so dense that we couldn't see through the trees:* woods, wood, thick growth of trees and undergrowth, wooded area, woodland, bush, wildwood; stand, grove, thicket, copse, coppice; wilderness, jungle.

◇ *Word origin: Forest* comes from Latin *foris*, meaning "out of doors." This same Latin word also gives us our word *foreign.*

foretell *v. Perhaps certain gifted persons can foretell the future:* predict, prophesy, foresee, prognosticate, divine, augur, forecast; apprehend, foreknow; presage, forebode, portend; tell fortunes, cast a horoscope, soothsay, act the seer.

forethought *n.* **1** *One needs forethought to live within one's means:* careful planning, prudence, carefulness, foresight, providence, far-sightedness, sagacity, shrewdness; caution, heed, wariness, circumspection. **2** *Part of the game is to answer impulsively, without forethought:* deliberation, prior thought, discretion, consideration, premeditation; precaution, prudence, anticipation.

Ant. 1 unpreparedness, carelessness, neglect, improvidence. **2** impulsiveness, spontaneity.

foreword *n. In the foreword the author states his intentions in writing the book:* preface, introduction, introductory statement, preamble, prologue; prelude.

◇ *Usage note:* See FORWARD.

forfeit *n.* **1** *You'll have to pay a forfeit if you fail to keep the appointment:* penalty, fine, damages, assessment, forfeiture.

—*v.* **2** *She forfeited the match when she refused to play. He forfeited his freedom when he was convicted of the crime:* lose because of some offence, surrender, yield, default; squander, waste, let slip, miss, allow to slip through the fingers.

◇ *Word origin: Forfeit* comes from Latin *foris* (outside) + *facere* (to do), hence to do something taken "outside" what is right.

◇ *Spelling tip:* Remember, *forfeit* forfeits the *i* before *e* except after *c* rule, hence spelt *for-fEIt.*

forge *n.* **1** *The blacksmith's forge was so hot that we couldn't stand near it:* furnace, hearth; blacksmith's shop, smithy, ironworks.

—*v.* **2** *The smith forged the horseshoe with great skill:* hammer out, beat into shape, shape, form, fabricate, make, manufacture, fashion, produce, turn out; devise, contrive. **3** *My signature on the cheque was forged:* sign falsely, imitate fraudulently, counterfeit, falsify, fabricate; copy, imitate, simulate.

◇ *Word origin: Forge* comes originally from Latin *fabrica*, workshop. It entered English during the Middle Ages, from the Old French word *forger.*

forgery *n.* **1** *He made a fortune by the forgery of paintings:* fraudulent imitation; falsification, counterfeiting, misrepresentation; deception, fraudulence. **2** *The curator of the museum discovered that the Greek vase was a forgery:* counterfeit, fraud, fake, sham; put-up job, hoax.

forget *v.* **1** *Don't feel hurt because she forgets your name:* fail to recollect, not remember, escape the memory, be forgetful of, be unable to recall, let slip from the memory of; neglect, slight, disregard. **2** *I hope he doesn't forget the plane tickets:* leave behind, overlook, fail to take, omit unintentionally; think no more of, pass over, dispense with, be done with, consign to oblivion, let bygones be bygones.

Ant. 1 remember, recollect, recall; reminisce, think back on, bring to mind, acquire, learn, retain; treasure, mind.

◇ *Word origin: Forget* comes from Old English *forgietan*, forget, from *for-* (un-) + *gietan* (grasp), i.e. "to miss or lose mental grasp" on something.

forgetful *adj. She's so forgetful that she has to make a note of everything:* apt to forget, absent-minded; heedless, neglectful, inattentive, oblivious, unmindful, negligent, mindless, careless, remiss; amnesiac.

Ant. retentive, unforgetting, unforgetful, attentive, careful, mindful.

forgive *v. We must forgive our enemies if we ourselves expect forgiveness:* pardon, excuse, absolve, cease to feel resentment against, make allowances for, bear with; think no more of, allow for; bury the hatchet; remit the penalty of; acquit, clear, exonerate, exculpate, condone, pass over, overlook; discharge, set free, release; *Informal* wipe the slate clean, let bygones be bygones.

Ant. blame, condemn, censure, charge.

◇ *Word origin: Forgive* comes from Old English *forgiefan*, forgive, from *for-* (away) + *giefan* (give), i.e. grant, remit, pardon. The word is connected with the German *vergeben*, to forgive, and with equivalent words in other Germanic languages because Christian missionaries during the Dark Ages used the now-lost ancestor-word to translate Latin *perdonare*, to pardon, forgive.

forgo *v. Because of other expenses, I'll have to forgo a new suit:* give up, do without, relinquish, renounce; surrender, yield, waive; abstain from, refrain from, eschew, skip, abnegate; sacrifice.

◇ *Word origin: Forgo* comes from Old English *forgān*, to pass over something.

fork *n.* **1** *Set the table with knives and forks:* pronged implement, eating utensil; pitchfork; trident. **2** *When you get to the fork in the road, bear right:* division, branching, branch, bifurcation, divergence, separation, intersection, junction; crotch, angle, bend, elbow; turning-point.

—*v.* **3** *Fork the bales onto the trailer:* pierce, take

hold of with a fork, stab, skewer, impale. **4** *The river forks just before it reaches the town:* diverge, divide, bifurcate, branch, branch out, split, ramify.

◇ *Word origin: Fork* comes from Latin *furca,* pitchfork.

forlorn *adj.* **1** *She's always forlorn since her children married and moved away:* unhappy, depressed, dejected, despondent, dispirited; broken-hearted, woebegone, bereft, bereaved, disconsolate, miserable, comfortless, hopeless, despairing, desperate, inconsolable; abject, pitiable, wretched, pathetic. **2** *We stayed at a forlorn little inn outside the town:* forsaken, deserted, solitary; desolate, dreary, dismal; friendless, lonesome, lonely, lone; destitute, abandoned, helpless, forgotten.

Ant. **1** happy, cheerful, elated, hopeful. **2** thriving, bustling.

◇ *Word origin: Forlorn* comes from Old English *forlēosan,* to forsake.

form *n.* **1** *The biscuits were cooked in the form of squares:* shape, outline, figure, pattern, contour; figuration, configuration; formation, conformation; structure, format, design, style, plan. **2** *This coat really fits my form:* body, figure, anatomy, build, physique, person; being, presence. **3** *When the cement has hardened, the form is removed:* mould, cast, frame, framework, matrix. **4** *Ice is merely water in another form:* appearance, phase, aspect, manifestation, image, likeness, semblance, guise; incarnation. **5** *The ant is a form of insect:* type, variety, kind, sort; genus, species, genre, class; description, denomination; model, brand, character, stamp. **6** *You paint well, but your work lacks form:* order, system, structure, orderliness, harmony, arrangement, regularity; shapeliness, proportion, symmetry. **7** *They didn't follow the traditional form of the marriage service:* prescribed method, order, format, rule, habit, proceeding, practice, liturgy, formality, ceremony, rite, ritual; formula, style, mode; way, manner. **8** *It's not good form to insist on talking about oneself:* social behaviour, manners, deportment, practice, conduct, custom, usage, propriety, decorum; etiquette, conventionality. **9** *If she's on form, she can win the match easily:* trim, fettle, fitness, shape, top condition, healthy condition.

—*v.* **10** *Form the plaster with your hands and allow it to harden:* fashion, shape, mould; carve, sculpt, cut, sculpture, chisel, model; rough-hew, hew, block out; cast, stamp, pattern; construct, structure, fabricate, forge, build; produce, make, create, devise, put together, manufacture; found, set up, establish. **11** *The sofa is formed of three separate sections:* compose, make up, constitute; serve to make up. **12** *He formed the habit of peering over his glasses:* develop, acquire, contract, pick up.

formal *adj.* **1** *The Queen took the salute at the formal march-past:* ceremonial, official, conventional, ritualistic, regular, customary; external, outward, perfunctory. **2** *"Your signature on the lease will make our agreement formal," said the landlord:* definite, settled, fixed; explicit, positive; proper, in due form, authoritative; legal, lawful. **3** *Her Royal Highness's manner with commoners is gracious but quite formal:* reserved, decorous, proper, strict, cool; prim, strait-laced, prudish; stiff, starched, stilted; rigid, inflexible, uncompromising; solemn, pompous; ceremonious, punctilious. **4** *He kept a black bow-tie and dinner jacket for formal occasions:* dressy, stylish, grand, smart; solemn, fancy, full-dress.

Ant. informal, casual, easy-going, unceremonious.

> **Exploring the Word**: Latin *forma,* form, gives us *form; conform,* to be in the same "form" with something else; *formal* and *formality,* which refer to social forms; *formula,* literally a "little form," a short, symbolic written form of a chemical or mathematical statement, and *formulate,* to form, make, or express; *inform,* which originally meant to form or shape another's mind or character by teaching; *reform,* to form again, refashion; and *uniform* (Latin *unus,* one), one in form, alike, or a dress or costume having one form or style. Latin *forma* is related to Greek *morphē,* from which we get our words *amorphous,* formless; *morphology,* the study of the formation and inflection of words; *Morpheus,* the Latin poet Ovid's name for the god of dreams (because dreams are the shapes seen by the dreamer) — we have long used *Morpheus* (like "sandman") as a facetious word for sleep or drowsiness; hence from *Morpheus* we get the name of the opium-derivative pain-killer *morphine* (in older usage called *morphia*).

formality *n.* **1** *The old man bowed and shook the child's hand with mock formality:* observance of form, conventionality, propriety, decorum, etiquette, punctilio; reserve, coolness. **2** *Once the terms had been hammered out, the signing of the treaty was just a formality:* ritual, rite, custom, convention, rule of procedure, ceremony, ceremonial, mere form, motion.

Ant. informality, ease, casualness.

formation *n.* **1** *A formation of planes thundered overhead:* ordered group, configuration, arrangement, constellation, set; structure, composition, make-up. **2** *The Pilgrim Fathers' goal was the formation of a colony in the New World:* creation, establishment, development, organization, genesis, generation; production, manufacture, fabrication, building.

formative *adj. One learns a lot during the formative years of adolescence:* impressionable, susceptible, accessible, sensitive; plastic, shaping, determinative.

former *adj.* **1** *In former days this was a fashionable* *restaurant:* past, prior, bygone, gone by; elapsed, lapsed, gone, passed away; ancient, old-time, of yore. **2** *He had two daughters, Alice and Sarah, the former of whom married an archaeologist:* first-mentioned, beforementioned, first-named; aforementioned, aforesaid. **3** *The house was built by her former husband:* previous, earlier, anterior, preceding, prior; antecedent, foregoing; erstwhile, quondam; *Informal* ex; *Archaic* whilom.

Ant. 1 modern, coming, future. **2** latter, succeeding, following. **3** ensuing, subsequent; present.

formerly *adv. She was formerly head of a large department store:* once, at one time, in time past, originally, previously; long ago, of old, of yore, anciently, hitherto, lately, ere now; *Archaic* whilom.

◇ *Usage note:* Don't become careless in your pronunciation or spelling and confuse *formerly* and *formally. Formerly,* of course, means previously, some time ago; *formally* means in a formal way or manner. Thus, *The chief of police was formerly an army sergeant. You're dressed too formally for a picnic.*

formidable *adj. A charging rhinoceros is a formidable sight:* awesome, imposing, impressive; fearful, terrifying, alarming, dreadful, menacing, threatening; overwhelming, terrific, overpowering; difficult, demanding, dangerous; taxing, onerous, mammoth.

◇ *Word origin:* A *formidable* opponent is feared or dreaded. *Formidable* comes from Latin *formidare,* to dread.

formula *n.* **1** *What's your formula for success?:* prescription, recipe, rule, principle, precept. **2** *The magician recited a secret formula:* incantation, rigmarole, set phrase, saying, verbal form, chant; cliché, platitude, pleasantry, cant.

"Matter — a convenient formula for describing what happens where it isn't."

—*Bertrand Russell*

---

formulate *v. So far, he has not been able to formulate his new plan:* express clearly, state, systematize; frame, draft, compose; specify, particularize, itemize; devise, invent.

forsake *v.* **1** *He held her close and swore never to forsake her:* desert, abandon, leave, quit, vacate, cast off; abdicate, resign, lay down; fling away, part with, jettison, dispose of; flee, depart. **2** *His new wife persuaded him to forsake his old drinking habits:* renounce, forswear, give up, have done with, repudiate, spurn, abandon; relinquish, yield, surrender, waive, drop; reject, discard; disclaim, disavow; deny, go back on.

fort *n. There are a number of disused forts along Britain's coast:* fortress, fortification, stronghold; bulwark, bastion, castle, citadel, fastness; garrison, base, station, camp.

forte *n. He can play classical and pop music, but his real forte is jazz improvisation:* strong point, special gift, speciality, particular talent, strength, chief excellence; natural turn, unusual aptitude, bent, knack.

◇ *Pronunciation tip: Forte,* referring to one's strong point, is generally pronounced as two syllables, *FOR-tay.* It should not be confused with *forte,* which means "loud" and is pronounced exactly the same: *The record-player was kept forte all evening.*

forth *adv.* **1** *From this day forth you are my best friend:* forward, onward, ahead, outward, on to the end. **2** *He brought forth a proposition that we all liked:* into consideration, to notice, into view, before one's attention; out of concealment, from retirement, from confinement.

◇ *Usage note:* Don't confuse *forth* and *fourth. Forth* means onward or forward in space or time: *to go forth. Fourth* is next after third: *the Fourth Estate.*

forthcoming *adj. His forthcoming play is about the Garden of Eden:* about to appear, coming, approaching; imminent, impending. **2** *Financial assistance from his friends is always forthcoming:* ready as needed, available, at hand, handy; open-handed, co-operative, helpful.

forthright *adj. Don't ask his opinion unless you're ready for a forthright answer:* frank, open, blunt, outspoken, candid, direct, plainspoken, straightforward; painfully truthful, not mincing matters, downright; *Informal* calling a spade a spade.

Ant. furtive, secret, underhand; dishonest, untruthful, deceitful.

forthwith *adv. We said good night and left forthwith:* immediately, without delay, at once, directly, instantly, right off, straight away, quickly, promptly.

fortification *n. There were fortifications along the border to discourage invaders:* fortress, fort, citadel, garrison, bastion, tower, bulwark, stronghold; breastwork, earthwork.

fortify *v.* **1** *The medieval town was fortified with a high wall and a deep moat:* strengthen against attack, defend with fortifications, protect, secure, shield; fortress, bulwark, garrison. **2** *The wooden beams were fortified with steel rods:* make strong, strengthen, reinforce, add strength to, brace, shore up, buttress; harden, stiffen. **3** *The bridegroom took a brandy to fortify himself for the ceremony:* sustain, make strong, build up, support, strengthen, buoy up, boost, hearten, cheer, reassure; encourage, embolden, urge on; stimulate, invigorate. **4** *The bread is fortified with various vitamins. The punch is well fortified with rum:* enrich, add nutrients to; add alcohol to, lace.

Ant. 2 weaken, undermine, debilitate, impair. **3** demoralize, dishearten, unnerve, discomfit.

fortitude *n. It takes a lot of fortitude to sail round*

the world single-handed: endurance, courage, strength of mind, moral strength, resoluteness, mettle; spirit, firmness, resolution, determination, prowess, pluck, tenacity; hardihood, dauntlessness, fearlessness, intrepidity, heroism; valour, bravery, boldness; nerve, dash, daring; *Informal* guts, grit, nerve, spunk, backbone.
Ant. cowardice, weakness, faint-heartedness.

fortress *n. The soldiers attacked the fortress:* large fortified place, fort, citadel, stronghold, fortification, acropolis; bastion, bulwark, buttress.

fortuitous *adj. The impromptu celebration was the result of a fortuitous meeting with an old friend:* chance, accidental, random, unexpected; undesigned, unpremeditated, not planned, unintentional, inadvertent, unintended, casual; stray, hit-or-miss, haphazard, incidental; not meant, never thought of, adventitious; lucky, happy, fortunate.
Ant. pre-arranged, planned, purposed, intentional, premeditated.
◇ *Usage note:* Technically, *fortuitous* does not mean lucky, or fortunate, or favourable. It means "happening by chance," whether good or bad. Thus, careful speakers and writers do not use *Under more fortuitous circumstances the business would have succeeded* but use *favourable* or *fortunate* here instead.

fortunate *adj.* **1** *That irritating man is fortunate in having such a tolerant wife:* lucky, having good fortune, blessed, favoured; successful, booming, flourishing, happy, felicitous; rich, prosperous, well-to-do, well-off; *Informal* sitting pretty. **2** *It was a fortunate day when we opened that shop:* bringing good luck, auspicious, propitious, favourable, advantageous, profitable, resulting favourably; well-timed, timely, opportune, convenient; promising, encouraging, providential; palmy, bright, rosy, fair, benign, halcyon.
Ant. **1** unlucky, unfortunate. **2** ill-starred, baleful, unhappy, miserable, disastrous, calamitous.
◇ *Word origin:* See FORTUNE.

"Fortune hath somewhat the nature of a woman; if she be too much wooed, she is the farther off." —*Charles V of Spain quoted by Sir Francis Bacon*

---

fortune *n.* **1** *Gold prospectors could make a fortune overnight if they hit a rich vein:* immense amount of money, wealth, riches, ample stock of wealth; affluence, prosperity, opulence, easy circumstances; bonanza, windfall, godsend; substance, property, capital, estate, means; revenue, income; treasure, mint, gold mine, pile. **2** *Let's leave it to fortune where we spend our holiday:* fate, destiny, luck, chance, accident, fortuity, haphazard; good luck, lady luck; kismet. **3** Usually **fortunes** *His fortunes have been more down than up over the last few years:* lot, portion, destiny, fate, luck, condition in life, circumstances; star.
Ant. **1** poverty, destitution, indigence. **2** design, intent, intention, purpose.
◇ *Word origin: Fortune* and *fortunate* come from Latin *fortuna,* whose source is the Latin word *fors,* meaning chance.

fortune-teller *n. A fortune-teller told her that she would marry a handsome foreigner:* clairvoyant, crystal-gazer, palmist, chiromancer, gipsy; soothsayer, oracle, prophet, sibyl, augur.

forum *n.* **1** *The issues will be discussed at the forum next month. He left the House to seek a new forum for his ideas:* public meeting-place, public arena, assembly place; platform, rostrum, outlet, medium, lecture room. **2** *There is a forum on drug addiction tonight at 8 p.m.:* open discussion, symposium, seminar, debate, colloquium.
◇ *Word origin:* If you gossip, swap news items, or discuss politics when you meet friends in the supermarket, you are doing what the Romans did in the market-places. *Forum* is Latin for an outdoor market-place. Because people met and talked at such market-places, the word *forum* came to mean any place for an assembly or political discussion.

forward Also **forwards** *adv.* **1** *The cars moved forward very slowly:* ahead, onward, in advance, in front, toward the front, forth, frontwards, before; toward the future. **2** *The proposal was brought forward at our last meeting:* forth, into consideration, into discussion, into prominence; out, into view.
—*adj.* **3** *The forward motion of the queue was barely perceptible:* moving ahead, advancing, onward; frontal, fore; anterior; progressive, go-ahead, forward-looking, up-to-date; enterprising. **4** *Mother thought his behaviour was rather forward:* bold, brash, impudent, presumptuous, immodest, self-assertive, presuming, over-confident; fresh, impertinent, cheeky, insolent, unmannerly; brazen, shameless, offensive, barefaced; intrusive.
—*v.* **5** *We asked the postman to forward our letters:* send forward, readdress, send on, pass on, relay, re-route. **6** *The civic leaders helped to forward the project:* advance, help to progress, promote, further; assist, back, champion, accelerate, hasten, spread, quicken.
Ant. **1** backward, to the rear. **3** backward, regressive. **4** retiring, modest. **6** hinder, impede, obstruct, bar, block.
◇ *Usage note: Forward* is always correct, as an adjective or as an adverb. *Forwards* is correct only as an adverb. Thus, *The soldiers took a forward* (never "forwards") *step,* but *They stepped forward* (*forwards* is also correct here). To avoid problems, stick to *forward* and you'll always be right. Incidentally, don't confuse the adjective and adverb *forward,* toward or at the front, with the noun

foreword, the preface of a book, the part *before* the regular *word.*

foster *v.* **1** *Early experience with bullies in school fostered in him a hatred of tyrants:* encourage, promote, further, forward, advance, accommodate, aid, nurture, help forward, help onward; advocate, support, back, take up the cause of, befriend, patronize; side with, favour, countenance, sanction; foment, stimulate. **2** *They have fostered several children of various races:* rear, bring up, raise, rear up; nurse, mother, care for, tend, take in, feed; nourish, nurture, support, sustain; cherish, treasure, hold dear, harbour, protect.

Ant. 1 oppose, combat, resist, withstand; curb, restrain, inhibit.

◇ *Word origin: Foster* comes from Old English *fōstrian,* to nourish, from *fostor,* food (*foster* and *food* come from the same *food*-word in Germanic).

foul *adj.* **1** *The slaughterhouse was filled with a foul odour:* disgusting, loathsome, obnoxious, putrid, stinking, malodorous; hateful, odious, revolting, repulsive. **2** *Take off those foul clothes and let me wash them:* dirty, soiled, filthy, nasty, unclean; begrimed, besmeared, bedraggled; smeared, stained, sullied; muddy, grimy, grubby; squalid, sordid. **3** *I wish we didn't have to go out in this foul weather:* stormy, squally, blustery, gusty; wet, rainy, drizzly, misty; foggy, murky, cloudy; muddy, turbid. **4** *Many were shocked by his foul language:* coarse, vulgar, lewd, smutty, indecent, obscene; profane, blasphemous; indelicate, immodest, unseemly, gross; abusive, insulting. **5** *It was a neighbourhood accustomed to foul crimes:* heinous, abominable, infamous, notorious; disgraceful, contemptible, detestable; vile, wicked, evil, monstrous, base, scurvy, nefarious, villainous, atrocious, flagitious. **6** *The ship was delayed for an hour because of a foul anchor:* tangled, entangled, ensnared, befouled, encumbered, impeded, choked.
—*v.* **7** *Persons allowing their animals to foul the footpaths will be prosecuted:* make foul, dirty, befoul, sully, soil, begrime, besmirch, pollute. **8** *Masses of seaweed had fouled the anchor:* tangle, clog, entangle, befoul, ensnare.

Ant. 1 fair, fragrant, pleasing, **2** clean, spotless, stainless. **3** fair, clear. **4** mild, modest, seemly, pure. **5** admirable, exemplary; pleasant; honourable. **7** cleanse, purify; honour. **8** clear, untangle.

◇ *Usage note:* Some people have difficulty sorting out *foul* and *fowl. Foul,* of course, means disgusting, evil, or refers to something that is out of bounds or against the rules. A *fowl* is a chicken or any related bird, such as a turkey, duck, or goose. Thus, *a foul smell, a foul pass. One more foul and you're out of the game,* but *It's neither fish nor fowl!*

found *v.* **1** *His grandfather founded the business in 1909:* establish, institute, organize, bring about, set up, originate, create, develop, give rise to, start, set going; settle, colonize. **2** *Most of her arguments were founded on fact:* base, rest, sustain, locate, ground. **3** *The house was founded on solid rock:* build, construct, erect, raise, rear.

◇ *Word origin: Found* and *foundation* come from Latin *fundus,* base, bottom. The same Latin word also gives us *fundamental.*

foundation *n.* **1** *First the builders poured a solid foundation of cement:* base, substructure, underpinning, ground, groundwork, bed, bottom, lowest layer, hard core, support, foot, pedestal; basement, cellar; rock. **2** *The charges of fraud against the corporation proved to be without foundation:* basis, base, justification, cause, reason, rationale; root, ground, groundwork, source, origin, commencement; purpose, motive; premiss, assumption, underlying principle, infrastructure. **3** *He left money for the foundation of a music school:* founding, establishment, institution, setting up, creation; settlement. **4** *The foundation provides money for hospitals and medical research:* institution; charity, fund; philanthropy, benefaction, endowment.

◇ *Word origin:* See FOUND.

founder[1] *v.* **1** *The ship foundered during an Atlantic storm:* sink, go down, go under, go to the bottom, swamp; capsize, shipwreck; run aground. **2** *The company foundered during the last recession:* fail utterly, come to grief, collapse, abort, miscarry, perish, succumb; break up, fall apart, go under; come to nothing, go up in smoke; turn out badly. **3** *His horse foundered as they came down the mountain-path:* go lame, stagger, limp, hobble, reel; trip, stumble, tumble, fall, lurch, topple, plunge, sprawl; break down; *Informal* come a cropper.

◇ *Word origin: Founder* comes from an Old French verb *fondrer,* to sink, from Latin *fundus,* bottom. The same Latin word gives us *foundation.*

◇ *Usage note:* See FLOUNDER.

founder[2] *n. Our company is managed by the son of the founder:* originator, creator, builder, organizer, planner, architect, benefactor, strategist; author, father.

fountain *n.* **1** *The coloured lights playing on the fountains were spectacular:* jet, stream of water; gush, flow, spout. **2** *Explorers traced the River Nile to its several fountains in Central Africa:* source of stream, fountain-head, well-spring, head of a stream, well, spring, fount; reservoir. **3** *Ancient Greece was a fountain of wisdom and philosophy:* origin, source; genesis, beginning; birth, derivation, first principles; reason, cause; supplier, purveyor, feeder.

◇ *Word origin: Fountain* comes from Latin *fons,* fountain, spring of water. The same Latin word gives us *font.*

foxy *adj. He's so foxy that I always wonder if I'm being cheated:* cunning, crafty, clever, artful,

wily, tricky, guileful, sharp, canny, shrewd, shifty, astute; sly, stealthy, insidious, devious, oblique, underhand; deceitful, deceptive; designing, intriguing, conniving.
Ant. straightforward, above-board, forthright; candid, open, plain, frank; artless, guileless, ingenuous, naïve.

foyer *n. The audience waited in the foyer before being allowed into the cinema:* antechamber, vestibule, ante-room, hall; lobby; entrance porch, loggia.
◇ *Word origin: Foyer* ultimately comes from the Latin word *focus*, which meant "hearth," hence a gathering place or meeting-place. Thus our words *foyer* and *focus* both come from Latin *focus*, hearth, and, in completely different contexts, both mean a gathering place, meeting-place. See also FOCUS.

fraction *n.* **1** *I can understand how to add up whole numbers, but I'm stumped by fractions:* part of a whole number, fractional part; section, segment, piece, portion, subdivision; ratio, quotient, proportion. **2** *Not more than a fraction of the members were present:* small part, bit, few; particle, fragment, trifle, morsel; shaving, cutting, chip; scrap, crumb.

> "Produce! Produce! Were it but the pitifullest infinitesimal fraction of a product, produce it in God's name!" — *Thomas Carlyle*

fractious *adj. Don't be fractious when I ask you to do something:* cross, irritable, peevish, ill-tempered, grouchy, snappish, fretful, querulous, irascible; touchy, huffy, shirty, waspish, petulant, shrewish, pettish; quarrelsome, unruly, refractory, rebellious, wayward, perverse, contrary, disputatious; recalcitrant, wilful, unmanageable.
Ant. complaisant, amiable, good-humoured, genial, agreeable, good-natured.

fracture *n.* **1** *When she fell, she suffered a fracture of her wrist:* break, severance, rupture, cleavage; breach, separation, division; split, rift, fault, crack.
—*v.* **2** *A serious misunderstanding fractured their friendship:* break, crack, split, sever; disrupt, breach, rend, cleave.

> **Exploring the Word:** The Latin verb *frangere*, to break, gives us *fracture*, a break; *fragment*, a piece broken off; *fraction*, a minute quantity or (in arithmetic) part of a whole number; *fragile* and *frail*, easily broken, delicate, weak; *fractious*, irritable, and *refractory*, unruly (from an obsolete meaning of *fraction:* "discord, dissension"); *infringe*, to break into, violate; and *infraction, infringement*, violation.

fragile *adj.* **1** *These wine glasses are much too fragile for every-day use:* easily broken, dainty, breakable; delicate, brittle, shivery, splintery; crumbly, friable, crisp; ephemeral, evanescent. **2** *She has been in fragile health all winter:* frail, infirm, delicate, feeble, weak, slight, decrepit; tender, soft; flimsy, rickety, sleazy, dilapidated, tumbledown, unsubstantial.
Ant. tough, strong, stout, sturdy; elastic, resilient, flexible; hardy, tenacious; durable, lasting.

fragment *n.* **1** *The archaeologists examined the fragments of ancient pottery:* part broken off, piece, segment, section, remnant, fraction, portion; chip, sherd, shard, bit, snip, morsel, crumb, shred, scrap; trace, vestige, survival.
—*v.* **2** *The police tried to fragment the mass of demonstrators so that they could tackle the ringleaders:* disunite, break apart, break up, splinter, shatter; divide, separate; chop up, cut up; crumble, chip, disintegrate.
Ant. 2 unite, bring together, combine.

fragmentary *adj. He could give us only a fragmentary account of the meeting:* incomplete, scrappy, piecemeal, disconnected; broken, fractional, detached, not entire, scattered.

fragrance *n. Do you remember the fragrance of lilacs after the rain?:* fragrant odour, perfume, scent, aroma; bouquet, aura, redolence, incense, balm.
Ant. stench, stink, effluvium, miasma, offensive smell.
◇ *Word origin:* See FRAGRANT.

fragrant *adj. The roses imparted a fragrant smell to the whole room:* sweet-scented, sweet-smelling, redolent, odorous, odoriferous, aromatic, perfumed; balmy, spicy.
Ant. fetid, malodorous, stinking.
◇ *Word origin: Fragrant* and *fragrance* come from Latin *fragrare,* to smell.

frail *adj.* **1** *The climber dangled in mid-air, held by one frail rope:* easily broken or destroyed, fragile, brittle, breakable, shivery, splintery, crumbly; rickety, dilapidated; sleazy, flimsy, insubstantial; perishable, delicate; vulnerable, fallible. **2** *Her health has been frail for some months:* slight, weak, delicate, feeble, not robust, fragile, weakly; infirm, decrepit.
Ant. 1 strong, stout, sturdy, stalwart, tough. **2** healthy, sound, hale, robust, vigorous.

frailty *n. A liking for flattery was one of his frailties:* weakness of character, moral weakness, fault, sin, vice, failing defect, blemish, flaw, weak point, fallibility, imperfection, weak side, foible, susceptibility.
Ant. strength, virtue.

frame *n.* **1** *Wouldn't this picture look better in a black frame?:* mounting, case, housing; border, setting, backing, edging, rim. **2** *The wooden frame of the house is already in place:* framework, skeleton, structure, framing, form, scaffolding, casing, mould, body. **3** *John is a man of large frame:* physique, build, figure, shape, anatomy; system, scheme, constitution, make, construction; cast; outline, contour, set. **4** *A good dinner always puts him in a pleasing frame of mind:* attitude, state, mood, humour, nature, temperament, disposition, temper.

—*v.* **5** *A new set of by-laws was framed by the board:* devise, conceive, contrive, invent, plan; draft, sketch, indite; concoct, scheme, hatch; formulate, map out, design; organize, systematize. **6** *He says he was framed by his ex-wife:* incriminate unjustly, give false evidence against.

◇ *Word origin:* A *frame* provides an enclosing border or support for a picture, window, house, etc. It comes from the Old English *framian,* to provide for or construct.

franchise *n.* **1** *At first, the franchise was restricted to male property owners aged 21 or over:* right to vote, voting power, ballot, suffrage, enfranchisement. **2** *Many companies competed for the franchise to expand dealings in the pharmaceutical industry:* right, privilege, authorization, permission, official sanction; grant, charter; prerogative; freedom, immunity.

◇ *Word origin: Franchise* comes from Old French *franc,* free. It originally meant a right, privilege, or licence to do something freely, as to vote, explore new territory, or start a business.

frank *adj. She decided to be frank in rejecting his proposal:* candid, plain-spoken, direct, outspoken, straightforward, free, downright, forthright, straight from the shoulder; bold, round, plain, unreserved, sincere, open, genuine, natural, honest, above-board; ingenuous, artless; undisguised, transparent, evident, clear, apparent, unmistakable, unambiguous, unequivocal; manifest, distinct, patent, explicit.

Ant. reticent, evasive, indirect, reserved, close, covert, secretive; dissembling, underhand, crafty, disingenuous.

◇ *Word origin: Frank* comes from Old French *franc,* free. The same word also gives us *Frankish* (of the Salian *Franks*), *France,* and *French.* The Salian *Franks* were a Germanic people who conquered Roman Gaul around A.D. 500. In *Frankish* Gaul only the conquering people, their descendants, and those under their protection had full freedom, so the ethnic name acquired the sense "free." In Germanic the name meant "Javelins" — the javelin was their national weapon when they invaded Gaul. The political and military successes of the *Franks* reached their height with the reign of Charlemagne, founder of the Holy Roman Empire (A.D. 800), whose reign witnessed the earliest documents of a new language: *French.*

frantic *adj. There was a lot of frantic activity just before the royal visitors arrived:* excited, agitated, hectic; frenzied, distracted, overwrought, beside oneself, distraught, nervous; raging, impassioned, rabid, raving, furious, infuriated; wild, violent, ungovernable; crazy, mad, insane, deranged, delirious, berserk.

Ant. calm, collected, cool, unruffled, composed.

◇ *Word origin: Frantic* originally meant insane or delirious. It comes from Greek *phrēn,* mind, which also gives us *frenzy* and *phrenology,* the doctrine that the conformation, bumps, and ridges of a person's skull can indicate his mentality and personality.

fraternal *adj. There was always a lot of fraternal affection between the boys:* brotherly, kindred, friendly, amicable, social; hearty, warm-hearted; loving, devoted, affectionate; related, consanguineous.

Ant. hostile, antipathetic, inimical.

◇ *Word origin: Fraternal, fraternity,* and *fraternize* come from the Latin word for brother, *frater.*

fraternity *n.* **1** *One of the writer's favourite themes is the fraternity of mankind:* brotherliness, brotherhood, brotherly relation, kinship, interrelation; consanguinity, ties of blood, blood connection, propinquity. **2** *Nowadays the old fraternities are forgotten in favour of the unions:* society, circle; league, alliance, federation, confederacy, coalition, united body; clique, coterie, clan, brotherhood; guild, company, union, association.

fraternize *v. Soldiers were forbidden to fraternize with local inhabitants:* mingle, keep company, associate, mix, hob-nob, consort, band together, co-operate, combine, unite, coalesce, confederate; sympathize, harmonize, concur.

Ant. shun, avoid, keep away from.

fraud *n.* **1** *He was charged with fraud, for selling deeds to land which didn't exist:* fraudulence, swindling, cheating, trickery, deceit, deception, dishonesty, misrepresentation, sharp practice, duplicity, guile, cozenage, double-dealing, chicanery, treachery; craft, artifice, subterfuge, dissimulation, machination, imposture, stratagem; sham, hoax, ruse, trick, swindle, humbug. **2** *He is a complete fraud and certainly isn't who he says he is:* imposter, charlatan, mountebank, sham, fake, counterfeit, pretender; knave, rascal, rogue; quack, cheat, swindler, bluffer, con man.

Ant. 1 fairness, good faith, honesty, integrity.

◇ *Word origin: Fraud* comes from Latin *fraus,* deceit.

fraudulent *adj. Fraudulent business practices, such as short-changing customers, are against the law:* deceitful, dishonest, deceptive, treacherous, underhand, guileful, crafty, wily, tricky, unprincipled, dishonourable, cunning, knavish; crooked, cheating; spurious, sham, bogus, false, counterfeit.

fraught *adj. The expedition was fraught with danger:* filled, full, laden, charged, abounding, loaded, teeming, replete, pregnant, heavy; attended, accompanied.

Ant. devoid, lacking, wanting, empty.

◇ *Word origin: Fraught* comes from a form of

Middle Dutch *vracht*, freight. Thus our words *fraught*, filled, laded, and *freight* have the same origin.

fray[1] *n.* **1** *Several young hooligans were involved in the fray:* quarrel, fight, dispute, disagreement, tiff, controversy, squabble, bickering, fuss, set-to, altercation, contention, dissension; fracas, commotion, tussle, rumpus, scuffle; wrangle, brawl, riot, mêlée, tumult. **2** *The fray intensified when fresh troops arrived:* battle, conflict, contest, fight, combat, warfare; affray, skirmish, engagement.

◇ *Word origin: Fray*[1], a fight, is just a shortened form of the older *affray*, which is from Latin *ex-* (out of) + Frankish *frithuz* (peace), "out of peace," i.e. a disturbance of the peace.

fray[2] *v. Just look how the cuffs of this shirt have frayed!:* ravel, become tattered, wear out, become threadbare; strain, chafe, fret, rub.

◇ *Word origin: Fray*[2], to unravel, comes from Latin *fricare*, to rub.

freak *n.* **1** *The bearded lady is a freak:* monstrosity, monster, oddity, curiosity, deviation, aberration, abnormality, marvel, wonder; abnormal organism, sport. **2** *All this rain is a freak of the weather:* twist, quirk, vagary, irregularity; kink, whim, caprice, turn; fancy, humour, whimsy; craze, fad.

—*adj.* **3** *The cars were involved in a freak accident:* odd, strange, queer, unusual, erratic, freaky, freakish, peculiar, bizarre.

free *adj.* **1** *Most of the former French colonies in Africa are now free nations:* self-governing, autonomous, self-directing. **2** *The Russian serfs and American slaves became free at just about the same time:* emancipated, freed, liberated, enfranchised, at liberty, manumitted, delivered, released; unshackled, unfettered, unbound, unconfined, unconstrained, unbridled, unhampered, unmuzzled, unrestrained; bondless, unchained, unattached; fancy-free, uncommitted, footloose. **3** *Not very many imports are free of all duty. Her nature is free of jealousy:* exempted from, exempt from, not liable to, immune to, excused from, released from, absolved of; unaffected by, devoid of, lacking in. **4** *You are free to go now:* allowed, permitted, able, at liberty. **5** *A free dish is given with each £10 order:* complimentary, without cost, gratis, for nothing, costless, gratuitous, chargeless. **6** *Tie a knot in the free end of the rope:* loose, unattached; not in use, spare, extra; idle, unoccupied, available. **7** *Sometimes his free manner seems merely rude:* open, abandoned, uninhibited, unrepressed, unrestrained, uncontrolled, familiar, informal, easy, expansive, unceremonious; forward, unreserved, bold, audacious, over-familiar, daring; confident, assured, fearless lax, careless; licentious, wanton, dissolute. **8** *Very few people are free with their money:* generous, free-handed, liberal, open-handed, giving, lavish, prodigal, bounteous, big, big-hearted, handsome, bountiful, munificent. **9** *The corridors should be kept free of furniture:* clear, not littered, unobstructed, uncluttered, unencumbered, unimpeded, unblocked, unclogged.

—*adv.* **10** *The barn door was swinging free in the high wind:* without restriction, freely, loosely; leisurely, idly, carelessly. **11** *The first 100 customers will be admitted free:* without charge, at no cost, gratis.

—*v.* **12** *The enemy freed 12 of the prisoners:* set free, liberate, make free, set at liberty, release, let loose, let go, emancipate, manumit, enfranchise, exempt; parole, discharge; redeem, save, ransom; unchain, uncage, unleash, unshackle, unfasten. **13** *He hoped to free his people from hunger:* release, disengage, extricate, rid of.

Ant. **1** occupied, dependent. **2** subservient. **6** bound, engaged, busy, preoccupied. **7** reserved, restrained, restricted. **8** stingy, close, niggardly. **9** clogged, obstructed, cluttered. **12** imprison, gaol, intern, incarcerate, confine, restrain, inhibit, restrict, limit.

◇ *Usage note:* ***Free*** and *for nothing* are interchangeable in some sentences: ***He let me have the tickets free*** or ***He let me have the tickets for nothing.*** Don't blend the two, however, and use "for free," which is not considered good usage.

"...in our country we have those three unspeakably precious things: freedom of speech, freedom of conscience, and the prudence never to practise either of them."

—*Mark Twain*

---

freedom *n.* **1** *The little country will gain its freedom next year:* political independence, autonomy, self-determination, sovereignty, self-government; civil liberty, enfranchisement, emancipation, manumission; liberation, release, exemption from control. **2** *I like this jacket because it gives me more freedom:* ease of movement, elbow-room; latitude, scope, sweep, margin, range, play, swing; unrestricted use, wide berth. **3** *Alone at last, they could now speak with freedom of their love:* openness, frankness, abandon, abandonment, absence of reserve, unreservedness, candour, unconstraint; informality, naturalness; bluntness, directness, forwardness, downrightness. **4** *The teacher resented the freedom with which the student addressed her:* boldness, impudence, licence, disrespect, rudeness, impertinence; impropriety, indecorum.

Ant. **1** dependence, restriction; bondage, servitude, slavery, serfdom; imprisonment, captivity. **3** restraint, caution, reluctance, respectfulness, decorum.

freeze *v.* **1** *Salt water freezes at a lower temperature than fresh water:* become solid, solidify, turn to ice, harden; chill, cool, refrigerate; become glaciated, congeal; frost. **2** *I can't skate any more, I'm frozen:* benumb, chill, stiffen with cold; nip, bite, sting, pierce; anaesthetize. **3** *When we heard the scream, we froze in our tracks:* become immobile, become paralysed, stop; halt, arrest; chill with fear, terrify.

—*n.* **4** *The weatherman is predicting a freeze tonight:* frost, chill, below-freezing temperature. **5** *I was due for a rise when they put a freeze on wages:* lawful control, ceiling, restriction.

freight *n.* **1** *Nowadays the railways earn most of their profit from freight:* transport of goods, shipment of merchandise, truckage, cartage, portage, conveyance, trans-shipment. **2** *Coal trucks can carry many tons of freight:* goods, lading, cargo, load, charge, burden; luggage, baggage.

—*v.* **3** *The ship was freighted with machinery and grain:* load, lade, charge, burden; weigh down.

◇ *Word origin: Freight* comes from Middle Dutch *vrecht*, freight, and is ultimately related to *fraught.*

frenzy *n.* **1** *The baboon shook the bars of its cage in a frenzy of rage:* fit, seizure, transport, outburst, access, furore, delirium; madness, fury, distraction, hysteria; obsession, craze, mania. **2** *She was in a frenzy because fifteen people were coming to dinner:* mental agitation, turmoil, state; mad rush, great haste.

Ant. 2 calm, composure, collectedness, coolness, equanimity; sobriety, sanity, judgement.

◇ *Word origin: Frenzy* originally meant insanity or delirium. It comes from Greek *phrēn*, mind, which also gives us *frantic.*

frequency *n. He uses slang words with great frequency. The frequency of the banging meant that we couldn't sleep all night:* frequent occurrence, repetition, recurrence, reiteration, iteration, persistence.

frequent *adj.* **1** *We take frequent walks through the park:* occurring often, oft-repeated, at short intervals, numerous; continual, recurrent, habitual, reiterative incessant, perpetual. **2** *During the summer we were frequent guests in their home:* regular, constant, habitual; daily, everyday; ordinary, common, familiar; wonted, customary; usual, accustomed.

—*v.* **3** *On Sundays we frequent the art galleries:* haunt, go to frequently, attend regularly, go often to, resort to, visit repeatedly, be seen at regularly.

Ant. 1 occasional; few, scanty. **3** shun, avoid, eschew, steer clear, keep away, spurn.

frequently *adv. Matilda and I frequently have dinner together:* often, oft-times, many times, repeatedly; recurrently, constantly, continually, incessantly, perpetually, over and over again; usually, habitually, customarily, generally, ordinarily.

Ant. rarely, seldom, hardly ever, infrequently.

fresh *adj.* **1** *They have fresh bread every morning at the bakery:* newly made, not stale, recent; well-preserved, unfaded, unspoilt, in good condition, unwithered, unwilted, not deteriorated, undecayed; (*variously*) green, hot, sweet; unworn, unused; undimmed, untarnished. **2** *There is a lot of fresh material in his new play:* new, original, not used before, novel, brand-new; unusual, unfamiliar, untried, unaccustomed; rare, strange, unique; modern, modernistic, new-fashioned, newfangled; recent, late, just out, up-to-date. **3** *It was so good to taste fresh meat and fresh water again:* not salted, unsalted; not preserved, unpickled, unsmoked, undried, uncured. **4** *She was still fresh after working all day:* fit, alert, keen, lively, ready, active, energetic, unworn, not fatigued, unwearied; refreshed, freshened, rested, invigorated; unimpaired, unabated. **5** *Have you ever noticed what fresh complexions country girls have?:* wholesome, clear, youthful-looking; rosy, ruddy; blooming, gleaming, sparkling, glowing; fair, bright, flourishing. **6** *Open the window and let in a little fresh air:* pure, refreshing, cool; chill, nipping, bracing, stinging, cutting, biting; stiff, brisk, keen. **7** *She was sent to her room for being fresh:* impudent, cheeky, pert, saucy, insolent; forward, presumptuous, smartalecy, flippant, nervy; bold, brassy, assuming; obtrusive, meddlesome.

Ant. 1 stale, old. **2** trite, ordinary, hackneyed, stereotyped, shop-worn. **3** salted, preserved, tinned. **4** weary, fatigued, exhausted; dull. **5** sickly, pallid, faded. **6** stale, impure, musty. **7** sweet, amiable, charming, well-mannered.

fret *v.* **1** *It won't help to fret about the problem:* worry, brood, agonize, fume, stew, chafe; be peevish, be angry, be vexed, be irritated, be fretful; mope, lament, pout, pine, sulk; distress, gall, vex, ruffle, irritate. **2** *Constant use had fretted the sandal strap to breaking-point:* wear away, abrade, erode, corrode, rub, excoriate, gnaw, eat; tatter, fray.

—*n.* **3** *As she spoke we could see that she was in a fret:* vexation, annoyance, displeasure, irritation, peevishness, fretfulness; disquiet, discomposure, fidgets, sulks.

◇ *Word origin: Fret* comes from Old English *fretan*, to eat up. By the 1200's the word was being used figuratively in the sense "worry." Old English *fretan* was originally a compound of *fra-* (*for-*, *"altogether, out"*) + *etan*, to eat, with cognates or relatives in other Germanic languages. Its Modern German cognate *fressen*, to eat or feed (said of animals), is also used figuratively of annoyance or anxiety.

friction *n.* **1** *Friction with the air causes damage to planes flying at high speeds:* rubbing, abrasion, grating, fretting, chafing; attrition; resistance, counteraction. **2** *Reporters made the most of the friction between the two delegates:* conflict, opposition, discord, disagreement, clash of opinion, dissension, antagonism, resentment, bad feeling, bad blood; strife, quarrel, contention.

◇ *Word origin: Friction* comes from Latin *fricare,* to rub.

friend *n.* **1** *A friend and I hitch-hiked across Europe last summer:* acquaintance, comrade, companion, chum, confidant; partner, buddy, pal, crony, mate; playmate, playfellow; consort; bedfellow, intimate; boy-friend, girlfriend, escort, beau; lover, mistress, favourite, paramour. **2** *There was a special performance for friends of the orchestra:* patron, supporter, backer, benefactor; well-wisher, encourager; advocate, defender, partisan, adherent. **3** *Can we count on our friends to support the motion?:* ally, colleague, fellow, associate; co-partner, partner, co-worker; confrère, brother, follower, retainer, minion; henchman, myrmidon.

Ant. 1 foe, enemy. **2** antagonist, opponent, adversary. **3** rival, competitor.

friendly *adj.* **1** *He said that he was giving me a friendly warning:* kindly, kind, helpful, well-disposed; amiable, neighbourly, amicable; loving, familiar, affectionate, kind-hearted, cordial, genial, warm-hearted; ardent, devoted, intimate; sympathetic, gracious, generous, chummy, companionable, clubby, convivial. **2** *Several friendly nations came to the conference:* allied, not hostile, on good terms, being friends, fraternal, brotherly; hospitable, social, accessible, affable. **3** *A friendly wind helped the boat across the finishing-line:* favourable, helpful, auspicious, propitious, salutary, advantageous, beneficial, benign, fortunate, opportune.

Ant. 2 belligerent, hostile, contentious. **3** unfavourable, sinister, inauspicious.

friendship *n.* **1** *John and I have maintained our friendship for thirty years:* acquaintanceship, fellowship, association as friends, relationship of friends, companionship, comradeship, brotherhood, friendly relations, fraternity; close tie, intimacy, familiarity. **2** *The two nations signed a treaty of perpetual friendship:* good feeling, friendliness, harmony, accord, concord, amity, comity, amicableness, consonance, understanding, sympathy, good fellowship, cordiality, unity, neighbourliness, goodwill, solidarity.

Ant. 1 enmity, animosity, hostility, spite, antipathy, antagonism. **2** strife, conflict, combat.

fright *n. The child turned and ran in fright from the growling dog:* fear, alarm, terror, panic, fear of danger, consternation; scare, perturbation; dread, apprehension, dismay, trepidation; affright, horror; concern, anxiety, misgiving; cold feet, funk; fear and trembling, intimidation, reign of terror, disquietude; quaking, tremor, flutter, quivering, palpitation.

Ant. bravery, boldness, courage, fortitude, stout-heartedness.

frighten *v. He jumped out of the cupboard and frightened the daylights out of me:* alarm, scare, make afraid, throw into a fright, terrify, terrorize, shock, horrify, disturb, with fear, petrify, affright, frighten, startle; *Archaic* affray; intimidate, daunt; excite, agitate, disquiet.

Ant. calm, soothe, comfort, reassure.

◇ *Usage note:* See AFRAID.

frightful *adj.* **1** *As the full moon rose, frightful howls pierced the air about the cemetery:* horrible, horrendous, horrid, terrible, awful, fearful, shocking, appalling, dreadful, alarming; terrific, horrific, fearsome; lurid, grisly, ghastly, macabre, gruesome, sinister, baleful. **2** *The most frightful dog came bounding out at us:* offensive, loathsome, nasty, insufferable, hideous, disgusting, detestable; revolting, repulsive, repellent, abominable; monstrous, freakish, ogreish. **3** *Informal She really is a frightful snob:* very great, terrific, terrible, extreme, awful, dreadful, insufferable.

Ant. 1 calming, soothing. **2** beautiful, attractive. **3** slight, partial, moderate.

frigid *adj.* **1** *With the central heating out of order the house was frigid:* cold, freezing cold, bitterly cold, freezing, icy; gelid, glacial; cool, chilly; bleak, raw, bitter, nipping, piercing, biting, cutting. **2** *She seemed polite enough, but her manner was distinctly frigid:* stiff, unresponsive, distant, forbidding, aloof; prim, formal, rigid, austere, frosty, cold, cool, chilly, icy, strait-laced.

Ant. 1 hot, burning, sweltering, stifling. **2** cordial, friendly, warm, hospitable; ardent, passionate, impassioned.

◇ *Word origin: Frigid* comes from Latin *frigere,* to be cold, which also gives us our word *refrigerate.*

frill *n.* **1** *She liked to add little frills to her aprons and nighties:* ruffle, gathering, flounce, fringe, edging, furbelow. **2** *Why can't she just serve dinner without all those silly frills?:* ornament, decoration, added touch, embellishment; affectation, superfluity; air, mannerism.

fringe *n.* **1** *How would this shawl look with a six-inch fringe?:* edging, trimming, ornamental bordering, border, tassel, skirting, hem, margin, selvage; mane; edge, periphery, limit, frontier.

—*v.* **2** *A ring of grass fringed the pool:* border, edge, skirt; surround, enclose; decorate, embellish.

frisk *v.* **1** *George loves to frisk about on the lawn with the dogs:* romp, frolic, caper, gambol, cavort, lark, prance, dance, bound, bounce, cut capers; disport, trip, sport, jump about; skip, leap, jump, spring, hop. **2** *The officers frisked the two suspects at the road-block:* search, examine, inspect; check quickly, look over; ransack, rummage through.

◇ *Word origin:* See FRISKY.

frisky *adj. That pony may be too frisky for the children:* lively, animated, spirited, agile, vivacious, nimble, active; spry, sportive, playful, frolicsome, in high spirits, peppy, rollicking; waggish, prankish, mirthful, jocular.
Ant. demure, sedate; pensive, meditative; stodgy, stolid.
◇ *Word origin: Frisky* and *frisk* come from French *frisque,* lively, playful.

frivolity *n. While their money lasted, they wined and dined their friends with gay frivolity:* giddiness, flightiness, levity, lightness, emptiness, folly; triviality, frippery, fickleness, flippancy, airiness; wantonness, thoughtlessness, abandon; dallying, play, whimsy, sport, jest, fun.
Ant. seriousness, staidness, sedateness; gravity, solemnity; soberness, earnestness.

> "How rare, how precious is frivolity! How few writers can prostitute all their powers! They are always implying 'I am capable of higher things'." —*E. M. Forster*

frivolous *adj.* **1** *Once a year she bought something frivolous just to please herself:* impractical, trifling, trivial, worthless, imprudent, improvident, ill-considered, unimportant, insignificant, pointless, silly, petty, paltry; slight, piddling, flimsy, niggling, minor; empty, airy, light, frothy, light-headed, flighty, careless; vain, self-indulgent, extravagant. **2** *Why would she marry such a frivolous young man?:* flighty, superficial, unserious, silly, hare-brained, light-minded; flippant, insouciant; rattle-brained, dizzy, shallow; careless, heedless; foolish, senseless, fatuous; brainless, barmy, witless, stupid; inane, silly, nonsensical.
Ant. 1 important, vital. **2** mature, adult; sensible, serious, earnest; grave, solemn.
◇ *Word origin: Frivolous* and *frivolity* come from Latin *frivolus,* meaning empty, trifling, worthless, silly.

frock *n.* **1** *It's just a little frock that my dress-maker made:* dress, gown, suit, coat, cloak, robe, smock, blouse. **2** *The monks wore frocks of coarse homespun:* clerical garb, canonicals, vestment, monk's robe; cassock, soutane, surplice, chasuble.

frolic *n.* **1** *The clowns were full of frolic:* fun, gaiety, merriment, merry-making, mirth, recreation, amusement; sport, play, festivity, entertainment; tomfoolery, buffoonery; jollity, joviality, pleasantry; antic, gambol, spree, romp, caper, lark, escapade, skylarking, prank.
—v. **2** *The lambs were frolicking in the sunshine:* romp, frisk, skip, caper, gambol, sport, disport, play merrily, amuse oneself, make merry; cut capers, act up, play pranks.
◇ *Word origin: Frolic* comes from the Dutch *vrolijk,* merry, glad.
◇ *Spelling tip:* Remember, the final *c* in *frolic* becomes *ck* in *frolicked* and *frolicking.*

front *n.* **1** *The front of the house faces the street:* face, forward part; façade, frontage. **2** *The soldiers were shipped to the front as replacements:* head, lead, top, beginning; fore; advance guard, trenches, front rank, vanguard, front lines. **3** *She maintained a calm front throughout the ordeal:* external appearance, demeanour, carriage, mien, air, bearing, presence; mask, pretence, façade.
—adj. **4** *We sat in the front row:* located in front, fore, anterior; first, beginning, initial.
—v. **5** *The clubhouse fronts on to the lake:* face, look out, look forward, stand opposite to, give on, regard.
Ant. 1, 2, 4 back, rear.
◇ *Word origin: Front* comes from Latin *frons,* forehead. This same Latin word gives us *confront,* literally "to stand in front of," *affront,* and *effrontery.*

frontier *n.* **1** *Soldiers guard the frontier against invasions:* border, boundary, boundary line; limits, verge, edge, perimeter, extreme, confines.
Ant. interior, settled region.
◇ *Word origin: Frontier* is related to *front,* literally the part of a country that fronts onto another.

frost *n. We may have a frost tonight, so cover your tomato plants:* below-freezing weather, cold spell, chill; frozen moisture, covering of ice, ice crystals; hoar-frost, rime.

> "I leant upon a coppice gate
> When Frost was spectre-grey,
> And Winter's dregs made desolate
> The weakening eye of day." —*Thomas Hardy*

froth *n.* **1** *Wind whipped the waves into a green froth:* foam, spume, scum, head, fume, fizz, bubbles; lather, suds, yeast; white-cap, surf. **2** *Critics dismissed the play as a bit of froth:* trivia, frippery, trumpery, flummery, frivolity, triviality, nonsense; *Informal* bosh, fiddle-faddle, balderdash; trash, rubbish.

frown *v.* **1** *When she frowns, you know she's very angry:* wrinkle the forehead, scowl, knit the brow, glower, look displeased, glare, look stern; mope, sulk, pout, fret; ponder, muse. **2** *Many people frown on that kind of behaviour:* disapprove of, view with disfavour, look disapprovingly on, discountenance, look askance at; show disapproval of, show displeasure at, look down on.
—n. **3** *With a frown he examined his son's school report:* frowning look, scowl, glower, black look, glare.
Ant. 1 smile, show pleasure, express satisfaction, show kindliness. **2** approve, support, advocate, foster, cherish; favour, countenance.

frozen *adj.* **1** *The ship remained frozen in the*

ice-fields for months. Keep the meat frozen until you are ready to cook it: ice-bound, obstructed, clogged, immobilized; stymied, stalemated; refrigerated, chilled, cooled, iced, gelid, solidified by cold. **2** *When my toes feel frozen, I know that it's time to go inside:* benumbed, numb, cold; chill, chilly; gelid, icy, glacial; frost-bitten; wintry, hibernal; arctic, polar.

Ant. 1 thawed, melted. **2** warm, hot; torrid.

frugal *adj.* **1** *The frugal Scotsman never takes a taxi when he can walk:* economical, thrifty, unwasteful, prudent with money, sparing, economy-minded, penny-wise; parsimonious, tight, penny-pinching, stingy, niggardly; ascetic, abstemious. **2** *It was a frugal dinner, but very nourishing all the same:* scant, not abundant, slim, sparing, skimpy.

Ant. 1 extravagant, wasteful, inprudent, spendthrift. **2** luxurious, lavish, profuse.

fruit *n.* **1** *The Harvest Festival table overflowed with all the fruits of the earth:* produce, product, crop, yield, production, harvest; young, offspring, progeny. **2** *I hope the old man lives to enjoy the fruits of his labour:* result, product, consequence, outgrowth, upshot, outcome, issue, effect; return, profit, benefit, advantage; revenue, remuneration, emolument, earnings; award, reward.

◇ *Word origin:* Do you enjoy eating *fruit?* Or have you ever said that a man should enjoy the *fruits* of his labour? If so, your concept of *fruit* matches the original Indo-European meaning of the word—"agricultural produce/enjoyment." The Latin word from which *fruit* is derived is *fructus,* meaning use and enjoyment, produce, income. Related Latin words are *fruges,* the fruits of the earth, produce of fields and orchards, and *frui,* to enjoy, delight in. From forms of these Latin words we get our words *frugal* (Latin *frugalis* originally had the connotation "used in the best way," i.e. sparingly) and *fruition,* which originally meant enjoyment, peaceable possession. Derived from the same Indo-European root are Modern German *brauchen,* to use, and Old English *brūcan,* to enjoy, use as food. This survives in our word *brook,* to tolerate, stomach, as in the sentence *We're getting married now and will brook no interference with our plans.*

fruitful *adj.* **1** *Cherry trees here in the city are seldom fruitful:* productive, fecund, prolific, fructiferous; blooming, yielding, fertile, abounding in fruit; fruit-bearing. **2** *The anonymous tip proved fruitful, and the suspect was captured:* profitable, productive, advantageous, effective, successful, efficacious.

Ant. 1 unfruitful, barren, sterile, infertile, unproductive. **2** fruitless, pointless, useless, vain, futile, abortive, ineffectual; scarce, scanty.

fruition *n. The plan should reach fruition in another year:* fulfilment, achievement, realization, attainment; satisfaction, gratification, actualization, materialization, consummation; maturity, ripeness.

◇ *Word origin:* See FRUIT.

fruitless *adj.* **1** *Further investigations proved fruitless:* unfruitful, pointless, useless, bootless, unsuccessful, unavailing, empty, hollow, vain, futile; ineffective, ineffectual, inefficacious; unprofitable, profitless, nugatory; worthless; abortive, inoperative; inept, incompetent. **2** *Why did we ever move to this fruitless land?:* unfruitful, barren, infertile, arid, sterile; unproductive, unprolific.

Ant. 1 useful, profitable, fruitful; effective, worthwhile, productive. **2** fertile, fecund; abundant, prolific, fructiferous.

frustrate *v. Steady rains frustrated our efforts to put in the flowers:* hinder, defeat, thwart, baffle, foil, circumvent, prohibit, inhibit, bring to naught, nullify, cancel, make of no avail, render invalid, make null and void, check, impede, block, bar; suppress; undermine, cut the ground from under; forestall, balk, obstruct, prevent, counter. **2** *Giving the child problems he can't solve will only frustrate him:* discourage, fluster, upset, dispirit, disappoint, disconcert, dishearten; cripple, hamstring, clip the wings of.

Ant. 1 foster, promote, further, forward, advance; incite, instigate, abet, foment. **2** encourage, hearten, cheer; satisfy, gratify.

frustration *n. Without public support our efforts will end in frustration:* defeat, failure, futility, non-success, non-fulfilment, foiling, thwarting, arrest, hindrance, balking, inhibition, interference, bafflement; contravention, counteraction, obstruction; disappointment, dissatisfaction, let-down, chagrin, discomfiture.

fry *v. I always fry potatoes in hot fat with a bit of onion:* cook, sauté, brown, grill, frizzle, fricassee; French fry, deep fry.

fuel *n.* **1** *Factories have been urged to switch from coal to a cleaner fuel:* combustible material; (*variously*) wood, coal, coke, oil, natural gas; gas, electricity, petroleum. **2** *The newspaper article provided him with fuel for his speech:* material, fodder, ammunition, inspiration; sustenance, means, wherewithal, impetus.

—*v.* **3** *We have to fuel the furnace once a day:* provide with fuel, replenish with fuel, fill up, stoke up, charge, recharge; sustain.

◇ *Word origin: Fuel* is from Latin *focus,* meaning hearth. This Latin word also gives us our words *focus* and *foyer,* places where light rays or people gather, as at a hearth.

fugitive *n.* **1** *The fugitive was wanted by police in several countries:* runaway, deserter, outlaw; refugee, escapee; exile, expatriate; renegade, apostate; rover, wanderer, itinerant, straggler; vagrant, vagabond, nomad; tramp, loafer.

—*adj.* **2** *St. Paul urged the fugitive slave to return*

to his master: escaping, escaped, fleeing, running away, flying. **3** *Poetic The fugitive hours were gone and would not return:* fleeting, short-lived, transitory, evanescent, transient, fugacious, ephemeral; brief, momentary, passing, impermanent; unstable, errant, elusive, volatile, flitting; hurried, cursory, hasty, summary; short, temporary; fading, shifting.
Ant. 3 lasting, permanent, durable; changeless, immutable; endless, eternal.
◇ *Word origin:* A *fugitive* flees from justice, arrest, or pursuit. The word comes from Latin *fugere*, to flee.

fulfil *v.* **1** *The dream of a world without war has yet to be fulfilled:* carry out, accomplish, achieve, realize, effect, implement, effectuate, bring to pass, bring about; establish, execute, consummate; perfect, bring to perfection. **2** *Don't be lax about fulfilling your obligations:* obey, perform, do, abide by, keep, discharge, comply with, adhere to, be faithful to, live up to; keep faith with; redeem; observe, follow, heed. **3** *The thesis will fulfil the requirements for your M.A.:* satisfy, suit, meet, fill out, make good, answer.
Ant. 1 neglect, ignore, slight, overlook, disregard; fail in. **3** fall short of, fail to meet; disappoint, dissatisfy.
◇ *Spelling tip:* Some people try to spell *fulfil* as if they were combining *full* and *fill.* Don't. Both *L*'s are single in *fuLfiL.* But the second *L* is doubled in *fuLfiLLed* and *fuLfiLLing,* though not in *fuLfiLment.*

fulfilment *n.* **1** *The little house in the country was the fulfilment of all her dreams:* realization, accomplishment, effectuation, implementation, attainment, achievement; execution, establishment, completion, crowning, culmination; finishing touch. **2** *What fulfilment could there ever be in a job as a typist?:* satisfaction, contentment, gratification; pleasure, delight, happiness, contentedness.
◇ *Spelling tip:* See FULFIL.

full *adj.* **1** *Add a full cup of chopped nuts. The child is full of energy:* filled, heaped, brimming, brim-full, flush; replete, abounding, fraught, crammed, bursting, packed, laden, loaded, chock-full; teeming, swarming, saturated; filled up, well-supplied, well-stocked; sated, surfeited, stuffed, gorged, glutted. **2** *Have you got a full supply of firewood?:* complete, entire, whole, thorough, maximum, total; intact, unabridged, plenary; mature, perfect, up to the mark. **3** *The dress has a full skirt:* ample, capacious, wide, broad, voluminous; comprehensive, all-inclusive; large, big; round, rotund, shapely, plump; rich, resonant.
—*adv.* **4** *He knew full well what I was trying to say:* very, quite, perfectly; exactly, precisely.
Ant. 1 empty, void; vacant, devoid, blank, exhausted. **2** partial, incomplete, qualified; altered, abridged. **3** tight, restricted; limited, exclusive; thin, meagre, angular, faint.

fully *adv.* **1** *Are you fully aware of what may happen?:* completely, entirely, wholly, totally, altogether, quite; perfectly, in all respects, in every respect; from first to last, throughout, from top to toe, from head to foot; positively, utterly, at all points; substantially, on the whole; every inch, heart and soul. **2** *Is he fully supplied with the materials for the job?:* sufficiently, amply; abundantly, plentifully, copiously; richly.

fume *n.* **1** *The fumes from his cigar made dining with him disagreeable:* smoke, haze, exhalation; vapour, gas, billow, waft; unpleasant odour, reek, stench; scent; miasma.
—*v.* **2** *The chimney fumed in great black billows:* smoke, send forth fumes, puff, smoulder, emit, exude, belch forth; exhale; smell, reek, stink, stench. **3** *When he put down the phone, he was really fuming:* display anger, rage, seethe, lose one's temper, get steamed up, rant, rave, fly off the handle, explode, flare up, foam, boil, flame up.
◇ *Word origin: Fume* comes from Latin *fumus,* smoke.

fun *n.* *We had great fun playing tag in the swimming-pool:* enjoyment, gaiety, pleasure, amusement, merriment, diversion; entertainment, recreation, distraction, relaxation; joking, jest, playfulness, waggishness, jollity, mirth, good humour, joviality; cheer, frolic, whoopee, skylarking, tomfoolery, buffoonery; game, sport, play, horseplay, romp, antic, prank, lark, spree, escapade, revelry, high jinks, good time; *Slang* ball, gas.
Ant. misery, melancholy, woe, gloom, tedium.

"Work is much more fun than fun."
—*Noël Coward*

---

function *n.* **1** *The main function of the kidneys is to purify the blood:* purpose, role, activity, operation, job, business, task, duty; capacity, power, faculty; province, sphere, office, niche, place, scope, range, field; concern, objective, raison d'être. **2** *It was a rather large function with all sorts of dignitaries and celebrities in attendance:* social gathering, fête, gala, affair, festivity, party, entertainment, reception, soirée; dinner party, feast, banquet; ceremony, occasion.
—*v.* **3** *This armchair also functions as a day-bed:* serve, act, perform, do duty; operate, behave, work, answer a purpose, help, benefit, render a service, serve one's turn.
◇ *Word origin: Function* and *functional* come from Latin *fungi,* to perform. Incidentally, our word *fungi* has nothing to do with this word but is the plural of *fungus,* from Latin *fungus,* mushroom, which goes back to the same Mediterranean (pre-Indo-European) source as Greek *sphongos,* sponge.

functional *adj.* *Is that oil lamp functional or*

merely decorative?: working, operative, operable, functioning; useful, serviceable, practical, utilitarian.

fund *n.* **1** *The family contributed weekly to a Christmas fund:* sum of money, accumulated amount, savings, accumulation, bank; nest-egg. *Slang* kitty; pool, pot; foundation, endowment, investment. **2** *That girl is a fund of information:* store, supply, stock; repository, reservoir, well, fount, spring; treasure, storehouse, horde, reserve; mine, lode, vein.
—*v.* **3** *We're hoping that the government will fund the project:* finance, pay for, underwrite, foot, float; support, endow, patronize.

Ant. **1** expenditure, outlay, outgo, disbursement; payment, remuneration.

◇ *Word origin: Fund* comes from Latin *fundus,* bottom, foundation, piece of farmland. Old French *fonds* gives our English word the added denotations of "capital" or "stock." Our words *found* (to establish), *foundation,* and *fundamental* also come from Latin *fundus,* and in fact our word *bottom* is cognate with it.

fundamental *adj.* **1** *His book is on the fundamental principles of banking:* basic, underlying, essential, first, primary, elementary; key, crucial, vital, central; major, principal, main, chief; cardinal, indispensable, integral.
—*n.* **2** *Have you mastered the fundamentals of retail selling?:* principle, basic, primary rule, essential, axiom, element, component; base, basis, foundation, corner-stone; groundwork.

Ant. **1** advanced; superfluous, accidental; secondary, subordinate, lesser.

funds *n. pl. I'd like to help, but I'm momentarily out of funds:* money, cash, cash in hand, wherewithal, means, resources, assets, capital, property, wealth, finances, income; *Slang* the ready, lucre, dough, brass, lolly, dibs, pelf, bread, scratch.

funeral *n. The funeral consisted of a Requiem Mass and a grave-side service:* rites, obsequies, requiem, memorial service, interment, burial, entombment, inhumation; cremation; wake.

◇ *Word origin: Funeral* goes back to Latin *funus, funera,* death, funeral, funeral rites.

funereal *adj. From the doctor's funereal expression, I expected the worst:* sad, mournful, gloomy, dismal, doleful, woeful, grieving, solemn, dirgeful, sombre, dreary, depressing; weepy, woebegone, lachrymose, lugubrious, cheerless, long-faced, grim, grim-faced; desolate, broken-hearted.

Ant. happy, gay, cheery, merry, lively, joyous, festive.

funnel *n.* **1** *Use a funnel to pour the oil into the bottle:* cone-shaped utensil; channel, conduit, duct, shaft. **2** *The steamship has four large funnels:* smoke-stack; chimney, smoke pipe, stove-pipe, ventilator, flue, air shaft.
—*v.* **3** *They funnel most of their income into investments:* pour, concentrate, channel, focus, direct.

funny *adj.* **1** *It's a very funny story, but I daren't repeat it:* comical, amusing, humorous, diverting, laughable, hilarious, absurd, ridiculous, ludicrous; witty, droll, comic, facetious, waggish, jocular, jocose, sporting, jesting, antic, mirthful, merry; farcical. **2** *That's a funny way to speak of a relative:* odd, strange, weird, curious, bizarre, queer, peculiar.

Ant. **1** serious, humourless; solemn, grave; mournful, melancholy.

fur *n. Her new suit is trimmed with fine fur:* pelt, animal skin; hair, fleece, down.

furious *adj.* **1** *She gets furious whenever you mention her weight problem:* enraged, irate, angry, mad, irascible, hot under the collar, infuriated, maddened, provoked, raging, wrathful, fuming; rabid, frenzied, wild, fanatical; unbalanced, frenetic. **2** *A furious gale blew the ship towards the rocky shore:* tempestuous, turbulent, fierce, intense, violent, vehement, stormy, raging, tumultuous, rampant; fiery, savage, passionate; ungovernable, unrestrained; reckless, heedless, wild.

Ant. **1** calm, serene, pleased, placated. **2** mild, calm, tame.

◇ *Word origin:* See FURY.

furnace *n. Why isn't the furnace sending out any heat?:* heater, heating system; oven, stove, incinerator; forge, boiler, kiln.

◇ *Word origin: Furnace* comes from Latin *furnus,* oven.

furnish *v.* **1** *The company will furnish each contestant with a free ticket:* provide, equip, supply, stock, accommodate; endow, vest; purvey, render; favour, indulge; provision; give, bestow on. **2** *The house was furnished entirely with handmade items:* equip, appoint, outfit, fit out, array, fit up; rig; accoutre, dress; gird, arm, prepare.

◇ *Word origin: Furnish* and *furniture* come to us from Old French *furnir,* to equip, fit out, which goes back to a now-lost Frankish word related to our word *frame.*

furniture *n. Some articles of furniture were lost when we moved:* household goods, house fittings, movables, appointments, chattels, furnishings.

furore *n.* **1** *The doctor's new book has caused quite a furore. A Calvinist phrase for God's anger is "the furore of His wrath":* commotion, uproar, excitement, to-do, reaction, noise; rage, fury, fit of anger, passion, frenzy, madness, mania, agitation, raving; lunacy, insanity; transport, fervour, fanaticism. **2** *The latest furore is for frisbees:* craze, vogue, fad, rage, mania, enthusiasm, fashion.

◇ *Word origin:* See FURY.

furrow *n.* **1** *The plough dug a series of furrows across the field:* trench, channel, depression,

cut, rut, groove, corrugation, trough, ditch, track; rift, crevice, crack, fissure, cleft. **2** *The furrows on his brow showed deep concentration:* wrinkle, crease, deep line, crow's-foot, ridge.
—*v.* **3** *In April we furrowed the fields for spring planting:* plough, trench, dig. **4** *Years of worry had furrowed her face:* wrinkle, line, seam, pucker, knit.

further *adv.* **1** *The Carters live a few houses further down the street:* farther, yonder, at a greater distance, more remotely, farther on, more in advance; beyond, abroad, afar off, out of range. **2** *Let's not discuss the matter any further. Let me say further that I couldn't agree with you more:* more, additionally; again, yet, too, likewise, also; besides, furthermore, moreover; over and above, to boot.
—*adj.* **3** *Harry and Joan live in the further of those two houses over there:* more distant, yonder, farther, farther on. **4** *Where can I get further information?:* additional, supplementary, more, extra, supplemental; spare, other, auxiliary, ancillary; new, fresh; contributory, accessory.
—*v.* **5** *His support furthered my career:* forward, aid, assist, help, advance, encourage; foster, back, back up, champion, promote, propagate, work for, favour, stand by; lend a hand, contribute to, strengthen; hasten, quicken, expedite, speed, accelerate, oblige, accommodate.
Ant. 1, 3 nearer, closer. **5** slow, retard; hinder, frustrate, thwart, impede, obstruct.
◇ *Usage note:* See FARTHER.
◇ *Word origin:* Both *further* and *farther* come from Old English *furthor,* "more far." During the Middle English period (1100–1450) *furthor* split into the variants *further* and *farther,* each of which developed its own special meanings over the years. But they are still near-synonyms, and we use them with just about equal frequency.

furtherance *n. She is active in the furtherance of our cause:* advancement, advance, promotion, support, aid, succour, help, assistance, lift; patronage, favour, interest; advocacy, championship, defence; countenance, co-operation.
Ant. opposition, hindrance, restraint; defeat, destruction.

furthermore *adv. She has no brains and furthermore she's devoid of talent:* also, moreover, besides, in addition, too, additionally, as well, likewise; *Informal* to boot, into the bargain; over and above, what's more.

furtive *adj. I could tell by his furtive glances at his watch that he wished to go:* secret, secretive, surreptitious, stealthy, hidden, clandestine, covert; masked, veiled, shrouded, cloaked, private, secluded, unrevealed, unseen; confidential, mysterious, undercover; collusive, conspiratorial; sly, shifty, wily, crafty, underhand, sneaking, shady, elusive, evasive.
Ant. forthright, straightforward, aboveboard; unconcealed, unreserved; public, undisguised, brazen, barefaced.
◇ *Word origin: Furtive* literally means "stolen," as in the phrase *stolen kisses,* i.e. stealthy. It comes from Latin *furtivus,* stolen, from *furtum,* theft, secret action, from *fur,* thief.

"Beware the fury of a patient man."
—*John Dryden*

---

fury *n.* **1** *He smashed his fist into the wall in a drunken fury:* rage, unrestrained anger, frenzy, furore, wrath, ire, choler; outburst, fit, tantrum, huff, dudgeon; acerbity, acrimony, virulence, gall, spleen. **2** *Darwin felt the full fury of the storm:* might, force, violence, fierceness, vehemence, ferocity, intensity, severity, turbulence; assault, attack; impetuosity, headlong rush; bluster, excitement. **3** *He wondered if she would turn into a noisy fury like her mother:* spitfire, she-devil, violent person, hell-cat, shrew, termagant, virago, vixen, she-dragon.
Ant. 1 calm, serenity, tranquillity, quietude, peacefulness, composure, placidity, ease of mind, equanimity. **3** angel.
◇ *Word origin: Fury, furious,* and *furore* come from Latin *furere,* to rage, rave.

fuse[1] *v.* **1** *The heat of the fire caused the silverware to fuse:* smelt, run together, blend by melting together, liquefy by heat, melt. **2** *The chairman must fuse dissenting elements into a strong united party:* consolidate, merge, blend, mingle, intermingle, join, link, combine, incorporate; solidify, federate, amalgamate, league, band together, confederate; assimilate, coalesce, associate.
Ant. 2 separate, disunite, disperse, diffuse.

> **Exploring the Word**: *Fuse* (to melt, pour together) and *foundry* (a place where metal is melted and poured) come from Latin *fundere,* to melt. The same Latin word gives us *confuse* and *confound,* to pour or melt together; *diffuse,* poured out, "spread out thin"; *effusive,* pouring forth, gushy; *funnel,* a device used for pouring, a "pourer"; *fusion,* something melted together, as a group or aggregate; *futile,* literally poured out, melting away, hence useless; *infuse,* to pour in; *profuse,* poured fully, hence copious, lavish, abundant; *refuse,* literally to pour back, reject; *refund,* to pour back or pay back money; *suffuse,* to overspread; and *transfusion,* a pouring across, as blood from one person to another.

fuse[2] *n. The bomb had a long fuse that delayed the explosion:* detonator, igniting tube, ignition, firing material, wick, torch, blue touchpaper.

fusion *n.* **1** *After fusion the metal will be recast:* smelting, melting, liquefaction; dissolving.

2 *Success in business depends on the fusion of many diverse talents:* combination, blending, blend, union, merging, amalgamation, synthesis, unification; commixture, commingling, intermixture; federation, confederacy, confederation, league, alliance, association, coalescence, coalition.

fuss *n.* **1** *Let's have a simple wedding with as little fuss as possible:* bustle, ado, anxious activity, stir, to-do, flutter, flurry, pother, bother; commotion, hurly-burly, disturbance, hubbub, confusion, turmoil, turbulence, perturbation; ceremony, ceremoniousness, pomp, superfluity; fret, stew, fidget; worry, agitation; much ado about nothing, storm in a teacup; fluster, flap, hustle, scurry.

—v. **2** *Too nervous to sit still, she got up to fuss about in the kitchen:* stir, bustle, busy oneself, potter, pother; tinker, fool, fidget, flutter about. **4** *Don't waste energy fussing over such a minor matter:* fume, fret, worry; nit-pick, nag; carp, cavil, quibble, niggle; trouble, take pains, labour. **5** *He can be fussed by the least little thing:* fluster, disconcert, rattle, confuse, flurry; annoy, bother, pester, put into a fuss, trouble, perturb; excite, agitate.

Ant. **1** inactivity, peace, tranquillity, simplicity.

fussy *adj. She's very fussy when it comes to planning a menu:* particular, hard to please, exacting, demanding, meticulous, nit-picking, finicky, finical; painstaking, assiduous, fastidious, squeamish, scrupulous; critical, pernickety, old-maidish, crotchety; bustling, busy, nervous; cluttered, ornate.

futile *adj. His efforts to save the business were futile:* useless, fruitless, vain, profitless, idle, worthless, valueless, bootless, unprofitable; ineffective, ineffectual, unsuccessful, unavailing, abortive, nugatory; trifling, trivial, insignificant, empty, petty, frivolous, unimportant.

Ant. effective, fruitful, successful; profitable, useful, worthy; important, significant.

future *n.* **1** *In future you'd better get his permission first:* time to come, time from now on, futurity; hereafter, tomorrow, morrow, by-and-by, offing. **2** *Has the job any future?:* outlook, prospect, chance for advancement, opportunity; anticipation, expectation; hope.

"Concerts in England have no future; I have no future; nobody has any future."
—*Sir Thomas Beecham*

— adj. **3** *Our future plans are still indefinite:* from now on, in prospect, coming, to come, impending, prospective, eventual, projected, ultimate, anticipated, hereafter; following, subsequent, ensuing, succeeding; later, latter, after.

Ant. **1** past, time gone by, antiquity. **3** past, gone, bygone, former, previous.

◇ *Word origin: Future* comes from Latin *futurus,* a future form of *esse,* to be.

fuzz *n. The scarf left fuzz all over my jacket:* fluff, lint, bits of thread, down, downy fibres.

fuzzy *adj.* **1** *These peaches have a very fuzzy skin:* downy, linty, fluffy; frizzy, woolly; pubescent. **2** *When the lens isn't focused, you get a fuzzy picture:* blurred, indistinct, unclear, ill-defined, out of focus, not clear, indefinite; shadowy, dim, obscure; misty, hazy, murky, foggy; confused.

Ant. **1** smooth, slick. **2** clear, sharp, in focus, precise, distinct, detailed.

G

gab *n. Informal A good salesman should have the gift of the gab:* small talk, glib speech, chatter; blarney, baloney, balderdash; gossip, chit-chat; idle talk, patter, prattle.

gadget *n. This new gadget peels potatoes in a jiffy:* contrivance, device, tool, contraption, mechanical invention; newfangled object, novelty, gimmick; attachment; accessory; *Slang* doodah, thingumajig, thingumabob.

gag *v.* **1** *The robbers tied him up and gagged him with a towel:* stop up the mouth of, silence, hush; suppress, smother, stifle, muzzle, choke; bottle up, close off, stop.

—n. **2** *The burglar stuffed a handkerchief in her mouth as a gag:* restraint on mouth to prevent outcry, stoppage, block; closure. **3** *Slang The comedian only told one funny gag:* joke, practical joke, hoax, jest, horseplay, foolery, facetiousness.

"Give us courage and gaiety and the quiet mind; spare to us our friends, soften to us our enemies."
—*R. L. Stevenson*

---

gaiety *n.* **1** *When she tossed back her head and laughed, the whole room seemed to share her gaiety:* gay spirits, cheerfulness, vivacity, joyousness, high enthusiasm, good humour, high spirits, liveliness, animation; jauntiness, effervescence, sprightliness, sportiveness, festive spirits, airiness; elation, exhilaration; frolic, amusement, celebration, merry-making, fun. **2** *We feasted our eyes on the gaiety of the opening parade:* brightness, colourfulness,

showiness, brilliance; gaudiness, garishness; frippery, frumpery; tinsel, glitter, show.
Ant. 1 sadness, melancholy, misery, despair, gloom; gloominess, despondency.

gain *v.* **1** *You will gain experience if nothing more in that job:* acquire, obtain, secure, achieve, attain, get; gather, collect, get possession of, capture, bag, net; reap, win, glean; pick up, procure. **2** *Last week I gained another five pounds:* acquire, put on, add, build up. **3** *After battling against the blizzard, we finally gained our destination:* attain, reach, arrive at, hit, come to; fetch, overtake, close with. **4** *The doctors say that she continues to gain:* improve, recover, make progress; thrive, prosper, flourish; bloom, blossom.
—n. **5** Often **gains** *The taxes will be high on this year's gains:* earnings, winnings, profit, compensation, wages, salary, bonus, income, revenue, remuneration, dividend; proceeds, produce, yield; plus, favourable balance. **6** *The gain in volume this year is nearly 10 per cent:* increase, return, accretion, increment, addition, accumulation; advantage, improvement, attainment, plus; leap, jump.
Ant. 1 lose, forfeit. **4** fail, decline, worsen. **5** loss, forfeiture, detriment; damage, injury; privation, deprivation.

"Play not for gain but for sport."
—George Herbert

---

gainfully *adv. How long has he been gainfully employed?:* profitably, lucratively, productively, remuneratively; usefully.

gait *n. She walked with the straight-backed gait of a woman of fashion:* walk, stride, step, pace, tread; carriage, bearing, deportment.
◇ *Word origin:* A *gait* is a particular way of walking or running. It comes from Old Norse *gata,* path, street.

gala *adj.* **1** *It's a gala occasion when the Smiths have a party:* festive, celebratory, glittering, ceremonial, gay; splendid, sumptuous, opulent, grand, spectacular, magnificent, majestic; glamorous, fancy-dress, star-studded.
—n. **2** *At the swimming gala all the best performers appeared:* celebration, festive occasion, festival, party, benefit.
◇ *Word origin: Gala* comes from Italian *gala,* holiday dress, festive clothes. It may come from Arabic *khil'a,* presentation garment. Or it may come from Old French *galer,* to make merry, from a now-lost Frankish word related to our words *gallant, well,* and *weal.*

gale *n.* **1** *We thought that we'd never reach port in that gale:* strong wind, hurricane, blow; gust, squall, tempest, cyclone. **2** *When I told her my predicament, she went into gales of laughter:* uproar, outburst, gust, flurry; stir, commotion, fit, agitation, tumult.

gall[1] *n.* **1** *He has a lot of gall expecting me to finish his work:* impudence, effrontery, audacity, temerity, assurance, brazenness; brass, nerve, cheek; insolence, presumption, sauciness, high-handedness. **2** *Of their former friendship there is nothing left but gall:* bitterness, bile, rancour, spleen, venom, animosity, virulence, malignity, acrimony.
◇ *Word origin: Gall*[1] comes from Old English *gealla,* bile, gall, which goes back to an Indo-European root meaning "to shine." The connection is that bile (the fluid secreted by the liver) is yellow. (Bile is a bitter fluid long associated with anger and bitterness. In fact the same Indo-European root gives us our word *yellow.*) The Latin and Greek words for *gall* also stem from this root. They are *fel* and *kholos,* respectively. From Greek *kholos* we get *choler, cholera,* and *choleric.*

gall[2] *v.* **1** *My shins were galled by walking through those brambles:* chafe, make sore, rub sore, abrade, bruise; flay, score, excoriate. **2** *It galls me that she does nothing and then gets all the credit:* annoy, irritate, irk, provoke, gripe, vex, miff, exasperate, fret, displease, exacerbate, harass, rile, anger, ruffle, enrage, nettle; incense, affront, offend; sting, injure; *Slang* bug.
Ant. 2 delight, please highly, amuse.
◇ *Word origin: Gall*[2] comes from Latin *galla,* gallnut or oak-apple (a harmless swelling in plant tissue caused by insects, microorganisms, or external injury). *Galla* also meant "a female of Gaul" (present-day France, then a Roman province), whilst at the same time it meant a harsh, inferior table wine used by the common people. The Romans loved puns, and these homonyms (different words spelt alike) provided good material.

gallant *adj.* **1** *Custer's army made a gallant last stand:* brave, valiant, heroic, noble, chivalrous, courageous, dauntless, fearless, intrepid, daring, bold; valorous; lion-hearted, stalwart, stout-hearted; high-spirited, plucky, game, resolute. **2** *The gallant young man is popular with the women:* chivalrous, cavalier, courtly, attentive, dashing, mannerly, courteous, polite, gentlemanly, suave, urbane, well-bred; considerate, thoughtful, kindly, obliging.
—n. **3** *The town's gallants meet at the coffee-house:* cavalier, dandy, dashing young man, blade; *Slang* masher; fop, Beau Brummel.
Ant. 1 cowardly, fearful, afraid, ignoble. **2** impolite, discourteous, ill-mannered, rude, churlish, boring.
◇ *Word origin: Gallant* comes from the Old French verb *galer,* to make merry. Thus, a gallant man originally was one who made merry, loved life, and was full of good spirit.
◇ *Pronunciation tip: Gallant* has two pronunciations. When used to mean "brave, courageous," the adjective is pronounced with stress on the first syllable: *GAL-unt.*

When used to mean "courtly, dashing," the stress is on the second syllable: *guh-LANT*. The noun is also stressed on the second syllable.

gallantry *n.* **1** *The soldier was rewarded for his gallantry in action:* bravery, heroism, valour, dashing, courage, courageousness, fearlessness, dauntlessness, intrepidity, derring-do, daring; spirit, pluck, mettle, nerve, prowess, determination, resoluteness; *Slang* grit. **2** *His gallantry made him an ideal escort:* courtly attention, courtliness, chivalry, good manners, politeness, courtesy; good breeding, gentility, suavity, urbanity.

Ant. 1 cowardliness, cowardice; irresolution. **2** boorishness, loutishness, churlishness; discourteousness, discourtesy, rudeness, ungraciousness, inattentiveness.

gallery *n.* **1** *The monastery garden was surrounded by a gallery:* covered walk, roofed promenade, arcade, portico, colonnade, cloister, passageway, piazza, loggia, stoa; triforium, ambulatory. **2** *The old-time ham actors loved playing to the gallery:* balcony; *Slang* grandstand, bleachers. **3** *The gallery is having a show of new French art:* art gallery, picture gallery, exhibition hall, salon; art museum.

◇ *Word origin: Gallery* comes from Medieval Latin *galeria*, porch.

gallop *n.* **1** *The big, black horse took the fence at full gallop:* fast gait; rapid ride, run, fast clip, mad dash; jog, trot, sprint.

—*v.* **2** *The horse galloped away before I could catch it:* go at a full gait, run, race; ride at a fast gait, ride at full speed. **3** *The boy galloped away to join his friends:* race, run, rush, hurry, hasten, make haste, hie, dash, speed, tear along, tear off, bowl along; bolt, bound, spring, fly, scurry, dart; *Informal* flit, scamper, whisk, whizz, skim, scuttle, scud, sprint, shoot.

Ant. 1 slow gait. **2** amble, walk. **3** crawl, creep, walk, saunter, amble.

gallows *n.* *The highwayman was hanged on the gallows at noon:* scaffold, gibbet; (*loosely*) noose, rope, halter, Tyburn tree.

galore *adv.* *The farmers have had rain galore this whole year:* in abundance, in great quantity, aplenty, to spare, as much as desired, *French* à gogo.

Ant. in short supply.

◇ *Word origin: Galore* is from Irish *go leōr*, which means "enough," an expression popularized in English by Sir Walter Scott.

galvanize *v.* **1** *Batteries were hooked up to galvanize the doorbell:* electrify, charge, energize, activate, stimulate, treat. **2** *The alarm galvanized the firemen into action:* arouse, excite, stimulate, stir, move, electrify, bring to vitality, quicken; infuse new life into, vitalize, fire, inspire, thrill, wake, awaken, spur on, rally, provoke.

Ant. 2 lull, soothe, pacify; dull, deaden.

◇ *Word origin: Galvanize* comes from the last name of Luigi Galvani, 1737–1798, an Italian physiologist whose experiments led to the discovery that chemical action could produce electricity. It is this "galvanic" action that is used in batteries.

gambit *n.* *Pretending to be sick was only a gambit to gain sympathy:* manœuvre, ploy, stratagem, scheme, trick, feint, ruse, artifice; opening move, initial play; voluntary sacrifice.

◇ *Word origin: Gambit* comes to us from Old French *gambet*, a tripping up. Its root is Late Latin *gamba*, meaning leg, which also gives us *gambol* and *gambade*, a horse's leap.

gamble *v.* **1** *He gambles on horses and at dice:* bet, wager, play for money; have a flutter, try one's luck, tempt fortune. **2** *I'll gamble on his honesty and lend him the money:* take a chance, risk, hazard, speculate, chance; back, trust in, have blind faith in.

—*n.* **3** *Opening a restaurant now would be a big gamble:* risk, hazard, uncertainty, speculation, venture; leap in the dark, random shot, toss-up, blind bargain.

Ant. 2 be conservative, conserve; play safe. **3** surety, sure thing, safe bet.

◇ *Word origin: Gamble* is from the Old English *gamenian*, to play. It is related to the word *game*.

gambol *v.* *The lambs gambolled in the field:* romp playfully, skip about, dance about, frolic, frisk, sport, caper, cut capers, cavort, prance, jump about, rollick; leap, bound, spring, bounce, vault.

"'The game', he said, 'is never lost till won.'"
—*George Crabbe*

---

game *n.* **1** *Hide-and-seek is a favourite children's game:* play, amusement, diversion, pastime, sport, entertainment, recreation, distraction; fun, merriment, frolic, merry-making, gaiety, festivity; lark, romp, antic, gambol, spree. **2** *Who won the football game?:* match, contest, athletic contest, competition, tournament, tourney. **3** *A good hunter always has game on the table:* wild animals, wildfowl, fish; hunted meat; prey, quarry.

—*adj.* **4** *He was a game fighter even when he was losing:* resolute, determined, plucky, unflinching, willing, dauntless, intrepid, courageous, brave, fearless, spunky, spirited, heroic, valiant, valorous, gallant; daring, cocky. **5** *Ever since my skiing accident I've had a game leg:* disabled, incapacitated, lame, crippled, halt, limping, bad, *Informal* gammy; deformed, crooked, hobbling.

Ant. 1 work, toil, labour; duty; job, chore, business. **4** irresolute; fearful, afraid, cowardly. **5** healthy, strong, well.

◇ *Word origin: Game* comes from Old English *gamen*, sport, play, which in turn comes from a root in Common Germanic meaning "to enjoy."

gamut *n. Her acting covers the whole gamut from comedy to tragedy:* full range, complete scale, entire sequence, compass, sweep, scope, reach, complete series; series of gradations, graded series.
◇ *Word origin: Gamut* comes from Medieval Latin *gamma ut. Gamma* was the first note in the early musical scale and *ut* was the last, thus *gamma ut* meant from the first to the last note of the scale.

gang *n.* **1** *Most of my old gang of friends have left town:* crowd, group, band, flock, pack; clique, circle of friends, coterie; friends, comrades, chums, companions; *Informal* mates, pals, cronies; associates, neighbours; fellow members; schoolmates, class-mates; co-workers, fellow workers, crew. **2** *A gang of highwaymen held up the stage-coach:* band, mob, company, troop, party, pack, body; ring. **3** *The gang of workers finished the railway line in record time:* crew, squad, shift, team, relay; troop, company, detachment, phalanx.
◇ *Word origin: Gang* originally meant "a going," from the Old English verb *gangan,* to go. It later took on connotations of going together and hence of a group.

gangster *n. Gangsters tried to take control of the local night-clubs:* mobster, hoodlum, racketeer; syndicate member, mafioso; crook, brigand, felon, ruffian; *Informal* hooligan, tough, hood.

gaol Also **jail** *n.* **1** *He was sentenced to three months in gaol:* prison, penal institution, prison house, house of correction; *Slang* lock-up, jug, can, clink, cooler; remand home, Borstal; police station, detention centre, halfway house, pound; *Military* guardhouse, guardroom, block hole, *Naval* brig; dungeon, keep, cell, Bastille.
—*v.* **2** *The police gaoled him with the rest of the protesters:* imprison, incarcerate, confine, lock up; hold in custody, take or make prisoner, take in, bring in, arrest, put under arrest, capture, seize, apprehend, arraign; *Informal* book, nab; *Slang* run in, pinch, collar.
Ant. 2 release, liberate, free, parole.
◇ *Word origin: Gaol* comes from Vulgar Latin *caveola,* little cage, based on Latin *cavea,* cage. Sometimes, the word is spelt *jail.* The reason for the alternative is this: 300 years ago some dialects pronounced *gaol* with a hard *g,* as in *goal,* and others as in the way we do today. The latter pronunciation prevailed, but the original spelling is still retained.

gap *n.* **1** *We could see the house through a gap in the wall:* opening, breach, empty space, hole, gape, aperture; crack, crevice, fissure, cleft, chink, break, slit, slot, cut, fracture, divide; puncture, rent, rift, gash, notch, cavity. **2** *After his ridiculous remark, there was a gap in the conversation:* blank space, interval, pause, void, vacuum, interim, lacuna, hiatus; break, interruption, intermission, recess, interlude. **3** *How much of a gap is there in their ages?:* difference, disparity, divergence.
◇ *Word origin: Gap* and *gape* come from Old Norse *gapa,* gap, abyss.

"Come on now, all you young men, all over the world. You are needed more than ever now to fill the gap of a generation shorn by the war."
— *Winston Churchill*

---

gape *v.* **1** *The audience gaped as the magician sawed the girl in half:* stare open-mouthed, stare in wonder, stare stupidly, show astonishment, regard with awe, gawk, stare, look excitedly, peer, gaze. **2** *The shirt gapes where the button came off:* part, separate, split, fly open, cleave, expand, open wide, spread out.

garb *n. The nurse's garb was very becoming:* uniform, outfit, apparel, attire, dress, costume, clothing, clothes, garments, togs, rig; raiment, habiliments, habit, vesture, vestment; gown, robe, suit, wardrobe, finery, gear, livery, trappings.
◇ *Word origin: Garb* is the dress characteristic of an occupation, office, or rank, the most suitable or even graceful dress for that occupation or office, and comes from Medieval French *garbe,* "gracefulness." This French word *garbe* itself once meant "a sheaf of grain," which is very graceful.

garbage *n.* **1** *Put the garbage out for the dustman:* refuse, kitchen scraps; rubbish, trash, waste; swill, offal, carrion. **2** *Informal Why do you carry all that garbage around in your pockets?:* junk, useless things, odds and ends, rubbish, litter, debris.
Ant. 2 valuables, treasure.

garble *v. Somehow his instructions were garbled, and he went to the wrong address:* confuse, jumble, mix up, be unclear, misunderstand; distort; fragment.
Ant. make clear, clarify, straighten out.
◇ *Word origin: Garble* goes back to Arabic *gharbala,* to sift, put through a sieve. Thus we might say someone's words are so *garbled* it sounds as if he were talking through a sieve.

garden *n.* **1** *Don't plant your garden with ill-assorted flowers:* garden plot; (*variously*) flower garden, vegetable garden, kitchen garden, herb garden, rock garden, lawn, plot. **2** *The historic house and gardens are closed to the public at sunset:* small park, estate, botanical garden, zoological park, natural park. **3** *The settlers made a garden out of the desert:* fertile region, agricultural region; paradise, Eden, oasis, Arcadia.
—*v.* **4** *First thing every morning he gardens for an hour or so:* cultivate a garden, plant a garden, tend a garden, work in a garden, work the soil, use one's green fingers.

gargantuan *adj. They bought a gargantuan house with at least 30 rooms. King Henry VIII had a* *gargantuan appetite:* gigantic, enormous, immense, huge, great, unbelievably big; vast, colossal, tremendous, mammoth, massive, stupendous, monstrous; titanic, herculean, elephantine, prodigious, amplitudinous; overgrown, hulking, towering.

Ant. small, little, tiny, diminutive, miniature; dwarfish, puny, pint-sized; compact, meagre, scant, paltry, trivial, niggling.

◇ *Word origin:* This word comes from *Gargantua*, the peace-loving giant with an enormous appetite who is the hero of Rabelais's satire *Gargantua* (1534).

garish *adj. That garish dress is inappropriate for church:* gaudy, loud, flashy, showy, bright; over-elaborate, too colourful, extremely ornate, tastelessly showy, ostentatious, pretentious, cheap, brassy, obtrusive; tawdry, vulgar, flaunting, tinsel.

Ant. sedate, conservative, unobtrusive, modest; plain, simple, sombre; refined, tasteful, elegant.

◇ *Word origin:* Something that is *garish* causes people to stare at it, so *garish* is based on Middle English *gaure,* to stare.

garment Often **garments** *n. Overcoats and other winter garments are on sale:* article of clothing; apparel, attire, garb, dress, raiment, habit, vestment, habiliment.

◇ *Word origin: Garment* and *garnish* comes from Old French *garnir,* to garnish, prepare. Thus when we *garnish* a lamb chop or put *garments* on ourselves, we are doing substantially the same thing, preparing or dressing up.

garnish *v.* **1** *The chef garnished the lamb chops with sprigs of mint:* embellish, decorate, adorn, ornament, trim, beautify, deck, bedeck, array, spruce up, furbish, festoon, set off, smarten, gild, embroider, emblazon; *Informal* dress up, doll up, deck out.

—*n.* **2** *The ham was given a garnish of parsley:* decoration, embellishment, adornment, ornament, trim, trimming, festoon.

Ant. 1 strip, make bare, denude, deprive, divest.

garret *n. The poet lived in poverty in an unheated garret:* attic, loft; top floor, floor under the eaves.

Ant. basement, cellar.

garrison *n.* **1** *The garrison faced starvation during the long siege:* soldiers stationed at a fort, detachment; (*variously*) division, brigade, regiment, squadron, platoon, battery, escadrille. **2** *The army built a garrison to defend the town:* fort, fortification; military camp, military base.

—*v.* **3** *The troops were garrisoned near the field of battle:* place on duty, station, assign to, put on duty in a garrison. **4** *The town was garrisoned by a detachment of the king's militia:* occupy with troops, provide with a garrison; guard, watch over, secure, patrol.

◇ *Word origin: Garrison* comes from Old French *garison,* based on the verb *garir,* to defend, to watch. This same word is the basis of the word *garret,* which originally meant "watch-tower."

garrulous *adj. She's so garrulous that you can't get a word in edgeways:* talkative, loquacious; wordy, windy, long-winded; gabby, voluble, chattery, chatty, prattling, prating, babbling; gossipy.

Ant. reticent, taciturn, quiet, reserved, close-mouthed, tight-lipped; terse, concise.

◇ *Word origin: Garrulous* comes from Latin *garrulus,* talkative. Thus the meaning of this word has not changed for more than two thousand years!

gas *n.* **1** *Helium is a gas used in balloons. The army developed a deadly nerve gas:* gaseous mixture; vapour, fume. **2** *Slang The play was really quite a gas:* amusing or funny thing, joke, laugh, lark.

gash *n.* **1** *The gash in his cheek required ten stitches:* long cut, slash, gaping wound, incision; split, cleft, slit, crack, fissure, rent.

—*v.* **2** *The flying glass gashed her arm severely:* make a long cut in, cut deeply, slash, make an incision in, incise, lacerate, slice; split, slit, cleave, rend, tear, hack; carve, quarter, dissect.

gasp *v.* **1** *The long-distance runner gasped for air:* struggle (*for breath*) with open mouth, inhale frantically, labour for breath; suck in (*air*), breathe convulsively; have difficulty breathing, respire laboriously; gulp, pant, wheeze, puff, catch the breath. **2** *The victim gasped out the name of his attacker:* utter with gasps, exclaim in short breaths, speak breathlessly, blurt, vociferate, cry hurriedly.

—*n.* **3** *Her words came in gasps and were barely audible:* sudden short breath, convulsive breathing, sharp inhalation, gulp.

◇ *Word origin: Gasp,* to open the mouth and take in the breath suddenly, comes from Old Norse *geispa,* yawn.

gastronomy *n.* **1** *The famous chef wrote a book on gastronomy:* art of good eating, epicurism, pleasures of food and drink. **2** *Mr. Eguchi's new restaurant offers French gastronomy in a Japanese setting:* culinary practices; style of cooking and serving.

"Paris is the capital of gastronomy."

—*Eugene Fodor*

---

gate *n.* **1** *Close that gate or the cows won't stay in the pasture:* enclosure door, entrance to a pen, opening through a fence; portal, gateway, hatchway. **2** *We bought our tickets for the football match at the gate:* entrance door; box office, turnstile, ticket seller's booth. **3** *The pond won't fill with water until the gate is closed:* sluice; tap, valve, spigot.

gather *v.* **1** *Storm-clouds gathered on the horizon.*

Gather the men together and we'll start the march: assemble, get together, bring together, marshal, muster, accumulate, collect, amass, mass, group, convene, cluster, come together, bunch together, concentrate, congregate; pile up, stack, heap up, lump together, stockpile. **2** *From your remarks, I gather that you're not happy here:* infer, deduce, assume, be led to believe, conclude; learn, understand, observe.
—*n.* **3** *The dress had tiny gathers at each shoulder:* fold, pucker; pleat, ruffle, shirr.
Ant. 1 disperse, dissipate; separate.

gathering *n. The party was the largest social gathering of the season:* assembly, meeting, party, conference, conclave, convocation, convention; company, crowd, throng, assemblage, accumulation, congregation, aggregation, multitude, turn-out; *Informal* gang, pack, mob, bunch, drove, flock, horde, crush, press; collection, concentration, convergence.

gauche *adj. He's so gauche that he even addressed the director as "Old Boy":* ill-mannered, uncouth, socially awkward, unpolished, lacking in social graces, inelegant, too informal, tasteless, ungentlemanly, unmannerly, unrefined, uncultured, ill-bred; proletarian, plebeian; ungraceful, inept, blundering, clumsy, heavy-handed, bungling, maladroit.
Ant. polite, well-mannered, well-bred, elegant, polished, gracious, formal, tasteful, refined; graceful.
◇ *Pronunciation tip:* The correct pronunciation of *gauche* is *gōsh.*
◇ *Word origin: Gauche* comes from French *gauche* meaning left-handed, hence clumsy.

gaudy *adj.* **1** *She wears such gaudy clothes that she must have no taste at all:* garish, flashy, loud, showy, fancy; cheap, vulgar, worthless, tasteless, tawdry, flimsy, sham, bespangled, tinsel. **2** *A good circus has to be gaudy:* colourful, showy, eye-catching, striking, ostentatious, glaring, pretentious; brilliant, dazzling, glittering, vivid, intense; sparkling, lustrous.
Ant. 1 sedate, conservative, quiet; modest, tasteful, refined, elegant, unpretentious, subtle. **2** dull, lack-lustre, colourless.
◇ *Word origin: Gaudy* comes from Old French *gaudir,* to be merry, based on Latin *gaudere,* to rejoice.

gauge *v.* **1** *Can you gauge the distance to the top of that hill?:* estimate, judge, appraise, ascertain, guess; evaluate, calculate, adjudge, rate, assess.
—*n.* **2** *This gauge registers the pressure in pounds:* measuring instrument, measuring device, measure, meter; standard, criterion, yardstick. **3** *What gauge is that railway?:* size, measurement, internal diameter, inner measurement, inner dimension, bore.
◇ *Word origin: Gauge* comes from Old French *gauger,* to measure.

gaunt *adj.* **1** *Illness has left him pale and gaunt:* very thin, emaciated, scrawny, haggard; lanky, skinny, bony, lean, lank, slender, scraggy, spindly, spare, raw-boned, spindle-shanked; starved, cadaverous, wasted, withered, pinched, skeletal, shrivelled. **2** *It's gaunt country once you leave the main road:* bleak, desolate, deserted, barren; grim, forbidding.
Ant. 1 plump, fat, chubby, stout, portly, corpulent, obese, rotund, well-fed; sleek. **2** lush, luxurious, blooming, inviting; bustling, active.

gawk *v. Stop gawking and call a doctor straightaway!:* stare stupidly, gape, gawp, look with astonishment; gaze, peer.

gay *adj.* **1** *Martha is a gay, fun-loving person:* cheerful, cheery, happy, light-hearted, merry, joyous, joyful; jolly, sunny, lively, vivacious, sparkling, sprightly, gleeful, in good spirits, buoyant, dashing, sportive, insouciant, effervescent, frolicsome, jovial, jocular, jocose, hilarious, humorous, waggish; festive, convivial, social, jubilant, frivolous, playful, rejoicing, elated, exultant, glad, gladsome, blithe, genial, smiling, airy, bright; jaunty, skittish, frisky, animated, spirited, coltish, volatile; *Slang* fun. **2** *What a gay new hat!:* bright, colourful, showy, brilliant, vivid, intense, glowing, lustrous; particoloured, multi-coloured, variegated; eye-catching, sumptuous, splendid; glittering, flamboyant, theatrical.
Ant. 1 grave, serious, sombre, sedate, staid, solemn, sober; cheerless, joyless; quiet, still, silent; unhappy, morose, grim, miserable; heavy, sad, melancholy. **2** dull, colourless, sombre, drab, lack-lustre; sedate, conservative.
◇ *Spelling tip:* People sometimes forget that the *y* of *gay* becomes *i* in *gaily* and *gaiety.* (Usually a final *y* preceded by a vowel does *not* become an *i* when a suffix is added, but *gay* is an exception.)

gaze *v.* **1** *My father often used to gaze into the distance:* look steadily, look intently, look fixedly, contemplate, stare, watch, eye, keep one's look fixed, rivet the eyes, look deeply, look earnestly, strain one's eyes; study, peruse; look with wonder, gape, ogle, peer, scrutinize, survey, inspect, examine, pore over, witness, observe; glance, scan, behold, regard, peek; glare, glower, lower.
—*n.* **2** *He turned his gaze to the horses on the right:* intent look, stare, steady look, scrutiny.

gear *n.* **1** *This large gear turns the small one to rotate the cylinder:* toothed wheel, cog-wheel; flywheel, cam. **2** *The scuba diving gear is in the car boot:* equipment, paraphernalia, outfit, things, accessories, apparatus, trappings; implements, instruments, tackle, rig, tools, contrivances; personal effects, belongings, property; apparel, clothing, clothes, attire, dress, garments, garb; *Informal* togs.

◇ *Word origin: Gear* comes from Old Norse *gervi*, equipment, gear.

gem *n.* **1** *The queen's crown was set with diamonds, rubies, and other gems:* jewel, precious stone; semi-precious stone. **2** *The critics say that his new play is a gem. She really is a gem to go to all this trouble:* jewel, prize, treasure, wonder, marvel, one in a thousand; *Slang* peach, dear, doll, sweetheart.

genealogy *n. She can trace her genealogy back to the thirteenth century:* family tree, ancestry, lineage, list of forbears, family descent, extraction, derivation, pedigree; stock; line, house, birth.

◇ *Word origin: Genealogy* comes from the Greek word *geneālogiā*, "tracing of one's descent." This was a favourite pastime, and everybody who was anybody could claim descent from the gods and heroes. Greek *geneā*, race, is related to Latin *genus*, kind, from which we get our word *genus*.

general *adj.* **1** *General elections will be held next month. I have a general idea of how a car works:* comprehensive, collective, overall, generic, basic, taken as a whole; sweeping, blanket, extensive, panoramic; vague, non-technical, imprecise, inexact; not special, not particular, not specific, not limited, non-exclusive; unspecified, miscellaneous, not partial. **2** *The suggestion met with general approval:* widespread, popular, prevalent, prevailing, common, universal, broad, public, pandemic; world-wide, ecumenical. **3** *His general mood is pleasant enough:* usual, customary, regular, habitual, normal, natural, typical, accustomed, wonted; ordinary, everyday, conventional, frequent; current, prevalent, prevailing, most common.

Ant. 1, 2 specific, concrete, definite, particular, individual; exact, precise, special, distinctive. **3** exceptional, rare, singular, uncommon, unusual, extraordinary, infrequent; peculiar, odd.

◇ *Word origin: General* comes from Latin *generalis*, of one kind, from *genus*, kind. The word has descended into the modern European languages from Latin thanks to the antonym *general/specific* or *genus* as opposed to *species*, a distinction first set up by the Greek philosopher Aristotle.

generality *n.* **1** *Please stop speaking in generalities and be specific:* general statement, sweeping statement, generalization; abstract thought, vague notion, imprecise thinking, unorganized idea; undetailed plan, inexact presentation. **2** *The generality of his knowledge is awesome:* universality, all-encompassing reach, far-flung scale; collectiveness, miscellaneousness; indiscriminateness. **3** *It's a generality that people want to improve their lot:* general rule, generalization, widespread principle, universal thing; obvious statement, truism, cliché, platitude.

Ant. 1 specific, detail. **2** specialization; limit.

generalize *v. Do you know enough about today's youth to generalize about them?:* infer, conclude, judge, form an opinion; speak in generalities, make a sweeping statement, make a generalization.

generally *adv.* **1** *Dinner is generally served at 7 p.m. in this house:* usually, ordinarily, in general, as a rule, for the most part, in most cases, in the usual course of things, habitually; often, frequently, repeatedly, currently; always, universally; extensively. **2** *Women, generally speaking, live longer than men:* without reference to particular persons or things, without particularizing, without noting the individual exceptions; for the most part, in the main, on the whole, largely, mainly, chiefly, principally, mostly.

Ant. 1 rarely, as an exception, occasionally, in a few cases, unusually, especially, particularly. **2** specifically, individually.

generate *v.* **1** *This plant generates enough electricity for the entire city. The vicar tried to generate enthusiasm for the plan:* produce, cause, make, form, bring about, engender, effectuate, induce, institute, bring into existence; construct, fabricate, invent, fashion, contrive, coin, originate; develop, evolve, occasion. **2** *The human race was generated by Adam:* beget, father, sire, spawn; procreate, create; breed, reproduce, engender, propagate; proliferate, fructify, fecundate; impregnate, fertilize, bear, yield.

Ant. 1 extinguish, end, terminate, annihilate, kill, stifle, crush, quash.

◇ *Word origin:* The basis of our word *generate* is Latin *generare*, to procreate, beget. Related words are Latin *genus*, race, stock, birth, Greek *genos* (which means the same as Latin *genus*), and our word *kin.* These words all descend from the same Indo-European root.

generation *n.* **1** *Adam's generation populated the earth:* progeny, issue, offspring; family, tribe, race, clan, house, line, lineage, breed, strain, stock; kin. **2** *The biology class studied the generation of fruit flies:* process of generating, reproduction, propagation, procreation, engendering, begetting, breeding; fertilization, impregnation; proliferation. **3** *The generation of ideas is a valuable talent:* creation, origination, production, formation, genesis; causation; development, growth, evolution.

generous *adj.* **1** *Your father was very generous to give you so much money:* open-handed, willing to give, free-handed, large-hearted, ungrudging; lavish, liberal, munificent, princely, bountiful, bounteous, unrestricted, unstinting, unstinted, sparing no expense; extravagant, prodigal, effusive; charitable, beneficent, philanthropic, free-giving, hospitable. **2** *This restaurant serves unusually generous portions:* plentiful, ample, bounteous, large, copious, abundant, liberal; overflowing,

plethoric. **3** *Aunt Helen had a most generous spirit:* unselfish, humane, humanitarian, considerate, benevolent, noble, altruistic; accommodating, obliging; big-hearted, large-hearted, magnanimous; high-minded, lofty; honourable.
Ant. 1 stingy, tight, tight-fisted, close-fisted, cheap, niggardly, miserly, parsimonious, illiberal, penurious, avaricious, covetous, selfish. **2** small, little, tiny; scarce, measly, scanty, minimal. **3** mean, ignoble, small, petty, churlish, rapacious, greedy.
◇ *Word origin: Generous* comes from Latin *generosus*, of good family.

genesis *n. A news item about a freak accident was the genesis of her story:* origin, beginning, creation, birth, inception, root, generation, begetting, engendering.
Ant. end, termination, finish.

genial *adj. The host's genial manner put everyone at ease:* cordial, friendly, good-natured, congenial, amiable, gracious, affable, agreeable, pleasant, convivial, neighbourly, companionable, sociable, social, courteous, civil, warm, happy, glad, hearty, expansive, kind, kindly, cheerful, sunny, vivacious, merry, cheery, jovial, jolly, jocund, gay, in good spirits, sparkling, mirthful, bright, light-hearted, festive, joyous, joyful; jaunty, lively.
Ant. unfriendly, unpleasant, ungracious, unsympathetic, cool, cold; rude, discourteous, uncivil; harsh, sullen, morose; cutting, sarcastic, sardonic, ironical, cheerless, caustic.
◇ *Word origin: Genial* comes from Latin *genialis*, of the bridal bed (because the Romans dedicated it to the *genii*, or guardian spirits, of the newly-weds). Thanks to this pleasant association, the word took on the additional connotations of pleasant, delightful, joyous, jovial, and festive.

"At least once a year everyone is a genius."
—*G. C. Lichtenberg*

---

genius *n.* **1** *Einstein was a great scientific genius:* mental giant, mastermind, brilliant intellect, prodigy; *Slang* brain, mind, whizz-kid, ace; master, expert, mine of information, walking encyclopaedia. **2** *Rembrandt's genius is obvious in his paintings. You have a genius for getting into trouble:* natural talent, creative power, faculty, gift, knack, natural endowment, aptitude, penchant, wizardry, proclivity, bent, propensity, flair, predilection, turn of mind; insight, perception, percipience, intuition; imagination, invention, ingenuity; wisdom, intelligence, sagacity, understanding, wit.
Ant. 1 idiot, imbecile, half-wit, moron; oaf, fool, simpleton, dunce, dolt; numskull, blockhead, booby, nit-wit, ninny, nincompoop; *Slang* nutter. **2** ineptitude.
◇ *Word origin: Genius* comes from Latin *genius*, guardian spirit.

genre *n. Shakespeare's play* Macbeth *is an example of the tragic genre of drama:* style, category, kind, class, sort, genus, species; fashion, description; school.
◇ *Word origin: Genre* comes from Latin *genus*, kind, which also gives us *general* and *genus*.

genteel *adj.* **1** *My aunt Mary was the most genteel woman I ever knew:* refined, well-bred, courteous, mannerly, polite, civil, well-spoken, ladylike, gentlemanly, courtly, decorous, poised; polished, cultured, cultivated, urbane; aristocratic, thoroughbred, patrician, of gentle blood. **2** *White gloves are correct at such a genteel gathering:* elegant, stylish, fashionable, modish, suited to high society, élite, high-class; *Slang* hoity-toity, high-falutin, high-hat, swanky, ritzy, high-toned; over-refined, pretentious.
Ant. 1 unrefined, uncultured, inelegant, unpolished; impolite, discourteous, boorish, unmannerly, uncivil, rude; plebeian, low-class, low-bred, ill-bred. **2** unaffected, plain, natural, simple, unsophisticated, unfashionable, inelegant.
◇ *Word origin: Genteel* goes back to Latin *gentilis*, of the same stock, well-born. It was at one time a variant of *gentle* (noble).

gentle *adj.* **1** *She was a gentle woman who wouldn't hurt a fly:* gentle-hearted, kindly, kind, peaceful, compassionate, tender-hearted, tender, sympathetic, mild, meek; tolerant, benign, lenient, indulgent, merciful; thoughtful, considerate. **2** *She gave the baby a gentle pat on the back. A warm, gentle breeze was coming off the sea:* mild, soft, light, easy, slight; quiet, calm, serene, tranquil, placid; balmy, moderate, temperate, not violent, not rough, not severe; bland, smooth, untroubled, low. **3** *Is that horse gentle enough for the children to ride?:* docile, tame, manageable, easily handled, tractable; domesticated, broken, harmless, subdued, pacific, peaceful, calm.
Ant. 1 hard; cruel, unkind, heartless, hard-hearted, rough, harsh, offensive, aggressive. **2** rough, harsh, hard, intense, powerful, strong, sharp, violent, immoderate; sudden, abrupt. **3** wild, fierce, savage, intractable; unmanageable.
◇ *Word origin: Gentle*, like *genteel*, goes back to Latin *gentilis*, of the same race or clan, well-born. The same word was applied by the Latin Church Fathers to pagan Romans and is the source of our word *gentile* (non-Jewish). Also related in the sense of "elegant, gentlemanly" is our word *jaunty*.

gentleman *n.* **1** *A gentleman would never use such language!:* well-mannered man, honourable man, refined man, civilized man, polished man; man of social position, man of good family or breeding, man of gentle birth, aristocrat, patrician; *Slang* gent, toff, nob; cavalier, caballero, don, hidalgo, chevalier, squire, esquire. **2** *Are you the gentleman who read*

the gas-meter last month?: man, young man, fellow, chap, *Slang* bloke, guy.
Ant. 1 brute, lout, churl, boor, cad, scoundrel, dastard, bounder, rat.

gentry *n. Fox-hunting is a sport associated with the gentry:* aristocrats, aristocracy, upper class, society, gentlefolk, élite, country gentlemen.
Ant. lower class, working class, bourgeoisie, plebeians, commoners, *Slang* hoi polloi.
◇ *Word origin: Gentry* is from Old French *genterise,* people of good family, and is ultimately based on Latin *gens,* clan, which also gives us *genteel* and *gentle.*

genuine *adj.* **1** *Is the bracelet genuine gold?:* real, authentic, true, bona fide, actual, honest, legitimate, true-blue, solid, pure, sterling, unalloyed, unadulterated, 100 per cent. **2** *The audience applauded with genuine enthusiasm:* sincere, true, unaffected, earnest; frank, candid, open, straightforward, honest, heartfelt, natural; ingenuous, naïve, artless, guileless, unsophisticated, simple, plain.
Ant. 1 fake, false; artificial, phoney, bogus, counterfeit, imitation, ersatz, fraudulent, simulated, feigned, sham, spurious. **2** insincere, affected, hypocritical, pretended, fake, false, phoney, artificial.
◇ *Pronunciation tip:* The proper pronunciation is *GEN-u-in* not "gen-u-wine."
◇ *Word origin: Genuine* is from Latin *genuinus,* inherent in one's nature, inborn. Thus "the genuine article" was born or made that way.

germ *n.* **1** *Cover your mouth when you cough so that you won't spread germs:* microbe, virus, microorganism, bacterium, bacillus; *Informal* bug. **2** *It's only the germ of an idea, but you ought to develop it:* beginning, first stage, spark, rudiment; origin, source, root, fountain-head, seed, embryo. **3** *Wheat germ is very health-giving:* bud, sprout, offshoot; seed, ovule, ovum; egg, embryo; nucleus, germ-cell, spore.
Ant. 2 outcome, upshot, result; end, termination, consummation.

germane *adj. That's an interesting point, but it's not germane to our discussion:* pertinent, relevant, appropriate, applicable, apt, connected, relative, material, related, native, proper, intrinsic; apropos, appertaining, suitable, fitting, fit, to the point, to the purpose.
Ant. irrelevant, inappropriate, unrelated, immaterial, unconnected, extraneous, incompatible, extrinsic, incongruous, inconsonant; foreign, alien.

germinate *v. Put the seeds in wet sand until they germinate:* sprout, put out shoots, push up, vegetate, spring up, generate, burgeon, shoot; bud, flower, bloom, blossom, open.
Ant. wither, die, perish; stagnate.
◇ *Word origin: Germinate* comes from Latin *germinare,* to sprout. It is based on *germen,* sprig, sprout in Latin, from which we also get our word *germ.*

gestation *n. The period of human gestation is 9 months:* full term of a pregnancy, life from conception to birth, pregnancy, maturation; development, evolution, incubation, generation, epigenesis.
◇ *Word origin: Gestation* is from Latin *gestare,* to carry young.

gesticulate *v. The driver gesticulated for the police car to stop:* gesture; signal, motion, wave the hand, make a sign, beckon, indicate; (*variously*) shrug, nod, nudge, wink.
◇ *Pronunciation tip:* Like *gesture, gesticulate* is pronounced with a soft *g* that sounds like a *j,* thus *jes-TIC-u-late.*

gesture *n.* **1** *The speaker's gestures seemed unrelated to his speech:* bodily movement, hand and arm movement, gesticulation, pantomime; signal, sign, motion, indication, dumb show; (*variously*) shrug, nod, wave, nudge, touch, wink. **2** *He said that he would help, but I'm sure it was only a gesture:* polite action, empty offer, formality, courtesy, flourish, demonstration. —*v.* **3** *She was gesturing so excitedly that I knew something was wrong:* gesticulate, signal, motion, wave, beckon.
◇ *Pronunciation tip:* Remember that the *g* in *gesture* properly receives a soft, or *j,* sound to rhyme with the *g* in *gem.* Thus, the word is properly pronounced as *JES-tyur.*
◇ *Usage note:* A *gesticulation* is an excited or emphatic motion of the body, such as the waving of one's arms. A *gesture* is a more controlled, calmer motion of the hands or head to express an idea or feeling, as a nod of the head or the raising of a finger. Thus, *The man's shouts and gesticulations caused the passers-by to stand and stare,* but *The lecturer made a gesture of quiet and the room grew still.*

get *v.* **1** *Get a copy of the book from the library. You'll get a spanking when your father comes home:* obtain, acquire, attain, receive, procure, fetch, pick up, come by, go after, secure, come into possession of, glean, meet with; achieve, win, gain, earn, realize, net, bag, reap, take; inherit, succeed to, pocket. **2** *Our house gets awfully warm in the summer:* become, come to be, get to be, change to, be changed to, grow, turn, turn to, turn into, be converted into, wax. **3** *Did you have time to get the car washed this morning? What time should I get lunch?:* have done, cause to be done, have, make ready, fix, prepare. **4** *I tried to get you, but your phone was engaged. What time does the bus get to Victoria?:* reach, communicate with, contact; arrive, come to, get in to; meet with, transport. **5** *Sorry, I didn't get your name. He didn't get the point of the joke:* understand, comprehend, grasp, learn, perceive, hear, catch; take in, fathom, work out, follow, sense. **6** *It gets me why she suddenly decided to sell the house:* baffle, bewilder, perplex, puzzle, confound, confuse, mystify; upset, annoy, irritate, disconcert, *Slang* beat. **7** *The Operatic*

Society got the alderman to serve as honorary chairman: persuade, induce, influence, prevail upon, enlist, dispose, incline; coax, wheedle, bring round, sway, win over, talk round, suborn; predispose, move, prompt. **8** *The goblins will get you if you don't watch out:* seize, grab, capture, lay hold of, take, snatch, grasp, collar, grip; ensnare, entrap. **9** *The teacher got chicken-pox from the students:* catch, contract, be afflicted with, suffer from, come down with.

Ant. 1 give, give up; dish out, mete out; avoid, forgo, eschew, forswear; lose, relinquish, abjure. **2** stay, remain. **4** leave, separate from; avoid. **5** misunderstand. **6** make sense, be logical to; please, comfort, calm. **7** dissuade. **8** let go, give up, release, free. **9** cure, heal, mend.

◇ *Usage note:* It *gets* very easy to over-use *get.* Try to think of a synonym that is correct for the use you are going to make of it, and that way, your meaning may become more precise.

ghastly *adj.* **1** *I was really alarmed by her ghastly complexion:* ghostlike, ghostly, death-like, corpselike, cadaverous; deathly pale, pallid, ashen, colourless, wan, pasty, blanched; lack-lustre, glassy, haggard, livid. **2** *It was the most ghastly accident that I've ever seen. The rug was a ghastly shade of green:* hideous, revolting, gruesome, grisly, repellent, repulsive, loathsome, ugly, dreadful, horrible, horrendous, horrid, odious, terrifying, frightful, terrible, shocking, appalling, grim, forbidding, dismal; uncanny, weird, fearful.

Ant. 1 ruddy, robust, healthy, fresh, blooming. **2** attractive, appealing, beautiful, lovely, charming, enticing.

◇ *Word origin: Ghastly* comes from Old English *gāstlīc,* spiritual, from *gāst,* soul, ghost.

ghost *n.* **1** *The former owner's ghost is believed to haunt the house:* spirit of a dead person, disembodied spirit, departed spirit; phantom, apparition, phantasm, wraith, spectre, supernatural being, shadow, shade, *Slang* spook; manifestation, materialization; banshee, sprite, demon, chimera, goblin, hobgoblin; phantasma, *German* doppelgänger. **2** *Since the tragedy, she's been a ghost of her former self. There was just a ghost of her perfume left in the room:* trace, suggestion, hint, semblance; shadow.

◇ *Word origin: Ghost* comes from Old English *gāst,* soul, ghost.

"How many children, and how many men, are afraid of ghosts, who are not afraid of God!"
— *Thomas Babington Macaulay*

---

ghostly *adj. A ghostly light seemed to be moving through the trees:* ghostlike, spectral, phantom, phantasmal, phantomlike, unearthly, supernatural; *Slang* spooky; shadowy, illusive; weird, eerie, uncanny, unreal; ghastly, pale.

Ant. earthly, natural.

giant *n.* **1** *Is it true that Jack climbed the beanstalk and slew the giant?:* imaginary being of huge stature, colossus, titan, Brobdingnagian, Gargantua, Goliath. **2** *Our rugger team didn't have a chance against those giants:* tall person, tall thing, colossus, titan; *Slang* whopper, spanker, thumper, strapper.

Ant. 1 dwarf, pigmy. **2** *Slang* shorty, half-pint, titch.

gibberish *n. With some words missing and others misspelt, the message was pure gibberish:* meaningless talk, senseless writing, nonsense, unintelligible language, babble, drivel, gabble, inarticulate talk, meaningless words, foolish talk; *Informal* balderdash, stuff and nonsense, bosh, twaddle, fiddle-faddle, flapdoodle, hocus-pocus, double-talk, mumbo-jumbo, blather.

◇ *Pronunciation tip:* The *g* in *gibberish* may be pronounced either soft, as in *gem,* or hard, as in *go.* Thus both *JIB-ber-ish* and *GIB-ber-ish* are correct, though the first is widely preferred.

gibe Also **jibe** *n.* **1** *She bore her sister's gibes throughout her childhood:* taunt, taunting, jeer, criticism, sarcastic remark, sarcasm, cutting remark, scoff, sneer, ridicule, mockery, derision; quip, wisecrack; *Informal* slings and arrows; *Slang* knock, brickbat.

—*v.* **2** *The children gibed at her because of her dirty face:* jeer, taunt, poke fun, make fun of, scoff, mock, tease, ridicule, laugh at, deride, sneer, twit, chaff, flout, rail at; *Slang* rag, roast, needle.

Ant. 1, 2 compliment, praise. **2** applaud; salute.

◇ *Word origin: Gibe* comes from Old French *giber,* to play roughly, treat roughly.

giddy *adj.* **1** *The medicine made her feel giddy and she had to sit down:* dizzy, light-headed; feeling faint, faint, fainting, affected with vertigo, vertiginous, reeling, whirling, swimming. **2** *We viewed the parade from the giddy heights of the 20th floor:* causing dizziness, dizzying, awesome, overpowering. **3** *How can such a serious man be interested in such a giddy girl?:* flighty, frivolous, capricious, erratic, fickle, changeable, impulsive, fitful, volatile, unsteady, inconsistent; careless, thoughtless, reckless, irresponsible, silly, mercurial, inconstant, fanciful, whimsical, vacillating, harum-scarum, hare-brained, rattle-brained, befuddled, muddled.

Ant. 1 steady, stationary, steady on one's feet. **2** steadfast, determined, resolute, single-minded; serious, earnest; calm, serene.

◇ *Word origin: Giddy* comes from Old English *gydig,* meaning possessed by a god, insane. Over the centuries the word has been watered down to mean "dizzy" or rushing about irrationally from one thing to another.

gift *n.* **1** *The office makes a yearly gift to the British Heart Foundation. He claimed that the stolen money was a gift from his employer:* present, something given; award, donation, favour, tip, gratuity, boon, benefaction; bonus, prize, grant, fee, consideration, premium; hand-out, largess, alms, dole, contribution, offering, aid, help; bribe, sop, graft, tribute; legacy, bequest, dot, dowry, dower, endowment. **2** *Mother has a gift for making people feel at home. To be able to paint so well is a real gift:* special ability, talent, capacity, natural endowment, aptitude, flair, genius, knack, faculty, capability, facility; qualification, attribute, quality, power, forte, aptness, virtue, property, turn, bent; skill, expertise, ingenuity, adroitness, proficiency, competency, craft, power.

Ant. **1** penalty, fine, forfeiture.

◇ *Word origin:* A *gift*, that which is given, is based on Old English *giefan*, to give.

gifted *adj.* **1** *The composer is also a gifted pianist:* talented, naturally endowed, fitted for, cut out for, at home as; ingenious, clever, inventive, able, adroit, resourceful; facile, proficient, accomplished, skilled, capable, qualified, expert, master, masterly, polished, practised, finished, experienced; deft, quick, handy, slick; *Slang* crack, wizard. **2** *The youngest attends a school for gifted children:* especially intelligent, unusually clever, bright, brilliant, having a high I.Q.

Ant. **1** talentless; amateur, unskilled, inept. **2** retarded, backward, dumb, dull, slow, slow-witted, slow-learning.

gigantic *adj. China is a gigantic country, sprawling over 3½ million square miles:* very large, huge, vast, enormous, immense, giant, colossal, mammoth, massive, monstrous, tremendous, stupendous, jumbo, elephantine; mighty, unwieldy, ponderous, hulking, strapping, bulky, lumpish, lubberly, towering, voluminous; large-scale, prodigious; gargantuan, herculean, titanic.

Ant. small, little, tiny, miniature, compact; *Slang* teeny-weeny, itsy-bitsy; infinitesimal, microscopic; feeble, puny, weak; petty, insignificant; dwarfish, pigmy.

giggle *v.* **1** *Why do teenage girls giggle so much?:* laugh in a silly way, laugh nervously, titter, twitter, simper, snicker, snigger.

—*n.* **2** *Her nervous giggle annoys me:* silly laugh, titter, snigger, snicker, simper.

gild *v.* **1** *The decorator gilded the mirror to match the gold in the wallpaper:* coat with gold leaf, paint gold, gold-plate. **2** *She gilds the truth to make it more palatable:* embellish with minor lies, exaggerate, twist; gloss over, slant, stretch, bend.

gimcrack *n. She has a shelf full of little gimcracks:* knick-knack, bauble, gewgaw, trinket, ornament, curio, bagatelle, kickshaw, what-not; thingumabob, thingumajig, contrivance, plaything, toy.

gingerly *adv. We walked gingerly over the newly waxed floor:* very carefully, cautiously, warily, guardedly, charily, watchfully, circumspectly, vigilantly, prudently, discreetly, timidly, heedfully; suspiciously, daintily, delicately, fastidiously, mincingly, finically, squeamishly.

Ant. boldly, confidently; rashly, brashly, carelessly, heedlessly.

gird *v.* **1** *The warriors girded their loins and prepared for battle:* encircle with a belt, bind with a girdle, girdle, strap, belt, lace round; tie, secure; hitch, truss, tighten, fasten. **2** *Enemy troops girded the city:* surround, encircle, ring, encompass, hem in, circumscribe, circle, loop; enclose, confine, wall in, hedge in, pen; besiege, lay siege, blockade. **3** *Gird yourself for some bad news:* brace, steel, strengthen, fortify, sustain, prepare; harden, stiffen, buttress.

girdle *n.* **1** *The woman needs a girdle with that tight dress:* corselet, corset, foundation garment, belt, bodice; stays. **2** *The king wore a girdle of gem-studded velvet:* waistband, sash, belt, cummerbund; circlet, girth, cincture; surcingle, baldric. **3** *A girdle of trees enclosed the park:* ring, belt, circle, band, hedge, boundary, hem, contour.

girl *n.* **1** *The school is for girls from the age of 12 to 18. The eldest girl is a doctor now:* young female, schoolgirl, miss, lass, lassie, colleen, ingénue; daughter, female child; unmarried woman, maiden, maid, virgin, damsel, demoiselle; *Informal* nymph, wench, minx, baggage, nymphette, soubrette; *Slang* chick, bird, bit of fluff, kitten. **2** *We need a girl once a week to help with the housework:* maid, maidservant, domestic, female servant, hired woman, hired girl, home help, cleaning woman, cleaning lady, female employee, au pair, help, maid-of-all-work; cook, scullion; lady's maid, handmaid. **3** *Freddy's girl won't be in town for the dance:* girl-friend, sweetheart; fiancée, betrothed, affianced; darling, lady love, angel, innamorata; mistress.

"I want a girl just like the girl that married dear old dad." — *William Dillon*

---

girlish *adj. She's lost her girlish figure over the last ten years:* girl-like, maidenlike, maidenly, sylphlike, youthful.

Ant. matronly, mature, womanly.

girth *n.* **1** *The girth of the tree-trunk was over 100 inches:* circumference, perimeter, length round. **2** *Tighten the girth or the saddle will slip:* saddle-girth, saddle-band.

gist *n. The gist of his long speech was that he is against the proposal:* essence, main idea, main point, essential part, sense, force, significance, substance, sum and substance, implication, theme, burden, effect, drift; core, heart, centre, pith, kernel, marrow, meat, spirit, import, purport.

give *v.* **1** *What can I give you for your birthday?:* present, present to, make a gift, make a gift of, bestow, offer, donate; grant, accord, deliver freely, hand over; award, confer; commit, entrust. **2** *Most people give to some charity at Christmas. She gave her brother the bulk of her estate:* contribute, donate, make a gift, bestow, consign, apportion, allot, dispense, distribute, subscribe, assign, settle money upon, transfer money or property to, entrust, vouchsafe, make over, vest in, enrich; endow, bequeath, leave; *Slang* hand out, shell out, fork out. **3** *Give your hat to the cloakroom attendant:* place in someone's care, give over, hand over, entrust; present, accord. **4** *Give me one good reason why I should do that. She gave a cry that brought us all running:* put forth, show, provide, present, issue, convey, afford; utter, emit, offer, give vent to, voice, articulate, pronounce. **5** *Would you give me that magazine on the table, please?:* hand to, accommodate with, provide with, supply with, equip with, present, furnish, deliver, hand over, indulge with, favour with, proffer, tender, offer. **6** *The shop will give you £10 for your old golf-bag. She gave the porter a tip for carrying her suitcase:* pay, compensate, recompense, remunerate, allow, exchange, dispose of, requite; tip, bribe, grease the palm of; hire, buy; grant, accord, confer, hand over, dispense, distribute, present; *Slang* shell out, fork out. **7** *She gave them notice that she was leaving on the 15th:* notify, announce, let know, communicate, impart; present, issue, render. **8** *The assignment gave him a chance to prove his talents:* permit, allow, grant, enable; present, offer, accord, provide, supply, furnish, proffer, afford, confer, impart, vouchsafe, deign, concede; admit, yield. **9** *He gave himself to the job with tremendous enthusiasm:* apply, devote; surrender, attach, lose oneself in, lend, offer; addict. **10** *The branch gave under the weight of the heavy snow:* give way, break down, collapse; slacken, loosen, unbend, ease, relax, relent, bend; retreat, move back, recede; shrink, become soft, sink, deliquesce. **11** *Our picture window gives onto the patio:* open on; lead on to, afford an entrance; look out on, provide a vista.
—*n.* **12** *A good mattress shouldn't have much give:* flexibility, resilience; bounce, springiness.
Ant. 1–8 receive, get, take, accept, keep, retain, withhold, hold; take back, withdraw, recall. **11** shut off, block, hide, screen, mask, conceal, obscure.

glacial *adj. A glacial wind blew from the north. She greeted us with a glacial stare:* cold, chill, freezing, frigid, bone-chilling, polar, arctic, icy, frozen, frosty, wintry, gelid; raw, bitter, piercing, biting; hostile, antagonistic, disdainful, contemptuous.
Ant. hot, warm, mild, balmy; friendly, cheery.
◇ *Word origin: Glacial* comes from Latin *glacies,* ice.

glad *adj.* **1** *We were so glad that you could visit us:* happy, delighted, pleased, elated, joyful, joyous, gleeful, cheerful, exhilarated, contented, rejoiced; *Slang* tickled, tickled pink. **2** *Where were you when you received the glad news?:* happy, delightful, pleasing, elating, joyous, joyful, joy-giving, exhilarating, cheerful, blissful, gratifying, entrancing, cheering.
Ant. 1 sad, unhappy, melancholy, sorry, sorrowful, depressed, displeased, dejected, miserable; disappointed, discontented. **2** depressing, sad, unhappy, unpleasant, displeasing.
◇ *Word origin:* A *glad* face is a happy, shining face. It comes from Old English *glæd,* shining.

glamorous *adj. Jean Harlow was a glamorous film star of the 1930's:* fascinating, charming, bewitching, enchanting, captivating, alluring; attractive; exciting, charismatic.
Ant. unglamorous, unexciting, colourless, unattractive, dull, drab.

glamour *n. Do you still think there's any glamour in the advertising business?:* fascination, excitement, adventure, romance, challenge; attractiveness, allure, charm, enchantment, magnetism; magic, illusion, glitter.
◇ *Word origin:* We get *glamour* from a Scottish variant of *grammar,* in the sense of occult learning or *gramarye,* "grammarie," magic. Sir Walter Scott revived and popularized both of these words. A parallel development in French is *grimoire,* book of magic ("grammar").

glance *v.* **1** *He glanced at the newspaper and threw it aside:* look quickly, see briefly, view momentarily, observe quickly, scan, cast a brief look, snatch a glance, catch a glimpse of, glimpse, regard hastily; peek, peep. **2** *Stones and other missiles will only glance off the bullet-proof windows of this limousine:* rebound, ricochet, career, bounce; graze, brush, shave, skim, slip, touch, kiss.
—*n.* **3** *Have you got time for a glance at this report?:* quick look, brief look, quick view, glimpse; peek, peep, squint.
Ant. 1 study, contemplate, scrutinize, peruse, inspect fully. **3** long look, perusal, thorough examination, close scrutiny, full inspection.

glare *n.* **1** *The glare of the headlights almost blinded us:* harsh light, gleam, glint, flash, flare, glitter, glisten, blaze, flame; brightness, luminosity, radiance, glow, resplendence; gloss, sheen, shimmer, sparkle. **2** *He ignored his wife's glare and went on with the story:* angry look, reproving look, black look, dirty look, threatening look, piercing stare, glower, scowl.
—*v.* **3** *The sunlight glared on the ice:* shine harshly, reflect brightly, glitter, flare, gleam, glimmer, dazzle; sparkle, glisten, shimmer, glow, flash, blaze; radiate, twinkle, flicker.

4 *The teacher glared at the impertinent boy:* stare angrily, look fiercely, scowl, look black, glower, lower.

glaring *adj.* 1 *Those glaring lights hurt my eyes:* harsh, bright, strong, brilliant, intense, dazzling, flaring, piercing, penetrating; glittering, shimmering; vivid, resplendent. 2 *This bill contains a glaring error in addition:* conspicuous, obvious, blatant, unconcealed, unmistakable, undisguised; outrageous, audacious, gross, rank.

Ant. 1 soft, subdued. 2 hidden, concealed, inconspicuous; subtle, discreet.

glass *n.* 1 *Pour the milk into a clean glass:* drinking-vessel, tumbler, goblet; beaker, chalice. 2 *Drink eight glasses of water every day:* glassful, tumblerful.

◇ *Word origin: Glass* comes from Old English *glæs*, glass, which has the following close relatives: *gloss, gleam, glint, glimmer, glitter, glisten, glare,* and *glow*.

glaze *v.* 1 *How much did it cost to glaze that big window after it broke? The potter glazed the bowl after it was dry:* glass over, fit with glass, cover with glass; put a glassy finish on, enamel, coat with a glaze. 2 *My eyes began to glaze after four hours of reading:* become glassy, film over, blur, grow dim.

—*n.* 3 *The glaze is baked on the pottery at a very high temperature:* glossy coating, glazing, vitreous surface, gloss, finish, enamel, varnish.

◇ *Word origin: Glaze* comes from Middle English *glasen*, to *glass* (a window) or *glaze* (cover with a vitreous substance).

gleam *n.* 1 *The searchlight sent its gleam into the night sky:* beam, ray, streak, glow, glitter, glimmer; spark, sparkle, flash. 2 *A good waxing will give the old table a fine gleam:* sheen, lustre, gloss, brightness, gleaming, radiance, effulgence, brilliance, coruscation, glitter. 3 *The soldiers got an occasional gleam of humour from their sergeant:* trace, ray, inkling, glimpse, bit, drop, jot, iota, speck, grain, hint, least bit, tiny bit, glimmer, flicker.

—*v.* 4 *The car's headlights gleamed in the distance:* shine, glow, flash, glare, flare, shimmer, glitter, glisten, glimmer, sparkle, glint, scintillate, coruscate; blink, flicker, twinkle.

Ant. 1 darkness. 2 dullness, tarnish.

"Cold upon the dead volcano sleeps the gleam of dying day." —*Alfred, Lord Tennyson*

---

glean *v. The historian gleaned his material from old books and documents:* gather piecemeal, discover gradually, collect little by little, pick up, cull, accumulate, amass, gather, scrape together, harvest.

glee *n. The children shouted with glee when they saw the presents:* merriment, gaiety, joy, joyfulness, joyousness, exhilaration, exultation, rapture, delight, gladness, ecstasy; jollity, hilarity, mirth, laughter, jollification, cheerfulness, joviality, jocularity; playfulness, liveliness, sprightliness, sportiveness.

Ant. sadness, gloom, dejection, depression, melancholy, misery; *Slang* the blues, the dumps.

gleeful *adj. The boy gave a gleeful shout when he received the puppy:* happy, elated, glad, joyous, delighted, merry, gay, joyful, jolly, exultant, cheerful, exhilarated, mirthful, jovial, jocund, light-hearted, lively.

Ant. sad, gloomy, dejected, melancholy.

glen *n. The trip includes a sightseeing tour through the mountains and glens of Scotland:* narrow valley, dell, dale, vale, hollow, bottom.

Ant. height, peak, summit, mountain, hill.

glib *adj. The salesman had a glib answer for every question:* facile, flippant, quick, suave, ready, smooth, smooth-tongued, fluent, voluble, nimble of speech, ready of tongue, easy of manner; insincere, devious; slippery, oily, unctuous.

Ant. considered, sincere, deliberate, artless, guileless; hesitant, hesitating; halting, silent, quiet, taciturn.

◇ *Word origin: Glib* means being more facile than sincere, being smooth or slippery in talk or manner. The word comes from Middle Low German *glibberich*, slippery.

glide *v.* 1 *The hawk spread its wings and glided down towards the mountain:* soar, float, coast, sail, drift, flow. 2 *The dancers glided gracefully over the floor:* move smoothly, move effortlessly, slide, float, flow, skim, slip; skate, glissade; roll, drift, stream. 3 *Isn't it amazing the way the years glide by?:* slip, pass quickly, go unnoticed, roll, steal, drift, run; elapse, proceed, issue.

Ant. 1 fall, plummet, sink. 2, 3 lurch, stagger, flounder, stumble, trip, hobble, shuffle.

glimmer *n.* 1 *The candle made only a glimmer in the vast room:* faint gleam, small glow, flickering light, shimmer, glimmering, twinkle; ray, scintilla. 2 *There is still a glimmer of hope that the drought will end this week:* trace, gleam, flickering, drop, speck, grain, bit, hint, glimpse, intimation, fleeting view.

—*v.* 3 *The lights of the town glimmered in the distance:* shine, shine faintly, flicker, twinkle, flash, blink; gleam, sparkle, glitter, glisten, shimmer, scintillate, coruscate; glare, glow, flare, beam.

Ant. 1 glare, flash, flare, blaze.

◇ *Word origin: Glimmer* comes from Middle English *glimeren*, to shine.

glimpse *n.* 1 *The huntsman caught only a glimpse of the deer before it ran into the woods:* fleeting look, quick look, brief look, brief sight, momentary view, quick view, glance; peep, peek, squint.

—*v.* 2 *We glimpsed the diplomats as the procession passed:* see fleetingly, see briefly, catch a glimpse of, espy, sight briefly, view momentarily; peep at, peek at.

Ant. 1 long look, survey, observation,

scrutiny, inspection. **2** survey, observe closely, scrutinize, study, inspect; drink in.

glisten *v. The street glistened in the rain:* shine, sparkle, glitter, scintillate, coruscate, shimmer, glow, glimmer, gleam, glint, twinkle, flicker, radiate.

glitter *v.* **1** *The diamond glittered in the light:* sparkle, shine, glisten, gleam, glow, glimmer, flash, glint, radiate, flare, twinkle. —*n.* **2** *A good polishing will restore the candlestick's glitter:* lustre, shine, sheen, gleam, glow, sparkle, fire, radiance, brilliance, splendour; beaming, refulgence. **3** *Theatregoers love the glitter of the opening night:* glamour, splendour, grandeur, pomp, show, showiness, pageantry, display, tinsel; excitement, thrill, electricity.

Ant. **2** dullness. **3** drabness, dullness, dreariness, monotony.

gloat *v. Be a good winner and don't gloat over your victory:* crow over, vaunt, brag, revel in, glory over, exult, preen oneself, rejoice selfishly, relish maliciously, be over-pleased; strut, swagger.

Ant. regret, deplore; belittle, disparage, deprecate, slight, detract from, deride, scoff at, sneer at; *Slang* run down, knock, put down.

◇ *Word origin:* When one *gloats* over something, one grins over it. *Gloat* comes from Old Norse *glotta*, to grin.

global *adj. Another global war could destroy mankind:* world-wide, universal, intercontinental, international; general, widespread, comprehensive, all-encompassing, unlimited, unbounded, all-out.

Ant. local, neighbourhood, regional, sectional, provincial, parochial; limited, restricted, confined, circumscribed.

globe *n.* **1** *The earth is not a true globe but is slightly larger near the equator:* sphere, spherical body, spheroid, spherule, ball, orb, globule. **2** *Sandy's travels took her all over the globe:* planet, celestial body, world, Earth.

gloom *n.* **1** *A log fire quickly dispelled the gloom:* darkness, dark, blackness, dimness, dinginess, murkiness, murk, gloominess; shadows, shade, cloudiness, dusk, duskiness, obscurity. **2** *Don't let defeat fill you with gloom:* depression, low spirits, despondency, dejection, sadness, melancholy, cheerlessness, unhappiness, moroseness, heavy-heartedness, heaviness of mind; doldrums, blues, mopishness, disconsolateness, despair, hopelessness, forlornness, distress; woe, misery, oppression, sorrow, grief, dolour.

Ant. **1** light, brightness; daylight, sunlight, radiance. **2** joy, glee, delight, happiness, gladness, cheerfulness, high spirits, merriment, mirth, jollity, smiles.

◇ *Word origin:* Both *gloom* and *glum* grew out of Middle English *glomben*, to look sullen. However, the "darkness" meaning of *gloom* is John Milton's innovation — it appears nine times in his poetry and has been a literary word for "darkness" ever since. As for *glum*, Samuel Johnson describes it as follows in his *Dictionary* (1755): "a low cant word formed by corrupting *gloom.*"

gloomy *adj.* **1** *It was a gloomy winter's day:* dark, dim, dull, dismal, dreary, murky, shaded, shady, shadowy, sombre, cloudy, overcast, sunless, dusky. **2** *Can't you snap out of that gloomy mood?:* sad, unhappy, downcast, dejected, melancholy, despondent, depressed, cheerless, glum, doleful, dispirited, low-spirited, disheartened, heavy-hearted, down-hearted, moody, morose, crestfallen, chap-fallen, woebegone, mopish, dismal, dreary, grim, desolate, sombre, morbid, funereal, in the doldrums; discouraged, pessimistic, miserable, sorrowful, heartsick, forlorn, disconsolate, comfortless; frowning, dour, sour, ill-humoured; *Slang* down in the mouth, down in the dumps.

Ant. **1** bright, light, sunny; radiant, brilliant, dazzling. **2** happy, glad, cheerful, joyful, jolly, joyous, gleeful, merry, jovial, jocund, blithe, gay, high-spirited, light-hearted, smiling, delighted; *Slang* on top of the world.

glorify *v. Wesley wrote hymns to glorify God. His new book glorifies the outdoor life:* give glory to, pay homage to, exalt, venerate, revere; deify, idolize, canonize, adore, worship, bow down and worship, enshrine, consecrate, beatify, elevate, ennoble, dignify, immortalize, burn incense to, light candles before; praise, laud, extol, honour, celebrate, make more splendid, add lustre to, sing the praises of; glamourize, romanticize.

Ant. desecrate, profane, defile, dishonour, debase, defame, degrade; condemn, mock.

glorious *adj.* **1** *What a glorious spring day!:* gorgeous, beautiful, wonderful, marvellous, splendid, fine, great, grand, excellent, superb, delightful, divine; sparkling, brilliant, dazzling, shining, radiant, resplendent, glowing, lustrous. **2** *Beethoven's Ninth Symphony is a glorious piece of music:* sublime, noble, magnificent, grand, supreme, majestic, august, imposing, impressive, stately, dignified, distinguished, famous, eminent, noted, celebrated, honoured, pre-eminent, renowned, illustrious, notable, praiseworthy.

Ant. **1** awful, horrible, horrid, ugly, unpleasant, dull, drab, dreary, gloomy; *Slang* lousy. **2** minor, unimportant, unimpressive, trivial, trifling; undistinguished, unknown.

glory *n.* **1** *The Psalmist sang to the glory of God:* adoration, worship, homage, veneration, praise, thanksgiving, gratitude, benediction, blessing, admiration. **2** *The old soldier had won glory on the field of battle:* honour, renown, fame, eminence, pre-eminence, illustriousness, esteem, repute, distinction, celebrity, notability, prestige, mark, name. **3** *The glory*

of the Cheddar Gorge can best be seen for miles around on a clear day: grandeur, splendour, magnificence, majesty, gloriousness, resplendence, impressiveness, sublimity, stateliness, nobility, dignity, solemnity, excellence.
—*v.* **4** *The mother gloried in her son's success:* take pride, rejoice proudly, revel, take delight; be boastful, pat oneself on the back, preen oneself, plume oneself, boast, vaunt.
Ant. 1 blasphemy, profanity. **2** dishonour, disgrace, shame, infamy, ignominy, disrepute; condemnation, malediction, curse. **3** ugliness, meanness, triviality, paltriness.

"To the glory that was Greece
And the grandeur that was Rome."
—*Edgar Allan Poe*

---

gloss *n.* **1** *The wax imparted a high gloss to the table-top:* lustre, shine, sheen, polish, glow, gleam, radiance, brightness, glossiness, brilliance, shimmer, luminousness.
—*v.* **2** *The chair was glossed to give it an expensive look:* shine, polish, give a sheen to; glaze, varnish, enamel, lacquer, japan, veneer. **3** *Parents tend to gloss over their children's mistakes:* smooth over, treat lightly, mitigate; explain away, rationalize, excuse, whitewash, cover up, disguise, colour, veil, mask, cloak.
Ant. 1 dullness, dull film. **3** exaggerate, overemphasize, blow up; accept, recognize, face.
◇ *Word origin:* A *gloss* is a shine that flashes in the light almost as if the surface were burning or giving off sparks. It is related to Old Norse *glossi*, blaze.

glow *n.* **1** *The glow from the embers warmed us:* soft light, gleam, afterglow, glimmer, shimmer, flicker, radiation; low flame, soft heat, heat, warmth. **2** *The long rest brought a glow back to her cheeks:* colour, warmth, brightness, intensity, vividness, reddening; flush, bloom, blush. **3** *The glow of her smile made the guests feel very welcome:* warmth, radiance; enthusiasm, fervour, ardour, earnestness, eagerness, gusto.
—*v.* **4** *The remains of the fire glowed for hours. The hands of this watch glow in the dark:* burn softly, smoulder; shine, gleam, glitter, shimmer, be incandescent, be fluorescent, glisten, twinkle, flicker. **5** *The boy glowed with pride when he caught a fish:* radiate, fill, flush, blush, thrill, tingle; feel intensely, be enthusiastic about, be eager, be animated.
Ant. 2 paleness, pallor, whiteness, wanness, ashenness, greyness, dullness, drabness. **3** coldness, chill, coolness, iciness; indifference, dispassionateness, half-heartedness.

glower *v. The policeman glowered at the driver who was causing a jam:* scowl, look angrily, look fiercely, glare, frown, lower, look black, stare sullenly; pout, sulk.
Ant. smile, grin; laugh, snicker, smirk.

glowing *adj.* **1** *The children had glowing cheeks after their walk in the snow. The room was decorated in glowing shades of red:* ruddy, flushed, red; bright, vivid, luminescent, florid, hot, flaming. **2** *The critics wrote glowing reviews of the new play:* enthusiastic, rave, raving, fervent, ardent, ecstatic; thrilling, sensational, exciting, stimulating, passionate, rhapsodic.
Ant. 1 pale, pallid, white, wan, ashen, grey, colourless, dull, drab. **2** unenthusiastic, cool, dispassionate, half-hearted, so-so; dull, boring; scathing, cruel, brutal, venomous, stinging, vitriolic.

glut *v.* **1** *Many people glut themselves with turkey and stuffing at Christmas:* stuff, gorge, cram, fill, overfeed, eat to excess, overeat, satiate, eat one's fill, eat out of house and home, gluttonize, gormandize; devour, gulp, gobble, gobble up, bolt, wolf. **2** *The manufacturer glutted the market with cheap pocket radios:* oversupply, flood, deluge, overload, saturate, supersaturate, sate, surfeit, jade; choke, clog, congest, obstruct.
—*n.* **3** *During a petrol shortage, big cars become a glut on the market:* oversupply, overabundance, superabundance, saturation, supersaturation, surplus, excess, superfluity, surfeit, drug, burden, load, overdose, plethora, clog, obstruction.
Ant. 1 starve; nibble. **2** undersupply, empty. **3** scarcity, shortage, paucity, dearth, want, lack, scarcity.
◇ *Word origin: Glut* comes from Old French *gloutir*, to swallow, from Latin *glutire*, to gulp down, from which we also get *glutton* (Latin *glutto*). Related are Latin *gula*, throat, from which we get our word *gullet*, and Old English *ceolu*, throat, from which we get *jowl* (dewlap).

glutton *n. Most gluttons are overweight:* voracious eater, overeater, trencherman, gourmand, gormandizer, gorger; *Slang* pig, hog, gannet.
Ant. small eater, fussy eater, dainty eater, finicky eater; dieter.

gluttony *n. High blood pressure can be the result of gluttony:* excessive eating, voracity, voraciousness, ravenousness, gormandizing, gourmandism; rapacity; *Slang* hoggishness, piggishness, eating like a pig.
Ant. dainty eating, eating like a bird; dieting.

gnarled *adj. That gnarled oak tree is 100 years old. The old farmer had large, gnarled hands:* knotty, knotted, full of knots, covered with knurs, snaggy, leathery, wrinkled, weather-beaten, rugged; contorted, twisted, distorted, crooked.
Ant. smooth, sleek, unblemished; unwrinkled, silky; straight.
◇ *Word origin: Gnarled* is a variant of *knurled*, from *knurl* knot or bump, as on a tree trunk. *Gnarled* first occurred in Shakespeare and was a favourite 19th-century literary word.

gnash *v. He gnashed his teeth in anger:* grind

together, hit together, bite and grind, strike together, chomp, gnaw.

gnaw *v.* **1** *The boy gnawed an apple while he watched television:* munch, eat away at, chew, nibble, nibble at, chomp, crunch, bite, masticate; graze, browse, ruminate. **2** *Her unfair decision gnawed at her conscience:* trouble, worry, torment, rankle, distress, chafe, fret, grate, gall, harrow, eat at.

gnome *n. In fairy-tales gnomes always guard hidden treasure:* dwarf, troll, shrivelled little old man; elf, goblin; sprite, pixie, leprechaun.

◇ *Word origin: Gnome* comes from Modern Latin *gnomus*, a term for "pygmy" coined by the Swiss alchemist and physician Paracelsus (1493–1541).

go *v.* **1** *What time will you go to the shops today? On your marks, get set, go!:* move toward, set out for, start for, begin, proceed, progress, be off, advance, make headway, go on, get on, wend, repair, stir; press onward, forge ahead, gain ground, sally forth. **2** *Please go now, I'm getting tired:* leave, depart, go away, take one's departure, withdraw, retire, decamp, move out, move away, quit; *Slang* scram, beat it, take off, scarper, blow, split; steal away, steal off, slip off, sneak off, take French leave, flee, fly, take flight. **3** *Does this road go to the city? This belt won't go round my waist:* lead, extend, reach, stretch to, spread to. **4** *Is the machine going properly now?:* work, operate, function, run, be operative, act, perform; be in motion. **5** *Time goes so fast when you're having fun:* pass, pass by, go by, elapse, lapse, expire, flow, slide, glide by, slip away. **6** *Most of my money goes in rent. The award goes to a different actor each year:* be used, be applied, be given, be awarded, be contributed. **7** *How did things go at the office today?:* turn out, go out, fare, take place, come to pass, transpire; result, end, terminate, fall out. **8** *Where do these cups go? That green hat doesn't go with your blue dress:* fit, have a place, belong; be compatible, be suited to, agree, harmonize, accord, blend; conform with, comport, tally. **9** *Elizabeth prefers to go by the name of Betty. How does that old saying go?:* be known, be considered, be reckoned; be stated, be phrased, be expressed.

—*n.* **10** *The job requires a man with a lot of go:* ambition, drive, energy, vigour, vim, vim and vigour, vitality, force, spirit, animation, vivacity, verve, pep, dash, élan, life, mettle, enterprise; *Slang* get up and go. **11** *Let me have a go at fixing it:* try, attempt, turn, chance, whirl; effort, trial, endeavour, experiment.

Ant. 1 stay, remain; arrive, finish, end. **2** arrive, come, move in. **4** be inoperative, be broken; stop. **5** stand still. **6** be unused; keep, retain. **8** mismatch, be incompatible, be unsuited, disagree. **10** laziness, lifelessness, lethargy.

◇ *Usage note:* The basic forms of the verb *to go* are, of course, *go* (present), *went* (past), *gone* (past participle): *She goes today, She went yesterday, She has gone before.*

goad *n.* **1** *The drovers used goads to keep the herd moving:* prod, cattle-prodder, prick, pointed stick. **2** *Fear of failure can be a goad to hard work:* incentive, stimulus, stimulant, driving motive, spur; inducement, encouragement, instigation, whet, fillip.

—*v.* **3** *His wife goaded him to ask for a rise:* prod, urge, exhort, constrain, incite, spur, drive, stir up, arouse, *Slang* egg on; stimulate, impel, propel, move, press, set on.

Ant. 2 detriment, curb. **3** deter, keep back, hold back.

goal *n.* **1** *His goal in life is to own his own business:* aim, objective, ambition, purpose, intention, design, end, target. **2** *The striker hammered the ball into the goal:* scoring area; basket, wicket, goal-line, boundary. **3** *The hockey team scored three goals in the first half:* point, mark; try, basket, wicket.

goat *n.* **1** *The farmer raised sheep and goats:* (*variously*) billy-goat, nanny-goat, nanny, buck, kid. **2** *Don't go near him — the old goat!:* lecher, lewd person, fornicator, debauchee.

gobble *v.* **1** *Did you hear that turkey gobbling in the night?:* gabble, cackle, gaggle, caw. **2** *The secretaries gobbled their lunch and ran back to the office:* gulp, gulp down, bolt, bolt down, swallow quickly, eat quickly, devour, stuff, cram down.

goblin *n. Eat your spinach or the goblins will get you!:* wicked elf, evil sprite, bogyman, bogy, demon, gremlin, troll, ogre.

◇ *Word origin:* What could a *goblin* have to do with *cobalt?* Both go back to an ancient Germanic word that meant "household ruler," i.e. household god. With the Christianization of the Germans, the old gods went underground; the term for household god became Middle High German *kobolt*, "underground goblin," name given to *cobalt* ore by miners in the belief that it was injurious to silver ores in which it occurred. The word passed into Old French — a 12th-century author gives *Gobelinus* as the name of a *goblin* haunting Evreux, France. The word passed into English on the eve of the Hundred Years' War.

God *n.* **1** *In the beginning God created the heavens and the earth:* Lord, Our Father, God Almighty, the Almighty, the Supreme Being, the Deity, the Creator; the Godhead, the Omnipotent, the Omniscient, the All-Merciful. **2** Usually **god.** *Apollo was the Greek god of sunlight:* deity, divine being, ruling spirit, divinity.

Ant. 1 the Devil, Prince of Darkness, Spirit of Evil, the Foul Fiend; Satan, Mephistopheles, Lucifer, Beelzebub; *Slang* Old Nick, Old Harry. **1, 2** mortal, human, human being, flesh and blood.

◇ *Word origin:* Our word *god* goes back via Germanic to Indo-European, in which a corresponding ancestor form meant "invoked one." The word's only surviving non-Germanic relative is Sanskrit *hū*, invoke the gods, a form of which appears in the *Rig Veda*, most ancient of Hindu scriptures: *puru-hūtās*, "much-invoked," epithet of the rain-and-thunder god Indra.

"If the concept of God has any validity or use, it can only be to make us larger, freer, and more loving." —*James Baldwin*

God-forsaken *adj. The little deserted town was a God-forsaken place:* desolate, deserted, remote; neglected, abandoned; bleak, wretched, lonely.

godless *adj. Bombing the defenceless town was a godless act. In time he repented his godless life:* evil, wicked, depraved; blasphemous, irreligious, sacrilegious, ungodly, impious, profane, heathen, unhallowed, unsanctified, unrepentant, unrighteous.

Ant. godly, pious, religious, holy; sacred, hallowed, consecrated, sanctified; inspired.

godly *adj. The old patriarch was a wise and godly man:* devout, pious, reverent, religious, righteous, devoted, God-loving, God-fearing, pietistic, believing, faithful, pure in heart, saintly, holy, divine, spiritual; sacred, hallowed, consecrated, sanctified.

Ant. ungodly, godless, atheistic, irreligious, sacrilegious, impious, unrepentant, profane, heathen; evil, wicked, depraved.

gold *n.* **1** *Many prospectors found gold in the hills of California:* (*variously*) gold-dust, nugget, bullion, ingot, bar, *Chemistry* aurum. **2** *The school's colours are green and gold:* bright yellow, yellow, gilt. **3** *He tries to appear mean, but he really has a heart of gold:* goodness, kindness, beauty, purity; goodwill, beneficence, humanity.

golden *adj.* **1** *The child has blue eyes and golden hair. A golden sunset:* bright-yellow, gold-coloured, gold, aureate, blond; gilt, gilded; bright, shining, resplendent. **2** *Year after year he waits for a golden opportunity to be presented to him:* advantageous, opportune, favourable, timely, promising, auspicious, propitious, seasonable, well-disposed, *Slang* rosy. **3** *Good health and peacefulness can make old age the golden years of one's life:* joyous, most joyous, happy, happiest, glorious, most glorious, best, blest, delightful, beatific; flourishing, halcyon, palmy; most precious, most valuable, priceless, richest.

Ant. **1** black, dark, brunette, dull. **2** unfavourable, inauspicious, untimely, unpromising. **3** worst, sad, saddest, wretched, most wretched; lean, poorest.

good *adj.* **1** *Sir Thomas More was a wise and good man. Florence Nightingale was renowned for her good deeds:* virtuous, worthy, honourable, morally excellent, righteous, upright; honest, reliable, conscientious; moral, wholesome, praiseworthy, exemplary; religious, pious, devout, pure, innocent, unsullied, untainted; humane, considerate, benevolent, kind-hearted, kind, kindly, gracious, sympathetic, well-disposed, altruistic, beneficent, obliging. **2** *Have you been a good boy today?:* dutiful, obedient, proper, seemly, well-mannered, decorous, well-behaved, orderly. **3** *Where can we get a good steak? Antony Powell's novels are particularly good:* satisfactory, excellent, fine, great, wonderful, splendid, first-rate, choice, select, sound, capital, tiptop; worthy, worthwhile; valuable, precious, priceless; admirable, commendable, *Slang* crack. **4** *The office needs another good typist:* skilled, skilful, capable, efficient, proficient, adroit, thorough; top-notch, first-rate, excellent, first-class, ace. **5** *Milk is good for you. It's a good day for swimming:* beneficial, healthful, healthy, salutary, advantageous; suitable, appropriate, favourable, right, proper, fitting, fit, qualified, useful, adequate, becoming, adapted, deserving. **6** *Have a good time on your holiday. An entertainer has to have a good personality:* enjoyable, pleasant, agreeable; cheerful, lively, sunny, genial, convivial, sociable, companionable. **7** *Why don't you wear your good suit to the party?:* best; new, newest, smartest, most dressy, most stylish, expensive, valuable, precious, priceless. **8** *I would cash his cheque if I could be sure it was good:* valid, bona fide, sound, real, genuine, authentic, honest, legitimate, proper; worthwhile, valuable. **9** *The old farm is a good mile from here. She spends a good deal of time playing bridge:* full, complete, solid, entire; considerable, large, fairly great, substantial, sizeable, ample; adequate, sufficient.

—*n.* **10** *No one's all bad — everyone has some good in him. More people should concern themselves with doing good:* goodness, virtue, merit, worth, value, excellence, kindness, righteousness, moral qualities; righteous acts, moral acts. **11** *You must try harder for the good of the team:* benefit, advantage, gain, profit, prosperity, good fortune, success, welfare, interest, well-being, improvement; service, favour, good turn, boon; enjoyment, happiness, wealth; blessing, godsend, prize, windfall.

Ant. 1-8, 10, 11 bad. **1** evil, wicked, sinful, dishonourable, immoral, dishonest, unreliable; unworthy, unwholesome, blameable; sullied, fallen, corrupt, corrupted, tainted; mean, cruel, unkind, ill-disposed, selfish. **2** improper, unseemly, ill-mannered, indecorous, naughty, mischievous. **3** unsatisfactory, unsatisfying, awful, second-rate, unsound, valueless, worthless. **4** unskilled, incompetent, inefficient, amateurish, awful, horrible, *Slang* lousy. **5** disadvantageous; wrong, improper, unfitting, unseemly, unsuitable, inappropriate, unqualified, useless, inadequate; unbecoming, undeserving. **6** awful, *Slang* lousy; unpleasant, disagreeable; dull, boring, cheerless, drab. **7** worst, valueless, worthless; informal, sporty, old, oldest. **8** phoney, counterfeit, sham, fraudulent, bogus; false, invalid, unsound, dishonest, worthless. **9** scant, short, incomplete; small, insubstantial; inadequate, insufficient. **10** evil, wickedness, badness, sinfulness, meanness, baseness; immorality, dishonesty, corruption, cruelty. **11** detriment, loss; failure, ill fortune; decline.

◇ *Usage note:* See WELL.

good-bye *interj.* **1** *Good-bye and write me as soon as you get settled:* farewell, so long, bye, bye-bye, cheerio, adieu, God be with you, Godspeed; till we meet again, be seeing you, see you later; *French* au revoir; *Spanish* adios; *Italian* arrivederci *Informal* ciao; *German* auf Wiedersehen; *Japanese* sayonara.
—*n.* **2** *He gave her a rose at their last good-bye:* farewell, parting, leave-taking, separation.

Ant. **1** hello, good morning. **2** meeting, greeting, welcoming; reunion.

◇ *Word origin: Good-bye* is a contraction of the phrase "God be with you."

goodness *n.* **1** *She was a gentle woman of exceeding goodness:* moral excellence, worth, honour, righteousness, honesty, integrity, merit, wholesomeness, probity; virtue, virtuousness, morality, rectitude, purity, innocence, benevolence, kindness, kindliness, generosity; piety, devotion; propriety, decorum. **2** *Eat the carrot raw if you want to get all its goodness:* benefit, advantage, value, worth, usefulness, profit, service; flavour, nutrition, nourishment.
—*interj.* **3** *Goodness, what a big cake!:* gracious, goodness gracious, mercy, heavens, Good Lord, well I never; *Slang* wow, wowee, gee, gee whiz, boy, oh boy, crikey, blimey, gosh, say, cor, hey.

Ant. **1** badness, evil, wickedness, sinfulness, immorality, dishonesty, unwholesomeness, corruption, worthlessness. **2** detriment, disadvantage, drawback.

goods *n. pl.* **1** *The removal men put all our goods in the van:* possessions, property, worldly goods, movables, effects, chattels; paraphernalia, trappings, appurtenances, things, gear. **2** *All the shop's goods are protected by insurance:* merchandise, stock, wares, articles of trade, commodities.

"When a strong man armed keepeth his palace, his goods are in peace."
—*St Luke* xi. 21

---

gore *n. Aunt Rose thinks there's too much gore in bullfighting:* bloodshed, butchery, slaughter, carnage; blood, dried blood, clotted blood.

◇ *Word origin: Gore,* clotted or dried blood, comes from Old English *gor,* mud or filth.

gorge *n.* **1** *The waterfall was at the far end of the gorge:* steep valley, canyon, chasm, ravine, gully, defile; hollow, abyss, crevasse, gap; glen, dell, dale, vale. **2** *The dog had a chicken-bone caught in its gorge:* throat, gullet, craw, oesophagus; mouth, muzzle. **3** *It makes my gorge rise to see someone behave so badly:* disgust, revulsion, repugnance, repulsion, nausea; anger, wrath, blood, ire, animosity, hatred.
—*v.* **4** *The children gorged themselves on cake and sweets:* stuff, fill, glut, sate, cram, satiate; over-eat, over-indulge, eat greedily, indulge, gormandize, gluttonize; swallow greedily, devour, gulp, gobble, bolt.

◇ *Word origin: Gorge* goes back to Latin *gurges,* whirlpool.

gorgeous *adj. You never saw such a gorgeous mink coat in all your life. What a gorgeous day!:* beautiful, attractive, good-looking, lovely, exquisite, stunning, ravishing, splendid, elegant, magnificent, grand, fine, sumptuous, rich-looking, imposing, impressive, splendiferous, opulent, luxurious, costly; shining, brilliant, dazzling, bright, glittering, resplendent.

Ant. ugly, hideous, unsightly, unattractive, repulsive, plain, homely, cheap, tawdry, trashy, shoddy, scrubby, sorry; drab, dull; dreary, gloomy, murky, dismal, sombre, bleak, grey.

◇ *Word origin: Gorgeous* goes back to Old French *gorgias,* elegant.

gory *adj.* **1** *The hunter's knife was gory. The gory feud lasted for years:* bloody, blood-stained, blood-soaked, stained with gore, covered with gore; bloodthirsty, murderous, sanguinary. **2** *The gory tale gave the children nightmares:* bloody, scary, blood-curdling, frightening, terrifying, horrifying; *Slang* creepy.

gospel *n.* **1** Often **Gospel** *Ministers devote their lives to preaching the gospel. A Gothic translation of the Gospels was made around the year 360:* the tidings of salvation proclaimed by Jesus Christ, the good news; any of the first four books of the New Testament: Matthew, Mark, Luke, or John. **2** *Her husband's opinions are gospel as far as she's concerned:* the whole truth; ultimate truth, the final word, the last word; doctrine, creed, credo.

◇ *Word origin: Gospel* comes from Old English *gōdspel,* good news.

gossip *n.* **1** *A career can be ruined by malicious gossip:* groundless rumour, hearsay, whispering behind one's back, backbiting, scandal-mongering, scandal; idle talk, prattle, twaddle, babble, tattle, tittle-tattle; comment, report, news. **2** Also **gossiper** *She's such a gossip you daren't tell her anything:* idle tattler, tale-bearer, idle talker, rumour-monger, scandalmonger, tattle-tale, blabbermouth, tattler, chatterbox, busybody, babbler, chatterer; snooper, meddler, magpie.

—*v.* **3** *Don't you hate people who gossip about their friends?:* spread rumours, go about tattling, talk idly, tattle, prattle, prate, gabble, blab, talk one's head off, give one an earful; snoop, pry, meddle, stick one's nose in other people's business; *Slang* muck-rake.

Ant. 3 keep quiet, keep mum, keep a secret, keep one's lips sealed, keep one's counsel.

◇ *Word origin: Gossip* comes from Old English *godsibb*, godparent. From this original meaning of "sponsor at baptism," and hence "close associate," *gossip* gradually came to mean an idle talker.

gourmand *n. A gourmand is somebody who likes good food and plenty of it:* trencherman, bon vivant, gormandizer, glutton, big eater; *Slang* pig, hog.

Ant. small eater, dainty eater, choosy eater, fussy eater; dieter.

◇ *Word origin: Gourmand* comes from Old French *gourmand*, glutton. Being inclined to a more indulgent view of gluttony than their neighbours, Frenchmen have always used *gourmand* as a term of approval.

gourmet *n. A gourmet always wants the best food, not the most:* epicure, gastronome, gastronomist, connoisseur.

◇ *Pronunciation tip: Gourmet* should be pronounced goor-may, never "goor-met."

◇ *Usage note:* A *gourmet* is a fastidious devotee of good food and drink; a *gourmand* is one who takes hearty pleasure in good eating. Thus, the *gourmet* insists on quality, the *gourmand* on quality *and* quantity.

◇ *Word origin:* In his *Dictionnaire de la Langue Française* (1885), Emile Littré defines *gourmet* as "a subtle gourmand." He also gives "wine connoisseur" and "wine-taster" as modern senses of *gourmet* in French. The original French meaning was "wine merchant's apprentice."

govern *v.* **1** *Canada is governed by a prime minister and his cabinet:* administer, manage, rule, direct, head, lead, control, guide, steer, pilot, supervise, superintend, oversee, exercise authority over, be at the helm of; *Informal* be in the driver's seat, pull the strings. **2** *She's never been able to govern that malicious tongue of hers:* control, restrain, check, hold in check, curb, bridle, inhibit, hold in hand, keep under control; discipline, command, rule, dominate, boss. **3** *What factors governed your decision?:* guide, influence, sway, lead, steer, incline, rule.

Ant. 1 be subject; follow, comply, obey, submit. **2** let loose, give free rein to; encourage.

◇ *Word origin: Govern* comes from the Latin *gubernare*, to steer a ship. A cliché dating back to the ancient Greeks has it that those who govern "steer the ship of state."

government *n.* **1** *Society could not exist without government:* governing system, rule, administration, authority, law, management, control, regulation, command, direction, guidance, supervision; state, dominion, statesmanship, reins of government. **2** *The prime minister and his government will resign and new elections will be held:* governing body, administration, regime.

◇ *Pronunciation tip:* Don't be careless. Do pronounce the first *n* in *goverNment.* The sloppy pronunciation "gover'ment" is so common that many people even misspell the word by leaving out the *n.* So when you spell and pronounce it remember that first *n: goverNment.*

gown *n.* **1** *The bride wore a white satin gown:* formal dress, long dress, fancy dress, party dress; dress, frock; nightgown, nightdress. **2** *Every graduate wore a cap and gown:* academic garb, robe, academic dress, academic attire.

◇ *Word origin: Gown* goes back to Medieval Latin *gunna*, fur-lined robe worn by members of the academic professions.

grab *v.* **1** *He jumped up from the table, grabbed his hat and ran to the bus stop:* seize, snatch, grasp, pluck, lay hold of; clutch, grip, hold, clasp; capture, catch, nab, collar, bag.

—*n.* **2** *The boy made a grab at the frog, but it jumped away:* sudden grasp, snatch, lunge, pass.

Ant. 1 let loose, let go of, release, free; drop, put down, set.

grace *n.* **1** *It's difficult to walk up and down stairs with grace:* gracefulness, elegance, supple ease, lissomeness, willowiness, fluidity; beauty, comeliness, pulchritude, good looks. **2** *As a girl she learned the graces required of a good hostess:* charming quality, endowment, accomplishment, skill; charm, refinement, culture, cultivation, polish, urbanity, suavity, elegance, mannerliness, manners, decorum, etiquette, propriety, tact, taste. **3** *The monks prayed daily for grace:* God's favour, God's love, divine goodness, divine influence, charisma; holiness, sanctity, saintliness, devoutness, moral strength; virtue, piety, excellence, merit, love, felicity. **4** *By the king's grace, the traitor was permitted to leave the country:* mercy, pardon, clemency, lenience, forgiveness, charity, reprieve, indulgence, mercifulness. **5** *Drivers have two weeks' grace to renew their licences:* extra time, exemption, reprieve, dispensation, indulgence.

—*v.* **6** *Borders of flowers graced the paths in the park:* adorn, decorate, beautify, ornament, embellish, set off, garnish, deck, bedeck; spruce up, smarten, dress up, enhance, enrich. **7** *His Eminence graced the banquet by his presence:* dignify, honour, glorify, elevate, aggrandize, exalt, favour, endow.

Ant. 1 clumsiness, awkwardness, inelegance, gawkiness, stiffness, ugliness. **2** bad habit, inelegance, boorishness, bad manners, tactlessness, tastelessness. **4** disfavour, ill will, enmity, animosity; sternness, harshness, cruelty. **6** desecrate, ruin. **7** insult, dishonour, shame.

graceful *adj. She just isn't graceful enough to be a good dancer:* easy-moving, naturally supple, limber, lithe, willowy, sinuous, lithesome, lissome, light-footed; attractive, comely, lovely, beautiful; delicate, elegant, sylphlike.
Ant. clumsy, awkward, ungainly, ungraceful, graceless, inelegant, gawky, lumbering, ponderous, stiff; ugly, homely, plain.

gracious *adj.* **1** *She was the most gracious hostess I've ever known:* kindly, courteous, cordial, amiable, affable, good-natured, hospitable, obliging, civil; polite, chivalrous, courtly, pleasant; kind, friendly, kind-hearted, charitable, humane, tender, compassionate, benevolent, benign, benignant, merciful, lenient, clement.
—*interj.* **2** *Gracious, what an ugly house!:* Good heavens, Good Lord, mercy, goodness, goodness gracious, my.
Ant. 1 ungracious, uncordial, unpleasant, ill-natured, haughty, unfriendly, cold, cool, remote, stiff, unkind, discourteous, rude, impolite, brusque, curt, gruff, surly, sullen; cruel, mean.

> **Exploring the Word:** *Grade, gradual,* and *graduate* come from Latin *gradus,* step. Thus a *grade* is a mark or level of attainment in school, *gradual* means step-by-step, to *graduate* from university is to complete a step in one's education; a *graduated thermometer* is one marked off in steps or degrees of temperature and to *degrade* is to reduce in rank or status. The past participle of Latin *gradi,* to step, is *gressus,* stepped. The *gress-* of *gressus* forms the stem on which are based: *aggression,* a stepping to attack; *congress,* literally a group that comes together, hence an assembly; *digress,* to step away from the main topic of discussion; *egress,* a going out or exit; *regress,* a stepping back, as to an earlier place or stage, and *retrogress,* also taking a backward step; and *transgress,* to step beyond the bounds prescribed by religious or secular law.

grade *n.* **1** *The lorry had a hard time going up the steep grade:* incline, slope, gradient, ramp, inclined plane, acclivity, declivity; hill, bank. **2** *These pearls are of the highest grade. He hopes that he will soon be promoted to a higher grade:* rank, degree, level, standing, place; order, class, status, station, position; estate, condition, caste; stage, step, sphere; quality, value, intensity, brand, pitch. **3** *The boy got a grade B in the spelling test:* mark; rating.
—*v.* **4** *Poultrymen grade their eggs from small to extra large:* classify, sort; rank, order, gradate, value, rate, brand. **5** *The teacher spent all weekend grading the children's essays:* mark, give a grade to, rate. **6** *Grading the road should minimize its slipperiness:* level, even, make horizontal, smooth, flatten.

gradual *adj. Your work has shown a gradual improvement:* slow but steady, progressive, regular, continuous, successive, graduated, slow, gentle, steady, deliberate; piecemeal, step-by-step, little-by-little, inch-by-inch, drop-by-drop.
Ant. sudden, abrupt, precipitate, instantaneous, overnight.

graduate *n.* **1** *Our French teacher is a graduate of the Sorbonne:* holder of a degree, recipient of a diploma.
—*v.* **2** *I want to work in industry when I've graduated:* obtain a degree, be awarded a diploma, pass out, complete one's studies. **3** *The measuring cup is graduated in ounces:* mark with gradations, divide into degrees, calibrate, grade, measure out.
—*adj.* **4** *The teacher is taking a graduate course in mathematics:* post-graduate, post-baccalaureate.
Ant. 1 drop-out. **2** fail exams. **4** undergraduate.

graft[1] *n.* **1** *The graft on the apple tree is thriving:* inserted shoot, implantation, transplant, splice; slip, sprout, scion.
—*v.* **2** *The surgeon grafted skin from the patient's back onto his burned arm. The hawthorn branch was grafted onto an older tree:* implant, transplant, ingraft; inset, infix, join; plant, bud.
◇ *Word origin: Graft*[1] comes from Latin *graphium,* stylus, which in turn comes from Greek *graphein,* to draw or write. The original connection in meaning arose when someone likened the shape of a shoot for grafting to that of a stylus or pencil.

graft[2] *n. Steps were taken to abolish graft in local government:* corruption, bribery, plunder; pay-offs, bribes, hush-money, rake-off, kick-back, spoils; *Slang* payola.
◇ *Word origin: Graft*[2] may come from the slang phrase *hard graft,* "hard work." Or it may come from a figurative extension of *graft*[1] — by accepting a bribe a corrupt civil servant *grafts* something extra onto his regular income.

grain *n.* **1** *Farmers produce millions of tons of grain to feed the nation:* edible seed plants, cereal; (*variously*) wheat, rye, barley, oats, corn, maize, millet. **2** *The grain was separated from the stalks by beating:* kernel, seed, ovule; cereal, grist; (*variously*) wheat, rye, barley, oats, corn, maize, millet. **3** *The grains of sand run through the hourglass:* particle, granule; bit, pellet. **4** *There isn't a grain of truth in his assertion:* bit, speck, particle, trace, spark, iota, jot, dot, scintilla, whit, tittle, atom, crumb, molecule, mite, morsel, fragment, granule; trifle, touch, pinch, dash, modicum.
Ant. 2 chaff, stalks.
◇ *Word origin: Grain* can be traced back to the Latin *granum,* seed.

grand *adj.* **1** *What could be more grand than Buckingham Palace?:* magnificent, majestic, stately, monumental, august, imposing, elegant, impressive, distinguished, striking, splendid, superb, glorious, noble, sublime, lofty, imperial, palatial, royal, luxurious, sumptuous, opulent; fancy, dashing, showy; pretentious, ostentatious; large, big, huge, mammoth. **2** *The queen received her subjects in a grand manner:* stately, majestic, regal, noble, august, exalted, lofty, dignified, elevated, lordly, royal, kingly, queenly, princely; grandiose, pompous; *Slang* high-falutin. **3** *Going to the races is a grand idea:* good, splendid, excellent, wonderful, fine, great, terrific, marvellous, fabulous, superb, sensational, smashing, admirable, first-rate, choice; *Slang* A-1, fab, keen, super, out-of-this-world, out-of-sight, real cool, groovy. **4** *He became Grand Master of the Masonic Lodge:* main, chief, head, supreme, highest-ranking. **5** *When they told us the grand total of our bill I was stunned:* complete, full, all-embracing, comprehensive, all-inclusive.

Ant. 1 petty, paltry, trivial, trifling, measly, puny, small, little, meagre, unimposing, insignificant; unimportant, secondary, incidental, inferior. **2** undignified, common, low-class, boorish; base, mean, contemptible, small. **3** bad, poor, unsound, wretched, worthless, inferior, second-rate; *Slang* rotten, terrible, awful, lousy.

◇ *Word origin: Grand* comes from Latin *grandis*, full-grown, tall, great.

grandeur *n. The painting shows the grandeur of the royal palace in 1850:* magnificence, majesty, splendour, stateliness, sublimity, nobility, glory, impressiveness; pomp, state, augustness, solemnity, dignity; importance, celebrity, eminence, fame, distinction, excellence, lustre, loftiness.

Ant. paltriness, triviality, pettiness, smallness; insignificance, unimportance, inferiority, commonness, meanness.

"So nigh is grandeur to our dust,
So near is God to man."
—*Ralph Waldo Emerson*

grandiloquent *adj. The grandiloquent speech went on for over an hour:* high-flown, high-sounding, flowery, grandiose, pompous, bombastic, inflated, turgid, swollen, stilted; magniloquent, lofty, rhetorical; *Slang* high-falutin.

Ant. simple, direct, unaffected, low-key; base, lowly.

grandiose *adj. Renting a chauffeur-driven limousine was just one of his grandiose ideas:* grand, high-flown, flamboyant, splashy, theatrical, pretentious, pompous, affected; *Slang* high-falutin.

◇ *Word origin: Grandiose* came into English through French from an Italian word *grandioso*, originally from Latin *grandis*, tall, great. It was first used in English by the novelist Thackeray in 1840, though the much rarer *grandiosity* is recorded one year earlier.

grant *v.* **1** *The general granted us permission to visit the military base. The government will grant land to anyone willing to farm it:* give, allow, consent to, permit, bestow, accord, confer, vouchsafe, agree to; allot, allocate, present, donate, cede, assign, award, endow; dispense, deal out, apportion. **2** *Are you ready to grant that I was right?:* concede, admit, accede to, allow, consent, vouchsafe, yield.

—*n.* **3** *The student lived on a grant from the government:* allotment, appropriation, present, presentation, gift, donation, award, bursary, scholarship, endowment, benefaction, contribution, bestowal, largess; bequest, subsidy, offering, allowance, assignment, gratuity, tribute; concession, indulgence, favour, boon.

Ant. 1 refuse, deny, withhold, withdraw. **2** refute, disagree.

graphic *adj.* **1** *The reporter wrote a graphic description of the accident:* vivid, realistic, illustrative, pictorial, picturesque, well-drawn, well-delineated, forcible, striking, trenchant, explicit, clear, distinct, expressive, descriptive. **2** *The museum has an exhibition of the graphic arts:* visible, seen; written, drawn, painted, printed.

Ant. 1 unrealistic, unpicturesque, indefinite, hazy, obscure, vague, dull; impressionistic, expressionistic. **2** abstract; performing.

Exploring the Word: Greek *graphē*, writing (or drawing), and the related verb *graphein*, to write (or draw), give us *graph* and *graphic; anagram*, a word "written anew" by rearranging its letters; *diagram*, lines drawn across each other; *grammar*, literally the art of letters, i.e. the study of language; *epigram*, originally an inscription but now something worth inscribing, as a brief, witty poem or a pithy remark; *epigraph*, an inscription on an ancient monument (hence *epigraphy*, the science of inscriptions) or a brief quotation at the beginning of a literary work; *programme*, originally a written announcement put before the public, later a printed schedule or list of events or performers, as of a theatrical performance, and then the performance itself; and, of course, such words as *telegram* and *telegraph* (Greek *tēle*, afar), writing or messages sent afar by wire or radio; *cablegram*, an overseas telegram sent via underwater cable; *phonograph* (Greek *phōnē*, sound), an early type of record player; and *photograph* (Greek *phōs*, light), literally a "light-drawing."

grapple *n.* **1** *The sailors used a grapple to retrieve the chest from the bottom of the sea:* grappling-hook, grapnel, large hook.

—*v.* **2** *The friends thou hast, grapple them to thee*

with hoops of steel: hold, hold tightly, clasp, fasten, make fast, grasp, grip, clutch, seize, catch, lay hold of. **3** *Every man has to grapple with the problem of what he wants to do in life:* struggle, contend, combat, fight, wrestle, take on, do battle, encounter, engage, face, tackle, meet, confront, breast, try to overcome; *Slang* get one's teeth into.

Ant. **2** free, let loose, let go, release. **3** avoid, evade, side-step, run away from.

◇ *Word origin: Grapple* comes from Old French *grapil*, hook, from Old Provençal *grapa*, hook. A *grapa* was used for harvesting *grapes.* English *grape* originally meant "bunch of grapes" (as does the related French *grappe*). These words all descend from a now-lost Germanic term for a hooked tool used in the wine harvest.

grasp *v.* **1** *She grasped the letter and held it to her breast:* seize, seize upon, grab, snatch, catch, catch at, take, take hold of, lay hold of; hold, clutch, clasp, grip, clinch; grapple. **2** *The student couldn't grasp what the teacher was trying to explain:* comprehend, understand, catch on to, get, take in, perceive, fathom, follow, master, *Slang* savvy; sense, infer, deduce. *—n.* **3** *Take a firm grasp on the rope and pull. The mother held the child tightly in her grasp:* grip, hold, clasp, clutch; clutches, embrace, handclasp; seizure, seizing, gripping. **4** *Soon a full partnership will be within his grasp:* reach, power, control, compass, scope, range, sweep, sway. **5** *The course will improve the students' grasp of algebra:* comprehension, understanding, perception, ken, knowledge, mastery, talent, skill, sense.

Ant. **1** drop, release, free, let go, let loose, relinquish, surrender. **2** misunderstand.

grasping *adj. She's more than ambitious, she's grasping:* greedy, avaricious, rapacious, predatory, covetous, selfish, mercenary, venal, wolfish, hoggish.

Ant. unselfish, altruistic, generous, largehearted, public-spirited.

grate[1] *n. Let's build a fire in the grate:* fire-place, hearth, fire-box.

"Only that film, which fluttered on the grate,
Still flutters there, the sole unquiet thing."
—S. T. Coleridge

◇ *Word origin: Grate,* a lattice-like framework, comes from the Latin *cratis*, lattice.

grate[2] *v.* **1** *The car's bumper grated against the kerb:* scrape, rasp, grind, rub, scratch, abrade; screech, scream, jangle, buzz, burr, clack. **2** *Grate the cheese and sprinkle it on top:* shred, pulverize. **3** *His rudeness is beginning to grate on my nerves:* chafe, jar, gnaw at, irritate, annoy, rankle, gall, irk, vex, go against the grain.

Ant. **1** slip, slide, glide. **3** calm, soothe, pacify, quiet, settle.

grateful *adj. We were grateful for your long, informative letter:* thankful, full of gratitude, deeply appreciative, gratified; obliged, obligated, beholden, indebted.

Ant. ungrateful, unappreciative, disobliged.

gratification *n.* **1** *Collecting stamps gives him tremendous gratification:* satisfaction, pleasure, enjoyment, comfort, solace; happiness, delight, joy, relish, gladness, elation, exhilaration, glee, jubilation, thrill, kick, bliss, rapture, transport, enchantment, ecstasy. **2** *The gratification of his appetite keeps him fat:* gratifying, satisfying, indulgence, humouring, soothing, pleasing.

Ant. **1** frustration, disappointment, dissatisfaction; sorrow, sadness, gloom, pain. **2** control, discipline, curbing, restraint; denial, abnegation.

gratify *v.* **1** *Winning the tournament gratified the golf champion:* give satisfaction to, satisfy, give pleasure to, please, delight, make glad; regale, gladden, exhilarate; divert, entertain, refresh, recreate; thrill, interest, take one's fancy, amuse, tickle one's fancy, entrance, suit, transport, enrapture, enthral, enchant. **2** *Will you have some sherbet to gratify your sweet tooth?:* satisfy, indulge, humour, pamper, coddle, favour; give in to, appease, soothe, flatter, compliment.

Ant. **1** frustrate, disappoint, dissatisfy, displease, offend; sadden, pain. **2** control, discipline, curb, restrict, deny.

grating[1] *n. The entrance to the vault was blocked by a grating:* framework of bars, gate of bars, grate, grille, grid, gridiron; open latticework, trellis, lattice; tracery, fretwork, fret, filigree.

◇ *Word origin:* A *grating*, a *gridiron*, and a *grill* are similar in pattern. All are based on Latin *cratis*, meaning wickerwork or lattice.

grating[2] *adj.* **1** *The iron door made a grating sound as it closed:* rasping, scratching, raspy, creaky, squeaky, harsh, shrill, jangling, piercing, high-pitched, strident, raucous, discordant, jarring, cacophonous. **2** *His incessant chatter can be grating on the nerves:* annoying, irritating, disagreeable, unpleasant, displeasing, offensive; exasperating, vexatious, exacerbating.

Ant. **1** musical, melodic, mellifluous, soft. **2** pleasing, pleasant, agreeable; calming, soothing.

gratitude *n. How can I express my gratitude for all your help?:* gratefulness, appreciation, thankfulness, thanks, acknowledgement, recognition, obligation, beholdenness; giving thanks, thanksgiving.

Ant. ingratitude, ungratefulness, thanklessness, unthankfulness.

gratuitous *adj.* **1** *His gratuitous insults flabbergasted me:* uncalled for, unprovoked, unwarranted, unjustified, groundless, unfounded; unproven, baseless, conjectural, presumptive; wanton, irrelevant. **2** *The flood victims are greatly indebted for the gratuitous help of nearby*

towns: free, free of cost, gratis, given without charge, obtained without payment, for nothing, complimentary, unrecompensed, without compensation; voluntary, unasked for, freely bestowed, spontaneous, willing.
Ant. 1 justified, warranted, provoked; well-founded, well-grounded, proven, real, relevant. **2** paid, compensated; compulsory, involuntary.

> **Exploring the Word:** Latin *gratus,* dear, pleasing, gives us *grateful* and *gratitude,* full of favour, full of kindness for benefits received, appreciation; *gratify,* to please; *gratuitous* and *gratis,* done as a favour, free; *gratuity,* money given for a personal service, tip; *congratulate,* to express pleasure at the achievement of another; *ingrate,* one who is not grateful; and *ingratiate,* to bring oneself into another's favour; *graceful,* full of pleasing beauty or form, and *grace,* (1) pleasing beauty or form, (2) a prayer of thanksgiving before a meal, (3) the favour of God toward man, *God's grace,* or (4) the state of being pleasing to God, *a state of grace.*

grave¹ *n. The funeral procession arrived at the grave:* excavation for burial, burial-place, place of interment, last resting-place; tomb, mausoleum, vault, crypt, catacomb, cenotaph, ossuary.

grave² *adj.* **1** *His sister was happy and carefree, but he was always grave:* solemn, sedate, serious, earnest, thoughtful, subdued, quiet, dignified, sober, staid; sombre, gloomy, dour, frowning, grim-visaged, long-faced; sage, philosophical. **2** *The international situation is becoming a matter of grave concern:* serious, critical, crucial, urgent, pressing, acute, important, vital, momentous, of great consequence, consequential, significant, weighty, life-and-death.
Ant. 1 carefree, gay, joyous, happy, sunny, smiling, merry, boisterous; frivolous, facetious, flippant, flip, trifling, undignified; devil-may-care, dashing, exciting. **2** frivolous, unimportant, uncritical, inconsequential, insignificant, petty; mild.

graveyard *n. There are only a hundred tombstones in this graveyard:* cemetery, burying-ground, memorial park, churchyard, necropolis, charnel-house, ossuary; potter's field; *Slang* bone-yard.

gravitate *v.* **1** *The wet leaves gravitate to the bottom of the pool:* settle, settle down, sink, descend, fall. **2** *We naturally gravitate toward people who are kind to us:* be drawn, be attracted, have a natural tendency, have a proclivity for, be prone to, incline; lean toward, tend, move, head, point toward.

gravity *n.* **1** *An apple falls down instead of up because of gravity:* gravitation, gravitational attraction, mutual attraction of objects, pull of the earth. **2** *The surgeon announced his decision with the utmost gravity:* seriousness, solemnity, solemnness, earnestness, thoughtfulness, dignity, sobriety, sedateness, staidness, gloominess, sombreness, grimness, calmness, serenity, tranquillity. **3** *The economic situation has reached a point of extreme gravity:* seriousness, urgency, concern, critical nature, crucial nature, danger, emergency; importance, import, moment, significance, consequence, consideration, magnitude, enormity.
Ant. 1 anti-gravity; escape velocity, momentum. **2** levity, frivolousness, frivolity, facetiousness, flippancy, thoughtlessness; gaiety, merriment, glee, joy, happiness. **3** inconsequentiality, unimportance, insignificance, pettiness.

graze¹ *v. The cows grazed in the pasture:* eat grass, feed on herbage, browse, crop; turn out to pasture, pasture.
◇ *Word origin:* Graze¹ comes from the Old English *græs,* grass.

graze² *v.* **1** *The child grazed his knee on the top step:* scrape, scratch, skin, abrade, rasp, rub, grind; touch lightly, brush, skim, glance.
—*n.* **2** *Put a little ointment on that graze:* scrape, scratch, abrasion.
◇ *Word origin: Graze²,* to scrape lightly, may come from *graze¹,* to eat growing grass, since a cow's mouth appears to scrape the ground whilst eating.

grease *n.* **1** *Pour off some of the bacon grease before you fry the eggs. Put some grease on that squeaky door hinge:* fat, dripping, lard, tallow; oil, lubricant; ointment, salve, unguent, balm.
—*v.* **2** *How often do you grease your car?:* lubricate, oil, apply grease to, smear with grease, lard; anoint.

greasy *adj.* **1** *Wash this greasy plate again:* grease-covered, oily, lardaceous, buttery; slippery, slick, slithery. **2** *This bacon is too greasy:* lardy, fat, fatty, grease-filled.
Ant. 2 lean.

great *adj. Great crowds of people came to the sale:* vast, immense, enormous, huge, large, big, tremendous, gigantic, colossal, stupendous, mammoth, prodigious, voluminous, gross, monstrous, cyclopean, titanic, gargantuan; many, countless, multitudinous, abundant, unlimited, boundless, inexhaustible, manifold. **2** *He felt great happiness:* extreme, pronounced, decided, considerable, strong, high, extravagant, inordinate, prodigious. **3** *It is a great decision for one person to have to make:* important, of much consequence, consequential, significant, weighty, heavy, momentous, grave, serious, critical, crucial. **4** David Copperfield *is one of the great books of the 19th century. Bradman was a great cricketer. This concerto is great!:* outstanding, superb, remarkable, superior, superlative, magnificent, notable, prominent, distinguished, glorious, leading, famous, noted, renowned, chief, illustrious, eminent, celebrated, esteemed; fine, good, excellent, marvellous; grand, splendid, wonderful, fabulous, fantastic, terrific, sensational, smashing, choice, first-rate; *Slang* A-1, fab, super, it, out of this world, out-of-sight, way out, groovy, real cool; expert, proficient, skilful, crack, able, apt, adroit; *Informal* the bee's knees. **5** *Our minister is a great man:* fine, noble, high-minded, of lofty character, magnanimous, altruistic, humane, loving, generous, kind, gracious.

Ant. 1-4 small, little, tiny, diminutive, puny; insignificant, petty, paltry, trivial, trifling, measly, mean. **2** mild, weak, some. **3** unimportant, inconsequential, inconsiderable, insignificant, secondary, incidental. **4** poor, bad, worse, inferior, wretched, worthless, *Informal* rotten, terrible, awful, *Slang* lousy; second-rate, unnotable, undistinguished, average, inexpert, unskilled, inept. **5** mean, base, ignoble, low-minded; hateful, wicked, inhumane, unkind.

greatly *adv. His health has greatly improved:* very much, tremendously, immensely, enormously, vastly, largely, immeasurably, infinitely, mightily, powerfully, abundantly, considerably, remarkably, markedly, notably.

Ant. little, insignificantly, mildly, somewhat.

greed *n. The pirate's greed led him to cheat his partners out of their share:* greediness, money-hunger, avarice, avariciousness, covetousness, selfishness, cupidity, rapacity, rapaciousness, piggishness; itching palm.

Ant. generosity, munificence, liberality, altruism, unselfishness, benevolence.

greedy *adj.* **1** *Greedy men cannot be trusted:* money-hungry, avaricious, grasping, acquisitive, covetous, rapacious, predatory, selfish, mercenary, *Informal* hoggish. **2** *The greedy animals crowded round the feeding-trough:* ravenous, gluttonous, voracious, insatiable, famished, hungry; devouring, gormandizing; *Informal* hoggish, piggish, swinish. **3** *How refreshing to see a student who is greedy for knowledge!:* eager, avid, full of desire, keenly desirous, ardent, fervent, burning, thirsting, hungry, craving, impatient, anxious.

Ant. 1 generous, munificent, liberal, altruistic, unselfish, benevolent. **2** sated, full. **3** uncaring, apathetic, indifferent.

◇ *Word origin:* People have been *greedy* for centuries. *Greedy* comes from an Old English word *grædig,* though very similar words occur in the historical records of most Germanic lands.

green *adj.* **1** *These green walls are hideous!:* green-coloured, (*variously*) yellow-green, chartreuse, lime, lime-green, apple-green, olive, olive-green, greenish, grass-green, verdant, pea-green, forest-green, sage-green, cobalt-green, jade, emerald, sea-green, eau-de-Nil, blue-green. **2** *The apples are still too green to pick. Green wood warps easily:* unripe, immature, not fully aged, underdeveloped, undeveloped; young, tender, unfledged, crude; raw, unseasoned, not dried, not cured; untanned, unsmoked, unmellowed. **3** *The army makes men of green recruits:* inexperienced, callow, raw, untrained, rough, undisciplined, crude, awkward; unpolished, unsophisticated, unversed, immature; unskilled, inexpert, ignorant, uninformed; gullible, easily fooled, credulous.

—*n.* **4** *The village shops were built round the green:* village green, common, heath, lawn, grassy area, turf, sward, greensward, verdure; campus; putting-green, golf-course.

Ant. 2 ripe, mature, matured, aged, developed, seasoned, finished. **3** experienced, mature, sophisticated, seasoned, skilled, expert, trained.

◇ *Word origin: Green* is related to *grass* and *grow.* All three words may have been the same in Common Germanic.

greet *v.* **1** *The host greeted his guests at the door:* welcome, bid welcome, salute, hail, meet, accost; recognize, tip one's hat to, doff the cap to, speak to, smile upon. **2** *The class greeted my suggestion with boos and hisses:* meet, receive, welcome, accept.

Ant. 1 ignore, shun, give the cold shoulder to; bid farewell, wave good-bye.

greeting *n.* **1** *The greeting of all the guests took more than an hour:* welcoming, welcome, saluting, salutation, salute, reception; introduction, presentation. **2** Often **greetings** *When you see Jane, give her my greetings:* salutation, hello, regards, respects, remembrance, friendly message, felicitations, well-wishing, best, best wishes, good wishes.

gregarious *adj. A gregarious person loves parties:* sociable, social, outgoing, convivial, extroverted, companionable, friendly; vivacious, lively, talkative.

Ant. unsociable, solitary, introverted.

grey *adj.* **1** *Grey walls would set off your paintings better. His face was drawn and grey:* neutral, pearl-grey, greyish, silver, silvery, slate, dun, drab, dove-coloured, mouse-coloured; ashen, ashy, livid, pale, hoary. **2** *It's another grey winter's day:* gloomy, dismal, sombre, dark, murky, overcast, sunless, cloudy, clouded, foggy, misty. **3** *He was already grey at 30:* grey-haired, grey-headed, silver-haired, hoary-headed, grizzly; pepper-and-salt.

Ant. 2 bright, clear, sunny.

grief *n. No one could console them in their grief:* grieving, sorrow, sadness, heart-break, heartache, misery, agony, wretchedness, suffering, anguish, distress, despondency, despair, desolation; affliction, tribulation, woe.

Ant. consolation, comfort, solace; joy, happiness, bliss, cheer, delight, enjoyment, gaiety, gladness, glee, rejoicing.

grievance *n. The workers demanded a committee to*

handle grievances: complaint, *Slang* beef; injustice, wrong, disservice, hurt, iniquity, outrage, injury; *Informal* bone to pick.
Ant. benefit, privilege, boon; compliment.

> **Exploring the Word:** *Grave,* serious, solemn, "heavy," and *gravity,* seriousness, weightiness, also (since Isaac Newton) the force whereby two bodies attract each other proportionate to their mass, come from Latin *gravis,* heavy, which also gives us *aggravate,* to make heavy with care, to make more burdensome; *grieve,* to have a heavy heart, *grief* and *grievance,* that which gives one a heavy heart or is a heavy burden, something that oppresses or weighs one down, and *grievous,* heavy, burdensome, distressing.

grieve *v.* **1** *The nation grieved for its war dead:* feel grief, mourn, weep, lament, sorrow, be sad, be anguished, be heavy-hearted, rue, wail, shed tears, cry, cry one's eyes out, sob, moan, bemoan. **2** *The loss of the pet grieved the child:* sadden, make sorrowful, make unhappy, distress, agonize; pain, break the heart, make the heart bleed, wound the feelings of, cut to the quick; torture, harass, discomfort, oppress, deject, depress, disquiet, afflict.
Ant. 1, 2 console, comfort, solace, soothe, ease. **1** rejoice, delight in, enjoy, be happy about, be glad of. **2** delight, please, gratify, gladden, cheer, amuse, entertain.

grievous *adj.* **1** *The death of Martin Luther King in 1968 was a most grievous loss:* tragic, sorrowful, sad, heart-breaking, woeful, agonizing, distressing, painful, lamentable. **2** *The number of grievous crimes keeps increasing. She suffered a grievous injury:* very bad, grave, severe, serious, heavy, harsh, acute, critical, crucial, significant; appalling, atrocious, heinous, iniquitous, shocking, outrageous, monstrous, nefarious, shameful, deplorable, glaring; intolerable, insufferable, unbearable, harmful, distressing, lamentable, burdensome, destructive, calamitous.
Ant. 1 delightful, pleasant, pleasing, welcome, joyous, happy, glad; laughable, amusing, entertaining. **2** trivial, trifling, facetious, frivolous, unimportant, inconsequential, insignificant, mild, light.
◇ *Pronunciation tip:* The proper pronunciation of *grievous* has only two syllables. It should be pronounced *GREE-vus,* not "GREE-vee-us."

grill *n.* **1** *Cook the sausages under the grill:* griddle, gridiron, grid, grating, crossbars; broiler.
—*v.* **2** *Let's grill the steaks over charcoal:* broil, cook. **3** *Informal The police grilled the suspect about the missing jewels:* interrogate, question, pump, give third degree; cross-examine.
◇ *Word origin: Grills, gratings* and *gridirons* have rectangular patterns and come from the Latin *cratis,* wickerwork, lattice.

grim *adj.* **1** *The boss has looked grim all morning:* sombre, gloomy, austere; sullen, grumpy, sulky, scowling, morose, cantankerous; stern, severe, harsh, fierce, ferocious, unyielding, unrelenting, relentless, merciless, cruel, brutal, heartless, vicious, inhuman, fiendish; obstinate, implacable, determined, resolute, inexorable. **2** *The subject is much too grim to make jokes about:* horrible, ghastly, sinister, grisly, frightful, horrid, hideous, gruesome, macabre, lurid, dreadful; repellent, repulsive, repugnant, forbidding, loathsome, appalling, foul, odious, revolting, shocking, squalid, ugly.
Ant. 1 happy, cheerful, joyful, gay, merry; lenient, benign, merciful, sympathetic, soft, easy, kind, kindly, amiable, amenable, congenial, genial. **2** pleasant, pleasing; attractive.

grimace *n.* **1** *She made a grimace when I mentioned his name:* face, wry face, ugly expression of distaste, contemptuous face, sneer.
—*v.* **2** *The boy grimaced when his father said he couldn't borrow the car:* make a face, scowl, glower, lower.
◇ *Pronunciation tip:* Most people pronounce *grimace* as *GRIM-us,* stressing the first syllable. However, *gri-MACE* is equally acceptable, and is in fact the older standard pronunciation.

grime *n. It takes strong soap to wash the grime out of clothes:* oily grit, dirt, soil, soot, smut, filth, smudge.

grind *v.* **1** *Most of the wheat will be ground into flour:* pulverize, powder, granulate, mill. **2** *It is possible to grind knives by scraping them on a step:* sharpen, whet, file, rasp; polish, abrade. **3** *The child grinds his teeth in his sleep:* grate, rasp, gnash, grit.
—*n.* **4** *Informal: Writing this report every month is a real grind:* chore, drudgery, dull task, laborious work, hard job.
Ant. 2 dull, take the edge off. **4** easy job, enjoyable task, pleasure, joy, *Slang* piece of cake.

> "Though the mills of God grind slowly, yet they grind exceeding small."
> —*H. W. Longfellow*

grip *n.* **1** *The carpenter held the hammer securely in his grip:* grasp, clutch, clasp, hold. **2** *He shook my hand with an iron grip:* hand-clasp, handshake; gripping power. **3** *The woman was in the grip of a strong emotion. A navigator must have a good grip of mathematics:* grasp, control, hold, retention, clutches, mastery, domination; understanding, comprehension, perception. **4** *The sword has a golden grip:* handle, hilt. **5** *Grandmother travelled with a trunk and two grips:* valise, suitcase, bag, travelling-bag, satchel, Gladstone.
—*v.* **6** *He gripped the hammer and started nailing*

the wood together: grasp, seize firmly, clutch, clench, hold fast, hold tight; seize hold of, catch hold of, seize, grab, snatch. **7** *The reporter's account of the trial gripped the readers' interest:* hold, retain, take hold on, spellbind, rivet, attract, impress.

◇ *Word origin: Grip,* like *grapple,* comes from the Old French *grapin,* hook.

gripe *n.* **1** Often **gripes**. *Green apples gave him the gripes:* stomach-ache, belly-ache, colic, cramps, spasm; affliction, distress, twinge, pang, pain, twitch. **2** *The foreman wouldn't listen to the workers' gripes:* grievance, protest, complaint, faultfinding, whining, grousing, grumbling; *Slang* beef, squawk.
—*v.* **3** *The waitress griped about the small tip:* complain, grumble, mutter, whine, find fault, grouse, grouch, fret, cavil, carp, rail, protest, *Slang* beef, squawk, bellyache, *Yiddish* kvetch.

Ant. 2 complaint, flattery. **3** thank, express appreciation; compliment on.

grisly *adj. It was the most grisly crime the town had ever known:* gruesome, horrible, horrid, horrendous, hideous, ghastly, macabre, lurid, frightful, dreadful, shocking, gory, abominable, grim; abhorrent, repugnant, repellent, revolting, repulsive, loathsome, foul, odious, appalling.

Ant. pleasant, pleasing, innocuous, attractive, charming, nice.

◇ *Usage note:* Don't confuse *grisly,* "gruesome, causing horror," with *gristly,* "full of gristle," the cartilage of meat. Thus, *The guillotine is a grisly instrument. This meat is gristly.* Remember that *gristle* and the meat it may be in both have *t's.* Another word that may be confusing is *grizzly,* with two *z's,* meaning grey or streaked with grey: *a grizzly beard, a grizzly bear.*

◇ *Pronunciation tip: Grisly* and *grizzly* are pronounced exactly alike, *GRIZ-lee. Gristly* is pronounced *GRIS-lee.*

grit *n.* **1** *Wipe the grit off the windscreen:* soot, dirt, dust, filth, muck. **2** *It took a lot of grit to cross the plains in a covered wagon:* spunk, pluck, fortitude, courage, nerve, guts, mettle, backbone; determination, tenacity, doggedness, perseverance, resolution, indomitable spirit, stamina.
—*v.* **3** *The patient gritted his teeth in pain:* grind together, rub, grate, scrape, rasp, gnash.

Ant. 2 faint-heartedness, cowardice, timidity; faltering, wavering, hesitation, vacillation.

groan *v.* **1** *The patient groaned as he was lifted onto the stretcher. The class groaned when the teacher set the homework:* moan, whimper; grumble, murmur, wail, lament; roar, howl, bellow, bleat; bemoan. **2** *The old gate groaned on its hinges:* creak, resound harshly; squeak, screech.
—*n.* **3** *With a groan the boxer realized he had lost:* moan, whimper, sorrowful murmur, wail. **4** *We could hear the groan of the roof under the weight of the snow:* moan, creak, crack, squeak.

groom *n.* **1** *The groom led the horse to the barn:* stable-boy, ostler; footman. **2** *The groom waited at the altar for the bride:* bridegroom; newly married man, husband.
—*v.* **3** *The jockey groomed his horse with loving care:* curry, curry-comb, brush, comb, rub down. **4** *The girl spent hours grooming herself before the party:* clean up, wash, make tidy, make neat, spruce up, primp, preen, comb, freshen, refresh; dress. **5** *The prince is being groomed for other duties:* prepare, prime, make ready; train, educate, indoctrinate, familiarize with; initiate, drill, exercise, practise.

groove *n.* **1** *The groove on the school desk is for pens and pencils:* rut, furrow, gutter, channel, trench, flute, hollow; cut, cutting, scoring, score, corrugation. **2** *A holiday is a good time to get out of one's groove and do something different:* rut, habit, fixed routine, set way of doing things, beaten path, matter of course; convention, second nature, usage, procedure, rule, practice, custom, use.

Ant. 1 ridge, bump.

◇ *Word origin: Groove,* furrow, is related to *grave,* excavation for a burial.

grope *v.* **1** *I groped for the light switch in the dark room:* feel about, fumble, probe; fish for, paw, move blindly, feel one's way, move stumblingly. **2** *He groped for the right answer to the problem:* search blindly, fumble, probe; venture, try one's luck, see how the land lies, send up a trial balloon, put out a feeler.

gross *adj.* **1** *The firm's gross profit was over a million pounds last year:* total, whole, entire, aggregate; total before deductions, before expenses, before taxes. **2** *The accident was caused by gross negligence:* flagrant, downright, sheer, utter, complete, total, plain, glaring, obvious, manifest; rank, outrageous, unmitigated, unqualified, unequivocal. **3** *His gross remarks made us cringe:* coarse, crude, unrefined, vulgar, indelicate, improper, offensive, unseemly; lewd, lascivious, lecherous, carnal, smutty, foul-mouthed, earthy, ribald, indecent, obscene, licentious, sordid. **4** *The man was so gross he could hardly get through the door:* fat, obese, overweight, heavy; big, large, bulky, unwieldy, huge, great, vast, immense, enormous, monstrous, gigantic, massive, stupendous, colossal, prodigious, titanic, gargantuan.
—*n.* **5** We buy our pencils by the gross: twelve dozen; large quantity, dozens.
—*v.* **6** *A popular film can gross 5 million pounds:* earn, take in, make a gross profit of, pick up, reap; *Slang,* bag, bring in.

Ant. 1 net; total after deductions, total after expenses. **2** partial, mitigated, qualified. **3** delicate, dainty; refined, cultivated, elegant; decent, proper, inoffensive, chaste. **4** thin, slim, svelte; small, little, tiny, petite. **6** net, clear.

grotesque *adj.* **1** *These grotesque statues are relics of prehistoric times:* distorted, deformed, oddly shaped, misshapen, unnatural, fantastic, weird, bizarre, fanciful, strange, outlandish, peculiar, eccentric, incongruous; wild, extravagant, exotic, rococo, baroque. **2** *She never appreciated his grotesque humour:* outlandish, absurd, odd, distorted, fantastic, antic, wild, extravagant, weird, bizarre, preposterous; *Slang* far-out, way-out.

Ant. 1 well-proportioned, graceful, classic; realistic, natural, naturalistic; familiar. **2** routine, average, standard, normal, typical, unimaginative; down-to-earth.

◇ *Word origin:* The Italian *grotto,* a cave used as a shrine, gives us our word *grotesque,* which originally referred to the fantastic statues and other decorative forms found in such caves. Thus *grotesque* literally means "like the things one sees in a grotto".

grotto *n. The poet had constructed for himself a pleasant grotto in which he could pass long afternoons:* cavelike shrine, grot; catacomb; cavern, cave, recess, hollow.

grouch *n.* **1** *Why did you have to be a grouch and spoil the party?:* complainer, grumbler, sulky person, pouter, ill-humoured person, sullen person, moper, *Slang* wet blanket, killjoy, spoil-sport.

—*v.* **2** *It doesn't do any good to grouch about the bad weather:* complain, find fault, gripe, grumble, mutter, whine, cry, grouse, cavil, carp, rail, protest; *Slang* beef, belly-ache; sulk, fret, pout, mope.

Ant. 1 charmer, flatterer, Prince Charming; life and soul of the party. **2** compliment, flatter.

"Though more than half the world was his,
He died without a rood his own;
And borrowed from his enemies
Six foot of ground to lie upon."
—*W. M. Thackeray of Napoleon Bonaparte*

---

ground *n.* **1** *After that bumpy flight it's good to be back on the ground:* the earth, firm land, terra firma; dry land. **2** *The ground must be ploughed in early spring:* earth, soil, dirt, sod, turf, loam. **3** Sometimes **grounds** *Houses should be built on high ground. Now that you've seen the house, I'll show you the grounds:* tract of land, land, terrain; region, habitat, area, territory, realm, province, district, domain, sphere; property, real estate, estate, lawns, gardens; campus; farm, field, acres. **4** Usually **grounds** *What grounds have you for dismissing him?:* basis, cause, reason, motive, excuse; purpose, rationale, object, account, principle, occasion, considerations, arguments, inducement, call; reason why, pros and cons, the whys and wherefores. **5 grounds** *Put the coffee grounds in the bin:* sediment, dregs; settlings, deposit.

—*v.* **6** *A storm grounded the ship on a sand-bar:* run aground, beach, strand, founder. **7** *Your accusation must be grounded on facts:* base, establish, fix firmly, support, settle, found, set, secure, confirm, organize, institute. **8** *All applicants must be well grounded in mathematics:* instruct, train, teach, familiarize with, educate, indoctrinate, inform, initiate; drill, exercise, practise, discipline, prepare.

Ant. 1 the air, the sky; the sea, the ocean, water. **6** float; launch.

groundless *adj. The accusation is groundless and can't be backed up by facts:* without basis, baseless, unjustified, unjustifiable, unwarranted, unfounded, unsupported, without reason, without cause, without foundation, uncalled for, needless, idle, gratuitous, illogical, not following, imaginary, chimerical, unreal, flimsy, empty; unproved, false, fallacious, faulty, erroneous, untrue.

Ant. well-founded, reasonable, justified, logical, true, proven, provable, supported, real, substantial.

groundwork *n.* **1** *The framers of Magna Carta laid the groundwork on which our freedom is based. Constant practice is the groundwork for success in playing the piano:* foundation, basis, base, ground, grounds, underpinning, bedrock, corner-stone, root, tap-root, spring, cradle, origin, source; first principles, fundamental, fundamentals. **2** *It will take a lot of groundwork before we can start a new business:* preparation, planning, preliminary steps; apprenticeship, learning, training, practice, indoctrination.

group *n.* **1** *A group of students asked to see the principal:* assemblage, aggregation, gathering, collection, congregation; crowd, band, throng, party, company, cluster, bunch, pack, gang, troop, detachment; horde, swarm, herd, flock. **2** *Children and the elderly are two groups who watch TV regularly:* class, classification, variety, species, branch, division, subdivision, section; set, faction, clique, circle, coterie, association, league, brotherhood, fraternity; family, tribe, clan.

—*v.* **3** *Group the children together according to age:* sort, organize, range, marshal, line up, align, arrange, combine, cluster, co-ordinate, classify, class, assign, sift, catalogue, place, file, register, alphabetize, index, size; grade, graduate. **4** *At every party the same people group together:* associate, fraternize, mingle, cluster, marshal, hob-nob, keep company, consort.

Ant. 1, 2 individual. **3** separate, disperse, scatter.

grove *n.* **1** *We had our picnic in a quiet grove:* thicket, copse, coppice, woodland, cluster of trees, small wood, spinney, brake; shrubbery, pinery; forest. **2** *The house looks out over an orange grove:* cluster of trees, plantation.

grovel *v. I hate to see a man grovel before his superiors:* humble oneself, demean oneself, be servile, behave abjectly, cower, cringe; fawn,

toady, crawl, kowtow, stoop, snivel, truckle, lick the boots of, bow and scrape.
Ant. be proud, be haughty, hold one's head high; domineer, intimidate, browbeat.
◇ *Word origin:* To *grovel*, to lie down or crawl before one's superiors, is from the Middle English phrase *on gruff*, face down, on all fours.

grow *v.* **1** *My goodness, how that child has grown!:* become larger, grow taller, spring up, shoot up, fill out; expand, increase, swell, widen, stretch, spread, extend; magnify, amplify, aggrandize. **2** *Orange trees won't grow in this climate:* develop, mature, come to fruition, ripen; germinate, vegetate, sprout, bud, fructify, blossom, flower, bloom. **3** *This looks like good soil for growing wheat:* cultivate, raise, produce, propagate, breed; sow, plant, till, farm, garden. **4** *The report shows how our business has grown this year:* thrive, flourish, progress, develop, prosper, succeed, advance, improve, enlarge, increase, expand, rise, surge, wax, boom, mushroom, rocket. **5** *The patient grew weaker every day:* become, get, come to be. **6** *Playing with the orchestra helped him to grow as a musician:* mature, develop; obtain experience, get practice, have training; become worldly, become sophisticated.
Ant. 1, 4 shrink, decrease, diminish, lessen, dwindle. **2** die, fail, decline, decay. **4** decline, slacken, subside, wane.

growl *v.* **1** *The dog growled when the stranger came close:* snarl, bark menacingly. **2** *The boss won't growl at you for asking for a rise:* snap, speak harshly, reply gruffly, complain, grumble, grouse, gripe, fret; mutter, murmur, groan, grunt, whine, croak.

growth *n.* **1** *It's fascinating to watch the growth of a child. Has that cherry tree reached its full growth?:* natural development, development; advancement, advance, progress, improvement; maturity, matureness, prime. **2** *The growth of our business has been phenomenal. The city's growth must not be encouraged:* expansion, increase, development, extension, increment, enlargement, encroachment, surge, spread, swell, amplification, augmentation, urban sprawl; progress, improvement, advancement, advance, prospering, flourishing, rise, success. **3** *Is all this wheat just one season's growth?:* crop, production, cultivation, produce, flowering, planting, sowing, propagation. **4** *The doctor removed a small growth from the patient's chin:* mass of tissue, lump, polyp, cyst, hump, tumour; excrescence.
Ant. 2 decrease, decline, lessening, dwindling, shrinking, shrinkage, slackening, subsiding, retreat, backsliding, failure; stagnation.

grudge *n.* **1** *Do you still bear him a grudge for cheating you?:* ill will, resentment, hard feelings, malice, spite, malevolence, rancour, pique, aversion, dislike, animosity, animus. —*v.* **2** *I don't grudge her her good fortune, but she should share it with others:* begrudge, envy, resent, be provoked at, be indignant at, cast a jaundiced eye at.
Ant. 1 appreciation, thankfulness, goodwill, friendliness, liking. **2** celebrate, be pleased for.

gruelling *adj. Working down a mine is a gruelling job:* tiring, exhausting, fatiguing; hard, punishing, racking, torturous, brutal.
Ant. easy, soft, *Slang* cushy; enjoyable, pleasant; exhilarating, exciting.

gruesome *adj. The gruesome story of graves and ghosts frightened the child:* horrible, horrifying, hideous, horrid, horrendous, grisly, gory, ghastly, frightful, spine-chilling, bloodcurdling; revolting, repulsive, repellent; grim, forbidding, shocking, fearful, terrible, macabre.
Ant. pleasing, pleasant, cheery, cheerful, appealing, benign, sweet, sentimental.
◇ *Word origin: Gruesome* is based on the Scottish word *grue*, to shudder.

gruff *adj.* **1** *The sergeant always gave a gruff answer to the soldiers' questions:* surly, brusque, curt, blunt, short, abrupt, stern, bluff; uncivil, rude, impolite, discourteous, ungracious, insulting; snarling, grumpy, grouchy, bearish, sour, crabbed, churlish; caustic, tart, sharp, waspish, ill-humoured, ill-natured, ill-tempered, sulky, sullen, peevish, bristling, crusty. **2** *A slight cold had given the speaker a gruff voice:* hoarse, husky, rough, harsh, throaty, rasping, guttural; cracked, croaking, ragged, raucous.
Ant. 1 pleasant, kind, sweet, good-humoured; courteous, polite, civil, gracious. **2** smooth, mellifluous, rich.
◇ *Word origin: Gruff* comes from Dutch *grof*, rough, coarse, rude.

grumble *v.* **1** *The handyman wouldn't do anything without grumbling:* grouse, fret, murmur discontentedly, mutter, complain, gripe, growl, chafe, find fault. **2** *My stomach begins to grumble around lunch-time:* rumble, whine, gurgle, croak, *Informal* talk back.

grumpy *adj. Many people are grumpy when they first wake up:* surly, ill-tempered, grouchy, sullen, sulky, irritable, disgruntled, ill-humoured, cantankerous, peevish, pettish, out of sorts, testy, out of humour, in a bad temper, in a bad mood, sour; churlish, ill-disposed, moody, splenetic, crusty.
Ant. in a good mood, in good humour, pleasant, sweet, kindly disposed.

guarantee *n.* **1** *The new car has a one-year guarantee:* warranty, written promise of quality, written assurance of durability; surety, endorsement, guaranty, affirmation, pledge, assurance, avowal, word, word of honour, security, testimony; bond, bail. **2** *Beauty is no guarantee of happiness:* assurance, promise.

—*v.* 3 *The manufacturer guaranteed the new furnace for five years:* give a guarantee on, warrant, vouch for; assure, endorse, insure, underwrite, sponsor; avow, testify. 4 *The travel brochure guarantees that you'll have the time of your life. Buying a train ticket doesn't guarantee you a seat:* promise, pledge, give one's word, vouch for, assure, affirm, allege, avow, attest, swear, stand behind; be responsible for, make oneself answerable for, make certain, answer for, become surety for, bind oneself, contract.

guaranty *n.* 1 *Howard gave his guaranty that I would repay the loan:* warrant, warranty, pledge, guarantee, formal assurance, security, surety, insurance, endorsement, covenant, promise; contract, agreement, voucher. 2 *The bank can't give the loan without some kind of guaranty:* collateral, security, pledge; bail, bond; deposit.

◇ *Usage note:* The nouns *guaranty* and *guarantee* may be used correctly as synonyms of each other. However, it is more precise to use *guaranty* in referring to assurance for the repayment of a loan or to the collateral for such a loan.

guard *v.* 1 *Three soldiers guarded the prince whenever he left the palace. Wear a hat to guard your face against the sun:* protect, safeguard, shield, shelter, defend; watch over, keep safe, preserve, secure; save; attend, tend, mind, escort, conduct, convoy. 2 *Policemen guarded the prisoner throughout the trial:* keep under surveillance, keep watch over, keep under close watch, keep from escaping.

—*n.* 3 *The guard won't let anyone through the gate without a pass:* sentinel, sentry, watchman, watch-dog; body of defenders, garrison, patrol, picket, watch, convoy, escort; protector, bodyguard, defender; guardian, custodian, gatekeeper, door-keeper, concierge. 4 *All hockey players should wear shin-guards:* shield, screen, safe-guard; defence, protection, security, preservation.

Ant. 1 expose to danger, endanger, threaten; menace, imperil.

◇ *Word origin: Guard* comes from Old French *garder* and is related to Old English *weardian*, to guard.

> "The virtue which requires to be ever guarded is scarcely worth the sentinel."
>
> —*Oliver Goldsmith*

guardian *n.* 1 *The Church is the guardian of the faith:* protector, preserver, keeper, custodian, defender, guard, trustee, shepherd, curator, conservator, watch-dog, vigilante, warder; guard, escort, bodyguard, sentry, picket, sentinel, patrol, convoy, champion, safeguard, attendant, conductor. 2 *Children may go on the trip only with the consent of their parents or guardians:* legal custodian, protector, patron, benefactor; guardian angel, champion, advocate, friend at court.

Ant. 1 enemy, foe, opponent, attacker; traitor. 2 ward, protégé.

guess *v.* 1 *You win a prize if he doesn't guess your weight correctly:* judge correctly, estimate correctly, correctly answer, answer with the facts; divine, work out; speculate, conjecture, risk an opinion on, hazard a supposition, hypothesize, make a stab at.

—*n.* 2 *My guess is that the job will take four hours:* estimate, supposition, assumption, speculation, opinion, belief, view, hypothesis, conjecture, presumption, surmise, prediction, suspicion, feeling, divination, theory, guesswork, postulation, postulate.

Ant. 1 know, prove. 2 certainty, fact.

guest *n.* 1 *How many guests are coming to dinner?:* invitee, visitor, caller, friend; company. 2 *The motel can accommodate 400 guests:* (*variously*) boarder, lodger, sojourner, diner; patron, customer, paying customer, tenant, habitué, frequenter; patient, inmate.

Ant. 1 host, hostess.

◇ *Word origin: Guest* can be traced back to Old Norse *gestr*, stranger, and is related to Latin *hostis*, originally "stranger." *Hostis* came to mean "army" in later Latin and came into English in the Biblical phrases *Lord of hosts* and *hosts of heaven.* (Our word *host* for one who lodges or entertains another comes from Latin *hospes*, which meant "guest," "host," and "stranger.")

guffaw *n. He let out a guffaw when I finished telling the joke:* burst of laughter, peal of laughter, hearty laugh, boisterous laugh, roar of mirth, howl, scream, shout of merriment; *Slang* horse-laugh, belly-laugh.

◇ *Word origin: Guffaw*, like *buzz* and *hiss*, originated as an imitation of the sound it represents.

guidance *n.* 1 *The young man sought guidance in the choice of a career:* counsel, advice, help; information, instruction, intelligence, enlightenment, pointer, tip, clue, hint. 2 *Funds will be spent under the committee's guidance:* direction, leadership, management, conduct, auspices; escort, protection, lead.

guide *v.* 1 *The hunters need someone to guide them through the jungle:* lead, pilot, steer, show the way to, direct, conduct; escort, usher, accompany, convoy, shepherd. 2 *Can the pilot guide the plane to a safe landing? My father guided this business to success:* manœuvre, manipulate, manage, handle, direct, conduct, control, command, engineer, steer, lead, pilot, regulate; rule, govern, preside over, oversee, superintend, have charge of.

—*n.* 3 *Their guide through the mountains was a young Indian:* pilot, escort, convoy; conductor, leader, helmsman, steerer, director, usher; marshal, shepherd, attendant, chaperon. 4 *Let your conscience be your guide. That old tree is a*

guide to where the gold lies hidden: counsellor, adviser, monitor, mentor, teacher, master; model, example, rule, pattern; landmark, signpost, marker, beacon, guiding light, pole-star, lodestar.
Ant. 1 misguide, mislead. **3** follower. **4** disciple, imitator, pupil.

guild *n. The musicians formed a guild to present concerts:* professional organization, association, society, league, fraternity, alliance, company, corporation, incorporated society, federation, confederacy, order, coalition; union, trade union.

guile *n. He's full of guile, so take care he doesn't cheat you:* slyness, trickery, trickiness, cunning, craft, craftiness, artifice, chicanery, wiliness, artfulness, strategy, sharp practice; deceit, treachery, duplicity, fraud, deception, dishonesty, *Slang* hanky-panky; tricks, stratagems.
Ant. candour, frankness, honesty, sincerity, veracity, truthfulness.

guileless *adj. The child gave a guileless answer to the question:* straightforward, candid, frank, open, honest, sincere, truthful, above-board; artless, undesigning; ingenuous, naïve, unsophisticated, innocent, simple, unaffected, unselfconscious; harmless, innocuous, unoffending.
Ant. sly, cunning, deceitful, crafty, tricky, deceptive, artful; treacherous, fraudulent.

guilt *n.* **1** *The prosecuting lawyer tried to establish the suspect's guilt:* guiltiness, guilty conduct, criminality, culpability; wrongdoing, misconduct, misdoing, misdeed, misbehaviour, wrong, turpitude, transgression; sinfulness, sin, vice; trespass, delinquency, dereliction. **2** *Nothing could erase the guilt from his conscience:* guilty feeling, shame, disgrace, self-disgust, humiliation, degradation, dishonour, infamy; stigma, blot, black mark.
Ant. 1 innocence, blamelessness, righteousness, sinlessness, good deed, virtue. **2** pride, honour, self-respect.

guilty *adj.* **1** *The jury found the defendant guilty:* justly charged, having committed a crime, culpable, blameable, blameworthy, responsible for a wrongdoing. **2** *The thief sought forgiveness for his guilty acts:* criminal; immoral, sinful, wrong, corrupt, erring, offensive. **3** *His guilty look gave him away:* sheepish, hangdog; contrite, sorry, regretful, ashamed, conscience-stricken.
Ant. 1-3 innocent. **1** blameless. **2** moral, righteous, virtuous. **3** proud, noble.

guise *n. The king travelled throughout the land in the guise of a monk:* dress, attire, costume, habit, clothing, clothes, garb, fashion; disguise, pretence, appearance, semblance, masquerade.

gulf *n.* **1** *A hurricane is forming in the Gulf of Mexico:* large bay, estuary, arm of the sea, firth, fiord, inlet, cove. **2** *The earthquake left a gulf in the fields. The gulf between the two friends widened:* chasm, abyss, crevasse, canyon, gully, opening, rent, cleft; rift, split, separation.
◇ *Word origin: Gulf* goes back to Greek *kolpos*, bay. Today a gulf and a bay are still the same thing, an area of an ocean or a sea partially enclosed by land, but we call the biggest bays *gulfs*.

gullible *adj. The youth was so gullible he parted with all his money to a total stranger:* easily fooled, easily deceived, easily cheated, easily duped; over-trusting, unsuspicious, credulous, trusting, trustful; naïve, innocent, unsophisticated, inexperienced, green, simple.
Ant. cynical, suspicious, untrusting, hard to convince; sophisticated, worldly.

gully *n.* **1** *When snow melts in the mountains the gully is flooded:* ravine, gap, small valley, dell, combe, defile, gorge, small canyon. **2** *The road was constructed with a gully on each side:* ditch, drainage ditch, gutter; furrow, trench.

gulp *v.* **1** *I was so thirsty I gulped three glasses of water. The boy gulped down his lunch and ran out to play:* swallow in large mouthfuls, swallow eagerly, swallow greedily, swill, guzzle, swig, quaff, toss off; bolt, devour.
—*n.* **2** *There's just one gulp of milk left in the glass:* mouthful, swallow, swig, large draught.
Ant. 1 sip, drink daintily; nibble, eat daintily.
◇ *Word origin: Gulp*, like *buzz, guffaw*, and *hiss*, is of imitative origin, i.e. it imitates the sound it represents.

gun *n.* **1** *The hijacker was arrested for the illegal possession of a gun:* firearm, small arms; (*variously*) revolver, pistol, automatic, twelve-bore, .22, six-shooter, Colt, rifle, shot-gun, carbine, Winchester, musket, fowling piece, muzzle-loader, blunderbuss, flintlock, petronel, machine-gun; *Slang* gat, shooting-iron, piece, equalizer. **2** *The anti-tank guns were wheeled into place:* cannon, field piece, artillery piece, big gun, ordnance; (*variously*) mortar, howitzer, Big Bertha, Long Tom.
—*v.* **3** *Keep hidden, because they'll be gunning for you:* hunt, go after, shoot, expect to shoot; try, attempt, aim.
◇ *Word origin:* When large cannon are given such personal names as Big Bertha (during World War I) or Long Tom (during World War II), word history is repeating itself. The word *gun* itself is taken from the Old Norse nickname for a big catapult, *Gunnhildr* (a Scandinavian feminine name). The oldest known mention of *Gunnhildr* occurs in the Exchequer Accounts of 1330–31 in which "a large catapult named *Dame Gunilda*" is listed.

gurgle *v.* **1** *The cider gurgled from the jug into the glass:* flow noisily, bubble, burble, babble, plash, sputter, ripple.
—*n.* **2** *We listened to the soothing gurgle of the brook:* gurgling, bubbling, babble, burble.

◇ *Word origin: Gurgle* is a variant of *gargle,* which came from Latin *gurgulio,* gullet.

gush *v.* **1** *Oil gushed from the well:* flow forth, pour out, spurt, spout, stream, jet, well, burst forth, rush forth, issue, run, splash, squirt. **2** *She gushed so much I didn't get a word in edgeways:* talk effusively, be over-enthusiastic, chatter, babble, burble, gab, prattle, blather, blabber, prate, rattle on, run on, jabber, flatter excessively.
—*n.* **3** *A gush of water came out when the pump started:* sudden outflow, outpouring, spurt, torrent, stream, jet, spout, squirt, splash, rush, outburst. **4** *Do we have to listen to that gush about your school-days?:* foolish talk, boring talk, mawkishness, sentimentalism, emotionalism; nonsense, stuff and nonsense, twaddle, blabber, drivel, rubbish, chatter, blab; *Slang* hot air, gas, baloney, bull, tripe.
Ant. 1 drip, trickle, dribble, ooze. **2** be close-mouthed, be uncommunicative. **3** drip, trickle.

gust *n.* **1** *A gust of wind scattered the leaves:* puff, blast, breeze, wind; zephyr, squall, flurry, blow. **2** *A loud gust of laughter came from the next room:* burst, outburst, outbreak, sudden rush, explosion, paroxysm, fit.
—*v.* **3** *When the wind gusts this way it's no good for sailing:* blow in bursts, blow intermittently, puff, blast.

gusto *n. The hungry man ate with gusto:* hearty enjoyment, relish, zest, enthusiasm, fervour, zeal, delight, pleasure, appreciation, savour, satisfaction, appetite; personal liking, individual taste.
◇ *Word origin: Gusto* comes from Latin *gustus,* taste, and is related to the French word *goût* (as in the cliché *Chacun à son goût,* "Everyone to his taste"). Important Germanic cognates of these are our words *choice* and *choose.*

gut *v.* **1** *The pheasants must be gutted before they're cooked:* eviscerate, clean, disembowel. **2** *Fire gutted several houses in the road:* destroy the interior of; lay in ashes, level, ravage, raze, consume, lay waste, lay in ruins.
—*n.* **3** *Sheep gut is used to make violin strings:* intestines, entrails, viscera; lower alimentary canal, bowels. **4** *Slang You're getting a big gut from overeating:* stomach, abdomen; paunch, belly; bay window, beer belly, spare tyre. **5** **guts** *Slang It really took guts to face up to that bully:* courage, bravery, boldness, mettle, spunk; daring, spirit, nerve, audacity, dash, bravado.

guttural *adj. The actress was known for her guttural voice:* throaty, husky, deep, low; hoarse, harsh, gruff; thick, inarticulate.
Ant. nasal, high-pitched, high, squeaky.
◇ *Word origin: Guttural* comes from Latin *guttur,* throat.

guzzle *v. Don't guzzle your tea!:* drink greedily, gulp down; swill down, swig, toss off, quaff, tipple; eat greedily, bolt, devour.
Ant. sip, drink daintily; nibble, eat daintily.
◇ *Word origin: Guzzle* comes via Old French *gosier,* from Latin *guttur,* throat, which also gives us *guttural.*

gyrate *v. The figure-skater gyrated faster and faster:* spin round, rotate, revolve, circle, twirl, whirl, turn round, wheel, spiral, swirl, pirouette.
◇ *Word origin: Gyrate* comes from Greek *guros,* circle, which also gives us *gyroscope.*

H

habit *n.* **1** *Moles have the habit of burrowing in the earth. Where did the habit of shaking hands originate?:* practice, behaviour pattern, custom, convention, matter of course, routine, beaten path, rut, groove; characteristic tendency, trait, proclivity, peculiarity, inclination, wont, second nature; rule, observance, manner, mannerism. **2** *George has an awful habit of picking his teeth:* way, practice, acquired mode of behaviour, habitual action, fixed practice, confirmed way; leaning, inclination, predisposition, predilection, partiality, fondness, propensity, prevailing tendency. **3** *Each order of nuns wears its own special habit:* dress, attire, costume, garment, garb, apparel, raiment, clothes, clothing, outfit, uniform, robe, vesture, livery; gear, trappings, accoutrements, habiliments.
◇ *Usage note: Habit, custom,* and *fashion* all refer to a way of behaving or doing that has become usual. *Habit* usually is used to refer to one person's behaviour: *Jim has the bad habit of biting his fingernails. Custom* is used especially to refer to rules of conduct followed by a group: *In Spain, the custom is to eat the main meal at midday. Fashion* is used to refer to invented styles that may change more frequently than customs: *The current fashion is to eat steak rare rather than well done.*
◇ *Word origin: Habit* comes from Latin *habitus,* meaning both "condition" and "dress", since in ancient times one's dress usually represented one's condition or position in life.

habitat *n.* **1** *The Western plains of North America were the habitat of the bison:* natural home, natural locality, native environment, area of distribution; terrain, territory, range, domain, realm, milieu, environment, haunt, place, spot, locale, setting, region, zone, precinct; *Slang* stamping ground. **2** *The hermit's habitat was a crude cabin:* dwelling, dwelling-place, place of abode, abode, domicile, habitation; home, housing, lodging, lodgement, quarters; *Slang* digs, roost, pad.

"Habit converts luxurious enjoyments into dull and daily necessities." —*Aldous Huxley*

---

habitation *n.* **1** *These tenements are not fit for habitation:* occupancy, tenancy, occupation, dwelling, lodging, lodgement, residence; abode, temporary stay. **2** *Their mountain habitation is far from the city's noise:* abode, place of residence, dwelling, dwelling-place, home, habitat, place of abode, domicile, haunt, residence, house; housing, lodging, shelter, quarters; *Slang* digs, roost, pad. **3** *The pioneers built a habitation near the mouth of the river:* settlement, community, colony.

habitual *adj.* **1** *Singing in the bath is habitual with him. Grandfather sat in his habitual place near the fire:* customary, usual, accustomed, regular, normal, natural, common, fixed, established, traditional, typical, wonted, familiar, expected, conventional; routine, recurrent, inveterate, confirmed; continual, incessant; by force of habit, second nature. **2** *Harold has become an habitual borrower:* chronic, confirmed, inveterate, constant, addicted, continual, frequent, repeated, periodic, recurrent, established, ingrained, deep-seated, deep-rooted, perpetual, systematic, methodical.

Ant. 1 rare, uncommon, unusual, exceptional, abnormal, extraordinary, strange, unexpected, occasional. **2** infrequent, sporadic, irregular, unconfirmed.

habituate *v. Working on the farm habituated him to rising early:* accustom, make used to, indoctrinate, inculcate; break in, inure, harden, instil, imbue, adapt, discipline, initiate, season, train, school, drill.

habitué *n. Mildred is an habitué of the city's museums:* frequenter, regular patron, frequent visitor, constant customer; *Informal* regular.

◇ *Pronunciation tip:* One hears *habitué* pronounced both as *ha-bit-you-AY* and *ha-BIT-you-ay. Ha-BIT-you-ay* is the preferred pronunciation.

hack[1] *v.* **1** *He hacked at the logs with his hatchet. Carve the turkey nicely—don't hack it:* cut roughly, cut, chop, hew, chip, mangle, mutilate, lacerate, gash, slit, slash. **2** *The boy's been hacking ever since he caught cold:* cough repeatedly, cough drily, emit short coughs, rasp; *Slang* bark.

◇ *Word origin: Hack*[1], to cut or chop, comes from Old English *haccian*, to cut to pieces.

hack[2] *n.* **1** *Grandfather had no carriage but hired a hack for his journey:* saddle-horse, medium-sized horse, common horse, carriage horse, hackney; *Slang* nag; worn-out horse; hired horse, horse for common hire; cart-horse, shaft-horse, dray-horse, draught horse, work-horse. **2** *The need for money turned a talented writer into a hack:* scribbler, penny-a-liner, Grub Street writer.

Ant. 1 thoroughbred; pony.

◇ *Word origin: Hack*, meaning a horse for hire, is just a short form of *hackney* (which was also the name given to a kind of coach that plied for hire, and to the medium-sized horse used to pull it). The literary *hack* who does mediocre writing gets his name from the horse, since both could be hired cheaply to do routine work.

"There are a thousand hacking at the branches of evil to one who is striking at the root." —*H. D. Thoreau*

---

hackneyed *adj. The play had a hackneyed plot:* commonplace, routine, common, stale, trite, banal, inane, insipid, vapid, stereotyped, threadbare, pedestrian, stock, worn-out, worn, well-worn, shop-worn, platitudinous, conventional, ordinary, moth-eaten, humdrum, uninspired, unimaginative; dull, jejune.

Ant. original, new, fresh, novel, imaginative, unusual, uncommon; striking.

haggard *adj.* **1** *The sailor was haggard from his long, lonely voyage:* tired-looking, hollow-eyed, gaunt, care-worn, woebegone; exhausted, spent, weary, fatigued, tired, drooping, fagged, toil-worn, worn, wasted, overwearied, flagging; *Slang* flaked out, dead beat, pooped. **2** *She was haggard with fright and we hardly recognized her:* wild-eyed, wild-looking, wild, frenzied, overcome, overwrought, upset, raging, ranting, harassed, harrowed.

Ant. 1 brisk, energetic, vigorous, jaunty, bright-eyed, well-rested; hale, hale and hearty, glowing with health, robust, sleek. **2** calm, serene, tranquil.

◇ *Word origin: Haggard* comes from Old French *hagard*, wild hawk, untamed hawk.

haggle *v.* **1** *The women were haggling over the price of fish:* dicker, bargain, barter, higgle, beat down. **2** *We always haggle over who should wash up:* squabble, quibble, bicker, wrangle, quarrel, dispute.

hail *v.* **1** *An old friend hailed me from across the street. The host hailed the guests at the door:* call to, shout at, cry out to, address, greet, accost, salute; welcome, receive, usher in, shake hands with, make welcome, bid one welcome. **2** *The people lined the streets to hail the returning heroes:* acclaim, cheer, applaud, exalt, honour, glorify, eulogize, extol, panegyrize, esteem, compliment, commend.

—*n.* **3** *Through the fog we heard a hail from another ship:* shout, call, accosting, calling out, hello, salutation, greeting, salute.

Ant. 1 ignore, avoid, cut. **2** condemn, rebuff, insult, criticize, boo, hiss.

hair *n.* **1** *She has the most beautiful red hair I've ever seen:* head of hair, tresses, locks, curls, ringlets, bangs; *Slang* mop, mane; (*of animal*) coat, fur, pelt, fleece; wool, down, mane. **2** *The car missed the pedestrian by a hair:* narrow margin, hair's breadth.

hairy *adj. Keep that hairy dog off the couch!:* hirsute, shaggy, bushy, woolly, furry, fleecy.

half *n.* **1** *Pay half now and the rest later. You've only heard half the story!:* one half, one of two equal parts, fifty per cent; part, fraction, portion, section, some.

—*adj.* **2** *The dog eats half a pound of meat every day. His testimony was full of half-truths:* one-half, halved; partial, fractional, incomplete, divided; inadequate, imperfect, limited, insufficient, deficient, meagre, slight, scanty, skimpy; moderate, middling, tolerable, passable.

—*adv.* **3** *You're only half trying:* partially, partly, in part, after a fashion, inadequately, insufficiently, slightly, barely, feebly, weakly, faintly; relatively, fairly, moderately, passably, tolerably, comparatively, rather; pretty nearly, all but.

Ant. 1 whole, total, sum total, all, aggregate, entirety. **2** whole, complete, entire, full. **3** wholly, completely, entirely, fully, totally; strongly, adequately, sufficiently.

half-hearted *adj. He acknowledged the gift with a half-hearted thank-you:* unenthusiastic, indifferent, lack-lustre, perfunctory, cool, cold, spiritless, faint, tame, lukewarm, passive, unaspiring, irresolute, neither hot nor cold, neither one thing nor the other; listless, apathetic, languid, phlegmatic.

Ant. whole-hearted, enthusiastic, animated, eager, spirited, zealous, moved, avid, warm, emotional, concerned, excited; ambitious, aspiring, energetic, red-hot.

half-way *adv.* **1** *The house is half-way up the hill:* midway, half the distance, in the middle.

—*adj.* **2** *York is the half-way point on the journey:* middle, midway, intermediate, medium, median, midmost, middlemost, equidistant, between two extremes.

half-wit *n. Who was the half-wit who left the refrigerator door open?:* fool, dunce, blockhead, dolt, ninny, nitwit, dim-wit, numskull; feeble-minded person, moron, imbecile, idiot, simpleton, mental defective, mental deficient, dullard.

hall *n.* **1** *Martha's room is at the far end of the hall:* hallway, corridor, passageway, passage. **2** *Leave your boots and umbrella in the hall:* entrance hall, entry, lobby, vestibule; waiting-room, reception-room, ante-room, ante-chamber. **3** *The concert will be given in the Albert Hall:* concert hall, auditorium, assembly room, meeting-place, amphitheatre, chamber, club room; dining hall, banqueting hall.

hallowed *adj. The church graveyard is hallowed ground:* sacred, consecrated, dedicated; holy, blessed, sanctified, sacrosanct.

Ant. profane, unsanctified.

◇ *Word origin: Hallowed* literally means "holied". Both *hallow* and *holy* come from Old English *hālig*, which means "holy" because the first Christian missionaries to England used the word as a vernacular equivalent both of Latin *sanctus*, holy (or holy man, saint), and Latin *sacer*, sacred. Among pagan speakers of Old English, *hālig* had a variety of interesting meanings: propitious, of good augury; inviolate, taboo; uninjured, whole, healthy. In fact, our words *health* and *whole* are closely related to *holy*, as are the Germanic feminine names *Helga* and *Olga*.

hallucination *n. The high fever gave her hallucinations. You didn't see a ghost, it was just an hallucination:* delusion, fantasy, illusion, mirage, apparition, chimera, aberration, vision, dream, nightmare.

◇ *Word origin: Hallucination* is based on Latin *alucinari*, to wander in thought or speech.

halo *n.* **1** *The saint was painted with a halo over his head:* ring of light, aureole, nimbus, corona, radiance. **2** *Does a halo around the moon mean bad weather?:* chromosphere. **3** *One always feels a kind of halo surrounding royalty:* atmosphere of glory, magnificence, splendour, resplendence, radiance, luminousness, lustre, illustriousness, majesty, dignity, grandeur, holiness, sanctity, sublimity, spiritual aura, solemnity.

◇ *Word origin:* Our word *halo* has a surprisingly earthy origin. It comes from Greek *halōs*, circular threshing-floor.

halt *v.* **1** *The hikers halted at the stream to refill their flasks:* stop, come to a stop, come to a standstill, pull up, draw up, wait, rest, pause, tarry, linger, suspend, interrupt; terminate, quit, cease, discontinue, leave off; *Informal* knock off, shut up shop, shut down, hang fire, break off, call it a day, wind up; brake, check, rein in, throttle down, heave to. **2** *Officials are working hard to halt inflation:* stop, end, bring to a standstill, defeat, choke off, prohibit, extinguish, prevent, cut off, vanquish, suppress, overthrow, overturn, put down, subdue, rout, quell, quash, crush, scotch; curb, check, hinder, impede, repress, restrict, restrain, balk, thwart, stem, stall, stay, delay, abate, frustrate, foil, hamper, hold in check, bridle, block, inhibit; *Slang* throw a spanner in the works, spike one's guns, cut the ground from under.

—*n.* **3** *The proceedings came to a halt around noon:* stop, cessation, standstill, discontinuance, suspension, termination, close, end; recess,

intermission, respite, interval, pause, rest, interruption, delay, interlude; *Informal* breather, breathing-space, break.
—*interj.* **4** *Halt! Who goes there?:* stop, stand still, don't move, come to a halt.
Ant. 1, 2 continue, go ahead, proceed; begin, start, resume. **2** support, encourage, forward, maintain, aid, abet, bolster, boost. **3** beginning, start; resumption, continuation. **4** proceed! move on! pass!

halve *v. Halve the apple and we'll share it. Prices were halved during the sale:* cut in half, split in two, divide equally, bisect; lessen by one half, reduce 50 per cent.
Ant. double, increase 100 per cent.

hamlet *n. The boy grew up in a hamlet of 200 people:* small village, village, village without a church.
Ant. metropolis, city, megalopolis.

hammer *n.* **1** *The only tools in the house are a hammer and screwdriver:* (*variously*) claw-hammer, tack-hammer; mallet, sledge-hammer, steam-hammer, pile-driver, rammer; gavel.
—*v.* **2** *Hammer a hook in the wall and hang the picture on it:* nail; hit, pound, knock, pummel, whack, tap, punch, bang, drive. **3** *The blacksmith hammered a horseshoe from the red-hot metal:* forge, form with a hammer, beat out; fashion, shape, make.

hamper *v. Lack of equipment is hampering our work:* hinder, impede, interfere with, hold up, encumber, inhibit, thwart, frustrate, balk, stall, restrain, restrict, retard, curb, check, stem, block, obstruct, fetter, shackle, muzzle, gag, hamstring.
Ant. help, aid, assist, further, promote, forward, expedite, speed, accelerate, hasten, encourage, bolster, boost.

hand *n.* **1** *Aren't your hands cold with no gloves on?:* manual extremity; palm, fist; *Slang* paw, mitt. **2** *The foreman hired three new hands last week:* labourer, hired hand, hired man, man, worker, workman, working-man, employee, aid, helper, menial, handyman; member of a crew. **3** *Give me a hand with this ladder:* help, assistance, aid, support, lift. **4** Usually **hands.** *The condemned man's fate is in the governor's hands:* care, keeping, charge, custody, control, possession, power, hold, authority, command, management, guidance, dominion, jurisdiction, supervision, domination, auspices. **5** *Aunt Edna writes a beautiful hand:* handwriting, penmanship, script, calligraphy, longhand. **6** *Give the young singer a great big hand:* round of applause, burst of applause; ovation.
—*v.* **7** *Hand me the newspaper, please:* give, pass, hand over, present, deliver, convey, turn over to, furnish with; *Informal* reach. **8** *Remember how Sir Walter Raleigh handed Queen Elizabeth across the puddle?:* give a hand to, hold out a helping hand to, help, assist, guide, aid, do a good turn for, minister to, come to the aid of.
Ant. 2 employer, boss, foreman, overseer, supervisor.

handful *n. Only a handful of people attended the dance:* small number, few, smattering, sprinkling, scattering; small quantity, tiny amount, minimum, scant amount, modicum, thimbleful.
Ant. horde, mob, crowd, throng, a large number, a lot.

handicap *n.* **1** *Her lack of a university degree is a definite handicap:* drawback, disadvantage, detriment, impediment, restriction, limitation, obstacle, barrier, stumbling-block, difficulty, inhibition, burden, encumbrance, inconvenience. **2** *It takes great fortitude to learn to live with a handicap:* physical disability; (*variously*) lameness, loss of a limb, blindness, deafness, speech impediment.
—*v.* **3** *Being overweight will handicap a boy in sports:* hinder, hold back, hamper, impede, encumber, retard, burden, restrict, limit, place at a disadvantage, inhibit, thwart, suppress, repress; restrain, curb.
Ant. 1 advantage, benefit, asset, edge, boost, boon. **3** help, benefit, give an advantage to, assist, aid, forward, promote, further, boost.
◇ *Word origin:* The word *handicap* comes from the name of a 17th-century lottery game called "hand in cap," in which players held forfeits in a cap.

handle *n.* **1** *Give me the rake with the long handle. The door handle just fell off:* shaft, shank, hilt; holder, grip, pull, knob.
—*v.* **2** *Don't handle the tomatoes, you'll bruise them!:* take in the hands, pick up, hold; finger, knead, pinch, poke, touch, feel; stroke, caress, fondle, massage; *Slang* paw, maul. **3** *The pilot really knows how to handle an aeroplane:* control, steer, guide, manœuvre, pilot; operate, run, work, manipulate, ply, use, utilize, employ, bring into play, manage, command. **4** *Can the new employee handle this job? Rembrandt handled lighting with dramatic effect in his paintings:* manage, deal with, cope with, take care of; command, control, manipulate, conduct, treat. **5** *The hardware department handles a complete line of power tools:* sell, offer for sale, carry, stock, deal in, trade in, traffic in, market.

"Take things always by their smooth handle." — *Thomas Jefferson*

---

handsome *adj.* **1** *Bill and Jane have four handsome children. What a handsome room!:* good-looking, attractive, fine-looking, sightly, comely, easy on the eye, easy to look at, lovely, exquisite, beauteous, beautiful, pretty, bonny, fair; splendid, tasteful, elegant, stately, impressive, imposing, well-formed, well-proportioned, well-arranged. **2** *The waiter received a handsome tip:* generous, liberal, bountiful;

ample, considerable, sizeable, sufficient, abundant, moderately large. **3** *Caring for the motherless child was another of his handsome deeds:* gracious, generous, bountiful, unselfish, noble, magnanimous, big-hearted, princely; humanitarian, benevolent, merciful, benign, compassionate.

Ant. 1 ugly, unattractive, unprepossessing, unsightly; tasteless, inelegant; ill-proportioned, unshapely. **2** ungenerous, illiberal, stingy, niggardly, miserly, cheap; small, meagre, skimpy, scant. **3** mean, base, selfish, ignoble.

◇ *Word origin: Handsome* (*hand* + *-some*) meant "handy, easy to handle" during the reign of Henry VIII. In a typical use in this sense, a writer of the 1520's remarks that the long sword of the Germans was not so *handsome* as the Roman short sword. The first writers to use the word in its modern meaning were the poets Edmund Spenser and Shakespeare in the 1590's. In their usage, as in ours, *handsome* applied mainly to good-looking boys and men. *Handsome* in the sense of princely, noble, magnanimous was originally a figurative extension of the "good-looking" sense. *Handsome* as in *a handsome tip* or *a handsome piece of work* was once only American English but may now be heard anywhere in the English-speaking world.

handy *adv.* **1** *Keep the flashlight handy in case the fuse blows again:* accessible, close at hand, ready to hand, at hand, on hand, at one's elbow, within easy reach, easily accessible, available, obtainable, near, convenient, nigh, on call, in readiness, on tap, at one's beck and call.

—*adj.* **2** *Father was never very handy at fixing things:* skilful, expert, adroit, dexterous, deft, nimble-fingered, competent, proficient, capable, adept, accomplished, clever, efficient. **3** *This electric food-mixer isn't very handy:* easy to use, convenient to handle, manageable, wieldy, useful, practical, serviceable, helpful.

Ant. 1 out of the way, hard to get at, inaccessible, unavailable, inconvenient, remote, far. **2** clumsy, awkward, unskilled, all thumbs. **3** clumsy, awkward, unwieldy, cumbersome, inconvenient; useless, impractical.

hang *v.* **1** *After you have cleaned the windows, hang the curtains. This picture hangs over the mantelpiece:* suspend, fasten from above, append, attach, affix; dangle, swing freely, be pendent, depend. **2** *The murderer was condemned by the judge to be hanged:* execute by hanging, send to the gallows, die on the gallows, lynch; *Slang* string up. **3** *His whole career hangs on his passing the exam:* depend, be dependent, be contingent, rest, turn upon, hinge, be subject to, lie in, pivot on, repose in. **4** *The child hung his head in shame:* let droop, dangle, bow, lower, drop, incline, bend forward, bend downward, sag; lean over, trail.

—*n.* **5** *Informal If you get the hang of needle-point I wish you'd teach me:* knack, understanding, grasp; gist, point, meaning, thought.

Ant. 1 take down, detach. **4** lift, raise.

◇ *Usage note:* (1) *Hang* has two basic meanings: *to hang a picture* or another object, and *to hang a man.* The past tenses are different for the two meanings: a picture, curtains, door, etc., are *hung*, but a human being, and only a human being, is *hanged.* Thus, *Have you hung the curtains yet?*, but *The highwayman was hanged at dawn.* (2) Don't forget that a *hangER* is one who hangs something or an object used for hanging: *a paper-hanger, Hang your coat on this hanger.* A *hangAR* is an aeroplane shed: *The plane was wheeled into the hangar for repairs.*

hankering *n. The old man had a hankering to see his boyhood home again:* longing, craving, desire, yearning, hunger, thirst, urge, itch, aching, pining.

haphazard *adj. You can't work in such a haphazard way if you want to get the job done:* unmethodical, disorganized, unsystematic, chaotic, unorganized, disordered, disorderly, random, arbitrary; careless, unthinking, casual, chance, slapdash, fitful, sporadic, catch-as-catch-can, hit-or-miss, on-and-off; aimless, purposeless, undesigned, undirected, unpremeditated, accidental.

Ant. organized, methodical, systematic, orderly, ordered; careful, thoughtful, designed, planned, arranged, premeditated, purposeful, considered, deliberate.

happen *v.* **1** *When did the accident happen?:* take place, occur, come about, come to pass, ensue, transpire, result, befall, eventuate; arise, spring up, crop up, come into existence, present itself, appear. **2** *I happen to be a close friend of the mayor:* have the fortune to be, have the luck to be; be the case, turn out. **3** *What will happen to her now?:* become of, befall, be one's fate, fall to one's lot, be one's fortune; be experienced by, be borne by, be endured by, be suffered by.

happening *n. It was an unfortunate happening:* event, occurrence, incident, episode, affair, experience, matter, proceeding, occasion, circumstance, chance, adventure, advent, case; accident, vicissitude, *Slang* just one of those things.

happiness *n.* **1** *Imagine our happiness at having all the children home for Christmas!:* gladness, joy, delight, felicity, contentment, content, sense of well-being, pleasure, enjoyment, satisfaction, light-heartedness, rejoicing, elation, jubilation, high spirits, bliss, beatitude, blessedness, rapture, ecstasy, gaiety, exultation, transport, exuberance; merriment, cheer, cheerfulness, cheeriness, glee, jollity, mirth. **2** *Her grandchildren are her greatest happiness:* pleasure, satisfaction, gratification, blessing, comfort.

Ant. 1 unhappiness, sadness, sorrow, grief,

woe; depression, despondency, low spirits, misery, anguish, distress, discomfort. **2** bane, annoyance; calamity, misfortune, thorn in one's flesh, cross to bear.

happy *adj.* **1** *I'm so happy that you could visit us. My birthday was a happy occasion:* glad, pleased, delighted, content, contented, gratified; *Slang* tickled, tickled pink; gay, cheerful, in high spirits, elated, joyous, overjoyed, exhilarated, blissful, rapturous, ecstatic, exultant, gleeful, transported, rhapsodic, jubilant, flushed with pleasure, exuberant, in the seventh heaven; pleasant, pleasing, delightful, gratifying, cheering, joyful. **2** *Wasn't it a happy coincidence that I bumped into you?:* fortunate, lucky, auspicious, favourable, felicitous, propitious; convenient, opportune, meet, timely, seasonable, fitting, fit, advantageous, agreeable.

Ant. 1 sad, unhappy, sorry, sorrowful, displeased, discontented; despondent, forlorn, miserable, gloomy, melancholy, depressed, joyless, mournful, sombre; down in the mouth, down in the dumps. **2** unfortunate, unlucky, luckless, inauspicious; unfitting, unseasonable.

harass *v.* **1** *The retreating army was harassed by the enemy:* attack repeatedly, raid frequently, assault continually, beset, besiege. **2** *If you'll stop harassing me I can finish this work:* torment, pester, badger, harry, worry, disturb, annoy, irritate, distress, bother, irk, vex, plague, hound, discommode, exasperate, tease, bait, heckle, hector, browbeat, bully, intimidate, cow.

◇ *Pronunciation tip:* Today, *harass* may be pronounced either as *ha-RASS* or as *HAR-ass,* but *HAR-ass* is preferred.

◇ *Word origin:* To *harass* someone is to annoy or pursue him relentlessly. It comes from Old French *harer,* to set dogs on.

harbinger *n. The returning swallows are the harbingers of spring:* herald, precursor, forerunner, indication, announcer, signaller, proclaimer; first sign, omen, portent, token, clue, symbol.

◇ *Pronunciation tip:* The *g* in *harbinger* is soft, like a *j.* Thus *HAR-bin-jer* is the proper pronunciation.

◇ *Word origin:* Originally a *harbinger* was a courier who rode in advance of a travelling party to arrange for lodging (from Old French *herberge,* shelter or lodging). The English word *harbour,* meaning "shelter" or "refuge", is closely related to it.

harbour *n.* **1** *The disabled ship was towed into harbour:* port, protected anchorage; (*variously*) dock, pier, wharf, quay, cove, bay, creek, roadstead, haven, inlet, basin; destination, goal, terminus, terminal point.

—*v.* **2** *The suspect is accused of harbouring an escaped convict:* give refuge to, shelter, conceal, give a hiding-place to, shield, protect, care for, keep safe; quarter, house, lodge, billet, take in, keep. **3** *For years she harboured resentment against her stepmother:* nurture, foster, nurse, bear in the mind, hold, maintain, retain, feel, cling to; brood over, muse over.

◇ *Word origin: Harbour* is closely related to Old French *herberge,* shelter, and is based on Old English *herebeorg,* "refuge for an army".

hard *adj.* **1** *This toffee is so hard that no one can chew it:* firm, solid, hardened, rock-like, stony, steely; rigid, stiff, unmalleable, inflexible, unpliable. **2** *A hard blow knocked the boxer down:* strong, powerful, forceful, heavy, fierce, severe, violent. **3** *The teacher asked a hard question. It is a hard book to read:* difficult, arduous, laborious, strenuous, tough, exacting, formidable, troublesome, burdensome, wearisome; baffling, confusing, puzzling, perplexing, bewildering, unfathomable, cryptic; complex, complicated, involved, intricate, impenetrable, knotty. **4** *That new employee is really a hard worker:* industrious, energetic, vigorous, enterprising, assiduous, diligent, persevering, persistent, unremitting, indefatigable, untiring, unflagging; earnest, zealous, eager, conscientious, willing, spirited, animated. **5** *We work for a hard master:* strict, stern, severe, unyielding, stubborn, uncompromising, stringent, unbending; hard-hearted, cruel, cold, implacable, unrelenting, merciless, pitiless, inexorable, unremitting, callous, impervious, unsparing, ruthless, thick-skinned, hardened, insensitive; inhuman, brutal. **6** *This has been a hard winter. Many families had a hard time during the Depression:* severe, harsh, rough, difficult; unpleasant, disagreeable, distressing, oppressive, disheartening, burdensome, onerous, intolerable, unbearable, tormenting; harmful, hurtful, lamentable, sad, melancholy. **7** *Hard feelings existed between the neighbours. The lawyers exchanged hard words:* hostile, belligerent, unfriendly, antagonistic, bellicose; mean, ugly, bitter, vicious, rancorous, venomous, malicious, acrimonious, vindictive, spiteful, sullen, cantankerous, unkind, critical, insulting.

—*adv.* **8** *The ice is frozen hard:* solid, solidly, firm, firmly, tight, tightly, rigid, stiff, closely. **9** *It rained hard. Hit the ball hard:* forcefully, forcibly, powerfully, strongly, heavily, fiercely, severely, violently, intensely, sharply, vigorously. **10** *The farmer worked hard to gather the hay before the rains came. The student studied hard:* industriously, vigorously, rigorously, energetically, arduously, laboriously, furiously, intently, intensely, with all one's might, unsparingly, unceasingly, steadily, diligently, persistently, untiringly, determinedly, assiduously, unflaggingly, conscientiously, resolutely, earnestly, eagerly, keenly, seriously, closely. **11** *Mother took the bad news very hard:* emotionally, to heart, with strong feelings, with much sorrow, distressfully, severely, painfully, agonizingly; with much anger, angrily.

Ant. **1-3, 5, 6, 8** soft. **3, 5, 6** easy. **1** mushy; flexible, pliant, pliable, malleable. **2** weak, light, mild. **3** light, simple, uncomplicated, straightforward, clear, direct; easy as pie. **4** lazy, lethargic; lax, careless. **5** soft-hearted, lenient, permissive, yielding, kind, kind-hearted, warm-hearted, merciful, sensitive, humane, gentle. **6** mild, pleasant, agreeable, enjoyable, good, salubrious. **7** friendly, loving, amiable, warm, kind, sweet, good; complimentary. **8** loose, loosely, lightly. **9** softly, weakly, gently, mildly, lightly, faintly. **10** easily, effortlessly; lazily, lethargically. **11** calmly, unemotionally, mildly, placidly, serenely.

◇ *Word origin: Hard* comes from Old English *hard,* and is related via Frankish to French *hardir,* to make hard, from which we get our word *hardy.* (It is also related to the *-hard* or *-ard* final syllables of the Germanic masculine names *Bernard, Gerard, Leonard,* and *Richard.*) It also has an important cognate in *Greek: kratos,* strength, power, from which our *-crat* and *-cracy* word-endings, such as *democrat* and *democracy,* are derived. Their root meaning is reflected in the slogan "Power to the People".

hard-headed *adj. The job requires a hard-headed businessman:* practical, objective, pragmatic, realistic; unemotional, unfeeling, impersonal, sensible, tough-minded; not easily deceived, not easily ruffled, cool, cool-headed, self-controlled, poised, *Slang* unflappable.

Ant. soft-hearted, idealistic, impractical, theoretical, philosophical; emotional, volatile, hot-headed, excitable.

hard-hearted *adj. Only a hard-hearted person would fail to be sympathetic:* cruel, cruel-hearted, unfeeling, heartless, merciless, remorseless, unsparing, unforgiving, uncaring, insensitive, indifferent, unsympathetic, cold-blooded, ruthless, unpitying, pitiless, cold, hard, callous, thick-skinned, inhuman, brutal.

Ant. kind, loving, sweet, compassionate, sympathetic, soft-hearted, warm-hearted, understanding, sensitive, warm, gentle, humane, merciful, forgiving.

hardly *adv.* **1** *There is hardly a foot of water in the well. It is hardly possible that such a thing could have happened:* scarcely, barely, only, just, not quite, almost not, faintly; rarely, uncommonly, infrequently, not often. **2** *That was hardly the way to greet a friend!:* by no means, not by any means, certainly not, in no manner, in no way, not at all.

Ant. **1** fully, easily, amply, more than, well over, abundantly; often, frequently, commonly, usually. **2** by all means, certainly, really, truly, undoubtedly, indubitably.

hardship *n.* **1** *His family endured great hardship during the war:* suffering, affliction, misfortune, adversity, ordeal, misery, unhappiness, grief, sorrow, travail, sadness, woe, wretchedness, agony. **2** *Having another mouth to feed would be a great hardship just now:* privation, burden, handicap, encumbrance, difficulty, load, problem, millstone round one's neck, load, cross to bear.

Ant. **1** comfort, ease, happiness; good fortune, benefit. **2** help, aid, blessing, boon, relief, load off one's back.

hardy *adj. One has to be hardy to work as a forester:* robust, rugged, sturdy, hearty, strapping, able-bodied, strong, tough, vigorous; healthy, fit, physically fit, hale, in good condition, in fine fettle.

Ant. delicate, frail, fragile, dainty, soft, weak, feeble, sickly, debilitated.

harlot *n. Thieves and harlots frequented the café:* prostitute, whore, strumpet, trollop, bawd, doxy, jade, street-walker, scarlet woman, painted woman, fallen woman, Jezebel, call-girl; *Slang* tart, pro; kept woman, floosie, mopsy.

◇ *Word origin: Harlot* comes from Old French *herlot,* vagabond, knave.

"Samson with his strong body had a weak head, or he would not have laid it in a harlot's lap." —*Benjamin Franklin*

---

harm *n.* **1** *They were accused of doing him bodily harm. The drought did a lot of harm to the crops. Bad publicity did a lot of harm to the actor's career:* injury, hurt, damage, suffering, pain, agony, trauma; impairment, detriment, mischief, adversity, hardship, misfortune, ill, destruction, abuse, defacement, deterioration, scourge, calamity, havoc, devastation. **2** *What's the harm in having a little fun?:* wrong, wickedness, evil, sin, sinfulness, iniquity, immorality, vice, villainy; malice, malevolence, maliciousness.

—*v.* **3** *Don't harm your eyes by reading in dim light. Will this cleaning fluid harm the furniture?:* impair, injure, hurt, wound, maim, ruin, cripple, pain, abuse, maltreat, do violence to, misuse, ill-use; damage, blemish, mar, spoil, deface, disfigure; debase, degrade, undermine; wrong, aggrieve.

Ant. **1** good, benefit, help, aid, assistance; boon, blessing. **2** goodness, righteousness, blessing. **3** benefit, help, aid, assist; improve, better, ameliorate.

harmful *adj. Follow the directions carefully, or this medicine may be harmful:* injurious, dangerous, deleterious, hurtful, destructive, damaging, unwholesome, unhealthy, unhealthful, detrimental, adverse, bad, pernicious, baneful.

Ant. beneficial, good, helpful, wholesome, healthful, healthy; harmless, safe.

harmless *adj. Grass snakes are harmless reptiles:*

safe, not dangerous, not hurtful, non-toxic, without risk; inoffensive, gentle, peaceable, mild, blameless, innocent, uncorrupt, guiltless, innocuous, unobjectionable.

Ant. harmful, dangerous, unsafe, destructive, unhealthy, injurious, unwholesome.

harmonious *adj.* **1** *Harmonious sounds drifted across the fields. The room was decorated in harmonious shades of blue and green:* melodious, sweet-sounding, mellifluous, euphonious, sweet, dulcet, agreeable, agreeably combined, matching, compatible, harmonizing, co-ordinated, consistent, unified, synchronized. **2** *The two families' relations were very harmonious:* like-minded, in agreement, in harmony, in accord, compatible, congenial, agreeable, amiable, amicable, sympathetic, friendly.

Ant. **1** harsh, grating, unmelodious, cacophonous; clashing, incompatible, contrasting, unco-ordinated, inconsistent. **2** incompatible, unlike, different, discordant, unfriendly.

harmony *n.* **1** *The interior decorator chose the rugs and curtains for their harmony:* pleasing consistency, co-ordination, compatibility, agreement, concord, correlation, parallelism, matching, mutual fitness, balance, symmetry, order, proportion, unity, organic totality. **2** *Bob and I worked together in harmony for years:* agreement, accord, concord, unanimity, like-mindedness, conformity, unity, amicability, amity, congeniality, sympathy, compatibility, fellowship, friendship, co-operation, mutual regard, peace; good understanding, harmonious relations, concurrence in opinions.

Ant. **1** incongruity, inconsistency; conflict, disproportion. **2** disagreement, enmity, opposition, conflict, contention, dissension, antagonism, hostility.

◇ *Word origin: Harmony* is having everything or everyone joined together agreeably. It comes from the Greek *harmozein,* to fit together.

harness *n.* **1** *Put the harness on the shire-horse and hitch him to the plough:* tackle, trappings; (*variously*) halter, bit, bridle, reins, straps, traces, caparison, tugs.

—*v.* **2** *Harness the pony and we'll go for a ride in the trap:* put in harness, hitch up, yoke, saddle, rig up. **3** *The mill-wheel harnesses the energy of the river:* control and use, direct to a useful purpose, render useful, make productive, turn to account; restrain, curb, muzzle, bridle, rein.

harridan *n. The old harridan screamed at the children for sitting on her doorstep:* disagreeable old woman, crone, old crone, shrew, hag, virago; *Slang* battle-axe, witch.

◇ *Word origin: Harridan* comes from a 17th-century French slang word, *haridelle,* "worn-out horse, jade".

harrowing *adj. After that harrowing experience I shook for a week:* distressing, disturbing, tormenting; frightening, fearful, alarming, chilling, blood-curdling, terrifying, nerve-racking, threatening, dangerous.

harry *v.* **1** *Pirates often harried the coastal towns:* attack repeatedly, raid frequently, beset; raid, plunder, sack, pillage, terrorize. **2** *She was harried by doubts of his honesty. The carpenter could finish the job more quickly if you didn't harry him:* trouble, torment, distress, haunt, disturb, bother, worry; harass, pester, gall, badger, annoy, irritate, irk, vex, plague, hound, exasperate, distract; tease, bait, hector, heckle, ride, intimidate, bully.

Ant. **2** soothe, quiet, comfort, console, solace; support, help, aid, encourage.

◇ *Word origin: Harry* comes from Old English *hergian,* to despoil with an army (Old English *here,* army).

harsh *adj.* **1** *What a harsh voice the speaker has! The harsh light hurt my eyes:* unpleasant, piercing, jarring, grating, shrill, rasping, hoarse, strident, scratchy, discordant, raucous, unmusical, unharmonious, cacophonous, glaring, over-bright, too bright. **2** *Snow White received harsh treatment from her stepmother. The critics had nothing but harsh words for the new play:* cruel, pitiless, ruthless, merciless, unsparing, severe, stern, ungentle, unkind, abusive, vindictive, heartless, hardhearted, brutal; bitter, caustic, hard, rough, sharp, uncharitable.

Ant. **1** soft, gentle, mild, smooth, pleasant, pleasing, agreeable, soothing; harmonious, mellifluous. **2** kind, gentle, sweet, loving, merciful, charitable.

◇ *Word origin: Harsh* may come from Danish *harsk,* rancid, or it may come from Middle Low German *harsch,* hairy, rough.

harum-scarum *adj. You should know better than to ask some harum-scarum kid to do the job:* disorganized, undependable, unreliable, inconsistent, erratic, careless, unsettled; foolish, reckless, giddy, scatter-brained, rattle-brained, feather-brained, hare-brained, flighty, impulsive, impetuous, absent-minded, confused, bewildered; unplanned, haphazard.

Ant. organized, well-planned, careful, efficient, consistent, settled, serious, methodical, responsible, conscientious.

◇ *Word origin: Harum-scarum* is from an old jingle *hare 'em, scare 'em* in which *hare* is a nonsense word.

harvest *n.* **1** *The neighbouring farmers gathered to help with the harvest:* harvesting, reaping, crop-gathering; (*variously*) mowing, cutting, picking, haymaking. **2** *There was a large apple harvest this year:* crop, yield, season's growth, produce; gathering, collection, accumulation, gleaning. **3** *The new medicine is the harvest of 30 years' research:* result, product, fruit, fruition, reward, benefit, proceeds, gain, re-

turn, yield, gleaning, reaping; aftermath, outgrowth, output.
—*v.* **4** *Try to harvest the fruit before the first frost:* gather, reap, pick, pluck, mow, cut, get in; collect, amass, accumulate.
Ant. 4 plant, sow, seed.

hassle *n.* **1** *Slang There was a hassle over who should pay for the broken window:* squabble, quarrel, argument; fight, struggle, tussle, battle, conflict, contest.
—*v.* **2** *Slang If the police hassled the pick-pockets more, maybe they would disappear from the streets:* harass, harry, persecute, hound, bother, badger, annoy.
◇ *Word origin: Hassle* may be a combination of *haggle* + *tussle.*

haste *n.* **1** *The contract says the work must be completed with all possible haste:* speed, tempo, speediness, hurry, rush, swiftness, quickness, hurriedness, rapidity, fleetness; expedition, dispatch. **2** *Haste makes waste:* undue speed, careless hurry, precipitateness; recklessness, rashness, impetuousness, impulsiveness.
Ant. 1 slowness, delay, procrastination, plodding, sluggishness, leisureliness, lagging, hanging back. **2** deliberation, care, carefulness, sureness, reflection, calmness.

hasten *v.* **1** *She gobbled down her lunch and hastened to her appointment:* hurry, rush, speed, make haste, race, run, hustle, dash, scurry, fly, whisk, jump, sprint, bolt, dart, scuttle, flit, scamper, hurry up, lose no time, make time, go at the double, go like lightning; *Slang* go hell for leather, go full blast, step on the gas, step on it; work against time, make short work of. **2** *An electric typewriter would hasten the work:* accelerate, speed up, expedite, quicken, push forward, precipitate, advance, promote; hurry on, urge on, drive on, incite, impel, egg on.
Ant. 1 move slowly, creep, crawl; plod, shuffle; lag, procrastinate, dally, dawdle. **2** slow, slow down, delay, decelerate, slacken, retard, impede, inhibit, check, arrest, curb, hold back.

hastily *adv.* **1** *There wasn't much time, so I dressed hastily:* quickly, speedily, fast, hurriedly, promptly, straightaway, post-haste, apace; *Slang* pronto, at the double, like a shot, like greased lightning, hell for leather, before one can say Jack Robinson. **2** *Don't make important decisions hastily:* too quickly, rashly, recklessly, impetuously, impulsively, precipitately, thoughtlessly, summarily, carelessly, heedlessly, on the spur of the moment.
Ant. 1 slowly, at a snail's pace. **2** deliberately, carefully, thoughtfully, calmly.

hasty *adj.* **1** *A hasty search turned up the missing ear-ring:* fast, quick, hurried, rapid, speedy, swift, prompt, fleet, quick as a flash; cursory, brief, rushed, fleeting, passing, momentary, breathless, superficial. **2** *One often regrets hasty decisions. Your hasty temper will get you into trouble one of these days:* unduly quick, rash, impetuous, impulsive, reckless, hurried, headlong, heedless, abrupt, precipitate, without deliberation.
Ant. 1 slow, leisurely, plodding; long, protracted, detailed, meticulous, thorough, exhaustive. **2** deliberate, careful, considered, studied, thoughtful, premeditated.

"'The people may eat grass': hasty words, which fly abroad irrevocable, — and will send back tidings." —*Thomas Carlyle*

---

hatch *v. The thieves hatched a plan to rob the bank:* think up, devise, concoct, plot, plan, contrive, make up, formulate, conceive, design, evolve, create, frame, invent, fabricate, improvise, originate, construct, fashion, *Slang* dream up, cook up; manufacture, bring forth, produce, give birth to.

hate *v.* **1** *Those girls have hated each other since their school-days. I hate mice!:* dislike, despise, detest, abhor, loathe, abominate, hold in contempt, bear malice toward, be hostile to, not be able to bear, have no use for, recoil from, shrink from, be repelled by, be sick of, be tired of; *Slang* give one a pain, give one a pain in the neck. **2** *Mother hated to move from such a nice neighbourhood:* be sorry, be reluctant, be unwilling, feel disinclined to, be averse to, shrink from, not care to, would rather not, not have the heart to, dread, wish to avoid, have no taste for, have no stomach for, wince at, regard as distasteful.
—*n.* **3** *Never trust a man who is full of hate:* hatred, dislike, distaste, disliking, aversion, loathing, repugnance, abomination, abhorrence; enmity, hostility, detestation, rancour, malice, antipathy, animosity, animus, venom, malevolence, resentment, vindictiveness, revengefulness, acrimony.
Ant. 1-3 love, like. **1** be fond of, delight in, regard highly, esteem, treasure, prize, cherish, dote on, be attracted by. **2** be pleased, enjoy, relish, fancy, prefer, be inclined; wish, hope. **3** liking, fondness, affection, devotion, amity, goodwill.
◇ *Usage note: Hate, detest, abhor,* and *loathe* all mean to dislike greatly. *Hate* is often the result of jealousy or past experience and can lead to violence: *Cain hated Abel. Detest* often refers to a feeling about a type or class of person or thing and implies a fundamental clash of beliefs, personalities, etc.: *I detest Communism. Winston Churchill detested lazy people. Abhor and loathe* suggest that one is repelled, with *abhor* referring somewhat more to abstract things and *loathe* to emotional reactions: *Nature abhors a vacuum. My sister just loathes snakes.*

hateful *adj.* **1** *What a hateful thing to do!:* offensive, disgusting, detestable, contemptible, repugnant, repellent, loathsome, despicable, revolting, deplorable, abhorrent, foul, odious, obnoxious, abominable, monstrous, ugly, nasty, vile, unpleasant, distasteful, sickening; mean, villainous, infamous, heinous, atrocious, insufferable, wicked, sinful; irritating, objectionable, intolerable, unbearable, unendurable. **2** *Did you see that hateful look she gave me?:* full of hate, expressing hate, evil, forbidding, scornful, contemptuous, disdainful.

Ant. 1 commendable, likeable, desirable; pleasing, pleasant, charming, attractive, wonderful, lovable, good, sweet, kind, beautiful. **2** friendly, loving, affectionate, devoted, kind, sweet, pleasant.

hatred *n.* **1** *The old man's hatred of people has made him a recluse:* dislike, disgust, aversion, hate, loathing, abomination, abhorrence, distaste, detestation, repugnance, revulsion. **2** *Such hatred can only lead to bloodshed:* hostility, enmity, malice, rancour, animosity, antipathy, animus, malevolence, ill will, venom, resentment, vindictiveness, revengefulness, acrimony, bitterness, bad blood.

Ant. 1, 2 love, affection, fondness, devotion, liking, attachment, affinity, attraction. **2** friendliness, amity, goodwill, kindness.

haughty *adj. Her high social position has made her haughty:* arrogant, proud, scornful, disdainful, contemptuous, overbearing, high and mighty, high-handed, lordly, aloof, officious; snobbish, conceited, condescending, patronizing, hoity-toity, swollen-headed; *Slang* stuck-up, snooty, uppity, uppish, high-hat, high-falutin.

Ant. humble, modest; hail-fellow-well-met; *Slang* one of the boys; servile, subservient, obsequious, self-effacing.

◇ *Word origin: Haughty* is based on French *haut,* high. This same word is found in the French phrases *haute couture,* high fashion, *haute cuisine,* fine cooking, and *haut monde,* high society.

haul *v.* **1** *The fisherman hauled the fish into the boat. The tractor hauled the load away:* pull, drag, draw, heave, yank, jerk, wrench, lug, tug; carry, transport, move, convey, fetch, bring, take, remove.

—*n.* **2** *Give a haul on this rope to get the anchor loose:* pull, tug, yank, jerk, heave, wrench. **3** *The bank robbers got away with a £10,000 haul. The fisherman had a huge haul of fish:* take, catch, yield, gain, takings; profit, capture, reward, booty, spoils, swag, bag.

haunt *v.* **1** *As a girl, she used to haunt the local cinema:* frequent, visit often, go to repeatedly, beat a path to; hover about, loiter near, linger around; *Slang* hang around, live in. **2** *Memories of her childhood haunted her:* obsess, weigh on, prey on, beset, trouble, torment, distress, disturb, worry, plague; frighten, terrify, terrorize.

—*n.* **3** Often **haunts** *The snack-bar was one of the students' haunts:* resort, gathering-place, meeting-place, rendezvous, stamping-ground, retreat; (*of animals*) lair, den, burrow, hole, cave, nest.

haven *n. The ship sought a haven from the storm:* shelter, refuge, retreat, sanctuary, asylum, hide-out; harbour, port.

havoc *n. The storm wreaked havoc on the town:* widespread damage, destruction, devastation, ruin, rack and ruin, disaster, catastrophe, cataclysm, ruination, calamity, upheaval.

hazard *n.* **1** *Are you aware of the hazards of mountaineering?:* danger, risk, peril, threat, endangerment, imperilment, pitfall, jeopardy. **2** *By hazard he took a wrong turning and discovered a short cut:* chance, accident, fluke, luck, stroke of luck, good fortune; mishap, mischance, misfortune, coincidence.

—*v.* **3** *If I may hazard a guess, she's at least 50. I'll hazard a quid on the bingo game:* venture, chance, dare, risk, submit, throw out, advance, volunteer, offer, proffer; presume, dare say, suppose, guess, theorize, speculate, conjecture, hypothesize; gamble, bet, wager, stake, take a chance, chance it, tempt fate, trust to luck. **4** *Don't hazard your reputation by supporting that crook:* endanger, risk, imperil, jeopardize, threaten, expose.

Ant. 1 protection, safeguard, safety. **2** design, plan, calculation, premeditation. **4** protect, safeguard, make safe, preserve.

◇ *Word origin: Hazard* was originally a gambling term. It comes from Arabic *al-zahr,* a die (one of a pair of dice), and *hazard* is still our word for a dice game that Americans call "craps". From being the name of a game of chance the word took on more general meanings of any chance, risk, peril, or danger.

hazardous *adj.* **1** *These steep stairs are hazardous:* dangerous, unsafe, perilous, precarious, risky. **2** *Prospecting for gold is a hazardous way to earn a living:* chancy, precarious, unsure, uncertain, unreliable, insecure, speculative, dubious, doubtful, shaky, untrustworthy; unsound, unstable.

Ant. 1 safe, secure. **2** sure, certain, reliable, sound, stable.

haze *n.* **1** *The mountain was barely visible through the haze:* mist, fog, smoke, pall; cloud, vapour, film, veil, screen, cloak, mantle. **2** *Look where you're going — don't walk about in a haze!:* state of confusion, daze; befuddlement, muddle, bewilderment, fogginess.

hazy *adj.* **1** *It was another of those hazy autumn days:* misty, foggy, smoky; overcast, murky, veiled; dusky, bleared, bleary, blurry, filmy, faint. **2** *We have only a hazy idea how to get to your house:* vague, general, indefinite, ill-defined, uncertain, unclear, nebulous, faint, dim; confused, foggy, muddled.

Ant. 1 clear, bright; light, sunny. **2** clear,

certain, sure, detailed, well-defined, explicit.

head *n.* **1** *She has a good head for arithmetic:* mind, brain, mentality, intellect, I.Q., *Slang* grey matter; talent, gift, bent, genius, aptitude, capacity, ability, perception, understanding, apprehension, discernment, judgement, cleverness, acuteness, quickness of mind. **2** *The original founder is still head of the organization:* leader, chief, director, boss, administrator; *Slang* big shot, guiding light; (*variously in business*) chairman of the board, chairman, chief executive officer, chief executive, president, manager, superintendent, foreman, supervisor; (*variously in government*) dictator, king, queen, monarch, sovereign, ruler, tsar, potentate, suzerain, president, prime minister, premier; (*variously in the armed forces*) commander-in-chief, general, captain, commandant, commander, admiral, commodore, field marshal, marshal. **3** *The tallest boy stood at the head of the line. The studious girl came head of her class:* front, first place, forward part, front rank, forefront, lead, highest rank, place of honour. **4** *The head of the Ganges is in the Himalayas:* source, origin, beginning, birthplace, rise, fountain-head, spring, wellspring, fountain, font, well. **5** *Her burst of anger brought matters to a head:* climax, turning-point, crisis, peak, extremity, utmost extent, conclusion, termination, culmination, inevitable result, end, fruition. **6** *The head of a pin is the blunt end, but the head of a spear is the sharp end:* upper end, top, peak, tip, apex, crown, crest, vertex, acme, zenith, summit, pinnacle.

—*adj.* **7** *Take the bills to the head bookkeeper:* chief, highest-ranking, managing, principal, main, foremost, first, highest, leading, dominant, supreme, superior, prime, premier, pre-eminent, paramount; governing, commanding, ruling, controlling. **8** *The prince rode in the head car of the cavalcade:* first, lead, leading, front, fore, foremost, headmost, highest, top, topmost, uppermost, primary, most prominent.

—*v.* **9** *Didn't Princess Margaret head the list of patrons?:* lead, be at the head of, be first, precede, lead the way, take the lead, be in the vanguard; start, begin, initiate, inaugurate, launch, introduce. **10** *When the president died the vice-president was chosen to head the firm:* be head of, direct, supervise, manage, take charge of, administer, superintend, lead, conduct, command, govern, control, rule, be master of, have authority over, officiate at, preside over, be at the helm, take the reins, be in the driver's seat. **11** *Head the boat toward the shore. When the rain stops let's head for the picnic grounds:* steer, aim, turn, drive, pilot, guide, direct; move toward, direct one's course, go in the direction of, go to, proceed to, make for, start off for, make a bee-line for.

Ant. **2** follower, subordinate; (*variously*) cog, menial, drone, underling, worker, hired hand, labourer, working man, enlisted man. **3** end, foot, bottom, tail, last place, lowest rank. **4** mouth; end, foot. **6** bottom, foot. **7** lowest, inferior, subordinate. **8** last, end, trailing, hindmost; bottom, bottommost. **9** follow, go behind, be last, bring up the rear; end, finish, terminate, conclude. **10** follow, be subordinate, be inferior. **11** move away, retreat, withdraw.

headstrong *adj. She's so headstrong that she's bound to get into trouble:* wilful, bent on having one's own way, impulsive, rash, reckless, incautious, imprudent, hot-headed, intractable, ungovernable, froward, refractory, uncontrollable, contrary, defiant, unmanageable, incorrigible, unruly, recalcitrant; stubborn, obstinate, bull-headed, pigheaded, mulish, obdurate.

Ant. subservient, pliant, impressionable, manageable; cautious, deliberate, methodical.

heady *adj.* **1** *This is very heady punch, so watch your step:* intoxicating, potent, strong, hard. **2** *Being offered such a good job was very heady news:* exciting, exhilarating, intoxicating, thrilling, stirring; tempting, inviting, alluring, seductive, tantalizing.

Ant. **1** non-intoxicating, non-alcoholic, weak, soft. **2** depressing, disappointing, melancholy.

heal *v.* **1** *This salve will help to heal the wound. The doctor claimed to have healed a hundred similar cases:* cure, make well, get well, make whole, heal up, knit, mend; return to health, recover, recuperate, improve, convalesce. **2** *That long talk healed many of our differences:* reconcile, conciliate, settle, compose, rectify, right, set to rights, make harmonious, restore good relations; alleviate, soothe, relieve, salve.

Ant. **1** wound, hurt, injure, harm; reopen, break; make worse, get worse.

◇ *Word origin:* To *heal* comes from Old English *hǣlan*, to make whole.

health *n.* **1** *How is the old man's health?:* physical condition, general condition. **2** *You mustn't do anything to jeopardize your health:* good health, healthfulness, freedom from disease, clean bill of health; well-being, hardiness, robustness, vigour, strength, stamina, hardihood.

Ant. **2** sickness, illness, disease, ailment; weakness, debility, frailty.

◇ *Word origin: Health* comes from Old English *hāl*, whole, healthy.

healthful *adj. There's nothing more healthful than a brisk walk every day:* healthy, good for one's health, wholesome, conducive to health, health-giving, salubrious, salutary, invigorating, nutritious, beneficial, nourishing.

Ant. unhealthy, unwholesome; detrimental, deleterious, dangerous.

healthy *adj. All the children are healthy and happy:* in good health, enjoying good health, able-bodied; hale, hearty, sound, strong, robust, hardy, vigorous, sound in wind and limb, in fine fettle, *Slang* in the pink.
Ant. sick, sickly, ill, infirm, diseased, unhealthy, ailing; feeble, frail, weak, delicate, fragile, unsound, debilitated.
◇ *Usage note:* Both *healthy* and *healthful* are widely used to mean "good for one's health". However, many writers and speakers insist that a distinction be made between these two words: *healthful* for contexts where the meaning is "promoting good health" and *healthy* where the meaning is "enjoying good health". Thus, *Regular exercise is very healthful,* but *You're looking healthy these days.*

heap *n.* **1** *This heap of dirty clothes is for the laundry:* pile, stack, mass, mound, cluster, bundle, batch, bunch; accumulation, collection, gathering, assemblage, agglomeration, aggregation; jumble, mess. **2** *Informal* **heaps** *I had heaps of presents on my birthday:* large amount, a lot, lots, good deal, great deal, load, abundance, profusion, great number, multitude, plenty, considerable amount, mass, oceans, floods; *Informal* stacks, lashings, pots, reams, volumes, swarms; *Slang* oodles.
—*v.* **3** *Rake the leaves and heap them by the garage:* pile, pile up, group, bunch, bundle, amass, mass, lump; collect, gather, concentrate. **4** *The boss usually heaps work on me just when it's time to go home. The boy heaped his plate with turkey and salad:* load, load up, pile, supply abundantly, give in profusion, shower upon, pour upon; fill, inundate, flood, deluge, engulf; accord, assign, award, present.
Ant. **2** few, hardly any. **3** scatter, disperse, dissipate, dispel.
◇ *Word origin: Heap* comes from Old English *hēap,* meaning "a big heap or pile" and also "a big crowd of people". The word has been used colloquially as in sense **2** above for more than 300 years.

hear *v.* **1** *A large audience heard the concert last night:* listen to, be among the listeners at, be present at, be a spectator at, appear at, attend, witness, look on, be in the audience. **2** *I hear that you're moving to France:* understand, find out, be informed, be told, receive news, be led to believe, be made aware of, receive information, learn, gather, discover, ascertain; receive a letter; receive a phone call; *Slang* hear tell. **3** *Hear our plea, O Lord!:* listen to, heed, favour, approve, receive, hearken to, accede to, grant, admit, acknowledge; concede, acquiesce, give assent, be favourably disposed to. **4** *The judge will hear the case next month:* judge, try; officially investigate, examine, inquire into.
Ant. **3** ignore, reject, disapprove, disagree with, condemn.

hearing *n.* **1** *The board of governors is granting the parents a hearing on their complaints next month:* opportunity to be heard, interview, conference, audience, consultation, council; official investigation, inquiry, examination, review, probe; questioning, interrogation. **2** *The mother didn't realize the child was within hearing:* earshot, hearing distance; range of hearing, carrying distance, reach of one's voice, sound.

hearsay *n. It's only hearsay that the chairman is going to resign:* rumour, gossip, report, talk, idle talk.

heart *n.* **1** *The old lady had a warm heart where children were concerned. Did you know in your heart that you'd never return?:* feelings, emotion, sentiment, nature, temperament, mood, disposition, humour; innermost feelings, true nature, soul. **2** *The child's sad story won our hearts:* sympathy, compassion, tenderness, gentleness, soft-heartedness; tenderness, affection, fondness, love; tolerance, indulgence, forgiveness, charity, clemency. **3** *I wanted to argue with him, but I hadn't the heart:* courage, enthusiasm, desire, spirit, firmness, resoluteness, fortitude, pluck, spunk, gameness, resolution; bravery, valour, fearlessness, stout-heartedness, daring, boldness, audacity, audaciousness, gallantry, manfulness; *Slang* guts, backbone, stomach. **4** *The heart of the problem is a shortage of funds:* essence, core, root, source, base, main part, soul, nucleus, centre, kernel, pith, quintessence; essentials, fundamentals, rudiments, principles, foundation; *Slang* nitty-gritty, brass tacks. **5** *The dentist's surgery is in the heart of town:* centre, central part, middle, hub, busiest part, inner part, interior.
Ant. **2** dislike, hatred, hate, enmity; hard-heartedness, cruelty. **3** timidity, cowardice, fear, yellow streak; shyness. **4** minor part, supplement, accessory; side issue, irrelevancy. **5** outskirts, periphery, environs.
◇ *Word origin: Heart* goes back to Old English *heorte,* heart. Cognate words are Greek *kardia,* and Latin *cor,* heart. All of these derive ultimately from the Indo-European word meaning "heart", whose root, reconstructed as *kerd-*, also gives us *creed* and *credo.*

"For Mercy has a human heart,
Pity a human face." — *William Blake*

---

hearth *n.* **1** *Sweep the hearth before stoking the fire:* fireplace, fireside, chimney corner. **2** *After weeks of travelling the salesman was happy to return to his own hearth:* home, abode, household, house, family life, family circle.

heartless *adj. Refusing food to that poor man was a heartless thing to do:* cruel, cruel-hearted, cold-hearted, hard-hearted, callous, unfeeling, insensitive, unkind, unmoved, unstirred, unresponsive, unsympathetic, unmerciful,

pitiless, unpitying, uncaring, brutal, savage, ruthless, inhuman, cold-blooded.
Ant. kind, generous, humane, compassionate, sympathetic, sensitive, merciful, sweet, soft-hearted, warm-hearted.

hearty *adj.* **1** *The Smiths always give their guests a hearty welcome. Sounds of hearty laughter came from the next room:* sincere, genuine, wholehearted, warm; profuse, ample, effusive, generous, thorough, complete, unrestrained, unbounded, unreserved; vigorous, enthusiastic, zestful, heartfelt, lively. **2** *The children are all lively and hearty:* healthy, well, physically fit, hale, sound, vigorous, hardy, strong, robust.
Ant. 1 half-hearted, lukewarm, mild, cool, cold, stiff. **2** sickly, ill, unhealthy, delicate, frail, weak, puny; feeble, debilitated.

heat *n.* **1** *Father can't stand the heat of August:* hotness, warmness, warmth, high temperature; hot weather, warm weather; hot spell, oppressive heat. **2** *Don't make any decisions in the heat of anger:* stress, passion, fervour, fervency, excitement, intensity; height, climax; enthusiasm, eagerness, thrill, zeal, ardour; rapture, transport.
—v. **3** *Heat the stew and we'll have supper:* make hot, warm, bring to the boil, warm up, heat up; (*variously*) cook, reheat, simmer, stew, roast, braise, steam, bake, fry, broil, boil, grill, sauté.
Ant. 1 cold, coldness, coolness, cold temperature; cold wave, cold spell. **2** composure, calmness, coolness. **3** cool, let cool, cool off, chill; freeze.

heated *adj. The men had a heated argument about politics:* vehement, impassioned, passionate, fervent, excited, emotional, intense, stormy, tempestuous, raging, hot, fiery, violent, furious, angry, inflamed, irate, infuriated, bitter.
Ant. dispassionate, calm, mild, peaceful, quiet; friendly, sociable.

heathen *n.* **1** *Dr. Smith is a Baptist missionary among the heathen. The Bible translates the Hebrew term "goy" (non-Jewish nation) as "heathen". The Fula are Muslims and regard their animist neighbours as heathens:* (*variously*) non-Christian, infidel: non-Jew, idolator, gentile, goy; non-Muslim, unbeliever; any uncivilized denier of the God of the Old Testament; (*loosely*) pagan, savage, polytheist, barbarian, uncivilized native. **2** *Informal Heathen though he was the old man never tired of boasting about his sculptor son:* ignoramus, boor, troglodyte.
Ant. 1 (*variously*) Christian, true believer; Jew, adherent of Judaism; Muslim, adherent of Islam, believer.
◇ *Word origin: Heathen* goes back to Old English *hǣthen*, pagan, literally "heath-dweller" and hence "savage", because living on uncultivated land. It acquired its earliest religious associations during the 4th century A.D. thanks to the Bible translations into Gothic by Ulfilas, and the term "heathen" for *gentile* (Old Testament) or *pagan* (New Testament) became universal in the Germanic tongues. In the religious sense the word has always had both *heathens* and *heathen* as plurals, according to whether one is talking about them as individuals or as a group. Incidentally, our word *hoyden* (a bumptious, saucy girl) comes from the same root via Middle Dutch *heiden*, heathen.

"My ideas of civility were formed among heathens." —*Charles Dickens*

---

heave *v.* **1** *Heave this box onto the top shelf:* hoist, haul up, pull up, drag up, draw up, yank up, lift, raise, elevate, boost; pry, lever. **2** *Heave the rocks into the ravine:* throw, pitch, fling, hurl, cast, toss, sling, let fly, propel, fire, launch, *Slang,* chuck, bung. **3** *The grave-digger heaved a great sigh of relief when the work was done:* utter wearily, breathe heavily, emit, exhale, eject, discharge, blow, puff; groan, moan, sob; retch, vomit. **4** *The old man's chest heaved alarmingly as he gasped for breath:* expand and contract, palpitate, surge; expand, swell, dilate, thrust up, bulge, be thrown upward, tilt up, arch; draw a deep breath, pant.
Ant. 1 lower, take down, put down, pull down.
◇ *Word origin: Heave* is from Old English *hebban,* to lift, raise, haul up. It is cognate with Latin *capere,* to take, from which we get our words *capacious,* able to take large quantity; *capacity,* ability to take; and *captive,* one taken, a prisoner.

heaven *n.* **1** Often **Heaven** *May her soul rest in Heaven:* paradise, abode of God and his angels, dwelling-place of the righteous after death, our eternal home, the hereafter, afterlife, next world, world to come, world beyond; life everlasting, eternal bliss, life beyond; the kingdom of Heaven, the heavenly kingdom, the City of God, the heavenly city, the Holy City, the Celestial City, our Father's house, the abode of saints, Elysium, Elysian fields, Island of the Blessed, Isle of the Blessed, Zion, New Jerusalem, Abraham's bosom; Valhalla; Olympus; the happy hunting-ground. **2 the heavens** *The astronomer scanned the heavens through the telescope:* the sky, the firmament, the starry heavens, the vault of heaven, the celestial expanse, the celestial sphere; space, outer space, ether. **3** *Our weekend in the country was heaven:* complete happiness, bliss, sheer bliss, seventh heaven, heaven on earth, supreme happiness, paradise, ecstasy, perfection, rapture, Shangri-la, utopia, dreamland, enchantment, glory, delight.
—interj. **4** *Heavens, what a gigantic birthday cake!:* well, I'll be blowed, goodness, good

gracious, goodness gracious, mercy on us, my stars, my oh my, my word.

Ant. 1 hell, hades, the infernal regions, the underworld, the nether world, the abyss, eternal damnation, eternal fire; limbo. 3 hell, pure hell, agony, misery, torment.

◇ *Word origin: Heaven* comes from Old English *heofon,* Heaven, the heavens, which goes back to a now-lost Common Germanic word meaning "arch of the Sky".

heavy *adj.* 1 *What a heavy suitcase!:* weighty; cumbersome, cumbrous, burdensome, bulky, unwieldy, big, large, hefty. 2 *The thunder was followed by heavy rain. The boat foundered in the heavy seas. Have you always been a heavy smoker?:* abundant, profuse, copious, extensive, excessive, intemperate, unrestrained, immoderate, inordinate, unstinting, extravagant, full, large, considerable; violent, strong, fierce, savage, forceful, raging, tempestuous, turbulent, rampaging, furious, seething, unrelenting, unremitting, roaring; hard, intense. 3 *The taxes on personal property are getting heavy. Going bankrupt was a heavy blow to his pride:* burdensome, oppressive, hard to endure, onerous, harrowing, grievous, harsh, distressing, unbearable, intolerable, unendurable; damaging, injurious, detrimental, ruinous, calamitous, destructive, deadly, crushing, pernicious, deleterious. 4 *My friends, it is with a heavy heart that I speak to you tonight:* sorrowful, sad, gloomy, melancholy, full of care, pained, distressed, depressed, woeful, agonized, miserable, doleful, burdened; cheerless, joyless, downcast, dejected, forlorn, desolate, disconsolate, mournful, grieving, crestfallen, laden with sorrows, grief-stricken, tearful, stricken. 5 *The job carries heavy responsibilities. This philosophical work is too heavy for me to enjoy:* serious, weighty, grave, solemn, momentous, important, overwhelming, of great import, of great consequence, consequential, impressive, awesome, imposing, notable, significant, noteworthy; profound, deep, difficult, complex; tedious, laborious, tiresome, wearisome; dreary, dull, monotonous, pedantic. 6 *I recognized his heavy step on the stairs:* ponderous, lumbering, clumsy, lumpish, leaden, slow, sluggish, lethargic; listless, torpid, lazy, lifeless, apathetic, languid, phlegmatic. 7 *The boy is so heavy that he needs extra-large shirts. Heavy lines on the map indicate main roads:* fat, obese, stout, portly, plump, corpulent, overweight, hefty; thick, bulky, broad, massive; coarse, gross, dense, rough; rugged, sturdy.

Ant. light. 1 lightweight; compact, handy. 2 moderate, mild, soft, gentle, calm, weak; small, scant, sparse, slight, thin, little, skimpy, trifling, trivial. 3 easy, light, bearable, acceptable. 4 happy, gay, cheerful, exuberant, joyful, buoyant. 5 trivial, trifling; frivolous, gay; unimportant, insignificant, inconsequential; entertaining, exciting. 6 agile, brisk, spry, quick, rapid, buoyant, active. 7 thin, skinny.

heckle *v. Several students heckled the speaker:* jeer at, harass, harry, badger, bait, molest, bully, mock, hector, twit, taunt, hound, chivvy, hoot, shout down, boo, hiss.

◇ *Word origin: Heckle* was originally a variant of *hackle,* a board with a set of teeth for cleaning flax or hemp. It has long meant to tease a person as if with such an instrument. *Hackle* may also denote one of the erectile hairs on the necks of some birds and animals, so *Don't get your hackles up* means *Don't let your hair stand on end* (with anger). Both *heckle* and *hackle* are by-forms of the older *hatchel,* flax comb, which is in turn closely related to our word *hook.*

hectic *adj. Moving day was rather hectic:* frenetic, frantic, tumultuous, turbulent, furious, feverish, wild, mad, stormy, headlong, break-neck.

Ant. calm, serene, tranquil, relaxing, restful, peaceful.

hedge *n.* 1 *The new owner planted a hedge round the garden:* fence of shrubs, hedgerow, row of bushes; fence, wall, barrier, border, ring, bound, margin, circumference, delineation. 2 *A savings account is a hedge against misfortune:* protection, guard, insurance; compensation, counterbalance.

—*v.* 3 *We planted lilacs to hedge the lawn:* enclose, surround, border, bound, edge, encircle, outline, fence, wall, ring, shut in, hem, hem in; limit, delineate, demarcate, mark off. 4 *Answer the question fully — don't hedge:* equivocate, evade, be evasive, temporize, duck, dodge, beg the question; *Informal* beat about the bush.

hedonist *n. "Eat, drink, and be merry with no thought of tomorrow" is the code of a hedonist:* pleasure seeker, libertine, profligate, voluptuary, dissipater, debauchee, sensualist, Sybarite.

Ant. puritan; moralist.

◇ *Word origin: Hedonist* comes from Greek *hēdonē,* pleasure.

heed *v.* 1 *Heed the doctor's advice or you'll be sorry:* follow, be guided by, mind, obey, accede to, defer to, yield to, concur, comply with, hold to, be ruled by, bow to, submit to, observe, respect; take notice of, listen to, consider, bear in mind, pay attention to, take note of, give ear to, give a thought to, take to heart.

—*n.* 2 *I warned him, but he paid me no heed:* attention, notice, regard, mind, mindfulness, care, observation, attentiveness, heedfulness, carefulness, prudence, precaution, pains; conscientiousness, scrupulousness, meticulousness, fastidiousness; perusal, study, examination, scrutiny.

Ant. 1 ignore, disregard, slight, neglect, overlook; reject, refuse, turn a deaf ear to, be inattentive to, treat frivolously. **2** inattention, disregard, mindlessness; carelessness, neglect, thoughtlessness.

heedless *adj. Heedless people have the most accidents:* careless, thoughtless, mindless, unmindful, negligent, neglectful, unthinking, inattentive, oblivious, unobserving, unobservant, unwatchful, unwary, unconcerned, unaware, unheeding; remiss, slack, lax, improvident, imprudent, incautious, rash, impetuous, reckless; hare-brained, scatter-brained, foolish, witless; frivolous, happy-go-lucky.

Ant. careful, cautious, wary, mindful, attentive, heedful, thinking, thoughtful, observant, watchful, vigilant; concerned, aware, alert.

height *n.* **1** *The mountain rises to a height of 3,000 metres:* altitude, elevation, upward extent; tallness, highness, loftiness. **2** *The house on the height has a commanding view of the town:* hilltop, vantage point, promontory, eminence; mountain, hill, highland, fell, down, cliff, bluff, mound, rise, knoll, plateau; pinnacle, summit, peak. **3** *Her remark was the height of rudeness:* extremity, utmost degree, limit, ultimate, maximum, peak; pinnacle, high point, summit, zenith, acme, apex, apogee, culmination; supremacy, perfection, consummation, flowering, heyday.

Ant. 1 depth, lowness. **2** valley, canyon, chasm, ravine, abyss; lowland. **3** depth, low point, nadir; minimum.

◇ *Pronunciation tip:* In the Middle Ages, the pronunciation of this word varied between *highth* and *height.* The pronunciation (and the spelling) *highth* enjoyed a great vogue during the 17th century, the word becoming thus analogous in form to *depth, breadth,* and *width.* Milton uses it in *Paradise Lost.* But Shakespeare and the Bible consistently use *height,* so *height* won.

heinous *adj. The murder was a most heinous crime:* atrocious, abominable, abhorrent, repugnant, repulsive, reprehensible, despicable, deplorable, horrid, shocking, monstrous, inhuman, gross, detestable, loathsome, foul, hideous, contemptible, distasteful, objectionable, outrageous; disgusting, revolting, vile, sickening, nasty, beastly; infamous, villainous, iniquitous, nefarious, vicious, terrible, odious, ghastly, offensive; scandalous, outrageous, disgraceful; sinful, wicked, evil.

Ant. good, beneficial, worthwhile, attractive, charming, admirable, laudable, praiseworthy, meritorious; lovable, pleasing, pleasant.

◇ *Word origin: Heinous* comes from Old French *haïneus,* hateful, which comes from *haïr,* to hate.

heir Fem. **heiress** *n. The millionaire's only heir was his son:* beneficiary, inheritor, (*fem.*) inheritress, inheritrix; heir apparent, heir presumptive.

hell *n.* **1** Often **Hell** *The preacher warned us about punishment in Hell:* abode of the damned, infernal regions, lake of fire, bottomless pit, the pit, the abyss, the lower world, the underworld, the nether world, the shades below, place of the lost, home of lost souls, Satan's kingdom, kingdom of the Devil; everlasting fire, hell-fire; (*variously*) Gehenna, hades, inferno, perdition. **2** *Her life has been hell since her husband fell ill:* torment, anguish, agony, wretchedness, suffering, misery; despair, hopelessness, grief, martyrdom, remorse.

Ant. 1, 2 heaven, paradise. **2** bliss, joy, rapture, enchantment, happiness, ecstasy.

◇ *Word origin: Hell* comes from Old English *hel,* from Germanic *haljō,* "hidden place", and is closely related to Old Norse *Hel,* the underworld, also a name of the Norse goddess of death. Cognate Germanic words are *hall, Valhalla, hull, hole, hollow, holster,* and *helmet* — all of which descend in one way or another from the root ideas of covering and concealment. Cognate with these are Latin *celare,* to conceal, *cella,* store-room (from which we get our words *cell* and *cellar*), *occulere,* to hide (from which we get *occult,* i.e. "hidden"), and Greek *kaluptein,* from which we get the older traditional title of the Revelation of S. John, the last book of the New Testament: the *Apocalypse,* literally, the "Uncovering".

help *v.* **1** *Ted helped his brother to build the bookcase. Please help the needy:* assist, give assistance to, aid, lend a hand, give a helping hand, co-operate with, collaborate with, contribute to, serve; support, back, champion, advance, uphold, further, promote, side with, endorse, encourage, advocate, take the part of, stand by, give moral support to, maintain, intercede for; *Slang* stick up for; befriend, guide, advise, minister to, succour, console, nurture; be of advantage; give to, contribute to; *Slang* chip in for. **2** *Help me — I can't swim!:* save, rescue, aid, come to the aid of, snatch from danger, extricate, retrieve. **3** *The injections helped the patient's hay fever:* relieve, alleviate, cure, soothe, calm, mitigate, remedy, improve, lift, put at ease, ameliorate, correct, make healthy, make whole, bring through, bring round, do a world of good for; rectify, mend.

—n. **4** *The movers need some help in lifting the piano. The mayor needs the help of the local party members to be re-elected. The city must give more help to the poor:* assistance, aid, helping hand, co-operation, collaboration, service; support, backing, advancement, promotion, furtherance, endorsement, encouragement, contribution, gift, protection, friendship, support; benevolence, guidance, advice, care, welfare, good offices, kind regard. **5** *The*

cook is in charge of the daily help: employee, worker, workman, labourer, hand, hired hand, assistant, helper, hired helper; (*variously*) farm-hand, domestic, servant, maid, apprentice, underling, menial, retainer, au pair, factotum; staff, crew, work-force, force. **6** *Aspirin may be a help for that headache:* cure, remedy, corrective, preventive, restorative, aid, relief, balm, salve.

Ant. 1 hinder, impede, obstruct, hold back, block, bar, frustrate, thwart, foil, balk; oppose, fight, side against, discourage; *Slang* put down. **2** harm, hurt, injure, attack; kill, let die. **3** make worse, aggravate, irritate, discomfit. **4** hindrance, obstruction, block, bar, opposition, discouragement. **6** bane, aggravation, irritant.

helper *n.* **1** *The carpenter and his helper built the garage in two days:* assistant, aid, mate, aide-de-camp, adjunct, right-hand man, right hand, man Friday, girl Friday, helping hand; auxiliary, deputy; apprentice. **2** *The doctor needs a helper to take over half his practice:* partner, colleague, associate, accomplice, confederate, collaborator, co-worker, confrère. **3** *The women's club needs more helpers to make the charity ball a success:* backer, supporter, patron, benefactor, angel, good Samaritan, fairy godmother, advocate, champion.

henchman *n. The film producer never went anywhere without several henchmen:* right-hand man, lieutenant, retainer, squire; bodyguard, attendant; hireling, minion, flunkey, lackey, yes-man, hanger-on; *Slang* stooge.

◇ *Word origin: Henchman* comes from Old English *hengst* (horse) + *man* (man, i.e. groom). Thus a *henchman* was originally the groom who took care of one's horse.

henpecked *adj. The aggressive woman berated her henpecked husband:* wife-ridden, under the thumb of one's wife; submissive, meek, timid, docile, unassertive, browbeaten, obedient.

Ant. manly, dominating, *Spanish* macho; forceful, aggressive, assertive.

herald *n.* **1** *The herald announced the king's approach:* messenger, town crier, proclaimer, courier. **2** *Shakespeare called the lark the "herald of the morn":* forerunner, harbinger, precursor, envoy, predecessor, foregoer, usher; omen, sign, warning, token, indication, indicator, symbol, clue; forecast, portent.

—*v.* **3** *Trumpets heralded the king's approach:* announce, proclaim, report, foretell, make known, give tidings of, divulge, reveal, usher in; inform, communicate, publish, publicize, advertise, bruit abroad, give voice to.

◇ *Word origin:* Is there a connection between the word *herald* and the name *Harold?* There is: both go back to a Common Germanic word meaning "army commander".

herculean *adj.* **1** Sometimes **Herculean** *The herculean wrestler easily won the match:* strong, powerful, mighty, muscular, strong as Hercules, strapping, rugged, burly, brawny, sturdy, robust, hefty; hard, tough. **2** *Moving the boxes from the attic to the basement was a herculean task:* strenuous, laborious, arduous, exhausting, wearying, fatiguing, toilsome, burdensome, difficult, onerous.

Ant. 1 weak, feeble, frail, delicate. **2** easy, effortless, relaxing, restful.

◇ *Word origin: Herculean* comes from the name of the mythical Hercules, renowned for his great strength and for his performance of 12 gigantic labours (the Labours of Hercules).

◇ *Pronunciation tip:* The preferred pronunciation of *herculean* is *her-kew-LEE-an.* It is also correct to say *her-KEW-lee-an.*

herd *n.* **1** *A herd of antelope thundered across the plains:* pack, drove, flock, bunch, group, cluster, gathering. **2** *There was a great herd of bargain-hunters at the sale:* crowd, mob, throng, horde, swarm, drove, bunch, gang, band, pack, press, mass, host, tribe, flock, cluster, army, troop, legion; gathering, group, assemblage, assembly, company, body, multitude, number, lot, congregation, convocation, conclave, collection, array, party.

—*v.* **3** *The drovers herded the cattle into the pens:* drive, guide, force, goad, spur, lead. **4** *The teacher herded the boys into the playground before the games began:* bring together, collect, muster, round up, assemble, gather, call together; crowd, cluster, huddle, bunch, come together, flock together, rally, group, convene.

hereafter *adv.* **1** *Hereafter, I'll take your advice:* after this, from now on, in future, henceforth, henceforward, subsequently, from this time forth; at a later date, at a later time, one of these days, ultimately.

—*n.* **2** *The pious man expected his reward in the hereafter:* afterlife, next world, life after death, future life, life beyond the grave, world to come, heaven, heavenly kingdom, paradise.

Ant. 1 heretofore, hitherto, before this, before now, before, in the past. **2** mortal life, here, here and now.

hereditary *adj.* **1** *Is baldness hereditary?:* inherited, inheritable, heritable; inbred, inborn, congenital. **2** *The family has a large hereditary fortune:* inherited, handed-down, ancestral; traditional, established.

Ant. 1, 2 acquired. **2** earned, saved.

◇ *Usage note:* See CONGENITAL.

◇ *Word origin: Hereditary* comes from Latin *hereditas,* inheritance, based on Latin *heres,* heir, which also gives us *heir* and *heritage.*

heresy *n. Pope Leo X excommunicated Martin Luther for heresy. A businessman who speaks in favour of lower profits is speaking heresy!:* heretical beliefs, apostasy, heterodoxy, unorthodoxy, unsound doctrine, fallacy, unorthodox belief, unorthodox opinion, nonconformity, irreligion, dissension, iconoclasm.

Ant. orthodoxy, catholicity; convention, conformity, traditionalism.

◇ *Spelling tip: Heresy* can be a spelling problem. You'll get it right if you say it slowly to yourself, then write each syllable carefully, *her-e-sy.*

heretic *n. In former times the Inquisition burned heretics at the stake:* dissenter, apostate, misbeliever; nonconformist, recusant, renegade; backslider, recreant.

Ant. orthodox believer, true believer, adherent.

heretical *adj. Can any church tolerate heretical ideas? Some of the painter's ideas about art seem a bit heretical:* unorthodox, contrary to accepted standards; unconventional, iconoclastic, nonconforming, radical.

Ant. orthodox; conventional, conforming.

◇ *Word origin: Heretical* comes from Greek *hairetikos,* able to choose, from *hairein,* to choose. Related words in classical writings denote the founding of new philosophical schools and the act of siding with one against others. The Romans called such new systems of thought *haereses* ("heresies"), and the Church Fathers early adopted the word in the sense of "unorthodox doctrine", which it has had ever since.

"It is the customary fate of new truths to begin as heresies and to end as superstitions."

— *T. H. Huxley*

---

heritage *n. Fair play is part of our heritage:* tradition, birthright, inheritance, patrimony; estate, family possession, legacy.

hermit *n. The hermit left his cave to go into the village only once a year:* recluse, solitary; religious recluse, eremite, anchorite, desert saint, cenobite, monastic.

◇ *Word origin: Hermit* goes back to Greek *erēmitēs,* desert dweller, religious *hermit* in the desert. (Greek *erēmia* means "desert, waste land".) The deserts of the Middle East have long been the home of religious *hermits* representing Judaism, Christianity, and Islam. The Essenes (of the famous Dead Sea Scrolls) were *hermits* in this sense, as was John the Baptist.

hero Fem. **heroine** *n.* **1** *Odysseus was a legendary Greek hero:* brave man, valorous man, man of courage, champion, fearless fighter, intrepid warrior; great man, noble man, chivalrous man, gallant; daredevil, daring man; legendary person, idealized person, popular figure, idol, star, man of the hour. **2** *The hero gets the girl at the end of the film:* leading man, principal male character, protagonist, male lead, main actor, male star.

Ant. villain. **1** coward, dastard, poltroon. **2** antagonist; villain.

◇ *Word origin: Hero* comes from Greek *hērōs,* hero, whose root meaning is "protector".

heroic *adj.* **1** *King Arthur's heroic deeds are the subject of many stories:* brave, courageous, valiant, valorous, dauntless, undaunted, fearless, lion-hearted, stout-hearted, intrepid, resolute, unflinching, bold, daring; noble, gallant, chivalrous; legendary, mythological, mythical, Homeric. **2** *The opera* Lohengrin *is in the heroic style:* classic, grand, epic, elevated, dignified, exalted; highbrow, extravagant, grandiose, high-flown; ostentatious, pretentious; exaggerated, inflated, bombastic.

Ant. 1 cowardly, faint-hearted, afraid, timid, timorous, irresolute, wavering; ignoble, mean, base, craven. **2** simple, straightforward, unadorned; earthy, lowbrow.

heroism *n. Daniel's heroism in the lions' den is well known:* bravery, courage, courageousness, valour, dauntlessness, fearlessness, lion-heartedness, boldness, daring, fortitude; gallantry, nobility, chivalry.

Ant. cowardice, timidity; baseness.

hesitant *adj. Why were you so hesitant about asking for help?:* hesitating, reluctant, half-hearted, faltering, lacking confidence, hanging back; undecided, doubtful, indecisive, uncertain, halting, unsure, irresolute, wavering, vacillating, shilly-shallying. *Slang* sitting on the fence.

Ant. eager, willing, avid, keen; resolute, determined, steadfast, staunch, firm, certain, sure, confident, decisive, decided.

hesitate *v.* **1** *The driver hesitated at the crossroads, then turned right:* pause, stop briefly, halt, falter; be undecided, be uncertain, be unsure, be irresolute, waver, vacillate, shilly-shally, dilly-dally, straddle the fence. **2** *I hesitate to pay so much for a suit:* shy at, be unwilling, boggle at, begrudge; hang back, be reluctant, balk, shrink from, think twice, scruple.

Ant. 1 go pell-mell, go headlong, continue; be decisive, decide, be firm, be certain, be sure, be confident. **2** welcome, do willingly, embrace, be determined, resolve.

◇ *Word origin: Hesitate* comes from Latin *hæsitare,* to stammer.

heterogeneous *adj. It was a heterogeneous group of rich and poor, old and young:* mixed, varied, diversified, diverse, assorted miscellaneous, motley, variegated, composite; dissimilar, unlike, unrelated, disparate, divergent.

Ant. homogeneous, uniform; same, like, alike, identical, similar.

◇ *Word origin: Heterogeneous* comes from Greek *hetero-* (other, different) + *genēs* (kind), thus "other kind" or "different kinds".

hew *v. The farmer spent a day in the woods hewing timber. The statue was hewn from one large block of marble:* chop, hack, cut, cut down, chop down, sever, lop, prune; carve, chisel, cut out, sculpture, form, shape, fashion, mould, devise, model.

hiatus *n. There was a hiatus of two years before the student went back to college:* lapse, interval, interim, break, space, gap, blank, interruption, disruption, lacuna.

hide *v.* **1** *Hide your money in your shoe:* conceal, secrete, keep out of sight, prevent from being seen, prevent from being discovered, put in concealment, cache, seclude. **2** *The robbers hid in a cave:* lie concealed, be hidden, hide out, conceal oneself, remain in a hiding-place, keep out of sight, lie low, go into hiding; *Slang* go underground. **3** *I can't hide my feelings. Fog hid the mountain:* conceal, obscure, cover, veil, screen, cloak, curtain, shroud, cloud; repress, suppress; mask, disguise.

Ant. 1, 3 reveal, show, expose, display, exhibit, parade, flaunt; find, discover, uncover. **2** find. **3** divulge, disclose, bare, unmask, unveil; admit, confess, avow, lay open.

◇ *Word origin: Hide,* to conceal, comes from Old English *hȳdan,* to hide. *Hide,* animal skin, is from Old English *hȳd,* skin, hide. Both come from the same Indo-European root and are cognate with Latin *cutis,* skin, which gives us our words *cutaneous* and *cuticle,* and Old French *hutte,* which gives us our word *hut.* The idea underlying all these words is that of cover or covering.

hideous *adj. What a hideous wallpaper! Every day we hear of some hideous crime:* ugly, grotesque, dreadful, horrid, repulsive, awful, abhorrent, abominable, frightful, ghastly, revolting, appalling, shocking, repellent, macabre, gruesome, horrendous, horrible; monstrous, loathsome, detestable, disgusting, sickening, vile, odious.

Ant. beautiful, lovely, pleasant, pleasing, charming, captivating, entrancing, appealing.

◇ *Word origin: Hideous* comes from Old French *hideus,* ugly.

high *adj.* **1** *Modern cities are notable for their many high buildings:* tall, lofty, towering, soaring, high-reaching, sky-scraping, cloud-capped. **2** *The car was travelling at high speed. Prices have never been so high:* great, extreme, excessive, inordinate, unreasonable, undue, intemperate, immoderate; extravagant, exorbitant, exaggerated, unrestrained, uncurbed, unbridled. **3** *He holds a high position in the government. The spy was guilty of high treason. One must have high ideals:* important, serious, elevated, lofty, top, eminent, exalted, consequential, significant, notable, distinguished, prominent, pre-eminent, illustrious, august, superior, imposing, leading; prime, primary, foremost, chief, main, principal, capital, predominant, uppermost; peerless, ascendant, grand, excellent, noble. **4** *The speaker had a very high voice:* high-pitched, soprano, in the upper register; shrill, sharp, strident, piercing, ear-splitting. **5** *John has been in high spirits all day:* excited, elated, exuberant, exhilarated, exultant; merry, joyful, joyous, gay, cheerful, light-hearted, playful, jubilant, overjoyed, jolly, gleeful, jovial, mirthful.
—*adv.* **6** *The hawk was circling high in the sky:* at great altitude, at great height, way up, far up, aloft.

Ant. low. **1** short, stunted, dwarfed. **2** moderate, mild, average, reasonable, routine, reduced; subdued, suppressed, restrained. **3** low-ranking, lowly, unimportant, inconsequential, insignificant, undistinguished; secondary, common, routine, average; menial; debased, degraded, ignoble. **4** low-pitched, bass, alto; deep, husky, gruff, hoarse. **5** sad, cheerless, gloomy, joyless, depressed, dejected, melancholy; angry, annoyed, irritable.

high-flown *adj. The young man had high-flown ideas about saving the world. The delegate made a tedious, high-flown speech:* lofty, elevated, grandiose; proud, self-important, lordly, presumptuous; pretentious, extravagant, inflated, high-flying, pompous, florid, high-sounding, sententious, exaggerated, flamboyant; bombastic, magniloquent, orotund, grandiloquent; *Slang* high-falutin.

Ant. down-to-earth, practical, realistic, pragmatic; straightforward, simple, to the point; terse, concise.

highland *n.* Often **Highlands** *This tartan skirt was made in the Highlands of Scotland:* uplands, hill-country, tableland, plateau, mountainous region, heights, downs, fells, headland; rise, promontory, ben.

Ant. lowlands; valley.

highlight *n.* **1** *Rembrandt used highlights to focus attention in his paintings:* spot of intense light, strong illumination; focal point, prominent detail. **2** *The highlight of the children's holiday was the visit to Whipsnade:* climax, outstanding part, main feature, memorable part, high point, peak, most interesting aspect.
—*v.* **3** *The Chancellor's speech highlighted the need for reduced tariffs. The portrait highlighted the queen's necklace:* emphasize, stress, accent, accentuate, give prominence to, underline, focus attention on; make light, make bright.

Ant. 1 shadow. **2** low point; disappointment. **3** de-emphasize, play down, gloss over, slight, neglect, overlook.

high-minded *adj. Such a high-minded person would never lie:* honourable, honest, fair, ethical, principled, sincere, truthful, just, scrupulous, conscientious, upright, worthy, uncorrupt, square-dealing; noble, idealistic, lofty.

Ant. unprincipled, unworthy, dishonourable, dishonest, unfair, unethical, corrupt, unscrupulous, ignoble, mean, base, low.

high-strung *adj. Thoroughbred horses are often high-strung:* nervous, excitable, easily agitated, tense, uneasy, skittish, jumpy, wrought-up, restless, impatient, nervy.

Slang jittery, uptight; neurotic, over-sensitive, moody.

Ant. calm, collected, placid, even-tempered; *Slang* cool.

hijack *v. At five o'clock we heard that the plane had been hijacked and flown to Cuba:* take over, force to travel to a new destination, hold up, seize, (usually, of an aeroplane); divert, overpower, commandeer, re-route.

hike *v.* **1** *The Boy Scouts hiked out to the reservoir:* march, tramp, journey on foot, walk; trudge, roam, wander, rove, ramble; *Informal* hoof it, leg it, go by Shanks's pony.
—*n.* **2** *After the hike to the river the walkers camped for the night:* march, tramp, journey on foot, walk.

hilarious *adj.* **1** *The comedian told several hilarious stories:* very funny, laugh-provoking, comical, uproarious, hysterical, riotous, highly amusing, laughable, rollicking. **2** *Everyone at the party had a hilarious time:* lively, jubilant, jovial, jolly, gay, gleeful, joyous, mirthful, high-spirited, exuberant, exhilarated, jocund, joyful, merry, rollicking; boisterous, noisy, vociferous.

Ant. 1 sad, serious. **2** dull, gloomy, depressed; quiet, sedate.

◇ *Word origin: Hilarious* comes from Greek *hilaros,* cheerful. The original English form (17th century) was *hilarous;* the present form was coined by Sir Walter Scott because it sounded better with the extra *i.*

"I was that man — in a dream:
And each world's night in vain
I patient wait on sleep to unveil
Those vivid hills again."

— *Walter de la Mare*

---

hill *n.* **1** *The park is on a hill overlooking the town. The lorry went up the hill in first gear:* hilltop, knoll, foothill, rise, hillock, hummock, promontory, dune, fell, bluff, cliff, highland, height, elevation, eminence; slope, incline, acclivity, hillside, climb, gradient, ramp, bank; declivity. **2** *Make a hill round each bean plant:* mound of earth, mound; heap, pile.

Ant. 1 low ground, valley, canyon, gorge, gully, ravine, bottom, basin, hollow, dale, glen, vale.

hinder *v. Heavy snow hindered the bus's progress. Lack of practice hindered the team:* delay, slow down, hold up, hold back, detain, arrest, stall, check, curb, hamper, retard, encumber, obstruct, block, impede, restrain, handicap, inhibit, frustrate, interfere with, make difficult; stifle, stymie, thwart, foil, hobble, fetter, spike, hamstring, put a spoke in the wheel.

Ant. help, aid, support, further, advance, promote, benefit, encourage; expedite, facilitate, accelerate, speed, hurry, hasten, quicken.

◇ *Word origin:* the basic meaning of *hinder* is to keep back or *behind.*

hindrance *n. Lack of education could be a hindrance to your career:* impediment, stumbling-block, obstacle, obstruction, handicap, encumbrance, restriction, limitation, constraint, restraint, retardant, difficulty, bar, snag, catch, curb; barrier, blockade, clog, barricade, fetter, shackle.

Ant. help, aid, benefit, assistance, support, furtherance, advancement, spur, boon.

hinge *n.* **1** *This door has a squeaky hinge:* hinged joint, pivot.
—*v.* **2** *The whole business hinges on the committee's decision:* depend, hang, revolve round, be subject to, rest, turn, pivot, swing; be due to, result from, arise from, emanate from.

◇ *Word origin: Hinge* and *hang* both come from Old English *hangian,* to hang. Shakespeare was the first to use *hinge* as a verb (as in sense **2** above).

hint *n.* **1** *Give me a hint so that I can solve the riddle. There was a hint of anger in the statement:* clue, inkling, notion, idea, tip, tip-off, pointer; suggestion, indication, insinuation, implication, innuendo, allusion, intimation, impression, whisper, indirection, slight knowledge; *Informal* word in the ear, word to the wise. **2** *There was just a hint of garlic in the salad:* trace, little, slight amount, touch, whisper, smattering, bit, pinch, grain, iota, jot, suspicion, *French* soupçon.
—*v.* **3** *She hinted that it was time we left:* suggest, intimate, imply, signify, insinuate, indicate, *Informal* tip off.

Ant. 2 abundance, profusion, plethora, amplitude; excess, surplus. **3** assert, declare, announce, state in no uncertain terms.

Word origin: The first recorded uses of *hint* are in Shakespeare. Its origin is unknown.

hire *v.* **1** *The skipper hired two more hands for the voyage:* employ, engage, give employment to, retain, appoint, secure, obtain, get, procure. **2** *During our holidays we hired a boat and went fishing:* rent, charter, lease, let, engage.
—*n.* **3** *The new farm-hand is worth every penny of his hire:* salary, wages, pay, compensation, remuneration, stipend, fee, emolument, recompense, income, receipts, payment, profit, reward, gain, earnings; cost, charge, rent.

Ant. 1 discharge, dismiss, let go, cashier; *Slang* sack, fire, give the boot, show the door.

hireling *n. The gangster sent his hirelings to rob the bank:* menial, minion, flunkey, lackey, retainer; henchman. *Slang* stooge, thug, hatchet man, strong-arm man.

hirsute *adj. Cavemen are often pictured as muscular and hirsute:* hairy; unshaven, unshorn, bearded, bewhiskered, whiskered; bushy, woolly, shaggy, downy, bristled, bristly, prickly.

Ant. hairless, clean-shaven; bald, close-cropped.

hiss *v. The audience hissed the villain of the play:* boo; hoot at, shout down; heckle, catcall, jeer at, scoff at, deride, mock, sneer at, revile; *Slang* give the raspberry.

Ant. applaud, clap, cheer, shout approval.

historic *adj. Plymouth Hoe is a historic spot. November 11, 1918 is a historic day:* important in history, famed, well-known, renowned, memorable, celebrated.

Ant. unimportant, unknown, uncelebrated, ordinary.

◇ *Usage note:* Don't confuse *historic* and *historical. Historic* means famous in history, celebrated: *a historic occasion, Waterloo is a historic battlefield. Historical* merely means concerned with history: *a historical novel, the local historical society.*

historical *adj. The book is based on historical events. It is a historical fact that George Washington had false teeth made of wood:* in history, of history, grounded in history; authentic, actual, real, true, documented, recorded, chronicled, supported by historical evidence; bygone, ancient, belonging to the past, past, former.

Ant. present-day, current, contemporary; fictional, fictitious, legendary, mythical, fabulous.

history *n.* **1** *The 1830's were a decade of history. Today's history is being made in Washington, London, and Moscow:* important events, major events, world events, national events, local events; political change, military action, human progress, development, growth, change; an interesting past, an unusual past; actual events, unalterable facts. **2** *The local librarian is writing a history of Cornwall:* narration of past events, factual story of the past, chronicle, account, record, saga, epic, annals; portrayal, recapitulation, review, résumé; narration, narrative, story, tale. **3** *At one time in history, all this land belonged to the king:* the past, former times, bygone days, bygone times, olden times, old times, the old days, days of old, days of yore, yesteryear, yesterday; tradition.

Ant. **1** current events. **1, 2** fiction, fantasy, legend, myth, fable. **3** the present, today, now; the future, time to come.

◇ *Word origin: History* comes from Greek *historiā*, story.

hit *v.* **1** *The boxer hit his opponent with a hard right to the jaw. The golfer hit the ball 200 yards down the fairway:* strike, deal a stroke, deal a blow, smash, knock, jab, punch, smack, slap, slam, poke, thwack, lambaste, *Slang* paste, clout, sock, belt, wallop, whack, clip, baste, bash; trounce, pummel, drub, pound, beat, flog, thrash, batter, pelt, flail; smite, club, batter, cudgel. **2** *The van hit the car at the junction:* collide with, smash into, bump, butt, bang into; strike together. **3** *The arrow hit the target. Informal The leading car hit 120 miles an hour on the straight:* strike, succeed in striking, go straight to, make a bull's-eye, send to the mark; attain, connect with, reach, achieve, realize, arrive at; effect, execute, bring off. **4** *The bad news hit everyone hard:* affect, touch, move, impress; overwhelm, overcome, crush, upset, hurt, devastate, shatter, abash; arouse, rouse, incite, provoke, quicken, stir, inflame. **5** *Our troops and planes will hit the enemy at dawn. The back-bencher's speech hit at government spending:* attack, strike, strike out at, assault, assail, mount an offensive; denounce, damn, criticize, censure, condemn, revile, lash out at, reproach; *Slang* rap.

—*n.* **6** *Jim is still recovering from that hit on the head:* blow, impact, bump, knock, strike, rap, tap, cuff, bang, thump, thwack; *Slang* clip, wallop, whack, bat, swat, clout, smash, crack, belt, sock; smash, pasting, jab, punch, smack, slap. **7** *The new play is the biggest West End hit in years:* success, popular success, sensation, triumph, winner; victory, boon, find, coup, blessing, godsend.

Ant. **1** caress, pat; block, parry, deflect. **2** miss. **3** miss, miss the mark; fail. **5** retreat, withdraw, surrender, give up; defend, support, champion, praise, acclaim, applaud, compliment. **7** failure, fiasco; *Slang* washout, flop.

◇ *Word origin: Hit* comes from Old Norse *hitta*, to come upon, to meet with.

hitch *v.* **1** *Hitch these two ropes together. Hitch the ox to the plough:* tie, tether, loop, loop together, make fast, couple, attach, fasten, connect, bracket, yoke, clamp, secure; put in harness, harness. **2** *Hitch up your socks:* pull, tug, yank, raise, haul, draw, jerk.

—*n.* **3** *The horse was tied with a hitch to the post:* knot, loop; attaching, joining, coupling, connection, fastening, tying. **4** *The bowler gave a hitch to his trousers before delivering the ball:* pull, tug, yank, jerk. **5** *The programme went off without a hitch:* mishap, mischance, mistake, difficulty, complication, problem, catch, snag; trouble, delay, halt, obstacle, stumbling-block, restraint, hindrance, restriction, curb, stop, check, interruption; handicap, limitation.

Ant. **1** untie, unfasten, uncouple, loose, loosen. **2** pull down.

hither *adv. Come hither and let us have a look at you:* here, over here, to this place, to the speaker, forward, onward, on, near, nearer, close, closer, close by, nearby.

Ant. thither, yon, there; away, farther, farther away.

hitherto *adv. Hitherto I have always liked your work:* till now, until now, up to now, thus far, up to this point, before this, heretofore, hereto, to the present time.

Ant. henceforth, henceforward, hereafter, in future, after this, subsequently.

hive *n. The swarm followed the queen bee to a new*

hive. The stock-exchange was a hive of activity: swarm of bees, colony, cluster; busy place, hub, centre, heart, beehive, apiary, powerhouse.

◇ *Word origin:* Hive comes from Old English *hȳf*, hive, which is related to Old Norse *hufr*, a ship's hull, Latin *cupa*, cask (from which we get *cupola*), Greek *kupē*, mouse-hole, and Sanskrit *kupas*, hole.

hoard *n.* **1** *The mountaineer kept a hoard of tinned food at the hut:* stockpile, cache, store, supply, reserve, fund; gathering, accumulation, collection, pile, heap, mass, amassment, quantity.
—*v.* **2** *Before rationing in World War II, some people hoarded sugar:* stockpile, store away, put by, lay up, cache, save up, store, amass, accumulate, collect, buy up, acquire.
Ant. **2** distribute, dispense, scatter, disperse; waste, squander, dissipate.
◇ *Usage note:* Don't confuse *hoard* and *horde.* To *hoard* is to save, accumulate, or store away, or it denotes an accumulation stored away for safe-keeping: *to hoard gold, A hoard of food was found in the cave.* A *horde* is a crowd: *A horde of Tartars invaded Europe.*
◇ *Word origin: Hoard* comes from Old English *hord*, meaning "treasure". Thus when we speak of a "treasure hoard", we are using the original meaning of the word.

hoarse *adj. The actor's cold made his voice hoarse:* husky, harsh, rasping, raspy, scratchy, rough, gruff, cracked, throaty, guttural.
Ant. full, rich, sweet, mellow, melodious, melifluous.

hoary *adj.* **1** *The old prospector's hair and beard were hoary. The fields were hoary with snow:* grey with age, white with age; white, whitened, grey, greyed. **2** *That's a hoary tale that my grandfather used to tell!:* old, ancient, aged; antique, out-of-date, dated, passé, *Slang* old hat.
Ant. **2** brand-new, new, modern, up-to-date, recent, *Slang* with-it.
◇ *Word origin: Hoary* comes from *hoar* as in *hoar-frost*, which goes back to Old English *hār*, grey-haired. The ancestor-word in Germanic also meant grey-haired, with the additional significance of "venerable", hence "master", from which Modern German derives *Herr*, meaning "Lord", "Sire", (and nowadays) "Mister".

hoax *n.* **1** *Telling the boy he could catch whales in that pond was just a hoax:* mischievous deception, humorous deception, absurd story, exaggerated tale, false alarm, yarn, tall story, fiction; spoof, trick, chicanery, deception, fake, cheat, humbug, canard, hocus-pocus.
—*v.* **2** *The radio audience was hoaxed into believing that Martians had landed:* hoodwink, deceive, delude, take in, fool, trick, mislead, bluff; defraud, swindle, cheat, bilk, dupe, gyp, cozen, gull; *Slang* bamboozle, con.
Ant. **1** truth, true story, fact, factual account. **2** undeceive, enlighten.
◇ *Word origin: Hoax* is probably a contraction of *hocus-pocus.*

hobble *v.* **1** *Hobble the horse so that it won't run away:* fetter, shackle, bind, manacle. **2** *The skier hobbled around on crutches for a month after the accident:* limp, halt, walk lamely; shuffle, lumber, stumble, shamble, stagger, toddle.
—*n.* **3** *Tie the hobble round the horse's rear legs:* fetter, shackle, manacle. **4** *After his stroke the old man walked with a hobble:* limp, lame gait, uneven gait, jerking motion, stumbling motion, shuffle, stagger.
Ant. **2** run, prance, walk briskly. **4** jaunty step, even gait.

"Young man, get a hobby; preferably get two, one for indoors and one for out; get a pair of hobby-horses that can safely be ridden in opposite directions." —*A. Edward Newton*

---

hobby *n. Stamp-collecting is an educational hobby:* diversion, pastime, leisure-time activity, relaxation, amusement, entertainment, pursuit, avocation, divertissement.
Ant. work, job, vocation.

hocus-pocus *n.* **1** *The magician said some kind of hocus-pocus and a rabbit appeared. The children much enjoyed the magician's hocus-pocus:* magic formula, magic words, chant, incantation, mumbo-jumbo, abracadabra; magic spell, charm, spell, bewitchment; conjuring tricks, magic, sleight of hand, legerdemain, prestidigitation. **2** *There's too much hocus-pocus going on in local politics:* deception, trickery, deceit, dishonesty, humbug, hoax, delusion, sham, rubbish, bunkum, fakery; cheat, swindle, confidence trick; *Slang* hanky-panky, flim-flam, hog-wash, fiddle-faddle, poppycock, bosh, flapdoodle, moonshine, tommy-rot, stuff and nonsense, con trick, bull.
◇ *Word origin: Hocus-pocus* is ultimately based on a pseudo-magical Latin formula, *hax pax max Deus adimax*, made up by students during the 16th century.

hoi polloi *The chairman's wife is too proud to rub shoulders with hoi polloi:* the common people, the plebs, the proletariat, the proles, the working class; the lower orders, the masses, the crowd, the mob, the herd, the multitude, the lower classes, the vulgar, the rank and file, every Tom, Dick, and Harry; riff-raff, rabble, *French* canaille.
Ant. aristocrats, the blue-blooded, the upper class, high society, the ruling class; the intelligentsia, the illuminati, the Beautiful People.
◇ *Word origin: Hoi polloi* is Greek for "the many". The expression arose during the Peloponnesian War (431-404 B.C.) and was first used in extant writings by the historian

Thucydides and the philosopher Plato, referring to the common people of Athens. Plato's antonym for *hoi polloi* was "the more refined". Thucydides' antonym was closer to the truth: "the more propertied".

hoist *v. Hoist the flag to the top of the pole:* raise, raise up, pull up, uplift, lift, elevate, heave, take up, bear up, bear aloft.

Ant. lower, pull down, drag down.

hold *v.* **1** *Hold the money tightly. The mother held the baby. A pile of sandbags held the bridge:* keep in the hand, have in the hand, grasp, clutch, grip, clasp; keep in the arms, embrace, enfold; carry, bear, take; support, uphold, brace, prop, shore. **2** *The glue didn't hold. This rope won't hold in a strong wind:* stick, stick fast, cling, adhere, cleave; remain tied, remain bound, stay fixed; lock, unite, clinch, stay, resist breaking. **3** *This box holds a pound of chocolates. Will that filing cabinet hold all these papers?:* have a capacity of, contain, accommodate, take in, include, enclose. **4** *Please hold your applause until the last performer has finished. The police are holding the suspect:* restrain, contain, control, defer, postpone, repress, suppress, suspend, withhold, desist from, hold back, hold off, hold up, hold in check, hold down, forestall, stall, hinder, inhibit, frustrate, thwart, check, curb, stay, keep, halt, block, prevent, limit, restrict; detain, confine. **5** *Please hold my seat until I return. The airline is holding two tickets for you:* keep, retain, reserve, set aside; watch, protect, guard; keep valid, be in force. **6** *He's too lazy to hold a job. The governor has held office for ten years:* keep, maintain, hold down; have, possess, occupy. **7** *The club will hold its monthly meeting next Tuesday:* conduct, carry on, have, execute, engage in, join in; preside over, direct, manage. **8** *We hold these truths to be self-evident. I will hold you responsible for all damage:* maintain, assert, affirm, declare, profess, deem, consider, regard, think, believe, conceive, count, reckon, suppose, presume, assume, understand, surmise, conclude, deduce; propose, submit, offer, put forth, put forward, advance, present, tender, venture, advocate, urge; bind, obligate, enforce.
—*n.* **9** *Take a firm hold on this line:* grasp, grip, clasp, clutch; embrace. **10** *The climber couldn't find a hold to climb any higher:* foothold, toehold, handhold, stand, anchorage, advantage; leverage, purchase. **11** *Her brother has always had a strong hold over her. Legal documents give the present owner a legitimate hold on the property:* influence, controlling force, control, sway, domination, dominance, mastery, rule, command, power, ascendancy; bond, attachment; possession, ownership.

Ant. **1** let go, let loose, put down, let drop; hand over, give over, give. **2** come undone, come unstuck, let go; come untied, loosen, let loose, break, give way. **4** give, bestow, accord, grant, tender, offer, release, let loose, free, let go. **5, 6** give over, turn over, give up. **5** cancel, let lapse. **7** cancel, call off; postpone. **8** disavow, disclaim, deny, refute, repudiate, controvert, reject, abjure, forswear, gainsay.

hole *n.* **1** *The boys watched the cricket match through a hole in the fence:* opening, aperture, breach, open space; break, gap, rent, slit, crack, slot; puncture, perforation. **2** *The bomb left a big hole in the ground. Set a trap over that mouse hole:* hollow place, depression, cavity, concavity, indentation, excavation, pocket, orifice; cave, cavern, tunnel, pit, shaft, dug-out, crater; den, lair, earth, burrow. **3** *The police discovered several holes in the suspect's alibi:* fault, flaw, discrepancy, inconsistency.

Ant. **1** cover, plug, stopper, closure. **2** projection, protuberance, prominence, convexity, mound.

◇ *Usage note:* If a shirt or a theory has *holes,* it is *holey.* Don't confuse this word with *holy,* sacred, or *wholly,* completely.

◇ *Word origin:* See HELL.

holiday *n.* **1** *Easter is considered a high holiday:* holy day; feast day; celebration, jubilee, fiesta, fête; vacation, vacation day, day of rest. **2** *I hope to have a holiday in Paris in the spring:* recreation, leisure, leave, furlough, recess, stay at the seaside or in the country, tour, trip abroad, excursion, honeymoon, outing.
—*adj.* **3** *The whole town was in a holiday mood:* festive, celebrating, gala, merry-making, gay, joyous, joyful, cheery, cheerful.

Ant. **2** work. **3** serious, sombre, sad, gloomy.

◇ *Spelling tip: Holiday* is a shortened form of the term *holy day* and thus has only one *l: hoLiday.*

"I have a great confidence in the revelations which holidays bring forth."

—*Benjamin Disraeli*

---

holiness *n. Please remove your hats out of respect for the holiness of the shrine. Islam denies the divinity of Jesus without disputing his holiness:* sanctity, sacredness, blessedness, saintliness.

Ant. worldliness, secularity.

◇ *Usage note: Holiness* is used as a title for various religious dignitaries, the best-known of whom are the Pope and the Dalai Lama. Thus: *His Holiness Pope Paul VI.* (The correct opening salutation in a letter to either is *Your Holiness.*)

hollow *adj.* **1** *These chocolate eggs are all hollow:* empty inside, empty, unfilled, not solid, vacant. **2** *The boy has a thin frame and hollow cheeks:* concave, rounded inward, curving inward, sunken, cavernous, depressed, indented. **3** *His voice was hollow:* dull, expressionless, unresonant, non-resonant, muted, sepulchral; deep, low, rumbling, reverberating. **4** *The victory, won at too great a price, proved hollow:* meaningless, unavailing, empty, vain, false, pointless, specious, deceptive, fruitless, profitless, useless, futile, unprofitable, worthless, valueless, unsatisfactory, disappointing, nugatory, inconsequential. —*n.* **5** *More gravel is needed to fill the hollow in the drive:* depression, concavity, cavity, hole, indentation, pocket, ditch, furrow, rut, dip, sink; dent, dimple; void, vacuum; cave, cavern, crater, crevasse. **6** *Let's have a picnic down in the hollow:* valley, dale, dell, vale, glen. —*v.* **7** *Hollow out the turnip and make a Hallowe'en lantern:* gouge out, scoop out, dig out, empty out, excavate; groove, channel.

Ant. **1** solid, full, filled, occupied. **2** convex, protruding, rounded, raised. **3** vibrant, resonant; expressive. **4** worthwhile, profitable, useful, valuable, meaningful, significant; satisfying, gratifying, pleasing. **5** protuberance, projection, bump, hump, mound, knob. **6** hill, hillock, mountain, rise, hummock, knoll, bluff, height.

◇ *Word origin:* See HELL.

holocaust *n.* **1** *The mob set fire to the police archives, but some files escaped the holocaust:* conflagration, deadly fire; devastating blaze; bonfire. **2** *Millions of Jews perished in the Nazi holocaust:* devastation, ruin, havoc, ravage; vast slaughter, massacre, carnage, killing, annihilation, genocide, mass murder, butchery.

◇ *Word origin: Holocaust* is from Greek *holos* (whole) + *kaustos* (burnt), thus whole burnt offering.

◇ *Usage note:* This word was first used in its figurative sense of "complete destruction" by Milton. In its original Biblical sense of "whole burnt offering", *holocaust* denotes a profoundly solemn act. Its present-day sense likewise suggests events that are of the utmost gravity: *During the Cold War everyone feared an atomic holocaust.*

holy *adj.* **1** *The Bible and the Koran are considered holy books:* of divine character, of divine origin, divine, divinely inspired, pertaining to God, from God, sacred, heavenly, spiritual, religious, from above, heaven-sent. **2** *Francis of Assisi was a most holy man:* saintly, godly, dedicated to God, devoted to God, spiritual, pure, pure in heart, sinless, angelic, immaculate, unstained, profoundly good, moral, righteous, guileless, uncorrupted, undefiled, unspotted, faithful, virtuous, unworldly; devout, pious, religious, reverent. **3** *In those days suicides could not be buried in holy ground:* consecrated, hallowed, sacred, blessed, sanctified; sacrosanct, inviolable, religious, solemn, venerated; worshipped, adored, revered.

Ant. unholy. **1, 2** secular, worldly, earthly, human; profane, sacrilegious, irreligious, blasphemous, impious; sinful, wicked, evil, corrupt, immoral, impure. **3** unconsecrated, unsanctified, unhallowed, desecrated.

Holy Spirit, Holy Ghost *n. The Trinity consists of the Father, the Son, and the Holy Spirit. Praise Father, Son, and Holy Ghost:* presence of God, third person of the Trinity, Comforter, Paraclete; *Latin* spiritus sanctus, *Greek* hagion pneuma.

◇ *Usage note:* During the past generation many Christians have adopted the expression *Holy Spirit* in place of *Holy Ghost,* although the latter has been hallowed by 1300 years of continuous use, ever since the first Christian missionaries to the Saxons rendered *spiritus sanctus* as *se hālga gāst.* Because both Latin *spiritus* and the original Greek *pneuma* mean "breath" or "spirit", early Christians meant thereby to liken the presence of God to a supernatural *breath. Spirit* (closely related to our words *inspire* and *respiration*) is thus a better translation. *Ghost* has always also meant "soul of a dead person, spook". In Anglo-Saxon times the word had spooky pagan overtones, as well—Old English *gāst,* ghost, underlies our words *ghastly* and *aghast.* Related words in other Indo-European languages have the same basic connotation of terror. All the way from Vedic India (roughly 2000 B.C.) to pagan Iceland (Christianized about A.D. 1000), high-sounding relatives of our word *ghost* evoked the most frightening aspects of wrathful and terrifying gods.

homage *n. This statue was erected in homage to the town's war heroes:* honour, respect, reverence, regard, veneration; praise, tribute, exaltation, glorification, esteem, devotion, deference, obeisance; worship, adoration, adulation.

Ant. dishonour, disrespect, irreverence; condemnation, blame, criticism.

◇ *Word origin: Homage* is based on Latin *homo,* man, and originally was the formal allegiance that a vassal owed his lord.

home *n.* **1** *My uncle is planning to make his home in Devon when he retires:* house, residence, place of residence, dwelling, dwelling-place, domicile, abode, bungalow, place of abode; *Informal* place where one hangs one's hat, home sweet home, **2** *Alaska is the home of the Kodiak bear:* habitat, haunt, abode, habitation, native land, native region, natural environment; *Slang* stamping-ground. **3** *The old woman spent her last years in a home for the aged:* institution, residence; (*variously*) nursing home, sanatorium, hospital, orphanage, asylum, old people's home; refuge, haven.

◇ *Usage note:* Avoid using *home* in the following way: *We saw a nice home for sale in Northampton.* Say *house* instead.

homely *adj.* **1** *The mother is beautiful, but the daughter is homely:* plain-looking, plain, not good-looking, ordinary, drab, unattractive. uncomely, unhandsome, graceless, ungraceful. **2** *Even though he is extremely famous, he*

hasn't forgotten his homely manners. What a warm, homely room!: plain, simple, unassuming, unpretentious, unaffected, ordinary, everyday, familiar, natural, artless, unsophisticated, rustic, provincial, homespun; home-like, snug, cosy, comfortable.
Ant. elegant, grand, splendid, regal, courtly, refined; pretentious, affected, ostentatious, sophisticated.

homicide *n.* **1** *After the death of his brother, the man was charged with homicide:* murder, manslaughter, slaying, bloodshed, foul play; (*variously*) parricide (*killing one's parent or close relative*), matricide (*killing one's mother*), patricide (*killing one's father*), fratricide (*killing one's brother*), fœticide (*abortion*), infanticide (*killing an infant*), uxoricide (*killing a wife*), regicide (*killing a king*). **2** *In Anglo-Saxon times a homicide often paid blood money to the relatives of the person he had killed:* murderer, slayer, killer, manslayer, man killer.
◇ *Word origin: Homicide* is from Latin *homo* (man) + *cidere* (to cut, to kill).

homogeneous *adj. It was a homogeneous crowd of teenage girls, all wearing jeans and sweaters:* of the same kind, all alike, of a piece; uniform, unmixed, unvarying, unadulterated; constant, pure; akin, kindred, similar.
Ant. heterogeneous, mixed, varied, varying, different, diverse, divers, various, divergent.
◇ *Word origin: Homogeneous* goes back to the Greek words *homos* (same) + *genos* (kind), hence of the same kind.

honest *adj.* **1** *An honest man. Honest dealings:* law-abiding, ethical, truthful, decent, upright, fair, just, righteous, honourable, virtuous, principled, conscientious, scrupulous, blameless, proper, reasonable, faithful, true-blue, tried and true, reputable, fair and square, square, straight, straight as a die, above-board, open and above-board, as good as one's word, honest as the day, *Slang* on the level, on the up-and-up; legal, legitimate, lawful. **2** *Give me an honest answer. I expect an honest day's work. Have some bread and butter; real, honest to goodness dairy butter:* true, truthful, frank, straightforward, candid, blunt, plain-spoken, forthright, clear-cut, trustworthy, dependable, reliable, solid; valid, genuine, real, authentic, bona fide. **3** *The youth has an honest face. She appreciated my honest praise:* sincere, open, frank, candid, plain, guileless, ingenuous, unaffected, innocent, artless, unsophisticated; reserved, undisguised.
Ant. dishonest. **1** unethical, untruthful, unfair, unrighteous, dishonourable, bad, immoral, unprincipled, unscrupulous, unfaithful, improper; illegal, illegitimate, unlawful, corrupt, fraudulent; crooked, base, low, vile. **2** false, lying, untruthful, deceitful, unreliable, untrustworthy, undependable, fake, treacherous, invalid, counterfeit. **3** guilty, insincere, artful, deceitful, hypocritical, disguised, secretive.
◇ *Word origin: Honest* comes from Latin *honos*, honour.

honesty *n. Are you questioning my honesty?:* truthfulness, integrity, trustworthiness, veracity, word, sincerity, uprightness, rectitude, incorruptibility, honour, reputability, faithfulness, morality, scruples, principles, fairness, just dealing, square dealing, straight dealing, good name; innocence, guilelessness.
Ant. dishonesty, crookedness, corruption, deceitfulness, deception, untruthfulness, falseness, falsity, lying, mendacity, trickery, fraud, chicanery, duplicity, insincerity, deceit, guile; unfairness.

"The louder he talked of his honour, the faster we counted our spoons."
—*Ralph Waldo Emerson*

---

honour *n.* **1** *George Washington was a man of honour:* honesty, high-mindedness, principle, honourableness, probity, decency, uprightness, nobleness of mind, scrupulousness, faithfulness, conscientiousness, sincerity, trustworthiness; honesty, integrity, virtue, fairness, justness, truthfulness, truth, veracity, rectitude, goodness, constancy. **2** *I was taught to show honour to my elders. My great-grandfather won honour in the Boer War:* respect, esteem, regard, deference, reverence, homage, veneration, admiration, approbation, tribute, adoration, worship, glorification, exaltation; fame, glory, acclaim, renown, greatness, importance, high standing, distinction, prestige, repute, commendation, praise, recognition, note, notability, celebrity, credit, eminence, prominence, illustriousness, good report, good name, a feather in one's cap. **3** *It's an honour to meet you:* privilege, compliment, pleasure, favour; grant, authorization, permission, sanction, power, right, leave, liberty.
—*v.* **4** *Honour thy father and thy mother:* esteem, revere, venerate, respect, value, regard, admire, praise, laud, extol, commend, exalt, glorify, worship, have regard for, look up to, think much of, show deference to, pay homage to, pay tribute to, bow down before. **5** *His Majesty will honour us with a visit:* confer honour upon, give one the privilege of, favour, compliment, grant, dignify, glorify. **6** *Will the bank honour this cheque?:* take, accept, credit, acknowledge; make payment on, pay, redeem, cash, credit, make good.
Ant. 1-5 dishonour. **1** bad character, meanness, lowness, baseness, dishonesty, unscrupulousness, insincerity. **2** low regard, disrespect, contempt, disdain, scorn, shame, disgrace, disrepute, condemnation, infamy, ignominy, degradation, debasement, bad name. **3** insult, disfavour. **4** condemn, hold in

contempt, disrespect, disdain, scorn, insult, defame, shame, degrade, debase, discredit, slight, disobey. **5** insult, offend, affront. **6** refuse, reject; refuse payment on; *Slang* bounce.

hoodwink *v. The stranger hoodwinked several of us into investing in a non-existent oil-well:* deceive, trick, dupe, cheat, swindle, defraud, victimize, cozen, gull; *Slang* rook, bamboozle; fool, hoax.

hook *n.* **1** *The waterlogged chest was raised from the sea with a hook:* grapple, grapnel, gaff, crook, bill, billhook, pot-hook, fluke, crampon. **2** *The dress is fastened with a hook and eye:* link, fastening, bracket, coupling. **3** *Hang your hat on the hook in the hall:* peg, knob, nail.
—*v.* **4** *Hook the french window when you come in:* fasten, latch, secure, make fast, make secure; buckle, hitch. **5** *The fishermen were hooking bass as fast as they could get their lines in the water:* catch, take, bag, nab, seize, grab; (*variously*) net, snare, ensnare, trap, capture; *Informal* collar.
Ant. **4** unhook, unfasten, unlatch. **5** let go, loose; throw back.

hooligan *n. A gang of hooligans wrecked the football train:* rough, ruffian, tough, thug, rowdy, mugger, juvenile delinquent, vandal; *Slang* punk; gangster, gunman, crook, desperado; *Slang* hoodlum, strong-arm man.
◇ *Word origin: Hooligan* seems to have an Irish origin, deriving probably from a music-hall song about a rowdy Irish family, which was popular in the 1890's.

hoot *v.* **1** *The owl hooted all night. The train hooted in the distance:* screech, shriek, scream, howl, wail, shrill, whoop, ululate; moan, whistle, blow, honk. **2** *The crowd hooted its disapproval. The students hooted the speaker:* howl, shout, cry out, sing out, bellow, heckle, proclaim, bawl, wail, screech, scream, roar, yelp, whoop, yowl, din, chorus; boo, jeer, hiss, ridicule, scoff at, mock, cry down, sneer at, snicker at, taunt, deride, catcall; *Slang* give a raspberry.
—*n.* **3** *The speaker was greeted with a chorus of hoots:* boo, jeer, hiss, catcall, sneer, snicker, taunt, cry of disapproval, caterwaul, *Slang* raspberry; shout, shouting, wail, wailing, screech, screeching, scream, screaming, yelp, whoop, yowl, outcry; uproar, tumult, commotion, racket.
Ant. **2** hail, cheer, applaud, clap, give a standing ovation; encourage, yell bravo, *Slang* root for; welcome, salute, acclaim. **3** cheer, applause, clapping, standing ovation; encouragement, shout of bravo, hurray, hurrah, huzzah; welcome, acclamation.

hop *v.* **1** *The rabbit hopped across the field. The boy hopped over the puddle and ran down the path:* jump, spring, leap, bound, vault, bounce, skip; prance, gambol, frisk, bob, caper, romp, trip; jump over on one foot, leap over, spring over, vault over, skip over.
—*n.* **2** *With one hop the frog was back in the pond:* jump, spring, leap, bound, vault, skip, bounce.

hope *n.* **1** *Today's young people give me hope for the future:* faith, confidence, belief, assurance, reassurance, encouragement, trust, reliance, conviction, optimism, expectation, great expectations, expectancy, anticipation, assumption, presumption. **2** *Father's fondest hope is to retire to Cornwall:* desire, wish, aspiration, ambition, longing, craving, yearning, hunger, dream, day-dream, fancy, heart's desire, *Informal* hankering. **3** *Our only hope is that the coastguard heard our SOS:* chance of survival, possible way out, help, rescue, salvation, saving grace.
—*v.* **4** *I hope you're feeling better. The Johnsons hope to buy a new house next year:* trust, feel sure, be confident, desire, wish, intend to, aspire, look forward to, count on, expect, contemplate, anticipate, reckon on, long for, crave, yearn for, hunger for, dream of, day-dream, have one's heart set on, be bent upon, have an eye to, have a fancy for, *Informal* hanker after. **5** *The doctors are doing all they can; now we can only hope:* be hopeful, have faith, hope for the best, trust in the Lord, trust; look on the bright side, take heart, be optimistic.
Ant. **1** dread, despair, despondency, hopelessness, distrust, doubt, disbelief. **4** doubt, deem unlikely, despair of. **5** despair, dread, expect the worst.

hopeful *adj.* **1** *The team is hopeful that it will win the championship:* full of hope, in hopes, expectant, anticipative, optimistic, confident, assured, trusting. **2** *The patient's good appetite was a hopeful sign of recovery:* promising, favourable, propitious, auspicious, heartening, reassuring, cheering, encouraging, fortunate, of good omen.
Ant. **1** despairing, dejected, despondent, pessimistic, down in the mouth. **2** discouraging, depressing, unpromising, unfavourable, inauspicious, disheartening, unencouraging, adverse, unfortunate.

hopefully *adv. To travel hopefully is better than to arrive:* expectantly, confidently, optimistically, sanguinely.
◇ *Usage note:* The practice of using *hopefully* as a synonym for *I hope* has become alarmingly common. The sentence *hopefully we will meet again on Thursday* is not good English. Use the adverb only to mean *with hope in one's heart,* as in *she started each day hopefully.*

hopeless *adj.* **1** *It's a hopeless situation:* without hope, past remedy, incurable, beyond recall, irrevocable, irreversible, irreparable, irredeemable, irretrievable, impossible, beyond help, lost, futile, vain, useless, pointless. **2** *The wrestler felt hopeless when he saw how big his opponent was:* without hope, pessimistic, despairing, dejected, abject, despondent, disconsolate, depressed, down-hearted, downcast; sad, forlorn, heart-broken, heavy-hearted, sick at heart, sorrow-stricken, grief-stricken; down in the mouth, melancholy.

Ant. 1, 2 hopeful. **1** promising, encouraging, optimistic, favourable, propitious, auspicious, heartening, reassuring, rosy; remediable, curable, redeemable, retrievable. **2** full of hope, confident, assured, encouraged, heartened, expectant, gay, cheerful, happy, uplifted, light-hearted, joyful.

horde *n. Every summer the valley was invaded by hordes of grasshoppers:* multitude, host, crowd, throng, mob, bunch, crush, drove, assemblage, assembly, gang, party, congregation, company, gathering; tribe, legion, band, troop.

◇ *Usage note:* See HOARD.

◇ *Word origin: Horde* goes back to Turkish *ordū*, army, camp. The word originally referred to the *horde* of Mongols who invaded Europe under Genghis Khan. The same word gave its name to *Urdu*, the principal language of Pakistan.

horizon *n. The course in philosophy opened up new horizons for the student:* limit of experience, limit of knowledge, frontier, world, domain, area, range, vista, outlook, sphere, expanse, compass, perspective, stretch, field, bounds, prospect.

◇ *Word origin: Horizon* is from Greek *horizōn*, separating circle, apparent line between earth and sky. The term is one of hundreds that have entered our vocabulary directly from the works of the philosopher Aristotle.

horizontal *adj.* **1** *Draw a horizontal line from one side of the page to the other:* parallel to a base line, parallel to the horizon, level, parallel to the ground, level with the ground; flat, plane, even, plumb, flush. **2** *After he wrenched his back he had to stay horizontal for a week:* recumbent, prone, supine, reclining, prostrate, lying down, *Informal* flat on one's back.

Ant. 1 vertical, up and down; inclined, uneven. **2** upright, on one's feet, standing.

horn *n.* **1** *The young goat was just beginning to grow horns:* antler, antenna; spike, point. **2** *A modern symphony orchestra usually contains four horns:* (*brass instrument: variously*) French horn, cornet, trumpet, trombone, tuba, bugle, baritone, sousaphone, euphonium, saxhorn, flügelhorn.

horrendous *adj. Informal Don't tell the children such horrendous stories:* horrible, horrid, awful, dreadful, appalling, frightful; revolting, repulsive, repellent, horrifying, ghastly, gory.

Ant. pleasing, pleasant, attractive, agreeable.

◇ *Word origin:* See HORROR.

horrible *adj. The accident was a horrible sight. The sewer emitted a horrible smell. What a horrible thing to say!:* gruesome, harrowing, revolting, repulsive, sickening, awful, disgusting, loathsome, terrible, vile, repellent, hideous, nauseating, distasteful, detestable, disagreeable, unpleasant, unsavoury, foul, rank, nasty, bad, abhorrent, odious, obnoxious, abominable, unbearable, insufferable, appalling, dreadful, atrocious, monstrous, ghastly, shocking, frightful, forbidding, horrid, unspeakable, disquieting, despicable.

Ant. pleasing, pleasant, agreeable, attractive, appealing, delightful, wonderful, good, charming, enchanting, fetching, lovely.

horrify *v. Try not to horrify Mother with such gruesome stories:* shock, terrify, frighten, affright, petrify, make one's flesh creep, make one's hair stand on end; disgust, sicken, repel, revolt, appal, nauseate, make one sick, make one turn pale; daunt, dishearten, disconcert, disquiet, dismay.

Ant. charm, enchant, please, delight; gladden, reassure, calm, soothe.

horror *n.* **1** *I have a horror of snakes:* fear, terror, dread, panic, apprehension, alarm, trepidation, dismay; aversion, loathing, abhorrence, detestation, abomination, hatred, distaste, disgust, dislike, antipathy, repugnance, revulsion, repulsion. **2** *The horrors of war are beyond description:* cruelty, outrage, inhumanity, crime, atrocity; awfulness, hideousness, terribleness, misery, distress, wretchedness, hardship, suffering, anguish, torment, discomfort, privation, affliction, woe.

Ant. 1 liking, affinity, delight, love, attraction. **2** pleasure, delight, gratification, happiness, joy, wonder, reward, goodness, benefit, boon.

◇ *Word origin: Horror* and *horrendous* come from Latin *horrere*, to bristle, as with fear or anger.

hors d'oeuvre *n. Hors d'oeuvre and cocktails were served on the patio before dinner:* appetizer, canapé, titbit; (*variously*) little sandwich, finger sandwich; *Italian* antipasto.

◇ *Word origin:* We have borrowed *hors d'oeuvre* directly from French. Literally it means "out of the work" or "out of the main course". You may well find it on your English menu written as *hors d'oeuvres*, but in French it is an invariable noun and has no plural.

◇ *Pronunciation tip: Hors d'oeuvre* is pronounced *or-DURV(R)*, with silent *h*.

horse *n.* **1** *Saddle the horse:* (*young*) foal, yearling; (*female*) filly, mare, brood-mare; (*male*) colt, stallion, sire, stud, gelding; (*variously*) steed, charger, mount, galloper, racehorse, trotter, pacer, mustang, Arab, Dartmoor pony, bronco, cart-horse, thoroughbred, draught-horse, palfrey, dobbin, hackney, hack, jade, nag. **2** *The king's army had 1,000 foot soldiers and 200 horse:* cavalry, cavalrymen, soldiers on horseback, horse-soldiers, mounted troops, troopers, mounted warriors, dragoons, yeomanry, lancers, hussars, cossacks.

Ant. 2 infantry, foot-soldiers.

horseman *n.* **1** *A good horseman can ride any horse well:* rider, rider on horseback, equestrian, (*fem.*) equestrienne; jockey, postillion; (*variously*) horse breeder, trainer, groom, stable owner, stable keeper, stable-man, stableboy, hostler, ostler. **2** *A detachment of horsemen rode into battle:* cavalry soldier, cavalryman, horse-soldier, trooper, dragoon, yeoman, lancer, hussar, cossack.

hose *n. The shopper bought two pairs of nylon hose:* stockings, hosiery; socks, tights.

hospitable *adj.* **1** *Fred and Jane are always very hospitable to their guests:* gracious, cordial, genial, friendly, warm, amicable, welcoming, open-handed. **2** *I pride myself on being hospitable to new ideas:* receptive, accessible, open, open-minded, approachable, agreeable, responsive, amenable, tolerant.

Ant. 1, 2 inhospitable. **2** narrow-minded, unreceptive, unapproachable, unresponsive, intolerant.

◇ *Pronunciation tip: Hospitable* and *inhospitable* may be pronounced so that either the *HOS-* or the *-PIT-* is accented. Thus both *hos-PIT-a-ble* and *HOS-pi-ta-ble* are correct, as are both *in-hos-PIT-a-ble* and *in-HOS-pi-ta-ble.* If you have to make a choice, probably *hos-PIT-a-ble* and *in-hos-PIT-a-ble* are more frequently heard.

hospital *n.* **1** *The young doctor was house surgeon at the local hospital:* medical centre, clinic, polyclinic, infirmary, sick bay. **2** *Our local council is building a new hospital for the mentally disturbed:* (*variously*) asylum, sanatorium, nursing home, home, general hospital, isolation hospital, maternity home, cottage hospital, mental home, psychiatric hospital.

host[1] Fem. **hostess** *n.* **1** *Fred was host at the Old Boys' dinner. A good hostess makes her guests comfortable:* master of ceremonies, mistress of ceremonies; party-giver, welcomer. **2** *Your host, John Smith, hopes your stay at the hotel will be a pleasant one:* hotel manager, hotel keeper, innkeeper, hotelier, proprietor, (*fem.*) proprietress, landlord; restaurant manager, receptionist, maître d'hôtel, head waiter, head waitress.

Ant. 1, 2 guest. **2** lodger, boarder, traveller; diner; customer, patron.

host[2] *n. A host of barbarians attacked the city:* multitude, horde, swarm, troop, legion, army, drove, array, throng, *Informal* lot; band, group, party, gathering, body, convention, meeting, congress, confluence, conclave, company, convocation, congregation; mob, crowd, gang, crew.

Ant. handful, sprinkling, small group, scattering.

hostile *adj.* **1** *The town was surrounded by hostile troops. The hostile forces fought for possession of the mountain pass:* enemy, belligerent, opposing, opposed, fighting, battling, contending, clashing, warring, at war; dissident, on bad terms, at odds, at loggerheads, with crossed swords. **2** *A hostile look. Hostile words:* belligerent, angry, antagonistic, contrary, contentious, quarrelsome, bristling, disputatious, argumentative, disagreeing; malicious, vicious, malevolent, venomous, spiteful, bitter, malignant, malign, mean, ugly; unfriendly, unkind, unsympathetic, ill-disposed, ill-natured, disagreeable, incompatible, cranky, cantankerous, snappish, truculent, testy, touchy; cold, chilly, icy.

Ant. 1 friendly, peaceful. **2** friendly, approving, agreeable, amiable, amicable, cordial, congenial, sweet, kind, kindly, warm, sympathetic.

> **Exploring the Word**: *Host* and *hostess* refer to a person who entertains a guest and come from Latin *hospes*, guest. The same Latin word gives us *hotel* and *hostel*, as a *youth hostel*, a place where a guest stays; *hospital*, which originally meant an inn for pilgrims and other travellers; and *hospitable* and *hospitality*, referring to graciousness in welcoming and entertaining guests. In biology, a *host* is a living plant or animal from which a parasite, the uninvited "guest", obtains nourishment or protection. *Host*[1] and *host*[2] go back to the same Indo-European root which gives us our word *guest* — the root meaning "stranger who may be one's host or one's guest". A well-known cognate is Russian *gospodin*, "sir". Incidentally, the Eucharistic *host* is not related to any of the foregoing words but comes from Latin *hostia*, sacrifice. In classical usage, *hostia* referred to sacrificial animals; early Christian writers took it over as the term for the Eucharistic bread, or host. The ultimate origin of this word is unknown.

hostility *n.* **1** (*usually* **hostilities**) *Hostilities broke out between Germany and France in 1939:* war, warfare, act of war, state of war, warring, fighting, fight, conflict, combat, military operation, battle, battling, clash; contest, fray, fracas, scuffle, feud, duel, dispute, contention, argument, altercation, dissidence, disagreement, bickering. **2** *I can't understand his hostility to our suggestions:* belligerence, animosity, antagonism, antipathy, enmity, opposition, contrariness; anger, malice, viciousness, malevolence, bitterness, spleen, unfriendliness, ill will, rancour, hatred, hate, vindictiveness, venom.

Ant. 1 peace; truce, treaty, alliance. **2** agreement, approval, sympathy, goodwill, amity, fellow-feeling; love, friendship, amiability, cordiality, congeniality.

hot *adj.* **1** *I detest hot weather. You're hot after all that exercise. Bake the biscuits in a hot oven:* very warm, uncomfortably warm, warm, sweltering, sultry, torrid; at high temperature, heated; simmering, steaming, burning, boiling, broiling, scalding, scorching, blistering, searing, baking, roasting, sizzling, piping hot, fiery, smouldering; melting, molten, red-hot, white-hot, incandescent. **2** *Put some of this hot sauce on the barbecued chicken:* piquant, peppery, highly seasoned, sharp, nippy, biting, pungent. **3** *You'd better learn to control that hot temper of yours:* intense, violent, furious, raging, vehement, agitated, fierce, fiery, ardent, passionate, fervid, frenzied, feverish, stormy, tempestuous, hectic, excited, emotional, animated, earnest, wrought-up, ungovernable. **4** *The police are hot on the trail of the robbers:* very close, following very closely, in close pursuit, near. **5** *Is there any hot news on the election results?:* late, latest, new, recent, up to the minute, fresh. **6** *Informal This is going to be the hottest new style of the year:* popular, most popular, successful, sought after, fast-selling; attractive, good, top, excellent.

Ant. 1 cold, chilly, chilled, cool, cooled, frigid, freezing, icy, frosty. **2, 3** mild, bland. **3** peaceful; unemotional, objective, dispassionate. **4** cold. **5** old, out-of-date, old hat, stale.

"I believe in getting into hot water. I think it keeps you clean." —*G. K. Chesterton*

---

hotchpotch Also **hodgepodge** *n. The garden is just a hotchpotch of bushes and weeds:* jumble, mess, confusion, mixture, muddle, miscellany, conglomeration, medley, mélange, hash, patchwork, mix, composite, potpourri.

◇ *Word origin: Hotchpotch* is a variant of *hotchpot,* an Anglo-Norman legal device for combining the property of several parties so that it could be divided equitably.

hotel *n. The hotel can accommodate 300 guests:* inn, lodging, hostel, hospice; motel, pub.

hound *n.* **1** *The hounds cornered the fox at the edge of the woods:* hunting dog, beagle, foxhound; dog, canine; *Slang* mutt, doggy; (*young*) pup, puppy, whelp.

—*v.* **2** *The debt collector hounded the poor man until he paid the debt. Don't keep hounding me to cut the grass!:* chase, pursue, track, trail, stalk, dog, follow, hunt, tail; nag, keep after, keep at, hector, harass, harry, badger, worry, annoy, needle.

Ant. 2 run from, flee, escape, evade, elude.

◇ *Word origin: Hound* is from Old English *hund,* dog. Until early Modern English it was the regular generic term for "dog". See Word origin under DOG.

hour *n.* **1** *At what hour did you tell them to come?:* time, particular time, fixed time. **2** *When is your lunch hour?:* period, interval, span, space. **3** *The rock singer is the teenage idol of the hour:* present time, current moment, day.

◇ *Word origin: Hour* comes from Greek *hōra,* season, time of day, period of time, hour.

house *n.* **1** *The new house has four bedrooms and a box-room:* home, dwelling, dwelling-place, residence, abode, domicile, habitation; (*variously*) cottage, country house, town house, mansion, manor house, terraced house, semi-detached, bungalow. **2** *You woke up the whole house!:* household, family. **3** *He was the last ruler of the House of Hapsburg:* royal family, noble family, line, dynasty, clan; lineage, ancestry, family tree, ancestors, strain. **4** *A church is a house of worship:* building, meeting-place, gathering-place; (*variously*) church, temple, theatre, opera house, concert hall, auditorium, hippodrome, hall. **5** *The actors counted the house from behind the curtain:* audience, spectators. **6** Often **House** *The bill was passed by the lower House and sent to the Lords:* House of Commons, Commons, House of Lords, Lords, congress, lower chamber, legislature, assembly, council. **7** *John works for a commercial house now:* business firm, company, concern, firm, business, organization, corporation, partnership; store, shop.

—*v.* **8** *Many villagers volunteered to house the flood victims:* lodge, shelter, harbour, quarter, board, billet, put up, accommodate; furnish with a house. **9** *The vintage car was housed in a barn:* store, garage, shelter, keep, contain, accommodate.

Ant. 8 evict, eject, oust, expel. **9** discard, throw away.

household *n.* **1** *Our neighbours have a large household. Mother takes care of the household:* family, family circle, house; home, domestic establishment, hearth.

—*adj.* **2** *How much are your household expenses? This is a good household soap:* for a family, housekeeping; for a house, for home use.

housewife *n. It's hard to combine a business career with being a housewife:* homemaker, wife; housekeeper, family manager, home economist.

◇ *Word origin:* Housewife comes from Old English *hūs* (house) + *wīf* (wife). *Hussy* is a different form of the word *housewife* and this same root, *hūs,* house, is also found in *husband.*

housing *n.* **1** *Many families are in need of better housing:* house, home, dwelling, domicile; abode, shelter, lodging, lodgement, quarters, accommodation, residence, habitation. **2** *That machine should be protected by a metal housing:* case, covering, enclosure, shield, sheath, jacket, envelope.

hovel *n. Do you mean to say that he has lived in that hovel for forty years?:* wretched dwelling, broken-down residence, cramped shelter, ramshackle building; *Slang* dump, hole; shanty, shack, slum.

Ant. mansion, palace, show-place, villa, castle, manor.

◇ *Word origin: Hovel* comes from Middle English *hovel,* shed. The word is of otherwise unknown origin — it cannot be traced back further.

hover *v.* **1** *The helicopter hovered over the trees:* pause in flight, hang suspended, hang, poise, float; flutter, flit, flitter. **2** *I can't stand anyone hovering near me when I'm working:* linger about, hang about, hang around, wait near at hand, attend, haunt. **3** *The patient hovered between life and death:* waver, hang, pause, falter, hang in doubt, see-saw, fluctuate, vacillate.

Ant. 1 fall, sink, drop. **2** leave alone; depart, go away, withdraw, retreat.

howl *v.* **1** *The dog howled all night:* yelp, bay, cry, bark. **2** *To howl with pain. To howl with glee:* cry out, yell, shout, bellow, roar, shriek, scream, hoot, yowl, yelp, wail.

—*n.* **3** *The mournful howl of a wolf woke the campers. A howl of protest went up when the result was announced:* cry, bay, yelp, bark, whine; outcry, clamour, uproar, yell, shout, bellow, roar, shriek, scream, yowl, hoot, wail, groan.

Ant. 2, 3 whisper, murmur, mutter.

hub *n. London was the hub of the Empire:* centre, axis, pivot, core, focal point, heart, focus, middle.

hubbub *n. What was all that hubbub about?:* uproar, pandemonium, tumult, rumpus, fuss, to-do, hullabaloo, disturbance, stir, commotion, hue and cry, disorder, turmoil, bedlam, ferment, fuss, perturbation, agitation, pother; racket, noise, clamour, din, hurly-burly, babble.

Ant. quiet, quietness, serenity, calm, calmness, tranquillity, peacefulness, repose, equanimity, stillness, hush.

◇ *Word origin: Hubbub* comes from an Old Irish war cry *abu!* which comes from Old Irish *buide,* victory.

huddle *v.* **1** *The campers huddled round the campfire for warmth:* crowd together, throng, cluster, gather closely, flock together, press together, converge, collect, herd. **2** *The lost boy was found huddled up in a doorway:* curl up, snuggle, nestle, cuddle, make oneself small.

—*n.* **3** *The executives went into a huddle before the stockholders' meeting:* gathering, conference, meeting, discussion, confab, session, putting together of heads. **4** *Please sort out that huddle of clothes in the middle of the floor:* heap, jumble, mass, mess, muddle, hotchpotch; crowd, group, bunch; confusion, disarray, disorder.

Ant. 1 disperse, scatter. **2** stretch out, stand up.

hue *n. The bedroom is painted in pale hues of green and gold:* colour, shade, tint, tincture, tone; cast, tinge.

◇ *Word origin: Hue* is from Old English *hīw,* appearance.

hue and cry *n. A great hue and cry went up when they found they had been robbed:* clamour, hullabaloo, uproar, outcry, bellow, roar, yell, shout, yowl, shriek; cry of alarm, alarm; howl of protest, dissenting shout.

◇ *Word origin: Hue* is from legal Anglo-Norman (the French imported to England by William the Conqueror and used here as the official language for several hundred years following 1066): *hu* (outcry) *e* (and) *cri* (cry) — the outcry calling for help to pursue a felon. Over the years *hu e cri* became *hue and cry.*

huffy *adj. Jane tends to be huffy when she doesn't get her own way:* easily offended, touchy, angry, irate, waspish, quarrelsome, ill-humoured, resentful, querulous, petulant, churlish, snappish, testy, irritable, peevish, grumpy, cross, curt, rancorous, hard to live with, out of sorts, sulky, surly, sullen, resentful, offended, wounded, hurt, moping, glowering, disgruntled, discontented, moody, morose; *Slang* shirty, in a lather.

Ant. calm, soothed; good-humoured, cheerful, sunny, gay, friendly, pleasant.

hug *v.* **1** *They hugged the child before putting him to bed:* embrace, hold, clasp, press to the bosom, hold close, squeeze, cuddle, snuggle, nestle; cling together. **2** *The road hugs the side of the mountain:* keep close to, cling to, follow closely, parallel closely, hover near.

◇ *Word origin: Hug* is probably from Old Norse *hugga,* to console.

huge *adj. As is suggested by its name, the Colossus of Rhodes was huge. She spent a huge amount of money on that coat:* extremely large, immense, enormous, vast, colossal, giant, gigantic, titanic, mammoth, monstrous, elephantine, jumbo, gargantuan, leviathan, herculean, cyclopean, Brobdingnagian; massive, great, overwhelming, staggering, stupendous, imposing, mighty, spectacular, monumental, extravagant, prodigious.

Ant. small, little, tiny, dwarfish, minute; *Informal* wee, tiddly, itsy-bitsy; microscopic, infinitesimal; petty, puny, insignificant.

hulking *adj. The gorilla is a great hulking animal:* bulky, heavy, massive, powerful, big, husky, oversized, massive, ponderous.

◇ *Word origin: Hulking* comes from *hulk,* big clumsy ship, from Greek *holkas,* heavy cargo ship, derived from *helkein,* to tow (the term seems originally to have denoted a type of barge).

hull *n.* **1** *Don't throw the peanut hulls on the floor. The freighter's hull is made of steel plates:* husk, shell, skin, pod, coating, shuck, peel, rind, case; epidermis, carapace, integument, tegmentum; body of a ship.

—*v.* **2** *Hull a bowlful of peas:* shell, husk, shuck.

◇ *Word origin: Hull* comes from Old English *hulu,* husk, pod. The word is related to *hole, hollow,* and *hell.*

hum *v.* **1** *Do you know the tune I'm humming?:* croon, drone, intone. **2** *The engine hummed pleasantly as the plane reached cruising speed:* whirr, purr, drone, thrum, vibrate; buzz. **3** *The market hummed as trading began:* be busy, be active, bustle, thrive, be in full swing.

—*n.* **4** *The steady hum of the motor indicated that the car was working properly:* whirring, whirr, drone, droning, purring, purr, vibration; buzzing, buzz; murmur, faint sound.

human *adj.* **1** *To err is human. We all belong to the human race:* characteristic of mankind, like man; of man, of men, mortal, manlike, anthropoid. **2** *If you must dismiss the employee do it in a human way:* sympathetic, compassionate, humane, gentle, merciful, kindly; personal, individual; humanitarian.
—*n.* **3** *Wolves will not usually attack humans:* human being, person; man, Homo sapiens.
Ant. 1 non-human; god; animal. **2** inhuman, beastly, brutish, unsympathetic, cruel; impersonal.
◇ *Word origin: Human* goes back to Latin *humanus*, human, related to Latin *homo*, man. The root meaning of *homo* is "earthling", and it is related to the familiar Latin word *humus*, earth, soil, which also gives us our words *exhume, humble,* and *humiliate.* Also related is Greek *chthōn*, earth, which gives us our word *autochthonous* ("originally dwelling") as in the sentence *The Aborigines are the autochthonous inhabitants of Australia.* Another related word is Old English *guma*, man, which gives us *bridegroom*, literally "bridesman".

humane *adj. Helping that family was a very humane thing to do:* kind, kindly, compassionate, sympathetic, benevolent, warm-hearted, merciful, pitying, human, humanitarian, generous, philanthropic, magnanimous, unselfish.
Ant. inhumane, cruel, inhuman, brutal, barbarous, uncivilized, merciless, unmerciful, pitiless, ruthless; unkind, unsympathetic.

humanity *n.* **1** *The Nazi war criminals were condemned for crimes against humanity:* the human race, mankind, man, humankind, Homo sapiens; mortals, human beings, people. **2** *Our humanity unites us:* humanness, human nature, mortality. **3** *There is great humanity in all the writing of Tolstoy:* kindness, kindliness, compassion, sympathy, gentleness, tenderness, benevolence, warm-heartedness, charity, fraternal feeling, fellow-feeling, brotherly love, goodwill, humaneness, mercy, love.
Ant. 1-3 inhumanity. **3** unkindness, cruelty, brutality, ruthlessness.

humble *adj.* **1** *Many famous people are surprisingly humble:* modest, unassuming, unpretentious, unpresuming, without arrogance, unostentatious; demure, gentle, meek; subservient, obsequious, deferential. **2** *It was a humble but nevertheless a comfortable house. The managing director began in a very humble job:* poor, low, lowly, modest, wretched, shabby, miserable, inferior; plain, simple, common, ordinary, undistinguished, obscure, inglorious, insignificant, inconsequential, unimportant; low-ranking, plebeian.
—*v.* **3** *The king's forces were humbled by the peasants' revolt:* bring down, put down, subdue, chasten, make humble, bring low, humiliate, abash, put to shame, embarrass, disgrace, mortify, shame, take down a peg; conquer, crush, degrade, pull down, derogate, trample underfoot, dishonour, demean, abase, debase, make lowly, cast dishonour upon.
Ant. 1 proud, arrogant, haughty, immodest, pretentious, vain, vainglorious, pompous, lordly, overbearing, snobbish, conceited, superior, boastful, assuming, ostentatious, presuming, presumptuous. **2** rich, wealthy, sumptuous, elegant; superior, out of the ordinary, distinguished, glorious, famous, important, significant, consequential, high, high-ranking, aristocratic. **3** exalt, raise, elevate, magnify, aggrandize.
◇ *Word origin: Humble* comes from Latin *humilis*, low, lowly, which is derived from the same root as *humus*, ground, and *homo*, man, "earthling".

"From the highest to the humblest tasks, all are of equal honour; all have their part to play." —*Winston Churchill*

---

humbug *n.* **1** *By means of humbug, the swindler sold the worthless jewels as genuine:* deception, deceit, trick, trickery, fraud, cheat, flimflam, swindle, artifice, double-dealing, forgery, fake, counterfeit, imposture, dodge; pretence, pretension, sham, make-believe, spoof, hoax, fiction. **2** *His speeches are always full of humbug:* pretence, pretentiousness, pretension, sham, hypocrisy, flummery, equivocation, mendacity, lying, lies, falsification, falsehood; nonsense; *Informal* bunk, bunkum, balderdash, blather, claptrap, hocus-pocus; *Slang* hokum, bull, blarney. **3** *The humbug tried to pass himself off as a lawyer:* fraud, quack, fake, faker, impostor, charlatan, mountebank; swindler, cheat, cheater, confidence man, con man, sharper, trickster; liar, fibber, perjurer, hypocrite.
—*v.* **4** *He humbugged me into believing his story:* deceive, trick, delude, fool, hoax, bamboozle, mislead, beguile, hoodwink, dupe, cheat, swindle, cozen, gull, take in; lie, fib; falsify, fabricate, misrepresent.
—*interj.* **5** *Christmas? Bah! Humbug!:* nonsense, rubbish, balderdash; *Slang* hooey.
Ant. 2 truth, truthfulness; the genuine article. **4** undeceive, disabuse.

humdrum *adj. It was just another humdrum day:* dull, boring, monotonous, run-of-the-mill, uninteresting, routine, dreary, tiresome, tedious, wearisome, wearying, lifeless, flat, insipid, trite, trivial, banal, commonplace, hackneyed, mediocre, uninspired, uninspiring, indifferent, unexciting, uneventful, unvarying, common, ordinary, unexceptional.

Ant. stimulating, exciting, provocative, entertaining, interesting, lively, gay, animated, exceptional, extraordinary.

humid *adj. It's so humid today that my clothes are sticking to me:* muggy, sticky, sultry, steamy, damp, moist, dank, clammy.

Ant. arid, dry, moistureless.

◇ *Word origin: Humid* goes back to Latin *umere*, to be moist, which also gives us *humidity, humidor*, and *humour.*

humiliate *v. I was so humiliated when I couldn't remember her name:* embarrass, make ashamed, shame, mortify, chagrin, abash, humble, disgrace, dishonour, discomfit, chasten, crush, subdue, debase, degrade, bring low, bring down a peg.

Ant. honour, make proud, elevate, exalt, elate, please.

humiliation *n. When accused of lying, she flushed with humiliation:* embarrassment, shame, mortification, chagrin, discomfiture; disgrace, dishonour, degradation, debasement.

Ant. pride, honour.

humility *n. With true humility he thanked the others for their help:* modesty, humbleness, unpretentiousness, lack of pride, self-abasement, diffidence, demureness meekness, shyness, timidity, bashfulness.

Ant. pride, arrogance, haughtiness, pretentiousness, vanity, vainglory, pomposity, disdain, snobbishness, conceit, superiority, boastfulness, presumption, superciliousness.

humorous *adj. The play was so humorous that the audience laughed all through it:* funny, comic, comical, full of humour, witty, droll, mirthful, laughable, amusing, side-splitting, rib-tickling, waggish, whimsical, jocular, jocose, farcical, satirical; ludicrous, ridiculous, nonsensical.

Ant. unfunny, grave, serious, solemn, sober; sad, melancholy; earnest, matter-of-fact.

humour *n.* **1** *The humour of the situation made us all laugh:* funniness, comedy, comicality, ridiculousness, ludicrousness, drollery, nonsense, jocularity, jocoseness, jocosity. **2** *The book is cheerful and full of humour:* jokes, joking, wit, wittiness, witticisms, gags, wisecracks, jests, jesting, foolery, fooling, foolishness, tomfoolery, raillery, ridicule, buffoonery, waggery, comedy, high comedy, low comedy, broad comedy, slapstick, low humour, broad humour, burlesque, farce, caricature, parody, travesty, satire, whimsy, word-play, puns. **3** *Dad is always in a good humour on pay-day:* mood, temper, disposition, spirits, frame of mind.

—*v.* **4** *You have to humour him when he's in one of those moods:* give in to, indulge, pamper, flatter, spoil, baby, go along with, comply with, put up with, suffer, tolerate, appease, soothe, placate, mollify, cajole.

Ant. 1, 2 seriousness, gravity, solemnity, sobriety; sadness, grief, sorrow, melancholy. **4** stand up to, oppose, fight; aggravate, rouse, arouse, excite.

◇ *Word origin:* In ancient physiology, a *humour* was any of the four body fluids (blood, phlegm, yellow bile or choler, and black bile or melancholy) which were believed to influence a person's health and temperament (hence "good humour" and "bad humour"). Latin *umere*, to be moist (which gives us *humid, humidity, humidor*) is closely related to *humour.*

hump *n.* **1** *The Arabian camel has one hump, the Bactrian camel has two;* protuberance on the back, hunch; bulge, lump, bump, mound, prominence, swelling, convexity, projection, excrescence; knob, knurl.

—*v.* **2** *When the puma humps its back, it will attack:* arch, hunch, raise in a hump, lift, bend, put up; tense. **3** *Just hump this suitcase into the hall, please:* carry, lift; shoulder, hoist; *Slang* lug.

hunch *n.* **1** *I have a hunch that Jack will be there after all:* intuition, feeling, premonition, presentiment; idea, good idea, suspicion, inkling, clue, glimmer.

—*v.* **2** *The boy hunched his shoulders against the wind:* bend, hump, arch, tense.

hunger *n.* **1** *This meal ought to satisfy your hunger. Hunger is a major problem in the drought-stricken areas of Africa:* desire for food, hungriness, appetite, ravenousness, voracity; famine, starvation, malnutrition, lack of food. **2** *The hunger for power has created many tyrants:* craving, greed, greediness, desire, lust, itch, yearning, appetite, thirst, hankering; fondness, liking, love, relish.

—*v.* **3** *A good student hungers after knowledge:* long for, desire, crave, burn for, have an appetite for, wish, want, thirst after, lust after, yearn for; itch for, pant for, hanker after.

Ant. 1 satiety, fullness; overeating. **2** repulsion, revulsion, disgust, repugnance, loathing, abhorrence, aversion, detestation, hatred.

hunk *n. The boy broke off a large hunk of bread and ate it:* chunk, piece, block, lump; *Informal* wad, gobbet; quantity, portion, mass.

hunt *v.* **1** *November is a good time to hunt deer:* shoot, go after, chase, track, stalk, trail, seek; drive out, ferret out. **2** *Police are hunting an escaped convict in this area:* pursue, chase, track, trail, trace, follow the trail of, follow the scent of, look for, search for, try to find, look high and low for, go in quest of, follow; turn everything upside down, leave no stone unturned, peer into every corner; explore, probe, inquire into.

—*n.* **3** *The hunt is expected to begin at sunrise:* chase, hunting; fox-hunt, riding to hounds, course, coursing.

hurdle *n.* **1** *The favourite cleared the last hurdle and galloped towards the finish:* barrier, obstacle (*in*

steeplechasing) fence, hedge, wall. **2** *The oral is the student's last hurdle before he graduates:* obstacle, barrier, difficulty, hindrance, impediment, obstruction, stumbling-block, snag, interference.
—*v.* **3** *The athlete hurdled the last fence and ran to victory:* jump, leap, vault, bound, spring over, clear.
◇ *Usage note:* Don't confuse *hurdle* and *hurtle.* A *hurdle* is a barrier or obstacle; *to hurdle* something is to jump over it; it is used both literally (of hurdles, or fences) and figuratively (i.e., of difficulties): *The horse jumped over the hurdle. The athlete hurdled the fence.* To *hurtle* means to go very fast, speed: *The car hurtled down the road. The bicycle hurtled into the pedestrian.*

hurl *v. The last competitor in the field events hurled the discus 60 metres:* throw, fling, cast, sling, pitch, heave, toss, let fly; propel, launch, discharge, fire off; *Slang* chuck.
Ant. catch, capture, seize; grasp, clutch, grab; take, receive.

hurrah Also **hurray, hooray** *interj.* **1** *Three cheers for the team — hip, hip, hurrah!:* good, fine, wonderful, excellent, great, bravo, heaven be praised, hallelujah, hosanna.
—*n.* **2** *Thousands of hurrahs greeted the marathon walkers when they entered the stadium:* shout of joy, cry of acclaim, cheer, bravo, exultation; acclaim, congratulation, salute; *Archaic* huzza, huzzah.

hurricane *n. The hurricane struck the town with winds of 135 miles per hour:* violent tropical storm, (*in the western Pacific*) typhoon; tempest, windstorm, cyclone, monsoon.
◇ *Usage note:* A *hurricane* is a violent rainstorm that starts over the ocean in the tropics, covers a large area, and is accompanied by winds blowing in a circular pattern at over 73 miles an hour; a *typhoon* is such a storm in the Western Pacific and the China seas. A *tornado* has whirling winds which form a funnel-shaped cloud that causes destruction in a narrow path. A *cyclone* is a *tornado* and is also used to refer to a considerably larger low-pressure weather system surrounded by a circular flow of wind.
◇ *Word origin: Hurricane* comes to us from Spanish *huracán.* The word entered Spanish from the Carib Indians in the West Indies.

hurry *v.* **1** *Hurry home before it gets dark:* go quickly, come quickly, move fast, move hastily, hasten, make haste, speed, speed up, accelerate, rush, hustle, get a move on; bolt, dart, dash, scurry, scuttle, scramble, whizz, push on, press on, cover the ground, go like the wind, go like a shot, lose no time, *Slang* make tracks, step on it, step on the gas, get cracking. **2** *Don't hurry the cook or she'll spoil the dinner:* urge on, goad, prod, drive on, push on, pressure, egg on; rush, hustle, speed up, accelerate.
—*n.* **3** *There was so much hurry at the last minute that she forgot her hat:* rush, haste, scurry; hustle and bustle, fuss, flurry, flutter, hurry-scurry, tumult, turmoil, commotion, ado.
Ant. 1 delay, slow down, slacken; procrastinate, dawdle, dally; move slowly, creep, crawl. **2** delay, slow, slow down, retard, detain. **3** slowness; composure, calmness.

hurt *v.* **1** *These new shoes hurt. My feet hurt:* pain, ache, smart, sting, burn; torment, distress, agonize, torture. **2** *The driver hurt himself badly in the accident. Don't put that hot cup on the table; it will hurt the varnish:* injure, harm, disable, maim, cripple, lame, mangle, mutilate, impair, damage, maul; bruise, cut, scratch, scar, mar, mark, disfigure, deface. **3** *A sloppy appearance hurt the youth's chances of getting a job:* hamper, impair, hinder, hold back, encumber, impede, retard, restrain, limit, frustrate, inhibit, weaken, obstruct, oppose, spike, check, thwart, foil, block, preclude, exclude, balk, forestall; decrease, lessen, reduce, diminish, lower, narrow, minimize. **4** *It hurts me when you talk like that:* offend, sting, wound one's feelings, aggrieve, grieve, distress, trouble, cut to the quick.
—*adj.* **5** *The boy came home with a hurt knee:* injured, bruised, cut, scratched; scarred, marked; disabled, crippled, lame; mangled, mutilated, damaged; painful, aching, smarting. **6** *She's hurt because she wasn't invited to the party:* offended, resentful, indignant, pained, wounded, injured, stung, piqued, crushed; distressed, crestfallen, dismayed, disheartened, aggrieved, mortified, chagrined; morose, melancholy, heartbroken, miserable, wretched, heartsick, dejected.
—*n.* **7** *This lotion will make the hurt go away:* pain, soreness, ache, sting, discomfort. **8** *He never got over his hurt at being rejected:* pain, discomfort, sting, pique, resentment, mortification, embarrassment, chagrin, aggravation, annoyance; distress, suffering, misery, dismay, dejection, grief, heartbreak, wretchedness, torment, agony.
Ant. 1 relieve, alleviate, assuage, soothe. **2** heal, cure; repair, fix, restore. **3** help, aid, abet, benefit, forward, promote, advance, expedite; increase, multiply, heighten, widen. **4** console, calm, soothe; please, compliment, compensate. **5** relieved, alleviated, assuaged, soothed; healed, cured; repaired, restored. **6** consoled, calmed, complimented, soothed, placated. **8** happiness, pleasure, joy, delight, ecstasy; pride, satisfaction.
◇ *Word origin: Hurt* comes from Old French *hurter,* to hit.

hurtle *v. The motor cycle hurtled along the road at 70 miles an hour:* speed, fly, race, plunge, rush, spurt, shoot, tear, scoot, whizz, run, hie, whisk, gallop, scamper, scurry, scuttle, bolt, dash, dart, bound; go like the wind, go like a shot, go hell for leather.

Ant. crawl, creep, inch, drag, go at a snail's pace.
◇ *Usage note:* See HURDLE.

husband[1] *n. Her husband is a stockbroker:* spouse, mate, man, consort, *Slang* hubby, old man; groom, bridegroom; married man.
Ant. bachelor; wife.

husband[2] *v. A nation must husband its natural resources:* conserve, preserve, use sparingly, manage wisely; save, set aside, retain, keep, maintain; hoard, accumulate, amass.
Ant. waste, squander, spend.

> **Exploring the Word:** Our word *house* comes from Old English *hūs,* which also gives us both the word *husband* (literally a housedweller, householder) and the work most early householders did, *husbandry,* farming. *Home* comes from Old English *hām,* a house with land, and a collection of such houses was called a *hamlet* (and such cities as *Nottingham, Birmingham,* etc., still contain the word *ham,* house, a collection of houses). *Cabin* comes from Late Latin *capanna,* hut, while *shack* comes from the Aztec Nahuatl word for a wooden hut, *xacalli* (pronounced "shacalli"). *Bungalow* is from Hindustani *banglā,* meaning Bengalese, a house in the Bengalese style. *Mansion* comes from Latin *manere,* to dwell, which also gives us *manor,* the most important dwelling in an area, and, via Scottish, *manse,* a homestead. *Penthouse* comes from Latin via Old French *apentis,* appendage, as to a building, while *apartments* are a separate suite of rooms *apart* from others in the same building.

hush *interj.* **1** *Hush! Someone's coming!:* be quiet, be still, be silent, quieten down, silence, quiet; *Informal* shut up, shush, pipe down, keep mum.
—*v.* **2** *The mother hushed the baby by rocking it:* quiet, shush, quell, silence, still; soothe, calm, mollify.
—*n.* **3** *There was such a hush in the empty house, it was eerie:* silence, stillness; quiet, peacefulness, tranquillity.
Ant. 3 racket, din, noise, clamour.
◇ *Word origin: Hush* comes from Middle English *husssht,* "Shush!"

husky *adj.* **1** *The husky boy carried the heavy package easily:* big, strong, robust, muscular, brawny, sturdy, strapping, burly, thickset, solid, broad-shouldered, powerful, athletic, strong as an ox; stout, overweight, plump. **2** *The teacher's voice is husky because she has a cold:* hoarse, harsh, rough, coarse, rasping, grating, guttural, throaty, croaking, cracked.
Ant. 1 small, puny, weak; thin, slim, underweight. **2** shrill.
◇ *Word origin: Husky* comes from *husk,* and may refer to the toughness of *husks,* or in its sense of "hoarse" may have originally meant "dry as a husk."

hussy *n. That hussy had the nerve to flirt with my husband!:* strumpet, brazen woman, brash girl, saucy miss, minx; loose woman, bawd, woman of easy virtue, adulteress, trollop, baggage, wanton; prostitute, harlot, whore, lewd woman, fallen woman, scarlet woman.

hustle *v.* **1** *If you're going to be ready in time, you'd better hustle:* hurry, hasten, make haste, rush, speed up, move quickly, bolt, dart, dash, scurry, scuttle, scoot, scramble, get a move on, step on it, fly, lose no time. **2** *Informal A salesman has to hustle for a living:* be aggressive, work energetically; *Slang* be an eager beaver, be on the ball. **3** *When the man started to fight, they hustled him out of the bar:* push, shove, nudge, elbow, prod, jostle, shoulder, throw, toss.
—*n.* **4** *There's always a hustle in the kitchen before dinner:* energetic action, bustle, stir, hurry, scurry, rush, flutter, flurry, fuss, tumult, turmoil, commotion, scramble, hubbub, ado, hurry-scurry.
Ant. 1 procrastinate, dawdle, dally. **2** relax, take it easy. **4** calmness, composure; peace, quiet, tranquillity.
◇ *Word origin: Hustle* comes from Middle Dutch *husselen,* to shake, to toss.

hut *n. In summer the shepherd lived in a hut near the high pasture:* shed, lean-to, log cabin, cabin, shieling, barn, chalet, shack, shanty, hutch.
Ant. mansion, palace, castle, manor.

hutch *n. The boy cleaned out the rabbit-hutch once a week:* pen, coop, cage, enclosure, shed, sty, cote, stall, crib.

hybrid *n. Mules are a hybrid, the offspring of a male donkey and a female horse. The play was a hybrid of tragedy and farce:* cross-breed, half-breed; mixture, composite, amalgam; six of one and half a dozen of the other, neither one thing nor the other.
Ant. thoroughbred.
◇ *Word origin: Hybrid* comes from Latin *hibrida,* mongrel or hybrid (animal). The word was used for one born of a Roman father and a foreign mother, or a freeman and a slave.

hygienic *adj. Public drinking-fountains are not very hygienic:* clean, sanitary, germ-free, sterile, disinfected, pure, unpolluted, uncontaminated, disease-free, aseptic; healthful, healthy, salutary, salubrious, wholesome; harmless, uninjurious.
Ant. unsanitary, contaminated, dirty, impure, polluted; unhealthy, harmful.

hymn *n. The church service ended with a hymn:* song in praise of God, anthem, psalm, devotional song; song of praise.

hyperbole *n. "She's as big as a house" is an example of hyperbole:* overstatement, exaggeration, extravagant statement, figurative statement, stretch of the imagination, figure of speech, metaphor.
Ant. understatement.
◇ *Word origin: Hyperbole* comes from Greek

huper (over) + *ballein* (to shoot), to overshoot the mark, exceed, hence exaggerate.

hypocrisy *n. The M.P. showed his hypocrisy by saying that he was for the bill and then voting against it:* insincerity, falsity, two-facedness, duplicity, *Slang* phoniness; dishonesty, deceit, mendacity.

Ant. sincerity, truthfulness, honesty, forthrightness.

hypocrite *n. You must be a hypocrite to say that you like her hat, and then laugh at it behind her back:* insincere person, false person, two-faced person, *Slang* phoney; deceiver, dissembler.

◇ *Word origin: Hypocrite* comes from Greek *hupokritēs,* stage actor, hence one who plays a part.

hypocritical *adj. It would be hypocritical to praise bad work:* insincere, false, two-faced, dishonest, deceitful, deceptive, feigning, feigned, counterfeit, false, *Slang* phoney.

Ant. sincere, heartfelt, unfeigned, genuine, honest; forthright, plain-spoken.

hypothetical *adj. The medical students were asked how they would treat a hypothetical case and were marked according to their responses:* supposed, assumed, theoretical, speculative, conjectural, possible, imaginary, suppositional, postulated; conditional, uncertain, questionable, dubious.

Ant. real, actual, true; certain, proved, proven, demonstrated, tested, tried, confirmed, established, substantiated, verified, corroborated, evidential.

hysteria *n. The doctor gave her an injection to calm her hysteria:* emotional outburst, hysterics, fit, frenzy; uncontrolled fear, uncontrolled weeping.

hysterical *adj.* **1** *Both parents grew hysterical when they couldn't find their child:* overcome with fear, distraught, beside oneself, distracted, uncontrollable, frenzied, crazed, overwrought, raving, worked-up, wrought-up; *Informal* carried away, crazy, out of one's mind. **2** *The hysterical thing about the joke is how the comedian tells it:* wildly funny, uproarious, comical, laughable, farcical, ridiculous, absurd, ludicrous, amusing, droll.

Ant. 1 calm, composed, poised, self-possessed. **2** sad, sombre, serious, grave, melancholy.

I

iconoclast *n. He's an iconoclast who insists on attacking organized religion:* dissenter, rebel, nonconformist, radical, revolutionary.

Ant. conformist, assenter.

◇ *Word origin: Iconoclast* literally means an image-breaker. It comes from Greek *eikōn* (image) + *klastēs* (breaker). *Iconoclasm,* "image-breaking," was originally a policy of the Byzantine emperor Leo the Isaurian, who in A.D. 726 banned religious statues, icons, and other pictures, as well as candles, crosses, and holy medals — on the theory that these "images" were a hindrance to the conversion of Jews and Muslims.

icy *adj.* **1** *Drive carefully — the roads are icy:* frozen over, glazed, slippery, sleety; cold, frigid, frozen, freezing, bitterly chilly, wintry, arctic, raw, bitingly cold, frosty, gelid. **2** *An icy reception greeted the late arrivals. She gave me an icy stare:* hostile, unfriendly, cold, without warmth or feeling, frigid, frosty, distant, impassive, aloof, haughty, cool, unemotional, cold-hearted, glacial, chilly, chilling.

Ant. 2 warm, friendly, gracious, sympathetic, cordial.

idea *n.* **1** *The idea of equating material advancement with success is slowly changing:* concept, mental picture, notion, thought, something believed, insight, interpretation, apperception, appreciation, conception. **2** *We need to have some idea of the cost:* hint, inkling, clue, indication, intimation, impression, approximation, notion, suggestion. **3** *The council approved the commissioner's idea for improving traffic conditions:* proposal, suggestion, approach, solution, recommendation. **4** *My idea of a holiday involves sun, sand, and sea:* view, feeling, understanding, sentiment, opinion, outlook, conviction, belief.

◇ *Word origin: Idea* comes from Greek *ideein,* to see.

> "Positive ideals are becoming a curse, for they can seldom be achieved without someone being killed, or maimed, or interned."
>
> —*E. M. Forster*

ideal *n.* **1** *The ideals of a free nation include liberty and justice for all:* aim, objective, goal, ultimate aim, ultimate end, highest goal; level of perfection, highest attainment, summum bonum. **2** *Sir Laurence Olivier is the ideal of many actors:* model, hero, idol, inspiration, perfect model, standard of excellence; exemplar, last word, ultimate, criterion, paradigm, pattern, archetype; primary aim, objective, dream, chief hope, target of one's efforts.
—*adj.* **3** *The meadow is an ideal place for the children to play:* perfect, absolutely suitable, meeting every need or desire, exemplary,

optimal, excellent, faultless, impeccable, matchless.

idealism *n. Not even this bitter disappointment crushed his idealism:* belief in noble goals, persistent hopefulness, optimism, meliorism; wishful thinking, romanticism, utopianism.
Ant. realism, pragmatism, cynicism.

idealist *n.* **1** *It is the idealists among us who try to aid humanity:* persistent optimist, perfectionist. **2** *There are few idealists in politics:* utopian, visionary, romantic, romanticist, dreamer, star-gazer.
Ant. 1, 2 pragmatist, realist, cynic.

identical *adj. Identical chairs flanked the fireplace:* twin, duplicate, exactly alike, perfectly matched, indistinguishable, precisely corresponding, alike feature for feature; very same, one and the same, self-same; exactly as before, none other than.
Ant. diverse, different, disparate, contrary, divergent; distinct, separate, unlike.

identification *n.* **1** *Identification of the jewels was made by the owner:* establishment of identity; recognition, verification, confirmation, pinpointing, ascertainment; detection, revelation. **2** *The candidate's identification with graft and crime cost him the election:* assumed relationship, connection, association, affiliation. **3** *A driving-licence is adequate identification:* certificate of identity, credentials; (*variously*) proper papers, passport, identity card, identifying badge, label, or button; item or means of recognition.

identify *v.* **1** *You can identify me by a green carnation in my lapel:* recognize, know, determine, place, designate, pick out, tell the identity of, be sure of, verify, specify. **2** *The world identifies Mrs. Pankhurst with female emancipation:* associate, combine, attach by association, think of in connection, mention in the same breath, put in the same category; consider the same, consider to be intimately connected, regard as representative of. **3** *The audience identified with the main character:* put oneself in the place of, feel empathy for, respond sympathetically towards, take the point of view of.
Ant. 1 mistake, confuse, overlook. **2** confuse, dissociate.
◇ *Word origin: Identify* comes from Latin *idem* (the same) + *-ficare* (to make), to make the same, to match up with something known. The same Latin word, *idem,* the same, gives us *identical* and *identity,* "sameness" or unity of character.

identity *n.* **1** *Fingerprints established the suspect's identity:* name, individuality, unique personal nature, delineation. **2** *The identity of these two ideologies is hidden by their different names:* exact similarity, exact likeness, duplication, precise correspondence; oneness, accord, harmony, rapport, unanimity. **3** *Many people in a large city feel a loss of a sense of identity:* individuality, distinctness of character, self, personality, self-perspective, distinctiveness, differentiation, personal uniqueness, social role.
Ant. 2 difference, separateness, distinctness, contrariety.
◇ *Word origin:* See IDENTIFY.

ideology *n. Communist ideology is impossible for individualists to accept:* set of beliefs, body of concepts, principles, ideals, doctrine, theory, dogma, programme, rationale, ethos, political philosophy.
◇ *Word origin: Ideology* comes from French *idéologie,* "system or science of ideas" (from Greek *ideā,* "idea," i.e. ideal form, model + *-logia,* -logy). Not surprisingly, this word was originally part of the vocabulary of the French Revolution, first appearing in print, both in English and in French, in 1796.

idiocy *n.* **1** *Idiocy can be congenital or caused by some early childhood disease:* cretinism, mongolism. **2** *It would be idiocy to antagonize such an influential politician:* folly, senselessness, stupidity, absurdity, foolishness, foolhardiness, fatuity, abject silliness, inanity, asininity, insanity, utter rashness, suicide.
Ant. common sense, sense, sanity, wisdom, sagacity, judiciousness.

idiom *n.* **1** *Foreigners often have trouble with idioms like "draw a bath":* phrase, characteristic expression, unique grammatical or semantic construction. **2** *The play suffers in its translation from French into the Spanish idiom. The symphony is written in the modern jazz idiom:* language, mode of expression, characteristic style, parlance, speech; colloquialism, localism, dialect, argot, patois, vernacular, jargon, slang; lingo.
◇ *Word origin: Idiom,* an expression peculiar to a language, region, or group, comes from Greek *idios,* one's own, which also gives us *idiot* and *idiosyncrasy.*

idiosyncrasy *n. Wearing ear-muffs indoors is one of her idiosyncrasies:* peculiar trait, quirk, unusual characteristic, oddity, mannerism, unusual habit, peculiarity, anomaly, eccentricity, distinction; personal mark.
◇ *Spelling tip: Idiosyncrasy* has an unusual idiosyncrasy of its own; it has two *-sy*'s in it: *idioSYncraSY.*
◇ *Word origin:* See IDIOM.

"To generalize is to be an idiot."
—*William Blake*

---

idiot *n.* **1** *An idiot has a mental age of three or four:* helplessly feeble-minded person, mental defective, cretin. **2** *The fire started because some idiot ignored the "No Smoking" sign:* foolish person, fool, simpleton, half-wit, dolt, ninny, ass, blockhead, nitwit, nincompoop, imbecile, booby, dunce, numskull.
Ant. 1 genius, mastermind, prodigy.

◇ *Usage note:* Technically, an *idiot* has the lowest intelligence of the various types of the mentally deficient, ranking below *imbecile* and *moron*, having the lowest IQ, and being incapable of learning connected speech. See also MORON.

idiotic *adj. Not seeing a doctor was just idiotic!:* stupid, empty-headed, absurd, asinine, moronic, imbecilic, stupidly clumsy or careless, ridiculous, rattle-brained, doltish, half-witted, foolish, foolhardy, senseless.

Ant. intelligent, sensible, thoughtful, sage, wise, brilliant, commonsensical.

idle *adj.* **1** *The factory closed and left hundreds of employees idle:* unemployed, lacking work, inactive, doing nothing, not working, unoccupied, out of work, redundant, jobless. **2** *The fuel shortage has left many aeroplanes idle:* not in operation, not being used, unused, not operating, doing nothing, gathering dust, inactive; fallow. **3** *Spring makes everyone feel idle:* lazy, indolent, sluggish, slothful, languid, somnolent, enervated, lethargic, at leisure, inert, torpid, drowsy, listless, otiose. **4** *Don't waste time on idle gossip:* baseless, worthless, empty, vapid, unsubstantiated, petty, trifling, trivial, valueless, vain, useless, unproductive; fruitless, futile, bootless, pointless, aimless, unimportant, good-for-nothing.

—*v.* **5** *We idled the summer away swimming and playing tennis:* fritter, spend in idleness, pass lazily, while, fiddle away, potter, loaf, fool away, laze, waste.

Ant. 1 active, employed, working, occupied, busy. **2** operative, operating, functioning, actuated, working, active. **3** energetic, industrious, busy, wide-awake, active. **4** important, meaningful, profitable, worthwhile, significant, advantageous, productive, beneficial, useful, purposeful, effective, fruitful.

◇ *Usage note: Idle, idol,* and *idyll* can cause confusion. *Idle*, of course, means "not active": *Just because you're old doesn't mean you have to be idle!* An *idol* is an image of a god or of a person greatly admired: *The pagans worshipped idols. Clarke Gable was a matinée idol.* An *idyll* is a literary work about simple, pastoral scenes or a charmingly rustic life, etc.: *Tennyson wrote many idylls.*

◇ *Word origin: Idle* comes from Old English *īdel*, worthless.

idol *n.* **1** *The temple was filled with golden idols:* religious effigy, icon, graven image, simulacrum; artifact, relic. **2** *Rudolf Valentino was a famous matinée idol:* popular hero, popular figure, public favourite; inspiration, adored person, guiding light; person towards whom one directs one's aspirations; godlike figure.

◇ *Usage note:* See IDLE.

◇ *Word origin: Idol* comes from Greek *eidōlon*, image, idol. The same Greek base gives us *idyll* (a poem "imaging" scenes of rustic life).

idolatry *n.* **1** *Idolatry was commonplace in many early pagan religions:* worship of an object, image-worship, reverence of idols, idolization. **2** *Only a millionaire could satisfy that woman's idolatry of jewels:* inordinate love, worship, adoration, obsession, preoccupation, excessive fondness, passion, devotion, veneration, single-minded attention, infatuation, senseless attachment, madness, mania.

idolize *v.* **1** *Some cults idolize the sun:* worship, adore, reverence, bow down before, deify, apotheosize. **2** *The boy idolized his father:* adore, love to excess, worship, dote loyally upon, treasure, give up one's heart to, prize; *Slang* be smitten, be mad about.

Ant. 2 despise, scorn, disdain.

idyllic *adj. The grazing cows made an idyllic picture:* peaceful, rustic, pastoral, arcadian, sylvan, bucolic, charmingly simple, unspoiled, romantic.

ignite *v.* **1** *A cigarette stub ignited the straw:* set on fire, set fire to, fire, kindle, light, inflame, touch off. **2** *The wood must be dry to ignite easily:* catch fire, catch on fire, burn, take fire, blaze, flame.

Ant. 1 stifle, extinguish, quench, douse.

◇ *Word origin: Ignite* comes from Latin *ignis*, fire.

ignoble *adj. The assassination was one of history's most ignoble deeds:* despicable, infamous, heinous, shameful, dishonourable, base, contemptible, nefarious, vile, dastardly, low, unconscionable, foul, degraded, mean, depraved, cowardly, pusillanimous, craven, degenerate, disgraceful, debased, discreditable, unworthy, indecent.

Ant. admirable, commendable, laudable, meritorious, lofty, sublime, glorious, splendid, distinguished, honourable, superior, exalted, grand, notable, fine, worthy, praiseworthy.

◇ *Word origin: Ignoble* comes from Latin *in-* (non-) + *gnobilis*, well-known, illustrious.

ignominious *adj. The army's disorganized retreat was ignominious:* humiliating, shameful, inglorious, disgraceful, wretched, degrading, abject, sorry, low, dishonourable, causing dishonour, discreditable, disreputable, grievous, unbearable.

Ant. creditable, honourable, reputable, estimable, worthy.

◇ *Word origin: Ignominious* comes from Latin *in-* (non-) + *gnomen* (name, good name), hence deprived of one's good name, disgraced.

ignoramus *n. Jim is quite knowledgeable but pretends to be an ignoramus:* know-nothing, lowbrow, illiterate, moron, idiot.

◇ *Pronunciation tip:* Although *ignoramus* is often pronounced *ig-nuh-RAH-mus*, the generally accepted pronunciation is *ig-nuh-RAY-mus.*

◇ *Word origin: Ignoramus* means "We do not know" in Latin.

ignorance *n. Poverty, disease and ignorance remain major world problems. Ignorance of the law is no excuse:* illiteracy, lack of knowledge or education, lack of learning, backwardness, mental darkness; unawareness, obliviousness, unenlightenment, confusion, want of perception, unacquaintance, unfamiliarity.

Ant. knowledge, education, wisdom, sense, learning, erudition; comprehension, insight, perception, empathy, understanding.

ignorant *adj.* **1** *The mountain villagers are an ignorant but peaceable people:* uneducated, unlearned, illiterate, lacking knowledge, unschooled, unlettered, unenlightened, untaught, untrained, untutored; naïve, unworldly. **2** *The father was ignorant of the child's fears:* uninformed, unknowing, innocent, unaware, unperceptive, unknowledgeable, blind to, uncognizant, in the dark about. **3** *That was an ignorant remark for someone who claims to be an expert:* unintelligent, shallow, irresponsible, insensitive, foolishly uninformed; fatuous, asinine, dumb, stupid.

Ant. 1 educated, instructed, learned, well-informed, wise, lettered, literate, cultured, cultivated. **2** aware, conscious, informed, briefed, knowledgeable, knowing. **3** sagacious, perceptive, astute, knowledgeable, wise, brilliant, sage.

ignore *v. He always ignored the speed limit on the motorway:* take no notice of, refrain from noticing, disregard, be oblivious to, pay no attention to, turn one's back, pay no heed to, shut one's eyes to, brush aside, scorn, slight, eschew, give the cold shoulder to; pass over, skip, omit, overlook.

Ant. heed, acknowledge, notice, note, regard, recognize, mark, attend.

ill *adj.* **1** *Is he ill enough to need a doctor?:* sick, sickly, unwell, ailing, unsound, poorly, diseased, unhealthy, indisposed; failing, invalid, laid up, under the weather. **2** *The perpetrator of this ill deed will be apprehended. Let's disregard any ill comments that are aimed at us:* evil, harmful, wicked, vile, foul, peevish, surly, cross; malicious, unkind, vengeful, acrimonious. **3** *The unusually heavy rainfall was an ill omen for the travellers:* unfavourable, boding bad luck, sinister, disturbing, unpropitious, unlucky, inauspicious, threatening, foreboding, ominous.
—*n.* **4 ills.** *She would be happiest helping to cure the ills of humanity:* affliction, ailment, disease, plague, complaint, malady, infirmity; woe, trouble, sorrow, slings and arrows, misfortune, trial. **5** *They remain a forgiving people, despite the ill done them:* wickedness, malice, evil, mischief, abomination, cruelty, abuse, outrage, ill-treatment, ill-usage, harm, injury, damage, malefaction.
—*adv.* **6** *The country can ill afford to wage a large-scale war:* scarcely, hardly, barely; by no means, nowise, noway.

Ant. 1 well, hale, healthy, strong, vigorous, robust. **2** kind, generous, selfless; favourable, complimentary, flattering. **5** good, beneficence, decency, honour, kindness. **6** well, easily, effortlessly, handily.

◇ *Usage note:* The adverbial form of *ill* is often joined by a hyphen to the past tense of a verb to create a new adjectival form. In such cases the *ill-* element may take on a variety of meanings for which synonyms can be substituted. For example, *He enjoyed his ill-gotten gains:* evilly, wrongly, wickedly, dishonestly; *Your criticism of our business methods was ill-received:* unfavourably, adversely; *The decision to sell was ill-timed:* inopportunely, inauspiciously, unpropitiously.

illegal *adj. Parking a car on a pedestrian crossing is illegal:* unlawful, against the law, not legal, prohibited, unsanctioned, proscribed, forbidden, banned, illicit, unauthorized; illegitimate, criminal, actionable, outlawed; against the rules.

Ant. legal, licit, lawful, authorized, permissible.

illegible *adj. Parts of the document are faded and illegible:* unreadable, impossible to read, indecipherable, undecipherable, unintelligible; obscured, hard to make out.

Ant. legible, readable, clear, intelligible.

◇ *Spelling tip:* Some people can't remember whether this word ends in *-able* or *-ible.* Remember that your two *i*'s (eyes) judge whether something is *IllegIble* or not.

"What is it to me if my neighbour's grandfather were a Syrian, or his grandmother illegitimate?" —*Jeremy Taylor*

---

illegitimate *adj.* **1** *The agency made illegitimate use of public money:* illegal, improper, not legitimate, unwarranted, unlawful, illicit, unauthorized, lawless, unsanctioned, prohibited. **2** *The king's illegitimate son could not inherit the throne:* bastard, natural, base-born, misbegotten.

Ant. 1 legitimate, lawful, legal. **2** legitimate.

ill-fated *adj. The ill-fated ocean liner* Titanic *was the subject of a film:* unfortunate, doomed to disaster, ill-omened, ill-starred, doomed, luckless, blighted, unlucky, destined to end unhappily, hapless.

illicit *adj. The police began a drive against illicit drug-trafficking:* unlawful, not legal, illegal, illegitimate, impermissible, not permitted, criminal, felonious, lawless, prohibited, improper, unauthorized; clandestine; *Informal* under-the-counter, black-market.

Ant. licit, lawful, legal, legalized, legitimate, permissible, above-board.

◇ *Usage note:* Don't confuse the adjective *illicit,* meaning "not legal," with the verb *elicit,* meaning "to draw out." Thus, *The police are cracking down on illicit gambling,* but *The detective elicited a confession from the criminal.*

illiterate *adj.* **1** *Many of the world's people are completely illiterate:* unable to read and write, unlettered, ignorant, uneducated, unlearned, not educated, unschooled. **2** *That illiterate report must have been prepared by an idiot:* badly written, ungrammatical, childish, amateurish, ludicrously bad, unscholarly, unreliable, witless, incoherent. **3** *I am illiterate on the subject of modern art:* unknowledgeable, ignorant, uninstructed, untutored, uninitiated, unversed, uninformed, unenlightened.

Ant. literate, taught, instructed, educated, schooled, informed, knowledgeable, expert.

illness *n. An undiagnosed illness put him in hospital:* sickness, malady, disorder, disease, ailment, infirmity, disability, affliction; complaint, malfunction; ill health, poor health.

Ant. health, robustness, wholesomeness, salubriousness, salubrity, hardiness.

illuminate *v.* **1** *Torches illuminated the picnic areas:* light up, fill or supply with light, light, illumine, irradiate, cast light upon. **2** *Footnotes illuminated the difficult passages of the text:* clarify, explain, make understandable or lucid, make clear, throw light on, elucidate, enhance, spell out; give insight into; edify, instruct; exemplify.

Ant. 1 darken, obliterate, becloud, benight, cloud, obscure.

◇ *Word origin: Illuminate* comes from Latin *in-* (thoroughly) + *luminare* (to light), from *lumen,* light, which also gives us *luminous* and *luminary.*

illumination *n.* **1** *The illumination of the stage came from footlights:* illuminating; irradiation, illumining, lighting up. **2** *The library's reading-rooms need better illumination:* lights, lighting, light fixtures, lighting equipment; source of light. **3** *He sought illumination from the works of the great philosophers. Illumination of the public is a major aim of the ecology group:* enlightenment, knowledge, perception, insight, wisdom, comprehension; information, instruction, edification, education.

Ant. 1 darkening, adumbration, dimming, obscuring.

illusion *n.* **1** *Mirrors give an illusion of greater space to a room:* semblance, misleading visual impression, optical illusion, unreality, deceiving appearance; false image, mirage; chimera, hallucination, delusion, deception; hocus-pocus, humbuggery. **2** *The illusions of youth fade with maturity:* false belief, false idea, erroneous impression, mistaken idea, delusion, misconception, misimpression, fallacy, misapprehension, fancy, caprice, vagary.

Ant. 1 reality, substantiation, actuality, truth.

◇ *Usage note:* See ALLUSION.

illusory *adj. The illusory state of tranquillity soon erupted into war:* unreal, illusive, deceptive, delusive, false, fallacious, spurious, misleading, imaginary, fanciful, unrealistic, hallucinatory, sham, counterfeit; ostensible, apparent, seeming.

Ant. substantial, real, true.

illustrate *v.* **1** *The company's bank statements illustrate its success:* make clear, explain, make intelligible, elucidate, throw light on, illuminate, define, clarify; emphasize, bring home, point up; demonstrate, show. **2** *The artist illustrated the book with pen-and-ink drawings:* ornament, provide with illustrations, adorn with pictures, portray, delineate; paint or draw illustrations for; represent, picture.

◇ *Word origin:* When we *illustrate* something, we try to make it clear by means of drawings or examples. The word comes from Latin *in-* (thoroughly) + *lustrare* (to illuminate). Also related are our words *lustre* and *illustrious.* All of these have the same root as Latin *lumen,* light.

illustration *n.* **1** *The magazine has illustrations in black and white and in colour:* picture, photograph, portrayal, drawing, figure, image; plate. **2** *The speaker gave an illustration of the dangers of poor nutrition:* example, instance, typical, occurrence, pertinent case, representative sample, specimen, exemplification.

illustrious *adj.* **1** *Roger Bannister was an illustrious athlete:* highly notable, famous, famed, eminent, renowned, celebrated, widely admired; of the first rank, distinguished, honoured, acclaimed. **2** *Dame Flora Robson has had an illustrious career in the theatre:* distinguished, brilliant, splendid, lustrous, glorious, magnificent; exemplary, matchless, peerless.

◇ *Word origin:* See ILLUSTRATE.

image *n.* **1** *Chagall often uses contorted images of fiddlers in his paintings:* representation, likeness, facsimile, copy, picture, effigy, portrait, figure, delineation, depiction; artistic or mechanical reproduction, photograph, semblance, simulacrum. **2** *The image of the trees in the lake made a lovely picture:* reflection, mirroring, reflected appearance, likeness, semblance, countenance, visage. **3** *Only a faint image of the encounter remains:* memory, recollection, concept, idea, mental picture. **4** *The girl is the very image of her mother:* copy, duplicate, reproduction, replica, double, facsimile, incarnation. **5** *The writer used the image of silk to describe the girl's hair:* literary comparison; figure of speech; simile; metaphor; symbol. **6** *The missionaries rebuked the natives for worshipping images:* idol, fetish, icon, statue, effigy, graven image.

◇ *Word origin: Image* comes from Latin *imago,* copy, imitation, representation (related to Latin *imitari,* to imitate).

imaginary *adj.* **1** *All the characters in the book*

are imaginary: unreal, invented, made-up, fictitious, fanciful; illusory, fantastic, fabulous, mythical, legendary, factitious, dreamed up; sham, counterfeit; *Slang* bogus, phoney.
—*n.* **2** *The heroine of* Through the Looking-Glass *confuses the imaginary with the real:* fanciful, romantic; fiction, fancy, illusion, delusion, figment, make-believe.
Ant. 1 real, actual, corporeal, true, factual.

imagination *n.* **1** *Fairy-tales often help to develop a child's imagination:* inventiveness, fancy, invention; creativity, creative thought; power to picture mentally. **2** *With a little imagination we should find a solution:* resourcefulness, thought, ingenuity, inventiveness, thoughtfulness, creativeness, enterprise, creative use of resources; cunning, astuteness.
◇ *Word origin:* See IMAGINE.

imaginative *adj. An imaginative set designer can always enhance a play. The artist's imaginative use of colour delighted the critics:* original, creative, inventive; inspired, clever, ingenious; off the beaten track; unusual, out of the ordinary; enterprising, resourceful.
Ant. unimaginative, unromantic, literal, uninventive, ordinary, pedestrian, commonplace, unoriginal, uncreative, uninspired, prosaic, mundane, run-of-the-mill.

imagine *v.* **1** *Try to imagine being on the moon:* picture, pretend, conceive, project, visualize, envisage, fantasize. **2** *I imagine you are tired from the journey:* presume, gather, assume, suppose, should think, believe, conjecture, infer, surmise; take for granted; suspect, fancy.
◇ *Word origin:* To *imagine* is to form a mental image. Both *imagine* and *imagination* come from Latin *imago*, image, imitation. Also related are *imitate* (from Latin *imitari*, to represent, imitate) and *emulate* (from Latin *aemulari*, to imitate or vie with, emulate).

imbecile *n.* **1** *The captain was an imbecile to set sail in this storm:* fool, foolish person, idiot, nitwit, half-wit, ass, booby, numskull, simpleton, dunce, nincompoop, ninny, blockhead, dolt.
—*adj.* Also **imbecilic 2** *Lending someone your passport is an imbecilic thing to do:* foolish, stupid, asinine, silly, absurd, inane; careless, mindless, thoughtless.
◇ *Usage note:* Technically, an *imbecile* is midway between the helpless *idiot* and the more intelligent *moron*, has a mental age of from three or four to seven or eight years, and is capable of some basic activities. See also MORON.
◇ *Word origin: Imbecile* comes from Latin *imbecillus*, weak or feeble, hence mentally weak.

imbibe *v. During the hot summer our family imbibed gallons of iced tea:* consume, drink, quaff, ingest, swallow; *Informal* tope, tipple, guzzle, swig, sup, toss down; partake, wash down.
◇ *Word origin: Imbibe* comes from Latin *bibere*, to drink, which also gives us *beverage* and *bib*.

imbue *v.* **1** *Churchill imbued Englishmen with enormous patriotism:* inspire, fill, endow, impress, instil, inculcate, infuse, ingrain; fire, animate. **2** *Sunset imbued the Caribbean skies with delicate colours:* tinge, tint, colour, tincture, bathe, steep, suffuse, permeate, pervade.
◇ *Word origin: Imbue* is from Latin *imbuere*, to wet, stain.

imitate *v.* **1** *Be yourself and don't imitate others:* follow the pattern of, copy in manner, fashion oneself after, mirror, take as a model, simulate, follow in the steps of, emulate, reproduce the image of. **2** *The comedian imitated W. C. Fields:* mimic, impersonate, act in imitation of, ape, represent, mime, parody, caricature; *Informal* take off. **3** *The vinyl upholstery imitates real leather:* simulate, have the appearance of, copy, reproduce closely, duplicate, pass for, look like, counterfeit.
◇ *Word origin: Imitate* and *imitation* come from Latin *imitari*, to imitate, make an image or copy of.

imitation *n.* **1** *The fabric isn't real silk; it's only an imitation:* simulation, copy of an original, counterfeit, fake, semblance, reproduction, facsimile, similarity; duplication. **2** *He can do imitations of every nationally known public figure:* impersonation, impression, burlesque, mimicry, parody, take-off, travesty, representation, adaptation, aping.
—*adj.* **3** *Conservationists urge the wearing of imitation fur:* simulated, fake, ersatz, make-believe, mock, sham; synthetic, artificial, man-made.
Ant. 3 real, actual, true, genuine.

immaculate *adj.* **1** *The maid kept the house immaculate:* spotless, spick and span, impeccably clean and neat; unstained, stainless, untarnished, unsullied, shipshape. **2** *The Minister's record is immaculate:* above reproach, faultless, morally blameless, pure, clean, virtuous, guiltless, perfect, unexceptionable, unimpeachable, intact, flawless, irreproachable, unsullied; innocent, sinless, saintly, chaste, virgin, virginal.
Ant. 1 dirty, filthy, spotted, unclean, stained, sullied. **2** impure, corrupt, sinful, contaminated, defiled, polluted, tainted, spotted, filthy, tarnished, sullied, impeachable, blameworthy.
◇ *Spelling tip: Immaculate* children wash both hands and spell *iMMaculate* with two *m*'s.
◇ *Word origin:* An *immaculate* room is a spotless one. The word comes from Latin *in-* (non-) + *maculatus* (spotted). *Macula* means "spot" or "blemish" in Latin.

immaterial *adj.* **1** *What people wear to the party is immaterial. The testimony is immaterial to these* *hearings:* of no importance, not relevant, irrelevant, inconsequential, insignificant, extraneous, unimportant, of minor importance, trifling, trivial, matter of indifference, having no bearing, of little account. **2** *The medium claims that she is in contact with the immaterial world:* spiritual, incorporeal, noumenal, bodiless, insubstantial, unsubstantial, impalpable, intangible, unbodied, unearthly, ghostly, ethereal, evanescent, spectral, disembodied, shadowy, extrasensory, mystical.

Ant. 1 relevant, significant, germane, important, essential, vital, crucial. **2** material, physical, real, tangible, corporeal, palpable, earthly.

immature *adj.* **1** *The larva or caterpillar is the immature stage of the butterfly:* embryonic, unripe, young, youthful, rudimentary, infantile, pubescent, unformed, half-grown, not mature, unfinished; unmellowed, out of season, green. **2** *Some adults remain emotionally immature:* childish, juvenile, callow, puerile, infantile, babyish; *Informal* wet behind the ears.

Ant. 1 mature, adult, ripe, mellow, developed, fully-fledged. **2** adult, mature, grown-up, responsible.

immeasurable *adj. These rocks have been here for an immeasurable time:* beyond measure, limitless, inestimable, incalculable, measureless, immense, unlimited, illimitable, infinite, unbounded, boundless, unfathomable; interminable, endless, inexhaustible.

Ant. measurable, finite, limited, circumscribed, restricted, bounded, specific; exact.

immediate *adj.* **1** *Please send an immediate answer:* prompt, undelayed, instant, instantaneous, express, done without delay, sudden, swift, speedy, punctual. **2** *The shopping centre is in the immediate neighbourhood. The immediate past:* next, near, adjacent, close, local, nearby, nearest, proximate, contiguous, nigh, not distant; recent.

Ant. 1 delayed, postponed, leisurely, unhurried, slow, relaxed, late, tardy. **2** distant, peripheral, far, remote.

immense *adj. The Atlantic Ocean is immense. We cooked an immense quantity of food:* vast, enormous, monstrous, stupendous, great, tremendous, huge, massive, gigantic, prodigious, Brobdingnagian.

Ant. small, little, tiny, minute, diminutive, petite, sparse, spare.

◇ *Word origin: Immense* comes from Latin *in-* (un-) + *mensus* (measured), hence immeasurable.

immerse *v.* **1** *Immerse the cloth in the dye for twenty minutes:* submerge, dip, lower, dunk, duck, douse, drench, steep, soak, bathe, sink, plunge. **2** *The entire family is immersed in scientific research:* involve deeply, absorb, occupy, be caught up in, engage, engross, preoccupy with, concentrate on.

◇ *Word origin: Immerse* comes from Latin prefix *in-* (in) + *mergere* (to dip), which also gives us *emerge* and *submerge.*

immigrate *v. Many Italians immigrated to the United States and Canada:* migrate, move to, relocate in; settle, colonize.

Ant. emigrate; leave, depart from.

imminent *adj. My departure is imminent. The mountain climbers were in imminent danger:* impending, approaching, close at hand, near, near at hand; threatening, perilous, menacing.

Ant. distant, future; delayed.

◇ *Usage note:* See EMINENT.

immobile *adj.* **1** *Bolt the table to the floor to make it immobile:* immovable, fixed, stationary, fast, secure, steadfast, riveted, rooted, unbudgeable, stable; rigid, stiff. **2** *A back injury kept him immobile for weeks:* incapacitated, laid up, motionless, not moving, still, quiet, quiescent, static, at rest, stock-still, immobilized.

Ant. 1 mobile, portable, movable, transportable. **2** active, vigorous, up and about, on the move.

immoderate *adj. The young men consumed an immoderate amount of wine and fell asleep:* excessive, extravagant, prodigious, unreasonable, unbridled, inordinate, uncalled-for, intemperate, extreme, exorbitant, unconscionable, undue, unrestrained, gargantuan, mind-boggling.

Ant. moderate; temperate; restrained, curbed, checked, inhibited; reasonable, rational, prudent, cautious, judicious, sensible.

immodest *adj.* **1** *Clothing once thought immodest is acceptable today:* indecorous, revealing, indecent, indelicate, shameless; lewd, loose, suggestive, risqué; coarse, gross, wanton, unchaste. **2** *The actor made immodest claims about his talent:* vain, exaggerated, inflated, pompous, conceited, high-sounding, brazen, self-centred, self-aggrandizing, braggart, bombastic, boastful, pretentious, peacockish.

Ant. 1 modest, decent, delicate, decorous, pure, chaste. **2** modest, humble, restrained.

immoral *adj. Selling drugs to children is immoral. The court banned two immoral films:* unethical, unprincipled, corrupt, evil, wrong, vicious, wicked, profoundly bad, iniquitous, sinful, infamous, nefarious, heinous, profligate, dissolute; sexually arousing, lewd, prurient, debauched, depraved, obscene, licentious, salacious, indecent; pornographic; *Informal* dirty, blue.

Ant. moral, upright, virtuous, law-abiding, conscientious, good, honourable, chaste, pure, clean, inoffensive.

◇ *Usage note: Immoral* and *amoral* sound somewhat alike but have quite different meanings. *Immoral* means "wicked, violating morality": *All Murder is immoral. Amoral* means "lacking a knowledge of right and wrong": *Wild Animals are Amoral, they can't be blamed for killing their prey.* Remember: *All Murder is iMmoral, Wild Animals are Amoral.*

immortal *adj.* **1** *Humans long to be immortal. The immortal works of Beethoven are listed by opus number in the Kinsky Beethoven-Verzeichnis:* undying, not mortal, eternal, everlasting, divine, deathless, imperishable, lasting for all time, enduring, abiding.
—*n.* **2 Immortals** *In ancient Greek mythology the Immortals dwelt on Mount Olympus:* the gods, (*specifically*) the members of the Greek and Roman pantheon. **3** *Chaucer is one of the immortals of literature:* monumental figure, titan, giant, demigod, great name, illustrious name.
Ant. **1** mortal; transitory, fleeting, fugitive, ephemeral, evanescent, transient, short-lived, passing; fly-by-night.

"To make a speech immortal you don't have to make it everlasting." —*Leslie Hore-Belisha*

---

immovable *adj.* **1** *The entrance is blocked by an immovable rock:* unmovable, fixed, set, settled, fast, secure, immobile, stationary, unbudgeable, fastened. **2** *The director was immovable in his determination to end the strike:* unyielding in purpose, unchangeable, stubborn, obdurate, not to be put off, fixed, inflexible, stolid, inexorable, unbendable, adamant, resolute, dogged; unfeeling, impassive, unimpressionable, heartless, steely, cold-hearted, icy, cold, unsympathetic, unimpressible, detached.
Ant. **1** movable, portable, transportable, yielding. **2** flexible, persuadable, open-minded, reasonable, irresolute, changeable.

immune *adj.* **1** *The inoculations made the children immune to measles:* resistant, unsusceptible, protected, safe, invulnerable, unthreatened by, not in danger of. **2** *Income from certain shares may be immune from taxation:* exempt, free, not affected by, not liable to, not subject to, at liberty, clear, not vulnerable.
Ant. **1** subject, vulnerable, susceptible; unprotected, unsafe. **2** subject, liable.

imp *n.* **1** *The forest was said to be full of mischievous imps:* small demon, evil spirit, sprite, elf, little goblin, little devil, leprechaun. **2** *The little imp has hidden my glasses again:* mischievous child, harmlessly naughty child, devil, demon, rascal, urchin, hoyden.
◇ *Word origin: Imp* is ultimately derived from Greek *emphyein,* to implant. In English, *imp* meant first a graft or shoot of a plant, then a child, and finally a mischievous child or young demon.

impact *n.* **1** *The impact of the car cracked the telegraph-pole:* collision, crash, smash, violent blow, force, concussion, jolt. **2** *The full impact of the news hit us only after several days:* effect, brunt, burden, shock, thrust; implication, repercussion.

impair *v. The water shortage impaired the city's fire-fighting capacity:* hinder, damage, mar, vitiate, harm, cripple, subvert, injure, lessen, weaken, enfeeble, decrease, undercut, detract from, reduce; enervate, debilitate, worsen.
Ant. improve, amend; repair; better, ameliorate, enhance, facilitate, increase.
◇ *Word origin: Impair* is ultimately derived from Latin *pejor,* worse, which also gives us our word *pejorative.*

impale *v.* **1** *The tribesmen impaled their victims upon wooden stakes:* fix on a stake, stick, run through. **2** *The collector impaled the butterflies on pins before framing them:* transfix, affix, tack, pin, stick.

impart *v.* **1** *The prime minister imparted the news of his trip at a press conference:* make known, tell, pass on, communicate, relate, confide, mention, reveal, disclose, divulge, share. **2** *The red curtains impart a certain elegance to the room:* confer on, bestow on, give, lend, grant, render, contribute, deliver, offer, dispense, consign, accord, afford.

impartial *adj. Try to remain impartial until you have heard both sides of the story:* unbiased, fair, just, objective, equitable, non-partisan, disinterested, dispassionate, open-minded, even-handed, neutral, unprejudiced, fair-minded.
Ant. partial, prejudiced, influenced, swayed, affected, biased, slanted, bigoted, unfair, unjust.

impasse *n. The education authority and the teachers' union have reached an impasse:* deadlock, stalemate, blind alley, bottle-neck, cul-de-sac, dead end; snag; dilemma, quandary, standstill.

impassioned *adj. The leader roused the protesters with an impassioned speech:* ardent, fervent, excited, inspired, passionate, heated, earnest, eager, zealous, fiery, stirring, rousing, forceful.
Ant. dispassionate, objective, cool, impassive, apathetic, indifferent, detached.

impassive *adj. The chairman maintained an impassive manner throughout the furious debate:* emotionless, unemotional, unmoved, imperturbable, dispassionate, aloof, stoical, untouched, stony, calm, cool, sedate, unperturbed, unimpressible, inscrutable, impervious, stolid, apathetic, phlegmatic, unimpressionable, insensible, indifferent.
Ant. responsive, emotional, passionate, excited, perturbed.

impatient *adj. The class was impatient for the holidays to begin. The teacher became impatient with the inattentive students:* restless, nervous, edgy, tense, irritated, excitable, fussy, restive; enthusiastic, eagerly desirous, feverish,

highly-strung, rabid, passionate, hurried, ardent, itchy, anxious; peevish, irritable, irascible, testy, annoyed, touchy, intolerant.
Ant. patient; composed, imperturbable, unruffled, cool; calm, serene, tranquil, placid, restful, quiet; gradual, slow; unperturbed.

impeccable *adj. She has impeccable taste in clothes. His character is impeccable:* flawless, faultless, immaculate, free from imperfection, unblemished, perfect, irreproachable, irreprovable, unassailable, blameless, above criticism, unexceptionable, unimpeachable.
Ant. deficient, defective; superficial, shallow, uncritical, cursory; culpable, blameworthy; faulty, tarnished, stained, corrupt, flawed.
◇ *Word origin: Impeccable* comes from Latin *in-* (not) + *peccare* (to sin). Latin *impeccabilis* means "sinless."

impede *v. A brick shortage impeded construction of the house:* delay, slow down, block, interfere with, interrupt, check, retard, obstruct, hinder, thwart, arrest, side-track, stall, stymie, deter, hamper, hold back, halter, disrupt.
Ant. assist, promote, advance, further, forward; help, aid.

impediment *n. Lack of confidence is an impediment to success. He suffers from a speech impediment:* delay, slowing down, block, stumbling-block, interference, obstruction, hindrance, interference, handicap, obstacle, drawback, detraction; defect, flaw, deformity.
Ant. advantage, bolster, help, aid.

impel *v. Financial pressures impel the firm to cut back on spending:* force, require, drive, push, compel, urge, necessitate, prompt, prod, constrain, spur, goad, incite.
Ant. restrain, curb, check, inhibit, hinder.

impending *adj. The dark clouds suggest an impending storm:* approaching, immediate, coming, due any moment, imminent, oncoming, forthcoming, in prospect, brewing, looming; threatening, menacing.

impenetrable *adj.* **1** *The dense hedge of thorns formed an impenetrable barrier round the castle:* impervious, inviolable, unenterable, impassable, invulnerable, inaccessible; solid, thick, dense, sealed. **2** *The motive for the crime was impenetrable:* incomprehensible, defying interpretation or understanding, insensible, elusive, mysterious, unfathomable, inscrutable, inaccessible, insoluble, impalpable, inexplicable, intangible, obscure, puzzling.
Ant. **1** pierceable, penetrable, vulnerable, enterable, accessible, passable. **2** understandable, fathomable, soluble, explicable, clear, obvious, lucid.

imperative *adj. It is imperative that we reach the doctor:* urgent, vitally important, essential, of the utmost necessity, requisite, necessary, needful, mandatory, compulsory, pressing, unavoidable, crucial, critical.
Ant. unnecessary, unimportant, avoidable, non-essential; non-obligatory.
◇ *Word origin: Imperative* comes from Latin *imperativus*, "specially ordered," from *imperare*, to command. Also related are our words *imperial* and *empire.*

imperceptible *adj. The difference between the two colours is imperceptible:* undetectable, unnoticeable, not readily apparent, inconsiderable, subtle, minimal, unappreciable, minute, small, scant, insignificant, hidden, indistinct, unperceivable; academic, slight, minor; infinitesimal.
Ant. manifest, obvious, clear, perceptible, palpable, noticeable, distinct.

imperfection *n.* **1** *The price of the coat was reduced because of a few minor imperfections:* defect, flaw, blemish, fault, impairment, faulty detail, deformity, shortcoming, weakness. **2** *The architect was disturbed by the imperfection of the construction:* faultiness, imperfectness, falling short, inadequacy, insufficiency, fallibility, incompleteness.
Ant. **2** perfection, perfectness, completeness, faultlessness.

impermanent *adj. Physical beauty is impermanent and fades with age:* fleeting, transitory, unenduring, evanescent, ephemeral, unstable, passing, not fixed, transient.
Ant. permanent, immortal, stable, fixed.

impersonal *adj.* **1** *These suggestions are impersonal and not directed towards anyone in particular:* general, all-encompassing, applicable to all; impartial, objective, detached, disinterested; perfunctory, remote, impassive. **2** *A machine is an impersonal object:* inanimate, inorganic; inhuman, soulless, spiritless, lifeless, dead.
Ant. **1** personal, specific. **2** personal, animate; human, alive, vital.

impersonate *v.* **1** *Detectives sometimes impersonate drug addicts:* pretend to be, pose as, dress up as, get oneself up as, take the role of, represent oneself as, act the part of, masquerade as, pass oneself off as. **2** *It was Bill who was to impersonate the lion in* Androcles and the Lion: portray, play the part of, imitate, represent, personify, mimic, mime, copy, take off, ape.

impertinent *adj.* **1** *The impertinent youth was sent out of the room:* rude, unmannerly, disrespectful, insolent, impudent, presumptuous, arrogant, uncivil, brazen, peremptory, brassy, insulting, discourteous; *Informal* cheeky, fresh. **2** *The judge ruled the testimony impertinent to the case:* irrelevant, extraneous, unimportant, immaterial, not pertinent, extrinsic, not germane, beside the point, unrelated, inappropriate.
Ant. **1** polite, respectful, mannerly, deferential. **2** pertinent, relevant, germane, related; important, vital, crucial.

imperturbable *adj. The usually imperturbable man showed signs of fear:* unexcitable, calm, collected, cool, serene, undisturbed, unflustered, level-headed, sedate, composed;

unsusceptible, impervious, impassive, unanxious, nerveless; *Slang* unflappable.

Ant. perturbable, choleric, touchy.

impervious *adj.* **1** *The firemen wore masks that were impervious to the acrid smoke:* impenetrable, impermeable, inaccessible, allowing no passage to, unapproachable; sealed or closed against; invulnerable. **2** *The beautiful actress seemed impervious to the usual ravages of age:* immune to, protected against; untouched by, unmarked by. **3** *The witness clung to his story and seemed impervious to reason:* unmoved by, unaffected by, untouched by, closed to.

Ant. 1 susceptible, vulnerable. **2** open, exposed, susceptible, sensitive, liable, prone.

impetuous *adj.* **1** *The impetuous man is constantly falling in love. Inviting everyone to spend the weekend was an impetuous move:* rash, impulsive, hasty, headlong, precipitate; abrupt, unpremeditated, capricious, unexpected. **2** *The storm approached with impetuous speed:* headlong, violent, precipitate, forcible, rampant, stormy, vehement; relentless, inexorable.

Ant. 1 cautious, wary. **2** moderate, leisurely, slow, mild.

◇ *Word origin: Impetuous* and *impetus* both come from Latin *impetere*, to attack. *Impetuous* means tending to act or attack suddenly, on impulse; *impetus* is the force, energy, or motivation behind an act or attack.

impetus *n.* **1** *The impetus of the car carried it into the back of the lorry:* momentum, forward motion, force. **2** *Children need an impetus to study:* stimulus, stimulation, spur, motivating force, impulsion, propulsion, boost, drive, momentum, force, start, push, prod; incentive, motivation.

impinge *v. I hate to impinge upon your privacy:* encroach, intrude, infringe, trespass, transgress, violate, obtrude.

impish *adj. The impish boy is constantly teasing his brother:* implike, mischievous, puckish, elfin, playfully naughty, sportive, roguish, prankish.

implacable *adj. It was impossible to negotiate with such an implacable enemy:* irreconcilable, unappeasable, inexorable, unamenable, intractable, unpacifiable, uncompromising, relentless, unrelenting.

Ant. reconcilable, appeasable, yielding, lenient, relenting, forbearing, indulgent, tolerant, flexible.

implausible *adj. No one was taken in by that implausible excuse:* unlikely, improbable, incredible, unbelievable, illogical, unreasonable, doubtful, barely conceivable, preposterous, senseless, ridiculous, outrageous, far-fetched.

Ant. plausible, credible, believable, reasonable, likely, conceivable, sensible.

implement *n.* **1** *What implements are needed for gardening?:* tool, utensil, instrument, device, article, piece; equipment, materials.

—*v.* **2** *Donations are needed to implement our child-care programmes:* put into effect, begin, activate, enact, start, set in motion, carry out, fulfil, achieve, accomplish, realize.

implicate *v. The suspect implicated two others in the robbery:* involve, associate, connect, ensnare, embroil, entangle; incriminate, inculpate.

Ant. dissociate; exclude, eliminate, rule out; extricate, disentangle, untangle, disconnect; acquit, exculpate.

implication *n.* **1** *The journalists discussed the political implications of the war:* ramification, suggestion, outcome, effect, overtone, intimation, inference, consequence, significance, connotation, innuendo. **2** *We were judged guilty by implication:* association, connection, involvement, entanglement.

implicit *adj.* **1** *Victory was implicit in the early election returns:* implied, hinted, suggested, tacitly expressed; inferred, deducible, understood. **2** *The crew had implicit faith in the captain's judgement:* innate, inherent, unquestioning, absolute, complete, profound, certain, resolute, unshakable, unreserved, steadfast, staunch.

◇ *Usage note:* See EXPLICIT.

implore *v. The prisoner implored the king for mercy:* beg, beseech, entreat, urge, plead with, obtest, supplicate, go to on bended knee.

Ant. order, demand, command.

◇ *Word origin: Implore* comes from Latin *in-* (thoroughly) + *plorare* (to weep), hence to invoke tearfully.

imply *v.* **1** *The doctor's frown implied that something was wrong:* indicate, suggest, hint, insinuate, intimate. **2** *A fair trial implies an unbiased jury:* presuppose, indicate, bespeak, betoken, presume; signify, mean, denote, evidence.

◇ *Usage note: Imply* and *infer* are not synonyms. *Imply* means to suggest or hint: *The police implied that the crime was solved. Infer* means to conclude or derive from: *Since the police implied* (suggested, hinted) *that the crime was solved, I inferred* (concluded) *that they would soon arrest the culprit.*

impolite *adj. It's considered impolite for a man to wear a hat indoors:* discourteous, ill-bred, ungenteel, unmannerly, rude, indecorous, unfitting, uncivil, inconsiderate, not polite, disrespectful, impolitic.

Ant. polite, courteous, mannerly, civil, respectful, considerate.

import *n. The import of the situation hit me like a ton of bricks:* significance, importance, meaning, burden, implication, connotation, thrust, moment, ramification, overtones.

importance *n.* **1** *The importance of loving care to a child cannot be over-emphasized:* value, significance, import, weightiness, weight, momentousness, relevance, essentialness, worth, seriousness, consequence, moment. **2** *The visitor must be of great importance:* rank, position, influence, esteem, repute, stature, eminence.

Ant. 1 unimportance, pettiness, triviality, paltriness, insignificance; nothingness, immateriality. **2** unimportance, insignificance.

important *adj.* **1** *The speech was an important one in the campaign:* meaningful, consequential, significant, weighty, momentous, great, influential, serious, imperative, distinctive, notable. **2** *Pablo Picasso was one of the century's most important painters:* leading, foremost, major, pre-eminent, remarkable, prominent, influential, esteemed; distinctive, original, creative, seminal.

Ant. 1 unimportant, inconsequential, inconsiderable, indifferent, insignificant, minor, unnecessary, needless, negligible, non-essential, secondary, trivial. **2** unimportant, insignificant, undistinctive, minor.

"Every individual has a place to fill in the world, and is important, in some respect, whether he chooses to be so or not."

—*Nathaniel Hawthorne*

---

impose *v.* **1** *The police imposed a curfew until the disturbance was over. Tariffs have been imposed on all foreign goods:* institute, lay on, introduce, place on, set, levy; *Slang* slap on. **2** *Don't try to impose your wishes on us:* force, inflict, enact, establish, prescribe, dictate, command, apply, peddle, thrust upon; *Informal* palm off.

Ant. lift, remove.

imposing *adj. The Post Office Tower is an imposing structure:* impressive, majestic, grand, outstanding, striking, massive, towering, awe-inspiring, commanding, stately.

Ant. unimposing, unimpressive, ordinary.

impossible *adj.* **1** *It's impossible to reach the airport in this traffic:* out of the question, not possible, unfeasible, impracticable, unachievable, unattainable; beyond belief, beyond reason, unimaginable, inconceivable. **2** *That child is impossible! Inflation is an impossible problem:* intractable, stubborn, unyielding, intransigent, unmanageable; intolerable, insufferable, unbearable; unsolvable, insoluble, unanswerable.

Ant. 1 possible, likely, probable, feasible.

impotence *n. The cut-back in government finance leaves the project in a state of impotence:* weakness, powerlessness, ineffectiveness, ineffectuality, inefficacy, helplessness, incapacity, disability, paralysis.

Ant. capacity, vigour, ability, power, potency, strength, effectiveness, efficacy.

impotent *adj. Low morale can render an army impotent. His reply was an impotent shrug:* unable to function; ineffective, powerless, weak, disabled, helpless, paralysed; feckless, hapless.

Ant. potent, powerful, puissant, forceful, vigorous.

◇ *Pronunciation tip: Impotent* should be pronounced so that the first syllable is stressed. Thus, *IM-puh-tent,* not "im-PO-tent."

impoverished *adj.* **1** *Money and food were sent to the impoverished drought victims:* poor, destitute, abject, sorely wanting, without material resources, impecunious, indigent, without means, down-and-out, marked by extreme poverty, pauperized, needy. **2** *The land became impoverished from years of irresponsible use:* exhausted, worn out, used up, wanting, depleted, bereft, sterile, effete, barren, drained, unproductive.

Ant. 1 rich, affluent, wealthy, well-to-do, well-off. **2** fertile, fecund, fructuous, rich, productive.

impractical *adj. Running a household without a budget is impractical. Why did he marry such an impractical person?:* unrealistic, unwise, unintelligent, lacking foresight, bungling, disorganized, loose-ended, helter-skelter; starry-eyed, romantic; sloppy, careless.

Ant. sound, sensible, down-to-earth, practical, pragmatic, clear-eyed, realistic, systematic.

impregnable *adj. Minefields and barbed wire made the position virtually impregnable. The prosecution had an impregnable case:* invincible, unattackable, invulnerable, unassailable; powerful, strong, sturdy, mighty, potent.

Ant. vulnerable, frail, flimsy, assailable, weak, defenceless.

impregnate *v.* **1** *Pavlov impregnated the laboratory animals by means of artificial insemination:* make pregnant, cause to conceive, get with young, cause to bear offspring; fructify, fecundate, inseminate, fertilize. **2** *Impregnate the cloth with cleaning fluid:* saturate, wet, moisten, soak, imbrue, permeate, drench, steep, infuse, dampen, suffuse, inundate.

impression *n.* **1** *The new headmaster made a bad impression on the parents:* effect, impact, sensation, feeling; reception, influence, imprint. **2** *I had the impression that you were ready to leave:* feeling, opinion, belief, understanding, idea, notion, surmise, conviction. **3** *The suspect's shoes had left deep impressions in the mud:* imprint, impress, mark, outline, track, indentation, stamp, mould, trace, contour.

impressionable *adj. The early years of a person's life are the most impressionable:* easily influenced, receptive, susceptible to impressions, sentient, passible, affective, emotionally affected; suggestible, gullible.

impressive *adj. Kangchenjunga is an impressive sight:* imposing, thrilling, awe-inspiring, moving, soul-stirring, exciting, grand, majestic, striking, august, overpowering, outstanding, memorable, unforgettable.

Ant. unimpressive, unimposing, ordinary, unmoving, uninspiring, unmemorable.

imprison *v. The bank robber was imprisoned for 20 years:* place in prison, confine, incarcerate, gaol, place in confinement, shackle, hold captive, restrain, encage, coop up, fence in, constrain, pen, entomb, immure.
Ant. free, release, liberate.

improbable *adj. Rain seems improbable on such a clear day. His explanation was an improbable one:* not probable, unlikely, unforeseeable; unreasonable, implausible, illogical.
Ant. probable, likely; reasonable, plausible, logical.

impromptu *adj.* **1** *Our guest delivered an impromptu speech:* improvised, unprepared, extempore, unrehearsed, done on the spur of the moment, unexpected, sudden, offhand, unpremeditated, makeshift, spontaneous, impulsive; *Slang* off the top of one's head, off the cuff.
—adv. **2** *Don't be surprised if they ask you to sing impromptu:* without warning, without advance notice, on the spot, with no preparation, off the cuff, extemporaneously, at a moment's notice, then and there.
Ant. 1 considered, planned, prepared, rehearsed, premeditated, deliberate.
◇ *Word origin: Impromptu* comes from the Latin phrase *in promptu,* in readiness. The expression is related to and contains the word *prompt.*

improper *adj. Blue jeans would be improper for the form outing:* not suitable, inappropriate, unfit, unseemly, unbefitting, malapropos, irregular, out of place, inapt, unconformable, contrary to accepted standards, unbecoming, indecorous; out of tune, unharmonious, ill-suited, being at odds; indecent, lewd.
Ant. proper, right, correct, decorous, decent, fitting, apropos; *French* comme il faut, de rigueur.

improve *v.* **1** *Practice will improve your bowling technique. The patient improved under the new treatment:* make better, help, make more desirable or attractive, better, correct, repair, enhance, ameliorate, make improvements to; develop beneficially, recuperate, come round, take a turn for the better, gain ground, rally. **2** *Retired people can improve their lives by doing voluntary work:* enrich, enhance, put to good use, employ to a good or useful end, turn to account, make productive, cultivate, increase the resources of, develop.
Ant. 1, 2 impair; worsen; injure, harm, damage, mar.

improvement *n.* **1** *There has been little improvement in the air-pollution problem:* betterment, amelioration, beneficial development, progress, upswing, gain. **2** *Putting a new roof on the house is a valuable improvement:* enhancement, repair, reconstruction, reclamation, additive, amendment, emendation, reform. **3** *Electric typewriters are certainly an improvement on the manual sort:* refinement, betterment, advance, advancement, progression, step forward, overtaking.

improvident *adj. The improvident heir quickly spent the family fortune:* thriftless, spendthrift, unparsimonious, unthrifty, extravagant, wasteful, prodigal, lavish; imprudent, shortsighted, reckless, negligent.
Ant. provident, cautious, thrifty, penny-wise; prudent, farsighted, foresighted.

improvise *v. The singer forgot her words and had to improvise. We improvised bookcases out of tea chests:* perform without preparation; invent offhand, make up, extemporize, come up with, do a makeshift job, throw together, ad lib; make do.

imprudent *adj. It was imprudent of the doctor to discuss his patients. It's imprudent to drive with those worn tyres:* incautious, unwise, rash, inadvisable, indiscreet, ill-advised, ill-considered, thoughtless, injudicious; heedless, untoward, foolish, foolishly impulsive, foolhardy; unthinking, mindless; *Slang* crazy, dopey, mad, bananas.
Ant. prudent, wise, thoughtful, judicious, cautious, careful, discreet.

impudent *adj. The impudent child antagonized her teachers:* rude, brash, disrespectful, insolent, discourteous, impolite, shameless, brazen, impertinent, pert, forward, bumptious; *Informal* fresh, cheeky, smart-alecy.
Ant. respectful, courteous, polite, deferential.
◇ *Word origin: Impudent* comes from Latin *in-* (not) + *pudens,* "feeling shame," from *pudere,* to be ashamed. Also related is our word *impudicity,* shamelessness.

impulsive *adj.* **1** *The impulsive force of the wind drove the boat from its mooring:* pushing forward; propelling, propellant, impelling, driving; forceful, forcible. **2** *The impulsive teenagers jumped into the pool fully clothed. What an impulsive act!:* rash, capricious, whimsical, notional, devil-may-care, unpredictable; spur-of-the-moment, impromptu, offhand, unpremeditated, unplanned, involuntary, spontaneous, impetuous, extemporaneous.
Ant. 1 curbing, arresting, halting. **2** deliberate, premeditated, considered, cautious, circumspect, calculating, planned, rehearsed, contrived.

impunity *n. The children can pick raspberries here with complete impunity:* freedom from punishment, freedom from harm; immunity, clearance; absolution, dispensation; privilege, prerogative, exemption.
Ant. blame, retribution, hazard; culpability, punishment, loss, harm, danger, risk.
◇ *Word origin: Impunity* comes from Latin *in-* (not) + *poena* (penalty), hence without penalty, unpunished. Latin *poena* also gives us our words *pain, punish,* and *subpoena.* All of these words are ultimately derived from Greek *poinē,* punishment, expiation.

impure *adj.* **1** *Our lungs are black from breathing* *impure air:* dirty, unclean, defiled, polluted; filthy, foul, sullied, vitiated, tainted, contaminated, noxious, noisome, unwholesome. **2** *The addition of an alloy made the gold impure:* adulterated, degraded, debased, devalued, depreciated; unrefined. **3** *The minister chastised his son for using impure language:* immoral, improper, indecorous, indelicate, unchaste, immodest, licentious; smutty, dirty, lustful, lecherous, libidinous, prurient, salacious, obscene, lewd, indecent.

Ant. 1-3 pure. **1** clean, unpolluted, untainted, uncontaminated, wholesome. **2** unmixed, unadulterated, unalloyed; perfect. **3** chaste, wholesome, moral, decent, decorous, clean, proper.

impurity *n.* **1** *The impurity of the water made it unfit to drink:* taintedness, pollution, uncleanness, foulness, contamination, unwholesomeness, defilement, corruption, dirtiness, filth. **2** *Milk is pasteurized to rid it of impurities:* adulterant, contaminant, foreign matter; adulteration, alloy, taint, dross.

Ant. 1 purity, cleanness, wholesomeness.

impute *v. The critics imputed the failure of the play to poor direction:* charge, ascribe, refer, attribute, assign, set down to, lay at the door of, relate, see as a result.

inaccessible *adj. The island is inaccessible except by boat. State papers are inaccessible to the public:* unapproachable, unreachable; beyond access, hopelessly remote, unattainable, unobtainable, not at hand.

Ant. accessible, reachable; approachable; attainable, obtainable.

inaccuracy *n.* **1** *The inaccuracy of the news report was disgraceful:* inexactness, faultiness, incorrectness, fallaciousness, unreliability, imprecision, unclarity. **2** *The novel was full of historical inaccuracies:* error, mistake, slip, fallacy, blunder; erratum; *Slang* howler, boob.

Ant. 1 accuracy, correctness, reliability, faultlessness, exactness, precision, preciseness.

inaccurate *adj. An inaccurate description threw the police off the track:* incorrect, faulty, erroneous, full of errors, wrong, false, fallacious, unreliable, imprecise, inexact; wide of the mark; mistaken; not on target, off the track, off, off target.

Ant. accurate, correct, true, faithful, flawless, exact.

inactive *adj.* **1** *Those office machines have been inactive since the computer was installed:* idle, inoperative, inert, quiet, still, dormant, on the shelf, out of service, unused, static. **2** *The inactive life of the tropics began to bore the couple:* sluggish, idle, torpid, languid, easy-going, somnolent, low-intensity, low-key, indolent, lazy, slothful, dormant, quiet, sedentary, dull, leisurely, otiose.

Ant. 1 active, operative, operating, functional. **2** active, bustling, dynamic, busy, industrious, vigorous.

inadequate *adj.* **1** *Coal stocks are inadequate for a long winter:* not adequate, deficient, insufficient, less than necessary or required, wanting, below par, short, scanty. **2** *If you feel inadequate to the job, go out and get some useful experience:* incompetent, incapable, unqualified, unfit, too raw, inept, not up to, not equal to, imperfect, unfitted.

Ant. 1 adequate, sufficient, abundant, enough. **2** adequate, qualified, equal, experienced.

inadvertent *adj. The newspaper apologized for the inadvertent omission:* unintentional, unintended, not on purpose, accidental, unmeant, unthinking, involuntary, unpremeditated.

Ant. deliberate, premeditated, intentional, studied, considered, conscious, aware.

inadvisable *adj. It would be inadvisable to approach him whilst he's still angry:* unwise, injudicious, imprudent, ill-advised, not advisable, impolitic, inopportune, risky, chancy, inexpedient.

Ant. advisable, wise, prudent, politic, judicious, opportune, expedient.

inalienable *adj. Freedom of assembly is an inalienable right:* inviolable, unassailable, absolute, unimpeachable, unforfeitable, sacred, sacrosanct, inherent; protected, defended.

inane *adj. He was so ill at ease that he could only make inane remarks about the weather:* foolish, senseless, vapid, silly, absurd, vacuous, void of intelligence, shallow, pointless, asinine, nonsensical, empty, ridiculous; unthinking, unintelligent; stupid, idiotic, meaningless, fatuous.

Ant. meaningful, sensible, sound, thoughtful, intelligent, wise, sage, deep, profound.

◇ *Word origin: Inane* comes from Latin *inanis*, empty.

> "Like a God-created, fire-breathing Spirit-host, we emerge from the Inane; haste stormfully across the astonished Earth; then plunge again into the Inane." — *Thomas Carlyle*

inapplicable *adj. Your idea is exciting but inapplicable to our present needs:* not applicable, irrelevant, unsuited, unsuitable, not pertinent, not apt, inappropriate, unfit, incompatible, not germane, inapposite.

Ant. applicable, suitable, suited, relevant, germane, pertinent, appropriate, apposite.

inappropriate *adj. Wearing shorts to church is completely inappropriate:* unsuitable, unsuited, improper, out of place, incongruous, unfitting, inapt, incompatible, in bad taste, indecorous, infelicitous, unbecoming, out of fashion.

Ant. appropriate, fitting, proper, felicitous, suitable, meet, fit, decorous, becoming.

inarticulate *adj.* **1** *The man answered with a strange inarticulate sound:* incoherent, unintelligible, mumbled, babbled; blurred, garbled, indistinct, confused. **2** *Fear made him totally inarticulate:* incapable of speech, mute, dumb, tongue-tied, speechless, wordless; paralysed. **3** *The sophisticated actor was surprisingly inarticulate in private:* hesitant in speech, uncommunicative, poorly spoken, inexpressive.

Ant. 1 articulate, clear, intelligible, coherent, distinct. **2** articulate. **3** expressive, glib, voluble.

inattentive *adj. The singer was offended by the inattentive audience. An inattentive driver is a menace on the road:* showing no interest; not attentive, careless, negligent, thoughtless, unmindful, heedless, absent-minded, distracted, forgetful, unaware, day-dreaming.

Ant. attentive, heedful; mindful, careful, aware.

inaugurate *v.* **1** *The city inaugurated the clean-air campaign with a parade:* begin formally, launch, set in action, undertake, initiate, institute, embark upon, usher in, set up, start, *Informal* kick off. **2** *The new professor will be inaugurated in June:* induct formally into office, invest with office; induct, instate, instal ceremoniously.

Ant. 1 terminate, end, conclude, finish.

◇ *Pronunciation tip:* By pronouncing *inaugurate* properly as *in-AWG-yuh-rate*, not "in-auger-rate", you will more easily remember its correct spelling, *inaug-U-rate.*

◇ *Word origin:* When we *inaugurate* a new official or a new business, it has little to do with religion. Yet *inaugurate* comes from Latin *inaugurare,* "to sanctify a place or person by ceremonial consultation of the flight of birds." Originally a technical term of the Roman religion, this word is related to *auger* and *augury.*

inauspicious *adj. I'm afraid you have picked an inauspicious moment to arrive:* ill-chosen, badly timed, ill-omened, unpropitious, unfavourable, unlucky, unpromising, unfortunate, infelicitous, disastrous.

Ant. auspicious, favourable, propitious, fortunate, lucky, happy, providential, well-timed, hopeful, promising.

inborn *adj. Children seem to have an inborn love of music:* inherent, innate, inbred, congenital, constitutional, natural, native, intuitive, intrinsic; basic, fundamental.

Ant. acquired, learned, conditioned, taught, inculcated.

incalculable *adj.* **1** *The number of galaxies in the universe is incalculable:* beyond counting or calculation, too great to be calculated, too numerous to count, inestimable, countless, measureless, immeasurable, uncountable, incomputable, innumerable, infinite. **2** *The future is incalculable:* unknowable in advance, unforeseeable, uncertain, dubious, unpredictable.

Ant. 1 calculable, estimable, measurable, countable, computable; limited, finite. **2** calculable, predictable, certain, foreseeable, knowable.

incandescent *adj.* **1** *As electrical force increased, the wire became incandescent:* glowingly hot, luminously hot, white-hot; brilliant, blindingly bright. **2** *The language of the play was incandescent. The young man has an incandescent charm:* brilliant, electrifying, galvanic, electric; dynamic, magnetic, scintillating, high-powered, glowing, radiant.

◇ *Word origin: Incandescent* comes from Latin *in-* (in) + *candescere* (to glow white, gleam). Also related are our words *candid, candle,* and *candour.*

incapable *adj.* **1** *Incapable management ruined the company:* unskilled, inept, incompetent, inferior, unfit, unqualified, untrained, inadequate, inefficient, ineffective. **2** *He would be incapable of committing such a cruel deed:* lacking the mettle for, unable, powerless, helpless, impotent.

Ant. 1, 2 capable, able. **1** competent, qualified; efficient, effective, skilled.

incapacitate *v. A back injury incapacitated the athlete for the whole season:* disable, render incapable, undo, make powerless, make unfit; cripple, paralyse, enfeeble, lay up, put out of action; disqualify.

incarcerate *v. Soviet authorities often incarcerate political offenders in mental institutions:* imprison, gaol, confine, immure, intern, commit; pen, restrain; *Slang* coop up.

Ant. free, release, liberate.

◇ *Word origin: Incarcerate* is derived from Latin *in-* (in) + *carcer* (gaol).

incense *v. The unruly class incensed the teacher:* enrage, inflame, anger, make angry, infuriate, madden, make indignant, provoke, *Informal* rile, nettle.

incentive *n. Profit-sharing is a good incentive for employees:* motivation, spur, stimulus, inducement, lure, enticement, *Informal* carrot, come-on; inspiration.

Ant. deterrent, prohibition, warning, dissuasion.

◇ *Word origin:* To give someone an *incentive* is literally to get them to sing to your tune, to sing in the tune you want them to. *Incentive* comes from Latin *in-* (in) + *canere* (to sing).

inception *n. An address by the headmaster to the whole school marked the inception of the new term:* commencement, beginning, start, birth, onset, arrival, inauguration; outset, début.

Ant. termination, end, ending, completion, finish, finishing, conclusion.

incessant *adj. Her incessant complaints are tiresome to everyone:* constant, ceaseless, continuous, continual, unceasing, unremitting, perpetual, everlasting, persistent, interminable, unbroken, unrelenting, uninterrupted.

Ant. intermittent, periodic, sporadic, occasional; rare, infrequent.

◇ *Word origin: Incessant* comes from Latin *in-* (not) + *cessare* (to cease), which also gives us *cease.*

incident *n.* **1** *The incident has long since been forgotten:* particular event, episode, affair, occasion, occurrence, happening; small disturbance, scene, contretemps, clash.
—*adj.* **2** *The problems incident to starting a new business are numerous:* occurring naturally, related, arising from, happening in the course of, going along with, incidental, connected with, likely to happen.
◇ *Word origin: Incident* comes from Latin *incidere,* which is made up of *in* (in) + *cadere* (to fall), and so an *incident* is something that literally falls into, or happens, to you.

"Death is only an incident in life."
—*William De Morgan*

---

incidental *adj. The incidental costs of the car added up to a large sum:* secondary, extraneous, accessory, minor, subordinate; unexpected, unlooked-for.
—*n.* **2 incidentals.** *When you are travelling, be sure to take along a small suitcase for incidentals:* minor items, accessories, appurtenances, extras; odds and ends, minutiae.
Ant. 1 essential, fundamental, basic.

incidentally *adv. Incidentally, the Joneses may come with us if they like:* by the way; in passing, connected with that, by the by, apart from the main subject, apropos, speaking of that, while we're on the subject.
◇ *Pronunciation tip: Incidentally* is formed from *incidentAL + LY*; it is pronounced and spelt *inciDENTally* — although you may come across the spelling "incidently" in books and records before about 1820.

incipient *adj. An incipient sore throat kept the child at home. She is an incipient actress:* beginning, becoming apparent; nascent, inchoate, half-formed, developing; barely starting; promising, budding, embryonic, fledgling.
Ant. realized, achieved, finished, full-blown; accomplished.

incisive *adj.* **1** *An incisive command stopped the dog in its tracks:* keen, sharp, biting, crisp, brisk, curt, cutting, piercing, acute, mordant, trenchant, express, summary. **2** *Oscar Wilde was known for his incisive wit:* penetrating, cutting, analytic, acute, precise; shrewd, well-aimed, perceptive, probing, penetrating, trenchant, intelligent, sharp.

incite *v. The dictator's cruel decree incited the people to open rebellion:* rouse, activate, stimulate, actuate, arouse, urge on, inflame, provoke, foment, excite, agitate, egg on; stir, stir up, fire, drive, impel, goad, prompt.
◇ *Word origin: Incite* comes from Latin *in-* (thoroughly) + *citare* (to set in motion, rouse). The same Latin verb gives us *cite* and *recite.*

inclement *adj. Inclement weather forced us to postpone the picnic:* stormy, violent, rough, severe, tempestuous, foul, nasty.
Ant. clement, mild.

inclination *n.* **1** *The engine has an inclination to race. People have an inclination to loaf about in hot weather:* tendency, propensity, penchant, leaning, proneness, predilection, proclivity, preference, disposition, predisposition; fondness, bent, liking. **2** *The minister accepted the plan with an inclination of his head:* nod, bow, bend, bending, lowering, inclining. **3** *There is a steep inclination in the road ahead:* slant, rise, dip, slope, acclivity, incline, rake, pitch, hill, gradient.
Ant. 1 dislike, antipathy, disinclination.

incline *v.* **1** *The whole family inclines to rise early:* tend, have a mind to, have a preference, prefer, enjoy, like, lean toward. **2** *Older people incline to slow down:* tend, be apt, be likely, have a propensity, seem, be wont to. **3** *The roof inclines over the porch:* slope, slant, tilt, rake, decline, cant, pitch, lean. **4** *Incline your body from the waist when you bow:* bend forward, lean, bend, tilt, bow.
—*n.* **5** *The house is perched upon an incline:* slope, hill, gradient, pitch, cant, inclined plane, acclivity.
Ant. 1 dislike, hate, abhor, be disinclined.
◇ *Word origin:* Both *incline* and *inclination* come from Latin *in-* (on) + *clinare* (to lean), which also gives us *decline* and *recline.*

include *v. The meal includes an aperitif, main course, dessert, and coffee:* contain, comprise, embrace, enfold, cover, take in, incorporate, comprehend, involve, entail, subsume.
Ant. exclude; eliminate, rule out, omit, leave out, forget.

incoherent *adj. His account of the robbery was hysterical and incoherent:* disjointed, unintelligible, rambling, confused, bewildering, irrational, inconsistent, unclear, nonsensical, muddled.
Ant. coherent, intelligible, logical, connected, rational, consistent.

income *n. In addition to his salary, he had a small income from investments:* revenue, earnings, livelihood, means, wages, salary, emolument.
Ant. expense, disbursement, outlay.

incomparable *adj. Have you seen the incomparable beauty of Lake Windermere?:* peerless, matchless, unequalled, unrivalled, unapproachable, inimitable, superlative, transcendent, beyond compare.
Ant. ordinary, fair, mediocre, second-rate, average, inferior, run-of-the-mill.
◇ *Pronunciation tip:* See COMPARABLE.

incompatible *adj.* **1** *The partners were too incompatible to stay in business together:* inharmonious, uncongenial, antagonistic, lacking rapport, at variance, at odds, mismatched, clashing, disagreeing. **2** *That raucous voice is incompatible* *with her fragile appearance:* inconsistent, contrary, incongruous, jarring, discordant, at odds, contradictory, unsuited, not going well with, inappropriate.

Ant. compatible, accordant, consonant, consistent, congenial; harmonizing, harmonious, agreeing, appropriate.

incompetent *adj. The incompetent typist had to retype the letter five times:* inept, untrained, lacking ability, ineffectual, ineffective, inefficient, unfit, incapable, inexpert, unqualified.

Ant. competent, apt, expert, efficient.

incomplete *adj. My set of china is still incomplete:* unfinished, lacking a part, partial, not total, containing omissions, broken, fragmentary; wanting, defective, deficient.

Ant. complete, finished, whole, unbroken.

incomprehensible *adj. Physics is incomprehensible to me:* baffling, bewildering, beyond understanding, ungraspable, beyond comprehension, unintelligible, confusing, unfathomable, abstruse, impenetrable.

Ant. comprehensible, understandable, clear, plain, intelligible.

"The nearer we get to any natural object the more incomprehensible it becomes."

—*G. C. Lichtenberg*

---

inconceivable *adj. It's inconceivable that people should be starving in such a wealthy country:* unthinkable, unbelievable, incredible, beyond belief, contrary to reason or belief; highly unlikely, unimaginable, strange, improbable, impossible to comprehend.

Ant. conceivable, believable, credible, plausible, reasonable, likely, imaginable, probable, comprehensible.

◇ *Spelling tip: Inconceivable,* like *conceive,* follows the basic spelling rule of "*i* before *e* except after *c*", hence *inconcEIvable.*

inconclusive *adj. The committee's inconclusive findings left the case up in the air:* undetermined, indeterminate, unresolved, unsettled, eluding settlement, indecisive, not definite, still doubtful, unconvincing.

Ant. conclusive, decisive, definite.

incongruous *adj.* **1** *Ordinary clothes look incongruous on the beach:* inappropriate, odd, outlandish, out of keeping, out of place, unsuitable, not harmonious; *Slang* far-out. **2** *The witness's incongruous testimony puzzled the jury:* conflicting, contrary, at variance, incompatible, contradictory, inconsistent, irreconcilable, discrepant, disagreeing.

Ant. 1 congruous, fitting, suitable, appropriate, consonant, consistent, accordant, agreeing, harmonious, becoming.

inconsequential *adj. The matter is too inconsequential to worry about:* trivial, trifling, of no moment, valueless, slight, unimportant, of no consequence, insignificant, nugatory, meaningless, piddling, petty.

Ant. consequential, important, momentous, significant, meaningful, crucial.

inconsiderate *adj. It was inconsiderate of him to play the music so loud:* thoughtless, rude, impolite, insensitive, uncaring, unkind, uncharitable, disregardful, ungracious; rash, unthinking, remiss, negligent, careless, tactless, lacking regard.

Ant. considerate, thoughtful; kind; polite.

inconsistent *adj.* **1** *His dissolute life is inconsistent with his puritan upbringing:* incompatible, dissonant, inharmonious, inaccordant, inconsonant, discrepant, contrary, contradictory, not in agreement, incongruous, irreconcilable. **2** *An inconsistent parent can make a child feel insecure:* erratic, unstable, constantly changing, wayward, inconstant, changeable; fickle, unpredictable, irresolute, variable, vacillating, changeful.

Ant. 1 consistent, consonant, coherent, compatible, congruous; according or accordant, agreeing, tallying, corresponding or correspondent, suitable. **2** consistent, unchangeable; stable, reliable; constant, steady.

inconspicuous *adj. The star preferred to remain inconspicuous by wearing a very simple dress:* unnoticed, unnoticeable, unobtrusive, attracting little attention, not outstanding; unassuming, modest; unapparent, dim, muted.

Ant. conspicuous, noticeable; striking, prominent, egregious.

incontrovertible *adj. The eyewitness's testimony was incontrovertible:* undeniable, indisputable, irrefutable, apodictic, beyond question, unquestionable, established, past dispute, unarguable.

Ant. disputable, questionable, debatable.

inconvenient *adj. It's inconvenient to have to work at the week-end:* inopportune, untimely, bothersome, troublesome, tiresome, awkward, annoying; burdensome, distressing.

Ant. convenient, opportune, timely; advantageous, helpful.

incorporate *v. The committee incorporated the investigator's findings in its report:* include, embody, work in, consolidate, fuse, amalgamate, introduce into, assimilate.

incorrect *adj. The article was filled with incorrect statements:* wrong, erroneous, untrue, mistaken, false, fallacious, inaccurate.

Ant. correct, right, accurate, true.

incorrigible *adj. The incorrigible boy was in and out of approved schools for years:* uncontrollable, unmanageable, unruly, beyond saving, past changing, beyond help, intractable; delinquent, hardened, hard-core, thoroughly bad.

Ant. correctable, manageable, tractable, amenable.

incorruptible *adj. The incorruptible policeman even refused a free cup of coffee:* pure, righteous, upright, honest, reliable, beyond corruption, above temptation, trustworthy, unbribable.

Ant. corruptible, bribable, corrupt, dishonest, unreliable.

increase *v.* **1** *Travel increases one's knowledge of the world:* make greater or larger, enlarge, expand, enrich, add to, augment, advance, enhance. **2** *The membership increased by 50 per cent:* enlarge, become larger, swell, expand, burgeon, grow, wax, become more numerous, multiply.

Ant. decrease, diminish, lessen, reduce, abate, dwindle; shorten, abridge, abbreviate, curtail, retrench; contract, condense, shrink, deflate, decline, lower.

incredible *adj. For such a tiny woman she had an incredible appetite:* unbelievable, remarkable, unimaginable, awesome, hardly credible, inconceivable, preposterous, absurd, far-fetched, amazing, astounding, astonishing.

Ant. credible, believable, unremarkable; ordinary, usual, common.

◇ *Usage note: Incredible* means hard to believe; *incredulous* means hard to convince, sceptical. Thus, *His story of rescuing six drowning men was incredible!* but *We were incredulous when we heard his story.*

◇ *Spelling tip:* Some people are never certain whether *incredible* ends in *-able* or *-ible*. Remember that your two eyes may look at something and find it *IncredIble*, with two *i*'s.

> **Exploring the Word:** *Incredible* means unbelievable. It comes from Latin *credere*, to believe, trust, which also gives us *credit*, belief in the truth of something, trust that someone will repay a debt, and *creditor*, one who trusts another to repay him a debt; *credulous*, willing or too willing to believe; *credence*, belief; *creed*, a formal statement of belief; *credo*, a set of beliefs; and *credential*, proof that allows one to believe another's identity, authority, or experience.

incredulous *adj. The judge was incredulous when the defendant stated his bizarre alibi. She gave me an incredulous glance:* dubious, sceptical, unwilling to believe, not believing, distrustful, doubtful, suspicious; showing disbelief.

Ant. credulous, believing, trustful, trusting.

◇ *Usage note:* See INCREDIBLE.

incur *v. Do not incur unnecessary debts. The naughty child incurred his nanny's wrath:* contract, become liable for, bring into being, assume, bring on, acquire, fall into, become subject to; arouse, incite, stir up, involve, provoke, bring out.

incurable *adj. Rabies is an acute and, in many cases, incurable disease. Jim is an incurable optimist:* beyond cure, having no remedy, irremediable, cureless, uncorrectable; incorrigible, relentless, ceaseless, unflagging, inveterate, dyed-in-the-wool, hopeless.

Ant. curable, correctable, remediable.

incursion *n. The enemy made a second incursion into the neighbouring lands:* invasion, foray, attack; assault, encroachment, impingement, raid; forcible entry, inroad, push; advance forward or into.

indebted *adj.* **1** *The restaurant is heavily indebted to the bank:* under obligation, in debt, burdened with debt; financially burdened; chargeable, accountable. **2** *We are indebted to you for your loyal support:* obligated, bound, beholden, bounden; deeply appreciative, grateful, full of thanks, thankful.

Ant. 1 unobligated, free and clear. **2** unobligated, unbeholden, ungrateful, unthankful.

indecent *adj.* **1** *It seemed indecent to talk business at the funeral:* unseemly, improper, lacking common decency, indiscreet, unbecoming, rude, ignoble, ill-bred, uncivil, offensive, vulgar, in bad taste. **2** *The indecent film was banned:* immoral, immodest, obscene, pornographic, lewd, licentious, bawdy, salacious; arousing lust, prurient, unwholesome, *Informal* smutty, dirty, filthy, blue.

Ant. 1, 2 decent. **1** proper, seemly, becoming, tasteful, appropriate; polite, civil. **2** chaste, pure, modest, virtuous, moral, ethical; high-toned, elegant, tasteful.

indecisive *adj.* **1** *The result of the race was indecisive, and we had to run it again:* not decisive, inconclusive, unsettled, indeterminate, doubtful, dubious, disputable, debatable; unclear, confusing. **2** *An indecisive man could never run this firm:* irresolute, vacillating, hesitant, hesitating, wavering, weak, mercurial, half-hearted, uncertain, blowing hot and cold, wishy-washy.

Ant. 1 decisive, conclusive, firm, clear; indisputable, undebatable, certain. **2** decisive, resolute, certain.

indecorous *adj. Her flimsy dress seemed indecorous for the garden-party. We were shocked by her indecorous behaviour:* immodest, unbecoming, unseemly, unfitting, improper, unsuitable, inappropriate, not in good taste; ill-bred, low-class, gross; wicked, sinful; reprehensible, blameworthy.

Ant. decorous, decent, nice, demure; ceremonious, formal, conventional, standard, proper, suitable.

indeed *adv. The garden is indeed beautiful:* in fact, truly, in reality, without question, for sure, veritably, in truth, really, to be sure, with certainty, positively, strictly speaking, joking apart, as a matter of fact, to tell the truth, to be honest, in point of fact, actually, coming right down to it.

indefatigable *adj. The new man is an indefatigable worker and will go far:* tireless, persistent, inexhaustible, persevering, unwearying, diligent, sedulous. unflagging, untiring.

◇ *Word origin: Indefatigable* is a direct borrowing from Latin *indefatigabilis*, tireless, indefatigable, a word coined by the philosopher Seneca. From *fatigare* (to tire) we also get our word *fatigue.*

indefensible *adj.* **1** *The village proved indefensible and fell in a matter of hours:* unable to withstand attack, vulnerable, defenceless; open to attack, unprotected, pregnable, vincible. **2** *Her purchase of a mink coat was an indefensible waste of money:* inexcusable, beyond justification, unjustifiable, unspeakable, unpardonable, without reason or rationale; open to criticism, improper, untenable.

Ant. 1 defensible, invincible, invulnerable, protected. **2** defensible, justifiable, excusable, pardonable, reasonable, rational, tenable.

indefinite *adj.* **1** *The shop will be closed for an indefinite period:* unspecified, having no fixed limit, undetermined, indeterminate, unknown, inexact, inexplicit; illimitable, measureless, limitless. **2** *I gave him an indefinite answer:* unsettled, uncertain, indistinct, vague; not clearly defined, dim, ill-defined, amorphous, indecisive, doubtful, tentative, obscure, ambiguous, unsure.

Ant. 1 definite, clear-cut, certain, limited, known, specific. **2** certain, definite, settled, sure, unambiguous.

indelible *adj. The book left an indelible impression on me. The ink made an indelible stain:* vivid, permanent, unforgettable, lasting, memorable; permanently fixed, ineradicable, unerasable, irremovable, incapable of being deleted or wiped out, ingrained.

◇ *Word origin: Indelible* comes from Latin *in-* (non-) + *delebilis* (blottable). The Latin word *indelebilis* was coined by the poet Ovid with the phrase *indelebile nomen,* "imperishable name."

indelicate *adj.* **1** *His indelicate manners are the result of a rough upbringing:* coarse, crude, rude, unrefined, unbecoming; clumsy, awkward. **2** *That was an indelicate story to tell in mixed company:* offensive, lacking good taste, indiscreet, unrefined; immodest, crude, indecent, vulgar, suggestive, risqué, broad, obscene, coarse, gross, rude, improper.

Ant. 1 delicate, refined, seemly, decorous, smooth, polite, polished. **2** decent, chaste, refined, discreet, proper.

indentation *n.* **1** *You can identify some trees by the indentations of the leaves. The map shows numerous indentations along the coastline:* cut, notch, incision, cavity, furrow, score; recess, concavity, niche, pocket, bay, inset. **2** *High heels had made indentations in the linoleum:* dent, pit, channel, furrow, depression, nick.

Ant. bump, protuberance, projection, prominence.

◇ *Word origin:* An *indentation* is literally a *dent in* something.

independence *n. The American colonies won their independence from England:* emancipation, liberty, self-determination, self-government, freedom from control, sovereignty, self-reliance, liberation, autonomy.

Ant. dependence; subordination, subjection; servitude, slavery, bondage; reliance, dependency.

independent *adj.* **1** *Children should be encouraged to be independent thinkers:* self-reliant, uncontrolled, on one's own, autonomous, free, self-directing, individualistic, uncoerced; unconstrained, free from the control or influence of others. **2** *Many people would like to see Scotland as an independent country:* free, self-governing, autonomous; self-determining, sovereign. **3** *The medical college is independent of the university:* separate, not joined to or associated with, unattached to, distinct from, exclusive, apart from, unconnected with. **4** *The inheritance made him independent for life:* solvent, well-to-do, well-off, in easy circumstances, well-fixed, affluent, *Informal* well-heeled.

Ant. 1 dependent; influenced, controlled, directed; subordinate, subject, tributary, subservient, servile, slavish, subject, attached, interrelated. **4** dependent, reliant, beholden, attached.

◇ *Spelling tip:* A truly *independent* person pays his own rent. Remember: pay *rENT,* be *independENT.*

indescribable *adj. The artistry of Michelangelo's* Pietà *is indescribable:* beyond description, inexpressible, beyond words, ineffable, beggaring description; indefinable; overwhelming, unutterable.

indestructible *adj. Toys for toddlers should be as indestructible as possible:* unbreakable, damage-resistant, infrangible, enduring, durable, permanent, everlasting, imperishable, incapable of being destroyed.

Ant. destructible, perishable, breakable, unenduring, fragile, frangible, friable.

indeterminate *adj. The acting superintendent will serve for an indeterminate time:* unspecified, undetermined, unstipulated, uncertain, unfixed in extent or amount, not clear, unresolved, vague, undefined; ambiguous, problematic, perplexing, indefinite.

Ant. specified, precise, definite, certain, determined, fixed, defined.

"—Where the statue stood
Of Newton, with his prism and silent face,
The marble index of a mind for ever
Voyaging through strange seas of thought
alone." — *William Wordsworth*

---

index *n.* **1** *The poems are listed by the author in the index:* alphabetical list, catalogue, register, glossary. **2** *Overeating is often an index of emotional stress:* sign, token, indication, symptom, clue, evidence, manifestation, proof, mark.

◇ *Usage note:* The plural of *index* may be our usual English plural *indexes* or the originally Latin plural *indices* (pronounced *IN-di-seez*). Both are correct.

◇ *Word origin:* The *index* finger is the

forefinger, and *index* is the Latin word for forefinger.

indicate *v.* **1** *The patient's pallor indicates anaemia:* be a sign of, be symptomatic of, show, denote, imply, point to, suggest; evince, bespeak, reveal, symbolize, signify, stand for, represent. **2** *Indicate where the pain is with your finger:* point out, point to, specify, direct attention to. **3** *A barometer indicates air pressure:* show, make known, register, reveal, tell, establish, record.

indication *n. There was no indication this morning that it would rain:* sign, hint, intimation, signal, manifestation, token, warning, evidence, mark, clue, suggestion, foretoken, symptom, gesture, demonstration; portent, augury, omen, boding, foreboding, premonition, presage; signifying, telling, indicating, designation, mention, showing, pointer.

indicative *adj. Fever may be indicative of an infection:* suggestive, indicatory, characteristic, evidential, symptomatic, expressive, significant, emblematic, symbolic, representative, denotative, connotative, designative.

indifference *n.* **1** *He would have preferred anger to her cold indifference:* unconcern, absence of feeling, lack of interest, disinterest, neglect, inattention, impassiveness, impassivity, nonchalance, aloofness, carelessness, negligence, insensibility, insensitivity, disdain, insouciance, apathy, coldness. **2** *Religion is a matter of indifference to many of today's youth:* unimportance, triviality, no import, insignificance, paltriness, inconsiderableness.

Ant. **1** concern, warmth, sensibility; attention, interest, eagerness, caring. **2** importance, magnitude, significance, greatness.

indifferent *adj.* **1** *The writer was indifferent to criticism, good or bad:* unconcerned, not caring, insensible, without interest, impervious, uninterested, insusceptible, detached, unmindful, impassive, unmoved, insouciant, apathetic, nonchalant, cool, aloof. **2** *The actor's indifferent performance left the audience unimpressed:* perfunctory, mediocre, not very good, uninspired, ordinary, so-so, rote, commonplace, neither good nor bad, medium, middling, fair, modest, moderate, passable, average, betwixt and between; falling short of any standard of excellence, second-rate, rather poor.

Ant. **1** avid, eager, keen, agog; interested, sensitive, susceptible, caring, sympathetic, responsive, compassionate, enthusiastic. **2** choice, notable, remarkable, exceptional, rare, first-class, superior, excellent, fine.

indigenous *adj. The indigenous flora of New Zealand is remarkably beautiful:* native, growing naturally, aboriginal, originating in, characteristic of, endemic, home-bred, home-grown, autochthonous.

Ant. naturalized; exotic; foreign, alien, extraneous, imported.

indigent *adj. Many indigent people receive State aid:* needy, destitute, in want, lacking the necessities of life, poor, in need, poverty-stricken, impoverished, penniless, without resources, badly off, moneyless, without food and clothing; *Informal* unable to keep the wolf from the door, hard-up.

Ant. wealthy, moneyed, rich, affluent, comfortable, solvent, flush.

indignant *adj. The actress was indignant at the columnist's personal questions:* incensed, offended, angry, infuriated, displeased, piqued, peeved, resentful, irate, provoked, riled, vexed, wrathful, fuming; *Informal* miffed, huffy, put off, put out, worked up, mad, on one's high horse, steamed up, wrought up.

Ant. pleased, delighted.

◇ *Word origin: Indignant* is ultimately derived from Latin *indignari,* to think unworthy. Latin *dignus,* worthy, is also found in our words *dignity* and *dignitary.* Our word *indignant* was created from Latin *indignari* by the poet Edmund Spenser for the following phrase in the *Faerie Queene* (1590): "full of fierce fury and indignant hate."

indignation *n. Reports of child abuse aroused public indignation:* resentment, displeasure, righteous anger, annoyance, vexation, dismay, irritation, pique, umbrage, ire, choler, animus, rage, wrath, fury, uproar.

Ant. calm, pleasure, serenity, composure, complacency, approval.

indignity *n. The prisoners suffered many indignities:* abuse, insult, mistreatment, injury to dignity, outrage, affront, insult to one's self-respect, humiliation, injustice, contemptuous treatment, offence, dishonour, discourtesy, rudeness, slur, *Informal* slap in the face.

Ant. dignity, honour, respect, deference, compliment, courtesy.

indirect *adj.* **1** *We took a long, indirect route to the beach:* devious, roundabout, winding, rambling, circuitous, meandering, oblique, zigzag, digressive, crooked, tortuous. **2** *The offer of a job was an indirect outcome of their meeting:* incidental, unintentional, unintended; ancillary, secondary, derivative; distant, remote. **3** *The politician's indirect answers angered the press:* evasive, not straightforward, discursive, oblique, rambling, digressive, circuitous, roundabout, vague, hedging.

Ant. **1** direct, straight. **2** direct, connected, primary. **3** direct, forthright, straightforward.

indiscreet *adj. Repeating a secret is indiscreet:* imprudent, incautious, injudicious, uncalled-for, improvident, uncircumspect, unbefitting, unseemly, foolhardy, impolitic, tasteless, ill-judged, thoughtless, unwise, careless, tactless, untactful.

Ant. discreet, judicious, prudent, circumspect, cautious, politic, tactful.

indiscriminate *adj.* **1** *The boy's indiscriminate choice of friends got him into trouble:* promiscuous, undiscriminating, unchoosy, random, unselective, undistinguishing, choosing at random, haphazard, hit-or-miss, without rhyme or reason. **2** *The indiscriminate collection of furniture made the room look cluttered:* haphazard, random, unsystematic, disorganized, slapdash, jumbled, thrown together, motley, mongrel, confused, aimless, chaotic; *Informal* higgledy-piggledy.

indispensable *adj. A good director is indispensable for a successful film:* essential, crucial, vital, imperative, absolutely necessary, needed, required, requisite, not dispensable, needful, obligatory, mandatory, compulsory; fundamental, basic.

Ant. dispensable, expendable, disposable, unnecessary, non-essential.

◇ *Spelling tip: Indispensable* ends with *-sable.* Remember this sentence: *Sable coats are indispenSABLE.*

indisposed *adj.* **1** *One of the guests was indisposed with a cold and so couldn't come:* ailing, ill, laid up, slightly sick, taken ill, not oneself, unwell, bedridden; already engaged, occupied, *Informal* under the weather. **2** *She was indisposed to accept the dull job:* averse, not disposed, reluctant, hesitant, disinclined, unwilling, not predisposed, loath, not in favour of, opposed.

Ant. 1 healthy, hardy, hale, well, hearty, sound. **2** disposed, eager, avid, keen, anxious, willing, desirous, inclined.

indistinct *adj. The radio programme was indistinct because of the atmospherics. The figure on the horizon was indistinct:* muffled, vague, not distinct, unintelligible, unclear, inaudible, weak, faint, not clearly defined, not clearly perceptible; obscure, ill-defined, indefinite, cloudy, murky, shadowy, clouded, out of focus, dim, nebulous, blurred, muddy; indecipherable, illegible; uncertain, mysterious, enigmatic, puzzling, hidden, indeterminate, ambiguous; incomprehensible, incoherent, confused.

Ant. distinct, intelligible, comprehensible, clear, audible, articulate, well-defined, perceptible, definite.

indistinguishable *adj. One twin is indistinguishable from the other. The sign was indistinguishable in the fog:* not differentiable, identical with, not distinguishable; a carbon copy of, a perfect likeness of, *Informal* the spitting image of; indiscernible, unclear, imperceptible, unobservable, unnoticeable, inconspicuous, not capable of being made out, invisible, unapparent, indistinct, obscure.

Ant. distinguishable, differentiable; separate, unidentical, different; discernible, perceptible, observable, noticeable, visible, apparent, distinct, clear.

individual *adj.* **1** *Students can apply for individual tuition:* special, especial, separate, particular, exclusive, personal, private, independent, singular, one's own, specific, exclusive, personalized. **2** *The model has an individual way of dressing:* special, distinctive, unusual, original, personal, different, uncommon, unconventional, singular, characteristic, distinct, unique, peculiar to oneself.

—*n.* **3** *Everyone should be accepted as an individual:* person, somebody, single human being, self-determined being, distinct person, unique entity, autonomous being.

Ant. 1 general, universal, group, collective, common. **2** conventional, ordinary, common, indistinct.

individuality *n. The actor's individuality makes him interesting:* independent nature, uniqueness, distinction, particularity, singularity; unique character, specialness.

"No member of a crew is praised for the rugged individuality of his rowing."
—*Ralph Waldo Emerson*

---

indoctrinate *v. The instructor thoroughly indoctrinated his class in political theory:* teach, inculcate, instruct in a doctrine, initiate, train, school, educate, familiarize with, drill, give instruction to, infuse, instil, implant.

indolent *adj. The indolent student stayed in bed until midday:* lazy, slothful, habitually idle, inactive, shiftless, slack, sluggish, inert, lethargic, listless, lumpish, lackadaisical, dawdling, dilatory.

Ant. industrious; busy, diligent, conscientious, assiduous, sedulous; energetic, strenuous, vigorous, active.

◇ *Word origin: Indolent* is formed from Latin *in-* (not) + *dolere* (to feel pain, grieve), hence "without pain" (original sense in English) or "taking no pains," i.e. "lazy" (present sense in English). Latin *dolere* also gives us *condolence, dolorous,* and *doleful.*

indomitable *adj. The coach's indomitable spirit helped the team to victory:* invincible, indefatigable, unconquerable, invulnerable, unyielding, insuperable, unassailable, staunch, steadfast, formidable, unwavering, irrepressible, resolute, stubborn, dogged, unflinching, fearless, dauntless, unshrinking, intrepid, stalwart, courageous, undaunted, persevering, doughty, valiant, cast-iron.

Ant. yielding, weak, feeble, languid, wavering, faltering, flinching, shrinking, cowardly.

◇ *Word origin: Indomitable* is formed on Latin *in-* (not) + a form of the verb *domare,* to subdue, tame. Our words *dominate* and *domestic,* by the way, do not come from the same root. Latin *domare* (to tame) is, however, cognate with our (originally Germanic) word *tame.*

indorse *v.* See ENDORSE.

indubitably *adv. She will indubitably come:*

unquestionably, certainly, without doubt, undoubtedly, for sure, for certain, doubtless, of course, without question.

induce *v.* **1** *My arguments induced him to vote for the amendment:* coax, persuade, influence, prompt, dispose, incline, prevail upon, bring round, encourage, get, sway, win over, prevail on. **2** *Alcohol can induce a loosening of the tongue:* bring on, give rise to, lead to, occasion, prompt, cause, bring about, produce, motivate, inspire, sow the seeds of, set in motion, effect, instigate, incite, activate, actuate, provoke, arouse.

Ant. 1 dissuade, prevent, disincline, deter, hinder, restrain. **2** deter, hinder, stop, halt, curb, suppress.

inducement *n. The biscuit was an inducement to the dog to perform:* incentive, enticement, allurement, incitement, goad, spur, bait, stimulus, inspiration, motive, ground, cause, reason, provocation, temptation, persuasion, instigation, attraction.

Ant. deterrent, discouragement.

indulge *v. The nurse indulged the spoilt child too much. He indulged his fondness for cherries:* cater to, serve, go along with, oblige, gratify, accommodate, give way to, yield to, give loose rein to, treat, appease, yield to the desires of, pamper the whims of, pander to, mollycoddle, humour to excess, spoil, cosset.

Ant. deny, forbid, thwart, disappoint, discipline, abstain from.

indulgence *n.* **1** *Rich desserts are an indulgence that the overweight can't afford:* luxury, something indulged in, self-indulgence, extravagance, excess, self-gratification, intemperance, immoderation; dissipation, profligacy, debauchery. **2** *The pilot asked for the passengers' indulgence during the delay:* sufferance, understanding, tolerance, forgiveness, forbearance, patience, lenience, compassion, permissiveness, allowance, kindness, graciousness, benignity.

Ant. 1 abstinence, self-sacrifice, repression, restraint. **2** condemnation, castigation, reprehension.

indulgent *adj. A nursery-school teacher may be somewhat indulgent:* lenient, tolerant, understanding, forbearing, humouring, forgiving, permissive, easy-going, complaisant, clement, pampering, sparing, patient, yielding, obliging, benign, conciliatory.

Ant. strict, stern, severe, rigorous, stringent, harsh, rough, austere, intolerant, unmerciful, unforgiving, demanding.

industry *n.* **1** *Heavy industry suffers during an energy crisis:* business, commerce, manufacture, trade. **2** *The clerk was rewarded for his industry:* hard work, zeal, diligence, industriousness, sedulousness, application, go, labour, assiduity, bustle, hustle, enterprise, energy, perseverance, toil, patient plodding, indefatigability, activity, assiduousness.

◇ *Word origin: Industry* is from Latin *industria*, diligence.

inebriated *adj. Both men were too inebriated to drive:* drunk, under the influence, intoxicated, tipsy, drunken, drunk as a lord; *Slang* plastered, in one's cups, well-oiled, sozzled, tight, high, loaded, paralytic, blotto, stoned, smashed.

Ant. sober.

> **Exploring the Word:** *Inebriated* comes from Latin *in-* (thoroughly) + *ebrius*, drunk. Also related is our word *sober*, from Latin *sobrius*, not drunk. A 4th-century A.D. grammarian claimed that *ebriety* (drunkenness) was derived from the state of coming out of (*e-*) the wine pot (*bria*) — which conjures up visions of a flushed, glassy-eyed jack-in-the-box, and is very pleasant although most unlikely. Latin *bria* (wine pot) occurs only once in the whole of classical Latin — in the above summarized text! All of which leaves the history of the word *inebriated* as muddled as the state denoted by it.

ineffective *adj. The air-conditioner was ineffective in such a crowded room. He proved to be an ineffective administrator:* of little use, not much good, not producing results; inefficient, unproductive, weak, powerless, inadequate, useless, impotent, inoperative; incapable, worthless.

Ant. effective; effectual, efficacious, efficient; useful, profitable, capable, productive, adequate.

◇ *Usage note:* See EFFECTIVE.

ineffectual *adj. Charles I was a brave king but an ineffectual ruler:* inept, incompetent, ineffective, inefficient, unsatisfactory, inefficacious, unprofitable, useless, unavailing, not up to par, unsuccessful, unproductive, profitless, vain, futile; weak, impotent, hapless, feeble, inadequate, lame.

Ant. effectual, efficacious, effective, profitable, fruitful, useful, successful, productive, gainful; efficient, satisfactory, competent, adequate.

◇ *Usage note:* See EFFECTIVE.

inefficient *adj. The inefficient operation cost the firm a lot of money:* ineffective, incompetent, slipshod, ineffectual, slack, unproductive, inadequate, not efficient, wasteful of time or energy, inefficacious, inept, good-for-nothing, indifferent; futile, pointless.

Ant. efficient, competent, able, capable, qualified; skilful, skilled, proficient, expert, adept; effectual, efficacious.

ineligible *adj. Poor marks made the student ineligible to sit the exam:* unqualified, disqualified, not eligible, unentitled, unfit, unacceptable, unsuitable.

Ant. eligible, qualified, suitable, fit.

inept *adj.* **1** *The soldiers were brave but inept:* inefficient, incompetent, unskilled, untrained, unqualified, without dexterity, bungling, ineffective, inefficacious, ineffectual, awkward, clumsy, maladroit. **2** *The speaker's inept comparison simply bewildered the audience:* out of place, unapt, pointless, empty, inane, inappropriate, unsuitable, unfitting, foolish, senseless, asinine, silly, fatuous, nonsensical.

Ant. **1** efficient, skilful, apt, qualified, dextrous, competent, talented, effectual, effective, adroit, efficacious, able. **2** apt, germane, appropriate, pointed; sensible.

inequality *n. Women are fighting against sexual inequality in the business world:* unfairness, inequity, lack of equality, imparity, favouritism, prejudice; irregularity, difference, diversity, variableness, changeableness, dissimilarity, unequalness, dissimilitude, disparity, disproportion, inconstancy, divergence, unlikeness.

Ant. equality, fairness, impartiality, regularity, sameness, similarity, similitude, constancy, likeness.

inert *adj. The man was so inert that he seemed dead:* motionless, static, inactive, quiescent, still, passive, inanimate, impassive; listless, phlegmatic, sluggish, dull, numb, leaden, supine, slack, torpid, languid.

Ant. dynamic; animated; active, alert, kinetic, brisk, lively, energetic, vigorous.

◇ *Word origin: Inert* comes from Latin *iners: in-* (not) + *ars* (skill), unskilled, inactive. From Latin *ars* (skill, art) we also get our words *art, artifact,* and *artificial.*

inertia *n. Blame your inertia on the hot weather:* inertness, listlessness, sluggishness, languor, disinclination to move, passiveness, inactivity, laziness, inaction, lethargy, lassitude, apathy, indolence, supineness, passivity, torpor, dullness, stupor, weariness.

Ant. activity, action, liveliness, energy, vigour, vitality, animation.

inevitable *adj. Traffic delays are inevitable at a holiday week-end:* inescapable, unavoidable, unpreventable, ineluctable, destined, certain, written in the book of fate, fated, sure, sure to happen, ineludible.

Ant. escapable, avoidable, eludible, evadable, preventable; uncertain, indeterminate.

◇ *Word origin: Inevitable* comes from Latin *inevitabilis: in-* (not) + *evitare* (to avoid), hence unavoidable.

inexcusable *adj. Her rudeness was inexcusable:* unpardonable, unforgivable, indefensible, unjustifiable, unallowable, intolerable, unbearable.

Ant. excusable, pardonable, justifiable.

inexpensive *adj. The restaurant serves good, inexpensive meals:* low-priced, not expensive, popularly-priced, costing little, nominally priced; reasonable, moderate, cheap, good at the price; *Informal* light on the wallet.

Ant. expensive, costly, high-priced.

◇ *Usage note:* See CHEAP.

inexperienced *adj. The crew felt unsafe with such an inexperienced pilot:* unseasoned, unskilled, inexpert, unpractised, untrained, unschooled, uninitiated, untutored; untried, unfledged, green, callow, fresh; unfamiliar, unversed, unaccustomed, unconversant, unacquainted; unsophisticated, naïve, raw, immature.

Ant. experienced, skilled, practised, seasoned, trained, expert, schooled, conversant, versed, accustomed; sophisticated, worldly, worldly-wise.

inexplicable *adj. The flying-saucer sighting was inexplicable:* unexplainable, unfathomable, unsolvable, incomprehensible, unaccountable, insoluble, undecipherable; mysterious, mystifying, abstruse, puzzling, perplexing, enigmatical.

Ant. explicable, explainable, intelligible, fathomable, solvable, comprehensible, accountable, soluble; reasonable, understandable, obvious, clear.

infallible *adj. The designer has an infallible eye for colour. It looked like an infallible escape plan:* faultless, flawless, free from error, unerring, incapable of error, unfailing, not liable to err, free from mistake, unimpeachable, apodictic, absolutely trustworthy, impeccable, perfect, inerrant, irrefutable, incontrovertible; dependable, foolproof, sure, reliable, assured, positive, perfect.

Ant. **1** fallible, questionable, dubious, contestable, untrustworthy, controvertible, refutable, doubtful, unreliable, uncertain, unsure, undependable.

infamous *adj. Bluebeard was an infamous character. I was shocked by her infamous behaviour:* notorious, disreputable, having a bad reputation, villainous, of evil fame, of ill repute, nefarious, outrageous, dishonourable, vile, scandalous, shameful, ignoble, foul, heinous, monstrous, evil, wicked, opprobrious, disgraceful, base, damnable, odious, perfidious, detestable, abhorrent, sordid, recreant, abominable, low, iniquitous, treacherous, shamefully bad, corrupt, scurrilous, immoral, sinful, knavish, profligate.

Ant. illustrious; glorious, splendid, sublime, reputable, honourable, good.

◇ *Pronunciation tip: Infamous* should be pronounced so that the first syllable is stressed: *IN-fuh-mus,* not "in-FAME-us."

infantile *adj. Temper tantrums in an adult are infantile:* babyish, suitable to an infant, characteristic of an infant, childish, childlike, juvenile, infantlike, infantine.

Ant. mature, adult, manly, womanly, grown-up.

infatuated *adj. Many men were infatuated with the beautiful young widow:* enamoured, bewitched by, inspired with blind love for, inflamed by, beguiled by, spellbound by, carried away by, having a crush on, intoxicated by, smitten

by, deprived of common sense by, obsessed by, entranced by, captivated by, charmed by, enraptured by, enthralled by.
◇ *Word origin: Infatuated* comes from Latin *infatuatus*, "befooled." Latin *fatuus*, foolish, also gives us our word *fatuous*.

"I may not here omit those two main plagues, and common dotages of human kind, wine and women, which have infatuated and besotted myriads of people. They go commonly together." —*Robert Burton*

---

infect *v.* **1** *The flu virus infected almost the entire class:* contaminate, taint, poison, blight. **2** *The director's bad mood infected the whole cast:* touch, influence, spread among, affect adversely, work upon, have an effect on, spread through, leave its mark on.

infectious *adj.* **1** *Measles is an infectious disease:* catching, communicable, virulent, germ-laden, epidemic, inoculable, spreading, infective, contagious, *Informal* catchable. **2** *The children's gaiety was infectious:* catching, contagious, tending to affect others, irresistible, compelling, captivating.
Ant. 1 non-contagious, non-communicable, incommunicable.

infer *v. The jury inferred from the testimony that the defendant was lying:* conclude, deduce, reckon, reason, judge; opine, guess, conjecture, speculate, gather, consider probable, glean, suppose, surmise, form an opinion, deem, presume.
◇ *Usage note:* See IMPLY.

inferior *adj.* **1** *Brass is inferior to gold. A private is inferior to a sergeant:* worth less than, of lower quality than, less valuable than; lower in rank than, of less importance than, subordinate, subservient, secondary, junior, subsidiary. **2** *Many sausage makers use inferior meat:* poor, substandard, low-quality, low-grade, second-rate, less valuable, of less excellence, indifferent, mediocre.
Ant. 1 superior, higher, senior, greater. **2** superior, first-rate, first-class, top, prime, fine, excellent.

infernal *adj.* **1** *The poet wrote of the infernal world of Satan:* hellish, Plutonian, Stygian, lower, nether. **2** *He should try to control that infernal temper:* damnable, hellish, devilish, horrible, fiendish, diabolical, demoniacal, awful, terrible, heinous, black, cursed, execrable, flagitious, vicious, accursed, malicious, nefarious, atrocious, vile, abominable, monstrous, iniquitous, horrendous.
Ant. 1 supernal, angelic, celestial, heavenly.
◇ *Word origin: Inferior* is Latin for "lower." Its basic form *inferus*, low, is also the base of our word *infernal* — thus the phrase *infernal regions* literally means the *lower regions*.

infidel *n. Richard I and Saladin considered each other to be infidels:* unbeliever, heathen, pagan, idolater, non-believer in God, atheist, apostate, heretic; savage, barbarian.
Ant. believer.
◇ *Usage note: Infidel*, "unbeliever," comes from Latin *infidelis*, unfaithful. The word was first applied to the Saracens against whom Englishmen and other Christians were crusading in the Holy Land. The word is also used, from the Muslim point of view, to denote non-Muslims, especially Christians. *Infidel* has also sometimes been used in the sense of "(Christian) heretic" or "atheist," but the word has always been mainly associated with the hostile relationship between Christianity and Islam.

infidelity *n.* **1** *Infidelity was the cause of the divorce:* adultery, breaking of the marriage vows, marital faithlessness, unfaithfulness, betrayal, disloyalty. **2** *Infidelity to any of the organization's tenets will not be tolerated:* non-observance, non-adherence, breach, falsity, disregard, transgression, violation.
Ant. 1 fidelity, faithfulness, loyalty.

infinite *adj.* **1** *Learning to ski requires infinite patience. Man's will to survive is infinite:* enormous, great, immense, tremendous; immeasurable, vast, measureless. **2** *The universe seems infinite:* boundless, interminable, limitless, unlimited; illimitable, unbounded, uncircumscribed, endless, knowing no limit, without end, inexhaustible; incalculable, measureless.
Ant. 1 small, little, limited. **2** finite; circumscribed, definitive, restricted, limited, bounded, measurable.

infinitesimal *adj. The punch contained only an infinitesimal amount of alcohol:* tiny, inconsiderable, microscopic, imperceptible, immeasurably small, diminutive, puny, minute, extremely small, *Informal* wee; inappreciable, negligible.
Ant. enormous, vast, infinite, huge, immeasurable, large, great.

infirm *adj. The old man was too infirm to work:* weak, feeble, frail, weakened, unsound, ailing, decrepit, enfeebled, doddering, poorly, worn, helpless, failing, ailing, sickly, fragile, ill, debilitated, strengthless, powerless, enervated, disabled, emaciated.
Ant. hale; strong, sturdy, stalwart, stout; healthy, robust, sound.

infirmity *n.* **1** *Age and infirmity finally finished her:* disability, ailment, debility, infirmness, debilitation, malady, illness, disorder, indisposition, physical weakness, frailness, sickness, loss of health, lack of strength, handicap, fragility. **2** *Some infirmity of character led the policeman to take a bribe:* failing, moral weakness, deficiency, flaw, defect, fault, frailty, vulnerability, imperfection; instability, unstableness.
Ant. 1 strength, vigour, healthfulness, soundness. **2** strength, perfection; stability.

inflame *v. Rudolph Valentino inflamed thousands of silent-film addicts. The agitator tried to inflame the mob:* excite, electrify, intoxicate, arouse, provoke, rouse, fire, excite the passions of, incite, stir up, stimulate, agitate, work up, heat up, enkindle, craze; rile, incense, enrage, madden.

Ant. extinguish (a passion), quench, allay, cool, calm, pacify, quiet, suppress.

inflammable *adj.* **1** *Don't light matches near inflammable liquids:* flammable, easily set on fire, capable of being set on fire, combustible, ignitable, incendiary. **2** *An inflammable temper got the man in trouble:* fiery, volatile, excitable, sensitive, inflammatory, easily roused, incendiary, highly-strung, choleric, impetuous, precipitate, over-hasty.

Ant. **1** non-flammable, uninflammable. **2** placid, calm, easy, passive, even, cool.

◇ *Usage note:* See FLAMMABLE.

inflammatory *adj. The speaker's inflammatory remarks almost started a riot. The argument created an inflammatory situation:* provocative, fiery, incendiary, rabble-rousing, enraging, inciting, rabid, arousing, tending to stir up strong feelings, intemperate, rebellious, insurgent, revolutionary, mutinous, demagogic; combustible, inflammable, explosive, fulminating, volcanic.

Ant. soothing, calming, pacifying.

inflate *v. Use a bicycle-pump to inflate the balloons:* fill up, puff out, blow up, be blown up, swell, pump up, fill with air or gas, distend, dilate.

Ant. deflate, empty, flatten.

◇ *Word origin: Inflate* comes from Latin *in-* (in) + *flare* (to blow).

inflexible *adj.* **1** *Marble is an inflexible material:* unbending, unyielding, rigid, hard, firm, solid, not flexible, fixed, taut, stiff, unplastic, unmalleable. **2** *The committee was inflexible in its opposition to our request:* unchangeable, rigid, unyielding, unbending, hidebound, obstinate, obdurate, intractable, stubborn, tenacious, pigheaded, mulish, dogged, headstrong, determined, adamant, adamantine, resolute, uncompromising, inexorable, implacable, unwavering, immovable; impervious, iron-bound, stringent, hard and fast, firm, immutable.

Ant. **1** flexible, elastic, resilient, supple, springy; pliable, pliant, yielding, plastic, malleable, ductile; fluid, liquid; expansive, buoyant, soft. **2** amenable, tractable, docile, biddable, flexible, yielding, changeable, compromising, irresolute, undetermined.

inflict *v. The hurricane inflicted severe damage on the island. Don't inflict any of your problems on me!:* lay on, visit upon, put upon, impose, cause to suffer, bring to bear, perpetrate, wreak; *Slang* unload, dump.

Ant. spare, remove, alleviate, withdraw, suspend.

influence *n.* **1** *Some pressure groups have too much influence on the Government:* weight, sway, power, pull, effect, pressure, hold, potency, mastery, ascendancy, authority, domination, dominion, control, leverage, advantage, prestige; *Slang* clout.
—*v.* **2** *My father influenced me to accept the job:* induce, persuade, impel, act upon, work upon, move, prompt, provoke, stir, inspire, incite, arouse, actuate, sway, exercise influence on, have a bearing on, play a decisive role in, incline, dispose, predispose, guide, be guided; bring pressure to bear on.

Ant. **1** ineffectiveness, impotency. **2** dissuade, restrain, hinder, impede.

influential *adj. The citizens' lobby was influential in changing the election laws:* effective, instrumental, having influence, effectual, forceful, powerful, efficacious, important, momentous, potent, puissant, strong, weighty; leading, moving, inspiring, activating.

Ant. uninfluential, weak, ineffective, ineffectual, unefficacious, inoperative, inconsiderable, unpersuasive, ineffectual, powerless, impotent, unimportant.

influx *n. The influx of holiday-makers enlivened the town. April brought an influx of warm air:* inflow, inundation, flowing in, indraught, infiltration, ingress, entry, incursion, arrival, converging.

Ant. outflow, outpouring, exit, egress, exodus.

inform *v.* **1** *The police must inform the prisoner of his legal rights:* tell, apprise, notify, let know, give notice to, advise, make known to, report to, give knowledge of, give information, acquaint, familiarize, send word to, disclose to, forewarn, communicate to, declare to, mention to, enlighten, edify, serve notice on, signify to, announce to, indicate to, tip off, *Slang* clue up. **2** *Who informed on the killer?:* denounce, give damaging evidence, furnish incriminating evidence, report an offence, tell on, tattle; *Slang* snitch, squeal, blab, rat, grass.

◇ *Word origin: Inform* is from Latin *informare,* to give form to. Latin *forma,* form, also gives us *form* and *formation.*

informal *adj. The party will be informal, so you needn't dress up:* casual, simple, without formality, unceremonious, unofficial, easy, unconstrained, natural, not formal, easy-going, off-hand.

Ant. ceremonious, formal, official.

information *n. Information on witchcraft can be obtained from the library:* data, material, news, knowledge, report, facts, evidence, tidings, account, fact-finding; (*variously*) documents, papers, notes, materials; announcement, notice, intelligence, enlightenment; briefing, notification.

informer *n. The informer's identity was kept secret:* police informant, *Slang* nark, squealer, blabber, squeaker, rat, traitor, Judas.

infraction *n. He had his driving-licence revoked for too many infractions of the speed limit:* violation, breaking of a law, infringement, breach, transgression, trespass, encroachment; disobedience, unobservance, non-observance; insubordination; peccadillo.

infrequent *adj. Fortunately, her attacks of asthma are infrequent:* occasional, rare, seldom, not regular, few and far between, sporadic, uncommon, unusual, few, not habitual, happening at long intervals, seldom happening.
Ant. frequent, usual, customary, ordinary, common, habitual.

infringe *v.* **1** *Pirating the book infringed the author's copyright:* violate, transgress, commit an infraction of, act contrary to, disobey, commit a breach of, break, contravene. **2** *Don't infringe on my territory:* trespass, encroach, intrude, invade, impinge, overstep; interfere with, *Slang* barge in.

infuriate *v. The child's stubbornness infuriated its mother:* anger, make angry, inflame, madden, enrage, rile, kindle wrath, incense, provoke, exasperate, make furious, outrage, offend, aggravate, lash into a fury, chafe, try one's temper; *Informal* get one's goat.
◇ *Word origin: Infuriate, furore,* and *fury* are all based on Latin *furere,* to be insane, to be madly in love.

infuse *v. The glowing reviews infused the performers with confidence. If only he could infuse some enthusiasm into his work!:* instil, inspire, imbue, fortify; pour into, impart to, insinuate, introduce into, cause to penetrate, inculcate, inject into, breathe into.

ingenious *adj. Not even the experts could work out the magician's ingenious escape:* clever, cunning, artful, inventive, masterful, stunning, deft, adroit, masterly, expert, exhibiting ingenuity, brilliant, shrewd, crafty, resourceful, original.
Ant. unoriginal, pedestrian, unimaginative, artless, unskilful, uninventive, unresourceful, clumsy, maladroit.
◇ *Usage note: Ingenious* and *ingenuous* are a pair of words that look and sound alike and catch out many people. *Ingenious* means clever, imaginative; *ingenuous* means frank, open, naïve; unsophisticated. Thus, *Digital watches are ingenious devices. Children are more ingenuous than adults.*
◇ *Word origin:* See INGENUITY.

ingenuity *n. The student showed ingenuity when solving the difficult maths problem:* cleverness, skill, skilfulness, inventiveness, resourcefulness, imagination, aptitude, good thinking, adroitness, ingeniousness, imaginativeness, adeptness, flair, mastery, expertise, know-how, brains, sharpness, dexterity, deftness, cunning, shrewdness, facility, astuteness.
Ant. awkwardness, clumsiness, dullness, stupidity, unskilfulness, inability, ineptitude, maladroitness.
◇ *Word origin: Ingenuity, ingenious,* and *ingenuous* all come from Latin *ingenuus,* native. Latin *ingenuus* developed the further connotations of "well-born" (hence candid and unsophisticated) and "inborn" (hence talented, *ingenious*). Latin *ingenium* means both "unaffected natural disposition" and "genius" — both the *ingenious* and the *ingenuous.*

ingrained *adj. The boy had an ingrained fear of heights:* fixed, inborn, inbred, inherent, innate, deep, deep-seated, deep-rooted, constitutional, rooted, indelible, thorough, intrinsic, inveterate, confirmed, firm.

ingratiating *adj.* **1** *His ingratiating manner endeared him to his superiors:* winning, engaging, captivating, personable, likeable, magnetic, attractive, appealing, enchanting, congenial, winsome, persuasive, charming, amiable, genial, pleasing, cordial, affable, sweet, lovable, gracious, friendly, good-humoured. **2** *His smile is false and his voice sickeningly ingratiating:* unctuous, gushing, oily, oleaginous, fulsome, smarmy, obsequious; self-serving, falsely disarming; presumptuous.
Ant. 1 forbidding, austere, unattractive, unappealing, displeasing, unpleasant, abrasive, unlovable, charmless.

ingredient *n. What ingredients went into the soup? Hard work is a vital ingredient of success:* element, component, constituent, integral part; feature, factor, essential, contributor, principle.

inhabit *v. No one has inhabited that island for over 100 years:* reside in, live in, dwell in, occupy, take up one's abode in; people, populate.

inhabitant *n. The inhabitants were evacuated from the flooded village:* resident, native, dweller, occupant, occupier, denizen, inmate, tenant; boarder, lodger; citizen, villager.

inhale *v. The fireman inhaled a dangerous amount of smoke:* breathe in, inbreathe, suck in, draw into the lungs, snuff, sniff, respire.
Ant. exhale, expire.
◇ *Word origin: Inhale* is built on Latin *in-* (in) + *halare* (to breathe), from which we also get our words *exhale* (to breathe out) and *halitosis* (bad breath).

inherent *adj. Freedom of religion is an inherent part of any democracy:* essential, innate, inseparable, hereditary, native, intrinsic, inborn, deep-rooted, inveterate, natural, inbred, ingrained, constitutional, inalienable.
Ant. foreign, alien, extrinsic, adventitious; subsidiary, superficial, supplemental.
◇ *Word origin: Inherent* comes from Latin *in-* (in) + *haerere* (to hang or stick) — *inhaerere,* to *inhere.* From Latin *haerere* we also get our words *adherent, adhesive, cohere,* and *cohesive.*

inheritance *n. A large inheritance made him independently wealthy:* legacy, bequest, estate, devise, bestowal, heritage, endowment; birthright, patrimony.

inhibit *v. The medicine inhibited the spread of the disease:* prevent, hold back, arrest, hinder, impede, restrain, suppress, check, stop, repress, smother, muzzle, harness, block, control, obstruct, curb, constrain, gag, restrict, hold in leash; forbid, prohibit, enjoin, bar.
Ant. allow, let, permit, suffer, further, encourage, support, abet.
◇ *Word origin: Inhibit* is from Latin *inhibere*, to check, to hold in, to row (a boat) backwards, based on the elements *in-* (in) + *habere* (to have, to hold).

"Criticism is never inhibited by ignorance."
—*Harold Macmillan*

inhibition Often **inhibitions** *n. He has absolutely no inhibitions about disagreeing with his boss:* mental reservation, guardedness, self-consciousness, mental block, holding back of an action or thought, misgiving, inhibiting or restraining influence, reserve, restriction, constraint, restraint of action; impediment, obstruction, blockage, stricture, constriction, check.
inhuman *adj. The inhuman treatment of mental patients shocked the public:* cruel, unfeeling, merciless, pitiless, heartless, cold-hearted, brutal, ruthless, barbarous, barbaric, monstrous, cold-blooded, savage, malevolent, vicious, satanic, hard-hearted, brutish, demoniac, diabolical, malignant, venomous, fiendish.
Ant. human, humane; benevolent, kind, humanitarian, charitable, altruistic, sympathetic, compassionate, tender.
inimitable *adj. Many have tried in vain to copy the painter's inimitable style:* matchless, unmatched, incomparable, unique, incapable of being imitated, peerless, unparalleled, rare, unequalled, nonpareil, beyond compare, unrivalled; consummate, superlative, supreme.
Ant. common, ordinary, imitable.
iniquity *n.* **1** *The iniquity of torture is universally recognized:* unfairness, gross injustice, dishonesty, violation of one's rights, immorality, unrighteousness, inequity, unjustness. **2** *The corrupt politician's iniquities should not go unpunished:* wickedness, wrong, wrongdoing, evil, evil-doing, sin, transgression, infamy, miscreancy, knavery, roguery, villainy, flagrancy; abomination, sinfulness, depravity, corruption, outrage, immorality, vice, profligacy, turpitude.
Ant. 1 justice, fairness, integrity, virtue, probity, honesty, uprightness, goodness, morality.
initial *adj. Our initial move must be to obtain the board's approval:* opening, starting, beginning, first, commencing, primary, introductory, incipient, initiatory, inaugural, maiden; original, primal.
Ant. last, ultimate, ending, final, closing, terminal.
◇ *Word origin: Initial,* like *initiate,* is from Latin *initium,* beginning, from *inire,* to go in.
initiate *v.* **1** *The museum initiated the fund-raising drive with a special exhibition:* begin, set afoot, start, be started, set going, get going, open, be opened, get under way, enter upon, commence, launch, be launched, originate, institute, found, set the ball rolling, kick off, inaugurate, take the lead, set up, break the ice, lay the foundation, establish, lead the way, lay the first stone, blaze a trail. **2** *The Rotarians initiated 12 new members:* induct, usher in, receive, admit with special rites, inaugurate, instal, give entrance to, take in, bring in, introduce, invest. **3** *A year in Florence initiated the girl into the art world:* introduce, familiarize with, acquaint with; accustom to, habituate to.
Ant. 1 consummate; fulfil, execute, accomplish, achieve, terminate, conclude, finish, end, complete. **2** refuse, reject, expel.
◇ *Word origin:* See INITIAL.
initiation *n.* **1** *An initiation ceremony will be held for all new members:* initiating, formal admission, introduction, induction, ushering in, admittance, entrance. **2** *The composer owed his initiation into the world of music to his father:* introduction, indoctrination, inculcation, guidance. **3** *Who was responsible for the initiation of hostilities?:* commencement, opening, beginning, genesis, inception, outset, onset, start, starting, beginning, introduction, inauguration, outbreak.
Ant. 1 expulsion, rejection, exit. **3** end, finish, completion, finalization, termination, closure.
initiative *n.* **1** *The council took the initiative in closing the park to cars:* lead, first step, first move, leading action, introductory act. **2** *Florence Nightingale was a woman of great initiative:* enterprise, leadership, forcefulness, dynamism, ability to initiate action, originality, creativity, power to begin, aggressiveness; *Slang* get-up-and-go.
inject *v. Try to inject some new life into the party:* insert, put, interject, throw in, interpolate, introduce, infuse, instil; force; *Slang* pump.
injure *v. The boy injured his shoulder. Heavy drinking can injure one's health. A scandal is bound to injure someone's reputation:* harm, do injury to, wound, damage, do harm to, cause harm to, afflict, hurt, mar, impair; bruise, deface, disfigure, mangle, lacerate, maim, deform, mutilate, lame; wrong, violate, abuse, ill-treat, maltreat, affront, offend, misuse, sting, sully, stain, vitiate, malign, debase, spoil, blemish, scathe.
Ant. soothe, heal, pacify; aid, help, assist, benefit.
injurious *adj. Smoking is injurious to the lungs. Poor administration is injurious to a business:*

hurtful, damaging, harmful, detrimental, destructive, deleterious, noxious, ruinous, calamitous, pernicious, disastrous, corrosive, abusive; inimical, adverse.
Ant. beneficial, helpful, advantageous, salutary; profitable.

injury *n. A severe head injury left the fighter unconscious for days. The harsh review was an injury to the singer's pride:* hurt, harm, wound, damage, bruise, mutilation, cut, lesion, gash, contusion, stab, blow, affliction, scratch, laceration; abuse, blow, injustice, outrage, indignity, affront; defamation, vilification, detraction, impairment, aspersion, disservice.

injustice *n. The newspaper led a campaign against injustice to non-members of the union. Many injustices are committed in the name of progress:* unjustness, unjust action, unfairness, inequality, bias, prejudice, partiality, inequity, bigotry, favouritism, partisanship; wrong, disservice, infraction, injury, iniquity, wrongdoing, infringement, sin, persecution, unfair treatment, encroachment, tyranny, transgression, offence, foul play, evil, malpractice.
Ant. justice, equity, fairness, fair play, impartiality, lawfulness, rectitude, right, righteousness, equality.

inkling *n. Did you have any inkling that he was coming? There was never any inkling of scandal about her:* idea, vague idea, hint, suspicion, tip, clue, suggestion, notion; glimmering, cue, intimation, conception, supposition; whisper, insinuation, innuendo.
◇ *Word origin: Inkling* comes from Middle English *inkle,* to mutter.

inlet *n. Anchor the boat in the inlet in case there's a storm:* cove, harbour, bay, gulf, estuary; narrows, waterway, strait, bight, fiord, firth.

inn *n. We'll find a cosy inn to stay in for the night:* public house, pub, lodge, lodging-house, road-house, hotel, hostel, pension, hospice, hostelry, tavern.
◇ *Word origin: Inn* comes from Old English *inn,* house. It is related to *in* and *indoors.*

"For the world, I count it not an inn, but an hospital; and a place not to live, but to die in."
—*Sir Thomas Browne*

---

innate *adj. Mozart had an innate feeling for music. An innate flaw doomed the plan right from the start:* native, natural, inborn, inherent, inbred, instinctive, intuitive, natural, ingrained, intrinsic, essential, congenital, constitutional, inherited, hereditary, indigenous.
Ant. acquired, learned; accidental, adventitious, incidental, fortuitous; assumed, affected, cultivated, fostered, nurtured; unnatural.
◇ *Word origin: Innate* is from Latin *innatus,* inborn. Latin *nasci,* to be born, is also the basis of *nativity, native,* and *nation.*

inner *adj.* **1** *The party crossed a courtyard and entered the inner part of the palace:* interior, inward, inside, internal, central, middle. **2** *The secret was locked in the inner recesses of his mind:* more secret, more intimate, unobvious, hidden, private, esoteric. **3** *Most people struggle for inner peace:* spiritual, psychological, mental, psychic, emotional.
Ant. 1 outer, outward, outside, exterior, external, outermost, open. **2** outer, external, open, public, obvious, exterior, exoteric.

innermost *adj. She confided her innermost thoughts to me:* most personal, most intimate, most private, deep-rooted, farthest inward, secret, deepest, inmost, deep-seated.
Ant. surface, superficial.

innocence *n.* **1** *The defendant's innocence is presumed until guilt is established:* guiltlessness, freedom from moral wrong, inculpability, blamelessness, impeccability, sinlessness, incorruption, clean hands, stainlessness; chastity, purity, spotlessness, immaculateness. **2** *The girl has the sweetness and innocence of a child:* simplicity, artlessness, ingenuousness, guilelessness, freshness, freedom from cunning or trickery, naïvety, purity, chastity.
Ant. 1 guilt; offensiveness, contamination, sinfulness, impurity, corruption, wrongness. **2** artfulness, guile, cunning, trickery, wiliness, disingenuousness, worldliness.

innocent *adj.* **1** *The jury found the defendant innocent:* guiltless, inculpable, blameless, faultless, free from moral wrong, above suspicion; sinless, irreproachable, upright, unimpeachable. **2** *Jill is an innocent soul:* guileless, open, unsuspicious, naïve, unworldly, unsophisticated, simple, artless, ingenuous, childlike, honest, uncorrupt, uncorrupted, spotless, unblemished, clean, impeccable, undefiled, stainless, spotless, pristine, unstained, unsullied, virtuous, pure, immaculate, virginal, chaste. **3** *The question was innocent. An innocent prank turned into disaster:* well-meant, meaning no harm, harmless, intending no damage, unmalicious, innocuous, inoffensive, unoffending.
—*n.* **4** *Herod's slaughter of the innocents is recounted in the second chapter of Matthew:* young child, baby, little one, tiny tot. **5** *The fox's favourite trick was to feign the innocent:* unsophisticated person, artless one, (*fem.*) ingénue.
Ant. 1 guilty, culpable, blameworthy, responsible; immoral, iniquitous, nefarious, sinful, unlawful, vicious, vile, wicked, evil, wrong; impure, tainted. **2** worldly, sophisticated, disingenuous, dishonest, artful, scheming; corrupt, sullied. **3** harmful, malicious, offensive.
◇ *Word origin: Innocent* is based on Latin *in-* (not) + *nocere* (to harm). Also based on this Latin verb are our words *innocuous* and *nuisance.* Closely related, because from a common Latin root, are our words *internecine,*

noxious, obnoxious, and *pernicious*. (Also related is Greek *nekros*, corpse, from which we get *necrophilia* and *necrosis*. All these words go back to an Indo-European root word meaning "death.")

innocuous *adj.* **1** *The women exchanged innocuous gossip over lunch:* harmless, not damaging, painless, not injurious, innocent, inoffensive. **2** *The play was innocuous and quickly forgotten:* meaningless, vapid, insipid, empty, barren; trite, banal, commonplace.

Ant. **1** hurtful, deleterious, harmful, wanton, insidious, obnoxious, damaging, injurious, offensive, malicious. **2** powerful, trenchant, compelling, impressive.

innovation *n. The innovation of jet flight has made the world seem smaller:* introduction, institution, establishment, inauguration, commencement; departure from the old, introduction of new methods, modernization, drastic change, breaking of precedent; new measure, novelty, alteration, latest thing, latest fashion; *French* dernier cri.

◇ *Word origin:* An *innovation* is something new. It comes from Latin *innovatio*, renewal, renovation. This is based on *novus*, new, which also gives us *novice, novel*, and even *nova* (a star that has recently flared up).

innuendo *n. The gossip column was full of innuendoes about famous people:* insinuation, veiled allusion, intimation, whisper, oblique hint, sly suggestion, implication, indirect reference, overtone.

◇ *Word origin:* An *innuendo* is an oblique comment or subtle suggestion. The word is from Latin *nuere*, to nod.

innumerable *adj. There are innumerable stars in the sky:* countless, incalculable, myriad, numberless, incapable of being counted, numerous, multitudinous, too many to be counted, unnumbered.

Ant. numerable, countable, computable; few, sporadic.

inoffensive *adj. The smell of petrol is strong but inoffensive:* harmless, not objectionable, unoffending, tolerable, innocuous, endurable, sufferable; innocent, neutral; safe.

Ant. offensive, harmful, objectionable, offending, obnoxious; noxious.

inopportune *adj. I'm afraid I caught you at an inopportune moment:* inconvenient, untimely, ill-timed, incommodious, badly timed, inappropriate, unpropitious, unsuitable, unseasonable; awkward, troublesome; undesirable, unfavourable, disadvantageous, inauspicious, unfortunate, ill-advised.

Ant. opportune, timely, convenient, appropriate, propitious, suitable, commodious; favourable, auspicious, fortunate.

inordinate *adj. An inordinate amount of time was spent discussing details:* excessive, immoderate, extravagant, disproportionate, lavish, undue, unreasonable, unconscionable, superabundant, exorbitant, superfluous, overmuch, extreme, intemperate, unnecessary, profuse, unrestrained, wanton, overflowing, supersaturated, surplus, needless, uncalled-for, irrational; outrageous, scandalous, disgraceful, deplorable, shocking.

Ant. temperate, moderate; restrained, inhibited; rightful, equitable, reasonable, sensible.

inquire Also **enquire** *v.* **1** *The pilot inquired about the weather conditions:* ask, query, seek information, question, make inquiry. **2** *The reporter inquired into the allegations of fraud:* investigate, probe, explore, study, look into, look deeper, inspect, examine, search, look behind the scenes of, scrutinize, look over, track down, *Informal* check on.

Ant. **1** reply, answer, respond, rejoin, retort; inform.

inquiry Also **enquiry** *n.* **1** *The murder inquiry was handled by the chief of London's C. I. D.:* investigation, seeking for truth, examination, inquisition, hunt, scrutiny, search, probe, study, reconnaissance, inquest, quest, exploration, research, inspection, survey. **2** *Personnel made an inquiry about the applicant's previous job:* query, question, interrogation, quiz.

◇ *Word origin: Inquiry* comes, ultimately, from Latin *in-* (in) + *quaerere* (to ask), which also gives us *query* and *question.* It entered English from French some time after the Norman conquest.

◇ *Usage note:* See QUERY.

inquisitive *adj.* **1** *The student is bright and inquisitive:* eager for knowledge, searching, intellectually curious, inquiring, fond of investigation, investigative, questioning. **2** *The inquisitive woman was always prying into her neighbour's affairs:* prying, interfering, meddling, over-curious, unduly curious, intrusive, too curious, meddlesome, snooping; *Informal* snooping, nosey.

Ant. **1** indifferent, unconcerned, incurious, uninterested, apathetic, inattentive.

insane *adj.* **1** *The psychiatrists declared the killer insane. The letter made her insane with jealousy:* mentally deranged, not sane, not of sound mind, mad, crazed, crazy, lunatic, unsound, demented, maniacal, out of one's mind, bereft of reason, not in touch with reality, mentally disordered, unbalanced; (*variously*) psychotic, manic, schizophrenic, paranoic; *Informal* out of one's wits, out of one's mind, touched, mad as a hatter, mad as a March hare, stark staring mad, unhinged; *Slang* daft, round the bend, off one's chump, potty, bonkers, loco, bats, batty, nuts, bats in the belfry, nutty, nutty as a fruitcake, balmy, loony, off one's rocker, cracked, zany; raving, frenzied, wild, berserk. **2** *It's completely insane to fly in this weather:* idiotic, senseless, unreasonable, foolish, dumb, imbecilic, mad, crazy; imprudent, injudicious; absurd, ridiculous, insensate; bizarre, eccentric.

Ant. 1, 2 sane; sensible, judicious, wise, sapient, prudent, sound, reasonable.

insanity *n.* **1** *She feared that insanity ran in the family:* mental illness, madness, mental disorder, derangement, raving, loss of reason, unsoundness, aberrance, aberration, craziness, lunacy, (*variously*) dementia, mania, psychosis, paranoia, schizophrenia, monomania, hallucination. **2** *Few people dispute the insanity of nuclear war:* idiocy, senselessness, foolishness, absurdity, madness, craziness, folly, unreasonableness.

Ant. 1 sanity, good sense, rationality, reason, intelligence, soundness.

"All power of fancy over reason is a degree of insanity." —*Samuel Johnson*

---

insatiable *adj. The fat man has an insatiable appetite:* unappeasable, voracious, incapable of being satisfied, unquenchable, unsatisfiable, insatiate, bottomless, implacable; omnivorous.

Ant. satiable, appeasable, satisfiable, quenchable.

inscrutable *adj. The mythological Sphinx had an inscrutable face:* unknowable, incomprehensible, indecipherable, not easily understood, impenetrable to understanding, unfathomable, mysterious, mystifying, arcane, past comprehension, beyond interpretation, puzzling, perplexing, baffling, inexplicable, unsearchable, enigmatic, elusive, unintelligible, unreadable, unrevealed; *Informal* poker-faced, dead-pan; hidden, concealed, veiled, masked.

Ant. obvious, palpable, plain, clear, manifest, open, evident, patent; penetrable, comprehensible, understandable; intelligible, explainable, self-evident, familiar, explicable, readable, knowable, revealing, transparent, lucid.

◇ *Word origin: Inscrutable* comes from Latin *in-* (not) + *scrutari* (to examine), hence not capable of being examined. Latin *scrutari* also gives us *scrutiny* and *scrutinize.* The Latin word *inscrutabilis* (inscrutable) first appears in one of the letters of Saint Augustine, with reference to "the inscrutable justice of God."

insecure *adj.* **1** *The battalion held an insecure position on the hill:* unsafe, endangered, exposed to danger, in danger, vulnerable, defenceless, exposed, ill-protected, unshielded, unprotected, unsheltered, risky, perilous, precarious, hazardous, on slippery ground, not out of the woods, under fire, dangerous, critical. **2** *The foundations of the house are insecure:* not firm, unsteady, shaky, unstable, dilapidated, weak, wobbly, frail, unreliable, rickety, unsound, ramshackle, tottering, built upon sand, in a bad way, dangerous.

Ant. 1 secure, safe, invulnerable, protected, shielded, sheltered, steady, trustworthy. **2** stable, sound, reliable, firm.

insecurity *n.* **1** *The engineers warned us about the insecurity of the bridge in a storm:* insecureness, instability, precariousness, shakiness, unsteadiness, vulnerability, defencelessness, unsafeness, danger. **2** *A basic feeling of insecurity kept the boy from making friends:* lack of assurance, lack of confidence, uncertainty, lack of sureness, lack of self-reliance, self-doubt, doubt, dubiousness, doubtfulness, diffidence, incertitude, apprehensiveness. **3** Often **insecurities** *The insecurities of the venture kept investors away:* peril, hazard, danger, cause for alarm, risk, pitfall, contingency.

Ant. 1 security, secureness, stability, invulnerability, safeness. **2** security, assurance, sureness, confidence, certitude. **3** security, safeness, sureness, certainty.

insensitive *adj. He was always insensitive to the feelings of others. The fisherman's hands were insensitive to the cold:* unaware of, not sensitive, indifferent, unconcerned, uncompassionate; hardened, unfeeling, callous, blasé, cold; unaware of feeling, not capable of feeling, impervious, insensible, insensate, dead, numb.

Ant. sensitive, compassionate, tender; susceptible, subject, prone, open, exposed, hypersensitive.

inseparable *adj. The blind man and his dog are inseparable:* constantly together, always in each other's company, attached, extremely intimate; not to be separated, incapable of being parted, indivisible, unseverable, indissoluble.

Ant. separable, unattached, divisible, sunderable, severable, soluble.

insert *v. Insert the key in the lock. He inserted a comment in the margin:* place in, put in, infix, set in, embed, inject, inlay, inset, put between, wedge in, push in, intersperse, slide in, infuse, interlard, press in, thrust in, stick in, stuff in, tuck in, drive in, *Informal* pop in; introduce, interpolate, interpose, interject, intrude, enter, add.

Ant. extract, disengage, detach, withdraw, remove, draw.

◇ *Word origin:* To *insert* originally meant to plant a seed by inserting it into the ground. It is from Latin *in-* (in) + *serere* (to sow). In classical times, Latin *inserere* came to mean "to ingraft" and hence "to insert." From the time of Augustus Caesar on, a newly derived form, *insertare,* became the regular Latin word for "to insert."

inside *n.* **1** *The inside of the cabinet is papered:* interior, inner part, inner space, interior part, inner surface, inner side.

—*adj.* **2** *The leading horse was on the inside track:* inner, innermost, inmost, inward; internal, interior. **3** *I have inside information on the plans for the bank robbery:* private, confidential, cliquish, for the elect or knowledgeable, secret, esoteric, intimate, internal.

Ant. **1** outside, exterior. **2** outside, outer, exterior, outermost, external, outward. **3** outside, public, open, exoteric.

insidious *adj.* **1** *We were taken in by her insidious plan:* devious, treacherous, deceitful, guileful, intending to entrap, crafty, tricky, sly, wily, cunning, foxy, artful, contriving, underhand, perfidious, crooked, slippery, shady, designing; surreptitious, subtle; false-hearted, disingenuous. **2** *Corruption within the government was insidious and widespread:* secretive, stealthy, surreptitious, underhand, undercover, furtive, sneaking, clandestine, covert, undetected, concealed, disguised; pernicious, deleterious.

Ant. **1** upright, forthright, artless, ingenuous, straightforward, sincere, open, honest, candid. **2** open, conspicuous, innocuous, obvious; harmless.

insight *n.* *The teacher had unusual insight into children's emotions:* perception, spontaneous understanding, apprehension, acumen, innate knowledge, penetration, discernment, intuition, penetrating judgement, immediate cognition, perspicacity, perspicaciousness, perceptiveness, perceptivity, instinctive knowledge, intuitiveness, clear understanding, comprehension.

Ant. obtuseness, blindness.

"But tasks in hours of insight will'd
Can be through hours of gloom fulfill'd."
—*Matthew Arnold*

---

insignia *n.* *Sew the insignia onto the shoulder of the uniform:* emblem, badge of office, distinguishing mark of honour, decoration, patch, sign, mark of authority, ensign of royalty, symbol; (*variously*) bar, star, wings, medal, epaulette, chevron, stripe.

◇ *Usage note:* Technically, *insignia* is plural, but today it is used and accepted both as singular and plural: *The insignia of rank is (are) worn on the uniform's left sleeve.*

insignificant *adj.* *This problem was insignificant compared with the others that she faced:* unimportant, inconsiderable, petty, negligible, trivial, of little account, of no consequence, inconsequential, having little meaning, paltry, nugatory, of no moment, small, minute, minuscule, trifling, meaningless, meagre, irrelevant, not vital, worthless, immaterial, flimsy, puny, non-essential, indifferent, niggling, not worth the trouble, beneath consideration, second-rate, piddling, not worth mentioning, *Informal* small fry.

Ant. significant, considerable, important, momentous, large, meaningful, essential, vital, appreciable; relevant, material.

insincere *adj.* *His insincere offer fooled nobody:* hypocritical, dishonest, dissembling, deceitful, disingenuous, emotionally dishonest, two-faced, uncandid, untruthful, untrue, guileful, disingenuous, dissimulating, fraudulent, perfidious, mealy-mouthed, devious, lying, evasive, equivocal.

Ant. sincere, honest, candid, truthful, true.

insinuate *v.* **1** *The article insinuated that the boxer was bribed:* imply, suggest, hint slyly, allude remotely to, intimate, whisper, let fall. **2** *The social climber insinuated herself into the group:* ingratiate, push artfully, worm one's way, gently incorporate, introduce subtly, wheedle, inject, insert.

Ant. **1** deny. **2** withdraw, remove, retreat; alienate.

◇ *Word origin: Insinuate* is based on Latin *in-* (in) + *sinus* (curve): *insinuare,* to wind in. Latin *sinus,* curve, is also the basis of *sinuous, sinus* (a curved or folded cavity in the cranial bones), and even of the word *sine* in trigonometry (referring to an acute angle, bend, or curve of a right-angled triangle).

insipid *adj.* **1** *An insipid play like that won't last more than three weeks:* uninteresting, pointless, stupid, dull, characterless, banal, wearisome, bland, boring, trite, vapid, inane, barren, drab, prosiac, jejune, lifeless, zestless, arid, monotonous, lean, empty, commonplace; *Slang* wet, wishy-washy, namby-pamby. **2** *The unsalted vegetables tasted insipid:* flat, tasteless, stale, unappetizing.

Ant. **1** interesting, zestful, pungent, spirited, spunky, provocative, engaging, lively, stimulating, exciting, piquant, colourful. **2** pungent, piquant, spicy; fiery, peppery, gingery; savoury, tasty, palatable, appetizing.

◇ *Word origin:* An *insipid* meal is dull; it has no flavour; it is *not sapid. Insipid* comes from Latin *in-* (not) + *sapidus,* sapid. Besides the somewhat literary word *sapid* (tasty), we also get our words *savour* and *savoury* from Latin *sapere,* to taste, savour.

insist *v.* **1** *She insisted that she heard somebody in the house:* maintain, state firmly, asseverate, assert positively, vouch, contend, claim, hold, assert, aver, take a firm stand, stress, stick to one's story, repeat, reiterate, stand one's ground, be pertinacious, persist, be determined; protest, remonstrate. **2** *The doctor insisted that Don stop smoking:* demand, advise firmly, urge, lay down the law, require, exhort, command, be emphatic, be firm about, press earnestly; warn, caution, admonish.

Ant. **1** deny, **2** beg, plead, ask, request.

◇ *Word origin:* When we *insist* on something, we stand on our rights or stand up to someone. *Insist* comes from Latin *in-* (on) + *sistere* (to cause to stand still, to stand firm), which is also the basis of our words *consist* and *desist.*

insolence *n.* *The foreman refused to put up with the worker's insolence:* insulting rudeness, impertinence, unmannerliness, disobedience, disrespect, overbearing contempt, overweening pride, lordliness, audacity, hauteur, arrogance, disdain, haughtiness, imperiousness, superciliousness, presumption, incivility, impoliteness, brazenness, bumptiousness, effrontery, gall, impudence, insulting disobedience.

Ant. deference, modesty, respect, politeness, bashfulness, humility, mannerliness, civility.

insolent *adj. The insolent child must be punished:* disrespectful, insulting, impertinent, rude, impolite, impudent, unmannerly, audacious, brazen, bumptious, outrageous, arrogant, presumptuous, defiant, overbearing, haughty, supercilious, disdainful, contemptuous, galling, *Informal* cheeky, fresh.

Ant. respectful, deferential; submissive, courteous, polite, civil, complimentary, mannerly.

◇ *Word origin:* When we say that we are not used to such *insolent* behaviour, we are using *insolent* in its original meaning. The word is from Latin *in-* (un-) + *solens* (accustomed), and *insolens* originally meant "unaccustomed, contrary to custom, unusual." The word later acquired the additional connotation "insolent" in Latin.

insolvent *adj. The company became insolvent and had to declare itself bankrupt:* incapable of discharging liabilities, penniless, unable to satisfy creditors, unable to pay one's bills, short of money, destitute, ruined, out of money, bankrupt, impoverished, moneyless; *Informal* broke, unable to make ends meet, down-and-out.

Ant. solvent, wealthy, flourishing, thriving, moneyed, rich, *Informal* flush.

inspect *v.* **1** *Ask the mechanic to inspect the tyres. How often does the auditor inspect your books?:* examine, scrutinize, look over carefully, look carefully at, look intently at, regard carefully, view closely and critically; investigate, reconnoitre, peruse, observe, contemplate, peer at, eye; explore, pore over, scan, survey, probe. **2** *The visiting president inspected the troops:* review, view formally, survey formally, examine officially.

Ant. 1, 2 ignore, overlook.

"Genius is one per cent inspiration and ninety-nine per cent perspiration." —*Thomas Edison*

---

inspiration *n.* **1** *The painter's inspiration was drawn from nature. Love was Robert Browning's greatest inspiration:* incentive, stimulus, influence, inspiring action, incitement, motivation, motive, prompting, compulsion, spur, encouragement, impulse, creative impulse. **2** *Newton discovered the laws of gravity in a flash of inspiration:* flash, creative thought, idea, afflatus, divine afflatus, fancy, flight of fancy, revelation.

Ant. 1 depressant, discouragement, disenchantment, deterrent.

inspire *v.* **1** *Shakespeare has inspired generations of playwrights:* stimulate to creation, be an ideal for, fill with life or strength, infuse with inspiration, influence, exalt, illumine, illuminate, impel, motivate, prompt, occasion, galvanize, encourage, embolden, animate, vivify, fire, inspirit, hearten, enliven, quicken; cause, be responsible for. **2** *A fair and kind employer inspires loyalty:* arouse, rouse, enkindle, engender, encourage, stimulate, prompt, induce, stir, excite, promote, inspirit, give rise to, provoke, cause, produce, occasion.

Ant. 1 stifle, put off, discourage. **2** stifle, kill, discourage, suppress.

instability *n. His instability makes him a poor job prospect:* unstableness, lack of stability, lack of firmness, fluctuation, unsteadiness, inconstancy, vacillation, irresolution, indecision, insecurity, wavering, frailty, changeability, capriciousness, changeableness, fitfulness, flightiness, inconsistency, mercurialness, vulnerability, weakness.

Ant. stability, security, constancy, strength, steadiness, resolution, consistency.

install *v.* **1** *The builders installed a new boiler:* place in service, lodge, establish, station, set in place, put in, locate, plant, arrange, situate, move in, make operative; embed, lay. **2** *The club installed the new officers last night:* introduce into office, establish in an office or position, induct, invest, instate, receive, usher in, initiate, inaugurate, seat, crown, ordain.

Ant. 1 remove, dislodge. **2** dismiss, retire.

◇ *Word origin:* To *install* something is to seat it in its place. *Install* comes from Latin *in-* (in) + *stallum* (seat, place). *Stallum* (stall) is a Medieval Latin word of Germanic origin, connected with our word *stall* (which is from Old English *steall*, stall).

instalment *n.* **1** *How many instalments did it take to pay off the loan? The first instalment of his book was very exciting:* payment, successive portion, amount due, money payable; section, fragment, division, chapter, segment, issue. **2** *The instalment of the phone didn't take long:* installing, installation, putting in, establishing in office or position, establishment, stationing, placing in service, locating, laying, connecting, wiring up.

Ant. removal, detachment.

instance *n. I can't think of a single instance when Mother was unfair:* example, illustration, case, case in point, circumstance, time, occasion, exemplification; sample, antecedent, object lesson, specimen, prototype, precedent.

instant *n.* **1** *The clap of thunder lasted only an instant:* split second, very short time, moment, minute; twinkling, jiffy, flash, trice. **2** *We liked each other from the first instant we met:*

specific moment, particular time, point in time, very minute, second.
—*adj.* **3** *The telegram asked for an instant reply:* immediate, quick, prompt, instantaneous; sudden, abrupt, unhesitating; on the spot, split-second. **4** *Spaceships are stocked with a variety of instant foods:* pre-mixed, pre-cooked; ready-to-use.
Ant. 1 aeon, age, eternity. **3** delayed, hesitant, slow.

instantaneous *adj. His death was instantaneous; he felt no pain:* immediate, sudden, extremely fast, happening in an instant, imperceptibly fast, unhesitatingly quick, prompt, abrupt, direct; quick as a flash, speedy, swift, rapid.
Ant. delayed, slow, gradual.

instantly *adv. The boss wants the job done instantly!:* at once; without delay, without hesitation, immediately, promptly, quickly; right now, here and now, in a flash; *Informal* quick as a wink, this minute, on the spot, pronto.
Ant. later, in the future; at one's leisure.

instead *adv. The roast beef is all gone, so have a chop instead:* as a substitute or equivalent, as a replacement, as an alternative, rather, in its place, in lieu of that.

instigate *v. Dissidents tried to instigate a rebellion:* provoke, urge; bring about, incite, start, begin, initiate, spur, goad, prompt, stimulate; foment, stir up, kindle, set in motion.
Ant. repress, restrain, discourage, stop, suppress.

instil *v. The couple instilled a love of music in their children:* impart, introduce gradually, inculcate, implant, inspire, induce; sow the seeds of, engender.
Ant. remove, eliminate, eradicate, drain, extirpate.
◇ *Word origin: Instil* comes from Latin *in-* (in) + *stillare* (to trickle, drop), literally to put in by drops. Latin *stillare* also gives us our words *distil* and *still* (as in speaking of the device in which whisky is *distilled*).

instinct *n.* **1** *Their natural instincts led the pigeons back to the roost:* natural or inbred behaviour, natural tendency, nature, native aptitude, inborn drive; blind knowledge, blood knowledge, intuition, mother wit. **2** *Some people have an instinct for saying the right thing:* aptitude, gift, genius, natural sense, faculty, intuition, knack, natural inclination, proclivity, predisposition, capacity, tendency.
Ant. 1 learned behaviour, experience, reason, deliberation, judgement.

instinctive *adj. The will to survive is instinctive:* innate, inherent, inborn, resulting from instinct, intuitive, inspired, natural, native, unlearned, unacquired; involuntary, spontaneous, automatic, impulsive; deep-seated, ineradicable.
Ant. learned, acquired, voluntary, deliberate, wilful.

institute *v.* **1** *The government instituted a consumer protection agency:* establish, inaugurate, begin, found, originate, set up, bring into being, organize, constitute. **2** *The police instituted a new investigation:* start, initiate, inaugurate, introduce, put into effect, prescribe, pass, enact, ordain; undertake, get under way, get going, commence.
—*n.* **3** *The university plans to establish an institute for Chinese studies:* institution, school, college, academy, professional school, graduate centre, establishment; association, society, foundation.
Ant. 1 abolish, end, terminate, conclude, close, finish, complete. **2** halt, stop, close, finish, wind up, terminate, end.

institution *n.* **1** *The institution of slavery was once widespread. Our annual fête has become a local institution:* custom, established practice, convention, unwritten law, ritual, habit, usage, fixture. **2** *Strong financial institutions are the foundation of a sound economy:* company, organization, establishment, association, organized society, foundation. **3** *Our city boasts many excellent institutions:* institute, school, academy, college, university, seminary. **4** *He should be locked up in an institution:* lunatic asylum, madhouse, mental hospital, *Slang* nut-house, loony-bin; prison.

"Individualities may form communities, but it is institutions alone that can create a nation."
—*Benjamin Disraeli*

---

instruct *v.* **1** *A private tutor instructed the prince and princess:* teach, tutor, educate, school, train, drill, indoctrinate, coach, catechize. **2** *Instruct the passengers on customs regulations:* give information to, apprise, brief, advise, acquaint, inform, enlighten. **3** *The captain instructed the soldiers to retreat:* command, direct, order, enjoin authoritatively, bid.
Ant. 1, 2 misinform, mislead, deceive, neglect.
◇ *Word origin:* To *instruct* a person is to build knowledge or skill in him. The word comes from Latin *in-* (in) + *struere* (to build), which also gives us *structure* and *construction.*

instruction *n.* **1** *Instruction of recruits was the responsibility of the sergeant:* instructing, teaching; education, guidance, coaching, training, tutoring, tutelage, indoctrination; pedagogy. **2** usually **instructions** *The instructions for assembling the toy are all very clear:* direction, information, guide-line, prescription, recommendation, explanation, specification, advice, rule; lesson, maxim, precept, motto, moral, homily.
Ant. 2 misinformation, misdirection.

instrument *n.* **1** *All surgical instruments must be sterilized before use:* implement, tool, device, utensil, appliance, apparatus, contrivance, machine, mechanism; gadget. **2** *A police force is an instrument for preserving law and order:* agency, agent, means, medium; expedient;

instrumentality; tool. **3** *The lawyers will draw up all the necessary instruments:* legal document; contract, deed, charter, paper, grant.

Ant. 2 obstruction, bar, stop, preventive; counteragent, opponent, neutralizer.

instrumental *adj. The newspaper was instrumental in bringing the problem to the public's attention:* helpful, serving as a means, useful, effective, effectual, active, contributory, valuable, conducive, assisting; decisive, crucial, vital, essential.

Ant. ineffectual, useless; insignificant, negligible.

insubordinate *adj. Insubordinate troops were tried by court-martial:* disobedient, refractory, insolent, defiant, intractable, recalcitrant, uncompliant, unsubmissive, unruly, rebellious, fractious, mutinous; disorderly, ungovernable.

Ant. obedient, docile, submissive, subdued; servile; obsequious.

insubstantial *adj.* **1** *The experience seemed as insubstantial as a dream:* unreal, immaterial, intangible, bodiless, impalpable; baseless, groundless, imaginary, visionary, apparitional; airy, gossamer, ethereal. **2** *The chair is too insubstantial to hold an adult:* slight, frail, flimsy, weak, fragile; shaky, unsound, unstable. **3** *The donation was insubstantial but all the same welcome:* modest, trifling, paltry, small, inconsiderable, trivial, piddling.

Ant. 1-3 substantial. **1** real, material, tangible, palpable. **2** sturdy, hardy, sound, strong, stable. **3** large, great, considerable.

insufferable *adj. That child is an insufferable brat:* unendurable, intolerable, unbearable; dreadful, insupportable, unspeakable; detestable, disgusting, hateful, outrageous, abominable.

Ant. pleasant, pleasing, attractive, charming, appealing, disarming, ingratiating.

insufficient *adj. The old car has insufficient power to get up the hill. He had insufficient funds to set himself up in business:* inadequate, scanty, deficient, wanting, lacking, not enough; unsatisfactory; impotent, incompetent.

Ant. sufficient, adequate, competent, enough, satisfactory.

insular *adj. Living outside the mainstream of modern life had made the villagers insular and suspicious:* narrow, narrow-minded, bigoted, biased, illiberal, prejudiced, limited; provincial, parochial, isolated, insulated.

Ant. broad-minded, liberal, catholic, cosmopolitan, sophisticated, worldly.

◇ *Word origin: Insular* comes from Latin *insula*, island. *Insulate, insulation, isolate,* and *isle* are also based on Latin *insula*, as is our word *insulin* (named after the anatomical "Islands of Langerhans," which are clusters of cells in the pancreas that are involved in secreting the substance).

insult *v.* **1** *The angry students insulted the teacher:* treat with contempt, be rude to, slight, offend, treat insolently, abuse, scorn, deride, be discourteous to; cut, affront, disparage. —*n.* **2** *The speaker's patronizing words were an insult to the audience:* affront, slight, offence, indignity, rudeness, discourtesy, outrage, cheek, impudence; lèse-majesté.

Ant. 1 please, flatter, praise. **2** compliment, flattery, honour, homage.

◇ *Pronunciation tip:* Some people fail to distinguish properly between the two different pronunciations of the word *insult:* one for the noun and the other for the verb. The noun, an *insult*, should be clearly stressed on the first syllable: an *IN-sult.* The verb, to *insult*, should be clearly stressed on the second syllable: to *in-SULT.*

> **Exploring the Word:** Latin *salire*, to leap, jump, gives us *insult*, just as we speak of "jumping on someone" or "jumping down somebody's throat" when we criticize harshly or insult; *assault, assail,* and *sally*, to leap towards someone in attack, a leaping to the attack; *desultory*, jumping from one thing to another, hence disconnected, unmethodical, random; *exult*, to jump forth or "jump for joy" as we say nowadays; *resilient*, capable of jumping or springing back to a former shape, elastic; *result*, literally a jumping back from the edge, going no farther, hence the end or final outcome; and *salient*, leaping out to be noticed, very noticeable, important.

insulting *adj. The reviewer's criticism was unnecessarily insulting:* rude, discourteous, impolite, uncivil, insolent, offensive, abusive; derogatory, invidious, defamatory, vicious.

insurance *n. Does the company pay medical insurance?:* financial protection against loss, assurance; indemnity, cover, policy; security, warranty, guarantee.

insure *v. The owner insured the house for £40,000:* obtain insurance for, cover by insurance; guarantee against loss or risk; secure, underwrite.

Ant. imperil, jeopardize.

◇ *Usage note:* See ENSURE.

insurgent *n.* **1** *Insurgents tried to overthrow the government:* rebel, resister, mutineer, insurrectionist, dissident, renegade, revolter, revolutionary; guerilla, partisan. —*adj.* **2** *Insurgent activities will be dealt with harshly:* revolutionary, rebellious, mutinous, breakaway, dissident; lawless, insubordinate, disobedient, disorderly.

Ant. 1 patriot, loyalist. **2** obedient, loyal, patriotic, subordinate.

◇ *Word origin:* An *insurgent* rises in revolt against authority and an *insurrection* is such a rising or rebellion. The words come from Latin *in-* (against) + *surgere* (to rise), which also gives us *surge.*

insurmountable *adj. The odds against our winning seemed insurmountable:* incapable of being overcome, beyond reach, too great, insuperable, hopeless; unconquerable, unbeatable.
Ant. surmountable, beatable.

insurrection *n. The insurrection within the prison was suppressed by the prison warders:* revolt, rebellion, insurgence, mutiny, riot, rising, uprising, outbreak.
Ant. obedience, submission, subsidence, acquiescence.
◇ *Word origin:* See INSURGENT.

intact *adj. The vase that he dropped remained intact:* undamaged, in one piece, whole, unbroken, integral, complete, perfect; in good shape, without a scratch, unimpaired, unhurt, uninjured, sound, safe.
Ant. impaired, damaged, injured, marred, broken, shattered.

intangible *adj.* **1** *The soul is intangible:* incapable of being touched, untouchable, immaterial, abstract, ethereal, insubstantial, impalpable, imperceptible. **2** *An intangible feeling of disaster filled the room:* vague, elusive, fleeting, evanescent, transient, fugitive, imperceptible, shadowy.
—*n.* **3** *The complex plan is full of intangibles:* abstraction, imponderable, accidental or unpredictable happening, unforeseen turn of events.
Ant. 1, 2 tangible, palpable, perceptible; material, concrete, physical.

integral *adj.* **1** *This hedge forms an integral part of the landscaping:* essential, necessary, indispensable, component, constituent, inherent, basic, requisite.
Ant. 1 peripheral, unessential, unimportant, unnecessary.

integrate *v.* **1** *All the department reports should be integrated into one annual statement:* blend, combine, mix, mingle, merge, bring together, fuse, intermix, unite. **2** *The city was ordered to integrate all public services:* make available to every race; open for use by all; desegregate.
Ant. 1 disperse, scatter, separate, divide. **2** segregate, separate.
◇ *Word origin: Integrate* comes from Latin *integer,* whole. Hence, *integrate* means to bring together into a whole, to unify.

integration *n.* **1** *An electronic sound system represents the integration of thousands of components:* combination, combining, mixing, blending, fusion, synthesis, union. **2** *Martin Luther King was a leading advocate of racial integration:* desegregation, assimilation.
Ant. 1 separation, dispersion. **2** segregation, separation, apartheid.

integrity *n.* **1** *The integrity of the judge is unquestioned:* honesty, probity, uprightness, moral soundness, moral stature, principle, character, virtue, purity, rectitude, decency, self-respect, straightforwardness, morality. **2** *The integrity of a building depends upon a sound foundation:* structural soundness; unimpaired condition, reliability, completeness; wholeness, completeness, strength, unity, coherence, cohesion.
Ant. 1 duplicity; deceit, venality, corruption, dishonesty, immorality. **2** flimsiness, shakiness, fragility, faultiness, uncertainty, unsoundness.

intellect *n.* **1** *It is man's intellect that distinguishes him from the beasts:* intelligence, mental power, power of comprehension, power of thinking, understanding, reasoning, faculty, cognition, cognitive power, *Informal* brains; sense, mind, rationality, consciousness, perception; wisdom. **2** *That fellow is a good athlete but not much of an intellect:* thinker, intellectual, *Slang* brain; wit.
Ant. 1 emotion, instinct; muscle. **2** idiot, moron.

intellectual *adj.* **1** *Chess is a highly intellectual game. I admire her intellectual achievements:* cerebral, of the mind, using the intellect, mental, abstract; academic, scholarly. **2** *The intellectual girl won a research grant:* intelligent, scholarly, studious; *Informal* bookish, brainy; reasoning, thoughtful, rational.
—*n.* **3** *Bertrand Russell appealed to all sorts of people, not just intellectuals:* person interested in ideas; thinker, academic, scholar; pundit, sage, savant; mandarin, highbrow; *Slang* brain, boffin, egghead.
Ant. 1 physical, material, fleshly. **2** unintellectual, illiterate, unlearned, ignorant, stupid. **3** lowbrow, idiot, moron.

intelligence *n.* **1** *The prime minister's intelligence and wit enlivened his press conferences:* intellect, mental power, comprehension, understanding, mental skill, power of reasoning, wisdom, acumen, sagacity, shrewdness, perspicacity, *Informal* brains. **2** *Intelligence that an enemy attack was imminent reached the divisional commander:* information, news, knowledge, advice, notice, report, notification, advisement, *Slang* dope, gen; tidings.
Ant. 1 ignorance, stupidity, misapprehension, dullness. **2** concealment, suppression; misinformation.

intelligent *adj. An intelligent person would have spotted the flaws in his argument:* thoughtful, thinking, bright, clear-headed, sensible, well-informed, sage, wise, perspicacious, perceptive, brilliant, keen, quick, knowing, sagacious, quick-witted, prudent, astute, canny, sharp, shrewd, *Slang* brainy, smart.
Ant. unintelligent; foolish, idiotic, stupid, dumb; irrational, unreasonable.

intelligentsia *n. The dictator gaoled the intelligentsia of his country:* educated class, intellectual leaders, intellectual élite; thinkers, intellectuals, ivory tower academics, academic community.
Ant. masses, hoi polloi; bourgeoisie.
◇ *Word origin: Intelligentsia* comes to us via

Russian from Latin *intelligentia,* intelligence. The Russian word means "intellectuals collectively, the intellectual class."

intend *v. What do you intend to do today?:* plan, aim, contemplate, have in mind, mean, determine, propose, design, set as a goal, aspire, project, resolve.

intense *adj.* **1** *The heat from the furnace is intense:* extreme, very great, concentrated, acute, sharp, strong, powerful, forceful, considerable, forcible, potent, violent, keen. **2** *The patient has an intense desire to recover:* fervent, earnest, passionate, ardent, strong, powerful, extreme, deep, vehement, burning, deeply felt, emphatic.

Ant. 1 weak, mild, moderate, gentle. **2** subdued, relaxed, easy, moderate, casual, indifferent, cool, weak, mild.

intensify *v. Lying down only intensified the pain:* increase, heighten, quicken, aggravate, make more intense, sharpen, reinforce, strengthen, magnify, boost, deepen, worsen, redouble.

Ant. reduce, lessen, diminish, mitigate, allay; abate; moderate, qualify; alleviate, lighten, relieve.

intensity *n.* **1** *The intensity of the light depends on the wattage of the bulb:* magnitude, power, strength, depth, severity. **2** *The intensity of the play left the audience numbed:* passion, emotion, ardour, fervour, vehemence, energy, vigour, strength, power, force, potency, earnestness, zeal, forcefulness.

Ant. 2 relaxation, languor, coolness, indifference, weakness.

intent *n.* **1** *The prisoner was charged with intent to kill:* intention, design, purpose, plan, determination, premeditation, aim, end. **2** *The intent of the speech escaped no one:* meaning, significance, purport, import, burden, drift; gist, substance.

—*adj.* **3** *The man's intent gaze caused the girl to lower her eyes:* steady, steadfast, intense, fixed, highly attentive, undistracted, piercing; concentrated, preoccupied, engrossed, absorbed. **4** *She was intent on having her own way:* set, bent, insistent, earnest, tenacious, resolved, determined, unbending, unwavering.

Ant. 1 accident; chance, luck, fortune. **3** unsteady, wavering, wandering; casual, indifferent.

intention *n. His intention is to spend a month in Spain:* plan, aim, intent, objective, design, purpose, goal, resolution, target, object, resolve, end, determination.

"Hell is paved with good intentions."
—*Samuel Johnson*

---

intentional *adj. The newspaper "slip" was intentional:* deliberate, intended, done on purpose, planned, purposeful, designed, premeditated, contemplated, voluntary, calculated.

Ant. accidental, fortuitous, inadvertent, unintentional, unplanned.

intercede *v.* **1** *Relatives interceded on behalf of the disowned son:* offer support or help, lend a helping hand, put in a good word for, use one's influence; speak up, plead. **2** *A neutral nation volunteered to intercede in the interests of achieving peace:* arbitrate, mediate, act as intermediary, serve as go-between, intervene, interpose, step in.

Ant. 1, 2 withdraw, remain aloof, remain neutral.

intercept *v. Try to intercept the letter before it falls into the wrong hands. He tried to intercept a forward pass:* seize, get hold of, detain, stop, block the passage of, catch, nab, take, grab, deflect, re-route, cut off; ambush.

Ant. transmit, relay; hasten, expedite; admit, permit.

interchangeable *adj. In some cities abroad, bus and underground tickets are interchangeable. Football and soccer are interchangeable terms:* switchable, tradeable, exchangeable, transposable; equivalent, closely similar, synonymous, corresponding, parallel, analogous.

Ant. unswitchable; unlike, opposite.

intercourse *n.* **1** *The war stopped commercial intercourse between the two nations:* communications, dealings, trade, traffic, relations, connection, exchange, correspondence, commerce; conversation, discourse, talk, communion, colloquy, parley. **2** *Pregnancy is a result of intercourse:* sexual relations, copulation, coitus; coupling, pairing; *Informal* sex.

interest *n.* **1** Often **interests** *His interests include reading and tennis:* preferred activity, absorption, engrossment, pursuit, avocation, preoccupation; pastime, hobby. **2** *The politician's routine speech aroused little interest among political observers:* notice, attention, concern, curiosity, regard; suspicion. **3** Sometimes **interests** *A good leader should act in the interests of all his people:* behalf, benefit, service, advantage, good. **4** *The family has an interest in a chain of hardware stores:* share, portion, stake, part, investment, holding, partial ownership. **5** *The loan was made at 6 per cent interest:* profit, bonus, yield, dividend, gain.

—*v.* **6** *Geology interests him:* absorb, engage the attention of, preoccupy, excite the curiosity of, divert, attract; touch, affect. **7** *The teacher tried to interest the students in current events:* concern, involve, engage.

Ant. 2 unconcern, indifference. **3** disadvantage, detriment. **6** bore, *Slang* turn off.

◇ *Word origin: Interest* means "it makes a difference, it is important" in Latin.

interesting *adj. The magazine's issue on marriage was especially interesting:* absorbing, stimulating, arresting, striking; attractive, entertaining, engaging, pleasing; fascinating, riveting; curious, suspicious.

Ant. uninteresting, dull, boring, flat, tedious.

◇ *Word origin: Interesting* comes from French *intéressant* (from the same Latin idiom *interest*, "it is important") and was first used by the 18th-century critic and aesthetician Shaftesbury in the sense of "important" (still its primary sense in French) and shortly thereafter by Laurence Sterne in its now usual sense of "apt to excite interest."

interfere *v.* **1** *The television interferes with my concentration:* conflict, be a hindrance to, be inconsistent, not be conducive to, counter, get in the way, be an obstacle to, frustrate, jar. **2** *Don't interfere in other people's problems:* mix, meddle, step in, rush in, intrude, intercede; *Slang* butt in, stick one's oar in.
Ant. 1 aid, help, assist.

interim *n.* **1** *The meeting doesn't start until noon, so in the interim I can make some phone calls:* intervening time, interval, interlude, meantime.
—adj. **2** *An interim government was appointed until new elections could be held:* temporary, provisional, temporal, tentative, stop-gap, *Latin* pro tempore.
Ant. 2 permanent.
◇ *Word origin: Interim* means "meanwhile" in Latin.

interior *adj.* **1** *The interior walls of the hut were unpainted:* internal, inmost, inner, innermost, inside, located within, inward.
—n. **2** *The interior of the house is spacious and bright:* internal part, inside, inner space. **3** *The terrorized tribes fled to the interior:* remote regions, inland parts, hinterland, heartland.
Ant. 1 exterior; outer, outward, outside, external. **2** exterior, outside. **3** coast, borders.
◇ *Word origin: Interior* is (in Latin) the comparative derived from *inter*, within, hence literally means "more within." The superlative form *intimus*, "innermost," gives us our word *intimate*, as in the phrase *intimate friends*.

interject *v. The speaker interjected a few jokes into his lecture:* insert, throw in, put in, interrupt with, interpose, interpolate, inject, force in, introduce, slip in, sneak in.
Ant. extract, remove, withdraw.

interloper *n. The host had the interloper thrown out:* intruder, outsider, trespasser; gate-crasher, uninvited guest, meddler, interferer, invader, persona non grata.
◇ *Word origin: Interloper* comes from Latin *inter-* (between) + Middle Dutch *loopen* (to run), hence one who runs between or intrudes.

interlude *n. My evening at home was a pleasant interlude in a hectic week:* interval, intervening period, respite, intermission, recess, pause, breathing-space, let-up; episode, event, incident.
◇ *Word origin: Interlude* is from Latin *inter-* (between) + *ludus* (play), hence a period or feature coming between two parts of a play — the interval or intermission.

intermediary *adj.* **1** *Leicester was our intermediary stop between London and York:* intermediate, bridging, midway. **2** *The intermediary agent in the dispute is to be a neutral diplomat:* mediating, acting as mediary, arbitrating, serving as mediator.
—n. **3** *He served as intermediary in the labour management dispute:* mediator, arbitrator, middle-man, intermediate, go-between; referee, umpire, adjudicator.

intermediate *adj.* **1** *The intermediate part of the journey took us through Hungary:* middle, midway, intermediary, half-way, mid, midmost, median, mediate, transitional, intervening. **2** *This piano piece is of intermediate difficulty:* medium, moderate, average, middling, so-so; fair, mediocre.
Ant. 1 first; last. **2** beginning; advanced.

interment *n. The interment took place at the local cemetery:* burial, burial ceremony, entombment, inhumation, funeral.
Ant. exhumation.

interminable *adj. People began to walk out during the interminable speech:* endless, unending, without a stop, tediously long, long-drawn-out, prolix, long-winded, illimitable, infinite, incessant.
Ant. brief, short, fleeting.

intermission *n. The emergency crew worked all night without intermission. The play has two 15-minute intermissions:* interval, interim, period of respite, pause, stoppage, suspension, halt, interlude, stop, rest, break, recess; hiatus, gap.
Ant. continuance, prolongation, uninterruptedness.

"Pleasure is nothing else but the intermission of pain." —*John Selden*

---

intermittent *adj. The weatherman predicted intermittent rain:* recurrent, spasmodic, periodic, stopping and starting, stop-go, discontinuous, off and on, on-again-off-again, fitful, irregular.
Ant. steady, unceasing, continuous.

internal *adj.* **1** *The bleeding must be coming from an internal injury:* interior, located inside, inner. **2** *The nation's internal affairs are in utter turmoil:* domestic, home, governmental, administrative, executive, sovereign, political.
Ant. 1 outer, exterior, external, outside. **2** foreign.
◇ *Word origin: Internal* comes from Latin *internus*, internal.

international *adj. International trade benefits all the participants:* between nations, involving two or more nations, cosmopolitan; world-wide, universal.
Ant. national, domestic.

interpret *v.* **1** *The psychiatrist interpreted John's ghastly dream:* explain, make clear, explicate, explain the meaning of, assign a meaning to, decipher, define, elucidate, throw light

upon; unravel, puzzle out, work out, piece together. **2** *I interpreted her smile as signifying approval:* understand, construe, take, accept, make out, decipher, see, read, account for. **3** *Please interpret the comments of our foreign guest:* translate, re-phrase in one's native language; restate, paraphrase, reword, render.
Ant. **2** mistake, confuse, confound, misconceive, misunderstand.

interrogate *v. The police interrogated the witness about the accident:* question, probe, examine, cross-examine; investigate, test, catechize, ask, query; *Informal* grill, give the third degree.
Ant. answer, retort, respond.
◇ *Word origin: Interrogate* comes from Latin *inter-* (between) + *rogare* (to ask), hence to ask questions between two sides, to question formally.

interrupt *v.* **1** *A news flash interrupted the quiz programme:* stop, break off, halt temporarily, cause to stop, break in on, discontinue, cut in on, disturb, interfere with, obstruct the course of. **2** *Breakwaters interrupt the long stretch of beach at intervals:* block partially, interfere with, break the continuity of, disconnect, intersect, disjoin, punctuate.
Ant. **1** continue, resume.

interruption *n. The interruption was caused by a group of hecklers:* halt, pause, stop, discontinuity, obstruction, hindrance, disconnection, interference; break, gap, hiatus, lacuna, intermission, rift, interlude.
Ant. continuance, resumption.

intersect *v.* **1** *A beam of light intersected the darkness of the room:* cut across, cross, traverse, pass through, pass across, bisect, divide, transect. **2** *The roads intersect a mile from here:* cross, interconnect, criss-cross, meet and cross, have a common point; meet, come together, overlap.

intersection *n. The collision occurred at the intersection of the A31 and the ring road:* junction, meeting-point, crossroads, crossing, interchange, corner, fork.

interval *n.* **1** *An interval of almost a year passed before another meeting took place:* intervening period, interim, pause, recess, interlude, intermission; season, spell, hiatus, interruption. **2** *The trees were planted at intervals of about six feet:* space, opening, gap, interspace, separation, spacing.
◇ *Word origin: Interval* literally means "between the ramparts." It comes from Latin *inter-* (between) + *vallum* (rampart), which also gives us our word *wall.*

intervene *v.* **1** *Much had happened during the years that intervened:* occur between times, pass, take place, come to pass, befall. **2** *The referee intervened before the players hurt each other:* step in, interpose, intrude, interfere, mediate, arbitrate, intercede, come between, interrupt, *Slang* butt in.

intervention *n. The policeman's intervention broke up the fight. The two countries will not accept outside intervention:* stepping in, breaking in, mediation, intermediation, interposition, arbitration, intercession; interference, intrusion, *Slang* butting in.

interview *n.* **1** *He was listening to an interview on the radio:* conversation, talk, chat; round-table conference, question-and-answer session, questioning. **2** *Don't be late for your interview, or you won't get the job:* professional examination, evaluation, personal appraisal, consultation; conference, meeting, parley.

intestines *n. pl. Most digestion takes place in the intestines:* alimentary canal; insides, entrails, viscera, bowels, *Informal* guts, innards.

intimate[1] *adj.* **1** *Only the couple's most intimate friends were invited:* close, bosom, cherished, dear, familiar, nearest and dearest. **2** *Some feelings are too intimate to discuss:* deeply personal, innermost, confidential, private, guarded. **3** *An intimate knowledge of drugs enabled him to help the addicts:* detailed, deep, in-depth, thorough, personal, direct, experienced, first-hand, close.
—*n.* **4** *Many famous writers were among Gertrude Stein's intimates:* close friend, close associate, confidant, familiar; *Informal* chum, crony, pal, mate.
Ant. **1** distant, remote. **2** open, public, known. **3** superficial, limited, slight. **4** stranger, outsider; enemy, foe.
◇ *Pronunciation tip: Intimate,* the adjective, and *intimate,* the verb, are both pronounced with stress on the first syllable. However, the verb also has a long *ā* in the last syllable. Thus, *We are IN-ti-mit friends,* but *Don't IN-ti-mate that you know the true story.*

intimate[2] *v. The report intimated that more was involved than met the eye:* hint, suggest, imply, indicate, insinuate, allude, refer to indirectly, rumour.
Ant. state, declare, assert, proclaim.
◇ *Pronunciation tip:* See INTIMATE[1].

intimation *n. There are intimations that the director may be replaced:* hint, suggestion, innuendo, indication, veiled comment, rumour, allusion, insinuation, sign, portent.

intimidate *v. The gang tried to intimidate the bank manager:* terrorize, terrify, scare, make afraid, make timid, make fearful, fill with fear, alarm, subdue, bully, daunt, brow-beat; compel by threats, coerce.
Ant. encourage, inspire, imbolden; reassure.

intolerable *adj. The noise of the drilling is intolerable:* unendurable, unbearable, insupportable, insufferable; excruciating, racking, agonizing; abominable, hateful, abhorrent; unreasonable, excessive, outrageous.
Ant. tolerable, bearable, endurable, comfortable; reasonable.

intolerance *n.* **1** *Racial intolerance is one of the* *greatest evils in the world today:* bigotry, bias, prejudice, narrow-mindedness, lack of forbearance; xenophobia, chauvinism, racialism. **2** *Albinos have a high level of intolerance for bright light:* low-tolerance, inability to bear, hypersensitivity; weak spot; *Informal* no stomach.

Ant. 1 tolerance, compassion, forbearance, liberality. **2** tolerance, endurance.

"Conquest brings self-conceit and intolerance, the reckless inflation and dissipation of energies." —*Havelock Ellis*

---

intolerant *adj. Some pious church-goers are intolerant of other religions:* not tolerant, bigoted, prejudiced, narrow-minded, closed-minded, hostile, resentful, jealous, mistrustful; xenophobic, chauvinistic.

Ant. tolerant, liberal, forbearing, broad-minded.

in toto *adv. The writer insisted that the study be published in toto:* as a whole, in its entirety, uncondensed, uncut, entirely, unabridged, outright, completely, totally, in all, all together.

Ant. abridged, condensed, cut, in part, incompletely.

intoxicated *adj.* **1** *How could she become intoxicated after only one glass of wine?:* drunk, inebriated, drunken, *Informal* in one's cups, high, tight, tipsy, *Slang* blotto, smashed, loaded, paralytic, well oiled, stoned, plastered, sozzled, stewed. **2** *The couple were intoxicated by the beauty of the night:* transported, rapt, enthralled, infatuated, delighted, elated, exalted, entranced, enchanted, exhilarated.

Ant. 1 sober. **2** bored, indifferent.

◇ *Word origin: Intoxicated* comes from Latin *intoxicare,* to poison, to drug. From Latin *toxicum,* poison, we also get our words *toxic* and *toxin.*

intractable *adj. The intractable child refused to obey:* stubborn, perverse, headstrong, hard to cope with, obstinate, wilful, unmanageable, obdurate, incorrigible, mulish, unruly, fractious, refractory, ungovernable, contumacious, unmalleable, inflexible.

Ant. tractable, obedient, docile, submissive, subdued; compliant, acquiescent, amiable.

intransigent *adj. The intransigent strikers refused to negotiate:* uncompromising, stubborn, intractable, obdurate, irreconcilable, iron-willed, unyielding, immovable, unbudgeable, inflexible.

Ant. compromising, yielding, flexible, open-minded, acquiescent, compliant.

◇ *Word origin: Intransigent* comes from Latin *in-* (not) + *transigere* (to agree).

intrepid *adj. Intrepid commandos led the raid:* fearless, bold, valiant, brave, courageous, heroic, dauntless, resolute, doughty, daring, adventurous, undismayed, valorous.

Ant. cowardly, timid, fearful, cautious, prudent.

◇ *Word origin: Intrepid* literally means "unshaken by fear." It comes from Latin *in-* (not) + *trepidus* (alarmed, agitated).

intricate *adj. The intricate computer requires a skilled operator:* complicated, complex, sophisticated, involved, difficult to understand; *Informal* tricky, knotty; full of detail or difficulties, entangled; devious.

Ant. easy, simple, straightforward, effortless; obvious, plain, clear, patent.

◇ *Word origin:* An *intricate* knot is difficult to untangle, an *intricate* puzzle difficult to solve. *Intricate* comes from Latin *in-* (in) + *tricae* (difficulties).

intrigue *v.* **1** *Fairy-tales intrigue most children:* interest greatly, fascinate, appeal strongly to, arrest, attract, absorb, enthral, arouse the curiosity of, capture the imagination of, fire, tickle one's fancy, titillate. **2** *The barons intrigued against the king:* plot, conspire, machinate, manœuvre craftily, scheme, collude. —*n.* **3** *Politics is a game full of intrigue. The intrigue was exposed:* scheming, machination, secret plotting; underhand or secret dealings; knavery, double-dealing, sharp practice, behind-the-scenes manipulation, plot, scheme, conspiracy. **4** *King Arthur discovered the intrigue between Queen Guinevere and Sir Lancelot:* love affair, romance, amour.

Ant. 1 bore. **3** sincerity, candour, honesty, openness, straightforwardness.

◇ *Word origin:* Difficult things *intrigue* us and secret *intrigues* cause difficulties. *Intrigue* comes to us from Italian *intrigare,* but its basic elements are Latin *in-* (in) + *tricae* (difficulties). These same Latin word elements also give us *intricate.*

intrinsic *adj. Their acting is good, but the play has little intrinsic value:* essential, innate, inherent, basic, fundamental, underlying, ingrained, inborn, native, natural, indigenous, per se.

Ant. extrinsic, accidental, incidental; added, appended; extraneous, alien, acquired.

"It isn't etiquette to cut anyone you've been introduced to. Remove the joint!" —*Lewis Carroll*

---

introduce *v.* **1** *Introduce me to your friends:* give an introduction, make acquainted, make known, present. **2** *A visit to the museum introduced the class to modern art:* bring knowledge to, acquaint, inform, expose, make familiar, initiate. **3** *He wanted to introduce an alternative to the plan:* propose, advance, offer, put forward, present, originate, create, bring into notice; urge, sponsor, recommend. **4** *The MC introduced the programme with a few jokes:* start, begin, lead off, lead into, *Informal* kick off. **5** *Saint Patrick introduced Christianity to the Irish:* bring in, show, make familiar, import, bring into practice, institute, establish. **6** *Shakespeare always introduced some comic relief into his tragedies:* put in, insert, interpolate, infuse, add, interject, interpose, *Informal* throw in, bung in.

Ant. 3 withdraw, remove, eliminate, exclude, delete, excise.

introduction *n.* **1** *The union fought against the introduction of automation:* introducing, instituting, institution, bringing in; conducting, ushering in; presentation; insertion. **2** *Make the introductions while I take the coats:* presentation, acquaintanceship, meeting of strangers. **3** *Modern introductions were resented by the older employees:* innovation, change, novelty. **4** *The book's introduction is brief:* preface, prefatory material, preamble, foreword, opening part, opening; prelude, precursor; preliminary speech, opening remarks, prologue.

Ant. 1 extraction, elimination, removal, withdrawal; completion, end, termination. **4** epilogue, afterword.

introductory *adj. The manufacturer made an introductory offer at a lower price:* serving to introduce, preliminary, acquainting, initiatory, prefatory, precursory.

Ant. final, conclusive, terminal.

introvert *n. An introvert spends much time alone:* reserved person, withdrawn person; self-contained person; introspective person, inner-directed person; loner, unsociable person, thinker, contemplative, brooder.

Ant. extrovert, outgoing person.

intrude *v.* **1** *The judge intruded his prejudices upon the case:* thrust, interject improperly, interpose, push, impose. **2** *Don't intrude in a family dispute:* enter uninvited, thrust oneself in, obtrude, interfere, intervene, interlope, come uninvited, trespass, encroach.

intruder *n. An intruder broke into the house last night:* unlawful entrant, interloper, interferer, intervener; gate-crasher, thief, trespasser, encroacher.

Ant. guest.

intuition *n. Intuition told me that he would not turn up. My intuition turned out to be correct:* innate knowledge, immediate cognition, instinct, instinctive feeling; extra-sensory perception; telepathy, clairvoyance, precognition, second sight; insight, guesswork, sixth sense; *Informal* hunch, flash.

Ant. ratiocination, reasoning, deduction.

intuitive *adj. The child has an intuitive appreciation of music:* innate, instinctive, intuitional, natural, native, constitutional, inborn, inbred; resulting from intuition, based on a hunch; non-rational, extra-sensory, telepathic, psychic, clairvoyant.

Ant. acquired, learned, rational.

inundate *v.* **1** *Flood waters inundated the valley:* engulf, overflow, fill with water, overspread, submerge, flood, deluge, drown. **2** *The visiting astronaut was inundated with invitations:* swamp, glut, flood, saturate, overcome; load down, overburden, overwhelm.

Ant. 1 drain dry, reclaim, desiccate, parch.

◇ *Word origin: Inundate* comes from Latin *in-* (in, on) + *unda* (wave), so the word means literally "to cover by a wave."

invade *v.* **1** *Germany invaded many neighbouring countries in World War II:* overrun, enter by force, swarm over, infest, enter as a conquering power, encroach upon, enter as an enemy, march into, strike at, attack. **2** *Tourists invaded the city:* enter *en masse*, overrun, engulf, flood, descend upon. **3** *An epidemic of measles invaded the school:* strike, overspread, spread throughout, permeate, penetrate, infect. **4** *The state must not invade the freedom of the church:* intrude on, infringe upon, encroach on, trespass, violate, restrict, limit; *Informal* chip away at.

Ant. 1, 2 abandon, relinquish, vacate, evacuate. **3** bypass. **4** respect, honour.

◇ *Word origin:* To *invade* is to enter or go into a foreign country by force; an *invasion* is the act of so doing. The words come from Latin *in-* (in) + *vadere* (to go). Latin *vadere* (to go) is connected with Old English *wadan* (to go), from which we get our word *wade.*

invalid[1] *n.* **1** *The invalid is confined to a wheelchair:* chronically ill person, disabled person, enfeebled person, stricken person, valetudinarian; (*variously*) cripple, paraplegic, paralytic.

—*adj.* **2** *We engaged a nurse to look after our invalid mother:* infirm, enfeebled, unable to care for oneself, debilitated, disabled, sick, sickly, ailing, unwell, valetudinarian, incapacitated, powerless, weak, weakened.

Ant. 2 strong, well, healthy, vigorous.

◇ *Pronunciation tip:* See INVALID[2].

invalid[2] *adj. This document is invalid unless it is officially stamped. That is an invalid argument:* not valid, void, null, nugatory, useless, forceless, ineffective, good-for-nothing, worthless; inoperative; dead-letter; unconvincing, illogical, fallacious, unsupported, unsound, false.

Ant. valid, sound, legal, legitimate; correct, forceful, logical.

◇ *Word origin: Invalid* comes from Latin *in-* (not) + *validus* (powerful), which also gives us *valid, validate, valiant,* and *valour.*

◇ *Pronunciation tip: Invalid* meaning "infirm, disabled" or "a disabled person" is pronounced *IN-va-lid,* with the stress on the first syllable. *Invalid* meaning "worthless" is stressed on the second syllable, *in-VAL-id.*

invalidate *v. Unauthorized alterations invalidated the passport. Inaccuracies invalidated the speaker's argument:* make invalid or worthless, make void, nullify, vitiate, annul, abrogate, cancel, deprive of legal force; weaken, discredit, undercut, undermine, refute.

Ant. validate, certify, authorize; strengthen, enhance.

invaluable *adj. These manuscripts are invaluable to scholars and should be in a museum:* priceless, beyond price, very precious, of great worth, very valuable, inestimable; rare, choice.

Ant. worthless, valueless.

invariable *adj. The students respected the teacher's invariable fairness:* constant, unfailing, uniform, unwavering, unvarying, immutable, unchanging, changeless, unchangeable, always the same, consistent.

Ant. variable, changing, changeable, varying.

invasion *n.* **1** *The military invasion was timed to take place at dawn:* infiltration, penetration, incursion, aggression, assault, attack, raid, inroad; onslaught. **2** *The illegal search was an invasion of their civil liberties:* encroachment, breach, intrusion, infringement; trespass, overstepping, usurpation.

Ant. 1 evacuation, retreat. **2** respect, honouring.

◇ *Word origin:* See INVADE.

invective *n. Harsh invective poured from the speaker's mouth:* bitter language, harsh words, verbal abuse, venom, vilification, insult, contumely, execration, sarcasm; vituperation, denunciation, revilement, censure, rant, railing, billingsgate.

Ant. praise, honour, commendation.

invent *v.* **1** *Alexander Graham Bell invented the telephone:* originate, create, develop, contrive, devise, put together, fabricate, formulate; *Informal* think up, come up with. **2** *He invented some story about the train being derailed:* make up, concoct, conceive, fabricate, contrive, conjure up, coin; *Informal* cook up, trump up.

Ant. 1 copy, imitate, reproduce.

"Inventions that are not made, like babies that are not born, are rarely missed."

—*J. K. Galbraith*

---

invention *n.* **1** *The invention of a space rocket took many years:* inventing, creation, fabrication, origination, discovery; production, development. **2** *The electric toothbrush is a clever invention:* contrivance, gadget; implement, device, apparatus, machine, contraption; design. **3** *Mozart is famous for melodic invention:* inventiveness, resourcefulness, originality, imagination, ingenuity, creativity, fertility. **4** *The alibi was pure invention from start to finish:* fabrication, sham, fake, dissimulation, forgery, concoction, fiction, lie, prevarication, trumpery.

Ant. 3 uninventiveness. **4** truth, fact.

◇ *Word origin:* Like many *in-* words, *invention* is of Latin origin. It comes from *in-* (in) + *venire* (to come), literally to come into or upon something for the first time.

inventory *n. The company's inventory lists 2,000 items. The inventory was in perfect condition:* stocklist, catalogue, roster, roll, index, schedule, register; objects or items represented on the list, stock, merchandise, goods, supply.

inverse *adj. The baby cried in inverse proportion to the amount of food it was given:* reversed, back to front, converse, backward, right-to-left, bottom-to-top, inverted, opposite, indirect, contrary.

Ant. forward; direct.

inverted *adj. In an inverted position, a 9 looks like a 6:* turned upside-down, reversed in position, inverse, bottom up.

Ant. upright, right side up.

invest *v.* **1** *Everyone should invest some time in community service:* devote, give, allot, apportion, set aside, appoint. **2** *Only the union committee is invested with the power to call a strike:* endow, supply, license, enable. **3** *The singer invested her songs with a bitter-sweet sadness:* endow, infuse, imbue, colour, clothe, fill, enrich. **4** *The designer invested the performers with sumptuous costumes:* clothe, garb, dress, cover, array, adorn.

Ant. 1, 2 withhold, deny. **2** withdraw.

◇ *Word origin:* When we *invest* money in a business, we literally provide or clothe it with money; when we *invest* power in a politician, we provide or clothe him or her with power. *Invest* comes from Latin *in-* (in, on) + *vestire* (to clothe, provide with vestments), which also gives us our word *vest.*

investigate *v. The police are investigating the murder:* inquire into, explore, examine closely, study, scrutinize, research, probe, look into, search into, delve into; question, query, ask about; sift, pore over, dissect, analyse, anatomize; survey.

Ant. conjecture, guess; ignore.

◇ *Word origin:* Sherlock Holmes *investigated* many cases by following the footprints left at the scene of the crime. That's exactly what an *investigator* should do, because *investigate* comes from Latin *in-* (in, into) + *vestigium* (footprint, track, trace), literally "to follow footprints," hence to search into something.

investigation *n. The investigation may take many months:* inquiry, investigating, thorough examination, search, study, scrutiny, probe, research, fact-finding; analysis, dissection, anatomy.

investment *n.* **1** *The man became rich through making wise investments:* investing, allotment of funds, capital spending, stock acquisition; financial transaction. **2** *Each partner's investment was £5,000:* money invested, contribution, offering, share; risk, venture, stake, ante.

inveterate *adj. Inveterate romantics are always falling in love:* confirmed, steadfast, constant, habitual, established, inured, hardened, ingrained, deep-rooted, deep-seated, die-hard,

adamant; incurable, unregenerate, unreconstructed.
Ant. undeveloped, incipient; reformed.
◇ *Word origin:* An *inveterate* spendthrift is one confirmed in his habit by long experience, an *inveterate* custom is an old one. The word comes from Latin *in-* (very) + *vetus* (old). Latin *vetus*, old, also gives us our word *veteran*, literally "old one."

invidious *adj. Distinguishing my work from her own was an invidious comparison:* insulting, causing envy or hard feelings, inciting ill will, offensive, slighting; malevolent, malicious, vicious, spiteful.
Ant. fair, just, placating; flattering.

invigorating *adj. An early morning swim is always invigorating:* refreshing, restorative, strengthening, energizing, bracing, healthful, stimulating, rejuvenating, quickening.
Ant. tiring, weakening.

invincible *adj. The Maginot Line was thought to be invincible. His invincible sense of humour helped him through hard times:* unconquerable, impregnable, insurmountable, insuperable, totally secure; irrepressible, unbeatable, undefeatable.
Ant. conquerable, vulnerable.
◇ *Spelling tip: Invincible* is spelt with three *i's;* there is no "-able" in it. Remember, *I* am *InvIncIble.*

invisible *adj. H. G. Wells wrote a famous story about an invisible man:* not visible, not perceptible to the eye, imperceptible, undiscernible, unapparent, unseeable, unseen; covert, obscure, hidden.
Ant. visible, apparent, plain.

invitation *n.* **1** *Have the party invitations been sent out yet?:* request for someone's presence, summons, solicitation, offer, call, bid. **2** *Gloomy thoughts are an invitation to depression:* inducement, lure, enticement, temptation, open door; bid, call, summons; challenge.
Ant. 1 rebuff, repulse, response, reply.

invite *v.* **1** *Invite the family to stay for the week-end:* request the presence of, summon courteously, urge, call, bid. **2** *The new hotel invited suggestions from the guests:* request politely, ask formally; encourage, welcome, solicit. **3** *Some people seem to invite disaster:* tempt, induce, attract, entice, lure, court, encourage, welcome; *Informal* ask for; act so as to cause.
Ant. 2, 3 repel, forbid, discourage.

inviting *adj. This is an inviting room. His proposal that we go swimming was an inviting one:* tempting, attractive, appealing, alluring, enticing, warm, welcoming.
Ant. uninviting, unattractive, forbidding, repellent.

invocation *n. The priest read a solemn invocation calling on divine blessing for the new church:* entreaty to a supernatural power, prayer, appeal, supplication, orison, petition, plea, summoning.

invoke *v.* **1** *The sinner invoked the Lord's forgiveness:* entreat, call upon, petition, implore, appeal for, supplicate, pray for; beg, beseech, importune, ask for. **2** *The minister invoked an old and forgotten act:* put into effect, have recourse to, resort to, use, implement, employ, apply, introduce. **3** *The medium tried to invoke the spirits of the dead:* summon by incantation, call forth, conjure.

involuntary *adj. She gave an involuntary shiver:* spontaneous, reflex, unintentional, unconscious, instinctive, automatic, inadvertent.
Ant. willing, voluntary, intentional.

"Any man's death diminishes me, because I am involved in Mankind; and therefore never send to know for whom the bell tolls; it tolls for thee." —*John Donne*

---

involve *v.* **1** *The plan involves the co-operation of both young and old:* include, contain, be a matter of, comprise; entail, depend on, imply. **2** *Treaty obligations involved the country in the war:* cause to be associated, implicate, embroil, entangle, mix up. **3** *The minister is heavily involved in preparing new anti-monopoly legislation:* absorb fully, preoccupy, commit, engage, wrap up.
Ant. 2 extricate, disentangle, liberate, release. **3** disengage.

inward Also **inwards** *adv.* **1** *The door opens inward:* towards the inside, towards the interior, interiorly. **2** *Nostalgia turned his reflections inward:* toward one's private thoughts, into the mind or soul, inwardly.
—*adj.* **3** *The explorers discovered an inward passage. He has achieved inward peace:* directed towards the inside, ingoing, incoming, leading inside, going in, inner-directed, interior; personal, private, mental, spiritual, inner.
Ant. 1, 2 outward, outside. **3** outer, exterior, superficial.
◇ *Usage note: Inward* is always correct, as an adjective or as an adverb. *Inwards* is correct only as an adverb. Thus, *The thief suffered inward* (never "inwards") *convulsions*, but *The ship headed inward* (or *inwards*) *to port.*

iota *n. There's not an iota of truth to the story:* faint degree, small amount, particle, jot, ounce, tiniest quantity, scintilla, spark, bit, spot, speck.
Ant. mass, lot.
◇ *Word origin: Iota* is *iōta*, a letter in the Greek alphabet corresponding to our letter *i.* Greek *iōta* also gives us our word *jot.* Our figurative use of the word dates from Jesus' famous declaration recorded in Matthew 5: 18: "Till heaven and earth pass, one jot or one tittle shall in no wise pass from the law, till all be fulfilled." In the Greek original of that passage, the word for "jot" is *iōta.*

irascible *adj. The irascible old man is constantly picking quarrels:* easily angered, cantankerous, choleric, waspish, bad-tempered, hot-tempered, irritable, quarrelsome, splenetic, cross, testy, cranky.

Ant. good-natured, amiable, gentle, mild, placid, serene, tranquil, easy-going.

◇ *Word origin:* See IRE.

irate *adj. The long wait at the check-out counter made the shoppers extremely irate:* angry, furious, enraged, infuriated; irritated, annoyed, livid, vexed, indignant, *Informal* mad.

Ant. good-humoured, tolerant, tranquil.

ire *n. The strike stirred up the community's ire:* anger, rage, outrage, fury, umbrage, wrath, indignation, resentment, choler.

Ant. goodwill, patience, forbearance, forgiveness.

◇ *Word origin: Ire* comes from Latin *ira,* anger, which also gives us *irate, irascible,* and *irritate.*

iridescent *adj. The jewel shone iridescent in the sun's rays:* changeable in colour, colourful, glowing, shiny, reflecting many hues, rainbowlike, opalescent, prismatic.

Ant. blanched, neutral, colourless, dingy, dull, lustreless.

◇ *Spelling tip: Iridescent* can be hard to spell. You'll get it right if you pronounce it slowly to yourself and then spell all the syllables carefully: *Ir-i-deS-cent.*

◇ *Word origin: Iridescent* literally means "displaying the colours of the rainbow." It comes from Greek *iris* (rainbow) + the Latin suffix *-escent* (being, beginning to be). Our word *iris,* meaning the coloured part of the eye and the colourful flower, comes from the Greek word. In Greek mythology, *Iris* was the goddess of the rainbow, an attendant of Zeus, and a messenger of the gods.

irk *v. Our late arrival irked the performers:* annoy, irritate, vex, gall, ruffle, bother, pester, provoke, *Informal* rile.

Ant. please, delight, cheer; overjoy.

ironic Also **ironical** *adj.* **1** *His tone when he praised that awful play was ironic:* mocking, sarcastic, expressing or filled with irony, sardonic, facetious; insincere, pretended; derisive, biting, cutting, stinging, sneering, caustic, abrasive. **2** *It's ironic that so many pacifists have died violent deaths:* incongruous, inconsistent, contradictory, surprising, unexpected, implausible; curious, strange, odd; *Informal* funny, weird.

Ant. **1** sincere, straightforward, direct. **2** natural, predictable, expected.

irony *n.* **1** *Swift's humour is full of irony:* double meaning, facetiousness, sarcasm, mockery. **2** *What an irony to be offered three jobs in one week after being out of work for a year!:* incongruity, contrariness, absurdity, unexpected outcome, reverse state of affairs.

Ant. **1** sincerity, straightforwardness, directness.

◇ *Usage note:* See SARCASM.

irrational *adj.* **1** *Animals and fish are irrational creatures:* incapable of logical thought, unthinking, unreasoning. **2** *Both your fears and your behaviour are irrational:* unsound, illogical, unreasonable, not based on reason, baseless, nonsensical, absurd, foolish, specious, ill-advised.

Ant. **1, 2** rational. **2** reasonable, wise, sensible, logical.

irreconcilable *adj. The partner's differences seem irreconcilable:* beyond reconciliation, unadjustable, unbridgeable, intransigent, implacably hostile, unappeasable; inconsistent, incompatible, opposed.

Ant. reconcilable, appeasable.

irrefutable *adj. The argument for increased benefits is irrefutable:* undeniable, not refutable, incontrovertible, indisputable; proof positive, unquestionable.

Ant. refutable, disputable, moot.

irregular *adj.* **1** *Braces straightened the child's irregular teeth:* uneven, crooked, out of line, unaligned; not smooth, rough, broken, bumpy; asymmetrical. **2** *Wearing shorts to the office is highly irregular:* non-conforming, unconventional, unusual, uncharacteristic, unexpected; improper, unsuitable, inappropriate, unfitting, indecorous; eccentric, peculiar, queer, odd, singular; abnormal, aberrant, anomalous; unsystematic, unmethodical, haphazard, desultory.

Ant. **1** regular, even, smooth, uniform. **2** regular, normal, typical; usual, customary; legitimate, proper, common, established; methodical, orderly, systematic, uniform.

"A poor relation — is the most irrelevant thing in nature." —*Charles Lamb*

---

irrelevant *adj. The question is interesting but irrelevant to the problem:* unconnected, unrelated, beside the point, inapt, immaterial, non-pertinent, impertinent, malapropos, extraneous, foreign, neither here nor there, not germane.

Ant. relevant, pertinent, related.

irreligious *adj. Communists are assumed to be irreligious people:* not religious, not holding religious beliefs, unbelieving, lax, godless, atheistic, agnostic, impious, profane, ungodly.

Ant. religious, pious, devout.

irreparable *adj. The hurricane caused irreparable damage:* beyond repair or salvage, uncorrectable, irreversible, beyond redress, irremediable, remediless.

Ant. reparable, salvageable, reversible, remediable.

irrepressible *adj. Nothing could dampen the boy's irrepressible enthusiasm:* unrestrainable, uncontrollable, unquenchable, undamped; bubbling, ebullient, overflowing, vibrant, galvanic, boisterous, tempestuous, full of life.

Ant. repressible, restrainable; depressed, damped, feeble, flaccid.

irreproachable *adj. The judge's record for fairness is irreproachable:* beyond reproach or criticism, above reproof, without fault, flawless, blameless, faultless, inculpable, impeccable; unblemished, stainless, unspotted, unimpeachable.

Ant. reproachable, flawed, blameworthy, faulty.

irresistible *adj.* **1** *He felt an irresistible urge to run away:* overwhelming, not resistible, not withstandable, overpowering, overmastering. **2** *The box of chocolates was irresistible:* extremely tempting, enticing, alluring, not to be resisted, tantalizing, seductive, beckoning, highly desirable.

Ant. 1 resistible, withstandable, weak. **2** resistible, unattractive.

◇ *Spelling tip:* It may seem conceited, but you will spell this word correctly if you just say, "*I* am *IrresIstIble.*"

irresolute *adj. His irresolute nature made him a poor manager:* indecisive, wavering, hesitating, hesitant, faltering, unsettled, doubtful, undecided, uncertain, changeable, vacillating, fickle, weak, unsteady, unresolved.

Ant. resolute, determined, unwavering, decisive; decided, certain.

irresponsible *adj. She was an irresponsible mother to leave the children alone in the house. Turning down the scholarship was an irresponsible thing to do:* careless, not responsible, undependable, unreliable, indifferent, immature, untrustworthy, thoughtless; imprudent, incautious, reckless, rash, ill-considered, injudicious, over-hasty; foolish, hare-brained.

Ant. responsible, careful, thoughtful, trustworthy, dependable.

irreverent *adj. The vicar said that it was irreverent to talk in church:* disrespectful, lacking reverence, impious, profane, blasphemous; impudent, brazen, shameless, saucy, sacrilegious; disparaging, slighting, critical, sceptical, debunking.

irrevocable *adj. The decision to close the business is irrevocable:* final, conclusive, not subject to reversal, unchangeable, not commutable, irreversible, unalterable.

Ant. reversible, changeable, alterable.

irritable *adj. The heat made everybody irritable:* bad-tempered, ill-humoured, easily irritated, easily annoyed, easily angered, irascible, easily vexed, touchy, over-sensitive, testy, peevish, waspish, impatient, snappy, pettish, fretful.

Ant. easy-going, amiable, good-natured, agreeable, genial, affable.

◇ *Spelling tip:* The two *r's* can cause you to become *iRRitable.*

irritate *v.* **1** *The child's whining irritated the nurse:* annoy, vex, anger, make angry, make impatient, peeve, provoke, exasperate, irk. **2** *Woollen clothing will irritate the rash:* make painful, aggravate, make sensitive, inflame, make sore, make swollen, rub against, chafe.

Ant. 1 appease, mollify, placate, pacify; gratify, please, delight. **2** soothe, balm, ease.

◇ *Word origin:* See IRE.

island *n.* **1** *The island lies a mile off shore:* isle, islet, atoll. **2** *The library is an island of quiet, away from the hustle and bustle of the town:* sanctuary, refuge, shelter, haven, place of tranquil isolation, isolated spot, oasis, enclave.

◇ *Word origin: Island* is an Old English word that for many years was spelt *iland.* The *s* was added in the 15th century because people associated the word with *isle. Isle,* itself, comes to us via Old French from Latin *insula,* island, which also gives us *insular, insulate,* and *isolate* (which means literally to make an island of something).

isolate *v. Research workers have isolated and identified the virus:* separate, segregate, place apart, set apart, insulate, quarantine, seclude, sequester; disconnect, detach.

Ant. join, unite, combine, mix.

◇ *Word origin:* See ISLAND.

issue *n.* **1** *The motor vehicle licensing department handles the issue of driving-licences. The magazine comes out in monthly issues:* giving out, granting; sending out, putting forth, issuance, distributing, dispensation; number, edition, publication. **2** *Taxation was the main issue in the parliamentary elections:* problem, question, dispute, matter for discussion, point of debate, matter to be settled, matter in dispute. **3** *There was little hope that the negotiations would have a happy issue:* result, consequence, outcome; yield, product. **4** *The king's legal issue inherited the throne:* offspring, progeny, children, descendants, heirs, heritors, posterity. **5** *The issue of water from the cracked pipe grew so serious that we called the fire brigade:* outpouring, gush, discharge, outflow, effluence, drainage, eruption.

—*v.* **6** *Lava issued from the volcano:* pour forth, go out, emanate, flow out, spout, gush, erupt, pass out, emerge. **7** *The post office issued the new stamps last week:* put in circulation, circulate, distribute. **8** *The authorities issued food to the flood victims:* give out, distribute, dispense, allot. **9** *Her insecurity issues from an unhappy childhood:* result, proceed, follow, ensue, grow out of, rise, arise, emerge, emanate, stem, spring, originate.

Ant. 3 start, beginning, inception, cause. **4** parent, sire. **7** withdraw, revoke, repeal. **8** withhold, withdraw. **9** cause; start, begin, initiate.

◇ *Word origin: Issue* originally meant "to go forth" or "that which goes forth." It comes from Latin *ex-* (out, out of) + *ire* (to go).

itch *v.* **1** *I itch all over after that walk in the forest:* have an itch, feel the need to scratch, prickle, tickle, crawl, creep. **2** *The girl itched to see the*

world: long, yearn, hanker, have an urge, crave, desire, pine, ache.
—*n.* **3** *I have an itch on my back:* prickling sensation, tingling, itchiness, prickliness. **4** *Most people have an itch for romance:* strong wish, desire, yearning, restless urge, hankering, craving.

item *n.* **1** *There are ten items on my shopping-list:* article, notation, entry, detail, unit, thing, matter, subject, point. **2** *There is an item on the kidnapping in today's paper:* report, news article, notice, piece, story, feature, account, dispatch.
◇ *Word origin: Item* was once mainly used in its original Latin meaning of "moreover" or "also" to introduce a new statement, entry, or clause in a list, contract, or formal piece of writing.

itemize *v. Please itemize the materials we shall need to build the garage:* list individually, individualize, state one by one, particularize, detail, state item by item, enumerate, spell out, specify.
Ant. combine, group, *Informal* lump together.

itinerant *adj. Itinerant minstrels were a common sight during the Middle Ages:* wandering, wayfaring, peripatetic, roving, migrant, travelling, nomadic, footloose, vagrant, transient.
Ant. stationary, settled, resident.

"The Germans are sending over professors of English to trace out the imaginary itinerary of Joyce's imaginary Mr Bloom through the different pubs he is supposed to have visited."
—*George Boyle*

itinerary *n.* **1** *Leave your itinerary so that we can reach you in case of emergency:* travel plan, schedule, detailed plan for a journey, list of places to be visited, timetable, route, circuit. **2** *Father kept a lively itinerary of the trip:* logbook, record of a journey, travel record, journal, account, diary.
◇ *Word origin: Itinerary* comes from Latin *itinerari,* to journey about.

J

jab *v.* **1** *All through the game he kept jabbing me in the side:* poke, nudge, tap, prod, dig, stab, strike, rap, hit, goad, elbow.
—*n.* **2** *His left jabs had taken their toll by the sixth round:* poke, short punch, quick thrust, cut, stroke, stab, dig, swing; hit, blow; *Slang* belt, sock, clip, pasting, lick, swat.

jabber *v.* **1** *She was jabbering on about nothing in particular and bored everyone to tears:* babble, chatter, talk aimlessly, talk idly, maunder, prattle, prate, blather, drivel, blab, talk nonsense, utter drivel, clack, ramble, gibber, rattle.
—*n.* **2** *Her endless jabber was infuriating:* jabbering talk, gibberish, nonsense, drivel, idle talk, maundering, ranting, prattle, chatter, blabber, babble, prating, patter, blather, gab, twattle, clack, palaver, raving, gossip, chit-chat, gushing, twaddle, cackle; *Slang* gas, hot air.
◇ *Word origin:* The word *jabber* imitates the noise it represents — fast, unintelligible talk.

jacket *n.* **1** *You need a light jacket for the cool days of spring:* short coat, (*variously*) sports coat, blazer, smoking-jacket, dinner-jacket, anorak, wind-cheater. **2** *The notebook was protected by a plastic jacket:* outer covering, wrapper, wrapping, cover, envelope, casing, case, coat, enclosure, sheath.
◇ *Word origin: Jacket* can be traced back to the Old French word for a peasant's smock, *jaque. Jacket* is the diminutive of this word.

jaded *adj.* **1** *The film dealt with the same old jaded themes of betrayal and revenge:* shop-worn, worn-out, tired, played out, over-used, stale; fatigued, exhausted, wearied, dog-tired, spent, over-wearied, tired out. **2** *Parisians are said to be jaded and unimpressible:* blasé, bored, surfeited, spoiled, cloyed, dulled, satiate, satiated, sated, glutted, over-indulged.
◇ *Word origin: Jaded,* worn-out or exhausted, comes from the old word *jade,* an old, worthless horse.

jagged *adj. I've got a jagged tooth that has to be filed down:* rough, snaggy, irregular, having uneven notches or points, indented, crenulated, ragged on the edges, jaggy, uneven, broken; knifelike, serrated, notched, sharp-toothed, saw-toothed, nicked, ridged, zigzag; angular, craggy, rugged, cragged, pointed; spiny, spinous, bristly, thorny; studded, spiked, barbed.
Ant. smooth, even, regular; level.

jam *v.* **1** *He jammed his clothes into the old suit-case. The people were jammed into the small lift:* press, cram, crowd, stuff, pack, over-crowd; squeeze, insert forcefully, ram, sandwich, wedge; work in, force in, edge in, worm in, foist in; put between. **2** *The car picked up speed when she jammed down the accelerator:* hit suddenly, push, thrust, press, bear down on. **3** *The accident jammed the main road for three hours. The gun has jammed:* block, obstruct, congest, stick, suspend, stall, arrest, interrupt,

stop, cease; become unworkable, get stuck, malfunction, break down temporarily.
—*n.* **4** *I'd rather walk than be stuck in a traffic jam:* impassable mass of objects or persons, crowd, multitude, throng, sea, agglomeration, mob, horde, pack, flock, herd, swarm, host, drove, army; crush, push, press. **5** *Informal He's in an awful jam over his mortgage:* fix, trouble, mess, predicament, strait, plight, dilemma, quandary; *Slang* pickle, scrape, pinch, hot water.

jangle *v.* **1** *Gold and brass bracelets jangled on her wrist as she gesticulated:* rattle, clang, clatter, clank; tintinnabulate, chime, jingle, ring, make a plangent sound, reverberate; sound harshly, sound discordantly, make a racket, clash, crash. **2** *The children's constant screaming jangles my nerves:* upset, jar, irritate, grate on.
—*n.* **3** *The jangle of the alarm bell woke the sleeping soldiers:* rattle, clang, clatter, clank, racket, clangour, wild pealing, harsh ringing, din, reverberation; cacophony, jumble of sound, confusion of noise.
Ant. 3 silence, quiet.

jar[1] *n. There were jars of sweets on the shelves of the shop:* large earthen or glass vessel, crock, pot, jug, bottle, canister, flask, decanter, urn, demijohn.

jar[2] *v.* **1** *The noise of the drill jarred on my nerves:* grate on, send a shock through, sound discordantly, cause to vibrate painfully, grind, set on edge, chafe. **2** *The earthquake jarred the city and the surrounding countryside:* shake, vibrate harshly, rock, cause to quake, jolt, cause to quiver, agitate, make tremble, convulse, joggle, stir, upheave.
—*n.* **3** *The jar of the alarm made him leap out of bed:* harsh sound, rattle, clang, clatter, clank, racket, clashing, crash, clangour, din, reverberation; cacophony, discordance, bray, brawl, blare, blast, buzz, bleating. **4** *The jar of the explosion was felt for miles around:* concussion, reverberation, shake, jolt, agitation, impact, crash, shock, quake.
Ant. 2 soothe, calm, quiet.

jargon *n.* **1** *A trainee solicitor must learn to understand the elliptical jargon of the law:* specialized or professional language, idiom, parlance, phraseology, vocabulary, usage, vernacular, argot, lingo, cant, shibboleths. **2** *The report was full of esoteric jargon and completely useless:* meaningless writing or talk, nonsense, gibberish, verbiage, grandiloquence, stuff and nonsense, prattle, drivel, prate, blather, twaddle, blabber, babble, jabberwocky, rigmarole, rubbish, humbug, fustian, tommy rot; *Slang* bunkum, balderdash, hog-wash, bosh, flapdoodle, abracadabra, poppycock, hocus-pocus, fudge, moonshine, gobbledygook, bull, baloney, piffle. **3** *He learnt to converse in the native jargon:* simplified language, vernacular, lingo, dialect, patois, brogue, pidgin, lingua franca.

jaundiced *adj.* **1** *We take a jaundiced view of her professed naïvety:* sceptical, cynical, doubting; blasé, bored, satiated. **2** *Other people's good luck always makes him rather jaundiced:* jealous, envious, covetous, green-eyed; resentful, hostile, feeling ill will, mistrustful, suspicious, doubting.
Ant. 1 credulous, believing, trusting.
◇ *Word origin: Jaundiced* comes from Latin *galbus*, yellow. *Jaundice* is an abnormal condition in which the skin and the whites of the eyes turn yellow; it is usually associated with diseases of the liver.

jaunt *n. He had collected many souvenirs from his jaunts in all parts of the world:* short trip, excursion, tour, outing, expedition, ramble, adventure, flight; *Informal* spin, stroll, promenade, airing.

jaunty *adj. It was pleasant to meet such a jaunty, smiling young man:* light-hearted, high-spirited, buoyant, bouncy, perky, sprightly, vivacious, airy, breezy, free and easy, carefree; sporty, debonair, dapper, high-stepping, spruce, neat, trim; *Informal* natty.
Ant. staid, sober, sedate, dignified; dull, lifeless, pessimistic.

jealous *adj.* **1** *She was jealous of her friend's good figure:* envious, resentful, covetous, green-eyed, grudging. **2** *She was extremely jealous of her boy-friend. They were ridiculously jealous of their social position:* possessive, suspicious, mistrustful, mistrusting, wary, anxious, concerned, regardful, watchful, apprehensive; conscious of, obsessed with, unduly proud of, zealous in maintaining or guarding something, mindful.
Ant. 1 trusting, trustful, **2** indifferent, uncaring.
◇ *Word origin:* A *jealous* person is overzealous of his position. *Jealous* comes from Greek *zēlos*, zeal, which also gives us *zealous.* Thus the two words "rhyme" in meaning and origin as well as in sound.

jeer *v.* **1** *They jeered at the first speaker:* deride, sneer, mock, revile, laugh at, taunt, hoot, ridicule, scorn, harass, hound, make game or sport of, poke fun at, heckle, hector, gibe rudely, scoff, flout; hiss, boo, whistle at, whoop, catcall; *Slang* knock, rag, give the raspberry.
—*n.* **2** *The jeers from the crowd caused the speaker to leave the platform:* jeering utterance, derision, taunt, mockery, contumely, slur, barb, yell of contempt, hoot, insult, aspersion, abuse, obloquy, scoff, scoffing.
Ant. 1 applaud, cheer. **2** encouragement, adulation, applause.

jeopardy *n You'll put yourself in jeopardy by irritating a man like that:* danger, peril, openness to danger, imperilment, vulnerability, hazard, endangerment, unsafety, liability, risk, precariousness, insecurity.
Ant. security, safety.

◇ *Word origin: Jeopardy* comes from Old French *jeu parti,* "split game," i.e. a draw in which the next move will decide the game. (The word was originally a term in chess.)

jerk *n.* **1** *He gave a firm jerk on the rope and pulled in the rowing-boat. His hand moved in jerks because of his anger:* pull, snap, tug, yank; shake, twitch, quiver, spasm, fit, reflex, start, trembling, tic.
—*v.* **2** *He jerked at my lapel. His hands jerk when he's irritated:* pull, tug, twist, thrust, pluck, yank, wrench; shake, convulse, twitch, quiver, tremble.

jest *n.* **1** *We don't need your jests at the moment, thank you:* facetious remark, joke, jape, gibe, quip, wisecrack, crack, pleasantry, pun; *Informal* gag, trick, prank, game; witticism, bon mot.
—*v.* **2** *He jests at scars that never felt a wound:* crack jokes, joke, quip, banter, fool, tease, act up, play the fool, laugh; *Slang* horse around.
◇ *Word origin: Jest* was originally a variant spelling of *gest,* an exploit or a tale of adventure and romance. Only later did it come to mean an exploit or a tale to provoke laughter.

jester *n. Royal jesters brought welcome respite from the court formalities:* clown, fool, zany, buffoon, joker, wag, motley fool, madcap, funny man, merry-andrew, Punchinello, *Informal* card; harlequin, wearer of the cap and bells; (*variously*) mime, pantomimist, mimic, mimer, mummer, comedian, comic, wit, humorist.

jet *n.* **1** *The firemen turned jets of water on the blaze:* stream, stream of liquid, fountain, spurt, spray, spout, squirt, swash, shoot, flush, gush. **2** *Swinging the jet to the right, he watered the lawn with the long hose:* spout, nozzle, spray, sparger, sprinkler; atomizer, syringe.
—*v.* **3** *Oil suddenly jetted out of rig number four:* spout, spurt, stream, shoot, shoot out, spray, squirt, issue, discharge, break or burst forth, gush, fountain, rush up, surge, vomit forth.

jettison *v. During the storm the crew jettisoned much of the ship's cargo:* throw overboard, toss overboard, pitch over, throw over, cast off, throw off ballast; eliminate, discard, throw out, dump, scrap, unload, eject.

jewel *n.* **1** *The jewels were kept in the safe:* precious stone, cut and polished stone, gem, stone. **2** *She appeared at the reception wearing her finest jewels:* ornament, piece of jewellery, bangle, bauble, bead, trinket, (*variously*) necklace, earring, ring, tiara, locket, bracelet, pendant, brooch. **3** *She was a jewel among secretaries:* treasure, prize, gem, one in a thousand, one in a million, first-rater, ace; *Informal* top-notcher, pearl, pearl of great price, pure gold, find, honey, dear, apple of one's eye, salt of the earth; *Slang* the tops, humdinger, winner, knock-out; work of art, masterpiece.
◇ *Word origin: Jewel* comes from Latin *jocus,* joke, sport, play. A jewel is thus a "plaything."

jewellery *n. Her jewellery was insured for half a million pounds:* jewels, gems, precious stones, adornments, personal ornaments, regalia; articles of gold, silver, or gems; trinkets, bangles, costume jewellery.

jiggle *v. He jiggled the key in the lock to try to get the door open. Please stop jiggling!:* shake, wiggle, joggle, agitate, jostle; wriggle, fidget, bounce, twitch, jerk.
◇ *Word origin:* To *jiggle* is to move rapidly up and down or from side to side, as in dancing a jig, and the word *jiggle* actually comes from the jig. *Jig* itself comes from Old French *gigue,* a fiddle. (German *Geige,* violin, is related.)

> **Exploring the Word:** The Latin word *jacere,* to throw, cast out, gives us *jet,* a sudden spurt of liquid, air, etc., cast out from a source, and *jettison,* to throw cargo overboard. It also gives us *abject,* thrown away, so mean or despicable as to be thrown away, as an *abject coward*; *adjacent,* literally thrown next to something else; *conjecture,* a thought or idea thrown out for discussion; *dejected,* thrown down in spirit, or "downcast," as we would say; *eject* and *ejaculation,* to throw out, discharge; *inject,* to throw in, and *injection,* that which is "thrown in," as vaccines by a hypodermic needle; *interjection,* literally something thrown between other things, as a word "interjected" between others; *object* and *objection,* to throw something in the way or something that is thrown in the way; *project,* to throw forward, plan; *projectile,* something to be thrown forward or discharged; and *projector,* used to "throw" the image of a slide, film, etc., on to a screen; and *subject,* literally "to throw under," hence to bring under control or domination, or that which is controlled or dominated, as a *king's subjects* or a *school subject,* or to be thrown under or forced to "undergo" an experience, as to be *subjected to insults.*

jilt *v. She jilted him a week before the wedding:* cast off a lover or sweetheart, break an engagement, break off with, break one's word or promise; forsake, leave, leave in the lurch, desert; betray, let down, break one's heart.

jingle *v.* **1** *His keys jingled in his pocket:* jangle, ring, clank, clink, clatter, tinkle.
—*n.* **2** *The jingle of bells announced the arrival of the ice-cream van:* ringing, clang, tinkle, tintinnabulation, jangle, reverberation. **3** *That jingle has been played to death on the radio recently:* a catchy poem or song, singing commercial, commercial tune, ditty, singsong advertisement; facetiae, burlesque poem or verse, trivial verse, doggerel, limerick.
◇ *Word origin: Jingle* was created to imitate

the light ringing or tinkling sounds it represents.

jinx *n. It seemed as if there were a jinx on her holiday:* evil spell, evil eye, curse, plague, ill wind, malevolent charm; nemesis, bugbear, bugaboo.

job *n.* **1** *It was my job to see that all orders were carried out quickly:* work, task, responsibility, charge, assignment, duty, business, affair; commission, mission, chore, errand, undertaking, function, role, part, stint, concern, care, trust; enterprise, activity, exercise, performance, accomplishment, achievement. **2** *He took a job as a night-watchman:* post of employment, position, situation, engagement, appointment, place, opening; means of support, occupation, career, living, livelihood, business, line of business; capacity, role, part, function, office; profession, vocation, field, province, calling, pursuit, métier, trade, craft, kind of work. **3** *They were paid according to the number of jobs they completed:* unit of work, assignment, contract, commission; completed effort, piecework, lot, allotment, quota, portion, share, output, product.

jocular *adj. He was a jocular man, especially in the company of women:* humorous, light-hearted, given to joking or jesting, sportive, witty, jocose, facetious, jolly, jocund, jovial, merry, gay, mirthful, laughter-loving, full of fun, playful, rompish, prankish, roguish, frolicsome, waggish; entertaining, amusing, droll.
Ant. grave, earnest, sober, solemn.
◇ *Word origin: Jocular* goes back to the Latin word for joke, *jocus.*

jog *v.* **1** *The pony cart jogged down the bumpy road:* trot, bounce, jar, rock, jiggle, jounce, shake, jostle, joggle, bob, jerk. **2** *The mention of his name jogged my memory:* nudge, stir, activate, energize, actuate, stimulate, prompt, animate, set going.
—*n.* **3** *Give the pendulum a little jog to start the clock:* jerk, pull, twist, wrench, shake, twitch; *Informal* yank, tug.

join *v.* **1** *We joined the pieces of material by sewing their edges together:* bring together, connect, conjoin, fasten, tie together, marry, couple, bind, fuse, unite, piece together; splice, merge, mix, blend, combine, pool; chain, link, bridge. **2** *Use some paste to join the broken ends:* cement, glue, stick together, stick, hold fast, attach, paste; cohere, bind, connect, unify, unite, solder, fix. **3** *Two rebel groups joined forces to overthrow the government:* unite, ally, combine, merge, bring together, consolidate; federate, amalgamate, conglomerate, associate, confederate, syndicate; hold together, get together, meet, fraternize, cooperate. **4** *We joined the country club:* become a member of, associate oneself with, sign up with, enrol in, enlist in, enter, subscribe to. **5** *The living-room joined the patio:* adjoin, border on, verge on, be adjacent to, conjoin, be contiguous with; connect with, meet, reach, touch, abut; hug, skirt, scrape, brush, graze.
Ant. 1, 2 disjoin; part, separate, sever, sunder; detach, disengage; disentangle, untangle, divide, disconnect. **4** leave, resign, quit.

joint *n.* **1** *He suffers from arthritis in his leg joints:* part where joining occurs, place of joining, connection, articulation, juncture, junction, hinge; nexus, link, knot; (*variously*) ankle, hock, knuckle, knee, elbow.
—*adj.* **2** *The canvassing was a joint effort by both organizations:* mutual, common, shared, sharing or acting in common, community, communal, hand-in-hand, collaborative, collective, co-operative, coalitional, conjoined, conjunctive; combined, allied, united, corporate, unified, associated, associate, consolidated; like-minded, unanimous.
Ant. 2 individual, solitary, lone.

jointly *adv. They took care of that problem jointly:* together, in common, by combined action, conjointly, mutually, by mutual consent, collectively, in conjunction, in association, unitedly, in unison; *Informal* arm in arm, hand in hand, side by side.
Ant. separately, individually, on one's own.

"Nothing reveals a man's character better than the kind of joke at which he takes offence." —*G. C. Lichtenberg*

---

joke *n.* **1** *A lampshade on his head was his idea of a joke:* jest, pleasantry, diversion, playful or mischievous trick or remark, play of wit, horseplay, facetiousness, whimsy, frolic; practical joke, gag, jape, monkey business, prank, caper, frolic, antic, lark; funny story, anecdote, shaggy-dog story, bon mot, wit, witticism, pun, quip, badinage, repartee, wisecrack, banter, satire, parody, lampoon, farce, travesty, burlesque. **2** *He was the joke of the town because of his tough-guy dress:* object of joking or ridicule, butt, laughing-stock; simpleton, fool, buffoon, clown, town fool, village idiot, bumpkin. **3** *The job was so easy it was a joke:* trifle, nothing, mere nothing, snap of the fingers, child's play, lark, farce, no great matter, a little thing, nothing to speak of, nothing worth mentioning.
—*v.* **4** *He was always joking about when there was work to be done:* jest, clown, crack jokes, play the fool, frolic, gambol; *Slang* mess about, horse around, wisecrack. **5** *They joked about his ineptitude:* poke fun at, make jokes about, mock, ridicule, make merry with, laugh to scorn, make game of, gibe at, laugh at, smile at, chortle, laugh up one's sleeve, snicker, deride, pooh-pooh, scoff at, jeer at; play a practical joke upon, send on a fool's errand, put on, dupe, gull, take in, fool, tease; *Slang* roast.
◇ *Word origin: Joke,* like *jocular,* comes from Latin *jocus,* joke.

joker *n.* **1** *Bunter was the form joker:* clown, jester, comedian, funny man, wit, wag, life and soul of the party, madcap, zany, humorist, punster, mimic, buffoon.

jolly *adj. We had a jolly time at the party. She's my jolliest aunt:* happy, merry, gay, mirthful, funny, gleeful, delightful, rollicking, jocund, jocular, jovial, merry, droll, high-spirited, playful.
Ant. solemn, grave, serious; lugubrious, morose, dour, saturnine.

jolt *v.* **1** *The news of his illness really jolted me out of my complacency. The bumpy road caused the old car to jolt and rattle:* startle, disturb, perturb, upset, take aback; shake, jar, shake up, shock, stun, *Informal* throw; jerk, jog, bump, bounce, convulse, joggle, jump, bob, jiggle, jostle.
—*n.* **2** *The news about her nephew was a jolt to her. We were shaken by the jolts of the train going over the points:* shock, jar, start, thunderbolt, trauma; set-back, reversal, shaking, bounce, jounce, twitch, jerk, joggle, jostle, jog, bump, lurch, agitation, jiggle, quiver, quake.

jostle *v. The students jostled each other on the staircase as they went to their classes:* shove, bump, push roughly, hit against, collide, run against, shoulder, elbow, butt, push, knock against, prod, jab, poke.

jot *v.* **1** *She jotted down the main points that the ecologist was making:* write quickly, put down, take down, set down, make a note of, make a memorandum of, note, scribble; list, record, register, enter.
—*n.* **2** *The fact that he was leaving didn't upset me a jot:* the least bit, one little bit, one iota, speck, whit, bit, dot, mite, trace, trifle, particle, snip; modicum, scintilla, snippet.
◇ *Word origin: Jot* and *iota* were originally the same word. In the 17th century calligraphers began writing the capital *I* so elaborately that it developed into our *J*, which became a consonant while *I* remained a vowel. Many words now spelt with *j* were formerly spelt with an *i*.

journal *n.* **1** *She kept a journal of her activities:* daily record, diary, register, chronology, almanac, record, daybook, notebook, calendar, chronicle, memorandum, record book, memory book, year-book, history, scrapbook, album; memoirs, autobiography, confession; *Naval* log, log-book; *Bookkeeping* ledger, account book. **2** *He is always writing articles for learned journals:* magazine, publication, periodical, monthly, quarterly, annual; newspaper, paper, gazette, chronicle, tabloid, sheet, daily, weekly.
◇ *Word origin: Journal* comes from Latin *diurnus*, daily, hence a daily record. *Journey*, *diary*, and *diurnal* (occurring by day, belonging to the day, the opposite of nocturnal) are also based on this same Latin word.

journey *n.* **1** *His journeys took him all over the world:* travelling, trip, tour, walk, expedition, trek, excursion, outing, jaunt, wandering, divagation, peregrination, roving, odyssey, pilgrimage, quest; flight, voyage, course of travel, cruise; route, itinerary, transit, circuit, passage, way.
—*v.* **2** *He journeyed round the world:* travel, tour, make a trip, divagate, peregrinate, trek, fly, voyage, sail, navigate, cruise, course, ramble, roam, rove, wander, pilgrimage, wend, meander, tramp.
◇ *Word origin: Journey* originally meant a day's travel. It comes from Latin *diurnus*, daily. See also JOURNAL.

jovial *adj. King Cole was a kind, jovial man:* cheerful, merry, gay, mirthful, gleeful, cheery, blithe, jocund, jolly, hearty, jocular, jocose, sunny, buoyant, delightful, sportive, playful, frolicsome, fun-loving, laughing, humorous, hilarious, rollicking.
Ant. saturnine, dour, morose, gloomy, lugubrious, melancholy.
◇ *Word origin:* A *jovial* person should certainly be good-natured because *jovial* means "born under the influence of Jove," the benign chief god of the Roman pantheon.

jowl *n. Squirrels can carry nuts in their jowls:* jaw, cheek, flesh of the lower face, mandible, muzzle (*of an animal*), *Informal* chops.
◇ *Word origin: Jowl* comes from an Old English word *ceafl.* At first sight the two words look very distant, but here is a list of some of the intervening forms, which help to show how *ceafl* became our *jowl*: *cheafl, chavel, chawle* and *jowle.* The *j* did not appear until the 17th century, and the reasons for some of these changes are not entirely understood.

joy *n.* **1** *She was filled with joy upon the birth of her grandchild:* delight, happiness, gladness, exultation, satisfaction, rapture, fullness of heart, ecstasy, elation, excitement, cheerfulness, glee, gaiety, exhilaration, delectation, jubilation, enjoyment, pleasure, contentment. **2** *Her children were the joy of her life:* cause of gladness, source of pride or satisfaction, treasure, prize, pride, precious possession.
Ant. 1 sorrow, misery, despair, unhappiness, grief. **2** bane, trial, tribulation.

joyful *adj.* **1** *He was joyful to see his brother again:* delighted, jubilant, happy, glad, pleased, exultant, cheerful, elated, full of joy, ecstatic, overjoyed, enraptured, transported, beside oneself with joy, gladsome. **2** *The birth of the baby was a joyful event:* happy, gladsome, pleasing, heart-warming, causing or bringing joy, delightful, blessed, rosy, cheerful, bright, pleasurable, heartening, gratifying.

joyous *adj. Their 50th wedding anniversary was a joyous occasion:* happy, glad, gladsome, joyful, wonderful, rapturous, gay, merry, cheerful, light-hearted, gratifying, pleasurable, heartening, heart-warming, delightful.
Ant. sad, unhappy, joyless.

jubilant *adj. When he won first prize, he was jubilant:* joyful, overjoyed, ecstatic, flushed with excitement or pleasure, in good or high spirits, exultant, rejoicing, rapturous, delirious, radiant, enraptured, exuberant, elated, exhilarated; cheerful, joyous, merry, mirthful, gay, gladdened, glad, gladsome, delighted, smiling, laughing, happy, gleeful, pleased, gratified, jolly, light-hearted, cheery; blithe, blithesome, buoyant, rhapsodic, enrapt, charmed, captivated, intoxicated; *Informal* happy as a lark, merry as a cricket, walking on air, tickled pink, happy as the day is long.
Ant. doleful, sorrowful, despondent, sad, melancholy, *Informal* down in the dumps.

judge *n.* **1** *They asked him to be a judge at the cake-making contest:* official, arbitrator, arbiter, moderator, juror, adjudicator; critic, reviewer, censor; referee, umpire. **2** *She was a good judge of character:* critic, assessor, appraiser, evaluator, connoisseur.
—*v.* **3** *He has judged many cases in his 25 years on the bench:* rule on, settle, pass sentence, pronounce judgement on, administer justice, adjudge, adjudicate, arbitrate, sit in judgement on, determine, decide, find, announce a verdict; conduct, try, review, hear; referee, umpire. **4** *I can't judge which one I like better. He judged the time to be about noon:* decide, ascertain, find, resolve, determine, discern, distinguish; estimate, surmise, guess, conjecture, suppose, believe, assume, imagine, fancy; adjudge, consider, regard, deem, conclude; infer, deduce; *Informal* reckon. **5** *She was always judging people according to their taste in clothes:* appraise, rate, rank, assess, value, weigh, gauge, size up, analyse.

judgement *n.* **1** *In the jury's judgement he was guilty as charged:* decision, finding, ruling, verdict; decree, sentence; adjudication, arbitration. **2** *She always had poor judgement in picking friends:* discretion, taste, judiciousness, discernment, discrimination; perceptiveness, perception, sense, shrewdness, acumen, percipience. **3** *The reviewer's judgement was that the play would be a success:* opinion, appraisal, belief, conviction, conclusion, deduction, persuasion, estimate, valuation, assessment, view.

judicial *adj.* **1** *His guilt or innocence will be decided by judicial process:* judiciary, jurisdictional, juristic, legal, official. **2** *He acted in a very judicial manner both inside and outside the court:* judgelike, magistral, magisterial, majestic, imposing, impartial, distinguished, befitting a judge.
◇ *Usage note:* See JUDICIOUS.

judicious *adj. That was not a particularly judicious way of handling the interview:* sensible, wise, sagacious, sage, perspicacious, sound of judgement, discriminating, discerning, astute, knowing, sound, level-headed, reasonable, clear-sighted, acute, shrewd, sober, sober-minded, percipient; diplomatic, politic, tactful, thoughtful, reflective, prudent, well advised.
Ant. injudicious, imprudent, unsound; tactless, thoughtless, unreasonable.
◇ *Usage note: Judicial* refers to a judge or to an official decision made by a judge: *The lawyers awaited the judicial decision of the Chief Justice. Judicious* refers to any wise, sensible, or well-considered decision, speech, or act: *The doctor's decision to operate proved to be judicious.*

> **Exploring the Word**: The Romans had two words for law, *jus* and *lex*. From Latin *jus* we get: *judge*, one who speaks the law; *judicial*, of the law, legal; *jurisdiction* (Latin *dicere*, to speak), the area in which a law or legal position is "spoken" or applied; *jurisprudence* (Latin *prudentia*, knowledge), knowledge or the philosophy of the law; *jurist*, one who practises the law, as a judge or lawyer; *justice*, that which is legally right; *jury*, those sworn to hear legal evidence; and *injury*, not lawful, not just, a violation of another's rights. From *lex*, law, we get *legal*, of the law; *loyal*, law-abiding, oath-keeping, hence faithful; and *legislation*, from *legis latio*, literally the bringing forward of a law.

jug *n. She filled the jug with wine:* vessel, pitcher, ewer, jar, urn, crock, decanter, bottle, flagon, carafe, demijohn, tankard, mug, container.

juggle *v.* **1** *He was able to juggle five plates and sing at the same time:* practise jugglery, keep aloft, keep objects in play. **2** *The accountant juggled the company's books and embezzled thousands of pounds:* manipulate, falsify, misrepresent, modify, disguise, reorganize, meddle with.

jumble *v.* **1** *Someone has jumbled the files, and now I can't find anything:* mix confusedly, mix up, throw together, toss at random, pitch, strew about, turn topsy-turvy, scatter, pile up, shuffle, heap, bunch.
—*n.* **2** *His room was a jumble of clothes, newspapers, and beer bottles:* confusion, mixture, disarray, tangle, muddle, medley, conglomeration, mix, accumulation, aggregate, mélange, miscellany; mess, chaos, clutter, tumble, hotchpotch, gallimaufry, farrago, pot-pourri, stew, salmagundi, mishmash, patchwork, olio; *Informal* something the cat brought in, everything but the kitchen sink.
Ant. **1** separate, isolate; order. **2** order, system, arrangement.

jump *v.* **1** *He not only avoided cracks in the pavement — he jumped over them:* leap, hop, skip, vault, spring, bounce, pitch, bound; buck, prance, gambol. **2** *The car jumped the railings and went over the cliff:* skip, go over, hurdle, overrun, not be held back. **3** *She jumped whenever someone*

came up behind her: start, flinch, wince, recoil. **4** *The professor was always jumping from one topic to another:* skip, pass, digress, switch, change abruptly, move quickly. **5** *The price of meat jumped ten pence in one month:* increase or rise suddenly, climb rapidly, rocket, zoom up.
—*n.* **6** *One jump and you'll be over the fence:* bound, leap, vault, skip, hop, spring. **7** *Though it was only a small jump, his horse landed in the ditch:* obstacle, obstruction, barrier, barricade, impediment, hurdle. **8** *In May there was a considerable jump in sales:* sudden rise, increased volume, upturn; surge, swift increase, boost, increment, augmentation.

junction *n. The policeman directed the traffic at the junction of the two main roads:* convergence, juncture, link-up, joining place, conflux, concurrence, confluence, joining, connecting point, crossroads, intersection, fork.

Exploring the Word: Latin *jungere*, to yoke, join, gives us *join, joint, junction*, and *juncture*. It also gives us *enjoin* and *injunction*, to ask, or a requirement, that someone join in doing something; *junta*, a group of people joined together for a secret purpose, as to take over a government; *adjoin*, to join to, and *adjunct*, something joined to something else; *conjugal*, pertaining to those joined in marriage; *conjunction*, used in grammar to refer to words that connect or join together other words, phrases, and clauses, and *conjugation*, which refers to joined-together classes of verbs; and *subjugate*, literally to put under the yoke. *Jungere* also gives us *jugular vein*, because it is the vein passing the point where the collar bones are *joined* to the spine.

juncture *n.* **1** *At that juncture, he decided to proceed with his original plans:* point of time, occasion, moment, interval, pass; critical point, crisis. **2** *We placed the wiring at the juncture of the two walls:* junction, joining, joint, connection, seam, mutual edge, closure, point of contact, meeting, intersection. **3** *The signs were put at the juncture of the two mountain paths:* intersection, convergence, confluence, joining place, joining, junction, link-up, connection.

jungle *n. Tarzan lived in the jungle. Some parts of this city are no better than a jungle:* rain forest, wilderness, wild impenetrable land, unexplored territory, virgin forest, bush, wild, swampy forest; undergrowth, dense vegetation; uncivilized territory, lawless region, savage environment.
Ant. civilization, civilized territory.
◇ *Word origin: Jungle* comes to us via Hindustani *jangal*, jungle, from Sanskrit *jungala*, wilderness.

junior *adj.* **1** *I spoke to Mr. Smith junior:* younger, minor. **2** *He was the junior member of the committee:* lesser, subordinate, lower, secondary, inferior, minor, second-string; more recent, newer, later.
Ant. 1, 2 senior, elder, older; superior.
◇ *Word origin: Junior* is the comparative form of Latin *juvenis*, young, hence "younger," which also gives us *juvenile* (youthful), *juvenilia* (works produced by an author or artist in youth), and *rejuvenate* (to make young again). Latin *juvenis* (young) comes from the same Indo-European root from which are derived our originally Germanic native-English words *young* and *youth*.

junk *n. We took all the junk out of the basement:* rubbish, litter, discarded material, clutter, trash, debris, refuse, waste, odds and ends, cast-offs, oddments, rummage, scrap, *Slang* garbage.

jurisdiction *n.* **1** *The university had no jurisdiction since the crime happened outside the hall of residence:* judicial right, lawful power, authority, prerogative, legal right, say, control, dominion, command, sway, rule. **2** *The sheriff's jurisdiction was only within his own county:* extent of authority, scope of power, overlordship, province, dominion, hegemony, domain, district, circuit, sphere, compass, zone, range, reach, scope, bounds, beat, quarter, area, latitude, field.

just *adj.* **1** *He was a just man who listened to both sides of each complaint:* fair, equitable, even-handed, fair-minded, impartial, unbiased, unbigoted, unprejudiced; trustworthy, honest, moral, upright, uncorrupt, good, decent, blameless, ethical, principled, scrupulous, upstanding, high-minded, righteous, honourable, conscientious, above-board, open to reason; disinterested, dispassionate, objective. **2** *He had just cause for anger:* reasonable, sensible, justified, justifiable, sound, balanced, logical, based on knowledge and understanding; well-grounded, well-founded, firm, solid, strong. **3** *All in all, I think life imprisonment was a just sentence:* deserved, fair, justified, equitable, justifiable, worthy, merited, due, condign; suitable, appropriate, fitting, proper, befitting; logical, reasonable, adequate, acceptable.
—*adv.* **4** *I have just seen her:* a brief time ago, a moment ago, but a moment before, a little while ago; a short time ago, not long ago, recently, lately, only now. **5** *The roast came out just right. That's just what he told me, too:* exactly, precisely, in all respects, completely, fully, entirely, perfectly, absolutely, quite. **6** *He just managed to gain second place:* by a narrow margin, narrowly, by a hair's breadth, barely, by a little, only just, no more than, hardly scarcely. **7** *He was just a poor man:* only, nothing but, merely, but, no more than, simply, at most.
Ant. 1-3 unjust. **1, 2** devious, corrupt; untrue, dishonest, prejudiced, unfair, unreasonable, partial, unlawful, inequitable. **3** undeserved, unfit, inappropriate.

justice *n.* **1** *In the name of justice, all men should be* *equal before the law:* righteousness, goodness, probity, right, uprightness, fairness, fair play, rightness, justness, equity, equitability, equitableness, honour, truth, honesty, integrity, virtue. **2** *He had justice on his side:* legality, right, proper cause, legitimacy, lawfulness, the law, constitutionality; justification. **3** *Is there no justice after a crime like this?:* due punishment, reparation, penalty, chastisement, correction, atonement, amends, redress, satisfaction, just deserts, compensation, payment, remuneration.

Ant. 1-3 dishonesty, favouritism, inequity, injustice, partiality, unfairness, unlawfulness, unreasonableness, untruth, wrong.

justify *v. In some cases the end justifies the means:* vindicate, excuse, prove right, show to be just, warrant, support, validate, uphold, sanction, confirm, sustain, bear out, defend, account for, explain, make explanation for.

jut *v. The pier jutted out over a shallow bay:* extend, protrude, stand out, project, beetle, thrust forward, stick out, poke out, bulge, overhang, shoot out.

◇ *Word origin:* A rock can *jut* or stick out of a mountainside in somewhat the same way as water can *jet* or spout out of a hose; both are thrust out or thrown forward. *Jut* arose 500 years ago as a variant of *jet.*

juvenile *adj.* **1** *The film was aimed at a juvenile audience. He acted in a very juvenile manner for a grown man:* young, youthful, adolescent, junior; immature, childish, infantile, puerile, callow, boyish, girlish, babyish.

—n. **2** *Property may not be owned by a juvenile:* minor, youth, stripling, child, infant.

Ant. 1 adult, mature, matured, grown-up, fully-fledged; senile; manly, womanly. **2** adult, older person.

◇ *Word origin: Juvenile* comes from Latin *juvenis,* a young person, which also gives us *juvenilia, junior,* and *rejuvenate.* It was first used by Francis Bacon in an essay which was published in 1625.

K

keen *adj.* **1** *The knife was old, but the blade had a keen edge:* sharp, fine, finely honed, sharp as a razor, razorlike, paper-thin. **2** *He had the keenest faculties and a phenomenal memory:* sharp, shrewd, astute, acute, penetrating, incisive, alert, quick-witted, clever, discerning, perspicacious, discriminating. **3** *We were keen on going to the picnic. He had a keen appreciation of art:* eager, enthusiastic, impatient, excited; intense, fervid, ardent, earnest, fervent, avid, zealous, impassioned, fierce.

Ant. 1, 2 blunt, dull, obtuse. **3** apathetic.

keep *v.* **1** *We kept all the gifts Aunt Mary gave us. He kept the family name:* retain, hold, possess, preserve, maintain, conserve, *Informal* hang on to. **2** *Try to keep your clothes in the wardrobe. They kept a supply of fancy towels in their shop:* hold, store, place, deposit, accumulate, heap, stack, pile; have, lay in, furnish, carry, stock. **3** *She kept her niece for a week while her sister was ill:* care for, take care of, look after, mind; extend hospitality to, have as a guest; guard, watch over, safeguard, keep an eye on. **4** *Peter Peter Pumpkin Eater had a wife and couldn't keep her:* support, provide for, supply with the necessities of life, sustain, pay for, maintain. **5** *Keep everybody away from the accident! The parade kept the traffic from moving:* hold, hold back, keep back, restrain; encumber, stall, retard, impede, inhibit, arrest, constrain, prevent; obstruct, block, hinder, bar, hamper, hamstring, cramp, clog, hobble, tie up, shackle; detain, delay, hold up, deter. **6** *He kept at his studies and graduated with distinction:* continue, carry on, keep up, persist in; stay, abide, stick, remain, stand, maintain, be constant, persevere, endure, be steadfast. **7** *We always keep the religious holidays. See that you keep the law:* observe, hold, pay heed to, celebrate, solemnize, honour, ritualize, commemorate; obey, comply with.

—n. **8** *He earned his keep by doing odd jobs:* room and board, board and lodgings, sustenance, daily bread; subsistence, support, living, livelihood, maintenance. **9** *The ruins of the medieval keep were still standing after 600 years:* fortress, stronghold, donjon, fortification, fort, citadel, castle, tower.

Ant. 1 discard, abandon, give up, lose. **5** release, liberate, free; speed, expedite, hurry. **7** ignore, disregard.

◇ *Word origin: Keep* is from Old English *cepan,* to observe, to see, to comply with. *Keep* in the sense of "stronghold inside a castle" was introduced by Sir Philip Sidney into English in his classic romance *Arcadia* (1590).

keeper *n.* **1** *Only the keeper was allowed inside the animal cages:* gamekeeper, attendant, guard. **2** *He was the keeper of the art collection. Am I my brother's keeper?:* curator, caretaker, guardian, warden, custodian, retainer, conservator; governess, chaperon, duenna, nurse, nursemaid, wet-nurse; protector, bodyguard, guardian angel; guard, sentinel, sentry, escort; gaoler.

keepsake *n. She kept the partially-torn photograph as a keepsake of her lover:* memento, memory, token of remembrance, souvenir, remembrance, token, reminder, relic; symbol, emblem.

keg *n. Kegs of beer were delivered to the pub:* barrel, cask, drum, butt, vat, tank, container, tun, tub, puncheon, hogshead, kilderkin.

kerchief *n. She wrapped a kerchief round her head:* scarf, muffler, cloth, handkerchief, neckerchief, cravat, neckcloth.

◇ *Word origin: Kerchief,* a square of fabric for covering the head, comes from Old French *covrir* (to cover) + *chief* (head).

kettle *n. The water boiled in the kettle:* tea-kettle, pot, pan, saucepan, cauldron, crucible, tub, vat, tureen, boiler.

key *n.* **1** *He used his key to open the door:* opening device, opener; (*variously*) latchkey, master-key, passkey, skeleton key, house key. **2** *Her story provided the key to the mystery:* crucial determinant, solution, explanation, answer, meaning, translation, interpretation, elucidation, resolution, finding, explication, light, exposition; cue, clue, indicator, indication, indicant; point, pointer. **3** *The instruments were tuned to the key of E. The arrangement involved her singing in different keys:* tonality; scale, mode.

—*v.* **4** *We tried to key the programme to a younger audience:* adjust, fit, suit, adapt, address, direct, gear.

kick *v.* **1** *The footballer kicked the ball over the goal:* strike with the foot, punt, boot, hit, strike. **2** *Shot-guns often kick back after firing:* recoil, spring back, jump back, fly back, rebound. **3** *The landlord kicked him out of his flat for not paying the rent:* eject, throw out, cast out, turn out, remove, send packing, show the door, evict, oust from, send about one's business; *Slang* give the boot to, boot out. **4** *Informal I have always kicked against Bill's ideas:* complain, fuss, make a fuss, protest, grouch, object, remonstrate, grumble, find fault, grouse, fret, fume, growl, *Slang* gripe, beef.

—*n.* **5** *He gave the ball a hard kick:* a hit with the foot, boot, stroke; act of kicking. **6** *The kick of the shot-gun made him fall backward:* recoil, kick-back, springing back, rebound, return, reaction, backlash. **7** *Slang Sailing gave him quite a kick:* thrill, pleasure, excitement, amusement, fun, enjoyment; great satisfaction, gratification. **8** *Slang The spices really gave the salad a kick:* flavour, pungency, high seasoning, tang, intensity, punch, sparkle, snap, dash, piquancy; pep, verve, zest, vigour, vim, power, force, vitality, life, animation.

kid *n.* **1** *The kids were kept in the smallest field:* young goat, yearling; billy-goat, nanny-goat. **2** *The gloves were made of kid:* goatskin, goat-hide, goat-leather. **3** *Informal The kids had a great time at the party:* child, little one, youngster, tot, moppet, shaver, lad, kiddywink; juvenile, adolescent, teenager; baby, infant.

—*v.* **4** *Slang They kidded him because he grew a beard. She was only kidding him when she said she'd marry him:* tease, plague, harry, make fun of, mock, laugh at, make sport of, jest, hoax, make game of, *Slang* rag, rib, ride; ridicule, fool, mislead, delude, trick, deceive, hoodwink, gull, bamboozle, cozen, beguile, bluff.

Ant. 3 adult, grown-up.

kill *v.* **1** *The prisoners killed a warder during the escape:* murder, slay, slaughter, cut down, put to death, assassinate, butcher, massacre, shoot down, shoot, mortally wound, injure fatally, end the life of, take the life of, dispatch, put an end to, get rid of, do in, do away with, silence, wipe out, exterminate, put to sleep, deal death to, shed blood, spill blood, execute; *Slang* knock off, bump off, finish off, (*variously*) strangle, garrotte, smother, asphyxiate, gas, suffocate, drown, poison, electrocute, hang, lynch, string up, bring to the gallows, behead, guillotine, bring to the block, decapitate, cut the throat of, burn to death, burn at the stake, put to the sword, put to the knife, run through, dismember, hack or chop to pieces, tear limb from limb, draw and quarter, disembowel. **2** *Her constant nagging quite killed his ambition:* extinguish, defeat, destroy, ruin, break, check, put a stop to, halt, stay, quell, stifle, smother, finish off.

Ant. 1, 2 enliven, bring to life, revitalize.

killing *n.* **1** *The killing of the two children made the headlines:* murder, slaying, annihilation, homicide, manslaughter, massacre, violent death, death by violence, slaughter, carnage, elimination, extermination, decimation, butchery, bloodshed, capital punishment, execution, electrocution, fatality; (*variously*) shooting, stabbing, strangulation, strangling, garrotting, guillotining, decapitation, lynching, hanging, poisoning, impalement, flogging to death, beating to death, stoning to death, burning to death; patricide, matricide, regicide, fratricide, sororicide, uxoricide, infanticide, suicide; crucifixion, martyrdom, immolation. **2** *Grandfather was lucky enough to make a killing on the stock-market:* stroke of luck, master-stroke, success, coup, windfall, bonanza; *Slang* big hit, smash hit; cleaning up, clean-up.

—*adj.* **3** *He raised his sword for a killing blow:* lethal, mortal, deadly, causing death, deathly, fatal, death-dealing. **4** *He had a killing toothache:* extremely painful, excruciating, murderous, devastating.

kind[1] *adj. Although he tried to appear gruff, he was basically a kind man:* kindly, benign, generous, good-hearted, tender-hearted, soft-hearted, tender, gentle, compassionate, merciful, good-natured, affectionate, charitable, warm-hearted, big-hearted, sympathetic, understanding, well-meaning, considerate, thoughtful; amiable, obliging, cordial, gracious, accommodating, amicable, friendly, neighbourly, good-humoured, well-disposed, gentle, polite, courteous, civil.

Ant. unkind, cruel, harsh, merciless, severe.

kind[2] *n. What kind of dessert do you like best?:* sort, type, brand, variety, style, description; cast, mould, nature, genus, genre, designation, breed, ilk, strain, caste.

kind-hearted *adj. Her kind-hearted deeds showed her to have a generous nature:* kind, kindly, benign, good-hearted, tender-hearted, compassionate, kindly disposed, charitable, philanthropic, good, warm-hearted, soft-hearted, good-natured, sympathetic, generous, humanitarian, humane, loving, affectionate, gentle, gracious, warm, merciful, accommodating, helpful; understanding, thoughtful, considerate, well-meaning, well-intentioned, altruistic, amicable.

Ant. hard-hearted, cold-hearted, cold, selfish, unkind, cruel, harsh, severe, unsympathetic.

kind-heartedness *n. Her kind-heartedness was shown in the many things she did for other people:* kindness, kindliness, benefaction, goodness, goodness of heart, tenderness, compassion, kindly nature, good nature, unselfishness, sympathy, understanding, benevolence, magnanimity, charitableness, philanthropy, altruism, humanitarianism, humaneness, love for mankind, goodwill, goodwill towards one's fellow men, humanity, mercy; graciousness, consideration.

Ant. unkindness, cruelty, meanness, selfishness, indifference, cold-heartedness.

kindle *v.* **1** *He kindled the logs in the fireplace:* enkindle, ignite, set on fire, set fire to, cause to start burning, light, apply a match to, *Informal* stick a match to. **2** *The orphan's plight kindled the woman's maternal instincts:* stir, arouse, rouse, stir up, inspire, call forth, waken, awake; enkindle, fire, stimulate, agitate, intensify, provoke, induce, incite, inflame, excite, invigorate, quicken, animate; sharpen, whet, foment, urge, prod, goad.

Ant. 1, 2 smother, stifle, extinguish, quench.

kindling *n.* **1** *We sent the boys to collect kindling for the bonfire:* tinder, firewood, material that burns easily, fuel; (*variously*), brush, brushwood, twigs, small branches, paper, shavings. **2** *The kindling of the logs in the fireplace brought warmth to the room:* setting fire to, igniting, ignition, enkindling, burning, flaming, lighting, firing, combustion.

kindly *adj.* **1** *He was a kindly man, helping those less fortunate than himself:* kind, benign, good, generous, warm-hearted, soft-hearted, affectionate, devoted, tender, compassionate, gentle, charitable, merciful, sympathetic, philanthropic, benevolent, magnanimous, warm, humanitarian, big-hearted, humane, friendly, understanding, patient, considerate, tender-hearted, good-natured, well-meaning, neighbourly; amiable, gracious, cordial, good-humoured, courteous, amicable.

—*adv.* **2** *The nurse behaved kindly towards her patients:* benignly, generously, warm-heartedly, warmly, soft-heartedly, affectionately, tenderly, compassionately, gently, charitably, mercifully, sympathetically, philanthropically, benevolently, magnanimously, humanely, big-heartedly, understandingly, considerately, tender-heartedly, good-naturedly, well-meaningly, amiably, cordially, graciously, good-humouredly, amicably, well-manneredly, civilly.

Ant. 1 unkindly, malevolent, malign, malicious, spiteful, unsympathetic; mean, cruel, harsh, severe. **2** unkindly, malevolently, malignly, maliciously; spitefully, unsympathetically, meanly, cruelly, harshly.

kindness *n.* **1** *One often depends on the kindness of strangers:* kindliness, benevolence, generosity, benefaction, beneficence, mercy, charity, charitableness, philanthropy, humanity, humanitarianism, humaneness, magnanimity, goodness, goodness of heart, sympathy, compassion, unselfishness, consideration, understanding, patience, toleration, tolerance, grace, graciousness; goodwill, goodwill towards one's fellow men, brotherly love, friendly feelings, warm feelings. **2** *I've never forgotten her past kindnesses to me:* kind act, humane gesture, kindly gesture, good deed, act of charity, act of generosity, good turn, act of grace, generosity, benefaction, bounty, gift, favour, kind office, help, aid, assistance, generous treatment.

Ant. 1 unkindness, malevolence, harshness, cruelty, severity, sternness, roughness, austerity. **2** cruel or unkind act, evil deed.

"Kindness is very indigestible. It disagrees with very proud stomachs."

—*William Makepeace Thackeray*

---

kindred *adj. We were kindred spirits and entirely compatible:* like, allied, closely related, similar, corresponding, alike, matching, resembling; united, harmonious, agreeing, accordant, congenial, sympathetic, *Spanish* simpático; consanguine, intimately related.

Ant. alien, unrelated, uncongenial, different.

◇ *Word origin:* See KIND[2].

king *n. We arrest you in the King's name:* monarch, ruler, sovereign, liege lord, His Majesty, suzerain, crowned head, anointed ruler, royal personage, the anointed, royal person, potentate, protector, defender of the faith, emperor.

◇ *Word origin: King* comes from Old English *cyng* (pronounced *king*), which originally meant "son of the royal *kin*."

◇ *Usage note:* See PRESIDENT.

kingdom *n. He ruled his small kingdom fairly and justly:* realm, nation, country, dominion, domain, land, territory, state, principality, duchy, dukedom, empire, monarchy.

kink *n.* **1** *He brushed the kinks out of the horse's mane:* twist, tangle, coil, crimp, crinkle, frizz, knot, frizzle. **2** *It took us two days to smooth out all the kinks in our plan:* complication, hitch, defect, rough spot, difficulty, flaw, imperfection, loose end, tangle, knot. **3** *An excessive fondness for black was the only kink in his personality:* peculiarity, eccentricity, oddity, mental twist, twist, idiosyncrasy, quirk, queerness, weirdness, foible; freakishness, singularity, vagary.

◇ *Word origin: Kink* comes from Dutch *kink*, hitch (in a story), twist, kink. It was originally a navigational term. Its earliest English sense is as a twist in a ship's rope. By the later 18th century it had started to be used in a wider context.

kinsman *n. She awaited the arrival of her kinsmen from Spain:* relative, blood relative, relation, blood relation, kin, sib, fellow countryman, fellow citizen; (*variously*) father, mother, sister, brother, aunt, uncle, grandmother, grandfather, cousin, child, offspring, son, daughter, heir, parent.

kiss *v. She kissed her aunt fondly when she arrived:* touch with the lips, greet with a kiss, kiss the cheek, kiss the hand, osculate; *Archaic* buss.

◇ *Word origin: Kiss* comes from Old English *cyssan* (pronounced *kissan*), which is in turn derived from a now-lost word in Common Germanic that was ancestral to Modern Germanic *kuss* and *küssen*. This word has always meant exactly the same thing.

kit *n. He took his repair kit from the garage and started to overhaul the engine:* set of tools, instruments, implements, utensils; equipment, supplies, devices, gear, outfit, necessaries, provisions; things, paraphernalia, accoutrements, trappings, impediments, furnishings, rig.

◇ *Word origin: Kit* is from Middle Dutch *kitte*, tankard — an important item in any medieval drinking man's *kit*.

kitchen *n. All meals were prepared in the kitchen:* room equipped for cooking, scullery, galley, cookhouse, *French* cuisine, *Spanish* cocina; bakery, bakehouse.

◇ *Word origin: Kitchen* is from Latin *coquina*, kitchen (derived from *coquere*, to cook). Thus *cook* and *kitchen* have the same Latin root. The originally French word *cuisine* (kitchen, style of cooking) is also related, as in the Italian *cucina*.

knack *n. I wish I had the knack of cooking. He had a knack for foreign languages:* skill, talent, facility, gift, ability, aptitude, adroitness, dexterity, dexterousness, finesse, expertise, genius, faculty, flair, natural endowment, cleverness, ingenuity, quickness, readiness, proficiency, efficiency, competence, capability, capacity, forte, bent, inclination, propensity, turn.

Ant. ineptitude, clumsiness, awkwardness; disability.

knave *n. The knave cheated her out of her savings:* rascal, scoundrel, blackguard, rogue, varlet, reprobate, culprit, scallywag, scamp, rapscallion, cad, rotter, bounder, wretch, good-for-nothing; *Slang* rat, cur, dog, con man, phoney.

Ant. hero, gentleman.

◇ *Word origin: Knave* is an example of a word whose meaning has become devaluated or debased over the centuries (a process technically called *pejoration*). A *knave* was originally any youth, and later meant a young male servant. It comes from Old English *cnafa*, page.

kneel *v. Don't forget to kneel at the altar:* bow, bend the knee, bow down, genuflect, fall on one's knees, curtsy; make obeisance, prostrate oneself; (*variously*) kowtow; salaam, fall at the feet of.

knick-knack *n. She had little knick-knacks on shelves all over the house:* small object, trifle, bagatelle, bauble, trinket, toy, plaything, gewgaw, gimcrack, thingumajig, frippery, bric-à-brac, *French* bibelot.

knife *n.* **1** *It's very difficult to get a knife sharpened properly these days:* cutting tool, blade, cutter, cutlery; (*variously*) pocket-knife, penknife, jack-knife, paring knife, switch-blade knife, bowie knife, skinning knife, hunting knife, bread-knife, table-knife, carving knife, surgical knife, scalpel, palette knife, flick-knife, pruning knife, machete, stiletto, dirk, dagger.

—*v.* **2** *The thugs knifed him in the attempted robbery:* cut, stab, wound, lacerate, cut apart, slash, mutilate, cut down, run through, pierce.

"A man may as well open an oyster without a knife, as a lawyer's mouth without a fee."

—*Barten Holyday*

---

knight *n. We read about King Arthur and the Knights of the Round Table:* soldier, man-at-arms, warrior, fighter, fighting man, arms bearer, horseman, equestrian, Templar; defender, protector, guardian, champion, paladin, hero, vindicator, brave person, gallant, cavalier; gentleman, man of rank.

◇ *Word origin: Knight* is an example of a word whose meaning has become glorified over the centuries (a process technically known as *melioration:* compare *knave*). A *knight* was originally any youth and later meant a military follower. The word comes from Old English *cniht*, boy.

knit *v.* **1** *She knitted scarves whilst she was convalescing:* weave, do needlework, interweave, twist, intertwine, stitch, tat, plait, braid, crochet. **2** *Our common interests knitted the group together:* draw, draw together, ally, join, connect, unite, unify, bind, link. **3** *He knitted his brow in contemplation:* wrinkle, knot, crease, furrow.

◇ *Word origin:* If you have *knots* in your *knitting*, be reassured that to *knit* and to *knot* have always been closely related. Both come from Old English *cnyttan*, to tie.

knob *n.* **1** *We replaced the knobs on all the doors:* rounded handle, handle, handhold, hold, grip; lever, latch. **2** *We used sandpaper to smooth out the knobs on the wood:* lump, hump, knot, knurl, knur, snag, bulb, tubercle, nub, node, convexity, protuberance, protuberancy, protrusion, bulge, swell, swelling, polyp, projection, prominence.

knock *v.* **1** *There was definitely somebody there when he knocked at the door:* rap, tap, hit, strike, bang, thump, thud. **2** *They knocked the building down to make room for the new road:* pound, demolish, smash, batter, hammer, raze. **3** *The assailant knocked the man to the ground:* hit, strike, smite, slam, slap, pummel, pound, beat, thwack, kick, push, jostle, dash, cuff, swat; *Informal* belt, batter, crack, smack, clout, wallop, sock. **4** *Informal The critics knocked her last play:* criticize, find fault with, belittle, disparage, deprecate, peck at, cavil, carp at, abuse, lambaste, cry out against, decry, reprehend, inveigh against, censure, cut to pieces, condemn; *Slang* rap, murder. —*n.* **5** *His amnesia was caused by a knock on the head:* stroke, hit, thump, thwack, bang, tap, rap, pat, slap; blow, smack, whack, punch, cuff, smash, bump, glancing blow, crash, crack; *Informal* sock, clip, clout, bat, lick. **6** *Informal You have to take certain knocks in life:* set-back, failure, defeat; reprehension, censure, condemnation, criticism, fault-finding.

knot *n.* **1** *The rope was tied in a knot:* interlacement, twist, loop, braid, plait; (*variously*) slip-knot, sheet-bend, half hitch, hitch, hawser fastening, reef knot, running knot, surgeon's knot, figure-of-eight knot, flat knot, single knot, double knot, overhand knot, midshipman's knot, hangman's knot, bowline knot, granny. **2** *The sweater was decorated with small knots of embroidery:* ornament, rosette, loop, braid, frogging, star; shoulder knot, epaulette. **3** *Knots of flowers grew by the fence:* cluster, bunch, clump; gathering, circle, group, assemblage, collection; bundle, pack, lump, heap, pile, mass. **4** *She wore her hair in a knot:* bun, chignon, braid, plait, top-knot, French roll, tuft.

◇ *Word origin: Knot* comes from Old English *cnotta*, knot, which is related to Old English *cnyttan*, to tie, which gives us our word *knit*.

knotty *adj.* **1** *We panelled the play room with knotty wood:* knobby, full of knots, gnarled, nodular, unsmooth, rough, uneven, rough-grained, coarse, coarse-grained, rugged, bumpy, knurled; flawed, blemished, snaggy. **2** *He deliberated for hours over the knotty problem:* difficult, thorny, tricky, complex, problematical, complicated, hard, tough, perplexing, puzzling, intricate, baffling, ticklish, troublesome.

Ant. 1 smooth. **2** plain, simple, obvious, easy.

know *v.* **1** *How did you know I'd be here? He knew the job was difficult:* be certain, be sure, apprehend, realize, discern, be positive, be confident, have no doubt, feel certain, be assured, have knowledge, have information about, be informed, recognize, perceive, notice, see, be cognizant of, be wise to; understand, make out, be aware of; be intelligent, be smart, be sagacious; *Archaic* wot of. **2** *He knew the lay-out of the room:* have knowledge of, have in one's head, be acquainted with, be familiar with, have at one's finger-tips; *Informal* have pat; know inside out, know backwards, know by rote, know by heart, know full well. **3** *We know many people in show business:* be acquainted with, be familiar with, enjoy the friendship of, be on good terms with, be close to, be on intimate terms with; *Informal* be thick with, rub shoulders with, be on a good footing with; have dealings with. **4** *You really ought to know by now when you can tease him and when you can't:* distinguish, identify, be able to distinguish, discern, discriminate, make out, perceive; perceive differences, recognize differences, tell one from the other.

Ant. 1 be ignorant or illiterate, overlook, misunderstand, misconstrue. **3** be unacquainted with, be unfamiliar with.

knowing *adj. She gave us a knowing look when the subject was broached:* meaningful, significant, expressive, eloquent, fraught; conscious, aware, perceptive.

Ant. blank, dull, empty.

"Bodily exercise, when compulsory, does no harm to the body; but knowledge which is acquired under compulsion obtains no hold on the mind." —*Plato*

---

knowledge *n.* **1** *I was surprised by the breadth of her knowledge:* learning, scholarship, erudition, education, wisdom, intelligence, ken, schooling, cultivation, enlightenment, information, *Informal* book-learning. **2** *He had no knowledge of his past actions:* awareness, realization, consciousness, perception, sense, cognizance, recognition, familiarity, memory, inkling, comprehension.

Ant. 1 ignorance, illiteracy, inexperience, misunderstanding, unfamiliarity, unawareness.

knowledgeable *adj. He was quite knowledgeable about current events:* well-informed, abreast of, conversant with, cognizant of, acquainted with, no stranger to, versed in, at home in, familiar with, *French* au courant, au fait.

known *adj. The mystery man was a known star of stage and screen. It is a known fact that he was once a millionaire:* recognized, acknowledged, familiar, popular, celebrated, famous, well-known, noted; apparent, obvious, evident, palpable, manifest, self-evident, plain, distinct, patent, definite, common.

Ant. unknown, unfamiliar, unrecognized; secret, unpublished, unrevealed.

kudos *n. Informal His brave deeds brought him kudos from the high command. You won't gain any kudos from that cowardly retreat:* glory, praise, laudation, admiration, honour, high regard, esteem, prestige, celebratedness, fame, celebrity, repute, renown, distinctive mark.

◇ *Usage note: Kudos* is a long-neglected word recently revived by journalists seeking a fresh synonym for "glory, plaudit, honour."

◇ *Pronunciation tip: Kudos* may be pronounced either *KOO-doss* or *KEW-doss.*

◇ *Word origin: Kudos* comes from Greek *kudos,* glory. The word originated in the 18th century slang of Oxford and Cambridge universities.

L

label *n.* **1** *All the items in the sale had special labels on them:* tag, ticket, sticker, sign, stamp, mark, name, seal, docket, brand, tally; identification, designation, classification, appellation, specification, inscription; earmark.
—*v.* **2** *Make sure you label all the test-tubes:* mark, note, tag, ticket, docket, mark off; name, classify, describe, title, define, denominate, characterize, put a mark on, earmark, brand.

◇ *Word origin:* In Old French *label* means "ribbon" and may go back to Dutch *lap,* rag, patch.

labour *n.* **1** *Much labour went into the building of the pyramids:* exertion, effort, industriousness, laboriousness, plodding, menial work, manual labour, travail, struggle, sweat of one's brow. **2** *Most of the firm's labour is idle:* manpower, employees, workers, work-force, labourers, blue-collar workers. **3** *She went into labour two weeks early:* birth pangs, birth throes; parturition, accouchement.
—*v.* **4** *He laboured in the mines for 30 years:* work, drudge, toil, travail, sweat, slave, work like a slave, struggle, work day and night, *Informal* work one's fingers to the bone, grind away, plug away; occupy oneself with, busy oneself with, employ one's time. **5** *He laboured under unfortunate delusions of grandeur:* smart under, suffer, agonize, be the victim of, be affected by, be troubled by, be burdened by.

Ant. 1 rest, repose, relaxation, leisure, respite, ease. **4** rest, relax.

◇ *Word origin: Labour* is the Latin word for toil, distress.

> "There is no real wealth but the labour of man." —*Percy Bysshe Shelley*

laboured *adj.* **1** *The old man moved in a laboured manner:* ponderous, heavy, stiff, wooden; difficult, strained, forced, cramped, halting; awkward, maladroit, clumsy. **2** *His so-called witticisms are so laboured:* strained, forced, contrived, unnatural, unspontaneous, drawn-out, heavy, ponderous; self-conscious.

Ant. 1, 2 easy, natural, simple, light.

labourer *n. He began his career as a labourer in South America:* workman, worker, labouring man, working man, navvy, toiler, manual worker, wage-earner; hand, hired man, menial, hired hand, hireling, drudge, plodder, site worker, handyman.

lace *v.* **1** *The child has learnt to lace up his shoes:* tie, fasten, secure, bind, close, draw together, tie up, tighten, make fast; make taut, strap, truss, tether, lash, braid. **2** *Somebody has laced the punch with rum:* add spirits to, flavour, make more tasty, spice up, suffuse, infuse, fortify, strengthen, intermix, *Informal* spike.

Ant. 1 unlace, untie, unfasten.

◇ *Word origin:* Both *lace* and *lasso* come from Latin *laqueus,* noose, snare. *Lace* is, literally, a network of dainty nooses.

lacerate *v. The broken glass lacerated her arm:* slash, cut, lance, gash, puncture, wound, stab, slice, tear, rip, sever, scratch, scar, deface; hurt, inflict pain, give pain, pain, torment, distress, torture, agonize, excruciate.

◇ *Word origin: Lacerate* comes from Latin *lacerare,* to mangle.

lack *n.* **1** *His lack of a university education rankled as he grew older. A lack of food caused her to grow weak:* want, absence, deficiency, need; neediness, privation, deprivation; scarcity, scantness, dearth, shortage, exhaustion, depletion; omission.
—*v.* **2** *He lacked the connections necessary to get his business started:* miss, need, be short of, fall short of, want, be found wanting, be deficient in, be inadequate, be insufficient, be missing, fail to reach the mark, be short.

Ant. 1 sufficiency, adequacy, competence;

abundance, copiousness, plentifulness; excess, superfluity, surplus, plethora. **2** have, hold, possess, own, enjoy.

◇ *Word origin: Lack* goes back to Middle Low German *lak,* deficiency.

lackadaisical *adj. He was lackadaisical and his boss knew it. She dressed in a lackadaisical manner:* indifferent, mindless, listless, lifeless, lax, inanimate, spiritless, unexcited, unexcitable, uninspired, unambitious, unaspiring, unmotivated, idle, loafing, dilly-dallying; languid, lethargic, phlegmatic; uninterested, indifferent, unconcerned.

Ant. animate, spirited, excited, inspired, ambitious, intense, diligent.

◇ *Word origin: Lackadaisical* comes from Shakespeare's phrase *alack the day* ("Oh woe the day of disgrace or failure").

lackey *n. The king was always surrounded by his lackeys:* attendant, servant, assistant, helper, retainer, employee, hireling, minion, underling, inferior, slave, menial, flunkey; follower, mercenary; (*variously*) waiter, usher, page, squire, steward, butler, valet, cupbearer.

laconic *adj. Although his speeches were laconic, they were informative:* short, concise, brief, succinct, terse, compact, condensed, sparing of words, pointed, to the point, summary; curt, blunt.

Ant. voluble, wordy, loquacious, garrulous, verbose, windy.

lad *n. Our news-boy was an enterprising lad:* boy, youth, youngster, young man, schoolboy; stripling, shaver, sprig, kid; young fellow, young chap.

◇ *Word origin: Lad* comes from Middle English *ladde,* boy, "kid." It is of unknown origin. In some present-day dialects the word is still much used in direct address ("Come along now, my lad"). This was its original use.

lady *n.* **1** *Her bearing and appearance indicated that she was a lady:* well-bred woman, respectable woman, woman of refinement, woman of good family, gentlewoman; wife, spouse. **2** *The ladies were dressed in their finest gowns:* woman, matron, female. **3** *The lady of the manor received us graciously:* woman of rank, noblewoman, peeress, aristocrat; (*variously*) duchess, countess, viscountess, marchioness, baroness.

◇ *Word origin:* A *lady's* place was originally in the kitchen baking bread. *Lady* literally means "bread-kneader," from Old English *hlāf* (loaf, bread) + *daege* (kneader). If modern women are disturbed by this origin for *lady,* they should remember that a *lord* was not originally a lord and master but meant "a keeper of the loaves."

ladylike *adj. That wasn't a very ladylike thing to say:* (*of a woman*) well-bred, well-mannered, polite, courteous, mannerly, genteel, decorous, refined, dignified, well brought up; cultured, polished, cultivated, proper, respectable, civil.

Ant. unladylike, ill-bred, ill-mannered, impolite, discourteous, unmannerly, rude, unrefined, uncultured, hoydenish.

◇ *Spelling tip:* People sometimes forget that the *y* in *lady* does not change to *i* in the word *ladylike.* Remember: *ladY, ladYlike.*

lag *v.* **1** *The smallest boy always lags behind:* trail, drag behind, drag, be behind, linger, loiter, dawdle, tarry, delay, be slow, slacken, hang back, inch along, limp, trudge, falter, stagger, halt; procrastinate, dally, take one's time, dilly-dally, be idle, be late, be tardy, be overdue.

Ant. 1 lead, go ahead, hurry along.

lair *n. The fox was caught in his lair with the carcass of the chicken he had stolen:* den, retreat, resting-place, sanctuary, hide-out, lie, haunt, covert; hole, burrow, cavern, hidey-hole, earth, sett.

◇ *Word origin:* A *lair* is where an animal beds down. The word comes from Old English *leger,* bed.

laissez-faire Also **laisser-faire** *n. The new administration will adopt a policy of laissez-faire towards industry:* non-intervention, non-interference, let-alone principle, let-alone policy; unconcern, indifference; live and let live, leave well alone, let them be.

◇ *Word origin:* We have taken the term *laissez-faire* directly from French *laissez* (let) + *faire* (do), hence let others (in trade and industry) do as they will, without governmental controls, a policy of non-interference.

lame *adj.* **1** *He walked with an elegant cane, but he was not lame:* crippled, disabled, limping, halt, maimed, infirm, hobbled; game, unsound, deformed; feeble, faltering, weak, halting. **2** *His lame excuse did not withstand close questioning:* weak, feeble, inadequate, clumsy, insufficient, deficient, flimsy, wanting, failing, unconvincing, unpersuasive, ineffectual, unsatisfactory.

Ant. 2 bold, convincing, effectual, effective.

"Youth is nimble, age is lame."
—*William Shakespeare*

---

lament *v.* **1** *Tennyson lamented the death of his friend in a poem:* mourn, weep, bewail; deplore, show concern for, complain about, express pity for, regret, sympathize with, commiserate with, condole with.

—*n.* **2** *We could hear her laments through the closed door:* lamentation, sob, plaint, cry, moan, wail, outcry, keening, ululation, wail, whimper; mourning. **3** *The minstrels chanted their laments before the king:* dirge, song of lamentation, threnode, death song, funeral music, requiem.

◇ *Word origin: Lament* comes from Latin *lamentum,* weeping, wailing. Shakespeare first recorded the noun in English.

◇ *Pronunciation tip: Lamentable* should be pronounced by stressing the first syllable. Thus, *LAM-en-ta-ble* is correct.

lamp *n. I need a better lamp to read by:* light; (*variously*) electric light, battery lamp, gas light, oil-lamp, lantern, reading-light, head-light, ceiling light, ceiling fixture, standard lamp, table-lamp, night-light, chandelier, wall-light, spotlight, floodlight, searchlight, beacon, sun-lamp, heat-lamp.
Word origin: Lamp comes from Greek *lampē*, torch, lamp, related to *lampein,* to shine.

lampoon *n.* **1** *The magazine lampoon on the present political scene was outrageous:* satire, burlesque, parody, mockery, spoof, travesty, farce, pasquinade, diatribe, caricature; *Informal* send up, take-off, put-on.
—*v.* **2** *The school magazine lampooned the current administration:* satirize, parody, burlesque, caricature, make fun of.
◇ *Word origin:* An old French drinking-song gave us the word *lampoon,* a sharp but humorous attack or spoof. The song's refrain was the word *lampons,* "let us drink." Perhaps early sarcastic remarks were followed by the refrain, either to toast the wit who had said it or for the wit and his target to drink together as friends again.

lance *n. All the king's soldiers were equipped with lances:* spear, javelin, pike, halberd, shaft, harpoon, gaff.
◇ *Word origin: Lance* is from Latin *lancea,* a light spear. Romans were aware that *lancea* was not a native Latin word and wondered where it did come from. Some thought it came from a language spoken in pre-Roman Spain. Others thought it derived from Greek *longkhē,* spear; we may never know the true derivation.

land *n.* **1** *We live on the land, not the sea:* ground, earth, dry land, mainland, terra firma. **2** *This land is good for growing vegetables. We own land in Essex:* ground, soil, earth, subsoil, dirt, loam, humus; terrain; real estate, realty, property, real property, grounds, acres. **3** *He wanted to visit the land his father came from:* country, nation, commonwealth, state, republic, dominion, realm, empire, domain, kingdom, colony, settlement; region, territory, terrain, zone, area, district, section, vicinity, location; fatherland, motherland, homeland, native land, native soil, the old country. **4** *If you stood on the roof, you would see the land for miles around:* country, county, district, countryside, region, province, shire, canton, riding, parish, ward, acreage, acres, fields, tract, terrain, grassland, cornfield, wheat field, farmland, meadow, lea, pasture, grass, park, lawn, green, village green.
—*v.* **5** *We landed at Luton airport on schedule:* come in for a landing, descend, come down, alight, light, settle; *Informal* set down; make a three-point landing. **6** *The ship landed on Saturday:* dock, come to land, put into port, make port, arrive at land, anchor, reach land, put into the harbour, put in, drop anchor, moor, tie up; put into shore, set foot on dry land, make land, debark, disembark, lay anchor. **7** *His conduct will land him in gaol one day. He landed six new accounts:* lead one to, carry one to, bring one to; lay hold of, catch, gain, secure, get, win over, clinch, seize, grab, capture, *Informal* nab; take, snare, net.
◇ *Word origin: Land* comes from Old English *land,* "land" (in most of that word's present day senses and a few more meanings which it no longer has). The root meaning seems to have been "open land, common." Our word *lawn* comes from the related Middle English *laund,* pasture.

landlord *n. The landlord collected the rent personally every month:* landholder, land-owner, property owner, owner, possessor, holder, freeholder, householder; lord of the manor; squire.
Ant. tenant, lessee, renter.
◇ *Word origin:* Today *landlords* usually own and rent houses or buildings to others. Originally, in feudal times, a *land lord* was truly a lord of the land, a nobleman who owned land or a manor under a grant from the king.

landscape *n.* **1** *One look at the landscape persuaded him to settle there:* natural scenery, scenery, scenic view, scene, view, vista, spectacle, panorama, sight. **2** *She preferred a good landscape to a portrait:* painting or drawing of countryside, scenic representation, rural scene.

lane *n. There were many narrow lanes in the village:* narrow thoroughfare, path, passageway, footpath, way, road, roadway, drive, alley, alleyway, passage, pass, bypath, course, route, trail, access, approach, byway.

language *n.* **1** *He spoke the language of his country:* speech, tongue, vocabulary, idiom, vernacular, mother tongue, native tongue, *Informal* lingo; dialect, patois, jargon; slang, colloquialism, cant, argot. **2** *The inarticulate student has problems with language:* oral communication, self-expression, reading and writing, verbal intercourse, discourse, spoken language, elocution, public speaking; words, vocabulary. **3** *I never could understand the language of the law:* vocabulary, wording, phraseology, speech, prose, parlance, verbiage, expression, idiom, rhetoric, use of words; manner of speaking or writing, diction, idiom, mode of expression, jargon. **4** *Watch your language — there are ladies present!:* profanity, cursing, swearing, imprecation, profane talk, *Informal* cussing.
◇ *Word origin:* A literary word for *language* is "tongue." The ancients also used this image, as our word *language* comes from Latin *lingua,* tongue. From *lingua* we also get our words *linguistics, lingo,* and *lingua franca.*

languid *adj.* **1** *The illness made him feel languid:* faint, feeble, weak, weary, drooping, sickly, declining, indisposed, debilitated, unhealthy, unsound, unstable, doddering, infirm, on the decline, fatigued, exhausted, enervated, worn-out, spent; rickety, shaky, trembling; lackadaisical, languorous, sluggish, torpid, apathetic, inert, inactive, supine. **2** *It was one of those hot, languid days when moving about was an effort:* sluggish, listless, inanimate, inert, apathetic, lifeless, lethargic, languorous, spiritless, dull, heavy, torpid, slow, leaden.

Ant. 1 strong, tireless, active, energetic, vigorous, robust.

◇ *Word origin:* See LANGUISH.

languish *v.* **1** *He lost his accustomed vigour and languished in the tropical climate:* go into a decline, droop, faint, diminish, wilt, wither, deteriorate, give away, break down, wane, ebb, waste away, become ill, take sick, sicken, go downhill, dwindle, fail. **2** *He languished for the sight of his family:* pine for, sigh for, be desirous of, yearn for, hunger for, hunger after, long for, thirst for; *Informal* have a hankering for; desire, covet, hunger, thirst.

Ant. 1 luxuriate, thrive, prosper, flourish, bloom.

◇ *Word origin:* Both *languid* and *languish* come from Latin *languere,* to be weary.

lanky *adj. Although his brother was stocky, he himself was extremely lanky:* lank, tall and thin, lean, bony, scrawny, skinny, raw-boned, angular, gaunt, spare, gangling.

Ant. burly, husky, brawny, muscular, sinewy; plump, portly, rotund, chubby, fleshy, stocky, stout, fat, short, full, rounded.

lap *v.* **1** *The kittens lapped up the milk:* lick, lick up, tongue, drink, sip. **2** *From the beach chalet we could hear the waves lapping on the shore:* ripple, slosh, wash, splash, plash, babble, murmur, bubble, gurgle.

◇ *Word origin: Lap* comes from Old English *lapian,* to lap up. The same Indo-European root is present in Latin *lambere,* to lick, from which we get our literary word *lambent,* flickering (like flames licking over a surface) or luminous (like eyes in which fire is reflected).

lapse *n.* **1** *His lapse of manners was unforgivable:* breach, disregard, dereliction, error, slight mistake, omission, slip, peccadillo, oversight, fault, flaw, negligence, delinquency, laxity, infraction, blunder, faux pas, *Informal* boner; loss, failure, failing, shortcoming, fall, forfeiture. **2** *His lapse into drunkenness followed a long run of bad luck:* decline, descent, downfall, drop, backsliding, relapse, regression, wane, slump, deterioration, degeneration, falling off. **3** *After a lapse of a century, the custom has been revived:* elapsing, period, interval, process of time, interval, interim, interlude; intermission, interruption, respite, pause, recess, *Informal* break; hiatus, gap.

—*v.* **4** *He lapsed into a coma and never recovered:* fall, slip, decline, sink, collapse; worsen, backslide, relapse, recede, deteriorate, degenerate, wither, sag, droop; drop, slump down. **5** *The guarantee lapsed two months ago:* expire, become obsolete, run out, terminate, lose validity, fall into disuse.

◇ *Word origin: Lapse* comes from Latin *lapsus,* slip, error.

larceny *n. The thief was charged with larceny:* stealing, theft, robbery, burglary; pilferage, pilfering, purloining, misappropriation, looting, sacking, depredation, absconding, embezzlement, extortion, bilking, cheating, swindling, defalcation, fleecing, fraud, forgery, plagiarism; house-breaking, shoplifting, safe-cracking; petty larceny, petit larceny, grand larceny.

◇ *Word origin: Larceny,* the unlawful removal of the property of others, comes to us via Anglo-French *larcin,* from Latin *latro,* mercenary. (In all times and climes, *mercenaries* have been notorious as plunderers.)

larder *n. The cook kept the tinned food in the larder:* pantry, food cupboard, buttery, supply room, store-room, spence, still-room.

◇ *Word origin:* Originally a *larder* was a storehouse for bacon. *Larder* and *lard* both come from Latin *lardum,* lard, bacon fat.

"It's as large as life, and twice as natural!"
—*Lewis Carroll*

---

large *adj. They lived in a large house. He was given a large allowance. He had a large capacity for learning. He was of large build:* big, huge, great, grand, massive, immense, enormous, gigantic, spacious, capacious, vast, roomy, expansive, sizeable, imposing, Brobdingnagian; substantial, considerable, ample, goodly, liberal, unstinted, copious, extravagant, exorbitant; comprehensive, extensive, wide, broad, sweeping, far-reaching, unlimited, limitless, boundless, high; mighty, towering, hulky, strapping, heavy, rotund, obese, fat, portly, plump, overgrown, outsized, ponderous, monstrous, giantlike, colossal, gargantuan; magnificent, stupendous; *Informal* king-sized, man-sized.

Ant. small, little, tiny, diminutive, minute; brief, inconsiderable, infinitesimal; narrow, paltry, petty, scanty, sparse, short, trifling, trivial, slight, slender, slim, thin, pint-sized.

◇ *Word origin: Large* comes from Latin *largus,* ample, generous, which also gives us *largess;* the musical directions *largo* (drawn out, extended) and *larghetto* (fairly slow).

largely *adv. He owed his success largely to hard work:* mostly, mainly, chiefly, for the most part, by and large, on the whole, primarily, principally, generally, predominantly, to a great extent, greatly, substantially, considerably; extensively, widely.

largess Also **largesse** *n. She was known for her largess to those less fortunate:* generosity, benefaction, kindness, benevolence, bounty, philanthropy; donation, gift, offering, bestowal, boon, favour, assistance, aid, help, charity, mercy, benignity; reward, payment, remuneration, gratuity.

◇ *Word origin:* See LARGE.

lark *n. The banker went to the amusement arcade for a lark:* escapade, frolic, fling, spree, caprice, whim; *Informal* joke, kick, high old time; trick, prank, antic, caper, game, sportiveness.

lascivious *adj. He was blackballed by the club for lascivious conduct:* indecent, obscene, lewd, immoral, improper, lustful, ribald, bawdy, prurient; filthy, vulgar, gross, coarse, indelicate, salacious, squalid, foul, dirty, dirty-minded, impure, unwholesome, immodest, lecherous, sordid, lurid; shameless, wanton, unblushing, licentious, depraved, ruttish.

◇ *Word origin: Lascivious* is from Latin *lascivus,* lustful. Our originally Germanic word *lust* is in fact related to the Latin *lascivus,* lustful, and so is the old word *list* (to desire), as in *If your ladyship list.*

lash[1] *v. The robbers lashed the bank manager to a chair:* tie, bind, tie up, fasten, secure, leash, rope, make fast, truss, pinion, strap; tether, brace, moor, attach, fix, hitch.

lash[2] *n.* **1** *The pirate captain beat his crew with a lash:* whip, scourge, cat-o'-nine-tails; strap, thong. **2** *The criminal was sentenced to 50 lashes:* whip blow, stroke, hit, stripe.

—*v.* **3** *The wagon driver lashed the horses:* whip, whip up, flog, thrash, lambaste, flail; horsewhip. **4** *Rain lashed against the window-pane:* beat, strike, smack, hit, knock, buffet, pound, hammer.

lass *n. All the young lasses were there in their prettiest dresses:* girl, young woman, schoolgirl, maiden, maid, female, miss, virgin; wench, damsel, colleen, lassie, lovely, pretty.

lassitude *n. His lassitude was caused by overwork:* weariness, weakness, debility, sluggishness, fatigue, tiredness, exhaustion, lack of energy, enervation, lethargy, inertia, feebleness, indolence, faintness, torpor, torpidity, drowsiness, languor, languidness, supineness, prostration, dullness, droopingness; apathy, indifference, ennui, doldrums, boredom.

Ant. vigour, energy, strength, robustness, freshness; verve, spirit, vitality; *Informal* get-up-and-go, push, vim, pep.

◇ *Word origin: Lassitude* is a state of extreme fatigue or torpor. It comes from Latin *lassus,* tired.

last[1] *adj. The hero is shot in the last act. She always had to have the last word. He was the last boy in the line:* final, conclusive, concluding, terminal, ultimate, extreme, farthest, furthest, utmost; rearmost, hindmost, behind, at the end, trailing, tagging along, bringing up the rear.

—*adv.* **2** *Our horse came last in the race:* after all the others, after, behind, at the back of, in the rear, trailing, in last place. **3** *The speaker came to his main point at last:* finally, in the end, in conclusion, ultimately, eventually, once and for all, terminally.

—*n.* **4** *He was the last of my list of volunteers:* final one, concluding person or thing; rearmost one. **5** *At the last, you will not be able to repent!:* end, conclusion, crucial time, closing, ending, finish, terminus, finale; crack of doom, end of the world, doomsday, Day of Judgement, Armageddon.

Ant. 1 first, foremost, opening, introductory, initiatory; best, highest. **2** first, ahead of all others, in front. **4** first.

◇ *Word origin: Last*[1] comes from Old English *latost,* superlative form of *laet,* late, hence latest.

last[2] *v. How long did the film last? These shoes have lasted a year:* continue, go on, persist, extend, hold good, exist, survive, endure, stay, stand, remain, carry on, hold out, maintain, keep, persevere, abide, live; wear, stand up, hold up; outwear, outlive.

Ant. fail, die; end, stop, terminate, expire, depart, fade, cease; wear out, *Informal* give out, crack up.

◇ *Word origin: Last*[2] comes from Old English *lǣstan,* to follow a track, continue on course, continue. (Old English *lāst* means footstep, track—hence the shoemaker's *last.*)

lasting *adj. The diplomats tried to conclude a just and lasting peace. He had a lasting interest in art:* enduring, abiding, continuing, durable, long-term, permanent, never-ending, lifelong, long-lived, protracted; continuing a long time, of long duration, firm, steadfast, constant, incessant, perpetual, unceasing, indissoluble, indestructible; deep-rooted, deep-seated, established, firmly established, solid; persistent, lingering, chronic; eternal, immortal.

Ant. fleeting, fugitive, passing, transitory, transient, short-lived, ephemeral, momentary.

lastly *adv. Lastly, let me stress the importance of everyone's co-operation in this plan:* finally, in conclusion, in the end, at last, after all; all things considered, on the whole, taking everything into consideration, all in all, to sum up.

Ant. firstly, at the outset, in starting, in the beginning, at first.

latch *n.* **1** *Please be sure the latch on the door is secure:* lock, catch, bolt, bar, fastening; hasp, clamp, hook, snap, loop, buckle, button, clip, clinch.

—*v.* **2** *Latch the gate carefully so that the cows won't get out:* lock, bolt, fasten, secure, make fast.

Ant. 2 unlock, unlatch, unfasten, loose.

◇ *Word origin: Latch* comes from Old English

læccan, to seize; it has no cognate in other Germanic languages, and is of ultimately uncertain origin.

late *adj.* **1** *He was always late for appointments. The film was late starting because of projection difficulties:* tardy, overdue, unpunctual, dilatory, behind time; slow, delayed, detained, postponed, put off, held up. **2** *He was a late addition to the crew:* recent, new, fresh, newborn. **3** *She was an admirer of the late President:* lately dead, recently deceased; departed, passed on, gone.

—*adv.* **4** *He arrived late for his appointment:* behind time, after time, behindhand, tardily, dilatorily.

Ant. 1 early, punctual, prompt, timely, ahead of time. **2** old, seasoned. **3** alive, still living, existing, extant. **4** early, ahead of time, in advance, beforehand.

lately *adv. I've taken to making my own clothes lately:* recently, of late, not long ago, a short time ago; just now, presently, currently.

Ant. at first, originally.

latent *adj. Many of our deepest desires remain latent:* dormant, sleeping, quiescent, inactive, passive, suspended, in abeyance, abeyant, potential, undeveloped, unaroused, not manifest, hidden, concealed, covert, intangible, unapparent, unexposed, inconspicuous, unexpressed.

Ant. activated, realized, developed; manifest, expressed, apparent, evident, obvious, conspicuous.

◇ *Word origin: Latent* means not yet visible or developed, still hidden. It comes from Latin *latens,* hidden (from *latere,* to lie hidden). Related is the Greek word *lēthē,* forgetfulness (because the past is thereby *hidden*). The word is familiar to us because it gave its name to the mythical river of forgetfulness, *Lethe.*

> "Men have a much better time of it than women. For one thing, they marry later. For another thing, they die earlier."
>
> —*H. L. Mencken*

later *adv.* **1** *The others will join us later:* afterwards, at a subsequent time, in a while, thereafter, in time, presently, subsequently, tardily, thereupon, after a while, in sequel, successively, since, next, behind, from that moment, in the course of time.

—*adj.* **2** *The later arrivals had to stand at the back:* subsequent, ensuing, successive, following, succeeding, consequent, consecutive. **3** *The later works are the composer's best:* occurring late in time, mature; more recent, most recent; towards the end, latter.

Ant. 2 earlier, antecedent, prior, beforehand.

◇ *Usage note: Later* (one *t*) means more late, after some time: *See you later. Latter* (two *t*'s) means the second of two, the second mentioned: *I like both whisky and beer but I prefer the latter.* It's easy to remember: *Later* means more late and has *late* in it; *laTTer* means the second of *two* and has two *t's* in it.

lather *n.* **1** *This shampoo makes a lot of lather:* foam, shaving foam, froth, head, suds, soapsuds; spume, scum. **2** *The horse was exhausted and in a lather:* sweat, foam, froth.

—*v.* **3** *Lather your hair well before rinsing it:* soap, soap up; make froth, make foam.

◇ *Word origin: Lather* comes from Old English *lēathor,* washing soda. (Washing soda is a sodium carbonate found in nature as *natron*—a white, powdery substance which has been used since prehistoric times as an ingredient of soaps and bleaching agents.)

latitude *n. The progressive school allowed great latitude in the selection of courses:* scope, freedom of action, freedom of choice, free play, amplitude, range, liberality, full swing, sweep, margin, independence, unrestrictedness, lack of restraint, licence.

◇ *Word origin: Latitude* goes back to Latin *latus,* wide.

latter *adj.* **1** *Of your two examples, I prefer the latter:* second-mentioned, more recent, latest, later; ensuing, successive, succeeding, subsequent; last-mentioned, last; modern. **2** *Rain is predicted for the latter part of the day:* later, final, last, end, ending, terminal.

Ant. 1 former, earlier, previous; early, first, beginning. **2** first, initial, beginning, opening, commencing.

◇ *Usage note:* See LATER.

laudable *adj. Generosity is a laudable trait:* praiseworthy, estimable, admirable, commendable, worthy of admiration, deserving of esteem, meritorious, exemplary, unimpeachable, creditable, noble, sterling.

Ant. contemptible, lowly, base, unworthy, execrable, blameworthy, ignoble.

laugh *v.* **1** *The clown made the children laugh with joy:* chuckle, giggle, express mirth, roar with laughter, roar, chortle, guffaw, snicker, titter, snigger, cackle, break up, split one's sides, roll in the aisle, howl.

—*n.* **2** *The comedian finally got a laugh out of the unresponsive audience:* guffaw, giggle, chortle, burst of laughter, roar, cackle, peal of laughter, mirth, glee, snicker, snigger.

Ant. 1 scowl, glower, frown; cry, mourn. **2** scowl, glower, frown; cry.

laughable *adj. The situation was so absurd that it was laughable:* hilarious, funny, amusing, arousing laughter, worthy of laughter, risible, droll, merry, diverting, witty, comic, comical, farcical, side-splitting, rib-tickling, tickling; worthy of scorn or derision, ludicrous, ridiculous, silly, stupid, asinine, inane, preposterous, outlandish, outrageous, dopey, grotesque, foolish, absurd.

Ant. solemn, serious, grave, sombre, morose, sad, melancholy.

laughing-stock *n. You'll be the laughing-stock of the whole school in that silly outfit:* joke, butt, fool, ass, figure of fun, dupe, fair game.

launch *v.* **1** *The shipyard workers launched the freighter with a great splash:* set afloat, send down the skids, put to sea, slide from the stocks, set into the water. **2** *The firm launched the new product with a big advertising campaign:* inaugurate, begin, start, introduce, unveil, première; embark upon, set forth on, venture upon; institute, found, establish. **3** *We will launch the moon-shot tomorrow:* shoot, discharge, let fly, thrust forward, hurl, propel, project, cast forth, catapult, throw, eject, set in motion, impel, send off, fire off, fire.

Ant. 1 beach, ground; dock. **2** terminate, stop, withdraw, scrap. **3** withhold, retain, hold back.

launder *v. We'll have to launder these dirty overalls:* wash, clean, cleanse, scrub, soak, rinse, scour, wash and iron, wash out.

◇ *Word origin: Launder* and *laundry* go back to Latin *lavare,* to wash. This same Latin word gives us *lavatory* (literally "a place for washing") and *lave* (an older, chiefly literary word for "to wash").

lavish *adj.* **1** *He gave away his inheritance with too lavish a hand. Such lavish praise was hardly deserved:* free, profuse, plenteous, plentiful, extravagant, generous, effusive, prodigal, bounteous, bountiful, without limit, overwhelming, intemperate, sumptuous, opulent, luxuriant, lush, plush, over-liberal, excessive, profligate, immoderate, unsparing, unstinting, munificent, great-hearted, sumptuous; impetuous, wild, exuberant.

—v. **2** *The prince lavished money on show girls:* squander, spend freely, waste, dissipate, give excessively, bestow generously, give in profusion, over-indulge, pour out, shower, play Croesus with, fritter away.

Ant. 1 meagre, parsimonious, sparing, scanty, frugal, cheap, thrifty, provident, stingy, niggardly, tight-fisted, miserly. **2** withhold, stint, retain; begrudge.

◇ *Word origin: Lavish* comes from Old French *lavasse,* a downpour (of rain). Its source is Latin *lavare,* to wash, which also gives us *launder.*

law *n.* **1** *The legislature passed a law against racial discrimination:* rule, governing principle, regulation, mandate, commandment, established dictate, decree, legal form, enactment, precept, edict, standing order, statute, ordinance, canon, by-law, act, bill. **2** *Man cannot live without food and laws:* system of laws, collection of rules, rules of conduct, code; lawful behaviour, conformity to rules, civil peace, orderliness, legal process and provision, justice, due process of law, legality, writ. **3** *Newton's laws of motion form the foundation of classical mechanics:* principle, standard, criterion, axiom, postulate, dogma, precept, fundamental, convention, working rule, generalization, model, formulation, theorem, truth, absolute, invariable. **4** *Will you go in for law or medicine?:* jurisprudence, the practice or profession of a lawyer, legal profession. **5** *There was so much commotion that the neighbours called the law:* police, law-enforcing agency; *Slang* fuzz, copper.

Ant. 2 chaos, anarchy, caprice, disorder.

◇ *Word origin: Law* comes from Old English *lagu,* code of rules. The word is related to our word *lay,* to set down. The law is something that has been "set down."

lawful *adj.* **1** *Parking on a zebra crossing is never lawful:* legal, sanctioned by law, legally permitted, authorized, legitimate, legalized, legitimized, within the law, statutory, licit, allowed, permissible. **2** *The lawful owner claimed the car:* rightful, proper, acknowledged by law, authorized, legally entitled, legitimate, prescribed, legally recognized, granted, entitled, due.

Ant. 1 unauthorized, unlawful, illegal, illicit, forbidden. **2** pretended, disputed, illegitimate.

lawless *adj.* **1** *We must try to wipe out the lawless activities of the mob:* unlawful, contrary to law, indifferent to law, anarchic, law-breaking, illegal, illegitimate, transgressive; insubordinate, disobedient, defiant, non-compliant. **2** *A lawless crowd stormed the embassy:* disorderly, rebellious, mutinous, unruly, uncontrollable, ungoverned, chaotic, insurgent, disorganized, terrorist, refractory, riotous. **3** *At what period did Britain stop being lawless and uncivilized?:* having no laws, anarchic, heedless of law, ungoverned, chaotic, unrestrained, unbridled, wayward, free-wheeling, wide open, out of hand, wanton, licentious.

Ant. 1 obedient, lawful, law-abiding, orderly, compliant, licit, legitimate. **2** civilized, docile, restrained, disciplined, regimented, orderly. **3** well-governed, law-abiding, well-run.

lawn *n. The lawn needs mowing:* grass, greensward, grassy ground, sward, grass plot, park, meadowland, green field, terrace.

◇ *Word origin: Lawn* comes from Old French *lande,* heath, moor. An originally Celtic word, it is related to our Germanic word *land.*

lawyer *n. The court appointed a lawyer for the accused:* solicitor, barrister, attorney-at-law, counsellor, counsel, Q.C., advocate, legal adviser, counsellor-at-law, prosecutor, special pleader, *Informal* silk.

Ant. client, accused, defendant.

◇ *Usage note:* A *lawyer* is anyone who has the training and certification to practise law. An *attorney-at-law* is a lawyer who has been given the authority to act in legal matters for another. *Attorney* itself means in English specifically "one appointed to act for another in business or legal matters". It is only in the U.S.A. that it is used of any qualified lawyer who has a client. Legal *counsel* is a lawyer or group of lawyers engaged to advise a client or to conduct a case in court: *My solicitor prepared the contract. My counsel will argue my case in the court. Counsel* is also the term by which a judge often addresses or refers to a trial lawyer: *Will counsel for the defence please call his next witness?* In actual everyday use, however, *lawyer* and *counsel* overlap and may in most circumstances be used interchangeably—but it's still interesting to know some of the traditional distinctions between them.

lax *adj. The coach was too lax about training, and the team did poorly:* negligent, neglectful, irresponsible, slack, loose, heedless, careless, unheeding, slipshod, remiss, yielding, indifferent, unconscientious, undutiful, unmindful, indifferent, casual, uncaring, unconcerned, thoughtless, oblivious.

Ant. firm, scrupulous, strict, rigid, conscientious, unyielding, disciplined, severe, stern, austere, stringent.

> **Exploring the Word**: Latin *laxus*, loose, gives us *lax*, slack, *laxative*, a medicine to loosen the bowels, and *relax*, to slacken, to make less tight. The same Latin word also gives us *lease*, to *lease* property to another for his use during a stated period of time; *release*, to let loose; and *leash*, a line that lets a dog move freely on a slack lead.

lay[1] *v.* **1** *Lay the packages on the table:* put, place, set down, set, rest, repose, deposit, cause to lie. **2** *The tornado laid the house flat:* prostrate, knock down, level, fell, beat down, knock over, floor, ground, raze, throw to the ground. **3** *The nominating committee laid its proposals before the board:* forward, present, offer, proffer, enunciate, elucidate, make a presentation of, place, put. **4** *I'll lay you odds he will be late:* wager, bet, gamble, hazard; give odds. **5** *A turtle lays many eggs at once:* produce, bear, deposit, oviposit. **6** *Lay the cartons one on top of another. The tiles were laid in a geometric pattern:* place, arrange, set, align, lay out, dispose, assemble. **7** *It's a mistake to lay too much emphasis on success:* place, put, assign, allot, allocate, give, lend, apply; attribute, impute. **8** *The prisoners laid an elaborate plan to escape:* arrange, formulate, form, make, devise, concoct, organize, plan, hatch, put together.

Ant. 1 elevate, raise, lift. **2** pick up, set standing, erect, raise, lift. **3** withhold, withdraw, hide, keep secret. **6** disarrange, confuse, muddle.

◇ *Usage note:* See LIE.

◇ *Word origin: Lay*[1] comes from Old English *lecgan,* to cause to lie.

lay[2] *adj.* **1** *She serves as a lay teacher at the convent school:* non-ecclesiastical, secular, non-clerical, laical. **2** *The patient's lay diagnosis was close to the doctor's:* non-professional, unprofessional, amateur, inexpert, partly informed, non-specialist.

Ant. 1 ordained, ecclesiastical, clerical, church. **2** professional, expert, specialized.

◇ *Word origin: Lay*[2] comes from Greek *lāos,* common people.

layer *n. A layer of smog settled over the city. The gateau has three layers:* thickness, plate, leaf, sheet, coat, stratum, tier, slab, stage, zone, level, storey, bed; ply, lamina, scale.

lazy *adj.* **1** *She's too lazy to clean out the house:* idle, unwilling to work, shiftless, indolent, inert, inactive, slothful, slack, listless, lax, unindustrious. **2** *The river seems lazy today:* sluggish, lethargic, torpid, languid, langorous, slow-moving; easy-going, sleepy, drowsy.

Ant. 1 industrious, quick, energetic, active, assiduous, diligent. **2** active, brisk, stimulated, swift.

◇ *Word origin: Lazy* comes from Middle Low German *lasich,* languid, lazy.

> "There is to me something profoundly affecting in large masses of men following the lead of those who do not believe in men."
>
> —*Walt Whitman*

---

lead *v.* **1** *The tug will lead the liner into the harbour:* guide, show the way, steer, draw, direct, head, command, conduct, pilot, convey, shepherd, marshal, precede, go before. **2** *The candidate's integrity and strength led the voters to support him:* influence, persuade, attract, incline, induce, allure, lure, charm, tempt, seduce, draw, entice. **3** *The path leads down to the river:* proceed, direct, guide, advance, go, stretch, extend, aim. **4** *The vice-chairman will lead the meeting. The centre-forward leads the football team:* direct, moderate, conduct, manage, preside over, control, head, command, domineer. **5** *That nation leads in industrial output:* excel, rank first, outstrip, outdo, surpass, come first, set the pace; pioneer. **6** *The drum major led the parade:* go first, head, be in advance, top. **7** *He leads a full and active life:* pass, conduct, pursue, experience, live, have, undergo, go through. **8** *The accident led to many lawsuits:* result in, produce, branch into, tend toward, issue in, bring on.

—n. **9** *The black horse took the lead. Your candidate has a slight lead:* precedence, precedency, advance, first place, foremost position, antecedence, priority; edge, margin, advantage; plurality. **10** *The police haven't a single lead:* clue, hint, guide. **11** *Most of the clergy followed the lead of the archbishop:* guidance, model, example, direction, indication, leadership. **12** *A versatile actor is needed to play the lead:* leading role, star part; protagonist, hero, principal performer, leading man, leading lady.

Ant. 1 tail, trail. **2** disincline. **5** lag, trail.

◇ *Word origin: Lead* comes from the Old English verb *lǣden,* to cause to go.

leaden *adj.* **1** *His arms felt leaden from the heavy burden:* heavy, weighed down, numbed, deadened, torpid, languid, sluggish, listless, unwieldy, cumbersome, hard to move, inert; burdened, careworn, depressed, gloomy, glum. **2** *The sky was leaden before the storm:* dark, grey, greyish, darkened, sombre, murky, gloomy.

Ant. 1 light, feathery; active, energetic; strong, vital. **2** light, bright, clear.

leader *n. Harold was named leader of the fund-raising committee:* head, director, conductor, chief, chieftain, supervisor, commander, manager, captain, foreman, boss; forerunner, front-runner, pace-setter, pace-maker, pioneer, guide, pathfinder, trail-blazer; *Slang* bigwig, kingpin; magnate, mogul, tycoon; patriarch, godfather; master, prophet, mentor, guru.

Ant. follower, adherent, henchman, partisan, disciple.

leadership *n.* **1** *The Deputy Prime Minister took over the leadership of the country:* administration, directorship, managership, governorship, domination, hegemony, sway, stewardship, guardianship, superintendency, guidance, lead, supremacy, primacy, mastership, captaincy, headship; helm, wheel, reins. **2** *The boy showed qualities of leadership at a tender age:* ability to lead, initiative, managerial skill, authoritativeness, command, supremacy, pre-eminence, charisma; self-assurance, self-reliance.

leading *adj.* **1** *Monet was one of the leading French Impressionist painters:* foremost, most influential, most important, most significant, head, supreme, chief, prominent, notable, nonpareil, great, ranking, sovereign, prime, pre-eminent, unrivalled, unparalleled, unchallenged, principal, dominant, main, top, topmost, paramount, outstanding, stellar. **2** *Some people believe that the Rolling Stones will always be the leading pop group:* foremost in position, advance, first, prime, initial, pace-setting, advanced. **3** *My leading motive in writing the book was to enlighten the public:* principal, primary, guiding, directing, controlling, governing, ruling, motivating, prime, underlying, basic, essential, quintessential.

Ant. 1-3 secondary. **1** subordinate, inferior, supernumerary, minor, lesser, rank and file. **2** following, hindmost. **3** incidental, superficial.

leaf *n.* **1** *The leaves of most plants are green:* frond, cotyledon, blade, needle, bract, petal. **2** *The old book's leaves are dry and crumbling:* page, sheet, leaflet, folio. **3** *The leather-bound book is decorated with gold leaf:* foil, lamination, sheet of metal, lamella. **4** *The table has three leaves which can be extended:* insert, inset, extension.

—*v.* **5** *Forsythia bushes leaf in early spring:* produce leaves, green, turn green. **6** *Leaf through the book and look at the illustrations:* turn pages quickly, flip, thumb, glance, browse, skim, riffle.

league *n.* **1** *Several nations formed a defence league. Faust was in league with the Devil:* alliance, association, group, collaboration, confraternity, partnership, guild, confederacy, confederation, federation, coalition, union, fraternity, society, co-operative; conspiracy, cabal. **2** *The local schools formed a mid-week football league:* alliance, association, network, co-operative, group of competing teams.

—*v.* **3** *The feminist groups leagued together to support a woman teacher who had been sacked:* combine, merge, unite in a league, band, consolidate, ally, confederate, join forces.

Ant. 1 disunion, separation, secession. **3** divide, separate, part, secede.

Exploring the Word: Football players, lawyers, lovers, doctors, and musicians should be interested in the Latin verb *ligare,* to bind. It gives us *league,* a group bound together by common interests, as *The Football League; liable,* bound by responsibility, apt to be bound, and *liability,* responsibility, vulnerability, as a *legal liability; liaison,* a love affair; *ligament,* fibrous tissue binding or connecting bones and supporting organs; and *ligature,* a binding, in writing and printing a character of two "bound" or connected letters; and to a musician a slur indicating that a group of notes is sung or played as one connected phrase.

leak *n.* **1** *Water poured in through a leak in the ship's hull:* opening, gash, hole, aperture, puncture, fissure, crevice, cleft, crack, interstice, perforation, rupture, chink, break, breach, rent, fault, rift, rip. **2** *The leak was so slight that we barely noticed it:* leaking, leakage, draining, drain, outflow, efflux, seepage, escape, ebb.

—*v.* **3** *Both the roof and the basement leak during heavy rain. The car leaks oil:* admit leakage, be permeable, exude, seep; discharge, vent, ooze, filter, let enter or escape. **4** *An informant leaked the news to the press:* divulge, reveal, disclose, let out, make public, give away, let slip, confide, allow to become known; *Slang* blab, spill.

Ant. 4 conceal, hide, suppress.

lean[1] *v.* **1** *The exhausted runner leaned against the fence:* rest, rest one's weight, support oneself, prop oneself, recline. **2** *See how the trees lean in the wind:* bend, incline, tilt, slant, list, cant, slope; lurch. **3** *Many people lean on a personal philosophy in times of misfortune:* rely, depend, have faith in, seek solace in, resort to, take assurance from, set store by, trust in. **4** *Most of the writer's works lean towards satire. Children today lean towards casual clothes:* tend, prefer, aim, have a propensity for, be partial to.

Ant. 1, 2 stand erect, straighten up. **3** reject, withdraw from.

lean² *adj.* **1** *Lean meat is better for you than fatty meat. The prisoners looked lean and pale:* not fat, thin, spare, skinny, slender, willowy, svelte, slim, skeletal, angular, spindly, lank, lanky, raw-boned, scraggy; emaciated, gaunt, weedy, scrawny. **2** *The firm made lean profits during the early years:* meagre, scant, scanty, inadequate, small, poor, spare, insufficient, exiguous, thin, modest, slender.

Ant. 1 fatty, brawny, fleshy, burly, plump, portly. **2** full, rich, abundant, plentiful, ample, profuse.

leap *v.* **1** *The young deer were leaping about in the park:* jump, spring, bound, hop, hurtle, bounce, gambol, prance, caper, frisk, romp, cavort. **2** *The thief leapt over the wall and escaped:* jump, jump across, spring, vault, bound, hop, hurtle. **3** *Don't leap to any conclusions:* rush, hasten, jump, arrive prematurely, make unjustified assumptions, come hastily.

—*n.* **4** *The boy cleared the fence in one leap:* bound, jump, spring, hurtle, hop, vault, saltation; *French* jeté.

Ant. 1 walk, run, crawl.

learn *v.* **1** *Some people learn languages easily. All students here must learn to swim:* master, pick up, acquire knowledge of; receive instruction in, become able. **2** *We must try to learn the answer:* find out, determine, discover, detect, unearth, uncover, ascertain; *Informal* ferret out. **3** *When did you learn of Mary's divorce?:* hear, find out about, get to know, become apprised, become familiar with, become informed. **4** *The actor had trouble learning his part:* memorize, commit to memory, con.

Ant. 1 forget; teach, instruct. **4** forget.

◇ *Usage note:* Some people don't distinguish between *learn* and *teach.* The distinction is a fairly recent one. Until the mid-18th century there was nothing wrong with a sentence such as "The teacher learned the children to count." Then, for no discoverable reason, *learn* in the sense of "teach" retreated from educated society, and is now only used in a jocular or colloquial vein.

◇ *Word origin: Learn* comes from Old English *leornian,* to learn, to teach. It is closely related to the word *lore.*

learned *adj. All these books were donated to the library by a learned woman:* wise, informed, educated, schooled, accomplished, erudite; profound, deep, scholarly, well-educated, cultivated, cultured, literate, well-read, knowledgeable.

Ant. illiterate, unlettered, uneducated, unlearned, ignorant.

◇ *Pronunciation tip: Learned,* in the sense of "erudite", is pronounced as two syllables: *LUR-ned.*

leash *n.* **1** *Tie the dog's leash to the fence:* strap, lead, harness, curb, rein, line, tether, rope.

—*v.* **2** *Leash the dog if you're going on the beach. Leash your anger until you've heard the whole story:* restrain, fasten, control, curb, harness, tether; hold in, suppress, contain, stifle.

Ant. 2 unleash; unharness, release, vent.

leave *v.* **1** *Leave the room at once! The circus left town this morning:* go away from, separate from, quit, retire from, be off, depart, set out, go, exit, bid farewell, move on, move away from, embark from, decamp, fly, flee, abscond, venture away from, absent oneself; *Informal* weigh anchor; *Slang* shove off, push off, take off, split. **2** *Leave that window open, please. Just leave the dishes on the table:* let stay, let remain, keep, maintain, retain, sustain. **3** *The boy left school in the middle of the year:* abandon, forsake, depart from, surrender, relinquish, desert, leave behind, yield, give up. **4** *Leave the diagnosis to the doctor:* yield, entrust, allot, consign, give over, resign, cede, waive, eschew, forgo, release, surrender, commit, assign. **5** *The cigarette left a bad taste in my mouth:* result in, produce, deposit, generate, cause. **6** *He leaves a wife and three grown-up sons:* leave behind, be survived by. **7** *The man left most of his money to charity:* bequeath, bequest, legate, will, commit, assign, consign, allot, apportion, endow.

—*n.* **8** *The minister asked leave to take the floor:* permission, consent, allowance, indulgence, sanction, approval, endorsement, understanding, tolerance, sufferance, concession. **9** *He took his leave after thanking the host:* parting, departure, farewell, going, retreat, leave-taking, withdrawal. **10** *The platoon goes on leave for two weeks:* holiday, sabbatical, respite, liberty, recess, time off, vacation, furlough.

Ant. 1 arrive, come, appear, emerge. **3** persist, gain, hold, retain, stay, continue. **4** assume, take over. **5** remove, erase, eradicate. **8** rejection, refusal, denial, forbiddance, prohibition, interdiction. **9** stay, continuance, persistence; arrival. **10** duty.

lecherous *adj. His lecherous behaviour scandalized the whole town:* lustful, lewd, libidinous, oversexed, lascivious, salacious, prurient, satyrlike, randy, erotic, lubricious, ruttish, goatish.

Ant. prudish, strait-laced, puritanical.

lechery *n. Don Juan led a life of lechery:* hypersexuality, carnality, lust, lustfulness, promiscuity, excessive sexual desire, salaciousness, lewdness, prurience, lasciviousness.

Ant. purity, chasteness, celibacy.

lecture *n.* **1** *The sociology class heard a lecture on prison reform:* talk, address, speech, discourse, oral presentation, disquisition, oration; sermon, preachment, homily, reading, narration. **2** *Mother gave us a lecture on keeping our rooms neat and tidy:* rebuke, reprimand, admonitory speech, harangue, chastisement, admonishment, moralizing talk, cautionary speech, warning, remonstrance, censure,

talking-to, dressing down, reproof, reproach, chiding.
—*v.* **3** *The detective lectured in the local schools on drug abuse:* talk, give a talk, speak, expound, discourse. **4** *The doctor lectured his patient about smoking too much:* reprove, rebuke, take to task, harangue, rail at, scold, admonish, criticize at length, censure, chide, upbraid, moralize, preach, sermonize, hold forth.
Ant. 4 praise, compliment, applaud, laud.

Exploring the Word: Latin *legere* has three related meanings: (1) to read, (2) to choose, and (3) to gather. In its "read" meaning, *legere* gives us *lecture,* a talk read from notes; *lectern,* a reading table; *legible,* able to be read, readable; and *lesson,* a reading for study. In its "choose" meaning, it gives us *elect,* to choose, and *predilection,* a deliberately-chosen preference; *elegant,* chosen with grace or taste; *eligible,* able to be chosen; and *élite,* the chosen ones, the pick; *intelligent,* able to choose or make a distinction between things; *select,* to choose; and *neglect,* literally to leave unchosen, hence to disregard. In its "gather" meaning, *legere* gives us *collect,* to gather together; *legion,* troops gathered or chosen; and even *sacrilege* (Latin *sacer,* sacred), literally to "collect" (i.e. steal) sacred objects from a temple or shrine.

ledge *n.* **1** *The climbers advanced across a rocky ledge:* shelf, projection, offset, outcropping, sill, step, foothold. **2** *Potted plants lined the ledge in the living-room:* shelf, sill, mantel, mantelshelf, mantelpiece.

leer *n.* **1** *The stranger's leer frightened the children:* lewd look, lustful look, lascivious stare, ogle, goggle, sly glance, evil look, impolite gaze, insulting stare.
—*v.* **2** *The sailors leered at every passing girl:* stare suggestively, give the glad eye, look knowingly, look with insulting familiarity, ogle, glance wantonly, look with a leer; smirk, fleer.

leeway *n. We have a great deal of leeway to make up:* lost time, arrears, shortfall, backlog.

left-over *n.* **1** *The canal project is a left-over from the previous regime. Save the left-overs for the dogs:* residue, excess, remainder, surplus, residual, legacy, oddments, crumb, scrap, survivor, carry-over; remaining food, remaining odds and ends, leavings, waste.
—*adj.* **2** *Use the left-over roast to make hash:* remaining, residual, surplus, excess; unused, uneaten.

leg *n.* **1** *The girl continued skipping on one leg:* lower extremity, limb, member; *Slang* stick, stump, shank, pin; (*bones*) femur, fibula, tibia. **2** *One leg of the chair is cracked:* prop, support, upright, brace; post, column, pillar. **3** *We're on the last leg of our journey at last:* portion, segment, part, stage, section, lap, stretch.

legacy *n.* **1** *The man left his entire art collection as a legacy to the museum:* bequest, devise, gift; inheritance, estate. **2** *The Ionic style of architecture is a legacy from ancient Greece:* heritage, tradition; left-over, remaining portion, survivor, vestige, carry-over, transmission; heirloom; hand-me-down.
◇ *Word origin:* See LEGATION.

legal *adj.* **1** *The judge's son hopes to enter the legal profession. A legal question:* of law; juridical, jurisprudential, juristic; forensic, judicial, adjudicatory; court-room. **2** *Is it legal for bankers to serve on the municipal finance committee? Double parking is not legal:* permitted by law, lawful, permissible, rightful, sanctioned, constitutional, valid, licit, legitimate; fair, within bounds; *Slang* cricket, kosher.
Ant. 2 illegal, unlawful, illegitimate, illicit.

legality *n. The legality of the tax deduction is in question:* lawfulness, legitimacy, accordance with law; validity, licitness, constitutionality.
Ant. illegality, unlawfulness, illegitimacy, illicitness.

legation *n. The country's legation is housed near the United Nations building:* diplomatic mission, consulate, delegation, ministry.
◇ *Word origin: Legation* goes back to Latin *legare,* to send, send as a deputy, which also gives us *legacy* and *delegate.*

legendary *adj.* **1** *Len Hutton played many legendary innings for England:* famous, familiar to all, famed, known by tradition, storied, proverbial, worthy of legend, celebrated. **2** *King Arthur is a legendary figure:* fabled, mythic, mythical, figuring in legends, fanciful, imaginary, unverifiable, fabulous, apocryphal, fictitious, unsubstantiated, unauthenticated.
Ant. 1 unknown. **2** historical, authenticated, genuine.

legerdemain *n.* **1** *The magician's legerdemain drew a gasp from the audience:* sleight of hand, prestidigitation, deftness, adroitness; juggling, jugglery. **2** *The coalition was accomplished by a brilliant piece of political legerdemain:* deception, trickery, artfulness, cunning, adroit manipulation, manœuvring.
◇ *Word origin: Legerdemain* is from Old French *leger de main,* literally "light of hand."

legible *adj. The new edition is in larger, more legible type:* readable, easily read, plain, visible, decipherable, distinct, clear, neat.
Ant. illegible, undecipherable, unreadable, unclear, indistinct.

legion *n.* **1** *The ancient Roman legion had from 3,000 to 6,000 foot-soldiers:* military force, army, division, brigade, troops, corps.
—*adj.* **2** *Mahatma Ghandi's followers were legion:* multitudinous, numerous, numberless, countless, myriad, very many.

legislation *n.* **1** *Legislation is the duty of a parliament:* lawmaking, making law, passage of law. **2** *Equal rights legislation has occupied the House for many months:* legislative law, ordinance, enactment, regulation, bill, statute, amendment, act.

legislator *n. Members of Parliament and other legislators should be answerable to their constituents:* lawmaker, member of a legislature, representative, delegate, councillor, assemblyman, alderman; *American* senator, congressman, congresswoman.

> **Exploring the Word**: The Romans had two words for law, *lex* and *jus*. From *lex* we get *legal*, lawful, pertaining to the law; *legitimate*, lawful; *legislator* (Latin *legis lator*, one who brings forward a bill). From *jus* we get *justice*, *juridical*, *jurisprudence*, and *jury*.

legislature *n. How members of the legislature voted should be made known to the public:* law-making body; (*variously*) parliament, senate, congress, assembly, council, diet, Dáil, Tynwald; house, chamber.

legitimacy *n. The legitimacy of the nephew's claim to the estate is in question:* legality, validity, lawfulness, rightfulness, correctness, appropriateness, genuineness, authenticity.
Ant. illegitimacy, illegality, unlawfulness.

legitimate *adj.* **1** *Which prince is the legitimate heir to the throne?:* lawful, rightful, true, legal, licit. **2** *The workers' grievances are legitimate and must be remedied:* genuine, justified, authentic, believable, plausible, logical, sound, well-founded, just, tenable, valid, reasonable, fair; proper, correct, appropriate.
Ant. 1 unlawful, illegal; fraudulent, sham, false. **2** unfounded, unjustified, unsound, unfair.

leisure *n. Reading is a pleasant occupation for one's leisure:* free time, spare time, time off, idle hours, periods of relaxation, ease, relaxation, recreation, respite, rest, repose, diversion.
Ant. duty, work, occupation, employment, labour, business; obligation, responsibility, burden.
◇ *Word origin: Leisure* comes from Latin *licere*, to be permitted, which also gives us *licence* and *licentious*.

"Leisure is the mother of philosophy."
— *Thomas Hobbes*

---

leisurely *adj.* **1** *We went for a leisurely stroll after dinner:* relaxed, restful, unhurried, without haste, slow-moving, slow, idle, casual; languid, lackadaisical.
—*adv.* **2** *We walked leisurely, looking in all the shop-windows:* unhurriedly, slowly, lingeringly, without haste.
Ant. 1 hasty, rushed, rapid, fast, brisk. **2** hurriedly, quickly, rapidly, fast.

lend *v.* **1** *Can you lend me five pounds until payday?:* loan, allow to use temporarily, make a loan of; *Informal* let one have, trust one for; advance. **2** *A fireplace lends cosiness to a room:* impart, furnish, give, invest, supply, contribute. **3** *The community lent its full support to the mayor's plan:* contribute, give freely, put at another's disposal.
Ant. 1 borrow. **2** deprive. **3** refuse, withhold, keep.
◇ *Usage note:* See LOAN.

length *n.* **1** *The length of the track is one mile:* reach, span, distance from end to end, extent, measure, longitude, range, compass, measurement. **2** *The lot is 200 feet in length and 50 feet in width:* longer dimension, longer side, lengthiest part; *Informal* the long way. **3** *The length of the film is two hours:* duration, extent, time; magnitude, period, stretch, term, elapsed time. **4** *We'll need several lengths of string to tie the package:* piece, portion, segment, section, run, stretch.
Ant. 2 width, breadth, depth.

lengthy *adj. Be prepared for a lengthy speech after dinner:* very long, of great length, extended, prolonged, protracted, elongated, extensive; discursive, long-winded, windy, garrulous, wordy, rambling, prolix, drawn-out, padded, digressive; interminable.
Ant. short, brief, limited; condensed, concise, succinct, terse, to the point.

lenient *adj. The judge gave the prisoner a lenient sentence. This time I am going to be lenient with you:* mild, soft, sparing; merciful, clement, tender-hearted, indulgent, tolerant, forbearing, easy-going, kind-hearted, moderate, charitable, compassionate, sympathetic, benevolent, liberal, permissive, forgiving.
Ant. harsh, stern, exacting, rigid, rigorous, stringent, strict, severe, cruel, merciless.
◇ *Word origin: Lenient* comes from Latin *lenis*, soft, mild.

less *adv.* **1** *Father likes to take the less frequented roads:* to a smaller extent, in a more limited way; little, meagrely, barely.
—*adj.* **2** *The film had less success than expected:* smaller, not as great, more limited, slighter, not so significant.
—*n.* **3** *People have been imprisoned for less:* a smaller amount, lesser action, less serious offence.
Ant. 1-3 more. **2** greater, larger.
◇ *Usage note: Less* tells *how much;* it applies to uncounted amounts, quantities, or masses of non-separable things: *less money, less water, less population. Fewer* tells *how many;* it applies to separate items, units, or parts that can be counted: *fewer pennies, fewer lakes, fewer people.* The simplest way is to remember: *less* of one thing, *fewer* of two or more things.

lessen *v. Talking things out lessened the tension. The fury of the storm is lessening:* decrease, diminish, abate, dwindle, sink, reduce, shrink, contract, lower, depreciate, slacken, ease, wane, ebb, abridge; alleviate, lighten, mitigate; dilute, thin.

Ant. increase, raise, lengthen, enlarge, extend, heighten, multiply, mount, build.

lesser *adj.* **1** *The opera was pleasant, but it's one of the composer's lesser works:* smaller, less important, secondary, slighter, humbler, inferior, minor.

—*adv.* **2** *He is the lesser known of the two actors:* to a smaller degree, less, secondarily.

Ant. 1 major, larger, primary, superior. **2** greater, primarily.

lesson *n.* **1** *The test will cover lessons 1 to 5 inclusive:* exercise, segment, assignment, matter to be learnt, student's task, study, instruction, homework. **2** *The singer began taking lessons at the age of 12:* class, instruction, drill, learning session. **3** *Her faith throughout the tragedy was a lesson to all:* example, model, exemplar, notice, instruction, study, guide, moral, message, warning, admonition, deterrent, example, caveat, remonstrance, caution, rebuke, punishment. **4** *The lesson for today is from Paul's Epistle to the Ephesians:* reading, recitation from the Scriptures.

Ant. 3 misguidance, deception, bad example.

let *v.* **1** *Let the porter carry the bags:* permit, allow, authorize, warrant, license, approve, give assent to; sanction, endorse; suffer, leave, tolerate. **2** *The family let the house for July and August:* rent, lease out, hire out, sublease, sublet. **3** *Let the passengers know that the plane will be late:* cause, make, enable, allow, permit, grant, empower.

Ant. 1 forbid, prohibit. **2** buy; sell.

lethal *adj. Too many sleeping-pills can be lethal:* deadly, fatal, mortal, killing, mortally toxic; dangerous, destructive; virulent, poisonous, venomous.

Ant. harmless, wholesome, healthful.

◇ *Usage note:* See DEADLY.

◇ *Word origin: Lethal* comes from Latin *lethalis*, deadly, whose root is *letum*, death.

lethargic *adj. The hot, humid climate made everyone lethargic:* lazy, drowsy, sleepy, languid, indolent, idle, dull, somnolent, enervated, debilitated, dispirited, torpid, lacklustre, sluggish, slothful, indifferent, passive, inert, listless, apathetic.

Ant. energetic, vigorous, alert, active, responsive, bright, spirited; energized, animated, stimulated.

lethargy *n. My profound lethargy made work impossible:* languor, lassitude, apathy, drowsiness, sluggishness, dullness, inactivity, inertia, torpor, torpidity, laziness, indolence, listlessness, sloth, slothfulness.

Ant. vigour, alertness, liveliness, activity, eagerness.

letter *n.* **1** *There are 26 letters in the alphabet:* orthographic character, alphabetic character, written symbol. **2** *A letter was sent out asking for contributions:* epistle, dispatch, missive, note, message; memorandum, document, certificate; love-letter, billet-doux. **3** *Both sides obeyed the letter if not the spirit of the agreement:* actual terms, specific details, literal wording, strict meaning, substance, exact sense, literalness, preciseness. **4 letters** *He was a man of letters with no interest in current affairs:* literary accomplishment, learning, erudition, scholarly attainment; literature, belles lettres.

Ant. 3 spirit, tenor, heart.

level *adj.* **1** *The floors of the old house are remarkably level:* flat, even, horizontal, flush, plane; uniform, consistent; lacking roughness or unevenness, smooth, unwrinkled; on an even keel; parallel to the horizon, in line with the horizon. **2** *The water rose level with the first landing. Supply is about level with demand:* even, on a line, aligned; equivalent to, comparable to, on a par with; together, tied, neck and neck.

—*n.* **3** *The water rose to the level of the porch:* height, elevation, vertical position, plane. **4** *The whole class is preparing for examinations at Advanced Level:* stage, standard, rank, grade, position, achievement. **5** *The men's clothing department is on ground level. They discovered fossils in the lowest level of rock:* floor, storey, landing, elevation; layer, bed, stratum, zone, vein.

—*v.* **6** *The bulldozer levelled the road before the tarmac was laid:* grade, make even, even out, make horizontal, align, plane, flatten, smooth, equalize. **7** *A tornado levelled the entire village:* flatten, raze, knock down, topple, lay low, wreck, tear down, reduce, devastate. **8** *The hunter levelled his gun at his quarry. You should level an accusation at the suspect:* aim, direct, point.

Ant. 1 slanted, tilted, uneven, warped, bumpy, hilly; vertical. **2** below, above. **6** roughen, furrow. **7** raise, erect; build, construct.

◇ *Word origin: Level* comes from Latin *libella*, little balance.

> **Exploring the Word**: Latin *levis* light, gives us: *levity*, light-heartedness; *leaven*, an agent, such as yeast, for making dough rise and become light; *levitation*, rising up and floating in the air; *levy* to raise or call up troops, to impose a tax or fine; *elevate*, to raise, *elevation*, a raised place, and *elevator*, that which raises; *lever*, a simple tool for prising up or raising things; *levee* an assembly or reception (originally held by a prince or nobleman on rising from bed in the morning); and *alleviate*, to lighten pain or trouble.

levity *n. The situation is too grave for levity:* frivolity, lightness, lightheartedness, mirth, whimsy, lack of earnestness or seriousness, hilarity, foolishness, silliness, giddiness,

jocularity, flippancy, flightiness; pleasantry.
Ant. gravity, seriousness, sobriety, earnestness, solemnity, dignity.

levy *n.* **1** *The government authorized a levy on all cigarette sales:* duty, excise, tax, assessment, fee, toll, imposition, tariff. **2** *National leaders demanded a levy of troops to meet the danger:* conscription, call-up, muster.
—*v.* **3** *The court levied a fine on the defendant:* impose, demand, exact, assess, charge; collect.

lewd *adj. The film was considered lewd by some people. He uttered a lewd remark:* obscene, indecent, vulgar, lustful, lecherous, bawdy, ribald, risqué, pornographic, lascivious, excessively erotic, libidinous, wanton, licentious, libertine, immoral, salacious, prurient.
Ant. chaste, decent, modest; proper, prim, pure, moral.
◇ *Word origin: Lewd* is from Old English *lǣwede*, lay (as opposed to clerical), unlearned — hence ignorant, vulgar. The additional connotation of "lascivious" has been attached to the word since about 1400.

liability *n.* **1** *Heavy liabilities forced the company into liquidation:* debt, obligation, indebtedness, debit, arrear, burden, duty, responsibility. **2** *Shyness would be a liability in politics:* disadvantage, drawback, onus, burden, obstacle, handicap, minus, impediment, shortcoming, stumbling-block, inconvenience.
Ant. 1, 2 asset. **2** bonus, plus, advantage, head start, boon.

liable *adj.* **1** *Compulsive eaters are liable to obesity:* vulnerable, susceptible, open, exposed, subject, prone, inclined, disposed sensitive, ripe for. **2** *The man was liable for his wife's debts:* legally responsible, answerable, accountable, chargeable, obligated. **3** *If you disagree with him, he's liable to get annoyed:* likely, apt, inclined, prone.
Ant. 1 exempt, immune. **2** unaccountable, exempt. **3** unlikely, disinclined.
◇ *Usage note:* See LIKELY.

"For a woman to have a *liaison* is almost always pardonable, and occasionally, when the lover chosen is sufficiently distinguished, even admirable; but in love as in sport, the amateur status must be strictly maintained."
—*Robert Graves*

liaison *n.* **1** *Our officers had close liaison with the general staff. The negotiator acted as liaison between labour and management:* contact, connection, communication, intercommunication; alliance, bond, link, co-ordination, union, co-operation, interchange, mediator, go-between. **2** *For years the countess had kept up a secret liaison with a cabinet minister:* love affair, illicit romance, amour, entanglement, intrigue; *French* aventure.

liar *n. A compulsive liar finds it impossible to tell the truth:* falsifier, prevaricator, fabricator, perjurer; fibber, story-teller.
◇ *Spelling tip:* Along with *beggAR*, and *scholAR*, *liAR* is one of the three most common words ending in *-ar* that people sometimes want to write incorrectly, with an *-er*. Remember, all three of these words, including *liAR*, end in *-ar*.

libel *n.* **1** *The actor brought a suit aginst the gossip columnist for libel:* printed slander, defamation, malicious falsehood, calumny, aspersion, obloquy; unjust accusation.
—*v.* **2** *The candidate claimed that his opponent had libelled him in the article:* vilify, malign, slur, derogate, discredit, slander, defame, revile, disparage, blacken, calumniate, asperse.
Ant. 1 vindication, apology. **2** vindicate, apologize, retract; set the record straight.
◇ *Usage note:* See SLANDER.
◇ *Word origin: Libel* originally meant a defamatory pamphlet. It is based on Latin *libellus*, little book, from *liber*, book. Our word *library* also comes from Latin *liber*, book.

liberal *adj.* **1** *Liberal legislators hoped to improve the lot of the masses:* progressive, reformist, advanced, free-thinking; latitudinarian; left of centre; moderate. **2** *Try to keep a liberal attitude and listen to both sides:* fair-minded, open-minded, broad-minded, tolerant, forbearing, magnanimous, unbigoted, unprejudiced, unbiased, impartial; enlightened, humanitarian. **3** *Adorn the room with a liberal display of flowers:* abundant, generous, lavish, open-handed, unsparing, extravagant, bounteous, bountiful, handsome, munificent, prodigal, unstinting, plenteous, ample. **4** *The chairman gave a liberal interpretation of the rules:* lenient, broad, unrigorous, not strict, casual, lax, flexible, tolerant, open to reason, not literal.
—*n.* **5** *Liberals did not like the government's conservative policies:* progressive, reformer, latitudinarian, libertarian; non-extreme, moderate.
Ant. 1 conservative, reactionary, right-wing, left-wing. **2** intolerant, narrow, bigoted, biased, prejudiced, provincial, limited. **3** skimpy, inadequate, small, cheap. **4** strict, unbending, fixed, inflexible, rigid, literal. **5** extremist, conservative, reactionary, right-winger, leftist.

liberate *v. The allied armies liberated France from the Nazis. Try to liberate yourself from preconceived ideas:* set free, deliver, release, discharge, disencumber, emancipate, redeem, absolve; rescue, extricate, divorce, let loose, let go, let out.
Ant. imprison, intern, confine, restrict, limit; entrap, enthral, enslave.

libertine *n.* **1** *Casanova is known both as a literary figure and as a libertine:* profligate, debauchee,

rake, voluptuary, reprobate, lecher, roué, sensualist, seducer; immoralist, moral iconoclast, immoral person.
—*adj.* **2** *His libertine behaviour shocked the staid community:* immoral, dissolute, loose, unchaste, licentious, lewd, lustful, wanton, lascivious, libidinous, lecherous, morally unrestrained, profligate.
Ant. 1 prude, puritan. **2** strait-laced, moral, virtuous, chaste.

> **Exploring the Word**: *Liberty* means freedom and to *liberate* means to set free. Both words come from Latin *liber*, free, which also gives us: *liberal*, giving freely, given freely, free from traditional political views; *libertine*, which in ancient Rome meant a freed slave (Latin *libertinus*, freedman) and has come down to us to mean one who is too free from moral convention or restraints; *livery*, originally the clothing freely given by a master to his servant, now a uniform worn by a servant or attendant; and *deliver* to set free or hand over, as in *deliver us from evil* and *to deliver a package.*

liberty *n.* **1** *The constitution guards the liberty of the people:* freedom, self-determination, independence, autonomy; right, privilege. **2** *William Wilberforce sought to give slaves their liberty:* freedom, manumission, emancipation, liberation, delivery; citizenship, enfranchisement. **3** *Employees have the liberty of using all the museum facilities:* freedom, permission, sanction, leave, licence, dispensation; carte blanche. **4 liberties** *The fresh boy takes too many liberties with his elders. He takes liberties with the truth:* familiarity, licence, impropriety, undue intimacy; distortion, misrepresentation, violation, misuse, falsification.
Ant. 1 tyranny, despotism; restraint, constraint, compulsion, duress, coercion. **2** slavery, subjugation, captivity, imprisonment, restraint, enslavement. **4** propriety, judiciousness, rigorousness.

licence *n.* **1** *The restaurant applied for a licence to sell wine:* authorization, leave, liberty, permit, allowance, sanction, warrant, privilege, carte blanche, grant, admission, free passage, freedom, dispensation, franchise. **2** *The date on the licence indicates that it expired a month ago:* permit, certificate, pass, passport, visa, safe conduct. **3** *Too much licence was taken in translating the book:* liberty, departure from rule, deviation from custom, nonconformity, freedom, privilege; laxity, looseness, latitude, slackness; audacity, brazenness, presumptuousness. **4** *Too much permissiveness may lead beyond liberty to licence:* abused freedom, indifference to others' rights, irresponsibility, licentiousness, recklessness, temerity, presumption, arrogant self-indulgence, debauchery, libertinism, anarchy, lawlessness, disorder.
Ant. 1 prohibition, denial, restriction. **3** strictness, restraint. **4** restraint, constraint, restriction, moderation, sobriety, submission.

license *v. We have been licensed to sell both wines and spirits:* authorize, issue a licence to or for, certify, warrant, empower, enable, allow, let, sanction, accredit, commission; approve, endorse.
Ant. prohibit, forbid; restrain, curb, check; disallow.
◇ *Word origin: License, licence* and *licentious* all come from Latin *licere*, to be permitted.

licentious *adj.* **1** *The ruler's licentious practices led to a popular uprising:* irresponsible, unrestrained, amoral, unconstrained, excessive, lawless, unprincipled, unscrupulous, prodigal, ungoverned. **2** *The licentious exhibition was closed by the police:* lewd, libertine, lustful, lecherous, lascivious, immoral, libidinous, lubricious, debauched, wanton, abandoned, loose, promiscuous, smutty, salacious; goatish, profligate, dissolute, depraved, dissipated, ruttish, brutish; *Informal* dirty, sleazy, blue.
Ant. 1 law-abiding, lawful, responsible, principled, scrupulous. **2** chaste, pure, proper, moral.
◇ *Word origin:* See LICENSE.

lick *v.* **1** *Lick the ice-cream cone so that it won't drip:* pass the tongue over, touch with the tongue, tongue, lap, collect with the tongue. **2** *The first flickers of fire licked the dry timber:* pass lightly over, lap, touch; ignite, fire, kindle. **3** *Informal If City don't lick the Rovers, I'll not watch them again:* defeat, beat, conquer, vanquish, overcome, overthrow, overpower, subdue, subjugate, rout, outmatch, master; *Informal* trounce, clobber.
—*n.* **4** *Informal May I have a lick of your lollipop?:* taste, sample; lap, suck. **5** *Informal That yellow car was moving at a fair lick:* speed, pace, velocity.

lie[1] *n.* **1** *The testimony was a pack of lies from beginning to end:* falsehood, prevarication, falsification, untruth, fib, fiction, invention, fabrication, story, false story, perjury, deception, deceit, misrepresentation, equivocation.
—*v.* **2** *The witness lied to the jury:* perjure oneself, prevaricate, falsify, speak falsely, fabricate, tell untruths, forswear oneself; fib, embellish, embroider, romance, stretch the truth.
Ant. 1 truth, veracity, fact.

lie[2] *v.* **1** *Lie here until the dizziness passes:* recline, rest, repose, be supine, be flat, be prone, sprawl, loll, lounge, stretch out. **2** *The king lies now in his final resting-place:* be buried, be interred, repose. **3** *The village lies north of here. The responsibility lies with the driver:* be placed, be located, be found, exist, remain, abide, rest, stay, inhere, belong, be present, be established, obtain; range, extend.

Ant. 1 rise, arise, stand; be active, go, change.
◇ *Usage note:* People sometimes have a hard time getting *lie* and *lay* straight. *Lie* is an intransitive verb (does not take an object) meaning to recline: *I am going to lie down. Lay* is a transitive verb (takes an object) meaning to put something down: *Please lay the plate down.* The confusion occurs because the past tense of *lie* is *lay,* while the past tense of *lay* itself is *laid!* Thus, *Lie down on the couch, I lay down on the couch yesterday,* but *Please lay the plate down now, He laid the plate down here yesterday.*

"Life is an offensive, directed against the repetitious mechanism of the Universe."
—*A. N. Whitehead*

life *n.* **1** *There are many forms of life on earth:* living thing, living being, creature, organism, animal, plant; animate existence, being, substantiality, subsistence. **2** *Many lives were lost in the explosion:* human, human being, person, individual, soul. **3** *The mayfly has an average life of 24 hours:* lifetime, term of existence, life span, life expectancy; survival, longevity, duration. **4** *Her life has been one of great accomplishment. Hermits lead a quiet life:* career, lifework, path, course; existence, mode of living. **5** *The author's life of Michelangelo was made into a film:* biography, autobiography, story, life story, memoir. **6** *The new musical bursts with life and humour:* liveliness, vitality, animation, spirit, energy, zest, vivacity, vigour, verve.
Ant. 1 death, lifelessness, nothingness. **6** lifelessness, spiritlessness, dullness, flatness.

lifeless *adj.* **1** *The poor animal lay lifeless in the road:* dead, without life, defunct; deceased, departed, late; inert, inactive; inanimate. **2** *Plays often make dull, lifeless films:* static, lacking vitality, dull, spiritless, torpid, vapid, colourless, boring; stiff, wooden, flat, hollow.
Ant. 1 living, alive; animate, **2** animated, vital; active, dynamic, live, spirited.

lift *v.* **1** *Please lift the packages onto the counter. Lift up your head and pay attention:* hoist, heave, move upward, raise, elevate, raise up, rear, uplift, boost. **2** *The government lifted the ban on tourist travel:* cancel, revoke, rescind, put an end to, remove, banish, countermand. **3** *The encouraging letter lifted our hopes:* elevate, uplift, exalt, raise, give a boost to. **4** *With the onset of rain, the smog lifted from the city:* rise, disperse, dissipate, scatter, vanish, disappear, float away, be dispelled; ascend, soar, move upward. **5** *Informal Someone lifted his wallet:* steal, take, thieve, pilfer, pinch, purloin, filch, swipe, snatch, make off with, pick, palm, pocket; appropriate.
—*n.* **6** *The employer's praise gave the staff a lift:* sense of well-being, rising of spirits; encouragement, enheartenment, reassurance, boost, inspiration, elation, uplift; *Slang* shot in the arm.
Ant. 1 lower, drop. **2** establish, impose. **3** lower, disappoint, depress, crush, dash. **4** hang, descend, fall. **6** let-down, blow.
◇ *Word origin: Lift* is from Old Norse *lypta,* to raise in the air. It is related to *loft* and *lofty.* The modern German word *luft,* air, comes from the same ancestor-word.

light[1] *n.* **1** *Light from the setting sun filled the darkened room:* radiance, illumination, shine, luminosity, brightness, blaze, glare, glow, lustre, sparkle, brilliance, effulgence; beam, sunbeam, moonbeam. **2** *Switch on a light so that we can see better:* source of light; (*variously*) lamp, lantern, beacon, torch, candle. **3** *Try to see the problem in a new light:* approach, aspect, manner of understanding, viewpoint, attitude, slant, side, vantage point, direction, angle, frame of reference. **4** *The new facts throw some light on the matter:* elucidation, understanding, information, enlightenment, insight, illumination. **5** *Have you got a light for my pipe?:* means of ignition; match, lucifer, lighter; flame. **6** *Helen Keller was a light and inspiration to all sightless people:* model, exemplar, guide, paragon, shining example, guiding light, beacon.
—*adj.* **7** *The room is not light enough for reading:* bright, well lighted, having light, illuminated, luminous, radiant, brilliant, sunny, aglow. **8** *The living-room walls are light yellow:* pale, light-toned, not deep or dark, light-hued, fair, bleached; blond, blondish.
—*v.* **9** *Light a fire for warmth:* ignite, set burning, set fire to, fire, catch fire, conflagrate, flame, spark, kindle. **10** *Light the auditorium during the interval. To light one's way:* illuminate, illumine, give light to, irradiate, flood with light, brighten, floodlight; clarify. **11** *A smile lit up his face:* brighten, make cheerful, lighten, radiate, make radiant, cause to shine. **12** *Light some lamps in here:* turn on, switch on, put on.
Ant. 1 dark, darkness; shadow, shade, dusk, dimness. **4** obscurity, mystery, cloud, shadow. **7** dark, dim, gloomy, dusky. **8** dark, deep. **9** extinguish, put out, damp, douse, quench. **11** darken, cloud, dull.
◇ *Usage note:* Either *lighted* or *lit* can be used as the past tense and past participle of *light;* both are correct and may be used interchangeably in all contexts.

"The mind of the bigot is like the pupil of the eye; the more light you pour upon it, the more it will contract." —*Oliver Wendell Holmes*

light[2] *adj.* **1** *The suitcase is surprisingly light:* lightweight, not heavy, not burdensome, weightless; gossamer, buoyant, ethereal. **2** *A light breeze stirred the curtains. We had reasonably light rainfall for the month:* small, inconsequential, barely perceptible, inconsiderable, moderate, slight, puny, faint. **3** *Let's see a light* *film for a change:* light-hearted, amusing, funny, gay, carefree, frivolous, sprightly, non-intellectual, trifling; trivial, paltry, superficial, petty, inconsiderable, slight. **4** *I heard a light tap at the window:* soft, moderate, slight, faint, gentle. **5** *She is a very light dancer:* light-footed, airy, graceful, sylphlike. **6** *A light dinner is recommended for easy digestion:* small, spare, frugal, modest in quality, not rich, slight, meagre, scanty, restricted, not heavy, abstemious. **7** *The beautiful day put us in a light mood:* high-spirited, gleeful, jolly, sportive, jaunty, jubilant, happy, merry, bright, cheerful, gay, buoyant. **8** *Some light exercise is recommended during convalescence:* easy, simple, manageable, effortless, moderate, untaxing.

Ant. 1, 2, 4, 5, 6, heavy. **1** burdensome, weighty. **2** strong, substantial. **3** serious, intense, deep, profound. **4** forceful. **5** clumsy. **6** rich, gluttonous. **7** serious, despondent, sombre. **8** hard, strenuous, taxing.

light[3] *v.* **1** *The butterfly lit on a leaf:* come to rest, alight, stop, land, perch, fall, settle, roost. **2** *I lit upon the ring while cleaning the drawers:* chance, discover, meet with, stumble on, encounter, come across, come upon, happen upon, find.

lighten[1] *v. More lamps will lighten the gloomy room:* brighten, cause to become lighter, light up, irradiate, illuminate, make bright, become light; scintillate, blaze, flare, flash, coruscate.

Ant. darken.

lighten[2] *v.* **1** *We dropped ballast to lighten the balloon:* make lighter, make less burdensome, reduce in weight, unload, ease, buoy up, unburden, disburden. **2** *Extra help lightened the maid's work:* ease, lessen, reduce, make less harsh, mitigate, disencumber, alleviate, relieve, assuage, allay, abate, moderate, temper. **3** *My sister's phone call lightened our mood:* lift, gladden, elate, inspire, revive, enliven, buoy, uplift.

Ant. 1 weight. **2** increase, heighten, intensify, aggravate. **3** depress, sadden, oppress, weigh down.

light-hearted *adj. The children were light-hearted on the last day of school:* cheerful, cheered, gay, carefree, merry, joyous, jolly, joyful, glad, sunny, airy, free and easy, blithe, lively, buoyant, effervescent, sprightly, sanguine.

Ant. heavy-hearted, cheerless, sad, depressed, dejected, despondent, melancholy, morose, glum, gloomy.

lightly *adv.* **1** *The visitor tapped lightly on the door:* gently, hesitantly, weakly, faintly, timidly, softly. **2** *The cake is lightly sprinkled with sugar:* thinly, slightly, meagrely, sparingly, sparsely, moderately. **3** *Respect is not won lightly:* easily, facilely, readily, without effort. **4** *Step lightly over the rocks:* nimbly, gingerly, airily; quickly, swiftly, buoyantly. **5** *Responsibility must not be undertaken lightly:* carelessly, thoughtlessly, without concern, unconcernedly, frivolously, indifferently, slightingly, blithely, blandly, flippantly.

Ant. 1 heavily, firmly, forcefully. **2** heavily, thickly, abundantly. **3** with difficulty, arduously. **4** heavily, awkwardly, ploddingly, slowly, ponderously. **5** carefully, seriously, earnestly.

like[1] *adj. The boys reacted in a like manner. The brothers have like personalities:* identical, similar, akin, much the same, comparable, corresponding; congruent, matched, analogous, cognate, equivalent, equal, uniform, parallel; selfsame; allied, related, resembling.

Ant. unlike, dissimilar, different, diverse, divergent.

like[2] *v.* **1** *Most children like music:* enjoy, take pleasure in, find agreeable, relish, fancy, be partial to, dote, savour, relish. **2** *The students like the new head of department:* esteem, admire, find agreeable, have a friendly feeling for, be partial to, be fond of, fancy, approve, endorse; favour, support; *Informal* have a crush on. **3** *Would you like to join us?:* care, think fit, feel inclined, wish, want, have a mind, choose.

—*n.* **4 likes** *Everyone has different likes and dislikes:* partialities, favourites, inclinations, prejudices, preferences.

Ant. 1-3 dislike. **1, 2** hate, abhor, detest, loathe, abominate.

likeable Also **likable** *adj. She has an outgoing and likeable personality:* pleasing, genial, attractive, easily liked, charming, winsome, lovable, pleasant, amiable, agreeable, engaging, appealing, complaisant; nice, sympathetic; *Spanish* simpático.

Ant. unlikeable, displeasing, unpleasant, hateful, odious, repellent, repulsive.

likelihood *n. There is a strong likelihood of rain today:* prospect, probability, stong possibility, good chance, reasonableness.

Ant. improbability, unlikelihood.

likely *adj.* **1** *An accident is likely to happen at that junction:* inclined, apt, probable, liable, destined. **2** *Your story is a likely one:* plausible, credible, reliable, believable, reasonable. rational, seemingly truthful, verisimilar. **3** *The park is a likely spot for the picnic:* suitable, fit, proper, befitting, appropriate, qualified. **4** *The former half-back is a likely person for the coaching job:* promising, able, apt.

—*adv.* **5** *We will most likely be late:* probably, presumably, in all probability.

Ant. 1 unlikely, **2, 3** doubtful, dubious, questionable, problematic. **4** unpromising.

likeness *n.* **1** *The artist sketched a good likeness of my father:* portrait, picture, representation, image, study, model, delineation, rendition, portrayal; replica, facsimile. **2** *There is a likeness between the brothers:* resemblance, similarity, similitude, semblance, agreement; correspondence, analogy, affinity.

Ant. 2 dissimilarity, difference, divergence, disparity.

liking *n. Most children have a liking for animals:* affinity, preference, taste, appetite, inclination, proclivity, partiality, affection, fancy, fondness, penchant, leaning, predilection, soft spot, weakness.

Ant. dislike, disinclination; hatred, abhorrence, loathing, repugnance, aversion.

"If we treat people too long with that pretended liking called politeness, we shall find it hard not to like them in the end."

—*Logan Pearsall Smith*

---

limber *v. Exercise will limber you up:* make limber, loosen, relax.

limit *n.* **1** *The climbers had reached the limit of their endurance:* end, furthest bound, greatest extent, end-point, breaking-point, ultimate. **2** Often **limits** *These stakes mark the limits of the property:* edge, border, boundary, rim, fringe, frontier, margin, confines, periphery, perimeter. **3** *Is there a speed limit on this clearway?:* limitation, restriction, maximum, greatest number allowed, ceiling, top; restraint, check, curb; quota.

—*v.* **4** *The nation must limit land development:* restrict, restrain, confine, delimit, curb, check, bound, keep within bounds, narrow, inhibit; define, prescribe, circumscribe, qualify.

limited *adj. Each branch of government has limited powers:* defined, delimited, confined, special, bounded, circumscribed, specified, finite; narrow, cramped, restricted, minimal.

Ant. unlimited, unbounded, unrestricted, limitless.

limitless *adj. The country's natural resources are not limitless:* endless, unlimited, unending, unbounded, boundless, without measure, measureless, infinite, without limit.

Ant. limited, circumscribed, bounded, restricted, restrained, measured.

limp[1] *n.* **1** *The war wound left him with a pronounced limp:* lameness, halting walk, jerky step, halt, lame movement, falter, hobble.

—*v.* **2** *The injured player limped off the field:* hobble, falter; crawl, skulk.

◇ *Word origin: Limp* comes from a shortening of Old English *lempheált*, lame, halt.

limp[2] *adj. The runner went limp with exhaustion:* slack, loose, flabby, drooping, floppy, flaccid, lax, lacking vitality, lacking firmness, dead tired, weak, lethargic, enervated, exhausted.

Ant. stiff, rigid, strong, hardy, robust.

limpid *adj. We could see ourselves in the limpid stream. He is a master of limpid prose:* lucid, clear, transparent, translucent, pellucid; vitreous, crystalline; perspicuous, unambiguous.

Ant. muddy, murky, cloudy, opaque.

line *n.* **1** *Draw a line under the misspelt words:* underscore, long thin mark, score, long stroke, stripe, dash, streak, slash; demarcation, border, outline, contour. **2** *Her face bore lines of worry:* wrinkle, mark, crease, furrow, crow's-foot. **3** *The children stood in line until the teacher said they could move:* queue, file, rank, tier, series, column, range, procession. **4** *Drop us a line during your travels:* note, brief message, letter, postcard, card, report, word. **5** *Any deviation from the party line brought swift reprimands:* policy, stance, position, ideology, doctrine, idea, intention, scheme, system; course of action, belief, method; purpose, direction. **6** *The calf comes from a long line of prize cattle:* lineage, stock, genealogy, race, family, house, strain, ancestry, breed. **7** *The shipping line is in financial trouble:* transit company, transport service or company, transit route. **8** *Public relations is his line:* occupation, business, profession, vocation, calling, pursuit, métier, trade, means of living, livelihood, craft. **9** *The fishing line became entangled in seaweed:* cord, strand, thread, cordage; cable, rope; towing-line. **10** *The gale brought the power lines down:* circuit, conductor, conduit, power supply, electrical system. **11** **lines** *The play does not try to be original but follows traditional lines:* pattern, habitual or fixed idea, convention, principle, model, example, general form or notion, routine. **12** *Soldiers in the line suffer the most casualties:* front line, firing-line, fighting front, front, vanguard; trenches, barricades; defensive perimeter.

—*v.* **13** *Line the pages for the graph both horizontally and vertically:* rule, mark or rule with lines; score, draw, inscribe. **14** *People had lined up in front of the theatre:* queue up, arrange in a line, align, array, form in a line, rank, marshal, file.

> **Exploring the Word**: What do *lingerie* and an *ocean liner* have in common? They have a remote common ancestor in Latin *linum*, flax. This word gives us *linen*, made of flax, *lining* and, via French, *lingerie*, things made of linen; *lint*, a small fluff of flax or linen; and *line* (from the Latin *linea*, originally a linen thread, later any thread). From this last we get *lineage* and *lineal*, referring to the "line" of a family's descent; *linear*, in a straight line, straight; and such terms as *bee-line* and *ocean liner* (which sails in a direct line from one port to another, without intermediate stops for picking up or unloading cargo).

lineage *n. He is from a family of ancient lineage:* extraction, line, stock, pedigree, descent, heredity, genealogy, ancestry.

◇ *Spelling tip: Line* drops the *e* to become *linage* when referring to the lines in a newspaper column or other written matter. It is then pronounced as two syllables: *LIE-nij.*

Our local newspaper carries £3,000 worth of advertising linage. Line keeps the *e* to become *lineage* when referring to ancestry or pedigree. It is then pronounced as three syllables: *LIN-ee-ij. The lineage of this dog includes two Crufts champions.*

linger *v.* **1** *The last guests lingered until 2 a.m.:* stay, remain, tarry, persist, delay departure, wait, dawdle, dilly-dally, procrastinate, dally; loiter, lag, trail, *Informal* hang around. **2** *He lingered on long after he could function normally:* last, persist in living, survive, hang on, die slowly, cling to life.

Ant. **1** leave hastily, rush, depart, disappear.

◇ *Word origin: Linger* comes from Old English *lengen,* to make long, delay.

"Knowledge comes, but wisdom lingers."
—*Alfred, Lord Tennyson*

---

linguist *n.* **1** *Mr. Kerenyi is our resident linguist—he speaks eight languages:* multilingual person, polyglot; interpreter, translator. **2** *The Orientalist Sir William Jones was among the first modern linguists:* linguistics expert, language scholar; (*variously*) philologist, etymologist, lexicographer, semanticist, grammarian.

liniment *n. The liniment eased the player's aching shoulder:* ointment, medicated lotion, soothing liquid preparation, balm, unguent, emollient, salve.

◇ *Word origin: Liniment* comes from Latin *linire,* to smear on.

link *n.* **1** *The bracelet is formed of silver links:* section of a chain, bond, ring, loop, joint. **2** *Old friends are a link with the past:* tie, bond, connecting part, connection, interconnection, junction, splice, association, relation, liaison, relationship.

—*v.* **3** *Fingerprints linked the suspect with the crime:* connect, conjoin, interconnect, tie, tie in, couple, combine, bind, fuse, unite; group, bracket, associate, relate, implicate, involve.

Ant. **3** separate, sever, divorce, split, divide; clear, vindicate.

liquid *adj.* **1** *The river shone like liquid gold in the rays of the setting sun:* fluid, melted, thawed; molten.

—*n.* **2** *The patient could only take liquids:* drink, beverage, liquid substance, fluid, potable.

Ant. **1** solid, gaseous; hard, frozen, congealed. **2** solid; vapour, gas.

◇ *Spelling tip:* The second *i* in *liquid* changes to *e* in *liquefy.*

◇ *Word origin: Liquid* comes from Latin *liquere,* to be liquid, which also gives us *liquor, liqueur,* and *liquidate.*

liquidate *v.* **1** *The inheritance allowed him to liquidate his debts:* settle, pay, discharge, dispose of, clear, pay off, account for, put to rest, abolish, erase, cancel. **2** *He decided to liquidate his restaurant business and start afresh:* close down, settle the affairs of, wind up, conclude, terminate. **3** *The dictator brutally liquidated all opponents:* assassinate, kill, murder, eradicate, annihilate, exterminate, demolish, destroy, abolish, do away with, break up; *Slang* rub out, finish off.

◇ *Word origin:* To *liquidate* one's debts is to clear them up, to clear the balance sheet. *Liquidate* comes from Latin *liquidare,* to make liquid, to clear up, from *liquere,* to be liquid, which also gives us *liquid, liquor, liquefy* and other related words.

liquor *n.* **1** *You must be of legal age to buy spirituous liquor:* alcoholic beverage, alcoholic drink, spirits, intoxicants, distilled spirits; (*variously*) whisky, Scotch, bourbon, rye, gin, rum, vodka, brandy, beer, lager, perry, mead, potheen; *Slang* booze. **2** *Use the liquor from the roast for the gravy:* liquid, juice, drippings, broth, extract.

◇ *Usage note: Liquor* means any alcoholic beverage, or whisky, and is usually made from distilling grain mash. *Liqueur* is a sweet alcoholic beverage, as a cordial, usually served after meals, and is generally made by adding sugar syrup and flavouring to distilled spirits. Thus, *The still-owner made potato liquor,* but *Aunt May had a sip of cherry liqueur after dessert.*

◇ *Word origin:* See LIQUID.

lissome *adj. This year's champion in the Ladies' Singles is a lissome teenager named Jill. The dancer moved with lissome grace:* lithe, limber, supple, flexible, pliant, lithesome, nimble, agile, slender, graceful, light-footed.

Ant. rigid, stiff, wooden, inflexible; clumsy, awkward.

list[1] *n.* **1** *Make up a shopping-list. Has the club got a list of all its members?:* written series, register, roster, roll, muster, inventory, record, slate; index, schedule, enumeration, table, catalogue.

—*v* **2** *List all the things you need from the grocer's:* write in a series, record, write down, catalogue, tabulate.

◇ *Word origin: List*[1] comes from Italian *lista,* strip of paper, later a roll of names.

list[2] *n.* **1** *The ship has a list to port:* tilt, leaning, lean, inclination, slant, slope.

—*v.* **2** *The freighter listed as the cargo shifted:* tilt, lean, slant, heel over, tip, careen.

listen *v. Please listen carefully:* attend, hark, list, heed, make an effort to hear, pay attention, give heed, take notice, keep one's ears open, give ear, note carefully, prick up one's ears, strain one's ears, *Informal* be all ears, lend an ear; eavesdrop, listen in, overhear.

Ant. be deaf to, turn a deaf ear to; ignore, neglect, disregard, pay no heed to, take no notice of.

listless *adj. Many people feel listless on rainy days:* sluggish, lifeless, lazy, indolent, lacking zest, inactive, dull, spiritless, leaden, lethargic, phlegmatic, soporific, torpid, sluggish,

down; apathetic, uninterested, indifferent, unconcerned, mopish, languid, dreamy.
Ant. lively, energetic, active, wide-awake, spirited; alert, interested, attentive.

litany *n.* **1** *The priest led the congregation in the Litany:* ceremonial prayer, prescribed prayer, formal prayer, invocation with responses, prayer of supplication. **2** *She gave us a long litany of her woes:* recital, recitation, account, repetition, description, narration, recapitulation.
◇ *Word origin: Litany* comes from the Greek word for supplication, *litaneiā.*

literal *adj.* **1** *The students were asked to make a literal translation of the French story:* faithful, exact, precise, word-for-word, as close as possible to the original, verbatim, strict, accurate, direct, true, undeviating, *Latin* ad litteram. **2** *The general wanted a literal report on the enemy's strength:* accurate, precise, factual, truthful, categorically true, without exaggeration, exact, correct, reliable, unimpeachable, trustworthy, honest, dependable, authoritative, undisputed, meticulous, scrupulous, conscientious, authentic, actual, real. **3** *He's so literal-minded that he never knows when I'm kidding:* matter-of-fact, prosaic, unimaginative, taking everything at face value.
Ant. 1 free, liberal, general, figurative. **2** inaccurate, incorrect, wrong, erroneous, false, non-factual, untruthful, unreliable, untrustworthy; careless, hazy, inexact, sloppy. **3** figurative; imaginative.
◇ *Usage note: Literally* means "in an exact sense, actually": *Few people have been literally scared to death. Figuratively* means "as a figure of speech, as an image or exaggeration to make one's point": *We were scared to death, figuratively speaking.*

literary *adj. The literary club meets once a month:* of literature, of writings, of belles lettres, of books; fond of books, addicted to reading, bookish; artistic, poetic; intellectual, literate, lettered, belonging to the literati.
Ant. uneducated, unlettered, untutored, untaught, unschooled, unenlightened.

literate *adj.* **1** *Only a few of the nation's peasants are literate:* able to read and write, proficient in reading and writing. **2** *A television news correspondent should be a highly literate man:* educated, learned, well-informed, well-read, literary, lettered.

literature *n.* **1** War and Peace *is one of the classics of Russian literature:* literary work of lasting value, artistic writing, belles lettres, letters, classics. **2** *We delved into all the literature on colonial furniture:* writings, works, books, papers, treatises, dissertations, theses; lore, scholarship.
◇ *Word origin: Literature, literal,* and *literate* come from Latin *littera,* letter of the alphabet. Thus *literature* is enduring or artistic writing or "letters," *literal* means following the exact words or meaning "to the letter," and *literate* means able to read and write, knowing one's letters.

lithe *adj. A pole-vaulter should be strong and lithe:* limber, supple, flexible, pliant, lissome, agile, nimble, graceful.
Ant. rigid, stiff, wooden, inflexible; clumsy, awkward.
◇ *Word origin:* A very *lithe* person moves as if he were made of rubber. In Old English *līthe* means "soft." By Chaucer's day (late 14th century) the word acquired its present sense of "supple."

litter *n.* **1** *Good campers don't leave litter on the campsite. What's this litter of clothes on the bedroom floor?:* scattered rubbish, rubbish, trash, refuse, debris; leavings, junk, mess, heap, jumble, pile. **2** *The Alsatian bitch had a litter of five puppies:* group of animals born at one birth; offspring, young, issue, progeny. **3** *The wounded were carried into the hospital on litters:* stretcher, portable bed, portable couch. **4** *The squirrel made a litter of dried leaves:* bed, nest, lair; bedding, pallet.
—*v.* **5** *Thoughtless holiday-makers had littered the beach with cigarette packets and beer cans. The reporter's desk was littered with news releases:* strew with rubbish, clutter with trash, strew, clutter, scatter; heap, pile, jumble.
Ant. 5 clean up, pick up; organize, order, arrange, tidy, tidy up, neaten.
◇ *Word origin: Litter* comes from Latin *lectus,* bed, hence our meaning of *litter* as stretcher. Since an animal giving birth does so in its bed, stall, or box, *litter* took on the meaning of the young brought forth at one birth. Early beds were stuffed with straw that easily got scattered, hence our meaning of *litter* as scattered rubbish or clutter.

little *adj.* **1** *The old man lived in a little house in the woods. The little dog followed the boy everywhere:* small, diminutive, petite, pint-sized, pocket-sized, miniature, wee, tiny, minute, *Slang* itsy-bitsy, itty-bitty; undersized, dwarfish, stunted; pygmy, elfin, Lilliputian; microscopic, infinitesimal. **2** *A little group met to play bridge every Friday. The doctor has little hope for her recovery. There is little milk left in the jug:* small, scant, meagre; skimpy, hardly any, not much, scarcely any, short, insufficient, deficient; few and far between, to be counted on one's fingers. **3** *The tourists only spent a little time in Italy:* brief, short, hasty, quick, fleet, passing; short-lived, momentary. **4** *She had a little cold last week, but she's fine now:* trivial, mild, slight, inconsequential, negligible, insignificant, unimportant, trifling, faint, piddling, paltry, of no account. **5** *The criticism all came from people with little minds:* narrow, petty, mean, short-sighted, opinionated, inflexible; worthless, unworthy, inferior, third-rate, mediocre, commonplace, run-of-the-mill.

—*adv.* **6** *I little thought he would take me seriously. The old woman slept little. The children visit the parents little now:* not at all, never, by no means, not in a thousand years; in only a small amount, in a small degree, not much, slightly, scarcely, hardly, somewhat; rarely, not often, seldom.
—*n.* **7** *Just put a little on each plate:* small amount, small quantity; pittance, next to nothing, minimum, drop, crumb, iota, jot, dot, whit, bit, speck, fragment, particle, dash, pinch, trifle, modicum, drop in the ocean, trace, hint, suggestion.
Ant. 1, 2, 4 big, large, great, immense, huge, monstrous, enormous, colossal, giant, giant-sized. **2, 3** much, more than enough, abundant, ample, plentiful. **3** long. **4** major, important, momentous, grave, serious, considerable, significant, consequential. **5** broad-minded, farsighted. **6** always, certainly, surely, assuredly; much. **7** lot, much, many.

"If a little knowledge is dangerous, where is the man who has so much as to be out of danger?" —*Thomas Huxley*

liturgy *n. The church has used the same liturgy for hundreds of years:* ritual, religious ceremony, form of public worship, collection of formularies for public worship, rite, particular arrangement of services; services, worship, service, mass, eucharist, communion, sacrament.

liveable Also **livable** *adj.* **1** *Some of the houses are barely liveable in:* suitable for living in, habitable; homey, snug, cosy, comfortable, *Informal* comfy. **2** *A few luxuries make life more liveable:* worth living, worthwhile, agreeable, enjoyable, pleasant, satisfying, gratifying; bearable, tolerable, endurable, acceptable, passable.
Ant. 1 uninhabitable, unsuitable. **2** unpleasant, unsatisfactory; unbearable, intolerable, unendurable, painful, disagreeable.

live[1] *v.* **1** *Was he still living when the doctor arrived?:* be alive, have life, draw breath, breathe, have being; exist, be, be animate; see the light of day, come into existence, walk the earth. **2** *Grandmother lived to the age of 93. The flowers will live longer if you put them in water. Tennyson's poetry will live for ever:* remain alive, survive, endure, prevail, cling to life, persist, hold on, abide; stand, obtain, escape destruction, be permanent. **3** *How can anyone live on that salary? Can he live as a painter?:* subsist, support oneself, provide for one's needs, maintain life, get along, make ends meet, make one's living; acquire a livelihood, earn money, follow a particular occupation, get ahead. **4** *The castaways lived on fish and coconuts:* subsist, feed, be nourished, survive, get along, be supported; thrive, flourish; increase, multiply. **5** *How long have you lived at this address? I've always wanted to live in North Wales:* reside, be in residence, dwell, abide, make one's abode, make one's home, lodge, stay, billet; settle, remain, take root, pass one's life.
Ant. 1, 2 die, pass away, expire, perish. **2** wither, fade, languish, decline, decay; depart, vanish. **3** be destitute, be indigent. **4** starve to death, starve.
◇ *Word origin:* It is interesting to note that *live*[1], the verb, comes from Old English *lifian* (to live) while *live*[2], the adjective, has a separate history, being a shortening of *alive.*

live[2] *adj.* **1** *The laboratory is conducting experiments with a dozen live monkeys:* alive, living, quick, animate, breathing, existent; vital, physical, corporeal, incarnate, bodily, fleshly. **2** *Housing is still a live issue:* pertinent, of present interest, active, burning, pressing, prevalent, prevailing; current, present-day, up-to-date, still in use, happening, going on, at hand, at issue, in question. **3** *Use tongs to handle those live embers:* burning, afire, fiery, blazing, ablaze, aflame, flaming, aglow, glowing, alight, ignited; hot, red-hot, white-hot.
Ant. 1 dead, defunct, deceased, departed. **2** inactive, dormant, out-of-date, old hat.
◇ *Word origin:* See LIVE[1].

livelihood *n. Can he earn a livelihood writing poetry? Farming has been the family's livelihood for three generations:* living, adequate income, means of support, maintenance, subsistence, sustenance, source of income; occupation, vocation, calling, business, line of work, trade, profession, career, métier; job, situation, position; venture, undertaking, enterprise.
Ant. destitution, indigence; avocation, hobby, entertainment, recreation, fun.
◇ *Word origin: Livelihood* literally means one's way of life. It comes from Old English *līf* (life) + *lād* (way).

lively *adj. He may be 80, but he's still lively. The band played a lively tune:* spirited, brisk, sprightly, vivacious, animated, full of life, full of spirit, eager, excited, enthusiastic, buoyant; active, vigorous, alert, peppy, perky; ardent, fervent, vivid, excitable.
Ant. lifeless, inactive, dull, slow, sluggish, phlegmatic, leaden, listless, apathetic; decrepit, disabled, debilitated.

livery *n. The footmen wore red and gold livery:* uniform, costume, servant's uniform, vestments, regalia, garb, attire, clothing, raiment.
◇ *Word origin: Livery* was originally the free clothing or uniform given to male servants and retainers. It comes from Latin *liber,* free, which also gives us *liberty, liberal, libertine,* and *deliver* (literally "set free").

livid *adj.* **1** *The skin was livid where he had been* *struck:* black-and-blue, discoloured, purple; bruised, contused. **2** *Her insulting remark made me absolutely livid:* enraged, incensed, furious, infuriated, raging, fuming, mad, angry, indignant, *Slang* steamed up, hopping mad; outraged, exasperated, vexed, riled, galled, provoked.

Ant. 2 mollified, assuaged, forgiving; delighted, enchanted, enraptured, blissful, overjoyed, happy, content, pleased.

living *adj.* **1** *Are your grandparents still living? Every living creature has a place in nature's scheme:* alive, live, existing, existent, quick, breathing, this side of the grave; animate, in the flesh, fleshly, bodily, embodied, incarnate, material, corporeal, organic; on the face of the earth, under the sun. **2** *English and French are living languages. The ideals of our ancestors are part of our living heritage:* still in use, alive, live, active, operative, existent, extant, of present interest, up-to-date, going on; surviving, enduring, prevailing, persisting, remaining, permanent.

—n. **3** *The sheer joy of living makes up for one's troubles:* existing, existence, life, being, having life, drawing breath, subsisting, subsistence, animation. **4** *Such reckless living can ruin your health:* way of life, mode of living, lifestyle. **5** *My next-door neighbour makes a good living growing tomatoes. What do you do for a living?:* income, subsistence, sustenance, livelihood, means of support, maintenance; occupation, vocation, calling, business, trade, profession, career, line of work, job, work, employment; venture, undertaking, enterprise.

Ant. 1, 2 dead, deceased, expired, defunct, lifeless. **1** inanimate, inorganic. **2** vanishing, perishing, obsolescent; out-of-date, inactive. **3** dying, expiring. **5** destitution, indigence; avocation, hobby, entertainment, recreation, fun.

load *n.* **1** *It took three loads of gravel to cover the drive. The plane can carry a ten-ton load:* quantity carried; (*variously*) wagonload, load, carload, planeload, shipload; cargo, shipment, freight, lading, haul; capacity, contents. **2** *The walls of the building carry the load of the roof. That's a load off my mind!:* quantity supported, burden, weight, dead weight, encumbrance, pressure; care, trouble, worry, oppression, misery, depression, affliction, tribulation; misfortune, unhappiness, unhappy lot.

—v. **3** *The men loaded up the van with strawberries:* fill, lade, pile, pack, heap, stack, stuff; weight, burden. **4** *She's been loaded down with family responsibilities all her life:* weigh down, burden, overwhelm, oppress, afflict, trouble, worry, vex, try; hamper, encumber, handicap, hinder.

Ant. 2 support; solace, consolation. **3** unload, empty, lighten, unpack. **4** free, liberate.

loaf *v.* *Don't just sit there and loaf — get to work!:* waste time, idle, do nothing, kill time, fritter time away, take it easy, laze about, dally, loll, lounge about, twiddle one's thumbs, be lazy, malinger, star-gaze, day-dream.

Ant. work, toil, labour, slave.

loafer *n.* *That loafer won't even look for a job!:* lazy person, idler, malingerer, ne'er-do-well, shirker, wastrel, sluggard, lazy-bones, layabout, punk.

Ant. hard worker, worker, working man, labourer.

◇ *Word origin: Loafer* comes from Dutch *landloper*, literally one who lopes over the land, a vagrant. Our great-grandparents then shortened *loafer* to *loaf* to describe what a loafer does. Our other word *loaf* (of bread) comes from the Old English word for bread, *hlāf*.

loan *n.* **1** *My neighbour asked for the loan of our binoculars:* permission to borrow, lending; advance, advancing, giving credit, accommodation. **2** *The bank arranged a loan of £500 for house improvements:* sum of money lent, thing lent, thing borrowed; credit, mortgage, advance.

—v. **3** *I shall ask the bank to loan me £100:* lend, permit to borrow, advance, allow; mortgage, credit.

Ant. 3 pay back, give back, return.

◇ *Usage note:* The verbs *loan* and *lend* are interchangeable when the meaning is to give the temporary use of something. Thus *Loan me five pounds* is just as correct as *Lend me five pounds. Loan* is more precisely used when speaking of money and *lend* when speaking of objects: *The bank loaned him £5,000 to start his business. Jane lent me her cookery book.* However, this is not a rule, and either *loan* or *lend* may be used in either case.

◇ *Spelling tip:* It's easy to spell *loan,* but spelling *mortgage* can be a problem. Most MORTals pay off a *MORTgage* sometime in their lives, and both words begin with mort. Thus, remember the *t* when you spell *morTgage.* However, don't pronounce this *t*; it is silent. The pronunciation is *MOR-gij.*

loath *adj.* *The salesman is loath to accept a job in a new area:* unwilling, averse, reluctant, disinclined, indisposed, opposed, resisting, set against, against, hostile, inimical.

Ant. willing, anxious, eager, keen, avid, enthusiastic, desirous, wanting.

◇ *Word origin:* See LOATHE.

loathe *v.* *He's an art critic who loathes modern art:* detest, hate, despise, dislike, find disgusting, abominate, abhor, deplore, be unable to bear, have a strong aversion to, have no stomach for; scorn, disdain, eschew, keep clear of, shrink from, recoil from, draw back from, blench from, flinch from, shy away from, view with horror.

Ant. love, adore; like, relish, fancy, dote on, enjoy; desire, crave, hanker after, long for.

◇ *Usage note:* See HATE.
◇ *Word origin: Loathe* and *loath* come from Old English *lāthian*, to be hateful.

loathsome *adj. The villain of the play was completely loathsome:* detestable, hateful, despicable, disgusting, abominable, abhorrent, revolting, repugnant, nasty, obnoxious, offensive, sickening, odious, nauseating, rank, mean, invidious, distasteful, foul.
Ant. lovable, adorable, likeable, engaging, attractive, alluring, charming, delightful.

lobby *n.* **1** *Wait in the lobby of the building until the rain stops:* vestibule, entrance-hall, foyer, porch, reception-hall, ante-room, waiting-room, reception-room, antechamber.
—*v.* **2** *The health group has recently been lobbying for a ban on cigarette advertising:* advocate strongly, urge legislative action, solicit votes, seek to influence members of a law-making body, exert influence, bring pressure to bear, *Informal* pull strings.
◇ *Word origin: Lobby* comes from Medieval Latin *lobia*, porch, gallery. Also related are *lodge* (a hut in the woods), *loge* (a box, gallery, or upper porchlike balcony of a theatre), and *loggia* (an open, roofed gallery or porch supported by columns).

"And as imagination bodies forth
The forms of things unknown, the poet's pen
Turns them to shapes, and gives to airy nothing
A local habitation and a name."
—*William Shakespeare*

---

local *adj. The mayor is a local celebrity:* townwide, city-wide, regional, sectional, provincial, neighbourhood, territorial, native, home-grown; geographically restricted, limited, confined, narrow, urban, insular, parochial.
Ant. international, world-wide, national, nation-wide; foreign, exotic.

locale *n. The play's locale is London:* setting, place where events occur, location, locality, site, spot, area, quarter, zone, vicinity, region, neighbourhood, section, province.

locality *n. The two factories are in the same locality:* neighbourhood, area, district, section, province, zone, quarter, vicinity, region, territory, location; locale, place.

locate *v.* **1** *The police are trying to locate the missing man:* find, discover the whereabouts of, track down, ferret out, search out, unearth, uncover, detect, hit upon, come upon, light upon, stumble on, meet with, lay one's hands on. **2** *The fire station is located in Duke Street. The dentist carefully located the filling in the cavity:* situate, place, establish, set down, seat, deposit, put, fix, station, post.
Ant. 1 lose, shake; hide, conceal. **2** dislodge, displace.

location *n. No one knows the location of Captain Kidd's hidden treasure. This corner would make a good location for a petrol station:* whereabouts, position, site, spot, place, situation, locale.

> **Exploring the Word**: Latin *locus* (place) has been borrowed directly into Modern English to designate various highly technical concepts of "place" in certain exact sciences such as mathematics and genetics. The word is also used in the phrase *locus classicus*, "classical place," which is the term for a standard passage (originally in classical literature) that elucidates a word or subject: *The* locus classicus *attesting the presence of Christians in Rome during the first century A.D. is in the* Annals *of Tacitus. Locus* also gives us some common words, as: *locate*, to find or to be in a specific place; *location*, *locality*, and *locale*, all meaning place; *local*, a native of a place, a nearby public house; *locomotion*, moving, or the ability or means of moving from one place to another, and *locomotive*, causing motion, or that which moves things from one place to another; *dislocate*, to put or be out of place; and *allocate*, to put in a place for a specific purpose, to set aside.

lock[1] *n.* **1** *The front door needs a stronger lock:* fastening device, securing device, fastening; (*variously*) bolt, padlock, safety-catch, latch; clasp, hook, clamp, catch. **2** *The ship passed through several locks in the canal:* canal gate, dock gate, floodgate, sluice-gate, dam.
—*v.* **3** *Be sure to lock the office door when you leave:* fasten, secure, (*variously*) bolt, padlock, bar. **4** *You should lock the jewels in a safe. The convicts were locked up in their cells:* secure, lock up, keep under lock and key; shut in, confine, gaol, imprison, incarcerate, cage, pen, coop up, impound, put behind bars. **5** *The men locked arms and sang Auld Lang Syne:* join, entwine, link, interlink, unite, intertwine; clinch, grip, hold, grasp, clasp, grapple, seize, hold, grab, embrace.
Ant. 3 unlock, unbolt, unbar, unfasten; open. **4, 5** free, release, let go.

lock[2] *n. Grandmother still has a lock of my baby hair in her scrap-book:* tress, ringlet, curl, tuft, bang, quiff, forelock.

lodge *n.* **1** *The gatekeeper lived in a lodge near the main entrance:* cabin, cottage; hut, shelter; hotel, motel, chalet, resort, camp; country house.
—*v.* **2** *The travellers lodged in motels every night. The guest-house can lodge five persons:* stay, put up, obtain lodgings, sojourn, camp; furnish with lodgings, house, billet, bed, quarter, shelter, harbour. **3** *The coin rolled across the floor and lodged in a crack:* catch, become fixed, be positioned. **4** *Tell the manager I want to lodge a complaint:* submit, file, register, enter formally, place on record, make known.
◇ *Word origin: Lodge* comes from Old French

loge, summer-house, hut. It is related to Medieval Latin *lobia*, porch, gallery, which gives us *lobby*.

lodging *n.* Usually plural. *Will you have lodgings for tonight?:* temporary quarters, place to stay, overnight accommodation, a room, bed for the night, temporary sleeping accommodation.

loft *n.* **1** *The artist rented a loft to use as a studio. The church has a beautiful organ loft:* attic room, attic, garret mansard; top floor, balcony, gallery; belfry.
—*v.* **2** *The batsman lofted the ball into the outfield:* throw high, hit high, strike in a high arc, sky.
Ant. 1 basement, cellar. **2** ground.
◇ *Word origin: Loft* comes from Old English *loft*, air, sky, hence that which is up in the air, as an upper room. This word is related to *lift*. Its German equivalent *Luft*, air, is familiar in the name of the *Luftwaffe*, the German air force during World War II, and is also to be found in the names of various German, Scandinavian, and Icelandic airlines.

lofty *adj.* **1** *Lofty towers flanked the town gate:* soaring, towering, tall, high, elevated, high-reaching. **2** *Despite his lofty position the Duke was quite happy to drink out of an old mug:* exalted, imposing, stately, elevated, dignified, majestic, sublime, noble; high, high-ranking, mighty, important, distinguished, leading, illustrious, eminent, pre-eminent, glorious, great. **3** *I didn't like her lofty treatment of the visitors:* proud, haughty, arrogant, lordly, disdainful, scornful, aloof, distant, remote, cold, high-and-mighty, *Slang* hoity-toity; snobbish, imperious, patronizing, condescending, self-important, conceited; *Informal* puffed-up, stuck-up, snooty.
Ant. 1 low, short, stunted, dwarfed. **2** lowly, undignified, debased, mean, ignoble, degraded, cheap; low, low-ranking. **3** modest, unassuming, humble; friendly, cordial, hospitable, warm, receptive, open.

log *n.* **1** *The cabin was built of logs:* length of tree trunk, part of branch; block, stump. **2** *The time of departure was entered in the ship's log:* log-book; (*loosely*) record book, journal, calendar, diary, docket, schedule, account.
◇ *Word origin: Log* comes from Middle English *logge*, log, and cannot be traced back any further. In its "log-book" sense the word has been traced to Arabic *lauh*, tablet. *Log* in this sense has passed into Dutch, German, Danish, Swedish, and even French. (In French it is spelt *loch*, pronounced "luck.")

logic *n.* **1** *Lawyers should be well-versed in logic:* science of reasoning, syllogistic reasoning, inductive reasoning, organized thinking, dialectics, deduction. **2** *There is no logic in her argument:* good sense, sound judgement, organized reasoning, reason, chain of thought, sense, coherence, cogency.

logical *adj.* **1** *The plan was presented in a logical manner:* consistent, well-organized, coherent, rational, sound, reasonable, intelligent; relevant, pertinent, germane; valid, deducible. **2** *He is the logical choice for our M.P.:* reasonable, likely, most likely, plausible, intelligent, enlightened, sensible.
Ant. 1 illogical, inconsistent, unorganized, incoherent, irrational, unreasonable; intuitive, instinctive. **2** illogical, unlikely, implausible.

> **Exploring the Word:** *Logic* comes from Greek *logikē technē*, art of discourse, art of reasoning. From this we get *logical* and from the same Greek base *logos*, discourse, speech, word, we get *prologue* (Greek *pro*, before), literally "foreword," hence an introduction to a speech, play, or book; *epilogue* (Greek *epi-*, in addition), an addition to the main discourse, hence an addendum or short concluding section of a speech, story, or the like; and even *apology*, from the Greek *apologia* (Greek *apo-*, off, from), a discourse in defence, a speaking "off" of something — the most famous example of the word in this sense is Plato's *Apology*, a highly polished literary version (by Plato) of the "apology" pronounced by Socrates while on trial for his life before the Athenian Assembly in 399 B.C.

loiter *v. A suspicious character was loitering in the hall:* linger idly about, hang around, hover around; skulk, lurk, slink; loll, idle; tarry, dilly-dally, dally, dawdle, shilly-shally, loaf.
Ant. hasten, hurry, scurry, scuttle, scamper.
◇ *Word origin: Loiter* comes from Middle English *lotere*, to dawdle. Large numbers of vagrants made their way from Holland to England during the 15th century, and the word came with them — its Middle Dutch equivalent is *loteren*, to wag about.

loll *v.* **1** *He's been lolling around the house all day. Sit up straight, don't loll in your chair:* lounge, loaf, idle, dawdle, languish, take it easy, relax; recline, lean, slouch, slump, sprawl, flop over. **2** *The horse's tongue lolled as the animal gasped for breath:* dangle, droop, hang loosely; flop, flap, sag, drop, drag.
◇ *Word origin: Loll* comes from Middle Dutch *lollen*, to lull to sleep. Related words are *lull* and *lullaby*; Latin *lallare*, to sing a lullaby, which gives us the technical term *lallation*, pronouncing *r* as *l*, something that the Chinese are popularly supposed to do when speaking English; Greek (and English) *glossolalia*, "speaking in tongues," from *glossā*, tongue, language + *lalein*, to speak; *lament*, from Latin *lamentum*, cry of grief; *loon* (the diving bird) from Old Norse *lōmr*, which is thought to be so-called from its laughlike cry. *Loll* in the sense of "letting (the tongue) hang out" was coined by Shakespeare in *Cymbeline* (Act 5, Scene 3) in a passage

describing a battle: "... the enemy full-hearted, lolling the tongue with slaught'ring, having work more plentiful than tools to do't...."

lonely *adj.* **1** *Robinson Crusoe spent many lonely days on the desert island before Man Friday appeared:* by oneself, solitary, without company, unaccompanied, unattended, companionless; secluded, withdrawn, reclusive, eremitic, unsocial. **2** *The visiting nurse cheered the lonely invalids:* forlorn, depressed by solitude, lacking companionship, friendless, lonesome, forsaken, isolated. **3** *The cabin was built in a lonely spot:* isolated, secluded, remote, desolate, deserted, lonesome, unpopulated, uninhabited, unfrequented.

Ant. **1** accompanied, together. **2** popular, befriended. **3** crowded, mobbed, populous, frequented, teeming, swarming, bustling.

long[1] *adj.* **1** *There will be a long wait until the next bus:* lengthy, extended, prolonged, protracted, spun out; interminable, unending. **2** *Alaska has a long coastline:* lengthy, extended, elongated, protracted, far-reaching, outstretched.

—n. **3** *It won't rain for long:* a long time, an extended period.

—adv. **4** *His election was long anticipated. It was below freezing all winter long:* throughout a period of time; over an extended period; during the time, throughout the period. **5** *The river is nearly 100 miles long:* in length, from end to end.

Ant. **1, 2** short, brief; little, small. **1** momentary, short-lived, quick. **2** abridged, abbreviated, curtailed, compressed.

◇ *Word origin: Long*[1] comes from Old English *lang*, which also gives us our word *length*.

long[2] *v.* *The old man longs for the good old days:* yearn, crave, hunger, thirst, hanker, sigh, pine, have a desire, hope, wish, aspire, have one's heart set on, be bent upon.

Ant. despise, detest, loathe, abhor, abominate, hate, deplore, be repelled by; spurn, scorn, disdain, eschew, reject, renounce, forsake, refuse.

longing *n.* **1** *After travelling abroad for so many months she had a longing to see her own home town again:* strong desire, yearning, craving, hungering, thirst, wish; aspiration; *Informal* urge, hankering, yen.

—adj. **2** *The child gave a longing look at the chocolate cake:* desirous, yearning, craving, hankering, hungering, wishful, pining, languishing, ardent.

Ant. **1** indifference, unconcern, apathy; loathing, disgust, hatred, abhorrence, antipathy, repulsion, revulsion. **2** uninterested, indifferent, unconcerned, apathetic, cold, cool; loathing, disgusted, hateful, scornful.

look *v.* **1** *Look at the flock of geese up there. Look at all the facts before reaching a conclusion:* see, watch, turn the eyes upon, fix the eyes on, regard, contemplate, stare, gape, glance, peep, scan, peek, behold, give attention to, study, scrutinize, survey, examine. **2** *Mother looks angry this morning. You look just like your father:* appear, seem, show, present evidence, exhibit, manifest, strike one as being, have the expression, cut a figure, carry the appearance. **3** *The house looks towards the lake:* face, front, have a view of, be directed, be situated opposite.

—n. **4** *Let's have a look at the new car:* glance, glimpse, peek, peep, visual examination, once-over, contemplation, survey, scrutiny, visual search, reconnaissance, stare, view, observation, sight, gaze, ogle, glare. **5** *Why such a woebegone look? The boss had a happy look on his face:* appearance, general aspect, countenance, presence, mien, expression, demeanour, air, guise, cast, bearing.

Ant. **1** be blind, be unseeing; close one's eyes to, overlook, miss, pass over, neglect, ignore, disregard.

loom *v.* *The Malvern hills loomed high on the horizon:* tower, soar; emerge, come into view suddenly, rise, appear; stand forth, stand out.

Ant. vanish, disappear, melt away, fade away, dissolve from view.

loop *n.* **1** *There are lots of loops in this embroidery:* circle, spiral, whorl, convolution, twirl, coil; eye, eyelet, ring, noose, opening, loophole, aperture; bend, twist, curve.

—v. **2** *Loop the rope over the post and make it fast:* wind round, bend, twist, turn, curve round, circle, coil, curl; roll, furl; plait, braid.

loose *adj., adv.* **1** *Her hair hung loose over her shoulders. The dog ran loose in the yard. The loose papers blew off the desk:* unbound, untied, unfastened, free, freed, freely, liberated; untethered, unchained, unfettered, unyoked, unleashed, uncaged, unimprisoned; unattached, unconnected, unjoined. **2** *Is that shirt loose enough? He likes to wear his coats loose:* slack, free, not fitting tightly, not binding, not tight, not fastened; loosely.

—adj. **3** *Years of loose living made him soft:* wanton, profligate, abandoned, dissipated, debauched, wild, fast, dissolute, licentious, immoral, libertine, lewd, unbridled, unconstrained, unchaste, rakehell. **4** *Her logic is too loose to make much sense:* inexact, unexacting, imprecise, inaccurate, vague, careless, slack, heedless.

—v. **5** *Loose the hounds. They loosed the prisoners' bonds and set them free:* untie, untether, unbind, unfasten, loosen, unloose, undo; free, set free, release, let go, liberate; unbridle, unshackle, unchain, unleash, unmanacle, unhandcuff; slacken.

Ant. **1** tied, bound, secured, fastened, tethered, fettered, chained; restrained, leashed, curbed. **2** tight. **3** moral, abstemious, virtuous, chaste, disciplined, Spartan, puritanical. **4** precise, exact, accurate, clear, meticulous. **5** tie, bind, fasten, tether, fetter, chain, manacle, handcuff; capture, cage, imprison.

loot *n.* **1** *The pirate ships were loaded with loot:* spoils, plunder, booty, stolen goods; *Slang* boodle, haul, swag.
—*v.* **2** *While the police were kept busy in one part of the town, local hooligans were looting shops on the other side:* plunder, pillage, sack, ransack, raid, rob, fleece, strip, pilfer.
◇ *Word origin: Loot* comes to us from Hindi *lūt*, booty, spoils, based on Sanskrit *luptra*, plunder.

loquacious *adj. He's so loquacious that I can't get a word in edgeways:* talkative, garrulous, wordy, verbose, windy, long-winded; prating, chatty, chattery, chattering, prattling; *Informal* gabby, blabby.
Ant. silent, reserved, taciturn, close-mouthed, uncommunicative, reticent.

lord *n. The serfs vowed to do battle for their lord:* king, ruler, sovereign, monarch; master, superior, chief, commander; feudal superior, seignior, land-owner, landholder, proprietor.
◇ *Word origin:* The *lord* of the house is actually "the keeper of the bread." *Lord* comes from Old English *hlāfweard* (*hlāf*, bread, loaf + *weard*, keeper, ward), for the lord was literally the keeper of his men's bread, providing it for them in return for their faithful service.

lordly *adj.* **1** *A lordly feast was provided:* fit for a lord, grand, majestic, regal, magnificent, elegant, sumptuous, stately, princely; lofty, imposing, magisterial, noble; eminent, august, exalted, dignified. **2** *His lordly manners angered everyone:* haughty, arrogant, lofty, proud, disdainful, scornful, aloof, distant, remote, cold, high-and-mighty, hoity-toity, snobbish, imperious, patronizing, condescending, conceited, self-important, *Informal* stuck-up, puffed-up, snooty; tyrannical, despotic, domineering, dictatorial, bossy.
Ant. **1** lowly, plebeian, humble, modest, mean, abject. **2** modest, unassuming, humble; servile, submissive, gentle, mild.

lore *n. The villagers spend hours talking about local folk-lore:* popular knowledge, traditional knowledge, anecdotal knowledge; practical knowledge.

lose *v.* **1** *The man lost his wallet. The enemy lost three ships in the naval battle. The ice skater lost his balance:* suffer loss of, incur the loss of, be deprived of, misplace, mislay; miss, be thrown off. **2** *Don't lose your way in the storm. We lost all track of time:* stray from, miss, confuse; forget, ignore, fail to heed. **3** *The team played well, but lost the game:* be defeated in, be the loser, fail to win, suffer defeat in, fail, have the worst of it, forfeit, take a licking, come out second best.
Ant. **1** keep, retain, hold; save, preserve; find, recover, get back. **2** find, keep. **3** win, have the best of it.

loss *n.* **1** *The loss of the ship ended his career as a captain:* wreck, wrecking, destruction, demolition, ruin, annihilation; extermination, extirpation, extinction, eradication; abolition, dissolution, removal. **2** *Can the company bear the loss of a million pounds? He suffered a temporary loss of memory:* forfeiture, deprivation, privation, bereavement, expenditure, riddance; amount lost, number lost. **3** *How did the boxer take the loss of the fight?:* losing, failure to win, defeat, undoing, overturn, vanquishment; *Slang* pasting. **4** *The loss of her purse caused her much inconvenience:* losing, misplacing, mislaying, being without.
Ant. **1** saving, preservation. **2** gain, acquisition; restoration, recovery, reimbursement. **3** winning, win. **4** finding, recovery.

lost *adj.* **1** *The lost ring was never found. The family searched the whole neighbourhood for the lost dog:* missing, mislaid, misplaced, gone out of one's possession; vanished, strayed, stray, astray, absent, lacking. **2** *The lost hikers asked the policeman for directions:* gone astray, unable to find one's way, off-course. **3** *How many planes were lost in the battle?:* destroyed, wrecked, demolished, ruined, wiped out, abolished, obliterated, annihilated, exterminated, eradicated, extirpated; killed, murdered, perished. **4** *Try to make up for lost time:* wasted, misapplied, squandered, misdirected, misused. **5** *She gazed at the sunset, lost in thought:* absorbed, preoccupied, engrossed.
Ant. **1** found, recovered, reclaimed, returned. **3** saved, preserved.

lot *n.* **1** *The boys drew lots to determine who should play first:* straw, counter. **2** *It was her lot to suffer throughout her life:* fate, allotted portion, share; apportionment, allowance, ration, measure, quota, proportion, allotment. **3** *The neighbours bought a lot to build a house on. Lot 23 was all we wanted at the auction:* parcel of land, plot, property, tract, piece of ground, portion of land, article offered for sale, piece, portion. **4** *We all like ice cream, so give everyone a lot:* great deal, much, many, *Informal* lots, lots and lots, oceans, oodles; *French* beaucoup.
◇ *Usage note: A lot of* and *lots of* are both informal but generally acceptable: *The library has a lot of books, The library has lots of books.* In more formal use, however, some people prefer to use *many, much,* or some other word for *lot* or *lots*, as: *The library has many books* or *The library has a great many books.*
◇ *Word origin: Lot* comes from Old English *hlot*. German, Dutch, and the Scandinavian languages all have words closely resembling *lot*, originally meaning a counter used in keeping score or assigning a duty or reward, hence the drawing of lots. Later *lot* came to mean that which befalls one in life, by

chance, from which we get the game *lotto* and the word *lottery*.

loud *adj.* **1** *Who is making those loud noises?:* noisy, ear-splitting, deafening, clamorous, resounding, sonorous, booming, thundering, blatant, intense; vociferous, loud-mouthed. **2** *What a loud sports jacket!:* garish, gaudy, flashy; bright, vivid, colourful; showy, ostentatious.

Ant. 1 soft, subdued; quiet, silent, inaudible. **2** sedate, sombre, dull, colourless, conservative.

lounge *v.* **1** *On Sundays a lot of people just like to lounge around. The passengers lounged in deckchairs:* loaf, idle, take it easy, do nothing, relax, lie, pass time idly, fritter away time, kill time, dawdle, dally, dilly-dally; recline, stretch out, laze, loll, sprawl, slump, slouch; rest, sleep, slumber.

—n. **2** *Shall we meet in the lounge at three?:* reception-room, reception-hall, vestibule; sitting-room, reading-room.

lousy *adj.* **1** *The mattress is lousy and must be fumigated:* pediculous, infested with lice. **2** *Slang That was a lousy thing to do to anyone. It was a lousy joke:* mean, shabby, nasty, crummy, unethical, unkind, vicious, dreadful, unpleasant; inferior, bad, terrible, rotten, awful, second-rate.

lout *n. That lout doesn't even know that you're supposed to thank your hostess:* boor, churl, clod, oaf, dunce, clown, jerk, booby, dullard, dummy, bumpkin; *Informal* nutter.

Ant. gentleman, sophisticate, dandy, swell.

lovable *adj. Isn't that the most lovable puppy?:* adorable, winsome, endearing, engaging, winning, enchanting, lovely, charming, delightful, super, sweet, cuddly, darling.

Ant. hateful, detestable, odious, obnoxious, abominable, abhorrent, loathsome, repugnant, revolting, repellent, offensive.

love *n.* **1** *The engaged couple swore undying love. She felt a great love for her parents and her country:* passion, passionate affection, the tender passion, rapture, amorousness, ardour, amour, infatuation; devotion, adoration, fondness, tenderness, affection, affectionate regard, warm personal attachment, warm feeling, sentiment, emotion, esteem, admiration; friendship, amity, brotherhood, fellow-feeling, compatibility, affinity, sympathy, concord, congeniality, cordiality; charity, goodwill, benevolence, solicitude. **2** *He has always had a love of good food:* strong liking, fondness, devotion, relish, taste, predilection, attachment, penchant, leaning, partiality, inclination, proclivity, weakness, turn, bent, mind. **3** *He's lonely because his love is out of town this weekend. The theatre was his first love, but he became a radio announcer:* beloved, loved one, inamorata, true-love, paramour, lover, mistress, flame, light of one's life; sweetheart, darling, dear, dearest, precious, angel, sweetie, honey; boy-friend, beau, fellow, man; girl-friend, girl, woman; fondness, attachment, penchant, choice.

—v. **4** *Romeo loved Juliet. W. B. Yeats loved his country. Love thy neighbour:* have a passionate affection for, be filled with rapture by, feel amorous towards, be infatuated with, be enamoured of, be devoted to, adore, be fond of, feel tenderness towards, lose one's heart to, hold dear, regard affectionately, feel warmly towards, admire, esteem, treasure, cherish; sympathize with, feel goodwill towards, feel solicitude for. **5** *I've always loved opera:* like immensely, be fond of, be devoted to, relish, delight in, fancy, take pleasure in, enjoy, appreciate, savour, bask in, rejoice in, revel in, luxuriate in; *Slang* get a kick out of; have a penchant for, have a leaning towards, have a partiality for, have an inclination towards, be drawn to, have a weakness for.

Ant. 1–3 hate, hatred, dislike, distaste, aversion, abhorrence, repugnance, repulsion, disgust, loathing, abomination, detestation, contempt, scorn. **1** animosity, antipathy, antagonism, acrimony, animus, bitterness, resentment, hostility, opposition, malice, ill will, incompatibility, uncongeniality. **3** enemy, foe, rival. **4, 5** hate, dislike, abhor, be disgusted by, loathe, abominate, detest, scorn. **5** find distasteful, be averse to, find repugnant.

lovely *adj. What a lovely dress! The new nurse is a lovely person. We had a lovely time at the party:* attractive, handsome, beautiful, adorable, exquisite, elegant; delightful, charming, enchanting, fascinating, pleasing, pleasant; winsome, winning, lovable, sweet, captivating, alluring, engaging, endearing, irresistible, fetching; good, fine.

Ant. ugly, hideous, unattractive, tasteless; hateful, detestable, odious, obnoxious, offensive, distasteful, abominable, abhorrent, loathsome, repugnant, revolting, repelling, awful, bad.

lover *n.* **1** *The starlet's latest lover is a Hollywood director:* paramour, mistress; beloved, loved one, innamorata, true-love, love, sweetheart; dear, darling, sweetie, honey; boy-friend, beau, fellow, swain, lover-boy, admirer, man; girl-friend, girl, woman. **2** *Art lovers flocked to the opening of the gallery:* devotee, enthusiast, aficionado; fan, fanatic; *Slang* nut, freak, maniac.

loving *adj. She gave her husband a loving look. The child has a very loving nature:* affectionate, fond, tender, amorous, ardent, enamoured, amatory, devoted; warm, sympathetic, caring, kind, friendly, warm-hearted, solicitous, benevolent.

Ant. unloving, hateful, distasteful, disgusting, contemptuous, scornful, angry, hostile; indifferent, unconcerned, aloof, detached, cold, chilly, frigid, mean, cruel.

low *adj.* **1** *Low clouds hid the tops of the skyscrapers. It's hard to sit gracefully in these low chairs:* near the ground, not far above the horizon, low-lying; unelevated; near the floor, low-slung; lower. **2** *A line of low hills was seen in the distance. The main Post Office is in a low, two-storey building:* short, of less than average height, having little elevation, squat, stumpy, stubby, dumpy, snubbed, sawed-off, truncated; small, little. **3** *The low areas were inundated by the high tide:* low-lying, below sea-level, near sea-level, unelevated, coastal; concave, sunken, depressed; underwater, submerged, deep, undersea, submarine; underground. **4** *I've been feeling low all week:* unhappy, depressed, dejected, disheartened, despondent, doleful, downcast, down, melancholy, gloomy, dispirited, glum, lethargic; *Informal* in the doldrums, blue, down in the mouth. **5** *The winning ticket had a low number. The student passed with low marks. He works for low pay because he loves the job:* small, little; lowly, humble, insignificant, inconsequential, unimportant, low-ranking, paltry, trifling, common, mediocre, inferior. **6** *How could anyone do such a low thing?:* mean, base, vile, awful, terrible, scurvy, despicable, ignominious, dishonourable, unworthy, contemptible, abominable, repulsive, repugnant, heinous, cruel, brutal, outrageous, scandalous, disrespectful, nefarious, scoundrelly, corrupt, unethical, wicked, evil, cowardly, dastardly; degraded, depraved, sordid, squalid, gross, coarse, vulgar, obscene, dirty; *Slang* crummy, caddish. **7** *Speak in a low voice:* subdued, hushed, muffled, muted, quiet; whispered, murmured, faint, feeble; soft, gentle, soothing; low-pitched, of a low tone.
—*adv.* **8** *Bend down low. Speak low:* in or to a low position, prone, prostrate; to a low degree; in a low tone, quietly, softly; deep.
Ant. 1–5, 7, 8 high. **2** tall, lofty, soaring, towering. **3** elevated. **4** happy, elated, cheerful, gay, enthusiastic, peppy, full of pep, energetic, alert; *Informal* bright-eyed and bushy-tailed. **5** superior, grand, lofty, elevated, exalted, eminent, consequential, significant, important, illustrious, high-ranking, above average. **6** wonderful, fine, admirable, commendable, praiseworthy, laudable, meritorious, creditable, honourable, worthy, uplifted, angelic; courteous; brave. **7** loud, noisy, strong, raucous; high-pitched.

lower[1] *v.* **1** *The carpenter should lower that shelf about two feet. Lower the blind to keep out the sun. The deer lowered its head to drink from the pond:* make lower, decrease the height of, drop, pull down, let down, take down, put down, depress; submerge, immerse, duck, sink. **2** *We must lower our expenses:* decrease, reduce, diminish, make less, curtail, pare, pare down, cut, shorten, abbreviate, prune, lop off, render less, subtract from, detract from, deduct. **3** *Please lower your voice. Can you lower those bright lights a little?:* tone down, soften, subdue, make less intense, dim, damp, muffle, mute, repress.
—*adj.* **4** *What people really want is lower taxation:* reduced, decreased, diminished, lessened, curtailed, pared, pared down.
Ant. 1–3 raise. **1** elevate, lift up, pull up, hoist. **2** increase, enlarge, inflate, boost, magnify, amplify, augment, aggrandize; extend, protract, prolong. **4** higher, increased, enlarged.
◇ *Pronunciation tip:* See LOWER[2].

> **Exploring the Word**: Literature, drama, and opera have given us several well-known words for lovers, lady-killers, and philanderers. *Lothario* comes from the name of the rake in Nicolas Rowe's play *The Fair Penitent* (1703). *Romeo*, of course, comes from Shakespeare's tragedy *Romeo and Juliet* (1596) and Gounod's opera based on it (1867), though the story of the young lovers doomed by their families' feud, and the name *Romeo* and his sentimental, romantic character, appeared in several plays and poems before Shakespeare wrote his famous version. *Don Juan* (the *Juan* is pronounced "hwan" except when reading Byron's *Don Juan* — Byron pronounced it *Don JOO-an*) comes from the name of a legendary Spanish libertine who has had an extremely active literary life, appearing in works by Dumas père, Balzac, Flaubert, Pushkin, Molière, Bernard Shaw (the "Don Juan in Hell" section of *Man and Superman*), and Byron (his epic satire *Don Juan* bears only a slight resemblance to the legend), as the title of a tone poem by Richard Strauss, and, most brilliantly of all, as the hero of Mozart's opera *Don Giovanni*. *Casanova* comes from the name of G. J. Casanova de Seingalt, 1725–98, an Italian adventurer who acquired lasting fame thanks to his *Memoirs*, which describe his life as a gambler, charlatan, and amorous adventurer throughout Europe.

lower[2] *v. The boss lowered when he saw all the workers standing around talking:* scowl, glare, look sullen, give a dark look, frown, sulk, glower.
◇ *Pronunciation tip: Lower*[1], meaning "to pull down" or "decreased," is pronounced *LOW-er*. *Lower*[2], meaning "to scowl or frown," is pronounced *LOU-er* and rhymes with "tower."

lowly *adj. The firm's director was not ashamed of his lowly origins. He rose from lowly birth to become the queen's consort:* humble, simple, modest, unassuming, unpretentious, obscure, low-bred, low-born, baseborn, plebeian, proletarian, ignoble.

loyal *adj. The king rewarded his loyal supporters. A good friend is always loyal:* faithful, steadfast, true, constant, trusty, trustworthy, devoted, dependable, unwavering, unswerving, staunch, firm, dutiful, true-blue, tried and true.

Ant. disloyal, false, faithless, unfaithful, perfidious, treacherous, untrustworthy; rebellious, traitorous, treasonous.

◇ *Word origin: Loyal* comes from Latin *legalis*, legal. The connection with the idea of *legality* is this: *loyal* originally meant "faithful to one's legal obligations."

loyalty *n. Once he took the vow his loyalty never wavered:* faithfulness, steadfastness, constancy, trustworthiness, devotion, dependability, staunchness, allegiance, adherence, fealty.

Ant. disloyalty, falsity, falseness, faithlessness, inconstancy, perfidiousness, perfidy, treachery; sedition, rebellion, insurrection.

lozenge *n. Take a throat lozenge to stop your cough:* pastille, small confection, troche; cough-drop, small medicated sweet, tablet, pill.

◇ *Word origin: Lozenge* literally means "diamond-shaped" and comes from a Gaulish word meaning "slab, flat stone," which made its way into Late Latin as *lausiae*, "slates." Early cough lozenges (in the 1500's) were diamond-shaped — hence the modern meaning.

lucid *adj.* **1** *The witness gave a lucid account of what happened:* clear, easily understood, crystal clear, intelligible, understandable, articulate, comprehensible; precise, direct, straightforward, accurate, specific, well-organized, to the point, apposite, positive, certain. **2** *Although often delirious, the patient has some lucid moments:* clear-headed, clear-thinking, normal, rational; responsive, perceptive.

Ant. 1 unintelligible, incomprehensible, vague, indistinct, unclear, ambiguous, equivocal, garbled, mystifying. **2** confused, muddled, irrational; unresponsive, unperceptive.

◇ *Word origin: Lucid* comes from Latin *lucere*, to shine, to be shining clear or sparkling clean.

"You see this yer Dow
Hed the worst kind of luck;
He slipped up somehow
On each thing that he struck."
—*Francis Brett Hart*

---

luck *n.* **1** *As luck would have it, we arrived just as they were leaving:* fortune, fate, destiny, kismet; chance, occasion, accident, Lady Luck, wheel of fortune. **2** *With a little luck the team would have won. Did you have any luck in finding a job?:* good luck, good fortune, happy accident, piece of luck, smile of fortune; success, victory, triumph.

Ant. 1 design, cause and effect. **2** bad luck; failure, defeat.

lucky *adj.* **1** *I suppose I'm just not lucky:* fortunate, blest with good luck, in luck, favoured, blessed, born under a lucky star. **2** *It was a lucky accident that the train was late. This is your lucky day!:* fortunate, opportune, timely, beneficial, good, happy, felicitous, providential, auspicious, propitious, favourable, bringing good luck, of good omen, promising.

Ant. 1, 2 unlucky, unfortunate, ill-favoured. **2** untimely, detrimental, bad, unhappy; inauspicious, unfavourable, unpromising, sinister, ominous.

lucrative *adj. The eldest brother now has a very lucrative job:* profitable, money-making, remunerative, well-paid, gainful, high-income.

Ant. unprofitable, low-paid, unremunerative.

◇ *Word origin: Lucrative* comes from Latin *lucrum*, gain, which also gives us *lucre*, as in the expression "filthy lucre."

ludicrous *adj. It was so ludicrous to see the child throw away the banana and try to eat the skin!:* ridiculous, absurd, crazy, outlandish, preposterous, nonsensical; amusing, laughable, comic, comical, funny, farcical; *Slang* wild, far-out.

Ant. sensible, logical; tragic, grave, solemn, serious, sad, sorry, doleful, dolorous, melancholy.

◇ *Word origin: Ludicrous* comes from Latin *ludere*, to play, which also gives us *illusion* (literally that which plays with or makes sport of our ideas, impressions, or concepts).

lug *v. Lug these boxes up into the attic:* drag, tote, carry, carry with difficulty, transport; pull, tow, draw, tug.

◇ *Word origin: Lug* is related to Swedish *lugga*, to pull by the hair.

luggage *n. Are you going to carry your luggage or find a porter?:* baggage, bags, suitcases, trunks.

◇ *Word origin:* As any traveller with a heavy suitcase knows, *luggage* is so called because it is what one *lugs* around whilst travelling.

lull *v.* **1** *The mother lulled the child to sleep:* soothe, quiet, calm, pacify, hush, still, quell, subdue, compose, assuage, mollify, ease.
—*n.* **2** *There was a sudden lull in the conversation. This is just the lull before the storm:* hush, quiet, temporary stillness, brief silence, quiet interval, pause, break, interlude, interruption, halt, hiatus, gap, caesura, lacuna, short rest, respite, recess, breather, breathing-space; calm, calmness, tranquillity.

Ant. 1 excite, arouse, rouse, aggravate, provoke, incite. **2** continuation, resumption; flow, gush, spurt; excitement, tumult, turbulence, violence.

lumber[1] *n. The attic is the place where we store all our lumber:* cumbrous material, unused furniture, junk.

◇ *Word origin:* What does lumber have to do with Lombardy? In medieval times, the region of Lombardy (whose capital is Milan) was a financial centre and *Lombard* came to mean a banker, money-lender, or pawnbroker, and later to mean stored articles, as those left for collateral or in pawn. From this meaning of stored items we get our word *lumber*, furniture no longer needed and stacked away. Incidentally, Lombard Street in London is so named because many banks and financial offices are located there.

lumber[2] *v. The hippopotamus lumbered into the water:* waddle, trudge, move clumsily, move heavily, plod, clump, shamble, shuffle.

luminary *n.* **1** *The sun is only one of thousands of luminaries in the sky:* light, luminosity, body that gives off light; source of light, illuminator. **2** *Many luminaries attended the opening of the opera season:* celebrity, famous person, eminent person, personage, dignitary, notable, *Slang* bigwig, big shot, V.I.P., somebody.

◇ *Word origin:* See LUMINOUS.

luminescent *adj. Children love to watch the luminescent light of fireflies:* glowing, aglow, luminous, gleaming, glimmering, shimmering; glistening, twinkling, flickering; fluorescent, phosphorescent, not incandescent, glowing without heat.

Ant. incandescent, caused by heat, hot.

luminous *adj. The watch has a luminous dial:* reflecting light, luminescent, radiant, irradiated, glowing, illuminated, shining; shining in the dark.

◇ *Word origin: Luminous, luminescent,* and *luminary* come from Latin *lumen,* light. Our unit for measuring the flow of light is called a *lumen,* and the Latin word also gives us *illuminate* (literally, to light thoroughly).

lump *n.* **1** *Break up these large lumps of soil:* mass, gob, chunk, clod, clump, cake, hunk. **2** *How did you get that lump on your head?:* bump, swelling, protuberance, knot, knob, node, nodule, knurl, protrusion, excrescence; tumour, tumescence, growth.

—*v.* **3** *Lump all our money together and let's see how much we've got:* heap, pile, unite, mass, amass, gather, bunch, batch, group, compile, assemble, aggregate, collect; combine, merge, pool, fuse, mix, blend.

Ant. **1** granule, grain, particle, bit. **2** depression, cavity, concavity, hollow, indentation, dent, pit, dip, dimple. **3** scatter, disperse; separate, divide.

lunacy *n.* **1** *Modern medicine and psychiatry can prevent certain forms of lunacy:* insanity, insaneness, madness, mental derangement, psychopathic condition. **2** *It's sheer lunacy to drive so fast:* folly, foolishness, foolhardiness, imprudence, absurdity, silliness, senselessness, craziness; imbecility, idiocy, stupidity.

Ant. **1** sanity, reason. **2** good sense, prudence.

lunatic *n.* **1** *The lunatic was committed to a mental asylum:* madman, maniac, insane person, deranged person, crazy person; psychopath, demoniac; *Slang* nut, cuckoo, loony.

—*adj.* **2** *The man's lunatic behaviour is a menace to society:* insane, crazy, mad, deranged, demented, maniacal, unhinged, unbalanced, daft, irrational, non compos mentis, of unsound mind, mentally ill, senseless, reasonless; *Slang* round the bend, crackers, bonkers, potty, nutty, cracked, crack-brained, batty, screwy, loony, cuckoo, touched, loco, off one's rocker, touched in the head, out of one's mind, not all there, not right in the head, not in one's right mind; psychotic, psychopathic.

Ant. **2** sane, sound, rational, reasonable; *Slang* all there.

◇ *Word origin:* Insanity was once thought to be controlled by the moon and its phases. *Lunatic* literally means "moonstruck", subject to the changes of the moon, and comes from Latin *luna,* moon, from which we also get our word *lunar.*

lunge *n.* **1** *The boxer made a lunge at his opponent:* charge, rush, plunge, thrust; lightning attack, jab, stab, pass, swing, swipe, cut.

—*v.* **2** *The swordsman lunged at the foe:* thrust, jab, stab, strike at, hit at; attack, charge, pounce, make a pass, set upon, fall upon.

Ant. **2** recoil, step back; parry.

◇ *Word origin:* To *lunge* literally means to extend or elongate one's arm or body forward. It comes from French *allonger,* to make longer, and is related to our word *long.*

lurch *v. The sailor lost his balance when the ship lurched. The sick man lurched forward and then fell:* roll, pitch, list, tilt, incline, heave, keel, slant, toss, swerve; jerk forward, lunge, plunge; stagger, stumble, sway, reel, totter.

lure *n.* **1** *Is cheese really a good lure for mice? The fisherman used a metal lure that looked like a minnow:* bait, decoy; trap, snare. **2** *The sale of television sets was just a lure to get cusomers into the store:* enticement, allurement, inducement, allure, attraction, temptation; blandishment, cajolery, bribe; *Slang* come-on, carrot.

—*v.* **3** *The decoys lured the ducks to the pond. The travel brochure lured me into taking a Caribbean holiday:* entice, allure, attract, tempt, tantalize, fascinate, beguile, seduce; coax, cajole, persuade, induce.

Ant. **1** repellent. **3** revolt, repel, deter.

◇ *Word origin: Lure* comes from an Old French word of Germanic origin, *loirre,* bait.

lurid *adj.* **1** *The painting was full of lurid colours:* fiery, bright-red, flaming, bloody, sanguine, scarlet, carmine, rubicund; glaring, glowing, shining. **2** *The book told a lurid tale of crime in the big city:* sensational, graphic, dramatic, vivid, melodramatic, wildly emotional; appalling, shocking, grim, ghastly, eerie, gory, bloodcurdling.

Ant. 1 pale, watery, pastel. 2 mild, light-hearted, gay, sunny, breezy, jaunty, carefree.

lurk *v. The thief lurked in the shadows:* skulk, slink, prowl, sneak, lie in wait, lie concealed, hide, lie in ambush; go furtively.

luscious *adj. Nothing is more luscious than wild strawberries:* delicious, mouth-watering, succulent, sweet and juicy, delectable, appetizing, flavourful, tasty, savoury, toothsome; fragrant, scented, perfumed, aromatic.

Ant. sour, acid, vinegary, tart, bitter; bland, flavourless, tasteless.

◇ *Word origin: Luscious* is probably a shortening of *delicious.*

"I dote on myself, there is that lot of me and all so luscious." —*Walt Whitman*

---

lush *adj.* 1 *The grass looked very lush after the rain:* luxuriant, flourishing, dense, prolific. 2 *Our suite at the Ritz is exceptionally lush:* luxurious, grand, sumptuous, plush, elegant, magnificent, elaborate, ornate, splendid, fancy; *Slang* posh.

Ant. 1 sparse, thin, meagre, scanty; barren, arid. 2 plain, simple, crude, Spartan.

lust *n.* 1 *The dictator's lust for power knew no bounds. Lust is one of the seven deadly sins:* passion, strong desire, craving; bodily appetite, fleshly desire, sexuality, libidinousness, lasciviousness, lewdness, salaciousness, satyriasis, nymphomania, carnality, lechery.

—*v.* 2 *The old miser still lusts after money. Phaedra lusted after Hippolytus and caused his death:* desire intensely, crave, have a passion for, covet, hunger for; seek sexually, be lascivious, be libidinous, be lewd, be lecherous.

Ant. 1 unconcern, apathy. 2 be indifferent; spurn, disdain, scorn.

◇ *Word origin: Lust* comes from Old English *lust,* pleasure, desire, appetite, sexual desire. (In Modern German the corresponding word is *Lust,* which means "pleasure, fun.")

lustre *n.* 1 *This polish brings out the lustre of the silver:* shine, gleam, sheen, gloss, brightness, brilliance, resplendence, sparkle, radiance, refulgence, glow, glimmer, glitter, dazzle; radiation, luminosity, luminousness. 2 *Winning the Nobel prize added even more lustre to the poet's name:* glory, distinction, illustriousness, fame, prestige, honour; merit, notability.

Ant. 1 dullness; tarnish. 2 ignominy, dishonour, shame, infamy, disrepute.

◇ *Word origin: Lustre* and *lustrous* come to us via Italian *lustrare,* to light up, from Latin *lucere,* to shine. The same Latin word gives us *lucid* and *illustrate.*

lusty *adj. Robin Hood led a group of fine, lusty men:* hearty, full of life, vigorous, robust, virile, husky, brawny, strapping, healthy, sound; exuberant, whole-hearted, unrestrained, uninhibited, irrepressible.

Ant. lifeless, dull, lethargic, listless; effete, exhausted, feeble, weak, infirm, decrepit, frail, sickly.

luxuriant *adj.* 1 *The jungle had a luxuriant growth of vines:* lush, flourishing, dense, profuse, abundant, overgrown, teeming. 2 *The building is covered with luxuriant scroll-work:* elaborate, ornate, fancy, elegant, magnificent, splendid, extravagant, luxurious, grand, sumptuous; florid, flowery.

Ant. 1 sparse, thin, meagre, scanty; barren, arid. 2 plain, simple, unadorned.

◇ *Usage note:* See LUXURIOUS.

luxuriate *v. After a week of adventure the campers luxuriated in hot baths and soft beds:* bask, delight, indulge in, relish, rejoice in, wallow in, live in luxury.

luxurious *adj.* 1 *The house is full of luxurious carpets:* expensive, costly, rich, grand, elegant, sumptuous; enjoyable, comfortable, pleasurable, gratifying, pleasure-giving. 2 *She's very fond of luxurious living:* costly, extremely comfortable, wealthy, given to luxury; loving luxury, indulgent, over-indulged, pampered; effete, decadent.

Ant. 2 ascetic, austere, Spartan, deprived; frugal, thrifty, economical, sparing, temperate; poor, squalid.

◇ *Usage note:* Beware of confusing *luxurious* and *luxuriant. Luxurious* means "characterized by luxury": *A Rolls-Royce is a luxurious car. LuxuriANT* means "*abundANT*, growing profusely": *The garden had luxuriant foliage.*

luxury *n.* 1 *She's lived in luxury all her life:* luxuriousness, material abundance, extreme comfort; high standard of living, wealth, riches, affluence; *Slang* high living. 2 *A long hot bath can be pure luxury:* delight, enjoyment, pleasure, satisfaction, gratification, bliss, heaven, paradise. 3 *Buying a new coat before the old one had worn out would just have been a luxury:* extravagance, indulgence, non-necessity, non-essential.

Ant. 1 poverty, penury, destitution, straitened circumstances; deprivation, austerity, need, want, difficulty, distress. 2 deprivation, privation, hardship, affliction, burden, trial, infliction, misery. 3 necessity.

lynch *v. The mob lynched the suspected murderer:* hang, gibbet, execute without due process of law; *Informal* string up.

◇ *Word origin: Lynch* is originally an American word. It comes from *Lynch's law,* the name of a compact drawn up by Captain William Lynch of Virginia and his neighbours in 1780 by which they enabled themselves to deal summarily with horse-stealers, counterfeiters, and others. As to the nature of the punishment to be meted out, the compact simply states, "We will inflict such corporeal punishment on him or them, as to us shall seem adequate to the crime committed or the damage sustained."

lyric Also **lyrical** *adj.* **1** *The playwright has a lyric gift:* songlike, melodious, musical, melodic, lilting, sweet-sounding, mellifluous, mellifluent; poetic.
—*n.* **2** Often **lyrics** *If you don't know the lyrics of the song, just hum the tune:* words of a song; poem expressing a poet's own thoughts.
◇ *Word origin: Lyric* comes from Greek *lyra*, a lyre, the small harplike instrument played while held upright in the lap. (The Greeks used the lyre to accompany poetry and song.)

M

macabre *adj. The macabre story of headless ghosts frightened the children:* gruesome, grim, ghastly, horrible, frightful, frightening, horrid, dreadful, horrific; eerie, weird, ghostlike.
Ant. pleasant, beautiful, lovely, appealing, inviting, delightful.
◇ *Pronunciation tip: Macabre* should always be pronounced so that the second syllable is stressed, *ma-KAH-bruh, ma-KAH-ber,* or, sometimes, *ma-KAHB.*
◇ *Word origin: Macabre* comes to us from Old French *danse macabre,* dance of death, literally "dance of the Maccabees." Why did "dance of the Maccabees" mean "dance of death"? Perhaps because of a now-lost miracle play based on the Old Testament Apocrypha story of the Maccabees, a family who led a bloody war of liberation against the Syrians which lasted for almost 30 years. (The war ended in 142 B.C. with the establishment, of an independent Jewish state which was to be ruled by the descendants of the original Maccabees until the Roman conquest of 63 B.C.) There is much that is *macabre* in the tale of the Maccabees.

Machiavellian *adj. The prime minister has a Machiavellian scheme to get himself appointed the young king's guardian:* scheming, designing, self-serving, underhand, amoral, treacherous, perfidious, unscrupulous, cunning, crafty, devious, deceitful, false-hearted.
Ant. naïve, ingenuous, open, candid, frank, straightforward.
◇ *Word origin:* Machiavellian comes from the name of the Florentine diplomat Niccolò Machiavelli, 1469-1527, whose book *The Prince* outlined ruthless ways to get and keep political power.

machination *n. By a series of machinations one partner gained complete control of the business:* scheme, intrigue, design, crafty plan, rule, conspiracy, plot, artifice, device, stratagem, manœuvre, contrivance, ruse, dodge.
◇ *Pronunciation tip:* The *ch* in *machination* may be pronounced either *k* or *sh: mak-i-NA-tion* or *mash-i-NA-tion.*

machine *n.* **1** *The washing-machine needs repairing:* apparatus, appliance, device, mechanism, mechanical contrivance. **2** *The M.P. has a well-oiled political machine working for his re-election:* organization, body, force, association, combine, union, society, pool, trust, faction, group, gang, ring, club, set, coterie, army, corps; structure, machinery, system, set-up.
◇ *Word origin: Machine, machinery,* and *machination* come from Greek *mēchanē,* machine, contrivance. The same Greek word gives us *mechanical* and *mechanics.*

machinery *n.* **1** *The ship's machinery is being overhauled:* mechanical equipment, mechanism, apparatus, gear, contrivances; tools, tackle. **2** *He is defying the machinery of school authority:* system, organization, structure, set-up, make-up; *Slang* wheels.

macrocosm *n. The earth is but a speck in the macrocosm:* cosmos, universe, the great world, creation, nature; heavens, firmament.
Ant. microcosm.
◇ *Word origin: Macrocosm* comes from Greek *makros* (great, large) + *kosmos* (world, universe), which also gives us *cosmic, cosmos, cosmopolitan* (at home anywhere in the world), and *microcosm* (literally "little world").

mad *adj.* **1** *I was mad at missing my bus:* angry, furious, irate, enraged, infuriated, incensed, wrathful, exasperated, provoked, miffed, fuming, foaming at the mouth, boiling over, seeing red, flushed with anger, in high dudgeon, livid, wild, wrought up, worked up, riled, in a huff, up in arms; *Informal* shirty, hopping mad. **2** *Van Gogh had periods during which he was completely mad:* insane, crazy, demented, lunatic, crazed, deranged, maniacal, unbalanced, irrational, unhinged, bereft of reason, daft, balmy, not quite right, not all there, out of one's mind, not right in one's upper storey; *Slang* crackers, round the bend, nuts, nutty, nutty as a fruit-cake, cuckoo, cracked, screwy, have a screw loose, off one's rocker, touched, loco; non compos mentis, *Informal* non compos. **3** *The two sisters are mad about tennis. He's been mad about her for months:* enthusiastic, wild, excited, fanatic, avid, devoted to, frenzied, impassioned, ardent; infatuated, in love with, beside oneself, distracted, distraught.

Ant. 1 appeased, mollified. 2 sane, sound, rational. 3 calm, cool, collected, composed, unexcited, uncaring, nonchalant; disdainful.

◇ *Usage note:* For decades, purists have been telling people that *mad* means "insane" and not to use it to mean "angry." Nevertheless, *mad* certainly does mean "angry," and expressions such as *I'm mad with him, She's mad because she wasn't invited to the party* are quite common.

◇ *Word origin: Mad* is a shortened form of Old English *gemād,* insane.

"When we remember we are all mad, the mysteries disappear and life stands explained." —*Mark Twain*

---

madam *n. Madam, it is a pleasure to serve you:* lady, madame; matron, dowager, Mrs., *French* madame, *Spanish* señora, *Italian* signora, *German* Frau; *Archaic* dame, mistress.

◇ *Word origin: Madam* is from Old French *ma dame,* my lady, which also gives us *madame.* The similar Italian phrase *ma donna,* my lady, gives us *madonna.*

made *adj. Can you tell us how this chair was made?:* manufactured, fabricated, produced, constructed, built, assembled, formed; created, composed, developed.

madhouse *n.* 1 *Two inmates escaped from the madhouse:* insane asylum, lunatic asylum, mental hospital, mental institution, psychopathic hospital; *Slang* loony-bin, nuthouse. 2 *I can't do any work — this place is a madhouse:* bedlam, scene of pandemonium, uproar, turmoil, wild confusion.

madman *n. Only a madman would rage and fume like that:* lunatic, insane person, maniac, deranged person, crazy person, demoniac, psychopath.

maelstrom *n.* 1 *The canoe was caught in the maelstrom:* whirlpool, rapids, vortex, swirl, eddy, white water, undertow. 2 *He's involved in the maelstrom of politics:* confusion, disorder, upheaval, tumult, uproar, pandemonium, bedlam, madhouse.

◇ *Word origin: Maelstrom* is from Dutch *maalen* (to whirl around, grind) + *stroom* (stream).

magazine *n.* 1 *You must be pleased to have got an article published in the magazine:* periodical, journal; (*variously*) weekly, monthly, quarterly. 2 *There was an explosion in the ship's magazine:* powder-magazine, powder-room, munitions-room; arsenal, military storehouse, military depot.

◇ *Word origin: Magazine* is from Arabic *makhāzin* storehouse; a powder-*magazine* is where gunpowder is stored and a *magazine* for readers is a storehouse of information.

magenta *n. The evening sky was a deep magenta:* reddish purple, purplish rose, fuchsia; maroon, vermilion; crimson, carmine.

◇ *Word origin: Magenta,* the dye, was discovered just after the French victory in 1859 over Austria at Magenta in Italy, and named to celebrate it.

maggot *n. The cheese was full of maggots:* larva, grub, worm, meal-worm.

◇ *Word origin: Maggot* comes from Old Norse *mathkr,* worm.

magic *n.* 1 *Some Haitians still practise magic:* black magic, voodoo, voodooism, sorcery, occultism, the black art, wizardry; witchcraft, witchery, demonology; spell, conjuration, divination. 2 *The magician thrilled the audience with his feats of magic:* prestidigitation, legerdemain, sleight of hand, hocus-pocus, jugglery. 3 *There was magic in the great man's presence:* animal magnetism, fascination, captivation, charisma, charm, enchantment, lure, allurement, entrancement.

Ant. 1 science, facts and figures.

◇ *Word origin: Magic* can be traced all the way back to Old Persian *magus,* member of the priestly caste of the Medes and Persians. The Magi, "wise men from the east," who came to Bethlehem bearing gifts to pay homage to the infant Jesus (Matthew 2: 1–12) were, of course, members of this caste.

magician *n.* 1 *Merlin was the famous magician at King Arthur's court:* wizard, sorcerer, shaman, warlock; witch-doctor, medicine-man; alchemist. 2 *Harry Houdini was a famous magician in vaudeville:* prestidigitator, sleight-of-hand artist, expert in legerdemain, escape artist; conjurer, juggler.

magistrate *n. His driving offence came up before the magistrates, but he elected to be tried by Judge and jury:* justice of the peace, *Informal* J.P.; minor judge, judicial officer, civil officer, prefect, police judge.

◇ *Word origin: Magistrate* comes from Latin *magister,* master, and later meant any minor judicial officer.

magnanimous *adj. Only a truly magnanimous man could forgive such insults:* forgiving, free of vindictiveness, generous, large-hearted, liberal; charitable, beneficent, philanthropic, altruistic, unselfish, princely.

Ant. unforgiving, vindictive, resentful, small, petty, selfish; parsimonious, miserly.

◇ *Word origin: Magnanimous* and *magnanimity* come from Latin *magnus* (great, large) + *animus* (spirit), literally having a large mind or spirit.

magnate *n. Lord Beaverbrook was a magnate of the newspaper industry:* leader, dominant person, great man, important person, VIP, influential person, notable, celebrity, *Slang* bigwig, big shot, big gun; nabob, tycoon, industrialist, giant of industry.

◇ *Pronunciation tip:* A *magnate* is not a magnet! Be sure to pronounce *magnate* as *MAG-nate.*

magnetic *adj.* 1 *The North Pole has a strong*

magnetic force: of a magnet, of magnetism. **2** *She has a magnetic personality:* attractive, fascinating, persuasive; captivating, charismatic, enchanting, alluring, entrancing, charming, irresistible, inviting, seductive.
Ant. 1 antimagnetic. **2** repellent, repulsive.
◇ *Word origin: Magnet* comes from Greek *Magnēs lithos,* "the stone of Magnesia," an ancient city in Asia Minor, from which magnesium oxide was exported. This substance is best known to us as the white powder used in the laxative, milk of Magnesia.

magnetism *n.* **1** *Magnetism makes a compass needle point north:* magnetic force, magnetic attraction. **2** *You could feel the magnetism of the singer's personality:* attraction, fascination, captivation, charisma, hypnotic appeal, enchantment, charm, enticement, allure, allurement, animal magnetism, lure, mesmerism, seduction.
Ant. 1 repulsion. **2** repulsiveness, repellency.

magnificent *adj. Mozart's* Don Giovanni *is a magnificent opera:* splendid, superb, grand, glorious, extraordinary, wonderful, fine, elegant, exquisite, noble, majestic, imposing, commanding, stately, august, transcendent, brilliant, resplendent.
Ant. modest, ordinary, undistinguished, unimposing, unassuming, humble, mean, lowly, ignoble, poor, tawdry, trifling, trivial, petty, paltry, bad; *Slang* awful, lousy.

magnify *v.* **1** *This microscope magnifies the object 500 times:* enlarge optically, increase the apparent size of, *Informal* blow up. **2** *She tends to magnify all her problems beyond recognition:* enlarge, expand, amplify, inflate, heighten, stretch, maximize, boost, double; *Informal* blow up, puff up; exaggerate, depict extravagantly, overstate, enlarge upon, overrate, embroider. **3** *The Bible says that we must magnify the Lord:* laud, praise, acclaim, exalt, extol, glorify, revere, adore, worship, reverence.
Ant. 1, 2 reduce. **2** diminish, decrease, deflate, lessen, lower, minimize, constrict, shrink; understate, underplay; belittle, deprecate.

magnitude *n.* **1** *The auditorium is a building of great magnitude:* size, extent, expanse, dimensions, proportions, mass, bulk, amplitude, volume, measure; bigness, hugeness, enormity, largeness, vastness, immensity; brightness. **2** *The professor is a scientist of considerable magnitude:* eminence, distinction, renown, repute, fame, celebrity, importance, consequence, significance, greatness.
Ant. 1 smallness, diminutiveness, meanness. **2** insignificance, unimportance, paltriness, triviality, triflingness.
◇ *Word origin: Magnitude* comes from Latin *magnus,* large, which also gives us *magnify, magnanimous,* and *magnificent.*

maid *n. It takes two maids and a gardener to keep up that big house:* housemaid, maid-servant, female servant, domestic, hired girl, (*variously*) nursemaid, parlourmaid, lady's maid, between-maid; cook, char, *Slang* tweeny.
◇ *Word origin:* See MAIDEN.

maiden *n.* **1** *The prince fell in love with a fair young maiden:* girl, lass, maid, virgin, lassie, colleen, damsel, demoiselle, soubrette, ingénue.
—*adj.* **2** Also **maidenly** *Her maiden blushes were most becoming:* girlish, youthful, chaste, virginal; unmarried. **3** *The* Titanic *sank on her maiden voyage. The new Member made his maiden speech in the House today:* first, initial, inaugural, original, introductory, initiatory.
Ant. 1 matron, dowager, lady, madam, grande dame. **2** matronly; unchaste; married, wedded, espoused.
◇ *Word origin: Maiden* and its short form *maid* come from Old English *mægden,* virgin, young woman.

mail[1] *n.* **1** *Did we get any mail this morning?:* post; (*variously*) letters, postcards, packages. **2** *The mail has been slow lately:* postal service, mail delivery, post-office service; air mail, surface mail.
—*v.* **3** *Mail the cheque today:* post, put in the post, get out, drop in a letter-box; send by post, send by mail.
◇ *Word origin: Mail* is still delivered in a mail-bag or pouch. *Mail* comes from Old High German *malha,* pouch, wallet, sack.

mail[2] *n. Sir Lancelot donned his coat of mail:* armour, arms, suit of mail, flexible armour of interlinked rings, defensive armour.

main *adj. The administrative office is in the main building. The main thing is to keep costs down:* leading, principal, central, chief, head, primary, foremost, prime, capital, predominant, paramount, outstanding, pre-eminent, supreme; vital, essential, necessary, indispensable, requisite, important, critical, crucial, urgent, pressing, consequential; special, particular.
Ant. subordinate, secondary, dependent, collateral, auxiliary, ancillary; unimportant, insignificant, trivial, minor, lesser, least, nonessential.

mainly *adv. The book is mainly about the author's childhood:* chiefly, principally, mostly, primarily, predominantly, for the most part, most of all, above all, in the main, on the whole, in great measure, first and foremost.
Ant. secondarily, subordinately; partially, slightly, least of all, minimally.

mainstay *n. He was the mainstay of the local theatre:* chief support, principal reliance; pillar, pillar of strength, prop, anchor.

maintain *v.* **1** *The two class-mates maintained their friendship for the next forty years:* keep, keep up, keep alive, keep going, continue, sustain, preserve, conserve, uphold. **2** *How can they maintain such a large house? The candidate maintained his position despite stinging criticism:* take care of, support, provide for, keep, keep up, care for, finance; stand by, defend, uphold. **3** *Each driver maintained that the accident was the other's fault:* declare, affirm, assert, state, insist, contend; hold, swear, avow, aver, profess, allege, claim.

Ant. 1 end, terminate, conclude, discontinue, drop, finish, abolish, dissolve, suspend, break off. **2** give up, relinquish; abandon, desert. **3** retract, disavow.

◇ *Word origin: Maintain* comes from the Latin phrase *manu tenere* (*manus*, hand; *tenere*, to have), to hold, to hold in one's hand.

maintenance *n.* **1** *Our foreign policy involves the maintenance of friendly relations with all countries. The Clerk of Works was responsible for the building's maintenance:* preservation, conservation, keeping, safe-keeping, safeguarding, protection; upkeep, repair. **2** *After the divorce he paid £200 a month for the maintenance of the children:* support, upkeep, subsistence, sustaining, sustenance, living, livelihood, keep.

Ant. 1 destruction, dissolution, eradication, abolition, termination, discontinuance, suspension.

◇ *Spelling tip:* There is no "maintain" in *mainTENance.* Remember this sentence: *A pounds worth of mainTENance may save you TEN pounds in repairs later.*

majestic *adj. In the distance rose the majestic Alps:* stately, august, grand, imposing, impressive, magnificent, splendid, glorious, superb, sublime, noble, lofty, elegant; regal, imperial, royal, princely; distinguished, famous, esteemed, illustrious, eminent, renowned.

Ant. modest, ordinary, unimposing, unassuming, humble, lowly, mean, ignoble, tawdry, paltry, undistinguished.

majesty *n. The majesty of the occasion thrilled us all:* grandeur, splendour, magnificence, dignity, augustness, elevation, loftiness, stateliness, glory, gloriousness, impressiveness, illustriousness, elegance, nobility, lustre, solemnity, sublimity.

Ant. meanness, shabbiness, paltriness, lowness; degradation, disgrace, shame, debasement.

◇ *Word origin: Majesty* comes directly from French *majesté*, which was derived from the Latin *major.* It first occurred in English in the early 14th century, referring to God. Later in the century, it came also to be applied to mortal sovereigns.

major *adj.* **1** *The major part of the job is done:* greater, larger, main, principal, chief. **2** *William Wordsworth is a major poet. Industrial unrest is one of the major problems of our time:* leading, primary, foremost, predominant, principal, chief, main, capital, prime, paramount, outstanding, pre-eminent, supreme, most important, important, serious, significant, consequential; essential, vital, necessary, indispensable, requisite, critical, crucial, urgent, pressing.

Ant. 1 lesser, smaller. **2** minor, lesser, subordinate, secondary, collateral, auxiliary, ancillary, insignificant, unimportant, trivial, trifling, inconsequential, non-essential.

◇ *Word origin: Major* is the Latin word for greater, larger, more important. This same Latin word gives us *majority, majesty,* and *mayor.*

majority *n.* **1** *The majority of the union members voted to strike:* mass, bulk, greater part, preponderance, lion's share, more than half the total, greater number. **2** *She reaches her majority in three years:* legal age, coming of age, seniority, adulthood.

Ant. 1 minority, lesser part. **2** childhood, infancy.

"Until a movement shews itself capable of spreading among brigands, it can never hope for a political majority."

—*George Bernard Shaw*

---

make *v.* **1** *The factory makes shirts and blouses. This shirt is made of cotton:* manufacture, construct, produce, fashion, form, fabricate, assemble, create, compose, devise, shape, frame, build, erect. **2** *Don't make trouble. That makes me furious! He made a speech:* cause, produce, bring about, effect, engender, foment, beget; cause to be; deliver, utter, speak, pronounce. **3** *I won't go and you can't make me!:* compel, force, oblige, constrain, require, impel, dragoon, press. **4** *Laws are made to be obeyed:* establish, put into effect, draw up, pass, enact, legislate; render, fix, appoint. **5** *We have to make Edinburgh by evening. Hurry or you won't make the train:* reach, attain, arrive at; meet, arrive in time for, catch.
—*n.* **6** *What make of car did you buy?:* kind, brand, mark.

Ant. 1 destroy, demolish, wreck, ruin, raze. **2** end, conclude; terminate, abolish, dissolve. **3** ask, beg, plead, entreat. **4** repeal, revoke, nullify, abolish, cancel, set aside. **5** leave, depart, withdraw from; be late for, miss.

makeshift *adj. The campers slept in a makeshift lean-to. This is only a makeshift plan until we've decided what to do:* stopgap, temporary, expedient, make-do, stand-by, tentative, substitute.

malady *n. The old woman has been afflicted by one malady after another all winter:* ailment, sickness, illness, disorder, disease, complaint, affliction, indisposition, infirmity.

Ant. health, healthfulness, haleness.

malaise *n. Mother isn't really sick, but she's suffered from a feeling of malaise all winter:* vague discomfort, minor complaint, twinge, throb, pang; discomposure, uneasiness, lassitude.

malcontent *adj.* **1** *She knew he was a malcontent young man when she married him:* habitually unsatisfied, dissatisfied, discontented, hard to please, faultfinding, restive, disgruntled,

restless, uneasy; glum, morose, sullen, grumpy, grouchy, sour, irritable, dejected, downcast, despondent.
—*n.* **2** *Did the new employee have a real grievance or is he just a malcontent?:* complainer, fault-finder, grumbler, grouch, growler, repiner; insurgent, rebel.
Ant. 1 contented, content, satisfied, happy, cheerful; complacent, easy-going, untroubled, unconcerned, unworried. **2** optimist.

> **Exploring the Word:** Here's a group of words that go from bad to worst. The Latin *malus*, bad, its comparative form *pejor* (worse), and its superlative *pessimus* (worst) give us: *malady*, something bad that one has, an illness or physical disorder; *malign*, to speak ill of someone; *malefactor*, one who does bad or evil things; *malevolent*, wishing ill to others; *malpractice*, bad practice, specifically improper or negligent medical treatment; *malaise*, the state of being ill at ease; *malaria*, literally "bad air"; the French expression *mal de mer*, "sea-badness," i.e. seasickness; and such words as *malcontent* and *maladjusted*. The Latin comparative and superlative give us: *pejorative*, literally "making worse," having a derogatory or disparaging meaning; *impair*, to make worse; and *pessimist*, one who looks on the worst side of things.

male *adj.* **1** *On average, male babies weigh more than female ones at birth:* masculine, of the sex that fathers young; manly, manlike.
—*n.* **2** *Males are generally taller than females:* a male person or animal; man, youth, boy; (*variously*) stallion, tom-cat, billy-goat, bull, cock, ram.
Ant. 1, 2 female, woman. **1** feminine.
◇ *Word origin: Male* comes from Latin *masculus*, male, from which we also get *masculine.*

malediction *n. The patriarch uttered a malediction against the rival clan:* curse, imprecation, evil spell, anathema; denunciation, fulmination, proscription.
Ant. benediction, blessing; eulogy, praise, compliment.

malevolent *adj. What a malevolent remark!:* malicious, showing ill will, ill-disposed, spiteful, ill-intentioned, malignant, sinister, acrimonious, venomous, resentful, vicious, rancorous, revengeful, malign; surly, sullen, ill-natured.
Ant. benevolent, benign, magnanimous, kind, gracious, friendly, amiable, warm-hearted.

malformed *adj. The tree has a malformed trunk:* misshapen, deformed, not straight, distorted, contorted, twisted, irregular, grotesque.

malice *n. He showed no malice towards anyone:* ill will, evil intent, malevolence, maliciousness, spitefulness, spite, grudge, rancour, resentment, animosity, acrimony, enmity, hate, venom, bitterness; evil disposition, uncharitableness, hard-heartedness.
Ant. benevolence, goodwill, charity, friendliness, amiability, kindness, graciousness.
◇ *Word origin: Malice, malicious,* and *malign* come from Latin *malus*, evil, which also gives us *malignant.*

malicious *adj. She was the victim of a malicious rumour:* vicious, spiteful, malevolent, ill-disposed, vindictive, revengeful, resentful, rancorous, hateful, invidious, acrimonious.
Ant. benevolent, benign, friendly, amiable, amicable, kind, kind-hearted, well-disposed.

malign *v.* **1** *A fair politician should debate the issues and not just malign his opponent:* slander, defame, speak ill of, revile, abuse, belittle, disparage, derogate, denigrate, deprecate, vilify, inveigh against, backbite, blacken the reputation of, traduce; *Informal* run down, put down.
—*adj.* **2** *We guessed that some malign influence was behind our misfortunes:* evil, bad, harmful, injurious, detrimental, deleterious, pernicious, baneful, noxious; ominous, sinister, black, malignant, malevolent, threatening, menacing, malicious, hateful.
Ant. 1 praise, extol, eulogize, compliment, commend. **2** benign, benevolent, good; kind, friendly, amiable, warm-hearted.

malignant *adj.* **1** *The doctors removed a malignant growth:* deadly, pernicious, virulent; fatal, toxic, poisonous. **2** *Such malignant gossip must be stopped before it ruins somebody's reputation:* malicious, malevolent, ill-disposed, vindictive, resentful, revengeful, spiteful, rancorous, hateful, vicious, invidious, acrimonious, bitter, venomous, hostile, fiendish, diabolical, evil, evil-minded.
Ant. 1 non-malignant. **2** benevolent, benign, friendly, amiable, amicable, kind, kind-hearted, well-disposed.
◇ *Word origin: Malignant* comes from Latin *malus*, evil, which also gives us *malign, malice,* and *malicious.*

mall *n. We walked some way down the shady side of the mall:* promenade, esplanade, tree-lined walk; square, plaza, piazza, court, quadrangle, yard, parade-ground, circus; arcade, colonnade, cloister.
◇ *Word origin:* The Mall and Pall Mall are two well-known London streets, stretching from Trafalgar Square to Buckingham Palace and to St James's Street. Pall Mall got its name because part of it was once an alley where the 17th-century game *pall-mall* (wooden ball and mallet) was played, a game in which a wooden ball was driven by a mallet (from Latin *malleus*, hammer) along an alley and through a raised ring.

malleable *adj.* **1** *Tin is a malleable metal:* workable, easily shaped, easily wrought; ductile, tractable, plastic, pliant, flexible. **2** *Since* *young children are malleable, one must be careful what one says in front of them:* impressionable, easily influenced, mouldable, tractable, teachable, manageable, governable, docile; adaptable, flexible, pliable, compliant.

Ant. 1 rigid, stiff, hard, firm; unyielding, inflexible, unbending, inelastic. **2** refractory, intractable, recalcitrant, ungovernable.

◇ *Word origin: Malleable* comes from Latin *malleus,* hammer, which also gives us *mallet* and *maul.*

malnutrition *n. Children in the drought-stricken area suffered from malnutrition:* undernourishment, lack of proper nutrition; starvation, emaciation.

malpractice *n. The doctor was sued for malpractice:* professional negligence, improper professional conduct, professional dereliction.

Mammon *n. Too many people worship Mammon these days:* wealth, riches, possessions, money, material goods, affluence, the god of money.

◇ *Word origin: Mammon* comes from Aramaic *māmōnā,* riches.

mammoth *adj. The Great Pyramids are mammoth structures:* enormous, huge, immense, monstrous, gigantic, colossal, very large, mighty, great, whopping, monumental, mountainous, prodigious, gargantuan, herculean, cyclopean, stupendous, tremendous.

Ant. small, little, tiny, miniature, minute, dwarfish; *Informal* wee, pint-sized; *Slang* itsy-bitsy, itty-bitty.

man *n.* **1** *Man cannot live by bread alone:* mankind, the human race, men and women, human beings, humankind, people, humanity, Homo sapiens. **2** *Every man must follow his own beliefs:* individual, person, human being, human, living being, living soul, soul, one; anyone, somebody, someone. **3** *The average man is taller than the average woman:* male, masculine person; gentleman, chap, fellow; *Slang* bloke, guy, gent. **4** *The minister pronounced them man and wife:* married man, husband, spouse, *Informal* hubby, old man. **5** *Hire a man to look after the garden:* handyman, workman, hired hand, hand, labourer, day labourer; employee, worker; manservant, male servant, boy, waiter, footman, butler, gardener, male retainer; assistant, helper, right-hand man; male follower, subject, liegeman, henchman.

—*v.* **6** *The crew was ordered to man the lifeboats:* attend, staff, take up one's position in, take one's place at, get to one's post; supply with hands, furnish with men, people; equip, fit out; garrison.

Ant. 3 woman, female. **4** bachelor; widower.

◇ *Word origin: Man* comes from Old English *mann,* man. The word has many relatives in the Indo-European languages. Among them are *minx,* from Low German *minsk,* hussy; the Yiddish word *mensch,* good chap, from Old High German *mensch,* man; and *muzhik,* a peasant in Tsarist Russia, from Russian *muzh,* man.

manacle *n.* **1** Usually **manacles** *The officer put manacles on the prisoner's hands:* handcuffs, hand-fetters, irons, shackles, chains, bonds, *Slang* bracelets.

—*v.* **2** *The policeman manacled the thief and took him to gaol:* handcuff, fetter, tie one's hands, put in chains, put in irons, shackle, *Slang* put bracelets on.

Ant. 2 unbind, unfetter, unchain; set free, free, liberate, turn loose, let go.

manage *v.* **1** *She seems so young to manage three children and that big house:* run, direct, oversee, superintend, have charge of, take care of, look after, watch over, supervise, head, administer, conduct, preside over, rule, govern, control, command, order, dominate, guide, steer, pilot, be at the helm, hold the reins. **2** *It's hard to manage a sailing-boat in a narrow inlet:* manipulate, manœuvre, handle, control, work, operate, make go, run; guide, steer; use, wield, ply. **3** *How will you manage without a job?:* survive, get along, get on, fare, shift, keep one's head above water, weather the storm. **4** *We haven't much time to do the job, but we'll manage it:* succeed, accomplish, deal with, cope with, cope, work out, bring about.

Ant. 1 be under the care of, follow. **3** be destitute, starve. **4** fail, botch, bungle, spoil, make a mess of, muff, make a hash of.

◇ *Spelling tip:* Remember that *manage* keeps its final *e* in *manageable* and *unmanageable.*

Exploring the Word: *Manage, manageable, management* and *manager* come from Latin *manus,* hand. Thus, to *manage* literally means to handle; *manageable* means capable of being handled; *management* is the handling of people or of business or political affairs; and a *manager* handles such affairs. Latin *manus,* hand, also gives us *command,* to give into someone else's hands, as by an order; *emancipate,* to free the hands, hence to free from bondage or slavery; *manacle,* handcuff; *mandate,* a charge or authorization putting responsibility in someone's hands; *manipulate,* to handle; *manual,* done by hand, *as manual labour,* or a handbook, as an *instruction manual; manufacture,* to make by hand, which is how everything was once made; and *manuscript,* literally writing done by hand.

management *n.* **1** *The owner's son took over the management of the business. The plan failed owing to bad management:* administration, supervision, direction, overseeing, superintendence, generalship; operation, guidance, regulation, conduct, conducting, command, control, ordering, charge, running, handling, care, rule; planning, organization; strategy, tactics, manipulation; dealing, negotiation, transaction. **2** *Management has vetoed your suggestion:* executives, executive board,

executive committee, administrators, the administration, supervisors, supervisory board, board of directors, directors, bosses; *Slang* bigwigs, big shots, big guns, top brass.
Ant. 2 labour; staff, employees, workers.

manager *n.* **1** *The manager deals with staff problems in this store:* head, boss, supervisor, foreman, superintendent, overseer, proprietor, executive director, administrator, majordomo, chief; agent, impresario. **2** *Only a good manager can run a household on thirty pounds a week:* planner, organizer, schemer; tactician, manipulator, negotiator.
Ant. 1 employee, worker, labourer, *Slang* flunkey.

mandate *n.* **1** *British mandates should be governed with a light hand:* protectorate, dependency, mandated territory, subject territory. **2** *Work on the new bridge will begin as soon as an official mandate is received. At the last election, the Government was given a mandate for trade union reform:* order, edict, decree, command, dictate, bidding, behest, directive, direction, instruction, authorization, authority, approval, sanction, charge, requisition, commission.
Ant. 2 petition, request, entreaty, supplication, appeal, solicitation, suit.

mandatory *adj. Attendance at the Sunday service is no longer mandatory for students:* compulsory, required, requisite, obligatory, not optional, binding, called for; essential, imperative, necessary, needful.

mangle *v. The dog's leg was mangled in the accident:* mutilate, maim, disfigure, maul, crush; cut, lacerate, tear, slash; injure, damage, harm, hurt, lame, impair.

mania *n.* **1** *Hitler's mania is often cited as the cause of World War II:* madness, violent derangement, insanity, lunacy, fanaticism, dementia; frenzy, delirium, raving, rage, hysteria, delusion, hallucination, aberration. **2** *Kim has a mania for collecting sea shells:* passion, craze, craving, enthusiasm, exaggerated love, infatuation; obsession, monomania, fixation.
Ant. 1 sanity, rationality; self-control, equanimity, stability, level-headedness, coolness, cool-headedness, calmness.
◇ *Usage note:* A *mania* is a compulsive craving, enthusiasm, or love of something: *What do you do with a husband who has a mania for watching football on TV?* On the other hand, a *phobia* is a compulsive fear of something: *He has one phobia — he's terrified of heights.*
◇ *Word origin: Mania* and *maniac* come from Greek *mania,* madness, raging.

maniac *n. They arrested some maniac for starting the fire. That maniac should be arrested for speeding:* madman, lunatic, crazy person, insane person, deranged person; *Slang* nut, nutter; loony; psychopath; reckless person, fool, simpleton, ass, nitwit, half-wit.

manifest *adj.* **1** *The principal's displeasure was manifest:* obvious, clear, evident, self-evident, plain, apparent, patent, visible, noticeable, palpable, unmistakable, transparent, unconcealed, undisguised; open, frank, candid. —*v.* **2** *The boss manifested his disgust with a scowl:* indicate, show, exhibit, reveal, express, disclose, make known, demonstrate, evince, evidence, display, divulge, make visible, unveil, uncover, hold up to view, bare, expose.
Ant. 1 hidden, concealed, suppressed, masked, obscured, vague, cryptic, inconspicuous, unseen. **2** hide, conceal, cover up, mask, cloak, bury, obscure, camouflage.
◇ *Word origin: Manifest* and *manifestation* are from Latin *manifestus,* literally struck by the hand, hence evident, plainly apparent. It is based on Latin *manus,* hand.

manifestation *n. A sore throat is one manifestation of a cold. The political rally was a huge manifestation of support for the candidate:* indication, symptom, evidence, proclamation, revelation; demonstration, show, display, exhibition, expression, presentation.

manifold *adj. A housewife has manifold responsibilities:* many, numerous, multitudinous, multiple, myriad, innumerable; varied, diversified, diverse, complex, multifarious.
Ant. few, scant, limited; simple, uncomplicated, uniform.

manipulate *v.* **1** *The magician manipulated the cards and the ace vanished:* handle, finger; feel, pinch, stroke, pat, massage, squeeze. **2** *Do you know how to manipulate a computer?:* operate, work, use, employ, handle, manage, control; wield, ply, drive. **3** *The treasurer was arrested for trying to manipulate the company's financial records:* tamper with, change fraudulently, manage by crafty means, influence deviously, control illegally, direct unethically, *Slang* cook; deceive, defraud.

"Mankind are an incorrigible race. Give them but bugbears and idols — it is all that they ask."
— *William Hazlitt*

---

mankind *n. Is mankind in danger of extinction?:* the human race, humankind, the human species, man, men and women, humanity; people, persons, society.

manly *adj* **1** *The boy has a very manly voice:* masculine, male, virile, manful. **2** *Football is a manly sport. Every soldier must do his duty in a manly fashion:* vigorous, hardy, strong, robust, husky, sturdy, muscular, athletic, brawny, strapping, powerful, stalwart; brave, courageous, daring, bold, resolute, stout-hearted, valiant, fearless, staunch, indomitable, plucky, self-reliant; noble, heroic, chivalrous, gallant, gentlemanly.
Ant. 1 unmanly, effeminate, womanish; boyish, juvenile, youthful, puerile, childlike,

childish, babyish. **2** weak, frail, feeble; cowardly, faint-hearted, irresolute; villainous, dastardly.

◇ *Usage note:* See MASCULINE.

manna *n. Our fathers ate manna in the desert:* miraculous food, spiritual nourishment, divine sustenance; boon, bonanza, sudden gain, unexpected gift, award, reward.

◇ *Word origin: Manna* was the food miraculously supplied to the Israelites in the wilderness as they fled from Egypt, according to Exodus 16: 14-36, hence our expression "manna from Heaven." Since they didn't know what this miraculous food was, they called it *manna*, from the Aramaic phrase *mān hū*, meaning "What is it?" (This at least is the traditional explanation of the word, and there is no other explanation.) Some scholars have suggested that manna may have been a saplike substance obtained from the flowering ash and related plants.

manner *n.* **1** *I love duck cooked in the Chinese manner:* way, style, mode, fashion, method, custom, practice, habit; guise, aspect, appearance, character. **2** *Her manner seemed rather uneasy:* behaviour, conduct; bearing, carriage, air, presence, deportment, demeanour. **3** *What manner of man is he?:* kind, type, sort, variety; classification, genre, species, category, breed, race, strain, stamp, brand, caste, make, form, mould; grade, rank.

◇ *Usage note: Manner* is a handy word, but don't use it in long clauses to replace simple adverbs. For example, *He worked in a hasty manner* can be expressed more simply as *He worked hastily.*

mannerism *n. Uncle Ned has an annoying mannerism of scratching his head while he talks. Her American accent is just a mannerism picked up on her visit to Washington:* peculiar action, habit, habitual gesture, distinctive way, characteristic style, eccentricity, idiosyncrasy, singularity; affectation, pose, affected gesture, mannered style, artificiality, pretence, pretension; airs.

mannerly *adj. The older boy's mannerly conduct was a shining example to the younger children:* polite, well-mannered, courteous, well-behaved; refined, well-bred, genteel, courtly, gallant, chivalrous.

Ant. unmannerly, rude, impolite, ill-mannered, gauche, boorish.

manners *n. pl.* **1** *His bad manners are inexcusable. Mind your manners:* social behaviour, behaviour, decorum, deportment. **2** *Don't they teach you any manners at that school?:* good manners, politeness, etiquette, courtesy, deference; refinement, polish, gentility, gallantry, courtliness, politesse.

Ant. 2 rudeness, impoliteness, bad manners, discourtesy, boorishness.

manœuvre *n.* **1** *The generals planned the manœuvre carefully:* troop movement, troop deployment; movement of warships, planes, armoured vehicles, etc.; training exercise. **2** *The prime minister thwarted the opposition's manœuvre to gain control of the government:* scheme, stratagem, gambit, move, ploy, tactic; plot, artifice, device, contrivance, machination, trick, dodge, intrigue.

—*v.* **3** *The ships manœuvred to block the channel. Can you manœuvre the car into that parking space?:* deploy, move; manipulate, steer, pilot, guide. **4** *The vice-president is manœuvring to displace the president of the company:* contrive, work surreptitiously, bring about in an underhand way, pull strings; scheme, plot, plan artfully, devise a way, intrigue, *Informal* finagle.

mansion *n. The old mansion down the road has been turned into a casino:* impressive house, imposing dwelling; manor, manor house, villa, château.

Ant. hovel, shack, hut, cabin, cottage, *Slang* hole.

manslaughter *n. She was charged with murder but got away with manslaughter:* accidental murder, unpremeditated killing, killing without malice aforethought: (*loosely*) murder, killing, homicide, spilling of blood.

mantle *n.* **1** *The actress wore a velvet mantle over her gown:* cloak, cape, tunic, wrapper; scarf for the head and shoulders, mantilla. **2** *A mantle of fog settled over the city:* covering, cover, veil, cloak, mask, envelope, curtain, screen, cloud, film, shroud.

◇ *Usage note:* Don't confuse *mantel* and *mantle.* A *mantEL* is a shelf above a fireplace: *Put the clock on the mantel.* Remember, a fireplace *mantEL* is a *shELf. A mantLE* is a cloak or hood, anything that covers or conceals: *The monk wore a mantle over his head.*

manual *adj.* **1** *The sports car has manual transmission:* hand-operated, non-automatic. **2** *Years of manual labour had hardened his muscles:* physical, done by hand, requiring physical strength.

—*n.* **3** *She bought a manual of home repairs:* handbook, guidebook, instruction book; text-book, primer, workbook.

Ant. 1 automatic; machine-operated, electric. **2** mental, intellectual.

manufacture *v.* **1** *The company manufactures toys:* produce, mass-produce, make, fabricate, mould, form, devise; assemble, put together, construct, build. **2** *You'll have to manufacture some kind of excuse:* invent, fabricate, make up, concoct, create, think up, *Informal* cook up.

Ant. 1 destroy, demolish.

manure *n. The manure heap is behind the barn:* dung, animal excrement, animal droppings; fertilizer; compost, dressing.

manuscript *n. He showed me the manuscript of his new play:* script, written document; typescript.

many *adj.* **1** *I've told you many times that I hate* *liver:* numerous, innumerable, numberless, countless, myriad, multitudinous; several, various, divers, sundry.

—*n.* **2** *Many are called but few are chosen:* a considerable number, a lot, lots, a heap, heaps, piles, scores, dozens, numbers; a liberal quantity, a profusion, an abundance.

Ant. 1 few, rare, infrequent, once or twice. **2** few, hardly any, a handful; none, none at all.

map *n.* **1** *This is a map of the Channel Islands:* topographical chart, chart, graph, projection, elevation; plot, diagram, plan, representation.

—*v.* **2** *The expedition will map the South Pole:* make a map of, chart. **3** *The agency mapped out an advertising campaign for the new product:* plan, project, prepare, devise, design, contrive, arrange, plot, lay out, organize, ready.

◇ *Word origin: Map* comes from the Medieval Latin term for a map, *mappa mundi,* literally "cloth of the world," since early maps were made of cloth. Thus our word *map* comes from the Latin *mappa,* cloth, which also gives us our word *napkin,* literally "little cloth" (in Old French the *m* was changed to an *n.*).

mar *v.* **1** *An unsightly scratch marred the table:* disfigure, blemish, deface, damage, hurt, scar, mark, nick, scratch, stain; ruin, destroy. **2** *A series of flat notes marred her singing:* spoil, taint, blemish, impair, hurt, detract from, make imperfect, diminish; defile, blight.

Ant. 1 beautify, embellish, adorn, decorate, ornament; restore. **2** improve, enhance, restore.

marauder *n. The marauders raided several coastal towns:* plunderer, pillager, ravager, despoiler, spoiler; pirate, buccaneer, privateer, freebooter; roving band of outlaws, guerrilla.

march *v.* **1** *First World War veterans will march at the head of the parade. March straight upstairs and change those wet clothes!:* parade, walk with measured steps, walk in step, walk in a procession, file by; go, go directly, walk, step, tramp, proceed.

—*n.* **2** *The soldiers had a ten-mile march before lunch. The students have organized a march from the rally to the football field:* hike, tramp, trek, group walk; parade, procession. **3** *The book describes the march of civilization from ancient Egyptian times up to the present-day:* progress, progression, development, advance, advancement, rise, growth. **4** *The band concert closed with a Sousa march:* piece of music in march time; martial music, military tune; funeral march.

mare *n. The mare recently had a foal:* female horse, brood-mare.

margin *n.* **1** *The student wrote notes in the margins of the book:* border, boundary, edge, rim, verge, confine, bound, fringe. **2** *There is no margin for error in his plan:* latitude, safeguard, extra amount, added quantity, extra room, allowance, play, flexibility.

Ant. 1 centre, middle, interior.

marginal *adj.* **1** *The book has small marginal illustrations:* in the margin, on the edge, along the border. **2** *The advantage of this plan over that is marginal:* barely profitable, not the main consideration, slight, inconsiderable.

marine *adj.* **1** *The school had an excellent course in marine biology:* oceanic, sea, salt-water; of the sea, aquatic. **2** *The steamship company's lawyer was a specialist in marine law:* maritime, of ships, naval, nautical; seagoing, ocean-going, seafaring.

Ant. 1 terrestrial, land, dry-land; fresh-water.

◇ *Word origin: Marine* comes from Latin *marinus,* sailor, of the sea, from Latin *mare,* sea, which also gives us *mariner, maritime,* and *marinate* (to pickle in salt water).

mariner *n. The old mariner had sailed the seas for 40 years:* sailor, seaman, seafarer, seafaring man, able-bodied seaman; *Slang* salt, jack, tar, Jack tar, sea-dog, bluejacket; navigator, pilot, helmsman.

Ant. landlubber.

marionette *n. The marionettes were called Punch and Judy:* puppet, articulated puppet, puppet on strings, *Italian* fantoccino.

◇ *Word origin: Marionette* comes from an Old French diminutive of the name *Marie.* The word originally designated a small image of the Virgin Mary.

marital *adj. The couple celebrated 25 years of marital bliss:* wedded, married, of marriage, matrimonial, conjugal, nuptial, connubial.

Ant. single, unmarried, unwed, unwedded.

◇ *Word origin:* See MARRY.

maritime *adj.* **1** *The admiral is an expert in maritime history:* marine, naval, nautical, of ships, of the sea, of sea trade, seagoing, sea-faring; oceanic, aquatic. **2** *Nova Scotia is one of Canada's Maritime Provinces:* coastal, bordering on the sea; engaged in sea trade, making a living from the sea.

Ant. 1 land, terrestrial, dry-land; fresh-water., **2** inland.

◇ *Word origin:* See MARINE.

mark *n.* **1** *What made those marks on the wall?:* spot, streak, line, stain; scratch, scar, cut, nick, dent, impression, pock, pit, notch, score; bruise, blemish. **2** *This vase bears the mark of a famous potter. Everyone stood as a mark of respect when the headmaster entered the room:* hallmark, sign, symbol, stamp, label, badge, emblem, brand, colophon, imprint; token, symbol, indication, evidence, measure, symptom, proof. **3** *The student received more than the pass-mark in all subjects:* grade, rating. **4** *If that was meant to be an apology, your words were wide of the mark. The employee's work has been below the mark this week:* target, goal, objective, intent, point, track, bull's-eye; standard, criterion, yardstick, touchstone.

—*v.* **5** *That wet glass will mark the table:* spot, streak, stain; scratch, scar, cut, nick, dent, leave an impression on, pock, pit, notch, score; bruise, blemish; mar, deface, disfigure, harm, injure; make a line on, write on, write in. **6** *The teacher marked the examination papers:* correct, judge, rate, grade. **7** *X marks the spot:* indicate, reveal, disclose, show, point out, designate, denote, signify, stand for; characterize, typify, symbolize, evidence, evince, suggest, betoken, manifest, be a sign of, distinguish, differentiate; label, stamp, brand. **8** *Mark my words!:* heed, attend, pay attention to, mind, note, regard.

Ant. 5 clean, remove, obliterate, erase; repair. **7** hide, conceal, mask, veil, cover, screen, disguise, camouflage. **8** ignore, overlook, disregard.

marked *adj. She is a woman of marked intelligence:* outstanding, distinct, conspicuous, striking, noticeable, obvious, prominent; exceptional, uncommon, extraordinary, unique, singular, special, particular, definite, decided.

Ant. ordinary, commonplace, everyday, undistinguished, routine, run-of-the-mill, mediocre.

market *n.* **1** *We buy our vegetables at the village market. There's a new fruit market on the corner:* market-place, wholesale market; grocer's shop, grocery; meat market, butcher's shop. **2** *Over a million shares of stock were traded on the market:* stock-market, stock exchange, kerb market, *French* bourse; financial centre; commodity market.

—*v.* **3** *The inventor is trying to market his new product:* sell, vend, merchandise, retail, *Informal* peddle, hawk; put up for sale, dispose of.

Ant. 3 buy.

◇ *Word origin: Market* and *mart* come from Latin *merx*, merchandise, wares, which also gives us *mercantile, merchant,* and *merchandise.*

marksman *n. A good hunter has to be a good marksman:* sharpshooter, good shot, good sniper, crack shot, dead shot, sure shot.

maroon[1] *v. The pirates' victims were marooned on a small island:* strand, cast ashore, put ashore, abandon, desert, forsake, *Informal* leave high and dry.

◇ *Word origin: Maroon* comes from an American Spanish word *cimarrón*, a fugitive slave. The word was first used in English during the 17th century, when the noun *maroon* meant a type of escaped black slave, living wild in the highlands and forests of the West Indies. Soon after that, the verb came to be used in its present sense, but if we remember how it came to have this sense, we will understand more easily the mysterious flavour of the phrase "marooned on a desert island"!

maroon[2] *adj. My new winter coat is maroon:* brownish red, wine, magenta, plum, terra-cotta.

◇ *Word origin: Maroon*[2] comes from French *marron*, chestnut, hence literally chestnut-coloured.

marriage *n.* **1** *They have been through a lot together in their forty years of marriage:* matrimony, marital state, wedlock, holy wedlock, conjugal union, connubial state, nuptial state. **2** *The marriage will take place in June:* wedding, marriage ceremony, nuptials, nuptial rites, tying the knot, leading to the altar, ringing of wedding bells.

Ant. 1 divorce, annulment; single life, bachelorhood, spinsterhood.

◇ *Spelling tip:* If you're married, this is an easy word to spell. Just remember "there's an *I* in *marrIage.*" Remember also that *marriage* keeps its final *e* in *marriagEable* and *unmarriagEable.*

marry *v.* **1** *He married a girl from his home town:* wed, get married to, take in marriage, espouse, exchange wedding vows with, lead to the altar, bestow one's hand upon, take for a husband, take for a wife, take for better or for worse; *Slang* get spliced, get hitched, tie the knot. **2** *The minister has married over 400 couples:* wed, join in marriage, join in wedlock, unite in holy wedlock, make one.

Ant. 1 divorce, get an annulment from.

◇ *Word origin: Marry, marriage,* and *marital* come from Latin *maritus*, married, joined.

"Marriage is popular because it combines the maximum of temptation with the maximum of opportunity." —*George Bernard Shaw*

---

marsh *n. The bird-watchers built a hide in the marsh:* swamp, bog, fen, slough; marshland, wetlands, quagmire, morass.

marshal *n.* **1** *The U.S. marshal always gets his man:* law officer; sheriff. **2** *The track-marshal ensured that the race was fairly run:* chief, leader, director, supervisor, manager, organiser, arranger. **3** *The oldest general was appointed marshal of the armies:* Field Marshal, Commander-in-Chief, generalissimo, chief officer, *French* maréchal.

—*v.* **4** *The general marshalled his army for battle. Marshal your arguments before debating:* gather, collect, muster, assemble, mobilize; arrange, order, organize, group, deploy, array, align, line up, draw up.

Ant. 4 scatter, disperse; disorganize.

◇ *Word origin: Marshal* comes from Old High German *marah* (horse) + *scalh* (servant), a horse servant, groom, and later a household official of a royal court. Old High German *marah*, horse, is also related to our word *mare* (female horse).

mart *n. My father still remembers the time when he had a stall at Lincoln mart:* trade centre, trading centre, exchange; market-place, market; trade fair, trade show, exposition, show.

◇ *Word origin:* See MARKET.

martial *adj.* **1** *The town was under martial law. The veteran had a martial bearing:* military; soldierly, soldierlike. **2** *The country maintains a martial attitude toward its neighbours:* warlike, belligerent, disposed to war, hostile, militant, combative, bellicose, pugnacious, contentious; military-minded.
Ant. **1** civilian, civil. **2** peaceful, conciliatory.
◇ *Word origin: Martial* literally means "pertaining to Mars," the Roman god of war.

martinet *n. The boss is such a martinet that he'll lecture you for coming in two minutes late:* taskmaster, severe disciplinarian, hard master, tyrant, despot, dictator, drill-sergeant, drillmaster, *Slang* little Caesar.
◇ *Word origin: Martinet* comes from the name of Jean *Martinet*, a 17th-century French general who invented a new system of military drill.

martyr *n. The early Christian Church had many martyrs:* person willing to die or suffer for a cause; person killed for his beliefs; one who undergoes great suffering; one venerated for dying or suffering.

martyrdom *n. The painting depicts the martyrdom of St. Sebastian:* the suffering of a martyr, death of a martyr; suffering, agony, anguish, torment, torture, ordeal, affliction; (*literary*) crown of thorns, bitter cup, cup of sorrow.
Ant. ecstasy, bliss, joy, pleasure, happiness, delight, gratification.

marvel *n.* **1** *His speech was a marvel of tact:* miracle, wonder, phenomenon, wonderful thing, supreme example; rarity, spectacle.
—*v.* **2** *The tourists marvelled at the beauty of the Lake District:* be awed, be overwhelmed, be struck with wonder, be staggered, be amazed, be astonished, be stupefied, gape.
Ant. **1** commonplace. **2** be bored; take in one's stride.

marvellous *adj. It was a marvellous party:* wonderful, splendid, lovely, superb, outstanding, great, grand, fine, first-rate, fabulous, heavenly, divine, fantastic, extraordinary, stupendous, sensational, colossal, magnificent, remarkable, *Slang* super, A-1, smashing, fab.
Ant. terrible, awful, lousy, bad; ordinary, commonplace, routine, everyday, run-of-the-mill.

masculine *adj. He likes to show off his masculine physique:* manly, male, manful, virile; strong, vigorous, robust, sturdy, hardy, husky, powerful, muscular, strapping, brawny, athletic; brave, courageous, resolute, daring, bold, stout-hearted, fearless, valiant, staunch, indomitable, plucky, intrepid, self-reliant, forceful.
Ant. weak, unmanly, effeminate, womanish, girlish; female, feminine, womanly, ladylike, womanlike.
◇ *Usage note:* The qualities or characteristics called *masculine* or *manly* in a man may be called *mannish* if present in a woman; in fact, *mannish* applies exclusively to women, just as *womanish* and *effeminate* apply to men only. All three words are used as epithets of disparagement.

mash *v.* **1** *Mash the potatoes and add cream and butter:* puree, reduce to pulp, crush, squash, smash.
—*n.* **2** *The horses are fed a mash of bran and oats:* pulpy mass, soft mixture, mush.

mask *n.* **1** *The children wore Hallowe'en masks. Each guest has to wear a mask:* false face; face covering, domino; face guard. **2** *The jokes were a mask to hide his sadness:* cover, cover-up, screen, cloak, shroud, veil, curtain, blind; disguise, camouflage.
—*v.* **3** *The bank robbers masked their faces:* cover, put a mask over, obscure, hide, disguise. **4** *A row of trees masked the scrap-yard from the eyes of passing motorists. She tried to mask her feelings:* hide, conceal, shield from view, cover, screen, veil, cloak, shroud, curtain, keep secret; camouflage, disguise.
Ant. **2** revelation, disclosure, display, manifestation, demonstration, show, exhibition. **3** unmask. **4** reveal, disclose, divulge, expose, show, display, exhibit.
◇ *Word origin:* Clowns throughout history have worn masks or painted their faces to look funny and grotesque. Our word *mask* comes from Arabic *maskharah*, buffoon. This same Arabic word also gives us *masquerade* and even *mascara*.

masquerade *n.* **1** *The masquerade was the biggest party of the year:* masked party, masked ball, mask, masque; French *bal masqué;* harlequinade. **2** *His laughter is just a masquerade so that you won't know how disappointed he is:* cover, cover-up, mask, screen, veil, cloak, shroud; camouflage, pretence, pretext, subterfuge, guise, trick, artifice, ruse.
—*v.* **3** *All this time he's been masquerading as a real doctor!:* go under the guise of, pass oneself off as, pretend to be, falsely claim to be; go disguised as.
Ant. **2** revelation, disclosure, display, manifestation, demonstration, show, exhibition. **3** unmask, find out; expose, reveal to be.
◇ *Word origin:* See MASK.

mass[1] *n.* **1** *Einstein studied the relationship of energy to mass:* the quantity of matter in a body; (*loosely*) matter, material; weight. **2** *That hill is actually one solid mass of coal:* block, lump, chunk, hunk, knot, clot, cake, concretion. **3** *The club members gathered a mass of used clothing for the jumble sale. A mass of people jammed into the arena:* pile, heap, stack, pyramid, batch, lot, clump, bundle, pack, bunch; accumulation, cumulation, collection, assemblage, gathering, group, body, aggregate, aggregation, assortment, conglomeration; crowd, throng, mob, congregation, host, horde, corps, troop, crush, press, jam. **4** *The mass of*

public opinion is in favour of the present licensing laws: greater part, majority, bulk, main body, lion's share.
—*v.* **5** *Protesters massed in front of the town hall:* collect, amass, gather, assemble, consolidate, congregate, accumulate; pile, heap, stack, bunch.
Ant. **2** fragment, bit, chip, piece, portion, morsel. **3** scattering. **4** minority. **5** disperse, scatter, spread.

Exploring the Word: Today we usually want our bread and cakes to be light. However, it seems likely that the Greek barley-cake called *māza* must have been very thick and heavy, because it has given us such words as *mass, massive,* and *amass.* Greek *māza* has also been erroneously linked with *matzo,* the Jewish unleavened bread traditionally eaten during the Passover. There is actually no connection between the two words.

mass[2] *n.* Often **Mass** *St. Patrick's Cathedral is famed for its midnight Mass on Christmas Eve:* celebration of the sacrament, Communion service, Holy Communion, holy sacrament, celebration of the Lord's Supper, Eucharist; offering of bread and wine, consecration of the elements.
◇ *Word origin: Mass* comes from Latin *missa,* dismissed, in the phrase *Ite, missa est,* "go, you are dismissed," said by the priest after the Eucharist is ended. In Late Latin Christian use, *missa* acquired the meaning "Eucharist."

massacre *n.* **1** *The brutal massacre of Jacobites at the battle of Culloden earned the Duke of Cumberland the nickname of "The Butcher":* mass slaughter, mass murder, indiscriminate killing, butchery, carnage, blood-letting.
—*v.* **2** *Herod's soldiers massacred the male infants of Bethlehem:* slaughter en masse, kill at random, butcher, decimate; put large groups to death, perpetrate genocide.
◇ *Word origin: Massacre* comes from an Old French word *maçacre,* a slaughter-house, shambles, and the ultimate derivation of this word is unknown. Despite the seemingly obvious connection between *massacre* and the *mass* of people who are killed in one, the two words are totally unrelated, and the similarities are merely fortuitous!

"Soap and education are not as sudden as a massacre, but they are more deadly in the long run."
—*Mark Twain*

massage *n.* **1** *A brisk massage restores the body's vigour:* rub-down; rubbing, kneading, stroking, manipulation.
—*v.* **2** *Massage your cheeks so that they won't get frost-bitten. He massaged his jaw thoughtfully:* rub, knead, chafe, stroke, handle, finger.

masses *n. pl. The masses are the true makers of history:* the common people, the crowd, the mob, the multitude, the many, hoi polloi, the common herd, the great unwashed; the working class, the proletariat, proles, plebeians, plebs, the riff-raff, rabble, the man in the street, the rank and file, every Tom, Dick, and Harry.
Ant. the élite, the aristocracy, the gentry, the upper class, nobility, society, high society, the crème de la crème, the Beautiful People, the intelligentsia, the cognoscenti, the illuminati; the middle class, the bourgeoisie.

massive *adj. A massive rock formation blocked the end of the valley:* immense, huge, gigantic, monstrous, enormous, mammoth, colossal, great, stupendous, cyclopean, titanic, gargantuan, elephantine, whopping; monumental, impressive, imposing, vast, extensive, towering; hulking, heavy, ponderous, weighty, bulky, solid, substantial.
Ant. small, little, tiny, diminutive, minute; petty, trivial; flimsy, slight, frail, slender, light.

master *n.* **1** *The dog obeyed his master. Cortés was master of the Aztec empire:* owner, lord, conqueror, ruler. **2** *Father was definitely the master in our house; I had to see the master after the lesson:* head, head man, boss, chief, leader, dominant person, authority, overlord; teacher, tutor; governor, director, supervisor, manager, overseer, supervisor, superintendent. **3** *The first mate was studying to become a master:* ship's captain, skipper, commanding officer. **4** *Grandfather was a master at carpentry:* expert, master hand, skilled artist, wizard, genius, virtuoso, *Slang* ace, whiz-kid.
—*adj.* **5** *Father and Mother have the master bedroom:* main, chief, principal, primary, prime, paramount, most important, predominant, supreme, choice, best. **6** *A cabinet-maker must be a master craftsman:* expert, skilled, masterly, proficient, first-rate, deft, able, accomplished, finished, talented, gifted, *Slang* ace, crack, A-1.
—*v.* **7** *You must learn to master your temper:* conquer, subdue, overcome, triumph over, control, regulate, govern, manage, dominate, tame, curb, suppress, check, bridle. **8** *He could never master mathematics:* grasp, learn thoroughly, be adept in, be skilled at, be proficient in, excel at, get the hang of.
Ant. **1** slave; subject, vassal, servant, **3** crew; able-bodied seaman. **4, 6** amateur, novice, tiro. **5** minor, lesser, unimportant. **6** amateurish, incompetent, inept, unskilled, untalented, unaccomplished; bungling, clumsy. **7** surrender to, yield to, capitulate to, give in to, give way to.
◇ *Word origin: Master* comes from Latin *magister,* master, which also gives us *magistrate.*

masterful *adj.* **1** *He showed a masterful grasp of*

the problem. The violinist gave a masterful performance: masterly, skilful, skilled, expert, virtuoso, deft, able, accomplished, finished, superb, excellent. **2** *She could only love a masterful man:* strong-willed, self-confident, self-reliant, resolute, dynamic, forceful; commanding, domineering, bossy, authoritarian.

Ant. 1 amateurish, incompetent, inept, unskilled, untalented, unaccomplished, bungling, clumsy. **2** weak, wishy-washy, irresolute, meek, spineless.

mastermind *v.* **1** *The police know who masterminded the robbery:* plan, organize, conceive, engineer, direct.

—n. **2** *The advertising manager is the mastermind behind our new marketing policy:* planner, organizer, engineer, initiator, moving force, director. **3** *It will take a mastermind to solve this problem:* genius, mental giant, brilliant intellect, sage, wizard, pundit; expert, specialist, virtuoso, master, master hand, authority, past master, old hand.

Ant. 3 idiot, moron, imbecile, simpleton, fool; amateur, incompetent, novice, tiro.

"Everything great in the world is done by neurotics; they alone founded our religions and created our masterpieces."

—Marcel Proust

---

masterpiece *n. Rembrandt's paintings are masterpieces:* great work of art, masterwork, classic, monument, prize, jewel, treasure, paragon, nonpareil, *Latin* ne plus ultra, *French* chef d'oeuvre.

mastery *n.* **1** *The sergeant had complete mastery over his men:* control, command, domination, dominance, leadership, supremacy, superiority, sway, rule, upper hand, whip hand. **2** *It takes years to gain a mastery of Japanese:* expert knowledge, expert skill, proficiency, ability, adroitness, deftness, grasp, acquirement, attainment, achievement, accomplishment.

Ant. 1 subservience, submission, obedience. **2** incompetence, ineptness.

masticate *v. Masticate each bite thirty times before swallowing:* chew; champ, munch, gnaw, nibble.

Ant. swallow whole, gulp, bolt.

◇ *Word origin: Masticate* comes from Greek *mastikhan,* to gnash the teeth, from Greek *mastax,* jaw.

match *n.* **1** *The blue shirt and blue and grey tie are a good match:* matching pair, corresponding twosome; mate. **2** *Bill is no match for his brother at chess:* equal, equivalent, peer; parallel, counterpart. **3** *Who won the tennis match?:* game, contest, competition, tournament, meet, event.

—v. **4** *The curtains match the rug. These two pieces of the jigsaw puzzle don't match:* harmonize, correspond, be alike, suit, fit, go well with; combine, fit together, pair, couple, connect, join, unite, yoke, link together; agree, be equal, adapt. **5** *The promoters matched the young boxer with a more skilful fighter:* pit against, oppose, set against, put in competition with; contend, enter the lists with, vie with.

Ant. 1 mismatch. **2** unequal, superior; inferior. **4** clash with, differ from; be unequal, be a mismatch.

◇ *Word origin: Match,* an equal, comes from Old English *gemæcca,* mate, fellow. Our other word *match,* used to make a light or light a fire, comes from Latin *myxa,* lamp-wick.

matchless *adj. The vase is of matchless workmanship:* incomparable, supreme, unmatched, unparalleled, unequalled, unrivalled; peerless, unsurpassed, unexcelled, crowning, superior, paramount, pre-eminent, foremost; rare, priceless, invaluable, inestimable, sterling, exemplary.

Ant. comparable, equalled, surpassed, excelled; average, mediocre, common, commonplace, ordinary, everyday; inferior, lesser, lower, cheaper, second-class.

mate *n.* **1** *The zoo is looking for a mate for its female panda. Her mate seems to like her cooking:* one of a pair of mated animals; spouse, helpmate; husband, *Informal* hubby; wife, better half. **2** *Informal I had a drink with my friend and his mates at a local pub:* chum, pal, crony, buddy, friend, companion, comrade, co-worker, fellow worker, associate, colleague, partner; classmate; room-mate; messmate. **3** *The mate gave orders to swab the decks:* first mate, second mate; ship's officer below the rank of captain, master mariner.

—v. **4** *Some animals will not mate in captivity:* pair off; couple, copulate, cohabit.

◇ *Word origin: Mate* comes from Middle Low German *gemate* (*ge-,* together + *mat(e),* food, meat), hence your mate is literally your messmate. The same Germanic word is the ancestor of our word *meat.*

material *n.* **1** *The material of the earth's crust is very old:* matter, substance, stuff, elements. **2** Often **materials** *The price of building materials has gone up:* supplies, stores, stocks; timber, bricks and mortar; equipment, machinery, tools. **3** *Mother bought some material to make a dress:* fabric; piece goods, cloth, linen. **4** *The reporter is collecting material for an article:* facts, figures, observations, impressions, quotations, notes; references, citations.

—adj. **5** *What do we know of the material universe?:* physical, formed of matter, tangible, substantial, substantive, essential, materialistic, concrete; bodily, corporeal. **6** *He made a material contribution to the work:* significant, important, substantial, consequential, essential, vital, indispensable; relevant, pertinent, germane, direct; grave, serious, weighty, momentous.

Ant. 1 spirit, soul; mind, intellect. **5** non-material, intangible; spiritual. **6** insignificant, unimportant, insubstantial, inconsequential, trifling, piddling, inessential, dispensable, superficial; irrelevant, facetious, cavalier.

◇ *Usage note: Material* is anything of which something can be made: *building material, dress material. Matériel* usually means supplies, stock in trade, equipment: *The army needs weapons and matériel.* Remember, *materiAL* means *fAbric, matériEL* means *suppliEs.*

◇ *Word origin: Material,* and its various derivatives, such as *materialism, materialist, materialize, materially,* and *matériel,* comes from Latin *materia,* matter, stuff, which also gives us our word *matter.*

materialism *n. Crass materialism causes people to forget spiritual values:* love of possessions, love of material things, concern for comfort, pursuit of wealth; acquisitiveness, covetousness.

Ant. asceticism; idealism.

materially *adv.* **1** *Were things materially different in the old days?:* significantly, substantially, essentially, vitally, emphatically, considerably, to an important degree, seriously, in the main, for the most part. **2** *Materially, the family is quite successful:* financially, monetarily, concerning material things, with regard to material comforts; in substance, tangibly, palpably, corporeally.

Ant. 1 insignificantly, unsubstantially, on the surface, superficially; hardly, scarcely, barely, little. **2** spiritually; intellectually.

materialize *v.* **1** *The party never materialized:* occur, take place, come into being, come to pass, come into existence, come about, happen. **2** *The ghost of Christmas Past materialized in front of Scrooge. A lorry suddenly materialized out of the fog:* appear, loom, assume a physical form, appear out of thin air, become visible.

Ant. 2 disappear, vanish, vanish into thin air.

maternal *adj.* **1** *She showed her daughter's picture with maternal pride:* motherly, of a mother, motherlike; doting, fond; shielding, sheltering, protective. **2** *My maternal grandmother was a small woman:* related through one's mother, on one's mother's side of the family; matrilineal.

Ant. 2 paternal.

◇ *Word origin: Maternal* and *maternity* come from Latin *mater,* mother.

maternity *n. Maternity can be very rewarding:* motherhood, being a mother; child-bearing, childbirth, delivery, parturition, labour, accouchement; pregnancy.

mathematical *adj.* **1** *He's some kind of mathematical genius:* of mathematics, of higher mathematics; computational. **2** *The hostess planned the seating arrangements with mathematical precision:* precise, exact, accurate, scientific, well-defined, meticulous, scrupulous, punctilious, rigid.

Ant. 2 careless, heedless, thoughtless, sloppy, inaccurate, inexact, loose, lax.

matinée *n. There will be two evening performances and a matinée of* Macbeth: afternoon performance; early performance, early show.

◇ *Word origin: Matinée* was originally a French word that can be traced (via French *matin,* morning) to the Latin phrase *matutina tempora,* morning time, early in the day. Thus a *matinée* is a performance of a play, showing of a film, etc., early in the day, now usually in the afternoon before a later evening performance. From the same source comes our word *matins,* morning prayers.

matriarch *n. My grandmother was the matriarch of our family:* female head, female chieftain, female ruler, female leader, materfamilias.

matrimony *n. Young couples should enter into matrimony seriously:* marriage, marital state, sacrament of wedlock, holy wedlock, conjugal union, connubial state, nuptial state.

Ant. divorce, annulment; single life, bachelorhood, spinsterhood.

matron *n.* **1** *Most of the club members are matrons, though young girls are welcome:* married woman, middle-aged woman, stately woman, dowager, madam, dame. **2** *When the boys are ill they go and see the matron:* female supervisor, overseer, superintendent; directress, mistress, domestic head, chief nurse.

Ant. 1 girl, maid, maiden, lass, young woman.

◇ *Word origin: Matron* comes from Latin *mater,* mother, as does *maternal.*

"Nothing matters very much, and very few things matter at all."

Attributed to *Arthur, Lord Balfour*

---

matter *n.* **1** *The physical world is composed of matter. He has some foreign matter in his eye:* material, substance, stuff, elements; object, thing. **2** *The book contains some rather controversial matter:* subject matter, text, subject, content, theme, topic, thesis, gist, sense, purport, drift, argument, essence, sum and substance; printed matter, written matter. **3** *The matter was resolved amicably. There's that little matter of the money you borrowed:* affair, business, situation, transaction, thing, proceeding, episode, occurrence, experience, adventure, scrape, circumstance, event, happening. **4** *It is no matter that he didn't phone:* importance, consequence, significance, import, moment, difference. **5** *What's the matter?:* trouble, difficulty, cause of distress; predicament, emergency, crisis, exigency, dilemma, quandary, perplexity, strait; obstacle, impediment, *Informal* fix, snag.

—*v.* **6** *It matters very much:* be of importance, be of consequence, count, be of concern, be noteworthy; import, signify, carry weight, have influence.

Ant. 1 spirit, soul; mind, intellect. 4 insignificance, unimportance, meaninglessness. 5 solution, answer, resolution. 6 be unimportant, be inconsequential, be of no concern.
◇ *Word origin: Matter,* like *material,* comes from Latin *materia,* matter, stuff.

mature *adj.* 1 *He's a mature man who can make his own decisions:* grown, matured, fully developed, completely grown, grown-up, full-grown, of age, adult, middle-aged, in one's prime; experienced, practised, seasoned; marriageable, nubile, womanly; manly, virile; ripe, full-blown. 2 *When the plan is mature we will proceed:* completed, perfected, ready, finished, fully-fledged.
—*v.* 3 *Girls mature earlier than boys:* maturate, reach maturity, come of age, become adult, grown up, develop; ripen, bloom; mellow.
Ant. 1 immature, undeveloped, half-grown, underaged, young, juvenile, adolescent, childish, childlike, youthful, boyish, girlish; green, *Slang* wet behind the ears; callow, unfledged; unripe. 2 incomplete, unperfected, unfinished.
◇ *Word origin: Mature* comes from Latin *maturus,* ripe, mature. Also in Latin, the plural form *maturi* designates adults as opposed to children (*pueri*).

"Immature artists imitate. Mature artists steal." —*Lionel Trilling*

---

maturity *n.* 1 *The body reaches maturity earlier than the mind:* adulthood, maturation, manhood, womanhood, full growth, full development; legal age, age of consent, majority; ripeness, full bloom; completion, perfection, readiness, fulfilment, culmination. 2 *This job calls for a man with a great deal of maturity:* experience, practice, seasoning; level-headedness, composure, mature judgement, matureness, responsibility.
Ant. 1 immaturity, youthfulness, boyishness, girlishness, childishness, juvenility, puerility, callowness; incompletion, imperfection, crudeness. 2 irresponsibility, faulty judgement; excitability, hot-headedness.

maudlin *adj. Dickens was a great writer despite his maudlin plots:* over-emotional, weakly sentimental, mawkish, teary, lachrymose, gushing, tearful, *Informal* gushy, mushy, slushy.
Ant. realistic, matter-of-fact, unemotional, unsentimental.
◇ *Word origin: Maudlin* comes from the name of Mary *Magdalene,* who is often depicted with her eyes swollen from weeping over Jesus, which in the picture-language of medieval iconography signified "tearful repentance."

maul *v. The boy somehow got into the lion's cage and was mauled horribly:* paw roughly, lacerate, beat, beat up, rough up, thrash, bruise, mangle.
◇ *Word origin: Maul* comes from Latin *malleus,* hammer, which also gives us *mallet* and *malleable.*

mausoleum *n. This is the mausoleum of the royal family:* magnificent tomb, family tomb.
◇ *Pronunciation tip:* The *s* in *mausoleum* may be pronounced either *s* or *z*: *maw-suh-LEE-um* or *maw-zuh-LEE-um.*
◇ *Word origin: Mausoleum* literally means a tomb as large and stately as that of King Mausolus of Caria, whose large tomb at Halicarnassus in Asia Minor, erected about 350 B.C., was regarded as one of the Seven Wonders of the World.

mauve *adj. The garden was full of mauve irises:* light purple, bluish purple, lilac, lavender, puce, plum, violet.
◇ *Pronunciation tip:* The preferred pronunciation of *mauve* is *mōv,* rhyming with *clove.*

maverick *n.* 1 *The cowboys rounded up the mavericks for branding:* unbranded calf, yearling; unbranded cow; motherless calf. 2 *The young minister was regarded as a political maverick:* nonconformist, individualist, independent thinker, one's own man; dissenter, dissident.
◇ *Word origin: Maverick* was originally an American word. It comes from the name of Samuel *Maverick* (1803–70), a Texas cattle owner who neglected to brand his cattle. According to legend, he claimed that since his cattle could be identified by having no brand, all unbranded cattle must be his.

maw *n.* 1 *The farmer crammed grain down the goose's maw:* gullet, throat, œsophagus, mouth; jaws, muzzle. 2 *Food is partially digested in a bird's maw:* crop, craw, first stomach of a bird.

mawkish *adj. Mother tends to get mawkish when she speaks of her childhood:* sentimental, oversentimental, maudlin, lachrymose, tearful, teary, *Informal* mushy, gushy.
Ant. unsentimental, unemotional, matter-of-fact.

maxim *n. "A stitch in time saves nine" is a popular maxim:* adage, aphorism, axiom, proverb, apothegm, truism, old saw; motto, guiding principle, rule.
◇ *Word origin:* A *maxim* is literally a saying of the greatest importance. It comes from Latin *maximus,* greatest. (The word actually arose from the Medieval Latin phrase *propositio maxima,* "greatest proposition," i.e. fundamental axiom — this became French *maxime,* axiom, and so passed into English.)

maximum *adj. The plane can fly at a maximum altitude of 75,000 feet. The car was going at its maximum speed:* greatest possible, greatest, utmost, top, highest, maximal; supreme, unsurpassed, paramount, foremost.
Ant. minimum, minimal, least possible, least, lowest, bottom.
◇ *Word origin: Maximum* comes from Latin *maximus,* greatest.

maybe *adv. Maybe we'll see you tomorrow:* possibly, perhaps, perchance, peradventure, mayhap; God willing, wind and weather permitting.

maze *n. The messenger boy got confused in the maze of offices:* labyrinth, complex, network, tangle, convolution, complex puzzle.

◇ *Word origin: Maze* was formed by shortening *amaze.* It is that which *amazes* or confuses us.

meadow *n. Cows were roaming the meadow:* grazing land, grassland, pasture, savanna, pasturage, green, mead, meadowland; forage, herbage.

meagre *adj. The campers took only a meagre supply of food:* scanty, scant, slight, little, skimpy, scrimpy, sparse, bare, slender, slim, thin, lean; inadequate, insubstantial, insufficient, wanting, short, stinted, spare, scarce.

Ant. ample, abundant, plentiful, copious; adequate, sufficient, substantial.

◇ *Word origin: Meagre* comes from Latin *macer,* lean, which also gives us *emaciated.*

meal[1] *n. It's time for the midday meal. This restaurant is known for its Chinese meals:* repast, spread, feast, banquet, refreshment, nourishment; food, cuisine, cooking, fare, victuals, bill of fare, menu, diet, *Slang* nosh, eats, grub, chow.

meal[2] *n. Simple pancakes can be made out of meal and water:* ground grain, flour; (*variously*) cornmeal, oatmeal, groats, bran, grits, farina.

mean[1] *v.* **1** *Father didn't mean to be a clerk all his life, but that's the way it turned out:* intend, have in mind; propose, plan, purpose, aspire to, want, wish, dream of, think of, resolve, determine upon, aim at, drive at, have in view. **2** *What does "antidisestablishmentarianism" mean? A damp breeze from the sea usually means rain:* denote, signify, express, stand for, symbolize, say, portend, foretell; indicate, point to, imply, suggest, intimate, hint at, betoken. **3** *Did she really mean it?:* say truly, speak sincerely, feel honestly, express genuinely.

Ant. 2 hide, conceal, mask. **3** lie, pretend, feign, counterfeit.

mean[2] *adj.* **1** *The shoes were of mean quality. He has some mean job at the local factory:* low, low-grade, poor, inferior, cheap, second-rate, flimsy, sleazy, gimcrack, jerry-built, trashy, rubbishy, squalid, wretched, miserable, sordid; menial, low-ranking, low-paying, trifling, petty, unimportant, trivial, paltry, piddling, insignificant, inconsequential, small. **2** *How could anyone be so mean?:* malicious, vicious, malign, malevolent, evil, villainous, base, petty, low, small-minded, shameful, contemptible, despicable, disgraceful, dishonourable, vile, nasty, disagreeable, rude, cruel, hard-hearted, merciless, pitiless, inhumane, inhuman, unfeeling, unsympathetic, uncaring, unfair. **3** *He's a mean man though very rich:* stingy, miserly, pinch-penny, close-fisted, niggardly, penurious, ungenerous, illiberal, tight, close, cheap; greedy, grasping, avaricious, venal, hoggish, selfish, self-seeking, mercenary.

Ant. 1 high, good, superior, excellent, superb, splendid, first-rate, choice, premium, deluxe; high-ranking, important, consequential, significant, big. **2** kind, good-hearted, warm, good, sweet, gentle, humane, sympathetic, compassionate; noble, honourable, praiseworthy, pleasing, attractive, agreeable, wonderful. **3** generous, liberal, openhanded, bountiful, munificent, princely; unselfish, altruistic.

mean[3] *n.* **1** *His income is £2,000 above the national mean. Can't we strike a mean and find a house that's not too big or too small?:* average, norm, par, median, rule; happy medium, balance, compromise, midway point.

—*adj.* **2** *The mean income of British families is over £4,000 a year:* average; normal, regular; commonplace, run-of-the-mill.

Ant. 2 extreme, ultimate; best, highest, greatest, most; worst, lowest, smallest, least.

◇ *Usage note:* In maths, the *mean* is the average found by adding the values and dividing by the number of values. Thus, the mathematical mean of the five numbers, 1, 2, 3, 4, 100 is (1+2+3+4+100) ÷ 5, or 22. The *median* is merely the middle number or the mid-point of a series of numbers. Thus the mathematic median of the five numbers 1, 2, 3, 4, 100 is 3, the middle number in the series, since two numbers are below it and two are above.

meander *v. The path meanders up the hill. The tourists meandered through the old section of the castle:* wind, circle, loop, zigzag, snake, undulate, spiral; wander, ramble, go aimlessly, stray, rove.

Ant. go straight, go directly, make a bee-line.

◇ *Word origin: Meander* comes from the old name of the *Meander,* a river noted for its winding course. The modern name for the river is the *Menderes,* located in what is now western Turkey and flowing into the Aegean.

meaning *n. Look up the meaning of the word in the dictionary. Did that long speech have any meaning at all? Since his wife died his life has had no meaning:* denotation, sense, signification; significance, substance, sum and substance, content, subject matter, essence, gist, pith, meat, upshot; implication, drift, suggestion, intimation, indication, hint, pointer; intention, intent, purpose, purport, thrust, force, burden, goal, aim, point, object; value, worth, end; view, design, scheme, plan.

Ant. meaninglessness, insignificance, irrationality, absurdity.

meaningful *adj.* **1** *She gave her husband a meaningful look:* pointed, significant, purposeful, having meaning, eloquent, expressive, deep, portentous, pregnant, designing, suggestive, explicit, pithy. **2** *Every man should look for meaningful work to do:* worthwhile, useful, substantial, significant, consequential, important, serious, meaty; gratifying, emotionally satisfying.

Ant. 1, 2 meaningless, superficial, senseless, facetious. **2** worthless, useless, unsubstantial, insignificant, inconsequential, unimportant, trifling, trivial, paltry.

meaningless *adj.* **1** *Italian is meaningless to me. It seems to be a completely meaningless riddle:* unintelligible, incomprehensible, incoherent, impenetrable, inexpressive, undecipherable, illegible; puzzling, baffling, inscrutable, inexplicable, mystifying, perplexing, bewildering, enigmatic. **2** *Thoreau felt that many people live meaningless lives:* without meaning, without purpose, purposeless, worthless, valueless, useless, insubstantial, aimless, insignificant, inconsequential, unimportant, inessential, trivial, trite, paltry, piddling, shallow, senseless, frivolous, facetious, foolish, fatuous, absurd, stupid, nonsensical, idiotic, preposterous.

Ant. 1, 2 meaningful. **1** intelligible, comprehensible, understandable, coherent, expressive, clear, obvious, evident, manifest, pithy, trenchant; legible, decipherable. **2** purposeful, worthwhile, valuable, useful, substantial, significant, momentous, consequential, important, deep, sensible.

means *n. pl.* **1** *Many elderly people have not the means to travel. Only a man of means could afford a house as big as that:* money, resources, wherewithal, funds, pounds, income, revenue, *Slang* lolly, dough, bread; wealth, riches, substance, capital, property, affluence, easy circumstances. **2** *Taking a plane is the quickest means of getting there:* way, method, mode; resort, avenue, course, alternative; measure, process, modus operandi.

meantime *n. I'll call you on Sunday, but in the meantime say nothing:* interim, interval, the period between, the intervening time.

meanwhile *adv. Meanwhile, across town, things were humming. Meanwhile, don't call us, we'll call you:* at the same time, concurrently; during the intervening period, in the interim, meantime, for the time being.

measurable *adj. The distances to the furthest stars are measurable:* computable, reckonable, capable of being measured, mensurable, determinable, appraisable, assessable.

Ant. immeasurable, indeterminate.

measure *v.* **1** *Did you measure the windows before buying the curtains? The table-cloth measures 18 feet by 20:* ascertain the dimensions of, find the size of, size, pace off, plumb, sound; time, clock; to be the size of, be long, be wide. **2** *It's hard to measure the importance of good manners:* evaluate, value, assess, appraise, gauge, survey, judge.
—*n.* **3** *The measure is given in centimetres. Hold the measure up to the box:* measurement, unit of measurement; (*variously*) gauge, rule, scale, yardstick. **4** *Flood victims received a full measure of aid:* share, allotment, quantity, amount, portion, quota, allowance, extent, degree, range, scope; necessary amount, required amount. **5** *He loved her beyond measure:* limit, limitation, bound, restraint, moderation, temperance. **6** *The measure is now before Parliament:* act, bill, proposal, law, enactment; plan, scheme, design, project, proposition. **7** *What measures were taken to prevent fires?:* course, means, step, method, resort, proceeding, procedure.

measured *adj.* **1** *The cars raced over a measured mile:* predetermined; precise, exact, verified. **2** *The dignitaries advanced with a measured tread:* uniform, steady, regular, equal. **3** *His reply was stated in measured phrases:* studied, deliberate, premeditated, intentional, calculated, well-planned, carefully thought out, cold-blooded.

Ant. 2 haphazard, irregular, random. **3** spontaneous, rash, reckless, emotional, on the spur of the moment, unplanned.

measurement *n.* **1** *The measurement of individual intelligence is very difficult:* measuring, mensuration, surveying, sounding, plumbing; evaluation, assessment, appraisal, gauging, estimation, reckoning. **2** *What are the measurements of the living-room rug?:* dimension, size, breadth, depth, length, height, width, area; capacity, volume, content; mass, weight; magnitude, amplitude, extent.

"Meat eaten without either mirth or music is ill of digestion." —*Sir Walter Scott*

---

meat *n.* **1** *Veal is a very tender meat:* edible animal flesh, animal tissue or organs. **2** *The weary travellers were given meat and drink:* food, nourishment, victuals, sustenance, edibles, comestibles, fare, provisions, grub, provender. **3** *The meat of his argument is that poverty cannot be cured by government aid:* gist, point, essence, substance, core, heart, kernel, nut, nucleus.

◇ *Word origin: Meat* comes from Old English *mete.* Its Germanic ancestor *mat(e)*, meat, food, also gives us our word *mate,* literally "food-sharer," hence a companion or spouse.

mechanical *adj.* **1** *She doesn't understand anything mechanical:* run by machinery, having to do with machinery; machine-driven, automatic, self-acting. **2** *His gratitude seemed rather mechanical. Blinking is a mechanical action of the eyelids:* perfunctory, routine, unfeeling, impersonal, cold, machinelike; automatic, instinctive, involuntary, unconscious, unthinking.

Ant. 1 manual. **2** genuine, sincere, heartfelt, whole-hearted, personal, warm; voluntary, conscious, thinking.
◇ *Word origin: Mechanical* and *mechanism* come from Greek *mēchanē*, machine.

> **Exploring the Word:** The names for our various kinds and cuts of meat are interesting to explore. Latin *bos*, cow, gives us *beef* (via French *boeuf*) as well as *bovine* (a name for a cow, Bossy), and *Bovril* (trade name of a packaged beef broth). *Veal* comes from Old French *viel*, calf; *pork* comes from Latin *porcus*, pig, while *bacon* is from Old High German *bacho*, ham, and our word *ham* is from an Old English word meaning thigh or thigh and buttocks of an animal. *Lamb* also is an Old English word, while *mutton* comes from Old French *molton*, sheep. *Sausage* comes from Latin *salsus*, salted, while the seasoned sausage of mixed meats, *baloney*, was named after Bologna, Italy, *frankfurters* after Frankfurt, Germany, and *hamburgers* after Hamburg, Germany, each of these types of sausage being associated with the cities they are named after. *Steak* comes from Old Norse *steik*, "stick" (because originally roasted on a spit), while a *chop* is a cut of meat chopped from a larger cut.

mechanism *n. The tin-opener is a simple mechanism. The mechanism of this toy train is faulty:* apparatus, tool, instrument, implement, utensil, contrivance, appliance, machine; works, machinery, motor.

medal *n. The war hero received many medals for bravery:* citation, decoration, medallion, ribbon, award of honour; trophy, prize; award.
◇ *Usage note:* See MEDDLE.

meddle *v. No one asked him to meddle in this affair:* interfere, intervene, intrude, concern oneself unasked, interlope, pry into, *Informal* butt in, horn in, poke one's nose into; tamper with.
Ant. keep out.
◇ *Usage note:* Don't confuse these four words: *meddle* (to interfere), *mettle* (courage), *medal* (an award), *metal* (a chemical element). Thus: *Please, Dad, don't meDDle in my affairs! It takes a lot of meTTle to fight tigers, This medal is an award for bravery, Tin is a metal.*

mediate *v. The lawyer tried to mediate between the company and the union:* arbitrate, negotiate, moderate, intervene, intercede, settle a dispute, bring to terms, effect an agreement, bring about an agreement; make peace between, conciliate, reconcile, restore harmony, step in, umpire, referee.
◇ *Usage note:* To *mediate* in a dispute is to try to find a middle ground or compromise on which both sides may agree: *The United Nations mediated in the quarrel between Greeks and Turks in Cyprus.* A *mediator*, of course, suggests such compromises, acts as a go-between, and tries to get both sides to agree. To *arbitrate* means to hear both sides of a dispute and then make a decision: *The union and the company asked the government to arbitrate in their dispute.* An *arbitrator* thus acts like a judge and determines which side is right. *Binding arbitration* means that the two sides have agreed to, or are forced to, accept the arbitrator's decision.

mediation *n. The dispute was settled by mediation:* arbitration, compromise, adjustment, conciliation, give-and-take, settlement of difficulties, coming to terms; negotiation, discussion, parley, intervention, intercession.

mediator *n. Who will act as mediator in the dispute?:* arbitrator, negotiator, moderator, reconciler, go-between, intermediary, referee, umpire, peacemaker.
◇ *Usage note:* See MEDIATE.

medical *adj. Medical research may find a cure for cancer. Some herbs have medical value:* relating to medicine, medicinal, curative, healing, therapeutic, remedial, restorative, sanative, health-bringing, salutary.
Ant. unhealthy, unhealthful, toxic, poisonous, virulent.
◇ *Word origin: Medical, medicine,* and *medication* come from Latin *medicina/medicus*, medicine, physician, both of which are based on the verb *mederi*, to heal.

medication *n. The doctor prescribed some medication:* remedy, medicine, medicament, healing application, curative substance; tonic, restorative, palliative, balm; panacea, nostrum, elixir.

medicine *n.* **1** *What kind of medicine are you taking?:* curative agent, medication; drug, pill, remedy, nostrum, tonic, restorative; balm, salve. **2** *Where did the doctor study medicine?:* science of medicine, practice of medicine, healing art, medical treatment, therapeutics, materia medica.
Ant. 1 poison, toxin, bane.
◇ *Word origin:* See MEDICAL.

medieval *adj. Chaucer wrote in the late medieval period:* of the Middle Ages (the period between A.D. 476 and approximately 1450), pre-Renaissance.
◇ *Word origin:* The *medieval* period in European history is the Middle Ages, 476–1450, i.e. the period between the collapse of the western Roman Empire, ending Classical Antiquity, and the Renaissance. *Medieval* comes from Latin *medius* (middle) + *aevum* (age).

mediocre *adj. The student tries hard, but his work is mediocre. He seems content with a mediocre job:* ordinary, run-of-the-mill, undistinguished, commonplace, pedestrian, indifferent, passable, tolerable, so-so, fair-to-middling, betwixt and between, average, medium, normal, common; unimportant, inconsequential, insignificant, negligible, inconsiderable, inappreciable, petty, slight, trifling,

paltry, meagre; inferior, second-rate.
Ant. extraordinary, uncommon, distinctive, distinguished, unique, unexcelled, unsurpassed, unrivalled, incomparable; superior, fine, excellent, superb; important, significant.
◇ *Usage note: Average* suggests no better or worse than the majority, neither superior nor inferior: *The grade of C means that the student did average work, The man was of average height. Mediocre* also means "not unusually good or bad, commonplace," but has a connotation of inferiority: *The teacher can't stand mediocre work, The critics condemned the play as mediocre.*
◇ *Word origin: Mediocre* and *mediocrity* come from Latin *medius*, middle, which also gives us *mean, medium, median, middle*, and *mid*. Our phrase *golden mean* is a literal translation of the Roman poet Horace's phrase *aurea mediocritas*, "happy medium, the way of common sense between extremes."

mediocrity *n. The old poet decried the mediocrity of today's writing:* commonplaceness, indifference, ordinariness, unimportance, insignificance, pettiness, paltriness, meagreness, triviality; low-quality, inferiority, poorness.
Ant. distinction, uniqueness; importance, significance, consequence; excellence, superiority, greatness, brilliance.

"The world is a republic of the mediocrities, and always was." —*Thomas Carlyle*

---

meditate *v.* **1** *Modern men don't set aside enough time to meditate:* think, reflect, think quietly, think seriously, ruminate, muse, contemplate, ponder, study, cogitate, deliberate, collect one's thoughts, dwell upon, turn over in one's mind, mull over. **2** *The councillor is meditating a reply to his critics:* plan, devise, concoct, contrive, consider, propose, have in view, aim at, dream of, aspire to.
Ant. 1 act, do.

medium *n.* **1** *Fish live in an aqueous medium:* environment, surroundings, atmosphere; setting, milieu. **2** *There has to be a medium between good and bad:* middle ground, midcourse, middle way; compromise, moderation, happy medium, mean, golden mean, balance. **3** *Television can be an excellent medium for education:* agency, means, way, mode, form, channel, instrument, vehicle, tool, avenue, instrumentality, organ. **4** *The medium supposedly called forth her long dead uncle:* spiritualist, psychic, clairvoyant, fortune-teller, diviner, crystal-gazer; go-between, intermediary, intermediate.
—*adj.* **5** *The boy is of medium height for his age:* average, common, normal, ordinary, middling, moderate.
Ant. 2 extreme limit. **5** extreme, utmost, extraordinary, uncommon, distinctive, undue, unique, unusual, unreasonable.
◇ *Usage note:* The plural of *medium* may be either the Latin *media* or the English *mediums*. One usually speaks of people who claim to communicate with the spirit world as *mediums: She consulted several mediums.* On the other hand, one usually refers to means, agencies, and artistic forms as *media: The painter works in oils, water-colours, and other media.* Today, *media* is also used to refer to the communications industry, newspapers, magazines, and television and radio networks: *The media are covering the election thoroughly.*
◇ *Word origin: Medium* comes from Latin *medius*, middle, which also gives us *middle, mid*, and *mediocre.*

medley *n. The band played a medley of march tunes:* miscellany, mixture, assortment, pot-pourri, mêlange, pastiche, mosaic, patchwork; jumble, hotchpotch, *Informal* mishmash, hash, mess.

meek *adj. The bossy woman was blessed with a meek husband. The meek shall inherit the earth:* submissive, deferential, complaisant, docile, yielding, acquiescent, unresisting, compliant, spineless, spiritless, weak-kneed, lamblike; humble, mild, gentle, modest, unassuming, unpretentious, retiring, tolerant, tender-hearted.
Ant. domineering, bossy, wilful, overbearing, self-assertive, bold, forward, presumptuous; spirited, *Informal* rebellious, insubordinate, unyielding; arrogant, lordly, proud, immodest, pretentious.
◇ *Word origin: Meek* comes from Old Norse *mjūkr*, soft.

meet *v.* **1** *I'd like you to meet my brother:* be introduced to, be presented to, become acquainted with; welcome, greet. **2** *I met an old school friend today. A policeman could meet danger at any minute of his working day:* come across, encounter, run into, bump into, come into contact with, light upon; confront, face, come into the presence of, speak with. **3** *The club meets at a different member's home each week:* assemble, convene, gather, collect, congregate, rally, muster, come together. **4** *To join the army, one must meet certain physical standards. Father was poor, but he always met his financial obligations:* fulfil, comply with, satisfy, observe, abide by, adhere to, execute, carry out, perform, discharge, heed, obey, be faithful to, follow, acknowledge, respect, keep one's pledge; equal, come up to, answer, match. **5** *Turn left where the avenue meets the main road. The two properties meet at the bottom of the valley:* cross, intersect, unite with, converge with; adjoin, abut, border.
Ant. 1 become estranged. **2** avoid, elude, escape, miss. **3** adjourn; disperse, scatter, dispel. **4** fail, fall short of; renege. **5** diverge.

meeting *n.* **1** *Our meeting was arranged by a mutual friend. The two lawyers had an argument at* *their very first meeting:* introduction, presentation; encounter, confrontation; date, engagement, rendezvous, tryst, assignation. **2** *The chairman called the meeting to order:* gathering, assembly, group, convocation, conclave, council, congress, caucus; conference, convention, get-together.

melancholy *n.* **1** *Rainy days give me a feeling of melancholy:* melancholia; depression, gloom, gloominess, dejection, despondency, disconsolateness, despair, forlornness, moodiness, low spirits, doldrums; *Slang* blues, dumps.
—*adj.* **2** *Hamlet was a melancholy man:* suffering from melancholia; depressed, gloomy, dejected, despondent, disconsolate, forlorn, glum, moody, mopish, doleful, downhearted, heavy-hearted, discouraged, dispirited, downcast, cheerless, heartsick, sick at heart, unhappy, morose, languishing, *Slang* down in the dumps, down in the mouth, blue. **3** *What a melancholy day!:* depressing, gloomy, dreary, sombre, dismal, desolate, joyless, plaintive, mournful, funereal; dolorous, doleful; unfortunate, calamitous.
Ant. 1 exhilaration, joy, delight, pleasure, cheer, happiness, gladness. **2** exhilarated, joyous, joyful, cheerful, light-hearted, happy, glad, vivacious, gay, lively, sprightly, merry. **3** exhilarating, joyous, delightful, cheerful, happy.
◇ *Word origin: Melancholy* comes from Greek *melanos* (black) + *cholē* (bile), black bile, the "humour" once believed to cause depression. See HUMOUR.

mêlée *n. Rival fans started a mêlée on the way to the football match:* brawl, row, fracas, fray, set to, scuffle, scrap, tussle, altercation, commotion, rumpus, disorder, riot.
◇ *Pronunciation tip: Mêlée* is, of course, pronounced *MEL-ay.* The stress is usually on the first syllable.

mellifluous *adj. We heard mellifluous bells across the lake:* sweet-sounding, sweet-toned, euphonious, mellifluent, musical, harmonious, sweet, dulcet, melodious, mellow, soft, smooth; resonant, full-toned.
Ant. harsh, discordant, grating, jarring, raucous, hoarse, unmusical.

mellow *adj.* **1** *This is a good mellow cheese:* ripe, mature, matured; full-flavoured, full-bodied, luscious, sweet, delicious; soft, rich.
—*v.* **2** *Age and responsibility mellowed the callow youth:* mature, season; make more understanding, make sympathetic, make compassionate, make more tolerant, soften, smooth the rough edges.
Ant. 1 unripe, immature, green; raw, sour, biting, harsh. **2** harden, brutalize, make callous, make unfeeling, make stubborn.

melodic *adj. The composer has quite a melodic gift:* of melody, creating melody, full of melody; melodious, tuneful, lyric.
Ant. unmelodic.

melodious *adj.* **1** *The girl has a very melodious voice:* sweet-toned, mellifluous, mellifluent, euphonious, musical, sweet, dulcet, mellow, soft, smooth; clear, rich, full-toned, resonant, ringing. **2** *The operetta was very melodious:* tuneful, full of melody, melodic, lyric.
Ant. 1 harsh, discordant, grating, jarring, raucous. **2** unmelodic, untuneful, cacophonous, unharmonious.

melodramatic *adj. The play was criticized for its melodramatic ending:* exaggerated, overtheatrical, sensational, stagy, sentimental, over-emotional, overwrought, mawkish, maudlin, histrionic, *Slang* hammy, corny.
Ant. realistic, matter-of-fact; understated, low-key, deadpan.
◇ *Word origin: Melodramatic* comes from Greek *melos* (song) + *drama* (drama), formerly a romantic drama with sensational incidents and usually including music and songs.

melody *n.* **1** *I'll hum the melody and you try to guess the words:* tune, air, strain, theme; song, aria, ballad, ditty. **2** *The success of a popular composer depends on his melody:* tunefulness, melodiousness, musicality, musical invention, melodic gift, melodic invention; euphony, mellifluence, sweetness of sound, timbre.
Ant. 1 harmony; rhythm. **2** dissonance; harshness, discordance, clashing, jarring.
◇ *Word origin: Melody* and *melodic* come from Greek *melos* (song) + *-ōdiā* (singing).

melt *v.* **1** *When the sun came out the snow melted quickly:* dissolve, liquefy, thaw. **2** *When the police came the crowd melted away:* dissipate, scatter, dispel, dwindle, fade, dissolve, disappear, evaporate, vanish; waste away. **3** *One week melts into the next:* blend, fuse, merge, pass, shade, fade, dissolve. **4** *The little boy's tears melted her heart:* touch, soften, disarm, make gentle, affect, arouse pity; appease, conciliate, mollify, propitiate.
Ant. 1 freeze, solidify; congeal, jell, set, harden. **2** accrue, gather, grow. **4** harden, make callous.

"I don't want to belong to any club that would accept me as one of its members."
—*Groucho Marx*

member *n.* **1** *Her lower members were numb with cold:* extremity, appendage; (*variously*) limb, leg, foot, toe, arm, hand, finger, digit; (*animals*) wing, pinion, tail; part, organ; (*plants*) shoot, bough, branch. **2** *All the members of the committee were present:* constituent, person who belongs to a group; component, element, part, piece, section, segment, portion, fragment, ingredient.
◇ *Word origin: Member* comes from Latin *membrum,* limb, arm, leg, body member.

membership *n.* **1** *Women are denied membership of the men's bowling league:* fellowship, league, affiliation, partnership, connection. **2** *The membership of the club is now 500:* roster, personnel, body of members, number of members; community, company, association; society, fraternity, brotherhood, club, fellowship.

membrane *n. The toes of a frog are connected by a membrane:* web, covering tissue; film, thin sheet, thin skin, envelope; integument, pellicle.

◇ *Word origin: Membrane* literally means "limb coating" and comes from Latin *membrum,* limb.

memoir *n. The duchess's memoirs caused a sensation:* autobiography, diary, journal, recollections, reminiscences, confessions, biography, intimate biography, life, life story.

memorable *adj. The visitors spent a memorable week in the Canadian Rockies. T. S. Eliot's* The Wasteland *is one of the most memorable poems of the 20th century:* unforgettable, notable, noteworthy, impressive, illustrious, famous, celebrated, distinguished, eminent, prominent, important, significant, momentous, historic, outstanding, salient, remarkable, extraordinary, striking, stirring, red-letter.

Ant. unmemorable, forgettable, unimpressive, undistinguished, unimportant, insignificant, mediocre, commonplace, ordinary, pedestrian, prosaic, banal, trite, trivial, run-of-the-mill.

◇ *Word origin:* See MEMORY.

memorandum *n. He sent us a memorandum about the meeting:* memo, reminder, note, brief report, jotting; list of items, agenda.

◇ *Usage note:* Since *memorandum* is a Latin singular, its traditional plural is *memoranda.* But in modern usage *memorandums* is equally acceptable. Thus, we may correctly say or write either *The executive wrote three memoranda* or *three memorandums.*

◇ *Word origin:* See MEMORY.

memorial *n.* **1** *This statue is a memorial to the town's war dead:* monument, testimonial. **2** *Friends gathered at a memorial for the late statesman:* tribute, homage, commemorative service, memorial service.

—*adj.* **3** *A memorial plaque in honour of the first minister of this church was installed in the chapel:* commemorative, monumental, testimonial.

memory *n.* **1** *Can a person improve his memory?:* recall, ability to remember, power of recollection, mental retention, remembrance, remembering. **2** *Mother has lovely memories of her youth:* recollection, mental impression, reminiscence, remembrancer, memento, souvenir, keepsake, reminder, token, memorial, commemoration, testimonial. **3** *He is gone, but his memory remains to guide the living:* fame, renown, eminence, reputation, repute, glory, prestige, distinction, esteem, honour, estimation, name, note, mark, regard, respect.

Ant. 1 forgetfulness. **2** amnesia; a total blank. **3** oblivion, nothingness, void, non-existence.

◇ *Word origin: Memory, memorable, memento, memorandum,* and *memorial* all come from Latin *memoria,* memory, which also gives us our words *memoir, memorabilia,* and *remember.* (Latin *memoria,* memory, is based on Latin *memor,* mindful.)

menace *n.* **1** *Icebergs are a menace to ships in the North Atlantic:* threat, danger, peril, hazard, jeopardy, risk, endangerment, imperilment, pitfall, cause for alarm.

—*v.* **2** *Overeating can menace a person's health. The hooligan menaced the local shop-keepers:* endanger, imperil, be a hazard to, jeopardize, risk; terrify, intimidate, threaten, terrorize, bully, browbeat, cow, daunt.

Ant. 1 blessing, benefit, boon, advantage. **2** benefit, help, aid, promote, further, advance; protect, guard, safeguard; soothe, console, calm.

mend *v.* **1** *A good tailor can mend that coat. The broken bone is starting to mend:* repair, fix, put in order, restore, renovate, recondition, touch up, retouch, patch, darn; heal, knit, cure, remedy. **2** *The judge warned the youth to mend his ways:* correct, reform, improve, better, ameliorate, meliorate, amend, rectify, revise.

Ant. 1 damage, harm, injure, lacerate, tear, break, split; spoil, ruin, destroy.

mendacity *n. There's so much mendacity in the world that one doesn't know whom to believe:* lying, falsehood, falsity, untruthfulness, falsification, prevarication, misrepresentation; deceit, deception, duplicity, dishonesty, hypocrisy, perfidy, double-dealing, fraud, chicanery, insincerity.

Ant. truth, truthfulness, veracity, frankness, openness, forthrightness; honesty, trustworthiness, uprightness, sincerity.

mendicant *n. The streets of Tangier are full of mendicants seeking alms. The Capuchins were founded as an order of mendicants:* begging monk, begging friar; beggar, street beggar, alms-seeker, cadger.

◇ *Word origin: Mendicant* comes from Latin *mendicus,* beggar, which is based on Latin *mendum,* physical defect. The connection is obvious — the original *mendici* of ancient Rome were cripples.

menial *adj.* **1** *No job is too menial for a hungry man. His menial behaviour disgusts me:* lowly, low, humble, ignoble, mean, abject; servile, subservient, slavish, obsequious, fawning, grovelling, truckling, cringing, sycophantic, *Informal* boot-licking.

—*n.* **2** *The king was surrounded by menials who did his every bidding:* servant, flunkey, lackey, underling, subordinate; employee, apprentice, helper; slave, drudge, drone; sycophant, toady.

Ant. 1 noble, dignified, autocratic, aristocratic, high, elevated; overbearing, haughty, domineering, bossy, proud, conceited. **2** master, lord, overseer, superior, chief, commander, boss.

mental *adj.* **1** *He got the answer by mental arithmetic:* of the mind, in the mind, done with the mind, intellectual, intelligent, cerebral, rational; psychic, psychological; abstract, metaphysical, subjective. **2** *How many mental patients does the hospital care for?:* mentally ill, mentally disturbed, psychotic, neurotic; insane, crazy, lunatic, disordered, disturbed, unbalanced, *Slang* nutty, cracked, psycho.

◇ *Word origin: Mental* and *mentality* come from Latin *mens,* mind, which also gives us *demented* (out of one's mind) and *dementia praecox* (a former term for schizophrenia), literally "precocious (premature) madness," i.e. pre-senile madness.

mentality *n. Contrary to popular belief, chess does not demand a high mentality. The girl has the mentality of a much older child:* intellect, mental ability, intelligence, mental power, mental endowment, mind, brains, *Informal* grey matter; perception, judgement, understanding, discernment, perspicacity, acumen, wisdom, sagacity.

mention *v.* **1** *Before closing I want to mention all those who contributed so generously. I hate to mention this, but—:* allude to, speak of briefly, refer to, touch upon; name, specify, cite, disclose, make known, divulge; hint at, intimate, imply, insinuate; state, remark, tell, tell of, report, recount, narrate.

—n. **2** *No mention was made of her illness:* allusion, suggestion, indication, hint, insinuation, inkling, reference, remark, statement, utterance, communication, advice, announcement, notice, notification, report, specification, observation, designation, acquaintance, enlightenment.

Ant. 1 omit, be silent about; forget, neglect, disregard, slight, ignore, drop, suppress. **2** omission, avoidance, neglect, silence, suppression.

mentor *n. The boy accepted the guidance of his friend and mentor:* adviser, counsellor, preceptor; teacher, instructor, tutor; monitor, guide, guru.

◇ *Word origin:* According to Homer's *Odyssey,* when Odysseus (Latin name: Ulysses) left home for the Trojan War, he appointed his wise counsellor Mentor to look after his son Telemachus. From this legendary guardian *Mentor* comes our word *mentor.*

mercenary *adj.* **1** *Does he love his wealthy mother or only pretend to for mercenary reasons?:* selfish, greedy, venal; monetary, money-motivated, for gain, for pay; acquisitive, grasping, avaricious, covetous.

—n. **2** *Much of the fighting was done by mercenaries:* hired soldier, paid soldier in a foreign army, soldier fighting for spoils.

Ant. 1 idealistic, selfless, unselfish, altruistic; generous, liberal, philanthropic, benevolent, munificent.

◇ *Word origin: Mercenary* comes from Latin *merces,* reward, wages. Also related is Latin *merx,* merchandise, which gives us *merchant, merchandise,* and *market.*

merchandise *n.* **1** *This shop has the best merchandise in town:* manufactured goods, goods, wares, stock, stock in trade; commodities, staples; effects, belongings.

—v. **2** *There's no point in manufacturing an item unless you can merchandise it:* sell, market, distribute; trade, deal in, buy and sell, carry on commerce in, do business in, traffic in; advertise, publicize, *Slang* huckster, hawk.

◇ *Spelling tip:* People sometimes forget that *merchandise* has an *s* in it, and not a *z.* Remember that *merchandise,* with an *s,* is to *sell,* with an *s*: *merchandiSe — Sell.*

◇ *Word origin:* See MERCENARY.

"Chrysanthemums from gilded argosy
Unload their gaudy scentless merchandise."
—*Oscar Wilde*

---

merchant *n. He is a widely travelled diamond merchant. Some of the local merchants donated goods for the fair:* salesman, dealer, wholesaler, purchaser, broker, jobber, trader; shopkeeper, retailer, tradesman, storekeeper, peddler, hawker, chandler, monger, street vendor.

◇ *Word origin:* See MERCENARY.

merciful *adj. The Judge had a reputation for being merciful:* compassionate, humane, exercising mercy, kind, lenient, clement, sparing, sympathetic, forgiving, pitying, kind-hearted, understanding, feeling, benign, beneficent.

Ant. merciless, unfeeling, uncompassionate, cruel, inhumane, hard-hearted, pitiless.

merciless *adj. The killer was merciless:* pitiless, ruthless, unmerciful, inhumane, hard-hearted, cold-blooded, inhuman, unrelenting, relentless, cruel, fell; harsh, severe, unsparing, heartless, unpitying, callous.

Ant. merciful, humane, forgiving, kind-hearted, clement, lenient.

mercurial *adj. He is so mercurial that he constantly changes his political outlook:* flighty, impulsive, changeable, inconstant, erratic, fickle, unstable, unpredictable, capricious, mobile, kinetic, fluctuating, variable, protean, impetuous, lively, electric, spirited, irrepressible.

Ant. unchanging, stable, fixed, phlegmatic.

◇ *Word origin: Mercurial* literally means like *Mercurius,* Mercury, the fleet-footed and cunning Roman messenger of the gods and himself patron god of travellers, artisans, orators, merchants, and thieves.

mercy *n.* **1** *The caretaker showed no mercy to trespassers. He begged for mercy:* compassion, kindness, forbearance, benevolence, pity, clemency, sympathy, humaneness, soft-heartedness, humanity, tolerance, charity, commiseration, grace, fellow-feeling, tender-heartedness, forgiveness, lenity, leniency, lenience. **2** *What a mercy he escaped the fire!:* good thing, piece of luck, lucky break, blessing.

Ant. 1 pitilessness, cruelty, harshness, rigour, severity, sternness, implacability, inhumanity, brutality.

mere *adj. It's a mere trinket:* common, ordinary, inconsiderable, insignificant, trifling, commonplace, mundane, nugatory, paltry, negligible, unappreciable, uneventful; nothing else but, nothing more than, pure and simple, utter, plain, bare, sheer, scant, unmitigated, bald.

merge *v. The two failing companies eventually merged:* combine, amalgamate, consolidate, fuse, become one, converge, blend, join, intermix, coalesce, synthesize, unite, interfuse, interconnect, interlock, confederate, associate, band together, link up.

Ant. separate, diverge, sever, part, disjoin, disband.

> **Exploring the Word:** *Merge, emerge, immerse,* and *submerge* come from Latin *mergere,* to immerse, plunge, dip. Thus to *merge* is to immerse or combine with something else, and a business *merger* is an immersion of one business into another or a combining of two companies; *emerge* (Latin prefix *e-,* out) literally means to "plunge out," and an *emergency* is a sudden coming forth of something calling for immediate action; *immerse* (Latin prefix *im-,* in) means to plunge or dip in; and *submerge* (Latin prefix *sub-,* under) means to plunge or dip under, as a submarine *submerges* beneath the surface.

merit *n.* **1** *There is great merit in dealing fairly with your employees. She is a person of some merit:* value, worth, worthiness, virtue, advantage, benefit, justification; efficacy, credit, quality, stature, ability, worthiness, talent, distinction.

—*v.* **2** *The suggestion merits serious consideration:* deserve, be entitled to, rate, be worthy of, have a right to, warrant, invite, prompt, have claim to, earn.

Ant. 1 fault, defect, worthlessness, weakness, imperfection, discredit.

◇ *Word origin: Merit* comes from Old French *merite,* the source of which is Latin *mereri,* to deserve.

meritorious *adj. He was praised for his meritorious service as Governor-General:* commendable, laudable, praiseworthy, noteworthy, exceptional, deserving of reward or commendation, worthy, creditable, well carried out, estimable, excellent, exemplary, admirable.

Ant. unexceptional, unpraiseworthy, unworthy, discreditable, undeserving, dishonest, dishonourable, ignoble, unchivalrous, ungenerous.

merriment *n. You never saw such unbridled merriment at a party!:* mirth, laughter, gaiety, jollity, hilarity, frolic, fun, good fun, good spirits, revelry, glee, sportiveness, amusement, cheer, gleefulness, celebration, joviality, jocularity, light-heartedness, liveliness, jocundity, festivity, merrymaking, high spirits, levity, good humour, jubilation, skylarking, exhilaration, conviviality, *Informal* whoopee.

Ant. cheerlessness, joylessness, distress, misery, mourning.

merry *adj. We joined the merry crowd:* gay, jolly, cheerful, happy, cheery, gladsome, gleeful, jovial, joyous, sportive, carefree, mirthful, jocular, frolicsome, fun-loving, light-hearted, jocund, lively, high-spirited, vivacious, laughing, skylarking, festive, convivial, rollicking, animated, revelling, sprightly.

Ant. sad, unhappy, gloomy, disconsolate, dismal, dejected.

◇ *Word origin: Merry,* like *mirth,* comes from Old English *myrig,* pleasant, happy.

mesmerize *v. They say that Hitler mesmerized his audiences:* spellbind, bewitch, magnetize, entrance, enthral; hypnotize, put in a trance, control another's mind.

◇ *Word origin: Mesmerize* comes from the name of the Austrian physician Friedrich Anton *Mesmer* (1733–1815), who first widely publicized hypnotism in public demonstrations in Vienna around 1775.

mess *n.* **1** *Pick up that mess of dirty clothes:* clutter, unsightly accumulation, jumble, litter, hotchpotch, confused mass, hash, mish-mash, conglomeration; untidy condition, dirty state, disorder, disarray. **2** *How did you get into a mess like that?:* predicament, muddle, difficulty, plight, mix-up, confusion, fix, pickle, situation, quandary, strait, stew, scrape, pinch, trouble, *Informal* hot water, pretty kettle of fish; dilemma, imbroglio, crisis. **3** *The fight happened in the officers' mess:* mess-hall, dining room, refectory, dining-hall, cafeteria.

◇ *Word origin:* Originally a *mess,* or the Old French *mes,* was any course of a meal (if you have been to Spain or Mexico you may have eaten an *entre mes* or *entremes,* "entrance course," or appetizer). From this original meaning we now have both our meaning *mess* as disorder or dirty or untidy things (perhaps from the dishes and left-overs of meals with many courses) and *mess* meaning a quantity of food, as in a "mess of beans" or "mess of greens" as well as *officers' mess,* a group of people who regularly eat together, their actual meal, or the place in which they eat.

message *n.* **1** *I received a message that she would be late:* notice, report, word, statement, news, communication, communiqué, intelligence, tidings, dispatch, missive, note, letter, bulletin. **2** *The play has a serious message:* point, theme, central idea, purport, moral.

messenger *n. The messenger brought your note today:* carrier, bearer, deliverer, delivery boy, delivery man, courier, go-between, emissary, envoy.

messy *adj.* **1** *I can't find anything on this messy desk:* disordered, cluttered, untidy, littered, chaotic, disarranged, confused, jumbled, topsy-turvy; bedraggled, sloppy, dishevelled, unkempt, slatternly, frowzy, blowzy, grubby. **2** *She found herself in a messy spot:* awkward, difficult, unpleasant, embarrassing, tangled, inextricable, unenviable, ugly, uncomfortable, tricky.

Ant. 1 ordered, neat, tidy, clean. **2** pleasant, comfortable, enviable.

metamorphosis *n.* **1** *There are four stages in the metamorphosis of a mosquito:* transformation, change of form, mutation, transmutation, structural evolution, transfiguration, series of changes, modification, conversion, transmogrification. **2** *This once-confident man underwent a complete metamorphosis after his business failure:* change in appearance or behaviour, personality change, transformation, alteration, radical change, startling change, permutation.

◇ *Word origin: Metamorphosis* comes from Greek *meta-* (beyond, after) + *morphē* (form), hence a transformation into something else.

"One thing that literature would be greatly the better for
Would be a more restricted employment by authors of simile and metaphor."
—*Ogden Nash*

---

metaphor *n. In poetry the rose is often a metaphor for love:* image, representation, figurative expression, poetic equivalent, sensory symbol, figure of speech, analogy, parallel, equivalence.

◇ *Usage note:* A *metaphor* is a statement that says that one thing *is* another by way of emphasizing a likeness or quality. Thus, *She's an angel* and *He's a lion in battle* are metaphors. A *simile* makes a comparison between two things by using the words *as* or *like.* Thus, *She's as good as an angel* and *He fights like a lion* are similes.

◇ *Word origin: Metaphor* comes from Greek *meta-* (beyond, after) + *pherein* (to carry), something carried beyond another, hence a figure of speech in which one object is carried beyond, put behind, or likened to another as if it were that other, as "The soldier was a lion in battle."

metaphysical *adj.* **1** *Trying to define God led us to even more metaphysical questions:* philosophical, speculative, abstract, unanswerable, intellectual; ultimate, essential, universal, eternal, fundamental, basic; ontological, cosmological, epistemological, existential; esoteric, mystical. **2** *Their argument was too metaphysical for me to follow:* abstract, intangible, vague, impalpable, lofty, high-flown, abstruse, oversubtle, recondite, deep, *Slang* far-out.

Ant. 1 physical, material, mundane. **2** concrete, tangible, clear, comprehensible, down-to-earth.

◇ *Word origin: Metaphysical* was first coined to describe Aristotle's later writings. It comes from Greek *meta-* (beyond, after) + *Physika* (Aristotle's treatise called *Physics*), hence Aristotle's writings "after his *Physics.*" We now use the word *metaphysical* to refer to any philosophical theories that go beyond the physical world, to those that transcend the physical sciences. (Aristotle's system of thought dealing with non-physical realities is in fact set out in the famous work which his ancient editors called the *Metaphysics.*)

mete *v.* Usually **mete out** *The money was meted out only after it had been carefully counted:* allocate, disburse, distribute, dispense, measure out, administer, deal out, dole out, allot, divide, assign.

◇ *Word origin:* To *mete* out means to allot, distribute, or measure out. It comes from Old English *metan,* to measure.

meteoric *adj. Many a rock singer has enjoyed a meteoric rise to success:* flaming, fleetingly bright, transiently brilliant, fiery, flashing, blazing; rapid, speedy, fast, swift, unabated, sudden, instant; unstoppable, inexorable, ineluctable.

Ant. slow, sluggish, gradual, inconspicuous, obscure.

◇ *Word origin: Meteoric,* like *meteor,* comes from Greek *meteōros,* high in the air.

method *n.* **1** *What guitar method did you study?:* system, technique, procedure, approach, process, way, course, means, scheme, form, routine, usage, programme, formula, fashion, modus operandi. **2** *There's method in his madness:* purpose, plan, design, order, scheme, system, efficacy, viability.

◇ *Word origin: Method* comes from Greek *meta-* (beyond, after) + *hodos* (way), hence after the regular way, following the prescribed or systematic way. The Greek *meta-*, beyond, after, also gives us such words as *metamorphosis, metaphor, metaphysical,* and *metatarsus* (the part of the foot after the tarsus, or ankle).

methodical *adj. He is methodical even when he's on holiday:* systematic, deliberate, precise, orderly, well-regulated, exact, tidy, uniform, regular, neat, careful, meticulous; logical, analytical; businesslike.

Ant. unmethodical, desultory, random, haphazard, casual, hit-or-miss, confused, disordered, chaotic, jumbled.

meticulous *adj. Our meticulous housekeeper never forgets a thing:* fastidious, scrupulous, exact, minutely careful, solicitous about details, painstaking, precise, finical, finicky, fussy, particular; punctilious.

Ant. careless, inexact, imprecise, sloppy, negligent.

◇ *Word origin:* A *meticulous* person fears failure if he misses a detail or doesn't take pains with minor matters. Its source is Latin *metus,* fear.

mettle *n. Their daring shows the Norsemen's mettle:* courage, hardy temperament, nerve, spirit, gameness, grit, pluck, valour, backbone, intrepidity, spunk, fearlessness, audacity, fortitude, vigour, bravery, gallantry, vim, enthusiasm, determination, resolution, heroism, derring-do, boldness, temerity, manliness, *Informal* guts.

◇ *Usage note:* See MEDDLE.

microbe *n. Doctors who tracked the cause of disease were called microbe hunters:* germ, virus, microscopic organism, micro-organism, bacillus, bacterium; (*variously*) parasite, spirochæte, streptococcus, staphylococcus, zygote, gamete.

◇ *Word origin: Microbe* literally means "little life." It is from Greek *mikros* (little, small) + *bios* (life).

"Think of the inexpugnable retreats for microbes prepared by Michelangelo in the curls of Moses' beard!" —*Aldous Huxley*

---

microscopic Also **microscopical** *adj.* **1** *The flu virus is microscopic. You need a microscopic lens to see it:* so small as to be invisible without a microscope, infinitesimal, immeasurably small, atomic; of a microscope. **2** *I can't read this microscopic print:* very little, tiny, minute, diminutive, imperceptible, extremely small, *Informal* teeny, titchy.

Ant. 1, 2 large, huge, immense; perceptible; macroscopic.

◇ *Word origin: Microscopic* comes from *microscope,* whose roots are the Greek *mikros* (little, small) + *skopein* (to watch), hence a *microscope* is an instrument to observe very small things, and *microscopic* means so small as to be visible only under a *microscope.*

middle *adj.* **1** *The middle section of the motorway was opened two years ago but they still have not finished the final section:* central, mid, midway, halfway, midmost, medial, middlemost, median; intermediate, not extreme, main.
—*n.* **2** *The painters moved the furniture to the middle of the room:* centre, midpoint, central part, midst, main part; core, heartland, heart, hub, nucleus. **3** *She wrapped the scarf around her middle:* waist, midriff, stomach, belly, *Slang* tummy, gut. **4** *Are you in the middle of something?:* midst, course, process, act, throes.

Ant. 1 beginning, end, initial, final, extreme. **2** edge, periphery, outskirts.

◇ *Word origin: Middle* and *mid* come from Old English *middel,* middle.

middling *adj. He had only middling success as an architect:* average, ordinary, mediocre, moderate, moderately good, so-so, fair, unremarkable, medium, just satisfactory, pretty good, indifferent, run-of-the-mill; second-rate, minimal.

midst *n.* **1** *They wanted the picnic to be in the midst of the forest:* heart, middle, centre, middle part, hub, bosom, thick, depths, deepest part, core. **2** *She felt ill in the midst of the ceremony:* heart, thick, most critical time, most important part, core, nucleus; half-way through, midway through.

mien *n. He had the mien of someone important:* bearing, air, demeanour, manner, behaviour, carriage, presence, deportment, attitude, style, appearance, aspect, countenance, visage, look, feature, semblance, expression.

◇ *Word origin: Mien* is a short form of *demean* or *demeanour.*

might *n. The tank battle was a test of armoured might:* power, force, strength, potency, prowess, vigour, puissance, robustness, durability, forcefulness, energy, competence, brawn, toughness, sturdiness, capability, capableness, lustihood, muscle; influence, *Slang* clout.

Ant. weakness, inability, feebleness.

mighty *adj.* **1** *He was a mighty warrior:* powerful, strong, hardy, vigorous, robust, stout, lusty, indomitable, stalwart, sturdy, potent, puissant, overpowering, invincible, forceful, able; courageous, brave, bold, valorous, valiant; strapping, brawny, husky, manful. **2** *The mighty iceberg came into view:* huge, enormous, of great size, immense, massive, extremely large, titanic, colossal, gigantic, vast, monstrous, majestic, monumental, imposing, prodigious, monolithic, gargantuan, stupendous, towering, Brobdingnagian, elephantine.

Ant. 1 feeble, weak, impotent. **2** small, tiny, unimposing, negligible, unimpressive.

migrate *v.* **1** *When did the Irish migrate to the United States?:* emigrate, immigrate, trek, journey, transplant oneself, relocate. **2** *Many birds migrate south every winter:* move periodically or seasonally, go elsewhere, depart with others.

◇ *Word origin: Migrate* comes from Latin *migrare,* to move, migrate. The same Latin verb gives us *immigrant* (one who moves into one country or region from another) and *emigrant* (one who moves out of a given country or region to go elsewhere).

mild *adj.* **1** *Her mild disposition is a marvel in this chaotic office:* gentle, calm, serene, placid, smooth, easy-going, good-tempered, docile, bland, easy, tranquil, moderate, pacific, pleasant, complaisant, forbearing. **2** *That coat is too heavy for such a mild day:* temperate, moderate, warm, balmy, not extreme, not severe, springlike, summery, pleasant. **3** *This mild soap won't irritate your skin. Please make my drink a mild one:* not strong, not sharp, soothing, soft, delicate, uninjurious, emollient, not severe, not astringent.

Ant. 1–3 harsh, severe. **1** fierce, unkind, unpleasant; stormy, turbulent; piquant, biting, bitter, savage, rough, wild, violent. **2** stormy, intemperate, cold. **3** strong, sharp, astringent, powerful.

milestone *n.* **1** *The ancient road was dotted with crumbling milestones:* road marker, signpost, mile-post. **2** *Their moving to the country proved to be a milestone in her life:* significant event, crucial occurrence, turning-point; decisive achievement, memorable moment, jubilee, red-letter day; anniversary.

milieu *n. His natural milieu is that of musicians:* environment, culture, setting, background, backdrop, *mise-en-scène*, element, scene, preferred company.

◇ *Pronunciation tip: Milieu* is a French word that remained almost intact when it was borrowed into English. A close approximation to the correct pronunciation is *meal* + *yer*, with the final *r* dropped.

◇ *Word origin: Milieu* is an environment or surroundings, literally the place one is in the middle of. It comes from Old French *mi* (middle) + *lieu* (place). French *lieu*, place, is also found in our expression "in lieu of," meaning in place of, and in *lieutenant*, one who acts for or in place of a king, captain, or other superior in his absence, although in this word we pronounce the *lieu* as *left*.

militant *adj. His political outlook is more militant than conciliatory:* combative, aggressive, belligerent, contentious, uncompromising, assertive, extreme, defiant, pugnacious, disputatious; engaged in or favouring warfare, warlike, military, paramilitary, fighting, war-mongering, bellicose, martial.

Ant. moderate, concessive; peaceable, pacific, pacifist, non-combative.

◇ *Word origin:* See MILITARY.

military *adj.* **1** *The military might of the superpowers is awesome:* armed, martial, war-making, combative; defensive. **2** *The old soldier never lost his military demeanour:* soldier-like, soldierly, strict, well-disciplined, crisp, Spartan. **3** *He hated all military routine:* regimented, regulated, systematized.

—n. **4** *The military took over the government of Greece:* army, armed forces, soldiers, standing army, militia, troops; generals, military establishment.

◇ *Word origin: Military* and *militant* come from Latin *miles*, soldier. The same Latin word also gives us *militia*.

Exploring the Word: Many military ranks are based on ancient words. *Admiral* comes from Arabic *'amīr a'ālī*, high commander, from which we also get *emir*. The rank of *commander*, one who commands, is from Latin *com-*, completely, thoroughly + *mandare*, to order, be in charge. An *ensign* was so-called because he carried a flag or wore one as insignia, from Latin *in-*, in + *signum*, rank. *Colonel* comes from Italian *colonnello*, "column-leader," while *major* is Latin for "greater," i.e. "higher-up." *Captain* is from Old French *capitaine* and *corporal* from Italian *capo*, both of which come from Latin *caput*, head, chief. *Lieutenant* is from French *lieu*, place + *tenant*, one who holds, hence one who holds or takes the place of a superior in his absence or has authority in lieu of another. *Sergeant* is from Old French *sergent*, one who serves, from Latin *servire*, to serve, and *private* is from Latin *privatus*, private individual — as opposed to one holding the "office" of *officer*.

mill *v.* **1** *We watched them mill the grain into flour:* grind, pulverize, crush, reduce to powder, granulate; shape, finish, groove, or polish with a milling tool. **2** *The crowd was milling around the railway station:* roam, meander, wander or converge en masse, move around aimlessly, swarm, teem.

◇ *Word origin: Mill*, originally a machine or building for grinding or crushing, comes from Latin *mola*, millstone.

"... more water glideth by the mill
Than wots the miller of." —*Shakespeare*

mimic *v.* **1** *Back in the barracks he would mimic their platoon sergeant:* ape, imitate, impersonate, parrot; mirror, echo, simulate, counterfeit, copy, reproduce.

—n. **2** *The boy is an incredible mimic:* imitator, impressionist, aper, copyist, feigner, *Informal* copy-cat.

◇ *Spelling tip:* Remember that the final *c* in *mimic* becomes *-ck* in *mimicked* and *mimicking*.

mince *v.* **1** *Mince the celery for the ham salad:* dice, chop finely, cut into tiny particles, cut into small pieces, shred, grate. **2** *I can't stand the way she minces around here:* pose, posture, put on airs, give oneself airs, attitudinize; affect daintiness, affect delicacy, affect primness. **3** *He is direct and never minces his words:* soften, moderate, mitigate, refine, palliate, spare, soften one's speech, qualify, be mealy-mouthed about, hold back, gloss over.

mind *n.* **1** *Fear of failure was in the back of his mind:* brain, intellect, mental capacity, apprehension, intellectual faculties, brains,

thinking apparatus, grey matter; reason, judgement, reflection, comprehension, understanding, sense, intelligence, rationality, ratiocination, cognition, awareness, perception, percipience. **2** *The shopkeeper behaved as though he had lost his mind:* mental balance, sanity, reason, faculties, rationality, understanding, judgement, sense, *Slang* wits, nous. **3** *To my mind he's extremely offensive:* judgement, opinion, point of view, outlook, reaction, response, way of thinking. **4** *The judge's mind is made up:* opinion, conclusion, consideration, judgement, intent, intention, thought, notion, impression, sentiment, conception, liking, will, propensity, choice, inclination. **5** *The old scrap-book brought his childhood to mind:* remembrance, memory, consciousness, recall, inward attention, recollection, retrospection, reminiscence, contemplation. **6** *Spring makes it hard to keep one's mind on work:* attention, concentration, thought, thinking, focus, preoccupation.
—*v.* **7** *Good drivers are always careful to mind the speed limit:* obey, heed, pay attention to, observe, follow, comply with, submit to, bow to, acquiesce to, adhere to, be careful concerning, be wary of, regard, note, be conscious of, take cognizance of, watch, notice, take notice of. **8** *My son can mind the shop for me:* tend, attend to, look after, take care of, take charge of. **9** *Tell her to mind how she uses that drill:* be cautious, be careful, take care, be wary about, watch. **10** *I don't mind your being a little late:* dislike, object to, resent, feel offended about, disapprove of, feel inconvenienced by, look askance at; shrink from, recoil from, turn up the nose at, have an aversion to, abhor, detest, hate.
Ant. **1** body. **2** insanity, irrationality. **7, 8** neglect, ignore, disregard.

"Man's mind stretched by a new idea never goes back to its original dimensions."
—*Oliver Wendell Holmes*

---

mindful *adj. Be mindful of the danger involved:* attentive to, alert to, regardful, heedful, thoughtful, careful, watchful, aware, cautious, observant, alive to, circumspect, wary; taken up with, occupied with, engrossed in, absorbed in, preoccupied with.
Ant. mindless, heedless, inattentive, oblivious, unaware, incautious, unobservant, thoughtless.

mindless *adj.* **1** *His mindless behaviour is disturbing:* witless, asinine, stupid, unintelligent, unthinking, nonsensical, obtuse, disregardful, unreasoning, ridiculous, simple-minded, doltish, cretinous, imbecilic, idiotic, insane. **2** *She is mindless of the feelings of others:* insensitive to, careless, regardless, thoughtless, unattuned, oblivious, heedless, indifferent, apathetic, inconsiderate, indiscriminate, unaware, inattentive, unheeding, neglectful, unobservant.
Ant. **1** intelligent, reasoning, thinking, reasonable, sane. **2** mindful, sensitive, considerate, aware, attentive, observant.

mine *n.* **1** *There was a fire in the coal mine:* pit, excavation, tunnel, shaft, quarry. **2** *His mine of anecdotes is inexhaustible:* supply, reserve, stock, store, fund, hoard, accumulation, cache, treasure, wealth, abundance. **3** *A bomb-disposal officer tried to detonate the mine:* underground or underwater explosive, booby trap, land mine.
—*v.* **4** *How much coal did the men mine last year?:* excavate, extract, take from the earth, remove from a mine, scoop out; dig for. **5** *The soldiers mined the enemy fort:* burrow under, tunnel under, dig under; lay explosives under, booby-trap.

mingle *v.* **1** *The thousand sounds of the city at night mingle in a curious melody:* blend, mix, intermix, combine, intermingle, merge, commingle, interfuse, fuse, interweave, amalgamate, intertwine, intersperse, interlard. **2** *A good host mingles with his guests:* socialize, join, mix, associate, circulate, intermix, fraternize, *Informal* hob-nob, rub shoulders with.
Ant. **1** separate, part, divide, dissolve. **2** stay aloof, stay separate, avoid.

miniature *adj. We saw an exhibition of miniature paintings:* small-scale, diminutive, tiny, little, elfin, pocket-size, lilliputian, pygmy, minute, microscopic, microcosmic.
Ant. large, full-size, oversize, enlarged, big, gigantic.
◇ *Pronunciation tip:* You may pronounce *miniature* either as *MIN-e-uh-chur* or as the shorter *MIN-uh-chur.* Both are correct. But when you write it be sure to spell it fully: *minIAture.*

minimal *adj. That loafer does a minimal amount of work:* minimum, least possible, lowest acceptable, smallest permissible, scarcely satisfactory, nominal, unappreciable, token.
Ant. maximal, maximum.

minimum *n.* **1** *These new floors require a minimum of care:* least possible amount, smallest amount possible, least possible degree, modicum, lowest quantity.
—*adj.* **2** *The mill owners still pay less than the minimum wage:* lowest amount allowed; least, smallest, least possible; basic, base.
Ant. **1, 2** maximum, largest, greatest.

minister *n.* **1** *They resented a minister who brought politics to the pulpit:* clergyman, preacher, pastor, chaplain, cleric, priest, parson, ecclesiastic, padre, father, vicar, reverend, rabbi, abbé, evangelist, revivalist. **2** *He sold his business before he became Minister of Agriculture:* head of governmental department, usually cabinet member.
—*v.* **3** *He ministered to his wife's every need:* attend to, be solicitous of, serve, answer,

oblige, tend, take care of, accommodate, care for; pander to, cater to.
Ant. 1 layman, congregant.

Exploring the Word: Latin *minuere,* to make smaller, diminish, lessen, gives us *miniature,* small; *minimum* and *minimal,* the smallest possible; *diminish,* to make smaller, become smaller; *mince,* to make smaller by chopping finely, to dice; *minutiae,* things of small importance; *minion,* a "small" or unimportant person who serves another, and *filet mignon,* the small (dainty or tender) centre of the fillet of tenderloin of beef. A *minute quantity* is a very small one and a *minute* of time is a small part (now 1/60th) of an hour, but the *minutes* of a meeting have nothing to do with time and are so-called because they are written in tiny or *minute* handwriting to be transcribed later in a larger, clearer hand. Also related to Latin *minuere,* to make smaller, lessen, is the Latin verb *ministrare,* to serve, to be subordinate to, from which we get our words *minister, ministration, administer, administration, minor, minus,* and *minimum.* Thus a *minister* serves others, as a *Protestant minister* or a *Minister of Education,* and *ministration* is the act of serving or the aid rendered; an *administrator* also attends to or assists in his job, which is to *administer,* serve, attend to, and an *administration* is a group that does this, as a *political administration;* a *minor* is literally one who is lesser, hence now means one who is under legal age. (The neuter form of the same word is *minus,* less, preserved in our arithmetical term *minus.*) Finally, Latin *minimus,* least, gives us our word *minimum,* smallest amount.

minor *adj.* **1** *He received only minor injuries:* small, insignificant, slight, light, unimportant, petty, inconsiderable, trivial, paltry, nugatory, trifling, piddling, imperceptible, inconsequential, lesser, secondary, subordinate. —*n.* **2** *They can't serve drinks to minors:* child, youngster, teenager, youth, adolescent, kid, *Legal* infant.
Ant. 1 major, greater, main, important, significant. **2** adult, elder; grown-up.
◇ *Usage note:* Do not confuse the word *minOr* and *minEr.* A *minOr* is a yOung person. A *minEr* works in a minE.

minority *n.* **1** *The minority doesn't have a chance in this election:* smaller portion, less, lesser, smaller amount. **2** *He will inherit the money when he has passed his minority:* immaturity, adolescence, boyhood, girlhood, *Legal* infancy.

minstrel *n.* **1** *In the Middle Ages there were many wandering minstrels:* troubadour, singer, songster, itinerant musician, bard, poet, player, serenader, entertainer, lyrist; versifier, poetaster. **2** *The minstrel put on his make-up:* comedian, singer, dancer, song-and-dance man, music-hall artist, interlocutor.

minute[1] *n.* **1** *My watch is five minutes slow:* sixty seconds, sixtieth part of an hour. **2** *This will only take a minute:* moment, second, instant, flash, jiffy, twinkling, trice, a short time.
Ant. 2 for ever, ages, aeons.

minute[2] *adj.* **1** *The scratch was almost too minute to see:* little, extremely small, imperceptible, tiny, diminutive, infinitesimal, miniature, lilliputian, fine, scant, microscopic, minikin, petite, *Informal* teeny, wee; slight, negligible, inappreciable, trifling, puny, inconsiderable, insignificant, petty. **2** *The second doctor made a minute study of the illness:* exhaustive, meticulous, close, detailed, scrupulous, itemized, precise, conscientious, careful, strict, exact.
Ant. 1 tremendous, huge, vast, monstrous, great, enormous, grand. **2** general, quick, tentative, rough, superficial.
◇ *Pronunciation tip: Minute*[1], meaning "sixty seconds," is pronounced *MIN-it. Minute*[2], meaning "extremely small," is pronounced *my-NUTE.*

minutiae *n. pl. He concerns himself with the minutiae and not the substance:* trivia, trivialities, minor details, trifles, bagatelles, odds and ends, particulars, particularities.

miracle *n.* **1** *Only a miracle could save the Children of Israel from Pharaoh's soldiers. Atheists don't believe in miracles:* divine act, supernatural happening; wonder, marvel, prodigy, mystery; portent, sign, omen. **2** *Picasso's work is a creative miracle:* marvel, wonder, phenomenon, prodigy, sensation, spectacle, masterpiece.

miraculous *adj.* **1** *The Revelation of St. John the Divine records a miraculous vision:* divine, supernatural, visionary, wonderful, phenomenal, prodigious, supernormal; wonder-working, thaumaturgical, magical; mysterious, inexplicable. **2** *The wounded man made a miraculous recovery:* extraordinary, exceptional, remarkable, wonderful, marvellous, spectacular; amazing, astonishing, astounding; unbelievable, incredible; phenomenal, preternatural.
Ant. 1, 2 ordinary, normal. **1** human, natural, mundane, of this world. **2** routine, unexceptional, predictable, run-of-the-mill.

mirage *n. The travellers found that the oasis was only a mirage:* optical illusion, illusion, phantasm, unreality, imagined image, fancy, hallucination, delusion, wishful thinking, misconception.

mire *n.* **1** *The wagon was stuck in the mire:* mud, muck, ooze, slime, slush, sludge; quagmire, bog, marsh, fen.
—*v.* **2** *The children were mired from head to toe:* spatter, soil, begrime, besmirch, cake, smear, muddy.
◇ *Word origin: Mire* comes from Old Norse *myrr,* swampy ground, bog.

mirror *n.* **1** *She spends hours admiring herself in the mirror:* looking-glass, reflecting-glass, glass, cheval glass. **2** *She is a mirror of virtue:* model,

example, exemplar, paragon, pattern for imitation, standard, epitome, paradigm.
—*v.* **3** *The pond mirrors the surrounding trees:* reflect, show, manifest, image.

> **Exploring the Word**: Etymologically speaking, it is perfectly natural to *admire* oneself in a *mirror* since *mirror* literally means that in which one may admire oneself! *Miracle, marvel, mirage, mirror* and *admire* come from the Latin verb *mirāri*, to wonder at, admire. A *miracle* and a *marvel* are things which cause wonder; to *marvel* at something is to wonder at it; *marvellous* means causing wonder, wonderful, miraculous; a *mirage* is an atmospheric reflection to be wondered at.

mirth *n. A student rag-week combines money-raising and mirth:* merriment, amusement, jollity, hilarity, gaiety, joviality, glee, laughter, cheerfulness, good spirits, levity, jocundity, jocularity, festivity, drollery, merrymaking.
Ant. sadness, dejection, depression, melancholy, misery, moroseness.
◇ *Word origin: Mirth,* like *merry,* comes from Old English *myrig,* pleasant, happy.

misadventure *n. The poor kid has had one misadventure after another:* mishap, misfortune, reverse, failure, disaster, calamity, catastrophe, unfortunate accident, adversity, casualty, débâcle, set-back, mischance, stroke of ill luck, bad break, ill.

misanthropic *adj. His unhappy childhood fostered his misanthropic personality:* antisocial, unfriendly, unsociable, distrustful, unneighbourly, inhospitable, morose, unpersonable, cynical, surly, discourteous, unaccommodating, unapproachable, unresponsive, cold, distant.
Ant. personable, amiable, amicable, loving, sociable, cordial; humanitarian; philanthropic, charitable.

misapprehension *n. We shared a misapprehension about the completion date:* misunderstanding, misconception, miscalculation, misinterpretation, false impression, breakdown of communications, misjudgement, mix-up, misconstruction, mistake.

misappropriate *v. He was indicted for misappropriating public funds:* misuse, embezzle, steal, peculate, misapply, channel selfishly, put to a wrong use, abuse, misemploy, bilk, mulct, defalcate, swindle, *Informal* dip one's hand into the till.

misbehave *v. If you misbehave once more you're going home!:* play up, disobey, behave improperly, deport oneself badly, do wrong, transgress, show poor manners, be rebellious, be defiant.
Ant. behave, toe the line.

misbehaviour *n. Her misbehaviour was an embarrassment to her parents:* bad behaviour, bad conduct, misconduct, impropriety, delinquency, disrespect, playing up; misdemeanour, offence, dereliction, lapse, transgression, trespass, misdeed, indiscretion, bad manners, impudence; unmanageableness, obstreperousness.
Ant. good conduct, discretion, mannerliness.

miscarriage *n.* **1** *The miscarriage of our plans was a great blow:* failure, undoing, misfire, failing, unrealization, collapse, breakdown, default, non-fulfilment, *Informal* botch, swizz, wash-out, frustration, casualty, shipwreck, scotching, short-circuiting, going awry. **2** *His wife had two miscarriages:* premature still-birth, spontaneous abortion, disruption of pregnancy.

miscellaneous *adj. The junk shop is filled with miscellaneous goods:* varied, assorted, of mixed character, various, different, heterogeneous, motley, of many categories, diversified, diverse, divers, of every description, sundry.
Ant. homogeneous, uniform, identical.
◇ *Spelling tip:* Don't forget the *cell* in *misCELLaneous* and in *misCELLany.*
◇ *Word origin: Miscellaneous* comes from Latin *miscere,* to mix, from which we also get *mix* and *mixture.*

mischance *n. It was my mischance that the car ran off the road:* misfortune, bad luck, unfortunate occurrence, ill luck, ill lot, mishap, adversity, accident, misadventure, infelicity, ill wind.

mischief *n.* **1** *The child has a lot of mischief in him:* naughtiness, rascality, devilment, sportiveness, tendency to tease, devilry, devilment, prankishness, sauciness, roguery; capriciousness, wilfulness. **2** *We fear he is up to serious mischief:* wrongdoing, knavery, scheming, plotting, malice, villainy, wrong, foul play, injury, depravity.

mischievous *adj.* **1** *The mischievous boy is very appealing:* naughty, impish, prankish, teasing, playfully annoying, elfin, elfish, playful, frolicsome, sly, roguish, devilish, sportive, waggish. **2** *Her mischievous interference caused a lot of unhappiness:* wicked, vicious, spiteful, malicious, malign, malignant, gratuitous, uninvited, uncalled for, annoying, vexing, injurious, destructive, harmful, pernicious, wicked, noxious, exacerbating, deleterious, detrimental.
◇ *Pronunciation tip:* The proper pronunciation of *mischievous* is one mark of a careful speaker. The word has only three syllables, not four, and should be stressed on the first syllable: *MIS-chi-vus,* not "mis-chee-vee-us."

misconception *n. Many people have misconceptions about astrology:* misapprehension, erroneous idea, mistaken notion, error, misinterpretation, fallacious notion, misunderstanding, delusion, misconstruction, misjudgement, misinformation, misrepresentation.

misconstrue *v. I'm sorry you misconstrued my*

meaning: misinterpret, take in a wrong sense, construe wrongly, misapprehend, mistranslate, distort, mistake, misunderstand, misjudge, miscalculate.

Ant. understand, apprehend.

miser *n. The miser wouldn't contribute a penny:* penny-pincher, stingy person, skinflint, tightwad, skimper, niggard, hoarder.

Ant. spendthrift, profligate, spender.

◇ *Word origin:* A *miser* lives miserably for the sake of saving money. It is a Latin word meaning "miserable," and is also the root of *miserable* and *misery.*

miserable *adj.* **1** *Their living conditions are miserable:* wretched, impoverished, very poor, deplorable, lamentable, sorry, pathetic, unbearable, sordid, mean, shabby, degraded, desperate, scurvy, pitiable, second-rate, beggarly, rubbishy, needy, hapless, feckless, unfortunate, inferior; contemptible, despicable. **2** *The loss of his dog made him miserable. Her face had a miserable expression:* forlorn, unhappy, heart-broken, woeful, crestfallen, disconsolate, wretched in mind, doleful, dolorous, broken-hearted, sorrowful, desolate, crushed, woebegone, despondent, dejected, heartsick, down in the mouth, grieved, mournful, depressed, cheerless, chapfallen, heavy-laden, sad. **3** *We were disappointed by his miserable performance:* sorry, deplorable, inept, abysmal, far from satisfactory, atrocious, appalling, abject; contemptible, despicable.

Ant. 1 comfortable, good, respectable. **2** happy, gay, joyous, cheerful. **3** admirable, laudable.

miserly *adj. She's so miserly that she won't give anything to anyone:* parsimonious, stingy, avaricious, mean, tight, tight-fisted, scrimping, penurious, pinching, penny-pinching, frugal, illiberal, close-fisted, selfish, ungenerous, greedy, niggardly, near, grudging, mean.

Ant. generous, unselfish, charitable, extravagant, prodigal, profligate.

"I am acquainted with sad misery
As the tann'd galley-slave is with his oar."
—*John Webster*

---

misery *n.* **1** *The misery of war is something that no one wants to experience:* sorrow, affliction, distress, trouble, suffering, woe, wretchedness, hardship, exaction, ordeal, trial, tribulation, privation, misfortune, catastrophe, disaster, calamity. **2** *I can't seem to shake off this feeling of misery:* wretchedness, heartache, desolation, extreme unhappiness, sorrow, sadness, grief, suffering, agony, woe, melancholy, distress, anguish, despair, torment, depression, dejection, despondency. **3** *The failure of her second marriage was another misery to her:* sorrow, chagrin, regret, blow, curse, *Informal* bitter pill, bad scene, bad news.

Ant. 1 luxury, ease, comfort. **2** happiness, joy, contentment, pleasure, enjoyment. **3** boon, comfort, benefit.

misfortune *n.* **1** *At times the 1960's seemed to be a decade of misfortune:* trouble, bad luck, hard luck, ill fortune, hard times, calamity, adversity, hardship. **2** *The half-back's injury was a misfortune for the whole team:* blow, calamity, mishap, catastrophe, disaster, unfortunate accident, tribulation, trouble, reverse, affliction, set-back, downfall, tragedy, loss, misery, ruination, casualty, misadventure, piece of bad luck.

Ant. 1 good luck, good fortune. **2** stroke of luck, relief.

misgiving *n.* Usually **misgivings** *We had misgivings about flying near mountains in such weather:* anxiety, fear, doubt, mental reservations, apprehension, foreboding, presentiment, lack of confidence, worry, suspicion, disquiet, qualm, scepticism, uncertainty, dread, alarm, mistrust, dubiousness, dubiety, doubtfulness, second thoughts.

Ant. confidence, trust, assurance, certainty.

misguided *adj. He was thoroughly misguided in his notions about language teaching:* mistaken, misled, in error, faulty, misdirected, misadvised, ill-advised, erroneous, led astray, off-course, injudicious, adrift, misinformed, *Informal* on the wrong scent, on the wrong track, wide of the mark, in the woods, at sea, off course.

mishap *n. Try to get through this manœuvre without one of your usual mishaps:* misadventure, unfortunate accident, disaster, casualty, set-back, miscarriage, difficulty, misfortune, slip-up, botch, snag, fiasco.

misinform *v. She misinformed me about the cost:* mislead, give incorrect information to, apprise inaccurately, misguide, deceive.

misjudge *v. I misjudged the time the detour would take. I'm afraid I misjudged her abilities:* miscalculate, estimate incorrectly, judge wrongly, fail to anticipate, overestimate, misconceive, underestimate, misconstrue, exaggerate, understate, misunderstand; judge unfairly, show poor intuition about, err about.

mislead *v.* **1** *Morning sunshine misled us into thinking it would be a warm day:* misguide, deceive, misinform, lead into error, misdirect, lead astray. **2** *I was misled by the man's respectable appearance:* delude, deceive, seduce, beguile, entice, inveigle, take in, take advantage of, victimize, play false, gull, dupe, hoodwink, betray, bamboozle, fool, double-cross, *Informal* lead down the garden path, string along.

◇ *Usage note:* See DECEIVE.

misnomer *n. In the services, "gun" is considered a misnomer for "rifle":* unsuitable term, misapplied name, inapplicable title, wrong designation, misnaming, wrong nomenclature, malapropism, bastardization.

misplace *v.* **1** *It's pouring and I've misplaced my* *umbrella:* mislay, lose, lose track of. **2** *Don't misplace your confidence by trusting that irresponsible man:* place unwisely, entrust wrongly, abuse.

misrepresentation *n.* **1** *His misrepresentation of the facts caused trouble:* misstatement, distortion, falsification, falsifying, doctoring, adulteration, altering, incorrect picture, twisting, exaggeration. **2** *The cartoon is a cruel misrepresentation of our Prime Minister:* bad likeness, wrong impression, poor likeness, incorrect picture, mockery, travesty; burlesque, caricature.

miss *v.* **1** *The batsman missed the ball:* fail to hit, fail to reach, fail to strike; fall short, fail to attain, miss the mark, fly wide, fail to light upon; fail to receive, fail to obtain. **2** *We missed the start of the film:* fail to catch, fail to be present at, fail to meet, fail to get; be distracted from, be late for, be absent from. **3** *He missed his only chance:* let slip, let pass, let go, fail to take advantage of, forgo, go without, disregard, pass over, overlook, neglect, surrender, *Informal* blow, muff. **4** *She missed her deadline on Wednesday:* fail to perform, fail to meet, fail to accomplish. **5** *When did you first miss the jewels?:* notice the loss of, note the absence of. **6** *The child misses his mother:* want, long for, pine for, lack, feel the loss of, feel the absence of, yearn for. **7** *I just missed burning my hand:* avoid, avert, escape. **8** *I missed what you said because of the noise. He missed my meaning:* fail to perceive, fail to hear, fail to understand, fail to get, fail to see, lose. **9** *The dry-cleaners missed the spot on the collar. We missed the turn in the dark:* overlook, pass by, leave out, disregard, neglect, slip up on, pass over, gloss over; bypass, overrun, overshoot.
—*n.* **10** *After three misses he gave up trying to hit the target:* failure, failure to hit, failure to reach, false step, default, error, slip, miscue, blunder; omission, neglect, oversight, delinquency, mistake, loss.
Ant. **1** hit, reach, strike, attain, obtain. **2** catch, meet, get, make. **3** seize, grasp, accept. **4** meet, fulfil, accomplish, make. **8** catch, hear, overhear. **10** hit, success.

"As some day it may happen that a victim
must be found,
I've got a little list—I've got a little list
Of society offenders who might well be
underground,
And who never would be missed—
who never would be missed."
—*W.S. Gilbert*

missile *n. The missile hit right on target:* projectile, shell, object or weapon that is thrown or shot; (*variously*) stone, spear, javelin, lance, harpoon, arrow, dart; guided missile, rocket.

mission *n.* **1** *The diplomat was sent on a mission of great secrecy. The mission to blow up the bridge failed:* charge, assignment, undertaking, enterprise, quest, task, commission, mandate, job, purposive military operation. **2** *The head of the Irish mission is on home leave. Our church mission in Africa needs medicines:* delegation, legation, diplomatic representative, missionary post, ministry. **3** *He believed that his mission was to work with drug addicts:* calling, pursuit, life's object, objective, end, principal task; raison d'être.

Exploring the Word: The Latin verb *mittere*, to send, let go, leads us into a vast complex of words, including: *missile*, something, as a rock, ball, or rocket, that can be sent forth or thrown; *mission*, that which one is sent forth to do, or a group sent forth to accomplish it, as a *religious mission* or a *United Nations peace-keeping mission*, and *missionary*, one sent forth to propagate or spread religion; *message* and *missive*, a communication or letter sent forth; *admit* (noun *admission*) to allow; *commit*, to send with another, to entrust to another's care, *commission*, something sent forth or entrusted, and *commission/committee*, a group sent together to accomplish something; *demise*, literally a sending-off, hence death; *dismiss*, to send away; *emit*, to send out, send forth, and *emission*, something given forth as a gas, and *emissary*, one sent forth on a mission, agent; *intermission*, something sent between two parts or events, as a break, and *intermittent*, having periods when something is sent between, with pauses between, stopping from time to time; *omit*, to let go, leave out, and *omission*, that which is left out; *permit* (noun *permission*), to allow to be sent through, to let something take place, to allow; *premiss*, an idea or hypothesis sent out before others as a basis of argument or reaching a conclusion; *promise*, a pledge or assurance sent from one person to another, and *compromise*, something promised together, a mutual promise or pledge two people or groups send out to each other; *remit* (noun *remission*), to send back something owed, to refer to another authority; *submit* (noun *submission*), to send or place under the will of another; *transmit* (noun *transmission*), to send a message across a distance from one person or place to another.

misspent *adj. He regretted especially his misspent youth:* missapplied, wasted, spent foolishly, thrown away, idled away, profitless, squandered.
Ant. productive, fruitful, unwasted, profitable.

misstate *v. He was accused of misstating the facts of the case:* state wrongly, state falsely, misreport, state misleadingly, falsify, misrepresent, misquote, alter, distort, pervert, give a false impression of; garble, confuse.

mistake *n.* **1** *Anyone can make a mistake:* error, misstep, wrong action, slip, slip-up, boner,

blunder, miscalculation, slip of the tongue, gaffe, oversight, faux pas, *Informal* bloomer.
—*v.* **2** *Did you mistake the margarine for butter?:* confuse, identify incorrectly, take one for another, wrongly accept, confound, mix up, misidentify. **3** *Unfortunately she mistook his intentions:* misunderstand, miscalculate, misinterpret, misconstrue, misapprehend, misread, misjudge.

"You've always made the mistake of being yourself." —*Eugène Ionesco*

---

mistaken *adj.* **1** *My belief in his integrity was, alas, mistaken:* wrong, erroneous, in error, false, fallacious, incorrect, inaccurate, faulty, at fault, unfounded, unsound, unjustified, untrue, groundless, ungrounded, illogical. **2** *She's mistaken about the name of the pub:* in error, making a mistake or misjudgement, deceived, *Informal* at sea, off course, on the wrong scent.
Ant. 1 wise, accurate, true, well-advised, sound, logical. **2** correct, accurate, right, logical.

mistreat *v. The general was accused of mistreating prisoners:* maltreat, ill-treat, abuse, oppress, persecute, misuse, treat unjustly, harm, harass, wrong, hound, manhandle, outrage, brutalize, bully, torment, molest, violate, assault, injure, harass.

mistress *n.* **1** *She is mistress of the manor:* female head, wife of the lord, lady, female owner. **2** *Does his wife know he has a mistress?:* lover, paramour, concubine, kept woman, inamorata, girl-friend, lady-love. **3** *"Mistress" is an archaic form of address for "Miss, Mrs., or Ms.":* Madam, Miss, Ms, Mrs.
◇ *Word origin:* A *mistress* is a woman in a position of authority, as over a household, a school—or a man. *Mistress* is the feminine form corresponding to *master.* Our *Mrs.* and *Miss* are both contractions of *mistress.* (*Ms.* is a blend of *Mrs.* and *Miss.*)

misty *adj. The park was misty with light rain:* hazy, clouded by mist, vaporous, dewy, foggy, steamy; overcast, murky, cloudy, nebulous.
Ant. clear, unclouded.

misunderstand *v. He was offended only because he misunderstood her meaning:* misconstrue, misinterpret, understand wrongly, take in a wrong sense, misjudge, misapprehend, mistake, misread, miscalculate, miss the point of, put a false construction on.
Ant. understand, apprehend, perceive.

misunderstanding *n.* **1** *His misunderstanding of the recipe resulted in a lop-sided cake:* misreading, mistake as to meaning, misconception, failure to understand, misapprehension, misinterpretation, misconception, false impression, misjudgement, miscomprehension. **2** *The brothers' heated misunderstanding spoilt the family party:* quarrel, disagreement, dispute, difference, rift, argument, discord, dissension, contretemps, conflict, squabble, altercation, wrangle, *Informal* barney, set-to.

"Misunderstandings are best prevented by pen and ink." —*William Hone*

---

misuse *n.* **1** *Writing reports was a misuse of her creative talent:* misemployment, wrong use, misappropriation, misapplication, waste, improper utilization, ill use; prostitution, perversion, squandering, abuse, desecration, corruption; ill-treatment, maltreatment, mistreatment, profanation.
—*v.* **2** *She misuses so many words that it almost seems to be done on purpose:* use improperly, misapply, use wrongly, misemploy; profane, prostitute, pervert, corrupt, put to wrong use. **3** *An arrogant man generally misuses his friends:* ill-treat, ill-use, abuse, wrong, mistreat, hurt, harm, take advantage of, exploit, injure, outrage, debase, maltreat.
Ant. 3 respect, esteem, honour, cherish, treasure, prize, appreciate.

mitigate *v. There's no way to mitigate the effect of that unfavourable report:* lessen, relieve, moderate in severity, alleviate, abate in intensity, palliate, soften, assuage, allay, soothe, weaken, mollify, ameliorate, ease, blunt, reduce, lighten, diminish, temper.
Ant. increase, augment, heighten, enhance, strengthen.

mix *v.* **1** *Mix flour and water to make paste. He never mixes business with pleasure:* combine, commix, join, put together, blend, unite, incorporate, interfuse, mingle, intermingle, commingle, compound, fuse, intermix, interlard, interweave, intersperse, intertwine, alloy, amalgamate; merge, coalesce. **2** *Did you mix the cream into the sauce?:* add, admix, put in, include, introduce, incorporate; fold, stir, whip, beat. **3** *He never mixes with the ground crew:* fraternize, associate, consort, socialize, hob-nob, club, be on intimate terms with, join.
—*n.* **4** *We got good results with this cake mix:* mixture, combination of ingredients; mingling, fusion, assembly.

mixed *adj.* **1** *They are a people of mixed blood:* mingled, alloyed, composite, combined, put together, fused, blended, intermixed, interwoven; hybrid, mongrel, adulterated, half and half. **2** *It's a mixed collection:* diversified, variegated, of various kinds, not pure, motley, heterogeneous, miscellaneous, hybrid, conglomerate, made up of different kinds. **3** *That story shouldn't be told in a mixed crowd:* consisting of persons of both the sexes, heterogeneous. **4** *My reaction was mixed:* indecisive, ambivalent, tending both ways, inconclusive, neither here nor there, uncertain, equivocal.

Ant. 1 unmixed, pure, isolated, straight, unblended. **2** unmixed, homogeneous. **3** male, female, homogeneous.

mixture *n. Green is a mixture of blue and yellow. His painting is a grotesque mixture of styles:* intermixture, combination, blend, admixture, union, fusion, amalgamation, adulteration; association, mix, alloy, amalgam, composite, compound, medley, stew, hodgepodge, jumble, hash, salmagundi, mélange, commixture, pastiche, pot-pourri, mishmash.

"O Mirth and Innocence! O milk and water!
Ye happy mixtures of more happy days."
—*Lord Byron*

---

mix-up *n.* **1** *I'm late because there was a mix-up in the time:* misunderstanding, mistake, miscomprehension, misjudgement, miscalculation, failure in communication. **2** *Informal Did you hear about the big mix-up during the prize-giving?:* disorder, fracas, imbroglio, mess, row, confusion.

moan *n.* **1** *The patient's moans kept her room-mate awake:* groan, wail, lament, plaint.
—*v.* **2** *He moaned when he read the bill:* groan, grumble; bemoan, lament, wail, bewail.

mob *n.* **1** *The police tried to control the mob:* riotous throng, disorderly crowd, rabble, horde, crush of people, gathering, assembly. **2** *The politician withstood the heckles of the angry mob:* common people, masses, rank and file, hoi polloi, populace, proletariat, plebeians, lower classes, rabble, multitude, *Informal* the great unwashed, herd. **3** *They say he's a member of the mob:* band or gang of criminals, gangsters, underworld network, syndicate, mafia.
—*v.* **4** *The kids mobbed the star when he left the theatre:* surround noisily, swarm around, flock about, converge on, crowd round.
◇ *Word origin:* Years ago *mob*, meaning a crowd of people, was considered an uneducated, slang word used only by those who didn't know it was a shortening of the Latin phrase *mobile vulgus*, literally the moving crowd, the fickle crowd. In fact, Jonathan Swift, author of *Gulliver's Travels*, wrote against using it in 1710, believing that cultivated people should use the full Latin term.

mobile *adj.* **1** *He converted his bus into a mobile library:* movable, transportable, travelling, not permanent. **2** *The Gipsies are historically a restless, mobile people:* moving readily, moving easily, itinerant, active, kinetic; rootless, wandering, nomadic, footloose.
Ant. 2 immobile, immovable, firm, set, steady, permanent.

mobilize *v. We may have to mobilize the reserves for the invasion:* muster, activate, assemble for action, make operative, organize, call to arms, put in motion, tap in emergency.
Ant. immobilize, disband, disarm, disorganize, retire.

mock *v.* **1** *She mocked his awkward marriage proposal:* ridicule, make fun of, scorn, treat with contempt, be contemptuous of, deride, revile, jeer at, taunt, assail with ridicule, spurn, make sport of, laugh at, scoff at, sneer at, poke fun at; imitate, ape, copy, burlesque, parody, caricature, mimic. **2** *His irresponsibility mocked my trust in him:* disappoint, frustrate, let down, show up, belie, insult, profane.
Ant. 1 praise, honour, laud. **2** fulfil.

mockery *n.* **1** *Mockery was the only outlet for his jealousy:* ridicule, ridiculing, derision, scoffing, scorn, disrespect, raillery; burlesque, mimicry, contemptuous imitation, travesty. **2** *The disclosure of bribery made a mockery of the contest:* sham, joke, laughing-stock, farce; travesty, burlesque.

mode *n.* **1** *His mode of doing business is offensive to me:* manner, way, fashion, course, method, practice, means, system, rule, approach, procedure, form, process, style, technique. **2** *She dressed in an old-fashioned mode:* style, custom, fashion, manner, cut, appearance, taste, way, trend, vogue.

model *n.* **1** *The investors disapproved the model of the proposed shopping centre:* replica, miniature representation, prototype, representation, pattern, facsimile, simulacrum, copy, dummy, mock-up. **2** *The angelic child is a model of perfection:* archetype, paragon, standard, ideal, paradigm, example, exemplar, mirror, pattern, criterion. **3** *Who was the model for Goya's* Olympia*? She's a photographic model:* source, subject, real-life version, prototype; mannequin. **4** *What model is your sewing machine?:* design, style, version, type, variety.
—*adj.* **5** *We looked at the model answers:* demonstrational, representative, simulated. **6** *He tries to be a model father:* perfect, worthy of imitation, ideal, exemplary, peerless.
—*v.* **7** *She models herself after her mother:* fashion, form according to a model, create in emulation, mould, give shape to, design, shape, cast, build, outline. **8** *The children modelled animals out of papier mâché:* form, shape, build, fashion, cast, mould, give form to. **9** *Will you model this coat for Mr. Jones?:* display, show, wear as a demonstration, sport.
Ant. 6 imperfect, flawed, unworthy.

moderate *adj.* **1** *We did only a moderate amount of business today:* average, medium, middling, modest, of medium quantity or extent, ordinary, mediocre, passable, fair; inexpensive, medium-priced. **2** *His moderate approach to the crisis kept everyone calm:* reasonable, temperate, mild, judicious, rational, not violent, dispassionate, unruffled, gentle, calm, cool, sober, peaceable, measured, careful.
—*n.* **3** *He's a political moderate:* middle-of-the-roader, mainstreamer, centrist.
—*v.* **4** *He might succeed better if he would moderate his shrill voice:* temper, control, soften, tone down, curb, make less severe, lessen, sub-

due, tame, abate, diminish, hush, restrain.
Ant. 1 immoderate, excessive, extreme, inordinate, unusual; expensive. **2** unreasonable, extreme, intemperate, hysterical, violent, ruffled, radical, wild. **3** extremist, radical. **4** intensify, heighten, increase.

> **Exploring the Word**: *Modern*, in the most recent manner, comes from Latin *modus*, manner, measure, which also gives us *mode*, a manner of doing something; *modify* and *modulate*, to change the manner or measure of something; *moderate* and *modest*, keeping within reasonable measures or limits and *moderation*, the act of so doing; *model*, something built to a scale measure, as a *model aeroplane*, or following the approved manner, as a *model of decorum*; *commodious*, with the right measurements, hence roomy or spacious enough, and such words as *commode* and *commodity*, both again referring to things being the right measure. Hence, a *commode* is literally that which is convenient, and a *commodity* was originally something convenient, then something profitable, and thus now means a movable "convenience" or basic article of trade that can be bought and sold.The same Latin *modus* is present in the term *modus operandi*, manner of operation, the method of proceeding.

moderation *n. Moderation in eating should keep your weight down:* temperance, abstemiousness, restraint, avoidance of extremes, forbearance, continence, economy, temperateness, frugality, self-control, moderateness; abatement, lessening, abating, allaying, alleviation, diminution, relaxation, mitigation, palliation, remission.
Ant. excess, intemperance, increase.

modern *adj. I'd rather stay in a modern hotel. She collects modern art:* new, contemporary, present-day, up-to-date, modernized, 20th-century, streamlined, of our time; recent, current, contemporaneous, in vogue.
Ant. antique, ancient, old, archaic, obsolete, past, antiquated, former, old-fashioned.

"The man who is ostentatious of his modesty is twin to the statue that wears a fig-leaf."
—*Mark Twain*

---

modest *adj.* **1** *Considering how he won the award, he should be more modest about it:* unassuming, humble, meek, not boastful, unassertive, self-effacing, unpretentious, free from vanity, devoid of egotism, unpretending. **2** *She served a modest but tasty meal:* simple, plain, unpretentious, unshowy, limited, unostentatious, quiet, unobtrusive. **3** *He made only a modest donation:* moderate, nominal, not excessive, not extravagant; medium-priced, inexpensive. **4** *She's too modest to be seen in a bathing costume:* reserved, discreet, bashful, shy, self-conscious, constrained, quiet, timid, demure, coy, diffident, blushing, shrinking, timorous, proper, strait-laced, prim, circumspect, prudish, puritanical.
Ant. 1 immodest, vain, boastful, ambitious; showy, pretentious, egotistic, ostentatious, fancy. **3** generous, magnanimous. **4** shameless, brazen, barefaced, impudent; immodest, indecent, indelicate, indecorous, unseemly, improper.

modesty *n.* **1** *I respect modesty, but I don't like coyness:* humility, humbleness, freedom from vanity, reserve, self-effacement, lack of self-importance, lack of boastfulness, restrained behaviour, restraint, freedom from presumption, constraint. **2** *The modesty of their home belies their great wealth:* simplicity, unpretentiousness, plainness, naturalness, lack of ostentation, inexpensiveness, reasonableness. **3** *Her modesty kept her from wearing a mini-skirt:* reserve, bashfulness, shyness, constraint, timidity, demureness, coyness, diffidence, timorousness, reticence, propriety, decency or reserve in dress; prudery.
Ant. 1 immodesty, boastfulness, self-conceit, pride, sauciness, arrogance, vanity, confidence, egotism, presumption, vainness, assurance, boldness, haughtiness. **2** extravagance, pretentiousness, showiness, ostentation. **3** immodesty, indecency, forwardness, impropriety.

modicum *n. If he had a modicum of intelligence, he'd accept the offer:* minimum, drop, jot, small quantity, mite, bit, pinch, trifle, small amount, dash, little bit, particle, tinge, sprinkling, touch, speck, snatch, fraction, grain, iota, handful, crumb, morsel, whit, atom, scrap, ounce, inch.

modify *v.* **1** *They modified their plans so that the cost would not be so enormous:* alter, vary, change, make different, adjust, give a new form to, transform, transmute, convert, refashion, rework, redo, reshape, remould, remodel, reorganize, revise, adapt, transmogrify. **2** *You'll have to modify the height of the table to make it fit:* reduce, moderate, modulate, temper, restrain, tone down, narrow, lower, remit, soften; qualify, limit, restrict, condition, control, adjust.

modulate *v.* **1** *Please modulate the sound on the TV:* adjust, attune, tune, reduce, regulate, change, turn down, tone down, moderate, lower, soften, temper. **2** *He modulated his voice when he spoke of the tragedy:* change, temper, vary in tone and accentuation, vary the inflection, inflect in the voice.

mogul *n. The cinema moguls discussed the industry's finances:* magnate, tycoon, important person, powerful figure, notable, tsar, lord, baron, personage, man of distinction, influential person, giant, *Slang* big shot, bigwig, VIP.
◇ *Word origin: Mogul* originally referred to

the Great Mogul, emperor of the Mogul Empire founded in India in 1526. (The founders of the Mogul Empire were *Mongols* who had been converted to Islam, and the word *Mogul* is an old variant of *Mongol.*)

moist *adj. She decided that the pastry was too moist and added some more flour. Her moist expression belied her indifference:* damp, wettish, slightly wet, wet; muggy, humid, dewy, dank, rainy, drizzly, drippy, vaporous; tearful, aqueous, misty, lachrymose.

Ant. dry, arid.

moisture *n. The sun will take the moisture out of the clothes:* dampness, moistness, wetness, damp, wet, wateriness; humidity, mugginess, dankness, dew, vapour; perspiration, sweat, exudate.

molest *v. That big bully is always molesting the children:* bother, harass, annoy, pester, disturb, harry, torment, beset, distress, trouble, fret, irritate, irk, worry, abuse, harm, attack, ill-treat, hurt, assault, injure, maltreat; sexually abuse.

mollify *v. Flowers would not mollify her anger:* appease, calm, moderate, placate, quell, lessen, mitigate, allay, reduce, palliate, conciliate, make less violent, decrease, soften, pacify, soothe, tone down, quiet, lighten, temper, abate, ease, assuage, curb, lull, blunt.

Ant. exasperate, exacerbate, agitate, stir, increase.

◇ *Word origin: Mollify* comes from Latin *mollis* (soft) + *facere* (to make), literally to make soft, hence to make less angry or violent.

molten *adj. The molten lava ran down the mountain:* liquefied, melted, smelted, igneous, magmatic.

moment *n.* **1** *I'll be with you in a moment:* minute, instant, twinkling, short period of time, second, jiffy, flash, split second, trice. **2** *At this precise moment I can't answer your questions:* point of time, the present time, instant, particular time, juncture. **3** *Your opinion is of great moment to me:* consequence; import, importance, worth, significance, weight, gravity, value, concern, interest, weightiness.

Ant. 3 insignificance, unimportance, triviality, inconsequence, unconcern.

◇ *Word origin:* See MOMENTUM.

"He knew the precise psychological moment when to say nothing." —*Oscar Wilde*

---

momentary *adj. It was only a momentary infatuation:* temporary, transitory, passing, fleeting, brief, short, short-lived, transient, ephemeral, fugitive.

Ant. permanent, lengthy, lasting, long-lived.

momentous *adj. The conference was a momentous occasion for both countries:* important, of great portent, significant, of great consequence, essential, critical, crucial, influential, eventful, fateful, earth-shaking, consequential, salient; grave, serious, ponderous, weighty.

Ant. unimportant, insignificant, trivial, trifling, inconsequential.

momentum *n. The spinning-top was losing momentum:* force, impetus, impelling force, energy, moment, property of a body that keeps it in motion, impulse, thrust, push, drive, headway, propulsion, velocity, speed.

◇ *Word origin: Momentum* is the Latin word for movement. It also gives us *moment,* which is literally a point in the movement of time.

monarch *n. The monarch was ousted by a military coup:* hereditary sovereign, prince; (*variously*) king, potentate, ruler, emperor, tsar, Kaiser, pharaoh, shah, khan, chieftain, doge, emir, rajah; (*fem.*) queen, princess; empress, tsarina, Kaiserin, ranee.

monastery *n. The monks have vowed never to leave the monastery:* place of contemplation, retreat, cloister, convent, abbey, nunnery, priory, friary; community of monks, community of nuns.

monastic *adj. A monastic life is unsuitable for gregarious people:* of monks, of monasteries; contemplative, solitary, monkish, secluded, cloistral, cloistered, eremitic, hermit-like, sequestered, celibate, recluse.

monetary *adj. The monetary value of the treasure is staggering. Is he having monetary problems?:* in money, pecuniary, financial, fiscal, measured or valued in terms of money.

"Money is like a sixth sense without which you cannot make a complete use of the other five." —*W. Somerset Maugham*

---

money *n.* **1** *The money stolen from the bank was never recovered. Beads are used as money in some cultures:* currency, cash, funds, revenue, paper money, coin, coinage, specie, hard cash, proceeds, assets, capital; *Informal* wherewithal, *Slang* dough, bread, lolly, readies, green; medium of exchange, measure of value, buying power, legal tender, payment. **2** *They live as though they have money:* wealth, affluence, financial independence, hereditary wealth, riches, lucrative investments, great income, no financial problems.

◇ *Word origin: Money* and *monetary* come from Latin *moneta,* meaning money, mint.

moneyed *adj. That restaurant caters for a very moneyed crowd:* wealthy, affluent, rich, prosperous, well-to-do, well-off, well-heeled, opulent, flush, elegant, *Informal* flashy, posh.

mongrel *adj.* **1** *The author depicts a nightmarish world of the future populated by mongrel subhumans:* mixed, of mixed breed, half-breed, cross-bred, hybrid; bastard, anomalous.

—*n.* **2** *The little mongrel is the smartest of all the puppies:* non-pedigree dog, cur, an animal of mixed breed, hybrid, half-breed, offshoot, cross-breed, *Slang* mutt.

Ant. 1, 2 pure-bred, thoroughbred. 1 pedigree.

◇ *Word origin: Mongrel* comes from Old English *gemang*, mixture, crowd. Our word *among* also comes from this Old English word.

monitor *n.* 1 *The teacher left a monitor in charge when she left:* disciplinarian, overseer, stand-in, invigilator, *Informal* watch-dog. 2 *I watched the programme on the director's monitor:* television set, studio television receiver, TV set, TV, scanner, pick-up, screen; warning device, sensor, *Informal* telly.
—*v.* 3 *He monitored all of the televised debate to be sure the contestants received equal coverage:* watch attentively, observe critically; censor.

◇ *Word origin: Monitor*, like *admonish*, comes from Latin *monere*, to warn or advise.

monk *n. He gave up a lucrative business career to become a monk:* brother, holy man, religious, prior, friar, abbé, abbot; hermit, recluse, anchorite, cenobite; Desert father.

◇ *Word origin:* Originally a *monk* was a religious hermit, one who lived and worshipped completely by himself. *Monk* comes from Greek *monos*, alone, solitary.

monkey *n.* 1 *The zoo has a little monkey that looks almost human:* primate, ape, simian, baboon. 2 *He made a monkey of me on the tennis court:* fool, dupe, ass, laughing-stock, butt, clown, buffoon, *Slang* jerk.
—*v.* 3 *I monkeyed about with the pin-ball machine until I broke it:* meddle, toy, tamper, trifle, fool, fiddle, play around, mess around; tinker.

◇ *Spelling tip: Monkey* becomes plural simply by adding an *s: monkey — monkeys.*

◇ *Word origin:* No one knows for sure where the word *monkey* comes from. One possibility is that it comes from the Spanish word *mona*, meaning female ape; another is that it may come from Dutch *monnik*, a monk, because some monkeys, such as the Capuchin, have brown-capped heads resembling the skull-caps which certain orders of monks used to wear; a third possibility is that it comes from the name *Moneke*, son of Martin the Ape in the old folk-tale *Reynard the Fox.*

monologue *n. We had to listen for an hour to a veritable monologue about her wonderful grandchild:* soliloquy, speech, oration, discourse, holding forth, address, expatiation, screed.

Ant. dialogue, conversation.

◇ *Word origin: Monologue* comes from Greek *monos* (alone) + *-logos* (speech), hence a speech by one person, especially to himself or with no one else interrupting. *Dialogue* comes from Greek *dia-* (across) + *-logos* (speech), literally "cross talk" between two or more people.

monopolize *v.* 1 *The government forbade them to monopolize the textile industry:* control, dominate, have a monopoly of, obtain exclusive possession of, corner, appropriate, own, absorb, take over, consume. 2 *The hostess completely monopolized her star guest:* appropriate, dominate, arrogate, take up, take advantage of, pre-empt.

Ant. 2 share, divide.

◇ *Word origin:* A business *monopoly* is the control of a commodity or service by one firm or person, with the resulting power to fix prices and eliminate competition. The word comes from Greek *monos* (alone) + *pōlein* (to sell), hence to sell alone, i.e. without competition.

monotonous *adj.* 1 *They'll diversify his job to make it less monotonous:* unvaried, boring, dull, dreary, humdrum, repetitious, flat, colourless, tedious, tiresome, wearisome, prosaic, pedestrian, routine, mundane, uninteresting, banal, dry, stodgy, routine, jejune, plodding, insipid. 2 *The preacher's monotonous voice put me to sleep:* without inflection, with a narrow range, droning, singsong, toneless, flat, soporific, somniferous, dull, torpid.

Ant. 1 varied, diversified, interesting.

monster *n.* 1 *This two-headed calf is a real monster:* deviant, variant, freak, freak of nature, *Latin* lusus naturae; phenomenon, anomaly, curiosity, oddity, wonder, marvel; miscreation, abnormality, monstrosity. 2 *Medusa is my favourite monster:* mythical or legendary being, semi-human creature; (*variously*) Chimera, Gorgon, dragon, gargoyle, Hydra, incubus, succubus, mermaid, satyr, Harpy, Fury, centaur; bogyman, zombie, vampire, Frankenstein, werewolf, Jekyll and Hyde, golem, ghoul. 3 *In the wrong hands freedom can become a monster:* dangerous creation, destructive force, uncontrollable force, threat. 4 *The murderer of the two princes in the Tower must have been a monster:* fiend, demon, devil, beast, brute, wretch, villain, scoundrel, cutthroat, savage, barbarian, blackguard, caitiff. 5 *Believe it or not, this 90-pound monster was supposed to be a toy poodle:* giant, mammoth, titan, colossus.

Ant. 1 commonplace, everyday thing, routine thing. 3 boon, blessing. 4 paragon, saint. 5 dwarf, midget, pygmy, shrimp, pip-squeak.

◇ *Word origin: Monster* actually comes from Latin *monere* to warn or advise, from which we also get our words *admonish* and *monitor.* To the Romans, a *monstrum* (monster) was a divine portent. Later it came to mean a prodigious being bearing such a portent, hence a freak.

monstrous *adj.* 1 *Two monstrous sharks crossed the bow of the boat:* huge, enormous, immense, gigantic, mighty, gargantuan, giant, titanic, tremendous, colossal, mammoth, hulking, stupendous, prodigious, Brobdingnagian; ghastly, revolting, gruesome, grisly, hideous, horrible. 2 *What a monstrous lie!:* outrageous, cruel, vicious, flagrant, egregious, fiendish, heinous, evil, horrid, obscene, villainous, nefarious, odious, atrocious, satanic, diabolical, shocking, scandalous; outright, utter, obvious, bald.

monument *n.* **1** *That statue is a monument to our war dead. His writings are a monument to the struggle of his people:* memorial, testament, testimonial, remembrance, memento, witness, token, commemoration, reminder. **2** *A monument was placed over the grave:* memorial, shrine; tombstone, gravestone, cenotaph.

◇ *Word origin:* A *monument* is built to remind us of a person or event. It comes from Latin *monere*, to remind.

monumental *adj.* **1** *The Great Sphinx is a fascinating example of Egyptian monumental art:* monolithic, cyclopean; statuary; gigantic, colossal, massive, heavy, huge, larger than life. **2** *Bradman's monumental innings of 452 will be remembered for many years:* historic, epoch-making, classic, immortal, enduring, memorable, lasting, awesome, stupendous, unprecedented. **3** *Speaking down to the people was a monumental mistake:* egregious, colossal, immense, decisive, inestimable; fatal, horrendous, catastrophic, shattering, mind-boggling.

Ant. **1** small, tiny, delicate, dainty, light, miniature. **2** unimportant, insignificant, petty, worthless; everyday, ephemeral.

mood *n. This balmy weather puts me in a cheerful mood. I'm just in one of my moods:* humour, disposition, state of mind, temper, frame of mind, mental state, feeling, emotional state, predisposition; state of dejection, depression, melancholia, melancholy, gloominess, low spirits, doldrums, *Informal* dumps, blues; state of irritation, vexation, hypersensitivity.

◇ *Word origin: Mood* comes from Old English *mōd*, mind. Incidentally, the grammatical *mood* of a verb (imperative, indicative, or subjunctive mood) has nothing to do with its state of mind, but is a completely different *mood*, a variant of the word *mode*, from Latin *modus*, manner or form.

moody *adj.* **1** *Such a moody person can depress everyone:* melancholy, dejected, gloomy, pessimistic, lugubrious, despondent, saturnine, morose, morbid, dismal, brooding, mopish, unhappy, *Slang* down-in-the-mouth; mean, irritable, irascible, sulky, ill-humoured, sullen, testy, surly, peevish, crabby, temperamental. **2** *I'm too moody to know what I'll feel like doing next week:* changeable, fickle, variable, unpredictable, inconstant, inconsistent, flighty, notional, mercurial, temperamental, capricious, volatile, erratic, whimsical, impetuous, impulsive.

Ant. **1** happy, joyful, cheerful; amiable, optimistic, compatible. **2** stable, constant, consistent, steady.

moor[1] *v. Let's moor at the next dock for the night. They moor the aircraft to the deck with ropes:* tie up, dock, anchor, berth, secure; fix firmly, affix, fasten, tether, anchor, tie down, attach.

Ant. untie, unfasten, cast off, set adrift.

moor[2] *Hounds pursued the escaped convict across the moor:* moorland, waste land, heath, wold, down, fell, upland; marsh, fen.

moot *adj. Whether life exists on other planets is a moot question:* debatable, questionable, unsettled, subject to argument, disputed, disputable, arguable, undecided, unresolved, conjectural, controversial, eristic.

Ant. indisputable, self-evident, axiomatic.

◇ *Word origin:* A *moot* point is one that is debatable or open for discussion. The word comes from Old English *mōt*, a formal meeting of freemen, especially a judicial assembly. A *moot court* is a mock court for the argument and trial of hypothetical cases, a practice court in which law students argue or debate cases.

mope *v. Stop moping and cheer up!:* sulk, languish, be dejected, fret, be gloomy, brood, pine, repine, lament, grieve, be downcast, pout, wear a long face.

moral *adj.* **1** *He was asked to give his legal opinion, not to make a moral judgement:* ethical, of right and wrong, of proper conduct, personal. **2** *It was not exactly moral for a practising lawyer to offer a bribe:* ethical, right, proper, virtuous, honourable, noble, estimable, meritorious, principled, just, fair, above-board; pure, honest, high-minded, saintly. **3** *By declaring him sane, the jury implied that he had a moral sense:* ethical, able to distinguish between right and wrong. **4** *He turns every subject into a moral discussion:* of morals, didactic, sermonizing, homiletic, preaching, moralizing, tendentious.

—*n.* **5** *Every story he tells has a moral:* lesson, message, tag, moral teaching; saying, proverb, maxim, adage, epigram, aphorism, motto.

Ant. **2** immoral, unmoral, amoral, wrong, sinful, unjust, unfair, dishonest, unethical, improper, dishonourable, unprincipled.

◇ *Usage note: Moral* and *morale* are a pair that catch some people out. *Moral* means "decent, adhering to the laws of God and man," or a point or lesson: *Grandfather was an honest, moral man. The moral of the story is that money can't buy happiness. Morale* means a state of mind or attitude in terms of confidence and courage: *After the defeat, the army's morale was low.*

◇ *Word origin: Moral* is from Latin *mores* manners, morals.

morale *n. The team's morale is on the increase:* spirit, mental attitude, level of optimism, moral strength, confidence, self-confidence, self-assurance, resolution, esprit de corps.

◇ *Usage note:* See MORAL.

morality *n.* **1** *I'm not concerned with the morality of the question:* ethical values, ethics, right or

wrong. **2** *It's obvious from his ruthless behaviour that he has no sense of morality:* goodness, righteousness, virtue, rectitude, honour, uprightness, fairness, probity, integrity; code of ethics, ethical philosophy, set of values. **3** *Her private morality is her own business:* sexual behaviour, habits, chasteness, modesty, tastes.
Ant. 2 immorality, wickedness, dishonour.

morass *n. I'll have to wade through that morass to find the ball:* marsh, slough, bog, quagmire, swamp, fen.
◇ *Word origin: Morass, marsh,* and *moor* were originally the same word, probably related to our now rare word *mere,* lake, which comes from Latin *mare,* sea.

morbid *adj. Cheer up, and don't be so morbid! His love of cemeteries is morbid:* depressed, gloomy, glum, sad, morose, brooding, self-absorbed, dour, saturnine, moody, melancholic, lugubrious, despondent, sombre; grim, pessimistic; unwholesome, preoccupied with death, suggesting an unhealthy mental state.
Ant. cheerful, optimistic, vital, life-centred.

> **Exploring the Word:** Latin *mori,* to die, and *mors,* death, give us *mortal,* meaning both deadly, as a *mortal wound,* and one who is subject to death, not a god, hence a human; *immortal,* not subject to death, as in the sentence *The Greeks believed their gods to be immortal,* or deathless, living for ever in memory or fame, as *the immortal plays of Shakespeare; mortality,* our mortal nature, and also large-scale loss of life, and *mortality tables,* which list for insurance companies the probable death rates or life-expectancy rate of various categories of people; *morbid,* diseased or sick, as before dying; *moribund,* dying, near death; *mortuary,* a place for the dead; and *mortify,* literally to make dead, kill, thus when we are mortified about making a mistake, we are truly "ashamed to death," and when a monk fasts to *mortify the flesh,* he hopes to kill his fleshly appetites.

more *adj.* **1** *I have more cakes should we need them:* extra, additional, other, added, supplemental, supplementary, further; spare, reserve.
—*adv.* **2** *He is more energetic than his sister:* to a greater extent or degree. **3** *If I have to work more tonight, I'll collapse:* further, longer, additionally.
Ant. 1, 2 less. **1** fewer.

moreover *adv. Bicycling is good exercise; moreover, it doesn't pollute the air:* further, besides, also, more than that, what's more, furthermore, too, in addition.

moribund *adj. Many of the early customs were moribund by the turn of the century:* dying, doomed, waning, stagnating, dying out, near death, fading out, being phased out, on its last legs.

morning *n.* **1** *I found it difficult to get up in the morning:* morn, daybreak, dawn, sunrise, break of day, daylight, first light, crack of dawn. **2** *He'll deliver the groceries some time this morning:* forenoon, before 12 noon.
—*adj.* **3** *We always have a very light morning meal:* early, of the morning, forenoon.
Ant. 1, 2 afternoon, evening; dusk, sunset.

moron *n. His exam results are so bad that you'd think he was a complete moron:* fool, dope, ass, nitwit, ninny, dunce, twerp, dummy, loony, nut, oaf, numskull, idiot, dim-wit, imbecile, half-wit, mutton-head, bonehead, dumbbell, nincompoop, booby, sap, jackass.
Ant. genius, brain, mastermind, wizard, whiz kid.
◇ *Usage note:* Technically, a *moron* is a person with the mildest degree of mental deficiency, having a mental age of from 7 to 12 years or an IQ of 50 to 75, and hence can perform all basic activities adequately. An *idiot* is a person with the most mental deficiency, having a mental age of only 3 or 4 years. He has an IQ in the lowest measurable range, and is incapable of performing basic activities or of learning connected speech. An *imbecile* has a mental level between that of an idiot and a moron, a mental age of 3 or 4 to 7 or 8 years, and can perform some basic activities.
◇ *Word origin: Moron* comes from Greek *mōros,* stupid, foolish.

morose *adj. I felt very morose after reading that sad story:* depressed, low, sad, melancholy, moody, glum, dour, *Informal* blue, down in the dumps; saturnine, mopish, gloomy, despondent, mournful, solemn; sullen, sulky, cross, surly, testy, waspish, sour, churlish, grumpy, ill-tempered, irascible.
Ant. cheerful, blithe, happy, good-natured, pleasant, genial, amiable, friendly.

morsel *n. You must taste just a morsel of this cake:* nibble, titbit, taste, bite, crumb, snack, sliver, sip, piece, nip, drop, small amount, mouthful; bit, scrap, touch, speck, little piece, segment, scintilla, trace, whit, modicum, fragment, iota, particle, grain, drop.
◇ *Word origin:* A *morsel,* of course, is a little bite of food. It's the diminutive of Old French *mors,* a bite, which derives from Latin *mordere,* to bite, source of our word *mordant,* biting.

mortal *adj.* **1** *Desire, like all things mortal, passes swiftly:* human, earthly, corporeal, mundane; fleeting, ephemeral, temporal, transitory. **2** *He received a mortal blow:* fatal, lethal, deadly, causing death. **3** *We were in mortal terror of being found out:* extreme, severe, intense, enormous, deep, grave, unimaginable, living.
—*n.* **4** *He was a strange and lonely mortal:* human being, person, creature, individual, *Informal* type, character.
Ant. 1 immortal, undying, everlasting, eternal, divine, perennial.

mortality *n.* **1** *Man's mortality is all too obvious in* *time of war:* transience, impermanence, evanescence, ephemerality, transitoriness. **2** *The mortality from the earthquake was devastating:* human loss, loss of life, fatality, carnage, bloodshed, death toll.

Ant. 1 immortality, permanence; divinity.

mortify *v.* **1** *Forgetting the introductory remarks really mortified me:* shame, horrify, embarrass, appal, chagrin, discomfit, abash, disconcert, make red-faced. **2** *It is good for the soul to mortify oneself periodically:* deny, discipline, self-discipline, be abstinent, practise continence, practise rigorous austerities; fast, do penance. **3** *The wound will mortify without care:* become gangrenous, fester, rot, decay, putrefy; make rotten, cause to decay.

Ant. 1 gratify, satisfy, make confident, make proud. **2** indulge, satisfy.

most *adj.* **1** *Of the three girls, Susan has the most freckles:* the greatest in number, degree, or quantity; maximum; in the majority.

—*n.* **2** *Give the winner the most:* largest amount, maximum; the majority.

—*adv.* **3** *That's the most beautiful cake I have ever seen:* in the greatest degree, extremely, to the greatest extent, very, in the highest degree, best.

◇ *Usage note:* Strictly speaking, *most* means "more than half." In formal speech and writing you should not use *most* as a synonym for *almost.* Thus, *Which of the candidates will win most of the votes?*, but *Almost* (not *"most"*) *everyone enjoyed the party.*

mostly *adv. The guests are mostly friends of the bride:* primarily, chiefly, for the most part, largely, mainly; especially, specially, particularly, principally; as a rule, most often, generally, greatly.

mother *n.* **1** *A mother can be a girl's best friend:* female parent, *Informal* mum, mummy, mamma, mammy, ma, mama, old lady, old woman, *Formal* mater. **2** *Necessity is the mother of invention:* origin, source, well-spring, stimulus, inspiration.

—*v.* **3** *She mothered two children and adopted a third:* bear, give birth to, bring forth, beget, produce, conceive, breed. **4** *She mothers her plants as she does her children:* care for, rear, raise, tend, mind, nurse, nurture, protect, indulge.

◇ *Word origin: Mother* is a basic kinship term. It is *Mutter* in German and *madre* in Spanish. Over two thousand years ago it was *mater* in Latin and *mētēr* in Greek, while the Sanskrit word was *mātr.* Historical linguists have reconstructed the Indo-European word as *māter-* (the hyphen means that the word-ending, if any, is uncertain). The original Indo-European language is now dated by experts as prior to the fifth millennium B.C. The "mother" word has thus been with us in forms very much like its present English form for the past six or seven thousand years (at least!) and no doubt a good deal longer.

motherly *adj. The sergeant is almost motherly to the young recruits:* maternal, tender, kind, loving, gentle, sheltering, protective, indulgent, devoted.

Ant. unmaternal, unkind, unloving.

motif *n. My wallpaper will have a French Provincial motif:* style, theme, artistic theme, subject, treatment, idea, shape, form, design, pattern, figure.

motion *n.* **1** *Put the engine in motion. He was enthralled by the water's ceaseless motion:* movement, mobility, motility, act of moving, kinesis; drift, passage, stir, flow, stream, flux, progress, action. **2** *I proposed a motion to take the minutes of the last meeting as read:* formal proposal, suggestion, request, proposition, recommendation.

—*v.* **3** *He motioned us to our seats:* signal, beckon, nod, gesture, gesticulate.

Ant. 1 rest, repose, stillness, immobility; quiet, quiescence, stasis.

> **Exploring the Word**: *Motion, move, mobile* (capable of being moved, easily moved), and *motor* (a mover of other things) all come from Latin *movere,* to move. This same Latin base gives us *commotion,* moving thoroughly, hence agitation, tumult; *demote,* to move down in rank or importance; *emotion,* an outward movement of feelings; *mobilize,* to put into motion, make active, make ready for war, and *demobilize,* to take out of action, movement, or service; *motive* and *motivation,* that which moves a person to some action or behaviour; *promote,* to move forward, advance, and *promotion,* an advancement, a move in favour of someone; *remove,* to move back or away, to take away, and *remote,* moved far away in place or time, distant.

motionless *adj. When the curtain rises, the dancers are motionless:* still, stationary, inert, without motion, immobile, immovable, unmoving, quiescent, calm, at rest, fixed, at a standstill, stable, tranquil, inactive, static; transfixed, riveted to the spot, frozen; lifeless, idle, dead.

Ant. mobile, active, alive.

motivation *n. His motivation was so strong that we didn't believe he could fail:* motive, reason, impulse, impetus, cause, driving force, impulsion, causation, provocation.

motive *n. What was his motive for committing the crime?:* reason, purpose, object, cause, intention, occasion, design, thinking, grounds, rationale; inducement, incentive, enticement, stimulus, prompting, instigation, spur, incitement, inspiration; goal, aim, end.

motley *adj.* **1** *It's amazing how well such a motley group got along:* varied, different, heterogeneous, disparate, composite, mixed, assorted, miscellaneous, variegated, sundry, diversified, unlike, incongruous, dissimilar, divergent, hybrid. **2** *I'm covering my sofa with a*

beautiful motley fabric: of different colours, varicoloured, chequered, multicoloured, polychrome, dappled, pied, piebald, particoloured, speckled, watered, tabby, brindled, kaleidoscopic, mottled, iridescent, harlequin.
—*n.* **3** *The dancers wore motley:* varied colours, patchwork, rainbow pattern; clown's costume, jester or buffoon's garish apparel, clownish trappings.
Ant. 1 uniform, homogeneous, identical, like, similar. **2** monochromatic, solid, plain.

mottled *adj. The draperies are a mottled fabric of yellow, green, and pink:* motley, particoloured, variegated, multicolour, piebald, polychromatic, iridescent, kaleidoscopic, pied, varicoloured, flecked, brindled, blotchy, specked, speckled, stippled, tabby.

mould[1] *n.* **1** *I made the mousse in my new copper mould:* cast, form, shaper; matrix, die. **2** *I like the angular mould of the sculpture:* shape, contour, line, formation, form, structure, frame, construction, cut, conformation, outline, turn, configuration. **3** *Women of her mould are easy to see through:* quality, type, ilk, sort, kind, character, stamp, kidney, make, brand.
—*v.* **4** *He moulded a rabbit out of clay:* model, shape, form, cast, fashion, create, knead, sculpt, figure, construct, pattern. **5** *Higgins tried to mould the cockney girl into an elegant lady:* form, fashion, remodel, turn, render, convert, transform, transmute, develop, bring along, train, make, transfigure.

mould[2] *n. The bread was covered with green mould:* fungus, mildew, blight, rust, lichen.

mound *n.* **1** *The archaeologist excavated an ancient burial mound:* pile, rampart, ridge, barrow, embankment, bulwark, earthwork. **2** *Only a tank could handle the mounds on that terrain:* knoll, hillock, hill, dune, mount, hummock, undulation, bump.
Ant. 2 dip, valley, dell, sink-hole, trough.
◇ *Word origin:* See MOUNTAIN.

mount *v.* **1** *You'll have to mount the ladder to reach the top shelf:* ascend, climb, go up, climb up, scale, get over, climb over. **2** *The death toll mounted for days after the fire:* rise, ascend, go up, increase, intensify, grow, soar, swell, surge, wax, multiply, augment. **3** *The Arab mounted the camel and rode away:* climb up on, get astride, get upon, straddle. **4** *The Navy mounted 8-inch guns on its warships. He mounted the diamond in a platinum setting:* install, fit, equip, outfit, rig, fit out; put in position on, set into, affix, frame, fix, set, set off.
—*n.* **5** *He urged his mount onwards:* riding animal; horse, saddle-horse, steed, charger; (*variously*) pony, elephant, camel.
Ant. 1 drop, descend. **2** fall, decline, lessen, decrease, diminish. **3** dismount.

mountain *n. The north face of the mountain was scaled for the first time:* peak, massif, natural elevation of the earth's surface, very high hill, fell, range, highland, height, bluff, ridge, mount, alp; volcano.
◇ *Word origin: Mountain, mound,* and *mount* come from Latin *mons,* mountain.

mountebank *n.* **1** *That miracle remedy the mountebank sold me was only coloured water:* quack, quacksalver, medicine man, charlatan, huckster. **2** *The investors were taken in by a clever mountebank:* confidence man, confidence trickster, fraud, swindler, cheat, sharper, con man, twister, operator, flimflammer.
◇ *Word origin:* A *mountebank* was originally a quack who sold home-made or patent medicines to people at fairs. He would climb up on his bench or platform and gather a crowd by his patter. Why was he called a *mountebank?* Because he made himself seem impressive by climbing up on his bench or platform. The word comes from Italian *montare* (to mount) + *in* (on) + *banco* (bench), hence *mountebank* means "mount a bench," as this charlatan always did.

mourn *v.* **1** *She's still mourning his death after all these years:* grieve for, express grief, lament, weep over, despair, be sorrowful, bewail, wail, pine, languish, cry, wail, weep, keen. **2** *I really mourn the loss of that old sweater:* regret, rue, deplore, bemoan.
Ant. 1 rejoice, exult, laugh, triumph.

mourning *n.* **1** *I know you miss him, but all this mourning doesn't help anyone:* grief, woe, grieving, lamentation, lamenting, bereavement, sorrow, despair; period of mourning. **2** *He wore mourning for his deceased wife:* weeds, crêpe, black, black apparel.
Ant. 1 rejoicing, celebration, merry-making.

mouth *n.* **1** *Open your mouth and close your eyes:* oral opening, jaws, oral cavity, facial orifice. **2** *The mouth of the jar was chipped:* opening, aperture, lips, rim. **3** *The regatta was held at the mouth of the River Exe:* inlet, bay, estuary, place where a river flows into another body of water, outlet, portal, wide opening, jaws.
—*v.* **4** *All he does is mouth pompous truisms. She mouthed the words as the record played:* pronounce, speak, declare, say, voice, propound; feign speech, feign singing, shape words, mime.

move *v.* **1** *Please move out of the way:* shift, stir, budge, change position, change place, proceed, advance, go; transpose, carry, pass, remove, transport, switch, bear, convey, transmit, drift. **2** *She moved here at the beginning of term:* transfer, relocate, change residence, change one's abode, shift, transplant. **3** *The clock doesn't move:* go, have motion, function, operate. **4** *Curiosity moved me to open the box:* cause, influence, induce, lead, impel, get, prompt, incite, drive, inspire, provoke, persuade, stimulate, motivate. **5** *I was truly moved by his tears:* touch, affect; arouse, rouse, excite, stir, sway, interest, impress, impassion, fire, strike. **6** *I move that we accept the proposal:*

propose, suggest, recommend, request, ask, urge, exhort, plead. **7** *Let's move before it's too late:* get started, start off, go, go ahead, begin; strike, attack.

—*n.* **8** *One move and I'll shoot!:* movement, motion, gesture, stirring, budging. **9** *Selling your car was a good move:* action, deed, act, manœuvre, ploy, measure, stroke, step. **10** *It's your move:* turn, opportunity, *Informal* go.

Ant. 1 stop, stay, arrest. **4** prevent. **5** untouched, unmoved, unimpressed.

movement *n.* **1** *The room shakes with his every movement:* motion, change of position, locomotion, stirring, progress, agitation, action. **2** *His movement was not in time with the music:* bodily rhythm, motion, steps, gestures, execution. **3** *The army's movements were kept secret:* activity, operation, manœuvre. **4** *We're starting a movement to clean up the city:* drive, crusade, undertaking, programme, measure, effort. **5** *The first movement of Beethoven's Fifth Symphony is familiar to most music-lovers:* section, part, division. **6** *This watch has a 21-jewel movement:* mechanism, action, works.

Ant. 1 inertia, stasis, quiescence.

movie *n. That movie is now being shown on TV:* motion picture, film, cinema, moving picture, picture show, picture, feature, *Slang* flick.

moving *adj.* **1** *It has no moving parts:* movable, capable of moving, mobile, motile, interacting; motor, locomotive. **2** *What's the moving force behind the team?:* motivating, spurring, inspiring, stimulating. **3** *The song was so moving that it made me cry:* touching, exciting, affecting, stirring, impressive, poignant.

Ant. 1 stationary, immobile, unmoving, still. **3** unaffecting, unexciting, unimpressive.

much *adj.* **1** *We have much work ahead of us:* abundant, ample, plenteous, sufficient, considerable, appreciable, copious, plentiful, plenty of, a lot of. **2** *In spite of all the publicity, the actress is not much to look at:* impressive, worthwhile, consequential, noteworthy, striking, special, satisfying.

—*n.* **3** *He doesn't think I've done much:* appreciable amount, great deal, good deal, sufficiency, quantity; lots, loads, heaps, scores, reams.

—*adv.* **4** *The professor is much revered:* greatly, decidedly, indeed, to a great degree, far; excessively, tremendously, exceedingly. **5** *He looks much the same as you:* somewhat, rather, nearly, approximately, about, almost. **6** *Do you go there much?:* often, frequently, regularly, many times, habitually, a lot.

Ant. 1 little, small, scarce, few. **1, 3** little. **2** unimportant, inconsequential, trifling, unsatisfying.

muck *n.* **1** *The pipes beneath the sink were clogged with muck:* mud, filth, dung, sewage, slops, rubbish, slime, mire, ooze, waste, *Informal* gunge, gunk. **2** *There is far too much muck in this book:* disgusting material, rudery, unwarranted nonsense, pornography, licence, filth, dirt, rubbish.

◇ *Word origin:* Because of the different connotations of these two meanings, *muck* is today a word which has to be used with caution. It comes from Middle English *muk*, dung, and this sense can on occasions cause such expressions as "to muck about" seem mildly vulgar. Very early on, *muck* was used of money, and although this sense is now obsolete, the ideas are associated in the phrase *where there's muck, there's brass.* A *muck-raker* is a journalist who exposes scandals, figuratively raking through dunghills for his bits of scandal or rumour. *Muck-rakes* were, of course, ordinary farm rakes in the old days.

muddle *v.* **1** *I muddled up the ingredients and had to begin again:* confuse, mix up, ruin, botch, bungle, blunder, mess, spoil, fumble, *Informal* muff, foul up; *Slang* fluff, blow, goof up. **2** *The drug muddled me so much that I forgot where I was:* stupefy, mentally confuse, mix up, nonplus, daze, throw, confound, rattle, bewilder; boggle, act confusedly.

—*n.* **3** *He's in too much of a muddle to be of any help. Her affairs are in a terrible muddle:* confused state, upset, pother, haze, fog, daze; jumble, mess, disorder, disarray, chaos, disarrangement, clutter.

◇ *Word origin: Muddle* comes from the word *mud*, and means to make muddy, stir up mud.

muffle *v.* **1** *Don't forget to muffle yourself against the cold:* wrap, cloak, swaddle, swathe, cover, enclose, conceal, mask, veil, envelop, shroud, gag. **2** *The interrogator muffled the prisoner's screams with a gag:* repress, suppress, cut off, silence, block off, blot out, quiet, hush, still, quell, dull, deaden, soften.

◇ *Word origin:* To *muffle* means to put on a muff or mittens to keep the hands warm. It comes from Old French *moufle*, muff, mitten. To *muffle* a sound is to deaden it by wrapping it in something, like a muff.

mug *n.* **1** *Give the baby a mug of milk:* cup, jug, tankard, tumbler, toby, toby jug, chalice, beaker, goblet, flagon. **2** *Slang He's got an ugly mug:* face, visage, countenance, kisser, phiz, mush.

◇ *Word origin:* Our drinking *mug* comes from Scandinavian *mugg*, pitcher, jug. *Mug* meaning face, a police photograph of a face (*a mug shot*), a man, dupe, or criminal, comes from the old practice of making drinking-mugs to resemble faces. For example, the toby jugs which some people collect are beer or ale mugs made in the form of an old man or a stout Englishman wearing a three-cornered hat.

muggy *adj. This muggy weather gives me head-*

aches: humid, sultry, vaporous, steaming, oppressive, stuffy, misty, close, sweltering.
◇ *Word origin: Muggy* comes from Old Norse *mugga,* drizzle.

mule *n. The miner used a mule to carry his equipment:* half donkey-half mare; (*loosely*) ass, donkey, jackass, hinny.
◇ *Word origin: Mule* comes from Old English *mūl* and Old French *mul,* both from Latin *mulus,* offspring of a jackass and a mare. This word comes from a very ancient Mediterranean language — the horse-breeding Indo-Europeans did not have mules, apparently.

mull *v.* Usually **mull over** *I'll mull over your proposal and let you know:* ponder, consider, reflect on, think about for a while, give thought to, meditate, weigh, ruminate.
◇ *Word origin:* When you *mull over* a problem, you are literally grinding it up in your mind—the word itself may well come from Middle English *mullen,* pulverize, crumble.

multifarious *adj. My multifarious duties make my work interesting:* varied, diverse, different, diversified, various, divers, variegated, manifold, motley, miscellaneous, sundry, heterogeneous, of many kinds, mixed, numerous, many, several.

multiply *v.* **1** *Our rabbits multiplied so fast that we had difficulty in finding homes for them:* procreate, propagate, reproduce, proliferate, breed, increase, beget, generate. **2** *Her anxieties multiplied until they could no longer be endured:* increase, enlarge, magnify, intensify, augment; add to, enhance, raise, extend, spread, heighten.
Ant. 2 decrease, diminish, lessen, wane, reduce, abate, shrink; divide.
◇ *Word origin: Multiply* and *multitude* both come from Latin *multus,* much. The *-ply* in *multiply* is from Latin *plicare,* to fold. This same Latin verb also gives us *complex* (folded over on itself, twisted into folds) and *duplicate* (folded over into two).

multitude *n. The multitude awaited the champion's arrival. A multitude of problems delayed the construction project:* crowd, throng, mob, legion, horde, scores, mass, array, conflux, host, large amount, great number, heap, pile, flood, drove, army, pack, herd, myriad.

mum *adj. Keep mum about the surprise party:* silent, still, quiet, wordless, close-mouthed, secretive, mute, tacit.

mumble *v.* **1** *I mumbled to conceal my lack of information:* mutter, murmur, utter indistinctly, speak inarticulately, speak incoherently, stammer, hem and haw, mouth.
—*n.* **2** *He gave a mumble of disapproval:* indistinct utterance, mutter, inarticulate sound, grunt, growl, murmur, snort.
Ant. 1 articulate, enunciate.

mundane *adj. Artists often have trouble with the mundane affairs of life:* ordinary, prosaic, commonplace, worldly, terrestrial, earthly, down-to-earth, day-to-day, everyday, practical, petty.
Ant. heavenly, celestial, ethereal, empyrean, unearthly, unworldly, spiritual.
◇ *Word origin: Mundane* comes from Latin *mundus,* world.

municipal *adj. We should consider this a municipal undertaking:* civic, community, city, parochial, administrative, public.
◇ *Spelling tip:* Your *municiPAL* government is your local government and should be your *pal.*
◇ *Word origin: Municipal* and *municipality* come from Latin *municipium,* a provincial town whose citizens enjoyed Roman citizenship during the Roman republic and empire. Derived from this word is the term *municeps,* citizen of such a locality. In late republican times the term acquired the additional meanings "local, provincial."

municipality *n. Our suburb is at last becoming a fully-fledged municipality:* self-governing district, town, city, township, parish, village.

munificence *n. The munificence of its patrons has kept the theatre alive:* generosity, bountifulness, liberality, benevolence, beneficence, benefaction, largess, bounty, bounteousness, humanitarianism, philanthropy, charity, charitableness, patronage.
Ant. parsimoniousness, stinginess, penny-pinching, niggardliness, miserliness.

munificent *adj. The park is just one of their munificent gifts to the city:* generous, liberal, open-handed, free, benevolent, beneficent, bountiful, bounteous, altruistic, kindly, philanthropic, humanitarian, charitable, gratuitous; lavish, profuse, extravagant.
Ant. stingy, penurious, mean, niggardly.
◇ *Word origin: Munificent* literally means giving gifts. It comes from Latin *munus* (gift) + *facere* (to make).

murder *n.* **1** *Matricide is the murder of one's mother:* homicide, assassination, manslaughter, killing.
—*adj.* **2** *Informal This heat is murder!:* unbearable, intolerable, oppressive, agonizing; very difficult, impossible, formidable.
—*v.* **3** *According to the historians he murdered his rival in cold blood:* kill, slay, assassinate, commit homicide, butcher, finish off, dispatch, slaughter, cut down, *Slang* knock off. **4** *The comedian gets laughs by murdering the English language:* use incorrectly, abuse, mangle, misuse, bastardize, corrupt.
◇ *Word origin: Murder* comes from Old English *morthor,* murder. The word is akin to Latin *mors* (stem *mort-*) death, which gives us *mortal, mortuary, morbid, moribund,* and *murrain.*

murderer *n. The murderer was executed for his crime:* killer, assassin, slayer, homicide; butcher, cut-throat.

murky *adj. I can't see anything in this murky light:* dark, dim, gloomy; hazy, misty, foggy,

cloudy, vaporous, dusky, overcast, obscure, lowering; dreary, sombre, dismal, cheerless.
Ant. bright, clear, unobscured.

murmur *n. Listen to the murmur of the brook:* purl, low sound, rumble, soft utterance, whisper, undertone, rustle, babble, purr, hum, lapping, drone, sough, mumble; mutter, complaint, grumble, lament, whimper, sigh.
◇ *Spelling tip:* The final *r* of *murmur* remains just one *r* in *murmuRing.*

muscle *n.* **1** *James exercises to develop his muscles:* biceps, flexor, sinew, tendon, thew. **2** *It'll take a lot of muscle to move this piano:* power, might, brawn, muscular strength, potency, thew, force, grit, puissance, energy, vigour, stamina, virility.
◇ *Word origin:* When you were a little child, did anyone ever flex his biceps and tell you that large rippling bulge was a mouse under his skin? That a muscle looks like a mouse under the skin is a very old idea, going back to Indo-European times. *Muscle* is from Latin *musculus,* little mouse, diminutive of Latin *mus,* mouse. Greek *mūs,* mouse, is also the regular word for "muscle" and so appears in scientific writings, starting with Hippocrates. In Germanic, the same signification (both "muscle" and "mouse") belongs to Old High German, Old English, and Old Norse *mūs.*

muscular *adj. All that tennis has made me quite muscular:* strong, husky, powerful, brawny, tough, strapping, athletic, sinewy.

muse *v. The old man mused over the harsh finality of life. If we buy a car, I mused, then we can't afford the trip abroad:* meditate, ponder, deliberate, speculate, ruminate, contemplate, cogitate, reflect; think reflectively, say reflectively.
◇ *Word origin:* When we sit and *muse,* we are trying to work something out in the same way that a dog tries to work out or scent something by pointing its *muzzle* in the air. *Muse* is very probably related to Old French *musel,* muzzle. Incidentally, our other word *muse,* the guiding spirit inspiring artists, comes from the *Muses* of Greek mythology, the nine daughters of Zeus and Memory, each of whom presided over one of the arts of the Greeks. Our words *music* and *museum* also come from these nine Muses.

mushroom *v. The small village quickly mushroomed into a town:* grow, expand quickly, proliferate, burgeon, increase, shoot up, sprout.
◇ *Word origin: Mushroom* comes from Old French *mousseron,* which probably goes back to a now-lost Gallo-Roman word for *moss.*

music *n.* **1** *Shall we have some music during dinner?:* harmonious sound, euphony, harmony, minstrelsy, song, tune, melody. **2** *He handed out the music to the orchestra:* printed music, score, sheet music.

musical *adj. The piece of bamboo makes a musical sound:* melodious, melodic, euphonious, harmonious, tuneful, dulcet, sweet, pleasant-sounding, lyric.
Ant. unmusical, discordant, inharmonious, unmelodious, cacophonous.

"Without music life would be a mistake."
—*Nietzsche*

---

musty *adj.* **1** *The musty curtains had to be thoroughly aired:* mildewed, mouldy, stale, dusty, fusty, damp, dank, dirty, stuffy, frowsty. **2** *I've heard that musty joke a dozen times:* hackneyed, stale, worn, worn-out, ancient, old, threadbare, banal, antiquated, commonplace, trite, familiar, *Informal* tired, old hat.
Ant. 2 new, novel, fresh, original.
◇ *Word origin: Musty* is probably a variant of the obsolete word *moisty,* moist.

mutation *n. Mutation caused genetic changes in the animal. This pink rose is a mutation of the red variety:* change, alteration, permutation, variation, metamorphosis, transformation, transmogrification, deviation, transfiguration, modification; anomaly, mutant.
◇ *Word origin:* A *mutation* is a change, especially a variation in a plant or animal caused by a new combination or modification of genes and chromosomes. The word comes from Latin *mutare,* to change.

mute *adj.* **1** *In horror stories the mad scientist's assistant is usually mute:* dumb, speechless, voiceless, aphasiac. **2** *He is mute on the subject of religion:* non-committal, silent, non-vocal, unwilling to speak, mum, reticent, close-mouthed, tight-lipped, uncommunicative; reserved, tacit, quiet, speechless, inarticulate. **3** *My name has a mute "e" in it:* unsounded, silent, unarticulated, unuttered, unpronounced.
Ant. 2 expansive, informative, loquacious. **3** audible, pronounced, articulated.

mutilate *v. The assassins often mutilated their victims:* butcher, maim, cut to pieces, lacerate, cripple, lame; deprive of bodily part, cut off, amputate, truncate, excise, dismember.
◇ *Word origin: Mutilate* comes from Latin *mutilus,* maimed (said of those who cut off a thumb to escape military service) or dehorned (said of a horned animal which has lost one or both horns).

mutual *adj.* **1** *He is a mutual friend of ours:* shared by two parties, interchangeable, common, coincident, correlative, joint, interactive, related. **2** *He loves me, and the feeling is mutual:* reciprocated, reciprocal, interchanged, returned.
Ant. 1 distinct, uncommon. **2** unreciprocated, unshared, disparate.

muzzle *v.* **1** *The judge ordered him to muzzle his dog:* harness, gag, bridle; curb, bind, check, rein in. **2** *The chairman tried to muzzle the opposition speakers:* silence, quiet, still, stifle, gag.

◇ *Word origin: Muzzle* comes from Old French *musel*, snout of an animal. Because an animal appears to be thinking or trying to catch a scent when it puts its *muzzle* or *musel* in the air, this word probably gives us our verb to *muse*, to ponder.

myriad *adj. Myriad treasures are believed to be buried beneath the sea:* innumerable, multitudinous, countless, boundless, measureless, infinite, incalculable, immeasurable, untold, limitless, manifold, uncounted, endless.

Ant. few.

◇ *Word origin: Myriad* comes from Greek *mūrias*, meaning 10,000.

mysterious *adj. There is something mysterious about her early childhood:* strange, puzzling, enigmatic, cryptic, secret, inscrutable, obscure, hidden, covert, clandestine, baffling, impenetrable, perplexing, secretive, undercover, sphinxlike, cloudy, inexplicable, surreptitious, unfathomable, dark, unknown, supernatural, undecipherable.

Ant. clear, plain, apparent, manifest, palpable.

mystery *n.* **1** *The mysteries of their religion uplifted them:* sacred rites, things unexplainable, mysticism, occultism, sacramental rite, symbolism, ineffability, holy of holies. **2** *The first one to solve the mystery of the lost glasses wins a prize:* puzzle, problem, secret, riddle, conundrum, enigma, obscurity. **3** *Her mystery makes her charming:* enigmatic manner, ineffability, ineffableness, mysterious quality, elusiveness, mystification, secrecy, ambivalence, quizzicality, vagueness.

mystical Also **mystic** *adj. The mystical element of the play came across well:* mysterious, inscrutable, obscure, unknowable, enigmatic, abstruse, esoteric, cabalistic, symbolic, symbolical, secretive, hidden, occult, cryptic; otherworldly, transcendental, ethereal.

mystify *v. I like it, and yet exactly why still mystifies me:* bewilder, fool, elude, confound, perplex, puzzle, baffle, *Slang* bamboozle, beat.

> **Exploring the Word**: From Greek *mustērion*, secret rite, we get *mystery*, something that is not known or not told, and *mysterious*, unknown, unexplained, secret. From the related Greek *mustēs*, an initiate, we get *mystic*; and from *mystic* we get *mystify* (the *-fy* is from Latin *facere*, to make), to make secret, hence to confuse or confound. All of these are based on Greek *mueîn*, to initiate, which comes from *muein*, to close the lips, keep mum.

myth *n.* **1** *Things happen every day that remind us of the classical myths:* story, legend, tale, fairy-tale, fable, allegory, parable. **2** *Her alleged trip to Cornwall was an utter myth:* fiction, made-up story, fantasy; falsehood, lie, fib, tall story, prevarication, canard, hearsay, story, hoax, yarn. **3** *The myth that the earth was flat was argued for many years before Columbus:* illusion, delusion, falsehood, error, shibboleth.

Ant. **1** historical fact, real-life occurrence. **2** truth, fact, actuality.

◇ *Word origin: Myth* comes from Greek *mūthos*, story. *Mythology* is from Greek *mūthos* (story) + *-logiā* (study).

mythical Also **mythic** *adj.* **1** *The French painters were drawn to historical and mythical subjects:* legendary, fabled, about myths, mythological. **2** *Jennifer has a mythical horse:* imaginary, fantasized, fictitious, fabricated, unsubstantial, illusory, unreal, pretended, conjured-up.

Ant. **2** real, actual, real-life.

mythological Also **mythologic** *adj. The poem is weighted down with mythological allusions:* drawn from mythology; legendary, mythical, mythic, unreal, unfactual, fabulous, imaginary, fictitious, fantastic, imagined, illusory.

N

nadir *n. Being thrown out of Mary's house was the nadir of my career as a Don Juan:* lowest point, apogee, zero, bottom, rock-bottom.

Ant. peak, apex, zenith, high point.

◇ *Word origin: Nadir* is from Arabic *nadīr es-sent* "opposite the zenith." (Arabic *samt* gives us our word *zenith*.)

nag *v.* **1** *I'll go if you'll just stop nagging:* pester, harass, badger, harp, hector, upbraid, scold, nettle, irritate, annoy, plague, importune, bedevil, pick on, heckle, devil, goad, rail at, peck at, bicker, *Slang* hassle. —*n.* **2** *That woman is a frightful nag:* scold, shrew, virago, termagant, harpy, tartar, battle-axe, Xanthippe; vixen, fury.

◇ *Word origin: Nag* comes from Scandinavian *nagga*, to gnaw, chew repeatedly. Our other word *nag*, an old or worthless horse, probably comes from Old English *hnægan*, to neigh, since that's all a *nag* is good for.

nail *v. We nailed all the shutters closed for the winter:* hammer, pin, fasten, fix, secure.

◇ *Word origin: Nail* comes from Old English *nægl*, finger-nail. Later, when carpenters' nails came into being, they were so-called because they resembled (finger) *nails* in shape and sharpness.

naïve Also **naive** *adj.* **1** *Her big eyes and naïve questions made everyone feel protective towards her:* innocent, unaffected, unsophisticated, childlike, unspoilt, simple, artless, unjaded, plain, ingenuous, guileless, unassuming, natural, candid, open, unworldly. **2** *Don't be so naïve as to be taken in by their lies:* gullible, foolish, immature, credulous, unsuspecting, unsuspicious, unwise, green, simple, unwary, susceptible.

Ant. 1 sophisticated, disingenuous, jaded, blasé. **2** artful, sly, suspicious.

◇ *Word origin: Naïve* and *naïveté* come from French *naïf,* natural, inborn, which comes from Latin *nasci* to be born. The same Latin word gives us our words *native* and *nation.*

naïveté Also **naïvety, naivety** *n. His naïveté was obvious from the way he told everyone his life story:* innocence, artlessness, ingenuousness, candour, simplicity, naturalness, frankness, unaffectedness; credulity, wide-eyedness; inexperience, callowness, greenness; foolishness, simple-mindedness, childishness.

Ant. sophistication, worldliness, experience.

◇ *Word origin:* See NAÏVE.

naked *adj.* **1** *Naked bathing is not allowed on this beach:* nude, unclad, undressed, unapparelled, unclothed, undraped, disrobed, bared, *Informal* in the buff, in one's birthday suit. **2** *We picnicked right there on the naked sand:* uncovered, bare, laid bare, exposed, wide-open. **3** *The naked truth is that I don't want to go:* plain, simple, unvarnished, frank, blatant, sheer, bald, patent, pure, palpable, manifest, perceptible, unqualified.

Ant. 1 dressed, covered. **2** euphemized, embellished, exaggerated.

name *n.* **1** *Her name is Amanda. The scientific name of the blackbird is* Turdus merula: appellation, cognomen, title, designation; signature, denomination; term, taxonomy, nomenclature. **2** *The name for him is speedy!:* nickname, chief characteristic, sobriquet, epithet, label.
—*v.* **3** *What will you name the new baby?:* call, christen, baptize, designate, *Informal* tag, label. **4** *When will they name a successor?:* choose, delegate, appoint, nominate, commission, ordain, select, specify.

nameless *adj.* **1** *The new company is as yet nameless:* unnamed, having no name, undesignated, without a name, untitled. **2** *The best entry was by a nameless poet:* unknown, anonymous; obscure, unhonoured, unheard-of, minor.

Ant. 2 famous, well-known, renowned.

nap *v.* **1** *The baby naps every afternoon. Don't be caught napping when the monthly report is due:* doze, take a short sleep, drowse, slumber, have a catnap, doze off, drift off, drop off, nod, rest, *Informal* snooze, have forty winks; not pay attention, be off guard, be unaware.
—*n.* **2** *That six-minute nap really refreshed me:* short sleep, catnap, slumber, rest, doze, siesta, *Informal* shut-eye, forty winks.

narcotic *n. The doctor prescribed a narcotic to ease the pain:* drug, opiate, anaesthetic, medicine, medication, medicament, soporific, pain-killer, sedative, tranquillizer, medicinal drug.

◇ *Word origin: Narcotic* comes from Greek *narkōtikos,* numbing, from *narkē,* torpor, numbness.

> **Exploring the Word**: *Name* comes from Latin *nomen,* name, which also gives us: *denomination,* literally "the name written down" as of the value on a banknote or a religion or sect entered on a list; *misnomer,* a wrong name, a "misname"; *nominal,* in name only, not actually; *nominate,* to name for an office or duty, *nomination,* the act of naming someone for an office or duty, as a political candidate, and *nominee,* the one named, as to run for public office; *nomenclature,* the "names" or words used to describe something, hence the vocabulary or terminology of a specific field; *noun,* in grammar, a word used as the name of a thing, action, or quality, and *renown,* literally a name sounded over and over again, hence fame or reputation; and the French expression *nom de plume,* pen-name, and *nom de guerre,* war-name, both terms being used to mean a pseudonym.

narrate *v. They would narrate tale after tale round the camp-fire:* tell a story, set forth, recount, relate, chronicle, detail, give an account of, describe, recite, render.

◇ *Word origin: Narrate, narration,* and *narrative* come from Latin *narrare,* to relate, tell.

narration *n. I will do the narration of the tour if you'll run the projector:* story-telling, relating, speaking, telling, recitation, recital, description.

narrative *n.* **1** *The true narrative of his life was more exciting than fiction:* story, tale, chronicle, statement, account, report, recital. **2** *Doesn't his narrative remind you of Hemingway's?:* story-telling, technique of writing, fictional style; dialogue.
—*adj.* **3** *The life of St. Francis is the subject of many narrative paintings:* telling a story, involving story-telling, anecdotal, having a plot, episodic, historical.

narrow *adj.* **1** *The handle of the brush is long and narrow:* slim, not wide, slender, fine, attenuated, tapered. **2** *How can anyone work in such narrow confines?:* small, pinched, close, scant, cramped, tight, scanty, restricted, confined, squeezed, compressed, constricted. **3** *It's hard to reason with such narrow minds:* bigoted, biased, opinionated, provincial, isolated, narrow-minded, illiberal, set, dogmatic, parochial, shallow, intolerant, hidebound; conservative, reactionary.

Ant. 1 broad, wide. **2** spacious, ample, big. **3** open, liberal, receptive; radical.

narrow-minded *adj. The narrow-minded city fathers refused approval for the dance:* provincial, bigoted, strait-laced, prudish, opinionated, narrow, parochial, conservative, reactionary, one-sided; unworldly, unsophisticated.

Ant. broad-minded, inquisitive, tolerant.

narrows *n. pl. The aircraft-carrier was too big to pass through the narrows:* strait, narrow part of a body of water, passage, neck, channel, canal, pass, isthmus; ravine.

nasty *adj.* **1** *What's that nasty smell?:* foul, odious, awful, nauseating, repellent. **2** *Telling on your brother was a nasty thing to do:* vicious, beastly, mean, abominable, hateful, vile, horrible. **3** *Firing people is a nasty business:* unpleasant, distasteful, disagreeable, disgusting, awful, revolting.

Ant. 1, 3 pleasant, enjoyable, nice. **2** kind, sweet, admirable, honourable.

◇ *Word origin: Nasty* comes from Middle Dutch *nestig,* filthy. The original meaning is thought to have been "nesty," i.e. like the nest of a dirty bird.

native *adj.* **1** *When he retired, he went back to live in his native land:* of one's place of birth, of one's homeland, natal, home, paternal. **2** *His native musical ability impressed his teachers:* inherent, inborn, innate, inbred, inherited, hereditary, intrinsic, basic, congenital, elemental, natural, endemic, ingrained, instinctive. **3** *To save money, we'll use only native building materials:* local, national, indigenous, autochthonous, domestic, home-grown.

—n. **4** *The natives were friendly to the explorers:* aborigine, original inhabitant; primitive, savage. **5** *He is a native of Glasgow:* one born in a specific place, lifelong inhabitant, national, resident, citizen, countryman, countrywoman.

Ant. 1 adopted. **2** acquired, learned. **3** imported, foreign. **5** foreigner, alien.

natural *adj.* **1** *The natural history course included a study of local rocks:* of nature, earthly, terrestrial. **2** *The Giant's Causeway is a natural phenomenon:* naturally occurring, formed naturally, native, formed over time, made by nature. **3** *It takes natural talent and lots of hard work. It's natural to be upset by his tantrums:* instinctive, inborn, inherent, native, god-given, intuitive; normal, characteristic, essential, to be expected, regular. **4** *The actress hasn't one natural gesture:* unaffected, spontaneous, genuine, straightforward, plain, unstudied, unmannered, unpretentious.

Ant. 2 unnatural, artificial. **4** affected, assumed, counterfeit, feigned, calculated.

nature *n.* **1** *I'd like to leave the city and rediscover nature:* the natural world, world apart from man, created world, physical world, creation, earth, globe; cosmos, universe. **2** *A cat is by nature very clean:* instinct, constitution, disposition, bent, humour, mood; birth, character, spirit, essence; trait, characteristic, property, peculiarity, feature. **3** *What is the nature of your business?:* kind, variety, sort, type, category, style, stamp, particularity.

> **Exploring the Word:** *Nation, nature, naïve, native,* and *nativity* come from Latin *nasci* (past participle *natus*), to be born. Thus a *nation* was originally a body of persons having a common origin. What we do by *nature,* or what is *natural* or comes *naturally* was born within us or as part of us. *Naïve* literally means as innocent and unsophisticated as when newborn, and *naïveté* means newborn innocence. *Native* refers to a person born in a particular place, *nativity* means birth, and the *Nativity* is, of course, the birth of Jesus or a work of art depicting the newborn Christ child in the manger in Bethlehem. The same Latin base also gives us *natal,* of birth, and *pre-natal,* prior to birth; *innate,* inborn; *pregnant,* literally before giving birth; and even *puny,* which originally meant born after, youngest, hence weak or small, from Old French *puisne: puis* (after) + *ne* (born) and ultimately from Latin *postius* (later) + *natus* (born); *cognate,* literally born together, hence kindred, related; *nascent,* being born, beginning to exist, just developing; *renaissance* (or *renascence*), a rebirth — the European *Renaissance* was a rebirth and flowering of learning, arts, and letters.

naughty *adj.* **1** *If you're naughty, you won't get any dessert:* bad, devilish, disobedient, misbehaving, mischievous, wilful, perverse, bad, obstinate, fractious, disrespectful. **2** *His jokes are funny but naughty:* off-colour, bawdy, vulgar, rude, dirty, pornographic, blue, ribald, risqué.

◇ *Word origin: Naughty* comes from the word *naught,* nothing, and literally means "nothing, no-good," hence mischievous, disobedient.

nausea *n.* **1** *The pitching and rolling of the ship filled me with nausea:* sickness, upset stomach, queasiness, biliousness; (*variously*) travel-sickness, motion-sickness, car-sickness, seasickness, airsickness. **2** *I felt nothing but nausea for that kind of politicking:* disgust, revulsion, repulsion, contempt, loathing.

◇ *Word origin:* If you've ever been seasick, you might guess where the word *nausea* originated: from the Greek *nausiā,* literally "ship sickness," seasickness — from Greek *naûs,* meaning "ship."

nauseate *v. The food they served would nauseate a vulture:* sicken, make sick, upset, make bilious, make sick to the stomach; disgust, repulse, revolt, offend, repel.

nauseated *adj. Several people became nauseated*

after eating the tainted food. Weren't you nauseated by that speech?: sick to the stomach, sick; disgusted, revolted, repelled, upset.

nauseous *adj.* **1** *Rotten eggs are nauseous. His sense of humour is nauseous:* sickening, disgusting, unappetizing, repulsive, revolting, repellent, upsetting. **2** *I felt nauseous before the ship even sailed:* sick, nauseated, upset, queasy, sick in one's stomach.

nautical *adj. He dressed in a nautical get-up for a sail:* seagoing, of the sea, marine, oceanic, maritime, boating, aquatic, yachting, naval.

> **Exploring the Word:** Greek *naûs,* ship, and its Latin equivalent *navis,* ship, give us *navy,* ships, warships, *naval,* of ships, of warships; *nautical,* of ships, of the sea; *navigate,* literally to direct a ship on its course; and *nausea,* which literally means "ship sickness," what we call seasickness today.

navigate *v.* **1** *We navigated the channel in record time:* cross, sail across, cover the body of water, sail, cruise, ride, voyage, sail over, ride across, fly. **2** *He was trained to navigate at Dartmouth:* chart a course, plot a course; sail, manœuvre.

navigation *n. My course didn't include night navigation. His navigation of the globe took two years:* art of sailing, seamanship, piloting, sailing, navigating, travelling, boating, cruising, voyaging.

navy *n. The small country has no navy, only merchant ships:* warships, naval forces, fleet, armada, flotilla, convoy.

near *adv.* **1** *She came near when I called:* close, close by, proximately, in propinquity, hereabouts, at close quarters, alongside, next door, close to home.
—*adj.* **2** *A storm is near, I'm afraid:* close, imminent, impending, looming, approaching, threatening.
—*prep.* **3** *Are you near the end of the book?:* close to, proximate to, in the vicinity of, not far from, in range of, in sight of.
—*v.* **4** *Throw out the lines when you near the dock:* approach, come close to, move towards, come up to, draw near, advance towards, close with.
Ant. **1** distant, remote, far.
◇ *Word origin:* Originally *near* was the comparative of *nigh,* close, and meant "nearer."

"And help us, this and every day,
To live more nearly as we pray."
—*John Keble*

---

nearly *adv. I'm nearly ready to go:* about, almost, approximately, all but, just about, practically.

nearness *n. It's the nearness of the museum that attracts me:* closeness, proximity, propinquity, contiguity, adjacency, immediacy; handiness, availability, accessibility; intimacy.
Ant. remoteness, distance.

neat *adj.* **1** *He keeps his desk neat and tidy:* orderly, straight, shipshape, organized, uncluttered; immaculate, clean. **2** *He plays a neat but unimaginative game:* efficient, competent, purposive, intelligent, controlled, dextrous, methodical, systematic, succinct, concise, correct, accurate. **3** *Slang What a neat idea for jeans!:* great, exciting, striking, imaginative, ingenious, original, groovy.
Ant. **1** messy, disorderly, untidy, disorganized, cluttered. **2** inefficient, uncontrolled, incompetent. **3** bad, awful, terrible, lousy.

nebulous *adj. Our plans for the trip are still nebulous:* vague, hazy, unclear, obscure, cloudy, dim, indistinct, confused, ambiguous, uncertain, intangible, impalpable, indefinite, uncertain.
Ant. distinct, definite, precise.
◇ *Word origin: Nebulous* comes from Latin *nebula,* cloud. We still use the Latin word *nebula* in astronomy to refer to certain vast cloudlike masses of gaseous matter.

necessarily *adv. The clouds are very low but this still doesn't necessarily mean it's going to rain:* automatically, naturally, inexorably, inevitably, axiomatically, accordingly, compulsorily, of necessity, of course, perforce, unqualifiedly, incontrovertibly.

necessary *adj. Take whatever tools are necessary to get the job done:* required, needed, needful, requisite, indispensable, essential, called for, fitting, desired, wanted; imperative, urgent, crucial.
Ant. unnecessary, dispensable, non-essential, optional.

necessitate *v. The extra guests necessitated our taking two cars:* require, make necessary, enforce, cause, oblige, demand, impel, force, constrain, create a need for, compel; prescribe, call for.

necessity *n.* **1** Often **necessities** *We'll take only the bare necessities for the camping trip:* something needed, essential, indispensable, requirement, exigency, must. **2** *What's the necessity of leaving so early?:* urgency, demand, pressure, need.

need *n.* **1** *The old man has a daughter who looks after his needs:* want, requisite, requirement, necessity, demand, exigency; wish, longing; essential, desideratum. **2** *Many of our citizens are in desperate need:* poverty, want, neediness, penury, indigence, impecuniosity, destitution, pennilessness; reduced circumstances, extremity, distress, straits; insolvency, bankruptcy.
—*v.* **3** *The boy needs a heavy coat for this sort of weather:* require, lack, want, demand, find necessary, find indispensable; have use for, have need of, call for, have occasion for; exact, necessitate, make a demand of; crave, yearn for.

Ant. 2 wealth, affluence; superfluity, excess.

needless *adj. Taxi-cabs are a needless expense:* unnecessary, uncalled-for, superfluous, dispensable, gratuitous; useless, unavailing, pointless, redundant, pleonastic; excessive, over-abundant.

Ant. essential, obligatory, required, needful; useful, beneficial.

needy *adj. There are many needy families in the city:* poor, penniless, destitute, indigent, impoverished, poverty-stricken, badly off, *Slang* broke, hard-up, down-and-out, skint.

Ant. rich, affluent, wealthy, well-to-do, well-off.

nefarious *adj. He was punished for his nefarious deeds:* evil, vile, infamous, atrocious, wicked, bad, foul, abominable, base, low, odious, iniquitous, execrable, despicable, detestable; vicious, depraved; unmentionable, unspeakable; hellish, devilish, infernal, ungodly; ghastly, beastly; scandalous, villainous, heinous; shameful, disgraceful, opprobrious, dishonourable.

Ant. good, honest, honourable, just; exalted, noble; admirable, praiseworthy, laudable.

◇ *Word origin:* A *nefarious* deed is an extremely wicked one, violating the laws of God and man. *Nefarious* comes from the Latin prefix *ne-* (not) + *fas* (divine law), hence against divine law.

negate *v. This year's losses negate last year's profits:* nullify, invalidate, void, reverse; quash, squash, quell; vanquish, defeat, overthrow, overwhelm, destroy, wipe out, blot out; deny, abrogate, revoke, gainsay, retract, disavow; rebut, refute, contradict; disallow, set aside; veto, repeal; disown, disclaim, repudiate.

Ant. affirm, confirm, attest to, ratify, endorse, corroborate, reinforce, support.

negative *adj.* **1** *The vote was overwhelmingly negative:* indicating "no," disapproving, refusing, declining, rejecting, opposing, opposed; disagreeing, objecting, dissenting, demurring. **2** *You can't learn anything with a negative attitude:* antagonistic, unco-operative, opposed, contrary, inimical, at odds, dissident; doubtful, dubious, sceptical; reluctant, unwilling, unenthusiastic; gloomy, bleak, dark, pessimistic, fatalistic, jaundiced, *Informal* downbeat, blue.

Ant. 1 affirmative, positive, assenting; agreeing, approving; concurring. **2** positive, optimistic, cheerful.

◇ *Word origin: Negative* and *negate* come from Latin *negare,* to deny.

neglect *v.* **1** *He's been neglecting his bills for months:* ignore, disregard, overlook, take no notice of, take no note of; let ride, let slide, let slip, slight, pass over, pass up, let pass, omit, let go; forget, fail, lose sight of, be remiss, be inattentive; pass by, shirk; abandon, shake off.

—*n.* **2** *Neglect of his studies caused him to fail:* inattention, disregard, non-preparation; neglectfulness, laxity, laxness, negligence, remissness, idleness, dereliction, slackness, non-compliance; indifference, carelessness, fecklessness, passivity; inaccuracy, slovenliness, inexactness; slight, omission, default, oversight; unfulfilment, under-achievement.

Ant. 1 attend to, take care of, perform, notice, appreciate, regard, value, prize. **2** attention, care, notice; regard, esteem, consideration, respect.

neglectful *adj. Lately he's been neglectful of his family:* negligent, careless, thoughtless, remiss, heedless, forgetful, unmindful, unthinking, unheeding, inattentive, unobservant, unwatchful, oblivious, disregardant; lazy, slack, procrastinating; respectless, disregardful, happy-go-lucky, devil-may-care, indifferent; inconstant, untrue, unfaithful; improvident, thriftless.

Ant. attentive, thoughtful, considerate, regardful, careful.

négligé Also **negligee** *n. Her trousseau included a black négligé:* dressing-gown, robe, wrapper, housecoat, kimono, bathrobe, peignoir.

negligent *adj. He crashed into a parked car and was charged with negligent driving:* neglectful, careless, indifferent, forgetful; inconsiderate, thoughtless; unthinking, unmindful, unheeding, heedless, remiss, lax; inattentive, unobservant; untidy, slovenly.

Ant. careful, strict, rigorous; thoughtful, considerate, attentive, mindful, heedful.

negligible *adj. The interest on my small savings is negligible:* unimportant, trifling, inconsequential, insignificant, trivial, petty, paltry, piddling, small.

negotiate *v.* **1** *The Arab and Israeli leaders met to negotiate a settlement:* confer over, discuss, transact, arrange, bargain for, contract; agree to arbitration, come to terms, settle, meet half-way, adjust differences; haggle, barter, dicker. **2** *I'll need a hand to negotiate these steps:* cope with, get over, handle, deal with, manage, make. **3** *Keep those bonds in a safe place because anyone can negotiate them:* sign over, transfer, convey, make over, transmit; pass, deliver, turn over, pass over; hand over, consign; redeem, cash, cash in.

◇ *Word origin: Negotiate* comes from Latin *negotium,* business, whose elements are the Latin prefix *neg-* (not) + *otium* (leisure).

neigh *v. The horse neighed as though to hurry us up:* whinny, *Archaic* hinny.

◇ *Spelling tip:* See NEIGHBOUR.

◇ *Word origin: Neigh* comes from Old English *hnaegan,* neigh, which also gives us *nag,* an old or worthless horse, a horse only good for neighing. (*Neigh* and its Old English form are imitative of the horse whinny they represent.)

neighbour *n.* **1** *Perhaps you can borrow an axe*

from the neighbours. Canada and the United States are neighbours: person who lives nearby; adjoining country, borderer; friend, acquaintance, associate.
—*v.* **2** *Canada and Mexico neighbour the U.S.A.:* border, border on, adjoin, conjoin, abut; touch, meet, be near, verge upon; come into contact with, connect with.
◇ *Spelling tip: Neighbour* and *neigh* are often misspelt, even though they are part of the spelling rule *"i* before *e* except after *c* or when sounded like *a* as in *neighbour* and *weigh."* There is that *a* sound in *neighbour* and *neigh*, of course, so they are spelt *nEIghbour* and *nEIgh.*
◇ *Word origin: Neighbour* comes from Old English *nēah* (near) + *gebūr* (dweller), one who lives near.

neighbourhood *n.* **1** *She had to move out of that tough neighbourhood:* district, quarter, place, area, vicinity, community, part, purlieus, side, ward, confines, environs, parish. **2** *His debts are in the neighbourhood of a thousand pounds:* range, approximate amount, area, sphere, environs.

neighbouring *adj. They're visiting here from the neighbouring town:* nearby, adjacent, adjoining, close by; contiguous, abutting, bordering, lying close, close, near, next, at hand, near at hand; surrounding, circumjacent.
Ant. distant, faraway, far-off, remote.

neighbourly *adj. The townsfolk were quite neighbourly when we moved here:* friendly, courteous, sociable, polite, amiable, kindly, kind, civil, hospitable, warm-hearted, affable, considerate, helpful, cordial, well-disposed, gracious, obliging, amicable, *Informal* chummy, matey.
Ant. antagonistic, uncivil, unfriendly, remote, hostile.

nemesis *n. Billy the Kid finally met his nemesis when Pat Garrett went gunning for him:* undoing, destruction, overthrow, ruin, downfall, *Informal* Waterloo; justice, vengeance, punishment, revenge; avenger, punisher, instrument of fate; rival, match.
◇ *Word origin: Nemesis* was the Greek goddess of vengeance and retribution. Her name derives from Greek *nemein*, to dispense.

neologism Also **neology** *n. Quisling is a neologism for traitor:* nonce word, coinage.
◇ *Word origin:* A *neologism* is a new word or phrase. It comes from Greek *neo-* (new) + *logos* (word).

neophyte *n. The neophyte learned the ropes very fast:* beginner, apprentice, novice, probationer, newcomer, learner; tenderfoot, greenhorn, student, pupil; convert, proselyte, entrant, disciple, novitiate.
Ant. veteran, old hand, expert.
◇ *Word origin: Neophyte* comes from Greek *neo-* (new) + *phytos* (planted), newly planted, hence a recent convert, novice, beginner.

nerve *n.* **1** *It takes a lot of nerve to work as a steeplejack:* courage, boldness, fearlessness, pluck, grit, mettle, endurance, determination, fortitude, hardihood, stoutheartedness, coolness, hardiness, steadiness, tenacity, dash, intrepidity, bravery, strength, resoluteness, *Informal* spunk, guts, backbone; gameness, spirit, confidence, self-assurance, self-reliance; valour, gallantry, derring-do. **2** *She had some nerve to say that!:* gall, insolence, presumption, arrogance, impertinence, impudence, effrontery, *Slang* brass, crust, sauce, cheek; assurance, assumption; sauciness, flippancy, brazenness.
Ant. **1** cowardice, faint-heartedness, weakness, frailty, feebleness.
◇ *Word origin: Nerve* comes from Latin *nervus*, meaning sinew, nerve. (*Nervous* thus literally means "sinewy" and was so used by older English poets.)

"Macbeth is not sufficient proof that a nervous bloke should not commit a murder."
—*James Bridie*

---

nervous *adj. She's so nervous that she jumps at the slightest noise:* excitable, jumpy, jittery, shaky, highly-strung, sensitive, touchy; ruffled, disturbed, uneasy, excited, tremulous, skittish, fidgety, neurotic, unsettled, trembling, unstrung, tense; anxious, hysterical, wild, delirious, fearful, apprehensive, timorous, feverish; alarmed, startled; peevish, irritable, impatient.
Ant. steady, calm, tranquil, peaceful; constant, even, equable, uniform; confident, bold; serene.

nervousness *n. She's taking pills now for her nervousness:* excitability, flutter, shaking, hysteria, quivering, trembling, twitching; hypersensitivity, touchiness, timorousness, timidity; perturbation, disturbance, agitation, irritability, irascibility; tension, tremor, fidgetiness; stage fright, apprehension, anxiety, *Informal* the shakes, the creeps, the fidgets.
Ant. calm, composure, coolness, equanimity.

nestle *v. The kitten nestled in the child's arms:* lie snug, snuggle, lie, lie close, dwell, stay, remain; embrace, clasp, enfold, fondle, nuzzle, cuddle, huddle, bundle, caress, coddle, pet, cosset; live, lodge, inhabit, occupy.
◇ *Word origin: Nestle* is based on our word *nest*, and literally means to nest, snuggle up as in a nest.

net[1] *n.* **1** *A low net stretched across the tennis-court:* mesh, netting, meshwork, web, network, lattice-work, lattice; screen, screening; grid, gridiron; grate, grating; grill-work, grille; snare, trap.
—*v.* **2** *They spent the afternoon netting butterflies:* capture with a net, ensnare, snare, enmesh, trap, entangle; apprehend, seize, take, catch,

lay hold of, get hold of, take captive, take prisoner, capture; snag, snap up, clasp, clutch, grab, grip.

net[2] *v. How much did the business net last year?:* realize in profit, gain, earn, clear a profit of, clear above expenses; accumulate, gather, pick up, collect, gather in, bring in, acquire, obtain, take in.

nether *adj. Sinners are condemned to the nether regions of Hell:* lower, below, under, inferior, subjacent, downward; basal, bottom.
Ant. upper, higher, above.

neurotic *adj. He has a neurotic fear of the dark:* unhealthy, nervous, anxious; psychoneurotic, disturbed, abnormal, unstable, sick, distraught, overwrought, emotionally disordered; obsessive, intense, immoderate.
◇ *Word origin: Neurotic* originally meant "pertaining to the nerves, nervous." It comes from the Greek word for sinew or nerve, *neuron.*

neuter *adj. Some types of insects are neuter:* asexual, sexless, neutral; barren, fallow, sterile, infertile, impotent; spayed, gelded, fixed.

neutral *adj.* **1** *Ireland was a neutral nation in World War II:* non-belligerent, noncombatant, uncommitted, detached, non-participating, non-interventionist, nonpartisan, non-interfering. **2** *My uncle was neutral on the subject of women's rights:* impartial, disinterested, unbiased; indifferent, unconcerned, uninvolved; withdrawn, dispassionate, remote, aloof, unaffected; of two minds, fence-sitting; pacifist, peaceful, peaceable. **3** *We painted the room a neutral colour:* indefinite, in between, middle, medium, intermediate, half-and-half; mean, normal, average; without hue, achromatic.
Ant. 1 belligerent, active, participating, interfering. **2** partial, interested, biased, predisposed; decided, decisive. **3** positive, affirmative.
◇ *Word origin: Neutral* and *neuter* come from Latin *neuter,* neither. Hence they mean belonging to neither side or going to neither extreme.

neutralize *v. A good defence will neutralize the attack:* render ineffective, frustrate, counterbalance, nullify, negate, offset, check, block, stymie; annul, cancel, stop, halt, impede, prevent; defeat, overcome, suppress, overpower; disable, incapacitate.

never *adv. I'll never speak to her again:* at no time, nevermore, not ever, under no circumstances, on no occasion, not at all, *Poetic* ne'er.
Ant. always, for ever, eternally, evermore.

nevertheless *adv. He's charming; nevertheless I don't entirely trust him:* nonetheless, on the other hand, in spite of that, yet, but, regardless, anyhow, however, notwithstanding, though, although, in any event, even so, for all that, contrarily, contrariwise, be that as it may, when all is said and done, at all events.
◇ *Usage note: Nevertheless* is a good word, but unfortunately it is being replaced by *however.* Thus most people would say or write *It snowed heavily — however* (or just *but*) *we still drove to Chester.* That is acceptable, but *It snowed heavily — nevertheless we still drove to Chester* is the more formal way to express the idea. Use *however* or *but* in this context if you wish — but it is a pity to ignore a splendid word like *nevertheless.*

new *adj.* **1** *Did you see Sam's new car?:* recently acquired, of recent make, brand-new, just out, spanking new, up-to-date, modern, current, up-to-the-minute, newly or lately issued, *Informal* newfangled; novel, original, late, fresh, recent. **2** *We have several new clerks this week:* untried, unseasoned, unessayed, unaccustomed, unfamiliar; unused, unexercised, unventured; uncharted, unexplored; remote, out-of-the-way; untouched, ungathered, uncollected, *Informal* green, wet behind the ears. **3** *He says he feels like a new man:* restored, reinvigorated, renewed, renovated, revivified, reborn, recreated, regenerated, refreshed; fixed, repaired; rebuilt, reconstructed, remodelled; resumed, reopened; changed, altered.
Ant. 1 old, ancient, antique; stale, hackneyed, trite, passé, outmoded, old-fashioned; aged, elderly. **2** used, experienced; familiar.

newcomer *n. She and her husband are newcomers to our town:* recent arrival, stranger, outsider; entrant, comer; foreigner, immigrant, alien; novice, tiro, neophyte; intruder, trespasser, interloper.

newly *adv. Don't sit on the newly-painted chair:* freshly, recently, lately, anew, afresh, of late, not long ago, just now.

news *n. pl. Did you hear the news about the election?:* information, intelligence, tidings, bulletin, communiqué, announcement, disclosure, account; report, release, dispatch, story, article, piece; low-down, exposé, revelation, divulgence, exposure, dope; statement, *Informal* flash; message, word, rumour, talk, gossip, hearsay, chatter, mention, babble; scandal, libel, slander, dirt.

nib *n.* **1** *The nib of the pen is gold-plated:* point, tip, end; apex, vertex, top, pinnacle, tiptop; upper end, height; extreme, extremity.
◇ *Word origin: Nib* is a variant form of *neb* and comes from Old English *nebb,* beak of a bird.

nibble *v.* **1** *She sat there nibbling a biscuit:* eat sparingly, eat in small bites, gnaw; munch, crunch, chew; nip, peck, peck at.
—n. **2** *I'll just try a nibble of this cheese:* bite, taste, small piece, morsel, titbit; crumb, speck, particle, fragment.

nice *adj.* **1** *That was a nice party you gave:* good, fine, pleasant, agreeable, excellent, pleasurable; amusing, marvellous, divine, fantastic, lovely, enchanting, wonderful, entrancing, *Informal* great, super, hunky-dory. **2** *We think Helen is a nice person:* friendly, sympathetic, warm-hearted, good, kind, agreeable, amiable, cordial, genial, congenial, pleasant; charming, attractive, interesting, delightful, gracious; understanding, compassionate; winning, pleasing; cheerful, likeable. **3** *A nice girl would never go there:* proper, refined, well brought up, virtuous, respectable, genteel, well-bred, correct, ladylike, seemly. **4** *The cabinet-maker does nice work. You must be careful to recognize the "nice" distinction between food-preparation and cookery:* careful, painstaking, scrupulous, precise, meticulous, skilful, sensitive, exact; correct, accurate, methodical, unerring; strict, rigorous; subtle, delicate, deft; fastidious, finicky, fussy, punctilious, over-conscientious.

Ant. 1 dreadful, miserable, awful; unpleasant, disagreeable. **2** unfriendly, unkind, mean. **3** coarse, vulgar, ill-bred, vicious. **4** sloppy, crude, rough, careless, haphazard, undiscriminating, inaccurate.

◇ *Usage note: Nice* is a nice word and it's nice to use but not nice to overdo it! *Nice days, nice kings, nice paper, nice dogs, nice books, nice films, nice meals* — it all becomes very vague. *Nice* is often used to mean *pleasant,* and *pleasant, pleasing, agreeable, friendly, kind* are just a few synonyms that could be used instead. A *sunny* (*clear, cloudless, warm*) day, an *interesting* (*exciting, gripping, charming, amusing*) book or film, etc. Do look for more precise, specific, colourful words to use in place of *nice.*

◇ *Word origin: Nice* originally meant "innocent, simple, not aware of the bad things of the world," as in our expression "a nice girl." It comes from Latin *ne-* (not) + *scire* (to know).

"O! it's nice to get up in the mornin',
But it's nicer to lie in bed."
—*Sir Harry Lauder*

---

nicely *adv. Your arrival was nicely timed. You've made that sweater very nicely:* carefully, accurately, faultlessly, exactly, precisely, unerringly; happily, fortunately, opportunely; critically, fussily; fastidiously; attractively, neatly; pleasantly.

Ant. carelessly, haphazardly, sloppily; unfortunately; unattractively, unpleasantly.

nicety *n.* **1** *She understands the niceties of furnishing a home:* subtlety, delicacy, finer point, subtle detail, small distinction, particularity; good taste, tastefulness, flair; cultivated taste, culture, cultivation, refinement, refined feeling, fine feeling; polish, finesse, fastidiousness, grace, elegance, tact. **2** *Notice the nicety of the artist's brushwork:* meticulousness, attention to detail, delicacy, exactness, precision, preciseness, care, accuracy, attention; subtlety, minute attention, elaborateness, sensitivity; insight, penetration, acumen, perspicacity, discrimination.

Ant. 2 coarseness, roughness, crudeness, inaccuracy, sloppiness, slovenliness, haphazardness.

niche *n.* **1** *The statue was placed in a niche on the staircase:* recess, alcove, nook, cranny, cubbyhole, depression, hole in the wall; snug place, dug-out, cove, cavity; corner, hollow. **2** *He found his niche in the foreign service:* proper place, calling, suitable occupation, congenial job, vocation, trade, métier, *Slang* berth.

◇ *Word origin: Niche* comes from Latin *nidus,* nest.

◇ *Pronunciation tip: Niche* may rhyme with *hitch* or *leash.*

nick *n.* **1** *This vase has a nick on the base:* score, notch, cut, scratch, snick, mar, scoring, mark, chip, dent, indentation, jag; wound, injury, incision, scar; cleft, depression, gouge; marking.

—*v.* **2** *He nicked his chin whilst shaving:* cut, notch, scratch, snick, lacerate, score, gash, injure, scar, damage, dent; mar, deface, mark.

◇ *Word origin: Nick* could be a variant form of our word *knock.*

nickname *n. His nickname is "Bunter" because he is fat:* sobriquet, familiar name, cognomen, diminutive, *Slang* monicker, handle; appellation, designation, pseudonym, epithet; childhood name, pet name, baby name.

◇ *Word origin:* A *nickname* has nothing to do with a nick. It comes from Middle English *an ekename,* meaning added or substituted. The *eke-* part of Middle English *ekename,* nickname, means "addition." It survives in our old-fashioned poetic word *eke,* meaning "also."

niggardly *adj.* **1** *Don't be so niggardly with the mayonnaise:* stingy, miserly, parsimonious, close-fisted, tight, mean, cheap, stinting, ungenerous, illiberal, grudging, sparing, hard-fisted, close, penurious; frugal, saving, thrifty; grubbing, mercenary. **2** *That was a niggardly gift for an old friend:* wretched, mean, insufficient, paltry, poor, sorry, beggarly, second-rate, meagre, scanty, scrubby, measly; cheap, flimsy, tawdry, miserable, contemptible, shabby.

Ant. 1, 2 bountiful, liberal, generous, munificent, handsome; profuse, lavish, prodigal, copious, ample, abundant, bounteous, plentiful.

nigh *adv.* **1** *Evening draws nigh:* near, close, within sight, within view. **2** *She is nigh on 80 years old:* almost, nearly, practically, verging on, on the brink of.

—*adj.* **3** *The time for repentance is nigh:* close, close at hand, at hand, near; close by, handy; in the vicinity, adjacent, neighbouring, bordering.

Ant. 3 far, distant, remote, removed.

night *n. The guard is on duty during the night:* night-time, dark, darkness, tenebrousness; hours of sleep, bedtime; evening, nightfall, dusk; small hours, early morning; murkiness, obscurity.

nightly *adj.* **1** *The theatre gives a nightly performance. Nightly shadows enveloped the house:* night, evening, night after night; nocturnal, night-cloaked, night-mantled, night-veiled; dark, obscure.

—*adv.* **2** *The restaurant is open nightly:* every night, night after night; at night, by night, nocturnally, through the night.

Ant. 1, 2 daily, during the day, every day. **1** diurnal. **2** diurnally.

nightmare *n. The child awoke suddenly from a nightmare:* bad dream; frightening vision, hallucination; incubus, succubus.

◇ *Word origin:* A *nightmare* has nothing to do with a *mare,* meaning a horse, but with an obsolete word *nihtmare,* meaning a female incubus. The *-mare* part of the word comes from Old English *mare,* witch.

nihilism *n. His rejection of all philosophies amounted to nihilism:* disbelief in anything, scepticism, universal doubt, agnosticism, amorality; nothingness, emptiness, non-existence; anarchism, radicalism, iconoclasm; lawlessness, irresponsibility, licence, chaos; terrorism; alienation, anomy.

Exploring the Word: *Nihil* is the Latin word for "nothing." From it we get *nihilism,* "nothing-ism," creed of many 19th-century bomb-throwing anarchists; *annihilate* to bring to nothing, destroy; *annul,* to reduce to nothing, put an end to, and *nil,* nothing, none, naught.

nil *n. My interest in the plan is nil:* non-existent, none, naught, nothing whatever, zero.

nimble *adj. He was nimble enough to jump the fence. A nimble mind:* agile, light-footed, nimble-footed, spry, supple; animated, spirited, swift, quick, mercurial, fleet-footed, speedy, lively, sprightly, active, quick as lightning, fleet, rapid, quick moving; light, deft, skilful, dextrous; expert, proficient; prompt, ready.

Ant. clumsy, slow, awkward, dull, heavy, inert, inactive; lethargic, lazy, indolent.

◇ *Word origin:* A *nimble* mind is quick to grasp ideas and nimble fingers can grab things quickly. *Nimble* comes from Old English *nīman,* to grasp, take.

nincompoop *n. Slang That nincompoop put the papers in the wrong file:* ninny, dunce, hare-brain, feather-brain, scatter-brain, simpleton, blockhead, jackass, bonehead, rattle-brain, noodle, fool, duffer, fathead, chump, cretin, ass, dunderhead, numskull; dim-wit, dolt, nitwit, half-wit; moron, idiot, imbecile; dope, dummy, jerk, clot, *German* dummkopf.

◇ *Word origin:* No one knows for sure where our word *nincompoop* comes from but it seems likely that it comes from the first two words of the Latin phrase *non compos mentis,* not of sound mind.

nip *v.* **1** *John nipped his finger with the pliers:* pinch, tweak, squeeze; clutch, seize, snag, grab, snare, grasp, clasp, grip, snatch; snap, compress. **2** *Don't nip any stalks off the plant till it's finished flowering:* cut off, lop, snip, cut, clip, dock, crop; cut short, abbreviate, curtail, shorten; snap, crack, shear, sever, sunder. **3** *The government nipped the rebellion in the bud:* check, cut off, curtail, put an end to, demolish, finish off, quash, deal a knock-out blow to, destroy, ruin, crush; blast, thwart. **4** *A sharp wind nipped our cheeks and noses:* freeze, chill, frost; pierce, bite, cut; chill, benumb, make one shiver.

nobility *n.* **1** *The nobility favoured the king's abdication:* noble classes, upper classes, aristocracy, ruling classes, élite, peerage, lords, patricians, patriciate; royalty; high society, *Informal* Beautiful People, upper crust, the Establishment, blue blood, *French* noblesse. **2** *He is remembered for the nobility of his character:* greatness, superiority, sublimity, exaltedness, dignity, loftiness, stateliness, mightiness; distinction, eminence, grandness, grandeur, prestige; pre-eminence, supremacy, primacy; majesty, splendour, magnificence. **3** *Documents disclosed the nobility of his birth:* nobleness, aristocracy, gentility, exalted condition, high rank, high station, distinction, breeding, high breeding.

Ant. 1 lower classes, peasantry, plebeians, obscurity, insignificance, meanness. **2** lowness, meanness, baseness, ignobility.

◇ *Word origin:* See NOBLE.

noble *adj.* **1** *The minstrel boy was really of noble birth:* exalted, high-born, patrician, gentle, high, high-ranking, aristocratic, distinguished, pure-blooded, blue-blooded, thoroughbred, superior; princely, royal. **2** *In keeping with his noble character, he left his fortune to charity:* great, lofty, selfless, superior, magnanimous, excellent, exemplary, elevated, eminent; moral, virtuous, upright, meritorious, incorruptible, just, trustworthy, honourable, estimable, worthy, reputable, high-principled, honest, ethical. **3** *Noble mansions line the river-bank:* stately, grand, majestic, lordly, baronial, imposing, impressive, splendid, magnificent, superb, handsome; awesome, awe-inspiring; glorious, supreme, sublime; famed, renowned, famous, pre-eminent; dignified, courtly, lordlike, distinguished; lofty, regal, imperial.

—*n.* **4** *Many of the nobles joined the uprising:* aristocrat, nobleman, patrician, grandee, peer, lord, thoroughbred; gentleman, chevalier, knight, cavalier, squire; great man, man of distinction, personage.

Ant. 1 lowborn, lowly, humble, plebeian, peasant, mean. **2** ignoble, base, selfish, despicable, contemptible, vulgar, doubtful, dishonest. **3** insignificant, modest, drab, mean, paltry, plain. **4** peasant, commoner, serf; scoundrel.

◇ *Word origin: Noble,* like *nobility,* comes from Latin *nobilis,* noble, which originally meant "well-known, renowned."

nocturnal *adj. Some animals are nocturnal and are never seen in daylight at all. Nocturnal clouds portended a storm:* night, night-time, of the night, active by night, nightly; night-cloaked, night-veiled, night-hidden; dark, obscure, darkling.

Ant. diurnal, daily, by day.

nod *v.* **1** *She nodded to us from across the room:* incline the head, bow one's head, bend the neck, make obeisance; shake up and down, lower and raise, bob; acknowledge, recognize, give salutation, greet, salute, hail, say hello. **2** *The judge nodded his assent:* express with a nod, indicate by nodding, reveal, show, signify, signal, beckon, motion, sign, gesture; agree, consent, assent, concur. **3** *We began to nod as the speech dragged on:* doze, fall asleep, go to sleep; drop off, fall off; drowse, be torpid or languid, be inactive; be forgetful, be negligent, lapse, let up.

—n. **4** *His nod means a higher bid:* quick bowing of the head; signal, sign, gesture.

node *n.* **1** *The trunk of the oak tree is full of nodes:* knot, woody formation, burl, joint, bud, lump, bump, nodule, prominence, protuberance, swelling, knob, bulge, button, hump; tumescence, excrescence.

◇ *Word origin: Node* comes from Latin *nodus,* knot. *Nodule* is the diminutive form of this Latin word and hence means "little knot."

nodule *n. The roots of the bean plant are covered with nodules:* knob, outgrowth, protuberance, bump, lump, node, stud, knot, sac; projection, protrusion, prominence; swelling, tumescence, bulge; excrescence.

> "... pray do not imagine that those who make the noise are the only inhabitants of the field."
> —*Edmund Burke*

noise *n.* **1** *Those planes make an awful noise:* sound, din, racket, clamour, uproar, pandemonium, clatter, bedlam, tumult, babel, hullabaloo, blare, wail, boom, blast, bang, rumble, rumbling; barrage, thunder, cannonade; hubbub, commotion, stir, ado; discharge, report, reverberation, echo; dissonance, cacophony; roar, vociferation; bluster, caterwauling; shouting, brawling.

—v. **2** *Don't noise it abroad, but he's retiring:* spread as news, circulate, repeat, pass, voice, rumour, bruit, *Slang* blab.

Ant. 1 quiet, silence, hush, stillness; peace, calm; harmony, melody.

noisy *adj. The streets are always noisy at 5 p.m.:* loud, rackety, clamorous, deafening, ear-splitting, uproarious, turbulent, blaring, strident, boisterous, thunderous, thundering, tumultuous, tempestuous, raging, stormy, resounding; alive, animated, lively; furious, rampageous; grating, jarring, harsh-sounding; dissonant, discordant; blatant, clangorous; shrill, piercing, cacophonous.

Ant. quiet, silent, subdued, hushed, still; melodious, tuneful.

nomad *n. Many Lapps were nomads until the U.S.S.R. cut off their migration route:* wanderer, itinerant, mover, rambler, roamer, strayer, migrator, migrant, traveller, rover, vagabond, bohemian, gipsy, knight of the road, stray, straggler; refugee, runaway, renegade; immigrant, emigrant.

◇ *Word origin: Nomads* are (in the original sense of the word) tribes or groups of people who move from place to place with the seasons to find new grazing lands for their cattle, sheep, or camels. The word comes from Greek *nemein,* to graze. The related Greek word for "one who migrates with grazing animals" is *nomas.* Its plural form *nomades,* "pastoral people," is used by Herodotus and other Greek writers to designate the Scythians and the Arabians.

nomadic *adj. The Bedouins of Arabia are a nomadic people:* travelling, wandering, roaming, roving, migratory, itinerant, strolling, peregrinating vagabond, peripatetic, vagrant.

nom de plume *n. Charles Dodgson's nom de plume was "Lewis Carroll":* pen name, writing name; pseudonym, assumed name; false name, alias.

◇ *Word origin: Nom de plume* is a French phrase literally meaning "pen-name." Incidentally, *nom de guerre* is the French phrase meaning "name of war," a war-name, hence an assumed name, especially as used on secret missions or when one is in danger.

nomenclature *n. In the nomenclature of botany, a tomato is a berry:* terminology, phraseology, vocabulary, terms; naming, nomination, appellation, designation, taxonomy; language, jargon, lingo.

nominal *adj.* **1** *He is just the nominal head of the company; the deputy chairman really runs it:* titular, ostensible, in name only, so-called, theoretical, official; purported, professed; pretended, suggested; baseless, groundless; puppet. **2** *There will be a nominal charge for admission:* small, low, minimum, moderate, reasonable, inexpensive, low-priced, cheap; unsubstantial, insignificant.

Ant. 1 veritable, actual, real, true. **2** considerable, substantial.

nominate *v.* **1** *I nominate Bill for club president:* name as a candidate, propose, suggest, recommend, put forward; label, tag, call, term, style. **2** *The Prime Minister nominated him to be Ambassador to France:* name, pick, choose; authorize, place in authority, elevate, elect, install, select, invest.

nomination *n. He has a good chance of winning the nomination:* choice of a candidate, selection, election, designation; submission of a name, suggestion; appointment, installation; accession, inauguration, investiture.

nonchalant *adj. How can he be so nonchalant in all this trouble?:* unconcerned, blasé, unheeding, imperturbable, unexcited, unemotional, unmoved, unaffected, unstirred, unruffled, cool, collected; offhand, casual, easy-going; indifferent, apathetic, lazy, uninterested, insouciant; withdrawn, dispassionate, unmindful, heedless, insensible; languid, phlegmatic, listless, lethargic, indolent, idle, careless; slack, lax.

Ant. concerned, moved, affected, stirred; anxious, agitated.

◇ *Word origin:* A *nonchalant* person shows little excitement or desire. He is cool toward things. The word comes from Latin *non* (not) + *calere* (to be warm).

non-committal *adj. She gave me a non-committal answer:* indefinite, vague, evasive; reserved, guarded, cautious, wary, careful, circumspect; tentative, ambiguous, temporizing; safe, cool, politic, prudent, discreet; mute, mum, unspeaking.

Ant. definite, decisive, positive, conclusive.

nonconformist *n. The Pilgrims were nonconformists who went to America to avoid persecution:* dissenter, individualist, loner, free spirit, liberated person, protester, heretic, rebel, revolutionary, radical, iconoclast; eccentric, exception, original, oddity; insurgent, maverick, deserter, renegade; free thinker, bohemian, vagabond, beat, hippy, *Informal* character, *Slang* oddball, crackpot, odd fish, weirdo, freak, nut, card.

nondescript *adj. The thief was so nondescript that no one could recall his face:* undistinctive, usual, ordinary, vague, unexceptional, unimpressive, undistinguished, stereotyped.

Ant. distinctive, unusual, extraordinary, vivid, unique.

nonentity *n. We hear that she has married a nonentity:* nobody, unimportant person, mediocrity, small-fry, nothing, nullity, *Informal* small beer, light-weight; Tom, Dick or Harry.

Ant. celebrity, somebody, VIP.

non-essential *adj.* **1** *Beer and cigarettes are non-essential items:* inessential, unnecessary, not vital, unimportant; extraneous, superfluous, irrelevant, subsidiary, incidental, accidental, extrinsic, peripheral, secondary; dispensable, disallowable, unconnected, beside the point, impertinent, inappropriate; insignificant, trivial, inconsequential, inconsiderable.

—*n.* **2** *The new budget cuts out all non-essentials:* unessential thing, unnecessary item, incidental; luxury, (*plural*) trimmings, trivia.

Ant. 1 vital, essential, important; apt, appropriate; significant.

non-partisan *adj. Adoption agencies should be non-partisan:* unaffiliated, non-political, politically independent; unbiased, unprejudiced; impartial; unswayed, uninfluenced; equitable, fair, just; uninvolved, disinterested, unimplicated; impersonal, objective; free-thinking, unbigoted.

Ant. partisan, political; biased, prejudiced; unfair, unjust, inequitable.

nonplus *v. The child was nonplussed by all the TV cameras:* confuse, confound, muddle, baffle, bother, abash, disconcert, discountenance, disturb, upset, dismay, embarrass, faze; perplex, puzzle, bewilder, stump, mystify; flabbergast, astound, dumbfound, put at a loss, astonish; stop, halt, bring to a standstill, stymie, deadlock, balk, foil.

◇ *Word origin:* When you are *nonplussed*, you are at a mental standstill, speechless, or at a loss. The word comes from the Latin phrase *non plus*, no further.

"Nine-tenths of existing books are nonsense, and the clever books are the refutation of that nonsense." —*Benjamin Disraeli*

---

nonsense *n. If you're going to talk nonsense, I won't listen:* foolishness, folly, ridiculousness, absurdity, stupidity, inanity, senselessness, silliness, childishness; fooling, tomfoolery, joking, monkey business, horseplay, high jinks, antics; ludicrousness, meaninglessness, facetiousness; triviality, frivolity, extravagance, flummery, trifles; prattle, babble, chatter, blather, drivel, gibberish, *Informal* twaddle, bunk, trash, garbage, rubbish, hog-wash, moonshine, rot, fiddle-faddle, piffle, flapdoodle; bombast, claptrap, balderdash, bosh, *Slang* baloney.

Ant. sense, common sense, wisdom; fact, reality, truth; gravity, seriousness, reason.

nook *n. He peered into every nook and cranny:* recess, niche, corner; depression, cubby-hole, cavity, dug-out; cove, snug place, inglenook, retreat, haven, lair; hiding-place, den, hide-out.

noon *n. The workers took their lunch at noon:* midday, twelve o'clock, twelve noon; noonday, high noon, noontide, lunch-time; zenith, meridian, highest point.

◇ *Word origin: Noon* comes from the Latin *nona hora,* the ninth hour, and originally meant the ninth hour after sunrise, or almost 3 p.m.

norm *n. A Beta plus is the norm in our grading system:* standard, average, rule, type; pattern, model, par; yardstick, criterion, measure.

◇ *Word origin:* See NORMAL.

normal *adj. His growth is quite normal for that age:* standard, average, usual, ordinary, expected, natural, regular; conformable, conforming, consistent; typical, par, representative, conventional; constant, steady, unchanging; steadfast, reliable, dependable; in good order, well-regulated, in shape, fit, sound, healthy; continuous, uninterrupted; incessant, unceasing, unremitting, unchanging, uniform; sane, reasonable, rational, right-minded; middling, mediocre.

Ant. abnormal, unusual, exceptional, irregular; peculiar, rare, singular, uncommon; unprecedented, remarkable; unnatural.

◇ *Usage note: Normality* is commonly used to denote a normal physical or mental state: *Psychotherapy might help restore him to normality. Normalcy* is used chiefly in the U.S.A. to denote a normal, healthy state of affairs politically and economically: *After the war the country slowly returned to normalcy.* This use of *normalcy* was coined by the American President Warren Harding. The newspapers reacted violently, for in the view of many, *normalcy* was a "barbarism" for *normality.* But he said he had looked it up in the dictionary. He probably had. It was there — it goes back to the 1850's, in the mathematical sense. (Incidentally, the first recorded use of *normality* was by Edgar Allen Poe, in 1848.)

◇ *Word origin: Normal* and *norm* come from Latin *norma*, ruler, carpenter's square. Thus the *norm* is the ruler or the standard and what is *normal* follows the ruler or the standard measure.

north *adj.* **1** *That north wind is really chilling:* coming from the north, northerly; northern; polar, arctic; northernmost; upper.

—adv. **2** *Leaving the city, we headed north:* toward the north, northward; northerly.

nostalgia *n. Those old recordings give him a feeling of nostalgia:* longing for the past, bitter-sweet memory; remembrance; homesickness, longing for home; pining, languishing; regret, remorse, wistfulness.

◇ *Word origin: Nostalgia* comes from Greek *nostos* (home-coming) + *algos* (pain). The word is first recorded in 1770, when it was used as a medical term for melancholia caused by homesickness.

nostrum *n. This is an old nostrum my grandmother used to treat stomach-ache:* remedy, medicine, formula, medicament; physic, balm, elixir, drug, potion; treatment, cure, cure-all, panacea; dose, draught, prescription; patent medicine.

◇ *Word origin:* Patent medicines containing secret ingredients formerly bore the label *nostrum* (Latin for "ours," i.e. "of our own make").

nosy Also **nosey** *adj. Don't be so nosy — this doesn't concern you:* inquisitive, curious, prying, intrusive, snooping.

notable *adj.* **1** *There is a notable difference in their ages:* conspicuous, marked, pronounced, noticeable, salient, outstanding, remarkable, striking. **2** *A notable doctor performed the operation:* renowned, reputable, famed, famous, celebrated, prominent, eminent, well-known.

—n. **3** *The convention attracted many notables:* celebrity, dignitary, luminary, personage, *Informal* VIP, bigwig, *Slang* star, toff.

Ant. 1 vague, ill-defined; imperceptible, concealed, hidden. **2** unknown, anonymous, obscure, little known.

notably *adv. The turn-out at the lecture was notably small:* strikingly, markedly, noticeably, outstandingly, prominently, conspicuously, visibly; distinctly, unmistakably.

notch *n.* **1** *He made a notch on the tree for each day that passed:* nick, cut, dent, indentation, score, scoring. **2** *This restaurant is a notch above the others:* degree, level, grade, *Slang* cut.

—v. **3** *We notched our heights on the tree trunk:* nick, score, cut, mark, scratch.

"What in May escaped detection,
August, past surprises,
Notes, and names each blunder."
—*Robert Browning*

---

note *n.* **1** *Make a note to get some more milk:* memorandum. **2** *Drop Mary a note to thank her:* brief letter, message, epistle, missive, communication; dispatch, communiqué; memorandum, *Informal* line. **3** *He paid the bill in £5 notes:* banknote, paper money; legal tender, money, currency; voucher, certificate, treasury note; draft, bank draft; promissory note, mortgage note, *Slang* smacker. **4** *Take note of the lavish table decorations:* regard, notice. **5** *Several persons of note were at the party:* importance, consequence, distinction, prominence, eminence, notability, reputation, fame, renown, celebrity.

—v. **6** *Note his name and address in your book:* make a note of, record, set down, put down, enter, write, write down, jot down, make a memorandum of, make an entry of. **7** *We noted his reluctance to testify:* notice, mark, perceive, take cognizance of, give attention to, take notice of, be aware of, be conscious of.

Ant. 4 inattention, indifference, heedlessness, aloofness, unconcern. **5** obscurity, insignificance. **7** ignore, disregard, overlook.

noted *adj. A noted surgeon operated on him:* famous, renowned, eminent, celebrated, well-known, distinguished, prominent, illustrious, reputable; remarkable, notable, noteworthy, outstanding.

Ant. unknown, obscure, undistinguished; notorious, infamous.

noteworthy *adj. The book is a noteworthy addition to our library:* distinguished, outstanding, sig-

nificant, important, remarkable, notable; substantial, considerable.
Ant. negligible, trivial, inconsequential.

> **Exploring the Word:** *Note* comes from Latin *notare,* to note, mark, which also gives us *notation,* a note, set of symbols, or a sign or figure that notes something; *annotate,* to make notes on or about something, to add notes to; *notice,* to note in one's mind; *notion,* a mental note, opinion, belief, or idea; *notify,* literally to make a note to another, to make something known to another as by a note; *denotation,* that which is noted down as a word's specific or explicit meaning, as in a dictionary, and *connotation,* that which is noted together with or in addition to a word's specific meaning, hence an added meaning it suggests, as in an individual's mind depending on his personal experience ("winter" has a good connotation to a skier and a bad one to a sunbather); *notable,* worthy of note, a person noted for his deeds or importance, or easily noted, conspicuous; *notorious* and *notoriety,* widely noted or widely known, and generally disapproved; and *notary public,* originally a public writer of official notes, now usually one who witnesses signatures of official "notes" or documents.

nothing *n.* **1** *There is nothing for dinner. His latest play is nothing:* naught, no thing, nullity; insignificance, obscurity; trash, stuff, rubbish; bubble, air; bauble, bagatelle, trifle, gewgaw, trinket; trivia, inconsequence. **2** *Multiply 2 by 0, and the answer will be nothing:* zero, nought, cipher, love, *Slang* duck's egg, nix.
◇ *Usage note: For nothing* meaning "free, without cost, gratis," is perfectly acceptable, as in *He let me have the tickets for nothing.*

notice *n.* **1** *The plan is not worth our notice:* attention, regard, cognizance, heed. **2** *Did you receive any notice about the sale?:* information, mention, notification, specification; intelligence, knowledge, *Slang* gen, dope; statement, declaration, communication, disclosure; poster, handbill, circular, leaflet; pamphlet, brochure; advertisement, announcement. **3** *She gave two weeks' notice before she left:* warning, notification. **4** *The paper gave the play a bad notice:* review, critique, appraisal, rating.
—*v.* **5** *Did you notice her engagement ring?:* see, catch sight of, observe, eye, take in, take notice of, mark, *Slang* get a load of.
Ant. 1 oversight, disregard, neglect, slight, connivance, omission, heedlessness; misinformation, ignorance. **5** ignore, slight, overlook, disregard, neglect; misjudge.

noticeable *adj. There's a noticeable difference in our totals:* definite, clear, plain, distinct, evident, obvious, conspicuous, unmistakable; striking, noteworthy, perceivable, perceptible, appreciable, observable, manifest, palpable.

notify *v. You will, of course, notify us of the next rent increase:* inform, acquaint, advise, tell, apprise; warn, brief, instruct.

notion *n.* **1** *I have no notion of what he means:* idea, concept, suspicion. **2** *I never knew anyone with such odd notions:* belief, opinion; whim, quirk, caprice, fancy; whimsy, conceit, humour, vagary, fancy, eccentricity.

notorious *adj. The guest was really a notorious jewel thief:* infamous, nefarious, arrant; widely known, renowned, notable, celebrated, outstanding.

nought *n. Eight followed by three noughts represents the number 8,000:* zero, ought; a cipher (0); nothing, nil, *Slang* blob.
◇ *Word origin: Nought* comes from Old English *nōwiht,* no whit or nothing.

nourish *v. They needed good food to nourish their bodies:* nurture, feed, sustain.
Ant. starve, undernourish.
◇ *Word origin: Nourish* comes from Latin *nutrire,* to breast-feed, to nourish, which also gives us *nutrition, nurture,* and *nurse.*

nourishment *n. She's beginning to recover now and take a little nourishment:* food, sustenance, nutriment, nutrition, viands, victuals, comestibles, food and drink, *Slang* eats, chow, grub.

novel *adj. That's a novel way to do your hair:* unusual, original, new, different, out of the ordinary, uncommon, singular, unique.
Ant. usual, customary, run-of-the-mill, habitual, ordinary, common, familiar, venerable, ancient, old-fashioned, time-honoured, traditional.
◇ *Word origin: Novel, novelty,* and *novice* all come from Latin *novus,* new. Thus something *novel* is new or unusual and a *novel* is a book-length piece of fiction created (hence unique and "new") by the author, a *novelty* is something new or unusual, and a *novice* is a person new at something, a beginner or recent convert.

novelty *n.* **1** *There's little novelty in his writing:* originality, newness, uniqueness, innovation. **2** *The shop sells novelties to tourists:* trinket, gewgaw, gimcrack, bagatelle, bauble, knick-knack; token, souvenir, memento.

novice *n. He's a novice on the football field:* beginner, tiro, learner, apprentice, newcomer; greenhorn, tenderfoot, amateur; pupil, student, disciple.
Ant. master, old hand, past master, professional, *Informal* pro.
◇ *Word origin:* see NOVEL.

noxious *adj. The room was filled with noxious fumes:* harmful, poisonous, deleterious, injurious, baneful, damaging, pernicious, hurtful; putrid, putrescent, noisome, foul, foul-smelling, abominable, beastly, revolting, loathsome, disgusting.
Ant. wholesome, beneficial; sanitary, salutary, salubrious.

◇ *Word origin: Noxious* comes from Latin *noxa*, harm. The related Latin word *nocere*, to harm, also gives us *innocent* (not having harmed) and *nuisance*.

nuance *n. This poem admirably expresses different nuances of feeling:* subtle change, nice distinction, delicate distinction; nicety, shade, subtlety, refinement, delicacy, fineness, finesse; keenness, sharpness, discernment.

◇ *Word origin:* A *nuance* is a shade of feeling or meaning, a subtle variation. The word comes from French *nuer*, to show variations of shade like a cloud (ultimately derived from Latin *nubes*, cloud). *Nuance* was first used in our language by Horace Walpole (1717-1797), in a letter written in 1781.

nub *n.* **1** *Put a nub of coal on the fire:* hump, knot, lump, knob, node; bulge, swelling, tumescence, protuberance, prominence, projection. **2** *The nub of the question is whether he is guilty or innocent:* essence, heart, core, kernel.

◇ *Word origin: Nub* is a variant form of *knob*.

nucleus *n. Retired employees make up the nucleus of the club:* core, nub, heart, kernel, centre.

Ant. exterior, face, integument; outer shell; appearance, features.

◇ *Word origin: Nucleus* means kernel or inner part in Latin, just as it does in English. The word is a diminutive form of *nux*, nut. (Latin *nux* and English *nut* are ultimately derived from a common Indo-European ancestor-word.)

nude *adj. The nude statue caused considerable comment:* naked, stark naked, bare, unclad, mother-naked, undressed, exposed, unclothed, unarrayed, unadorned, uncovered, wearing nothing, *Informal* stripped to the buff, without a stitch; *Slang* raw, in one's birthday suit.

Ant. clothed, covered, dressed, apparelled, clad.

◇ *Word origin: Nude* comes from Latin *nudus*, naked.

nudge *v. She nudged me at all the funny lines:* elbow, poke, jab, punch; bump, jostle, jolt, jog; push, touch, shove; motion, signal, indicate; dig in the ribs.

"The liberty of the individual must be thus far limited; he must not make himself a nuisance to other people." —*John Stuart Mill*

---

nuisance *n. That noisy fan is a real nuisance:* annoyance, bother, pest, bore, irritation, aggravation; inconvenience, botheration; worry, fret; scourge, affliction; handicap, misfortune; grievance, vexation; plague, pestilence, blight, curse; trouble, hurt, torment, burden.

Ant. pleasure, delight, satisfaction, benefit, blessing, gratification, happiness, joy.

◇ *Word origin:* A *nuisance* is anything that annoys or is a little harmful. The word comes from Old French *nuisance*, injury, and is ultimately derived from Latin *nocere*, to injure.

null *adj. The contract is null and void because the employer has broken it:* invalid, inoperative, non-existent, worthless, valueless, no good.

Ant. valid, lawful, binding.

◇ *Word origin: Null* comes from Latin *nullus*, none. (The neuter form of the same Latin word, *nullum*, means "nothing.")

nullify *v. Such an out-of-date law should be nullified:* repeal, abrogate, void, make void, cancel, annul, declare null and void, abolish; set aside, retract, revoke, rescind.

Ant. enact, decree, legislate, ratify, confirm; establish, institute.

numb *adj. My thumb was numb after I hit it:* unfeeling, insensate, benumbed, insensible, dead, deadened.

number *n.* **1** *Assign a number to each box:* numeral, figure, character, symbol, integer, cipher, digit; round number, even or odd number; amount, quantity, sum, aggregate, tally, total. **2** *A large number of guests came to the reception:* quantity, multitude, company, assembly, group, crowd, *Informal* mob, mass, bunch, herd, swarm; abundance, preponderance; indefinite number, indeterminate number; a good many, a great number; scores, quantities; host, army; bevy, array. **3** *There's a story about her in the current number:* issue, edition; book, magazine, quarterly; chapter, section, part, division; paragraph, passage.

—*v.* **4** *Number the pages in sequence. The guests numbered more than a hundred:* give a number to, enumerate; cipher; paginate, foliate, numerate; tally, tot up, reckon, count, total; compute, calculate; estimate, make an estimate of.

Ant. 2 scarcity, fewness, scantiness, paucity; want, lack; shortage, insufficiency. **4** guess, hazard, hypothesize, theorize, conjecture; lump, mass.

◇ *Usage note:* (1) For the differences between *number* and *amount*, see the Usage note at AMOUNT. (2) For the differences between *number* and *numeral*, see the Usage note at NUMERAL.

◇ *Word origin: Number, numeral* and *numerous* come from Latin *numerus*, number, which also gives us *enumerate* (to count out) and *innumerable* (not countable, too numerous to be counted).

numeral *n. The numerals on the clock are painted gold:* number, symbol, character, figure, cipher, digit, integer; cardinal number, Arabic or Roman numeral.

◇ *Usage note:* In technical use, a *numeral* is any character, symbol, letter, or word used to represent a number. Thus the number *two* can be represented by the following numerals: *2, II, ii.* The numbers *18* and *81* are different but contain the same *numerals*,

8 and *1*. In general — that is, non-technical use — *number* is often used for *numeral* and is completely acceptable.

numerous *adj. The bride and groom received numerous gifts:* many, in profusion, copious, abundant, plentiful, a multitude of.

Ant. few, scarcely any, not many.

◇ *Word origin:* See NUMBER.

numskull Also **numbskull** *n. Slang The numskull didn't even know the alphabet!:* dunce, ninny, scatter-brain, blockhead, bonehead, dolt, half-wit, duffer, moron, dummy, dunderhead, silly ass, dim-wit, dullard, nitwit, idiot, imbecile, cretin, ass, noodle, fathead, fool, simpleton, jerk, dope, clot, sap, dummkopf, nincompoop.

nuptial *adj. The nuptial ceremony was very brief:* matrimonial, wedding, marital; conjugal, connubial, hymeneal.

◇ *Word origin: Nuptial* comes from Latin *nuptiae*, nuptials, from *nubere*, to marry, which also gives us *nubile*, marriageable.

nuptials *n. pl. The nuptials were held in the bride's parish:* wedding, marriage, marriage ceremony, marriage service, wedlock, exchange of vows.

nurse *n.* **1** *The children were left with their nurse:* (*variously*) trained nurse, hospital nurse, registered nurse, private nurse, matron, sister; district nurse, public health nurse; governess, nanny, nursemaid; nursery-maid, nursery nurse, wet-nurse; guardian, attendant. —*v.* **2** *His wife nursed him back to health:* tend, care for, minister to, attend to; doctor, treat, remedy. **3** *The mother cat refused to nurse her kittens:* suckle, feed at the breast, wet-nurse, give suck to; succour, nourish, feed; foster, nurture, cultivate. **4** *He's been nursing a grudge for weeks:* keep in mind, bear in mind, have in mind; harbour, nurture, encourage, foster, promote.

Ant. neglect, disregard, slight; starve, kill, destroy.

◇ *Word origin: Nurse* comes from Latin *nutrire*, to breast-feed, to nourish. This same Latin verb gives us *nourish, nutriment, nutrition, nurture*, and *nursery* (a place where children or plants are nourished).

nursery *n.* **1** *The children spent their mornings at the nursery:* nursery school, day nursery, playgroup, kindergarten, day-school, infant school; playroom, schoolroom. **2** *We bought a small tree at the nursery:* greenhouse, botanical garden, arboretum, cold frame, conservatory, forcing-house; breeding-place, hotbed, incubator.

nurture *v.* **1** *The book told us how to nurture the puppy:* feed, nourish, foster, tend, sustain, maintain, look after, strengthen; provision. **2** *The school is responsible for nurturing the child's mind:* train, discipline, develop, prepare, cultivate, tutor, school, educate, teach, instruct; bring up, rear, breed, raise.

Ant. **2** neglect, overlook, slight; disregard, ignore; deprive, dispossess.

◇ *Word origin:* See NURSE.

nut *n.* **1** *A bowl of nuts stood on the table:* edible kernel; seed, stone. **2** *Slang You must be off your nut to do such a crazy thing:* head, mind, senses, reason, sanity, *Informal* top. **3** *Slang That nut should be locked up:* eccentric, crackpot, crank, odd fish, freak; madman, lunatic, maniac, loony; idiot; psychopath.

nutriment *n. They invented a synthetic nutriment for space-men:* food, nourishment, foodstuff, *Slang* eats, chow; nutrition, sustenance, subsistence, provisions, aliment; provender, feed, forage, mess, fodder, fare; groceries, viands, eatables, board, daily bread.

◇ *Word origin:* See NURSE.

nutrition *n. A balanced diet gives one the proper nutrition:* food, nourishment, nutriment, foodstuffs, eatables, diet, sustenance; groceries, provisions, rations, subsistence, *Slang* chow, grub; provender, pasturage, forage, fodder; silage, feed.

◇ *Word origin:* See NURSE.

nutritious *adj. The diet is nutritious but low in calories:* nourishing, nutritive.

nuzzle *v. The child nuzzled the kitten:* cuddle, coddle, snuggle, nestle, caress, embrace, fondle; pet, cosset, pat; kiss.

◇ *Word origin:* To *nuzzle* is literally to rub one's nose against someone. *Nuzzle* is an old diminutive form of the word *nose* (as in *nozzle*).

nymph *n. The painting showed nymphs and shepherds at play:* female nature spirit, naiad, dryad, sylph, wood-nymph.

◇ *Word origin: Nymph* comes from Greek *numphē*, bride, young girl, female nature spirit.

O

oaf *n. That oaf wouldn't know a good job if he saw one:* dolt, lout, boob, booby, dunderhead, numskull, bonehead, blockhead, dunce, dullard, simpleton, twerp, ninny, nitwit, clod, ignoramus, nincompoop, moron, idiot, imbecile, half-wit, *Slang* jerk, sap, dope, dummy.
Ant. genius, intellectual, pundit, sage, guru, *Slang* egghead, boffin.

oasis *n.* **1** *The road went through several oases in the desert:* watering-place, water-hole; fertile area, green spot. **2** *The library was an oasis of quiet:* haven, refuge, harbour, sanctuary, asylum, shelter.
Ant. 1 desert, arid region.

oath *n.* **1** *Every peer of the realm swears an oath of allegiance to the Queen:* vow, promise, avowal, pledge, adjuration, affirmation, attestation. **2** *The carpenter let out a stream of oaths when he hit his thumb with the hammer:* curse, profanity, blasphemy, obscenity, expletive, *Informal* cuss, swear-word; swearing, imprecation, malediction.
Ant. 2 benediction, blessing; prayer, invocation.

"Oaths are the fossils of piety."
—*George Santayana*

---

obdurate *adj.* **1** *The child was obdurate in refusing to eat vegetables:* stubborn, obstinate, intractable, unyielding, inflexible, adamant, immovable, wilful, headstrong, pig-headed, mulish; unmanageable, uncontrollable, ungovernable. **2** *The tyrant was obdurate in his treatment of prisoners:* unmoved, uncaring, unfeeling, harsh, merciless, unmerciful, unpitying, pitiless, unsympathetic, uncompassionate, unsparing, untouched, inexorable; hardened, callous, cruel, cold-blooded, hard-hearted.
Ant. 1 obedient, agreeable, compliant, flexible, amenable; manageable, docile, tractable. **2** compassionate, sympathetic, caring, feeling, merciful, pitying, relenting, soft-hearted, kind, gentle, tender.
◇ *Word origin: Obdurate* comes from Latin *ob-* (against) + *durus* (hard), hence hardened against. Latin *durus*, hard, also gives us *durable, duration* (the period of time during which anything is hard enough to last), and *duress* (hard treatment which forces someone to do something, coercion).

obedience *n. The dog was sent to school to learn obedience:* compliance, dutifulness, submissiveness, submission, docility, acquiescence, deference, tractability, yielding, ductility, subjection; allegiance; conformity, compliance, accordance.

obedient *adj. An obedient child does as he's told:* obeying, dutiful, compliant, submissive, yielding, docile, acquiescent, faithful, loyal, law-abiding, devoted, deferential, governable, tractable.
Ant. disobedient, disobeying, insubordinate, rebellious; contrary, perverse, wayward, recalcitrant, refractory, intractable, unruly, contumacious, disrespectful, undutiful, arrogant, unyielding, obstinate, obdurate, stubborn, ungovernable, unmanageable.

obeisance *n. The knights made obeisance to the queen. The king expects obeisance from all his subjects:* bow, curtsy, kneeling, genuflection, prostration; homage, deference, respect, veneration, esteem, regard, reverence, honour, obedience, humility, humbleness, self-abasement; loyalty, fidelity, fealty, allegiance.
Ant. disrespect, disregard, dishonour, irreverence; disloyalty, treachery.

obese *adj. The boy is too obese and should go on a diet:* fat, overweight, gross, corpulent, heavy, stout, tubby, pudgy, plump, fleshy, chubby, portly; paunchy, rotund, pot-bellied, big-bellied.
Ant. skinny, thin, slim, slender, scrawny, lean, spare, angular, raw-boned, lank, lanky, gaunt.
◇ *Word origin:* A person becomes *obese* by eating everything or all he wants. *Obese* comes from Latin *ob-* (completely) + *edere* (to eat).

obey *v. A good citizen obeys the law:* keep, comply with, be ruled by, follow orders, submit to, respect, observe, be regulated by, abide by, conform to, be governed by, mind, heed; acquiesce, toe the line, submit to, bow to, yield to, succumb to, accede to.
Ant. disobey, defy, revolt, rebel, mutiny, resist, refuse, be insubordinate.

object *v.* **1** *Mother objects to cigar-smoking:* be averse to, take exception to, disapprove of, oppose, protest, be at odds with, balk at, look askance at, frown on, demur from, shudder at, revolt at; dislike, loathe, shrink from, abhor, abominate, criticize, condemn, denounce, remonstrate against, cavil at, carp at, find fault with, *Slang* knock.
—*n.* **2** *A bright moving object appeared in the sky at sunset:* thing, article, body, form, phenomenon; device, gadget, contrivance, *Slang* thingumajig, thingumabob, dingus, what's-its-name. **3** *The principal has been the object of much criticism:* target, recipient, cynosure; victim, butt, dupe, prey, quarry. **4** *What is the object of the research?:* aim, goal, purpose, point, intent, intention, objective, design, end, target, mission, use; significance,

reason, sense, meaning, explanation, substance, principle, essence, gist, pith, cause, motive, incentive, inducement, basis.

Ant. 1 approve, agree, welcome, admit, greet with open arms, accept, comply, concur, assent, consent, acquiesce, accede; like, love, fancy, relish, praise, applaud, laud, admire, compliment.

◇ *Pronunciation tip: Object* is, of course, correctly pronounced one way as a noun and another way as a verb. The noun is stressed on the first syllable, an *OBject: What's that OBject in the sky?* The verb is stressed on the second syllable, to *obJECT: I obJECT to the motion and will vote against it.*

objection *n.* **1** *Father's objection was that the trip was much too expensive:* complaint, criticism, opposing reason, counter-argument, protest, exception, demur, cavil, *Slang* moan, beef. **2** *The boy kept the dog despite his sister's objection:* disapproval, opposition, disagreement, dissention, reservation, disapprobation.

Ant. 2 approval, consent, agreement, endorsement, support, countenance, approbation.

objectionable *adj. He apologized for his objectionable behaviour:* unacceptable, intolerable, unbearable, unendurable, disagreeable, unpleasant, displeasing, inappropriate, unseemly; offensive, obnoxious, nasty, foul, abominable, vile, odious, revolting, disgusting, abhorrent, loathsome, despicable, distasteful.

Ant. acceptable, agreeable, likeable, pleasant, pleasing, appropriate, seemly, fit, meet.

objective *adj.* **1** *It's very difficult to give objective criticism:* impartial, unprejudiced, detached, dispassionate, impersonal, unbiased, fair, just, uncoloured, open-minded, disinterested, unswayed, uninfluenced; real, actual. —*n.* **2** *Her objective is to get a university education:* aim, goal, purpose, object, intent, intention, design, end, mission; destination, target, mark.

Ant. 1 subjective, personal, biased, prejudiced, warped, unjust, unfair; abstract, theoretical.

obligation *n.* **1** *He has an obligation to help support his parents:* duty, responsibility, a favour owed, debt, indebtedness, liability, onus, charge, care, constraint, accountability, answerability. **2** *The manufacturer has not fulfilled the terms of his obligation:* agreement, contract, compact, bond, commitment, pledge, oath, promise, word, understanding; warranty, guarantee.

Ant. 1 choice, freedom.

obligatory *adj. Paying taxes is obligatory:* compulsory, mandatory, binding, required, requisite, imperative, necessary, unavoidable.

Ant. non-compulsory, voluntary.

oblige *v.* **1** *Having been to their party, we were obliged to invite them to ours. The will obliges the heirs to live in the family mansion:* obligate, to be duty-bound, require, demand of, necessitate, make, impel, constrain, bind, compel, force, coerce. **2** *The pianist obliged the guests with a short recital:* accommodate, favour, do a favour for, do a service for, put oneself out for; help, aid, assist, support, serve.

Ant. 1 free, unfetter, liberate, release, acquit; persuade, induce. **2** disoblige, inconvenience.

◇ *Word origin: Oblige* and *obligation* come from Latin *ob-* (toward, against) + *ligare* (to bind), thus to *oblige* a person is to bind him by a command, promise, or doing him a service or favour, and an *obligation* is the duty which binds him.

obliging *adj. A very obliging assistant waited on me:* accommodating, helpful, co-operative, solicitous, well-disposed; sympathetic, friendly, amiable, agreeable, good-natured, cheerful, complaisant, courteous, polite.

Ant. disobliging, unaccommodating, unco-operative, unhelpful, ill-disposed, inconsiderate; rude, discourteous, curt, surly, sullen.

oblique *adj.* **1** *Draw an oblique line from one corner of the paper to the opposite:* diagonal, slanting, slanted, inclined, sloping, tilted, aslant; askew, awry. **2** *The poem contains an oblique reference to Queen Elizabeth I:* indirect, masked, veiled, cloaked, sly, underhand, furtive, sneaking, implied, hinted, suggested.

Ant. 1 vertical; horizontal. **2** direct, frank, open, straightforward, forthright, candid, blunt, obvious, unveiled.

obliterate *v.* **1** *The bombardment obliterated the town:* annihilate, destroy, raze, level, wipe out. **2** *The rubber obliterated the writing. Try to obliterate the incident from your mind:* erase, expunge, wipe out, rub out, delete, abolish; strike out, cross out, cancel, blot out.

Ant. 1 construct, create, raise up; reconstruct, restore, rehabilitate. **2** write; add, keep.

◇ *Word origin:* To *obliterate* literally means to write over something so that it cannot be seen or read. It comes from Latin *ob-* (against) + *littera* (letter), which also gives us *letter, literate* (able to read and write the letters of the alphabet), *literal* (according to the letter), and *literature* (creative letters or letters of lasting importance).

"And if I drink oblivion of a day,
So shorten I the stature of my soul."
—*George Meredith*

---

oblivion *n.* **1** *The writer, once popular, is now relegated to oblivion:* obscurity, limbo, a forgotten state, disregard, insignificance. **2** *Non-religious people believe that death brings complete oblivion. He sought oblivion in drink:* nothingness, non-existence, the void, blankness; forgetfulness, obliviousness, unconcern, unconsciousness, insensibility, blotting out.

Ant. 1 fame, popularity, celebrity, immortality. **2** being, existence, life; remembrance, reminiscence, recall, recollection, reminder, memory.

◇ *Word origin: Oblivion* comes from Latin *oblivisci*, to forget.

oblivious *adj. Concentrating on his work, the draughtsman was oblivious of the noise. How can you be so oblivious of her rude remarks?:* unaware of, unconscious of, undiscerning, insensible, unobservant, unmindful, heedless of, unconcerned, forgetful.

Ant. aware, conscious, cognizant; heedful, concerned, troubled, worried, annoyed.

obnoxious *adj. She's charming, but her husband is obnoxious:* offensive, objectionable, disagreeable, unpleasant, displeasing, nasty, nauseating, repugnant, foul, vile, odious, revolting, disgusting, abominable, loathsome, despicable, abhorrent, repellent, hateful, detestable; unseemly, inappropriate, unbearable, unendurable, intolerable, insufferable.

Ant. agreeable, pleasant, pleasing, delightful, charming, engaging, likeable, alluring, enchanting; acceptable, appropriate, seemly, fit, meet, in good taste.

◇ *Word origin:* Today *obnoxious* merely means disagreeable or offensive. It used to mean harmful, dangerous, and comes from Latin *ob-* (toward) + *noxa* (harm, injury), which also gives us *noxious* (bad for the health).

obscene *adj. The court must decide whether the book is obscene or not:* indecent, morally offensive, pornographic, prurient, lewd, lascivious, salacious, vulgar, dirty, filthy, *Slang* smutty, blue.

Ant. decent, modest, chaste, innocent, clean.

◇ *Word origin: Obscene* comes from Latin *obscaenus,* ill-boding (a term of augury). The Latin word acquired connotations equivalent to its English meaning during the first century A.D.

obscenity *n.* **1** *Many objected to the obscenity of the book:* indecency, pornography, lewdness, prurience, lasciviousness, salaciousness, vulgarity, dirtiness, smuttiness, filthiness. **2** *His speech was full of obscenities:* vulgarity, profanity, obscene expression, taboo word, *Slang* swear-word, four-letter word.

Ant. 1 decency, modesty, chastity, innocence.

obscure *adj.* **1** *The point of his speech was obscure:* unclear, not easily understood, hidden, vague, uncertain, indefinite, indefinable, inscrutable, unfathomable, puzzling, perplexing, enigmatic, cryptic, confusing, confused. **2** *The bus stopped at an obscure little village:* unknown, little known, nameless, unheard-of, unsung, forgotten, unrenowned, unnoted, insignificant, inconsequential, unimportant, out-of-the-way, inconspicuous. **3** *An obscure figure could be seen through the fog:* indistinct, faint, dim, shadowy, murky, cloudy, dusky. —*v.* **4** *The large building obscured the hills behind:* hide, conceal, cover, block, eclipse; veil, blur, cloud, becloud; fog, befog; shroud, curtain, cloak, screen; mask, disguise; overshadow, shadow, darken. **5** *The suspect tried to obscure the case against him:* confuse, obfuscate, muddle, befuddle, make hard to understand.

Ant. 1 clear, lucid, plain, transparent, obvious, evident, manifest, apparent, explicit, intelligible; straightforward, unmistakable. **2** well-known, famous, renowned, prominent, eminent, celebrated; important, major, significant. **3** distinct, conspicuous, prominent, well-defined; bright, light. **4** reveal, disclose, show, expose, exhibit. **5** clarify, explain.

obsequious *adj. The boss prefers obsequious underlings:* servile, fawning, toadying, sycophantic, subservient, menial, ingratiating, deferential, slavish, cringing, cowering, mealy-mouthed, truckling, *Slang* bootlicking, kowtowing.

Ant. domineering, overbearing, lordly, proud, haughty, arrogant, impudent, brash, bold, assertive, forceful, aggressive.

observance *n.* **1** *Observance of the rules is important in this game:* obeying, following, compliance, adherence, attending, attention, heeding, keeping, regard, observation. **2** *Christmas is one of our religious observances:* ceremonial, commemoration, celebration, feast, solemnity; ceremony, ritual, rite, custom, practice, formality.

Ant. 1 non-observance, disobeying, non-compliance, inattention, disregard, omission.

observant *adj. Be observant for signs of danger:* watchful, vigilant, alert, on the look-out, awake, careful; mindful, attentive, heedful, regardful, conscious.

Ant. unobservant, inattentive, oblivious; unmindful, heedless, indifferent, unconcerned.

observation *n.* **1** *This telescope is used for the observation of distant stars. Not even the slightest clue escaped the detective's observation:* observing, watching, viewing, seeing, beholding, eyeing, glimpsing, spotting, inspection, detection, examination, surveillance, scrutiny, survey, probe, search; notice, attention, interest, heed, watchfulness, heedfulness, cognizance. **2** *The doctor examined the patient and wrote down his observations. The speaker had some witty observations to make about modern politics:* finding, first-hand information, discovery, description, diagnosis; remark, comment, statement, reflection, view, idea, opinion, theory, judgement, pronouncement, assertion, commentary.

observe *v.* **1** *Thousands observed the ship leaving the harbour. Did you observe anything suspicious?:* see, watch, view, behold, peer at, catch sight of, stare at, make out, inspect, survey, glimpse, espy, spot, ogle, eye; notice, note, discover, detect, perceive, mark, heed, regard, pay attention to, size up, take stock of. **2** *She observed that we were already late:* remark, comment, state, say, mention, announce, assert, declare; opine, reflect, theorize. **3** *Observe the rules:* obey, comply with, conform to, follow, heed, abide by, adhere to, fulfil, keep, be guided by, acquiesce in, defer to, carry out, execute, perform, respect. **4** *How many holidays do we observe?:* celebrate, commemorate, honour; sanctify, consecrate, solemnize; recognize, acknowledge.

Ant. 3 disobey, disregard, neglect. **4** profane.

obsessed *adj. He was obsessed with the idea of winning the race:* possessed, beset, dominated, controlled, having a fixation, maniacal, haunted, overwhelmingly desirous, overwhelmingly fearful, *Slang* hung up on.

obsession *n. Becoming a millionaire is an obsession with him:* overwhelming fear, all-encompassing desire, fixation, fixed idea, mania, phobia, quirk, neurotic conviction, ruling passion, monomania; *French* idée fixe.

obsolescent *adj. Propeller-driven passenger planes are obsolescent:* becoming obsolete, becoming out-of-date, disappearing, declining, passing out of use, dying out, on the way out.

Ant. new, novel, modern, late, latest; fresh, up-to-date, current, new-fashioned, fashionable, in vogue, newfangled; in, mod, with-it.

obsolete *adj. Women's bloomers are obsolete:* out-of-date, out of fashion, out of use, passé, old-fashioned, outdated, outmoded, antiquated, antique, archaic, bygone.

obstacle *n. A stone wall was the last obstacle in the steeplechase. Lack of education is an obstacle to success:* barrier, barricade, hurdle, blockade; impediment, obstruction, hindrance, curb, stumbling-block, bar, limitation, restriction, stoppage, block, snag, catch, problem, difficulty.

Ant. help, aid, benefit, boon, spur, expedient, furtherance, support, encouragement.

◇ *Word origin: Obstacle* comes from Latin *ob-* (against) + *stare* (to stand).

"A fool is better than an obstinate man."
—*Thomas Fuller*

---

obstinate *adj. The family was too obstinate to evacuate the house when the flood began:* stubborn, obdurate, unyielding, unbending, inflexible, wilful, self-willed, headstrong, mulish, unreasonably stubborn, pig-headed; resolute, steadfast, staunch, dogged, tenacious; intractable, unmanageable, uncontrollable, ungovernable, refractory, recalcitrant.

Ant. compliant, complaisant, yielding, pliant, amenable, flexible; irresolute, undecided, wavering, wishy-washy; tractable, manageable, docile, obedient, submissive.

◇ *Usage note:* See STUBBORN.

obstreperous *adj. That obstreperous child must be punished!:* disorderly, unruly, uncontrolled, unrestrained, disobedient, unmanageable, ungovernable, uncontrollable; rampaging, uproarious, noisy, loud, boisterous, clamorous, vociferous.

Ant. orderly, restrained, obedient, well-behaved, manageable, tractable, docile; quiet, calm.

◇ *Word origin: Obstreperous* comes from Latin *ob-* (toward) + *strepere* (to make noise), literally to make noise at someone.

obstruct *v.* **1** *A fallen tree obstructed the road. A fat spectator obstructed our view of the stage:* bar, barricade, block, blockade, debar, shut off, stop, dam up, choke off, close, close off, plug up; hide, eclipse, cover, shroud, mask, cloak. **2** *Lack of funds obstructed the project:* delay, hinder, impede, curb, inhibit, stall, retard, check, hobble, restrict, limit; stop, block, arrest, halt, frustrate, thwart, stifle, throttle, suppress, bring to a standstill.

Ant. 1 unblock, clear, open. **2** help, aid, benefit, further, promote, advance, support, encourage, spur, expedite, facilitate, accelerate.

◇ *Word origin: Obstruct* comes from the Latin prefix *ob-* (before) + *struere* (to build, pile up), hence to build or pile up an obstacle in front of something. Latin *struere,* to build, also gives us *construct* (to build together), *structure* (that which is built), and *destroy* and *destruction* (to "build down," "un-building").

obstruction *n. There must be an obstruction in the drain-pipe:* obstacle, barrier, blockage, block, stoppage, stop, barricade, impediment, hindrance, hitch, check, curb, bar, snag.

Ant. clearing, opening, freeing, unblocking; help, aid, assistance.

obtain *v.* **1** *Where does one obtain a driving-licence in this city? Where did you obtain your knowledge of Chinese history?:* acquire, get, attain, secure, procure, come by, pick up, get hold of; receive, earn, gain, glean, gather, achieve, get one's hands on, gain possession of, take, pick up. **2** *The same rules obtain for everyone:* be in force, hold, stand, prevail, exist, be the case.

Ant. 1 lose, be deprived, forgo, relinquish, forfeit, surrender; give, grant, bestow, present, offer, proffer, confer, dispense, distribute, deliver, assign.

obtrusive *adj.* **1** *Don't be so obtrusive in other people's affairs. It's hard to be polite to obtrusive people:* interfering, intruding, intrusive, prying, meddlesome, meddling, *Informal* nosy; interrupting; trespassing; forward, aggressive, brash, presumptuous, impertinent, familiar. **2** *The red chair is too obtrusive for this room:* prominent, conspicuous, salient, outstanding, sticking out; jutting out, protruding, projecting, bulging, protuberant.

Ant. 1, 2 unobtrusive. **1** reserved, reticent, modest, unassuming, diffident, demure, timid, shy. **2** inconspicuous; concave, indented, hollow.

obtuse *adj.* **1** *An obtuse angle is one of over 90°:* not sharp, not pointed; blunt, blunted, dull, unpointed, unsharpened. **2** *She's so obtuse that she never gets the point:* dull, dense, slow, slow-witted, thick, stupid, ignorant, simple; uncomprehending, insensitive, insensible, imperceptive, thick-skinned.

Ant. **1** acute, sharp, pointed. **2** intelligent, bright, smart, clever, quick-witted, keen, sharp, alert, sensitive.

obviate *v. The suspect's confession obviates the necessity for an investigation:* avert, avoid, make unnecessary, do away with, preclude, prevent; forestall, divert, parry, side-track, ward off, stave off, fend off, *Informal* nip in the bud.

Ant. necessitate, require, make essential, oblige, impel, cause, make unavoidable.

obvious *adj. Her displeasure was obvious:* evident, clear, plain, unmistakable, discernible, distinct, palpable, conspicuous, apparent, patent, manifest, undeniable, glaring, striking, *Informal* plain as the nose on your face; visible, unconcealed, not hidden, unmasked, unveiled, undisguised.

Ant. concealed, hidden, obscure, unclear, indistinct, inconspicuous, unapparent, imperceptible, invisible.

occasion *n.* **1** *This year's F.A. Cup final was quite an occasion:* event, special event, important event, occurrence, happening, episode, situation, incident, experience, adventure, venture; affair, celebration, time. **2** *I want to take this occasion to thank you:* particular time, opportune time, opportunity, suitable time, convenient time, instance, circumstance, chance, opening. **3** *There was no occasion for such behaviour:* reason, cause, justification, provocation, motive, motivation, ground, grounds, base, basis, explanation, rationale. —*v.* **4** *The remark occasioned a burst of applause:* cause, elicit, bring about, prompt, lead to, provoke, inspire.

◇ *Spelling tip:* You will *succeed* in spelling *occasion* correctly if you remember that both *SuCCeed* and *oCCaSion* have two *c*'s and one *s*.

occasional *adj. The weather was good except for an occasional shower. She likes an occasional glass of wine:* taking place from time to time, recurring, now and then, sporadic, fitful, spasmodic, intermittent, random, scattered, infrequent, incidental, uncommon, rare.

Ant. constant, continual, continuous, incessant; customary, habitual, usual, regular, routine.

occasionally *adv. They occasionally drop in to see us. It snowed occasionally but not enough for skiing:* at times, sometimes, from time to time, now and then, every now and then, once in a while, infrequently, seldom, hardly ever, rarely, once in a blue moon; intermittently, sporadically, periodically.

Ant. always, constantly, continually, continuously, incessantly; often, frequently, regularly, again and again, over and over again, habitually, customarily, generally, ordinarily, usually.

occult *adj. The fortune-teller claims to have occult powers. The club has an occult initiation rite:* supernatural, magic, mystic, secret, mysterious, dark, arcane, private, revealed only to the initiated, unrevealed, undisclosed, hidden, concealed, obscure, veiled, shrouded.

occupancy *n. The flat had been cold throughout his occupancy. The lease gives us occupancy of the house until the New Year:* tenancy, occupation, habitation, inhabitancy, possession, use, tenure.

Ant. eviction, dispossession, dislodgement; vacancy.

occupant *n. The new occupants of the house will move in tomorrow. Many of the early occupants of Norwich were French merchants:* dweller, resident, tenant, inhabitant, occupier; lessee, renter, lodger; settler, colonist, native.

occupation *n.* **1** *He gave his occupation as bus driver:* job, trade, business, line of work, line, profession, work, capacity, vocation, craft; employment, livelihood, living; calling, pursuit, walk of life, life-work, career, sphere, activity; forte, speciality, specialization, métier. **2** *The World War II German occupation of France lasted four years:* military occupation, military control, foreign rule, subjugation, subjection, control, seizure, conquest, possession.

"There are worse occupations in this world than feeling a woman's pulse."

—*Laurence Sterne*

---

occupy *v.* **1** *Business occupies his mind most of the time. Grandmother occupies her time by knitting:* fill, fill up, engage, take up, employ, busy, engross, absorb, monopolize, saturate, permeate, pervade, overrun, concern, amuse, entertain. **2** *Enemy troops occupied the country:* take possession of, have control, hold in thrall, conquer, subjugate, enslave. **3** *The Smiths occupy the house on the corner. Is anyone occupying this seat?:* dwell in, reside in, be the tenants of, inhabit, lodge in, live in; sit in, use, hold, possess, be in, be on, be situated in.

Ant. **2** liberate, free. **3** vacate, quit, leave, evacuate; relinquish, give up, hand over.

occur *v.* **1** *When did the accident occur?:* happen, take place, come about, come to pass, come off, befall, transpire, ensue, result, eventuate. **2** *Tuberculosis occurs most often in damp climates:* appear, arise, rise, turn up, crop up, spring up, emerge, develop, materialize, show itself, manifest itself, be found, be met with. **3** *It didn't occur to me that you would object:*

enter one's mind, cross one's mind, suggest itself, *Slang* hit, strike.
Ant. 1 be avoided, be evaded, be thwarted, be nipped in the bud. **2** disappear, vanish, fade away, be suppressed.
◇ *Spelling tip:* Remember that *oCCur* has a double *c.*

occurrence *n. It was the strangest occurrence I can remember:* happening, event, incident, instance, episode, experience, business, situation, venture, adventure, affair, occasion; appearance, emergence, unfolding, development, manifestation, materialization.
◇ *Spelling tip:* The *oCCuRRence* of two *c*'s and two *r*'s in this word makes it unusual.

ocean *n. The ship crossed the ocean in five days:* sea, high sea, deep, briny deep, main, water, flood, *Slang* pond.
◇ *Word origin:* To the Greeks, *Okeanos* was both a vast sea thought to encircle the earth and the giant god who ruled it and all the other seas. (From this word we get our word *ocean.*)

odd *adj.* **1** *1, 3 and 5 are odd numbers:* not divisible by two, not even. **2** *What an odd shell!:* unusual, strange, queer, uncommon, out of the ordinary, unique, peculiar, singular, rare, curious, bizarre, freakish, outlandish, quaint, funny, weird, *Slang* far-out. **3** *What shall I do with this odd sock?:* being one of a pair but having no mate, unmatched, single; leftover, surplus, remaining. **4** *The youth earned pocket-money doing odd jobs:* various, sundry, miscellaneous; occasional, casual, irregular, sporadic, spasmodic, periodic, spare, extra.
Ant. 1 even. **2** common, ordinary, usual, familiar, customary, habitual, regular, typical, normal, natural, unexceptional. **3** matched, paired, mated. **4** regular, constant, steady, permanent, full-time.
◇ *Word origin:* The Old Norse word *oddi* meant the third point or tip of a triangle. From this we took our concept of an *odd* number, and only later did *odd* take on the additional meaning of unusual.

oddity *n. An egg with two yolks is an oddity. We were puzzled by the oddity of the painting:* rarity, phenomenon, curiosity, wonder, marvel, sight, freak, rara avis; strangeness, singularity, peculiarity, individuality, uniqueness, unusualness, outlandishness, freakishness; bizarreness, queerness, eccentricity, unnaturalness, abnormality.

odious *adj. The Nazi concentration camps were the most odious places in history:* evil, vile, abominable, hateful, hated, despicable, contemptible, detestable, invidious, heinous, repulsive, repugnant, revolting, disgusting, loathsome, obnoxious, infamous, offensive, nasty, foul, nauseating, rotten, sickening, monstrous, hideous, objectionable, intolerable, unendurable, unbearable.
Ant. likeable, attractive, lovable, delightful, charming, pleasing, pleasant, agreeable, acceptable.

odour *n. I love the odour of freshly-roasted coffee. What's that dreadful odour?:* smell, aroma; scent, fragrance, perfume, essence, bouquet; stench, stink, effluvium.
◇ *Usage note:* See SMELL.
◇ *Word origin: Odour* is an originally Latin word. It hasn't changed in meaning since the Romans used it 2,000 years ago.

offal *n. The hunters took the meat and left the offal for the vultures:* remains, carrion, carcass, entrails, innards; garbage, refuse, waste, rubbish, trash, debris, leavings, dregs, residue.
◇ *Word origin: Offal* is actually the waste parts that "fall off" a butchered animal. The word comes from *off + fall.*

offence *n.* **1** *For what offence was he arrested?:* crime, misdeed, misdemeanour, felony, breach of conduct, infraction, violation, malfeasance, delinquency sin, transgression, wickedness, peccadillo, lapse, slip, shortcoming; outrage, enormity, atrocity, evil deed. **2** *She meant no offence by the remark:* insult, affront, disrespect, insolence, impudence, rudeness, umbrage, harm, abuse, embarrassment, humiliation, indignity, outrage, slap, snub, taunt, gibe.
Ant. 1 innocence, guiltlessness. **2** pleasure, delight, gratification, satisfaction.

offend *v.* **1** *He apologized for having offended her:* affront, displease, insult, wound, disgust, antagonize, anger, incense, inflame, madden, annoy, vex, aggravate, irritate, exasperate, rankle, nettle, rile, miff, fret, gall, chafe, pique, disgruntle. **2** *She prayed that she would never offend:* sin, err, transgress, misbehave, lapse, stray from the straight and narrow, fall from grace.
Ant. 1 please, delight, beguile, captivate, charm, enchant, win over; soothe, calm, conciliate.
◇ *Word origin: Offend* and *offence* come from Latin *ob-* (against) + *fendere* (to hit), literally to hit against someone. It is thus semantically analogous to our slang expression "knock": *Don't knock* (i.e. belittle, hence be offensive about) *your neighbour's religion!*

offensive *adj.* **1** *The youth's language was offensive:* insulting, disrespectful, insolent, impudent, rude, abusive, embarrassing, unmannerly, uncivil, ungallant; objectionable, rank, obnoxious, disgusting, unpleasant, disagreeable, distasteful, abominable, revolting, nasty, foul, horrid, hideous, repulsive, ugly, loathsome, repugnant, abhorrent, detestable, sickening, nauseating, intolerable, insufferable. **2** *Offensive troops charged the hill position:* attacking, attack, assault, assaulting, assailing, belligerent, aggressive, charging, storming, bombarding.
—n. **3** *The team took the offensive and won:*

attack, assault, onslaught, onset, aggression, initiative.

Ant. 1 polite, courteous, respectful, deferential, diffident, civil, conciliatory; pleasing, pleasant, delightful, charming, agreeable, attractive, captivating, winning. **2** defensive, defending, resisting. **3** defensive.

offer *v.* **1** *She offered us some of her cakes:* proffer, tender, present, place at one's disposal, bestow on, bestow. **2** *May I offer a suggestion? The neighbours offered to help:* propose, submit, render, advance, suggest, put forth, propound, volunteer, hold out, extend, make a motion, bring forward, be willing. **3** *They offered their house for sale:* put on the market, put up.
—*n.* **4** *Shall I accept his offer of help?:* proposition, proposal, offering, bid, invitation, submission, overture, suggestion.

Ant. 1, 2 retain, retract, withdraw, withhold, deny; accept, take, receive; reject, refuse, decline. **4** withdrawal, retraction, revocation; acceptance, reception; refusal, denial.

Exploring the Word: Latin *ferre,* to carry, bring, put, is the base of many English words, including: *confer,* to bring together, consult together, and *conference,* a meeting of people who have been brought together; *defer* and *deference,* to bring oneself down before another (to bow down before another) and respect shown to another; *differ, different,* and *difference,* to carry oneself apart, hence to be different, to disagree, apartness or disagreement; *infer,* to carry in the mind, hence to deduce or reason; *offer,* to put before someone, to present, and *proffer* (Latin *pro-*, in favour of + *offer*), to put before someone for acceptance; *prefer* and *preference,* to carry or choose something before another, hence to like it better, that which is chosen; *refer,* to carry back to another person, a book, etc., for information, *reference,* the person, book, etc., referred to, *referee,* one to whom a dispute is carried for settlement, and *referendum,* a proposal that a government carries to the voters for their decision; *suffer,* to carry under pain, hence to be burdened or miserable; and *transfer* (Latin *trans-*, across), to carry across from one person to another.

offhand Also **offhanded** *adj.* **1** *The M.P. asked the reporters not to quote his offhand remarks:* impromptu, extemporaneous, ad-lib, off-the-cuff, off-the-record, off the top of one's head, improvised, unpremeditated, unprepared, unplanned, spontaneous, chance, casual, random. **2** *He answered in a far too offhand manner:* casual, careless, thoughtless, glib, heedless, haphazard, nonchalant, unconcerned; facetious, cavalier, relaxed.

Ant. 1 prepared, planned, premeditated, studied. **2** serious, intent, sober, grave, responsible, careful, thoughtful.

office *n.* **1** *He held office in the last Government as Foreign Secretary:* position, post, job, capacity, function, occupation, role, commission, appointment. **2** usually **offices** *Did he appreciate your good offices?:* favour, service, help, assistance; duty, function, task. **3** *Now that the decorations were finished, the office was a pleasant place to work:* place of work, room set aside for work, department, counting house, booking-office, enquiry-office, local branch of large organization.

official *n.* **1** *The company officials determine policy. The governor is a public official:* office-holder, officer, executive, director, manager, administrator, supervisor; functionary, dignitary, agent; chairman, administrative head.
—*adj.* **2** *The Queen's official duties included the state opening of Parliament. There will be an official inquiry into the matter:* formal, administrative, vested; authorized, approved, sanctioned, authoritative, certified, accredited, authentic, warranted, licensed.

Ant. 1 underling, hireling; employee. **2** unofficial, unauthorized; informal, casual.

officious *adj. It's hard to be an executive without being officious:* obtrusive, intrusive, interfering, meddlesome, meddling, prying, poking one's nose in, offering gratuitous advice or services, overbearing, domineering, self-important, self-assertive, high-handed, high and mighty; pompous, patronizing, throwing one's weight about.

Ant. inobtrusive, in the background.

offset *v. His A in maths offset the D in art. Inflation will offset the pay-rise:* compensate for, make up for, counteract, counterbalance, balance; cancel out, nullify, neutralize, equalize, *Informal* knock out.

offspring *n. The dictionary defines* mule *as "offspring of a male ass and a mare." The old man's offspring are wrangling over the estate:* children, progeny, descendants, issue, increase; child, descendant, heir, scion; young, brood, family, litter, fry, spawn.

often *adv. How often do you visit your parents? It rains often at this time of the year:* frequently, regularly, repeatedly, habitually, periodically, recurrently, over and over again, time and again, again and again, generally, commonly, as a common thing, continually, constantly, oft, oftentimes, oft-times.

Ant. never; rarely, seldom, infrequently, occasionally, irregularly, now and then, once in a blue moon, hardly ever.

ogle *v. Every man on the beach ogled the starlet because of her figure:* stare at greedily, gaze at with desire; stare at, gape at, gawk at, gawp at, goggle at, scrutinize, eye, give the glad eye, give the once-over, leer at.

◇ *Word origin: Ogle* comes from Low German *oegen,* to look at, to eye. (The German word for "eye," *auge,* is also related — both to *ogle* and to *eye.*)

ogre *Fem.* **ogress** *n.* **1** *I used to revel in stories* *about fearful ogres:* man-eating giant, monster, fiend, brute; bugbear, bogyman. **2** *The new supervisor is a real ogre:* tyrant, martinet, dictator, despot, slave-driver.

◇ *Spelling tip: Ogre* ends in *-re*, not *-er*. Remember this sentence: *The ogRE had REd eyes.*

◇ *Word origin:* If you were ever afraid of *ogres* as a child, it was probably due to the 17th-century French writer Charles Perrault, who coined the word *ogre* and described these hideous man-eating giants in his compilation of fairy tales, in which he rewrote and gave their now traditional form to many older stories and folk-tales, including the stories of Bluebeard, the Sleeping Beauty, and Cinderella. How did he invent the word *ogre*? He probably based it on *Orcus*, the Roman god of death and of hell.

oil *n.* **1** *Oil and water won't mix:* non-volatile, viscid liquid; (*variously*) mineral oil, fuel oil, whale oil, vegetable oil, cooking oil, motor oil, lubricant; melted grease, melted fat; liniment, ointment, unguent, balm, salve; pomade, hair oil.
—*v.* **2** *Oil that squeaky hinge. She oiled herself with sun-tan lotion:* lubricate; cream, grease, anoint, salve, cream, lard.

◇ *Word origin: Oil* comes from Greek *elaion*, which was olive oil, the only kind of oil commonly known in the Graeco-Roman world.

ointment *n. Every first-aid kit should contain an ointment for burns:* unguent, balm, salve, emollient, liniment, lotion.

◇ *Word origin: Ointment* comes from Latin *ungere*, to anoint, which also gives us *anoint* and *unguent*.

old *adj.* **1** *She's forty years old:* of age. **2** *Father's an old man now. What an old car!:* elderly, aged, hoary, grizzled, grey-headed, grey with age, white with age, venerable; antiquated, ancient, vintage, time-worn, age-old, antique, old-fashioned, out-of-date, outdated, archaic, obsolete, obsolescent. **3** *She and I are old friends. Do you remember the good old days?:* of long standing, long established, time-honoured, traditional, age-old, of the past, from the past, of yore, bygone. **4** *This old coat doesn't fit any more. That's an old joke:* worn-out, outworn, decrepit, dilapidated, used, much-used, time-worn, weathered, *Slang* beat-up, weather-beaten, deteriorated, battered, ramshackle, crumbling, tumbledown, run-down, broken-down; familiar, hackneyed.

Ant. 2-4 new, recent, current, late. **4** young, immature; brand-new, spanking new, modern, novel, up-to-date, modish, newfangled, new-fashioned, fashionable, *Slang* mod, with-it.

◇ *Usage note: Old* may be used to refer both to people and to things: *an old man, an old house. Elderly* refers only to people and suggests someone between middle and old age: *Though an elderly man, he does a full day's work.*

old-fashioned *adj.* **1** *It may be a new dress but it looks old-fashioned to me:* out-of-date, out of fashion, outmoded, unfashionable, behind the times, out of style, passé, from time gone by, antiquated, antique, outdated, obsolete, *Slang* corny. **2** *She's an old-fashioned girl:* having time-honoured values, conservative, traditional; time-honoured, old-time, long-standing.

Ant. 1 modern, up-to-date, current, in style, newfangled, new-fashioned, fashionable, in vogue, up-to-the-minute, chic, modish, à la mode, avant-garde, *Slang* mod, with-it.

omen *n. Some people believe a black cat crossing your path is a bad omen. Let's hope this glorious weather is a good omen for our holiday:* augury, sign, token, portent, auspice; indication, harbinger, herald, precursor, presage, foretaste, straw in the wind, writing on the wall.

◇ *Word origin: Omen* is an originally Latin word meaning "prognostic sign in divination," from which we also get *ominous* (serving as an ill omen, threatening) and *abomination* (something of ill omen).

ominous *adj. Ominous black clouds caused us to head the boat towards the harbour:* threatening, menacing, sinister, dismaying, disquieting, portentous, unpromising, unpropitious, unfavourable, inauspicious, ill-starred, portending evil, unlucky, ill-omened.

Ant. encouraging, promising, favourable, propitious, auspicious.

omission *n.* **1** *The omission of the student's name from the pass list was an oversight. There are sins of commission and sins of omission:* leaving out, exclusion, non-inclusion, elimination, exception; neglect, negligence, delinquency, oversight. **2** *The catalogue has numerous omissions:* something omitted, exclusion, neglected item, thing overlooked, gap, hole.

Ant. 1, 2 inclusion; addition, supplement.

omit *v.* **1** *Be sure not to omit anyone's name from the list:* leave out, exclude, except, miss, skip, pass over, forget about, preclude, jump, ignore, elide, delete, drop, excerpt, cut, set aside. **2** *You omitted to tell me to buy bread:* neglect, fail, forget, overlook, let slip, ignore, avoid, shun, slight, bypass, leave undone.

Ant. 1 include, put in, add. **2** remember, recollect, recall.

omnipotent *adj. The Jews were the first nation on earth to worship a single omnipotent deity:* all-powerful, almighty, supreme.

Ant. powerless, helpless, impotent.

omniscient *adj. The Bible teaches that God is omniscient:* all-knowing, all-seeing, having infinite knowledge, all-wise; supreme, pre-eminent, infinite.

Ant. ignorant, unknowing, unaware, fallible, deceivable.

once *adv.* **1** *She was once my best friend. Once dinosaurs walked these plains:* formerly, at one time, previously, some time back, some time ago, in times past, long ago, once upon a time, in other days, in the old days, in the good old days, years ago, ages ago; heretofore, hitherto. **2** *We've been to France only once:* a single time, on one occasion; once and for all, for the nonce.
Ant. 1 in future, in time to come, after this, hereafter. **2** never, not at all, at no time; repeatedly, frequently, numerously, regularly, incessantly, continually.

"And Earth is but a star, that once had shone." —*James Elroy Flecker*

---

one *adj.* **1** *Put one piece of cake on each plate. He's the one man who can do it:* single, individual, a, an, sole, lone, solitary, only, singular, unique, unrepeated; entire, whole, complete.
—*pron.* **2** *One never knows what may happen:* a person, an individual, a man, a human being, a creature, somebody, someone, you, a body, a soul, a mortal, a thing.
◇ *Usage note: One another* and *each other* are used interchangeably today. Traditionally, however, *one another* applies to more than two people, while *each other* applies to only two people. Thus, *The people of Greenland and Tierra del Fuego must learn to understand one another*, but *He and his wife loved each other.*
◇ *Word origin: One* comes from Old English *ān*, one, which also gives us *an* and its shortened form *a*, and is also the basis of our word *only* (literally *one-ly*).

> **Exploring the Word:** *Omnipotent, omniscient, omnipresent, omnivorous, omnibus* and *bus* all go back to Latin *omnis*, all. Thus *omnipotent* means all-powerful; *omniscient* (Latin *sciens*, knowing) means all-knowing; *omnipresent* means being everywhere; *omnivorous* means eating food of all kinds, eating both flesh and plants; and *omnibus* (the Latin for "for all") means a collation or anthology of all or various things and a passenger vehicle for many people — which we have shortened to get our word *bus*.

onerous *adj. Holding down two jobs can be an onerous task:* oppressive, burdensome, hard to endure, not easy to bear, distressing, painful, wearisome, taxing, exhausting, crushing, heavy, grievous.
Ant. easy, light, simple, effortless, trivial.
◇ *Word origin:* See ONUS.

only *adv.* **1** *Only Jennifer was left in the room:* alone, by oneself, by itself, solely, exclusively, individually, singly, without others, as the only one, without anything further. **2** *She sees him only on Fridays:* no more than, merely, just, simply, purely: barely, nothing but, at least, to such an extent.
—*adj.* **3** *That was the only apple left. She's the only woman to have been elected mayor of this town:* lone, sole, solitary, individual, single, singular, exclusive, unique, alone, one and only; unparalleled, unrepeated, unmatched.
Ant. 1 together, collectively, among, amongst. **3** many, several, numerous, innumerable, multitudinous, myriad, manifold.
◇ *Word origin:* See ONE.

onset *n.* **1** *The onset of the disease was barely noticeable:* start, beginning, outset, commencement, inauguration, initiation, outbreak; inception, genesis, birth, infancy, founding, incipience. **2** *The bombardment began the final onset of the war:* attack, assault, onslaught, offensive, raid, thrust, push, sally, charge, onrush, incursion, invasion, storming.
Ant. 1 end, close, conclusion, termination; old age, death. **2** defence, resistance, counter-attack.

onslaught *n. They found it impossible to beat back the onslaught of the crowd:* attack, assault, charge, thrust, push, raid, sally, onset, onrush, blitz, blitzkrieg; offensive, advance, invasion, incursion, aggression.
Ant. defence, resistance; counter-attack.

onus *n. The onus is on the prosecution to prove the suspect guilty:* burden, responsibility, obligation, weight, load, strain, encumbrance, liability, duty.
◇ *Word origin: Onus* in Latin means "burden, cargo, embryo, excrement, trouble, tax." This hard-working word also gives us *onerous* (burdensome) and *exonerate* (to free from the burden of blame or responsibility).

onward *adv.* Also **onwards 1** *Onward, march! The ship sailed onwards through the night:* forward, ahead, toward the front, frontward, toward one's goal, along, en route, on the way.
—*adj.* **2** *The plane's onward movement was slowed by adverse winds:* forward, moving ahead, frontward, advancing, progressive, ongoing.
Ant. 1, 2 backward. **1** backwards; aback, to the rear. **2** retreating, regressive.
◇ *Usage note:* Could *Onward Christian Soldiers* also correctly have been *Onwards Christian Soldiers?* Yes, but the use of *onward* and *onwards* is tricky. *Onward* is always correct, as an adjective or as an adverb. *Onwards* is correct only as an adverb. Thus, *The army's onward* (never "onwards") *march continued,* but *The army marched onward* (or *onwards*). If you stick to *onward*, you'll always be right.

ooze *v.* **1** *The water oozed from between the pipes:* seep, exude, trickle, dribble, drip, leak, drain, filter; bleed, sweat.
—*n.* **2** *You should not have waded through the mud and the ooze:* soft mud, slime, sludge, silt, muck, mire, alluvium; secretion, exudation, seepage, leakage.

Ant. 1 gush, stream, flood, cascade, pour, flow, effuse.

◇ *Word origin: Ooze* comes from Old English *wāse,* slimy mud, which is related to Latin *virus,* slime, animal semen, venom, or sharpness (of brackish sea-water or bad wine). This word was long ago borrowed directly from Latin into English by medical writers, giving us our words *virus* and *virulent.*

opaque *adj.* **1** *Varnish is transparent, and paint is opaque. The once-clear mountain stream is now polluted and opaque:* non-transparent, non-translucent, impenetrable to light; dark, dull, murky, clouded, hazy, muddy, muddied. **2** *The report was written in long, opaque sentences:* hard to understand, unclear, impenetrable, incomprehensible, difficult, obscure, abstruse, unintelligible, unfathomable.

Ant. **1, 2** clear. **1** transparent, translucent, pellucid; shiny, bright, sparkling, gleaming. **2** lucid, intelligible, comprehensible.

◇ *Word origin: Opaque* comes from Latin *opacus,* dark.

open *adj.* **1** *An open window. An open boat. With open arms:* not shut, unshut, not closed, unclosed, ajar, agape, gaping, yawning, not covered, uncovered, coverless, unenclosed, unsealed, unfastened, unlocked; extended, unfolded; welcoming. **2** *The boat headed for the open sea. Hunting is easiest in open country:* expansive, wide, unbounded, unfenced, unobstructed, uncluttered, exposed, clear; uncrowded, uninhabited, not built up. **3** *The shop is open from 9 till 5:* doing business, open for business, open to the public, available, accessible. **4** *She's a very friendly, open person:* open-hearted, forthright, sincere, natural, plain, artless, straightforward, honest, candid, outgoing, extrovert, frank, direct. **5** *A juror must keep an open mind:* impartial, objective, unprejudiced, unbiased, unbigoted, disinterested, impersonal, fair, just; receptive, responsive.

—*v.* **6** *Please open the door. Open the book at page 78. They can't open the road until the snow is cleared:* unclose, throw open, set ajar, move aside, swing aside; unlock, unfasten, unbar, unseal; unfold, expand, lay open; clear, unblock. **7** *We'll open the meeting with a prayer:* begin, commence, start, initiate, inaugurate, originate, launch, embark upon, set in motion, get the ball rolling; institute, found, create, undertake, establish. **8** *What time does the building open?:* open to the public, become available for use, permit access, afford entrance, receive customers, start business.

Ant. **1–3** closed. **6–8** close. **1** shut; covered, enclosed, sealed, fastened, locked; folded. **2** restrict, shut in, bounded, protected, narrow; obstructed, crowded, cluttered. **3** unavailable, inaccessible, out of bounds, shut. **4** introverted, reticent, reserved, withdrawn. **5** prejudiced, biased, bigoted, subjective; unfair, unjust; stubborn, obdurate. **6** shut; lock, fasten, bar, seal; fold; block, obstruct. **7** end, conclude, finish, terminate, shut down.

opening *n.* **1** *The bugs come through the opening for the pipes:* hole, break, breach, gap, aperture, rent, rift, slit, cleft, crack, fissure, gash, slot, tear, vent, chink. **2** *The opening of the motorway is scheduled for next year. The book's opening is dull, but the last chapters are interesting:* inauguration, initiation, launching, installation; beginning, start, commencement, first part, preface, prelude, overture, introduction, *Slang* kick-off, send-off. **3** *We have an opening for a filing clerk:* job, vacancy, place, space, opportunity, possibility, chance, occasion situation, position, *Informal* spot.

Ant. **1** obstruction, blockage. **2** closing, close, termination, end, ending, conclusion, finish, finale, finis, postscript.

operate *v.* **1** *Do you know how this toaster operates? Can you operate a photocopier?* work, function, run, perform; manage, superintend, oversee, be in charge of. **2** *The doctor says he may have to operate:* perform surgery, perform an operation, *Informal,* open up.

> **Exploring the Word:** *Opus* is the Latin word for work. We use it to mean a literary or musical work and its plural, *opera,* to refer to a work of musical drama. The Latin verb form *operari,* to work, gives us *operate* and *operation.* We also use two Latin expressions based on *opus* and *operari: magnum opus,* major or chief work, and *modus operandi,* manner of working, operating method.

operation *n.* **1** *The students watched a printing-press in operation. All his time is devoted to the operation of his business:* action, performance, operating, running, working, conduct, procedure, activity, pursuit; supervision, management, superintendence, overseeing. **2** *How long has the plan been in operation?:* action, effect, force, influence, exertion; agency, instrumentality. **3** *The doctors say the operation was a complete success:* surgery.

opinion *n. It's my opinion that the plan won't work:* belief, estimation, sentiment, judgement, view, impression, conviction, persuasion, notion, conclusion, idea, surmise, suspicion, conception, assumption, thinking, conjecture, speculation, theory.

Ant. fact, reality, actuality, certainty; act, deed, event, occurrence, happening.

◇ *Word origin: Opinion* comes from Latin *opinare,* to think.

opinionated *adj. He's too opinionated to consider other people's views:* cocksure, closed-minded, stubborn, bull-headed, headstrong, inflexible, unyielding, unbending, dogmatic, uncompromising.

Ant. open-minded, broad-minded, unbiased,

unprejudiced, receptive, objective, impartial.

opponent *n. The candidate criticized his opponent's record:* opposition, rival, competitor, adversary, contender, antagonist, foe, enemy, assailant.

Ant. ally, colleague, co-worker, team-mate, helper, accomplice, mate, friend, supporter, promoter, backer.

opportune *adj. Now, before interest rates increase, would be an opportune time to buy a new house:* timely, well-timed, advantageous, favourable, appropriate, suitable, fitting, apt, seasonable, proper, propitious, auspicious, expedient, convenient, profitable, fortunate, lucky, happy, felicitous.

Ant. inopportune, unfavourable, inappropriate, unsuitable, improper, unseasonable, unfortunate, inconvenient, untimely.

opportunity *n. A summer in France gave her an opportunity to learn French. I'd like to take this opportunity to thank everyone for helping:* chance, good chance, favourable time, time, occasion, moment, means, opening.

◇ *Word origin: Opportunity* and *opportune* come from the Roman sailors' term for a favourable wind. They are from Latin *opportunus* (*ob-,* toward, + *portus,* port), blowing towards port (said of an *opportune* wind).

"This I set down as a positive truth. A woman with fair opportunities and without a positive hump, may marry whom she likes."

—*William Makepeace Thackeray*

---

oppose *v. Several of the speakers opposed the project:* act in opposition to, speak against, fight, combat, battle, contend against, contest, struggle against, resist, defy, be set against, take a stand against, *Slang* slam.

Ant. support, aid, help, abet, champion, defend, advance, promote, advocate, foster, back.

opposite *adj.* **1** *The two houses are on opposite sides of the street:* facing, opposed, other; reverse, converse. **2** *We have opposite views on politics:* opposing, opposed, conflicting, differing, contradictory, contrary, antithetical, antagonistic, adverse; counteractive, counter.

Ant. 1 same. **2** alike, like, identical, uniform, similar, analogous, synonomous, agreeing, consistent, corresponding, parallel.

opposition *n.* **1** *I don't understand his opposition to the plan:* resistance, contention against, disagreement, disapproval, rejection, aversion, negativism, defiance, contrariety, antagonism, hostility, enmity. **2** *The opposition was quick to reply to the charge:* opponent, competitor, rival, adversary, contender, antagonist, foe, enemy, other side.

Ant. 1 support, backing, approval, aid, help, assistance, advancement, promotion. **2** supporter, backer, promoter; ally, friend, colleague, helper.

oppress *v.* **1** *She was oppressed by her many woes:* trouble, vex, worry, burden, weigh down, tax, try; depress, dispirit, cast down, dishearten, deject, discourage, sadden, pain, grieve, sorrow. **2** *The tyrant oppressed the conquered peoples:* tyrannize, hound, persecute, treat harshly, abuse, maltreat.

Ant. 1 unburden, relieve, ease; gladden, cheer, cheer up, hearten, encourage.

oppressive *adj.* **1** *The occupation by foreign troops was extremely oppressive:* tyrannical, despotic, repressive; cruel, brutal, harsh, severe, hard-hearted. **2** *Obligations are often oppressive. Very hot weather can be oppressive:* burdensome, onerous, wearing, trying, troublesome, worrisome, vexing, pressing; depressing, discouraging; painful, grievous; uncomfortable, distressing, unbearable.

Ant. 1 humane, kind, gentle, compassionate, benevolent, tender, lenient, merciful, just. **2** soothing, relieving, gladdening, joyful, pleasant, pleasing, encouraging, comforting; comfortable.

opprobrious *adj.* **1** *The paper made an opprobrious attack on punk rock:* condemnatory, damning, denunciatory, hypercritical, censorious, faultfinding; abusive, vituperative, derogatory, scurrilous, acrimonious, malicious, malevolent, maligning, vilifying, vitriolic, fulminating, reviling. **2** *The officer was reprimanded for his opprobrious conduct:* disgraceful, dishonourable, shameful, disreputable, objectionable, unbecoming, deplorable, reprehensible, base, outrageous, shocking, scandalous, infamous, nefarious, heinous, despicable, corrupt, wicked.

Ant. 1 complimentary, flattering, approving, praising, laudatory, uncritical. **2** honourable, noble, meritorious, upright, ethical, principled, virtuous, moral; becoming, praiseworthy, worthy, laudable, estimable, noteworthy.

optimism *n. Nothing can daunt his cheery optimism:* confidence, sanguineness, hopeful outlook, hoping for the best, hopefulness, bright outlook, looking on the bright side, encouragement, cheerfulness, trust in the future, happy expectancy.

Ant. pessimism, cynicism; gloom, gloominess, glumness, depression, despondency.

◇ *Word origin: Optimism, optimist,* and *optimum* come from Latin *optimus,* best. Hence *optimism* is a disposition to look on the best or bright side of things or to believe that everything is for the best.

optimistic *adj.* **1** *The shareholders are optimistic about the company's future:* confident, sanguine, cheerful, disposed to take a favourable view, viewed favourably, hopeful, heartened, enthusiastic, encouraged, happily expectant, buoyed up. **2** *There are optimistic signs for the company's future:* promising, auspicious, propitious, favourable, encouraging, bright, heartening, full of promise, roseate, rose-coloured.

Ant. 1, 2 pessimistic. **1** cynical; despairing, depressed, despondent, discouraged, glum, gloomy. **2** unpromising, inauspicious, unfavourable, discouraging, disheartening.

optimum *n.* **1** *Atmospheric conditions are at the optimum for a space probe:* ideal, peak, height, best point, most desirable, perfect degree, crest, zenith, perfection, quintessence, acme. —*adj.* **2** *The experiment was conducted under optimum conditions:* ideal, best, perfect, most favourable, prime, choice, select, first-rate, first-class, flawless, faultless, unexcelled, superlative, supreme, capital, *Slang* A 1.

◇ *Word origin:* See OPTIMISM.

option *n.* **1** *Every voter should exercise his option:* franchise, free will, right of choosing, freedom of choice, will, self-determination, voice, decision, discretion. **2** *She has the option of entering university or starting her professional career:* choice, alternative, selection, election; preference, partiality, liking, predilection, pleasure, will. **3** *The publisher has an option on the author's next book:* first claim, right to buy, first choice to buy, right of first refusal, privilege.

Ant. 1 compulsion, coercion. **1, 2** requirement, obligation, necessity, *Informal* must.

◇ *Word origin: Option* and *optional* come from Latin *optare*, to choose.

optional *adj. The car has a heater, of course, but air-conditioning is optional:* left to one's choice, individually decided, elective, voluntary, non-obligatory, not required, volitional, unforced, discretionary, discretional; available at additional cost.

Ant. mandatory, obligatory, required, compulsory.

opulence *n.* **1** *The opulence of the pharaoh's palaces was awe-inspiring:* great wealth, riches, affluence, fortune, prosperity, ample means; luxuries, lavishness. **2** *The opulence of the food served at the banquet overwhelmed the guests:* abundance, profusion, copiousness, plenty, plentitude, amplitude, bounty, overflowing quantity, wealth, cornucopia; elegance, lavishness, richness, sumptuousness.

Ant. 1 poverty, indigence, want, privation, impecuniousness, impecuniosity. **2** scarcity, scarceness, paucity, scantiness, dearth, lack, want, insufficiency.

opus *n. The author's latest opus is his best yet:* work, piece, production, product, composition, creation, handiwork, brain-child, invention, effort, attempt.

oracle *n. The oracle prophesied famine and war:* divine utterance, message, prophecy, revelation, inspiration; medium, prophet, seer, augur, soothsayer, sage, diviner; predictor, adviser, infallible guide, person, source of wisdom or knowledge.

oral *adj.* **1** *Each pupil had to stand up and give an oral report in front of the class:* spoken, vocal, uttered, articulated, using speech, viva voce, (*loosely*) verbal. **2** *Is it an oral vaccine or one given by injection?:* swallowed, ingested, taken into the body through the mouth.

Ant. 1 written; unspoken, silent, tacit.

◇ *Usage note:* Do not confuse *oral* with *aural. Oral* means having to do with the mouth or with speech: *The teacher conducted an oral examination. The dog obeys both oral commands and hand gestures. Aural* means having to do with the ear or the sense of hearing: *Hearing-aids overcome some aural deficiencies.*

> **Exploring the Word**: *Oracle*, *orator*, and *adore* come from Latin *orare*, to speak, to pray. Thus an *oracle* is one who speaks wisdom or prophesies; an *orator* is a public speaker and an *oration* a speech (usually an elaborate public speech). *Oratory* is the art of public speaking (in churches, an *oratory* is a small or private chapel for saying prayers, while an *oratorio* is a musical composition on a sacred theme for orchestra, chorus, and solo voices); and *adore* literally means to pray to, hence worship. The related Latin noun *os* (stem *or-*), mouth, gives us *oral*, meaning of or pertaining to the mouth (as in the term *oral medicine*) or consisting of spoken words (an *oral report*), and *orifice*, a mouthlike opening.

oration *n. The students had to learn by heart Mark Antony's funeral oration from* Julius Caesar*:* address, formal speech, eulogy, talk; discourse, declamation, monologue, sermon, lecture, panegyric, *Informal* spiel, screed.

orator *n. Edmund Burke was one of Ireland's best known orators:* speaker, elocutionist, rhetorician, declaimer, *Informal* spell-binder; public speaker, speech-maker, lecturer.

oratory *n. Winston Churchill was known for his oratory:* rhetoric, eloquence, delivery, declamation; grandiloquence, bombast, grandeur of style; art of public speaking, speech, elocution.

orb *n. Her necklace was a string of crystal orbs:* sphere, ball, globe, globule.

Ant. cube; square.

orbit *n.* **1** *The satellite was launched into orbit round the moon:* course, track, trajectory, path, way, route, channel.

—*v.* **2** *The earth orbits the sun once in 365¼ days:* circle, revolve around, travel around, circumnavigate.

◇ *Word origin: Orbit* and *orb* come from Latin *orbis*, circle, wheel, sphere. Thus *orbit* literally means the track or rut of a wheel, the path of a circle or sphere. Our word *exorbitant* literally means out of the track, off course, or as we would say, an exorbitant price is one that is "out of line."

orchestra *n.* **1** *The orchestra played a Mozart symphony:* company of musicians, ensemble, band, chamber orchestra, symphony orchestra.

◇ *Word origin: Orchestra* comes from *orchēstra,* "dance space," a circular space for a chorus of dancers, in front of the stage in a Greek theatre. An *orchestra pit* is still the place for theatre musicians to play and is immediately in front of the stage.

ordain *v.* **1** *He was ordained priest two years ago:* confer holy orders upon, name, invest, frock, consecrate; appoint, commission, delegate, depute, elect. **2** *The king ordained that all forests should belong to the crown:* decree, rule, pronounce, will, prescribe, instruct, determine, adjudge, order, dictate, command, pass judgement; enact, legislate.

Ant. 1 unfrock, defrock; discharge, dismiss, relieve of one's duties, impeach. **2** countermand, revoke, rescind, reverse, annul, void, invalidate, cancel; repeal, nullify, overrule.

ordeal *n. Being lost on the moors for a week was an ordeal for the campers. The nation is just recovering from the ordeal of war:* nightmare, trial, harsh experience, trying experience, oppression, worry, vexation, trouble, burden, care, concern, pressure, strain, stress, tribulation, misery, torment, distress, agony, suffering, anguish, wretchedness, affliction, pain; unhappiness, sorrow, grief, heartache, tragedy, calamity.

Ant. delight, joy, happiness, elation, gladness, jubilation, ecstasy, rapture, bliss; relief, ease.

◇ *Word origin:* An *ordeal* is a trying experience, a test of one's character or endurance that seems to be dealt out to one by fate. It comes from Old English *or-* (out) + *dæl* (a deal), that which is dealt out to one.

order *n.* **1** *Loyal troops obeyed the duke's orders:* command, dictate, decree, rule, pronouncement, instruction, bidding, law, commandment, demand, dictum, imperative, ultimatum, ukase, fiat. **2** *The files are kept in alphabetical order:* arrangement, organization, classification, system, categorization, tabulation, designation, codification, grouping, neatness, tidiness, orderliness; form, structure, pattern, framework. **3** *The chairman tried to maintain order:* quiet, calm, law and order, peace and quiet, silence, peacefulness, harmony, tranquillity; control, discipline. **4** *Fish are a lower order of life than birds. Her singing talent is of the highest order:* classification, class, category, division, kind, species, family, caste, station, breed, sort, type; quality, calibre, position, standing, rank, status, degree, grade. **5** *The girl joined a religious order:* society, sisterhood, brotherhood, organization, fraternity, sorority, guild, house, body, society, association, alliance, group, club, lodge, confederacy, company, federation. —*v.* **6** *She ordered the dog to sit:* command, bid, direct, instruct, charge, decree, dictate, adjure, enjoin, ordain, call for. **7** *Let's order dessert when the waitress comes back:* request, call for, ask for, book, engage, reserve, contract for, agree to, purchase, authorize the purchase of.

Ant. 1 request, plea, entreaty, supplication. **2, 3** disorder, confusion. **3** anarchy. **6** plead, entreat, supplicate, beg.

> **Exploring the Word**: Latin *ordo,* row, series, rank, arrangement, gives us: *order* and *orderly,* referring to conditions in which everything is in its proper row or arrangement (*a religious order* is a grade or rank of clergymen); *ordinary,* literally according to or of the established or common order or arrangement; *ordinance,* a rule or order, as a municipal decree or law; and *ordain,* to decree or order.

orderly *adj.* **1** *Keep your cupboards orderly:* neat, tidy, spruce, shipshape, uncluttered, systematic, organized, methodical, classified, in a regular sequence. **2** *Let's proceed in an orderly manner:* disciplined, restrained, controlled, well-behaved, quiet, well-mannered, peaceable, peaceful, law-abiding.

Ant. 1, 2 disorderly. **1** messy, sloppy, unsystematic, disorganized, cluttered. **2** undisciplined, chaotic, uncontrolled, unregulated, riotous.

ordinance *n. The ordinance forbids fireworks inside the city boundary:* law, rule, regulation, statute, by-law; command, decree, edict, canon, fiat, dictum, order, enactment, writ, mandate, commandment, bull.

◇ *Usage note:* Don't confuse *ordinance,* a municipal law or a decree, with *ordnance,* military weapons and combat matériel. *The city council passed an ordinance against jaywalking,* but *The ordnance is stored in the arsenal.* Remember, *a cIty ordInance.*

ordinarily *adv. Ordinarily we eat breakfast at seven:* usually, generally, normally, customarily, commonly, as a rule, by and large, as a matter of course, in most instances, on average, conventionally, habitually.

Ant. rarely, infrequently, hardly ever, as an exception, occasionally, sporadically.

ordinary *adj.* **1** *It was an ordinary lunch of soup and a sandwich. He's not a hero, just an ordinary man:* common, commonplace, usual, average, customary, standard, normal, everyday, routine, familiar, typical, conventional, traditional, habitual, unexceptional, stereotyped, run-of-the-mill. **2** *The novelist's latest book is quite ordinary:* undistinguished, commonplace, mediocre, indifferent, unimpressive, uninspired, unimaginative, pedestrian, run-of-the-mill, so-so; uninteresting, dull, humdrum; unimportant, inconsequential, insignificant, trivial.

Ant. 1, 2 extraordinary, exceptional, outstanding, distinguished, unusual, unique, uncommon, rare, unfamiliar, novel, atypical, unconventional. **2** superior, impressive, imaginative, inspired; important, consequential, significant, exciting.

ordnance *n. The battle was lost through lack of proper ordnance:* artillery, cannon, field-guns; military weapons and equipment, war matériel.

organ *n.* **1** *The organ played as the bride came down the aisle:* pipe-organ, reed-organ, harmonium; hand-organ, barrel-organ, hurdy-gurdy. **2** *The heart is one of the body's vital organs:* functional part, bodily part, bodily structure. **3** *This paper is an official organ of the teachers' union:* journal, publication, trade journal, group publication, magazine; instrument, vehicle, agency.

◇ *Word origin: Organ* and *organism* come from Greek *organon,* instrument, engine, machine.

organic *adj.* **1** *Organic compounds form the basis of life. Organic gardening uses no manufactured chemicals:* containing carbon; of living things, living, alive, animate, quick; natural, non-synthetic. **2** *The patient has an organic malfunction:* of an organ, physiological, physical, anatomical, constitutional. **3** *The final chapter was part of a larger organic whole:* unified, ordered, harmonious, well-organized, patterned; systematic, planned, methodical, designed.

Ant. 1-3 inorganic. **3** haphazard, chaotic.

organism *n.* **1** *The amoeba is a very simple organism:* living thing, creature, animal, physiological unit; plant, organic structure. **2** *The army is an extremely complex organism:* organized body, organization, system, network, whole, entity, complex; institution, corporation, federation, association, society.

organization *n.* **1** *The organization of the business took two years:* formulation, forming, formation, incorporation, constitution, co-ordination, arranging, structuring, assembly, making. **2** *The most striking thing about this abstract painting is the organization of the shapes and colours:* arrangement, structure, design, pattern, composition, grouping, ordering, harmony. **3** *The British Medical Association is a professional organization of doctors:* association, society, fraternity, federation, union, club, fellowship, order, league, group, alliance, corps, party; business organization, business, establishment, firm, company, corporation, outfit; sect.

Ant. 1 dissolution, disbanding, break-up. **2** disorganization, confusion, chaos.

organize *v.* **1** *Let's organize a debating society:* form, formulate, establish, originate, found, create, set up, put together, lay the foundation of, develop. **2** *I'm trying to organize these dresser drawers:* arrange, systematize, make orderly, order, neaten, tidy, tidy up; classify, catalogue, co-ordinate, categorize, group, codify, tabulate, index, file.

Ant. 1 dissolve, disband, dismember, break up. **2** disorganize, disorder, confuse, mess up.

orgy *n. We're planning a quiet New Year's Eve party, not an orgy!:* wild revelry, wild party, wanton celebration, drunken festivities, debauch, carousal, saturnalia, bacchanalia.

◇ *Word origin: Orgy* comes from Greek *orgia,* secret rites, referring to the rites practised by the initiated in the worship of Demeter at Eleusis, in the Orphic mysteries, and in the cult of Dionysus (Bacchus), god of wine and fertility. The word literally means "services" and is related to *organon* (tool) from which we get our *organ*-words. It is also related to Greek *ergon,* work, and to Old English *weorc,* from which we get our word *work.*

orient *n.* **1 the Orient** *We visited Japan and two other countries in the Orient:* Asia; eastern Asia, the Eastern Hemisphere, the Far East. —*v.* **2** *The first days of training are meant to orient the recruits to army life:* accustom, familiarize, relate, acclimatize, reconcile, make feel at home. **3** *You can orient yourself by remembering that the big hill is due north:* locate, situate, set, fix, take one's bearings, find, place with reference to the points of the compass, determine one's direction.

Ant. 1 The Occident; Europe, the Americas, the Western Hemisphere. **2** estrange, alienate. **3** disorient, lose, confuse.

◇ *Word origin: Orient* comes from Latin *sol oriens,* the rising sun, hence the direction of the rising sun, the east. *Orientation* literally means facing the east, and the *orientation* of a church means its alignment on an east-west axis so as to have its altar in the eastern end.

orientation *n.* **1** *New employees must go through a period of orientation before they can be expected to understand their job:* familiarization, acclimatization, finding one's feet, adjustment. **2** *The winding trail caused the hikers to lose their orientation. The orientation of the building is such that the early morning sun shines on the façade:* sense of direction, direction; alignment, location, situation.

Ant. 1 estrangement, alienation; confusion, bewilderment, perplexity, mystification.

origin *n.* **1** *The origin of the flood was three weeks of torrential rain. The reporter traced the story back to its origin:* source, cause, basis, base, foundation, derivation, reason, principle, agent, generator; originator, creator, father, mother, author, producer, prime mover, spring, fountain-head, tap-root, root, ground. **2** *The students are studying the origins of jazz in America:* beginning, birth, genesis, inception, commencement; emergence, evolution, early development, growth, rise, derivation. **3** *The family is of Scandinavian origin:* extraction, descent, ancestry, parentage, family, lineage, house, stock, race, strain, breed, line; birth, nativity.

Ant. 1 end, finish, termination, conclusion. 2 death, fall, extinction, finis. 3 posterity, issue, progeny, offspring.

◇ *Word origin: Origin* and *original* come from Latin *origo*, source, beginning.

original *adj.* 1 *Philadelphia was the original capital of the United States. The original idea was good, but now the plan is too complicated:* first, initial, earliest, inaugural, introductory; basic, fundamental, essential, underlying, formative, germinal, seminal; aboriginal, primordial, primeval, primary, primal. 2 *She won an award for the most original design:* having originality, imaginative, creative, inventive, ingenious, fresh, novel, new, new-fashioned, unique, unusual, different, bold, daring, out of the ordinary, extraordinary, singular; uncommon, unfamiliar, strange, atypical, unconventional, unorthodox, *Informal* newfangled.

—*n.* 3 *Many steam engines have been built since, but this is the original:* prototype, first or earliest model, pattern, example, basis, first form.

Ant. 1 last, latest, final; superficial. 2 unoriginal, common, commonplace, usual, typical, conventional, traditional, ordinary, average, standard, normal, familiar, banal, trite, stale; old, old-fashioned, antiquated, *Slang* old hat; derivative, borrowed, copied. 3 copy, reproduction.

originality *n. The design for the building shows a great deal of originality:* imagination, creativity, inventiveness, ingenuity, individuality, freshness, newness, novelty, uniqueness, boldness, daring, unconventionality.

Ant. unoriginality, routinism, commonness, conventionality, averageness, familiarity, banality, cliché, triteness, predictability; derivativeness.

originally *adv.* 1 *We come originally from Sheffield:* by origin; by derivation, by birth. 2 *The dress originally cost £14:* at first, initially, at the outset, in the beginning. 3 *The house is decorated quite originally:* imaginatively, creatively, inventively, uniquely, differently, unusually, in an original way, unconventionally.

Ant. 2 finally, in the end. 3 conventionally, traditionally, typically, routinely, unimaginatively, predictably, tritely.

originate *v.* 1 *The Reformation originated in Germany. The river originates from a spring in the hills:* begin, start, commence, proceed, emanate; arise, rise, derive, come, germinate, flow, issue, spring up, crop up, sprout, emerge, stem; be based in. 2 *He is credited with originating a new printing process:* create, invent, devise, initiate, inaugurate, formulate, fabricate, father, conceive, design, draft; found, establish, organize, develop, evolve.

Ant. 1 end, conclude, terminate, finish, close, stop, cease. 2 copy, imitate, follow.

ornament *n.* 1 *We bought ornaments for the Christmas tree:* decoration, adornment, trimming, accessory, embellishment, trim, frills, garnish; ornamentation, finery, beautification, enrichment.

—*v.* 2 *The seamstress ornamented the dress with lace:* adorn, decorate, bedeck, festoon, trim, furbish, deck, trick out, garnish, gild; embellish, beautify.

ornate *adj. The gold frame is much too ornate for that simple picture:* elaborate, lavish, fancy, sumptuous, showy, flashy, flamboyant, ostentatious; decorated, adorned, embellished, baroque, rococo.

Ant. simple, plain, bare, unadorned, unembellished, undecorated.

> **Exploring the Word:** *Ornate, ornament,* and *adorn* all have an *orn* because they come from Latin *ornare,* to adorn. Thus *ornate* means adorned or over-adorned, an *ornament* is something used to adorn something else, and *adorn* retains the basic meaning of the Latin word.

orthodox *adj.* 1 *Old people cling to their orthodox beliefs:* traditional, established, following established doctrine, accepted, inveterate, authoritative, official, approved, religious, pious, devout. 2 *Such orthodox thinking will not lead to a new solution to the problem:* conventional, traditional, customary, conformable, commonplace, usual, routine, standard, fixed, established, regular, ordinary, usual; narrow, circumscribed, limited.

Ant. 1, 2 unorthodox. 1 heretical, radical, liberal, heterodox, unconformable. 2 unconventional, unusual, uncommon, unique, original, novel; eccentric, nonconformist, independent.

◇ *Word origin: Orthodox* comes from Greek *orthos* (right) + *doxa* (opinion, thinking). Greek *orthos*, right, also appears in *orthography* (spelling or writing) and *orthopaedics* (surgery correcting or making right deformities of the skeletal system).

ossify *v. At what age does cartilage ossify?:* harden into bone, fossilize; (*loosely*) harden, stiffen, become rigid, become fixed.

ostensible *adj. Bill is now the ostensible head of the company, but his father is still the real boss:* titular, nominal, apparent, outward, seeming, alleged, avowed, declared, professed, manifest, perceivable, visible; pretended, assumed, feigned, specious, illusory.

Ant. real, true, actual, genuine, de facto.

ostentatious *adj. Grandfather warned us not to be ostentatious with our money. The dress is too ostentatious to wear to a reception:* flaunting wealth, fond of display, showing off, grandiose, highflown; conspicuous, pretentious, flamboyant, flashy, showy, gaudy, garish, loud, florid, overdone, exaggerated, obtrusive.

Ant. modest, reserved, conservative, sombre, sedate; inconspicuous, simple, plain.

ostracize *v. After the scandal her old friends ostracized her:* shun, snub, refuse to associate with, reject, exclude, shut out, banish, disown, blacklist, blackball, give one the cold shoulder, turn one's back on, *Slang* cut.
Ant. welcome, accept, acknowledge.

other *adj.* **1** *I'll take this and one other suit on holiday:* additional, more, further, added, extra, spare, supplementary, auxiliary. **2** *Doesn't this dress come in other colours? Wait until you hear the other side of the story before blaming anyone:* different, additional, more, dissimilar, unlike, contrasted, differentiated; opposite, reverse, contrasting, contradictory, contrary, alternative, remaining.
◇ *Word origin: Other* comes from Old English *ōther*, which also gives us *either*. Incidentally, our word *or* is a contraction of *other*.

otherwise *adv.* **1** *Leave now; otherwise you'll be late:* if not, or else; under other circumstances, on the other hand. **2** *She could not phrase the question otherwise. I think otherwise:* differently, in another manner; in opposition, in disagreement, in defiance, contrarily, contrariwise, inversely, in reverse. **3** *He's too fat; otherwise he would be nice-looking:* in other respects, excluding this, barring this, excepting this, apart from this.
Ant. 2 similarly, alike, correspondingly.

oust *v. The umpire ousted the arguing player from the game. The lazy employee was ousted from the job:* expel, eject, remove, banish, put out, throw out, kick out; dismiss, discharge, cashier, fire, unseat, *Slang* axe, sack, show the door, give the boot, send packing.
Ant. admit, invite, ask in, welcome; hire, engage, employ, appoint.

outbreak *n. Police quelled the outbreak of violence. There has been an outbreak of measles in the school:* outburst, burst, eruption, explosion, outpouring, display, demonstration; sudden appearance, rapid spread, epidemic.
Ant. waning, ebbing, recession, decrease, decline, subsidence.

outburst *n. His outburst of anger shocked us all:* burst, eruption, outbreak, explosion, outpouring, display, demonstration.
Ant. suppression, repression, control, restraint, stifling.

outcast *n.* **1** *The one-time star became an outcast:* exile, deportee, refugee, expatriate, displaced person, man without a country; pariah, castaway; outlaw, fugitive, runaway; lonely wanderer, roamer, rover, homeless man, vagabond, derelict, destitute person.
—*adj.* **2** *The Salvation Army hostel was a haven for outcast families:* homeless, evicted, neglected, despised, forsaken, unwanted, rejected, discarded, expelled, castaway, ousted, banished.

outcome *n. What was the outcome of your interview?:* result, consequence, effect, upshot, issue, end, fruit, *Slang* pay-off.

outcry *n. The sentry's outcry warned the troops. There was a great outcry among consumers when prices rose:* crying out, cry, cry of alarm, cry of distress, cry of protest, shout, scream, shriek, caterwauling, screech, howl, yell, roar, bellow, whoop, yowl, yelp; clamour, uproar, commotion, noise, clangour, hubbub, hue and cry, hullabaloo; protest, complaint, objection, remonstrance.
Ant. whisper, murmur; quiet, stillness, calm, silence, tranquillity; assent, concurrence, ratification.

outer *adj. The outer surface is walnut veneer. The house is in the outer suburbs:* exterior, external, outward, outside, without; farther out, extreme, remote, outlying, peripheral.
Ant. inner, interior, internal, inward, inside, within; central, close-by, close-in, nearby, adjacent.

outfit *n.* **1** *Mother bought a new outfit for Easter. A scuba diving outfit includes tanks, hose, mask, and flippers:* ensemble, costume, set of clothing, get-up, wardrobe, habit; equipment, gear, paraphernalia, trappings, accoutrements, *Slang* rig.

outgoing *adj.* **1** *Put the letter with the outgoing mail:* outbound, going out, outward bound, leaving, departing, retiring. **2** *A good hostess should be warm and outgoing:* friendly, gregarious, genial, social, extroverted, sympathetic, cordial, warm, warm-hearted.
Ant. 1 incoming, arriving, entering. **2** cold, austere, indifferent, distant, reserved, retiring, withdrawn.

outgrowth *n.* **1** *The police investigation is an outgrowth of numerous complaints:* result, consequence, upshot, natural development, product, issue, fruit; end, conclusion, culmination, sequel, after-effect, aftermath, offshoot. **2** *The tree has outgrowths of fungus and mushrooms:* shoot, sprout, offshoot, outcrop, excrescence; protuberance, projection, bulge, node, knob, knot.

outing *n. The family enjoyed an outing to the beach last week-end:* excursion, pleasure-trip; hike, tramp, ramble, walk; drive, ride, tour, spin, jaunt, airing.

outlandish *adj. Did you ever see such an outlandish hat?:* preposterous, incredible, outrageous, odd, bizarre, fantastic, freakish, eccentric, queer, weird, strange, curious, peculiar, unusual, unconventional, unimaginable, unbelievable, inconceivable, unheard-of, unparalleled, *Slang* far-out.
Ant. commonplace, ordinary, everyday, routine, normal, familiar, standard, usual, run-of-the-mill.
◇ *Word origin:* When you think about it, *outlandish* has an obvious history. It means "like the customs of an *outlander* or foreigner."

outlaw *n.* **1** *A posse was formed to track down the outlaws:* criminal, fugitive, felon, bandit,

desperado, highwayman, miscreant; outcast, pariah.
—*v.* **2** *The new regulation outlaws the sale of bicycles without headlights:* make unlawful, forbid, prohibit, ban, bar, proscribe, exclude, deny, disallow, suppress, stop, interdict.
Ant. 2 legalize, permit, allow; encourage, foster, welcome.

outlay *n. Building the swimming-pool required an outlay of several thousand pounds:* expenditure, spending; amount spent, disbursement, outgo, cost, expense, charge.
Ant. profit, gain, yield, income.

outlet *n.* **1** *Switzerland has no outlet to the sea:* opening, egress, passage, channel, avenue; exit, gateway, gate, portal, door; duct, conduit. **2** *The child needs an outlet for all that energy:* vent, means of expression, means of satisfying, way of getting rid of, escape.
Ant. 1 entrance, ingress, entry.

outline *n.* **1** *The hunter could see the outline of the deer against the trees:* profile, silhouette, contour, delineation, lineation; boundary line, limits, tracing, perimeter, periphery. **2** *Just tell me the outline of the story now and fill in the details later:* synopsis, summary, résumé, brief report, brief, general sketch, thumb-nail sketch, condensation, digest, abridgement, abstract, review, recapitulation.
—*v.* **3** *Outline the figure in red. Outline the story before trying to write it down:* draw a line round, trace, delineate; diagram, write a synopsis, sketch out, plan, plot.
Ant. 1 bulk, mass, substance, volume; centre, core, heart.

outlook *n.* **1** *The outlook from the top of the mountain is breath-taking:* view, vista, prospect, sight, aspect, panorama, spectacle, scene, picture. **2** *His outlook has become quite pessimistic:* attitude, frame of mind, point of view, viewpoint, view, perspective. **3** *The experts say that the business outlook for next year is good:* prospect, expectation, anticipation, forecast, assumption, presumption; probability, chance, promise.
Ant. 3 hindsight; recapitulation.

outlying *adj. A new shopping centre is being built in an outlying area of the town. Some of the outlying districts have no bus service:* outer, exterior, peripheral; remote, distant, far-off.
Ant. central, inner, internal, core; nearby, near, neighbouring, close by, adjacent.

outrage *n.* **1** *Bombing the church was an outrage:* atrocity, inhumane act, act of brutality, wanton violence, barbarity, barbarousness, iniquity, enormity, monstrosity, gross offence, gross crime; evil, wrong, transgression, gross indecency; desecration, profanation. **2** *Such a lie is an outrage to anyone who loves the truth:* insult, affront, indignity, expression of contempt, disrespect, slap in the face.
—*v.* **3** *The speaker's remarks outraged the audience:* anger, incense, enrage, infuriate, madden, provoke, arouse, exasperate, gall, rile, ruffle, make one's blood boil, make one see red, steam up, get one's back up; insult, affront, make indignant, offend, shock, scandalize, disquiet, discompose.
Ant. 3 calm, soothe, quiet, pacify.
◇ *Word origin: Outrage* comes from Old French *outrage*, excess, violent action, outrage. The *out-* part of the word comes from Latin *ultra*, beyond (the -age is just a noun ending). People have always used this word to describe bad and "far-out" actions and the angry responses they provoke.

outrageous *adj.* **1** *The gang committed several outrageous crimes:* atrocious, vile, base, heinous, grossly offensive, iniquitous, monstrous, barbarous, inhumane, inhuman, brutal, foul, despicable, contemptible, wicked, nefarious, horrifying, odious, reprehensible, unspeakable. **2** *I've never heard such an outrageous remark in my life!:* offensive, abusive, shameless, shocking, scandalous, disgraceful, insulting, insolent, rude, disrespectful, contemptuous, scornful; infuriating, maddening, galling, exasperating. **3** *The price of the repairs was outrageous:* monstrous, extreme, unreasonable, preposterous, flagrant, unwarranted, unconscionable, gross, rank, exorbitant, immoderate, immense, excessive, enormous.
Ant. 3 reasonable, moderate, mild, minor, trivial, paltry; equitable, fair, just; tolerable.

outright *adj.* **1** *That statement was an outright lie:* utter, complete, total, downright, entire, full, unmitigated, unqualified, undiminished, unreserved, unconditional, absolute, sheer, thorough, thoroughgoing, out-and-out.
—*adv.* **2** *She was outright incapable of doing the job:* utterly, altogether, completely, absolutely, downright, thoroughly, entirely; openly, visibly, patently, manifestly, demonstrably. **3** *The driver was killed outright:* instantly, immediately, at once, on the spot, promptly, forthwith.
Ant. 1 partial, incomplete; qualified, conditional. **2** somewhat, partially. **3** later, eventually, ultimately, finally, in due course.

outside *n.* **1** *The outside of the house is painted white. The outside of the sweet is chocolate:* exterior, surface, outer side, façade, face; covering, case, sheath, skin, coating.
—*adj.* **2** *The outside walls are brick:* outer, exterior, external, outward, outermost, outdoor. **3** *National policy should not be determined by outside influences:* extraneous, foreign, alien, non-native, non-domestic, unfamiliar, strange. **4** *There's an outside chance it may rain today:* remote, distant, faint, obscure, slight.
—*adv.* **5** *Put the cat outside:* outdoors, out-of-doors, on or to the outside.
—*prep.* **6** *We took a journey outside the city:* beyond the bounds of, distant from, beyond the confines of.

Ant. 1, 2 inside, interior. **1** centre. **2** inner, inmost, innermost, inward, internal. **3** native, domestic; familiar, known. **5** indoors. **6** inside.

outspoken *adj. She's so outspoken that she's hurt the feelings of all her friends:* plain-spoken, blunt, frank, direct, straightforward, forthright, candid, unsparing; artless, ingenuous, guileless, undissembling, undissimulating.

Ant. tactful, diplomatic, gracious, judicious, reticent, guarded.

outstanding *adj.* **1** *This is one of the outstanding paintings of the Renaissance period:* foremost, eminent, prominent, famed, celebrated, distinguished, famous, renowned, best known, remarkable, memorable, unforgettable, striking, notable, noteworthy; exemplary, exceptional, extraordinary, marvellous, most impressive, magnificent, great, phenomenal. **2** *The outstanding bills must be paid by the first of the month:* unpaid, not yet settled, due, in arrears, uncollected, payable, owing.

Ant. 1 commonplace, routine, ordinary, usual, everyday, run-of-the-mill; trite, banal. **2** paid, settled, collected.

outward *adj.* **1** *There is no outward sign that the patient is improving. His outward appearance was calm but he was seething inside:* external, exterior, outer, outside, surface, superficial, visible, perceivable, perceptible, apparent, ostensible; evident, manifest, observable.

—*adv.* Also **outwards 2** *The ship was outward bound. This door opens outward, not inward:* out, toward the outside, away, from here.

Ant. 1, 2 inward. **1** internal, interior, inner, inside, inmost, innermost; invisible, imperceptible, unobservable. **2** in; toward the inside.

◇ *Usage note: Outward* is always correct, as an adjective or as an adverb. *Outwards* is correct only as an adverb. Thus, *His outward* (never "outwards") *appearance was calm,* but *The ship headed outward* (or *outwards*) *to deeper water.* If you stick to *outward,* you will always be right.

outwardly *adv. She was outwardly pleased with the idea:* to all appearances, apparently, evidently, seemingly, ostensibly, on the face of it, manifestly, visibly, clearly.

Ant. inwardly, secretly.

outweigh *v.* **1** *The boxer outweighed his opponent by ten pounds:* weigh more than, be heavier than, exceed the weight of. **2** *The good points outweigh the bad:* exceed, surpass, predominate, overshadow, eclipse, override, rise above, be more important than, prevail over, take precedence over.

outwit *v. The shop outwitted the robbers by putting fake jewels in the display case:* out-smart, outmanœuvre, take in, trick, fool, foil, thwart, baffle, circumvent; trap, ensnare.

ovation *n. The singer was greeted with a standing ovation:* enthusiastic applause, cheers, cheering, acclamation, acclaim, tribute; hurrah, hurray, huzza.

Ant. jeering, taunts, catcalls, hoots, booing.

over *adv.* **1** *Please look this contract over:* from beginning to end, from top to bottom, all through, all over; from head to foot, from cover to cover; from stem to stern, from end to end; along the course of. **2** *Will there be any left over?:* remaining, in addition, in excess, on top of the rest, beyond a certain amount, into the bargain, to boot; too, else, also; extra, over and above. **3** *Is the meeting over?:* at an end, finished, ended, concluded, done, terminated, completed, settled; lapsed, elapsed, expired, passed away, no more, gone, past, bygone. **4** *I guessed the amount, but Jim was over by £10:* in excess, in addition, above, extra, additional, excessive, surplus, too great, superfluous.

Ant. 2, 4 under, below, short, deficient, wanting, lacking. **3** begun, started, commenced; in progress.

"It's over, and can't be helped, and that's one consolation." —*Charles Dickens*

---

over-abundance *n. There is an over-abundance of tomatoes this year:* abundance, superabundance, excess, surplus, over-supply, superfluity, profusion, plethora, supersaturation, surfeit, glut, embarrassment of riches.

Ant. shortage, scarcity, dearth, scantiness, insufficiency, lack, want.

overall *adj. The overall situation is encouraging:* total, general, complete, comprehensive, all-inclusive, all-embracing, long-term, sweeping, panoramic, extensive, widespread; long-range.

overbearing *adj. He's so overbearing that no one wants to work for him:* arrogant, high-handed, self-assertive, self-important, cocky, lordly, high-and-mighty, know-it-all, disdainful, imperious, domineering, dictatorial, autocratic, tyrannical, despotic; egotistical, haughty, pompous, conceited, *Informal* stuck-up, snooty, high-hat.

Ant. modest, unassuming, humble, demure, meek, shy, timid, subdued, deferential, subservient; receptive, sympathetic, compassionate, gracious.

overcast *adj. The forecast is overcast skies and a little rain:* cloudy, overclouded, sunless, grey, dull, dreary, gloomy, leaden, murky; misty, foggy, hazy.

Ant. cloudless, unclouded, clear, sunny, brilliant, bright.

overcome *v. One day we shall overcome racial intolerance. She was overcome with grief:* conquer, best, get the better of, master, vanquish, defeat, beat, lick, suppress, overthrow, put down, overwhelm, overpower, subdue, crush, quell, prevail over, triumph over, transcend.

Ant. surrender to, give in to, capitulate to, submit to; give up, admit defeat.

over-confident *adj. The chess player was over-confident so that he played carelessly:* too confident, too sure of succeeding, self-assured, cocksure; impudent, presumptuous, brash, immodest, cheeky.

Ant. self-effacing, fearful, modest, sheepish, shamefaced.

overdo *v.* **1** *A little exercise is fine, but don't overdo it:* do to excess, carry too far, not know when to stop, be intemperate in; overtax oneself by; indulge oneself in. **2** *A simple "thank you" is enough; don't overdo it:* exaggerate, overstate, stretch a point, *Informal* lay it on thick; magnify, intensify, expand, amplify, embroider, gild, overact, overplay, *Slang* ham it up.

Ant. **2** understate, minimize, slight, neglect.

overdue *adj. Your visit here is long overdue:* past due, belated, late, tardy, unpunctual, behind time, behindhand, delayed, slow, dilatory, long delayed.

Ant. early, ahead of time, beforehand, premature.

overflow *v.* **1** *Turn the water off or the bath-tub will overflow. The flood overflowed the river valley:* flow over, run over, be filled to overflowing, spill, slop over; overspread, inundate, flood. —*n.* **2** *There is an overflow of cheap ball-point pens on the market:* over-abundance, superabundance, surplus, excess, superfluity, profusion, over-supply, plethora, copiousness, flood, glut.

Ant. **2** lack, want, scarcity, shortage, dearth, paucity, deficiency, insufficiency, inadequacy.

overhaul *v.* **1** *I tried to overhaul the lorry on the next bend but it was going too fast:* overtake, pass, catch up with, catch, beat. **2** *How much will it cost to overhaul the motor?:* renovate, revamp, rebuild, reconstruct, remodel, take apart and put back together, inspect and repair.

overhead *adv.* **1** *There was a large skylight overhead. Look overhead!:* over one's head, above one's head; upward, up above, above; aloft, atop, on top.
—*adj.* **2** *Turn on the lamps and the overhead light:* ceiling, roof; overlying, overhanging; uppermost, upper, superior, topmost.
—*n.* **3** *To increase profits the business must reduce its overheads:* operating expenses, general expenses.

overjoyed *adj. She seemed overjoyed to see us:* delighted, deliriously happy, jubilant, elated, joyous, gratified, enthralled, exultant, exuberant, enchanted, ecstatic, transported, *Informal* carried away, tickled pink, happy as the day is long, happy as a lark.

Ant. disappointed, unhappy, sad, depressed, dejected, downcast, sorrowful, despondent, blue.

overlook *v.* **1** *How could you overlook paying the rent?:* forget, neglect, leave undone, leave out, not trouble oneself about, omit, miss, slight, pass over, pass up, skip. **2** *She overlooks most of his faults:* ignore, disregard, regard indulgently, pass over, blink at, wink at; excuse, forgive, shrug off, forget about, think no more of, let bygones be bygones, let ride. **3** *The house overlooks the river:* have a view of, look over, give on, look out on, survey; tower above, command.

Ant. **1** remember, pay attention to, concentrate on, keep in mind. **2** complain, carp, nag, cavil, criticize, censure, find fault with, view with disfavour.

"The art of being wise is the art of knowing what to overlook." —*William James*

---

overpower *v.* **1** *The speaker overpowered the audience with the force of his argument:* overcome, overwhelm, affect strongly, move, sway, influence. **2** *He overpowered his assailant and called the police:* subdue, overcome, get the better of, best, get the upper hand over, master, overwhelm, conquer, vanquish, defeat, worst, bear, triumph over, crush, quell.

Ant. **2** surrender, give up, give in, capitulate.

overrate *v. The critics certainly overrated that show:* overpraise, overestimate, overesteem, rate too highly, overvalue, overprize, praise undeservedly, make too much of, attach too much importance to.

Ant. underrate, underestimate, undervalue; belittle, minimize.

overrule *v.* **1** *The court overruled the council's objection:* disallow, rule against, reject, override, dismiss, preclude, set aside, waive, eject, throw out, deny, veto, refuse, repudiate, invalidate, countermand, overturn, repel, revoke, cancel, annul, nullify, make null and void. **2** *One member wanted to raise the fees but the rest of the club overruled him:* prevail over, outvote, outweigh, bend to one's will.

Ant. **1** accept, allow, permit, approve, grant, authorize, favour; sustain, support, promote, champion, back.

overrun *v. The Vandals of northern Europe overran the Roman Empire. Weeds overran the garden:* swarm over, infest, surge over, rove over, run riot over, overspread, pour in on, overwhelm, invade; raid, invade, swoop down on; sack, pillage, plunder, loot, despoil; engulf, inundate, deluge; overgrow, choke, flourish in.

oversea Also **overseas** *adv.* **1** *Millions of American soldiers fought overseas in World War II:* abroad, in foreign lands, across the sea, beyond the sea; in foreign service.
—*adj.* **2** *Are you interested in an overseas job? Our overseas shipments go by freighter:* foreign, external, alien, exotic; transoceanic, ultramarine.

Ant. **1** at home, on native soil. **2** domestic, internal, native, indigenous.

oversee *v. While the owner is gone, his assistant*

will oversee the business: supervise, superintend, have charge of, handle, attend to, see to; administer, manage, direct, run, boss, command, govern, rule, guide, watch, preside over, carry on, pilot, steer, be at the helm of.

overshadow *v.* **1** *Heavy clouds overshadowed the mountain:* cast a shadow over, eclipse, shade, darken; obscure, hide, conceal, cover, screen, mask, shroud, veil, fog. **2** *His famous father overshadowed him:* outshine, eclipse, dwarf, tower over, render insignificant by comparison, diminish the importance of, steal the limelight from.

oversight *n. Did you mean to leave the door unlocked or was it an oversight?:* omission, mistake, blunder, heedless mistake, careless error; slight negligence, neglect, carelessness, laxity, inattention, thoughtlessness, heedlessness, disregard.

Ant. care, attention, heed, heedfulness, diligence, alertness, vigilance, meticulousness, scrupulousness.

overt *adj. There was no overt hostility between the two men:* apparent, obvious, noticeable, visible, observable, ostensible, plain, open, easily seen, perceptible, perceivable, palpable, evident, revealed, manifest.

Ant. covert, unrevealed, unnoticeable, invisible, hidden, concealed, covered, masked, secret, undisclosed, disguised; private, personal.

◇ *Word origin: Overt* is from the Old French word for "opened."

overtake *v.* **1** *The champion slowly overtook the rest of the field:* come abreast of, catch up with, catch, come up beside, gain on, reach, approach, run down; pass, overhaul, go by. **2** *The storm overtook the sailors before they could reach port:* take by surprise, come upon suddenly, befall, catch unprepared, catch off guard.

Ant. 1 fall back from, lose ground to.

overthrow *v.* **1** *The rebels conspired to overthrow the regime:* overturn, topple, bring down, cast down from power, put an end to by force, overcome, overpower, defeat, abolish, undo, crush, do away with.

—*n.* **2** *The overthrow of the dictator was greeted with cheers:* toppling, bringing down, casting out of power, undoing, downfall, defeat, overturn, abolition; revolution, rebellion, insurrection, mutiny.

Ant. 1 preserve, conserve, maintain, uphold, support, keep, perpetuate; defend, protect, guard. **2** preservation, perpetuation; defence, protection.

overtone *n. There were overtones of distrust in his voice:* suggestion, intimation, insinuation, hint, implication, connotation, slight indication, innuendo, drift, colouring, hue.

overture *n.* **1** *The opera was preceded by a short overture:* prelude, introduction, prologue; foreword, preface, preamble; beginning. **2** *The losing army made overtures of peace:* opening move, preliminary offer, receptive sign, invitation, approach, bid, offering, advance, tender, motion, signal, gesture, suggestion, proposal, proposition.

Ant. 1 finale, close; epilogue, afterword, coda. **2** rejection, spurning, repudiation, rebuke.

overwhelm *v.* **1** *Invading armies overwhelmed the town:* overrun, overpower, overcome, overthrow, defeat, vanquish, subjugate, conquer, beat; quash, crush, quell, bury, swamp, engulf, inundate. **2** *Sorrow overwhelmed the family:* overcome, overpower, devastate, crush, stagger, confound, bowl over.

Ant. 1 surrender, capitulate, give up, give in; rescue, deliver, save. **2** leave unaffected, leave indifferent; encourage, lift.

overwrought *adj. He was overwrought after the bitter argument:* over-excited, excited, agitated, wrought up, worked up, carried away, near hysteria, riled, greatly disturbed, distracted, inflamed, wild, frenzied, wild-eyed, uneasy, perturbed, ruffled; nervous, highly strung, over-sensitive, touchy.

Ant. calm, tranquil, placid, unruffled, serene, unexcited, untroubled, cool, composed, *Slang* unflappable.

owe *v. After the latest loan the business will owe the bank £10,000. You owe your parents more respect:* be in debt, be indebted to, be obligated, have a loan from; be under obligation to, be bound in gratitude, be beholden to.

Ant. repay, pay back, reimburse, liquidate, amortize, compensate.

own *adj.* **1** *Bring your own tennis-racket. What I do with my spare time is my own business!:* belonging to oneself, belonging to itself; personal, private, individual, particular.

—*v.* **2** *Has the youth ever owned a car before?:* possess, have possession of, be in receipt of, be the owner of, have, retain, keep, maintain, hold. **3** *She would never own up to a mistake. Society must own the right of every man to speak his mind:* admit, acknowledge, confess to, concede, disclose, tell; grant, allow, yield, consent to, recognize; avow, assent, concur, acquiesce.

Ant. 1 someone else's, another's. **3** deny, disown, disclaim, repudiate, abjure; deprive, divest, disallow, refuse, withhold.

P

pace *n.* **1** *Take three paces forward. The horse moved at an easy pace:* step, stride, gait, tread, slow gait, walk, amble, saunter. **2** *The work progressed at a slow pace:* rate, speed, velocity, motion, momentum, flow, gait.
—*v.* **3** *She paced the floor, waiting for the phone to ring. The horse paced around the ring:* walk nervously back and forth across; walk, go at a slow gait, amble, stroll, saunter.
Ant. 1, 2 trot, canter, run.

pacify *v. The king pacified the mob with promises of reform:* appease, calm, quiet, bring to a state of peace, soothe, placate, assuage, compose, mollify; restore to peace, restore harmony, conciliate, reconcile, settle differences, bring to terms, heal the breach.
Ant. make hostile, anger, enrage, madden, inflame, agitate, aggravate, provoke; begin hostilities, start a fight.
◇ *Word origin: Pacify* comes from Latin *pax* (peace) + *facere* (to make).

pack *n.* **1** *I carried my own pack on my back but it was heavy going. It seems that the whole story is a pack of lies!:* package, packet, parcel, bundle, kit, box, container; batch, bunch, set, lot, heap, mass, cluster, clump; accumulation, collection, assortment, miscellany. **2** *A pack of wolves haunted the place at night:* crowd, throng, group, horde, mob, multitude, swarm, flock, herd, drove, covey, pride, bevy, gaggle.
—*v.* **3** *Spectators packed the stadium. Pack these books up and put them in the attic:* fill, load, jam, cram, stuff; bundle, bunch, batch, group, gather, assemble, wrap up, tie, bind, truss.
Ant. 3 unpack, empty; unwrap, untie, unload.

package *n.* **1** *How much is this package of detergent? Have you still got the package that this came in?:* pack, parcel, packet; bundle, box, container, kit, wrappings.
—*v.* **2** *Nowadays they package the lettuce in Cellophane:* wrap, wrap up, pack, encase; display in a container.

pact *n. Seven countries signed the trade pact:* treaty, international agreement, agreement, compact, contract, concordance, concordat; bond, covenant, alliance, understanding.
◇ *Word origin: Pact* comes from Latin *pactus*, agreed. This is derived from *pacisci*, to make a covenant. The word is related to Latin *pax*, peace.

pad *n.* **1** *That carpet needs a pad under it. Get a pad to lie on:* cushion, cushioning, padding; mattress, bolster. **2** *Each student should have a pencil and pad:* tablet, writing tablet, notebook; desk pad, memorandum book, memo pad.
—*v.* **3** *The removal men padded the furniture with mattresses and canvas:* cushion, protect; upholster; stuff, fill. **4** *The author padded the book with long quotations:* fill out unnecessarily, expand needlessly, enlarge excessively, amplify freely, stretch out, inflate, fatten, blow up, puff out.

pagan *n.* **1** *The pagans worshipped the gods of fire and rain:* one who is not a Christian or Jew or Muslim; heathen, infidel, idolator, idol worshipper, totemist, polytheist; non-believer, atheist.
—*adj.* **2** *The pagan idols were destroyed by the missionaries:* heathen, heathenish, idolatrous, polytheistic; barbarian.
Ant. 1 Christian, Jew, Muslim; true believer, believer. **2** Christian, Jewish, Muslim, monotheistic, Christianized, civilized, enlightened.
◇ *Word origin:* The Romans considered those who lived in outlying villages as uncouth, uneducated people who didn't know much about culture, manners, or religion. *Pagan* comes from Latin *paganus*, rustic, peasant. The term is derived from Latin *pagus*, the country, rural district. From the 2nd century on, Latin *paganus* had the additional meaning of "civilian, non-soldier." Early Christians were fond of military metaphors, regarding themselves as soldiers of Christ. So they applied the "non-soldier" word to those who had not enlisted in the Church militant.

pageant *n. The pageant commemorates the founding of the town:* spectacle, elaborate performance, show, extravaganza; ceremony, ritual, pomp, rite, tableau; procession, parade.

pageantry *n. The pageantry of the coronation was spectacular:* display, pomp, pageant, ceremony, spectacle, ritual, rite; grandeur, magnificence, splendour, glitter, show, showiness, extravagance, ostentation, flair, *Slang* splash.
◇ *Word origin:* The word *pageantry* was invented by Shakespeare: "What pageantry, what feats, what shows, what minstrelsy, and pretty din the regent made . . . to greet the King." (*Pericles*, Act 5, Scene 2.)

pain *n.* **1** *I have a pain in my shoulder:* ache, aching, soreness, hurt, hurting, smarting, pang, throb, twinge, pinch, stitch, discomfort, malaise. **2** *May this country never again know the pain of war:* suffering, distress, anguish, agony, torment, torture, ordeal, hell, misery, grief, woe, heartache, heart-break, sorrow, sadness, affliction, wretchedness, unhappiness.
—*v.* **3** *Does your ankle still pain you?:* hurt, ache, smart, throb, sting, discomfort. **4** *The child's constant tantrums pained his mother:* distress, agonize, torment, torture, make miserable, trouble, worry, disturb, grieve, sadden; dis-

please, annoy, vex, gall, harass, rile, chafe, pique, exasperate, try one's patience.

Ant. 1 comfort, relief. **2** delight, joy, pleasure, sweetness, satisfaction, gladness, enjoyment, ecstasy, happiness, rapture, comfort, peace, solace. **3** relieve, ease, comfort. **4** delight, please, gladden, enchant, enrapture, captivate, charm, satisfy, gratify; comfort, solace.

◇ *Word origin:* The word *pain* is related to Greek *poinē*, penalty, fine. Thus our old expression "on pain of death," meaning "under penalty of death," used the word in an old sense. Since a penalty or fine is distressing and unpleasant, the word took on its modern sense of "distress, suffering."

painful *adj.* **1** *The child has a painful earache:* aching, very sore, agonizing, excruciating, throbbing, smarting, stinging, sharp, piercing, hurtful, torturous, racking, distressful; hurtful, afflictive. **2** *It was my painful duty to inform the next of kin:* unpleasant, distressing, disagreeable, distasteful, difficult, trying, gruelling, disturbing, disquieting; grievous, lamentable, sad, sorrowful, pathetic, dire, dismal, dreary.

Ant. 1 painless; soothing, comforting, alleviating, relieving. **2** pleasant, pleasurable, delightful, enjoyable, agreeable, happy, gratifying, satisfying.

painstaking *adj. After years of painstaking research a cure was found:* careful, thorough, thoroughgoing, conscientious, scrupulous, meticulous, punctilious, precise, exacting, diligent, persevering, assiduous, earnest, industrious, energetic, strenuous.

Ant. careless, haphazard, slapdash, *Informal* catch-as-catch-can; neglectful, negligent, feckless, heedless, thoughtless; half-hearted, lazy, frivolous.

pair *n.* **1** *What a lovely pair of shoes! The farmer hitched the pair of oxen to the wagon:* two matched items, set of two, team, brace, yoke, span. **2** *The bride and groom are a good-looking pair:* couple, duo, twosome; match, combination.
—*v.* **3** *Pair the socks and put them in the drawer:* match, match up, mate, pair off, couple, combine, unite.

◇ *Usage note: Pair* generally means one pair only, one set of two. Its preferred plural is *pairs: Helen bought two pairs of shoes.* In informal English one may say "two pair," but it's wiser to stick to *two pairs* and be on the safe side.

◇ *Word origin: Pair* comes from Latin *par*, equal.

pal *n. George and I were pals at school:* buddy, bosom friend, chum, comrade, companion, boon companion, crony, friend, intimate, intimate friend, confidant, shadow, mate; confrère, partner, *Informal* chum; accomplice, associate, colleague.

◇ *Word origin: Pal* is from Romany, the language of the Gipsies, in which it means "brother, mate." It can be traced all the way back to Sanskrit *bhartr*, brother. Thus, *pal* and *brother* mean the same and come from the same Indo-European source.

palace *n. Buckingham Palace is one of the residences of the Royal Family:* royal residence, castle; mansion, stately residence, manor house, château.

pale[1] *adj.* **1** *She looks so pale, she must be ill:* colourless, white, pasty, ashen, ash-coloured, wan, pallid, sallow, drained of blood, cadaverous, deathly, death-like, ghost-like, ghastly. **2** *The walls were painted pale green:* light, light-coloured, bleached, whitish, light-toned.
—*v.* **3** *She paled when we told her the news:* become pale, blanch, whiten.

Ant. 1 ruddy, rosy-cheeked, rosy, rubicund, high-coloured, florid, flushed. **2** dark, deep, vivid. **3** flush, blush.

◇ *Word origin: Pale*[1], *pallid*, and *pallor* come from Latin *pallere* to be pale, *pallidus*, and *pallor*, paleness. Also related is our word *appal* (literally to shock into becoming pale).

"Shall I, wasting in despair,
Die because a woman's fair?
Or make pale my cheeks with care,
'Cause another's rosy are?"

—*George Wither*

---

pale[2] *n. Pales were driven into the ground to slow down the enemy:* stake, post, picket, paling, upright, palisade.

palisade *n. The fort was surrounded by a palisade:* fence of stakes, fence of pales, enclosure, fence, close, stockade, bulwark, rampart.

pall[1] *n. The smoke from the fire cast a pall over the town. The bad news cast a pall over the party:* dark covering, darkness, dimness; gloom, melancholy, depression, moroseness, cheerlessness, oppression, desolation.

Ant. light, brightness; joviality, gaiety, joy, cheer, merriment, exuberance, exhilaration, high spirits.

◇ *Word origin: Pall*[1] comes from an Old English word *pæll*, cloak. From this, we can see that the original idea of a "pall of smoke" was a cloak-like mass of smoke hanging in the sky, and cutting out the sunlight.

pall[2] *v. We used to think Monopoly was fun, but now it's beginning to pall:* become boring, become dull, be tiresome, become tedious, weary, sicken, cloy; sate, satiate.

Ant. interest, excite, create enthusiasm, delight.

pallor *n. The old man's pallor indicates some serious illness:* paleness, pallidness, colourlessness, whiteness, pastiness, ashen colour, wanness, bloodless colouring, cadaverous colour, grey complexion.

Ant. ruddy complexion, ruddiness, flush.

◇ *Word origin:* See PALE[1].

palpable *adj. There is a palpable difference in their ages:* tangible, obvious, plain, clear, noticeable, discernible, manifest, perceivable, perceptible, recognizable, definite, distinct, evident, unmistakable; feelable, touchable.
Ant. intangible, unnoticeable, indiscernible, imperceptible, indistinct.
◇ *Word origin: Palpable* and *palpitate* come from Latin *palpare*, to touch. Thus *palpable* means easily perceived by the sense of touch, and *palpitate* means trembling, quivering, as if after having been touched.

palpitate *v. My heart is palpitating after all those stairs:* throb, pound, pulsate rapidly, beat quickly, pulse rapidly, flutter, quiver, quaver, go pit-a-pat; vibrate, shake, tremble, shiver.

palsied *adj. The old woman's palsied hand could hardly hold the glass:* palsy-stricken; shaking, trembling, quaking, uncontrollable.
◇ *Word origin: Palsy* is the inability to control movement, as a trembling of the hands, jaw, or other parts of the body. It comes from Greek *paralyein*, to disable, which also gives us *paralysis*.

paltry *adj. The waiter was furious at being given such a paltry tip. He worked his way up from a paltry job to become director of the company:* petty, trifling, trivial, of little value, piddling, puny, measly, minute, shabby, scrubby, sorry; unimportant, insignificant, inconsequential, inconsiderable, wretched, inferior, poor, not worth mentioning.
Ant. important, significant, consequential, essential, major, valuable, worthy, considerable, grand, magnificent.
◇ *Word origin: Paltry* comes from Low German *paltrig*, ragged, rag, hence literally valueless as a rag.

pamper *v. She pampers her husband as if he were a child:* spoil, indulge, cater to, cater to one's every whim, humour, give in to, cosset, mollycoddle.
Ant. be stern with, lay down the law; mistreat; maltreat, abuse, tyrannize, domineer, oppress, intimidate, bully.
◇ *Word origin: Pamper* comes from Low German *pamperen*, to treat luxuriously, especially to feed with rich food.

pamphlet *n. This sixteen-page pamphlet tells you how to care for your new car:* booklet, brochure; (*loosely*) leaflet, circular, folder, throw-away; tract, monograph.
◇ *Word origin:* One of the best sellers of the 12th century was *Pamphilus seu de Amore*, an unbound, pamphlet-sized Latin amatory poem (actually a love manual containing the sensational story of an old bawd). This was so popular that other similar-sized works became known as "pamphlets," after the first word of the title of this work.

panacea *n. There is no panacea for the world's problems:* cure-all, universal cure, sovereign remedy; easy solution, simple solution, final answer.
◇ *Word origin: Panacea* is Greek for "universal remedy." In ancient times the word was used as a name for various healing herbs or their juices; it was also the Pythagorean name for the number six.

pandemonium *n. Pandemonium broke out when the teacher left the room:* tumult, turmoil, chaos, bedlam, disorder, wild confusion, commotion; uproar, clamour, racket, din, hubbub, hullabaloo.
Ant. order, peace, quiet, calm, tranquillity.

Exploring the Word: Greek *pâs* (neuter singular *pân*), all, is found in many words, including: *panacea*, a cure-all; *pandemic*, common to all, universal, nation-wide; *pandemonium* (Greek *daimōn*, demon), the "abode of all devils" — originally a name made up by the poet John Milton, who named the palace of Satan in Hell *Pandemonium* in his *Paradise Lost; panegyric* (Greek *ēguris*, assembly), a eulogy to all assembled persons, hence a public eulogy; *panorama* (Greek *horama*, view, sight), a view in all directions; *pantheism* (Greek *theos*, god), the worship (or toleration) of all the gods of the various cults (as in late Roman times and present-day India), and also the belief that God is in all things, and *Pantheon*, a temple to all the gods (or a commemoration or list of all the gods or all the heroes of a nation); *pantomime* (Greek *mimos*, imitator), a play in which the actors use all gestures and no speech; and such combinations as *Pan-American*, relating to all of North and South America.

pander *n.* **1** *The waterfront is frequented by panders and prostitutes:* procurer, go-between, pimp; *Slang* ponce, mack; *French* souteneur, maquereau.
—*v.* **2** *The society columnist panders to the public's love of gossip:* cater, minister, serve, administer to, purvey, indulge, toady, truckle, be servile, be subservient.
◇ *Word origin: Pander* comes from *Pandaro*, name of the intermediary between the lovers Troilus and Cressida at the siege of Troy, as told by the Italian writer Boccaccio. The story was twice recast in English versions — as a long narrative poem by Chaucer and as a play by Shakespeare.

panegyric *n. The retiring chairman received a panegyric from his successor:* eulogy, laudation, praise, homage, tribute, extolment, commendation, compliment, encomium, good word.
Ant. condemnation, denunciation, censure, reproach, vituperation, diatribe.

panel *n.* **1** *The control panel of a modern jet is very complex. A light fixture was placed in the centre of each wall panel:* surface section; compartment, partition, piece, pane, insert, divider, bulkhead. **2** *A panel of artists will judge the contest:* expert group, advisory group, select group, jury; discussion group.

◇ *Word origin: Panel* comes from the diminutive of Latin *pannus,* piece of cloth, hence literally means a little piece or section, and later a small group of people, selected to hold a discussion, judge a contest, etc. Latin *pannus* also gives us *pane.*

pang *n. She felt a pang of regret at leaving home. Except for a slight pang his headache was gone:* twinge, brief sensation; ache, pain, throb, smart, pinch, prick, sting, distress, discomfort; agony, anguish, suffering.

Ant. pleasure, delight, gratification, satisfaction, enjoyment, joy, happiness, comfort, solace, relief.

panic *n.* **1** *Panic swept through the swimmers as they saw the shark approaching:* terror, overwhelming fear, fear and trembling, alarm, hysteria, scare, fright, affright, cold sweat; horror, dread, apprehension, anxiety, trepidation, nervousness, perturbation, consternation, confusion.

—*v.* **2** *In case of fire, don't panic:* give way to panic, succumb to fear, become hysterical, be overwhelmed by dread; *Slang* fall apart, go to pieces, go berserk.

◇ *Spelling tip:* Remember that the final *-c* in *panic* becomes *-ck* in *panicked, panicking,* and *panicky.*

◇ *Word origin: Panic* literally means "fear caused by the god Pan," the Greek god of forests, flocks, and shepherds, having the horns and hoofs of a goat, and believed to be able to cause a feeling of sudden fear in humans whenever he wished. It was probably reassuring for an ancient Greek to be able to say that he hadn't run away or become alarmed through cowardice, but merely because the god Pan had "panicked" him.

panorama *n. The look-out tower gave us a panorama of the distant valleys. The book presents an excellent panorama of modern history:* sweeping view, scenic view, scene, scenery, prospect, tableau, picture, perspective, survey, overview, bird's-eye view, diorama; overall picture, long view.

pant *v.* **1** *After running for a quarter of a mile he was sweating and panting:* breathe hard, gasp for breath, gasp, huff, puff, blow, wheeze. **2** *All his life he panted after wealth and luxury:* long for, yearn for, lust after, hunger for, crave, desire, want, covet, hope for, wish for, aspire to, sigh for; *Informal* itch for, set one's heart on, hanker after.

—*n.* **3** *The dog's breathing was just a series of irregular pants:* gasp, short intake of breath, puff, huff, wheeze.

◇ *Word origin: Pant* is indirectly related to *phantom.* The word comes from Late Latin *phantasiare,* to gasp, as at seeing a phantom. The basis of this is in turn Greek *phainein,* to show, from which are derived our words *phantom* and *fantasy.* The word is *not* related to *pants* (short for *pantaloons* — for that word origin, see PANTS). But the inevitable comic association of the two words drove *pant* (desire) out of the language of elevated style. Here is a classic example of its older poetic use: "As the hart panteth after the water brooks, so panteth my soul after thee, O God." (Psalm 42.)

pants *n. pl.* **1** *This sports jacket will match those pants nicely:* trousers, pair of trousers, slacks, breeches; *Informal* trews, jeans. **2** *The child could put on his own vest and pants but needed help with his outer garments:* underpants, drawers, briefs, smalls, shorts, panties, rompers, knickers.

◇ *Word origin:* What do *pants* have to do with lions, saints, and clowns? *Pantaleon* literally means "all lion" (Italian, *leone,* lion), hence very courageous. This appellation was given to Saint Pantaleone, patron saint of Venice. The saint's name came to be used as a nickname for a Venetian. Later, in Italian comedy, one clown always played a skinny, foolish old Venetian merchant, butt of the other clowns' pranks, and was called *Pantalone* or *Pantaloon,* the Venetian. His costume included trousers, which were soon called *pantaloons* after him (as in modern times, most clowns wore baggy pants). Thus, from the name "all lion" given to a saint, to a Venetian, to a clown playing a Venetian, to the trousers that the clown wore, we got *pantaloon,* and, after all that, shortened the word to get *pants.*

pap *n.* **1** *Mothers used to feed infants pap:* mush, mash, gruel, cereal, soft food, paste, pulp. **2** *Informal How can anyone write such pap?:* childish nonsense, drivel, triviality, trivia, rubbish, rot, twaddle, junk, tosh, bosh, balderdash, *Slang* flapdoodle.

papal *adj. When he was in Rome he received the papal blessing:* of the pope, pontifical, apostolic.

◇ *Word origin: Papal* comes from Medieval Latin *papa,* which comes from Greek *papas,* term for one's own father. In many Latin countries, *papa* is still the word for the Pope — the identical word *papa* that many English-speaking children used to use in referring to their father. By a curious accident, the ancient Greeks had two forms of the word for use in direct address, *papa* and *pâ,* probably pronounced very much the same as our words *papa* and *pa.*

paper *n.* **1** *Always bring a pen and paper to class. The picnic plates were made of water-resistant paper:* (*variously*) writing paper, notepaper, stationery, letter-paper, bond, carbon paper, onion-skin; cardboard, parchment, tissue-paper, tissue, tracing-paper, foolscap; wrapping-paper, pad; printing paper, newsprint, stock, pulp; wallpaper. **2** *This paper gives you the title to the property:* document, instrument, certificate, deed, record, writing. **3** *What does the paper say about tomorrow's weather?:* newspaper, journal, gazette, tabloid, news, chronicle; daily, weekly, monthly; publication, periodical, trade paper. **4** *Each student must write a paper on a special subject:* composition, essay, article, report, work, opus; manuscript, typescript, draft; White Paper. —*v.* **5** *When did you last paper this room?:* wallpaper; line with paper, cover with paper.

◇ *Word origin: Paper* comes from Latin *papyrus,* the plant whose long, tough stems were first used by the Egyptians in making paper. The Greeks called paper *papuros* (the Latin form comes from this), but the word is not of Greek origin. One would expect it to come from Egyptian, but it doesn't. Like many things from Egypt, the ultimate origin of the word *paper* remains a mystery.

par *n.* **1** *For the first time the firm's income and expenses are on a par:* equal footing, parity, equality, evenness, equilibrium, equivalency; balance, stability, level, identity, sameness, identicalness. **2** *I'm feeling below par today:* average, normal, usual, standard, *Informal* the norm.

parade *n.* **1** *Over a dozen bands are marching in the St. Patrick's Day parade:* procession, march, march past, review; cavalcade, caravan, motorcade, column, line, progression, train, string. **2** *I've never seen such a parade of jewellery as there was at the party:* show, display, array, exposition, demonstration, spectacle, flaunting, vaunting, ostentatious display; pageantry, pomp.

—*v.* **3** *Parisian workers will parade on May Day:* march in a procession, march; go in a column, defile. **4** *She loves to parade her knowledge:* show off, make a show of, display, make a display of, vaunt, flaunt, sport, be ostentatious with; *Slang* put on an act, put on airs; strut.

Ant. **2** suppression, hiding, concealing, masking, cloaking. **4** suppress, secrete, hide, conceal, mask, cloak, veil.

◇ *Word origin: Parade* comes from Spanish *parada,* exercise ground, practice area.

paradigm *n.* *They always held his brother up as a sort of paradigm:* model, ideal, paragon, example, exemplar, pattern, standard, criterion, yardstick; prototype, archetype, sample.

"England is a paradise for women and hell for horses." —*Robert Burton*

---

paradise *n.* **1** *Adam and Eve dwelt in Paradise. Hawaii is called an island paradise:* Eden, Garden of Eden; Utopia, Shangri-la; Land of Cockaigne; nirvana, heaven. **2** *On a hot day a shaded garden is sheer paradise:* delight, bliss, joy, enjoyment, ecstasy, rapture, heaven, pleasure, happiness, satisfaction, gratification, seventh heaven.

Ant. **2** misery, torment, hell, agony, torture, pain.

◇ *Word origin: Paradise* literally means a Persian king's garden. It is from Old Persian *pairidaēza,* enclosed park. We get it via Biblical Greek *paradeisos* Eden, Heaven. The word, in the sense of "garden," entered Hebrew from either Persian or Greek as *pardēs.* In modern Hebrew usage the same word means "orange orchard."

paradox *n.* *It's a paradox, but the older she gets the younger she seems:* self-contradictory statement; seeming contradiction, incongruity, anomaly, inconsistency, oddity; enigma, puzzle, riddle, poser, seeming absurdity.

Ant. rule, axiom, maxim, truism, aphorism, proverb.

◇ *Word origin: Paradox* comes from Greek *para-* (contrary to) + *doxa* (expectation, opinion, thinking).

paragon *n.* *Aunt Sue has always been a paragon of virtue:* model, example, exemplar, prototype, archetype, paradigm, apotheosis, idea, pattern, standard, criterion, yardstick.

◇ *Word origin: Paragon* comes from Greek *para-* (beside) + *akonē* (whetstone), hence something sharpened against another, something made excellent in comparison with another.

parallel *adj.* **1** *Parallel lines never meet:* running side by side, coextensive, lying side by side, equidistant; alongside, abreast. **2** *Stamp-collecting and coin-collecting are parallel hobbies:* similar, like, alike, analogous, comparative, comparable, collateral, corresponding, akin, correlative; twin, equivalent.

—*n.* **3** *The speaker pointed out the parallel between the French and the Russian Revolutions:* comparison, analogy, likeness, correlation, identification, relation, connection, parallelism, resemblance, similarity, coincidence. **4** *The Navy's able-bodied seaman is the parallel of the Army's private:* counterpart, equivalent, equal, corollary, match, correspondent, correlative, analogue, same, twin.

—*v.* **5** *Your educational background parallels mine:* be equivalent to, be similar to, be alike, compare with, be comparable to, correspond to, be analogous to, amount to the same thing, duplicate, equal, match.

Ant. **1** non-parallel. **2** dissimilar, unlike, distinct, different, divergent, disparate. **3** dissimilarity, difference, divergence, unlikeness, disparity. **4** opposite, reverse, counter. **6** be dissimilar, be unlike, differ, diverge.

◇ *Spelling tip:* You will spell *parallel* properly if you remember that it has two *paraLLel l's* in the middle and only one *l* at the end.

◇ *Word origin: Parallel* comes from Greek *para-* (beside) + *allēlos* (one another).

paramount *adj.* *Speed in finishing the job is of*

paramount importance: main, chief, foremost, utmost, greatest, pre-eminent, highest, predominant, dominant, preponderant, supreme, principal, capital, essential, superior, peerless, leading, cardinal, outstanding, unmatched, incomparable, transcendent.

Ant. secondary, subordinate, least, smallest, negligible, insignificant, inconsequential, unimportant, slight, trifling, minor.

◇ *Word origin: Paramount* comes from Old French *par* (by) + *amount* (above), superior. It comes from the ranking terminology of the feudal system.

paranoid *adj. He has become paranoid about any criticism of his work:* paranoiac, affected by paranoia; having a persecution complex, having delusions of grandeur; over-suspicious, unreasonably distrustful.

◇ *Word origin: Paranoid* comes from Greek *paranoos,* beside oneself, distracted, from *para-* (beside) + *noûs* (mind). The Greek word was coined by the poet Aeschylus.

parapet *n. The defenders of the castle fought from behind parapets:* defensive wall, breastwork, earthwork; rampart, bulwark, battlement, abutment.

◇ *Word origin: Parapet* comes from Latin *parāre* (prepare, ward-off) + *pectus* (the breast), a breast-high wall or defence work. Latin *pectus,* breast, also gives us *pectoral,* of or pertaining to the breast or chest, as the *pectoral muscles* or, on fish, the *pectoral fins.*

paraphernalia *n. Bring along your fishing paraphernalia:* equipment, gear, outfit, implements, accoutrements, rig, stuff, regalia, apparatus, supplies, things, provisions, trappings, utensils, tackle, harness, fittings, material; personal effects, effects, properties, belongings, furnishings.

◇ *Word origin: Paraphernalia* was originally a legal term for a wife's personal goods which did not come to her husband as part of her dowry, such as clothing, furniture, silverware, heirlooms, and other property that legally belonged to her if she left her husband or that reverted to her own family when she died. It comes from Greek *para-* (beside) + *phernē* (bride's dowry).

paraphrase *v. You needn't quote his exact words, just paraphrase what he said:* restate, reword, state in other words, state in one's own words; recapitulate; *Slang* recap, rehash.

Ant. quote, state verbatim.

parasite *n.* **1** *Spray the plant to rid it of parasites:* living thing that nourishes itself on another organism. **2** *Don't be a parasite, earn your own living:* beggar, cadger, sponger, free-loader, leech, bloodsucker; loafer, slacker, shirker, dead-beat, *Slang* slug.

◇ *Word origin: Parasite* comes from Greek *para-* (beside) + *sitos* (food), one who eats food beside one, literally one who eats at another's table.

parcel *n.* **1** *Send this parcel air-mail:* package, packet, bundle, pack, bale. **2** *This parcel of land consists of 18 acres:* lot, tract, plot, piece of land, property.

—*v.* **3** *The estate was parcelled out to the heirs:* apportion, distribute, divide, allot, allocate, disperse, dispense, dole out, deal out, partition, carve up, split up.

◇ *Word origin: Parcel* is from the diminutive of Latin *pars,* part, hence a little part, a distinct portion.

parch *v. The east wind had parched the land:* dry out, dry up, dessicate, shrivel, evaporate, dehydrate; wither, scorch, char, burn, blister, sear, singe, bake.

Ant. wet, moisten, water, flood, inundate.

parchment *n. Ancient manuscripts were written on parchment:* sheepskin, goatskin; scroll, polished brown paper, parchment paper.

◇ *Word origin: Parchment* literally means "skin of Pergamum," the ancient city in Asia Minor, where the art of preparing sheepskin for writing was invented. The city of Pergamum no longer exists, but the town of Bergama, Turkey, is on the same site.

pardon *n.* **1** *We asked his pardon for the unintentional rudeness. May God grant you pardon for your sins:* forgiveness, forbearance, indulgence; absolution, mercy, remission, deliverance, grace; release, exculpation, amnesty.

—*v.* **2** *Pardon the interruption:* forgive, excuse, forbear, indulge; overlook, disregard, blink at, wink at, shrug off, forgive and forget, let bygones be bygones. **3** *The convict was pardoned after serving five years of his sentence:* absolve, vindicate, exonerate, exculpate, grant amnesty; remit the penalty of, reprieve, set free, release, discharge.

Ant. 1 punishment, penalty, retaliation, retribution, vengeance, revenge, reparation, redress, condemnation, guilt. **2** punish; penalize, fine, discipline, correct. **3** condemn, doom, censure, blame, chasten, castigate, chastise, rebuke, admonish.

◇ *Word origin: Pardon* comes from Latin *per-* (through) + *donare* (to give), hence to grant, to grant forgiveness. The Latin verb *donare* is also the basis of *donate, donation,* and *donor.*

pare *v.* **1** *Pare the apple and then slice it:* peel, skin, strip, trim, shuck, shell, hull, husk. **2** *To increase profits the firm must pare costs:* cut, cut down on, slash, shave, trim, reduce, decrease, lessen, diminish, lower, curtail; shrink; crop, lop, dock, clip, shear.

Ant. 2 increase, inflate, enlarge, advance, raise, elevate, boost, step up.

"Children and subjects are much seldomer in the wrong than parents and kings."
—*Lord Chesterfield*

---

parent *n. To have good children one must be a good parent. The Wright brothers' aeroplane is the* *parent of the modern jet:* mother, father; dam, sire, begetter, procreator; ancestor, progenitor, predecessor, precursor, forerunner, antecedent; prototype, original, model, exemplar.

parenthetical *adj. The essay contains too many parenthetical sentences. Stick to your speech and don't make parenthetical remarks:* in parentheses, in brackets, bracketed; incidental, interposed, inserted, intervening, aside, casual, extraneous, impertinent, irrelevant, immaterial, superfluous.

pariah *n. After the scandal he left his native land and became a pariah:* outcast; exile, expatriate, man without a country, stray, vagabond, rover, roamer, wanderer; outlaw.

◇ *Word origin: Pariah* comes from Tamil *paraiyan,* hereditary drummer, from *parai,* drum. The *pariahs* were thus originally a caste of drummers. The Tamils are an ancient people still numerous in southern India and Ceylon.

parish *n.* **1** *The main road crosses the boundary of the parish at the next bridge:* township, subdivision of a county, community, neighbourhood. **2** *The new priest will soon be arriving in the parish. The priest asked his parish to pray for peace:* church district, division of a deanery or diocese; congregation, fold, flock.

◇ *Word origin: Parish* and *parochial* come from Greek *para-* (beside) + *oikein* (to dwell), hence a neighbourhood and later a district of a diocese. In *parochial* we give the *ch* the original Greek *k* sound (the Greek *oikein*), while in *parish* it has changed to *sh.*

parley *n. The two prime ministers will have a parley to discuss peace:* discussion, conference, meeting, council, exchange of views, diplomatic consultation, talk, conversation, palaver, discourse, *Slang* confab; peace talk, negotiation, arbitration, mediation.

◇ *Word origin: Parley* comes from the French word for to speak, *parler.* In English, it usually connotes talking with an enemy or an antagonist, as has been the case since the word entered our language in the sixteenth century. One of the first times the word was used was in this sentence of military comment: *Castles that come to parley, are commonlie at the point to (sur) render.*

parochial *adj.* **1** *The parochial boundaries are marked by ruined walls:* parish; church, religious. **2** *The candidate's views are too parochial for him to become a national leader:* local, regional, sectional, provincial, insular, countrified, small-town; narrow-minded, limited, narrow, petty, small, little, illiberal, hidebound.

Ant. 2 international, world-wide, universal, national; sophisticated, cosmopolitan; broad-minded, open-minded, liberal; broad, sweeping, all embracing.

◇ *Word origin:* See PARISH.

parody *n.* **1** *The student drama society gave a hilarious parody of* Hamlet*:* burlesque, take-off, ludicrous imitation, caricature, lampoon, satire, travesty.

—*v.* **2** *Everyone laughed when the comedian parodied the writer's drawl:* burlesque, caricature, mimic, lampoon, satirize, *Informal* take-off.

◇ *Word origin: Parody* comes from Greek *para-* (beside) + *ōdē* (song, poem), an imitation of a song or poem to be put beside the original for humorous comparison.

Exploring the Word: *Parley, palaver, parlance, parliament, parlour, parole* and *parable* all come from Latin *parlare,* to talk together, confer side by side (based on Greek *para-* beside + *ballein,* to throw, hence to throw together, place side by side). Thus a *parley* is a conference, as of two enemies brought side by side; *palaver* means a discussion conducted side by side, as we would say "face-to-face"; *parlance* is the speech of a group who live or work side by side, as *legal parlance;* a *parliament* is an assembly for discussion, deliberation, or legislation, especially when composed of several groups, political parties, or representatives of various areas meeting side by side; a *parlour* is a room for receiving callers and where people may talk privately, side by side; *parole* comes to us via French *parole d'honneur,* word of honour; and a *parable* is a short narrative making a moral point by comparison (side by side) of society with natural or homely things.

parrot *n.* **1** *Can that parrot talk?:* tropical bird of the order *Psittaciformes;* (*variously*) macaw, cockatoo, parakeet. **2** *The child is such a parrot; he repeats everything he hears:* mimic, mimer, imitator, *Slang* copy-cat; monkey, ape.

—*v.* **3** *She parrots every view her husband has:* repeat mindlessly, echo, reiterate, chorus; imitate, mimic, ape.

◇ *Word origin:* Both *parrot* and *parakeet* are said to come from French dialectal forms of the name *Pierre* (diminutive form: *Pierrot*), which in turn comes from Latin *Petrus,* Peter. Why did people call their *parrots* and *parakeets* by nicknames based on the name Peter? No one knows for sure. Perhaps it was because these birds "talk" and Saint Peter spread the gospel of Christ in speaking and writing.

parry *v. The fencer parried his opponent's thrust. The actress parried all questions about her personal life:* fend off, ward off, repulse, repel, beat off; dodge, shun, avoid, elude, avert, side-step, duck, circumvent, fight shy of, keep at a distance.

Ant. receive, take, welcome, face, confront, meet.

parsimonious *adj. Because the old couple were parsimonious they never had to ask for financial help:* frugal, saving, thrifty, economical, sparing, penny-pinching; miserly, tight-fisted, close, close-fisted, niggardly, ungenerous, stingy, money-grubbing.

Ant. extravagant, spendthrift, wasteful; lavish, liberal, munificent, generous, open-handed.

part *n.* **1** *There are three parts to the machinery of government: executive, legislative, and judicial. This looks like part of a broken cup:* section, portion, division, subdivision, sector, branch, department, unit, component, element, member, constituent, ingredient, region; piece, segment, fragment, fraction, scrap, shred, bit, sliver, chip, shard, sherd, snippet, cutting, slice, crumb, morsel, *Slang* hunk; item, detail. **2** *The young actress took the part of Joan of Arc:* role, character; impersonation, personification, guise, disguise. **3** *What was your part in the proceedings?:* role, function, capacity, share, concern, charge, care, place, business, assignment, job, chore, task, duty. —*v.* **4** *The curtain parted and the show began. The rope parted and the load fell to the ground:* open, separate, disengage, disunite, divide; detach, disconnect, disjoin, break apart, split, slit, sunder, sever, rend, tear, tear asunder; cleave, break. **5** *It's time to part:* depart, go, go away, leave, take one's leave, go one's way, set forth, set out, start out, take one's farewell, say goodbye, tear oneself away, get up and go, be on one's way; *Slang* mosey along, push off; end a relationship, break off, call it a day.

Ant. **1** whole, entirety, totality; mass, bulk, quantity. **4** unite, combine, join, close; hold, cling, stick, adhere. **5** arrive, come, appear; stay, remain, abide, tarry, linger.

partake *v. All the children will partake in the festivities. Everyone partook of the sumptuous meal:* share, take part, share in, enjoy, savour, sample, participate, engage in, join in, play a part in.

Ant. be excluded; abstain, forswear, forbear, forgo, refrain from, refuse, decline, eschew, relinquish, set out, pass up.

partial *adj.* **1** *This is only a partial list of the books needed:* incomplete, fractional, fragmentary, unfinished, uncompleted, inconclusive. **2** *He's too partial to be a fair judge:* partisan, biased, prejudiced, predisposed, slanted, prepossessed, subjective, one-sided, unbalanced, interested; unjust, unfair, inequitable.

Ant. **1** complete, entire, whole, total, full, final, finished. **2** impartial, unbiased, objective, balanced, disinterested, unprejudiced, equitable.

partiality *n.* **1** *The referee's partiality toward the home team was obvious:* bias, prejudice, predisposition, slant, one-sidedness, partisanship, favouritism. **2** *Father had a partiality for strawberry ice cream:* fondness, liking, inclination, predisposition, predilection, weakness, love, taste, affinity, propensity, penchant, fancy, bent, leaning, tendency, attraction, proclivity; choice, preference.

Ant. **1** impartiality, objectivity, disinterest; justice, fairness. **2** dislike, disinclination, distaste, disgust, abhorrence, aversion, loathing, revulsion, detestation, antipathy.

> **Exploring the Word:** Latin *pars* (stem *part-*), part, gives us many, many words, including: *part, partial* (being a part, favouring one part or side, hence biased), *impartial* (not being a part, not favouring one side, unbiased), and *partisan* (one who takes a part or advocates one side of an issue); *particle,* a small part; *particular,* referring to a part or specific thing, concerned with small details; *partake* and *participate,* both literally mean to "take part"; *partner* (one who has or is a part, as of a business) and *party* (one who takes a part, as *the guilty party* or *the party to a crime*), or a group or gathering of people who take part in a social gathering, as *birthday party,* or for some political cause, as the *Conservative Party; partition,* to divide something into parts, or a wall or divider that does so. Latin *pars,* part, is also the basis of such words as *apart,* separated into parts; *apartments* pl., a suite of rooms (as at a seaside resort); *compartment,* one of several parts which share a larger space, as of a sleeping-car on a train or part of a drawer or container; *depart,* literally to take part away, and *department,* a part or division away from the main body; *impart,* to give a part of or to share something with another, as to give or share information or news; and *repartee,* literally one's part or side given again, hence a reply. Latin *pars,* part, also gives us *parcel,* a small part or portion, as of land, or a small quantity wrapped up; *portion* (a part), *apportion* (to divide into parts, give parts), *proportion* (the relation or comparative size of parts), and *disproportionate* (not equally divided into parts, not shared equally).

partially *adv. The work is only partially finished:* partly, in part, moderately, incompletely, fractionally, piecemeal, somewhat.

Ant. all, completely, entirely, wholly, totally.

participate *v. No professionals may participate in the amateur tennis tournament:* take part, engage in, join in, be a participant, perform, play a part, partake, share, form a part of, *Slang* have a finger in.

Ant. be excluded; abstain, forswear, forgo, forbear, refrain from, eshew, sit out, pass up.

particle *n. A particle of rock was wedged beneath the door. There's not a particle of truth in that statement:* small piece, small fragment, speck, grain, shred, scrap, crumb, morsel, jot, iota, atom; trifle, trace, snippet, inch, whit, tittle, scintilla, modicum, mite.

particular *adj.* **1** *The shops are closed on that particular day. Golf is his particular passion:* specific, exact, explicit, express, special, especial, fixed, concrete, individual; definite, well-defined, distinct, single, personal, separate, sole, particularized, itemized, detailed. **2** *She's so particular that no one can please her:* hard to please, critical, demanding, exacting, choosy, fussy, finicky, *Informal* pernickety; strict, fastidious, meticulous, painstaking, scrupulous, punctilious.

—*n.* Usually **particulars** **3** *The lawyer must know all the particulars of the case:* detail, specific, item, fact, circumstance, event.

Ant. **1** general, universal; vague, unspecified, indefinite, undefined, impersonal. **2** easy to please, uncritical, undemanding, indifferent, heedless, inattentive; careless, slipshod, slapdash, haphazard, sloppy, inexact, carefree.

◇ *Pronunciation tip:* You should be more *particular* in your pronunciation than to leave out the *u* in *particUlar.*

particularly *adv.* **1** *The coffee is particularly good today:* especially, exceptionally, unusually, extraordinarily, strikingly, markedly, notably, eminently, supremely, prominently; mainly, principally. **2** *He particularly asked that you be there:* in particular, explicitly, expressly, especially, specially, definitely, distinctly.

partisan *n.* **1** *Their own partisans cheered the local team:* supporter, follower, adherent, sympathizer, champion, backer, upholder, enthusiast, fan, zealot, devotee, well-wisher. **2** *Even after the country was defeated, partisans fought the invaders in the hills:* freedom fighter, guerrilla, irregular, insurgent, (American) bushwacker, jayhawker.

—*adj.* **3** *The speaker vowed not to engage in partisan politics:* favouring one political party, predisposed towards one group, favouring a cause, partial, biased, prejudiced, one-sided, slanted, unbalanced, subjective.

Ant. **1** detractor, defamer, censor, critic, backbiter, knocker; opponent, foe, adversary, rival, contender. **3** non-partisan, bipartisan, unbiased, impartial, unprejudiced, disinterested, objective, broad-minded, open-minded.

partition *n.* **1** *The partition of Vietnam was one of the causes of the long and bitter war there:* division, dividing, separation, severance, splitting, parting; distribution, apportionment, allotment, allocation, assignment, demarcation, segregation. **2** *Put up partitions to separate the living and dining areas:* dividing wall, non-supporting wall, wall, divider, separator, panel, screen, barrier, fence, *Nautical* bulkhead.

—*v.* **3** *The dormitory was partitioned into cubicles:* divide, subdivide, separate, split up; distribute, disperse, dispense, apportion, allot, allocate, assign, parcel out, deal out, mete out.

partly *adv. The back door is only partly closed:* partially, in part, fractionally, to a degree, in some measure, somewhat, incompletely, not wholly, to a limited extent; comparatively, relatively, in a manner of speaking, after a fashion, vaguely.

Ant. fully, wholly, completely, entirely, totally.

partner *n.* **1** *The business is owned by two partners. Take your partners for a waltz:* joint owner, co-owner, co-partner; associate, colleague, fellow worker, confrère, collaborator, accomplice, confederate, team-mate, assistant, helper, aid; accessory; friend, fellow, comrade, ally, companion, buddy, chum, pal, mate; sharer, partaker, participant. **2** *Are you sure you want him for your partner for life?:* spouse, mate, helpmate; husband; wife, better half.

party *n.* **1** *The family is giving a party on Grace's birthday:* social function, social gathering, gathering of friends, gathering, celebration, festivity, fête, get-together, affair, reception, at home, soirée, *Slang* bash, blow-out, do, beano. **2** *Is there need for a new political party? Police sent out a rescue party to bring back the injured hiker:* alliance, federation, confederacy, league, coalition, conclave, faction, coterie; group, crew, team, band, body, company, squad, corps, unit, force; gang. **3** *Both parties are to appear before the judge:* participant, participator, perpetrator, (*legal use*) participant in a lawsuit, (*variously*) contestant, litigant, petitioner, plaintiff, claimant, accused, defendant, appellant, respondent.

◇ *Usage note:* A *party* means a group of persons: *A party of four registered at the hotel. The search-party found the missing child. Party* does not mean one person except in the legal sense (the guilty party) or in telephone operator's use ("Your party does not answer"). Don't use *party* when you mean a *person,* a *stranger,* a *human being,* a *man,* a *woman.* Say and write *Marilyn went out with the same man again last night,* not "Marilyn went out with that certain party again last night."

"Party is the madness of many, for the gain of a few." —*Jonathan Swift*

---

pass *v.* **1** *She never passes without stopping to say hello. The guard allowed the visitor to pass:* go by, go on, go past, go beyond, go ahead, go onward, move onward, progress, proceed. **2** *Time passes quickly on holiday. Wait for the rain to pass:* go, go by, go away, elapse, glide by, slide by, slip by, flow, proceed, progress; pass away, be over, end, terminate, expire, die away, die, fade away, melt away, blow over, peter out, run its course, vanish, disappear, dissolve, evaporate, depart, leave. **3** *Mother passes her time knitting:* spend, expend, use, consume, employ, engage, busy, occupy, fill, take up, devote. **4** *Dick has already passed his father in height:* surpass, exceed, go by, go beyond, go ahead, best, excel, outshine, eclipse, overshadow, outstrip, outdo, top, cap. **5** *Did you pass the chemistry examination?:* reach a satisfactory standard in, complete successfully, satisfy, qualify, meet, get through, achieve, accomplish, finish, come up to scratch, stand the test, attain the standard of. **6** *Parliament is expected to pass the bill:* enact, legislate, establish by law, vote approval on, approve, ratify, authorize, sanction, decree, ordain, legalize, accept; affirm, confirm. **7** *Please pass me the salt. Pass the news along. The scrum-half passed the ball to his winger, who scored the try:* hand, hand over, hand along, give, present, turn over, let have, convey, transfer, transmit, deliver, throw, toss, hit, kick.

—*n.* **8** *The excursion through the Brenner Pass was lovely:* mountain pass, gap, gorge, canyon, ravine, gully; passageway, pathway, way, course, route, avenue; channel, straits, narrows, canal. **9** *The soldier had a week-end pass. Retired players get season passes to all the matches:* permission to be absent, permission to leave, furlough; free ticket, complimentary ticket, right of passage, permit, authorization. **10** *Things have come to a pretty pass!:* state of affairs, situation, juncture, predicament, complication, difficulty, exigency, plight, strait, extremity, quandary.

Ant. **1, 2** stop, halt, cease, standstill, pause, wait; withdraw, retreat. **2** begin, start, commence; continue. **3** waste, squander. **4** fall behind, pull back. **5** fail, fall short. **6** vote down, defeat, reject, veto; disapprove. **7** hold, keep, retain. **8** peak, summit; barrier, obstacle.

◇ *Usage note:* The past tense and past participle of the verb *pass* are spelt *passed*: *The car will pass the lorry — it passed the lorry yesterday — it has passed it before.* Do not write the completely different word *past* when you mean *passed. Past* is an adjective; it means "gone by," "already having happened." See the Usage note at PAST for more examples.

passable *adj.* **1** *Are the roads passable in all this snow?:* traversable, fit for travel, clear, open, unobstructed; crossable, navigable, fordable. **2** *This suit is worn, but it's still passable. The film wasn't great, but it was passable:* presentable, respectable, reasonable, pretty good, better than nothing, admissible, tolerable.

Ant. **1** impassable, impenetrable, closed, blocked, obstructed. **2** inadequate, unacceptable, insufficient; exceptional, extraordinary, unusual, uncommon.

passage *n.* **1** *The newspaper quoted a long passage from the speech:* section, portion, piece, extract, clause, paragraph, sentence, column, verse, chapter. **2** *The hunters needed a guide for their passage through the jungle. Bon voyage and have a pleasant passage:* progression, passing, movement; journey, voyage, excursion, expedition, tour, trip, trek, transit; right to pass; cost of transport by sea, ship's fare. **3** *Passage of the bill depends on public support:* passing into law, enactment, legislation, ratification, approval, authorization, legalization, sanction, endorsement, acceptance; affirmation, confirmation. **4** *Is there a passage through the mountains? The house has an underground passage:* pass, passageway, way, course, route, path, road, corridor, hallway, aisle, tunnel, canal, channel; access, approach, right of access.

Ant. **3** veto, defeat, rejection, voting down. **4** barrier, obstacle, obstruction.

passageway *n. Don't leave your roller-skates in the passageway:* corridor, hallway, hall, passage, aisle, tunnel; access, entrance, entry, alley, exit, doorway, gateway; path, walk, pavement, *Nautical* gangway, companion-way.

passé *adj. The idea of a chaperon for a courting couple is passé:* out of fashion, old-fashioned, out-of-date, outdated, démodé, antiquated, antediluvian, quaint; ancient, antique, archaic, obsolete, stale, hoary, *Slang* prehistoric; lapsed, disused, retired, outworn, faded, past.

Ant. modern, new, novel, current, up-to-date, new-fashioned, newfangled, *Slang* mod, hip, with-it, *French* au courant, à la page, dans le vent.

◇ *Word origin:* In French, *passé* is the past participle of the verb *passer,* to pass. Hence it literally means "passed." It is also used just as we use it in English.

passion *n.* **1** *He could never put any passion into his singing:* emotion, feeling, warmth, heart, ardour, fervour, fire, intensity, sentiment, rapture, transport, ecstasy, intoxication, enthusiasm, earnestness, gusto, eagerness, vehemence. **2** *The newspapers called it a crime of passion:* lust, sexual desire, sexual appetite, carnality, carnal love, fleshly, desire; amorousness, love. **3** *Skiing is my current passion:* obsession, craze, mania, fancy, rage, craving, urge, desire, hunger, thirst; idol, beloved, loved one, infatuation, flame, inamorata.

Ant. **1** apathy, indifference, coldness, coolness, frigidity, unconcern.

passionate *adj. The two groups had a passionate debate. The groom gave the bride a passionate kiss:* impassioned, fervent, fervid, ardent, emotional, earnest, intense, fiery, fierce, furious, raging, tempestuous, excited, wrought-up, inflamed, feeling, heartfelt, enthusiastic, hot, heated, vehement, intoxicating, ecstatic; loving, amorous, desirous, lustful, sensuous, carnal, erotic, *Slang* sexy.

Ant. dispassionate, cold, cool, apathetic, passive, lethargic, indifferent; calm, soothing.

passive *adj. The townspeople remained passive throughout the occupation:* submissive, inactive, unassertive, impassive, compliant, docile,

acquiescent, yielding, inert, quiescent, lifeless, listless, dormant, non-resistant, unresisting; patient, resigned, enduring.
Ant. active, domineering, dominant, forceful, assertive, dynamic, energetic, alive, alert.

> **Exploring the Word:** Greek *pathos*, suffering, feeling, gives us *pathos*, the quality in literature and art that arouses feelings of sorrow or pity; *pathetic*, arousing pity or sadness, as does another's suffering, and *apathetic*, without feelings or emotions; *pathological*, caused by a disease a person suffers, or relating to the branch of medicine treating of diseases and their suffering; *sympathy* (Greek *sun-*, together), suffering or feeling with another; *antipathy* (Greek *anti-*, against), a feeling of aversion against someone or something. The Latin equivalent of Greek *pathos* is *passio* (coined by the Latin translator of Acts 1: 3, according to which Christ "showed himself alive after his *passion* [Greek *pathos*, Latin *passio*] by many infallible proofs"). Latin *passio*, suffering, and the verb on which it is based, *pati*, to suffer, give us our words *passion*, intense feeling or suffering, *passionate*, feeling intensely, *compassionate*, feeling the suffering of others, and *dispassionate*, free from feelings or passions, hence objective, impartial; *passive*, literally "suffering" action upon oneself, hence willingly submissive or inactive, and *impassive*, not feeling emotions.

past *adj.* **1** *The time for action is past. Forget past mistakes and start afresh:* gone by, passed away; elapsed, expired, ended, finished, gone, departed, dead and gone; belonging to the past, bygone, ancient, historical, former, previous, earlier, prior.
—*n.* **2** *The old man loved to talk about the past:* days gone by, days of yore, days of old, yesteryear, former times, previous times, times gone by, long ago, ancient times, olden times, ancient history, history, events gone by.
—*adv.* **3** *Did you see a car go past?:* by, across one's field of vision; beyond, through.
Ant. 1 future, coming, later; present, now, begun, started, arrived. **2** future, time to come, days to come, tomorrow; present, today, now, this day and age.
◇ *Usage note:* Some people have difficulty separating *past* and *passed*. *Past*, of course, is an adjective meaning "having already happened" or a noun meaning "time gone by": *Father aged a lot this past year, Forget the past. Passed* is the past tense of the verb *to pass: The car passed the lorry at 70 miles an hour, Bill passed the bar exams, You haven't passed round the plate of cakes.*

pastel *n.* **1** *Many of the artist's drawings are done in pastels:* colouring stick; (*loosely*) colouring pencil, chalk, crayon.
—*adj.* **2** *The bedrooms were painted in pastel colours:* pale, faint, soft, light, muted, dim, washed-out, faded.
Ant. 2 bright, deep, dark, strong, vibrant.
◇ *Word origin:* A *pastel* is a crayon made of a dried pigment-containing paste. It comes from the diminutive form of Italian *pasta*, paste, hence little paste, which is what holds the pigment or colouring matter together in a stick-like form.

pastime *n. Stamp-collecting is an agreeable pastime:* diversion, hobby, avocation, spare-time activity, relaxation, distraction, amusement, entertainment, fun, play, sport, game.
Ant. business, work, occupation, calling, employment, profession, job, chore, labour.
◇ *Spelling tip:* Beware! *Pastime* (*past* + *time*) has lost one of its *t's*. The only correct spelling is with one *t: pasTime.*

pastor *n. The pastor preached a lively sermon last Sunday:* minister, priest, preacher, parson, rector, clergyman, vicar, curé; padre, father, chaplain.
◇ *Word origin:* One often hears a *pastor* called a "shepherd" and his congregation his flock. *Pastor* is actually the Latin word for shepherd, feeder of a flock. *Pastoral* thus means pertaining to shepherds, rustic, rural. Related is the Latin *pascere*, to graze, from which our word *pasture* is derived.

pastoral *adj.* **1** Daphnis and Chloe *is a pastoral tale written for city people. The orchestra played Beethoven's "Pastoral Symphony":* bucolic, rustic, rural, portraying country life, depicting the life of shepherds; arcadian, idyllic. **2** *The new minister will take up his pastoral duties next month:* ministerial, ecclesiastical, clerical; priestly, episcopal, sacerdotal.
Ant. 1 worldly, sophisticated, cosmopolitan; urban, urbanized, city, citified, metropolitan. **2** secular, lay.

pasty *adj.* **1** *Breakfast was a pasty mess of hot oatmeal:* like paste, gluey, gummy, sticky, doughy; starchy, glutinous, *Slang* gooey. **2** *The sick man had a pasty complexion:* pale, ashen, ashy, wan, colourless, pallid, chalky, white, peaked, anaemic, bloodless, ghostlike, deathly, grey.
Ant. 1 dry, powdery. **2** ruddy, rosy, florid, rosy-cheeked, rubicund.

pat *v.* **1** *The children wanted to pat the rabbit:* pet, stroke, caress.
—*n.* **2** *She gave the pillow several pats:* light blow, gentle stroke, tap, small spank; hit, thwack, slap, thump, rap. **3** *Put a pat of butter on each plate:* little slab, small square, cake, dab, daub.
—*adj.* **4** *The salesman had pat answers to all my objections:* glib, facile, ready, easy, slick, smooth, flippant, contrived, rehearsed. **5** *There are no pat solutions to all the world's problems:* perfect, ideal, exact, precise; appropriate, apposite, fitting, pertinent, suitable, apt, apropos, easy, simple; satisfactory.

Ant. 4 sincere, well-considered, thoughtful, serious, impromptu, spontaneous. 5 imperfect, inexact; irrelevant, unsuitable; difficult; unsatisfactory.

patch *n.* 1 *The child's jeans had a patch at the knee:* mend, repair, small piece of material sewn on, reinforcement. 2 *We chased the rabbits out of the cabbage patch. There was a patch of ice on the road:* plot, garden, tract, lot, field, clearing; area, spot, stretch, expanse, zone.
—*v.* 3 *Do you know how to patch an inner tube?:* mend, cover with a patch, repair, fix, darn, sew up, reinforce.

patent *n.* 1 *Edison held the patent on the early phonograph:* government registration of an invention, certificate of invention, inventor's exclusive rights; registry, licence, permit.
—*adj.* 2 *Try some of this new patent medicine:* protected by patent, trade-marked, copyright; needing no prescription. 3 *The charge against him was a patent falsehood:* obvious, manifest, evident, open, plain, overt, express, palpable, decided, indubitable, downright, unreserved, glaring, unmistakable, pronounced, conspicuous, striking, rank, flagrant, bold, glaring, gross, prominent, clear, distinct, bald, undisguised, unconcealed, *Informal* plain as the nose on one's face, plain as a pikestaff.
—*v.* 4 *How long does it take to patent an invention?:* obtain a patent for, register as an original invention, obtain an inventor's exclusive rights to.
Ant. 2 unpatented. 3 imperceptible, subtle, hidden, concealed, disguised, questionable, dubious, equivocal, ambiguous, vague.
◇ *Word origin:* A *patent lie* is one that is open to everyone's view, while an inventor's *patent* is a protection so that he may bring his invention out into open view without its being appropriated by someone else. *Patent* comes from the Latin *patere,* to lie open.

paternal *adj. His father never gave him much paternal affection:* fatherly, fatherlike, of a father, from the father's side of the family; of a parent, parental, tender, benevolent, solicitous; concerned, interested, watchful, vigilant.

pathetic *adj. The orphan's plight really was quite pathetic:* pitiful, moving, affecting, touching, poignant, plaintive, distressing, arousing sympathy, calling forth compassion; to be pitied, piteous, pitiable, lamentable, sorrowful, rueful, sad, doleful, miserable, woeful, wretched, deplorable, grievous.
Ant. amusing, funny, laughable, comical, humorous, ludicrous, ridiculous, droll, entertaining.

pathos *n. The story was told with so much pathos that I wept all through it:* pathetic quality, power to affect, ability to touch, ability to arouse sympathy, poignancy, plaintiveness, sadness, feeling, sentiment, sentimentalism, sentimentality, pitiableness, anguish, heartache, agony, misery, distress, woe, desolation.
Ant. comicality, amusement, humour, fun.
◇ *Usage note: Pathos* (its adjective is *pathetic*) is a quality, as in literature and art, that arouses feelings of pity or sorrow: *If you enjoy a good cry, you'll like the pathos of this film. Bathos* is the sudden shift in speech or writing from a lofty level to a commonplace one, for contrast or humour, or overdone sentiment that has become melodramatic or maudlin: *The actors played the old tear-jerker for bathos and got lots of laughs.*

patience *n.* 1 *Have patience, the train will be here soon:* calm endurance, forbearance, uncomplaining nature, sufferance, long-suffering, imperturbability, equanimity, longanimity, fortitude; composure. 2 *It takes a good deal of patience to learn to type:* persistence, perseverance, diligence, application, tenacity, determination, resolution, indefatigableness, tirelessness, stamina, industry, staying power.
Ant. 1, 2 impatience. 1 restlessness, agitation, exasperation, fretfulness, irritation, frenzy, nervousness, peevishness, passion. 2 vacillation, irresolution.

"My patience is now at an end."
—*Adolf Hitler*

---

patient *n.* 1 *The doctor has several patients waiting to see him:* person under medical care, case; sick person.
—*adj.* 2 *Just be patient; I think you're next:* persevering, enduring, long-suffering, forbearing, unperturbed, serene, composed; persistent; persevering, diligent, determined, tenacious, resolute, tireless, indefatigable, industrious, unflagging, unfaltering, unwavering, unswerving, undaunted, dogged, dauntless.

patrician *n.* 1 *Patricians were noblemen of ancient Rome:* aristocrat, noble, peer, lord, knight, earl, baronet, gentleman.
—*adj.* 2 *The old gentleman still retains his patrician manners:* aristocratic, noble, lordly, princely, imposing, stately, dignified, genteel, well-bred, upper-class, high-born.
Ant. 1 peasant, commoner, working man, member of the proletariat, hoi polloi. 2 peasant, plebeian, common, vulgar, ignoble, proletarian, working-class, lower-class, lowborn; bourgeois, middle-class, low-brow, philistine.

patron *n.* 1 *If patrons have any complaints, they should see the manager:* customer, client, buyer, shopper; frequenter, habitué; spectator, attender. 2 *There will be a reception for patrons of the museum:* sponsor, supporter, backer, benefactor, (*fem.*) benefactress, promoter, philanthropist; protector, defender, helper, advocate, champion, upholder, encourager, sympathizer, well-wisher, friend, *Slang* angel.

Ant. **1** employee. **2** protégé, (*fem.*) protégée, ward.

> **Exploring the Word**: Greek *patēr*, Latin *pater*, mean father and are related to Old English *fæder*, father. Latin *pater* gives us *paternal*, of a father, fatherly, related through one's father, and *paternity*, fact of being a father, descent from a father; *patron*, originally a fatherlike guardian or protector of a young page at a royal court and only later a supporter (*a patron of the arts*) or a steady customer of a shop; and *pattern*, which literally means a fatherlike model for a youth to emulate, hence a model or an original to be followed or imitated. Related to Greek *patēr*, father, and *papas*, one's own father, are our informal words for father, *pa* and *papa*, and such terms as *Pope*, father of the Roman Catholic Church, *papal*, and *padre*, a chaplain. A *paternoster* is the Lord's prayer or an "Our Father" (Latin *pater*, father + *noster*, our) and our word *patter*, glib talk, rapid talk, is short for *paternoster*, from the rapid repetition of this prayer. Latin *pater*, father, gave the Romans *patria*, fatherland, country. From the cognate Greek *patris*, fatherland, we get *patriot*, one who loves his fatherland, and *patriotic*, characterized by love of one's country; Greek *patēr* gives us *patriarch*, the leader of a family or clan who rules by paternal right; and Latin *pater* gives us *patrician*, a nobleman in ancient Rome; *compatriot*, a fellow member of one's fatherland, *expatriate*, one who lives outside his fatherland, and *repatriate*, literally to restore someone to his fatherland.

patronage *n.* **1** *The restaurant welcomes the patronage of anyone suitably attired:* business, trade, buying, purchasing, commerce, custom, dealing; clientele, customers, patrons, clients. **2** *The scholarship fund depends on the patronage of the Old Boys:* financial support, support, sponsorship, charity, benefaction, philanthropy, backing, help, aid, assistance, favour; protection, advocacy, encouragement, friendship. **3** *The Minister controls patronage in this Department:* political favours, political appointments, government contracts.

patronize *v.* **1** *I'll never patronize that shop again:* do business with, trade with, shop at, buy from, frequent, be a customer of, be a client of. **2** *Don't patronize me. I'm not a child!:* treat in a condescending way, act in a superior way toward, assume a lofty attitude toward, act disdainfully toward, indulge unnecessarily.

Ant. **2** flatter, toady to, be subservient to.

patter *v.* **1** *The rain pattered on the window:* pat, beat, tap, rap, thrum, go pitter-patter; spatter, sprinkle.

—*n.* **2** *The parents heard the patter of tiny feet down the stairs:* pattering, pitter-patter, pat, tap, tapping, drumming; beat, palpitation.

pattern *n.* **1** *The cloth had a checked pattern:* design, decorative design, motif; form, shape. **2** *A good seamstress can make a dress without a pattern:* guide, design, plan, draft, model; original, archetype, prototype, stereotype; standard, criterion, example, paradigm, exemplar, sample, illustration, specimen, ideal, apotheosis, paragon.

—*v.* **3** *The youth patterned his life on Ghandi's:* model, fashion, shape, mould, form, make resemble; imitate, emulate, copy, mimic, follow, simulate, parallel, duplicate.

paunch *n.* **1** *The baby racoons clung to their mother's paunch:* stomach, abdomen, *Informal* tummy. **2** *A little exercising would reduce that paunch:* pot-belly, belly, *Slang* corporation, bread-basket, gut, pot.

◇ *Word origin: Paunch* comes from Latin *pantices*, guts.

pauper *n. After paying these bills I'll be a pauper!:* poor person, bankrupt, down-and-out; charity case, beggar, starveling, mendicant.

Ant. rich man, millionaire, magnate, tycoon, Midas, Crœsus, plutocrat.

◇ *Word origin: Pauper* comes from a Medieval Latin legal phrase *in forma pauperis*, "in the character of a poor man," i.e. entitled to sue in a court of law without paying costs.

pause *n.* **1** *After a brief pause the speaker continued:* stop, halt, rest, break, cessation, interval, hiatus, let-up, gap, suspension, stoppage, discontinuance, interlude, intermission, interim, interruption.

—*v.* **2** *The runners paused to catch their breath:* stop briefly, halt, cease, rest, let up, break off; hesitate, wait, delay, deliberate.

Ant. **1** continuity, continuation, progress, progression, advancement. **2** continue, proceed, progress, advance.

pave *v. One lane is closed while they're paving the road:* surface, resurface, face; tar, asphalt, tarmac, macadamize.

◇ *Word origin:* To *pave* a road one must ram down, crush, or roll out asphalt, gravel, or concrete to make a smooth surface. Both *pave* and *pavement* come from Latin *pavire*, to ram down.

pavilion *n. The reception was held in a pavilion on the lawn. The players retired to the pavilion when rain stopped play:* tent; tentlike building, light open structure, temporary building; exhibition hall, exposition building.

◇ *Word origin: Pavilion* comes from Old French *paveillon*, tent, which comes from Latin *papilio*, butterfly (because the curtains of Roman tents looked like butterfly wings).

pawn[1] *v.* **1** *The unemployed reporter pawned his typewriter to pay the bill:* give as security, pledge, raise money on, borrow on, mortgage.

—*n.* **2** *He demanded her wrist-watch as a pawn for the loan:* security, pledge, assurance, bond, guarantee, guaranty.

Ant. 1 redeem.

◇ *Word origin: Pawn*[1] comes from an Old Frisian word (the Germanic language of the Dutch province of Friesland) *pand*, meaning pledge.

pawn[2] *n. He was merely the pawn of the racketeers:* instrument, puppet, tool, dupe, *Slang* cat's-paw; lackey, flunkey, underling, hireling, henchman.

Ant. leader, chief, head, boss, *Slang* kingpin.

◇ *Word origin: Pawn*[2], an insignificant person or a chess piece of the lowest rank, comes from Old French *paon*, foot soldier. (Spanish *peon* is also related.) It comes from Medieval Latin *pedo*, foot soldier, from Latin *pes*, foot.

pay *v.* **1** *They paid the cashier and left. Please pay this bill by the end of the month:* give money owed to, give money for; pay in full, remit, settle, square accounts, foot, honour, meet, liquidate, make good, *Informal* open one's purse; *Slang* shell out, come across, cough up, stump up, chip in. **2** *It doesn't pay to waste time:* be advantageous, be worthwhile, be useful, benefit, compensate, repay, serve, bear fruit, be a good investment, stand one in good stead. **3** *How much does that job pay? Does it pay to invest in gilt-edged stocks now?:* offer as remuneration, offer as compensation, offer as wages, bring in, reimburse; profit, yield, return, be a good investment. **4** *Please pay attention. He paid her a compliment on her cooking:* give, grant, render, extend, proffer, present.

—*n.* **5** *How much tax do they take out of your pay?:* wages, salary, earnings, pay-packet, income; compensation, recompense, fee, payment, reimbursement, stipend, emolument.

Ant. 1 collect, receive; owe, be in debt. **2** be disadvantageous, be worthless, be useless, be futile. **3** charge, cost. **4** withhold, retain, suppress, repress; receive.

◇ *Word origin:* Did you ever *pay* a bill or debt in order to appease or keep peace with a friend, a shop, or a bank you owed money to? The concept of paying to appease or keep peace is an old one, for *pay* comes from Old French *payer*, to pay, to appease, which is ultimately from Latin *pax*, peace.

payment *n.* **1** *Payment of the bill may be by cheque or money order. The bookkeeper is in charge of all payments:* paying, remittance, settlement, liquidation, defrayal, discharge, outlay, expenditure, disbursement, debt, spending. **2** *Father makes a payment on the mortgage every month. What does he want in payment for that old car?:* instalment, partial payment, remittance, premium; remuneration, compensation, recompense, reimbursement, fee, pay, salary, allowance, contribution.

Ant. 1 non-payment, non-remittance; income, profit, return, credit.

peaceful *adj.* **1** *I want my children to be brought up in a peaceful world. Sweden is a peaceful nation:* free from war, non-warring, peacetime; peaceable, peace-loving, inclined toward peace, pacific, pacifistic, non-belligerent. **2** *Union and management reached a peaceful settlement of their differences:* amicable, friendly, without violence, non-violent, without hostility, free from strife, harmonious, agreeable. **3** *It's so peaceful in the woods:* quiet, still, silent, tranquil, serene, restful, calm, placid, undisturbed, untroubled.

Ant. 1 warring, wartime; belligerent, bellicose, hostile, warlike. **2** violent, hostile, strife-torn, bitter, antagonistic, angry, unfriendly. **3** noisy, loud, raucous, tumultuous; disturbed, perturbed, disquieted, agitated, upset, nervous, restless.

peak *n.* **1** *The mountain peak was covered with snow:* summit, pinnacle, tip, apex, crest; apogee. **2** *We drove through town at the peak of the rush-hour:* culmination, climax, maximum point, highest degree, acme, zenith, crest, flood.

—*v.* **3** *Athletes who peak too early soon fall off:* reach a maximum or crest, climax, culminate.

Ant. 1 base, bottom, foot, foundation.

◇ *Word origin: Peak* was originally a variant of *pike*, a hill with a pointed summit, as in the *Peak* District of Derbyshire. The word also reproduces Spanish and Portuguese *pico* and was thus applied to the *Peak* of Tenerife.

peaked *adj. The suit of armour included a peaked helmet:* with a peak, pointed, pointy, spiked, tapered; spiny, spiky.

peaky *adj. The patient was recovering but still looked peaky:* pale, wan, ashen, white; sickly, ailing, ill, weak, debilitated, wizened; thin, lean, skinny, scrawny, gaunt, emaciated, pinched, haggard, drawn.

Ant. hearty, hale, hale and hearty, healthy; robust, hardy, sturdy, husky, strapping, brawny; ruddy, rosy-cheeked, florid, flushed, blushing.

◇ *Word origin: Peaky* has nothing to do with *peaks* (pointed tops of things). It comes from an old verb to *peak,* to look ill, as in the Shakespearean phrase *peak and pine,* i.e. look sick and languish.

peal *n.* **1** *The peal of church bells filled the air. A peal of thunder woke us:* ringing, ring, reverberation, resounding, clang, knell, tintinnabulation; clap, crash, crack, roar, blare, boom, blast, rumble, roll.

—*v.* **2** *All the bells in town pealed at noon:* ring, reverberate, resound, clang, toll, knell, tintinnabulate; crash, crack, roar, blare, boom, blast, rumble, roll.

◇ *Word origin:* The *peal* of bells calls people to church or to a gathering. It is from Old French *apeler*, to call, and is closely related to our word *appeal.*

peck[1] *v.* **1** *The bird pecked at the breadcrumbs:*

strike with the beak, bore with the beak, pick up with the beak; tap, strike, thump, pat. **2** *The child just pecked at his food:* pick at, nibble, play with.
—*n.* **3** *Her husband gave her a peck on the cheek and left for the office:* light kiss, absentminded kiss, *Slang* smack; tap, rap, stroke, light jab.
Ant. 2 devour, gobble, wolf down, gulp, bolt.

peculiar *adj.* **1** *Every bell has its own peculiar sound:* particular, individual, distinctive, distinct, distinguishing, characteristic, representative, unique, singular, exclusive, private, personal, special, specific. **2** *What a peculiar hat!:* odd, queer, strange, unusual, curious, quaint, outlandish, unconventional, freakish, weird; eccentric, bizarre, idiosyncratic, erratic, capricious, whimsical, *Slang* far-out.
Ant. 1 common, general, unspecific, universal, indistinctive. **2** commonplace, usual, ordinary, expected, conventional, familiar, everyday.
◇ *Word origin: Peculiar* and *peculiarity* come from Latin *peculium,* private property, whose base is Latin *pecu,* cattle, money.

peculiarity *n.* **1** *The peculiarity of this particular stamp is the way the perforations have been left off:* feature, trait, distinguishing quality, uniqueness, characteristic, quality, singularity, particularity, distinction, mark, badge, **2** *Wearing no other colour than blue is only one of her peculiarities:* eccentricity, idiosyncrasy, odd trait, oddity; freakishness, strangeness, weirdness, queerness, bizarreness, unorthodoxy; abnormality.
Ant. 1 universality, common quality, general thing. **2** conventionality, normalcy.

pedagogue *n.* (now usually used contemptuously) *He was a lover of learning, but a tiresome pedagogue:* teacher, schoolteacher, schoolmaster, educator, tutor, instructor, professor.

pedant *n. Is the professor really a brilliant scholar or just a pedant?:* ostentatious man of learning; bookworm, plodding scholar, doctrinaire scholar; stickler, purist, dogmatist.

pedantic *adj. When you ask him a question you get a pedantic answer:* ostentatiously learned, pompous, academic, scholastic, didactic, doctrinaire, bookish, stilted, dogmatic, hairsplitting, meticulous, particular.
Ant. succinct, pithy, straightforward; vague; general, comprehensive.

peddle *v. The boy peddles newspapers at the street corner. Stop peddling gossip all over the office!:* hawk, vend, sell, carry about for sale; dispense, deal out, dispose of.
Ant. buy, purchase, get, obtain, acquire.

pedestrian *n.* **1** *Pedestrians have the right of way at zebra crossings:* walker, hiker, traveller on foot, stroller, *Informal* foot-slogger.
—*adj.* **2** *The city built a pedestrian precinct in the shopping centre:* for pedestrians, for walking; ambulatory, perambulatory, perambulating; peripatetic, itinerant. **3** *His newest play is quite a pedestrian affair:* unimaginative, mediocre, commonplace, ordinary, prosaic, banal; dull, uninteresting, humdrum, tedious, unexciting, unimportant, inconsequential, insignificant.
Ant. 1 driver, vehicle. **2** vehicular, for vehicles. **3** imaginative, exciting, interesting, intriguing, fascinating, compelling; important, significant, consequential, outstanding, remarkable, noteworthy.

> **Exploring the Word**: *Pedal, pedestal, pedestrian, pawn, peon, biped, impede, expedite,* and *expedition* all come from Latin *pes,* foot. Thus a *pedal* is a lever operated by the foot; *pedestal* comes to us via Italian *pie di stallo,* foot of a stall, hence a base or support; and a *pedestrian,* of course, is one who goes on foot. *Pawn* and *peon* were originally the same word and meant a foot soldier, the lowest-ranking soldier; a *biped* (Latin *bi-,* two) is an animal with two feet; *impede* literally means to put the feet in shackles, hence to stop or slow someone, while *expedite* literally means to take the feet out of shackles, hence to speed up or dispatch something, and an *expedition* is going out on foot, hence a journey or march. A *pedicure* (Latin *curare,* to care for) is a cosmetic treatment of the feet and toenails. *Pied-à-terre* is French for a temporary or secondary lodging, and literally means "one foot on the ground." Our word *pedigree* is from French *pié de grue,* foot of a crane, because the three lines denoting succession in *pedigrees* resemble the three-toed foot of a crane! A *tripod* (three feet) gets its name from the related Greek word *poûs,* foot. Finally, our English word *foot* goes back to Old English *fōt,* foot. All three — Latin *pes,* Greek *poûs,* and Old English *fōt* — go back to a common Indo-European ancestor word meaning "foot."

pedigree *n. The poodle had an impressive pedigree:* record of ancestry, official record of descent, family tree, genealogical table; line of descent, descent, lineage, ancestry, family, parentage, line, derivation.

"I'm always sorry when any language is lost, because languages are the pedigree of nations." —*Samuel Johnson*

---

peep[1] *v.* **1** *No peeping! The girl peeped round the door and asked us in:* peek, look surreptitiously, steal a look, look from hiding; peer, give a quick look, give a cursory look, glimpse, skim. **2** *The sun finally peeped out from behind the clouds:* peer out, come partially into view, begin to appear, emerge, come forth.
—*n.* **3** *The hunters just got a peep at the deer before it disappeared into the woods:* quick look, glimpse, glance, peek.

Ant. **1** scrutinize, inspect, examine, observe, contemplate; stare. **2** disappear, submerge, hide. **3** good look, examination, inspection.

peep[2] *n.* **1** *The children were delighted by the peeps of the chicks. One more peep out of you and you'll get a spanking!:* peeping, cheep, chirp, tweet, twitter, chirrup, squeak; word, sound, whisper, mutter, whimper, murmur.

◇ *Word origin: Peep,* chirp, was coined to imitate the sound it represents.

peer[1] *v.* **1** *She peered at the neighbours from behind the curtain:* look, gaze, stare, gape, peep, peek, squint. **2** *The moon peered out from behind a cloud:* appear, come into view, emerge, become visible.

peer[2] *n.* **1** *The defendant was tried by a jury of his peers:* equal, compeer; fellow citizen. **2** *The peers of the realm defied the king's edict:* nobleman, noble, lord; aristocrat, gentleman, patrician, *Slang* nob.

Exploring the Word: *Peer* comes from Latin *par,* equal, hence one's *peers* are one's equals in social status, age, education, talent, etc. In particular, *peer* has the added meaning of those who are equal in being nobles and have an equal voice in the House of Lords. Such *peers* include dukes, marquises, earls, viscounts, and barons, and the *peerage* are such noblemen collectively, their rank or office, or a book (as Burke's *Peerage*) containing a genealogical list of the nobility. *Peerless,* of course, means without a peer or equal, hence unequalled, of unequalled excellence. *Disparage* also comes from Latin *par,* equal, and means to do away with or lower another's "equality" or rank, hence to downgrade or treat with contempt.

peerless *adj. Paganini usually played with peerless artistry:* unsurpassed, matchless, unmatched, unequalled, incomparable, unrivalled, inimitable; superlative, surpassing, supreme, consummate, pre-eminent, transcendent; faultless, flawless.

Ant. commonplace, ordinary, mediocre, routine, indifferent, pedestrian; inferior, poor, second-rate.

peeve *v. What peeves me is the way she takes her friends for granted:* annoy, provoke, gall, irritate, chafe, exasperate, irk, vex, nettle, aggravate, rile, fret, perturb, *Slang* bug, give one a pain, give one a pain in the neck.

Ant. please, delight, charm, enchant, captivate, enrapture.

peevish *adj. Father gets peevish when he's kept waiting:* cross, irritable, testy, grumpy, grouchy, ill-humoured, sulky, petulant, snappish, fractious, cantankerous, cranky, churlish, huffy, pettish; mean, ill-natured, ill-tempered, splenetic, quarrelsome, querulous.

Ant. agreeable, easy-going, good-natured, pleasant, genial, amiable.

peg *n. The violin strings are wound round pegs and tightened:* pin, spike, skewer, nail, toggle; cleat, fastener, thole, thole-pin, dowel.

pellet *n. The rat poison comes in very small pellets:* ball, drop, bead, globule, marble, pea, pill; pebble, stone.

◇ *Word origin: Pellet* comes from a Romance diminutive of Latin *pila,* ball, hence little ball. (The classical diminutive *pilula* gives us our word *pill* and is first used in that sense by the naturalist Pliny — 1st century A.D.)

pelt[1] *v. After the thunder, the rain pelted down. The boys pelted the tin can with stones:* hit, strike, batter, shy, sling, hurl at, snowball, throw at, rap, pepper.

pelt[2] *n. The coat was made of leopard pelts. The goat had a greyish pelt:* animal skin, skin, hide; coat, fleece.

◇ *Word origin: Pelt*[2], the skin of an animal with the hair left on, comes (ultimately) from Latin *pellis,* skin.

pen[1] *n. How many sheep are in the pen?:* enclosure, fold, pound, paddock, compound, stockade; cage, coop, corral, sty, crib, hutch, stall.

◇ *Word origin: Pen*[1] comes from Old English *pinn,* pin, peg, perhaps because early *pens* were made of pegs stuck in the ground, or another way to *pen* an animal was to tie it to a peg or pin. Incidentally, the root-word *pen* in *penitentiary* has nothing to do with keeping prisoners penned up but has to do with the "pen-" in *penal, penalty,* and *penitence,* from Latin *poena,* penalty.

pen[2] *n.* **1** *The contract must be signed with a pen, not a pencil:* fountain pen, quill; ball-point pen. —*v.* **2** *She penned a note to her mother:* write, write in ink, write by hand, scribble, scrawl, pencil; compose, draft.

◇ *Word origin: Pen*[2] comes from Latin *penna,* wing, feather, plume, since early pens were feathers or quills. Latin *penna* also gives us *pinion* (wing, feather), *pennant* (a long, narrow feather-shaped flag), and *pennate* (having wings or feathers).

penal *adj. Devil's Island was a famous penal colony:* of punishment, disciplinary, punitive, corrective, penalizing, punishing, castigatory, retributive; of gaols, of prisoners.

"Crime is only the retail department of what, in wholesale, we call penal law."
—*George Bernard Shaw*

penalty *n. The sign read "No litter. Maximum penalty £50":* punishment, forfeiture, retribution, infliction, assessment, suffering; fine, forfeit, handicap, disadvantage.

Ant. reward, prize.

penchant *n. The fat youth had a penchant for rich desserts:* fondness, partiality, liking, strong inclination, fancy, preference, predilection, proclivity, propensity, leaning, attraction, taste, relish, tendency, affinity, disposition,

proneness, prejudice, bias; flair, bent, turn, knack, gift.
Ant. hatred, dislike, loathing, aversion, abhorrence, disinclination, repulsion.

> **Exploring the Word**: *Penalize* (to punish or fine), *penalty* (a punishment or fine) and *penal* (referring to gaol, or gaols, as a place of punishment), all come from Latin *poena*, punishment, fine (related to Greek *poinē*, which means the same). The same base gives us *punishment* itself; *pain*, literally torment or punishment, as in the phrase "under pain of death"; *punitive*, inflicting punishment or a fine, and *impunity*, freedom from punishment, fine, or the usual consequences; and *subpoena* (Latin *sub-*, under), which is a judicial writ requiring a person to appear in or present evidence to a court "under penalty" for refusing to do so. Outside the field of law and in the context of religion, this same base gives us *penance*, undertaking penalties to atone for or receive absolution for a sin; *penitence*, the penalty or amends undertaken with accepting guilt; and *repent*, literally to be punished by feeling regret and remorse for one's sins and hence to reform.

pendent Also **pendant** *adj. The necklace was a gold band with pendent diamonds:* hanging, suspended, dangling, pendulous, pensile, swinging.

pending *adj. Their divorce case is still pending, but it should go through soon:* awaiting decision, awaiting settlement, undetermined, undecided, unsettled, in the air, in suspense; imminent, in the offing.

pendulous *adj. The pendulous vines made the jungle impassable:* hanging, suspended, dangling, pendent, swinging, pensile; drooping, sagging.

penetrate *v.* **1** *The nail easily penetrated the soft wood:* pierce, puncture, cut into, bore, prick, perforate; cut through, pass through, traverse. **2** *The foul smell penetrated the entire house:* pervade, permeate, saturate, impregnate, seep in; enter, invade, infiltrate. **3** *Were you able to penetrate the author's symbolism?:* understand, comprehend, perceive, discern, fathom, get, get to the bottom of, work out, unravel, see through, catch; decode, decipher.
Ant. 1 ricochet, rebound, glance off.

penetrating *adj.* **1** *Ammonia has an extremely penetrating smell:* piercing, sharp, stinging, caustic, biting, acrid, strong, pungent, harsh, reeking; heady, redolent; pervading, pervasive, permeating, saturating. **2** *The book is a penetrating study of the labour movement:* keen, sharp, sharp-witted, perceptive, discerning, thoughtful, perspicacious, shrewd, astute, intelligent, smart, clever, percipient, trenchant; alive, alert, aware.
Ant. 1 mild, sweet. **2** obtuse, unperceptive, uncomprehending, thoughtless, shallow, dull, stupid, dumb; indifferent, apathetic.

penetration *n.* **1** *The heavier the arrow the greater its penetration into the target:* power of penetrating, foray, passage, invasion, intrusion, infusion, access; perforation, piercing, boring, puncturing. **2** *She showed great penetration in analysing the problem:* insight, keenness, sharpness, perception, discernment, perspicacity, shrewdness, astuteness, intelligence, cleverness, quickness, grasp.
Ant. 2 obtuseness, stupidity, shallowness, dullness.

penitence *n. If a sinner feels penitence, he can be forgiven:* repentance, remorse, compunction, regret, humiliation, contrition; penance, attrition, expiation, atonement.
Ant. impenitence, unrepentance, obduracy; hardness, callousness.

penitent *adj.* **1** *Those who were penitent obtained absolution:* penitential, repentant, contrite, atoning, remorseful, self-reproaching, apologetic, sorry, conscience-stricken, regretful.
—*n.* **2** *The penitents were saying their prayers at early Mass:* a penitent person, one who is remorseful for sin or fault; devotee, pilgrim.
Ant. 1 impenitent, unrepentant, obdurate; remorseless, callous.

penniless *adj. Bad investments have left him penniless:* moneyless, destitute, poverty-stricken, impoverished, indigent, poor, needy; insolvent, ruined, bankrupt, wiped out; *Slang* broke, flat broke, stony, skint, bust.
Ant. rich, wealthy, affluent, moneyed, well-heeled. *Slang* loaded.

pensive *adj. What did you say to put him in such a pensive mood?:* quietly thoughtful, reflective, introspective, musing, dreaming, daydreaming, dreamy; sad, wistful, melancholy, solemn, serious, sombre, grave.
Ant. frivolous, joyous, happy, cheerful, gay, jovial, carefree, light-hearted.
◇ *Word origin: Pensive* comes from Latin *pensare,* to think, weigh.

"Pensive poets painful vigils keep,
Sleepless themselves to give their readers sleep."
—*Alexander Pope*

---

pent-up *adj. The children need to work off their pent-up energy:* repressed, suppressed, stifled, penned-up, penned-in, hedged-in, boxed-up, bottled-up, stored-up, held back, reined in, confined, checked, inhibited.

penury *n. She lived in penury during her last years:* poverty, impoverishment, want, indigence, need, privation, destitution, straitened circumstances, dire necessity; financial ruin, insolvency, bankruptcy.
Ant. wealth, prosperity, opulence, luxury, elegance, abundance, affluence.

people *n. pl.* **1** *Will people ever live 200 years?:*

human beings, humans, mortals, men and women, individuals, human kind, Homo sapiens, mankind, humanity. **2** *The people of Birmingham want better schools. My people came from Ireland:* citizens, citizenry, inhabitants, population, populace; family, ancestors, relatives, kin, kinsfolk. **3** *A politician must appeal to the people:* the public, the common people, the rank and file, the masses, the multitude, the millions, the man in the street, one and all; commoners, the common run; the lower classes, the lower orders, the working class, the working man, the mob, the rabble, the herd, the crowd, the great unwashed, hoi polloi.

Ant. 3 nobility, aristocracy, gentry, upper classes, élite, landed gentry.

◇ *Usage note:* See PERSON.

◇ *Word origin: People* comes from Latin *pŏpulus,* people. (Latin *pōpulus* — pronounced with a long *o* — means "poplar.")

pep *n. She's always full of pep when she starts to work:* vigour, vim, vitality, verve, energy, dash; *Informal* go, get-up-and-go; animation, vivacity, spirit, enthusiasm, life, gusto, liveliness.

◇ *Word origin: Pep* is a short form of *pepper,* and originally meant spicy, quick-tempered.

peppery *adj. This soup is too peppery:* highly seasoned, spicy, hot, piquant, fiery, pungent, sharp.

Ant. bland, mild, tasteless, insipid.

perambulate *v. Every evening the local people perambulate around the plaza:* walk, stroll, saunter, promenade, amble, ramble, pace, tour.

◇ *Word origin: Perambulate* comes from Latin *per* (through) + *ambulare* (to walk). An *ambulatory patient* is, of course, one who can walk, and our word *ambulance* comes from French *hôpital ambulant,* "walking (moving) hospital."

perceive *v.* **1** *Only an artist could perceive the fine shades of colour in the painting:* notice, be aware of, detect, note, discern, make out, recognize, distinguish, apprehend, discover; observe, see, hear, smell, taste, feel, sense. **2** *She gradually perceived that her parents had been right:* understand, comprehend, apprehend, grasp, gather, realize, know, conclude, deduce, gain insight into; *Slang* savvy, get.

Ant. 1 overlook, ignore, miss, pass over.

perceptible *adj. The difference in their height is hardly perceptible:* perceivable, discernible, noticeable, apparent, detectable, observable, visible, discoverable, ascertainable; obvious, evident, manifest, distinct, conspicuous, clear, plain, palpable, tangible, prominent, notable, unmistakable, well-defined; unconcealed, unhidden.

Ant. imperceptible, indiscernible, unnoticeable, unapparent, undetectable, inconspicuous; concealed, hidden, obscured.

◇ *Spelling tip:* Some people hesitate to write this word because they aren't sure whether it ends in *-able* or *-ible.* Remember that for something to be within your *perceptIon,* it must be *perceptIble.*

perception *n. A good driver must have a keen perception of distance:* discernment, awareness, sense, faculty, apprehension, conception, recognition, comprehension, cognizance, consciousness, detection, discrimination, understanding, grasp.

perceptive *adj. She is very perceptive about the moods of others:* understanding, full of insight, sensitive, responsive, aware, discerning, penetrating; intelligent, keen, sharp, astute, acute, sensible, quick, quick-witted.

Ant. insensitive, obtuse, callous, indifferent; stupid, thick, slow-witted, dull, dumb.

perch *n.* **1** *The bird sat on its perch and sang lustily:* roost, roosting-place; resting-place, rest, seat.

—*v.* **2** *The boy perched in the tree and called to his friends:* sit, roost, rest, settle; light, alight, land.

◇ *Word origin: Perch* comes from Latin *pertica,* pole. Our other word *perch* (the speckled fish) comes from Greek *perkē,* perch. The word is related to Greek *perknós,* dusky, specked, said of grapes or olives when beginning to ripen. It is similar to the Welsh *erch,* speckled, and to quite a few other names of spotted and pied animals in various Indo-European languages.

"'Hope' is the thing with feathers
That perches in the soul." —*Emily Dickinson*

---

perdition *n. Sinners may suffer eternal perdition:* damnation, condemnation, loss of heavenly salvation, loss of one's soul; everlasting punishment, hell-fire, Hell.

◇ *Word origin: Perdition* comes from Old French *perdicuin,* destruction, ruin, which is ultimately derived from Latin *perdere,* destroy.

peremptory *adj.* **1** *He was half-way up the tree when a peremptory order stopped him:* absolute, final, irrevocable, irreversible, incontrovertible, undeniable, unquestionable, decisive, unequivocal; unavoidable, obligatory, imperative. **2** *She's much too peremptory to co-operate with others:* domineering, overbearing, authoritative, dictatorial, assertive, aggressive, lordly, magisterial, masterful, imperious, high-handed; opinionated, closed-minded, dogmatic, biased.

Ant. 1, 2 indecisive. **2** submissive, unassertive, passive, docile, tractable, compliant, meek; co-operative, open-minded.

perennial *adj. He sat there with that perennial grin on his face:* perpetual, everlasting, permanent, constant, persistent, incessant, unceasing, ceaseless, continual, continuous, never-

ending, unremitting; fixed, changeless, unchanging, immutable, durable, imperishable, indestructible, lasting, long-lasting, undying, unfailing, long-lived.
Ant. temporary, occasional, sporadic, intermittent, periodic, evanescent; perishable, transient, fleeting, ephemeral, temporal.

perfect *adj.* **1** *Can you draw a perfect circle?:* exact, accurate, precise, true, pure, correct in every detail, flawless, unerring, strict, scrupulous, faithful. **2** *The athlete was in perfect health. The child has been a perfect angel all day:* faultless, flawless, without defect, unblemished, unimpaired, undamaged; complete, whole, entire, unbroken, finished, absolute, thorough, pure, consummate, unqualified, unmitigated, impeccable, matchless, unequalled, unrivalled, ideal, supreme, peerless, superlative, sublime; blameless, untainted, immaculate.
—*v.* **3** *The scientist perfected a method of desalinating seawater:* bring to perfection, develop, complete, achieve, accomplish, effect, realize, evolve, fulfil, consummate.
Ant. 1, 2 imperfect. **2** faulty, flawed, defective, blemished, impaired, ruined, spoiled, damaged, incomplete, deficient, unfinished; partial, mixed, impure, qualified; inferior, poor, bad, worthless, *Informal* awful, *Slang* lousy.

"Culture is then properly described not as having its origin in curiosity, but as having its origin in the love of perfection."
—*Matthew Arnold*

---

perfection *n.* **1** *The roast was cooked to perfection:* perfectness, excellence, faultlessness, flawlessness, superiority, sublimity, ideal state; exactness, accurateness, precision, purity. **2** *The perfection of the jet engine took many years:* development, completion, achieving, accomplishment, realization, evolution, fulfilment, consummation.

perfectly *adv.* **1** *The cake was baked perfectly:* to perfection, superbly, wonderfully, flawlessly, without fault, without defect, without blemish, impeccably. **2** *She's perfectly capable of taking care of herself:* entirely, thoroughly, completely, totally, fully, wholly, altogether, quite, utterly, absolutely, consummately, supremely, infinitely, pre-eminently, to the nth degree; downright, positively.
Ant. 1 imperfectly, faultily, defectively, poorly, badly. **2** not; incompletely, partially; mistakenly, erroneously, inaccurately.

perfidious *adj. Judas Iscariot's perfidious act made his name a byword for treachery:* treacherous, traitorous, deceitful, false, disloyal, faithless, treasonable, dishonourable, untrustworthy, unscrupulous; dishonest, corrupt, untruthful, undependable, lying, cheating; *Informal* sneaky, double-dealing, shifty, *Slang* two-faced.

perform *v.* **1** *A skilled worker can perform the task easily:* do, accomplish, carry out, execute, perpetrate, achieve, effect, realize, attain, fulfil, bring to pass, bring about, finish, consummate, discharge, dispose of, meet; *Slang* pull off, polish off. **2** *All of the musicians performed admirably. The actors performed* Twelfth Night: play, present, render; act, enact, take part in; tread the boards.
Ant. 1 fail, founder, neglect, forsake.

performance *n.* **1** *He failed miserably in the performance of his duty:* discharge, accomplishment, execution, performing, doing, acquittal, exercise, transaction, fulfilment, realization, attainment, conduct, achievement, dispatch, perpetration, effectuation; completion, consummation. **2** *The theatre gives two performances a day:* show, presentation, rendering, production, exhibition; (*variously*) play, concert, opera, ballet, recital, entertainment, spectacle, ceremony.

perfume *n.* **1** *Who's wearing that spicy perfume? Magnolias have a wonderful perfume:* fragrance, scent, essence; aroma, odour, bouquet.
—*v.* **2** *Those beautiful roses perfume the whole garden:* imbue with odour, give fragrance to, scent, sweeten.
Ant. 1 stench, stink, smell.
◇ *Word origin: Perfume* comes from Latin *per-* (thoroughly) + *fumus* (smoke), literally thoroughly smoked, full of smoke or vapour. The same Latin base gives us *fume.*

"Foreign smells are less intolerable than foreign perfumes." —*William Hazlitt*

---

perfunctory *adj. That was certainly a perfunctory "hello" he gave us:* indifferent, casual, uninterested, offhand, careless, unconcerned, cursory, inattentive, lax, hasty, superficial, routine, mechanical, half-hearted, lukewarm, apathetic, spiritless, listless, passionless; negligent.
Ant. careful, thorough, thoughtful, diligent, assiduous, attentive, warm-hearted, effusive, spirited, ardent, keen, zealous.

peril *n. Does he understand the perils of rock-climbing?:* risk, danger, hazard, jeopardy, pitfall, threat, menace, cause for alarm; vulnerability, exposure to danger, openness to attack, defencelessness, insecurity, uncertainty, unsafety.
Ant. safety, security, secureness, certainty, surety; invulnerability, unassailability, impregnability.

perilous *adj. The flood-waters were perilous to cross:* risky, hazardous, dangerous, fraught with danger, unsafe, ominous, threatening; uncertain, unsure, chancy, insecure, vulnerable, shaky, slippery, precarious.

perimeter *n. Trees were planted on the perimeter of the garden:* periphery, border, borderline, circumference, bounds, confines; margin, edge.

Ant. centre, middle, hub, heart, core, kernel, nucleus.

period *n.* **1** *The children's lunch period is from twelve to one. Dinosaurs roamed the earth in an earlier period:* time, span of time, interval, interlude, duration, term, season; era, epoch, age, aeon. **2** *The suspect's confession put a period to the investigation:* end, stop, close, finish, termination, limit, discontinuance, halt, cessation, finale, coup de grâce, *Slang* curtain.

◇ *Word origin: Period* and *periodical* come from Greek *periodos,* a going around, a cycle or part of a cycle. Thus a *period* is a portion or fixed interval of time or a punctuation mark dividing writing into sentence-sized portions. A *periodical* is a publication, such as a magazine, that is published at fixed intervals of time.

periodic Also **periodical** *adj. She makes periodic visits to the hairdresser:* repeated, recurrent, frequent, regular, routine, at fixed intervals, cyclic, seasonal.

periodical *n. The library subscribes to scores of periodicals:* publication; (*variously*) newspaper, paper, magazine, journal, bulletin, review, daily, weekly, monthly, quarterly, annual.

periodically *adv. You should have your eyes examined periodically:* regularly, routinely, at fixed intervals, repeatedly, often, frequently; occasionally.

periphery *n. Many houses have sprung up on the periphery of the town:* outskirts, fringes, suburbs, boundary, edge, perimeter, circumference, border.

Ant. centre, middle, hub, heart, core, nucleus.

perish *v. Dozens perished in the storm. The ancient Aztec culture has perished now:* die, expire, pass away; become extinct, cease to exist, wither away, decay, come to ruin, crumble, be destroyed.

Ant. be born, come into being, arise, appear; thrive, flourish, proliferate, prosper, fructify.

◇ *Word origin: Perish* comes from Latin *per-* (away) + *ire* (to go), to go away, hence to pass from existence.

perishable *adj. Perishable foods must be kept refrigerated:* subject to decay, subject to spoiling, decomposable, unstable; short-lived, fleeting, transitory, ephemeral, evanescent.

Ant. non-perishable, stable, durable, long-lived, lasting.

perjury *n. The witness lied to the jury and was charged with perjury:* giving false testimony, lying under oath, false swearing.

perky *adj. We all like her because she's so perky:* jaunty, pert, lively, gay, vivacious, animated, sprightly, spirited, full of spirit, alert, saucy, brisk; cheerful, elated, happy, sunny, smiling, light-hearted, free and easy.

Ant. passive, lethargic, spiritless, sluggish, phlegmatic; sombre, grave, serious, dour, sullen, gloomy, glum, sour, morose, sad, cheerless.

permanent *adj. They built a permanent monument to the hero. Are these dyes permanent?:* lasting forever, lasting, perpetual, everlasting, eternal, infinite, endless, undying, never-ending, unending, immortal, deathless, abiding, indestructible, imperishable, unyielding, unalterable, unfailing, changeless, immutable; long-lasting, long-lived, durable, enduring, unfading, constant, stable.

Ant. impermanent, temporary, brief, fleeting, momentary, finite, mortal, passing, short, short-lived, transitory, fugitive, unstable, variable, changing, inconstant, ephemeral, evanescent.

◇ *Word origin: Permanent* comes from Latin *per-* (through) + *manere* (to remain), to remain throughout, to stay to the end.

permeate *v. That cigar smoke permeates the whole house:* penetrate, pass through, soak through, seep through; pervade, saturate, diffuse throughout, infuse, fill, imbue.

Ant. bounce off, ricochet, glance off, slide off.

◇ *Word origin: Permeate* comes from Latin *per-* (through) + *meare* (to pass).

permissible *adj. Hearsay is not permissible evidence in court. Is smoking permissible in the theatre?:* permitted, allowed, allowable, tolerated, admissible, acceptable; sanctioned, authorized, granted, licensed, lawful, legal, legitimate, licit.

Ant. forbidden, prohibited, banned, disallowed, proscribed; unauthorized, unlawful, illegal, illicit.

permission *n. May I have permission to use the car? The Commanding Officer must give his permission for all leave:* leave, consent, assent, approval, acquiescence, concession, agreement, compliance, approbation; authorization, sanction, dispensation, indulgence, endorsement, grant, licence, permit.

Ant. refusal, denial, prohibition, ban, prevention, interdiction.

permissive *adj. Should parents be strict or permissive?:* indulgent, lenient, assenting, consenting, acquiescent, tolerant, forbearing; allowing, permitting, granting; unproscriptive, unprohibitive.

Ant. strict, rigid, authoritarian, domineering, proscriptive; refusing, denying, forbidding, withholding, grudging.

permit *v.* **1** *Will you permit me to ask a question? The rules do not permit players to step out of bounds:* let, allow, give permission, give leave to, give assent to, consent to, tolerate, suffer, endure, bear with, put up with, let pass, approve, condone; authorize, sanction, endorse, license.

—*n.* **2** *Have you a fishing permit?:* licence, official permission, authorization, warrant, authority, sanction.

pernicious *adj. The common cold is usually not a pernicious disease. Her gossip may be amusing but it is also pernicious:* harmful, injurious, serious, destructive, damaging, deleterious, detrimental, dangerous, disastrous, deadly, fatal, mortal, toxic, venomous, poisonous, noxious, malignant.

Ant. harmless, innocuous; beneficial, advantageous, helpful; healthful, healthy, wholesome, salutary, salubrious.

◇ *Word origin: Pernicious* comes from Latin *per-* (thoroughly) + *nex* (death), hence destructive, injurious.

perpetrate *v. Only a madman would perpetrate such a crime:* commit, perform, carry out, execute, do, enact, transact, bring about, pursue, *Slang* pull off.

perpetual *adj. The will provided a fund for perpetual care of the park. I'm tired of your perpetual nagging:* lasting for ever, lasting, permanent, everlasting, eternal, abiding, enduring, constant, sustained, endless, never ending, unending; continuous, ceaseless, incessant, unceasing, interminable, uninterrupted, unremitting, inexhaustible, repeated, continual.

Ant. temporary, impermanent, brief, fleeting, momentary, passing, short-lived, transitory, transient, ephemeral.

perpetuate *v. We must perpetuate the free-enterprise system:* cause to endure, make last, make perpetual, make everlasting, eternalize, memorialize; preserve, save, sustain, maintain, continue.

Ant. destroy, obliterate, annihilate, exterminate, abolish, stamp out, snuff out; forget, ignore; avoid, eschew.

perplex *v. Mathematics perplexes me:* puzzle, baffle, confuse, bewilder, mix up, confound, dumbfound, muddle, befuddle, nonplus, stump, mystify; rattle, throw into confusion, *Informal* make one's head spin.

persecute *v. The Pilgrim Fathers went to America after being persecuted for their religious beliefs:* harass, harry, annoy cruelly, pursue continually, oppress, tyrannize, plague, harrow, hector, hound, bully, badger, bait; torment, maltreat, abuse.

Ant. pamper, indulge, humour; favour, accommodate; support, uphold, champion, back.

◇ *Usage note:* See PROSECUTE.

persevere *v. Talent is worthless unless you persevere in developing it:* persist, be steadfast, be determined, be resolved, be resolute, be obstinate, work unflaggingly, not give up, keep on, maintain one's efforts, work hard, keep at it; *Informal* plug away, hammer away, bang away, stick at it, stick to one's guns, hang on.

Ant. be irresolute, waver, vacillate, shilly-shally, falter, let down; give up, give in.

persist *v. Despite hardships, she persisted in her efforts to get a university education:* persevere, work unflaggingly, maintain one's efforts, pursue relentlessly, be tenacious, not give up, stop at nothing, be obstinate, hold steadfast, stand fast, be determined, be resolute, keep at it, not yield, work day and night; *Informal* stick to it, stick to one's guns, hang on, move heaven and earth, leave no stone unturned, not take "no" for an answer, never say die.

Ant. be irresolute, waver, vacillate, shilly-shally; falter, quit, give up, surrender, stop, cease, end, leave off, die, expire, wither away, fade, shrivel.

persistent *adj.* **1** *With persistent effort we can finish on time:* stubborn, determined, obstinate, tenacious, relentless, obdurate, dogged, persevering, steadfast, resolute, unfailing, unswerving. **2** *Her persistent criticism made everyone weary:* constant, unrelenting, unceasing, incessant, continual, continuous, endless, perpetual, eternal, sustained, interminable, inexhaustible, unremitting, unshakeable; lasting, enduring, abiding.

person *n. I find him a strange person:* individual, human being, human, being, mortal, living soul, soul, living body, body.

◇ *Usage note:* In strict usage, *people* is used in referring to an indefinite number of individuals and *persons* where a precise number is specified. Thus, *The auditorium seats hundreds of people,* but *The capacity of the restaurant is limited to 47 persons.*

◇ *Word origin: Person* comes from Latin *persona,* an actor's mask or character, an assumed personality. We still use the Latin *persona* to mean a character in a play, and psychologists still use it to mean a personality assumed by an individual for psychological concealment or defence.

personable *adj. We need a personable girl at the reception desk:* agreeable, affable, having a pleasing personality, likeable, friendly, amiable, warm, charming, attractive, pleasant, cordial, well-mannered, complaisant, tactful, diplomatic, amicable, sympathetic, well-disposed.

Ant. unpleasant, surly, ill-natured, sullen, rude, discourteous.

"It is as great a spite to be praised in the wrong place, and by a wrong person, as can be done to a noble nature." —*Ben Jonson*

---

personal *adj.* **1** *The library contains the captain's personal papers:* private, own, individual, intimate, exclusive, special, particular, privy; inward, inwardly felt, subjective. **2** *The doctor lectured the class on personal hygiene:* bodily, physical, corporeal.

◇ *Usage note:* Don't confuse *personal* and *personnel. Personal* means of, for, or belonging to a particular person: *personal property. Is this a business call or a personal one? A personal problem is depressing him. Personnel* refers to the people employed on a job or having to do with workers: *The factory transferred 50 of its key personnel to the Sydney office. The shop steward is having personnel problems with the younger workers.*

◇ *Pronunciation tip: Personal* is stressed on the first syllable: *PUR-suh-nul. Personnel* is stressed on the last syllable: *pur-suh-NEL.*

personality *n.* **1** *Can one develop an agreeable personality?:* outward character, disposition, temperament, make-up, nature; identity, individuality, distinctiveness. **2** *An entertainer has to have a lot of personality:* charm, personal attraction, friendliness, agreeableness, amiability, affability, magnetism, charisma.

personify *v. For him, Elizabeth Taylor personified the ideal of female beauty:* embody, represent, exemplify, incorporate, characterize, express, symbolize; externalize, incarnate, personalize.

◇ *Word origin: Personify* comes from Latin *persona* (actor's mask or character) + *facere* (to make), literally to make or represent a character, to represent as a human being.

personnel *n. All personnel will receive an extra week's holiday:* employees, workers, staff, staff members, members, work-force, associates.

◇ *Usage note:* See PERSONAL.

◇ *Pronunciation tip:* See PERSONAL.

perspective *n.* **1** *Primitive artists often paint without perspective:* the art of conveying distance, sense of depth. **2** *From the top of the hill you can get a perspective of the entire park:* panoramic view, bird's-eye view, overview, vista, scene, view, outlook, prospect. **3** *I've been so close to the problem that I can't see it in perspective:* broad view, overview, comprehensive view, viewpoint, sense of proportion.

perspicacious *adj. The critic's remarks about the book were very perspicacious:* discerning, perceptive, astute, shrewd, penetrating, acute, keen, sharp, keen-sighted, clear-headed, clear-sighted, alert, awake, sagacious.

Ant. undiscerning, dull, dull-witted, stupid, thick-headed; dense, doltish, vacuous.

persuade *v. Can't we persuade you to come to the party?:* induce, influence, move, get, prevail upon, convince, win over, bring round, talk into, sway, prompt, coax, wheedle, cajole, inveigle; lure, tempt, entice.

Ant. dissuade, discourage, deter, repel, inhibit; forbid, prohibit.

persuasive *adj. A good politician must be a persuasive speaker:* convincing, compelling, forceful, believable, plausible, credible; effective, influential, winning, seductive, inviting, alluring, coaxing.

pert *adj.* **1** *Don't be pert to your elders:* impudent, impertinent, insolent, brash, flippant, flip, fresh, saucy, nervy, brazen, brassy, audacious, smart-alecy, impolite, discourteous, insulting. **2** *The old lady walked with pert little steps:* lively, sprightly, brisk, perky, spry, dapper, alert, wide-awake, quick, energetic.

Ant. **1** shy, bashful, meek, retiring, demure, modest, reserved; respectful, diffident, polite, courteous.

pertinent *adj. Your argument is very pertinent and I shall bear it in mind:* relevant, to the point, germane, material, appropriate, fitting, concerning the matter at hand, befitting, apt, applicable, suitable, apropos, meet; related, congruent, concerned, connected, corresponding, consistent.

Ant. irrelevant, immaterial, inappropriate, unfitting, unsuited, unsuitable; unrelated, incongruous, unconnected, foreign, alien, discordant.

perturb *v. The teacher was perturbed by the student's lack of interest:* disturb, trouble, worry, distress, disquiet, upset, discompose, disconcert.

pervade *v. The aroma of fresh coffee pervaded the house:* permeate, spread through, diffuse throughout, saturate, fill, infuse, imbue, penetrate.

perverse *adj. She takes a perverse delight in disagreeing with absolutely everyone:* contrary, stubborn, obstinate, obdurate, inflexible, balky, hard-headed, wrong-headed, mulish, dogged, pigheaded; headstrong, wilful, wayward, intractable, disobedient, rebellious.

Ant. co-operative, complaisant, pliant, flexible; agreeable, good-natured, accommodating, obliging, amiable.

pervert *v. He perverts history because of his extreme political views:* distort, warp, contort, abuse, misuse, corrupt, misrepresent, misapply, put a false interpretation on, falsify; debase, desecrate, corrupt, subvert, degrade, deprave.

perverted *adj. The child has a perverted sense of humour:* distorted, twisted, warped, contorted, unbalanced, misconstrued, misconceived, misunderstood; false, faulty, untrue, fallacious, unsound, erroneous, imperfect; degraded, depraved, debased, corrupt, unnatural, abnormal, aberrant.

Ant. sound, true, valid, balanced, correct, natural, normal; good, straight, worthy, commendable.

"Pessimism is only the name that men of weak nerves give to wisdom." —*Mark Twain*

---

pessimism *n. The pessimism in his writing is too depressing:* gloomy outlook, seeing only the gloomy side, belief that bad prevails; despair, hopelessness, discouragement, downheartedness, gloom, gloominess.

Ant. optimism, hopefulness, courage, dauntlessness, enthusiasm, cheerfulness.

pessimist *n. A pessimist never expects anything to turn out well:* defeatist, one who sees only the

bad side, one who believes that bad prevails; *Slang* prophet of doom, scaremonger, sabre-rattler, sourpuss, killjoy, spoil-sport, wet blanket.
Ant. optimist, utopian, incurable romantic, Pollyanna.
◇ *Word origin: Pessimist* comes from Latin *pessimus*, worst. The word comes to us from *pessimism*, the doctrine that this world is the worst of all possible worlds, as set forth in 1819 by the German philosopher Schopenhauer in response to *optimism* (from Latin *optimus*, best), the doctrine that the present world is the best of all possible worlds, as propounded by the German mathematician and philosopher Leibnitz in 1710.

pest *n. The spray gets rid of mosquitoes and other pests. That child is a real pest!:* troublesome insect, troublesome animal, destructive plant; annoying person, nuisance, scourge, blight, bane, annoyance, irritation, vexation, curse, *Informal* thorn in one's side, *Slang* pain in the neck.
◇ *Word origin: Pest,* like *pestilence*, comes from the Latin word for plague, *pestis*.

pester *v. He's always pestering me to help him with his homework:* bother, annoy, torment, badger, plague, provoke, harass, harry, hector, nag, vex, irritate, irk, fret, nettle, disturb, trouble, worry, bait; try one's patience, get on one's nerves.
◇ *Word origin: Pester* has nothing to do with *pest*. It comes from Old French *empestrer*, to tie up (an animal) for grazing. Late Latin *pastura* (pasture) is the base on which the Old French word was formed.

pet *n.* **1** *Does a dog make a better pet than a cat?:* household animal, house pet. **2** *Mother loved us all, but Jim was her pet:* favourite, darling, baby, *Slang* apple of one's eye; dear, beloved, loved one, sweetheart.
—adj. **3** *Improving the local park is the mayor's pet project:* favourite, choice, favoured, preferred, cherished, dearest, dear to one's heart.
—v. **4** *Don't be afraid to pet the dog, he won't bite:* pat, stroke, caress, fondle.

petition *n.* **1** *The petition to keep the school open had 500 names:* formal request, appeal, entreaty, plea; proposal, suit, solicitation; application, requisition; prayer, supplication, invocation, beseeching, orison; imploring.
—v. **2** *The condemned man petitioned the governor for clemency:* ask, beg, sue, beseech, entreat, call upon, appeal to, apply to, request of, plead with, urge, press, seek; pray, supplicate, invoke.

petrified *adj.* **1** *After thousands of years of absorbing minerals from water, the trees became petrified:* stony, rocklike, hard as a rock, solidified, turned to stone; hard, hardened, dense, solid. **2** *She stood there, petrified with fear:* paralysed, frozen, stupefied, dumbstruck, dumbfounded, numb, numbed, benumbed, dazed, shocked, terror-stricken, spellbound, *Informal* scared stiff.
◇ *Word origin: Petrified* comes from Latin *petra* (rock) + *facere* (to make), hence made into rock, turned to stone.

petty *adj.* **1** *Don't bother the supervisor with such petty matters:* trivial, trifling, insignificant, unimportant, inconsequential, minor, paltry, slight, small, puny, piddling, niggling, flimsy, inconsiderable. **2** *It was petty of her not to accept the apology:* small-minded, narrow-minded, mean, ignoble, shabby, ungenerous.
Ant. **1** important, major, consequential, significant, momentous, considerable. **2** broad-minded, large-hearted, magnanimous, generous, tolerant.

petulant *adj. When he doesn't get his way, he can be quite petulant:* peevish, fretful, irritable, cross, snappish, sullen, sulky, surly, grumpy, grouchy, testy, huffy, pettish, irascible, fractious, gruff, cantankerous, sour, crotchety, crabbed, bearish, ungracious, ill-natured, ill-tempered, out of sorts, thin-skinned, touchy, tetchy, uncivil; faultfinding, complaining, contentious, quarrelsome.
Ant. agreeable, pleasant, good-natured, cheerful, happy, smiling, complaisant, co-operative, content, gracious, amenable.

phantom *n. Had he actually seen his long-lost brother in the fog, or was it only a phantom?:* apparition, spectre, ghost, phantasm, phantasmagoria, dream, mirage, chimera, figment of the imagination, hallucination, illusion, vision.
◇ *Word origin:* See PHENOMENON.

phase *n.* **1** *The disease was discovered in an early phase:* stage, condition, degree, level, step, development, point of development, juncture. **2** *Examine every phase of the problem:* aspect, facet, feature, side, angle, slant, circumstance, view, attitude, appearance.

phenomenal *adj. John Stuart Mill was a man of phenomenal intelligence:* extraordinary, exceptional, outstanding, remarkable, superior, super, surpassing, uncommon, unusual, unprecedented, unparalleled, stupendous, prodigious, unique, singular, unheard-of, incredible, miraculous, marvellous, spectacular, fantastic, sensational, astonishing, amazing, overwhelming.
Ant. ordinary, common, unexceptional, usual, routine, normal, standard, average, customary, accustomed.

phenomenon *n.* **1** *Snow is a natural phenomenon of winter:* occurrence, happening, visible fact, natural event, part of existence, contingency, thing, actuality, fact of life, proceeding, occasion, incident, episode. **2** *Beethoven was a phenomenon among musicians:* rarity, marvel, miracle, wonder, remarkable person, exceptional thing, exception, singularity, sensation, nonpareil, curiosity.

◇ *Usage note:* The plural of *phenomenon* is *phenomena*: *The phenomena were observed by astronomers throughout the world.*
◇ *Word origin: Phenomenon* comes from Greek *phainein*, to show, which also gives us *phantom, fantasy*, and *diaphanous.*

"Physics tries to discover the pattern of events which controls the phenomena we observe."
—*Sir James Jeans*

---

philanthropic *adj. The orphanage is just one of her many philanthropic causes:* charitable, alms-giving, eleemosynary, benevolent, humanitarian, generous, magnanimous, munificent, beneficent.
Ant. misanthropic; miserly, niggardly.

philanthropist *n. Andrew Carnegie was a true philanthropist, giving away millions to charity:* benefactor of charities, contributor, donor, giver, alms-giver, humanitarian, Good Samaritan, *Slang* do-gooder.
Ant. misanthrope; miser, niggard.

> **Exploring the Word**: *Philanthropy* literally means love of mankind, from Greek *phil-* (loving) + *anthropos* (man). Greek *anthropos* also gives us such words as *misanthrope*, one who hates mankind, *anthropology* (Greek *-logy*, science or study of), the study of man, his origin and physical and cultural development, and *anthropoid*, mankind, resembling man, as an *anthropoid ape;* and *anthropophagy*, cannibalism (Greek *phagein*, to eat).

philanthropy *n. Many organizations benefited from the wealthy man's philanthropy:* charity, charitableness, humanitarianism, alms-giving, benevolence, beneficence, generosity, large-heartedness, unselfishness, public-spiritedness, goodness, open-handedness, liberality, bounty.

philistine *n.* **1** *He's too much of a philistine to patronize the arts:* lowbrow, vulgarizer, cultural ignoramus, barbarian, savage, yahoo; bourgeois, conformist, conventionalist.
—*adj.* **2** *For a university professor he certainly made some philistine remarks:* uncultured, uncultivated, unrefined, uneducated, ignorant, untutored, unlettered, uninformed; lowbrow, bourgeois, conventional, conformist, commonplace, prosaic; anti-intellectual.
Ant. 1 intellectual, highbrow; *Slang* egghead.
◇ *Word origin:* The *Philistines* were a race of warlike people of ancient Philistia, southwest of Palestine. Because they were devoted to war and military discipline, they had little time or inclination for culture; thus today a *philistine* is a person without culture or good taste, or one who follows convention blindly.

philosopher *n. Plato and Socrates were leading philosophers of Ancient Greece:* student of basic truths, seeker of universal laws; lover of wisdom, seeker after truth, wise man, sage; logician, rationalist, reasoner, philosophizer, thinker, dialectician, theorizer.
◇ *Word origin: Philosopher* and *philosophy* come from Greek *philos* (loving) + *sophos* (wise). Thus a *philosopher* is a lover of wisdom, and *philosophy* is the love of wisdom.

philosophic Also **philosophical** *adj.* **1** *The problem demands a philosophic approach:* reasonable, logical, rational, judicious, thoughtful, sagacious; theorizing, theoretical, abstract, learned, erudite. **2** *She's very philosophical about all her bad luck:* stoic, stoical, cheerful, resigned, fatalistic, patient, impassive, unemotional, self-restrained, composed, calm, serene, tranquil, unperturbed, unruffled, unexcited, quiet.
Ant. 1 illogical, irrational, thoughtless, careless, ill-considered; scientific, practical, factual, pragmatic. **2** emotional, excited, impulsive, hot-headed, rash, reckless, unrestrained; upset, perturbed, distraught.

philosophy *n.* **1** *The judge's hobby is philosophy:* study of basic truths, search for universal laws, seeking after wisdom, love of wisdom; logic, rationalism, reason, reasoning, thought, thinking, philosophizing, theorizing, ideas; aesthetics, metaphysics. **2** *The book analyses the philosophy of Bertrand Russell. My philosophy is live and let live:* system of beliefs, beliefs, convictions, conception, doctrine, basic idea, principle; opinion, view, viewpoint, attitude to life. **3** *Accept the bad news with philosophy:* stoicism, resignation, fatalism, patience, cheerfulness, forbearance, calm, restraint, impassivity, composure, serenity, imperturbability, tranquillity.

"A little philosophy inclineth man's mind to atheism, but depth in philosophy bringeth men's minds about to religion."
—*Francis Bacon*

---

phlegmatic *adj. We've never had a row because he is so phlegmatic:* unemotional, unimpassioned, undemonstrative, imperturbable, unconcerned, unexcitable, cool, calm, serene, tranquil, impassive, stoical; spiritless, listless, languid, lethargic, sluggish, dull, passive, unfeeling, insensitive, indifferent, apathetic, nonchalant.
Ant. emotional, passionate, excited; active, alert, lively, animated, energetic, interested.

phobia *n. She has a phobia about heights:* unreasonable fear, terror, horror, dread, apprehension, overwhelming anxiety; *Slang* bugbear, bugaboo.
Ant. love, liking, fondness, fancy, bent, relish, penchant, inclination, predilection.
◇ *Usage note:* If you're not clear on the very real differences between a *phobia* and a *mania*, see the Usage note at MANIA.

phoney Also **phony** *adj.* **1** *The counterfeiter made*

phoney five-pound notes: not genuine, fake, counterfeit, forged, sham, spurious, bogus, mock, pretended; artificial, imitation, synthetic, false, fraudulent, deceptive, trick, unreal, pseudo, unauthentic, untrue.
—*n.* **2** *He says he's a doctor, but I'm sure he's a phoney. This painting isn't a Rembrandt, it's a phoney:* fake, sham, fraud, counterfeit, imitation, make-believe, synthetic, fraud, forgery.
Ant. 1 real, authentic, genuine, original, bona fide, true. **2** the genuine article.

phrase *n.* **1** *The speaker chose his phrases carefully:* expression, words, turn of phrase, word group, utterance, remark, locution. **2** *In the words of the old phrase, "Time flies":* figure of speech, saying, expression, truism, proverb, maxim, aphorism, cliché, colloquialism, dictum; idiom, locution.
—*v.* **3** *The way he phrased the question I couldn't understand it:* express, word, put into words, find words, couch, put, state, declare, impart; say, voice, utter, enunciate, communicate, verbalize, articulate.

physical *adj.* **1** *No one knows how large the physical universe is:* material, existing, natural, tangible, substantive, solid, concrete, real, actual, apparent, external, essential. **2** *He renounced the physical world and devoted himself to spiritual exercises:* of the body, bodily, human, corporeal, corporal, living, fleshly, animal, carnal, sensual.
Ant. 1 non-material, intangible. **2** spiritual, moral; mental, intellectual.
◇ *Word origin: Physical, physique, physiognomy, physic,* and *physician* all come from Greek *physis*, nature.

physiognomy *n. A person's physiognomy was formerly thought to reveal his character:* features, outward appearance, countenance, visage, face; shape, profile, outline, contour, silhouette, configuration, façade.

"It's only the pick of the Army that handles the dear little pets." —*Rudyard Kipling*

---

pick *v.* **1** *It took her an hour to pick a dress that suited her:* select, choose, decide upon, settle upon, single out, fix upon, elect, opt for. **2** *Will you pick some flowers for the dinner-table?:* pluck, pull off, pull out, detach, crop, cut; gather, collect, harvest.
—*n.* **3** *This pup was the pick of the litter:* choice, the best, prize, preference, favoured one, elect, élite, flower, cream, *French* crème de la crème.
Ant. 1 reject, refuse, decline, spurn, scorn, disclaim, repudiate. **3** the worst, the booby prize.

picket *n.* **1** *One of the pickets in the fence was loose:* stake, palisade, pale, pointed stick, paling; post, upright, stanchion; tether, restraint. **2** *The picket warned the sleeping troops that the enemy was creeping near:* forward look-out, look-out, sentinel, watch, sentry, guard, patrol. **3** *The pickets prevented workers from entering the factory:* striker, protester, boycotter, rebel.
—*v.* **4** *A white fence picketed the yard on three sides:* enclose, fence, pen in, shut in, wall in, hedge in, hem in; restrict, restrain. **5** *The workers voted to picket the plant:* demonstrate against; (*loosely*) strike, walk out, go out, boycott, blockade.

pickle *n.* **1** *Would you like pickles with that sandwich?:* pickled cucumber, cucumber pickle; (*variously*) sweet pickle, dill pickle, gherkin, sour pickle, kosher dill, mixed pickle, mustard pickle. **2** *Informal If the car runs out of petrol on this lonely road, we'll be in a pickle:* predicament, difficulty, tight spot, plight, jam, fix, mess, difficult position, extremity, emergency, mess, scrape; *Slang* hot water, pretty pickle, pretty pass, fine kettle of fish.
—*v.* **3** *Grandmother used to pickle peaches:* preserve in brine, preserve in vinegar, corn, marinate; treat with diluted acid.

picture *n.* **1** *This is a picture of the view from our hotel window:* representation, delineation, portrayal, illustration; drawing, painting, sketch, study, etching; photograph, photo, snapshot; daguerreotype. **2** *There's a good picture on at the local cinema:* motion picture, moving picture, film, *Slang* flick, *American* movie. **3** *She is the picture of her mother as a girl:* likeness, image, duplicate, copy, facsimile, double; *Slang* spitting image, carbon copy. **4** *He was the picture of health:* perfect example, model, paragon, mirror, exemplification, personification, essence, embodiment.
—*v.* **5** *The painter pictured the general sitting on a horse:* portray, represent, depict, illustrate, feature, delineate; paint, draw, sketch; photograph. **6** *Can't you just picture Mother on a surf-board!:* imagine, see, envision, call to mind, see in the mind, conceive of, fancy, believe.
◇ *Pronunciation tip:* Some people tend to pronounce *piCture* as if it were the same as a water *pitcher.* Be careful to pronounce the *c* when you say this word: *PIK-cher.*

picturesque *adj. On national holidays the Bavarian peasants wear picturesque costumes:* quaint, exotic, colourful, striking, distinctive, interesting, imaginative; attractive, charming, beautiful, artistic.
Ant. everyday, usual, commonplace, uninteresting, drab, dull, flat, tame, insipid; unattractive, inartistic.

piddling *adj. The clerk got a piddling rise of 50p. a week:* trifling, trivial, insignificant, inconsequential, unimportant, minute, paltry, petty, skimpy, slight, measly, modest, niggardly, small, little, puny, flimsy.
◇ *Word origin: Piddling* is based on the verb to *piddle,* to dawdle, to trifle.

piebald *adj. The piebald horse had patches of white, brown, and black:* dappled, mottled, spotted, speckled, flecked; variegated, many-coloured, particoloured, motley, multi-coloured, many-hued.

◇ *Word origin: Piebald* comes from *pie* (meaning a magpie) + *bald* (having white feathers or fur on the head, as a *bald* eagle), and means "spotted with white and black" like a magpie's head plumage.

piece *n.* **1** *Cook the beans with a piece of salt pork. The glass broke into pieces:* portion, quantity, amount, share, slice, cut, chunk, hunk, lump; pat, blob, bit, fraction, scrap; fragment, shard, part, shred, sliver; swatch, length, cutting, paring; component, member, section, segment, division. **2** *This is a foul piece of treachery. This chair is an antique piece. The workers are paid by the piece:* instance, example, case, specimen, sample; unit, item, article, member, thing, entity. **3** *The pianist played a piece by Chopin. The dramatist is writing a new piece for the theatre. Did you read this piece in today's paper?:* selection, composition, work, creation, study; play, drama, sketch; story, article, essay, review, item.
—*v.* **4** *Do you think you can piece together this torn curtain?:* patch, patch up, mend, repair, restore, fix.

Ant. **1** all, everything, total, sum total, entire amount, entirety, the whole; nothing, none, zero, nought, nullity. **4** tear, break, pierce, crack, shred.

pierce *v.* **1** *The nail completely pierced the tyre:* perforate, puncture, penetrate, make a hole in, bore through, cut through, pass through; stick, prick, stab, spear, spike, lance. **2** *Her angry words pierced his heart:* sting, hurt, pain; cut, wound; affront, grieve, distress.

Ant. **1** glance off; patch, block, stop up. **2** soothe, calm, quiet; please, delight, gladden, cheer, gratify.

piercing *adj.* **1** *We heard her piercing voice across the road:* shrill, grating, screeching, shrieking, strident; loud, ear-splitting, ear-shattering, deafening. **2** *She fixed him with a piercing gaze. What a piercing sound!:* sharp, keen, penetrating, searching, probing; biting, cutting, intense, fierce, furious, raw, bitter, cruel, caustic; angry, painful, hurtful, agonizing, torturous, excruciating.

Ant. **1, 2** calm, soothing. **1** mellifluous, melodic; quiet, low. **2** vague, easy; pleasant, delightful, cheering, gratifying.

piety *n.* *The old woman expressed her piety by attending church daily:* piousness, religiousness, devoutness, devotion, godliness; reverence, respect, loyalty, dutifulness, humility; religiosity.

Ant. impiety, sacrilege, ungodliness, irreverence; disrespect, disloyalty.

◇ *Word origin: Piety* and *pity*, and also *pious*, come from Latin *pietas* and *pius*, meaning dutifulness and dutiful respectively. Incidentally, our noun *Pietà*, a painting or sculpture depicting the Virgin Mary mourning over the dead body of Jesus in her arms, is borrowed directly from Italian which has the same Latin base.

pig *n.* **1** *The farmer raises cows, chickens, and pigs:* hog, swine, porker, runt, (*male*) boar, (*female*) sow; (*young*) piglet, suckling pig, *Informal* piggy. **2** *Informal We ate so much we made pigs of ourselves:* glutton, ravenous eater, large eater, gourmand, gourmandizer.

◇ *Word origin:* We might think that the slang term for a policeman, a *pig*, is very modern. However, it has been in existence since at least the early nineteenth century. One slang dictionary from 1812 contains this entry: *Pigs or Grunters*, police runners.

pigheaded *adj.* *He's so pigheaded you can't reason with him:* stubborn, obstinate, wrong-headed, bull-headed, unyielding, unbending, inflexible, opinionated, obdurate, deaf to advice, blind to reason, mulish, dogged; wilful, insistent, contrary, perverse, recalcitrant, refractory.

Ant. complaisant, flexible, open-minded, agreeable, tractable, docile, amiable, co-operative, obliging.

pigment *n.* *Add some red pigment to give the paint a pinkish tint:* colour, colouring, colouring matter, tint, dye, dyestuff.

pike *n.* *The king's sentry barred the doorway with his pike:* lance, bill, halberd, pole-axe, spear, spike; javelin; harpoon.

◇ *Word origin: Pike* comes from Old French *piquer*, to pierce, and is related to our verb *to pick.* The fish called a *pike* gets its name from its pointed snout.

pile^1 *n.* **1** *A pile of dirty clothes lay by the washing-machine. He made a pile of money on the stock-market:* heap, stack, mass, batch, pyramid, mound; accumulation, collection, assortment, lump, aggregation, hoard, store; large amount, quantity, profusion, abundance.
—*v.* **2** *Pile the leaves in the corner of the garden:* heap, mass, amass, stack, assemble; accumulate, collect, gather, agglomerate.

Ant. **2** scatter, disperse, strew, spread, broadcast.

◇ *Word origin: Pile*^{1} and *pillar* come from Latin *pila*, pillar or pier.

pile^2 *n.* *The carpet has a soft, thick pile:* nap, shag; surface, plush, fleece, grain, warp, fibrousness.

◇ *Word origin: Pile*^{2} comes from Latin *pilus*, hair. From the same Latin base is derived the nickname of the enlisted man in the French Army of World War I, *poilu*, literally "hairy one."

pile^3 *n.* *Piles were driven into the ground to support the building:* piling, support, post, upright, stake, beam.

◇ *Word origin: Pile*^{3} comes from Latin *pilum*, a heavy javelin used by Roman foot soldiers.

pilgrimage *n. Devout Muslims must make a pilgrimage to Mecca:* religious journey, devotional excursion.

> "To let friendship die away by negligence and silence, is certainly not wise. It is voluntarily to throw away one of the greatest comforts of this weary pilgrimage." —*Samuel Johnson*

pillage *v. The barbarians pillaged the town of all its wealth:* plunder, raid, sack, loot, rifle, rob, despoil, strip, fleece, ravage, maraud.
◇ *Word origin: Pillage* comes from French *piller*, to plunder.

pillar *n.* **1** *The porch is supported by six immense pillars:* column, post, upright, support, pile, piling, shaft, stanchion; pilaster. **2** *Father was a pillar of the church for over thirty years:* mainstay, tower of strength, corner-stone, important person, leading light, rock, support, champion; *Slang* VIP, somebody, big wheel.
◇ *Word origin:* See PILE[1].

pilot *n.* **1** *The flying school passes out a hundred pilots a year:* flyer, aviator, airman, aeronaut; *Slang* erk. **2** *Samuel Clemens (better known by his pseudonym "Mark Twain") was a Mississippi river-boat pilot:* helmsman, steersman, coxswain; guide, driver, leader.
—*v.* **3** *It's hard to pilot a boat in these rough waters. Tourists need a guide to pilot them through the Casbah:* steer, be at the helm of, be at the wheel of, handle the tiller of, keep on course, control, manage, handle, navigate; direct, lead, conduct, escort, guide, accompany.
◇ *Word origin: Pilot* comes from Italian *pilota.* The word for "pilot" in the harbour service of Byzantium was probably *pēdōtēs*, from Greek *pēdon*, oar, rudder. Latin-speaking mariners from the West heard and transcribed the word as *pilotus.*

> "The philosopher is Nature's pilot. And there you have our difference: to be in hell is to drift: to be in heaven is to steer." —*George Bernard Shaw*

pin *n.* **1** *The dressmaker used a pin to fasten the pattern to the cloth:* (*variously*) straight pin, safety-pin, nappy pin; hat-pin; skewer, prong thole-pin, dowel. **2** *Did you see the diamond pin she got for Christmas?:* brooch, clasp, clip, medal, badge, decoration.
—*v.* **3** *The children played Pin the Tail on the Donkey:* attach with a pin, affix, secure, fasten, clasp. **4** *The policeman pinned the thief's arms behind him:* pinion; hold fast, hold down; restrain, bind, fasten.

pinch *v.* **1** *The girl pinched her little brother's arm out of meanness. These shoes pinch my feet:* tweak, squeeze, nip; cramp, crimp, compress, tighten, crush. **2** *Slang The officer pinched the driver for going through a red light:* arrest, take into custody, apprehend, run in, *Informal* collar, nab, catch, grab, capture. **3** *Slang The thief pinched his pocket-book and ran:* steal, snatch, swipe, snitch, lift, crib, purloin, filch.
—*n.* **4** *The old man gave the boy a playful pinch on the cheek:* tweak, nip, squeeze. **5** *Add a pinch of salt:* bit, speck, mite, jot, iota, spot, snip, trace, tittle. **6** *Most Western Europeans have never felt the pinch of hunger. I could help you out at a pinch:* strait, plight; emergency, crisis, predicament, difficulty, necessity, exigency, squeeze, clutch, jam, pickle.

pine *v.* **1** *She pined for her native land:* yearn, long, hanker, sigh, languish; crave, hunger for, thirst after, desire, covet; *Informal* pant for. **2** *After so much heart-break she just pined away:* fail in health, decline, waste away, languish, wither, wilt, droop, flag; die, expire.
◇ *Word origin: Pine* comes from Latin *poena* (Greek *poinē*), punishment, penalty, which also gives us our word *pain.*

pinnacle *n.* **1** *The climbers reached the pinnacle of the mountain. A writer who wins the Nobel prize has reached the pinnacle of success:* highest point, peak, summit, apex, zenith, height, top, tip-top, acme, crown, cap. **2** *The church tower carries four pinnacles:* spire, steeple, belfry, bell tower, campanile.
◇ *Word origin:* Does a distant mountain peak look like a wing-tip to you? It comes from the diminutive of Latin *pinna*, wing, hence a small wing.

pin-point *n.* **1** *The castle was just a pin-point in the distance:* dot, spot, speck, jot, iota.
—*v.* **2** *Engineers are trying to pin-point the cause of the trouble:* locate exactly, detect precisely, zero in on; describe precisely, detail, characterize.

pioneer *n.* **1** *Pioneers from the West cleared the forest 100 years ago:* first settler, early immigrant, colonist; frontiersman, explorer. **2** *William Morris was a pioneer in the car industry:* leader, trail-blazer, forerunner, pathfinder, founder, founding father, father, establisher; predecessor, antecedent, precursor; herald, harbinger.
—*v.* **3** *Dr. Barnard pioneered transplant surgery:* be a leader, blaze the trail, lead the way, show the way, start, establish, found, discover, invent, create, develop.

pious *adj.* **1** *His parents were pious churchgoers:* devout, religious, dedicated, faithful, reverent, reverential, worshipful; godly, spiritual, holy, divine, saintly, sainted. **2** *The revivalist's pious statement that the meek shall inherit the earth was felt by some to be hypocritical:* sanctimonious, holier-than-thou, unctuous, pietistic, self-righteous; hypocritical, insincere.
Ant. 1 impious, irreverent, irreligious, ungodly, godless, unholy. **2** humble, meek; sincere, genuine.

pipe *n.* **1** *The pipe behind the stove is for the gas:* tube, conduit; conveyor; main, duct, conductor.

—*v.* **2** *The birds began piping at daybreak:* whistle, sing, cheep, peep, trill, warble, twitter, chirp, tweet; play a flute, play a bagpipe, play a bo's'n's pipe.

◇ *Word origin: Pipe,* like *fife,* goes back to Latin *pipare,* to cheep, imitative of a bird's sound. The earliest pipes were musical instruments resembling flutes and fifes that sounded like bird-calls, and we still speak of the *pipes* (bagpipes) and the *pipes of Pan* as such instruments today. Because these were long hollow tubes, *pipe* was next used to refer to any such tube, ranging from water-pipes and sewer-pipes to pipes used for smoking.

piquant *adj.* **1** *In Mexico, turkey is served with a piquant sauce:* pungent, spicy, sharp, tangy, zesty, savoury, highly seasoned, hot, peppery, strongly flavoured; bitter, acid, biting, stinging, piercing, mordant. **2** *The play sparkled with piquant dialogue:* lively, peppy, sharp, zesty, vigorous, spirited, scintillating, sparkling, clever, bright, stimulating, animated, rousing, interesting, provocative, trenchant, incisive; racy, salty, spicy, peppery.

Ant. 1 bland, mild. **2** banal, inane, insipid, tame, jejune, uninteresting, boring, dull.

◇ *Word origin: Piquant* and *pique* both come from French *piquer,* to sting, prick, provoke. As in English, the French word is used in both good and bad senses.

pique *v.* **1** *It always piques him not to be consulted:* displease, offend, affront, hurt one's feelings, annoy, irritate, vex, irk, gall, nettle, provoke, exasperate, disquiet, perturb; *Informal* put one's back up, miff, peeve, put one's nose out of joint. **2** *The book piqued my interest:* arouse, kindle, stimulate, rouse, provoke, excite, stir, quicken, spur, goad.

—*n.* **3** *She flounced out of the room in a fit of pique when he made that remark:* resentment, hurt feelings, displeasure, annoyance, irritation, vexation, exasperation, indignation, ire, umbrage, discomfort; grudge, spite, malice, vindictiveness, ill feelings; embarrassment, humiliation, mortification.

Ant. 1 please, delight, gratify, satisfy, compliment. **2** deaden, dull, kill, quench.

pit *n.* **1** *Dig a pit and bury the debris. The wood is full of pits and needs sanding:* hole, hollow, hole in the ground, cavity, crater, depression; gully, trough; indentation, gouge, concavity, furrow, dent, dimple, notch, dip, pock; scar, pock-mark.

—*v.* **2** *The stiletto heels are pitting the parquet floor:* gouge, dent, indent, nick, notch, pock, scratch, scar. **3** *The managers want to pit the champion against an unknown competitor:* match, set against, oppose, put in competition; contrast, juxtapose.

Ant. 1 mound, lump, bump, protuberance.

pitch *v.* **1** *The Boy Scouts pitched their tent near the stream:* set up, raise, erect; set, place, fix, plant, establish, locate, station. **2** *He pitched the ball over a wall:* throw, hurl, heave, fling, cast, toss, lob, chuck, sling, fire, propel, shy, let fly. **3** *The fisherman lost his balance and pitched into the lake:* fall headlong, fall headfirst, fall, topple, tumble. **4** *The boat pitched in the storm:* rock from front to back, toss, plunge, lurch, bob, shake, jolt, jerk, oscillate, undulate.

—*n.* **5** *The roof has a steep pitch:* slope, incline, grade, cant, angle. **6** *He had played on bad pitches before, but never on one with such a slope:* playing area, sports ground, field, track. **7** *Her voice has a very high pitch:* tone, sound; harmonic, speed of vibration. **8** *The children had reached a high pitch of excitement:* level, degree, point; height, peak, apex, summit, zenith, pinnacle, crown, top. **9** *The pitch of the ship threw the passengers off balance:* forward plunge, headlong fall, dip, rocking, lurch, lurching, bobbing, oscillation, undulation.

pithy *adj. An epigram should be short and pithy:* to the point, meaningful, forceful, expressive, trenchant; concise, terse, succinct.

Ant. diffuse, vague; wordy, verbose, rambling, turgid.

pitiful *adj.* **1** *The pitiful sobs of the child softened our hearts:* pitiable, piteous, arousing pity, deserving pity, heart-rending, heart-breaking, moving, touching, poignant, pathetic; sad, lamentable, distressing, mournful, plaintive, miserable, forlorn, doleful. **2** *The thief made a pitiful attempt to justify the crime. The play wasn't just bad, it was pitiful!:* contemptible, deserving of scorn, miserable, despicable, pitiable, wretched, worthless, shabby, poor, sorry, abject, measly, insignificant, paltry, dreadful, abominable.

Ant. 1 happy, cheerful, merry, glad, joyous, joyful. **2** commendable, praiseworthy, laudable; noble, lofty, sublime, exalted, dignified, great, grand, glorious; delightful, endearing, lovable, charming.

◇ *Usage note: Pitiable, pitiful,* and *piteous* all mean arousing pity, but in increasing degrees. A *pitiable* event or words can arouse some pity but the situation is not tragic: *The child raised a pitiable cry for more ice cream. Pitiful* refers to something that calls forth a strong feeling of pity and compassion: *The war orphans' plight was pitiful. Piteous* refers to something that moves one to tears or is completely heart-rending: *The starving child gave a piteous cry for food.* Despite these sophisticated shades of meaning, *pitiful* is the word most often used for all occasions and for all degrees of pity.

pitiless *adj. He beat the dog with pitiless brutality:* merciless, heartless, without pity, unmerciful, unpitying, unsparing, hard-hearted, cold-blooded, relentless, unrelenting, ruthless, cruel, brutal; unmoved, unresponsive, indifferent, untouched, insensitive, uncaring.

Ant. merciful, sparing, relenting, soft-hearted, compassionate, benign, kind; concerned, caring, responsive, touched.

pittance *n. He puts most of his money in the bank and tries to live on a mere pittance:* small amount, trifle, modicum, minimum, little, crumb, mite; trifling sum, small allowance, minimal wage.

◇ *Word origin: Pittance* comes from Old French *pitance,* a monk's allotment of food. It is ultimately derived from Latin *pius,* dutiful, which also gives us *piety, pious,* and *pity.*

pity *n.* **1** *The sad story aroused eveyone's pity. It's a pity he didn't finish the course:* sympathy, compassion, commiseration, condolence; cause for sorrow, regret, sad thing, shame; *Informal* crying shame. **2** *The tyrant showed no pity:* mercy, charity, clemency, lenience, kindliness, humanity, tenderness, lenity, soft-heartedness, indulgence, forbearance, magnanimity.

—*v.* **3** *I pity the flood victims:* feel sorry for, have compassion for, commiserate with, sympathize with, lament, feel for, bleed for, weep for.

Ant. **1** anger, rage, wrath, fury; scorn, disdain, indifference, apathy, unconcern. **2** cruelty, brutality, hard-heartedness, harshness, inhumanity, mercilessness, pitilessness, ruthlessness; severity.

"Pity is the best taught by fellowship in woe."
—*Samuel Taylor Coleridge*

---

pivot *n.* **1** *The hands of the watch rotate on a pivot:* pin or shaft about which something turns; (*loosely*) axis, axle, swivel, hinge, fulcrum.

—*v.* **2** *The gyroscope pivoted on its stand:* rotate, revolve, wheel, swivel, circle, spin, twirl, turn, swing round, whirl, pirouette. **3** *The passage of the bill pivots on the Liberals' support:* depend, hang, rely, be contingent on, hinge on, revolve round, turn, focus, centre, be in the hands of.

pivotal *adj. The pivotal point of his speech came when he mentioned immigration. The Welsh language must be preserved because of the pivotal position it occupies in the community:* decisive, crucial, critical, climactic, determining, vital.

placate *v. No one can placate him when he's angry:* calm, soothe, pacify, mollify, assuage; appease, propitiate, win over, conciliate.

place *n.* **1** *Is there any suitable place to put this bowl of flowers?: Beware of that slippery place on the pavement:* space, spot, niche, point; site, location, position, whereabouts, *Law* venue. **2** *There's a place in the High Street that has great reductions:* establishment, concern, business, store, shop, company, firm. **3** *He was given an important place in the newly formed Cabinet:* position, situation, post, appointment, job, office, station, commission; function, duty, rank. **4** *We're having a party at my place. He retired to a little place in the country:* residence, home, abode, house, dwelling, domicile, habitation, quarters, premises, rooms, office, building, *Informal* digs; farm, plot, land, property. **5** *Jo'burg is a nice place to visit. This is the place where the storm did so much damage:* city, town, village; state, county, township, borough, district, neighbourhood, vicinity, area, province, region, locality, locale, zone, quarter; country, territory.

—*v.* **6** *Place the chair in that corner:* put, set, rest, stand, situate, position, plant, deposit, settle, array, locate, ensconce, install; fix, affix, attach; house, lodge, harbour, shelter. **7** *The employment agency placed her with an insurance firm:* get a job for, find work for, appoint, assign, install, commission, invest. **8** *I remember her name but I can't place her:* identify, remember, recognize, classify, pigeon-hole, set in context.

Ant. **6** remove, take away, dislodge, dislocate; detach, take off.

placid *adj. The chalet overlooks a placid mountain lake. She has an amazingly placid disposition:* calm, quiet, tranquil, peaceful, serene, restful; untroubled, unruffled, smooth, undisturbed, collected, composed, undemonstrative, unexcited, unexcitable, imperturbable; gentle, mild.

Ant. turbulent, agitated, rough; excitable, excited, tempestuous, emotional, passionate, impassioned, impulsive, disturbed, perturbed.

plague *n.* **1** *In the 14th century the plague killed one-third of the population of Europe:* bubonic plague, Black Death; widespread epidemic, pandemic, fatal epidemic, pestilence; contagious disease, epidemic disease, infection, *French* peste. **2** *The plague of locusts swept over the land:* affliction, scourge, hardship, misery, agony, suffering, woe, trouble, burden; evil, curse, bane, blight, cancer.

—*v.* **3** *The mistake plagued him for years:* torment, trouble, distress, worry, disquiet, perturb, persecute, harass, disturb, bother, vex, harry, chafe, fret, badger; pain, aggrieve, afflict, embarrass, haunt, prey on one's mind; try the patience of, get on one's nerves, go against the grain.

plain *adj.* **1** *The figures aren't plain enough to read:* clear, distinct, legible, discernible, conspicuous, obvious, prominent, visible, apparent, glaring, pronounced, striking, outstanding, vivid, clear-cut, well-defined, well-marked, manifest, palpable. **2** *Please rephrase the question in plain English:* easily understood, simple, clear, straightforward, direct, explicit, specific, unambiguous, unmistakable, understandable, comprehensible, unequivocal. **3** *The plain truth is that he doesn't like you:* honest, frank, blunt, candid, open, sincere, forthright, straight, undisguised, undiluted,

naked, bald, bare, unembellished, unvarnished, unadorned; plain-spoken, outspoken, unreserved. **4** *Most of her relations are plain country folk. The hostess wore a plain blue dress:* simple, unaffected, unpretentious, unassuming; modest, everyday, ordinary, average, common, matter-of-fact; obscure, undistinguished, commonplace; unadorned, undecorated, unornamented, ungarnished, without frills. **5** *The girl had a good figure but a plain face:* homely, ordinary, dull, not beautiful, unhandsome, unattractive, unlovely, uncomely, having plain features, not striking.
—*n.* **6** *The family crossed Salisbury Plain to see Stonehenge:* flat land, level tract of country, grassland, table-land, plateau, open country.
Ant. 1 indistinct, vague, blurred, illegible, indiscernible, inconspicuous; hidden, concealed. **2** obscure, abstruse, complex, difficult, indirect, ambiguous, incomprehensible; affected, pretentious. **3** deceptive, evasive, disguised, veiled, indirect. **4** affected, pretentious, assuming, snobbish; sophisticated, worldly, distinguished; decorated, ornamented, adorned, fancy, frilly. **5** beautiful, gorgeous, good-looking, attractive, comely, handsome.
◇ *Usage note:* Don't confuse *plain* and *plane. Plain* means clear, straightforward, simple, or a clear expanse of level, treeless land: *plain English, the plain truth, good plain food, cowboys riding the Western plain* (or *plains*). A *plane* is a flat geometrical surface, or a short form of the word "aeroplane."
◇ *Word origin: Plain,* like *plane,* comes from *planus,* the Latin word for "flat."

plainly *adv.* **1** *Although wealthy, she dresses very plainly:* simply, unpretentiously, unaffectedly, unassumingly, modestly, ordinarily; without adornment, without ornamentation. **2** *It's plainly the newest house on the estate:* clearly, obviously, conspicuously, prominently, markedly, visibly, strikingly, vividly, discernibly, manifestly, undeniably, unquestionably, undoubtedly, doubtless, definitely, without doubt, beyond doubt. **3** *She stated quite plainly that she didn't want to go:* clearly, distinctly, explicitly, directly, unmistakably, unambiguously, comprehensibly, unequivocally, honestly, frankly, bluntly, candidly, openly, baldly, positively.

plaintive *adj. The widow gave a plaintive wail at the graveside:* sad, mournful, sorrowful, lamenting, moaning, melancholy; doleful, dolorous, heart-rending, rueful, lugubrious, pathetic, piteous, pitiful.

plan *n.* **1** *The city council has a plan for building a covered market. The builder must follow the architect's plan:* scheme, programme, proposal, suggestion, idea, conception, proposition, procedure, method, way, strategy; design, blueprint, sketch, map, diagram.
—*v.* **2** *The entertainment committee will plan the dance:* organize, devise, make arrangements, make preparations, conceive, think out, plot, contrive, prepare, fabricate, design; form, frame, outline, shape; block out, lay out, project, map out, diagram. **3** *Do you plan to stay late?:* intend, aim, purpose, propose.
◇ *Usage note:* The expression *advance planning* is a redundancy, since *planning* is the laying out of a future course; therefore "advance" is unnecessary.

"A perfect Woman, nobly planned,
To warn, to comfort, and command."
— *William Wordsworth*

---

plane *n.* **1** *The roof was a perfect plane:* flat surface, level surface. **2** *The discussion was continued on a high plane:* level, elevation, standing, condition, position, status, station, degree. **3** *The plane took off from the airport at noon:* aeroplane, aircraft; jet, *Slang* bird.

plant *n.* **1** *We came here to study the life of plants. Are these plants tomatoes or beans?:* vegetation, flora, herbage; (*variously*) tree, flower, bush, shrub, vine, herb, weed, wort, grass, moss, algae, fungi; seedling, slip, vegetable. **2** *The workers at the plant belong to the union:* factory, shop, works, yard, mill, foundry; business, establishment.
—*v.* **3** *Don't plant potatoes before mid-April:* put in the ground, sow seed, broadcast, scatter, set in, set out; transplant.

plaster *n.* **1** *The painter will fill those holes with plaster before painting the wall:* pasty mixture of gypsum or lime, sand, and water; calcined gypsum, grout, stucco, powdered gypsum; plaster of Paris. **2** *The boy stuck a plaster on his grazed knee:* sticking-plaster, adhesive plaster, dressing, bandage, lint.
—*v.* **3** *Will it take long to plaster the ceiling? The boy plastered the bread with butter:* cover with plaster; coat, smear, spread thickly, overlay, lather, daub, bedaub.

plastic *adj.* **1** *Clay is a very plastic substance:* capable of being moulded, easily moulded, shapable, formable, pliable, malleable, pliant, ductile, flexible, yielding, elastic, supple, soft.
—*n.* **2** *Is this real leather or just plastic?:* mouldable substance; synthetic organic compound.
Ant. 1 hard, rigid, stiff, inflexible, inelastic.
◇ *Word origin:* The important feature of both *plastic* and *plaster* is that they can be moulded or formed into almost any shape before becoming hard. The words come from Greek *plastikos,* mouldable.

plate *n.* **1** *Put the plate in the dishwasher:* dish; serving dish, platter. **2** *Stay for lunch, and I'll give you a plate of stew:* serving, helping, platter, platterful, portion, dish.

plateau *n.* **1** *The village stands in the middle of a*

grassy plateau: elevated plain, table-land, table, wold; highland, upland.
Ant. 1 valley, vale, ravine; combe, gully, savannah, swamp, lowland.

> **Exploring the Word**: What do a *plate, platter, plateau, platform,* and a *platitude* have in common? They are all flat and come from Vulgar Latin *plattus,* flat (a borrowing from Greek *platus,* broad). In Old French *plate* was a flat sheet of metal (we still speak of *tin-plate* and *armour-plate* on tanks, war-planes, and battleships). *Plate* later came to mean a dinner plate (such plates were originally made of metal, too). A *platter,* of course, is just a big plate; a *plateau* is a large area of high, flat land; a *platform* is a flat form or surface raised above the floor, as for a speaker to stand on; and a *platitude* is a flat, dull, or commonplace statement. Greek *platus,* broad, from which all of the foregoing are ultimately derived, also gives us *platypus,* the semi-aquatic mammal so-called because flat-footed (Greek *poûs,* foot) and the name of the Greek philosopher *Plato* (427-347 B.C.). His original name was Aristocles but he was nicknamed *Platōn* ("Broad-shouldered") when a teenager, and the nickname stuck.

platform *n.* **1** *The mayor got up on the platform and welcomed us:* speaker's platform, stage, stand, rostrum, dais, pulpit. **2** *He adopted Votes for Women as the first plank of his political platform:* programme, policy, plan, set of principles, goal; campaign promises.

platitude *n. The speech was dull and full of platitudes:* trite remark, stereotyped expression, cliché, banality, commonplace, truism, hackneyed saying, threadbare phrase, *Slang* chestnut, bromide, old familiar tune, same old story.

platoon *n. The lieutenant was put in charge of an infantry platoon:* three or more sections; (*loosely*) unit, detachment, group, force, team, crew, corps, band, body.
◇ *Word origin:* A *platoon* is figuratively a "ball of men." The word comes from French *peloton,* group of men, which is derived from Old French *pelote,* ball, and ultimately from Latin *pila,* ball.

plaudit *n.* Usually **plaudits** *The play won the plaudits of the critics:* praise, approval, acclaim, commendation, approbation, compliment, rave, bouquet; applause, cheer, cheering, hurrah, hallelujah.
Ant. condemnation, jeer, taunt, hoot, *Slang* brickbat, rap, knock, slam, dig; boo, hiss, raspberry.

plausible *adj. Did you find the ending of the story plausible?:* believable, probable, credible, likely, persuasive, reasonable, conceivable, possible, justifiable, acceptable, logical, sound, sensible, valid.
Ant. unbelievable, improbable, incredible, unlikely, implausible, unreasonable, inconceivable, impossible, illogical.

play *n.* **1** *I have decided not to act in the school play this year:* drama, stage play, dramatic piece, dramatic performance; (*variously*) comedy, tragedy, farce, melodrama; show, spectacle, extravaganza, pageant, entertainment. **2** *All work and no play makes Jack a dull boy:* amusement, recreation, entertainment, diversion, fun, merry-making, pleasure, enjoyment; caper, romp, lark, gambol, frolic, jest, sport. **3** *There's too much play between the door and the frame:* free motion, freedom of movement, swing, sweep; room, space, elbow-room, scope.
—*v.* **4** *The children play indoors when it rains:* engage in games, amuse oneself, entertain oneself, divert oneself, have fun, make merry, enjoy oneself, gambol, romp, revel, frisk, frolic, sport, cavort, caper, skylark, antic, disport, while away the time; trifle, toy. **5** *The teams will play each other on Saturday. He played rugger for his college:* contend against, compete with, vie with, perform in a game; participate in a sport, take part, be in a team. **6** *Can you play the piano? Who's going to play Lady Macbeth?:* perform on, perform; act, act out, act the part of, take the part of, impersonate, personify, enact, represent.

"A little work, a little play
To keep us going — and so, good day!"
—*George du Maurier*

---

playboy *n. The spoilt son grew up into a playboy:* pleasure seeker, night-club habitué, party-goer, good-time Charlie, profligate, hedonist, rake, lecher, womanizer, ladies' man, Lothario, Casanova, Don Juan, *Slang* wolf.
Ant. ascetic, monk, puritan; hermit, recluse.

player *n.* **1** *The boy wants to be a football player when he grows up. Hide-and-seek can be played by as many players as one wants:* team member, performer, athlete; participant, contender, competitor, contestant, opponent, antagonist, adversary. **2** *The players included several local actors:* actor, actress, Thespian, trouper, mummer, cast (*pl.*).

playful *adj. Kittens are very playful. It was just a playful remark:* full of play, frolicsome, frisky, lively, rollicking, coltish, sprightly, sportive; not serious, amusing, jesting, humorous, mirthful, capricious, waggish, impish, prankish, fun-loving, light-hearted.
Ant. sedate, serious, sombre, grave, morose, despondent, gloomy, glum.

plea *n.* **1** *Their plea for aid went unanswered:* appeal, entreaty, prayer, suit, petition, supplication, solicitation, beseeching, begging, adjuration, request. **2** *His plea was that he had been unavoidably detained:* excuse, defence, explanation, argument, justification, vindication, apology, extenuation; pretext.

plead *v. She pleaded with the traffic warden not to give her a parking ticket:* beg, beseech, implore, entreat, appeal to; petition, importune, solicit, enjoin, supplicate, adjure.

pleasant *adj.* **1** *Have a pleasant weekend. It was a pleasant spring day:* agreeable, pleasing, pleasurable, enjoyable, gratifying, satisfying, lovely, charming, attractive, inviting, felicitous, good, fine, nice; mild, gentle, soft. **2** *The new doctor is a pleasant young man:* likeable, congenial, genial, friendly, affable, amiable, cheerful, good-humoured, good-natured, cordial, warm, amicable, tactful, polite.

Ant. **1** unpleasant, displeasing, disagreeable, distasteful, wretched, distressing, miserable, horrible, bad, awful. **2** unlikeable, unfriendly, cold, offensive, repulsive, ill-humoured, ill-natured, rude, impolite, ill-mannered.

pleasantry *n. There wasn't much conversation, only an exchange of pleasantries:* polite remark, good-natured remark, greeting, salutation; quip, jest, witticism, sally, bon mot, joke, humorous remark, jape, *Slang* wisecrack.

please *v.* **1** *The boy's good manners pleased his elders:* gladden, delight, give pleasure to, make happy, gratify, satisfy, suit, content, elate, charm, fascinate, enthral, entrance, enrapture, thrill; tickle; amuse, divert, entertain. **2** *The income allows her to live as she pleases:* like, wish, choose, desire, want, will, be inclined, elect, prefer, opt.

Ant. **1** displease, dissatisfy, repel, disgust, offend; sadden, depress, grieve; anger, madden, incense, annoy, provoke, pique, vex, nettle, chafe.

◇ *Word origin: Please, pleasant,* and *pleasure* come from Latin *placere,* to be pleasing, which also gives us *complacent* (with a pleasant outlook, not disturbed) and *implacable* (not able to be pleased or appeased).

pleasing *adj. The audience found the show pleasing. An entertainer should have a pleasing personality:* pleasurable, gratifying, satisfying, enjoyable, gladdening, delightful, amusing, diverting, entertaining; attractive, agreeable, inviting, likeable, winning, captivating, charming, fascinating; friendly, affable, amiable, congenial, genial, cheerful, good-natured, good-humoured, polite, mannerly, well-mannered.

Ant. displeasing, unpleasant, unacceptable, unattractive, disagreeable, distasteful, disgusting, unlikeable.

"Life affords no higher pleasure than that of surmounting difficulties." —*Samuel Johnson*

---

pleasure *n.* **1** *The gift gave the child a great deal of pleasure:* enjoyment, happiness, joy, delight, gratification, cheer, bliss, elation, exultation, rapture; gaiety, mirth, light-heartedness, merriment, jubilation, high spirits. **2** *All they seek in life is pleasure:* amusement, fun, gratification, diversion, entertainment, recreation, festivity, gaiety. **3** *What's your pleasure, coffee or tea?:* desire, choice, like, wish, will, inclination, preference, option.

Ant. **1** displeasure, unhappiness, sorrow, sadness, suffering, pain, affliction, misery, anger, vexation. **2** work, labour, toil; self-denial, abstinence. **3** necessity, duty, obligation, compulsion; coercion.

plebeian *adj.* **1** *She has such a plebeian taste in furniture:* vulgar, coarse, common, lowbrow, low-class, non-U, unrefined, uncultivated, uncultured, commonplace, popular, banal, ordinary, low, mean, base; of the common people, low-born, proletarian, working-class.

—*n.* **2** *He may act like an aristocrat, but at heart he's a plebeian:* common man, commoner, average man, average citizen, one of the masses; proletarian, man in the street.

Ant. **1** highbrow, refined, cultivated, cultured, educated; upper-class, aristocratic, royal. **2** aristocrat, élite, patrician, noble, nobleman, peer, lord; intellectual, highbrow.

pledge *n.* **1** *I gave him my pledge that I would vote for him:* vow, solemn promise, oath, word, assurance, adjuration, avowal, troth; agreement, pact, compact, covenant, contract. **2** *The pawnbroker took the camera as a pledge for the loan:* security, warranty, guaranty, surety, collateral; pawn, bond, bail.

—*v.* **3** *I pledge allegiance to the Queen:* promise solemnly, promise, vow, swear, bind by an oath, assert, guarantee, warrant, give one's word.

plentiful *adj. The town has a plentiful supply of food:* abundant, profuse, copious, bountiful, bounteous, prolific, lavish, ample, abounding, plenteous, lush, liberal, generous, large, unsparing, unstinted, infinite, inexhaustible.

Ant. scant, scanty, sparse, inadequate, insufficient, deficient, scarce, skimpy, sparing, small.

"The rich is happy in the plenty giv'n,
The poor contents him with the care of Heav'n." —*Alexander Pope*

---

plenty *n.* **1** *The car has plenty of room for everybody:* an abundant supply, ample amount, a full measure, abundance, sufficiency, profusion, plenitude, good deal, great deal, a wealth, enough and to spare, *Slang* lots, oceans, worlds, oodles, stacks, masses. **2** *For the New Year we wish you peace and plenty:* prosperity, good times, affluence, well-being, riches, wealth, luxury, opulence.

Ant. **1** scarcity, sparsity, dearth, lack, shortage, scantiness, insufficiency, paucity, inadequacy, deficiency. **2** poverty, indigence, hard times.

pliable *adj.* **1** *Before making the chair seat, soak the rushes to make them pliable:* flexible, easily bendable, pliant, plastic, resilient, elastic, springy; supple, lithe, limber. **2** *Be careful what you teach to young children whose characters are still pliable:* impressionable, pliant, compliant, receptive, willing, responsive, flexible, easily influenced; accommodating, manageable, adaptable, submissive, yielding, acquiescent, tractable.
Ant. **1** stiff, rigid, unbending. **2** stubborn, obstinate, inflexible, unyielding, wilful, headstrong, dogged, intractable, dogmatic, unadaptable, obdurate.

> **Exploring the Word**: Latin *plicare,* to fold, bend, double over, gives us many words, including words for being easily folded, bent, or flexible, as *pliable, pliant,* and *supple*; words referring to folds, twists, or layers or to increasing the number of something as if by folding it into two or more sections, as *pleat, plait, ply, duplex, double, duplicate, triple, quadruple, multiply,* and *replica*; words referring to folded things as being involved or confusing, as *complex* and *complexion, complicate,* and *perplex*; and a further group of words meaning unfolded or folded out, as if to reveal, explain, or use something fully, as *deploy,* to spread out, *display, explicit, explicable, explain,* and *exploit.*

plight *n. The plight of the people in the drought-stricken area has not improved:* condition, situation, circumstance, state; poor condition, distressing situation, dangerous circumstances, predicament, extremity, distress, trouble, difficulty, vicissitude, trial, tribulation; crisis, impasse, emergency, exigency, scrape, pinch, *Slang* pickle, straits, fix, jam, muddle.

plod *v.* **1** *The soldiers plodded through the mud:* trudge, walk heavily, drag, lumber, shuffle, waddle. **2** *The youth just plodded along at his piano lessons:* work slowly, drudge, toil, grind, struggle; persevere, be resolute, stick at it, peg away, *Slang* plug away, grub.
◇ *Word origin: Plod* was coined to imitate the sound of a heavy step, probably of a horse.

plot[1] *n.* **1** *The government uncovered a revolutionary plot:* conspiracy, intrigue, secret plan, evil plan, scheme, machination, manœuvre, design, stratagem. **2** *The plot of the novel is too silly to relate:* story, story-line, tale, narrative, incidents, yarn, plan, action, design.
—*v.* **3** *The criminals were plotting to rob the bank:* conspire, scheme, intrigue, design, plan, contrive, manœuvre, collude, be in collusion. **4** *The navigator plotted the ship's course:* chart, map, compute, calculate, determine; mark, draw, sketch, outline, diagram, draft.

plot[2] *n. Tomatoes will grow easily on this plot:* area of ground, patch; lot, tract, field, clearing, allotment.

plough *v.* **1** *We will plough the field soon after the last frost:* dig up, turn up, spade, dig, break, break up, loosen, work; furrow, harrow, cultivate, *Slang* bulldoze. **2** *The ship ploughed through heavy seas to port:* push, press, plunge, drive, cut, shove, forge.

pluck *v.* **1** *Please don't pluck the flowers by the roots:* pick, pull out, pull off, pull at, draw; jerk, grab, yank, snatch; uproot, extirpate.
—*n.* **2** *The boxer showed a lot of pluck by fighting back even though he was badly hurt:* spirit, mettle, courage, bravery, valour, boldness, daring, *Slang* spunk, grit, guts; resolution, temerity, determination, resolve, fortitude, doggedness, perseverance, persistence, tenacity.

plug *n.* **1** *Stop up the leak with a plug:* stopper, stopple, bung, cork.
—*v.* **2** *We plugged the hole temporarily with putty:* stop up, close, shut off, stanch, cork, fill up, stuff.

plumb *n.* **1** *The fisherman used a plumb to find the depth of the lake:* plumb-line, plummet, lead; plumb bob, level.
—*v.* **2** *The geologist plumbed the depths of the ocean. She tried to plumb the depths of his mind:* take soundings, sound, fathom, measure, test, cast the lead; probe, penetrate, gauge, examine.
◇ *Word origin: Plumb* comes from Latin *plumbum,* lead, referring to the lead weight fixed to the end of a line for use in finding the exact perpendicular, sounding the depth of water, etc. Our word *plumber* has the same Latin base, because the Roman *plumbarius* was a lead worker.

plummet *v. The hawk plummeted toward the earth:* plunge, fall, fall headlong, drop straight down, dive, tumble, descend abruptly.
Ant. rise, ascend, shoot upward.

plump[1] *adj. She's not grossly fat, but she's plump:* chubby, pudgy, somewhat fat, fleshy, stout, portly, stocky, rotund; rounded.
Ant. slender, slim, lean; thin, skinny, scrawny, lanky, skeletal, cadaverous.
◇ *Word origin: Plump*[1] comes from Flemish *plompe,* dull, blunt, thick.

plump[2] *v.* **1** *The youth plumped down in the chair and went to sleep:* drop, plop, flop, plunk, sprawl, collapse; spill, fall heavily, tumble.
—*adj.* **2** *The suspect answered with a plump denial of the charge:* direct, straightforward, forthright, outright, downright, blunt, abrupt; unswerving, undeviating, firm, solid.

plunder *v.* **1** *The invading soldiers plundered the town:* sack, pillage, loot, raid, rifle, rob, pilfer, ravage, maraud, despoil, fleece, strip.
—*n.* **2** *The pirate ship was filled with plunder:* loot, booty, pillage, spoils, pilferings, filchings, prize, *Slang* swag, haul.
◇ *Word origin: Plunder* now means property stolen by soldiers in a war. The word comes from Middle Dutch *plunde,* household goods.

plunge *v.* **1** *The blacksmith plunged the red-hot*

horseshoe into a bucket of water. The boys plunged into the swimming-pool: dip, thrust, cast, douse, immerse, duck; submerge, submerse, descend, sink; dive, jump, leap, throw oneself, fall headlong, tumble, pitch. **2** *The fireman plunged into the building:* rush, dash, run, dart, charge, speed, hurtle, bolt, sprint, scramble, lunge, hasten, scurry, scuttle, hustle, whisk, tear, shoot, fly, streak, scuttle; surge, push, press, drive, swarm. **3** *The boat plunged in the high seas:* pitch, toss, lurch, heave, reel, rock, jerk, roll, sway, tumble about, prance about. —*n.* **4** *The sky-diver had a plunge of more than 20,000 feet before his parachute opened:* drop, fall, dive, headlong rush, jump, leap.

Ant. **1** emerge, rise, withdraw, take out. **2** stroll, amble, crawl.

plus *prep. One plus six equals seven:* added to, in addition to, and.
—*adj. You must remember to put a plus sign in front of it:* additional, extra, mathematical sign. **2** *It does have a plus factor in that there are four bedrooms:* added, supplementary, extra, additional, other; helpful, useful, advantageous, beneficial.
◇ *Word origin: Plus* is Latin for "more."

ply[1] *n. The rug-wool is four-ply:* layer, thickness, sheet, plate, leaf, sheath, lamina, slice; strand, twist, plait.

ply[2] *v.* **1** *The old woman plied her bobbins in making lace:* employ, wield, put to use, utilize, manipulate, operate, work, handle. **2** *Father still plies his trade as a carpenter:* practise, carry on, exercise, follow, work at, labour at, pursue, occupy oneself with, persevere at, bend one's efforts to, devote oneself to. **3** *The salesman plied his customers with food and drink. Reporters plied the candidate with questions:* besiege, press, thrust upon, urge upon, prevail upon, supply persistently, offer repeatedly. **4** *The ship plies between Hong Kong and Singapore:* travel regularly, make repeated trips, go back and forth; sail, navigate, run, fly.
◇ *Word origin: Ply*[2] is a short form of *apply.*

pocket *n.* **1** *Have you any change in your pocket? The briefcase has two pockets for papers:* pouch-like part of a garment; compartment, envelope, receptacle, *Archaic* placket; chamber, cavity, hollow; pouch, bag, sack; purse, handbag, pocket-book. **2** *The prospector finally found a pocket of silver in the hill:* isolated mass; vein, lode, pit, strip, streak, strain.
—*v.* **3** *The ticket-seller was gaoled for pocketing the box-office takings:* steal, pilfer, put into one's pocket, appropriate, arrogate, usurp, help oneself to, take possession of, embezzle; attain, get, obtain, come by, gain, receive.
—*adj.* **4** *A pocket camera is easy to carry:* pocket-size, for carrying in the pocket, small, little, miniature; for the pocket.

pocket-book *n. He made a short note of the proceedings in his pocket-book:* notebook, diary; accounts book, jotter, memo pad.

pod *n. The peas must be stripped from the pods:* husk, jacket, hull, shell, shuck, sheath, case, seed case, seed-vessel.

> **Exploring the Word**: *Pocket, pouch, poke,* and *poached* all come from French *poche,* pocket, pouch. A *pocket* and a *pouch* are almost the same thing — though a *pocket* is usually part of a garment, a built-in *pouch; poke* is another word for pocket or for a small carrying bag, as in our expression *to buy a pig in a poke,* which means to buy something without first seeing it; and a *poached* egg is so-called because during the cooking the white forms a pouch round the yolk.

poem *n. Rudyard Kipling wrote some of the best remembered poems in the English language:* verse, rhyme, verse composition, jingle, doggerel; (*variously*) ballad, ode, sonnet, madrigal, lyric, idyll, song, limerick.
◇ *Pronunciation tip:* Very few people today make the mistake of leaving out the *e* in *poEm.* That makes the mispronunciation "pōm" even more grating to most listeners. Remember: *PO-em.*
◇ *Word origin: Poem* comes from Greek *poiēma,* work, especially poetic work. Thus, when we speak of a *poem* by Robert Frost as "a work by Robert Frost," we are using the same concept the Greeks did. (Greek *poiēma,* poem, poetic work, derives from the verb *poieein,* to make, create, invent, write poetry.)

poet *n. Gerard Manley Hopkins was belatedly recognized as the greatest poet of the late nineteenth century:* maker, singer, writer of poetry; (*variously*) lyrist, lyric-writer, song-writer, librettist, improviser, reciter, minstrel, balladeer, ballad monger, troubadour, versifier, rhymer, rhymester, Poet Laureate.
◇ *Usage note:* In antiquity the poet Sappho (of Lesbos in the 7th century B.C.) was spoken of as the female counterpart of Homer. Greeks and Romans referred to Homer as "the poet" and to Sappho as "the poetess." In present-day usage, however, the feminine form *poetess* has lost favour, as have *authoress* and *aviatrix.*

poetic Also **poetical** *adj. T. S. Eliot's plays have many poetic qualities:* lyric, lyrical, imaginative, rhythmic, metrical, musical, melodic, songlike, lilting, melodious.

Ant. unpoetical, prosaic, routine, realistic, commonplace, matter-of-fact, unimaginative.

poetry *n. Most of Alexander Pope's poetry is written in heroic couplets:* verse, metrical composition, poesy, rhyme; versification.

poignant *adj. The poignant words brought a tear to every eye. The critic wrote a poignant review of* Lassie Come Home: moving, affecting, touching, heart-rending, pitiful, pitiable, piteous, distressing, woeful, grievous,

lamentable, pathetic, rueful, doleful; cutting, piercing, penetrating, sharp, pungent, piquant.
Ant. unaffecting, unmoving, cold, blunt, unfeeling; insipid, trite, vapid, banal, superficial.
◇ *Pronunciation tip:* The pronunciation of *poignant* can be a real stumbling-block because the *g* is silent. Thus, the correct way to say the word is *POIN-yant,* not "poig-nant."

point *n.* **1** *Have you got a pencil with a sharper point? The lighthouse is on the northern point of the island:* sharp end, tapered end, tip, nib; spike, pike, apex, prong; projection, protuberance, prominence, extension, offshoot, promontory, outgrowth, spur. **2** *The freezing-point of water is 32 degrees Fahrenheit:* degree, stage, position, condition, place; limit, mark. **3** *At that point the audience got up and left:* instant, moment, time, very minute, juncture. **4** *I think I missed the point of his story:* main idea, purpose, object, end, reason; gist, essence, heart, kernel, pith, core, meat, marrow, sum and substance. **5** *There's no point in arguing any further:* sense, reason, cause, object, objective, aim, intention, purpose, end, value, use. **6** *Here's a point you may have overlooked:* detail, item, particular, aspect, feature, quality. **7** *The team won by two points:* score, tally; unit, number; (*variously*) run, goal, game.
—*v.* **8** *Point the gun at the target:* aim, train, direct; steer, guide, turn, bend, slant, level. **9** *His odd conduct points to an ulterior motive:* indicate, suggest, imply, signify, intimate, hint at; portend, foreshadow, presage, bode, argue; testify; demonstrate, manifest, prove.
◇ *Word origin: Point* and *poignant* come from Latin *pungere,* to prick. A *point* is a sharp tip with which to prick or make a dot and *poignant* means painful or sharp, piercing, both having the connotation of a painful prick.

pointer *n.* **1** *The guide used a pointer to indicate the towns on the map. The pointer on the speedometer showed sixty miles an hour:* indicator, guide, stick; hand, arm, needle. **2** *The old hand gave the youth a few pointers before starting him on the job:* piece of advice, bit of information, hint, suggestion, recommendation; admonition, caution, warning.

pointless *adj.* **1** *Fencers are required to use pointless foils:* without a point, unpointed, rounded, obtuse; blunt, dull, worn down, not edged, unsharpened. **2** *Further discussion on this matter would be pointless:* useless, purposeless, unproductive, unprofitable, bootless, unavailing, meaningless, fruitless, futile, worthless, aimless, invalid, ineffectual; unreasonable, illogical, absurd, ridiculous, irrelevant, senseless, inapplicable, beside the point.
Ant. 1 pointed, sharp. **2** useful, profitable, meaningful, fruitful, productive, beneficial, worthwhile, valid, invaluable; appropriate, fitting, proper, to the point; reasonable, logical, sensible; desirable, advisable.

poise *n.* **1** *A good hostess needs a lot of poise:* assurance, self-confidence, self-command, self-control, presence of mind, presence, aplomb, equanimity, calm, composure, *French* savoir faire, sang-froid.
—*v.* **2** *The matador poised the sword above his head, then drove it into the bull:* balance, be in equilibrium; hold aloft, raise, elevate.

poison *n.* **1** *Strychnine is a deadly poison:* toxic chemical, harmful chemical, bane; (*loosely*) venom, toxin, harmful drug. **2** *Hate is a poison for which there is no antidote:* evil, harm, curse, bane, disease, cancer, malignancy, malignity, canker, plague, pestilence; outrage, enormity, abomination, corruption.
—*v.* **3** *Tainted food can poison your system. The Borgia family poisoned many people:* kill with poison, harm with poison, give poison to; infect, contaminate, disease, make sick, impair, weaken, debilitate. **4** *Industrial waste is poisoning the atmosphere. Don't allow evil thoughts to poison your mind:* contaminate, pollute, taint, adulterate; corrupt, defile, degrade, corrode.
Ant. 1 antidote. **2** good, benefit, salve, balm.
◇ *Word origin: Poison,* like *potion* and *potable,* comes from Latin *potare,* to drink. The Latin noun based on this verb, *potio,* originally meant any medicinal draught or potion, but by late republican times was increasingly used in the specialized sense of "poison."

poke *n.* **1** *The master gave the new boy a poke in the ribs:* jab, thrust, punch, hit, prod, jolt, dig, thump.
—*v.* **2** *Stop poking me with your elbow:* prod, jab, dig, nudge, jolt, thrust, push, butt, hit, punch, stick, stab, gore.

police *n.* **1** *Call the police!:* law-enforcement organization, police force, law-enforcement officers, policemen, constabulary, *Informal* cops, gendarmes, men in blue, fuzz.
—*v.* **2** *Several watchmen police the factory at night:* patrol, guard, protect, go on one's beat; maintain law and order, keep in order, regulate, control.

policeman *Fem.* **policewoman** *n. Ask the policeman where the opera-house is:* police officer, officer, officer of the law, law-enforcement officer, *Informal* copper, bobby, arm of the law, gendarme, *Slang* cop, dick, flatfoot, fuzz; (*variously*) patrolman, man on the beat, motorcycle policeman, traffic cop; detective, inspector, police sergeant, constable.

policy *n. The store's policy is to exchange merchandise rather than to give cash refunds. The Foreign Secretary carries out foreign policy:* practice, procedure, course of action, mode of management, line of conduct, system, programme, routine, habit, custom, rule, behaviour, way, method, principle, style; plan, scheme, strategy, tactics, design.

polish *v.* **1** *Polish the silver before the guests arrive:* shine, buff, rub up, burnish, smooth, sand, pumice; wax, gloss, varnish, glaze. **2** *The Minister spent several days polishing his speech:* perfect, refine, improve, enhance, round out, touch up, emend, correct.
—*n.* **3** *Use brown polish on these shoes:* wax, shining substance, gloss, varnish, glaze, oil; abrasive, sandpaper, pumice, rouge. **4** *Four years of drama school gave her considerable polish:* culture, cultivation, refinement, elegance, grace, finesse, suavity, urbanity; good manners, politeness, politesse, courtesy, gentility, *Slang* class.
Ant. 1 tarnish, oxidize, discolour, dull, corrode, erode. **3** remover, eraser. **4** boorishness, clumsiness, awkwardness; indecorum, gaucheness, uncouthness.
◇ *Word origin: Polish* and *polite* come from Latin *polire,* to polish, smooth, or refine. Thus, when we say that a *polite* person has polished manners or that *politeness* smooths out social relationships, we are employing the same image for *politeness* that the ancient Romans used.

Exploring the Word: *Police* goes back to Greek *politeia,* polity, government, administration, which is based on Greek *polis;* city. (*Politics* comes from the related *Politika;* public matters, politics, title of a famous book by Aristotle.) In early modern times, *police* meant "state policy," especially with reference to the relationship between government and those governed. Around 1750 the word came to mean "law enforcement" with the establishment of the first modern *police* force in France. Every police force on earth today can trace its ancestry back to a model of that 18th-century Parisian prototype. The word *policeman* was first used in England following the passage of the controversial Metropolitan Police Act in 1828. Its leading sponsor was the Home Secretary, Sir Robert ("Bobby") Peel, whose name is preserved in the term *bobby.* A *bobby*'s official rank is that of *constable.* This word goes back to Late Latin *comes stabuli,* literally "count of the stable" or "chief equerry," title of many a medieval king's right-hand man — *Constable* of France, Lord High *Constable* of England. By 1400 the word also acquired its present meaning. *Sheriff* comes from Old English *scīrgerēfa,* literally shire-reeve, a representative of the Anglo-Saxon kings in a shire or county.

polite *adj.* **1** *What a polite young man!:* courteous, well-mannered, mannerly, well-behaved, civil, respectful, diffident, gentlemanly, courtly, gallant. **2** *Such boorishness is not accepted in polite society:* refined, cultured, polished, genteel, well-bred, civilized, elegant, fashionable, high, élite, patrician.
Ant. 1 rude, impolite, discourteous, ill-mannered, unmannerly, uncouth; insulting, impudent, impertinent. **2** unrefined, uncultured, ill-bred, unpolished, crude, boorish.

"A politician will do anything to keep his job — even become a patriot."
— *William Randolph Hearst*

politician *n. The Minister is a skilled politician:* professional in party politics, politico, political careerist; office-seeker, office-holder, public servant, legislator, statesman.

politics *n. pl.* **1** *The history of European politics is an interesting subject:* political science, art of government, administration of public affairs, practice of government; affairs of state, government policy, statecraft, statesmanship. **2** *The Liberal and the Tory had an argument about politics:* political views, political matters, party policy, party leadership, political manœuvres.
◇ *Usage note:* This plural noun is usually construed as singular, which means that it takes a singular verb: *Politics is the art of the possible.*

poll *n.* **1** *The election will begin at six a.m. when the polls open:* voting place, polling booth; voting list; voting, vote, returns, tally, figures. **2** *An independent poll shows that 60 per cent of the people favour comprehensive schools:* public opinion poll, Gallup poll, public survey, census, count; public opinion.
—*v.* **3** *We polled the members about the change in the rules:* take a vote on, register the vote of, solicit the vote of, canvass, sample the opinion of, count heads. **4** *The winning candidate polled over twenty-five thousand votes:* receive a vote; register, tally.
◇ *Word origin: Poll* comes from Middle Dutch *polle,* the top of the head, head. Thus, a voting *poll* is a way to "count heads," a *poll tax* is sometimes still called a "head tax," and when a farmer *polls* a cow, he cuts or trims the horns that are on the top of its head.

pollute *v. All those waste products are polluting the river:* contaminate, befoul, foul, dirty, soil, sully, make filthy; defile, profane, desecrate, debase, deprave.
Ant. purify, cleanse, clarify, purge.
◇ *Word origin: Pollute* comes from Latin *polluere,* to defile.

pollution *n. The new law will reduce air pollution:* contamination, contaminating, befouling, fouling, dirtying, soiling, defiling; uncleanness, foulness, adulteration; pollutant, impurity.

pomp *n. The coronation of the new king was performed with great pomp:* stately display, ceremony, solemnity, pageantry, splendour, grandeur, magnificence, brilliance, glory; flourish, style, show, display; pompousness, ostentation, pretentiousness, showiness, affectation.

◇ *Word origin:* A *pomp* was originally a pagan procession or pageant. The word comes from Greek *pompē*, a procession in honour of a god. In Roman imperial times the word had the additional sense of "triumphal procession."

pompous *adj. He was a pompous, officious little bureaucrat:* self-important, ostentatious, pretentious, haughty, arrogant, patronizing, snobbish, condescending, overbearing, presumptuous, *Informal* uppish, puffed-up; vain, conceited, egotistic, supercilious, vainglorious, proud, imperious, blustering, swaggering, grandiose, lordly, high and mighty, affected, mannered, snooty.
Ant. simple, modest, inglorious; dull.

pond *n. We fed the ducks on the pond:* small lake, pool, tarn; lagoon, water-hole; basin.
◇ *Word origin:* A fish *pond* and a dog *pound* are literally the same word, both modern derivations of Old English *pund*, an enclosure or pen for animals. To *impound* something is, of course, to shut it up, as in a pound.

ponder *v. He pondered the problem for many hours:* consider, meditate on, reflect on, contemplate, think over, give thought to; cogitate, cerebrate, ruminate, deliberate, study, concentrate upon, puzzle over, examine, *Informal* put on one's thinking-cap; mull over, muse, reflect, speculate, wonder, brood over.

> **Exploring the Word**: Latin *pondus,* weight, gives us *ponder,* to weigh in the mind; *ponderous,* having great weight, heavy, lumbering; *preponderance,* superior in "weight," influence, or importance; and *pound,* a unit of weight, and a monetary unit which used to be equal to a specific weight of gold.

ponderous *adj.* **1** *The men struggled with the ponderous equipment:* heavy, weighty, burdensome, awkward, cumbrous, cumbersome, unwieldy; massive, bulky, enormous, big, large, *Informal* hefty. **2** *The ponderous woman needed help in getting up from the chair:* heavy, awkward, ungraceful, lumpish, hulking, graceless, lumbering, bovine, corpulent. **3** *His ponderous speech put everyone to sleep:* dull, heavy, heavy-footed, laboured, lustreless, boring, unexciting, dreary, unlively, sluggish; long-winded, wordy, tedious, droning, monotonous, wearisome.
Ant. 1 light, weightless; small, tiny, dainty. **2** graceful, light on the feet; dainty. **3** exciting, absorbing, lively; short, terse, brief, concise, succinct, to the point.

pontifical *adj.* **1** *The Pope excommunicated the Archbishop for defying his pontifical authority:* belonging to the Pope, churchly, priestly, ecclesiastical, clerical, episcopal, apostolic. **2** *He can't make a simple statement without seeming pontifical:* pompous, pretentious, condescending; imperious, overbearing.

pool *n.* **1** *Deer often come to drink at the pool. The corpse lay in a pool of blood:* pond, lake, tarn, mere, (*variously*) fish-pond, millpond, swimming-pool; puddle, splash. **2** *He was employed as a member of our typing pool:* group, association, combine, coalition, confederation, cooperative, collective, union. **3** *Who won the football pools this week?:* stakes, lottery, kitty, jackpot, bank.
—*v.* **4** *We pooled our resources and got the job done quickly:* combine, merge, amalgamate, share, consolidate, band together, unite, ally.
◇ *Word origin: Pool* comes from French *poule,* meaning a stake, a collective heap, and originally meaning a hen, because a hen lays an egg a day, forming a *pool* or collective heap.

poor *adj.* **1** *He was so poor that he couldn't even afford the fare:* poverty-stricken, indigent, insolvent, destitute, impoverished, penniless, moneyless, pauperized, bankrupt, impecunious, *Slang* broke; needy, in need, in want, in straits, strapped, *Informal* badly off, hard up, on the rocks. **2** *The land was too poor to produce crops:* unfertile, infertile, barren, sterile; desolate, forlorn, meagre, bare, exhausted, depleted, empty; uncultivable, fallow, unproductive, dead, wasted, worked out. **3** *It was a poor imitation of the real thing. His poor performance caused him to fail the scholarship. It was a poor attempt to win her affection:* inferior, inadequate, deficient, defective, imperfect, wanting, faulty, lacking something, devoid of; paltry, wretched, sorry, meagre, beggarly, indifferent, worthless, fruitless, vain, futile, unprofitable, unworthy. **4** *The poor man never knew what hit him:* pitiable, unfortunate, unlucky, pathetic, miserable, wretched, sorry; distressed, unhappy, sad, grieving.
—*n.* **5** *The state must care for the poor:* the unfortunate, the needy, the penniless, the destitute, the indigent.
Ant. 1, 2 rich. **1** affluent, wealthy, moneyed; fortunate, lucky, *Informal* well-off, *Slang* in the money, in clover; comfortable. **2** fertile, productive, fecund, cultivable, fruitful, fructiferous. **3** worthy, superior, excellent. **5** the rich, the affluent, the wealthy.

pop *v.* **1** *One of the balloons popped:* explode, burst; boom, bang, discharge, detonate, crack, snap. **2** *The magician had real rabbits popping out of his hat:* appear, materialize, issue forth suddenly, burst, arise, come.
—*n.* **3** *We heard a pop and the champagne cork bounced off the ceiling:* explosion, detonation, bang, blast, report, crack, burst. **4** *I love ginger pop:* soda-water, soft drink, fizzy drink, *(variously)* lemonade, ginger beer.
◇ *Word origin: Pop,* a sharp explosive sound, was coined to imitate the sound, and the drink *pop* is so named because of the carbonated pop that it makes when you open a bottle of it.

poppycock *n. Informal Don't tell me you actually believe that poppycock!:* balderdash, bunkum, bosh, tosh, nonsense, stuff, rubbish, trash, hog-wash, rot, gibberish, *Slang* jabberwocky, twaddle, blather, prattle, fustian, tommy rot, wish-wash, fiddle-faddle, flapdoodle; rigmarole, *Slang* gobbledygook; absurdity, drivel, inanity, froth, flummery, abracadabra, hocus-pocus, moonshine, hooey, fudge, baloney.

popular *adj.* **1** *Mary was a popular girl:* sought-after, well-received, in favour, in demand, accepted; preferred, approved, well liked, favourite, admired; well-known, celebrated, famous. **2** *Taxes are always a popular issue. The goods are on offer at popular prices:* public, of the people, general, communal, community, civic, democratic, social, sociological, civil, national; inexpensive, affordable, cheap.
Ant. **1–2** unpopular. **1** in disfavour, unaccepted; unliked, odious, displeasing.

popularity *n. The comedian enjoyed great popularity during the 30's and 40's:* favour, acceptance, approval, vogue, fashion, fame, reputation, celebrity, repute, note, notability; glory, *Informal* kudos; acclamation, esteem, regard, admiration; notoriety.

population *n. The population of the city rose by 20 per cent:* inhabitants, number of people; citizenry, public, citizens, body politic, commonality; people, folk, populace.
◇ *Word origin: Population, popular,* and *people* come from Latin *populus,* the people. Latin *vox populi* means "the voice of the people," hence public sentiment.

populous *adj. Cities are more populous than rural areas:* full of people, full of inhabitants, populated, peopled, crowded, teeming, swarming, thronged, densely inhabited.

pore[1] *v. He pored over the report, looking for the slightest error:* read, study, ponder, examine, scrutinize, peruse, scan, run the eye over; study, consider, search, probe, delve into, explore, survey, review.

pore[2] *n. Pimples occur when pores of the skin become clogged. Pumice is a rock with many pores:* tiny opening, hole, orifice, aperture, outlet.

porous *adj. Sponges are porous:* absorbent, permeable, penetrable, pervious; honeycombed, sievelike, cellular, riddled, lacy; spongy.

port *n. The ship will reach port tomorrow morning:* seaport, harbour, dock, pier, wharf, quay, landing, anchorage, mooring, dry dock; shelter, refuge, haven; destination.

portable *adj. I have a portable television set:* transportable, movable, haulable, conveyable, cartable, liftable; compact, folding, pocket, small, light, manageable, easily carried, handy, convenient, pocket-sized.

portal *n.* Usually **portals** *Many great men have passed through these portals:* entrance, door, gate, gateway, doorway, approach, entry, threshold, arch, portcullis, vestibule, portico.

portend *v. The unemployment statistics portend bad times ahead:* foretell, forecast, augur, bode, prophesy, predict, prognosticate; herald, signify, point to, warn of, forewarn, give token of, presage, betoken, denote, suggest, forbode, foreshadow, foretaken, bespeak.

portent *n. The dark clouds were portents of a thunderstorm:* warning, sign, forewarning, boding, foreboding, threat, dire prospect; omen, sign, token, augury, presage, harbinger.

portentous *adj.* **1** *Neighbouring countries viewed the dictator's speech as portentous:* foreboding, threatening, intimidating, ominous, menacing, alarming, frightening; significant, fateful, prophetic; unpropitious, inauspicious. **2** *She was a pianist of portentous talent:* prodigious, stupendous, amazing, astonishing, surprising, remarkable, extraordinary, incredible, superlative, exceptional, superb.

Exploring the Word: Latin *portus* originally meant passageway, doorway, and later both gateway and harbour. From its meaning of harbour or gateway we get *port* and the *port* in *seaport* and *airport.* From its meaning of doorway, passageway, we get *portal* and the *port* in *porthole* and *portside* (the left side of a ship as one faces forward, because the deck-house entrance and loading doors and gates were on this side in ancient vessels). This meaning also gives us *hall porter,* originally a gatekeeper or doorkeeper; *porch,* a covered space at the entrance to a building, *portico,* entrance or open space covered by a roof on columns, and *porte cochere,* a rooflike covering over an entrance, drive, or courtyard to shelter people getting in and out of vehicles. *Portugal* was originally called *Portus Cale,* the region behind the *port* city of *Cale,* and *port* wine is so called after the Portuguese city of *Oporto* or *Porto,* which was the shipping centre for it.

porter *n. The porter took our luggage into the air terminal:* luggage carrier, attendant, carrier, transporter, bearer, conveyer, conductor; (*in the Far East*) coolie.
◇ *Word origin:* The *porter* who carries a traveller's luggage in a hotel or at a railway station gets his name from Latin *portare,* to carry. There is a dark-brown alelike malt beer called *porter* because it was apparently once the favourite drink of *porters* in hotels and at railway stations.

"That best portion of a good man's life,
His little, nameless, unremembered acts
Of kindness and of love."
— *William Wordsworth*

portion *n.* **1** *A portion of the contract dealt with royalties:* part, section, division, segment, sector; piece, fragment; measure, quantity, amount, sum. **2** *Her portion of the inheritance amounted to £50,000:* part, division, allowance, allotment, share, apportionment, allocation; serving, helping, ration, percentage, *Slang* cut. **3** *We must all accept our portion of life:* fortune, lot, destiny, fate, doom, luck, kismet, *Greek* moira; God's will.

portly *adj.* *He was a portly gentleman with an enormous appetite:* large, substantial, heavy, fat, big, corpulent, obese, fleshy, plump, rotund, stout, round, full, stocky, burly, chubby, tubby, endomorphic.
Ant. thin, slender, trim.

portrait *n.* **1** *A portrait of his wife hung over the fireplace:* painting, sketch, drawing, photograph, picture, likeness. **2** *From her portrait of you, I thought that you'd be much shorter:* description, verbal picture, word painting, personal report, thumb-nail sketch, impression, graphic account, depiction, representation, vignette, cameo.

portray *v.* **1** *The artist portrayed her as almost saintly:* depict, describe, picture, delineate, model; sketch, draw, illustrate, paint, carve, sculpture, photograph. **2** *Who portrayed King Lear?:* enact, play, represent, characterize, impersonate, pose as, simulate; imitate, mimic, ape. **3** *The author portrayed his father as a vicious drunkard:* describe, depict, characterize, represent, detail; figure, set forth, narrate, delineate, picture.

pose *v.* **1** *He posed the model by the window, with the light behind her:* position, arrange, group, order, set, line up. **2** *She loves to pose when men are around:* posture, act self-consciously, act affectedly, show off, give oneself airs. **3** *He posed as a reporter to get in:* pretend to be, pass oneself off as, impersonate. **4** *Allow me to pose several questions:* state, put forward, submit, set forth, postulate, advance, throw out, present, propose, propound, bring up, suggest.
—*n.* **5** *He nervously assumed a stiff pose next to the fireplace:* attitude, posture, position, stance, bearing, carriage; mien, cast, air, mannerism, style.

posh *adj.* *Slang We were invited to a posh party at their country house:* elegant, fancy, refined, high-class, classy, chic, smart, stylish, extravagant, lavish, swanky, ritzy, chichi.
◇ *Word origin:* One explanation of the origin of the word *posh* is that it is from the phrase *p(ortside) o(ut), s(tarboard) h(ome)* — referring to the preferred, most expensive staterooms on the shady side of ships plying between England and India. It makes a good story and certainly *may* be the origin of *posh*, but there's much room for doubt.

position *n.* **1** *The hilltop was a perfect position for the watch-tower:* place, location, locus, situation, disposition; locality, site, station. **2** *The sprinters lined up in a tense crouching position:* posture, stance, pose, attitude. **3** *The guards were in position at all the exits:* one's station, usual or proper place. **4** *A man in his position might have done the same thing:* situation, predicament, condition, state, circumstances, plight; standing, place. **5** *She was a woman of high position:* standing, status, station, elevation, prominence, eminence, distinction, importance, prestige, consequence, notability, class, caste, place, order. **6** *I held an important position in the textile company:* job, place, career, post, capacity, function, role, charge, appointment, assignment, responsibility, duty, commission, office. **7** *What's your position on foreign aid?:* opinion, viewpoint, outlook, point of view, stand, frame of mind. **8** *He had a good position after the first three throws:* location, vantage, place, placing, standing, ground.
—*v.* **9** *She positioned the rooks on the wrong squares:* put, place, arrange, array, set; pose, stand, fix, situate, locate, lodge, deposit.

Exploring the Word: Latin *ponere*, to place, and its derivative *positio*, place, position, give us several dozen English words, including: *position*, to place, or a place; *positive*, literally firmly placed, hence sure, affirmative; *posture*, the position or carriage of the body or a mental position or attitude; *pose*, an assumed position, as for a photographer or an affected mental position or attitude; and the *post* in *military post*, *post of employment*, and *post office*, referring to a place or position occupied by troops, a worker, or an office-holder, and to a place where letters are *posted* or placed. The same base gives us *appose* and *juxtapose*, to place next to, place beside, as for comparison; *compose* and *compound* to put together, create by combining things; *composition* and *compost*, a work so created, a mixture of decaying organic substances; *component*, one of the parts put together, and *composure*, a state of calm when one has all one's thoughts and feelings together; *depose*, to place down, put down, *deposit*, something put down, as money in a bank, and *depot*, a place where things are put down or left, a warehouse; *dispose*, to put in a particular place or arrangement, and *disposition*, the arrangement or final settlement itself, or one's nature or tendency, the arrangement or attitude towards life put together by one's personality.

positive *adj.* **1** *He gave a positive answer to the question:* affirmative, conclusive, firm, absolute, decisive, unqualified, definite, definitive, leaving no doubt, unequivocal, explicit, corroborative, confirmatory, undisputed, irrefutable, incontrovertible. **2** *She was positive that she had seen him:* sure, certain, undoubting, confident, assured, cocksure, dead certain, convinced. **3** *He always has some positive ideas on company policy:* practical, practicable, effective, constructive, useful, helpful, serviceable, applicable; beneficial, gainful, good, salutary, contributory. **4** *What we need is some positive thinking!:* forward-looking, optimistic, progressive, affirmative, co-operative. **5** *Informal She's a positive sweetheart:* real, honest-to-goodness, absolute, complete, veritable, total, thoroughgoing. **6** *His positive ways made him hard to live with:* dogmatic, opinionated, narrow, autocratic, overbearing, dictatorial; obdurate, unchangeable, immovable; assertive, self-assured, *Informal* cocksure.

Ant. 1 negative, inconclusive, qualified, indefinite, disputable. **2** unsure, tentative, doubting, uncertain. **3** negative; impractical, speculative; wild, foolish, useless. **4** pessimistic; conservative, reactionary; neutral, indifferent; vain, idle. **6** amenable, tractable, self-effacing.

positively *adv.* **1** *She positively identified him as the attacker:* absolutely, unhesitatingly, unquestionably, indisputably, decidedly, definitely, unmistakably, indubitably; emphatically, categorically, without qualification, affirmatively, assuredly, confidently, certainly. **2** *It's positively the worst play I've ever seen:* quite definitely, literally, unquestionably, without doubt, assuredly, absolutely.

possess *v.* **1** *They possess the house and eight acres of land:* own, have, have title to, hold, occupy, maintain. **2** *She possesses a beautiful singing voice:* have, be endowed with, be blest with, boast; command; enjoy. **3** *Nazi Germany possessed much of Europe during World War II:* conquer, vanquish, overrun, grab, control, occupy, absorb, take over, acquire. **4** *He was possessed with the desire to own the house:* dominate, control, influence, obsess, consume; fascinate, fixate, mesmerize, enchant, be eaten up, hypnotize, bedevil, bewitch; dominate, make insane, drive crazy.

possession *n.* **1** *He's had possession of the adjoining ground for 10 years. Possession is nine-tenths of the law:* possessing, owning, ownership, proprietorship, vested interest; occupation, occupancy, control, hold, title, tenure. **2** *He was a poor man with few possessions:* belongings, goods, asset, material thing, effect, resource, accoutrement. **3** *These islands were once possessions of Spain:* dominion, territory, province, protectorate. **4** *With his usual self-possession, he answered all the questions:* presence of mind, self-control, composure, even temper, calmness, unexcitability, coolness, placidity, sang-froid, poise, equanimity, equilibrium; control, command.

possibility *n.* **1** *What's the possibility of having a sunny weekend?:* chance, likelihood, probability, hope, odds. **2** *There's always the possibility that he won't come:* chance, eventuality, risk, hazard, gamble, contingency. **3** *That idea has great possibilities:* potentiality, promise, prospects; feasibility, practicability, workability.

possible *adj.* **1** *Here, for instance, is one possible educational programme:* potential, contingent, conceivable, thinkable, imaginable, hypothetical; credible, thinkable, worth consideration, reasonable, compatible; admissible, cognizable. **2** *Anything is possible with that man:* capable of being done, within reach, attainable, obtainable, achievable, practicable, workable, feasible, performable, manageable, conceivable; capable of happening.

Ant. 1, 2 impossible. **1** inconceivable, unimaginable, improbable; incredible, unthinkable, unreasonable, incompatible; unlikely. **2** unobtainable, inaccessible; unfeasible.

◇ *Usage note:* A thing is *feasible* if it can be done; it is *possible* if it can happen or come about; and it is *probable* if it is likely to happen or come about. Thus, *Climbing Mt. Everest is feasible* (it can be done), but *The weather report says rain is possible* or *probable* (*possible*—it can happen, there's some chance, or *probable*—it is likely to happen, there's more than a 50 per cent chance).

possibly *adv.* **1** *Possibly we'll meet again soon:* perhaps, maybe, it may be, could be, conceivably, as luck may have it, perchance, God willing. **2** *They give you all the food you can possibly eat for £5:* conceivably, normally, at the most. **3** *She couldn't possibly have left without me:* by any means, in any way, at all, by the remotest chance.

post[1] *n.* **1** *He spent the morning putting new posts along the back fence:* stake, picket, upright, pale, support, column, shaft, pole, mainstay, brace, splint, pile.

—*v.* **2** *As soon as the Vice-Chancellor posted the news, students began to gather in the hall. I'll keep you posted on further events:* put up, fasten up, pin up, publish, place in public view; make known, announce, broadcast, circulate, declare, disclose, report, advertise; proclaim; inform, notify, instruct, advise, acquaint, apprise, enlighten.

◇ *Word origin: Post*[1], an upright piece of timber or other support, and *poster,* originally an advertisement or notice for affixing to a *post,* come from Latin *postis,* door-post.

post[2] *n.* **1** *The policeman was at his post until midnight:* place of duty, station, round, beat, routine. **2** *He held an important post in the company:* job, position, office, situation, place, spot, station, seat; capacity, role, function, part; assignment, appointment. **3** *He returned to the post with a message for the general:* military camp, base, headquarters; settlement.

—*v.* **4** *Post two soldiers at each gate:* station, situate, install, place, put, fix, set, establish; quarter, lodge, house, camp, settle; locate.

posterity *n.* *They preserved his writings for posterity:* future generations, succeeding ages, history; offspring, descendants, heirs, progeny; family, young, children; descent, lineage, succession.

postpone *v. Would it be possible to postpone the party till next week?:* defer, delay, hold over, adjourn, reserve, remand, suspend; stay, keep back, table, shelve.

"The care of posterity is most in them that have no posterity." —*Francis Bacon*

postulate *v.* **1** *He postulated first that good and evil exist in all men:* propose, put forth, submit; assume, take as an axiom, presume, take for granted, presuppose; conjecture, guess, hazard, surmise, theorize, hypothesize, speculate.
—*n.* **2** *He believed the postulate that virtue is its own reward:* premiss, assumption, fundamental principle, presumption, presupposition, axiom, theorem, theory, hypothesis.

posture *n.* **1** *These exercises will improve your posture:* stance, carriage, bearing, pose, shape, contour; set, attitude, mien. **2** *The meeting took on a different posture after his moving speech:* mood, tone, tenor, aspect, air, attitude, state, case, phase; situation, circumstance, predicament.

potent *adj.* **1** *This drug is a potent remedy:* powerful, strong, mighty, forceful, vigorous, overpowering, formidable, efficacious. **2** *Hitler was a potent demagogue:* influential, convincing, impressive; forceful, powerful, forcible, dynamic.
Ant. **1, 2** impotent, weak; ineffectual, inefficient. **1** weak. **2** unconvincing, ineffective, unimpressive.

potential *adj.* **1** *Always be on the look-out for potential dangers:* possible, conceivable, latent, concealed, hidden, lurking, covert, unapparent; unrealized, dormant, quiescent, passive; unexerted, unexpressed, implicit, undisclosed.
—*n.* Also **potentiality** **2** *You're wasting your potential on this job:* ability, possibilities, capability.
Ant. **1** actual, real, manifest.

pot-pourri *n.* **1** *She kept a jar of pot-pourri on the dressing-table:* aromatic mixture of dried petals. **2** *The last concert of the Proms was a musical pot-pourri:* medley, mixture, mélange, pastiche, miscellany, hotchpotch, mosaic, patchwork; salmagundi, motley.
◇ *Pronunciation tip: Pot-pourri* (hash, mess) is pronounced *poe-poo-REE,* not "pot-pouree."
◇ *Word origin:* French *pot-pourri* literally means "rotten pot," i.e. a highly seasoned mixture of meat and vegetables cooked together.

pouch *n. She kept her cigarettes in a leather pouch:* bag, sack, satchel, receptacle, container; (*variously*) pocket, wallet, purse, pocketbook, handbag, reticule; haversack, kit, ditty-bag, duffle bag.

pounce *v.* **1** *The hawk pounced on the field mouse:* swoop down on, fall upon, drop from the sky, plunge, strike at, spring upon, fly at, dash at, snatch; surprise, take unawares, ambush.
—*n.* **2** *With one pounce, the leopard had killed its prey:* swoop, downward rush, spring, leap, jump.

pound *v.* **1** *He pounded so hard on the window that it broke. The boxer pounded his opponent:* strike, hammer, drum, beat, batter, bang, *Informal* clobber; pummel, maul, trounce, thump, thwack, clout, cudgel, smack, wallop; drub, lambaste, thrash, paste, fustigate, beat black and blue. **2** *His head was pounding from the heat and the noise:* throb, beat, pulsate, palpitate. **3** *The miller pounded the grain into a fine powder:* pulverize, crush, crumble, grind. **4** *They pounded down the stairs:* stomp, thunder, march, tramp, clomp.

pour *v.* **1** *The wine-waiter poured champagne into the glasses:* let flow, decant; tap, draw off; spill, squirt, effuse, slop; ladle out. **2** *He worked so hard that perspiration poured from him:* stream, issue, flow, gush, spout, cascade; seep, ooze, dribble, drop, drip; drain. **3** *It poured for 40 days and nights:* rain heavily, rain hard, rain in torrents, *Informal* rain cats and dogs, come down in buckets, come down in sheets; flood, deluge, drench.

pout *v. Stop pouting and do as I tell you:* sulk, look sullen, grimace petulantly, have a hang-dog look, make a long face, scowl, fume, brood, brood over, fret, mope; be out of humour, frown, glower, lower.

poverty *n.* **1** *The family lived in poverty:* privation, need, destitution, indigence, penury, impoverishment, pennilessness, insolvency, bankruptcy, pauperism; want, lack. **2** *There's a poverty of acting talent today:* lack, deficiency, insufficiency, shortage, dearth, paucity, scarcity, deficit, meagreness.
Ant. **1** affluence, luxury, opulence, comfort; richness. **2** abundance, sufficiency, overabundance, plethora.

"Poverty is no disgrace to a man, but it is confoundedly inconvenient." —*Sydney Smith*

power *n.* **1** *The doctors restored her power of speech:* faculty, capability, capacity, competence, aptitude, talent, skill, genius, attribute, qualification, gift, endowment, property, quality. **2** *You could see the power in his big hands:* strength, force, might, potency, energy, puissance, powerfulness, pressure, muscle, brawn, iron grip; vigour, vitality. **3** *The manager has the power to fire an employee on the spot:* right, prerogative, status, influence, sway, prestige, authority, licence. **4** *The cardinal was the real power behind the throne. The Western powers turned down the Soviet proposal:* authority, ruler; major nation, dominant state. **5** *The lights flickered as the power was reduced:* electricity, hydroelectric power.

—*v.* **6** *Electricity powers all our appliances:* give energy to, energize, activate, operate, supply with power.

Ant. 1 incapability, incapacity. **2** weakness, impotence, feebleness; enervation, listlessness.

powerful *adj.* **1** *The athlete should have a powerful body:* strong, able-bodied, mighty, potent, indomitable, unconquerable, invincible; vigorous, robust, sturdy, hardy, brawny, husky, athletic, muscular, strapping, stalwart, stout, Herculean. **2** *He's a powerful speaker:* commanding, authoritative, cogent, forceful, high-powered, energetic, rousing, moving, exciting, emphatic, incisive, intense, effective.

powerless *adj.* **1** *Samson was powerless after Delilah had cut his hair:* helpless, without strength, impotent, feeble, feckless, weak, debilitated incapacitated, disabled, prostrate, crippled, infirm. **2** *The town was left powerless and had to surrender:* defenceless, unarmed, pregnable, vulnerable.

practical *adj.* **1** *Let me give you some practical advice:* useful, sound, sensible, realistic, functional, solid, down-to-earth, serviceable, utilitarian, pragmatic, pragmatical, systematic, efficient, businesslike; judicious, hard-headed, unsentimental, unromantic, matter-of-fact. **2** *As a practical fund-raiser he knows how to get people to be generous:* working, practised, seasoned, veteran, experienced, versed, accomplished, proficient, skilled, skilful, qualified, able, expert; trained, instructed.

Ant. 1, 2 impractical, unpractical. **1** theoretical, speculative, unsound, injudicious. **2** inexperienced, unversed, unqualified.

◇ *Word origin: Practical, practice, practise,* and *pragmatic* come from Greek *prattein,* to do.

practically *adv. He was such a good friend that he was practically a member of the family. I'm practically ready:* virtually, in effect, essentially, nearly, in the main, almost, just about, all but, substantially; fundamentally, basically, to all intents and purposes.

practice *n.* **1** *With practice he could speak French fluently:* training, drill, repetition, discipline, preparation, seasoning, exercise, rehearsal. **2** *The new methods were not put into practice until last year:* operation, action, use, usage, effect, execution, performance, exercise, application, play. **3** *It was her practice to rise every morning at dawn:* custom, wont, habit, rule, procedure, routine, process, method, mode, manner, fashion, way, ritual, ways, conduct, observance, tendency, modus operandi. **4** *His shady practices got him a prison sentence:* method, action, deed, manœuvre, trick, ruse, dodge, device.

practise *v.* **1** *He practised the piano every day:* rehearse, drill, discipline, train; familiarize oneself with, become proficient at, prepare for, qualify. **2** *Why don't you practise what you preach?:* perform, do, carry out, follow, put into practice, put into action, apply, use, utilize, live up to, turn to use, bring into play, set to work. **3** *He's only practised dentistry for a year:* perform in, work at, engage in, pursue, be engaged in.

praise *n.* **1** *He had nothing but praise for his son:* good words, compliments; appreciation, approbation, acclaim, congratulation, commendation, approval, laudation; admiration, regard, esteem, respect; applause, accolade, plaudit, cheer, hurrah; eulogy, panegyric, encomium, tribute, testimonial. **2** *The congregation raised their voices in fervent praise:* worship by hymn-singing, adoration.

—*v.* **3** *The mayor praised him for his philanthropic activities:* commend, laud, approve, acclaim, extol, congratulate, compliment, applaud, cheer; panegyrize, eulogize, exalt, *Slang* build up. **4** *Praise the Lord:* worship, celebrate, glorify, exalt; revere, venerate, honour.

praiseworthy *adj. His praiseworthy deed earned him a special citation:* worthy, estimable, excellent, exemplary, commendable, admirable, laudable, meritorious.

prance *v. She pranced around the room when she heard the good news:* dance, skip, cavort, caper, gambol, romp, frolic; leap, spring, jump, vault; bounce, bound, frisk.

pray *v.* **1** *I pray daily for your good health:* make devout petition to God, commune with God, address the Lord, offer a prayer, say one's prayers, invocate; fall on bended knee. **2** *I pray you, have mercy!:* beg, beseech, entreat, implore, plead, supplicate, make an entreaty for, cry to; ask earnestly, request, solicit, call upon, petition, urge, sue, bid.

prayer *n.* **1** *The priest led the congregation in prayer:* litany, orison, praise, thanksgiving, adoration, worship, glorification. **2** Often **prayers** *You're the answer to my prayers!:* hope, dream, aspiration; request, appeal, plea, petition, solicitation; supplication, invocation; entreaty, suit, beseechment.

"Prayer is and remains always a native and deepest impulse of the soul of man."

— *Thomas Carlyle*

---

preach *v.* **1** *He devoted his life to preaching the word of God:* sermonize, proclaim, discourse, evangelize. **2** *Practise what you preach:* advocate, urge, profess, press urgently, exhort, propagate, stand for, hold forth, declare, pronounce, expound, promulgate, exhort; prescribe.

◇ *Word origin:* To *preach* comes from Latin *praedicare,* to proclaim (the Gospel).

preacher *n. He started his career as a local preacher:* clergyman, minister, churchman, ecclesiastic, evangelist, reverend, pastor, man of the cloth, prebendary, parson, vicar, curate, chaplain, padre, *Informal* sky pilot; sermonizer.

precarious *adj.* **1** *The situation was precarious politically:* vulnerable, uncertain, problematical, ticklish, uncontrolled, critical, insecure, touch-and-go, not to be depended upon, unreliable, undependable, doubtful, dubious, questionable. **2** *Freelance journalism can be a precarious occupation:* hazardous, risky, perilous, unsafe, chancy, unsteady, unstable, shaky; alarming, sinister.
Ant. 1 certain, sure, secure, dependable, reliable, unquestionable. **2** safe, steady, stable.
◇ *Word origin: Precarious* comes from Latin *precarius*, obtained by begging. Originally it meant obtained only at the will of the grantor and by entreaty, hence the extended meaning of "uncertain, transitory," which we have inherited from the Latin writers, Ovid and Seneca, whose works were enormously influential in Europe throughout the medieval and Renaissance periods.

precaution *n. Take every precaution so as not to catch cold:* safety measure, caution, care, safeguard, defence; protection, security; forethought, provision, foresight, anticipation, carefulness, heedfulness, circumspection.

precede *v. A dance-drama preceded the star performance:* go before, go ahead of, come before, take place before, go on before; antedate, antecede.
◇ *Spelling tip:* To *cede* means to yield or surrender, so that someone else may *precede* you or go first. Thus there is a *cede* in *precede: preCEDE.*

precedence Also **precedency** *n.* **1** *My family takes precedence over my business:* priority in importance, pre-eminence, predominance, preference, prevalence.
◇ *Usage note: Precedence* is the fact or right of being ahead in rank, place, or time: *A major takes precedence over a captain. Paying our bills must take precedence over buying a new TV set.* A *precedent* is an act or decision used as a guide for later ones: *George Washington's truthfulness set a precedent for all children who chop down cherry trees! The decision in Regina vs. Smith is a legal precedent that the judge must consider.*

precedent *n. As first woman executive in the company, she felt she had set a precedent:* example, pattern, model, guide-line, standard, criterion.

preceding *adj. The preceding message was prerecorded:* previous, earlier, prior, foregoing, preliminary, precursory, antecedent; preexistent, first-named, first-mentioned, aforesaid, aforementioned, abovementioned, former.

precious *adj.* **1** *She owned many precious antiques:* costly, dear, expensive, high-priced, valuable, priceless, invaluable, inestimable, beyond price, not to be had for love or money; rare, choice, exquisite. **2** *A family is a precious blessing in life:* valuable, highly esteemed, cherished, choice, treasured, prized, valued, beloved, adored; sweet, darling, adorable, lovable. **3** *Her poems are appealing, but a bit precious:* excessively nice, dainty, affected, over-refined, fastidious, prissy, fussy, particular, meticulous, finical.

precipice *n. The path ends at the precipice, which has a 50-foot drop:* cliff, cliff edge, ledge, escarpment, bluff, palisade, crag, declivity.
◇ *Word origin: Precipice, precipitate,* and *precipitation* come from Latin *prae-* (before) + *caput* (head), hence head first, headlong. Thus a *precipice* is a place having a steep headlong descent; to *precipitate* is to bring about hastily or make a headlong plunge, while *precipitation* is something that falls headlong from the sky, such as rain, snow or hail.

precipitate *v.* **1** *Scarlet fever precipitated the poor man's death:* hasten, bring on, quicken, expedite, speed up, accelerate, advance, spur. **2** *The explosion precipitated tons of snow from the mountain:* throw, hurl, thrust, cast, fling, propel, drive, launch, catapult, discharge, let fly.
—*adj.* **3** *Don't be too precipitate in your choice, otherwise you might make a mistake:* hurried, hasty, abrupt, rushed, proceeding rapidly, speedy; headlong, reckless, rash, incautious, foolhardy, imprudent, thoughtless, impetuous, impulsive.

Exploring the Word: Latin *caedere*, to cut, gives us *precise* and *precision*, literally to foreshorten and foreshortening, respectively, hence conciseness and exactness; *incision*, a cutting in, a cut, *incisive*, cutting (in the sense of penetrating, sharp, keen), as an *incisive remark*, and *incisor*, one of eight front teeth in man especially adapted for cutting; *concise*, literally cut through, hence "cut," i.e. abbreviated, terse, as a *concise statement; decisive* and *decision*, cut down to the end, hence conclusive, a conclusion or judgement, and *decide*, to cut or pare down to the final answer or opinion, to determine, settle; and *excise*, to cut out.

precise *adj.* **1** *Can't you be more precise in your answers?:* exact, specific, strict, clear-cut, express, definite, explicit, accurate, incisive, unequivocal, to the point, distinct, literal; careful, painstaking, meticulous, fastidious. **2** *He had precise ways of doing things and refused to change:* exact, particular, unbending, inflexible, meticulous, distinct, rigid, strict.
Ant. 1 inexact, implicit, indefinite, ambiguous, equivocal, indistinct, vague, nebulous; careless, heedless, loose, lax, incautious. **2** flexible, changing, haphazard.

precision *n. He wrote the report with care and precision:* exactness, preciseness, accuracy, meticulousness, scrupulous care, attention; authenticity, factualness, truthfulness, fidelity.

precocious *adj. She's such a precocious little girl!:* uncommonly smart, mature, advanced, bright, quick, clever, apt.
Ant. slow, backward, retarded, stupid.
◇ *Word origin:* A *precocious* child is literally one who is "done" or cooked early! Precocious comes from Latin *prae-* (before, early) + *coquere* (to cook), hence our modern meaning of one who is unusually developed or advanced for his age.

preconception *n. Your preconceptions about Southerners are way off the mark:* prejudgement, predisposition, fixed idea, notion, presumption; bias, prejudice.

precursor *n. The polite letters were only precursors to blackmail:* vanguard, advance guard, forerunner; harbinger, messenger; usher, herald; predecessor, antecedent; sign, token, mark, omen, portent, warning; symptom.

predatory *adj. The pirates were predatory and unpredictable:* rapacious, predacious, plunderous, thievish, marauding, pillaging, larcenous.

predestination *n. It was predestination that we met and fell in love:* fate, fortune, kismet, destiny, providence, what must be, God's will, inevitability, force of circumstances; preordination, predetermination.
Ant. accident, chance.

predetermined *adj. The final vote at the conference was pretty well predetermined:* already settled, foreordained, pre-planned, decided, predestined, calculated, premeditated, prearranged, deliberate, intentional, planned, destined, fated.

predicament *n. How did I ever get into such a predicament?:* trying situation, dilemma, dangerous condition, trouble, crisis, difficulty, imbroglio, perplexity, sad plight, strait, quandary, *Informal* hot water, jam, scrape, fix, bind, mess, hornet's nest, pinch, pickle.

predict *v. I predict that you will meet a handsome stranger:* prophesy, forecast, foretell, foresee, divine, read the signs, anticipate, envisage; betoken, presage.

prediction *n. It's uncanny, but all her predictions have come true:* prophecy, soothsaying, forecast, foretelling, crystal-gazing, augury, portent, divination; anticipation, announcement, proclamation, declaration.

predilection *n. I have a predilection for rich desserts:* preference, predisposition, partiality, proneness, proclivity, propensity, leaning, penchant, bent, inclination, tendency; love, liking, fondness, fancy, desire, taste, hunger, appetite, relish; prepossession, prejudice, bias, favour.
Ant. aversion, disinclination, dislike, hatred.

predispose *v. His mother's work as a nurse predisposed him to become a doctor:* incline, dispose, make of a mind to, bias, prejudice, sway, influence, prevail upon, prompt, induce, persuade, urge, encourage; seduce, win over, entice, lure, tempt.

predominant *adj. At the conference, French and German were spoken but English was predominant:* more frequent, prevailing, prevalent, dominant, important, major, reigning, sovereign, chief, main, leading, supreme, paramount; controlling, authoritative, ruling, influential, ascendant, powerful, strong, forceful, potent, vigorous.
Ant. subordinate, secondary; minor, unimportant, inferior; uninfluential, weak.

pre-eminent *adj. Even as a youth, Mozart was pre-eminent among composers:* foremost, superior, supreme, paramount, second to none, unequalled, consummate, unrivalled, unparalleled, unsurpassed, matchless, peerless, incomparable, best, greatest, dominant, predominant; eminent, renowned, illustrious, famous, famed, celebrated, honoured, distinguished.

prefer *v.* **1** *I prefer thrillers to romances:* choose rather, like better, fancy, single out, adopt, pick out, elect, make a choice of, select, have rather, favour, pick and choose, opt, make one's choice, think better, take to, fix upon. *Archaic He was preferred to the rank of lieutenant:* promote, raise in office, advance in rank, graduate, elevate; aggrandize, exalt, dignify, ennoble.
Ant. 1 dislike, reject, eschew; hate, loathe, detest, abhor.
◇ *Spelling tip:* Remember that the single *r*-ending in *prefer* doubles in *prefeRRed* and *prefeRRing.*

"People say that life is the thing, but I prefer reading." —*Logan Pearsall Smith*

---

preference *n.* **1** *Do you have a preference for a particular food?:* partiality, first choice, liking, fancy, predilection, inclination, predisposition, bias, prejudice, proclivity, proneness, propensity; option, selection, pick. **2** *Graduates generally get preference over schoolboy candidates for jobs:* favouring, precedence, advantage, favoured treatment, priority; ascendancy, predomination, supremacy.
Ant. 1 dislike, aversion, eschewal; hatred, abhorrence.
◇ *Pronunciation tip: Preference* is always stressed on the first syllable. Thus, *PREF-er-ence,* never "pre-FUR-ence."

pregnant *adj.* **1** *She was pregnant with their first child:* with young, parturient, gravid, gestating, with child, having a baby, *Informal* expecting, in the family way; about to become a mother. **2** *The poem was pregnant with meaning:* full, replete, filled, fraught, abounding, teeming, plenteous, rich; fruitful, fertile, prolific, luxuriant, fecund, copious; productive, proliferous, fructiferous; life-giving; meaningful, important, provocative, significant, weighty, seminal, momentous; suggestive, full of possibilities, impressive, forceful, potential.

prejudice *n.* **1** *Her prejudices were many, her reasons few:* bias, preconception, slant, prejudgement, predisposition, one-sidedness, narrow-mindedness, bigotry; intolerance, unfairness, discrimination, partiality, predilection, favouritism. **2** *Will you be able to judge without prejudice to the defendant?:* impairment, injury, detriment, damage, harm, hurt, ill; loss, disadvantage.
—*v.* **3** *He successfully prejudiced the audience against his opponent:* affect with a prejudice, influence against, sway, bias; predispose, jaundice, poison, infect, taint, contaminate. **4** *His attempt to escape seriously prejudiced any hopes of parole:* damage, harm, hurt, injure, mar, impair, spoil.

preliminary *adj. The judge held a preliminary hearing:* preparatory, initiatory, preparative, introductory, prelusive, prelusory, precursory.
Ant. final, concluding; subsequent, following.
◇ *Word origin: Preliminary* comes from the Latin prefix *prae-* (before) + *limen* (threshold), "before the threshold" — the word is not classical. *Praeliminarius* (preliminary) belongs to the Modern Latin vocabulary which arose during the late Middle Ages.

prelude *n.* **1** *Months of training were a necessary prelude to the championship bout:* preliminary, introduction, preparation; opening, preamble, preface, prologue. **2** *The pianist played several of Chopin's preludes:* short instrumental piece, brief musical selection; overture, introductory movement.

premature *adj.* **1** *The candidate's announcement of victory was premature:* too soon, too early, hasty, abortive, overhasty, too advanced, precipitate; untimely, ill-timed, inopportune, unseasonable. **2** *After six months she gave birth to a premature baby:* unripe, undeveloped, immature, raw, green; unfledged, unprepared, unready, callow; incomplete, embryonic, unhatched, vestigial; rudimentary.
Ant. 1 on time, well-timed, timely, opportune; too late, overdue. **2** mature, ripe; overripe.

premeditated *adj. He was charged with premeditated murder:* pre-arranged, predesigned, predetermined, predevised, studied, planned; deliberate, conscious, intended, intentional, calculated, considered, contrived, wilful, voluntary; in cold blood, with malice aforethought.

premise *n.* **1** Also **premiss** *It was the lawyer's premiss that his client was innocent:* hypothesis, basis for reasoning, proposition, argument, postulate, principle, theory; assumption, presumption, presupposition. **2 premises** *The police think that the thief is still on the premises:* buildings and grounds, property, site; immediate area, vicinity, environs.
◇ *Usage note:* When used to mean a proposition that serves as a basis for an argument or that helps form a conclusion, *premiss* is the more frequent spelling, though either form may be used both in the singular and the plural: *The premiss of the law is that a man is innocent until proved guilty. From the two premises that everyone has to eat and that few people grow their own food, I would conclude that most people patronize their local grocer's.* However, when referring to real-estate property, a building, or part of a building, only the plural form of *premise, premises,* is used, never the singular. *These premises are protected by a burglar alarm.*

premium *n.* **1** *Since I bought a bigger car my insurance premium has increased:* a regular fee paid in return for insurance cover or for instruction in a trade or profession; fee, due, subscription. **2** *Tickets for the Cup Final can be bought, at a premium:* inflated rate, overpayment, increased value, appreciation, consideration. **3** *I put a premium on punctuality:* high value, great stock, priority.

premonition *n. She had a premonition that he had been injured:* forewarning, foreboding, prediction, omen, presage, sign, augury, auspice, token, foretoken; indication, presentiment, feeling, *Informal* hunch, idea.

preoccupy *v. I was too preoccupied to hear the bell:* engross, occupy wholly, absorbed, immerse, arrest, engage the attention, take up, make uppermost in the mind, wrap up; fascinate.

preparation *n.* **1** *He insulated the house in preparation for winter:* anticipation, precaution, prior measure, safeguard, provision, timely care; prudence, foresight, forethought, expectation. **2** *The preparation of the banqueting hall took six hours:* getting ready, preparing. **3** Usually **preparations** *We had only a week to make preparations for the wedding:* plan, arrangement, measure, preliminary. **4** *The chemist suggested a preparation to relieve the ache:* concoction, composition, prescription, mixture, elixir, tincture, dressing; confection, prepared food. **5** *His earlier preparation made him perfect for the job:* experience, qualification, training, apprenticeship, instruction, direction, education, guidance, tutelage, teaching, seasoning.

"To be prepared for war is one of the most effectual means of preserving peace."
—*George Washington*

---

prepare *v.* **1** *We prepared the playroom for the party:* ready, make ready, get ready, fix, adapt, arrange, rearrange. **2** *Prepare yourself to take advantage of opportunity. They prepared for the worst:* ready, prime, be resolved, make provision for, provide, be prepared, be ready; take steps, clear for action, put things in order, set one's house in order.

preponderance *n. The preponderance of factory buildings made the city ugly:* predominance, prevalence, profusion, domination, majority, greater numbers, mass, bulk, lion's share, plurality; excess, superabundance, glut, surplus, oversupply, surfeit, plethora, redundance.

prepossessing *adj. She was a lovely, prepossessing young woman:* attractive, striking, charming, pleasant, engaging, nice, personable, winsome; alluring, fascinating, bewitching, captivating, inviting, tantalizing, enchanting, entrancing, beguiling.
Ant. unprepossessing, unpleasant; uninviting.

preposterous *adj. That's the most preposterous idea I've ever heard:* outrageous, ridiculous, ludicrous, absurd, fatuous, foolish, silly, imbecilic, asinine, stupid, inane, nonsensical, laughable, irrational, unreasonable, bizarre, *French* outré.
◇ *Word origin: Preposterous* literally means "before-behind." It comes from Latin *prae-* (before) + *posterus* (behind), hence back to front, with the cart before the horse, as it were.

prerequisite *adj.* **1** *The standard phone call is prerequisite to any personal meeting with him:* required beforehand; required, mandatory, called for, necessary, imperative, essential; indispensable, demanded, *French* de rigueur. —*n.* **2** *Several years' experience is the minimum prerequisite for this job:* requirement, something needed beforehand, qualification, postulate, necessity, need, requisite, condition, exigency, stipulation, demand, *Latin* sine qua non.

prerogative *n. You have the prerogative of changing your mind:* privilege, warrant, right, licence, claim; liberty, freedom, advantage, exemption; birthright, rightful power, authorization, legal power; grant, due, franchise; choice, option.
◇ *Word origin: Prerogative* comes from the Latin phrase *praerogativa tribus,* literally "prerogative (first-voting) tribe," a term applying to the tribe to which it fell by lot to vote first in the Comitia (the assembly of the Roman people, voting by tribes, which met on the Campus Martius). In imperial times the Latin word acquired its present sense of preference, privilege, prerogative.

"Reason to rule, but mercy to forgive;
The first is law, the last prerogative."
—*John Dryden*

prescribe *v. The by-laws prescribed that membership should be limited. The doctor prescribed plenty of rest:* legislate, rule, direct, specify, stipulate, dictate, order, enjoin, command, decree, ordain, require, impose, demand; institute, appoint, establish, settle, set, fix, assign; recommend, urge, require.

Exploring the Word: *Prescribe* and *prescription* come from Latin *prae-*, before, + *scribere,* to write, hence to write a rule or direction that must be followed, or the written order for a medicine before it can be taken. Many abbreviations and symbols are used in medical prescriptions that come from Latin and Greek and are hard for a layman to understand. Here are some of the most common ones:

℞ is merely the abbreviation of the Latin word *recipe,* "take," followed by the formula for compounding a medicine.
A.C. on a prescription means "before meals," from Latin *ante cibum.*
B.I.D. on a prescription means "twice a day," as it is the abbreviation of Latin *bis in die.* Similarly *t.i.d.* means "three times daily" (Latin *ter in die*) and *q.i.d.* means "four times daily" (Latin *quater in die*), whilst *p.r.n.* means "when required" or "according to circumstances" (Latin *pro re nata*).
GTT. on a prescription means "drops" (Latin *guttae*).
AQ. means "water" (Latin *aqua*).
ADD. on a prescription is just the doctor's quick way of instructing the pharmacist to add something or to add up so much to make a specific quantity, from Latin *adde,* add.

presence *n.* **1** *Your presence at the meeting will help our cause:* attendance; existence, being, substantiality, subsistence; entity, life. **2** *There is a spy in our presence:* company, midst; neighbourhood, immediate circle, group. **3** *The speaker was a man of poor presence. He had a certain presence that made women fall in love with him:* personal appearance, features, lineaments, aspect, favour, look, figure; charisma, compellingness, character, vitality; air, manner, bearing, carriage, deportment, demeanour, mien, expression. **4** *I can feel the presence of something evil in this old house:* spirit, shadow, ghost, curse, manifestation, spectre, incorporeality, phantasm, wraith, apparition, revenant, vision, phantom.

present[1] *adj.* **1** *The present state of affairs changes matters somewhat:* current, existent, contemporary, at the moment, contemporaneous, now, prevalent, immediate, instant, coeval; now under consideration. **2** *All the students are present today:* here, in attendance, not absent, not away, accounted for; in, at hand, nearby, near, about, in the room, *Informal,* on the spot, on hand; nigh, vicinal; existing in a place or thing, embedded, unremoved, implanted, rooted, ensconced.
—*n.* **3** *I live in the present, not the past:* now,

nowadays, here and now, today, this day and age, the time being, the moment.

Ant. **1** past; future. **2** absent. **3** the past, the future.

present² *v.* **1** *It is my honour to present you with this token of our esteem. He presented the school with a cheque for a thousand pounds:* give, give a gift to, confer, bestow, award, grant, accord, hand over; make a present of, donate, place at one's disposal, provide, supply; proffer, offer, propose, submit, put forward, advance, tender; give away, give out, mete out, dole out, render; contribute, *Informal* chip in. **2** *Please present your first witness:* summon, call up, introduce, show, exhibit, display, produce, bring on; offer, proffer, tender, bring forward, draw forth. **3** *He presented his views and then sat down:* state, assert, declare, apprise of, tell, impart, make known, give by way of information, give notice of, communicate; propound, asseverate, frame, allege, profess, cite, pronounce, aver, hold forth; recount, relate, recite, deliver, read, *Informal* come up with; advance, offer, proffer, tender, propose, put forth, expound. **4** *Kindly present your bills on the first of the month:* submit, hand in, give over, turn in, surrender.

—*n.* **5** *I received many presents on my birthday:* gift, offering, thing presented; donation, endowment, bequest, legacy, benefaction, boon, largess, gratuity, perquisite, tip, grant, oblation, fee; alms, liberality, bounty.

presentable *adj.* **1** *She looked quite presentable in her evening gown:* becoming, proper, fit to be seen, suitable, acceptable, decent; fashionable, stylish, modish. **2** *The house was presentable but far from immaculate:* good enough, passable, respectable, not bad, suitable, decent, unobjectionable, so-so, tolerable, acceptable, better than nothing, fair-to-middling.

presentation *n.* **1** *He feels nervous about his presentation at court to receive the C.B.E.:* ceremonious introduction, reception. **2** *The subject of the book is interesting but the presentation is poor:* arrangement, exposition, submission, production, show, demonstration, exhibition, display; materialization, appearance, unfoldment, unfolding, exposure, disclosure. **3** *The cheque was the nicest presentation of all:* gift, present, bestowal, largess, grant, boon, oblation; benefaction, favour, gratuity, tip, compliment; fee; liberality, bounty.

presently *adv.* *The speaker will begin presently:* soon, pretty soon, shortly, anon, forthwith, directly, before long, in a while, after a while, in no time, any time now, in a short time.

preservation *n.* *We must strive for the preservation of our national heritage:* conservation, saving, salvation; safeguarding, safe keeping, protection, defence, maintenance.

Ant. abandonment, decay, ruin, destruction.

preserve *v.* **1** *We must preserve our redundant churches:* keep safe, guard, protect, watch over, shield, shelter, conserve, save, defend, safeguard, maintain, keep intact, secure, keep sound, nurse, foster. **2** *You can have strawberries in winter if you preserve them in deep freeze:* (*variously*) bottle, conserve, store, *Informal* put up; seal, insulate; freeze, refrigerate; cure, smoke, salt, season, marinate, corn, pickle; dehydrate, dry; embalm, mummify.

—*n.* **3** Often **preserves** *I like peach preserves at lunch-time:* jelly, jam, conserve, confection, compote, marmalade, comfit, sweetmeat, sweet. **4** *No hunting is allowed in the game preserve:* wildlife enclosure, sanctuary, shelter, refuge, park.

◇ *Word origin: Preserve* and *preservation* come from Latin *prae-* (before) + *servare* (to keep), literally to "forekeep," hence to protect, keep in safety or for the future.

preside *v.* *The Lord Chief Justice will be presiding at the trial. Father always presided over dinner:* be in authority, hold the chair, be at the head of, hold authority; wield authority, chair, preside at the board, preside at a meeting; direct, conduct, control, govern, administrate, administer, rule, command, *Informal* boss; supervise, manage, superintend, keep order, regulate; watch, overlook, oversee; host.

president *n.* **1** Usually **President** *The President addressed the nation:* executive officer, chief executive, chief of state, head of the nation, head of government, commander-in-chief, chief magistrate, first citizen. **2** *He succeeded his father as president of the company:* chief officer, chief official, head, chairman, ruler.

◇ *Usage note:* Words such as *president, prime minister, premier, governor, mayor, alderman, councillor, professor, doctor, senator, congressman, king* and *prince* are capitalized when used as the title of a specific official or when the identity is unmistakable: *President Kennedy, Doctor Johnson, King Henry IV. Did you hear Alderman Jackson's statement? The President will deliver the inaugural address.* When not used as a specific title or when not accompanied by the name of the official, these words are often spelt with a small letter: *A president does not have the power of a king. Most countries have a prime minister, but not all have a president.*

press *v.* **1** *Press the reject button. Press one clove of garlic:* push; depress, push down, force down, thrust down, push in, flick; condense, compress, mash, crush, reduce, squeeze, cram, jam, stuff, force, strain. **2** *The tailor pressed the trousers:* iron, smooth, steam, flatten, hot-press; calender, mangle. **3** *She pressed the puppy to her bosom:* hold closely, hug, squeeze, fold in one's arms, embrace, clasp. **4** *The problem pressed us sorely for weeks:* trouble, oppress, burden, bear upon, weigh heavily upon, bear down upon. **5** *He keeps pressing me for money:* beg, implore, importune, urge repeatedly,

entreat, plead, enjoin, supplicate, appeal, exhort; dun, tax; beset, tap; urge insistently, prod, urge with force, compel, constrain, insist on, put the screws on; exact, extort, force from, hound, pressurize, bear down on, set on. **6** *The fans pressed around the pop group:* crowd, press in upon, surge, swarm, throng, mill, assemble, congregate, come together, gather, flock together, collect, cluster, herd, huddle. **7** *I'm a little pressed for time:* push, rush, hurry, be in short supply of, constrict, be hard put.
—*n.* **8** *Censorship infringes the freedom of the press:* newspapers, journals, periodicals, pamphlets, books, printed matter. **9** *The press weren't allowed into the meeting:* reporters, journalists, newspaper-men, the Fourth Estate. **10** *The manuscript goes to press next week:* printing-press, letterpress, printing machine; machine for compressing; printing, publication, final form. **11** *A press of fans greeted her at the stage door:* crowd, throng, mob, multitude, swarm, bunch, host, horde, pack, drove, legion, army, body, heap, crush.

Exploring the Word: *Press* and *pressure* come from Latin *pressare*, to press. *Printing-presses* are so named because they press paper against an inked plate, which is how newspapers are printed and why reporters are often called *ladies and gentlemen of the press*. Latin *pressare* also gives us *compress* (Latin *com-*, together), to press together; *depress* (Latin *de-*, down), to press down, lower, lower one's spirits; *express* (Latin *ex-*, out), to press out, to give an outward indication, as in *expressing one's views* or going out directly or rapidly, as an *express train; impress* (Latin *im-*, thoroughly, completely), to press thoroughly, hence to leave a mark or *impression* on something or someone; *oppress* (Latin *ob-, op-*, against), to press against, hence to force or burden; *repress* (Latin *re-*, back), to press back, keep back; and *suppress* (Latin *sub-, sup-*, under), to press under, hence to put down, quell, or conceal, as to *suppress a rebellion* or *suppress the news*.

pressing *adj. It was a pressing engagement and I couldn't avoid it:* urgent, imperative, vital, necessary, critical, crucial, essential, indispensable, needed, needful, exigent, important; insistent, crying, clamouring, importunate, demanding.
Ant. unnecessary, non-essential, dispensable, unimportant; regular, customary, routine.

pressure *n.* **1** *The pressure inside the submarine was almost unendurable:* air pressure, compression, compaction, squeeze; weight, heaviness, gravity, density. **2** *Having to cope with so many problems put him under great pressure:* stress, strain, tension, difficulty, adversity, straits, trouble, trial, grievance, load, care, oppression, burden, affliction, anxiety, distress. **3** *The pressure his father applied got him his position with the company:* influence, sway, pull, weight; power, potency, force, bias, interest. **4** *The pressures of business were too much for him:* press, urgency, exigency, hurry; stress, strain, pinch; compulsion, coercion; need, necessity, want; demand, requirement.

prestige *n. He was an author of international prestige:* fame, celebrity, glory, renown, reputation, prominence, note, repute, mark, notability, distinction, significance, account, import, importance, consequence, pre-eminence, eminence, honour, esteem, regard, report.

presume *v.* **1** *Dr. Livingstone, I presume?:* assume, take for granted, take it, believe, postulate, posit, think likely, suspect, imagine, conceive, fancy; suppose, surmise, gather, deduce, have it. **2** *She presumed to write to him in her daughter's name:* dare, take leave, take a liberty, make free, venture, make bold, be so bold, act presumptuously, have the audacity. **3** *She presumed on his good nature:* rely too much, take undue advantage of, impose.
◇ *Usage note:* See ASSUME.
◇ *Word origin: Presume, presumption,* and *presumptuous* come from Latin *prae* (before) + *sumere* (to take, to use), hence to anticipate or (in later use) to venture, to take for granted.

presumption *n.* **1** *Your presumption that he'd be here was wrong:* assumption, premiss, belief, supposition, postulate; speculation, guess, surmise, conjecture; preconceived opinion, presupposition, prejudgement, preconception. **2** *It took a great deal of presumption to insult the ambassador at his own party:* audacity, brass, effrontery, arrogance, gall; *Informal* cheek, nerve; *Slang* lip; impertinence, impudence, insolence, rudeness, flippancy, presumptuousness, pride, haughtiness, egotism; boldness, daring, forwardness.
Ant. 2 respect, deference, politeness.

presumptuous *adj.* **1** *It was presumptuous of the young back-bencher to challenge the leadership so soon:* bold, audacious, daring, over-confident, over-familiar, forward, nervy, shameless, brash, brazen, brassy, fresh, cocky. **2** *Her presumptuous airs made her disliked by many:* haughty, proud, snobbish, assuming, over-bearing, lofty, patronizing, pompous, lordly, imperious; disdainful, contemptuous, domineering, dictatorial, arrogant.

pretence *n.* **1** *The stage murder looked real, but it was only pretence:* make-believe, pretension, fake, hoax, invention, fabrication, imposture, counterfeit; trick, trickery, deceit, deception. **2** *By an elaborate pretence, the detective infiltrated the smuggling ring:* deception, subterfuge, guile, feint, camouflage, pretext, disguise, mask, cloak, cover. **3** *Her manners were modest and devoid of all pretence:* show, pretentiousness, showing off, ostentation, display, fanfaronade, ostentatiousness, affectedness,

affectation, false show, airs; boasting, bragging, vaunt, bombast, bluster, pomposity.
Ant. 1 reality, actuality, fact. **2** truthfulness, honesty. **3** simplicity, sincerity, candour, frankness, ingenuousness, openness.

pretend *v.* **1** *Let's pretend we're grown-ups!:* make believe, take a part, fill a role, imagine, fancy, suppose; mimic, impersonate, masquerade, act, play-act. **2** *She pretended to have a headache so that she wouldn't have to go:* feign, fake, affect, put on, assume, simulate, imitate, make a show of; counterfeit, sham, dissimulate, dissemble, put on a false front. **3** *How can you pretend to speak the language when you don't know the simplest rules of grammar?:* affect, claim, purport, dare, presume.

pretension *n.* **1** *His pretension to the crown was invalid:* claim, right, title, pretence; aspiration, ambition. **2** *She talked of her aristocratic friends with great pretension:* ostentation, affectation, hypocrisy, pretence, airs, showing off, ostentatiousness, grandioseness, display, show, showiness, pretentiousness; pomp, bombast, self-importance, pomposity.

pretentious *adj. He was a pompous, pretentious man. Her grave is marked by a large, pretentious monument:* showy, ostentatious, pompous, fatuous, bombastic, pedantic, boastful, flaunting, overbearing, affected, unnatural, insincere, presuming, assuming; lofty, airy, snobbish, *Informal* high and mighty, hoity-toity, stuck-up; puffed-up, blown-up, inflated, exaggerated, theatrical, stagy; flashy, tawdry, ornate, gaudy, garish, florid, extravagant, overdone; self-glorifying, self-important, self-praising, smug.
Ant. unpretentious, modest, unaffected, natural, unassuming; plain, simple.

pretext *n. She used the ringing of the doorbell as a pretext to hang up the phone:* excuse, alleged reason, professed purpose, basis, ground, pretence, bluff, feint, pretension; justification, vindication.

pretty *adj.* **1** *She's such a pretty girl!:* attractive, beautiful, pleasing to the eye, lovely, comely, bonny, handsome, good-looking, beauteous, sightly, pulchritudinous, well-favoured, fair, goodly; delicate, dainty, graceful; captivating, alluring, fetching, charming, engaging; well-proportioned, symmetrical, shapely, well-set, well-made.
—adv. **2** *It was a pretty poor turn-out for the meeting:* moderately, fairly, rather, somewhat.
Ant. 1 unattractive, ugly, plain, unsightly, clumsy, graceless, unseemly; unshapely, unsymmetrical.
◇ *Usage note: **Pretty*** is commonly used in informal speech to mean somewhat, moderately, or fairly, as in the sentence ***He's a pretty good negotiator.*** Pedantic writers on style have tried to restrict the usage to colloquial use, but numerous examples of it in formal published writings may be found dating back as far as the turn of the century.
◇ *Word origin: Pretty* comes from Old English *praetig,* sly, deceitful. Since sly people often try to disguise their deceit by being especially charming or pleasant, *pretty* came to mean charming or pleasant and later graceful and good-looking.

prevail *v.* **1** *A feeling of political indifference prevailed throughout the country:* abound, exist generally, be current, be widespread, obtain, exist, be prevalent. **2** *Abstract Expressionism prevailed in the big international art exhibitions of the 1950's:* predominate, be prevalent, preponderate, abound; have sway, hold sway, rule, reign. **3** *The better fighter prevailed:* triumph, be victorious, win, be a winner, be the victor, gain the palm, win the laurels; prove superior, succeed, conquer, overcome, carry the day, *Informal* bring home the bacon.

"The truth is great and shall prevail,
When none cares whether it prevail or not."
—*Coventry Patmore*

prevailing *adj.* **1** *The prevailing fashion in evening wear was the caftan:* current, popular, in style; widespread, prevalent, general, usual, customary, normal, conventional, accustomed; definite, fixed, established, set. **2** *The prevailing colours in her drawing-room are green and blue:* principal, main, prevalent, dominant, predominant, preponderant.
Ant. 1 dated, out-of-date, old-fashioned; unusual, rare, uncommon. **2** infrequent, minor, subordinate, lesser, inferior.

prevalent *adj. Vandalism is prevalent in city parks:* common, frequent, frequently occurring, prevailing, general, widespread, abundant, extensive; habitual, usual, normal, conventional, everyday, commonplace, familiar, customary.
Ant. infrequent, rare, unusual, uncommon.
◇ *Spelling tip: Prevalent* has an *a* in the middle and ends in *ent: prevAlent.*

prevent *v. Vitamin C is supposed to prevent colds. We prevented him from committing a gross error:* keep from occurring, defend against, counteract, fend off, hold back, stave off, ward off; block, bar, dam, deter, thwart, frustrate, foil, anticipate, balk, arrest, nip in the bud, forestall, avoid, preclude, avert; stop, halt, obviate, veto, prohibit, forbid, rule out; intercept, side-track, turn aside, deflect, draw off, turn away.
Ant. permit, allow, encourage, urge, incite.

prevention *n. Prevention of forest fires is up to you. You should be inoculated as a prevention against polio:* avoidance, stoppage, hindrance, inhibition, restraint, preclusion; obviation, elimination, defeat; frustration, thwarting, forestallment, interception.

previous *adj. Have you any previous experience?* prior, preceding, earlier, early; foregoing, foregone, former, before, aforesaid, aforementioned.

Ant. subsequent, consequent, succeeding, following, later.

◇ *Usage note: Previous* and *prior* may be used interchangeably in general use: *Previous to 1970, Prior to 1970; On a previous occasion, On a prior occasion.* In legal use, however, *prior* has the specific meaning that something else may take precedence: *There is a prior claim to the estate, If the prior marriage was legally dissolved then the second one is legal.*

prey *n.* **1** *The huge bird flew off with its prey in its claws:* quarry, game, kill, food; victim; quest, prize. **2** *She was the prey of unscrupulous lawyers:* victim, dupe, target, gull; *Slang* pigeon, fall guy, cat's-paw, sucker.
—*v.* **3** *Stronger animals prey upon weaker ones:* feed upon, devour, consume, eat, feast upon, fatten upon, gorge oneself upon; live off; fasten upon, fasten oneself to, parasitize, infest; suck the blood of.

price *n.* **1** *What's the price of that car? He must pay the price of his folly:* cost, face value, amount, charge, expenditure, expense, outlay; selling price, current price, market value, list price, retail price, wholesale price; value, worth, exchange value; penalty, punishment.
—*v.* **2** *The coat was priced at £50. We priced a number of Mediterranean holidays:* assess, evaluate, set a price on, appraise, value, cost.

priceless *adj. He owned many priceless antiques:* without price, beyond price, invaluable, valuable, precious, dear, highly-priced, costly, expensive, worth a king's ransom; irreplaceable, rare; incomparable, peerless; cherished, prized, treasured, valued.

Ant. worthless, cheap, inexpensive; common.

pride *n.* **1** *She took great pride in her son's success:* satisfaction, pleasure, enjoyment, delight, joy, happiness; gratification, comfort. **2** *A man with such pride rarely loses his temper in public:* self-esteem, dignity, self-respect, honour. **3** *If you cannot admit that you are wrong, you are guilty of pride:* self-importance, egoism, egotism, vanity, conceit, self-love, self-glorification, vainglory; immodesty, smugness, self-satisfaction; show, display, ostentation, parade, pomp, airs, pretension; swagger, arrogance, haughtiness, superciliousness, pomposity, imperiousness.
—*v.* **4** *He prided himself on his perfect self-control:* be proud of, be pleased with, have a feeling of pride in oneself, be satisfied with, be delighted at, be gratified at.

Ant. 3 humility, modesty, meekness.

prig *n. Don't be such a prig — let your hair down and enjoy the party!:* prude, puritan, Victorian, *Informal* Mrs. Grundy, stuffed shirt; hypocrite, bigot; pretender; pedant, formalist.

prim *adj. She was a prim, old-fashioned schoolteacher:* particular, fussy, precise, strict, proper, tidy, fastidious, strait-laced, puritanical, prudish, squeamish; priggish, prissy, starched, unbending, inflexible, stiff-necked, no-nonsense, stuffy, haughty, smug.

Ant. careless, loose, untidy; informal, easy-going, relaxed, carefree.

primary *adj.* **1** *He did well in primary school and even better later:* first, introductory, beginning, initial, elementary, preparatory; rudimentary, nascent. **2** *Your primary duties are outlined in this job-description:* chief, main, principal, fundamental, basic, key, cardinal; prominent, predominant, dominant, ruling, star, leading, greatest, highest, utmost; important, necessary, vital, essential. **3** *Love and hate are primary emotions:* primitive, primordial, primal, primeval; initial, original, prime, beginning, first; basic, fundamental, elementary, seminal, rudimentary, key, basal; native, indigenous, natural, inherent, innate; oldest, earliest.

Ant. 1 secondary, following, subsequent, succeeding, ensuing, later. **2** lesser, unimportant, subordinate, inferior; indirect, supplementary.

> **Exploring the Word:** Latin *prior* means former, previous, and gives us *prior* and *priority. Prior* was originally the comparative of Old Latin *pri,* before (equivalent to *primus,* first, foremost). From it we get: *prime,* chief, first-rate; the first element in the noun phrase *prima donna* (Italian for "first lady"), the leading female singer of an opera company; *primary,* first, elementary, e.g. *primary colours,* the colours on which all others are based; *primer,* a first or beginning reading book; *primeval,* belonging to the first or earliest ages (Latin *aevum,* age), as *This is the primeval forest; primitive,* first, earliest, early; *prince,* the first or principal person, hence a male monarch or his son; *principal,* first in rank or importance, chief, the head of a school or other organization; and *principle,* a first or basic rule, truth, cause, or essence.

prime *adj.* **1** *He's the prime suspect in the murder case:* primary, chief, main, principal, cardinal, most important, leading, predominant; ruling, pre-eminent; greatest, highest, maximal, crowning, paramount, superlative, supreme, utmost; unsurpassed, unmatched, matchless, best, without peer, peerless; important, necessary, essential, vital. **2** *Only prime cuts are sold at this shop:* superior, quality, of the best quality, Grade A, choice, specially selected, select, first-class, unparalleled; *Slang* A1, top-drawer, ace, top-hole. **3** *The prime cause of our malaise is greed:* basic, fundamental, elementary, rudimentary, elemental, basal, essential; intrinsic, inherent, innate, congenital; native, indigenous, natural; primal, oldest, earliest, original,

first. **4** *Spring is the prime season for planting:* best, preferred, most advantageous, most favoured, choice; timely, in good time, opportune, convenient; fit, seemly, suitable, fitting, propitious, befitting, expedient, well-timed, provident, auspicious, lucky; in good season, seasonable, early, bright and early.
—*n.* **5** *She married in her prime:* peak, perfection, ideal level, excellence; full strength, greatest strength; height, zenith, heyday, best days; maturity, full flowering, blossoming, bloom, flower, full beauty, pink.
—*v.* **6** *Her mother primed her for a life on the stage:* prepare, ready, fit, make ready, put into readiness, get ready, adapt, adjust; groom, coach, train, instruct, breed, raise, educate, school, tutor; inform, fill in, guide, prompt, brief.
Ant. 1 secondary, lowest, least important. **2** the worst, second-class, third-rate. **4** untimely, inconvenient, unsuitable, inauspicious, unfit; unseasonable.

primitive *adj.* **1** *Space travel is still at a primitive stage of development:* early, earliest, original, first, primary; beginning, elementary, introductory; undeveloped, unrefined, crude, rudimentary. **2** *The Eskimos of the far north are primitive people:* uncivilized, native, aboriginal, backward; antique, archaic. **3** *He adopted a primitive style of painting:* unsophisticated, simple, uncomplicated; artless, uncultivated, unskilled, unlearned. **4** *The pioneers had to endure quite primitive living conditions:* uncomfortable, inconvenient, crude; bare, Spartan, austere, ascetic.
Ant. 1 advanced, later; developed, sophisticated, refined. **2** civilized, modern. **3** sophisticated, artful, fashionable. **4** comfortable, elaborate.

principal *adj.* **1** *He's the principal shareholder:* chief, leading, foremost, most important, supreme, superior, capital, pre-eminent, dominant, prominent, predominant, outstanding, controlling, most considerable, main, cardinal; primary, prime, first; fundamental, essential, basic; greatest, ultimate, paramount.
—*n.* **2** *The principals were gathered on stage for the rehearsal:* star, leading man, leading lady, protagonist, featured player, *Informal* first fiddle. **3** *She was sent to the principal's office:* head of a school or college, headmaster, headmistress, master, dean, preceptor; person in authority, chief person, chief authority, superior. **4** *How much interest will there be on a principal of £5,000?:* original sum, original investment, capital sum, invested sum, fund; money.
Ant. 1 least important, inferior, minor, least powerful, weakest, inconsiderable; secondary, auxiliary, subsidiary, supplementary.
◇ *Usage note:* See PRINCIPLE.

principle *n.* **1** *He studied the principles of psychology:* rule, truth, law, assumption, precept, fact, basis, fundamental, rudiment, proposition, element, formula; regulation, canon, code, direction, dictum; theorem, axiom, maxim. **2** *His principles wouldn't allow him to work on Saturday:* belief, article of faith, credo, tenet, theory, creed; dogma, doctrine, religious belief, scruple, way of thinking, system of belief; teaching, view, attitude, position. **3** *He is too much a man of principle to compromise:* morality, standards, ethics, uprightness, honesty, probity, scruples; honour, integrity, incorruptibility, sense of honour; righteousness, rectitude, respectability; goodness, virtue, morals; conscientiousness.
Ant. 3 immorality, dishonesty; dishonour.
◇ *Usage note:* A *princip*LE is a *ru*LE or general truth, as in morality or ethics: *In principle, I'm against government controls, A judge must be a man of high principle.* Most other meanings are spelt *princi*PAL. A *princi*PAL runs a college and should be a *pal* to the students. A *principal* in any group takes a leading part. In your savings account, *principal* is the capital which earns interest. Thus, *The principal announced the examination results, Drinking is a principal cause of road accidents, A principal of £500 earns 6% interest a year.*

prior *adj. Sorry, I'd love to go, but I have a prior commitment. Prior to her coming here she was in Paris:* previous, preceding in time, pre-existing, pre-existent, earlier, former; precursory, going before, foregoing, prefatory, preparatory; aforementioned, aforesaid.
Ant. subsequent, following.
◇ *Usage note:* See PREVIOUS.

priority *n. This project has priority over all others:* precedence, greater importance, preference, urgency, immediacy, the lead, precedency, pre-eminence; antecedence, seniority, superiority, ascendancy.

prison *n. He was sent to prison for armed robbery:* gaol; penal institution, house of detention, penitentiary, reformatory, house of reform, house of correction, internment centre; dungeon, tower, bastille, penal colony, *Slang* jug, stir, can, cooler, choky, clink.

"The first prison I ever saw had inscribed on it: 'Cease to Do Evil; Learn to Do Well'; but as the inscription was on the outside, the prisoners could not read it." —*George Bernard Shaw*

privacy *n.* **1** *A hidden microphone in a person's home is an invasion of privacy:* privateness, seclusion, security, integrity; solitude, solitariness, isolation, dissociation; retirement, withdrawal, retreat. **2** *The generals planned the coup in privacy:* secrecy, privity, secret, clandestineness.

private *adj.* **1** *This is private property:* privately owned, personal, special, exclusive, express, restricted, closed, limited, confined, fixed;

not public. **2** *Plans for the take-over were kept private:* confidential, clandestine, privy, secret, inviolate; unofficial; undercover, covert, classified, undisclosed, concealed, unrevealed, hidden, underground, buried, invisible; sub rosa, hush-hush; mysterious, cryptic, obscure, esoteric, indistinct, dark. **3** *He retired to his private retreat in the mountains:* secluded, isolated, remote, desolate, reclusive, privy, sequestered, lonely, solitary, lonesome, unfrequented.

Ant. 1, 2 public. **1** unrestricted, open, general, unlimited, unconfined. **2** known; official; disclosed, unconcealed, revealed; *Informal* out in the open. **3** unsecluded, frequented, visited.

privation *n. I could not bear the privations of army life:* hardship, lack of comfort, misery, deprivation, squalor; need, neediness, want, lack; poverty, impoverishment, indigence, penury, impecuniousness, pauperism, exigency, mendicancy, destitution, beggary, bankruptcy, reduced circumstances.

Ant. ease, comfort, wealth, riches, affluence, success, good luck; sufficiency, gain, acquisition.

privilege *n.* **1** *Big businesses enjoy certain privileges that smaller ones do not. It is my privilege to serve you:* right, prerogative, prerequisite, birthright, freedom, liberty; licence, franchise, title, charter, patent; advantage, favour, boon, benefit; honour, pleasure.

privileged *adj. They belong to that privileged group of people who enjoy the "good life." Talks between lawyer and client are privileged and cannot be divulged:* limited, special; exempt, free, immune, excused; allowed, granted, permitted, licensed, sanctioned, warranted, empowered, entitled, authorized; unaccountable, not liable.

prize[1] *n.* **1** *She won second prize in a beauty contest:* award, trophy, medal, cup; reward, guerdon, premium; ribbon, decoration, blue ribbon, laurels, crown. **2** *As a secretary she was a prize:* jewel, pearl, gem, diamond, pure gold, treasure, masterpiece, champion; *French* crème de la crème; *Slang* honey, peach.

—*adj.* **3** *Her prize recipe was printed in the newspaper:* winning, honoured, award-winning.

—*v.* **4** *She prized him for his good sense and understanding:* value, set store by; admire, respect, look up to, honour, esteem, regard, like, hold in esteem, appreciate; hold in affection, treasure, hold dear, cherish.

◇ *Word origin: Prize* is a variant of our word *price* and literally means something "of price" given as an honour or award.

prize[2] Also **prise** *v* **1** *We prized open the locked door with a crowbar:* force, break, work, lever, crack, jimmy. **2** *You'll never prize anything out of me!:* force, wring, squeeze; wrench, tear, wrest, extract; worm, winkle, ferret.

probable *adj. The weather forecast suggests that showers are probable. He's a probable candidate:* likely, possible, promising, presumable, presumptive, supposed; encouraging, assuring, seeming, ostensible, apparent; *Informal* on the cards; credible, logical, reasonable, plausible, conceivable, believable.

◇ *Word origin: Probable,* like *probe, proof,* and *prove,* comes from Latin *probare,* to test, prove, and literally means tested but leaving some room for doubt, hence likely.

probably *adv. We shall probably leave on Sunday:* in all probability, most likely, in all likelihood, as likely as not, presumably, supposedly.

probe *v.* **1** *Scientists probed the causes of the earthquake:* investigate, look into, inspect, pry into, delve into; scrutinize, study, examine, test; question, inquire, interrogate, quiz, query; hunt, pursue, follow up, seek after. **2** *The surgeon probed for the bullet in the man's back:* look for, seek, explore with a probe, search; *Informal* fish for, rummage; penetrate.

—*n.* **3** *His probe into the bribery charges proved futile:* investigation, inspection, exploration, examination, inquiry, inquest, study, search, research, survey, analysis, trial, test, review.

problem *n.* **1** *I need help in solving this maths problem. They ran into marital problems:* question, query, poser, puzzle, riddle, conundrum; difficulty, disagreement, disputed point.

—*adj.* **2** *The problem child needs special care. She had problem hair:* unruly, difficult, hard to manage, uncontrollable, unmanageable; intractable, incorrigible, stubborn.

Ant. 2 perfect, model, manageable.

◇ *Word origin: Problem* comes from Greek *pro-* (forward, toward) + *ballein* (to throw), something thrown forward for discussion, or as we would say, an idea "tossed out" for debate.

"It is the first of all problems for a man to find out what kind of work he is to do in this universe." — *Thomas Carlyle*

problematic Also **problematical** *adj. She has already taken her driving test six times, so it is problematical whether she will ever pass:* uncertain, unsettled, undetermined, enigmatic, unknown; perplexing, paradoxical, puzzling; difficult, troublesome, worrisome, doubtful, questionable.

Ant. certain, settled, known, undisputed, unquestionable.

proceed *v.* **1** *Proceed to the next lights, then turn left. Please proceed with your work:* go, go forward, move ahead, move forward, go ahead, move on, go on, continue, carry on, progress, advance, make one's way; press on, push on, keep moving. **2** *After everyone was seated, the* *chairman proceeded to announce his plans:* undertake, set out, begin, commence, start; take action, act, move, operate, function, work. **3** *His destitution proceeded from unwise spending:* result, arise, issue, take rise, come, follow, ensue, succeed, be caused, spring, flow, emanate, start, derive, be derived, be produced, originate, grow, stem.

Ant. 1 retreat, go backward, get behind; discontinue, stop; regress, lose ground; stop moving.

◇ *Spelling tip:* Only three common words in the English language end in *-ceed: proceed, exceed,* and *succeed* (along with their various forms, such as *proceeded, exceeds, succeeding,* etc.). Keep these three *-ceed* words in mind: *proCEED, exCEED, sucCEED.*

proceedings *n. pl.* **1** *Minutes of the proceedings were written down by the club secretary:* activity, happenings, occurrences, transactions, events, incidents, operations, affairs, matters, actions, goings-on, doings. **2** *His lawyer is representing him in the proceedings:* legal action, legal process, lawsuit, suit, action at law; litigation, trial, case, cause. **3** *He carefully read the proceedings of the last meeting:* minutes, records, account, report, returns, description, memoranda, archives.

proceeds *n. pl. The proceeds of the bazaar will go to needy families:* profit, gain, receipts, yield, income, revenue, earnings, assets; reward, remuneration, returns; money, lucre, pelf, winnings, takings, pickings.

process *n.* **1** *Sherlock Holmes discovered the murderer by a process of elimination:* method, system, manner, practice, procedure, mode; course of action, plan, scheme, project, line of action, policy, ways and means; measure, step; usage, function. **2** *Adolescence is the process of development from childhood to maturity:* procedure, set of changes, proceeding, passage, course, movement, motion, transformation; unfolding; flux, flow, change, progress, progression.

—*v.* **3** *Grocers' shops sell many foods that have been processed:* prepare, treat, convert, alter, transform; (*variously*) freeze, preserve, freeze-dry, smoke, dehydrate, dry, tin. **4** *We will process your order at once:* fulfil, take care of, fill, ship, handle, deal with, dispose of.

procession *n. The procession moved slowly down the main street:* parade, march, caravan, cavalcade, cortège, train, file, rank, column, array, line; sequence; course; passage, progression, progress, succession.

proclaim *v. The salesman proclaimed that his tonic would cure all ills:* declare, announce, herald, make known, make manifest, make public, broadcast, give out; promulgate, assert, affirm, set forth, state, profess; publish, advertise, circulate, blaze abroad, publicize, trumpet, blazon, call out, blare, cry, sing out, hawk about; tell, voice; report, enunciate, communicate; release, divulge, reveal.

Ant. retract, recall; suppress, repress, conceal, secrete.

proclivity *n. She has a proclivity towards unpunctuality:* propensity, leaning, inclination, disposition, affection, liking, proneness, tendency, predilection, penchant, bent, bias, prejudice, predisposition, turn of the mind; appetite, desire, impulse; *Informal* soft spot.

Ant. dislike, aversion, hatred, loathing, disinclination.

procrastinate *v. Stop procrastinating and finish your homework!:* put off action, postpone, wait till tomorrow; hesitate, hold back, hang back, lag, be dilatory; delay, stall, play for time, temporize, kill time, dally, tarry, loiter, dilly-dally, dawdle, waste time, twiddle one's thumbs, linger, drag one's feet.

Ant. expedite, hasten, hurry, speed, speed up.

◇ *Word origin: Procrastinate* means "to put off until tomorrow." It comes from Latin *pro-* (forward) + *cras* (tomorrow).

procure *v. He was able to procure a Rembrandt etching from the art dealer:* obtain, acquire, get, secure, get into one's hands, lay hands on, attain, achieve, come by; take possession of, receive, pick up; take, appropriate, help oneself to, seize, commandeer; win, earn, gain; get together, accumulate, gather; buy, purchase; cause to occur, effect, bring about, contrive,elicit, induce, evoke, incite.

prod *v.* **1** *The shepherd prodded the sheep with his staff:* poke, jab, prick, flog, whip, lash, needle; shove, push; accelerate, quicken, speed, propel. **2** *The teacher tried to prod the pupils into taking more interest:* impel, stir, incite, excite, stimulate, instigate, prompt; actuate, rouse, stir up, set in motion, move, animate, encourage, motivate; urge, exhort, goad, provoke, egg on, nag, spur, bear down upon, pressurize.

prodigal *adj.* **1** *He had nothing left of his inheritance because of his prodigal ways:* wasteful, spendthrift, unthrifty, over-liberal, profligate, extravagant, exorbitant, lavish, excessive, gluttonous; improvident, dissipating, inordinate, intemperate, immoderate, reckless, impetuous, precipitate, wanton. **2** *The prodigal amount of spawn laid by the fish ensured the survival of the species:* bountiful, profuse, abounding, abundant, plentiful, bounteous, ample; lush, luxuriant, lavish, exuberant, generous; numerous, countless, numberless, innumerable, multitudinous; teeming, swarming, myriad, replete, copious.

—*n.* **3** *The prodigal went through money as if it were water:* spendthrift, squanderer, spender, wastrel, profligate.

Ant. 1 thrifty, frugal, economical, cautious, miserly, stingy; provident, temperate, moderate. **2** scarce, scanty, deficient, scant, meagre, sparse, few, limited.

◇ *Word origin: Prodigal* comes from Latin

prodigere, to drive forth, use up, waste. From this word are derived Latin *prodigus*, spendthrift, and the very rare word *prodigalitas*, on which we base our words *prodigality* and *prodigal*. These are in no way related to *prodigious* and *prodigy*.

prodigious *adj. His knowledge of music was prodigious. A prodigious collection of modern art was on display:* exceptional, rare, singular, extraordinary, uncommon, unique, impressive, striking, noteworthy, renowned; surprising, startling, amazing, astounding, astonishing, dumbfounding, overwhelming, wonderful, remarkable, marvellous, wondrous, miraculous; enormous, vast, huge, immense, far-reaching, large, terrific, big, great, monumental, mighty, stupendous, tremendous, gigantic, colossal, monstrous, grand; inconceivable, unimaginable, unthinkable; unaccustomed, unwonted, unprecedented.

Ant. unexceptional, ordinary, common, usual; unimpressive, unremarkable; small, negligible.

prodigy *n. Mozart was a prodigy who could read, play and improvise music at the age of 5:* gifted child, great talent, young genius, *German* Wunderkind; genius, wizard, master, master-mind, expert, whiz-kid; marvel, wonder, sensation, phenomenon, *Informal* stunner; rare bird, rarity, *Latin* rara avis.

◇ *Word origin: Prodigy* comes from Latin *prodigium*, prophetic sign, omen, portent, marvel. The word literally means "a fore-speaking" — the *-ig-* part is related to the *-age* in *adage*, "a speaking to." It is NOT related to *prodigal*.

produce *v.* **1** *They're thinking of producing a new synthetic fibre:* make, create, manufacture, construct, fashion, shape, compose, devise, fabricate, turn out, frame, evolve, form, concoct, conceive, develop; originate, institute, found, give birth to, beget, generate, invent, procreate, give life to, hatch, bring into being, bring into existence, bring into the world. **2** *The land produces enough to feed us:* provide, supply, furnish, give, bear, yield, afford; flower, sprout, bloom, bear fruit. **3** *Can you produce evidence to clear him?:* show, exhibit, present, show forth, present for inspection, bring into view, advance, cause to appear, put on view, hold up to view, manifest, bring forward, bring in, adduce, evince, set forth, bring out, bring to light, display, put on display; materialize, reveal, divulge, uncover, disclose, unveil, discover, unmask, make plain, *Informal* come up with. **4** *Dim lights and soft music are supposed to produce a romantic atmosphere:* cause, effect, give rise to, set up, put into effect, put in force, effectuate, bring about, bring off; achieve, accomplish, bring to pass, carry into execution.

—*n.* **5** *He has a stall where he sells groceries and farm produce:* agricultural products, staple commodities, fruit and vegetables, greengroceries, foodstuffs.

Ant. 3 conceal, hide, withhold. **4** prevent.

production *n.* **1** *Japan is famous for the production of transistor radios:* making, producing, manufacture, manufacturing; building, construction, formation, origination, creation, fabrication; execution, effectuation, performance, fulfilment. **2** *Several new productions will appear in the West End this season:* presentation, theatrical performance, show, drama, play, stage show, entertainment, musical; motion picture, film, cinema; carnival, circus. **3** *After the production of an eyewitness, the man was convicted of murder:* introduction, appearance, showing, exhibit, display, materialization, show, presentation, manifestation, demonstration; disclosure, revelation.

productive *adj.* **1** *He was a director of a very productive firm:* producing, creating, creative, accomplishing much, prolific, effectual, efficacious; active, busy, vigorous, dynamic. **2** *Through irrigation the desert was turned into productive land:* fruitful, fertile, fecund, proliferous, prolific, fructiferous; luxuriant, rich, plentiful, plenteous, copious, teeming, producing in abundance, yielding. **3** *It was not a productive venture for him:* profitable, remunerative, gainful, worthwhile, paying, money-making. **4** *After being released from prison he became a productive member of society:* useful, contributing, valuable, invaluable.

Ant. 1–4 unproductive. **1** inactive; ineffectual. **2** unfertile, barren, sterile, unfruitful; poor, unyielding. **3** unprofitable, ungainful. **4** useless.

profane *adj.* **1** *His profane language made the women blush:* irreverent, blasphemous, ungodly, godless, sacrilegious, irreligious, impious, unholy; foul, filthy, nasty, vile, abusive; wicked, evil, sinful, shameless, unchaste, unseemly, impure; crude, coarse, vulgar, obscene, lewd, bawdy, ribald, off-colour. **2** *Both sacred and profane music were played at the memorial service:* secular, non-religious, lay, temporal, worldly, earthly, terrestrial.

—*v.* **3** *The infidels profaned the holy place:* desecrate, debase, abuse, commit sacrilege, blaspheme; offend, outrage; misuse, ill-use, waste; pollute, pervert, contaminate, prostitute, violate; mock, revile, scorn.

Ant. 1, 2 sacred, religious, spiritual. **1** holy, reverent, divine; decorous, proper, clean; delicate, seemly.

◇ *Word origin: Profane* and *profanity* come from Latin *pro-* (in front of) + *fanum* (temple), i.e. outside the temple, hence not sacred.

profess *v.* **1** *He professed to be a member of the aristocracy:* claim, allege, lay claim, assume, purport; dissimulate, dissemble, sail under false colours, make a pretence of, pass oneself off, make out; simulate, act, pretend, put on, sham, feign, counterfeit, fake. **2** *He professed himself content with the payment:* confess, admit, own, acknowledge, affirm, confirm, certify, avow, vouch, aver, asserverate, depose; declare, state, proclaim, propound, announce; allege, assert, put forward, offer, advance; tell, say, enunciate; hold forth, contend, maintain. **3** *He professed Catholicism:* declare one's faith in, embrace, believe in, practise.

profession *n.* **1** *What profession will you be studying for?:* occupation, line of work, line, business, job, field, speciality, employment, work, vocation, walk of life, career, calling, métier, pursuit, undertaking, endeavour; office, position, situation, post, field, sphere; practice, service, industry, trade, craft. **2** *She wanted to marry a man in one of the professions:* branch of learning, higher discipline; (*variously*) the Church, law, medicine, the Armed Services, teaching. **3** *He made a profession of eternal gratitude:* declaration, statement, announcement, pronouncement; acknowledgement, confession, affirmation, confirmation, deposition, testimony, attestation; avowal, averment, promise, word, word of honour, troth, plight, pledge, vow, guarantee, assurance; assertion, claim, allegation.

Ant. 1 avocation, hobby; trade.

◇ *Word origin: Profession, profess,* and *professor* come from Latin *pro-* (before) + *fateri* (to avow, declare), hence to *profess* is to declare openly before others, a *profession* is one's declared occupation, and a *professor* is one who declares publicly, as in a lecture-hall.

professional *adj.* **1** *Professional athletes are not allowed to take part in the Olympics:* paid, receiving pay, in business as. **2** *You had better get professional advice before buying stocks or bonds:* highly skilled, competent, knowledgeable, practised, expert, experienced, adept, well-trained, well-informed.

—*n.* **3** *Their house was decorated by a professional:* expert, specialist, authority, adept.

Ant. 1, 3 amateur **2** incompetent, inept.

proficient *adj. She was a proficient typist:* skilled, capable, competent, able, good, adroit, deft, apt, adept, dextrous; expert, clever, sharp, masterly, masterful, efficient, effective, ready, quick, handy; trained, practised, accomplished, experienced, professional; talented, versatile.

Ant. unskilled, incapable, inept, incompetent, bad, maladroit, unaccomplished.

profile *n.* **1** *A profile of the Queen appears on our coinage:* outline, contour, delineation, lineaments, configuration, form, shape, figure; side view, side, half face, silhouette; skyline; picture, portrait, sketch, drawing. **2** *The journalist used to write weekly profiles of men in the news:* biography, short biography, tale, character sketch, vignette.

◇ *Word origin: Profile* comes from Latin *pro-* (forward) + *filum* (thread, line), hence outline.

profit *n.* **1** *Did you make any profit last year?:* gain, return, realization; (*variously*) gross profit, net profit, clear profit, marginal profit; money, remuneration, income, revenue, pay, earnings; proceeds, receipts; consideration, compensation, financial reward. **2** *Gaining good qualifications will be to your profit:* advantage, benefit, interest, advancement, gain, improvement; good, benefaction, boon, favour; service, utility, use, avail, account, value.

—*v.* **3** *Attending those extra classes profited me:* benefit, help, serve, avail, stand in good stead. **4** *You must learn to profit by experience:* make good use of, make the most of, be better for, be improved by, learn a lesson from, reap the benefit of, make use of, utilize, use, put to good use. **5** *He hoped to profit from his investments:* make money, earn, gain.

"Such truth as opposeth no man's profit nor pleasure is to all men welcome."

— *Thomas Hobbes*

---

profitable *adj.* **1** *Selling that piece of property was a profitable venture for me:* gainful, rewarding, yielding profit, paying, money-making, remunerative, lucrative, well-paying; fruitful. **2** *Travel can be a profitable experience:* worthwhile, rewarding, productive, favourable, beneficial, advantageous, salutary, serviceable, useful; valuable, invaluable.

profligate *adj.* **1** *No decent human being wants to have anything to do with one who leads such a profligate life:* dissolute, debauched, depraved, dissipated, degenerate, degraded, immoral, wicked, iniquitous; wanton, loose, abandoned, promiscuous, wild, fast, unprincipled, licentious, lascivious. **2** *Your profligate ways are depleting your fortune:* wasteful, prodigal, extravagant, lavish, unthrifty, spendthrift, improvident; unrestrained, unbridled, reckless.

—*n.* **3** *I won't let my daughter go with that profligate!:* reprobate, profligate person, rake, debauchee, degenerate, *French* roue, libertine, pervert, sinner, wrongdoer; spendthrift, wastrel, prodigal.

Ant. 1 moral, decent, upright; kind, good, virtuous, chaste.

◇ *Word origin: Profligate* comes from Latin *pro-* (forward) + *fligare* (to fling, dash, hurl), to dash to the ground, destroy, hence one who flings down virtue, decency, or money.

profound *adj.* **1** *That was a very profound statement:* deep, thoughtful, wise, sagacious, sage, penetrating, piercing, learned, erudite, intellectual, scholarly, educated; knowledgeable, comprehensive, recondite, omniscent, all-knowing; philosophical, reflective, thoughtful, well-considered, sober, serious, sober-minded; informed, well-informed, knowing, enlightened. **2** *His death had a profound effect on her:* deep, severe, extreme; thorough, thoroughgoing, far-reaching, radical, utter, complete, consummate, penetrating, out and out, piercing, pronounced, decided, positive. **3** *Please accept my most profound apologies:* deeply felt, heartfelt, keenly felt, sincere, heart-stirring, strongly felt, deep-seated, soul-stirring, moving; hearty, intense, keen, acute, abject.

Ant. 1 shallow, superficial, unwise, stupid, unlearned, uneducated, unknowledgeable, thoughtless, inconsiderate; uninformed, unenlightened; imprudent. **2** slight, superficial, shallow, surface, external. **3** insincere, shallow, hollow.

profuse *adj.* **1** *She gave profuse thanks for our contribution. If the rain keeps off, it will be a profuse harvest this year:* generous, munificent, abundant, bountiful, bounteous, copious, ample, rich, lavish. **2** *Your profuse spending has left you almost penniless:* wasteful, unthrifty, prodigal, improvident, spendthrift, intemperate, inordinate, immoderate, excessive, lavish, extravagant.

Ant. 1 meagre, scanty, inadequate, exiguous, sparse, cheap, stinting, skimpy, illiberal, close-fisted. **2** thrifty, penny-pinching, provident, temperate, moderate.

profusion *n. The garden boasted a profusion of flowers:* great amount, great quantity, multiplicity, abundance, multitude; superfluity, extravagance, excess, waste.

"Books are not absolutely dead things, but do contain a potency of life in them to be as active as that soul was whose progeny they are."

—*John Milton*

---

progeny *n. The castle passed into the hands of the duke's progeny and is still owned by the same family today:* descendant, offspring, young, child, children, issue, offshoot; heir, heirs, scion, family, kin, kindred, blood, clan; posterity, race, stock, lineage, breed, line.

programme *n.* **1** *Today's programme includes a tour of the Roman Baths:* schedule, order of events, things to be done, agenda, plan, order of business, curriculum, syllabus; timetable; card, bill, prospectus; book, slate, calendar, bulletin. **2** *The ushers gave everyone a programme of the evening's performance:* list of players, dramatis personae, list of selections; notice, sketch, outline. **3** *New programmes appear on television in the autumn:* show, presentation, production; series.

—*v.* **4** *The computer will only produce the desired result if it has been correctly programmed:* schedule, arrange, set, instruct; design, intend, expect.

progress *n.* **1** *We made swift progress toward the mountains. He made progress with his work:* headway, forward movement, advancement, advance, furtherance; accomplishment, achievement; development, betterment, improvement, success. **2** *Has the new nation's progress been too fast?:* development, growth, rise, promotion; enrichment, enhancement, improvement; forward motion. **3** *No one will be admitted whilst the play is in progress:* process, development, course, unfolding, action, movement, stride.

—*v.* **4** *He progressed within the company so fast that he was made a director in two years:* advance, proceed, move ahead, continue ahead, shoot ahead, go forward, get ahead, make headway, gain, make strides, gain ground, get on. **5** *Have you progressed far in your studies?:* advance, improve, become better, get better, take a turn for the better, grow better, make progress, make strides, make headway; increase, climb, mount; develop, grow, mature, grow up, ripen.

Ant. 1 regression; failure, decline, retreat, retrogression, relapse, recession. **4** move backward, regress, retrogress, recede, go backward; lose ground, lose, get behind. **5** become worse, grow worse.

◇ *Pronunciation tip:* Some people fail to distinguish properly between the two different pronunciations of the word *progress*, one for the noun and the other for the verb. The noun should be clearly stressed on the first syllable: *You must make more PROGress if you're going to finish the work on time.* The verb *to progress* should be clearly stressed on the second syllable: *Show your pass and proGRESS through the gate.*

progression *n. The film showed the progression of events leading up to the incorporation of Austria in the Third Reich in April 1938:* sequence, succession, consecutiveness, continuance, order, series, continuation, continuousness; string, chain, strain; course, run; progress, advancement, furtherance, advance, forward movement.

progressive *adj.* **1** *He was an up-and-coming, progressive committee-man:* concerned with progress, supporting change; dynamic, forward-going, forward-looking, going ahead; advancing, advanced; enterprising, up-to-date; radical, reformist. **2** *It was a progressive disease and he would suffer more and more:* advancing step-by-step, gradual, increasingly severe, steadily going on; travelling, spreading, ongoing.

—*n.* **3** *Many young politicians are progressives:* radical, reformist; activist; populist.

Ant. 1, 3 reactionary, conservative.

prohibit *v.* **1** *The law prohibits double-parking:* forbid, disallow, proscribe, say no to, negate, disqualify, deny, veto. **2** *He threw himself in front of the door and prohibited us from leaving:* prevent, inhibit, check, obstruct, impede, limit, hinder, block, curb, hamper, bar, interfere with; delay, stay, stop, preclude, obviate; ban, suppress, repress, withhold; restrict, enjoin, restrain.

Ant. 1, 2 permit, let, allow, suffer, tolerate; authorize, order. **1** endure, bear; command, consent to, give permission, license. **2** direct, empower, give consent, give leave; further.

◇ *Word origin: Prohibit* and *prohibition* come from Latin *pro-* (in front of) + *habere* (to hold), to hold in front, hold back, hinder.

prohibitive Also **prohibitory** *adj. Prohibitive laws discouraged the drug trade. The project was abandoned because the costs were prohibitive:* inhibitive, restrictive, circumscriptive, enjoining, restraining, forbidding; suppressive, repressive; preventive, injunctive; hindering, obstructive, disallowing, disqualifying, inadmissible, unacceptable.

project *n.* **1** *My project this year is to refurnish the house:* undertaking, job, task, work, activity, assignment; plan, design, scheme, intention, ambition, aim, objective, goal.

—v. **2** *Could you project a new marketing technique for us?:* plan, design, draft, outline, propose, devise, frame, contrive, concoct, invent, map out. **3** *Ledges project about one foot all round the building:* extend, jut out, stand out, stick out, protrude, overhang, beetle, bend over. **4** *Remember to project your voice so that you can be heard in the back row:* transmit, throw, throw out, cast, fling; eject, ejaculate, emit, expel, discharge, send; shoot, propel, hurtle, launch, fire. **5** *Can you project next month's sales?:* forecast, plan ahead, predetermine, extrapolate, calculate, reckon, predict.

◇ *Pronunciation tip: Project* is, of course, correctly pronounced one way as a noun, a *project,* and another way as a verb, *to project.* The noun is stressed on the first syllable, a *PROJ-ect: Our school PROJect was to decorate the gym.* The verb is stressed on the second syllable, *to pro-JECT: Can you proJECT how much the trip will cost you?*

projection *n.* **1** *The narrow projection scarcely provided a foothold:* ledge, shelf, extension, overhang, extrusion, protrusion, protuberance, bulge, ridge, bump. **2** *His projection shows what the population is likely to be in 1999:* estimate, estimation, prediction, prospectus, forecast, extrapolation.

proletariat *n. Lord Nuffield rose from the proletariat to become a big businessman:* working class, labouring classes, labourers, rank and file, wage-earners, the common people, the masses, the people, the crowd; the multitude; commonalty, commoners, commonage; *Greek* hoi polloi; *Latin* plebs, populus, vulgus mobile; *Disparaging* lower classes, lower orders, the herd, the horde, the mob, rabble, the great unwashed, *French* canaille.

Ant. upper class, aristocracy, upper crust, gentry, nobility.

◇ *Word origin:* The *proletariat,* the working class, comes from Latin *proletarius,* the propertyless and lower class of the ancient Roman state. The Roman word was based on Latin *proles,* offspring, because — having no property or status — *proletarians* were considered useful to the state only because they bred children.

proliferate *v. Rabbits proliferated after they were introduced into Australia:* multiply, increase, reproduce rapidly, breed quickly, procreate, regenerate, propagate, pullulate, teem, swarm; hatch, breed.

◇ *Word origin:* See PROLIFIC.

prolific *adj.* **1** *My pet hamsters were so prolific that they soon needed a larger cage:* reproductive, proliferous, proliferative, breeding, propagating, fertile, fruitful, yielding, fecund, procreative, multiplying, progenitive, germinative. **2** *Haydn was a prolific composer who wrote 104 symphonies:* very productive, creative.

Ant. 1 barren, unfruitful, unproductive, infertile, sterile. **2** unproductive.

◇ *Word origin: Prolific* and *proliferate* come from Latin *proles* (offspring) + *facere* (to make).

prolong *v. We had to prolong our stay for another week:* lengthen, extend, make longer, stretch, elongate, attenuate, protract, draw out; maintain, sustain, continue, perpetuate, spin out, drag out; slow down, hold back, delay, retard.

Ant. curtail, shorten, abridge, abbreviate, lessen; expedite, hurry.

prominence *n.* **1** *His prominence in the musical world is established:* eminence, distinction, importance, pre-eminence, fame, renown, prestige, celebrity, notability, reputation, name; conspicuousness, salience, noticeability, significance; brilliance, greatness, illustriousness; grandeur, nobility, majesty, splendour; respectability, honour, dignity; mark, credit, popularity, notoriety; weight, influence, significance, might, superiority. **2** *Her beauty was marred by the slight prominence of her teeth:* projection, extrusion, protuberance, bulge, convexity, process, excurvature, excrescence, tumescence, rising, swelling, protrusion, hump, knurl, bump, knob, lump, node. **3** *The house was built on a prominence overlooking the sea:* high point, height, promontory, precipice, pinnacle, summit, crest, cliff; elevation, high place, peak, mountain, hill, knoll, rise, hillock, rising ground, mound, hummock, tor, dune; overhang, bluff, extension, outcrop, headland, spur.

prominent *adj.* **1** *They opened a shop on the most prominent site in town:* conspicuous, evident, noticeable, apparent, easily seen, salient, obvious, definite, well-marked, pronounced, remarkable; discernible, recognizable; glaring, staring, arresting, striking. **2** *He has a* *prominent nose:* jutting out, extended, jutting, protruding, protrusive, standing out, protuberant, bulging, projecting, convex, swelling, swollen. **3** *He's a prominent archaeologist:* important, prestigious, pre-eminent, illustrious, distinguished, honoured, respected, well-known, leading, eminent, outstanding, renowned, celebrated, notable, famous.

Ant. 1 inconspicuous, unnoticeable, indefinite; unrecognizable; secondary, insignificant, minor, indistinguishable, indistinct, unimportant. **2** receding, concave, indented. **3** unimportant, undistinguished, unknown.

promiscuous *adj.* **1** *Countless students enjoyed her promiscuous hospitality:* indiscriminate, uncritical, indiscriminative, undiscriminating, undiscerning, unselective, indifferent, random, unmeasured, undirected, helter-skelter, haphazard, desultory, casual, careless, aimless. **2** *The cupboard contained a promiscuous array of things:* mixed, heterogeneous, intermixed, mixed together, mixed-up, mingled, commingled, composite, miscellaneous, variegated, motley; diverse; sweeping, wholesale; jumbled, scrambled, disorderly, disordered, disorganized, disarranged; chaotic, perplexed, confused. **3** *She could never live down her reputation as a promiscuous girl:* wanton, loose, wild, immoral, unchaste, unvirtuous, impure; licentious, lewd, lascivious, dissipated, of easy virtue, immoral, morally loose.

Ant. 1 discriminating, discerning, selective, critical, distinguishing; careful, prudent. **2** unmixed, unmingled; orderly, neat, ordered, organized, arranged. **3** moral, upright, temperate, modest, chaste, virtuous, pure.

◇ *Word origin: Promiscuous* comes from Latin *pro-* (thoroughly) + *miscere* (to mix). Latin *promiscuus,* indiscriminate, is used in the same senses as our word *promiscuous,* except insofar as the latter refers to sexual *promiscuity.* The Latin word's only reference to sex is an indirect one, in the phrase *conubia promiscua,* mixed marriage — i.e. between patricians and plebeians.

promise *n.* **1** *Give me your promise that you'll never do that again:* word, pledge, word of honour, vow, oath, troth, plight, avowal, covenant, agreement, stipulation; assurance, guarantee, warrant, warranty; declaration, profession. **2** *The young viola player is full of promise:* potential, good prospects, cause for hope.
—v. **3** *I promise never to tell anyone:* give a promise, take an oath, give one's word, pledge, vow, plight, aver, avow, vouch, guarantee, assure, warrant; covenant, agree, undertake, be bound, commit oneself, plight one's troth, make an avowal, swear, swear an oath, assert under oath. **4** *The skies promise better weather in the morning:* indicate, give hope of, make one expect, lead one to expect, hint at, suggest, betoken, augur, imply; hold a probability, be probable.

promising *adj. He's a promising new painter. It was a promising start in a new field:* giving promise, full of promise; favourable, hopeful, reassuring, assuring, encouraging; rising, advancing, up-and-coming; inspiriting, bright, cheerful, cheering, rosy, optimistic, happy; propitious, auspicious, of good omen, lucky, fortunate, looking up.

Ant. unfavourable, unpromising, discouraging.

promontory *n. The house was on a promontory overlooking the sea:* headland, high point of land, point, neck of land, spur, ness, cape, peninsula, embankment; projection, overhang, precipice; cliff, height.

promote *v.* **1** *He was in town to promote his new book:* publicize, advertise, help the progress of, forward, help forward, further, advance, urge forward, *Slang* push, plug; work for, render a service to, work toward, clear the way for, ease, expedite; speak for, advocate, foster, encourage, support; cultivate, refine, develop, improve upon, enhance; aid, help, assist, abet. **2** *They promoted the corporal to the rank of sergeant:* advance in rank, raise, elevate, upgrade; prefer.

Ant. 1 impede; hinder, obstruct, prevent.

promotion *n.* **1** *The salesman's promotion to general manager occurred without much ceremony:* advancement in position or rank, elevation, rise, upgrading, preferment. **2** *The group were in town for the promotion of their new album:* advertising, advertisement, publicity, *Slang* ballyhoo; advancement, furtherance, promulgation, advance, progress, encouragement, boosting.

Ant. 1 demotion, degradation. **2** denigration, discouragement.

prompt *adj.* **1** *Thank you for your prompt attention to the matter:* instant, immediate, quick, instantaneous, unhesitating; punctual, timely, on time, sharp, eager, zealous, lively.
—v. **2** *Whatever prompted you to act in such a way?:* spur, impel, induce, inspire, stimulate, actuate, stir, excite, inspirit, activate, incite, move, motivate, instigate, goad, provoke, cause, occasion; push, thrust, press, propel, drive, force; incline, dispose, influence, determine, persuade. **3** *If the actor forgets his lines someone in the wings will prompt him:* cue, assist one's memory, supply with a cue; remind, jog the memory, prod, set back on the track; assist, help out, put words in one's mouth.

Ant. 1, 2 remiss, lax, slack; dilatory, hesitating, slow, late, tardy. **2** inactive, sluggish, unready, inattentive, unobservant; inanimate; inefficient; unresponsive. **3** discourage, dissuade, deter.

promulgate *v. T. H. Huxley promulgated Darwin's theory of evolution:* set forth, expound, present, communicate, enunciate, elucidate; teach publicly, instruct, explain, interpret; sponsor, foster, promote.

prone *adj.* **1** *She's prone to giggling at the most inopportune moments:* inclined, susceptible, liable, tending, disposed, predisposed, apt, subject, accustomed, habituated. **2** *He was lying prone on the couch, fast asleep:* flat, face down, recumbent, level, prostrate, horizontal.
Ant. 1 averse, disinclined. **2** erect, upright, vertical, face up, supine.
◇ *Usage note: Prone* actually means lying flat on the stomach, face downwards, whilst the reverse is *supine*, lying flat on the back, face up.
◇ *Word origin: Prone* is ultimately derived from Latin *pro-*, forward. Latin *pronus*, bending forward and downward, is the antonym of Latin *supinus*, bending over backwards. Latin *pronus* also means "inclined" as in English (sense **1** above).

prong *n. Forks have three or four prongs:* tine, point, projection; hook, tooth, horn, branch; spur, spike, barb.

pronounce *v.* **1** *Foreigners find it hard to pronounce certain words in English:* articulate, speak, say, enunciate, vocalize, sound; give forth, utter, emit; frame, form. **2** *I now pronounce you man and wife:* declare, proclaim, announce, state, voice, orate; judge, pass judgement.
◇ *Spelling tip:* Don't confuse the word *proNUNciation* with the word *proNOUNCE.* They are pronounced and spelt differently, each being spelt — and pronounced — exactly as it sounds.

> **Exploring the Word**: The Latin *nuntiare*, to announce, report, gives us *announce; denounce*, literally to announce down, to degrade by an announcement or report; *enunciate*, literally to announce out, hence to speak out, speak distinctly; *pronounce* and *pronouncement*, literally announce forth, formal declaration; and *renounce*, to take back one's original announcement or declaration.

pronounced *adj. He speaks with a pronounced Scottish burr:* decided, distinct, unmistakable, broad, definite, well-defined, clear-cut, unquestionable, positive, clearly indicated, clear, plain, noticeable, obvious, conspicuous; apparent, strongly marked, outstanding, arresting, vivid, bold; patent, evident, recognizable, unhidden, visible, manifest, undisguised.

pronouncement *n. The prisoner stood and heard the pronouncement of his sentence:* official statement, formal statement, announcement, declaration, proclamation, decree.

proof *n.* **1** *Did you have any proof that your alibi was true?:* conclusive evidence, corroboration, verification, certification, grounds, documentation, ratification, substantiation, confirmation, attestation. **2** *Will your theory stand up to proof?:* trial, test, probation, essay, assessment, scrutiny, examination, ordeal, weighing. **3** *The editor corrected the proofs:* (*in printing*) trial impression, proof sheet, galley proof, galley.
◇ *Word origin:* See PROBABLE.

prop *n.* **1** *Beams were used as props to keep the wall from collapsing:* support, mainstay, pillar, buttress, reinforcement, stanchion, sustainer, supporter, stay, brace.
—*v.* **2** *They propped up the stage scenery with several braces:* support, shore up, hold up, brace, shoulder, buttress, underpin. **3** *She propped the broom against the chair:* rest, lean, set, stand.

propagate *v.* **1** *It's necessary for the species to propagate itself in order to stay in existence:* multiply, reproduce, proliferate, breed, progenerate, procreate, increase, generate, engender, beget, give birth, hatch, spawn. **2** *The missionaries propagated the teachings of Christianity throughout the islands:* spread, disseminate, make known, promulgate; publish, publicize, issue, give to the world, broadcast, noise abroad, trumpet, blazon; circulate; make public, give currency to, bring into the open, put forth, purvey, report, notify, proclaim, preach, give out; tell, repeat, enunciate, air, communicate, impart, herald; whisper about, rumour, hint abroad; scatter, disperse, bestrew, sow, spray; instil, implant, inculcate.
Ant. 1 reduce, diminish, decrease; extinguish. **2** hush up, silence, suppress, repress, stifle.
◇ *Word origin: Propagate* comes from Latin *propagare*, to cause (a plant) to increase or spread by means of slips, from *propages*, slip, shoot, offspring. The word *propaganda* (based on *propagate*) comes from the title of the *Sacra Congregatio de Propaganda Fide* (Sacred Congregation for Propagating the Faith), a Congregation of the Roman Curia founded by Pope Gregory XV in 1622 and charged with overseeing the church's foreign missions; hence, *propaganda* became associated with a systematic effort to spread the Roman Catholic faith, then with any systematic effort to persuade people to support or adopt any particular opinion or course of action.

propagation *n.* **1** *The "multiplication" spoken of in the first chapter of Genesis is what we now call "propagation of the species":* reproduction, procreation, breeding; siring, begetting; giving birth, pregnancy, gestation, bearing, yielding; hatching, laying, spawning; generation, engendering. **2** *The Ministry of Information was concerned with the propagation of false information:* spreading, dispersion, diffusion, dissemination, circulation, distribution; transmission, publication, issuance.

propel *v. The bow serves to propel the arrow:* shoot, catapult, eject, set in motion, impel, drive forward, drive, force, push forward, push, prod, shove, goad, poke; start, launch, thrust, precipitate; send, discharge, project, toss, cast, hurl, pitch, heave, sling.

propensity *n. Children have a propensity for getting into mischief:* inclination, leaning, tendency, proclivity, predilection, liking, partiality, weakness, preference, penchant; attraction, affinity, sympathy, favour, pleasure, taste, fancy; turn, bent, predisposition, bias, disposition.

Ant. disinclination, aversion, loathing, dislike, hatred, antipathy, displeasure.

proper *adj.* **1** *I was never taught the proper way to hold a pencil:* right, correct, appropriate, suitable, fitting, applicable, pertinent, germane, relevant; apropos, fit, apt, meet, conformable; conventional, orthodox. **2** *Use proper language in the company of ladies:* decorous, decent, becoming, seemly, befitting, fitting, suitable, fit, acceptable; polite, courteous; modest, nice. **3** *Please go to your proper places:* individual, own, assigned, respective, particular, specific; distinguishing, peculiar, distinctive, characteristic, typical, appropriate, marked, representative. **4** *The city proper is half the size of the metropolitan area:* strictly defined, in the limited sense, within legal limits, officially bounded, per se; express, particular, precise, correct, true.

Exploring the Word: Latin *proprius*, one's own, gives us *property*, both in the sense of a quality or attribute (because *proper* to one thing and not others) and in the sense of "ownership," and *proprietor*, an owner; *proper*, *propriety*, and *appropriate*, referring to that which is native or proper to one's own self or to society; and *expropriate*, to take from one's possession and give to the state.

properly *adv.* **1** *You conducted yourself properly:* in a proper manner, appropriately, suitably, aptly, acceptably; decently, decorously, politely, tastefully; conventionally. **2** *If you do it properly the first time, you won't have to do it again:* correctly, exactly, right, without error, accurately, precisely, perfectly.

property *n.* **1** *I leave all my property to my son:* belongings, effects, possessions, goods; estate, wealth, assets, resources, holdings, chattels; appointments; funds, means, investments, stock, treasure, capital, moneys; right of possession, ownership, title, proprietorship. **2** *We're interested in buying property in Ireland:* land, real estate, realty, acres, acreage, grounds, estates, territory. **3** *One of the properties of water is to expand when it freezes:* quality, aspect, characteristic, trait, feature, particularity, attribute; peculiarity, idiosyncrasy, singularity, individuality; mark, point, badge, earmark.

prophecy *n.* **1** *She had the gift of prophecy and was rarely wrong:* foretelling the future, prediction, forecasting, soothsaying, forecast, divination, prognostication. **2** *Her prophecies nearly always came true:* prediction, forecast, prognostication; augury, portent; revelation, sign from God.

◇ *Usage note:* Don't confuse the noun *a prophecy*, a prediction or divine discourse, with the verb *to prophesy*, to predict, to foretell with supernatural powers. Thus, *The hermit's prophecy is that the world will come to an end this year*, but *The hermit said, "I prophesy that the end of the world is at hand."*

prophesy *v. The soothsayer prophesied that Caesar would meet his doom:* predict, foretell, forecast, divine, soothsay, prognosticate, premonish, warn, foresee, augur, portend, apprehend, forbode.

"The best qualification of a prophet is to have a good memory." —*Lord Halifax*

prophet *Fem.* **prophetess** *n.* **1** *He claimed to be a prophet of the Lord:* revealer of the word of God, proclaimer of holy truth; evangelist, inspired spokesman, guide, intercessor, interpreter, preacher. **2** *Is she really a prophetess or is there a trick in her prophecies?:* predictor, foreteller, forecaster, seer, prognosticator, prophesier, sibyl, sage, soothsayer, oracle, diviner, augur; crystal-gazer, fortune-teller; sorcerer.

◇ *Word origin: Prophet, prophecy,* and *prophesy* (Greek *pro-*, before, + *phanai*, to speak) come from Greek *prophētēs*, a (divinely inspired) predictor.

proponent *n. She was a proponent of women's rights:* advocate, supporter, exponent, champion, spokesman, spokeswoman, enthusiast, apologist, representative; defender, vindicator, backer, partisan, upholder, votary, patron, friend.

proportion *n.* **1** *The proportion of gin to vermouth in a martini is three to one:* relative amount, relationship, ratio, balance, distribution, correlation, correspondence. **2** *The size of the furniture should be in proportion to the size of the room:* proper relation, balance, symmetry, perspective, proportionality, ideal distribution, evenness, consistency, commensuration, correspondence; harmony, agreement. **3 proportions** *The proportions of the room allowed us to put in a grand piano:* dimensions, size, extent, measurements, area, scope, expanse, range, span, spread, width, breadth; amplitude, magnitude, volume, capacity, greatness, bulk, mass. **4** *A large proportion of the report was written by someone else:* part, amount; division, segment, fraction, share, portion; ratio, quota, percentage, measure, lot, degree.

Ant. 2 disproportion, unevenness, inconsistency, disparity; disagreement, contrast, disharmony.

proposal *n.* **1** *The member put forward a proposal to improve public transport:* recommendation, proposition, plan, programme, course, scheme, resolution, line of action; plot, design, conception, idea, stratagem; prospectus, prospect, presentation, outline, draft, sketch, theory. **2** *I've decided to accept their proposal and spend the summer holidays on their yacht:* invitation, proposition, offer, suggestion, motion, appeal, proffer, bid, nomination, presentation, overture; marriage proposition, suit.

propose *v.* **1** *He proposed a brand new system of accounting. He proposed his new neighbour for membership of the club:* recommend, suggest, present, submit, tender, proffer, come up with, offer for consideration, introduce, bring forward, put forward, put forth, advance, propound, set forth. **2** *She proposes to move within the month:* plan, intend, set about, mean, design, plot, scheme, undertake, venture, purpose, determine, expect, aspire, aim, hope, contemplate, have in mind, have in view, have a mind. **3** *He proposed to her on bended knee:* make an offer of marriage, pay suit; ask for one's hand, affiance; *Informal* pop the question.

proposition *n.* **1** *The man wanted to buy our house and made us an attractive proposition:* offer, proposal, offer of terms, deal, bargain; negotiation, agreement, stipulation, contract, guarantee, assurance. **2** *The members voted on two major propositions:* proposal, suggestion, recommendation, scheme, resolution, plan, undertaking; subject, topic, issue, question, matter, point.

propriety *n. Always conduct yourself with propriety:* correctness; courtesy, decorum, good behaviour, decorousness, dignity, good manners, etiquette, formality, gentlemanly or ladylike behaviour, respectability; savoir-faire, appropriateness, becomingness, applicability, fitness, suitableness, seemliness, aptness, rightness.

prosaic *adj. The guests exchanged prosaic remarks and glanced at their watches:* dull, flat, tiresome, dry, stale, unimaginative, vapid, pedestrian, plebeian, hackneyed, platitudinous, uninteresting, unentertaining, tedious, monotonous, dull, spiritless, jejune, trite, common, matter-of-fact, humdrum, usual, routine, ordinary; prosy, wordy, unpoetical.

Ant. exciting, imaginative, fascinating, interesting, entertaining, spirited; uncommon, unusual, extraordinary; poetical.

proscribe *v. During the Renaissance the church proscribed scientific works like those of Galileo:* denounce, condemn, censure, disapprove, repudiate; curse, damn, anathematize; outlaw, prohibit, forbid, interdict, ban, excommunicate; banish, exile; boycott.

Ant. allow, permit, encourage, aid.

◇ *Usage note: Proscribe* means to ban something, as by decree: *My religion proscribes the use of alcohol and other stimulants.* Don't confuse this word with *prescribe*, which means to recommend, as for health reasons: *The doctor prescribed a strong medicine.*

prosecute *v.* **1** *They are prosecuting him for murder:* try, put on trial, arraign, indict, bring before a court, bring to justice, bring to trial; sue, bring action against, bring suit against, prefer charges against, go to law, take to court. **2** *The detective prosecuted his search for the ringleader throughout London:* persevere in, be resolute in, stick to, keep at or on, persist in, continue, prolong, maintain, sustain; follow up, pursue, go on with, carry on, wage, see through.

◇ *Usage note: Prosecute* and *persecute* are too close in sound not to be confusing. *Prosecute* means to try by law, bring to trial: *The PROsecuting counsel will PROsecute the accused. Persecute* means to oppress or harass persistently: *The Romans PERsecuted the early Christians.*

prospect Usually **prospects** *n.* **1** *The prospects for world disarmament aren't too good:* chances, outlook, probability of success, likelihood, probability; anticipation, foretaste, expectation, hope, promise. **2** *I am excited at the prospect of visiting Quebec:* expectation, contemplation, anticipation, expectancy, hope, ambition; plan, design, proposal. **3** *The prospect from the balcony was breath-taking:* view, vision, picture; scene, vista, panorama; outlook, aspect. **4** *The salesman worked hard to find some new prospects:* potential client, potential customer, candidate, possibility.

—*v.* **5** *He prospected for diamonds in Rhodesia:* explore, seek, search; go after, look for; work a mine.

prospective *adj.* **1** *The prospective merger of the two companies has excited everyone:* future, coming, impending, approaching, to come, close to hand, to be, forthcoming, about to be, eventual, destined; in prospect, in view, foreseen, on the horizon, expected, looked-for, intended, hoped-for, in expectation; in the wind, looming, threatening. **2** *Is she a prospective customer?:* likely, potential, promising.

prosper *v. The business prospered under new management:* thrive, gain, get on, get ahead, make good, be fortunate, fare well, come off well, run smoothly; be successful, flourish, succeed; advance, increase, progress, flower, bear fruit, fructify; make one's fortune, grow rich.

Ant. fail, lose, be unfortunate, be unsuccessful; decrease, be fruitless; grow poor.

◇ *Word origin: Prosperity* is just around the corner — at least everyone hopes it is. *Prosper, prosperity,* and *prosperous* come from Latin *prosper*, fortunate, answering to one's hopes (from *pro-*, for, + *sperare*, to hope).

prosperity *n. He enjoyed his new prosperity:* success, well-being, affluence, thriving condition, material comfort, ease, prosperousness; good fortune, run of luck, good luck, profit, advantage, gain, advance, progress, advancement; affluence, wealth, bounty, opulence, luxury, abundance, plenty; blessings, welfare; palmy days, halcyon days, golden age, good times.

Ant. want, poverty, indigence, destitution, misfortune, bad luck, disadvantage; failure, reverses, adversity; shortage, depression.

"Peace be within thy walls, and prosperity within thy palaces." —*Psalms CXXII. 7*

---

prosperous *adj.* **1** *He had the well-fed look of a prosperous businessman:* successful, thriving, flourishing; fortunate, lucky; rich, opulent, wealthy, affluent, moneyed; well-to-do, comfortable, well-off, in easy circumstances; *Slang* on easy street. **2** *The auction got off to a prosperous start:* auspicious, propitious, providential, fortunate, of good omen, lucky, timely, opportune; good, favourable, promising, well-disposed, heartening, hopeful, encouraging, cheering, reassuring, pleasing; bright, rosy, golden, smiling, sunny, fair, happy.

Ant. **1** unsuccessful, unfortunate, unlucky; failing; poor, impoverished; defeated, beaten. **2** unpropitious, unfortunate, inauspicious, unlucky, untimely, inopportune; bad, unfavourable, unpromising.

prostitute *n.* **1** *The police tried to clear the area of pimps and prostitutes:* whore, harlot, slut, street-walker, lewd woman, loose woman, fallen woman, jade, bawd, hussy, strumpet, trollop, call-girl; courtesan; *Informal* floozie, tart, brass.

—*v.* **2** *The poet prostituted her talent, writing greeting-card verses:* debase, cheapen, sell out, corrupt, pervert, spoil, defile, debauch; abuse, misuse, misemploy, misdirect, misapply; profane, desecrate.

prostrate *v.* **1** *The slaves were forced to prostrate themselves before the king:* bow down, kneel down, abase, kowtow, fall to one's knees. **2** *The wrestler prostrated his opponent:* throw flat, flatten; overthrow, overcome, *Informal* floor.

—*adj.* **3** *The prostrate slaves didn't get up until after the king left:* lying flat, lying full length, lying face down, stretched out, laid out, prone, horizontal, recumbent, flat; bowed low, supplicating, beseeching, crouching, on bended knee, on one's knees. **4** *She was prostrate after hiking so far on that hot day:* overcome, worn out, bone weary, dead tired, exhausted, prostrated, spent, *Informal* fagged, whacked, on one's last legs, flaked out.

prostration *n.* **1** *The slaves showed honour to the king by their humble prostration before him:* act of prostrating; bow, genuflection, kneeling; submission, subjection, lowliness, abasement. **2** *In his prostration and grief he wasn't able to cope with the funeral arrangements:* exhaustion, weakness, weariness, enervation, dejection, depression; paralysis, impotence, helplessness, depth of misery, desolation, despondency, desperation, despair, anguish, woe, distress, wretchedness, heartache, sorrow, misery, grief.

protect *v. The troops were there to protect the townspeople. Use an umbrella to protect yourself from the rain:* guard, shield, defend, watch over, safeguard, secure, take care of, care for, tend, look after; shelter, cover, hide, veil, screen; keep, maintain, sustain, conserve, save, preserve.

Ant. attack, assault, assail; expose.

◇ *Word origin: Protect* and *protection* come from Latin *pro-* (before) + *tegere* (to cover), hence to shield or take precautions against attack or harm.

protection *n.* **1** *A policeman's first duty is the protection of the people:* protecting, guarding, safeguard, defence, championship, preservation, safe keeping, guardianship, custody, charge, care, keep, conservation, saving; support, aid, assistance; immunity, safety, security. **2** *An umbrella serves as a protection against the rain:* protector, shield, guard, preserver, safeguard, security; buffer, fence, wall; cover, shade, screen, shelter; asylum, refuge, preserve, sanctuary.

protective *adj.* **1** *Camouflage is man-made protective coloration:* protecting, guarding, safeguarding, safe keeping, preventive, defensive. **2** *He felt protective towards his younger sister:* sheltering, shielding; watchful, vigilant, heedful, careful, solicitous; fatherly, motherly, paternal, maternal, sisterly, brotherly, big-brotherly, avuncular, grandfatherly, grandmotherly.

protest *n.* **1** *The student protest was organised as part of the campaign for bigger grants:* demonstration, march, picketing, boycott, sit-in, strike; opposition, dissent, contradiction; dispute, disagreement, dissidence, resistance, disaffection, difference of opinion, demur, discountenance, remonstrance, remonstration, deprecation, renunciation, formal complaint, disclaimer; objection, protestation; *Informal* kick, beef, gripe.

—*v.* **2** *Consumer groups are protesting against higher prices:* complain, express disapproval, cry out, object, take exception; oppose, disapprove, dissent, beg to differ, disagree, differ in opinion, contradict, deny, controvert. **3** *The defendant protested his innocence:* assert, vow, avow, declare, contend, insist, announce, put or set forth, put forward, propound, hold out, maintain, offer; profess, speak, state, enunciate, pronounce; testify, attest, affirm, asseverate, aver, assure, allege, avouch.

Ant. **1** endorsement, agreement, sanction;

acquiescence, approval. **2** approve, agree, sanction, endorse, acclaim, subscribe to.

◇ *Pronunciation tip: Protest* is, of course, correctly pronounced one way as a noun, *He made a PRO-test to the referee* (stress the first syllable), and another way as a verb, *He pro-TEST-ed loudly to the police* (stress the second syllable).

protocol *n. In accordance with protocol, the Foreign Secretary met the visiting diplomat at the airport:* diplomatic or court etiquette; proprieties, code of behaviour, good form, decorum, formality, manners, usage, customs, standards, conventions, dictates of society.

◇ *Word origin: Protocol* comes from Greek *prōtokollon*, the first sheet glued to a papyrus roll or to the inside cover of a book, with a table or enumeration of the book's contents explaining any restrictions as to who should or should not know of them. The word is based on Greek *prōtos* (first) + *kolla* (glue).

protract *v. The ceremony was protracted by many long-winded speeches:* prolong, extend, lengthen, draw or stretch out, drag out, spin out, keep going, keep up.

protrude *v. Nails protruded from the board and had to be removed in the interests of safety:* jut out, project, stand out, stick out; bulge, swell, belly, push forward.

protuberance *n. On his cheek he has a large protuberance which looks like a boil:* bulge, swelling, prominence, projection, excrescence, *Archaic* protuberancy; knob, bump, hump, knot, lump, node, knurl; convexity, excurvature, roundness, bow; elevation, rising, ridge, welt, weal.

proud *adj.* **1** *He was a proud man who resisted his friends' offers of help:* independent, self-sufficient, dignified, scrupulous, honourable, self-respecting; strict, punctilious, principled, high-minded; lofty, elevated, reserved, distinguished; fine, admirable, august. **2** *I'm so proud of you!:* filled with pride, pleased, satisfied, gratified, contented, delighted, happy. **3** *He was one of those proud, boastful men that you couldn't bear listening to:* conceited, vain, smug, self-satisfied, self-important; prideful, self-praising, bragging, boastful, braggart, egotistical, swollen, vainglorious, know-all, complacent; pompous, overbearing; assuming, affected, puffed-up, inflated, bloated; arrogant, insolent, flaunting; patronizing, condescending, supercilious, disdainful, contemptuous, intolerant; haughty, aloof, snobbish, lordly, high and mighty, imperious; *Informal* uppish, uppity, snooty, cocky, stuck-up; *Slang* toffee-nosed, high-hat. **4** *It was a proud time for his parents when he received his diploma:* glorious, exalted, elevated, euphoric. **5** *The young aristocrat bore a proud name:* stately, noble, majestic, magnificent, great, lordly, grand, august; revered, venerable, storied, cherished.

Ant. 1 humble, lowly, submissive; ignoble, dishonourable, undignified, servile, cringing, abject. **2** ashamed, displeased, dissatisfied, discontented. **3** humble, unassuming, modest, unobtrusive, meek, unpresuming, deferential. **4** ignominious, humiliating. **5** base, ignoble.

prove *v.* **1** *The testimony of eyewitnesses proved that he was innocent. This document proves that she has a legal claim to the estate:* verify, establish, substantiate, bear out, uphold, support, sustain, corroborate, document, witness, authenticate, confirm, affirm, attest, certify, warrant, testify to; justify, make good, validate, ascertain, show clearly, demonstrate, manifest, evidence. **2** *He devised a system for proving new marketing techniques:* test, try, try out, put to the test, verify, make trial of, subject to trial; check, analyse, examine, probe, look into. **3** *It proved a waste of time:* result in, turn out to be, be found to be, end up, wind up, eventuate, result.

Ant. 1 disprove, refute, discredit, rule out.

◇ *Usage note:* Both *proved* and *proven* are correct as the past participle of *prove*, though *proven* is rather literary, except in Scotland where it frequently occurs in a legal context, of a case *not proven*.

◇ *Word origin:* See PROBABLE.

proverb *n. He lives by the proverb, "Early to bed and early to rise makes a man healthy, wealthy, and wise":* popular saying, adage, maxim, aphorism, truism, accepted truth; epigram, precept, apothegm, saw, axiom, moral; dictum, mot, byword, motto; cliché.

"A proverb is no proverb to you till your life has illustrated it." —*John Keats*

---

provide *v.* **1** *Was he able to provide you with the information? The Red Cross provides food and shelter for victims of disaster:* furnish, give, place at one's disposal, offer, submit, present, tender, impart, render; yield, produce, grant, confer, bestow, donate, contribute, afford, pay, allow, accord, award, deliver, dispense; arm, equip, fit, outfit, supply. **2** *He worked hard to provide for his old age:* prepare, make plans, take measures, anticipate needs; get ready, make ready, provision; arrange, plan, accumulate, save up; make arrangements, make provision, cater. **3** *The contract provides that he shall be recompensed for any loss that he incurs:* state, stipulate, postulate, specify, require.

Ant. 1 deprive, withhold, refuse, disallow. **2** neglect, overlook.

◇ *Usage note:* Both *provided* and *providing* may be used as a conjunction to introduce a conditional clause: *We shall go abroad next year, providing* (or *provided*) *we have the money. Provided* is preferred in formal use.

provident *adj. He was a provident man who made*

careful preparation for his future: far-sighted, well-prepared, far-seeing, foreseeing, wise, thoughtful, discreet, judicious, discerning; cautious, wary, precautious, careful; ready, equipped; prudent, frugal, thrifty, economical, saving, parsimonious, chary.
Ant. improvident, unprepared, short-sighted; injudicious, undiscerning; incautious, unwary; imprudent, wasteful, uneconomical, reckless.

> **Exploring the Word**: Latin *videre*, to see, gives us many, many words, such as *vision, visual, visible, view*, and the like. Putting the Latin prefix *pro-*, before, in front of Latin *videre*, to see, gives us a whole group of additional words, including: *provide*, to foresee, hence to fill a need beforehand, make ready for the future, which is what a *provident* person or a good *provider* does; while *Providence* (or Divine Providence) is used as a synonym for *God*, alluding to the Deity's all-foreseeing care over the cosmos. On the other hand, *improvident* and *improvise* refer to not seeing beforehand and to speaking or acting without a pre-arranged script or plan. *Provisions* refer to food or supplies stocked to fill a foreseeable need; *provision* and *proviso* refer to conditions, stipulations, or clauses making conditions that are contingent on foreseeable happenings in the future, as in a contract. *Provisional* refers to things set up for temporary immediate need, it being foreseen that their *definitive* form may be different (such as a *provisional* government, a *provisional* appointment, or a *provisional* agreement).

province *n.* **1** *British Columbia is a province of Canada:* administrative division, state, territory, region, area, section, part. **2** *It's within his province to issue authorization:* area, field, sphere, territory, capacity, function, office, jurisdiction, domain, job, authority; responsibility, charge, business, duty, assignment, station, place, role, scope of duties.

provincial *adj.* **1** *Such scandal was not often reported in the provincial newspapers:* of a province, regional, territorial, local. **2** *She was a farm girl with simple provincial manners:* rural, country, countrified, rustic, bucolic; unsophisticated; homespun, homely, rude, rough; *Disparaging*, crude, gauche; unpolished, unrefined, clumsy, loutish, boorish, oafish; clownish, awkward, agricultural, clod-hopping, gawky. **3** *The townspeople looked on with a provincial distrust of foreigners:* narrow, parochial, insular.
Ant. 1 standard, national. **2** urban; sophisticated, courtly, urbane, fashionable, polished, refined, smooth. **3** cosmopolitan.

provision *n.* **1** *Provision of shelter was the Red Cross's main concern for the victims of the disaster:* providing, supplying, furnishing, giving, endowment, donation. **2 provisions** *Provisions were kept in the storehouse:* supplies, food, eatables, edibles, comestibles, sustenance, stores, groceries, victuals, viands, provender; feed, forage, fodder. **3** *He made provision for their welfare in his will:* arrangement, anticipation, provident measures or steps, prearrangement, forethought, wherewithal; provident care, precaution, preparation, readiness. **4** *According to the provisions of this agreement, you must continue to work for them for another 2 years:* proviso, requisite, requirement, obligation, stipulation, condition, term, article, clause; restriction, limitation, reservation, modification, qualification; *Informal* string.

proviso *n. His will left everything to his daughter, with the proviso that she should not marry:* condition, restriction, limitation, qualification, modification, stipulation, requirement; clause, amendment, addition, rider; *Informal* string.

provocation *n. She flared up at the slightest provocation:* cause, motivation, incitement, goad, spur, prodding, stimulation, stimulus, vexation, irritation, pique, annoyance, perturbation, aggravation; excitation, slight, affront, offence.

provocative *adj.* **1** *Jack's provocative remark started an angry argument:* provoking, annoying, aggravating, irritating, vexing, vexatious, irksome. **2** *She wore a very provocative dress:* seductive, tempting, tantalizing, captivating, intriguing, entrancing, enchanting, alluring, attractive, sexy; exciting, intoxicating, thrilling, stimulating, arousing, irresistible, inviting.

provoke *v.* **1** *Her constant nagging provoked him:* anger, enrage, incense, outrage, infuriate, madden, irritate, vex, agitate, annoy, gall, aggravate, irk, exasperate, rile, try one's patience, chafe, grate, move to anger, work into a passion, make one's blood boil, put out of humour, put out; *Slang* get one's goat, get under one's skin, get one. **2** *The cad's foul language provoked rage in the honest girl's breast:* cause, prompt, excite, incite, inspire, impel, instigate, induce, compel, arouse, stimulate, rouse, stir, animate, move, motivate. **3** *The race provoked his love of competition:* arouse, stimulate, bring on, give rise to, cause, produce, bring about, effect, actuate, motivate, prompt, pique, put in motion, galvanize, foment, incite, generate, create, establish; stir, stir up, rouse, awaken, call forth, elicit, fire, inflame, kindle, quicken, excite, evoke.
Ant. 1 gratify, assuage, calm, soothe, mollify, ease, propitiate, please.

prowess *n.* **1** *Richard the Lion Heart was known for his prowess in battle:* bravery, valour, courageous deeds, heroism, fearlessness, intrepidity, gallantry, courage, grit, nerve, daring, boldness, derring-do, dauntlessness;

strength, might, power, vigour, fortitude, stamina, endurance, mettle, spirit, hardihood, *Informal* spunk, *Slang* guts. **2** *She showed great prowess as a businesswoman:* ability, skill, skilfulness, competence, aptitude, know-how, knack, talent, facility, genius, accomplishment, adeptness, expertise, proficiency.

Ant. 1 cowardice, cowardliness, fear, timidity, meekness. **2** incompetence, ineptness.

prudent *adj. A prudent investor buys only sound shares:* wise, sensible, careful, showing good judgement, judicious, expedient, discerning, sagacious, sage, politic, sapient, level-headed, well-advised, rational, sane, self-possessed; thoughtful, considerate, reflecting, prudential, provident, heedful, vigilant, wide-awake, cautious, wary, circumspect, shrewd, guarded, chary; prepared, discreet, far-sighted; frugal, thrifty, saving, economical, sparing.

Ant. imprudent, indiscreet, unwise, irrational; thoughtless, inconsiderate, improvident, careless, heedless, reckless, rash, incautious, wasteful, extravagant, uneconomical.

prudish *adj. She is too prudish to enjoy that comedian's off-colour jokes:* prim, extremely proper and modest, over-modest, priggish, puritanical, prissy, strait-laced; precise, fastidious, finical, particular; timid, shy, demure, skittish, shockable, Victorian, squeamish; smug, sanctimonious, self-righteous, punctilious, pedantic, mincing; stilted, starched, stuffy, old-maidish.

prune *v.* **1** *He spent the afternoon pruning the hedge:* trim, clip, snip, thin, thin out, shear, cut, crop, lop. **2** *It's an editor's job to prune a manuscript:* reduce, trim, cut; abridge, condense, abbreviate; simplify, clarify.

pry *v. Stop prying into my affairs!:* snoop, poke, butt, nose, poke one's nose in, interfere, peek, peer; probe, explore, delve, inquire, search.

pseudo *adj. He is too middle-class to be anything but a pseudo revolutionary:* false, spurious, mock, pretended, feigned, make-believe, fictitious, counterfeit, sham, bogus, fraudulent, fake, phoney; self-styled, *French* soi-disant.

Ant. genuine, real, authentic.

psyche *n. C. G. Jung had much to say about the human psyche:* soul, mind, spirit, make-up, personality, self; ego, super-ego, id; subconscious, unconscious, anima.

psychic *adj.* **1** *A dream is a psychic event:* mental, psychological; cerebral, intellectual; spiritual. **2** *The medium claimed to have psychic powers:* extra-sensory, preternatural, telekinetic, supernatural, occult, mystic; telepathic, clairvoyant.

—*n.* **3** *She claimed to be a psychic:* clairvoyant, seer, telepath; prophet, soothsayer, diviner, augur; medium, spiritualist; *French* voyant, (*fem.*) voyante.

psychology *n. Students of psychology try to predict behaviour. The psychology of a hermit differs from that of a pop star:* mental processes, mind, make-up, attitude, feeling, head; *Informal* what makes one tick.

◇ *Usage note: Psychology* is the science dealing with the mind, mental processes, and behaviour, and a *psychologist* studies these things. *Psychiatry* is the branch of medicine concerned with psychic problems requiring therapy, and a *psychiatrist* is a doctor specializing in *psychotherapy*. A common form of psychotherapy is *psycho-analysis*, a technique developed at the turn of the century by the Viennese physician Sigmund Freud. Today most *psycho-analysts* are also psychiatrists. It is usual to refer to the technique as "analysis" and its practitioners as "analysts."

Exploring the Word: *Psychology* and the language of love owe a great debt to the Greek myth of the troubled love-life of the beautiful maiden *Psyche*, her lover *Eros*, with whom she was finally united, and his jealous mother *Aphrodite*. *Psyche* got her name from Greek *psychē*, breath of life, and was finally accorded a place among the *Immortals* as goddess of the soul, the spirit, or the breath of life. From this and her troubled life we get our words *psyche*, *psychic*, *psychiatry*, *psychology*, *psychosis*, *psychotic*, and *psychopath*. From Psyche's lover, *Eros*, the god of love, and the Greek word *erōs*, love, we get *erotic* and *erogenous*. Eros was known as *Cupid* to the ancient Romans (Latin *cupido*, passion), from which we get *cupidity*, a passion for possessions or wealth. From Eros's jealous mother, *Aphrodite*, the goddess of love, we get *aphrodisiac*. She was known as *Venus* to the ancient Romans, which gives us the nickname for an alluring woman, the name of the planet *Venus*, the names of several beautiful but deadly plants, as the *Venus's fly-trap*, and finally the term *venereal disease* (literally, "disease of Venus").

psychotic *adj.* **1** *Hitler had psychotic tendencies, which brought disaster on the civilized world:* insane, psychopathic, lunatic; mad, demented, deranged; *Slang* loony, crazy, nutty, bonkers.

—*n.* **2** *Psychiatrists try to help psychotics to recover their lost sanity:* insane person, psychopath, madman, lunatic, maniac, neurotic, schizophrenic, *Slang* nut-case, loony.

public *adj.* **1** *Public opinion favours tax reform. A librarian is a public servant:* common, general, popular, societal, social; political, civic, civil; state, national, nation-wide, country-wide. **2** *The zoo and gardens are public:* open to everyone, free to all, used by all, shared, not private or exclusive; unrestricted, available, accessible, passable, unbarred, unenclosed, unfenced, unbounded, not circumscribed, unobstructed; communal, community-owned. **3** *The investigator made public his findings:* widely known, familiar to many people, notorious, recognized, acknowledged, disclosed, divulged, open, overt, outward, unabashed, unashamed, plain, frank, obvious, conspicuous, evident, visible, unconcealed, exposed, apparent, undisguised, revealed, patent, manifest, observable, discernible, perceivable, in sight or view, in broad daylight.

—n. **4** *The museum is open to the public:* people, everyone, populace, community, nation, population, citizenry, commonalty, society, body politic, proletariat, folk, bourgeoisie, multitude, masses, hoi polloi, rank and file, mob. **5** *The concert-going public is well served by good orchestras:* following, attendance, audience, followers, those interested; buyers, purchasers, clientele, trade, patrons; constituency, supporters.

Ant. 1 private, personal, individual. **2** private, proprietary, exclusive, restricted, unavailable, inaccessible, barred, secluded, closed. **3** secret, unknown, unrecognized, hidden, unrevealed, mum.

publicity *n. The book received good publicity:* public notice, attention, currency, report, notoriety; circulation, promulgation, advertising, salesmanship, promotion; information, propaganda; build-up, write-up; *Informal* ballyhoo, plug, puff, boost, blurb.

publicize *v. He was in town to publicize his new book:* promote, make known, make public, bring to public notice, give currency, spread word of, advertise, sell, circularize, proclaim, acclaim, announce, broadcast, herald, boost, sell, propagate, promulgate; *Informal* ballyhoo, push, plug.

publish *v.* **1** *The company has published all of that author's works:* print for sale, send to press, issue, bring out, put out. **2** *Don't publish that — it's strictly off the record:* print, make generally known, announce, make public, publicize, give publicity to, promote; disclose, release, give out, vent, air, broadcast, give to the world, tell, communicate, utter, impart, divulge, diffuse, disseminate, spread, propagate, promulgate, circulate; proclaim, declare, trumpet, herald, advertise, placard.

Ant. 2 conceal, hide, secrete; muffle, smother; bury, suppress; withhold, keep secret.

pucker *v.* **1** *Lemons make your mouth pucker up. The curtains were puckered at the top:* draw together, contract, shrink; pinch, crease, purse, compress, squeeze; wrinkle, crinkle; gather, tuck, make a pleat.

—n. **2** *She sewed little puckers in the romper:* fold, tuck, gather, pinch, pleat, crease, wrinkle, crinkle, crumple, rumple, ruffle.

pudgy Also **podgy** *adj. All those sweets have made him pudgy:* fat, stout, chunky, chubby, stocky, plump, rotund, thickset, tubby, roly-poly, squat, stubby, short and fat, dumpy.

puerile *adj. Stop being so puerile and act your age!:* childish, foolish, silly, immature, infantile, simple, childlike, callow, juvenile, green, raw; irrational, senseless, inane, nonsensical, ridiculous, frivolous, vapid, harebrained; trivial, piddling, worthless.

Ant. adult, mature; rational; intelligent.

puff *n.* **1** *The locomotive let off puffs of steam:* short blast, abrupt emission, sudden gust, whiff, breath, exhalation, flurry, small cloud, wisp. **2** *Her sleeve had a slight puff to it:* swelling, rising, bulge, bunching, elevation, node, inflammation, distention, inflation, dilation, bow, convexity, hump, protuberance, extension, protrusion, protuberancy, excrescence, tuberosity. **3** *Informal That speech was just a puff for his book:* commendation, sales talk, euphemism, praise, laudation, flattery, encomium, flummery, puffery, panegyric, much ado about nothing, advertisement, blurb, publicity; bluster, exaggeration, bombast; *Informal* plug, boost, ballyhoo.

—v. **4** *After running the mile, he was huffing and puffing:* breathe hard, be out of breath, pant, heave, wheeze, gasp, exhale, blow, be winded. **5** *The dragon puffed out fire:* blow in puffs, send forth, emit, discharge. **6** *He puffed on his pipe:* draw, suck, inhale; smoke. **7** *The prisoners' stomachs were puffed out from malnutrition:* be inflated, be distended, swell, blow up, inflate, expand, extend, distend, dilate, stretch, bloat.

"The pipe, with solemn interposing puff,
Makes half a sentence at a time enough."
— *William Cowper*

---

puffy *adj. Next morning his face was puffy with bruises:* swollen, inflated, puffed-up, bulging, inflamed, distended, expanded; round, corpulent, fat, fleshy.

pugnacious *adj. When he drank too much, he'd become quite pugnacious:* quarrelsome, given to fighting, antagonistic, unfriendly; aggressive, combative, defiant, warlike, hostile, menacing, militant; contentious, belligerent, bellicose, fractious, disputatious, argumentative; threatening, with teeth bared; with a chip on one's shoulder.

Ant. peaceful, calm, friendly, accommodating.

◇ *Word origin: Pugnacious* and *pugilist* come from Latin *pugnus,* fist.

pull *v.* **1** *The child pulled a red wagon:* haul, drag, lug, tug, draw; take in tow, tow; trail, trawl. **2** *He pulled a cord and the butler appeared:* tug, jerk, grab, yank. **3** *The dentist may have to pull out that infected tooth:* draw, remove, detach, withdraw; extract, wrest, wring; uproot, extirpate, dig, weed. **4** *The actor pulled his rival to pieces:* criticize, comment unfavourably upon. **5** *Pull over!:* go, move, drive. **6** *She pulled a muscle in her back:* strain, stretch, twist,

wrench, sprain. **7** *The promoters hoped to pull record crowds:* draw, attract; lure, entice.
—*n.* **8** *She gave the dog's leash a pull:* tug, jerk, yank, shake. **9** *He couldn't resist the pull of her charm:* pulling power, drawing power; lure, allure, attraction, attractiveness, influence, enticement, fascination, appeal, allurement; gravity, magnetism.
Ant. 1, 2, 8 push, shove. **3** insert, plant. **7** repel.

pulsate *v. Her heart was pulsating with excitement:* expand and contract rhythmically, throb, beat, palpitate, vibrate, reverberate, thump, pound, pulse, undulate, oscillate, tick, quiver, flutter, shake, shiver, quaver, shudder, tremble; wave, waver; come and go, alternate, ebb and flow.

pulse *n.* **1** *The ship's engine beat with a steady pulse:* throb, regular beat, rhythm, cadence, pulsation, palpitation, recurrence, undulation, stroke, vibration, oscillation.
—*v.* **2** *When he got angry, the veins in his temple pulsed:* beat, throb, palpitate, pulsate, thump, vibrate; quiver, shudder, tremble, oscillate.

pulverize *v. The mill pulverizes grain:* reduce to powder or dust, grind, pound, granulate, atomize, mince, crush, crunch, crumble, crumb, mill.
◇ *Word origin: Pulverize,* like *powder* and *pollen,* comes from Latin *pulvis,* powder, dust.

punch *n.* **1** *He gave the bully a punch in the mouth:* blow, hit, jab, thrust, clout, stroke, cuff, thump, box, poke, knock: *Informal* chop, sock; *Slang* haymaker.
—*v.* **2** *He punched the man in the nose:* hit with the fist, strike, smite, box, thwack, whack, jab, poke, pelt, wallop, clobber, clout, swat, cuff, clip; *Informal* sock, plug, paste; baste, pummel, pound, beat.
◇ *Word origin: Punch,* to strike sharply, as with the fist, is a variant of *pounce,* to emboss metalwork with a design hammered on the reverse side. *Punch,* a tool for perforating leather, stamping a design, etc., is short for *puncheon. Punch,* the beverage made of wine or spirits and fruit juices, comes from Sanskrit *pañchan,* five, from the five original ingredients: tea, sugar, lemon, water, and arrack (an Oriental spirit distilled from rice and molasses).

punctual *adj. He was always punctual for appointments:* on time, not late, early, in good time, well-timed, prompt, ready, regular, steady, constant; quick, expeditious, instant, immediate, instantaneous; seasonable, timely; *Informal* on the dot.
Ant. unpunctual, late, tardy; behind time.

punctuate *v.* **1** *He did not bother to punctuate the telegram:* mark with punctuation marks; insert the stops, separate, break. **2** *He punctuated his argument with phrases in his native Spanish:* interrupt, break, intersperse, pepper, lace, sprinkle, scatter.

puncture *n.* **1** *A puncture in the balloon made it collapse:* hole, break, rupture, opening, perforation, nick, cut; wound, bite, sting.
—*v.* **2** *She punctured her finger with a sewing needle:* pierce, make a hole in, prick, pink, stick; wound, cut, nick. **3** *Bad reviews punctured the young actor's ego:* deflate, depreciate; let down, knock down, shoot down, bring back to earth.

Exploring the Word: What do *puncture, punctual,* and *punctuation* have in common? They all come from Latin *punctus,* sting, pin-point, point. Thus, to *puncture* is to pierce with, or as if with, a pointed instrument. A *punctual* person arrives "on the dot." Many *punctuation* marks consist of or contain points or dots, as the full stop or period (sometimes also called *point*) as well as the exclamation mark and colon. (In Early Modern English, "pointing" a sentence meant punctuating it.) The verb form of Latin *punctus* is *pungere,* to pierce or sting. From *pungere* we get our word *pungent* — a pungent odour is sharp and acrid (like the smell of a car tyre burning), whereas a pungent taste may be delicious, a combination of hot and spicy with a hint of sourness, and a pungent remark may be amusingly spicy and to the point, or it may be unpleasantly caustic even if apropos.

pungent *adj.* **1** *The ribs were served with a hot pungent sauce:* sharp-tasting, highly flavoured, savoury, spicy, flavourful, piquant, flavoursome, palatable, tasty, highly-seasoned, salty, peppery, hot; nippy, tangy, strong, stimulating, sharp; sharp-smelling, acrid, sour, acid, tart, astringent, vinegary, caustic, bitter, acetous, biting, stinging, smarting, penetrating. **2** *His pungent remarks made him quite a few enemies:* sharp, piercing, pointed, acute, trenchant, keen, poignant; stinging, biting, mordant, caustic, invidious, cutting, incisive, penetrating, sarcastic, smart, wounding, tart, acrimonious, bitter; stimulating, stirring, provocative, tantalizing, racy, spicy, scintillating; sparkling, brilliant, clever, snappy, keen-witted, witty.
Ant. 1 bland, mild; unsavoury, unpalatable, tasteless; weak, unstimulating. **2** dull, mild, moderate, inane, vapid; pointless.

punish *v. His father punished him for disobeying:* subject to a penalty, penalize, chastise, correct, discipline; sentence, imprison, fine; give one his deserts; rebuke, reprove, admonish, castigate, chasten, take to task, dress down; avenge, take revenge, take vengeance on, bring to account, get even with, retaliate, settle accounts with; whip, flog, beat.
Ant. excuse, pardon, forgive; exonerate, absolve, vindicate; praise, laud, reward.

punishment *n. For a punishment, you'll get no pocket-money for two weeks:* penalty, penance, penal, retribution, penalization, payment, price, deserts; fine, forfeit, damages, redress, reparation, discipline, correction, chastisement, castigation, chastening, (*variously*) spanking, whipping, flogging, flaying, crucifying, hanging.

"In nature there are neither rewards nor punishments — there are consequences."
—*Robert Ingersoll*

puny *adj. Oliver Twist was an underfed, puny child:* small and weak, undersized, underdeveloped, slight, pint-sized, sawn-off, little, lilliputian, miniature, diminutive, tiny; weakly, sickly, poor, feeble; thin, fragile, emaciated, delicate, frail, infirm.
Ant. large, great, robust, healthy, strong, vigorous; colossal, gigantic.
◇ *Word origin: Puny* comes from Old French *puisné,* younger, literally late-born (*puis,* after, + *né,* born). The word acquired its sense of "diminutive" from the widely held (and incorrect) assumption that late-born young tend to be undersized.

pupil *n. She taught a class of 27 pupils:* student, learner, schoolgirl, schoolboy, coed; undergraduate, scholar; beginner, novice, tiro, initiate, probationer, apprentice, disciple.
Ant. teacher, master, mistress, tutor.
◇ *Word origin: Pupil* comes from Latin *pupillus,* meaning a ward or orphan under the care of a guardian (Latin *tutor,* guardian, tutor); the word only later came to mean a person under the tutelage of a teacher. *Pupillus,* orphan, comes from *pupus* (boy) and *pupa* (girl), terms of endearment used in speaking to or of little children in ancient Rome. *Pupa* also means "doll" in Latin (the French word *poupée,* doll, is derived from it). The *pupil* of the eye is named from the tiny image ("doll") of oneself seen in reflection in another's eye. Our word *puppet* is also derived from the "doll" meaning of Latin *pupa,* as is our word *pupa* for the quiescent (doll-like) stage in the development of a metamorphic insect such as a bee or a butterfly.

puppet *n.* **1** *The children enjoyed the puppets:* animated doll, marionette, manikin; glove puppet; doll, toy. **2** *Emperor Maximilian of Mexico was denounced as a mere puppet of Napoleon III:* tool, creature, pawn, cat's-paw, dupe, instrument; lay figure, figure-head; man of straw, jackstraw; hireling, flunkey, servant, henchman.

purchase *v.* **1** *We purchased a new car:* acquire, buy, pay for, pick up.
—*n.* **2** *We're pleased with our purchase:* acquisition, buying, acquirement; buy. **3** *The strong ropes gave us good purchase for getting up the side of the cliff:* advantage, hold, leverage; footing, foothold, toe-hold, support; means of exerting power, influence, edge.
Ant. 1 sell, dispose of, liquidate, convert into cash. **2** sale, selling; disposal; liquidation.
◇ *Word origin: Purchase* comes from Old French *purchacier,* to seek after, literally "to go hunting for" — the *-chase* in *purchase* is the same as our word *chase* (hunt).

pure *adj.* **1** *These animals were bred from pure stock. Have you ever breathed pure oxygen?:* unmixed, full-strength, unadulterated, unmodified, unalloyed, unmingled, neat, straight; perfect, faultless, flawless, undefiled, uncorrupted, untainted, unblemished, unmarred; clean, fresh, immaculate, uncontaminated, uninfected, unpolluted, disinfected, antiseptic, germfree, sterilized, sterile, sanitary, healthful, wholesome, fit for consumption; purebred, of unmixed descent, thoroughbred, pedigree, pure-blooded. **2** *It was pure luck that he was at home when we called:* mere, sheer, stark; absolute, complete, whole, entire, full, utter, downright, out and out, positive, perfect; unqualified, thorough. **3** *She was a pure and wholesome girl:* innocent, guiltless, sinless, decent, uncorrupted, moral, righteous, ethical, upright; virtuous, chaste, undefiled, virgin, virginal, unsullied, unspoiled, spotless, immaculate, untainted, untarnished, unblemished, inviolable, inviolate; blameless, above suspicion, unimpeachable, true, sincere, guileless, angelic. **4** *The academy debated the distinction between pure and applied sciences:* theoretical, abstract, hypothetical, conjectural, speculative, fundamental, basic, higher.
Ant. 1–3 impure. **1** adulterated, alloyed, mingled; imperfect, flawed, corrupted, tainted, blemished; unclean, dirty, contaminated; infected, polluted, unsterilized, unhealthful; mixed. **2** qualified. **3** guilty, culpable, sinful, corrupt, corrupted, immoral; unvirtuous, unchaste, defiled, sullied, spoiled, spotted, tarnished, blemished, contaminated; impeachable, untrue, insincere; immodest, indecent, filthy, gross, lewd, obscene. **4** applied, practical.

purely *adv.* **1** *It's purely a matter of taste. The lecture was purely technical:* only, solely, merely, simply, essentially; completely, entirely, totally, absolutely, fully, wholly. **2** *She always conducted herself purely and with propriety:* virtuously, chastely, virginally, incorruptibly, morally, innocently, cleanly, admirably, worthily, in all honour; piously, devoutly; cleanly, flawlessly, faultlessly.
Ant. 2 immorally, dishonourably, unwholesomely, impiously. **3** impurely, faultily.

purge *v.* **1** *The new Chief Constable has promised to purge the police department:* clean up, cleanse, purify, clean out, sweep out, shake up. **2** *Stalin purged his enemies from the Party:* remove, get rid of, do away with, oust, dismiss, liquidate, eliminate, expel, uproot, discharge, rout out; eradicate. **3** *She was purged of*

her sins and devoted the rest of her life to prayer and good works: wash, cleanse; obtain absolution, pardon, forgiveness, or remission for.
—*n.* **4** *Stalin conducted a purge of the officer corps:* purging, clean-up, shake-up, purification. **5** *The medicine was an effective purge:* laxative, purgative, physic, emetic, enema.

purify *v. Purify the water before drinking it:* make pure, disinfect, sanitize, clear, clarify, (*variously*) boil, chlorinate, filter, distil.
Ant. contaminate, pollute, dirty, infect.

puritanical *adj. D. H. Lawrence crusaded against puritanical censorship:* strict, severe, austere, puritan, prim, prissy, prudish, priggish, strait-laced, stiff-necked, stilted, stiff, stuffy, rigid, dogmatic, fanatical, narrow, bigoted.
Ant. permissive, broad-minded, latitudinarian.

purity *n.* **1** *Exhaust fumes are a threat to the purity of the air we breathe:* pureness, clearness, clarity, lucidity, limpidity; cleanliness, cleanness, immaculateness, immaculacy, brilliance; excellence, fineness; homogeneity, uniformity. **2** *She was a woman of exemplary purity and goodness:* guiltlessness, guilelessness, innocence, clear conscience; modesty, chastity, temperance, virginity, chasteness, virtuousness, virtue, decency, uprightness, morality, rectitude; piety, holiness, saintliness, sanctity; integrity, honesty, incorruptibility, honour; simplicity, plainness, directness.
Ant. 1, 2 impurity, impureness. **1** contamination, cloudiness; diversity. **2** vice, immodesty, unchasteness, immorality.

purport *v.* **1** *The letter purported to be from the general himself:* claim, profess; declare, allege, or assert oneself.
—*n.* **2** *What is the purport of your visit here?:* meaning, import, significance, signification, implication, sense, reason, rationale, bearing; intention, purpose, design, end, aim, object, objective, intent, burden, point; gist, substance, drift, tenor, trend.

purpose *n.* **1** *The purpose of a cat-door is to let the cat go in and out at will:* object, objective, function, point, rationale, intention, intent, raison d'étre; meaning, reason, sense, aim, design. **2** *His purpose was to graduate from medical school and become a great surgeon:* goal, aim, ambition, aspiration, object, objective, mission, intent, intention, target, resolution, plan, motive, design, scheme, project, proposal; disposition, desire, wish, expectation, hope. **3** *He walked with a stride full of purpose:* resolve, determination, resolution, motivation, will, fixed intent.
—*v.* **4** *He purposed to become one of the world's leading conductors:* intend, mean, resolve, aim, aspire, drive at, persist, persevere; design, propose, plan, determine, conclude; endeavour, take upon oneself, set about, undertake, elect, choose; commit oneself, decide, make up one's mind; think to, contemplate, have a mind to.
Ant. 3 purposelessness, aimlessness; inconstancy.

"Your purpose in life is simply to help on the purpose of the universe."
—*George Bernard Shaw*

---

purposeful *adj. He was a hard-working man whose every action was purposeful:* deliberate, intentional, calculated, conscious, considered, studied, premeditated; resolute, decided, resolved, determined upon.
Ant. aimless, purposeless, vacillating, irresolute, faltering, wavering; undecided, unresolved, undetermined.

purposely *adv. I left the door open purposely:* deliberately, on purpose, intentionally, with intent, calculatedly, expressly, designedly, by design; knowingly, advisedly, consciously.
Ant. accidentally, unintentionally, inadvertently, unknowingly, unconsciously, unthinkingly, unwittingly, by chance.
◇ *Usage note: Purposely* means on purpose, intentionally, not by accident: *She purposely ignored me at the party. Purposefully* means carefully or with a specific goal in mind: *The seamstress sewed purposefully all night in order to finish the dress for the wedding.*

purse *n.* **1** *Keep the money in your purse:* handbag, pocket-book, bag; money-bag, wallet, pouch. **2** *The purse for the next race is £25,000:* prize, award, stake; winnings, treasury, fund, coffer.
—*v.* **3** *The sour taste made her purse her lips:* pucker, wrinkle, knit; pleat, pinch, gather, fold; bunch, contract.
◇ *Word origin: Purse* comes from French *bourse* (Latin *bursa*, Greek *bursa*), a purse, a skin or hide used as a purse. A *purser* was formerly a naval paymaster or keeper of the purse; today he is an officer having charge of the accounts of a vessel, keeping valuables for passengers, etc. French *bourse* also gives us *disburse* and *bursar.*

pursue *v.* **1** *The policemen pursued the bank robbers:* chase, follow in hot pursuit, go after, give chase to, race after, run after; chase after, track, trail. **2** *She pursued the goal of perfection in her art:* seek, try for, try to accomplish, aspire to, aim for or at, contrive to gain, be determined upon; push toward, strive for, labour for, be intent upon, set one's heart upon, be after. **3** *He pursued his studies with seriousness:* engage in, carry on, perform.

push *v.* **1** *Push the button if you want the lift:* press, exert force on, move. **2** *The celebrity pushed past the reporters and got into his car:* make one's way, work, drive, press, force one's way; struggle, shove, elbow, squeeze, worm, wiggle, wedge, shoulder, nudge; ram, butt, hustle, jostle, fight, forge. **3** *We always have to push him to do his homework:* urge, encourage, egg on, goad, incite, prod, spur, instigate, rouse, inspire, induce, arouse, animate, motivate, impel, prompt, stimulate, provoke, propel, move, sway, persuade, importune, exhort; hound, dun, bear down hard upon, harass, browbeat, heckle, badger, harry, coerce, constrain, compel, force, drive, prevail upon; *Informal* put the screws on. **4** *The salesman pushed the new product at every opportunity:* promote, publicize, propagandize, advertise, make known, boost; *Informal* plug. **5** *The child pushed his fingers into the mud up to his wrist:* stick, thrust, drive, shove, stuff, plunge.

—*n.* **6** *Give the gate a push and it will open:* shove, nudge, prod, jolt. **7** *Informal The president of the company was a man with a lot of push:* energy, vitality, drive, go, vigour, vim and vigour, ambition, determination. **8** *The army's push into enemy territory was successful:* thrust, advance, incursion, inroad, foray.

Exploring the Word: *Pulse* and *pulsate* refer to the driving of the blood through the circulatory system and come from Latin *pulsare,* to beat, pulse (derived from the base of Latin *pellere,* to push, drive). The same base gives us *push; propel, propeller,* and *propulsion* (Latin *pro-,* forward), which refer to driving or pushing forward; *compel* and *compulsion* (Latin *com-,* thoroughly, completely), to drive, force, that which drives, an inner drive; *dispel* (Latin *dis-,* away), to drive away; *expel* and *expulsion* (Latin *ex-,* out), to drive out, the act of driving out; *impel* and *impulse* (Latin *im-,* forward), to drive forward, that which urges on; *repel, repulse,* and *repulsion* (Latin *re-,* back), to drive back, a driving back, and a feeling that forces one back or away.

pusillanimous *adj. The brave hero scared off the pusillanimous villain:* cowardly, lily-livered, faint-hearted, mean-spirited; timorous, fearful, apprehensive; spiritless.

Ant. courageous, brave, valorous; bold, daring, spirited.

put *v.* **1** *Put the milk in the refrigerator. Put the files in alphabetical order:* place, set, rest, lay, position, deposit. **2** *The sergeant put the soldier to work on spud-bashing:* assign, set, employ. **3** *He was put under arrest by the policeman:* place, bring. **4** *The invading forces put our army on the defensive:* drive, force, throw. **5** *I don't put much faith in his promises:* assign, place, fix, set, lay, attribute, ascribe, impute. **6** *Let me put it to you this way:* express, phrase, word, state; articulate, enunciate. **7** *The plan was put to the members for consideration:* propose, submit, offer, bring forward, present; throw out, pose. **8** *The athlete put the shot about 40 feet:* throw, heave, pitch, cast.

Ant. 1 remove, raise, withdraw, displace, misplace, transpose, transfer, change.

putrid *adj. That awful smell was caused by putrid meat:* spoilt, rotten, decomposing, decaying, bad, purulent, putrefied, putrescent, tainted, rancid.

Ant. pure, clean, wholesome, uncontaminated, fresh, untainted, good.

"Let schoolmasters puzzle their brain,
With grammar, and nonsense, and learning,
Good liquor, I stoutly maintain,
Gives genius a better discerning."
—*Oliver Goldsmith*

puzzle *v.* **1** *The murder case continued to puzzle the police:* perplex, nonplus, bewilder, confuse, confound, baffle, mystify, stump, flummox, bamboozle; outwit, foil, hoodwink. **2** *I keep puzzling over his strange behaviour:* wonder, mull, brood, ponder.

—*n.* **3** *The murder case was a puzzle to the detective:* mystery, problem, dilemma, bewilderment, bafflement, mystification, perplexity, complication, difficulty, enigma, conundrum, riddle.

pygmy *n.* **1** *The side-show featured a giant and a pygmy billed respectively as the tallest and smallest men in the world:* midget, dwarf, manikin, lilliputian, Tom Thumb; shrimp, mite, runt, elf, homunculus.

—*adj.* **2** *The zoo acquired a pygmy hippopotamus:* dwarf, dwarfish, miniature, diminutive, midget, toy, tiny, undersized, elfin.

◇ *Word origin: Pygmy* comes from Greek *pugmē,* a measure of length, commonly given as the distance from a man's elbow to his knuckles. From this unit of length is derived the name of the *Pugmaîoi,* a fabulous race of dwarfs on the upper Nile, said by Homer to have been warred upon and destroyed by cranes. From this we get our name for the small forest people (ranging less than five feet tall) of equatorial Africa.

Q

quack *n.* **1** *When the orthodox methods of Harley Street couldn't help his back trouble, he resorted to quacks:* ignorant pretender, medical impostor, fake doctor, charlatan.
—*adj.* **2** *He was a quack psychiatrist:* fake, fraudulent, phoney, sham, counterfeit.
◇ *Word origin: Quack*, fake doctor, is a short form of *quacksalver*, from Dutch *kwakzalver*, charlatan. Dutch *kwakken* means to *quack*, so the word may originally have meant "one who *quacks* boastfully, like a duck, about his *salve* and other medical remedies."

quagmire *n.* **1** *The horses were stuck in the quagmire:* soft muddy ground, marsh, bog, swamp, fen, morass, mire, quag, slough, sludge, ooze, sump. **2** *You'll need more than diplomacy to get out of that quagmire:* predicament, difficulty, critical situation, crisis, dilemma, perplexity, Gordian knot, quandary, involvement, intricacy, entanglement, strait, imbroglio, scrape, jam, fix, mess, muddle, morass, mire, quicksand, hot water, pickle, pinch.

quail *v. We all quailed when the headmaster suddenly entered the room:* shrink with fear, blanch, lose courage, be cowardly, take fright, show a yellow streak, have cold feet, lose heart, lose spirit, run away, turn tail, shy, fight shy, cower; quake, shudder, tremble, shake, shiver in one's shoes, shake in one's shoes.

quaint *adj. We enjoyed the quaint custom of the village:* charmingly old-fashioned, out-of-the-way, picturesque, old-time, antiquated; unusual, strange, odd, bizarre, queer, eccentric, outlandish, peculiar, singular, curious, unique, original, unconventional, uncommon, rare, singular, extraordinary; droll, fanciful, whimsical.
Ant. modern, new, newfangled, modish, up-to-date, fashionable.

quake *v.* **1** *The people quaked with fear when their village was invaded:* shake, shudder, quaver, stand aghast, tremble, shiver, blanch, quail, quiver.
—*n.* **2** *The quake caused much damage:* earthquake, tremor, seismic disturbance. **3** *A quake of fear passed through him:* quiver, shiver, thrill, shudder, trembling, wave, ripple, spasm, throb.

qualification *n.* **1** *Only applicants with the proper qualifications will be considered:* requisite, prerequisite, requirement; eligibility, fitness, suitability; competency, capability, ability, capacity, faculty, endowment, talent, accomplishment, achievement, aptitude, gift, skill, property; attribute, forte; standard; credential, bona fide, certification. **2** *The contract has several qualifications which apply to both parties:* limitation, restriction, reservation, stipulation, condition, postulate, provision, proviso; exception, exemption, escape clause; objection; modification, arrangement.

qualified *adj.* **1** *Take that dog to a qualified vet:* experienced, trained, competent, practised, versed, knowing; eligible, fit, fitted, equipped, suited, meet, equal; capable, adept, able, talented, skilled, skilful, accomplished, expert; certified, licensed, authorized; efficacious, proficient, efficient. **2** *He gave a qualified answer when I asked for definite assurances:* limited, indefinite, conditional, provisional, reserved, guarded; restricted, limited, hedging, equivocal, ambiguous.
Ant. 1 inexperienced, untrained, unpractised.

qualify *v.* **1** *Two years of experience qualified him for promotion. She didn't qualify for the semifinals:* make fit, make eligible, fit, train, ground, prepare, adapt, ready, condition, equip, make competent or capable, enable, endow; license, sanction, permit; empower, entitle, authorize, give power, commission; certify, legitimate; be eligible, measure up, be accepted; *Informal* have what it takes. **2** *Father said no initially but later qualified his answer:* limit, restrict, restrain, circumscribe, narrow; modify, moderate; alter, adapt, adjust, accommodate; temper, soften, assuage, mitigate, abate, ease, diminish, reduce. **3** *Broadly speaking, adjectives are words that qualify nouns:* describe, characterize, modify.

quality *n.* **1** *She has a quality of kindness that appeals to everyone:* characteristic, attribute, trait, mark, feature, aspect, property; character, nature, constitution, disposition, temperament; qualification, capacity, faculty. **2** *The furniture was of poor quality:* value, worth, calibre, degree of excellence, grade, rank, class, merit. **3** *You could tell that he was a man of quality by his dress and behaviour:* social status, rank, family, position, high station, standing, blood; eminence, distinction, dignity.
Ant. 3 inferiority, low rank, low station.
◇ *Usage note: Qualitative* refers to *quality*, to the nature or value of something: *An antique dealer must have good qualitative judgement. Qualitative chemical analysis shows that water is made up of hydrogen and oxygen.* On the other hand, *quantitative* refers to quantity, to the amount or size of something: *Test your quantitative judgement by guessing how many beans are in the jar. Quantitative chemical analysis shows that water has two atoms of hydrogen to one of oxygen.* Remember: *QUALitative* refers to *QUALity*, *QUANTitative* refers to *QUANTity*.

qualm *n.* **1** *He had no qualms about robbing the poor:* scruple, misgiving, compunction, twinge of conscience, reservation; hesitation, reluctance, unwillingness, indisposition, disinclination. **2** *Already on the boat-train I felt a qualm, and by the time I got aboard ship I was seasick:* queasiness, faintness, dizzy spell, giddiness, vertigo, nausea, turn, sick feeling.

Ant. 1 willingness, inclination.

quandary *n. She was in such a quandary that she didn't know to whom to turn:* dilemma, difficulty, predicament, strait, impasse, crisis, pinch, fix, entanglement, plight, imbroglio, involvement, morass, mire, pickle, jam, scrape, hot water.

quantity *n. Put a small quantity of sugar into the batter:* amount, sum, number; measurement, measure, size, extent, extension; abundance, aggregate, multitude; volume, mass, magnitude, bulk, greatness, amplitude, area, vastness, expanse, length; dosage, dose, portion, share, proportion, quota, apportionment, allotment.

◇ *Word origin: Quantity* comes from Latin *quantus*, meaning "how much?" This also gives us *quantitative*, having to do with size or amount, and *quantum*, a certain amount.

quarantine *n.* **1** *The health officials put the ship's crew in quarantine:* isolation, sequestration, medical segregation, *French* cordon sanitaire. —*v.* **2** *Doctors quarantined the cholera victims:* isolate, confine, segregate, sequester.

◇ *Word origin: Quarantine* comes to us via Italian *quarantina* from Latin *quadraginta*, meaning 40. In the past, 40 days of isolation were imposed upon ships, persons, and goods arriving at a port when suspected of carrying an infectious disease, this being considered enough time for any disease to run its course.

quarrel *n.* **1** *The couple's quarrel was so loud that the police were called:* dispute, squabble, bickering, argument, conflict, scrap, tiff, fuss, row, misunderstanding, falling out, open variance, difference, contradiction; disagreement, breach of the peace, dissension, strife, contention, discord, dissidence, controversy. **2** *My quarrel is with the lack of facilities here:* dispute, cause for complaint, complaint, objection, bone of contention, apple of discord. —*v.* **3** *The couple quarrelled constantly and finally got a divorce:* disagree angrily, argue, bicker, wrangle, fuss, have words, raise one's voice, squabble, be at odds, dispute, be at variance, be at loggerheads, differ, dissent; altercate, brawl, contend, fight, row, be at each other's throats; fall out, misunderstand; clash, jar, feud, conflict; cavil, nag, carp, raise a complaint, find fault, pick a quarrel.

Ant. 1 agreement, accord, accordance, concurrence, concord, concordance, harmony; understanding; peacefulness, congeniality. **3** agree, accord, concur, coincide, consent, assent.

quarter *n.* **1** *A quarter of the population voted for him. Insurance premiums are due every quarter:* one of four equal parts, fourth part, one-fourth, fourth, 25 per cent; three months. **2** *Throughout the Latin quarter, Spanish is the predominant language. The troops attacked the city from all quarters:* area, place, part, location, locality, locale, district, region, province, zone, territory, terrain; specific place, spot, station, position, situation; sphere, domain, realm; direction, point of the compass, side. **3** Usually **quarters** *We must find quarters before nightfall:* lodging, lodgings, housing, place to stay, place to live, board, shelter, billet, digs. **4** *The king gave no quarter to traitors:* mercy, pity, clemency; leniency, compassion, humanity, sympathy, indulgence.

—*v.* **5** *Peel and quarter the apples:* cut into quarters, slice four ways. **6** *Visiting diplomats are always quartered at the embassy:* furnish with quarters, billet, lodge, house, install, put up; place, station, post.

quash *v.* **1** *The dictator's army quashed the rebellion:* suppress, put down, crush, smash, quell, squash, quench, subdue, repress; stop, put an end to, extinguish, exterminate, obliterate, annihilate, ruin, destroy, wreck, devastate, strike out, blot out, delete, cancel, expunge, erase, efface, dissolve, eradicate, dispel, extirpate; undo, overturn, overthrow, overwhelm. **2** *The appeal court quashed the previous ruling on the case:* set aside, annul, nullify, void, abrogate, declare null and void, invalidate, vacate; overrule, override, countermand; retract, rescind, recall, revoke, reverse, repudiate.

◇ *Word origin: Quash* comes from Latin *quassare*, to shatter, smash to pieces.

quasi- *prefix. The vegetarian restaurant offered a quasi-steak, made of soya but no meat:* almost, near, virtual; somewhat, part, half-way, semi-; apparent, seeming, resembling.

◇ *Word origin: Quasi* is Latin for "nearly."

quaver *v.* **1** *Her voice quavered when she heard the sad news. I quaver when speaking to large audiences:* shake, quiver, shiver, tremble, shudder, quake; wave, wobble, totter, teeter, falter, waver; wriggle, writhe; oscillate, sway, vibrate, pulsate, throb, beat; trill.

—*n.* **2** *The broadcaster's voice had a quaver in it as he announced the sad news:* tremulous shake, quavering tone, tremor, trembling, quiver, throb, vibration; trill, vibrato, tremolo.

quay *n. The fishing boat landed at the quay:* landing-stage, wharf, pier, dock, mole, jetty; waterfront, basin, marina.

◇ *Pronunciation tip: Quay*, like *cay*, is properly pronounced *key*.

queasy *adj. Greasy food makes me queasy. I felt queasy about going to the headmaster's study:* sick to the stomach, sickish, nauseous, giddy, nauseated, disposed to vomit; bilious, nauseating, sickening; qualmish, uneasy, uncomfortable, uncertain, troubled, upset.

queen *n. Elizabeth I was the beloved queen of England:* female monarch, king's consort, princess; *Latin* regina, *French* reine, *Spanish* reina, *Italian* regina, *German* Königin.

queer *adj.* **1** *Her queer way of dressing attracted the stares of passers-by:* strange, odd, funny, unusual, uncommon, peculiar; bohemian, unconventional, nonconforming, unorthodox, eccentric, erratic, *French* outré; extraordinary, exceptional, original, unique, rare; irrational, unbalanced, crazy, unhinged, touched, daft; unparalleled, unprecedented, unexampled; abnormal, unnatural, outlandish, freakish, bizarre, weird, grotesque, exotic; fantastic, preposterous, absurd, ludicrous, laughable, ridiculous, comical, droll, fanciful, capricious; curious, quaint, off the beaten track, out of the way; astonishing, remarkable. **2** *He gave some queer answers to the policeman's questions:* suspicious, doubtful, questionable, irregular, far-fetched; *Informal* shady, fishy. **3** *Heights give me a queer feeling:* queasy, slightly ill, qualmy, faint, dizzy, giddy, light-headed, reeling, vertiginous.
—*v.* **4** *Informal His cheating in the exam queered his chances of a scholarship:* ruin, wreck, spoil, thwart, damage, harm, impair, injure, disrupt.
Ant. **1** common, regular, conventional, customary, orthodox, ordinary, unexceptional, unoriginal; normal, natural; rational, sane. **2** straight, believable. **4** help, aid, boost, enhance.
◇ *Word origin: Queer* probably comes from German *quer,* oblique, slanted, hence out of the usual or straight course.

"Now, my suspicion is that the universe is not only queerer than we suppose, but queerer than we *can* suppose . . . I suspect that there are more things in heaven and earth than are dreamed of, in any philosophy."
—*J. B. S. Haldane*

---

quell *v. The dictator quelled the uprising:* crush, put down, put an end to, quench, quash, extinguish, ruin, destroy, stamp out; vanquish, wreck, conquer, defeat, beat down, worst, rout; overcome, overpower, overthrow, overwhelm; subdue, subjugate, suppress; reduce, scatter, disperse.
Ant. encourage, foster, foment, defend; enlarge.

quench *v.* **1** *Iced tea will quench your thirst on hot days:* satisfy, satiate, sate, appease, slake. **2** *The firemen quenched the blaze:* extinguish, put out, blow or stamp out, stifle, smother; dampen, cool suddenly, douse; crush, quell, put down, suppress, annihilate.

querulous *adj. She divorced her nagging, querulous husband:* complaining, grumbling, peevish, fretful, disagreeable, faultfinding, finicky, fussy, finical, exacting, difficult, obstinate; dissatisfied, discontented, resentful, long-faced, sour; whining, whiny, shrewish, petulant, pettish, crabbed, grouchy, captious, disputatious, splenetic, irascible, quarrelsome, nettlesome, irritable, cross, cranky, touchy, testy, waspish.
Ant. uncomplaining, agreeable, good-tempered, complacent; contented, satisfied, pleased; genial, cheerful, easy, calm, equable.

query *n.* **1** *Direct all queries to your nearest dealer:* question, inquiry; matter in dispute, problem, issue, question at issue; request, demand; inquisition, investigation, inquest; examination, interrogation; search, quest.
—*v.* **2** *The police queried him about his alibi on the night of the crime:* ask, question, put a query to, inquire of, make inquiry, quiz, interrogate, seek by asking, sound out; investigate, subject to examination, examine, look into, inspect; catechize. **3** *I query his trustworthiness:* consider questionable, question, doubt, have doubts about, suspect, harbour suspicions, distrust, mistrust, impugn; dispute, controvert, challenge, impeach.
◇ *Usage note:* Both *query* and *inquiry* may refer to questions: *The librarian at the information desk handled all queries* (or *inquiries*) *about books. Make inquiries about the airline's flights to Delhi; when they leave, when they arrive, how much a ticket costs, and if lunch is served on board. Inquiry,* however, is also used to refer to a full-scale investigation: *The Ministry of Transport held an inquiry into the rail crash.*

Exploring the Word: *Quest, question,* and *query* come from Latin *quaerere,* to seek, ask. The same base gives us *acquire, acquisition,* and *acquisitive,* to get by seeking, that which is sought and obtained, and seeking possessions; *conquer,* to seek out and obtain completely; and *conquest,* that which has been sought out and obtained; *exquisite,* literally much sought after, hence desirable, appealing, fine, rare; *inquire,* to ask into, and *inquiry* and *inquest,* an asking into, an investigation; *request,* literally to ask again, and *require, requirement, requisite,* and *requisition,* referring to seeking something because it is needed.

---

quest *n.* **1** *The knights of King Arthur's Round Table set out on their quest for the Holy Grail:* search, pursuit, exploration, hunt, seeking, crusade, journey, enterprise, adventure.
—*v.* **2** *Jason quested after the Golden Fleece:* seek, search; pursue, hunt.

question *n.* **1** *Did you ask him a question?:* something asked, request for information, query. **2** *The question was put to the vote:* matter of discussion, issue, point in dispute, moot point, question at issue, subject of investigation, proposal, proposition, motion, subject; bone of contention; uncertainty, misgiving, doubt, dubiety, objection; dispute, controversy. **3** *I'd like to travel more, but there's always the question of money:* problem, difficulty, consideration, matter, *Informal* rub.

—*v.* **4** *Stop questioning me about my personal business!:* ask, inquire of, query, quiz, interrogate, put questions to, sound, *Informal* pump; grill, put through the third degree, examine, cross-examine, bombard with questions, subject to examination, investigate, look into; test, drill, catechize. **5** *I question his capacity for leadership:* consider questionable, be uncertain of, lack confidence in, doubt, have one's doubts about, call in question; hesitate to believe, harbour suspicions about, suspect; distrust, mistrust, impugn; refuse to believe, disbelieve; take exception to, challenge, oppose, dispute.

Ant. 1, 4 answer, reply. **1** response. **3** solution, explanation. **4** respond. **5** trust, be certain of, have confidence in, have no doubts about; believe.

◇ *Usage note:* The phrase *the question as to whether* has needless words. Use either *the question is, whether,* or *the question whether.* Thus, instead of *The question as to whether we shall go or not remains,* use *The question whether we shall go or not remains* or *Whether we shall go or not is undecided.*

◇ *Spelling tip:* Remember that it takes two or more questions to make a *questionnaire* and that there are two *n's* in *questioNNaire.*

quibble *v.* **1** *Pedants tend to quibble over the precise meanings of words:* raise trivial objections, carp, nag, cavil, niggle; pick a fight, spar, fence; be evasive, dodge the issue, equivocate.

—*n.* **2** *A quibble over exact wording delayed passage of the bill:* trivial objection, cavil, petty distinction, nicety; evasion, equivocation, dodge, shift, shuffle, distraction, delaying tactic; subtlety, subterfuge; white lie, prevarication, pretence, artifice, duplicity.

◇ *Word origin: Quibble* comes from Latin *quibus,* to whom, which was used vaguely in so many legal documents and phrases (we use it in "to whom it may concern") that it came to mean an evasion of a specific name or truth, hence an evasive point or distraction, a trivial difference.

quick *adj.* **1** *After a quick courtship they got married:* brief, rapid, fast, abrupt, sudden, precipitate, headlong; fleet, swift, whirlwind, hasty, expeditious, accelerated. **2** *She ran with quick steps to the house when it started raining:* rapid, speedy, fast, expeditious, precipitate, brisk, swift, fleet, hasty, hurried; flying, nimble-footed, light-footed, winged; brisk, spirited, lively, sprightly, agile, spry, nimble, frisky, animated, active, energetic, vigorous, vivacious. **3** *My son is a quick learner and always comes top of the class:* quick-witted, bright, apt, intelligent, discerning, perspicacious; smart, clever, acute, keen, astute, sharp, alert, wide-awake, vigilant; sagacious, brainy; prompt, eager, shrewd, penetrating; expert, skilful, facile, able, dextrous, adroit, deft, adept. **4** *He has a quick tongue, but is usually sorry afterwards,* excitable, impetuous, impulsive, highly strung, impatient; irritable, sharp, keen, snappish, fiery, peppery, hot-blooded, hot-tempered, irascible, choleric, splenetic; waspish, petulant; testy, touchy, temperamental.

Ant. 1-3 slow. **1** long, lingering, gradual. **2** deliberate; sluggish, lazy, lethargic; heavy; inert, inactive; dull, wearisome. **3** dull, unintelligent, stupid, unresponsive, slow-witted; inexpert, unskilful, maladroit; sluggish, lazy. **4** calm, patient; restrained, temperate.

◇ *Word origin: Quick* comes from Old English *cwic,* living, alive. From "alive," the meaning changed to "lively," responding readily or eagerly, alert (a *quick* mind), and then to swift, occurring in a short time. We still find *quick,* meaning alive, living flesh, or living feelings in the phrase *the quick and the dead* or *cut to the quick.*

"And inasmuch as feeling, the East's gift,
Is quick and transient—comes, and lo, is gone—
While Northern thought is slow and durable."
—*Robert Browning*

quicken *v.* **1** *Is there any way in which we can quicken the preparation of dinner?:* make more rapid, speed, accelerate, expedite, hasten, hurry, hurry on, precipitate, hustle; further, advance, propel, drive, rush, dispatch; press, urge, egg on, impel. **2** *A good debate can quicken one's mind:* excite, stimulate, activate, stir, pique, provoke, spur, goad, rouse, arouse, affect, instigate, galvanize, kindle, incite, enkindle, inspire, inspirit, fire; actuate, vitalize, vivify, animate, enliven, energize, revive, invigorate, move, sharpen, refresh.

Ant. 1 slow down, slacken, check, delay, hinder, impede, obstruct, retard. **2** deaden; put to sleep, enervate, dull.

quiet *adj.* **1** *It was so quiet that you could hear a pin drop. Why are you so quiet this evening?:* making no sound, silent, noiseless, soundless, hushed, soft, low, calm, not busy or active; reticent, saying little, taciturn, reserved, uncommunicative, mum, speechless, inarticulate, voiceless, mute. **2** *My summer vacation was anything but quiet:* restful, untroubled, unruffled; calm, mild, halcyon, serene, tranquil, peaceful, peaceable, pacific, placid. **3** *The dog lay quiet at his master's feet:* inactive, inert, passive, undisturbed, becalmed, at rest; dormant, sleeping, slumbering, dozing, comatose, lethargic; still, motionless, immobile, at a standstill, stock-still; unmoved, fixed, stable, stationary, immovable, stagnant. **4** *He was a quiet man who didn't let small things upset*

him: gentle, clement, mild, meek, docile, not rough or turbulent, retiring, easy-going, contented; sedate, composed, cool-headed, phlegmatic, collected, steady, unexcitable, imperturbable, unperturbed, patient; humble, modest, moderate, temperate; unobtrusive, undemonstrative, unimpassioned, dispassionate, even-tempered. **5** *The quiet décor of her home made you feel comfortable and at ease:* not showy or loud, plain, simple, unostentatious, unassuming, unpresumptuous, unpretentious; not bright, soft, mellow, subdued.
—*v.* **6** *The teacher tried to quiet the students:* make quiet, silence, still, hush, mute; stifle, muffle, smother; bridle one's tongue. **7** *The aspirin seemed to quiet the headache:* relieve, allay, mitigate, palliate, comfort, soothe, soften, alleviate, mollify, assuage, settle, set at ease, compose, calm, pacify, tranquillize; dull, blunt, deaden; lessen, decrease, weaken; still, abate, lull, quell, subdue, bring to a standstill; stay, stop, curb, check, arrest, put a stop to, suspend, discontinue, terminate, bring to an end.
—*n.* **8** *In the quiet of my room I tried to think things out:* quietness, silence, still, stillness, hush, lull, quietude, soundlessness, noiselessness, muteness; calm, calmness, tranquillity, serenity, peace, peacefulness, placidity, rest, repose, relaxation; ease, gentleness.
Ant. 1 noisy, talkative, verbose, loquacious. **2** excited, troubled, ruffled, agitated, upset, perturbed, turbulent. **3** active, busy, disturbed, restless, agitated, disquieted; awake, alert. **4** turbulent, violent, mercurial, excitable, perturbable, impatient; immoderate, intemperate, passionate, high-spirited. **5** obtrusive, demonstrative, conspicuous, showy, blatant, loud, ostentatious, pretentious; bright, harsh, glaring. **6** stir, agitate, disturb, perturb. **7** worsen, heighten, enlarge, strengthen, intensify, increase. **8** noise, din, activity, disturbance, commotion.

quietly *adv.* **1** *I want you to sit quietly:* silently, soundlessly, noiselessly, mutely, softly; speechlessly, inaudibly. **2** *He waited quietly for his mother to return:* patiently, calmly, serenely, contentedly; composedly, collectedly, unexcitedly, unperturbedly, placidly, tranquilly, peacefully, pacifically; tamely, meekly, mildly; moderately, temperately; undemonstratively, dispassionately. **3** *She was a quietly pretty woman:* unobtrusively, unpretentiously, unostentatiously, unassumingly, without ceremony; modestly, humbly, unboastfully, diffidently, bashfully; coyly, demurely.

quip *n. Dorothy Parker was known for her quips:* clever remark, witty saying, witticism, retort, repartee, wisecrack, *French* bon mot; banter, badinage, sally, spoof, riposte; play on words, word-play, pun, epigram, double entendre; cutting remark, crack, sarcasm, jest, taunt, gibe, jeer, raillery, jape, joke, gag.

quirk *n.* **1** *Wearing that silly hat everywhere was a quirk of hers:* peculiarity, oddity, eccentricity, idiosyncrasy, crotchet; odd fancy, foible, caprice, vagary, whimsical notion, whimsy, whim; aberration, abnormality; kink, fetish. **2** *By a quirk of fate the brothers found themselves on opposite sides during the Civil War:* sudden twist, turn, freak accident.

"He is no wise man who will quit a certainty for an uncertainty." —*Samuel Johnson*

---

quit *v.* **1** *He wants to quit the urban rat race and buy a farm in the country:* leave, go away from, take off, depart, get away from, withdraw, drop out, retire from; take wing or flight, skip or flee the coop. **2** *You can't quit your job now:* resign, leave a job, have done with, renounce, reject, disavow, disown, relinquish, let go, part with, give up, abdicate; abandon, forsake.
—*adj.* **3** *I wish I could be quit of these responsibilities!:* released from obligation, clear, free, rid, exempt, absolved, discharged; exculpated, exonerated, acquitted, all straight; clear of debt, owing nothing.
Ant. 1 arrive at, come to; remain, stay. **2** keep, maintain.

> **Exploring the Word:** *Quiet, quit,* and *quite* look and sound so much alike because they all come from Latin *quietus,* quiet, rest, which gives us *quiet. Quit* literally means "at rest," hence to stop, cease, leave, or resign. *Quite* was a Middle English variant of *quit,* and from the meaning of "completely stopped" or "ended" came to mean totally, noticeably. The related Latin verb *quiescere,* to be quiet, gives us *quiescent,* quiet, while the Latin phrase *quietus est,* it is quit, for ever put to rest, gives us our *quietus,* as in the slang phrase to put the *quietus* on something, that is to silence, suppress, or kill it.

quite *adv.* **1** *It is not quite dawn yet. The bottle is quite empty:* totally, completely, entirely, wholly, *Latin* in toto; fully, at all points, altogether; perfectly, utterly, positively; exactly, precisely; outright, out and out, in all respects, throughout. **2** *It was quite a bargain:* actually, in fact, really, surely, in reality, indeed, truly, verily, in truth, veritably; certainly, assuredly; absolutely. **3** *He was quite rude:* to a considerable extent, exceedingly, extremely, remarkably, very, excessively, considerably, in a great degree, to a high degree, highly; vastly, hugely, enormously, exceptionally, unusually. **4** *I suppose that she is quite pretty, but that's about all!:* relatively, moderately, to a certain extent.

quiver *v.* **1** *The building quivered as the explosives went off:* shake slightly, shudder, tremble, shiver, quake, quaver, vibrate, convulse, twitch, jump, jerk, jolt; palpitate, pulsate,

throb; oscillate, fluctuate; wriggle, wobble, totter; be agitated, pant.
—*n.* **2** *He could tell by the quiver in her lower lip that she was about to cry:* quivering, tremulous motion, vibration, tremble, shiver, shudder, shake, tremor, flutter, flicker; quaver, convulsion, seizure; throb, pulsation, palpitation; tic, spasm, twitching.

quixotic *adj. He had the quixotic idea of challenging all his enemies in turn to a duel:* extravagantly chivalrous, absurdly romantic, fanciful, impulsive, whimsical; chimerical, dreamy, sentimental, poetic, head-in-the-clouds, utopian, idealistic, impractical; fantastic, wild, madcap, preposterous, absurd, ridiculous.
Ant. realistic, down-to-earth, practical, serious.
◇ *Word origin: Quixotic* refers to the extravagant idealism of Don *Quixote*, the man from La Mancha, hero of the Spanish novelist Miguel de Cervantes' satiric romance *Don Quixote de la Mancha* (published 1605–1615). The name of the laughable, lovable, and often admirable Don *Quixote* comes from Spanish *quixote*, thigh-piece of a suit of armour.

quiz *v.* **1** *The teacher quizzed the children on history. Father quizzed my boy-friend about his intentions:* question, examine, subject to examination, test; query, ask, inquire of, sound, put to the proof; interrogate, investigate, cross-examine, *Informal* pump.
—*n.* **2** *The history quiz consisted of 10 questions:* test, examination, exam; investigation, interrogation, questioning, inquest, inquisition, inquiry; cross-examination.

quota *n. Each salesman has a quota of business to bring in each month:* portion, share, proportion; allotment, apportionment, distribution, allocation, assignment; quantity, measure, ration, percentage; minimum.
◇ *Word origin: Quota* comes from shortening the Medieval Latin phrase *quota pars*, how great a part, how great a share of a total. Also *quot*, how many.

R

rabble *n.* **1** *The railway station was swarming with a rabble of kids on their way to camp:* mob, swarm, disorderly crowd. **2** *"Rabble" is an insulting term for "common people":* commoners, proletariat, lower classes, the masses, rank and file, populace, the great unwashed, riff-raff, hoi polloi, the herd, *German* Lumpen proletariat, *French* canaille.
Ant. 2 aristocracy, upper classes, nobility, élite, high society.

rabid *adj.* **1** *Rabid dogs were destroyed by police on the Continent last year:* suffering from rabies, hydrophobic, foaming at the mouth. **2** *The enemy came on in a rabid "human wave" assault and we had to fall back:* fanatical, wild, raging, frenzied, frantic; maniacal, berserk, crazed. **3** *She is a rabid football fan:* zealous, fervent, ardent.

race *n.* **1** *It rained on the day of the stock-car races:* competitive trial of speed, contest, rally, competition, heat.
—*v.* **2** *I'll race you from here to the corner. Stirling Moss and Jim Clark raced cars professionally:* run a race, enter in a race, engage in a contest of speed, compete in a race; operate. **3** *She overslept and had to race to the office:* hasten, hurry, run, run like mad, hie oneself, rush, hustle, make a mad dash, hotfoot it, dart, fly, dash.
Ant. 3 go slowly, crawl, creep.

racket *n.* **1** *Who's making all that racket?:* loud noise, din, shouting, caterwauling, babel, clamour, clangour; commotion, clatter, uproar, vociferation, roar; hubbub, tumult, hullabaloo, hurly-burly, rumpus; pandemonium, disturbance, stir, turmoil, banging around, turbulence. **2** *The dishonest moneylender operated a racket:* illegitimate enterprise or occupation, game, underworld business undertaking. **3** *Informal What's your racket?:* business, occupation, line, *Slang* game.
Ant. 1 quiet, silence, tranquillity, peace.
◇ *Word origin: Racket*, a confused noise or commotion, may possibly have been coined to imitate the sound of the rattle of dice. (There was a medieval dice game called *racket.*) Racket (illegitimate enterprise) is short for *grab-racket*, a 19th-century criminal slang term for various modes of swindling. The word went underground for a generation or so, then suddenly reappeared, together with *racketeer* and *racketeering*, during the U.S. Prohibition era. As late as 1928, *racketeering* was sufficiently unfamiliar to British readers to require the following definition in the *Daily Express:* "'Racketeering' is the new word that has been coined in America to describe the big business of organized crime."

raconteur *n. A toast-master should be a practised raconteur:* skilled storyteller, anecdotist, narrator, spinner of yarns, teller of tales, fabulist, romancer.

racy *adj.* **1** *Women were fascinated by him because of his racy life-style:* vigorous, exhilarating, heady, zesty, zestful, keen, energetic, spirited, fast, lively, animated, exciting, stimulating, buoyant, sparkling, glowing. **2** *It's quite a racy novel:* suggestive, lurid, risqué, bawdy, ribald, off-colour, salacious, prurient, erotic.

Ant. unexciting, dull, flat, bland, insipid, flat, stale, jejune.

radiance Also **radiancy** *n.* **1** *One of the gems had a deep, subtle radiance:* lustre, sparkle, glitter, dazzle, iridescence, lambency, gleam, sheen, splendour, resplendence, brightness, brilliancy, brilliance, luminosity, effulgence, refulgence, luminousness, coruscation, incandescence. **2** *Her face positively glowed with radiance when she won first prize:* animation, joy, happiness, rapture.

Ant. 1 dullness, dimness, murkiness, darkness. **2** sadness, glumness, dourness.

Exploring the Word: From the ancient wheel to *radio, rayon,* and atomic *radioactivity* seems a long way, but in fact it is not. The Latin word for a spoke of a wheel is *radius,* which gives us our word *radius, ray, radiate, radiant, radiance, radio* (short for *radio-telegraphy,* the transmission and reception of certain electromagnetic rays), *radioactivity* (the spontaneous emission of certain electromagnetic rays) and *radium* (so-named because it emits such rays). The trademark name *Rayon* was coined from *ray* because of the synthetic fabric's thin raylike filaments. (Incidentally, *rayon* is actually the French word for *ray.*)

radiant *adj.* **1** *The sky was radiant yesterday:* shining, bright, sunny, giving off rays of light, luminous, effulgent, refulgent, lustrous, glowing, aglow, incandescent; glittering, gleaming, dazzling, brilliant, sparkling, scintillating, flashing. **2** *The bride looked radiant. The lover gave his sweetheart a radiant smile:* bright with joy, beaming, glowing, happy, elated, ecstatic, overjoyed, joyous, blissful, rapturous, pleased, delighted.

Ant. 1 dull, dark, sombre, dismal, murky, lustre-less, sunless, shadowy, cloudy, gloomy, overcast, black. **2** sad, sorrowful, unhappy, disconsolate, gloomy, sombre, joyless, cheerless; displeased, unpleased.

radiate *v.* **1** *The electric heater radiated warmth. Heat radiated from the fire:* emit heat, light, or other radiation; give out, circulate, give off, beam, shed, transmit; diffuse, scatter, disperse, disseminate, shed, pour, spread, spread out, carry. **2** *Spokes radiate from the hub of the wheel:* branch out, spread, diverge, go in all directions.

Ant. 1 absorb, soak up. **2** converge, come together, move together, meet, focus, centre, concentrate, close in, zero in.

radical *adj.* **1** *There are radical differences between binary and decimal numeration:* basic, fundamental. **2** *Disbanding the company seemed a rather radical step:* severe, extreme, immoderate, drastic, precipitate, rash, inordinate. **3** *When a society is polarized, the radical Left confronts the radical Right and there's nobody in between:* favouring drastic reforms, extreme, extremist, militant, revolutionary.

—*n.* **4** *When we use "radical" as a noun, we usually mean a left-winger:* revolutionary, extremist, left-wing militant; rebel, firebrand, free-thinker, anti-establishmentarian.

Ant. 1 superficial, negligible, inessential, trivial. **2, 3** conservative, moderate, middle-of-the-road. **4** right-winger, reactionary.

◇ *Word origin: Radical* comes from Latin *radix,* root. Hence, a *political radical* wants to change the very roots of a governmental system, whilst in mathematics a *radical* is a quantity that is the root of another, and in chemistry a *radical* is a group of atoms that act as a basic unit or root in a compound. Latin *radix,* root, also gives us our word *eradicate* (to root out, hence to destroy completely). Our word *root* is also distantly related to Latin *radix.*

ragamuffin *n. Ragamuffins scavenged the war-torn streets for scraps of food:* urchin, guttersnipe, street arab, hoyden, *French* gamin, (*fem.*) gamine; tatterdemalion, sloven, wretch; beggar, tramp, derelict, itinerant, vagabond, rag-picker, vagrant.

◇ *Word origin:* The original *ragamuffin* was not a street urchin but a demon *Ragamoffyn* in *Piers Plowman* (1393) by the English poet William Langland.

rage *n.* **1** *His rage over the crime was beyond words. The defeated fighter stamped up and down in a rage:* violent anger, wrath, extreme agitation, frenzy, indignation; fury, choler, vehemence, temper, furore, excitement; resentment, animosity, bitterness, spleen, madness, perturbation, ire, umbrage, high dudgeon, displeasure, irritation, pique; passion, violent emotional state, rampage, storm, frenzy, temper, tantrum, ferment, paroxysm. **2** *Big ear-rings are the rage now:* object of widespread enthusiasm, prevailing taste, current style, fashion, vogue, mode, craze, mania, fad, the latest thing, the "in" thing, the last word, *French* le dernier cri.

—*v.* **3** *She raged when her jewels were stolen whilst under police protection:* speak with anger, act with fury, storm, throw a fit, flare up, fly off the handle, lose one's temper, show violent anger, be violently agitated, be furious, vent one's spleen, blow one's top, explode, blow up, fulminate, rant, roar, raise Cain, fume, seethe, boil, rave, froth at the mouth, lose one's cool. **4** *The war raged for several years:* continue violently, go at full blast.

Ant. 1 calm, calmness, coolness, equanimity;

pleasure, gratification, joy, delight. **3** be pleased, be gratified; remain unruffled, keep one's cool.

ragged *adj.* **1** *The ragged children begged the tourists for money:* clothed in tatters, wearing worn clothes, dressed in rags, seedy. **2** *He wore a ragged old coat:* worn to rags, worn-out, worn, tattered, shaggy, shabby, torn, rent, threadbare, frayed, tatty, battered, shredded, the worse for wear, patched, shoddy. **3** *Jane's nerves were ragged by Sunday morning:* overtaxed, strained, exacerbated, aggravated, at breaking-point, run down.

raid *n.* **1** *In AD 844, the Normans began raids on the Spanish coasts:* surprise attack, sudden assault, razzia, onset, predatory incursion, inroad, foray. **2** *Nobody move — this is a raid!:* authorized police break-in, round-up.
—*v.* **3** *Tonight we raid Calais! Many night-clubs in Soho were raided:* attack, assault, swoop down on, invade, storm, enter suddenly, make a raid on.

rail[1] *n.* **1** *The boy leant against the iron rail:* horizontal support, bar, railing, barrier, fence, banister. **2** *I'm afraid of flying — I prefer to go by rail:* railway, train.
◇ *Word origin:* A *rail* is a thin, straight bar. It comes from Old French *reille,* itself derived from a variant form of Latin *regula,* a straight bar, from which we also get our word *rule,* a straight measuring rod and an inflexible principle.

rail[2] *v. He was always railing against the government:* vociferate, inveigh, fulminate, speak harshly, declaim, scold, talk angrily, raise one's voice, vituperate, rant, rant and rave, rage; shout abuse, take on, carry on; scream, gnash one's teeth, foam at the mouth, raise a hue and cry, *Slang* blow up, blow one's top.

"Sunshine is delicious, rain is refreshing, wind braces up, snow is exhilarating; there is no such thing as bad weather, only different kinds of weather." —*John Ruskin*

---

rain *n.* **1** *Rain doesn't seem likely at the moment:* rainfall, precipitation, (*variously*) drizzle, mizzle, sprinkle, cloudburst, rain-storm, shower, downpour, drench, deluge, torrent. **2 rains** *We don't see many tourists when the rains come:* the rainy season, monsoon. **3** *A rain of pamphlets fell from the plane:* shower, deluge, spate, plethora.
—*v.* **4** *It rained for 40 days and 40 nights:* (*variously*) pour, shower, drizzle, sprinkle, *Slang* come down in buckets, rain cats and dogs, come down in sheets. **5** *The mill chimneys rained black soot on the city:* shower, drop, send down, shed. **6** *He rained gifts on his future bride:* lavish, shower.

raise *v.* **1** *The carpenter raised the shelf above the reach of children. The dressmaker raised the hem of the dress:* erect, put up, elevate, lift. **2** *The building was raised on level ground:* build, set up, construct, erect, put up. **3** *The farmer raises cows and sheep. We want to raise our children to be decent men and women:* grow, breed, produce, cultivate, develop, nurse, nurture, foster; rear, bring up. **4** *That discussion raised my hopes:* excite, stimulate, pique, sharpen, rouse, arouse, awaken, summon up, stir up, spark, urge, spur, inspire, boost, kindle, inflame. **5** *There's one point I'd like to raise:* put forward, bring up, advance. **6** *The landlord raised my rent:* increase, make higher, inflate, jack up. **7** *We're trying to raise funds for the Red Cross:* collect, solicit, canvass, obtain, bring in, procure, amass. **8** *The curfew was raised:* lift, end, terminate.
Ant. 1 lower, let down, drop; sink, depress. **2** destroy, ruin, raze, demolish, wreck, smash, tumble, level. **4** quell, quash, put to sleep, calm, soothe. **5** suppress, keep quiet, pass over in silence. **6** decrease, lessen, cut, reduce, diminish. **8** start, begin, initiate, establish, effect; reinstate.
◇ *Usage note:* Don't confuse *raise* and *rise. Raise* means to lift something or to grow or breed something: *All those in favour raise their hands. It's easy to raise tulips. Rise* means to get up (of one's own accord, not to be lifted) or to grow higher (not just to grow): *The sun will rise at 4.57 a.m. tomorrow. Please rise when the judge enters the court. The bread won't rise unless you add yeast.* Incidentally, don't confuse *raise,* to lift up, with *raze,* to demolish. A demolition crew *razes* a building.

rake[1] *v.* **1** *Rake the soil round the bole of the tree:* scrape, scarify, harrow, hoe; comb, scour, ransack, go over with a fine-tooth comb. **2** *Army bullets raked the get-away car:* sweep with gunfire, enfilade, pepper.

rake[2] *n. Don't have anything to do with that rake, young lady!:* dissipated man of fashion, voluptuary, sensualist, libertine, roué; lecher, seducer, womanizer, Don Juan, Lothario, Casanova, immoralist, debauchee, prodigal, profligate; rascal, rogue, playboy.
◇ *Word origin: Rake[2]* and *rakish* come from *rakehell* (profligate gentleman), a word which enjoyed great currency between 1550 and 1725. It derives from the old phrase *to rake hell* — a *rake* being such a wicked fellow that you would have to "rake Hell" to find his like.

rakish *adj.* **1** *He's a rakish young man:* loose-living, dissolute, dissipated, immoral, debauched. **2** *He wore his hat at a rakish angle:* jaunty, sporting, breezy, sauntering, airy, dashing, cavalier, debonair, gallant, bumptious, swaggering.

rally *v.* **1** *The teacher rallied the group before setting out for the museum:* reassemble, bring together again, reconvene, reunite, call together, unite, assemble, collect, gather, muster. **2** *His brothers rallied to his side when he was in* *trouble:* come to the aid or support of a person or cause, rush, be at beck and call. **3** *The patient rallied after taking the new medicine. The team rallied in the second half:* recover strength, revive, get well, get better, recuperate, improve, convalesce, *Archaic* recruit; take a turn for the better, pick up, pull through, come round, get one's second wind, catch up, score.

—*n.* **4** *Will you be attending tonight's political rally?:* gathering, caucus, mass meeting, convention, assembly, congregation, convocation, *Slang* powwow. **5** *The patient's sudden rally surprised the doctors:* recovery, revival, recuperation, renewal of strength, restoration, convalescence, improvement.

Ant. **1** disband, dissolve, dismiss, discharge, release, disperse. **2** desert, abandon, forsake. **3** lose strength, become weaker, get worse, take a turn for the worse, sink, fail. **5** relapse, loss of strength, collapse.

ram *v.* **1** *He rammed the stake through the rotting wood:* drive, force, jam, thrust, push firmly; strike, hit, beat, hammer. **2** *The car rammed into a tree:* slam, crash, smash, run into, hurtle; dash, batter, butt, bump.

ramble *v.* **1** *We like to ramble around the neighbourhood on sunny afternoons:* wander, stroll, saunter, meander, perambulate, traipse, rove, drift, roam, gad, gad about, range, gallivant. **2** *The road rambles through a thick wood:* meander, zigzag, snake, wind, twist, go hither and thither or here and there.

—*n.* **3** *She likes taking a ramble through the woods on sunny afternoons:* idle walk, stroll, saunter, traipse, roam, hike.

rambling *adj. In a rambling two-hour speech the dictator promised to restore democracy:* digressive, discursive, circuitous, prolix, diffuse, disjointed, uneven.

Ant. concise, to the point, direct.

rampage *n.* **1** *The gang went on a rampage and shot several people:* violent spree, jag of violence.

—*v.* **2** *The terrified elephants rampaged through the jungle:* move or behave violently, storm, rage; go berserk, run amok.

◇ *Word origin: Rampage,* a violent dashing about, and *rampant,* wild, unchecked, come from Old French *ramper,* to stand menacingly on the hind legs (as of a bear or lion). From this we also get our words to *romp,* to frolic boisterously, and *rompers,* a style of child's play-suit. The original connotation of a beast rearing up on its hind legs is still found in referring to coats of arms in heraldry, where *rampant* refers to a figure of a beast of prey shown in profile, standing on its hind legs with the forelegs elevated, as in the description of a coat of arms having "a lion rampant on a field of blue."

rampant *adj.* **1** *Malaria is still rampant in some swampy regions:* widespread, rife, prevalent, unchecked, unrestrained, raging, ungovernable, uncontrollable. **2** *The knight's coat of arms showed two leopards rampant on an azure field:* (of a four-legged animal) standing on the hind legs, standing up, erect.

Ant. **1** restrained, curbed, checked.

◇ *Word origin:* See RAMPAGE.

rampart *n. The enemy attacked the outer ramparts of the fort. The hill served as a rampart protecting the town from floods:* protective barrier, defensive wall; fortification, barricade, protective wall, bulwark, earthwork, breastwork, parapet, bastion.

ramshackle *adj. They took shelter in a ramshackle old barn:* shabby, deteriorating, dilapidated, falling to pieces, tumbledown, run-down, crumbling; rickety, unsteady, unstable, tottering, shaky.

Ant. new, modern, well-built; steady.

◇ *Word origin:* An old variant form of our verb to *ransack* was to *ramshackle.* A house rickety enough to look as if it had been ripped up by marauders was said to be of a *ramshackled* appearance. By the early 19th century the *-d* had been dropped from the end of the word, and the connection with *ransack* long since forgotten.

rancid *adj. Our tea was served with ghee, a liquid butter with a rancid taste:* rank-tasting, rank-smelling, gamy; old, strong, high.

Ant. fresh, pure.

rancour *n. A victim of injustice is bound to be full of rancour:* resentment, bitterness, ill feeling, ill will, hostility, antagonism, spleen, acrimony; hatred, animosity, spite, spitefulness, animus, antipathy, enmity, hate.

Ant. amity, goodwill, friendship, friendliness, amicability.

random *adj. The two friends had a random encounter in the street. Father likes to take random walks round about the town:* occasional, chance, unintentional, unplanned, undesigned, unpremeditated, unintended, unexpected, fortuitous, accidental, hit-or-miss, offhand, casual, off the cuff, haphazard, aimless, adventitious, stray.

Ant. deliberate, planned, intended, premeditated.

range *n.* **1** *The company puts out a large range of products:* variety, scope, gamut, selection. **2** *Hiring and firing are within the range of his responsibilities. The enemy plane flew out of the range of our guns:* sphere, field, orbit, domain, province, reach, limit, radius, bounds, purview. **3** *The Drakensberg range:* chain of mountains, ridge, sierra, massif. **4** *She cooks excellent meals on the old kitchen range:* cooker, cooking-stove, oven.

—*v.* **5** *Her children's ages range from three to eighteen:* extend, run, stretch, reach. **6** *He spent the summer ranging the countryside:* rove, wander, roam, explore.

rank[1] *n.* **1** *It was a terrible play — of the very lowest rank:* grade, quality, class, order, type, sort.

2 *His rank allowed him to join some exclusive clubs. The captain was promoted to the rank of major:* social standing, position, class, standing, status, estate; echelon, professional grade, level, classification. **3** *Soldiers stood in ranks for inspection:* line, row, file, column.

—*v.* **4** *Buying a boat ranks low on my list of priorities:* have rank, take rank, be ranked, have place, be classed, stand, rate, come out. **5** *The plates were ranked in order on the dresser:* arrange in rows, set in order, line up.

rank² *adj.* **1** *The island was covered with rank greenery:* overgrown, overabundant, luxuriant, lush, lavish, dense, profuse, tall, high-growing, jungly, tropical, wild. **2** *Throw all the rank food out, then get that refrigerator mended!:* strong-smelling, ill-smelling; rancid, foul; stale, off. **3** *It was a rank insult:* utter, absolute, total, complete, sheer, bald, unmitigated, downright, flagrant, arrant, rampant, glaring; gross, crass, coarse, filthy, nasty, scurrilous; outrageous, monstrous, atrocious.

Ant. **1** spare, scanty, sparse. **2** fresh, sweet-smelling, unspoiled.

◇ *Word origin: Rank²* comes from Old English *ranc,* strong. Hence, a *rank smell* is a strong one, *a rank growth* of weeds is a strong or flourishing one, *rank injustice* is a strong or complete injustice.

rankle *v. His harsh words rankled:* irritate, gall, chafe, rile, pique, fester, go down badly.

Ant. please; soothe.

◇ *Word origin: Rankle* comes ultimately from Greek *drakōn,* snake, and in medieval medical usage meant an ulceration or abscess (because a typical abscess burns like a snakebite). Greek *drakōn* is also the basis of our word *dragon.*

ransack *v.* **1** *We ransacked the attic for grandmother's photograph album:* rummage through, rake, comb, search, turn upside down, scour. **2** *Vandals ransacked the cathedral:* pillage, sack, vandalize, plunder, loot, rifle, raid, despoil, ravage, gut, strip.

rap *v.* **1** *The teacher rapped his knuckles until they were sore. We rapped at the door, but there was no answer:* tap, thump, drum, knock. **2** *The officer rapped out a command:* utter abruptly, bark, speak sharply. **3** *Informal The critics rapped the new play:* criticize, knock, come down on, *Slang* pan, clobber.

—*n.* **4** *We heard a rap at the door:* light quick blow, knock, tap, bang. **5** *Informal I refuse to take the rap for something you did:* blame, responsibility, adverse consequences.

Ant. **3** praise, eulogize, laud, flatter, rave about.

rapacious *adj. The pirates of old were a rapacious lot. His rapacious ways made him wealthy but friendless:* plundering, marauding, ransacking, thievish, pillaging, looting, predatory; greedy, avaricious, covetous, grasping, mercenary; insatiable, voracious, wolfish, ravenous.

rapid *adj. She made a rapid departure. It was an age of rapid strides in science:* quick, fast, fleet, swift, speedy; hasty, hurried, instant; brisk, active; expeditious, precipitate, prompt; feverish, agitated, rushing, galloping, flying; accelerated, unchecked.

Ant. slow, leisurely, gradual; deliberate; lazy, dilatory.

rapidly *adv. He was rapidly becoming the nation's number one T.V. star. She ran rapidly up the stairs:* swiftly, fast, speedily, expeditiously, with rapid strides, apace, quickly, at a great rate, by leaps and bounds, overnight, at full speed; briskly, hurriedly, hastily, pell-mell, helter-skelter, as fast as one's legs will carry one, like a house on fire, like a shot, in top gear.

Ant. slowly, gradually.

rapport *n. He enjoys great rapport with all his children:* relationship, camaraderie, affiliation, fellowship; connection, link, interrelationship.

◇ *Pronunciation tip:* Pronounce this word *ra-PORE.* The pronunciation, in which the final *-t* is silent, reflects the fact that the word was recently borrowed from French (*rapport,* relationship).

> **Exploring the Word**: *Rapture, rapt, rape, rapacious, ravish, ravage, ravenous, rapid, ravine,* and *surreptitious* all come from Latin *rapere,* to take by force, seize and remove. Thus, *rapture* and *rapt* refer to being seized or carried away by pleasure or a lofty emotion; *rape* means to take by force in a sexual sense, and *rapacious* means given to seizing or taking, hence grasping, greedy, predatory; *ravish* can mean either to cause rapture or to rape, but *ravage* means to plunder, to pillage and burn, lay waste. *Ravenous* literally means so hungry that one desires to seize food, by force if necessary; *rapid* refers to fleeing with something taken or seized, hence quick, swift; *rapids* literally are swift, rushing water, while a *ravine* is a gorge cut by such water.

rapt *adj.* **1** *She was a rapt listener:* engrossed, enthralled, absorbed, interested, attentive, intent. **2** *There was a rapt expression on his face whenever he looked at his sweetheart:* transported, ecstatic, rapturous, enchanted, enraptured, spellbound, enrapt, charmed, intense, bewitched, captivated, moonstruck, awed, entranced, fascinated, delighted; bemused, dreamy.

Ant. **1** uninterested, disinterested, detached, indifferent, incurious; bored.

rapture *n. Seeing Rome for the first time filled the young visitor with rapture:* ecstasy, joy, felicity, delight, bliss, beatitude.

Ant. unhappiness, sorrow, woe, misery.

rare *adj. Friends like him are rare:* seldom found, seldom to be met with, hard to find; scarce, few, few and far between, infrequent, uncommon, unusual, exceptional, out of the ordinary.

Ant. plentiful, many, bountiful, abundant; ubiquitous, profuse, manifold, often found, easy to find; frequent, habitual, regular.

◇ *Word origin: Rare* comes from Latin *rarus,* rare, infrequent. Our word *rare,* as in a *rare steak,* comes from Old English *hrēr,* half-cooked. Oddly, the word applied only to eggs until the 18th century, and *rare-done* or *rare-boiled* meant the same as "poached" and "soft-boiled." Nowadays it is most frequently heard in reference to the amount one wishes one's steak to be cooked!

rarely *adv. He rarely studied, yet he passed every exam:* seldom, not often, hardly ever, scarcely ever, infrequently, on rare occasions, only occasionally; hardly; once in a while, once in a blue moon.

Ant. often, frequently, always, continually, ordinarily, usually.

rascal *n.* **1** *That rascal was always playing practical jokes on us:* mischievous person, trickster, prankster, scamp, imp, devil, scallywag, rapscallion. **2** *Her second husband was something of a rascal:* rake, rogue, devil, delinquent, reprobate, rakehell.

◇ *Word origin: Rascal* comes from Old French *rascaille,* scabby, scruffy, mangy folk, i.e. the "great unwashed." The word ultimately derives from Latin *radere,* to scratch, which also gives us our word *rash* as in *skin rash.*

rash *adj. I think you were rash to accept his proposal. Hotspur was a rash young man:* precipitate, abrupt, hasty, premature, imprudent, injudicious, indiscreet, incautious; brash, irresponsible, reckless, headlong, impulsive, impetuous, adventurous, ungoverned, uncontrolled, unchecked, ill-advised; careless, heedless, thoughtless, unthinking; harebrained, devil-may-care; foolhardy, foolish.

rate *n.* **1** *She can read at the rate of 100 words a minute:* speed, pace, tempo. **2** *The rates at the hotel ranged from £10 to £15 per night:* price, charge, figure, fee, dues; cost, expense, levy, tariff, toll; assessment.

—*v.* **3** *I rate that performance one of the best I've ever seen:* classify, class, rank, count, measure, estimate; regard, deem, look on.

rather *adv. I was rather surprised at her behaviour:* to a certain extent, quite, very, pretty; somewhat, a bit, slightly, in some degree, comparatively, relatively, fairly, in some measure, moderately, *Informal* sort of, kind of; after a fashion, more or less.

ratify *v. A majority is needed to ratify the new resolutions:* confirm, validate, approve, uphold, affirm, make valid, authenticate, make good, endorse, acknowledge, sanction; settle firmly, authorize, certify, *Informal* O.K.; consent to, agree to, accede to.

Ant. veto, disapprove, refute, disagree to; invalidate, disavow, repudiate.

ratio *n. The ratio of hydrogen to oxygen in water is 2 to 1:* proportional relation, interrelationship, proportion, proportionality, equation, fixed relation; arrangement, distribution, apportionment.

ration *n.* **1** *Each flood victim was provided with a stated daily ration of food:* share, allotment, apportionment, provision; measure, dole, due. **2 rations** *The besieged fort had rations for two more days:* provisions, stores, food, provender.

—*v.* **3** *If the fuel shortage continues, will petrol have to be rationed?:* distribute by restricted allotments, apportion, allocate, allot, mete out.

rational *adj.* **1** *It was a rational plan and bound to succeed:* based on reason, sound, reasonable, logical; solid, wise, sage, sagacious; judicious, advisable, perspicacious; credible, feasible, plausible. **2** *The doctors found him to be rational and so able to stand trial:* sane, compos mentis, in one's right mind, lucid, normal, sound, responsible, *Slang* all there.

Ant. 1, 2 irrational, unreasonable, unsound, insane.

rationale *n. I simply don't understand the rationale of his plan:* basis, underlying reason, logic, foundations, grounds; reasoning, philosophy, key concept.

rationalize *v.* **1** *The boy's mother rationalized his bad behaviour as rebellion against unjust authority:* justify, account for, make allowance for, make excuses for, excuse, explain away, put a gloss upon, palliate, whitewash. **2** *They were unable to rationalize the apparent miracle:* explain, interpret rationally; account for objectively, bring into conformity with reason.

rattle *v.* **1** *The engine rattled. The earth tremor rattled the dishes in our cupboard. The old car rattled down the street:* clatter, clink, clank, roll loosely, jar, shake, bounce, clatter. **2** *He rattled on about his various ailments:* chatter, maunder, prate, blather. **3** *Any mention of the accident rattled her:* shake, upset, disturb, perturb, agitate, jangle, faze, discomfit, fluster, flurry, discompose, disconcert, distract, throw; nonplus, bewilder, confuse.

—*n.* **4** *The rattle of the windows was caused by the wind:* clacking, clatter, clang, clank.

Ant. 3 calm, compose, soothe, settle, relax.

raucous *adj. Don't speak in such a raucous voice! The raucous yelling of the crowd could be heard streets away:* harsh, rough, jarring, grating, hoarse, grinding, jangling; discordant, strident, cacophonous, inharmonious, dissonant, stertorous, blaring, loud, ear-splitting; shrill; piercing.

Ant. soft, mellow, mellifluous, soothing.

ravage *v. The invaders ravaged the countryside:*

cause widespread damage to, ruin, lay in ruins, raze, gut, lay waste, waste, wreck, desolate, destroy, demolish, devastate, rape, spoliate, despoil, shatter; pillage, plunder, maraud, sack, loot, strip, ransack, raid, overrun.

◇ *Usage note: Ravage* means to destroy or wreck: *A hurricane ravaged the island. Ravish* means two separate things: (1) to fill with delight, to be ravishing: *The opera ravished the audience;* (2) to abduct or to rape: *The soldiers ravished the female captives.*

rave *v.* **1** *The distraught man went on raving until finally he was led away:* rant, rage; babble, ramble; make delirious utterances. **2** *Father raved when I disobeyed him:* storm, fume, be furious, be mad, go on, be angry, lose one's temper, flare up, explode, thunder; sputter, bluster, run or go amok, *Slang* fly off the handle, blow one's top. **3** *He raved about Brando's performance:* speak glowingly, gush, effervesce, bubble, wax, go on and on, expatiate, rhapsodize; rant, carry on.
—*n.* **4** *His book has received raves from all the critics:* an extravagantly good review, rave review, an extremely favourable criticism, *Informal* kudos, good press, compliments, words of praise, high praise, flattery.
—*adj.* **5** *The critics gave rave notices to that new play:* laudatory, highly favourable.
Ant. **3** cavil at, deplore. **4** condemnation, disapproval, *Slang* knock. **5** condemning, faultfinding; bad, disparaging.

ravenous *adj. Scrooge epitomised ravenous greed for money. The children were ravenous after going all day without eating:* predatory, ravening, rapacious, covetous, greedy, avaricious, grasping, insatiable, insatiate; hungry, voracious, starving, famished; gluttonous, piggish.

ravish *v.* **1** *The slave-traders ravished babes from their mothers' arms:* seize and carry away by force, make off with, snatch. **2** *As it says in the Bible, their houses shall be spoiled and their wives ravished:* rape; outrage, violate, abuse, deflower, defile. **3** *She was ravished by the sight of her first grandchild:* transport, enrapture, enthral, overjoy, delight, gladden, cheer, captivate, enchant, charm, entrance, fascinate; tickle pink, *Slang* knock-out.
Ant. **3** displease, disgust, provoke, rile, pique,
◇ *Usage note:* Senses **1** and **2** above are nowadays rare except in highly literary contexts.

ravishing *adj. You look simply ravishing, my dear:* enchanting, alluring, charming, entrancing, captivating, bewitching; very pleasing, delightful, gorgeous, splendid, beautiful, sensational, *Slang* smashing.
Ant. terrible, awful, disgusting, repulsive.

raw *adj.* **1** *The main ingredient of steak tartare is raw chopped beef:* uncooked, unprepared, unbaked; underdone, under-cooked, rare. **2** *The raw materials arrived at the factory by the trainload:* natural, crude, unrefined, unprocessed, rough, not manufactured, not finished, basic. **3** *The raw forces of the country people were no match for the well-trained invaders:* untrained, unskilled, undisciplined, unpractised, unexercised, undrilled, unprepared, inexperienced, inexpert, amateurish, uninitiated, unseasoned, untried, untested, undeveloped, crude, unrefined; untaught, ignorant; fresh, green, unfledged, immature, unripe, callow, young. **4** *These are the raw facts:* frank, plain, brutal, unembellished, unvarnished, bare. **5** *It's rather raw outside, so dress warmly:* chilly, damp, bleak; cold, harsh, nipping, pinching, biting, piercing, cutting, bitter, numbing, freezing; inclement, blustery, windswept.
Ant. **1** cooked, prepared; baked; done, well-done, well-cooked. **2** refined, manufactured, wrought, finished. **3** trained, skilled, disciplined, practised, experienced, professional. **4** embellished, gilded, smoothed over, edulcorated. **5** warm, balmy, fair, sunny, mild.

raze *v. They're going to raze this building to the ground to make way for the new bypass:* tear down, pull down, level, fell, flatten, knock down, break down, dismantle, reduce; wreck, smash, demolish, destroy, ruin, wipe out, obliterate, remove.

reach *v.* **1** *When will we reach Cape Town? Can you reach his hand?:* arrive at, get to, come to, make, get as far as, set foot in or on, land at, enter, *Slang* make, *Nautical* put in or into; succeed in touching, contact, touch, go to, attain, get hold of, seize, grasp, secure, get to, come to. **2** *He reached for the phone and quickly dialled a number:* stretch, stretch out, extend; strain after something, grab at; make an effort. **3** *You can reach me at this number:* contact, get, find, get in touch with, communicate with. **4** *Record sales this week reached well into the thousands. The temperature reached the 90's:* extend, climb, spread; approach, move, amount to, go to, hit.
—*n.* **5** *A man's reach should exceed his grasp:* capacity, range, compass, scope, extent; act of reaching, stretch; grab, grasp, clutch.

reaction *n.* **1** *Water encourages the reaction of iron and oxygen to form rust:* chemical change, chemical transformation; nuclear change in an atom, change in the nucleus of an atom. **2** *What was her reaction when you proposed to her?:* response, reply, answer, counteraction, reflex. **3** *After radical political reform the forces of reaction are always a danger:* (*variously*) resurgent, conservatism, right-wing comeback, counter-revolution, restoration, backlash.

reactionary *adj.* **1** *Metternich's reactionary policy could not stop the movement for political and social reform:* reversionary, regressive, counter-revolutionary, die-hard, right-wing, ultraconservative.

—*n.* **2** *The baron was a reactionary who favoured a return to the feudal system:* ultra-conservative, right-winger, counter-revolutionary, die-hard.

read *v.* **1** *He can read several languages. Can you read the Morse code?:* apprehend, understand, construe, comprehend, discern, perceive; make out the meaning or significance of, translate, interpret, explain; study, pore over, scan, analyse, decipher. **2** *I read an interesting article in yesterday's newspaper:* peruse, scan, glance or run the eye over, note, study; pore over. **3** *The actor read his lines well:* utter, render in speech, speak aloud something written, recite; give a public reading or recital; deliver, present. **4** *Although it was a comedy, you could read biting social comment into the actors' lines:* adduce, extrapolate, construe. **5** *The thermometer now reads 50 degrees. The invitation read "Open house — come one, come all!":* have a certain wording, be worded, say, go; show, indicate.

"When I am dead, I hope it may be said:
'His sins were scarlet, but his books were read.'"
—*Hilaire Belloc*

---

readily *adv.* **1** *The younger mechanic readily fixed the car. The call to arms was met readily:* promptly, immediately, at once, straight away, instantly, quickly, expressly, in no time, without delay, speedily, pronto; easily, without difficulty, effortlessly, smoothly, with no effort, hands down; on the spur of the moment, at short notice, at the drop of a hat. **2** *She readily accepted his proposal of marriage:* willingly, without reluctance or demur, in a ready manner, freely, graciously, with good grace, with goodwill, ungrudgingly.
Ant. 1, 2 unreadily. **1** slowly, with difficulty. **2** unwillingly, reluctantly, grudgingly.

ready *adj.* **1** *It took us several hours to get the gymnasium ready for the school dance. I'll be ready to help you whenever you need me:* completely prepared, in readiness, set, all set, duly equipped, fitted out, furnished; in condition for immediate action or use, fit, serviceable, in working order; immediately available for use, accessible, present, at hand, handy, on hand, on tap, in harness, primed; punctual, speedy, expeditious, prompt; equal to, up to; mature, ripe. **2** *I'm always ready to make new friends:* willing, eager, disposed, inclined, prone, pre-disposed, apt. **3** *He was a ready pupil, quickly learning all his tutor had to teach him and more:* prompt in understanding or comprehending, acquisitive, perceptive, discerning, quick in perceiving, attentive, alert, wide-awake, bright, astute, sharp, acute, keen, cunning, shrewd, showing quickness, quick-witted, clever, ingenious, resourceful; skilful, artful, masterly, expert, dextrous, apt, adroit, deft, facile, versatile. **4** *The bank was ready to foreclose unless he could raise enough money to pay off the mortgage:* likely at any time or moment, liable; tending; on the verge of, on the brink of, at the point of, set, just about. **5** *The country was made ready for war:* prepare, put in order, equip, fit out.
Ant. 1-4 unready. **1** unprepared, unequipped, unfurnished; unfit, out of order; unavailable, inaccessible, unhandy; tardy, late, slow, inexpeditious; immature. **2** unwilling, loath, disinclined, indisposed, reluctant, hesitant. **3** slow, plodding, pedestrian, unexceptional.

real *adj.* **1** *This jacket is made of real leather:* genuine, actual, authentic, bona fide. **2** *This is the real story:* true, factual, valid, veritable, unquestionable, veracious, truthful; actual, well-grounded, solid, substantial, substantive, tangible; rightful, legitimate; absolute, positive, certain, unadulterated, unalloyed, unvarnished. **3** *His love was real:* sincere, not affected, unaffected, genuine, unfeigned; true, honest, pure, unadulterated.
Ant. 1-3 unreal, fake, false. **1** imitation, counterfeit, factitious. **2** imagined, imaginary. **3** insincere, affected, feigned, faked.

realistic *adj. He was realistic about his failure. It was such a realistic landscape that one could almost walk into it:* pragmatic, down-to-earth; true-to-life, natural, naturalistic, lifelike, graphic, descriptive, depictive; real, authentic, genuine, truthful, faithful, precise.
Ant. unrealistic, impractical, idealistic, romantic, fanciful.

realize *v.* **1** *I don't think you fully realize the importance of his speech:* comprehend, apprehend, understand, gather, grasp, get, fathom, appreciate, absorb, feel strongly; perceive, see into, penetrate, make out, discern; be cognizant of, recognize, cognize; conceive, imagine. **2** *He realized his fondest dream when he won the Booker prize:* actualize, fulfil, complete, consummate, bring to pass, bring about, effectuate, carry out, execute, carry through, work out, discharge, do, produce, perform; attain, get, achieve, accomplish, make good. **3** *She realized very little by selling those stocks:* get as profit, gain, acquire, profit, clear, net, obtain a return, make money, make capital of, accomplish.

really *adv. Did he really say that? Really, he's the most exasperating person I know:* actually, in fact, truly, truthfully, genuinely; literally, indeed; surely, certainly, positively, unquestionably, absolutely, categorically.

realm *n.* **1** *His realm extended half-way into Asia:* dominion, kingdom, domain, empire, royal domain, monarchy, demesne, land, country; nation, state. **2** Also **realms** *That plan is not beyond the realm of possibility:* sphere, province, orbit, region, field.

rear[1] *n.* **1** *Please move to the rear of the bus! Her window looks out on the front lawn, mine overlooks the park in the rear:* back, end, tail end, heel,

stern, hind part, back part, postern, posterior; after part, area or position behind. **2** *Three companies made up the rear:* last or back part of an armed force, rearguard.
—*adj.* **3** *The rear end of the car was dented, but we had no trouble getting the boot open:* at, of, in, or near the back; back, hindmost, aftermost, after, posterior, rearmost; dorsal; aft.
Ant. **1** front, fore, forefront, forepart; foreground; frontage. **2** front rank, front lines, advanced guard, vanguard. **3** front, frontmost, forward, foremost, leading.

rear[2] *v. The boy was reared by his aunt:* bring up, raise, care for; train, cultivate, develop, nurture, nurse, foster.

reason *n.* **1** *There was no reason for her rudeness:* cause, occasion, motive, grounds, justification, explanation, rationale. **2** *Use the reason that God gave you:* brains, faculties, wit, comprehension, apprehension, understanding, perception, head, intelligence, intellect, perspicacity, acumen, sense, common sense, penetration, awareness, discernment, insight, *Slang* grey matter, gumption, nous. **3** *An obstinate person will not listen to reason:* common sense, logic, reasoning, appeal to reason, argumentation, exhortation. **4** *There is no reason in a madman:* rationality, soundness of mind, reasonableness, mental balance, sanity, normality, sense, lucidity, clear-headedness.
—*v.* **5** *The solution is there if you care to reason it out:* think through, work out, solve.
Ant. **4** irrationality, unsoundness, mental unbalance, insanity, abnormality, incoherence.
◇ *Usage note:* Try to avoid the construction *the reason is because* by rephrasing your sentence or by using *the reason* or *the reason that* instead. Thus say and write *The reason we're late is that our car broke down* (or better still *We're late because our car broke down*), not "The reason we're late is because our car broke down."

reasonable *adj.* **1** *Your proposal sounds reasonable, but we'll have to talk about it further:* judicious, wise, sensible, intelligent; logical, rational; sane, sound, credible, plausible, probable, possible, likely; well-grounded, well-founded, admissible, justifiable, understandable; legitimate, proper, suitable, fitting, equitable, fair, just. **2** *Be reasonable in your dealings with people and you'll be respected:* of good sense or sound judgement, exercising reason, rational, logical, thinking, understanding, thoughtful, reflective; just, fair, impartial, objective, judicious, level-headed, patient, cool-headed; moderate, prudent, circumspect; intelligent, sensible, wise, knowing, sage. **3** *It was a reasonable request. My rent is reasonable:* not exceeding a reasonable limit, not unlikely, not excessive, not extreme, natural, predictable, moderate, lenient, temperate, fair, just, equitable.
Ant. **1-3** unreasonable, irrational, unintelligent, unsound, impossible; unjust, unfair, outrageous.

> **Exploring the Word:** *Reason, rational, rationale,* and *rationalize* all refer to conscious thought or calculating. *Rate, ratio,* and *ration* refer to calculating, in a more mathematical way, in order to determine a price, percentage, or share. All these words come from Latin *ratio,* reason, account, and its adjective *rationalis,* endowed with reason, as in the sentence *Homo est animal rationale:* "Man is a rational animal." Our legal word *arraign* has this same base and means to call into court to answer an indictment, to accuse someone for a specific reason.

reasoning *n.* **1** *Dr. Johnson's powers of reasoning were quite formidable:* ratiocination, logic, thought, thinking; deduction, inference, analysis, penetration. **2** *Can't you understand our reasoning here?:* argument, train of thought, rationale, analysis, interpretation, ground, basis.

reassure *v. Reassure the child that he has your confidence:* personally assure, bolster, inspire hope in, encourage, inspirit, uplift, buoy up, cheer; comfort, set one's mind at rest.
Ant. dishearten, discourage, disconcert.

rebel *n.* **1** *The rebels were arrested and tried for treason. The film director was a rebel amongst his peers:* insurgent, insurrectionist, traitor, turncoat, deserter; secessionist, seceder, separatist, anarchist; revolutionist, revolutionary, resister; iconoclast, nonconformist, dissenter, malcontent, upstart.
—*v.* **2** *The peasants rebelled but were ultimately powerless:* resist lawful authority, rise up, take arms against an established order, oppose by force, revolt, mutiny, riot. **3** *He rebelled at the idea of teaching young children:* be repelled by, turn away from, pull or draw back from, flinch, wince, quail, react, shrink, shy, recoil, be unwilling, avoid.

rebellion *n. The junta soon crushed the leftist rebellion:* insurrection, revolt, insurgency, revolution, mutiny, uprising, upheaval.
Ant. resignation, submission.

"A little rebellion, now and then, is a good thing, and as necessary in the political world as storms in the physical." —*Thomas Jefferson*

---

rebellious *adj. The king retaliated against the rebellious barons by confiscating their lands. Many children are rebellious during their teens:* defiant, disobedient, insubordinate, intractable, refractory, contrary, recalcitrant, pugnacious, fractious, contumacious, quarrelsome; up in arms, mutinous, seditious, insurgent, insurrectionary, revolutionary, turbulent, truculent, unruly, unmanageable, ungovernable, uncontrollable, disorderly, alienated.

Ant. patriotic, loyal, dutiful, deferential; obedient, unresistant, subordinate, subservient.

rebuff *n.* **1** *She met his innuendo with a sharp rebuff:* rejection, refusal, putting off; repulse, snub, slight, cold shoulder, *Slang* put-down, slap in the face.
—*v.* **2** *Elizabeth rebuffed Mr. Collins' proposal:* snub, slight, reject, spurn, ignore, disregard, cold-shoulder, refuse, deny, decline, *Slang* turn down; check, keep at a distance, put off.
Ant. 1 welcome, acceptance, encouragement, come-on, come hither; spur, aid. **2** welcome, encourage.

rebuke *v.* **1** *The clerk was harshly rebuked for misplacing some important files:* scold, upbraid, reproach, admonish, take to task, reprimand, reprove, chide, remonstrate with, lecture; censure, berate, call down, dress down, *Slang* bawl out, take down a peg; find fault with, blame, tear off a strip.
—*n.* **2** *The sharp rebuke came as a complete surprise:* scolding, reprimand, remonstrance, admonishment, upbraiding, admonition, reprehension, reproach, reproof, reproval, tongue-lashing; disapproval, censure, castigation, chiding, berating, *Slang* bawling out, dressing down.
Ant. 1, 2 praise. **1** laud, applaud, congratulate; commend, compliment, approve. **2** laudation, commendation, compliments, approval; *Informal* pat on the back, congratulation.

recalcitrant *adj. The recalcitrant youth needed more understanding teachers:* stubborn, obstinate, unwilling, unsubmissive, headstrong, mulish, pigheaded, bull-headed, wilful, contrary, balky, intractable, perverse, wayward.
Ant. obedient, compliant, amenable, submissive, yielding; controllable, manageable, governable.

recall *v.* **1** *I'm sorry, I don't recall your name:* recollect, remember; recognize, place. **2** *They recalled some reserve units when war broke out:* reactivate, remobilize, call back; reinstitute, revive, reanimate.
—*n.* **3** *All the facts I learnt then are lost beyond recall. She has total recall for lists of numbers:* recollection, memory, remembrance; faculty of memory, ability to remember.

recapitulate *v. The newscaster recapitulated the Prime Minister's speech:* summarize, repeat in essence, sum up; reiterate, recount, repeat, relate, restate, reword, rephrase.

recede *v. As he got older his hair began to recede. The floodwaters have receded:* retreat, go back, withdraw, regress, abate, ebb, subside; retire, retreat, retrogress.
Ant. advance, proceed, move forward.
◇ *Spelling tip: Cede* means to yield or surrender. To *recede* is to yield or surrender and then withdraw, as the tide does. Thus *recede* ends in *cede, reCEDE.*

receipt *n.* **1** *This bill is payable upon receipt:* arrival, receiving, reception, recipience, admission, admittance, acceptance, acquisition, possession. **2** *The delivery-man asked me to sign a receipt:* written acknowledgement of payment or goods received, voucher, release, discharge, transferral. **3 receipts** *We opened a shop and our first day's receipts exceeded our expectations:* amount or quantity received, profits, net profits, return, returns, gain, proceeds, share, takings, gate; *Slang* cut, revenue, income, earnings; pay, wages, payment, reimbursement, remuneration, emolument. **4** *Archaic This mince pie is made according to an old family receipt:* recipe, formula.

receive *v.* **1** *Have you received my cheque yet? The patient received the best of care:* get, acquire, secure, come by, be in receipt of, obtain, be given. **2** *The hotel receives guests from all over the world:* accommodate, take in; admit, put up. **3** *The prisoners received harsh and unfair treatment:* encounter, meet with, experience, go or pass through, have inflicted on one, submit to, be subjected to, undergo, sustain, suffer. **4** *Madam is not receiving callers today. He was received with open arms:* be at home to, entertain, admit; welcome, greet, meet. **5** *The book was well received by the critics and the public:* regard, accept, approve, react to, adjudge.
◇ *Spelling tip:* This is one of the most frequently misspelt words in the English language. You will always spell it right if you remember the basic spelling rule, "*i* before *e* *except after c* (or when sounded like *a* as in *neighbour* and *weigh*)." Thus, *c* is followed by *e* and *i: reCEIve.*

recent *adj. I was surprised to see so recent a film on television. The bicycle is a recent purchase. In recent times the price of almost everything has gone up:* new, modern, up-to-the-minute, contemporary, up-to-date, lately made, late; novel, fresh; not long past, of yesterday, latter-day.
Ant. old-fashioned, dated, old, long past, remote, long ago.

receptacle *n. Throw your litter in that wire receptacle in the corner:* holder, container, depository, repository, receiver, carrier; box, bin, basket, skip, hopper, hamper, compartment; vessel.

reception *n.* **1** *I couldn't fathom her cool reception — what had I done?:* act of receiving one, welcome, greeting, recognition. **2** *We had a big reception for the new ambassador:* affair, social gathering; party, fête, soirée, *Informal* do.

receptive *adj. The inventor hoped to find the examiner at the Patent Office in a receptive mood:* favourably disposed, open-minded, accessible, approachable, amenable, hospitable, responsive, interested, susceptible.
Ant. unreceptive, illiberal, unresponsive, closed-minded, narrow-minded, prejudiced, biased.

recess *n.* **1** *Parliament has risen for its summer*

recess: suspension of business, intermission, break, coffee-break, respite, rest, breathing-space, hiatus, pause, lull, *Informal* let-up; interim, interlude, interval; holiday, vacation. **2** *The safe was set in a recess of the wall:* receding part of space, indentation, hollow, break, fold; alcove, cell, nook, niche, slot, pigeon-hole, corner, bend; cleft, gorge, gap, pass. **3 recesses** *Outwardly he appeared forgiving, but in the recesses of his mind he planned revenge:* inmost part, depths, penetralia.

reciprocal *adj. Our relationship is based on reciprocal respect. Britain and France made reciprocal trade agreements:* mutual, common; shared; interdependent, returned, given in return, exchanged, equivalent, give-and-take, one for one; complementary, bilateral, corresponding, interrelated, interchangeable, interchanged, linked.

Ant. one-way, unilateral.

"Kindness is generally reciprocal; we are desirous of pleasing others because we receive pleasure from them." —*Samuel Johnson*

---

reciprocate *v. He reciprocated his friend's admiration. They've invited us to dinner so many times that we must reciprocate:* return, feel, give in return, give or take mutually, requite, interchange; respond, return the compliment, act likewise, make return.

recital *n.* **1** *She gave her first public recital at the Town Hall when she was 14:* solo musical performance, concert. **2** *His recital of the poem was flawless. Did she give you a recital of her woes?:* recapitulation, narration, recitation, rendition, delivery, performance, reciting; narrative, telling, talk, discourse, dissertation; report, description, detailed statement, particulars, graphic account; public reading, oral exercise.

reckless *adj. He was fined for reckless driving:* incautious, heedless, unheeding, unmindful, careless, irresponsible, thoughtless, regardless, inconsiderate, mindless, unthinking, neglectful, negligent, unwatchful, unwary, unaware, oblivious, inattentive, unconcerned; wild, daring, cavalier, daredevil, devil-may-care, volatile; precipitate, rash, unsolicitous, indiscreet, imprudent, uncircumspect, hasty, impulsive, fickle, unsteady; foolhardy, foolish, insensible; flighty, madcap, scatter-brained, hare-brained, giddy.

Ant. cautious, heedful, mindful, careful, wary, aware, observant, thoughtful, regardful, responsible, deliberate.

reckon *v.* **1** *The wages were reckoned according to the number of hours worked:* count, add, add up, total, tally, balance, figure, calculate, compute, estimate. **2** *Because we are happy and healthy we reckon ourselves fortunate. He reckoned that we were only a few miles from our destination:* regard, esteem, consider, deem, think, judge, adjudge, estimate; count, account, class, rank, rate, appraise, assess, value; determine, surmise, estimate, come to or arrive at a conclusion regarding, decide, guess, speculate. **3** *Informal I reckon you'll be able to leave the hospital soon:* guess, fancy, expect, presume, surmise, suppose, imagine. **4** *I didn't reckon on his arriving two days ahead of time:* count, bank, plan, bargain. **5** *If you come home late you'll have me to reckon with!:* deal, cope, handle.

reckoning *n.* **1** *A reckoning was made of all outstanding accounts:* count, total, tally, adding, sum, calculation, computation; estimate, estimation; statement of an amount due, bill, account, charge, settling of an account. **2** *Both Christianity and Islam predict a time of reckoning for mankind:* judgement, last judgement, doom.

recline *v. She was reclining on a couch:* lie back, lie down, rest in a recumbent position, repose; lean, take one's ease, lounge, loll, sprawl.

◇ *Word origin:* ***Recline*** comes from Latin *re-* (back) + *clinare* (to lean), to lean back, hence to lie back, lie down. The same Latin verb gives us *decline* and *incline.*

recognition *n.* **1** *In this disguise, you can walk into your own home without a chance of recognition even by your loved ones:* identification, act of being recognized. **2** *Some artists gain recognition only after death. The controversy over the new regime held up recognition for several years:* acceptance, acknowledgement, understanding, comprehension, notice; act by which one government recognizes the existence of another, validation, diplomatic relations.

recognize *v.* **1** *I didn't recognize you in that disguise:* know, identify, place, make out, discern, pick out, sight, spot. **2** *We recognize your financial problems, but your account is overdue:* be aware of, appreciate, understand, comprehend, respect, acknowledge, realize, see, discern, make out; admit, know. **3** *Portugal recognized Guinea-Bissau in 1974:* establish diplomatic relations with, acknowledge.

Ant. 2 ignore, overlook, turn one's back upon, close one's eyes to.

recoil *v.* **1** *Spiders always made her recoil:* draw back, hang back, start, shrink back, jump back, retreat, blench, quail, revolt; wince, flinch, demur, falter, shirk, blink, fail; cower, cringe. **2** *The cannon recoiled sharply when it went off:* fly back, spring back, bound back, jump back, kick.

"It is hard, if not impossible, to snub a beautiful woman — they remain beautiful and the rebuke recoils." —*Winston Churchill*

---

recollect *v. I can't recollect where we met:* recall, call to mind, remember, place.

recommend *v.* **1** *The supervisor recommended me for promotion:* put forward, present as worthy

of, mention favourably, speak well of, favour, endorse, advocate, vouch for. **2** *The doctor recommended a change of scenery:* urge, suggest, propose, advise, prescribe, order, counsel.
Ant. **1** mention unfavourably, disapprove. **2** forbid.
◇ *Spelling tip:* If something is good enough to *recommend* to a friend, it is worth having two *m*'s: *recoMMend.*

recommendation *n. It was on your recommendation that we appointed that new typist:* commendation, good word, behest, approval, endorsement, reference, *Slang* plug.
Ant. condemnation, disapproval, rejection.

recompense *v.* **1** *The company recompensed him for working overtime:* compensate, remunerate, pay, reimburse, repay, reward.
—*n.* **2** *This money isn't enough recompense for all the time and effort I put into the job!:* compensation, remuneration, payment, reparation, repayment, return, reward, indemnification.

reconcile *v.* **1** *Father was unable to reconcile my brothers:* conciliate, propitiate, restore to friendship, reunite. **2** *A pacifist cannot be reconciled to war:* conciliate, win over, persuade, resign. **3** *We had better reconcile the accounts:* settle, set straight, make up, square; harmonize, fix up, patch up, rectify, adjust, correct.

reconnaissance *n. Reconnaissance of enemy territory showed a heavy concentration of artillery:* inspection, survey, scrutiny, observation, reconnoitring, scouting, investigation, exploration; surveillance.

record *v.* **1** *You should record precious comments like that:* write down, set down in writing, put or place on record, make an entry of, register, transcribe, take down, note, copy, inscribe for posterity, jot down, make a memorandum of; enter, catalogue, list, enrol, post, admit, introduce, log; chronicle; register, tape. **2** *A cardiograph records the heartbeat:* register, show, indicate.
—*n.* **3** *A record of each child's birth was kept in the family Bible:* account, report, document, register; docket, file; journal, annals, chronicle, archive, history, proceedings; note, memorandum, memo, jotting. **4** *His employment record has always been good. He has no record with the police:* facts known about a person or thing, history, report of actions, account; background, experiences, adventures; conduct, performance, career. **5** *Mark Spitz broke several world swimming records at the 1972 Olympics:* best performance known, top performance, greatest achievement of its kind to date, unbeaten mark, unsurpassed example, best rate attained.
Ant. **1** erase, obliterate, cancel, delete; disregard, omit.

recoup *v. He went back to the baccarat table hoping to recoup his losses:* regain, win back, retrieve, redeem, recover, replace; make up for, make good, make amends for, redeem; provide an equivalent for.
◇ *Word origin: Recoup* comes from the French prefix *re-* (back) + *coup* (a sudden blow, stroke), hence to recover or make up a loss with a sudden stroke. French *coup*, a sudden blow, stroke, is also in *coup de grâce* (final blow, finishing stroke) and *coup d'état* (a quick stroke of policy, especially the seizure of power).

recover *v.* **1** *The army was unable to recover any of the territory that it had lost. The stolen jewels were finally recovered:* get back, retrieve, recoup, regain, find, repossess, reclaim, redeem, recapture, reconquer, win back; make up for, make good, restore, offset, balance, compensate. **2** *She's at home now recovering from the operation:* return to good condition, regain strength, be restored to health, get well, recuperate, convalesce, return to health, take a turn for the better, improve, heal, mend; rally, come round, pull through; regain control of oneself, be oneself again, revive, revivify, resuscitate, rejuvenate, restore, pick up.
Ant. **2** relapse, fail, grow worse.

recreation *n. What's your favourite recreation?:* diversion, leisure activity, pastime, play, hobby, sport, entertainment, amusement, avocation; diversion, relaxation.
◇ *Word origin:* Because of the pronunciation, we often forget that *recreation* is literally a *re-creation*, a creating again, hence a refreshment of body or mind by pleasurable exercise or amusement. (However, don't confuse the pronunciation of the common word *recreation* with that of the somewhat literary word *re-creation*, as in the sentence *A good translation must be a re-creation of the original.*)

rectify *v. The accounting error was rectified before the ledgers were audited:* right, set right, put right, make right, correct, adjust, regulate, straighten, square; mend, amend, emend, fix, repair, revise; remedy, redress, cure, reform.

recumbent *adj. One sleeps in a recumbent position:* lying down, prone, prostrate, supine, flat, stretched-out, horizontal; reclining, leaning.
Ant. upright, erect, standing, standing-up, vertical; sitting.

recur *v.* **1** *If the headache recurs, you should have your eyes tested:* occur again, repeat; return, come again, reappear; resume, persist, continue. **2** *The good times of my college days frequently recur to me:* come back, return to mind, flash across the memory, be remembered, haunt one's thoughts.

recurrent *adj. I had a recurrent dream about a sunflower:* frequent, periodic, intermittent, regular, appearing again, reappearing.

red *adj.* **1** *She wore red lipstick:* blood-coloured; (*variously*) maroon, wine, ruby, vermilion, crimson, cardinal, scarlet, cherry, rosy, rose;

pink, coral, flame. **2** *Her red cheeks showed her embarrassment:* blushing, reddened, ruddy, flushed, rosy, florid, blooming, rubicund, glowing, inflamed, flamin burning.

"He redeemed his vices with his virtues."
—*Ben Jonson*

redeem *v.* **1** *Present this pawn ticket and you can redeem your ring:* buy back, repurchase; ransom; reclaim, recover, retrieve, regain, repossess, recoup. **2** *By getting the work done on time he redeemed his promise to me:* keep, fulfil, make good; discharge. **3** *She worked every weekend to redeem the lost time:* make up for, cover, defray, compensate for, make good, settle; make amends for, atone for, satisfy, recover, regain, retrieve. **4** *The preacher went about the countryside trying to redeem lost souls:* rescue, save, deliver from sin and its consequences, evangelize, turn from sin, set straight again; convert, reform.

Ant. 1 lose, forfeit, yield, give up. **2** break; shun, disregard, violate.

◇ *Word origin: **Redeem**, redemption,* and *ransom* come from Latin *re-* (back, again) + *emere* (to buy), to buy back. Hence, to *redeem* means to regain possession of by paying a price, as to *redeem* a mortgage, to fulfil a promise, make amends, or rescue from sin and its "price" or penalties; in Christian theology, *redemption* is salvation from sin through the atonement of Christ (who has paid for one's sins); and to *ransom* is to secure the release of a prisoner for a price.

redress *n.* **1** *Redress of a sort is obtained when a court grants damages to a victim of fraud:* reparation, compensation, recompense, payment, indemnification, restitution, rectification, amends, satisfaction, easement, relief.

—*v.* **2** *The king redressed past injustices by granting the peasants land:* correct, right, set right, rectify, make reparation for, compensate for, make retribution for, amend, make up for; reform; remedy, ease, relieve.

reduce *v.* **1** *We've reduced the price of the coat from £100 to £65:* lessen, diminish, discount, mark down, slash, cut. **2** *It's easy to reduce if you simply watch what you eat:* lose weight by dieting, slim, diet, trim down, slenderize. **3** *The military court reduced the major to the rank of captain. Poverty reduced him to begging for a living:* lower in rank, demote, *Slang* bust, break; force, lower. **4** *The hurricane reduced the house to a shambles:* bring down, leave in; damage, bring to destruction. **5** *Water reduces the potency of alcohol:* minimize, lessen, lower, cut down, dilute, thin, water, blunt the edge of, dull; modulate, tone down, moderate, temper, ease, abate, mitigate, assuage, soften; checkmate, retard, slow down, curb, check; debilitate, atrophy, weaken, devitalize, enfeeble, cripple, incapacitate, undermine.

Ant. 1, 3 increase. **1** add to, augment, enlarge, extend, mark up. **2** gain weight, put on pounds. **3** promote, elevate. **5** heighten, enhance, strengthen.

redundant *adj.* **1** *Many city churches become redundant when the population moves to the suburbs:* not needed, surplus to requirements, empty, neglected; out of work, dismissed. **2** *The story doesn't need all this redundant background material:* superfluous, overflowing, extra, excess, surplus, superabundant, inordinate.

reek *n.* **1** *The reek of rotti vegetables came from the rubbish dump:* unpleasant smell or odour, stink, stench, effluvium. **2** *You could hardly breathe for the reek of incense and spiced tobacco:* fume, emanation, cloud of smoke.

—*v.* **3** *She reeks of cheap perfume:* smell strongly, give off, smell, be malodorous, stink, smell to high heaven. **4** *The newly upturned clods reeked in the sun:* smoke, fume, steam.

◇ *Usage note:* See SMELL.

◇ *Word origin: **Reek*** comes from Old English *rēocan,* to give off smoke. This original sense is preserved in the old Scottish saying, *Lang may your lum reek* ("Long may your chimney smoke," i.e., may you live a long and prosperous life).

reel *v.* **1** *The boxer reeled and grabbed his opponent's shoulder:* rock, move uncertainly, stagger, totter, teeter, wobble, sway, stumble, lurch, pitch, roll. **2** *He knew he'd been drugged when everything started to reel around him:* turn round and round, rotate, whirl, swirl, spin, revolve, sway, waver. **3** *I was reeling after getting off the Big Wheel:* feel dizzy, be giddy, be in a vertiginous state, experience vertigo.

refer *v.* **1** *After filling in the forms I was referred to the personnel manager:* direct, send. **2** *We referred the proposal to the board of directors:* hand over, submit, deliver, transmit, pass. **3** *The speaker referred to the past to make his point:* advert, make reference; allude, mention. **4** *Please refer to the last page of the book for the answers:* go, turn to; consult.

refine *v.* **1** *The purpose of an oil refinery is to refine crude petroleum:* strain, filter, process, free from impurities, purify, cleanse. **2** *As he grew more practised, his style refined:* develop, improve, grow more delicate, become finer or more elegant.

Ant. 1 contaminate, adulterate. **2** coarsen.

refined *adj.* **1** *Neat's-foot oil is a highly refined organic product used to dress leather:* purified, clean, clarified. **2** *Jane Austen's novels are full of refined people with refined manners:* well-bred, free from coarseness, genteel, gentlemanly, ladylike, courtly, polite, courteous, mannerly; discriminating, fastidious, elegant, cultured, cultivated, civilized, polished, suave, finished; urbane, gentle, graceful, delicate.

Ant. 1, 2 unrefined. **1** impure, unpurified. **2** ill-bred, coarse, boorish, common, philistine, ungenteel, ungentlemanly, unladylike, unmannerly; undiscriminating; inelegant, uncultured, graceless.

refinement *n.* **1** *You could tell she was a woman of refinement by her courteous behaviour:* fine sensibilities, fineness, cultivation, urbanity, culture, finish, finesse, elegance, grace, polish, tastefulness, discrimination, discernment, fastidiousness; dignity, gentility, breeding; suavity, urbanity, *French* savoir faire; graciousness, gentleness, delicacy; politeness, civility, courtesy, good manners, courteousness, propriety; nicety, example of refined manners. **2** *This plant was set up for the refinement of crude oil:* purification, cleaning, cleansing, filtration, distillation. **3** *With a few refinements your essay would be excellent:* improvement, revision, rectification, amendment; development, amelioration, enhancement, betterment; advance, progression, advancement, step up, step forward.

Ant. **1** vulgarity, coarseness, tastelessness, gracelessness, discourtesy.

reflect *v.* **1** *The still water reflected the full moon:* mirror, cast back from a surface, cause to return or rebound, send back, throw back, return, give back or show an image of, image, copy, imitate, reproduce. **2** *His cowardice reflected shame on his family:* cast, throw, bring upon, bring as a result of one's actions. **3** *The book reflected the author's own thoughts on the matter:* show, display, express, exhibit, bring to light, reveal, disclose, uncover, expose, manifest, set forth, present, demonstrate, register, represent, mirror. **4** *Failure to pay your bills reflects upon your credit rating:* affect, have an ill effect, bring discredit, undo, undermine, betray, cast or bring reproach, condemn. **5** *Reflect for a moment — is what you mean to do the right thing?:* think, think carefully, deliberate, reason, ponder, consider, study, muse, meditate, contemplate, speculate, revolve in the mind, mull over, cogitate, ruminate, cerebrate, dwell upon, concentrate.

Ant. **1** absorb, keep, retain. **3** conceal, mask, hide, cover.

reflection *n.* **1** *She studied her reflection in the mirror:* image, mirror image, optical counterpart. **2** *He gave much reflection to the problem but still had no answer:* serious thought, deliberation, thought, consideration, attention, thinking, pondering, meditation, musing, pensiveness, study, concentration, rumination, cogitation, cerebration. **3** *The book included reflections by various people involved in the incident:* thought, notion, idea, sentiment, conviction, opinion, impression, view. **4** *Your brother's irresponsibility is no reflection on you:* statement or action that brings doubt or blame by association, derogation, insinuation, imputation, unfavourable observation or remark, slur, reproof, reproach, disparagement.

reform *n.* **1** *Reform of the whole set-up is urgently needed:* correction, rectification, reformation, amendment.
—*v.* **2** *How can an indifferent society reform desperate men? The ex-offender had reformed and was now a productive member of society:* change for the better, better, improve, correct, rectify, set straight again, restore, rehabilitate, remodel, rebuild, remedy, repair; revise, convert, be converted, progress; mend, amend, repent, atone, abandon evil conduct, mend one's ways, turn over a new leaf, set one's house in order.

refrain *v.* *For better health you must refrain from eating too much:* abstain, restrain oneself, keep oneself, hold off, desist, stay one's hand, curb oneself; forbear, forgo, renounce, eschew, avoid.

Ant. indulge in, be intemperate; continue, persist, go ahead.

◇ *Word origin:* ***Refrain***, to abstain from, comes from Latin *refrenare*, to check or curb (desire). Latin *refrenare* is based on *frenum*, bridle, from which is also derived French *frein*, bridle, braking device, car brake.

refresh *v.* **1** *The travellers stopped at an inn to refresh themselves. A shower always refreshes me on hot days:* freshen, invigorate, brace, vivify, restore, recruit, strengthen, enliven, revive, renew, energize, rejuvenate, cool off, recreate, reanimate. **2** *Please refresh my memory as to where we've met before:* prompt, prod, jog, arouse, rouse, stimulate, stir up, activate, quicken; revive, renew, awaken.

Ant. **1** weaken, tire, weary, fatigue.

refreshment *n.* **1** *The hostess served refreshments after the tennis matches:* food and drink, nourishment, snack, sandwich, collation, meal, lunch, appetizer, hors d'oeuvre, *Informal* pick-me-up, eats; beverage, drink, thirst-quencher, bracer, restorative, refresher, cocktail, drinkable, potable, potation. **2** *She looked forward to winter for the refreshment of long walks in snowy weather:* invigoration, restoration, reinvigoration, recreation, relaxation, rejuvenation.

"Patriotism is the last refuge of a scoundrel."
—*Samuel Johnson*

---

refuge *n.* **1** *We took refuge under an awning when it started to rain:* shelter, sanctuary, protection. **2** *Churches and schools were refuges to the flood victims. North America has long been a refuge for exiles from the Old World:* place of shelter, haven, retreat, sanctuary, asylum, resort; harbour, harbourage, anchorage, home, port in a storm. **3** *Drinking was his refuge from unpleasant reality:* resort, hide-out, means of self-defence, bolt-hole, escape, help in distress.

Ant. **1** exposure, peril, danger, threat, menace; insecurity.

refund *v.* **1** *The government refunded the excess tax*

that I had paid: give back (money), return, reimburse, pay back, repay, recompense, make compensation for, remunerate, remit, make restitution for.
—*n.* **2** *I'd like to return this merchandise for a refund or credit:* rebate, repayment, reimbursement, remittance; amount repaid.
Ant. 1 withhold.

refurbish *v. Refurbishing the old house has made it habitable again:* renovate, fix up, spruce up, remodel, improve, renew, do up, restore, recondition, overhaul, repair, mend; clean, tidy up, freshen.

refusal *n. His refusal was final — we couldn't make him change his mind:* rejection, denial, negation, declining, non-acceptance, non-consent, non-compliance, unwillingness; veto.

refuse[1] *v. Because of a prior engagement we had to refuse the invitation. I wouldn't refuse help to an old friend. We had a pass but were still refused admittance:* not accept, decline, say no to, reject, turn down, forbid, prohibit, disallow, withhold, deny.
Ant. approve, accept, consent to, permit, allow, agree to, give.

refuse[2] *n. The refuse was unloaded at the municipal tip:* rubbish, trash, garbage, waste, junk, litter.
◇ *Pronunciation tip: Refuse*[2] is a noun, pronounced *REFuse: Throw the REFuse in the dustbin. Refuse*[1] is a verb and is pronounced *reFUSE: I reFUSE to answer your question.*

refute *v. The accused was given no opportunity to refute the accusations:* disprove, confute, give the lie to, invalidate, counter, rebut, answer, challenge, contradict.
Ant. prove, vindicate, support, confirm, corroborate, substantiate.

regain *v. If you don't sue now, you'll never regain your property. The patient never regained consciousness:* recover, retrieve, repossess, get again, gain anew, get back, retake, reclaim, recapture, recoup, redeem, win back.

regal *adj. A regal welcome awaited us at the farm. She was a lady of regal bearing:* royal, kingly, queenly, noble, princely, lordly, proud, kinglike, princelike, queenlike; fit for a king or queen; stately, majestic, splendid, magnificent, grand, imposing, august.

regale *v.* **1** *The fool regaled the king's court with his nonsense:* amuse, entertain, divert. **2** *We regaled the dignitaries with the best dishes the chef could cook:* feed sumptuously, feast, serve nobly, wine and dine, fête, ply; lionize.

regard *v.* **1** *I regard that programme as one of the worst I've ever seen:* consider, look upon, view, see, think, judge, account, believe, hold, put down, reckon, estimate, rate. **2** *Prince Hal regarded his father's advice and later, as Henry V, proved to be an able ruler:* heed, follow, accept, respect, esteem, show consideration for, consider, mind, note well, pay attention to, listen to, hearken to. **3** *His work is highly regarded by other painters:* value, esteem, think highly of, think well of, respect, look up to, admire, hold a high opinion of. **4** *The condemned prisoner regarded the jury with a look of outraged innocence:* gaze at, look at, view, look upon, contemplate, behold, eye, turn one's eyes towards, cast the eyes on; scan, survey, watch, scrutinize, take the measure of, take in.
—*n.* **5** *He had little regard for his parents' feelings:* thought, consideration, concern, attention, notice, note, observation, heed, mind, care, meditation, reflection; respect, esteem, admiration, estimation, appreciation. **6** *In that regard, at least, we agree:* respect, matter, point, subject, aspect, detail; reference, relation, connection.
Ant. 1–5 disregard. **2, 3** reject, repudiate, despise, scorn, disrespect, spurn, ignore, think badly of, look down on, disparage, detest, loathe, dislike. **4** look away from, shun, ignore. **5** heedlessness, indifference, contempt.
◇ *Usage note: As regards, in regard to,* and *with regard to* are all acceptable phrases, but can usually be replaced by the shorter *regarding, concerning,* or *about.* Thus, *As regards* (or *in regard to,* or *with regard to*) *the contract, the second paragraph must be changed* are all acceptable, but the sentence could better begin with *Regarding the contract. . . , Concerning the contract. . . ,* or *About the contract. . . .*

regardless *adv. Informal I knew it was futile, but I talked to him regardless:* nevertheless, nonetheless, anyway, anyhow, for all that, in spite of everything.

"Alas, regardless of their doom,
The little victims play!
No sense have they of ills to come,
Nor care beyond today." —*Thomas Gray*

---

regenerate *v.* **1** *The congregation was spiritually regenerated by the preaching of the evangelist:* reform, rejuvenate, uplift, make a new man of. **2** *Bumper harvests regenerated hopes of resolving the economic crisis:* generate anew, give new life to, revive, renew, reawaken, resuscitate, resurrect, revivify; inspirit, restore, retrieve. **3** *Certain worms can regenerate after being cut in half:* grow back an injured or lost part; revivify.

regimentation *n. Daily life in Albania is said to be characterized by strict regimentation:* discipline, order, uniformity, control, regulation, system, method, rigour, rigorousness, orthodoxy, regimen, doctrinaire approach.

region *n.* **1** *My cousin lives in a mountainous region:* area, territory, space, expanse, tract, range, country, land, district, zone, province. **2** *He is a well-known authority in the region of physics:* area, field, sphere, domain, realm.

register *n.* **1** *We signed the hotel register when we arrived:* record book; ledger, day-book, diary,

log, log-book, visitors' book. **2** *A register next to the turnstile indicated the number of people who had gone through:* dial, meter, indicator, gauge; recorder, calculator, counter. **3** *The singer's voice had a wide register:* range, scale, compass.
—*v.* **4** *The court stenographer registered the trial proceedings:* write down, record, put in writing, put on the record, make a record of, note down, set down, take down. **5** *I registered at a hotel near the bus station. You must register in order to be able to vote:* enrol, sign up, check in, enlist. **6** *The Geiger counter registered a high concentration of radioactive particles. His face registered disappointment at losing the contest:* show, indicate, exhibit, disclose, mark, point to, record; portray, express, betray, betoken.

Exploring the Word: Although *rex* is Latin for king, its derivative form *regalis*, kingly, of a king, is more important in forming English words, including: *regal*, fit for a king, stately; *regalia*, a king's emblems, insignia, and clothing, as the crown, sceptre and robe, hence fine clothing or fancy trappings; *royal*, of a king, his family, or rank; *realm*, a king's domain. The related Latin *regnum*, reign, give us our word *reign*, the time or period of a king's rule or to hold and exercise royal power. Incidentally, *Reich*, as in *Third Reich* (the Nazi state under Hitler, 1933–45), is German for realm. It is related to our word *rich* (the rich are powerful) and is related to but not derived from Latin *rex*. All of these "king" words are also related to Hindi *rājā*, a rajah, title of certain Indian princes or kings. They go back to an Indo-European word (of which *reg-* was the stem) designating a tribal king.

regress *v.* **1** *As he got older, his mind regressed further into the past:* go back, move backward, withdraw, reverse, retrogress, revert, retreat, recede, back, fall, fall back, pass back.
—*n.* **2** *Soviet shipping has guaranteed rights of ingress and regress through the Dardanelles:* return, exit.
Ant. **1** progress, advance; climb, rise, ascend. **2** ingress, entrance.

"I think I don't regret a single 'excess' of my responsive youth — I only regret, in my chilled age, certain occasions and possibilities I didn't embrace." —*Henry James*

regret *v.* **1** *You'll regret having said those words! He regretted his decision:* be sorry for, feel sorrow for, feel remorse for, be ashamed of, be remorseful, rue, be rueful, rue the day, repent, bemoan, deplore, bewail, moan, mourn, grieve at, lament, weep over, feel distress over, reproach oneself for, have second thoughts about, *Informal* eat humble pie, eat one's words.
—*n.* **2** *I've never had any regrets over anything I've done:* sorrow, grief, remorse, remorsefulness, regretfulness, rue, ruefulness, compunction, contrition, apology, apologies, repentance, grievance, lamentation; disappointment, dissatisfaction, anguish, woe, qualm, reservation, scruple, pang of conscience, twinge, second thought; self-condemnation, self-reproach; heartache.
Ant. **1** feel happy for, rejoice, laugh at; feel satisfaction over. **2** remorselessness, impenitence, satisfaction, pleasure, contentment.

regrettable *adj. Overpopulation has caused a regrettable situation. I find your tactlessness regrettable:* lamentable, pitiable, unhappy, grievous, woeful, unfortunate, deplorable.
Ant. happy, joyous; fortunate, successful, lucky, fortuitous.
◇ *Usage note:* A person is *regretful*, full of regret, expressing regret: *Father was regretful because he couldn't send us to a public school. He refused the offer regretfully:* A thing, an incident, or an event is *regrettable*, causing regret: *The shooting of an innocent bystander is the most regrettable part of the story.*

regular *adj.* **1** *Getting up at dawn is part of his regular routine:* usual, normal, customary, typical, ordinary, common, commonplace, familiar, daily, steady, constant, habitual, undeviating, invariable, unvarying, unchanging, set, fixed, established. **2** *Jim's a regular customer. She made regular entries in her diary:* consistent, habitual, frequent, recurrent, recurring, periodic, periodical. **3** *The golfer held his club in the regular manner:* orthodox, correct, proper, classic, established. **4** *Informal Charlie is a regular ladies' man:* thorough, real, absolute, complete. **5** *The model had small, regular features:* uniform, even, smooth, well-proportioned, fine, symmetrical, well-balanced.
—*n.* **6** *Informal The barmaid knew all the regulars by their first names:* regular customer, regular client, habitué, old faithful, reliable, dependable.
Ant. **1–3, 5** irregular. **1** unusual, abnormal, unconventional, exceptional, rare, uncommon, variable, inconsistent, inconstant, varied, deviating, varying; sloppy, disorderly, unmethodical. **2** occasional, infrequent, rare. **3** erratic, unorthodox. **4** phoney, fake. **5** uneven, variable.

regulate *v.* **1** *The policeman regulated traffic at the crossroads:* control, handle, manage, superintend, supervise, oversee, monitor, guide, direct. **2** *Please regulate the sound on that radio:* adjust, fix, moderate, balance, modulate, tune.
Ant. **1** confuse, disrupt, disorganize; neglect, set free, decontrol.

regulation *n.* **1** *The function of a thermostat is the regulation of temperature:* adjusting, adjustment, handling, control. **2** *It's against regulations to leave camp without permission. Radio* *broadcasting is subject to government regulation:* rule, ordinance, decree, standing order, direction, statute, dictate, order, command, edict, commandment.

rehabilitate *v.* **1** *The social worker tried to rehabilitate the juvenile delinquents:* restore to society, straighten out, re-educate, set straight; redeem, save. **2** *The old ship was rehabilitated and used as a floating university:* salvage, renovate, make over, remake, reconstruct, restore, fix, readjust, refurbish, recondition. **3** *The king rehabilitated the banished earl:* restore, reinstate.

rehearse *v.* **1** *The actors rehearsed their parts. The conductor rehearsed the musicians before the first night:* prepare, practise, ready, drill, train, go over, run through; read one's lines, study one's lines. **2** *A spokesman for the immigrant workers rehearsed their grievances at the hearing:* repeat, recite, give a recital of, recount, relate, narrate; reiterate, retell.

reign *n.* **1** *Robin Hood is said to have lived during the reigns of King Richard the Lionheart and King John:* rule, tenure, regnum, incumbency, government, regime, sovereignty. **2** *Under the reign of wise teachers, he learned quickly:* influence, dominance, tutelage.

—*v.* **3** *Queen Victoria reigned for over 60 years. Chef Henri reigns supreme in the restaurant's kitchen:* have royal power, wear the crown, occupy the throne, sit on the throne, exercise sovereignty; rule, govern, hold authority, exercise authority, hold sway, command.

◇ *Spelling tip: Reign, rein,* and *reindeer* follow the spelling rule of "*i* before *e* except after *c* or when sounded like *a* as in *neighbour* and *weigh.*" There is that *a* sound in *reign, rein,* and *reindeer,* so they are spelt *rEIgn, rEIn,* and *rEIndeer.*

◇ *Usage note:* Because *reign, rein,* and *rain* are pronounced alike, some people find it hard to sort out their different spellings. *Reign* refers to the rule of a *soveREIGN: The reign of Queen Elizabeth I was from 1558 to 1603. Some day the Prince of Wales will reign as king.* A *rein* is one of the straps forming part of the bridle used to govern a horse: *Hold on to the reins tightly.* Last but not least, R-A-I-N, *rain* is what runs down dRAINS.

"To reign is worth ambition though in hell:
Better to reign in hell, than serve in heav'n."
—*John Milton*

---

reimburse *v. You will be reimbursed for any supplies you have to buy:* pay back, refund, repay, remunerate, indemnify, square up, compensate, recompense.

rein *n.* **1** Usually **reins** *Use the reins to lead the horse:* part of bridle. **2** *A heavy person should keep a tight rein on his appetite:* restraint, check, hold, bridle, harness.

—*v.* **3** *You must learn to rein in your temper:* control, check, curb, hold back, bridle, harness; restrict, limit, suppress; watch, keep an eye on.

◇ *Spelling tip* and *Usage note:* See REIGN.

reinforce *v. The troops reinforced the fort for the battle. That concrete is reinforced with steel beams:* make stronger, strengthen, support, buttress, prop, bolster, brace up.

Ant. weaken, debilitate; diminish, lessen, harm, hurt.

reject *v.* **1** *She rejected his proposal of marriage. The board rejected all our ideas:* refuse, say no to, decline, turn down; shrug off, dismiss, turn from, repudiate, repel, repulse, rebuff, disdain, spurn, disallow, deny.

—*n.* **2** *These convicts are society's rejects:* cast-off, castaway, discard; flotsam.

Ant. **1** accept, say yes to, pay attention to, receive willingly, approve, countenance, be in favour of, agree with; allow, permit; select. **2** treasure, prize.

rejection *n. The publisher's rejection of his manuscript depressed him:* refusal, rejecting, declining, rebuffing, scorning, spurning, disdain, dismissal, rebuff.

Ant. acceptance, approval, selection, espousal, affirmation.

rejoice *v. He rejoiced in his good fortune. The people rejoiced when the new king was crowned:* be glad, be happy, be pleased, be transported, be delighted, be overjoyed, exult, glory, delight, sing for joy, be elated, make merry, revel, celebrate.

Ant. be sad, be unhappy, mourn, lament, grieve.

rejoicing *n. The streets were filled with rejoicing after the victory:* celebration, festivity, revelry, revelling, merry-making, mirth, merriment, liveliness, gaiety, jubilee, jollity, good cheer; happiness, gladness, jubilation, jubilance, joyfulness, delight, pleasure; exultation, elation, ecstasy; triumph, cheering.

rejuvenate *v. The old man tried to rejuvenate himself by taking hormones:* make youthful again, restore, put new life into, reinvigorate, revive, resuscitate, revitalize, reanimate, restore, revivify.

Ant. age, make older; tire, weary, fatigue; weaken, debilitate.

relapse *v.* **1** *The boy relapsed into his old ways as soon as he was home from Borstal:* fall back, slip back, sink back, turn back, revert, backslide, regress, retrogress, lapse.

—*n.* **2** *Just when we thought he had recovered, he suffered a relapse. To avoid a relapse, the former addict moved to a place where drugs were not available:* lapse, fall, reversion, return to illness, turn for the worse, falling back, retrogression, reverse, regression, backsliding, decline, recurrence.

relate *v.* **1** *The witness related what he had seen:* tell, recount, recapitulate, give an account of, report, detail, particularize, describe, make known, reveal, disclose, divulge, impart, convey, communicate, state, say, utter, speak, narrate, recite. **2** *Can you relate what happened in your childhood to your present state of mind? His remarks related to the topic under discussion:* connect, associate, attach, link, refer, have reference, pertain, concern, be relevant, appertain, apply, belong. **3** *It's unfortunate when a father and son can't relate to each other:* feel close, have rapport, interact well, communicate, be sympathetic, be responsive, feel empathy with.

Ant. **1** keep to oneself, keep secret. **2** dissociate, disconnect,. separate, divorce, detach; be unconnected, be irrelevant.

relation *n.* **1** Also **relationship** *There's no relation between our department and the local government department:* connection, tie-in, tie, link, bond, interrelationship, association, affiliation, dealings. **2** *He's a distant relation of mine:* relative, kin, kinsman. **3** *Your remarks bear no relation to this conversation:* regard, connection, reference, bearing, relevance, concern, pertinence, application, applicability. **4** *Her relation of the fairy-tale fascinated the youngsters:* narrating, narration, telling, recital, recitation; narrative, account, report, description, version, retelling.

Ant. **1** disconnection, dissociation, independence.

relative *n.* **1** *Most of my relatives were able to attend the family reunion:* relation, cognate, kinsman, kinswoman, kinsfolk, kin, kith, kith and kin, people, family, folks, blood relative, flesh and blood, connection, clan, tribe.

—*adj.* **2** *He weighed the relative advantages of buying a house and renting a flat:* comparative, comparable, dependent, not absolute, relational. **3** *He's had experience in electronics and other relative fields:* related, correlated, correlative, connective, connected, associated, affiliated, allied, interrelated, interconnected. **4** *The slides were relative to the art lecture:* pertinent, appropriate, pertaining, having reference or regard, relevant, referable, respective, applicable, germane.

Ant. **1** stranger, alien, foreigner. **2** absolute. **3** unconnected, unrelated. **4** irrelevant, remote, inappropriate.

◇ *Usage note: Relative* and *relation* may be used interchangeably: *One of my relatives* (or *relations*) *is coming to dinner. Relatives, relations, kin, kinsfolk* are synonyms, but in actual use the first two terms apply especially to the outside relatives of *nuclear families* (husband, wife, and children), whereas the *kin* words hark back to the days of *extended families* (husband, wife, children, and other close relatives all making up one household). *Kin* is also used in the singular in the sense of "blood relation, kinsman or kinswoman," as in the sentence *He's no kin of mine.*

relax *v.* **1** *A good massage always relaxes me. Relax and enjoy yourself:* make less tense, loosen up, calm, soothe; cool off, unwind, unbend, ease up, let up. **2** *The regulations can be relaxed only under unusual circumstances. The general didn't relax his cruel treatment of the prisoners:* make less severe, make less strict, slack, slacken, loosen, make lax, bend, unbend, ease, decrease. **3** *The doctor told him to relax for a month or so before going back to work:* rest, take it easy, enjoy oneself, take a holiday; be idle, idle, be lazy, laze, loaf about, lie around.

Ant. **1** tense, tighten, alarm, alert, bear down. **2** tighten, intensify, heighten, increase. **3** work, be busy, be active.

relaxation *n.* **1** *A relaxation of the rules permitted outsiders to compete in the contest:* remission, easing, loosening, bending, abatement, slackening. **2** *What do you like to do for relaxation?:* recreation, enjoyment, fun, amusement, entertainment, diversion, pleasure, refreshment; pastime, avocation, hobby, sport, games; rest from work, repose, leisure.

Ant. **1** tightening, stiffening. **2** work, toil, labour, strain.

release *v.* **1** *The convict was released from prison after serving his sentence:* free, set free, liberate, let out, discharge, set at liberty. **2** *The driver started the engine, released the brake, and was on his way:* relieve; set loose, loose, untie, unloose, unfasten, unbind; disengage, detach, extricate. **3** *Don't release this news to the public until we give you the go-ahead. The new film will be released next month:* distribute, circulate, present.

—*n.* **4** Amnesty *fights for the release of political prisoners:* releasing, liberating, freeing, liberation, setting free, emancipation, setting loose, letting go, extrication, dismissal. **5** *The new film's date of release has not yet been decided:* distribution, publication, circulation.

Ant. **1** imprison, incarcerate; detain, hold, keep. **2** fasten, engage. **3** withhold, suppress, hide. **4** imprisonment, incarceration, internment, detention, holding.

relent *v. Father objected at first but then relented and let us go camping by ourselves:* grow lenient, grow less severe, become milder, soften, unbend, yield, give in, let up, give way, capitulate, have pity, be merciful, give quarter, come round.

relentless *adj. He was relentless in his pursuit of fame and fortune. The general was relentless in meting out punishment:* unrelenting, remorseless, implacable, inexorable, unyielding, inflexible, uncompromising, undeviating, adamant, harsh, hard, stern, severe, stiff, rigid, rigorous, ruthless, pitiless, merciless.

Ant. relenting, remorseful, yielding, flexible, pliant, compromising; kind, sparing, gentle, compassionate, feeling, pitying, merciful, lenient, soft-hearted, sympathetic, forgiving.

relevant *adj. The film was relevant to what was being discussed in class:* related, pertinent, referring, associated, concerning, connected, cognate, intrinsic, tied in, allied, bearing, germane, material, significant, appropriate, apposite, applicable, apropos; apt, suitable, suited, fit, fitting, to the point, to the purpose, on the subject.

Ant. irrelevant, unrelated, unconnected; inappropriate, inapplicable, immaterial, extraneous, extrinsic, foreign, alien, beside the point.

◇ *Spelling tip:* Beware! *Relevant* has two *e's* and one *a*, it ends in *-ant*.

reliable *adj. The* Oxford Dictionary of English Etymology *is a reliable source of information about the derivation of words. Jim is not a reliable employee:* dependable, unfailing, trustworthy, trusty, responsible, solid, sound, true, tried and true.

Ant. unreliable, undependable, irresponsible, untrustworthy.

◇ *Word origin:* See RELY.

reliance *n. I place no reliance on anything that he says he'll do:* trust, confidence, dependence, faith, credence, credit, belief, assurance.

Ant. distrust; uncertainty.

relic *n. In the attic, we found relics of our grandmother's childhood:* remembrance, keepsake, token, memento, souvenir, records, reminder, fragment, remnant, scrap, vestige, trace; antique, heirloom, artefact.

relief *n.* **1** *In some cases of extremely painful injury, morphine is the only relief. For relief of headaches take aspirin:* easement, alleviation, assuagement, palliation, amelioration, mitigation, reduction, remedy, cure, panacea, balm, anodyne, antidote, palliative, lenitive. **2** *Much to the student's relief, the exam was postponed:* peace of mind, release from anxiety, cheer, encouragement, elation. **3** *My holiday in Hawaii was a welcome relief from work:* respite, rest, break.

Ant. 1 discomfort, aggravation; oppression. **2** anxiety, upset, depression, mental suffering, discouragement. **3** hardship, burden.

relieve *v.* **1** *The ointment relieved her itching. His humorous remark relieved the tension in the room:* ease, lighten, mitigate, alleviate, assuage, solace, palliate, appease, pacify, mollify, temper, abate, allay, subdue, soothe. **2** *I was relieved to hear that you were all right:* reassure, free from fear, comfort, calm, console, solace, cheer, encourage. **3** *Public funds relieved the poverty-stricken families:* bring help to, aid, help, succour, assist, support. **4** *His arduous programme was relieved by frequent though brief breaks:* break up, punctuate, mark, interrupt; set off, put in relief, contrast. **5** *The night watch relieved the afternoon watch at 6 p.m. The general was relieved of his command:* remove, take away, release, let out, replace, free; spell, take the place of, take over.

Ant. 1 increase, intensify, heighten, aggravate. **2** alarm, discourage, concern. **3** burden, oppress.

religion *n.* **1** *As she grew old, religion meant more and more to her. Art for art's sake was Mallarmé's religion:* belief in God or gods, deism, theism, faith, belief, religious faith, worship, adoration, devotion, reverence, veneration, homage; piety, devoutness, godliness, religiousness, spirituality; theology, doctrine, dogma, cult, creed, canon. **2** *Moses was the great lawgiver of the Jewish religion:* system of faith, system of worship; creed, denomination, sect, cult, persuasion, affiliation, church.

Ant. 1 atheism, godlessness, impiety, irreligion, irreverence, sacrilege, unbelief.

"Science without religion is lame, religion without science is blind." —*Albert Einstein*

---

religious *adj.* **1** *He went to Sunday school for religious instruction. The revolutionary government forbade anyone to hold religious services:* spiritual, holy, sacred, theological, divine, denominational, devotional, doctrinal, scriptural. **2** *Though he wasn't a religious man, he believed there was a greater force controlling his destiny:* religious-minded, devout, spiritually-minded, godly, God-fearing. **3** *She was religious about always arriving on time for an appointment:* conscientious, unswerving, constant, staunch, steadfast, undeviating, unerring, faithful, devout, devoted, scrupulous, exact, rigid, fastidious, meticulous, punctilious, fanatical; ardent, whole-hearted.

Ant. 1, 2 irreligious. **1** secular. **2** impious, unfaithful, irreverent, profane, unbelieving, godless; atheistic, agnostic, free-thinking. **3** unconscientious, feckless, unreliable, inconstant.

relinquish *v.* **1** *He relinquished all rights to the property. Edward VIII relinquished his throne to marry Mrs. Simpson:* renounce, repudiate, deny, disclaim, dismiss, lay aside, shed, cast off, discard, put aside; surrender, cede, give up, deliver up, hand over, yield; forgo, forbear, waive, sign away; resign, abdicate, quit, withdraw from, leave, vacate, forsake, abandon, turn one's back on, wash one's hands of, rid oneself of, drop. **2** *Parents are sometimes reluctant to relinquish the authority they have over their children:* release, let go, give up, break off.

Ant. keep, retain, hold, cling to; sustain, maintain.

relish *n.* **1** *He has a relish for parades and carnivals:* liking, partiality, fondness, love, appreciation; enjoyment, zest, want, desire, wish, longing, penchant, propensity, predilection, hankering, fancy, taste, palate, stomach. **2** *A spirit of adventure gives relish to life:* pleasure, delight, satisfaction, gratification, enjoyment, ebullience, exuberance, enthusiasm; pleasing quality, zest, gusto, savour, tang, taste, flavour, accent, piquancy, fillip. **3** *Give me a hot dog with mustard and relish:* condiment,

(*variously*) gentleman's relish, pickles, tomato sauce, chili sauce, Worcester sauce, horse-radish sauce, chutney, piccalilli.
—*v.* **4** *I don't relish the idea of telling him the bad news:* like, have a liking for, love, fancy, dote on, take pleasure in, delight in, rejoice in, enjoy, be pleased with, appreciate, luxuriate in, *Informal* be crazy about, go much on, get a kick out of, *Slang* dig.
Ant. 1 dislike, hatred, distaste. **2** displeasure, dissatisfaction; distaste. **4** dislike, hate, loathe.

reluctant *adj. King John was reluctant to sign the Magna Carta in 1215:* unwilling, loath, averse, disinclined, indisposed; hesitant, diffident, shy.
Ant. eager, enthusiastic, keen, willing, desirous, inclined.

rely *v. If you ever need a friend, you can rely on me:* depend, be dependent, feel sure of, rest, lean, count, bank, reckon, give credence, swear, bet, place one's trust in.
◇ *Word origin: Rely, reliable, reliance,* and *religion* come from Latin *re-* (again) + *ligare* (to bind), to bind again, hence to bind strongly. To *rely* on someone is to be *bound* strongly to him by trust or confidence; likewise, *religion* is the *bond* between God and man.

remain *v.* **1** *He gave large sums of money to charity but preferred to remain anonymous. Her love for him remained all through her life:* stay, continue, persist, go on, linger, hang on, hold up, endure, abide, last, survive, subsist, prevail, remain alive. **2** *She told the children to remain in the car while she went into the store. Only my brother now remains at home:* stay, stay behind, stay in the same place, not move, not stir, wait, *Informal* stay put, stand, stick; be left, be left behind, be left over.
Ant. 1 leave, die, pass, disappear. **2** go, leave, depart.

remark *v.* **1** *I remarked that she looked very pretty:* observe, say, say in passing, mention, comment. **2** *Have you remarked his curious accent?:* mark, note, notice, take notice of, take note of, make note of, perceive, see, look at, behold, observe, espy, regard, survey, view; pay heed, give heed to, mind, pay attention to, fix the mind on, contemplate.
—*n.* **3** *Your remarks may have hurt her feelings:* commentary, reflection, comment, observation, word. **4** *The book was so bad it's not even worthy of remark:* consideration, note, notice, attention.

remarkable *adj. His remarkable feats of courage earned him a mention in dispatches.* Gone With the Wind *is a remarkable film:* noteworthy, notable, conspicuous, unusual, singular, phenomenal, signal, extraordinary, exceptional, outstanding; distinguished, striking, impressive.
Ant. ordinary, usual, common, commonplace, everyday, unsurprising; mediocre, unexceptional; undistinguished, insignificant, unimpressive.

remedy *n.* **1** *I'll tell you my favourite remedy for a cold:* cure, medicine, relief, nostrum, medicament, medication, treatment. **2** *Optimists saw in the League of Nations a remedy for the ills of the world:* corrective, preventive, panacea, cure-all, help, aid, assistance, relief, redress.
—*v.* **3** *Those pills will do nothing to remedy your sinus infection. It is easier to prevent than to remedy an injustice:* cure, heal, effect a remedy, relieve, ease, calm, alleviate, palliate, assuage, ameliorate, soothe, make easy, mitigate, mollify; restore to health, make sound, put into good condition, set right, fix, regulate, improve, make better, help, aid, repair, mend; correct, rectify, restore, redress, right, amend, emend.
Ant. 1 toxin, poison; disease. **3** aggravate, heighten, intensify, worsen, make worse.

remember *v.* **1** *I don't remember her name, but her face is familiar:* recall, call to mind, recollect; keep in mind, have in mind, retain the thought of, not forget, bear in memory, bear in mind. **2** *He remembered his faithful butler in his will:* take note of, appreciate, recognize, take care of, do something for; reward, tip.
Ant. forget, disregard, ignore, neglect, overlook.
◇ *Word origin: Remember, remembrance,* and *reminiscence* are based on Latin *memor,* mindful, and other related Latin words from which we get our words *memory, memorable, memento, memoir, memorandum, memorabilia,* and *memorial.*

remembrance *n.* **1** *Have you any remembrance of your childhood?:* memory, recall, remembering, recollection, reminiscence, retention in the mind; recognition, nostalgia. **2** *The photograph was a remembrance of her wedding-day:* reminder, souvenir, favour, keepsake, relic, memento, token; memorial, commemoration.
Ant. 1 forgetfulness, obscurity, oblivion.

remind *v. That story reminds me of an experience I had long ago:* bring to mind, bring back to, suggest to, bring to recollection, awaken memories of, put in memory, put in mind.
◇ *Word origin: Remind* is a word wholly created on English soil. It means literally to *mind* again and is in fact composed of the two native elements *re-* and *mind.* It is first recorded in 1645.

reminisce *v. Old friends like to reminisce about the "good old days":* remember, recollect, hark back, think back, look back, exchange memories, swap remembrances, tell old tales; reflect, ponder, muse, mull.

reminiscent *adj. Your experience is reminiscent of one that I had some time ago. The fire glowing on the hearth put us in a reminiscent mood:* remindful, similar to, analogous to; remembering, recollecting, retrospective, nostalgic.

Ant. forgetful, oblivious, unremembering.

remiss *adj. He was sacked for being remiss in his duties:* careless, negligent, lax, undutiful, unmindful, unthinking, thoughtless; sloppy, slipshod, slack, loose; slow, dilatory, indolent, slothful, lazy, laggard, lackadaisical, shiftless, loafing, idle, inactive; neglectful, forgetful, inattentive, indifferent, uncaring, oblivious, unwatchful.

Ant. careful, dutiful, attentive, diligent; neat, meticulous, scrupulous.

remit *v.* **1** *Please remit the balance due upon receipt of this bill:* send in payment, pay; make good, reimburse, compensate, put to rights; discharge, send, forward, dispatch, ship, transmit. **2** *Christ remitted the sins of the penitent thief:* forgive, pardon, excuse, overlook, pass over, absolve, clear. **3** *The cold wave finally remitted its icy grip on the city:* diminish, decrease, moderate, reduce; slacken, slack, relax.

Ant. 1 withhold. **2** condemn, accuse, punish. **3** increase, strengthen, intensify, heighten.

remnant *n. Some pieces of pottery were the only remnants found of the ancient civilization. A patchwork quilt is made up of remnants of cloth:* remainder, left-over, trace, monument, vestige; piece, bit, bits and bobs, scrap, fragment; remains, odds and ends; leavings, discard, residue, residuum, survival.

remorse *n. The killer had no remorse for what he had done:* regret, regretfulness, rue, feelings of guilt, self-reproach, self-reproof; compunction, qualm, pangs of conscience, second thoughts; contrition, repentance, penitence; sorrow, grief, lamentation, anguish.

Ant. satisfaction, guiltlessness, pride.

◇ *Word origin: Remorse* comes from Latin *re-* (again) + *mordere* (to bite), a biting again, constant biting, hence a feeling of pain after something is over.

"One man's remorse is another's reminiscence."
—*Ogden Nash*

---

remote *adj.* **1** *He dreamed of travelling to remote South Sea islands:* far, far-off, far away, distant, far-removed, a long way off, out of the way; exotic, alien, strange, foreign. **2** *He lived in a remote part of the forest:* secluded, set apart, isolated, God-forsaken, solitary, sequestered, segregated, separate; out of the way; lonely, alone, quiet. **3** *Space travel seemed only a remote possibility to our parents:* distant, slight, faint, slim; unlikely, doubtful, dubious, implausible. **4** *He seemed remote, uninterested in the conversation:* removed, distant, stand-offish, aloof, detached, far-away, far-off.

Ant. 1 close, near, nearby; familiar. **2** prominent; busy. **3** immediate, imminent; accessible, approachable, attainable. **4** attentive, interested, involved, alert.

remove *v.* **1** *Remove those muddy shoes! The rioters were forcibly removed from the plaza:* take off, doff; take away, take out, dislodge, expel, oust, eject, evacuate, cart off, take away, sweep out, carry off. **2** *The casualty had to have his leg removed:* amputate, cut away, chop off, cut off, lop off. **3** *He removed his desk to another office. They have decided to remove to a warm climate:* move, transfer, transport, transplant; displace, change, shift; depart, leave, go away, take leave, quit, vacate, withdraw, make an exit, retreat, retire, emigrate. **4** *Bleach removes colour. Remove my name from your mailing list:* wipe out, get rid of, take out, erase, extract, eliminate, cancel, delete, blot out, drop. **5** *The corrupt official was removed from office:* dismiss, discharge, unseat, sack, *Slang* kick out, boot out.

Ant. 1 put on, don, put back. **2** join, unite, combine; keep, retain, detain, hold. **3** keep, sustain, maintain, hold, retain; hang on, stay, remain. **4** install, establish, set.

rend *v.* **1** *The lightning rent the tree. And the earth did quake, and the rocks rent:* rip, tear, split, rive, divide, rupture, cleave, sunder, sever, dissever, splinter, fracture, break, crack, break into pieces, shatter, fall to pieces. **2** *Rend your heart, and not your garments! They spit on us, they rend us with their scorn:* lacerate, afflict, sear, pain, tear, rip, cut, hurt, wound. **3** *An explosion rent the air:* split, pierce with sound. **4** *This debate has rent our community so long, there soon won't be anything left to rend:* tear, disintegrate; divide, polarize, split, splinter.

Ant. 1 join, reunite, unite, bind, secure; mend, heal.

◇ *Word origin: Rend* comes from Old English *rendan*, to tear.

◇ *Usage note: Rend* typifies a class of words we all know but rarely use except in highly formal speech or writing — "high style," as some writers on language call it. Several of the above illustrative sentences come from the Authorized Version of the Bible. Be careful when you use this word, because it doesn't always ring true when used in a present-day context.

render *v.* **1** *A long recuperation rendered him healthy again:* cause to be, make, cause to become. **2** *The piano concerto was rendered flawlessly:* do, perform, play, execute, interpret. **3** *We call on you to render assistance:* give, present, make available, tender, accord, grant, donate; supply, dispense, deal out, dole out, hand out, allot, *Informal* come across with, shell out, fork over. **4** *He was obliged to render a large sum in arrears of taxes:* pay as due; make restitution of, remit, make payment of, make requital, pay back, give in return, requite. **5** *The troops refused to render up their position:* give up, yield, surrender, cede, turn over, relinquish, hand over. **6** *The Greek word translated as "charity" in the Authorized Version is rendered differently in the Revised:* translate, construe, interpret.

Ant. **3** withhold, refuse, keep, retain. **4** hold, keep, hang on to.

◇ *Word origin:* See RENT.

rendezvous *n.* **1** *We have a rendezvous at noon. The lovers arranged a secret rendezvous:* agreement to meet, pre-arranged meeting, date, appointment, engagement, encounter, assignation, tryst, tête-à-tête. **2** *The Chinese restaurant was our rendezvous:* meeting-place, gathering place, stamping-ground, focal point.

—*v.* **3** *The two patrols rendezvoused at noon:* meet by appointment, get together; tryst; assemble, gather, muster.

◇ *Pronunciation tip: Rendezvous* retained its French pronunciation, more or less, when borrowed into English: *RAHN-day-voo.* Used as a plural (no change in spelling), the noun is pronounced *RAHN-day-vooz.* The past tense of the verb, *rendezvoused,* is pronounced *RAHN-day-vood;* the present participle, *rendezvousing,* is pronounced *RAHN-day-vooing.*

rendition *n. Can you imagine a Japanese rendition of* Jingle Bells*?:* rendering, translation, interpretation, arrangement, version, reading, performance.

renegade *n.* **1** *He was considered a renegade when he switched political parties:* traitor, deserter, slacker, betrayer, turncoat; recreant, apostate, heretic, forsaker; rebel, insurgent, quisling, rat, mutineer; backslider; runaway, fugitive, outlaw.

—*adj.* **2** *The renegade policeman became a gangster:* traitorous, apostate, recreant, unfaithful.

Ant. **1** adherent, follower, loyalist.

◇ *Word origin:* A *renegade* is a traitor who has denied his country, faith, etc.; and to *reneg(u)e* is to deny or renounce a promise (in card games it is called "revoke," that is to fail to follow suit when able to do so). Both *renegade* and *reneg(u)e* come from Latin *re-* (again) + *negare* (to deny).

renege Also **renegue** *v. It's bad form to renege on a bet:* break a promise, break one's word, go back on one's word, fall back, back out, turn one's back, withdraw, pull out, *Informal* get cold feet.

Ant. fulfil, carry out, stand by.

renew *v.* **1** *We renewed our old friendship:* begin again, resume, continue, take up again, pick up; re-establish, reinstate. **2** *Do you want to renew our contract?:* extend, continue, prolong, sign again, offer again, maintain, retain. **3** *He tried hard to renew his faith:* revive, rejuvenate, regenerate, reinvigorate, revitalize, refresh, save, salvage, redeem. **4** *A good shampooing renewed the soiled carpet:* restore, rejuvenate, revitalize, make sound, put back into shape.

Ant. **1** forget, discontinue, end. **2** discontinue, cancel, let lapse, drop. **4** age, depreciate, wear out.

renounce *v. He renounced all rights to the throne. Consider carefully before renouncing your faith:* give up, relinquish, resign, abdicate, give up claim to, cede, part with, quit, forgo, eschew, waive; abandon, abnegate, wash one's hands of, cast aside, put aside, lay aside, dismiss; repudiate, abjure, forswear, recant, abrogate, deny, disavow, disclaim, reject, disown, cast off, write off, turn from, discard.

Ant. avow, assert, proclaim, maintain, uphold, defend, claim; keep, retain, hold, accept, approve, acknowledge.

renovate *v. The new owner set about renovating the rickety old building:* repair, mend, fix, improve; make over, remake, revamp, modernize, remodel, restore, refurbish.

◇ *Word origin: Renovate* comes from Latin *re-* (again) + *novare* (to make new), to make new again, which is derived from *novus,* new. The same Latin base gives us *novice, novel,* and *innovation.*

renown *n. Paderewski and Pablo Casals were musicians of renown:* fame, repute, reputation, popularity, note, notoriety, celebrity; eminence, distinction, mark.

Ant. obscurity, unpopularity; disrepute, infamy, shame, disgrace.

renowned *adj. Robert Browning was a renowned poet:* celebrated, well-known, popular, famous, famed, notable, noteworthy, noted, prominent, outstanding, acclaimed, eminent, distinguished.

Ant. obscure, forgotten, unpopular, insignificant, undistinguished.

rent[1] *n. Rent for the flat is due on the first of every month:* rental, payment; dues, fee.

—*v.* **2** *We rented the caravan to a young couple. They rented a cottage for their holiday:* sell the use of, let, rent out, lease; buy the use of, hire, charter, lease.

◇ *Word origin: Rent[1]* is payment *rendered* for the use of another's building, land, or other property. Both *rent* and *render* come from Latin *re-* (back) + *dare* (to give), to give back, compensate, pay.

rent[2] *n* **1** *I tried to sew up the rent in my dress:* opening, rip, tear, tatter, rift, hole, rupture, fissure, cleft, chink, breach, crack, slit; chasm, gash, gap, hiatus, crevasse; split, fracture. **2** *The two opposing factions caused a rent in the party:* breach, break, rift, split, division, schism, cleavage.

renunciation *n. The preacher urged renunciation of the things of this world:* renouncing, rejection, repulsion, spurning, refusal, repudiation, abnegation; denial, disavowal, disclaiming, eschewing, forgoing, abandonment, relinquishment, forswearing, abjuration, giving up.

Ant. acceptance, retention.

repair[1] *v.* **1** *These shoes will have to be repaired:* mend, restore, set right, make good, recondition, refurbish, renew, rebuild, patch. **2** *I'd like to repair the loss you have sustained:* make up, remedy, redress, rectify, patch up, mend, amend, emend, correct.

—*n.* **3** *You could always get the repair done by Uncle Jim:* repairing, mending, patching, reconditioning, rebuilding; refurbishing, overhaul. **4** *The child's clothes were in a poor state of repair:* general condition, state, shape.

Ant. 1 break, destroy, ruin. **2** aggravate, exacerbate, worsen, deepen. **3** destruction, breaking.

◇ *Word origin: Repair* comes from Latin *re-* (again) + *parare* (prepare) hence to prepare again, make ready for use again after damage or wear.

repair[2] *v. The ladies repaired to the drawing-room:* withdraw, retire, remove, move, betake oneself, go.

reparation *n. He made reparation by paying for the goods that he had damaged:* amends, redress, restitution, requital, return, quittance, satisfaction, peace-offering.

repartee *n. A good comedian should be skilled in repartee:* witty reply, witty retort, bon mot, clever rejoinder, snappy come-back, riposte; badinage, persiflage, word-play, bandying of words, banter.

repast *n. A hearty repast was laid before the travellers:* meal, table, board, banquet, feast, spread; food, provision, victuals, nourishment, refreshment.

repay *v. We can never repay your kindness. She repaid him for his insult by not inviting him to the party:* pay back, reimburse, make restitution, recompense, remunerate, indemnify, refund, requite, reward, make requital, make retribution, give in exchange, return, return the compliment, match; make a return for, pay in kind, reciprocate; get back at, get even with.

repeal *v.* **1** *Parliament repealed the ancient law:* cancel, abrogate, abolish, annul, nullify, void, declare null and void, invalidate, set aside, revoke, rescind.

—*n.* **2** *The year 1846 marked the repeal of the Corn Laws:* abrogation, cancellation, abolition, termination, annulment, nullification, voiding, invalidation, revocation.

Ant. 1 confirm, re-establish; validate. **2** confirmation, re-establishment; validation.

◇ *Word origin: Repeal* comes through Old French *r(e)-* (back) + *apeler* (to summon, call), to summon back, call back, hence to rescind or revoke a law, from Latin *re-* + *ad* (to) + *pellere* (to drive).

repeat *v.* **1** *Please repeat the question. Repeat after me:* restate, say again, reiterate; echo, imitate, mimic. **2** *She repeated what she had heard to her mother:* tell, relate, recite, retell, recount, quote, pass on. **3** *History repeats itself. The choral society will repeat their concert next week:* duplicate, perform again, reproduce.

—*n.* **4** *Today's lecture was a repeat of yesterday's:* repetition, reiteration, duplication, re-run.

repel *v.* **1** *The defenders of the fort repelled the attackers. Boric acid crystals repel cockroaches:* push back, force back, drive back, rout, beat back, repulse, rebuff; dispel, scatter, disperse, chase away, put to flight, drive away; *Informal* send packing; keep off, hold off, ward off, fend off, forfend, stave off, throw off, resist, be proof against, foil, frustrate, deflect, withstand, oppose; keep at bay, keep at arm's length, check, keep out. **2** *The gory scene repelled me:* disgust, repulse, revolt, be offensive to, be repugnant to, put off, go against one's grain; sicken, nauseate, turn one's stomach, make one's flesh creep, set one's teeth on edge, make one shudder; offend, alienate, *Slang* turn off.

Ant. 1, 2 attract, draw. **2** please, delight, captivate, invite, fascinate, entrance, enchant.

repellent *adj.* **1** *This fabric is water-repellent:* repelling, resisting; impermeable, proof. **2** *The sight of meat is repellent to some vegetarians:* repugnant, repulsive, disgusting, distasteful, abhorrent, offensive, revolting, loathsome.

◇ *Usage note: Repellent* as in sense **1** above is always used in combination *with another word: water-repellent, insect-repellent, etc.* It may also be used as a noun in this sense: *"Vapona" is a repellent to be hung up in order to keep off flies.*

repent *v. The killer never repented of the crime he committed. Repent, for the kingdom of heaven is at hand:* regret, deplore, be grieved for, lament, bewail, weep over, bemoan; feel remorse, be ashamed, be regretful, reproach oneself, be sorry, rue; be penitent, be contrite.

"Never go to France
Unless you know the lingo,
If you do, like me,
You will repent, by jingo." —*Thomas Hood*

---

repentance *n. Saint Augustine wrote about his own repentance for a misspent youth:* remorse, regret, grief, sorrow; self-reproach, self-condemnation, compunction, guilt, pangs of conscience; penitence, contrition.

Ant. contentment, complacency, impenitence.

repercussion *n.* **1** *Are you aware of the repercussions that could occur if we carry out this plan?:* result, effect, side-effect, after-effect, reaction, reverberation, backlash, boomerang effect, recoil. **2** *The repercussion of the blast could be heard for miles:* reverberation, concussion, echo.

repetition *n. The play was a repetition of a theme used twenty years ago:* repeat, retelling, restatement, reiteration.

◇ *Spelling tip: Repeat* has an *-ea-* in it, but *repetition* has only an *e.* If you say the two words to yourself carefully before you spell them you will get them right: *re-peat, re-pe-ti-tion.*

repetitious *adj. I found the lecture boring and repetitious:* repetitive, wordy, prolix
Ant. concise, pithy, succinct, terse.

replace *v.* **1** *He replaced Mr. Jones as director:* take the place of, fill the place of, step into the shoes of, succeed, supersede, supplant, displace, take over from, substitute for, spell. **2** *Replace those books on the shelf:* put back, put back in place, return, restore.

replenish *v. Our dwindling supplies were replenished when the new shipment arrived:* fill up again, refill, restock, reload, replace, renew, restore.
Ant. dissipate, empty, drain.

> **Exploring the Word:** Latin *plere,* to fill, gives us *complete, complement, replete* (filled up), *replenish* (to fill again), and *supply* (to fill up with what is needed). It also gives us *accomplish* and *comply,* to perform fully, fulfil; *compliment,* which originally meant to supply as a gift, something given; *deplete,* to "unfill," exhaust, empty; *expletive,* an interjection or exclamation used to fill out or emphasize a sentence; *implement,* to fill in, perform, fulfil, or a tool, piece of equipment, etc., used to fill a function; and *supplement,* that which fills up a need or lack, as a *vitamin supplement.*

replete *adj. The proofs arrived replete with misprints. The diners were replete after the eight-course dinner:* abundantly filled, filled to repletion, abounding, teeming, fraught, well-stocked, loaded, crammed, jam-packed, full to bursting, brimming; stuffed, full, gorged, sated, satiated, surfeited.
Ant. empty, bare, barren; hungry, starved, famished.

replica *n. We asked the artist for a replica of the portrait, so that we could both have a copy:* duplicate, close copy, carbon copy, imitation, facsimile, replication, reproduction, model.

reply *v.* **1** *Please reply to the question. I replied that I had never been there:* answer, respond, rejoin, make rejoinder, retort, come back with, counter, react.
—*n.* **2** *I'm waiting for a reply to my question. His only reply was an angry stare:* response, answer, retort, rejoinder, counter, reaction; acknowledgement.
Ant. 1 question, demand, ask. **2** request, question; invitation.

report *n.* **1** *His report of the battle won the editor's commendation. Copies of the annual report were sent to the shareholders:* account, description, version, relation, narration, story, write-up, summary, record, article, news story, press release. **2** *The messenger brought in a secret report from France:* dispatch, message, communiqué, note, memorandum, missive. **3** *The report that he was going to resign was false:* information, word, gossip, hearsay, rumour, talk. **4** *We could hear the report of cannons in the distance. The pistol went off with a sharp report:* noise, sound, boom, discharge, detonation, bang, crack.
—*v.* **5** *The newspaper reported the death of the statesman:* announce, communicate, relate, tell, divulge, disclose, reveal, state, recount, recite, put in writing, write down, put on record, describe, detail. **6** *He reported the student for misconduct:* denounce, inform against, expose, tell on, complain about. **7** *The soldier reported for duty:* present oneself, appear; *Informal* show up, clock in.
Ant. 5 keep secret, withhold, conceal.

repose *n.* **1** *A full day's work earned him an evening of repose:* rest, respite, ease, tranquillity, calm, quiet, peacefulness, relaxation, leisure, inactivity.
—*v.* **2** *After lunch Father reposed in the hammock:* rest, be at rest, lie, lie at rest, recline; relax, be calm, settle.

repository *n. The warehouse served as a repository for the store's additional merchandise:* storage place, depository, magazine, storehouse, warehouse, depot.

reprehensible *adj. Assassination is a reprehensible crime:* condemnable, unworthy, objectionable, shameful, disgraceful; heinous, villainous, opprobrious, nefarious, foul, infamous, despicable, ignoble, base, vile, wicked, evil, bad; unpardonable, inexcusable, unjustifiable; deserving of blame, deserving censure, censurable, blameable, blameworthy, culpable, guilty.
Ant. admirable, laudable, praiseworthy, blameless, unobjectionable, pardonable, forgivable.

"The smallest atom of truth represents some man's bitter toil and agony."
—*H. L. Mencken*

---

represent *v.* **1** *In Morse code, dots and dashes represent letters:* stand for, symbolize, designate, denote, stand for, be the equivalent of, express, indicate, be, mean, equal, serve as; typify, characterize, emblematize, betoken. **2** *Her lawyer represented her at the sale of the estate. The foreign minister represented his country at the conference:* act in place of, stand in the place of, act as a substitute for, be proxy for, be an agent for, be deputy for, be in the position of; speak and act for. **3** *His drawing represented a Parisian café:* portray, depict, show, show a likeness of, picture, illustrate, sketch, outline, delineate, describe; state, present. **4** *She represented her friend as being much prettier than she was:* describe, depict, give an account of, portray, delineate. **5** *Which actor represented Hamlet? The man represented himself as a leading surgeon:* portray, impersonate, appear as, appear in the character of, enact, act the part of; pose as.

representative *n.* **1** *The lawyer acted as her*

representative at the hearing: agent, deputy, emissary, envoy, proxy, delegate, substitute, proctor, surrogate, spokesman, *Informal* mouthpiece. **2** *Each local Institute sends one representative to the A.G.M.:* member of a legislature, legislator, delegate; assemblyman, assemblywoman, member of parliament, M.P.

—*adj.* **3** *The lion is representative of the feline family:* serving to represent, typifying, symbolic, symbolical; exemplary, exemplifying, typical, illustrative, descriptive, emblematic, delineative, denotative. **4** *Every democracy is proud of its own representative form of government:* representational, republican, democratic, elected, elective; delegated, delegatory, deputed. **5** *The pollsters questioned a representative sample of the population:* representing the whole, balanced, varied, cross-sectional.

repress *v.* **1** *It is often a mistake to repress one's true feelings:* hold back, keep in check, keep down, curb, check, restrain, inhibit, hold in, hold back, suppress, hide, conceal, mask, cloak, cover, veil, stifle, muffle, smother, strangle; pen up, bottle up, shut up, box up. **2** *Seasoned mercenaries were hired to repress the rebellion:* crush, quash, quell, subdue, put down, squash, silence.

Ant. 1 let out, release, express. **2** encourage, incite, foment.

reprimand *n.* **1** *The motorist received a reprimand and a fine from the magistrate for speeding:* sharp reproof, reproval, rebuke, reproach, admonition, admonishment, upbraiding, scolding, remonstrance, castigation, chiding, dressing-down, berating, trimming, censure, criticism, obloquy, opprobrium, rebuff, denunciation, disparagement, *Informal* rap on the knuckles, rocket, lecture.

—*v.* **2** *The teacher reprimanded the class for being noisy:* reprove severely, rebuke, admonish, reproach, scold, upbraid, rail at, chastise, castigate, chide, berate, trim, dress down, call to account, take down, tell off; *Informal* tear off a strip, give a rap on the knuckles; give a tongue-lashing, take to task, lecture, raise one's voice against, denounce, dispraise, disparage; reprehend, reprobate, revile, criticize, censure.

Ant. 1 commendation, compliment, applause, approval. **2** commend, compliment, praise, applaud, approve.

reproach *v.* **1** *He was gently reproached for his rude behaviour:* find fault with, chide, admonish, reprimand, rebuke, reprove; criticize, censure, condemn, stigmatize, malign, vilify, revile, blame; scold, upbraid, rail at, castigate, charge, tongue-lash, call to account, take to task; disparage, denounce, asperse; shame, disgrace.

—*n.* **2** *Her behaviour was above reproach. The workers feared their supervisor's reproaches:* blame, rebuke, reproof; remonstrance, scolding, upbraiding, criticism, censure, hard words, tirade, diatribe. **3** *The youth's bad behaviour is a constant reproach to his parents:* cause of blame, badge of infamy, stigma, taint, blemish, stain, blot, spot, tarnish, slur; indignity, insult, offence; shame, humiliation, degradation, embarrassment, scandal, disgrace, dishonour, discredit.

Ant. praise, commend, applaud, compliment. **2** commendation, compliment, praise, applause, honour. **3** honour, credit.

reprobate *n.* **1** *The old reprobate never reformed:* wicked person, degenerate, profligate, roué, prodigal, rake, rakehell, immoralist, voluptuary, wanton, abandoned person; rascal, scamp, black sheep, rapscallion, rotter; miscreant, sinner, transgressor, evil-doer, wrongdoer, outcast, castaway, untouchable, pariah, derelict.

—*adj.* **2** *He was a reprobate person with no redeeming qualities:* corrupt, incorrigible, depraved, profligate, degenerate, dissolute, abandoned, shameless; wicked, evil, evil-minded, low, base, bad, vile.

Ant. 1 angel, paragon, saint. **2** pure, virtuous, righteous, saintly, angelic.

reproduce *v.* **1** *The machine in the hardware department can reproduce a key in two minutes. The bird-watcher could reproduce the call of over fifty birds:* make a duplicate of, duplicate, replicate, copy, match, represent; repeat, re-echo, mirror, reflect; imitate, counterfeit, forge. **2** *Rabbits reproduce quickly:* produce young, produce offspring, procreate, propagate, generate, proliferate, give birth, beget, sire, bring forth, multiply, breed, spawn.

reproduction *n.* **1** *Wealthy Romans collected reproductions of Greek statues:* copy, carbon copy, likeness, duplicate, replica, facsimile, representation; imitation, simulation. **2** *We studied the processes of reproduction in the biology class:* generation, propagation, procreation, proliferation, multiplication, breeding.

Ant. 1 original, prototype.

reproof *n. He received a gentle reproof from his girl-friend for forgetting to shave:* rebuke, reproach, remonstrance, scolding, reprimand, chiding, criticism, censure, condemnation.

Ant. approval, commendation, praise, reward.

reprove *v. When the child giggled, her mother reproved her with a stern look:* reproach, rebuke, chide, reprimand; censure, scold.

Ant. praise, applaud, encourage.

republic *n. Andorra is a small mountain republic between France and Spain:* republican nation, state having representative government, popular government, democracy, nation enjoying constitutional government.

◇ *Word origin: Republic* comes from Latin *res* (thing) + *publicus* (of the people, public, citizens), the thing of the public, hence a state or nation that belongs to the people or the citizens. A *republican* is thus one who advocates or upholds a republic, a country or government belonging to the people, and from this word Americans have named their Republican Party.

"Alike were they free from
Fear, that reigns with the tyrant, and envy, the
vice of republics." —*H. W. Longfellow*

---

repudiate *v.* **1** *The new government repudiated the treaty signed by the former rulers:* reject, disavow, deny, disclaim, protest; rescind, reverse, revoke, repeal, retract, void, nullify, annul, declare null and void, abrogate, cancel, abolish, dissolve. **2** *The man repudiated the religion he was born into and became an atheist:* disown, disavow, reject, cast off, discard, wash one's hands of, abandon, desert, forsake.

Ant. **1** accept, approve; adopt, espouse. **2** acknowledge, accept, embrace.

repugnant *adj.* **1** *What a repugnant smell! The very thought of eating squid is repugnant to me:* repellent, offensive, causing disgust, disgusting, nauseating, sickening, repulsive, foul, nasty, vile, obnoxious, revolting, objectionable, unacceptable, undesirable, disagreeable, unpleasant; distasteful, unpalatable, unsavoury, unappetizing; odious, hateful, loathsome, detestable, abhorrent, abominable, insufferable. **2** *Lying and cheating are repugnant to my way of thinking:* contrary, opposed, adverse, counter, antipathetic, uncongenial.

Ant. **1** attractive, pleasant, tasteful, unobjectionable, desirable, agreeable, favourable. **2** consistent, harmonious, compatible.

repulse *v.* **1** *The army repulsed the attacking forces:* repel, throw back, drive back, beat back. **2** *The neighbours repulsed our offers of friendship:* reject, refuse, rebuff, turn one's back on, be deaf to, be cold to, spurn, stand aloof from, avoid, shun, shrink from, recoil from; *Informal* cold-shoulder.

—*n.* **3** *Her repulse of his proposal depressed him:* refusal, rebuff, rejection, spurning, shunning.

Ant. **2** welcome, accept, encourage. **3** encouragement, acceptance, welcome.

repulsion *n. Spiders fill me with repulsion:* revulsion, repugnance, disgust, distaste, indisposition, disinclination; dislike, antipathy, detestation, aversion, loathing, hatred, abomination, abhorrence.

repulsive *adj. His table manners are repulsive:* repugnant, repellent, offensive, disgusting, obnoxious, nauseating, nasty, vile, objectionable, disagreeable, distasteful, loathsome, detestable, abominable, odious.

Ant. attractive, agreeable, pleasant, tasteful.

◇ *Usage note: Repugnant, repulsive,* and *repellent* all mean inducing feelings of disgust or dislike, and in decreasing order of disgust. *Repugnant* refers to a deep-seated aversion, especially to something contrary to or inconsistent with one's own beliefs or feelings, as to a type or a general idea: *All war is repugnant. My sister finds fat men repugnant. Repulsive* suggests a strong sense of personal disgust and loathing, especially on an individual or personal level, which may even change at a later date: *The smell of sewage is repulsive. At first my sister found him repulsive, but now she likes him. Repellent* is not as strong as the other two words, suggesting somewhat less disgust and usually being about less serious things: *Chewing-gum is repellent to me.*

reputable *adj. If you want good service, go to a reputable dealer:* respectable, creditable, trustworthy, held in good repute, reliable, of good name.

Ant. disreputable, untrustworthy, shady.

◇ *Pronunciation tip: Reputable* and *disreputable* should be pronounced so that the *REP-* is stressed. Thus *REP-yu-ta-ble* and *dis-REP-yu-ta-ble.*

reputation *n. The scandal badly injured her reputation. That critic has a reputation as an excellent judge of talent:* standing, stature, repute, name.

repute *n.* **1** *Hazlitt was an essayist of high repute:* respectability; standing, reputation, renown, prominence, fame, celebrity, notoriety.

—*v.* **2** *He was reputed to be a heavy gambler:* consider, regard, hold, esteem, estimate, judge, deem; believe, think, suppose, account, reckon, view, say.

request *n.* **1** *Put in a request for a transfer to another department. This is not a request, it's an order!:* application, solicitation, petition.

—*v.* **2** *The judge requested the prisoner to withdraw. He requested her hand in marriage:* ask, ask for, apply for, call for; solicit, bid for, seek, sue for, press one's suit for, petition for, make entreaty for, entreat, desire.

require *v.* **1** *What material do you require to complete the job?:* need, stand in need of, have need of; want, lack, miss; desire, hope for, wish for, long for, crave. **2** *The subpoena requires you to appear in court:* command, charge, enjoin, order, oblige, constrain, compel, direct, dictate, bid. **3** *This plan requires secrecy:* necessitate, make imperative, entail, imply.

Ant. **1** dispense with, forgo.

requirement *n.* **1** *Experience in a related field is a requirement for this job:* prerequisite, essential, requisite, must, desideratum, qualification, *Latin* sine qua non. **2** *The product met all the requirements set by the government:* guide-line, specification, standard, criterion.

requisite *adj.* **1** *He has the requisite qualifications for this job:* required, mandatory, compulsory, obligatory, prerequisite, necessary, essential, imperative, needed, indispensable.

—*n.* **2** *A good head for heights is a requisite for*

high-rise construction work: prerequisite, requirement, need, necessity, essential, must, desideratum, *Latin* sine qua non.

Ant. 1 unnecessary, superfluous, inessential, superfluity, luxury.

rescind *v. The judge rescinded the court's previous decision:* revoke, reverse, retract, repeal, recall, take back, invalidate, countermand, overrule, counterorder, override, set aside, discard, get rid of, sweep aside; void, annul, abrogate, abolish, declare null and void, nullify, cancel, quash, dissolve.

Ant. uphold, support; validate.

rescue *v.* **1** *The fireman rescued three people from the burning building:* save, recover, extricate, deliver.

—n. **2** *A solicitor arranged for the rescue of the hostage. The survivor attributed his rescue to quick work by the lifeboat men:* rescuing, saving, recovery, liberation, deliverance, freeing, extrication, release, salvage.

Ant. 1 abandon. **2** loss, abandonment.

research *n.* **1** *You may conduct the research for your paper in the library:* inquiry, investigation, search, fact-finding, analysis, scrutiny, study, inspection, examination, probe, exploration, scholarship.

—v. **2** *The scientist researched the cause of the disease:* do research on, study, investigate, conduct an examination into.

resemblance *n. You bear a striking resemblance to Harold Wilson. There's no resemblance between the two paintings:* likeness, similarity, closeness in appearance, affinity, similitude, semblance, analogy, correspondence, parallel.

Ant. unlikeness, dissimilarity, difference.

resemble *v. I resemble my mother, but my brother resembles my father:* bear a resemblance to, look like, appear like, favour, take after, be like, be similar to, correspond to, be akin to, parallel.

resent *v. I resent that remark!:* feel anger at, be indignant at, be provoked by, be in a huff about, be piqued at, view with dissatisfaction; dislike, feel displeasure at, be offended at, take exception to, take amiss, take offence at, take umbrage at, be insulted by, be jealous of, bear a grudge against.

Ant. like, approve; welcome.

resentment *n. Her words were full of hatred and resentment:* indignation, bad feelings, anger, outraged spirit, ire, crossness, bad temper, dudgeon, huff, asperity, ill will, rancour; acrimony, bitterness, acerbity, sourness, soreness, irritation, irritability; pique, wounded pride, umbrage, offence, hurt feelings, displeasure; animosity, animus, malice, vindictiveness, vengefulness, spite; jealousy.

reservation *n.* **1** *I have no reservation about hiring him. The professor accepted the student provisionally, subject to certain reservations:* reluctance, doubt, hesitancy, uncertainty; compunction, scruple; qualification, strings, condition, stipulation, provision, proviso. **2** *We made a reservation for a week in June at the hotel:* accommodation, booking, pre-arrangement, appointment, date, reserved place.

reserve *v.* **1** *It's often wise to reserve judgement. Reserve your strength for the race this afternoon:* keep, keep back, withhold, retain, hold, keep as one's own; preserve, spare, conserve, save, husband, lay up, store up, salt away, hoard up, amass, stock, stock-pile, put by for a rainy day; postpone, delay, put aside, shelve, table. **2** *Telephone in advance to reserve a room:* set apart, pre-arrange, provide for, engage, book; schedule.

—n. **3** *Keep the equivalent of six months' earnings as a reserve:* emergency fund, contingency fund, reservoir, savings, nest-egg, hoard, stockpile. **4** *A man of reserve seldom shows emotion:* reticence, reservedness, aloofness, retiring disposition.

—adj. **5** *We're running on reserve power:* stored-up, unused, extra, spare, additional; second-string, back-up.

Ant. 1 give, grant; squander, splurge, spend; throw away, waste. **4** sociability, warmth, affability, conviviality, openness, frankness.

Exploring the Word: *Reserve, reservation,* and *reservoir* come from Latin *re-*, back, + *servare,* to keep. Thus to *reserve* is to keep something back and a *reserved* person keeps back his emotions; a *reservation* is an agreement to keep back or hold a hotel room, seat on a plane, etc., for someone and a wildlife *reserve* is a tract of land held back for the keeping of wild animals either in, or in an approximation to, their native habitat; while a *reservoir* is for holding back a supply of something, usually water for a city.

reserved *adj.* **1** *Be sure to get reserved seats:* kept in reserve, retained, booked, taken, engaged, spoken for, bespoken. **2** *The Cornish are supposed to be reserved, but we found them warm and friendly:* reticent, aloof, self-contained, undemonstrative, inhibited, constrained, formal, ceremonious, strained, distant, stand-offish, unsocial, unsociable, unresponsive, uncommunicative.

Ant. 1, 2 unreserved. **2** demonstrative, open, uninhibited; sociable, warm, affable.

reservoir *n.* **1** *The reservoir supplies the city's water:* water reserve; basin, mill-pond, well, fount, cistern. **2** *Tacitus described Rome as the reservoir into which all things infamous and shameful flowed:* tank, receptacle, container, repository, depository. **3** *The labours of scholars have put at our disposal an immense reservoir of facts:* supply, store, reserve, fund, stock, accumulation, pool, stockpile.

reside *v.* **1** *I reside in Bangalore. Jim and Meg reside at the Grand Hotel when they come up to Town:* dwell, live, have residence, have one's abode, keep house, lodge, sojourn. **2** *Does goodness reside in generosity to others?:* lie, rest, exist, belong, be present, be inherent, be ingrained, be intrinsic.

residence *n. His office is in town, but his residence is in the suburbs. I dread taking up residence in a new town. After a residence of ten years in Rio, she moved to Lisbon:* home, house, homestead, household, lodging, quarters, dwelling, dwelling-place, habitation, domicile, abode, address, place, flat, room, *Informal* digs, *French* pied à terre, *Slang* pad; stay, sojourn.

resident *n. I'm a resident of Toronto. We joined the residents' committee:* inhabitant, dweller, citizen, denizen, townsman, local; tenant, occupant, lodger.

residue *n. A residue of coffee grounds remained in the pot:* remainder, remains, leavings, dregs, residuum, remnant, rest, balance.

resign *v.* **1** *He resigned his position in the company:* give up, step down from, quit, relinquish, leave, abdicate. **2** *You must resign yourself to the fact that you'll never be rich or famous:* submit, reconcile.

resignation *n.* **1** *His resignation left a vacancy on the board of directors:* leaving, retirement. **2** *He accepted his defeat with resignation:* submission, submissiveness, passiveness, non-resistance, acquiescence, equanimity, stoicism, fatalism, patience.

Ant. **1** retention. **2** rebellion, resistance, protest.

resilient *adj. Rubber is very resilient. He's so resilient that his troubles never seem to get him down for long:* rebounding, elastic, flexible, springy, supple, rubbery; expansive, rapidly recovering, buoyant, resistant, irrepressible; hardy, tenacious, adaptable.

Ant. inflexible, stiff, rigid, tense; flaccid.

"I can resist everything except temptation."
—*Oscar Wilde*

---

resist *v.* **1** *He made an attempt to resist his attackers. This material resists stains:* fight against, oppose, strike back, beat back, fight, combat, contest, withstand, make a stand against, hold out against, bear up against, stand up to, weather, repel, counter, counteract, stop, stem, thwart, baffle, balk, foil, frustrate. **2** *Try to resist your craving for chocolates and other rich foods:* not give in to, abstain from, refrain from, say no to, refuse, reject; turn down.

Ant. **1, 2** give in to, surrender to, submit to. **1** yield, comply with, succumb to, capitulate, acquiesce. **2** indulge in, enjoy.

◇ *Usage note:* A *resister* is a person who resists: *I shall continue to be a staunch resister against these modern fads.* A *resistor* is an electrical device for introducing resistance into an electrical circuit: *This old television set needs some new tubes, condensers, and resistors.*

◇ *Word origin: Resist* comes from Latin *re-* (back) + the verb *sistere* (to stand, stop), to back by standing firm, withstand. The same Latin verb gives us *cease, desist,* and *insist.*

resistance *n. The proposal met with resistance from the villagers. Resistance movements sprang up all over Nazi-occupied Europe:* opposition, contention, non-compliance, obstinancy, recalcitrance; rejection, rebuff, refusal, obstruction; struggle, armed struggle, insurgency, national liberation movement; insurrection, mutiny, rebellion.

resolute *adj. He was a serious, resolute student. Lord Beaverbrook was a resolute and energetic leader:* determined, purposive, set in purpose, deliberate, steadfast, staunch, tenacious, pertinacious, earnest, zealous, industrious, assiduous, steady, diligent, vigorous; persevering, relentless, persistent, dogged, untiring, unflagging, indefatigable; unyielding, unwavering, unfaltering, unflinching, inflexible, uncompromising, undeviating, unswerving, unbending, strong-minded, strong-willed, stern, stubborn, obstinate, intrepid.

Ant. irresolute, unresolved, doubtful, undecided, undetermined, unsteady, vacillating.

resolution *n.* **1** *The resolution was passed by two votes:* motion, formal proposition, proposal. **2** *Have you made a New Year resolution?:* resolve, promise, intent, intention, purpose, plan, design, ambition; objective, object, aim, goal. **3** *He lacked the resolution to get through medical school:* resoluteness, firmness of purpose, fixed purpose, persistence, determination, tenacity, resolve, will-power, perseverance, resilience, steadfastness, stability, steadiness, constancy, stamina, staying-power, endurance; zeal, earnestness, energy, indefatigability, mettle, spirit, aggressiveness, follow-through. **4** *He was faced with the resolution of a difficult matter:* solution, resolving, clearing up, working out, sorting out, settlement.

"Good resolutions are simply cheques that men draw on a bank where they have no account."
—*Oscar Wilde*

---

resolve *v.* **1** *We resolved to visit Grannie at least once a year:* make up one's mind, dedicate oneself to, determine, decide, form a resolution, purpose, plan, intend, design, set out. **2** *We can resolve the matter to your satisfaction:* clear up, settle, solve, find the solution to, explain, answer, elucidate. **3** *The jury was trying to resolve whether the defendant was guilty or innocent:* determine, settle, vote on, decide, adjudge, make up one's mind.

—*n.* **4** *It is our resolve never to surrender this fortress:* determination, resolution, fixed intention, purpose. **5** *Man is of soul and body formed for deeds of high resolve:* resoluteness, resolution, steadfastness, firmness.

◇ *Word origin: Resolve, resolute,* and *resolution* come from Latin *re-* (again) + *solvere* (to loosen). To resolve a problem is "to loosen" it so that something can be decided. Latin *solvere,* to loosen, also gives us *solve* and *dissolve.*

resonant *adj. For such a skinny person he's got an amazingly resonant voice:* full, rich, vibrant, sonorous, ringing; stentorian, bellowing, resounding, reverberant, booming, orotund, thunderous.

resort *v.* **1** *Even saints have been known to resort to violence:* have recourse to, bring into play, avail oneself of, apply, take up, exercise, make use of, employ, use, utilize.
—*n.* **2** *We stayed at a resort in the Pyrenees:* holiday place, tourist centre, spa, watering-place, retreat. **3** *In the face of defeat, suicide was the samurai's last resort:* recourse, expedient; avail, hope, chance.

resound *v. Church bells resounded throughout the Alpine valley:* peal, ring, sound, reverberate, tintinnabulate, clang, fill the air, echo.

resource *n.* **1** *Escape was the only resource left to him:* recourse, expedient, wherewithal, means of supplying. **2** Usually **resources** *We pooled our resources and bought a boat:* wealth, capital, funds, assets, money, revenue, income, collateral, wherewithal; belongings, effects, possessions.

resourceful *adj. He was a clever and resourceful young man:* inventive, creative, imaginative, innovative, original, ingenious, smart, bright, sharp, cunning, shrewd, artful; adroit, skilful, able, competent, capable, effectual, proficient, ready, enterprising.
Ant. unresourceful, uninventive, uncreative, artless; unskilful, incompetent, incapable.

respect *n.* **1** *In that respect you're perfectly right:* detail, point, particular, matter, circumstance, feature, point of view, aspect, regard. **2** *In respect of your request, five pounds will be credited to your account:* relation, regard, reference, concerning, connection, bearing. **3** *He had great respect for his stepfather. Reporters have no respect for anyone's privacy:* regard, deference, veneration, reverence, esteem, appreciation, affection; praise, laudation, admiration, approval; notice, recognition; consideration. **4** **respects** *It is proper to call on a new neighbour to pay one's respects:* expressions of friendship or esteem, compliments, consideration, tribute, fealty, regards, greetings, remembrances.
—*v.* **5** *Respect your elders!:* honour, esteem, do honour to, revere, venerate, pay deference to, defer to, have respect for, regard, pay attention to; look up to, be appreciative of, understand, set store by, admire, value, cherish, prize. **6** *I respect your desire for privacy but I am obliged to intrude. They respected the artist's last wishes and burned his letters:* consider, treat with consideration, treat with forbearance, refrain from interfering with, show consideration for, appreciate, regard, honour, comply with, obey, heed, follow, abide by, observe, adhere to, be faithful to, acknowledge.
Ant. **2, 3, 5** disrespect, disregard. **3** irreverence, contempt, scorn, disdain. **5** pay no attention to; think little of, have a low opinion of, scorn, hold in contempt, disdain. **6** neglect, ignore, disregard, disdain, abuse.

respectable *adj.* **1** *My parents are respectable people. Can't you behave in a respectable manner?:* worthy of respect, worthy, reputable, estimable, honourable, noble, dignified, upright, honest, above-board; proper, decent, decorous, correct; becoming, presentable; refined, polished, courtly, civil, polite. **2** *He earns a respectable salary:* ample, sufficient, fairly good, fairly large, considerable, fair, moderate, proper, passable, satisfactory, admissible, decent, worthy.
Ant. **1** unworthy, disreputable, dishonourable, ignoble, improper, indecent, indecorous, unbecoming, unpresentable; unrefined, impolite. **2** small, poor, paltry, inadequate, demeaning.

respectful *adj. You can be respectful without being obsequious:* deferential, polite, courteous, showing politeness, mannerly, gracious, civil; decorous, reverent, reverential; ceremonious, formal, attentive, obliging, accommodating, winning, amiable, personable, genial.
Ant. disrespectful, impolite, discourteous, uncivil, unmannerly, unrefined, ungracious, irreverent, indecorous; heedless, hostile, antagonistic.
◇ *Usage note: RespectFULLY* means in a *respectFUL* or polite way: *Please speak more respectfully to your parents. RespectABLY* means in a manner able to be respected, in a worthy or proper manner: *We may have been poor, but we were always respectably dressed. RespectIVELY* means in a specified order, one after the other: *Your bank balances for May and June were £50 and £60 respectively.*

respiration *n. Tadpoles use gills in respiration. In yoga you learn to control your respiration:* breathing, respiratory action.

respite *n. The producer gave the cast a short respite before the next scene. The condemned prisoner's lawyer got him a respite:* rest period, recess, break, breathing-space, intermission, pause, lull, let-up; reprieve, stay of execution, delay, extension, temporary suspension.

resplendent *adj. The light of the chandelier made her modest necklace look positively resplendent:* refulgent, brilliant, bright, sparkling, dazzling, splendid; gleaming, coruscating, glittering, glowing, radiant, beaming, blazing; luminous, lustrous, lambent.
Ant. dull, lustreless, lacklustre, grey, sombre, dimmed, flat, matt.

respond *v.* **1** *He did not respond to the question:*

reply, answer, give an answer, speak up. **2** *The Mountain Rescue team is quick to respond to a call for help:* react, act in response, reply.

> **Exploring the Word**: *Respiration* comes from Latin *re-*, back, again + *spirare*, to breathe, hence to breathe again and again. The Latin *spirare* also gives us *aspire*, literally to breathe on something, or (in the language of the Authorized Version) "to pant after" something, i.e. to desire or want something badly; *conspire*, literally to breathe together, i.e. to plot or scheme together; *expire*, to emit the breath, to breathe one's last, and hence to come to an end; *inspire*, to breathe life into, and *inspiration*, that which breathes life into an idea, project, or the like; *perspire* and *transpire*, both of which originally meant to breathe through the pores or give off waste through the pores as by sweating, but now *perspire* has pre-empted this meaning for animals and *transpire* for plants; in ordinary colloquial use *transpire* has come to mean "to take place."

response *n.* **1** *What's your response to these charges?:* answer, reply; rebuttal, counterstatement, countercharge; retort, return, rejoinder, riposte, come-back. **2** *The master's response to our plan was encouraging:* reaction, impression, acknowledgement, feedback.
Ant. **1** query, question. **2** proposal, proposition.

responsibility *n.* **1** *He accepted all responsibility for the mistake:* liability; accountability, answerability, blame, burden, culpability. **2** *Taking care of a family is a big responsibility:* charge, trust, function, task, burden, obligation, duty, order. **3** *I recognize her brilliance but question her responsibility:* dependability, reliability, trustworthiness.
Ant. **3** unreliability, undependability, untrustworthiness.
◇ *Spelling tip:* This is similar to the spelling tip for *responsible.* Remember: "*I* bear the responsibility for my own fate," and there are three *I*'s in *responsibility.*

responsible *adj.* **1** *Parents are responsible for the welfare of their children:* accountable, duty-bound, liable, answerable, under obligation. **2** *A Cabinet appointment puts one in a responsible position:* requiring maturity and ability, important, challenging, demanding; administrative, executive. **3** *Who's responsible for this mess?:* liable to be called to account, culpable, guilty, at fault. **4** *Betty is a responsible young lady:* conscientious, reliable, dependable, trustworthy, creditable; capable, mature, self-assured, adult, of age.
Ant. **1, 2, 4** irresponsible. **1** unaccountable, under no obligation. **4** unconscientious, immature, unreliable, undependable, untrustworthy.
◇ *Spelling tip:* Remember: "*I* am responsible for my own fate," and there is an *I* in *responsible.*

responsive *adj. You weren't responsive enough at the interview. If we are not responsive to beauty, we shall miss a lot in life:* reactive, sharp, quick to answer, alive, awake; susceptible, impressionable, sensitive, sympathetic, compassionate, understanding, aware of.
Ant. unresponsive, apathetic, silent; slow to respond; impassive, dead, insensitive, unsympathetic.

rest[1] *n.* **1** *We took a short rest before starting off on the second lap. If you have a cold, take aspirin, drink fluids, and get plenty of rest:* relief from work or exertion, respite, break, recess, pause, lull, intermission, interruption, suspension, quiet spell, breathing-space; *Informal* breather; vacation, holiday; ease, relaxation, leisure; peace, quiet, stillness; sleep, slumber, hibernation; bed-rest, nap, siesta; *Slang* snooze, forty winks. **2** *After a long illness he was finally laid to rest:* death, one's final peace, repose, the grave, demise, end, departure, decease, cessation. **3** *The ball came to rest inches from the corner pocket:* state of motionlessness, standstill, halt, stop. **4** *The judge put the gavel on a small wooden rest:* supporting device, holder, support, prop, base, stand, platform, trivet.
—*v.* **5** *The hikers rested awhile. You can rest now, we're home. The runners rested their legs:* relax, take one's ease, be at ease, take a breather, pause, let up; settle down, be quiet, be at peace; lie down; *Informal* cool one's feet, recline, loll, repose; sleep; give rest to, ease, laze, lounge, loaf. **6** *The skiers rested at the bottom of the hill. Shall we let the matter rest?:* come to a standstill; stand, lie, be, remain. **7** *He rested the box on the chair:* set down, deposit, set, place, lay; lean, prop. **8** *The success of the plan rests on your co-operation:* be founded, be based, depend, rely, hang, hinge; be found, reside, be, exist, lie.
Ant. **1** unrest, restlessness; work, toil, activity, stir, excitement, disquiet.

"Absence of occupation is not rest,
A mind quite vacant is a mind distress'd."
—*William Cowper*

---

rest[2] *n.* **1** *You may have the rest of the pie. Some agree with Jim, but the rest of us agree with Sam:* remains, remainder, remaining part, complement, that which is left, that which remains, remnant, residue, residuum, the others.
—*v.* **2** *Rest easy:* remain, go on being, continue to be, keep, stay.

restful *adj. I like a restful holiday:* relaxed, comfortable, giving rest, soothing, full of rest; unagitated, undisturbed, peaceful, tranquil, serene, calm, placid, quiet, pacific.
Ant. restless, unrelaxed, uncomfortable; agitated, disturbing, busy.

restitution *n. Restitution must be made for the loss of these paintings:* redress, satisfaction, atonement, amends, reparation, remuneration, compensation, recompense, indemnification, indemnity, reimbursement, requital, repayment, paying back, reinstatement; *Law* replevin.

restless *adj.* **1** *The patient has had many restless nights. Jimmy is a restless child:* restive, wakeful, sleepless, insomniac, fitful, awake, unquiet; agitated, uneasy, disquieted, ill at ease, uncomfortable; nervous, jittery, highly strung, jumpy, fidgety, worried, fretful, anxious, hyperactive, excitable, impatient. **2** *For many years Ulysses was a restless wanderer:* always in motion, never at rest, on the go, on the move, transient, incessant, unsettled.

Ant. 1 restful, quiet, undisturbed, easy, comfortable, relaxed, carefree.

restore *v.* **1** *Angela, the monitor, finally shouted to restore quiet in the classroom:* bring back, get back, recoup, recover, retrieve, rescue, reclaim; reinstate, re-establish, reinstall; recreate. **2** *We restored the antique desk. Mother restored the old jacket by putting patches on the elbows:* reconstruct, rebuild, recondition, rehabilitate, refurbish, convert, renew, renovate, remodel, make over, do over, fix, mend, repair, patch up, retouch, touch up. **3** *The thermal treatments were quite effective in restoring her:* bring back to health, bring round, rally, pull through, make well, rehabilitate, set on one's feet; strengthen, energize, stimulate, exhilarate, reinvigorate, revitalize, revive, reanimate, revivify, resuscitate, refresh; cure, remedy, heal, treat, medicate, mend, dose. **4** *He was later restored to his former rank:* put back, reinstate, reinstitute, re-establish, reinstall; return, bring back, give back.

◇ *Word origin: Restore,* like *rest*[2] and *restaurant,* comes from Latin *restaurare,* to rebuild, repair, renew. Our words to *store,* a *store,* and *storehouse* come from the same word. The key concept underlying all of these words is *renewal* of the things being stocked — the laying up of a *store* of goods. *Store* in the sense "large shop" is only about 200 years old.

restrain *v. The leash restrained the dog:* keep under control, suppress, contain, withhold, hold back, inhibit, temper, chasten, restrict, limit, check, curb, bridle, arrest, muzzle, gag, constrain, hold, prevent, curtail, stop; bind, shackle, fetter, trammel, pinion, harness.

restrict *v. The French police are legally entitled to restrict anyone's movements as they please. Firemen tried to restrict the area of the blaze:* confine, constrain, restrain, suppress, hold back, check, curb, impede, frustrate, thwart, cramp, hamper, obstruct, inhibit, prevent; keep within limits, limit, hold, circumscribe; narrow, constrict.

restriction *n.* **1** *Copyright restrictions forbid our photocopying this paper:* curbing, limitation, control, regulation. **2** *It is a club with rigid restrictions on its membership:* rule, regulation, provision, proviso, condition, stipulation, qualification, reservation, requirement.

result *v.* **1** *His lameness resulted from an accident:* arise, ensue, eventuate, happen, stem, owe to, derive, originate, turn out, issue, spring. **2** *Her singing lessons resulted in her getting a part in a musical:* culminate, wind up, end up, pan out. —*n.* **3** *What were the results of the medical tests? The fire was the result of carelessness:* finding, decision, verdict, opinion, judgement, determination, resolution, solution, report; consequence, outcome, effect, upshot, reaction, development, product, after-effect, aftermath, outgrowth, sequel, fruit, issue.

Ant. 1 originate, prompt. **3** cause, determinant; antecedent, origin, source, root.

resume *v. Please resume what you were doing:* take up again, begin again, go on with, proceed, continue, recommence.

◇ *Word origin: Resume* comes from Latin *re-* (again) + *sumere* (to take), to take up again.

resurgence *n. There has been a resurgence of violence in the city:* revival, appearing again, rising again, rebirth, renaissance, recrudescence, return, renascence, re-emergence.

Ant. passing away, decline, fading.

retain *v. Concentrated study will help you to retain knowledge:* keep, hold on to, maintain, keep possession of, possess, grasp, absorb, hold; keep in mind, bear in mind, commit to memory, fix in the mind, remember, recall, recollect, call to mind; have at one's fingertips.

Ant. discard, lose, surrender, relinquish, abandon.

retaliate *v. When one of their soldiers was killed, the army retaliated by killing hostages:* counter, reciprocate, exact retribution, return like for like, repay in the same coin, give measure for measure, give one a dose of his own medicine, exact one's pound of flesh; return, repay, requite, return the compliment; pay back, pay off, avenge, revenge, take revenge, take vengeance.

◇ *Word origin: Retaliate* comes from Latin *re-* (back) + *talio* (punishment in kind, from *talis,* of such a kind), hence punishment in kind returned for injury or wrong, revenge.

retard *v. Lack of sunlight retards growth in many organisms:* slow up, slow down, impede, delay the progress of, detain, check, block, obstruct, clog, fetter, hamper, hinder, baffle, inhibit, arrest, prevent; delay, hold up, prolong, draw out, drag, slacken, decelerate.

Ant. speed, speed up, accelerate, expedite, quicken, hasten, rush; advance, further.

reticent *adj. T. E. Lawrence became an increasingly reticent man:* taciturn, quiet, uncommunicative, silent, sparing of words, close-mouthed, tight-lipped; reserved, retiring, shy, diffident, self-contained, restrained, closed.

Ant. voluble, talkative, communicative, unreserved, expansive, inclined to speak freely, candid, frank, open, plain.

◇ *Word origin: Reticent* comes from Latin *re-* (again) + the verb *tacere* (to be silent), to be silent again. Related to the same Latin verb is our word *taciturn.*

retire *v.* **1** *For relaxation he retires to a cottage in the Cotswolds:* go away, betake oneself, depart, retreat, withdraw, remove, resort. **2** *I'm tired, so I'll retire now:* go to bed, turn in, go to sleep, lie down to rest, call it a day; *Informal* doss down, hit the hay, flake out. **3** *He retired from the army:* withdraw from public life or business, give up office, resign, remove from active service, secede, abdicate, drop out.

Ant. **2** get up, arise; wake up, awaken. **3** join, sign on, enlist.

◇ *Word origin: Retire* and *retiring* come from French *retirer,* pull back. Hence to retire is to draw back or go away, as for privacy or rest, or to withdraw from business or active service. A *retiring* person is a shy, modest person, who draws back from other people or activities.

"The minor longs to be at age, then to be a man of business, then to make up an estate, then to arrive at honours, then to retire."

—*Joseph Addison*

---

retiring *adj. Bill's a rascal with a deceptively retiring manner:* withdrawn, uncommunicative, unsocial, reticent, quiet; shy, bashful, modest, demure, shrinking, meek, sheepish, timid, timorous; unassuming, inconspicuous, unassertive, humble, unpretentious; reserved, self-contained.

Ant. outgoing, gregarious, sociable, bold, brazen, brassy, forward, audacious, *Informal* pushy.

retort *v.* **1** *"Same to you!" he retorted:* reply sharply, counter, return, rejoin, rebut; give answer, say, respond, answer, come back with, fire back.

—*n.* **2** *Her retort left me with nothing more to say:* sharp reply, pointed answer, counterblast, rebuttal, quip, rejoinder, witty reply.

retract *v.* **1** *You must retract that statement or defend it with your life:* withdraw, take back, recant, recall, rescind, revoke, repeal, reverse, abnegate, abrogate, disavow, disown, disclaim, deny, abjure, renounce, forswear. **2** *The point of a ball-point pen retracts:* draw back, pull back, peel back, draw in, recede, retreat, withdraw, recoil; reel in.

Ant. **1** offer, proffer. **2** poke out, protrude.

retreat *n.* **1** *The general ordered a retreat:* strategic withdrawal, falling back, pulling back, backing out, retirement, evacuation, flight, departure, get-away, escape. **2** *His retreat from social life was absolute:* withdrawal, retirement, seclusion, solitude, isolation, immurement, reclusion; hibernation, rustication. **3** *They spent their honeymoon in a mountain retreat:* place of seclusion, privacy, or refuge; resort, haunt, refuge, asylum, sanctum, sanctuary, den, haven, shelter, harbour, port.

—*v.* **4** *He retreated from reality:* withdraw, retire, fall back, move back, fall to the rear, draw back, back away, recoil, shy away, shrink, make a retreat, depart, go, leave, make a get-away, escape, turn tail, make oneself scarce; flee, abscond, bolt, take flight.

Ant. **1** advance, charge. **2** entrance; participation. **4** advance, move forward, rush to, meet head on, engage.

retribution *n. There will be retribution for his heinous crimes:* requital, retaliation, justice, satisfaction, redress, amends, restitution, return, reparation, reciprocation, recrimination, reprisal, penalty, punishment, reward; recompense, vengeance, revenge, an eye for an eye and a tooth for a tooth, measure for measure, just deserts.

retrieve *v. Interpol is busy trying to retrieve the stolen painting:* recover, regain, get back, get back again, find again, recoup, reclaim, repossess, redeem, recapture, rescue; fetch, go and get.

retrospect *n. His youth was more enjoyable in retrospect than it had actually seemed at the time. Each instalment of the serial story begins with a retrospect of the preceding chapter:* contemplation of time past, review, retrospection, remembrance, reminiscence, flashback, looking backward; second thought, reconsideration, afterthought, hindsight.

return *v.* **1** *We thought that spring would never return. When will you return from Cyprus?:* come back, go back, reappear, recur. **2** *The electorate will return their favourite candidate to office. The thief returned the missing jewels:* send back, bring back, put back, restore; reinstate, reinstall, re-establish. **3** *Permit me to return the compliment:* give back, repay, give in recompense, give in turn, requite, reciprocate. **4** *The stocks returned more than ten per cent a year:* repay, yield, provide, earn, be profitable, give interest, render. **5** *The jury is expected to return its verdict shortly:* announce, deliver, come to, render.

—*n.* **6** *News of the astronauts' safe return to earth was delayed. Police announced the return of the stolen goods:* returning, coming back, homecoming, arrival, advent; reinstatement, restoral, re-establishment, restoration, recovery, retrieval; putting back. **7** *We're dreading the return of rationing:* returning, recurrence, reappearance, reversion, happening again. **8** *The bonds yielded a handsome return:* profit, income, revenue, earnings, proceeds, yield, interest, gain, reward, advantage, benefit, compensation, gross.

Ant. **1** depart, leave, go away, disappear. **2** retain, keep, hold, withhold; remove. **4** lose, be unprofitable. **6** departure, leaving, removal.

reveal *v. Further investigation revealed previously hidden facts:* make known, divulge, give out, disclose, impart, unearth, bare, lay bare, bring to light, unmask, unveil, expose, uncover, make public; publish, come out with, let out, betray, give inside information, point out, *Slang* give the low-down; lay open to view, display, show, exhibit; manifest, evidence, unfold.

Ant. conceal, hide, keep secret, veil, mask, cover.

◇ *Word origin:* To *reveal* literally means to draw a veil back so that something can be seen, and a *revelation* is literally an *unveiling.* Both words come from Latin *re-* (back) + *velum* (veil).

revel *v.* **1** *She revelled in the notoriety resulting from her rival's divorce case:* take great pleasure, derive pleasure from, rejoice, take delight, delight, enjoy, relish; indulge, wallow in, bask in, be in seventh heaven. **2** *The villagers revelled far into the night:* make merry, indulge in festivities, celebrate, take one's pleasure, *Informal* paint the town red; carouse, roister, have one's fling, go on a spree; frolic, gambol, romp, caper.

revelation *n.* **1** *"Spilling the beans" means confessing or making a startling revelation:* disclosure, divulgation, divulgence, divulgement; confession, admission; bombshell, exposure, exposé; discovery, unveiling. **2** *Revelations concerning sin and baptism form the subject of an early Christian book titled* The Shepherd*:* vision, apocalypse, prophecy, revelatory writing.

Ant. cover-up, concealment, veiling, smokescreen.

◇ *Word origin: Revelation* is based on the same Latin word elements as *reveal,* but comes to us directly from Latin *revelatio* (unveiling) which is a translation of Greek *apokalupsis* (*apocalypse* — literally also "unveiling"). Both words come down to us because they are alternative titles of the *Revelation to John,* or *Apocalypse,* also known as the *Book of Revelation,* the visionary description of the coming and reign of the Messiah which forms the conclusion of the New Testament.

revelry *n. The streets were filled with revelry after the victory:* boisterous festivity, revelling, merry-making, celebrating, celebration, jollity, jollification, conviviality, exultation, festival, carnival, jamboree; carousal, roistering, high jinks, spree.

revenge *v.* **1** *I shall be revenged on you for this!:* inflict punishment in return for a wrong done, exact expiation, take vengeance for, take revenge, avenge; wreak one's vengeance, have one's revenge, make reprisal for, vindicate, take an eye for an eye, give tit for tat, return like for like, undertake a vendetta, demand one's pound of flesh; reciprocate, retaliate, requite, repay, pay back, recompense.

—*n.* **2** *He sought revenge for the harm they had done him:* vengeance, paying back, retaliation, reprisal, satisfaction, retribution, requital, repayment, eye for an eye, tooth for a tooth.

◇ *Usage note: Revenge* refers to retaliation for a wrong done to oneself: *I'll revenge myself for what you did to me! My revenge was sweet. Avenge* and *vengeance* refer to retaliation for a wrong done to others. *I avenged my father's murder, I sought vengeance for my father's murder.*

reverberate *v. Our voices reverberated in the cave. The sound of the bells reverberated through the valley:* carry, echo, resound, ring, vibrate, be reflected, boom, rumble, thunder.

revere *v. One of the Ten Commandments enjoins us to revere our parents:* honour, treat with veneration, venerate, defer to, show honour and devotion to, reverence, look up to, show deep regard for, respectfully cherish, deeply respect.

Ant. disrespect, dishonour; despise, scorn, mock, contemn, snap one's fingers at.

◇ *Word origin: Revere, reverence,* and *reverent* come from Latin *re-* (again) + *vereri* (to fear), hence to regard with profound awe or respect, to venerate. The title *Reverend* before a clergyman's name is a title of such respect.

"Revere thyself, and yet thyself despise."
—*Edward Young*

---

reverence *n. Aeneas' reverence for his father was one of our Latin teacher's favourite themes:* deep respect, esteem, regard, honour, homage, deference, veneration, admiration, adoration, devotion, worship; awe, fear; devoutness, piety, gesture indicative of deep respect, observance; genuflection, prostration, religiosity.

Ant. irreverence, disrespect, disregard, dishonour; hatred.

reverie *n.* **1** *The child stopped crying and fell into a reverie:* day-dream, brown study, dreamy spell. **2** *Did you have reveries about what you'd do when you grew up?:* fantasy, flight of fancy, musing, day-dream, dream, extravagance, castle-building, castles in the air, castles in Spain, wishful thinking. **3** *She sat at the window, deep in reverie:* meditation, abstracted preoccupation, musing, dreamland, woolgathering.

reverse *adj.* **1** *Sign your name on the reverse side of the contract:* turned backward, reversed, opposite, backward, converse, inverse, inverted, back, rear.

—*n.* **2** *His answer was just the reverse of what we expected:* contrary, opposite, antithesis, counter, counterpart, converse, inverse. **3** *On the reverse are lines for your comments:* back, rear, other side, posterior, tail. **4** *He's entitled to some success after all those reverses:* reversal, change for the worse, adversity, set-back, upset, disappointment, mischance, misfortune, mishap, hardship, trouble, hard times; frustration, failure, defeat.

—*v.* **5** *If you'll reverse the placard you'll see what I mean:* turn round, turn over, turn upside down, up-end, upturn, turn topsy-turvy; turn inside out, invert, transpose. **6** *The umpire never reversed a decision:* change, undo, unmake, revoke, rescind, repeal, retract, recall, recant, withdraw; overrule, override, set aside, countermand, invalidate, nullify, annul, declare null and void, void, negate, cancel, abrogate.

Ant. **3** obverse, front. **4** advance, benefit. **6** ratify, uphold, stick to.

revert *v. Pressure of work made him revert to his old habit of smoking:* go back, return, turn back, regress, retrogress, backslide, lapse, relapse, fall back on.

review *n.* **1** *The review in the* Daily Telegraph *damned the book with faint praise:* critique, criticism, critical piece, notice, commentary, evaluation. **2** *He had his poems published in a literary review:* magazine, journal. **3** *The committee has met for a final review of the facts:* examination, re-evaluation, reassessment, reconsideration, recapitulation, study, scrutiny, rehash, contemplation of past events, retrospection, reflection, survey. **4** *The soldiers were in full uniform for the review:* military inspection, presentation, formal examination, military display; parade, procession; show, exhibition, exposition, demonstration.

—*v.* **5** *Let's review the situation:* look at again, go over again, look over again, re-evaluate, re-examine, reassess, reconsider, retrace, hash over, scrutinize, study; reiterate, run over, recapitulate; restate briefly, summarize, sum up. **6** *The local paper will review the new play:* write a critique of, criticize, evaluate, report on, comment upon, discuss in a critical review, pass judgement on, analyse.

revise *v. Ben Jonson tells us that Shakespeare never had to revise a manuscript:* correct, change, alter, modify, edit, rewrite, redo, amend, rectify, emend, doctor, overhaul, recast, review, tinker with, fix up, revamp; bring up to date, make an up-to-date version of, update.

revision *n. Revisions were made to bring the text up to date. The poet published a final revision of his works in his old age:* change, alteration, modification, correction, improvement, emendation, amendment; revised version, recension, edition.

revive *v.* **1** *The smelling-salts revived her:* restore to consciousness, bring back to life, resuscitate. **2** *His interesting lecture revived my enthusiasm for ornithology:* bring back to life, reanimate, rouse again, reawaken, infuse new life into, give new life to, refresh, freshen, renew. **3** *The repertory company revived plays from 30 years ago:* present again, bring back into use, produce again, set going again, bring back into notice, make operative again, resurrect; *Slang* dig up, drag up; restage, reproduce, repeat.

revoke *v. The authorities will revoke your licence if you get another endorsement for speeding. There's a campaign afoot to revoke current restrictions on immigration:* withdraw, take back; negate, annul, nullify, invalidate, void, declare null and void, cancel, abrogate, abolish, expunge, erase, quash, do away with; repeal, rescind, reverse, recall, call back, retract; override, overrule, countermand, set aside, disallow, dismiss, abjure, renounce, disclaim, repudiate.

Ant. restore, give, grant; authorize, validate.

revolt *v.* **1** *Several tribes revolted against the new government policy:* rise, rebel, rise up, mutiny. **2** *The violence in the film revolted me:* disgust, repel, repulse, offend, go against, sicken, make one sick, nauseate, turn the stomach; make the flesh creep, horrify, appal, shock, distress, *Slang* turn one off.

—*n.* **3** *The peasants' revolt was put down by the dictator's troops:* rebellion, active resistance against authority, insurrection, insurgency, uprising, coup, putsch, revolution, opposition, disorder, mutiny, sedition, dissent, factiousness.

Ant. **1** give allegiance to, give loyalty to, support, bow, submit to. **2** attract; delight, amuse, please, fascinate.

> **Exploring the Word:** *Revolve* comes from Latin *re-*, back, again, + *volvere*, to turn, roll, hence to turn round. Latin *volvere*, to turn, also gives us *convolution*, a turning, coil; *evolve*, to roll out, to unfold or develop, and *evolution*, that which unfolds, development; *involve*, to roll up in, envelop, hence to include, affect, or complicate; *revolt*, literally to reverse, and *revolution*, literally a complete reversal, as of a political regime. Related English words are *whelk* (the mollusc, so-called because of its spiral shell), *willow* (the tree, because its twigs are flexible, "willowy"), *wallow* (to roll, as in mud), *well* (a spring, because the water bubbles up and rolls out of it), and *waltz* (because the dancers perform revolutions on the dance floor).

revolting *adj. It was a revolting spectacle:* disgusting, repulsive, repellent, repugnant, disagreeable, offensive, objectionable, foul, distasteful, obnoxious, nasty, vile, odious, invidious, horrid, shocking, appalling, horrible, horrific, grim, frightful, dreadful, sickening, nauseating, abhorrent, abominable, loathsome, hateful; malodorous, noxious, noisome, stinking.

Ant. pleasant, agreeable, attractive, delightful, unobjectionable; sweet-smelling, fragrant; palatable.

revolution *n.* **1** *Wagner brought about a revolution in music and musical taste:* complete change, radical departure, basic reformation, big shift. **2** *The Russian Revolution occurred on November 7th, 1917. Hitler attempted a Nazi revolution in 1923:* overthrow of an established regime, replacement of an old regime, coup d'état, coup, putsch. **3** *The American Revolution took place between 1775 and 1783:* (*variously*) revolutionary war, armed struggle, war against an established regime, insurrection, uprising, rising, rebellion, revolt, mutiny. **4** *The earth makes one revolution round the sun each year:* revolving, circling, movement in an orbit, circumvolution, circumrotation. **5** *The "78 RPM" on the old record means "78 revolutions per minute":* single turn, rotation, gyration.

Ant. 1 reaction, retrogression, regression. **2, 3** counter-revolution, countercoup, reaction, restoration, backlash.

revolutionary *adj.* **1** *Revolutionary factions wanted a complete overthrow of the government:* opposed to the established order, revolutionist, radical, extremist, insurrectionary, insurgent, rebellious, mutinous, subversive, seditious, dissenting. **2** *The inventor had a revolutionary idea:* radically innovative, fundamentally novel, unprecedented, very advanced.

Ant. 1 reactionary, counter-revolutionary; loyalist, conservative. **2** old, usual.

revolve *v. The moon revolves round the earth:* move in orbit, go round, circle, circumrotate, turn, gyrate, wheel.

revulsion *n. Descriptions of the murder aroused feelings of revulsion in all of us:* strong disgust, repugnance, aversion, abhorrence.

Ant. attraction, fascination, relish, taste.

◇ *Word origin: **Revulsion*** comes from Latin *re-* (back) + *vellere* (to pull), a drawing back, as in disgust.

reward *n.* **1** *A large reward is offered for the return of the ring. Eventually evil-doers get their just reward:* prize, compensation, recompense, payment, bounty, guerdon, remuneration, quid pro quo, award, consideration, premium, bonus; token of appreciation, deserts, wages, due, reckoning, what is coming to one.

—*v.* **2** *If you do well in Spanish I'll reward you with a trip to Spain. Nero was well enough rewarded for his crimes:* repay, requite, recompense, compensate, remunerate, take care of.

Ant. 1 penalty, fine, damages, punishment. **2** punish, penalize.

rhetoric *n.* **1** *Cicero was a master of rhetoric. Flaubert was a strong believer in the principles of rhetoric:* art of speaking or writing, rules of composition, classic style. **2** *Churchill's "Blood, sweat, and tears" speech is a masterpiece of rhetoric:* effective use of formal language, verbal communication, elocution, discourse, oratory, eloquence, high style, mannered language. **3** *The speaker resorted to rhetoric but said nothing of importance:* eloquence, magniloquence, grandiloquence, figures of speech, hyperbole, euphism, empty phrases, *Slang* hot air, wind, hocus-pocus, hokum, eyewash, hooey, bunkum.

◇ *Word origin: **Rhetoric*** comes from the Greek phrase *rhētorikē tekhnē*, the technique or art of (public) speaking.

◇ *Usage note:* A skilled practitioner or teacher of the classical art of *rhetoric* is a *rhetorician*, or *rhetor*. The term, *rhetor*, however, is usually reserved for a teacher of eloquence or professional public speaker of Graeco-Roman times. One of the ancient *rhetors'* (or *rhetoricians'*) many inventions was the *rhetorical question.* A rhetorical question is a question asked for effect rather than for an answer—for example: *Do you want to lose the shirt off your back and end up in the workhouse?*

rhetorical *adj.* **1** *The ancients loved rhetorical fireworks, so popular speakers were idolized like present-day pop stars:* flamboyant, high-flown, bombastic, grandiloquent, oratorical, eloquent, showy, inflated, windy, grandiose, magniloquent, silver-tongued, extravagant, high-sounding, ornate, aureate, florid, flowery, embellished, euphuistic. **2** *Carlyle's language is often so heavily larded with rhetorical words it is impossible to understand:* used for stylistic effect, expressive, decorative, ornamental. **3** *The politician took a copy of his speech and made a few rhetorical changes for ease of delivery, balance and effect:* stylistic, elocutionary; verbal, linguistic, discursive; disputative, disputatious, argumentative.

rhythm *n. Rhythm is a basic component of music and language. Our diet follows the rhythm of the seasons:* fluctuation, recurrence, natural flow, recurrent alternation, flow pattern, time, movement, metre, measure, accent, beat, stress, cadence, number, rhythmic pattern, accentuation, emphasis, swing, lilt, syncopation.

◇ *Word origin: **Rhythm*** comes from Greek *rhuthmos*, rhythm, regular recurrence, time (in the sense of "keeping time"). The word is related to Greek *rhein*, to flow.

ribald *adj. It's a revue with racy songs and ribald humour:* bawdy, lewd, risqué, vulgar, blue, indecent, crude, rude, coarse, uncouth, earthy, unrefined, gross, shocking, lascivious, licentious, libidinous, racy, wanton, rakish, raffish, prurient, suggestive.

◇ *Usage note: **Ribaldry*** is bawdy but wholesome. *Lewdness* is salacious, and unwholesome. ***Ribald*** always implies a jolly, "Wife of Bath"-style approach to sex. *Lewd* has a variety of mainly unpleasant connotations, ranging from "foul-mouthed and dirty-minded" to "morbidly obsessed with sex."

rich *adj.* **1** *I'm not rich but I'm not poor either:*

well-off, wealthy, affluent, rolling, well-to-do, flush, moneyed, on easy street, propertied, prosperous, well-heeled, *Informal* in clover. **2** *Rich silks and other materials were brought back from the Orient:* valuable, estimable, highly valued, precious, opulent, luxurious, sumptuous, splendid, prodigal, lavish, expensive, costly, fine, priceless. **3** *Plum pudding is a rich dessert:* heavy, filling, full-bodied; sweet. **4** *The carpets were a rich red. His voice was a rich baritone:* intense, lush, dark, deep, bright, vivid; resonant, deep-toned, sonorous, euphonious, mellow, mellifluous. **5** *Our home was always rich in love and understanding:* abundant, abounding. **6** *South Devon has acres of rich farmland:* productive, fruitful, fertile, fecund, loamy, luxuriant, lush.

Ant. 1, 5, 6 poor. **1** impoverished, destitute, penniless, indigent, impecunious, penurious, needy, poverty-stricken. **2** worthless, valueless, inexpensive, cheap. **3** bland, dull, flat. **4** weak, flat, dull; high-pitched, tinny. **5** wanting, lacking, scarce, rare, scanty, meagre. **6** unproductive, unfertile, unfruitful, barren, sterile, dry.

rickety *adj.* **1** *My younger brother spent the summer rebuilding a rickety old barn:* tumbledown, shaky, unsteady, wobbly, tottering, broken-down, deteriorated, dilapidated, decrepit. **2** *In the welfare state we rarely see rickety children:* suffering from rickets, decrepit, weak-jointed, feeble, frail, fragile, infirm, debilitated, weak, weakly, tottering, withered, wasted.

Ant. 1 sturdy, steady, solid, sound.

rid *v. I want to rid this city of corruption! Shall I ever be rid of this cold?:* free, purge, clear, unburden, disburden, disencumber, disabuse, liberate.

Ant. burden, encumber, take on, adopt.

riddance *n. The insecticide company promised complete riddance of the black-fly. He's gone, and good riddance:* clearing out, clearance, removal, ejection, expulsion, dislodgement; relief, deliverance, freeing.

Ant. encumbrance, adoption.

ride *v.* **1** *Do you know how to ride a bicycle?:* manage, control, handle. **2** *The bicycle rode roughly on the bumpy road. He rode a motor-cycle to the station. The politician rode on a wave of popularity:* move, move along, travel, progress, journey; transport, drive, carry, support; move along, be supported, be carried.

rider *n. A rider was attached to the will:* additional clause, addition, amendment, codicil, supplement, appendage, suffix, affix, adjunct, addendum, appendix, attachment.

ridge *n.* **1** *The village is just over that ridge:* hill, rise, crest, hillock, mound, knoll, bank, edge, bluff, promontory. **2** *A sandy beach at low tide often has ridges:* rib, ripple, crinkle, crimp, wrinkle, corrugation, rim, fret, bar, weal, welt, wale.

ridicule *n.* **1** *The new bridge was generally an object of ridicule:* mockery, sneering, derision, derogation, disparagement, gibe, aspersion, scorn, sarcasm, taunt, jeer, snicker, ribbing, teasing, caricature, burlesque, travesty, lampoonery.

—*v.* **2** *His classmates ridiculed him:* make fun of, make sport of, poke fun at, mock, mimic, imitate insultingly, laugh at, laugh to scorn, sneer at, scoff at, belittle, treat with disrespect, deride, disparage, humiliate, taunt, jeer, gibe at, twit, guy, rib, tease, make a butt of, make sport of, play tricks on, make a monkey of, caricature, burlesque, lampoon, parody.

Ant. 1, 2 praise, honour; respect. **1** homage, veneration, deference.

ridiculous *adj. That's the most ridiculous thing I've ever heard!:* absurd, ludicrous, preposterous, asinine, nonsensical, foolish, silly, idiotic, fatuous, inane, irrational, destitute of reason, unreasonable, senseless, frivolous; incredible, astonishing, fantastic, outlandish, queer, odd, grotesque, bizarre, laughable, comical, funny, droll, amusing; *Informal* hysterical, farcical, crazy, nutty, screwy.

"There is always something ridiculous about the passions of people whom one has ceased to love." —*Oscar Wilde*

---

rife *adj.* **1** *These marshlands were once rife with mosquitoes:* teeming, swarming, alive, thick, populous, crowded, packed, stocked up, *Informal* bursting; dense, close, solid, studded. **2** *Poverty is rife in the inner city:* prevalent, general, prevailing, predominant; extensive, universal, widespread, epidemic, current, far-reaching; pandemic.

rifle *v. The burglar rifled the safe:* search and rob, rob, plunder, go through, pillage, ransack, ravage, sack, loot, despoil, spoliate.

rift *n.* **1** *The blast created a rift in the rock face:* cleft, split, crack, fissure, fracture, break, chink, breach, rent, cut, slit, aperture, gash, rupture; chasm, crevice, gap, cranny, fault, crevasse, abyss, defile, gully, gorge, ravine. **2** *There should be no rifts between good friends:* division, breach, rupture, break, misunderstanding, disagreement, quarrel, falling out.

right *adj.* **1** *Nannies inculcate right conduct:* good, exemplary, proper, decent, morally excellent, virtuous, nice, fitting, seemly, right-minded, moral, upright, righteous, honest, above-board, ethical, scrupulous, honourable, unimpeachable, correct, punctilious, meet, square, fair and square, even-handed; equitable, just, fair. **2** *That's not the right way to do it. Mussolini did not have the right answer:* valid, allowable, admissible, satisfactory; correct, accurate, free from error, unmistaken, perfect, infallible, exact, precise, true, factual, veracious, veridical, truthful. **3** *He's*

not in his right mind: rational, normal, regular, sane, sound, reasonable. **4** *The right time to act is now:* most appropriate, suitable, seemly, fitting, proper, becoming; desirable, favourable, preferable, convenient, opportune, advantageous, ideal. **5** *From these three identical "Rembrandts" pick out the right one, i.e., the original:* actual, genuine, real, authentic; definite, clear-cut, certain; unquestionable, irrefutable, undisputed, incontestable; rightful, lawful, legal, licit, legitimate, valid.
—n. **6** *The Bourbon pretender pressed his right to the throne. You have the right to remain silent:* just claim, legal title, legal claim, moral claim, justification, birthright, inheritance; power, privilege, prerogative, liberty, licence, freedom, grant, permission, sanction; authority, legal power, authorization, jurisdiction. **7** *The defendant does not know right from wrong:* good, virtue, goodness, righteousness, moral excellence, good behaviour, good actions, morality, morals; integrity, honour, nobleness, uprightness, propriety, rectitude, probity; what ought to be, what should be. **8** Often **rights** *He bought the rights to the play:* ownership, deed, proprietorship, authorization, warrant, interest in property.
—adv. **9** *Losing no time, he went right to the heart of the matter:* directly, promptly, straight, completely. **10** *You have guessed right at last:* correctly, appropriately, suitably, properly, accurately, perfectly; exactly, precisely, just. **11** *Everything came out right in the end:* well, favourably, satisfactorily, *Informal* O.K. **12** *I'll be right there:* immediately, at once, directly, presently, in a moment.
—v. **13** *A crane was used to right the toppled statue:* set upright, stand up, restore to the proper position. **14** *The nationalist side wants to right many old grievances. The court ruling will right some existing injustices:* correct, put right, amend, solve, put in order; vindicate, redress, recompense, make restitution for, make up for.
Ant. 1, 2, 4, 5, 7, 10, 11 wrong. **1** bad, sinful, iniquitous, nefarious, improper, indecent, unvirtuous, immoral; dishonest, unethical, unscrupulous, dishonourable; unjust, unfair, false, illegitimate. **2** unsatisfactory; incorrect, inaccurate, mistaken, invalid, erroneous, erring, imperfect, inexact, fallacious, untrue, unfactual, false, untruthful. **3** irrational, abnormal, insane, unsound. **4** inappropriate, unsuitable, unseemly, unfitting, unbecoming; undesirable, unfavourable, inconvenient, disadvantageous. **5** false, fake, phoney, sham, counterfeit, fraudulent; indefinite, uncertain, questionable, contestable, unlawful, illegal, illicit, illegitimate. **7** evil, badness, venality, villainy, sinfulness, corruption, transgression, iniquity, bad behaviour, immorality; dishonour, impropriety. **9** indirectly, circuitously, slowly; incompletely. **10** incorrectly, improperly; inaccurately, imperfectly. **11** badly, unfavourably, poorly. **13** set down, put down; make crooked, topple.

righteous *adj. The colonial governor, while severe, was a righteous man:* moral, honourable, ethical, honest, upright, just, fair, equitable, good; godly, pious, devout, God-fearing, religious, reverent, holy, spiritual, pure in heart; virtuous, chaste, incorrupt, unsullied, innocent.
Ant. unrighteous, immoral, bad, evil, wicked, sinful, villainous, dishonourable, disreputable, dishonest, corrupt, unscrupulous, unprincipled, false, iniquitous, unjust, unfair; ungodly, irreligious, unholy, irreverent, unvirtuous.

rightful *adj. The rightful heir to the throne is the Crown Prince:* having a right, having a just claim, deserving, right, true, proper, correct, legitimate, legal, lawful, held by a just or legal claim, allowed, sanctioned, authorized, valid, constitutional, designated, prescribed, inalienable, deserved, appropriate, fitting, condign.
Ant. unrightful, untrue, improper, incorrect, illegitimate, illegal, unlawful, usurping.

rigid *adj.* **1** *If the wood is too rigid it may splinter. Don't be so rigid — relax:* stiff, unyielding, inflexible, unpliant, unbending, inelastic, fixed, hard, set, firm, tense, taut; wooden. **2** *The sergeant is a rigid disciplinarian:* strict, stringent, hard, stern, severe, harsh, austere, sharp, rigorous, exacting; stubborn, unrelenting, obdurate, uncompromising, inflexible, unbending, unyielding, strong, firm, fixed, set, cut and dried, clear-cut; strait-laced, formal, puritanical.
Ant. 1, 2 flexible, yielding. **1** pliant, supple, limber, bending, mobile, elastic, plastic. **2** lenient, soft, tolerant, indulgent, merciful, lax; informal.
◇ *Word origin: Rigid* and *rigour* both come from Latin *rigere,* to be stiff. *Rigour* is often used to mean stiffness of opinion or temper, strictness, severity. *Rigor mortis* means "the stiffness of death," and the French expression *de rigueur* means compulsory or required by etiquette or good form, an inflexible or "stiff" rule of good manners.

rigorous *adj.* **1** *The training involved rigorous exercises:* demanding, challenging, trying, stern, austere, harsh, exacting, tough, very harsh, severe, strict, stringent. **2** *The Babylonians were capable of rigorous accuracy in their computations:* exact, accurate, correct, precise, scrupulous, meticulous, punctilious.

rim *n. The wagon wheel had an iron rim. We stood on the rim of the crater:* outer edge, border; brim, verge, brink, ledge, lip.
Ant. core, centre, hub, inside.

ring[1] *n.* **1** *The dancers formed a ring round the maypole:* circle, perimeter, circumference,

loop, circuit, hoop; cordon. **2** *The police rounded up a ring of international jewel thieves:* gang, band, party, cabal, syndicate, combine, league, cartel, federation, bloc.
—*v.* **3** *She instructed the pupils to ring the correct answer:* draw a ring around, circle, encircle, circumscribe. **4** *Ring the castle so that no one can escape:* surround, encircle, encompass; enclose, seal off; blockade, besiege.

ring[2] *v.* **1** *The church bells rang for the evening service:* sound, resound, reverberate, vibrate, fill the air, tintinnabulate, chime, peal, clang, knell, toll, jingle, jangle, tinkle; strike. **2** *You have to ring for service:* call, summon, signal, buzz. **3** *The street rang with gunfire:* reverberate, resound, echo.
—*n.* **4** *The ring of bells filled the air:* ringing sound, resonance, reverberation, tintinnabulation, chime, peal, clang, ringing, striking, vibration, toll, knell, tinkle, ting-a-ling. **5** *His story had a suspicious ring to it:* quality, sound, tone, aura.

riot *n.* **1** *The police tried to quell the riot:* public disturbance, disorder, violence, breach of the peace, lawlessness; tumult, strife, turbulence, outburst, turmoil, trouble, Donnybrook, rumpus, mêlée, commotion, uproar, pandemonium, confusion; revolt, rebellion, insurrection, uprising.
—*v.* **2** *The dissidents rioted in the capital:* break the peace, raise an uproar, be violent, kick up a row, run amok, run riot, rampage, take the law into one's own hands, rebel, resist, revolt, mutiny, rise in arms, arise.

rip *v.* **1** *She ripped the drawing in half:* tear, rend, slash, rive, cleave, rupture, shred. **2** *His shirt ripped at the seam:* tear open, split, burst, sever.
—*n.* **3** *Sew up that rip in your shirt:* tear, rent made by ripping, split, cut, slash, laceration, rift, incision, cleavage, fracture, fissure, slit.

ripe *adj.* **1** *Are the tomatoes ripe?:* fully-grown, fully-developed, mature, maturated; mellow, seasoned. **2** *The time is ripe for our departure:* come, due; timely; ideal, perfect; consummate, complete, accomplished, finished; fully-prepared, fit, primed, ready.
Ant. **1** unripe, unready, underdeveloped, undeveloped, immature, green, unseasoned. **2** incomplete, unaccomplished, unprepared, unfit, untimely, unready.

rise *v.* **1** *He rose from the chair. I rise at dawn:* get up, stand, arise; get out of bed, meet the day. **2** *The people rose up against tyranny and injustice:* arise in opposition, rebel, revolt, resist, mutiny; go to war, take up arms; take the law into one's own hands; disobey, defy; strike, stand up, meet, face. **3** *Hot air rises. The mountains hereabouts rise to 2000 feet:* go up, move upward, ascend, climb; mount, soar, spire, tower; extend directly upward, slope upward. **4** *Food prices rose sharply. The temperature kept rising:* increase, become greater, rocket, spiral, surge, become larger, swell, burgeon, become louder. **5** *He quickly rose to a position of importance:* reach a higher level or rank, rise in the world, work one's way up, be successful; climb, go up, succeed, prosper, thrive, flourish. **6** *Our hopes rose after hearing the good news:* soar, surge, mount, grow, improve, lift, elevate, balloon.
—*n.* **7** *His rise in the company was meteoric:* rising, advance; progress, advancement, headway; growth, increase in rank, climb. **8** *The consumption of convenience foods is on the rise. I forecast another rise in the minimum lending rate:* increase, upswing, march; addition, gain, augmentation, enlargement, expansion, extension.
Ant. **1, 3-7** fall. **1** sit, sit down; lie down, retire. **3-6** sink, descend, drop, plunge. **4** decrease, decline, shrink, lessen, abate. **6** descent. **8** decrease, drop, plunge, decline, lessening, contraction, downturn.
◇ *Usage note:* See RAISE.

risk *n.* **1** *You're taking a serious risk, driving so fast. Buying land that you haven't even seen is a risk:* hazard, peril, danger, imperilment, endangerment, jeopardy; chance, venture, speculation, gamble, uncertainty.
—*v.* **2** *It's wicked to risk other people's lives:* endanger, jeopardize, put in jeopardy, imperil, put in peril. **3** *If we stop, we'll risk missing the train. It's foolish to risk money on a throw of the dice:* take the chance of, run the chance of; venture, hazard, speculate, dare, try one's luck, tempt Providence, have a fling at.

"It is only by risking our persons from one hour to another that we live at all"
— *William James*

---

risky *adj.* *Stunt driving is a risky occupation:* hazardous, perilous, dangerous, fraught with danger, unsafe, precarious, daring, venturesome, adventurous, daredevil; uncertain, ticklish, chancy, hit-or-miss, haphazard.
Ant. safe, secure, certain.

risqué *adj.* *The risqué story made her blush:* ribald, improper, bawdy, indecorous, indecent; indelicate, immodest, immoral; racy, suggestive, salacious, lascivious, lewd, licentious, offensive, rude, vulgar, coarse, gross, dirty, obscene, smutty, pornographic, blue.
◇ *Word origin: Risqué* is a form of the French verb *risquer*, to risk.

rite *n.* *The marriage rites were performed by a priest. The local tribes have curious initiation rites:* formal act or procedure, ceremony, liturgy, ritual, service; solemnity, observance.

rival *n.* **1** *Although the boxers were rivals in the ring, they were really good friends:* competitor, contestant, disputant, contender, opponent, adversary, antagonist, foe, enemy.
—*adj.* **2** *The rival companies tried to outsell one another:* contending, competing, opposing.

—*v.* **3** *The two teams rivalled each other for the championship:* compete with, contend with, try to win from, clash with, do battle with, fight, strive. **4** *Nothing can rival her cooking:* be an equal of, equal, be a match for, match, touch, approach; excel, surpass, outdo, eclipse, outshine.

Ant. 1 ally, friend; associate, helper, assistant, supporter, champion, abettor, backer. **2** allied, non-competing. **3** aid, assist, help, support, back.

◇ *Word origin: Rival* comes from Latin *rivalis,* "living near the same river or stream," hence a competitor for the same water, fish, and game.

road *n. They live down the road:* way, thoroughfare, boulevard, avenue, street, roadway, motorway, bypass, service road, private road, trunk road, arterial road, highway, turnpike, throughway, byway, trail, lane, path.

◇ *Word origin: Road* comes from Old English *rād,* journey, akin to Old English *ridan,* to ride. Thus our words *road* and *ride* have the same source.

roam *v. Troubadours roamed throughout medieval Europe:* travel, ramble, rove, range, meander, jaunt, gad, stray, gallivant, traipse, tramp, peregrinate, divagate.

roar *v.* **1** *The lions roared. The crowd roared for more:* howl, bellow, bay, growl, cry; thunder, boom, resound; shout, scream, bawl, cry aloud, yell, vociferate, bluster, clamour. **2** *We roared at the clown's antics:* laugh loudly, guffaw; howl, hoot.

—*n.* **3** *We heard the roar of a lion. The roar of aeroplane engines announced a coming air raid:* cry, howl, bellow, bay, growl, grunt, snort; yell, outcry, bawl, shout, shriek, scream, bluster, clamour, rumble, boom, uproar, outburst, thunder, roll, racket, blare, din, noise.

rob *v. The looters robbed us of everything they could lay hands on. To get rich quick, they decided to rob a bank:* hold up, raid; (*loosely*) steal from, thieve, burgle, ransack, pillage, pilfer, sack, forage, despoil, plunder, loot; filch, steal, seize, purloin, rifle, lift, carry off, appropriate, help oneself to; skin, swindle, bamboozle, bilk, fleece, embezzle.

◇ *Word origin:* See ROBE.

robber *n. The robber stole things that you wouldn't have expected him to take:* thief, bandit, outlaw, crook, brigand; (*variously*) burglar, cat burglar, mugger, safe-breaker, shop-lifter, embezzler, con man, sharper, swindler, larcenist, plunderer, highwayman, marauder, raider, pirate, buccaneer, despoiler, looter, pickpocket.

robe *n. Long robes are worn by men and women in the Middle East:* gown; (*loosely*) dress, garment, costume, vestment, habit; (*variously*) dressing-gown, housecoat, négligé, smock, kimono, christening robe.

◇ *Word origin:* It is said that *robe,* like *rob,* comes from Old French *robe,* meaning booty or plunder, because robes or clothing were the most frequent booty of ancient soldiers and raiders who would strip their defeated enemies or victims. Taking a person's clothing delayed his pursuit until he could reclothe himself.

robust *adj. Such strenuous exercises could only be endured by a robust person:* hale, hardy, strong, tough, powerful, mighty, potent, forceful, puissant; healthy, well, wholesome, sound, healthful, hearty, fit, in fine fettle, able-bodied, rugged, sturdy, firm, athletic; virile, muscular, brawny, sinewy, wiry, husky, strapping; vigorous, lusty, stalwart, stout, staunch, energetic, active.

Ant. weak, unhealthy, infirm, unsound, unfit, sickly, frail, feeble, delicate, anaemic, slender, thin, emaciated.

◇ *Word origin:* When we say a person is *robust,* we are literally saying that he is as "strong as an oak." *Robust* comes from Latin *robustus,* oaken, oaklike. (*Robur* is Latin for *oak.*)

rock[1] *v.* **1** *The boat rocked on the rough seas:* sway to and fro, move backward and forward, move from side to side; swing, toss, roll, pitch, flounder; wobble, totter, bob, quake, shake, convulse, agitate; undulate, oscillate. **2** *The explosion rocked the valley. The scandal rocked the community:* shake, jar, convulse; disturb, upset, stun.

—*n.* **3** *The rocking of the cradle quieted the baby:* undulation, sway; wobbling, tottering, bobbing; shaking; convulsion.

rock[2] *n. There are dangerous rocks in the road:* stone, boulder; (*variously*) crag, cliff, reef; pebble, flint.

rod *n.* **1** *He stuck the rod into the ground and when the onlookers started digging, water gushed forth:* stick, staff; (*variously*) wand, baton, sceptre, mace, cane, crook, alpenstock, caduceus, stanchion, stake, pale, pole, swagger-stick; fishing-rod. **2** *Spare the rod and spoil the child:* stick, cudgel; (*variously*) switch, birch, cane, rattan, lash, whip, scourge; (*loosely*) punishment, penalty, retribution.

rogue *n. He's nothing but a rogue who'd sell his own mother!:* dishonest person, deceiver, fraud, mountebank, rotter, rascal, scoundrel, scamp, rapscallion, cur, good-for-nothing, wretch, knave, varlet, blackguard, villain, snake in the grass, bad man, bounder, evildoer, malefactor, miscreant, reprobate, cad; mischief-maker; scallywag, scamp, devil.

role *n.* **1** *What role did the actress play?:* part, characterization, impersonation, representation, personification; pose, posture, guise. **2** *In his role as usher, he requested those present in court to stand:* capacity, function, duty, service, chore, task, assignment, post; job, work.

roll *v.* **1** *Roll the ball to me. Roll over, Fido!:* turn over and over; turn, revolve, rotate, gyrate; spin, go round, swirl, whirl; wheel, swing, flip, turn. **2** *The car rolled to a stop. The tide rolled in:* wheel, coast; flow, swell, billow, surge. **3** *The thunder rolled round the hills:* boom, crack, rumble, thunder, roar, sound, resound, reverberate, echo. **4** *Roll the socks together in pairs:* wind, curl, coil, loop, twist, twirl, furl, knot, entwine, wrap; form into a ball. **5** *The ship rolled on the rough seas:* rock, undulate, toss, tumble, tumble about; lurch, reel, sway, pitch, move from side to side.
—*n.* **6** *The players watched the roll of the dice. You'll get used to the roll of the sea:* rolling, turning, tumble, toss, throw; rocking, tumbling, tossing, undulation. **7** *Archaeologists found rolls of papyrus in the ruins:* scroll, tube, cylinder, spool, reel. **8** *The teacher read out the roll of new boys:* list, register, catalogue, inventory, roster, muster, schedule. **9** *The roll of thunder presages a storm:* rumble, rumbling, boom, booming, thunder, drumming, drumbeat, reverberation.

Exploring the Word: From Latin *rota*, wheel, we get many words, mostly via Old French. Some of these are: *rotate, rotary, roll, roller, enrol* (to put a name on a roll), *control* (to keep a "counter roll," or record, as of accounts by a *controller*), an actor's *role* (because his part was originally written on a scroll or roll of paper), *roly-poly* (a round person or pudding), *roulette* (literally "little wheel"), and *roué* (literally "a debauchee worthy of torture on the wheel,") said of his companions by Philip, Duke of Orleans, Regent of France, around 1720). A Spanish form, *rueda*, gives us *rodeo*, cattle ring, round-up. The adjectival forms, Latin *rotundus* and French *rond*, circular, give us *rotund* (rounded, plump), *rotunda* (a circular building or hall under a dome), *round, around, surround,* and many musical and verse forms, as *roundelay, rondel,* and *rondeau.*

rollicking *adj. We had a rollicking time at the picnic:* joyous, happy, gay, merry, cheerful, gleeful, mirthful, hearty, rip-roaring, jolly, jovial, jocular, jocund, hysterical, devil-may-care; lively, spirited, free and easy, full of play, frolicsome, frolicking, playful, romping, gambolling, sprightly, bright, sparkling, sunny.
Ant. joyless, unhappy, sad, sorrowful, sorry, distressing, depressing, cheerless, mirthless; dull, sombre, gloomy.

romance *n.* **1** *She liked to read romances:* love-story; novel, fiction, melodrama, made-up fanciful story, fairy-tale, fantasy. **2** *Shakespeare immortalized the romance of Romeo and Juliet:* love affair, affair of the heart, relationship, affair, attachment; amour, idyll, tender passion; courtship, flirtation. **3** *Much of what she says is pure romance:* invention, wishful thinking, self-delusion, imagination, illusion, flight of fancy; exaggeration, concoction, fiction, fabrication; *Informal* tall story, fishing story, cock-and-bull story, moonshine, bosh. **4** *Are you drawn by the romance of far-away places?:* romantic quality, exoticism, appealing quality, allure, pull, fascination, call.
◇ *Word origin: Romance* and *romantic* come from Latin *Romanicus*, Roman, written in the "Roman" languages, or Latin. The first *romances* were so-called because they were written in French, a "Roman" or *Romance* language, and since these stories were long narratives of love and adventure, *romance* came to mean not only such stories but love affairs and adventures themselves.

"All history, so far as it is not supported by contemporary evidence, is romance."
—*Samuel Johnson*

---

romantic *adj.* **1** *Judy Garland made many romantic films:* concerning romance, conducive to romance, idyllic, sentimental; melodramatic. **2** *They're such a romantic couple!:* loving, amorous, ardent, enamoured, passionate, impassioned, warm-hearted, fond, devoted; sentimental, tender, sensitive; ardent, fervent; *Informal* mushy, soppy. **3** *Don't get carried away with romantic notions:* high-flown, idealized, impractical, improbable, rhapsodical; unreal, unrealistic, idealistic, flighty, whimsical, extravagant, fanciful, imaginary, dreamy, visionary; fantastic, preposterous, quixotic.
Ant. 1-3 unromantic. **1** realistic, prosaic, uninspiring. **2** unloving, unimpassioned, dispassionate, cold-hearted; unsentimental, insensitive; unaffectionate.

romp *v. The children romped in the park:* play in a lively manner, frolic, run about, frisk, caper, gambol, disport oneself, sport, jump about, skip, hop.
◇ *Word origin:* See RAMPAGE.

room *n.* **1** *Go to the room at the end of the hall. There were no rooms to be had at the inn:* chamber, cubicle, compartment; lodging, lodging place. **2** *That cabinet takes up too much room:* space, extent, range, scope, expanse, territory, area, volume, elbow-room. **3** *There's no room for error here:* chance, place, provision, allowance, margin.

roomy *adj. The caravan looks small but is really quite roomy:* spacious, capacious, commodious, ample, expansive; wide, long, lengthy, broad, extensive, large, vast, immense, big, huge, boundless, unlimited.
Ant. small, tiny, uncomfortable, closed-in, cramped; short; bounded, limited, confined.

root *n.* **1** *The root of a flower is as delicate as its petals. Don't pull out your hair by the roots:* under-

ground part, stem, embedded part, bulb, tuber; radicle, radix; hidden base; lower part, bottom. **2** *Let's get to the root of the matter:* basic part, basic element, fundamental, essential element, most important part, base, foundation. **3** *The roots of his neurosis go back to childhood:* origin, source, spring, fount, fountain, foundation, basis, ground; starting-point, motive, determining condition, reason, rationale; rise, mainspring, occasion, inception, beginning, commencement, start.
—*v.* **4** *Root the bulbs in potting compost. Are you rooted to that spot?:* fix, set, establish; fasten, stick, nail, bind.

◇ *Word origin:* See RADICAL.

rostrum *n. The speaker stepped up to the rostrum:* stage, platform, dais, stand, pulpit, lectern, podium, soap-box, stump.

◇ *Word origin: Rostrum* is Latin for beak, especially a beaklike protuberance on the prow of a galley used for ramming enemy ships. In the Roman forum, these beaklike rams captured from enemy ships were used to decorate the speaker's platform, and thus today *rostrum* means a speaker's platform or pulpit.

rosy *adj.* **1** *My darling has such rosy cheeks:* pink, blushing, reddish, reddening, flushed, flushing, blooming, ruddy, rubicund, rubescent, florid, glowing, inflamed, high-coloured. **2** *The future looks rosy:* rose-coloured, hopeful, cheerful, cheering, inspiriting, encouraging, promising, full of promise, reassuring, hopeful, optimistic, looking up, bright, auspicious, favourable, of good omen, propitious, felicitous; confident.

Ant. 1 pale, pallid, ashen, grey, whitish; sickly. **2** cheerless, discouraging, unpromising, hopeless, pessimistic, inauspicious; insecure, unsure.

rot *v.* **1** *The unrefrigerated food rotted:* spoil, go bad, decay, decompose, putrefy, disintegrate, wither up, moulder; go to pieces, fall into decay, deteriorate, degenerate, break down, crumble. **2** *Immoderate quantities of drink and ambition rotted his mind:* pervert, debase, defile, warp, deprave; infect, poison; corrupt, pollute, contaminate, tamper with; taint, stain; mar, impair, damage, injure, harm, hurt.
—*n.* **3** *The rot has only just begun to set in:* rotting, decay, rottenness, dry rot, decomposition, deterioration, disintegration; putrescence, putrefaction, putridity, purulence; contamination, corruption. **4** *Slang You don't believe that rot, do you?:* nonsense, tommy rot, bosh, bunkum, balderdash, poppycock, gobbledygook, twaddle, stuff and nonsense, moonshine, flapdoodle, inanity, absurdity, flummery, fiddle-faddle, trash, rubbish, gibberish, jabber, drivel, blather.

rotate *v.* **1** *The moon rotates round the earth:* move round a centre, turn on an axis, turn, revolve, spin, roll, circulate, whirl, gyrate, twirl, twist, swirl, wheel, eddy, pirouette, pivot, swivel. **2** *Farmer Brown rotated his cereal and root crops:* alternate, change, take turns, interchange, act interchangeably; go from one to the other.

rotten *adj.* **1** *Don't buy rotten fruit!:* decomposed, decayed, putrid, putrefied, putrescent, purulent, tainted, mouldering, worm-eaten, bad, rancid, fetid, reeky, foul, rank. **2** *To clear a department of rotten officials is more easily said than done:* dishonest, corrupt, deceitful, insincere, faithless, unscrupulous, dishonourable, disgraceful, contemptible, treacherous, untrustworthy, double-dealing, two-faced, devious, villainous, iniquitous, scurvy, crooked, criminal, vicious, venal, mercenary; immoral, indecent, dissolute. **3** *Informal That was a rotten trick:* very bad, base, contemptible; unpleasant, nasty, dirty, filthy, scurrilous, unforgivable.

Ant. 1 wholesome, untainted, fresh, pure, good. **2** honest, scrupulous, honourable, trustworthy; moral, decent, incorruptible.

rotund *adj.* **1** *A cushion is of a generally rotund shape:* round, globular, bulbous, rounded, spherical, ball-like, circular, ring-like; ovoid, egg-shaped, ovate, curved. **2** *The rotund woman needed to lose weight:* plump, fat, obese, full-fleshed, corpulent, fleshy, chubby, pudgy, lumpish, stout, portly, pot-bellied.

Ant. 1 angular, square, edged. **2** thin, slender, slim, lean, lank, lanky, skinny, gaunt, scrawny, raw-boned, emaciated, angular.

rough *adj.* **1** *Raw wool is a rough material. We rode over rough terrain:* coarse, not smooth, uneven, jagged, ragged, rough-hewn, irregular, broken, craggy, unlevel, bumpy, rocky; (*variously*) rugged, scratchy, knotty, stubbly, scaly, scabrous, chapped, gnarled. **2** *Football is a rough game. We sailed in rough seas:* violent, rigorous, rugged; tough, violently disturbed, agitated, choppy, turbulent, turbid, roiled, tumultuous, tempestuous, stormy, raging; untamed, wild, savage, ferocious. **3** *Ten lashes is pretty rough punishment:* sharp, harsh, tough, austere, stringent, severe, ungentle, hard, unfeeling, cruel, brutal; inconsiderate; extreme, drastic. **4** *The tramp had a rough manner:* boorish, rude, ill-mannered, unmannerly, ungentlemanly, uncourtly, ungenteel; unpolished, unrefined, raw, inelegant, ill-bred, ungracious, uncouth; bearish, loutish, churlish, crusty, gruff, bluff, surly, gauche, awkward, clumsy; blunt, brusque, gruff, abrupt; coarse, vulgar, indelicate, crude; callow, green. **5** *The gipsies have lived a rough life:* without ordinary comforts, uncomfortable, unluxurious; difficult, unpleasant, tough, rugged, hard, austere. **6** *This is just a rough plan:* not elaborated, unfinished, incomplete, not perfected, imperfect, crude, hastily done; quick, hasty; vague, sketchy, general, rudimentary, preliminary, approximate, not exact, inexact, vague, imprecise. **7** *He had a rough voice:* gruff, husky, raspy, rasping, hoarse, grating, jarring, raucous, strident, harsh; inharmonious, discordant, cacophonous, unmusical.

—*v.* **8** *If you go to camp you'll learn to rough it:* endure hardship, live "rough", do without luxuries. **9** *The prisoner said that the others had roughed him up:* treat violently, manhandle, push around, physically intimidate, beat, thrash; *Slang* beat up, do over. **10** *The writer roughed out his next novel:* indicate in rough form, prepare hastily, do roughly, draft, outline, sketch out.

Ant. 1, 2, 4, 5 smooth. **1** smooth-surfaced, regular, unbroken, level, plain, flat; soft, silky, satiny, velvety. **2** calm, easy, gentle, tender; tranquil, quiet; tamed, mild, halcyon. **3** soft, mild, kind, lenient, just, considerate. **4** polite, courteous, civil, well-mannered, mannerly, gentlemanly, courtly, genteel; polished, refined, urbane, elegant, well-bred; gracious, gentle; graceful, delicate, sophisticated. **5** comfortable, luxurious, velvety, easy, cushy, pleasant, plush, nice. **6** elaborated, finished, complete, perfected, detailed, specific, exact, precise.

round *adj.* **1** *Oranges are round:* circular, globular, globoid, orbed, spherical, spheroid, ball-shaped; rounded, curved. **2** *He was a short, round man:* rotund, full-fleshed, obese, corpulent, fat, full-formed, plump, chubby, pudgy, stout, portly. **3** *Give me a round dozen and I'll pay cash:* entire, full, whole, complete; unbroken, intact, undivided; thorough, total. **4** *He spoke in round tones:* full and rich, sonorous, resonant, smooth, flowing, fluent; harmonious, mellifluent.

—*n.* **5** *A round of parties ushered in the New Year. Let's order a round of drinks:* complete course, circle, series, succession, procession, progression, cycle. **6** Often **rounds** *The postman made his rounds:* circuit, beat, watch, route, course.

—*v.* **7** *The coach rounded the bend:* travel round, go round, make a circuit, skirt.

Ant. 1 angular, rectangular, square, many-sided, polygonal. **2** slim, thin, slender, skinny, lean, lank, gaunt, angular, raw-boned, emaciated. **3** incomplete, broken, imperfect, divided. **4** rough, gruff, harsh, hoarse, grating, jarring, shrill, strident; inharmonious.

◇ *Usage note: Round* may be used to mean with a revolving or circular motion, or during an entire period. Thus, *The racing car drove round the track; He lives in a caravan all the year round. Around,* however, means on every side; round about. Thus, *Fireweed flourished all around the city's bomb-sites.*

roundabout *adj. He arrived at the solution in a roundabout way:* indirect, meandering, circuitous, sinuous, rambling, erratic, discursive, tortuous, devious, oblique, zigzag, winding; circumlocutory, wordy; random, desultory.

Ant. straight, direct.

rout *n.* **1** *Napoleon's army suffered a complete rout at Waterloo:* disastrous defeat, total repulse, ruin, beating, drubbing, licking, disorderly retreat, disorderly flight, complete dispersal; panic, chaos, disorganization.

—*v.* **2** *Joan of Arc routed the English at Orleans:* put to flight, scatter, throw into confusion; repel, drive off, repulse, chase away, drive away; defeat, vanquish, worst, overpower, overthrow, overcome, crush, subdue, quell; drub, lambaste, beat, thrash; *Informal* lick, trim, flatten.

route *n.* **1** *Which route are you taking to Devon?:* way, course, itinerary; pass, road for travel, direction, passage. **2** *A postman's route can be a long trek:* fixed course or territory, beat, circuit.

—*v.* **3** *Cars were routed round the accident:* send by a particular route, forward by a specific route; direct, ship, dispatch, remit, transmit; detour, divert.

◇ *Pronunciation tip:* The pronunciation of *route* is *ROOT*.

◇ *Usage note:* Don't confuse *route, rout,* and *rote.* A route is a course or road to be travelled, a usual course, or to send by a specific course: *What's the shortest route to Devon? The AA routed us through Chester.* To *rout* is to defeat completely: *Aston Villa routed Blackburn Rovers 4-0.* A *rote* is a fixed way of doing something, as by memory or without thought: *He knew the poem by rote, but he didn't understand it.*

routine *n.* **1** *Getting up at dawn is part of his daily routine:* regular procedure, practice, established usage, custom, ordinary way; method, system, arrangement, order, operation, formula, technique.

—*adj.* **2** *A routine medical check-up is advisable at your age:* customary, conventional, usual; regular, typical, normal. **3** *The book has a routine plot:* predictable, unexceptional, dull, habitual, boring, periodic, tedious, ordinary, run-of-the-mill.

Ant. 2, 3 special, uncustomary, unusual, irregular, abnormal, different, exceptional, extraordinary.

> "We need some imaginative stimulus, some not impossible ideal such as may shape vague hope, and transform it into effective desire, to carry us year after year, without disgust, through the routine work which is so large a part of life." — *Walter Pater*

rove *v. My grandfather loved to rove about the countryside:* wander about, roam, ramble, meander, gad about, range, stroll, gallivant, traipse; prowl.

row[1] *n. Rows of tulips lined the borders. The tin soldiers stood in a row:* line; file, tier, queue, string; series, sequence, succession, rank, range, chain, column; train.

row² *n. We had a bit of a row but quickly made it up:* noisy dispute, quarrel, tiff, difference, squabble, altercation, words, wrangle, wrangling, scrape, scrap, brawl; fracas, mêlée, imbroglio, disorder, contretemps.

rowdy *adj. The rowdy boys were chased by the police:* boisterous, disorderly, unruly, rowdyish, raffish, mischievous; lawless.

Ant. peaceful, law-abiding, orderly, gentle; refined, mannerly, decorous.

royal *adj.* **1** *Some of the royal family of Spain are resident in Portugal:* regal, sovereign, monarchic. **2** *The Duke treated us to a royal feast:* fit for a king, regal; majestic, august, stately, imposing, magnificent, grand, splendid, resplendent, superb; lavish, munificent.

rub *v.* **1** *These sandals rub my heels:* chafe, abrade, make rough. **2** *He rubbed his aching legs with liniment:* massage, knead, stroke; handle, touch, finger, pass the fingers over; manipulate, move with pressure against something. —*n.* **3** *The masseur gave my back a rub:* rubbing, rub-down, massage, kneading, handling, manipulation, stroke, stroking. **4** *The plan is good, but how to make it succeed — there's the rub:* annoying circumstance, hitch, catch, problem, obstacle, secret, trick, thing, impediment, difficulty, trouble, strait, hindrance, hardship; pinch, set-back.

rubbish *n.* **1** *Throw the rubbish out:* refuse, trash, garbage, waste matter, junk, debris, litter, worthless material, dross, offal, jetsam. **2** *Informal I don't believe that rubbish:* nonsense, gibberish, inanity, balderdash, rot, rigmarole, drivel, bosh, flapdoodle, twaddle, babble, blather, silliness, idiocy.

ruddy *adj. The farmer had a ruddy complexion:* rosy, rosy-cheeked, reddish, florid, flushed, blushing; of a red colour, rubicund, roseate, sanguine.

Ant. pale, pallid, wan, colourless, ashen, grey, sallow.

rude *adj.* **1** *Rude behaviour will not be tolerated:* discourteous, inconsiderate, uncourteous, uncivil, disrespectful, impolite, impudent, insulting, abusive, impertinent, peremptory, insolent, saucy, fresh; unmannerly, bad-mannered, ungentlemanly, unladylike, uncourtly, ungallant, ungracious, undignified, ill-bred; indelicate, indecorous, indecent, profane; brusque, blunt, abrupt, gruff, surly, sullen, sulky, crusty; callow, green, uncouth. **2** *We put up a rude shelter and huddled under it:* roughly made, crude, roughly-built, rough-hewn, slapdash, makeshift, uneven, rough, rugged, scraggy, raw. **3** *Some people pride themselves on their rude and brusque way of speaking:* blunt, without refinement, coarse, unrefined, inelegant, unpolished, artless, without culture, uncultured, ungraceful, awkward, gauche, clumsy; gross, uncouth, vulgar, boorish, loutish, churlish; uneducated, untaught, unlearned, untutored, untrained, ignorant, illiterate; primitive, rustic, provincial, countrified, homely, rustic, wild, uncivilized, brutish.

Ant. 1 courteous, polite, respectful, considerate; mannerly, well-mannered, gentlemanly, ladylike, courtly, urbane, suave, gallant, gracious, dignified, well-bred; decorous, decent, affable, sociable, cordial, amiable, civil. **2** well-made, well-built, well-formed; wrought, fashioned, formed, shapely, finished, even, smooth, slick. **3** refined, elegant, polished, artful, cultured, graceful; educated, taught, learned, tutored, trained, literate; urbane, civilized.

◇ *Word origin: Rude* and *rudimentary* come from Latin *rudis*, rough. Thus *rude* means rough in manners, and *rudimentary* means rough in the sense of being unfinished or elementary.

rudimentary *adj.* **1** *My first piano teacher gave me a rudimentary knowledge of music:* elementary, basic, fundamental, concerning first principles, initial, primary, primitive, formative. **2** *A tadpole is a rudimentary frog:* incompletely developed, undeveloped, prototypal, incomplete, imperfect, premature, simple; immature, vestigial, primitive.

Ant. 1 advanced. **2** completely developed, developed, complete, perfect, mature.

rue *v. I rue the day I met you!:* feel sorrow over, be sorry for, regret, wish undone, lament, mourn, bemoan; deplore.

ruffian *n. The ruffian frightened everyone in the neighbourhood:* brute, bully, tough, villain, scoundrel, rogue, knave, blackguard, ugly customer, cut-throat; rowdy, roisterer, hooligan, hoodlum; *Slang* hood; mugger, thug, gangster.

ruffle *v.* **1** *The wind ruffled my hair:* dishevel, disorder, disarrange, wrinkle, rumple, roughen, ripple. **2** *The slight accident ruffled his composure:* disturb, trouble, upset, disquiet; perturb, disconcert, discompose, unsettle, confuse; agitate, excite, aggravate. —*n.* **3** *The wind made ruffles on the pond:* disturbance, agitation, wave, ripple. **4** *The shirt had ruffles on the collar and cuffs:* pleat, flounce, frill, ruche, ruff, fold, gathering.

Ant. 1 arrange, order; smooth. **2** compose, calm, settle.

rugged *adj.* **1** *Afghanistan is rugged mountainous territory:* rough, uneven, irregular, craggy, cragged, jagged, rocky, rock-strewn, bumpy. **2** *The old sailor had a rugged face:* wrinkled, furrowed, lined, worn, weathered, weather-beaten, hard-featured, rough-hewn, coarse. **3** *John Wayne portrayed a rugged cowboy:* hardy, hale, robust, vigorous, sturdy, stalwart, able-bodied, tough; husky, brawny, wiry, muscular, well-knit, sinewy, athletic; virile, masculine. **4** *The Outward Bound course was a* *rugged test of our endurance. A shepherd in the hills leads a rugged life:* harsh, tough, difficult, hard, severe, stern, trying, taxing, arduous, onerous, laborious; rude, unrefined, uncultivated, graceless, uncouth.

Ant. 1 even, smooth, regular, level; easy, soft. **2** smooth, unmarked, delicate, youthful, refined, pretty. **3** weak, frail, fragile, sickly, puny, skinny, slim; effeminate. **4** gentle, tender; refined, graceful, elegant, cultivated.

ruin *n.* **1 ruins** *We saw the ruins of an ancient Mayan temple in Mexico:* remains, remnants, wreckage; fallen structure, shell. **2** *The boat went to rack and ruin:* disintegration, decay, disrepair, wreckage; pot, seed. **3** *Moral laxity was the ruin of the Roman Empire:* downfall, fall, undoing, breakdown, ruination, crack-up, failure, defeat, overthrow; decay, disintegration, dissolution, destruction, devastation, doom.

—*v.* **4** *The fire ruined the carpet. The scandal ruined his chances of advancement:* bring to ruin, reduce to wreckage, demolish, destroy, wreck, shatter, pull to pieces, devastate, lay waste, gut, ravage, raze, level, fell, cut down, pull down, upset, overthrow, overturn, defeat, crush, quell, quash, squash, spoil, harm, put an end to. **5** *The stock-market crash ruined many investors:* make poor, reduce to poverty, bankrupt, impoverish, bring to want, beggar, pauperize, break.

Ant. 3 construction, creation, building up; success. **4** construct, build, build up; improve, help, enhance. **5** enrich, profit.

rule *n.* **1** *You must obey the rules of the game:* law, regulation, order, ordinance, decree, canon, precept, principle; maxim, axiom, adage, golden rule, rule of thumb, doctrine. **2** *Promptness is the rule here:* practice, method, system, routine, custom, policy, normal condition. **3** *There's no set rule for us to follow in this case:* guide, guide-line, precedent, criterion, model, precept, form, formula, prescription; standard, convention. **4** *George I's rule lasted 13 years:* reign, kingdom, sovereignty, suzerainty, regime, dominion, empire; control, command, authority, direction, administration, leadership, domination, supremacy, sway, influence, jurisdiction, government.

—*v.* **5** *Queen Victoria ruled Great Britain for almost 64 years:* reign, control, command, govern, regulate, direct, administer, manage, run; exercise dominion over, have authority over, lead, be at the head of, head; sway, influence, dominate, domineer, prevail, predominate, have the upper hand. **6** *The chairman ruled that he was out of order:* decide, determine, conclude, settle, resolve, establish, find, judge, adjudicate, adjudge, pass judgement upon; declare, pronounce, decree.

ruler *n.* **1** *King Wenceslas was a wise and beloved ruler:* leader, commander, head of state, (*variously*) sovereign, monarch, crowned head, emperor, king, queen, prince, tsar; lord, viceroy, suzerain; potentate, sultan, emir, shah, pharaoh, sheikh, chieftain, rajah, khan, shogun; president, chairman, governor, manager, director, administrator, supervisor, controller, co-ordinator; chief, head, boss. **2** *Use a ruler to measure the width of that cloth:* rule, yardstick, straight-edge, measure, tape-measure; slide-rule.

> **Exploring the Word**: Latin *regere*, to rule (closely related to *rex*, king) gives us our words *rule* and *ruler*. From *regere*, to rule, we also get *correct*, to guide or direct out of error; *direct* to supervise, hence to point out; *incorrigible*, unrulable; *regent*, one who rules during a king's absence, minority, or disability (an office known in medieval times as *rector regi et regni*, "rector" i.e. governor of king and realm — our word *rector* likewise comes from *regere*); *regime*, a ruling system or body, government, and *regimen*, a systematic, closely ruled course of living; *regiment*, a body of troops under the direction of an officer; *region*, a country or territory under one rule; *regular*, according to the rule, and *regulate*, to control or manage according to rules; and *erect*, to direct upward or outward, build.

rumble *v.* **1** *Grandfather's voice rumbled heartily when he laughed:* boom, reverberate, resound, roar, thunder, roll.

—*n.* **2** *The rumble of cannon could be heard in the distance:* roar, thunder, boom, booming, resonance, reverberation, roll.

ruminate *v. He ruminated on the courses of action open to him:* ponder, mull, brood, think, reflect, meditate, cogitate, deliberate, contemplate, think over, bring up again for consideration, consider, study, muse, speculate.

◇ *Word origin:* To *ruminate* means two things, to chew the cud as cows and other *ruminants* do, and to meditate or "chew over" something in the mind. The word comes from Latin *ruminare*, to chew over.

rummage *v. They liked to rummage through junk shops:* search thoroughly, look through, examine, explore, poke around, delve into, sift through; disarrange, ransack, turn over.

◇ *Word origin: Rummage* comes from Old French *arrumer*, to stow cargo in a ship's hold, which at one time involved a great deal of rearranging to fill the hold with as much as possible whilst giving the ship proper ballast. A *rummage sale* is a sale of items culled from a mass of secondhand, unclaimed, or overstocked articles, equivalent to a jumble sale.

rumour *n.* **1** *I don't believe any of those rumours about the Joneses:* unverified information, story, supposition, gossip, whisper, hearsay, insinuation, innuendo, talk, tale, *Slang* scuttle-butt.

—*v.* **2** *It was rumoured that the beggar was really a millionaire in disguise:* whisper, gossip, put about, bandy about, intimate, insinuate; circulate, spread abroad, put into circulation, report.

rump *n. The rider gave the horse a slap on its rump:* hindquarters, rear, posterior, rear end, buttocks, backside, bottom, croup, seat, dorsum, *French* derrière.

rumple *v. He rumpled his suit by sleeping in it:* wrinkle, crumple, crease, crinkle, crush, pucker, corrugate, ruffle; disarrange, disorder, dishevel, tousle.

run *v.* **1** *I've got to run for my bus:* go quickly, step quickly, make off rapidly, move swiftly, race, dart, sprint, jog, trot, dash; hustle, hasten, hurry, hie, scamper, scurry, rush, scramble; speed, tear along, fly, bound. **2** *It's been a nice visit, but now we have to run. The robbers took the money and ran:* leave, take flight, flee, fly, bolt; steal away, escape, decamp, abscond, take to one's heels, beat a retreat; *Informal* skedaddle, scarper, take off. **3** *The bus runs daily from the village green:* go, ply. **4** *The stream runs down the valley:* flow, pour, stream, course, roll, glide, sweep along; surge, issue; wander, meander. **5** *He ran the car into a ditch:* cause to move, drive, propel, thrust, push, impel; direct, navigate, manœuvre, pilot. **6** *Teach me how to run the business:* operate, manage, direct, supervise, oversee, co-ordinate; head, preside over, boss. **7** *She ran her fingers over the smooth material:* pass, glide. **8** *The film ran for 97 minutes:* extend in time, go by, pass, elapse, last, endure; proceed, move on, go, continue, advance. **9** *The little pond ran dry:* become, get. **10** *How much will the repairs run to?:* cost, amount to, total, add up to. **11** *Her red blouse ran in the wash:* bleed, lose colour, mingle colours. **12** *Will these tights run?:* come unravelled, separate, tear, ladder. **13** *The prices run from £5 to £200:* vary, extend, be, go. **14** *They ran the advertisement in the paper for two days:* print, publish; display; make copies of. **15** *She's not afraid to run a risk:* incur, bring on, court, invite; be liable to, be exposed to; encounter, meet, meet with; fall into. **16** *The ice cream ran in the warm sun:* dissolve, melt, become fluid, liquefy; vanish, disappear, evanesce, decompose, disintegrate.

—*n.* **17** *We took a run round the track:* running, trot, canter, gallop, jog, sprint, dash. **18** *Let's take a run out in the car:* drive, outing, trip, excursion, journey, pilgrimage, voyage, tour. **19** *I'm darning a run in my old sweater:* unravelled place, ladder. **20** *I can't keep up with the run of national events:* course, passage, tendency, direction, drift, flow, progress, onward movement. **21** *You have the run of my office:* freedom, unrestricted use. **22** The Mousetrap *has had the longest West End run to date. Gamblers always hope for a run of good luck:* continuous performance; series, course, continuance, continuation, perpetuation, duration; period, stretch, streak, spell, while. **23** *The children are building a rabbit run:* enclosure, pen. **24** *We've had nothing exciting — just the usual run of applicants:* class, kind, sort, genre, type. **25** *The team only scored ninety runs during the whole day:* point in cricket made by traversing length of pitch, score, tally.

Ant. **1** walk, crawl. **2** remain, stay. **8** stop, halt, cease. **16** solidify, congeal, harden. **17** walk, saunter. **22** discontinuance, stoppage.

rupture *n.* **1** *A rupture in the water-main flooded the street:* breaking, bursting, break, burst, split, fracture, crack, fissure, rent, severance, cleavage, cleft. **2** *What caused the rupture between the two wings of the party?:* break, rift, breach, schism, separation, dissociation, disunion, disagreement, dissension, discord; friction, clash.

—*v.* **3** *The membrane was ruptured:* break, burst, break up, crack, puncture, dissever, come apart, part, snap, sunder, divide. **4** *What ruptured their friendship?:* cause a break in, cause a breach in, disrupt, disunite, divide, break up.

Ant. **2** union; understanding, agreement; continuity. **4** unite, heal, knit.

rural *adj. We left the city for our rural home:* country, pastoral, bucolic, rustic, countrified, provincial.

Ant. urban, city, citified, cosmopolitan.

ruse *n. The telephone call was just a ruse to get me out of the way:* stratagem, machination, manœuvre, crafty device, contrivance, artifice, subterfuge, trick, hoax, deception, deceit, dodge, blind, feint.

rush *v.* **1** *We've got to rush to the hospital:* speed, race, hasten, hie, hurry, run, dash, tear, scramble, dart, hustle, scurry. **2** *The operation could not be rushed:* speed up, accelerate, dispatch, expedite, perform hastily, finish with speed; work against time, hurry. **3** *Don't rush me!:* hurry, spur on, whip, urge, goad, drive; pressure, pressurize, push, press, keep at. **4** *Don't rush into marriage:* go carelessly, go headlong, act thoughtlessly, leap, plunge, precipitate oneself. **5** *The enemy rushed the town:* attack suddenly, charge, descend upon, have at.

—*n.* **6** *The first shoppers made a rush for the bargain counter:* run, dash, charge. **7** *We have time to eat without any rush:* haste, speed, dispatch, urgency.

—*adj.* **8** *This is a rush job:* urgent, emergency, top priority.

Ant. **1** walk, crawl. **2** slow. **7** leisure; dawdling, idling.

rust *n.* **1** *The old sink pipes were full of rust:* corrosion, oxidation; stain, blight, rot, decay. **2** *Her carpet was a lovely shade of rust:* reddish-yellow, reddish-brown, russet.

—*v.* **3** *Exposed iron will rust. His talents had rusted over the years:* corrode, oxidize; decay, weaken with disuse, decline, deteriorate, crumble, atrophy.

"It is better to wear out than to rust out."
—*Bishop Richard Cumberland*

rustic *adj.* **1** *Ambridge is a rustic community:* country, rural, provincial, pastoral, bucolic. **2** *The country folk around here have down-to-earth rustic manners:* simple, plain, unsophisticated; rough, countrified, rude, unpolished, unrefined, inelegant, uncouth, crude, loutish, coarse, churlish, boorish; awkward, gauche, cloddish.
—*n.* **3** *Jock is a rustic from the highlands:* country person, countryman, provincial, peasant, bumpkin, yokel, clodhopper.
Ant. **1** urban, cosmopolitan. **2** sophisticated, fancy, polished, refined, elegant, courtly, urbane, citified. **3** sophisticate, cosmopolitan.

rustle *v.* **1** *The taffeta skirt rustled as she walked:* move with soft sounds, swish, hiss, stir, rub.
—*n.* **2** *We listened to the rustle of the leaves:* rustling, whispering sound, swish, hiss.
◇ *Word origin: **Rustle**,* to move with a succession of light rubbing sounds, comes from the Old English *hrūxlian,* to make a noise.

rusty *adj.* **1** *The bottom of the boat was rusty:* covered with rust, rusted, corroded; rotten, mouldy, tainted. **2** *My German is a little rusty:* out of practice, no longer fluent, sluggish, inept through neglect or loss of habit.

rut *n.* **1** *The heavy tanks left ruts in the road:* deep track, depression, furrow, hollow, ditch, trench, trough, tread, groove. **2** *It's time you changed your job, you're in a rut!:* fixed way of life, dull routine, monotonous round, narrow orbit, pattern, habit.
—*v.* **3** *Farm wagons rutted the road after the rain:* dig into, furrow, depress, hollow, groove, mark, channel, score.
◇ *Word origin: **Rut**,* a track worn by a wheel, or a settled routine, is a variant form of *route.* Thus in the old days one could follow the *route,* or the *rut,* to the next town. Our other word *rut,* mating season, heat, comes from Latin *rugire,* to roar, and originally referred solely to the bellowing of stags in the rutting season and, by extension, to the rutting time of deer.

ruthless *adj. Attila the Hun was a ruthless tyrant:* without pity, unmerciful, merciless, pitiless, unpitying, unforgiving, without compassion, unfeeling, heartless, hard-hearted, harsh, cruel, unsparing, remorseless, relentless, unrelenting; inhuman, vicious, barbarous, savage, ferocious, brutal, brutish, cold-blooded, murderous, deadly, bloodthirsty, sanguinary.
Ant. merciful, pitying, compassionate, forgiving, kind, tender, gentle, sparing, lenient, remorseful, humane.

S

Sabbath *n. But the seventh day is the sabbath of the Lord thy God:* Sabbath day, day of rest, day of worship, (*Christian Church*) Lord's Day, Sunday.
◇ *Usage note:* Except when directly quoting the Bible, in which *Sabbath* is spelt with a lower-case *s* (*sabbath*), you should spell the word with an upper-case *S* (*Sabbath*) in accordance with universal custom. The *Sabbath* falls on Sunday amongst all Christian sects except the Seventh-Day Adventists — on Saturday among Jews and Seventh-Day Adventists, and on Friday amongst Muslims.
◇ *Word origin: Sabbath* comes from Hebrew *shabbāth,* rest, the seventh day of the week, appointed in the Ten Commandments as a day of rest and worship to be observed by the Jews ("Remember the sabbath day, to keep it holy"), now Saturday; hence, in subsequent Christian usage, the Lord's Day, as observed by Christians, Sunday. The same Hebrew word gives us *sabbatical,* pertaining to the seventh year during which ancient Jews were required to refrain from tilling the soil in order to "rest" it — hence our modern *sabbatical,* a year's or a term's leave awarded to teachers in some educational institutions occasionally for study, travel, etc.

sabotage *n.* **1** *The enemy agent was arrested on charges of sabotage:* undermining of a cause, subversion; malicious destruction, malicious disruption.
—*v.* **2** *Enemy agents sabotaged the munitions factory:* undermine, conspire against, subvert, damage from within; disable, paralyse, cripple, retard, incapacitate, destroy, disrupt.

sack[1] *n. Give me a sack of potatoes. Santa brought a sack of toys:* bag, (*variously*) pouch, knapsack, rucksack, haversack, gunny-sack, duffle-bag.
◇ *Word origin: Sacks* were originally made of coarse cloth similar to that used in making *gunny-sacks. Sack* comes from Hebrew *sag,* sack, sackcloth. In the Bible, *sackcloth and ashes* refers to wearing rough sackcloth garments and sprinkling ashes on the head as marks of pĕnance or sorrow. The expression *to sack,* meaning to loot, comes from the use of

sacks by looters as a convenient means of carrying the stolen articles. *Sachet* is French for "little bag," specifically, a small ornamented bag for perfumed powder or the like.

sack[2] *v.* **1** *The invaders sacked the village:* pillage, plunder, loot, ransack, tear up, pull apart, lay waste, despoil, spoil, prey upon, raid, maraud, steal from, rob.

—*n.* **2** *The sack of Palmyra took place in A.D. 273:* plundering, pillage, rapine, ravishment, ravage, devastation, depredation, waste, despoliation; raid, marauding.

sacred *adj.* **1** *Ethelred asked to be buried in sacred ground:* consecrated, hallowed, blessed, sanctified, holy. **2** *Salzburg is sacred to Mozart-lovers:* venerable, awe-inspiring, revered. **3** *The sacred books of the Essenes are contained in the Dead Sea Scrolls:* religious, ecclesiastical, hieratic, church; scriptural, holy, Biblical; hallowed, divinely inspired.

Ant. **1** unconsecrated, profane. **3** profane, secular, lay, temporal.

sacrifice *n.* **1** *The pagans made sacrifices to their gods:* offering, oblation, homage; ritual slaughter, immolation. **2** *Parents often make sacrifices for their children:* relinquishment, cession, concession, renunciation, surrender.

—*v.* **3** *The ancient Greeks sacrificed lambs or calves before engaging in battle:* make a sacrifice of, offer up, make an offering of; immolate. **4** *We decided to sacrifice a holiday for a new car:* give up, relinquish, forgo, forfeit, waive, renounce, surrender, cede.

sacrilege *n.* *It is sacrilege to start a fight in a church:* profanation, desecration, misuse of sacred things; blasphemy, profanity, profaneness, impiousness, impiety, irreverence; sin, wickedness, sinfulness, violation, outrage.

◇ *Spelling tip:* There is no *d* in *sacrilege.* If you think it is *sacrilege* to say the mild oath "damn!," then don't even put its *d* in *sacrilege.*

sacrosanct *adj.* *The burial grounds were considered sacrosanct:* sacred, consecrated, hallowed, sanctified, solemn, holy, godly, religious, spiritual, divine, heavenly, celestial; inviolable, immune from attack.

sad *adj.* **1** *I was sad when I learnt of her misfortune:* unhappy, cheerless, joyless, grieved, grief-stricken; dispirited, downcast, low, crestfallen, heavy-hearted, chap-fallen, disconsolate, desolate, despondent, melancholy, inconsolable, depressed, dejected; *Informal* down in the mouth, down in the dumps, blue; distressed, miserable, pessimistic, troubled, full of care, despairing, broken-hearted, hurt, crushed; wretched, forlorn, sorrowful, doleful, mournful. **2** *It was such a sad story that I cried:* pitiful, touching, pathetic, lamentable, dismal; lachrymose, maudlin. **3** *Her sad circumstances made me unhappy:* unfortunate, grievous, serious, grave, calamitous, grim, dismal, solemn; lamentable, heart-breaking, heart-rending, woeful, mournful, distressing; trying, taxing, difficult, hard, adverse, troublesome; tragic.

Ant. **1** happy, cheerful, smiling, joyful, glad, spirited, light-hearted, pleased, merry, optimistic. **2** happy, amusing, cheery, bright. **3** easy, fortunate, lucky, prosperous, successful.

Exploring the Word: Latin *sacer,* sacred, gives us *sacred; consecrate,* to make sacred; *desecrate,* to make or treat as "unsacred," to profane; *sacrament,* originally an offering and accompanying oath to the gods; *sacrifice,* a sacred offering, hence an offering or something given up or destroyed; *sacrilege* (Latin *legere,* to gather), literally the stealing of sacred objects, hence the violation of sacred things; *saint,* a sacred person; *sacristan,* a church official in charge of sacred vessels, and the variant of this word, *sexton,* a church official in charge of maintaining church property, ringing the bell, and digging graves. The related Latin *sanctus,* holy, gives us *sanctity; sanctify,* to make holy; *sanctuary,* a holy place; *sanction,* to give holy approval, hence to authorize, approve, allow; and *sanctimonious,* which originally meant holy, saintly, but has come to mean making a hypocritical show of holiness or pretence of righteousness, assuming a "holier-than-thou" attitude. *Sacrosanct* combines both Latin *sacer,* sacred, and *sanctus,* holy, to mean sacred, not to be touched or changed.

sadistic *adj.* *He was a sadistic killer. The prisoners received vicious punishment at the hands of their sadistic captors:* deliberately cruel, brutal, vicious, fiendish, perverse, perverted, bloodthirsty.

◇ *Word origin: Sadistic,* taking pleasure in inflicting pain, comes from the name of the French man of letters and libertine, Count D. A. F. de *Sade,* commonly known as the Marquis de Sade, 1740–1814, who described numerous perversions, notably the inflicting of pain on others, in his writings, and advocated sexual violence as a way of life. The opposite term *masochistic,* deriving pleasure from one's own pain or humiliation, comes from the name of the Austrian novelist Leopold von Sacher-*Masoch,* 1835–95, who described this aberration in his writings.

safe *adj.* **1** *The crystal was safe in its protective casing:* secure, out of danger, safe and sound, out of harm's way; unharmed, unhurt, undamaged, unscathed, unscratched, unbroken, intact. **2** *The streets aren't safe at night:* secure, protecting, protected, guarded, defended, invulnerable, unexposed. **3** *Five thousand pounds is a safe estimate:* cautious, prudent, circumspect, conservative, modest,

discreet, non-committal, wary; sure, certain, realistic. **4** *The taxi company wants to hire a safe driver. The train is a safe means of transport:* not dangerous, dependable, reliable, trustworthy, to be trusted; sure, steady, firm, stable, sound; harmless, innocuous.
—*n.* **5** *Put your valuables in the safe:* locked box, storage box, safe-deposit box; vault.
Ant. 1 harmed, damaged; imperilled; jeopardized, at risk. **2** unsafe, dangerous, risky, hazardous, perilous. **3** wild, risky, extravagant; impetuous; speculative. **4** unsafe, undependable, unreliable; harmful, risky, pathogenic; lethal, toxic.

sag *v.* **1** *The mattress sagged in the middle:* bend downwards, droop, slump, sink, drop, descend, plunge, give way, settle; sway, keel, list, dip, lean, pitch, tilt. **2** *My mother's coat sagged on me:* droop, flop, flap, hang loosely, billow. **3** *Her spirits sagged as the night wore on:* weaken, diminish, decline, lose strength, break down; flag, weary, tire; fail, fizzle out.

saga *n. The Icelanders would sit round their fires at night listening to sagas of their heroes. The name of Captain Scott is famous in the saga of Antarctic exploration:* long narrative, heroic tale, epic, legend, adventure; chronicle, history; yarn, romance.

sagacious *adj. The professor was a sagacious man. We pray that the Court will reach a sagacious decision:* wise, shrewd, knowing, astute, intelligent, judicious, discriminating, sage, sapient, perspicacious, discerning, perceptive, practical, prudent; smart, clever, brainy, nimble-witted, sharp, acute, canny, calculating; sensible, sound, rational, tactful, discreet, diplomatic.
Ant. stupid, ignorant, dumb, obtuse, foolish, silly.

sage *n.* **1** *The king commanded his sages to answer the difficult problem:* wise man, magus, pundit, mage, philosopher, savant, scholar, guru, mandarin.
—*adj.* **2** *He was sage in judgement:* wise, shrewd, prudent; sensible, sound, sagacious, knowing, astute, intelligent.
Ant. 1 fool, idiot. **2** stupid, foolish, senseless.

sail *n.* **1** *Hoist the sail before we enter the open sea:* canvas sheet used on ship to catch the wind, mainsail; rigging. **2** *We went for a sail round the islands:* sailing trip, cruise, voyage, boat ride; journey by water, excursion.
—*v.* **3** *We sailed round the world on a 60-foot schooner. The ship sailed at noon:* cruise, go by water, navigate, ride the waves, skim, scud, steam; set sail, set out on a voyage, put to sea, shove off, weigh anchor, get under way. **4** *The balloon sailed upwards:* float, fly, drift, glide.

sailor *n. The old sailor had worked on many ships:* mariner, seaman, deck-hand, seafarer, seafaring man, navigator, voyager, *Informal* Jack tar, tar, salt, sea-dog.

sake *n.* **1** *For the sake of your family, don't take so many risks:* good, benefit, consideration, well-being, welfare, care, interest, concern, cause, behalf, regard, account, respect; advantage, profit, gain. **2** *For argument's sake, let's assume that the earth is flat:* end, purpose, object.

"The maid-servant, the sailor, and the schoolboy, are the three beings that enjoy a holiday beyond all the rest of the world."
—*J. H. Leigh Hunt*

---

salary *n. I would not consider a job with a salary of less than £350 per month:* fixed payment for work, wages, pay, earnings, income; stipend, allowance; remuneration, recompense.
◇ *Spelling tip:* Students sometimes misspell *salary*, not being sure that it ends in *-ary* rather than "-ery." Remember that both *pAy* and *sAlAry* only have *a*'s for vowels.
◇ *Usage note:* A *salary* is a fixed sum of money paid regularly to professional people, executives, and white-collar workers, while *wages* are payments, often based on an hourly rate, to artisans, members of skilled trades, factory workers, and labourers. Thus a teacher, company executive, filing clerk, etc., receives a fixed monthly *salary*, while a carpenter, an assembly-line worker, miner, or the like, receives hourly or weekly *wages*. Since the advent of assembly lines, unions, and almost full employment, many artisans, factory workers, and labourers receive weekly paycheques, but we still tend to call this money *wages*, rather than *salary*, considering it as a sum comprising distinct elements, such as an hourly regular rate, plus overtime or night-work payment. A salary is a more stable amount of money paid monthly, or at regular intervals above this.

> **Exploring the Word:** *Sailors* are so-called from Old English *segl*, sail. *Seaman* comes from Old English *sæ*, sea, lake, while *mariner* is from Latin *marinus*, sailor, which in turn comes from Latin *mare*, sea. A sailor is called a *salt* because he sails on salt water, i.e. the sea, and a *tar* from the tarred cloth or *tarpaulin* used to cover cargo (and at one time "tarpaulin" was a slang term for an American sailor's wide-brimmed storm hat).

sale *n.* **1** *My agent arranged the sale of the house:* selling, transfer, exchange. **2** *We're having a spring sale of winter coats:* disposal of goods at reduced prices, reduction, discount, cut; bargain, special offer.
Ant. 1 purchase, acquisition.

salient *adj. We stationed a look-out on the nearest salient point. The plan has several salient points in its favour:* prominent, protruding, obvious, conspicuous, standing out, jutting out, striking, noticeable, easily noticed, palpable, outstanding, manifest, flagrant, egregious, arrant, glaring, marked, pronounced, important, remarkable, notable, noteworthy; considerable, substantial.

Ant. low-lying, depressed; inconspicuous, minor, trifling.

sallow *adj. A gaunt man with a sallow complexion coughed in the corner:* yellowish, yellow, sickly, tallow-faced, anaemic, bilious; pale, wan, ashen, pallid, washed-out, brownish complexioned, green at the gills.

Ant. ruddy, rosy, flushed, blooming.

sally *n.* **1** *Joan of Arc was captured during a sally outside the walls:* sortie, thrust, counter-attack, bursting forth, foray, raid, attack. **2** *We made a lightning sally into the country and back:* excursion, journey, expedition, trip, outing. **3** *Her quick sally made us laugh:* clever remark, bon mot, ready reply, witticism, repartee, banter, badinage, retort, quip, wisecrack.

—*v.* **4** *The troops sallied forth and broke through the encirclement:* rush out, break out, issue suddenly, pour, surge, flow, spring; attack, charge, take the offensive, seize the initiative.

salon *n.* **1** *Large parties are held in the salon:* large room, drawing-room, hall, gallery. **2** *Alfred will be opening a new beauty salon in London soon:* stylish shop, beauty parlour, establishment.

◇ *Usage note:* Don't confuse *salon* (the last syllable rhymes with *John*) and *saloon* (the last syllable rhymes with *June*). *Salon* has an elegant connotation, as of a drawing-room or stylish shop: *The mansion has a large salon,* or *a beauty salon.* A *saloon* usually refers to a large room set aside for a particular activity, such as playing billiards, or drinking.

salt *n.* **1** *Please pass the salt and pepper:* sodium chloride; crystals obtained from sea-water or other saline solution, as brine. **2** *Her witty remarks added a little salt to the conversation:* wit, humour, pungency, piquancy; seasoning, smack, spice, savour, flavour. **3** *People like your grandmother are the salt of the earth:* best, quintessence, choice, pick, select, elect, cream.

—*v.* **4** *The stew tastes flat; you'd better salt it:* season, flavour, savour, spice. **5** *We salted the meat to preserve it:* cure, brine, marinate, pickle, corn, souse. **6** **salt away** *He's been salting away money for years:* save, store up, put away, lay away, set aside.

salubrious *adj. The part of the town near the railway station isn't very salubrious:* healthful, healthy, health-promoting, good for one, salutary, beneficial, wholesome, life-giving; clean, fresh, bracing, invigorating.

Ant. unhealthful, unhealthy, harmful, unwholesome, insalubrious, deleterious.

salute *v.* **1** *He saluted us heartily:* address, greet, hail, welcome; make obeisance to, bow to, nod to, wave to. **2** *I salute my opponent's courage:* applaud, cheer, praise, honour, respect, pay tribute to, take one's hat off to.

—*n.* **3** *The hero acknowledged the salutes of the crowd with a wave of his hand:* expression of goodwill, salutation, greeting, recognition, honour, homage, reverence; applause, accolade, laudation, acclamation.

Exploring the Word: *Salt* has been very important in human history and Latin *sal,* salt, *salsus,* salted, give us *salary, sauce, soused, sausage,* and *salad,* as well as *salt* and *saline.* Thus *salary* is so-called because it was originally money paid to Roman soldiers to buy salt, "salt-money." *Sauce* was originally any salty seasoning, and a *saucer* was a small dish to hold it; *soused* originally meant pickled in salt water, so calling a drunk "soused" is the same as calling him "pickled"; *sausage* is so-called because it is meat and meal heavily seasoned or preserved with salt; and a *salad* is a dish of salted vegetables; *silt* originally referred to a salty deposit or swamp; *saltpetre,* a form of potassium nitrate used in gunpowder, is from Latin *sal petrae,* rock salt; and, of course, Latin *sal,* salt, appears in our own words *salt, saline* (salty, containing salt) and as *sal* in the names of various patent medicines. Our expression *to take something with a grain* (or *pinch*) *of salt* also comes from Latin, and we sometimes use the Latin phrase: *I advise you to take the Secretary's latest remarks* cum grano salis.

salvage *n.* **1** *We're trying to finance the salvage of the Titanic:* recovery, reclamation, retrieval. **2** *The salvage was piled up on the pier:* property saved from destruction, reclaimed materials, remains, scrap, debris; flotsam and jetsam.

—*v.* **3** *We salvaged the cargo from the sunken ship:* save, rescue, retrieve, recover, rehabilitate, restore.

"I do not wish to be accused of inventing a new heresy to the effect that salvation depends on getting a first in classics." —*T. S. Eliot*

salvation *n.* **1** *Think on your eternal salvation, friend!:* saving of the soul from sin, redemption, deliverance; election, grace. **2** *Prayer was her salvation in times of stress:* means of surviving, protection, lifeline, mainstay, support, rock. **3** *A loan from a friend helped in the salvation of his business:* saving, rescue, preservation, salvage, retrieval, reclamation, recovery, survival.

Ant. **1** perdition, damnation, condemnation. **2** downfall. **3** destruction, loss.

same *adj.* **1** *This is the same dress as I wore to the other party:* identical, selfsame, one and the same, alike, twin, like, of like kind; similar. **2** *Carol's house and Jane's have the same number of rooms:* corresponding, equivalent, parallel; equal, on a par, on even terms. **3** *You're still the same person I knew ten years ago:* unchanged, invariable, consistent, uniform.

Ant. **1-3** different. **1** dissimilar, other. **3** changed, variable, inconsistent.

◇ *Usage note:* Business English often uses *same* as a pronoun for *it* or *they*. This usage isn't really businesslike or effective, in fact it sounds rather ridiculous. Thus, don't write "The parts have been received and same will be shipped to you immediately." Write instead, *The parts have been received and* (*they*) *will be . . .* The famous World War II message "Sighted Sub Sank Same" has a fine pithy alliteration. In formal use, however, the technically correct message would have been "Sighted Sub, Sank It," which just goes to prove that breaking rules of good usage can be worthwhile and expressive at times.

sample *n.* **1** *The sketches were merely samples of her work. The doctor took a sample of the patient's blood:* representative, specimen, example, illustration, instance, cross-section, portion, segment, exemplification, pattern, model, paradigm.

—*v.* **2** *She made us sample her cooking:* judge by a sample, test, examine partake of, taste, experience.

sanctimonious *adj. A true believer doesn't have to be sanctimonious about his beliefs. Our professor's always coming up with sanctimonious pronouncements:* making a show of sanctity, affectedly holy, belligerently pious, aggressively devout, self-righteous, pharisaical, holier-than-thou; solemn, overblown, pretentious, pompous, canting.

sanction *n.* **1** *We received sanction to proceed with our plans:* approval, endorsement, assent, consent, permission, authorization; leave, liberty, licence, authority; ratification, confirmation, support. **2** *The international community imposed sanctions on Rhodesia for what it considered her illegal political actions:* penalty, pressure, punitive measure, coercion.

—*v.* **3** *Our plan wasn't sanctioned by the board of directors:* approve, endorse, authorize, legitimate, license, allow, permit, countenance, accept, agree to, favour, support.

Ant. **1** disapproval, refusal, ban, prohibition. **2** incentive, encouragement. **3** disapprove, reject, ban, prohibit.

sanctuary *n.* **1** *Build ye the sanctuary of the Lord God:* holy place, consecrated place, holy of holies, place of worship, house of prayer, house of God, church, temple, chapel, shrine, retreat; sanctum, sanctum sanctorum. **2** *The air-raid shelter was a sanctuary against the bombs. The outlaw claimed sanctuary in the church:* refuge, haven, safe place; safety, protection, asylum, shelter, immunity from pursuers hiding-place, cover. **3** *The island is maintained as a sanctuary for endangered species of wildlife:* protected area, reserve, preserve, park.

sane *adj.* **1** *The killer was declared sufficiently sane to stand trial:* of sound mind, reasonable, in possession of one's faculties, compos mentis, clear-headed, sober, balanced, responsible, rational, lucid; *Slang* all there. **2** *We can hardly consider that a sane argument!:* reasonable, well-founded, sensible, judicious, sagacious, logical, far-sighted; credible, plausible.

Ant. **1** insane, unsound, mentally ill, non compos mentis, deranged, mad, irrational. **2** insane, senseless, stupid, foolish, injudicious, unreasonable, incredible, implausible.

sanguine *adj.* **1** *He had a sanguine outlook on life:* optimistic, hopeful, confident, happy, cheerful, sunny, bright; light-hearted, buoyant, in good spirits. **2** *Her cheeks were sanguine with excitement:* red, reddish, ruddy, crimson, scarlet; florid, rubicund, flushed, rosy, inflamed, glowing, blooming.

Ant. **1** pessimistic, doubtful, gloomy, depressed, despairing, heavy-hearted, dispirited, morose. **2** pale, ashen, pallid, white.

◇ *Usage note: Sanguine* and *sanguinary* both come from the Latin *sanguis*, blood, but have completely different meanings. Today, *sanguine* usually means cheerful or confident (because such people were once thought to have especially rich or healthy blood), or sometimes it is used to mean ruddy or having the colour of or like blood. Thus, *The head of the Chamber of Commerce has a sanguine disposition* (cheerful, confident). *Sanguinary* means accompanied with much bloodshed, or bloodthirsty. Thus, *At Thermopylae the Spartans made a heroic and sanguinary stand. Genghis Khan was a man of sanguinary disposition.*

sanitary *adj. The Department of Health checks on sanitary conditions. We cannot decorate the bathroom until the sanitary fittings are installed:* conducive to health and cleanliness; connected with bathrooms, lavatories, plumbing, etc.; health promoting, healthful, salubrious, healthy, wholesome; sterile, clean, germ-free, disease-free, hygienic, disinfected, aseptic, prophylactic.

Ant. unhealthy, unwholesome; unsterile, dirty.

sanity *n. She managed to keep her sanity throughout the ordeal:* mental health, soundness of mind, saneness, mental balance, normality; soundness of judgement, reason, rationality, sense, lucidity, clear-headedness, coherence.

Ant. insanity, insaneness, madness, derangement; irrationality, incoherence.

"Sanity is a madness put to good uses."
—*George Santayana*

---

sap *v. The ordeal sapped his energy and broke his spirit:* deplete, reduce, rob; weaken, undermine, tax, wear, enervate, enfeeble, exhaust, devitalize; break down, impair, cripple, afflict; subvert, destroy, ruin, devastate; bleed, drain.

sarcasm *n. His sarcasm hurt her feelings:* ridicule, irony, derision, contempt, mockery, scoffing; cutting remark, sneer, taunt, gibe, jeer, jest.
Ant. compliment, praise, enthusiasm, appreciation.
◇ *Usage note: Sarcasm* and *irony* are both used to ridicule or criticize, and always show up the weakness or vanity of others or of ideas. The difference between *sarcasm* and *irony* depends upon the tone of voice used for the remark and on the intention behind it. *Sarcasm* is usually the more bitter and can taunt or show contempt. *Irony* is usually more gentle and subtle than *sarcasm* and always asserts the opposite of what is really meant.

sarcastic *adj. He gave a sarcastic reply. Sarcastic people tend to lose friends quickly:* ironic, contemptuous, mocking, derisive, taunting; biting, cutting, piercing, stinging, caustic, acerbic, sardonic, scornful, sneering, disparaging.

sardonic *adj. He watched his enemies turn against each other, with sardonic amusement:* sarcastic, cynical, sneering, mocking, contemptuous, derisive, scornful, disparaging; caustic, biting, taunting, jeering.

Satan *n. Satan is the ruler of Hell:* the Devil, the Prince of Darkness, the Evil One, the Serpent, The Tempter, Beelzebub, Lucifer, Mephistopheles, The Foul Fiend, Old Nick, Old Scratch; Belial.

satanic *adj. This book reveals all about the satanic practices of witches:* befitting Satan, hellish, diabolical, demoniacal, demonic, infernal, devilish, fiendish, fiend-like; malicious, malignant, malevolent, bad, wicked, evil, infamous, inhuman, heinous, vicious, cruel, vile, sadistic; black.
Ant. angelic, heavenly, divine, benevolent, good, humane, kind.

sate *v. The huge meal sated our hunger:* satisfy fully, satiate, fill; glut, stuff, surfeit, gorge.

satellite *n.* **1** *How many satellites does Jupiter have?:* moon. **2** *The king's satellites accompanied him everywhere:* attendant, assistant, follower, disciple; companion, crony, retainer, servant; vassal, menial, underling, puppet, hanger-on, parasite, toady, sycophant. **3** *In the rhetoric of the Cold War, dependent allies of the superpowers have been termed their satellites:* client state, vassal, tributary, puppet.
◇ *Word origin: Satellite* comes from Latin *satelles,* attendant, bodyguard. In astronomy a *satellite* is a smaller body, a moon, attending upon and revolving round a larger, and thus the name is also given to the modern man-made satellites launched from Earth.

satire *n. Voltaire's* Candide *is a famous satire. The play is full of satire:* comic criticism, parody, take-off, send-up, burlesque, lampoon, travesty, caricature; mockery, ridicule, derision; pointed wit, sarcasm, irony, acrimony; raillery, banter, persiflage.
◇ *Word origin:* The word *satire* comes from Latin *lanx sature,* fruit salad, which phrase the ancient Romans later used to mean a medley or mixture, and still later applied to a discursive poem about a number of subjects. From this last we get *satire,* a piece of writing ridiculing various vices and follies, hence wit used to expose follies, ridicule.

satirical *adj. He wrote a satirical piece on the government:* ironically critical, sardonic, sarcastic, ironical; derisive, mocking, sneering, scornful, bitter, caustic; comic, humorous, tongue-in-cheek.

satisfaction *n.* **1** *He gets a good deal of satisfaction out of his garden. The matter will be resolved to your entire satisfaction:* pleasure, comfort, gratification, happiness, fulfilment, pride, content, contentment. **2** *The owner of the shop received satisfaction for the damage:* reimbursement, repayment, compensation, recompense, restitution, remuneration, payment, remittance; settlement, quittance, damages, deserts; requital, redress, rectification, justice, amends, atonement, correction, reckoning, answering, measure for measure.
Ant. 1 dissatisfaction, grief, shame, unhappiness, discontent.

satisfactory *adj. The actress gave a satisfactory performance but could have done better:* good enough, adequate, suitable, sufficient, acceptable, passable, up to standard, up to the mark.
Ant. unsatisfactory, inadequate, bad.

> **Exploring the Word**: *Satisfy, satiate,* and *sate* come from Latin *satis,* enough (*satisfy* is Latin *satis,* enough + *facere,* to do, hence literally to do enough). The same base gives us *saturate* (Latin *satur,* full of food, sated), to fill completely, as by soaking; and via Old French *assets,* literally "enough" (cf. Modern French *assez,* enough) to pay one's debts. A Germanic cognate of Latin *satis,* enough, is our word *sad,* from Old English *sæd,* literally sated, having had a surfeit of bad news or of worldly things.

satisfy *v.* **1** *Nothing satisfies her any more! Do you satisfy the entry requirements for the training college? The cold water satisfied our thirst:* make content, content, please, mollify, pacify, gratify, delight; meet, fill, fulfil, serve, suffice, be adequate to, answer; sate, satiate, slake, quench, appease, remove, put an end to. **2** *We satisfied all the claims that he could reasonably make:* pay off, settle, discharge, clear, annul; pay, remit, repay, reimburse, recompense, compensate, requite. **3** *His persuasive talk still didn't satisfy me that the plan would succeed:* convince, free of doubt, persuade, assure, reassure.
Ant. 1 dissatisfy, displease, annoy; intensify, worsen. **3** dissatisfy, dissuade.

saturate *v.* **1** *Heavy rain saturated the ground:*

soak thoroughly, drench, souse, douse, steep, immerse, submerge. **2** *His mind is saturated with Shakespeare:* fill, infiltrate, cover, permeate, suffuse, pervade, impregnate.
Ant. 1 drain, dry.

saucy *adj.* **1** *Her saucy remarks raised many eyebrows:* impudent, insolent, impertinent, forward, audacious, bold, brash, brazen, unabashed, barefaced, flippant, cheeky, fresh, smart-alecy, cocky; rude, impolite, discourteous, disrespectful. **2** *She was a saucy little girl:* pert, lively; high-spirited. **3** *Narcisse is modelling a saucy spring outfit:* jaunty, trim, smart, natty, spruce.

saunter *v.* **1** *He sauntered into the house as if nothing had happened:* walk casually, amble, stroll, promenade; wander, ramble, roam, meander; straggle, loiter.
—n. **2** *We took a slow saunter round the park:* stroll, leisurely walk, amble, ramble, promenade.

savage *adj.* **1** *The poor man received a savage beating from the thugs:* ferocious, fierce, brutal, barbaric, brutish, cruel, unkind, merciless, unmerciful, pitiless, sadistic, ruthless, relentless, bloody, murderous. **2** *If you love savage beasts, leave them alone:* untamed, wild, undomesticated. **3** *Early explorers were confronted by the savage tribesmen of the interior:* uncivilized, primitive, uncultivated, uncultured, heathenish, barbaric, barbarous. **4** *Savage winds whipped about the climber's head:* violent, harsh, rough, rugged.
—n. **5** *If this is civilization, give me the savages any day! Do you believe in the myth of the noble savage?:* primitive, aborigine, aboriginal, barbarian. **6** *Lock that savage up and throw away the key!:* fierce person, brute, fiend, maniac, barbarian, *Informal* animal; hooligan, hoodlum, ruffian, yob; boor, yahoo.
Ant. 1 kind, merciful, lenient, gentle, tender. **2** tame, domesticated. **3** civilized, cultivated, cultured. **4** mild, soft, calm. **5** civilized person.

"Whenever you save 5s. you put a man out of work for a day." —*J. Maynard Keynes*

---

save *v.* **1** *The firemen saved the family from burning to death:* rescue, recover, free, deliver, preserve, protect, safeguard, spare, salvage, redeem, help. **2** *You'll save electricity by turning off the lights that aren't in use:* conserve, preserve, husband, spare. **3** *I'm saving this dress for a special occasion:* set aside, store, reserve, set apart, withhold, hold, keep, conserve, preserve, put away. **4** *Save your voice for tonight's performance:* treat carefully, keep safe, conserve, protect, take care of, look after, safeguard, shield, defend, watch over, guard. **5** *You must learn to save if you want to provide for the future:* be thrifty, avoid spending, curtail expenses, economize, retrench; provide for a rainy day, lay up, lay by, hoard, amass, accumulate, deposit, bank, heap up, garner, stock.
Ant. 1 endanger, imperil, risk, hazard. **2** use, consume, waste. **3** use, spend. **4** expose, risk, endanger. **5** spend, be extravagant.

saving *adj.* **1** *His one saving grace was his sense of honour:* redeeming, redemptory, reclaiming, restoring, compensating, reparative.
—n. **2** *If you buy one now you'll benefit from a saving of 20%:* amount saved, reduction in cost, price-cut, discount. **3 savings** *It took all our savings to buy the house:* money laid aside, store of money, financial reserve, funds, bank deposit; nest-egg.

saviour *n.* **1** *Simon Bolivar was the saviour of the South American peasants:* protector, champion, defender, guardian; rescuer, deliverer, liberator, emancipator, freer; redeemer, guiding light. **2 Saviour** *The birth of the Saviour is celebrated on Christmas Day:* Christ, the Messiah, Redeemer, Prince of Peace, the Son of God.

savoir faire *n. Diplomats need a great deal of savoir faire:* social grace, social skill, tact, aplomb, graciousness, finesse, smoothness, adroitness, discretion; poise, complaisance; presence, assurance, composure, self-possesssion; polish, suavity, urbanity, worldliness.
Ant. awkwardness, clumsiness, ineptness, maladroitness.

savour *n.* **1** *This cake has the savour of nutmeg:* taste, flavour, tang, spice, piquancy, pungency; smell, aroma, odour, scent, fragrance; smack, relish, zest. **2** *His words had the savour of vengeance:* character, nature, particular quality, characteristic, property, particularity, distinctive feature, peculiarity, trait, quality; substance, essence, gist, spirit, soul.
—v. **3** *Her sauce savoured of garlic. This plan savours of treason:* taste, smell, smack, have a touch, show traces, have the hallmark, be suggestive. **4** *We ate the stew slowly, savouring it:* enjoy, relish, like, take pleasure in, delight in, luxuriate in, rejoice in, appreciate. **5** *He had savoured the effects of power during his first term in office:* experience, taste, sample, try.

savoury *adj.* **1** *Do you prefer sweet or savoury biscuits?* tasty, appetizing, mouth-watering, aromatic, fragrant, odorous; pungent, piquant, salty, not sweet, tangy, delectable, delicious, luscious, tasteful, palatable, full-flavoured, flavorous, *Informal* scrumptious, yummy. **2** *He wasn't a very savoury character:* reputable, respectable, in good odour, inoffensive, honest; attractive, alluring, charming.
Ant. 1 ill-tasting, tasteless, sweet, insipid, malodorous, smelly. **2** unsavoury, disreputable, shady.

say *v.* **1** *How dare you say such a thing to me! He said he wouldn't go. What did the telegram say?:* speak, tell, utter, give utterance to, voice, put into words, vocalize, articulate; express, word, mouth, phrase; state, declare, pronounce, announce; remark, comment, mention; communicate, convey; come out with, let out, divulge, repeat, reveal, make known, disclose. **2** *The actors said their lines perfectly:* recite, read, speak, deliver, render, pronounce, articulate, repeat, rehearse, perform, do. **3** *I'd say it's about two o'clock:* guess, suppose, surmise, assume, hazard a guess, conjecture, imagine; judge, reason; dare say; be sure, be certain, feel convinced. **4** *It's been said that he's an impostor:* report, rumour, spread, circulate, bruit, noise abroad, put out, allege, hold, maintain; contend, hint, imply, intimate, suggest, insinuate.

—n. **5** *We should all have a say in the running of our government:* right to speak, voice, participation; vote, franchise. **6** *You've had your say, now sit down:* opportunity to speak, chance; comment, expressed opinion; *Slang* twopenny worth.

Ant. 1 be quiet about, suppress.

saying *n.* *"A bird in the hand is worth two in the bush" is an old saying:* expression, proverb, saw, adage, maxim, truism, aphorism, dictum, motto, precept, apothegm, epigram, byword, moral.

scale[1] *n.* **1** *Scrape the scales of paint off the ceiling before repainting it:* thin piece, flake; plate. **2** *A scale of rust covered the steel plate:* coating, film, thin covering, skin, lamina, membrane, layer, crust, shell.

—v. **3** *You have to scale the fish before cooking it:* scrape, scour. **4** *Scale the old paint off the ceiling:* chip off, flake, shave, rub off; shell, peel, husk.

◇ *Word origin:* A *scale,* one of the thin bony membranous outgrowths on the skin of a fish, comes from Old French *escale,* husk, shell. In fact, the Old French base is distantly related to our word *shell.*

scale[2] *n.* **1** Often **scales** *Weigh the flour on the scales:* weighing machine, balance.

—v. **2** *The baby scaled six pounds seven ounces at birth:* have a weight of, weigh.

scale[3] *n.* **1** *What's the scale of that ruler? I know how to convert Fahrenheit to the centigrade scale:* gradation, graduation, calibration, rule; measure. **2** *We were all graded on a scale from 1 to 10:* classification, range, series, progression; spread, spectrum, continuum, order, ladder. **3** *What is the scale of your map?:* proportion, ratio. **4** *The opera singer could sing in several scales:* register, range, octave; key.

—v. **5** *Come with me and I'll teach you how to scale a rock face:* climb up, climb over, go up, ascend, surmount, rise, progress upward, work upward. **6** *Management agreed to scale wages according to the job specifications:* adjust, regulate, set; vary according to a scale.

◇ *Word origin: Scale,* meaning to climb to the top of (as by steps or rungs) or a progressive series of numbers, notes, sounds, or classifications (*to scale a wall, the Fahrenheit scale, musical scale, a wage scale*) comes from Latin *scala,* a ladder, akin to *scandere,* to climb. The same Latin base also gives us *scan,* to separate verse into metrical feet, to pass the eyes over quickly from point to point.

scamper *v.* **1** *The children scampered out of the house when the rain had stopped:* run, hasten, fly, hurry, race, sprint, dart, dash, scuttle, flit, zip, scurry; *Informal* scoot, skedaddle.

—n. **2** *The child left the house with a scamper:* quick run, dash, sprint, hasty run; scurry, zip. **3** *The dogs enjoyed a scamper in the open field:* frolic, running about playfully, gambol, frisk, romp.

scan *v.* **1** *The look-out scanned the horizon for a sight of land:* examine, peruse, pore over, scour, probe, scrutinize, inspect, study, size up, take stock of; search, explore, sweep, survey, check. **2** *He only scanned the letter before passing it back to his wife:* read hastily, glance at, browse through, skim. **3** *The English teacher taught the class how to scan poems:* divide into feet, show the metrical structure of; analyse.

scandal *n.* **1** *The Dreyfus Affair was the most famous political scandal in French history:* public disgrace, revelation of misconduct, exposure of wrongdoing, embarrassment, sensation, exposé. **2** *She brought scandal upon her family by her outrageous behaviour:* dishonour, disgrace, disesteem, embarrassment, discredit; shame, outrage; smirch, stain, stigma, blot, debasement, odium, ignominy, opprobrium. **3** *I will not listen to this scandal!:* malicious gossip, slander, libel, aspersion, defamatory talk, obloquy, calumny, detraction, disparagement, revilement, vituperation, abuse.

Ant. 2 honour, esteem, credit, praise.

◇ *Word origin: Scandal,* like *slander,* comes from Greek *skandalon,* a cause of tripping, hence a way of tripping a person up or bringing him into disgrace.

"Love and scandal are the best sweeteners of tea." —*Henry Fielding*

---

scandalous *adj.* **1** *I am shocked by his scandalous behaviour:* disgraceful, shameful, disreputable, highly improper, offensive, shocking, outrageous, reprehensible. **2** *That magazine is full of scandalous stories:* slanderous, libellous, scurrilous, defamatory, gossiping.

Ant. 1 proper, reputable, decent. **2** kind, praising, laudatory, sweet.

scant *adj.* **1** *The surveyors found only a scant water supply:* limited, meagre, deficient, insufficient, inadequate; small, short, paltry, sparse. **2** *My gaoler offered me a scant cupful of water:* not full, bare, incomplete. **3** *Since the husband died, the family has been scant of money:* ill-supplied, in need, short.

—*v.* **4** *The general refused to scant the men's rations:* limit, stint, hold back, skimp on, reduce, cut.

Ant. 1 plentiful, profuse, abundant, ample, adequate. **2** full, overflowing. **3** well-supplied. **4** be lavish.

scanty *adj. The beggar shivered in his scanty clothes:* inadequate, scant, insufficient; meagre, thin, slender, sparse, small, modest, short, stunted, undersized.

scar *n.* **1** *He had a scar on his arm from an old accident. She bore the scars of an unhappy childhood. The boat has been painted and its old scars covered:* mark left by an old wound, cicatrix, wound, seam, stitch-mark, pit, pock; dent, gash; defect, flaw, blemish.

—*v.* **2** *Falling on the rocks scarred his legs and arms. An unhappy childhood can scar you for life:* leave a scar on, wound, cut, scratch, gash, lacerate, mutilate, mangle; mark, bruise, deface, disfigure; hurt, impair, damage; influence, affect.

◇ *Usage note:* See SCARE.

scarce *adj.* **1** *Qualified workmen were scarce during the strike:* in short supply, hard to find, hard to obtain; wanting, deficient, not abundant, not plentiful. **2** *Peregrine falcons are now fairly scarce in England:* rare, rarely seen, unusual, uncommon, exceptional.

Ant. 1 abundant, plentiful. **2** numerous, common.

scarcely *adj.* **1** *We scarcely had time for breakfast:* hardly, barely, slightly, faintly, only just, no more than, not easily. **2** *He was scarcely the type of person needed for the job:* definitely not, certainly not, in no manner, in no way, by no means, not at all, not in the least, hardly, on no account.

scarcity *n.* **1** *The scarcity of supplies was alleviated when new shipments arrived:* insufficient supply, insufficiency, shortage, scantiness, lack, dearth, deficiency, want, paucity, thinness. **2** *Uranium is extremely expensive because of its scarcity:* rarity, infrequency of occurrence, rareness, scarceness, sparsity, uncommonness, sparseness, fewness.

scare *v.* **1** *The thunder and lightning scared the child:* fill with fear, strike terror into, make afraid, frighten, terrify, startle, terrorize, horrify, make one's flesh crawl, make apprehensive, panic, intimidate, harrow, daunt, disquiet, give a turn, disconcert, dishearten; become frightened.

—*n.* **2** *The smell of gas gave me a scare:* sudden fright, start, sudden terror, alarm, shock, panic; shake, palpitation, shiver, turn, nervousness, consternation; *Slang* jitters, the willies.

Ant. 1 reassure, calm, comfort. **2** calm, reassurance.

◇ *Usage note:* Don't confuse *scare* and *scar* or their other forms. To *scaRE* means to frighten or to make afraid; thus, *scaRE — scaRing — scaRed: Did that ghost story scare you? The scarecrows are for scaring away the birds. Don't be scared of the bogyman.* To *scaR* means to mark, and a *scaR* is a mark left on the skin or a surface, as after the healing of a wound or damage; the forms of the verb are *scaR — scaRRing — scaRRed: That wound may leave a scar. Stop scarring the furniture with your shoes. His face was badly scarred in the accident.*

scatter *v.* **1** *We scattered the rat poison around the floor of the cellar:* spread loosely, distribute, disperse, throw, strew, sprinkle, spatter, cast, sow; circulate, broadcast, disseminate. **2** *The crows scattered when the farmer shot at them. A loud noise scattered the pigeons:* disperse, flee; dispel, dissipate, rout, chase away.

Ant. gather, collect.

scatter-brained *adj. The playboy was so scatter-brained that he never had a serious thought. Going to Monte Carlo was a scatter-brained idea:* hare-brained, muddle-headed, rattle-brained, bird-brained, feather-brained, light-minded, empty-headed, flighty, madcap, giddy, silly, zany, dizzy, stupid; absent-minded, forgetful; foolish, foolhardy, wild, reckless, rash, careless, imprudent, devil-may-care; irresponsible, unsteady, unstable; *Informal* crazy, nutty.

Ant. serious, intense, intelligent; careful, prudent; responsible, steady, stable.

scavenger *n.* **1** *Vultures are scavengers:* carrion-eater. **2** *The street urchins were scavengers, roving the gutters:* salvager; collector, magpie, one who searches amongst dustbins, beggar, gutter snipe.

◇ *Word origin:* A *scavenger* is an animal or bird, such as a vulture, that looks for and feeds on dead animal flesh. Most such animals and birds have extremely keen eyesight. The word comes from Flemish *scauwen*, to look at.

"Thro' all the drama—whether damned or not—
Love gilds the scene, and women guide the plot."
—*R. B. Sheridan*

---

scene *n.* **1** *Criminals are said to return to the scene of the crime:* setting, site, location, locale, locality, whereabouts; place, spot, position, region. **2** *The setting of the sun over the lake was a beautiful scene:* vista, view, vision, sight, panorama, picture, show, display, spectacle; survey. **3** *She made a scene and upset the children:* display of temper, embarrassing spectacle, fuss, to-do, commotion. **4** *The scene of the story is Victorian England:* setting, locale; backdrop, background, scenery. **5** *We missed the first few scenes of the play:* episode, part, division, sequence; act.

◇ *Word origin: Scene, scenery,* and *scenic* come from Greek *skēnē*, tent, meaning a tent used as a stage, which formed the backdrop of ancient dramas. Our word *scenario,* the outline plot of a play or film, also comes from this Greek word for a stage tent. The *proscenium* is the part of a stage in front of the curtain (from the Greek prefix *pro-,* before, + *skēnē,* tent, literally the part "in front of the tent").

scenery *n.* **1** *The scenery on the mountain is breathtaking!:* landscape, terrain; general appearance, view, spectacle, vista. **2** *He painted scenery for the local operatic society's productions:* stage setting, backdrops, backgrounds, scenes, sets.

scent *n.* **1** *The scent of lemons filled the grove:* smell, odour, aroma, fragrance, bouquet, essence, perfume. **2** *The dogs followed the scent of the escaped convict. The thief managed to throw his pursuers off the scent:* odour left in passing; trail, track, course, path, pursuit, spoor.
—*v.* **3** *The hounds scented the fox and were off. The scout scented danger:* smell, sniff, breathe, inhale; get wind of, get a hint of, detect, distinguish, recognize, discern, suspect; trace, trail, track. **4** *She used lemon juice to scent her hair:* fill with an odour, give odour to, perfume, aromatize.
◇ *Usage note:* See SMELL.

sceptic *n. He's too much of a sceptic to take anything simply on trust:* doubter, doubting Thomas, questioner, scoffer; agnostic.
◇ *Word origin: Sceptic* and *sceptical* come from Greek *skeptesthai,* to examine, consider, and the derivative term *skeptikos,* a "considerer" or disciple of Pyrrho of Elis who lived from approximately 360-270 B.C. and taught that absolute knowledge is unattainable and that judgements must be continually questioned in order to attain relative certainty. This doctrine is called *scepticism.*

sceptical *adj. Ignorant people were sceptical of Columbus's theory that the earth was round. Nineteenth-century philologists tended to be too sceptical:* inclined to question, questioning, dubious, doubting, doubtful, unsure, uncertain, unconvinced, incredulous; disbelieving, scoffing, hypercritical.
Ant. convinced, sure, certain, confident, unquestioning, undoubting believing, credulous.

schedule *n.* **1** *What's on the schedule for today? Retailers have several price schedules:* list of events, agenda, calendar, programme, roll; list, table.
—*v.* **2** *The secretary is trying to schedule the month's appointments. We're scheduled to appear in court on Tuesday:* set the time for, fix, plan, book; appoint, set down, fit in, put down.
◇ *Spelling tip:* This word ends in *-ule,* as does the word *yule.* Remember, *I have a busy YULEtide schedULE.*
◇ *Pronunciation tip:* Don't forget that the first syllable of *schedule* is pronounced *shed-,* not *sKed-.*

scheme *n.* **1** *He suggested several schemes to increase sales:* plan, design, programme, project, course; method, means, system, way, device, procedure, policy; strategy, tactics. **2** *The robbers devised a scheme to hold up the mail train:* secret plan, conspiracy, plot, manœuvre, ruse, shift; contrivance, connivance; intrigue, stratagem, machination. **3** *The airport contains an original scheme of criss-crossing runways:* arrangement, system, grouping, organization, network, disposition. **4** *Follow this scheme to make the model aeroplane:* schematic diagram, outline, delineation, lay-out, sketch, design, drawing; chart, map.
—*v.* **5** *For months they had schemed to overthrow the government:* plan secretly, plot, conspire, connive; contrive, devise, concoct, study, design; frame, organize, manœuvre, machinate, intrigue; *Archaic* complot.
◇ *Word origin: Scheme* comes from Greek *schēma,* a plan, form.

scheming *adj. We were deceived by a scheming con man:* conniving, designing, contriving, calculating; Machiavellian, crafty, arch, sly, wily, artful, slippery, insidious, cunning, shrewd, tricky, intriguing.
Ant. naïve, artless, ingenuous.

scholar *n.* **1** *The new headmaster is an eminent scholar:* learned person, erudite person, sage, wise man, man of letters, pundit, savant, mandarin; academic specialist, humanist, intellectual; *Slang* boffin, egghead, brain. **2** *Several young scholars enrolled for the advanced mathematics course:* pupil, student, learner, studier, matriculant; schoolboy, schoolgirl, undergraduate, postgraduate, *Slang* bookworm.
Ant. 1 dunce, dolt; ignoramus, illiterate.
◇ *Spelling tip:* Some people make the mistake of spelling this word with an *-er* ending rather than the correct *-ar* ending. Remember: *scholARs ARe in school.*
◇ *Word origin:* See SCHOOL.

scholarly *adj. The Library at Alexandria was organized by scholarly people. Scholarly disputes can be rather dull at times:* erudite, learned, educated, academic, intellectual, lettered, liberal, humane.

scholarship *n.* **1** *Scaliger was renowned for his classical scholarship:* academic attainments, knowledge gained by study, learning, erudition, education, enlightenment, intelligence; thoroughness, accurate research, sound academic practice. **2** *He won a scholarship to the University of Cambridge:* aid granted to a student, grant, endowment, maintenance for a student, stipend; fellowship, exhibition, bursarship.
Ant. 1 stupidity, idiocy, foolishness.

scholastic *adj. A certain portion of our taxes is put aside for scholastic purposes. The sages engaged in scholastic disputation:* of schools, educational, academic; scholarly, instructional.

school *n.* **1** *The children go to school every morning by bus:* place for instruction; academy, institute; (*variously*) kindergarten, primary school, grammar school, prep school, private school, public school, comprehensive school, technical school, Sunday school, day school, boarding school, college, university, seminary. **2** *The old school refused to accept new ideas:* group of people who think alike, order, faction, denomination; way of thinking, thought, system, method, style, view; persuasion, doctrine, theory, faith, belief; *Informal* bunch, crowd.
—*v.* **3** *She was schooled in the ways of the mystics:* teach, train, instruct, educate.
◇ *Word origin:* If you are attending some classes during your leisure time, you understand the original meaning of *school. School* and its forms *scholar, scholarly, scholarship, scholastic,* etc., come from Greek *scholē,* leisure, studies undertaken during leisure time. The other word *school,* as a *school of porpoises,* is an old Dutch word meaning crowd, company, troop.

science *n.* **1** *We studied several sciences at school. Chemistry is a science:* natural phenomena, empirical knowledge, organized knowledge, systematic knowledge; field of systematic inquiry. **2** *The science of rugby is inborn, not learned. We had the procedure down to a science:* art, technique, method, discipline; finished execution, skill, aptitude, acquirement, finesse, facility.
◇ *Word origin: Science* and *scientific* come from Latin *scientia,* knowledge. Also akin are our Latinate words *conscience* and *conscious.*

"Science is the greatest antidote to the poison of enthusiasm and superstition."
—*Adam Smith*

---

scintillating *adj. Conversation at the party was scintillating:* sparkling, lively, animated, ebullient, exuberant, brilliant, stimulating, glittering; charming, bright, witty.
Ant. dull, boring, lack-lustre.
◇ *Word origin: Scintillating* comes from Latin *scintilla,* spark; hence it means "sparkling."

scoff *v. She scoffed at his attempts to improve himself:* mock, ridicule, deride, poke fun at, laugh at; deride, make sport of, make light of, make game of; flout, taunt, jeer, revile, rail at, run down; *Slang* knock, put down.
Ant. praise, compliment, exalt; applaud, cheer.

scold *v.* **1** *Dad scolded me for coming home late:* rebuke, upbraid, reprove, reprehend, remonstrate with, reprimand, chide, dress down, set down, take to task, bring to book, haul over the coals, put on the carpet, criticize, castigate, censure, blame angrily, berate, lash out at; find fault, nag, carp at, rail at, complain about.
—*n.* **2** *That old scold never has anything nice to say:* constant faultfinder, complainer, nagger, shrew, virago, termagant.
Ant. 1 praise, honour, compliment, applaud.
◇ *Word origin: Scold* comes from Old Norse *skald,* a satirist, poet who writes satire.

scoop *n.* **1** *The shop assistant used a scoop to put the toffees in a bag:* hand shovel; ladle, dipper, spoon. **2** *It was* The Herald *that actually came up with the scoop:* exclusive news story.
—*v.* **3** *The shopkeeper bent over to scoop out toffees for his smallest customers:* dish out; lade out, ladle, lift out, shovel, spoon; empty with a scoop, bail, clear, clean. **4** *The bulldozer scooped out a deep hole:* hollow, dig out, excavate, burrow, render concave, gouge.

scope *n.* **1** *The ministry is no place for a man of limited scope:* range or extent of view, vision; application, bearing; effect, force, influence, competence, breadth of knowledge, reach, grasp; aim, purpose, goal, motive, intention, ambition, destination, determination. **2** *The scope of his property was enormous:* extent in space, area, span, stretch, spread, extension, compass, bounds, reach, confines. **3** *Give your child's creativity a wider scope:* space for movement or activity, opportunity for operation; free course, rein, latitude, margin, range, field, room, elbow-room, vent; freedom, liberty.

scorch *v. An iron that is too hot may scorch your clothes. The hot weather scorched the grass:* burn the surface of, singe, sear; shrivel with heat, wither, parch, scathe, char; dry, dehydrate; blacken, discolour.
◇ *Word origin: Scorch* comes from Old Norse *skorpna,* to dry up, shrivel.

score *n.* **1** *The score is 2-0. Who made the final score?:* record of points made, tally; (*variously*) point, goal, run, try. **2** *My score in the test was 95:* test result, mark, grade. **3** *The tree trunk had many scores in it:* notch, incision, nick, scratch, mark, groove, cut, slash, gash, slit. **4** *"Fourscore and seven years ago . . .":* (set of) twenty. **5 scores** *Scores of people attended the special performance:* large numbers, multitudes, throngs, hosts, lots, legions, droves, swarms. **6** *I have to pay off this score before spending any more money:* amount owed, amount due, account, bill, obligation, charge, debt; grievance, grudge, difference. **7** *Informal He's a naïve kid who has no idea what the score is:* facts, reality, truth, true situation. **8** *He wrote the scores for many successful musicals:* music (for a play, motion picture, etc.); written form of a musical composition.
—*v.* **9** *How many goals did he score in that football game?:* make, gain, tally, register; pile up, amass. *Informal* knock up. **10** *I found the page but the sentence had been scored out:* cross out, cancel, put a line through. **11** *No good scout would score a tree trunk with a knife:* notch, scratch, cut, groove; mar, damage, deface. **12**

Our team is sure to score a resounding victory: achieve, win, strike, register. **13** *She learned how to score a musical composition at the conservatory:* orchestrate, arrange.

◇ *Word origin: Score* comes from Old Norse *skor,* a notch, especially a tally-notch. The word also means "twenty" in Old Norse.

scorn *n.* **1** *She regarded weaker people with scorn:* contempt, scornfulness, disdain, haughtiness, arrogance; opprobrium, derision, contumely; scoffing, sarcasm, mockery, ridicule.
—*v.* **2** *He scorned those who did not follow him into battle. The union leaders continue to scorn all the management's attempts to reconciliation:* look down on, esteem lightly, be contemptuous of, despise, curl one's lip at, hold in contempt, disdain, treat with disdain, refuse to recognize, not countenance, care nothing for; spurn, refuse, rebuff, reject, repulse; ignore, disregard, refuse to deal with, have nothing to do with, refuse to listen to, turn a deaf ear to; ostracize, spit upon.

Ant. 1 affection, deference, respect, esteem. **2** esteem, revere, look up to, admire; accept.

◇ *Usage note:* See CONTEMPT.

scoundrel *n. That scoundrel would sell his own mother!:* villain, rogue, cur, snake in the grass, ruffian, blackguard, twister, knave, varlet, cad, rotter; mountebank, good-for-nothing, ne'er-do-well; thief, crook, swindler, sharper; rascal, scamp, rapscallion, scallywag; turncoat, carpet-bagger, rat.

"Every man over forty is a scoundrel."
—*George Bernard Shaw*

---

scour[1] *v. Use wire wool to scour the kitchen sink. Mother made me scour the cutlery:* clean by rubbing, scrub, scrape, wash vigorously; abrade, polish, burnish, buff; shine, brighten.

scour[2] *v. He scoured the bookshops in search of a particular volume of poetry. We scoured the countryside looking for the lost child:* search through, comb, scan, rake, ransack range over, pass over, traverse; move swiftly over, race through.

◇ *Word origin: Scour,* to search through hastily or move swiftly, comes from Old Norse *skura,* to rush, run. Our other word *scour,* to wash thoroughly, as with steel wool, comes from Latin *ex-* (out, off) + *curare* (to take care), .to take care to get something out, hence to take care to wash out or off.

scourge *n.* **1** *The cruel captain used a scourge on disobedient sailors:* whip, lash, flail, cat-o'-nine-tails, strap; switch, birch, rod, cane. **2** *Lack of rain is the scourge of certain parts of India and Africa. Genghis Khan was the scourge of Asia:* cause of plague, bane, curse, terror; affliction, vexation.
—*v.* **3** *Captain Bligh scourged his crew without mercy:* flog, whip, lash, flail, thrash, beat; punish, discipline, flagellate; cane, switch, strap, birch, give the stick. **4** *Public figures sometimes fear being scourged by the press:* criticize severely, castigate, chastise, chasten, take to task, excoriate, haul over the coals, censure, *Slang* blast.

scout *n.* **1** *The scout reported that there was trouble on the road ahead:* person sent ahead, guide, reconnoitrer, vanguard, advance guard; pilot, escort. **2** *The Rovers' centre-forward was first discovered by a talent scout:* person employed to discover new talent, recruiter.
—*v.* **3** *Just scout around to see if anyone's hiding:* search, delve, pry, peer; make reconnaissance, reconnoitre, survey, observe, put under surveillance; spy, spy out.

◇ *Word origin:* We are used to thinking of a *scout* as one who is sent out to observe and get information, as of an enemy, rival sports team, etc. However, *scout* originally meant one who gets information by listening. The word comes from Old French *escoute,* listener.

scramble *v.* **1** *We scrambled for cover from the sudden rain:* scurry, rush, race, run. **2** *The three of us scrambled for the loose ball:* scuffle, struggle, vie, fight, strive, engage, scrimmage, combat, battle, come to blows, scrap, tussle, collide, clash. **3** *A child can scramble eggs. In our code we scramble letters so that words are unrecognizable:* stir together; mix together, mix up, jumble up, garble, disarrange, shuffle, disorganize, confuse, disorder; mess up, bring into disorder, upset, throw into confusion, unsettle, disturb, scatter.
—*n.* **4** *We made a scramble for cover when it started raining:* rush, race, run. **5** *There was a scramble to recover the loose-ball:* scuffle, struggle, tussle, competition, scrimmage.

◇ *Word origin: Scramble* is probably a variant of the word *scrabble,* to strive, gather hurriedly, scrape or scratch as with the paws.

scrap[1] *n.* **1** *There wasn't a scrap of evidence to convict him. Scraps of bread were thrown to the birds:* small piece, small quantity, fragment, fraction, trace, sliver, particle; minimum, modicum, glimmer, smattering, sprinkling; bit, morsel, speck, dab, drop; atom, molecule, jot, iota, grain, crumb. **2** *The old copper pipes were sold for scrap:* discarded material, reclaimable material, unwanted metal, junk; refuse, trash.
—*v.* **3** *We decided to scrap the old car. The plan would cost too much, and must be scrapped:* put on the scrap heap, sell as scrap; discard as worthless, cancel, abandon.

Ant. 3 keep, repair, maintain.

scrap[2] *n. Informal* **1** *The bully received a black eye in the class-room scrap:* fight, brawl, row; free-for-all, mêlée, brouhaha.
—*v.* **2** *Those two will scrap at the least provocation!:* fight, quarrel, brawl, row, come to blows.

scrape *v.* **1** *I slipped and scraped an elbow;* graze, bruise, abrade, grate; scuff, skin. 2 *The hungry troops tried to scrape together some food:* collect with difficulty, dig, forage, get by hook or by crook; secure, procure, acquire, obtain, pick up, glean, gather, amass. 3 *Don't scrape your finger-nail across the blackboard!:* grate, rasp, grind, scratch. 4 *We scraped for years to buy that house:* economize, be frugal, save, scrimp, stint, pinch pennies; 5 *We just scraped through the exam by the skin of our teeth:* squeeze, pass with difficulty.

—*n.* 6 *How did you get that scrape on your arm?:* skin injury, abrasion, bruise; mark, score, gash, groove. 7 *Her violent temper often got her into scrapes:* troublesome situation, predicament, difficulty, tough spot, tight spot, dilemma, pretty pickle, plight, straits; fight, scuffle, tussle, confrontation.

scratch *v.* 1 *The car was only scratched in the accident:* make a mark on, graze, score, scrape, streak; cut, gash, lacerate; mar, blemish; damage slightly. 2 *I've always wanted a scratcher to scratch my back:* scrape, rub, dig at; claw; relieve the itching of. 3 *He scratched a match along the stone:* draw along a rough surface, rub, scrape; strike. 4 *Scratch that last paragraph. Scratch his name from the finals:* strike out, cancel, cross out, delete, draw the pen through, withdraw, eliminate, remove, rule out, blot out, expunge, exclude, omit, erase, rub out. 5 *The scout scratched a map in the sand with his stick:* draw crudely, scrawl, scribble; incise, cut, etch. 6 *Her finger-nails scratched against the blackboard:* sound harshly, scrape, grate, rasp, grind.

—*n.* 7 *How did you get that scratch on your nose?:* slight flesh wound, laceration, abrasion, cut, gash.

scrawny *adj. That hulking great man was once a scrawny boy:* extremely thin, spindly, skinny, spare, lean, sinewy, lank, lanky; bony, gaunt, raw-boned; scraggy; puny, undersized, stunted; fleshless, skeletal, emaciated, drawn, wasted, attenuated.

Ant. fat, plump, chubby, brawny, muscular.

scream *v.* 1 *She screamed when she saw the dead body:* shriek, howl, cry out, wail; screech, squawk, yowl, yelp, squeal, bellow, roar, 2 *We screamed for help:* shout, yell, call out loudly, cry out, bawl.

—*n.* 3 *We heard screams in the night. During the war you got used to the scream of sirens:* loud, shrill cry, shriek, outcry, shout, yell; screech, squeal, whine, wail, yelp, squawk; bellow, roar; lamentation.

screen *n.* 1 *She changed clothes behind a screen:* partition, room-divider, curtain, lattice. 2 *The fog acted as a screen for the smugglers:* concealment, protection, cover, coverage, veil, mask, curtain, shroud, cloak, mantle; buffer, safeguard, defence. 3 *Sir Laurence Olivier is a star of stage and screen:* motion pictures, films, cinema, the silver screen, movies; the film industry. 4 *Slowly the vital information came up on the screen:* monitor, television screen, receiver.

—*v.* 5 *Sun-glasses will screen your eyes from the harmful rays:* shield, shelter, protect, defend, secure, safeguard, guard; cover, shroud, shade, veil; keep hidden, conceal, hide from sight; withhold, secrete, keep secret. 6 *The Personnel Department is here to screen applicants:* examine for suitability, evaluate, vet, rate, grade; eliminate, get rid of, throw away, discard, throw out, eject, weed out; separate, sift, cull, filter, strain; sort, arrange, order, group, class. 7 *The film will be screened at 9 o'clock tonight:* project, show, present; see, view, preview.

screw *n.* 1 *Use these screws to put the table together:* fastener, threaded nail, bolt. 2 *The ship's screws stopped and it drifted helplessly:* propeller; driver.

—*v.* 3 *Screw this coat hook on to the door. Screw the vice tighter:* fasten, bolt, rivet, attach, join, clamp; adjust, tighten; twist, turn. 4 *She screwed up her eyes in an attempt to see the shooting star:* twist, twist out of shape, contort, distort, pervert, warp; deform, misshape, garble; knot. 5 *The troopers screwed the information out of him somehow:* wring, wrench, wrest, force, exact, extort, twist, squeeze.

◇ *Word origin: Screw* comes from Old French *escroue*, literally a female screw or the threaded nut to be fitted on a bolt or screw.

scrimp *v. We scrimped for years until the house was finally paid for:* be sparing, skimp, be frugal, be parsimonious, be stingy, pinch, stint, save, be penurious, pinch pennies, cut corners, economize; dole out sparingly, use sparingly.

script *n.* 1 *She has a neat, precise script:* handwriting, hand, cursive; penmanship, calligraphy. 2 *The script was delivered to the director ahead of schedule. Several changes were made in the script:* manuscript, written text; dialogue, lines, book, scenario, libretto, score.

Scripture, Holy Scripture *n.* Often **the Scriptures, the Holy Scriptures** *The text for the sermon was a couple of verses from Scripture:* sacred writings, Holy Writ, inspired writings; the Bible, the Word of God, the Gospels, Old Testament, New Testament, *Informal* The Good Book; *Judaism* the Hebrew Scriptures, (*variously*) the Torah, the Law, the Pentateuch, the Septuagint.

scrub[1] *v.* 1 *Scrub your back with this long-handled brush:* rub clean, scour.

—*n.* 2 *She gave the floors a good scrub:* scrubbing, scouring; cleaning by rubbing.

scrub[2] *n. The land was cleared of scrub and dead wood:* low trees, bush, brushwood, stunted vegetation.

scrumptious *adj. Informal That was a scrumptious roast!:* delightful, delicious, flavourful, tasty, delectable, flavoursome, savoury, ap-

petizing, mouth-watering, luscious, juicy, succulent, tender; agreeable, enjoyable, pleasant, pleasing.
◇ *Word origin: Scrumptious* is probably just a humorous variant of *sumptuous.*

scruple *n.* **1** *He's a greedy person with no scruples when it comes to making a profit:* principle, ethics, moral restraint, compunction, misgiving; conscience, conscientiousness, scrupulousness, concern, care; qualm, anxiety, hesitation, uncertainty, apprehension, doubtfulness, protestation; squeamishness. —*v.* **2** *She scrupled when it came to disobeying her father:* be ethical, have principles, hesitate, refrain, demur, pause, hang back, blench, balk, halt; waver, fluctuate, falter; have a qualm, feel qualms, be qualmish, have a bad conscience, be timorous, shy, fight shy, take exception.
◇ *Word origin: Scruple* and *scrupulous* come from Latin *scrupulus,* a small sharp stone, hence a small sharp pang of conscience, gnawing doubt or uncertainty. The Roman statesman, man of letters, and orator Cicero, 106-43 BC, was the first to use this word in the modern figurative sense of a gnawing uneasiness or anxiety.

scrupulous *adj. He's a sharp but fairly scrupulous businessman. The scientist described his observations with scrupulous accuracy:* having scruples, principled, honest, conscientious, honourable, upright; painstaking, sedulous, deliberate, careful, cautious; exact, exacting, precise, meticulous, fastidious, punctilious; dutiful.
Ant. unscrupulous, dishonest, unprincipled; careless, reckless, inexact.

scrutinize *v. The building inspector scrutinized the structure's foundation:* examine closely, study, look at closely, peruse, regard carefully, *Slang* give the once-over; inspect carefully, survey, look over, take stock of; inquire into, investigate, pry into, peer into; search, explore, probe.
Ant. neglect, disregard, overlook; glance at.

scrutiny *n. His testimony was given close scrutiny:* examination, attention, study, investigation, inspection, perusal, close look, critical regard, watch, surveillance.

scuffle *v.* **1** *The boys scuffled in the school corridor:* struggle, fight, scrap, tussle, spar, jostle; come to blows, exchange blows, clash. —*n.* **2** *The scuffle in the playground was soon over:* struggle, scrap, tussle, row, fight, brawl, imbroglio; mêlée, Donnybrook, free-for-all, fracas; rumpus, commotion.
◇ *Word origin: Scuffle,* like *scuff,* comes from Old Norse *skūfa,* to shove.

scum *n.* **1** *Don't use the pool until the scum is cleared off:* surface, film, dross, deposit, slag, refuse. **2** *According to the eyewitness the demonstrators were the scum of society:* lowest of the low, trash, rubbish, dregs.

scurrilous *adj. W. C. Fields was celebrated for his scurrilous remarks. The old fellow was scurrilous but good-natured:* slanderous, derogatory, disparaging, detracting, derisive, reviling, contemptuous, insulting; coarsely abusive, coarse, gross, low, churlish, shameless, indecent, indelicate; vulgar, foul-mouthed.
Ant. decent, proper, delicate, refined, well-bred, polite.
◇ *Word origin: Scurrilous* comes from Latin *scurra,* "city slicker," gallant, dandy, elegant, debauchee. This word also means "parasite" or "droll" in the suite of wealthy persons. The word is also used of various kinds of buffoons, jesters, and clowns.

scurry *v.* **1** *The bathers scurried across the hot sand towards the water:* move quickly, run with light steps, scamper, scramble, scuttle, make tracks, rush, speed, hasten, hurry, hie, hustle, scoot, spring, skim, race, tear along. —*n.* **2** *We lifted the rock and watched a scurry of insects:* scamper, hasty running; rushing, hurrying, scooting; dispersal, scattering; haste, bustle, confusion.

scurvy *adj. The crew were a scurvy bunch of cut-throats:* mean, low, base, vile; contemptible, dishonourable, ignoble, worthless.
Ant. honourable, dignified, noble.

scuttle *v.* **1** *The captain scuttled his ship rather than see it captured by the enemy:* sink, send to the bottom, send to Davy Jones's locker; sacrifice, abort, discard, dispatch, scrap. **2** *The crab scuttled across the sea-bed:* scurry, hurry, hasten, scamper, speed, scramble.

sea *n.* **1** *My dream is to sail the seven seas in a schooner. Many Muscovites spend their holidays at resorts on the Black Sea. The small boat struggled in a turbulent sea:* ocean, deep, main, waves, waters, the briny deep; large body of water, bay, gulf, bight, lake. **2** *The business manager was deluged with a sea of complaints:* great deal, great quantity, multitude, flood, spate, ton, leap, heap, pile, welter, lots, mass, legion, host, swarm, flock, scores, abundance, profusion.
Ant. 1 land, terrain, terra firma.

seal *n.* **1** *The document bore the king's seal:* figure, emblem, mark, symbol, distinctive design, insignia, stamp, impression, imprint, brand; signet, imprimatur hallmark, colophon, trade mark. **2** *The envelope's seal was torn open:* fastening device, fastener; gummed flap. —*v.* **3** *You must seal the document with the king's insignia:* affix seal to, close with a seal; certify, authenticate, confirm, verify, ratify, validate, endorse; affirm, approve, sanction, accept, O.K. **4** *We sealed our agreement with a handshake:* settle, conclude, make final; fix, establish, determine. **5** *The jars were sealed with cellophane:* close, secure, fasten; shut, shut up, lock; plug, stop, stop up, cork, dam.
◇ *Word origin:* A *seal* was originally a device for reproducing the impression of a person's

crest or symbol on melted wax, used to close a letter or document. This seal proved the document's authenticity, whilst the unbroken wax proved that no one else had opened and read the recipient's private message. The word comes from Latin *sigillum*, small picture. (The word is a diminutive of *signum*, sign.)

seam *n.* **1** *Sew the split seams of the shirt:* line of stitches, juncture, joining, junction, joint, suture; interface. **2** *Seams appeared on the dried-up river-bed:* wrinkle, incised line, furrow, scar; fissure, chink, crevice, break, breach, rupture, opening, crack, cleft, gap. **3** *The prospectors found a seam of coal:* layer, stratum, vein, lode.

—*v.* **4** *Seam those two pieces and your skirt is finished:* join together in a seam, stitch together; suture. **5** *Worry had seamed his forehead:* furrow, wrinkle, mark, line, cut into, incise, notch.

seamy *adj. Policemen often see the seamy side of life:* unpleasant, nasty, disagreeable, coarse, sordid, rough, raw, dirty, dark, squalid.

Ant. pleasant, nice, agreeable; gentle, tender.

◇ *Word origin: Seamy* literally means full of seams, as the wrong side of a garment, hence its metaphorical application to the wrong side of things, the aspects of life we should prefer not to see.

sear *v.* **1** *The flames seared her arms when she tried to put out the fire:* burn, scorch, char, singe; cauterize. **2** *The bitter experience of betrayal seared his soul for ever after:* harden, scar, case-harden, steel.

search *v.* **1** *We carefully searched the attic for the old family album. The campers searched for a good place to pitch their tent. Police searched everyone present at the scene of the crime:* examine, scrutinize, explore, scour, scout out, investigate carefully, look over, inspect, overhaul, study, survey, check, probe, sift, comb, drag, look into, pry into, delve into, pore over, ransack, rummage, turn inside out, turn upside down, leave no stone unturned snoop, fish; hunt, look, cast about, seek, quest, frisk.

—*n.* **2** *After a lengthy search we found the earliest patent for an electric blender. A search of the cottage produced several unlicensed guns:* examination, inspection, scrutiny, study, close look, check, investigation, probe, inquiry, exploration; hunt, pursuit, quest; drag-net; tracer.

◇ *Word origin: Search* comes from Latin *circare*, to go round, explore, whose base is Latin *circus*, ring, circle.

season *n.* **1** *Spring and autumn are my favourite seasons. Peaches are out of season now. The young people have so much fun during the holiday season:* division of the year, (*variously*) spring, summer, the dog days, autumn, Indian summer, winter, quarter; appropriate time, peak time, prime; period, term, stage, spell, interval, duration.

—*v.* **2** *She seasoned the stew with sage. His new play was seasoned with wit and humour:* flavour, spice, leaven, lace; enliven, heighten, colour, accent, enhance, embellish, ornament. **3** *The actor was seasoned by years of performing:* improve by experience, train, practise, discipline, drill; break in, tame; refine, mellow, temper; accustom, inure, adapt; inform, shape, finish. **4** *The carpenter taught us how to season wood:* age, dry, ripen, temper, mature, prime, cultivate, condition, prepare.

◇ *Usage note: Seasonal* means occurring at or affected by a certain season: *The bird-watchers observed the seasonal migration of geese. Fruit-picking is seasonal work: Seasonable* means in keeping with the season: *Hot weather is seasonable for August. I love the seasonable good cheer of Christmas.*

seasoning *n.* **1** *This stew needs more seasoning:* flavouring, spice, condiment, relish, herb; (*variously*) salt, pepper, allspice, basil, thyme, oregano, rosemary, mace, sage, marjoram, clove, parsley, dill, paprika, garlic, onion, cinnamon, nutmeg, ginger. **2** *We must allow the youngsters a couple of years' seasoning in the second eleven:* training, practice, preparation, orientation, familiarization; ripening, maturation; ageing; drying.

seat *n.* **1** *Won't you come in and have a seat? I forgot to reserve seats at the opera:* (*variously*) chair, sofa, couch, divan, bench, cushion, place, box. **2** *The naughty child received several slaps on his seat:* buttocks, rear end, hindquarters, bottom, haunches, rump, posterior, croup, *French* derrière; *Informal* backside, behind. **3** *Hollywood is the seat of the film industry. London is the seat of government:* centre, hub, axis, nucleus; heart, core; capital. **4** *The castle was the seat of a noble family. The heart is regarded as the seat of the emotions:* residence, home, house, dwelling, abode, domicile, housing, address, quarters; site, locale, location, habitat; family seat, ancestral hall. **5** *He lost his seat in Parliament:* place in a select group, membership; incumbency.

—*v.* **6** *Please seat young Charles on your lap:* place on a seat; settle, situate, provide with a seat; cause to sit, show to a seat.

◇ *Word origin: Seat* comes from old Norse *sæti* seat (residence), and is closely akin to the word *sit*.

secede *v. I do not wish to incite groups to secede from the Established Church:* withdraw, leave, pull out, quit, retire, resign, have done, disaffiliate, apostacize.

Ant. join, federate.

◇ *Spelling tip: Cede* means to yield or transfer. *Secede* means to yield or transfer away, to withdraw from a union or group. Thus *secede* ends in *cede, seCEDE.*

seclude *v. The old hermit secluded himself to escape the outside world:* place apart, keep apart, separate, dissociate, place in solitude, shut off, isolate, sequester, retire, retire from sight, hide, go into retreat.

secluded *adj. The naturalist built himself a secluded hut in the forest. The ascetic led a secluded life:* isolated, sheltered, sequestered, cloistered; unvisited, seldom visited, unfrequented, remote, out-of-the-way, solitary, lonely, withdrawn, reclusive; shut in, confined; hidden from view, covert, shut away, private, screened off.

Ant. accessible, frequented; sociable; public, open.

seclusion *n. The millionaire went into seclusion to avoid interviewers. The mountain chalet presented ideal seclusion for quiet holidays:* isolation, solitude, hiding, concealment, retreat, reclusion, withdrawal, sequestration, cloister, retirement.

second[1] *adj.* **1** *He was second in line. She was second in her class:* next after the first; runner-up. **2** *They had a second house on the coast:* another, one more, additional. **3** *Every second person was chosen:* alternate, alternating, other. **4** *The film was a second feature in the programme:* inferior, subordinate, second-rate, second fiddle, surpassed, exceeded, out-done.

—*n.* **5** *He was the second to be chosen:* second one; runner-up. **6** *My second will call on you to arrange the duel:* helper, assistant, aid, attendant, lieutenant; agent, representative, deputy, delegate; substitute, alternate, stand-in, understudy, proxy.

—*v.* **7** *I second the nomination!:* support, endorse; back, stand by, back up, uphold; side with, subscribe to, favour, work for, advocate; promote, encourage, further, advance; help, assist, aid, abet.

◇ *Word origin: Second* comes from Latin *secundus,* following, which is closely akin to Latin *sequi,* to follow, which also gives us *sequence* and *sequel.* The unit of time, a *second,* equal to one-sixtieth of a minute, comes from the Latin way of reckoning time by *prima minuta* and *secunda minuta,* meaning the first minute or division of time (a minute) and the second minute or division of time (a second).

second[2] *n.* **1** *He ran the race in 45 seconds:* one-sixtieth of a minute. **2** *I'll be there in a second!:* moment, mo, minute, instant, jiffy, trice, flash; *Informal* bat of an eye, twinkling, shake, shake of a lamb's tail.

secondary *adj. Pat's at secondary school, but I'm still at my primary:* next after the first, second; following, subsequent, consequent, resultant. **2** *That problem is secondary to the one now facing us:* lesser, inferior, smaller, minor, lower; subordinate, ancillary; mediocre, second-rate, middling, second-best, second-string, second fiddle. **3** *"Moonlighting" means having an extra job as a secondary source of income:* other, alternate; subsidiary, auxiliary; not primary, not original; back-up.

Ant. **1-3** primary, first. **1** preceding. **2** superior, larger, bigger, major. **3** sole; original.

secrecy *n. The plotters were sworn to secrecy. She confessed under the seal of secrecy:* secretiveness, silence, uncommunicativeness, muteness, confidentiality, closeness; covertness, clandestineness, mystery, stealth, furtiveness, underhandedness, surreptitiousness, dark dealing; private, solitude, concealment, privacy, hiding, sequestration, seclusion.

secret *adj.* **1** *The president was elected by a secret ballot. A secret room was discovered behind the bookcase. The patent medicine is based on a secret formula:* private, confidential, unrevealable, unrevealed, undisclosed, unpublished, hush-hush; hidden, concealed, unseen, invisible, camouflaged, secluded; undercover, disguised; covert, clandestine, surreptitious; unknown, mysterious, mystic, dark, esoteric, arcane, occult. **2** *He's a devious, secret person and I don't trust him:* keeping knowledge to oneself, secretive, close-mouthed, tight-lipped, mum, discreet; mysterious; furtive, stealthy, hugger-mugger.

—*n.* **3** *Can you keep a secret?:* confidential information, confidential matter, confidence. **4** *Captain Cousteau lectured on the secrets of the deep:* mystery, enigma, puzzle. **5** *What's your secret for looking so young?:* formula, key, recipe, unguessed-at reason, special method.

Ant. **1, 2** open. **1** public, revealed, disclosed; obvious, evident, apparent, undisguised well-known, ordinary. **2** candid, frank, straightforward.

secrete *v. The escaped convicts secreted themselves in a cave until the police had driven past:* hide, conceal, cache, *Informal* stash; cloak, curtain, screen, veil, disguise; keep secret.

Ant. reveal, show, display, exhibit.

secretive *adj. She was secretive about where she'd been last night:* unrevealing, uncommunicative, tight-lipped, close-mouthed, silent, mum, mute; reserved, discreet, reticent, taciturn, sparing of words; sly, stealthy, furtive, evasive, surreptitious, underhand, covert, mysterious, cryptic, enigmatic.

Ant. open, communicative, talkative; candid, frank, plain, straightforward, direct.

sect *n. The Mennonite sect was founded during the 16th century:* religious subgroup, denomination, persuasion, school of thought, affiliation, religious creed, religious order, cult; division, faction.

section *n.* **1** *Do you separate your grapefruit sections with a knife? The class is divided into three sections:* part, division, piece, segment, portion; share, instalment, allotment, measure, proportion; chapter, passage. **2** *The smoking section of this theatre is to the right of the aisle. The residential section of the city is spacious and airy:* district, area, side, vicinity, province, sphere, region; sector, department; zone, ward; territory, range, terrain. **3** *A section of tissue was sent to the lab for microscopic examination:* slice, cross-section, cutting; specimen, sample.

> **Exploring the Word**: *Section, segment,* and *sector* come from Latin *secare,* to cut. They all literally mean a cutting or a piece cut off. The same Latin verb also gives us *bisect* (Latin *bi-*, two), to cut in two; *dissect* (Latin *dis-*, apart), to cut apart; *intersect* (Latin *inter,* between), to cut between, cut across, and *intersection,* the crossing of two streets; and *vivisection* (Latin *vivus,* alive), the dissection of live animals for purposes of medical research.

sector *n. Which sector of the economy has been hardest hit by the recession? After World War II, Berlin was divided into four sectors:* administrative division, zone, district; theatre, area, sphere of action.

secure *adj.* **1** *She felt secure only when both doors were locked. The child doesn't feel secure in his new school:* free from danger, free from harm, safe, unthreatened, invulnerable, protected, defended, sheltered, out of danger; carefree, reassured, easy, at ease, composed, self-possessed, confident. **2** *The citadel was secure:* unattackable, unassailable, impregnable. **3** *His shackles were secure:* firmly fastened; set, fixed, tight. **4** *Your future with the company is secure:* sure, certain, assured, guaranteed, definite, positive, absolute; *Slang* in the bag. —*v.* **5** *First he secured a good site for his new business:* obtain, procure, acquire, get, get hold of, get possession of. **6** *They say that our missiles and bombers secure us from attack:* free from harm, make safe, safeguard, defend, protect, shelter, ensure. **7** *The bank required collateral to secure the loan agreement:* ensure, guarantee. **8** *The boat was secured to the dock:* make fast, fix firmly, fasten, lash tight, batten down, tie down, bind.

Ant. 1–4 insecure. **1** unsafe, endangered, threatened, in danger; unsure, uneasy, anxious. **2** weak, vulnerable. **3** loose, unfixed. **4** unsure, uncertain, unassured, indefinite; unsettled, undetermined; precarious. **5** lose, give up. **6** endanger, imperil, harm, leave unprotected. **8** loose, unloose, untie.

◇ *Word origin: Secure* comes from Latin *se-* (apart, without) + *cura* (care). Latin *cura,* care, also gives us *accurate* (done with great care), *care,* and *cure.*

security *n.* **1** *My family's health and security are of the utmost importance to me:* freedom from danger, freedom from harm, protection, safety, safe keeping; preservation, maintenance, support, care, keep. **2** *The airport's system of security requires that every passenger be searched:* defence, safeguards, safety measures, protective devices; police, guards, troops. **3** *The hostages were used by the robbers as security for escape:* assurance, guarantee, surety, pledge, bond, warranty; collateral; deposit. **4** *You can look forward to your future in the company with security:* secureness, assurance, confidence, certainty, positiveness, sureness, absoluteness, definiteness, decisiveness; trust, peace of mind, reliance, promise, hope, faith, conviction. **5** Usually **securities** *Your negotiable securities should be locked up:* stocks, bonds, certificates of title to property.

sedate *adj. The governess was a middle-aged, sedate woman. We spent a sedate evening at home:* calm, composed, unruffled, collected, level-headed, self-possessed, self-controlled, cool, cool-headed, imperturbable, impassive, undemonstrative, unexcited serious, steady, solemn, sober, grave; poised, dignified, decorous, reserved, staid; tranquil, subdued, quiet, still.

Ant. nervous, perturbed, disturbed, impassioned, agitated, excited, noisy, active, restless, unsteady; flighty, frivolous, gay.

sedative *adj.* **1** *Phenobarbitone is prescribed for its sedative effects:* soothing, calming, comforting, easing, tranquillizing, soporific, composing; palliative, calmative, allaying, alleviative, assuasive, lenitive; anodyne, analgesic. —*n.* **2** *The doctor gave the distraught woman a sedative:* tranquillizer, calmative; analgesic, anodyne, palliative, alleviative, mitigator, lenitive, assuasive; narcotic, opiate.

sedentary *adj. You may find that being a telephone operator is too sedentary a job:* sitting, seated, inactive, unmoving, unstirring, inert, fixed, stationary; quiescent, resting, still.

"Henry has always led what could be called a sedentary life, if only he'd even got as far as actually sitting up." —*Henry Reed*

---

sediment *n. Sediment remained at the bottom of the coffee-pot. After the flood the streets were covered with sediment:* settlings, grounds; dregs, leavings, remains, residue; dross, scum; debris, waste, slag.

seduce *v.* **1** *The vile man tried to seduce the young girl:* persuade to do wrong, lure, entice, lead astray; corrupt, defile, debauch, deflower, violate, ravish; deprave, pervert, disgrace, dishonour; abuse, ruin. **2** *The homeless dog seduced us into adopting it. The audience was seduced by the star's radiance:* attract, turn one's head, win over, conquer, persuade, overcome the resistance to, entice, charm, tempt, lure, allure, captivate.

Ant. 1 persuade to do right; save, protect; honour. **2** repel, repulse; disgust; dissuade.

seductive *adj. The starlet always wore a seductive dress:* alluring, enticing, sexy, provocative, voluptuous, come-hither; attractive, charming, disarming, enchanting, bewitching.

Ant. repulsive, repellent; drab, staid, prim.

see *v.* **1** *Can you see what that sign says? Did anyone* *see the accident? What you see is what you get!:* make out, discern, distinguish, recognize; behold, observe, witness; hold in view, have in sight, notice, look at, regard, spot, catch sight of, sight, glimpse, spy, espy, descry; view, survey, contemplate, take in; eye, set one's eyes on, stare at, gaze at; *Slang* get a load of. **2** *Now do you see why I did it?:* perceive, understand, comprehend, apprehend, appreciate, grasp, take in, fathom, get the drift; know, be cognizant of, realize, be aware of, be conscious of. **3** *I can't see you as a mother:* visualize, envisage, picture, conceive, make out; regard, consider. **4** *Let me see what I can do:* find out, ascertain, determine; consider, meditate, contemplate, ruminate, give thought to. **5** *The soldiers saw action in Malta:* undergo, experience, go through. **6** *See that you arrive on time!:* make sure, take care, make certain, see to it, watch, mind, observe. **7** *Please come to see us again soon. I can see the applicants tomorrow:* call on, visit; meet, encounter, run into; speak to, consult, confer with; receive, attend to, entertain, listen to, interview. **8** *How long have you two been seeing each other?:* court, woo; keep company with. **9** *John always sees me to the door:* escort, accompany, attend, walk.

Ant. 1 neglect, overlook, disregard, ignore. **2** misunderstand, mistake, be unaware of.

◇ *Usage note:* The basic forms of the verb *to see* are *see* (present), *saw* (past), *seen* (past participle): *He sees it today. He saw it yesterday. He has seen it before.* The past participle *seen* must always be used with *have, has, was,* or *were;* thus *I have seen it* — not "I seen it." *He has seen it* — not "He seen it."

seed *n.* **1** *The child planted marigold seeds in the window-box:* grain, pit, stone, ovule; seedling. **2** *A good teacher can plant the seeds of knowledge in her students:* source, origin, basis, germ, embryo, beginning. **3** *I will make thy seed as the dust of the earth:* descendants, progeny, issue, offspring, children; heirs, posterity.

—*v.* **4** *I'm seeding some of my land with grass:* sow with seed, plant. **5** *Seed the raisins before you put them in the cake:* remove the seeds from; pit.

seek *v.* **1** *The police are seeking information as to the whereabouts of the robbers:* try to find, search for, look for, track down, look into, dig for, probe for, investigate, explore, examine, scrutinize, inspect; nose out, ferret out, pursue, be after, hunt, fish for, sniff out, trace. **2** *Dick Whittington set out to seek his fortune. His lawyers are seeking a new trial:* try to obtain, strive for, aim for, aspire to, pursue; be after, go in for; request, inquire for, petition for, demand, call for; solicit, court, invite. **3** *We sought to change her mind, but she resisted our arguments:* try, attempt, endeavour, essay, set about, go about, try one's hand at, undertake, venture, *Informal* have a go at, have a bash at.

Ant. 1 neglect, ignore, abandon; avoid, shun; discard, relinquish, drop.

seem *v. He seems happy enough with his new job:* appear, look, give the impression of being, have the semblance of, look like, look as if, strike one as being.

seeming *adj. Her seeming indifference was only an act:* ostensible, apparent, evident, obvious; presumed, supposed, putative.

seemly *adj. Young people should address their elders in a more seemly manner:* suitable, proper, appropriate, in good taste, fitting, becoming, befitting, due, acceptable, correct, prudent, polite, courteous, decorous, right, decent, tasteful, refined; *French* comme il faut.

Ant. unseemly, unbecoming, improper, rude, impolite, impertinent, pert, forward.

seep *v. Rain seeped through the cracks in the roof:* leak, ooze, trickle, dribble, drip; suffuse, diffuse, penetrate, permeate, soak.

Ant. gush, flow, flood.

seethe *v.* **1** *The water in the hot springs was seething:* boil, bubble, churn, roil; simmer, stew, brew, cook. **2** *He seethed with anger because the train left him stranded on the platform:* be greatly excited, be agitated, be upset, be irate, be livid, be angry, be indignant, rage, rant, rave, boil, storm, breathe fire, fume, smoulder; carry on, foam at the mouth, bluster, raise a rumpus, stamp one's foot, throw a tantrum, raise Cain; *Slang* blow up, blow one's top, be in a tizzy.

segment *n.* **1** *She peeled the orange and offered me a segment:* part, piece, section, division, portion; instalment, increment; stage, leg.

—*v.* **2** *That rod has been segmented for easy storage:* divide into parts, section, cut up, split up; cleave, separate, disjoin, disunite.

Ant. 1 whole, entity, entirety. **2** combine, fuse; join, unite.

segregate *v. The librarian segregates very large books and puts them on separate shelves. School changing-room facilities segregate girls from boys:* separate, isolate, detach, divide, divorce, disunite, disconnect; keep apart, set apart, set aside, single out, sort out; seclude, insulate, quarantine.

Ant. unite, blend, mix, desegregate, integrate.

◇ *Word origin: Segregate* comes from Latin *se-* (apart) + *grex* (flock), apart from the flock, isolated.

seize *v.* **1** *He seized his gun and ran out to investigate. The military junta seized power:* take hold of, take possession of, grab, snatch, pluck, grasp, clutch, embrace, lay hands upon; acquire forcibly, take possession of by force; usurp, arrogate, commandeer; confiscate, impound, appropriate. **2** *She was quick to seize the meaning of his words:* grasp, comprehend, apprehend, understand, read, catch, gather, take in, glean. **3** *Uncontrollable laughter seized us:* overwhelm, overpower; possess. **4** *The* *escaped convict was seized outside the city:* capture, arrest, apprehend, take into custody, take captive; catch, nab, *Informal* bag, collar. **5** *Seize every opportunity you can if you want to succeed:* take advantage of, make use of, utilize, profit from, act upon.

Ant. 1, 4 let go of, release; relinquish, give up; free, liberate, let go, loose. **5** waste, let pass, pass by.

seizure *n.* **1** *The seizure of the explosives ended a three-month police search:* act of seizing, taking, grasping; capture, apprehension, arrest; snatching, usurpation; possession, appropriation, confiscation; commandeering, impressment; abduction, kidnapping. **2** *After his seizure, he needed round-the-clock care:* attack, convulsion, fit, stroke, visitation, paroxysm; onset, access, spell, episode, crisis.

seldom *adv. I seldom get a chance to read:* rarely, not often, not frequently, infrequently; hardly ever, now and then, occasionally, once in a while.

Ant. often, frequently, always.

select *v.* **1** *One must select one's golf clubs with consummate care. The decorator selected a delicate print for the wallpaper:* choose, pick, pick out, make one's choice, decide for, elect, single out, opt for, prefer; fix upon, settle upon, put aside, lay aside; *Informal* give the nod to. —*adj.* **2** *Only a select few were invited to the party:* choice, picked, privileged, chosen. **3** *We only stay at select hotels:* superior, first-rate, first-class, élite; choice, preferred; exclusive, *Informal* top-notch, four-star, A1, posh, fancy.

Ant. 1 reject, refuse, repudiate, spurn. **2** indiscriminate; random. **3** inferior, second-rate; modest, ordinary, unremarkable, undistinguished.

selection *n.* **1** *I made my selection, and the assistant charged it to my account:* choice, choosing, preference, pick, decision, election, option. **2** *There's very little selection of winter clothes in the spring:* variety, choice, range, option. **3** *The band played a selection of popular tunes:* selected number, collection, programme; medley, miscellany, potpourri.

selective *adj. Learn to be a selective customer:* choosy, choosing, carefully, discriminating, particular, fastidious, finicky, meticulous; cautious, careful.

Ant. unselective, promiscuous, careless, indiscriminate.

self-assured *adj. He was self-assured and bound to succeed:* confident, self-confident, assured, cocky, cocksure, brash.

Ant. self-doubting, insecure, unconfident.

self-centred *adj. A self-centred person isn't concerned with the needs of others:* selfish, self-seeking, self-absorbed, full of oneself, vain, self-concerned, wrapped up in oneself, self-important; egotistic, egoistic, egocentric, conceited, big-headed, narcissistic.

self-confidence *n. Repeated failure in school was harming the boy's self-confidence:* self-assurance, self-reliance, positive self-image, resolution, mettle, pluck, spirit, nerve; cocksureness, boldness, cockiness, gameness.

self-control *n. Counting to ten helps one to maintain self-control when one is extremely angry:* self-discipline, will-power, self-possession, composure, self-restraint, mental balance, level-headedness, presence of mind, soberness, firmness, soundness, stability, cool-headedness, sobriety, poise, savoir-faire, aplomb, unexcitability, imperturbability, sang-froid; patience, temperance, forbearance.

selfish *adj. You must learn to share and not be so selfish:* self-seeking, self-concerned, self-centred, egocentric, egotistic; greedy, rapacious, avaricious, covetous, venal, mercenary, grasping; uncharitable, ungenerous, illiberal, grudging, stingy, parsimonious, miserly, mean.

Ant. unselfish, selfless, considerate; generous, large-hearted, magnanimous, giving; altruistic.

self-reliant *adj. After her husband died, Mrs. Jones had to learn to be self-reliant:* independent, assured, self-confident, self-possessed, enterprising, spirited, plucky, mettlesome; resolute, hardy.

self-righteous *adj. Don't give me any of your self-righteous lectures!:* sanctimonious, righteous in one's own regard, smug, pharisaical, hypocritical, insincere, mealy-mouthed; pompous, pious, moralizing, pretentious, holier-than-thou.

self-satisfaction *n. We all feel self-satisfaction after a job well done:* satisfaction with one's accomplishments, pride, self-pleasure, self-content, complacency, self-approval, self-admiration; vanity; flush of success.

sell *v.* **1** *We sold the house for £15,000:* give up for a price, exchange for money; dispose of, dispense. **2** *He sells vacuum cleaners:* deal in, trade in, handle; offer for sale, put up for sale, put on sale, effect the sale of; vend, market, barter, peddle, hawk, traffic in. **3** *The toy manufacturer was sold on our new plastic material:* win the acceptance of, win over, persuade to buy, persuade to accept, convince, prevail upon, enlist. **4** *He sold his country for a promise of power:* betray, sell out, deliver up, take a bribe for, play false, deceive.

"Every one lives by selling something."
—*Robert Louis Stevenson*

---

semblance *n.* **1** *Her semblance of indifference was only an act. Let's try to maintain some semblance of order:* outward appearance, aspect, likeness, look, show, air, mien, bearing; unreal appearance, pretence, simulacrum. **2** *Zeus appeared to Europa in the semblance of a bull:* guise, appearance, image, representation, copy, duplicate, replica, reproduction, facsimile, cast, counterpart, likeness.

seminal *adj. The ideal of social equality was one of the seminal ideas of the French Revolution:* originating, original, primary, germinal, germinative; generative; creative, productive.

send *v.* **1** *Send this package by special delivery:* cause to go, have transported, have transmitted, dispatch, relay, forward, convey. **2** *The ship sent out a message for help:* transmit, project, broadcast, disseminate; give off, emit. **3** *We sent the man to the right address:* direct, refer, point the way to, indicate the route to, guide, show, lead, head, conduct. **4** *The mortars sent shells across the enemy lines:* propel, throw, deliver, shoot, hurl, cast, discharge, drive, emit, launch, fling, toss.

Ant. 1 hold, keep, retain; receive. **2** receive, get.

> **Exploring the Word**: Many of our words dealing with old age are based on Latin *senex*, old man; thus *senescent* means growing old, *senile* refers to the physical and mental weakness of old age, and *senior* means older. The predominantly American terms *senate* and *senator* have the same root — a *senato* is literally a respected *elder*. This same Latin base gives us several titles of respect to old men (or to any respected or dignified man), including *sir* and *sire* (and Spanish *señor*, Italian *signore*, and French *monsieur* and *Monseigneur* from *mon*, "my," hence literally "my sir" or "my lord," with *Monseigneur* being applied to the ecclesiastical hierarchy (bishops, cardinals, etc.). Our word *surly* was originally *sirly*, "sirlike," i.e. assuming lordly airs.

senile *adj. Though he was well past 80, he was by no means senile:* doddering, superannuated, doting, foolish, senescent, infirm, decrepit.
◇ *Pronunciation tip: Senile* should always be stressed on the first syllable: *SEE-nile.*

senior *adj.* **1** Often **Senior** *Mr. Jones, Junior, is the image of Mr. Jones, Senior:* older, elder, *French* père. **2** *Mr. Gray is a senior officer in this bank:* superior, higher in rank; above, over. **3** *It is my pleasure to introduce one of our most respected senior statesmen. Senior citizens may have concessionary bus tickets:* of long tenure, doyen; veteran; elderly, of pensionable age.
—*n.* **4** *My sister is the senior of the two of us:* one who is older, elder. **5** *The three vice-presidents are my seniors:* person of higher rank, superior, better.

Ant. 1–5 junior. **1** younger. **2** subordinate, inferior. **5** subordinate, inferior.

seniority *n. The Registrar became committee chairman by virtue of his seniority:* precedence, longer service, tenure, longevity; superiority in rank; greater age.

sensation *n.* **1** *After the accident he had no sensation in his left thumb:* perception, feeling, sensitivity, sensibility, perceptivity; consciousness, awareness, detection. **2** *I have a dizzy sensation:* impression, sense, perception, feeling. **3** *The moon landing in 1969 caused a world-wide sensation:* public excitement, uproar, stir, commotion, to-do, thrill, agitation; cause of excitement, thrilling event; hit; scandal.

sensational *adj.* **1** *The acrobat performed a sensational feat of daring:* outstanding, striking, spectacular, extraordinary, exceptional; exciting, thrilling, electrical, galvanic; dramatic; excellent, superb. **2** *The boy was reading a sensational paperback novel:* shocking, exaggerated, extravagant, emotional; lurid, cheap, meretricious.

Ant. 1 ordinary, common, everyday, routine; mediocre. **2** prosaic, dull.

sense *n.* **1** *The word "tactile" refers to the sense of touch:* faculty, function, feeling, sensation; (*variously*) touch, smell, taste, sight, hearing. **2** *A square meal gives one a sense of well-being:* impression, sensation, realization, awareness, recognition, consciousness. **3** *The teacher tried to inculcate a sense of beauty in his pupils:* appreciation, understanding, intuition. **4** *I can rely on his good sense:* mental ability, judgement, reason, mind, understanding, perspicacity, sagacity, wisdom, intelligence, reasonableness. **5** *There is no sense in crying over spilt milk:* value, worth, use, good, point, benefit, purpose, practicality, efficacy. **6** *A sense of impending doom overwhelmed us:* impression, awareness, intuition, premonition, presentiment; aura, atmosphere. **7** *Can you make any sense of these instructions? One sense of "secrete" means to hide or conceal:* meaning, signification, connotation, denotation, definition.
—*v.* **8** *The blindfolded prisoner could sense the change of atmosphere:* be aware of, perceive, feel; recognize, detect, discern. **9** *She was quick to sense his difficulty:* grasp, understand, apprehend, comprehend, take in, descry, see, note, perceive, espy, regard, discern, realize. **10** *We sensed that something was wrong:* have a vague impression, feel, suspect, divine, guess.

Ant. 4 stupidity, folly. **5** nonsense. **9** misunderstand; disregard, ignore, neglect, overlook, miss.

senseless *adj.* **1** *The punch on the head left the boxer senseless:* unconscious, without sensation, insensible, insensate; deadened, numb; knocked out. **2** *Leaving your job would be a senseless thing to do:* useless, meaningless, purposeless; stupid, witless, brainless, hare-brained, foolish, foolhardy, inane, silly, nonsensical, ridiculous, irrational, unreasonable, unwise, ill-advised, irresponsible, *Informal* crazy, dumb, nutty; without reason, illogical, groundless, meaningless, pointless, aimless; idle.

Ant. 1 conscious. **2** meaningful, worthwhile,

useful; sensible, smart, intelligent, clever, wise; rational, reasonable, sound, logical.

sensibility *n.* **1** *It is now possible to measure the sensibility of plants to light and heat:* ability to perceive, responsiveness, sensitiveness, sensitivity, perception. **2** *The way she dressed suggested the sensibility of a painter:* artistic responsiveness, aesthetic judgement, refined tastes; emotional make-up, temperament. **3** Often **sensibilities** *Learn to have regard for other people's sensibilities:* sensitivity, sensitiveness, susceptibility, feelings; thin skin, sore spot, Achilles' heel.

Ant. 1 insensibility, insensitiveness, insensitivity; deadness, dullness, numbness, unconsciousness.

sensible *adj.* **1** *Donald is a sensible young man. Our counsellor offered a sensible approach to the problem:* sound, showing good sense, intelligent, thoughtful, perspicacious; wise, sage, sagacious, far-sighted; discerning, discriminating, prudent, discreet, judicious, just; well-advised, well-grounded, logical, rational, reasonable, sane; plausible, credible, possible. **2** *Animals are quick to be sensible of danger:* aware, perceiving, perceptive, cognitive, cognizant; conscious, knowing, enlightened, informed, apprised. **3** *There has been a sensible increase in violence over the recent weeks:* perceptible, noticeable, discernible; tangible, palpable, detectable, visible; plain, apparent, evident, obvious. **4** *Are the natives of Tierra del Fuego sensible to extremes of heat and cold?:* capable of feeling or perceiving, sensitive.

Ant. 1 unsound, unintelligent, stupid, unwise, foolish, absurd, senseless, imprudent, indiscreet, injudicious; illogical, irrational, unreasonable. **2** insensible, unaware, ignorant, blind. **3** undetectable, unnoticeable, invisible. **4** insensible, insensitive.

sensitive *adj.* **1** *The tips of the fingers are particularly sensitive:* responsive, perceptive, sentient, sensing. **2** *Don't be so sensitive; I was only joking:* easily affected emotionally, easily offended or hurt, touchy, thin-skinned; delicate, impressionable, susceptible; perceptive, keen, acute. **3** *The cardiograph is a sensitive machine:* detecting slight change, delicate, fine; accurate, precise, exact; faithful. **4** *Careful! The bruise is still sensitive:* sore, tender, painful.

Ant. 2 hard, tough, coarse, thick-skinned, obtuse. **3** rough, inaccurate, approximate.

sensual *adj. Saint Paul reproves us for having sensual thoughts. He indulges his sensual enjoyment of good wine:* erotic, carnal, lustful, lewd, licentious, lecherous, sexy; earthy, fleshly, voluptuous, pleasure-seeking, hedonistic.

sensuous *adj. A meadow in spring is full of sensuous delights:* gratifying the senses, strongly appealing, delicious, exquisite, delightful.
◇ *Usage note: Sensuous* most often means powerfully appealing to the senses or to the aesthetic faculty: *the sensuous smoothness of polished jade. Sensual* often means appealing to the senses in a sexual or quasi-sexual way: *a sensual painting of a nude.* This distinction was in fact the original raison d'être of the word *sensuous.* The poet John Milton invented it in order to have a synonym of *sensual,* minus the association with sex. He used the word in an often-quoted formulation of what poetry should be: "simple, sensuous, and passionate."

sentiment *n.* **1** Often **sentiments** *We share the same sentiments on the matter:* opinion, attitude, point of view, viewpoint, feeling, thought, notion, idea. **2** *Resisting sentiment, she threw out all of her old letters:* feeling, emotion, sentimentality, nostalgia, tenderness, heart, softheartedness, emotionalism, romance, romanticism.

> **Exploring the Word**: *Sense, nonsense, sensation, sensitive, sensual, sensible,* and *sentiment* refer either to physical perception, mental perception, or both. They come from Latin *sentire,* to feel, and the related word *sensus,* feeling, perception (in both the physical and mental sense). The same Latin base gives us *sentinel* and *sentry,* whose duty it is to perceive danger and warn others; *scent,* to perceive by the sense of smell, a smell or odour; *consent* and *consensus* (Latin *con-,* together), to feel or think together or alike, hence agreement; *dissent* (Latin *dis-,* apart), to feel or think apart or differently, hence disagreement; and *sentence,* meaning both an expression of one feeling, as in writing, and a feeling or opinion, as when a judge passes a *sentence* on a convicted criminal.

sentimental *adj.* **1** *Sentimental films always make me cry:* emotional, mawkish, pathetic, romantic, romanticized; *Informal* tear-jerking, mushy. **2** *She becomes sentimental whenever she thinks of her childhood:* emotional, nostalgic; tearful, maudlin, lachrymose.

sentimentality *n. When the author prolongs the heroine's death for two chapters, he is guilty of sentimentality; Stop all of this sentimentality — you must face facts squarely:* emotionalism, mawkishness; sentimentalism, pathos, bathos; emotional nature, heart, temperament, *Slang* kitsch, schmaltz.

separate *v.* **1** *A barbed-wire fence separates the two farms. Separate the orange into sections:* keep apart, divide, mark off, come between, split, partition; subdivide, cut, sever, detach, break, sunder, bisect, part; disjoin, disunite. **2** *Separate the white clothes from the coloured before laundering:* set apart, put apart, segregate; sort out, remove, single out, isolate; pick out, cull, sift; distinguish. **3** *We separated after ten years of marriage. Bear left where the road separates:* go separate ways, go different ways, go

apart; divorce, split up; branch out, diverge, part, split, divaricate, bifurcate, fork, ramify, radiate, spread. **4** *The sponge cake separates easily in one's fingers:* come apart, break away, break apart; crack, split, part, crumble.
—*adj.* **5** *The suite consisted of four separate rooms:* not joined, not connected, disunited; not shared, single, individual, distinct; different, diverse, dissimilar. **6** *Our newspaper and our printing business form separate corporate entities:* independent, existing by itself, autonomous.
Ant. 1 join, attach, link, unite, engage, connect. **2** combine, unite, mix, merge, integrate, consolidate. **3** meet, merge; convene. **4** adhere, cling. **5** joined, connected, united; shared; alike, similar. **6** affiliated, merged, interdependent.
◇ *Spelling tip:* This is one of the most frequently misspelt words in the English language. Remember that it has two *a*'s: *sepArAte.*
◇ *Word origin: Separate* comes from Latin *se-* (apart) + *parare* (to prepare), hence to put or keep apart. The same Latin word elements give us *severe* and *several.*

separation *n.* **1** *Let us proceed to the separation of chaff from wheat:* separating, division, disjunction, disunion, disconnection, divorce, severance; detachment, dissociation; sorting, removal, segregation, isolation. **2** *Their separation at the railway station was emotional:* parting, farewell, goodbye, divergence, branching; estrangement, divorce; breach, break, split, schism. **3** *There is a separation of 100 yards between each telegraph pole:* gap, space, opening, distance, interval.

sepulchre *n. Each year, until the reign of Henry VIII, thousands of pilgrims visited the sepulchre of Saint Thomas à Becket:* tomb, crypt, vault, ossuary, reliquary, resting-place; mausoleum, cenotaph, necropolis, grave, burial place.
◇ *Word origin: Sepulchre* comes from Latin *sepulcrum,* burial place, tomb.

sequel *n.* **1** The Silver Spoon *is a sequel to John Galsworthy's* The White Monkey: continuation, follow-up. **2** *As a sequel to the encounter, he met the same beggar in an expensive restaurant later that night:* subsequent event, aftermath, upshot, offshoot, outgrowth, product; epilogue, postscript, addendum; conclusion, end, finish, dénouement, culmination; consequence, result, outcome.

sequence *n.* **1** *Hitler rose to power by a strange sequence of events:* progression, order, succession, arrangement; series, run, course, flow, train, string, chain; consecutiveness, successiveness. **2** *New employees had to attend a sequence of meetings on sales technique:* series, cycle, round; procession, parade, cavalcade, course.

sequester *v. The jury was sequestered while it deliberated over the murder case:* set apart, seclude, withdraw, isolate, separate, segregate, retire, put aside, confine, quarantine.

serene *adj. The woods were reflected in the serene lake:* calm, tranquil, peaceful, quiet, still, untroubled, halcyon, unruffled, smooth; sedate, dignified, unperturbed, placid, composed, undisturbed, unexcitable, unimpassioned, poised, cool, nonchalant; clear, fair, bright, unobscured, pellucid, limpid.
Ant. disturbed, troubled, rough, agitated; excitable, anxious, discomposed.

> **Exploring the Word**: *Sequence, sequel, sequester, second, sect, sue, suit, suitor,* and *suite* can all be traced back to Latin *sequī,* to follow. Thus *sequence* is the order of things that follow each other; a *sequel* is what follows, the following part or instalment of a story; *sequester* means to seclude, originally to set aside until a following or later time; *second* refers to something that comes after; a *sect* is a group that follows a particular faith; to *sue* a person literally means to follow a person around pleading for the righting of a wrong or a favour, hence suing or presenting a *suit* in court or a *suitor* who pleads his *suit* to a girl. A *suit* for wearing is so-called because the coat and trousers match or "follow" each other, and a *suite* of furniture, *hotel suite,* or *musical suite,* as the *Nutcracker Suite,* are so-called because the parts (items, rooms, or movements) match or follow each other.

serenity *n. Her own serenity contrasted with everyone else's anxiety:* calmness, placidity, tranquillity, peacefulness, quietude, quiescence, composure, implicit confidence, dignity, equanimity, collectedness, coolness, complacence, nonchalance, *French* sangfroid.
Ant. anxiety, uneasiness, alarm, discontent.

serf *n. The feudal landowners had many serfs in their service:* slave bound to the land; vassal, villein; bondman, thrall; peasant, cottar.
Ant. master, lord.
◇ *Word origin:* See SERVE.

serial *n.* **1** The Forsyte Saga *was my favourite television serial:* story presented in instalments.
—*adj.* **2** *Charles Dickens wrote many of his novels for serial publication:* in instalments, in successive parts; continued, continuous, consecutive, successive; regular, recurring; piecemeal. **3** *What is the serial number of that pound note?:* of a series, arranged in a series.

series *n. The northern counties were hit by a series of violent storms:* succession, progression, procession, sequence; set, cycle, chain, string, parade; group, number.

serious *adj.* **1** *The doctor emerged from the patient's room with a serious look on his face:* thoughtful, pensive, grave, solemn, frowning, long-faced, saturnine; sober, sedate, staid, grim, rueful; sad, dejected, downcast. **2** *If you're* *serious about becoming an actor, you must work hard:* sincere, earnest, not joking, not trifling, determined, decided, resolute, resolved, purposeful. **3** *Buying a house is a serious matter:* demanding careful thought, important, consequential, momentous, weighty, heavy, crucial; fateful, portentous. **4** *There's been a serious accident on the motorway. Europe is threatened with a serious fuel shortage:* dangerous, perilous, harmful, critical, severe, alarming, bad; incapacitating, crippling.

Ant. 1 thoughtless, careless; joyful, happy, jolly, gay, laughing, frivolous. **2** insincere, joking, trifling; undecided. **3** unimportant, insignificant, trivial. **4** slight, minor.

sermon *n.* **1** *The bishop preached a sermon from the pulpit:* speech containing religious instruction, exhortation, homily; preaching, preachment. **2** *Don't give me a sermon on punctuality just because I'm five minutes late:* long tedious speech, lecture, harangue, tirade; reproof, admonition, rebuke; dressing-down, tongue-lashing.

serpent *n.* **1** *The goddess is shown holding a serpent in each hand:* snake, reptile; (*variously*) adder, viper, asp, cobra, rattlesnake, smooth snake, grass snake. **2** *Don't trust that serpent:* traitor, trickster, deceiver, cheat, double-dealer; rogue, snake, snake in the grass; devil, the Devil, Satan.

serpentine *adj. A serpentine maze of tunnels and trenches provided shelter during the bombardments:* twisting, winding, snaking, meandering, tortuous, circuitous, devious, zigzag, roundabout, crooked, mazy, labyrinthine; spiral, convoluted, flexuous, sinuous.

servant *n.* **1** *The millionaire had 30 servants on his staff:* employee, attendant, retainer, helper, domestic, factotum; (*variously*) maid, valet, footman, chauffeur, cook, butler, hired man, hired girl, housekeeper; menial, flunkey, lackey, slavey, scullion; henchman, underling, minion; man, girl, man Friday, girl Friday; help. **2** *The mayor is a public servant:* public employee, public official, server; servitor.

Ant. 1 master, lord, employer.

serve *v.* **1** *The butler served him faithfully for 25 years:* work for, act as a servant to, be in the service of, attend, take care of, wait on. **2** *How may we serve you?:* be of help to, assist, render assistance, minister, tend, supply, provide for, aid, help, promote, further, oblige, attend; give aid or service, be of use. **3** *I have to serve on the jury next week. The convict has to serve his sentence:* go through a term of service, work, act, perform, do duty, hold an office, fill a post, officiate; go through, carry out, spend, pass, complete. **4** *She served in a restaurant during the evenings to help pay her way through university:* wait at table, work as a waiter or waitress. **5** *Dinner will be served in the main dining-room:* provide for customers or guests; supply with food, set food on a table. **6** *This light dinner will serve me:* be enough for, content, satisfy, suit, suffice, do. **7** *Her flat also serves as her office. The table will serve as a desk:* act, be of use, be used, be functional, function, be instrumental; answer the purpose, answer the requirements, *Informal* fill the bill. **8** *Her ingenuity has always served her well:* treat, work for, function for, avail. **9** *The lawyer arrived to serve a writ:* deliver, present, hand over.

Ant. 1 command, order; deceive, betray. **2** obstruct, hinder, thwart, oppose. **6** be insufficient for; dissatisfy. **7** be useless.

◇ *Word origin: Serve, service, servant, servile, servitude,* and *serf* all come from Latin *servus,* slave, servant.

service *n.* **1** Sometimes **services** *May I be of service to you? Your services are no longer required:* labour; effort, ministration; attendance, assistance, help, aid; benefit, advantage, usefulness, use, profit, accommodation; support, avail; employment, employ. **2** *The bus service is free to O.A.P.s:* use, provision, system, accommodation, facility, utility, convenience. **3** *I do agree that the British health service is excellent:* department, agency, bureau. **4** Usually **services** *Yes, he was in the services during World War II:* armed forces, army, navy, air force. **5** *Does your car need a service?:* repair, servicing, maintenance, mechanical work. **6** *The service in this restaurant is excellent:* attendance, waiting, accommodation, order-filling. **7** Often **services** *The dentist sent a bill for his services:* professional work, treatment. **8** *There is a church service this evening:* ritual, ceremony, ceremonial, rite, observance.

—*v.* **9** *The mechanic's gone to service a broken dishwasher:* repair, maintain, adjust, mend. **10** *That power generator services the entire Midland area:* serve, supply services to.

◇ *Word origin:* See SERVE.

serviceable *adj. The old coat is still serviceable:* usable, useful, utilitarian, functional, effective, operative, practical; durable, lasting, rugged, strong, tough.

servile *adj.* **1** *A servile attendant accompanied the millionaire everywhere, opening doors and lighting cigars:* slavish, submissive, fawning, abject; unctuous, oily; obsequious, truckling, toadying, cringing, sycophantic, scraping, grovelling, bootlicking. **2** *The luckless gentleman was at last reduced to servile labour:* befitting a slave, menial; in bonds, abject, slavish, subservient, humble.

Ant. 1 masterly, commanding, haughty.

servitude *n. To manumit means to release a slave or slaves from servitude. He was sentenced to ten years' penal servitude:* slavery, thraldom, bonds, bondage, oppression, subjugation, enslavement, fetters, shackles, chains; compulsory service, hard labour, imprisonment.

Ant. freedom, emancipation.

session *n.* **1** *Where was the first session of the United Nations General Assembly held?:* meeting, sitting, conference, convention, assembly, synod, conclave. **2** *We urge you to enrol for the spring session now:* period, term, semester, quarter; course, round, bout.

> **Exploring the Word:** Latin *sedere*, to sit, settle, gives us *sedate*, settled, calm, and *sedative*, a medicine that calms; *sedentary*, characterized by much sitting, settled in one place; *sediment*, matter that has settled to the bottom of a liquid; *session*, a sitting together, as of a legislative body, group of students, musicians, etc., for a specific purpose or activity; and *obsession*, (Latin *ob-*, on), literally something that "sits upon" one like a besieger (Latin *obsessio*, siege). Latin *sedere*, to sit, also gives us *assess* and *assize*, literally to sit in judgement, to estimate, fix a fine, try, hold an inquiry; *assiduous*, sitting down, hence persevering, unremitting, industrious; *dissident*, literally to sit apart (Latin *dis-*, apart), hence disagreeing, differing; *insidious*, sitting in ambush, hence beguiling, deceitful, stealthy; *preside* (Latin *prae-*, before), to sit before others as a chief executive, or as we say "*to chair*" a meeting; and *president*, the person chosen to sit before others as a chief executive, holding the chair of office; *reside*, to "settle down" in a place, *residence*, the place where one settles, and *resident*, one who settles in a place or house or figuratively sits in a chair there, as a *resident surgeon*.

set *v.* **1** *Set the package on the table:* put, place, position, move into position, lay, *Informal* plunk, plop; drop. **2** *Set the timer to go off in 20 minutes. Set the table. Can you set type?:* fix, adjust, regulate, calibrate; prepare, order, arrange, line up, align. **3** *Let the jelly set:* harden, become hard or firm, solidify, consolidate, gel, jellify, congeal, thicken. **4** *What time does the sun set?:* sink, pass below the horizon. **5** *I can't set a value on friendship:* place, assign, establish, assess, attach, confer; estimate, rate. **6** *She set a trap to catch the mice:* position, arrange, station, situate, install. **7** *Let's set the time of the meeting. I hate to set rules on anything:* decide upon, settle, fix, determine, establish, make, create; prescribe, decree, ordain. **8** *The play is set in Venice:* put in a setting, locate, represent, suppose to take place. **9** *The jeweller charges a lot of money to set diamonds in a bracelet:* fix, mount in a frame; imbed; ornament, stud. **10** *The composer set a prayer to music:* fit, arrange, adapt; style. **11** *The hunters set the dogs on the cornered bear:* urge to attack, release, unleash.
—*n.* **12** *The set of his chin suggested great tenacity:* setting, position, carriage, bearing, cut, line, profile; firmness, rigidity. **13** *Alice wants a chess set for Christmas:* group, collection, assortment, array, suit, outfit, kit, service. **14** *The so-called Beautiful People were yesterday's fashionable set:* group of persons, crowd, clique, faction, coterie, club, bunch. **15** *Do you want to buy a television set?:* apparatus, assembly, machine, complex, unit. **16** *Hollywood has many old film sets:* scenery, scene, setting, backdrop; studio; locale, location.
—*adj.* **17** *Have we got a set date for the party?:* definite, fixed, decided, firm, settled, prearranged, agreed upon; anticipated. **18** *At the meeting we stuck to the set questions and answers we had already agreed upon:* established, usual, customary, accustomed; stock, common, commonplace, conventional, everyday, routine, regular, habitual, familiar; banal, trite, hackneyed, stale. **19** *We're all set for the picnic:* arranged, ready, prepared. **20** *He's set in his ways:* stubborn, obstinate, steadfast, immovable, rigid, inflexible, frozen, hardened, stiff.

Ant. 1 remove, lift, pick up. **2** disarrange. **3** melt, soften. **4** rise. **7** change, break. **9** remove, extract. **17** undecided, tentative, vague. **18** unexpected, impromptu; unusual, uncommon, irregular. **19** unprepared. **20** flexible, adaptable.

◇ *Usage note:* For the differences between *set* and *sit*, see the Usage note at SIT.

settle *v.* **1** *Let's settle on a time for the meeting:* decide, agree, fix, choose, set, determine, establish. **2** *Let's settle matters between us once and for all:* put in order, dispose properly, arrange, bring to order; reconcile, resolve, clear up, straighten out, rectify, put to rest, work out. **3** *It's wise to try to settle one's accounts each month:* pay, discharge, acquit oneself of, dispose of, make good, clear, satisfy. **4** *My grandparents settled in Yorkshire:* move to, populate, establish oneself; colonize, put down roots, take root, lodge, inhabit, people, make one's home, set up house. **5** *The sedative quickly settled her nerves:* calm, bring to rest, soothe, quiet, compose, allay, pacify. **6** *Bits of cork settled at the bottom of the wine bottle:* deposit dregs, descend gradually, collect at the bottom, precipitate; clarify, clear. **7** *You'll have to give the foundations time to settle:* sink, drop, droop, sag, find one's level. **8** *The bird settled on a high branch:* come to rest; land, alight, light; perch; sit down.

Ant. 1 disagree. **2** disarrange; confuse. **4** wander; emigrate. **5** agitate, excite, disturb. **7** rise, ascend.

◇ *Word origin: Settle, settlement,* and *settler* come from Old English *setl*, seat. These words are closely related to *sit, set,* and *seat.*

settlement *n.* **1** *After the settlement of our differences, we became friends:* adjustment, arrangement, reconciliation, resolution, working out. **2** *The settlement of Iceland is recorded by Ari the Learned. This summer we intend to excavate an ancient, Anglo-Saxon settlement:* colonizing, colonization, peopling; community of settlers, colony, encampment, camp, post, outpost; small community, village, hamlet. **3** *His father had to take on the settlement of his gambling debts. The court awarded her a handsome settlement:* payment, satisfaction, liquidation, discharge, amortization, clearing, clearance, acquittance; adjustment, compensation; bequest, sum, amount.

settler *n. Early settlers had a difficult life:* pioneer, frontiersman; immigrant, colonist, colonizer.

sever *v.* **1** *His arm was severed in the accident:* cut in two, cut off, separate, part, amputate, dismember, lop off, truncate, bisect, cleave, split, slice, saw off; rive, rend, tear. **2** *Sometimes it's best to sever all family ties:* discontinue, dissolve, put an end to, do away with, disunite, disjoin, split up, break off, rupture.
Ant. 1 unite, join, bind. **2** continue; keep, maintain.

several *adj.* **1** *We received several replies to our inquiry:* more than two, some, a number of, a few. **2** *They had their several duties to perform:* separate, different, distinct, peculiar; individual, respective, own, particular, certain, specific, exclusive, special, express, private, personal, independent; single, distinctive; diverse, assorted, sundry.
—pron. **3** *There are several here that I don't know:* several persons or things, a few, a number.
Ant. 2 joint, combined, communal.

severe *adj.* **1** *Being put in the stocks was a severe punishment:* strict, harsh, rigorous, taxing, demanding, vigorous, rough, stiff; cruel, brutal, merciless, ruthless, unsparing; drastic, draconian. **2** *The general had a severe manner:* serious, stern, dour, strait-laced, grave, sober, grim, saturnine, sedate, sombre, austere, forbidding, cold. **3** *That coat is too severe to be worn to anything but a funeral:* restrained, plain, simple, conservative, uniform, unadorned, undecorated; chaste. **4** *The Irish potato famines of the 1840's were severe. The weatherman predicts severe cold:* intense, violent, extreme, unrelenting, raging, fuming; furious, fierce, savage, wild, brutal; turbulent, tumultuous; bitter, stinging, piercing, biting, cutting. **5** *Appendicitis can be a severe illness:* serious, painful, dangerous, distressing.
Ant. 1 gentle, lenient, merciful, mild, moderate; easy; kind, considerate. **2** affable, genial, sweet. **3** gay, cheerful; decorative. **4** gentle, mild. **5** tolerable; easy; pleasant, mild.

sex *n.* **1** *What sex is the baby?:* gender, sexual classification, sexual identity, reproductive function; masculinity, maleness; femininity, femaleness. **2** *The permissive society has had more effect on public attitudes towards sex than on private behaviour:* sexuality, generation, reproduction, procreation; sexual urge, sexual instinct, libido, Eros; sexual intercourse, love, love-making, coitus, coition, copulation.

sexual *adj. Sex hormones affect the growth and function of the sexual organs. Dr. Alfred Kinsey wrote a report on present-day sexual behaviour. Don't confuse love with mere sexual attraction:* genital, generative, procreative, venereal, copulatory, sex, coital; marital, conjugal, intimate; erotic, sexy, amatory, sensual, libidinous.

sexy *adj. The actor made the most of his sexy voice. The celebrated dancer wiggled in a sexy way:* erotic, voluptuous, provocative, flirtatious, coquettish, suggestive, seductive, come-hither.

shabby *adj.* **1** *The beggar's clothes were shabby. The house had grown shabby with age:* worn, ragged, raggy, threadbare, frayed, torn, tatty, the worse for wear; neglected, deteriorated, decaying, dilapidated, broken-down, ramshackle, tumbledown, rundown, seedy; impoverished, poverty-stricken. **2** *He was a shabby dresser:* slovenly, wearing worn clothes, ill-dressed; dirty, mangy, scruffy, tatty, sorry; impoverished, ragged, down at heel, down and out. **3** *The mental patients received shabby treatment:* unfair; mean, wretched, sorry, miserable, contemptible, ignoble, dishonourable, sordid, low, inferior, unworthy; ungenerous, meagre, cheap, poor, beggarly, illiberal, tight.
Ant. 1 pristine, new, neat, well-kept, well-to-do; grand, imposing. **2** well-dressed, fine, splendid; fashionable, chic. **3** fair, considerate, admirable, honourable; liberal, generous, handsome, lavish.

shackle *n.* **1** *Shackles were placed on the prisoner's hands and feet:* fetter, irons, chains, bonds; handcuffs, cuffs, manacle; hobble.
—v. **2** *Shackle the captives so that they cannot escape:* fetter, chain, manacle, handcuff, cuff, secure, bind, tie, tether, pinion. **3** *The soap-box orator told us that our minds are shackled by ignorance and superstition. Lack of money shackled his plans for retirement:* restrict, thwart, retard, block, hamper, hobble, cramp, hinder, frustrate, foil, limit, impede, curb, check, encumber, inhibit, circumscribe, stall, forestall, balk, bar, prevent, deter, hamstring.
Ant. 2 unshackle, unchain; free, release. **3** aid, help, abet, promote, foster, further.

shade *n.* **1** *It's cooler in the shade:* shadow, shadows; darkness, semi-darkness. **2** *We need a new shade for that lamp:* (*variously*) lampshade cover, shield, screen, hood, veil, curtain, awning, canopy, shutter. **3** *A lighter shade of blue will make the room seem larger:* hue, tone, tint, colour, cast. **4** *There's only a shade of difference between the two candidates:* small degree, trace, tinge, touch, bit, whit, jot, iota, particle, scintilla, atom, modicum, soupçon, suggestion, hint.
—v. **5** *An awning shaded the porch:* shield from the sun, shield from the light, screen; make shady, darken, dim.

Ant. 1 sunlight, sunshine, direct light, light, glare, brightness. **4** great amount, full measure, lot, abundance, *Informal* heap, reams. **5** light, lighten, illuminate, brighten; expose, uncover.

shadow *n.* **1** *No shadow is cast when the sun is directly overhead:* silhouette, reflection; penumbra. **2** Usually **shadows** *Someone was lurking in the shadows:* shade, partial darkness; gathering darkness. **3** *Only a shadow of doubt remained. He was only a shadow of his former self:* trace, shade, bit, slight amount, small degree, touch, tinge; suggestion, whisper, hint, ghost, faint image. **4** *The shadow of possible invasion hung over the country. The scandal left a shadow on his reputation:* threat, spectre, cloud; dark spot, blight, taint, blot, blemish, smirch, smudge, stain.
—*v.* **5** *Two detectives shadowed the suspect closely:* follow, tail, trail, dog, tag after, hound; track, stalk, pursue.

shady *adj.* **1** *It's cooler in the shady part of the garden:* shaded, shadowy. **2** *Don't do any deals with that shady character:* disreputable, questionable, suspicious, fishy, dubious; unethical, dishonest, crooked, devious, underhand.
Ant. 1 sunny, sunlit, bright, unshaded, exposed. **2** upright, honest, honourable, moral, ethical, proper, above-board, straight, *Slang* square.

shaft *n.* **1** *Grasp the knife firmly by the shaft:* handle, shank, hilt; spindle, trunk, stalk, stem. **2** *The archers sent their shafts whizzing through the air:* (*variously*) arrow, dart, quill, spear, lance. **3** *The candidates exchanged shafts in the debate:* sharp remark, barb, cut, gibe, insult, affront, aspersion, *Informal* brickbat. **4** *A shaft of light came through the window:* ray, beam, streak, stream, gleam, patch. **5** *The miners were lowered into the shaft. The smoke escaped up the shaft of the chimney:* excavation, cavity, pit, chasm, abyss; duct, vent, funnel, flue.

shaggy *adj. Shaggy dogs require frequent grooming. A shaggy rug covered the floor:* hairy, hirsute, unshorn, bushy, woolly; downy, tufted, long-haired, piled; whiskered, bewhiskered, bearded.
Ant. smooth, short-haired, close-cropped, shorn, flat-woven.
◇ *Word origin: Shaggy* comes from the noun *shag,* which originally meant rough, matted hair, though is now used mainly as a variety of finish on a carpet or cloth, and as a type of rough-cut tobacco. *Shaggy* is first recorded in English about the year 1590.

shake *v.* **1** *The house shakes when a train goes by. Shake the bottle well:* vibrate, quiver, quake, quaver, totter, wobble, sway, tremble, shudder, shiver, flutter, flicker, jiggle, joggle, jostle; agitate, mix. **2** *Don't shake your fist at me:* wave, brandish, flourish, swing. **3** *The mining disaster shook the town:* disturb, distress, unnerve, perturb; jar, jolt, rattle, unsettle, unstring, discompose, disquiet, ruffle, frighten; stun, startle, stagger, move, touch, affect, stir. **4** With **off** *The thief managed to shake off the police. I can't seem to shake off this cold:* escape from, get away from, elude; get rid of, rid oneself of, throw off, slough.
—*n.* **5** *Give the bottle a couple of shakes before pouring the juice:* jiggle, jog, bounce, jolt, jounce, flourish.
Ant. 3 calm, quiet, soothe, reassure, settle, compose, steady. **4** catch, capture, get; keep, retain.

shaky *adj.* **1** *Get down off that shaky ladder. I'm feeling a little shaky today:* unsteady, trembling, shaking, quivering, wobbly, tremulous, tottering, weak, unstable, flimsy, frail, fragile; unsafe, hazardous, insecure, precarious; nervous, jumpy, jittery, fidgety. **2** *His determination to become a lawyer seems rather shaky:* wavering, uncertain, unsure, dubious, unreliable, undependable, inconstant, vacillating, faltering, undecided, irresolute, unresolved, half-hearted, halting, hesitant.

shallow *adj.* **1** *The boat ran aground in shallow water:* shoal, of little depth, (*variously*) ankle-deep, knee-deep, waist-deep. **2** *They carried on a shallow conversation about parties and clothes:* superficial, insubstantial, frivolous, trivial, slight, inconsequential, unimportant, trifling, surface, skin-deep.
Ant. 1 deep, bottomless. **2** profound, serious, substantial, important, in-depth, intellectual, thoughtful, perceptive, keen, sharp.

sham *n.* **1** *Her illness was all a sham to gain sympathy:* fraud, fake, pretence, trick; imitation, counterfeit, copy, forgery, phoney, put-on.
—*adj.* **2** *The child's sham weeping fooled no one:* feigned, fraudulent, fake, pretended, phoney, false, make-believe, put-on; counterfeit, bogus, forged, imitation, artificial, synthetic, simulated, spurious.
—*v.* **3** *The girl's favourite trick was to sham tears:* pretend, feign, fake, simulate, put on, act, imitate, affect, assume.
Ant. 1 original, the genuine article, *Informal* the real McCoy, the real thing. **2** real, genuine, authentic, true; unfeigned, unpretended, natural.

shame *n.* **1** *The student felt great shame at having failed the exam:* guilt, remorse, self-disgust, self-abomination; embarrassment, mortification, chagrin, shame-facedness, unworthiness. **2** *The corrupt politician brought shame upon his party:* disgrace, dishonour, contempt, ignominy, humiliation, mortification, disrepute, disrespect, degradation, debasement, odium. **3** *The way he abuses his dog is a crying shame:* disgrace, scandal, stigma. **4** *What a shame that it rained on the day of the picnic:* disappointment, regretful thing, sorrowful happening.

—*v.* **5** *The class's unruly behaviour shamed the teacher:* embarrass, humiliate, mortify, disgrace, humble.
Ant. **1** shamelessness, pride, self-respect, glory, worthiness. **2** honour, credit, renown, glory, esteem. **5** do credit to, make proud.

"Its the same the whole world over,
Its the poor wot gets the blame,
Its the rich wot gets the pleasure,
Ain't it all a blooming shame."
—*1914-18 War Song*

---

shameful *adj. What a shameful thing to do!:* disgraceful, dishonourable, shameless, contemptible, ignoble, ignominious, opprobrious, inglorious, degrading, shocking, outrageous, despicable, deplorable, odious, reprehensible; dastardly, vile, villainous, base, mean, low, unworthy, iniquitous, heinous.
Ant. honourable, glorious, noble, worthy, praiseworthy, dignified, decent, virtuous, respectable; admirable, commendable, meritorious.

shameless *adj.* **1** *The shameless woman flirted with every young man she met:* without shame, disgraceful, dishonourable, degraded, abandoned, dissolute, immodest, wanton, promiscuous, loose, immoral, indecent, indecorous. **2** *He's a shameless liar:* brazen, forward, brash, barefaced, unblushing, unabashed, unreserved, audacious, flagrant.

shape *n.* **1** *The shape of Italy resembles a boot when you look at it on a map:* outline, contour, figure, silhouette, profile, conformation, configuration; form, build, physique. **2** *Just get your ideas into shape:* order, array, orderly arrangement, state of neatness. **3** *He's in good shape for a man of his age:* condition, physical condition, health, fettle.
—*v.* **4** *The potter shaped the clay into a vase, A good teacher helps to shape a child's character:* form, mould, model, fashion, frame; make, create, build, construct, develop.
Ant. **2** disorder, disarray, disarrangement, confusion, chaos. **4** destroy, ruin; warp.
◇ *Spelling tip: Shape* is easy to spell, but *misshapen* can be a problem because of its two *s's.* Remember *miS + Shapen=miSShapen.*
◇ *Word origin: Shape* comes from Old English *scieppan,* to create.

share *n.* **1** *George's share of the inheritance was £20,000:* part, portion, allotment, apportionment, allowance, quota, percentage, ration.
—*v.* **2** *Three doctors share the office:* own jointly, use jointly, receive together. **3** *Share the biscuits with your brother:* divide and give out, split, cut up, divvy up, apportion, allot, allocate, deal out, measure out, mete out.
◇ *Word origin:* See SHEAR.

sharp *adj.* **1** *Be careful with that sharp axe. Hammer the sharp end of the peg into the ground:* keen-edged, fine-edged, fine, not blunt, razor-sharp; pointed, piked, edged, cutting; serrated, toothed, bristly, thorny, spiny, prickly. **2** *After the storm there was a sharp drop in temperature. The sharp pain made the patient wince:* sudden, abrupt, precipitous, rapid; distinct, clear, clearly defined, extreme, acute, fierce, violent, keen, severe, intense, drastic, marked, excessive, immoderate, inordinate; vertical, steep, sheer, angular. **3** *This salad-dressing has a sharp taste:* biting, bitter, salty, acid, sour, tart, caustic, acrid; piquant, strong; cutting, piercing, nippy, stinging, nipping. **4** *She has such a sharp voice:* shrill, piercing, harsh, penetrating, raucous, strident; high, high-pitched, high-toned. **5** *It takes sharp eyes to see the flaw. He's old but his mind is still sharp:* keen, acute, perceptive, quick; shrewd, astute, clever, penetrating, alert, awake, wide awake. **6** *His sharp business dealings earned him a bad reputation:* wily, crafty, cunning, sly, foxy, artful, calculating, conniving, contriving, unscrupulous, unprincipled, unethical, deceptive, tricky. **7** *The angry men exchanged sharp words:* angry, harsh, scathing, unkind, spiteful, bitter, barbed, cutting, stinging; cruel, severe, vitriolic, rancorous, galling, venomous, acrid; abrupt, gruff, brusque, curt, blunt, crusty, bearish, crabbed.
—*adv.* **8** *Look sharp!:* sharply, keenly, acutely, alertly, quickly, closely, attentively. **9** *The meeting started at eight o'clock sharp:* promptly, punctually, on the dot, on the nose, on the button; precisely, exactly, *Spanish* en punto, *French* juste.
Ant. **1** dull, blunt; round, rounded, straight, bulbous. **2** slow, gradual; gentle, easy, moderate, indistinct, blurred, unclear. **3** bland, mild, flat, insipid; sweet. **4** soft, mellow, soothing; well-modulated, low. **5** dull, dim, slow; unperceptive, obtuse, uncomprehending, unaware. **6** direct, straightforward, out in the open, above-board, ingenuous, guileless, artless; ethical, honest, scrupulous, principled. **7** sweet, gentle, kind, tender, soothing; polite, courteous, friendly, warm, loving. **8** dully; inattentively, carelessly, distractedly. **9** more or less, *Spanish* más o menos, *French* plus ou moins.

sharpen *v. Sharpen the knife on the whetstone:* make sharper, edge, put an edge on; whet, hone, grind, strop.

shatter *v.* **1** *The plate shattered when it hit the floor:* break into pieces, break into smithereens, shiver, smash, crash, burst, explode, sunder, rive; splinter, crush, crumble, pulverize; break, crack, fracture, split. **2** *Bad marks shattered the student's chances of gaining a scholarship:* destroy, wreck, ruin, smash, devastate, crush, squash, demolish, scuttle, spoil, upset, topple, overturn.
Ant. **2** increase, improve, enhance, heighten.

shave *v.* **1** *Father finally shaved his beard. Shave off the top branches of that bush:* cut off, cut, clip, crop, lop, prune, trim, snip, barber, scissor, shear, fleece. **2** *The bullet just shaved his pursuer's cheek:* graze, scrape, glance, brush, skim, touch lightly.

shear *v.* **1** *An experienced hand can shear a sheep in less than a minute. Shear the dead branches from the tree:* cut the fleece from, fleece; cut, clip, crop, trim, lop, prune, snip, scissor, shave. **2** *Pétain was shorn of all his offices and honours:* deprive, relieve; take away, remove.

◇ *Usage note:* Don't confuse *shear,* to cut off, clip, with any of the meanings of *sheer,* transparent, pure or absolute, steep. Thus, *It's time to shear the sheep,* but *She wore a sheer silk dress. That's sheer nonsense. The cliff ends in a sheer drop of over 100 feet.*

◇ *Word origin: Shear* and *share* come from Old English *scieran,* to shear. A *share* is a part that has been "sheared off," as it were.

sheath *n. The pirate drew the dagger out of its sheath. The gramophone record came in a cellophane sheath:* scabbard; covering, sheathing, wrapper, wrapping, envelope, jacket, coat, coating, case, slip-case, casing, sleeve; membrane, skin, capsule, pod.

shed[1] *n. The farmer built a shed for his tractor next to the barn:* lean-to; tool-shed, tool-house; hut, shack, hovel, shanty.

◇ *Word origin: Shed*[1] is a variant of *shade,* hence a shelter, as from the sun.

shed[2] *v.* **1** *Don't shed any tears over that scoundrel. Can anyone shed some light on the situation?:* let fall, let flow, spill, pour forth, give forth, emit, radiate, exude, discharge, shower; throw, cast, spread, distribute, scatter, strew, disperse, disseminate, broadcast. **2** *Trees shed their leaves in autumn. An angora cat sheds more hair than a Siamese:* cast off, let fall, drop, discard, slough, doff, moult.

Ant. **1** suppress, repress, withhold, hold back, choke back, stop; gather, collect, amass.

◇ *Word origin: Shed*[2] comes from Old English *scēadan,* to separate.

sheepish *adj.* **1** *The sheepish mob followed the leader without question:* easily led, submissive, passive, docile, tractable, unassertive, obeisant, obedient, servile, subservient, unresisting, yielding. **2** *The man made a sheepish apology:* embarrassed, abashed, shamefaced, shy, ashamed, hangdog, chastened, chagrined, mortified, guilty, blushing; timorous, fearful, bashful, timid, meek, humble, diffident, shrinking.

Ant. **1** aggressive, strident, overbearing, assertive, masterful, independent; stubborn, obdurate, hard-headed, wilful; disobedient, intractable, unyielding. **2** brazen, brash, unabashed, unashamed, unblushing, barefaced, audacious, bold, immodest, confident, poised.

sheer *adj.* **1** *That dress is too sheer to wear without a slip:* transparent, thin, fine, diaphanous, gossamer, gauzy, filmy. **2** *The clowns drew cries of sheer delight from the children:* unmixed, unadulterated, pure, one hundred per cent, unalloyed; absolute, utter, total, complete, unlimited, unbounded, unrestrained, consummate, unconditional, unmitigated, unqualified, perfect, out and out. **3** *The Seven Sisters rise sheer from the sea near Beachy Head:* steep, vertical, perpendicular, straight up and down, bluff, sharp; abrupt, precipitous.

Ant. **1** opaque; thick, coarse. **2** mixed, impure, alloyed, adulterated, doctored; partial, fragmentary, incomplete, imperfect, conditional, mitigated, qualified, limited. **3** gradual, gentle, sloping; horizontal.

sheet *n.* **1** *Fresh sheets were put on the beds. A sheet of frost covered the windscreen:* article of bedlinen, coating, coat, layer, covering, blanket, film, sheath, overlay. **2** *Cover the desk with a sheet of formica:* square, rectangle, slab, panel, leaf, piece, plate, pane.

shell *n.* **1** *The turtle had an unusual pattern on its shell. Put the shells in the dustbin:* carapace, case, hull, husk, shuck, pod. **2** *Only the shell of the building stood after the fire:* framework, skeleton, hulk, walls and roof. **3** *Shells burst over the enemy camp. The gun holds six shells:* artillery shell, cartridge shell, cartridge, bullet, round, shot; cannon shell, grenade, bomb, missile, projectile, rocket.

—*v.* **4** *Please shell some walnuts for the cake:* hull, husk, shuck. **5** *Cannons shelled the fort:* fire on, bombard, rain shells on, pound, barrage, pepper.

shelter *n.* **1** *The umbrella gave little shelter from the heavy downpour. The ship sought shelter from the storm:* cover, shield, refuge, safety, haven, protection, asylum, sanctuary, security. **2** *Most of our money goes on food and shelter:* housing, lodging, quarters, dwelling-place, a roof over one's head.

—*v.* **3** *The overhanging roof sheltered us from the rain. Bonny Prince Charlie was sheltered by loyal Highlanders:* protect, shield, cover; guard, safeguard, defend; harbour, take in, house, care for, look after, give refuge.

Ant. **2** exposure. **3** expose, lay bare; expel, turn out, evict; betray, hand over.

◇ *Word origin: Shelter* comes from Old English *scēldtruma,* "shield-troop," i.e., phalanx.

shelve *v. The committee decided to shelve the project for the time being:* lay aside, put aside, postpone, put off, suspend, defer, table, hold in abeyance, pigeon-hole, *Slang* put on ice, freeze.

Ant. begin, start, initiate, commence; activate, reactivate, revive.

shepherd *n.* **1** *The shepherd tended the flock:* herdsman, herder. **2** *The Lord is my shepherd:* protector, guardian, shelter, shield, refuge; defender, keeper, custodian, safeguard, champion, benefactor, patron, provider.

—*v.* **3** *The herdsman shepherded his flock through the winter. The guide shepherded the tourists through the Louvre:* tend, herd, watch over, guard; guide, lead, pilot, direct, show, escort.

Ant. 1 cattle-thief, poacher. **2** enemy, foe, rival.

"The good shepherd giveth his life for the sheep." —*John 10: 11*

---

sheriff *n. Robin Hood plagued the Sheriff of Nottingham:* chief executive officer of the crown in a county; officer of the crown: mayor, councillor.

◇ *Word origin:* A *sheriff* is literally a *shire reeve,* the *reeve* (royal county official) of a *shire* (or county). The office has existed since Anglo-Saxon times (Old English *scīrgerēfa,* sheriff), but has undergone many changes over the past 1000 years.

shield *n.* **1** *The sword glanced off the knight's shield:* (*variously*) buckler, aegis, escutcheon. **2** *Dark glasses are an effective shield against the glare:* protection, protector, guard, safeguard, defence, buffer, cover, screen, shade, fender.

—*v.* **3** *Motor-cyclists should wear helmets to shield them from injury. The motor is shielded in a shock-proof housing:* protect, guard, safeguard, secure, preserve, keep, keep safe, shelter; house, harbour; screen, cover, shade.

Ant. 2 danger, risk, hazard. **3** expose, lay bare, uncover; endanger, risk, hazard.

shift *v.* **1** *Shift the sofa so that it faces the fireplace:* move, transfer; switch, transpose, change, exchange, interchange, vary; swerve, veer.

—*n.* **2** *A sudden shift in the wind warned of the coming storm:* change, variation, shifting, alteration, deviation, fluctuation, alternating, turning, move, switch, veering, swerve. **3** *Bob works on the day shift:* work period, stint, assignment, tour of duty, go. **4** *She wore a light shift over her bathing-suit:* straight, loose-fitting dress; camisole, chemise, slip.

shiftless *adj. This office has no place for a shiftless worker:* lazy, idle, inactive, lax, lackadaisical; careless, slothful, unconscientious, work-shy; good-for-nothing, ne'er-do-well.

Ant. ambitious, willing-to-work, energetic, industrious, active; conscientious, painstaking, scrupulous, careful.

shifty *adj. That shifty character needs watching:* crafty, foxy, cunning, sly, wily, scheming, contriving, conniving, sneaky, slippery, manœuvring, tricky, fast, deceitful, fly; evasive, unreliable, untrustworthy, treacherous.

Ant. open, straightforward, direct, artless, guileless; reliable, dependable, trustworthy, loyal.

shimmer *v.* **1** *A light shimmered in the distance. The beauty queen's lamé gown shimmered in the torchlight:* glimmer, twinkle, flicker, flutter, flash, blink, dance, sparkle, glisten, scintillate, coruscate, phosphoresce; gleam, glow, beam. **2** *The landscape shimmered in the heat:* quiver, quake, shiver, waver, vibrate, tremble.

—*n.* **3** *Through the telescope I glimpsed the shimmer of a far-distant star:* twinkle, glimmer, tremulous flickering, blinking, faint glimmering, wavering light.

shine *v.* **1** *The sun is shining. The diamond shone brightly:* emit light, shed light, reflect light, gleam, radiate, glow, beam, sparkle, shimmer, glitter, glisten, glister, twinkle, flicker, flash, blink, scintillate, coruscate, irradiate. **2** *Shine the silver before the guests arrive:* polish, gloss, wax; buff, burnish, rub up; brighten.

—*n.* **3** *We saw the shine of the night-watchman's flashlight:* light, illumination, gleam, glow, beam, glare, glint, glitter, glimmer, sparkle, shimmer, twinkle, flicker, flash, blink; luminosity, luminousness, incandescence. **4** *How does she get such a good shine on her silverware? Give these shoes a good shine:* gloss, lustre, glow, sheen, brightness, radiance, brilliance, dazzle; polish, polishing, shining, wax, waxing, burnishing.

Ant. 2 dull, darken, dim; tarnish. **3** dark, darkness, blackness; dimness, murkiness. **4** dullness, tarnish.

shiny *adj. The boy had a shiny new penny:* bright, brilliant, shining, gleaming, glistening, shimmering, sparkling, glittering, scintillating; luminous, radiant, lustrous, incandescent, effulgent; polished, burnished, glossy.

ship *n.* **1** *Rough seas delayed the ship:* large boat, vessel, craft; (*variously*) steamship, steamer, ocean liner, liner, yacht, sailing ship, tanker, freighter, cargo ship, tramp steamer, tramp, packet, cruiser, battleship, destroyer, carrier, aircraft-carrier. **2** *The whole ship was given a day's leave:* ship's company, crew, hands.

—*v.* **3** *Ship the merchandise by air:* transport, send, dispatch, route, forward.

◇ *Usage note:* See BOAT.

◇ *Pronunciation tip: Ship* is pronounced the way it's spelt, but three things that go with ships aren't: *gunwale* (the upper edge of the hull of a ship or boat), *boatswain* (a subordinate officer who calls the crew to duty with his whistle and has charge of the anchors, rigging, etc.) and *forecastle* (the forward part of the main deck). The *w* in *gunwale* is silent, so that it is pronounced *gun'l,* not "gunwale." Likewise, say *bos'n,* not "boatswain." *Forecastle* is telescoped into two syllables: *folk-s'l.* Indeed, we sometimes find these words spelt as they are pronounced: *gunnel, bo'sun* and *fo'c's'le;* but it is better to retain the traditional spelling.

shirk *v. Don't try to shirk your responsibilities:* get out of doing, avoid, evade, shun, duck, shrink from, side-step, dodge, escape, elude, ignore, neglect, eschew; malinger.

Ant. meet, face, confront; fulfil, perform, undertake, do, honour.

shiver *v.* **1** *The child shivered with the cold:* shake, tremble, shudder, quiver, quaver, quake.
—*n.* **2** *A shiver of fear ran through me when the lights went out:* tremble, shudder, quiver, quaver, tremor. **3** Often **shivers** *The goblet broke into shivers when I dropped it:* bit, piece, fragment, sliver, shard, sherd.

shock[1] *v.* **1** *The shock of the earthquake was felt for miles around:* impact, jar, jolt, rock, concussion; blow, collision. **2** *The king's abdication was a shock to the nation. Oh, you did give me a shock:* surprise, blow, unexpected blow, disturbance, consternation, trauma, jolt, jar, bolt out of the blue; scare, start, turn.
—*v.* **3** *We were shocked by the sad news. The parents were shocked by the child's foul language:* surprise, stun, stagger, shake, daze, stupefy, paralyse, jar, jolt, overwhelm, bowl over, give a turn; perturb, dismay, distress, disturb, upset, unsettle, disquiet, discompose, disconcert, astonish, astound, startle; appal, horrify, disgust, revolt, offend, outrage.
◇ *Word origin: Shock*[1] is related to French *choc,* collision, and *choquer,* to shock. In Old French, *choquer* means "to strike with fear," and this is thought to be the origin of our word *shock,* upset.

shock[2] *n. We collected the sheaves into shocks, using about twelve for each one:* collection of sheaves, stack, bundle, pile; rick, cock.
◇ *Word origin: Shock*[2] comes from Middle Dutch *schok,* a group of sixty (a *shock* being once apparently made up of sixty sheaves).

shock[3] *n. The baby was born with a shock of black hair:* bushy mass, crop, mop, mane, thatch.
◇ *Word origin: Shock*[3] may well be a metaphorical extension of *shock*[2] (stack of sheaves).

"Awaiting the sensation of a short, sharp shock,
From a cheap and chippy chopper on a big black block." —*W. S. Gilbert*

---

shocking *adj.* **1** *The failure of the bank was shocking news:* surprising, astounding, astonishing, startling, staggering, stupefying, jarring, jolting, overwhelming; disturbing, perturbing, upsetting, disquieting, unsettling, disconcerting. **2** *Grandmother thought it shocking for girls to wear shorts. The hospital's treatment of mental patients is shocking:* scandalous, disgraceful, outrageous, indecent, offensive; appalling; horrifying, horrible, horrid, terrible, awful, disgusting, frightful, monstrous, insufferable, abominable, reprehensible, detestable, abhorrent, repugnant, repellent, odious, foul, wretched, hideous, revolting, ghastly, gruesome, grisly.
Ant. 1, 2 unsurprising, expected; gratifying, satisfying, pleasing. **2** acceptable, decent; good, excellent, fine, wonderful, marvellous, glorious, worthy, capital; admirable, honourable, praiseworthy, commendable, laudable, attractive, pleasant, desirable, first-rate.

shoddy *adj.* **1** *The carpenter did a shoddy job:* inferior, poor, careless, sloppy, negligent, inefficient, haphazard, slipshod. **2** *Leaving his wife to do all the work was a rather shoddy thing to do:* nasty, mean, shabby, inconsiderate, low, low-down, base, reprehensible, contemptible, dirty; niggardly, miserly, ungenerous, stingy.
Ant. 1 excellent, first-rate, good, fine; precise, accurate, careful, meticulous, thorough, scrupulous, fastidious. **2** noble, gentlemanly, kind, thoughtful, considerate; sympathetic, compassionate.

shoot *v.* **1** *The policeman shot the mad dog:* hit, with a bullet, shell, *Informal* wing, riddle, pepper, spray, *Slang* plug, pelt, kill, pick off, snipe at, fell, blow out one's brains. **2** *Each archer shot three arrows at the target. The catapult shot hundred-pound rocks at the enemy. The reporters began to shoot questions at the councillor:* fire, open fire, discharge, let fly, hurl, propel, eject, sling, cast, fling, throw, toss, launch, catapult; detonate, explode, go off; bombard, shower, rain, pelt. **3** *The horses shot out of the starting-gate:* move suddenly, charge, spring, dart, bolt, dash, sweep, spurt, jump, leap; race, speed, fly, tear, rush, hurry.
—*n.* **4** *New shoots appeared in the bush:* new growth, young branch, sprout, bud; stem, sprig, tendril; offshoot.

shop *n.* **1** *The local dress shop is having a sale:* store, establishment, boutique, retail store; emporium, market, mart. **2** *The machines for repair are placed in the shop:* workshop, studio, atelier; factory, plant, works, mill.
—*v.* **3** *The newly-weds shopped for silver and china:* seek to purchase, go shopping for; window-shop, look, hunt, browse; buy, purchase, patronize.

shore[1] *n.* **1** *There are lighthouses all along the Eastern shore. We spend all our weekends on the shore:* coast, sea-coast, seaboard; sea-shore, seaside, beach, strand; bank, riverbank. **2** *Finally, the sailors sighted shore:* land, dry land, terra firma.

shore[2] *v. Heavy posts shored the roof of the tunnel:* support, prop, hold, hold up, brace, buttress, bolster; bulwark, underpin.
Ant. weigh down, burden, crush, overwhelm, push over, overturn.

short *adj.* **1** *Short hair is cooler for summer. A short person may have difficulty in reaching the top shelves:* not long; not tall, stubby, squat, truncated; stunted; small, little, pint-sized, pocket-sized, diminutive, slight, elfin, pygmy, lilliputian, dwarfish. **2** *Our summer holiday was far too short. The mayor gave a short speech:* brief, short-lived, quick, fleet, fleeting, momentary, hasty, summary, cursory; concise, terse, succinct, compact; abridged, abbreviated, condensed; curtailed. **3** *The tired salesman was short with the customers:* curt, brusque, abrupt, gruff, impatient, sharp; cross, snappish, testy; ill-tempered, impolite. **4** *The plane had only a short fuel reserve:* low, scanty, scant, sparse, scarce, meagre, skimpy, tight, niggardly, lean, slender, slim, thin; insufficient, deficient, wanting, lacking, limited, not abundant.

—*adv.* **5** *The driver managed to pull up short, and so avoid a nasty accident:* suddenly, abruptly, without warning, precipitously. **6** *The deadline was suddenly moved forward, and I was caught short:* unawares, without preparation, by surprise, without warning.

Ant. **1** long; tall, high, reedy, rangy. **2** long, longish, lengthy, protracted, attenuated, elongated, extended; interminable, unending. **3** patient; polite, civil, mannerly; verbose, wordy, long-winded. **4** adequate, sufficient, ample, plenteous, plentiful, abundant, superabundant, copious, well-stocked, inexhaustible, profuse, lavish; overflowing, excessive, overstocked. **5** slowly, gradually, gently.

shortage *n. There is a shortage of food in the flooded areas:* lack, want, deficiency, dearth, insufficiency, inadequacy, scantiness, scant supply, limited amount, scarcity, sparsity, sparseness, dearth, deficit, leanness.

Ant. abundance, superabundance, profusion, plenty, copiousness, plethora, sufficiency, adequacy; surplus, excess, overflow.

shortcoming *n. Narrow-mindedness is a serious shortcoming:* fault, flaw, defect, blemish, imperfection, failing, weakness, frailty, foible; drawback, handicap, failure.

Ant. advantage, strength, strong point, virtue, merit.

shorten *v. Can the tailor shorten the coat by this evening? Shorten the report by five pages:* make shorter, cut short, cut down, trim, clip, pare, prune, shave, shear; abbreviate, cut, abridge, condense, précis, reduce, decrease, foreshorten, diminish, lessen.

Ant. lengthen, elongate; extend, protract, expand, increase, enlarge, inflate.

shortly *adv. The guests will be arriving shortly:* soon, in a short time, in a little while, before long, by and by, presently, directly, anon, in a minute.

Ant. later, much later.

short-sighted *adj.* **1** *A short-sighted person usually needs glasses:* unable to see far, near-sighted, myopic; amblyopic, weak-eyed, purblind. **2** *It was short-sighted not to plan for the possibility of rain:* lacking foresight, improvident, imprudent, ill-advised, unthinking, injudicious, undiscerning, uncircumspect; careless, heedless, thoughtless, incautious, foolish.

Ant. **1-2** far-sighted. **2** foresighted, long-sighted, prudent, wise, sagacious, circumspect.

shot *n.* **1** *The shots quickly drew the police:* gunfire, report, discharge; volley, salvo, fusillade; detonation, blast, explosion. **2** *The cannon was out of shot:* ammunition, bullets, slugs, projectiles, balls. **3** *The hunter is an excellent shot:* marksman, shooter, rifleman, sharpshooter, sniper; archer, bowman. **4** *The golfer's tee-shot travelled two hundred yards down the fairway:* stroke, throw, toss; play, move; hit, drive. **5** *How about making a shot at the answer?:* attempt, try, chance, go; guess, conjecture, surmise, essay. **6** *A shot of penicillin should cure the infection:* injection; dose.

shoulder *n.* **1** *Someone tapped me on the shoulder:* part of the body between the neck and upper arm; scapula, clavicle. **2** *The wrecked car was left on the shoulder of the road:* edge, side, rim, margin, verge, border, brink, bank, skirt; crest, brow.

—*v.* **3** *The doctor shouldered his way through the crowd:* shove, elbow, push, thrust, lunge; jostle, bump. **4** *The eldest son shouldered the burdens of the family:* assume, undertake, take on, bear, carry on one's shoulders, take, carry, uphold, sustain, support.

Ant. **2** middle, centre, **4** shirk, shun, neglect, avoid, evade, eschew, duck, dodge.

"The easiest way to get a reputation is to go outside the fold, shout around for a few years as a violent atheist or a dangerous radical, and then crawl back to the shelter."

—*F. Scott Fitzgerald*

---

shout *v.* **1** *The drowning man shouted for help:* cry out, cry, call out, call, yell, scream, shriek, howl, roar, bellow, bawl, clamour, thunder, exclaim, rend the air; whoop, hoot, yelp, hollo, huzzah.

—*n.* **2** *The shout brought everyone running. A shout of acclaim went up when the hero appeared:* cry, outcry, call, yell, scream, shriek, howl, screech, roar, bellow, yelp; whoop, hoot, hollo, cheer, hurrah, huzzah; clamour, outburst, burst, chorus, hullabaloo, hue and cry.

shove *v.* **1** *Stop shoving! Shove the chair closer to the table:* push, prod, jostle, elbow, shoulder, crowd, nudge; thrust aside, bump, butt; propel, drive, force, impel.

—*n.* **2** *Someone gave me a shove from behind:* push, prod, thrust, boost, nudge; jostle.

show *v.* **1** *Does my slip show?:* be visible, be within view, come into view, appear, peep out; be noticeable, attract attention. **2** *The test will show how much each student knows:* reveal, disclose, make known, manifest, uncover, bare, lay bare, expose, unveil, bring to light; demonstrate, exhibit, display, prove, evidence, evince, suggest, intimate, hint at, represent, establish, bespeak; argue, testify to, attest, confirm, substantiate, certify, corroborate, bear out, bear witness to. **3** *Show me how this lock works:* explain, indicate, make clear, point out, make known to, inform, teach, instruct, coach, school, tutor. **4** *Show the guest into the study:* direct, lead, guide, usher, conduct. **5** *The judge showed leniency towards the prisoner:* grant, give, bestow, endow, tender, proffer, impart, lavish; dispense, favour, distribute.

—n. **6** *Many hands went up in a show of support. His face gave no show of fear:* display, demonstration, exhibition, sign, expression, token, mark, evidence, indication, manifestation, revelation, disclosure, testimonial, attestation, confirmation. **7** *The cattle were purchased at a recent show:* exhibition, exposition, fair; display, demonstration. **8** *There's a good television show on tonight. The local theatre has a new show this week:* programme, production, entertainment, performance; (*variously*) play, drama, comedy, musical, motion picture, picture, film, opera, operetta, ballet, stage show, vaudeville show, variety show, bill; spectacle, ceremony, pomp. **9** *Her headache was all show to avoid going to work. He likes to put on a show of wealth for his guests:* display, pretext, pretence, pretension, affectation, pose, sham, front, counterfeit; impression, effect, appearance, illusion, delusion; vaunting, flaunting.

Ant. 1 hide, conceal, secrete, withhold, suppress, be invisible, be unnoticeable. **2** hide, conceal, obscure, veil, mask, cloak, cover; disprove, deny, refute. **5** withhold, keep; withdraw. **6** hiding, concealing; disguise, camouflage.

shower *n.* **1** *It will take more than a shower to end the drought. A heavy shower turned the road into a quagmire:* brief fall of rain, sprinkle, drizzle, mizzle; downpour, cloudburst, torrent. **2** *A shower of acorns fell from the tree. A shower of contributions reached the Red Cross:* fall, pouring down, rain; deluge, flood, inundation, torrent, stream, rush, surge, profusion, plethora, wealth; salvo, volley, barrage, bombardment.

—v. **3** *The lawn-sprinkler showered the children. Is it supposed to shower today?:* sprinkle, spray, wet; rain, drizzle, mizzle. **4** *The grandparents showered gifts on the children:* give in abundance, bestow liberally, lavish, rain, deluge, pour, bombard.

show-off *n. Only a show-off would steer a bicycle with his feet:* exhibitionist, flaunter, swaggerer, strutter; egotist, braggard, braggadocio, boaster.

shred *n.* **1** *The machine tore the paper into shreds:* strip, ribbon, band; fragment, sliver, piece, bit, scrap, rag, tatter. **2** *There's not a shred of truth in the story!:* bit, particle, speck, grain, iota, jot, scrap, fragment, trace, atom, molecule, whit, spot, scintilla, hair.

Ant. 2 mass, pile, heap, heaps, oceans, *Informal* loads, oodles.

shrewd *adj.* **1** *He's too shrewd to be trusted in business matters:* sly, crafty, cunning, foxy, wily, cagey; artful, tricky, shifty, slippery, slick, smooth, disingenuous, contriving, designing, scheming, calculating, self-serving, machiavellian. **2** *Shrewd investors held their stock until prices rose again:* astute, smart, clever, sharp, sharp-witted, acute, keen, knowing, canny, discerning, quick, quick-witted, perceptive, sensible, far-seeing, far-sighted, probing, piercing, penetrating; wise, intelligent, sagacious, perspicacious, circumspect, prudent, cautious, careful, wary, prudent.

Ant. 1 straightforward, artless, guileless, ingenuous, candid, open, sincere, fair; innocent, naïve, unsophisticated. **2** dull, unknowing, ignorant, undiscerning, slow-witted, slow, near-sighted, short-sighted, imprudent, careless; dumb, stupid.

shriek *n.* **1** *The children greeted each other with shrieks of joy:* cry, outcry, call, yell, yelp, screech, squeal, howl, shout, scream, whoop, hoot, peal.

—v. **2** *The girl shrieked when she saw the mouse:* cry out, scream, screech, yell, yelp, squeal, howl.

shrill *adj. A radio announcer shouldn't have a shrill voice:* high, high-pitched, screeching, piercing, penetrating, strident, piping, loud, blaring, clamorous, raucous.

Ant. soft, mellow, mellifluous, dulcet, silver-toned, velvety, satiny; resonant, deep, low, well-modulated.

shrine *n. Every day the women come to pray at the shrine:* holy place, consecrated place, sacred tomb; altar, sanctuary, sanctum, chapel, church, temple, mosque.

◇ *Word origin: Shrine* comes from Latin *scrinium,* a case or chest, hence a receptacle for sacred relics. Later it came to mean a tomb or a chapel sanctified by the presence or the remains of a holy personage or dedicated to a holy personage.

shrink *v.* **1** *Will this sweater shrink when it is washed? A bad harvest caused the farmer's income to shrink:* become smaller, make smaller, make less, lessen, shrivel, shorten, draw together, contract, pucker, constrict, deflate, compress, condense; decrease, diminish, decline, curtail, reduce, dwindle, dry up, wane, ebb. **2** *The shy man shrank at the thought of being called upon to speak. The boy shrank from the expected blow:* draw back, hang back, recoil, cringe, cower, quail, shudder, shy, blench, flinch, wince, duck, retreat, withdraw, retire; demur, refuse, balk, bridle.

Ant. 1 stretch, swell, distend, dilate, inflate; increase, enlarge, amplify, grow, expand, mushroom, balloon. **2** welcome, meet head on, confront, stand up to.

shrivel *v. The peaches shrivelled in the sun:* shrink,

dry up, wither, wizen, wrinkle, pucker; parch, scorch.

shroud *n.* **1** *The body was wrapped in a silken shroud:* burial cloth, grave-clothes, winding-sheet, cerements, cerecloth, pall. **2** *A shroud of mystery surrounded the case:* cover, covering, cloak, blanket, sheet, veil, mantle, pall, screen, cloud.
—*v.* **3** *The negotiations were shrouded in secrecy:* wrap, clothe, swathe, cover, envelop, cloak, veil; hide, conceal.
Ant. **3** uncover, unveil, reveal, expose.

shudder *v.* **1** *The child shuddered with fear. The plane shuddered and went into a tail-spin:* tremble, shake, quiver, quaver, quake, shiver; twitch, jerk.
—*n.* **2** *She felt a shudder of fear when she remembered the accident:* trembling, tremor, shiver, quiver, quaver, shake, quake, flutter, throb, paroxysm, pulsation, pang, twitch, jerk.

shuffle *v.* **1** *Stop shuffling your feet!:* drag, scrape, slide, scuff, walk with clumsy steps, shamble. **2** *Shuffle the cards and deal:* jumble, disarrange, rearrange, mix, scramble; exchange the positions of, interchange.
—*n.* **3** *His injured knee caused him to walk with a shuffle:* dragging gait, sliding gait, clumsy step, scraping movement; limp.
Ant. **1** lift. **3** light step, high step.

shun *v.* *The recluse shunned all company:* avoid, evade, elude, dodge, keep away from, keep clear of, steer clear of, shy away from, fight shy of, shrink from, turn away from, circumvent; eschew, forgo, reject, boycott, ignore, have nothing to do with, have no part in.
Ant. welcome, embrace, encourage, seek, search out, solicit, court.

shut *v.* **1** *Shut the door. Shut the curtains:* close, secure, fasten, snap, clasp, latch, lock; draw to, draw, fold. **2** *Shut the cat in the kitchen for the night:* enclose, confine, constrain, cloister, closet, cage, coop, fence in, box, lock; barricade, impound, imprison, intern, incarcerate.
—*adj.* **3** *Is the window shut?:* closed, closed up; fastened, secured, latched, locked; drawn, drawn to.
Ant. **1** open, unshut, draw back; unfasten, unlock. **2** free, liberate, release, let out. **3** open, opened; unfastened, unlocked.

shy *adj.* **1** *The child was too shy to enjoy parties:* self-conscious, bashful, shrinking, timid, timorous, meek, reserved, reticent, demure, modest; fearful, apprehensive, tremulous, nervous, anxious. **2** *Always be shy of blaming the most obvious suspect immediately:* chary, wary, leery, suspicious, distrustful, cautious, careful.
—*v.* **3** *The horse shied at a shadow on the road:* jump back, draw back, recoil from, balk, spring aside, swerve, rear, dodge, shrink, blench, cower, flinch, wince.
Ant. **1** forward, brash, brazen, brassy; bold, fearless, unfrightened, unapprehensive. **2** rash, reckless, careless, unsuspicious, unsuspecting.

sick *adj.* **1** *The actor was too sick to perform. Grandfather has been sick for years. Are you going to be sick?:* ill, unwell, ailing, laid up, indisposed; infirm, sickly, invalid, afflicted, unsound, unhealthy, poorly, frail, delicate, weak; nauseated, vomiting, throwing up, queasy, under the weather. **2** *The missing child's parents are sick with worry:* deeply upset, greatly affected, stricken, afflicted, suffering, distressed, grieved, wretched, heart-broken, crushed, miserable, troubled, uneasy, disturbed, perturbed, disquieted, discomposed. **3** *I'm sick of the same old routine every day:* fed up with, disgusted with, tired, bored with; adverse to, repelled by, displeased with, revolted by.
Ant. **1** well, fine, tiptop; healthy, hale, hale and hearty, sound, unimpaired, strong, robust, vigorous, blooming, fit as a fiddle. **2** unaffected, untroubled, undisturbed, unperturbed, unconcerned, unworried, easy, tranquil, calm.

"They are as sick that surfeit with too much, as they that starve with nothing."
—*William Shakespeare*

---

sicken *v.* *The sight of blood sickened the medical student. Within a week the captured whale sickened and died:* make sick, make ill, nauseate, turn the stomach, disgust, revolt, repel, repulse, horrify, upset, offend, shock; become sick, fall sick.
Ant. cure, make well; please, delight, enchant, gratify.

sickening *adj.* *What's that sickening smell?:* causing sickness, nauseating; disgusting, vile, horrible, nasty, revolting, repugnant, repulsive, repellent, loathsome, abhorrent, distasteful, offensive.
Ant. curative; agreeable, mouth-watering, delightful, pleasant, pleasing, heavenly, wonderful, inviting, tempting, attractive, lovely, enchanting, alluring, captivating.

sickly *adj.* **1** *The sickly child missed many days of school. Did you notice her sickly complexion?:* ailing, in poor health, unhealthy, sick, ill, unwell, infirm, invalid, afflicted, unsound, frail, weak, delicate, poorly; pale, wan, ashen, drab, peaked, bloodless, leaden, cadaverous, lack-lustre. **2** *A sickly light shone through the half-drawn blind:* weak, feeble, faint, ineffective, unconvincing, lacking in fervour, insipid, spiritless, flat, uninspired, apathetic, torpid; simpering, smirking, snickering, sneaky, guilty, self-conscious, silly, namby-pamby, wishy-washy.

sickness *n.* **1** *The worker was absent owing to sickness. Chicken-pox is a common childhood sickness:* illness, ill health; disease, complaint, disorder, infirmity, ailment, malady, affliction; poor health, sickliness, unsoundness, invalidism, frailness, delicate health; disability. **2** *Rough seas caused much sickness among the passengers:* nausea, queasiness, vomiting, *Informal* throwing up.

side *n.* **1** *Stand by my side. Please write on both sides of the paper:* flank; lateral surface, flat surface, surface. **2** *Two sides of the property face the water. The boys stood at the far side of the room:* boundary, bound, limit, perimeter, border, edge, periphery, margin, rim, brim, skirt, hem; part, area, segment, section, sector, territory, region, division; half, quarter. **3** *Both teams wanted the best batsman on their side. Which side do you think will win the election?:* team; group, body, sect, faction, party, clique, coterie, circle; alliance, coalition, association, affiliation, federation. **4** *Let's hear the defendant's side of the story. Look at the problem from both sides:* position, stand, attitude, part, belief, opinion, cause, behalf; viewpoint, point of view, view, standpoint, aspect, angle, slant, light, phase, facet. **5** *Harry is related on my father's side of the family:* part of a family; line of descent, lineage, bloodline, strain, stock, house.
—*adj.* **6** *Plant the rose-bushes in the side bed:* at one side, on one side, lateral, flanking; fringing, bordering, marginal, skirting. **7** *Figure B shows the same device from the side view. He gave her a side glance:* from the side, towards the side, lateral; sideways, sidelong, oblique, indirect, askance. **8** *Does the job offer any side benefits? The car is parked in a side street:* minor, subordinate, lesser, incidental, secondary, subsidiary, insignificant, unimportant, inconsequential; related, accessory, collateral, contingent, allied.
Ant. **1** front, back; top, bottom, edge. **2** middle, centre, midpoint. **6** front, back, rear; top, bottom; centre, central, middle. **7** frontal, direct, headlong; rear. **8** major, main, primary, principal, prime, first, leading.

sideways *adv.* **1** *The pedestrian jumped sideways to avoid the cyclist. Try to slip sideways through the hole in the fence:* to the side, towards one side, from one side, sidewards; with one side forward, laterally, sidelong, edgeways, edgewise, aslant, obliquely.
—*adj.* **2** *The boy gave the girl a sideways look:* sidelong, oblique, lateral.
Ant. **1** forwards, backwards; head on. **2** direct, headlong.

sift *v.* **1** *Sift the brown sugar on to the biscuits. Dust sifted through the window frame:* sprinkle, scatter; drift, filter. **2** *It's hard to sift the facts from the lies in his story. The jury sifted through the transcripts of the trial:* separate, sort out, sort, winnow, screen; study, scrutinize, inspect, examine closely, probe, search, investigate, analyse, review.
◇ *Word origin: Sift* and *sieve* come from Old English *siftan* and *sife*, meaning "to sift" and "sieve," respectively. Also related are *seep* and *sip*. The basic root-sense in Germanic was "trickle, drip."

sigh *v.* **1** *The waitress sighed with weariness. He sighed, "Too bad":* let out one's breath, breathe loudly, moan, groan, sob; say with a sighing sound, whine, hiss. **2** *The soldiers sighed for their homes and families:* pine, yearn, long, brood; grieve, weep, lament, mourn, sorrow.
—*n.* **3** *The student gave a sigh of relief when the exam was over:* deep audible breath; moan, groan, sob, whine; hiss.

sight *n.* **1** *Wearing glasses will help poor sight:* eyesight, vision, visual perception. **2** *We waved until the car was out of sight:* range of vision, field of vision, eyeshot, view, ken, scrutiny, gaze, survey. **3** *The sight of land elated the ship's crew:* seeing, vision, appearance, visibility, viewing, glimpse, view. **4** *The sun setting over the sea was a sight to behold:* view, spectacle, display, pageant, exhibit, scene, image; place of interest, thing of interest. **5** often *Plural The rifle has new sights:* sighting device, peep-sight, bead; telescopic sights.
—*v.* **6** *The captain sighted a ship on the horizon:* see, descry, observe, glimpse, spot, catch sight of, spy, espy, perceive, behold, view.
Ant. **1** blindness.

sign *n.* **1** *A valentine is a sign of love. The dark clouds may be a sign of rain:* symbol, mark, figure, token, evidence, manifestation, emblem, badge, ensign; indication, indicator, omen, portent, prognostic, presage, warning, forewarning, forecast, herald, signal, clue, symptom, hint, suggestion, note, index; characteristic, earmark, trade-mark, trait, feature, stamp, brand. **2** *The guard gave the driver the sign to start. The winner made a thumbs-up sign:* signal, motion, gesture; go-ahead, wave, nod. **3** *A "For Sale" sign was in the window:* (*variously*) placard, advertising sign, electric sign, neon sign, signboard, signpost, billboard; road sign, street sign, milestone; name-plate.
—*v.* **4** *Please sign both copies of the contract. Please sign my autograph book:* write one's signature, set one's hand to, countersign, underwrite, undersign, endorse; autograph, inscribe.

signal *n.* **1** *The referee blew his whistle as a signal for the game to begin. Did the policeman give us a signal to go ahead?:* sign, indication, indicator, cue, warning, command; gesture, O.K., motion, nod.
—*adj.* **2** *The* Aeneid *is a signal example of literary epic as contrasted with oral epic:* singular, unique, exceptional, one-of-a-kind, distinctive, outstanding, extraordinary, exceptional, remarkable, noteworthy, notable, distinguished, eminent, illustrious, famous, honoured, renowned, impressive, important, consequential, significant, momentous,

considerable, memorable, unforgettable; conspicuous, striking, arresting, prominent, commanding.
—*v.* **3** *The conductor signalled the orchestra to rise:* motion, gesture, beckon, give a sign to.
Ant. 2 ordinary, commonplace, common, familiar, everyday, run-of-the-mill.

Exploring the Word: *Sign, signal, signature, insignia,* and *ensign* (a banner or flag) all come from Latin *signum,* sign, emblem, badge of office, distinguishing mark. This also gives us: *assign,* to distribute, appoint, or authorize as if by an official seal or signature; *consign,* to transfer possessions or authority officially, as with an official seal or signature; *design* and *designate,* to mark out, point out, appoint officially, as with an official seal or signature; *resign,* give back a badge of office, hence to leave a job, give up a position, etc.; *significant,* literally worthy of *insignia* or a badge of office, hence important, and *insignificant,* not worthy of a badge of office or official recognition, trivial, petty; and *signify,* to make a sign, indicate.

significance *n. The Torah has great significance for Jews. Do you understand the significance of the doctor's findings?:* consequence, importance, import, weight, meaning, implication, moment, portent, gravity, force, influence, authority, concern, interest, note, notability, eminence, prominence, distinction, excellence, value, merit, worth, virtue; sense, drift, intent, intention, aim, object, purpose, direction.

significant *adj.* **1** *The discovery of penicillin was an extremely significant event in medical history. Does the report give all the significant facts of the case?:* consequential, important, substantial, meaningful, material, principal, great, paramount, major, chief, main, prime, vital, critical, serious, portentous, influential, considerable, momentous, grave, noteworthy, notable, eminent, prominent, distinct, outstanding, remarkable, impressive, exceptional, signal, eventful. **2** *The hush was significant of the crowd's respect for the speaker. He gave her a significant look:* indicative, expressive, meaningful, suggestive, symbolic, symptomatic, emblematic, representative, demonstrative; eloquent, pregnant, cogent, telling, knowing.
Ant. 1 insignificant, inconsequential, unimportant, insubstantial, meaningless, immaterial.

signify *v. A white flag signifies surrender. Please signify your agreement by raising your hand:* be a sign of, stand for, mean, indicate, represent, connote, convey, express, manifest, evidence, evince, demonstrate, exhibit, show, proclaim, declare, announce, communicate, set forth, designate, disclose, reveal, tell, give notice of; imply, intimate, suggest, hint at, denote, typify, symbolize, bespeak, betoken, import, argue; portend, predict, prognosticate, augur, omen, forbode, foretell, foreshadow, presage, herald, promise.

silence *n.* **1** *The silence of the woods was broken by the cry of a bittern. Father's silence indicated his disapproval. Silence was the key to the young man's success:* quiet, quietness, noiselessness, soundlessness, stillness, hush; peace, calm, tranquillity, serenity, placidness, placidity, repose; speechlessness, muteness, dumbness; reserve, reticence, uncommunicativeness, taciturnity, secretiveness, close-mouthedness.
—*v.* **2** *The speaker tried to silence the angry crowd. There must be a way to silence the echoes in this room:* still, quiet, quieten, hush, calm, strike dumb, tongue-tie; deaden. **3** *The dictator has silenced his opponents by gaoling them. We must silence our fears and proceed:* gag, muzzle, choke off, suppress, repress, crush, quell, quash, put down, squash; stop, halt, stifle, check, curb, vanquish, overcome, defeat, rout, banish, subdue, conquer, extinguish, nullify, allay, quiet, still, put an end to, lay to rest.
Ant. 1 sound, noise, noisiness, din, roar, clamour, row, tumult, turmoil, commotion, agitation, excitement; speech, talking, talkativeness, verbosity, verboseness, loquaciousness, garrulousness, chatter, babel. **2** make noise; arouse, rouse, agitate, incite, stir up; make louder, amplify. **3** ungag, encourage, support, aid, help, abet, champion, broadcast, publicize.

"Silence is the unbearable repartee."
—*G. K. Chesterton*

silent *adj.* **1** *The cat moved on silent feet. The house was as silent as a morgue:* making no sound, having no sound, soundless, noiseless, quiet, still, hushed, muted, mute; idle, inactive, unstirring, lifeless, inert, quiescent, dormant, calm, peaceful, tranquil, serene, placid. **2** *The class was silent as the teacher explained the examination rules. Bill is the strong, silent type:* not speaking, saying nothing, wordless, mum, tongue-tied; speechless, mute, dumb; speaking little, untalkative, reticent, uncommunicative, close-mouthed, close-lipped, tight-lipped, taciturn, reserved; secretive, mysterious, discreet. **3** *The "p" in "psychic" is silent:* not pronounced, unpronounced, not sounded, unsounded, unvocalized, mute. **4** *The two nations have a silent understanding to come to each other's aid if either is attacked:* tacit, understood, implied, implicit, inferred, intimidated, insinuated, suggested, unspoken, unsaid, untalked of, unmentioned, unexpressed, undeclared, unarticulated; unpublished, unwritten, unrevealed, hidden, covert, concealed.
Ant. 1 noisy, clamorous; active, stirring, live-

ly, bustling, tumultuous, agitated, excited. **2** noisy, vocal, vociferous, talkative, talky, garrulous, loquacious, wordy, verbose, chatty, blabbering, babbling. **3** sounded, pronounced, articulated. **4** spelt-out, explicit, stated, declared, announced, expressed.

silly *adj.* **1** *It's silly to drive without fastening one's seat-belt. He's a vain, silly creature:* lacking judgement, foolhardy, irrational, senseless, unwise, ill-advised, unwary, irresponsible, ridiculous, pointless; foolish, dumb, stupid, simple-minded, witless, brainless, feather-brained, hare-brained, rattle-brained, addle-brained, muddle-headed; shallow, fatuous, idiotic, absurd, asinine, inane, childish, frivolous, frothy, giddy, mad, insane, crazy. **2** *That silly joke made everyone laugh:* ridiculous, nonsensical, preposterous, farcical, ludicrous, laughable; meaningless, purposeless, inconsequential, inappropriate, aimless, unreasonable.

Ant. **1** judicious, rational, sensible, wise, reasonable, sane, sound, smart, bright, clever, brainy, intelligent, perceptive, sharp, acute, sage; serious, deep, mature, stable. **2** serious, meaningful, purposeful, consequential, appropriate; sad, sorrowful.

◇ *Word origin:* Sometimes happiness leads to carefree laughter, giggling, and foolishness. The word *silly* comes from Old English *saelig,* happy, blessed.

silvan Also **sylvan** *adj. She loved the silvan beauty of the eastern part of the country:* woody, forest-like, woodland, Arcadian, wooded, timbered, forested, thicket-grown, forest-clad, overgrown, luxuriant, bushy, leafy, moss-carpeted.

> **Exploring the Word**: *Silvan* goes back to Latin *silva,* forest, a wood, which also gives us *silviculture,* the art of growing and tending trees; the names *Sylvia* and *Sylvester,* literally forest-girl and forest-boy; and the *-sylvania* ending in *Pennsylvania* and Count Dracula's beloved homeland *Transylvania.* (*Pennsylvania* is named after William Penn, hence *Penn* + *sylvania,* Penn's land abounding in forests, and *Transylvania* is from Latin *trans-*, across, + *sylvania,* woods, literally across the woods, the region on the other side of the forest.) Finally, Latin *silva,* woods, gives us (via French *sauvage*) our word *savage,* literally one who lives in the woods.

silver *n.* **1** *The prospector discovered a silver mine. The silver needs polishing:* white shining precious metal, argentine, argent, *Latin* argentum; articles made of silver, silverware, silver jewellery. **2** *I have only a pound note and some silver:* change, coins. **3** *The old man had silver hair:* greyish white, platinum.

similar *adj. The two dresses are similar but not identical. The two men have similar political views:* nearly alike, much the same, kindred, akin, parallel, like, equivalent, comparable, analogous, close, correspondent, corresponding, correlative, agreeing, approximate, resembling, allied, cognate.

Ant. different, dissimilar, unalike, unlike, disparate, diverse, opposite, opposed, contrary, contradictory, antithetical, disagreeing.

◇ *Usage note: Similar* means like but not identical; *same* means identical. Thus, *When the twins wore the same dresses no one could tell them apart,* but *The sisters wore similar cotton dresses; Jane's was blue and Helen's was red.* Do not use *similar* to mean "exactly the same" or "identical."

> **Exploring the Word**: Latin *similis,* like, alike, gives us *similar, dissimilar* (unlike), and *resemble,* as well as: *assimilate,* to include as part of oneself, make another like oneself, as immigrants are assimilated into a new country; *facsimile,* literally something made to be like something else, a copy; *semblance,* likeness, appearance; *simulate,* to make appear like something else, to counterfeit or feign; and *simile,* a figure of speech in which two things are said to be alike, as "Her eyes are like violets." Closely related is Latin *simul,* at the same time, which give us *simultaneous,* happening at the same time; *assemble,* to bring together at the same time; and *ensemble,* the people or things brought together at the same time, as musicians to play or a set of clothes worn together.

similarity *n. There's a strong similarity between these two paintings:* resemblance, likeness, correspondence, parallelism, kinship, similitude, semblance, sameness, comparability, equivalence, agreement, congruity, harmony, concordance, conformance, conformability, affinity, closeness, nearness, reciprocity.

Ant. dissimilarity, difference, dissimilitude, disparity, diversity, incongruity, discordance, disagreement.

simmer *v.* **1** *Simmer the sauce for five minutes. I hear the kettle simmering:* boil gently, stew, seethe; bubble, gurgle, burble. **2** *He simmered with anger:* seethe, fume, foam, boil, sizzle, burn.

simper *v. The children simpered behind the teacher's back:* snigger, snicker, smirk, giggle, titter; smile affectedly, grin self-consciously.

simple *adj.* **1** *There are three types of sentence: simple, compound, and complex. Even a child can solve this simple puzzle:* having few parts, not complex, uncomplicated, uninvolved, not elaborate; unsophisticated; basic, elemental, elementary, fundamental, rudimentary; easy, not difficult, manageable, soft. **2** *She wore a simple black dress to the reception. The old farmer led a simple life:* plain, not fancy, unadorned, undecorated, unembellished, untrimmed, modest, unaffected, unworldly, unpretentious; unsophisticated, natural, common, commonplace, ordinary, workaday; quiet, peaceful, rustic, homely, innocent, naïve, guileless, artless, ingenuous. **3** *The simple truth is that no one wants to do the job:* plain, honest, true, sincere, candid, naked, stark, bare, unadorned, unvarnished, downright, sheer, absolute, straight, unfeigned, open, artless, guileless; blunt, frank, direct, plain-spoken, straightforward, out-and-out. **4** *He's so simple that he'll believe anything you tell him:* innocent, naïve, artless, guileless, ingenuous, green, callow, unworldly, inexperienced, unsophisticated; dumb, stupid, simple-minded, slow, dense, dull, thick, thick-witted, obtuse, foolish, weak up top.

Ant. 1 complex, complicated, involved, intricate, elaborate, compound, sophisticated, advanced; difficult, hard, tough. **2** fancy, elaborate, ornate, adorned, decorated, embellished, pretentious, affected, ostentatious, flashy, showy; sophisticated, worldly, cosmopolitan; busy, hectic, bustling, confused, tumultuous. **3** dishonest, insincere, varnished, gilded, indirect, devious, artful, guileful; feigned, pretended, contrived. **4** worldly, sophisticated, knowing, wise, experienced; crafty, sly, cunning, foxy, clever, canny, shrewd, sharp, acute, keen, smart, bright, fast, quick on the uptake.

simpleton *n. Anyone who believes that nonsense is a simpleton!:* fool, numskull, nincompoop, dunce, oaf, ignoramus, dolt, ninny, booby, idiot, dummy, imbecile, ass, jackass, dope, donkey, *Slang* jerk, clot, stupe; rustic, twerp, greenhorn.

simplicity *n.* **1** *Modern architecture is marked by great simplicity. He spoke with great feeling and simplicity:* lack of complexity; easiness, obviousness, directness, straightforwardness, plainness, clarity, clearness, purity, restraint, cleanliness, lack of adornment, austerity, serenity. **2** *The child's simplicity was disarming:* openness, candour, directness, sincerity, honesty, guilelessness, truthfulness, artlessness, naturalness; innocence, naïvety, unworldliness, lack of sophistication.

Ant. 1 complexity, complicatedness, intricateness, difficulty; elaborateness, fanciness, ornateness, decoration, adornment, embellishment, pretentiousness, affectation, ostentation. **2** sophistication, worldliness; deviousness, insincerity, dishonesty, craftiness, untruthfulness, guilefulness, guile, slyness, cunning, conniving.

simply *adv. Give the directions as simply as possible. The poem is beautiful yet very simply expressed:* uncomplicatedly, plainly, directly, straightforwardly, explicitly, clearly, lucidly, intelligibly; without adornment, starkly, modestly, unaffectedly, unpretentiously, naturally, ingenuously.

simulate *v. She simulated tears to gain our sympathy:* feign, put on, pretend, counterfeit, affect, fabricate, fake, sham; act, play, pose, make believe, imitate, ape, mimic, copy.

simulated *adj. The coat is made of simulated leopard-skin:* imitation, synthetic, artificial, fabricated, man-made, pretend, make-believe, sham; fake, counterfeit, phoney, forged.

Ant. real, authentic, actual, natural, true, bona fide.

simultaneous *adj. The two armies made simultaneous offensives on two fronts:* occurring at the same time, concurrent, coincident, synchronous, concomitant; existing at the same time, coexistent, coexisting, contemporaneous, contemporary.

sin *n.* **1** *May God forgive you your sins. The school considers disobedience a sin:* ungodly act, immoral act, irreligious act, sinfulness, iniquity, transgression, trespass; wrong, wrongdoing, evil, evil deed, villainy, vice, misdeed, violation, breach, crime, offence, infraction, error, slip, lapse, shortcoming. **2** *It's a sin the way she wastes money:* shame, disgrace, scandal.

—*v.* **3** *Who has not sinned?:* offend against God, offend against morality, transgress, trespass, err, offend, fall, stray, do wrong, do evil, slip, lapse.

Ant. 1 virtue, goodness, righteousness, sinlessness, godliness, holiness, uprightness, probity; good, honesty, ethics, morality.

"That which we call sin in others, is experiment for us." —*Ralph Waldo Emerson*

---

sincere *adj. Her sadness seemed sincere. The youth made a sincere effort to reform:* free from pretence, unfeigned, undeceitful, unaffected, real, honest, natural, genuine, authentic, artless, guileless, ingenuous, candid, frank, straightforward, forthright, truthful; bona fide, earnest, whole-hearted, heartfelt, serious, in good faith.

Ant. insincere, feigned, pretended, deceitful, contrived, affected, devious, deceptive.

◇ *Word origin: Sincere* comes from Latin *sincerus*, pure. The *sin-* in this word is cognate with our word *same*, and the *-cerus* with the name of the goddess of agriculture *Ceres* and with the word *creare*, to create, grow. The root-meaning of *sincerus* is "of one growth." Even today we say of sincere people that they are "all of a piece."

sincerely *adv. The boy was sincerely sorry:* really, genuinely, honestly, truly, frankly, truthfully; earnestly, seriously, whole-heartedly.

Ant. insincerely, falsely, dishonestly, deceptively, untruthfully, deceitfully.

sincerity *n. Everyone was touched by the sincerity of her apology:* honesty, genuineness, earnestness, seriousness, candour, frankness, forthrightness, truthfulness, artlessness, straightforwardness, unaffectedness, ingenuousness, guilelessness, whole-heartedness, good faith.

sinful *adj. Stealing is sinful. The people of Sodom and Gomorrah were shamelessly sinful:* wicked, evil, unrighteous, unholy, impious, irreligious, iniquitous, immoral, profligate, corrupt, depraved, degenerate; villainous, vile, wrong, bad, heinous, despicable, wayward, errant, criminal, shameful, disgraceful.

Ant. sinless, righteous, upright, virtuous, moral, pure, godly; honest, ethical, honourable.

sing *v. The soprano sang beautifully. The birds sang all day:* utter musical sounds, intone, chant, croon, lilt, hum, perform a song, tell in song, make melody, tell in verse; warble, chirp, chirrup, trill, tweet, pipe, whistle.

singe *v. Stand clear of the fire, or you may singe your clothes:* scorch, sear, char, burn slightly, burn superficially.

singer *n. Caruso was a great singer:* vocalist, songster, songstress, crooner, diva, chantress, chanteuse, chorister; (*variously*) tenor, bass, soprano; contralto, baritone, countertenor, mezzo-soprano; prima donna; minstrel, troubadour, bard; song-bird.

> **Exploring the Word:** Many words for singers, voices, and musical parts come to us via Italian from Latin. Going in order from the highest to the lowest voice, these are: *soprano* from Latin *super*, above, hence above all others, highest; *mezzo-soprano* (Latin *medius*, middle + *soprano*), the female voice between soprano and contralto; *alto*, from Latin *altus* high, hence the highest adult male voice or sometimes the lowest female voice, which is usually called *contralto* (from Italian *contra*, against + *alto*); *tenor*, the male voice between alto and baritone, from Latin *tenere*, to have, to hold, that which holds the course or leads; *baritone*, which comes from Greek *barutonos*, deep-sounding; and, lowest of all male voices, *bass* or *basso*, from Late Latin *bassus*, low (which also gives us the woodwind instrument the *bassoon*). Regardless of her voice range, a woman opera star may be called a *prima donna*, Italian for "first lady" or a *diva*, "goddess," from the feminine form of Latin *divus*, divine.

single *adj.* **1** *Put a single rose in the vase:* one, only one, individual, solitary, lone, sole, singular. **2** *Is the new employee married or single?:* unmarried, unwed, spouseless, wifeless, husbandless, spinster, bachelor, *Slang* on the shelf.

Ant. 1 accompanied; several, some, many, numerous. **2** married, wed, wedded, *Slang* hitched.

singular *adj.* **1** *The youngster has a singular ear for music:* unique, rare, unusual, uncommon, exceptional, extraordinary, unequalled, unparalleled, matchless, unprecedented, peerless, surpassing, choice, select, superior; remarkable, noteworthy, wonderful, marvellous, prodigious. **2** *A singular glow came from the unidentified flying object:* unusual, unnatural, odd, strange, queer, peculiar, curious, freakish, bizarre, fantastic, outlandish, quaint, different, unconventional, eccentric, anomalous, unwonted, uncustomary, atypical, unfamiliar, abnormal, aberrant, unaccountable, extraordinary, out of the ordinary, off the beaten track.

Ant. 1, 2 common, commonplace, familiar, ordinary, usual, everyday, routine, conventional.

sinister *adj.* **1** *Sinister rumblings came from the volcano. The villain's sinister laugh rang out across the stage:* threatening, ominous, menacing, dire, frightening, fearful, alarming, disturbing, disquieting, dismaying; inauspicious, unpropitious, unfavourable, unpromising, adverse, unlucky. **2** *The government discovered a sinister plot to take over the country:* wicked, evil, villainous, vile, foul, treacherous, perfidious, malevolent, malign, malignant, insidious, Machiavellian, rascally, rank, dark, black, reprehensible, despicable, detestable, damnable, accursed, cursed, diabolical, infernal, hellish, devilish.

Ant. 1 calming, soothing, encouraging, heartening favourable, auspicious, promising, propitious, opportune, advantageous; beneficial, kindly, benevolent, benign. **2** noble, heroic, honourable, worthy, virtuous, just, high-minded, exemplary, righteous, upright, reputable, principled, ethical.

◇ *Word origin: Sinister* is Latin for "left." The word took on the meaning of ominous or malevolent because in augury omens seen on the left were considered unfavourable. In heraldry when describing coats of arms and the like, *sinister* is still used to mean "on the observer's left." Thus, *a lion sinister on a field of blue* would mean a lion occupying the left-hand portion of a blue background on a coat of arms.

sink *v.* **1** *The moon sank behind the mountains. The porch sinks a bit in the left corner:* descend, go down, lower, drop, fall, plunge; decline, dip, slant, slope, tilt, sag, droop, slump. **2** *The ocean liner* Titanic *sank in 1912. The anchor sank to the bottom and held the ship firm:* descend below the surface, submerse, submerge, go to the bottom, go under, go to Davy Jones's locker; become absorbed, seep, soak; engulf, drown. **3** *The farmer sank fence posts along the farm's boundary. The engineers sank a tunnel into the ground:* put down, set, lay, lower, bury; excavate, dig, bore, drill, drive, gouge, scoop out, hollow out. **4** *Prices sank to an all-time low. The patient's health seemed to sink overnight:* lower, decline, fall, lessen, diminish, drop, shrink, subside, go down, reduce, depreciate; deteriorate, degenerate, retrogress, regress, worsen, wane, ebb, slump, slip, languish, give way, droop, sag, go from bad to worse, go downhill, go to pot, go to the dogs. **5** *I never thought he'd sink to cheating at cards:* stoop, fall, descend, lower oneself, degrade oneself, debase oneself; succumb, give way, yield.

—*n.* **6** *Wash your hands in the sink:* basin, wash-basin, bowl, wash-bowl.

Ant. 1 rise, ascend, climb, mount, incline. **2** surface, emerge. **3** remove, dig up; fill in. **4** rise, increase, advance, ascend, climb, grow.

sinuous *adj. The sinuous trail wound up the mountainside:* full of turns, winding, curving, curved, bending, convoluted, folded, serpentine, twisted, twisting, coiling, meandering, zigzag, wandering, circuitous, roundabout, indirect, rambling, tortuous.

Ant. straight, direct.

◇ *Word origin: Sinuous,* like *insinuate,* comes from Latin *sinus,* curve, which also gives the geometric terms *sine* and *cosine* and the anatomical word *sinus* (a cavity or channel, formed by a bending or folding, as the cavities in the cranial bones at the top of one's nose).

sip *v.* **1** *Sip the coffee slowly until it cools down:* drink bit by bit, drink slowly, sup; sample, taste, savour.

—*n.* **2** *Try a sip of this lemonade:* small mouthful, small draught, dram, swallow, drop, thimbleful, sup, soupçon, nip, tot, drink, sample, taste.

Ant. 1 gulp, bolt, swill, swig, quaff, toss off. **2** gulp, swig.

siren *n.* **1** *The police siren woke everyone:* warning signal; (*variously*) alarm, whistle, horn. **2** Sometimes **Siren** *According to Homer, the Sirens lured Odysseus's companions to shipwreck and death. Watch out for that woman; she's a real siren:* nymph, sea nymph; seductress, enchantress, temptress, vamp, deceiver; bewitching woman, charmer.

sit *v.* **1** *Sit on this chair next to me. The bird sat on the topmost branch of the tree:* be seated, have a seat; squat, sprawl, loll; settle, perch, roost. **2** *The house sits high on a hill overlooking a lake. The old trunk sat in the attic for years:* be situated, be located, be established, be seated, be placed, stand, rest, lie; remain, stay, endure, reside, abide, linger. **3** *The committee sits twice a year. Have you ever sat on a jury?:* convene, be in session, assemble, meet, gather, conduct business; occupy a place, have an official seat, hold an official position; govern, rule, reign, officiate, preside, chair. **4** *One of my neighbour's daughters sat with the children:* babysit, watch, watch over, care for, take care of, mind, attend, teach, keep company, chaperon, nurse.

Ant. 1 stand; lie. **2** move, remove. **3** adjourn, disperse, scatter.

◇ *Usage note: Sit* is an intransitive verb (does not take an object) meaning to seat oneself, to be seated: *I sit on that chair while sewing. Set* is a transitive verb (takes an object) with several meanings, one of which is to put something down: *Set the teapot on the table.*

site *n. A new school occupies the site of the old railway station. I think Exmoor will make an excellent site for the film:* spot, place, ground, post, position, station; locale, locality, location, territory, region, area, province, section, sector, district, zone, field, scene, setting.

◇ *Usage note:* A *site* is where something is located, *to cite* is to quote or refer to something, as a passage in a book or a rule or law. Thus, *Schliemann found the site of ancient Troy, The plant site must be near a railway siding,* but *The lawyer cited the case of Rex v. Johnson.*

situate *v. The housing development must be situated near a bus route:* locate, place, position, put, establish, station, settle, install, lodge, ensconce, house; plant, post, stand; construct, build.

Ant. move, remove.

situation *n.* **1** *The international situation is steadily worsening. How did you ever get into such a bad financial situation?:* state of affairs, state, circumstances, condition, status, case, position, posture; predicament, plight, mess, fix, quandary. **2** *The shop is in an ideal situation to attract tourists:* position, location, locality, locale, spot, place, site, station, seat. **3** *The situation as sales manager entails a great deal of travelling:* job, position, post, assignment, place, seat, office, berth, capacity; role, function, duty, work, livelihood.

size *n.* **1** *The size of the pool is 40 feet by 20:* dimensions, measurement, extent, amplitude, stretch, proportions, area, volume, spread, expanse; magnitude, largeness, greatness, bigness, bulk, mass, scope; content, capacity. **2** *What was the size of the research grant?:* amount, quantity, sum, aggregate, total, totality.

—*v.* **3** *Size up the situation with care before making your decision:* appraise, assess, evaluate, estimate, have the measure of, *Slang* tape.

sizzle *v.* **1** *The steak sizzled on the grill:* hiss, sputter, spit, frizzle.

—*n.* **2** *We awoke to the smell of fresh coffee and the sizzle of hot sausages:* hissing, hiss, sputtering.

skeleton *n. The medical students studied a skeleton of the human body. Only the skeleton of the house was still standing after the fire:* bony framework, bones; frame, underlying structure, hulk.

Ant. skin; exterior, surface, covering, sheath.

◇ *Word origin:* To the ancient Greeks *skeleton* referred to a mummy. It is the Greek word for "dried," and the Greek phrase *skeleton soma* meant dried body, mummy.

sketch *n.* **1** *The artists made several sketches before beginning the final painting. The builder followed the architect's sketch:* drawing, preliminary drawing, preliminary painting; rough design, blueprint, graph, chart. **2** *The wages committee presented to the meeting a sketch of their long report:* outline, brief description, rough account, summary, abstract, précis, synopsis, digest. **3** *The actors amused the audience with several impromptu sketches:* skit, short play, scene, vignette, characterization; lampoon, take-off, burlesque, satire.

—*v.* **4** *A pavement artist sketched the passers-by:* make a quick drawing of, draw; rough out, draft. **5** *The historical article sketched the major events of the decade:* set forth briefly, describe quickly, outline, plot, summarize, abstract, map, mark out, picture, depict, delineate, portray, chart, graph, rough out.

sketchy *adj. The advertisement only gives a sketchy description of the property:* incomplete, cursory, rough, vague, bare, essential, outline, brief, short, hazy, slight, skimpy, slender, meagre, light, shallow, superficial, undetailed; unfinished, preliminary, provisional, preparatory, unpolished, unrefined, crude, rough-hewn.

Ant. complete, full, detailed, lengthy, long, in-depth, exact; finished, final, polished.

skid *n.* **1** *The car braked too quickly and went into a skid:* slip, sliding motion, slide; glissade. **2** *The heavy crates were packed on skids and taken to the warehouse:* runner, platform with runners; trolley.

—*v.* **3** *The lorry's wheels skidded on the wet road:* slide, slip, slip sideways, side-slip; glide, glissade, skip, skate, ski, skim.

skilful *adj. Only the most skilful pilots are employed by airlines. The bricklayer did a skilful job in building the wall:* skilled, expert, able, competent, capable, proficient, qualified, accomplished, professional, masterful, masterly, experienced, veteran, practised, trained, well-versed; apt, adept, adroit, dextrous, handy, facile, deft, talented, gifted, ingenious, clever, sharp, keen, cunning, slick.

Ant. unskilful, unskilled, inexpert, inept, incompetent, unqualified, unaccomplished, non-professional, amateurish, inexperienced, unpractised, untrained; unqualified; clumsy, awkward, bungling.

skill *n.* **1** *The antique cabinet had been made with great skill:* skilfulness, craft, adroitness, adeptness, expertness, deftness, dexterity, handiness, mastery, competence, artistry; acumen, cunning, cleverness, ingenuity, inventiveness. **2** *Have you the skill to ski down such a difficult slope?:* ability, capacity, prowess, faculty, facility, proficiency, experience, knowhow, knack; talent, gift.

Ant. 1 incompetence, ineptness, ineptitude, awkwardness, clumsiness. **2** inability, non-proficiency, inexperience.

skim *v.* **1** *Skim the cream off the top of the milk:* take up from the surface, scrape. **2** *The water-skier skimmed over the surface of the lake:* move lightly, glide, sweep, glissade, coast, skate, scud, skid, skip, float, sail, fly. **3** *Don't read the report word for word now, just skim through it:* read superficially, glance over, scan, flip, thumb, leaf.

Ant. 3 examine carefully, peruse.

skimp *v.* **1** *Don't skimp on the butter when making these biscuits:* be sparing of, be stingy with, scrimp, stint, slight, hold back, withhold. **2** *By skimping a little we can stick to our budget:* be frugal, use economy, economize, be stingy, cut expenses, be parsimonious, be niggardly, pinch, scrimp, stint, scrape along.

Ant. 1 lavish, squander, be generous with, be profuse with, pour on, load on. **2** be extravagant, overspend, squander, be thriftless.

skimpy *adj. Why did you give me such a skimpy portion of ice cream? That sweater is too skimpy to wear over a bulky shirt:* not large enough, small, tight, smallish, scant, scanty, spare, sparse, scrimpy, meagre, modest, slight, cramped; inadequate, insufficient, incomplete, wanting, inconsiderable.

Ant. big, too big, large, full, loose; abundant, profuse, copious, generous, lavish, considerable; adequate, sufficient.

> **Exploring the Word**: *Skin* comes from Old Norse *skinn*, animal skin. The Greek word for skin is *derma*, which gives us *epidermis*, the outer layer of skin; *dermatologist*, a doctor who treats disorders of the skin; and *pachyderm*, literally "thick skin," hence any of certain thick-skinned animals, as the elephant, hippopotamus, or rhinoceros.

skin *n.* **1** *Many Scandinavians have fair skin. The trappers sold bear skins to the trading post:* epidermis, body covering; complexion; hide, pelt, coat, fur, fleece. **2** *Tomatoes are quite safe to eat with their skins on:* peel, rind, husk, hull, shell, pod, jacket, case, casing, sheath, integument, outer coating.

—*v.* **3** *The hunter skinned the deer. The boy skinned his knee:* strip the skin from, remove the hide from, lay bare; scrape, bark, abrade.

skinflint *n. That skinflint wouldn't give a shilling to charity:* stingy person, miser, niggardly person, niggard, penny-pincher, Scrooge, *Slang* tightwad.

Ant. big spender, sport.

◇ *Word origin:* A *skinflint* is one so miserly or so against wasting anything that he would skin a flint (an exceptionally hard stone).

skinny *adj. The boy is skinny but surprisingly strong:* thin, slender, lean, scrawny, spindly, emaciated, spare, lank, lanky, angular, gawky, gangling, scraggy, gaunt, raw-boned, skeletal.

Ant. fat, obese, corpulent, plump, chubby, hefty, husky, rotund, fleshy, robust.

skip *v.* **1** *The little girls skipped down the path. The speaker skipped from one topic to the next, confusing* *everyone:* leap lightly, hop, jump, trip, bob, spring, bounce, bound, flit, prance, gambol, caper, romp; jump lightly over, leap over. **2** *The autobiography skips over the author's childhood and begins with his adolescence. Let's skip dessert and just have coffee:* pass over, omit, leave out, overlook, ignore, eschew, neglect, disregard, do without; evade, elude, dodge, shun, miss. **3** *The boy skipped school two days in a row:* be absent from, be absent from without excuse, play truant, cut.

—*n.* **4** *The ice skater made two little skips and then did a pirouette:* light jump, leap, bound, spring, hop, bounce; prance, gambol, caper.

Ant. 1 shuffle, lumber, drag, trudge, plod, waddle. **2** include, cover, put in, contain, refer to, take into account; confront, meet. **3** be present, attend.

skirmish *n.* **1** *The major battle is over but there are still skirmishes along the front:* brief fight, encounter, clash, engagement, action; brush, fray, affray, scrap, tussle, fracas, scrimmage, *Slang* set-to, run-in.

—*v.* **2** *The soldiers skirmished at the border:* fight briefly, clash, battle; struggle, scrimmage, brush, scrap, tussle, tilt, joust.

◇ *Word origin: Skirmish* comes from an archaic German verb meaning to fight with the sword. The same base gives us *scrimmage,* and also the name of *Scaramouch,* the boastful buffoon of commedia dell'arte whose name thus literally means "Skirmisher" or "Swordfighter."

skirt *n.* **1** *She wore a skirt and blouse. The dress has a full skirt:* (*variously*) underskirt, dirndl, crinoline, kilt; mini, maxi, midi.

—*v.* **2** *The road skirted the lake for a few miles:* pass along the edge of, border, flank, lie along; circle, encircle, circumscribe, enclose, hem in, envelop, gird, girdle, ring. **3** *Politicians tend to skirt round controversial questions:* avoid, evade, shun, fight shy of, keep away from; make a detour round, go round, circle, circumvent.

Ant. 1 slacks, trousers, pants. **2** diverge from, lead away from. **3** face, confront, meet.

skittish *adj. The stable boy tried to calm the skittish horse. Don't be so skittish; such levity is not becoming in this sober company:* easily startled, easily frightened, fearful, nervous, jumpy, jittery, fidgety, excitable; restless, restive, unsteady, shaky, fitful, impulsive, flighty, mercurial, volatile, unstable, playful, fidgety; frivolous, coquettish.

Ant. calm, relaxed, tranquil, serene, placid, unexcitable, composed, stable, steady, cool as a cucumber, unflappable; sober, sombre, grave, serious, heavy, ponderous, staid.

sky *n. There's not a cloud in the sky today. Astronomers scanned the sky for a sight of the comet:* atmosphere; upper atmosphere, the firmament, the heavens, the blue vault of heaven, arch of heaven, space, outer space.

◇ *Word origin: Sky* is the Old Norse word for "cloud" and later for "cloudy sky." Thus our connotation of *sky* is more optimistic than it was five or six hundred years ago, or perhaps English skies are less cloudy than those of Scandinavia and Iceland.

"I must go down to the seas again, to the lonely
sea and the sky,
And all I ask is a tall ship and a star to steer her
by." —*John Masefield*

---

slab *n. The walls of the building are made of slabs of marble. The boy helped himself to a large slab of pie:* thick flat piece, thick slice; hunk, chunk, wad; plank, board, slat; wedge.

Ant. bit, fragment, scrap, sliver, splinter, chip, shaving, shred.

slack *adj.* **1** *Keep the reins of the horse slack:* loose, relaxed, lax, limp, flaccid, not tight, not taut, not firm; pliant, flexible, flabby, baggy; free, untied, unfastened. **2** *The teacher was a slack disciplinarian. Living alone, he became slack about his appearance:* unexacting, lax, undemanding, not firm, easy, soft, loose, permissive; careless, slipshod, neglectful, negligent, dilatory, remiss, slapdash, offhand, inattentive, lazy, slothful, indolent, nonchalant, lackadaisical, thoughtless, unthinking, unconcerned, indifferent, heedless, unmindful. **3** *Business has been slack because prices are too high:* not busy, inactive, lethargic, listless, dull; slow, slow-moving, slow-paced, sluggish; leisurely, lazy, quiet.

—*adv.* **4** *The reins fell slack upon the horse's neck:* limply, loosely, freely, easily; sluggishly, slowly.

Ant. 1 tight, taut, rigid, stiff, firm, tense, inflexible; tied, fastened. **2** exacting, demanding, meticulous, firm, inflexible, hard; careful, diligent, attentive, sedulous, thoughtful, mindful, concerned, caring, heedful. **3** busy, active, brisk, quick, bustling, fast, fast-moving, rapid. **4** tight, tightly, tight-strung, taut, tautly, rigidly, stiffly, tensely, unyieldingly.

◇ *Word origin:* See SLAKE.

slacken *v.* **1** *Wait for the rain to slacken before you go out. Don't slacken your efforts when the job is only half done:* slack off, slow, slow down, abate, taper off, dwindle, ease, moderate, soften, weaken, mitigate, temper; relax, reduce, lessen, decrease, diminish, curb, check, arrest, restrain, limit, retard, inhibit, keep back. **2** *Don't slacken the reins or the horse may bolt:* loosen, loose, relax, untighten, slack, slack up on, let go limp, go limp; free, release, let go, let loose.

Ant. 1 quicken, increase, rise, accelerate. **2** tighten, draw tight.

slacker *n. Don't count on that slacker to do any of the work:* malingerer, shirker, dodger, laggard, loafer, idler, dawdler, procrastinator, dallier, loiterer, good-for-nothing, do-nothing, skiver, truant; slowcoach.

slake *v. The lemonade slaked my thirst:* quench, satisfy, sate, satiate, gratify, appease, relieve, mollify, assuage, allay, alleviate, decrease, take the edge off, curb, moderate, modify, ease, temper, mitigate; calm, soothe, compose, still, subdue, quell, hush, quiet, tranquillize, cool.

Ant. increase, heighten, intensify, stimulate, aggravate, inflame, fire, pique.

◇ *Word origin: Slake* comes from Old English *slacian,* to lessen, reduce, loosen, from *slaec,* slack. *Slacks* are so-called because they hang loosely from the hips and fit more loosely than trousers.

slam *v.* **1** *The housewife slammed the door in the saleman's face:* shut with force and noise, bang. **2** *Don't slam the cards down just because you have lost!:* slap, hit, throw; strike forcefully. **3** *The waitress slammed into the swinging door:* crash, bang; strike with violent impact, collide with, bump, smash.

—*n.* **4** *The slam of the shutters woke me:* bang, crash; act or sound of slamming.

slander *n.* **1** *When he called me a thief, I decided to sue him for slander:* defamation, falsehood; malicious fabrication, false spoken statement, distortion, misrepresentation.

—*v.* **2** *He slandered his opponent's good name:* defame, malign, vilify, revile; smear, sully, soil, besmirch.

◇ *Usage note: Slander* and *libel* both refer to defamation or unjustified attack on a person's reputation. A *slander* is spoken: *Did you hear him slander me in front of my friends?* A *libel* is written (published): *I'm suing the newspaper for libel.* Remember: *Slander is Spoken, Libel is Literary.*

slant *v.* **1** *The path slants down to the river here. Slant the desk top whilst you're writing:* incline, slope, angle, tilt; lean, list. **2** *The writer slanted the story in favour of the subaltern:* colour, bias, prejudice, distort, angle.

—*n.* **3** *The slant of the floor makes the table unsteady:* slope, tilt, rake, incline, pitch; slanting direction. **4** *Bertolt Brecht's plays have a political slant:* bias, prejudice, angle, view, viewpoint, leaning, attitude.

Ant. 1 straighten, level off. **3** evenness, level.

slap *n.* **1** *Her slap left red marks on his arm:* blow, smack, hit, whack, wallop, cuff. **2** *The Soviet attacks on Titoism were also a slap at China:* blow, insult, cut, rejection, snub.

—*v.* **3** *The baby slapped his sister when she tried to kiss him:* hit, strike, smack, cuff, whack, wallop.

slash *v.* **1** *Vandals slashed the paintings with knives:* cut, gash, rip, lacerate, slit, rend, slice. **2** *The shop intends to slash fur prices after Christmas:* cut, lower, drop, decrease, reduce drastically.

—*n.* **3** *Make broad slashes through the words to be deleted. The slashes in the tyres made the car unusable:* stroke, mark, cut, gash, rip, rent, laceration. **4** *The consumer welcomes a slash in meat prices:* cut, decrease, reduction, drop, lowering.

slate *n.* **1** *A floor of slate would suit the kitchen well:* dark blue-grey rock. **2** *I hang a slate in my kitchen for memos:* blackboard, tablet.

◇ *Word origin: Slate* comes from Old French *esclate,* chip, slab, slice, hence the rock slate that splits into thin, even slices. Such slices are used to write on; hence our expression *a clean slate* which is used figuratively to mean a fresh beginning, with all previous errors erased.

slaughter *n.* **1** *Methods employed in the slaughter of beef cattle are under attack by the RSPCA:* killing, butchering. **2** *The attack resulted in a slaughter of the unarmed villagers:* massacre, blood-bath, mass murder, wholesale killing, pogrom.

—*v.* **3** *I couldn't bear to watch them slaughter the cattle:* butcher, kill. **4** *The killer slaughtered the entire family:* slay, massacre, destroy, annihilate, exterminate, wipe out.

◇ *Word origin:* See SLAY.

slave *n.* **1** *There were more slaves than citizens in ancient Athens:* serf, vassal, bondservant, bondsman, thrall, chattel. **2** *He's a slave to alcohol:* addict, prey, victim. **3** *She's been a slave in that job and should have left the company long ago:* drudge, work-horse, toiler, plodder.

—*v.* **4** *Why do you slave at that unfulfilling job?:* drudge, toil, work like a slave.

Ant. 1 master, owner. **3** loafer, idler. **4** loaf, idle.

slavish *adj.* **1** *Slavish devotion to another person is self-destructive:* servile, subservient, slave-like, submissive. **2** *The painting is done in a slavish imitation of Van Gogh's manner:* literal, strict, exact; unimaginative, imitative, unoriginal.

Ant. 1 masterful, wilful, assertive. **2** original, imaginative, creative, inventive.

slay *v. David slew Goliath:* kill, slaughter, destroy, execute, annihilate, massacre.

◇ *Usage note:* The past tense of *slay* is *slew,* not "slayed." Thus, *The knight SLEW the dragon.* The past participle is *slain: The captain lies SLAIN after the battle.*

◇ *Word origin: Slay, slaughter* and *slug* come from Old English *slean,* to hit hard. The same Old English base gives us *onslaught,* literally a murderous assault, and *sledge-hammer,* literally a "heavy blow hammer" or a "slaying hammer."

sleazy *adj. That is a sleazy fabric, and it won't last long. His Gothic novel is a sleazy piece of writing:* flimsy, shoddy, insubstantial, shabby, tawdry; vulgar, cheap, squalid.

sleek *adj.* **1** *Your hair looks sleek and beautiful:* glossy, shiny, silky, satiny, lustrous. **2** *The baroness was invariably attended by a sleek gigolo:* smooth, suave, unctuous, oily, ingratiating, fawning.

sleep *n.* **1** *I was awakened from a sound sleep:* slumber, snooze, nap, doze. **2** *She went to her eternal sleep:* death, rest, peace.
—*v.* **3** *Everyone slept until dawn:* slumber, repose, nap, snooze, doze.

Exploring the Word: *Sleep* can be traced back to Old English *slæp,* sleep, and beyond that to a now-lost Indo-European ancestor word meaning something like "hanging loosely." From this same ancestor word comes our word to *slump,* which is what you do when you fall asleep sitting up. *Somnus* is Latin for sleep; *insomnia* means sleeplessness; *somnambulate* (Latin *ambulare,* to walk) means to sleep-walk; and *somnolent* means drowsy. The cognate Greek word for sleep is *hupnos,* from which we get *hypnotic* and *hypnotism.*

sleepy *adj.* **1** *I'm too sleepy to watch the end of the programme:* drowsy, weary, tired, fatigued, exhausted. **2** *There was little to do in the sleepy fishing village:* quiet, inactive, dull, peaceful.
Ant. 1 awake, energetic, spirited, animated, alert. **2** bustling, active, busy, thriving, lively.

slender *adj.* **1** *She admired his slender build:* slim, lean, willowy, skinny, slight, delicate, thin, narrow. **2** *The farm yielded only a slender crop this year:* little, small, meagre, scanty, spare. **3** *Your chance of winning is slender:* slim, slight, feeble, faint, weak, poor, remote.
Ant. 1 large, fat, thick, stout, bulky, heavy. **2** large, profuse, considerable, appreciable, prolific. **3** strong, considerable, solid.

slice *n.* **1** *Will you have a slice of pie?:* piece, portion, section, cut, segment.
—*v.* **2** *Slice the meat thinly:* carve, cut, shave; whittle, pare; divide, separate, cut off, sever, dismember, segment.

slick *adj.* **1** *A slick operator could sell anything:* sly, wily, cunning, tricky, clever, smooth-talking, fast-talking.
—*n.* **2** *The oil slick covered the beach:* film, coating, coat, scum.
—*v.* **3** *He slicked down his hair with oil:* smooth; make glossy.
Ant. 1 honest, open, ingenuous.
◇ *Word origin: Slick* belongs to a cluster of Germanic words deriving from an Indo-European root whose basic idea was "slimy." These words are: *sleek* (a variant of *slick*), *slime, slimy, slippery, slight* (the word originally meant "smooth" and "sleek," as well as "small"), *slip,* Yiddish *schlep* (to drag, as over a slippery surface), and *loam* (it is slimy and slippery).

slide *v.* **1** *The boy likes to slide down the banister:* glide, coast. **2** *The car slid into the ditch:* skid, slip, fall, veer, side-slip. **3** *The committee let the matter slide:* pass, slip, lapse.
—*n.* **4** *Let's go for a slide on the toboggan:* coast, glide; coasting, journey. **5** *They need a rubber mat at the foot of the slide:* chute, ramp, slope. **6** *Do you prefer prints or slides?:* small transparency, diapositive, lantern-slide, transparent plate.

"But wild ambition loves to slide, not stand,
And Fortune's ice prefers to Virtue's land."
—*John Dryden*

slight *adj.* **1** *Only a slight change in temperature is predicted:* small, little, modest, moderate, limited, restricted, imperceptible, unimportant, inappreciable, negligible, tiny, infinitesimal. **2** *He's too slight to play rugby football:* slim, slender, frail, lean, thin, spare, fragile.
—*n.* **3** *I was hurt by the obvious slight:* snub, insult, slap, cut, rebuff, incivility.
Ant. 1 considerable, great, big, substantial, appreciable, tangible. **2** husky, muscular, sturdy.

slim *adj.* **1** *Anything looks good on his slim figure:* slender, thin, lean, svelte, willowy. **2** *There's only a slim chance that the crash victims will survive:* slender, faint, remote, distant, slight, small, meagre.
Ant. 1 chubby, fat; broad, broad in the beam, wide, huge, elephantine. **2** great, strong, considerable.
◇ *Word origin: Slim* is from Middle Dutch *slim,* bad, bent, weak. Thus, a *slim* person was once a bent-over or weak person, and a *slim chance* is still a weak one.

slime *n. My boots are covered with slime from the marsh:* mire, muck, ooze, sludge; sticky mud.

slimy *adj.* **1** *The rain made a slimy mess of the yard:* mucky, gummy, sticky, viscous, glutinous. **2** *That slimy man gives me the creeps:* offensive, obnoxious, creepy; nasty, vile, repulsive, foul, putrid, loathsome.
Ant. 2 pleasant, appealing.

slink *v. We caught the thief slinking out the back way:* slip, creep, steal, skulk; move in a furtive manner.

slip[1] *v.* **1** *Slip the shoe onto your foot:* slide, glide; put. **2** *She slipped and fell down the stairs:* skid, slide, lose one's balance. **3** *We slipped away from the party unnoticed. Slip me the letter:* sneak, steal, go quietly; pass, hand stealthily. **4** *The years have just slipped by:* pass quickly, pass imperceptibly. **5** *The patient's condition is slipping:* fail, worsen, decline, sink, fall. **6** *The burglar slipped from my grasp:* escape; break away, get clear of. **7** *How did the news slip out?:* leak, escape, be revealed.
—*n.* **8** *She had a nasty slip on the icy pavement:* skid, slide; fall. **9** *That was an embarrassing slip about his brother's divorce:* blunder, indiscretion, imprudence, lapse, error, faux pas. **10** *The slip in the market has been devastating:* drop, fall, decline. **11** *You need a slip under that dress:* petticoat, underskirt, chemise. **12** *The boat came untied and drifted out of the slip:* berth,

dock, landing-stage. **13** *He gave me a slip from his plant:* cutting, sprig, sprout, shoot, offshoot. **14** *He scribbled on a slip of paper:* scrap, strip, shred, small piece; receipt, voucher, ticket.

Ant. 5 improve, rise. **10** rise, improvement, increase.

slippery *adj.* **1** *Be careful when you walk across this slippery floor. Wet soap is slippery:* slithery, smooth, waxy, greasy, oily, glassy, soapy. **2** *Don't trust that slippery character:* tricky, shifty, untrustworthy, unreliable, treacherous, foxy, sneaky, crafty, contriving.

Ant. 1 rough, coarse; dry. **2** trustworthy, reliable, steady, dependable, responsible.

◇ *Word origin:* See SLICK.

slipshod *adj. The cabinet was put together in a hurried, slipshod way:* careless, lax, sloppy; casual, thoughtless, offhand, slovenly, loose, untidy, messy.

Ant. careful, correct, meticulous, exact, fastidious; orderly, tidy, neat.

◇ *Word origin: Slipshod* literally means "wearing slip shoes," i.e., slippers or old shoes that are down at the heel and used as household "slop-abouts," hence the modern connotation of "sloppy, slovenly."

slit *n.* **1** *The coin fell through a slit in the floor:* cut, crevice, gash, incision, slash, crack, fissure.

—*v.* **2** *Slit holes in the mask for your eyes:* cut, slash.

slither *v. The belly-dancers slithered like snakes:* slide, glide; move with a side-to-side motion.

◇ *Word origin: Slither* comes from Old English *slidrian,* a frequentative form of *slidan,* to slide. "Frequentative" means "expressing repeated action." Thus, *slither* is an old frequentative of *slide,* meaning "to slide back and forth" or "slide and keep on sliding."

slogan *n. We need a new slogan for the advertising campaign:* motto, campaign cry, battle-cry, catch-phrase.

◇ *Word origin:* The Highland clans of Scotland gave us the word *slogan:* It comes from the Scottish Gaelic *slugah* (army) + *gairm* (yell), battle-cry, rallying cry.

"Definition of a slogan: a form of words for which memorability has been bought."

—*Richard Lisborne*

---

slop *v.* **1** *Don't slop water all over the floor:* slosh, splash, splatter, spill, swash. **2** *Have you slopped out the pigs yet?:* clean the living–quarters.

—*n* **3** *Carry this bucket of slops out to the pigsty:* swill, rubbish, waste, refuse.

slope *v.* **1** *The ski-run slopes down sharply here:* slant, incline, lean, tip, tilt, bend, bank.

—*n.* **2** *The meadow has a gentle slope:* slant, incline, down-grade, inclination, descent.

Ant. 1 flatten, level. **2** plane.

sloppy *adj.* **1** *I hate driving on these sloppy side-roads:* watery, sloshy, muddy, slushy, wet, sodden, swampy, marshy. **2** *We lost the match because of sloppy fielding:* weak, inattentive, half-hearted, unimpressive.

Ant. 1 dry. **2** careful, strong; adequate.

sloth *n. Her sloth keeps her from getting ahead in her job:* laziness, lethargy, indolence, lassitude, shiftlessness, torpidity, languor, phlegm, sluggishness, idleness.

Ant. energy, industriousness, diligence, assiduousness, activeness, get-up-and-go.

slouch *v.* **1** *Sit up straight and don't slouch!:* droop, slump, stoop.

—*n.* **2** *She'd look taller if it weren't for her slouch:* stoop, droop, slump. **3** *He's no slouch when it comes to helping with the dishes:* lazy-bones, laggard, sluggard, loafer, slacker, shirker, idler.

Ant. 1 straighten up. **3** go-getter, eager beaver, ball of fire.

slovenly *adj.* **1** *That outfit is too slovenly to wear to an interview for a job:* messy, sloppy, untidy, dirty, unclean, dowdy, slatternly, disorderly, unkempt. **2** *I shouldn't pay for the slovenly job he did on your shed:* slipshod, careless, slapdash, messy; indifferent, unconcerned.

Ant. 1 neat, tidy, trim, clean, orderly. **2** careful, meticulous, precise, conscientious, methodical, orderly.

slow *adj.* **1** *The old car made slow progress. He is a slow runner:* slow-paced, slow-moving, slow motion, snail-like, tortoise-like. **2** *Tree sloths climb with slow movements:* heavy, sluggish, torpid, lumpish. **3** *The patient made a slow recovery:* long, prolonged, extended, stretched-out, drawn-out, protracted, time-consuming, lingering, tarrying, delayed. **4** *My tenant's rent payments are always slow:* late, behind time, overdue, unpunctual, delayed, belated, backward. **5** *John is a slow worker:* plodding, dawdling, dilatory, procrastinating, laggard, sluggish. **6** *I'd be slow about accepting those terms. He's slow to take a stand:* hesitant, cautious; half-hearted, backward, dragging; indisposed, loath, disinclined, reluctant, averse. **7** *That game is a bit slow for my taste:* dull, tedious, boring, unexciting, uninteresting; slow-moving, sluggish, ponderous. **8** *Ticket sales are slow this month:* leisurely, unhurried, deliberate; inactive, quiet, not busy, not lively. **9** *Cousin Oscar is too slow for the advanced class:* slow-witted, dim-witted, dull-witted, slow on the uptake, backward, stupid, obtuse, dense, dumb, dim, dull; impercipient, unperceptive.

—*v.* **10** *The train slowed as it approached the station:* slow down, reduced speed, decelerate, lose momentum; flag, falter. **11** *The strike will slow production:* slow down, slow up, hold up, retard, check, curb, brake; handicap, hinder, obstruct, impede.

Ant. 1–3, 5 fast, quick, swift, speedy. **1** lightning-like. **4** prompt, punctual, on time.

6 eager, enthusiastic; inclined, disposed. **7** exciting, interesting; fast-moving. **8** hurried, hasty, active, busy, lively. **9** quick-witted, smart, bright, intelligent; perceptive. **10, 11** speed up, accelerate. **10** pick up speed. **11** spur, help, aid, abet.

◇ *Word origin: Slow* has been in the vocabulary of English- and indeed Germanic-speaking peoples since the earliest times. It comes from an Old English word *slāw*, which has cognates in many other Germanic languages.

sludge *n. They drained the sludge from the bottom of the tank:* mud, mire, dregs, muck, slime, slush.

slug *v. The two prize-fighters slugged each other brutally:* hit, strike, punch, whack, thump, smite, pound, clout, bat, belt, sock, bash, baste, lambaste, *Informal* thwack, *Slang* clobber.

sluggish *adj.* **1** *Hot weather makes me sluggish:* lethargic, listless, spiritless, soporific, phlegmatic; lazy, indolent, slothful; inert, inactive, lifeless, torpid. **2** *The turtles ran a sluggish race:* slow, unhurried, leisurely, protracted.

Ant. 1 active, energetic, industrious, animated, spirited, lively. **2** rapid, fast, quick, brisk.

◇ *Word origin: Sluggish* comes from an old word *slug*, meaning a slow, lazy person, which also gives us the snail-like garden *slug*, which in turn gives us *slug* meaning a bullet (because the original shape of a bullet was like that of a garden slug). This same word *slug*, a lazy person, is possibly also related to our word *slouch*.

slumber *v.* **1** *I was slumbering soundly when the alarm rang:* sleep; doze, snooze, nap. **2** *How long did the volcano slumber?* lie dormant, be inactive; hibernate, vegetate.

Ant. 1 be awake. **2** erupt; be active.

slump *v.* **1** *The dying man slumped to the pavement:* collapse, fall, drop, slip, give way, sag, tumble. **2** *Her work slumped because of personal problems:* dip, plunge, decline; fall off suddenly.
—*n.* **3** *I could tell from his slump how tired he was:* slouch, droop, sagging posture. **4** *The economy went into a severe slump:* lapse, decline; falling off, reverse, setback.

Ant. 2 improve, increase. **4** improvement, rise, upsurge, upturn.

◇ *Word origin: Slump* is related to Norwegian *slumpa*, to fall or sink. In English, it originally meant to fall or sink into a bog, a snowdrift, or the like.

slur *v.* **1** *I can't understand you when you slur your words together like that:* mumble, mutter, run together, pronounce indistinctly. **2** *She slurred over the unflattering comments:* overlook, skip, disregard, ignore, gloss over, pass over, let pass; treat with indifference. **3** *Don't slur my brother's reputation!:* blacken, smear, defame, malign, stain, taint, sully.
—*n.* **4** *Your slur makes it difficult for us to understand you:* mumbling, muttering, slurred speech, running-on of words, elision. **5** *The rumours cast a slur upon my good name:* stain, mark, spot, blemish, taint.

Ant. 1 enunciate. **2** stress, accentuate. **3** praise, laud, compliment. **4** enunciation. **5** compliment, praise.

◇ *Word origin: Slur* comes from a dialectal word meaning wet mud. This image of mud as being disparaging or malicious is a common one, as when we call gossip *mud-slinging*.

sly *adj.* **1** *The dealer won the game with a sly manœuvre:* wily, crafty, cunning, tricky, artful, conniving, sneaky, foxy, shrewd; mischievous, playful, cunning. **2** *She gave me a sly wink:* secret, furtive, private, covert, confidential.

Ant. 1, 2 open, direct, straightforward.

smack[1] *v.* **1** *She smacked him with her open hand:* slap, smite, hit, whack, spank; strike sharply.
—*n.* **2** *He gave the boy a smack on the leg:* slap, rap, blow, whack, spank, hit. **3** *He gave me a smack on the lips:* loud kiss, hearty kiss, buss.

Ant. 1 pet, caress.

◇ *Word origin: Smack*[1] (a slap, blow, or a sharp noise made by separating the lips while sucking in the breath) is from Middle Dutch *smacken*, to eat noisily. Our other word *smack*[2], meaning a taste, flavour, or hint of something, as in *This cake smacks of nutmeg* or *His story smacks of exaggeration*, comes from Old English *smaec*, taste, flavour.

smack[2] *n.* **1** *Without a smack of garlic that dish would be very dull:* trace, tinge; hint, suggestion, soupçon, taste, flavour. **2** *There's a smack of autumn in the air:* touch, trace, bit, suggestion, dash.
—*v.* **3** *This trifle smacks of rum. That excuse smacks of prevarication:* taste; smell; have a flavour.

"The God who looks after Small Things had caused the visitor that day to receive two weeks' delayed mails in one."

—*Rudyard Kipling*

---

small *adj.* **1** *Are you small enough to squeeze through the hole?:* little, tiny, petite; diminutive, undersized, slight. **2** *The business made only a small profit this year:* meagre, scanty, not great. **3** *Even the small details should be thoroughly checked:* minor, inconsequential, insignificant, trivial, superficial, unimportant, lesser, trifling; of no account. **4** *Someone with a small mind usually believes the worst:* mean, petty, narrow, opinionated, bigoted; provincial. **5** *The kitten uttered a small cry:* feeble, weak, fragile, faint.

Ant. 1, 2 large, big, great, vast, huge, immense, enormous; appreciable, substantial. **3** major, important, significant, consequential, vital. **4** big, generous, far-sighted, unbiased. **5** strong, powerful, solid, substantial; loud, noisy, heavy.

smart *adj.* **1** *It's easy to teach smart students:* intelligent, bright, sharp, keen, clever, quick, brainy, astute. **2** *These clothes are quite smart enough to wear to the party:* fashionable, chic, modish, elegant, stylish; trim, neat. **3** *He's always ready with a smart retort:* witty, clever, shrewd, sharp; smart-alec, brash, saucy. **4** *The marchers moved at a smart pace past the reviewing platform:* energetic, vigorous, quick. **5** *A red ant can give you a smart sting:* painful, sharp.
—*v.* **6** *Does your hand smart from the burn?:* hurt, sting, burn; feel pain, be painful. **7** *I still smart each time I think of his rudeness:* ache, suffer, wince, flinch, blench.
Ant. **1** dumb, dull, slow, dense, thick, stupid. **2** sloppy, frowzy; old-fashioned, dowdy; outmoded, passé. **4** crawling, slow.

smash *v.* **1** *He smashed the window with a brick:* shatter, break, splinter, disintegrate, demolish. **2** *The car smashed into a telegraph-pole. Informal She smashed him one with her fist:* crash, strike, hit, collide with; crack, break; batter, beat, *Slang* bash, clobber. **3** *Our tanks quickly smashed the enemy infantry:* rout, destroy, crush, demolish, shatter.
—*n.* **4** *He gave me a smash on the head:* blow, bang, clout, forceful hit. **5** *The vibrations from the car smash could be felt inside the house:* crash, collision, accident, pile-up, smash-up.

smashing *adj. Informal That's a smashing outfit you're wearing:* terrific, sensational, marvellous, wonderful, super, extraordinary, fabulous, fantastic, great.

smattering *n. He has only a smattering of French:* drop, bit, slight amount, dash, dab.

smear *v.* **1** *The painter smeared the walls with plaster:* spread, rub, daub, coat, cover; lay on. **2** *My clothes are smeared with mud:* stain, smudge, besmudge, splotch, soil, smirch, streak. **3** *Water smeared the ink:* blur, smudge; obliterate, make indistinct. **4** *My opponent tried to smear my reputation:* soil, stain, tarnish, mar, blacken, besmirch, blemish; malign, slander, denigrate, degrade, injure.
—*n.* **5** *You've got a lipstick smear on your cheek. That is a filthy smear on his good name!:* blotch, smudge, streak, splotch, stain, smirch; libel, slander, accusation.

smell *v.* **1** *We could smell the stew in the hall:* scent, sniff, nose, get wind of, be windward of, get scent of. **2** *The room smells of incense:* have a scent, give out an odour, emit an odour. **3** *This cheese smells!:* reek, stink, have an unpleasant odour, be malodorous, pong. **4** *I smell something funny about that plan:* detect, sense, perceive, feel, suspect.
—*n.* **5** *I love the smell of wistaria. A putrid smell drove us from the room:* aroma, scent, odour, fragrance; perfume, bouquet, whiff, emanation; reek, stench, fetor. *Informal* stink, pong.
◇ *Usage note: Scent, odour, smell, reek, stink,* and *stench* go from pleasant and neutral smells to very unpleasant ones. *Scent* refers to something that smells pleasant or delicate: *The scent of perfume. Roses scented the garden. Odour* and *smell* are neutral (and often ambiguous!) words that can be used for either pleasant or unpleasant things: *The smell* (or *odour*) *of the cake baking was very appetizing* or *The smell of rotten eggs* or *What's that smell* (or *odour*)*?*, which last can mean either a pleasant or an unpleasant one. A *reek* is a strong odour, unpleasant because it is too strong, though otherwise it might (or might not) be pleasant: *the reek of garlic, She reeks of perfume. Stink* is an informal, often insulting word for unpleasant smells: *The stink of Limburger cheese, You stink of onion! Stench* refers to the worst smells and suggests rot or decay: *The stench of manure.*

smelly *adj. Informal Take the smelly fish out of the refrigerator!:* stinking, malodorous, odorous, fetid, reeking, noisome, rank, putrid.
Ant. fragrant, sweet-smelling, fresh-smelling.

smile *n.* **1** *Wipe that smile off your face:* grin, smirk, simper.
—*v.* **2** *We smiled when we heard the good news:* grin, beam, show pleasure. **3** *Fortune smiles on those who are kind:* favour; shine; be benevolent towards.

smirch *v.* **1** *The chimney was smirched with years of grime:* besmirch, soil, smudge, dirty, begrime, besmudge, stain, smear. **2** *The gossip smirched his good standing in the community:* besmirch, tarnish, stain, damage, smear, sully, soil, blacken; slander, dishonour, discredit.
—*n.* **3** *There's a smirch on your white jacket:* stain, smudge, blotch, smear, spot. **4** *The incident was a smirch on her perfect record:* smear, blemish, stain, taint, blot; mark, stigma; discredit, dishonour.

smirk *n.* **1** *He gave a smirk when he heard her excuse:* sneer, simper, sarcastic smile, unpleasant grin.
—*v.* **2** *She smirked at my explanation:* sneer; simper.

smoke *n.* **1** *Smoke is coming out of the chimney:* sooty vapour; exhalation, fumes. **2** *Informal I like to have a smoke after dinner:* a spell of tobacco-smoking; something which is smoked; (*variously*) cigar, cigarette, pipe.
—*v.* **3** *Is the fireplace smoking?:* smoulder, fume; give off smoke, billow, reek. **4** *You can't smoke in this section of the theatre:* use tobacco; draw, suck, inhale, puff; light up, *Informal* have a drag.

smoky *adj.* **1** *You'd better clean that smoky oven:* smouldering, fuming; emitting smoke. **2** *I can't breathe in this smoky car:* smoke-filled, reeking. **3** *The walls are smoky from the incinerator:* sooty, dingy, grimy, smudgy, smoke-darkened.

smooth *adj.* **1** *The road is very smooth here. The fashion model has smooth skin:* even, flat, level; silky, velvety, sleek. **2** *Stir the mixture until it is*

smooth: without lumps. **3** *The toboggan made a smooth run down the mountain:* even, steady; without abrupt turns, without jerks, without breaks. **4** *The change-over in management was very smooth:* orderly, harmonious, well-ordered, well-regulated, methodical, uneventful, unproblematic, easy, calm, even, peaceful. **5** *Nothing seems to upset his smooth disposition:* even, calm, serene, peaceful, placid, easy-going, pleasant, mild, composed, collected, self-possessed. **6** *She is a smooth talker:* flattering, ingratiating, glib, facile. **7** *That's a smooth wine:* mellow, mild; without sharpness.
—*v.* **8** *Smooth the plaster before putting on the wallpaper:* make even, make level, flatten. **9** *Money smoothed her way to the top:* pave, open; prepare; ease; facilitate, help. **10** *He should smooth his sales manner:* refine, cultivate, polish, perfect soften, mellow, civilize. **11** *The leader was able to smooth the anger of the mob:* calm, soothe, mollify, appease, assuage, allay, mitigate.
Ant. **1** rough, bumpy, uneven, irregular. **2** lumpy. **3** jerky, uneven, bumpy, rough. **4** disorderly, difficult, turbulent, troublesome. **5** nervous, excitable. **6** rough, unpolished, abrasive. **7** harsh, sharp, pungent. **8** roughen, rough up. **9** hamper, hinder.

smother *v.* **1** *The killer smothered his victim with a pillow:* suffocate, asphyxiate, strangle, choke. **2** *Try to smother the flames with sand:* extinguish, snuff, deaden, quench. **3** *They smothered the child with love. The steak was smothered with mushrooms:* shower, wrap, surround; envelop in. **4** *We tried to smother our laughter:* hide, suppress, conceal, mask, quash; keep down, choke back.

smoulder *v.* **1** *The fire smouldered all night:* smoke; burn without flame. **2** *I smouldered for days after our argument:* seethe, burn inwardly; rage silently, fume.

smudge *n.* **1** *You have an ink smudge on your forehead:* smear, blot, stain, spot.
—*v.* **2** *She smudged her dress with chalk:* smear, stain, spot, dirty.
Ant. **2** clean, cleanse.
◇ *Word origin: Smudge* comes from Middle High German *smutzen,* to smear, make dirty, and is thus related to Modern German *Schmutz,* dirt, filth, to which our words *smut* and *smutty* are also akin.

smug *adj. He looked so smug about knowing the right answer:* self-satisfied, self-righteous, superior, virtuous.
Ant. unsure, uncertain, insecure.

smut *n.* **1** *Wipe the smut from the window sill:* soot, smudge, dirt, grime. **2** *The police promised to crack down on smut:* pornography, obscenity, lewd material, dirt, filth.

smutty *adj.* **1** *My hands are all smutty from the coal:* sooty, dirty, grimy, soiled. **2** *The children shouldn't read those smutty books:* dirty, lewd, obscene, vulgar, indecent; pornographic.
Ant. **1** clean, immaculate. **2** clean, pure, puritanical, strait-laced.

snag *n.* **1** *Our boat hit a snag in the water:* protrusion, projection stub, stump; hidden obstruction. **2** *The housing project encountered a few financial snags:* hindrance, obstacle, hitch; difficulty, block, stumbling-block, impediment, encumbrance, obstruction, barrier, bar.
—*v.* **3** *I snagged my stockings on the desk:* tear, rip; catch, grab, fasten upon.

snake *n.* **1** *Grass snakes are harmless:* serpent, viper, ophidian, reptile, reptilian. **2** *His behaviour showed that he was a snake:* sneak, traitor, untrustworthy person.

> **Exploring the Word**: The words *snake, reptile, serpent,* and *herpetology* (the study of snakes and related creatures) are all derived from roots which refer to the fact that snakes creep or crawl. *Snake* comes from Old English *snācan,* to creep (which also gives us *snail* and *sneak*); *reptile* comes from Latin *reptilis,* crawling, and *serpent,* from Latin *serpens bestia,* creeping beast; while *herpetology* comes from the Greek word for snake, *herpeton,* creeping thing. *Pythons* get their name from *Puthōn,* an ancient name of the Greek city of Delphi. *Puthōn* was also the name of that city's tutelary demon which in the shape of a monstrous serpent haunted nearby caves until killed by Apollo.

snap *v.* **1** *She snapped her fingers to gain the child's attention:* crack, click, pop. **2** *Snap the bolt tightly:* latch, catch, lock, secure, clasp; close. **3** *He snapped the stick in two:* break, crack, fracture. **4** *The crab snapped at my toe:* bite, nip, grab. **5** *The cadets snapped to attention:* jumped, clicked. **6** *She snapped at me when I tried to comfort her:* speak irritably, snarl, growl, bark, yelp.
—*n.* **7** *We could hear the snap of the twigs as they approached:* crack, click, pop. **8** *My dress snap is broken:* catch, clasp, fastener. **9** *The dog made a snap at my finger:* nip, bite, grab, snatch. **10** *We're having a sudden cold snap:* frost spell.
—*adj.* **11** *That was no snap decision on her part:* sudden, hasty, thoughtless, quick, careless, impulsive.

snare *n.* **1** *We caught a rabbit in the snare:* trap, noose, net. **2** *That advertisement is a snare for inexperienced people:* trap, pitfall, deception, entanglement; lure, bait, decoy.
—*v.* **3** *Indians snared rabbits with vines:* capture, ensnare, trap, entrap, hook, catch, seize.

snarl[1] *v.* **1** *Rover snarled when I took away his bone:* growl. **2** *The boy snarled at his mother:* snap, lash out, speak cynically.
—*n.* **3** *The terrier's snarl was frightening:* growl.

snarl[2] *v. The wind snarled the streamers on the float. An accident can snarl up traffic for hours:* tangle, entangle, twist, knot, disorder, jumble, muddle, confuse; hinder, clog, impede.

Ant. order, unsnarl, untangle, unscramble.

snatch *v.* **1** *The rescuer snatched the boy out of the sea:* grab, seize, grasp; pluck, nab, pull, wrest. **2** *Let's snatch an hour's sleep:* grab, catch, take.

—*n.* **3** *We only saw snatches of the show:* part, snippet, fragment, bit, piece.

sneak *v.* **1** *Let's sneak out during the last scene:* slip, steal. **2** *Can you sneak the puppy into the house?:* slip, spirit, smuggle.

—*n.* **3** *Don't trust that sneak:* tell-tale, informer; skulker, lurker, slinker; rascal, knave, bounder, rogue, scallywag, scoundrel, rapscallion, scamp, miscreant.

—*adj.* **4** *The newspaper gave us a sneak preview of the book:* surprise, secret, secretive, furtive, surreptitious, sly, underhand.

sneaky *adj. I'd be ashamed of playing such a sneaky trick:* underhand, sly, devious, treacherous, traitorous; secretive, furtive; mean, malicious, vicious.

Ant. open, above-board.

sneer *v.* **1** *The captive sneered at her attempt to be friendly:* scorn, mock, scoff, rebuff, jeer, deride, disdain.

—*n.* **2** *An ugly sneer was all we got for our trouble:* smirk, scoff.

snicker *v. The children snickered when the teacher tripped over:* giggle, titter, snigger, simper.

snide *adj. He was offended by her snide manner:* sarcastic, nasty, insinuating; mocking, scoffing, contemptuous.

sniff *v.* **1** *This cold makes me sniff constantly:* snivel, sniffle, snuffle, snuff. **2** *You must sniff this lovely perfume:* smell, whiff, snuff. **3** *He sniffed at the proposal:* disdain, disparage; mock, scoff, jeer.

—*n.* **4** *Her sniffs kept me awake:* sniffle, snuffle, snort. **5** *Did you get a sniff of that garlic?:* smell, whiff, odour, aroma.

snip *v.* **1** *Please snip these uneven strands of hair:* clip, cut, crop, lop, trim, prune.

—*n.* **2** *I heard the snip of the scissors:* click, clack, snap. **3** *Will you give me a snip of that material?:* scrap, swatch; bit, fragment, cutting, piece; sample. **4** *Informal This car is a snip at twenty pounds:* bargain, give-away.

snob *n. He's too much of a snob to mix with that earthy crowd. She's an intellectual snob:* social climber, élitist, stuck-up person, pretentious person, condescending person.

snobbish *adj. She's much too snobbish to stay at that ordinary hotel:* pretentious, disdainful, condescending, overbearing, superior, vain, haughty, *Informal* stuck-up, snooty, high-hat, toffee-nosed.

Ant. unpretentious, humble.

snort *v.* **1** *We ran when the bull began to snort:* grunt, pant, puff, blast, blow, huff, gasp; storm, rage. **2** *She snorted at our modest plan:* scoff, jeer, sneer, sniff.

—*n.* **3** *The pony gave a snort when she tried to saddle him:* grunt, gasp, pant, huff.

◇ *Word origin: Snort* seems to come from Middle Low German *snorren,* which also gives us *snore.*

snub *v.* **1** *The rich man snubbed his poor relations:* ignore, disdain, slight, scorn, rebuff; turn up one's nose at, cut, treat with contempt, give the cold shoulder.

—*n.* **2** *I was hurt by her pointed snub:* rebuff, slight, cut, repudiation, cold shoulder.

—*adj.* **3** *He had a snub nose:* short, blunt, stubby, retroussé.

snuffle *v.* **1** *Everyone seems to be snuffling from hay fever:* sniff, sniffle, snuff. **2** *The child finally snuffled out his story:* speak through a heavy cold.

—*n.* **3** *I've had this confounded snuffle all week:* sniff, light cold; wheeze.

◇ *Word origin: Snuffle,* to sniff or inhale through the nose, comes from Middle Dutch *snuffelen,* to snuffle. The pulverized tobacco *snuff,* which is inhaled into the nostrils or chewed, is short for the Dutch *snufftabak,* tobacco for snuffing.

snug *adj.* **1** *The cat was snug in its basket. The hunters found a snug cabin in the woods:* cosy, comfortable; sheltered, safe, secure; tranquil. **2** *These shoes are too snug:* tight-fitting, tight, close-fitting; skin-tight.

—*n.* **3** *We sat in the snug supping our beers:* bar-parlour, small room in public house.

Ant. **1** uncomfortable; unprotected. **2** loose.

◇ *Word origin: Snug* comes from Low German *snügger,* trim, as in the phrase *a trim ship,* i.e., a watertight, seaworthy, well-run ship. *Snuggle* means to lie *snug* or close, to nestle.

snuggle *v. The child snuggled in her mother's lap:* nestle, nuzzle, lie snug, cuddle, lie closely, curl up, nest.

soak *v.* **1** *The bedspread is soaking in the dye. Soak your feet in warm water and salt:* steep, bathe, wet, saturate. **2** *Paper towels will soak up the spilt milk:* absorb, take in, take up. **3** *The wet snow soaked through my boots:* seep, penetrate, permeate, enter, pervade. **4** *The full impact of the news will soak in later:* penetrate, pervade; sink in, be perceived, be absorbed, come home to.

soar *v.* **1** *The bird soared through the air:* wing, glide, float, fly. **2** *Rents have recently soared, and many tenants have had to move:* climb, rise, mount, rocket, increase swiftly; tower, thrust upward.

Ant. **1** fall, drop. **2** fall, drop, decrease, plummet, slump, sink.

sob *v.* **1** *The child sobbed hysterically:* weep, cry, blubber, whimper, wail, snivel.

—*n.* **2** *The sobs of the baby were so sad:* cry, whimper, plaint.

Ant. laugh, chortle.

sober *adj.* **1** *He was a sober man who seldom smiled:* solemn, serious, sombre, grave, sedate, staid. **2** *A funeral is a sober event:* grave, grim, sad, serious, solemn, sombre, sorrowful, joyless. **3** *The colours in this room are sober and* *depressing:* drab, subdued, dull, sombre, dreary. **4** *She is sensible and will give a sober opinion of the facts:* realistic, sound, dispassionate, moderate; prudent, judicious; level-headed, rational, cool, sane, steady. **5** *He joined Alcoholics Anonymous and has stayed completely sober for five years:* temperate, dry, abstemious, not drunk.

Ant. 1 gay, frivolous, light-hearted, merry. **2** happy, gay, joyous. **3** light, bright, showy, colourful, exciting, lively. **4** frivolous, unrealistic, immoderate, unsound, excessive, passionate, imprudent, injudicious. **5** drunk, intoxicated, inebriated.

"A sober man may become a drunkard through being a coward. A brave man may become a coward through being a drunkard."
—*G. K. Chesterton*

---

sociable *adj.* **1** *She's very sociable and loves parties:* gregarious, friendly, social, affable, chatty, extrovert, outgoing, gracious, neighbourly, agreeable. **2** *The meeting was as sociable as it was businesslike:* social, friendly, cordial, convivial.

Ant. 1 unfriendly, withdrawn, introvert, unsociable, cold, uncommunicative. **2** stiff, formal, businesslike; cut and dried.

social *adj.* **1** *This is just a social call:* friendly, sociable. **2** *My wife is a warm, social person:* sociable, gregarious, friendly, neighbourly, pleasant, agreeable. **3** *The ball was the social occasion of the year:* fashionable, smart, stylish, *Informal* in. **4** *Bees are social insects:* gregarious, co-operative, interdependent.

Ant. 1 business. **2** antisocial, unfriendly, cold. **3** unfashionable. **4** solitary, independent, reclusive, hermit.

◇ *Word origin: Social* and its various forms, such as *society* and *socialize,* come from Latin *socius,* companion, ally, which also gives us *associate* and *dissociate.*

society *n.* **1** *Drug addiction is a major concern of society:* humanity, humankind, mankind, the general public, civilized man. **2** *Victorian society was prudish compared with present-day society:* social order, community. **3** *She is president of the literary society:* group, body, club, association, organization, circle, alliance, league. **4** *Everyone who is anyone in society attended the wedding:* élite, aristocracy, nobility, gentry, blue bloods, high society, *Informal* the nobs.

sock[1] *n. Your socks don't match:* short stocking, ankle sock.

◇ *Word origin: Sock*[1], a short stocking, comes from Latin *soccus,* slipper, a very light shoe similar to that worn by ballet dancers.

sock[2] *v.* **1** *Informal He socked his opponent in the eye:* hit, strike, box, punch, slap, wallop, smack, smash, *Slang* belt, clobber.
—*n.* **2** *Informal I'll give you a sock on the jaw:* hit, punch, slap, wallop, smack, blow.

◇ *Word origin: Sock*[2], to strike, was perhaps coined to imitate the sound of a blow.

sodden *adj.* **1** *The football field was sodden from the previous night's rain:* drenched, saturated, soppy, sopping, soaked, soggy, wet through. **2** *This sodden soufflé must have too much liquid in it:* mushy, pasty, doughy, lumpy, heavy, soggy. **3** *He had a heavy sodden look on his face, as though he had drunk too much:* listless, dull, expressionless, besotted.

Ant. 1 dry. **2** light, fluffy, crisp.

◇ *Word origin: Sodden* is an obsolete past tense of the verb *seethe,* to boil, bubble, or soak, hence soaked or flabby and pale as if all the strength had been soaked out.

soft *adj.* **1** *A soft mattress is bad for one's spine. A soft wood is easier to carve:* pliable, pliant, supple, malleable; not hard, easily penetrated, easily moulded. **2** *This silk scarf feels so soft:* smooth, sleek, velvety, satiny, downy, furry, silky, silken. **3** *The doorbell is almost too soft to hear:* subdued, faint, muted, hushed, feeble; gentle, pleasantly low. **4** *Those soft colours are very soothing. The lovers walked hand in hand in the soft rain:* gentle, mild, subdued, tranquil, restful, quiet; delicate, pale, pastel; not sharp, low intensity, shadowed, harmonious, shaded, twilight. **5** *She had a soft spot in her heart for him:* tender, kind, lenient, tolerant, sympathetic, compassionate, pitying; sentimental. **6** *His muscles are soft from lack of exercise:* weak, flabby; incapable of great endurance; not strong. **7** *The word "giant" has a soft "g":* not sharp, not hard; having a breathy sound. **8** *Informal A soft assignment can be dull:* easy; requiring little effort.

Ant. 1, 5, 7, 8 hard. **1** unyielding, stiff, inflexible. **2** rough, harsh, course, abrasive. **3** loud, strong, noisy. **4** harsh, loud, sharp, glaring, bright. **5** unkind, unsympathetic. **6** strong, tough. **8** difficult, tough, rough.

soften *v.* **1** *The landlord asked us to soften the music:* lower, subdue, moderate; tone down, make softer, turn down. **2** *Soften the butter before adding it to the mixture:* make soft, melt. **3** *She tried to soften the blow:* lessen, temper, mitigate, cushion, palliate, mollify.

Ant. 1 raise, intensify, increase; louden. **2** harden, freeze, set. **3** heighten.

softly *adv. He speaks too softly to be heard. Children find it hard to move softly:* quietly, weakly; gently, easily, mildly.

Ant. loud, loudly, blaringly, noisily; roughly; harshly, toughly, unkindly.

soggy *adj.* **1** *The ground is soggy from the melting snow:* soaked, soppy, saturated, drenched, sodden. **2** *Too much liquid made the cakes soggy:* mushy, pasty, doughy, heavy, sodden.

Ant. 1 dry. **2** dry, fluffy, light.

soil[1] *n.* **1** *This soil is good for growing vegetables:* ground, earth, loam, humus. **2** *It's good to have my feet back on British soil:* earth, land, region, country, terra firma.

soil² *v.* **1** *She soiled the carpet with her muddy shoes:* dirty, stain, smudge, grime, smear, spot, muddy, blacken. **2** *His ugly innuendos soiled my reputation:* blacken, disgrace, tarnish, stain, ruin, sully, foul.
Ant. 1 clean, whiten, cleanse.

"It is in men as in soils, where sometimes there is a vein of gold which the owner knows not of." —*Jonathan Swift*

sojourn *v.* **1** *We sojourned with my parents over the summer:* abide, visit, (spend one's) holiday; stay in a place temporarily, reside for a time. —*n.* **2** *How long was your sojourn in Tibet?:* visit, stay, stopover, pause, holiday, vacation.
◇ *Word origin: Sojourn,* to stay for a short time, comes from Latin *sub* (under) + *diurnum* (day), less than a day. Our word *journey* has the same base and originally meant a day's travel.

solace *n.* **1** *We drew solace from the many notes of sympathy:* comfort, consolation, reassurance; relief in affliction, help in need.
—*v.* **2** *The minister's words solaced the grief-stricken widow:* console, comfort, calm, assuage, reassure, soothe.
Ant. 1 pain, distress, discomfort, anxiety, anguish. **2** pain, distress, discomfort, dishearten.

soldier *n.* **1** *Our soldiers will defend us against the enemy:* military man, enlisted man, warrior, fighting man, trooper, veteran. **2** *He is a soldier for Christ:* militant leader, zealot, fighter, follower, worker, servant.
◇ *Word origin: Soldier* comes from late Latin *solidus,* a gold coin, payment, and later a legionary receiving such payment. Thus our *soldier* gets his name from the pay of a Roman soldier.

sole *adj.* **1** *The hermit is the sole inhabitant of these woods:* only, exclusive, lone, solitary, single. **2** *He has sole responsibility for the child:* exclusive, undivided.
Ant. 2 shared, divided, joint.

Exploring the Word: *Sole, solo, solitary* and *solitude* come from Latin *solus,* alone, which also gives us: *solitaire,* a card game played by one person alone, or a diamond or other gem set by itself; *soliloquy* (Latin *loqui,* to speak), talking alone, as to oneself; *desolate,* completely alone, feeling completely alone; and *sullen,* sad and lonely, gloomy, in an ill humour.

solely *adv.* **1** *The boy was solely at fault for the broken window:* exclusively, alone, singly, single-handedly. **2** *Porpoises live solely in salt water. It was solely a case of mistaken identity:* exclusively, purely, uniquely, merely, only.

solemn *adj.* **1** *That solemn little girl never smiles:* sombre, staid, grave, sedate, sober; quiet in demeanour. **2** *He made a solemn decision never to drink again:* sombre, grave, earnest, serious; determined, sincere, steadfast, absolute. **3** *The inauguration was a solemn event:* formal, dignified, ceremonious, ceremonial, awe-inspiring. **4** *A baptism is a solemn rite:* holy, religious, sacred, spiritual.
Ant. 1 jovial, joyous, bright, lively, gay, happy, merry, spirited. **2** frivolous, half-hearted, insincere. **3** informal. **4** unholy, irreligious, sacrilegious.

solicit *v. They solicited our help in producing the school play. Campaign workers were busy soliciting votes:* seek, request, ask, appeal for, canvass, endeavour to obtain.

solicitous *adj.* **1** *He was solicitous about her problems at work:* concerned, thoughtful, anxious, attentive. **2** *The politicians do not seem particularly solicitous to proceed in this investigation:* eager, zealous, desirous, longing, ardent, intense, keen, avid, enthusiastic.
Ant. 1 unconcerned, undisturbed. **2** uninterested, unambitious, unenthusiastic.

solid *adj.* **1** *A rock is a solid object. This figurine is solid:* real, substantial, concrete, tangible; dense, massy, not hollow. **2** *We couldn't break through the solid line of tanks. What we want is a solid programme of entertainment with no commercials:* unbroken, impenetrable, impermeable; constant, continuous, uninterrupted, without breaks. **3** *Ice is solid, water is liquid:* hard, firm, solidified. **4** *This old house has a remarkably solid foundation:* firm, well-constructed, strong, well-built, lasting, tough, sturdy, rugged, durable, substantial. **5** *The curtains are solid green. The table is solid oak:* pure, unmixed, genuine, thorough, one hundred per cent, real. **6** *My ring is solid gold:* real, pure, complete, unalloyed. **7** *My father is a solid member of the community:* sound, stable, steady, reliable, dependable, trustworthy; sober, sensible, level-headed, rational. **8** *The city council was solid in its decision to build a shopping centre:* unanimous, undivided, united, agreed.
Ant. 1 hollow. **2** broken, permeable. **3** liquid, gaseous. **4** flimsy, shaky, unstable, unsteady, unsound. **5** mixed, variegated. **7** unsound, unstable, irresponsible, unreliable. **8** at odds, divided, undecided, split.

solidarity *n. A national emergency evokes solidarity among the populace:* closeness, unity, unification, union; harmony; co-operation; consolidation of interests and responsibilities.
Ant. divisiveness, factiousness, discord.

solitary *adj.* **1** *The stranger ate a solitary meal. The old fisherman leads a solitary life:* lone, lonely, lonesome, companionless; avoiding the society of others. **2** *The solitary boat looked tiny in the vast sea:* lone, isolated, single. **3** *The thieves hid in a solitary desert retreat:* secluded, cloistered, lonely, out of the way, deserted, hidden, concealed; desolate, remote, isolated, uninhabited.

Ant. 1 companionable; gregarious, sociable, social. **3** bustling, busy, well-travelled.

solitude *n.* **1** *The solitude of a hermit's life is not for me:* isolation, aloneness, loneliness, solitariness, desolation, seclusion, remoteness. **2** *The hunters never saw a soul in that arctic solitude:* waste, wilderness, lonely place, desert.

solution *n.* **1** *The solution of the crime took three years:* solving, resolving, resolution; unravelling. **2** *Have you found the solution yet?:* explanation, answer, key, cipher, resolution. **3** *A marinade is a solution of wine and spices:* emulsion, suspension; mixture, blend, pickle.

solve *v. The clever child solved the riddle quickly:* resolve, decipher, unravel, find a solution to, find the answer, find the key, untangle, work out.

solvent *adj.* **1** *After years of saving, he was finally solvent:* in good financial condition, able to pay debts, financially sound. **2** *This experiment will show you whether sugar is solvent in cold water:* dissolvable, dilutable, dissoluble, soluble.
—*n.* **3** *You need a solvent to soften that dried paint:* dissolving agent, dissolvent, diluent.
Ant. 1 bankrupt, broke. **3** hardener.

sombre *adj.* **1** *Why were schools painted in such sombre colours? Wednesday was a sombre day:* drab, toneless, gloomy, dark, cheerless, dreary, grim. **2** *His sombre voice told us that the news was bad:* grim, gloomy, depressing, mournful, grave, serious, sober, solemn.
Ant. 1 cheerful, gay, colourful, bright, sunny, lively. **2** cheerful, happy, gay, bright.

song *n.* **1** *The band played our favourite song:* ballad, aria, carol, hymn, melody, tune, ditty, number. **2** *The song of the robin woke me this morning:* piping, utterance, call, chirping, musical sound. **3** *I enjoy reading Keats's love songs:* poem, lyric, verse, lay.

sonorous *adj. The sonorous clang of the cymbals startled us:* resonant, full-toned, deep, vibrant, rich, reverberating, resounding, ringing.
Ant. weak, tinny.
◇ *Pronunciation tip: Sonorous* is usually stressed on the first syllable: *SON-a-rus,* though it may be stressed on the second: *suh-NOR-us.*

soothe *v.* **1** *He tried to soothe the irate crowd:* pacify, comfort, calm, tranquillize, console, moderate, placate, mollify, relieve, appease. **2** *The medication soothed her pain. The priest tried to soothe her doubts:* lessen, alleviate, relieve, ease, mitigate.
Ant. 1 upset, disturb, rouse, excite, disquiet. **2** increase, irritate.

soothsayer *n. A soothsayer predicted that I would inherit a fortune:* fortune-teller, seer, diviner, prophet, forecaster.
◇ *Word origin:* A *soothsayer* is one who says *sooth* (truth) and hence is a sayer of true things learnt by supernatural insight, one able to foretell events. *Sooth* (truth) is also in our word *forsooth,* in truth, certainly. It comes directly from Old English *sōth,* truth.

sop *n.* **1** *A doughnut is a good sop for coffee:* food for dipping or dunking. **2** *The small wage increase is a sop to the unions:* bribe, pay-off, hush-money, payola, tip, gratuity, baksheesh.
—*v.* **3** *Sop the cutlets in egg before flouring them:* dip, dunk, soak, drench, wet, saturate. **4** *Use your bread to sop up the sauce:* soak, absorb; take up. **5** *My clothes were sopping with rain:* soak, wet, drench; become wet.

sophisticated *adj.* **1** *The Duke of Windsor was a sophisticated world traveller:* seasoned, experienced, worldly, worldly-wise, cosmopolitan. **2** *The play was too sophisticated for most of the school children:* intellectual, cultured, cultivated, *Informal* highbrow; studied, artificial, precious, mannered. **3** *I can't understand how this sophisticated new equipment works:* complicated, complex, difficult, subtle, advanced.
Ant. 1 unsophisticated, unseasoned, simple, unworldly. **2** unsophisticated, provincial. **3** simple, old-fashioned, uncomplicated.

> **Exploring the Word:** *Sophisticated* means wise in the way of the world; a *sophomore* is a wise fool; and a *philosopher* is a lover of wisdom. These words are based on Greek *sophos,* wise. *Philosopher* (Greek *philos,* loving + *sophos,* wise); a lover of wisdom, has meant the same thing for thousands of years, whilst *theosophy* (Greek *theos,* god) is a system of thought professing to lead one to a knowledge of God through spiritual ecstasy, etc. Greek *sophos,* wise, also gives us *sophistry,* subtle reasoning or arguments, especially those so involved as to be deceptive; also the name of the Greek *Sophist* philosophers who were very skilled in subtle argument, a term which is now used to describe retailers of specious arguments, or *sophisms.*

soporific *adj.* **1** *His soporific voice almost put us to sleep:* hypnotic, somniferous, sleep-inducing, balmy, sluggish, heavy. **2** *This warm weather makes me soporific:* sleepy, sluggish, drowsy, slumberous; lethargic, lazy.
—*n.* **3** *Wine is a soporific for me:* sedative, hypnotic; sleep-inducer.
Ant. 1, 2 lively, animated. **3** stimulant.
◇ *Pronunciation tip: Soporific* is stressed on the third syllable: *sop-uh-RIF-ic.*

sopping *adj. Take off those sopping clothes!:* drenched, wet, saturated, soppy, soaked.

sorcery *n. The witch used sorcery to turn the girl into a mouse:* witchcraft, witchery, wizardry, black magic, enchantment, spell.

sordid *adj.* **1** *This sordid slum isn't fit for a pig:* filthy, squalid, unclean, dirty; rank, putrid, rotten. **2** *The prostitute wrote a book about her sordid life. The politician made a sordid business deal:* low, base, depraved, ignoble, vile, wicked, debauched, degraded, vulgar, gross, disreputable, corrupt.

Ant. 1 clean, fresh. 2 honourable, pure, noble.

sore *adj.* 1 *The nurse bandaged my sore toe:* painful, tender, aching, sensitive, smarting, irritated; hurting, hurt, bruised. 2 *Losing the election was a sore disappointment:* sharp, acute, harsh, painful, wounding; agonizing, distressing, unbearable. 3 *The farmers are in sore need of fuel:* severe, desperate, critical, extreme, great. 4 *Informal I'm afraid Bill is still very sore about your victory:* angry, irritated, irked, upset.
—*n.* 5 *Put some iodine on that sore:* inflammation, wound; sore spot.
Ant. 1 pain-free, painless. 2 painless. 4 happy, joyous, cheerful, glad, pleased.
◇ *Word origin:* We usually don't think of *sore* and *sorry* as being related, but *sorry* is simply a respelling of *sore* with a *-y* added. Thus in the same way as we have *filth-filthy, rain-rainy, stone-stony,* etc., we have *sore-sorry.* Both words come from Old English *sār,* painful, distressing, grievous.

sorely *adv. She is sorely in need of advice:* badly, severely, greatly, extremely, desperately, critically.

sorrow *n.* 1 *The staff felt sorrow at the news of his death:* sadness, unhappiness, woe. 2 *Too many sorrows crushed her spirit:* misfortune, trial, trouble, hardship, travail, disaster, catastrophe; bad fortune.
—*v.* 3 *I sorrow for you in your loss:* grieve, lament, despair, mourn; be sad.
Ant. 1 joy, gladness, delight, happiness. 2 good fortune, happiness, joy. 3 rejoice, revel.

"There are few sorrows, however poignant, in which a good income is of no avail."
—*Logan Pearsall Smith*

---

sorry *adj.* 1 *I'm sorry that I made you cry:* regretful, contrite, sorrowful, sad, unhappy; remorseful, repentant. 2 *Was she very sorry that she missed the party?:* sad, melancholy, crestfallen, sorrowful; grieved, unhappy, brokenhearted. 3 *What a sorry situation! The house is in a sorry state:* miserable, sad, pitiful, pitiable, deplorable, wretched, woeful; pathetic, ridiculous.
Ant. 1 happy, unrepentant. 2 happy, joyous, elated, cheerful. 3 wonderful, uplifting.
◇ *Word origin:* See SORE.

sort *n.* 1 *Is this the sort of car you want?:* kind, type; make, brand, species, variety, classification. 2 *Informal Trust him — he's a good sort:* person, individual.
—*v.* 3 *Let's sort out the names alphabetically:* arrange, group, list, classify, class, divide, organize, systematize, grade, order, catalogue, index, categorize; place in a category. 4 *They tried to sort the fakes from the originals:* separate, segregate, take from, sift.
◇ *Usage note:* The expression *sort of* to mean *somewhat* or *rather* is much used informally, but is unacceptable in formal writing. Thus, you may say *I felt sort of (somewhat, rather) ridiculous standing there without a shirt.* But remember that it is informal.

sot *n. The old sot wandered the streets begging for enough money for another bottle:* drunk, drunkard, alcoholic, soak; boozer, wino.
Ant. teetotaller, abstainer.

soul *n.* 1 *Her body died but her soul went to heaven:* spirit; spiritual part of a person, vital force. 2 *He loved her with his heart and soul:* being, spirit; inmost feelings, inner core. 3 *Won't someone help that poor soul?:* person, creature, individual; living being. 4 *The old farmer was the very soul of honesty:* essence, embodiment, quintessence. 5 *Some musicians lack soul:* inspiration, force, spirit, vitality.

sound[1] *n.* 1 *I love the sound of rain on the roof:* noise; that which is heard, sensation produced by hearing. 2 *He didn't like the sound of her suggestion:* drift, tone, tenor, suggestion, implication. 3 *Were you within sound of the explosion?:* range, earshot; hearing distance.
—*v.* 4 *The warning alarm sounded. Sound the gong for lunch:* make a noise, produce sound, cause to sound, produce noise. 5 *The cannons sounded the death of the general:* signal, announce. 6 *Her voice sounds happy:* seem, convey a certain impression. 7 *You must sound your words more clearly:* pronounce, articulate, enunciate, voice, utter.

sound[2] *adj.* 1 *Her heart is as sound as a drum:* robust, sturdy, strong, good, fit, hardy, healthy. 2 *The wiring in the old building is surprisingly sound:* undamaged, intact, unmarred; perfect; substantial, strong, well-built, lasting, sturdy, well-constructed; firm, solid, durable. 3 *She has a sound, growing business:* solid, strong, stable, solvent. 4 *You can depend on him to make a sound choice. The general presented a sound analysis of the situation:* sensible, solid, reliable, competent, sober, dependable, wise, penetrating, rational, reasonable, responsible. 5 *I was in a sound sleep when you called:* deep, untroubled. 6 *The officer gave him a sound reprimand:* thorough, thorough-going, severe, firm.
Ant. 1-4 unsound. 1 poor, ailing, weak. 2 damaged, defective. 3 failing, insolvent, insecure, shaky. 4 unreliable, incompetent, rash, irrational, irresponsible, frivolous. 5 light. 6 half-hearted.

sour *adj.* 1 *These pickles are too sour:* tart, acid, vinegary, tangy, sharp, keen; acerbic, astringent. 2 *Does the milk taste sour?:* spoilt, turned, fermented, rancid, curdled, bad; *(loosely)* off. 3 *The baby's clothes have a sour smell:* offensive, nasty, repugnant, distasteful, unsavoury, unpleasant. 4 *She glanced at the noisy child with a sour expression:* disagreeable, nasty, unpleasant, peevish, surly, choleric, bad-tempered, crabbed, jaundiced, dour; uncivil, sullen, ill-humoured, ill-tempered, waspish, tart, testy, irritable, grouchy.

—*v.* **5** *The cream soured in the boot of the car. Too much heat soured the wine:* spoil, become spoilt, ferment, become fermented, curdle, turn. **6** *A lonely childhood soured the boy. An unhappy romance soured her initial reaction to men:* embitter, ill-dispose, make disagreeable, make unpleasant, jaundice, make bad-tempered; make cynical, make pessimistic, prejudice, alienate, *Slang* turn off.

Ant. 1 sweet, bland, mild. **2** fresh, unspoilt. **3** sweet, pleasant, agreeable, savoury, fresh. **4** sweet, agreeable, pleasant, gracious, amiable, affable, good-natured, good-humoured.

source *n.* **1** *The reporter refused to name the source of his information. What is the source of his strength?:* origin, derivation, authority, basis; cause, antecedent, fountain, fount, spring, well-spring, root, foundation; father, author, begetter. **2** *The explorers searched for the source of the river:* beginning, rising, headwater, head, well-spring, place of issue, fount, fountain.

Ant. 1 outcome, result, effect, consequence, end, conclusion. **2** mouth, estuary, termination.

souse *v.* **1** *The abrupt downpour soused us:* wet thoroughly, drench, soak, saturate; douse, inundate, immerse, submerge, duck, dunk, dip. **2** *She soused the mushrooms in the marinade for two days:* pickle, steep, soak, marinate.

Ant. 1 dry.

souvenir *n. She kept the pine-cone as a souvenir of her weekend in the country:* memento, reminder, remembrance, relic, keepsake, token, trophy.

◇ *Word origin: Souvenir* is a French word meaning remembrance, memory, keepsake; it comes from the Latin prefix *sub-* (under) + *venire* (to come), hence to come into the mind.

sovereign *n.* **1** *He abdicated as sovereign of the tiny kingdom:* supreme ruler, monarch; king, queen, prince, emperor, empress, tsar, tsarina, potentate; crowned head, chief, chieftain, overlord, autocrat, lord.

—*adj.* **2** *No one questions the Queen's sovereign authority:* ruling, supreme, absolute; royal, monarchical, imperial, reigning; powerful, regal, all-powerful, prepotent, potent; kingly, queenly, princely. **3** *Your welfare is my sovereign concern:* principal, chief, paramount, leading, governing, ruling, supreme, utmost, main, uppermost, highest, dominant, major, prime. **4** *We have an ambassador in most of the world's sovereign states:* self-governing, independent, self-directing, self-ruling, autonomous.

Ant. 1 subject; peasant, serf. **2** subordinate; limited, partial. **3** minor, secondary, least, lowest.

◇ *Word origin: Sovereign* can be traced all the way back to Latin *super*, above, hence indicating the person above all others in a country.

sovereignty *n.* **1** *The sovereignty of the monarch was under attack:* power, dominion, authority, supremacy, command, control, ascendancy, sway, jurisdiction, predominance, paramountcy, primacy; kingship, lordship; throne, sceptre, crown. **2** *The United States of America declared its sovereignty in 1776:* independence, autonomy, self-determination, self-rule, home rule, self-government, freedom.

"Every succeeding scientific discovery makes greater nonsense of old-time conceptions of sovereignty." —*Anthony Eden*

---

sow *v.* **1** *Sow the marigold seeds in early spring:* plant, seed, scatter, strew, cast, broadcast, implant, sprinkle, set in. **2** *Her strange behaviour sowed suspicions of guilt in our minds:* plant, establish, inject, lodge, instil, introduce; spread, scatter, strew.

space *n.* **1** *The rocket was lost in space:* outer space, the void, the firmament, the heavens, sky, ether, nothingness, infinity, emptiness. **2** *We need more space to set up the equipment:* room, area, range, territory, expanse, scope, spread, amplitude, swing, field, margin, compass, reach, latitude, breadth, width, sweep. **3** *She has a wide space between her teeth:* gap, distance, span, chasm, separation, break, hiatus, interruption, interval, interstice, interspace, lacuna, omission, blank. **4** *Can you finish eating in the space of an hour?:* period, interval, span, duration, term. **5** *Luckily, there was an extra space on the plane:* seat, place, spot, reservation, accommodation.

—*v.* **6** *Space the paintings evenly along the wall. Space the meetings at hourly intervals:* place, arrange, organize, distribute, order, set out, line up, range, rank, mark out; schedule, time. **7** *He spaced the dancers so that they wouldn't bump into one another:* separate, keep apart, part, spread.

Ant. 2 confinement, limitation. **3** closure. **7** crowd, bunch.

spacious *adj. Our garden is spacious enough for a swimming-pool:* large, ample, wide, broad, sizeable, commodious, roomy; immense, expansive, vast, enormous.

Ant. small, cramped, crowded, close.

span *n.* **1** *The rescuers searched the entire span of the island. The span of human life is short:* distance, breadth, length, dimensions, reach, stretch, proportions, measure, scope, range, sweep, area, territory; extent, term, spell, duration, period, interval. **2** *The car stalled on the second span of the bridge:* arch, vault archway, trestle, wing, extension.

—*v.* **3** *The overpass spans the centre of town:* bridge, bridge over, cross, extend across, reach over, vault. **4** *Their friendship spanned a lifetime:* cover, reach over, stretch over, reach across; last, endure, survive.

spank *v.* **1** *Mother spanked her for running into the street;* slap, hide, thrash, tan, wallop; strike, beat, hit, flagellate, strap, belt, switch, whip, flog, cane, birch, slipper, *Slang* whop, lick.
—*n.* **2** *If you misbehave once more, I shall give you a spank:* slap, strike, hit, blow, wallop, belt, walloping, thrashing.

spare *v.* **1** *The king spared the prisoner:* save from death, leave uninjured, refrain from hurting, deal leniently with, forgive, give quarter to, show mercy, be merciful to, have mercy on, show consideration for; exonerate, liberate, release, free; let off, reprieve, pardon, acquit. **2** *The doctor tried to spare him from pain:* safeguard, protect, exempt, guard, shield, shelter, defend; save, relieve. **3** *I can spare some time now:* afford, part with, grant, give, let go of, dispense with, relinquish, forgo, cede. **4** *Spare your energy for the last lap:* conserve, withhold, not use, hold back, save, hoard, reserve, husband, lay up, set aside, amass, use frugally, keep. **5** *She never spares the butter when she's baking:* use frugally, use economically, economize on, be parsimonious with, limit, pinch, conserve, skimp on, stint, be niggardly with.
—*adj.* **6** *Has the house a spare room? I gave the beggar my spare change:* reserve, extra, auxiliary, supplementary, substitute, supplementary; unnecessary, superfluous, supernumerary, odd, additional, unused, surplus, unconsumed, extraneous, excess, left-over. **7** *The suit hung limply on his spare frame:* fleshless, lean, scrawny, thin, emaciated, gaunt, skinny, lank, lanky, skeletal, haggard, weedy, rangy; slight, meagre, skimpy, scanty, scant, slender.
Ant. **1** punish, condemn, destroy, hurt, harm, injure. **2** afflict, expose. **4** squander, use, spend. **5** squander, spend. **7** fat, fleshy, heavy, plump, large.

sparing *adj. She is sparing with the family's budget. The professor was sparing in his praise:* thrifty, economical, frugal, careful, saving, parsimonious, miserly, penurious, near, close-fisted, close, stinting, stingy, ungenerous, niggardly, tight-fisted; grudging, meagre, scanty, scant.
Ant. lavish, profuse, generous, open-handed.

spark *n.* **1** *A spark from the cigarette started the forest fire:* ignited particle, glowing particle, fiery particle; ember, brand, scintilla. **2** *Sparks flew from a short circuit in the toaster:* flash, flicker, sparkle, beam. **3** *The dog showed not a spark of interest in his food:* bit, iota, trace, jot, glimmer, atom, flicker.
—*v.* **4** *The fire is sparking:* throwing out sparks, sparkle, glitter gleam, flash. **5** *We need to spark off some ambition in the lazy boy:* stimulate, incite, arouse, excite, pique, provoke, stir, instigate.

sparkle *v.* **1** *Her diamond tiara sparkled like fire:* shine, glitter, glint, glisten, flicker, twinkle, gleam, shimmer, scintillate, dazzle, flash; coruscate. **2** *The champagne sparkled:* bubble, fizzle, effervesce, fizz, pop, foam, froth. **3** *The children sparkled with excitement:* scintillate, shine, be vivacious, be witty, be cheerful, rejoice, be gay, effervesce.
—*n.* **4** *I see a sparkle in the ashes:* glint, glitter, twinkle, flicker, shimmer, scintillation, glimmer, flash; ember, brand. **5** *Did you notice the sparkle in her eyes?:* gleam, radiance, brilliance, glow, dazzle, glimmer, glitter, light, glint, effulgence, luminosity, luminousness. **6** *His sparkle made him the life and soul of the party:* liveliness, animation, verve, dash, brilliance, élan, pep, vim; vivacity, life, exhilaration, ebullience, exuberance, vitality, spirit; quickness, alertness, briskness; cheerfulness, gaiety, jollity, cheer, effervescence.
Ant. **1** fade. **5** dullness, flatness. **6** dullness, tedium, cheerlessness, drabness, lethargy.

sparse *adj. Sparse trees provide poor shelter:* few, few and far between, thin, thinly distributed, scarce, infrequent, rare; scattered, sporadic, dispersed, spaced-out, diffuse, strewn; meagre, scanty, spare, exiguous, scant, skimpy.
Ant. plentiful, populous, crowded, numerous, dense, thick.

Spartan *adj. The monks lead a Spartan life:* plain, simple, austere, ascetic, frugal, stark; disciplined, rigorous, restrained, restricted, stiff, stern, exacting, severe, hard, stringent, inexorable, inflexible, self-denying.
Ant. fancy, self-indulgent, luxurious, lavish, undisciplined, unrestrained, spendthrift, hedonistic, soft, easy, *Slang* cushy; lax.
◇ *Word origin: Spartan* means typical of *Sparta,* the ancient Greek city, whose people were noted for their discipline, fortitude, and austere way of life.

spasm *n.* **1** *It was on the way home that she suffered the spasm. A spasm of pain contorted the wounded man's face:* cramp, seizure, crick; twitch, tic, jerk, convulsion, shudder, start, grip, paroxysm; throe, pang. **2** *What caused that brief spasm of tears?:* spell, fit, onset, burst, access, attack, frenzy, storm, flash, spurt, seizure, explosion, tempest, eruption.
◇ *Word origin: Spasm* belongs to a cluster of words derived from Greek *span,* to pull, tear, wrench, sprain. In the language of ancient Greek medicine, *spasma* meant a sprain or rupture of muscle fibre, while *spasmos* meant a convulsion, often specifically an epileptic seizure. *Spasmōdēs* meant subject to seizures, convulsive, *spasmodic.*

spasmodic *adj. She shows only spasmodic bursts of affection:* fitful, intermittent, periodic, fleeting, sporadic, capricious, desultory, flighty, mercurial, erratic, irregular, transient, inconstant, discontinuous.
Ant. constant, steady, regular, lasting.

spatter *v.* **1** *The painters spattered paint on the rug:*

splash, bespatter, splatter, sprinkle; spray, swash, slop, spurt; spot, mottle, fleck, stipple, speckle. **2** *Try not to spatter your dress with grease:* spot, stain, soil.

spawn *v.* **1** *Salmon swim up-river to their birthplaces to spawn:* deposit eggs, lay eggs. **2** *Lower species often spawn in great numbers:* reproduce, propagate, proliferate, multiply, teem, breed. **3** *These meetings spawn all kinds of revolutionary ideas:* engender, generate, give rise to, propagate, give birth to, produce, bring forth, beget, yield.
—*n.* **4** *The polluted water harmed the spawn of the trout:* eggs, seed; offspring, brood; product, yield, fruit.

speak *v.* **1** *The chief engineer speaks with an Italian accent:* talk, utter words, articulate, vocalize, sound, give utterance; enunciate, pronounce; mutter, mumble, murmur, whisper; call, shout, cry out; converse, confer, consult, exchange words, chat. **2** *She spoke her mind with abundant clarity:* express, say, make known, communicate, tell, state, declare, recite, convey, relate, impart, put into words, voice, give voice to; divulge, reveal, disclose, make disclosure, proclaim, announce, advise, air, report; imply, suggest, be expressive, indicate. **3** *Is the governor going to speak at the rally?:* give a speech, deliver an address, discourse, lecture; sermonize, preach; expound, orate, declaim, hold forth, harangue, expatiate, dilate. **4** *His letter spoke of his future plans:* mention, comment, refer, make reference, remark, treat, discuss, deal.
Ant. **2** repress, hide, conceal, suppress.
◇ *Word origin: Speak* comes from Old English *sprecan*, to speak. A close relative is German *sprechen*, to speak, as in the sentence *Sprechen Sie Deutsch?* Also related are Old English *spēc*, speech, and German *Sprache*, language.

speaker *n. The vicar is the opening speaker in our debate:* talker, lecturer, spokesman, orator, speechmaker; reciter, reader; preacher, sermonizer; rhetorician, declaimer, discourser; monologist; mouthpiece.
Ant. listener, audience.

spear *n.* **1** *The spear pierced his heart:* javelin, lance, harpoon, pike, bolt, dart, gaff.
—*v.* **2** *Have you ever speared trout?:* impale, stab, pierce, lance, spike, pike, gore, stick, transfix, spit, penetrate, puncture, prick.

spearhead *n.* **1** *The whale broke the spearhead off the harpoon:* point of a spear, iron. **2** *He was the spearhead of the conservation movement:* leader, establisher, pioneer, initiator, creator, spokesman, begetter, founder, prime mover, instituter, inaugurator, avant-guardist.
—*v.* **3** *Mrs. Pankhurst and others spearheaded the Woman's Suffrage Movement:* lead, pioneer, initiate, begin, start, launch, inaugurate, establish, originate, give birth to, institute, found, conceive, develop.

special *adj.* **1** *The carpenter uses a special machine for planing:* especial, certain, specific, distinct, specialized, particular; proper. **2** *This is a special day in my life:* out of the ordinary, unusual, uncommon, unique, select, distinctive, novel, unconventional, rare, singular, extraordinary, distinct, exceptional, especial, important, momentous, signal, outstanding, distinguished, noteworthy, remarkable, red-letter. **3** *The circus hired him for his special trapeze stunts:* distinctive, unique, peculiar; personal, individual, typical, representative. **4** *Your apple pie is a special favourite of mine. David is a very special friend:* particular, great, outstanding, especial, exceptional; close, devoted, staunch, fast, steadfast, ardent, good, intimate.
—*n.* **5** *Informal Today's special is the shoulder of lamb:* speciality, feature, star attraction, high point, highlight, *French* pièce de résistance; extravaganza; bargain, sale item.
Ant. **1** ordinary, all-purpose, general, unspecialized. **2** common, ordinary, undistinctive, unimportant, routine. **3** ordinary, unexceptional, usual.
◇ *Usage note: Special* and *especial*, *specially* and *especially*, mean almost the same thing. In modern use, *special* and *specially* are winning over *especial* and *especially*, because they are shorter and may be used both in an adjectival position before a noun and as a predicative adjective: *a special* (or *especial*) *offer. This offer is very special* (but not "especial"). Thus you need not worry about sticking to *special* and *specially* all the time, and your great grandchildren may find that *especial* and *especially* are not part of their vocabulary at all.

specialist *n. My cousin is a specialist in Chinese studies:* expert, connoisseur, master, consultant, skilled hand, past master, adept.
Ant. amateur, generalist.

"My speciality is being right when other people are wrong." —*George Bernard Shaw*

---

speciality Also **specialty** *n.* **1** *Will your speciality be psychology or sociology:* special field, focus, pursuit, special subject; special line of work, profession; hobby; faculty, aptitude, bent, talent, competence, genius, turn, endowment. **2** *The restaurant's speciality is home-made soup:* special, distinctive product, distinction, particularity, earmark, badge, mark, trade mark, stamp, feature, claim to fame, forte.

specific *adj.* **1** *What is the specific time of arrival? There are two specific questions we must answer:* precise, definite, exact, certain, fixed, specified, clearly stated, categorical, clear-cut, concrete, stated, unequivocal; confined, circumscribed, limited, bounded, pinned-down, tied-down, restricted; detailed, minute, determinate, relevant, pertinent, pointed, particular. **2** *A specific attribute of the*

elephant is its long trunk: especial, peculiar, special, distinctive, individual, unique, singular, particular, intrinsic, endemic, characteristic, typical, personal.
—*n.* **3** Often **specifics** *The specifics of the accident were hazy:* particular, item, fact, relevant point, detail, datum, circumstance. **4** *The doctor prescribed a specific for his stomach pains:* special remedy, medicine, cure, medication, physic, potion.
Ant. 1 approximate, indefinite, uncertain, vague, hazy; general. **2** common, undistinctive, general.

specification *n.* **1** *The numerous charges against him lacked appropriate specification:* itemization, particularization, enumeration; precision; particularity; clarity, detail; concreteness, substance. **2** *He fits all but one specification:* requirement, condition, stipulation, qualification, necessity.

specify *v. Please specify what the job will entail. The chef specified a dry white wine for the recipe:* state in detail, define, indicate, designate, enumerate, name, be specific about, stipulate, cite, adduce, itemize, denote, particularize, describe, define, set forth; call for, order.

specimen *n. This is a perfect specimen of a Red Admiral butterfly:* sample, model, representative, example, exemplar, instance, type, exemplification.

speck *n.* **1** *Is that a speck of dust on the page or a full stop?:* particle, grain, mote, bit; dot, spot, mark, speckle, fleck. **2** *I put just a speck of cream in my coffee. There's not a speck of truth in her statement:* trace, trifle, bit, modicum; whit, particle, mite, scintilla, iota, jot, hair, glimmer, shadow, pin, farthing.

spectacle *n.* **1** *The eclipse was a spectacle not to be missed:* marvel, wonder, phenomenon, curiosity; sight, scene; rarity, rare sight. **2** *The performers put on quite a spectacle:* exhibition, presentation, extravaganza, demonstration, production, exhibit, exposition, display, pageant, parade.

spectacular *adj.* **1** *Princess Anne's wedding was a spectacular affair:* magnificent, gorgeous, glorious, striking, elaborate, sumptuous, impressive, showy, eye-catching, splendid, opulent, ceremonious, grand, rich, stately; jewelled, bespangled; theatrical; fabulous, marvellous, astounding, overwhelming. **2** *The fireman made a spectacular rescue:* thrilling, daring, impressive, hair-raising, daredevil, dramatic, sensational.
—*n.* **3** *The Searchlight Tattoo was something of a spectacular:* spectacle, elaborate production, ostentatious show, extravaganza, gala.
Ant. 1 plain, unimpressive, modest, ordinary. **2** simple, easy.

spectator *n. Thousands of spectators jammed into the stands:* onlooker, observer, watcher, viewer, witness, eyewitness, beholder, sightseer; kibitzer; theatregoer, fan, aficionado; audience, gallery, house.
Ant. performer, entertainer.

> **Exploring the Word:** Knowing that the Latin verb *specere* means to look, look at, observe, one could work out the meaning of many of the dozens of English words based on it, including: *specimen*, a sample or example for examination; *spectacle*, something interesting to look at, a display, *spectacles*, eye-glasses, *spectator*, one who watches or beholds, and *spectacular*, well worth looking at, unusual, imposing; *spectre*, a vision of a ghost, apparition, and *spectral*, ghostlike; *spectrum* (Latin for "appearance, image, visible shape"), the band of visible wavelengths or colours; *speculate*, literally "to spy out the future" (From Latin *speculari*, to spy out, and *specula*, watch-tower, both derived from *specere*, to look), hence to theorize, conjecture; and *speculator*, one who tries to see into the future, as to make long-range or risky investments. The same Latin verb *specere*, to look, look at, is also the base of *aspect*, an appearance, view, or viewpoint; *auspicious* (ultimately from Latin *avis*, bird + *specere*, to look at), literally "shown to be favourable from watching the flight of birds," as by a Roman augur, hence promising success, favourable; *circumspect* (Latin *circum-*, around), looking around in all directions, hence cautious; *conspicuous*, (Latin *con-*, together), seen all together, not partially hidden, hence highly visible, attracting attention; *despise*, to look down on, regard with contempt, *despicable*, contemptible and *spite*, a shortened form of *despite*, a malicious desire to harm another out of contempt for him.

spectral *adj. Cobwebs gave the place a spectral atmosphere:* ghostly, spooky, phantom, incorporeal; eerie, unearthly, uncanny, weird, creepy, supernatural, other-worldly; gossamer, ethereal, unreal, wraithlike, insubstantial, chimerical, airy, vaporous, shadowy.
Ant. earthly, homely, tangible.

spectre *n. The children thought that they had seen a spectre in the deserted mansion:* ghost, phantom, spook, spirit, wraith, shade, apparition, demon, hobgoblin, sprite, ghoul, banshee, revenant, presence, phantasm.

speculate *v.* **1** *He often speculated about the purpose of life. Scientists only speculate about life on other planets:* meditate, consider, muse, contemplate, engage in thought, reflect, think, reason, deliberate, ponder, ruminate, study, cogitate, excogitate, wonder, brood; guess, surmise, conjecture, theorize, hazard an opinion, hypothesize, suppose, imagine, fancy, dream. **2** *He speculated in foreign exchange and lost a lot of money:* buy and sell riskily, play the market, wager, take a chance, hazard, trade hazardously, gamble, chance, venture.

speech *n.* **1** *We express ourselves through our speech and writing:* speaking, oral communication, talking, talk, articulation, utterance, voice, vocalization; conversation, dialogue, converse, discourse, verbal intercourse, parlance, confabulation, oral commerce, discussion; remarks, statement, spoken words, observation, pronouncement, expression, declaration, comment; palaver, prattle, chatter, gossip, chit-chat. **2** *The candidate delivered a moving speech to his workers:* address, talk, oration, sermon, lecture, declamation, discourse, recitation, diatribe, tirade, salutation, dissertation, appeal, harangue, exhortation, homily; soliloquy, monologue. **3** *Her speech is informal and full of colloquialisms:* style of speaking, manner of speaking, expression, utterance, rhetoric; articulation, pronunciation, enunciation, diction, elocution. **4** *The speech of the islanders is hard to understand:* language, dialect, tongue, idiom; jargon, slang, colloquialism.

Ant. **1** muteness, dumbness, speechlessness; silence.

speed *n.* **1** *He finished the job with amazing speed:* quickness, dispatch, celerity, alacrity, swiftness, expedition, rapidness, rapidity, briskness, haste, hastiness; fleetness, velocity, dash, hurry, rush, acceleration. **2** *The plane went faster than the speed of sound:* rate, velocity; tempo, momentum.

—*v.* **3** *The ambulance sped to the hospital:* hurry, rush, hasten, make haste, lose no time, tear, tear off, hurtle, plunge; run, scurry, race, hie, gallop, hustle, dart, bowl along, *Informal* go hell for leather, go helter-skelter, zip, zoom, flash, belt. **4** *We'll never get there if he doesn't speed up:* hurry up, hurry, quicken, hasten, spurt ahead, step up, pick up, put on a burst of speed, put on more speed, expedite, accelerate, *Informal* get a move on, step on it, step on the gas. **5** *Good fortune sped her on her climb to the top:* hasten, assist, help, aid, boost, promote, advance, further, favour, give a lift, expedite, propel, impel, push forward, move along, dispatch.

Ant. **1** slowness, delay, sluggishness. **3** creep, crawl, drag. **4** slow down. **5** hinder, slow, hamper, inhibit, block, bar.

◇ *Word origin: Speed* once meant success, prosperity. Because it was noted that success went to those who were alert and fast-acting, the word came to mean quickness.

speedy *adj. He made a speedy exit. She wished him a speedy recovery:* swift, fast, rapid, hurried, hasty, quick, headlong, precipitate, sudden, abrupt, fleet, running, brisk; ready, without delay, early, not delayed, summary, with dispatch, express, quick-fire, rapid-fire, lively.

Ant. slow, sluggish, dilatory, laggard, lagging; delayed, late, tardy.

spell[1] *v.* **1** *Children find Mediterranean hard to spell. B-a-b-y spells baby:* write the letters of, say the letters of; form a word, make up. **2** *Those dark clouds spell rain:* foretell, signify, mean, portend, indicate, typify, promise, forecast, denote, augur, stand for, betoken, suggest, symbolize, purport, bespeak, omen, forebode, imply, presage, herald, represent, amount to, connote.

◇ *Spelling tip: Misspell* is itself one of the most frequently misspelt words in the English language. There are two *s's* in it: *miS+Spell=miSSpell.*

◇ *Word origin: Spell*[1] comes from Old French *espeler,* to spell, from a now-lost Frankish word meaning to tell (and thus related to *spell*[2]). The Germanic peoples of the late Roman Empire and the Dark Ages following it were fascinated by writing and endowed letters with magical properties. Thus *spelling* or "telling" letters or runes was synonymous with casting *spells.*

spell[2] *n.* **1** *The fairy godmother's spell transformed the pumpkin into a coach:* charm, enchantment, magic formula, magic, incantation, voodoo, sorcery, witchery, invocation, mumbo-jumbo; abracadabra. **2** *Most women fall under the spell of his charm:* enchantment, fascination, rapture, glamour, bewitchment, allure, influence.

spell[3] *n.* **1** *The long spell of sentry duty exhausted him:* stretch, turn, period, tour, term, bout, time, course, duration, round, tenure, assignment, stint, trick, watch, go. **2** *Just rest for a spell:* while, bit; interval, break, respite, lull, recess, pause. **3** *We're expecting a cold spell:* period, wave, snap.

spellbound *adj. We were spellbound by the music:* fascinated, transported, rapt, enchanted, charmed, enraptured, entranced, bewitched, transfixed, possessed; breathless, speechless, wordless, dumbfounded, tongue-tied, awestruck, agape, open-mouthed.

Ant. unimpressed, indifferent, disenchanted.

spend *v.* **1** *They spend more money than they earn. What did you spend on that lamp?:* pay, pay out, expend, disburse, dispense, allocate, dole out, outlay, *Informal* give, *Slang* fork out, shell out. **2** *He spends too much energy worrying:* consume, employ, expand, devote, invest, use, squander, waste, dissipate. **3** *By the end of the tenth lap he had spent himself:* burn out, drain, use up, exhaust, destroy, consume, dissipate, deplete, impoverish, wear out, waste; scatter, empty. **4** *Let's spend tomorrow together:* occupy, pass, while away, take up, use, fill.

Ant. **1** earn, make, acquire, get, gain, take in; save, hoard, collect, gather. **2** save, conserve. **3** save, reserve, hoard, conserve, treasure up.

spendthrift *n.* **1** *He's a spendthrift and can't save a penny:* wastrel, big spender, squanderer, prodigal, profligate.

—*adj.* **2** *My spendthrift brother pays a fortune for his clothes:* extravagant, wasteful, improvident, wastrel, profligate, prodigal.

Ant. 1 *Slang* tightwad. **2** frugal, thrifty, penny-pinching, stingy.

spent *adj. He was completely spent after two weeks of hard labour:* exhausted, weak, weary, wearied, used up, played out, worn out, debilitated, tired out, done, powerless, strengthless, ready to drop, drooping, fatigued, *Slang* whacked, dead-beat; laid low, faint, on one's last legs, prostrate, enfeebled, done in, fagged out.

Ant. energetic, lively, strong, robust, vital.

spew *v. The volcano spewed out molten lava. The stove spewed smoke into the room:* vomit, disgorge, regurgitate, heave, throw out; cast up, spit out, eject, expel.

sphere *n.* **1** *A ball is a sphere:* globe, round body, ball, globular mass, spheroid, globule, orb. **2** *Poverty and slums were outside the rich boy's sphere:* orbit, domain, realm, area, pale, scope, compass, beat, territory; experience, knowledge.

◇ *Word origin: Sphere* comes from Greek *sphaira,* ball, sphere. The same Greek word gives us *atmosphere* (the sphere or body of gases surrounding the earth or other celestial body) and *hemisphere* (half a sphere).

spice *n.* **1** *Pepper is one of my favourite spices:* seasoning, pungent substance; condiment, flavouring, herb. **2** *He's bored and needs a little spice in his life:* zest, tang, flavour, piquancy, relish, excitement, pungency, savour, zip, snap, kick, accent.

Ant. 2 boredom, flatness, dullness.

spicy *adj.* **1** *Mexican food is too spicy for me:* pungent, hot, piquant, sharp, strong, redolent, peppery, nippy, fiery, tangy, zippy, snappy, aromatic, gingery. **2** *The comedian specialized in spicy remarks:* pungent, sharp, keen, piquant, witty, clever, spirited, provocative, pithy; sparkling, scintillating; piercing, trenchant, incisive, acute. **3** *That French film is too spicy for the children:* racy, ribald, risqué, scandalous, improper, indelicate, questionable, indecent, bawdy, salty, suggestive.

Ant. 1 bland, flat, tasteless, unsavoury, insipid. **2** bland, boring, dull, insipid, tedious, spiritless, lifeless. **3** proper, prudish.

spike *n.* **1** *Hammer the spike in straight:* large nail, pin, skewer, rivet, peg, stake. **2** *I tore my blouse on a spike of the fence:* point, prong, barb, tine; thorn, briar, spine, spur, bramble, bristle.

spill *v.* **1** *Be careful not to spill the tea. Tears spilled from her eyes:* cause to overflow, allow to run over, overturn, slop, slosh, waste; drip, fall, drop, run, flow, overflow, splash. **2** *The warrior spilled his opponent's blood:* let flow, shed, pour out. **3** *The horse spilled his rider:* dump, cause to fall, throw, toss. **4** *Informal I knew he'd spill the whole story!:* disclose, reveal, tell, *Slang* blab.

spin *v.* **1** *Few women spin their own yarn today:* make by twisting fibres; form into thread or yarn. **2** *Children love to spin tops. The dancer spun round and round:* twirl, whirl, turn, rotate, revolve, swirl, wheel, pirouette, gyrate. **3** *No one believed the fantastic tale he spun:* tell, narrate, render, relate, unfold, recount; invent, concoct, fabricate.

—*n.* **4** *Place your bets before the spin of the wheel:* turn, spinning, twirl, roll, rotation. **5** *We went for a spin round the town:* quick drive, rapid ride, turn, fast circle, whirl.

"Let the great world spin for ever down the ringing grooves of change."

—*Alfred, Lord Tennyson*

---

spine *n.* **1** *He broke his spine in a fall from a horse:* backbone, vertebral column, spinal column, vertebrae. **2** *Hedgehogs and porcupines protect themselves with their spines:* quill, horn, pointed projection, barb, spike, spur, point, prong, bristle, prickle; bramble, thorn, briar, needle.

spineless *adj. That man is too spineless ever to remonstrate with his boss:* timid, fearful, faint-hearted, weak, timorous, cowardly, pusillanimous, lily-livered, irresolute, chicken-hearted, cowering, spiritless, cringing, vacillating, weak-willed, weak-kneed, indecisive, wavering.

Ant. fearless, tough, strong, forceful, courageous, resolute.

spiral *n.* **1** *A coiled spring forms a spiral:* helix, screw, whorl, whirl, gyre, coil, corkscrew; curl, curlicue, ringlet.

—*adj.* **2** *A spiral staircase takes up less space than a regular one:* helical, corkscrew, screw-shaped, spiroid, curled, whorled, winding.

◇ *Word origin: Spiral* comes from the Latin *spiralis* which in turn comes from Greek *speira,* coil. The shrub *spiraea* is so called because of its spiral-like growth.

spire *n.* **1** *The view from the church spire was breath-taking:* steeple, belfry, turret, obelisk, minaret, tower, bell tower, shaft. **2** *The snow-capped spires were beautiful against the blue sky:* peak, crest, summit, cap, cone, point, pinnacle, apex, vertex, tip.

spirit *n.* **1** *They believe the spirit lives on after death:* soul, immortal part, vital essence; intellect, mind, psyche. **2** *The house was haunted by spirits:* ghost, shade, spook, apparition, spectre, phantom, phantasm, hobgoblin, wraith, banshee, presence; elf, fairy, bugbear, bugaboo, goblin, ghoul, sprite, dybbuk. **3** *The spirit is willing but the flesh is weak:* will, motivation, resolve, resolution; mind, heart, animus, impulse, urge. **4** **spirits** *He was deeply depressed and no one could lift his spirits:* mood, feelings, disposition, emotions, attitude, morale, sentiment, temper. **5** *Even the children lacked spirit on that gloomy day. The troops*

attacked with spirit: vigour, vim, zest, liveliness, animation, vitality, verve, élan, vivacity, enthusiasm, energy, eagerness; pluck, mettle, enterprise, drive, zeal, avidity; sprightliness, sparkle, ardour, fire, glow, warmth; courage, bravery, doughtiness, audacity, dauntlessness, stout-heartedness, daring, backbone, fortitude, boldness, stoutness, valour, staunchness, fearlessness, spunk, *Informal* guts, grit. **6** *The spirit of the country at present is one of disillusionment:* temper, feeling, disposition, frame of mind, vein, mood, humour, tone, tenor, turn of mind. **7** *We won because of our great team spirit:* allegiance, devotion, loyalty, attachment, bond, fervour, ardour, enthusiasm, feeling. **8** *I feel as bound by the spirit as by the letter of the agreement:* intention, significance, intent, meaning, essence, purport, substance; sense, gist, effect, purpose, aim.
Ant. 1, 3 body, flesh, materiality. **5** lifelessness, dullness, spiritlessness, timidity.

spirited *adj. The spirited horse will be a good racer. He gave a spirited reply:* high-spirited, full of spirit, lively, fiery; courageous, plucky, nervy, intrepid, fearless, bold.
Ant. spiritless, dispirited, timid.

spiritual *adj.* **1** *The medium tried to reach someone in the spiritual world:* ghostly, supernatural, supernal, psychic, metaphysical, phantom, incorporeal, immaterial, unearthly, otherworldly, spectral, insubstantial, intangible. **2** *Her spiritual beauty outshone her physical beauty:* of the soul, psychic, psychological, mental, cerebral, inner, innermost; moral, unworldly, unfleshy, Platonic. **3** *He devoted himself to the spiritual life:* religious, holy, godly, pious, devotional, divine, ecclesiastical, priestly, monastic, Christian, sanctified, churchly, celestial, heavenly; blessed, hallowed, consecrated, sacrosanct ascetic.
Ant. 1 physical, earthly, material, corporeal. **2** fleshly, bodily, physical, carnal, sensuous. **3** earthly, temporal, worldly; atheistic, sacrilegious.

spit[1] *v.* **1** *Don't spit on the pavement:* expectorate, spew, eject. **2** *The pan spat grease all over the stove. The fat was spitting furiously:* spew, spatter, throw out, eject, shower, scatter; pop, hiss, sputter. **3** *He spat out angry words at his tormentors:* fling, eject, throw, express violently; hiss, shriek.
—*n.* **4** *Wipe the spit off the child's chin:* saliva, sputum, spittle.
◇ *Usage note:* Many people are confused by the forms of the verb *to spit.* In general use, the verb may have the same form in all tenses. However, it is more usual to use the form *spat* for all past and perfect tenses, especially when it is used figuratively: *Today he spits; Yesterday he spat;* and *He has spat* or *He had spat. She spat insults at him. Why had he spat out the oath so defiantly?*

spit[2] *n.* **1** *Put the meat on the spit:* brochette, rod, skewer, turnspit. **2** *We went fishing from the end of the spit:* long narrow point of land, bar, peninsula, sandbank, headland, promontory, shoal; atoll, reef.

spite *n.* **1** *He tripped her up out of spite, not accidentally:* malice, gall, hatred, hate, vindictiveness, bitterness, ill will, venom, maliciousness, resentment, malignity, animosity, animus, malevolence, hostility, odium, antipathy, loathing, grudge, enmity, rancour, revengefulness, vengeance, vengefulness, detestation, bad blood.
—*v.* **2** *You came late just to spite me!:* treat maliciously, annoy, humiliate, mortify, pain, injure, misuse, hurt, wound, ill-treat; sting, gall, slap in the face, provoke, irk, harass, nettle, put out, irritate.
Ant. 1 kindness, kindliness, love, benevolence. **2** please, help, aid, assist, support, serve.

splash *v.* **1** *The diver splashed water all over the sunbathers:* splatter, spatter, shower, scatter, slosh, dash, fling; spread, strew, bestrew, cast, plash, disperse. **2** *The piglets splashed about in the muddy pen:* plunge, paddle, wallow, welter, bathe. **3** *He splashed his shirt with paint:* bespatter, spatter, splatter, shower, sprinkle, splotch, besmirch, soil, stain, daub, smear, streak, discolour. **4** *The waves splashed against the rocks:* wash, dash, hit, buffet, surge, toss, break, strike, smack, batter. **5** *The outbreak of war was splashed across the front page of the papers:* show prominently, blazon, broadcast.
—*n.* **6** *Splashes from the oars soaked his jacket:* flying liquid, spattering, splattering, shower. **7** *The news made quite a splash in society:* stir, commotion, ado, uproar; impact, effect.
◇ *Word origin:* When you drop a rock into water, do you hear a *splash* or a *plash?* Today, we use the word *splash* to imitate the sound, but not many decades ago people used the word *plash.* Since the sound itself hasn't changed, it's rather a mystery why a *plash* has become a *splash.*

splay *v.* **1** *He splayed his fingers on the floor to do a handstand:* extend, stretch out, spread out.
—*adj.* **2** *Ducks have splay feet:* spread out, broad, outspread, fan-shaped, fanlike; turned outwards. **3** *The walls of fortifications built by the Normans were very thick and often had splay windows:* irregular, tilted, aslant, sloping, inclined, slanted, slanting.
Ant. 1 narrow, compress. **2** narrow; straight. **3** flat, straight, level, even, symmetrical.

spleen *n. He was upset and vented his spleen upon his wife:* bad temper, rancour, spite, peevishness, venom, bile, gall, acrimony, animosity, animus, malice, ill humour, ill will, bitterness, enmity, resentment, hatred, vexation, resentment, hostility, irritability.
Ant. cheerfulness, happiness, good humour, joy.

◇ *Word origin:* The *spleen* was formerly thought to be the seat of emotions, which ranged from mirth to anger, hence to *vent one's spleen* meant to let the spitefulness out.

"A ship, an isle, a sickle moon —
With few but with how splendid stars."
—*James Elroy Flecker*

---

splendid *adj.* **1** *The queen wore splendid jewels. This is a splendid house:* beautiful, magnificent, *Informal* splendiferous, flashing, costly, superb, gorgeous, resplendent, dazzling, glittering, effulgent, brilliant: rich, ornate, gleaming; sumptuous, palatial, majestic, grand, elegant, imposing, regal, royal, stately, glorious. **2** *He has a splendid reputation as a statesman:* exalted, lofty, high, august, noble, elevated, illustrious, eminent, distinguished, peerless, imposing, glorious, pre-eminent, brilliant, surpassing. **3** *That's a splendid painting:* excellent, exceptional, outstanding, estimable, brilliant, surpassing, transcendent, marvellous, admirable, rare, fine, remarkable, terrific, wonderful.

Ant. 1 plain, sombre, tawdry, poor; beggarly, squalid. **2** inglorious, ignoble, mean, low, sordid, tarnished, ignominious. **3** ordinary, poor, unexceptional, unremarkable, mediocre, unexciting.

splendour *n.* **1** *The splendour of the jewels made my eyes blink. White teeth enhance the splendour of her smile:* brilliance, dazzle, luminosity, light, lustre, gleam, sheen, fire, glitter, burnish, shine, luminousness, radiance, effulgence, resplendence, irradiance, incandescence, intensity. **2** *We were dazzled by the splendour of the royal wedding. The splendour of the Niagara Falls is incomparable:* pomp, grandeur, gorgeousness, glory, resplendence, brilliance, beauty, magnificence, opulence, stateliness; sublimity, augustness, nobility pre-eminence, renown.

Ant. 1 dullness, paleness, pallidness, drabness. **2** plainness, dullness, drabness.

splice *v. Can you splice the broken ends of the rope?:* interweave, braid together, knit, plait, intertwine, interlace, connect, merge, graft; join together, wed.

Ant. cut, break, sever.

splinter *n.* **1** *Pull the splinter out with tweezers:* sliver, fragment, shiver, chip, needle.

—*v.* **2** *The carpenter splintered the wood when he drove in the nail:* split, shiver, sliver, shatter, crumble, disintegrate, pulverize, smash, break up; fly apart, fragment.

split *v.* **1** *Split the pineapple before peeling it. The board split as I sawed it:* divide lengthwise, bisect, halve; cleave, rive, hew; break, crack, snap. **2** *The strike split the union members into angry factions:* divide, disunite, rupture, part, sever, come between, set at odds, sow dissension, set against, segregate, alienate; disagree, differ, diverge, part company. **3** *When he bent over, he split his pants. The water pressure split the pipe:* tear, tear asunder, become torn; sunder, break, burst, rive, be riven, part, rupture, divide, break apart, dissever; shiver, splinter, fracture, snap, crack, give way. **4** *The robbers split the loot evenly:* share, parcel out, divide, divvy up, apportion, disperse, portion, allocate, partition, dispense, dole, deal, distribute, allot, mete, subdivide.

—*n.* **5** *Can you mend this split in my jacket?:* tear, rift, rent, breach, cleft, splitting, separation; break, crack, fissure, fracture, opening. **6** *A split in the party could lose us the election:* rupture, breach, cleavage, disunion, break, schism, dissension, cleavage, division; quarrel, rift, divorce, dissociation, falling out, difference, divergence, disagreement, alienation, estrangement, parting of the ways.

—*adj.* **7** *This split material is useless. A schizophrenic is sometimes said to have a split personality:* torn, severed, rent, ripped, riven; broken, segmented, ruptured, dissevered, splintered, fractured, cracked; divided, separated, dual, two-fold; mixed, varied; undecided, ambivalent.

Ant. 1, 2, 3 unite, join. **6** union, merger, junction, agreement, connection. **7** whole, unbroken, sound.

splurge *n. He'll regret that jewellery-buying splurge when he receives the bill:* indulgence, self-indulgence, binge, spree, bender; showy display, showing off.

splutter *v.* **1** *She spluttered a nervous apology:* sputter, stammer, stutter, mumble, jabber, gibber. **2** *The log was spluttering in the fireplace:* spit, hiss, seethe, sputter; spew, spray, spatter; expectorate, slobber.

◇ *Word origin:* The word *splutter* is a blend of *spl(ash)* and *(sp)utter.* In his famous *Dictionary* (1755), Samuel Johnson labels *splutter* "a low word."

spoil *v.* **1** *She spoiled the soup with too much salt. The rain spoilt her new dress:* ruin, botch, mess up, foul up, mar, bungle, impair, damage, muddle, blemish, flaw, blight, disrupt, disfigure, mutilate, destroy, harm, injure, deface. **2** *Food spoils more quickly without preservatives:* go bad, decay, rot, taint, become tainted, sour, putrefy, decompose, addle, deteriorate, mould, mildew, turn. **3** *He spoilt his son by giving him too much money:* over-indulge, pamper, over-gratify, coddle, molly-coddle, baby, humour.

Ant. 1 enhance, improve. **2** preserve, conserve, save. **3** deprive, overtax, discipline.

spoils *n. pl. To the victor go the spoils!:* benefits, prizes, loot, booty, plunder, swag, bounty; profits, take, acquisitions; perquisites, comforts, amenities; patronage.

◇ *Word origin: Spoil* comes from Latin *spolium*, booty, most often in classical usage occurring in the plural form *spolia*, spoils.

From the related verb *spoliare,* to strip, to rob; we get our words *spoil* (destroy) and *despoil* (plunder).

sponge *v.* **1** *Sponge the wound with an antiseptic before bandaging it:* swab, wash, rub, mop, moisten, clean, cleanse; blot, towel, dry. **2** *Informal He eats well by sponging on friends:* scrounge, obtain free, borrow, cadge, *Slang* freeload.

sponsor *n.* **1** *A large department store is the sponsor of the annual Christmas carnival. You must add the names of three sponsors to the application form:* promoter, financer, backer, advertiser; patron, angel, protector, guarantor, referee, supporter, defender, advocate, proponent, partisan, champion, upholder, guardian; godparent.
—*v.* **2** *Our local M.P. sponsored the new import legislation. Who will sponsor your admission into the club?:* back, finance, advocate, promote; champion, support, guarantee, warranty, uphold, stand up for, vouch for; set up, underwrite.
◇ *Word origin:* In Latin *sponsor* means bondsman, one who makes himself *responsible* for another's liability. Related is the verb *spondere,* to promise, which gives us our word *spouse.*

spontaneous *adj. Her remarks were spontaneous and obviously not planned:* unpremeditated, improvised, impulsive, impetuous, off the cuff, ad-lib, extemporaneous; natural, unstudied, uncontrived, ingenuous; extempore, impromptu, unprompted, unconstrained, voluntary, unplanned, free, gratuitous; offhand, unbidden, willing, independent, automatic, unhesitating, instinctive.
Ant. premeditated, studied, contrived, forced, planned, calculated, involuntary, constrained.

sporadic *adj. We've had only sporadic flurries of snow this month:* irregular, spotty, scattered, sparse, spasmodic, fitful, widely spaced, now and then, infrequent, periodic, fragmentary, intermittent, few and far between, meagre, few, thin, scarce, rare, uncommon; random, haphazard.
Ant. continuous, regular, steady, constant.

sport *n.* **1** *Tennis is a popular sport:* athletic pastime, physical activity, game, competition, contest, athletics; diversion, recreation, fun, distraction, entertainment, amusement, play, relaxation, hobby. **2** *The child's teasing was only sport:* play, jest, jesting, pleasantry, skylarking, trifling, kidding, jollity, gaiety, frolic, mirth, hilarity, antics, fun; joviality, merry-making, festivity; raillery, ridicule, mockery, scoffing, derision, chaff, badinage, persiflage, depreciation. **3** *The poor man has been the sport of Fortune all his life:* laughing-stock, butt, fair game, scapegoat, buffoon, joke, plaything. **4** *Informal Dick's a sport — he'll try anything:* game person, daredevil.
—*v.* **5** *The lambs were sporting in the meadow:* play, disport, amuse oneself, play games; make merry, dally, caper, gambol, revel, frisk, trip, cavort, frolic, rollick, lark, romp, skylark. **6** *He sported with her affection:* toy, trifle, take advantage of, play, be frivolous, play cat and mouse, deal lightly, treat cavalierly, take in, ill-treat, abuse, misuse. **7** *He sports an ivory-handled cane these days:* display, exhibit, show off, flourish, flaunt; carry, bear.
Ant. **1** business, job, duty, work. **2** cruelty, seriousness, respect, adoration. **4** coward, sissy, stick-in-the-mud. **5** work, toil.
◇ *Word origin:* Our word *sport* was originally a shortened form of *disport,* to divert, amuse.

spot *n.* **1** *There's a spot on your tie:* stain, mark, speck, splotch, smudge, soil, blot, daub, smirch, fleck, patch, speckle, blotch, dot, discoloration. **2** *The dishonourable discharge left a spot on his reputation:* disgrace, stain, blemish, brand, taint, blot, defect, flaw, stigma, slur, imputation, aspersion, reproach. **3** *We're going to build our home on this spot. I wish people wouldn't leave litter in beauty spots:* place, locality, locale, location, point, site, tract, situation, space, seat, locus, premises, position; part, region, district, area, territory, quarter, neighbourhood, station, section, sector. **4** *Informal All these expenses coming at once have put me in a spot:* bad situation, difficulty, plight, mess, fix, bind, predicament.
—*v.* **5** *Wine spotted the table-cloth:* stain, smudge, smirch, soil, sully, blot, dot, discolour, daub, speck, grime, blemish, smear, speckle, sprinkle, spatter, splash. **6** *I finally spotted a redshank:* locate, see, pick out, recognize, discover, light on, espy, spy, discern, detect.

spotless *adj.* **1** *The house was left in a spotless condition:* clean, unsoiled, unspotted, immaculate, unstained, unmarred, unsullied, untarnished, pure, perfect, unblemished, gleaming, shining, untainted, snowy. **2** *His military record was spotless:* perfect, unflawed, flawless, untarnished, immaculate, unblemished, untainted, unsullied, faultless, pure, clean, stainless, unmarred; impeccable, irreproachable, unexceptionable.
Ant. **1** filthy, dirty, messy, soiled. **2** tarnished, flawed, marred, blemished, tainted; reprehensible.

spotty *adj.* **1** *She has a spotty complexion from too much sun-bathing:* mottled, full of spots, dappled, spotted, flecked, freckled, variegated; blotchy, splotchy, pimply, scabious. **2** *The company's records are spotty; they never achieve a steady profit:* uneven, irregular, unmethodical, fitful, erratic, unsystematic, disorganized, variable, chequered, sporadic, intermittent, spasmodic, unsteady, capricious, desultory; inconstant, wavering, unreliable, undependable, uncertain.

Ant. 1 smooth, unmottled; clear. **2** even, regular, methodical, systematic, uniform, constant, dependable.

spout *v.* **1** *The whale spouted water from the blow-hole on its back. Lava spouted from the volcano:* spurt, discharge, emit forcibly, squirt, issue, spray, pour out, disgorge, vomit, spew, eject, expel, gush, jet, stream, flow, surge, shoot, well, exude. **2** *Informal He spouts about things he knows nothing about:* speak pompously, carry on, go on, pontificate, harangue, gush, hold forth, rant.

—*n.* **3** *Something's clogging the spout of the kettle:* outlet, vent, mouth, pipe, nose, tube, nozzle, lip, conduit, trough, snout, channel, waterspout, beak, sluice. **4** *A spout of water rose up before them:* jet, spurt, shoot, stream, fountain, gush, spray.

sprawl *v.* **1** *Her writing sprawled all over the page:* spread out, straggle, meander, stretch out, push out, reach out, wind, extend, branch. **2** *Don't sprawl at table:* slouch, stretch out, loll, flop, slump, languish, recline, sit awkwardly, lie awkwardly, lounge.

spray¹ *n.* **1** *The spray from the fountain kept us back. Perfume spray scented the air:* droplets, mist, splash, moisture, vapour. **2** *The shower's spray is broken:* sprayer, nozzle, rose, sprinkler, vapourizer, atomizer, syringe. **3** *The running boy kicked up a spray of sand:* barrage, shower, burst, fusillade, volley, discharge.

—*v.* **4** *She sprayed hairspray into her eye by mistake:* discharge, scatter, disperse, shower, sprinkle, spatter; atomize; moisten, dampen; coat, treat.

spray² *n. A spray of mistletoe hung over the doorway:* sprig, bouquet, nosegay, shoot, switch, twig, bough, posy, blossom.

spread *v.* **1** *Let's spread the blanket under that tree:* stretch out, open, unfold, untwine, unroll, unfurl, extend. **2** *She spread her toys all over the room. Their friendship spread over many years:* scatter, be scattered, bestrew, sprinkle, overspread, cast, distribute, diffuse, shed, strew, disperse; extend, stretch, cover. **3** *The radio spread the news as soon as it happened. The fire spread rapidly:* publish, communicate, circulate, divulge, make known, disseminate, proclaim, broadcast, propagate, make public, air, repeat, report, bruit, blazon, vent, noise abroad, publicize, herald, announce, distribute, issue, ventilate, trumpet, declare, promulgate, whisper about, radiate, diffuse; proliferate, penetrate, pervade, permeate; overrun, suffuse, advance. **4** *Spread the wax thinly on the floor:* apply, coat, lay, smear, besmear, overlay, bedaub, overspread, cover, cloak, pave; spray, spatter; plaster.

—*n.* **5** *The spread of the disease frightened the villagers:* spreading, increase, expansion, dispersion, enlargement, diffusion, dissemination, advance, circulation, amplification, radiation, pervasion, permeation, suffusion, proliferation. **6** *Those antlers have a spread of five feet:* stretch, reach, extent, extension, span, scope, range, distance, breadth, length, area, field, width, circuit, compass; expanse, open land, sweep, tract. **7** *Informal The caterers prepared a huge spread:* feast, array of food, table, banquet. **8** *The wedding had a big spread in* The Times: notice, coverage, write-up, report, article, account, story; printed advertisement.

Ant. 1 fold, roll up, wind, furl. **2** collect, pile up, gather. **3** suppress, conceal, hush; localize, confine; diminish, die, abate. **5** halting, check, abatement, diminishing.

spree *n. He had a bad hangover the morning after his spree. She went on a buying spree:* carouse, carousal, revel, revelry, bacchanal, orgy, debauch, *Informal* binge, bender, drunk; saturnalia, splurge, fling.

sprightly *adj. He's unusually sprightly for a man of 85:* animated, lively, alive, light-hearted, playful, vivacious, gay, buoyant, sportive, blithesome, blithe, spry, jolly, cheery, merry, jovial, active, dashing, jaunty, frolicsome, cheerful, breezy, keen, spirited, dynamic, nimble, brisk.

Ant. glum, lethargic, lifeless, sluggish.

spring *v.* **1** *He sprang out of bed when the alarm went off:* leap, bound, rise suddenly, jump, dart, vault, lunge, bounce, start, hop. **2** *Force is required to spring the mine:* release, trigger. **3** *Tourist shops sprang up throughout the resort. Shouts of protest sprang from the crowd:* rise, shoot up, arise, appear, mushroom, crop out; sprout, burgeon, pop up, loom, start up; pour, issue suddenly, burst forth, stream, flow, well, break forth, surge, rush, gush, jet, spout, spurt, shoot, emanate. **4** *I can't believe that Man springs from the apes:* descend, be brought forth, emanate, originate, come forth, be descended, proceed, derive, be derived, come into existence, stem, sprout, start, flow, arise, rise, germinate, begin, commence, issue, come, result, ensue.

—*n.* **5** *The dancer's high springs dazzled the audience:* jump, leap, saltation, vault, bound, skip, hop, caper, bounce, gambol, lunge; entrechat. **6** *Fine weather can put a spring into your step. There's no spring left in this tennis ball:* springiness, buoyancy, elasticity, kick, bounce, resiliency, elastic force, flexibility, reflex, stretch, recoil. **7** *The water at the spring was too cold to paddle in:* small stream, pool, hot spring, well, water-hole, watering-place, fount, fountain, well-spring; baths, spa.

Ant. 1 crawl, creep; land, alight, drop, fall. **4** end, finish, terminate. **6** inflexibility.

◇ *Word origin:* A *spring,* be it a leap, a coiled steel wire, a natural fountain or flow of water, or the season, goes back to Old English *springan,* to leap. A metal *spring,* of course, leaps back into place, a *spring* of water is a place where water leaps forth from the ground, and the season *Spring* leaps forth with blooms and blossoms.

sprinkle *v.* **1** *Sprinkle some castor sugar on the cake:* dust, scatter, dash, strew, bestrew; squirt, spray, water, spatter, splash, shower, diffuse, splatter. **2** *It's not really raining, just sprinkling:* shower, rain lightly, drizzle.

sprinkling *n. The recipe calls for only a sprinkling of dill:* sprinkle, modicum, droplet, minimum, dash, drop, soupçon, hint, touch, pinch.

sprint *v.* **1** *The players sprinted across the football field:* run, race, dash, tear, whisk, whiz, shoot, scamper, dart, rush.
—*n.* **2** *He crossed the finishing-line with a sprint:* dash, burst, spurt, kick.
Ant. 1 stroll, saunter, walk, creep, crawl. **2** walk, stroll.

sprout *v.* **1** *New buds sprouted from the pussy willow:* shoot forth, begin to grow, come up, burgeon, spring up, grow, come up, bloom, flower, blossom, put forth; spread, wax, multiply, germinate.
—*n.* **2** *Bean sprouts are very good for your health:* shoot, offshoot, sprig, outgrowth, germinated seed.

spruce *adj. You look so spruce in your new suit:* trim, tidy, neat, smart, chic, dapper, natty; spick and span, shipshape, well-groomed, kempt, elegant, *French* soigné.
Ant. sloppy, messy, seedy, shabby, down at heel.
◇ *Word origin: Spruce* was once spelt *pruce,* and meant from *Pruce,* i.e. Prussia. *Spruce trees* are so named because they were first known as being native to Prussia. When a person *spruces up* or a room looks *spruce,* neat, trim, it refers either to the neatness and symmetry of the tree or perhaps to the fineness of *spruce leather,* a very fine leather made in Prussia.

spry *adj. She's very spry for a woman of her age:* lively, sprightly, animated, frisky, light-footed, supple, active, nimble, brisk, agile, deft; spirited, jaunty, sportive, full of life, buoyant, vigorous, energetic, playful, vivacious, hearty, hale, full of spirit, quick.
Ant. doddering, slow, inactive, sluggish, lethargic.

spunk *n. Informal It took a lot of spunk to brave that sea:* guts, pluck, spirit, grit, nerve, courage, boldness, daring, bravery, mettle, fire, pepper, ginger, salt, gumption.
Ant. cowardice, timidity, fear, squeamishness.
◇ *Word origin:* Before it meant pluck or courage, *spunk* meant *punk,* rotten wood or other tinder used in lighting a fire. It comes from Irish *sponnc,* tinder, and can be traced all the way back to Greek *spongos,* sponge.

spur *n.* **1** *The cowboy dug his spurs into the horse:* boot, spike, goad, prodder. **2** *The encouragement was a helpful spur to his ego:* stimulus, incitement, inducement, incentive, stimulant, stimulation, goad, excitant, whet, provocation, impetus, prick, instigation, whip, fillip, motive, impulse, encouragement. **3** *This spur of the railway connects us with the city:* branch, arm, wing, leg, fork; tributary, feeder; siding.
—*v.* **4** *Her loving care spurred on his recovery:* stimulate, hasten, encourage; goad, prod.
Ant. 2 discouragement, hindrance, restraint, check, curb, deterrent.

spurious *adj. Imagine paying all that money for a spurious Rembrandt!:* not genuine, fake, forged, counterfeit, sham, imitation, unauthentic, bogus, phoney, fraudulent; simulated, feigned, mock, make-believe; false, hollow, fallacious, faulty, unsound, specious, illegitimate.
Ant. genuine, real, authentic; sound, legitimate, solid.

spurn *v. She spurned his love:* reject, turn down, scorn, disdain, refuse, repulse, repudiate, repel, look down upon, treat with contempt, contemn, cast aside, decline, sneer at, scoff at, disparage, trample upon, mock, flout, cold-shoulder, rebuff, turn up one's nose at.
Ant. welcome, embrace, accept, encourage.

spurt *v.* **1** *Blood spurted from the wound:* spout, jet, gush, issue, burst, spring out, stream, flow, pour out, surge, shoot, squirt, spray; emit, disgorge, discharge, vomit forth. **2** *Our horse spurted ahead just at the finishing-line:* speed, sprint, burst, lunge, tear, scoot, whiz, spring, dart, dash, rush.
—*n.* **3** *A spurt of water came out of the hose:* rush, jet, gush, stream, shoot, spout, sudden flow, squirt, fountain, ejection, spray. **4** *He threw the glass in a spurt of anger:* explosion, eruption, burst, outbreak, outburst, flash, outpouring, rush, access, gust.
Ant. 1 drip, ooze. **2** creep, crawl, dawdle, lag. **3** oozing, drip, dribble, drizzle.

"'Will you walk into my parlour?' said a spider to a fly;
''Tis the prettiest little parlour that ever you did spy.'"
— *Mary Howitt*

---

spy *n.* **1** *Foreign spies followed him to the airport:* espionage agent, secret agent, intelligence agent, undercover agent, fifth columnist, quisling; saboteur, agent provocateur; informer.
—*v.* **2** *Government agents spied on the enemy submarines:* watch secretly, keep watch, engage in surveillance, shadow, scout, reconnoitre; snoop, pry, peep. **3** *The dog spied a rabbit in the bush:* see, observe, discover, descry, glimpse, spot, catch sight of, sight, make out, detect, recognize, perceive, behold, notice, find, view, discern.

squabble *v.* **1** *They squabbled over who should pay the bill:* wrangle, quarrel, bicker, clash, dispute, differ; have words, argue, bandy

words, set to, lock horns, brawl, row, fight, contest, contend, battle, war, tiff.
—*n.* **2** *Their squabble was over a woman:* quarrel, tiff, dispute, difference, dissension, fight, disagreement, scrap; contention, words, argument, row, run-in, set-to, altercation, controversy.
Ant. 1 agree, concur, assent. **2** agreement, concurrence.
◇ *Word origin: Squabble* comes from the Swedish dialectal word *skvabbel,* to quarrel.

squalid *adj. These squalid slums breed disease:* unclean, foul, dirty, filthy, decayed, slovenly, reeking, nasty, sloppy, dishevelled, slatternly, horrid, run-down, tumble-down, deteriorated, dilapidated, ramshackle; degraded, wretched, sordid, rotten, miserable, poverty-stricken, abject, mean, shabby, battered, broken-down.
Ant. clean, attractive, well-kept, tidy.
◇ *Word origin: Squalid* and *squalor* come from Latin *squalere,* to be filthy, from *squalus,* filthy, scabby.

squalor *n. The poor man lives in unbelievable squalor:* wretchedness, foulness, filth, squalidness, uncleanness, dirtiness, dirt, nastiness, uncleanliness; ugliness, degraded condition, sordidness, meanness, abjectness, poverty, misery, neglect.
Ant. cleanliness, beauty, fineness, splendour, luxury, nobility.

squander *v. Don't squander your money on such a badly-made dress:* waste, throw away, misspend, dissipate, fritter away, misuse, *Slang* blow; lavish, run through, exhaust, spend like water, be prodigal with.
Ant. save, conserve, hoard.

square *n.* **1** *The sides of a square are of equal length:* quadrangle, quadrate, quadrilateral, box. **2** *The meeting was held in the village square:* market-place, large intersection, circus block; park; green, common. **3** *Slang Yes, my father is a bit of a square:* dull person, conservative, stick in the mud, old fogy; prig, prude.
—*v.* **4** *Square the material in four parts:* reduce to square form, block out, quadrate, set at right angles; form into right angles. **5** *That touchdown squared the score. This payment will square my debt:* even, level, make even, even up, balance; pay off, settle up, close, discharge, liquidate. **6** *Can you square those crooked pictures?:* align, make straight, straighten, even out, make level, make even; flatten, plane, smooth. **7** *Be certain your alibi squares with mine:* agree, tally, harmonize, blend, accord, fit, conform, match, correspond, be in unison, cohere, be congruous, concur, fall in, equal. **8** *Did you square your differences with your brother?:* settle, resolve, reconcile, heal, rectify, adjust, set right, reach agreement on, compose, arbitrate, patch up, arrange, mend, straighten out, mediate, clear up.
—*adj.* **9** *Company policy on maternity leave is fair and square. Are you being absolutely square with me?:* honest, just, equitable; truthful, candid, straightforward.
Ant. 3 hippie, hipster, mod, sophisticate. **6** make crooked, distort. **7** disagree, contrast, contradict. **8** entangle, prolong, worsen.

"A man who is good enough to shed his blood for the country is good enough to be given a square deal afterwards." —*Theodore Roosevelt*

---

squash *v.* **1** *She sat on his hat and squashed it:* smash, crush, flatten, press flat, compress, pulp, mash, ram down, squish; squeeze, jam, cram, crowd; compact, concentrate. **2** *The wage freeze squashed his hope of a rise:* put down, quell, quash, prostrate, crush, suppress, repress, dispel, dissipate, trample, upset, flatten, level, undermine, overthrow; destroy, annihilate, obliterate.
Ant. 2 aid, promote, enhance, support.

squat *v.* **1** *If you squat behind the table he won't see you:* crouch, bend the knees, sit on the heels; kneel; cringe, cower, lie low, shrink. **2** *The migrant workers squatted on the unused farm:* settle without title, dwell, establish oneself, set up house, move in, make a home, take up residence, encamp, locate oneself.
—*adj.* **3** *Her body is too squat to be attractive:* dumpy, stumpy, stocky, chunky, stubby, pudgy, thickset, square.
Ant. 3 lanky, tall, slim, reedy, willowy.

squawk *v.* **1** *The hen squawked when the farmer took her eggs:* scream, squall; blare. **2** *Slang The tenants squawked about the lack of heat:* complain, protest, grumble, gripe.

squeak *v. The mouse squeaked in the corner. The rusty hinges of the door squeaked when we opened it:* screech, squeal, shriek; cheep, peep, cry, shrill, chirp, yelp.

squeal *v.* **1** *The puppy squealed when I stepped on his tail:* wail, yelp, cry, shrill, screech, shriek, peep, cheep, scream, yell, squeak. **2** *Slang One of the thieves squealed to the police:* inform, turn informer, betray accomplices, *Slang* blab, sing, grass.

squeamish *adj.* **1** *She's too squeamish to see a peep-show:* priggish, puritanical, prudish, modest, prim, proper, easily shocked, demure, fastidious, strait-laced, coy, sanctimonious, mincing, finicky, finicking, finical, fussy. **2** *That film is too violent for someone so squeamish:* easily nauseated, qualmish, easily disgusted, weak-stomached, delicate, sick, sickish, queasy, nauseous.
Ant. 1 bold, immodest, brazen, brash. **2** coarse, tough, strong-stomached.

squeeze *v.* **1** *Squeeze the walnuts together to crack them:* press, compress; clutch. **2** *He squeezed the last bit from the toothpaste tube:* extract, press out, force out; elicit, wring, wrest, wrench; pry, pull out, tear out, draw out, withdraw, extricate; extort, compel, coerce. **3** *We* *squeezed our whole party into the lift:* crowd, cram, pack, jam, stuff, thrust, cramp, wedge; concentrate, compact, consolidate. **4** *Mother squeezed me tightly when I left:* hug, embrace, clasp, hold. **5** *Can you squeeze through that line of cars?:* press, push, force one's way, wedge, elbow, crowd, shove, shoulder, ram, drive, jostle, butt, edge.

—*n.* **6** *He gave her hand a squeeze. I managed to park, but it was a tight squeeze:* clasp, grasp, grip, hold, embrace, hug, clutch; pressure, crushing, compression, pinching, constriction; narrowing, crowding, stricture, wedge; bottleneck; passage, defile.

squelch *v.* **1** *The children squelched through the sunlit pools searching for crabs:* ooze, splash, drip, wade, wallow.

—*n.* **2** *The boots made a loud squelch in the marshy ground:* squelching sound, splash, plash, gurgle, ooze.

squirm *v.* **1** *The patient squirmed in pain:* turn, twist, contort, wriggle, writhe, wiggle, jerk, bend, twitch, pitch, toss. **2** *He squirmed with embarrassment:* show discomfort, be restless, writhe, shrink, blench, be upset, smart, flinch, wince, sweat, agonize.

squire *n.* **1** *The squire and his guests went hunting:* country gentleman, landowner, rich farmer; member of the gentry, lord of the manor. **2** *The ladies and their squires formed up for the quadrille:* escort, consort, attendant; gallant, cavalier, companion, *Informal* boy-friend.

—*v.* **3** *He squired her around town that summer:* escort, attend, court, accompany, take, chaperon, chauffeur.

squirt *v.* **1** *Juice from the grapefruit squirted in my eye:* spray, spurt, shoot, gush, spout, discharge. **2** *The elephant squirted water on the children:* spray, shower, spatter, sprinkle, splash, dash, besprinkle; shoot, discharge.

—*n.* **3** *The squirt from the water-pistol took me by surprise:* spray, jet, spurt, stream. **4** *Slang He's nothing but a little squirt!:* insignificant person, punk, piker, cretin, weed, runt.

stab *v.* **1** *The killer stabbed his victim with a carving knife:* jab, pierce, stick, spear, bayonet, impale, gore, wound, gash, cut, spike, lance, run through, thrust through, knife, transfix, lacerate, prick, spit, gouge, slash, cleave. **2** *Her bitter words stabbed him to the heart:* wound, hurt, injure the feelings of, pierce, cut, pain.

—*n.* **3** *The stab missed its target:* jab, thrust, lunge, dagger stroke, cut, prick, slash, wound, laceration, gash. **4** *I felt a sudden stab of remorse:* pang, prick, painful sensation, ache, sting, twinge, bite, shiver, thrill, qualm. **5** *Informal Just make a stab at writing a poem:* try, attempt, pass; trial, essay, endeavour.

Ant. 2 soothe, assuage, ease, comfort, please, delight.

stability *n.* **1** *Her stability enables her to face almost any problem:* steadiness, constancy, solidness, soundness, poise, aplomb, balance, equilibrium, evenness, reliability, stableness, steadfastness. **2** *I will vouch for the stability of the old staircase:* solidity, soundness, firmness, steadiness, solidness, security, fixedness. **3** *The young nation has not yet attained political stability:* permanence, fixity, firmness, unchangeableness, abidingness, durability, changelessness, continuity.

Ant. 1 instability, inconstancy, unsteadiness, weakness, unreliability, irresolution. **2** frailty, fragility, unsteadiness, weakness. **3** impermanence, changeableness, instability.

stable *adj.* **1** *He finally built a stable business:* established, reliable, durable, sound, secure, well-grounded, indissoluble, solid. **2** *The building has a stable foundation:* sound, sturdy, solid, steady, fixed, stationary, firm, safe, secure, immovable, anchored, moored. **3** *Our country has a stable government:* fixed, unchangeable, firm, unchanging, steady, abiding, persisting, enduring, constant, uniform, even. **4** *John is a stable employee:* reliable, steady, steadfast, true, staunch, loyal, stalwart, dependable, unwavering, firm, constant, faithful, unfaltering.

Ant. 1-4 unstable. **1** impermanent, shaky, unsound, unsteady. **2** frail, shaky, unsteady, unsubstantial, unsound. **3** changeable, alterable, variable, shaky, wavering. **4** unreliable, unsteady, mercurial, volatile, erratic.

stack *n.* **1** *Let's hide behind this stack of hay. They left me with a stack of dirty dishes:* pile, heap, bank, mass, clump, load; mound, mountain, bunch, accumulation, aggregation, batch, bundle. **2** *The ship had two huge stacks discharging smoke:* smoke-stack, chimney, flue, funnel.

—*v.* **3** *Stack the chips in equal piles:* heap, pile, arrange vertically, mound, bank; gather, bunch, lump, amass, assemble, batch, hoard, accumulate.

staff *n.* **1** *The old man needed his staff to climb the hill:* cane, stick, walking-stick, rod, crutch, pole, alpenstock; cudgel, wand, stave, bludgeon, truncheon, bat, shillelagh. **2** *The flag was raised only half-way up the staff:* pole, flag-pole, flagstaff, support. **3** *How many are on the hotel staff?:* force, crew, personnel, help, employees, group, team; assistants, advisers, retinue.

—*v.* **4** *How many employees will it take to staff this resort?:* make up the staff of, man, work, tend, manage, service.

◇ *Word origin: Staff* comes from Old English *staef*, stick, pole. Since everyone who owed allegiance to a king or lord served under the same flag or flagstaff, *staff* came to mean such a loyal group and thus today we have *general staff* and *office staff*. The female side of a family is called the *distaff* side from Old English *distaef*, the staff or pole for holding the flax or wool used in spinning, hence the side of the family who spins. (The opposite of *distaff* side is *spear* side, the side of the family that uses the spear, the male side.)

stage *n.* **1** *The rocket is in its final stage of development:* period, phase, level, step, grade. **2** *The actor almost fell off the stage:* raised platform, raised floor, *Slang* boards; rostrum, pulpit, dais, soap-box, scaffold, stump. **3** *The stage was his whole life:* dramatic profession, show business, theatre, stage playing, acting, drama, the footlights, *Slang* the boards. **4** *Europe was the principal stage for the Second World War:* spot, surroundings, scene of action, setting, locale, locality, arena, whereabouts, position, theatre, location, site, bearings.

—*v.* **5** *The cathedral staged a son et lumière in honour of the Queen's jubilee:* produce, put on the stage, present, put on; act, perform, dramatize, play.

stagger *v.* **1** *She staggered out of bed:* stumble, sway, wobble, reel, hobble, totter, lurch, shamble, blunder, waver. **2** *A punch like that would stagger an ox:* cause to sway, cause to reel, make unsteady, stun, knock silly, totter, throw off balance. **3** *The news of his death staggered the country:* stun, jolt, shock, nonplus, astound, astonish, shake, amaze, dumbfound, unsettle, disconcert, jar, bowl over, overwhelm, strike dumb, take away the breath of, stupefy, startle, flabbergast, bewilder, confound, give a turn, consternate. **4** *Stagger the seats so that everyone can see:* spread out, arrange in a zigzag order; alternate, overlap, take in turns.

Ant. **2** steady. **3** steady, stabilize; strengthen.

stagnant *adj.* **1** *Stagnant water is more likely to be noxious:* still, not running, not flowing, motionless, inert, lifeless, close, standing, unstirring, dead, quiet, quiescent, inactive, uncirculating; filthy, polluted, foul, tainted, putrid, putrefied, slimy, stale. **2** *The seaside resort becomes stagnant when the tourists leave:* lifeless, inactive, dull, listless, dormant, dead, sluggish, inert, static, languid, torpid, slow, leaden, lethargic; vegetative, lazy, supine, ponderous, dronish, monotonous.

Ant. **1** running, flowing, moving, circulating; clean, pure, fresh, unpolluted. **2** lively, active, busy, thriving.

stagnate *v. The air will stagnate if we don't get some ventilation. His mind stagnated after years of solitude:* remain motionless, cease to flow, lie still, be stagnant, not stir, stand still; putrefy, become foul, become contaminated, become polluted; become sluggish, vegetate, become dull, stop developing, stop growing, go to seed, deteriorate, go to pot; become inactive, lie idle.

Ant. flow, circulate; grow, bustle.

staid *adj. He's too staid for such a lively young wife:* sedate, sober, settled, sombre, subdued, serious, dignified, reserved, undemonstrative, solemn, stiff, quiet, earnest, demure, grave, complacent, priggish, prudish; decent, decorous, seemly.

Ant. exuberant, jaunty, wild, indecorous, flighty, demonstrative, playful, capricious, loose.

stain *n.* **1** *Will that stain come off your tie?:* spot, discoloration, blemish, tarnish, blot, smudge, soil, smear, blotch, splotch, speck, mark, taint, daub, smirch. **2** *His trial for embezzlement was a stain on his family's good name:* blot, spot, brand, stigma, blemish, taint, tarnish, flaw, imputation, soil, smudge, shame, disgrace, slur, dishonour. **3** *We need a dark stain on the floor:* tint, dye, colouring, dyestuff, tincture.

—*v.* **4** *The tomato sauce stained the table-cloth:* spot, discolour, blemish, smirch, tarnish, blotch, sully, soil, smear, smudge, mar, spoil, grime, daub, mark, splotch, blot. **5** *Stain the table before you varnish it:* dye, colour, tint, pigment. **6** *He stained his military record by getting drunk:* blemish, taint, disgrace, bring reproach upon, tarnish, defile, blot, blacken, impair, besmirch, foul, debase, stigmatize, dishonour, befoul, sully, drag in the mud, spoil, subvert, ruin, undermine, detract from; vilify, slander, discredit, denigrate, disparage, libel.

Ant. **2** honour, credit, accolade. **4** clean. **6** clear, honour, enhance.

stake *n.* **1** *One of the stakes in the fence is broken:* post, picket, pale, pole, peg, spike, pile, rod, bar; column, pillar, marker, standard. **2** *Ridley and Latimer were burned at the stake:* post to which heretics, evil-doers, etc., were tied to be burned to death. **3** *What is the stake in your poker game? In international finance the stakes are high:* money risked, hazard, bet, ante, wager, play; prize, pot, jackpot, reward, spoils, take, haul, booty, winnings, purse, pickings, loot, returns. **4** *He has a big stake in the new play:* share, investment, risk, interest, speculation, venture, hazard. **5** *I have no stake in the outcome of the trial:* personal concern, interest, involvement.

—*v.* **6** *The city engineer staked out the site for the new school:* mark off, delineate, mark out, outline, demarcate, define, delimit. **7** *Stake the sweet peas securely:* brace, support, hold up, prop, stay; tie to a stake, hitch, secure, fasten, tether, trammel, moor, make fast, fetter, lash, peg down. **8** *I'd stake my life on his honesty:* bet, wager, hazard, risk, chance, jeopardize, pawn, speculate, venture.

stale *adj.* **1** *These old peanuts taste stale. Open the windows and get rid of this stale air:* flat, not fresh, vapid, tasteless, savourless; fusty, musty, close, stagnant. **2** *His style of writing has become stale:* trite, banal, hackneyed, insipid, flat, vapid, arid, dull, common, commonplace, ordinary, mediocre, humdrum, unvaried, tedious, worn-out, prosaic,

threadbare, pedestrian, unimaginative, monotonous, uninteresting.
Ant. 1 fresh, crisp. **2** original, imaginative, varied.

stalemate *n. The stubborn negotiators reached a stalemate:* deadlock, impasse, tie, draw; halt, blockage, standstill.
Ant. decision.

stalk[1] *n. Hold the flower by its stalk:* stem, shaft, column, trunk, twig, pedicel.

stalk[2] *v.* **1** *The mugger stalked his victim. We stalked the eland through the long grass:* approach stealthily, pursue quietly, creep up on, sneak up on, track, hunt; steal, lurk, prowl; threaten, menace. **2** *She stalked angrily out of the room:* march, strut, walk stiffly, stamp, stomp, tramp. **3** *Fear stalked abroad at night:* haunt, go through, hang over, pervade.

stall *n.* **1** *The horse got out of its stall:* booth, cubicle, cell, compartment, coop, pen, confine, shed, stable. **2** *The fish stall hasn't opened yet:* booth, stand, arcade, shop, kiosk. **3** *We sat in the stalls at the opera:* seat on the ground floor of a theatre.
—*v.* **4** *The cows were stalled in the barn for the night:* confine, pen, put in a stall, install; bed down. **5** *The strike stalled our holiday plans. The cold weather made the car stall:* stop, bring to a standstill, be brought to a standstill, arrest, impede, check, paralyse, incapacitate, pull up, stop short, stop running, trammel, block, interrupt, obstruct, disable, hobble; delay, put off, postpone. **6** *The manager stalled for time while his secretary searched for the file:* delay, play for time, temporize; be evasive, equivocate.

stalwart *adj.* **1** *He's stalwart enough to lift the piano:* sturdy, robust, sound, strong, muscular, strapping, hardy, brawny, powerful, vigorous, rugged, hefty, able-bodied, hale, mighty, beefy, husky. **2** *The stalwart captain refused to desert the ship:* valiant, bold, heroic, intrepid, courageous, stout-hearted, lion-hearted, indomitable, gallant, brave, valorous, manly, strong-willed, unflinching, spunky, plucky, staunch, gritty. **3** *He demonstrated a stalwart belief in human rights:* unwavering, steadfast, staunch, stable, firm, unshakeable, resolute, constant, unswerving, unflagging, unbending, intransigent, uncompromising, indomitable, unfaltering, unflinching, undeviating, persistent, unyielding, undaunted, unshrinking.
Ant. 1 weak, feeble, frail, infirm, unsteady, shaky. **2** cowardly, fearful, timorous, faint-hearted, weak. **3** faithless, weak, shaky, flagging, deviating, half-hearted, uncertain, fragile, feeble, frail.
◇ *Word origin: Stalwart* is a Scottish variant of the obsolete word *stalworth,* literally "worthy from the base up." The word was introduced into modern English by Sir Walter Scott.

stamina *n. She hasn't the stamina for the long tour:* endurance, strength of constitution, vigour, sturdiness, vitality, stoutness, pith, energy, perseverance, staying power.

stammer *v. He stammered most when he was nervous:* speak with breaks and pauses, speak hesitantly, falter, stutter, stumble; sputter, hum and haw, fumble, mumble, splutter.

stamp *v.* **1** *The horse stamped the ground nervously. Peevishly she stamped her foot:* step on, thump, pound; crush, smash, trample. **2** Usually **stamp out** *They tried to stamp out the burning leaves:* extinguish, put out, crush, put down, quench, suppress. **3** *The soldiers stamped noisily through the town:* tramp, trudge, stalk, stride, strut, march. **4** *The bookbinder stamped the leather with a fleur-de-lis:* print, mark, imprint, brand, impress, engrave, seal, inscribe, label. **5** *His wild youth stamped him as the black sheep of the family:* mark, characterize, brand, identify; reveal, demonstrate, betray, exhibit, distinguish, manifest, display, expose, personify; stigmatize; type-cast.
—*n.* **6** *My date-stamp is broken:* engraved block, seal, die, mould, matrix, mint, intaglio, signet, punch. **7** *The cabinet is authentic and bears the stamp of the maker:* mark, engraving, character, seal, brand, hallmark, imprint, identification, signature, official mark, trade mark, authentication, emblem, label; ratification, endorsement, imprimatur, attestation, certificate, certification, voucher, validation, *Informal* O.K. **8** *The farmer is a kindly fellow, but his brother is a man of a different stamp:* mark, characteristic; type, variety, character, sort, kind, nature, order, make, strain, genre, cast, breed, brand.

stampede *n.* **1** *Twelve horses were killed in the stampede:* frenzied rush, headlong flight, rout, sudden scattering, panic; chaos, pandemonium. **2** *The fuel shortage caused a stampede to the filling stations:* race, rush, dash.
—*v.* **3** *The guests stampeded out of the burning hotel. They stampeded the box office for tickets:* take flight, flee, beat a retreat, scatter, rush, panic, take to one's heels; crowd round, overrun, flood, inundate, engulf.

stand *v.* **1** *We stood because there were no seats:* be upright, be erect, hold oneself erect, be on one's feet; rise, rise to one's feet, get up. **2** *Stand the ladder over here. The lamp stands next to the armchair:* put, place, be placed, set, set upright, be set upright, rear, raise, rest, put up, stick up, set on its feet, hoist, erect, mount. **3** *Please stand aside:* step, move, remove, take a position, shift, draw. **4** *He stands for home and country:* support, uphold, defend a cause, argue, champion, be in favour of, declare oneself for, commend, sanction, speak well or highly of, plead for, endorse, countenance, honour, advocate. **5** *A church has stood on the same spot for a thousand years. My decision stands:* be present, be located, be situated, rest, remain, exist, have its seat, stay, continue, be permanent; persist, prevail, remain in force, remain valid, hold. **6** *The sea-wall stood against the raging storm. I can't stand strong criticism:* endure, remain intact, abide, remain erect or whole, persist, sustain, survive, resist destruction, resist decay or change, prove good, hold, be indestructible, obtain, hold out, last, remain steadfast, remain firm, bear up, keep one's position, carry on, withstand, tolerate, take, suffer, undergo, brook, face, weather, stomach; stand one's ground, persevere, stand up against. **7** *He stands last in her affections:* be, rank, place. **8** *He stood lunch for the three of us:* pay for, undertake, provide, finance; treat.

—n. **9** *His feet ached from the two-hour stand:* standing, wait without a seat; stance. **10** *The army made a valiant stand against the fierce attack:* defence, resistance, effort, hold. **11** *What is the Minister's stand on the bill?:* position, point of view, policy, opinion, viewpoint, sentiment, standpoint, stance, disposition. **12** *Where's the vegetable stand?:* booth, stall, counter, kiosk; tent, pavilion.

Ant. 1 sit, lie, recline. **2** lay. **6** collapse, succumb, falter, waver, yield, give way. **9** repose, sit, sitting. **10** retreat, collapse, withdrawal.

standard *n.* **1** *New cars without seat belts do not meet government safety standards. Critics with different standards often disagree:* requirement, specification, criterion, guide-line, principle; prototype, measure, yardstick, touchstone, ideal, guide, canon. **2** *Two men carried the standard in the royal parade:* flag, pennant, banner, streamer, ensign, jack. **3** *The street will need six lamp standards to make it sufficiently light:* pillar, support, stanchion, upright, post, column; leg, foot; base, foundation.

—adj. **4** *What is the standard size of a twin bed?:* normal, basic, usual, customary, universal, accepted, common, ordinary, typical, regular, stock.

Ant. 4 abnormal, exceptional, irregular, unusual.

standing *n.* **1** *His standing in the community is high:* rank, order, position, place, station, grade, status, reputation. **2** *He finally paid a debt of ten-years standing:* duration, length of existence, continuance, age, tenure, time, term, life.

—adj. **3** *He looks bigger in a standing position:* vertical, upright, perpendicular, upended, stand-up, erect. **4** *Standing water breeds mosquitoes:* motionless, still, stationary, inactive, not flowing, inert, static, dormant, unstirring, stagnant, at rest, quiescent. **5** *They gave us a standing invitation:* fixed, continuing, immovable, permanent, perpetual, lasting, renewable.

Ant. 3 sitting, reclining, recumbent, lying. **4** flowing, moving, running.

star *n.* **1** *The stars are out tonight:* heavenly body, celestial body, planet, satellite; asteroid, meteoroid, meteor, comet, sun; constellation, galaxy, Milky Way, nebula. **2 stars** *If the stars are against us, we can achieve nothing:* fortune, fate, destiny, predestination, the future, signs of the zodiac, portents, omens; astrological chart. **3** *The stars of the film all came to the première:* principal actor, principal, lead; hero, protagonist; well-known actor, popular entertainer, main attraction, draw, starlet; superior performer, superstar, idol, immortal, god, goddess; (*variously*) prima donna, diva, prima ballerina, virtuoso, soloist; prominent figure, famous person, celebrity, luminary, eminence, notable, lion, mainstay, cynosure, VIP, bigwig.

—v. **4** *The late show tonight stars Sidney Poitier. With Olivier starring, the play is bound to succeed:* present in a leading role, feature, be a vehicle for; play the lead, take the leading role, head the cast, top the bill. **5** *I didn't exactly star in my first job:* do well, excel, shine, succeed, gain approval, attract attention, be conspicuous.

> **Exploring the Word:** The Greek word for *star* is *aster,* which gives us the *aster* flower, because it looks like a star; *astronomy* (Greek *nomos,* law), the study of the laws governing the stars; *astrology* (Greek *logos,* theory), "star theory" (actually, to the Greeks, *astrology* and *astronomy* were synonyms); *astronaut* (Greek *nautēs,* sailor), star sailor, space traveller: and *astrodome,* star dome, a transparent dome in which to observe the stars.

stare *v.* **1** *She was just staring into space. Don't stare at me!:* gaze intently, fix one's gaze, look intently, gape, ogle, peep, gawk, goggle; glare, lower, peer, watch; glower.

—n. **2** *Her icy stare sent a chill through me:* glare, fixed look, long glance, glower, staring, gaze, gape, gaping, ogling; scrutiny, inspection; once-over.

stark *adj.* **1** *Stark terror seized the passengers:* downright, bare, utter, plain, sheer, simple, pure, bold, patent, obvious, flagrant, absolute, complete, unmistakable, glaring, unmitigated, outright, palpable, arrant, evident, blunt, staring, conspicuous, gross, total, out and out, unalloyed, veritable, consummate. **2** *The room was as stark as a monk's cell:* bare, severe, naked, plain, unadorned, barren, chaste, austere, empty; cold, forsaken, harsh, grim, desolate, abandoned, vacant, forlorn.

—adv. **3** *The infant posed on the bearskin rug stark naked:* absolutely, fully, utterly, wholly, quite, downright, completely, altogether, entirely, clean, plain, out and out, plumb, to the nth degree, through and through.

Ant. 2 fancy, adorned, embellished; gay, bright; cosy, warm, inviting; cultivated.

◇ *Word origin: Stark* comes from Old English

stearc, stiff, harsh. Our word *starch*, to stiffen linen, is related.

start *v.* **1** *Let's start for the coast early:* commence, get going, begin to move, make off, set out, leave, set off, take off, venture out, sally forth, make tracks for, hit the road, depart, set sail, push off, embark. **2** *Start the engine and I'll be there in a moment:* set in operation, put in motion, set going, set in action; touch off, ignite, kindle, propel. **3** *She started her cookery course two days ago:* begin, commence, undertake, set about, embark on, enter upon, venture on, break ground, put into execution, take the first step, fall to, initiate, take up, plunge into, broach, turn one's hand to, make a beginning, buckle down. **4** *Lord Baden-Powell started the Scout movement in 1908:* initiate, be initiated, originate, be originated, institute, found, be founded, establish, launch, set up, inchoate, set moving, begin, inaugurate, create, give birth to, form, give rise to, introduce, lay the foundation of, touch off, usher in, fabricate, bring about, forge, propagate, engender, generate, beget, father, be the cause of. **5** *Suddenly a pedestrian started from between the cars. Blood started from the wound:* spring, move suddenly, bound, jump, rise suddenly, burst forth, leap; rush, issue suddenly, spurt, gush, erupt, break forth, issue, shoot, emerge; pop out. **6** *The shot started the birds:* flush, rouse, disturb, scatter; eject, displace, turn out, evict. **7** *I started when you touched my arm:* jump, twitch, jerk involuntarily, recoil, wince, blink, blench, shy, flinch.

—*n.* **8** *The start of the tour was hectic:* beginning, outset, commencement, first step, opening, onset, setting in motion; inauguration, inception, birth, creation, origin, genesis, dawn, initiation. **9** *She gave a start when I inserted the needle:* jump, spasm, jolt, jerk, wince, twitch, turn. **10** *All that money gives him a head start over his rivals:* lead, advantage, head start, edge, advance, odds, drop, jump, priority, leg up. **11** *My father gave him his start in life:* opening, chance, introduction, opportunity; support, aid, assistance, backing, advocacy.

Ant. 1 delay. **2** stall, turn off. **3, 4** end, finish, terminate, stop, cease. **8** end, finish, finale, termination; wind-up. **10** disadvantage, handicap.

startle *v. The knocking at the windows startled me:* frighten, surprise, disturb suddenly, cause to start, cause to jump, scare, alarm, disquiet, disconcert, faze, perturb, intimidate, discompose, upset, give a turn, jar, unsettle, take off one's guard.

Ant. calm, soothe, reassure, compose, settle.

starve *v.* **1** *The pot-holers starved before rescuers could get to them:* perish from hunger, die of hunger; go hungry, suffer from lack of food, famish, hunger, fast. **2** *The enemy soldiers starved the townspeople into surrendering:* cut off from food, weaken by lack of food, undernourish, underfeed, deprive of food; force by underfeeding. **3** *I am starving for some excitement in this miserable town:* hunger, yearn, long, be hungry, pine, crave, desire earnestly, thirst, lust, burn, languish, gasp, raven, aspire; deprive, make eager, make desperate, deny, refuse, cut off.

Ant. 1 glut, overeat, gorge. **2** feed, overfeed, surfeit, glut.

state *n.* **1** *Ice is water in its solid state. What is the financial state of his business?:* condition, position, constitution, form, guise, shape, phase, structure, aspect; circumstances, status, situation, posture; predicament, plight, pass. **2** *The royal family always appears in state:* high style, luxury, comfort; pomp, full dress, ceremony, ritual, formality. **3** *I was disturbed by his depressed state:* condition, attitude, mind, frame of mind, state of mind, spirits, morale. **4** *The prime minister resigned for the good of the state:* nation, republic, commonwealth, country, monarchy, dominion, kingdom, realm, land, principality; body politic, people, government.

—*adj.* **5** *The Duke attended two state functions this week:* ceremonial, official, governmental.

—*v.* **6** *He stated his case before a judge. Please state the exact time of arrival:* declare, express, propound, recite, recount, narrate, set forth, offer, present, put, explain; report, relate, describe, expound, elucidate.

Ant. 6 repudiate, deny, contradict, refute; disclaim.

stately *adj.* **1** *We were awed by Mount Fuji's stately splendour:* impressive, majestic, imposing, grand, regal, glorious, lofty, proud, magnificent, august, royal, imperial. **2** *The pavan was a stately dance:* formal, ceremonial, dignified, eminent, elegant, grandiose.

Ant. 1 unimpressive, humble, modest, poor. **2** ordinary, common, *Informal* jolly.

statement *n.* **1** *He made a flattering statement about her clothes:* utterance, avowal, pronouncement, speech, assertion, declaration, profession, claim, explanation, testimony, mention, comment, remark, observation, sentence. **2** *The company prepared a statement of its profits and losses:* report, record, account, announcement, specification, delineation; relation, exposition, recitation, recital; bill, invoice, account, tally, check, charge, tab, reckoning; balance sheet, count, accounting, valuation; communiqué, manifesto.

static *adj.* **1** *Life at college seemed static, and the student longed for a change:* inactive, motionless, stagnant, unmoving, inert, still, suspended, immobile, stationary, changeless, unchanging.

—*n.* **2** *There's a lot of static on the radio:* crackling, interference, atmospherics, static electricity.

Ant. 1 moving, mobile, kinetic; lively, spirited, vigorous, brisk, active.
◇ *Word origin: Static* (unmoving) comes from Greek *statikos,* meaning causing to stand. The word was introduced into scientific thought by Aristotle with his concept of *statikē arkhē* (principle of rest, static principle) as opposed to *kinētikē arkhē* (principle of motion, kinetic principle).

> **Exploring the Word:** Latin *stare,* to stand, and its particular forms *status* (stood) and *stans* (standing), give us a great many words, including: *stand; standard,* via Old French, so-called because people stood under such banners or flags, which came to represent a group or its criteria; *stance,* a way of standing; *staunch,* standing firm; *stanchion,* a "standing" or upright support; *state,* figuratively the way a person "stands," his "state of being" or "state of mind," and the expression of the way he stands is what he *states* or declares (a *statement*), while a *state* is a country or region that stands as a political entity. The same Latin base gives us *station,* place where one stands, as while waiting for a train or standing guard duty; *stationary,* standing in one place, standing still; *stay,* to stand in one place; *status,* a person's "standing," hence also rank, position, condition; *stature,* how high one stands, both literally and figuratively; *statue,* originally so-called because it stood on a pedestal; *stable, stabilize,* and *stability,* all referring to standing firm; *statistics,* which give the mathematical "standings" of something; *stage,* a platform where actors stand; *stamen,* the pollen-bearing organ of a flower, so-called because it stands within the floral envelope; *stamina,* the capacity to withstand exertion, hardship, or difficulty; the editorial word *stet,* meaning "let it stand," used when correcting manuscripts or galleys; and, via Italian, *stanza,* originally a standing still or stop in versification, hence the paragraph unit of a poem.

station *n.* 1 *All men to your stations!:* assigned place, position, post, location, placement, emplacement, spot, site. 2 *We met at the railway station:* terminal, terminus, depot, stop, halt. 3 *The thief was questioned at the police station. The fire station was painted red:* station house, headquarters. 4 *The rescue team took the injured child to a first-aid station:* facility, dispensary. 5 *His station in life is not what it was:* social standing, rank, position, status, place, footing, grade, condition, level, class, sphere, degree, importance, prestige, caste.
—*v.* 6 *The army stationed him in West Germany. The commissionaire was stationed at the exit:* assign, post; locate, place, install, ensconce.

stationary *adj.* 1 *It is easier to aim at a stationary target than at a moving one:* immovable, motionless, standing still, standing, immobile; fixed, riveted, firm, moored; inert, transfixed, stable, stock-still, dead-still. 2 *Business has been slow but our profits have remained stationary:* constant, unchanged, not changing, steady, stable, fixed, even, intact, undeviating, firm, uniform, unvarying, unchangeable, immutable.
Ant. 1 moving, mobile. 2 varying, changing, unstable, volatile, irregular; changeable.
◇ *Usage note: StationAry* means in one *plAce. StationEry* is writing *papEr* and is sold by a *stationEr.*

stature *n.* 1 *Napoleon was a man of small stature:* height, tallness, size. 2 *Such pettiness was surprising in a person of his stature:* rank, standing, place, position, high station, eminence, distinction, elevation, prominence, importance.
Ant. 2 low rank, inferiority, lowliness.

status *n.* 1 *His status in the community suffered from the scandal. Jewels symbolize status to some people:* position, rank, standing, footing, condition, estimation, station, caste, class, place; eminence, distinction, prestige, social superiority. 2 *What's the status of the peace talks?:* situation, state, condition.

staunch Also **stanch** *adj.* 1 *He's a staunch supporter of the church:* firm, steadfast, true, steady, zealous, strong, stout, solid, faithful, loyal, trustworthy, resolute. 2 *This is a staunch little cabin:* substantial, solid, sturdy, stout, rugged, well-built, well-constructed, sound. 3 *When the boys finished caulking the boat, they soaked her to make her staunch:* watertight, sound.
—*v.* 4 *The doctor applied a tourniquet to my arm to stanch the bleeding:* stop the flow of, check, dam, hold back, obstruct, stem, impede, contain.
Ant. 1 inconstant, unfaithful, fickle, capricious, lukewarm. 2 weak, shoddy, jerry-built, flimsy. 3 leaky.
◇ *Usage note: Staunch* is more commonly used than *stanch* to modify a noun. Thus, *a staunch supporter.* The opposite is true when this word is used as a verb: *to stanch the flow of blood.*

stay[1] *v.* 1 *She stayed until my mother came home:* remain, tarry, visit, hang around, linger. 2 *How long did they stay with you?:* remain, reside, dwell, abide, sojourn, take up quarters, lodge, live. 3 *Stay as sweet as you are!:* keep oneself, endure, continue to be, remain, go on being. 4 *Yoga is a difficult art, but if you stay the course, you'll learn it:* remain, continue, persist, persevere, hold out, carry on, stick; last out, see through. 5 *She stayed her tears until her lover was out of sight:* restrain, hold back, suppress, rein in, postpone, withhold, curb, check, keep in, stifle, quell. 6 *Athenians stayed the Persians at Salamis:* block, foil, frustrate, thwart, ward off, stem.
—*n.* 7 *How long was your stay at the seaside?:* sojourn, stop, temporary residence, halt, visit, vacation, holiday. 8 *The barrister won a*

stay of sentencing for his convicted client: postponement, delay, abeyance; reprieve.

Ant. 1 leave, go, depart. **4** give up, succumb. **5** loose, free, release, express. **6** fall to; surrender to.

stay[2] *n. One of the tent stays has come loose:* support; (*variously*) brace, prop, buttress, reinforcement, stanchion, standard, rest, rod, pole, guy, splint, shore, aim, rib, mainstay, block.

steadfast *adj.* **1** *The navigator steered the ship on a steadfast course. Pay steadfast attention to your teacher:* steady, fixed, undeviating, direct; unwavering, attentive, undistracted, unflinching, rapt, intent, keen, unfaltering, unflagging. **2** *Oliver Cromwell had a steadfast faith in God:* firm, resolute, indomitable, undaunted, intransigent, obstinate, tenacious, inflexible, unyielding, uncompromising, unchangeable, unchanging, unalterable, constant, deep-rooted, deep-seated, single-minded.

Ant. 1 deviating, wavering, flagging, faltering; fragile, unstable. **2** unreliable, irresolute, wavering, vacillating, capricious, half-hearted, changeable, fickle.

steady *adj.* **1** *Is that stool steady enough to stand on?:* stable, firm, substantial, immovable. **2** *With the monsoon came a steady rain. The drummer maintained a steady beat:* constant, unremitting, continuous, continuing, persistent, incessant, unending, unceasing, ceaseless; regular, even. **3** *He's a steady church-goer:* habitual, constant, frequent, regular, faithful, devoted, confirmed. **4** *She's steady in her commitment to her job:* steadfast, constant, undeviating, unwavering, firm, resolute, staunch, untiring, unfaltering, unflagging, persevering, tenacious, dedicated, devoted, unremitting, resolute, single-minded. **5** *He's a steady pupil who never scimps his homework. The chauffeur is a steady driver:* reliable, dependable, careful, serious, sober, deliberate, conscientious, methodical, stable; level-headed, cool-headed, sure.

—*v.* **6** *Steady that ladder for me, please:* stabilize, hold fast, secure.

Ant. 1 unsteady, shaky, unstable, insecure. **2** sporadic, intermittent, uneven, irregular, syncopated, broken, varying. **3** infrequent, irregular, rare, sporadic, occasional. **4** irregular; undependable, unreliable; ambivalent, in two minds, vacillating, irresolute, faltering, uncertain. **5** unsteady, unreliable, careless, frivolous, unsteady, shaky. **6** shake, rock, tip, tilt, wobble.

steal *v.* **1** *Someone stole a painting from the museum:* take, purloin, filch, pilfer, lift, snatch; make off with, abscond with, swindle, embezzle, extort, usurp, misappropriate; defraud; thieve, copy, crib, plagiarize; abstract, borrow, appropriate, imitate, help oneself to, *Slang* rip off, liberate, pinch, snitch, swipe. **2** *The children stole a look at the Christmas presents:* take secretly, sneak. **3** *Try to steal into the room without waking the children:* slip, slide, sneak, creep, tiptoe, pass stealthily, slink, skulk, pass unobserved. **4** *Time steals away quickly when you're having fun:* slip, pass, creep, slide, drift, elapse, escape, glide, happen gently, diffuse, flow, filter, flit, fly.

◇ *Word origin: Steal* and *stealth* come from Old English *stelan,* to steal. Originally *stealth* (*steal-th*) meant a stealing, a theft, and only later came to mean the sneaky manner of moving or behaving that is associated with theft.

stealth *n. When it comes to catching mice our cat is a model of patience and stealth:* covertness, secrecy, clandestine procedure, secretiveness, furtiveness, stealthiness, slyness, surreptitiousness.

Ant. openness, candidness.

steel *n.* **1** *The builders brought in a lot of steel for the new building:* tempered iron, steel articles. **2** *The knight plunged his steel into the dragon's throat:* blade, bayonet, sword, knife, sabre, foil, cutlass, dagger, dirk, rapier, machete, scimitar, falchion, broadsword.

—*v.* **3** *Here's some unpleasant news, so steel yourself for the blow:* brace, fortify, gird, nerve.

steep[1] *adj. The slope is too steep for us to climb:* close to vertical, sheer, precipitous, abrupt.

Ant. flat, gentle, gradual.

steep[2] *v.* **1** *She steeped the cucumbers in brine to pickle them:* soak, be soaked, immerse, be immersed, saturate, brew, souse, impregnate, suffuse, marinate. **2** *She steeps herself in the problems of her students. The village is steeped in history:* immerse, plunge, bury, saturate, engulf, drench, imbue, submerge, infuse, fill, pervade.

Ant. 1 drain.

> **Exploring the Word:** To *steer,* the *stern* of a ship, *starboard,* and *steerage* are all derived from Old English *steor,* rudder. Thus *steer* literally means to use the rudder; the *stern,* rear, of a ship is so-called because that's where the *steering* oar or rudder of Viking ships was; *starboard* (Old English *bord,* side), the right-hand side of a ship as one faces forward, was originally the side where the rudder handle or steering oar was; and *steerage,* the lower deck, is so-called because it was originally the part of a ship round the rudder or steering gear.

steer *v.* **1** *The captain steered the yacht into the harbour. He steered the team to victory:* sail, navigate, direct, guide, pilot, run, conduct, govern, lead, head, coach. **2** *The ship steered for the open sea:* proceed, head, sail, make, lay, lay a course, take a course, aim, bear, run, be bound, make a bee-line.

stem[1] *n.* **1** *The stem of my rose is broken:* main stalk; (*variously*) trunk, spear, shoot, cane, leaf-stalk, stock, spire, peduncle, pedicel,

tendril. 2 *Don't hold the wineglass by its stem:* shank.
—*v.* 3 *His back trouble stems from an old war wound:* come, derive, issue, result, proceed, arise, rise, originate, spring, ensue, grow.

stem[2] *v. Nothing could stem the glacier's irresistible advance. The government tried to stem the growing discontent of the people:* stop, hold back, curb, stay, restrain, check, quell, arrest, prevent, impede, dam, withstand, oppose, hold one's own against, staunch, thwart, stall, halt, block, surmount, hinder, bring to a standstill, retard, deter.
Ant. further, promote, encourage, stimulate, incite, excite, unleash.

stench *n. The stench of the abattoir is terrible:* stink, bad smell, offensive odour, reek.
Ant. fragrance, aroma, perfume.
◇ *Usage note:* See SMELL.

step *n.* 1 *With two steps she reached the crying child. He walks with a measured step:* footstep, pace, stride, gait; (*variously*) strut, hobble, shuffle, shamble, swagger. 2 *Did you hear a step in the attic?:* footfall, tread, stepping sound. 3 *Glazing is the final step in making pottery:* stage, phase, move, process, measure, proceeding, act, action, procedure. 4 *The promotion put him three steps from the top:* grade, level, stage, rank, rung, degree, point, gradation, period, span, remove. 5 *One of the back steps needs replacing:* stair, foothold, tread, rung; footing, purchase.
—*v.* 6 *The patient was able to step to the window:* move, walk, pace, tread, stride. 7 *Ouch! You stepped on my foot:* tread, tramp, trample.

stereotype *n.* 1 *She fits the stereotype of an "old maid":* conventional image, received idea, popular preconception, cliché, formula.
—*v.* 2 *The commentator stereotyped the protesters as "long-haired weirdies":* pigeon-hole, type-cast, type, categorize, crudely identify.
◇ *Word origin: Stereotype* was first used to mean a metal printing plate containing the hard, three-dimensional impression of type to be printed. It comes from Greek *stereos,* solid, three-dimensional. Because *stereotypes* were used to print the same thing over and over again, the word came to mean a hackneyed, conventional expression, then any repeated or typical custom, person, etc. Greek *stereos* also gives us *stereophonic* or *stereo,* referring to sound reproduction using two or more receivers or speakers giving the effect of hearing the sound from more than one direction, hence "three-dimensional" sound that surrounds the listener.

sterile *adj.* 1 *The infant was kept in a sterile incubator:* sterilized, disinfected, free from germs, pure, sanitary, uninfected, aseptic. 2 *The sterile couple adopted two children. The earth was rocky and sterile:* barren, infertile, childless; unfruitful, infecund, fallow, bare, empty, waste, desert. 3 *The negotiations proved sterile:* unproductive, unprofitable, worthless, fruitless, ineffective, profitless, unrewarding, ineffectual, bootless, impotent, abortive, vain, useless, unavailing.
Ant. 1 unsterile, infected, germ-ridden, insanitary. 2 fertile, prolific, productive; fecund, fruitful. 3 productive, profitable, fruitful, effective.
◇ *Word origin: Sterile* comes from Latin *sterilis,* barren.

stern *adj.* 1 *He's much too stern with his son:* severe, strict, hard, unfeeling, unreasonable, despotic, unmerciful, stringent, cruel, tyrannical, sharp, pitiless, harsh, coercive, cold-blooded, ruthless, austere, grim, brutal, ungentle, rigorous. 2 *The teacher gave him a stern look:* grim, austere, forbidding, hard, unkind, severe, serious, sombre, gloomy, cold, unapproachable, unsympathetic, sharp, rigid, grave, implacable, harsh, stiff, frowning, reproachful, reproving, admonishing.
Ant. 1 permissive, soft, lenient, flexible, gentle, benign, merciful, kind. 2 friendly, approachable, kind, smiling, amused, relaxed, warm, sympathetic.

stew *v.* 1 *I stewed the vegetables in a covered pan for an hour:* boil slowly, cook in water, simmer, seethe, steep. 2 *Informal They can do as they please, of course, but they'll be left to stew in their own juice:* suffer the consequences of one's action, agonize, fret.
—*n.* 3 *We had beef stew for dinner:* stewed food, ragout; mixture, miscellany. 4 *Informal She's in a stew because she can't find a baby-sitter:* state of worry, state, mental agitation, fuss, fret, flutter, tizzy, fluster.
◇ *Word origin: Stew* comes from Vulgar Latin *extufare,* to cook until steam comes out. (This in turn derives from Greek *tuphos,* hot vapour.) Thus, when we say a person is *in a stew,* we mean he's giving off steam.

steward *n.* 1 *His steward made poor investments for him:* financial manager, administrator, supervisor; overseer, bailiff, agent, executor, trustee, deputy, comptroller, controller, representative. 2 *She rang for the steward:* (*variously*) ship's attendant, aeroplane attendant, (*fem.*) stewardess; waiter.

stick[1] *n.* 1 *They made a bonfire of sticks:* branch, switch, twig, faggot. 2 *Grandfather walks with a stick. Bill carries a stick to ward off dogs:* cane, staff, ash-plant; baton, swagger-stick, wand, rod; bat, club, cudgel, shillelagh, caber, truncheon, bludgeon; cue; pole, shaft, stave, stake, skewer; sceptre, staff, caduceus, crook, crosier.

stick[2] *v.* 1 *Do you shoot tigers and stick pigs?:* spear, spike, stab, jab, prick, poke, pink, perforate, punch. 2 *He stuck a needle in my arm:* jab, thrust, dig, poke, insert, punch. 3 *Stick this bulletin on the notice-board:* fix, put, place, set, plant, fasten, tack, pin, affix, nail, attach. 4 *Can you stick the torn pieces together again?:* join;

(*variously*) glue, fasten, paste, seal, adhere, cement, fuse, affix, weld, bind. **5** *A bone stuck in my throat:* lodge, become fastened, catch, snag, be embedded. **6** *The bus stuck fast in the snow:* stall, mire, be unable to proceed, be tangled, hinder, check, block, immobilize, bind, trammel, hold, obstruct, curb, snarl, impede, constrain, shackle, scotch, thwart, hamper, balk, detain, inhibit, bar, back up, checkmate, stop. **7** *Stick to your guns!:* persist, be true, keep steadily at, hold, be faithful, be constant. **8** *The prizefighter stuck it out to the end, but lost on points:* endure, abide, stand, bear up under, last, continue, not give up, carry on. **9** *I was stuck over one word in the crossword puzzle:* stymie, balk, stump, bewilder, boggle, erk, puzzle, baffle, perplex, confuse.

Ant. **3** remove, dislodge, unfasten, untack, unpin, unscrew. **4** separate, detach, disengage. **6** release, free, unblock, untangle, unfasten.

◇ *Word origin:* The Indo-European root *steig-*, to stick, pointed, survives in Greek, Latin, and Germanic words, giving us *to stick*, to pierce or stab as with a pointed *stick*; and both *stitch*, a sudden piercing pain and *stitch*, to pierce fabric with a threaded needle; *stigma* (Greek for a tattoo mark), a mark of disgrace, and its plural form *stigmata*, marks resembling the wounds Christ received during the Crucifixion; and *instigate*, to goad, hence to provoke, incite. Incidentally, the *steaks* we eat are so-named from the *sticks* they were originally roasted on, i.e., *steak* was originally a term for skewered roast meat.

stickler *n. I'm a stickler for detail:* martinet, purist, fanatic; devotee, enthusiast, *Slang* nut, bug, crank; monomaniac, zealot.

◇ *Word origin:* A *stickler* for details has nothing to do with sticks. The word comes from Old English *stihtan*, to arrange.

sticky *adj.* **1** *Tar is sticky:* gummy, sticking, adhesive, adherent, gluey, tacky, viscid, viscous, clinging, gooey, glutinous, cohesive, gelatinous, mucilaginous. **2** *This sticky weather makes my hair frizz:* clammy, humid, muggy, damp, moist, wet, dank.

Ant. **1** slick, slippery. **2** dry, crisp.

stiff *adj.* **1** *The laundry has made this shirt too stiff:* starchy, rigid, crisp, inelastic. **2** *The steering-wheel is stiff. My back is stiff:* unyielding, tight, resistant, hard to move; unlimber, inflexible, tense, rigid, painful to move. **3** *A stiff breeze carried the boat onto a sandbank:* vigorous, strong, intense, forceful, pounding, persistent, steady, powerful, raging, keen, brisk, smart, spanking. **4** *We couldn't change his stiff determination to go:* stubborn, tenacious, firm, steadfast, decided, determined, strong, indomitable, fixed, staunch, unfaltering, unflinching, iron, steely, steeled, dogged, steady, unswerving, grim, obstinate, persistent, strong-willed, uncompromising, stern, constant, settled, resolute, resolved, intense; valiant, brave, unshaken, courageous. **5** *It's hard to relax in this stiff atmosphere. The lawyer nodded a stiff greeting:* cold, austere, formal, precise, stately, aloof, ceremonious, prim, wooden, stilted, starchy, cool, chilly, constrained, strait-laced, distant, *Slang* uptight. **6** *The acting was stiff, and the characterization lifeless:* wooden, graceless, forced, clumsy, awkward, uneasy, stilted, ungainly, inelegant, laboured, cold, unnatural, affected, mannered, artificial. **7** *That's a stiff assignment for a newcomer:* difficult, exacting, laborious, heavy, tough, hard, stringent, rigorous, formidable. **8** *He makes stiff demands on his employees. The asking price is too stiff:* steep, high, excessive, heavy, exorbitant, undue, inordinate, immoderate, unwarranted, extravagant. **9** *I don't think his offence deserved such a stiff penalty:* harsh, stern, severe, cruel, sharp, brutal, drastic, violent, fearful, austere, unreasonable, sore, awful, bitter, uncompromising, extreme, merciless, draconian, pitiless, ruthless, grievous. **10** *The whipped cream is not stiff enough:* thick, firm, solid, solidified, heavy, dense, viscid, viscous, jellied, gelatinous, clotted.

Ant. **1** soft, loose, yielding, bendable, supple, flexible, limp, pliant, pliable, elastic, malleable. **2** supple, loose, limber, relaxed. **3** gentle, easy, soft. **4** half-hearted, undecided, faltering, irresolute, shaky. **5** casual, informal, cosy, relaxed, unceremonious, warm. **6** smooth, graceful, easy, unforced, natural, unaffected. **7** easy, soft, cushy. **8** easy, simple, soft, moderate. **9** mild, moderate, permissive, soft, sparing, merciful. **10** thin, soft, mushy, liquid.

stifle *v.* **1** *The maniac stifled his victim with a cushion. It's stifling in these overheated cars:* asphyxiate, smother, choke, suffocate, strangle, throttle, garrotte; cause to gasp for air, swelter, gag. **2** *She stifled her laughter:* suppress, repress, curb, restrain, keep back, smother, muffle, check.

Ant. **2** release, express; encourage, further, foster.

◇ *Word origin: Stifle* comes from Old French *estouffer*, to smother.

still *adj.* **1** *The deer lay very still:* motionless, without movement, stationary, at rest, unstirring, unmoving, immobile. **2** *The restaurant was as still as a tomb:* silent, quiet, noiseless, soundless.

—*v.* **3** *The wind stilled at sunset:* grow calm, quiet; grow hushed, silent. **4** *Alcoholics Anonymous helps alcoholics to still their craving for drink:* restrain, overcome, repress, suppress. **5** *Gargantua ate and ate, but nothing stilled his hunger:* assuage, appease, gratify, pacify. **6** *Cesare Borgia stilled every uprising by wiping out whole regiments:* put an end to, restore order, put down, settle, silence, cause to cease.

Ant. 1 active, moving, disturbed, agitated, restless, turbulent. 2 noisy, loud.

stilted *adj. His introduction was stilted and self-conscious:* stiff, wooden, awkward, graceless, laboured, unnatural, pompous, starched, starchy, cold, mannered, ceremonious, rigid, prim, priggish, forced, artificial, constrained, *Slang* uptight.

Ant. relaxed, easy, graceful, informal, spontaneous, natural, unforced.

◇ *Word origin:* We usually forget that *stilted* literally means "on stilts," hence artificially elevated in speech or manner, pompous.

stimulant *n. Tea is a stimulant that keeps me awake at night:* energizer, tonic, bracer, excitant.

Ant. anaesthetic, narcotic, depressant, tranquillizer, *Slang* downer.

◇ *Usage note:* Many people use *stimulant* and *stimulus* interchangeably. To be accurate, you should know that a *stimulant* is a substance that temporarily quickens physical or psychological processes: *Coffee is a stimulant, The doctor gave the heart patient a stimulant.* A *stimulus* is anything that excites or provokes a response: *The promise of a bonus was a stimulus to the workers, Music can be a stimulus to day-dreaming.*

stimulate *v. Visiting the museum stimulated my interest in the Florentine painters:* arouse, excite, awaken, enkindle, fan, rouse, spur, actuate, prompt, stir, alert, animate, quicken, activate, initiate, incite, wake, inflame, vivify, inspire, inspirit, sharpen.

Ant. deaden; discourage, dull; calm, sooth, assuage.

◇ *Word origin: Stimulate, stimulant,* and *stimulus* come from Latin *stimulare*, to goad, as in herding animals.

stimulus *n.* 1 *Fear is a stimulus to the adrenal gland: (loosely)* stimulant, activator, energizer, excitant. 2 *Nothing is a greater stimulus to pride than success:* incentive, spur, incitement, inducement, goad, provocation, encouragement, fillip, quickener, motive, whet.

Ant. 1 repressant, depressant, suppressant. 2 discouragement, damper, deadener, stay, obstacle, handicap.

◇ *Usage note:* See STIMULANT.

sting *v.* 1 *A bee stung him on the arm:* prick, wound, stab, pierce, nettle, penetrate. 2 *The blowing sand stung the back of my legs. His abrupt reply stung her:* burn, pain sharply, chafe, hurt, cause to wince, irritate, prick, wound; anger, rack, pique, rasp, agonize, grate, offend, disturb, insult, provoke, inflame, rile, grip, gnaw, vex, nettle, incense, madden, torment, harrow, torture, infuriate, gall. 3 *My eyes are stinging from the smoke:* burn, feel sharp pain, smart, prick, wince, itch, twinge, tingle. 4 *His smug challenge stung her into action:* impel, incite, provoke, irritate, goad, prod, kindle, fire, excite, stir up, nettle, whip, egg on, shake, arouse, instigate, spur, actuate, quicken, lash, awaken, propel, motivate, pierce, prompt, move.

—*n.* 5 *Did you get the bee-sting out?:* stinging organ, prick, stinger, barb. 6 *The sting of a jellyfish can be very painful:* bite, wound, sore, burn, pinch, nip; pain, hurt, tingle, prickle, irritation. 7 *I am still smarting from the sting of her bitter words:* wound, pain, hurt, ache, blow, affliction, bite, irritation, gall, scourge, rub, venom, cut, vexation, bitter pill, bitter cup, bitter draught, cross, shock.

Ant. 2 soothe, caress; mollify, assuage, calm. 4 delay, hinder, obstruct, halt, thwart, deaden, paralyse. 7 balm, caress.

stingy *adj.* 1 *That stingy man won't contribute a penny:* miserly, tight, tight-fisted, close, penurious, parsimonious, close-fisted, niggardly, ungenerous, penny-pinching, mean, sparing, illiberal, stinting, frugal, cheese-paring. 2 *It's hard to support a family on such a stingy salary:* meagre, slender, scanty, scant, sparse, lean, scrimpy, skimpy, small, modest, insufficient, thin, paltry, piddling, niggardly, inadequate.

Ant. 1 generous, liberal, bountiful, munificent; prodigal, extravagant, lavish, charitable. 2 large, lavish, huge, profuse, ample, abundant, bountiful.

◇ *Word origin: Stingy* comes from *sting*, hence a *stingy* person is one who feels a sting every time he parts with money.

stink *v.* 1 *The stagnant swamp stinks!:* reek, emit a bad odour, smell to high heaven, be malodorous, offend the nostrils, give a bad odour. 2 *Slang That book really stinks:* be rotten, be boring, be worthless, be no good.

—*n.* 3 *The stink of sour milk filled the refrigerator:* stench, bad smell, unpleasant odour, reek, fetor.

Ant. 3 perfume, aroma, fragrance, sweetness.

◇ *Usage note:* See SMELL.

stint *v.* 1 *I'll have to stint my gifts to charity this year:* restrict, set limits to, give in small amounts, limit, cut down on, reduce, be sparing with, restrain, constrain, circumscribe, check, curb. 2 *One thing Mother never stints on is food:* be sparing, hold back, scrimp, be frugal, save, deny oneself, economize, pinch pennies, withhold, be parsimonious.

—*n.* 3 *She was assigned the most difficult stint. The band did a stint in Liverpool:* job, chore, task, duty, work period, term, assignment, part, turn, shift, quota; engagement.

◇ *Word origin: Stint* comes from Middle English *stynten*, to stop, to limit.

stipend *n. Parish clergy rarely enjoy a generous stipend:* income, allowance, fixed pay, salary, wage, emolument, remuneration, recompense.

stipulate *v. Our contract with the builder stipulates the maximum amount he can charge us:* specify, set forth, insist upon, state, designate, name, cite, make a point of, make provision; promise, pledge, guarantee, insure, grant, provide, allow, assure, agree, warrant.

stir *v.* **1** *The branches began to stir as the breeze came up:* move, rustle, shake, shiver, twitch, flutter, quiver. **2** *Stir the sauce:* move, scramble, mix, agitate, set in motion, commix, blend, mingle, intermix, commingle. **3** *You'd better stir if you want to catch the bus:* act, move; (*variously*) exert oneself, make an effort, bestir oneself, hustle, get moving, get a move on, scramble, bustle, be active, step lively, rush, scamper, hasten. **4** *The house-master's emotional pep talk stirred the boys:* rouse, arouse, inspire, move, excite, animate, awaken, inspirit, energize, electrify, kindle, quicken, vivify, work up, stimulate, fire, enflame, jolt, goad, provoke, start, spur, prod.

—*n.* **5** *She lay awake, listening to the stir of the willow branches above the tent:* stirring, moving, movement, rustle, rustling, sough. **6** *Don't forget to give the sauce an occasional stir:* stirring, mixing, prodding, agitation, mingling. **7** *The film company caused quite a stir in the village:* commotion, tumult, flurry, uproar, to-do.

Ant. **3** relax, settle down. **4** calm, pacify; lull, deaden. **5** stillness, immobility, quiet, silence.

stitch *n.* **1** *Make your stitches closer together:* loop of thread; suture. **2** *Every stitch she owns is at the dry-cleaner's:* bit of clothing, piece, garment, particle, shred, article, scrap. **3** *Plural The comedian had us in stitches:* uncontrollable laughter, guffaws, hoots. **4** *All that dancing gave me a stitch in my side:* pain, kink, pang, crick, twinge, twitch, tingle, ache, cramp.

—*v.* **5** *The tailor stitched the split seam in seconds:* sew, fasten with thread, mend, baste, seam, tack; embroider; suture.

◇ *Word origin:* See STICK[2].

stock *n.* **1** *The shop carries a large stock of gift-wrapping paper at Christmas:* supply, store, inventory, array, quantity, selection, assortment; cache, accumulation, stockpile, fund, reserve, hoard, provision, reservoir; wares, merchandise, goods. **2** *How much stock have you in the company?:* ownership, shares, capital, capital shares; investment. **3** *We're running low on feed for the stock:* livestock, cattle, domestic animals, herd. **4** *She comes from sturdy peasant stock:* descent, lineage, ancestry, strain, line, breed, parentage, heredity, birth, root, extraction, blood, race, house, tribe, progeniture, nationality, pedigree, caste, people, genealogy, family tree, clan, dynasty, origin, source, forebears. **5** *That rose is the finest of its stock:* breed, type, kind. **6** *Grab the rifle firmly by the stock:* handle, haft, grasp, shaft, butt, hold. **7** *You need a good rich stock for the gravy:* broth; bouillon.

—*adj.* **8** *Toothpaste is stock merchandise at a chemist's:* standard, basic, regular, staple. **9** *He got only a stock response to the suggestion that he sent to the governor:* routine, formal, form, pro forma.

—*v.* **10** *The landlord stocked the house with plenty of linen:* supply, furnish, appoint, equip, store, provide, fit out, accoutre, provision. **11** *Do they stock children's shoes?:* handle, keep in stock, offer.

Ant. **10** empty, drain, deplete.

stocky *adj. One brother is stocky and the other is tall and slim:* thickset, short and heavy, husky, solid, sturdy, chunky, squat, stout, stubby, dumpy.

Ant. slim, slender, lanky.

stodgy *adj.* **1** *We almost died of boredom at that stodgy resort. Much technical writing is needlessly stodgy:* dull, stuffy, humdrum, boring, tiresome, dreary, wearisome, tedious, lifeless; flat, prosaic, pompous, lumbering, prolix, clumsy, laborious, pedantic. **2** *It was hard to swallow that stodgy pudding:* indigestible, dull, starchy, heavy, thick, lumpy. **3** *He's too young to have such a stodgy outlook:* old-fashioned, antiquated, dated, passé, narrow, inflexible; staid, serious, stuffy.

Ant. **1** exciting, lively, interesting, vital, vivacious, animated. **2** light, fluffy, airy. **3** new, modern, up-to-date, flexible, *Slang* with-it.

stoic *n.* **1** *He's a stoic and never shed a tear at the news:* fatalist, quietist; man of stone, man of iron.

—*adj.* **2** *His stoical attitude helped us all to bear the tragedy:* detached, philosophic, impassive, unruffled, unimpassioned, imperturbable, calm, tranquil, dispassionate.

Ant. **2** uncontrolled, undisciplined, excitable, volatile, emotional, passionate, disturbed.

◇ *Word origin: Stoic* comes from the name of the *Stoic* school of philosophy, founded by the Greek philosopher Zeno about 308 BC. Zeno taught that wisdom lay in detachment from joy, pleasure, grief, and pain. Zeno and his followers were called *Stoics* after the *Stoa Poikilē*, or Painted Porch, at Athens where he and his successors taught. Located in the Agora (Market), which was the cultural and commercial centre of the Athenian world, the Painted Porch was so-called because of its many murals. These murals celebrated famous Greek victories: Theseus defeating the Amazons, the destruction of Troy, the Battle of Marathon, etc.

stoicism *n. We were impressed by his stoicism throughout the crisis:* impassivity, imperturbability, tranquillity, fortitude, philosophical attitude, fatalism.

Ant. emotionalism, excitability, hysteria.

stolid *adj. He's too stolid to show excitement about anything:* impassive, apathetic, sluggish, lethargic, phlegmatic, dull, obtuse, lumpish, dense.

Ant. excitable, emotional, passionate, energetic, lively, active, animated, acute.

stomach *n.* **1** *That heavy meal lies like lead on my stomach:* belly, abdomen, tummy; craw, crop, gizzard, maw; paunch, midriff, middle, *Slang* guts, pot, pot-belly, bread-basket. **2** *How can you have any stomach for lunch after that huge breakfast?:* hunger, appetite, taste, thirst, keenness, relish. **3** *I have no stomach for violent films:* liking, taste, appetite, disposition, keenness, desire, fancy, inclination, hunger, pleasure, affinity, leaning, attraction, proclivity, predilection, relish, partiality, mind, bent, temper, bias, sympathy, propensity, humour.

—*v.* **4** *The sick man couldn't even stomach liquids:* keep down, hold in the stomach, retain. **5** *He couldn't stomach the snobbery of some of the guests:* stand, bear, put up with, take, endure, suffer, bear with, tolerate, brook, abide, submit to, resign oneself to, reconcile oneself to, let pass, close the eyes to, overlook, make allowance for, pass over, be patient with.

Ant. **2** distaste, disrelish. **3** dislike, distaste, disinclination, abhorrence, aversion, displeasure. **4** regurgitate, vomit. **5** reject, condemn, discountenance.

◇ *Word origin: Stomach* comes from Greek *stomachos,* throat, gullet, from *stoma,* mouth.

stone *n.* **1** *The house is built of stone. The boys threw stones into the pond:* rock, pebble. **2** *She has a three-carat stone in her ring:* gem, precious stone, jewel, brilliant, birthstone, bijou. **3** *The stones have been removed from these cherries:* pit, kernel, seed, nut.

—*v.* **4** *Vandals stoned the new building, breaking all the windows:* throw rocks at, pelt with stones.

stony *adj.* **1** *You'll need shoes to walk on this stony path:* full of rocks, rocky, pebbly, bumpy, gravelly, craggy, jagged, uneven, coarse, rough, rugged. **2** *Coal is a stony substance, but it's not a rock:* stonelike, rocklike, rocky; (*variously*) adamantine, flinty, ossified, concrete, lithoid, marble, granite, fossilized, petrified, crystallized. **3** *Her tears couldn't move his stony heart:* unfeeling, insensible, unsympathetic, cold, hard-hearted, cold-hearted, merciless, austere, severe, soulless, unresponsive, icy, heartless, callous, obdurate, frigid, stern, stolid, passionless, unemotional, indifferent, flinty, hardened, blank, expressionless, cold-blooded, stoical, unyielding, heartless, inexorable, pitiless, chill, forbidding, indurate, steely, deadened, untouched, unaffected, uncaring, *Informal* hard-boiled; bloodless.

Ant. **1** smooth, even. **2** soft, flexible, yielding. **3** feeling, sensitive, sympathetic, warm, responsive, soft-hearted, tender-hearted, tender, compassionate, soft, mellow, friendly.

stoop *v.* **1** *She stooped to pick up a piece of paper:* bend down, lean over. **2** *He stoops from years of bending over a desk:* slouch, be round-shouldered, be bowed, be doubled over, lean forward. **3** *I can't believe he would stoop to such nonsense:* lower oneself, degrade oneself, descend, fall, deign, bow, condescend, resort, succumb, bend, prostrate oneself; acquiesce, concede, yield, submit.

—*n.* **4** *His stoop seemed more pronounced after his illness:* stooping posture, stooping carriage, slump, slouch, round-shoulderedness, bend, droop, sag.

Ant. **1** stand erect. **3** rise, ascend. **4** straightness, erectness.

> **Exploring the Word**: *Stone* comes from Old English *stān,* stone, and is the base of some interesting combinations. The *Stone Age* is the earliest known period in the cultural evolution of mankind, characterized by the use of stone tools and weapons (preceding the Bronze Age). A *stone* is a unit of weight equal to fourteen pounds. The prehistoric ceremonial structure made up of circular formations of huge dressed stones with lintels on Salisbury Plain in Wiltshire is called *Stonehenge,* literally "hanging stones," because of the way the stones seem to be balanced or "hung" on each other. A *stone bottle* is made of *stoneware,* a very hard pottery made of clay mixed with flint or sand. (Incidentally, the German word for *stone* is *stein,* and a *beer stein* is a stoneware mug for beer.) The American general "Stonewall" (Thomas Jonathan) Jackson, 1824–63, got his nickname because he was as resistant in battle as a stone wall, not giving an inch.

stop *v.* **1** *Stop or I'll shoot! Stop what you're doing. A tourniquet stops heavy bleeding:* halt, stay, stand fast, hold; discontinue, suspend, put an end to, cut short, bring to a standstill, postpone; check, suppress, block, stem, stall, interrupt the flow of, stanch, cut off; curb, rein in. **2** *The guards stopped him from escaping:* restrain, hinder, hold back, prevent, bar, obstruct, preclude, deter, thwart, hamper, frustrate. **3** *He stopped the leak with cement:* plug, caulk, close, block, fill, stop up, fill the holes in, close up, occlude, stanch, seal. **4** *The music stopped. The lightning stopped. The car stopped:* come to an end, cease, come to a halt, discontinue, conclude, finish, be over, desist, leave off, break off, terminate, run its course, run out, wind down, peter out, quit, hold, reach completion, come to a standstill, pause, intermit, lapse, pass away, draw to a close, expire, surcease; draw up, brake, stall, pull up, alight, become inactive, idle, falter, rest, stand; drop anchor. **5** *We stopped at a hotel for two nights:* sojourn, stay, rest, dwell, lodge, stop over, put up, abide, take up quarters, visit, tarry, repose, suspend one's journey.

—*n.* **6** *The strike caused a stop in production. We must put a stop to the fighting:* cessation, halt, halting, stoppage, suspension, arrest, break, discontinuation, desistance, leaving off, pause, respite, lapse, spell, interruption, lull, intermission, abeyance, wait, interlude, recess, interval, hiatus, breathing-space; end, standstill, ban, curb, block, prohibition. **7** *We made a stop at Mother's on our way to Scotland:* visit, stay, stop-over, sojourn, rest, respite, break, pause. **8** *I get off at the next stop:* stage; depot, station, terminus, terminal; destination.

Ant. 1 start, begin, commence, initiate, continue, set going, institute, originate, inaugurate. **2** speed, assist, expedite, facilitate, further, encourage, incite. **3** unplug, open, uncork, unseal. **4** start, begin, commence, continue, go on, proceed, progress, advance. **6** start, commencement, beginning; resumption.

◇ *Word origin: Stop* and *stuff* are both ultimately derived from Greek *stuppē*, tow, oakum (coarse hemp or flax fibre used for stuffing, caulking, and packing).

store *n.* **1** *Mother went to the store to buy some household things:* shop, market, mart, supermarket, department store, emporium, establishment. **2** *Our store of fuel is running low:* supply, provision, stock, pile, stockpile, hoard, inventory, stock in trade, reserve, wares, effects, fund, reservoir, quantity, cache. **3** *He lays great store by her advice:* faith, confidence, regard, value, credit, trust, reliance, dependence, estimation, esteem. **4** *He always has a store of marvellous anecdotes:* abundance, multitude, plethora, full measure, wealth, overflow, plenty, large quantity, legion, luxuriance, fund, richness, satiety, array, lot, volume, pack, host, profusion, copiousness, plenteousness, hoard, scores, riches, prodigality, multiplicity, exuberance, cornucopia.

—*v.* **5** *Squirrels store nuts for the winter:* save, stow away, keep, lay aside, put away, deposit, salt away, hoard, amass, reserve, lay up or by, husband, lay in, accumulate, hold, heap up, store up, cache, put in storage, put in mothballs, *Informal* stash.

Ant. 3 disbelief, distrust, scepticism, doubt, suspicion. **4** paucity, lack, poverty, dearth, skimpiness. **5** waste, spend, squander.

storm *n.* **1** *The islanders were warned that a storm was coming:* torrent, deluge, rainstorm, cloudburst, downpour; snowstorm, blizzard; windstorm, tempest, gale, squall, blow, hurricane, typhoon, cyclone; tornado. **2** *My criticism produced a storm of anger. The speaker caused a storm in the hall:* outburst, eruption, outbreak, burst, explosion, roar, tumult, disturbance, agitation, commotion, clamour, hubbub, turmoil, furore, flurry, uproar, row, stir, rumpus, upheaval, pother, to-do, ado, hullabaloo, brouhaha, fuss, tempest. **3** *The enemy took the place by storm:* sudden attack, violent assault, frontal attack, overwhelming onslaught.

—*v.* **4** *The wind stormed so hard that the telegraph poles were blown down:* rain heavily, snow heavily, blow violently. **5** *He stormed at the waiter and embarrassed everyone at the table:* rage, rant, rave, lose one's temper, complain furiously, bluster, carry on, rampage, raise hell, vent one's rage, fly into a rage, snarl, raise the devil, fume, *Slang* blow one's top, lose one's cool, fly off the handle. **6** *She stormed out of the house:* rush, stamp, rage, tear, tramp, stalk. **7** *Their only hope of victory was to storm the enemy camp at night:* charge, attack, assail, rush, strike, assault, make an onslaught, fall upon.

Ant. 1 calm, fair weather. **2** calm, peace, hush, tranquillity. **5** whisper, reason, cajole. **6** amble, saunter.

stormy *adj. Don't take the boat out in this stormy weather:* rainy; snowy; windy; turbulent, blustering, tempestuous, inclement, raging, squally, roaring, howling, wild, foul.

Ant. mild, calm, fair.

story *n.* **1** *His story of the incident contradicts mine. I saw your name in a newspaper story:* report, account, allegation, version, statement, word, testimony, tidings, article, news, information, dispatch, news item, piece, column. **2** *He won a fiction award for his short stories:* tale, narrative, romance, fable, yarn, sketch, allegory, anecdote, parable; plot, argument, legend. **3** *Informal I know you're just telling a story!:* lie, white lie, falsehood, fib, fabrication, prevarication; excuse.

◇ *Word origin: Story,* a narrative, like the word *history,* comes from Greek *historia,* narrative. This word was adopted by the Romans, and it is from Latin *historia* that we got such words as *history* and *story.*

stout *adj.* **1** *She's too stout to wear that clinging dress:* fat, corpulent, large, thickset, portly, rotund, plump, obese, big, round, heavy, tubby, fleshy, bulky, stocky. **2** *His stout self-confidence makes you feel you can depend on him:* brave, stout-hearted, courageous, heroic, dauntless, lion-hearted, valorous, valiant, intrepid, sturdy, daring, unshrinking, unflinching, stalwart, gallant, resolute, indomitable, plucky, doughty, fearless, confident, *Informal* spunky; steadfast, determined, staunch, resolved, firm, faithful, unwavering, true, unfaltering, steady, constant, inflexible, untiring, unshakeable, unswerving, enduring. **3** *We need a couple of stout young fellows to move the piano. You'll need stout boots for climbing:* sturdy, strapping, strong, husky, stalwart, hardy, robust, muscular, tough, vigorous, rugged, able-bodied, athletic, brawny, mighty, burly, fit, staunch, able, leathery, hefty, solid.

Ant. 1 lean, lanky, spare, skinny, slim, slender, thin. **2** cowardly, timid, irresolute, fearful, shrinking, apprehensive. **3** weak, frail, puny, feeble, fragile, unfit, unsound, flimsy, jerry-built, insubstantial.

◇ *Word origin: Stout* comes from Old French *estout*, bold, strong, as in the phrase *stout-hearted men.* Because strong men were often large and thickset, *stout* took on its newer meaning of "bulky, fat." The word is cognate with German *stoltz*, proud.

stow *v. Stow the potatoes in a cool dark place:* store, put, place, set, pack, ensconce, cache, tuck, stuff, jam, load, cram, salt away, deposit, *Informal* stash.

straight *adj.* **1** *They ploughed a straight furrow from the top of the field to the bottom:* direct, unbent, unswerving, undeviating, not curved. **2** *Make sure the rear-view mirror is straight:* square, even, level, adjusted, aligned. **3** *Give me a straight answer to my question:* straightforward, honest, candid, forthright, true, truthful, reliable, veracious, square, frank, clear, above-board, accurate, four-square, right, sound, trustworthy. **4** *We've had eight straight days of rain:* unbroken, solid, uninterrupted, continuous, successive, consecutive, incessant, sustained, ceaseless, persistent, unrelieved. **5** *His desk is always straight:* orderly, tidy, in order, neat, shipshape; co-ordinated, sorted out, arranged, methodical.
—*adv.* **6** *He spent years in prison, but now he seems to be going straight:* honestly, not criminally, not deviating from the path of good behaviour or the norm. **7** *Go straight to bed. Go straight home:* directly, immediately, instantly, forthwith; in a straight line, without wandering. **8** *Stand up straight:* straightly, erectly, upright; evenly, on a level, squarely.
Ant. 1 curved, crooked, indirect, winding, bent, zigzag. **2** crooked, uneven, awry. **3** unreliable, confused, false, ambiguous, qualified, evasive, equivocal. **4** broken, interrupted, discontinuous, non-consecutive. **5** messy, disorderly, untidy, disarranged, confused, disarrayed. **6** off the rails, in error. **7** eventually, later, afterward. **8** crookedly, unevenly, askew, awry.
◇ *Usage note: Straight* means not curved, not crooked, directly: *a straight line, a straight pin, Go straight home.* Do not use it to mean *strait*, a channel connecting two larger bodies of water: *the Strait of Magellan.*

straightforward *adj.* **1** *We took a straightforward route to the beach:* direct, straight. **2** *She gave a straightforward explanation of her mistake. He's completely straightforward in his business dealings:* open, candid, frank, honest, guileless, plain-spoken, above-board, forthright; trustworthy, square, upright, honourable, straight, ethical, scrupulous, creditable.
Ant. 1 indirect, roundabout, circuitous. **2** devious, sharp, disingenuous, unethical, unscrupulous, shady.

strain[1] *v.* **1** *If you strain the elastic any more, it will break:* draw tight, stretch, put under tension, pull, tug, make tense or taut, tighten; stretch, elongate, protract, distend, extend. **2** *The prisoner strained to get away from his captors:* struggle, heave, exert one's strength, make a supreme effort, huff and puff. **3** *The manufacturer strained to get his orders out on time. The doctor warned him against straining himself:* drive oneself, exert oneself, press, struggle, overwork, push to the utmost, work day and night, grind, over-exert, tax, overtax, fatigue, wear out, exhaust, burden, overburden, drudge, burn the midnight oil, work one's fingers to the bone, work like a slave, work like a horse, burn the candle at both ends, overdo, do double duty; try hard, bear down, buckle down. **4** *He strained his Achilles tendon whilst playing tennis:* pull, sprain, impair by stretching, injure, wrench, weaken, twist, hurt by over-exertion. **5** *Some cooks strain their gravy:* sieve, filter, screen, sift, winnow, purify, drain, refine.
—*n.* **6** *Too much strain broke the rope:* stress, pressure, force, tension. **7** *The strain of keeping awake was painful:* effort, exertion, struggle. **8** *A heating-pad might ease that muscle strain:* sprain, pull, injury, wrench, twist. **9** *He was under enormous strain during the trial:* tension, pressure, mental stress, hardship. **10** *It seems to me that I've heard that strain before. Jim whistled a familiar strain from Rodgers and Hart:* tune, song, melody, air.
Ant. 1 relax, loosen, slacken. **2** relax, yield. **3** idle; pamper, coddle. **7** effortlessness. **9** relaxation.

strain[2] *n.* **1** *He comes of a tough peasant strain:* parentage, ancestry, lineage, descent, stock, derivation, family, people, extraction, breed, heredity, line, blood. **2** *My uncle cultivated a rare strain of orchid:* type, breed, variety, kind, sort, group. **3** *A strain of musical talent seems to run in the family:* streak, hereditary character, vein, natural capacity, tendency, trait, predisposition, grain, genius, inclination, disposition.

strait *n.* **1** *Our boat went aground in the strait before we reached the sea:* narrow passage of water, narrows; channel. **2** Often **straits** *His gambling debts put him in awkward financial straits:* predicament, difficulty, plight, distress, embarrassment, extremity, *Informal* fix, pickle, hole, mess.
Ant. 2 ease, comfort, luxury.
◇ *Usage note:* See STRAIGHT.

strait-laced *adj. He's too strait-laced to be seen at a dance hall:* puritanical, proper, strict, prudish, prim, rigid, over-scrupulous, narrow; formal, reserved, inhibited, undemonstrative, stiff, austere, severe, *Slang* uptight, square.
Ant. loose, immoral; relaxed, uninhibited, broad-minded.

strand[1] *v.* **1** *The hurricane stranded the boat on the reef:* run aground, go aground, beach, drive ashore, leave ashore, ground; shipwreck.

2 *The loss of electricity left us stranded without heat. The bus left, and we were stranded in a strange town:* leave, leave high and dry, leave in the lurch.
— *n.* 3 *Hotels were going up all along the strand:* shore, coast, sea-shore, foreshore, beach, sea-coast, bank, riverside.

strand[2] *n.* 1 *Separate the rope into its individual strands. Weave a love-knot with a strand of hair:* filament, fibre, thread; cord, rope, string, tress, braid, twist. 2 *Father gave Mother a strand of pearls for her birthday:* string, necklace.

strange *adj.* 1 *His behaviour seems strange:* peculiar, odd, unusual, queer, extraordinary, abnormal, curious, singular, uncommon, eccentric, irregular, outlandish, unnatural, unconventional, bizarre, unaccountable, freakish, erratic, out-of-the-way, unaccustomed, fantastic, aberrant, anomalous, far-fetched. 2 *Not being able to speak the language made me feel strange:* out of place, uncomfortable, ill at ease, uneasy, awkward, disoriented, estranged, lost, discomposed, bewildered, foreign, alien, alienated. 3 *He is strange to this area:* foreign, alien, unknown, unfamiliar, unaccustomed, unused, new. 4 *This machine is strange to me:* unfamiliar, unknown, unexplored, untried, new.
Ant. 1 regular, conventional, normal, commonplace, run-of-the-mill, usual, common, accustomed, ordinary. 2 at home, comfortable, at ease, easy. 3 known, familiar. 4 familiar, known, used.
◇ *Word origin: Strange* and *extraneous* are based on the same word. They come from Latin *extraneus,* foreign, unfamiliar (Latin *extra,* outside). *Extraneous* has kept its *ex-* sound, while *strange* has come to us from Latin via French, in which the Latin *x-* sound changes to an *s-* sound.

"There is no excellent beauty that hath not some strangeness in the proportion."
—*Francis Bacon*

stranger *n.* 1 *Everyone at the party was a stranger to me:* unknown person. 2 *It's hard for a stranger to make friends in this town:* outsider, newcomer, foreigner, immigrant, alien.
Ant. 1 friend, acquaintance, mate, chum. 2 native, insider, resident, habitué.

strangle *v.* 1 *The killer strangled his victims with his bare hands:* choke, suffocate, stifle, smother, asphyxiate, throttle, garrotte. 2 *The dictator's first step was to strangle the free press:* stop, suppress, repress, stifle, throttle, choke off, burke, quell, put a stop to, check, crush, put down, snuff out, extinguish, muzzle, gag, smother.
Ant. 2 assist, further, encourage, promote, forward, abet, aid, help.

strap *n.* 1 *The strap on one of my ski boots broke:* fastening strip, thong, band, tie.
— *v.* 2 *Strap the suitcases on top of the car:* lash, tie, bind, truss, leash. 3 *He strapped the boy with a leather belt:* whip, thrash, beat, flog, belt, lash, flail, scourge.

strapping *adj. Informal That frail boy grew up to be a strapping man:* robust, sturdy, strongly built, husky, stalwart, hardy, muscular, brawny, powerful.
Ant. frail, weak, fragile, puny, delicate.

stratagem *n. The general's clever stratagem was successful against the enemy:* manœuvre, scheme, plan, plot, trick, intrigue, ruse, artifice, tactic, trickery, device, machination, game, deception, deceit, ploy, dodge, feint, blind, wile.

strategic *adj.* 1 *The strategic operation was agreed to by all the top brass. The army made a strategic retreat:* tactical, military; calculated; politic, diplomatic; planned, well thought-out, deliberate, clever, cunning, cautious, careful, guarded, prudent, precautionary, vigilant, wary. 2 *Refreshment stands were set up in strategic spots around the dance floor. Wait for the strategic moment, and then strike:* crucial, important, decisive, critical, vital, significant, momentous, key, principal, consequential, turning.
Ant. 1 non-strategic; unplanned. 2 unimportant, inconsequential, trifling.

strategy *n.* 1 *The strategy is to wear the enemy down by repeated attacks:* military plan, overall plan, grand design, scheme; tactics, manœuvring, devices, game, artifice, policy. 2 *He was an expert in strategy during the war:* military science, war planning, war policy, art of war. 3 *He needs to improve his strategy before he can call himself a good tennis player:* artfulness, craft, cunning, craftiness, wiles, artifice, game plan, tactics.
◇ *Usage note:* There's a nice difference between *strategy* and *tactics. Strategy* is an overall plan or campaign: *The team's strategy is to win the game using their wingers as much as possible. The general's strategy is to win the war with air power. Tactics* are the techniques or ploys used to carry out the plan: *At the second line-out the team's tactic is to throw the ball right over the line. One of the general's favourite tactics was to drop paratroops behind enemy lines.*
◇ *Word origin: Strategy, strategic,* and *strategem* come from Greek *stratos* (army) + *agein* (to lead), to lead an army, to be a general, hence *strategy* is a piece of generalship.

straw *n.* 1 *He was lazing in the sun chewing a straw. The glasses were packed in straw:* stem of grain; hay, chaff. 2 *May I have a straw for my drink?:* tube for sucking liquid; pipette.
◇ *Word origin: Straw* comes from Old English *streaw.* It is not known where *strawberries,* fruit of the genus Fragaria, got their name. A *strawberry blonde* is a woman whose hair colour is between strawberry (red) and blonde.

stray *v.* 1 *The kitten must have strayed from its mother:* go astray, wander, drift, straggle, lose

one's way. **2** *Her thoughts strayed to her childhood:* wander, drift, digress.
—*n.* **3** *The kind lady's house was always open to strays:* homeless person or creature, waif, lost person, lost animal, itinerant, vagabond, wanderer, drifter, straggler.
—*adj.* **4** *We adopted a stray dog:* straying, lost, misplaced. **5** *Only a few stray clouds dotted the sky:* scattered, set apart, separate, random.

streak *n.* **1** *You have a streak of paint on your forehead:* long smear, line, stripe, band; (*loosely*) smudge, blotch, splotch, smirch, blur, daub, blot. **2** *There are streaks of ore in the mountain:* layer, portion, vein, lode, bed, seam; level, stratum, plane. **3** *He has a mean streak:* vein, cast, strain, touch, element.
—*v.* **4** *The winning horse streaked past the finishing-line:* race, speed, rush, hurtle; whiz, tear, zoom, dart, dash, fly.
Ant. **4** creep, crawl, go at a snail's pace.

stream *n.* **1** *The stream is full of trout:* narrow river, streamlet, brook, beck, rivulet, rill, branch, run, watercourse, leak, tributary, feeder, freshet. **2** *A stream of water ran off the roof. A stream of traffic crossed the bridge. The child kept up a steady stream of talk:* flow, torrent, run, course, rush, race, current, spout, sluice, river, gush, onrush, jet, flux, surge, deluge, flood, tide; effusion, spate, profusion.
—*v.* **3** *Blood streamed from the wound. Vehicles streamed from the car-park:* flow, pour, run, issue, course, rush, surge, burst, spill, gush, spout, spurt, flood, fountain, shoot; move continuously, file, go on endlessly. **4** *The streets were streaming with tourists:* teem, abound, flow, overflow. **5** *The ribbons in her hair streamed behind her as she ran down the hill:* wave, float, flutter, blow, waft, stretch out, extend.

street *n. The child ran into the street. Our street has had a number of burglaries:* road; (*variously*) thoroughfare, roadway, square, highway, way, avenue, boulevard, lane, high street, main street, back street, alley, mews, terrace.
◇ *Word origin: Street* comes from the Late Latin phrase *strata via,* paved way. The Old English word for a Roman road is *strǣt.* This sense of the English word survives in the names of Watling *Street,* Ermine *Street,* Icknield *Street* (also known as the Icknield Way), and Stone *Street.* These "streets" are all old Roman roads which are still to be seen.

strength *n.* **1** *Has he enough strength to lift these weights? She has great strength of character:* power, vigour, might, muscles, hardiness, force, brawn, *Slang* beef; robustness, puissance, potency, sturdiness, stoutness, sinew, lustiness, stamina, endurance, vitality, pith, backbone; firmness, fortitude, toughness, solidity, vitality, spirit; tenacity, pluck, grit, mettle, bravery, stout-heartedness. **2** *What is the total strength of the enemy army?:* force, number, size. **3** *This medicine has lost its strength:* potency, power, force, efficacy, *Archaic* virtue. **4** *The clouds diminished the strength of the sunlight. The sauce has lost some of its strength:* intensity, concentration, purity, vitality. **5** *Her faith in God is her real strength. Maths is her main strength, languages her weakness:* source of power, support, security, anchor, mainstay, buttress, sustenance, succour; forte, strong point.
Ant. **1** weakness, frailness, powerlessness, impotence, spiritlessness, feebleness. **3** ineffectiveness, inefficacy, unsoundness. **4** flatness, dilution, adulteration. **5** frailty, flaw.

strengthen *v. His back strengthened with exercise. The new evidence strengthened his case:* make stronger, become stronger, give strength to, gain strength, grow stronger, reinforce; fortify, build up, buttress, support, brace, prop, shore up, sustain; harden, steel, restore, renew, enhance, improve.
Ant. weaken, debilitate, crush, enervate, destroy, devitalize.

strenuous *adj.* **1** *You shouldn't take such strenuous exercise:* laborious, taxing, exhausting, physically demanding, difficult; intense, vigorous, hard, uphill. **2** *He's a strenuous student and will do well at school:* energetic, dynamic, vigorous, zealous, active, industrious, intense, earnest, ardent, eager, enterprising, animated, spirited, assiduous, sedulous, diligent, hard-working, dogged, on one's toes, painstaking, indefatigable, untiring.
Ant. **1** easy, light, effortless. **2** lazy, indolent.

stress *n.* **1** *They place too much stress on money and position:* emphasis, importance, weight, consequence, significance, meaning, value, seriousness, prominence, worth, urgency, necessity, concern, consideration, moment. **2** *In the word* sawdust, *the stress is on the first syllable:* accent, accentuation, emphasis, beat. **3** *The bough couldn't bear up under the stress of the heavy snow. The stress of not knowing was too great for her:* strain, tension, force, burden, pressure, oppression.
—*v.* **4** *The speaker stressed the need for better education:* emphasize, lay emphasis on, accentuate, accent, underscore, underline, mark, assert positively, insist upon, feature, repeat, affirm, assert. **5** *Stress the second syllable in* today: accent, emphasize, accentuate.
Ant. **1** unimportance, insignificance, de-emphasis. **5** underplay, play down, understate; ignore, neglect, pass over.

stretch *v.* **1** *She stretched the clothes-line between two trees. Will this material stretch?:* distend, extend, draw out, pull out, widen, lengthen, deepen, protract, expand, be expandable, elongate; strain, make tense or tight, draw tight, draw taut, put under tension, be elastic, be extendable, bear extension. **2** *Stretch your hand through the window:* extend, put forth, reach, reach out. **3** *The road stretches across the* *mountains:* lie over, cover, extend, reach, spread, span, traverse. **4** *Let's stretch out on the sand for a while:* lie at full length; sprawl. **5** *The cat stretched and arched its back:* strain the body, draw out the muscles. **6** *I think you have stretched a point there. You stretch my patience too far:* exaggerate, strain, push to the limit, carry too far, push too far, overtax, overstrain, overwork, overburden, burden, overcharge, overtask, fatigue, tire, over-exert. —*n.* **7** *He did a long stretch in gaol:* spell, term, duration, period, stint, while. **8** *We drove fast along a stretch of empty motorway:* expanse, spread, run, tract, distance. **9** *The stretch has gone out of this waistband:* elasticity, elastic quality, resiliency, tautness, spring.

Ant. **1** shrink, loosen, relax, slacken, tighten, tauten, contract, condense, narrow, shorten. **2** withdraw, retract.

stricken *adj. The region has long been stricken with poverty. All hands were rescued from the stricken ship. The stricken animal was put out of its misery:* afflicted, smitten; (*variously*) ill, sick, taken sick, diseased, blighted, incapacitated, wounded, injured, hurt.

strict *adj.* **1** *Her father was strict and insisted that she be home by midnight. Our laws against speeding are very strict:* stern, rigid, severe, authoritarian, rigorous, uncompromising, austere, stringent, unyielding, exacting, inflexible. **2** *The army demands strict loyalty:* perfect, absolute, complete, exact, unerring, conscientious, fastidious, meticulous, scrupulous, nice.

Ant. **1** lax, lenient, indulgent, permissive; loose, flexible; broad, approximate. **2** loose, inattentive, careless.

stride *v.* **1** *He strode out of the house:* march, walk with long steps, take long steps, stalk, step. —*n.* **2** *He reached the house in a few strides:* pace, long step. **3** *The dancer moves with a graceful stride:* gait, step. **4** *He's made tremendous strides toward recovery:* step, advance, advancement, progress, headway, improvement.

strident *adj. His strident voice hurts my ears:* grating, harsh, piercing, jangling, jarring, raucous, discordant, rasping, grinding, shrill, dissonant, clashing, cacophonous, twanging.

Ant. soft, mellow, deep, dulcet, mellifluous.

strife *n. A history of strife has left its mark on this tiny nation:* conflict, dissension, turmoil, upheaval, trouble, unrest, disharmony, contention, disturbance, disquiet, convulsion, struggle, violence, warfare.

Ant. peace, accord, calm, agreement, harmony.

strike *v.* **1** *He struck me with his fist. Strike the nail as straight as you can:* hit, deal a blow to, bang, box, cuff, slap, club, thump, smash, pound, knock, tap, clap, bump, beat, cudgel, clout, slam, bat, sock, punch, wallop, pummel, pelt, smite, whack, buffet, hammer, clip, drub, belt; thrash, flog, batter, lash, whip, lambaste, scourge, flail, flagellate. **2** *The enemy struck at dawn:* attack, assail, hit, assault, charge. **3** *The speeding car struck a telegraph pole:* hit, dash against, meet head on, run into, hurtle against, knock into, bump into, beat against, ram, run or fall foul of, collide with. **4** *Heavenly music struck our ears:* reach, fall upon, hit; burst upon. **5** *The lateness of the hour suddenly struck us:* occur to, come to the mind of, dawn upon, reach. **6** *His enthusiasm struck his teacher favourably:* impress, affect, appear to, seem to. **7** *Prospectors finally struck gold. He struck upon the solution quite by accident:* hit, come, arrive, run, light, chance, meet, stumble, find, encounter, come upon, come across, reach, unearth, discover. **8** *The hagglers failed to strike a bargain:* reach, achieve, make, effect, arrange. **9** *The soldiers struck camp and slipped away:* take down, pull down, put away, fold up, take apart. **10** *Strike that statement from the record:* remove, cancel, eliminate, erase, eradicate, delete, wipe, cross out, scratch. **11** *The clock struck twelve:* sound, ring, chime, knell, toll. **12** *A blight struck the entire crop:* hit, afflict suddenly, assault, assail, affect severely, deal a blow to, devastate, smite. **13** *The transport workers struck just before Christmas:* go on strike, walk out. —*n.* **14** *The strike ended when the wage demands were met:* walk-out, work stoppage, industrial dispute; protest, boycott.

◇ *Word origin: Strike* comes from Old English *strīcan,* to stroke, rub, move.

striking *adj. She bears a striking resemblance to her mother:* remarkable, noticeable, notable, conspicuous, outstanding, impressive; astounding, extraordinary, surprising.

string *n.* **1** *The string round the package broke:* cord, thread, twine, strand, line, binding. **2** *Mother has a lovely string of pearls:* strand, rope, necklace. **3** *A string of children filed into the house. A string of hotels lined the beach:* procession, file, parade; row, chain, column, line, sequence, series, queue. —*v.* **4** *They strung these pearls too tightly:* thread, put on a string. **5** *String the hammock between the two trees:* stretch, extend, spread.

stringent *adj.* **1** *Stringent laws are needed to protect the consumer:* strict, stiff, rigorous, compelling obedience, inflexible, uncompromising, unyielding, harsh, severe, stern. **2** *He used the most stringent reasoning in defending his thesis:* forceful, cogent, effectual, severe, rigorous. **3** *Such a stringent budget allows for few luxuries:* tight, close, sparing, spare, frugal.

Ant. **1** flexible, loose; inaffective, relaxed. **2** ineffective, unconvincing, equivocal, unsound, inconclusive. **3** lavish, plentiful, ample, generous, liberal.

strip[1] *v.* **1** *The doctor told him to strip before getting on the scales:* unclothe, undress, remove one's clothes, disrobe, divest of clothing, undrape, doff; lay bare, unwrap, uncover, disencumber. **2** *We had to strip the old paint off the doors:* remove, shave, peel, flay, flake, draw off, pull off, tear, lay bare, skin, denude. **3** *They stripped the prisoners of their dignity:* deprive, rob, divest, denude. **4** *The pirates stripped the cargo ship:* plunder, ravage, sack, rob, despoil, loot, ransack, desolate, spoliate, lay waste, raid, steal from, rifle.

Ant. 1 dress, clothe, don; cover. **2** apply, put on. **3** invest, furnish.

◇ *Word origin: Strip*[1], to pull the clothing or covering from, comes from Old English *bestrīepan*, to plunder, despoil.

Exploring the Word: Our words *stringent* and *strait* (as in the *Strait of Magellan, strait-jacket,* and *strait-laced*) come from Latin *stringere,* to draw tight, press. *Stringent* means tightly bound to rules and regulations, strict. A *strait* (like the *Bering Strait*) is a channel between two larger bodies of water, while a *strait-jacket* is a jacket that can be tied tightly around a violent person to restrain him, and *strait-laced* originally meant enclosed in a tightly-laced corset, hence literally "uptight." Latin *stringere* also gives us: *astringent,* drawing together organic tissue or a preparation that does this, or causing the lips to draw together or pucker, as something sour; *constrict* and *constrain,* to draw together by force, to bind or restrain; *distress,* drawn apart, pulled asunder, hence suffering; *district,* a region or territory over which a government draws out or stretches its authority; *strain,* to bind as closely as possible, draw or pull beyond the limit, and *restrain,* to hold back, as by binding tightly.

strip[2] *n.* **1** *I need two strips of adhesive tape:* long narrow piece, slip, ribbon, band, stripe. **2** *The landing-strip was covered with snow:* airstrip, airfield, runway.

stripe *n.* **1** *Vertical stripes on a dress are slimming:* band, streak, line, bar, striation. **2** *His mother sewed the stripes on his uniform:* strip of material, tape, braid, ribbon; emblem of rank, insignia, chevron, bar.

"Fail I alone, in words and deeds?
Why, all men strive, and who succeeds?"
—*Robert Browning*

strive *v.* **1** *A desire to please his parents made him strive to do well:* struggle, try hard, attempt earnestly, exert oneself, make efforts, labour, do all one can, push, take pains, do one's utmost, strain; leave no stone unturned, do one's best, spare no pains, work like a Trojan, move heaven and earth; essay, undertake, endeavour. **2** *The beleaguered platoon strove against invincible odds:* fight, contend, vie, struggle, battle.

Ant. 1 take it easy.

stroke *n.* **1** *He felled his opponent with one stroke:* blow, punch, chop, whack, swat, sock, wallop. **2** *Give your hair 50 strokes with a brush every day:* brush, massage, light touch, caress. **3** *On the stroke of midnight she rushed from the ballroom:* striking, tolling, sounding, chime, ringing. **4** *The stroke left his right side paralysed:* paralytic stroke, brain haemorrhage, apoplectic fit, apoplexy, seizure. **5** *The letter Y ends with a downward stroke, known as a descender:* movement, flourish. **6** *He outmanœuvred the enemy by a bold stroke. A stroke of fate turned the beggar into a rich man:* hit, achievement, blow, feat, deed, transaction, coup; piece of luck, chance, fluke, coincidence, accident.

—*v.* **7** *The golfer stroked the ball into the cup:* hit lightly, tap, dribble, poke. **8** *He stroked her hair gently:* caress, pat, pet.

stroll *v.* **1** *A huge crowd strolled down the avenue:* walk slowly, amble, saunter, promenade, wander, dawdle along, ramble, meander.

—*n.* **2** *Will you join us for a stroll in the park?:* walk, amble, promenade, ramble, saunter, turn, tour, constitutional.

Ant. 1 run, race, hurry, dash, scurry.

strong *adj.* **1** *Is the boy strong enough to lift that box? There's a strong undertow in the river here:* powerful, having great strength, forceful, mighty, potent, puissant; muscular, sinewy, stalwart, stout, Herculean, burly, hardy, brawny, robust, healthy, tough, athletic, vigorous; severe, intense, violent. **2** *Getting on with people is one of his strong points:* able, competent, capable, skilled, well-qualified, well-endowed, proficient, advantageous. **3** *She was strong enough to overcome her handicap:* firm in spirit, resourceful, plucky, gritty, stalwart, stout, courageous, sturdy, sound, tough, tenacious, persistent, persevering; resilient, buoyant; tireless, indefatigable. **4** *He offered some strong reasons for abandoning the project:* convincing, compelling, forceful, powerful, moving, potent, effective, solid, sound, cogent. **5** *There's a strong similarity between the two cousins:* close, clear, distinct, definite, emphatic, unmistakable. **6** *Those colours are too strong for a bedroom:* bright, bold, loud, vivid, intense, fiery. **7** *His strong religious belief helped him through a bad time. The suggestion has strong support:* keen, fervent, intense, deep, deep-seated, zealous, ardent, vehement, earnest, impassioned, fervid, fierce, confirmed, assiduous, faithful, devoted, sedulous, diligent, high-spirited, animated, spirited. **8** *I like my coffee strong. The fortune-teller used strong perfume:* highly flavoured, sharp, potent, concentrated, undiluted, tangy, highly-seasoned, pungent, highly-spiced, piquant, savoury, tart, biting, hot.

Ant. 1 weak, frail, feeble, powerless, soft. **2** unqualified. **3** passive, spiritless, submissive. **4** unconvincing, ineffectual, unsound; meek, mild, conciliatory. **5** slight, vague. **6** faint, dull, colourless. **7** shallow, spiritless, faint, apathetic, lethargic, half-hearted, wavering, insecure, unfaithful. **8** diluted, watery; faint, subtle; bland, tasteless, insipid; soothing, balmy; odourless.

stronghold *n.* **1** *The plan was to attack the enemy stronghold at midnight:* fortified place, fortress, fortification, fort, bulwark, battlement, citadel, bastion, fastness, stockade, rampart, keep, hold, redoubt. **2** *Oxford is a stronghold of tradition:* centre, refuge, home, locale; bulwark, bastion, citadel, rampart.

structure *n.* **1** *A large structure is being created on the old fairground:* building, construction, edifice. **2** *The structure of the song is symmetrical:* arrangement, form, make-up, organization, composition, interrelation of parts, configuration, conformation, formation, design.
—*v.* **3** *They structured the programme to appeal to all ages:* put together, construct, organize, arrange, design, assemble.
◇ *Word origin: Structure,* that which is built, comes from Latin *struere,* to build. From it we also get *construct,* to build; *construe,* to build up a meaning, infer; *destruction* and *destroy,* literally building down, to build down or "unbuild"; and *obstruct,* literally to build in front of, to block.

struggle *v.* **1** *He struggled with the intruder. He struggled against those who opposed his plan:* battle, fight, join issue, combat, contend, compete, vie, tussle, scuffle, skirmish, tilt, brush, duel, engage, match, exchange blows, spar, cross swords, lock horns, brawl, jostle, grapple, scrap; clash, argue, oppose, resist, differ, feud, quarrel. **2** *She had to struggle to meet the deadline:* strain, push, work hard, do all one can, exert oneself, labour, strive, take pains, endeavour, spare no pains, move heaven and earth, do one's utmost, leave no stone unturned, work like a Trojan.
—*n.* **3** *The emperor lost 1000 men in the struggle:* fight, conflict, battle, combat, war, engagement, encounter, action, strife. **4** *It was a struggle to stay awake:* strain, grind, trial, labour, long haul, exertion, effort, push, pull, endeavour, stress.
Ant. **1** surrender, give in, yield, succumb. **4** push-over.

strut *v. He strutted into the restaurant as though he owned it:* swagger, walk pompously, parade, sail, peacock.
Ant. cringe, cower, slink, sneak.

stub *n.* **1** *The ashtray is full of cigarette stubs. I can't write with this pencil stub:* stump, butt, end, fag-end, broken remnant, remains; tail. **2** *Keep your ticket stubs:* torn ticket, cancelled ticket, counterfoil; payment voucher, receipt.
—*v.* **3** *He stubbed his big toe on the kerb:* strike accidentally, scrape, bump, knock. **4** *He quickly stubbed out his cigarette:* snuff, crush, put out, extinguish.
◇ *Word origin: Stub* and *stubborn* come from Old English *stubb,* tree stump. Hence a *stub* is any short projecting part or a short or broken remnant, as a *pencil stub* or *cheque stub. Stubborn* literally means as unyielding as a tree stump.

stubborn *adj.* **1** *She's too stubborn to give in:* obstinate, unmovable, immovable, unyielding, obdurate, tenacious, opinionated, indomitable, unbending, intractable, intransigent, perverse, refractory, recalcitrant, headstrong, self-willed, wilful, uncompliant, inflexible, ungovernable, mulish, pigheaded, bull-headed, dogged. **2** *He made a stubborn attempt to break the lock:* purposeful, persistent, resolute, sturdy, strong, forceful, concerted, whole-hearted. **3** *I can't shake off this stubborn cold:* hard to handle or manage; tenacious, resistant.
Ant. **1** pliable, adaptable, tractable, flexible; irresolute, yielding, docile, manageable; vacillating, wavering, undecided. **2** weak, feeble, frail, half-hearted. **3** manageable.
◇ *Usage note: Stubborn* and *obstinate* both mean fixed and unchanging in opinion or action. A *stubborn* person sometimes sticks to his course for good or idealistic reasons: *He has a stubborn faith in justice.* An *obstinate* person often seems unreasonably determined not to change: *Aunt Edith is obstinate about not allowing a television set in the house.*

student *n.* **1** *How many students attend the local polytechnic?:* pupil, learner, scholar, undergraduate, matriculant; collegian, commoner; schoolgirl, schoolboy. **2** *A good reporter is a keen student of human nature:* observer, examiner, spectator, reviewer, watcher, interpreter, analyst, commentator, reader.
Ant. **1** teacher, professor, tutor, lecturer, demonstrator, mentor, instructor.

> "The value of a really great student to the country is equal to half a dozen grain elevators or a new transcontinental railway."
> —*William Osler*

studied *adj. The studied casualness of the stranger's manner put us on our guard:* calculated, deliberate, intentional, premeditated.
Ant. spontaneous, impulsive, unplanned, instinctive.

studious *adj.* **1** *The studious sister rarely goes to parties:* devoted to study, scholarly, academic, intellectual, erudite, brainy, cerebral, bookish. **2** *He made a studious effort to make us feel welcome:* earnest, diligent, painstaking, purposeful, laborious, determined, intent.
Ant. **1** fun-loving, frivolous; unscholarly. **2** idle, indulgent, careless, inattentive, thoughtless, negligent, indifferent.

study *n.* **1** *She got married and never ever finished her studies:* pursuit of knowledge, learning, education, school work, academic work, scholarship, instruction, mental cultivation,

reading. **2** *The committee made a study of the root causes of civil disorders:* investigation, inquiry, survey, research, examination, search, consideration, analysis, scrutiny, inspection, exploration, probe. **3** *The dictionary is in the study:* library, studio, reading room, office, den.
—*v.* **4** *He's studying for his exams:* read, learn, educate oneself, school oneself, pursue knowledge, *Informal* cram, grind, swot. **5** *The committee will study the proposal thoroughly. Astronomers studied the heavens for the predicted new comet:* plunge into, read up on, delve into, investigate, examine, inquire into, consider, explore, observe, probe, survey, search through, research. **6** *He studied the directions for putting up the tent:* examine, read closely, look at carefully, pore over, survey, review, glance over, peruse, scrutinize.

◇ *Word origin: Study, student, studio,* and *stooge* come from Latin *studere,* to apply oneself, be diligent, hence our words *study, studious,* and one who studies, a *student.* A *studio* was originally a place to study, but in Italian it came to mean a place where young painters studied or practised under a master, hence our modern concept of an *artist's studio. Stooge* was originally a slang word for student, later for an apprentice or assistant, and thus came to mean an assistant to a comedian.

stuff *n.* **1** *Have you got the stuff you need to make the rug? Hope is the stuff that dreams are made of:* raw material, material, staple; matter, substance, component, constituent, ingredient; essence, inmost substance, quintessence. **2** *Informal I left some of my stuff in Mother's attic:* things, effects, gear, belongings, possessions, paraphernalia, tackle. **3** *Informal That story is nothing but a lot of stuff:* nonsense, stuff and nonsense, bunk, empty talk, humbug, balderdash, rubbish, foolishness, trash, hooey, hokum, twaddle. **4** *Informal Now get out there and do your stuff!:* best, utmost, darndest; thing, bit, tricks, act, performance.
—*v.* **5** *She stuffed the trunk with her summer clothes:* pile, fill, fill up, jam, cram, load, pack, wad, heap, burden. **6** *It seems barbaric to stuff animals for decorative purposes. He stuffed the cushions with down:* fill with stuffing, fill, pad. **7** *She stuffed herself with chocolate:* gorge, cram, overeat, feed gluttonously, gluttonize, overindulge, satiate, sate, make a pig of. **8** *Just stuff the laundry into the machine:* load, pack, thrust, jam, cram, crowd, stash, cache, wedge, store, stow.
Ant. **3** facts, truth. **5** empty, unpack. **8** take out, remove.

◇ *Word origin:* See STOP.

stuffing *n.* **1** *He used straw as stuffing for the dolls:* filling, padding, wadding, packing. **2** *I add walnuts to my stuffing for the turkey:* dressing, filling, forcemeat.

stuffy *adj.* **1** *The subway is unbearably stuffy in the summer:* close, unventilated, ill-ventilated, fusty, suffocating, stagnant, heavy, stifling, muggy, musty, sultry, sweltering, stale-smelling, oppressive, airless. **2** *My nose is stuffy:* congested, stopped up, stuffed up, clogged up, blocked up. **3** *We expected and got a stuffy response from that prig:* cold, reserved, strait-laced, prim, narrow-minded, sanctimonious, humourless, priggish.
Ant. **1** airy, well-ventilated, cool. **2** unclogged. **3** natural, warm, liberal, generous, enthusiastic.

stultify *v. Nothing stultifies a student's enthusiasm more than a dull teacher:* vitiate, make useless, cripple, hamstring, impair, reduce to absurdity, nullify, frustrate, suppress, thwart, inhibit.
Ant. arouse, encourage, spark, enliven, animate, spur, inspire.

◇ *Word origin: Stultify* comes from Latin *stultus* (foolish) + *facere* (to make), hence to make foolish.

stumble *v.* **1** *She stumbled over a stool in the darkened room:* trip, stagger, pitch forward; fall, take a spill, sprawl, lurch, topple. **2** *He stumbled out of the bar to look for a cab:* stagger, reel, walk unsteadily, totter, sway, flounder, hobble, shamble, pitch, roll. **3** *The actor stumbled over his lines:* blunder, slip up, make mistakes, falter; hash up, botch, mess up, bungle. **4** *I stumbled upon the answer to the riddle:* happen, fall, blunder, hit, come by chance.
—*n.* **5** *She broke her ankle in that stumble over the bike:* trip, stagger, misstep, spill, fall, topple.

stump *n.* **1** *We used the stump as a table:* tree stump, stub. **2** *After the extraction it was discovered that the dentist had left the stump of my wisdom tooth still in my jaw:* stub, butt, end.
—*v.* **3** *The crime stumped the entire murder squad:* mystify, baffle, dumbfound, perplex, foil, bewilder, confound, stymie, befog, confuse, nonplus, *Informal* bamboozle. **4** *Try not to stump up the stairs:* stamp, stomp, tramp, thud, clump, walk heavily.

stun *v.* **1** *The blow on the head stunned him for a few moments:* daze, stagger, stupefy, numb. **2** *Her sudden tantrum stunned us:* shock, dumbfound, stupefy, amaze, astonish, astound, flabbergast.

◇ *Word origin: Stun* and *stunning* come from the Latin prefix *ex-* (thoroughly) + *tonare* (to thunder, crash), hence to stupefy as by a thunderclap.

stunning *adj.* **1** *The fighter received a stunning blow on the head. The news was stunning:* dazing, stupefying, numbing; dumbfounding, amazing, astounding, shocking, startling, flabbergasting, astonishing, staggering. **2** *Her stunning outfit made everyone turn to look at her:* striking, strikingly attractive, beautiful, lovely, exquisite, electrifying.
Ant. **1** mild, harmless; expected, commonplace, ordinary. **2** plain, ordinary, run-of-the-mill, unimpressive, unremarkable.

stunt[1] *v. It used to be said that smoking would stunt one's growth:* check, dwarf, curb, stint, limit, delimit, restrain, restrict, cramp, stifle, suppress, abort.

Ant. increase, stimulate.

◇ *Word origin: Stunt*[1] to dwarf, was an Old English word meaning "dull" that was influenced in its sense-development by the cognate Old Norse *stutt* (probably *stuntr* in an earlier form of the language), meaning "short."

stunt[2] *n. That last stunt on the trapeze brought cheers from the crowd:* trick, act, feat, number, turn.

stupefy *v.* **1** *The fall from the ladder stupefied him:* daze, stun, shock, make punch-drunk, make one feel punchy. **2** *News of the bombing stupefied the nation:* daze, flabbergast, stagger, amaze, astound, dumbfound, astonish, confound, surprise, overwhelm, nonplus.

stupendous *adj.* **1** *What a stupendous idea!:* remarkable, astounding, extraordinary, wonderful, astonishing, marvellous, terrific, great, fabulous, unusual, prodigious, incredible, stunning, amazing, surprising, unexpected. **2** *The stupendous block of flats dwarfed the rest of the neighbourhood:* gigantic, huge, mammoth, vast, enormous, prodigious, tremendous, immense, massive, giant, colossal, very large, imposing, big, titanic, jumbo, very great, mighty, Herculean, Cyclopean, monstrous, gargantuan, elephantine.

Ant. 1 ordinary, unsurprising. **2** small, little, modest, diminutive, lilliputian, wee, tiny.

stupid *adj.* **1** *A stupid class is difficult to teach:* dull, dumb, brainless, witless, unintelligent, dense, simple-minded, simple, slow-learning, backward, weak-minded, doltish, rattle-brained, empty-headed; muddle-headed, dim-witted, duncelike, obtuse, oafish; idiotic, half-witted, imbecile, imbecilic, moronic, cretinous. **2** *The boy's stupid behaviour got him into trouble. The general made a stupid decision:* foolish, irresponsible, unwise, reckless, indiscriminating, imprudent, ill-advised, ill-considered, ill-judged, mistaken, absent-minded, heedless, foolhardy, thoughtless, unintelligent, idiotic, silly, childish, inane, senseless, nonsensical, unreasonable, inappropriate, fatuous, asinine; tactless, indiscreet, boorish. **3** *We left in the middle of the stupid show:* senseless, meaningless, absurd, silly, nonsensical, pointless, irrelevant, inept, inconsequential, preposterous, aimless, purposeless, asinine.

Ant. intelligent. **1** bright, clever, shrewd, quick, sharp, responsive. **2** smart, sensible, wise, thoughtful, tactful, prudent, well-advised, adult, mature, reasonable, canny, appropriate. **3** meaningful, interesting, deep, relevant, consequential, purposeful, sensible.

◇ *Word origin: Stupid, stupefy, stupor,* and *stupendous* all come from Latin *stupere,* to be amazed (from the fact that many stupid people go about wide-eyed and open-mouthed, as if in a state of unending amazement).

"The only thing that ever consoles a man for the stupid things he does is the praise he always gives himself for doing them."

—*Oscar Wilde*

---

stupor *n.* **1** *The drug caused a state more like a stupor than natural sleep:* stunned condition, near-unconsciousness, stupefaction, coma, numbness, somnolence. **2** *The defeated nation recovered from its stupor and began to rebuild:* torpor, apathy, inertness, inertia, lethargy, daze, coma.

sturdy *adj.* **1** *We need several sturdy men to push this car:* strong, mighty, muscular, rugged, powerful, robust, tough, burly, vigorous, stout, stalwart, forceful, sinewy, strapping, hardy, able. **2** *This chair is not sturdy enough to stand on:* solid, substantial, sound, strong, heavy, secure, tough, rugged, lasting, durable, well-constructed, well-made, well-built. **3** *He put up a sturdy fight to the end:* brave, courageous, gallant, resolute, stout-hearted, intrepid, valiant, unshrinking, spirited, stout, indomitable, undaunted, dauntless, heroic, firm, daring, invincible, doughty, plucky, dogged, high-spirited, fearless, unabashed, gritty, determined, stubborn, enduring, defiant, *Informal* spunky, gutsy.

Ant. weak. **1** frail, feeble, powerless. **2** fragile, unsubstantial, light, flimsy. **3** cowardly, fearful, irresolute, shrinking.

Stygian *adj. We descended the staircase to the Stygian depths of the castle's dungeon:* infernal, hellish; dreary, sombre, murky, dark, funereal, gloomy, dim, black, starless, tenebrous, unlighted.

Ant. Olympian, bright, light, cheerful, sunny, lighted.

◇ *Word origin: Stygian* and the river *Styx* ("the Hateful"), one of the five rivers surrounding Hades, come from Greek *stugein,* to hate.

style *n.* **1** *De Quincey's style is verbose and Hemingway's is terse:* typical mode of expression, manner, characteristic tone. **2** *The wealthy couple live in style:* luxury, elegance, pomp, comfort, affluence. **3** *He handled the awkward situation with style:* grace, smoothness, polish, aplomb, savoir-faire, charm, taste, flair, *French* élan. **4** *Platform shoes are back in style. Last year's style was too way-out for me:* fashion, vogue, currency, favour; trend, mode, rage. **5** *Which style of writing-paper do you prefer?:* type, kind, sort, pattern, model.

—*v.* **6** *She styled my hair in a page-boy:* design, arrange, give style to. **7** *He styles himself a revolutionary:* call, name, designate.

Ant. 1 substance, content, essence. **2** squalor, drabness, simplicity. **3** awkwardness, tastelessness, gaucheness.

◇ *Word origin: Style* and *stylish* come from Latin *stilus,* stylus, an iron-pointed peg or other instrument for writing on wax tablets, later one's individual manner of writing, hence manner, appearance, fashion. The spelling of *style* is based on a very old error. We should be spelling it *stile* (after Latin *stilus*) had not some writers of late antiquity imagined that the word was derived from Greek *stulos,* pillar. Greek *u* is transliterated as Latin *y,* so these writers respelt it *stylus,* and we have inherited their error.

stylish *adj. My aunt is a stylish dresser:* fashionable, chic, voguish, in vogue, modish, up-to-date, up-to-the-minute, latest, in fashion, à la mode, new, modern, smart, elegant, sophisticated, *Slang* with-it, swinging, trendy.

Ant. unstylish, unfashionable, passé, out-of-date, outmoded, dowdy, old-fashioned.

stymie *v. The riddle stymied us all:* stump, mystify, confound, puzzle, confuse; block, thwart, hinder, frustrate, obstruct.

◇ *Word origin:* In its literal sense, *stymie* is a golf term for a situation in which an opponent's ball lies directly between the player's ball and the hole, blocking it. Hence *stymie* has come to mean to frustrate or confound. (The verb to *snooker* means much the same in the game of snooker and has a similar transferred sense of "thwart".)

suave *adj. He's as suave as a diplomat:* urbane, smooth, polished, gracious, politic, civilized, diplomatic, charming, affable, mannerly, elegant; flattering, politic, diplomatic, ingratiating.

subconscious *adj. The thief must have had a subconscious desire to be caught:* subliminal, half-conscious, intuitive, instinctive, dawning, dim; automatic.

Ant. conscious, explicit, expressed, clear.

◇ *Usage note:* See UNCONSCIOUS.

subdue *v.* **1** *The police used tear-gas to subdue the rioters:* overcome, crush, master, quell, put down, overpower, down, still, smash, subject, subjugate, oppress, defeat, foil, overwhelm, thrash, drub, whip, trim, rout, triumph over, conquer, vanquish, get the upper hand over, trample, floor, overrun, surmount, break, bow, reduce, get the better of. **2** *His soothing words subdued her fears:* calm, reduce, curb, check, moderate, palliate, mellow, soften, temper, assuage, ease, allay, salve, soothe, tranquillize, slacken, mollify, relieve, appease, deaden, mitigate, ameliorate, meliorate. **3** *Try to subdue your laughter:* tone down, moderate, quieten down, mute, muffle, soften, soft-pedal.

Ant. 2 awaken, quicken, arouse, provoke, inflame, agitate, irritate. **3** vent, unleash.

subject *n.* **1** *Gothic architecture was the subject of the seminar:* topic, matter, subject matter, matter in hand, theme, substance, issue, motif, point at issue, question, point in question; concern, case, affair, business; thesis, text; gist, pith. **2** *How many subjects are you studying this term?:* branch of knowledge, field, study, discipline. **3** *The Queen has many loyal subjects:* follower, dependent, subordinate; liege, vassal; citizen.

—*adj.* **4** *We are subject to the law of the land:* bound by, owing allegiance, owing obedience; subservient, subordinate, at another's command, answerable, subjected, obedient. **5** *The date of our visit is subject to my firm's holiday schedule:* dependent upon, conditional upon, contingent on, stipulatory. **6** *He is subject to violent fits of temper:* susceptible, vulnerable, open, liable, prone, disposed, exposed, at the mercy of, in danger of.

—*v.* **7** *The hurricane subjected the islanders to devastating floods:* expose, put through, cause to undergo or experience, submit. **8** *His rude behaviour subjects him to frequent rebuffs:* make liable, lay open, bare, expose.

Ant. 3 sovereign, ruler. **5** independent, unrelated. **6** invulnerable, unsusceptible, undisposed. **8** exempt, protect.

◇ *Pronunciation tip: Subject* is, of course, correctly pronounced one way as a noun, a *subject,* and another way as a verb, *to subject.* The noun is stressed on the first syllable, a *SUB-ject: We'll discuss the SUB-ject later.* The verb is stressed on the second syllable, to *sub-JECT: The guards sub-JECT-ed the prisoner to harsh treatment.*

"I think that we should be men first, and subjects afterward." —*Henry David Thoreau*

---

subjective *adj. Bill has never done anything wrong, so I suppose my dislike of him is purely subjective:* personal, emotional, inner, individual, partial, partisan, biased.

Ant. objective, impersonal; external, concrete, tangible; impartial, unbiased.

subjugate *adj. Conquistadors subjugated the Aztecs:* conquer, subdue, make subservient, vanquish, overmaster, reduce to submission, lay one's yoke upon, bring under the yoke, dominate, quell, tame.

Ant. release, free, liberate.

◇ *Word origin: Subjugate* literally means "bring under the yoke" (Latin *jugum,* yoke). The original root meaning is "join," and, in fact, our word *join* comes from the same root as Latin *jugum* and English *yoke* (its Latin ancestor is *jungere,* to join). Also related is Sanskrit *yoga,* yoke, from which we get our word *yoga.* (Yoga is so-called because it *joins* or *yokes* body and mind.)

sublime *adj.* **1** *A classic example of the sublime style in prose narrative is the opening chapter of the*

Book of Genesis: lofty, exalted, imposing, elevated, noble, majestic, grand, stately, high, high-wrought, awe-inspiring. **2** *Her performance was sublime:* excellent, splendid, superb, very good, marvellous; estimable, praiseworthy; wonderful, great, terrific.
Ant. 1 low, ordinary, everyday, commonplace. **2** poor, bad, ordinary, mediocre.
◇ *Word origin: Sublime* and *sublimate* come from Latin *sub-* (under) + *limen* (lintel, threshold), to rise up from under the threshold into the air, hence elevated, lofty, supreme. In psychology, to *sublimate* means to convert unconscious drives and desires into acceptable social outlets.

submerge *v.* **1** *She submerged the clothes in the soapy water. The submarine submerged:* plunge, put or go under water, immerse, submerse, sink, souse, douse, go under, dive, go down. **2** *The raging waters submerged the tiny village:* inundate, cover with water, flood, engulf, cover completely, stream over, deluge, pour over, drown.
Ant. 1 surface, emerge. **2** uncover.

submission *n.* **1** *In a gesture of submission, the rebel kissed the king's feet. Her present submission is actuated solely by her fear of being punished:* submitting, yielding, giving in, surrender, capitulation; submissiveness, obedience, compliance, non-resistance, passivity, passiveness, meekness, tractability, tameness. **2** *The deadline for submission of entries is June 1st:* handing in, presentation, remittance, submitting, tendering.
Ant. 1 resistance, rebellion, mutiny; rebelliousness, disobedience, defiance.

submissive *adj. Stand up and fight for your rights instead of being submissive:* obedient, yielding, meek, unresisting, deferential, pliant, docile, compliant, complaisant, acquiescent, malleable, passive, capitulating, dutiful, unassertive, tractable, accommodating; truckling, toadying, obsequious, slavish, servile, fawning, ingratiating, subservient, crawling, bootlicking.
Ant. rebellious, disobedient, haughty, proud, arrogant, unyielding, defiant, refractory, resistant, assertive, masterful.

submit *v.* **1** *The captain submitted to his mutinous crew:* give in, give up, surrender, yield, succumb, accede, bow, resign oneself, capitulate, cede, bend, knuckle under, acquiesce, acknowledge defeat, kneel, stoop, lay down one's arms, defer, prostrate oneself, humble oneself, comply, hoist the white flag, throw up the sponge, throw in the towel. **2** *He submitted to hypnotism in order to stop smoking:* subject oneself, expose oneself, acquiesce, agree; resort. **3** *My cousin submitted his plans for a playground to the city council:* present, tender, put forward, put forth, commit, suggest, hold out, volunteer, offer, proffer. **4** *I submit that the prosecution's case is a tissue of lies:* suggest, claim, contend, assert, propose, argue.
Ant. 1, 2 resist, withstand, fight, defy. **3** withdraw.

subordinate *adj.* **1** *A private is subordinate to a corporal:* lower in rank, of low rank, inferior, outranked, junior, subaltern; subservient, ancillary, auxiliary, subsidiary, secondary, subject; lesser, lower.
—n. **2** *He treated his subordinates like slaves:* person of lower rank, inferior, assistant, junior, help, worker, dependent, attendant; servant, underling, hireling, lackey, menial.
Ant. 1, 2 superior, senior. **1** higher, primary; leading, prominent. **2** chief, master, leader, supervisor, boss.
◇ *Word origin: Subordinate* comes from Latin *sub-* (under) + *ordinare* (to order), set in a lower order, belonging to a lower rank.

sub rosa *adv. We were suspicious because the deal was made sub rosa:* confidentially, secretly, in secret, privately, in private, covertly, under the rose, behind closed doors, behind the scenes, off the record, *Informal* on the sly, on the quiet.
Ant. openly, publicly, overtly.
◇ *Word origin: Sub rosa* is Latin for "under the rose." A rose was the customary emblem of secrecy hung by the Romans over a secret meeting, from the myth that Cupid once gave Harpocrates, the god of silence, a rose in exchange for his promise to keep the secrets of Venus.

subscribe *v.* **1** *He subscribed generously to the new school:* pledge money, promise to give, contribute, donate, open one's purse strings, lend one's aid, help, *Informal* chip in. **2** *The lawyer invited his client to subscribe the affidavit:* sign, undersign, set one's name to, affix one's signature to. **3** *Do you subscribe to many magazines?:* have a subscription, receive a periodical by post. **4** *I don't subscribe to the idea that money brings happiness:* lend approval, assent, consent; go along with, hold with, support, endorse.
Ant. 4 be opposed, dissent.

subsequent *adj. The first volume cost £10, but all subsequent ones were £8:* ensuing, succeeding, following, successive.
Ant. previous, preceding.

subservient *adj.* **1** *His subservient attitude to his boss makes me wince:* excessively submissive, fawning, obsequious, toadying, servile, slavish, ingratiating, sycophantic, bootlicking, menial, cringing, docile, truckling, prostrate. **2** *A good leader's policies must be subservient to the needs of the people:* subordinate, subsidiary, subject, auxiliary, contributory, accessory, ancillary.
Ant. 1 domineering, overbearing, assertive, masterful, *Slang* bossy; disobedient, rebellious. **2** superior.
◇ *Word origin: Subservient* comes from Latin *sub-* (under) + *servire* (to serve), which also

gives us our words *serve, servant, service,* and *servitude.*

subside *v.* **1** *As the land subsides, the sea advances:* settle, sink; drop, cave in. **2** *My nervousness subsided when the plane landed. The crowds subsided:* diminish, lessen, abate, decrease, wane, moderate, ebb, calm, recede, melt away, let up, ease, shrink, dwindle.

Ant. 1, 2 rise; increase, swell. **2** grow, wax, heighten, intensify.

subsidiary *adj.* **1** *In addition to his salary, he receives subsidiary income from investments:* supplementary, supplemental, additional, extra. **2** *He never got beyond a subsidiary position in the firm:* secondary, junior, subordinate, lower, lesser, minor, inferior.

—n. **3** *This generator is a subsidiary to our main power supply:* auxiliary, addition, supplement, adjunct, accessory. **4** *He works for the corporation's subsidiary in Bolton:* subsidiary company, affiliate, division, branch.

Ant. 1, 2 primary, principal, main, chief, major, most important. **2** senior, leading, superior. **4** parent company, main office.

subsist *v. The survivors of the crash subsisted on coconuts and bananas:* live, survive, exist, stay alive, sustain oneself, nourish oneself, support life, feed oneself; eke out a living, keep body and soul together, make ends meet.

Ant. die, perish, starve.

subsistence *n. The few pounds he took home every Friday were barely enough for the family's subsistence:* survival, continued existence, maintenance, nourishment, sustenance, support, upkeep; livelihood, living.

substance *n.* **1** *Of what substance does a meteorite consist? There was a sticky substance on the floor:* material, matter, stuff; ingredient, constituent, element. **2** *Our fears had substance — the house was indeed on fire:* corporality, substantiality, corporeality, corporealness, reality, actuality; solidity, body, real content. **3** *The substance of her argument was that we had treated her unfairly:* burden, core, thrust, main point, essence, import, germ, soul, keynote, connotation, gist, basic idea, purport; intent, pith, marrow, heart; sum and substance, quintessence, backbone, sense, force. **4** *Our elderly grocer was not exactly a person of substance:* affluence, property, money, means, wealth, riches.

substantial *adj.* **1** *Turkey had a substantial tobacco crop this year:* sizeable, considerable, plentiful, plenteous, large, ample, big, full, abundant. **2** *For an unschooled man, he exhibits a substantial understanding of economics:* firm, solid, sound. **3** *The banker built himself a substantial house in Richmond:* big, bulky, monumental, massive.

Ant. 1 insubstantial, poor, meagre, small, paltry, inconsiderable, scanty. **2** slight, weak, unsound, feeble. **3** small, tatty, jerry-built; lightweight, slender.

substantiate *v. You haven't substantiated your argument at all:* verify, corroborate, prove, demonstrate, show to be true, authenticate.

Ant. disprove, refute, discredit, undermine, tear to shreds, explode.

substitute *n.* **1** *For celebrations, there is no substitute for champagne. The regular teacher is ill, so a substitute is teaching today:* alternate, replacement, deputy, supply, fill-in, surrogate, makeshift, stopgap, temporary, stand-by, understudy, locum, ersatz.

—v. **2** *She substituted a fake diamond for the original:* exchange, change. **3** *Her brother substituted as host while her husband was away:* fill in, take over, stand in, act.

—adj. **4** *The School Board hired a substitute teacher:* supply, surrogate, alternate, stand-in, replacement, temporary.

subterfuge *n. Why didn't they tell us immediately rather than resort to this subterfuge?:* scheme, artifice, trick, stratagem, dodge, deception, evasion, shift, smoke-screen, ruse, blind, machination, wile, imposture; sham, chicanery, deviousness, sneakiness, game-playing, intrigue, scheming, guile, duplicity, pretence, evasiveness, camouflage, sophistry, casuistry, make-believe.

Ant. straightforwardness, openness, honesty.

◇ *Word origin: Subterfuge* comes from Latin *subter-* (secretly under) + *fugere* (to flee), to escape secretly or "under cover," hence any stratagem to avoid detection or difficulty.

subtle *adj.* **1** *The message of the film was subtle and indirect. There's a subtle hint of garlic in the sauce:* understated, indirect, delicate, light, refined, fine. **2** *His subtle understanding of labour problems qualified him for the job:* fine, keen, sharp, astute, skilful, masterly, discriminating, discerning, sophisticated, perspicacious, clever, deft, expert, quick. **3** *I fall for that subtle ploy every time!:* sly, tricky, crafty, wily, foxy, cagey, cunning, artful, slick, designing, devious, deceptive, shifty, underhand.

Ant. 1 heavy-handed, blunt, obvious, direct. **2** unskilful, undiscerning, undiscriminating, unsophisticated. **3** obvious, artless.

◇ *Pronunciation tip: Subtle* is pronounced *suttle.* (*Suttle* is, in fact, Milton's spelling of the word.) Sixteenth-century humanists inserted the *b* to remind us that the word comes from Latin *subtilis.* They also introduced *subtile,* pronounced *suttle* or *sub-tle,* which is an archaic literary variant of *subtle.*

succeed *v.* **1** *The experiment succeeded. He didn't succeed in borrowing his father's car:* be fruitful, turn out successfully, be effective, be efficacious, do well, make a hit, bear fruit, click, hit, catch, strike oil, attain a goal, achieve one's aim, triumph, prevail, gain one's end, avail, win, hit the jackpot. **2** *He eventually succeeded as a playwright:* attain fame, prosper, attain wealth, come into one's own, make a hit, triumph, find fulfilment, gain one's end, strike oil. **3** *Louis XIV succeeded Louis XIII. Who will succeed to the throne?:* accede, move up, come next in order, become heir; assume the office of, take over, come into possession of, inherit; follow, come afterward, be subsequent to, take the place of, replace.

Ant. 1, 2 fail, flop, fall short, miss. **3** precede.

◇ *Spelling tip:* Only three common words in the English language end in *-ceed: succeed, exceed,* and *proceed.* Learn these *-ceed* words now: *sucCEED, exCEED, proCEED.*

succeeding *adj. The new law will apply to this and all succeeding cases:* subsequent, ensuing, consequent, successive, following, future, later, impending, coming, oncoming, posterior.

Ant. preceding, foregoing, earlier, previous, prior, former.

success *n.* **1** *The success of the school fête was greater than we could have hoped:* happy outcome, triumph, fulfilment. **2** *His success surprised those who remembered him as a poor student:* attainment, prosperity, good fortune, achievement, advancement, ascendancy, fame, eminence, conquest, triumph, affluence. **3** *Was the charity ball a success?:* well-received venture, hit, triumph, victory.

Ant. 1-3 failure, disaster, downfall, collapse.

"The secret of success is constancy to purpose." —*Benjamin Disraeli*

---

successful *adj.* **1** *Because the timing was perfect, the surprise was totally successful:* triumphant, effective, efficacious, achieved, fruitful. **2** *She is a successful businesswoman:* prosperous, flourishing, thriving, rich, well-off, affluent, wealthy; proven, acknowledged.

Ant. 1, 2 unsuccessful. **1** defeated. **2** unprosperous, failed.

succession *n.* **1** *The endless succession of parties wore us out:* series, procession, sequence, chain, round, cycle, run, train. **2** *His succession to the party leadership is in dispute:* taking over, assumption, accession, inheritance.

successive *adj. He underwent four successive operations in two weeks:* succeeding, following one after another, consecutive.

succinct *adj. His comments were detailed but succinct:* to the point, terse, expressed in few words, brief, direct, clipped, concise, neat, condensed, compact, sparing of words, epigrammatic, short, tight, summary, crisp, pithy, gnomic, aphoristic.

Ant. discursive, rambling, maundering, circuitous, prolix, wordy, verbose, long-winded.

succour *n.* **1** *The volunteers gave succour to the wounded:* help, sustenance, relief, aid, accommodation, helping hand, comfort, assistance, support, maintenance.

—*v.* **2** *The local vicar was always quick to succour those in need:* aid, assist, comfort, lend a hand to, help, relieve, support, sustain, nurture, wait on, minister to, nurse, take care of, render assistance to, back up, give a lift to, protect, shield, befriend.

succumb *v.* **1** *He succumbed after a long illness:* die, pass away, expire, go under. **2** *He finally succumbed to her pleading:* give in, yield, give way, submit, accede, capitulate, surrender; fall victim to.

Ant. 1 live, survive. **2** resist, fight, hold firm.

◇ *Word origin: Succumb* comes from the Latin prefix *sub-* (under) + *cubare* (to lie, sleep), hence to lie down.

sudden *adj. He came to a sudden stop. Don't make sudden decisions:* abrupt, quick, speedy, rapid, immediate, instant, instantaneous; hasty, impetuous, precipitate, rash; unlooked-for, unanticipated, unforeseen, unforeseeable.

Ant. slow, gradual; deliberate; foreseen, anticipated, expected.

◇ *Word origin: Sudden* comes from Latin *sub-* (under, underneath) + *ire* (to come or go), to come "under," i.e., stealthily. (Sudden events come without warning.)

suddenly *adv. Suddenly the lights went out:* abruptly, all of a sudden, without warning, all at once, unexpectedly, at short notice, on the spur of the moment, in an instant, before one knows it, on the spot, in the twinkling of an eye, in no time.

Ant. gradually, slowly, deliberately, not unexpectedly.

sue *v.* **1** *They sued the removal firm for ruining the furniture:* bring a civil action against, litigate against, institute legal proceedings against, prefer a claim against, start a lawsuit against. **2** *The condemned man sued for mercy:* beg, plead, beseech, entreat, appeal, make appeal to, importune, implore, supplicate, petition, pray.

suffer *v.* **1** *She suffered greatly as a child. Is he suffering much from his injuries?:* feel distress, lament, despair, go through a lot, bear the cross, pine, grieve; feel pain, agonize, ache, hurt. **2** *His work suffers when he has problems at home:* deteriorate, fall off, be impaired, drop off. **3** *If the watch wasn't insured, she'll have to suffer the loss:* endure, bear, sustain, go through, undergo, tolerate, bear with, withstand, stand, stomach, put up with.

suffering *n.* **1** *She refused to talk about her family's suffering during the war:* sorrow, distress, travail, heartache, heavy heart, grief, misery, dolour, woe, tribulation, care, anxiety, anguish, trial. **2** *The medicine should ease the suffering:* ache, pain, hurt, soreness, irritation, torture, affliction, agony, discomfort, pang, misery, twinge, distress, throe, torment.

Ant. 1 pleasure, joy, happiness.

sufficient *adj. Have we sufficient petrol for the journey?:* enough, adequate, ample, plenty, satisfactory, up to the mark, plentiful.

Ant. insufficient, deficient, inadequate, wanting, meagre, scant, not enough.

suggest *v.* **1** *I suggest that we leave early for the airport. The letter suggested that a new clinic should be built:* recommend, advocate, move, urge, advise, propose, bid, counsel, posit, submit, propound, advance. **2** *His restlessness suggested that his backache had returned:* intimate, hint at, imply, lead one to believe, indicate, give a clue.

suggestion *n.* **1** *I followed his suggestion that I should try to lose weight:* advice, prompting, counsel, urging, recommendation, exhortation; pointer, tip. **2** *There's only a suggestion of rum in this cake:* suspicion, shade, hint, trace, touch, dash, grain, taste, tinge, tint, soupçon, dab, sprinkling, feeling, intimation.

suggestive *adj.* **1** *This silly old song is suggestive of my youth:* reminiscent, evocative, expressive, allusive, remindful. **2** *His suggestive remarks shocked the young lady:* improper, lewd, indelicate, indecent, loose, shameless, wanton, seductive, sexual, licentious, risqué, bawdy; stimulating, prurient, provocative.

Ant. 2 decent, delicate, chaste, clean.

> **Exploring the Word:** *Suggest* comes from Latin *sub-* (under) + *gerere* (to carry, bear, conduct), hence to carry up from below, or "bring up," something, i.e., to mention, introduce, or propose it. Latin *gerere* also gives us: *belligerent* (Latin *bellum*, war), carrying on war; *congestion* (Latin *con-*, with), carrying or conducting with others, hence crowded, crowding; *gestate*, to carry young in the womb; *gesture* and *gesticulate*, to carry, conduct, or bear oneself, later to make a movement that is part of one's conduct; *ingest*, to carry in, as to ingest food by eating; and *jest*, originally that which is carried on, a deed or exploit, later a narrative of an exploit (a romantic adventure story), and finally any witty story or humorous remark.

suit *n.* **1** *His new suit doesn't fit well. John wore a sailor suit to the party:* set of garments, outfit; jacket and trousers, jacket and skirt; garb, clothing, costume, clothes, apparel, habit, habiliment, raiment, trappings, duds, get-up, attire, accoutrements, togs; livery, uniform. **2** *She responded graciously to her wooer's suit:* courtship, court, wooing, blandishment, addresses, love-making, attentions, overtures. **3** *His suit for mercy was very moving:* plea, appeal, solicitation, entreaty, begging, supplication, prayer, petition.

—*v.* **4** *The architecture of the house should suit the rugged landscape:* conform to, match, befit, fit, beseem, correspond to, be proper for, harmonize with, fall in with, agree with, square with, go along with, be appropriate to, be congruous with, tally with, accord with, dovetail with, comport with. **5** *Outdoor living suits you:* become, be appropriate for, befit, be suitable for, be becoming to, do one good. **6** *A later flight suits me even better:* be acceptable to, be convenient to, accommodate, content, oblige, be agreeable to, seem good to; make glad, gratify, satisfy, please, gladden.

Ant. 4 disagree with, be inappropriate to, not go with. **6** inconvenience, discommode.

◇ *Usage note:* Don't confuse *suit* (rhymes with *mute*) and *suite* (rhymes with *wheat*). A *suit* is a coat with matching trousers or skirt, a series of playing cards, a proceeding in a court of law, or the courting of a woman. Thus, *a blue serge suit. In the game of bridge, hearts and spades are the major suits. The managing director brought a suit against the embezzler. Romeo paid suit to Juliet.* A *suite* is a set of related rooms, matching furniture, or a musical composition: *Reserve the bridal suite at the hotel. The living-room suite included the sofa and the chair for only £299. Tchaikovsky's "Nutcracker Suite" is my favourite piece of music.*

suitable *adj. Is this dress suitable for such a formal affair? The minister's words were suitable to the sad occasion:* proper, appropriate, meet, fitting, fit, befitting, seemly, right, adequate, apt, qualified, cut out for, becoming, worthy, apropos, applicable, congruous, seasonable, relevant, pertinent, germane, commensurate.

Ant. unsuitable, inappropriate, unbecoming, improper, incompatible, dissonant, inconsistent, unfit, unseemly, out of place.

suitcase *n. I packed my suitcase last night:* bag; (*variously*) valise, grip, satchel, travelling-bag, overnight bag, Gladstone bag, portmanteau; duffle bag, rucksack, knapsack.

suitor *n. She had many handsome suitors in her youth:* beau, boy-friend, lover, admirer, love, flame, wooer, swain, sweetheart.

sulk *v. He sulked about not winning the race:* pout, be sullen, wear a long face, mope, show ill temper, be in a huff, be disgruntled, be resentful, be in a pet, grumble, fret, be out of humour, be miffed, fume, be put out, chafe, grouch, scowl, frown, glower, look glum.

sullen *adj. She couldn't appease the sullen child:* ill-tempered, gloomy, ill-humoured, brooding, grumpy, out of humour, out of sorts, surly, glowering, sulky, crabbed, resentful, grouchy, sour, morose, scowling, peevish, petulant, splenetic, sore, grim, ill-natured, temperamental, glum, saturnine, moody, unsociable, crabby, unamiable, cross, touchy.

Ant. cheerful, happy, gay, smiling, sociable, merry, amiable.

sultry *adj.* **1** *No one feels like working in this sultry weather:* sweltering, suffocating, stifling, oppressive, close, stuffy, warm and damp, humid, hot and moist, muggy, sweaty. **2** *The waitress brushed past the lorry driver with a sultry sidelong glance:* erotic, hot, voluptuous, sexy, sensual, provocative.

◇ *Word origin: Sultry* was originally a variant of the word *swelter.*

summarily *adv. The foreman summarily dismissed two of the workers:* at short notice, unhesitatingly, on the spur of the moment, precipitately, arbitrarily, without delay, on the spot, promptly, with dispatch, immediately, straight away, straightway, directly, at once, quickly, speedily, forthwith.

summary *n.* **1** *His summary of the case omitted the most important facts:* digest, concise statement, short version, brief, abstract, résumé, detailed outline, précis, survey, *Informal* rundown; abridgement, recapitulation, condensation, breakdown, epitome, syllabus, synopsis, sketch, abbreviation, sum and substance, analysis, aperçu.
—*adj.* **2** *He had time for only a summary report:* short, brief, hasty, concise, abridged, succinct, condensed, terse, curt, hurried; perfunctory, token, cursory. **3** *It was a summary verdict:* unceremoniously fast, rapid, done without consideration, peremptory, conducted without delay, hasty, quickly performed, instantaneous, sudden.
Ant. **2** complete, full, detailed, lengthy. **3** deliberate, considered, slow.

summit *n. From the base camp they reached the summit in twenty-six hours. He is now at the summit of his career:* peak, crest, highest point, apex, height, top, pinnacle, zenith, apogee; acme, crowning point, culminating point, culmination, climax.
Ant. base, bottom, depth, nadir, all-time low.

> **Exploring the Word**: We commonly add a column of figures from top to bottom, writing the total at the bottom, but the Romans added a column of figures from bottom to top. We still call the total of a column of figures the *sum,* from Latin *summus,* highest (literally the topmost number), from this Roman method of addition, and still speak of *summing up,* even though we have added down through a column of figures. Latin *summus,* highest, also gives us *summary,* a summing up of facts or important ideas, hence an abstract or boiled-down version. A *summit* is the highest part of a mountain, or the highest level or rank, as a *summit meeting* between heads of state.

summon *v.* **1** *Summon the police quickly!:* call for, beckon, send for, rouse; call together, muster, activate, call into action, gather, call out. **2** *The prosecutor summoned three witnesses:* call, command to appear, subpoena, serve with a writ. **3** *She had to summon all her strength to face them again:* call forth, call on, invoke, command, muster, call into action, gather, draw on, strain.
Ant. **1** dismiss, discharge.

sumptuous *adj. A sumptuous meal was served to the visiting dignitaries:* splendid, luxurious, magnificent, grand, regal, spectacular, elaborate, lavish, munificent, elegant, superb; dear, costly, expensive, rich, de luxe, *Slang* posh.
Ant. plain, ordinary, cheap.
◇ *Word origin: Sumptuous,* luxurious, showing lavish expenditure, comes from Latin *sumptus,* expenditure.

sunny *adj.* **1** *Let's sit in a sunny spot. Yesterday was a sunny day:* sunshiny, bright, sunlit; cloudless, shining, clear, brilliant, unclouded, fair, fine. **2** *The waiter didn't exactly have a sunny disposition:* amiable, affable, happy, smiling, cheerful, cheery, joyful, blithe, jolly, joyous, light-hearted, genial, sparkling, buoyant, optimistic, breezy, jovial, merry.
Ant. **1** shaded, dark, cloudy, overcast, gloomy, cheerless, grey, murky, sombre, wintry. **2** glum, gloomy, unhappy, morbid, unsmiling.

superb *adj.* **1** *His first novel was superb:* very fine, first-rate, excellent, magnificent, admirable, laudable, praiseworthy, A1, first-class, great, top-notch, top-drawer, of the first water, tip-top, *Slang* far-out. **2** *They put up for sale a superb Persian rug:* sumptuous, splendid, grand, magnificent, marvellous, luxurious, de luxe, gorgeous, exquisite, costly, rich, expensive, priceless, precious, elegant, choice, select, golden, elect, matchless, rare; majestic, breath-taking, imposing, peerless, regal, princely, stately, lordly.
Ant. **1** bad, awful, terrible, second-rate. **2** tawdry, ordinary, plain.

supercilious *adj. His small success made him supercilious and obnoxious:* haughty, self-important, lordly, pompous, disdainful, condescending, patronizing, arrogant, high and mighty, proud, overbearing, vainglorious, egotistical, magisterial, *Slang* stuck-up; uppity, snobbish, prideful.
◇ *Word origin:* Have you ever raised an eyebrow to express disbelief or contempt? If so, you can understand why the word *supercilious* comes from the Latin prefix *super-* (above) + *cilium* (the eyelid), the eyebrow, literally habitually raising the eyebrow.

superficial *adj.* **1** *The crack in the table is only superficial. Apart from superficial cuts and bruises, she is unhurt:* on the surface, outer, surface, exterior, skin-deep. **2** *She has only a superficial understanding of economics:* shallow, skin-deep, summary, incomplete, slight, faint, slim, flimsy, cursory, perfunctory, passing, partial, minimal, surface, nodding, desultory. **3** *He's too superficial to appreciate the tragedy of the situation:* frivolous, shallow, hollow, empty-headed, narrow-minded, lacking depth, mindless, silly, myopic, short-sighted, trite.
Ant. **1-3** deep, profound. **1** substantial, pervasive. **2** thorough, complete, total. **3** serious, intent, earnest, far-sighted.

superintendent *n. My father was appointed*

superintendent of the Child Welfare Society: supervisor, chief administrator; director, head, overseer, proctor, chief, custodian, guardian, foreman, boss, manager, warden, steward, headman.

superior *adj.* **1** *John Gielgud is a superior actor. The new butcher will give you a superior cut of beef:* excellent, exceptional, fine, notable, first-rate, incomparable, distinguished, pre-eminent, noteworthy, nonpareil, unrivalled, foremost, illustrious, peerless, inimitable, matchless; de luxe, choice. **2** *Her knowledge of French literature is superior to mine:* greater, better, more extensive, more advanced. **3** *His superior manner makes people resent him:* haughty, lordly, imperious, condescending, patronizing, snobbish, arrogant, high and mighty, vainglorious.
—*n.* **4** *His promotion was approved by his superiors:* senior, boss, chief, supervisor; leader, better, commander.
Ant. **1** inferior, lower, worse, poorer, lesser, unexceptional, undistinguished, mediocre, ordinary, average, second-rate, common, unremarkable; inconspicuous, obscure. **2** inferior, less, worse. **4** inferior, subordinate, employee; underling, minion.

"What the superior man seeks is in him; what the mean man seeks is in others."

—*Confucius*

---

superlative *adj. Our carpenter does superlative joinery:* most excellent, of the highest order, greatest, of the first water, superior, surpassing, best, supreme, magnificent, pre-eminent, foremost, transcendent, unsurpassed, expert, prime, surpassing all others, paramount, crack, exquisite, consummate, first-rate; matchless, incomparable, unrivalled, peerless, unequalled, unmatched, unparalleled, nonpareil.
Ant. inferior, poor, unexceptional, undistinguished.

supernatural *adj. The medium claimed to have supernatural powers:* preternatural, occult, mystic, transcendental, spiritual, psychic, paranormal, miraculous, superphysical.
Ant. natural, explainable, worldly.

supersede *v. This new drug will supersede all others in the treatment of the disease:* supplant, replace, take the place of, displace, succeed.
◇ *Spelling tip: Supersede* is one of the very few words in the English language that ends in *-sede.* Remember, *superSEDE* supersedes other words by ending in *-sede.*

supervise *v. Can you supervise a whole production line?:* superintend, watch over, oversee, look after, preside over, manage, direct, govern, survey, control, have charge of, administer, head, boss, handle.

supervision *n. My house was built under an architect's supervision:* direction, guidance, control, superintendence, surveillance, orders, management.

supervisor *n. Only the supervisor can authorize your leave:* overseer, manager, administrator, director, superintendent, foreman, boss, head, chief, steward, commander, man at the wheel.

supplant *v. Machines are supplanting men in many industries:* supersede, replace, take the place of, usurp the place of, displace, depose.

supple *adj.* **1** *The tubing is supple and fireproof:* pliant, flexible, plastic, tractable, bendable, pliable, elastic. **2** *She has the supple body of a gymnast:* lithe, limber, lissome, co-ordinated, graceful, adaptable, flexible, amenable, tractable, compliant, yielding, malleable.
Ant. **1** stiff, rigid, firm, inflexible. **2** stiff, awkward, graceless.

supplement *n.* **1** *The evening classes are a supplement to his regular course:* complement, annex, addition, augmentation, corollary, extra, extension, addendum, adjunct. **2** *The newspaper publishes a special travel supplement twice a year:* section, insert, attachment; appendix, addendum, rider, postscript, codicil, added part.
—*v.* **3** *He supplemented his earnings by taking a night job:* add to, extend, increase, augment.

supply *v.* **1** *The Red Cross supplied the hospital with blood. Who will supply the champagne?:* provide, furnish, outfit, stock, equip; present, give, contribute, bestow, yield, deal out, come up with, deliver, render, grant, provision.
—*n.* **2** *How will they arrange for a daily supply of food to the flood victims?:* provisioning, providing, furnishing, allocation; stock, reservoir, reserve, store, quota, provision, cache, fund. **3** Often **supplies** *What supplies shall we need for our climb?:* equipment, needed items, goods, material, items, provisions; gear, trappings, accoutrements; foodstuff.

support *v.* **1** *Buttresses support the damaged wall:* bear up, hold up; prop, bolster, uphold, brace, sustain, buttress, stay, shore up. **2** *That crate will never support your weight:* sustain, bear, hold. **3** *He has to support his mother and his sister:* maintain, provide for, subsidize, keep, finance, pay for, underwrite, back financially, foster. **4** *Her brother supported her throughout the tragedy:* help, sustain, succour, comfort, give hope to, aid, carry, be a source of strength, strengthen. **5** *I support his right to speak:* defend, back up, champion, uphold, stand up for, stick up for, second, advocate, go along with, say yes to, reinforce, espouse, sanction, favour, countenance; aid, boost, assist, further, patronize, bolster. **6** *Your testimony will support his plea of innocence:* verify, confirm, make good, establish, substantiate, corroborate, accord with, bear out, vouch for, accredit, clinch, warrant, attest to, endorse, bolster, guarantee, ratify. **7** *Mother* *refused point-blank to support disobedience:* endure, tolerate, put up with, suffer, abide, bear, brook, stand.

—*n.* **8** *These beams are the main support of the building. One of the roof supports is cracked:* holding up, buttressing; supporter, brace, prop, underpinning, post, buttress, abutment, shore, pile, pedestal, stanchion, bolster, pillar, column, pilaster, base. **9** *On her shoulders falls the responsibility for the support of the whole family. Joe provided emotional support for the children when their father died:* sustenance, maintenance, upkeep, livelihood, means, subsistence, keeping, nurture; comfort, succour, aid, help, strength, boost, encouragement, consolation, lift. **10** *The candidate did not ask for our support:* backing, patronage, aid, assistance, espousal, defence, advocacy, boost, promotion, furtherance, involvement.

supporter *n. He is a supporter of many liberal causes:* backer, upholder, defender, champion, patron, adherent, benefactor, disciple, well-wisher, partisan, advocate, ally, helper, follower, sympathizer.

Ant. adversary, antagonist, opponent.

suppose *v.* **1** *Suppose you're offered the job—will you accept it?:* assume, hypothesize, presume, predicate, posit, consider. **2** *I suppose you're all hungry?:* imagine, take for granted, presume, assume, judge, fancy, guess, conceive, suspect, divine, surmise.

supposition *n. That was only supposition. He acted on the supposition that the public would applaud his feat:* presumption, assumption, conjecture, opinion, predication, surmise, guess, guesswork, suspicion, belief, theory, thesis, notion, view, speculation, hypothesis, postulate, idea.

Ant. certainty, surety, fact, knowledge.

suppress *v.* **1** *The new government quickly suppressed the rebellion:* put down, overpower, crush, subdue, put an end to, quash, overcome, snuff out, squash, quench, quell, extinguish. **2** *It was all I could do to suppress my anger:* repress, withhold, stifle, keep back, check, control, smother, restrict, restrain, muffle, still, hold back, put a damper on, hold in leash, inhibit, keep in, curb. **3** *His father tried to suppress the scandal:* keep secret, keep private, cover up, conceal, hide, bury, silence.

Ant. **2** express, let out, unleash, pour forth, vent. **3** reveal, uncover, expose, broadcast.

supremacy *n. His supremacy on the tennis-court was unquestioned. The king's supremacy was in jeopardy:* pre-eminence, superiority, primacy, precedence, transcendency domination, power, sovereignty, mastery, absolute authority, ascendancy, power to command, absolute rule, supreme leadership, omnipotence.

supreme *adj.* **1** *In the oligarchy, his position was unquestionably supreme. The Pope is the supreme authority in the Roman Catholic Church:* sovereign, dominant, uppermost, front-ranking, first, highest, chief, principal, paramount, foremost, all-powerful, topmost, leading, ruling; commanding, prime, unqualified, absolute, unconditional, unlimited. **2** *The supreme craftsmanship of this vase makes it priceless:* perfect, consummate, nonpareil, peerless, superlative, matchless, unexcelled, incomparable, unsurpassed, unequalled, unparalleled, second to none, unmatched, unrivalled; extreme, immeasurable.

> **Exploring the Word**: *Super, superior,* and *supreme* come from Latin *super,* above, beyond. *Superior* is the comparative of *super* and means "higher" in both Latin and English. *Supreme* comes from the Latin superlative form *supremus,* highest. Thus, although we tend to forget it, *super, superior,* and *supreme* are the basic form, the comparative form, and the superlative form of the same word, just like high, higher, highest.

sure *adj.* **1** *I am sure of his loyalty:* confident, assured, fully persuaded, convinced, positive, certain, undoubting. **2** *This investment is a sure thing:* trustworthy, never-failing, reliable, worthy of confidence, unfailing, dependable, firm, steady, fast, solid, true, faithful; fail-safe, unfailing, infallible. **3** *She has a sure eye for colour:* unerring, certain, accurate, unfailing, flawless, infallible, dependable, reliable, steady, stable.

Ant. **1, 3** unsure. **1–3** uncertain. **1** insecure, unassured, unconvinced, doubtful, distrustful. **2** fallible, unsteady, inconstant, wavering, unworthy, faithless, undependable, untrue, unreliable. **3** erring, inaccurate, unreliable, unsteady, unstable.

surely *adv. The tortoise gets there slowly but surely. Surely you'll stay for dinner:* for certain, assuredly, without doubt, undoubtedly, certainly, doubtless, unquestionably, definitely, positively, indubitably, emphatically, by all means, come what may, without fail, no doubt, to be sure, infallibly, of course.

surface *n. The surface of the sphere is coated with aluminium:* outside, superficies, outer face, exterior; (*variously*) covering, shell, coat, finish, coating, veneer, crust, skin.

◇ *Word origin: Surface* comes from French *sur-* (above) + *face* (face), above the face or exterior part. Coming directly from Latin, the same word elements have given us our word *superficies,* surface.

surge *n. A surge of impatient shoppers poured into the store. Booksellers report a surge of interest in astronomy this year:* wave, swell, flood, rush.

◇ *Word origin: Surge* comes from Latin *surgere,* to rise. The same Latin verb gives us *insurgent* (one who rises up against authority) and *resurrection* (a rising again).

surly *adj. The local children were scared of the surly*

shopkeeper: sullen, rude, snarling, irascible, grouchy, discourteous, ill-humoured, bad-tempered, testy, crabbed, ill-natured, abrupt, cross, crusty, uncivil, grumpy, touchy, waspish, snappish, peevish, unfriendly, gruff, petulant, harsh, hostile, unamiable, sour, splenetic, bearish, choleric.
Ant. amiable, gracious, cordial, affable, genial, nice, pleasant, courteous, friendly, civil.

surmise *v.* **1** *I surmised that Robinson was up for promotion:* conjecture, imagine, guess, suppose, presuppose, think, presume, opine, judge, suspect, consider, theorize, believe, deem, infer, hypothesize, posit, conclude.
—*n.* **2** *It's only a surmise, but I think he'll barely win the contest:* guess, supposition, notion, idea, conjecture, opinion, speculation, assumption, hypothesis, *Informal* shot in the dark; presumption, belief, suspicion, thought.

surmount *v.* **1** *How shall we surmount that high wall?:* get over, scale, climb, top, clear. **2** *The obstacles he surmounted before becoming the leading baritone were formidable:* conquer, master, overcome, prevail over, vanquish, get the better of, triumph over.
◇ *Word origin: Surmount* comes to us through French *surmonter,* from Latin *super-* (over) + *mons* (mountain, hill).

surpass *v.* **1** *He surpassed the goal that he had set for himself:* exceed, go beyond, outdo, top, best, outstrip, beat, outdistance, leave behind, triumph over, go one better, outrun, transcend. **2** *This mousse au chocolat surpasses any dessert I've ever had in a restaurant:* excel, outdo, be superior to, rise above, outshine, eclipse, over-shadow, override, outclass, take precedence over, be better than.

surplus *n.* **1** *The government paid the farmers for their potato surplus:* oversupply, surfeit, superfluity, excess, overflow, plethora, overproduction, glut.
—*adj.* **2** *Some use should be found for surplus crops:* excess, extra, superfluous, left-over, residual.
Ant. 1 deficiency, shortage, insufficiency, inadequacy, dearth, paucity, lack.
◇ *Word origin: Surplus* comes from Latin *super-* (above, over) + *plus* (more), hence "overmore," i.e., overmuch.

surprise *v.* **1** *His facility with power-tools surprised us:* astonish, astound, nonplus, startle, amaze, flabbergast, take aback, strike with wonder, shock, stun, dumbfound, stagger, strike with awe, defy belief, leave open-mouthed, stupefy, confound, boggle the mind. **2** *Mother surprised me raiding the larder:* catch in the act of, come upon unexpectedly, take unawares, discover, catch off one's guard, burst in on. **3** *The outlaws surprised them in the forest:* ambush, assail suddenly, set upon, make a sneak attack on, take by surprise, fall upon, pounce upon, take unawares.
—*n.* **4** *The surprise was difficult to arrange. The promotion was a surprise:* something unexpected, bolt from the blue, bombshell, revelation. **5** *To my surprise a gigantic ape appeared at the door:* amazement, wonder, astonishment, wonderment, incredulity, shock.

surrender *v.* **1** *They were the last rebel contingent to surrender in the war:* give up, yield, submit, capitulate, concede, lay down arms, show the white flag, throw in the towel, throw up the sponge. **2** *She gradually surrendered her dream of becoming an actress. He surrendered all rights to the property:* give up, let go, abandon, relinquish, renounce, give over, yield, forgo, part with, forsake, vacate, waive, turn over, hand over, render, accede, cede, deliver up.
—*n.* **3** *The Allies broadcast the terms of the surrender. The surrender of the evidence was delayed:* yielding, capitulation, submission; relinquishment, giving up, delivery; forgoing, renunciation.
Ant. 1 resist, withstand, oppose. **2** retain, keep, hold on to.
◇ *Word origin: Surrender* comes from the same base as our word *render,* with the Anglo-French prefix *sur-* (over) in front of it. Hence, to render oneself or a possession over to someone else.

surreptitious *adj. The conspirators held a surreptitious meeting:* secret, secretive, stealthy, furtive, clandestine, hidden, covert, concealed, veiled.
Ant. open, above-board, candid, direct, straightforward.
◇ *Word origin: Surreptitious* comes from the Latin prefix *sub-* (under) + *rapere* (to seize by force), hence acting secretly.

surround *v. The firemen surrounded the burning building. A picket fence surrounds the yard:* encircle, circle, enclose, ring, encompass, girdle, gird, belt, compass, circumscribe, envelop, hedge, shut in, close in, hem in, fence in.
◇ *Word origin: Surround* comes to us via French, but its base is Latin *super-* (over) + *unda* (a wave), to be covered over with waves of water, hence to be completely enclosed. Latin *unda,* wave, also gives us *undulate,* to move like a wave or in waves.

surroundings *n. pl. It is important to work in friendly surroundings:* circumstances, environs, conditions; environment, habitat, setting, scene, ambience, milieu.

surveillance *n. The police have him under constant surveillance:* watch, observation, vigil.
◇ *Word origin: Surveillance* comes from French *surveiller,* to survey, from *sur-* (over) + *veiller* (to watch). Its base is Latin *vigilare,* to watch, which also gives us *vigil, vigilance,* and *vigilant.*

survey *v.* **1** *Let's survey the events leading up to the*

crime: review, look over, view generally, pass in review, consider, contemplate, scan, examine, inspect, scrutinize. **2** *The city engineer surveyed the property in order to amend the map:* measure, determine the extent of, verify the boundaries of, delimit, plot, graph, gauge, block out; fathom, plumb; reconnoitre, observe, scout.
—*n.* **3** *They held a survey of the most popular television programmes:* review, study, comprehensive view, overview, investigation, poll, canvass.

survival *n.* **1** *The explorer was an expert at survival in the wilderness:* living, keeping alive, subsistence. **2** *This custom is a survival from my great-grandmother's day:* relic, vestige, hangover, continuation, carry-over.
Ant. **1** death, extermination, extinction, eradication.

"Victory at all costs, victory in spite of terror, victory however long and hard the road may be; for without victory there is no survival."
— *Winston Churchill*

---

survive *v.* **1** *How long can the plane-crash victims survive in the Arctic? How many of the country's ancient customs survive?:* keep alive, continue to live, subsist, last, hang on, hold out; live on, persist, endure, continue, abide, subsist, be extant. **2** *Miraculously, they survived the bombing:* live through, come through alive. **3** *Insurance statistics show that most wives survive their husbands:* outlive, outlast, live longer than.
Ant. **1** perish, disappear. **2** succumb to. **3** pre-decease.

susceptible *adj.* **1** *An imprecise law is always susceptible of differing interpretations. Is the virus susceptible to treatment?:* open, prone, vulnerable, receptive to, capable of being affected by, sensitive to, disposed to, conducive to, liable to. **2** *He's susceptible to a woman's tears:* sensitive, alive to, responsive, easily moved by, vulnerable, readily impressed by, easily touched by, sympathetic, sensible.
Ant. **1, 2** unsusceptible. **1** immune, invulnerable. **2** insensitive, unresponsive, unmoved, invulnerable, insensible, resistant.
◇ *Usage note: Susceptible* used with the preposition *to* expresses a reaction to stimulus: *Artists are susceptible to beauty in every form; susceptible of*, however, is equivalent to capable of, or admitting: *His statement was susceptible of several interpretations.*

suspect *v.* **1** *He suspected her of insincerity. He suspected her sincerity:* mistrust, doubt, distrust, question, have no confidence in, have one's doubts about, harbour suspicions about, wonder about, misdoubt, be suspicious of, believe guilty. **2** *We suspect that they will be late:* imagine, conjecture, surmise, opine, guess, hypothesize, believe, posit, theorize, judge, presume, speculate, suppose, think.
—*n.* **3** *The suspect is being held at the police station for questioning:* suspected person, alleged culprit.
Ant. **1** trust, believe. **2** know, know for sure, be sure, be certain.

suspend *v.* **1** *Suspend the swing from the branch of the tree:* hang, dangle, swing, append, sling. **2** *I'll suspend judgement until all the facts are available:* put off, postpone, delay, defer, table, reserve, shelve, stay, withhold. **3** *They suspended construction during the strike:* discontinue, cease, stop, halt, arrest, interrupt, leave off, break off, bring to a stop, bring to a standstill, stop short, check, cut short, put an end to.

suspense *n.* *I can't stand the suspense of not knowing!:* uncertainty, incertitude, indecision, unresolved situation, indetermination, expectation, anticipation, being on pins and needles, being on tenterhooks, curiosity.
Ant. certainty, certitude, resolution.

suspicion *n.* **1** *Suspicion was taking its toll on the jealous wife:* distrust, mistrust, jealous apprehension, suspiciousness. **2** *I have my suspicions about his part in this case:* conjecture, feeling, idea, surmise, guess, supposition, hunch, hypothesis, notion.
Ant. **1** trust, trustfulness, belief, confidence; credulity.

suspicious *adj.* **1** *His behaviour was, to say the least, suspicious:* open to doubt, questionable, dubious, suspect, doubtful, slippery, ambiguous, untrustworthy, shady. **2** *The police are suspicious of his alibi because he already has a record:* inclined to suspect, mistrustful, distrustful, wary, doubting, incredulous, disbelieving, sceptical.
Ant. **1, 2** unsuspicious. **1** open, above-board, clear, unambiguous. **2** trusting, confident; credulous.

sustain *v.* **1** *These four posts sustain the entire building:* support, bear up, uphold, hold up, underpin, prop. **2** *The company was somehow able to sustain the severe fuel shortage:* bear, brook, endure, carry on under, hold out against, abide, stand, withstand, brave, tolerate. **3** *He sustained a terrible head injury:* suffer, undergo, experience. **4** *The runner was able to sustain the same pace for hours:* maintain, keep up, prolong, protract. **5** *The prisoners sustained themselves on bread and water:* nourish, maintain; nurture, feed, keep alive.

swagger *v.* *He swaggered brazenly across the room:* strut, stride insolently, sweep, parade.
Ant. slink, sneak, creep.

swallow *v.* **1** *Chew your meat thoroughly before you swallow it:* ingest; gulp, gobble, devour, gulp down; imbibe, guzzle, swig, down, swill, tipple, quaff. **2** *He swallowed his anger and went on working:* repress, hold in, suppress, keep back, withhold, hold back.
—*n.* **3** *Take a swallow of my lager:* mouthful, drink, gulp, nip, sup, sip, taste, bit.

swamp *n.* **1** *We saw alligators in the swamp:* marsh, bog, morass, quagmire, quag, fen, wetland, marshland, slough, moor, ooze.
—*v.* **2** *The huge wave swamped our canoe:* sink, submerge, fill; engulf, flood, wash over, inundate, envelop, deluge, swallow up. **3** *The evangelist was swamped with invitations to speak:* overwhelm, flood, besiege, engulf, beset, snow under.

swap *v. The boys swapped cigarette cards:* trade, exchange, barter, give and take.
◇ *Word origin:* Did you ever "strike" a bargain? If so, you were making a *swap. Swap* comes from Middle English *swappen*, to strike or slap, hence for two people to slap each other's hands to seal a bargain. From this custom we get both our idea of sealing a bargain with a handshake and our term "to strike a bargain."

swarm *n.* **1** *A swarm of locusts destroyed the crop. A swarm of fans ran onto the football ground:* multitude; drove, throng, horde, cloud, mass, herd, press, great number, stampede, host, crowd, myriad.
—*v.* **2** *The bargain-hunters swarmed into the store:* flock, surge, throng, crowd, herd, over-run, cluster, rush, mass, stream. **3** *The marsh was swarming with mosquitoes:* abound, teem.

sway *v.* **1** *The boat swayed on the stormy sea. The seasick passenger swayed with dizziness:* rock, list, move to and fro, swing, roll, oscillate, wave, undulate, pendulate, fluctuate, waver; reel, totter, wobble, stagger. **2** *The prospect of cold weather swayed them, and they decided to go south:* move, influence, prompt, persuade, motivate, rouse, lead, induce, bend the will of, stimulate, predispose, dispose, incite, encourage, spur, impel, prevail on, bring round. **3** *He has never swayed in his loyalty to his family:* fluctuate, vacillate, change, shift, vary, hesitate, alter, swerve, bend.
—*n.* **4** *The sway of the hammock made him feel queasy:* swaying, swinging, waving, pulsation, oscillation, undulation, fluctuation, back and forth, to-and-fro. **5** *The cabinet is completely under the sway of the Prime Minister:* control, authority, rule, domination, command, mastery, power, domain, jurisdiction, government, iron hand, dictatorship, reign, grip, suzerainty, hold. **6** *His father has too much sway over the boy:* influence, control, domination, hold, command, grip, direction, power, manipulation, *Slang* clout.

swear *v.* **1** *The witness swore to tell all he knew:* state under oath, take an oath, vow, vouch, avow, bind oneself by oath, certify, warrant, bear witness, attest, adjure, pledge oneself, aver, assert, promise. **2** *He swore them to silence:* cause to promise, bind by an oath, pledge. **3** *The boy swears like a trooper:* curse, use profanity, utter oaths, blaspheme, *Slang* cuss.

sweep *v.* **1** *Did you sweep up all the broken glass? Sweep the floor and make the beds:* brush, clean, hoover, whisk, gather. **2** *The winner swept past the finishing line:* race, dash, rush, dart, scurry, hurry, charge, scud, fly, zoom, swoop, tear.
—*n.* **3** *There's a long sweep of empty road before you come to the inn:* stretch, distance, spell. **4** *He cut the rope with one sweep of his knife:* swing, arc, stroke, swish, swoop.
◇ *Word origin: Sweep* and *swoop* derive from a common ancestor-word: a *swooping* bird *sweeps* its prey up in its claws.

sweeping *adj. The company's new director made sweeping changes in the office:* extensive, widespread, wide-ranging, broad, wholesale, radical, exhaustive, blanket, comprehensive, large-scale, thoroughgoing.
Ant. small, modest, trifling, trivial, limited, superficial, narrow, slight.

sweet *adj.* **1** *These biscuits are too sweet:* sweet-tasting, sugary; saccharine, cloying. **2** *There's a sweet spring only a hundred yards inland from the shore. Do you like sweet butter? This milk is too old to be still sweet:* not salt, not salty, freshwater, fresh, non-fermented, wholesome, not spoilt, not rancid. **3** *The soprano has a sweet voice:* melodious, dulcet, pleasing, mellifluous, tuneful, silver-toned, mellow, euphonious, smooth. **4** *The baby smells so sweet after his bath:* fragrant, fresh. **5** *The Jacksons are sweet people:* attractive, sympathetic, agreeable, nice, pleasant, good-natured, dear, kind, lovable, amiable, darling.
—*n.* **6** *Don't eat too many sweets:* confection, sweetmeat, (*variously*) toffee, caramel, chocolate, fudge, peppermint, barley sugar, butterscotch, dolly mixture, bull's eye, *Slang* gob-stopper.
Ant. **1** sour, acid, acerbic, bitter, nasty. **2** salt-water, salt, salty, salted; stale, rancid, sour, decaying, tainted, turned, off. **3** harsh, shrill; raucous, discordant, unmelodious, displeasing, unmusical, inharmonious, dissonant, strident. **4** stale, bad-smelling, rank. **5** disagreeable, unpleasant, unattractive, nasty, ill-natured, unlovable, unamiable; dreadful, awful.

sweetheart *n. Her sweetheart gave her a ring for Christmas:* love, beloved, true love, darling, lover; mistress, lady-love, lady friend, inamorata, girl-friend, boy-friend, beau, swain, suitor, gentleman friend; fiancé, (*fem.*) fiancée, *Slang* honey, old lady, old man, old flame.

swell *v.* **1** *His eye swelled painfully after the blow. The guest list swelled to 100 people:* distend, puff, puff up, grow, blow up, fatten, bulge, inflate, extend, bloat, thicken; expand, increase, lengthen, stretch, widen, spread out, burgeon, rise. **2** *The music swelled as the finale approached. The sea swelled as the storm neared:* intensify, amplify, heighten, rise, mount, throb; billow, surge, wax, heave.
—*n.* **3** *The clipper ploughed her way through the heavy*

swell: undulation of the surface of the sea; wave, billow; breaker, boomer, comber. **5** *The young man imagined himself as a swell, dressed in the latest fashion:* fashion-plate, smart dresser, dandy, fop, clothes-horse.

Ant. 1 shrink, contract, condense, compress, constrict. **2** decrease, diminish, lessen, fall, wane, lower, ebb away.

Exploring the Word: *Sweet* itself comes from an Old English word *swēte*; however, the various types of sweets which we know have many different countries of origin — some of which are quite exotic! Chocolate comes from an Aztec word *xocolatl* and *sugar* is originally a Sanskrit word — the product originated in India and was first brought to Europe by Arabs following the Moorish conquest of Spain (A.D. 720). The only sweetening known to the Greeks and Romans was *honey*. *Bon-bon* comes from French *bon-bon* — originally a baby-talk reduplication: "goody-goody!" *Liquorice* comes from Greek *glukurrhiza*, sweet-root, and is still made from a dried herbal root. *Caramel* comes from Medieval Latin *calamellus*, sugar-cane (introduced by the Arabs in Spain). *Lollipop* is from an old dialectal word *lolly*, tongue, + *pop*, popping noise. *Gumdrops* are drops of sweetened, flavoured, and coloured gum arabic; they were originally called "gum arabic drops" though gelatin is now used instead. *Jelly beans* are bean-shaped sweets with a gelatinous centre. *Molasses* comes from Late Latin *mellaceum*, must, new wine, which comes from Latin *mel*, honey. A highly refined, more palatable form of molasses is *golden syrup*, or *treacle*. In the apothecary's shop of 14th-century London, treacle had a quite different meaning — the word designated a special kind of medicine for poisonous bites originally imported from Byzantium where it was called *thēriakē*, "bite-remedy" (from Greek *thēr*, wild animal). The connection between the remedy and treacle is apparently that molasses was used as a vehicle for the medicine.

swelling *n. The ice-pack brought the swelling down:* swell, puffiness, distension, bulge, bump, lump, bruise, swell, protuberance.

swelter *v. We were sweltering on that stuffy bus:* be oppressed with heat, be hot, sweat, perspire, languish, *Informal* cook, fry, boil, broil.

Ant. freeze, shiver.

◇ *Word origin: Swelter* comes from Old English *sweltan,* to faint, to die; hence to faint or suffer from oppressive heat.

swift *adj. The thief made a swift exit:* hasty, fast, rapid, fleet, prompt, immediate, speedy, brisk, quick, expeditious, flying.

Ant. slow, sluggish, inexpeditious, late, tardy.

swill *v.* **1** *They swilled those drinks down in no time:* guzzle, drink greedily, gulp down, swallow noisily, quaff, soak up, swig, tipple, drain the cup.

—*n.* **2** *The farmer fed his pigs swill:* slop, liquid food, mash; refuse, garbage.

swindle *v.* **1** *He swindled his brothers out of their inheritance:* cheat, defraud, gyp, hoax, trick, fleece, cozen, bilk, do, gull, hoodwink, bamboozle, con, dupe, deceive, delude, rook. **2** *The company swindled money from its investors:* embezzle, mulct, steal, defalcate, *Slang* rip off.

—*n.* **3** *The housing development scheme was a pure swindle:* fraud, hoax, cheat, steal, gyp, embezzlement, trick, confidence trick, con trick, racket, *Slang* rip-off.

swindler *n. He seemed a distinguished-looking man, but he was a swindler:* embezzler; con man; crook, charlatan, fraud, cheat, faker, deceiver.

swing *v.* **1** *The pendulum stopped swinging:* move to and fro, oscillate, sway, rock, undulate, see-saw, move back and forth. **2** *Swing the plants from the wooden beams. The horse thief will swing if they catch him:* hang, be hanged, dangle, suspend, be suspended, drop, loop. **3** *Informal Can you swing us an invitation to the party?:* manage, manipulate, handle, accomplish, manœuvre, pull off, wangle, inveigle, extract. **4** *He swung round on his heel and walked out:* pivot, rotate, turn, whirl. **5** *The mayor tried to swing public opinion in favour of his plan:* influence, sway, decide, determine, rally, move, manipulate.

—*n.* **6** *The swing of the ship made everyone seasick:* swaying, rocking, listing, pitching, rolling, oscillation. **7** *It takes just one mighty swing of the bat to hit a six:* sweep, sweeping blow, stroke. **8** *The party was in full swing when we arrived:* activity, go, progress.

◇ *Usage note:* The past tense of *swing* is *swung*. Thus, *We swung on the swings all day yesterday.*

swirl *v.* **1** *A gust of wind swirled bits of paper down the street:* whirl, spin, twist, revolve, wheel, turn, roll, twirl; rotate, eddy, churn, gyrate, bowl. **2** *Riding the roller-coaster made my head swirl:* be dizzy, reel, spin, swim.

switch *n.* **1** *The teacher whipped the bad boy with a hazel switch:* rod, small branch, stick. **2** *The wiring's good and the bulb is brand-new but the switch doesn't work:* actuator device, box, lever, handle, button. **3** *The train was derailed when the switch failed:* shunting device, shunt, train switch. **4** *We had to make a sudden switch in our arrangements:* change, alteration, trade, shift.

—*v.* **5** *The cow switched its tail:* whisk, jerk, move, swing, lash. **6** *I switched wallets with my sister:* exchange, change, trade.

swollen *adj. Put an ice-pack on that swollen eye:* puffed-up, swelled, distended, bloated, inflated, bulging, puffy.

Ant. shrunken, contracted.

swoop *v.* **1** *The sea-gull swooped down on the fish:* descend, drop, plunge, sweep down, plummet, dive; spring, pounce, rush headlong. —*n.* **2** *With one swoop the falcon captured its prey:* dive, swooping, plunge, sweep, drop; pounce, rush.

◇ *Word origin:* See SWEEP.

sword *n. The duellists crossed swords:* blade, steel; (*variously*) sabre, rapier, steel, cutlass, foil, scimitar, épée, broadsword.

"The sword does not jest."
—*Charles XII of Sweden*

---

sycophant *n. Richard II surrounded himself with sycophants:* parasite, toady, flatterer, bootlicker, fawner, flunkey, stooge, hanger-on, yes-man, truckler, rubber stamp, slave, lackey, cat's-paw, tool, jackal, puppet.

◇ *Word origin:* Although *sycophant* nowadays means a flatterer, the Greek word from which it is derived means an informer, one who denounces others to the authorities. The word was later applied to the satellites of the rich and powerful as a term of abuse.

symbol *n.* **1** *In maths, x is the symbol for an unknown quantity:* sign, mark, figure, indication. **2** *The ring was a symbol of his love. The lion is often used as a symbol of courage:* emblem, token, badge, mark, representation, sign, figure.

◇ *Word origin: Symbol* and *symbolize* come from Greek *sun-* (together) + *ballein* (to throw), to throw together, put together, group under a token or mark. Hence, a *symbol* is something chosen to stand for a group of things.

symbolize *v. The dove symbolizes peace:* stand for, mean, represent, express, personify, connote, denote, emblematize, signify, betoken, symbol, signal, imply, allegorize, shadow forth.

symmetrical *adj. The formal garden is too symmetrical for my taste:* balanced, well-balanced, orderly, congruent, well-proportioned, regular.

Ant. asymmetrical, unbalanced, irregular, uneven, unequal, disorderly.

symmetry *n. William Blake, the poet, praised the tiger's "fearful symmetry". The snowflake is often cited as an example of perfect symmetry:* correspondence of parts, regularity, conformity, balance, proportionality, equilibrium, order, orderliness, harmony; beauty of form, form, shapeliness.

Ant. disproportion, disharmony, irregularity, disagreement, disparity, malformation.

sympathetic *adj.* **1** *The pupils take their problems to one of the more sympathetic teachers:* sympathizing, compassionate, understanding, sensitive, tender-hearted, commiserative, warm-hearted, soft-hearted, pitying, comforting, humane, kindly, merciful, benevolent, benign, benignant, feeling. **2** *His mother was not sympathetic to his plea to leave school:* favourably disposed, well-disposed, agreeable, approving, friendly.

Ant. 1, 2 unsympathetic. **1** uncompassionate, cold-hearted, inhumane, insensitive, pitiless, unpitying, unfeeling, unmerciful.

sympathize *v.* **1** *Her family sympathized with her desire to be a lawyer:* agree, be in accord, side, go along; understand, appreciate, approve, sanction, regard with favour, favour, back, support; bear goodwill towards, stand behind, take an interest in. **2** *I sympathize greatly with the bereaved man:* feel compassion for, be sorry for, feel for, have pity for, pity, empathize, feel sympathy for; identify with, grieve with, share the sorrow of, lament with, mourn with.

Ant. 1 disagree, oppose, fail to understand, misunderstand, disallow, reject.

sympathy *n.* **1** *There was an instant sympathy between the two men:* concord, accord, harmony, congeniality, understanding, agreement, rapport, affinity, communion, consonance, unanimity, concert, regard, amity, fellow-feeling, fellowship, friendship. **2** *He felt tremendous sympathy for the war orphans:* concern, compassion, feeling, commiseration, tenderness, empathy, grief, sorrow, pity. **3** *Your plan has my complete sympathy:* support, favour, sanction, approval, agreement, advocacy, well-wishing, partisanship, patronage.

Ant. 1 antipathy, hostility, misunderstanding, antagonism. **2** coldness, mercilessness, pitilessness, insensibility, indifference, unconcern. **3** disfavour, disapproval, opposition.

symposium *n. We attended a symposium on ecology:* conference, parley, round-table conference, colloquy, congress, meeting, synod, debate, *Slang* pow-wow.

◇ *Word origin:* In ancient Greece, a *sumposion* ("banquet") was a combination of a dinner and a drinking party. The word comes from Greek *sun-* (together) + *posis* (a drinking), drinking together. On one memorable evening of this sort in about 400 BC, Socrates and several famous Athenian friends had a lengthy round-table discussion concerning the nature of love. Plato's literary version of that evening is titled the *Symposium*, and from that title we get our word *symposium*, meeting for the discussion of a particular subject.

symptom *n. A rash is one symptom of scarlet fever:* signal, sign, indication, evidence, token, warning, mark.

◇ *Word origin: Symptom* comes from Greek *sun-* (together) + *piptein* (to fall), to befall simultaneously. Hence, a symptom is something that indicates something else, as a change in bodily functions indicates the presence of a disease. *Syndrome* comes from the

Greek *sun-* (together) + *dramein* (to run), things that run together, hence a group of symptoms indicating the presence and nature of a disease. Thus several related *symptoms* become a *syndrome.*

syndicate *n. A syndicate is buying up all the stock of the firm:* combine, alliance, league, federation, union, association, group, trust, cartel.

synonym *n. "Bloom" is a synonym for flower:* equivalent word, parallel word, analogue, equivalent; another name.

Ant. antonym, opposite.

> **Exploring the Word:** *Synonym* comes from Greek *syn-* (with) + *onuma* (name), literally "by-name," i.e. same-meaning word. (The term was coined by Aristotle, who in his *Rhetoric* defines *synonyms* as words having different forms but the same sense.) Greek *onuma*, name, also gives us *antonym* (Greek *anti*, against, opposite), an opposite name or word; *anonymous* (Greek *an-*, without, not), without a name; *pseudonym* (Greek *pseudos*, false), a false name, as an author's pen-name; and *homonym* (*Greek homos*, same), a word that looks and sounds like another but has a completely different meaning and origin (thus a *tear*, a rent and *tear*, a drop of water from the eye, are homonyms — they are the "same word," but completely different!).

synonymous *adj. "Grief" is synonymous with "sorrow":* equivalent, similar in meaning, alike, like, same, equal, coequal.

Ant. antonymous, opposite in meaning.

synopsis *n. It's a good idea to read a synopsis of the opera before going to it:* outline, summary, précis, epitome, argument, abstract, *Informal* run-down; aperçu, résumé.

◇ *Word origin: Synopsis* comes from Greek *sun-* (together) + *opsis* (view), an overall view, summary.

synthetic *adj. Synthetic suede is more durable than the real thing:* artificial, man-made, ersatz; fake, phoney, counterfeit.

Ant. real, authentic, genuine, natural, organic.

◇ *Word origin: Synthetic* comes from Greek *sun-* (together) + *tithenai* (to put), to put together or produce artificially.

system *n.* **1** *Her Majesty's Inspectors play an integral part in the education system. Music lovers appreciate a good hi-fi system:* combination of parts, organization, organized entity, overall unit, unit, structure, set-up. **2** *Don't wreck your system by overwork and lack of sleep!:* constitution, body, organism. **3** *The system underlying modern physics is not fully worked out:* theory, theoretical base, hypothesis, frame of reference. **4** *Does the new clerk understand the filing system?:* method, procedure, arrangement, scheme, programme, mode of operation, modus operandi, regimen, routine.

◇ *Word origin: System* comes from Greek *sun-* (together) + *histanai* (to make stand, set up). The word thus literally means "set-up" in its original sense.

systematic *adj.* **1** *The bank recommends that each family should have a systematic arrangement for saving:* planned, organized, systematized, orderly, ordered. **2** *His books are kept in a highly systematic way:* methodical, precise, orderly, well-organized, businesslike, tidy, neat, well-regulated, constant, regular.

Ant. 1, 2 unsystematic. **1** arbitrary, haphazard, random. **2** unmethodical, disorderly, disorganized, unbusinesslike, messy, sloppy.

◇ *Spelling tip:* Remember that *systematically* is spelt with two *l's: systematic* + *-ally.*

T

tab *n.* **1** *Buy file dividers with alphabetical tabs:* short strip, loop, eyelet, flap, tongue. **2** *Informal I wish you would mind your own business instead of keeping tabs on me:* check, observation, surveillance.

table *n.* **1** *Set the table with the best china. A radio stood on the table by the bed:* (*variously*) dining-room table, kitchen-table, breakfast-table, tea-table; stand, end-table, coffee-table, bedside table, display table, card-table. **2** *The squire had a big house and kept a good table:* board, spread, fare. **3** *The maths book contained a multiplication table. Find Chapter 3 by looking in the table of contents:* list, chart, tabular arrangement, tabulation, schedule, record, inventory, catalogue, register, roll, roster; synopsis, index, syllabus.

—*v.* **4** *The M.P. tabled a motion:* put forward for discussion, propose, suggest, enter.

◇ *Word origin: Table* comes from Latin *tabula*, board, writing tablet, picture. From *tabula* we also get our words *tablet* (writing pad) and *tableau. Tablet* acquired the additional sense "flat pill" in Elizabethan times. From *Tabloid*, a nearly 100-year-old trade mark for a tablet of condensed medication, we get our word *tabloid*, a small-format newspaper, so-called because of its condensed presentation.

tablet *n.* **1** *Each student should have pencils and a tablet of lined paper:* pad of paper, writing pad,

pad, memo pad. **2** *The statue had a bronze tablet listing the town's war dead:* plaque, panel, thin slab, surface, sheet, leaf, tablature. **3** *Take two aspirin tablets and go to bed:* flat pill, lozenge, troche, wafer, pellet, bolus, capsule.

taboo Also **tabu** *adj.* **1** *Eating pork is strictly taboo among orthodox Jews:* forbidden, banned, prohibited, proscribed, outlawed, anathema, unacceptable, disapproved, unthinkable, unmentionable, *German* verboten.
—*n.* **2** *The Polynesians have a taboo on mentioning certain sacred rites:* religious ban, social ban, ban, prohibition, proscription, interdiction.
Ant. allowed, permitted, permissible; approved, sanctioned, encouraged.
◇ *Word origin: Taboo* is from Tongan, the Polynesian language of the Tonga Islands, south-east of Fiji, in which it means "sacred."

tacit *adj. The neighbours had a tacit agreement not to park in front of each other's houses:* unexpressed, understood, implied, implicit, wordless, undeclared, unspoken, unstated.

taciturn *adj. He's so taciturn that no one knew whether he enjoyed the party or not:* reserved, reticent, sparing of words, uncommunicative, close-mouthed, tight-lipped, silent, secretive.
Ant. talkative, loquacious, voluble, garrulous, chatty, open, unreserved, wordy, verbose.

tack *n.* **1** *The calendar was fixed to the wall with tacks:* short nail; (*variously*) drawing-pin, carpet tack; tholepin, peg, spike. **2** *The yacht's sudden tack to starboard startled the passengers:* zigzag, change, swerve, shift, switch. **3** *If this plan doesn't work, we'll try a new tack:* course of action, approach, method, way.
— *v.* **4** *Tack the bulletin on the notice-board:* nail, pin; attach, fasten, affix. **5** *They tried to tack the highway measure onto the housing bill:* add, attach, affix, append, *Slang* slap, clap. **6** *The sailing-ship tacked to port:* change course, go about, veer, sheer, swerve, zigzag.
Ant. 4 untack, unpin; loosen, unfasten, take off, take down. **5** subtract, deduct, separate, detach, delete, cut.

tackle *n.* **1** *The sports shop had a window full of fishing tackle:* equipment, gear, paraphernalia, apparatus, trappings, rigging, accoutrements, appointments, implements; tools, instruments, material, appliances. **2** *The freighter was unloaded at the dock by heavy-duty tackle:* system of ropes and pulleys; (*variously*) hoist, lift, crane, derrick, winch, windlass, capstan, halyard, jenny. **3** *The policeman floored the rioter with a flying tackle:* throw, pinioning of the legs.
—*v.* **4** *The comedian wanted to tackle a serious role in his next film. The boys tackled the job of painting the room enthusiastically:* undertake, attempt, try, assay, endeavour, attack, take on, take up, accept, embrace, assume, devote oneself to, turn one's hand to, embark upon, engage in, set about, go about, enter upon, begin. **5** *The winger was tackled just short of the line:* seize and throw down, throw, wrestle to the ground, confront and gain possession of ball from, *Slang* rob.
Ant. 4 reject, spurn, shun, evade, forgo, forswear, eschew; postpone, set aside, shelve.

tact *n. The hostess showed enormous tact in handling a touchy situation:* diplomacy, delicacy, savoir-faire, suavity, suaveness, finesse, discretion.
Ant. tactlessness, crudeness, clumsiness, awkwardness, heavy-handedness, indiscretion, indelicacy, insensitivity.

Exploring the Word: *Tact, tactile, tangible, tangent,* and *tango* all come from Latin *tangere*, to touch, and the related *tactus*, sense of touch. Thus, *tact* is the right social touch; *tactile* means pertaining to the sense of touch; while *tangible* means capable of being touched, hence real; *tangent* means touching at a single point (in geometry a *tangent* is a straight line touching a curve at only one point), and *tangential* means touching slightly, hence only partly relevant. *Tango* comes to us from Argentina, where it means fiesta or dancing party, but goes back to a Spanish word meaning to touch or pluck the strings of a musical instrument. Latin *tangere* also gives us *attain*, to grasp, get; *contact*, touch; *contiguous*, touching, in close proximity; *contaminate*, to make impure by contact; and *contagious*, transmitted by contact.

tactful *adj. A diplomat must be very tactful. The tactful suggestion offended no one:* socially adroit, diplomatic, politic, smooth, suave, decorous, subtle, discreet, delicate, considerate, sensitive.
Ant. tactless, undiplomatic, unpolitic, unsubtle, indecorous, indiscreet; indelicate, tasteless, clumsy, untoward, awkward, gauche.

tactic *n. The best tactic is to confess and ask her forgiveness:* course of action, way, tack, method, scheme, policy, approach, means of getting one's way. **2** *Usually* **tactics** *The general's brilliant tactics won the battle:* manoeuvres, battle arrangements, military operations.
◇ *Word origin: Tactics* comes from the Greek phrase *hē taktikē tekhnē*, the art or science of arranging troops for battle. The word is derived from the verb *tassein*, to arrange.
◇ *Usage note:* For the distinction between *tactics* and *strategy*, see STRATEGY.

tag *n.* **1** *Each item on the shelves carries a printed price tag:* label, tab, ticket, slip, card, stub, mark, marker; pendant, appendage, attachment.
—*v.* **2** *The helpers tagged the jumble for the sale:* attach a tag to, label, ticket, mark; term, title, name. **3** *Just tag a postscript onto the end of the letter:* add, add on, tack on, attach, append, annex, affix; fasten, join to. **4** *Informal*

Must your brother tag along with us everywhere we go?: accompany, attend, follow, shadow, trail, tail, dog, heel, hound, hang on to the skirts of.

tailor *n.* **1** *A Savile Row tailor makes all Bill's clothes. The tailor shortened the trousers by two inches:* garment-maker, dressmaker, seamstress, costumier, clothier, *French* couturier.
—*v.* **2** *Her outfits are tailored by a famous couturier. We can tailor the house to suit the buyer's needs:* fashion, make, create, design, devise, shape, construct, build, produce, fabricate; alter, adapt, convert, change, transform; sew.
Ant. **2** destroy, tear up; leave alone, let be.

Exploring the Word: *Tailor, retail, detail, entail* and *tally* come from Late Latin *taliare,* via French *tailler,* to cut, cut up. Thus a *tailor* is one who cuts cloth and sews it into garments; *retail,* literally to cut again, refers to selling small quantities cut from a larger item, as fabric cut from a bolt, meat cut from a carcass, etc., (*wholesale* means to sell the undivided whole); a *detail* is a part cut off, a separate item, a minor item; *entail* literally means cut in, to involve; and a *tally* was originally a piece of wood on which notches were cut to keep account. Our word *tailings,* residue or leavings, as from a mine, also refers to small pieces cut off. (*Tail* has no relation to this base but comes from Old English *taegl,* tail, akin to various Germanic words meaning lock of hair, horse's tail, fringes, etc.)

taint *n.* **1** *The scandal was a taint on the family's good name:* stain, spot, blemish, blot, stigma, tarnish, smudge, smirch, flaw, defect, fault, imperfection.
—*v.* **2** *Rumours of bribery tainted the politician's reputation:* spoil, damage, ruin, sully, defile, debase, stain, spot, soil, tarnish, blemish, besmirch, dirty, smudge, smear, mar; become spoiled, go bad, putrefy, rot, turn.
Ant. **2** enhance, elevate, exalt, strengthen, reinforce, boost.

take *v.* **1** *Please take a few nuts from the bowl. Take the rope in your right hand and pull:* get, have, obtain, acquire, secure, avail oneself of, help oneself to; grip, grasp, clutch, clasp, hold, lay hold of, get hold of, lay hands on, seize, grab, snatch, nab. **2** *The army took control of the government. The thieves took all the money that was in the safe:* seize, grab, usurp, appropriate, misappropriate, capture, commandeer, confiscate, deprive of, divest; steal, purloin, filch, pocket, pilfer, cheat, bilk, fleece; loot, plunder, sack, pillage. **3** *Take this package to the post office. The teacher took the children on a tour through the art gallery:* deliver, carry, bring, bear, tote, lug, convey, transport, move, transfer; conduct, guide, lead, escort, usher. **4** *The customer tried on two dresses and took both. My sister has taken a house by the sea for the summer:* buy, purchase; rent, lease, hire, obtain, acquire, get, use, employ; catch. **5** *If you take 6 from 10, you are left with 4:* subtract, deduct, take away, remove, eliminate. **6** *We took your silence to mean that you agreed:* interpret, understand, regard, respond to, receive, look on, see, perceive, deem, suppose, believe, comprehend, hold, consider, conceive, conclude, deduce, ascertain, infer, make out, *Slang* read. **7** *Take the doctor's advice and do some exercises:* accept, comply with, accede to, agree to, consent to, assent to, heed, follow, mind, obey, mark, listen to, observe, respect, be ruled by, resign oneself to, go along with. **8** *It takes years of study to become a doctor. It took all his strength to lift the chair:* require, necessitate, need, demand, call for; use, use up, employ, consume, claim. **9** *She won't take any more of his insults:* endure, bear, stand, tolerate, suffer, stomach, brook, submit to, undergo, put up with. **10** *I take great pleasure in introducing our guest speaker:* feel, have, experience, know; derive, gain, attain, get, draw. **11** *Bill took the blame for his brother's mistake:* accept, assume, undertake, shoulder, draw. **12** *As soon as the injection takes, the patient should improve:* take effect, begin to work; work, succeed.
—*n.* **13** *The fisherman brought home a huge take:* catch, haul.
Ant. **1** give, put; let go, put down. **2** surrender, give up, yield, let go; return, restore, give back. **5** add, tack on. **7** reject, refuse, spurn, decline, veto, turn down, dismiss, renounce, repudiate, scorn. **11** forgo, forswear, avoid, evade, eschew. **12** fail, flop.

tale *n.* **1** *The author told a tale of intrigue and adventure:* story, narrative, narration, account, yarn, anecdote; (*variously*) novel, short story, romance, fable, legend, myth, epic, saga. **2** *The woman told tales to make her life seem glamorous. Don't tell tales out of school:* fib, lie, falsehood, untruth, fabrication, falsification, tall story, cock-and-bull story, fishing story; piece of gossip, scandal, rumour, hearsay, tittle-tattle.

talent *n. The girl seems to have a talent for drawing:* special ability, natural gift, gift, faculty, facility, endowment, genius, aptitude, capacity, proficiency, skill, knack, flair, turn, forte.

"Talent is that which is in a man's power; genius is that in whose power a man is."
—*James Russell Lowell*

talk *v.* **1** *Can the baby talk yet? We talked business for two hours:* utter words, speak, speak about; (*variously*) converse, exchange words, bandy words, communicate orally, discuss, chat, chatter, gossip, palaver, prattle, prate, babble, *Slang* rap, jaw, rattle on. **2** *You'd better talk to a lawyer:* confer, consult, speak, take

up; negotiate, parley. **3** *He's talking nonsense!:* utter, speak, say, express, intone, enunciate, state, proclaim, pronounce, deliver, declare; preach, pontificate.
—*n.* **4** *Let's have a little talk together:* conversation, chat, tête-à-tête, chit-chat, colloquy, confabulation; discussion, conference, consultation, parley, dialogue, *Slang* pow-wow, palaver, confab, rap. **5** *The speaker gave a short, humorous talk:* address, lecture, speech, oration, discourse, sermon; harangue, tirade, exhortation; declamation, recitation, utterance. **6** *There's been some talk about closing the office. Some people are all talk and no action:* gossip, rumour, hearsay, noise, report, word, *Slang* tittle-tattle, empty speech, hot air, empty words, blarney, verbiage, bunkum, prattle, chatter, chat, twaddle, blather, gab.
Ant. 1 be silent, be mute, be inarticulate; listen.

talkative *adj. The talkative guest monopolized the conversation:* loquacious, voluble, garrulous, chatty, *Slang* gabby; prolix, long-winded; wordy, verbose.
Ant. silent, mute, mum, speechless; reticent, reserved, taciturn, uncommunicative, secretive, close-mouthed, tight-lipped.

talker *n.* **1** *The history master is a marvellous talker:* conversationalist, converser; speaker, lecturer, orator, speech-maker, speechifier; spokesman, *Slang* mouthpiece. **2** *She's quite a talker—I couldn't get a word in!:* loquacious person, voluble person, garrulous person, chatterbox, chatterer, windbag, prattler, babbler, blatherskite; gossip, scandalmonger.

tall *adj.* **1** *The boy is four feet tall:* high, in height. **2** *Professional basketball players are all very tall. A tall mountain loomed over the valley:* of more than average height, long-limbed, big, lanky, rangy, gangling; high, lofty, towering, soaring, elevated. **3** *Informal The tale of catching a 100-pound fish is a pretty tall story:* hard to believe, implausible, incredible, unbelievable, preposterous, absurd, hard to swallow, exaggerated, embellished.
Ant. 1 wide, broad, long, deep. **2** short, squat, low, stubby, dwarfish; tiny, small, diminutive. **3** believable, credible, plausible, reasonable, unexaggerated, unembellished, unadorned; true, real, authentic.

tally *n.* **1** *The golfer added up the strokes on his tally:* score-card, score-pad. **2** *The final tally was 200 votes for and 150 against:* count, mark, score; total, sum, muster, census, poll.
—*v.* **3** *The judges tallied the scores:* record, mark down, register, list, catalogue, post; count, add, sum up, total, compute, calculate, tabulate, reckon. **4** *The cheque stubs don't tally with my bank statement:* match, square, correspond, agree, conform, accord, concur, harmonize.

tame *adj.* **1** *Even a tame monkey can become a dangerous pet. Bill is too tame to stand up for his own rights:* domesticated, domestic, broken; docile, gentle, mild, tractable, unresisting, submissive, subdued, pliable, pliant, complaisant, amenable, meek, timorous, timid. **2** *Country life was too tame for the boys from the city:* unexciting, uninteresting, dull, boring, tedious, prosaic, flat, lifeless; quiet, placid, serene, tranquil.
—*v.* **3** *Cowboys used to tame wild horses. She'd better tame that violent temper:* break, make docile, domesticate, subdue, train; control, conquer, overcome, master, dominate, govern, manage, restrain, repress, suppress, curb, bridle, rein, check, regulate, damp.
Ant. 1 wild, untamed, undomesticated, intractable, unsubmissive, stubborn, obdurate, strong-willed. **2** exciting, interesting, stimulating, spirited, lively, wild, frenzied, tumultuous.

tamper *v.* **1** *Don't tamper with other people's affairs:* meddle, interfere, intrude, intervene, horn in, butt in, poke one's nose into. **2** *Has anyone tampered with this lock?:* tinker, fool around, *Informal* mess around, monkey around, muck about.

tan *v.* **1** *It takes skill to tan cowhide:* convert to leather, treat with tanning solution. **2** *Fair-skinned people don't tan easily:* sun-tan; brown, bronze.
—*adj.* **3** *The walls are covered with tan wallpaper:* light-brown, brownish, yellow-brown, beige, tawny, sandy, cinnamon, roan, sorrel, khaki.
Ant. 2 fade; peel **3** dark-brown, mahogany.

tang *n.* **1** *The salad-dressing has too much of a tang of garlic:* strong taste, flavour, savour, pungency, bite, sharpness, sting, piquancy, tartness, acridness, acridity; smell, odour, reek, aroma, scent. **2** *There's a tang of autumn in the air:* trace, tinge, hint, touch, suggestion, bit, smack.
◇ *Word origin: Tang,* a penetrating flavour or smell, also means the shank of a sword blade or knife. The word comes from Middle English *tange,* serpent's tongue, insect's sting, probably from Old Norse *tangi,* point, sting.

tangible *adj.* **1** *A ghost is not a tangible thing:* palpable, touchable, material, solid, physical, corporeal, substantial. **2** *The jury needs tangible evidence in order to convict:* concrete, real, actual, material, verifiable, indubitable, positive, clear-cut, obvious, manifest.
Ant. 1 intangible, untouchable, impalpable; immaterial, ethereal, spiritual, incorporeal, disembodied.

tangle *v.* **1** *The strings of the puppet tangle easily. The wind tangled the girl's long hair:* twist, snarl, entangle, ravel, knot; disarrange, dishevel, tousle, jumble, disorder, rumple, ruffle.
—*n.* **2** *A deer was caught in the tangle of brambles. The negotiations were in a hopeless tangle:* snarl, knot, tanglement, entanglement, web, net, network, mesh, skein, jungle, labyrinth, maze; fix, impasse.

Ant. 1 untangle, unsnarl, unknot, unravel, loose, loosen, untwist; arrange, order, array, organize, straighten, disentangle.

tank *n.* **1** *A fifty-gallon tank supplies water to the kitchen and bath:* storage tank, vat, container, receptacle; reservoir, cistern, boiler; fish tank, aquarium. **2** *Each infantry company was supported by three machine-guns, a howitzer, and two tanks:* armoured vehicle on caterpillar tracks; armoured car.

◇ *Word origin:* The first recorded use in English of *tank* is in the following account of a voyage to India in 1616: "Besides their rivers they have many ponds which they call *tanques.*" Related words in various languages of India mean reservoir, cistern, pond. A military tank is so-called because of the secrecy surrounding the manufacture of the first British tanks during World War I. "Tank" was the code word for the armoured hulls whilst they were being built and shipped to France.

tantalize *v. The speaker tantalized us with tales of exotic lands and buried treasure:* torment with unobtainable prospects, tease, taunt, make one's mouth water, whet the appetite, tempt, titillate, lead on, intrigue; fascinate, bewitch, charm, captivate, entice.

Ant. satisfy, gratify, fulfil, appease.

◇ *Word origin: Tantalize* comes from the name of *Tantalus,* a mythical king who was condemned to Hades for his crimes on earth and made to stand in water that receded when he tried to drink, whilst at the same time he was unable to reach the fruit-laden branches above him.

tantrum *n. The child's tantrums were caused by frustration:* burst of temper, fit of passion, hysterics, outburst, fit, paroxysm, explosion.

tap[1] *v.* **1** *Rain tapped on the window-pane:* strike lightly, touch lightly, rap, pat, beat softly, peck, thud.

—*n.* **2** *I felt a tap on my shoulder and turned to see Bill grinning:* light strike, gentle blow, touch, stroke, pat, rap, peck.

tap[2] *n.* **1** *Who left the hot-water tap on?:* faucet, spigot, stopcock, cock, spout.

—*v.* **2** *The bartender tapped a new keg of beer:* put a tap in, unplug, unstopper, remove the stopper, uncork; open the stopcock of; draw liquid from, draw off, broach. **3** *The country must tap new sources of energy:* draw upon, use, utilize, employ, put to work.

tardy *adj.* **1** *It has been a tardy spring this year:* late, not on time, unpunctual, behind time, behindhand, belated; overdue, remiss, dilatory. **2** *The tardy progress of the work discouraged the foreman:* slow, slow-paced, sluggish, slack, creeping, crawling, leisurely, languid, snail-like; procrastinating, reluctant.

Ant. 1 punctual, on time, prompt; undelayed; early, premature. **2** fast, speedy, quick, rapid; industrious, eager, zealous.

◇ *Word origin: Tardy* and *tarry* come from Latin *tardus,* slow. *Retard* has the same base and literally means to "slow back," to delay.

target *n.* **1** *The arrow hit the centre of the target. The organization's target was to double its membership:* mark, object aimed at; objective, object, goal, aim, end, purpose, ambition; design, plan, intent, intention. **2** *Paul was the target of the practical joke:* butt, scapegoat, victim, prey, dupe, gull, pigeon, laughing-stock.

◇ *Word origin: Target* is the diminutive of Middle English *targe,* light shield, hence a small, round shield, which was probably the first target.

tariff *n.* **1** *The tariff on cigarettes has gone up:* duty, tax, export tax, excise tax, excise, assessment, impost, levy; list of import-export taxes, customs list, trade controls. **2** *The railways increased their tariff by ten per cent:* fare, freightage; (*loosely*) charge, rate, fee, price, cost, expense, rent, commission.

◇ *Spelling tip:* A *tariff* on imported goods can double their price, and *tariFF* has a double *f.*

tarnish *v.* **1** *Silver tarnishes easily:* oxidize, corrode, discolour, blacken, dull, dim, darken, lose lustre. **2** *The charge of fraud tarnished the firm's reputation:* discredit, degrade, defile, defame, vilify, stigmatize, denigrate, disgrace, dishonour, taint, stain, sully, spot, blemish, blacken, foul, befoul, smirch, besmirch, soil, blot, erode, dirty, dull, dim, darken, drag through the mud.

Ant. 1 shine, polish, burnish, clean; brighten. **2** enhance, glorify, credit, exalt.

tarry *v.* **1** *I mustn't tarry here a moment longer:* linger, dally, remain, stay, bide, abide, rest, pause, *Informal* hang around, cool one's heels. **2** *Don't tarry too long before coming to a decision:* dawdle, delay, wait, take time, be tardy, lag, procrastinate, put off, postpone, stave off, temporize, stall, hang back.

Ant. 1 leave, go, depart, be off, run, run along, move on, get moving. **2** rush, hurry, hasten, be quick, hustle, expedite, precipitate, spur.

◇ *Word origin:* See TARDY.

tart[1] *adj.* **1** *This lemon juice is very tart:* sour, sourish, sharp, astringent, acid, acrid, acetic, vinegary; piquant, pungent, bitter. **2** *The clerk's tart reply offended the customer:* sharp, caustic, cutting, biting, acerb, acrid, crusty.

Ant. 1 sweet, sugary, saccharine, cloying; mild, bland, mellow, flat. **2** sweet, kind, kindly, gentle, mild, pleasant, agreeable, benign, genial, polite, gracious, friendly, amiable, good-natured.

◇ *Word origin: Tart*[1] comes from Old English *teart,* sharp, rough.

tart[2] *n. The hostess served cream with apple tart:* individual pie, small fruit pie, open pie; pastry shell.

◇ *Word origin: Tart*[2] comes from Old French *tarte.*

task *n. Each child is responsible for certain household* *tasks:* chore, job, duty, work, labour, stint, mission, assignment, charge, errand, business.

> **Exploring the Word:** Latin *taxare,* to appraise something as by weighing it in the hand to see if it is solid, hence to rate or evaluate, gives us *tax,* a proportional assessment based on evaluation or appraising; *task,* originally perhaps an amount of work performed for one's lord in lieu of paying a tax; *taste,* originally to judge or appraise by touching with the tongue or taking into the mouth, as a *wine-taster* does (hence, *good taste* is good judgement in artistic or social things); and *taxi* (originally *taximeter cab,* then *taxi-cab,* and finally *taxi*), via French *taxe,* charge.

taskmaster *n. The major was a stern taskmaster:* martinet, slave-driver, tyrant, despot, dictator; master, boss, supervisor, superintendent, overseer, foreman, director, manager.

taste *v.* **1** *Can you taste the mint in the icing? This punch tastes just like pineapple juice:* experience the flavour of; savour, discern; have a flavour of, savour of, smack of. **2** *Taste some of this cake:* sample, eat a little of, take a bite of, try, test; drink a little of, take a sip of. **3** *At last he tasted the joys of success:* experience, partake of, encounter, meet, undergo, feel, enjoy, relish, savour, have a foretaste of.

—n. **4** *This cole-slaw has a sour taste:* flavour, savour, relish, smack, tang, piquancy. **5** *Have a taste of this delicious pie:* mouthful, bite, morsel, bit, crumb, sample, spoonful; sip, swallow, nip. **6** *Rachel has a taste for sweets. Modern furniture is more to my taste than antiques:* liking, predilection, propensity, leaning, inclination, penchant, bent, partiality, disposition, fondness, craving, hankering, longing, desire, fancy, yearning, whim, relish, appetite, thirst, hunger. **7** *Sylvia has marvellous taste in clothes. The comic's jokes were in poor taste:* aesthetic judgement, sense of beauty, discernment, artistic appreciation; sense of propriety, propriety, correctness, judgement, discrimination, insight, delicacy, decorum.

Ant. 3 miss. **6** distaste, dislike, disinclination, disrelish; hatred, abhorrence, loathing. **7** tastelessness; impropriety, indelicacy, coarseness, crudeness.

tasteful *adj. Everyone admired the tasteful décor:* showing good taste, aesthetic, artistic, attractive, elegant, exquisite, refined, cultured, handsome, beautiful.

Ant. tasteless, inelegant, ugly, loud, flashy, garish, tawdry, gaudy, unrefined, uncultured.

tasteless *adj.* **1** *The soup was rather tasteless:* having no taste, flavourless, unflavoured, without savour, bland, insipid, weak, flat, mild, watery. **2** *No one laughed at the tasteless joke. Her wardrobe seems completely tasteless:* lacking good taste, cheap, common, crude, rude, coarse, crass, gross, uncouth, improper, inappropriate, unseemly, unsuitable, insensitive, indelicate, indecent, indecorous, low, ribald, disgusting, distasteful, offensive, gaudy, flashy, garish, inelegant, unrefined, uncultured.

tasty *adj. The stew was quite tasty:* good-tasting, delicious, delectable, luscious, toothsome, *Slang* scrumptious, yummy; savoury, flavourful, flavoursome, full-flavoured, appetizing; piquant, spicy, well-seasoned, hot, zestful, tangy.

tatters *n. pl. The old vagrant was dressed in tatters:* shreds, rags; ragged clothing, torn clothes, cast-off clothes; patches.

taunt *v.* **1** *The bully taunted the smaller boy:* jeer at, jeer, mock, insult, tease, rag, gibe, twit, guy, snigger at, deride, sneer at, ridicule, make fun of, poke fun at, make game of; torment, provoke, harass.

—n. **2** *The older sister's cruel taunts reduced the little girl to tears:* jeer, mockery, insult, teasing remark, ragging, chaffing, gibe, derision, sneer, scoff, snigger, ridicule, sarcastic remark, scornful remark, slur, verbal abuse; tormenting, provocation, harassment.

Ant. 1 humour, flatter, jolly, coddle, court, pander to, truckle to, curry favour with, butter up; praise, compliment. **2** humouring, flattering, coddling, pandering, truckling, currying favour, buttering-up, praise, compliment.

taut *adj.* **1** *Keep the tape-measure taut:* drawn tight, tight, stretched out full, tense, not slack, not loose, rigid, unbending, inflexible, under strain, unrelaxed. **2** *The captain runs a taut ship:* well-regulated, orderly, businesslike, well-disciplined, tight, neat, tidy, trim, spruce, smart, shipshape.

Ant. 1 slack, loose, relaxed, flexible. **2** sloppy, slovenly, undisciplined, messy, untidy.

tawdry *adj. That tawdry dress will never do for church:* showy, flashy, flamboyant, garish, gaudy, loud, tasteless, inelegant, vulgar, crass, tatty, cheap, gimcrack, pretentious, ostentatious, conspicuous, obtrusive.

Ant. tasteful, elegant, refined, *Informal* classy, high-class, superior, stylish; simple, plain, quiet, reserved.

◇ *Word origin: Tawdry* is a quick way of saying *St. Audrey.* It comes from *St. Audrey's lace,* later slurred to *tawdry lace,* a type of cheap silk necktie sold at St. Audrey's Fair at Ely in the Middle Ages.

tawny *adj. Her tawny skin tans easily:* tan, bronze, yellowish-brown, light-brown, brownish, beige, fawn, sandy; dusky, swarthy, olive.

◇ *Word origin: Tawny* comes from French *tanné,* tanned.

tax *n.* **1** *The French kings used to levy a burdensome*

tax on salt: payment of money to support a government and its service; (*variously*) income tax, corporation tax, vehicle excise duty, value added tax, excess profit tax, capital transfer tax, estate duty, capital gains tax; impost, assessment, excise, levy, tariff, duty, custom, toll. **2** *Racing to catch the train was a tax on our nerves:* burden, strain, strenuous demand, load, exertion, drain; charge, obligation, duty.
—*v.* **3** *The government does not tax certain charitable foundations:* impose a tax on, assess, levy, exact a duty from. **4** *The over-active child taxed the nurse's patience:* burden, overburden, weigh, weight, lade, load, saddle, strain, overwork, tire, stretch, try; drain, exhaust, wear out, deplete.
Ant. **1** deduction, non-taxable income, allowance.

"Taxes are the price we pay for civilized society." —*Oliver Wendell Holmes, Jr.*

---

teach *v. M. La Farge teaches French at the local school. The professor prefers to teach post-graduate students:* give instruction in, conduct classes in, give lessons in, be employed as a teacher; give instruction to, conduct seminars in, give lessons to, lecture on, instruct, educate, school, tutor, coach, drill, exercise, discipline, supervise, prepare, prime; inform, enlighten, edify, indoctrinate, implant.
Ant. learn, study, attend school, college, university, etc., be educated.

teacher *n. The teacher dismissed the class:* (*variously*) schoolteacher, schoolmaster, master, schoolmistress, mistress, lecturer, instructor, professor, don, tutor, maestro, educator, preceptor, pedagogue, trainer, coach.

teaching *n.* **1** *The teaching of maths has changed drastically in the last decade. Audio-visual aids have revolutionized teaching:* instruction, instructing, schooling, tutoring, tutelage, training, preparation; the teaching profession, education, pedagogy. **2** *The teachings of Mao Tse-tung are revered in China:* precept, doctrine, dogma, principle, tenet.

team *n.* **1** *A team of oxen pulled the plough:* harnessed pair, yoked group; pair, set, yoke, tandem. **2** *A football team consists of eleven players:* sports team, side; (*football, cricket, hockey*) eleven, (*Rugby Union*) fifteen, (*netball*) seven. **3** *A team of heart specialists performed the surgery. He's a member of the government's economic advisory team:* group, staff, crew, band, gang, company, association, alliance, league, confederation, federation, coalition, combine, party, faction, circle, clique, coterie.
—*v.* **4** *The horses are teamed in pairs. Several charities teamed up to raise funds for the new hospital;* yoke, join, couple, rig; combine, unite, join together, band together, get together, ally, form an alliance, merge, incorporate, federate, unify, consolidate, amalgamate; co-operate, pool one's efforts.
Ant. **4** unjoin, unyoke, unhook, uncouple; separate, divide, part, go one's separate way.
◇ *Usage note:* Technically, *team* is a collective noun. It can be either singular or plural, depending on whether it is a unit or is composed of a number of individuals. Thus, you may say *The team is the best in the league* (as a unit) or *The team are driving to the match in their own cars* (as separate individuals).
◇ *Word origin: Team* and *teem* come from Old English *team*, offspring. A *team* is a number of related animals or people (related by working or playing together), and *to teem* means to be full to overflowing, as with children in a house.

tear[1] *n. A tear rolled down the child's cheek:* teardrop.

tear[2] *v.* **1** *The kitten tore a hole in the curtain. Silk stockings used to tear easily:* rip, rend, rive, split, slit, cleave, sever, sunder, shred, pull apart, come apart, pull to pieces, run, snag. **2** *The handbag-snatcher tore the bag from the woman's hand:* pull, grab, seize, wrench, pluck, snatch, yank. **3** *Political conflict has torn the nation:* divide, disunite, split, splinter, rend, disrupt. **4** *When the bell rang, the students tore out of the room:* speed, race, rush, hasten, run, bolt, dash, dart, sprint, spurt, shoot, fly, hie, scurry, scuttle, scoot, scud, whiz, gallop, sweep, whisk, plunge, scamper, scramble, skedaddle, hustle, go hotfoot, make tracks.
—*n.* **5** *The house has withstood many years of wear and tear:* damage, destruction, ravage, hard treatment, abuse, hard use; impairment, injury. **6** *Mother will sew up the tear in your shirt:* rip, rent, slit, split, hole; gap, break, breach, crack, rift, fissure, fault, rupture, opening.
Ant. **1** mend, repair, sew, stitch up. **3** unite, re-unite, bind, solidify, join, strengthen. **4** creep, crawl, amble, stroll, saunter, dawdle. **6** patch, mend.

tease *v.* **1** *Everyone teased her about her Irish brogue. Don't tease the cat or it will scratch you:* taunt, gibe, ridicule, mock, chafe, rag, needle, make fun of, laugh at, twit, guy, bait, goad, heckle, mimic, tantalize, torment; pester, plague, worry, provoke, annoy, irritate, bother, aggravate. **2** *My uncle was a tease, always making fun of us:* teaser, taunter, mocker, needler, tantalizer, tormentor.
Ant. praise, laud, compliment; humour, flatter; comfort, console, soothe, placate.
◇ *Word origin: Tease* comes from Old English *taesan*, to pull apart, pluck, a sense surviving in the hairdressing technique of *teasing* the hair.

technique *n.* **1** *The young artist has imagination but needs to improve his technique:* technical skill, form, skilfulness, craft, expertness, proficiency, facility, adroitness, know-how, knack.

2 *Doctors are developing a technique for treating diabetes:* procedure, method, way, technology, approach, manner, system.

Exploring the Word: In Greek, the word for carpenter is *tektōn.* The related word for metalworking and shipbuilding is *tekhnē,* which later came to mean any art or science. *Tektōn* gives us our word *architect* (Greek *arch-* master), master builder, and *tekhnē* gives us such words as *technical, technician, technique,* and *technology.* Thus, the concept of *technology* has always been synonymous with that of art and science. However, if an ancient Greek were to hear of the *Manchester University Institute of Technology* or indeed of any *Tech.,* he would assume they were schools for language study, because in Greek *tekhnologia* means systematic treatment of grammatical structures.

tedious *adj.* **1** *Cleaning out the basement was a tedious job:* time-consuming, long-drawn-out, slow, long; tiring, wearying, fatiguing, exhausting, irksome, burdensome, onerous, oppressive, laborious, dreary, dismal. **2** *The tedious play put the audience to sleep:* dull, boring, monotonous, unexciting, uninteresting, unimaginative, prosaic, humdrum, insipid, vapid, drab, dreary, dismal, dry, lifeless, tiresome, wearisome, jejune.

Ant. 1, 2 exhilarating, exciting, interesting, amusing, enthralling, stimulating. **1** quick, fast, short. **2** imaginative, stirring, lively, provocative, inspiring.

tedium *n. He couldn't face the tedium of twenty more years at the same job:* monotony, dullness, tediousness, sameness, routineness, boredom, rut, ennui, tiresomeness, drabness, dreariness.

Ant. excitement, interest, amusement, fascination, stimulation, liveliness, exhilaration; inspiration, challenge.

teem *v. Rome teems with tourists in the summer:* swarm, be overrun, overflow, abound, be full of, be inundated, brim, gush, bristle with, be well-stocked, burst at the seams.

Ant. be empty of, have a scarcity of.

◇ *Word origin:* See TEAM.

teeter *v. The plank teetered as the boys walked across it. After being hit, the boxer teetered and then fell:* wobble, totter, sway, see-saw, stagger, lurch, reel.

teetotaller *n. Max is a teetotaller himself but will offer his guests cocktails:* non-drinker, abstainer, prohibitionist.

Ant. drunk, drunkard, alcoholic, dipsomaniac, sot, *Slang* boozer, wino.

◇ *Word origin: Teetotal* comes from the word *total* with the initial *t* pronounced separately for emphasis, as if someone said "I practise total abstinence, T-total abstinence." Today we might say that a person practises total abstinence "with a capital T."

telepathy *n. He knew what I was thinking by telepathy:* thought-transference, sixth sense, second sight, extra-sensory perception, ESP; clairvoyance, spirit communication.

tell *v.* **1** *Tell the truth:* narrate, declare, relate, recount, give an account of, report, set forth, recite, speak, utter, state, say, pronounce, mention, enunciate, advise, acquaint, apprise, communicate, make known, impart, reveal, divulge, disclose, unfold, let fall, spout, publish, broadcast, spread abroad, bruit, blab, blazon, babble, inform, betray, breathe a word about, describe, chronicle, detail, depict, portray, sketch, paint a picture; confess, own. **2** *Fish lovers find it easy to tell fresh from frozen. Even the weatherman couldn't tell that the storm was coming:* tell apart, distinguish, discern, identify, make out, recognize, perceive, ascertain, find out, work out, calculate, reckon, apprehend, make out, see; predict, forecast, foretell. **3** *Tell the orchestra to begin:* direct, instruct, order, command, bid, ask, request. **4** *A six-year-old should be able to tell the time. The nun sat telling her beads:* recite, count, count off, number, enumerate; compute, calculate, reckon, estimate. **5** *Years of dissipation finally told on his health:* take effect, influence, have force, weigh, carry weight, take a toll of, be potent, register, be of account.

Ant. 1 keep quiet, keep mum, be mute, keep secret, hide, conceal; listen. **2** confuse, mix up.

telling *adj. The court's decision was a telling blow for the freedom of the press:* effective, effectual, efficacious, powerful, forceful, potent, weighty, momentous, trenchant, significant, influential, cogent, material, definite, definitive, decisive, decided, positive, conclusive, valid, solid, important, consequential.

Ant. ineffective, unimportant, immaterial, insignificant, meaningless, trivial, inconsequential, indefinite, indecisive.

tell-tale *n.* **1** *Don't expect that tell-tale to keep a secret:* talebearer; tattle-tale, tattler, blabbermouth, gossip, busybody, scandalmonger; informer, *Slang* squealer, grass.

—*adj.* **2** *There were tell-tale fingerprints on the jam jar:* revealing, give-away, betraying, divulging, disclosing, informative, enlightening; confirming, verifying, affirming.

temerity *n. How can he have the temerity to ask such personal questions? No one had the temerity to shoot the rapids:* audacity, insolence, gall, brazenness, brashness, nerve, cheek, brass, impudence, effrontery, forwardness, sauciness, freshness, impertinence, intrusiveness, pushiness, indiscretion, *Yiddish* chutzpah.

Ant. reserve, reticence, politeness, tact, discretion, meekness, bashfulness, shyness; timidity, cowardice, caution, wariness.

temper *n.* **1** *The mob was in no temper to listen to reason:* frame of mind, mood, disposition, humour. **2** *She stalked out of the room in a temper:* anger, rage, fury, wrath, ire, irritation, irritability, annoyance, vexation, bad humour, pique, peevishness, acrimony, choler, spleen, gall, bile, animus, dander, huffiness, irascibility, churlishness, dudgeon, indignation, displeasure, umbrage, passion, emotion, ferment. **3** *Don't make me lose my temper!:* good humour, kindly disposition; calmness, composure, equilibrium, balance, *Slang* cool. —*v.* **4** *It's a new process for tempering steel:* strengthen, harden, toughen, anneal. **5** *Mother tried to temper Father's anger with soothing words:* soften, moderate, allay, appease, pacify, tranquillize, mitigate, palliate, calm, compose, quiet, soothe, still.

Ant. **2** good will, good humour, calmness, composure. **3** bad humour, bad disposition, anger, rage, fury, indignation, wrath, ire, irritation, vexation, pique, peevishness; fit of emotion, ferment. **4** soften, weaken. **5** intensify, heighten, aggravate, excite, increase, stir, rouse, arouse, pique.

temperament *n. The child has an equable temperament. The young opera singer has a true artist's temperament:* disposition, nature, mood, frame of mind; temper, make-up, character, personality, spirit, soul; humour, tone, cast, quality, tenor, complexion, leaning, tendency, bent.

> **Exploring the Word**: Latin *temperare*, to mix in the proper proportion, gives us our word *temper* (both verb and noun) as in the phrases *to temper a critical remark with a smile* and *being out of temper*. *Distemper* is any of several diseases of animals, especially dogs, that can unbalance or derange them. Our words *temperament* and *temperamental* also refer to degrees of moderation (or immoderation). *Temperate* refers to moderation or mildness and to a moderate climate; *temperance* also refers to moderation in the consumption of (or even abstinence from) alcoholic beverages. *Temperature* refers to degrees of heat or cold (the chemist, Robert Boyle, introduced the word in its present-day sense in a work published in 1670, *Of the Temperature of the Submarine Regions as to Heat and Cold*). Returning to the arts and crafts, Latin *temperare* also gives us *tempera*, a painter's medium of a mixture of water and any of various substances, as egg yolk, glue, gum, etc.

temperamental *adj. She's as temperamental as a prima-donna:* highly-strung, excitable, moody, thin-skinned, sensitive, explosive, volatile, passionate, emotional, hot-headed, fiery, peppery, mettlesome, hysterical; unpredictable, capricious, erratic, fickle, unreliable, undependable, unstable; wilful, headstrong.

Ant. even-tempered, easy-going, cool, cool-headed, calm unexcitable, *Slang* unflappable; reliable, dependable, predictable, steady.

temperance *n.* **1** *Exercise temperance in giving advice to friends:* moderation, forbearance, self-control, restraint, prudence; abstention, self-denial. **2** *The restaurant is not licensed because the owner believes in temperance:* teetotalism, abstinence, abstemiousness, sobriety, prohibition.

Ant. **1, 2** intemperance, immoderation. **1** lack of restraint, abandon, indulgence, extravagance. **2** drinking, imbibing; alcoholism, dipsomania, boozing.

temperate *adj.* **1** *Be more temperate in your eating habits. A good teacher must be temperate in her criticism of her pupils' work:* self-restrained, self-controlled, moderate, unextravagant, sparing, sedate, sober, sane, rational, reasonable; calm, even, cool, cool-headed, level-headed, composed, collected, unruffled, steady, tranquil, easy-going, self-possessed, patient, dispassionate, unimpassioned. **2** *Mexico City has temperate climate:* mild, gentle, soft, moderate, clement, pleasant, mellow; balmy, sunny, warm.

Ant. **1, 2** intemperate, immoderate. **1** unrestrained, uncontrolled, extreme, excessive, abandoned, inordinate, unreasonable, extravagant, irrational; temperamental, excitable, passionate, impassioned, explosive, volatile, hot-headed, hysterical, frenzied, wild. **2** inclement, harsh, severe, unpleasant.

tempestuous *adj. Tempestuous winds sometimes endangered the ship. The two candidates had a long, tempestuous debate:* stormy, turbulent, raging, violent, furious, agitated, tumultuous; passionate, impassioned, emotional, frenzied, overwrought, wrought-up, hysterical, frantic, excited, fiery, hot, explosive, feverish.

Ant. calm, placid, peaceful; relaxed, unagitated, easy, serene, tranquil, quiet, cool-headed, unemotional, disinterested.

temporal *adj.* **1** *The Pope exercises spiritual rather than temporal authority:* civil, lay, secular, non-spiritual, non-clerical, non-ecclesiastical, profane. **2** *Most of us are too busy with temporal things to think about eternity:* non-eternal, temporary, transient, fleeting, passing, ephemeral, day-to-day, worldly, mundane, mortal, earthly.

Ant. **1** ecclesiastical, clerical; spiritual, sacred, religious. **2** eternal, everlasting, other-worldly, unearthly, heavenly.

temporary *adj. We took temporary quarters until the house was ready. The book enjoyed temporary fame:* momentary, brief, impermanent, passing, fleeting, transitory, transient, fugitive, short-lived, ephemeral, evanescent; stopgap, provisional, interim.

Ant. lasting, everlasting, permanent, durable, enduring, long-lived, persisting, protracted.

tempt *v.* **1** *Don't tempt a thief by leaving the keys in* *the car. That chocolate cake tempts me:* seduce, entice, inveigle, lure, allure, woo, bait, decoy; appeal to, attract, pull, invite, take one's fancy, whet the appetite, draw, intrigue, tantalize; captivate, bewitch, charm. **2** *Don't tempt providence by driving recklessly:* put to the test, fly in the face of, try, risk, provoke, incite, goad, rouse, arouse, prick.

Ant. 1 discourage, repel, repulse, disgust.

temptation *n. He couldn't resist the temptation of her rosy lips. Cooks must avoid the temptation to nibble:* tempting, allurement, lure, enticement, attraction, seduction, pull, draw, bait, inducement, incentive, incitement, stimulus, fascination, captivation, charm, spell.

tenacious *adj. He held my hand in a tenacious grip. She was tenacious in her belief and could not be swayed:* fast, firm, clinging, iron, hard, set; persevering, persistent, resolute, obstinate, determined, stubborn, obdurate, inflexible, uncompromising, immovable, unchangeable, unbending, inexorable, unwavering, unfaltering, unswerving, undeviating, adamant, steadfast, staunch, stalwart, constant, relentless, mulish, pigheaded, dogged.

Ant. loose, lax, limp, slack; unpersevering, undetermined, irresolute, flexible.

tenant *n. The landlord collects the tenants' rent monthly:* renter, lessee, leaseholder; lodger, paying guest, boarder; occupant, inhabitant, resident, dweller, denizen.

Ant. landlord, lessor.

tend[1] *v.* **1** *Children tend to like cosy corners:* be inclined, be disposed, have a tendency, be apt, be likely, be liable, have an inclination, lean, have a leaning, predispose, bid fair to. **2** *At the junction take the road that tends west:* lead, bear, extend, point, head, aim, be bound for, gravitate, move.

tend[2] *v. Who will tend the garden whilst you're away? A practical nurse should have experience in tending sick people:* attend to, care for, take care of, look after, keep an eye on, mind, watch over, watch; nurse, nurture, foster, wait on, minister to.

Ant. neglect, ignore.

tendency *n. He has a tendency to talk too much. Stock-market prices showed an upward tendency:* inclination, disposition, proclivity, proneness, propensity, trend, predisposition, readiness, penchant, bent, leaning, habit, set, drive, turning, drift, direction, course, gravitation, heading, aim.

Ant. disinclination, indisposition, aversion, reluctance, unreadiness, hesitancy.

tender[1] *adj.* **1** *The nurses bathed the patient with tender care. He sounds tough but he has a tender heart:* soft, gentle, delicate, dainty; kind, good, compassionate, sympathetic, considerate, understanding, thoughtful, caring, soft-hearted, warm-hearted, loving, affectionate, fond, sentimental, merciful, benevolent, benign, generous. **2** *I cooked the joint for hours but it still isn't tender:* soft, succulent, brittle, easily broken, fragile, delicate. **3** *She left home at the tender age of thirteen:* young, youthful, juvenile, under age, immature, inexperienced, unsophisticated, impressionable, callow, green. **4** *The area around the wound is very tender. Since the scandal, bankruptcy is a tender subject in this office:* sensitive, painful, requiring delicacy; sore, aching, swollen, inflamed, raw.

Ant. 1 tough, hard; mean, cruel, brutal, inhuman, sadistic, vicious, unsympathetic, unkind, inconsiderate, uncaring, hard-hearted, cold-hearted, hateful, merciless, pitiless, ruthless. **2** tough, hard, leathery, stiff. **3** old, elderly, advanced; full-grown, grown-up, mature, experienced, seasoned, practised, worldly, worldly-wise, sophisticated. **4** insensitive.

Exploring the Word: A *tenant*, a *lieutenant*, and a *tenor* have something in common. All come from Latin *tenere*, to hold. A *tenant* holds lands or property, a *lieutenant* is one who holds authority in *lieu* of another (as when a king, captain, or other superior is away), and a *tenor* is so-called because this voice originally sang or "held" the melody. The same Latin verb gives us *tenet*, a belief or principle held to be true; *tenacious*, holding tight; and *tenure*, the period during which one holds a position or office. Latin *tenere* is also the base of: *abstain*, to hold off, refrain; *contain*, to hold with, hold; *content*, that which is held; and *continent*, which literally means *container*, one of the "containers" or boundaries of the seven land masses of the globe (*incontinent* means not able to hold one's temper, not able to hold back one's desires); *detain*, to hold apart, as a prisoner is *detained* in a gaol, or to hold apart for the future, to delay; *entertain*, to hold the attention agreeably, as between less agreeable tasks; *maintain* (Latin *manus*, hand), to hold in the hand, hence to preserve, as *to maintain a building in good repair*, and later came to mean declare or affirm, to hold to a belief; *obtain*, literally to hold or reach toward, hence to get hold of; *pertain* and *appertain*, to hold or reach through, hence to relate or apply; and *pertinacious*, holding thoroughly or tightly, hence persevering, persistent.

tender[2] *v. If I may tender a suggestion to the committee—:* present formally, make formal offer of, proffer, prefer, submit, put forward, lay before, volunteer, give, hold out, advance, propound, propose, extend, suggest.

Ant. withhold; withdraw, retract.

tender-hearted *adj. The tender-hearted man wept at the news:* sympathetic, compassionate; soft-hearted, kind-hearted, considerate, understanding, thoughtful, gentle, mild, humane, benevolent, benign, merciful, generous.

Ant. hard-hearted, cold-hearted, mean,

cruel, brutal, sadistic, inhuman, vicious, merciless, pitiless, callous, unsympathetic, inconsiderate.

tenderness *n.* **1** *The tenderness of her touch soothed the child:* softness, gentleness, delicacy, mildness; kindness, kindliness, loving-kindness, compassion, sympathy, goodness, benevolence, beneficence, humanity, humaneness, mercifulness; fondness, warmth, affection, lovingness, love. **2** *The tenderness of the wound made walking painful:* sensitivity, soreness, painfulness, aching, rawness, smarting.

Ant. 1 hardness, toughness; cruelty, meanness, brutality, viciousness, unkindness, hard-heartedness, cold-heartedness, coldness, harshness, severity, mercilessness. **2** insensitivity.

tenet *n. The tenets of his religion exclude divorce:* belief, doctrine, dogma, way of thinking, credo, canon, teaching, conviction, persuasion, principle, maxim, rule, thesis, view, opinion.

tenor *n. Were you able to grasp the tenor of his speech?:* meaning, sense, import, significance, essence, content, substance, gist, drift, implication, connotation; intent, intention, object, purport, purpose, trend, direction, tendency.

tense *adj.* **1** *Keep the rope tense:* stretched tight, tight, taut, drawn, rigid, stiff; inflexible, unyielding. **2** *The witness was extremely tense:* nervous, strained, taut, drawn, wrought-up, high-strung, tremulous, uneasy, restless, restive, fidgety, jittery, excited, agitated, shaky, fearful, apprehensive, timorous, *Slang* uptight.

—*v.* **3** *Tense the reins and the horse will stop. The woman tensed at the sound of footsteps:* tighten up, draw up, make taut, stiffen, brace.

Ant. 1 relaxed, slack, loose, limp, flaccid; pliant, flexible. **2** relaxed, loose, calm, cool, collected, self-possessed. **3** relax, loosen.

tension *n.* **1** *Too much tension will break the string:* stretching, straining, stress, tugging, traction, pressure, pulling, exertion; spring, elastic force; tightness, tautness, rigidity, stiffness. **2** *She collapsed under the tension of waiting for the news. You could feel the tension when the two rivals walked into the room:* strain, stress, dread, anxiety, apprehension, nervousness, restiveness, trepidation, misgiving, fearfulness, perturbation, hostility, combativeness, suppressed anger, *Slang* bad vibrations.

Ant. 1 slack, looseness, laxness. **2** relief, relaxation, ease, calmness, serenity, tranquillity.

tentative *adj. Our holiday plans are still tentative:* unconfirmed, not settled, unsettled, not final, under consideration, open to consideration, subject to change, provisional, speculative, not definite, indefinite, undecided; experimental, trial, temporary, not permanent, ad interim, acting, probational, probationary, proposed.

Ant. confirmed, settled, final, set, firm, conclusive, definite, decided, closed, unchangeable.

> **Exploring the Word**: *Tent, legal tender, tendons* and *tensions* all come from Latin *tendere,* to stretch, extend, reach. *Tent* comes from late Latin *tenta,* "stretched." (If you ever pitched a tent, you will remember that it involves lots of stretching.) To *tender* something is to extend it or offer it (*to tender a reward*) and *legal tender* is that which can be legally offered in payment of a debt, as money. *Tendons* are sinews used to stretch out the limbs, and *tensions, tense,* and *intense* refer to stretching tightly, being stretched or under stress. Latin *tendere* gives us many other words including: *attend* and *attention,* to reach or be at a place, and the stretching of one's mind toward something; *contend* and *contention,* literally stretching together, striving with someone; *distend,* to stretch, stretch apart or bulge out; *extend* and *extent,* to stretch out, the farthest stretch or limit; *intend* and *intent,* to stretch out or strive for something and that which is stretched for; *ostentatious,* literally stretched out in front of others for display, showing off; *portend* and *portent,* to reach into the future, to warn or be an omen of what will happen; and *pretend, pretence,* and *pretentious,* to stretch before the fact, stretching the truth, a striving to create a false appearance.

tenuous *adj. Some legislators put forward a rather tenuous argument against the bill:* weak, flimsy, insubstantial, unsupported, slight, slim, thin, slender, frail, fragile, shallow, paltry, unconvincing, half-hearted, uncertain, indefinite.

Ant. strong, solid, valid, substantial.

◇ *Word origin: Tenuous* comes from Latin *tenuis,* thin. The same Latin base gives us *extenuating* (thinning out, hence tending to make less blameworthy, as *extenuating circumstances*) and *attenuate* (to make thin or fine, reduce in size or value).

tepid *adj. I want my coffee hot, not tepid! Such an accusation demands more than a tepid response:* lukewarm, warmish; moderate, mild, unemotional, half-hearted, indifferent, impassive, phlegmatic, languid, apathetic, nonchalant, lackadaisical.

term *n.* **1** *A doctor's secretary must be familiar with medical terms:* word, phrase, expression, idiom, technical word, technical expression; name, designation, appellation. **2** *The President of the Republic will complete his term of office next year. The lease is for a term of three years:* span of time, span, period, time, duration, course, spell, while, interval, stage, cycle; age, era, epoch, reign, administration, dynasty. **3** *One of the terms of the contract calls for high-grade steel in the construction:* stipulation,

condition, provision, proviso, clause, item, detail, requirement, pre-requisite, requisite, *Slang* catch, string. **4 terms** *He's on good terms with his employer:* relations, standing, footing, status, state, position, circumstance.
—*v.* **5** *The art critic termed the picture the worst of the year:* call, name, designate, dub, tag, style, characterize, cite.

terminal *adj.* **1** *Fore Street is the terminal stop on this bus route:* last, final, concluding, end. **2** *Doctors say he has terminal cancer:* causing death, mortal, fatal, deadly, lethal.
—*n.* **3** *We'll pick you up at the bus terminal:* station, depot, terminus, stand.
Ant. **1** first, initial; beginning, opening. **2** non-fatal, chronic; temporary, passing.

terminate *v. Let's terminate this meeting by ten p.m. The lease terminates in May:* bring to an end, come to an end, conclude, finish, stop, cease, close, wind up, complete, discontinue, expire, lapse, run out.
Ant. begin, start, commence, initiate, open; continue, pursue, extend.

termination *n. A few people lingered after the termination of the meeting:* end, ending, close, closing, conclusion, concluding, finish, wind-up, completion, cessation, finis, finale, expiration, lapse.
Ant. beginning, start, commencement, initiation, opening, inception.

terrain *n. The mountainous terrain was too rugged to cross without a guide:* topography, ground, area, region, territory, tract, countryside; surroundings, environment, milieu, setting, zone, district.

> **Exploring the Word:** Latin *terra,* dry land, earth, gives us some obvious words and some that aren't so obvious. The obvious ones include *terrain, territory, terrestrial, terrace* (originally a level area raised above a field or cut into a hillside, as for farming, and only later a level area, sometimes paved, next to a house and hence also a row of houses), and the Latin phrase we still use, *terra firma* (firm land, solid ground, as opposed to oceans and lakes or the air). The less obvious words that come from Latin *terra* include: *terrier,* because such dogs were used to pursue rabbits and the like in their burrows; *tureen,* originally any earthenware dish; *interment,* putting into the earth, burial; *subterranean,* underground; *terra cotta,* brown kiln-burnt clay, or pottery or a statue made of it; and even *Mediterranean,* literally "in the middle of the land," because the Mediterranean Sea is almost surrounded by dry land and was in the middle of the ancient world.

terrestrial *adj.* **1** *Although they can swim, polar bears are terrestrial animals:* land, ground, earth-bound; riparian. **2** *Terrestrial gravity is greater than lunar gravity:* of the earth, earthly, worldly, global, mundane.
Ant. **1** marine, aquatic, sea, water. **2** celestial, astral, lunar, cosmic, space.

terrible *adj.* **1** *A terrible storm destroyed many houses. We're paying a terrible rent now:* severe, fierce, intense, strong, harsh, brutal, rough; great, huge, tremendous, immoderate, extreme, excessive, inordinate, monstrous, enormous, terrific. **2** *What's that terrible smell?:* extremely bad, horrible, horrid, obnoxious, awful, hideous, repulsive, revolting, offensive, odious, distasteful, unpleasant, objectionable, intolerable, insufferable, appalling, hateful, bad, heinous, dire, ghastly, shocking, beastly. **3** *The roar of a lion can be a terrible sound:* alarming, frightening, terrifying, fearful, fearsome, harrowing, awful, dreadful, horrifying, formidable, distressing, upsetting, disturbing.
Ant. **1** mild, moderate, harmless, gentle; small, insignificant, paltry. **2** wonderful, excellent, fine, good, great, pleasing, pleasant, delightful, admirable, nice; worthy, praiseworthy, laudable, commendable. **3** comforting, reassuring, encouraging, settling, soothing, calming, easing.

terrific *adj.* **1** *A terrific explosion woke the whole town:* severe, intense, fierce, harsh, terrible, extreme, excessive, monstrous, great, enormous, huge, inordinate, immoderate, tremendous; frightening, terrifying, fearful, fearsome, alarming, harrowing, distressing, awful, dreadful, horrifying, upsetting, disturbing. **2** *You must read this book, it's terrific:* great, fine, good, wonderful, excellent, marvellous, sensational, fabulous, fantastic, stupendous, smashing, super, extraordinary, remarkable, exceptional, *Slang* super, fab, out of this world.
Ant. **1** mild, moderate, harmless, gentle, slight, insignificant, paltry; comforting, reassuring, encouraging, settling, soothing, calming, easing. **2** bad, terrible, awful, lousy, stinking, horrible, dreadful, hideous, revolting, unpleasant, appalling, distasteful.

terrify *v. The thunderstorm terrified the child:* fill with terror, frighten, scare, alarm, horrify, panic, petrify, unman, abash, daunt, cow, intimidate, overawe, make one's hair stand on end, make one's blood run cold, make one's skin creep; upset, disturb, appal, dismay, agitate, disquiet.
Ant. comfort, reassure, encourage, hearten, soothe, calm, ease, please, delight.
◇ *Usage note:* See AFRAID.

territory *n.* **1** *The mountainous territory was impassable in winter:* terrain, region, land, area, zone, district, sector, clime, tract, countryside, locale. **2** *The Aleutian Islands are part of Alaska's territory:* domain, realm, province, sphere of influence, dominion, commonwealth, state, nation, principality, kingdom, empire; protectorate, dependency, colony; bailiwick, pale, limits, confines, bounds.

terror *n. The rumble of the volcano caused terror among the natives:* fear, fear and trembling, fright, affright, horror, panic, alarm, dread; dismay, trepidation, perturbation, consternation, apprehension, awe, anxiety, agitation, disquiet, disquietude.
Ant. security, reassurance, encouragement, comfort, calm, quiet, tranquillity.

terse *adj. The terse statement that "war is hell" says it all:* brief and to the point, concise, pithy, succinct, crisp, incisive, pointed, neat, compact, condensed, compressed, clear, clear-cut, unambiguous, summary, trenchant, epigrammatic, axiomatic; brief, short, abrupt, curt.
Ant. rambling, circuitous, roundabout, diffuse, discursive, verbose, wordy, lengthy, long, long-winded; vague, confused, ambiguous.
◇ *Word origin: Terse* originally meant rubbed to a polish, clean. Only later did this expand to mean clearly stated. It comes from Latin *tergere*, to rub, polish, which also gives us *detergent*, a surface-acting chemical agent with a strong cleansing effect.

test *n.* **1** *Chemical tests showed the presence of potassium. The manœuvres will be a test of the army's effectiveness:* analysis, investigation; trial, try-out, dry run, dummy run, probe, check, feeler; proof, verification, confirmation, corroboration. **2** *The teacher gives us a test every Friday:* examination, exam, quiz; questioning, questionnaire, catechism.
—*v.* **3** *The teacher will test the class on spelling today. The drug company tested the new product for years before putting it on the market:* quiz, examine; analyse, investigate, probe, experiment with; try out, put to the proof, prove, verify, confirm, corroborate, substantiate, validate, send up a trial balloon, throw out a feeler.

testament *n.* **1** *His last will and testament directed that all his property go to his eldest son:* final written will; bequest, legacy, settlement. **2** **Testament** *The Apocrypha are Biblical writings belonging to neither Testament:* Old Testament, New Testament.

testify *v. The fingerprint expert was asked to testify at the trial. His hard work testified to his determination to succeed:* bear witness, give evidence, state as fact, swear; attest, show, indicate, signify, demonstrate, evidence, evince, manifest.

testimonial *n.* **1** *His former employer wrote him a glowing testimonial:* recommendation, reference, commendation, endorsement, citation; certificate, affidavit, deposition. **2** *The statue is a testimonial to a great general:* memorial, monument, tribute; medal, ribbon, trophy.

testimony *n.* **1** *The witness's testimony cleared the suspect:* declaration under oath, statement, attestation, avowal, averment, profession, acknowledgement, deposition, affidavit, evidence. **2** *Winning the scholarship is testimony of her intelligence:* evidence, witness, indication, demonstration, manifestation, verification, corroboration, confirmation, affirmation, certification, endorsement, documentation, proof.
Ant. 2 denial, disavowal, refutation, disproof, contradiction, rebuttal.

> **Exploring the Word**: Latin *testis*, witness, originally meant "third person standing by" (the *te-* was originally *tri-*, three, and the *-stis* meant "stander"), so-called because a witness is a third party in a litigation. From Latin *testis*, witness, we get: *testify*, to bear witness, act as a witness; *testimony* and *testament*, both meaning the declaration of a witness (each *Testament* of the Bible is so-called because it bears witness to a covenant between God and man); to die *intestate*, literally to die without having witnessed one's own will, hence to die without having left a valid will; *testes* (Latin plural of *testis*) and *testicles*, so-called because they bear witness to a male's virility. Latin *testis*, witness, also gives us *attest*, to bear witness to, affirm; *contest*, literally to bring together witnesses from both sides, hence a debate, dispute, or struggle; *detest*, literally to reject or refute someone's testimony, hence to be against or hate him; and *protest*, literally to come forward as a witness, hence to declare one's negative testimony publicly.

testy *adj. Too little sleep put her in a testy mood:* irritable, ill-humoured, quick-tempered, irascible, cross, cranky, grumpy, crabby, snappish, snappy, fretful, peevish, petulant, sullen, waspish, churlish, splenetic, choleric, snarling, cantankerous, contentious, touchy, temperamental, impatient, crusty, fractious, captious, cavilling, faultfinding, sharp-tongued, perverse, acrimonious, moody, *Informal* filthy.
Ant. good-natured, good-humoured, even-tempered, sweet, pleasant, amiable, genial, friendly, agreeable, kind, generous, patient, smiling, sunny.

tête-à-tête *n. No one wanted to interrupt the couple's tête-à-tête:* private conversation, intimate conversation, confidential talk, private interview; chat, talk, parley, confabulation.

tether *n.* **1** *The boy had a pet goat that he led around on a tether:* leash, halter; rope, chain, cord.
—*v.* **2** *The keeper tethered the monkey to its perch:* put on a leash, tie with a rope, tie, chain, fasten, secure; hobble.
Ant. 2 untether, unleash, untie, unchain, unfasten; release, free, loose, loosen.

text *n.* **1** *Did you just look at the pictures in the book or did you also read the text? All the city schools use the same history text:* main body of writing, words, wording, content; textbook, schoolbook, manual. **2** *The preacher took his text from*

Judges: sermon, subject, subject matter, theme, topic, thesis, argument; passage, quotation, verse, paragraph, sentence.
Ant. 1 illustration; notes, index, glossary; prologue, introduction, epilogue.

textile *n.* Usually plural, *Lancashire and Yorkshire acquired their wealth from textiles:* woven material, fabric, cloth, piece goods.

texture *n. Satin has a smooth texture. The fine texture of her hair makes it unmanageable:* weave, composition, structure, character, quality, make-up, surface, nap, grain, feel, look; fineness, coarseness.

thank *v.* **1** *Don't forget to thank the hostess:* express gratitude to, express appreciation to, make acknowledgement to, tender thanks to, be grateful to, bless.
—*n.* **2 thanks** *Let us express our thanks to God for this wonderful harvest:* gratitude, gratefulness, appreciation, thankfulness; benediction, blessing, grace.
Ant. 2 ingratitude, ungratefulness.
◇ *Word origin: Thank* comes from Old English *thanc,* thanks, thought. Thus there was once a semantic connection between *giving thanks* and *being thoughtful.*

thankful *adj. We were thankful for his help:* full of thanks, grateful, appreciative, feeling gratitude, expressing appreciation; obliged, beholden, indebted to.

thankless *adj.* **1** *No one wanted to take on the thankless task:* not likely to be appreciated, unappreciated, unacknowledged, unrewarded; unrewarding, fruitless, useless, profitless, vain, bootless; undesirable, unwelcome, uninviting, unpleasant, disagreeable, distasteful. **2** *A thankless employer inspires little loyalty:* ungrateful, ingrate, unappreciative, unthankful, thoughtless, inconsiderate, heedless, unmindful, ungracious; critical, faultfinding, cavilling.
Ant. 1 appreciated, acknowledged, rewarded; rewarding, fruitful, useful, desirable, pleasant, agreeable. **2** appreciative, grateful, thankful.

thaw *v.* **1** *The ice thawed in the sun:* melt, dissolve, liquefy, soften; warm, warm up. **2** *The little girl's smile thawed the crusty old man:* melt, warm, make friendly, make sympathetic, make affectionate, make forgiving; become genial, relax, unbend, break the ice, shed one's reserve.
—*n.* **3** *The spring thaw caused heavy flooding:* thawing, melting; period of above-freezing winter weather, first warm weather of spring.
Ant. 1 freeze, freeze solid, solidify, congeal, harden; cool, chill. **3** freeze, frost.

theatre *n.* **1** *The play was given in a small theatre off the Strand. Medical students watched the operation from a glass-enclosed theatre:* (*variously*) playhouse; cinema, picture house, amphitheatre, colosseum, arena, lecture hall, auditorium, lyceum. **2** *A good production of* Hamlet *is real theatre:* drama, stage entertainment, theatricals, show business; theatricality, histrionics. **3** *The entire theatre gave the star a standing ovation:* audience, spectators, house, auditorium, assemblage, assembly, gallery. **4** *The South Pacific was the theatre of much of the action in World War II:* field of operations, site, arena, stage, setting, scene, place.

"So long as there is one pretty girl left on the stage, the professional undertakers may hold up on their burial of the theatre."
—*George Jean Nathan*

---

theatrical *adj.* **1** *Most of the producer's friends belong to the theatrical world:* of the theatre, stage, film, entertainment, show-business, *Slang* show-biz; dramatic, thespian, histrionic. **2** *His manner is altogether too theatrical:* exaggerated, stilted, affected, artificial, stagy, unnatural, mannered; pretentious, ostentatious, extravagant, showy, flashy, grandiloquent, grandiose, magniloquent.

theft *n. He was arrested for jewel theft:* stealing; (*variously*) robbery, burglary, thieving, filching, pilfering, purloining, shop-lifting, hijacking, fraud, swindling, embezzlement, rustling.

theme *n.* **1** *Love is a major theme of Robert Browning's poetry:* subject, subject matter, topic, text, motif, thesis, general idea, focus, keynote, point, question, argument, proposition, premise. **2** *Can you whistle the theme from the overture to* Don Giovanni*?:* melody, strain, tune, air, song; theme song.
◇ *Word origin: Theme* and *thesis* come from Greek *tithenai,* to put. Hence, a *theme* is literally something put forth as a topic to be discussed, or a melody that is to be elaborated in a composition.

> **Exploring the Word**: Greek *theos,* god, gives us *theology* (Greek *logos,* science), "divine science," and *theocracy* (Greek-derived suffix *-cracy,* rule, government), government by God through a priest-king or priesthood; *atheism,* without God, i.e. the belief that there is no God; *monotheism* (Greek *monos,* single), belief in one God; *polytheism* (Greek *polus,* much, many), belief in many gods; and *pantheism* (Greek *pas, pan,* all), the doctrine that every part of the universe is a manifestation of God or worship of all gods of all cults (as in ancient Rome or modern India).

theology *n. After taking a degree in theology he taught comparative religion at a theological college:* divinity; (*variously*) science of divine things, religion, dogma, doctrine, system of belief.

theoretical *adj. The belief that the universe is expanding has been proved and is no longer theoretical:* consisting in theory, concerning theory, theoretic, conjectural, hypothetical, speculative, suppositional, postulatory, putative; abstract, academic, non-practical.

Ant. proved, proven, known, verified, corroborated, demonstrated, substantial, established; practical, applied.

theory *n.* **1** *Einstein developed the theory of relativity:* principle, law; science, doctrine, philosophy, ideology. **2** *The scientist's theory is that if matter exists, so must anti-matter. It's my theory that the dog will find its way home in a day or two:* idea, notion, concept, hypothesis, postulate, conjecture, thesis, speculation, surmise, supposition, guess, thought, opinion, persuasion, belief, presumption, judgement, conclusion, deduction, view.

Ant. 2 practice, application; proof, verification, corroboration, substantiation, demonstration, exhibition, example.

therapeutic Also **therapeutical** *adj. Aspirin isn't therapeutic but it does ease pain:* healing, curative, remedial, ameliorative.

therapy *n. Speech therapy corrected the child's lisp:* treatment, remedial procedure, healing, rehabilitation.

◇ *Word origin: Therapy* and *therapeutic* come from Greek *therapeuein,* to take care of, to serve as an attendant.

thereafter *adv. The door will be open until 4 o'clock; thereafter the key can be obtained from the verger:* after that, afterward, afterwards, subsequently, from that time on, from then on, thenceforth.

Ant. before, previously.

therefore *adv. The house was being demolished; therefore we had to move:* in consequence, consequently, so, hence, thus, ergo, for that reason, for which reason, on that account, on that ground.

thereupon *adv. The child murmured "good-night" and thereupon fell asleep:* then, thereon, forthwith, straight away, directly, immediately, suddenly, upon that, upon which, at once, without delay, in a moment, in the twinkling of an eye.

thesaurus *n. The thesaurus is on the shelf next to the dictionary:* dictionary of synonyms and antonyms, treasury of words, conceptual dictionary, semantic dictionary, word list.

◇ *Usage note:* The plural of *thesaurus* is *thesauri* (rhymes with "sore eye').

◇ *Word origin: Thesaurus* comes from Greek *thēsauros,* treasure house, strong-room, bank vault. Latinized during the life of Julius Caesar, the word acquired the figurative sense "storehouse of knowledge," and during the Renaissance it became the title of several great dictionaries of Greek and Latin. In more modern times *thesaurus* has been used to designate vocabularies of selected terms in special fields such as music or medicine. But what most people mean by a *thesaurus* nowadays is a book of synonyms and antonyms, whether arranged according to categories or in simple alphabetical order. This basic concept was invented by the English physician and scholar Peter Mark Roget (1779–1869) and first embodied in his monumental *Thesaurus of English Words and Phrases, classified and arranged so as to facilitate the Expression of Ideas and assist in Literary Composition (1852).*

thesis *n.* **1** *The engineer's thesis was that the new machinery would double production:* proposition, proposal, argument; theory, hypothesis, postulate, concept, notion, conjecture, speculation, surmise, supposition. **2** *You may take a post-graduate degree by examination or by presenting a thesis:* dissertation, long essay, paper, treatise, disquisition, discourse, formal composition, article, tract; critique, commentary; master's thesis, doctoral thesis.

thick *adj.* **1** *That little restaurant makes good thick sandwiches:* fat, deep, wide, broad, big, bulky; generous, lavish, unstinted, munificent, liberal. **2** *Thick smoke impeded the firemen. This gravy is too thick:* dense, heavy, impenetrable; viscous, viscid, gelatinous, glutinous, concentrated, condensed, compact, solid, coagulated, clotted. **3** *Grandfather spoke with a thick Irish brogue:* strong, decided, pronounced, extreme, great, heavy, intense, deep, profound. **4** *The illness made his speech thick:* inarticulate, indistinct, muffled, fuzzy, blurred; hoarse, husky, guttural, throaty. **5** *You'll never get that into his thick head!:* stupid, dumb, dense, obtuse, slow, slow-witted, dull, dull-witted, doltish, *Informal* wooden, fat-headed. **6** *Informal The two men are as thick as thieves:* close, intimate, chummy, familiar, friendly, inseparable, devoted; brotherly, sisterly. **7** *The air was thick with mosquitoes:* swarming, teeming, dense, profuse, overflowing, packed, crowded; abundant, copious, plenteous, heaped, piled.

Ant. 1, 2 thin. **1** slim, narrow, shallow, slight, lean, spare, small. **2** light, watery, runny, diluted. **3** slight, faint, weak, vague. **4** articulate, distinct, clear; shrill, shrieking. **5** smart, clever, intelligent, keen, sharp, quick, quick-witted. **6** distant, unfriendly, estranged, hostile. **7** bare, barren, bereft, empty.

thicken *v.* **1** *Add cornflour to thicken the sauce:* make thick, become thicker, make dense; set, clot, cake, congeal, coagulate, condense, gelatinize, jell. **2** *The plot thickens:* become more complicated, intensify, deepen, darken, muddy, muddle.

Ant. 1 thin, dilute, thaw. **2** solve, resolve.

thicket *n. The deer hid in the thicket:* thick bushes, bush, undergrowth, covert, shrubs, shrubbery; growth of small trees, brake, bracken, grove, copse, scrub, forest, wood.

thickset *adj.* **1** *The thickset trees hid the sun:* close-planted, close-set, dense, packed, solid, close. **2** *One brother was thickset and the other tall and thin:* stocky, husky, sturdy, chunky, bulky, stout; squat, stubby, stumpy, tubby, dumpy, roly-poly.

Ant. 1 scattered, dispersed, sparse. **2** slim, slender; tall, rangy, reedy, gangling, lanky.

thick-skinned *adj.* **1** *A rhinoceros is thick-skinned:* having a thick skin, pachydermatous. **2** *He's too thick-skinned to take offence at such an insult:* insensitive, insensible, unfeeling, unsusceptible, imperturbable, unmovable, callous, hardened, inured.

Ant. 1, 2 thin-skinned. **2** sensitive, feeling; concerned, caring, passionate, emotional; vulnerable, soft, fragile.

thief *n. The police caught the thief red-handed:* robber, burglar, bandit, crook; (*variously*) mugger, filcher, pilferer, purse-snatcher, purloiner, shop-lifter, pickpocket, sneak-thief, kleptomaniac, housebreaker, hijacker, highwayman, rustler; swindler, embezzler, defrauder.

"Many a man is saved from being a thief by finding everything locked up." —*E. W. Howe*

---

thievish *adj.* **1** *That thievish fellow is bound to wind up in gaol:* thieving, given to stealing, larcenous, light-fingered, dishonest. **2** *The boy's skulking, thievish manner aroused the shopkeeper's suspicions:* thieflike, stealthy, furtive, sneaky, surreptitious, secretive, sly.

Ant. 1 honest. **2** open, frank, direct, above-board, straightforward.

thin *adj.* **1** *The boy was thin for his age. A light-bulb filament is very thin:* lean, not fat, slender, slim, skinny, slight, scrawny, emaciated, gaunt, lanky, lank, spindly, fine, fine-spun, narrow, threadlike, delicate; fragile, sheer, transparent. **2** *This gravy is too thin:* watery, runny, diluted. **3** *That's a pretty thin excuse. His hair is getting thin on top:* weak, insubstantial, feeble, faint, inadequate, insufficient; scant, sparse, spare.
—*v.* **4** *Thin the tops of the bushes. The traffic begins to thin around 7p.m.:* make thin, thin out, prune, reduce, diminish, grow thin, curtail. **5** *Thin the paint so that it will spread more easily:* dilute, water, water down, qualify.

Ant. 1 – 3 thick. **1** fat, overweight, corpulent, chubby, rotund, plump, obese. **2** viscous, concentrated. **3** strong, substantial, solid, forceful, adequate, sufficient; full, abundant, dense, plentiful. **4, 5** thicken. **4** increase, grow, heighten.

thing *n.* **1** *A tin-opener is a very useful thing. What's that thing that fell out of the motor?:* object, article, gadget, *Slang* thingumajig, thingumabob, what's-its-name, what-d'ye-call-it, dingus. **2** *You mean thing, you! The kitten was such a sweet little thing:* creature, living being, person, human being, entity. **3** *What a wonderful thing to do! How are things with you?:* deed, act, feat, action; event, occurrence, eventuality, proceeding, happening, matter, affair, transaction, business, concern, circumstance. **4** *I want to say one thing about your behaviour. There's just one thing missing to make this perfect:* statement, thought; detail, particular, item, feature, point, aspect. **5** Often **things** *She hasn't a thing to wear to the dance. Pack your things and go:* article of clothing, suitable outfit; clothing, clothes, possessions, belongings, movables, effects, goods, equipment, paraphernalia; *Slang* gear.

think *v.* **1** *Think before you act. We've been thinking about you all day:* use one's mind, apply the mind, reason, reflect, cogitate, deliberate, turn over in the mind, mull over, ponder, contemplate, meditate, ruminate, have in mind, make the subject of one's thought, dwell on, brood, keep in mind, remember, recall, recollect, use one's wits, rack one's brain. **2** *I think it's going to rain. Mother thinks she'll fly to Canada:* believe, have an opinion, deem, judge, surmise, presume, anticipate, conclude, guess, suppose, reckon, expect, speculate; imagine, conceive, fancy; intend, purpose, propose, plan, mean, design, contrive.

Ant. 1 be thoughtless, act rashly, act unreasonably; forget, slip one's mind.

thinker *n. It will take a real thinker to work out the solution:* man of thought, intellect, sage, master-mind, wizard, mental giant, smart person, bright person, philosopher, intellectual, *Slang* boffin, brains, egghead.

Ant. man of action, dunce, dumb-bell, dummy, ninny, nincompoop, dope, idiot, imbecile, moron, *Informal* dunderhead, noodle.

thinking *adj.* **1** *This series is written for the thinking man:* rational, reasoning, reflective, thoughtful, contemplative, meditative, philosophical; intelligent, smart, bright, studious, educated, cultured, cultivated, sophisticated.
—*n.* **2** *The driver averted an accident by quick thinking. What is your thinking on the matter?:* using one's head, thought, brainwork, judgement, deduction; conclusion, belief, inference; view, concept, position, stand, impression, surmise; contemplation, meditation, reflection, consideration, rumination, study, deliberation, speculation, mental absorption. **3** *She crossed the street without thinking:* paying attention, using one's head, being heedful.

thin-skinned *adj.* **1** *Thin-skinned potatoes are best for boiling:* having a thin skin. **2** *Don't be so thin-skinned; learn to shake off criticism:* easily offended, sensitive, touchy, susceptible, squeamish; irritable, petulant, ill-tempered, peevish, irascible, testy, huffy, sullen, sulky, quarrelsome, cross, cantankerous, crabbed, grumpy.

Ant. 1, 2 thick-skinned. **2** insensitive, callous, hardened; even-tempered, sweet-tempered, good-natured, sweet, kind, happy, content.

thirst *n.* **1** *The tennis players worked up a tremendous thirst:* need of liquid, dryness in the mouth, thirstiness. **2** *A keen student has a thirst for knowledge:* desire, keenness, craving, hankering, yearning, hunger, appetite, voracity, stomach, lust, passion, itch, relish, fervour, ardour.
—*v.* **3** *The children thirsted for ice-cold milk:* be thirsty for, desire to drink, be thirsty, be parched. **4** *The avaricious man thirsted for wealth:* desire, covet, crave, hanker for, yearn, lust, itch, hunger, pant.
Ant. 2 lack of interest, apathy; dislike, distaste, hate, abhorrence, aversion, revulsion, repulsion. **4** scorn, disdain, be uninterested in, be apathetic toward; dislike, hate, detest, abhor.

thorn *n.* **1** *These rose-bushes have a lot of thorns:* sharp spine, spike, barb, spur, prickle. **2** *The jibes of the other children were a thorn in his flesh:* bane, curse, torment, affliction, infliction, care, woe, trouble, plague, scourge, sting, gall, bitter pill, nuisance, annoyance, vexation, crown of thorns, cross, sore point.

"And the heart that is soonest awake to the flowers
Is always the first to be touch'd by the thorns."
—*Thomas Moore*

thorny *adj.* **1** *This bush is very thorny:* full of thorns, overgrown with thorns; prickly, spiny, barbed, spiked, bristling. **2** *How to reduce a company's costs without making anyone redundant is a thorny problem:* difficult, full of difficulties, hard, tough, troublesome, dangerous, dire, formidable, sticky, ticklish, critical, crucial; complex, perplexing, involved, annoying, irksome, vexatious, trying.
Ant. 2 easy, simple, untroublesome.

thorough *adj.* **1** *She gave the house a thorough cleaning. The new employee seems to be a very thorough worker:* complete, thorough-going, careful, full, painstaking, meticulous, exhaustive, all-inclusive, all-embracing, definitive. **2** *The entire production was a thorough success:* perfect, pure, utter, sheer, total, entire, absolute, unmitigated, unqualified, downright, out and out; uniform, consistent, of a piece.
Ant. 1, 2 partial, incomplete. **1** careless, slipshod, sloppy, lackadaisical. **2** marred, mitigated, qualified, imperfect, with reservations.
◇ *Word origin: Thorough* is a variant of *through,* originally meaning "through and through."

thoroughbred *adj.* **1** *The farmer raises thoroughbred black Angus:* pure-bred, pure-blooded, full-blooded, unmixed, pedigree.
—*n.* **2** *This merino sheep is a true thoroughbred:* pure-bred animal, pure-blooded animal. **3** Sometimes **thoroughbred** *Ten thoroughbreds are entered in the Derby:* horse of the thoroughbred breed, racehorse. **4** *That girl is a thoroughbred through and through:* aristocrat, blue-blood, high class person.

thoroughfare *n. The shopping centre is located near the main thoroughfare south of the city centre:* through street, street, highway, main road, road, avenue, boulevard.
Ant. dead-end street, no through road, cul-de-sac; alley, lane, back-street, side-street.

thoroughly *adv.* **1** *Search the house thoroughly:* completely, fully, exhaustively, inclusively, from top to bottom, through and through, carefully, meticulously. **2** *We had a thoroughly good time:* perfectly, in all respects, utterly, entirely, totally, completely, absolutely, downright, out and out; uniformly, consistently, from beginning to end, throughout.
Ant. 1, 2 partially, incompletely. **1** carelessly, sloppily, inconclusively, lackadaisically. **2** imperfectly, somewhat, in part; slightly.

thought *n.* **1** *Give the matter careful thought. The man stared blankly, lost in thought:* thinking, mental activity, deliberation, cogitation, consideration, reflection introspection, meditation, contemplation, rumination, musing, reverie, thoughtfulness, brown study. **2** *What are your thoughts on the matter? The thought of measuring volume by displacement of fluid came as a sudden inspiration to Archimedes. Sir James Jeans made important contributions to scientific thought:* idea, notion; opinion, conclusion, judgement, belief, view, speculation, supposition, surmise, sentiment, fancy, imagination, concept, conception; doctrine, credo, tenet, dogma. **3** *It's not the gift, it's the thought that counts:* thoughtfulness, consideration, concern, caring, attention, kindness, kind-heartedness, regard.

thoughtful *adj.* **1** *The magazine contains a thoughtful article on the international situation. Why are you so quiet and thoughtful today?:* full of thought, serious, thinking, probing; contemplative, reflective, meditative, musing, introspective, pensive, wistful. **2** *What a thoughtful gift!:* considerate, kind, kind-hearted, neighbourly, solicitous, attentive, caring, loving.
Ant. 1, 2 thoughtless. **1** shallow, facetious, unthinking, heedless, rash, reckless, irresponsible, remiss. **2** inconsiderate, insensitive, unkind, mean, cruel, cold-hearted; rude, impolite, neglectful.

thoughtfulness *n. We appreciate your thoughtfulness in sending flowers:* consideration, kindness, kind-heartedness, solicitousness, attentiveness.

thoughtless *adj.* **1** *Several thoughtless mistakes cost the man his job:* unthinking, careless, heedless, inattentive, imprudent, improvident, ill-considered, ill-advised, neglectful; stupid, dumb, silly, foolish, scatter-brained, rattle-brained, hare-brained, absent-minded. **2** *Her thoughtless remark offended everyone:* inconsiderate, insensitive, rude, impolite, unkind, indiscreet, inadvertent, rash, reckless, unreflecting.

Ant. 1, 2 thoughtful. **1** intelligent, smart, wise, sage, prudent, provident, well-advised, thinking, careful, alert. **2** considerate, sensitive, diplomatic, kind-hearted, solicitous, polite, courteous, discreet.

thoughtlessness *n.* **1** *The driver's thoughtlessness caused the accident:* carelessness, inattention, inattentiveness, heedlessness, neglect, negligence, oversight, absent-mindedness, rashness, recklessness, imprudence. **2** *The son's thoughtlessness hurt his mother's feelings:* lack of consideration, unconcern, insensitivity, unkindness, rudeness, impoliteness.

thrash *v.* **1** *Teachers used to thrash disobedient pupils:* whip, spank, cane, switch, birch, strap; lash, beat, flog, flail, scourge, flagellate; lambaste, trounce, maul, drub. **2** *The child thrashed around so much that he fell off the chair:* toss, plunge, wiggle, squirm, writhe, flounce, tumble, joggle, jiggle, heave, jerk. **3** *Farmers used to thresh their wheat by hand:* separate the grains of, flail, separate the wheat from the chaff. **4** *Community leaders met with a police official to thrash out mutual problems:* thresh out, resolve, argue out, solve, conclude by discussion.

◇ *Usage note: Thrash* was originally a variant of *thresh.* We are still free to use either of the two forms in the idiom *to thrash* (or *thresh*) *out* (a problem, difference, or the like).

threadbare *adj.* **1** *It's time to throw out that threadbare sweater:* worn-out, frayed, ravelled, shabby, ragged, tatty, worn to a thread, the worse for wear. **2** *The television play had a threadbare plot:* well-worn, hackneyed, banal, trite, cliché-ridden, stock, over-familiar, well-known, commonplace, routine, everyday, conventional, prosaic, humdrum, jejune.

Ant. 1, 2 new, brand-new. **1** unused, unworn, good as new. **2** novel, fresh, unique, singular, exciting, surprising, different, unusual.

threat *n.* **1** *Threats don't scare me:* menacing statement, terrorizing statement, intimidation; ill omen, portent, warning sign, premonition, foreboding, writing on the wall. **2** *The threat of an economic depression hangs over the world:* menace, danger, risk, hazard, peril, jeopardy.

Ant. 1, 2 promise. **1** bribe, enticement, reward.

threaten *v.* **1** *The gangster threatened to burn down the store unless the owner paid extortion money. The foreman threatened the lazy worker with dismissal:* promise injury, promise harm; menace, intimidate, cow, terrorize; warn, forewarn. **2** *Flood-waters are threatening the town:* menace, endanger, imperil, jeopardize; be imminent, impend, hang over.

Ant. 1, 2 protect, defend, safeguard, guard.

threatening *adj.* **1** *The bully's threatening remarks frightened the little child:* menacing, terrorizing, sinister, intimidating; warning, forewarning. **2** *Threatening clouds appeared on the horizon:* ominous, menacing, sinister, baneful, grim, alarming, ill-omened, foreboding, forbidding, inauspicious, unpropitious, loury; imminent, impending, approaching.

threshold *n.* **1** *The cabin has a flat stone for a threshold. Don't just stand there on the threshold, come in!:* doorstep, sill, groundsel, limen; entrance, doorway, door, gateway, portal. **2** *The scientist is on the threshold of a great discovery:* brink, verge, edge.

Ant. 2 end, termination, conclusion, finish.

thrift *n.* *To save money for your old age you must practise thrift now:* economy, frugality, thriftiness, parsimony, parsimoniousness, sparingness, close-fistedness; moderation, reasonableness.

Ant. extravagance, prodigality, wastefulness; excess, immoderation, unreasonableness.

◇ *Word origin:* See THRIVE.

thrifty *adj.* *Even though she had plenty of money, the old woman was very thrifty:* economical, frugal, parsimonious, economizing, sparing, saving, close-fisted, tight-fisted, penny-wise.

Ant. extravagant, free-spending, prodigal, spendthrift, uneconomical, wasteful, improvident; open-handed, generous.

thrill *n.* **1** *A thrill runs up and down my spine every time "The Rose of England" is played:* rush of excitement, tingle, quiver, throb, tremble, tremor, glow, flush. **2** *Seeing the pyramids was a real thrill:* thrilling event, adventure, satisfaction, kick; thrilling story, exciting thing.
—*v.* **3** *The close soccer final thrilled the crowd:* electrify, galvanize, stir, rouse, arouse, stimulate, excite, inspire, fire; delight, enrapture, transport, impress, tickle.

Ant. 2, 3 bore. **2** *Slang* drag. **3** calm, soothe, lull; bore, weary; irk, annoy.

◇ *Word origin:* No one gets a *thrill* when a dentist *drills* his teeth. Yet the two words probably come from a common Germanic ancestor-word. *Drill* comes from Dutch *drillen,* to drill; *thrill* comes from Old English *thyrlian,* to pierce. The sense "to pierce with a sudden wave of emotion" was developed by Shakespeare and his contemporaries. In their usage, however, it referred to painful emotions such as fear, remorse, and the like.

thrilling *adj.* *Catching my first salmon was the most thrilling part of the expedition. The spy story was thrilling:* exciting, stirring, awesome, sensational, electrifying, riveting, engaging, fascinating, absorbing, provocative, tantalizing, titillating; delightful, pleasurable.

Ant. boring, dull, uninteresting, tedious, monotonous.

thrive *v.* **1** *The garden seems to thrive on the new fertilizer:* grow vigorously, flourish, wax, bloom, fatten. **2** *Now that the new road is finished, the shopping centre should thrive:* prosper, succeed, get ahead, get on, grow rich, boom; be successful, be fortunate, turn out well.

Ant. 1 languish, die, wither, fade. **2** fail, go bankrupt; be unsuccessful, be unfortunate.

◇ *Word origin: Thrive* and *thrift* come from Old Norse *thrīfa,* to grasp, grab. Thus, one who *thrives* is literally a "grabber," and *thrift* literally means "acquisitiveness."

thriving *adj.* **1** *The tomato plants are thriving and plentiful this year:* growing fast, blooming, blossoming, flowering, luxuriant, rank, lush. **2** *The pizza restaurant did a thriving business. One brother is poor, but the other is thriving:* flourishing, prospering, prosperous, successful, succeeding, busy, vigorous; wealthy, rich, well-to-do, well-off, *Slang* on Easy Street, in clover.

Ant. 1 languishing, dying, withering, fading. **2** failing, bankrupt, unsuccessful poor, moneyless, penniless, destitute, poverty-stricken, impoverished, badly off, indigent, broke, *Slang* in Queer Street.

throaty *adj. The actor had a very throaty voice:* husky, deep, low, base, full-toned, sonorous, resonant; guttural, thick, gruff, hoarse, grating, rasping, croaking, cracked, dry.

Ant. high, thin, shrill, squeaky.

throb *v.* **1** *Her heart throbbed with the strain of walking up the hill:* beat, beat abnormally fast, pulsate, palpitate, vibrate, flutter, quiver, tremble, shake, twitch, heave, pant.
—*n.* **2** *The throb of drums from the disco could be heard through the park. Her nervousness was shown by a slight throb in her voice:* throbbing, beat, beating, pulsation, pulse, palpitation, vibration, oscillation, reverberation; flutter, fluttering, quiver, quivering.

throes *n. pl.* **1** *The company is in the throes of moving to new offices. The country is in the throes of a revolution:* upheaval, tumult, turmoil. **2** *The young mother was in the throes of labour when she reached the hospital:* pangs, spasms, paroxysms; ordeal, anguish. **3** *The dying man received extreme unction immediately before the final throes set in. In its death throes the whale spouted blood:* paroxysm, convulsion, agony.

◇ *Word origin: Throe* comes from Old English *throwian,* to suffer, feel pain, and has been long used to refer to processes and experiences so agonizing as to seem comparable to the agonies of birth and death. Note also that the word is used solely in the plural.

throng *n.* **1** *The pre-Christmas sale attracted a throng of shoppers:* great number, multitude, crowd, horde, host, army, mass, swarm, flock, pack, jam, rush, crush, flood, deluge.
—*v.* **2** *Spectators thronged along the parade route:* crowd, jam, cram, pack, swarm, mass, bunch, flock, press, surge, stream, herd, huddle, mill; gather, congregate, assemble, collect, cluster, converge.

Ant. 1 smattering, sprinkling, few. **2** disperse, scatter, disband.

throttle *v.* **1** *That villain ought to be throttled. The dictator throttled the press, lest news of his regime's atrocities got out:* choke, strangle, garrotte; choke off, block, check, smother, gag, stifle, silence, seal off, shut off, stop. **2** *The young pilot had to learn to throttle more smoothly:* work a fuel lever, feed the flow of fuel to an engine; (*variously*) change speed, reduce speed, increase speed.
—*n.* **3** *Pull out the throttle on a cold morning to help start the engine:* fuel valve, fuel lever.

Ant. 1 breathe, breathe easily; announce, proclaim, broadcast, reveal, disclose. **3** brake.

through *adj.* **1** *Is the work through yet? Dinner was through by the time the guests arrived:* finished, done, completed, concluded, ended, terminated, past. **2** *There are several through trains from Paris to Zurich:* direct, long-distance; non-stop, express.
—*adv.* **3** *The tunnel is high enough to walk through. Please read the list through?:* in one side and out the other, from one end to the other; from beginning to end, from first to last, from A to Z, all the way, to the end.

Ant. 1 begun, started, initiated. **2** local.

throughout *adv. The factory was painted green throughout. Throughout the late Middle Ages, witches were mercilessly hunted:* all over, in every part, everywhere; all the time, from beginning to end, all the way through.

Ant. here and there, in some places, in some parts; now and then, some of the time.

throw *v.* **1** *Throw the ball back to the bowler! Throw a sweater over your shoulders — it's chilly:* fling, hurl, toss, cast, pitch, heave, sling, let fly, lob, chuck, shy; propel, impel, launch, project, hurtle; put, place, put in, put on, put around. **2** *The horse threw his rider:* throw off, throw down, cause to fall to the ground, unseat; knock down, floor.
—*n.* **3** *He won a coconut on his very first throw:* toss, hurl, fling, cast, pitch, heave, sling, shy, chuck, lob, delivery, shot. **4** *The stronger wrestler won by three throws:* act of causing someone to fall to the ground; act of throwing off.

Ant. 1, 3 catch. **1** receive; give, hand.

thrust *v.* **1** *Thrust this wedge under the door. The angry man thrust his way through the crowd:* shove, push, poke, prod, butt, drive, press, force, ram, jam, impel, propel. **2** *The duellers thrust and parried. The pirate thrust the sword into the captain's back:* wield a sword, place a sword; stab, pierce, plunge, jab, lunge.

—*n.* **3** *The parachute instructor gave the student a hard thrust out of the plane's door. The rocket has a million pounds of thrust:* shove, push, poke, prod, boost, impulse; propelling force, propulsion force, impetus, momentum. **4** *Saint George killed the dragon with one thrust:* sword thrust, stab, stroke, lunge, plunge, pass, riposte, swipe. **5** *Napoleon's armies made a thrust into Russia:* military advance, assault, attack, drive, sally, raid, foray, incursion, aggression.
Ant. 1, 3 pull, draw, drag. **2, 4** parry. **5** retreat, withdrawal.

"Some are born great, some achieve greatness, and some have greatness thrust upon them." — *William Shakespeare*

---

thud *n. The book fell to the floor with a thud:* dull sound, thump, clunk, bang, knock, smack.

thug *n. The two thugs robbed the old man:* ruffian, hooligan, hoodlum, hood; (*variously*) gangster, mobster, robber, bandit, murderer, assassin, mugger, cut-throat.
◇ *Word origin:* A *thug* was formerly(in India) a member of a fraternity of professional robbers and murderers. The word goes back to Sanskrit *sthaga*, robber.

thumb *n.* **1** *The baby sucked its thumb:* inside finger, short finger next to the forefinger.
—*v.* **2** *He thumbed through the address book looking for the number:* flip through, leaf through, glance through, run one's eye through; handle, finger. **3** *Informal The student thumbed his way across country:* hitchhike, hitch, hitch a ride.

thump *v.* **1** *The speaker thumped his fist on the desk for emphasis:* strike, beat, hit, pound, knock, whack, thwack, bang, punch, buffet, batter, pummel, lambaste, slap, cuff, clip, jab, poke.
—*n.* **2** *Did you hear a thump in the attic? A piece of plaster fell and gave him a thump on the head:* clunk, thud, bang; heavy blow, heavy fall, knock, rap, slam, smack, clout, swat, whack, hit.

thunder *n.* **1** *Thunder and lightning woke everyone before the rain started. The thunder of artillery could be heard in the distance:* loud rumbling noise accompanying lightning discharge, thunderbolt, thunderclap; rumbling, clap, explosion, discharge, roar, boom, crash, crack.
—*v.* **2** *It thundered dreadfully all night long. Applause thundered through the concert hall:* give forth thunder, discharge thunder; rumble, reverberate, echo, resound, roll, peal, explode, boom.

thunderstruck *adj. The town was thunderstruck by the scandal:* astounded, astonished, dumbfounded, flabbergasted, aghast, agog, agape, awed, awestruck, overcome, amazed, surprised, bewildered, confused, perplexed.
Ant. unmoved, unexcited, indifferent, apathetic, calm.

thus *adv.* **1** *Hold the golf club thus:* in this way, in this manner, like this, like so, so; as follows. **2** *Costs and overheads are up; thus prices must rise:* therefore, so, hence, wherefore, consequently, accordingly, for this reason, ergo.
Ant. 1 the other way, the reverse way. **2** but, however, nevertheless, nonetheless, even so, in spite of this.

> **Exploring the Word:** *Thunder* comes from Old English *thunor*, thunder. Related Germanic words include *Thor*, the Norse god of thunder and war, whose name gives us *Thursday*, literally "Thor's day." Also related is *blunderbuss*, a musket, from Dutch *donderbus*, literally "thunder box." The related Latin word is *tonare*, to thunder, which gives us *detonate*, literally to "thunder off," to go off with the noise of thunder, and *astonish* and *stun*, literally to give or cause wonder as thunder does (when we are astonished we still say that we are *thunderstruck*). Our word *thunder* is also related to the name of *Stentor*, the thunder-voiced herald in Homer's *Iliad* whose name gives us our word *stentorian*.

thwack *n.* **1** *The branch sprang back and gave him a thwack across the shoulders:* blow, whack, smack, wallop, thump, knock, slap, clout.
—*v.* **2** *The boy accidentally thwacked his brother with the board:* whack, strike, hit, bang, baste, smack, wallop, thump, slap.

thwart *v. The barbed wire will thwart an infantry assault:* stop, frustrate, foil, balk, check, hinder, obstruct, baffle, inhibit, prevent, bar, ward off, stave off.
Ant. encourage, help, aid, support, abet; hasten, increase, aggravate, multiply, magnify.
◇ *Word origin: Thwart* comes from Old Norse *thvert*, transverse. *Thwart* is, of course, the basis of our word *athwart*, across the course of.

tic *n. He had a tic in his right cheek:* involuntary twitch, facial twitch, twitch, *Medical* trigeminal neuralgia, spasm, tic douloureux.
◇ *Word origin: Tic* is short for French *tic douloureux*, painful twitch. In English-language usage *tic douloureux* (pronounced *tick doo-luh-rer*) is synonymous with *trigeminal neuralgia*, an excruciatingly painful neuralgia of the *trigeminus*, the chief facial nerve.

tick *v.* **1** *You can't even hear this clock tick:* make a slight, sharp sound; click, clack, tap; make a sharp sound over and over again, tick-tock, beat, vibrate, oscillate, swing. **2** *Tick off the items on this list:* check, mark; record, note, mark down, list, enter, register, chronicle.
—*n.* **3** *Is there a tick in the engine?:* ticking noise; slight, sharp repeated sound; tick-tock, click, clack, tap; vibration, oscillation, throb, pulsation. **4** *Put a tick by each item you want to order:* mark, stroke, line, dot; scratch, notch, nick.

ticket *n.* **1** *He had two tickets for the latest West*

End play. Please show your ticket to the stewardess when you board the plane: ticket of admission, voucher, coupon, entry permit, pass; stub. **2** *The driver got a ticket for speeding:* parking-ticket, traffic summons. **3** *The sales ticket says that the coat costs £50:* tag, label, slip, marker, card. **4** *Slang Yes, this is just the ticket:* desired object, thing.
—*v.* **5** *Ticket the merchandise before putting it on display:* provide with a ticket, put a ticket on, tag, label, mark.
◇ *Word origin: Ticket* comes from Old French *etiquet,* label. Our word *etiquette* comes from the same base.

tickle *v.* **1** *She tickled the baby under the chin:* stroke with the fingertips, stroke lightly, rub lightly, stroke, titillate. **2** *My jaw still tickles from the dentist's injection:* tingle, twitch, itch, prickle, sting, prick, throb. **3** *The comedian tickled the crowd with his jokes. The puppy's antics tickled the children:* amuse, regale, divert, enliven, gladden, cheer, delight, please, fascinate, enchant, captivate, enthral, entrance, excite agreeably, thrill, rejoice, gratify, do one's heart good.
—*n.* **4** *The little girl laughed when her uncle gave her a tickle:* teasing stroke, tingling rub. **5** *A cough-drop can ease that tickle in your throat:* tickling sensation, tingle, twitching sensation, itch, scratchiness, prickle, sting.

ticklish *adj.* **1** *Are you ticklish?:* sensitive to tickling, easily tickled, tickly tingling, itchy, scratchy, prickly. **2** *Bringing the two enemies together will be a ticklish job:* delicate, awkward, requiring tact, uncertain, critical; difficult, complicated, intricate, tricky, tough, hard, knotty, thorny.
Ant. 2 easy, simple.

tide *n.* **1** *The tide left delicate lines on the sandy beach. The tide left the driftwood high and dry on the beach:* twice daily rise and fall of the oceans; (*variously*) high tide, ebb-tide, neap-tide, flood tide, low tide, rip-tide, undertow; tidal water, tide-water, wave, current, flow. **2** *The tide of fortune may make you wealthy again. The tide of public opinion is now against the minister's plan:* rise and fall, ebb and flow, wax and wane; drift, current, tendency, movement, direction, state.

"Truly there is a tide in the affairs of men, but there is no gulf stream setting for ever in one direction."
—*James Russell Lowell*

---

tidy *adj.* **1** *Her desk was always tidy. The carpenter was a good example of a tidy worker:* neat, orderly, trim, shipshape, trig, in apple-pie order; methodical, systematic, meticulous, precise, careful, regular, regulated, businesslike; clean, immaculate, spotless. **2** *Informal That car must have cost a tidy sum of money:* considerable, fairly large, substantial, sizeable, ample.
—*v.* **3** *Tidy the living-room before the guests arrive:* tidy up, neaten, neaten up, put in order, straighten, straighten up, clean up, spruce up, arrange, array,
Ant. 1 messy, sloppy, untidy, slovenly, unkempt, disordered, disorderly, unmethodical, unsystematic, unbusinesslike, careless, slip-shod; filthy, dirty. **2** inconsiderable, unsubstantial, small, little, tiny. **3** mess, mess up, disarrange, disorder; dirty.

tie *v.* **1** *Tie the boat to the dock. Tie a knot in this string:* bind, fasten, make fast, attach, secure, engage, tether, clinch, truss, lash; draw together and knot, knot, make a bow. **2** *Great Britain and the United States are tied by a common language and mutual interests:* bind, fasten, attach, join, unite, connect, link, yoke, ally, couple, marry. **3** *I'd like to give you more time to finish the job, but I'm tied by the contract:* limit, confine, constrain, restrain, restrict, hinder, hamper. **4** *Two teams tied for first place:* make the same score, have the same record of wins and losses or points, draw, come out even, match, divide the honours.
—*n.* **5** *Hold back the curtain with a tie:* fastener for tying, cord, rope, string, line, cable, fastening, belt, band, cinch, girdle, cincture, sash, cummerbund. **6** *Men are supposed to wear jackets and ties to the party:* necktie, cravat; bow-tie, neckerchief. **7** *The two friends have strong ties. The applicant is said to have strong ties with the oil industry:* bond, link, affinity, connection, relation, relationship, kinship, affiliation, shared interest, mutual interest, allegiance; duty, obligation. **8** *The game ended in a tie. The result was a tie:* tied score, tied record, tied vote; draw, dead heat, photo finish. **9** *The builder added more ties to the structure:* brace, support, beam, rod, connecting-rod; cross-beam.
Ant. 1 untie, unbind, unfasten, loose, loosen, disengage, unknot. **2** detach, separate, divorce, disunite.

tier *n. Our seats were up in the second tier of the balcony. The wedding-cake had three tiers:* row, rank, line, file, level, range, bank; layer, storey, stratum, stratification.

tiff *n.* **1** *The couple had a tiff over which party to go to:* minor quarrel, petty quarrel, words, squabble, argument, dispute, wrangle, altercation, disagreement, difference, misunderstanding. **2** *Don't be in a tiff just because you didn't get your own way:* slight fit of anger, annoyed mood, huff, state, temper, tizzy, miff, rage, ill humour, bad mood.

tight *adv.* **tightly 1** *This lid is screwed on tight:* firmly, securely, solidly, closely **2** *Pull the rope tight:* taut, tense, stretched out, stretched as far as possible, rigid, stiff, drawn tight. **3** *This dress is tight-fitting:* too closely, closely, snugly, uncomfortably, constrictedly. **4** *The suitcase was packed tight:* full, to the brim, to bursting-point.

—*adj.* **5** *The material has a tight weave. Destroyers kept a tight formation during the manœuvre:* closely constructed, closely fitted, close, dense, compact, set closely together, solid, compressed, impermeable, impenetrable, impassable; firm, secure, packed. **6** *The sergeant maintained tight discipline. Hold the horse with a tight rein:* strict, firm, stern, rigid, rigorous, severe, exact, stringent, austere, stiff, inflexible, unyielding, uncompromising, tyrannical, dictatorial, harsh, taut, tense, rigid, stiff, stretched out. **7** *Unless he gets some money soon he'll be in a tight spot:* difficult, worrisome, troublesome, hard, hard-up, tough, onerous, burdensome, trying. **8** *The government believes that if money is tight inflation will stop:* scarce, difficult to obtain, scant, sparing, skimpy; insufficient, inadequate, deficient. **9** *Informal Our candidate won in a tight election:* nearly even, nearly equal, nearly tied, close, well-matched, neck and neck, nose to nose. **10** *Informal Don't be so tight with your money:* stingy, miserly, tight-fisted, close, close-fisted, parsimonious, frugal, niggardly, penurious, illiberal, ungenerous, sparing, grudging. **11** *Informal Uncle Alf had too much beer and got tight:* drunk, drunken, intoxicated, inebriated, tipsy, happy, plastered, blind, smashed, soused, loaded, pickled, stewed, pie-eyed, glassy-eyed, paralytic, stiff, stoned, zonked, high, in one's cups, over the top, lit-up.

Ant. 1–3, 5, 6 loose. **1–3** loosely. **1** insecurely. **2** slack, limp, free. **5** open, porous, airy, lacy, insecure. **6–9** easy. **6** lenient, indulgent, soft, relaxed, undemanding, permissive, unexacting, slack, lax, mild, informal, flexible, yielding, easy-going, free and easy, flexible. **7** comfortable, enviable. **8** abundant, plentiful, profuse, rife, ready, ample, sufficient. **9** uneven, runaway, landslide. **10** extravagant, spendthrift, thriftless, prodigal, squandering, wasteful, lavish; generous, open-handed, liberal, munificent, charitable. **11** sober, sober as a judge.

tighten *v. Tighten the nut on this screw. Tighten the clothes-line so that it doesn't sag:* make tight, make tighter, fix firmly, secure; draw tight, make taut, make tense, take up the slack; narrow, squeeze, contract, constrict, pinch.

Ant. loosen, loose, slacken, slack off, relax, ease, ease off; free, release, untie, open.

tightwad *n. Informal That old tightwad wouldn't give a penny to charity:* stingy person, skinflint, miser, niggard, money-grubber, penny-pincher, Scrooge.

Ant. spendthrift, prodigal, squanderer, wastrel, big spender, big-time spender; philanthropist, good Samaritan.

tilt *v.* **1** *Is the table uneven or does the floor tilt?:* slant, incline, lean, slope, tip, list, cant. **2** *The two knights tilted until one was unhorsed:* joust, fight on horseback with a lance; fight, oppose, contend against, battle, contest; fence, spar, skirmish.

—*n.* **3** *The tilt of the roof prevents snow from accumulating:* slope, slant, incline, cant, rake, pitch, grade. **4** *Don Quixote engaged in a famous tilt with a windmill:* joust, jousting match, tournament; fight, contest, combat, battle, skirmish, encounter, affray; dispute, argument, quarrel, altercation, squabble, row, brawl, tiff.

Ant. 1 be even, be flat, be plumb. **3** evenness, flatness.

timber *n. Stack the timber near the tool-shed:* wood for building; beams, planks, boards, lumber, logs.

timbre *n. The singer's voice had a pleasant timbre:* tone, sound quality, pitch, resonance.

◇ *Pronunciation tip: Timbre* is pronounced *TAM-bre.*

◇ *Word origin: Timbre* is a modern French word which is now commonly used in English. It is ultimately related to Greek *tympanon,* a kettledrum. In French, its meanings have developed from "a drum or tambourine," to "a kind of bell," to "the sound made by a bell," and finally to "the character or quality of musical sound."

"Gather ye rosebuds while ye may,
Old Time is still a-flying:
And this same flower that smiles today,
Tomorrow will be dying." —*Robert Herrick*

---

time *n.* **1** *Time and tide wait for no man. It's been a long time since we've seen each other:* the passage of time, duration, continuation of all existence; period, interval, span of time, elapsed time, spell, term, while, stretch. **2** Usually **times** *The Parthenon was built in ancient times. Toy spaceships are a sign of the times:* epoch, era, period, age, aeon; stage, season, cycle, day. **3** *The time is 2.30 p.m. It's time to go. Christmas-time is almost here. The time of the play was the 1890's:* particular point in time, appointed time, proper moment, appropriate period, high time; (*variously*) instant, moment, hour, part of the hour, day, part of the day, week, part of the week, month, part of the month, year, part of the year, season, term, decade, century, period. **4** *The average time of man is three score years and ten:* lifetime, years, days, period, phase, season, generation. **5** *I haven't the time to play golf:* leisure time, spare time, free time, liberty, opportunity, chance, freedom. **6** *A good time was had by all:* experience, occasion, period, event, episode, incident. **7** *The piece was written in waltz time:* tempo; rhythm, beat, measure.

—*v.* **8** *The runner was timed for the mile in four minutes flat. The enemy timed his attack perfectly:* measure the speed of, clock; measure the duration of; choose the time of. **9** *The marchers timed their steps to the drum-beat:* synchronize, keep time, set to the rhythm of, adjust, match.

timeless *adj. The astronomer pondered the timeless reaches of space. Styles come and go, but good taste is timeless:* without beginning or end, eternal, infinite, never-stopping, never-ending, unending, everlasting, interminable, perpetual, ceaseless, incessant, boundless, continuous; enduring; long-lasting, persistent, perdurable, durable, permanent, abiding, unchangeable, immutable, indestructible, immortal, undying, deathless.

Ant. brief, quick, short, short-lived, temporary, passing, fleeting, unenduring, evanescent, ephemeral, transient, transitory, impermanent, changing.

timely *adj. A timely loan saved the businessman from going bankrupt. I'd like to give you some timely advice:* occurring at the right time, well-timed, opportune, convenient, seasonable, prompt, punctual, providential.

Ant. untimely, inopportune, inconvenient, ill-timed, unseasonable, late, tardy.

timid *adj. The boy is as timid as a mouse:* lacking self-assurance, faint-hearted, fearful, timorous, apprehensive, cowardly, spineless, weak-kneed; shy, bashful, diffident, overmodest, humble, sheepish, retiring, shrinking, unassuming.

Ant. self-assured, confident, daring, audacious, stout-hearted, fearless, brave, bold, intrepid, courageous, adventuresome; brash, brazen, forward, impertinent, impudent, presumptuous, insolent, fresh, saucy, immodest, unabashed, shameless, cheeky.

timidity *n. His timidity prevented him from asking her to the dance:* timidness, timorousness, shyness, lack of self-assurance, faintheartedness, fearfulness, trepidation, cowardice, spinelessness; bashfulness, diffidence, modesty, humility, sheepishness, *Slang* cold feet, lack of guts.

Ant. self-assurance, self-confidence, daring, audacity, fearlessness, bravery, boldness, courage; brashness, brazenness, forwardness, impertinence, impudence, presumption, insolence, immodesty, cheek.

tinge *v.* **1** *Just one drop of ink tinged the water blue. His smile was tinged with cruelty:* colour slightly, colour, tint, dye, stain; touch, infuse, imbue, instil, lace, season, flavour.

—*n.* **2** *The wallpaper has just a tinge of orange. The book has a tinge of unpleasantness:* slight coloration, tint, shade, cast, stain; tone, touch, trace, hint, dash, vein, nuance, suspicion, flavour, taste, smack, soupçon.

tingle *v.* **1** *Don't your hands tingle in the cold?:* have a prickling sensation, sting, prickle, tickle.

—*n.* **2** *A tingle of excitement ran down his back:* prickling, thrill, tremor, flutter, rush, surge, throb, palpitation, pulsation.

◇ *Word origin:* When your hands *tingle* with cold do you feel as if they would make a bell-like metallic sound if you shook them? *Tingle* is a variant of *tinkle,* the sound that a small bell makes.

tinkle *v.* **1** *Sleigh-bells tinkled in the distance:* ring lightly, jingle, clink, chink, clank, chime, peal, ding.

—*n.* **2** *The tinkle of a bell summoned the butler:* light ring, jingle, clink, chink, clank, chime, peal, ding, ting-a-ling.

Ant. 1, 2 boom, roar, bang, thunder.

tinsel *n.* **1** *The children put the tinsel on the Christmas tree:* decorative foil, shiny metal strip, spangle, sequin, glitter. **2** *The showy offices are just tinsel — the firm is small and almost bankrupt:* show, decoration, gaudiness, ostentation; sham, pretence, masquerade, front, camouflage, gloss, false colours; showy thing, gaudy thing.

◇ *Word origin: Tinsel* comes through Old French *estincelle* from Latin *scintilla,* spark, hence glittering bits of cheap metal or foil.

tint *n.* **1** *The blouse was striped in several tints of blue:* shade, hue, tone, nuance, tincture. **2** *There is a tint of green in the rug:* tinge, trace, hint, suggestion, touch, flash, shade. **3** *Is her hair naturally blonde or does she use a tint?:* dye, stain, colouring.

—*v.* **4** *Why not tint your hair red?:* colour, stain, colour slightly, dye, tone, wash; tinge, frost.

tiny *n. The bush has tiny red berries on it:* small, little, minute, miniature, diminutive, minuscule, wee, *Informal* teeny, teeny-weeny, itsy-bitsy, weeny; undersized, pocket-sized, pint-sized, midget, pygmy, dwarfish, lilliputian.

Ant. large, big, huge, enormous, immense, mammoth, oversized, giant, gigantic, monstrous, colossal, gargantuan, titanic.

tip¹ *v.* **1** *The rowing-boat tipped up when the fat man got in:* tilt, slant, incline, lean, list, slope, cant. **2** Often **tip over** *The glass tipped over and milk ran down the table-leg:* overturn, topple over, tumble over, upset, upturn, capsize, up-end, turn turtle.

Ant. 1 be even, be flat, be plumb. **2** upright.

◇ *Word origin: Tip¹* comes from Middle English *typen,* to turn over, upset. *Tipsy,* slightly intoxicated, comes from this word *tip,* and literally means walking crookedly or at a tilt as if about to tip over.

tip² *n.* **1** *Have you got a needle with a finer tip? The tribe used flint tips on its arrows:* pointed end, tapering end, small end; point, head, prong, spike. **2** *The tip of the iceberg was over half a mile wide:* top, peak, apex, summit, crown, crest, pinnacle, cap; upper part, brow.

—*v.* **3** *The baton was tipped with gold:* furnish with a slender end, serve as a pointed end, top, cap, crown; sharpen, barb, hook, point.

tip³ *n.* **1** *Many people give the paper-boy a tip at Christmas:* gratuity, small gift of money for services rendered, small reward; perquisite;

French pourboire. **2** *Here's a useful tip on how to remove stains. The police got a tip that the bank would be robbed tonight:* hint, suggestion, pointer, clue, advice, word to the wise, warning, admonition; secret information, inside information, inside dope, tip-off, low-down. **3** *The golfer gave the ball a tip with his putter:* tap, light blow, weak blow, stroke, pat, push.

—*v.* **4** *Let's tip the waiter and leave:* give a gratuity, give a small gift of money for services rendered, reward. **5** *The goalkeeper just managed to tip the ball over the bar:* tap, hit lightly, strike weakly, stroke, pat.

◇ *Word origin:* Although the old story has it that *tip*³, as a waiter's gratuity, is an acronym for the phrase *t*(o) *i*(nsure) *p*(romptness), linguists doubt this. It seems to come from Dutch *tippen*, to tap, and refers to the tapping sound a coin makes when put on a table. The idea of secret or inside information, as a *tip* on a horse-race or a *stock-market tip*, refers to someone tapping another person on the shoulder to whisper the confidential information or hint.

tippler *n. W. C. Fields was quite a tippler:* heavy drinker, habitual drinker, hard drinker, sot, boozer, toper, imbiber, sponge, bibber, soak, tosspot; drunk, drunkard, alcoholic, inebriate, dipsomaniac, wino.

Ant. teetotaller, abstainer, non-drinker; moderate drinker, social drinker.

tipsy *adj. Even a little wine can make some people tipsy:* mildly drunk, slightly intoxicated, *Slang* high; drunk, drunken, intoxicated, inebriated, tight, happy, plastered, blind, smashed, soused, loaded, pickled, stewed, pie-eyed, glassy-eyed, paralytic, stiff, stoned, in one's cups, over the top, half seas over, lit-up.

Ant. sober, sober as a judge.

◇ *Word origin:* See TIP¹.

tirade *n. The principal delivered a tirade to the disobedient students. The political candidate let loose a tirade against his opponent:* long angry speech, harangue, diatribe, jeremiad, lecture, reprimand, scolding, dressing-down, fulmination; denunciation, condemnation, castigation, vilification, invective, vituperation, curse.

Ant. good word, short eulogy, panegyric, complimentary speech, praising speech, laudation, commendation, homage, paean.

◇ *Word origin:* A *tirade* is a volley of words, usually of censure. It comes from Italian *tirata*, volley, a discharge of firearms.

tire *v.* **1** *Climbing to the top of St. Paul's Cathedral tired the tourists:* weary, wear out, fatigue, exhaust, fag, whack; make sleepy. **2** *Her constant chatter tired everyone. I'm tired of the same old breakfast every morning:* bore, exhaust the patience of, be fed up with, be sick of, to lose patience, lose interest, irk, annoy, bother, disgust.

Ant. **1** refresh, stimulate; wake up. **2** delight, interest, excite, enchant, fascinate, please, soothe.

◇ *Word origin: Tire* comes from Old English *tēorian*, to weary. It does not appear in cognate Indo-European languages.

tired *adj. After a full day's work she was tired:* weary, wearied, fatigued, exhausted, worn out, all in, dog-tired, whacked-out, fagged, played out, *Slang* dead-beat; sleepy, drowsy.

Ant. energetic, full of go, peppy, fresh, refreshed; raring to go; wide-awake.

"Life is one long process of getting tired."

—*Samuel Butler*

---

tireless *adj. The winner of the marathon was a tireless runner. The chairman thanked the committee for its tireless efforts in organizing the dance:* untiring, never-tiring, unwearied; industrious, hard-working, unflagging, unfaltering, unswerving, unremitting, indefatigable, devoted, unceasing, steadfast, resolute, determined, staunch, steady, constant, persevering, determined, faithful.

Ant. half-hearted, lackadaisical, sporadic, random; flagging, faltering, wavering, irresolute.

tiresome *adj.* **1** *Working in that noise all day is very tiresome:* fatiguing, wearying, wearing, tiring, exhausting, fagging; arduous, laborious, tedious, hard, difficult. **2** *What a tiresome opera! Andrew's constant puns are getting tiresome:* boring, monotonous, uninteresting, dull, drab, dismal, tedious; annoying, bothersome, irksome, vexing, trying.

Ant. **1** refreshing; easy. **2** delightful, interesting, exciting, stimulating, fascinating, enchanting, pleasing, soothing.

tiro Also **tyro** *n. The old hand gave the tiro some tips on how to do the job:* beginner, novice, neophyte, tenderfoot, new recruit, initiate, apprentice, learner.

Ant. veteran, master, expert, professional.

titanic *adj. The explorer discovered a titanic mountain range. A titanic effort is needed to finish the job by Monday:* gigantic, huge, immense, vast, colossal, giant, monstrous, gargantuan; great, strong, stout, prodigious, mighty, Herculean.

Ant. small, little, tiny, minute, diminutive, minuscule, wee, teeny, teeny-weeny, itsy-bitsy, pocket-sized, pint-sized, midget, pygmy, dwarfish, lilliputian; weak, feeble.

titbit *n. These smoked oysters are delicious titbits. I know a juicy titbit of gossip about her:* delicate bit, morsel, mouthful, delicacy; choice bit, bit, item.

◇ *Word origin: Titbit* used at one time to be spelt *tidbit* (indeed, this spelling is the dominant one in America). It comes from English dialectal *tid*, small thing, plus *bit*, a small piece, two words meaning the same thing.

titillate *v. The hint of scandal titillated everyone's curiosity:* excite, tickle, tease, provoke, rouse, arouse, allure, tempt, seduce, entrance, captivate, attract, whet the appetite.
Ant. allay, quiet, quench, quell, still, dull, slake, blunt, satisfy, sate, satiate.

titillating *adj. Boccaccio's* Decameron *is titillating and bawdy but not pornographic:* provocative, exciting, alluring, tempting, suggestive, seductive.

title *n.* **1** *The full title of the book is* The Life and Strange Surprising Adventures of Robinson Crusoe, of York, Mariner*:* name, designation, appellation, epithet. **2** *Hilda's new title is "Senior Controller of Marketing Research." She fell in love with the Count only because of his title:* rank, occupational rank, position, status, station, condition, grade, place; title of nobility, lordly rank, nobility, noble birth. **3** *Who owns the title to the property?:* legal right, legal possession, right, possession, ownership, deed, claim. **4** *Joe Louis held the heavyweight title longer than anyone else:* championship, crown, laurel.
—*v.* **5** *The youth titled his poem "My Lost Love":* entitle, name, designate, term, dub, label, christen.

titter *v.* **1** *The audience tittered at the little joke:* laugh self-consciously, laugh nervously, giggle, laugh softly, chuckle, snigger, snicker, simper, smirk.
—*n.* **2** *That little titter of hers is annoying:* self-conscious laugh, nervous laugh, giggle, snigger, snicker, simper, smirk, chuckle, soft laugh, tehee.
Ant. 1, 2 roar, guffaw. **1** split one's sides, die laughing, roll in the aisles. **2** burst of laughter, horse-laugh.

titular *adj. The king was the titular head of state, but the prime minister held the reins of power:* in name only, in title only, nominal, theoretical, known as.
Ant. actually, really, in fact, for all practical purposes.

toady *v.* **1** *He gets good marks but that's only because he toadies to the teacher:* flatter to gain favour, curry favour, fawn, grovel before, kowtow to; *Slang* suck up to, butter up.
—*n.* **2** *Imperial Caesar is surrounded by a horde of flattering toadies:* sycophant, flatterer, fawner, lickspittle, truckler, yes-man, adulator, bootlicker; servile follower, flunkey, stooge, hanger-on, parasite.
Ant. 1 defy, confront, be hostile to, stand up to, oppose, resist, scorn, disdain, mock, taunt, twist the lion's tail. **2** defiant person, hostile person, opponent, enemy, foe, antagonist.
◇ *Word origin: Toady* is a short form of the earlier *toad-eater.* Sarah Fielding, sister of Henry Fielding, the author of *Tom Jones,* wrote the following classic explanation of the word's meaning in one of her novels written in 1744: "*Toad-Eater* is a metaphor taken from a mountebank's boy eating toads in order to show his master's skill in expelling poison. It is built on a supposition that people who are in a state of dependence are forced to do the most nauseous things that can be thought on, to please and humour their patrons."

toast *v.* **1** *Come and toast your feet by the fire:* warm, warm up, heat; dry. **2** *Toast the bread before making the bacon and tomato sandwiches. The children toasted chestnuts over the bonfire:* heat until crisp, brown; grill, cook over an open fire. **3** *Let's all toast the bride and groom:* drink in honour of, salute with a drink, drink one's health, clink glasses; honour, celebrate, compliment, commemorate.
—*n.* **4** *Poached eggs on toast make a good breakfast:* toasted bread, browned bread; a slice of browned, crisp bread. **5** *I propose a toast to our new chairman:* drink in honour of, drink to compliment, drink to commemorate.
Ant. 1 cool, cool off, chill.
◇ *Word origin: Toast* comes from Latin *tostus,* grilled, roasted. A *toast* to someone's health comes from the old custom of putting a piece of spiced toast in a glass of wine to enhance the wine's flavour and from the notion that the name of the person whose health is drunk will spice the wine like such a piece of toast.

today *n.* **1** *Today is March 22nd. The songs of today aren't as tuneful as they used to be when I was a boy:* the present day, this day; the present age, this epoch, this era, this time, modern times.
—*adv.* **2** *Let's go to the beach today. Children get a better education today than at any time in the past:* on this day; nowadays, now, in this day and age, in modern times, during the present age, in this epoch, in this era.
Ant. 1, 2 yesterday; tomorrow.

toddle *v. The child is just beginning to toddle:* take short, unsteady steps; walk unsteadily, waddle.
Ant. stride; run, skip, prance.

togs *n. pl. Informal Come on, put your togs on and we'll go out:* clothes, clothing, outfit, apparel, attire, duds.

toil *n.* **1** *After much toil the furniture was finally crammed into the removal van:* hard work, work, labour, effort, exertion, application, industry, pains, drudgery, sweat, elbow-grease; hardship, travail.
v. **2** *The farmer toiled in the field from dawn till dusk:* work hard, labour, drudge, slave, grub, sweat, exert oneself, apply oneself, work like a horse.
Ant. 1, 2 play. **1** amusement, entertainment, recreation, cavorting, ease; *Slang* messing about. **2** take one's ease, relax, enjoy oneself, amuse oneself, take one's pleasure, laze, loiter.
◇ *Word origin: Toil* has its origin in the

Latin verb *tudiculare,* to stir about. Thus etymologically, the first *toilers* were Italian peasants who pressed olives in a *tudicula.*

Exploring the Word: *Toga, togs, tile* and *thatch* come from Latin *tegere,* to cover. Thus a *toga* was a Roman's cover or garment, especially the Roman citizen's formal outer garment, from which we get our word *togs,* clothing. *Tiles* are also a cover, originally for a building, hence *roofing tiles,* and in Old English this word became *thatch,* used for *thatched roofs.* Latin *tegere,* to cover, also gives us *detect* and *detective,* to take the cover away, uncover, or one who uncovers a criminal; *protect,* literally to put a cover in front of, to shield or guard, and *protégé,* literally a person under another's protection.

token *n.* **1** *The employees gave their colleague a watch as a token of their esteem:* symbol, sign, expression, indication, mark, index, manifestation; reminder, memento, keepsake, souvenir, remembrance, testimonial. **2** *This fruit-machine accepts only tokens:* coinlike metal piece, *French* jeton.
—*adj.* **3** *Employing only one woman among fifty men is but a token recognition of the equal rights of both sexes:* superficial, passing, nodding, of no real value, symbolic, for show; minimal, serving as a sample, vestigial.
Ant. 3 real, actual, valuable, worthwhile, serious, equitable, deep.

tolerable *adj.* **1** *Such rude behaviour is not tolerable:* able to be tolerated, bearable, endurable, sufferable; acceptable, allowable, permissible. **2** *That restaurant has tolerable food, but I wouldn't recommend it:* fairly good, fair, passable, acceptable, adequate, innocuous, mediocre, average, ordinary, commonplace, indifferent, run-of-the-mill, so-so, middling, fair-to-middling, betwixt and between.
Ant. 1 intolerable, unbearable, unendurable, insufferable; unacceptable. **2** excellent, outstanding, wonderful, terrific, superior, great, choice, exemplary, noteworthy, memorable; awful, dreadful, terrible, lousy, bad.

"The responsibility of tolerance lies with those who have the wider version." —*George Eliot*

tolerance *n.* **1** *Some people have greater levels of tolerance to pain than others:* ability to tolerate, capacity to resist, power to endure, endurance. **2** *Tolerance among the races of the world is essential:* an understanding attitude, fair treatment, fairness, lack of prejudice, freedom from bigotry, democratic spirit, goodwill, brotherly love, fellow-feeling, live-and-let-live attitude; forbearance, patience, sufferance, compassion, sympathy, charity.
Ant. 1 sensitivity. **2** prejudice, bigotry, bias, predisposition, ill will, unfairness, discrimination; irritability, anger, irascibility.

tolerant *adj.* **1** *Can't you be tolerant of other religions?:* understanding, unprejudiced, unbigoted, fair, having goodwill, having brotherly love, liberal, broad-minded, moderate; forbearing, patient, compassionate, sympathetic, charitable. **2** *The teacher was too tolerant of disobedient behaviour:* lenient, permissive, indulgent, soft, easy, easy-going, forbearing, forgiving, uncomplaining, kind-hearted, soft-hearted, sparing.
Ant. 1 intolerant, prejudiced, bigoted, biased, unfair, illiberal, narrow-minded, closed-minded. **2** strict, rigid, harsh, stiff, severe, stern, exacting, uncompromising, unyielding, unbending, authoritarian, tyrannical, dictatorial, despotic.

tolerate *v.* **1** *I can't tolerate that loud music:* bear, endure, put up with, stand, take, suffer, abide, brook, stomach, submit to, undergo. **2** *The school cannot tolerate cheating in exams:* allow, permit, sanction, consent to, admit, recognize, vouchsafe, indulge, be soft on, be easy on, be sparing of, show mercy toward, wink at.
Ant. 2 forbid, prohibit, disallow, proscribe, disallow, ban, prevent, oppose.

toll *n.* **1** *Each car must pay a toll to cross the bridge:* fee, charge, payment, levy, impost, assessment, tax, tariff, tribute. **2** *The flood took a toll of a hundred lives:* loss, amount of loss, extent of damage, destruction, extermination, extinction, annihilation, sacrifice, penalty; undoing, disruption, depletion.

tomb *n. Archaeologists discovered many underground tombs on the uninhabited island:* burial chamber, vault, sepulchre, crypt, monument to the dead; burial place, grave.

tomfoolery *n. Stop this tomfoolery and get down to work!:* foolishness, silliness, prankishness, play, horseplay, monkey business, skylarking, nonsense, playing around, fooling around, messing around, mischief.
◇ *Word origin: Tomfoolery* comes from *Tom Fool,* a term formerly applied to buffoons. The original *Tom Fool* lived in Durham during the first half of the fourteenth century, and a Latin account book kept by the local authorities of that time makes frequent mention of disbursements for the upkeep of *Thomas fatuus* ("Thomas fool"), including a final one for his funeral in 1357.

tomorrow *n.* **1** *Tomorrow is Sunday. Today's youth will be the leaders of tomorrow:* the day after today, the morrow; the future, the next generation.
—*adv.* **2** *The county fair starts tomorrow. Tomorrow people will be spending their holidays on the moon:* on the day after today; in the future, in days to come.
Ant. 1, 2 yesterday; today.
◇ *Word origin: Tomorrow* comes from Old English *to* (at) + *morgen* (morning), literally "at the next morning."

tone *n.* **1** *The shrill tone of the factory whistle rent the air:* pitch, sound quality, sound, quality, timbre, tonality; note, musical interval of two semitones, overtone, harmonic; intonation, modulation, accent, stress, inflection, cadence, lilt. **2** *The tone of this letter is rather unfriendly:* attitude, mood, spirit, style, manner, means of expression, note, tenor, quality, temper. **3** *The coat is a light tone of green:* shade, tint, hue, cast, colour, chroma.

—*v.* **4** Often with **down** *Please tone your voice down:* pitch, sound, subdue, moderate, temper, modulate, soften; shade, tint. **5** *Exercise will tone your muscles. Some people take vitamins to tone up the system:* make firm, firm up, make supple, make more elastic, invigorate.

tongue *n.* **1** *Stick out your tongue:* organ of speech. **2** *The stranger spoke in a foreign tongue. Fear made him lose his tongue:* language, dialect, vernacular, patois, vocabulary; style of speech; power of speech. **3** *The shoe-lace caught on the tongue of his shoe. The tongue of this board fits into that groove:* flap, overhanging strip. **4** *The dock is just round that tongue of land:* point, spit, promontory. **5** *The scales' tongue finally rested at 2 pounds:* pointer, index, dial, finger, arm.

—*v.* **6** *To make a trill, tongue the whistle as you blow:* touch with the tongue, move the tongue against; lick, lap.

◇ *Word origin:* Our word *tongue* is related to Latin *lingua,* also meaning "tongue." During the Renaissance it was customary to refer to Hebrew, Greek, and Latin as "the three tongues," i.e. the three classical languages. In all three the word for the organ of speech also means "language." Greek *glōtta, glōssa,* tongue, gives us our words *glottal,* of the tongue, and *glossolalia,* the gift of tongues, i.e. the Pentecostal miracle whereby the Apostles "were all filled with the Holy Ghost and began to speak with other tongues, as the Spirit gave them utterance" (Acts 2: 4). Latin *lingua,* tongue, gives us our word *linguistics,* the science of language, and the word *language* itself.

tonic *n.* **1** *In the old days people took a tonic in the spring. Fresh air is a good tonic for melancholy:* strengthening medicine, restorative, stimulant, invigorant, analeptic, bracer, refresher, pick-up, pick-me-up. **2** *The melody began and ended on the tonic:* keynote; primary note of a diatonic scale.

tool *n.* **1** *A carpenter is only as good as his tools:* implement, hand-held instrument, instrument, device, contrivance, apparatus, appliance, machine, mechanism. **2** *A good education is a necessary tool for succeeding:* agent, means, medium, vehicle, intermediary, wherewithal. **3** *The author is just another of the Establishment's tools:* person used by another, instrument, pawn, puppet, dupe, hireling, stooge, cat's-paw.

tooth *n.* **1** *The dentist filled the tooth:* hard bony part growing from the jaw; (*variously*) incisor, molar, grinder, canine, bicuspid, wisdom tooth; fang, tusk. **2** *Who broke a tooth off this saw?:* serration; (*variously*) point, spike, tine, tang, spur, barb, thorn, cusp, nib.

top *n.* **1** *Let's climb to the top of that hill. There's a scratch on the top of the table:* highest point, summit, peak, apex, pinnacle, acme, zenith, tiptop; crest, crown, brow; upper surface, upper part. **2** *Where's the top to this bottle? The top of this box is torn:* lid, cap, cover; cork, stopper. **3** *Kay finished the term at the top of her class. Only a hard worker can reach the top:* highest rank, highest position, head, lead, first place, fore, van, front, place of honour.

—*adj.* **4** *Put the book on the top shelf. The car's top speed is 120 miles per hour:* topmost, highest, uppermost, upper; greatest, best. **5** *The top doctors in the country will attend the meeting:* highest-ranking, foremost, best, chief, principal, paramount, eminent, pre-eminent, renowned, noted, notable, celebrated, famous, greatest.

—*v.* **6** *Top the strawberries with whipped cream:* put a topping on, put a top on, put over, crown, cap, cover; complete, add a finishing touch to. **7** *The swimmer topped the world record by two-tenths of a second:* be at the top of, be greater than, surpass, exceed, better, best, excel, outdo, eclipse, beat, outshine, outstrip.

Ant. 1-4 bottom. **1** base, foot, nadir, lowest point; underside, underneath. **3** foot, end, tail-end, last place, rear. **4** lowest, lower; least, worst. **5** inferior, second-rate, inept, incompetent; unknown, anonymous. **7** trail, be at the bottom, be less than.

topic *n. The speaker's topic will be "poetry in the Modern World." That's not a fit topic for polite conversation:* subject, subject matter, theme, matter in hand; text, thesis.

topical *adj. The book is too topical to be of interest ten years from now:* about current matters, current, contemporary; local, localized, limited, restricted, particular.

Ant. historical, traditional; general, universal, comprehensive, all-inclusive.

topmost *adj. One apple grew on the topmost branch. The dentist had reached the topmost echelon of his profession:* top, highest, uppermost; supreme, chief, head, pre-eminent, leading, foremost, principal, paramount.

topple *v.* **1** *The vase toppled and was smashed to smithereens:* tip over, overturn, turn over, upset, fall over; fall, tumble, pitch forward. **2** *The rebels have toppled the regime:* overthrow, bring down, abolish; defeat, vanquish, overcome, overpower, crush, smash, shatter, quash, quell.

topsy-turvy *adv.* **1** *We turned the room topsy-turvy looking for the ring:* upside-down, inside out, into a confused state, in a disorderly state.

—*adj.* **2** *I've never seen such a topsy-turvy office:* confused, confusing, disorderly, disarranged, disorganized, untidy, messy, chaotic; upside-down, wrong side up, inverted, reversed.

Ant. 1, 2 right side up. **1** straight, into a state of order. **2** orderly, well-arranged, organized, tidy, neat, trim.

◇ *Word origin: Topsy-turvy* comes from the plural of *top* plus the obsolete verb *tervy,* to turn.

torch *n.* **1** *The campers lit torches from the campfire:* burning brand, brand, firebrand, flambeau; portable electric light. **2** *The rescuers needed an acetylene torch to cut through the wreckage:* portable device for producing a hot flame; welder's torch.

◇ *Word origin: Torch* comes from Old French *torche,* which goes back to Latin *torquere,* to twist, because medieval torches were made up of lengths of twisted straw dipped in wax.

torment *v.* **1** *Pain tormented him all day long. The thief was tormented by guilt:* cause to suffer, afflict, torture, rack, distress, pain; plague, worry, trouble, annoy, agonize, persecute, harass, harrow, vex, nag, irritate, pester.

—*n.* **2** *Mosquitoes and huge black flies caused the hikers much torment:* suffering, agony, torture, anguish, pain, distress, misery, worry, annoyance, irritation, despair; cause of suffering, source of agony, scourge, bane, curse.

Ant. 1, 2 delight, comfort, ease. **1** please, make happy; soothe, allay, assuage. **2** pleasure, happiness, joy.

torn *adj. The child wore a torn shirt:* ripped, rent, split, slit, ruptured; ragged, shredded, unravelled.

torpid *adj. The heat and lack of sleep made everyone torpid:* slow-moving, sluggish, inactive, inert, lethargic, lazy, listless, spiritless, indolent, languid, langorous, apathetic, passive, slow-thinking, dull; half asleep, sleepy, drowsy, somnolent; dormant.

Ant. quick-moving, active, energetic, vigorous, peppy, full of beans, animated, lively, spirited, alert, *Slang* sharp, bright-eyed; wide-awake.

torpor Also **torpidity** *Her torpor may be due to illness:* sluggishness, slow movement, inertia, lethargy, laziness, listlessness, lassitude, indolence, languor, apathy, passiveness, dullness; sleepiness, drowsiness; inactivity.

Ant. energy, vigour, vim, pep, go, animation, liveliness, alertness; wide-awakeness.

torrent *n.* **1** *The drought was broken by a torrent. The torrent carried the raft far downstream:* heavy rain, downpour, deluge, cloudburst, torrential rain, cascade, cataract, Niagara; fast-flowing stream, violent stream of water, strong current. **2** *The angry man let loose a torrent of swear-words:* stream, rapid flow, outburst, outpouring, discharge, rain, deluge, flood, volley, barrage, salvo, burst, eruption, rush.

Ant. 1 shower, sprinkle, drizzle.

◇ *Word origin:* Amazingly enough *torrent* and *torrid* both come from Latin *torrere,* to parch. A *torrid* clime is one that parches, a hot, sunny one, as in the *Torrid Zone.* A *torrent* is a turbulent stream, one that seems to "boil" with bubbles and white swirling water.

> **Exploring the Word**: *Torpid, torpor,* and *torpedo* come from Latin *torpere,* to be sluggish or numb, which is what our words *torpid* and *torpor* refer to. From the related Latin *torpedo,* numbness, came the name of the *torpedo,* or electric ray, a fish that paralyses with its sting, and then the *torpedo,* named (1807) by the inventor Robert Fulton, 1765-1815. Fulton's *torpedoes* were actually submarine mines which were towed or moored or, under some conditions, allowed to drift toward an oncoming enemy ship.

torrid *adj.* **1** *Nothing will grow in this torrid climate:* hot and dry, scorching, parching, burning, broiling, fiery, sultry, tropical. **2** *The film contains a torrid love scene:* passionate, impassioned, ardent, fervent, fervid, vehement, spirited, excited, hot, hot and heavy, heated, intense; amorous, erotic, sexy, lustful.

Ant. 1 cold, cool, chilly; mild, gentle. **2** dispassionate, unimpassioned, spiritless; serene, moderate, mild, cool, apathetic, lethargic.

tortuous *adj. A tortuous trail led up the mountain. The essay was so long and tortuous that I couldn't make sense of it:* winding, twisting, full of curves, circuitous, sinuous, serpentine, zigzag, meandering, crooked; labyrinthine, convoluted, complicated, involved, indirect, roundabout, devious, ambiguous, hard to follow.

Ant. straight, straight as an arrow, direct; straightforward, simple.

torture *v.* **1** *The secret police tortured the captive to obtain information:* subject to severe pain, put on the rack; mistreat, maltreat, abuse. **2** *After sentencing the man the judge was tortured by doubts:* cause anxiety, torment, distress, cause anguish; rack, harrow, wring, prick, smite.

—*n.* **3** *The dungeon was full of instruments of torture:* punishment by causing pain, extorting information by subjecting to pain, cause of severe pain, brutality. **4** *Waiting for news of the lost boy was sheer torture to his parents:* torment, agony, anguish, suffering, distress, ordeal, trial, infliction, cruelty.

Ant. 1 persuade, coax, cajole, wheedle, entice, flatter, charm. **2** set at ease, disburden, calm, quiet, relax; cheer, comfort, solace. **3** pleasure, comfort, contentment, mirth, gaiety, cheer. **4** joy, delight, ecstasy, rapture, happiness, enjoyment, gratification.

toss *v.* **1** *Toss the newspaper over here. The boys tossed a ball back and forth:* throw carelessly, throw, pitch, flip, fling, sling, heave, hurl, cast, lob, let fly, propel. **2** *The child tossed and turned in his sleep. The storm tossed the small boat at its anchor:* pitch, jerk, sway, rock, shake, agitate, roll, joggle, churn, tumble about, wiggle, wriggle, writhe, flounce, undulate, oscillate.

—n. **3** *I hope we win the toss:* pitch, throw (often, of a coin), heave, fling, sling, hurl, cast, lob, flip. **4** *With a toss of her head she walked away:* sudden upward raise, flounce, jerk, shake, flourish.

Ant. 1, 3 catch, grasp. **1** seize, snatch, clutch, take; hold, keep, retain.

Exploring the Word: *Torture* and *torment* come from Latin *torquere,* to twist, and the related *tortura,* twisting, writhing, torment. The latter term was used by Roman medical writers in the sense "excruciating pain." A *tortuous* road is a twisting, turning one. The word *torment* comes from Latin *tormentum,* a rack, i.e. a type of rack on which prisoners were stretched and twisted, in order to make them confess. The same Latin base gives us *contort,* to twist together; *distort,* to twist apart; *extortion,* twisting something out of someone; *retort,* to turn or twist a remark or criticism back at the original speaker; and *torque,* which in mechanics is the moment of force that causes twisting or rotation.

total *n.* **1** *Add up the bill and tell me the total:* sum, sum total, full amount, whole amount, whole, aggregate, totality, entirety.

—adj. **2** *The total cost was over a hundred pounds. The total population of the town was only two thousand:* entire, whole, complete, full, gross, integral. **3** *The party was a total success. The enemy suffered total defeat:* absolute, complete, utter, perfect, thorough, unconditional, unqualified, unlimited, undisputed, sheer, sweeping, comprehensive, downright, outright, out and out, *Slang* wholesale.

—v. **4** *Total the bill and add ten per cent. The number of deaths totals six hundred:* total up, tot up, add up, add, sum up, reckon, compute, calculate, figure up, figure, find the sum; add up to.

Ant. 1 subtotal, partial amount, part. **2, 3** partial, incomplete. **2** fractional. **3** slight, meagre, hollow, fragmentary; conditional, qualified, mixed, uneven, half-way; marred, defective, wanting. **4** subtract, deduct.

totalitarian *adj. Under Mussolini, Italy was a totalitarian country:* strictly controlled, undemocratic, unrepresentative, Fascist, Fascistic, dictatorial, despotic, tyrannous.

Ant. anarchistic; democratic, republican, representative, popular.

◇ *Word origin: Totalitarian* is based on our word *totality* and refers to a government that has *total* power over the people (with or without the people's consent), hence rules as one faction, considering all the people as one unit, and allows no dissent or individuality. The term arose during the 1920's and was first used with reference to Italian Fascism.

totally *adv. His story is totally false:* completely, utterly, entirely, from beginning to end, throughout, thoroughly, absolutely, unconditionally, without qualification, perfectly, downright, unmitigatedly.

Ant. partially, in part, incompletely, slightly, somewhat, conditionally, with qualifications.

tote *v. Informal Are you going to tote that suitcase all over Europe? The sheriff always toted a gun:* carry, carry around, lug, cart, drag, haul, move, fetch, convey, transport; carry on one's person, bear, pack.

totter *v. The old man tottered down the street. The glass tottered and fell:* walk unsteadily, waddle, stagger, stumble, reel, lurch, falter; wobble, sway, waver, teeter, shake, rock, oscillate, vacillate.

touch *v.* **1** *Reach out and touch the wall:* put the hand against, put a finger against, make contact with, handle, finger, paw, thumb, feel, stroke, rub, manipulate, caress, pet, stroke. **2** *The two buildings touch at this point:* be in contact, meet, join, unite, be contiguous, abut, adjoin, border, converge, come together, bring into contact. **3** *Don't touch the money in the savings account. The vegetarian won't touch meat:* use, utilize; consume; avail oneself of, resort to, have recourse to, have to do with, be associated with, deal with. **4** *The beggar's plea for food touched us deeply. The hero's speech touched the entire audience:* affect, move, impress, work, soften, melt, sadden; influence, sway, strike, inspire, thrill, excite, arouse, stir, fire, inflame, electrify. **5** *The discussion touched on the problem of higher costs:* mention, discuss briefly, deal with in passing, allude to, refer to, broach, hint at, bear upon, concern, pertain to; note, cite. **6** *No one in the family can touch Jeanette as a cook:* compare with, equal, match, rival, come up to, come near, keep pace with.

—n. **7** *He located the light switch by touch. The slightest touch will bruise the flower:* the sense of touch; feel, feeling; touching, stroke, handling, fingering, thumbing, manipulation, palpation, contact; caress, fondling. **8** *The salesman kept in touch with the office by phone. The old man is out of touch with today's attitudes:* communication, contact; awareness, familiarity, acquaintance, realization, understanding, comprehension, perception. **9** *The salad had a touch of garlic:* trace, tinge, tint, bit, pinch, dash, sprinkling, soupçon, smack, taste, speck, hint, suggestion, suspicion, intimation. **10** *This symphony shows the touch of a master:* technique, deftness, adroitness, hand, style, manner, method, skill, art, artistry,

form, mastery, finesse, flair, gift, finish, polish, virtuosity; guiding hand, influence, direction.

Ant. 2 separate, diverge. **4** leave one unaffected, leave unmoved, leave one cold; bore. **5** ignore, disregard, overlook, pass over, skip, omit, leave out, reject, slight.

"The spider's touch how exquisitely fine! Feels at each thread, and lives along the line." —*Alexander Pope*

---

touching *adj. The hero's funeral is the most touching scene in the play:* moving, affecting; emotional, dramatic, sentimental; saddening, sad, heartfelt, heart-breaking, heart-rending, distressing, poignant, tender, pathetic, sorrowful.

Ant. unmoving, unaffecting, unemotional.

touchy *adj.* **1** *She's touchy about her prerogatives, so be extra tactful. Why are you so touchy today?:* sensitive, easily offended, easily hurt, thin-skinned, concerned, resentful, bitter; irritable, huffy, grumpy, grouchy, cross, testy, crabby, peevish, snappish, petulant, surly, quick-tempered, irascible, cantankerous, querulous, captious, waspish. **2** *Both labour and management are angry, so the negotiator is in a touchy situation:* delicate, requiring diplomacy, requiring tact, sensitive, ticklish, awkward, critical, requiring caution, precarious, difficult, fragile.

Ant. 1 insensitive, thick-skinned, callous, hardened, inured, impervious, indifferent, unconcerned, nonchalant; sweet, good-humoured, happy, pleasant, cheerful, cheery, smiling, blithe, jaunty, friendly, even-tempered, in good spirits, light-hearted, sunny, **2** non-critical, easy, easily handled, stable.

tough *adj.* **1** *The table-top is made of very tough plastic. What a tough steak!:* strong, durable, hardy, sturdy, firm, resistant, rugged, solid, impenetrable, infrangible, heavy-duty; leathery. **2** *Digging a tunnel under the river will be a tough job. How to balance the government's budget without raising taxes is a tough problem:* difficult, hard, laborious, arduous, strenuous, toilsome, exhausting, onerous, formidable, exacting, troublesome, trying, grievous, irksome, hard-to-solve, baffling, bewildering, puzzling, perplexing, confusing, complicated, intricate, complex, involved, thorny, knotty, ticklish, enigmatic. **3** *Mr West is known as a tough teacher. The boss is a tough man to convince:* hard, stern, strict, firm, rigid, exacting, unyielding, uncompromising, inflexible, unbending, stubborn, obstinate, obdurate, perverse, adamant, hard-headed, dogged, mulish, bull-headed, pigheaded; crafty, wily, canny, cagey, calculating, cold. **4** *The bully's tough talk frightened the other boys:* rough, vicious, bloodthirsty, ruthless, mean, cruel, brutal, savage, barbaric, inhuman, cold-blooded, heartless, hard-hearted, hard, unfeeling, insensitive, unsympathetic, pitiless, callous.

Ant. 1, 2 soft. **1** weak, delicate, frail, fragile, flimsy, brittle, frangible, susceptible; tender. **2, 3** easy. **2** simple, effortless, slight. **3** lenient, indulgent, permissive, unexacting; accommodating, amenable, acquiescent, complaisant, compliant, compromising, flexible. **4** sweet, kind, humane, benign, gentle, mild, soft-hearted, sympathetic, compassionate, considerate, loving, merciful.

toupee *n. He bought a toupee to cover his bald spot:* small wig, hair-piece, wig, periwig, peruke.

◇ *Word origin: Toupee* comes from French *toupet*, tuft of hair, forelock. This comes from Old French *toup*, crown of the head. (Old French *toup* has the same Germanic origin as our word *top*.)

tour *n.* **1** *The neighbours are making a three-week tour of France and Italy:* (*variously*) circular journey, sightseeing trip, jaunt, excursion.
—*v.* **2** *The British Lions will tour New Zealand in the spring. The group is touring the North this summer:* visit, travel round, travel through, sightsee, holiday in, travel and perform at, travel and work at, inspect.

tousled *adj. Please comb that tousled hair of yours!:* uncombed, straggly, dishevelled, unkempt, disordered, rumpled, messy, untidy, tangled.

Ant. combed, brushed and combed; well-kempt, neat, tidy.

tow *v.* **1** *The car had to be towed to the garage. The winch towed the log out of the way:* haul, drag, drag along, pull, trail, lug; hoist, lift.
—*n.* **2** *The disabled motorboat got a tow from a Coast Guard launch:* act of towing, towing.

Ant. 1, 2 push, shove.

tower *n.* **1** *The town's water-tower was next to the reservoir. The city hall had a picturesque clock tower:* tall structure; (*variously*) water-tower, clock tower, bell tower, belfry, prison tower, guard tower, look-out tower; steeple, spire, turret, minaret, skyscraper, column, obelisk; castle, keep. **2** *Throughout the centuries Oxford has been a tower of learning. Throughout the trouble, Joe has been a tower of strength:* pillar, mainstay, bulwark, stronghold, rock, foundation, well-spring, fountain-head, refuge.
—*v.* **3** *Salisbury cathedral's spire towers into the sky. Charlemagne towered above other rulers of his day:* rise high, rise above, ascend, soar, mount, shoot up, loom, surge, extend above, overhang, overtop, overshadow, eclipse; surpass, exceed, outshine, transcend, outdo, outclass, leave behind.

Ant. 3 fall, sink, descend, drop.

◇ *Word origin: Tower,* like *turret,* comes from Latin *turris,* tower, a high, fortified tower. The *Tyrolean Alps* and the *Tyrol* region of western Austria and northern Italy get their names from their towering mountains, via the same Latin word. Our figurative use of the word *tower*, as in the phrase *tower of strength*, comes from the Bible: "The name of the Lord is a strong tower" (Proverbs 18: 10).

towering *adj.* **1** *The towering hills cast deep shadows across the valley:* high, tall, lofty, ascending, soaring, mounting, overhanging, alpine, cloud-swept, cloud-capped, snow-clad. **2** *Beethoven was a towering musical genius:* surpassing, supreme, transcendent, pre-eminent, paramount, foremost, principal, dominant, sublime, superior, extraordinary, incomparable, peerless, unexcelled, unequalled, unrivalled, unparalleled, without parallel, unmatched, matchless, second to none.

Ant. **1** low, low-lying, short, squat, dumpy, stubby, truncated; flat, deep, submerged. **2** lowly, lesser, inferior, sorry, poor, paltry, inconsequential, insignificant; ordinary, commonplace, common, average, mediocre, run-of-the-mill, everyday.

town *n.* **1** *The town has only one primary school:* small town, large village, small city; (*loosely*) village, hamlet, place, settlement. **2** *Aunt Edith has a bungalow at the seaside and a house in town. I've always lived in good old London town:* self-governing populated place, municipality, borough, township, parish; city, urban area, population centre, metropolis. **3** *The whole town turned out to welcome the returning heroes:* townspeople, inhabitants, citizenry, residents. **4** *The head office is in town, but there are branches in the suburbs:* main business district, business district, shopping district, city centre, inner city.

◇ *Word origin: Town* comes from Old English *tūn,* which originally meant an enclosure, as a hedge or fence, then a group of farm buildings within such an enclosure, and finally became our modern word *town.*

"Bournemouth is one of the few English towns that one can safely call 'her'." —*John Betjeman*

---

toxic *adj. Carbon monoxide is a toxic gas:* poisonous, poisoned, deadly, lethal; pernicious, noxious, unhealthy.

Ant. non-toxic, non-poisonous, non-lethal; healthy, clean, salubrious, refreshing, invigorating.

◇ *Word origin: Toxic* comes from the Greek phrase *toxikon pharmakon,* arrow-poison, i.e. a poison in which arrows were dipped (Greek *toxon* means bow, and its plural *toxa* means arrows). Poisoned arrows were much used by the ancients.

toy *n.* **1** *The boy's favourite toy was a clockwork car. A private plane is the rich man's latest toy:* plaything; bauble, trinket, gadget, gewgaw, gimcrack, trifle.

—*adj.* **2** *Toy trains are being replaced by toy racing-cars:* for play, for amusement. **3** *Toy poodles are among the most popular breed of dog:* miniature, diminutive, small-scale, small-size, midget, pygmy, stunted, dwarf; little, tiny, lilliputian.

—*v.* **4** *The teacher had an annoying habit of toying with a pencil whilst he lectured. He's just toying with her affections:* play, trifle, dally, fiddle, amuse oneself with.

Ant. **1** necessity; tool, instrument, utensil. **2** real, actual. **3** full-size; oversize, giant, large, big, huge, enormous, immense, colossal, gigantic, mammoth, gargantuan.

◇ *Word origin: Toy* comes from Middle English *toye,* dalliance, amorous sport, flirtation, hence the idiom *to toy with someone's affections.*

trace *n.* **1** *There is no trace of the missing jewels. These statues are the only traces of a once great civilization:* sign left behind, sign, mark, indication, evidence, relic, vestige, token, remains; trail, track, footprint. **2** *There was a trace of sadness in her smile. It rained a trace last night:* tinge, touch, hint, suspicion, suggestion, shade, flavour; small amount, little bit, bit, trifle, jot, iota, drop.

—*v.* **3** *Police are trying to trace the missing man. The post office is tracing the missing package:* follow the trail of, track, track down, hunt for, hunt, nose out, ferret out, search for, look for, seek; find, discover, come across, light upon, unearth, dig up, uncover. **4** *The book traces the history of modern art:* map, diagram, draw, outline, delineate, describe, depict, mark out. **5** *Trace the drawing on a piece of tissue-paper:* copy by drawing over, draw over, follow the outline of.

track *n.* **1** *The train left the tracks just outside the station. The garage door is off its track again:* rail, guide rail, parallel rails; (*variously*) railway line, tramway, permanent way. **2** *The guide followed the tracks of the elephants. Police are on the track of the criminal:* footprint, mark, sign, spoor; trail, path, scent. **3** *Try to get off on the right track in your new job:* course, path, tack, way; foot. **4** *The racing-cars sped round the track. The athlete excelled at both track and field events:* race-track, running-track; sports performed on a track.

—*v.* **5** *The hunters tracked the bear to its lair. Scientists are trying to track the lost satellite:* follow the track, follow the path, trail, follow; trace.

tract[1] *n. The plane flew over the snowy tract of the Antarctic. He owns a large tract of land in Queensland:* stretch, expanse, region, area, quarter, district, territory; plot, lot.

◇ *Word origin: Tract*[1] comes from Latin *tractus,* stretch, region, tract of land. In Latin the word is used as a synonym of *regio,* region.

tract[2] *n.* **1** *Young members of the sect hand out tracts on street corners:* pamphlet, leaflet, brochure, booklet. **2** Das Kapital *is Karl Marx's famous* *tract analysing the capitalist system:* treatise, essay, disquisition.

◇ *Usage note: Tract* in the sense "treatise" is archaic in speech but still current in formal writing. The expression has an old-fashioned flavour and may soon become obsolete.

tractable *adj. A seaside donkey must be extremely tractable:* easy to manage, manageable, easy to control, controllable, governable, obedient, trainable, teachable, docile, tame, submissive, compliant, yielding.

Ant. intractable, unmanageable, uncontrollable, ungovernable, disobedient, wild, unruly, refractory, headstrong, wilful, stubborn, obstinate.

trade *n.* **1** *Foreign trade kept the country's economy healthy. Members of the professions used to look down on people in trade:* commerce, buying and selling, business, mercantile business, business dealings, transactions, merchandising. **2** *Bricklaying was Father's trade. Jim is a carpenter by trade but he does sculpture, too:* manual occupation, skilled occupation, skilled labour, occupational skill, manual skill, craft, handicraft; occupation, profession, calling, vocation, line of work, line, business, pursuit, employment.

—*v.* **3** *I'd love to trade in this car for a pick-up truck:* exchange, swap, barter. **4** *Germany trades with all European nations:* carry on commerce, do business, buy and sell, deal. **5** *The ancient Phoenicians traded in many countries:* do business, exchange commodities, buy, deal.

tradition *n.* **1** *The concept of "fair play" is an old British tradition. Celebrating Christmas at Aunt Jean's is a family tradition:* handed-down belief, custom, habit, typical way, practice, convention, usage, unwritten law, order of the day. **2** *According to tradition, the author of the* Iliad *and the* Odyssey *was a blind poet named Homer:* legend, myth, folk-tale, tale, saga; folklore, lore, superstition.

Ant. **1** novelty, innovation, new idea, the latest thing; law, decree, dogma. **2** true story, biography, autobiography; fact.

◇ *Word origin: Tradition* comes from Latin *tradere,* to deliver, give over, hence the knowledge, customs, etc., transmitted from generation to generation. The same Latin verb also gives us *betray, treason* and *traitor,* referring to delivery or giving over of something to an enemy.

traditional *adj. Birthday cakes are a traditional part of birthday parties. The house was furnished with traditional furniture:* handed down from generation to generation, customary, typical, conventional, usual, habitual, fixed, inveterate, established, acknowledged; old, ancestral, historic.

Ant. new, modern, novel, original, innovative, unusual, unconventional.

traffic *n.* **1** *This road carries a lot of traffic at the rush-hour:* vehicular movement; (*variously*) cars, lorries, buses, trains, planes, ships. **2** *The nine o'clock flight to Paris carries a lot of traffic:* passengers, travellers, voyagers; (*variously*) riders, tourists, holiday-makers, excursionists, commuters; freight. **3** *Customs must suppress the illegal drug traffic:* transportation of goods, trade, dealings, business, enterprise, commerce, buying and selling, transactions; smuggling, bootlegging. **4** *The family has never had any traffic with criminals!:* dealings, relations, doings, contact, proceedings, intercourse.

—*v.* **5** *The bootlegger was arrested for trafficking in illegal whisky:* trade, deal, buy and sell, carry on commerce; smuggle, bootleg.

◇ *Spelling tip:* Remember that the final *-c* in *traffic* becomes *-ck* in *traffiCKing.*

tragedy *n.* **1** *The boy's death was a tragedy. The widow's life was full of tragedy. The hurricane was a major tragedy to most of the islands:* dreadful happening, sad thing, unfortunate affair, shocking misfortune, pathetic occurrence, affliction; misery, anguish, sorrow, grief, woe, heartache, unhappiness, heart-break, blow, grievous day; disaster, catastrophe, calamity. **2** *Shakespeare wrote comedies, histories, and tragedies:* play with a disastrous ending, play about the downfall of a great man or woman.

Ant. **1** blessing, boon, kindness, wonderful thing, good fortune; happiness, joy, pleasure, satisfaction, gratification, bliss, contentment. **2** comedy.

◇ *Word origin: Tragedy* literally means "goat-song." It is from Greek *tragos* (goat) + *ōidē* (song). The word originally designated a ritual dance, with singing, in which one or more of the participants played the part of a goat.

"In this world there are only two tragedies. One is not getting what one wants, and the other is getting it." —*Oscar Wilde*

---

tragic *adj.* **1** *The tragic accident took eight lives:* dreadful, unfortunate, appalling, heartbreaking, sad, lamentable, pathetic, pitiable, mournful, grievous, dreary, woeful, unhappy, shocking, awful, frightful, terrible, horrible; disastrous, calamitous, catastrophic, fatal, deadly. **2** *The matinée idol wanted to be a tragic actor:* of dramatic tragedy; serious, dramatic.

Ant. **1** fortunate, happy, felicitous, pleasant, satisfying, gratifying, agreeable, joyful, worthwhile, wonderful, lucky. **2** comic.

trail *v.* **1** *The petrol lorry trailed a chain below it to reduce static electricity. The kite's tail trailed in the air:* drag, drag along, drag behind, tow, draw; dangle, hand down, float, stream, flow. **2** *The little boy trailed along behind his father. The team trailed by one goal as they entered the final minute:* follow, lag behind, be behind, tread on the heels of, follow in the wake of, bring up the rear; move slowly, dawdle, poke; be losing, be down. **3** *Police trailed the thieves to their hide-out:* track, trace, follow, tail, hunt, hound, dog. **4** *Her voice trailed to a whisper:* diminish, dwindle, shrink, subside, fall, grow faint, grow weak, taper off, lessen, decrease, peter out.

—*n.* **5** *The dogs followed the trail of the fox. The police are on the trail of the kidnapper:* track, footprints, scent, spoor; sign, mark, trace, path. **6** *Follow the trail until you come to the hut:* path, footpath, pathway, beaten track, way; bridle-path.

Ant. **1** push, shove. **2** lead, go before; be winning. **3** flee, run away. **4** increase, rise, swell, grow, intensify, strengthen.

train *n.* **1** *The train is pulling into the station now. The long train of nomads spanned the horizon:* railway train; underground train; caravan, procession, column. **2** *What train of events led to the discovery?:* series, succession, sequence, progression, chain, line, set. **3** *The wedding gown had a long train:* trailing part, trail, queue, appendage, continuation, after-part. **4** *The king is always surrounded by his train:* retinue, attendants, entourage, cortège.

—*v.* **5** *You should train your dog not to bark. The country needs to train five thousand doctors a year:* teach good behaviour, teach a habit, discipline, domesticate, break; instruct, teach, educate, school, prepare. **6** *The boxer trained for a month before the fight:* exercise, get in shape, prepare, practise, rehearse. **7** *The army trained its cannon on the fort:* aim, point, direct, level, sight, bring to bear.

trait *n. Boldness and resolution are two of the traits of a good leader:* characteristic, quality, mark, distinguishing mark, earmark, attribute, feature; peculiarity, idiosyncracy, mannerism.

traitor *n. In time of war any traitor will be shot. Judas was a traitor to Christ:* one who betrays his country, one who commits treason, turncoat, renegade, serpent, snake in the grass, wolf in sheep's clothing; (*variously*) deserter, rat, mutineer, revolutionary, rebel; betrayer, deceiver, hypocrite, false friend, Judas, apostate, quisling.

Ant. patriot, loyalist; defender, supporter, true friend.

◇ *Word origin:* See TRADITION.

tramp *v.* **1** *We tramped for hours through the snow:* trek, hike, march, trudge, walk, traipse, footslog, slog; (*loosely*) wander, ramble, roam, rove, meander, perambulate, gallivant, peregrinate, prowl. **2** *We knew that you were back, because we heard you all tramp up the garden path:* stamp, walk noisily, tread heavily, trample.

—*n.* **3** *There's a tramp at the back-door asking for money:* drifter, wandering beggar, gipsy, vagrant, beachcomber, floater, knight of the road, itinerant.

trample *v. The cowboy was almost trampled in the stampede. Don't trample the new grass:* grind under foot, run over, crush, flatten, squash; step heavily upon.

> **Exploring the Word:** The closely-related Latin verbs *trahere* and *tractare*, to drag, draw, pull, handle, give us *train, tractor*, and *trawler*, all of which pull things; *trailer*, something pulled, and *trail*, to be pulled behind, to come behind, or a path or track as left by something pulled, as a *trail through the woods; traction*, pull or degree of pull; and *tractable*, easy to pull or lead, easily-handled, docile, and the verb to *train*, to lead, handle, make docile. The idea of dragging something over the ground, as a stick or plough, to leave a line or mark a boundary, not only gives us *trail*, but *trace* and *tract* of land and also *portrait* and *portray*, referring to pictures marking off the "boundary" of a person with a few lines, and *trait*, an individual characteristic or quality such as a portrait artist tries to catch with lines from his pen or brush. The sense "to handle" in both Latin *trahere* and *tractare* gives us our words: to *treat*, to handle in a certain way; *treatment*, the way something is handled; *maltreatment*, bad treatment, bad handling; *treatise*, a written treatment or handling of a subject; *entreaty*, a plea or supplication as a way of handling something; and *treaty*, which sets forth the way two countries will handle their affairs, as ending a war.

tranquil *adj. Twilight in the forest is a very tranquil period. Mother remained tranquil despite the confusion around her:* peaceful, calm, serene, restful, placid, still, quiet, unruffled, unexcited, composed, cool, undisturbed, mild, gentle.

Ant. agitated, disturbed, confused, busy, restless; excited, rattled, distracted.

◇ *Word origin: Tranquil* comes from Latin *tranquillus*, quiet. A *tranquillizer* is a drug that reduces nervous tension and anxiety, a medicine that makes a person tranquil or quiet. The term was introduced by Thomas De Quincey (1785–1859) in his *Confessions of an English Opium-Eater.*

transact *v. He transacts most of his business by phone:* carry on, carry out, conduct, exact, perform, do, execute, handle, accomplish, manage, discharge, achieve, settle, take care of.

transaction *n. Investors made millions on that real estate transaction:* business dealing, dealing, deal, piece of business, venture, enterprise, affair, operation, exchange, negotiation.

transcend *v.* **1** *That bizarre tale of men from Mars transcends belief:* exceed, go beyond, rise above, outdo, surmount, surpass, overstep, overleap. **2** *Cleopatra's beauty transcended that of all other women:* surpass, be greater than, be superior to, exceed, excel, outdo, overshadow, outshine, eclipse, outrival, outdistance, outrank.

transcendental *adj.* **1** *The mystic was concerned with transcendental realities:* metaphysical, transcending experience, spiritual, mental, intuitive. **2** *A number of people agree on the transcendental beauty of a Beethoven symphony:* extraordinary, unusual, uncommon, superior, great, exceeding, surpassing, elevated.

Ant. 1 physical, empirical. **2** ordinary, common, commonplace, usual, average; inferior, little.

transfer *v.* **1** *Let's transfer these files to the new cabinets. He transferred the ownership of the house to his wife:* move, remove, shift, relocate, change, convey, carry, bring, send, transport, transmit; consign, turn over, hand over, relegate, make over, deed, cede.
—*n.* **2** *The transfer of the ship's cargo onto the pier was halted by a severe storm:* transferring, transferral, transference, moving, removal, shifting, shift, relocation, relocating, conveying, carrying, bringing, sending, transportation, transporting, transmittal, shipment; consignment, delivering, relegation, deeding.

Ant. 1 keep, retain; leave. **2** keeping, retention.

transfix *v.* **1** *The harpoonist transfixed the whale with his first shot:* impale, skewer, spear, run through, fix fast, pin, stick, stab, spike, pierce, penetrate. **2** *The magician transfixed the children with his wonderful fire-eating act:* rivet the attention of, rivet, hold rapt, engross, hold, absorb, fascinate, spellbind, mesmerize, entrance, hypnotize, bewitch, captivate, intrigue, enchant; stun, astound, astonish; terrify.

◇ *Word origin: Transfix* comes from Latin *trans-* (across, over) + *figere* (to fasten).

transform *v. The caterpillar was transformed into a butterfly. The new owners transformed the old house into an hotel:* change, turn, convert, transfigure, transmute, alter, transmogrify, metamorphose; remodel, reconstruct, remould, recast, refurbish.

transgression *n. The sinner prayed that his transgressions would be forgiven. Eavesdropping is a transgression on another's privacy:* offence, sin, misdeed, evil deed, trespass, iniquity, wrongdoing, wrong, immorality, error; infraction, infringement, breach, encroachment, contravention, overstepping; crime, law-breaking.

Ant. virtue, morality, probity, righteousness, grace, good deed, merit; observance, compliance, adherence.

transgressor *n. The preacher warned all transgressors to repent. Transgressors of the speeding restrictions will be fined £100:* sinner, evil-doer, trespasser, offender; law-breaker, violator, wrongdoer, culprit, malefactor, miscreant, criminal.

Ant. innocent, exemplar; law-abider.

transient *adj.* **1** *Youthful beauty is transient:* temporary, transitory, fleeting, brief, momentary, ephemeral, evanescent, impermanent, unenduring, not lasting, perishable, short-lived, temporal, soon past, passing, here today and gone tomorrow. **2** *Many of these birds are transient visitors to these islands:* temporary, staying a short time, short-term, fleeting, passing through.

Ant. 1, 2 permanent. **1** lasting, long-lasting, undying, unfading, imperishable, perpetual, persistent, durable, abiding.

◇ *Usage note: Transient* means disappearing quickly, brief. Thus: *a transient thought, a transient worker. Transitory* means existing for a short time: *transitory pleasures, Mayflies are transitory creatures.*

transition *n. The transition from country life to city life is often difficult:* change, change-over, passing, passage, shifting, jump, leap, conversion, variation, transformation, transmutation; progression, gradation, graduation.

transitory *adj. His first love was a transitory summer romance that ended when school began:* temporary, transient, fleeting, brief, short-lived, passing, impermanent, not lasting, unenduring, evanescent, ephemeral, here today and gone tomorrow.

Ant. long, long-lived, lasting, persistent, durable, enduring, permanent, undying, abiding, everlasting, perpetual, eternal.

translate *v.* **1** *Chinese is a difficult language to translate into English:* render, convert; decode, decipher. **2** *It's time you translated your beliefs into actions!:* change, turn, transform, apply, convert, transmute; recast, alter. **3** *Please translate the medical diagnosis into terms that I can understand:* explain, interpret, simplify, elucidate, clarify, make clear, spell out; reword, paraphrase, rephrase, express differently.

translucent *adj. Stained-glass windows are translucent enough to admit some light:* semi-transparent, semi-opaque, pellucid, translucid.

Ant. opaque.

◇ *Usage note:* A *transparent* material allows light to pass through it and gives a clear view of objects on the other side of it. A *translucent* material allows some light to pass through but does not give a clear view of objects on the other side. Thus a regular window-pane is *transparent,* a frosted window is *translucent.*

transmission *n.* **1** *The police arrived in time to prevent the transmission of the secret documents:* transmitting, transfer, transferring, transference, passage, passing, handing over, changing of hands, transmittal, transmittance, sending, conveyance, dispatch, forwarding, transportation, delivery, remittance. **2** *Normal transmission will resume as soon as possible:* delivery, broadcast, programme; communication.

transmit *v.* **1** *A telegram will be the quickest way to* *transmit the message. Certain mosquitoes transmit malaria:* send, convey, deliver, relay, transfer, dispatch, issue, forward, ship, remit, pass on, carry, spread, disseminate, communicate. **2** *The station transmits from 6 a.m. until midnight:* broadcast, televise, send, relay a signal.

transparent *adj.* **1** *The water was so transparent that we could see the fish clearly:* clear, crystal clear, lucid, limpid, pellucid, glassy. **2** *Those transparent curtains will never keep the light out:* see-through, thin, sheer, gauzy, translucent, diaphanous. **3** *Her reason for leaving was transparent:* evident, self-evident, plain, obvious, apparent, perceptible, palpable, manifest, visible, patent; explicit, distinct, clear-cut, unmistakable, unambiguous, unequivocal.

Ant. 1, 2 opaque. **1** muddy, roiled. **2** thick. **3** imperceptible, unapparent, hidden, concealed, unrevealed, invisible, undetectable; indistinct, confused, vague, mysterious, mystifying.

transpire *v.* **1** *After a few days, it transpired that the accident had been more serious than was at first supposed:* become known, be discovered, be revealed, be disclosed, come to light, come out, make public, become public knowledge, get abroad, show its face, leak out. **2** *Informal Please tell us what transpires at the meeting:* occur, happen, come to pass, take place, be met with; befall, arise, present itself, chance, appear, turn up, crop up.

◇ *Usage note:* Originally *transpire* meant to exhale or give off a vapour, then it was used to refer to the revealing of a secret or the discovery of a fact: *When the sun came up it transpired that we had camped on the edge of a crevasse. At the book's end it transpired that the orphan was really the millionaire's son.* Today many people use *transpire* to mean "to happen." Many teachers and critics consider this usage improper, informal, or affected, so be warned that its use can let you in for some criticism.

transport *v.* **1** *It took all day to transport the furniture to the new office:* transfer, move, remove, convey, carry, transmit, take, bring, send, deliver, dispatch, fetch, bear, cart, tote, lug; ship, truck, freight. **2** *The beautiful music transported the audience:* carry away, move, thrill, enrapture, enchant, lift, enthral, entrance, overpower, make ecstatic, electrify, captivate, delight, charm, bewitch, *Slang* send.

—*n.* **3** *The transport of explosives is a dangerous business:* transporting, transportation, shipment, shipping, conveying, conveyance, moving, transfer, removal, carrying, sending, delivery, dispatch, bearing, carting, shifting. **4** *We had almost despaired when transport finally arrived:* vehicle, conveyance; (*variously*) ship, freighter, cargo ship, train, goods train, aeroplane, cargo plane, lorry, bus.

trap *n.* **1** *The rabbit was caught in a trap:* (*variously*) snare, springe, net, pitfall. **2** *Promising a fortune for nothing was just one of the con man's traps:* ruse, artifice, stratagem, wile, feint, ploy, device, machination, manœuvre; ambush, booby trap.

—*v.* **3** *Some cheese helped us to trap the mouse:* entrap, catch, snare, ensnare, enmesh, hunt down, lure, entangle. **4** *The engineers tried to trap the gas in the pipes but some escaped:* seal, stop, lock in, hold back, compartmentalize.

trappings *n. pl. The trappings of a king include his robe, crown, and sceptre. The house was filled with all the trappings for a party:* dress, garb, costume, raiment, attire, clothing, clothes, apparel, vesture, investment, outfit, habiliment; gear, accoutrements, paraphernalia, trimmings, effects, array, things, fittings, ornaments, decorations, embellishments, adjuncts.

trash *n.* **1** *Gather up the leaves and put them with the rest of the trash:* litter, rubbish, junk, rubble, refuse, garbage, waste matter, residue, sweepings, dregs, leavings, debris; worthless stuff, odds and ends, cast-offs. **2** *Don't waste your time reading that trash!:* worthless writing, worthless talk, junk, drivel, rot, hogwash, balderdash, twaddle, nonsense, foolishness. **3** *Informal Her son runs around with that trash from the other side of town:* disreputable persons, unsavoury element, shady types, scum, riff-raff, good-for-nothings, tramps, ne'er-do-wells, idlers.

Ant. 1 valuables, treasure. **3** élite, worthies.

travail *n.* **1** *The pioneer's life was full of hardship and travail:* toil, drudgery, hard work, backbreaking work, burdensome work, exertion. **2** *The travails of war left the country limp:* anguish, suffering, strain, stress, hardship, worry, distress, pain.

Ant. 1 ease, relaxation, rest, loafing. **2** comfort, pleasure.

◇ *Word origin: Travail* comes from Medieval Latin *trepalium*, a three-pronged instrument of torture.

"A man travels the world over in search of what he needs and returns home to find it."

—*George Moore*

---

travel *v.* **1** *Try to make the ball travel in a straight line:* move, proceed, progress, go, wend, press onward. **2** *We travelled to Greece and Turkey last summer. We travelled the distance in three hours:* take a trip, journey, tour, visit; pass over, traverse, cross, pass through; roam, rove, wander, trek, globe-trot, range; (*variously*) voyage, cruise, sail, drive.

Ant. 2 stay, remain, settle, remain stationary.

◇ *Word origin: Travel* used to be much more difficult than it now is. In fact, *travel* is just a variant of *travail*, pain, anguish, torturous labour!

traveller *n.* **1** *The airport was filled with summer travellers:* one who travels; (*variously*) tourist, journeyer, holiday-maker, wayfarer, walker, hiker, voyager, excursionist, tripper, sight-seer, globe-trotter, wanderer, itinerant, rover, vagabond, nomad, migrant, gipsy, pilgrim. **2** *How many travellers does your sales manager oversee?:* travelling salesman, commercial traveller, representative, drummer, *Informal* rep.

traverse *v.* **1** *The hikers had to traverse the shaky bridge one at a time:* cross, go across, move over, move along, travel over, travel, cut across; move through, negotiate, pass through. **2** *The fly-over traverses the old town:* cross, cross over, span, reach across, go across, extend over, reach over, bridge, intersect, run through.

travesty *n.* **1** *The comedian's travesty of a vicar giving his sermon was riotously funny:* ludicrous imitation, burlesque, spoof, take-off, parody, caricature, send-up, mockery, broad satire, farce. **2** *The entire trial was a travesty of justice:* mockery, perversion, shameful imitation, shameful example, misrepresentation, distortion, sham, disgrace.

◇ *Word origin:* Why is there a "vest" in *travesty*? Because it comes from Italian *travestirse,* to dress up in another's clothes or *vestments,* especially as a burlesque or parody.

treacherous *adj.* **1** *Brutus proved to be a treacherous friend to Caesar:* traitorous, untrustworthy, faithless, false-hearted, unfaithful, disloyal, untrue, deceitful, deceptive, false, perfidious, tricky, devious, two-faced. **2** *Freezing rain made the road treacherous:* dangerous, hazardous, unsafe, perilous, precarious, risky, slippery.

Ant. **1** loyal, true, true-blue, faithful, trusty, trustworthy, dependable, reliable. **2** safe, reliable.

treachery *n. The boss considers the buying of a rival product treachery to the firm:* disloyalty, treason, betrayal, faithlessness, untrustworthiness, falseness, deceit, deceitfulness, deception, perfidy, violation of faith, breach of faith, underhandedness, duplicity, trickery, double-dealing, double-cross, infidelity, apostasy.

tread *v.* **1** *Tread softly on the stairs so as not to wake the baby. Many religious pilgrims have trod this same path to the shrine:* walk, walk along, walk on, step, step on, trudge along, tramp, hike, stroll; roam, rove, range, prowl. **2** *The boys trod on the newly-planted flowers:* trample, stamp, crush under foot.

—*n.* **3** *We heard father's tread on the steps:* step, sound of footsteps, footstep, footfall; walk; manner of walking, gait, pace, stride.

◇ *Usage note:* The past tense of *tread* is *trod: Our ancestors trod this same path.* Its past participle is *trodden* or *trod: Dr. Livingstone visited parts of Africa where the foot of a white man had never trod. Look where the rabbits have trodden a path in the snow.*

treason *n. In time of war, treason is a crime punishable by death:* betrayal of one's country, aiding an enemy, sedition, subversion, rebellion, revolt, revolution, insurgence, insurrection, mutiny; disloyalty, treachery, perfidy, apostasy.

Ant. loyalty, patriotism; faithfulness, fidelity.

◇ *Word origin:* See TRADITION.

treasure *n.* **1** *The divers discovered the pirates' treasure in the sunken ship:* stored wealth, riches, hoard, store, deposit, *Slang* gold-mine; (*variously*) precious gems, jewels, gold, silver. **2** *That new secretary is a real treasure:* gem, jewel, paragon, pride and joy, apple of one's eye, pearl of great price, godsend.

—*v.* **3** *The boy treasured the teacher's good opinion above all else:* value, cherish, revere, esteem, prize, hold dear, count precious, regard, dote upon, care greatly for, bank upon.

Ant. **3** disclaim, scorn, disregard, hold for naught, take lightly.

treasury *n.* **1** *How much money is in the company's treasury?:* place where funds are kept, exchequer, repository, depository, storehouse, bank; vault, till, coffer, safe, strong-box, money-box. **2** *Does the library have a treasury of the poems of Robert Burns?:* collection, anthology, compendium, compilation, thesaurus.

◇ *Word origin:* See THESAURUS.

treat *v.* **1** *Her parents still treat her like a child:* act toward, behave toward, deal with, relate to, consider, look upon; manage, handle. **2** *You'll need a doctor to treat that wound:* try to cure, try to heal, doctor, attend, minister to, prescribe for, remedy, medicate, patch up, dress. **3** *The book treats the problems of economic development:* discuss, have as a subject matter, write about, expatiate on, address oneself to, speak about. **4** *The wood was treated with a termite repellent:* apply, cover, coat, imbue, impregnate. **5** *Father treated everyone to dinner at a restaurant:* entertain as a guest, take out, give, *Slang* stand; favour, grant; divert.

—*n.* **6** *After days of camping, a hot shower is a real treat:* pleasure, satisfaction, gratification, comfort, delight, joy, thrill. **7** *Going to the theatre is my birthday treat:* small gift of food, small gift; favour, grant; entertainment paid for by another.

treatise *n. The doctor wrote a treatise on alcoholism:* systematic work, detailed article, discourse, study, monograph, exhaustive paper, extensive piece, tract, tractate, manual, dissertation, report, memoir.

treatment *n.* **1** *All visitors should receive courteous treatment. The intermediary's sensitive treatment of the problem satisfied both sides in the dispute:* manner of dealing, handling, management, treating, manipulation, operation, conduct, approach, process, procedure, way, course. **2** *The doctors decided upon non-surgical treatment of* *the tumour:* medical care, cure, remedy, therapy, doctoring; regimen; application, medication, antidote.

treaty *n. The warring nations will soon sign a peace treaty:* international agreement, formal agreement, pact, compact, covenant, concordat, entente, understanding.

tremble *v. His hands were trembling from the cold. The girl's voice trembled and she started to cry:* shake, quiver, shiver, shudder, quake, quaver, waver, flutter, pulsate, palpitate.

tremendous *adj.* **1** *Tremendous gales devastated the crops. Building the bridge was a tremendous undertaking:* huge, gigantic, immense, colossal, enormous, extremely large, great, mammoth, giant, monstrous, gargantuan, elephantine, titanic, vast, towering; formidable, awesome, major, considerable, sizeable; important, consequential. **2** *Informal France is known for its tremendous restaurants:* wonderful, excellent, exceptional, extraordinary, marvellous, fantastic, incredible, amazing, first-rate, noteworthy, great, fabulous, fine, terrific, stupendous.

Ant. 1 small, little, diminutive, wee, undersized, miniature, dwarf, stunted, pygmy; easy, simple, minor, unimportant. **2** ordinary, fair, average, mediocre, unexceptional, unremarkable, run-of-the-mill; bad, poor, awful, terrible, lousy, second-rate.

> **Exploring the Word**: *Tremble, tremor,* and *tremendous* come from Latin *tremere,* to shake, tremble. *Tremble* and *tremor* retain this basic meaning while *tremendous* originally meant causing shaking or trembling due to awe or astonishment at the great size or force of something. The same Latin base also gives us the musical word *tremolo,* a rapid vibrating sound of one tone over and over again or a rapid alternating between two tones, giving a trembling effect, and *delirium tremens,* an acute delirium commonly known as the "D.T.'s" or "the horrors," caused by alcohol-poisoning.

tremor *n. The tremor in his hands was the only indication of his nervousness. A slight earth tremor was felt in Madrid today:* shaking, shake, trembling, tremble, quiver, quivering, shiver, shivering, shudder, waver, flutter, quavering, pulsating, spasm, paroxysm, throb, convulsion, palpitation, vibration; quake, jolt, shock, jar.

Ant. steadiness.

trend *n. Today's trend is towards less formal clothing:* fashion, mode, style; drift, direction, bent, tendency, leaning, inclination, propensity, proclivity, impulse.

trepidation *n. It's natural to have some trepidation before undergoing surgery:* apprehension, disquiet, uneasiness, anxiety, dread, alarm, fear, consternation, worry, disquietude, nervousness, *Informal* jitteriness, cold feet.

Ant. confidence, sureness, fearlessness, quietude, steadiness, calm, cool.

◇ *Word origin: Trepidation* comes from Latin *trepidus,* alarmed, agitated, which also gives us *intrepid,* not alarmed, hence bold, brave.

trespass *v.* **1** *The farmer threatened to shoot anyone who trespassed on his property:* enter unlawfully, intrude, infringe, invade, encrouch, impinge.

—*n.* **2** *The fishing-boat was seized for its trespass into restricted waters:* wrongful entry, unlawful entry, encroachment, intrusion, infringement, invasion. **3** *Forgive us our trespasses:* sin, wrongdoing, evil-doing, immorality, error, iniquity, transgression, misdeed, offence; misconduct, misbehaviour, infraction, overstepping the mark, delinquency.

Ant. 3 good deed, virtue.

trial *n.* **1** *The trial ended in acquittal for the defendants:* court case, litigation, judicial contest, hearing. **2** *The trial of the new plane was delayed by bad weather. The recipe didn't turn out well the first time, but I'll give it another trial:* test, testing, test run, try-out, trying, putting to the proof; try, attempt, essay, venture, go, shot, endeavour, effort, *Informal* spin, whirl. **3** *The poor man's life was full of trials and tribulations:* hardship, misfortune, trouble, distress, affliction, woe, misery, pain, adversity, burden, ordeal, vexation, suffering, wretchedness, agony, anguish, torment, care, worry, heartache, misadventure, accident, bad luck, cross to bear.

Ant. 3 ease, comfort, happiness, joy, delight, good fortune, good luck.

tribulation *n. Too many tribulations have left him a beaten man:* affliction, trouble, ordeal, suffering, wretchedness, misfortune, worry, care, hardship, heartache, agony, anguish, torment, pain, adversity, trial; woe, misery, distress, grief, vexation, sorrow, unhappiness; ill fortune, bad luck.

Ant. happiness, joy, delight, ease, comfort; good fortune, good luck.

tribunal *n. The case was tried before the highest tribunal in the land:* court, bar, bench, forum, seat of judgement, authority, judiciary, ruling body; judge's bench, judge's chair.

tribute *n.* **1** *We must give tribute to all those who helped make this a free country. The musician gave full tribute to his old teacher:* honour, respect, esteem, gratitude, acknowledgement, recognition; praise, compliment, commendation, laudation, eulogy, panegyric, extolling, encomium; testimonial, memorial. **2** *The pirates demanded tribute from the captured ship:* payment, settlement, ransom, bribe, peace offering, levy, excise, impost, assessment, tax, duty, toll, consideration, pay-off, blood-money, pound of flesh.

Ant. 1 dishonour, disrespect, ingratitude, disdain, scorn; blame, insult, condemnation, slur, slap in the face.

trick *n.* 1 *Pretending to be hurt is a trick many prize-fighters use:* ruse, device, deception, deceit, stratagem, machination, artifice, wile, feint, blind, manœuvre, ploy, gimmick, resort, hoax; underhand act, chicanery, sophistry, trap, fraud, imposture, subterfuge, contrivance, dodge, hocus-pocus. 2 *Telling someone that his shoe is untied is an old April Fool's trick:* prank, joke, gag, antic, bluff, practical joke, caprice, put-on. 3 *Can the dog do tricks? Here's a new trick that the magician did:* clever act, skilled act, stunt, feat, antic, number; magic demonstration, sleight of hand, piece of legerdemain. 4 *There's a trick to making good coffee:* knack, art, know-how, skill, deftness, gift, dexterity, adroitness, technique, secret.
—*v.* 5 *Dad tricked Mother into believing he had forgotten her birthday — then surprised her:* deceive, take in, trap, hoax, gull, dupe, bait, outmanœuvre, hoodwink, mislead, have, outwit, bamboozle, outfox, bluff; cheat, swindle, manipulate, flimflam.
Ant. 1 honesty, truth, sincerity, candour, frankness, openness, straightforwardness, guilelessness. 4 luck.

trickery *n. The con man obtained that money by trickery, not work:* deceitfulness, deceit, guile, chicanery, charlatanism, duplicity, deviousness, skulduggery, stratagem, wiliness, craftiness, artfulness, slipperiness, quackery, rascality, pretence, hocus-pocus, imposture, crookedness, deception, bunkum, flimflam, artifice, shiftiness.
Ant. honesty, straightforwardness, artlessness, candidness, candour, frankness, openness, uprightness.

trickle *v.* 1 *Blood trickled from the wound. The audience trickled back into the auditorium:* drip, dribble, seep, leak, exude, ooze; move slowly, pass bit by bit, go gradually.
—*n.* 2 *Only a trickle of water came out of the pipe:* dribble, drip, seepage, slow stream; little bit, small amount, small quantity.
Ant. 1 splash, gush, stream, course, pour, spurt, surge. 2 stream, gush, flood, surge, spurt; lot, lots, much, many.

tricky *adj.* 1 *Be careful of your opponent, he's pretty tricky:* crafty, sly, cunning, foxy, slippery, wily, rascally, artful, deceptive, underhand, shifty, devious. 2 *The old car is tricky to start. Working out a compromise between the two sides will be tricky:* difficult, complicated, hard to handle, touch-and-go, temperamental. 3 *Be careful crossing that tricky bridge:* unreliable, unstable, undependable, unpredictable, hazardous, unsafe, dangerous, risky.
Ant. 1 candid, straightforward, open, frank, artless, ingenuous, guileless, honest, truthful. 2 simple, easy. 3 reliable, dependable, stable.

trifle *n.* 1 *The lost ring was only a trifle. Don't cry over trifles:* trinket, bauble, gimcrack, knick-knack, bagatelle, gewgaw, plaything, toy; triviality, thing of no importance, small matter, unimportant matter, nothing. 2 *Is there anything left? A mere trifle:* small quantity, little, morsel, bit, mite, dash, dab, drop, nip, pinch, speck, scrap, sliver, crumb, fragment, trace, iota, jot, modicum, sprinkling, tinge, touch.
—*v.* 3 *He's just trifling with her affections:* treat lightly, deal lightly, amuse oneself, toy, play. 4 *We trifled too long at the fair:* dally, dawdle, linger, idle, dilly-dally, pass the time of day, loiter, kill time, waste time.
Ant. 2 lot, lots, loads, stacks, oodles.

trifling *adj. The owner offered but a trifling reward for the return of the lost dog:* insignificant, unimportant, inconsequential, trivial, negligible, small, slight, petty, puny, piddling, nugatory, miniscule, inconsiderable, niggling, nominal, token, inappreciable, beneath notice, not worthy of mention, worthless, paltry, sorry, beggarly.
Ant. important, significant, consequential, worthwhile, considerable, appreciable, large.

trim *v.* 1 *Be sure to trim the rose-bushes:* prune, clip, crop, pare, lop, shave, shear, cut. 2 *The seamstress trimmed the dress with red stitching:* decorate, ornament, adorn, deck, bedeck, array, garnish, embellish, furbish, trick out, beautify, bedizen, embroider. 3 *The loaders trimmed the load of the lorry so that it wouldn't be top-heavy. The crew trimmed the sails of the ship to achieve greater speed:* balance, distribute, arrange, adjust, equalize; change, shift, adjust to the direction of the wind.
—*n.* 4 *Your holiday seems to have kept you in good trim:* shape, condition, fitness, state, form, fettle. 5 *The lace trim on the bride's dress is over a hundred years old:* trimming, adornment, embellishment, decoration, garnish, ornamentation, border, piping. 6 *His sideburns need a trim:* trimming, cutting, levelling up, clipping, shearing, cropping, pruning, paring.
—*adj.* 7 *Eat less to achieve a trim figure:* lean, slim, slender, svelte, shapely, streamlined, well-proportioned, thin, lissome, shipshape, compact; fit, limber, supple, lithe, athletic.

trinket *n. We bought a few trinkets as souvenirs for the children:* trifle, bauble, small ornament, bit of jewellery, bagatelle, gewgaw, gimcrack, knick-knack, odds and ends, toy, plaything.

trip *n.* 1 *The trip was cancelled because of the snowstorm:* journey, voyage, excursion, outing, tour, jaunt, cruise, pilgrimage, expedition, foray, ramble.
—*v.* 2 *The boy tripped over a roller-skate and broke his arm:* stumble, fall over, miss one's footing, misstep, slip, cause to fall, throw off balance, lose one's balance, upset. 3 *The little girl can read easy words but trips on the hard ones. The hard maths problem tripped up most of the students:* make a mistake, err, blunder, slip

up, bungle, flounder, fluff, botch, muff; cause to make a mistake, cause to err, throw off, disconcert, confuse, fool, catch, catch off guard, outdo, hoodwink, outfox. **4** *She tripped down the stairs like a fairy princess:* skip, step lightly, tread gracefully, flounce, caper, bob, prance, dance, gambol, scamper, frolic. **5** *The machine won't operate unless someone trips this lever:* release, undo, pull, flip, throw, activate, set off.

trite *adj. The critics denounced the play for its trite plot:* banal, stale, hackneyed, pedestrian, worn-out, shop-worn, stereotyped, clichéd, commonplace, routine, run-of-the-mill, platitudinous, oft-repeated, threadbare, common, ordinary; silly, frivolous, shallow, unimportant.

Ant. original, fresh, unusual, novel, exciting.

◇ *Word origin: Trite* comes from Latin *tritus*, oft-trodden, beaten, frequented, common: *iter tritum*, the beaten track. The Romans also used the word figuratively as we do: *sermo trita*, trite, commonplace language.

triumph *n.* **1** *Helen Keller's triumph over deafness, blindness, and muteness was a miracle. The new opera is a complete triumph:* victory, success, conquest, mastery, ascendancy, superiority, accomplishment, attainment, achievement, *Informal* hit, smash hit, coup.

—v. **2** *The Allies triumphed over the Axis powers in World War II. Justice triumphs in the end:* be victorious, succeed, be successful, win, prevail, come out on top, get the better of, best, subdue, conquer, overwhelm, vanquish, overcome, surpass, gain the day, take the prize, have the best of it.

Ant. 1 defeat, loss; failure. **2** lose, succumb.

◇ *Word origin:* In ancient Rome, a *triumph* was the victory-procession of a general, conquering dictator, or successful consul into Rome. The word may go all the way back to Greek *thriambos*, a hymn or procession in honour of Dionysus, god of wine and fertility.

"He sicken'd at all triumphs but his own."
—*Charles Churchill*

---

triumphal *adj. Winning a gold medal in the Olympics was the triumphal moment in the athlete's career. The heroes were given a triumphal reception:* victorious, successful, ascendant, fulfilling, rewarding, gratifying; joyous, exultant; spectacular, proud, marking a triumph, triumphant.

triumphant *adj.* **1** *The triumphant team celebrated its victory:* victorious, winning, successful, conquering, champion, trophy-winning, prize-winning, laurel-wreathed, first-place. **2** *The triumphant fans poured onto the pitch:* rejoicing, celebrating, exultant, jubilant.

Ant. 1 defeated, beaten, unsuccessful. **2** despairing, disappointed.

trivial *adj. Don't let such trivial things upset you:* trifling, unimportant, inconsequential, petty, slight, piddling, paltry, insignificant, inessential, flimsy, nugatory, inconsiderable, small, little, slim, meagre, puny, niggling, beggarly, worthless, idle, foolish, inappreciable, of little value, incidental; everyday, ordinary, common, commonplace, pedestrian, trite, banal.

Ant. weighty, important, consequential, significant, essential, worthwhile, momentous, material, considerable, large, appreciable, substantial; unusual, extraordinary, uncommon, exceptional.

◇ *Word origin:* What's *trivial* about a roundabout or a place where three roads meet? *Trivial* and *trivia* come from the Latin prefix *tri-* (three) + *via* (road), a square or place where three roads meet, a place common to all roads, hence, commonplace, ordinary, insignificant.

troop *n.* **1** *A troop of Boy Scouts was camping by the river. A troop of shoppers descended on the department store looking for bargains:* band, unit, company; throng, horde, drove, crowd, swarm, herd, flock, gathering, assemblage, aggregate, congregation, collection, crush, press, army, bunch, gang. **2 troops** *The nation must keep its troops on constant alert:* soldiers, soldiery, army, armed force, military force, infantry, fighting men, militia; cavalry, cavalry unit; uniformed men, policemen, troopers.

—v. **3** *The children trooped into the yard in single file:* march, file, parade; walk briskly, stride, step, trudge, tramp.

◇ *Usage note:* A *troop* is a gathering, often an organized one, as a body of soldiers, policemen, or Boy Scouts. A *troupe* is a company of actors or other performers, of *troupers*. Thus, *a Boy Scout troop. Six troopers managed to ride away from the ambush*, but *a circus troupe. The old trouper still knew all the lines of* Macbeth.

trophy *n. The winning golfer received £1,000 and a silver trophy. The stuffed lion's head was the only trophy of his African safari:* (*variously*) cup, loving-cup, medal, blue ribbon, prize, citation, wreath, laurels, palm; testimonial, souvenir, relic, memento; spoil, booty.

◇ *Word origin: Trophy* and *tropic* both come from Greek *tropē*, a turn, also specifically a turning-back or repulse of an enemy in the field. In the case of *trophy*, the Greek word refers to a monument to commemorate the victory. In the case of *tropic*, the Greek word refers to the turning of the sun at the solstice (at its farthest point from the equator before turning back towards it).

tropical *adj. Bananas grow best in tropical climates:* in the tropics, of the tropics; hot and humid, torrid, sultry, stifling, sweltering.

Ant. arctic; cold, wintry, icy, chilly, cool.

trot *v. The horse trotted for a while, then went into a canter:* go at a gait between a walk and a gallop; jog, go briskly, walk smartly, step quickly.

Ant. gallop, run; plod, creep, crawl.

trouble *v.* **1** *The boy's lack of friends troubled his parents deeply. May I trouble you for a drink of water?:* distress, worry, upset, dismay, grieve, disquiet, make uneasy, agitate, perturb, concern, discompose, disconcert, unsettle, oppress, torment, plague, harry, depress; bother, disturb, inconvenience, annoy, pester, badger, harass, discommode, put out. **2** *Didn't you trouble to read the directions?:* exert oneself, make the time, make the effort, attempt, think, attend, heed. **3** *Grandmother's arthritis is troubling her again:* bother, afflict, affect, pain, annoy, vex, plague.
—*n.* **4** *Did you have much trouble getting tickets for the opera? Please take the trouble to read the contract thoroughly:* difficulty, bother, pains, inconvenience, annoyance, irritation, vexation, pother, fuss, strain, stress, struggle; effort, care, attention, exertion, work, labour. **5** *If you can't pay the bill, you're going to be in trouble:* difficulty, predicament, dilemma, quandary, entanglement, pass, pinch, strait, crisis, *Informal* scrape, mess, pickle, fix, hot water, deep water; challenge, competition, opposition. **6** *Throughout a lifetime of trouble God was her only salvation:* woe, misery, distress, pain, suffering, affliction, agony, tribulation, ordeal, hardship, trial, misfortune, adversity, disaster, burden, difficulty, reverse, setback, grief, sorrow, worry, blow, hard times, ill wind, rainy day. **7** *Political agitators tried to cause trouble:* unrest, instability, disorder, agitation, dissension, commotion, discord, row, disunity, disturbance, ferment, convulsion, embroilment; dissatisfaction, discontentment, discontent, strife. **8** *Back trouble prevents him from diving:* ailment, disability, defect, disorder, difficulty; breakdown, malfunction, snag.

Ant. 1, 3 relieve, ease. **1** calm, soothe, compose, please, delight. **3** assuage, mollify. **4** convenience, facility. **6** pleasure, delight, happiness, joy, ease, comfort; success, good fortune. **7** peace, peacefulness, calm, tranquillity, content, contentment; unity, accord, concord, harmony.

"Man is born unto trouble, as the sparks fly upward." —*Job* 5:7

---

troublesome *adj.* **1** *The youth was a troublesome student. Troublesome financial problems depressed him:* distressing, worrisome, bothersome, demanding, trying, taxing, disturbing, annoying, vexing, irksome, irritating, exasperating, tormenting, harassing, inconvenient, difficult, tough, cursed; disobedient, undisciplined, uncontrolled. **2** *The troublesome task of scraping the floors took days:* laborious, difficult, arduous, Herculean, onerous, oppressive, burdensome, cumbersome, unwieldly, unpleasant, disagreeable, fatiguing, tiresome, tiring, tedious, wearisome, hard, tough, heavy, knotty, thorny.

Ant. 1, 2 easy, simple, undemanding; pleasant, pleasing, delightful. **1** soothing, calming; obedient, disciplined, accommodating, congenial.

> **Exploring the Word**: A mob can cause *trouble. Trouble, turbulence, turbine,* and *turbo-jet* come from Latin *turba,* turmoil of a mob of people, with strong connotations of violence. This gives us our words *trouble* and *turbulence.* From the related Latin *turbo,* whirlwind, we get *turbine* and *turbo-jet,* so-called from their rotary propelling mechanisms. The same Latin base gives us *disturb,* to cause disorder, as *to disturb the peace,* and *perturb,* to confuse thoroughly.

trough *n.* **1** *Lead the horses to the water-trough:* boxlike receptacle, drinking-box; tray. **2** *The heavy rain made a trough in the hillside. The boat was in a trough between two waves:* depression, hollow, channel, watercourse, canal, furrow, trench, gully, gorge, ravine.

trounce *v. The sturdy man trounced his would-be assailant. The netball team trounced its opponents:* defeat decisively, win easily over, overwhelm, overpower, vanquish, beat, whip, drub, lick, trim, humble, carry the day, take care of, get the better of.

truce *n. The enemy rejected a Christmas truce, and the bombing continued:* temporary halt in fighting, cease-fire, suspension of hostilities, armistice; respite, lull, pause, rest, stay, break, interruption, breathing-space, discontinuance, stop, halt.

Ant. war, warfare, hostilities, fighting.

truck *n. The boys stowed away in one of the trucks of a goods train:* railway wagon, luggage barrow, bogie.

◇ *Word origin: Truck,* like *truckle* and *trundle,* comes from Greek *trokhos,* wheel. A *truckle* bed or *trundle* bed is a low bed on small wheels or casters for rolling under another bed.

truculent *adj. His truculent nature gets him into a lot of scrapes:* belligerent, bellicose, aggressive, pugnacious, hostile, defiant, fierce, nasty, ill-tempered, bad-tempered, ill-humoured, ill-natured, snarling; surly, cross, touchy, peevish, snappish, petulant, sour, ungracious, churlish, sulky, insolent, rude.

Ant. peaceful, gentle, kind, diffident, accommodating, friendly, gracious, amiable, affable.

trudge *v. The losing team trudged wearily off the field:* plod, walk wearily, drag, lumber, clump, shamble, march, tramp.

Ant. bound, skip, prance, scamper, trot.

true *adj.* **1** *Is it true that a tomato is a fruit? This is a* *true story:* in accordance with the facts, accurate, correct, right, exact, precise; factual, truthful, trustworthy, literal, strict, faithful. **2** *The table is a true antique. Albert Schweitzer was a true humanitarian:* genuine, authentic, real, valid, bona fide, legitimate, actual; positive, absolute, in the true sense of the word, unquestionable, true-blue, pure, simon-pure. **3** *You've been a true friend:* faithful, loyal, steadfast, trusty, devoted, firm, staunch, constant, dependable, reliable, unwavering, unswerving, steady. **4** *The true heir to the throne is in exile:* rightful, lawful, legitimate, legal, official, proper, just, bona fide, real. **5** *This skirt is not a true size 12:* normal, regular, even, typical, usual, real, full.

Ant. 1–5 false. **1, 3** untrue. **1** inaccurate, incorrect, wrong, fallacious, inexact; non-factual, fictitious, imaginary, figurative. **2** fake, phoney, counterfeit, bogus, spurious, imitation, artificial, synthetic. **3** faithless, disloyal, treacherous, deceitful, untrustworthy, unreliable, inconstant, undependable. **4** illegal, unofficial, unlawful, illegitimate. **5** abnormal, atypical.

truly *adv.* **1** *Mozart was truly a brilliant composer:* unquestionably, beyond question, beyond doubt, indubitably, no doubt, unequivocally, assuredly, verily, certainly, incontestably, without question, indisputably, absolutely, indeed, really, in truth, in actuality, in fact, surely, positively, definitely, to be sure. **2** *You quoted Hamlet's soliloquy truly:* accurately, correctly, exactly, precisely, literally, actually, factually. **3** *I'm truly sorry for the mistake. I love you truly:* sincerely, truthfully, honestly, really, genuinely, faithfully, upon my word, joking apart.

Ant. 1 questionably, dubiously, uncertainly. **2** inaccurately, incorrectly, inexactly, imprecisely. **3** insincerely, untruthfully, unfaithfully.

truss *v.* **1** *Truss the suitcases securely on top of the car. Truss the turkey and put it in the oven:* tie, secure, strap, bind, fasten, make fast, hitch; tie up, bind up, pinion, constrict, confine.

—*n.* **2** *The bridge was built on steel trusses:* braced framework, brace, support, prop, stay, shore, stanchion, beam.

Ant. 1 untie, loosen, unbind, unfasten, unhitch.

trust *n.* **1** *The people's trust in the government has been shaken:* confidence, faith, belief, credence, assuredness, reliance, certitude, sureness, conviction. **2** *The legacy was held in trust until the child came of age:* care, custody. **3** *Public office is a public trust:* responsibility, charge, obligation, duty.

—*v.* **4** *Trust in God. Don't trust anything that this scheming gossip says:* have faith in, put confidence in, believe, rely on, depend upon, count upon, look to, place oneself in the hands of, swear by, pin one's faith upon; credit, accept, take on faith, give credence to, subscribe to. **5** *I trust that the accommodation will be satisfactory:* presume, assume, expect, hope, be confident, anticipate, feel sure, contemplate, reckon upon, count on, take for granted.

Ant. 1, 4 mistrust, distrust, doubt. **1** disbelief, incredulity, suspicion, uncertainty, misgiving, scepticism. **4** disbelieve, discredit.

◇ *Usage note: Trust, faith,* and *confidence* all describe a high regard for another person. *Trust* refers to belief in another's actions, that he will act morally or ethically: *A good mother can trust her children to do right. Can you trust him with the money? Faith* is more of a belief in the inner qualities of a person than in how he will act: *The mother had faith that her son would succeed in the future. Confidence* is less deep than trust or faith and often depends on one's past experience of a person and his judgement rather than his morals or ethics: *The boss has confidence that his assistant can do the job.*

trusting *adj. The confidence trickster defrauded the trusting widow of her life savings:* trustful, believing, unsuspicious; credulous, gullible.

Ant. distrustful, doubting, suspicious, sceptical.

trustworthy *adj. Only trustworthy people can be considered for such a high position:* responsible, dependable, reliable, trusted; faithful, loyal, true, true-blue, steadfast, honourable, high-principled, honest, ethical, above-board, upright, incorruptible, scrupulous.

Ant. untrustworthy, irresponsible, undependable, unreliable, disreputable; unfaithful, disloyal, treacherous, dishonourable, dishonest, crooked, corrupt, unscrupulous.

truth *n.* **1** *The detective was determined to get at the truth. I'm not certain of the truth of his story:* facts, reality; truthfulness, trueness, veracity, verity, reliability, authenticity, actuality, trustworthiness, fidelity, integrity, faithfulness, accuracy, exactness. **2** *The mortality of man is an unquestioned truth:* fact, proven principle, verity, reality, law.

Ant. 1, 2 untruth. **1** untruthfulness, falseness, falsity, mendacity, deceit, deception, dishonesty, inaccuracy. **2** fiction, fabrication, delusion, fallacy, error.

"In order that all men may be taught to speak truth, it is necessary that all likewise should learn to hear it." —*Samuel Johnson*

---

truthful *adj.* **1** *Edith is too truthful to lie about anything:* honest, veracious, sincere, guileless, artless, undeceitful, candid, frank, open, straightforward, above-board. **2** *The witness gave a truthful account of the incident:* factual, in accordance with the facts, true, honest, correct, accurate, reliable, authentic, trustworthy, faithful, scrupulous, precise, exact, meticulous, unvarnished, unadulterated.

Ant. 1, 2 untruthful. **1** lying, deceitful, deceptive, dishonest, insincere. **2** false, untrue, dishonest, inaccurate, fictitious, fabricated, fallacious, incorrect.

try *v.* **1** *Please try to finish the job by Friday:* attempt, strive, endeavour, make an effort, set one's sights on, essay, aim, seek, undertake. **2** *The pilots were eager to try the new plane. Have you tried that new toothpaste?:* test, put to the test, prove, make trial of, tackle, have a fling at, have a go at, take a crack at; sample, use, partake of, avail oneself of. **3** *I wouldn't try water-skiing without a life-jacket:* risk, venture, take a chance on, undertake. **4** *The case was tried at the Old Bailey:* hear and decide, adjudicate, adjudge, sit in judgement, deliberate. **5** *The unruly children tried our patience:* strain, tax to the limit, put to a severe test.
—*n.* **6** *The contestant has one more try at the answer:* attempt, effort, endeavour, opportunity, turn, *Informal* shot, go, bash, crack, fling, whack. **7** *Give the new dishwasher a try and see if you like it:* trial, test.
◇ *Usage note: Try to* is a standard, formal, preferred usage: *Try to get home on time.* "Try and" is acceptable only in informal speech and writing. Thus try to avoid such constructions as "Try and get home on time."

trying *adj. Mother looks as though she's had a trying day:* difficult, tough, hard, arduous, taxing, irksome, troublesome, onerous, burdensome, distressing, irritating, vexing, exasperating, aggravating, harrowing, tiresome, wearisome, tedious, fatiguing.

tsar Also **czar** *n. The tsar of Russia was overthrown in 1917:* emperor, ruler, overlord; (*loosely*) monarch, sovereign, caesar, king; despot, tyrant, dictator.
◇ *Word origin: Tsar* is a Russian word derived from Latin *Caesar,* which is also the base of the German word *Kaiser.*

tube *n. A rubber tube was used to siphon water from the fish-tank. Buy a tube of toothpaste:* pipe, cylinder, conduit, hose; cylindrical container.
◇ *Word origin: Tube* comes from Latin *tubus,* tube, pipe. *Tubus* also designates a kind of trumpet used at Roman sacrifices; the *tuba* was the straight battle-trumpet (so-called to differentiate it from the curved *cornu,* horn, also a war-trumpet of the Romans).

tuck *v.* **1** *Tuck the scarf into your collar:* stick, insert, thrust, stuff, shove, cram, put; gather, gather in, roll up. **2** *Tuck this blanket round the children:* wrap snugly, cover snugly, enwrap, swaddle, swathe, shroud.
—*n.* **3** *The tailor made the waist of the trousers smaller by taking in a tuck:* gather, pleat, pucker, ruffle, crinkle.

tuft *n. The drought left the lawn with only a few tufts of grass. The bird had a beautiful blue tuft on its head:* cluster, bunch, wisp, bundle, batch, sheaf, clump; topknot, crest, plume.

tug *v.* **1** *Tug hard at the door handle:* pull, yank, jerk, draw, wrench, wrestle; haul, drag, tow.
—*n.* **2** *Give the drawer a tug and it will open:* pull, yank, jerk.
Ant. 1, 2 push, shove, poke.

tumble *v.* **1** *Jack and Jill tumbled down the hill:* fall head over heels, fall, roll, topple, go sprawling, stumble. **2** *The acrobats tumbled over the stage:* do forward rolls, somersault, cartwheel, flip, do acrobatics, bounce. **3** *A clothes-dryer works by tumbling the clothes:* toss, whirl, mix, shuffle, stir up, jumble. **4** *The temperature tumbled to 30 degrees last night:* drop, fall, plunge, dive, descend.
Ant. 4 rise, ascend, soar, increase.
◇ *Word origin: Tumble* comes from Old English *tumbian,* to leap, dance, do a cartwheel. The drinking-glass *tumbler* is so-called because the base was originally rounded so that it would not stand upright by itself.

tumult *n. The tumult in the streets awakened us:* uproar, commotion, hullabaloo, clamour, din, bedlam, pandemonium, hubbub; disturbance, turmoil, confusion, bustle, agitation, excitement, ado.
Ant. peace, quiet, stillness, calm, serenity, tranquillity.

tune *n.* **1** *The wood-winds carry the tune in this part of the composition. Irving Berlin wrote this tune:* melody, theme, motif; song, air, strain, ditty, number. **2** *The piano is out of tune. The design of the house is in tune with modern architectural thinking:* pitch; agreement, harmony, accord, concord, concert, conformity, *Informal* step, line.
—*v.* **3** *The violinist tuned the violin for the next piece. How long is it since you've had this engine tuned? You'll get a better picture if you tune the television set:* adjust to the correct pitch, pitch; adjust for proper functioning; adjust for proper reception, adjust the tone, adjust.

turbid *n. The landslide partially filled the lake and left its waters turbid:* unclear, murky, clouded, cloudy, stirred up, full of sediment, roiled, muddy; disturbed, agitated, unsettled.
Ant. clear, crystal clear, limpid, clean; calm, placid, smooth.

turbulent *adj. The sea is too turbulent for sailing. The turbulent meeting ended in a slanging-match:* disturbed, agitated, tumultuous, tempestuous, blustering, violent, raging, fierce, stormy, furious; restless, chaotic, disorderly, uproarious, clamorous, unruly, boisterous, riotous.
Ant. calm, smooth, placid, quiet, orderly.

turgid *adj.* **1** *The wound was red and turgid:* swollen, puffed up, puffy. **2** *The writer's turgid prose is hard to read:* pompous, bombastic, overblown, inflated, pretentious, hyperbolic, grandiloquent; ostentatious, showy, florid, flowery, ornate.
Ant. 1 shrunken, puckered. **2** simple, modest, restrained, reserved; concise, succinct, pithy, plain-spoken.

◇ *Usage note:* Don't confuse *turgid* and *turbid. Turgid* means puffed out, swollen, or bombastic, as language: *The headmaster gave a turgid speech. Turbid* means muddy or cloudy: *a turbid river.*

turmoil *n. Ever since Mother went into hospital the house has been in a turmoil:* state of confusion, confusion, disturbance, chaos, disorder, mess; tumult, commotion, uproar, pandemonium, ferment, agitation, convulsion.

Ant. order, peace, peacefulness, state of calm.

turn *v.* **1** *Turn the wheel to the right. The path turns to the left after that big tree. Turn over or your back will get sunburnt:* revolve, rotate, move in a circle, spin, whirl, wheel, roll, swivel, gyrate, pivot; move round, pass round, shift, swerve, veer, wing, twist, curve, bend, flex; roll over, overturn, invert, reverse. **2** *In the autumn the leaves turn red and gold. He turned fifty on his last birthday. Public school turned the youth into a self-confessed cynic:* change, change to, become; transform, metamorphose, convert, alter, make. **3** *The outcome of the election turns on whether the voters believed the prime minister's speech or not. Everything turns on this last kick of the game:* be contingent on, be decided by, depend, hang, hinge, pivot, rest, reside, lie. **4** *Let's turn our attention to the matter at hand. You can always turn to me for help:* direct, apply, put; look, go, come. **5** *The speaker certainly knew how to turn a phrase:* make skilfully, perform, execute, deliver, accomplish; carry out, do. **6** *Kevin turned his ankle whilst ice-skating:* sprain, wrench, twist. **7** *Turn the prisoners loose. How could the old man turn his own son out of the house?:* send, cause to go, discharge; eject, throw, drive. **8** *Don't leave the milk out in the sun or it will turn:* sour, spoil, curdle, ferment, acidify. **9** *The cabinet-maker turned the legs on a lathe:* make round, cut into a round form, grind into a cylinder.

—*n.* **10** *Give the dial one turn to the left:* rotation, revolution, spin, swing, twirl, whirl, roll, swivel, pivot, gyration, twist; change of direction. **11** *The patient took a turn for the better:* change, shift, fluctuation, deviation, alteration. **12** *The road is full of sharp turns. Take two turns of the rope round the fence-post and tie a knot:* curve, bend, twist, zigzag, winding, arc; loop, coil. **13** *Has each child had a turn at riding the pony? Whose turn is it to keep watch?:* opportunity, chance, go, crack, shot, whack, round, fling, attempt, effort; time, stint, shift, spell, period. **14** *One good turn deserves another:* deed, act, action, service. **15** *Let's take a turn in the garden before going to bed:* short walk, walk, stroll, constitutional; short drive, ride. **16** *Oh! You did give me a turn!:* shock, start, surprise, scare, fright.

Ant. 2 remain, stay, continue to be. **7** keep, retain, hold; capture, catch, secure.

turncoat *n. The general ordered that the turncoat be shot:* traitor, renegade, Judas; deserter, rat.

Ant. patriot, loyalist.

turn-out *n.* **1** *There was a huge turn-out for the dance:* gathering, crowd, throng, assemblage, assembly, audience, representation. **2** *The factory produced a record turn-out this year:* output, production.

tussle *v.* **1** *The children tussled over the last piece of rock:* scuffle, fight, brawl; struggle, battle.

—*n.* **2** *He received a black eye in the tussle:* fight, scuffle, scrap, brawl, fracas, fray, mêlée, set-to, free-for-all; struggle, battle.

◇ *Word origin: Tussle* was originally a variant of *tousle.*

tutor *n.* **1** *A tutor helped me prepare for the Spanish exam:* coach, private teacher, instructor, master, teacher, mentor.

—*v.* **2** *The football coach tutors us in maths six hours a week:* teach privately, coach, instruct, give lessons in, teach, school, drill, prepare.

Ant. 1 pupil, student, disciple. **2** study, learn.

◇ *Word origin: Tutor* is the Latin word for a legal guardian and came to be used in English to mean an educational guardian.

twaddle *n. Everyone is tired of listening to her twaddle:* idle talk, silly talk, drivel, nonsense, rubbish, babble, chatter.

twang *n.* **1** *We heard the twang of a guitar from next door:* sharp vibrating sound, vibration, resonance, reverberation. **2** *She speaks with a strong nasal twang:* nasal sound, nasal resonance.

twilight *n.* **1** *I could hardly see in the twilight. Driving at twilight is dangerous:* evening, dusk, gloaming, half-light, edge of darkness; nightfall, sundown, eventide. **2** *The old man is in the twilight of his career:* decline, last phase, ebb.

Ant. 1 dawn, sunrise, daybreak. **2** advent, beginning, unfolding; peak, height, crowning point, climax.

twin *adj.* **1** *The twin sisters refused to dress alike:* born as one of a pair, forming a pair. **2** *Twin columns flanked the throne:* paired, matched, identical, duplicate, like, alike. **3** *The plan has a twin purpose:* double, dual, twofold.

twine *n.* **1** *Wrap the bundle with strong twine:* string, cord, double-stranded string, twisted thread; binding; rope, cable.

—*v.* **2** *She twined her hair into braids:* intertwine, interlace, weave, entwine, twist, plait, braid; wind, coil.

twinge *n.* **1** *I felt a twinge in my neck:* sudden sharp pain, pain, spasm, stab, pang, stitch; throb, twitch. **2** *Didn't you ever feel a twinge of regret about leaving school?:* pang, stab.

twinkle *v.* **1** *The pilot saw the lights of the city twinkling far below:* glimmer, shimmer, shine, flicker, flash, sparkle, gleam, glisten, glow, scintillate, blaze, flare.

—*n.* **2** *The sky was dark except for the twinkle of a distant star:* glimmer, shimmer, flicker, sparkle, gleam, glow, flare, flash.

twirl *v. The dancers twirled across the stage. The marching band was led by an old soldier twirling a* *baton:* spin, whirl, rotate, revolve, gyrate, pivot, twine.

twist *v.* **1** *Twist the tourniquet tighter. Twist the dial to the left:* wind, twine, intertwine, entwine, interlace, tangle, knot, ravel; coil, curl, roll, wrap; rotate, turn, swivel, pivot, whirl, spin. **2** *The river twists to the right in about a mile:* bend, curve, wind, arc, swing, swerve, veer, curl, snake, zigzag, meander. **3** *Aunt Louise twisted her ankle when she fell. The boy twisted the toy from his brother's hands:* sprain, wrench, turn, wrest, yank, pull. **4** *She twisted my words to suit her own purpose. His face was twisted in pain:* distort, contort, wrench out of shape.
—*n.* **5** *The visitor placed a twist of tobacco in his pipe:* roll, coil, plug, quid, lump, piece. **6** *Give the knob a twist:* turn, rotation, spin, whirl, wrench. **7** *The mountain road is full of twists:* bend, zigzag, winding curve, corkscrew curve, hairpin bend, convolution, involution. **8** *There's an unusual twist to the plot at the end of the book. An indoor picnic—there's a new twist!:* change, development, surprise, turn; notion, idea, approach, slant, treatment, way, system, method.
Ant. 1 untwist, unwind; straighten, uncoil, unroll, unwrap; untangle, disentangle, unknot, unravel.

> **Exploring the Word**: *Twist, twine, twill, tweed,* and *twin* all go back to Old English *twā*, two. *Twist* originally meant to wind two strands together (a *twist* of tobacco is still two strands wound round each other). *Twine* was originally so-called because it was composed of two strands twisted together. *Twill* is so-named because it is a fabric made of two threads twisted together. *Tweed* is simply the Scottish pronunciation of *twill,* which is "tweel," however the final *l* became a *d* because the pronunciation was influenced by the name of the river *Tweed* which flows through the district where Scottish *twill* is made. The same Old English word also gives us *twin, twain* (as in "never the *twain* shall meet" and "mark *twain,*" meaning "mark two fathoms in depth," from which the American writer Samuel Clemens got his pen-name Mark *Twain*), *between, betwixt,* and *twixt* (because these words always or almost always mean between *two* other things).

twitch *v.* **1** *The general's hands twitched in anger. Stop twitching and sit still!:* jerk, quiver, quaver, throb, shake, tremble; wiggle, squirm, writhe.
—*n.* **2** *Is the twitch in my eye noticeable?:* tic, involuntary movement, jerk, spasm, quiver, quaver, throb, shake, tremor; paroxysm.

twitter *v.* **1** *The wrens twittered madly when the cat came near their nest:* chirp, chirrup, cheep, chatter, peep.
—*n.* **2** *The twitter of birds filled the garden:* twittering, chirp, chirping, chirrup, chirruping, cheep, peep. **3** *Everyone was in a twitter over the wedding:* flutter, tizzy, flurry, fluster, whirl, bustle, ferment, stew, fuss, pother, uproar, turbulence.

tycoon *n. Lord Beaverbrook was one of the tycoons of the Press:* powerful businessman, wealthy businessman, magnate, mogul, nabob, potentate, captain of industry, industrialist, *Slang* bigwig, big gun, giant, boss.
◇ *Word origin: Tycoon* comes from the Ancient Chinese word for "emperor," which literally means "great prince." We didn't get the word directly from Ancient Chinese, however, but from the Japanese form *taikun*, a title applied to the shoguns (military leaders of Japan) prior to 1868.

type *n.* **1** *The horticulturist developed a new type of rose:* class, kind, sort, variety, category, order, species, genus, race, family, phylum, group, division, brand. **2** *Stan is one of the strong, silent type:* typical person, typical thing, individual example, specimen, model, sample; prototype, archetype. **3** *The wedding invitations were printed in fancy type:* typeface, printed letters, design, pattern, printing character, typography, fount.

typical *adj.* **1** *A typical day at the office begins at nine o'clock. Jane is a typical teenager:* representative, standard, normal, regular, usual, ordinary; true-to-type, conventional, orthodox; prototypal, model, exemplary. **2** *That sarcastic reply is typical of him:* characteristic, in character, to be expected, in keeping, true to type; distinctive, individual.
Ant. 1 atypical, abnormal, unrepresentative, irregular, unusual, uncommon, unique, singular, unconventional, strange, weird. **2** uncharacteristic, out of keeping, unexpected.

tyranny *n. The Russians revolted against the tyranny of the Tsar:* despotism, cruel authority, unjust rule, cruelty, harshness, severity, persecution, coercion; absolute rule, iron rule, reign of terror, dictatorship.
Ant. humanity, kindness, benevolence, fairness; democracy, freedom.

tyrant *n. The American colonies regarded King George III as a tyrant:* cruel and unjust ruler, despot, cruel master, uncompromising superior, slave-driver, taskmaster, martinet, bully, persecutor; absolute ruler, dictator.
◇ *Word origin: Tyrant* and *tyranny* come from Greek *turannos*, a lord, master, king, especially an absolute master or ruler.

U

ugly *adj.* **1** *One sister is beautiful, the other ugly. What an ugly dress!:* unattractive, unsightly, unseemly, unbecoming, ill-favoured, repulsive, hideous, frightful, grotesque, monstrous; evil-looking. **2** *His ugly disposition gained him few friends. What an ugly thing to do!:* nasty, quarrelsome, cantankerous, unpleasant, mean, hostile, belligerent, difficult; disagreeable, obnoxious, repulsive, offensive, dreadful, unbearable, disgusting, foul, odious, vile, abominable, abhorrent, sickening, horrid, horrible, repellent, repugnant. **3** *Ugly clouds gathered on the horizon:* forbidding, ominous, threatening, menacing, inauspicious, dangerous, troublesome.

Ant. **1** beautiful, pretty, handsome, attractive, fair, lovely, comely. **2** pleasant, agreeable, personable, good-natured, likeable, friendly; good, nice, sweet, attractive. **3** promising, auspicious, fortuitous.

◇ *Word origin: Ugly* comes from Old Norse *uggligr*, dreadful, fearful.

ulterior *adj. She definitely had an ulterior motive in offering to help:* hidden, covert, unrevealed, unexpressed, undisclosed, undivulged; selfish, self-serving, opportunistic.

Ant. obvious, manifest, evident, self-evident, plain; altruistic, public-spirited.

ultimate *adj.* **1** *The ultimate cost of the job was over a hundred pounds. Becoming a director is his ultimate goal:* final, last, resulting, terminal, definitive, conclusive, crowning, end, eventual, long-range. **2** *An Oscar represents the ultimate accolade for a film actor's performance:* greatest, utmost, highest possible, maximum, extreme, crowning, at the peak.

—n. **3** *That hat is the ultimate in ridiculousness:* height, final point, utmost, peak, apex, acme, high point, extreme, last straw.

Ant. **1** initial, first, beginning. **2** least, lowest, minimum.

umpire *n.* **1** *The crowd disagreed with the umpire's decision:* referee, judge; arbiter, arbitrator, mediator, negotiator, moderator, adjudicator, go-between.

—v. **2** *If you will umpire for twenty minutes, I'll take over for the rest of the game:* referee; judge, arbitrate, mediate, adjudicate, moderate.

◇ *Word origin:* An *umpire* is a third party settling disputes and enforcing rules between two equal teams or parties. The word comes from Old French *nonper*, third (from *non*, not + *per*, even, equal).

unabridged *adj. There's an unabridged dictionary on the library table:* not abridged, not shortened, full-length, complete, uncut, uncondensed.

Ant. abridged, shortened, condensed.

unacceptable *adj. Such behaviour is completely unacceptable:* not acceptable, not allowable, unsatisfactory, unsuitable, unseemly, improper, displeasing, unwelcome, insupportable, not up to scratch.

unaccountable *adj.* **1** *Many unaccountable things happened in that haunted house:* unexplained, inexplicable, baffling, strange, weird, peculiar, incomprehensible, unfathomable, mysterious; unusual, intriguing, extraordinary, astonishing, surprising, unheard-of. **2** *The driver was held unaccountable for the accident:* not responsible, not answerable, not accountable, not liable, blameless, innocent, inculpable, free, clear, excused.

Ant. **1** explainable, explicable, comprehensible; usual, ordinary, normal, natural. **2** accountable, responsible, answerable, liable, culpable, guilty, blameable, blameworthy.

unaccustomed *adj.* **1** *The unaccustomed sights of the Casbah were fascinating:* unusual, unfamiliar, uncommon, out of the ordinary, extraordinary, strange, foreign, quaint, unique, singular, curious, peculiar, odd, queer, bizarre, surprising, astonishing, unimaginable, startling, out-of-the-way, unheard-of, amazing, remarkable, fantastic, *Slang* wild; new, novel, original, rare. **2** *The poor man was unaccustomed to such luxury. I'm still unaccustomed to skiing on such steep slopes:* not used to, unused, not accustomed, unhabituated, strange, unacquainted, not given to; inexperienced, unpractised, untried, green, a novice at, unfamiliar with, unversed in, new to.

Ant. **1, 2** accustomed, familiar. **1** ordinary, common, regular, run-of-the-mill. **2** used to, well-acquainted, given to; experienced, practised, well-versed, seasoned.

unaffected *adj.* **1** *Users of paraffin stoves were unaffected by the coal shortage. Passers-by were unaffected by the beggar's plea:* not affected, not influenced, untouched, unbothered, undisturbed; unmoved, unstirred, unimpressed, unresponsive to, indifferent to, insensitive to, unconcerned, unfeeling, impervious to, unsympathetic to. **2** *The girl's unaffected manner charmed everyone:* natural, sincere, genuine, simple, wholesome, plain, open, honest, frank, candid, direct, straightforward, plain-spoken, unreserved, open-hearted, undesigning, guileless, ingenious; naïve, innocent, childlike, unsophisticated, unworldly.

Ant. **1, 2** affected. **1** influenced, touched, changed, disturbed; moved, stirred, responsive, interested, concerned, sympathetic. **2** unnatural, artificial, insincere, pretentious, assumed, *Informal* put-on, phoney; indirect, devious, scheming, designing, Machiavellian; sophisticated, worldly.

unanimous *adj. The members were unanimous in approving the project:* showing complete agreement, in complete accord, with no dissent; united, allied, harmonious, like-minded, accordant, consonant, of one mind, of the same mind.

Ant. not agreed, dissenting, discordant, disagreeing, unharmonious, inharmonious.

unapproachable *adj.* **1** *The wide moat made the castle unapproachable. The judge was a stern, unapproachable man:* inaccessible, unreachable, beyond reach, unattainable; remote, aloof, distant, austere, forbidding, intimidating, awesome. **2** *Shakespeare's genius as a playwright is unapproachable:* unequalled, unrivalled, matchless, unparalleled, peerless, incomparable, beyond compare, inimitable, unique, nonpareil; supreme, pre-eminent, superior, foremost, second to none.

unassuming *adj. Despite his wealth and position, he has an unassuming personality:* modest, unpretentious, not vain, without airs, easy-going, unostentatious, natural, simple, plain, homely, unobtrusive, unassertive, muted.

unavoidable *adj. Some mistakes are unavoidable. Paying taxes is unavoidable:* inevitable, inescapable, unpreventable, uncontrollable, fated, sure, certain; necessary, requisite, compulsory, obligatory, imperative, fixed.

unaware *adj. He was unaware of his secretary's true feelings for him:* unsuspecting, ignorant, unenlightened, unknowing, unconscious, unapprised, unacquainted, incognizant; unwarned, unalerted, heedless, in the dark about, off one's guard, unmindful.

Ant. aware, cognizant, knowing, conscious, acquainted, heedful, mindful, enlightened, suspicious, wary, on one's guard.

unawares *adv.* **1** *He drove into the ditch completely unawares:* unknowingly, unwittingly, inadvertently, unintentionally, unconsciously, accidentally, by accident, mistakenly, by mistake, involuntarily, by chance. **2** *The squall took us unawares:* unexpectedly, abruptly, without warning, suddenly, by surprise, like a bolt from the blue, like a thunderbolt, like a thief in the night, out of nowhere.

Ant. 1 knowingly, wittingly, intentionally, purposely, on purpose, consciously, voluntarily. **2** prepared, forewarned.

unbalanced *adj.* **1** *The scales are unbalanced. The unbalanced stack of books toppled over:* not balanced, unequal, uneven, unpoised, out of equilibrium, unadjusted, lopsided, leaning, unsteady, unstable. **2** *The actress portrayed a woman with an unbalanced mind:* mentally disturbed, unsound, deranged, demented, irrational, illogical, unsettled, unhinged, unstable, crazed, psychotic, psychopathic, warped, *Informal* cracked, daft, screwy, nutty, batty, not all there, loco.

unbearable *adj. The thought of losing the race was unbearable to him:* intolerable, insufferable, unendurable, unacceptable, insupportable, inadmissible, unthinkable.

unbecoming *adj.* **1** *Why did Claire wear such an unbecoming dress?:* unattractive, unappealing, ugly, tasteless, ill-suited, unsightly. **2** *The officer was demoted for unbecoming conduct:* unsuitable, improper, unsuited, inappropriate, unfitted, unbefitting, indecorous, unseemly.

unbending *adj. The captain is an unbending disciplinarian:* rigid, stiff, inflexible, unyielding, severe, firm, strict, tough, obstinate, stubborn, uncompromising, *Informal* hard as nails, stony-faced.

Ant. soft, easy, flexible, compromising, pliant, adaptable; wishy-washy.

unbiased *adj. It was difficult to find a completely unbiased jury:* unprejudiced, impartial, neutral, disinterested, open-minded, just, fair, uninfluenced, liberal, broad-minded, tolerant, unbigoted, undogmatic, fair-minded.

unblemished *adj. The actress has a fair, unblemished complexion. The police chief has an unblemished reputation:* flawless, perfect, unvitiated, immaculate, spotless, pure, uncontaminated, unadulterated, unsoiled, unmarred, unsullied, white as snow, clean as a whistle.

unbounded *adj. On seeing the pony, the boy's joy was unbounded:* boundless, unlimited, unrestrained, unconditional, unrestricted, absolute, unconstrained, uncontrolled, unbridled.

unbroken *adj.* **1** *After the storm only three of the windows remained unbroken:* (*variously*) uncracked, unshattered, unsmashed, unruptured; whole, intact, complete, entire, undivided, undiminished. **2** *The new year brought an unbroken series of successes:* continuous, uninterrupted, successive, consecutive; ceaseless, endless, incessant, continual, unremitting; progressive, sequential.

Ant. 1 broken, cracked, shattered, smashed, ruptured, damaged, incomplete. **2** intermittent, interrupted, occasional, irregular, fitful, uneven, disconnected.

unburden *v. I'll unburden you of those packages. The boy unburdened all of his troubles to his teacher:* relieve, disburden, free, unencumber, disencumber; disclose, confess, reveal, confide, *Slang* get off one's chest, get out of one's system; unbosom.

uncanny *adj.* **1** *Sherlock Holmes possessed uncanny powers of observation:* extraordinary, unimaginable, remarkable, unexampled, exceptional, astonishing, unbelievable, incredible, marvellous, fantastic, inspired, prodigious, unheard-of; intuitive. **2** *An uncanny silence pervaded the old mansion:* curious, mysterious, strange, uncomfortable, unnatural, eerie, weird, unearthly, *Informal* spooky.

Ant. 1 average, normal, common, usual, unexceptional, unremarkable, mediocre, run-of-the-mill. **2** natural, obvious.

◇ *Word origin: Uncanny* is the negative of *canny* (wary, shrewd, skilful), which comes from *can*, to be able, to know how. Thus *uncanny* literally means succeeding although appearing incapable of success.

uncertain *adj.* **1** *They are uncertain of the time at which they'll arrive. Whether the game will be held or not is uncertain:* not certain, not sure, unsure, not confident, doubtful, dubious; not definite, indefinite, speculative, unconfirmed, undecided, up in the air. **2** *An uncertain number of people were waiting. The outcome of the election is still uncertain:* indeterminate, unpredictable, not known exactly, undetermined, indefinite, indistinct, unclear, hazy, obscure, nebulous, doubtful, not fixed, unsettled, in question, debatable, disputable, questionable, conjectural. **3** *Uncertain weather postponed our trip to the beach. Uncertain people make poor leaders:* wavering, variable, vacillating, fluctuating, erratic, fitful, unresolved, irresolute, unsure, hesitant.

Ant. **1–3** certain, definite. **1** sure, assured, confirmed, decided, positive. **2** predictable, known, determined, clear, settled, indisputable, unquestionable. **3** firm, resolute, certain, staunch, unvarying, unwavering, unhesitating.

uncertainty *n.* **1** *The uncertainty of her answer made me most suspicious:* hesitancy, hesitation, indefiniteness, irresolution, unsureness, vagueness, indecision, doubt, ambiguity, vacillation, equivocation, ambivalence, confusion, perplexity, quandary, *Informal* shilly-shally. **2** *The future is full of uncertainties:* something uncertain, chance, gamble, odds, risk, variable.

uncharitable *adj. Scrooge was very uncharitable. The veteran violinist made several uncharitable comments about the young musician:* ungenerous, stingy, tight, niggardly, illiberal, parsimonious, mean, tight-fisted, close-fisted; ungracious, unkind, unfriendly, unfeeling, unsympathetic.

uncivilized *adj.* **1** *Some tribes in New Guinea are still uncivilized:* savage, barbaric, barbarous, untamed. **2** *What uncivilized manners!:* uncouth, brutish, churlish, rude, boorish, uncultured, unpolished, obnoxious, ill-bred, ungenteel, vulgar, uncultivated.

uncomfortable *adj.* **1** *These shoes are uncomfortable:* causing discomfort, causing distress, painful, bothersome, irritating, distressful. **2** *The boy felt uncomfortable with his new classmates:* uneasy, ill at ease, awkward, out of place, discomposed, edgy, nervous, disquieted, discomfited, troubled, on edge, confused, upset.

uncommon *adj.* **1** *A solar eclipse is an uncommon occurrence:* unusual, rare, infrequent, unfamiliar, unique, scarce, extraordinary, exceptional, unconventional, few and far between, novel, peculiar, curious, bizarre, *Informal* once in a lifetime. **2** *This rose has an uncommon loveliness:* exceptional, remarkable, outstanding, incomparable, unusual, unparalleled, notable, extraordinary; superior, superlative, matchless, peerless, unmatched, unexcelled, supreme.

uncommunicative *adj. Gwen shows her anger by being uncommunicative:* unsociable, reticent, taciturn, close-mouthed, withdrawn, retiring, reserved; speechless, inexpressive, mute, mum, silent, tongue-tied, dumb, secretive.

Ant. talkative, voluble, loquacious, garrulous, gregarious, sociable, communicative, open, extroverted, outgoing, expressive.

uncomplimentary *adj. The aging actress's remarks about the ingénue were uncomplimentary:* disapproving, disparaging, unadmiring, unflattering, insulting, critical, negative, derisive.

uncompromising *adj. The candidate must be a man of uncompromising integrity:* firm, strict, rigid, scrupulous; stiff, unrelenting, exacting, inflexible, immovable, unbending, unyielding, obdurate, inexorable.

unconcerned *adj. The public seems unconcerned about the impending fuel shortage. The children in the playground seemed unconcerned about the rain:* indifferent, oblivious, apathetic, insensitive, uninvolved, unaware, nonchalant, uncaring, unsympathetic, unfeeling, unmoved, unresponsive; aloof, distant, passionless, cold; serene, untroubled, unperturbed, unmindful, composed, impervious.

Ant. concerned, aware, mindful, involved, caring, interested, sympathetic, compassionate; anxious, worried, perturbed, troubled.

unconditional *adj. Only an unconditional surrender was acceptable to the Allies:* unlimited, unqualified, unrestricted, absolute, thoroughgoing, complete, entire, utter, conclusive.

Ant. conditional, provisional, restricted, qualified, limited; partial, incomplete, inconclusive.

unconquerable *adj. There is no such thing as an unconquerable fortress. The child has an unconquerable fear of dogs:* invincible, undefeatable, unvanquishable, unable to be overcome, insurmountable, unbeatable, invulnerable, impenetrable; inveterate, ingrained, innate.

unconscious *adj.* **1** *The boxer was unconscious for several hours after being knocked out:* without consciousness, senseless, insensate, without awareness, in a faint, in a coma, comatose, *Informal* out, out cold. **2** *She had an unconscious hostility towards her sister:* unrealized, incognizant, unsuspected, unknown, unmindful, latent, suppressed.

Ant. **1, 2** conscious, aware. **2** cognizant, knowing, active.

◇ *Usage note:* In psychology, the *unconscious* is that division of the psyche which is not in the field of awareness, including, for example, the blind impulses underlying much of our behaviour: *No one, not even a psychiatrist, can be aware of his own unconscious.* On the other hand, the *subconscious* is mental activity just below the threshold of consciousness. Of this we may become aware through psychotherapy, meditation, and other related techniques: *A psychiatrist can help you to understand your subconscious urge to overeat.*

unconventional *adj. Sixty years ago cars were an unconventional means of transport. Wearing jeans and sandals to the wedding was thought unconventional:* uncommon, unusual, extraordinary, exceptional, unaccustomed, atypical, rare, original, unique, irregular, quaint, newfangled, fantastic, strange, peculiar, odd, curious, queer, outlandish, bizarre; nonconformist, nonconforming, unorthodox, different, eccentric, individualistic, idiosyncratic, bohemian, freakish, weird, off the beaten path, off-beat, *Slang* screwy, nutty, crazy, kinky, far-out.

uncouth *adj. The other guests were offended by his uncouth manners:* crude, rude, boorish, crass, coarse, rough, gross, uncivil, callow, indelicate, loutish, brutish, impolite, ill-mannered, unmannerly, unrefined, uncivilized, barbaric; uncultivated.

Ant. refined, polite, genteel, cultivated, well-mannered, delicate, gentlemanly.

◇ *Word origin:* There was once a word *couth*, which meant known, but it died out of general use in the seventeenth century, leaving us with its negative form *uncouth*. This literally means unfamiliar, not well-known, hence outlandish, strange, and in modern times, having outlandish manners, crude, rude.

uncover *v.* **1** *She uncovered the sandwiches as the guests arrived:* remove the cover from, unwrap, undo, unsheathe; undress, disrobe, bare, undrape, strip, unclothe, denude. **2** *It was two young reporters who uncovered the whole plot:* bring to light, disclose, expose, reveal, lay bare, make known, unmask, make visible, dig up, dig out, unearth.

Ant. 1 cover, wrap, sheathe; dress, clothe, drape. **2** hide, conceal, cloak, veil, suppress.

unctuous *adj. His personality was unctuous and insincere:* too smooth, too suave, smug, ingratiating, flattering, sanctimonious, oily, slippery, smarmy, honeyed, fawning, servile, self-righteous, pietistic.

Ant. blunt, brusque, open, frank, candid, straightforward.

undaunted *adj. Although they trailed by two goals to one, the team remained undaunted. We must face the future with undaunted spirits:* not discouraged, unperturbed, undismayed, not put off; resolute, courageous, unshrinking, valiant, valorous, stalwart, intrepid, unflinching, stout-hearted, heroic, brave, fearless, indomitable, *Informal* plucky, gritty.

Ant. daunted, discouraged, perturbed, dismayed, disconcerted, irresolute, vacillating, meek, cowardly, fearful.

undecided *adj.* **1** *Our plans are still undecided:* not decided, undetermined, uncertain, unsure, indefinite, unsettled, unresolved, not final, pending, open, tentative, in abeyance, unformulated, vague, *Informal* up in the air. **2** *I'm still undecided about whom to vote for:* unsure, irresolute, indecisive, of two minds, open-minded, fluctuating, wavering, vacillating, dubious, *Informal* going round in circles, blowing hot and cold, humming and hawing, dithering.

Ant. 1, 2 sure, resolved. **1** decided, determined, certain, definite, settled, final, firm. **2** resolute, decisive, certain, steadfast, unwavering.

undemonstrative *adj. The father loved his children but was very undemonstrative:* reserved, inexpressive, not affectionate, not displaying emotions, unemotional, unresponsive, cold, impassive; stoical, self-controlled; repressed.

Ant. demonstrative, affectionate, emotional, responsive, unreserved, expressive, warm, outgoing.

undeniable *adj. That he's telling the truth is undeniable. Rembrandt's "Night Watch" is an undeniable masterpiece:* unquestionable, indisputable, incontestable, irrefutable, indubitable, beyond a doubt, incontrovertible, sure, certain, established, demonstrable, proven, decisive, conclusive, obvious, manifest, patent.

Ant. questionable, debatable, dubious, disputable, refutable, uncertain, indecisive, inconclusive, up in the air.

undependable *adj. When it comes to being on time, Sally is totally undependable:* not to be depended on, unreliable, untrustworthy, irresponsible, unpredictable, erratic, inconstant; variable, wavering, changeable, unstable, capricious.

Ant. dependable, reliable, responsible, trustworthy, predictable, exact, unchanging.

undercurrent *n.* **1** *Swimming in the cove was dangerous because of the undercurrent:* undertow, rip-tide, cross-current. **2** *You could almost feel the undercurrent of hatred in the room:* underlying attitude, hidden feeling, undertone, mood, atmosphere, aura, quality, intimation, suggestion, hint, sense, tinge, vibrations, *Informal* vibes.

underestimate *v. Never underestimate the power of a woman:* rate too low, undervalue, underrate, misjudge, miscalculate, undersell, sell short; disregard, dismiss, minimize, discredit, detract from, belittle, depreciate, disparage, deprecate, *Slang* put down.

Ant. overestimate, over-value, overrate, overstate, exaggerate.

undergo *v. She has to undergo minor surgery. The early settlers underwent many hardships:* go through, submit to, experience; withstand, stand, encounter, endure, sustain, weather, suffer, brave.

Ant. evade, shun, avoid, escape, forgo, sidestep, circumvent, steer clear of.

underground *adj.* **1** *The power cables for the new houses are underground:* buried, below the surface, subterranean. **2** *The spy never told his family about his underground activities:* secret, covert, undercover, clandestine, surreptitious, sub-rosa.

"The work an unknown good man has done is like a vein of water flowing hidden underground, secretly making the ground green."
—*Thomas Carlyle*

---

underhand Also **underhanded** *adj. He got the contract in an underhand manner:* unethical, unscrupulous, unprincipled, devious, tricky, sneaking, sneaky, surreptitious, stealthy, covert, evasive, furtive, conniving, cunning, crafty; illegal, dishonest, crooked, fraudulent, corrupt.

Ant. open, above-board, ethical, scrupulous, principled; legal, honest.

underling *n. The volunteer workers resented being treated like underlings:* menial, flunkey, hireling, servant, subordinate, minion, inferior, minor employee, domestic employee, hired hand; subject, vassal, serf, thrall, attendant.

Ant. executive, supervisor, boss, employer, chief, *Informal* governor.

undermine *v.* **1** *The escaped convicts had undermined the prison walls. The shifting sands undermined the foundation of the breakwater:* excavate under, tunnel under, burrow under; eat away at, erode, wear away the base of, riddle. **2** *She jealously tried to undermine our friendship. The crooked politician tried to undermine attempts at reform:* subvert, weaken, injure, cripple, ruin, destroy, *Informal* torpedo; render powerless, thwart, foil, frustrate, neutralize, hamstring, cut the ground from under.

Ant. 2 reinforce, strengthen, buttress, encourage, support, forward, help, aid, abet.

underscore *v. Underscore the titles of the books you want. The speaker underscored his words by banging his fist on the table:* underline, draw a line under; stress, emphasize, accentuate, press home, accent, point up, mark, bring out forcibly, intensify, draw attention to, heighten.

Ant. de-emphasize, moderate, skip over.

understand *v.* **1** *I didn't understand your message. She didn't understand what was happening to her:* grasp the meaning of, comprehend, absorb, make out, fathom, *Informal* get, *Slang* dig; know, recognize, appreciate, see, be aware, perceive, discern, apprehend, realize, grasp. **2** *He understood my letter to be a subtle warning:* interpret, see, read, take, take to mean. **3** *We understand that you'll be returning next year:* gather, hear, learn, presume, take for granted, take it, conclude, assume. **4** *I understand your not wanting to discuss the matter:* sympathize with, appreciate, can see, see the reasons for, accept.

◇ *Word origin:* Five hundred years ago one could have talked about "understanding (standing under) a tree in a shower." As one of Shakespeare's characters put it, "Why, stand under and understand is all one." Today, however, only the figurative meaning is used, and to *understand* means to have a comprehension or awareness of something or its meaning (as if one knew something from the bottom up, from having *stood under* it).

understanding *n.* **1** *Few people have any understanding of international law:* knowledge, grasp, comprehension, appreciation, cognizance, perception, awareness, apprehension. **2** *Because she has great understanding, people confide in her:* sympathy, compassion, appreciation, empathy, sensitivity, insight, perception, intuition. **3** *Management has finally reached an understanding with the employees:* agreement, meeting of minds, pact, concordance, compromise.

—*adj.* **4** *The youth was fortunate in having understanding parents:* sympathetic, compassionate, appreciative, responsive, sensitive, tolerant, perceptive, discerning, knowing.

Ant. 1 misunderstanding, incomprehension, ignorance. **2** insensitivity, lack of insight, obtuseness, aloofness. **4** unsympathetic, uncompassionate, unresponsive, unfeeling, insensitive; intolerant, strict, stiff, rigid.

undertake *v. Who will undertake the job of decorating the hall?:* set about, take on, assume, enter upon, embark on, tackle, agree to do, promise to do, obligate oneself to, commit oneself to, get involved in, attempt, strive, endeavour, essay; commence, begin, start.

Ant. abandon, drop, desist, decline, forswear, eschew, avoid; discontinue, stop.

undertaking *n. Building one's own house is a tremendous undertaking:* endeavour, enterprise, project, task, job, commitment, venture, pursuit, concern.

undertone *n.* **1** *They spoke in undertones so as not to wake the baby:* low tone, subdued voice, whisper, murmur, mumble. **2** *There was an undertone of danger in the air:* undercurrent, feeling, sense, quality, mood, colouring, implication, intimation, atmosphere, aura, suggestion, hint, trace, tinge, scent, flavour.

underworld *n.* **1** *Most gambling is controlled by the underworld:* criminal element, criminals, organized crime, gangsters, (*loosely*) the Mafia, **2** *Are sinners doomed to spend eternity in the underworld?:* Hell, Hades, limbo, abode of the damned, bottomless pit, infernal regions, lake of fire and brimstone, place of departed spirits, shades below; purgatory.

◇ *Word origin:* In 17th-century usage the phrase *the underworld* was sometimes used for the *world under* Heaven, the abode of "all creatures here below." In Greek and Roman mythology, the *underworld* was the abode of the dead, Hades (often represented as being underneath the surface or in the interior of the earth). In later use, the term meant the regions of Hell (Heaven has always been considered "up" and Hell "down"). From the connotation of the *underworld* as being the abode of sinners plus the concept of sinners and criminals being "beneath" honest society, we get our modern meaning of *underworld* as the part of society engaged in crime and vice, especially organized criminals.

undesirable *adj. The dock area was full of tramps and other undesirable characters. Declaring oneself to be bankrupt would be an undesirable step:* unsavoury, offensive, unworthy, unattractive, objectionable, distasteful, disagreeable, unwelcome, uninviting, unseemly, unsatisfactory; unacceptable, unsuitable, inadmissible, unwished-for, unwanted, unbidden, unpopular, disliked; inappropriate, unbefitting, unfit, improper, unbecoming.

undignified *adj. Arriving barefoot may have been undignified, but it was fun:* lacking dignity, indecorous, unbecoming, unseemly, inelegant, boorish, unladylike, ungentlemanly, unrefined, improper, unbefitting, tasteless, in bad taste; low, discreditable, unworthy, degrading, shameful, beneath one, beneath one's dignity, *Latin* infra dignitatem, *Informal* infra dig.

undisciplined *adj. Undisciplined children annoy everyone. The violinist had natural talent, but his playing was completely undisciplined:* unrestrained, wayward, wilful, obstreperous, wild, uncontrolled; undependable, unreliable, fitful, erratic, capricious, unsteady, inconstant, unpredictable; untrained, untaught, unschooled, untutored, unpractised, unfinished.

undisguised *adj. Her undisguised enthusiasm somehow won all of us over to the idea:* open, unconcealed, unhidden, obvious, evident, unmistakable, manifest, evident, distinct, pronounced, clear; unreserved, wholehearted, utter, out and out, complete, thoroughgoing, plain as the nose on one's face, plain as day.

undismayed *adj. The Wright brothers were undismayed by their first failures to fly and tried again. We were undismayed by his threats:* undiscouraged, not disheartened, still confident, undaunted, not disconcerted, unabashed; unalarmed, not apprehensive, unfrightened, unscared, unafraid, unintimidated, not cowed, not put off.

undisputed *adj. The will was undisputed by the deceased's relatives. Milton's genius is undisputed:* uncontested, not disputed, unquestioned, accepted; indisputable, incontestable, undeniable, freely admitted, granted, undoubted, beyond doubt, past dispute, irrefutable, without question, incontrovertible, a matter of fact, acknowledged, unquestionable, indubitable, conclusive, certain.

undistinguished *adj. The play was undistinguished, but the acting was good:* ordinary, commonplace, mediocre, unexceptional, unremarkable, usual, plain, prosaic, nothing to write home about, unexciting, run-of-the-mill, everyday.

undisturbed *adj.* **1** *She is easy-going and remains undisturbed when the children squabble:* unruffled, unperturbed, unagitated, unexcited, untroubled, unbothered; composed, placid, serene, peaceful, tranquil, equable, self-possessed, calm, cool, collected, steady. **2** *Give me an undisturbed hour and I'll finish the work. The accountant gave orders that the papers on his desk be left undisturbed:* uninterrupted, without interruption, quiet, of solitude; untouched, unmoved, not meddled with, left in order.

Ant. 1, 2 disturbed. **1** upset, perturbed, agitated, troubled, excited, nervous, ruffled. **2** interrupted, confused, busy; moved, meddled with, disordered.

undivided *adj. You may count on our undivided support in the coming election:* not divided, solid, whole, entire, complete, unstinting, wholehearted; unanimous, united, of one mind.

undo *v.* **1** *It's almost impossible to undo the harm you've done:* offset, reverse, cancel, nullify, erase, annul, wipe out, neutralize, void, repair, counterbalance, counteract; compensate for, make up for, rectify. **2** *Can you undo this knot?:* open, free, unfasten, loose, loosen; (*variously*) disentangle, unknot, unravel, unwrap, unfold, untie, unbind, unlace, disengage, unbutton, unchain, unlock, unhook. **3** *This undoes all of my carefully-laid plans:* ruin, destroy, subvert, undermine, end, eliminate, demolish, wipe out, defeat, overturn, invalidate, quash.

Ant. 1 do, accomplish, effect, realize, produce, commit, manage. **2** fasten, close, tie, knot, tangle, button, lock, hook, close. **3** enhance, help, aid, abet, further.

"Many a man's tongue shakes out his master's undoing." — *William Shakespeare*

---

undoing *n.* **1** *Poor management resulted in the undoing of all that we had accomplished:* reversal, cancellation, wiping out, erasure, negation, annulment, nullification, neutralization, invalidation, thwarting, counteraction, upset. **2** *A surprise attack brought about the undoing of the air force:* ruin, ruination, collapse, downfall, destruction, doom, defeat, breakdown, overthrow. **3** *Her other marks were good, but maths was her undoing:* cause of ruin, nemesis, downfall, weakness, jinx, Achilles' heel.

Ant. 1 realization, accomplishment, establishment, furtherance. 2 victory, success, triumph. 3 strength, strong point, speciality, forte.

undress *v.* 1 *The patient undressed in the examination room:* take off one's clothes, disrobe, unclothe, strip, uncover, undrape.
—*n.* 2 *The hostess was in a state of undress when the first guests arrived:* nakedness, nudity; disarray, carelessness of attire, dishabille.
Ant. 1 dress, clothe, robe, drape, cover.

undue *adj. The parents felt undue concern about the child's illness. The widow remarried with undue haste:* excessive, too great, inordinate, uncalled-for, unwarranted, unnecessary, too much, unjustified, needless, superfluous; improper, unsuitable, inappropriate, not fitting, ill-advised, unseemly, unmeet, indiscreet, unworthy, unbecoming, objectionable, impolite, in bad taste.
Ant. due, proper, necessary, needed, justified; suitable, appropriate, fitting, seemly, meet, well taken.

undying *adj. He vowed his undying love:* eternal, never-ending, unending, unceasing, perpetual, endless, everlasting, lasting, enduring, imperishable, perennial, perpetual, incessant, permanent, constant, continual, unremitting, unrelenting, indestructible, unfaltering, never-failing, untiring, undiminished, uninterrupted, steady; deathless, immortal.
Ant. temporary, unlasting, impermanent, passing, ephemeral, transitory, transient, fleeting, temporal, brief, momentary; mortal, dying.

unearth *v.* 1 *The treasure-seekers unearthed a buried chest:* dig up, dig out, excavate; exhume, disentomb, disinter. 2 *The police have unearthed new information on the case:* discover, uncover, find, dig up, ferret out, bring to light, root out, come up with; divulge, disclose, reveal, show, display, exhibit.
Ant. 1, 2 bury. 2 cover up, conceal, hide.

unearthly *adj.* 1 *There were unearthly lights glowing in the haunted house:* not of this earth, not of this world, supernatural, extramundane, ethereal, spectral, ghostly, phantom; incorporeal, disembodied, preternatural, weird, eerie, uncanny. 2 *What an unearthly time to call!:* strange, abnormal, unusual, absurd, extraordinary, extreme; terrible, horrendous, disagreeable, unspeakable, awful, unpleasant, ungodly.
Ant. 1 earthly, natural, mundane. 2 normal, usual, common, ordinary, typical; pleasant, agreeable.

uneasy *adj.* 1 *The driver was uneasy about setting out on the icy roads:* worried, disturbed, upset, apprehensive, troubled, perturbed. 2 *She felt uneasy with her new in-laws:* ill at ease, awkward, uncomfortable, strained, nervous, nervy, edgy, on edge, unsure, tense, constrained, disquieted, *Slang* uptight. 3 *I have an uneasy sensation in the pit of my stomach:* upsetting, queasy, bothersome, unpleasant, disturbing, uncomfortable, worrying, irksome, disquieting.

unemotional *adj. Unemotional people seldom laugh or cry. She gave him a quick unemotional kiss on the cheek:* unfeeling, passionless, impassive, indifferent, unconcerned, unresponsive, undemonstrative, cold, cool, remote, distant, reserved.

unending *adj. The rainfall in the tropics seems unending:* incessant, unceasing, never-ending, perpetual, constant, endless, eternal, permanent, perennial, enduring, lasting, everlasting, unremitting, steady, undiminished, unwavering, continual, continuous, uninterrupted.
Ant. brief, short, fleeting, momentary, transitory, transient, temporary, passing; sporadic, intermittent, unsteady, interrupted.

unenlightened *adj. The primitive tribe was totally unenlightened about the outside world:* uninformed, unknowledgeable, ignorant, unfamiliar with, unlearned, uninitiated, uninstructed, uneducated, in the dark.
Ant. enlightened, well-informed, knowledgeable, knowing, familiar, learned.

unequal *adj.* 1 *The two men do the same job but earn unequal salaries. Since the two teams are unequal, the game isn't exciting:* not equal, uneven, different, unmatched, unlike, dissimilar, not uniform, disparate. 2 *The unequal treatment of minority groups is against the law:* unfair, unjust, prejudiced, biased, bigoted.
Ant. 1, 2 equal. 1 even, matched, uniform, similar, like, alike. 2 fair, just, right, unprejudiced, unbiased, unbigoted.

unequalled *adj. She grew roses of unequalled beauty:* unsurpassed, unmatched, unparalleled, matchless, incomparable, beyond compare, unrivalled, unapproached, beyond comparison, second to none, unexcelled, supreme, paramount, peerless, consummate, *Latin* ne plus ultra.

unequivocal *adj. The evidence is unequivocal. His refusal is unequivocal:* decisive, unambiguous, clear, clear-cut, absolute, definite, final, certain, incontestable, incontrovertible, emphatic.
Ant. equivocal, ambiguous, indecisive, vague, doubtful, indefinite.

unerring *adj. The antique dealer has an unerring ability to spot a fake:* infallible, unfailing, faultless, certain, sure, precise, reliable, faithful, unchanging, constant.

unethical *adj. The lawyer was disbarred for unethical practices:* unprincipled, dishonourable, disreputable, shady, shoddy, underhand, devious, *Informal* dirty; unfair, wrong, unconscionable, dishonest, questionable, unworthy, ungentlemanly.

Ant. ethical, principled, honourable, reputable, honest, clean, fair, above-board, conscionable.

uneven *adj.* **1** *The table wobbles because the floor is uneven. The car jolted over the uneven road:* not even, not level, not flat, not plumb, slanted, angled, awry, sloping, tilted, bent, crooked, curved; unsmooth, bumpy, lumpy, craggy, jagged, rough, coarse. **2** *I wouldn't bet on such an uneven fight. The two fighters are uneven in style:* unequal, one-sided, unbalanced, lopsided, ill-matched, unfair, unjust; disparate, dissimilar, different, unlike.

Ant. 1, 2 even. **1** level, flat, straight, plane, smooth, uniform. **2** equal, well-matched, well-balanced, fair, just; similar, alike, like.

uneventful *adj. Our trip was quite uneventful:* not eventful, quiet, unexceptional, routine, ordinary, commonplace, average, usual, standard, conventional, insignificant; dull, tedious, boring, humdrum, monotonous, uninteresting.

unexcelled *adj. The team has an unexcelled record of ten wins and no losses. The beauty of the Taj Mahal is unexcelled:* unsurpassed, unbeaten, supreme, peerless, transcendent, superior, consummate, flawless, faultless; unequalled, unrivalled, matchless, unmatched, incomparable, beyond compare, unparalleled, unapproached, second to none.

unexpected *adj. Well, this is an unexpected development!:* unanticipated, unlooked-for, unforeseen, startling, astonishing, surprising, out of the blue; undesigned, unplanned, sudden, accidental, unintended.

unfailing *adj. The Bible is an unfailing source of inspiration. James has been an unfailing friend for over twenty years:* inexhaustible, endless, continual, continuous, constant, dependable, reliable, never-failing, faithful, unchanging, true, loyal, unwavering, steady, infallible, enduring.

Ant. undependable, unreliable, unfaithful, treacherous, disloyal, untrue, inconstant, wavering, unsteady, faulty, fallible.

unfair *adj. It's unfair to accuse anyone without evidence. The referee was unfair in favouring one of the teams:* not fair, unjust, not right, inequitable, unreasonable, *Slang* not cricket; partial, biased, unequal, dishonourable, one-sided, unconscionable, unscrupulous, unprincipled, unethical, underhand, dishonest, corrupt, dirty, foul, crooked.

unfaithful *adj.* **1** *An unfaithful employee sold the idea to a rival firm. King Henry VIII beheaded two of his wives for being unfaithful:* disloyal, treacherous, perfidious, untrustworthy, faithless, false, false-hearted, deceitful; adulterous, inconstant, untrue, unchaste. **2** *I'm afraid that portrait is a very unfaithful representation of his looks:* not accurate, inaccurate, erroneous, untrue, false, inexact, imperfect, faulty, distorted.

Ant. 1, 2 faithful, true. **1** loyal, trustworthy, steadfast, true-blue; constant, chaste. **2** accurate, correct, exact, perfect.

unfamiliar *adj.* **1** *The classical musician was unfamiliar with popular music:* unacquainted, not acquainted, unconversant, unaccustomed to, a stranger to, unexposed to, unversed in, unenlightened about, ignorant of, uninformed about, inexperienced in, unpractised in, unskilled in, uninitiated. **2** *This soup has an unfamiliar taste. The artist's name is unfamiliar to most people:* unknown, unusual, strange, curious, unique, different, new, novel, out-of-the-way, exotic, foreign; not well-known, little known.

Ant. 1, 2 familiar. **1** acquainted, conversant, accustomed, well-versed, versed, knowledgeable, experienced, practical. **2** common, commonplace, normal, everyday, average, run-of-the-mill; well-known, known, recognized.

unfavourable *adj. Icy roads made travelling conditions unfavourable. I fear he's in an unfavourable position with his employers:* not favourable, adverse, poor, unsuited, ill-suited, unpropitious, inauspicious, regrettable, unhappy, infelicitous, bad, disadvantageous, untimely, inconvenient, inopportune, unpromising, ill-favoured, unfortunate.

unfinished *adj.* **1** *It's five o'clock and the work is still unfinished:* not finished, uncompleted, incomplete, undone, unexecuted, unfulfilled; imperfect, immature, deficient, wanting. **2** *These unfinished sketches give a general idea of what the house will look like. Buy unfinished furniture and paint it yourself:* rough, sketchy, crude, deficient, wanting, unpolished, unrefined; (*variously*) unpainted, unvarnished, unstained, unlacquered, whitewood.

unfit *adj.* **1** *This water is unfit for drinking:* not fit, unsuited, unsuitable, not suited, inadequate, not designed, ill-contrived, ineffective, inefficient, not equal to, useless. **2** *The young boy is unfit to run that business:* unqualified, inadequate, incompetent, unprepared, unequipped, ill-equipped, incapable, unready, unequal, unsuited, not equal to, not up to, not cut out for, ineligible. **3** *The operation left her unfit for months:* unsound, unhealthy, debilitated, sick, sickly, frail, weak, delicate, disabled.

Ant. 1–3 fit. **1** suitable, adequate, useful, adaptable. **2** suited, qualified, competent, capable, able, equipped, prepared, ready, eligible. **3** healthy, sound, hale, in good health, strong, sturdy.

unflagging *adj. The home crowd cheered their team with unflagging enthusiasm. Her unflagging determination to be a concert cellist is admirable:* unfaltering, untiring, tireless, indefatigable, undrooping, unremitting, unswerving, steady, steadfast, firm, resolute, undeviating, fixed, unwavering, unshaken, unyielding, staunch, indomitable, relentless, uncompromising, persevering, constant, determined, undaunted, enduring, tenacious, persistent.

Ant. faltering, wavering, flagging, drooping, irresolute, relenting, compromising, half-hearted.

unflinching *adj. The captain's unflinching courage gave the passengers hope:* steady, unshaken, unshrinking, steadfast, unabashed, plucky, unfaltering, strong, gritty, game, fearless, firm, indomitable, unhesitating, unwavering, unswerving, undaunted, unyielding, resolute.

Ant. shaken, hesitant, faltering, weak, wavering, irresolute.

unfold *v.* **1** *Unfold the map and pin it onto the notice board:* spread out, open up, open out, stretch out, unwrap, unroll, unfurl. **2** *The leader began to unfold his plan to his followers:* reveal, make known, disclose, divulge, unveil, uncover, show, bare, lay open, set forth, present, tell, explain, expound, explicate, describe, recount, elucidate.

Ant. 1 fold, close, roll up, furl. **2** conceal, hide, cloak, veil; keep secret, keep mum about.

unforeseen *adj. The unforeseen snowstorm closed the railway for days:* unexpected, unpredicted, surprise, unanticipated, unlooked-for, sudden, abrupt, out of the blue; unplanned, unintended, accidental, surprising.

Ant. foreseen, expected, anticipated, looked-for, predicted; planned, intended.

unfortunate *adj. His unfortunate career seemed doomed from the start. Her unfortunate remark caused Father to dislike her:* unlucky, luckless, ill-starred, hapless, unhappy, ill-fated, infelicitous, cursed, unsuccessful, unblest, unprosperous; regrettable, wretched, sorry, disastrous, woeful, ill-advised, unpropitious, inopportune, untimely, ill-timed, inauspicious.

Ant. fortunate, lucky, happy, felicitous, successful, propitious, opportune, timely, auspicious.

unfounded *adj. Rumours that an escaped convict was on the plane proved to be unfounded:* baseless, groundless, without foundation, without substance, idle; false, untrue, erroneous, fabricated, spurious.

ungainly *adj. Claire is too ungainly to be a ballerina:* ungraceful, clumsy, awkward, uncoordinated, stiff, lumbering.

Ant. graceful, lithe, willowy, limber, supple, sylphlike.

◇ *Word origin: Ungainly*, awkward, is the negative of the dialectal word *gainly*, graceful, based on an old word *gain* that meant fit, favourable.

ungodly *adj.* **1** *His ungodly life was a disgrace to his family:* not religious, godless; impious, blasphemous; wicked, sinful, immoral, heinous, iniquitous, depraved, degenerate, dissolute, dishonourable, corrupt, villainous, rotten, base, vile. **2** *Informal They woke us at an ungodly hour!:* dreadful, awful, horrendous, outrageous, terrible, ghastly, unreasonable.

Ant. 1 godly, religious, pious, moral, good, virtuous, wholesome, honourable. **2** agreeable, pleasant, acceptable, reasonable.

unguarded *adj.* **1** *A politician must be careful not to make unguarded remarks:* indiscreet, undiplomatic, uncircumspect, incautious, unwary; unrestrained, over-candid, too frank. **2** *The unguarded camp was vulnerable to attack:* unprotected, unpatrolled, unwatched, defenceless, undefended.

Ant. 1, 2 guarded. **1** discreet, circumspect, cautious, wary, careful. **2** protected, patrolled, watched, defended.

unhappy *adj.* **1** *Why are you so unhappy?:* not happy, sad, sorrowful, despondent, depressed, dejected, downcast, heavy-hearted, doleful, gloomy, forlorn, melancholy, dispirited, joyless, crestfallen, woebegone, sombre, blue, long-faced, down in the mouth, mopish. **2** *Investing in that business was an unhappy venture. Telling the hostess that the pie was "almost perfect" was an unhappy choice of words:* unfortunate, hapless, unsuccessful, unwise, imprudent, foolish, injudicious, ill-advised, regrettable, sorry, infelicitous, adverse, poor, bad, unlucky, luckless, inappropriate, inapt, unsuitable, awkward, unseemly, unbecoming, unbefitting.

Ant. 1, 2 happy. **1** gay, cheerful, joyful, joyous, light-hearted, sunny, smiling, exuberant, effervescent, enthusiastic. **2** fortunate, successful, wise, prudent, shrewd, good, fine, wonderful, lucky, blessed, favourable; appropriate, apt, suitable, seemly, becoming, correct, befitting.

"Men who are unhappy, like men who sleep badly, are always proud of the fact."

—Bertrand Russell

---

unhealthy *adj.* **1** *He's been unhealthy since childhood:* sickly, sick, infirm, ailing, not well, unwell, in poor health, indisposed, poorly, feeble, weak, unsound; invalid, diseased. **2** *Pollution of any kind is very unhealthy:* harmful to health, noxious, hurtful, unwholesome, insalubrious. **3** *There's an unhealthy atmosphere of greed and corruption throughout the country:* demoralizing, harmful, morally bad, undesirable, destructive, corrupting, contaminating, degrading, depraved, morbid, negative, bad; hazardous, dangerous, perilous.

Ant. 1–3 healthy. **1** well, sound, strong, robust. **2** healthful, salubrious, salutary, wholesome, beneficial. **3** moral, positive, constructive, desirable, good.

unheralded *adj. The novel is an unheralded masterpiece:* unexpected, unanticipated, unsung, unacclaimed, unproclaimed, unrecognized, unpublicized.

unhesitating *adj.* **1** *The sergeant expects unhesitating obedience to his orders:* immediate, quick, instantaneous, prompt, without hesitation, without delay, ready, direct. **2** *Their unhesitating support was heart-warming:* unreserved, whole-hearted, unflinching, eager, without reservation.

unholy *adj.* **1** *The unholy alliance between pornography dealers and the police deserves to be investigated:* wicked, depraved, ungodly, sinful, immoral, heinous, iniquitous, corrupt, evil, villainous, dishonest, dishonourable; rotten, base, vile. **2** *The room, which had not been cleaned for a week, was in an unholy mess:* dreadful, shocking, awful, ungodly, horrendous, outrageous, unreasonable.

Ant. 1 moral, good, virtuous, honest, honourable, wholesome; godly, religious, pious. **2** agreeable, pleasant, acceptable, reasonable.

unidentified *adj. The perpetrator of the crime got away and is still unidentified. The guests agreed that the cake had a strange unidentified flavour:* unknown, nameless, anonymous, vague, unrecognized; unnamed, unspecified, undesignated, unlabelled.

Ant. known, named, recognized; specified, designated, labelled.

unification *n. We cannot speak of a united England until the unification of the provinces under one king in Anglo-Saxon times:* uniting, union, consolidation, consolidating, unity, alliance, combining, combination, confederation, coalition, coalescence, incorporation, amalgamation, fusion.

Ant. separation, division, splitting, disunion, disunity.

uniform *n.* **1** *My daughter has a new school uniform:* dress, apparel, attire, array; (*variously*) vestment, habit, livery, regalia, regimentals.

—*adj.* **2** *The windows in the house are all uniform. The residents were uniform in their attitude toward strangers:* alike, equal, identical, similar, consistent, consonant, of a piece, harmonious, agreeing, of one mind, conforming, at one, in accord, in step, in line. **3** *The acoustics are uniform throughout the auditorium:* the same, even, equal, unvarying, unvaried, undeviating, unchanging, unaltered, constant, regular, consistent.

Ant. 2, 3 different. **2** unalike, dissimilar, nonstandard, multiform, mixed; disagreeing, discordant, individual. **3** uneven, unequal, mixed, variable, inconsistent, irregular, erratic, deviating, changed, altered.

unify *v. A common allegiance to the Crown unifies the British Commonwealth:* unite, combine, form into one, join, consolidate, bring together, confederate, federate, incorporate, ally, coalesce, amalgamate, fuse, merge; link up, couple, blend, lump together.

Ant. disunite, separate, divide, part, split, cleave, sever, disband.

unimaginative *adj. Most of the costumes at the party were unimaginative:* uninspired, unoriginal; routine, uncreative, ordinary, derivative, prosaic, trite, commonplace, clichéd, run-of-the-mill, stock, pedestrian, boring, stale, hackneyed, usual, predictable, unromantic, dull, unexciting, uninteresting, vapid, humdrum, dreary.

Ant. imaginative, original, creative, inspired, extraordinary, unusual, different, fanciful, exciting, interesting, fresh, novel, new.

unimpeachable *adj. His unimpeachable record makes him a perfect choice for Lord Chief Justice. The reporter obtained his information from an unimpeachable source:* totally honest, beyond criticism, impeccable, irreproachable, above reproach, unassailable, beyond question, blameless, faultless, perfect, unmarred, unblemished, spotless, stainless, untainted, clean, undefiled, inviolate, pure, immaculate; reliable, trustworthy, unquestionable, solid, unchallengeable, infallible.

Ant. questionable, dubious, debatable, controversial, suspect, faulty, imperfect, tainted, untrustworthy, unreliable.

◇ *Word origin: Impeach* comes from Latin *in-* (in) + *pedica* (fetter, from Latin *pes,* foot). The verb derived from these word elements is *impedicare,* to catch, ensnare, entangle. *Unimpeachable* hence literally means "uncatchable" because one's honesty or accuracy is unquestionable or blameless.

unimportant *adj. Whether you wear the red or the blue dress is really unimportant! His brother-in-law has an unimportant job in the firm:* not important, inconsequential, of no consequence, insignificant, of no moment, immaterial, irrelevant, nugatory, non-essential, not vital; inconsiderable, negligible, minor, lesser, subordinate, inferior, trivial, trifling, paltry, meagre, slight, piddling, low-ranking, second-rate, mediocre.

Ant. important, consequential, significant.

uninhabited *adj. The house has been uninhabited for almost a year. The boat landed on an uninhabited island:* unoccupied, unlived in, vacant, empty, untenanted, derelict, unpopulated, unpeopled, unsettled, deserted.

Ant. inhabited, occupied, lived in; populated, peopled, settled.

uninhibited *adj.* **1** *Only uninhibited people would think of joining a nudist colony. Her uninhibited remarks embarrassed her friends:* unselfconscious, not shy, open; spontaneous, impulsive, impetuous, rash, instinctive, *Informal* fast; heedless, unwary, unguarded, incautious, careless, indiscreet; outspoken, candid, frank, unreserved, plainspoken, straightforward, forthright; reckless, madcap, capricious, headstrong, abandoned, free, free-spirited, daring, flamboyant, immodest. **2** *The uninhibited use of motor transport caused a petrol shortage:* free, unrestrained, unconstrained, uncontrolled, unrestricted, unchecked, unobstructed, unhampered, unstopped, unimpeded, unhindered, uncurbed, unbridled, unreined.

Ant. 1, 2 inhibited. **1** self-conscious, shy, bashful, retiring, sheepish, modest, demure; wary, guarded, cautious, careful, discreet, self-controlled; stiff, rigid, *Slang* uptight. **2** restrained, constrained, controlled, restricted, checked, hampered, hindered, curbed, bridled.

uninspired *adj.* **1** *The audience was left uninspired by the dull speech:* unmoved, unstirred, unimpressed, unexcited, unaffected, untouched, unemotional, unstimulated, uninfluenced. **2** *The programme was so uninspired that I fell asleep:* unimaginative, unoriginal, ordinary, prosaic, trite, commonplace, clichéd, run-of-the-mill, stock, pedestrian, stale, hackneyed, predictable, dull, unexciting, indifferent, uninteresting, vapid, humdrum.

Ant. 1, 2 inspired. **1** moved, stirred, impressed, excited, affected, touched, influenced, stimulated. **2** imaginative, creative, original, fresh, novel, new, extraordinary, unusual, different, exciting, interesting.

unintelligible *adj. She was crying so hard that her words were unintelligible. The code was unintelligible to anyone who didn't have the key:* impossible to understand, incoherent, inarticulate, incomprehensible, illegible, incapable of being understood, meaningless, unfathomable, baffling, confusing, puzzling, perplexing; undecipherable, impenetrable, insoluble.

Ant. intelligible, understandable, coherent, articulate, legible; comprehensible, clear, decipherable, soluble.

unintentional *adj. The boy didn't mean to bump into you; it was purely unintentional:* accidental, fortuitous, unpremeditated, undesigned, unplanned, not done purposely, unconscious, inadvertent, unthinking, unwitting, involuntary.

uninteresting *adj. Chess strikes me as a very uninteresting game:* boring, tiresome, dreary, dull, tedious, uneventful, monotonous, drab, wearisome, prosaic, dry, jejune, trite, insipid, vapid, uninspiring, insignificant, ordinary, lifeless, colourless, unsatisfying.

uninviting *adj. The house was drab and uninviting:* unappealing, unwelcoming, unalluring, unattractive, unpleasant, displeasing, undesirable, disagreeable, distasteful, offensive, unappetizing, annoying.

union *n.* **1** *The book is a perfect union of humour and seriousness. The union of hydrogen and oxygen forms water:* combination, mixture, amalgam, amalgamation, consolidation, joining, blend, merger, unity, uniting, oneness, marriage, wedding; fusion, synthesis, unifying, unification. **2** *The Act of Union of 1707 made both England and Scotland subject to one sovereign:* association, affiliation, alliance, league, partnership, corporation, federation, confederation, fraternity. **3** *Join the union and get a fair deal:* (*variously*) trade union, craft-guild, workers' association, guild.

Ant. 1 separation, division.

unique *adj. The tranquil beauty of the Mona Lisa is unique:* singular, distinctive, peculiar, *Latin* sui generis, the only one of its kind, by itself, incomparable, unrivalled, unparalleled, unequalled, matchless, unmatched, peerless, unapproached, unexampled, inimitable, nonpareil, surpassing.

Ant. commonplace, common, usual, everyday, ordinary, average, routine, typical.

◇ *Usage note:* The best speakers and writers use *unique* only to mean the only one of its kind, never as a synonym for unusual, rare, or outstanding. Thus, *The Petrified Forest is unique,* but *Golden eagles are rare* (not "unique") *in this part of the world. Riding the camel was an unusual* (not "unique") *experience. The film is outstanding* (not "unique") *in its portrayal of suburban life.*

unit *n.* **1** *The refrigerator needs a new cooling unit. Send the third unit to join the rear guard:* part, element, section, component, constituent, member, division; entity, whole, quantity, group, package, detachment. **2** *An ounce is a unit of weight:* measure, measurement, quantity, category, denomination, entity.

unite *v.* **1** *The school united its music and drama departments:* unify, combine, join, consolidate, confederate, federate, incorporate, ally, coalesce, amalgamate, fuse, merge, couple, blend, pool, lump together. **2** *The people must unite against the tyrant:* join together, join forces, link arms, stand together, organize, speak with one voice, close ranks.

Ant. 1 divide, separate, disunite, split, part, sever, disjoin, detach, disengage.

united *adj.* **1** *The united scarves stretched for fifty yards:* unified, combined, consolidated, incorporated, amalgamated, fused, merged, joined, coupled, blended, allied, collective, pooled, lumped together; leagued, federated. **2** *Her parents were united in their insistence that she go to university:* joined together, one, of the same opinion, unanimous, of one mind, in agreement.

Ant. 1, 2 divided. **2** split, on opposite sides of the fence, at odds.

unity *n.* **1** *Would the unity of the nation be destroyed by stronger regional government?:* oneness, wholeness, entity, unification, consolidation, amalgamation, fusion, synthesis, merger, joining, association, federation, confederation, affiliation, league, alliance, union, partnership. **2** *The new prime minister begged for unity between the warring factions:* accord, concord, peace, harmony, co-operation, friendship, amicableness, unanimity, understanding, goodwill, fellowship, compatibility, like-mindedness, rapport.

Ant. 1, 2 disunity. **1** independence, individuality, heterogeneity, isolation, division, separateness, separation, severance. **2** disagreement, discord, disharmony, enmity, ill will.

"Thy hand, great Anarch! lets the curtain fall,
And universal darkness buries all."
—*Alexander Pope*

---

universal *adj. Over-population is a universal problem:* concerning everyone, affecting all, world-wide, international, omnipresent, widespread, existing, everywhere; general, all-embracing, all-inclusive, catholic.

Ant. individual, personal, private, local, localized, parochial, limited, restricted, exclusive, confined, special, specific.

unkempt *adj. The child always has dirty nails and unkempt hair:* uncombed, tousled, dishevelled, ungroomed, untidy, messy, sloppy, disarranged, disordered, slovenly.

Ant. combed, well-groomed, neat, orderly, tidy.

◇ *Word origin: Unkempt* comes from *kemb,* an obsolete variant of the verb *comb.*

unkind *adj. It was unkind of you to cancel the party at such short notice:* inconsiderate, thoughtless, unfeeling, unsympathetic, insensitive, uncaring, unfriendly, ungracious, inhospitable, uncharitable, ungenerous.

unlikely *adj.* **1** *Snow seems unlikely today. He may be right this time, but it's unlikely:* not likely, improbable, questionable, unbelievable, scarcely conceivable. **2** *The fat youth was the most unlikely member of the cycling team:* unpromising, unpropitious, hopeless.

Ant. 1 likely, probable, unquestionable, sure, certain. **2** promising, propitious, encouraging.

unlimited *adj.* **1** *The king held unlimited authority:* limitless, unrestricted, unrestrained, unchecked, uncontrolled, absolute, total, totalitarian, complete, unconstrained, unqualified, all-encompassing, comprehensive. **2** *They flew over the unlimited reaches of the Arctic. Life has unlimited possibilities:* endless, limitless, boundless, unbounded, infinite, inexhaustible, vast, immense, huge, immeasurable.

Ant. 1 limited, restricted, controlled, confined, checked, constrained; partial. **2** finite, limited, bounded, small, little, minute.

unmanly *adj.* **1** *The Spartans considered retreat unmanly, regardless of circumstances:* faint-hearted, weak-kneed, lily-livered, weak-hearted, chicken-hearted, cowardly, timid, pusillanimous, *Slang* wet, yellow. **2** *The football coach despised ballet as an unmanly pursuit:* effeminate, womanish, sissy.

Ant. 1 courageous, brave, valiant, lion-hearted, stout-hearted; brash, bold, reckless. **2** masculine, manly, virile.

unmannerly *adj. Who was that unmannerly individual at the entrance? The children are too unmannerly to be invited to the party:* badly behaved, ill-mannered, ill-bred, ungracious, ungentlemanly, unladylike; discourteous, impolite, crude, gross, uncouth, coarse, boorish, loutish, uncivil, surly.

Ant. well-behaved, courteous, polite, gracious, well-bred, mannerly; gentlemanly, ladylike, refined, cultured.

unmask *v.* **1** *The guests will come in costumes and masks but everyone will unmask at midnight:* remove a mask; take off one's disguise. **2** *The investigation unmasked the true culprits:* reveal, expose, disclose, uncover, discover, unveil, bare, lay open, bring to light, betray.

unmatched *adj.* **1** *The necklace is made up of twenty unmatched diamonds:* not matched, unmatching, not paired, unlike, differing, not uniform, unequal, dissimilar, disparate, diverse, variable. **2** *The painting is of unmatched beauty:* matchless, unequalled, unparalleled, peerless, supreme, second to none, beyond compare.

Ant. 1 matched, matching, paired, like, uniform, equal, similar.

unmindful *adj. He's too unmindful of his responsibilities to be dependable:* negligent, remiss, heedless, unheeding, thoughtless, careless, oblivious, unaware, forgetful.

Ant. careful, heedful, aware, unremiss.

unmistakable *adj. His lack of sincerity was unmistakable. The girl has an unmistakable genius for music:* clear, obvious, evident, manifest, plain, distinct, patent, palpable, pronounced, prominent, glaring, conspicuous; undeniable, unequivocal, unquestionable.

Ant. vague, indistinct, dim, faint, unrecognizable, unclear, hidden, concealed.

unmitigated *adj.* **1** *August was a month of unmitigated hot weather:* unrelieved, unalleviated, unabated, unbroken, persistent, uninterrupted. **2** *He's an unmitigated liar!:* downright, out and out, absolute, unqualified, arrant.

Ant. 1 mitigated, relieved, alleviated, abated, eased, lessened, softened, mild, soft; sporadic, intermittent, random, occasional. **2** partial, incomplete, qualified, limited; reformed, redeemed, regenerate.

unmoved *adj.* **1** *Mother wants this chair left unmoved:* not moved, not shifted, left in place, not transplanted. **2** *After debating for hours both sides remained unmoved on the principal issues:* firm, steadfast, unwavering, unswerving, unshaken, unfaltering, inflexible, undeviating; staunch, determined, resolute, resolved, persistent, obstinate, dogged, uncompromising, relentless; devoted, dedicated. **3** *His appeal for a loan left me unmoved:* unaffected, untouched, calm, unstirred, indifferent, uninterested, undisturbed, unresponsive, unconcerned, uncaring; cold, stony-hearted, aloof, unpitying, unfeeling.

Ant. 1 moved, transferred, shifted. **2** shaken,

wavering, vacillating; compliant, flexible, yielding, adaptable, submissive. **3** moved, touched, stirred, affected, concerned, responsive, sympathetic.

unnatural *adj.* **1** *She has an unnatural craving for salty foods:* not natural, abnormal, aberrant, freakish, anomalous. **2** *Finishing school has taught her an unnatural way of talking:* artificial, affected, mannered, studied, forced, assumed, contrived, phoney, self-conscious.

Ant. 1, 2 natural, normal. **1** common, ordinary, typical. **2** unaffected, unpretentious, sincere, genuine, honest.

unnecessary *adj. There's no sense in taking unnecessary risks. Buying the second cake was unnecessary:* not necessary, needless, uncalled-for, dispensable, inessential, unrequired, expendable, gratuitous; too much, excessive, extra, surplus, excess, superfluous, supplementary, auxiliary.

unnerve *v. Being alone in the woods at night unnerved us:* upset, unsettle, unhinge, agitate, daunt, intimidate, frighten, scare.

Ant. encourage, reassure; nerve, steel.

unnoticed *adj.* **1** *The boy slipped through the gate unnoticed by the guard:* unseen, unobserved, undiscovered, unperceived; (*variously*) unheard, untasted, not smelt, unfelt. **2** *Everyone had such a good time dancing that the lack of refreshments went unnoticed:* overlooked, disregarded, unnoticed, unheeded.

Ant. 1, 2 noticed. **1** seen, observed, witnessed, discovered, perceived; heard, tasted, smelt, felt. **2** noted, heeded, marked.

unobtrusive *adj. An unobtrusive grey rug lay on the floor. Her father is an unobtrusive man:* inconspicuous, unpretentious, modest, unostentatious; unassuming, diffident, bashful, reserved, unassertive, retiring, shy.

Ant. conspicuous, prominent, eye-catching, glaring, noticeable; ostentatious, pretentious, assuming, bold, brash, brazen, assertive, extrovert.

unorganized *adj. These unorganized papers must be sorted and filed:* unordered, orderless, unsystematized, unsystematic, unarranged, random, casual, haphazard, confused, loose, helter-skelter, harum-scarum, chaotic, unclassified, aimless, disjointed, undirected.

Ant. organized, ordered, systematized, systematic, arranged, classified.

◇ *Usage note: Unorganized* means without any plan or order whatsoever: *Unorganized papers covered the author's desk, The recruits remained unorganized until they were divided into companies, platoons, and units. Disorganized* means having a bad, misused, or abandoned plan or order: *No business can be run with a disorganized filing system, Beaten and disorganized, the troops threw down their rifles and ran.* In other words, things are *unorganized* before they are put in order, but can be *disorganized* only after they have been in order.

unperturbed *adj. Napoleon was unperturbed in the face of defeat:* calm, cool, collected, composed, poised, unruffled, unexcited, undisturbed, untroubled, undismayed, level-headed, cool-headed, unimpassioned, nonchalant.

Ant. perturbed, excited, discomposed, upset, disturbed, troubled, dismayed, impassioned.

unpleasant *adj. This medicine has an unpleasant taste. What an unpleasant man!:* disagreeable, displeasing, distasteful, offensive, repulsive, repugnant, obnoxious, objectionable, unlikeable, unattractive, irksome, vexatious, noisome, nasty; ill-natured, churlish, ill-humoured, bad-tempered.

Ant. pleasant, pleasing, agreeable, attractive, likeable; congenial, good-natured.

unprecedented *adj. Customers came in unprecedented numbers:* hitherto unknown, unheard-of, unexampled, extraordinary, exceptional, novel.

Ant. familiar, usual, regular, normal, routine.

unpredictable *adj. The patient's behaviour is unpredictable:* not predictable, not foreseeable, erratic, unstable, fitful, variable, random, uncertain, eccentric, inconstant, arbitrary, changeable, mercurial, impulsive, capricious, whimsical, fanciful.

Ant. predictable, stable, constant, undeviating, reasonable.

unprejudiced *adj. A judge must be completely unprejudiced:* without prejudice, impartial, objective, unbiased, unbigoted, fair, fair-minded, just, uninfluenced, unswayed, undogmatic, disinterested, open-minded, broad-minded, non-partisan.

Ant. prejudiced, partial, biased, bigoted, unjust, unfair, closed-minded, narrow-minded, partisan.

unpretentious *adj. After becoming wealthy he lived in the same unpretentious house as before:* unassuming, simple, plain, modest, unostentatious, unelaborate, unobtrusive, humble, homely.

unprincipled *adj. His lying shows that he is completely unprincipled:* without principles, unscrupulous, unconscionable, amoral, conscienceless.

unqualified *adj.* **1** *The youth is completely unqualified to be an accountant:* lacking the qualifications, untrained, unschooled, uneducated, unskilled, inexpert, inexperienced, unprepared, ill-equipped; unfit, unsuited, incompetent. **2** *The play is an unqualified success:* absolute, total, complete, positive, consummate, utter, downright, thorough, through and through, out and out, unconditional, undisputed, run-away.

unquestionable *adj. The defendant's integrity is unquestionable:* beyond doubt, undeniable, irrefutable, proven, unequivocal, unimpeachable, definite, certain, sure, clear, plain, self-evident, evident, perfect, flawless, faultless, irreproachable, uncensurable.

unreal *adj. She lives in an unreal world of make-believe:* not real, non-existent, imaginary, imagined, illusory, illusive, chimerical, insubstantial, fictitious, legendary, fantastic; ghostly, shadowy, spectral, intangible, phantasmagorical, phantom, ethereal, dreamlike, dreamy, dream, airy, idealistic, never-never.

unreasonable *adj.* **1** *It's unreasonable to expect snow in July:* contrary to reason, senseless, irrational, illogical, absurd, far-fetched, preposterous, nonsensical. **2** *He's a spoilt, unreasonable young man:* obstinate, headstrong, stubborn, inflexible, unyielding, unbending, obdurate, mulish, bull-headed, pigheaded, unmanageable, hard to deal with, ungovernable, intractable; opinionated, blinkered, closed-minded, bigoted, biased, prejudiced, fanatical. **3** *Management considers the union's demands unreasonable:* excessive, too great, exorbitant, extravagant, inordinate, immoderate, unfair, unwarranted, unjustifiable, undue, uncalled-for.

Ant. 1–3 reasonable. **1** sensible, logical, plausible, rational, sober, wise, prudent. **2** complaisant, agreeable, flexible, tractable, open-minded. **3** moderate, temperate, restrained, equitable, fair, justified, warranted.

unrelated *adj.* **1** *The two men look alike but are in fact unrelated:* not related, not kin, not kindred; dissimilar, unlike. **2** *Such personal remarks are completely unrelated to the matter under discussion:* extraneous, irrelevant, unconnected, not germane, foreign, unassociated, unallied, inappropriate, inapplicable, incompatible.

Ant. 1, 2 related. **1** kin, akin; similar, like, equal. **2** relevant, pertinent, germane, connected, applicable, appropriate, associated.

unrelenting *adj. The Department of Health waged an unrelenting war against the epidemic:* relentless, unremitting, unrelieved, incessant, ceaseless, unbroken, endless, unabated, unwavering; steady, constant, unswerving, undeviating, unyielding, inflexible, unbending, rigid, adamant, tenacious, uncompromising, implacable, inexorable.

unreliable *adj.* **1** *Rumours are always unreliable:* undependable, not to be trusted; questionable, uncertain, fallible, undependable; phoney, fake, false, inaccurate, mistaken, erroneous. **2** *The new worker proved to be completely unreliable:* undependable, irresponsible, not conscientious, untrustworthy, deceitful; unstable, changeable, fickle, inconstant, capricious.

Ant. 1, 2 reliable, dependable. **1** certain, sure, unquestionable, infallible; real, genuine, authentic, correct, accurate, true, right. **2** responsible, conscientious, trustworthy.

unrepentant *adj. The sinner died unrepentant. Should unrepentant criminals be given life sentences?:* without repenting, not contrite, not penitent, unexpiated, unatoned; unregenerate, remorseless, unashamed; hardened, incorrigible, obdurate, callous.

Ant. repentant, penitent, expiated, atoned; contrite, regenerate, remorseful, ashamed.

unresolved *adj. Whether the budget will bring tax increases or not is still unresolved:* undetermined, unsettled, undecided, unanswered, unsolved, unascertained, pending, tentative; doubtful, vague, uncertain, questionable, moot, problematical, speculative; disputable, contestable.

unrestrained *adj. The audience roared with unrestrained laughter:* uncontrolled, unrestricted, unchecked, uninhibited, irrepressible, unrepressed, unreserved, unsuppressed, uncurbed, unbridled, unhampered, unfettered, unchecked, ungoverned, unhindered; unlimited, boundless, excessive, extravagant, inordinate, immoderate, intemperate, abandoned.

unruly *adj. The child is unruly because he's been spoilt:* disobedient, obstreperous, wild, wilful, unmanageable, ungovernable, uncontrollable, intractable, wayward, headstrong, perverse, refractory, fractious, contrary, unbridled, restive, rowdy, boisterous.

Ant. obedient, well-behaved, well-mannered, manageable, controllable, docile, tractable, submissive, compliant, sweet-tempered, agreeable; calm, reserved.

"The tongue can no man tame; it is an unruly evil."
—*James 3:8*

---

unsafe *adj. The bridge is unsafe for heavy loads. If the enemy attacks, this fort will be unsafe:* dangerous, not safe, hazardous, perilous, risky; treacherous, untrustworthy, unreliable, unprotected, vulnerable, exposed, undefended, unguarded, insecure.

Ant. safe, secure, immune from danger, reliable, trustworthy, guaranteed; protected, guarded, defended.

unsatisfactory *adj. The student's work was deemed unsatisfactory:* not satisfactory, unacceptable, unworthy, inept; inadequate, deficient, below par, unsuitable, inappropriate, unfit, inadmissible, ineligible.

unsavoury *adj.* **1** *The salad was limp and the dressing unsavoury:* flat, insipid, tasteless, without savour. **2** *The natives ate sheep's eyes and other unsavoury things:* distasteful, unpleasant, bad-tasting, unappetizing, unpalatable, nasty, foul, nauseating, disagreeable. **3** *He has an unsavoury reputation:* morally objectionable, unpleasant, bad, tainted.

Ant. 1, 2 savoury, appetizing, tasty, agreeable, pleasing. **3** virtuous, good, moral.

unscathed *adj. How could he come out of that accident unscathed?:* uninjured, unharmed,

unhurt, unscratched, untouched, unimpaired, whole, entire, perfect, sound, intact, in one piece.
Ant. hurt, injured, harmed, damaged.
◇ *Word origin: Unscathed* is the negative of the rarely-used verb to *scathe,* to injure, harm, assail verbally. We use the adjective derived from this verb in the expression *a scathing* (severely critical) *remark.*

unscrupulous *adj. An unscrupulous acquaintance sold them some worthless stocks:* unprincipled, dishonourable, devious, unethical, immoral, amoral, sharp, crooked.
Ant. scrupulous, principled, moral, ethical, honourable, honest, just, fair, trustworthy.

unseemly *adj. Everyone was shocked by his unseemly conduct:* improper, inappropriate, unbefitting, unbecoming, indecorous, ungentlemanly, unladylike, unsuitable, out of place, discreditable, undignified, unworthy, disreputable, reprehensible, tasteless, offensive, distasteful, vulgar, indelicate, incorrect, indecent, gross, crude, coarse, rude, discourteous, ill-mannered, boorish, churlish, loutish.
Ant. seemly, proper, appropriate, fit, befitting, becoming, suitable, dignified, tasteful, cultivated, polite, courteous, mannerly, genteel, gentlemanly, ladylike.

unselfish *adj. It was very unselfish of you to help us:* selfless, altruistic, generous, considerate, large-hearted, self-sacrificing, handsome, princely, charitable, benevolent, humanitarian, magnanimous.

unsettle *v. World conditions have unsettled the stock-market. The lawyer's questioning unsettled the witness:* make unstable, unbalance, disturb, perturb, upset, disorder; disconcert, confuse, bewilder, fluster, confound, ruffle, bother, agitate, unhinge, throw off balance, *Slang* rattle.

unshaken *adj.* **1** *The father's trust in his son is unshaken:* undaunted, unaffected, undisturbed, undeviating, unwavering, unfaltering, unswerving, unflinching, steadfast, determined, resolved, staunch, constant, stable, inflexible, uncompromising, tenacious, relentless. **2** *She remained unshaken as we told her the bad news:* cool, calm, composed, controlled, poised, self-possessed, level-headed, serene, unperturbed, untroubled, unmoved, unruffled, unemotional, unexcited.
Ant. 1, 2 shaken. **1** wavering, faltering; destroyed, ruined, demolished, smashed, shattered, undone. **2** disconcerted, upset, emotional, excited, uncontrolled, moved, perturbed, troubled, dismayed, ruffled.

unsightly *adj. Please clean up this unsightly mess:* ugly, unattractive, hideous, obnoxious, offensive, distasteful, repellent, repulsive, odious, horrid, revolting, sickening.
Ant. attractive, lovely, beautiful, appealing.

unsolicited *adj. She gave me her unsolicited opinion of my hat:* unasked for, unrequested, unsought, uninvited, gratuitous, volunteered; unwanted, unwelcome, unwished for, undesired, unnecessary; voluntary, unforced, free, spontaneous.
Ant. requested, sought, invited, solicited, desired, welcomed; courted.

unsophisticated *adj. It was refreshing to talk to the unsophisticated youth:* natural, ingenuous, artless, unworldly, unpretentious, open, unaffected, unassuming, candid, guileless, straightforward, unstudied, uncontrived, undissembling; naïve, green, innocent.

unsound *adj.* **1** *The old horse was thin and unsound. The doctors judged him to be of unsound mind:* unhealthy, sickly, diseased, crippled, defective, ailing, in poor health, infirm, unfit, invalid; feeble, weak, decrepit, drooping, languishing; mentally ill, deranged, insane, mad, unbalanced, unhinged, unsettled, disordered, confused, *Slang* off one's rocker. **2** *Too little cement was used in the foundations, making the building unsound:* not solid, shaky, unsteady, weak, unstable, unsubstantial, rickety, tottery; unsafe, hazardous, dangerous, precarious, risky, perilous, unreliable, uncertain, insecure. **3** *I think your reasoning is unsound:* not valid, unfounded, groundless, weak, shaky, fallacious, faulty, incorrect, wrong, erroneous, illogical, defective, spurious, marred, blemished, impaired, imperfect, flawed; senseless, irrational, foolish, absurd.
Ant. 1–3 sound, strong. **1** healthy, whole, well, fit, in good health, of strong constitution, vigorous, robust, hardy, hale and hearty, in the pink; sane, rational, reasonable, stable, clear-headed. **2** solid, sturdy, firm, safe, secure, durable, lasting. **3** valid, well-founded, convincing, cogent, correct, accurate, true, judicious, sensible, meaningful, reliable, authoritative.

unsparing *adj. The charitable woman was unsparing of her time and money:* ungrudging, unstinting, generous, bountiful, munificent, liberal, lavish, profuse, plenteous, abundant, extravagant, copious, plentiful, full; unconditional, unqualified, unlimited.

unspeakable *adj.* **1** *The Urals are a mountain range of unspeakable grandeur:* inexpressible, too wonderful to describe, indescribable, unutterable, inconceivable, unimaginable, incredible, overwhelming, astonishing, extraordinary, immense, huge, vast, enormous, great, prodigious. **2** *It was a crime of unspeakable horror:* too horrible to talk about, awful, shocking, frightful, fearful, unheard-of, repulsive, repellent, disgusting, odious, loathsome, abhorrent, nauseating, sickening, revolting, abominable, monstrous.

unspecified *adj. We agreed to meet at some unspecified time in the future:* unmentioned, unnamed, unannounced, unpublicized, undetermined, undefined, undesignated, unindicated, unstipulated, unsettled; vague, general, indefinite.

unspoilt *adj.* **1** *The girl was charming and completely unspoilt:* unpampered, not coddled; natural, artless, unaffected, unassuming, unpretentious, open, unstudied, unself-conscious, unsophisticated, unworldly, uncorrupted, trusting. **2** *The wilderness possessed an unspoilt beauty. The politician's reputation is unspoilt by scandal:* preserved, undamaged, unharmed, unimpaired, perfect; spotless, unspotted, unmarred, unblemished, unscarred, untouched, intact.

unstable *adj.* **1** *That ladder is too unstable to hold you:* unsteady, unsubstantial, shaky, wobbly, tottering; flimsy, rickety, fragile, frail, weak. **2** *The patient's condition was unstable. The youth has a very unstable personality:* fluctuating, not constant, changing, changeable, vacillating, shifting, unsteady; erratic, volatile, emotional, mercurial, unpredictable, irrational, fitful, inconsistent, insecure, irresponsible, fickle, capricious, fly-by-night.

unsuccessful *adj.* **1** *The army made an unsuccessful attempt to capture the enemy fort:* without success, futile, vain, useless, unavailing, unfruitful, fruitless, abortive, unproductive, ineffectual. **2** *No matter what business he tried, he was always unsuccessful. Restaurants have always been unsuccessful in this neighbourhood:* unlucky, hapless, unfortunate, ill-starred, luckless, unprosperous; thwarted, foiled, baffled; poor, moneyless, penniless, hard up, badly off; profitless, unprofitable, unremunerative.

Ant. 1, 2 successful. **1** victorious, winning, triumphant, unbeaten; useful, fruitful, productive, effective, worthwhile. **2** lucky, fortunate; prosperous, thriving, flourishing, rich, wealthy, well-to-do, well-off, affluent; profitable, remunerative.

unsuitable *adj. That dress is unsuitable for a wedding:* inappropriate, unbefitting, unfit, unfitting, improper, unbecoming, unseemly, out of place, out of keeping, out of character, unhappy, infelicitous, indecorous, incongruous, inconsistent, incompatible; unacceptable, inadmissible, inadequate, worthless, useless.

unsullied *adj. The girl's reputation is unsullied:* unsoiled, clean, spotless, untainted, untarnished, unblemished, unblackened, uncorrupted, uninjured, uncontaminated, unpolluted, undefiled.

unsurpassed *adj. Keats'* Endymion *is a poem of unsurpassed beauty:* supreme, consummate, superior, best, paramount, peerless, highest, greatest, transcendent, exceptional, unexcelled, incomparable, unparalleled, matchless, unmatched, unequalled, unrivalled.

unsuspecting *adj. She tried the new dish on her unsuspecting guests. The unsuspecting youth was easily cheated:* unsuspicious, unaware, off one's guard; credulous, trusting, believing; over-trustful, gullible, unwary, naïve, over-credulous.

Ant. knowing, heedful, aware, alert; suspicious, cautious, wary.

unswerving *adj. The general had an unswerving devotion to duty:* dedicated, faithful, devoted, steadfast, unwavering, undeviating, unflinching, unyielding, unfaltering, untiring, unflagging, inflexible, uncompromising, resolute, resolved, determined, single-minded, staunch, strong, firm, steady, unremitting, unshaken, undaunted.

Ant. wavering, faltering, flagging, irresolute, weak, faint, half-hearted.

untangle *v. Help me untangle this yarn. There was some confusion over delivery dates that the shipping clerk had to untangle:* unravel, disentangle, untwist, unsnarl; straighten out, clear up, solve, extricate.

Ant. tangle, entangle, snarl, twist.

untarnished *adj.* **1** *Wrap the silverware tightly to keep it untarnished:* unoxidized, unblackened, shining, bright, polished. **2** *The arbitrator should be a man of untarnished reputation:* spotless, unsoiled, unstained, untainted, unsullied, unblemished, unbesmirched, undefiled, unimpeachable, undisputed, faultless, flawless, immaculate, impeccable.

Ant. 1, 2 tarnished. **1** oxidized, blackened, dull. **2** tainted, sullied, soiled, blemished, stained, besmirched, defiled, questionable, damaged, marred, discredited.

untenable *adj. If you check the facts, you'll find that your argument is untenable:* indefensible, unmaintainable, unsustainable, unjustifiable, insupportable, baseless, groundless, unsound, invalid, illogical, erroneous, fallacious, faulty, spurious, specious, unreliable; questionable, debatable, contestable.

Ant. justified, sustained, supported, well-grounded; valid, reasonable, sound, logical; unquestionable, uncontestable.

unthinkable *adj. It would be unthinkable to go to the wedding uninvited:* out of the question, not to be considered, inconceivable, unimaginable, insupportable, unjustifiable, unwarranted.

unthinking *adj. His unthinking remark offended the visitors:* thoughtless, inconsiderate, heedless, careless, inadvertent, tactless, insensitive, undiplomatic, uncircumspect; senseless, mindless, witless, imprudent, negligent.

untidy *adj. Straighten up that untidy room. She is one of the most untidy people that I've ever met:* messy, disorderly, littered, cluttered, unkempt, chaotic, disarrayed, confused, topsy-turvy; slovenly, sloppy, dishevelled, slatternly, dowdy, frowsy, rumpled, tousled, bedraggled; careless, slipshod, unmethodical.

untimely *adj. Her next-door neighbours' untimely*

visit prevented her from finishing the job. Everyone was shocked by his untimely remark: ill-timed, mistimed, inconvenient, inopportune, unexpected, premature; inappropriate, unsuitable, unfitting, unseemly, unbecoming, unbefitting, imprudent, out of place, unhappy, infelicitous, unfortunate, ill-advised.

untiring *adj.* **1** *None of the competitors could catch up with the untiring runner in the lead:* not becoming tired, tireless, never tiring, unwearied, fresh. **2** *His untiring help has been a great blessing:* unflagging, indefatigable, unfaltering, constant, unremitting, unceasing, wholehearted, determined, persevering, staunch, steadfast, resolute, steady, patient, persevering, persistent, tenacious, relentless, diligent, sedulous, assiduous; devoted, dedicated, zealous, earnest.

Ant. 1 tiring, tired, weary, exhausted, fatigued, spent, *Slang* dog-tired, played-out, dead-beat. **2** flagging, faltering, wavering, irresolute, faint-hearted, lukewarm, indifferent, perfunctory, sporadic.

untold *adj.* **1** *The book reveals the hitherto untold story of the actress's private life:* unrevealed, secret, private, concealed, unknown, suppressed, withheld, hushed up; unsaid, unspoken, unexpressed. **2** *The earthquake left untold thousands of people homeless:* innumerable, countless, uncounted, numerous, myriad, undetermined, numberless, unnumbered; incalculable, immeasurable, limitless, unbounded, endless, infinite.

untrue *adj.* **1** *His story is completely untrue:* not true, untruthful, false, fallacious, falsified, groundless, unfounded, made up, fictitious, spurious, meretricious, fake, sham, fraudulent; incorrect, erroneous, inaccurate. **2** *King Henry VIII had two of his wives executed on the charge that they were untrue to him:* unfaithful, faithless, inconstant, adulterous, unchaste, promiscuous, false, perfidious; disloyal, dishonest, treacherous, double-dealing.

Ant. 1, 2 true. **1** right, correct, accurate, authentic, genuine, real, valid, legitimate, *Slang* straight. **2** faithful, constant, chaste, pure, virtuous; loyal, honest, trustworthy, incorruptible, dependable, honourable, righteous, truthful.

untrustworthy *adj. The report from the front is untrustworthy. His best friend proved to be untrustworthy:* unreliable, undependable, unauthenticated, questionable, fallible, uncertain; unfaithful, disloyal, faithless, dishonest, false, insincere, untruthful, untrue, unprincipled, devious, deceitful, unscrupulous, disreputable, corrupted, treacherous, inconstant, two-faced, perfidious, irresponsible, shifty, slippery, capricious, fickle.

unusual *adj. The shape of this leaf is unusual. Kevin married a girl of unusual beauty:* singular, rare, exceptional, extraordinary, remarkable, noteworthy, atypical, untypical, novel, phenomenal, unique, uncommon, unfamiliar, surprising; strange, curious, peculiar; unparalleled, unequalled, unprecedented, unmatched, incomparable, unheard-of, out of the ordinary, *Informal* off-beat.

Ant. usual, common, commonplace, ordinary, unremarkable, unexceptional, average, typical, familiar, routine, normal, natural, traditional, conventional, orthodox, stock.

unvarnished *adj. The unvarnished truth is that you'll never recover the money:* plain, frank, candid, direct, honest, sincere, straightforward, straight, straight from the shoulder; unembellished, unadorned.

Ant. embellished, exaggerated; hypocritical, evasive, insincere, dishonest.

unveil *v.* **1** *The mayor unveiled a new statue in the park:* uncover, unsheathe, uncloak. **2** *In his speech, the chancellor unveiled his new tax plan:* disclose, reveal, divulge, bare, make known, announce, broadcast, publish, bring to light.

Ant. 1, 2 veil. **1** cover. **2** conceal, hide, disguise, camouflage.

unwarranted *adj. Such strong criticism was completely unwarranted:* unjustified, uncalled-for, indefensible, unreasonable, inexcusable, unfounded, groundless, arbitrary; unauthorized, unsanctioned, unapproved, culpable, censurable, unlawful, illegal.

unwavering *adj. It takes years of unwavering determination to become a surgeon:* unswerving, unfaltering, untiring, unflagging, dedicated, single-minded, faithful, undeviating, unflinching, resolute, determined, steadfast, staunch, strong, firm, steady, persevering, unremitting, persistent, tenacious, uncompromising, unshaken.

unwelcome *adj.* **1** *Although she said we weren't interrupting, her coolness made us feel unwelcome. Because he was a proud man, his son's offer of a loan was unwelcome:* unwanted, unwished for, uninvited, undesirable, unacceptable, rejected, excluded, unpopular, outcast, uncared for; unnecessary, unessential, unrequired. **2** *Telling the boy he can't go to camp after all is an unwelcome task:* disagreeable, unpleasant, displeasing, distasteful, undesirable, thankless.

unwholesome *adj.* **1** *Stay away from unwholesome foods:* unhealthy, insalubrious, deleterious, harmful, detrimental; unnourishing, noxious, pernicious, poisonous, venomous, baneful, deadly, toxic. **2** *Unwholesome friends led the youth astray:* morally harmful, immoral, corrupting, evil, sinful, depraved, dishonourable, degrading, ruinous, corrupted, demoralizing, undesirable; dangerous, polluting, contaminating, filthy, foul.

Ant. 1, 2 wholesome. **1** healthy, salubrious; nutritious, hygienic, sanitary, healthful. **2** moral, uplifting, edifying, inspiring.

unwieldy *adj. That heavy axe is too unwieldy for a child:* hard to handle, not handy, awkward, clumsy, inconvenient, uncomfortable, incommodious, cumbersome, bulky, heavy, burdensome, weighty.

Ant. handy, convenient, comfortable.

unwilling *adj. Clive is unwilling to be transferred to central office:* reluctant, loath, disinclined, unfavourably disposed, undesirous, averse, opposed, resistant, recalcitrant, dissenting, demurring, unenthusiastic, not in the mood.

unwise *adj. Investing all the money in only one stock would be unwise:* imprudent, improvident, ill-advised, inadvisable, unsound, unreasonable, short-sighted, injudicious, foolish, senseless, unintelligent, reckless, foolhardy, silly, dumb, stupid, *Slang* crazy, bonkers.

unwitting *adj. The taxi-driver became an unwitting accomplice in the bank robbers' get-away:* unknowing, unaware, unintentional, inadvertent, unthinking, unmeant, accidental, unpremeditated, undesigned, unplanned, unexpected; involuntary, unconsenting.

Ant. witting, knowing, premeditated, voluntary, intentional.

unwonted *adj. The normally shy man spoke with unwonted boldness:* unaccustomed, atypical, unusual, unfamiliar, unexpected, rare, uncommon, exceptional, extraordinary.

Ant. accustomed, customary, habitual, typical, routine, usual, normal, standard, predictable.

unworldly *adj.* **1** *The unworldly young man was shocked by the greed of his associates:* unsophisticated, naïve, innocent, inexperienced, provincial, over-trusting, trusting, idealistic, callow, green. **2** *The monk set his mind upon unworldly things:* spiritual, holy, sacred, divine, pious, religious, devout, godly, solemn, pure, celestial, heavenly, transcendental, ethereal, unearthly, immaterial; metaphysical, intellectual, moral, ethical, philosophical, aesthetic.

unworthy *adj. Such conduct is unworthy of an ambassador:* inappropriate, unbefitting, unfit, improper, unbecoming, unseemly, unsuitable, unacceptable; ignoble, dishonourable, unethical, shameful, discreditable, disreputable, degrading, objectionable.

Ant. worthy, honourable, noble, commendable, admirable, praiseworthy; appropriate, fitting, befitting, proper, becoming.

unwritten *adj.* **1** *Until the invention of writing all language was unwritten:* not written down, not reduced to writing, unrecorded, unregistered; spoken only, oral, vocal, by word of mouth. **2** *In the old days it was an unwritten law that children spoke only when spoken to:* unformulated, unstated, unexpressed, implied, implicit, understood, inferred, tacit, assumed; traditional, customary.

unyielding *adj.* **1** *The new mattress was firm and unyielding:* stiff, hard, rigid, unbending, inflexible, unpliable, stony, wooden, rocklike, tough. **2** *The union is unyielding in its demands for higher pay:* unbending, inflexible, unwavering, firm, steadfast, resolute, determined, uncompromising, unswerving, undeviating, inexorable; persistent, stubborn, obstinate.

upbraid *v. The foreman upbraided the worker for being habitually late:* reproach, scold, rebuke, reprove, reprimand, censure, admonish, find fault with; berate, castigate, revile, denounce, dress down, *Slang* tear a strip off, slam.

Ant. praise, laud, compliment, commend, applaud, eulogize.

◇ *Word origin: Upbraid* comes from Old English *ūpbrēdan*, to throw (an accusation) up against (someone).

upheaval *n.* **1** *The mountain was created by a subterranean upheaval millions of years ago:* (*variously*) upthrust, volcanic eruption, earthquake, explosion, quake, flood, tidal wave, blow-up; cataclysm, catastrophe. **2** *The Depression caused an upheaval in many people's lives:* drastic change, disruption, revolution, disturbance, tumult, turmoil.

uphill *adv.* **1** *It's tiring to walk uphill:* up the slope of a hill, upward.

—*adj.* **2** *It's an uphill walk to the look-out tower:* going upward on a hill, ascending, rising, upward. **3** *Making a success of the business was an uphill struggle:* difficult, arduous, strenuous, hard, tough, exhausting, taxing, enervating, tiring, fatiguing, wearisome, wearying, burdensome, onerous.

uphold *v.* **1** *Six pillars upheld the roof:* hold up, carry the weight of, support, bear, carry, prop, prop up, sustain, brace, shore, shore up, buttress, bolster, underbrace, underpin, elevate, raise. **2** *All citizens are expected to uphold the laws of the land:* support, maintain, sustain, preserve, protect, defend, champion, advocate, stand up for; approve, endorse, confirm, acknowledge, corroborate, encourage.

uplift *v.* **1** *Listening to the sermon should uplift your thoughts:* raise, elevate, advance, better, improve, refine, upgrade, cultivate, civilize, edify, inspire.

—*n.* **2** *Lectures and good books can provide a moral uplift for everyone:* betterment, elevation, advancement, improvement, refinement, enrichment, edification, cultivation.

Ant. **1** degrade, debase; depress, demoralize. **2** degradation, debasement, lowering; dishonour, disgrace, discredit, ignominy.

upper *adj.* **1** *Put the book on one of the upper shelves:* top, topmost, high, higher; superior, greater. **2** *He wants to be promoted to the upper ranks of the business:* top, elevated, high, superior, eminent, major, important. **3** *The tribe lived on the upper reaches of the Congo:* northern, more northerly; inland, further from the sea.

uppermost Also **upmost** *adj.* **1** *The flat is on the uppermost floor of the building:* highest, top, topmost, loftiest, crowning. **2** *The captain's uppermost concern was the safety of his passengers:*

most important, chief, foremost, major, main, principal, predominant, leading, prime, primary, first, essential, paramount, pre-eminent, highest, dominant.

Ant. 1 lowermost, lowest, bottom. **2** least, last, lowliest, minor, slightest, inessential, insignificant.

upright *adj.* **1** *Some tribes bury their dead in an upright position:* erect, vertical, perpendicular, standing-up, up-ended. **2** *It's a pleasure to do business with an upright man:* honest, ethical, honourable, moral, principled, trustworthy, upstanding, righteous, reliable, high-minded, good, fair, just, above-board, *Slang* on the level, on the up-and-up.

—*n.* **3** *The porch is supported by a row of uprights:* post, pillar, column, shaft, support, prop, pier, pile, stanchion, standard, strut, rib; stake, picket, pale, pole.

Ant. 1 horizontal, prone, lying down. **2** dishonest, crooked, unethical, dishonourable, unprincipled, untrustworthy, unreliable, unscrupulous, shady. **3** beam, lintel, transverse.

uprising *n. Troops were called in to quell the uprising:* rebellion, revolution, revolt, insurrection, insurgence, mutiny; riot, outbreak.

uproar *n. The prime minister's resignation caused an uproar:* state of confusion, commotion, furore, stir, tumult, turmoil, disturbance, burst of excitement, to-do, pandemonium.

◇ *Word origin: Uproar* does not come from *roar* but from Dutch *oproer,* riot, mutiny, insurrection.

uproarious *adj.* **1** *Trafalgar Square is the scene of uproarious behaviour each New Year's Eve:* full of commotion, tumultuous, turbulent, riotous, disorderly, tempestuous, raging, stormy, intense, wild, furious; boisterous, noisy, clamorous, loud. **2** *The new play is an uproarious comedy:* very funny, hilarious, hysterical, side-splitting.

Ant. 1 quiet, calm, peaceful, serene, tranquil, placid. **2** sad, tragic, melancholy, tearful, doleful, gloomy; solemn, grave.

uproot *v.* **1** *Uproot all the weeds in the garden. We must uproot our bad habits:* pull up by the roots, extirpate, root out; do away with, cast out, banish, destroy, eliminate, abolish, exterminate, annihilate, wipe out. **2** *Floods and famine uprooted many of the country's people:* force to move, force out, displace, dislodge.

Ant. 1 plant; establish, institute, found, create, form, build; encourage, further, aid, abet.

upset *v.* **1** *The child upset her glass of milk:* overturn, turn over, up-end, invert; tip over, topple over, turn topsy-turvy, capsize. **2** *Losing the ring upset her badly:* disturb, distress, trouble, grieve, make miserable, annoy, bother, worry, perturb, unnerve, discompose, disconcert, discomfit, agitate, fluster, rattle; anger, enrage, incense, ire, irk, infuriate, pique, vex. **3** *The rain upset our plans for a picnic. The unexpected visit upset our schedule:* reverse, change; disorganize, disorder, confuse, muddle, jumble, mix up, cancel, turn topsy-turvy. **4** *The home team upset the league champions:* defeat a favourite, win against the odds; (*loosely*) defeat, be victorious over, overthrow, vanquish, overcome, overwhelm, overpower, crush, quash, demolish, smash.

—*adj.* **5** *The upset lorry blocked traffic for hours:* overturned, turned over, upside-down, up-ended, inverted, upturned, wrong side up, tipped over, capsized. **6** *Was she upset by my phone call?:* perturbed, disturbed, distressed, bothered, annoyed, worried, agitated, troubled, worried, grieved, disquieted, unnerved, overwrought, hysterical, angered, enraged, furious, incensed, mad, irked, vexed.

Ant. 1 right. **2** calm, quiet, pacify, put at ease, comfort. **3** settle, steady, stabilize; organize, order, arrange, straighten. **4** be defeated, lose. **5** right side up. **6** calmed, quieted, pacified, eased, comforted, composed, placated.

upshot *n. The upshot of the matter was that he was asked to resign:* outcome, result, conclusion, culmination, end, final development, eventuality, consequence; sequel, aftermath, outgrowth, after-effect, offshoot, *Slang* pay-off.

◇ *Word origin: Upshot* was originally an archery term, meaning the final shot in a match. This use of *up* to mean the end or conclusion is also found in such phrases as *The time is up* (concluded, run out, ended) and *The game's up* (finished).

upstanding *adj.* **1** *Only one of the twelve trees is now upstanding:* standing up, tall, erect; upright, straight, perpendicular, on end, vertical. **2** *Arthur is an upstanding member of the community:* upright, honourable, trustworthy, high-principled, virtuous, righteous, good, honest, ethical, moral, truthful, true.

urban *adj. Liverpool, Greater Manchester, Sheffield and Birmingham are large urban areas:* city, metropolitan, municipal, civic, heavily populated.

◇ *Word origin: Urban* and *urbane* come from Latin *urbs,* city, and its adjective *urbanus,* of a city. Although nowadays they have different meanings, *urbane* was originally used in the sense of our word *urban. Urban* first appeared in the early seventeenth century, and gradually began to displace *urbane,* which in turn developed the sense suave or polished (of manners).

urbane *adj. The new art director is a consummately urbane man:* suave, elegant, polished, smooth, sophisticated, cosmopolitan, civilized, refined, cultivated, gracious, courtly, gallant, genteel, chivalrous, gentlemanly, diplomatic, tactful, politic, courteous, mannerly, well-mannered, well-bred.

Ant. crude, coarse, rough, rude, boorish, unrefined, unpolished, uncultivated, unsophisticated, tactless, discourteous, impolite; rustic, cloddish, countrified, provincial.

◇ *Usage note:* Don't confuse *urbane* and *urban. Urbane* means refined, courteous, suave: *The ambassador is very urbane. Urban* means in or of a city: *Millions were spent on urban renewal. What was once farmland is now an urban area.* See also Word origin at URBAN.

urchin *n. The urchins threw snowballs at passing cars:* young rogue, mischievous boy, whippersnapper, imp, gamin, (*fem*) gamine, brat; homeless boy, street arab, young hooligan, young tough, juvenile delinquent, *Slang* guttersnipe; boy, lad, laddie, youth, youngster, stripling, young fellow, whelp, young pup.

Ant. young gentleman, little Lord Fauntleroy, sissy.

urge *v.* **1** *The riders urged their horses up the steep hill:* drive, goad, prod, spur, push, force, press, poke, prick, *Slang* egg on; hasten, speed, accelerate, quicken. **2** *She urged the members to pay their subscriptions promptly:* beseech, implore, plead with, exhort, petition, entreat, request, appeal to, supplicate, importune, press, prevail upon, solicit; coax, persuade, convince, sway. **3** *The Tory M.P. urged the adoption of his housing bill:* argue for, advocate, recommend, advise, counsel, prescribe, suggest, push for, champion, support strongly, back.

—n. **4** *Father has an urge to visit Africa. What strange urge caused him to leave his job?:* impulse, desire, yearning, longing, craving, hankering, itch, yen, wish, fancy, hunger, thirst, passion; motive, motivation, reason, incentive, stimulus, drive, provocation, dictate, inducement, prompting, pressure.

Ant. 1 hinder, hold back, deter, prevent, restrain. **2** order, demand, command, require, force, coerce; discourage. **3** oppose, object to.

urgent *adj.* **1** *The operator said that the call was urgent:* pressing, important, serious, requiring immediate attention, compelling, essential, grave, crucial, critical, momentous, weighty; imperative, obligatory, compulsory, necessary, required, indispensable. **2** *The charity made an urgent appeal for funds:* earnest, intense, ardent, heartfelt, wholehearted, demanding, insistent, zealous, fervent, passionate, spirited, pleading, beseeching.

Ant. 1 unnecessary, unimportant, trivial, paltry, insignificant, inconsequential, trifling, facetious. **2** weak, feeble, half-hearted, lukewarm, indifferent, perfunctory, spiritless, laconic, apathetic, impassive, nonchalant, lackadaisical.

usage *n.* **1** *Usage dictates that the host sit at the head of the table:* custom, tradition, convention, etiquette, practice, good form, normal procedure, habit; system, method, mode, manner. **2** *In slang usage "rip off" means "steal":* way of using words. **3** *Owing to careless usage, the car lasted for only two years:* use, treatment, care, handling, operation, employment, manipulation; management, control.

use *v.* **1** *Do you know how to use a chain saw? Please use the back door when making deliveries. You'll have to use all your strength to force that door open:* make use of, put to use, operate, employ, work, manipulate, handle, ply, wield; utilize, apply, exercise, exert, resort to, have recourse to, avail oneself of, take advantage of, profit by, capitalize on, make the most of, exploit. **2** *The car used too much petrol. She used all her money on gaudy jewellery:* consume, expend, spend; deplete, drain, exhaust, run through, devour, swallow up, sap; squander, waste, dissipate, fritter away, throw away. **3** *He complains that she has used him badly:* treat, behave toward, act toward, deal with; handle, manipulate.

—n. **4** *We've had a lot of use out of that old telly. The poet is noted for his use of alliteration:* service, serviceability, operation, usage, usefulness, employment, work, function, enjoyment; application, utilization, handling, exercise. **5** *What's the use of working so hard if no one cares? An electric typewriter would be of no use to me in getting this work done:* good, value, worth, profit, benefit, advantage, avail; usefulness, service, help, aid, convenience.

Ant. 2 save, conserve, preserve. **4** disuse, unemployment. **5** bad, detriment, disadvantage, loss, drawback, obstacle, hindrance, futility.

useful *adj. An electric blender is always useful in the kitchen:* practical, serviceable, functional, utilitarian; helpful, beneficial, advantageous, worthwhile, valuable, profitable; effective, convenient, handy, time-saving.

useless *adj. This knife is useless for cutting bread. It's useless to speculate what might have been:* of no use, unusable, worthless, unserviceable, non-functional, unhelpful, ineffectual, impracticable, inadequate, inefficient, incompetent, futile, fruitless, unavailing, unproductive, profitless, bootless.

usher *n.* **1** *The usher showed us to our seats:* one who escorts people to seats, escort; guide, conductor, leader, director; porter; doorkeeper, gatekeeper.

—v. **2** *The councillor ushered the visiting dignitaries into the Town Hall:* escort, guide, show, conduct, convoy, attend, direct, lead, squire. **3** *The rising sun ushered in a new day:* herald, introduce, announce, proclaim; precede, preface, inaugurate, launch, *Slang* ring in.

usual *adj. He handled the situation with his usual tact. The play had the usual boy-meets-girl plot:* customary, accustomed, expected, familiar, habitual, normal, wonted, established, well-established; typical, ordinary, routine, common, commonplace, regular, standard,

stock, traditional, conventional, orthodox, prescribed, oft-repeated, popular, run-of-the-mill, trite, hackneyed, threadbare.
Ant. unusual, uncommon, exceptional, unique, singular, individual, rare, extraordinary, unconventional, unorthodox, novel, new, fresh, out of the way, off-beat, *Slang* far-out.

"The maxim of the British people is 'Business as usual'." — *Winston Churchill*

---

usurp *v. The duke tried to usurp the throne. Little by little the assistant began to usurp his boss's authority:* seize illegally, take unlawfully, steal, grab; take for oneself, appropriate, pre-empt, arrogate, encroach upon, infringe upon.
Ant. give up, surrender, yield, relinquish, renounce.

utilitarian *adj. A good cloth coat is more utilitarian than a fur one:* useful, practical, serviceable, functional, sensible; efficient, workable, effective; convenient, handy, beneficial, advantageous, valuable, profitable; severely practical, unlovely, not luxurious.
Ant. useless, purposeless, pointless, nugatory.

utility *n.* **1** *Living in a flat we miss the utility of a basement and an attic:* usefulness, use, service, availability, function; benefit, advantage, aid, help, avail, convenience. **2** *What are your monthly bills for the basic utilities?:* public service; (*variously*) gas, electricity, telephone, public transport.
—adj. **3** *Ray is one of the two utility players in the squad:* alternate, substitute, surrogate, secondary; extra, accessory, non-specific, movable, additional, supplementary, auxiliary.
Ant. **1** uselessness, worthlessness, futility, folly; disadvantage, inconvenience, drawback. **3** main, primary, prime, first, first-class, original, basic, essential.

utilize *v. If we are to avoid an oil shortage we need more machines that can utilize solar energy:* use, make use of, put to use, employ, take advantage of, turn to account, make the most of, capitalize on, exploit, put into service, bring into play; avail oneself of, profit by, resort to, have recourse to.
◇ *Usage note: Utilize* does mean to make use of: *Can you utilize a computer in your work? Is there any way in which we can utilize this old bus in a children's play area?* However, don't say or write *utilize* as an elegant replacement for *use:* don't use it when a simple *use* will do. Thus, *The students will use* (not "utilize") *the new library often. The director used* (not "utilized") *his deciding vote.*

utmost *adj.* **1** *I have the utmost confidence in his ability. Secrecy is of the utmost importance:* greatest, maximum, highest; foremost, chief, major, main, principal, predominant, paramount, prime, primary, first, leading, sovereign, supreme, pre-eminent, cardinal, capital.
—n. **2** *The new cruiser provided the utmost in luxury:* ultimate, last word, best, acme, zenith, peak, tiptop, *Slang* tops, the most.

Utopia *n. Cornwall is my idea of Utopia:* ideal life, perfect bliss, supreme happiness; perfect place, heaven, seventh heaven, paradise, the Garden of Eden, Shangri-la.
Ant. hell, hell on earth.
◇ *Word origin: Utopia* comes from Sir Thomas More's *Utopia* (1516), which describes an imaginary island of that name having a perfect social and political system and providing an ideal, paradisiacal life for its inhabitants. Where did Sir Thomas More get the name *Utopia?* From Greek *ou* (not) + *topos* (place), hence "No-place."

utter[1] *adj. With Mother away the house is in utter confusion:* complete, total, absolute, sheer, thorough, downright, outright, out and out, entire, perfect, pure, unrelieved, unqualified, unmodified, unmitigated, unchecked.
Ant. partial, moderate, slight, relative, reasonable, limited, qualified, passable, tolerable.
◇ *Word origin: Utter*[1] and *utterly* come from the old English comparative of *ūt,* out, hence literally means "outer, toward the outer limits."

utter[2] *v. He sat there without uttering a word. Don't utter a word of this to anyone:* speak, say, voice, pronounce, articulate, enunciate, vocalize, talk, express, emit, deliver; disclose, reveal, divulge, tell, state, proclaim, declare.
Ant. be mute, remain silent, keep quiet, keep mum; keep secret, keep confidential, conceal.

utterly *adv. The party was utterly delightful:* thoroughly, entirely, fully, completely, totally, wholly, absolutely, perfectly, downright, outright, extremely, just, to the nth degree.
Ant. partly, partially, somewhat, moderately, a little, rather, reasonably, passably, fairly, tolerably.

uttermost *adj.* **1** *The explorers reached the uttermost limits of the ice-pack:* outermost, farthest.
—n. **2** *The oarsmen strained to the uttermost of their strength:* utmost, extreme limit, maximum.

V

vacancy *n.* **1** *He peered over the cliff-edge into vacancy:* empty space, void, gap, opening, hole, hollow, cavity, breach, fissure, crevice. **2** *The vacancy of the house dates from last year:* emptiness, vacantness. **3** *All of these guest-houses have signs up saying "No vacancies":* unoccupied place, vacant quarters, room to let, apartment to let, house to let, office to let; housing, lodging, abode. **4** *The personnel department is trying to fill a vacancy in the servicing department:* unfilled position, available job, post, opening, situation, place.
Ant. 2 occupation, occupancy.

> **Exploring the Word:** *Vacuum, vacuous, vacant, vacate, evacuate, void, avoid, vacation, vain, vanity* and *vaunt* all come from Latin *vacare,* to empty, and its adjectival form *vacuus,* empty. Thus a *vacuum* is an empty space, a *vacuity;* a *vacuous* remark is one empty of intelligence; *vacant* means empty, especially of occupants; and *vacate* and *evacuate* mean to make empty or vacant; while a *void* is an empty space and to *void* means to empty, or empty of force, to make invalid (as in the expression *null and void*), and *avoid* means to make empty by keeping away. *Vacation* comes from the same Latin base and literally means an empty period, i.e. a period unoccupied with work or duty, a holiday. *Vain, vanity,* and *vaunt* also come from the same base. *Vain* means empty of value, having no real basis, useless (as in the phrase *vain hopes*) or being puffed up with *vanity,* which means empty conceit, *vainglory;* finally, *vaunt* means to make an empty boast or ostentatious display.

vacant *adj.* **1** *Do you know of a vacant room? By the end of the game the terraces were almost vacant:* unoccupied, empty, unfilled, not in use, for rent, for lease, to let, tenantless; deserted, uninhabited, abandoned, forsaken; unfurnished, clear, open. **2** *Since retiring, Father has had many vacant hours to fill:* unoccupied, free, leisure, idle, unemployed, unengaged, unencumbered. **3** *Idle passers-by gave the arguing men a vacant stare:* blank, expressionless, uncomprehending, empty, vacuous, vapid, wooden, dull, dead-pan, poker-faced; incurious, indifferent, unconcerned, apathetic, aloof, detached, blasé.
Ant. 1, 2 occupied, filled, taken, engaged, full, booked-up, crowded, packed. **1** rented, leased, in use, inhabited; crammed, jammed. **2** busy, employed. **3** expressive, comprehending, meaningful, thoughtful, reflective; animated, alert, lively; interested, concerned, engrossed, rapt.

vacate *v.* **1** *We have to vacate these offices by December 31st:* give up possession of, give up, quit, leave, withdraw from, depart from, evacuate, empty; relinquish, surrender, hand over, resign, abdicate.
Ant. occupy, move into, take possession of, fill, possess, employ, retain, keep, hold, hang on to.

vacation *n. Most students try to find jobs during the summer vacation:* leave, rest, holiday, intermission; academic intermission, judicial intermission, recess; furlough, *Informal* time off, leave of absence, sabbatical, *French* vacances.
Ant. work-time, work; academic year, term-time; court session; active duty.

vacillate *v. He seemed certain about it yesterday, but today he's vacillating:* waver, be irresolute, hesitate, be unsettled, be doubtful, be changeable, fluctuate, falter, not know one's own mind, shilly-shally, hum and haw, blow hot and cold.
Ant. be determined, be resolute, be steadfast, be certain, be settled.
◇ *Spelling tip: Vacillate* means to waver between *two* opinions. Remember that *vacillate* also has *two l's.*

vagabond *n.* **1** *During the Depression of the 1930's many men became vagabonds:* wanderer, roamer, rover, rambler, wayfarer, itinerant, floater, nomad, gipsy, migrant; vagrant, tramp, *Archaic* knight of the road.
—*adj.* **2** *The students spent a vagabond year hitch-hiking through Europe:* wandering, roaming, roving, rambling, wayfaring, footloose, itinerant, nomadic, journeying, travelling, transient, drifting, straying, vagrant, homeless; carefree, bohemian.
Ant. 1 householder, tenant; worker, businessman. **2** non-travelling, settled, ensconced, resident.

"Vagrants who on falsehood live,
Skill'd in smooth tales, and artful to deceive."
—*Alexander Pope*

---

vagrant *n.* **1** *Police kept a close watch on the drunkards and vagrants:* person with no permanent address, homeless person; person with no means of support; itinerant, floater, wanderer, roamer, rover, vagabond, knight of the road, nomad, migrant; tramp; beggar, loafer.
—*adj.* **2** *The old prospector had led a vagrant life:* roaming, roving, rambling, wandering, itinerant, peripatetic, nomadic, vagabond; homeless.

vague *adj. The agreement between the two countries is vague, but diplomats are working out the details. The man was rather vague about his past:* not definite, indefinite, inexplicit, unclear, imprecise, ill-defined, undetailed, uncertain,

unsettled, undetermined, confused, unsure, fuzzy, hazy, nebulous, unspecific, unspecified, loose, general, random, casual.
Ant. definite, explicit, clear, clear-cut, precise, specific, distinct, well-defined, detailed, express, settled, determined, fixed.

Exploring the Word: Both a *vagabond* and a *vagrant* are wanderers, though *vagabond* can have a somewhat romantic connotation while *vagrant* has a less appealing one, that of a homeless person without visible means of support. Both words come from Latin *vagari,* to wander, which also gives as *vague,* literally wandering, drifting, hence inconstant, uncertain. *Astray* and *extravagant* both come from Latin *extra,* beyond, plus the Latin verb *vagari,* to wander, hence, to *go astray* or to *lead someone astray* means to wander or lead someone beyond acceptable limits or away from the right path into error or evil, while *extravagant* means having wandered beyond the bounds of need, reason, or good taste.

vain *adj.* **1** *Ruth is very vain about her appearance:* proud, too concerned, self-satisfied, self-admiring, conceited, arrogant, puffed-up, vainglorious, pompous, self-important, *Slang* stuck-up; egotistical, supercilious, boastful, disdainful, cocky, swaggering, dandyish. **2** *The rescuers made a vain attempt to reach the sinking boat. Playing cards seems a vain pastime to me:* unsuccessful, unavailing, useless, futile, fruitless, bootless, ineffectual, ineffective, unprofitable, profitless; nugatory, worthless, trifling, pointless, time-wasting, without merit, idle, foolish, silly, superficial.
Ant. 1 modest, humble, unconcerned, unsatisfied; meek, unsure, shy, bashful. **2** successful, victorious, useful, fruitful, effective, expedient, serviceable; profitable, beneficial, beneficient, worthwhile; serious, substantial, valid, worthy.
◇ *Usage note: Vain, vein,* and *vane* all sound alike and can cause problems. *Vain* means conceited or useless: *Don't be so vain, After one vain attempt to start the car, he gave up.* A *vein* is a blood-vessel: *varicose veins.* A *vane* is a direction-pointer: *a weather-vane.*

valedictory *adj. The graduation ceremony will end with a valedictory address by the most successful student:* farewell, parting, leave-taking, departing; final, last, terminal, ultimate, conclusive.

valiant *adj. No knight was more valiant than Sir Lancelot:* courageous, brave, dauntless, undaunted, intrepid, valorous, heroic, bold, fearless, unafraid, daring, unflinching, lion-hearted, stout-hearted, stalwart, resolute; chivalrous, gallant, knightly, noble, worthy.
Ant. cowardly, craven, fearful, faint-hearted.
◇ *Word origin: Valiant* has been used in English since the beginning of the 14th century. It came into English, as did many other words denoting a chivalrous, aristocratic and refined existence, from Old French, in this case from Old French *vailant.* It comes ultimately from Latin *valere* to be worth, and thus *worthy* is a modern synonym reflecting exactly the original meaning.

valid *adj.* **1** *Do you have a valid reason for being late? This seems to be a valid solution to the problem:* acceptable, suitable, proper, fitting, applicable, effective, accurate, truthful, genuine, sound, well-grounded, well-founded, substantial, realistic, logical, good, convincing, forceful, compelling, decisive, weighty, strong, powerful. **2** *Such a contract is not valid in this country:* legally binding, having legal force, legal, legalized, lawful, licit, being in effect, official, legitimate, authoritative, authentic, constitutional.
Ant. 1 unacceptable, unsuitable, improper, unfitting, unapplicable, ineffective, false, inaccurate, untrue, *Informal* phoney; bogus, sham, unfounded, baseless, insubstantial, illogical, unrealistic, unforceful, weak. **2** invalid, void, null, inoperative, illegal, unlawful, illicit, unofficial, illegitimate.

validate *v. You must sign the driving-licence to validate it:* make valid, make legally binding, make legal, legalize, make lawful, make official, authorize, certify, stamp, ratify; enact, confirm, countersign, witness, authenticate, verify, corroborate, substantiate, sanction, warrant; put into effect.
Ant. invalidate, cancel, void, annul, terminate.

validity *n.* **1** *His argument seems to have a great deal of validity:* soundness, grounds, factual foundation, substance, logic, convincingness, force, weight, strength, power, potency, accuracy, truthfulness, authenticity, conclusiveness; acceptability, suitability, applicability, effectiveness. **2** *The lawyer questioned the validity of the contract:* legality, legal force, power; authority, authenticity, legitimacy, right, properness, correctness.
Ant. 1 unsoundness, weakness, flaws, lies, falsity, inaccuracy, ineffectiveness. **2** illegality, illegitimacy.

valley *n. The town nestled in a valley:* low region between mountains, river-valley, river-basin, basin; dell, dale, glade, glen, hollow, bottom, dip, ravine, gully, gorge, defile, divide, chasm, chine, gap, cut.
Ant. mountain, mount, peak, cliff, bluff, slope, ridge, hill, hillock, hummock, knoll, rise, height.

valour *n. The soldier was decorated for his valour under fire:* bravery, courage, dauntlessness, fearlessness, heroism, boldness, daring, fortitude; mettle, grit, spunk, nerve, guts; pluck, gallantry, chivalry.
Ant. cowardice, fear, fearfulness, timidity, pusillanimity, baseness, ignobility.

valuable *adj.* **1** *Friendship is a most valuable asset throughout life. Let me give you some valuable advice:* invaluable, worthwhile, precious, important, significant, priceless, treasured, prized, valued, esteemed, admired, respected; useful, beneficial, helpful, advantageous, profitable, good, fruitful, serviceable, utilitarian. **2** *Her grandmother left her a valuable ring:* of great monetary value, costly, expensive, highly-priced, dear, precious, priceless.

Ant. 1 worthless, valueless, unimportant, insignificant, trivial, unesteemed, disliked; useless, pointless, fruitless, unprofitable, silly, trifling. **2** cheap, inexpensive, worthless.

◇ *Usage note: Valuable* means worth a great deal or very useful: *This is a valuable necklace, Ken is a valuable player to have in the team. Valued* means esteemed, cherished: *Louise is a valued friend.*

value *n.* **1** *Mother attaches a great deal of value to good manners. A knowledge of typing is of great value in this job:* merit, worth, importance, significance, esteem, respect, admiration; prestige, greatness, excellence, superiority; use, usefulness, benefit, help, advantage, profit, service, utility. **2** *The expert set a value of £10,000 on the painting:* monetary worth, face value, market price; amount, cost, charge, rate, appraisal, assessment, estimation. **3 values** *I've never understood his set of values. Primitive peoples have different values from ours:* ideals, standards, moral code, code of ethics, mores; institutions, customs, rules, beliefs, practices, conventions.

—*v.* **4** *The assessor valued the house at £40,000:* assess, assay, appraise, evaluate, set a value on; fix the price of, price, compute; count, weigh, judge, size up, reckon, rate. **5** *I value his opinion:* regard highly, prize, respect, treasure, esteem, hold in high esteem, cherish, revere, set store by, admire, appreciate.

Ant. 1 unimportance, insignificance, inferiority; disadvantage, worthlessness, uselessness. **5** disregard, be contemptuous of; undervalue, underestimate.

valued *adj. Jennifer was my most valued friend:* highly-regarded, esteemed, prized, treasured, respected, cherished, appreciated, revered.

◇ *Usage note:* See VALUABLE.

van[1] *n. All the furniture had been put into the removal van:* small lorry, lorry, truck, trailer, minivan, pantechnicon.

◇ *Word origin: Van[1]* is a shortened form of *caravan,* which besides meaning a group of animals or vehicles travelling together also means a covered vehicle such as a lorry. With the growth of the railway system in the 19th century, *van* came also to be applied to certain specific carriages or wagons, as the *luggage van* or the *guard's van.*

van[2] *n. Tanks were in the van of the army's advance. Maxine was in the van of women's liberation:* vanguard, advance guard, avant-garde, forefront, front rank, first line, foremost division, head; front of an army, scout, sentinel, picket.

◇ *Word origin: Van[2]* is a shortened form of *vanguard.*

vandal *n. Many of the city's buses were defaced by vandals:* wilful destroyer, despoiler; looter, plunderer, pillager, ravager, raider, marauder.

◇ *Word origin: Vandal* comes from the name of the *Vandals,* a Germanic people who ravaged Gaul, overran Spain and North Africa, and pillaged Rome in the 5th century A.D.

vanguard *n.* **1** *The vanguard was sent ahead to clear the woods of enemy snipers:* advance guard, avant-garde, van, front rank, forward troops, foremost division, first line, spearhead, forefront. **2** *The vanguard of the Cubist movement praised the merits of the young painter:* avant-garde, forefront, taste-makers.

◇ *Word origin: Vanguard* comes from French *avant* (before) + *garde* (guard), the advance guard.

vanish *v.* **1** *The aeroplane vanished into the clouds:* disappear, become invisible, be lost to sight, dematerialize. **2** *His anger vanished and he burst out laughing:* disappear, cease, expire, perish, end, terminate, die, die away, die out, fade away, evaporate, melt away, pass away, dissolve.

Ant. 1 appear, loom, come into view; materialize. **2** arrive, commence, begin, start.

vanity *n.* **1** *She is pretty, but that's no excuse for such vanity:* pride, conceit, self-conceit, self-love, self-admiration, self-praise, narcissism, egotism, vainglory. **2** *The minister's sermon was on the vanity of amassing worldly goods:* lack of real value, worthlessness, uselessness, emptiness, hollowness, inanity, folly, idleness, futility, fruitlessness, unsubstantialness, superficiality, sham, falsity; mirage, delusion. **3 vanity bag, case** *She took out her vanity bag and began powdering her nose:* compact, powder box.

Ant. 1 self-hate, self-abasement, masochism; humility, modesty, meekness. **2** value, worth, usefulness, meaningfulness.

"Vanity dies hard; in some obstinate cases it outlives the man." —*Robert Louis Stevenson*

---

vanquish *v. The king's army vanquished the rebels:* defeat, conquer, overcome, overpower, crush, overwhelm, triumph over, beat, thrash, drub, lick, rout, master, subdue, subjugate, quash, get the upper hand over.

Ant. be defeated, lose, surrender, capitulate, give up, yield, submit, succumb, bow down, knuckle under.

vapid *adj. What a vapid young man! She made some vapid remarks about the weather:* lifeless, dull, flat, insipid, bland, flavourless, empty; tame, uninspiring, unsatisfying, colourless, lame, limp, stale, characterless, pointless, meaningless.

Ant. lively, exciting, inspiring, satisfying, colourful.

◇ *Word origin: Vapid,* like *fade,* comes from Latin *vapidus,* stale.

vapour *n. A thin coat of vapour began to collect on the windscreen:* moisture, mist, dew, fog, steam; smoke, smog; fumes.

◇ *Word origin: Vapour* comes from the Latin word for steam, *vapor.* This also gives us our word *evaporate.*

variable *adj.* **1** *It was a cloudy day with variable winds. Her affections tend to be variable:* changeable, changing, shifting, fluctuating; fickle, fitful, spasmodic, unstable, capricious, wavering, inconstant. **2** *A studio can deal with a variable number of artists at one time — anything up to ten:* indefinite, unsettled, diverse, different, uneven, unlike; alterable, mutable.

—n. **3** *There are several variables that could change our plans:* changeable factor.

Ant. 1 constant, unchanging, stable, steady. **2** invariable, firm, settled, unalterable, immutable, alike. **3** constant.

variant *adj.* **1** *"Gramme" is a variant spelling of "gram":* derived, different, modified, altered, transformed, divergent.

—n. **2** *The song is just a variant of an old folk melody:* variation, different form, modification, alteration, transformation, departure; take-off, spoof.

Ant. 1, 2 original. **1** basic, fundamental, root, earliest, underived, intrinsic, prime, primary, first, preferred. **2** archetype, prototype, pattern, model, source.

variation *n. We need some variation in our daily routine:* variety, change, difference, diversity, innovation, modification, transformation, alteration, departure, variant, mutation, metamorphosis; disagreement, discrepancy, divergency, deviation; rate of change, amount of change.

Ant. uniformity, sameness, regularity, consistency, permanence.

varied *adj. The shop carries a varied selection of merchandise:* diversified; diverse; assorted, miscellaneous, variegated, heterogeneous, sundry, unlike, mixed.

Ant. uniform, standardized, homogeneous.

variety *n.* **1** *Variety is the spice of life:* change, diversity, diversification, difference, variation, dissimilarity, non-uniformity, unconformity. **2** *The Imperial War Museum has a wide variety of exhibits on display:* assortment, medley, miscellany, mixture, collection, mélange, pastiche, motley, multiplicity, heterogeneity, hotchpotch, jumble, hash, patchwork, omnium gatherum. **3** *The orchard grows several varieties of apple:* kind, type, sort, classification; class, category, breed, strain, stock, species, subspecies, genus, genre, brand, group, division, subdivision, denomination; race, tribe, family.

Ant. 1, 2 sameness, uniformity, homogeneity, standardization, conformity; similarity, likeness.

various *adj.* **1** *We've had various types of cars but we prefer an estate model:* different, sundry, varied, diverse, divers, assorted, dissimilar, miscellaneous, other. **2** *Various people have expressed disagreement with his proposal:* numerous, many, countless, innumerable, myriad, multitudinous, multifarious; several.

Ant. 1 same, like, alike, identical, uniform.

varnish *n.* **1** *What's the best kind of varnish for this chair?:* resin solution; stain, lacquer, gloss.

—v. **2** *Varnish the bookcase and give it a coat of wax:* stain, lacquer, gloss. **3** *She tends to varnish the truth to make a more interesting story:* gild, embellish, adorn, enhance, disguise; mitigate, soften, make allowance for, gloss over, excuse, smooth over; cover, conceal.

Ant. 3 be frank, be candid, be open; lay bare.

vary *v.* **1** *Let's vary the routine and drive to work by a different route:* change, alter, diversify, modify, shift. **2** *Television sets vary widely in price. This marigold varies from the norm in being minute:* differ, be unlike, contrast, fluctuate, alternate; deviate, diverge, depart, veer; disagree, disaccord, dissent.

Ant. 1 keep unchanged, keep uniform, regulate, standardize. **2** conform, be uniform, be similar, be alike, be constant, be stable, correspond, harmonize; agree, comply with, reconcile with, fall in with, go along with.

vast *adj. The camel caravan crossed the vast expanse of the Sahara:* extensive, wide, widespread, far-flung, far-reaching, boundless, unbounded, measureless, immeasurable, unlimited, limitless, endless, interminable, immense, huge, enormous, tremendous, stupendous, gigantic, colossal, very large, very big, monstrous; spacious, capacious, voluminous.

Ant. limited, narrow; small, little, tiny; moderate-sized, modest.

◇ *Word origin: Vast,* like *waste,* comes from Latin *vastus,* desert, waste, emptiness.

vault[1] *n.* **1** *The vault of the cathedral is 150 feet above the floor:* dome, arched roof, arched ceiling, arch; arcade, cupola. **2** *The bank doesn't open its vault until 9 a.m.:* strong-room; wall-safe, safe, strong-box. **3** *The squire was buried in the family vault:* burial chamber, mausoleum, crypt, sepulchre, tomb; ossuary, catacomb.

vault[2] *v.* **1** *The boy vaulted the fence and ran into the woods:* hurdle, jump, jump over, leap over, spring over, bound, clear; pole-vault.

—n. **2** *One vault and he was over the hedge and gone:* jump, leap, spring, bound, hurdle.

Ant. 1 crawl under, creep beneath.

vaunt *v. She always vaunts her father's wealth:* boast about, brag of, crow about, gloat over, exult in, talk big about, give oneself airs about, blow one's own trumpet; flaunt, show off, make a display of, strut.

Ant. decry, disparage, detract; conceal, repress, suppress, keep quiet about.

veer *v. The car veered suddenly to avoid hitting the dog. As the wind veered to the west it began to rain:* change direction (of wind, clockwise), swerve, wheel, turn, turn aside, shift, dodge, curve, drift, *Nautical* go about, come round, tack, yaw, jibe.

Ant. go straight, go in a straight line, make a bee-line for; hold course.

vegetable *n. Dinner includes soup, entrée, salad, and two vegetables:* edible herbaceous plant; legume, produce, greens.

> **Exploring the Word:** *Vegetable* comes from Latin *vegere,* to be lively, full of life, not because the Romans knew they were full of vitamins but because vegetables grew so vigorously. The names of specific vegetables are also interesting: *asparagus* comes from Greek *aspharagos,* shoot, sprout; *cabbage* is from French *caboche,* head, which goes back to Latin *caput* head, from which we also get *captain, capital,* and *decapitate; cauliflower* comes from modern Latin *cauliflora,* flowering cabbage; *lettuce* is from Latin *lactus,* milk, because of its milky juice (the same Latin word gives us *lactation*); while *onion* is from Latin *unio,* oneness, unity, union, and (in jewellers' language) "large pearl." Country people in Roman times also used the word in the sense "onion." *Parsley* comes from Greek *petrosel̄inon,* rock parsley (Greek *petrā,* rock + *sel̄inon,* parsley), perhaps because it grew along the rocky banks of a river; and *parsnip* is from Latin *pastinaca,* carrot + Old English *nāp,* turnip, hence literally is a "turnip carrot." *Potato* comes to us via Spanish from the Arawakan (a West Indies language) *batata,* a sweet potato; *tomato* also comes to us via Spanish, from the Nahuatl (Aztec) word for it, *tomatl;* while *spinach* comes to us also via Spanish from Arabic *isfināj.* Thus, the Spanish conquest of Latin America and the Caribbean islands brought us *potato* and *tomato,* while the Moors introduced *spinach* into Spain, whence it spread throughout Europe.

vegetation *n.* **1** *The abandoned property was overgrown with vegetation:* plant life, plants, flora, shrubbery, foliage, herbage, verdure, leaves; grass, weeds, vegetable growth. **2** *Complete vegetation is my idea of a real holiday:* inactivity, idleness, loafing, sloth, torpor, lethargy, sluggishness, languor, languidness, indolence, inert existence; dormancy, hibernation, rustication.

vehement *adj. He's a vehement supporter of progressive education:* ardent, fervent, fervid, intense, fierce, passionate, impassioned, emotional, excited, violent, furious, hot, hot-headed, fiery, frenzied, agitated, stormy, tempestuous; enthusiastic, zealous, vigorous, fanatic, fanatical, rabid, wild, eager, earnest.

Ant. indifferent, unconcerned, mild, weak, feeble, lukewarm, half-hearted, dispassionate, impassive, subdued, calm, cool, quiet, placid, serene.

◇ *Pronunciation tip: Vehement* is pronounced without the *h* sound, *VEE-a-ment.*

vehemently *adv. The two men argued vehemently:* ardently, fervently, intensely, passionately, excitedly, violently, furiously, fiercely, hotly, strongly, tempestuously, emotionally; enthusiastically, zealously, vigorously, fanatically, wildly, eagerly, earnestly.

Ant. indifferently, mildly, feebly, half-heartedly, impassively, calmly, coolly, quietly.

vehicle *n.* **1** *No vehicles are permitted inside the park:* conveyance, means of transport; (*variously*) motor vehicle, car, lorry, bus, train, plane, spacecraft, rocket, motor cycle, bicycle. **2** *Television has become a major vehicle for advertising:* medium, means, agent, agency, instrument, tool, intermediary, organ.

◇ *Pronunciation tip: Vehicle* is pronounced without the *h* sound: *VEE-ikle.*

veil *n.* **1** *The bride wore a veil of lace. A veil of fog covered the valley:* facial covering; cover, blanket, curtain, cloak, screen, cloud, mantle, shroud.

—*v.* **2** *A curtain of smog veiled the sun. The misleading report veiled the facts:* hide, conceal, cover, cloak, mask, screen, shroud, enwrap, envelop; dim, obscure, camouflage.

Ant. 2 expose, disclose, reveal, show, divulge; unveil, uncover, unwrap, strip, denude.

◇ *Spelling tip: Veil* follows the spelling rule of "*i* before *e* except after *c* or when sounded like *a* as in *neighbour* and *weigh.*" There is that *a* sound in *veil,* thus it is spelt *vEIl.*

vein *n.* **1** *He was so angry that the veins stood out on his forehead:* blood-vessel, capillary. **2** *There was a vein of coal running through the mountain:* stratum, stria, layer, seam, lode; streak, line, stripe, thread, rib. **3** *He spoke to the crowd in a humorous vein. The book has a vein of cynicism throughout:* mood, tone, manner, style; nature, character, disposition, complexion, temper, temperament, tendency, inclination, bent, predisposition, propensity, predilection; strain, streak, touch, hint.

—*v.* **4** *The dried mud was veined with cracks:* line, streak, mark, marble, stripe, furrow, rib, web, fleck.

◇ *Usage note:* See VAIN.

velocity *n.* **1** *Some hawks descend with terrific velocity on their prey:* rapidity, swiftness, speed, fleetness. **2** *The velocity with which the coup was*

carried out stunned the opposition: quickness, speediness, celerity, expedition.
◇ *Word origin: Velocity* comes from Latin *velox*, swift.

venal *adj. The venal politician had no thought of the public welfare:* willing to be bribed, bribable, corruptible, corrupt, dishonest; greedy, rapacious, avaricious, covetous, grasping, mercenary, money-grubbing, selfish, *Slang* shady, crooked, bent.
Ant. unbribable, incorruptible, honest; public-spirited, selfless, altruistic.
◇ *Usage note:* Don't confuse *venal* and *venial. Venal* means corruptible and implies greed that would lead one to sell one's honour and principles: *The venal magistrate was exposed and thrown in gaol.* On the other hand, *venial* means pardonable or forgivable: *A venial sin does not keep one out of Heaven.*

vend *v. The founder of this department store started by vending old clothes from a push-cart:* peddle, hawk, huckster, sell; retail, merchandise, deal in, trade in, market; auction, trade, barter.

vendor *n. The youth works as an ice-cream vendor at the fair. The company is the largest vendor of open ranges in the country:* seller, hawker, peddler, street peddler, huckster, monger, salesman, trader; retailer, wholesaler, dealer, merchandiser, supplier, purveyor; merchant, tradesman.
Ant. buyer, purchaser, customer.

veneer *n.* **1** *Apply a veneer of shellac to the coffee-table:* facing, façade, outer layer, layer, covering, coat, coating, overlay, wrapper, sheath, envelope, casing, jacket. **2** *Underneath her veneer of haughtiness she's actually very kind:* outward appearance, façade, front, show, mask, pretence.

venerable *adj. Bede, the theologian and historian (673–735), is called "the Venerable Bede":* worthy of respect, respected, venerated, revered, august, esteemed, honoured, admired; deserving respect because of age, elderly, aged, old, patriarchal, ancient, hoary, white-haired.
Ant. dishonourable, disreputable, shameful, ignominious, inglorious, infamous, dishonoured, discredited, disgraced; young, youthful, inexperienced, green, callow.

"I for one venerate a petticoat."
— *George Gordon Byron, Lord Byron*

---

venerate *v. As a child he venerated his grandparents:* revere, esteem, respect, honour, admire, idolize, adore, cherish, extol, glorify, look up to, treat with deference, pay homage to, worship, hallow.
Ant. scorn, disdain, contemn, despise, detest, hate, dishonour; disregard, slight, spurn.

vengeance *n. He swore vengeance for the murder of his brother:* revenge, reprisal, retaliation, avenging, retribution, revengefulness, a tooth for a tooth, an eye for an eye; vindictiveness, malevolence, implacability, ruthlessness.
◇ *Spelling tip:* The *-ea-* in *vengeance* can be a problem. If you remember that *avenge* ends in an *e* and add *-ance* to it you will get it right: (*a*) *vengE + Ance = vengEAnce.*

venial *adj. He wasn't perfect, but all his sins were venial ones:* forgivable, pardonable, excusable; justifiable, warrantable, allowable, defensible; slight, trivial, not serious.
Ant. mortal; unpardonable, unforgivable, inexpiable; inexcusable, unwarrantable, unjustifiable, indefensible; flagrant, infamous.
◇ *Usage note:* See VENAL.
◇ *Word origin: Venial* comes from Latin *venia*, forgiveness. Thus a *venial* sin is a lesser one that may be pardoned or forgiven, whilst a *mortal sin* is a greater one that incurs spiritual death unless repented of and forgiven.

venom *n.* **1** *The rattlesnake secretes venom through its fangs:* poisonous fluid; toxin, *Archaic* virus. **2** *He spewed out his venom in a series of poison-pen letters:* hate, hatred, bitterness, ill will, malevolence, maliciousness, malice, animosity, resentment, rancour, rancorousness, spite, spitefulness, acrimony, hostility, enmity, grudge, anger, ire, choler, spleen, gall; savagery, barbarity, brutality.
Ant. 1 antidote, antitoxin. **2** love, affection, friendliness, kindness, sweetness, goodwill, good feeling, amity, brotherly love, benevolence, humanitarianism, charity.

venomous *adj.* **1** *Some jellyfish are venomous:* poisonous, noxious, toxic; lethal, deadly, virulent. **2** *Why are some book reviews so venomous?:* spiteful, hateful, malicious, malevolent, resentful, rancorous, hostile, ill-disposed, malign, malignant; caustic, bitter, vicious, cruel, brutal, savage, bloodthirsty.
Ant. 1 non-poisonous, non-toxic. **2** loving, affectionate, friendly, kind, kindly, sweet, genial, benevolent, compassionate, charitable, magnanimous, forgiving.

vent *n.* **1** *Smoke poured out of the vent in the roof:* opening, outlet, aperture, vent-hole, hole, orifice, air hole; (*variously*) ventilator, chimney, flue, smoke-stack, spout, pipe; faucet, tap, spigot. **2** *The children need a vent for all that energy:* outlet, means of escape, means of exit. **3** *She gave vent to her wrath in a furious tirade:* expression, utterance, voice; declaration, disclosure, revelation, exposure.
Ant. 1 obstruction, closure, stoppage, impediment, check.

ventilate *v.* **1** *Open the window and ventilate the room:* provide with fresh air, circulate fresh air, air, air out; aerate, oxygenate. **2** *Members are asked not to ventilate club problems outside this meeting:* make widely known, broadcast, publicize, report, circulate, voice, declare, divulge, disseminate, spread abroad, spread, air, sow, bandy about, noise abroad; discuss, talk about, express, comment on, review, analyse, examine, criticize.

venture *n.* **1** *Speculating on the commodities market can be a costly venture:* endeavour, undertaking, enterprise, project; gamble, uncertainty, risk, speculation, plunge. —*v.* **2** *Nothing ventured, nothing gained:* risk, hazard, dare, chance, gamble, wager, undertake, endeavour, attempt, strive for, try. **3** *If I may venture an opinion, he'll never succeed:* advance, put forward, offer, proffer, tender, volunteer, submit, hold out; presume, take the liberty, make free with, make bold. **4** *Don't venture into the jungle without a guide:* travel, go, risk going, plunge.

Ant. 1 certainty, surety, security, stability, reliability; caution, safety, protection. **2** assure, secure, guarantee; save, safeguard, conserve, protect.

Exploring the Word: *Venture* and *venturesome* are shortened forms of *adventure* and *adventuresome,* which come from Latin *advenire* (Latin *ad-,* to + *venire,* to happen), hence something that comes to one, an occasion, especially something that comes with danger or risk. Latin *venire,* to come, to happen, gives us many words, including: *advent* and *event,* something that happens or comes to one; *avenue,* a way of coming, road, course; and *circumvent* (Latin *circum,* round), to move round something, side-step. Adding Latin *con-,* together, to *venire,* to come, to happen, gives us *convene,* to come together, assemble, *convenient,* coming together at the right time, and *inconvenient,* not coming at the right time; *convent,* a religious community where nuns live together; *convention,* a coming together of people or a custom or rule most people agree upon, and *conventional,* following customs established by general agreement.

venturesome *adj.* **1** *He's so venturesome that he'll try anything:* adventurous, ready to take risks, daring, bold, daredevil, audacious, rash, impulsive, impetuous, reckless, foolhardy; enterprising, ambitious, energetic, aggressive. **2** *Diving for sunken treasure is a very venturesome way of making a living:* dangerous, hazardous, risky, perilous, precarious, unsafe; uncertain, insecure, unsure, speculative, doubtful, dubious, questionable, ticklish, tricky.

Ant. 1 cautious, wary, timid, timorous, apprehensive, fearful, afraid, fearsome; reluctant, adverse, loath, unwilling. **2** safe, protected, guarded; certain, sure, secure, reliable, sound, dependable, stable, trustworthy, infallible.

veracity *n. I sometimes doubt his veracity. The veracity of the report is unquestionable:* truthfulness, adherence to truth, honesty, integrity, probity, candour, frankness, openness, sincerity, guilelessness, ingenuousness; truth, accuracy, correctness, exactness, verity, verisimilitude, exactitude.

Ant. untruthfulness, deception, deceit, duplicity, guile, mendacity; lie, falsehood, fiction, fabrication, error.

verbal *adj.* **1** *The book gives a good verbal picture of life in China. A verbal agreement is not as binding as a written contract:* of words, in words, expressed in words; (*loosely*) oral, spoken, voiced, vocal, unwritten. **2** *The "-ed" in "talked" is a verbal suffix:* of verbs; derived from a verb.

◇ *Usage note: Verbal* refers to both spoken and written communications. Thus *verbal orders* may be either spoken or written. If you want to be precise, don't use *verbal* to mean "spoken"—the word you want is *oral.* And the opposite of *written orders* or *written instructions* is not "verbal orders" or "verbal instructions" but *oral orders, oral instructions.* However, many people do use *verbal* to mean *oral,* and it is generally accepted in informal speech.

verbatim *adv., adj. The witness repeated the conversation verbatim. Give me a verbatim account of what was said:* word for word, exactly, in exactly the same words, letter for letter, chapter and verse; to the letter, literatim; literal, literally, exact, exactly, precise, precisely.

verbiage *n. The speaker bored everyone with his verbiage:* wordiness, long-windedness, verbosity, verboseness, volubility, grandiloquence, effusiveness, loquacity, rambling, garrulousness, prolixity.

verbose *adj. The chairman was so verbose that it took him an hour to tell a simple joke:* wordy, long-winded, voluble, effusive, grandiloquent, prolix, talkative, garrulous, loquacious.

Ant. terse, concise, succinct, pithy; reticent, curt, brusque.

verdict *n. Has the jury reached a verdict?:* decision, judgement, finding, opinion, determination, ruling, assessment, estimation, valuation, answer; adjudication, arbitration, arbitrament.

verge *n.* **1** *Buttercups and cowslips grew on the verge of the road. The child was on the verge of tears:* edge, border, brink, margin, rim, brim, hem, skirt, fringe, lip, ledge, flange; limit, bound, boundary, extreme, confine, end, terminus. —*v.* **2** *The farm verges on the parish boundary:* border, be on the brink, fringe, skirt, edge; be near, approach, approximate.

Ant. 1 centre, middle, midst, heart, depth.

verify *v. Several witnesses verified his alibi. Later findings verified the scientist's theory:* confirm, corroborate, substantiate, attest to, prove, establish, support, sustain; certify, guarantee, validate, authenticate, witness, document, testify to, vouch for, accredit.

Ant. disprove, deny, refute, dispute, confute,

contradict, controvert, gainsay, discredit; invalidate, subvert, falsify, misrepresent.

veritable *adj. The old professor is a veritable gold mine of information:* true, real, genuine, actual, bona fide, valid, authentic, absolute, complete, utter, positive, literal, unquestionable, unimpeachable, true-blue.

Ant. sham, spurious, feigned, false, deceptive, supposed, questionable, so-called, figurative.

vermin *n. pl.* **1** *The gamekeeper carried a .22 rifle to shoot vermin:* noxious animals and birds, pests; (*loosely*) mice, rats, snakes, voles, foxes, moles, weasels, owls, birds of prey, crows, etc. **2** *At night all sorts of vermin crawled out of the walls of the old house:* pestiferous insects, (*variously*) cockroaches, lice, fleas, bed-bugs, silver-fish, centipedes, termites, bugs, woodlice, spiders, ants.

vernacular *n.* **1** *The politician tried to appeal to the people by speaking in the vernacular:* common speech, everyday language, slang, natural speech, colloquial speech, informal speech; native language, native tongue, the vulgar tongue. **2** *The word "squealer" means "informer" in prison vernacular:* jargon, lingo, slang, cant, idiom, dialect, patois.

Ant. 1 formal speech, educated speech, literary language; foreign language, second language. **2** standard speech, received speech.

vernal *adj. The vernal equinox occurs on or about March 21st each year. Freesias are vernal flowers:* spring; springlike, fresh, new, green, youthful.

versatile *adj.* **1** *In order to repair barns, build fences, grow crops, and care for animals, a farmer must indeed be versatile. Leonard Bernstein is a versatile composer:* having many abilities, many-sided, all-round, multi-faceted, many-skilled, handy, adaptable, resourceful, protean; gifted, talented, accomplished, ingenious, proficient, clever, adroit, apt, able, expert. **2** *Have you seen this versatile new gadget for the kitchen?:* having many uses, having many applications.

Ant. 1, 2 specialized, limited.

verse *n.* **1** *Most of Shakespeare's works are in verse:* poetry, measure, meter. **2** *The child recited a verse:* little poem, rhyme, jingle. **3** *Let's sing the first and last verses of the hymn:* stanza, stave, strophe. **4** *The minister read several verses from the Book of Job:* division within a biblical chapter, passage of Scripture, line of Scripture.

versed *adj. The factory needs a man who's well versed in electro-engineering. The school turns out students versed in the classics:* experienced, practised, familiar with, having an intimate knowledge of, acquainted with, conversant with, at home with, skilled, skilful, expert, proficient, accomplished, competent, able, adept; schooled, taught, instructed, tutored, well-informed, well-read, enlightened, lettered, learned, scholarly, erudite.

Ant. inexperienced, unpractised, unfamiliar, unacquainted, green, raw, unfledged, callow, unskilled, unaccomplished, incompetent, inept; ignorant, untaught, unschooled.

version *n.* **1** *The two men gave different versions of the accident:* account, story, report, description, depiction, interpretation, side. **2** *The author wrote an up-to-date version of the Romeo and Juliet story:* rendering, adaptation. **3** *Keats read Chapman's version of Homer:* translation, rendering, paraphrase, re-creation.

vertical *adj.* **1** *The cliff rose in a vertical wall from the sea:* perpendicular, straight up and down, upright, sheer, plumb.

—*n.* **2** *The wall slants 10° from the vertical:* perpendicular, upright position, upright.

Ant. 1, 2 horizontal. **1** level with the ground; prostrate, flat, supine; slanting, sloping, inclined.

> **Exploring the Word:** Latin *vertere*, to turn, gives us dozens of words containing *-vert-* and *-vers-*, including: *versus*, against; *vertical*, turned up; *vertebra*, which originally meant a joint, where one bone "turns" on another, and hence *vertebrate*, an animal having a jointed backbone, and *invertebrate*, an animal that does not have such a backbone; *vertigo*, dizziness, a feeling that one's surroundings are turning round and round; *vertex*, the highest point or summit, where things "turn" from going up to coming back down: *vortex*, a mass of turning or swirling liquid or gas; *versatile*, turned towards many things, many-sided, hence having an aptitude for various things; *verse*, literally a "turn," hence a single metrical or rhythmical line, stanza, or self-contained passage, as in a poem, song, or piece of writing (as a *verse* from the Bible); *version*, an account told from a particular point of view, slant, or "turn"; and *verso*, the "turned" over or reverse side of a coin, medal, etc., or the left-hand page of a book or folded piece of paper.

vertigo *n. She felt a touch of vertigo and steadied herself against the wall:* dizziness, lightheadedness, swimming of the head, giddiness, reeling, unsteadiness, loss of equilibrium; fainting.

verve *n. The pianist played the concerto with tremendous verve:* liveliness, animation, spirit, vivacity, dash, vigour, energy, vim, élan, zip, gusto, zeal, relish, enthusiasm, eagerness, ardour, fervour, passion, fire, abandon, rapture, feeling, warmth, vehemence, force, drive, punch.

Ant. apathy, lethargy, languor, torpor, indolence, indifference, spiritlessness, calmness, half-heartedness, reluctance, dislike, disdain, scorn.

very *adv.* **1** *It was very nice of you to invite us:* extremely, exceedingly, quite, most, indeed, enormously, incalculably, truly, highly, greatly, supremely, hugely, superlatively, surpassingly, especially, eminently, wondrously, enormously, unduly, extravagantly, exorbitantly; terribly, awfully, frightfully, positively, powerfully, mighty, jolly. **2** *This is the very best bedspread we have in stock:* absolutely, decidedly, truly, unequivocally, entirely, completely, altogether, utterly, unconditionally.

—*adj.* **3** *That's the very girl I was telling you about:* same, selfsame, identical, precise, actual, exact; genuine, true, pure, real, authentic, unimpeachable, veritable, truthful; right, correct, literal. **4** *The very sight of clams makes him ill:* mere, sheer, simple, unqualified, unconditional, unmitigated; actual, bare, stark, plain; downright, utter.

◇ *Usage note:* Don't overuse *very.* You need not intensify or emphasize everything you say. Thus *We had a very good time, He's a very tall man, It very often rains in September* might lose little, if any, meaning or sincerity if you merely said *We had a good time, He's a tall man, It often rains in September.*

vessel *n.* **1** *The* Queen Elizabeth II *is one of the largest vessels afloat:* ship, boat, craft; liner, steamship, steamboat, ocean-liner, *French* paquebot. **2** *Cook the meat in a large vessel with a tightly-fitting lid:* utensil, receptacle, container; (*variously*) pot, bowl, jug, crock, jar, vase, tub, vat, barrel, keg, cask, butt, cauldron; glass, tumbler, cup, mug, carafe, flagon, goblet, beaker, tankard, decanter, flask; platter, dish, plate. **3** *The doctor said that I'd severed a vessel in my leg:* blood-vessel, vein, artery, capillary; duct, tube.

◇ *Word origin: Vessel* is from the diminutive of Latin *vas,* vessel, which also gives us our word *vase* and is found in such medical terms as *vascular* (pertaining to vessels or ducts in the body) and *vasectomy* (the surgical severing and/or tying-off of a small semen-conveying duct in the male, as a form of birth control).

vest *n.* **1** *Is the vest included with the suit?:* waistcoat, jacket, *Historical* jerkin, doublet. **2** *It's cold today, so you'll probably need a vest:* undershirt; T-shirt.

—*v.* **3** *The bishop was vested with ceremonial robes:* dress, robe, attire, clothe, garb, accoutre, apparel, array, bedeck, deck out, fit out, rig out; drape, enwrap, envelop. **4** *Most of the authority is vested in the board of directors:* place in control of, put into the hands of, put in the possession of.

Ant. 3 divest, strip, unfrock; disrobe, unclothe; uncover, expose, lay bare; dismantle.

◇ *Word origin: Vest* comes from French and Italian *veste,* whose source is Latin *vestis,* clothes, attire. The same Latin base gives us *vestment,* an article of clothing, especially an ecclesiastical garment or robe of state or office (a priest's *vestment* is the ritual garment worn during the celebration of the Mass).

vestal *adj.* **1** *In ancient Rome the vestal virgins tended the sacred fire in the temple of Vesta:* chaste, pure, virtuous, simple, unsophisticated, unworldly; undefiled, immaculate; maidenly, virgin, unmarried.

—*n.* **2** *The Vestals' house, known as the* Atrium Vestae, *was situated to the south-east of the Roman Forum:* virgin, maiden, chaste woman, pure woman.

"How happy is the blameless vestal's lot!
The world forgetting, by the world forgot."
—*Alexander Pope*

---

vested *adj. Each country has vested rights to the waters off its own shores:* permanent, complete, established, fixed, settled, indisputable, unquestionable, absolute.

vestibule *n. I waited in the vestibule until the butler announced me:* porch, entrance hall, entrance way, foyer, entry, lobby, antechamber, anteroom, waiting-room, lounge; hall, hallway, corridor, passage.

vestige *n. The diamond ring was the last vestige of her bygone wealth:* trace, remnant, sign, token, evidence, relic; record, memento, souvenir.

◇ *Word origin: Vestige,* like *investigate,* comes from Latin *vestigium,* trace, track, footprint.

vestments *n. pl. The priest was robed in white and purple vestments:* ritual garments, official attire, raiment, apparel, dress, garb, costume, outfit, regalia, clothing, clothes, livery, uniform, gear, trappings, accoutrements, *Informal* togs, rig.

◇ *Usage note:* Originally *vestment* was singular and meant outer garment, but writers so often used the plural form *vestments* to mean attire, clothing, that we seldom refer to one *vestment* today.

veteran *n.* **1** *We tried to find a veteran to coach the young golfers. The unit still possessed two veterans of the 1st World War:* expert, master, campaigner, *Informal* old hand, old-timer; elderly serviceman, long-serving soldier.

—*adj.* **2** *The veteran bookkeeper announced his retirement:* experienced, seasoned, long-practised.

Ant. 1, 2 beginner, apprentice, novice, tiro, greenhorn, tenderfoot; recruit, raw recruit.

veto *v.* **1** *The chairman has the right to veto any of the board's proposals:* reject, turn down, give the thumbs down to, deny, enjoin, prevent, forbid, disallow, prohibit.

—*n.* **2** *The chairman threatened to use his power of veto over the council's proposal:* rejection, refusal, denial, disallowing, disallowance, prevention, prohibition.

Ant. 1 ratify, sign into law, approve, endorse, sanction. **2** ratification, signing, approval, endorsement, sanction.

◇ *Word origin: Veto* is Latin for "I forbid." Thus when an American President *vetoes* a bill, he is literally saying "I forbid" it.

vex *v. Nothing vexes me more than your constant criticism:* annoy, irritate, nettle, pique, exasperate, anger, irk, provoke, rile, miff, ruffle, chafe, fret, ruffle one's feathers, displease, pester, bother, torment, gall, harass, harry, badger; trouble, distress, worry, disturb, upset, grieve, pain, *Slang* hassle.

Ant. please, delight, gratify, satisfy; calm, quiet, soothe, placate, pacify, appease, mollify, conciliate.

◇ *Word origin: Vex* comes from Latin *vexare,* to shake, agitate, injure.

viable *adj.* **1** *The foetus is considered viable at six months. Seed must be stored in a dry place if it is to remain viable:* capable of independent life, able to live, able to develop, able to thrive, capable of growing. **2** *If the plan doesn't succeed have you a viable alternative?:* workable, practical, usable, applicable, adaptable.

Ant. 1, 2 non-viable. **2** unviable, impractical, useless, unworkable, unusable.

viaduct *n. The railway viaduct arches over the old road:* overpass, span, ramp, flyover.

vial *n. Grandmother always carried a vial of smelling-salts in her handbag:* small medicine bottle, phial; (*loosely*) ampulla, ampoule.

◇ *Word origin: Vial* comes from Greek *phialē,* a broad, flat bowl or saucer for drinking or pouring libations. Greek physicians administered medicines in small saucer-shaped vessels, for which the term was also *phialē.* The shape has changed completely but the term has stuck: the present-day vial and the ancient *phialē* are both vessels for administering medicine.

vibrant *adj.* **1** *The leaves were vibrant in the breeze:* fluttering, vibrating, quivering, pulsing. **2** *The room was decorated in vibrant colours:* bright, brilliant, vivid, colourful, intense, deep, florid, loud, glowing, shimmering, glittering, luminous, lustrous, radiant, resplendent. **3** *The vibrant sounds of the violin carried the melody:* resonant, reverberant, resounding, sonorous, deep-toned, orotund, throbbing; bell-like, quivering, pealing, ringing. **4** *Critics agreed that the actress was charming and vibrant:* vivacious, lively, alive, vital, animated, spirited, electrifying, full of vigour, energetic, forceful, vehement, eager, enthusiastic, ardent, fervent.

Ant. 1 still. **2** dull, drab, greyish; pale, soft, pastel. **3** shrill, piercing, screeching. **4** listless, sluggish, phlegmatic, spiritless, boring, dull.

vibrate *v. The entire house vibrates when a big lorry goes by:* reverberate, quiver, quaver, quake, tremble, flutter, wobble; sway, waver, swing, oscillate, undulate, pendulate; palpitate, throb, pulsate, beat, ripple.

vibration *n. When the machinery is running you can feel the vibration in the floor:* tremor, quiver, quivering, quake, quaking, trembling, throbbing.

vice *n.* **1** *The prodigal led a life of vice and debauchery:* iniquity, (sexual) immorality, depravity, corruption, degeneracy, licentiousness. **2** *Gossiping is her only vice:* fault, shortcoming, failing, flaw, imperfection, blemish, defect, frailty, weakness, weak point.

Ant. 1 virtue, good morals, morality. **2** good point, accomplishment, attainment, strong point, gift, talent, facility, forte.

"What maintains one vice would bring up two children." —*Benjamin Franklin*

---

vice versa *adv. Do you want the soup before the salad or vice versa?:* the other way round, in reverse, in the opposite order, contrariwise, conversely.

vicinity *n. The shop is somewhere in the vicinity of the Church and the Red Lion:* proximity, neighbourhood, region, area, environs, adjoining region, propinquity.

vicious *adj.* **1** *That vicious dog ought to be on a leash:* ferocious, savage, fierce, violent, dangerous, untamed, wild, predatory, bloodthirsty; cruel, brutal, barbarous, treacherous, ill-humoured, ill-tempered, ill-natured, sullen, surly, churlish. **2** *It was one of the most vicious crimes of the century:* wicked, evil, atrocious, heinous, monstrous, villainous, fiendish, inhuman, foul, gross, base, vile, terrible, awful, bad, nasty, depraved, nefarious, immoral, abominable, offensive, abhorrent, horrid, shocking, diabolical, hellish. **3** *He made up a vicious story about me to spite me:* spiteful, malicious, rancorous, mean, nasty, malevolent, venomous, acrimonious, invidious, vindictive, pernicious, hateful, defamatory, libellous, slanderous.

Ant. 1 tame, friendly, playful, good-humoured, good-natured, sweet-tempered. **2** moral, virtuous, righteous, upright, good, noble. **3** sweet, genial, kind, kindly, complimentary, laudatory.

victim *n.* **1** *The fire claimed 43 victims:* fatality, dead; casualty, injured, wounded. **2** *One victim was swindled out of her life's savings:* quarry, prey, target, dupe, gull, sucker, *Slang* mark; butt, scapegoat, tool, pawn.

Ant. 2 offender, culprit, guilty party, crook.

◇ *Word origin: Victim* and *victimize* come from Latin *victima,* a sacrificial animal. To the early Romans, animal sacrifice had magical overtones; *victima* is related to our words *witch* and *wile* (which originally meant sorcery and divination).

victor *n. The victors won by a score of seven to two:* winner, champion, medallist, prize-winner.

victorious *adj. The victorious team celebrated throughout the night:* conquering, winning, triumphant, successful, champion, championship, prize-winning, vanquishing.

Ant. defeated, beaten, worsted; conquered, vanquished, overcome, repulsed.

victory *n. Each candidate expected victory in the election:* triumph, conquest, success, superiority, supremacy, ascendancy, the prize, laurels, the palm.

Ant. defeat, loss, failure, overthrow; retreat.

vie *v. The two teams are vying for the championship:* compete, contest, contend, struggle, challenge, fight, be a rival, tilt with.

Ant. co-operate, share; negotiate.

view *n.* **1** *The tourists crowded closer to get a view of the painting:* look, glimpse, peep, glance, peek, gaze, sight. **2** *His view of the game was obstructed by a pillar. Finally the ship came into view:* range of vision, vision, sight, ken. **3** *What a beautiful view!:* vista, outlook, scene, scenery, panorama, prospect, spectacle, perspective, bird's-eye view, landscape, picture, diorama. **4** *In my view this road just leads to the castle:* opinion, notion, feeling, sentiment, attitude, belief, conviction, conception, thought, theory, judgement.

—*v.* **5** *Thousands viewed the Trooping of the Colour. Have you viewed the museum's new coin collection?:* watch, see, look at, witness, observe, behold, eye, take in, scan, glance at, glimpse, note; gaze at, survey, inspect, examine, scrutinize, explore, study, contemplate, pore over. **6** *Experts view the situation with alarm:* think about, regard, consider, perceive, judge.

vigilance *n. Eternal vigilance is the price of liberty:* watchfulness, alertness, attention, heedfulness, heed, care, concern, guardedness, carefulness; caution, cautiousness, precaution, prudence, circumspection, forethought.

Ant. negligence, neglect, laxity, carelessness, unwariness, inattention, lackadaisicalness.

"There is nothing so much seduces reason from vigilance as the thought of passing life with an amiable woman."

—*Samuel Johnson*

---

vigilant *adj. The guards must be vigilant at all times:* alert, on the alert, watchful, wide-awake, attentive, heedful, observant, on the look-out; careful, cautious, prudent, guarded, circumspect, wary, chary, on one's guard, on one's toes.

Ant. negligent, neglectful, lax, slack, remiss, careless, heedless, inattentive, unmindful.

vigorous *adj. The gamekeeper was a vigorous man. Lawrence's writing is known for its vigorous style:* energetic, active, dynamic, forceful, vibrant, vital, spirited, strong, powerful, mighty, sturdy, muscular, brawny, virile, robust, hale, hardy; lusty, bold, aggressive, assertive, lively.

Ant. inactive, lethargic, languorous, indolent, apathetic, torpid, spiritless; weak, feeble, frail, effete, enervated.

vigour *n.* **1** *The leader of the expedition must be a man of great vigour:* energy, vitality, drive, verve, spirit, dash, vim, pep, zip; strength, force, might, power, robustness, hardiness; haleness, stamina. **2** *He presented his ideas with a great deal of vigour:* forcefulness, animation, enthusiasm, verve, vim, spirit, élan, liveliness, vivacity; ardour, fervour, zeal, fire, vehemence, intensity, earnestness, passion.

Ant. 1, 2 lethargy, apathy, torpor; weakness, feebleness. **1** frailty. **2** calmness, serenity, tranquillity.

vile *adj.* **1** *Rotten potatoes have a vile smell:* disgusting, offensive, revolting, repugnant, repulsive, repellent, nasty, obnoxious, odious, foul, objectionable, abhorrent, loathsome, unpleasant, bad, awful. **2** *Kidnapping is a vile crime:* vicious, sordid, gross, base, low, mean, ignoble, nefarious, wretched; wicked, evil, sinful, iniquitous, heinous, abominable, loathsome, ugly, shocking, invidious, contemptible, despicable, shameful, beastly, villainous, hateful, detestable, execrable; immoral, depraved, degenerate, perverted, disgraceful, degrading, humiliating. **3** *There's no excuse for using such vile language!:* vulgar, gross, coarse, filthy, smutty, lewd, obscene, foul-mouthed, salacious.

Ant. 1 pleasant, agreeable, attractive, appealing, appetizing, good, wonderful. **2** honourable, noble, elevated, exalted, sublime, admirable, worthy; moral, upright, righteous, sinless. **3** refined, polite, cultured; delicate, chaste.

◇ *Word origin: Vile,* like *vilify* and *revile,* comes from Latin *vilis,* cheap, tatty, inferior, hence base, vile.

village *n. The village consisted of a general stores, a pub, and seven houses:* small town, hamlet, settlement, farming village, rural community.

Ant. city, big city, metropolis, megalopolis, metropolitan area.

◇ *Word origin: Village* comes from Latin *villa,* farm, country house. In medieval times, a *village* was a group of farms that grew up round a *villa,* the manor house of a landowner. (French *ville,* city, has the same source — many villages grew into cities!)

villain *n. The villain in a melodrama always menaces the heroine. The villain cheated the old lady out of her life's savings:* wicked person, scoundrel, rascal, rogue, knave, rapscallion, varlet, rotter, cad, blackguard, cur, scallywag, caitiff; evil-doer, malefactor, miscreant, transgressor.

Ant. hero, protagonist, leading man; gentleman, worthy, champion.

◇ *Word origin: Villain* originally meant a rustic and comes from Old French *vilain,* a farm servant. Its source is the Latin *villa,* farmhouse or country house.

vim *n.* **1** *How can you be so full of vim so early in the morning?:* pep, vigour, energy, vitality, zip, snap, dash, animation, liveliness, vivacity, verve, *Slang* go. **2** *The team with the most vim and*

vigour will win: enthusiasm, spirit, zeal, fervour, ardour, intensity, fire, passion, vehemence; drive, power, punch, force; strength, might, potency.
Ant. 1, 2 lethargy, apathy, torpor.
◇ *Word origin: Vim* is a form of Latin *vis,* power, which is related to the verb *violare,* to use force on, injure, rape, which gives us *violence* and *violate.*

vindicate *v.* **1** *The suspect is sure that the jury will vindicate him:* exonerate, clear, absolve, acquit, excuse, exculpate. **2** *The headmistress's speech vindicated the teachers' right to go on strike:* uphold, support, defend, champion, advocate, maintain, assert; justify, bear out, corroborate, substantiate, bolster.
Ant. 1 blame, accuse, charge; convict. **2** counter, contradict, oppose, refute.

vindictive *adj. After being fired, the vindictive typist spread nasty rumours about the company:* vengeful, revengeful, avenging, punitive, retaliative, unforgiving, spiteful, malicious, malign, malevolent.
Ant. forgiving, relenting, generous, magnanimous.

vintage *n.* **1** *The 1961 Bordeaux wines were a great vintage:* wine of a particular year, grape-harvest for a particular year. **2** *It's a marvellous old lamp of 1890 vintage:* date, period, era, epoch.
—*adj.* **3** *This was a vintage year for export orders:* choice, prime, rare, outstanding, wonderful, fine, superior, excellent, great, sterling, prize. **4** *The garage owner owns a vintage Rolls-Royce:* antique, ancient, old, aged, old-fashioned, out-of-date.
Ant. 3 bad, inferior, awful, terrible, *Informal* lousy. **4** new, brand-new, modern, up-to-date.

violate *v.* **1** *The actress violated the terms of her contract and was sued by the producer:* break, disobey, infringe, contravene, act contrary to, transgress, disregard; trespass, encroach upon, trample on, invade. **2** *The revolutionaries violated the flag by tearing it down:* profane, desecrate, defile, commit sacrilege, blaspheme, dishonour; abuse, outrage, rape, ravish.
Ant. 1, 2 respect, honour. **1** obey, uphold. **2** revere; protect, defend.

violation *n. The driver was fined for a violation of the speed limit. Listening to someone else's telephone conversation is a violation of his privacy:* breach, infringement, infraction, transgression, trespass, encroachment; contravention, nonobservance, abuse; dishonouring, defilement, desecration, sacrilege.
Ant. obedience, compliance, honouring, revering, upholding.

violence *n.* **1** *The violence of the hurricane caused widespread damage:* force, might, impact, onslaught; fury, ferocity, fierceness, intensity. **2** *The violence of the murder shocked everyone:* physical force, brutality, bestiality, ferocity, ferociousness, savageness, savagery; desecration, profanation, outrage.
Ant. 1 mildness, weakness, feebleness; calmness. **2** gentleness, tenderness, humaneness.
◇ *Word origin: Violence, violent, violate* and *violation* all come from Latin *violare,* to violate, rape, injure.

"It is organized violence on top which creates individual violence at the bottom."
—*Emma Goldman*

---

violent *adj.* **1** *The violent earthquake left 3,000 homeless:* full of force, strong, intense, severe, furious, fierce, raging. **2** *She can't seem to control her violent temper. The patient became violent and had to be strapped to the bed:* tempestuous, vehement, strong, fierce, furious, ferocious, fiery, hot, passionate, hot-headed, raging, explosive, uncontrollable, ungovernable, unbridled, unruly, intractable, savage, murderous; wild, insane, maniacal, berserk, rampant. **3** *The rebel leader died a violent death:* resulting from the use of force, cruel, brutal, painful.
Ant. 1 mild, weak, feeble. **2** gentle, calm, composed, collected, cool, quiet, serene, tranquil, unruffled, pacific; sane, rational. **3** peaceful.

virgin *n.* **1** *The virgin vowed that she would never marry:* maiden, maid, damsel, lass, girl.
—*adj.* **2** *The area contained twenty square miles of virgin forest. This sweater is made of virgin wool:* natural, unused, untouched, unpolluted, uncontaminated; pure, unadulterated, unalloyed, unmixed; chaste.
◇ *Word origin: Virgin* comes from Latin *virgo,* maiden, virgin. We still use *Virgo,* the Virgin, as the name of a constellation and the sixth sign of the Zodiac, often represented as a young woman with flowing hair. The girl's name *Virginia,* of course, refers to *the Virgin,* Virgin Mary, mother of Jesus. English settlers in the New World named their colony of *Virginia* after *"The Virgin Queen,"* Elizabeth I, who ruled from 1558-1603.

virile *adj. How could such a big, virile man have such a high, piping voice?:* manly, masculine, manful; vigorous, forceful, masterful, strong, powerful, muscular, robust, mighty, hardy, husky, strapping, brawny; courageous, brave, stout-hearted, bold, fearless, undaunted, resolute, stalwart, valiant, heroic, audacious, lusty; potent, capable of fathering children.
Ant. effeminate, unmanly, womanish, emasculate, weak; feminine; impotent, sterile.

virtual *adj. His sending her a dozen roses was a virtual declaration of love:* tacit, implied, indirect, implicit; essential, practical.
Ant. explicit, direct, stated, expressed, definite, emphatic.

virtually *adv. With the boss off sick, the bookkeeper is virtually in charge:* substantially, practically, in essence, essentially, in effect, to all intents and purposes, in substance, for the most part, for all practical purposes.

virtue *n.* **1** *Virtue is its own reward:* moral goodness, morality, goodness, righteousness, uprightness, honour, honesty, integrity, probity, high-mindedness, rectitude. **2** *Honesty is but one of his virtues. A low operating cost is only one of the car's virtues:* moral quality, moral principle, strength, principle; benefit, advantage, value, reward, strong point, good point, favourable point. **3** *The queen's virtue is unquestioned:* chastity, purity, virginity, innocence, modesty; good behaviour, decency.

Ant. **1** vice, wickedness, evil, sinfulness, immorality, badness, dishonour, dishonesty, corruption. **2** weakness, weak point, frailty, failing, defect, deficiency, fault; disadvantage, drawback. **3** unchastity, promiscuousness, promiscuity, immodesty.

virtuoso *n. The violin virtuoso was only 12 years old:* expert, master, master-hand, genius, prodigy, *Slang* wizard, whiz-kid.

virtuous *adj.* **1** *Everyone should seek to lead a virtuous life:* morally good, moral, good, righteous, upright, honourable, high-principled; ethical, just; meritorious, praiseworthy, commendable, laudable, exemplary. **2** *Samson knew that Delilah was not a virtuous woman:* chaste, pure, virginal, innocent, continent, unsullied, modest, decent.

Ant. **1** wicked, evil, sinful, immoral, bad, dishonourable, dishonest, corrupt. **2** unchaste, promiscuous, loose, impure, immodest.

virulent *adj.* **1** *The virulent fever claimed many victims:* dangerously infectious, deadly, lethal, poisonous, toxic, venomous, pernicious; hurtful, harmful, deleterious, injurious. **2** *The spite of her virulent rival nearly ruined her:* malicious, spiteful, malevolent, rancorous, malign, bitter, resentful, acrimonious.

Ant. **1** harmless, non-poisonous, non-toxic, innocuous. **2** benign, kind, sweet, good, friendly, amiable; charitable, sympathetic, compassionate, merciful.

◇ *Word origin:* See VIRUS.

virus *n. The disease is caused by a virus:* micro-organism smaller than a bacterium; (*loosely*) germ, microbe, *Slang* bug.

◇ *Word origin: Virus* and *virulent* come from the Latin *virus*, sap, slime, ooze, and *virulentus*, full of sap, slime, or ooze, with the strong connotation that such substances were poisonous or noxious.

visage *n. She always has a cheerful visage. The travellers looked out at the bleak visage of a bare mountain:* face, features, countenance; appearance, look, aspect, semblance, image, mien, demeanour, air; profile, physiognomy.

vis-à-vis, *adv., adj.* **1** *That was the first time we'd chatted vis-à-vis in years:* face to face, tête-à-tête, eye to eye, side by side; together, in company; confidentially, privately.

—*prep.* **2** *Our income vis-à-vis expenses caused us to go bankrupt:* in relation to; as compared with, in contrast to, as distinguished from, as opposed to.

◇ *Word origin: Vis-à-vis* is French for face to face, from Old French *vis*, face, and Latin *visus*, sight. These words go back to the Latin verb *videre*, to see. Thus, although *vis-à-vis* means face to face, the figurative meaning is "eyeball to eyeball."

> **Exploring the Word**: Which Latin origin gives us the most English words? One candidate would certainly be Latin *videre*, to see, and its past participle, *visus*, seen. This base gives us *vision*, the sense of sight, sight, something seen actually or in the mind's eye; *visionary*, one who has visions, a foresighted person or an impractical dreamer; *visual*, of or serving the sense of sight, something designed to be seen or to convey information by being seen, as a picture or chart; *visualize* and *envisage*, to form a mental picture, see in the mind; *visible*, being seen, capable of being seen; *view* and *vista*, that which is seen or is in the range of sight; *visit* and *visitor*, a going to see, or one who goes to see, and *visitation*, a visit or coming as if to be seen, as of a ghost or bad luck; *visage*, the face or facial expression of a person, as seen by others; *visa*, a document, signature, or stamp certifying that an official "has seen" one's passport and that the traveller may proceed; and even *visor*, a protective shield for the eyes, as on a cap or helmet. The same Latin base gives us many, many other words, including: *advise* and *advice*, literally to see to, hence to notify or give counsel, or the counsel or suggestion given by one who "sees to" such matters; *clairvoyant*, via French, the alleged ability to see hidden, distant, or future things clearly; *evidence* (Latin *e*-, out), literally something that is set out to be seen, and *evident*, easily seen, out in the open.

viscera *n. pl. The internal organs of the body are known as the viscera:* intestines, bowels, insides, guts, entrails, *Slang* innards.

viscous *adj. Treacle is a liquid, but an extremely viscous one:* thick, viscid, sticky, gluey, gummy, glutinous, *Informal* gooey.

visibility *n.* **1** *The bright orange jacket gave the pedestrian high visibility:* capability of being seen, conspicuousness, prominence, discernibleness, clarity, perceptibility, distinctness, definition. **2** *Because of fog, the visibility is down to 200 feet:* field of observation, range of view, reach of sight; ceiling; horizon.

visible *adj.* **1** *The house was visible across the valley:* capable of being seen, observable, perceivable, perceptible, discernible, seeable, in sight, in view; clear, distinct, prominent, well-defined, in focus. **2** *Her dissatisfaction was visible. The man had no visible means of support:* plain, manifest, open, unmistakable, inescapable, revealed, salient, glaring, patent, conspicuous, marked, pointed, pronounced, blatant; obvious, noticeable, evident, apparent, palpable.

Ant. 1, 2 invisible, imperceptible, indiscernible, unapparent; hidden, concealed, obscured, buried.

◇ *Spelling tip:* Things may be *visible* to your two eyes (i's) and *visible* has two i's: *vIsIble.*

vision *n.* **1** *With such poor vision he really needs glasses:* eyesight, sight; perception, discernment. **2** *Urban planning requires great vision:* foresight, ability to plan ahead, ability to forsee, imagination. **3** *He has a vision of what the business will be like 20 years from now:* mental image, concept, conception, idea, notion; dream, day-dream, fancy, fantasy, illusion. **4** *As a child the saint saw a vision of the Virgin Mary:* apparition, supernatural appearance, materialization, revelation; ghost, phantom, spectre.

Ant. 1 blindness. **2** hindsight; shortsightedness. **3** reality, fact, actuality.

visionary *adj.* **1** *Is "peace on earth" just a visionary idea?:* impractical, idealistic, utopian, starry-eyed, dreamy; unreal, imaginative, imaginary, insubstantial, illusory, fanciful, fancied, unfounded, chimerical, delusive.

—*n.* **2** *Church authorities were sceptical of the visionary's claims:* person who has visions, seer. **3** *Columbus was a visionary who made the world accept his dream:* imaginative thinker, theorist, speculative thinker; dreamer, day-dreamer, idealist, utopian; fanatic, zealot.

Ant. 1 practical, realistic; substantial, material, real, true, actual, authentic.

visit *v.* **1** *We visited Auntie Mary this afternoon. The tourists visited the city museum:* pay a visit to, call on, drop in on, look in on; be a guest of, sojourn at, stay with, go to see. **2** *A series of misfortunes visited the family:* afflict, affect, assail, assault, attack, smite, punish, frequent, haunt.

—*n.* **3** *Some neighbours dropped in for a short visit:* stay, call; sojourn.

◇ *Word origin: Visit, visitor,* and *visitation* come from Latin *visitare,* to go to see, which was derived from Latin *videre,* to see.

"A man is like a phonograph with half-a-dozen records. You soon get tired of them all; and yet you have to sit at table whilst he reels them off to every new visitor."

—*George Bernard Shaw*

---

visitor *n. The visitor was ushered into the drawing-room by the butler. The Johnsons are entertaining visitors at the moment:* caller, guest, company; sojourner, transient; tourist, voyager, sightseer, traveller, journeyer, day-tripper.

vista *n.* **1** *At the end of the lane was a vista of the distant mountains:* view, perspective, prospect, outlook; scenery, landscape, panorama. **2** *The grim vista of years of boredom stretched before him:* mental picture, prospect, outlook, vision, view.

visual *adj. Many teachers make use of visual aids:* conveying visible information, relating to sight, for the eye, optical, optic, ocular; visible, seeable, perceptible.

visualize *v. I can't visualize the coat as you describe it:* envisage, imagine, see in the mind's eye, picture, conceive of; foresee, image, fancy, dream of, day-dream of.

vital *adj.* **1** *The patient's pulse and other vital signs are weakening:* life, living, animate, vivifying; alive, live, existing, breathing, viable, quick. **2** *She's one of the most vital people in the organization:* lively, energetic, animated, vibrant, dynamic, vigorous, spirited, forceful. **3** *This is one of the most vital issues now before Parliament:* important, significant, critical, crucial, urgent, pressing; serious, essential, necessary, indispensable, requisite, material, chief, basic, fundamental, paramount, cardinal, foremost, primary.

Ant. 1 dying, dead, inanimate. **2** lethargic, apathetic, torpid, listless, phlegmatic, uninvolved. **3** unimportant, insignificant, trivial, trifling, negligible, non-essential, unnecessary, dispensable, subordinate.

vitality *n. Good nutrition will improve your vitality:* strength, life force, vital power, the vital spark, animal spirits, energy, vigour, *Informal* pep, vim, zip; animation, enthusiasm, vivacity, liveliness, exuberance, zest, zeal, verve.

Ant. lifelessness, lethargy, torpor, listlessness, apathy.

vitriolic *adj. The film critic is notorious for his vitriolic reviews:* caustic, acid, acrimonious, acerbic, cutting, biting, scathing, withering, hypercritical, abusive, sarcastic, sardonic, satirical.

Ant. kind, sweet, friendly, affable, amiable, sympathetic, compassionate; mild, bland.

vivacious *adj. The vivacious girl was a good dancer:* lively, buoyant, full of life, animated, effervescent, bubbling, bubbly, sprightly, spirited, active; merry, gay, light-hearted, cheerful, cheery, sunny, bright, genial, convivial, jolly, frolicsome.

Ant. lifeless, languid, spiritless, lethargic, listless, impassive, stolid; sombre, melancholy, sad.

vivid *adj.* **1** *The barn was painted a vivid red:* bright, intense, brilliant, strong, rich, deep, distinct, conspicuous, garish, showy, loud, florid, gay, colourful; shining, shiny, radiant, luminous, luminescent, glowing, lustrous, effulgent, resplendent. **2** *He made the story so vivid that we all believed it. The youth has a vivid imagination:* lifelike, true to life, realistic, graphic, descriptive, dramatic, expressive, picturesque, moving, stirring; lively, energetic, vigorous. **3** *The tall blonde actress made a vivid impression when she walked into the room. The old professor has a vivid memory:* striking, strong, powerful, remarkable, astounding, astonishing, marvellous, extraordinary, memorable; clear, distinct, definite, unmistakable, inescapable, forceful, emphatic.

Ant. 1-3 dull, colourless, pale, drab, vague, indistinct, indefinite, nondescript; weak, faint, dim. **1** pastel; sombre. **3** average, usual, unremarkable, everyday, routine, run-of-the-mill.

Exploring the Word: Latin *vita,* life, and *vivere,* to live, give us *vital,* essential to life, full of life; *vitality,* liveliness, animation, energy; *vivacious,* lively, animated; *vivid,* full of life, life-like; *vitamin* (Latin *vita,* life + *amine,* a class of organic compounds derived from ammonia), one of a group of organic substances found in food and necessary for normal life processes; *viviparous* (Latin *parere,* to bring forth), bringing forth living young, bearing young, as opposed to laying eggs; *vivisection* (Latin *secare,* to cut), cutting into living animals in the laboratory for medical or other research; and *Vivat!,* literally Live!, Long live! as in "Vivat Regina!" The same base gives us, via the French, *bon vivant,* one who enjoys good living; *convivial,* literally fond of living in a group, sociable; *revive,* to bring back to life again, and *revival* something brought back to life again, as an old play, or a meeting to bring new life and vigour to religious beliefs; *survive,* to live beyond the death of another, to live beyond a specific experience, to continue to live, and is found, of course, in the Latin phrase *curriculum vitae,* literally "course of life," hence career or a résumé or biographical statement of one's date of birth, schooling, work experience, etc., and *aqua vitae,* water of life, which was alcohol in ancient chemistry (the Scandinavian drink *aquavit* also literally means "water of life").

vixen *n.* **1** *The vixen carried the rabbit back to her earth:* female fox. **2** *After a few months he discovered that he'd married a vixen:* ill-tempered woman, quarrelsome woman, shrew, scold, virago, termagant, fury; spirited woman, spitfire.

◇ *Word origin: Vixen* meant a she-fox long before it meant a quarrelsome or spirited woman. The Old English form of this word was probably *fyxen,* though unfortunately it is not attested in the literature of the period. By the 15th century, the form *fixen* is found, and this remains our modern word except that the initial letter was influenced by the fact that *f* was pronounced as *v* in the south of England. And so it is the old southern English word which we use today.

vocabulary *n.* **1** *The child has a very large vocabulary for his age. The English vocabulary is larger than that of French:* word stock, lexicon. **2** *The vocabulary of skiing is peppered with borrowings from German and Norwegian. The play is written in the vocabulary of the working man:* speech, language, vernacular, lingo, jargon, argot, slang, dialect, patois, phraseology, phrasing, terminology, style, idiom.

vocal *adj.* **1** *Don't strain your vocal cords. The teacher gives a lot of vocal praise but writes scathing comments on our reports:* of the voice, oral, spoken, voiced, vocalized, uttered, articulated. **2** *I prefer symphonies to vocal music:* sung, for singing; lyric, choral, operatic. **3** *She was extremely vocal about her dislike of the plan:* outspoken, plain-spoken, blunt, open, frank, forthright, candid, direct, voluble.

Ant. 1 written; unvoiced, unspoken, unsaid. **2** instrumental. **3** reserved, reticent.

vocalize *v.* **1** *It would be better if she would vocalize her fears rather than suppress them:* put into words, utter, speak, say, express, articulate, air, vent, ventilate. **2** *The air by Brahms was vocalized by the soprano soloist:* sing without words.

Ant. 1 suppress, pass over in silence, say nothing of, leave unsaid, reduce to silence, hush, hold one's tongue, keep secret. **2** sing words.

vocation *n. Nursing is a very satisfying vocation:* calling, profession, métier, field, career, pursuit, life-work; line of work, occupation, trade, job, employment, situation, assignment, task, stint, post, berth; role, station, estate.

Ant. avocation, hobby, distraction, diversion, spare-time pursuit.

◇ *Usage note:* It's easy to confuse *vocation* and *avocation.* A *vocation* is a person's main work, his occupation: *A doctor's vocation is medicine, Picasso's vocation was painting.* An *avocation* is a person's hobby or diversion: *The doctor's vocation is medicine, his avocation is painting.* (The distinction arises from the literal meaning of the Latin words on which *vocation* and *avocation* are based: *vocatio,* a calling; *avocatio,* a calling away, a diversion.)

vociferous *adj.* **1** *A vociferous group of boys rushed into the room:* crying loudly, loud, loud-voiced, clamorous, noisy, boisterous, uproarious; shrill, piercing. **2** *She was very vociferous in criticizing my plan:* demanding to be heard, strident, blatant; vocal, outspoken.

Ant. 1 quiet. **2** reticent, soft-spoken, subdued, calm.

vogue *n.* **1** *Will long skirts be in vogue this year? Big sun-glasses are all the vogue this summer:* fashion, style, prevailing taste; rage, fad, craze, the latest thing, the thing; custom, practice. **2** *The film* Gone With the Wind *still retains a great vogue:* popularity, acceptance, popular favour, currency.

◇ *Word origin: Vogue* is French for fashion, hence something that is *in vogue* is in fashion.

voice *n.* **1** *All that shouting caused him to lose his voice. Ted speaks with a deep voice:* vocal sound, speech, power of speech; mode of speaking, tone, delivery, intonation, modulation, articulation. **2** *Will the club members have a voice in choosing the speakers? Politicians must heed the voice of the people:* right to express an opinion, vote, say, role, part, participation, representation; will, desire, wish, opinion, choice, preference, option. **3** *The composition was written for voice and orchestra:* singer; (*variously*) tenor, soprano, alto, baritone, mezzo-soprano, contralto, counter-tenor, bass; singers.
—*v.* **4** *To pronounce "library" properly, you must voice both* r*'s:* pronounce, articulate, enunciate, vocalize, utter, speak. **5** *Please voice any objections you have now:* state, express, declare, proclaim, announce, communicate, utter, say, air, ventilate, vent, vocalize, divulge, disclose, reveal.
Ant. 1 dumbness, muteness, speechlessness, voicelessness. **5** keep silent, keep to oneself, keep one's own counsel, be quiet; suppress.

> **Exploring the Word:** *Voice, vocabulary, vocal, vowel, vouch,* and *vocation* all come from Latin *vox,* voice, and the related verb *vocare,* to call. *Voice* is from Latin *vox,* voice; a *vocabulary* is all the words "called out" or voiced in a language or by a person or group; *vocal* means having a voice, pertaining to the voice (as *vocal cords*); a *vowel* is a speech-sound made by the voice (consonants are sounded more in the mouth, by the lips, teeth, tongue, etc.); *vouch* and *avouch* mean to speak an assurance or to speak as a witness for someone, and a *vocation* is a person's "calling," his regular occupation.

void *adj.* **1** *The book was void of meaning. Suddenly the street was void of people:* devoid, empty, barren, blank, lacking, wanting; vacant, bare, destitute, clear, free; drained, depleted, exhausted, emptied. **2** *That violation makes the contract void:* invalid, not legally enforceable or binding, inoperative, null, nugatory.
—*n.* **3** *At one time outer space was believed to be a complete void:* empty space, emptiness, vacuum, vacuity, blank.
—*v.* **4** *The overloaded tanker voided oil from its hold:* discharge, evacuate, empty, emit, eject, purge, pass, drain, exhaust, throw out, pour out. **5** *Both parties want to void the agreement:* invalidate, revoke, cancel, nullify, annul, abolish, repeal, repudiate, renounce, recant, reverse, countermand, rescind.
Ant. 1 full, filled, fraught; occupied, cluttered, jammed, mobbed, packed, jam-packed. **2** valid, in effect, binding, enforceable, operative. **4** take in, fill, replenish. **5** validate, enforce; reiterate, strengthen.

◇ *Word origin: Void* comes from Latin *vacuus,* empty, the same Latin word that gives us *vacuum* and *evacuate.*

volatile *adj.* **1** *Volatile liquids must be kept in very tightly closed containers:* evaporating quickly, evaporable, vaporizing, vaporous; gaseous. **2** *The situation in the Middle East is volatile:* explosive, eruptive; unstable, unsettled. **3** *Richard is too volatile to stay in one job for very long:* changeable, erratic, unstable, unsteady, irresolute, fitful, spasmodic, undependable, inconstant, capricious, mercurial, fickle, flighty, giddy, frivolous; brash, reckless, wild, rash.
Ant. 1–3 stable. **2** calm, peaceful. **3** constant, consistent, steady, dependable, resolute, determined, cool-headed, self-controlled, serious, sober.
◇ *Word origin: Volatile* and *volley* come from Latin *volare,* to fly. Thus, a *volatile* liquid evaporates easily, or has vapour or steam that "flies away," whilst a person with a *volatile* temper has changeable moods or, as we would say, "flies off the handle" easily. A *volley* of bullets flies into the air, as does a ball that is *volleyed.*

volition *n. If you decide to climb the mountain, it must be of your own volition:* free will, will, choosing, choice, decision, resolution, discretion, option, determination.
Ant. coercion, compulsion, duress, force, necessity, unavoidability.

volley *n. The attack began with a volley of shots. A volley of criticism greeted the speaker's proposal:* salvo, fusillade, barrage, curtain of fire; outburst, burst, outbreak, shower, outpouring.

volume *n.* **1** *What is the volume of water in the tank? The box has a volume of one hundred cubic feet:* cubic content, space occupied, capacity; measure, size, dimensions, bulk, magnitude, extent, vastness. **2** *During the holiday season the post office handles a tremendous volume of mail:* quantity, mass, amount, aggregate, heap, abundance. **3** *The girl carried a slim volume of poetry under her arm. The encyclopedia is in twenty volumes:* book, treatise, tract, monograph, quarto, folio; tome. **4** *Please turn down the volume on that radio:* loudness, sound.
◇ *Word origin: Volume* and *voluminous* come from Latin *volumen,* a roll or rolled-up scroll. *Voluminous* literally means capable of filling several volumes or rolled-up surfaces.

voluminous *adj. The M.P. carries on a voluminous correspondence with his constituents:* of great volume, large, abundant, copious, ample, sizeable, massive.
Ant. small, minimal, slight, sparse, scant, skimpy, restricted.

voluntary *adj.* **1** *The hospital is supported by voluntary contributions:* free-will, optional, discretionary, non-compulsory, unforced. **2** *Blinking is an involuntary muscular action, whereas*

winking is voluntary: deliberate, done consciously, intentional, intended, willed.
Ant. 1 forced, compulsory. **2** involuntary, instinctive, unconscious, automatic; unintentional, unpremeditated.

volunteer *n.* **1** *Mother works on Tuesdays as a volunteer at the hospital:* charity-worker, unpaid worker, non-professional. **2** *Do volunteers make better soldiers than conscripts?:* voluntary recruit.
—adj. **3** *The town has a volunteer fire service:* of volunteers, by volunteers; voluntary; unpaid, non-professional.
—v. **4** *Three people volunteered to help decorate the gym for the dance:* offer willingly, offer, express willingness, step forward; take on a task willingly; place at one's disposal; be at one's service. **5** *I volunteered the observation that the plan had been tried before:* tell voluntarily, offer willingly, proffer, tender, present, extend, advance, put forward.
Ant. 1 forced labourer, appointed agent. **2** conscript. **3** paid, professional; commercial. **4** draft, force, coerce, compel, constrain, necessitate; requisition, levy, confiscate.

voluptuary *n. The old voluptuary spent his fortune on a succession of beautiful women:* sensualist, hedonist, seeker of sensual pleasures; bon vivant, epicure, gourmet, gourmand, gastronome; libertine, debauchee, sybarite, rake, roué, womanizer, seducer.
Ant. ascetic, self-denier, abstainer.
◇ *Word origin:* See VOLUPTUOUS.

voluptuous *adj.* **1** *Velvet has a voluptuous texture:* pleasing to the senses, sensuous, sensual; luxurious, soft, smooth. **2** *The wealthy playboy enjoyed a long and voluptuous life:* sensual, pleasure-seeking, pleasure-loving, self-indulgent, hedonistic, sybaritic; erotic, sexual, wanton, fleshly, carnal, licentious, lascivious, lustful, profligate, dissolute, debauched, dissipated.
Ant. 1 rough, coarse, unpleasant. **2** ascetic, abstinent, abstemious, self-denying, austere, puritanical.
◇ *Word origin: Voluptuous* and *voluptuary* come from Latin *voluptas,* pleasure.

vomit *v.* **1** *In treating most cases of poisoning, force the patient to vomit:* throw up, regurgitate, retch, bring up, disgorge, *Informal* puke, heave. **2** *The volcano vomited great clouds of smoke:* spew forth, eject, emit, expel, belch forth, disgorge.

voracious *adj. Teenagers often have voracious appetites. The boy has always been a voracious reader:* ravenous, ravenously hungry, gluttonous; insatiable, greedy, hoggish, omnivorous.
Ant. satisfied, satiated, sated, replete; apathetic, indifferent; delicate, fastidious.
◇ *Word origin: Voracious* comes from Latin *vorare,* to devour, which also gives us *devour* and *carnivorous.*

vortex *n. The swimmer was caught in the vortex and perished:* whirlpool, eddy, maelstrom; whirling mass, whirlwind.

votary *n. The student became a votary of French drama:* devotee, enthusiast, admirer, partisan, fan, fanatic, champion, zealot; disciple, follower, adherent, habitué.

> **Exploring the Word:** A citizen *voting* in an election and a nun taking her final *vows* are doing somewhat related things; both are affirming their beliefs. *Vote, votary, votive, devoted, devout, vow,* and *avow* come from Latin *vovere,* to vow, affirm, and *votum,* avowal, affirmation. Thus a *vote* is a formal affirmation or expression of one's opinion or will, as in politics, whilst a *vow* or *avowal* is a solemn or sacred affirmation or promise.

vote *n.* **1** *Father's vote usually went to the party in power. Put your vote in the ballot-box:* election choice, ballot selection; expression of opinion, choice, selection, preference, option, decision, determination, judgement, approval, voice, say; ballot, ticket. **2** *The vote will be held next Tuesday:* election, plebiscite, referendum, poll. **3** *When did women win the vote?:* right to vote, suffrage, franchise.
—v. **4** *Vote for the candidate of your choice:* cast a vote, cast a ballot; support by one's vote.

vouch *v. Can you vouch for Fred's integrity?:* swear to, attest to, affirm, confirm, guarantee, endorse, corroborate, verify, certify, witness, authenticate; support, uphold, maintain, sustain, back, back up.
Ant. refute, repudiate, deny, abjure, denounce.

vow *n.* **1** *The couple made their wedding vows before the parish priest. She took her vows as a nun before she was twenty:* solemn promise, pledge, oath, plight, troth, word, word of honour; solemn promise to God, religious pledge.
—v. **2** *They vowed to love each other throughout their lives. She vowed she would never play tennis again:* promise, pledge, pledge one's word, swear, resolve, contract; declare, assert, affirm, vouch, assure, emphasize, stress.

voyage *n.* **1** *The voyage to Iceland took seven days:* sea journey, cruise, passage, ocean trip, crossing, sail.
—v. **2** *The yachtsman spent a year voyaging round the world:* cruise, sail, journey by water, travel by water.
◇ *Word origin: Voyage* comes from Latin *viaticum,* the provision of necessities for a magistrate's official journey. Today, we still use the term *viaticum* to refer to the Eucharist given on the verge of death as preparation for the last journey. Note the *via* in the Latin *viaticum* — it, of course, means way or road.

vulgar *adj.* **1** *His vulgar manners shocked everyone:* lacking good taste, coarse, rude, rough, crude, gross, uncouth, low, base; ill-mannered, impolite, boorish, ill-bred, unrefined, uncultivated; indecent, obscene, pornographic, smutty, suggestive, disgusting,

rude, risqué. **2** *Is the inscription in Classical or Vulgar Latin? The vulgar herd never appreciated Gustave Moreau:* plebeian, proletarian, lowbrow, common, ordinary, popular, demotic.
Ant. 1 elegant, refined, cultivated, tasteful, polite, mannerly, delicate. **2** aristocratic, noble, high-born, patrician; educated, cultured, highbrow.
◇ *Word origin: Vulgar, vulgarity,* and *vulgate* all come from Latin *vulgus,* the masses, the populace.

vulgarity *n.* **1** *The vulgarity of the film was shocking:* bad taste, coarseness, crudeness, indecorum, indelicacy; indecency, smuttiness, obscenity, pornography. **2** *His vulgarity cost him many friends:* bad manners, rudeness, impoliteness, boorishness, tastelessness, lack of refinement, bad taste, commonness.
Ant. 1 good taste, tastefulness, decorum, delicacy, decency. **2** good manners, politeness, refinement, cultivation, good breeding, sensitivity.

vulnerable *adj. All those who have not been inoculated are vulnerable to the disease. The young girl has always been vulnerable to criticism:* open to attack, defenceless, unprotected, unguarded, exposed, exposed to harm, liable to harm, susceptible; easily hurt, thin-skinned, easily wounded, sensitive.
Ant. well defended, protected, guarded, unexposed, invincible, unassailable; impervious, insensitive, thick-skinned.
◇ *Word origin: Vulnerable* comes from Latin *vulnerare,* to wound.

W

waddle *v. She waddled down the street carrying a bag of groceries:* wobble, totter, toddle, sway.

wade *v.* **1** *He waded into the river to test the currents:* walk in water, walk in mud, ford. **2** *It took hours to wade through all that work:* trudge, trek, labour, toil, drudge, plough.
◇ *Word origin: Wade* comes from Old English *wadan,* to go. We still use this meaning when we say we are *wading through* a pile of papers, meaning going through them. *Waddle* is a derivative form of *wade* and means to walk as if wading; a duck *waddles* because it seems to be wading even when walking on dry land.

waft *v. The scent of pine wafted through the mountain air:* float, drift, blow, puff.
◇ *Word origin:* When a pleasant smell or sound is *wafted* through the air, it is borne or conveyed gently. The word comes from the old word *wafter,* an escort-ship that convoyed other ships safely into port.

wag¹ *v.* **1** *Heads wagged at the wedding announcement. The young Einstein caused beards to wag throughout the scientific community:* move from side to side, move up and down repeatedly, oscillate, move, stir, wave, shake, waggle, wiggle, switch, flutter, flicker, flick, twitch, wigwag.
—*n.* **2** *With a wag of his tail the dog went to the door:* switch, wave, shake, waggle, wiggle, flutter, flick, flicker, twitch.
◇ *Word origin: Wag¹* comes from Old English *wagian,* to stir, move, shake, rock back and forth. Our other word *wag²*, a joker or wit, is a shortened form of the old word *waghalter,* one who is likely to "wag" at the end of a halter or rope, a gallows-bird.

wag² *n. Some wag put a "just married" sign on the spinster's car:* joker, jester, clown, comedian, buffoon, life and soul of the party, wit, humorist, farceur, wisecracker, droll, *Slang* card.

wage *n.* **1** *The job is interesting, but it doesn't pay a living wage:* remuneration, compensation, recompense, salary, payment, stipend, fee, earnings, income, pay, revenue.
—*v.* **2** *England and Spain waged war for many years:* carry on, conduct, undertake, engage in, practise.

wager *n.* **1** *Thousands of people made wagers on the Grand National. The most common wager on a horse race is one pound:* bet; gamble, hazard, speculation; stake, venture, flutter, ante; pool, pot, jackpot; winnings.
—*v.* **2** *The gambler wagered £10 on each throw of the dice:* bet, make a bet, venture, hazard, risk, stake; gamble, speculate, take a chance, tempt fortune, try one's luck. **3** *I wager that they'll be on time:* bet, speculate, guess, hazard an opinion, assume, suppose, presume, imagine, fancy, conjecture, surmise, theorize.

waif *n. The waif was left on the steps of the orphanage:* homeless child, foundling, stray, ragamuffin, street arab, tatterdemalion.

wail *v.* **1** *The women of the town wailed over the war victims. The siren wailed and woke everyone:* utter a long mournful cry, cry, weep, keen, bemoan, groan, lament, bewail; cry out, howl, roar, yell, bellow, bawl, shout, caterwaul, rend the air, whine.
—*n.* **2** *A wail went up from the mourner's bench. The wail of air-raid sirens rent the night air:* mournful cry, plaint, loud weeping, wailing, keening, moaning, moan, lament, lamentation, groan; outcry, howl, roar, shout, yell, bellow, caterwaul, whine.

Ant. 1, 2 laugh. **1** be jubilant, be happy, celebrate; whisper, murmur. **2** laughter; shout of joy; whisper, murmur.

waist *n.* **1** *He's getting a bit thick round the waist:* middle part, mid-section, midriff, mid-region. **2** *The waist should be taken in another inch or so:* waistline, waistband; blouse, shirt, top, bodice.

◇ *Word origin: Waist* comes from Old English *wæst,* body size, akin to *weaxan,* to grow, because the body grows thicker both above and below it. This same Old English verb gives us to *wax,* to grow, thrive as in *The waxing and the waning of the moon.*

wait *v.* **1** *You'll have to wait until I finish this work. The contract is waiting for your signature:* bide one's time, remain inactive, *Informal* take it easy, cool one's heels, hold one's horses; linger, tarry, dally; remain ready, rest in expectation. **2** *Let the work wait until I get back from holiday. We waited dinner, hoping you would get here:* be postponed, be put off, be delayed, be tabled, be shelved, linger, hang fire. *—n.* **3** *The passengers had a wait of four hours between planes:* delay, suspension, stay, pause, halt, stop, stop-over, postponement, deferment, *Law* adjournment.

◇ *Usage note: Wait for* means to await: *I'll be late; please wait for me. Wait on* means to serve: *The salesman was trying to wait on two customers at once.*

waive *v.* **1** *The ambassador waived his right to diplomatic immunity and paid the fine:* relinquish a legal right, surrender, give up, give up claim to, forbear to insist on, yield, forgo, let go, not use, dispense with. **2** *The judge waived his final decision for 60 days:* postpone, defer, put off, put aside, lay over, shelve, stay.

Ant. 1 claim, demand, insist on, exact, assert, maintain, defend. **2** hasten, hurry, speed up.

waiver *n. The younger son signed a waiver giving up all claims to the property:* relinquishment, disclaimer, renunciation, abdication, abandonment, dismissal.

wake[1] *v.* **1** *She woke her father and told him the good news:* awake, awaken, waken, wake up, rouse from sleep. **2** *The newspaper article woke my interest in archaeology:* arouse, rouse, awaken, waken, stimulate, provoke, kindle, fire, stir, excite, enliven, quicken, galvanize, rally; revive, resuscitate.

—n. **3** *The wake was held at the home of the deceased:* all-night vigil over corpse before burial, all-night watch over the dead.

Ant. 1 put to sleep, go to sleep; soothe, quiet, hush. **2** allay, quell, appease, calm; sate.

◇ *Usage note: Wake, waken, awake,* and *awaken* have the same meaning and may be used interchangeably. *Waken* and *awaken* are perhaps the more formal of the words: *At what time will the queen awaken? Awake* and *awaken* are used somewhat more frequently in a figurative sense, when waking from sleep is not meant: *Her suspicions were awakened.*

wake[2] *n. Sea-gulls followed in the wake of the ship:* wash, track of a vessel, backwash; trail, path, course, train.

wakeful *adj.* **1** *Worry caused her to be wakeful much of the night:* unable to sleep, sleepless, unsleeping, awake, wide-awake, insomniac; restless, astir. **2** *The palace guards were ever wakeful:* alert, vigilant, watchful, wary, careful, heedful, observant; cautious.

Ant. 1 sleepy, somnolent, dozy, drowsy; sleeping, restful. **2** off-guard, unvigilant, heedless, unwary.

walk *v.* **1** *Let's walk round the lake. We got off the bus and walked the last few streets:* proceed by steps, go on foot, travel on foot; stroll, saunter, amble, perambulate, promenade, march, tramp, traipse, trek; trudge, take a turn, *Informal* foot it, go Shanks's pony.

—n. **2** *The guests took a long walk after dinner:* stroll, saunter, constitutional, promenade, perambulation, march, trek, hike, journey on foot. **3** *Have you ever noticed that bouncy walk of hers?:* way of walking, gait, step, stride. **4** *The walk in front of the house is covered with ice:* place for walking; (*variously*) pavement, path, trail, road, way, route, passage.

wall *n. Let's knock out this wall and make the room larger. Two prisoners escaped over the walls of the prison:* side of a room, partition; side of a building; fence, barrier, confine, barricade, rampart, stockade, parapet, battlement, breastwork, fortification, bastion.

wallop *v.* **1** *He walloped the child for running away. Wallop that ball as hard as you can!:* hit hard, strike hard, lambaste, clobber, belt, punch, smack, whack, slap, swat, cuff; beat, thrash, pummel, spank, buffet; whip, strap, switch, lash. **2** *Informal The opposition party was really walloped in the recent elections:* beat badly, defeat, trounce, rout, crush, clobber, best, worst, *Slang* lick, trim.

—n. **3** *The boxer was floored by a stout wallop on the chin:* hard blow, punch, hit, smack, swat.

wallow *v.* **1** *Pigs love to wallow:* roll in mud, lie in mud. **2** *She wallows in her luxury:* luxuriate, revel, enjoy selfishly, live self-indulgently; bask in, swim in, riot in, feast on, relish.

wan *adj.* **1** *The patient still looks thin and wan:* pale, sickly, pallid, white, pasty, colourless, sallow, ashen; cadaverous, ghastly. **2** *She made a wan attempt to smile at the tasteless joke:* weak, feeble, sickly, sad, half-hearted, forced, unconvincing, lame, limp, ineffective, ineffectual, unavailing.

Ant. 1 ruddy, rosy, rosy-cheeked, pink-cheeked, bonny, florid, flushed. **2** strong, forceful, convincing, effective.

◇ *Word origin: Wan* originally meant pale from unhappiness or gloominess. It comes from Old English *wann,* gloomy, dismal.

wand *n. The fairy godmother waved her magic wand:* rod, stick, staff, baton, sceptre.

wander *v.* **1** *The boy wandered through the neighbourhood, looking for his dog. The student wandered through Europe during the summer:* walk aimlessly, move about aimlessly, roam, ramble, meander, rove, range, prowl; travel, journey, trek, jaunt, *Slang* knock about. **2** *The little stream wanders through the woods:* meander, curve, twist, zigzag; swerve, veer, alter course. **3** *The goat wandered from the yard and never came back:* stray, become lost.

Ant. 1 stay, remain, settle; rest, pause, stop, halt. **2** go straight as an arrow, make a bee-line. **3** be found; come home, return.

wanderer *n. My people are a nation of wanderers, never content to settle down:* roamer, rover, rambler, nomad, itinerant; vagrant, vagabond, gipsy, tramp; wayfarer, journeyer, traveller, voyager, globe-trotter, gadabout.

Ant. stay-at-home, stick-in-the-mud.

wane *v.* **1** *The school's good reputation has started to wane. The old man's health began to wane:* fade away, fade, decline, dwindle, weaken, decrease, diminish, subside, abate, ebb, lessen; wither, waste, droop, sink.

—*n.* **2** *The 1950's saw the wane of the steam era:* fading away, fading, decline, decrease, dwindling, subsiding, abating, ebbing, lessening, recession, weakening, withering.

Ant. 1 appear, rise, increase, expand, advance, strengthen, grow, develop, wax, improve, flourish, thrive, soar, blossom, brighten. **2** rise, increase, expansion, advancement, strengthening, growth, development, waxing.

want *v.* **1** *I want a pink sweater and a skirt to match:* desire, wish for, crave, fancy, hope for, long for, yearn for, pine for, covet, hanker after, hunger for, thirst for, hunger after. **2** *The police want him for theft:* seek, search for, hunt; have a warrant for (the arrest of). **3** *This book wants mending:* need, require, lack, be without; be deficient in, be destitute of, fall short in, come short of. **4** *She has never wanted for money:* be needy, have a shortage of, be without, lack.

—*n.* **5** *Most people have simple wants:* need, necessity, requirement, demand. **6** *The country suffers from a want of water. In the 1930's many people were reduced to dire want:* deficiency, lack, scarcity, shortage, dearth, insufficiency, paucity, need; privation, hunger, hard times; poverty, destruction, impoverishment, pauperism, indigence, penury, pennilessness, impecuniosity, insolvency.

Ant. 1 be sated, be satisfied; have, own, possess, enjoy; refuse, reject, decline, repudiate, spurn, relinquish, give up, give away, surrender; loathe, hate, dislike. **6** plenty, abundance, copiousness; sufficiency, adequacy; wealth, opulence, affluence, luxury.

wanting *adj. The car was tested for safety and found wanting. A motive for the crime was wanting:* deficient, inadequate, lacking, insufficient; imperfect, defective, short; missing, absent.

Ant. 1 adequate, sufficient, passable; perfect, complete, full.

wanton *adj.* **1** *The juvenile delinquents were charged with wanton destruction of property:* deliberate, wilful, malicious, malevolent, unjustified, needless, uncalled-for, groundless, inconsiderate, heedless, careless, irresponsible. **2** *He was often seen in the company of wanton women:* of loose morals, immoral, abandoned, promiscuous, unchaste, lewd, lecherous, libertine, licentious; gross, obscene.

—*n.* **3** *The riverside pub was frequented by thieves and wantons:* immoral person, dissolute person, lewd person, debauchee, libertine, voluptuary, sensualist, sybarite; (*of a man*) lecher, seducer, adulterer, fornicator, womanizer, rake, roué, whore-master; (*of a woman*) hussy, trollop, slut, strumpet, whore, prostitute, harlot, concubine, tart.

war *n.* **1** *The First World War lasted from 1914 to 1918:* state of armed conflict, armed conflict, warfare, hostilities, military operations, clash of arms; fighting, battle, combat. **2** *The minister continued his war against corruption:* fight, struggle, attack, battle, combat, opposition, conflict.

—*v.* **3** *The country warred with its neighbours for years. The church must war against vice:* wage war, make war, be at war, carry on hostilities, battle with, fight, combat, contend, struggle, clash, exchange shots, declare war, go to war, take up arms, attack, invade, march against.

Ant. 1 peace, peace-time; neutrality; treaty, armistice, truce, cease-fire. **2** acceptance, approval, assent, compliance, sanction, agreement. **3** make peace, call a truce.

◇ *Word origin: War* comes from Old High German *werra*, strife, confusion.

ward *n.* **1** *He's standing for the council in our ward:* administrative district, voting district; municipal district, area, quarter, zone. **2** *The patient was taken to the isolation ward:* section of a hospital, pavilion; section of a prison. **3** *The orphan became a ward of court:* charge, dependent; protégé.

—*v.* **4** *The boxer fought desperately to ward off his opponent's blows. Is there any way in which the firm can ward off bankruptcy?:* turn aside, turn away, fend off, stave off, keep at bay, block, repel, beat off, defend against, guard against; avert, prevent, thwart, forestall, hold at arm's length.

◇ *Word origin: Ward* comes from Old English *weardian* to watch, watch over, guard, protect. Closely related to this is Old French *garder*, which is the base of our words *guard, guardian*, and even wardrobe.

warden *n.* **1** *There is a resident warden in charge of the old people's flats:* superintendent, manager, steward, administrator. **2** *The game-warden examined the hunter's licence:* keeper, ranger, guard, sentry, watchman, protector, guardian, warder, curator.

wardrobe *n.* **1** *She bought a new wardrobe to take on the cruise:* collection of clothes, supply of clothing; apparel, clothing, things to wear, outfit, attire, togs, garments; habiliments; trousseau. **2** *You had better put some moth-balls in the hall wardrobe:* clothes cupboard, closet, cupboard; chest, chiffonier, tallboy.

wares *n. pl.* *The silversmith showed us his wares:* articles or goods for sale, merchandise, stock-in-trade, supplies, staples, commodities.

warfare *n.* *Fierce warfare raged along the border for days:* state of war, war, armed conflict, hostilities, military operation, clash of arms, fighting, fight, battle, combat, conflict.

warm *adj.* **1** *April was a warm, sunny month. The freshly-baked loaf was still warm:* moderately hot, somewhat hot, lukewarm, tepid, heated, not cold; hot. **2** *Wear a warm sweater:* providing warmth, warming, keeping in the body's heat. **3** *The dining-room was decorated in warm colours:* bright, sunny, vivid, brilliant, glowing. **4** *Aunt Sue is a very warm person. The teacher had a warm smile for everyone:* loving, warm-hearted, affectionate, kind, kindly, kind-hearted, tender, tender-hearted, sympathetic, compassionate, friendly, outgoing, cheerful, joyful, joyous, pleasant, cordial, happy, affable, gracious. **5** *The question prompted a warm discussion:* lively, vigorous, animated, fervent, earnest, passionate, heated, enthusiastic, spirited, intense, vehement.

—*v.* **6** *Warm the soup whilst I make the sandwiches:* heat, heat up, warm up, make hot; cook, simmer. **7** *The child's happy smile warmed his heart:* cheer, make joyful or happy; arouse affection, arouse sympathy, thaw, melt.

Ant. 1–4, 6–7 cool. **1, 3, 4** cold. **1** chilly, frigid, icy, ice-cold. **3** dull, drab, austere. **4** unfriendly, frigid, remote, stand-offish, aloof, haughty; cruel, hard-hearted, cold-hearted, unsympathetic, uncaring. **5** lethargic, apathetic, torpid, dull, boring. **6, 7** cool off, chill, freeze. **7** alienate; depress, sadden.

warm-hearted *adj.* *The warm-hearted woman took in the stray cat:* kind, kindly, kind-hearted, tender-hearted, sympathetic, compassionate, affectionate, loving, warm, solicitous.

Ant. unkind, cold-hearted, hard-hearted.

warmth *n.* **1** *Come in and enjoy the warmth of the fire. The warmth of this thin blanket is amazing:* warmness, heat, hotness; feeling of being warm, warm sensation. **2** *Everyone responds to the warmth of her smile;* lovingness, warm-heartedness, kindliness, kindness, kind-heartedness, tender-heartedness, tenderness, sympathy, compassion, cheer, cheerfulness, joy, joyfulness, cordiality, affability, graciousness, happiness, friendliness. **3** *He expressed his views with a great deal of warmth:* heat, passion, fire, excitement, spirit, enthusiasm, vehemence, vigour, intensity, animation, earnestness, zeal, fervour, verve.

Ant. 1, 2 chill, coolness, coldness, iciness. **2** cruelty, hard-heartedness, cold-heartedness, sternness, austerity, severity; frigidity, remoteness, aloofness, unfriendliness. **3** lethargy, apathy, torpor, indifference; insincerity.

warn *v.* *The scout warned the fort of the imminent attack. I warned you not to buy that old car:* alert, forewarn, give warning of danger, alert to danger, put on one's guard, caution, notify, make aware, apprise, inform; advise, council, admonish.

warning *n.* *The sentry's warning woke the fort's defenders. Didn't you have any warning that the house was being sold?:* warning signal, warning sign, alarm, forewarning, notice; notification, intimation, hint, sign, token, omen, foretoken, presage; advice.

warp *v.* **1** *The dampness warped the floor-boards:* bend, twist, contort, distort, mis-shape, deform. **2** *Years of living alone had warped his personality:* pervert, twist, distort, corrupt, lead astray, debase, infect; misguide, bias, prejudice, mislead.

—*n.* **3** *This railing has a warp in it:* bend, twist, distortion, contortion, deformation. **4** *Bitterness gave her outlook a peculiar warp:* quirk, twist, bent, leaning, tendency, disposition, inclination, proneness, propensity, proclivity, predisposition, one-sidedness, partiality.

Ant. 1 straighten, straighten out, unbend.

warrant *n.* **1** *The police have a search warrant. There is a warrant for the suspect's arrest:* authorization, permit; licence.

—*v,* **2** *Such actions warrant a severe reprimand:* justify, provide grounds for, give sufficient reason for; permit, authorize, license. **3** *The manufacturer warrants that all parts are new:* guarantee, certify, vouch for, pledge, swear, attest, affirm, promise, vow, avow, assure, assert, declare, asseverate, aver.

warranty *n.* *Each vacuum cleaner has a 5-year warranty:* written guarantee; pledge, agreement, certificate.

◇ *Word origin: Warranty* and *guaranty* both come from the French word *garantie.*

warrior *n.* *The warriors marched off with Hannibal to the Punic Wars:* soldier, legionary, fighting man, man-at-arms, military man, fighter, combatant, infantryman, veteran, campaigner.

wary *adj.* *It does no harm to be wary of new acquaintances:* cautious, careful, guarded, suspicious, chary, heedful, watchful, vigilant, on one's guard, alert, wide-awake; discreet, circumspect, close-mouthed, prudent.

Ant. unwary, unsuspecting, unguarded, rash, reckless, foolhardy, careless, heedless, incautious; negligent, remiss.

wash *v.* **1** *Wash your hands and come to supper:* clean with soap and water, clean, cleanse; (*variously*) launder, rinse, scrub, mop, scour,

sponge, wipe, rub, bathe, shampoo; *Archaic* lave. **2** *You'd better wash that cut with some iodine:* bathe, wet, moisten, drench, soak, irrigate, immerse, flood, inundate. **3** *A large piece of driftwood was washed onto the beach:* be moved by the flow of water, float; move in waves.
—*n.* **4** *This bedspread could do with a good wash:* washing, cleaning, cleansing; (*variously*) laundering, mopping, scouring, bath, shower, shampoo, ablution; *Archaic* lavation. **5** *Mother does a big wash twice a week:* laundry, clothes washing; group of things laundered.

waste *v.* **1** *Don't waste time on non-essentials. A badly-tuned engine wastes petrol:* squander, dissipate, throw away, fritter away, expend needlessly, consume extravagantly, use up fruitlessly, devour, burn up, run through, deplete, empty, drain, exhaust; misuse, use unwisely, mis-spend, misapply, misemploy. **2** *Invading armies wasted the countryside:* lay waste, destroy, ruin, devastate, spoil, wreck, demolish, crush, smash, shatter, raze; despoil, ravage, pillage, plunder, loot, sack, strip, rob, prey upon. **3** *The old man's strength was wasting away:* fade, dwindle, decline, weaken, decrease, diminish, subside, abate, ebb, wane, wither, crumble, decay; droop, sink, die; disappear, evaporate, melt.
—*n.* **4** *Industrial waste must be prevented from polluting our rivers:* waste material, refuse, garbage, trash, rubbish, debris, litter, sweepings, dregs; excrement; offal. **5** *Collect all the waste and use it to stuff cushions:* remnants, leftovers, scraps, leavings. **6** *Such a routine job is an utter waste of her talents:* wastefulness, squandering, extravagance, needless expenditure, useless consumption, needless loss; misuse, misapplication, dissipation. **7** *The explorers spent months in the Arctic wastes:* wasteland, barren expanse, emptiness, void; (*variously*) wilderness, desert, arid region, tundra, steppe; *American* badlands. **8** *Nothing could stop the waste of the city by the barbarians:* destruction, ruin, ruination, devastation, wreck, wrecking, demolition, razing; ravage, despoliation, pillage, plundering, looting, sack.
Ant. 1 save, conserve, husband, economize; spend wisely, use well. **2** build, rebuild, restore; protect, defend, guard. **3** strengthen, develop, grow, improve, rally, increase, advance. **6** saving, economy, thrift, frugality.

wasteful *adj. It's wasteful to throw out bones that could be used in a soup:* squandering, prodigal; extravagant, uneconomical, thriftless.

watch *v.* **1** *He kissed her whilst no one was watching. Watch the magician and try to work out how he makes the rabbit disappear:* look, look on, look at, stare, stare at, gaze at, see, eye, keep an eye on, peep at, peer at, ogle; observe, notice, note, pay attention to, attend, mark, regard, rivet one's eyes on, examine, scrutinize, survey, contemplate, pore over. **2** *Watch for an empty seat and grab it:* look out for, be on the look-out, be on the alert, keep an eye out for. **3** *Watch where you're going! Watch that he doesn't cheat you:* pay attention, be careful, be cautious, be on guard, be wary, take heed, be chary. **4** *Who's watching the children whilst the parents are out? Watch your money or it will all be gone before pay-day:* look after, look out for, keep an eye on, tend, tend to, care for, take care of, mind, oversee, superintend; save, preserve, protect, guard.
—*n.* **5** *Keep a close watch on the kettle so that it doesn't boil over:* eye, surveillance, observance, observation, watchfulness, supervision, superintendence, attention, notice, heed, vigilance; look-out, alert, guard, survey. **6** *The watch is late making his rounds. The sailor was allotted the early morning watch:* watchman, guard, sentry, sentinel, patrol, foot patrol, picket, scout; period of time for standing guard, being on duty. **7** *This watch keeps good time:* wristwatch; pocket watch.
Ant. 2 overlook, ignore, disregard. **3** be rash, be reckless, be careless. **4** neglect. **5** inattention, disregard, heedlessness.

watchful *adj.* **1** *The scout kept a watchful eye on the valley below him:* alert, observant, vigilant, on the look-out, attentive, heedful, aware, mindful, ready, open-eyed, wide-awake. **2** *To live on a tight budget one must be very watchful of one's expenses:* careful, prudent, cautious, circumspect, wary, guarded, on one's guard, chary, canny, shrewd.
Ant. 1, 2 careless, inattentive, heedless, unaware, unmindful. **1** unobservant. **2** rash, reckless, unguarded, unwary, thoughtless.

watchman *n. The watchman saw the prowler and called the police:* guard, sentry, sentinel, watch, patrol, foot patrol; picket, scout, look-out.

water *n.* **1** *Eat properly and drink six glasses of water a day:* H_2O. **2** *The canoeist was out on the water all day:* (*variously*) sea, ocean, lake, pond, pool, river, stream.
—*v.* **3** *Water the flowers every morning:* supply water to; (*variously*) sprinkle, wet, moisten, damp, dampen, souse, soak, drench, douse, dip, submerge, immerse, splash, irrigate, flood, inundate, deluge. **4** *Water the livestock when you feed them:* give water to drink. **5** *The farmer was convicted of watering the milk.* Also **water down** *That bar waters down its drinks:* add water to, dilute, thin, adulterate, cut, qualify. **6** *My eyes water when I'm tired:* run, overflow, stream, fill with tears.
Ant. 2 land, dry land, terra firma. **3** dry, dry up; parch, dehydrate, desiccate; wipe up, sponge, blot, swab.

watery *adj.* **1** *The pirate went to a watery grave. What's that watery stain on the wall?:* of water, like water, wet, moist, damp, liquid, fluid, aqueous. **2** *This gravy tastes watery:* thin, diluted, watered-down, weak, adulterated. **3** *We all had watery eyes in that smoky room:* running, streaming, tearful, tear-filled, rheumy.

wave *n.* **1** *A big wave swamped the rowing-boat:* billow, breaker, swell, comber, boomer, white-cap, roller; ripple, undulation. **2** *Can strong magnets distort radio waves?:* pulse, pulsation, vibration. **3** *The captain led the first wave of soldiers up the beach:* moving row, advancing rank, file, line, string, train, column, tier. **4** *Her hair has a natural wave:* curve, series of curves, curl; coil, winding, spiral, roll, twirl. **5** *She gave me a wave from across the road. One wave of the teacher's hand silenced the class:* salutation, to-and-fro hand gesture of greeting; gesture, gesticulation, hand signal, motion, flourish. **6** *There's been a wave of selling on the stock exchange:* surge, rush, deluge, flood; rise, increase, heightening.

—*v.* **7** *The flag waved in the breeze. Don't wave that book in my face:* move to and fro, flutter, flap, swing, sway, shake, waver, tremble, quiver; oscillate, vibrate, undulate, pulsate; brandish, flourish, wield. **8** *The patrol car waved us to a stop:* signal, gesture, gesticulate.

waver *v.* **1** *The old woman wavered on the top step and nearly fell:* totter, reel, stagger, wobble, sway, falter, begin to give way. **2** *He never wavered in his determination to become a doctor:* falter, be irresolute, be undecided, be undetermined, be doubtful, vacillate, shilly-shally, hesitate, change, vary, fluctuate.

Ant. 2 be resolute, be steadfast, be certain, be determined, be decisive, stand firm.

wax *v. The Cabinet waxed enthusiastic over the new education programme. The moon is always the same size but it seems to wax and wane according to the light that it reflects:* grow, become; become larger, enlarge, increase, expand, develop, thrive, extend, widen, become fuller, fill out, swell, dilate, spread out, inflate, puff out, blow up, balloon.

Ant. wane, become smaller, diminish, decrease, contract, narrow, deflate.

way *n.* **1** *It's hard for a traveller to get used to foreign ways. Being brusque is just his way:* custom, practice, manner, habit, usage, form; behaviour, conduct, nature, wont. **2** *What's the best way to make coffee?:* method, means, process, procedure, manner, system, technique, course of action. **3** *I never seem to drive round your way nowadays:* direction; neighbourhood, vicinity, area, region. **4** *This is the shortest way to town. Hard work is the way to success:* route, course, road, path, pathway, trail, lane, pass, passage; distance. **5** *Make way for the king!:* space, room to advance, opening.

—*adv.* **6** *Informal Can't you see it way in the distance?:* far, far off, remotely.

waylay *v. Six highwaymen waylaid the coach:* ambush, fall upon from ambush, lie in wait for, lay a trap for; assail, assault, attack; lure, decoy, inveigle.

wayward *adj.* **1** *The judge sent the boy to a home for wayward youths:* disobedient, ungovernable, incorrigible, intractable, unruly, insubordinate, rebellious, refractory, troublesome; headstrong, self-willed, wilful, contrary, perverse, obstinate, stubborn, recalcitrant, balky, mulish. **2** *Her wayward locks escaped from under her bonnet:* fitful, erratic, changeable, undependable, inconsistent, capricious, flighty, inconstant, fluctuating; fickle, restive, mercurial, whimsical.

Ant. 1 obedient, manageable, docile, tractable, compliant. **2** steady, fixed, constant, regular, consistent, dependable.

weak *adj.* **1** *The flu victim was too weak to walk:* lacking strength, weakened, feeble, faint, frail, debilitated; exhausted, spent, wasted, enervated; shaky, unsteady, helpless. **2** *The walls are too weak to hold up the roof. He gave us a weak smile:* frail, flimsy, insubstantial, puny, shaky, unsteady, fragile, breakable, brittle, frangible, delicate. **3** *We need strong leaders, not weak ones. The cricket team has a weak fast bowling department:* powerless, spineless, cowardly, soft, timorous, irresolute, unmanly, effeminate, namby-pamby, wishy-washy; ineffective, ineffectual, inefficacious, inefficient, unsatisfactory, poor, lame. **4** *The arguments in favour of the proposal are very weak. The army's defeat leaves the country in a weak position:* vulnerable, exposed, defenceless, assailable, unprotected, unguarded, unsafe, wide open; untenable, unsupported, unconvincing, untrustworthy, lacking. **5** *Don't make the coffee too weak:* watery, thin, diluted, adulterated; tasteless, insipid.

Ant. 1-5 strong. **2-4** strengthened, sturdy, powerful. **1-3** steady. **1** vigorous, hardy, hale, hearty. **2** substantial, sound, solid, hefty; unbreakable; vivid, beaming, radiant, brilliant; ardent, eager. **3** forceful, aggressive, vigorous, energetic; firm, hard, tough, brave, bold, stalwart, staunch, manly; effective, able, capable, potent. **4** solid, sound, substantial, forceful, convincing, trustworthy, valid, good, satisfactory, effective; impregnable, invulnerable, unassailable, well-guarded, protected, safe, secure. **5** potent.

weaken *v. Lack of food weakened his resistance. Public support for wage restraint began to weaken:* make weak, impair, undermine, cripple, emasculate, unman, soften, soften up, expose; diminish, lessen, lower, sap, mitigate, moderate, exhaust, waste, devitalize, enervate, dilute, water down, thin, thin out; fail, flag, droop, dwindle, wane, fade, abate.

Ant. strengthen, increase, grow, develop, rise, improve, enhance, better; invigorate, energize, revitalize.

weakling *n.* **1** *Don't be afraid of that weakling, he won't stop you:* physically weak person, frail person, feeble person, physical wreck. **2** *Stand up for your rights and don't be such a weakling:* weak-willed person, coward, sissy, namby-pamby, milksop, drip, wet, molly-coddle.

weakness *n.* **1** *The patient's weakness is due to poor* *nutrition:* feebleness, lack of strength, frailty, debility, debilitation; shakiness, unsteadiness. **2** *Can't you see the weakness of his argument?:* fault, defect, deficiency, imperfection, insubstantiality, lack of force, ineffectiveness, lameness, flimsiness, failing, frailty; vulnerability, susceptibility, unconvincingness, untrustworthiness. **3** *Jerry has a weakness for sports cars:* passion, fondness, intense liking, penchant, propensity, proclivity, tendency, inclination, proneness, leaning, prejudice, bias, bent, *Informal* soft spot.

Ant. 1, 2 strength. **1** vigour, vitality, stamina; health, hardiness, soundness, sturdiness; power. **2** force, effectiveness, potency; validity, perfection, soundness, unassailability, impregnability, trustworthiness. **3** dislike, hatred, loathing, aversion, disgust, horror.

wealth *n.* **1** *His wealth is estimated at four million pounds:* quantity of money, riches, fortune, assets, resources, means, capital, property, goods, chattels. **2** *The family always enjoyed great wealth:* affluence, prosperity; luxury, luxuriousness, opulence, independence, easy circumstances, *Informal* easy street. **3** *There is a wealth of detail in the painting:* abundance, profusion, richness, copiousness, amplitude, fullness, bounty, fund, store, mine.

Ant. 2 poverty, penury, pauperism, destitution, indigence, privation, straitened circumstances, want, need, wretchedness. **3** want, lack, dearth, paucity, scarcity, shortage, scantiness, deficiency.

wealthy *adj. The débutante comes from a very wealthy family:* rich, prosperous, affluent, moneyed, well-to-do, well-off, well-heeled.

Ant. poor, impoverished, poverty-stricken, destitute, indigent, needy, down-and-out.

weapon *n.* **1** *The army had completed testing the new weapon:* arm, armament, instrument of war, lethal instrument, deadly weapon. **2** *Reduced spending is our best weapon against inflation:* defence, protection, guard, countermeasure, safeguard, security, bulwark; offensive, attack; means, measure, resource.

wear *v.* **1** *Are you going to wear your jeans or a dress? The policeman wore his uniform proudly:* dress in, clothe oneself in, carry on the person, put on, don, slip on, attire oneself in, fit oneself with, costume oneself, garb oneself, array oneself, wrap, swathe, shroud, swaddle. **2** *This sweater has worn thin at the elbows:* wear away, wear out; abrade, rub away, fray, frazzle, shred; erode, wash away; corrode, eat away. **3** *This coat wears better than any I've had:* resist abrasion, stand up to wear and tear; last, endure. **4** *The long wait wore everyone out:* exhaust, tire, fatigue, weary, drain; overburden, tax.

—*n.* **5** *There's a lot of good wear left in those shoes:* wearability, use, service; utility, utilization, employment, application, consumption. **6** *This shop has the best selection of beach-wear in town:* clothing, clothes, apparel, wearing apparel, attire, garments, costumes, togs, duds. **7** *You can see the wear on the corner of the rug:* worn place, rubbed place, deterioration, disintegration, disrepair, wear and tear; damage, injury, dilapidation.

weary *adj.* **1** *I'm always weary after my day's work:* tired, exhausted, fatigued, wearied, spent, worn-out, drained, done in, fagged-out, played-out, all in, dog-tired, ready to drop, *Slang* dead-beat, whacked; sleepy, drowsy. **2** *I thought that weary speech would never end:* tiring, fatiguing, wearying, wearing, tedious, exhausting; boring, monotonous, tiresome, wearisome, humdrum, dull, routine; soporific, somniferous. **3** *He's weary of her constant nagging:* tired, sick and tired, impatient, dissatisfied; dispirited, discontented, disgusted; bored, blasé, jaded.

—*v.* **4** *The long drive wearied the children:* tire, tire out, fatigue, exhaust, wear out, play out; overtax, overwork, overburden.

Ant. 1 refreshed, revivified, invigorated; energetic, full of go. **2** easy; refreshing, invigorating; interesting, exciting, amusing, delightful. **3** invigorated, refreshed; pleased, delighted, interested; patient, forebearing. **4** refresh, invigorate, revive; energize, enliven.

weather *n.* **1** *What's the weather like this morning?:* atmospheric conditions; (*loosely*) climate.

—*v.* **2** *Stack the wood and let it weather a bit before building the barn. Copper turns green as it weathers:* expose to weather, dry, season, toughen; bleach, tan; rust, oxidize. **3** *The sun weathered the paint:* harm by exposure to the weather. **4** *The ship weathered the hurricane with no casualties:* pass through safely, withstand, stand; brave, face, confront.

—*adj.* **5** *Don't build your house on the weather side of the hill:* windward, facing the wind.

weave[1] *v.* **1** *The Navajo Indians weave beautiful rugs. Weave the two strings together to make a stronger cord:* interlace, intertwine, interweave, twist, knit, entwine, braid, lace, plait, criss-cross. **2** *The composer wove three separate melodies into his composition:* interweave, combine, merge, blend, fuse, mingle, incorporate, unify, unite, join, link.

—*n.* **3** *The fabric has a beautiful herring-bone weave:* woven pattern; texture.

Ant. 1 unravel, untwist, disentangle. **2** isolate, segregate; separate, divorce, divide.

weave[2] *v. The small car weaved through the traffic. The river weaves through the woods:* zigzag, wind, curve, meander, writhe, snake, twist.

Ant. go straight as an arrow, make a bee-line.

◇ *Word origin: Weave*[1] comes from Old English *wefan* from which we get also *web. Weave*[2] probably comes from Middle English *weve,* to wave, which is related ultimately to Latin *vibrare* to vibrate. The past tense of *weave*[1] is *wove;* of *weave*[2] it is *weaved.*

web *n.* **1** *Why doesn't a spider get caught in its own web?:* spider's web; cobweb. **2** *Campers had to* *sleep under cotton webs because of the mosquitoes:* webbing, net, netting, mesh, screening, screen, gossamer. **3** *His whole story is a web of lies:* network, tissue, complex; labyrinth.

wed *v.* **1** *The couple will be wed in June. He will wed his secretary next month:* marry, join in marriage, unite in holy matrimony, make one, hitch, tie the knot, splice; take for husband, take for wife, espouse, take for better or for worse, lead to the altar. **2** *She is wedded to the idea of equal rights for women:* bind, attach, marry, commit, devoted, pledge; enamour of, captivate by, fascinate by, win over. **3** *Try to wed both these ideas into one story:* blend, combine, unite, weave, fuse, merge, incorporate, unify, tie.

Ant. 1, 3 divorce, separate. **3** isolate, segregate; unravel, disentangle.

wedded *adj.* **1** *The couple had fifty years of wedded bliss:* married, united in marriage, marital. **2** *The two states are wedded into one nation:* united, joined, bound, tied, connected, linked; fused, merged, unified, incorporated, blended. **3** *He seems wedded to his career as a journalist:* devoted, committed, bound, deeply attached.

Ant. 1, 2 separated, divorced. **1** single, solitary, unwed, unmarried; bachelor, spinster.

wedding *n.* **1** *It was the grandest wedding of the season:* wedding ceremony, marriage ceremony, marriage, nuptials, nuptial rite. **2** *How long is it before they celebrate their golden wedding?:* wedding anniversary; wedding-day, marriage day, the big day.

Ant. 1 separation, divorce.

wedge *n.* **1** *Here's a wedge that you can use as a doorstop. Buy a wedge of cheddar at the grocer's:* V-shaped block, chock; pie-shaped piece, chunk.

—*v.* **2** *Wedge the door open:* fix with a wedge, stop, check. **3** *She couldn't wedge another item into the suitcase:* cram, jam, stuff, crowd, ram, squeeze, pack, press.

wedlock *n. They were united in wedlock at the parish church:* marriage, matrimony, holy matrimony, nuptial state.

wee *adj. Put just a wee drop of brandy in the punch. The elf lived in a wee house in the enchanted forest:* tiny, very small, little, minute, minuscule, scant, scanty, *Informal* teeny, teeny-weeny, itsy-bitsy; diminutive, miniature, pocket-size, petite; undersized, dwarf, lilliputian.

Ant. big, large, huge, immense, enormous.

weed *n.* **1** *Pull up the weeds or the carrots won't grow:* unwanted or wild plant.

—*v.* **2** *First thing tomorrow I have to weed the garden. The trouble-makers must be weeded out and sent elsewhere:* remove weeds from, rid of weeds, hoe; root out, uproot, separate, eliminate, remove, eradicate.

◇ *Word origin: Weed* comes from Old English *wēod,* weed. Our other word *weed,* as in *widow's weeds,* comes from Old English *waed,* garment.

weep *v. Don't weep for the dead, for they are at peace. Susan is always weeping over her lost youth:* shed tears, cry, sob, wail, keen, whimper, snivel, mourn, bemoan, lament, grieve.

Ant. laugh, rejoice, smile, be happy, enjoy.

weigh *v.* **1** *When on a diet, weigh yourself every day. I weigh 10 stone. Weigh out half a pound of flour for the cake:* ascertain the weight of, determine the heaviness of, have a weight of; measure by weight; deal out by weight. **2** *Freezing rain weighed down the branches. The lies began to weigh on his conscience:* burden, be a burden, make heavy, bear down, press, overload, saddle, tax. **3** *All that talk of rich friends doesn't weigh with me:* have influence, be influential, carry weight, count, have importance, be potent, work upon, persuade, *Informal* cut any ice. **4** *The jury must weigh the evidence before reaching a verdict:* consider carefully, ponder, judge, adjudge, balance in the mind, contemplate, brood over, ruminate on, meditate upon, mull over, reflect upon; study, examine.

Ant. 2 lighten; alleviate, relieve, ease, allay.

weight *n.* **1** *The weight of the rafters caused the walls to give:* heaviness, poundage, tonnage, mass, ponderousness; relative density. **2** *That package is a heavy weight for a child to carry. He's beginning to feel the weight of his financial problems:* load, burden, stress, strain, pressure. **3** *The mayor's opinion carries great weight in this town. Tax reform is a matter of some weight:* importance, influence, import, magnitude, significance, consequence, value, consideration, emphasis, urgency, concern.

—*v.* **4** *The statue was weighted with a lead base:* add weight to, weigh down, make heavy, make heavier; ballast, burden, encumber, saddle, tax, load.

Ant. 1 weightlessness. **3** unimportance, insignificance. **4** lighten, buoy, lift up.

weighty *adj.* **1** *The goods wagon held a weighty shipment of ore:* heavy, massive, hefty; ponderous, cumbrous, cumbersome, burdensome. **2** *How long has she had to bear this weighty responsibility?:* burdensome, onerous, oppressive, crushing, trying, taxing, difficult, arduous, troublesome. **3** *This is a weighty problem with no quick answer:* important, significant, consequential, serious, grave, earnest, solemn; substantial, considerable; urgent, crucial, critical, pressing, vital, essential.

Ant. 1–3 light, lightweight. **2** easy, easy to bear. **3** unimportant, insignificant, trivial, trifling, paltry, slight, frivolous.

weird *adj.* **1** *Weird noises came from the haunted house at night:* eerie, mysterious, strange, unearthly, spooky, supernatural, ghostly, phantasmal; mystic, magical. **2** *She certainly has a weird sense of humour:* odd, queer, eccentric, bizarre, freakish, grotesque, abnormal, unconventional, unnatural, unorthodox, strange, curious, peculiar, unusual, outlandish, *Slang* crazy, nutty, wild, far-out.

Ant. 1, 2 natural, normal. **2** usual, everyday, customary, routine, regular, common, familiar, conventional, orthodox, run-of-the-mill, *Slang* square, straight.

welcome *n.* **1** *The guests received a warm welcome:* greeting, salutation, salute; reception.
—*v.* **2** *The mayor welcomed the visiting dignitaries at the airport:* greet, receive, bid welcome, meet; admit, usher in, treat hospitably, offer hospitality to, entertain, do the honours, embrace, hold out the hand to, shake hands with, roll out the red carpet; receive with open arms, accept eagerly.
—*adj.* **3** *The host made us all feel welcome. What a welcome surprise!:* gladly received, wanted, accepted, at home, comfortable, hospitably entertained; agreeable, delightful, pleasant, pleasing, gratifying, inviting, engaging, winning, enticing, charming. **4** *All guests are welcome to use the golf-course. You're most welcome — don't thank me:* given full right to, free to enjoy, admitted; under no obligation.

welfare *n.* **1** *Parents are concerned about the welfare of their children. I give you this advice for your own welfare:* well-being, happiness, good, good fortune, advantage, benefit, profit; health. **2** *How long has the family been on welfare?:* the dole, relief, public assistance.

well[1] *n.* **1** *They sank the well to a depth of 250 feet:* hole drilled in ground to obtain water, oil, etc. **2** *There's a natural well behind the cottage:* spring, pool, fountain.
—*v.* **3** *Petroleum suddenly welled out of the ground. Tears welled up in her eyes:* pour, flow, stream, surge, issue, run, rise, gush, spurt, spout, spring, jet, ooze.
◇ *Word origin: Well* comes from Old English *weallan,* to boil, bubble up, gush up, as water, oil, and natural gas do in some wells.

well[2] *adv.* **1** *Alison is getting along well at school. The poor man can't hear well:* adequately, satisfactorily, nicely, acceptably, fairly well, properly, agreeably; quite well, successfully, commendably, laudably, splendidly, advantageously, famously, capitally, first-rate; auspiciously, favourably, propitiously. **2** *Dust the room well:* thoroughly, fully, completely, carefully. **3** *We could not very well turn down her invitation:* properly, rightly, justly, fairly, correctly, suitably; readily, easily. **4** *The new play was well received by the critics:* favourably, kindly, approvingly, warmly, sympathetically, enthusiastically. **5** *The bracelet is worth well over a thousand pounds:* considerably, substantially, amply, abundantly, sufficiently, very much. **6** *Do you know your neighbours well?:* intimately, familiarly, personally.
—*adj.* **7** *The doctor says you'll be well again in a few days:* in good health, healthy, strong, robust, vigorous, sound, hale, hearty, in fine fettle, up and about; rosy-cheeked. **8** *It's as well the children didn't see what happened:* good, right, proper, fitting; fortunate. **9** *All is well with the family:* satisfactory, good, going well, faring well, happy, successful, prosperous, auspicious, felicitous: advantageous, favourable, promising, lucky.
Ant. 1, 2, 4 badly, poorly. **8, 9** bad. **1** unsatisfactorily, inadequately, imperfectly, unacceptably, unsuccessfully. **2** carelessly, indifferently, sloppily, incompletely. **3** unjustly, unfairly, incorrectly, improperly. **4** unfavourably, unkindly, disapprovingly, unsympathetically; unenthusiastically, mildly, coolly. **5** somewhat, not much, scarcely. **7** sick, sickly, ill, unwell, infirm, diseased, ailing; poorly; weak, feeble, frail. **8** wrong, improper, unfitting, unfortunate. **9** unsatisfactory, going badly, unsuccessful; inauspicious, unfavourable.
◇ *Usage note:* Beware of confusing *well* and *good.* Basically, *well* is an adverb and means in a satisfactory manner (or in good health) — it is the opposite of *badly.* Thus, *The job pays well. She plays bridge well but chess badly. Good* is an adjective meaning satisfactory or excellent — it is the opposite of *bad: He gets good pay for the job, She is a good bridge player but a bad golfer.*

well-being *n. We were greatly concerned for your well-being. Carrying a good-luck charm will not insure your well-being:* welfare, happiness, felicity, good; success, profit, advantage, benefit, luck, good luck, fortune, affluence, prosperity, ease, comfort; health.

welt *n. The blow from the falling branch left a large welt on the horseman's arm:* raised ridge on the skin, wale, weal, swelling, stripe, streak; lump, bump, mark, contusion.

welter *v.* **1** *The dog weltered happily in the muddy puddle:* wallow, grovel, tumble about.
—*n.* **2** *Sort this welter of dirty clothes for the laundry:* jumble, mass, heap, mess, pile, hotchpotch. **3** *It's hard to hear above the welter of street noises:* confusion, tumult, commotion, turmoil, hubbub, racket, bustle; turbulence, storm, tempest.

wend *v. It's time to wend our way home:* direct one's path, proceed, move along towards, betake oneself, hie to, steer towards, make.

wet *adj.* **1** *Take off that wet jacket:* wringing wet, soaked, soaking, drenched, dripping, sodden, sopping, waterlogged, watery, soggy, moist, damp, dampened; dank, humid, clammy. **2** *Wet weather is predicted for tomorrow:* rainy, showery, stormy. **3** *The little boy wrote his name in the wet sand:* liquid, liquefied, not dry, not dried; not set, not hardened.
—*n.* **4** *Air the house to get rid of the wet:* wetness, moisture, moistness, dampness, dankness, clamminess, condensation, exudation. **5** *Button up your raincoat before going out in the wet:* rain, rainy weather, rainstorm, storm, bad weather, shower; precipitation, water.
—*v.* **6** *Do you wet your hair before combing it?:* moisten, dampen, damp, sprinkle, splash,

soak, drench, immerse, submerge, dip, steep; water, irrigate, inundate.
Ant. 1-3, 6 dry. **1** bone-dry, parched. **3** dried; set, hardened; non-liquid, solid. **4** dryness. **5** dry weather, fair weather, good weather. **6** parch, desiccate, dehydrate, evaporate.

whack *v.* **1** *The child whacked the puppy with a rolled-up newspaper:* strike, smack, clout, clobber, hit, belt, slug, sock, wallop, slam, smite, pound, baste, slap, cuff, box.
—*n.* **2** *The falling board gave him an awful whack on the head:* hit, blow, smack, clout, knock, belt, sock, wallop, thump, rap, bang; punch, slap, cuff, box. **3** *Have a whack at opening this jar:* try, go, attempt, trial, turn, *Slang* bash, crack, stab; endeavour, venture.

wharf *n. The shrimping boats unloaded their catch at the wharf:* pier, dock, landing-stage, jetty.
◇ *Word origin:* Like many words beginning with *wh, wharf* comes from an Old English word starting with *hw, hwearf.* In the last thousand years, most words that once began in *hw* have undergone this spelling change.

wheedle *v. Mother tried to wheedle father into going to the party:* coax, cajole, flatter, inveigle, charm, beguile, lure, entice, *Slang* butter up.
Ant. force, coerce, bully, browbeat, cow, intimidate, dragoon, bulldoze.

wheel *n.* **1** *American Indians had not discovered the wheel by the time the European settlers arrived. The refrigerator is mounted on wheels:* disc mounted on an axle; roller, caster, drum; ring, circle, hoop, round, disc.
—*v.* **2** *He wheeled about and saw a figure in the doorway. Dancers wheeled gracefully on the ballroom floor:* turn quickly, turn round, pivot, rotate, revolve, spin, swivel, whirl; circle, gyrate, twirl, swirl, pirouette. **3** *I shall wheel my bicycle up the hill:* roll, push along on wheels.

wheeze *v.* **1** *An allergy can make a person wheeze and sneeze:* breathe audibly, breathe with a whistling sound; breathe hard, gasp, puff, huff and puff, pant; hiss, whistle, cough.
—*n.* **2** *The child had an asthmatic wheeze:* audible breath, whistling breath, gasp, puff, huffing and puffing, panting; whistle, hiss.

whelp *n.* **1** *The mother wolf led her whelps out of the den:* pup, puppy; cub. **2** *That young whelp needs a good whipping:* whipper-snapper, urchin, brat, mischievous boy, good-for-nothing; youngster, lad, youth, stripling, child, kid.

whet *v.* **1** *The woodsman stopped chopping to whet his axe on the grindstone:* hone, grind, strop, sharpen, put an edge on. **2** *The smell of cooking whetted my appetite. The very first paragraph of the book whets the reader's interest:* arouse, excite, stir, awaken, kindle, stimulate, animate, quicken, pique, provoke, induce, tempt, allure, entice, make eager, avid or keen.
Ant. 1 dull, blunt. **2** quench, satisfy, sate, satiate, extinguish, deaden; offend, slake, stifle, damp, dampen, cool.

whiff *n.* **1** *A whiff of air stirred the leaves:* breath, puff, slight gust, draught, zephyr, breeze. **2** *There's a whiff of honeysuckle in the air. Did you get a whiff of that awful cigar?:* faint smell, scent, aroma, bouquet; sniff, smell, breath.

"A whiff of grapeshot can, if needful, become a blast and tempest." —*Thomas Carlyle*

---

whim *n. The boy is spoilt, because his mother panders to his every whim. In Edith's case, becoming a vegetarian was no more than a whim:* fancy, fanciful notion, notion, quirk, whimsy, caprice, conceit, eccentricity, crotchet; sudden notion, urge, impulse, vagary.

whimper *v.* **1** *The child whimpered when he was spanked:* cry softly, sob brokenly, blubber; whine plaintively, snivel.
—*n.* **2** *T. S. Eliot wrote that the world will end "not with a bang but a whimper":* snivelling, whine, sobbing, sob.
Ant. 1 howl, bawl. **2** howl.

whimsical *adj.* **1** *Jeremy is much too whimsical to be a businessman:* fanciful, capricious, eccentric, quixotic; fickle, fitful, inconsistent, erratic, changeable, chimerical. **2** *Her essay on the feeding of husbands is pleasantly whimsical:* droll, amusing, waggish, fanciful, quaint.
Ant. 1 staid, serious, sedate, sober, practical, down-to-earth, pragmatic, matter-of-fact; steady, consistent.

whine *v.* **1** *The child was whining because he was lost:* cry plaintively, whimper, snivel, mewl. **2** *Don't whine about your low pay; ask for a rise:* complain, grumble, fret, grouse, gripe.
—*n.* **3** *The dog let out a piercing whine and scuttled away. A whine of anguish came from the bereaved woman:* whimper, plaintive cry, snivel; wail, moan, cry, sob; murmur, complaint, mutter.

whip *n.* **1** *Muleteers need long whips:* horsewhip, thong, lash, strap, scourge, rawhide, cowhide, cat-o'-nine-tails, switch, birch rod, rod.
—*v.* **2** *The boy was whipped for stealing:* horsewhip, flog, strap, scourge, lash, switch, birch, cane; flagellate; beat, spank. **3** *Slang The team really got whipped in its last game:* trounce, drub, maul, beat decisively, defeat soundly, vanquish, rout. *Slang* take apart, lick. **4** *The wind whipped through the trees:* lash, flick, flap; move violently, toss about. **5** *The thief whipped the pen from my hand and ran off:* snatch, jerk, whisk, jolt. **6** *Whip the cream and ladle it over the strawberries:* beat, whisk.

whirl *v.* **1** *The propeller began to whirl, and the small plane started down the runway:* turn, turn round, spin, rotate, revolve; twirl, pivot, gyrate, pirouette, wheel, circle, swirl. **2** *Looking down from that height made my head whirl:* spin, reel; feel dizzy, feel giddy.
—*n.* **3** *The colourful whirl of the dancers was beautiful to watch:* turning, turn, spin, spinning, rotation, revolving, revolution, twirl, twirling, pivoting, pivot, gyration, pirouette,

wheeling, circle, circling, swirling. **4** *Christmas weekend was nothing but a whirl of parties:* rapid round, dizzy round, dizzying succession, flurry, merry-go-round; dither, state of excitement.

whirlpool *n. The swimmers were warned away from the whirlpool:* whirling current, maelstrom, vortex.

whirlwind *n.* **1** *The whirlwind sucked up dust from the fields:* funnel-shaped column of rapidly-rotating air; dust-spout, waterspout.
—adj. **2** *The couple were married after a whirlwind courtship:* impetuous, headlong, breakneck, rash, impulsive, short, quick, speedy, rapid, swift, hasty.
Ant. 2 long, lengthy, plodding, leisurely; careful, thoughtful, well-considered.

whirr *v.* **1** *The machine whirred when he turned on the switch:* run with a humming sound; drone, hum, buzz, whisper, purr.
—n. **2** *We heard the whirr of the vacuum cleaner in the living-room:* drone, hum, buzz, whisper.

whisk *v.* **1** *Whisk the cotton off your coat:* brush, sweep lightly, flick. **2** *The visiting dignitary was whisked away to the council chamber before reporters could question him. The car whisked past the traffic lights:* rush, speed, hasten, move quickly; race, spurt, shoot, tear, fly, whiz, sweep, zip, hurry, scurry, sprint, scoot, dash, bolt, dart, spring, bound, bowl along. **3** *Whisk the egg-whites until they are stiff:* beat, whip.
—n. **4** *With a whisk of his napkin the waiter removed the crumbs from the table:* sweep, brush, flick. **5** *Either an egg-beater or a whisk may be used to whip the eggs and milk:* wire whisk.
Ant. 1 rub, scrape. **2** move slowly, crawl, creep, drag, inch.

whisky Also **whiskey** *n.* **1** *Whisky can be distilled from corn, rye, barley, or other grain:* (*variously*) Scotch, Irish, rye, bourbon, moonshine, *Irish* and *Scottish* usquebaugh, *Irish* poteen, (*loosely*) aqua vitae. **2** *Give me a whisky and soda, please:* shot or tot of whisky.
◇ *Usage note:* The spelling *whisky* is standard in Great Britain, and preferred in Canada and Australia. However, it is spelt *whiskey* in America and with reference to Irish *whiskey*.

whisper *v.* **1** *Whisper, so that no one else will hear. "I love you," he whispered:* speak softly, utter under the breath; murmur, mutter, sigh, breathe; confide, speak confidentially. **2** *People have been whispering about those two for months. Don't whisper it to a soul:* gossip, make an insinuation, spread rumour, rumour, intimate, hint; reveal, divulge, disclose, tell, blurt, blab, bruit. **3** *The wind whispered through the pines:* rustle, murmur, sigh; drone, hum.
—n. **4** *Don't talk above a whisper in here:* undertone, murmur, mutter; indistinct utterance. **5** *There has never been a whisper about the banker's integrity:* insinuation, innuendo, rumour, piece of gossip, gossip; hint, suggestion, inkling. **6** *Listen to the whisper of the wind. The Rolls-Royce makes only a whisper when running at full speed:* rustling sound, rustle, murmur, sigh; drone, hum, purr, buzz.
Ant. 1, 4 shout, scream, roar, bellow, yell, cry. **2** speak out; keep secret, keep confidential, keep under one's hat. **3, 6** roar.

whit *n. He wasn't a whit sorry for what he'd done. Put just a whit of mustard on the sandwiches:* least bit, little bit, speck, mite; dab, drop, dash, pinch, morsel, trifle, jot, dot, iota, modicum, scintilla; fragment, crumb, snip.
Ant. great deal, large amount, lot, heap, load.

white *adj.* **1** *Kathy has beautiful white teeth:* ivory, ivory-coloured, pearl, pearly, snow-white, snowy, alabaster, milky white, cream-coloured. **2** *She turned white with fear:* colourless, pale, pallid, blanched, bleached, wan, ashen, ashy, pasty, ghostly, cadaverous, bloodless, sallow, grey, leaden. **3** *White hair can look distinguished. The fruit bowl was made of white glass:* grey, silver, silvery, hoary, grizzled; cloudy, smoky, filmy, translucent, chalky, milky, off-white, frosted. **4** *White settlers took the Indian's land:* Caucasian, light-skinned; European; fair, blond. **5** *You told her a white lie when you said she looked beautiful:* harmless, unmalicious, benign, innocent. **6** *Her reputation is as white as snow:* pure, spotless, unblemished, unsullied, unstained, unspotted, stainless, clean, immaculate; chaste, innocent, undefiled, virtuous.
Ant. 1 black, jet black, jet, coal black, ebony, raven, inky. **2** ruddy, flushed, rosy, rosy-cheeked, red, pink, florid, high-coloured. **3** clear, colourless, transparent. **4** black, Negroid; red, Indian; yellow, Oriental, coloured. **5** harmful, corrupting, sinister, malicious, vicious, venomous, malevolent, malign, pernicious, destructive. **6** evil, wicked, bad, nefarious, notorious; black, blemished, sullied, stained, spotted, besmirched.

whiten *v.* **1** *Whiten those cricket boots properly! Use a stronger soap to whiten the wash:* make white, make whiter, colour white, frost, silver; clean, bleach, blanch, lighten. **2** *She whitened when she heard the bad news:* pale, blanch, turn pale, turn ashen, turn white.
Ant. 1 blacken; darken, dull. **2** flush, blush.

whitewash *v.* **1** *It's time to whitewash the basement walls again:* paint with a mixture of lime and water, paint white; bleach. **2** *The committee's report tries to whitewash the minister's misdeeds:* excuse, justify, vindicate, absolve, exonerate; cover up, gloss over, glaze over, make allowances for.

whittle *v.* **1** *The little boy loved to sit and whittle sticks:* cut away bit by bit, carve roughly, carve, pare, chip away at. **2** *The company has whittled down its debt by about half. Faster planes have whittled an hour off the transatlantic-crossing time:* reduce gradually, lessen, pare, cut, shave, slash, decrease, shorten, curtail, clip.

whiz Also **whizz** *v.* **1** *The sentry heard a bullet*

whiz past his head: whistle, swish, sizzle, whirr, whine, hiss, buzz, hum, drone. **2** *The powerful lorries whizzed past the slower cars:* speed, race, shoot, tear, fly, spurt, zoom, zip, sweep, whisk, scoot, rush, hasten, scurry, scud, scuttle, dash, dart, sprint, bolt, bowl along, make time, make tracks.
—*n.* **3** *The deer heard the whiz of the hunter's arrow and ran:* swish, whistle, whirr, whine, hiss, buzz, hum, drone. **4** Usually **whiz-kid** *Informal Jean's a whiz-kid at maths:* expert, adept, wizard, dab hand, genius; master, masterhand, skilled hand.

whole *adj.* **1** *The two boys ate a whole pizza by themselves. It rained for the whole week:* entire, complete, full, total, unabridged. **2** *Captive seals would still rather eat whole fish than pieces:* in one piece, entire, undivided, uncut, unbroken; complete, intact, undiminished. **3** *After a month of recuperation he's whole again:* sound, well, healthy, in good health, hale, robust, vigorous; unharmed, uninjured, unbroken, undiminished, perfect.
—*n.* **4** *Buying the house will take the whole of your savings:* entire amount, total, sum total, aggregate; bulk, major part, main part, body, essence, quintessence. **5** *The table and six chairs make up the whole. These items make up the whole contract:* totality, entirety, unit, ensemble, system, assemblage, completeness.
Ant. **1** partial, incomplete. **2** divided, cut up, cut, broken, fractional. **3** sick, sickly, ill, ailing, unwell, diseased, feeble, faint, frail; injured, hurt, broken, flawed, imperfect. **4, 5** part, piece, segment, division, portion. **5** component, element, constituent.

whole-hearted *adj. The plan has my whole-hearted support:* sincere, unfeigned, true, heartfelt, deeply felt, complete, unreserved, earnest, serious, enthusiastic, emphatic.
Ant. half-hearted, lukewarm, faint, indifferent, perfunctory, unenthusiastic.

wholesome *adj.* **1** *A wholesome diet is essential for energy and alertness. The wholesome climate of the area is to be recommended:* healthful, healthy, nutritious, nourishing, health-giving, strengthening, invigorating; sanitary, hygienic. **2** *Wholesome friends, it is hoped, will never lead the girl astray.* Little Women *is a very wholesome book:* morally healthy, moral, honourable, right-minded, responsible, virtuous, upright, nice, decent, pure, clean, clean-minded, innocent, uplifting, worthy, meritorious, exemplary, ethical, honest, principled, dutiful.
Ant. **1–2** unwholesome. **1** unhealthful, unhealthy, pernicious, harmful, detrimental, deleterious, noxious; unsanitary, unhygienic. **2** immoral, dishonourable, evil, evil-minded, wicked, sinful, bad, indecent, impure, dirty-minded, filthy, lewd, degrading, unworthy, unethical, dishonest, crooked, unprincipled.

wholly *adv. I'm wholly in agreement with you:* entirely, completely, fully, totally, *Latin* in toto; utterly, perfectly, altogether, as a whole, in every respect, from beginning to end.
Ant. partially, incompletely, in part, somewhat, imperfectly, in some respects.

whoop *n.* **1** *The Indian let out a blood-curdling war whoop:* shout, yell, scream, cry, shriek, roar, bellow, howl, screech, hollo, outcry, hue and cry; cheer, hurrah.
—*v.* **2** *The children whooped with joy:* shout, yell, cry, cry out, shriek, screech, scream, howl, roar, bellow, hoot, rend the air; cheer, hurrah; hollo.

whore *n. Daniel Defoe's novel* Moll Flanders *tells the story of a whore:* prostitute, woman of ill fame, woman of ill repute, fallen woman, harlot, bawd, hustler, strumpet, trollop, jade, doxy, woman of easy virtue, demimondaine, lady of the night, fancy woman, painted lady, Jezebel, tart, street-walker, chippy, call-girl, *Slang* pro; mistress, kept woman, courtesan, concubine; hussy, slut.
Ant. nice girl, good girl, honest woman, respectable woman, lady.

whorl *n. The petals of the flower are arranged in whorls about the centre:* spiral arrangement, circular arrangement, spiral, circle, coil, convolution, curl, roll, corkscrew, helix.

wicked *adj.* **1** *Wicked deeds must be repented of:* evil, sinful, immoral, bad, iniquitous, reprehensible, vile, foul, base, gross, low, heinous, abominable, atrocious, hellish, fiendish, devilish, satanic, nefarious, cursed, villainous, evil-hearted, infamous, vicious, malicious, malevolent, evil-minded, shameful, scandalous, dishonourable, disgraceful, corrupt, depraved, degenerate, monstrous. **2** *Wicked children should be punished:* naughty, mischievous, rowdy, impish, knavish, rascally, ill-behaved, incorrigible. **3** *I have such a wicked toothache. I'm in agony:* intense, severe, serious, acute, fierce, extreme, bad, raging, rampant, awful, dreadful, fearful, painful, bothersome, troublesome, galling.
Ant. **1** moral, wholesome, upright, righteous, honourable, good, noble, ethical, honest, principled, benevolent, worthy, exemplary. **2** well-behaved, well-mannered, obedient.

wide *adj.* **1** *How wide is this living-room? Pall Mall is very wide:* broad, spacious, large. **2** *The plane flew over the wide Arctic wastes. The group discussed a wide variety of subjects:* broad, extensive, vast, spacious, immense, great, boundless, far-flung, far-reaching, wide-ranging, widespread. **3** *Are the shoes wide enough for your feet?:* large from side to side, ample, roomy, commodious, capacious. **4** *The children's eyes were wide with excitement as Father Christmas led the parade down the street:* wide open, fully open; expanded, dilated; extended, distended; outstretched, outspread.

—*adv.* **5** *The dentist asked me to "open wide." Leave the door wide open:* fully, completely, as far as possible.

Ant. 1-4 narrow. **1** long; deep. **2** restricted, constricted, limited, small. **3** tight, cramped, confined. **4** shut, closed, contracted. **5** barely, narrowly; partially.

widen *v. They are going to widen High Street. You ought to widen your circle of acquaintances:* make wider, broaden, spread, spread out, stretch; enlarge, expand, extend.

Ant. narrow, close, take in; reduce, decrease, contract.

widespread *adj.* **1** *A widespread flu epidemic affected much of Britain:* affecting a large area, extending far and wide, far-flung, far-reaching, extensive, broad. **2** *She greeted her son with widespread arms:* wide open, open, fully extended, outspread.

Ant. 1 localized, narrow, restricted, confined, limited, small. **2** closed, folded.

wield *v.* **1** *Sir Lancelot was adept at wielding his sword:* handle, ply, manage, manipulate; brandish, flourish, wave, swing. **2** *The sales manager wields tremendous power in this company:* exert, exercise, employ, display, have, use.

wife *n. His wife is a schoolteacher:* spouse, consort, companion, marriage partner; better half, helpmate, mate, helpmeet, *Dialectal* woman, *Slang* missis, old woman, old lady; bride; married woman.

Ant. single woman, miss, spinster, old maid.

◇ *Usage note: Spouse, consort,* and *companion* may all mean either "husband" or "wife." In formal writing, *consort* is used mainly to refer to a royal spouse: *As Queen Victoria's husband, Albert of Saxe-Coburg-Gotha is referred to as the Prince Consort. Companion* is obsolete as a legal term for "marriage partner" but is frequently seen as a synonym for "spouse" in certain written contexts: *I dedicate this book to my dear companion and helper.*

wig *n. The bald man bought a wig. The woman has a long blonde wig for the evening and a short one for daytime:* toupee, hair-piece, *Archaic* periwig, peruke.

◇ *Word origin: Wig* is short for *periwig*, a style of wig worn by men in the 17th and 18th centuries, having hair combed smoothly back from the forehead and across the top and often ending in one to three cylinders of curls just above the collar, as seen in many portraits of George III and his courtiers.

wiggle *v.* **1** *Can you wiggle your ears? Sit still, child, and stop wiggling!:* wag, waggle, shake, twitch, jerk, flutter, quiver; squirm, writhe.

—*n.* **2** *The squirrel made a little wiggle with his tail and jumped to another branch:* jerk, twitch, wag, waggle, flutter, shake; squirming, wriggling, writhing.

wild *adj., adv.* **1** *Some wild ponies still live on Exmoor. A pack of dogs runs wild in these woods:* living in a natural state, untamed, undomesticated, unbroken; feral, savage. **2** *Have you ever eaten wild bilberries? Strawberries grow wild on this hill:* uncultivated; without cultivation, naturally, by themselves. **3** *Dartmoor National Park is a wild and wind-swept region. After the nomads left, the area grew wild again:* untouched by man, uninhabited, uncultivated, natural; rugged, waste, bleak, desolate, abandoned; wooded, forested, overgrown. **4** *Wild tribes still inhabit some of the islands. Aborigines still live wild in the jungle:* uncivilized, primitive, savage, barbaric; ferocious, fierce; in an uncivilized state, in a primitive state. **5** *We ran into wild seas on our third day out. The wind blew wild:* violent, furious, tempestuous, blustery, howling; rough, choppy, turbulent; wildly, violently, furiously. **6** *A group of wild youths vandalized the school. His blazing eyes and wild talk frightened everyone. The mob ran wild in the streets:* unrestrained, disorderly, undisciplined, ungovernable, lawless, unruly, violent; frantic, frenzied, fanatical, rabid, raging, raving, berserk, crazed, insane, maniacal, mad, demented, unhinged; wildly, without restraint, lawlessly, violently, rampantly, insanely, maniacally, madly. **7** *I made a wild guess at the answer. Is that another of his wild ideas to make us all rich?:* reckless, rash, uninformed, ill-advised, illogical; impractical, fantastic, bizarre, giddy, flighty, fanciful, madcap, hare-brained, rattle-brained, *Slang* nutty, screwy; wide of the mark.

—*n.* **the wild** or **wilds 8** *The outlaw roamed the wilds for weeks at a time:* wilderness, bush; barren area, waste land.

Ant. 1 domesticated, tame, broken. **2** cultivated, planted. **3** populated, inhabited, cultivated; bare, barren. **4** civilized, advanced; friendly. **5, 6** calm, mild, gentle, quiet; calmly, mildly, gently, quietly. **6** well-behaved, orderly, law-abiding, lawful, peaceful; serene, tranquil; rational, sane; politely, peacefully, serenely. **7** careful, thoughtful, well-advised; realistic, practical, logical.

wilderness *n. The hunting-lodge is far out in the wilderness:* wilds, bush, unsettled, remote or desolate area, outback; waste land, waste.

wile *n.* Often **wiles 1** *She used all her feminine wiles to get him to go to the dance:* sly trick, trickery, artifice, ruse, contrivance, machination, chicanery, stratagem, manœuvre, ploy, gambit, trap; cunning, artfulness, craftiness, guile, subtlety.

—*v.* **2** *Can't you wile father away from the television set for one evening?:* lure, entice, seduce, charm; coax, cajole.

Ant. 1 frankness, openness, artlessness, simplicity, candour, straightforwardness, ingenuousness.

wilful *adj.* **1** *It wasn't accidental manslaughter; it was wilful murder:* deliberate, purposeful, intentional, intended, planned, premeditated, studied, designed, contemplated. **2** *There's no use arguing with such a wilful person:* stubborn, obstinate, unyielding, uncompromising, inflexible, persistent, determined, headstrong, perverse, self-willed, intractable, obdurate, closed-minded, mulish, pigheaded, bull-headed; unruly, ungovernable, undisciplined.

Ant. 1 unintentional, unintended, accidental, involuntary, unpremeditated, unplanned. **2** compliant, acquiescent, manageable, submissive, amenable, agreeable; obedient, tractable, docile.

will *n.* **1** *No one stands a chance against her iron will. The team has a strong will to win:* will-power, force of will, moral courage, self-discipline, strength of purpose, conviction; determination, resolution, resoluteness; desire, wish. **2** *What is your will, my lord?:* desire, wish, preference, inclination, pleasure; longing, yearning, craving, hankering. **3** *The shop wishes to retain its customer's goodwill. Woe to anyone who incurs ner ill will:* feeling, personal feeling, disposition, attitude. **4** *He died without leaving a will:* last will and testament.

—v. **5** *You can succeed if you will it strongly enough:* be resolved for, resolve, desire, want, wish for, determine upon. **6** *The deceased willed his vast estate to his daughters:* bequeath, endow, bestow, leave as an inheritance, confer, convey at death.

Ant. 1 irresolution, indecision, vacillation, wishy-washiness, indifference. **2** dislike, hatred, disinclination; loathing, detestation. **5** be irresolute, be indecisive, vacillate.

willing *adj. I'm willing to go if you are:* favourably inclined, content, favourably disposed, amenable, agreeable, not averse, game; ready.

Ant. unwilling, disinclined, reluctant, loath, averse.

willowy *adj. Most ballerinas are willowy:* gracefully slender, lithe, lissome, supple, limber, pliant, flexible.

wilt *v.* **1** *The roses were beautiful for a week, then they wilted:* wither, droop, become limp; shrivel, die. **2** *The old man's strength wilted away. His courage wilted when he saw the enemy:* wither, fade, wane, ebb, recede, subside, sink, dwindle, diminish, languish, decline, weaken, decrease, deteriorate, degenerate, flag, sag.

wily *adj. He's too wily to be trusted:* devious, sly, cunning, crafty, foxy, tricky, scheming, designing, intriguing, artful, deceptive, underhand, treacherous, deceitful, guileful, shifty, crooked; shrewd, sharp, alert.

Ant. open, candid, frank, sincere, honest, straightforward, above-board; innocent, simple, artless, guileless.

win *v.* **1** *The team must win today. Unless the defenders are reinforced the invading troops will win:* be victorious, triumph, prevail, conquer, vanquish, overcome, master, carry all before one, win the day. **2** *The actor won an Oscar for his role in the film. The youth won his diploma in only three years:* earn, gain, attain, achieve, accomplish, realize, acquire, obtain, secure, get, procure, receive, collect, pick up; *Informal* bag, net. **3** *Saint Olaf won Scandinavian converts to Christianity. Opponents of the plan must be won over:* convince, persuade, influence, convert, induce, sway, prevail on, bring round.

—n. **4** *Four more wins and the team will clinch the championship:* victory, triumph, success, conquest; winning game, winning contest.

Ant. 1-3 lose. **1** be defeated, be beaten, fail, miss. **3** alienate, estrange. **4** loss, defeat; tie, draw.

wince *v.* **1** *The patient winced when he took the foul-tasting medicine. The boy winced when his father raised his hand in anger:* grimace, make a face, flinch, shudder, draw back, recoil, shrink, quail, cower, cringe.

—n. **2** *He was unable to control an occasional wince whilst the surgeon was setting his leg:* grimace, flinch, shudder, recoil, shrinking, quailing, cowering, cringing.

wind[1] *n.* **1** *Is there enough wind to fly a kite today?:* air current, breeze, zephyr, draught, gust, blast, whiff, puff, air. **2** *The wind blew down several trees:* heavy wind, windstorm, gale, blow; (*variously*) tornado, cyclone, hurricane, tempest, typhoon, whirlwind. **3** *In this passage the wind carries the melody:* wind instrument; (*variously*) oboe, clarinet, flute, piccolo, trumpet, trombone. **4** *The blow knocked the wind out of him:* breath, air. **5** *If the deer gets wind of us, he'll run into the woods. How could he have got wind of our plans?:* scent, smell; hint, suggestion, inkling, intimation, clue, whisper, information, intelligence, news, knowledge, tidings, report. **6** *The challenger says he'll knock out the champion in the first round, but that's a lot of wind:* empty talk, idle talk, boasting, bombast, bluster, mere words, bluff, braggadocio, fanfaronade, twaddle, *Slang* hot air, nonsense.

Ant. 1 calm, dead calm, calmness, stillness. **3** strings; percussion.

wind[2] *v.* **1** *The stream winds through the valley. The hikers wound their way up the hill:* curve, bend, snake, twist, zigzag, ramble, wander, meander. **2** *Wind the wire round the post. Wind the yarn into a ball:* coil, twist, curl, loop, twine, entwine, lap, fold; roll, twirl.

Ant. 1 go straight as an arrow, make a beeline.

window *n. The room has windows on three sides:* opening to admit air or light; dormer, casement, bay; transom, skylight.

◇ *Word origin: Window* comes from Old Norse *vindr* (wind) + *auga* (eye), literally "wind-eye," i.e. an opening for air to enter.

windy *adj.* **1** *March is usually a windy month. The house stands on a windy hill:* breezy, blowy, gusty, blustery; wind-swept. **2** *The headmaster always makes such long windy speeches:* long-winded, wordy, rambling, meandering, verbose, garrulous, talkative, loquacious, gabby; empty, bombastic, grandiloquent, rhetorical.

Ant. 1 windless; calm, still. **2** terse, concise, pithy, succinct, pointed, trenchant.

wing *n.* **1** *The goldfinch's wings are black with yellow bars. The petrol tanks are in the aeroplane's wings:* pinion, pennon, arm; supporting surface, flap, aileron. **2** *The master bedroom is in the east wing of the mansion:* section; annex, addition, extension, appendage, adjunct. **3** *The actors stood in the wings waiting to go on stage:* side part of the stage, coulisse. **4** *He belongs to the radical wing of the party:* faction, segment, side, fraternity, group, band, knot, clique, circle, set, coterie.

—*v.* **5** *The bird winged its way through the storm. The aircraft winged out over the Atlantic:* fly, soar, zoom; take wing, take to the air. **6** *The shot winged the escaping convict:* hit in the arm or wing; wound slightly, graze, nick, clip.

winner *n. The champion was the winner by a knock-out:* victor, champion, master, vanquisher, conqueror.

wipe *v.* **1** *Wipe your shoes on the mat. Wipe the crumbs off the table. Wipe wax on the scratched surface:* rub lightly; (*variously*) clean, swab, sponge, dust, mop, scrub, scour, rub off; dry, towel; remove, take off, clean off; rub on, apply. **2** *Informal She told him to wipe the grin off his face:* remove, take away from, banish, get rid of, erase, eradicate.

—*n.* **3** *It takes more than a wipe or two to clean the oven:* swipe, rub, swab, stroke, brush.

wire *n.* **1** *One of the connecting wires came loose:* metal thread, metal strand; electric wire, electric cable, filament. **2** *The message came by wire. We received a wire saying that they had arrived safely:* telegram, cable.

—*v.* **3** *Wire the lid to the box. Is the garage wired for electricity?:* attach by a wire, fasten with wires, bind with wires; equip with wiring, install wires in. **4** *Informal Please wire me when you arrive:* send by telegraph, cable.

wiry *adj. The child has black, wiry hair:* resembling wire, wire-like; stiff, brittle, kinky. **2** *The gymnast was a wiry young man of twenty:* sinewy, lean; strong and supple, agile, limber, pliant.

wisdom *n.* **1** *Learning facts does not necessarily give one wisdom:* good judgement, sagacity, understanding, profundity, judiciousness, discernment, comprehension, penetration, apperception, intelligence, brains. **2** *The class will discuss the wisdom of Plato:* philosophy, teachings, principles, ideas.

Ant. 1 folly, foolishness, stupidity, nonsense, absurdity, senselessness, silliness.

wise[1] *adj. The judge is a very wise man:* having good judgement, sagacious, understanding, profound, judicious, discerning, perceptive, intelligent, knowing, knowledgeable.

Ant. foolish, stupid, silly, injudicious, unwise.

wise[2] *n. Archaic This will in no wise infringe anyone's rights:* way, manner, respect.

wish *v.* **1** *I wish to retire next year. We wish you luck:* want, desire, hope, long, crave, yearn, pine, hunger, thirst, aspire, set one's heart upon; desire one to have, want to come about.

—*n.* **2** *He tries to satisfy her every wish. Helen's wish is to visit Rome:* want, desire, hope, longing, craving, yearning, urge, aspiration, ambition; hunger, thirst, appetite, whim, fondness, love, penchant, inclination, leaning, partiality, predilection. **3** *It is dangerous to go contrary to the king's wish:* request, command, will, desire, want. **4** Usually **wishes** *Please accept our sincere wishes:* good wishes, best wishes, felicitations, congratulations, compliments.

wishful *adj. He is still wishful of becoming a millionaire. His hope of going to Cambridge is just wishful thinking:* wistful, fanciful, dreamy-eyed, over-optimistic.

wistful *adj.* **1** *The child gave a wistful look at the sweet-shop window:* desirous, yearning, longing, craving, hankering, pining. **2** *Whenever she speaks of her youth, she has a wistful expression:* pensive, sadly thoughtful, reflective, musing, contemplative, meditative, introspective; melancholy, forlorn, sad, sorrowful, woebegone, doleful, mournful, disconsolate.

wit *n.* **1** *A good after-dinner speech must contain some wit. Dorothy Parker's writing is known for its wit:* cleverness, sense of humour, humour, drollery, levity, jocularity, funniness, waggery, quickness at repartee; brightness, sparkle, vivacity. **2** *Oscar Wilde's wit is apparent in everything he writes:* raillery, badinage, persiflage, banter, joking, witty sayings, witticisms, jokes, cracks, gags. **3** *The speaker is known as a wit:* witty person, humorist, joker, wag, gagster, comedian, wisecracker, jester, epigrammatist, punster; satirist. **4** *She showed a great deal of wit in handling the delicate situation:* intelligence, understanding, perception, comprehension, judgement, sense, good sense, common sense, wisdom, insight, penetration, perspicacity, acumen, sagaciousness, sagacity, discernment, astuteness, shrewdness, cunning, intellect, *Informal* brains, nous. **5 wits** *I was out of my wits with worry. Keep your wits about you when you're driving:* mind, sanity, composure, mental balance, cool-headedness; mental alertness.

Ant. 1 seriousness, gravity, solemnity, sobriety, dullness. **4** foolishness, stupidity, silliness, folly, dumbness, obtuseness.

witch *n.* **1** *The witch put an evil spell on the young princess:* devil's consort, sorceress, female magician; (*loosely*) seeress, prophetess, enchantress, temptress. **2** *She's nice but her sister's* *a witch:* hag, crone, harridan, ugly old woman, battle-axe, beldam, ogress; mean woman, shrew, virago, termagant, scold, fury, vixen.

witchcraft *n. The old woman was drowned for practising witchcraft:* worship of the Devil, the cult of Satan; sorcery, wizardry, black magic, black art, witchery, voodoo, voodooism, conjuration, casting of spells, divination, enchantment, fetishism.

withdraw *v.* **1** *He withdrew his hand from the back of her chair. Withdraw fifty pounds from the savings account:* remove, take away, take off; extract. **2** *The waiter withdrew after serving the meal:* retire, retreat, go away, go, move away, leave, depart, disappear, absent oneself, make oneself scarce, *Informal* buzz off, skedaddle, *Slang* split. **3** *I withdraw that last statement and ask that it be struck from the record:* retract, take back, recant; rescind, recall.

Ant. **1** put on; put in; sheathe. **2** arrive, come, come near, appear. **3** introduce, propose, advance, offer; repeat, reiterate.

withdrawn *adj. The child is so withdrawn that we're becoming concerned about her:* retiring, reserved, uncommunicative, shy, quiet, introverted, unsocial, unfriendly.

Ant. boisterous, extroverted, open, sociable, friendly, gregarious, gay.

wither *v.* **1** *Because of the drought, most of the fruit withered. Frosts withered the leaves until the trees were bare:* wilt, droop, shrivel, dry up, fade, dehydrate, desiccate, blast. **2** *She withered him with one scornful look:* shame, cut down, humiliate, blast, abash, mortify.

Ant. **1** bloom, flower, blossom; flourish, thrive. **2** praise, compliment.

◇ *Word origin: Wither* is a variant of the verb to *weather.* Hence to *wither,* to dry, droop, or die in the sun or air, really means to *weather,* be dried by the air or weather.

withhold *v.* **1** *The company withholds part of its employees' earnings for income tax:* hold back, hold, keep back, keep, retain. **2** *The witness was accused of withholding information:* hold back, keep back, conceal, hide, suppress, keep secret, hush up; *Informal* sit on.

Ant. **1, 2** give, provide, furnish. **1** grant, bestow, confer, yield, let go; let loose, free, promote, advance, encourage. **2** reveal, disclose, divulge, expose, lay bare.

◇ *Spelling tip:* When some people are writing rapidly, they sometimes forget the second *h* in *withhold. WitHHold* that impulse—two *h's* are needed.

withstand *v. A politician must be able to withstand public criticism. This dress material will withstand repeated washing:* stand up to, resist, endure, bear, suffer, tolerate, weather, defy; grapple with, cope with.

witness *v.* **1** *Did anyone witness the robbery?:* see in person, see, observe, view, behold, look on; note, mark, notice, perceive; attend, be present at. **2** *A notary public must witness the signatures on the contract. Severe damage witnessed to the force of the storm:* verify, certify, corroborate, authenticate, substantiate, document, validate, endorse, sign, countersign, initial; attest to, confirm, vouch for, testify to, give testimony of, evidence, establish, bear out.

—*n.* **3** *Were there any witnesses of the accident?:* eyewitness, onlooker, observer, spectator, looker-on, beholder. **4** *Counsel for the defence called his next witness:* person who gives testimony, person who gives evidence, testifier, attester, deponent. **5** *His worried look bears witness to the strain that he's under:* evidence, testimony, proof, confirmation, corroboration, verification, authentication, substantiation, documentation, validation.

witty *adj. Jonathan Swift's writings are both witty and profound:* amusing, clever, funny, humorous, quick-witted, comic, jocular, jocose, waggish, droll, whimsical; sparkling, bright, scintillating, brilliant.

Ant. serious, sombre; sententious, dull, dry; sad, melancholy.

wizard *n.* **1** *Merlin was King Arthur's wizard:* sorcerer, magician, conjurer, medicine-man; oracle, soothsayer; necromancer, diviner, clairvoyant. **2** *Informal That boy is a wizard at maths:* genius, prodigy, expert, adept, virtuoso, *Slang* whiz-kid; sage, wise man.

wobble *v.* **1** *This ladder wobbles when you stand on it:* sway, teeter, totter, be unsteady, reel, waver, shake, quake, shudder.

—*n.* **2** *Put something under the table-leg to stop the wobble:* sway, swaying, teetering, tottering, unsteadiness, wavering, shake, shaking, shuddering, quaking.

woe *n. Job's life was full of woe:* suffering, distress, affliction, trouble, misfortune, misery, trial, tribulation, wretchedness, torment, agony, torture, sorrow, grief, heartache, anguish, dejection, gloom, anxiety, worry, melancholy, depression, despair.

Ant. joy, delight, pleasure, good fortune, happiness, bliss, satisfaction.

woebegone *adj. The bankrupt man walked about with a woebegone look upon his face:* woeful, suffering, distressed, troubled, miserable, wretched, agonized, tortured, sorrowful, doleful, mournful, forlorn, grief-stricken, sad, anguished, dejected, gloomy, funereal.

Ant. happy, cheerful, elated, smiling, joyful.

woeful *adj.* **1** *The woeful news grieved the nation:* distressing, unhappy, tragic, wretched, agonizing, painful, cruel, sorrowful, doleful, grievous, sad, heart-rending, heartbreaking, depressing, crushing, disheartening, lamentable, deplorable, calamitous, disastrous, dreadful, catastrophic. **2** *I've never seen such a woeful bunch of applicants for any job:* of very poor quality, unpromising, unlikely, awful, hopeless, terrible, bad, dreadful, feeble, horrible, miserable, appalling.

Ant. 1 happy, joyous, joyful, delightful, glad, heartening, cheering, cheerful, ecstatic. **2** promising, likely, excellent, wonderful, fine.

woman *n.* **1** *The girl dreamt of the day when she would become a woman:* adult female, lady; (*variously*) dowager, matron; damsel, maiden, maid. **2** *Woman, like man, must strive for political freedom:* womankind, women, females, the female sex, the fair sex, the weaker sex. **3** *The queen's women helped her to put on the royal robe. A woman comes twice a week to clean:* handmaiden, chamber-maid, female attendant, lady-in-waiting, maid, maid-servant, housekeeper, cleaning woman, charwoman, char. **4** *According to the song "Frankie and Johnny," she was his woman but he done her wrong:* paramour, lover, mistress, concubine, kept woman; sweetheart, lady-love, beloved, darling, girl, girl-friend, flame; wife, fiancée, steady girl.

Ant. 1-4 man. **1** girl. **4** beau, boy-friend, *Slang* man, husband, fiancé.

◇ *Word origin: Woman* comes from Old English *wif* (wife) + *mann* (human being, man).

wonder *v.* **1** *I wonder what she sees in him. Joe says that he didn't do it, but I still wonder:* be curious about, be inquisitive; speculate, conjecture, question, be doubtful, be uncertain; meditate, ponder, cogitate. **2** *I wonder at her perennial youthfulness:* marvel, be wonderstruck, stand agog, be awed, be amazed, be dazed, be stunned, be stupefied, be dumbstruck, be surprised, be flabbergasted, gape, stare.

—*n.* **3** *The Table Mountain is one of the natural wonders of the world:* phenomenon, marvel, miracle, wonderful work, rarity, spectacle, sight. **4** *The audience watched the trapeze act in wonder:* amazement, astonishment, wonderment, awe, fascination, stupefaction.

Ant. 1 know, be sure, be certain, comprehend, understand, perceive, see, fathom, work out; ignore, not care, be uninterested. **2** be unmoved, accept as a matter of fact. **3** common occurrence, commonplace, cliché. **4** apathy, unconcern, indifference; boredom.

wonderful *adj.* **1** *The human brain is a wonderful organ:* causing wonder, awe-inspiring, miraculous, amazing, incredible, phenomenal, fabulous, fantastic, unique, singular, extraordinary, astonishing, astounding, staggering, fascinating, striking, surprising, spectacular. **2** *We had a wonderful time:* excellent, admirable, marvellous, magnificent, good, fine, great, terrific, first-rate, capital, tip top, smashing, super, sensational, fabulous, fantastic, superb, divine, *Informal* fab.

Ant. 1 ordinary, common, usual, mediocre, average, modest, paltry, indifferent, uninteresting. **2** awful, terrible, bad, dreadful, abominable, miserable, appalling, horrid, unpleasant, unpleasing, *Slang* beastly, lousy, frightful, grim.

woo *v.* **1** *Father wooed several girls before marrying Mother:* court, pay court to, seek the love of, seek the favours of, pay one's addresses to, pursue, chase, set one's cap at. **2** *The candidate knew how to woo the voters:* try to persuade, solicit the approval of, court, appeal to, pursue, address, sue, importune, curry favour with, *Slang* butter up.

wood *n.* **1** *The room was panelled in the finest wood. Throw some more wood on the fire:* timber, boards, planks, wall-board, weather-board, log, firewood, kindling. **2** Usually **woods** *The hut was in a clearing in the woods:* forest, woodland, wildwood, bush, brush, copse.

Ant. 2 prairie, grasslands, savanna, tundra, meadow, moor, mountain, fen, desert, clearing.

wooden *adj.* **1** *The books were packed in a large wooden crate:* made of wood, wood, frame. **2** *I was amazed how wooden she was on the dance floor:* stiff, rigid, unbending, inflexible, awkward, clumsy, ungainly, ungraceful. **3** *She gave the stranger a wooden stare:* expressionless, dull, vacant, lifeless, unemotional, impassive, dead-pan, poker-faced, glassy-eyed.

Ant. 2 lissome, supple, limber, lithe, pliant, pliable, flexible, graceful. **3** expressive, animated, lively, spirited, emotional, passionate, fervent.

word *n.* **1** *The baby said his first word today. Write your reply in as few words as possible:* meaningful combination of letters, articulate sounds, unit of discourse; term, expression, locution, appellation, designation, sobriquet. **2** *Just let me say a word of thanks:* brief statement, remark, comment, utterance, phrase, pronouncement. **3** *Jenkins, the boss wants to have a word with you:* short talk, chat, brief conversation, discussion, conference, consultation, audience, interview, tête-à-tête, chit-chat, dialogue, discourse, colloquy. **4** **words** *They had words in the lobby and started to fight in the hall:* angry words, argument, quarrel, dispute, bickering, wrangling, altercation, contention, *Informal* set-to, barney. **5** *She sent word that she had arrived safely. What's the latest word from the theatre of war?:* message, communication, news, information, report, tidings, intelligence; dispatch, bulletin, communiqué, letter, telegram, telephone call; rumour, gossip, hearsay, *Slang* scuttle-butt, tittle-tattle. **6** *Bill gave me his word that he would be here:* assurance, promise, word of honour, pledge, vow, avowal, assertion, declaration. **7** *The Commander gave the word to begin moving out:* command, order, direction, decree, notice, summons, dictate, edict, mandate; decision, ruling, ultimatum; signal.

—*v.* **8** *Try to word the letter in a friendly way:* phrase, put into words, find words for, express, articulate, voice, describe, explain.

wording *n. The wording of the law is ambiguous:* phrasing, phraseology, manner of expression, choice of words, language.

wordy *adj. Don't be so wordy; make the report as short as possible:* verbose, long-winded, windy, loquacious, garrulous, talkative, discursive, mumbling, roundabout, prolix, redundant, tautological; grandiloquent, bombastic, turgid, fustian, gushing, effusive, rhetorical.

Ant. concise, terse, succinct, pithy.

work *n.* **1** *It took a lot of work to make that cabinet:* labour, effort, industry, exertion, toil, endeavour, drudgery, trouble, manual labour, elbow-grease, sweat. **2** *Cleaning out the attic is your work for this week-end:* piece of work, job, task, chore, employment, pursuit, assignment. **3** *The man is unemployed and looking for work. The youth decided to make retailing his work:* employment, job, paying job; line of work, occupation, profession, business, vocation, line, métier, trade, craft, calling, pursuit; function, duty, office. **4** *This painting is one of Matisse's greatest works.* Treasure Island *is probably Robert Louis Stevenson's best-known work:* work of art, creation, composition, achievement, performance, handiwork, piece, product, production, endeavour, structure, output; (*variously*) painting, drawing, sculpture, book, opus, symphony, opera, concerto, song, building. **5** *The philanthropist will be long remembered for his good works:* deed, act, achievement, feat; exploit, enterprise, transaction. **6 works** *Before the days of pipelines, many towns used to have their own gasworks:* plant, factory, mill, foundry, yard, shop, workshop. **7 works** *The jeweller opened the case of the watch and cleaned the works:* internal mechanism, moving parts, contents, insides, *Slang* innards.

—*v.* **8** *The boy works part-time at the grocery. The mechanic had to work for hours to repair the car:* be employed, have a job, be occupied, do business, pursue a vocation; labour, toil, be industrious, exert oneself, apply oneself, endeavour, perform, drudge, slave, sweat, *Informal* use elbow-grease, put one's shoulder to the wheel. **9** *How does this machine work? It's a good idea, but it just won't work. I'll just work out this sum:* operate, function, perform, run, go, act; take effect, be effective, succeed; do, solve, execute, enact, transmit, achieve. **10** *Work the dough into a ball:* shape, form, fashion, mould, make, manipulate. **11** *Phil wants to work up to being a sales manager. The ship worked its way into the harbour:* make one's way, progress, move, manœuvre, win, achieve, gain. **12** *Even a great doctor can't work miracles:* bring about, produce, cause, effect; originate.

—*adj.* **13** *Put on work clothes before beginning the job:* for working, of working.

Ant. 1, 2, 8 play. **1** child's play; ease, leisure. **2** recreation, entertainment, fun; rest, relaxation. **3** unemployment; holiday, vacation, leave, retirement; avocation, hobby, spare-time activity. **8** entertain oneself, have fun, relax, take it easy. **11** remain, stay put, mark time. **12** nullify, counteract, reverse. **13** leisure, play.

worker *n. The plant employs 500 workers. The charity needs some more good workers to collect funds:* working man, workman, labourer, labouring man, proletarian; hired hand, hand; employee, job-holder, artisan, craftsman; doer, performer, producer, *Slang* eager beaver; drudge, plodder.

Ant. employer; unemployed person, old-age pensioner; idler, loafer, good-for-nothing, do-nothing, lazy-bones, day-dreamer.

working *n.* **1** *Working takes up about a third of the day:* labour, labouring, toil, industry, exertion, drudgery; employment, job, tasks, chores, assignments, business, profession, occupation, duty. **2** *Do you understand the workings of a watch?:* operation, action, functioning, performance.

—*adj.* **3** *Working mothers left their children at the day nursery:* employed, holding down a job, labouring. **4** *The job requires a working knowledge of Spanish:* usable, useful, practical, effective, operative, fluent.

Ant. 1 play, playing, recreation, fun, entertainment; rest, relaxation, leisure. **3** non-working, unemployed; retired, holidaying.

workmanship *n. The chair is a fine example of 18th-century workmanship:* craftsmanship, handiwork, manual skill, handicraft, handcraft; construction, manufacture, technique.

world *n.* **1** *China is the largest country in the world. Is there life on other worlds?:* the planet Earth, globe, the earth, wide world; planet, heavenly body, celestial object, star. **2** *Man cannot explain many things in the world:* creation, universe, cosmos, macrocosm; nature. **3** *The world must unite in the war against pollution:* mankind, humanity, men, the human race, humankind, people; the public, everyone, everybody. **4** *The sequoia is the tallest member of the plant world. The news shocked the world of science:* group, class, division, system, sphere, domain, realm; profession, industry. **5** *It's nice to get away from the world once in a while:* human affairs, society, social intercourse, day-to-day living; material matters, secular things, mundane interests, worldly things. **6** *The Egyptian pyramids are an outstanding achievement of the ancient world:* era, period, epoch, age, times, duration. **7** *A holiday will do you the world of good:* a great deal, large amount, *Informal* lots, lashings, oodles, loads, heaps.

Ant. 5 spiritual matters, aesthetic matters.

worldly *adj.* **1** *Worldly things meant nothing to the monk:* earthly, terrestrial, mundane, temporal, secular, profane; material, mercenary; physical, corporeal, fleshly. **2** *He's too worldly to be shocked by the scandal:* sophisticated, worldly-wise, blasé, knowing, experienced, callous, hard-boiled.

Ant. 1 spiritual, heavenly, celestial, divine,

holy, sacred; ethereal, transcendental, non-material. **2** innocent, naïve, unsophisticated, artless, ingenuous.

worm *n.* **1** *Worms are good bait for fish:* small legless elongated animal; (*variously*) earth- or tapeworm; intestinal worm, helminth. —*v.* **2** *The hunters silently wormed their way towards the herd of antelope:* creep, crawl, wriggle, inch, edge, steal, advance stealthily.
Ant. 2 run, dart, sprint, dash.

worn *adj.* **1** *Those tyres are too worn to be safe. Can you patch the worn place on this jacket?:* worn through, worn-down, worn-out, frayed, abraded, threadbare, worn to a thread, worn smooth, worse for wear; decrepit, dilapidated, shabby, weather-beaten, battered, tumbledown, rickety, seedy, time-worn; faded, dingy. **2** *The patient looked worn and pale:* exhausted, fatigued, worn-out, weary, wearied, spent, tired, dog-tired, haggard, played-out, ready to drop; weak, enfeebled, wasted, debilitated; pinched, drawn.
Ant. 1 new, brand-new, spanking new, none the worse for wear. **2** energetic, vigorous, peppy, alive, dynamic, refreshed, restored, rejuvenated.

worrisome *adj.* **1** *That boy is so worrisome he'll be the death of me:* causing worry, troublesome, aggravating, annoying, irritating, tormenting, vexing, trying, irksome, bothersome, disturbing, pesty. **2** *Aunt Sue is so worrisome that she never gives herself a moment's peace:* tending to worry, anxious, apprehensive, uneasy, despairing, fretful, fussy.
Ant. 1 soothing, calming, non-irritating. **2** confident, secure; carefree, nonchalant, devil-may-care, lackadaisical.

worry *v.* **1** *Mother always worries when the girls stay out late. Don't worry, tomorrow is another day:* be anxious, feel uneasy, be apprehensive, be disturbed, be troubled, be distressed, agonize, fret, despair, lose heart, be downhearted, be heavy-hearted, be afraid, dread, brood over. **2** *Lack of rain is beginning to worry the farmers. Stop worrying me and get on with your work:* make anxious, make uneasy, disturb, upset, perturb, agitate, trouble, distress, harass, harry, badger, hector, bother, pester, vex, beset, plague, torment, persecute. —*n.* **3** *The wayward boy caused his parents a lot of worry:* anxiety, uneasiness, apprehension, concern, misgiving, consternation, dismay, trouble, distress, bother, grief, anguish, torment, agony, misery, woe, difficulty, care, vexation. **4** *Our chief worry is that the game will be cancelled:* concern, care, problem, dread, *Slang* bugbear, bugaboo, *French* bête noire.
Ant. 2 comfort, solace, console, soothe, calm, allay. **3** certainty, assurance, security, trust, certitude; calm, composure, equanimity, serenity, tranquillity, placidity, quiet, peace of mind; comfort, solace.
◇ *Word origin: Worry* now merely means to be uneasy, feel anxiety, but it comes from a much stronger Old English verb, *wyrgan*, to strangle, or tear at the throat with the teeth.

worship *n.* **1** *The worship of idols is called "idolatry" in the Bible:* adoration, veneration. **2** *Worship is on Sunday at 11 a.m.:* divine service, religious service, public worship, evensong, matins. —*v.* **3** *Each religion worships God in its own way:* pray to, adore, revere, venerate, reverence; glorify, exalt, praise, extol. **4** *He has worshipped his elder brother since he was a boy:* idolize, adore, revere, dote upon, put on a pedestal.
Ant. 4 hate, detest, loathe, despise, scorn.
◇ *Word origin:* See WORTH.

worth *n.* **1** *A university education will be of great worth to you later:* use, usefulness, utility, benefit, value, good, merit, worthiness, importance, consequence, justification. **2** *The appraiser put a worth of a thousand pounds on the ring:* value, price, selling price, market price, current price, going rate; valuation, appraisal. **3** *His net worth is reckoned at over a million pounds:* assets, wealth, resources, real property, effects, estate.
Ant. 1 uselessness, fruitlessness, futility, worthlessness, inutility; drawback, handicap. **3** debts.
◇ *Word origin: Worth* and *worship* both come from Old English *weorth*, worth, value. *Worship* is composed of this word *weorth*, worth, + *-ship* (a suffix meaning condition, office, etc., as in *friendship* and *sportsmanship*), hence *worship* was originally the condition or office of being worthy, worthiness, dignity.

worthless *adj. The plot of land he bought proved to be worthless. Joe's ideas are usually worthless:* without value, useless, unusable, unavailing, unproductive, ineffectual, pointless, fruitless, bootless, futile, meritless, meretricious; unimportant, inconsequential, insignificant, trivial, paltry, piddling, undeserving, of no account, good-for-nothing, not worth a straw.
Ant. worthwhile, worthy, valuable, precious, profitable, useful, usable, utilitarian, productive, effective, fruitful; important, consequential, significant.

worthwhile *adj. Here's some worthwhile advice to any young businessman. So few plays are worthwhile nowadays:* valuable, worthy, profitable, useful, usable, beneficial, good; worth one's time, worth the effort.
Ant. worthless, unworthy, useless, pointless, time-consuming, unimportant, inconsequential, trivial, of no account.

worthy *adj.* **1** *The people gave generously in support of the worthy cause. The school has educated many worthy young people:* worthwhile, deserving, praiseworthy, laudable, commendable, admirable, estimable, excellent, good, meritorious, suitable, fit, fitting, befitting, appropriate, proper, creditable, honourable,

virtuous, reputable, upright, decent, respectable, noble, honest, reliable.
—*n.* **2** *The mayor and other local worthies were at the hearing:* notable, dignitary, person of distinction, great man, great woman, personage, name, immortal, luminary, a somebody, pillar of society, *Slang* VIP, bigwig, big shot, big name.
Ant. 1 unworthy, worthless, undeserving, useless, unproductive, ineffectual; dishonourable, disreputable, ignoble, dishonest, unethical, unreliable, untrustworthy. **2** member of the rank and file, nobody, anonym, small person, obscure person, obscurity; everyman; Tom, Dick, and Harry.

wound *n.* **1** *The punch left a wound over his left eye:* laceration, gash, cut, slit, lesion; contusion, bruise. **2** *The argument caused a wound that has never healed:* hurt feelings, trauma, provocation, irritation, vexation, pain, sting, distress, affliction, anguish, torment; hurt, injury, damage.
—*v.* **3** *The bullet wounded the policeman in the left arm:* lacerate, gash, cut, slash, tear, pierce, bruise; hurt, injure, wing. **4** *Her nasty remark really wounded him:* hurt the feelings of, offend, pain, sting, distress, grieve, mortify, torment; harm, damage, hurt, injure.
Ant. 3, 4 heal. **4** appease, assuage, calm, soothe, comfort.

wraith *n. The wraith was said to appear on the stairs at midnight:* ghost, spectre, apparition, phantom, phantasm, banshee, spook, materialization, revenant.

wrap *v.* **1** *Buy tissue-paper to wrap the gift. Wrap a bandage round his arm:* wrap up, enclose, enwrap, bundle, encase; bind, wind, fold. **2** *The valley was wrapped in a dense fog:* clothe, cover, envelop, enclose, swathe, enfold, surround, girdle, gird, shroud, cloak, veil, mask, hide, conceal.
—*n.* **3** Usually plural *Take some wraps in case the weather turns cool:* (*variously*) shawl, cloak, coat, stole, mantle, wrapper, scarf; sweater.
Ant. 1 unwrap, unbundle; unbind, unwind, undo. **2** uncover, expose, reveal, open.

wrapper Also **wrapping** *n. The gramophone record came in a colourful wrapper:* paper wrapping, envelope; covering, case, slip-case, casing, sheath, sleeve, jacket, container.

wrath *n. Don't contradict her or you'll feel the full force of her wrath:* anger, rage, fury, vexation, irritableness; ire, indignation, rancour, resentment, hostility, animosity, animus, displeasure, spleen, choler, gall, bile.
Ant. appeasement, calm; kindness, friendship, geniality, affability, tenderness, forgiveness, love.

wreak *v. The hurricane wreaked havoc on the town. The angry troops wreaked vengeance on the civilian population:* inflict, visit, work, execute; retaliate with, vent, indulge, give full rein to, unleash.
◇ *Word origin:* See WRECK.

wreath *n. The President of the Republic placed a wreath on the tomb:* garland, laurel, festoon; coronet, crown, chaplet, diadem.

wreck *v.* **1** *The aeroplane skidded off the runway and wrecked two hangars. Lack of money wrecked our holiday plans:* ruin, destroy, demolish, level, raze, smash, shatter, break, break to pieces, devastate, ravage, put an end to.
—*n.* **2** *The new owners let the house become a wreck. After the scandal, Henry became a complete wreck:* dilapidated structure, ruin, mess; sick person, ailing person, debilitated person; derelict, wretch. **3** *The wreck was towed into port for salvage:* shipwrecked vessel, stranded ship, derelict, damaged remains, ruins. **4** *Cuts in the budget mean the wreck of all our plans:* ruin, destruction, devastation, undoing, dissolution, disruption, overthrow, upset, break-up, crack-up; end, death, finish.
Ant. 1 build, create, construct, fulfil; save, salvage, preserve, conserve, protect. **4** formation, formulation, creation, fulfilment; preservation, salvage, saving, conservation.
◇ *Word origin: Wreck* comes from Old Norse *wrek*, wreckage, referring specifically to ships driven ashore by tempests.

wrench *v.* **1** *The policeman wrenched the knife from the attacker's hand:* twist, wrest, wring, force, pull, jerk, tear, rip. **2** *The footballer wrenched his ankle in the tackle:* twist, sprain, strain.
—*n.* **3** *The plumber took out a wrench and tightened a bolt on the pipe:* spanner, adjustable spanner. **4** *With one quick wrench he opened the jar:* twist, wring, jerk, pull; tear, rip. **5** *It's not a real wrench, only a slight sprain:* sprain, strain, twist.

wrest *v.* **1** *The bully tried to wrest the ball from the smaller boy's hands:* wrench, twist, wring, pull, jerk, tear, rip, force. **2** *The settlers found it hard to wrest a living from the rocky soil:* obtain, get, gain, attain, achieve, secure, earn, glean, extract, squeeze.
Ant. 2 yield, give, furnish, supply.
◇ *Word origin: Wrest* and *wrestle* come from Old English *wræstan*, to wrest.

wrestle *v.* **1** *Mother forbade the boys to wrestle for fear that they would tear their clothes:* engage in wrestling; tussle, scuffle, grapple. **2** *I've been wrestling with this problem for weeks:* struggle, grapple, strive, contend, labour, toil, battle, attempt to find a solution.
◇ *Word origin:* See WREST.

wretch *n.* **1** *The poor wretch was shivering in the doorway:* unfortunate, miserable being, unhappy person, sufferer; outcast, cast-off, homeless person, derelict, waif. **2** *The miserable wretch deserted his wife and children:* contemptible person, vile fellow, villain, scoundrel, rotter, worm, blackguard, rascal, rogue, knave, scallywag, varlet, swine, cur.
◇ *Usage note:* Don't confuse *wretch*, a pitiable or contemptible person, with *retch*, to make an effort to vomit. *The poor wretch lay there*

starving, but *The roll of the ship caused me to retch.*

wretched *adj.* **1** *The wretched man hadn't eaten for three days. Why does Jane have such a wretched look on her face?:* pitiable, pitiful, unfortunate; pathetic, miserable, unhappy, hapless, woebegone, forlorn, downcast, doleful, cheerless, crestfallen, despondent, disheartened, depressed, dejected, abject, broken-hearted, inconsolable, disconsolate, crushed, melancholy, sorrowful, gloomy, worried, low-spirited, despairing, hopeless, sick at heart. **2** *The wretched landlord refuses to have the furnace repaired. What a nerve to charge £5 for that wretched meal!:* contemptible, despicable, mean, miserable, vile, low, base, niggardly; inferior, worthless, sorry, awful, terrible, dreadful, rotten, abominable, *Informal* lousy, shabby, crummy.

Ant. 1 fortunate, enviable, prosperous, flourishing, successful, thriving; happy, cheerful, gay, carefree, light-hearted, jovial. **2** noble, admirable, excellent, good, wonderful, fine, great, worthy.

wring *v.* **1** *Wring the water out of your bathing suit before hanging it up to dry. He wrung my hand in gratitude:* twist, force by twisting; squeeze, press, compress, choke. **2** *Isn't there any way to wring the truth out of the suspect?:* force, coerce, wrest, wrench, extract. **3** *His sad story wrung our hearts:* affect sorrowfully, sadden, grieve, distress, agonize, rend, pain, pierce, stab.

Ant. 2 coax, wheedle, cajole, entice, beguile, inveigle, charm. **3** gladden, fill with joy, cheer, uplift.

wrinkle *n.* **1** *The shirt hadn't a wrinkle in it. After forty, many people get wrinkles round their eyes:* crease, rumple, crinkle, crimp, pucker, furrow, crumple, corrugation, fold, gather, pleat; crow's-foot. **2** *Informal Putting wheels on a bob-sleigh for summer use is a new wrinkle:* trick, device, gimmick, dodge, wheeze, idea, notion, fancy; viewpoint, point of view, slant.
—*v.* **3** *Hang up your dress so that it won't wrinkle:* crease, rumple, crinkle, crumple, pucker, crimp, furrow, fold, gather, pleat.

writ *n.* *The lawyer obtained a writ so that he could examine the company's books:* court order, mandatory order, sealed order.

◇ *Word origin: Writ*, a special piece of writing, comes from the same Old English verb as write, *wrītan.* The phrase *Holy Writ* is a synonym for the Scriptures, i.e. the Bible.

write *v.* **1** *Many six-year-olds already know how to write. Write your name and address at the top of the page:* be literate; set down, write down, jot down, record, put on paper, put in writing, put in black and white, scribble, scrawl, take pen in hand; transcribe, copy; inscribe. **2** *He wrote his first novel at seventeen:* compose, produce, turn out, dash off, *Informal* author, pen. **3** *The lawyer is writing a contract for the partnership:* draw up, draft, make out. **4** *Deceit was written all over his face:* be evident, be manifest, be conspicuous, be apparent, be patent, show, stand out, be visible.

Ant. 1 be illiterate; say, speak, tell. **4** hide, conceal, mask, cloak, veil.

writer *n.* **1** *I'm not much of a writer, so don't expect a letter. The boy can paint, but he's still a poor writer:* letter-writer; penman, scribe, calligrapher, scribbler, scrawler, quill-driver. **2** *Tolstoy was a famous Russian writer. He's a sports writer for the Mail:* author, professional writer; (*variously*) novelist, playwright, poet, essayist, reporter, journalist, columnist, scriptwriter, television writer, song-writer, librettist, *Informal* hack, penny-a-liner.

Ant. 2 reader; viewer; listener.

writhe *v.* *The patient was writhing in pain until the doctor gave him an injection:* twist about, flail, thresh, thrash, jerk, contort, toss about, squirm, wiggle, wriggle.

"Every kind of writing is good save that which bores."
—*Voltaire*

---

writing *n.* **1** *The actual writing of the report took about two days:* writing down, jotting down, putting on paper, composing, drafting, turning out, dashing off, *Informal* authoring, penning; transcribing, recording, copying, inscribing. **2** *I won't believe it until I see it in writing. Can you read his writing?:* written form, print, handwriting, penmanship, longhand, calligraphy. **3** *According to this writing, the deed is valid. The class is studying the writings of 18th-century novelists:* (*variously*) document, letter, diary, journal, composition, publication, book, work, volume, tome, opus, novel, play, story, poem, essay, report, column, manuscript, script, libretto.

Ant. 1, 3 reading; speech, talk, address.

wrong *adj.* **1** *Cheating is always wrong:* immoral, evil, wicked, sinful, bad, iniquitous, wrongful, dishonest, unethical, dishonourable; unlawful, illegal, illicit, felonious, crooked, criminal, unfair, unjust; unwarranted, unjustifiable, inexcusable, blameworthy, reprehensible. **2** *Three wrong answers and you will fail the test:* incorrect, erroneous, untrue, false, inaccurate, mistaken, faulty, fallacious, inexact, wide of the mark; illogical, unsound. **3** *Such dark wallpaper is all wrong for a nursery. Did I say the wrong thing?:* improper, incorrect, unsuitable, inappropriate, undesirable, unbecoming, unseemly, unfitting, unfit, unbefitting, indecorous, inapt, unhappy, infelicitous, incongruous, malapropos; indelicate, immodest. **4** *Something's wrong with the engine:* faulty, amiss, out of order, in bad condition, out of shape, out of gear, awry; ruined, *Slang* kaput. **5** *Iron the skirt on the wrong side:* inverse, reverse, opposite.
—*n.* **6** *A sane man knows the difference between right and wrong. He was condemned by the community for the wrong that he did:* immorality,

evil, wickedness, sinfulness, iniquity, unrighteousness, dishonesty, unlawfulness, illegality, unfairness, injustice; immoral act, evil deed, sin, vice, offence, crime, misdeed, wrongdoing, injury, villainy, transgression, trespass, *Informal* dirty trick.

—adv. **7** *You guessed wrong:* wrongly, incorrectly, erroneously, inaccurately, mistakenly.

—v. **8** *Does he really think that I wronged him?:* ill-treat, mistreat, maltreat, treat unjustly, treat unfairly, abuse, dishonour, harm, injure, hurt, ruin; cheat, defraud, bilk, swindle, fleece; impose upon, encroach upon.

Ant. 1–3, 5–7 right. **1** moral, virtuous, righteous, rightful, godly, good, honest, ethical, highminded, honourable, lawful, legal, just, fair; admirable, commendable, praiseworthy, worthy, meritorious, laudable. **2** correct, true, accurate, exact, precise, perfect; logical, sound, sensible. **3** proper, correct, suitable, appropriate, becoming, seemly, fit, fitting, befitting, meet, happy, felicitous. **6** morality, righteousness, goodness, godliness, honesty, highmindedness, lawfulness, legality, justice, fairness; virtue, good deed. **7** correctly, accurately, truly, exactly.

wrought *adj.* **1** *The woman bought a delicately wrought silver tray:* worked, made, crafted, handcrafted, constructed, manufactured. **2** *The tourist bought a grate of wrought iron in the native bazaar:* hammered, beaten.

◇ *Word origin: Wrought* is actually an archaic past tense and past participle of the verb to *work.* Thus, *wrought iron* is iron *worked* (forged or welded) into various shapes, and the Biblical sentence "He *wrought* evil in the sight of the Lord" means "He worked (or did) evil."

wry *adj.* **1** *When the foreman makes that wry face, he's displeased:* twisted, crooked, contorted, askew, awry, warped. **2** *His wry remark was meant to make her laugh, but it hurt her feelings:* ironic, cynical, sarcastic, caustic, bitter, perverse; amusing, droll, dry.

Ant. 1 straight, direct, symmetrical.

◇ *Word origin: Wry* comes from Old English *wrīgian,* to move, move slightly, tend. Our word *awry* is based on this word *wry.*

Y

yank *v.* **1** *The boy yanked the skipping-rope out of the girl's hand and threw it up into the tree. The dentist yanked out the tooth:* pull suddenly, jerk, tug, snatch, wrench; pull out, extract, draw out.

—n. **2** *Informal Give the door a good yank to open it:* pull, jerk, tug, wrench.

Ant. 1, 2 push, shove.

yap *v.* **1** *The little Pekingese yapped all night long:* bark shrilly, yelp, caterwaul. **2** *Marilyn is always yapping about some new diet. What's the opposition party yapping about now?:* talk incessantly, talk foolishly, chatter, jabber, gabble, babble, blather, prattle, rabbit on, rave, rave on, gush, blab, gossip, tattle; talk, lecture, scold, complain; converse, palaver.

—n. **3** *The puppy gave a series of yaps and ran out of the door:* shrill bark, yelp.

yard[1] *n. The children are playing in the yard:* ground surrounding a building, grounds; enclosure, compound, confine, close; courtyard, court.

yard[2] *n.* **1** *Will two yards of dress material be enough?:* three feet, 36 inches, .914 metre; *abbreviation* yd. **2** *Nautical The captain threatened to hang the mutineers from the yard:* yard-arm, horizontal spar.

yarn *n.* **1** *Buy some yarn and Aunt Judy will knit you a sweater:* spun thread, wool, knitting thread, weaving thread. **2** *The sailor told us some old whaling yarns:* tale, story, adventure story, narrative, account, adventure, experience.

year *n.* **1** *That incident happened two years ago. The company's fiscal year ends on October 15th:* period of 365 days (or in a leap year 366 days), 12-month period, 52-week period, period of the earth's revolution round the sun.

yearn *v. Do pregnant women really yearn for sour pickles?:* crave, have a strong desire, long, hanker, ache, hunger, thirst, wish, languish, pine, sigh, have a fancy for, set one's heart upon, be bent upon, have a passion for.

Ant. detest, despise, hate, loathe, abhor, abominate, be repelled by, recoil from.

yearning *n. The city-dweller had a yearning to return to the wide-open spaces:* craving, longing, hankering, hunger, thirst, ache, strong desire, fancy, wish, passion, aspiration, inclination.

yell *v.* **1** *The lost man yelled, hoping that someone in the woods would hear him. The crowd yelled and screamed with joy at the goal:* cry out, shout, scream, bellow, roar, howl, shriek, bawl, whoop, yowl, hollo, hoot, screech, squall, yelp, clamour, rend the air, raise one's voice.

—n. **2** *The girl gave a yell of delight when the doll's house was delivered. The angry yells of the crowd drowned the announcer's voice:* cry, outcry, shout, scream, bellow, roar, howl, shriek, whoop, hoot, screech, squeal, yelp, hollo, clamour; cheer, hurrah, huzzah; boo.

yellow *adj.* **1** *A yellow scarf would look nice with that dress:* yellow-coloured, lemon, canary, golden, ochre, mustard-yellow, saffron, yellow-orange, flaxen, straw-coloured, blond. **2** *Informal They said that if he didn't fight he was yellow:* cowardly, timorous, pusillanimous, craven, faint-hearted, afraid, frightened, *Slang* chicken, lily-livered, chicken-hearted. —*v.* **3** *Bleach keeps the white clothes from yellowing:* turn yellow; make yellow.

Ant. 2 brave, courageous, fearless, bold, daring, audacious, venturesome, unafraid, stout-hearted, lion-hearted, *Slang* game. **3** bleach, whiten, brighten.

yelp *n.* **1** *The dog gave a yelp when I stepped on his paw:* sharp cry, yap, howl, squeal. —*v.* **2** *The girls yelped with glee when the pop star appeared:* cry shrilly, scream, shriek, screech, squeal, clamour, hollo, shout; yap, howl.

yen *n. After two weeks of vegetarian meals, the man had a yen for a big thick steak:* craving, longing, hankering, yearning, hunger, thirst, appetite, aching, desire, fancy, wish, passion, aspiration, inclination, relish.

Ant. hatred, loathing, abhorrence, revulsion.

◇ *Word origin: Yen* comes from the Chinese (Cantonese) *yăn,* craving for opium or an opiate. The other word *yen,* the standard monetary unit of Japan, is taken from Chinese *yüan,* meaning "round," i.e. a round coin.

yes *adv.* **1** *Yes, you are right:* aye, yea, it is so, just so, true, granted, of course, surely, truly, verily, to be sure, assuredly, certainly, indeed, emphatically, no doubt, undoubtedly, doubtless, positively, precisely, exactly, so be it, amen; affirmatively, in the affirmative. —*n.* **2** *May we count on your yes?:* affirmative reply, affirmation, consent, assent, okay, O.K., acquiescence, acceptance, approval.

Ant. 1, 2 no, nay. **1** not so, untrue, wrong, false, of course not, no indeed, doubtfully, negatively, in the negative. **2** refusal, rejection, veto, disapproval.

◇ *Word origin: Yes* comes from Old English *gēa* (yea) + *sī* (third person singular subjunctive of *bēon,* to be).

yesterday *adv.* **1** *Where did you go yesterday?:* on the day preceding today. —*n.* **2** *Where is yesterday's paper?:* the day before today; yester-morn, yester-eve. **3** *Do you remember the hair-styles of yesterday?:* the recent past, bygone days, former times, the past, yester-year, the good old days, days of yore, time gone by, olden times.

Ant. 1, 2 tomorrow.

◇ *Word origin: Yesterday* comes from Old English *giestran* (yesterday) + *day.*

yield *v.* **1** *This old tree still yields apples every year:* bear, bring forth, produce, give forth, put forth; give birth to, beget, spawn, procreate, generate. **2** *The stock yields 8% interest a year:* return, generate, pay, provide, furnish, supply, render, give. **3** *The town soon yielded to the attackers. Don't yield to temptation:* surrender, give up, give in, give way, capitulate, submit, succumb, accede, acquiesce, resign oneself, truckle, bow down, *Slang* kotow, cave in. **4** *Cars entering the motorway must yield the right of way. Will the speaker yield five minutes of his allotted speaking time to the area manager?:* relinquish, grant, concede, give up, give, give away, defer, forgo, waive, renounce, forbear. **5** *The chair yielded under his weight:* give way, sag, droop, cave in, collapse, break, split. —*n.* **6** *Farmers had an exceptionally good yield this year:* harvest, crop, gleanings; produce, product. **7** *The current yield on gilts is 9¾%:* interest, return, earnings, payment, revenue.

Ant. 3 resist, oppose, combat, counter-attack, attack; repulse, repel. **4** keep, retain, maintain, reserve, hold on to; appropriate, take, seize, grab, arrogate, claim.

◇ *Word origin: Yield* comes from Old English *gieldan,* to pay. When we speak of investments yielding interest, we are using *yield* in this original sense; when we *yield* to someone else, we are paying homage to that person; and when a field *yields* crops, it is giving them forth in a manner similar to payment. Also related is our word *guild,* a craft association founded on contributions and dues. The root-meaning in all of these words is "pay, payment."

yoke *n.* **1** *The two oxen were put under the yoke. A rubber yoke held the two wires together:* double harness, coupler, collar, bond, clasp. **2** *It takes a yoke of oxen to pull that wagon:* pair, team, brace, couple. **3** *Wilberforce sought to free the slaves from their yoke:* bondage, slavery, enslavement, servitude; serfdom, vassalage, thraldom. **4** *The youth was not ready to bear the yoke of responsibility:* burden, weight, oppression, load, strain, pressure, tax, troubles, distress, trial, tribulation. —*v.* **5** *The farmer yoked the oxen to the plough:* couple, double-harness; hitch, harness. **6** *Should these parts of the toy yoke together? The nation's economic growth is yoked to that of its neighbours:* join, unite, couple, link, fasten.

Ant. 3 freedom, liberty, independence. **4** joy, pleasure, delight, enjoyment, comfort, satisfaction. **5** unyoke, uncouple, unhitch, unharness. **6** separate, divide, divorce.

◇ *Usage note: Yoke* and *yolk* sound alike but have entirely different meanings. Remember that *yoke* is a wooden frame for harnessing oxen together, something that binds or unites, and *yolk* is the yellow portion of an egg.

yokel *n. It's no good asking one of these yokels the way; they're all stupid:* country bumpkin, naïve rustic, clodhopper, peasant, country boy.

◇ *Word origin:* There are two origins given for *yokel.* The first is that *yokel* is a diminutive of *yoke* and refers to a rustic ploughboy with his yoke of oxen. The other is that the word comes from the dialectal word *yokel,* a green woodpecker.

yolk *n. Separate the yolks from the whites before beating the eggs:* egg-yolk, yellow.

Ant. white, albumen.

◇ *Word origin: Yolk* comes from Old English *geoloca,* yolk, akin to Old English *geolu*, yellow, from which we get our word *yellow.*

yonder *adj. Archaic Yonder barn is bigger than the near one:* more distant, farther, thither.

Ant. nearer, closer; nearby, close, at hand.

young *adj.* **1** *You're still young. The major's too young to be made a general:* youthful, not old; younger, junior, juvenile, under age, minor, childish, boyish, girlish, puerile, adolescent, teenage; immature, inexperienced, undeveloped, callow; growing, budding.

—*n.* **2** *Both young and old like ice cream:* young persons, young people, children, juveniles, youngsters, kids, youths, teenagers, adolescents. **3** *The mother tiger guards her young fiercely:* baby, child, cub, pup, whelp, kitten; offspring, issue, progeny, descendant.

Ant. 1, 2 old, aged, **1** elderly, older, elder, senior, grey, hoary, old-mannish, old-womanish, ancient, venerable; adult, mature, grown-up, experienced, ripe, fully-developed, full-grown. **2** the old, pensioners, senior citizens, oldsters, oldies, old-timers; adults, grown-ups, **3** parent, progenitor.

youngster *n. The youngsters are both at school:* child, boy, girl, youth, kid, young person, adolescent, juvenile, teenager; offspring, progeny, tiny tot, baby.

Ant. oldie, oldster, old-timer, senior citizen, pensioner, adult, grown-up.

youth *n.* **1** *I visited South America in my youth. She's trying frantically to maintain her youth:* early life, childhood, boyhood, girlhood, adolescence, growing years, teens, pubescence, juvenile period, minority, school-days, salad days, younger days, springtime of life, prime, bloom, heyday; youthful condition, youthful appearance. **2** *The youth ran away to join the circus:* boy, schoolboy, lad, youngster, child, kid, juvenile, minor, teenager, adolescent, young man, stripling, fledgling. **3** *The new TV programme is aimed at youth:* young persons, young people, the young, children, boys and girls, youngsters, kids, juveniles, teenagers, adolescents, the rising generation.

Ant. 1 old age, later life; adulthood, maturity. **2** man, old man, old codger; adult. **3** senior citizens, pensioners, oldies, old-timers; adults, grown-ups.

youthful *adj. The magician loved to perform before youthful audiences. It was just a youthful prank. Outside interests keep one youthful:* young, juvenile, adolescent, teenage; childish, boyish, girlish, puerile, immature, inexperienced, callow; young-looking, enthusiastic, lighthearted, young at heart.

Ant. old, aged, elderly, older, senior, hoary; adult, mature, grown-up, full-grown, experienced; old-mannish, old-womanish, ancient, old-fashioned; senile, decrepit.

yowl *v.* **1** *The cats were yowling on the back fence:* howl, wail, caterwaul, miaow, yelp, scream, shriek, screech, squeal, bawl, whine.

—*n.* **2** *The handyman let out a yowl when he hit his thumb with the hammer:* howl, wail, yelp, cry, shout, hollo, bellow, roar, scream, shriek, screech, squeal, whine, bawl, caterwaul.

yule *n. Yule-tide is a merry time for children:* Christmas season, Christmas, Christmastide; the feast of Christmas.

◇ *Word origin:* In Old English *gēol,* yule, meant Christmas Day.

Z

zany *adj.* **1** *I prefer zany comedy to sophisticated humour:* clownish, outlandish, foolishly comical, nonsensical, ludicrous, slapstick, daft, daffy, dizzy, crazy, mad, madcap, wild.

—*n.* **2** *Don't be such a zany; be serious for a change:* clown, buffoon, jester, comic, comedian, harlequin, buffo, pantaloon, farceur.

Ant. 1 droll, ironic, sarcastic, wry, dry.

◇ *Word origin:* In Venice the nick-name for *Giovanni* is *Zanni.* The name became associated with a type of buffoon who played humorous servants in early Italian comedy. From this clownish character, the zanni, we get our word *zany.*

zeal *n. The boys began the work of building a kennel with zeal. His political zeal prevented us from having a quiet discussion:* zest, gusto, eagerness, fervour, ardour, industry, enthusiasm, animation, vigour, verve, fierceness, earnestness, intentness, vehemence, passion, devotion, fanaticism.

Ant. apathy, indifference, impassivity, nonchalance, torpor, languor, listlessness.

◇ *Word origin: Zeal, zealot, zealous,* and *jealous,* all come from Greek *zēlos,* zeal. Ultimately derived from an Indo-European ancestor-word meaning "to be aroused," Greek *zēlos* has an interesting range of meanings: jealousy, emulation, fervour, ambition, pride, glory, spirit.

zealot *n.* **1** *You've got to be a real zealot to be a top-notch car salesman:* believer, enthusiast, partisan, champion, devotee, fan; go-getter, pusher, hustler, live wire, eager beaver.

2 *Religious zealots wanted the entire population to wear sackcloth and ashes:* fanatic, enthusiast, true believer, obsessed person; crank, freak.

zealous *adj. Bill is the most zealous worker in the whole office. The lawyer made a zealous plea for his client:* full of zeal, eager, fervent, fervid, vigorous, ardent, earnest, enthusiastic, animated, intense, fierce, vehement, passionate, impassioned, devoted, industrious; fanatic, rabid, raging, raving.

Ant. apathetic, languorous, torpid, listless, unenthusiastic, dispassionate, passionless, indifferent, lack-lustre, lackadaisical, nonchalant, dull, calm, cool, quiet, low-key.

◇ *Word origin:* See ZEAL.

zenith *n.* **1** *Is the North Star really at the zenith of the north pole?:* point in the sky directly overhead. **2** *Being elected M.P. was the zenith of his political career. The British Empire was at its zenith in the 19th century:* peak, highest point, high point, pinnacle, acme, summit, apex, apogee, maximum, best, culmination, culminating point, climax.

Ant. 1, 2 nadir. **2** lowest point, low point, depth, minimum, worst.

◇ *Word origin: Zenith* comes from Arabic *samt,* "path" in *samt arrās* (path over the head). A medieval scribe copied the word *samt* incorrectly making it "senit," which became our *zenith.*

zephyr *n. A soft zephyr whispered through the palm trees:* light breeze, gentle wind, breath of air, puff of air; west wind.

Ant. gust, blast, gale, squall, bluster, windstorm, tornado; east wind.

◇ *Word origin: Zephyr* comes from Greek *zephuros,* west wind, probably cognate with Greek *zophos,* the west, the dark quarter, hence Hades, the nether darkness, gloom.

zero *n.* **1** *Four subtracted from four leaves zero. All our efforts added up to zero:* nothing, nothingness, nought, cipher, *Tennis* love, *Cricket* duck; *symbol* o. **2** *The thermometer shows 2 degrees above zero:* the lowest positive point on a scale, 32 degrees Fahrenheit, zero degrees centigrade; lowest point, nadir.

—*adj.* **3** *Our chances of making a profit are zero:* amounting to zero, nil, non-existent, naught.

Ant. 1 infinity; something, everything. **2** zenith, highest point. **3** perfect, excellent.

◇ *Word origin: Zero* comes from Arabic *sifr,* which also gives us our word *cipher.*

zest *n.* **1** *Father has a great zest for living:* keen enjoyment, gusto, relish, appetite, zeal, eagerness, enthusiasm, verve, passion; exhilaration, thrill, delight, joy, pleasure, satisfaction. **2** *The special zest of this soup is due to the saffron:* flavouring, flavour, savour, taste, tang, piquancy, seasoning; spice, salt.

Ant. 1 apathy, weariness, dullness, distaste, disrelish, displeasure, aversion, abhorrence, repugnance, loathing.

◇ *Word origin:* If you want to add zest to your cooking, just add lemon peel. *Zest* literally means lemon peel (from the French *zeste*), used for flavouring.

Zion *n. King David of Judah ruled from Zion. The Lord hath founded Zion:* City of David, hill in Jerusalem on which the Temple was built; ancient Israel; the Jewish people.

◇ *Word origin: Zion* comes from Hebrew *tsīyōn,* hill, fortress. *Zion* was originally the hill in Jerusalem on which stood the temple and royal residence of David and his successors (the City of David). From its use in the Psalms the word came to refer to the Jewish people, and later to any place or community especially under God's rule (as Israel or the Christian Church), and to the heavenly Jerusalem or heaven.

zip *n.* **1** *The scout saw the flash of a gun and then heard the zip of a bullet:* hiss, whine, whistle, buzz. **2** *The show was interesting but had no zip to it:* energy, vim, vigour, go, pep, dash, verve, animation, vivacity, liveliness, life, spirit, effervescence, exuberance, zest, gusto, enthusiasm; power, drive, force, strength, intensity, punch, impact, *Slang* oomph. **3** *Hurry up and close the zip on your pocket:* zip-fastener.

—*v.* **4** *Just zip down to the shop and get a pint of milk:* run, go quickly, dash, dart, rush, nip, fly. **5** *Better zip up your jacket — it's cold outside:* zip up, fasten with a zip-fastener, close.

Ant. 2 lethargy, torpor, languor, sluggishness, lassitude, apathy, listlessness, coolness; dullness, weakness. **4** creep, crawl. **5** unzip.

◇ *Word origin: Zip* was coined to imitate a sound, as of a bullet flying through the air.

zone *n.* **1** *Most of the world's wheat is grown in the North Temperate Zone. It's against the law to build factories in this residential zone:* region, territory, area, belt; district, quarter, ward, sector, section, locality, location, tract.

—*v.* **2** Also **zone off** *The army has zoned off this area:* assign as a zone for a special purpose, segregate, divide into zones, designate as a zone.

◇ *Word origin: Zone* comes from the Greek *zōnē,* girdle, belt, hence the *Torrid Zone, North* and *South Temperate Zones,* and *Arctic* and *Antarctic Frigid Zones* which encircle the earth between specific parallels of latitude.

zoo *n. Berlin has one of the largest zoos in the world:* zoological garden, zoological park; menagerie, vivarium.

◇ *Word origin: Zoo* is the short term for *zoological garden.* The source word is Greek *zōon,* animal.

40/116/5